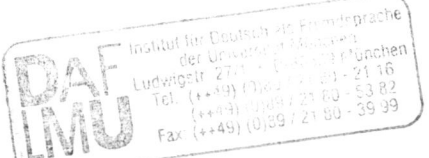

History of the Language Sciences
Geschichte der Sprachwissenschaften
Histoire des sciences du langage

HSK 18.1

# Handbücher zur Sprach- und Kommunikationswissenschaft

Handbooks of Linguistics and Communication Science

Manuels de linguistique et des sciences de communication

Mitbegründet von
Gerold Ungeheuer

Herausgegeben von / Edited by / Edités par
Armin Burkhardt
Hugo Steger
Herbert Ernst Wiegand

Band 18.1



Walter de Gruyter · Berlin · New York
2000

# History of the Language Sciences
# Geschichte der Sprachwissenschaften
# Histoire des sciences du langage

An International Handbook on the Evolution of the Study of Language from the Beginnings to the Present

Ein internationales Handbuch zur Entwicklung der Sprachforschung von den Anfängen bis zur Gegenwart

Manuel international sur l'évolution de l'étude du langage des origines à nos jours

Edited by / Herausgegeben von / Edité par
Sylvain Auroux · E. F. K. Koerner
Hans-Josef Niederehe · Kees Versteegh

Volume 1 / 1. Teilband / Tome 1



Walter de Gruyter · Berlin · New York
2000

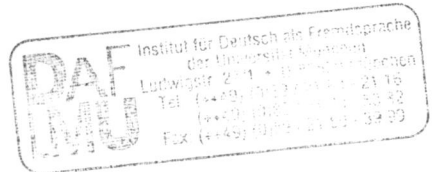

♾ Printed on acid-free paper which falls within the guidelines
of the ANSI to ensure permanence and durability.

*Die Deutsche Bibliothek – CIP-Einheitsaufnahme*

History of the language sciences : an international handbook on the evolution of the study of language from the beginnings to the present = Geschichte der Sprachwissenschaft / ed. by Sylvain Auroux .... – Berlin ; New York : de Gruyter
(Handbücher zur Sprach- und Kommunikationswissenschaft ; Bd. 18)

Vol. 1. – (2000)
ISBN 3-11-011103-9


Cover design: Rudolf Hübler
Typesetting: Arthur Collignon GmbH, Berlin
Printing: Oskar Zach GmbH & Co. KG, Berlin
Binding: Lüderitz & Bauer-GmbH, Berlin
Printed in Germany

## Contents / Inhalt / Table des matières

### Volume 1 / 1. Teilband / Tome 1


Editors' Foreword . . . . . . . . . . . . . . . . . . . . . . . . . . . . . . . . . . XXV
Vorwort der Herausgeber . . . . . . . . . . . . . . . . . . . . . . . . . . . . . . XXXVII
Préface des éditeurs . . . . . . . . . . . . . . . . . . . . . . . . . . . . . . . . . XLIX

I. The Establishment of Linguistic Traditions in the Near East
Die Anfänge sprachwissenschaftlicher Traditionen im Nahen Osten
La constitution des traditions linguistiques au Proche Orient

1. Erica Reiner, The Sumerian and Akkadian linguistic tradition . . 1
2. Joris F. Borghouts, Indigenous Egyptian grammar . . . . . . . . . . 5
3. Manfred Dietrich, Die Sprachforschung in Ugarit . . . . . . . . . . 14

II. The Establishment of the Chinese Linguistic Tradition
Die Anfänge der Sprachwissenschaft in China
La constitution de la tradition linguistique chinoise

4. Chung-ying Cheng, Classical Chinese philosophies of language: Logic and ontology . . . . . . . . . . . . . . . . . . . . . . . . . . . 19
5. David Branner, The Suí-Táng tradition of *Fǎnqiè* phonology . . . 36
6. David Branner, The rime-table system of formal Chinese phonology . . . . . . . . . . . . . . . . . . . . . . . . . . . . . . . 46
7. Alain Peyraube, Le rôle du savoir linguistique dans l'éducation et la société chinoise . . . . . . . . . . . . . . . . . . . . . . . . 55
8. Nonna V. Stankevič, La tradition linguistique vietnamienne et ses contacts avec la tradition chinoise . . . . . . . . . . . . . . . . 58

III. The Establishment of the Korean Linguistic Tradition
Die Anfänge der koreanischen Sprachforschung
La constitution de la tradition linguistique coréenne

9. Werner Sasse, Die traditionelle Sprachforschung in Korea . . . . . 63

## IV. The Establishment of the Japanese Linguistic Tradition
## Die Anfänge der Sprachforschung in Japan
## La constitution de la tradition linguistique japonaise


10. Roy Andrew Miller, The Japanese linguistic tradition and the Chinese heritage . . . 72
11. Stefan Kaiser, The first Japanese attempts at describing Chinese and Korean bilingualism . . . 77
12. Viktoria Eschbach-Szabó, Sprache und Denken in der japanischen Sprachforschung während der *Kokugaku* . . . 85
13. Viktoria Eschbach-Szabó, Die Frühzeit der neueren japanischen Sprachforschung: Vom *Kokugaku* zum *Kokugogaku* . . . 93
14. Frits Vos †, The influence of Dutch grammar on Japanese language research . . . 102
15. Roy Andrew Miller, The role of linguistics in Japanese society and education . . . 104
16. Roy Andrew Miller, Traditional linguistics and Western linguistics in Japan . . . 108


## V. The Establishment of Sanskrit Linguistics
## Die Anfänge der Sanskritforschung
## La constitution de l'étude du sanskrit


17. George Cardona, Pāṇini . . . 113
18. Hartmut Scharfe, Die Entwicklung der Sprachwissenschaft in Indien nach Pāṇini . . . 125
19. Madhav Deshpande, Indian theories on phonetics . . . 137
20. Jan Houben, Language and thought in the Sanskrit tradition . . . 146
21. George Cardona, The organization of grammar in Sanskrit linguistics . . . 157
22. Johannes Bronkhorst, The relationship between linguistics and other sciences in India . . . 166
23. Madhav Deshpande, The role of linguistics in Indian society and education . . . 173
24. Michael C. Shapiro, The Hindi grammatical tradition . . . 178
25. Vadim B. Kasevic, Indian influence on the linguistic tradition of Burma . . . 182
26. Bernard Arps, Indian influence on the Old Javanese linguistic tradition . . . 186


## VI. The Establishment of Dravidian Linguistics
## Die Anfänge der dravidischen Sprachforschung
## La constitution de la lingistique dravidienne


27. Jean-Luc Chevillard, Les débuts de la tradition linguistique tamoule . . . 191

28. Jean-Luc Chevillard, Le *Tolkāppiyam* et le développement de la tradition linguistique tamoule . . . . . . . . . . . . . . . . . . . . . . . . 194
29. Jean-Luc Chevillard, Les successeurs du *Tolkāppiyam*: le *Naṉṉūl*, le *Vīracōḻiyam* et les autres écoles . . . . . . . . . . . . . . . . . . . . 200

VII. The Establishment of Tibetan Linguistics
Die Anfänge der Sprachforschung in Tibet
La constitution de la linguistique tibétaine

30. Roy Andrew Miller, The early Tibetan grammatical treatises and Thon-mi Sambhoṭa . . . . . . . . . . . . . . . . . . . . . . . . . . . . 203
31. Pieter C. Verhagen, The classical Tibetan grammarians . . . . . . . 207
32. Pieter C. Verhagen, The influence of the Sanskrit tradition on Tibetan indigenous grammar . . . . . . . . . . . . . . . . . . . . . . . 210

VIII. The Establishment of Hebrew Linguistics
Die Anfänge der hebräischen Sprachforschung
La constitution de la linguistique de l'hébreu

33. Aaron Dotan, The origins of Hebrew linguistics and the exegetic tradition . . . . . . . . . . . . . . . . . . . . . . . . . . . . . . . . . 215
34. Irene Zwiep, Die Entwicklung der hebräischen Sprachwissenschaft während des Mittelalters . . . . . . . . . . . . . . . . . . . . . . . . . 228
35. Carlos del Valle, Hebrew linguistics in Arabic . . . . . . . . . . . . 234
36. Wout Jac. van Bekkum, Hebrew linguistics and comparative Semitic grammar . . . . . . . . . . . . . . . . . . . . . . . . . . . . . . 240

IX. The Establishment of Arabic Linguistics
Die Anfänge der arabischen Sprachforschung
La constitution de la linguistique arabe

37. Rafael Talmon, The first beginnings of Arabic linguistics: The era of the Old Iraqi School . . . . . . . . . . . . . . . . . . . . . . . . 245
38. Aryeh Levin, Sībawayhi . . . . . . . . . . . . . . . . . . . . . . . . 252
39. Michael G. Carter, The development of Arabic linguistics after Sībawayhi: Baṣra, Kūfa and Baghdad . . . . . . . . . . . . . . . . . . 263
40. Jean-Patrick Guillaume, La nouvelle approche de la grammaire au IVe/Xe siècle: Ibn Ǧinnī (320/932–392/1002) . . . . . . . . . . . 273
41. Gérard Troupeau, La période post-classique de la linguistique arabe: d'Ibn Ǧinnī à al-'Astarābāḏī . . . . . . . . . . . . . . . . . . . 280
42. Jonathan Owens, The structure of Arabic grammatical theory . . 286
43. Kees Versteegh, Grammar and logic in the Arabic grammatical tradition . . . . . . . . . . . . . . . . . . . . . . . . . . . . . . . . . 300
44. Jan Peters, Language and revelation in Islamic society . . . . . . . 307
45. Pierre Larcher, Les relations entre la linguistique et les autres sciences dans la société arabo-islamique . . . . . . . . . . . . . . . 312
46. Mohammed Sawaie, Traditional linguistics and Western linguistics in the Arab world . . . . . . . . . . . . . . . . . . . . . . . . 318

47. Adel Sidarus, L'influence arabe sur la linguistique copte . . . . . . 321
48. Robert Ermers, The description of Turkic with the Arabic linguistic model . . . . . . . . . . . . . . . . . . . . . . . . . . . . . . 325
49. Éva M. Jeremiás, Arabic influence on Persian linguistics . . . . . . 329
50. Nico Kaptein, Arabic influence on Malay linguistics . . . . . . . . . 333

X. The Establishment of Syriac Linguistics
Die Anfänge der syrischen Sprachforschung
La constitution de la linguistique syriaque

51. Rafael Talmon, Foreign influence in the Syriac grammatical tradition . . . . . . . . . . . . . . . . . . . . . . . . . . . . . . . . . 337
52. Riccardo Contini, The role of linguistics in Syrian society . . . . . 341

XI. The Establishment of Linguistics in Greece
Die Anfänge der griechischen Sprachforschung
La constitution de la linguistique en Grèce

53. Peter Schmitter, Sprachbezogene Reflexionen im frühen Griechenland . . . . . . . . . . . . . . . . . . . . . . . . . . . . . . . 345
54. Hans Arens, Sprache und Denken bei Aristoteles . . . . . . . . . . 367
55. Ineke Sluiter, Language and thought in Stoic philosophy . . . . . 375
56. Frédéric Lambert, La linguistique grecque chez les alexandrins: Aristophane de Byzance et Aristarque . . . . . . . . . . . . . . . . . 385
57. Vincenzo di Benedetto, Dionysius Thrax and the *Tékhnē* . . . . . . 394
58. David L. Blank, The organization of grammar in ancient Greece 400
59. R. H. Robins †, Greek linguistics in the Byzantine period . . . . . 417
60. Elmar Siebenhorn, Die Beziehungen der griechischen Sprachforschung zu anderen Disziplinen . . . . . . . . . . . . . . . . 424
61. Dirk M. Schenkeveld, The impact of language studies on Greek society and education . . . . . . . . . . . . . . . . . . . . . . . . . . 430
62. Vít Bubeník, Variety of speech in Greek linguistics: The dialects and the *koinè* . . . . . . . . . . . . . . . . . . . . . . . . . . . . . . 439
63. Mzekala Shanidze, Greek influence in Georgian linguistics . . . . 444
64. Jos Weitenberg, Greek influence in Armenian linguistics . . . . . . 447
65. Yannis Kakridis, Greek influence in the grammatical theory of Church Slavonic . . . . . . . . . . . . . . . . . . . . . . . . . . . . . 450

XII. The Establishment of Linguistics in Rome
Die Anfänge der Sprachforschung in Rom
La constitution de la linguistique à Rome

66. Daniel J. Taylor, Varro and the origin of Roman linguistic theory and practice . . . . . . . . . . . . . . . . . . . . . . . . . . . . . 455
67. Marc Baratin, À l'origine de la tradition artigraphique latine, entre mythe et réalité . . . . . . . . . . . . . . . . . . . . . . . . . . 459
68. Françoise Desbordes †, L'*ars grammatica* dans la période post-classique: le *Corpus grammaticorum latinorum* . . . . . . . . . . . . . 466

69. Carmen Codoñer, L'organisation de la grammaire dans la tradition latine . . . 474
70. James J. Murphy, Grammar and rhetoric in Roman schools . . . 484
71. Arpád Orbán, Augustin und die Sprache . . . 492

XIII. The Cultivation of Latin Grammar in the Early Middle Ages
Die Pflege der lateinischen Grammatik im frühen Mittelalter
La culture de la grammaire latine dans le Haut Moyen-Age

72. Roger Wright, The study of Latin as a foreign language in the Early Middle Ages . . . 501
73. Anneli Luhtala, Linguistics and theology in the Early Medieval West . . . 510
74. Louis Holtz, Alcuin et la redécouverte de Priscien à l'époque carolingienne . . . 525
75. Mark Amsler, The role of linguistics in early medieval education 532

XIV. Linguistic Theory in the Late Middle Ages
Sprachtheorien des späten Mittelalters
La théorie linguistique au Bas Moyen-Age

76. Irène Rosier-Catach, La grammaire spéculative du Bas Moyen-Age . . . 541
77. Corneille H. Kneepkens, Linguistic description and analysis in the Late Middle Ages . . . 551
78. Joel Biard, Linguistique et logique durant le Bas Moyen-Age . . . 560
79. Louis Kelly, Language study and theology in the Late Middle Ages . . . 572
80. Ludger Kaczmarek, Die Beziehungen der spätmittelalterlichen Sprachforschung zu anderen Gebieten . . . 584

XV. The Cultivation of Latin Grammar in the Late Middle Ages
Die Pflege der lateinischen Grammatik im Spätmittelalter
La culture de la grammaire latine dans le Bas Moyen-Age

81. Anne Grondeux, La *Grammatica positiva* dans le Bas Moyen-Age . . . 598
82. Anders Ahlqvist, The Latin tradition and the Irish language . . . 610
83. Ann T. E. Matonis, The Latin tradition and Welsh . . . 614
84. Valeria Micillo, The Latin tradition and Icelandic . . . 617

85. Kees Dekkers, Ælfric and his relation to the Latin tradition . . . 625
86. Sylvie Archaimbault, La tradition latine et les langues slaves dans le Bas Moyen-Age . . . 634
87. Hans-J. Niederehe, Sprachstudium und literarische Traditionen: Das Okzitanisch . . . 638

## XVI. The Classical Languages in the Age of Humanism
## Die klassischen Sprachen im Zeitalter des Humanismus
## Les langues classiques à l'époque de l'humanisme

88. Mirko Tavoni, The traditional study of Latin at the university in the age of Humanism . . . 650
89. Mirko Tavoni, The rediscovery of the classics in the age of Humanism . . . 657
90. Bernard Colombat, La réforme du latin à l'époque de l'humanisme . . . 661
91. Christian Förstel, L'étude du grec à l'époque de l'humanisme . . . 666
92. Sophie Kessler-Mesguich, L'étude de l'hébreu et des autres langues orientales à l'époque de l'humanisme . . . 673

## XVII. The Teaching of Languages in the 15th Through the 18th Centuries in Europe
## Der Fremdsprachenunterricht in Europa (15.–16. Jahrhundert)
## L'enseignement des langues du XVe au XVIIIe siècle en Europe

93. Konrad Schröder, Kommerzielle und kulturelle Interessen am Unterricht der Volkssprachen im 15. und 16. Jahrhundert . . . 681
94. Alda Rossebastiano, La tradition des manuels polyglottes dans l'enseignement des langues . . . 688
95. Claudio Marazzini, The teaching of Italian in 15th- and 16th-century Europe . . . 699
96. Otto Ludwig / Claus Ahlzweig, Der Unterricht des Deutschen im 15. und 16. Jahrhundert . . . 705
97. Barbara Kaltz, Der Unterricht des Französischen im 16. Jahrhundert . . . 711
98. Manuel Breva-Claramonte, The teaching of Spanish in 16th-century Europe . . . 717
99. Konrad Schröder, Der Unterricht des Englischen im 16. Jahrhundert . . . 723
100. Hartmut Bobzin, Der Unterricht des Hebräischen, Arabischen und anderer semitischer Sprachen sowie des Persischen und Türkischen in Europa (bis zum Ende des 18. Jahrhunderts) . . . 728
101. Konrad Schröder, Die Traditionen des Sprachunterrichts im Europa des 17. und 18. Jahrhunderts . . . 734

## XVIII. The Development of Grammatical Traditions for the Literary Vernaculars in Europe
## Die neuen Literatursprachen und die Herausbildung ihrer grammatischen Tradition
## Le développement des traditions grammaticales concernant les vernaculaires écrits de l'Europe


102. Claudio Marazzini, Early grammatical descriptions of Italian . . . 742
103. Miguel Angel Esparza Torres, Frühe grammatische Beschreibungen des Spanischen . . . . . . . . . . . . . . . . . . . . . . 749
104. Maria Leonor Carvalhão Buescu †, Les premières descriptions grammaticales du portugais . . . . . . . . . . . . . . . . . . . . . . . 756
105. Andres Max Kristol, Les premières descriptions grammaticales du français . . . . . . . . . . . . . . . . . . . . . . . . . . . . . 764
106. Monique Verrac, Les premières descriptions grammaticales de l'anglais . . . . . . . . . . . . . . . . . . . . . . . . . . . . . . . 771
107. Monika Rössig-Hager, Frühe grammatische Beschreibungen des Deutschen . . . . . . . . . . . . . . . . . . . . . . . . . . . . . 777
108. Geert Dibbets, Frühe grammatische Beschreibungen des Niederländischen (ca. 1550–ca. 1650) . . . . . . . . . . . . . . . . . 784
109. Helmut Schaller, Frühe grammatische Beschreibungen slawischer Sprachen . . . . . . . . . . . . . . . . . . . . . . . . . . . . . 792
110. Erich Poppe, Early grammatical descriptions of the Celtic languages . . . . . . . . . . . . . . . . . . . . . . . . . . . . . 800
111. Kaisa Häkkinen, Early grammatical descriptions of Finno-Ugric 806


## XIX. The Normative Study of the National Languages from the 17th Century Onwards
## Das normative Studium der Nationalsprachen ab dem 17. Jahrhundert
## L'étude normative des langues nationales à partir du fin du XVIe siècle


112. Rudolf Engler, Die Accademia della Crusca und die Standardisierung des Italienischen . . . . . . . . . . . . . . . . . . . 815
113. Peter von Polenz, Die Sprachgesellschaften und die Entstehung eines literarischen Standards in Deutschland . . . . . . . . . . . . 827
114. Jörg Kilian, Entwicklungen in Deutschland im 17. und 18. Jahrhundert außerhalb der Sprachgesellschaften . . . . . . . . . 841
115. Francine Mazière, La langue et l'État: l'Académie française . . . . 852
116. Ramon Sarmiento, Die Königliche Spanische Akademie und die Pflege der Nationalsprache . . . . . . . . . . . . . . . . . . . . . 863
117. Maria Leonor Carvalhão Buescu †, L'Académie des Sciences de Lisbonne . . . . . . . . . . . . . . . . . . . . . . . . . . . . . 870
118. Ingrid Tieken-Boon van Ostade, Normative studies in England 876
119. Even Hovdhaugen, Normative studies in the Scandinavian countries . . . . . . . . . . . . . . . . . . . . . . . . . . . . . 888

120. Jan Noordegraaf, Normative studies in the Low Countries . . . . 893
121. Sylvie Archaimbault, Les approches normatives en Russie (XVIIIe siècle) . . . . . . . . . . . . . . . . . . . . . . . . . . . . . . . 901
122. Jiří Kraus, Normativ orientierte Sprachforschung zum Tschechischen . . . . . . . . . . . . . . . . . . . . . . . . . . . . . . . 907
123. Jadwiga Puzynina, Normative studies in Poland . . . . . . . . . . . 912
124. Tiborc Fazekas, Normativ orientierte Sprachforschung in Ungarn . . . . . . . . . . . . . . . . . . . . . . . . . . . . . . . . . . . 916
125. Arnold Cassola, Normative studies in Malta . . . . . . . . . . . . . 919

## XX. The Study of 'Exotic' Languages by Europeans<br>Die Europäer und die 'exotischen' Sprachen<br>La connaissance des langues 'exotiques'

126. Even Hovdhaugen, The Great Travelers and the studies of 'exotic languages' . . . . . . . . . . . . . . . . . . . . . . . . . . . . . 925
127. Edward G. Gray, Missionary linguistics and the description of 'exotic' languages . . . . . . . . . . . . . . . . . . . . . . . . . . . . 929
128. Leonardo Manrique, Das Studium der autochtonen Sprachen Zentralamerikas: Nahuatl . . . . . . . . . . . . . . . . . . . . . . . 937
129. Wolfgang Wölck / Utta von Gleich, Das Studium der Eingeborenensprachen Südamerikas: Ketschua . . . . . . . . . . . . 950
130. Wolf Dietrich, Das Studium der Eingeborenensprachen Südamerikas: Guaraní . . . . . . . . . . . . . . . . . . . . . . . . . . 960
131. John Hewson, The study of the native languages of North America: The French tradition . . . . . . . . . . . . . . . . . . . . . 966
132. Elke Nowak, First descriptive approaches to indigenous languages of British North America . . . . . . . . . . . . . . . . . . 973
133. Wilhelm J. G. Möhlig, Das Studium der schwarzafrikanischen Sprachen . . . . . . . . . . . . . . . . . . . . . . . . . . . . . . . . . 980
134. Jean-Luc Chevillard, Das Studium der Eingeborensprachen des indischen Ozeans: Frühe Kontakte mit dem Sanskrit und den dravidischen Sprachen (entfallen)
135. Wei Chiao / Magnus Kriegeskorte, Das Studium der Sprachen des Fernen Ostens: Chinesisch . . . . . . . . . . . . . . . . . . . . . 991
136. Jean-Claude Rivière, La connaissance du malais et des langues de l'Océanie . . . . . . . . . . . . . . . . . . . . . . . . . . . . . . . . . 998

## XXI. Theories of Grammar and Language Philosophy in the 17th and 18th Centuries<br>Grammatiktheorien und Sprachphilosophie im 17. und 18. Jahrhundert<br>Théories grammaticales et philosophie de langage aux XVIIe et XVIIIe siècles

137. Claire Lecointre, Les transformations de l'héritage médiéval dans l'Europe du XVIIe siècle . . . . . . . . . . . . . . . . . . . . . . 1002

138. Jean Caravolas, Les origines de la didactique des langues en tant que discipline autonome . . . . . . . . . . . . . . . . . . . . . . . . . . 1009
139. Sylvain Aroux, Port-Royal et la tradition française de la grammaire générale . . . . . . . . . . . . . . . . . . . . . . . . . . 1022
140. David F. Cram / Jaap Maat, Universal language schemes in the 17th century . . . . . . . . . . . . . . . . . . . . . . . . . . 1030
141. Bernd Naumann, Die 'Allgemeine Sprachwissenschaft' um die Wende zum 19. Jahrhundert . . . . . . . . . . . . . . . . . . . . 1044

XXII. Ideas on the Origin of Language and Languages from the 16th to the 19th Centuries
Vorstellungen vom Sprachursprung und vom Ursprung der Sprachen (16.–18. Jahrhundert)
Conceptions de l'origine des langues et du langage du XVIe au XVIIIe siècle

142. Daniel Droixhe, Les conceptions du changement et de la parenté des langues européennes aux XVIIe et XVIIIe siècles . . . . . . . . 1057
143. Klaus D. Dutz / Ludger Kaczmarek, Vorstellungen über den Ursprung von Sprachen im 16. und 17. Jahrhundert . . . . . . . . 1071
144. Harald Haarmann, Die großen Sprachensammlungen vom frühen 18. bis frühen 19. Jahrhundert. . . . . . . . . . . . . . . . . . 1081

Volume 2 / 2. Teilband / Tome 2

XXIII. Studies of the Antecedents to and Connections between National Languages
Vorstellungen von der Entstehung der Nationalsprachen und ihren Beziehungen zueinander
Études des origines et des rapports des langues nationales

145. Werner Bahner, Frühe dialektologische, etymologische und sprachgeschichtliche Forschungen in Spanien
146. William Jervis Jones, Early dialectology, etymology and language history in German speaking countries
147. Jan Noordegraaf, Historical linguistics in the Low Countries: Lambert ten Kate
148. Even Hovdhaugen, The study of early Germanic languages in Scandinavia: Ihre, Stiernhielm
149. Robin Smith, Investigating older Germanic languages in England
150. Roger Comtet, L'étude des langues slaves en Russie: M. L. Lomonosov

151. Tiborc Fazekas, Die Entdeckung der Verwandtschaft der finno-ugrischen Sprachen

152. Rosane Rocher, The knowledge of Sanskrit in Europe until 1800

## XXIV. Historical and Comparative Linguistics of the Early 19th Century
## Die historische und vergleichende Sprachwissenschaft zu Beginn des 19. Jahrhunderts
## La linguistique historique et comparative au début du XIXe siècle

153. Kurt R. Jankowsky, The renewal of the study of the classical languages within the university system, notably in Germany

154. Kurt R. Jankowsky, The establishment of oriental language studies in France, Britain, and Germany

155. Jean Rousseau, La genèse de la grammaire comparée au début du XIXe siècle

156. N. E. Collinge, The introduction of the historical principle into the study of languages

157. Theodora Bynon, The synthesis of comparative and historical Indo-European studies: August Schleicher

## XXV. The Establishment of New Philologies in the 19th Century
## Die Herausbildung neuer Philologien im 19. Jahrhundert
## Le développement des nouvelles philologies au XIXe siècle

158. Jürgen Storost, Die 'neuen Philologien', ihre Institutionen und Periodica: Eine Übersicht

159. Pierre Swiggers, L'origine et le développement de la philologie romane

160. Uwe Meves, Die Entstehung und frühe Entwicklung der Germanischen Philologie

161. Karl Gutschmidt, Die Entstehung und frühe Entwicklung der Slavischen Philologie

162. Tiborc Fazekas, Finno-ugrische Philologie und vergleichende Grammatik

163. Rainer Voigt, Semitische Philologie und vergleichende Grammatik

## XXVI. Indo-European Philology and Historical Linguistics and their Legacy
## Indo-europäische Philologie, Historische Sprachwissenschaft und ihr Erbe
## La philologie indo-européenne et la linguistique historique et leurs legs

164. Kurt R. Jankowsky, The crisis of historical-comparative linguistics in the 1860s
165. Eveline Einhauser, Die Entstehung und frühe Entwicklung des junggrammatischen Forschungsprogramms
166. Kurt R. Jankowsky, Consolidation of the neogrammarian framework
167. Wilhelm J. G. Möhlig, Die Anwendung der 'vergleichenden Methode' auf afrikanische Sprachen
168. Robert A. Blust, The 'comparative method' applied to Austronesian languages
169. John Hewson, The 'comparative method' applied to Amerindian: The reconstruction of Proto-Algonkian
170. Catherine Bereznak/Lyle Campbell, The 'comparative method' as applied to other non-Indo-European languages

## XXVII. Language Typology, Language Classification, and the Search for Universals
## Sprachtypologie, die Klassifizierung der Sprachen und die Suche nach sprachlichen Universalien
## La typologie linguistique, la classification des langues et la recherche des universaux

171. Frans Plank, Language typology by the end of the 18th century
172. Jean Rousseau, La classification des langues au début du XIXe siècle
173. Manfred Ringmacher, Die Klassifizierung der Sprachen in der Mitte des 19. Jahrhunderts
174. Manfred Ringmacher, Sprachtypologie und Ethnologie in Europa am Ende des 19. Jahrhunderts
175. Regna Darnell, Language typology and ethnology in 19th-century North America: Gallatin, Brinton, Powell
176. George Yonek/Lyle Campbell, Language typology in the 20th century: From Sapir to late 20th century approaches
177. Bernard Comrie, Theories of universal grammar in the late 20th century

## XXVIII. The Analysis of Speech and Unwritten Languages in the 19th Century and its Continuation in the 20th Century
## Die Erforschung der lautlichen Äußerung und nicht verschrifteter Sprachen im 19. und die Fortsetzung im 20. Jahrhundert
## L'étude de la parole et des langues non-écrites pendant le XIXe siècle et sa continuation au XXe siècle


178. J. Alan Kemp, The development of phonetics from the late 18th to the late 19th century
179. Even Hovdhaugen, Field work and data-elicitation of unwritten languages for descriptive and comparative purposes: Strahlenberg, Sjögren, Castrén, Böthlingk
180. Enrica Galazzi, Physiologie de la parole et phonétique appliquée au XIXe et au début du XXe siècle
181. Wolfgang Putschke, Die Dialektologie, ihr Beitrag zur historischen Sprachwissenschaft im 19. Jahrhundert und Kritik am junggrammatischen Programm
182. Joachim Herrgen, Die Dialektologie des Deutschen
183. Marinel Gerritsen, The dialectology of Dutch
184. Graham Shorrocks, The dialectology of English in the British Isles
185. Tom M. S. Priestly, Dialectology in the Slavic countries: An overview from its beginnings to the early 20th century
186. J. Alan Kemp, The history and development of a universal phonetic alphabet in the 19th century: From the beginnings to the establishment of the IPA
187. Michael K. C. MacMahon, Modern language instruction and phonetics in the late 19th century


## XXIX. Approaches to Semantics in 19th and the First Third of the 20th Century
## Ansätze zur Semantik im 19. und im ersten Drittel des 20. Jahrhunderts
## Les approches à la sémantique au XIXe et au premier tiers du XXe siècle


188. Brigitte Nerlich, The renewal of semantic questions in the 19th century: The work of Karl Christian Reisig and his successors
189. Brigitte Nerlich, The development of semasiology in Europe: A survey from the second half of the 19th to the first third of the 20th century
190. Johannes Kramer, Die frühe Entwicklung des onomasiologischen Ansatzes in der Sprachwissenschaft und Lexikographie des 19. Jahrhunderts

191. Brigitte Nerlich, The study of meaning change from Reisig to Bréal
192. Wolfgang Settekorn, Die Forschungsrichtung 'Wörter und Sachen'
193. W. Terrence Gordon, The origin and development of the theory of the 'semantic field'

## XXX. Psychology and Physiology in 19th-Century Linguistics
Psychologische und physiologische Ansätze in der Sprachwissenschaft des 19. Jahrhunderts
La psychologie et la physiologie dans la linguistique du XIXe siècle

194. Clemens Knobloch, Die Beziehungen zwischen Sprache und Denken: Die Ideen Wilhelm von Humboldts und die Anfänge der sprachpsychologischen Forschung
195. David J. Murray, Language and psychology: 19th-century developments outside Germany: A survey
196. Gabriel Bergounioux, Le langage et le cerveau: la localisation de la faculté du langage et l'étude des aphasies
197. Clemens Knobloch, Psychologische Ansätze bei der Erforschung des frühkindlichen Spracherwerbs

## XXXI. Structural Linguistics in the 20th Century
Der europäische Strukturalismus im 20. Jahrhundert
Le structuralisme européen au XXe siècle

198. Manfred Kohrt/Kerstin Kuchaczik, Die Wurzeln des Strukturalismus in der Sprachwissenschaft des 19. Jahrhunderts
199. René Amacker, La dimension synchronique dans la théorie linguistique de Saussure
200. René Amacker, Le développement des idées saussuriennes par l'école de Genève: Bally, Sechehaye
201. Tsutomu Akamatsu, The development of functionalism from the Prague School to the present
202. Jørgen Rischl, The Cercle linguistique de Copenhague and glossematics
203. David G. Butt, Firth, Halliday, and the development of systemic-functional theories
204. Giorgio Graffi, The emphasis on syntax in the early phase of European structuralism: Ries, Jespersen, Mathesius, Guillaume, Tesnière
205. Heinz J. Weber, Die Entwicklung der Dependenzgrammatik und verwandter Theorien in der 2. Hälfte des 20. Jahrhunderts
206. Ulrich Püschel, Linguistische Ansätze in der Stilistik des 20. Jahrhunderts
207. John E. Joseph, The exportation of structuralist ideas from linguistics to other fields: An overview

## XXXII. Traditions of Descriptive Linguistics in America
Der amerikanische Deskriptivismus
La linguistique descriptive aux États-Unis

208. Stephen O. Murray, The ethnolinguistic tradition in 19th-century America: From the earliest beginnings to Boas
209. Stephen G. Alter, The linguistic legacy of William Dwight Whitney
210. Stephen O. Murray, Attempts at professionalization of American linguistics in the 20th century, and the role of the Linguistic Society of America
211. Victor Golla, The Sapirian approach to language
212. John G. Fought, The Bloomfield school and descriptive linguistics
213. John R. Costello, Tagmemics and the analysis of non-verbal behavior: Pike and his school
214. John Fought, Distributionalism and immediate constituent analysis in American linguistics
215. Sheila Embleton, Quantitative methods and lexicostatistics in the 20th century

Volume 3 / 3. Teilband / Tome 3
(Preview of Contents / Vorgesehener Inhalt / Table des matières prévus)

## XXXIII. Formalization Tendencies and Mathematization in 20th-Century Linguistics, Generative Grammar, and Alternative Approaches
Formalisierungstendenzen und Mathematisierung in der Sprachwissenschaft des 20. Jahrhunderts, die Generative Grammatik und ihre Alternativen
Les tendances vers la formalisation et la mathématisation des théories linguistiques au XXe siècle, la grammaire générative et ses alternatives

The axiomatic method in 20th-century European linguistics

Early tendencies of formalization in 20th-century American linguistics (e. g., Harris, Hockett)

Origin and development of the Chomskyan program: Generative linguistics to 1965

Le développement des grammaires catégorielles et applicatives: Bar-Hillel, Shaumyan

The development of stratificational grammar

The evolution of generative linguistics, 1965–1978

The development of Montague-Grammar

The development of case grammars in the 20th century (Fillmore, Simmons, Grimes, Shank)

Gouvernement et liage; principes et paramètres: la linguistique générative depuis 1978

The development of alternative approaches to generative linguistics: An overview (relational grammar, generalized phrase structure grammar, etc.)

Le développement des grammaires à orientation lexicale

## XXXIV. The development of Theories of Semantics, of the Lexicon, and Semantic-Based Theories in the 20th Century
## Die Entwicklung von Theorien zur Semantik, zum Lexikon und von semantisch orientierten Grammatiken
## Le développement des théorie de la sémantique, du lexique et des grammaires sémantiques

Die Zeichentheorie F. de Saussures und die Semantik im 20. Jahrhundert: Ein Überblick

Die Wortfeldtheorie unter dem Einfluß des Strukturalismus

Die Entwicklung der inhaltbezogenen Grammatik in Deutschland: Leo Weisgeber und seine Schule

Die europäische Onomasiologie in der zweiten Hälfte des 20. Jahrhunderts und ihr Verhältnis zur Semasiologie

Die sinnrelationale Semantik als Alternative zur Merkmalsemantik

Research on semantic change after Hermann Paul

The development of sentence-oriented semantic approaches within the generative framework

Semantic theories in 20th-century America: An overview of the different approaches outside of generative grammar: Nida, Goodenough, Lounsbury, Weinreich et al.

Semantic considerations in recent onomastic research: A survey

Semantik und Lexikographie im 20. Jahrhundert

Lexikologie als Theorie des Lexikons einer Grammatik: Eine Übersicht über neuere Entwicklungen

XXXV. Phonology and Morphology in the Later 20th Century
Jüngere Forschungen zur Phonologie und Morphologie
La phonologie et la morphologie au XXe siècle tardif

La phonologie générative jusqu'en 1975

La phonologie générative naturelle et la phonologie naturelle

Autosegmental phonology and underspecification theory

The development of lexical phonology

Le développement de la phonologie prosodique et de la phonologie métrique

Les théories morphologiques dans la linguistique de la fin XXe siècle

Morphologie comme formation des mots au XXe siècle: un survol

Jüngere Entwicklungen in der natürlichen Morphologie

XXXVI. The Study of Language Differenciation in the 20th Century
Die Erforschung der sprachlichen Variation im 20. Jahrhundert
L'étude de la différentiation linguistique au XXe siècle

Homogenität und Heterogenität der Sprache: Die Entwicklung der Diskussion im 20. Jahrhundert

Neuere Entwicklungen in der europäischen Dialektologie

Recent developments in North American dialectology

Die Erforschung der sozialen Variation von Sprachen: Ein Überblick zur Entwicklung in Europa

The analysis of social differenciation of languages: An overview of the development in North America

The development of creolistics and the study of pidgins

Kontaktlinguistik, Sprachkonfliktforschung und Sprachplanung: Überblick über die Tendenzen im 20. Jahrhundert

## XXXVII. Historical Linguistics in the Second Half of the 20th Century
Die historische Sprachwissenschaft in der zweiten Hälfte des 20. Jahrhunderts
La linguistique historique dans la deuxième moitié du XXe siècle

The place of historical linguistics in the age of structuralism

Konzepte von der Historizität von Sprachen und von Sprachgeschichte

The investigation of diachronic variety in languages: Traditions and recent developments

Les tendances et les traditions de la lexicographie de la seconde moitié du XXe siècle

The laryngeal and the glottalic theories

Modern theories of linguistic change: An overview

## XXXVIII. Critique of Traditional Linguistics and the Development of New Approaches to Language Analysis
Kritik an der traditionellen Sprachwissenschaft und Neuansätze in der Sprachforschung
Critiques et dépassement de la linguistique traditionelle et le développement d'approches neuves au langage

Die Sprachphilosophie Wittgensteins und die Sprachwisssenschaft in der zweiten Hälfte des 20. Jahrhunderts

The interface of linguistics and pragmatics: Its development during the second half of the 20th century

Die Rezeption und Weiterentwicklung der angelsächsischen Sprechakttheorie in der Sprachwissenschaft

Ursprung und Entwicklung der Textlinguistik

Die Rezeption der soziologischen Konversationsanalyse und Ansätze zu einer linguistischen Gesprächsforschung

Le développement des théories énonciatives: Antoine Culioli et son école

## XXXIX. 20th-Century Linguistics and Adjacent Fields of Study: Perspectives and Developments
## Die Sprachwissenschaft und ihre Nachbarwissenschaften: Ausschnitte aus der Entwicklung ihrer Beziehungen im 20. Jahrhundert
## La linguistique et les disciplines voisines au XXe siècle: Perspectives et développements


The ontology and epistemology of linguistics

Linguistics and semiotics I: The impact of Ogden & Richards' *Meaning of Meaning*

Linguistics and semiotics II: C. S. Peirce's influence on 20th-century linguistics

Linguistics and logic I: The influence of Frege and Russell on semantic theory

Sprachwissenschaft und Logik II: Der Einfluß der Quantorenlogik und ihrer Semantik auf die sprachwissenschaftliche Theoriebildung

Sprachwissenschaft und Philosophie I: Der Einfluß der Stereotypentheorie von Hilary Putnam und ihre Rezeption und Weiterentwicklung in der Semantik

Sprachwissenschaft und Philosophie II: Der Einfluß von H. P. Grice auf die Theoriebildung zur sprachlichen Kommunikation

La linguistique et la rhétorique: Un aperçu historique de leurs rapports reciproques au XXe siècle

Sprachwissenschaft und Psychologie I: Ein historischer Überblick über das Verhältnis von Sprache und Denken im 20. Jahrhundert

Linguistique et psychologie II: La théorie des prototypes d'Eleonore Rosch, sa réception critique à l'inténeur de la psychologie et sa réception dans la semantique linguistique

Le langage et les processus cérébraux I: La neurolinguistique du XXe siècle, de l'aphasiologie localiste aux sciences cognitives

Le langage et les processus cérébraux II: Un aperçu du développement de la pathologie du langage au XXe siècle

L'acquisition du langage I: Un aperçu du développement des conceptions de l'apprentissage d'une langue mère au XXe siècle

Language acquisition II: Second language acquisition research in the 20th century

La phonétique au XXe siècle: Un aperçu historique des tendances majeures de son développement

Sprache und Technologie: Die Entstehung neuer Anwendungsfelder sprachwissenschaftlicher Forschung im 20. Jahrhundert

La recherche concernant les langues spéciales et scientifiques: Un aperçu de son développement au XXe siècle

La traduction automatique I: Les premières tentatives jusqu'au rapport ALPAC

La traduction automatique II: Développements récents

Linguistics and artificial intelligence

Language and biology: A survey of problems and principles of biolinguistics

Integrational tendencies in linguistic theory

XL. History of Linguistics – The Field
Die Geschichte der Sprachwissenschaften: Umrisse der Disziplin
Le domaine de l'histoire de la linguistique

Hans-Josef Niederehe, Die Entwicklung der Geschichte der Sprachwissenschaft als Forschungsobjekt

Kees Versteegh, The study of non-Western traditions and its relationship to mainstream linguistic historiography

Sylvain Auroux, Théorie et méthodologie de l'histoire de la linguistique

E. F. K. Koerner, The history of linguistics, its professionalization, and its place within linguistics

XLI. Indexes / Register / Indexes

Index of names / Namenregister / Index des noms
Index of subjects / Sachregister / Index des matières
Index of languages / Sprachenregister / Index des langues

# Editors' Foreword

## 1. General introduction

### 1.1 Definition

In this Handbook the term 'history of the language sciences' will be used to denote the development of linguistic theories (ideas, proposals of analysis, explanations, methodological frameworks) as well as the organizational structures of their implementation, dissemination and teaching throughout the documented history of humankind. The regular use of the term 'linguistics' in this Handbook should not be taken as in any way implying a strict definition of the field. In a strict sense the term might be taken to be applicable only to the modern period in which linguistics was recognized as a separate discipline with its own well-defined principles of research and professional organization. However, in many linguistic traditions a special place was assigned within the general scheme of knowledge to the science that dealt with language. Even though the delimitation of this science with respect to topics and methods may differ between traditions, in a general sense these traditions are all related in that they regard language as a subject to be studied in its own right. 'Linguistics' will therefore be used as a general term for everything connected with the study of human speech. Obviously, the circumscription of the field itself is one of the topics to be dealt with in the analysis of its history, as will the subdivision of the field into various branches as well as its connection with other disciplines.

In most branches of linguistics an historical introduction surveying the development of the discipline has always been standard practice. Accordingly, most of the other handbooks in the present series contain historical chapters, whose main purpose is to sketch the development of a particular line of research leading up to contemporary commitments. This purpose differs, of course, from the one adopted in the present Handbook, which aims at the presentation of linguistic theories, of both past and present, in their own right. The focus in this presentation is on the explanation of their development, in terms of their own internal dynamic as well as in terms of external factors of social and cultural development in the society in which they are embedded.

As in all histories of a particular field, the relationship between the discipline to be studied, on the one hand, and the discipline which analyzes on a metalevel its methods, presuppositions and historical development, on the other, is a complex one. Linguistic historiography, as the discipline which analyzes the development of linguistics, has to be distinguished carefully from the object of its study. Although most historiographers of linguistics are themselves linguists, their goal must be different from that of linguists in that they attempt to explain the development of linguistics without passing value judgments of the theories involved. Typically, historiographers of linguistics aim at the elucidation of lines of development within the field within a particular cultural, socio-economic or political setting, and their interaction with other disciplines at different points in time, avoiding any kind of 'tunnel vision'.

Fundamentally, the aim of the historiography of linguistics differs from that of linguistics in that the historiographer does not aim at the elucidation of linguistic facts, but rather, at the elucidation of how scholars in different traditions approached the problems of language structure and language use. This also means that for the historiographer all approaches are equally relevant: there is no value scale in these approaches, let alone a cumulative development of the discipline up till the present time. For the historiographer, the past of the discipline cannot serve as the legitimation of its present state.

## 1.2 Scope

In the definition given above, the coverage of the Handbook has already been indicated as presenting all ideas about language and languages within the context of their development. It attempts to encompass as much as possible all studies, theoretical and practical, of language as a means of human communication throughout history. With the inclusion of practical studies we aim in particular at examining the work done in (pedagogical) grammar, lexicography, translation and any other activity concerned with language, analyzed as a function of the historical setting in which they took place.

There is one important exclusion to be mentioned here. The Handbook will only deal with those studies of language that have been laid down in written form of some kind. This means that so-called folk-linguistics has been reserved for other handbooks, such as the one dealing with Sociolinguistics. The same exclusion applies to empirical studies concerned with language attitudes: although language attitudes play an important role in the establishment of linguistic ideas and theories, they have been dealt with only insofar as they are mentioned explicitly in linguistic treatises.

Obviously, certain overlaps between individual handbooks in the present series have been inevitable. For instance, it is not always possible to distinguish sharply between the subject matter of the History of Linguistics and that of the Philosophy of Language, in particular in some of the non-Western traditions such as Chinese or Sanskrit, in which linguistics and philosophy of language are linked inextricably. As a result, both the present Handbook and the one dealing with the Philosophy of Language contain historical sections on major philosophical traditions dealing with language. In the case of the ancient Greek tradition, for instance, the work of Plato, Aristotle and the Stoics, or the work of the late medieval language philosophers is also studied in the present Handbook, though from the perspective of their relevance for the study of language, rather than merely touching upon the interface between philosophy and linguistics.

An important aspect of the present Handbook is its dedicated attempt at a complete coverage, both geographically and chronologically, of all linguistic traditions. This means that every effort has been made to go far beyond the traditional Eurocentric accounts which typically include a section on the work of the Sanskrit grammarians because (and only inasmuch as) they have become a point of interest to the discovery of the Indo-European language family, or a section on classical Arabic linguistics as an alibi rather than because a dedicated effort is made to break through the Western (claim to) hegemony. Alternatively, when non-Western traditions have been incorporated in recent years into general histories of linguistics, the emphasis has usually been on major figures, such as Pāṇini (for Sanskrit) or Sībawayhi (for Arabic). Our aim in the present Handbook has been to include as much as possible all linguistic traditions, both major and minor ones, in an effort to offer a picture that is as complete as possible of all different forms the study of language has taken throughout the centuries. Obviously, this ideal has not always been reached: for some traditions the documentation is insufficient. Thus, for instance, we were unable to include articles on the Ethiopian or the Cambodian linguistic tradition, to mention just two examples. In other cases, we were forced to cancel an article for purely practical reasons since it turned out to be impossible to find a competent author or the author we had invited could not deliver the article in time for inclusion in the Handbook.

A major problem has been the chronological delimitation of the Handbook with regard to the contemporary period. Although it would no doubt have been simpler to exclude recent developments in linguistics, we have decided not to take this course. It goes without saying that the historiographical analysis of contemporary linguistics can only be undertaken with special caution, even more so when those surveying the development of a given sub-branch of the field are also engaged in purely linguistic research and thus may find it difficult to detach themselves from their own research activities. In the subdivision of the subject matter in the final chapters of the Handbook and in the choice of authors we have tried to steer away as much as possible from biased accounts of modern currents and developments. At the same time, we believe that by presenting recent developments from a historiographical perspective we contribute towards a better understanding of the place and importance of a historical perspective to current pursuits within the discipline.

### 1.3 Themes

The editors of the present Handbook have attempted to deviate, as much as possible, from the traditional treatment that depicts the history of linguistics through a succession of great men, even if at times, especially for 19th and 20th century linguistics, such an approach imposed itself. However, it is not clear whether this would hold for earlier periods in the West or much earlier linguistic activity in the East. Even in cases where the articles focus on the contributions of individual linguists, the emphasis is on the specific themes, lines of linguistic thinking, research commitments and the connection of the individual linguist with the development of the tradition.

Given the enormous diversity, geographical, chronological, and thematic, of all the traditions involved, it is rather difficult to identify central themes that guide the approach taken here. However, we may point to the following considerations which underlie the selection of topics, the presentation of the subject matter as well as the organization and analysis of the material.

A central theme is the analysis of the development of linguistics in terms of 'mainstream' and 'undercurrent'. The organization of linguistic research in the Western tradition is such that, although it is possible to distinguish in each period research programs with a general validity for a large part of the scholarly community, there has never been a monopoly of one 'paradigm' over another. In contrast to the usual presentation of the history of the sciences, changes of direction do not normally take place in the form of sudden collapses of previous commitments and revolutionary innovations, but more often than not as a gradual alternation between 'mainstream' preoccupations and 'undercurrent' developments. This implies that along with the paradigm prevalent during a given period, other research programs (if such a modern concept can usefully be applied to earlier centuries) usually remain in force as more or less marginal movements within the scholarly community, at least one of which frequently returns to the foreground in the course of time and develops into a new 'mainstream' preoccupation.

In connection with the view of the history of linguistics just sketched, it is worth mentioning here that there appears to be at least one constant alternation between two diametrically opposed views on the methodology of the discipline of linguistics. Periods in which language is treated as an ideal structure, used in an ideal communicative situation with an ideal speaker/hearer, alternate with periods in which attention focuses on the variety and variability inherent in the phenomenon of speech. This alternation is very obvious in the 19th century, for example in the interaction between the comparative framework and the emergence of dialectology as the study of speech variety. The mainstream/undercurrent treatment of history suggests that both tendencies never completely supplanted each other, but always coexisted in varying degrees of monopolization vs. marginalization. In 20th-century linguistics one can observe a very similar alternation between the prevalent emphasis on the systematic and ideal structure of language and a seemingly growing interest in phenomena of variation in human speech and the function of language in actual communicative situations.

The mainstream/undercurrent dichotomy may also be seen to apply to more or less all linguistic activities in language departments all over the world. Regardless of the prevailing paradigms, linguists continue to occupy themselves with the grammar, history, lexicon, and structure of individual languages or language families. This, too, is part of the total picture of the history of linguistics, and must be included in a Handbook like the present, along with the practical aspects of linguistic study mentioned earlier.

One overriding concern has been the desire to avoid any kind of *Systemzwang* in the classification of the material and the subdivision in chapters and articles. The large number of contributors with differing backgrounds and areas of specialization should guarantee a broad choice of perspectives. Any attempt to force the analysis of the history of linguistics into a narrow classificatory scheme is bound to fail; such an attempt would distort the facts and obscure the developmental changes in each tradition. As mentioned above, a biographical approach has been avoided, but even so some articles have been included devoted to the achievements and ideas of one personality or one particular group of scholars within the context of an overall picture of the development.

The absence of a narrow organizational frame has another consequence for the presentation of the material. We have not made a choice between a data-oriented and a theory-oriented approach, since we believe that an exclusive choice in favor of either approach would have led to a biased perspective and a distorted picture of the linguistic activity in any culture. In some instances, it turned out to be more appropriate to focus on the results and products of a theory or a period; in other instances, the analysis of the methods, presuppositions and underlying principles of a research program provided a better picture of the tradition involved. Indeed, these two approaches complement each other in the analysis of the different trends and lines of developments in the history of the language sciences.

### 1.4 State of the art

Although the scope of the present Handbook is unprecedented, it builds on the result of earlier scholarship to some extent. As a separate discipline with its own professional organization, journals, and series, the historiography of the language sciences may be said to have started in the late 1960s and early 1970s. This does not mean that prior to the 1960s there were no histories of linguistics. In several non-Western traditions histories of the discipline were a standard component of the curriculum. Arab grammarians, for instance, made use of large biographical dictionaries in which the work of earlier grammarians was discussed. Such histories were dedicated exclusively to the history of one tradition only. In Western linguistics, historical introductions were usually connected with the treatment of specific languages or language groups, or in conjunction with studies devoted to particular linguistic topics, for instance phonology or semantics, where earlier endeavours were delineated.

Yet general surveys of the history of linguistic theory have been produced earlier than the 1960s, perhaps beginning with François Thurot's "Tableau des progrès de la science grammaticale" attached as *Discours preliminaire* to his 1796 translation of James Harris' *Hermes* (1751) which has been suggested to constitute "a first attempt at a historiography of grammar". Important historical accounts appeared by the mid-19th century, beginning with the 3-volume *Die Sprachphilosophie der Alten* by Laurenz Lersch (1838–41). Indeed, classical philology dominated the field, to the exclusion not only of traditions other than those of the Greeks, Romans, and possibly that of the Ancient Indians, but also of the more recent periods in the history of linguistic thought, from the Middle Ages to the present. A typical example of this is Steinthal's *Geschichte der Sprachwissenschaft bei den Griechen und Römern* (1863) which largely deals with language philosophy, not linguistics proper.

The last third of the 19th century witnessed the beginning of history-writing of these later periods in the works of Benfey (1869), Raumer (1870), Delbrück (1880, especially from the 4th ed. of 1904 onwards), and Bursian (1883), though generally conceived with a presentist bias. The Eurocentric treatment of past linguistic ideas has prevailed to the present day, though treatises on the development of Hebrew and Arabic grammar have begun to appear from the late 19th century onwards. Although the 1960s saw the publication of a fairly large number of textbooks devoted to the history of linguistics, it appears that only during the 1970s a greater awareness of the desirability of a much wider scope began to emerge. This newer trend is evident in the 2-volume *Historiography of Linguistics* undertaking published in 1975 as the last volume of the "Current Trends in Linguistics" series edited by Thomas A. Sebeok, which also includes surveys of linguistic traditions in the Far East and the Americas. It should be noted, however, that 'historiography' in most of the contributions to these volumes is understood as overviews of the "recent literature devoted to the history of the study of language" during the respective periods of Western linguistics or the non-Western traditions more generally, and not to actual history-writing as the term usually implies.

The present project follows instead the line of historiography of linguistic thought as has become more clearly articulated since the appearance, late in 1973, of the first journal exclusively devoted to the subject, *Historiographia Linguistica*. It was soon followed by the launching of regional as well as international societies for the history of the language sciences and the organization of scholarly meetings both in Europe and North America in which not only particular past linguistic theories were discussed and certain traditions presented but also questions of methodology and epistemology of historiographical research and presentation were addressed. The advances made in recent years in this field of study are best seen in the contributions to *Historiographia Linguistica*, the journals *Histoire – Épistémologie – Langage* (Paris, 1979–) and *Beiträge zur Geschichte der Sprachwissenschaft* (Münster, 1991–), and the proceedings of the triennial International Conference on the History of the Language Sciences (ICHoLS). The 1980s, finally, saw the publication of monographs devoted to questions of philosophy, theory, and method of linguistic historiography that have guided much of recent research. These debates are continuing.

About the time the present project was first discussed, Peter Schmitter launched his *Geschichte der Sprachtheorie* (Tübingen, 1987–), a monograph series covering various areas and periods in the history of linguistics, of which 4 have thus far been published (of altogether 9 projected volumes). With comparable goals, Sylvain Auroux has brought together a 3-volume *Histoire des idées linguistiques* (Brussels, 1990–2000), followed by a 5-volume *History of Linguistics* edited by Giulio Lepschy (London, 1994–). In the meantime, E. F. K. Koerner and R. E. Asher brought out their 500-page *Concise History of the Language Sciences: From the Sumerians to the Cognitivists* (Oxford, 1995), which not only offers a survey of the most important traditions but also a fairly up-to-date treatment of the various schools, theories, and strands in 20th-century linguistics not found in any of these multi-volume histories. We will have to wait until the publication of tome III of the present project for a fuller account of 20th-century linguistic science.

For information on the large majority of the main figures in the history of world linguistics the 1,000-page *Lexicon grammaticorum* (Tübingen, 1996), directed by Harro Stammerjohann, will be the main sourcebook for many years to come.

## 1.5 Structure of the Handbook

The Handbook has for the most part been organized in terms of chronological development. It was necessary to depart from this principle especially in the chapters devoted to the various non-Western traditions, which are depicted in parallel fashion, irrespective of chronology, although they often constitute independent traditions in geographically separate places. In some cases where the main impetus for the establishment of a tradition was derived from foreign influence, the treatment of this tradition has been connected with that of the mother tradition. This decision was taken, for instance, in the case of Armenian and Georgian linguistics, which are dealt within the chapter on the Greek tradition, or Coptic and Turkic linguistics, which are dealt with in the chapter on the Arabic tradition, and Vietnamese linguistics, which is dealt within the chapter on the Chinese tradition. Since most traditions at one time or another have undergone the influence of other traditions, this division has a certain arbitrariness and should not be taken as a judgment on the intrinsic value of the tradition in question.

The Greek and Latin traditions have been instrumental in the development of the Western linguistic tradition, but are treated here independently from their role in the post-Renaissance period. The indebtedness of post-Renaissance linguistics to Greek and Latin grammar is obvious, but the continuity between them has sometimes been exaggerated: there is certainly more to Greek and Latin grammar than just a preparation for mainstream Western linguistics. From the Greek and Latin linguistic traditions onwards chronological treatment has been kept more consistently down to the end of the Middle Ages.

Thereafter the Handbook describes the prevalent modes of Western linguistics, beginning with the period in which the Western European vernaculars began to be used both as objects and as media of research, i.e., as metalanguages. From this time onwards linguistic study is no longer concerned with a single language as object and as point of reference. The geographic spread of these ideas and research practices throughout Europe, the Americas and beyond after 1500, and their subsequent modification has severely tested a chronological treatment.

Another important change in the history of linguistics occurred during the 19th century through the development of comparative and historical linguistics as a dominant paradigm of the period. The shift towards synchronic linguistics at the beginning of the 20th century has become characteristic of the entire century. As the theories and methods of these two centuries have been exported to most of the non-Indo-European countries ever since they first emerged, they receive broad treatment in the present Handbook.

The presentation of the history of the language sciences in the West along established lines (Middle Ages, Renaissance, Enlightenment, 19th century, 20th century) has at times been challenged. In the present Handbook the chronological labels have been maintained for practical reasons; however, the subdivision into chapters has been determined by a thematic ordering of the subject, in terms of the mainstream/undercurrent dichotomy referred to above as well as other considerations of substance. For the most recent developments in linguistics a chronological ordering was, of course, out of the question; we have attempted here to concentrate on the methodological similarities and differences between existing theories as well as on the connections between linguistics and related disciplines (sociology, psychology, neurology, logic, mathematics, etc.). This aspect of the interrelatedness of linguistics within the human sciences is, indeed, one of the most characteristic features of modern linguistics.

## 2. Description of Individual Chapters

Chapter I deals with the Near Eastern traditions, in which the study of language mostly consisted in the study of the writing system and the lexicon. On the other hand, the coexistence of various stages of the language, or of several cultural languages, forced the specialists to occupy themselves with the codification of grammar as well.

Chapter II deals with the Chinese tradition. Most of the linguistic activities in China concentrated on phonology and lexicology, but in relation with philosophical theories a number of important ideas about the nature of the linguistic sign, both phonic and graphic, were developed. Preoccupation with language as a literary medium played, of course, an important role in Chinese society. Two linguistic traditions, namely, those of Korea and Japan, dealt with in Chapters III and IV, incorporated the Chinese heritage to a large extent. In the situation of bilinguialism which persisted in both areas, there was room for a contrastive analysis of grammatical systems. In the case of the Japanese tradition, an interesting aspect was the introduction of Dutch grammar as a model in the period called Rangakusha.

Chapter V is devoted to one of the major non-Western traditions, that of India. The Sanskrit tradition has received quite a lot of attention in recent linguistic literature, since it boasts the first attempt to give a complete description of a language with the help of a linguistic formalism, Pāṇini's *Astādhyāyī*. An important aspect of the Indian tradition is the relation between linguistics, logic and philosophy. Two sections are devoted to the use of the Indian model in Old Javanese and Burmese. Indian grammar played an important role in the development of the two linguistic traditions dealt with in Chapters VI and VII, devoted to Dravidic and Tibetan linguistics, in which indigenous elements were combined with the Indian heritage.

The Hebrew tradition, treated in Chapter VIII, was developed in connection with the exegesis of religious writings; in its later development it took over many elements from the Arabic tradition, to the extent where Arabic was even used as the primary medium. An important aspect of this tradition is that it contained the first attempt to establish a comparative relationship between the Semitic languages. In the Arabic tradition (Chapter IX), too, the relationship between language and religion was an important determinant in the development of ideas about the nature and origin of speech. Linguistics as a separate discipline began with the complete and systematic account of the language in Sībawayhi's *Kitāb*. The Arabic model was used for the description of other languages, such as Malay, Persian, Turkish and Coptic. The special interest of the Syriac tradition (Chapter X) is the fact that it combined elements from two linguistic traditions, Greek and Arabic.

In most histories of linguistics the Greek linguistic tradition (Chapter XI) is analyzed primarily in its role as the model for Latin and subsequently the entire Western tradition. In such an approach those aspects of the tradition that were not taken over tend to be neglected. What is aimed at here is a description of Greek linguistic tradition in its own right. The first sections are loosely ordered chronologically, highlighting, for the earlier period, the interdependence of philosophy and grammar and, for the later period, the philological tradition and the technical side of grammar on the basis of Dionysios Thrax' *Téchnè*. There are separate sections dealing with the role of grammar in education and the relationship between linguistics and other sciences. The translation of Thrax' *Téchnè* provided the point of departure for many indigenous traditions, such as Georgian, Armenian, Syriac and Old Church Slavonic.

The Greek tradition also served as an important model for the Latin tradition (Chapter XII), which culminated in the many treatises by Charisius, Donatus, and Priscian later assembled in the Corpus Grammaticorum Latinorum. These descriptions of Latin served as the starting point for the continuous traditions of the study of Latin in the early Middle Ages. Special sections in this Chapter are dedicated to grammar and rhetoric, and to the relationship between language and revelation in Christian theology. In the early Middle Ages (Chapter XIII) the cultivation of Latin was the determining factor in the development of linguistics. Special sections deal with linguistics and theology, linguistics and the system of sciences, and linguistics in society. In the later Middle Ages a distinction is made between the development of linguistic theory (grammatica speculativa) and the development of grammatical description (grammatica positiva). Speculative grammar (Chapter XIV) deals with the linguistic theory of the Modistae, and the relationship between linguistics and logic, theology, and other sciences in the late Middle Ages.

Chapter XV deals with the continuous tradition of the study of Latin in the late Middle Ages. A new development during this period was the use of the Latin model for various vernaculars, such as Irish, Welsh, Icelandic, English and Slavic languages. The last article of this Chapter describes the intrusion of vernaculars as literary language in poetics/stylistics. In subsequent Chapters the perspective changes and the vernaculars become languages in their own right which can be used at the metalinguistic level.

Chapter XVI deals with the re-awakening of interest in the classical languages, Latin *and* Greek, and the cultural content transmitted in these languages leads, in the course of the 15th century, to a reorientation in (Western) linguistics. It treats the caesura introduced by this shift in direction. Chapter XVII deals with the parallel development of an active interest, at first chiefly among merchants and soon thereafter among the aristocracy, in the vernaculars which Humanism had in effect revalorized, and a regular language learning process sets in. The transfer of humanistic ideas to the vernaculars paves the way for a grammatical (and lexical) description of vernacular literary texts (Chapter XVIII). The next step in the increased importance of the vernaculars is characterized by the development of rules and regulations for these languages, in effect to the establishment of a norm (Chapter XIX).

The discovery of the New World by Portuguese and Spaniards (and subsequently by the English, French and Dutch), which occurred about the same time as the re-awakening of interest in the classical languages, introduces Europeans to 'exotic' languages. These are first studied not for their own sake, but for practical, including political, reasons, notably for missionary purposes (Chapter XX). Only in the course of the 17th century is linguistic theory gaining attention; particularly in the 18th century do theoretical discussions take center space (Chapter XXI). The revalorization of the vernaculars and the declaration of their equal footing with the classical languages also leads to theoretical considerations; in the first phase of develpment these interests lead largely to discussions about the origin of languages (Chapter XXII). In the next phase these theoretical considerations lead to investigations into the origin and development of individual national languages. In this situation the relationship between these national languages takes on a special role (Chapter XXIII).

Chapter XXIV deals with the development and formal establishment of comparative-historical Indo-European linguistics in the first half of the 19th century, before the backdrop of a long-standing tradition of philological studies and literary interests in language, and with the establishment of academic positions and programs in this emerging field of study. Chapter XXV delineates the progressive professionalization of linguistics during the second half of the 19th century, including the establishment and proliferation of specialist journals, the creation of chairs for the 'new philologies', i.e., languages and language groups other than the traditional classical ones, Greek, Latin, and Sanskrit.

Chapter XXVI presents the evolution of the 'comparative method' developed within historical-comparative Indo-European philology for the reconstruction of earlier stages of languages and the assumed protolanguage. Further, it accounts for the application of the 'comparative method' to language families other than Indo-European, such as Finno-Ugric, African, Austronesian, and American Indian languages, since the second half of the 19th century.

Chapter XXVII delineates the vicissitudes in the evolution of ideas concerning the classification of languages according to morpho-syntactic organization of the early 19th century, through the development of sophisticated typological systems between 1850 (Steinthal) and 1921 (Sapir), to later 20th-century concerns for the discovery of structural unity within the diversity in languages worldwide, including the search for and the construction of universal grammars.

Chapter XXVIII depicts the development of methods of data elicitation in the 19th century and the parallel development of the scientific study of sound and sound production, the growing importance of phonetics in the teaching of modern languages, the establishment of universal alphabets for the transcription of unwritten languages, and the beginnings of dialectology. Chapter XXIX shows the evolution of the study of meaning in 19th-century linguistics, from the modest proposals made by Reisig and his followers, via the preoccupation with semantic change toward the close of the 19th century, and the 'Wörter und Sachen' approach in the first half of the 20th century. At the same time, contemporary work in dictionary-making is given its due. Chapter XXX deals with the early impact of psychology and physiology on linguistic studies in the 19th century, the relationship between linguistics and psychology especially in the work of Wundt, and emanating from the work of Broca, Wernicke and others, the development of research devoted to language and the brain, in particular the study of aphasia. Early investigations in first-language acquisition, too, reflect the emergence of psycholinguistics as an important area of interdisciplinary study.

Chapter XXXI is devoted to the evolution of the structural principle in European linguistics from its beginnings in the 19th century until the present day. Particular attention is given to the establishment of various post-Saussurean schools, trends, and research programs from the Geneva school at the beginning of the 20th century to the eventual exportation of structuralist concepts to other disciplines such as anthropology, sociology, literary theory, and psychology. Chapter XXXII traces the origin and development of the distinctly North American approach to language, its ethnolinguistic tradition developed during the 19th century as a result of the recognition of the importance of American Indian languages and the impact of Humboldtian ideas of language structure and perception, the establishment of anthropological linguistics, and the development of several parallel descriptive approaches. It also includes an account of the history of glottochronology and lexicostatistics as an outgrowth of the interest in establishing an historical dimension to languages without a written tradition.

Chapter XXXIII is devoted to the development of 20th-century linguistic theory in which the emergence of generative linguistics is central. It deals with the early formalization efforts of the 1940s and 1950s inside and outside of American descriptivist linguistics, and it depicts the influx of mathematical models and computer-assisted translation programs into linguistic theorizing and the various alternatives to Chomskyan linguistics, most of which take their cue from the generativist framework in one form or another.

Chapter XXXIV depicts the various traditions and trends in 20th-century semantics, only a small number of which can be traced back to Saussurean proposals. It includes articles on Firthian contextualism and generative semantics as well as on lexicology, lexicography, onomastics, etymology, and the influence of Peircian semiotics on semantic investigations, both synchronic and diachronic. Chapter XXXV accounts for the various strands of phonological and morphological inquiry in the later 20th century, from Chomsky & Halle's *Sound Pattern of English* (1968) to work in non-linear phonology and recent articulations of 'natural morphology', many of which respond to proposals made by Chomsky and his associates. However, other traditions in derivational morphology are treated as well.

Chapter XXXVI, essentially, illustrates the development of 'sociolinguistics' in the 20th-century from earlier work in dialectology to the thorough investigation of variation in language, both synchronically and diachronically. It begins with the debate over homogeneity and heterogeneity of language and ends with more recent trends in language-contact research, whether they be studies of pidgins and related forms of language development or problems in language planning around the globe. Chapter XXXVII assesses the resurgence of historical linguistics in the second half of the 20th century, following its initial decline as a result of the 'Saussurean revolution', and its impact on synchronic studies. It shows the revitalization of the field within the changed climate of opinion, the more recent research hypotheses in the field (such as the laryngeal and the glottalic theories), and the inroads made by creolistic and sociolinguistic studies on questions of language change. Chapter XXXVIII presents alternative – 'parole'-oriented – approaches to the various system-centered linguistic analyses described in the three preceding chapters, such as the Wittgensteinian emphasis on 'use of language', the development of speech act theory and pragmatics, text linguistics, discourse analysis, and various theories of enunciation.

Chapter XXXIX – by far the longest of the project – demonstrates the abandonment of the idea of autonomy of linguistics, advocated by Saussure and embraced by Chomsky, in favour of a multidisciplinary contact between and integration of the study of language with semiotics, philosophy, psychology, neurology, biology, artificial intelligence studies, and the impact of computer technology on translation, phonetics and other linguistic pursuits. At the same time the various applications of linguistic insight in other fields are reflected.

In the concluding Chapter XL, the editors, individually and complementing each other, map out their views on the origin, development and future of the history of the language sciences and detail their position with regard to questions of methodology and philosophy of linguistic historiography.

The Editors

# Vorwort der Herausgeber

## 1. Allgemeine Einleitung

### 1.1 Begriffsbestimmungen

Unter 'Geschichte der Sprachwissenschaften' wird in diesem Handbuch die Entwicklung sprachwissenschaftlicher Theorien und Vorstellungen von Erklärungs- und Analyseverfahren und methodologischen Abgrenzungen sowie die Herausbildung von organisatorischen Strukturen und Institutionen verstanden – sofern dies überhaupt dokumentarisch erfaßt werden kann – welche zur Verbreitung sprachwissenschaftlicher Kenntnisse beigetragen haben. Die Verwendung der Termini 'Sprachwissenschaft' bzw. 'Linguistik' sollte also keinesfalls dahingehend mißverstanden werden, als sei hierunter ein klar abgegrenzter Objektbereich zu verstehen. Eine solche Verwendung wäre für das Wesen der Sprachwissenschaft unserer Tage nur dort zutreffend, wo sie als eigenständige Disziplin mit eigenen, wohldefinierten Forschungsprogrammen und eigenen beruflichen Organisationsformen anerkannt und etabliert ist. In manchen Traditionen hatte die Sprachwissenschaft schon immer einen eigenen Platz innerhalb des allgemeinen Rahmens der Wissenschaften. Obgleich die genaue Abgrenzung der Sprachwissenschaft in Bezug auf ihre Themen und Methoden in jeder ihrer traditionellen Ausprägungen verschieden war, sind doch alle Traditionen durch ihre gemeinsame Betrachtung der Sprache als Wissenschaftsobjekt verbunden. Die Termini 'Sprachwissenschaft' bzw. 'Linguistik' werden in diesem Handbuch somit als generelle Bezeichnungen für all das verwendet, was mit dem Studium menschlicher Sprache zu tun hat. Die Abgrenzungen des Objektbereichs der Sprachwissenschaft(en), welche im Laufe der Jahrhunderte immer wieder anders vorgenommen wurden, werden dagegen im Zuge der Ausführungen zu ihrer Geschichte darzulegen sein, genau so wie ihre wechselvollen Kontakte mit anderen Disziplinen auch.

In den meisten Bereichen der Sprachwissenschaft ist es üblich geworden, umfassenderen Darstellungen einen historischen Überblick voranzustellen, welcher über die Entstehung und Herausbildung der Disziplin informiert. Ebenso gibt es auch in anderen Handbüchern dieser Serie historische Kapitel, deren Hauptziel es ist, die Herausbildung bestimmter Teildisziplinen darzulegen, welche zum aktuellen Stand und zu den derzeitigen Forschungsaufgaben geführt haben. In einem Handbuch zur Geschichte der Sprachwissenschaften ist dies aus einsichtigen Gründen nicht möglich, geht es hier doch darum, die Entstehung und Entwicklung sprachwissenschaftlicher Theorien in Geschichte und Gegenwart in ihrer Eigengesetzlichkeit und unter Rekurs auf interne und externe Faktoren darzustellen und zu erläutern.

Wie bei allen wissenschaftsgeschichtlichen Darstellungen ist auch hier die Beziehung zwischen der zu untersuchenden Disziplin auf der einen Seite und der Disziplin, die auf einer Metaebene ihre Methoden und Grundannahmen sowie ihre geschichtliche Entwicklung analysiert, recht komplex. Daher ist auch eine Geschichte der Sprachwissenschaften, welche die Entstehung und Entwicklung eben dieser Sprachwissenschaften analysiert, sorgfältig vom Objekt ihrer Untersuchungen zu unterscheiden. Auch wenn die meisten Historiographen der Sprachwissenschaften selbst Sprachwissenschaftler sind, so muß sich die historiographische Analyse in Zielsetzung und Blickrichtung doch von der sprachwissenschaftlichen Arbeit unterscheiden, und zwar so, daß historische Entwicklungslinien innerhalb der Sprachwissenschaften ohne Werturteile beschrieben werden. Somit geht es dem Historiographen letztlich um die Erhellung von Entwicklungstendenzen innerhalb eines konkreten kulturellen, sozioökonomischen bzw. politischen Rahmens auf der einen und um die Darlegung zeitweiliger Kontakte sprachwissenschaftlicher Forschungsrichtungen mit anderen Disziplinen auf der anderen Seite, auf alle Fälle aber um die Vermeidung eines 'Tunnelblicks'.

Die Aufgabe des Historiographen der Sprachwissenschaft ist grundsätzlich von der des Sprachwissenschaftlers verschieden, weil der Historiograph nicht auf die Erklärung linguistischer Tatsachen abzielt, sondern auf die Analyse der Behandlung dieser linguistischen Tatsachen, wie sie von Sprachwissenschaftlern in den verschiedensten Traditionen vorgenommen worden sind. Das heißt auch, daß für den Historiographen alle Annäherungsweisen prinzipiell gleichwertig sind und daß die Geschichte nicht als bloße kumulative Entwicklung bis zur gegenwärtigen Lage der Disziplin betrachtet werden kann: der Historiograph sollte somit vermeiden, die Vergangenheit als Legitimierung der Gegenwart zu benutzen.

### 1.2 Gegenstandsbereich

Bei der vorstehenden Begriffsbestimmung ist der Inhalt des Handbuches bereits ansatzweise umrissen worden. Es geht darin um einen Überblick über die Theorien und Vorstellungen, welche je von Sprache und Sprachen entwickelt worden sind. Es geht außerdem um die Kontexte, in denen dies geschah. Es wird also der Versuch unternommen, die Forschungen zur Sprache als Mittel menschlicher Kommunikation zu allen Zeiten so weit wie möglich zu erfassen und zu dokumentieren, seien diese nun theoretischer oder praktischer Natur. Schulgrammatiken und Sprachlehrbücher, Lexika und sonstige Werke sprachforscherischer Tätigkeiten werden in angemessenem Umfange berücksichtigt und hinsichtlich ihrer Bedeutung in der jeweiligen Zeit sowie hinsichtlich der sie leitenden Theorien beschrieben und gedeutet.

Eine wichtige Einschränkung besteht allerdings darin, daß das Handbuch nur solche Forschungen behandelt, welche in schriftlicher Form überliefert sind, so daß beispielsweise die sog. 'Volkslinguistik' nicht berücksichtigt wird. Ebenso werden auch Einstellungsfragen zur Sprache (*attitudes*) in diesem Handbuch nicht ausdrücklich erörtert. Obgleich sie eine wichtige Rolle in der Entwicklung von sprachwissenschaftlichen Theorien spielen, werden sie hier nur insofern behandelt, als sie in diesen Theorien erwähnt werden.

Selbstverständlich waren Überschneidungen mit einzelnen Handbüchern der Reihe im Einzelfalle nicht ganz zu vermeiden. So ist es beispielsweise nicht möglich, stets scharf zwischen der Geschichte der Sprachwissenschaften und der Sprachphilosophie zu unterscheiden, vor allem in einigen nichtwestlichen Traditionen, wie der chinesischen oder der das Sanskrit betreffenden, in denen Sprachwissenschaft und Sprachphilosophie immer fest verbunden waren. Deshalb finden sich historische Einleitungen zu den wichtigen philosophischen Traditionen sowohl in diesem, als auch in dem Handbuch zur Sprachphilosophie. So werden zum Beispiel die Werke von Platon, Aristoteles und der Stoiker sowie die der spätmittelalterlichen Sprachphilosophen erörtert, wenn auch lediglich hinsichtlich ihrer Bedeutung für die Sprachforschung, nicht aber hinsichtlich ihrer Berührungspunkte mit der Philosophie.

Ein wichtiges Charakteristikum dieses Handbuchs besteht darin, eine zeitlich und räumlich möglichst vollständige Darstellung aller sprachwissenschaftlichen Forschungsrichtungen anzustreben. Dies bedeutet gleichzeitig auch, daß wir über jene eurozentrische Blickweise hinausgehen wollen, welche die Sanskritgrammatik beispielsweise nur insofern berücksichtigt, als sie für die Entdeckung der indoeuropäischen Sprachfamilie von Interesse war. Unser Ziel in diesem Handbuch war es, so viele sprachwissenschaftliche Traditionen wie möglich einzubeziehen und sie in ihrer Eigenständigkeit zu behandeln. Leider war dieses Ziel nicht immer zu erreichen: für einige Traditionen gibt es einfach zu wenig dokumentierte Quellen. So ist es uns z. B. nicht gelungen, einen Aufsatz über die äthiopische oder die kambodschanische sprachwissenschaftliche Tradition aufzunehmen. In einigen Fällen sahen wir uns gezwungen, einen Aufsatz aus praktischen Gründen zu streichen. Teilweise war es uns nicht möglich, einen Autor ausfindig zu machen, teilweise lieferte ein eingeladener Autor nicht rechtzeitig ab.

Ein Problem stellte auch die chronologische Abgrenzung der zeitgenössischen Forschung in diesem Handbuch dar. Auch wenn es ohne Zweifel einfacher gewesen wäre, jüngste Entwicklungen einfach auszuklammern, so haben wir diesen Weg nicht eingeschlagen. Es dürfte sich aber von selbst verstehen, daß eine historische Analyse zeitgenössischer Sprachforschungen nur unter Wahrung gewisser Vorsichtsmaßnahmen betrieben werden kann. Dies gilt insbesondere dann, wenn diejenigen, die die Entwicklung auf einem Teilgebiet beschreiben, zugleich mit rein sprachwissenschaftlichen Forschungen auf ebendiesem Gebiet befaßt sind und daher möglicherweise nicht so leicht bereit sind, sprachwissenschaftliche Forschungen und wissenschaftsgeschichtliche Forschungen voneinander zu trennen. Mit dem Schlußkapitel des Handbuches, seiner Untergliederung, und mit der Wahl der Autoren haben wir versucht, dieser Gefahr entgegenzusteuern. Wir haben auch versucht, Grundannahmen und Prinzipien darzulegen, auf denen dieses Handbuch basiert. Wir sind jedenfalls der Überzeugung, daß eine Darstellung der zeitgenössischen Sprachwissenschaften unter historiographischem Blickwinkel zu einem besseren Verständnis eben dieser Forschungen beiträgt und ihre Bedeutung innerhalb des modernen Wissenschaftsbetriebes, aber auch innerhalb der Geschichte der Sprachwissenschaften, klarer hervortreten läßt.

### 1.3 Thematische Schwerpunkte

Die Herausgeber dieses Handbuchs haben versucht, von einer weitverbreiteten Darstellungsform von Wissenschaftsgeschichte, der 'Geschichte großer Persönlichkeiten', so fern wie möglich zu bleiben, selbst wenn diese Vorgehensweise, etwa bei der europäischen Sprachwissenschaft des 19. und 20. Jahrhunderts, manchmal schwer zu vermeiden war. Allerdings scheint es zweifelhaft, ob ein solcher Ansatz auch dann noch seine Tragfähigkeit behält, wenn es um frühe Epochen der Sprachwissenschaft geht. Auch dann, wenn ein Aufsatz die Beiträge individueller Sprachwissenschaftler hervorhebt, werden doch die spezifischen Themen, Gesichtspunkte und Forschungsprogramme einer bestimmten Tradition sowie die Beziehungen zwischen dem individuellen Sprachwissenschaftler und der Entwicklung dieser Tradition in den Vordergrund gestellt.

Angesichts der großen geographischen, chronologischen und thematischen Variationsbreite des Feldes möglicher Sprachforschungen fällt es nicht leicht, ein zentrales

Thema zu benennen, mit dem der hier gewählte Zugang vereinheitlichend beschrieben werden könnte. Trotzdem können nachfolgend einige Gesichtspunkte genannt werden, nach denen die Auswahl der Themen, die Präsentation des Stoffes sowie die Organisation und Analyse des Materials erfolgt ist.

Eine Art Leitmotiv bildet die Analyse von Entwicklungsgängen der Sprachwissenschaft in 'vorherrschende' und 'marginale' bzw. 'unterschwellige' Richtungen. Obwohl es bei den Sprachforschungen westlicher Tradition möglich wäre, für bestimmte Zeiträume Forschungsprogramme aufzuzeigen, welche für einen Großteil der gelehrten Welt eine Zeit lang Gültigkeit besessen haben, so kann doch nie vom Monopol eines 'Paradigmas' die Rede sein. In der Geschichte der Sprachwissenschaft lassen sich auch so gut wie keine Richtungsänderungen aufzeigen, die durch den plötzlichen Zusammenbruch früherer Forschungsprogramme oder durch irgendwelche 'revolutionären Entdeckungen' hervorgerufen worden wären. Statt dessen sind aber oft allmähliche Übergänge zwischen 'vorherrschenden' und 'unterschwelligen' Forschungsinteressen zu beobachten, weshalb hier parallel zum jeweils beschriebenen, vorherrschenden Paradigma andere Forschungsprogramme 'am Rande' ebenfalls weiterverfolgt werden. Diese nämlich können sich im Laufe der Zeit wieder in den Vordergrund drängen und dann zur 'herrschenden Lehre/Praxis' werden.

In Zusammenhang mit der hier skizzierten Auffassung von Wissenschaftsgeschichte kann auch darauf hingewiesen werden, daß es eine Art regelmäßigen Wechsel zwischen zwei gegensätzlichen Auffassungen des Zugangs zur Sprachforschung zu geben scheint. So lassen sich Zeiträume beobachten, in denen die Sprache gleichsam als ideales Werkzeug behandelt wird, das in idealen Kommunikationssituationen einem idealen Sprecher/Hörer dient. Diese werden dann abgelöst von Zeiten, in denen sich die Sprachforschung wiederum der sprachlichen Vielfalt und den Varietäten von Sprachen in Raum und Zeit zuwendet. Ein solcher Wechsel ist im 19. Jahrhundert zu beobachten, wo das Programm der vergleichenden Sprachwissenschaft durch die aufkommende Dialektologie in Frage gestellt wird. Die Unterscheidung zwischen einer 'vorherrschenden' und einer 'unterschwelligen' Richtung in der Geschichte der Sprachwissenschaft deutet an, daß keine der beiden Richtungen die andere jemals vollständig verdrängt, sondern daß sie jeweils nebeneinander betrieben werden, wobei sie auf der Skala zwischen 'vorherrschender Stellung' und 'Randerscheinung' immer wieder neue Plätze einnehmen können. In der Sprachwissenschaft des 20. Jahrhunderts scheint sich ein ähnlicher Positionswechsel abzuzeichnen, denn neben das offensichtlich vorherrschende Interesse an systematischen, idealen Strukturen der Sprache, tritt in jüngerer Zeit deutlich erkennbar wieder ein Interesse an sprachlichen Variationen sowie am Funktionieren der Sprachen in (komplexen) Kommunikationssituationen.

Die Unterscheidung zwischen 'vorherrschender' Lehre und 'unterschwelligen' Richtungen scheint auch auf sprachwissenschaftliche Institutionen anwendbar zu sein, denn unabhängig vom jeweils vorherrschenden Paradigma befassen sich diese recht oft weiterhin mit grammatischen Fragen in einem sehr praktisch verstandenen Sinne, mit Sprachgeschichte, mit dem Wortschatz, der Struktur einer Sprache oder mit Fragen der Sprachverwandtschaft, selbst wenn das dominierende Paradigma anderen Forschungsinteressen folgt. Auch das gehört in ein vollständiges Bild der Sprachwissenschaften und muß Berücksichtigung in einem Handbuch wie diesem finden.

Unser Bestreben war es darüber hinaus, bei der Anordnung der Materialien oder bei der Einteilung in Kapitel und Artikel jede Art von 'Systemzwang' zu vermeiden. Die große Zahl der Beiträger, welche aus den unterschiedlichsten Schulen kommen und dabei ihr spezifisches Fachwissen einbringen, sollte hinreichend Garantie dafür bieten, daß hier ein weites Spektrum von Perspektiven abgedeckt ist. Jeder Versuch, die Arbeiten zur Geschichte der Sprachwissenschaft in ein engeres Klassifikationsschema zu zwingen, muß Schiffbruch erleiden und zu verzerrten Darstellungen jener Abläufe und Veränderungen auf dem Gebiet der Sprachforschungen führen, welche im Laufe der Zeit stattgefunden haben.

Das Fehlen eines engen Organisationsrahmens hat eine weitere und, wie wir glauben, positive Konsequenz. Wir haben nicht zwischen einem 'datenorientierten' und einem 'theorieorientierten' Annäherungsverfahren gewählt, weil wir der festen Überzeugung sind, daß eine solche Wahl zu einem verzerrten Bild der Sprachwissenschaft in einem Kulturbereich führen würde. In einigen Fällen schien es angebracht, die Ergebnisse der Theorien hervorzuheben, in anderen Fällen ergab sich aus der Analyse der Methoden und Grundsätze eines Forschungsprogramms ein genaueres, schärferes Bild der jeweiligen Tradition. Beide Annäherungsverfahren ergänzen sich unserer Meinung nach somit bei der Darlegung von Entwicklungstendenzen in der Geschichte der Sprachwissenschaft.

### 1.4 Forschungsstand

Obwohl dieses Handbuch hinsichtlich der Breite seiner Anlage in gewisser Weise Neuland betritt, stützt es sich auf die Ergebnisse früherer Forschungen. Als eigenständige Disziplin mit Organisationsformen, Zeitschriften und Reihen ist die Geschichte der Sprachwissenschaft zwar erst zwischen dem Ende der sechziger und dem Beginn der siebziger Jahre in Erscheinung getreten. Das heißt nun aber nicht, vor den sechziger Jahren des 20. Jahrhunderts habe es überhaupt keine allgemeineren Überblicke über die Geschichte der Sprachwissenschaft gegeben. In manchen nicht westlichen Traditionen ist die Geschichte der Disziplin von jeher ein üblicher Bestandteil des Faches. Beispielsweise benutzen die arabischen Grammatiker ausführliche biographische Lexika, in denen die Schriften der früheren Grammatiker evaluiert wurden. Diese Art von Geschichtsschreibung widmete sich ausschließlich der Geschichte der eigenen Tradition. In der westlichen Sprachwissenschaft hingegen ging der Behandlung individueller Sprachen bzw. Sprachfamilien oder der Analyse von spezifischen linguistischen Problemen, z. B. in der Phonologie oder der Semantik, fast immer eine geschichtliche Einleitung voran, in der die historische Entwicklung des Problemkreises erörtert wurde.

Von einigen Forschern wurde François Thurots 'Tableau des Progrès de la Science Grammaticale', der als *Discours Préliminaire* zu einer 1796 publizierten Übersetzung des Hermes (1751) von James Harris erschien, als "erster Versuch einer Geschichte der Grammatik" bezeichnet. Umfangreichere wissenschaftsgeschichtliche Darstellungen erscheinen aber erst um die Mitte des 19. Jahrhunderts, wobei zunächst die dreibändige *Sprachphilosophie der Alten* von Laurenz Lersch (1838–1841) zu nennen wäre. Damals beherrschte die Klassische Philologie das Feld, was zur Folge hatte, daß außer der Tradition der Griechen und Römer, auch ansatzweise der Inder, alle anderen ausgeschlossen blieben, also auch die gesamte Sprachforschung vom Mittelalter bis zur Moderne. Ein typisches Beispiel hierfür ist auch Steinthals *Geschichte der Sprachwissenschaft bei den Griechen und Römern* (1863), welche zudem in erster Linie die antike Sprachphilosophie und nicht systematisch die Sprachforschung im eigentlichen Sinne behandelt.

Längere Perioden der Sprachwissenschaft finden erst in den historiographischen Arbeiten eines Benfey (1869), Raumer (1870), Delbrück (1880, namentlich ab der 4. Auflage von 1904 an) und Bursian (1883) Berücksichtigung, allerdings mit einseitiger Bevorzugung der Moderne. Eine eurozentrische Behandlung sprachwissenschaftlicher Vorstellungen und Ideen blieb bis in unsere Tage vorherrschend, obwohl es bereits seit Ende des 19. Jahrhunderts Abhandlungen über die Entwicklung der hebräischen und arabischen Grammatik gab.

Auch wenn in den sechziger Jahren des 20. Jahrhunderts eine stattliche Zahl von Hand- bzw, Lehrbüchern zur Geschichte der Sprachwissenschaften verlegt wurde, scheint sich ein echtes Interesse doch erst in den siebziger Jahren bemerkbar zu machen. Diese jüngere Entwicklung ist ablesbar an der zweibändigen *Historiography of Linguistics*, welche 1975 erscheint und die von Thomas A. Sebeok herausgegebenen *Current Trends in Linguistics* (Den Haag) beschließt. Sie enthält, außer den 'üblichen' Kapiteln, Überblicke über die sprachwissenschaftlichen Traditionen im Fernen Osten sowie in Nord- und Südamerika. Auffallend ist dabei allerdings, daß in vielen Beiträgen unter Wissenschaftsgeschichte eine Art Forschungsbericht zu 'jüngeren Publikationen zur Geschichte der Sprachwissenschaft' parallel zur westlichen Sprachwissenschaft verstanden wird, nicht aber eine eigenständige Forschungsaufgabe, wie man vielleicht erwartet hätte.

Das vorliegende Handbuch orientiert sich stattdessen an jenem Typus von Wissenschaftsgeschichte, der sich seit 1973, dem Erscheinungsjahr der ersten, ausschließlich der Geschichte der Sprachwissenschaften gewidmeten Zeitschrift, *Historiographia Linguistica*, immer klarer abzeichnet. Bald danach kam es auch zur Gründung von internationalen sowie regionalen Gesellschaften zur Geschichte der Sprachwissenschaften und zu ersten Tagungen und Kongressen, sowohl in Europa als auch in Amerika. Dort wurden nicht nur sprachwissenschaftliche Theorien der Vergangenheit bzw. einzelne Forschungstraditionen, sondern auch methodologische und epistemologische Fragen einer Geschichte der Sprachwissenschaften behandelt. Die Fortschritte, welche in den letzten Jahren gemacht wurden, lassen sich am besten an den Zeitschriften *Historiographia Linguistica, Histoire – Epistémologie – Langage* (Paris, 1979–) und den *Beiträge[n] zur Geschichte der Sprachwissenschaft* (Münster, 1991–), sowie an den Akten der in dreijährigen Abständen stattfindenden International Conference on the History of the Language Sciences (ICHoLS) ablesen. In den achtziger Jahren erscheinen schließlich auch Monographien zur Theorie und Methodologie der Sprachwissenschaftsgeschichte, welche die heutigen Orientierungen der Disziplin noch klarer hervortreten lassen.

Etwa gleichzeitig mit den ersten Diskussionen über das heutige Projekt lancierte Peter Schmitter seine *Geschichte der Sprachtheorie* (Tübingen, 1987–), eine Reihe von Monographien über verschiedene Gebiete und Perioden der Sprachwissenschaftsgeschichte. Von den 9 geplanten Teilen sind inzwischen 5 erschienen. Ein vergleichbares Ziel vertritt die 3-bändige Histoire des idées linguistiques, herausgegeben von Sylvain Auroux (Brussels, 1990–2000) und die 5-bändige *History of Linguistics*, herausgegeben von Giulio Lepschy (London, 1994–). In der Zwischenzeit erschien auch die 500-seitige *Concise History of the Language Sciences: From the Sumerians to the Cognitivists*, herausgegeben von E. F. K. Koerner und R. E. Asher (Oxford, 1995), die nicht nur einen Überblick über die wichtigsten Traditionen bietet, sondern auch über den aktuellen Forschungsstand der verschiedenen Schulen und Theorien der Sprachwissenschaft des

20. Jahrhunderts informiert. In anderen vielbändigen Handbüchern zur Geschichte der Sprachwissenschaft ist dies bisher noch nicht geschehen. Ein vollständigeres Bild dieser Periode wird erst im dritten Teil des hiesigen Handbuchs geliefert werden.

Auskünfte über die wichtigsten Persönlichkeiten in der Geschichte der Sprachwissenschaft sind zu finden in dem 1000-seitigen *Lexicon Grammaticorum*, herausgegeben von Harro Stammerjohann (Tübingen, 1996), das ohne Zweifel noch längere Zeit eine wichtige Quelle zur Geschichte der Sprachwissenschaft bleiben wird.

## 1.5 Aufbau des Handbuchs

Das Handbuch ist nach chronologischen Gesichtspunkten gegliedert. Abweichungen von diesem Prinzip erwiesen sich aber bei den ersten, den nicht westlichen Traditionen gewidmeten Kapiteln als notwendig, da sich die Sprachforschung in geographisch getrennten Räumen parallel und unabhängig von einander etabliert hat. Wo die Entwicklung einer Tradition am engsten mit fremdem Einfluß verbunden war, wurde diese Tradition im Rahmen der 'Muttertradition' behandelt. Dies betrifft zum Beispiel die armenische und georgische Tradition, die im Kapitel über die griechische Linguistik, die koptische und türkische Tradition, die im Kapitel über die arabische Linguistik oder die vietnamesische Tradition, die im Kapitel über die chinesische Linguistik behandelt werden. Solchen Entscheidungen haftet eine gewisse Willkür an, weil die meisten Traditionen irgendwann dem Einfluß anderer Traditionen unterworfen waren. Die hiesige Einteilung soll deshalb nicht dahingehend interpretiert werden als beinhalte sie ein Urteil über den Eigenwert der betroffenen Tradition.

Anschließend beschreibt das Handbuch die jeweils vorherrschenden Strömungen der westlichen Sprachwissenschaft, wobei es bei jener Zeit eine Zäsur setzt, in der die westeuropäischen Volkssprachen sowohl als Gegenstand der Sprachforschung als auch als Forschungsmittel, als Metasprachen, verwendet werden – der Renaissance. Von diesem Zeitpunkt an hat die Sprachforschung nicht mehr nur eine einzige Sprache als Untersuchungsgegenstand und Bezugsrahmen. Dies gilt natürlich nicht für die nichtwestlichen Traditionen, bei deren Beschreibung man heute oft von 'Klassik', 'Mittelalter' und 'Renaissance' redet und dabei Termini verwendet, die ursprünglich ausschließlich dazu dienten, Entwicklungen innerhalb der westlichen Hemisphäre zu beschreiben. Bei der Beschreibung nichtwestlicher Traditionen sollten sie dagegen vermieden werden, nicht zuletzt weil sie mit zu vielen Konnotationen verbunden sind, die auf Europa verweisen. Trotzdem kann auch hier von einer Zäsur gesprochen werden, einer Zäsur, welche durch den Import westlicher Sprachforschungen bewirkt wurde. Dabei kam es zu einer Mischung der einheimischen Sprachwissenschaft mit dem westlichen Modell. Mit der (in diesem Sinne verstandenen) 'Renaissance' übernimmt also das westliche Paradigma in der ganzen Welt eine vorherrschende Position, was eine einheitliche Darstellung der Sprachforschung in der nachfolgenden Zeit möglich macht.

Ein weiterer entscheidender Wandel in der Geschichte der Sprachforschung erfolgte im 19. Jahrhundert, wo sich die historisch-vergleichende Sprachwissenschaft zum vorherrschenden Paradigma der Zeit herausbildet. Mit der Hinwendung zur synchronischen Sprachforschung zu Beginn des 20. Jahrhunderts hebt schließlich die Geschichte des 20. Jahrhunderts an. Ihr, sowie der Geschichte der Sprachforschung im 19. Jahrhundert, wird der meiste Raum in diesem Handbuch gewidmet.

Bei den Unterteilungen der Zeiträume in einzelne Kapitel waren vornehmlich thematische Gesichtspunkte maßgeblich, wobei sowohl die oben erläuterte Unterscheidung von 'vorherrschender' Forschungsrichtung und 'unterschwelligen' Forschungsinteressen, als auch sonstige Erwägungen eine Rolle spielten. Für die Darstellung der jüngsten Entwicklungen im Bereich der Sprachwissenschaften kam eine rein chronologische Anordnung aus einsichtigen Gründen allerdings nicht mehr in Frage. Wir haben uns stattdessen auf methodologische Übereinstimmungen bzw. Divergenzen bei den in Frage stehenden Theorien konzentriert. Ferner haben wir auf Berührungspunkte zwischen den Sprachwissenschaften und ihren Nachbardisziplinen wie Soziologie, Psychologie, Neurologie, Logik, Mathematik, usw. geachtet, ist doch die wechselseitige Verbindung zwischen den Sprachwissenschaften und benachbarten Disziplinen eines der charakteristischen Merkmale der Sprachforschung unserer Zeit.

## 2. Erläuterungen zu den einzelnen Kapiteln

Die Sprachforschung des Nahen Ostens beschäftigt sich vornehmlich mit Problemen der Verschriftung und des Lexikons. Darüber hinaus bringt die Existenz unterschiedlicher Kulturdialekte und das Nebeneinander verschiedener Kultursprachen auch einen gewissen Zwang zur grammatischen Kodifizierung mit sich (Kapitel I).

Kapitel II behandelt die chinesische Sprachforschung. Hier stehen zwar Lautlehre und Lexikon im Mittelpunkt des Interesses, aber es kommt auch, im Zusammenhang mit philosophischen Erwägungen, zur Entwicklung von wichtigen Vorstellungen über die Natur des sprachlichen Zeichens (in seiner phonischen und graphischen Gestalt). Darüber hinaus spielt Sprache als literarisches Medium eine wichtige Rolle. Die chinesische Sprachforschung hat tiefgreifenden Einfluß auf die koreanische (Kapitel III) und die japanische Sprachforschung (Kapitel IV). Der für beide Sprachbereiche charakteristische Bilinguismus führt dort darüber hinaus zu konstrastiven Grammatikstudien. Interesse verdient auch die Übernahme niederländischer Grammatikmodelle im japanischen Sprachbereich während der Rangakusha-Zeit.

Die Sanskritsprachforschung, eine der bedeutendsten der vom Westen unabhängigen Sprachforschungsrichtungen, hat in der historiographischen Literatur viel Aufmerksamkeit erfahren. Ihr entstammt der erste Versuch einer vollständigen Sprachbeschreibung mit formal strenger Methode, Pāṇinis *Astādhyāyī*. Ein weiterer wichtiger Aspekt der Sanskritsprachforschung ist ihre Zuordnung zu Philosophie und Logik. Das Sanskritmodell hatte Auswirkungen für die Beschreibung des Alt-Javanischen und des Burmesischen (Kapitel V). In der dravidischen (Kapitel VI) und der tibetanischen Sprachforschung (Kapitel VII) verschmelzen eigene Traditionen mit dem Modell der Sanskritsprachforschung.

Die hebräische Sprachforschung entwickelt sich aus der Exegese religiöser Texte. In einer späteren Phase assimiliert sie manche Elemente der arabischen Tradition, welche schließlich vorherrschend wird. In diesem Zusammenhang ist auch ein erster Versuch zu verzeichnen, eine Beziehung zwischen den verschiedenen semitischen Sprachen nachzuweisen (Kapitel VIII). Auch in der arabischen Sprachforschung (Kapitel IX) ist die Beziehung zwischen Sprache und Religion entscheidend für die Entwicklung von Vorstellung über Ursprung und Wesen der Sprache. Eine eigenständige Sprachforschung beginnt hier mit Sîbawayhis *Kitâb* und der darin enthaltenen vollständigen, systematischen Darstellung des Arabischen. Sein Modell dient später zur Beschreibung anderer Sprachen, wie des Malaiischen, Persischen, Türkischen und Koptischen. Die syrische

Sprachforschung verdient Interesse namentlich deshalb, weil sie Elemente zweier Traditionen mit einander verbindet, der griechischen und der arabischen (Kapitel X).

In manchen Geschichten der Sprachwissenschaft wird die griechische Sprachforschung (Kapitel XI) hinsichtlich ihrer modellhaften Rolle für das Lateinische und für die gesamte westliche Tradition präsentiert. Dabei kommen jene Elemente üblicherweise zu kurz, welche nicht übernommen worden sind. Hier geht es dagegen um eine Darstellung, welche die griechische Sprachforschung an sich darstellt. Die ersten Abschnitte weisen nur eine chronologische Ordnung auf. Sie behandeln die wechselseitige Abhängigkeit von Philosophie und Grammatik in der Frühzeit und die philologischen Traditionen und die technischen Aspekte der Grammatik der späteren Zeit, welche auf der *Téchnè* des Dionysios Thrax basieren. Weitere Abschnitte behandeln die Rolle der Grammatik im Erziehungswesen sowie die Beziehung zwischen der Sprachwissenschaft und anderen Disziplinen. Übersetzungen der *Téchnè* stehen am Anfang vieler weiterer sprachwissenschaftlicher Traditionen, so die des Georgischen, Armenischen, Syrischen und Altkirchenslawischen.

Die griechische Sprachforschung ist auch ein wichtiges Vorbild für die lateinischen (Kapitel XII), welche ihren Höhepunkt mit den Arbeiten u. a. eines Charisius, eines Donats oder Priscians findet, deren grammatische Beschreibungen am Anfang einer langen Tradition von Lateinstudien im frühen Mittelalter stehen. Weitere Abschnitte dieses Kapitels sind dem Verhältnis von Grammatik und Rhetorik gewidmet, ferner die Beziehung zwischen Sprache und Offenbarung in der frühchristlichen Theologie. Im frühen Mittelalter (Kapitel XIII) bleiben die Lateinstudien bestimmender Faktor bei der Weiterentwicklung der Sprachforschung. In eigenen Abschnitten geht es um ihre Beziehung zur Theologie, ihre Position in der Wissenschaftssystematik und um ihre Rolle in der Gesellschaft. Im Hochmittelalter kommt es zu einer Unterscheidung zwischen Sprachtheorie (*grammatica speculativa*) und Sprachbeschreibung (*grammatica positiva*). Kapitel XIV behandelt die spekulative Grammtik der sog. Modisten sowie die Beziehung zwischen Sprachforschungen und Grammatik, Theologie und anderen Disziplinen.

Kapitel XV behandelt das Fortleben der vormodistischen Art der Sprachforschung, zum einen bei der Beschreibung des Lateinischen, zum anderen, ansatzweise, bei den ersten grammatischen Analysen verschiedener Volkssprachen, so des Irischen, Gälischen, Isländischen, Englischen und verschiedener slavischer Sprachen. Eine besondere Position nimmt dabei das Okzitanische (bzw. Provenzalische) ein, dem der letzte Abschnitt gewidmet ist; es ist Literatursprache und wird als solche von Katalonien und Kastilien bis Norditalien und Sizilien studiert und grammatisch und stilistisch beschrieben.

Die Rückbesinnung auf die klassischen Sprachen Latein *und* Griechisch und die in ihnen überlieferten Inhalte führt im Laufe des 15. Jahrhunderts zu einer Neuorientierung der (westlichen) Sprachwissenschaft; Kapitel XVI behandelt die damit eingeleitete Zäsur. Zeitlich in etwa parallel dazu entwickelt sich, zunächst vornehmlich bei Kaufleuten und dann bei Adeligen, ein praktisches Interesse an den, durch den Humanismus de facto aufgewerteten, Volkssprachen, und ein regelrechter Sprachlehrbetrieb setzt ein (Kapitel XVII). Die Übertragung humanistischer Vorstellungen auf die Volkssprachen bereitet den Weg zu einer grammatischen (und lexikalischen) Beschreibung volkssprachlicher literarischer Texte (Kapitel XVIII). Der nächste Schritt führt dann dazu, für die immer wichtiger werdenden Volkssprachen Regeln und Gesetze aufzustellen und eine Norm zu erarbeiten (Kapitel XIX).

Die Entdeckung der Neuen Welt durch die Portugiesen und Spanier (und bald darauf auch durch die Engländer, Franzosen und Holländer), welche etwa parallel zur Rückbesinnung auf die klassischen Sprachen erfolgt, bringt Europa in Kontakt mit 'exotischen' Sprachen, welche zunächst allerdings nicht um ihrer selbst Willen, sondern mit dem praktischen Ziel studiert werden, die neu entdeckten Welten zu missionieren (Kapitel XX). Sprachtheoretische Erwägungen gewinnen dagegen erst im Laufe des 17. Jahrhunderts wieder an Bedeutung; sie rufen namentlich im 18. Jahrhundert großes Interesse hervor (Kapitel XXI). Die Aufwertung der Volkssprachen und die Erklärung ihrer Gleichberechtigung mit den klassischen Sprachen führt ebenfalls zu theoretischen Überlegungen, welche zunächst in Abhandlungen über den Ursprung der Sprachen ihren Niederschlag finden (Kapitel XXII), die dann zu Forschungen zur Entstehung und Entwicklung einzelner Nationalsprachen überleiten, wobei den Beziehungen der einzelnen Nationalsprachen zueinander eine wichtige Rolle zukommt (Kapitel XXIII).

In der ersten Hälfte des 19. Jahrhunderts führt dann die Entstehung und Entwicklung der historisch-vergleichenden indoeuropäischen Sprachforschung zum Zurückdrängen der seit langem etablierten Tradition philologisch-literarischer Sprachstudien, wozu auch die Einrichtung von Lehrstühlen für dieses neue Forschungsgebiet entscheidend beiträgt (Kapitel XXIV). Diese Entwicklung greift bald auch auf die 'Neuphilologien' über, also auf neue Disziplinen, welche nicht mehr die klassischen Sprachen Griechisch, Latein und Sanskrit studieren, sondern jüngere Sprachen und Sprachengruppen. Auch hier kommt es zur Institutionalisierung und Professionalisierung durch die Einrichtung von Lehrstühlen und die Begründung neuer Zeitschriften (Kapitel XXV).

Innerhalb der historisch-vergleichend ausgerichteten indoeuropäischen Philologie entwickelt sich die 'vergleichende Methode' weiter zum Rekonstruktionsinstrument früherer Sprachstufen (und der mutmaßlichen Ursprache). In der 2. Hälfte des 19. Jahrhunderts wird diese Methode auch auf nichtindoeuropäische Sprachfamilien wie das Finno-Ugrische, auf afrikanische Sprachen sowie auf die austronesischen und amerikanischen Indianersprachen übertragen (Kapitel XXVI).

Die Klassifizierungsversuche von Sprachen nehmen im Laufe der Zeit immer neue Formen an, wobei im frühen 19. Jahrhundert zunächst morphosyntaktische Ansätze vorherrschen, die zwischen 1850 (Steinthal) und 1921 (Sapir) dann von komplexeren typologischen Verfahren abgelöst werden, die ihrerseits wieder durch die Suche nach einer strukturellen Einheitlichkeit aller Sprachen dieser Welt zurückgedrängt werden, wobei auch Fragen der Entwicklung einer Universalgrammatik mitspielen (Kapitel XXVII).

Im 19. Jahrhundert werden parallel hierzu Methoden der Datenerfassung bei schriftlich nicht fixierten Sprachen entwickelt sowie das wissenschaftliche Studium des Sprachlautes und der Lautproduzierung vorangetrieben. Damit gewinnt die Phonetik immer größerer Bedeutung, auch im Rahmen des Fremdsprachenunterrichts. Universelle Alphabete zur Aufzeichnung schriftloser Sprachen werden entwickelt und die Dialektologie nimmt ihren Aufschwung (Kapitel XXVIII). Aber auch semantische Forschungen gewinnen an Bedeutung. Hier reicht das Spektrum von den, eher bescheiden zu nennenden, Vorschlägen Reisigs über die Forschungen zum Bedeutungswandel am Ende des 19. Jahrhunderts bis hin zur Richtung 'Wörter und Sachen' am Anfang des 20. Jahrhunderts. Damit verbundene Arbeiten auf dem Gebiete der Lexikographie sind hier ebenfalls zu berücksichtigen (Kapitel XXIX). Schließlich sind auch Einflüsse von Psychologie und Physiologie auf die Sprachforschung des 19. Jahrhunderts zu verzeichnen, insbesondere im Werk von Wundt, Broca und Wernicke. Unter ihrem Einfluß entwickeln sich Untersuchungen zur Beziehung Sprache–Gehirn, insbesondere was Aphasie und Erstsprachenerwerb anbelangt (Kapitel XXX).

Die Wurzeln der strukturellen Sprachwissenschaft, welche gelegentlich mit dem Namen Saussures verbunden worden sind, reichen weit ins 19. Jahrhundert zurück. Im 20. Jahrhundert kommt es zur Herausbildung verschiedener Schulen und Forschungseinrichtungen, an deren Anfang die Genfer Schule steht. Strukturalistische Vorstellungen werden in der Folge auch für andere Humanwissenschaften bedeutsam, so die Anthropologie, Soziologie, Literaturtheorie und Psychologie (Kapitel XXXI). Nordamerika schlägt mit der Ethnolinguistik andere Wege ein. Auch sie hat ihre Wurzeln im 19. Jahrhundert, wo die Bedeutung der Indianersprachen für die Sprachforschung erkannt worden war. Die Sprachauffassung Humboldts war von entscheidender Bedeutung hierfür, wie auch die Anfänge einer anthropologisch orientierten Sprachforschung sowie die, getrennt von einander vorangetriebenen, Entwicklungen deskriptiver Ansätze. In diesem Zusammenhang kommt auch der Glottochronologie sowie der Lexikostatistik Bedeutung zu, kann man hierin doch den Versuch erblicken, bei Sprachen ohne Schrifttradition eine historische Dimension zu erschließen (Kapitel XXXII).

Zwischen 1940 und 1950 kommen neue Beschreibungsverfahren in und außerhalb Amerikas auf, welche durch den Versuch gekennzeichnet sind, Sprachen nach dem Vorbild der Mathematik mithilfe formaler Verfahren zu beschreiben. Die später aufkommende generative Sprachwissenschaft ist besonders charakteristisch hierfür. Mathematische Modelle sowie Arbeiten auf dem Gebiet der automatischen Übersetzung gewinnen damit immer größere Bededeutung für die sprachwissenschaftliche Theoriebildung, die sich in einer großen Zahl unterschiedlicher Entwürfe artikuliert, welche in mehr oder minder großem Maße der generativen Grammatik verpflichtet sind (Kapitel XXXIII).

Auch semantische Studien werden im 20. Jahrhundert in vielfältiger Form betrieben, aber nur ein kleinerer Teil davon geht auf Saussures Lehren zurück. Der Kontextualismus eines Firth und die generative Semantik können hier beispielsweise genannt werden, aber auch verschiedene Modelle der Lexikologie, der Lexikographie, Onomastik, Etymologie und jenen Arbeiten, die unter dem Einfluß der Semiotik von Peirce entstanden sind (Kapitel XXXIV). Ab Mitte des Jahrhunderts kommt es bei der Phonologie und Morphologie ebenfalls zu einer stärkeren Differenzierung in verschiedene Richtungen und Strömungen. Den Ausgangspunkt bilden Chomsky und Halles *Sound Pattern of English* (1968). Behandelt werden ferner Arbeiten von der 'nichtlinearen Phonologie' bis hin zur 'natürlichen Morphologie', von denen manche auf Vorschläge Chomskys und seiner Schule zurückgehen (Kapitel XXXV).

Die Dialektologie entwickelt sich im Laufe des 20. Jahrhunderts über Studien zu sprachlichen Varietäten zur Soziolinguistik. Die Entwicklung hebt an mit einer Debatte über Homogenität oder Heterogenität der Sprache und endet (vorläufig) bei der Sprachkontaktforschung, wobei das Spektrum des Forschungsinteresses von Pidgin- und Kreolsprachen bis hin zu Fragen der Sprachplanung reicht (Kapitel XXXVI). Als Folge der 'Saussureschen Wende' und dem damit eingeleiteten Aufschwung synchronischer Forschungen kommt es auf dem Bereich sprachhistorischer Forschungen in der ersten Hälfte unseres Jahrhunderts zunächst zu einer relativen Stagnation. Unter dem Einfluß neuer Forschungsannahmen (z. B. die Laryngal- und Glottal-Theorien) sowie angeregt durch die Resultate, welche die Kreolistik und Soziolinguistik bei Untersuchungen zum Sprachwandel erzielten, erfolgt ab der Mitte des Jahrhunderts dann wieder eine deutliche Neubelebung (Kapitel XXXVII). In den letzten drei Artikeln werden alternative ('parole'-orienterte) Ansätze zu den behandelten Forschungseinrichtungen dargestellt, u. a. derjenige Wittgenstein, der den Schwerpunkt auf den Sprachgebrauch legt, ferner Sprechakttheorie, Pragmatik und Textlinguistik, sowie Diskursanalyse und Aussagentheorie (Kapitel XXXVIII).

Im Kapitel XXXIX, dem längsten Kapitel des Handbuchs, geht um den Nachweis, daß die Vorstellung von der Autonomie der Sprachwissenschaft, welche seit den Anfängen des 20. Jahrhunderts nachdrücklich vertreten worden waren, heute zugunsten multidisziplinärer Sprachstudien, also im Hinblick auf eine Integration von Erkenntnissen auf dem Gebiet der Semiotik, Philosophie, Psychologie, Neurologie, Biologie, der Künstlichen Intelligenz, maschinelle Übersetzung usw. langsam aufgegeben wird. In dem Maße, wie die Sprachforschung sich aber anderen Disziplinen gegenüber als offen erweist, durchdringen sprachwissenschaftliche Kenntnisse auch diese Bereiche und werden hier fruchtbar.

Im abschließenden Kapitel XL legen die Herausgeber, ein jeder für sich, aber einander ergänzend, ihre Auffassung von Ursprung, Entwicklung und Zukunft der Geschichte der Sprachwissenschaften dar und erläutern ihre Position hinsichtlich der Methodologie und Epistemologie einer Geschichte der Sprachwissenschaften.

Die Herausgeber

# Préface des éditeurs

## 1. Généralités

### 1.1 Définitions

Dans ce manuel, sous le nom d''Histoire des sciences du langage' nous entendons tout aussi bien l'évolution des théories et conceptions linguistiques, des procédés d'analyse et des délimitations méthodologiques, que la formation de structures organisatrices et d'institutions qui ont contribué à l'expansion des connaissances linguistiques par l'histoire documentée de l'humanité. L'utilisation des termes 'sciences du langage' et/ou 'linguistique' ne doit pas porter à confusion; dans un sens étroit on pourrait soutenir que ce terme ne s'applique qu'à l'époque moderne, lorsqu'on a reconnu la linguistique en tant que domaine d'étude à part, avec ses propres principes nettement définis de recherche et d'organisation professionelle. Toutefois, plusieurs traditions linguistiques assignaient un statut particulier, parmi les diverses branches du savoir, à la science qui s'occupait du langage. Malgré le fait que les diverses traditions pouvaient différer les unes des autres quant aux limites de cette science du point de vue des sujets et des méthodes, de façon générale ces traditions sont liées les unes aux autres en ce qu'elles voient en le langage un objet digne d'intérêt en soi. Dans ce manuel, nous utilisons les termes 'sciences du langage' et/ou 'linguistique' essentiellement comme désignation générale pour tout ce qui a trait à l'étude du langage humain. Les délimitations du domaine d'objets des sciences du langage, qui n'ont pas cessé d'être remodelées au cours des siècles, seront présentées par rapport à leur histoire ainsi qu'à leurs relations mouvementées avec d'autres disciplines.

Dans la plupart des domaines de la linguistique, il est devenu d'usage de faire précéder les présentations encyclopédiques d'un aperçu historique qui donne des informations sur la création et la formation de la discipline (cf. les chapitres de ce type dans les manuels de la série où paraît cet ouvrage). Il s'agit habituellement de décrire la constitution de certains programmes qui ont conduit à l'état actuel et aux tâches présentes de la recherche. Pour des raisons évidentes, une telle pratique est impossible dans un manuel d'histoire des sciences du langage, puisqu'il s'agit de présenter et d'expliquer la création et l'évolution des théories linguistiques, dans leur passé comme dans leur actualité, en ce qu'elles ont de particulier. Dans cette présentation, on souligne l'explication de leur évolution du point de vue de leur dynamique interne propre comme du point de vue des facteurs externes que sont l'évolution sociale et culturelle de la société d'où proviennent ces théories.

Comme dans toute représentation historique des sciences, il y a des relations assez complexes entre, d'un côté, la discipline que l'on prend pour objet et, de l'autre, celle qui, à un niveau supérieur, analyse ses méthodes, ses hypothèses de base et son évolution. C'est pourquoi il importe de distinguer une histoire des recherches linguistiques, qui analyse leur création et leur évolution, et l'objet de ces recherches. Même si la plupart des historiens sont eux-mêmes des linguistes, l'analyse historique doit se distinguer, dans sa visée et son point de vue, des travaux de linguiste, afin de pouvoir décrire les lignes d'évolution internes sans que soient portés des jugements de valeur fondés sur d'autres théories. En fin de compte, le but de l'historien des sciences du langage est d'éclaircir des tendances évolutives à l'intérieur d'un cadre concret (culturel, socio-économique et/ou politique), ainsi que d'exposer les contacts temporaires de certaines directions de recherche avec d'autres disciplines. Mais, dans tous les cas, il faut éviter d'avoir des oeillères.

Essentiellement, les buts de l'historiographie de la linguistique diffèrent de ceux de la linguistique en ce que l'historiographe ne cherche pas à mettre en lumière des faits linguistiques, mais plutôt à mettre en lumière comment des penseurs appartenant à des traditions diverses ont affronté les questions de structure et d'usage linguistique. Ceci signifie également qu'aux yeux de l'historiographe toutes les approches se valent également: il n'y a pas d'hiérarchisation possible de ces approches en terme de leur valeur, encore moins un 'progrès' du domaine jusqu'à l'époque contemporaine. Aux yeux de l'historiographe, le passé du domaine ne peut servir à légitimiser son état actuel.

## 1.2 Envergure

Dans la définition qu'on vient de lire nous avons déjà esquissé les objectifs du manuel. Il s'agit de présenter une vue d'ensemble sur les théories et conceptions qui se sont jamais développées à propos du langage et des langues ainsi que les contextes dans lesquels elles se sont produites. Nous essaierons donc, autant que possible, de construire une représentation et de produire une documentation sur toutes les recherches concernant le langage conçu comme moyen de communication de par l'histoire, qu'elles soient de nature théorique ou pratique. Nous tiendrons également compte, de façon appropriée, des grammaires scolaires, des lexiques et d'autres ouvrages qui relèvent des activités de recherche linguistique, que nous décrirons et expliquerons en fonction de leurs rôles dans les activités humaines et de leurs théorisations implicites.

Il faut cependant mentionner une importante restriction. Le manuel ne traite que des recherches qui sont transmises par écrit. Cela signifie que ce que l'on nomme 'linguistique populaire', tout comme les prises de position envers les langues, doivent être réservées à d'autres manuels, par exemple, au manuel de sociolinguistique. La même restriction vaut pour les études empiriques portant sur les attitudes langagières: bien que les attitudes langagières jouent un rôle important dans la mise en place d'idées et de théories linguistiques, on ne les aborde que lorsqu'on les mentionne directement dans les écrits linguistiques.

Certes, dans quelques cas particuliers, on ne peut éviter des recoupements avec d'autres manuels de la série. Par exemple, il n'est pas possible de distinguer nettement l'histoire des sciences du langage et celle de la philosophie du langage; c'est particulièrement vrai dans le cas de certaines traditions non-occidentales, telles que la chinoise et la sanskrite, où sont liées de manière inextricable linguistique et philosophie du langage. Par conséquent, les deux manuels concernés contiendront chacun des sections sur certaines traditions philosophiques importantes par rapport au langage. Seront ainsi prises en compte dans ce manuel, par exemple, les traditions des Grecs anciens, notamment de Platon, d'Aristote ou des Stoïciens, ainsi que celle des grammaires spéculatives de la fin du Moyen Âge, eu égard à leur importance pour la recherche linguistique et non pour ce qui concerne la philosophie.

Une caractéristique importante de ce manuel est donc d'approcher d'une présentation à peu près complète dans l'espace et dans le temps de toutes les branches de la recherche linguistique. Ceci signifie également que nous voulons dépasser cette visée eurocentrique qui, le plus souvent, ne tient compte dans une section de la grammaire sanskrite uniquement parce que (et dans la mesure où) elle a présenté un intérêt dans la découverte de la famille des langues indo-européennes, ou alors ne tient compte dans une section de la linguistique arabe classique que pour se donner bonne conscience plutôt que pour briser l'hégémonie occidentale (autoproclamée). D'autre part, lorsqu'on a tenu compte récemment dans certaines histoires de la linguistique générale de certaines traditions non-occidentales, on a le plus souvent mis l'emphase sur les individus les plus importants, ainsi Pāṇini (dans le cas du Sanskrit) ou Sībawayhi (dans le cas de l'arabe). Notre but dans ce manuel a été de comprendre autant que possible toutes les traditions linguistiques possibles, tant majeures que mineures, nous efforçant d'offrir un panorama aussi complet que possible de toutes les diverses formes que l'étude du langage a prises au cours des siècles. Idéal que nous n'avons pas toujours atteint, évidemment: la documentation ne suffit pas dans le cas de certaines traditions. Ainsi, nous n'avons pu, par exemple, comprendre des articles sur les traditions linguistiques éthiopiennes ou cambodgiennes, pour ne mentionner que deux exemples. Dans d'autres cas, nous avons eu à laisser tomber un article pour des raisons purement pratiques, vu qu'il s'est avéré impossible de trouver un auteur compétent, ou alors l'auteur que nous avions invité ne pouvait terminer l'article à temps et de ce fait ne pouvait se trouver dans le Manuel.

L'un des problèmes que nous avons rencontrés a été de trouver une limite chronologique pour la recherche contemporaine. Même s'il était plus simple d'ignorer les tout derniers développements, nous n'avons pas choisi cette voie. Il va sans dire qu'on ne peut procéder à une analyse historique des recherches contemporaines que si l'on respecte un certain nombre de mesures de prudence, surtout quand ceux qui décrivent l'évolution d'un domaine entreprennent aussi des recherches dans ce domaine et, pour cette raison, ne sont peut-être pas tout à fait prêts à distinguer entre les recherches linguistiques et les recherches sur l'histoire des recherches linguistiques. Nous avons essayé, dans la dernière partie du manuel, par sa structure et par le choix des auteurs, de faire face et de présenter largement les hypothèses de base et les principes qui sont les fondements de l'ouvrage. En tout cas, nous sommes convaincus qu'une présentation des sciences du langage contemporaines d'un point de vue historique contribue à une meilleure compréhension et qu'elle souligne autant leur importance dans la recherche moderne que dans l'histoire de la discipline.

## 1.3 Les dominantes thématiques

Les directeurs de la publication sont tombés d'accord dès le départ sur ce qu'il ne fallait pas céder à une forme d'exposé largement répandue, l'"Histoire des grands personnages', même si ce procédé peut, çà et là, produire des résultats utilisables, comme c'est le cas pour la linguistique européenne des XIXe et XXe siècles. Mais il semble douteux qu'une telle approche garde encore sa valeur quand il s'agit des périodes plus anciennes de la tradition occidentale ou celles, plus anciennes encore, des traditions orientales. Même lorsque les articles traitent des contributions de linguistes en tant qu'individus, on souligne les thèmes propres, l'orientation de la pensée linguistique, la direction de la recherche et les liens unissant l'individu à l'évolution de la tradition.

Par rapport à l'immense latitude de variation géographique, chronologique et thématique dans le champ des recherches linguistiques possibles, il n'est pas facile de nommer un thème central qui pourrait décrire de façon unifiante l'accès que l'on a choisi. On peut, cependant, citer quelques aspects selon lesquels nous avons effectué le choix des thèmes, la présentation du contenu ainsi que l'organisation et l'analyse du matériau.

L'analyse de l'évolution des sciences du langage en branches 'dominantes', 'marginales' ou 'sous-jacentes' forme une sorte de leitmotiv. Quoiqu'il soit possible dans la tradition occidentale de dégager, pour certaines périodes, des programmes de recherche qui, pour une grande partie du monde cultivé, sont demeurés valables durant un certain temps, on ne peut jamais parler du monopole d'un 'paradigme'. Dans l'histoire des recherches linguistiques on ne peut pratiquement pas déceler de changements de cap qui soient provoqués par l'effondrement soudain des programmes de recherche précédents ou par de quelconques 'découvertes révolutionnaires'. Au lieu de cela, on observe souvent des transitions souples entre des intérêts de recherche 'dominants' et d'autres qui étaient 'sous-jacents'. C'est pour cette raison que, parallèlement au paradigme dominant, nous suivrons d'autres programmes de recherche 'marginaux', puisque ceux-ci, au fil du temps, passent à l'avant-plan et peuvent devenir la 'pratique et/ou théorie dominante'.

On peut faire remarquer, en rapport avec la conception de l'histoire des sciences ici esquissée, qu'il semble y avoir une sorte de balancement régulier entre deux conceptions opposées concernant la façon de procéder en abordant la recherche linguistique. On peut effectivement observer des périodes où la langue est traitée comme un outil idéal servant à un locuteur idéal dans des situations de communication idéales. Ces périodes sont ensuite relayées par d'autres périodes où la recherche linguistique se tourne à nouveau, dans l'espace et dans le temps, vers la diversité des langues et la variété linguistique. On peut remarquer une telle oscillation au XIXe siècle, au cours duquel le programme de la grammaire comparée est remis en cause par l'émergence de la dialectologie. La distinction entre une direction 'dominante' et une direction 'sous-jacente' signifie qu'aucune des deux ne fait jamais complètement disparaître l'autre mais qu'elles sont poursuivies parallèlement. C'est ainsi qu'elles peuvent occuper sans cesse de nouvelles places sur une échelle entre la 'position dominante' et le 'phénomène marginal'. Dans la linguistique du XXe siècle semble se profiler un changement de position de même type, car à côté de l'intérêt apparemment dominant pour les structures systématiques et idéales de la langue se manifeste clairement ces derniers temps un intéràt tant pour les variations linguistiques que pour le fonctionnement de la langue dans les situations (complexes) de communication.

La distinction entre théorie 'dominante' et directions 'sous-jacentes' semble également être applicable aux institutions linguistiques. Aujourd'hui, en dehors du paradigme dominant, ces institutions traitent assez souvent, en effet, des questions de grammaire dans un sens plus pratique, de l'histoire des langues, du 'trésor' d'une langue, de la structure d'une langue ou de questions de parenté, même si le paradigme dominant s'oriente vers d'autres intéràts de recherche. Cela aussi fait partie d'un tableau complet des sciences du langage et, dans un manuel comme celui-ci, on doit en tenir compte.

Notre but était, en outre, d'éviter toute sorte de 'contrainte induite par le système' lors du classement du matériel ou de la division en chapitres et articles. Le grand nombre des collaborateurs qui, venant des écoles les plus variées, apportent ainsi leurs connaissances spécifiques, devrait offrir des garanties suffisantes à ce qu'un large spectre de perspectives puisse s'exprimer. Toute tentative visant à enfermer les travaux sur l'histoire des sciences du langage dans un schéma classificatoire étroit est voué à l'échec; une telle tentative déformerait les faits et rendrait moins clairs les changements évolutifs dans chacune des traditions. Comme on a fait remarquer ci-dessus, on a évité l'approche biographique, mais malgré cela sont inclus des articles traitant des réussites et buts d'un individu ou d'un certain groupe de penseurs dans le contexte d'un examen d'ensemble de l'évolution de ladite tradition.

L'absence d'un cadre d'organisation étroit a une conséquence supplémentaire que nous croyons positive: elle préserve la possibilité de choisir entre une présentation de l'histoire des sciences du langage 'orientée vers les données et/ou les résultats' et une présentation 'orientée vers les théories'. Nous sommes convaincus qu'un choix exclusif pour l'une ou l'autre de ces possibilités doit conduire à biaiser la représentation. Dans certains cas, il est plus avantageux de privilégier ce qu'a engendré une théorie ou ce qu'a produit une époque; dans d'autres cas, une discussion des méthodes, principes et hypothèses d'un programme de recherche donne une image plus claire des traditions linguistiques. Les deux approches se complètent justement lors de la présentation des tendances de développement.

### 1.4 L'état de la recherche

Bien qu'il innove, en quelque sorte par la largeur de sa structure, notre ouvrage a la possibilité de s'appuyer sur les résultats de recherches antérieures. L'histoire des sciences du langage n'est apparue comme discipline autonome, dotée de ses propres formes d'organisation, de revues et de collections, qu'entre la fin des années 60 et le début des années 70. Cela ne veut pas dire qu'avant les années 60 il n'y ait eu aucune présentation générale de l'histoire des sciences du langage. Dans le cas de plusieurs traditions non-occidentales l'histoire du domaine faisait partie de l'apprentissage. Ainsi, les grammairiens arabes se servaient de gros dictionnaires biographiques on l'on traitait des travaux de générations antérieures de grammairiens. Ces histoires ne s'occupaient que de l'histoire d'une tradition. Dans la linguistique occidentale, les introductions historiques se rattachaient le plus souvent à l'examen de langues ou de groupes de langues particuliers, ou de pair avec l'examen de sujets linguistiques particuliers, par exemple la phonologie ou la sémantique, où l'on traçait dans leurs grandes lignes les travaux antérieurs.

L'ouvrage de François Thurot *Tableau des progrès de la science grammaticale*, qui fut publié comme "Discours préliminaire" de sa traduction (parue en 1796) du *Hermès* (1751) de James Harris, a été caractérisé par certains chercheurs comme la 'première tentative d'une histoire de la grammaire'. Ce n'est que vers le milieu du XIXe siècle que des présentations historiques plus vastes (parmi lesquelles il faudrait citer en priorité la *Sprachphilosophie der Alten* en 3 volumes de Laurenz Lersch, 1838–1841), seront publiées. La philologie classique était alors prépondérante; ce qui avait pour conséquence qu'à l'exception des Grecs, des Romains et, partiellement, des Indiens, toutes les autres traditions restaient exclues. Cette exclusion frappait dans sa totalité la recherche linguistique qui va du Moyen Age jusqu'aux temps modernes. On en trouvera un exemple typique dans la *Geschichte der Sprachwissenschaft bei den Griechen und Römern* (Steinthal 1863), qui finalement ne traite que de la philosophie du langage antique et non de la recherche linguistique au sens propre.

Ce n'est qu'avec les travaux historiques de Benfey (1869), Raumer (1870), Delbrück (1880, surtout à partir de la 4e édition de 1904) et Bursian (1883), que l'on tient compte des périodes récentes de la linguistique, mais avec une préférence unilatérale pour les temps modernes. L'orientation eurocentrique des conceptions et idées linguistiques est restée dominante jusqu'à nos jours, bien qu'aient paru depuis la fin du XIXe siècle des traités sur l'évolution des grammaires de l'hébreu et de l'arabe.

Même si un nombre important de manuels et de traité pédagogiques consacrés à l'histoire des sciences du langage a été publié dans les années 60 de notre siècle, il semble que ce soit seulement dans les années 70 qu'un véritable intérêt pour les traditions extra-européennes puisse être perçu. On peut constater cette évolution récente en lisant l'*Historiography of Linguistics* en 2 volumes, publiée en 1975 comme postface des *Current Trends in Linguistics* dirigés par Thomas A. Sebeok. Elle contient, outre les chapitres 'habituels', des aperçus des traditions linguistiques en Extrême Orient ainsi qu'en Amérique du Nord et du Sud. Il est frappant que, dans de nombreuses contributions, on entende par 'histoire' une sorte de rapport de recherche, en parallèle avec la linguistique occidentale, sur les 'publications récentes en histoire des sciences du langage', plutôt qu'un travail de recherche indépendant, comme on l'aurait peut-être attendu.

Notre manuel, à l'encontre de l'orientation que l'on vient de décrire, adopte le modèle du type d'histoire des sciences qui se profile de plus en plus nettement depuis 1973, année de publication de la première revue (*Historiographia Linguistica,* Amsterdam) entièrement consacrée à l'histoire des sciences du langage. Peu après cette parution furent fondées des sociétés internationales et régionales d'histoire des sciences du langage; les premiers séminaires et congrès eurent lieu en Europe et en Amérique. Lors de ces séminaires et congrès, on traitait non seulement des théories linguistiques du passé ou de traditions de recherche particulières, mais également des questions méthodologiques et épistémologiques posées par l'approche historique. La meilleure façon de constater les progrès qui ont été faits dans ce domaine, lors des dernières années, est de lire les revues *Historiographia Linguistica, Histoire Epistémologie Langage* (Paris, 1979–) et *Beiträge zur Geschichte der Sprachwissenschaft* (Münster, 1991–), ainsi que les actes de l'International Conference on the History of the Language Sciences (ICHoLS) qui, depuis 1978, a lieu tous les trois ans. Dans les années 80 ont été publiées des monographies consacrées à la théorie et à la méthodologie de l'histoire des sciences du langage qui illustrent encore mieux l'orientation actuelle de la discipline. Ces débats continuent toujours.

Vers l'époque où l'on commença d'abord à parler de l'actuel projet, Peter Schmitter donna le coup d'envoi à sa *Geschichte der Sprachtheorie* (Tübingen, 1987–), une série de monographies traitant de divers champs et périodes de l'histoire de la linguistique, dont 4 (sur 9 volumes prévus) ont été publiés jusqu'à maintenant. Avec des buts comparables, Sylvain Auroux a mis en place une *Histoire des idées linguistiques* (Bruxelles, 1990–2000) en 3 volumes, suivi d'un *History of Linguistics* (Londres, 1994–) en 5 volumes, sous la direction de Giulio Lepschy. Pendant ce temps, E. F. K. Koerner et R. E. Asher ont fait paraître leur ouvrage de 500 pages, *Concise History of the Language Sciences from the Sumerians to the Cognitivists* (Oxford, 1995), qui non seulement offre un tour d'horizon des plus importantes traditions, mais offre également une vue d'ensemble assez contemporaine des diverses écoles, théories et tendances de la linguistique du XXe siècle que l'on ne trouve dans aucune de ces histoires à plusieurs volumes. Pour un exposé plus détaillé des sciences du langage au XXe siècle, on devra attendre la publication du volume III de l'actuel projet.

Pour des renseignements sur la plupart des grands personnages dans l'histoire de la linguistique mondiale, le *Lexicon grammaticorum* de 1000 pages (Tübingen, 1996), sous la direction de Harro Stammerjohann, sera la principale source de renseignements pour bien des années à venir.

## 1.5 Structure du manuel

Nous avons organisé cet ouvrage, avant tout, selon une orientation chronologique. Néanmoins, il s'avérait nécessaire de dévier de ce principe pour les premiers chapitres, consacrées aux traditions non-occidentales, que l'on dépeint de façon parallèle, indépendemment de la chronologie, bien que ces recherches linguistiques du Moyen et et de l'Extrême Orient se sont établies, de façon parallèle et indépendante, en des lieux géographiquement séparés. Dans certains cas, lorsqu'une tradition a eu pour principal point de départ une tradition extérieure étrangère, on a traité de cette tradition du point de vue de la tradition-mère. Ainsi, on a pris cette décision dans le cas de la linguistique arménienne et géorgienne, dont on traite dans le chapitre sur la tradition grecque, ou la linguistique copte et turque, dont on traite dans le chapitre sur la tradition grammaticale arabe, et la linguistique vietnamienne, dont on traite dans le chapitre sur la tradition linguistique chinoise. Vu que la plupart des traditions, à un moment ou l'autre, ont subi l'influence d'autres traditions, cette division n'est pas sans un certain arbitraire et ne saurait être prise pour un jugement sur la valeur intrinsèque de la tradition examinée.

Les traditions grecques et latines ont joué un rôle-clef pour ce qui est de l'apparition de la tradition linguistique occidentale, mais on les examine ici sans prendre en considération leur rôle lors de la période suivant la Renaissance. La linguistique, après la Renaissance, a évidemment pris pour base la tradition latine et grecque, mais on en a parfois exaggéré l'importance: la grammaire grecque et latine ont été bien autre chose que des préparatifs en vue de l'apparition des courants principaux de la linguistique occidentale. C'est à partir des traditions linguistiques grecques et romaines, que l'ordre chronologique sera davantage respecté.

Le manuel passe ensuite aux courants dominants de la linguistique occidentale et établit une coupure avec la Renaissance, époque où les langues vernaculaires de l'Europe Occidentale sont devenues objets de recherche, moyens de recherche et métalangues. Désormais, la recherche linguistique n'a plus uniquement une seule langue comme objet et comme cadre de référence. Ce schéma n'est, bien évidemment, pas valable pour les traditions non-occidentales. Pour décrire ces traditions, on parle volontiers de nos jours d'époque 'classique', de 'Moyen Âge' et de 'Renaissance', utilisant des termes qui à l'origine servaient exclusivement à décrire les évolutions propres à l'hémisphère occidental. Ces termes devraient être évités pour la description des traditions non-occidentales, pas seulement parce qu'ils sont associés à trop de connotations qui renvoient à l'Europe. On peut cependant parler également d'une coupure à propos de ces traditions: elle a été causée par l'importation des recherches linguistiques occidentales, ce qui provoqua une fusion de la science linguistique locale avec le modèle européen. Avec la Renaissance (si l'on prend le terme en ce sens), le modèle occidental prend une position dominante à travers le monde, ce qui permet d'envisager une représentation unifiée de la recherche linguistique durant les périodes qui lui succédèrent.

Un autre tournant décisif dans l'histoire de la recherche linguistique eut lieu au XIXe siècle, lorsque la linguistique historique et comparative se dégagea comme paradigme dominant. Pour finir, l'histoire de notre siècle commence avec l'orientation vers la synchronie. C'est au XXe et au au XIXe siècles, que nous consacrons la plus large place dans ce manuel.

Les aspects thématiques ont présidé au découpage des périodes en chapitres; mais, autant la distinction entre branche 'dominante' et intérêts de recherche 'sous-jacents' que d'autres considérations substantielles y jouent également un rôle. En ce qui concerne la représentation des évolutions les plus récentes des sciences du langage, il n'est plus question, pour des raisons évidentes, d'un ordre purement chronologique. Au lieu de cela, nous nous sommes concentrés sur les points communs et les divergences méthodologiques des théories en question. Nous avons, en outre, prêté attention aux points de contact entre les sciences du langage et les disciplines voisines, comme la sociologie, la psychologie, la neurologie, la logique, les mathématiques, etc. Cette relation mutuelle entre les sciences du langage et les disciplines voisines est, en effet, l'une des caractéristiques les plus frappantes de notre temps.

## 2. Commentaires sur les différents chapitres

La recherche linguistique du Proche Orient s'occupe principalement de problèmes d'écriture et de lexique. En outre, l'existence de différents dialectes et la coexistence de différentes langues de culture impliquent une certaine contrainte de la codification grammaticale (chapitre I).

Le chapitre II traite de la recherche linguistique en Chine. La phonétique et le lexique sont ici les centres d'intérêt. Mais, dans le cadre de considérations philosophiques, il est aussi question de l'évolution d'importantes représentations de la nature du signe linguistique (dans sa forme phonique et graphique). La langue joue, en outre, un rôle capital en tant que médium littéraire. La recherche linguistique chinoise a eu une grande influence sur la Corée (chapitre III) et le Japon (chapitre IV). Le bilinguisme caractéristique de ces deux cas mène cependant à des études de grammaire contrastives. On s'intéresse aussi à l'emploi de modèles grammaticaux néerlandais pour la langue japonaise, lors de la période Rangakusha.

La science indienne, l'une des plus importantes parmi celles qui sont indépendantes de l'Occident, a suscité, ainsi que le sanskrit, un grand intérêt dans la littérature historiographique. C'est d'elle que provient la première tentative de description complète d'une langue (en l'occurrence le sanskrit), utilisant une méthode formelle stricte, l'*Asṭādhyāyī* de Pāṇini. Un autre aspect important de la recherche linguistique indienne est son association à la philosophie et à la logique. Le modèle indien (sanskrit) a eu des effets sur la description du javanais ancien et du burmesien (chapitre V). Dans le cas des recherches linguistiques consacrées aux langues dravidiennes (chapitre VI) et au tibétain (chapitre VII), les traditions propres se fondent plus ou moins avec le modèle adopté en provenance du sanskrit.

La recherche linguistique hébraïque se développe à partir de l'exégèse des textes religieux. Dans une phase postérieure, elle assimile certains éléments de la tradition arabe qui devient finalement dominante. On trouve également dans ce contexte une première tentative visant à démontrer la relation entre les différentes langues sémitiques (chapitre VIII). Dans la recherche linguistique arabe, la relation entre la langue et la religion est déterminante pour l'évolution des conceptions de son origine et de sa nature. Le *Kitāb* de Sībawayhi, qui contient une présentation complète et systématique de l'arabe, marque le début d'une recherche linguistique indépendante. Son modèle servira plus tard à la description d'autres langues, telles que le malais, le persan, le turc et le copte. La recherche syrienne est intéressante notamment dans le sens où elle combine des éléments de deux traditions, grecque et arabe (chapitre X).

Dans certaines histoires des sciences du langage, la recherche linguistique grecque est présentée en fonction de son rôle modèle pour le latin et pour la tradition occidentale toute entière. Les éléments qui n'ont pas été adoptés ultérieurement font habituellement figure de parents pauvres. Nous avons choisi, au contraire, une présentation qui illustre la tradition linguistique grecque en tant que telle. Les premières sections ne suivent qu'un ordre chronologique sommaire. Elles traitent de la dépendance mutuelle entre la philosophie antique et la grammaire ainsi que des traditions philologiques et des aspects techniques de cette dernière, qui, à une époque plus récente, sont fondés sur la *Téchnè* de Denys le Thrace. Les sections suivantes traitent du rôle de la grammaire dans le système éducatif et de la relation entre la science du langage et d'autres disciplines. Les traductions de la *Téchnè* sont à la base de beaucoup d'autres traditions linguistiques, comme celles du géorgien, de l'arménien, du syriaque et du vieux slavon liturgique.

La recherche linguistique grecque a aussi été un modèle important pour la latine (chapitre XII). Cette dernière atteint son apogée avec les travaux, entre autres, de Charisius, Donat ou Priscien dont les descriptions grammaticales constitueront pour le début du Moyen Âge le point de départ d'une longue tradition d'études latines. Les sections suivantes de ce chapitre sont consacrés à la relation entre grammaire et rhétorique, et entre langue et révélation dans la théologie des débuts du christianisme. Au début du Moyen Âge (chapitre XIII), les études du latin demeurent un facteur décisif pour l'évolution de la recherche linguistique. D'autres sections sont dédiés à leur rapport avec la théologie, à leur position dans la systématique des sciences et à leur rôle dans la société. Pendant le Haut Moyen Âge, on parvient à une distinction entre théorie linguistique (*grammatica speculativa*) et description linguistique (*grammatica positiva*). Le chapitre XIV traite de la grammaire spéculative de ceux que l'on appelle les modistes ainsi que de la relation entre les recherches linguistiques, la grammaire, la théologie et les autres disciplines.

Le chapitre XV traite de la survie du type de recherche linguistique pré-modiste, d'une part dans la description du latin, d'autre part dans le début des premières analyses grammaticales de différentes langues vernaculaires telles que l'irlandais, le gaélique, l'islandais, l'anglais et diverses langues slaves. La dernière section est consacrée à l'Occitan (ou Provençal) qui occupe dans ce cadre une position particulière; c'est une langue littéraire, elle est étudiée, décrite grammaticalement et stylistiquement en tant que telle depuis la Catalogne et la Castille jusqu'à l'Italie du Nord et la Sicile.

Le 'retour' aux langues classiques (latin et grec) et aux sources qui se sont exprimées dans ces langues conduit au cours du XVe siècle à une nouvelle orientation de la linguistique (occidentale); c'est au chapitre XVI qu'est traitée la rupture qui s'effectue ainsi. A peu près à la même époque se développe parallèlement, d'abord chez les marchands puis chez les nobles, un intérêt pratique pour les langues vernaculaires, revalorisées de fait par l'Humanisme; un apprentissage régulier de ces langues se met en place (chapitre XVII). La transposition des conceptions humanistes aux vernaculaires ouvre le chemin à une description grammaticale (et lexicale) de textes littéraires rédigés dans ces langues (chapitre XVIII). L'étape suivante mène à dresser, pour les vernaculaires dont l'importance ne cesse de croître, une liste de règles et de lois et à élaborer une norme (chapitre XIX).

La découverte du Nouveau Monde par les Portugais, les Espagnols, les Anglais, les Français et les Hollandais, qui a lieu à peu près au même moment que le retour aux langues classiques, met l'Europe en contact avec des langues 'exotiques', qui sont d'abord étudiées non pas en tant que telles, mais dans le but pratique d'évangéliser ces mondes nouvellement découverts (chapitre XX). Ce n'est qu'au cours du XVIIe siècle que les réflexions de linguistique théorique reconquièrent une signification; c'est, en fait, au XVIIIe siècle qu'elles suscitent un grand intérêt (chapitre XXI). La revalorisation des vernaculaires et l'explication de leur égalité avec les langues classiques conduit du même coup à des points de vue théoriques, qui apparaissent d'abord dans des traités sur l'origine des langues (chapitre XXI), conduisent ensuite à des recherches sur la naissance et l'évolution de langues nationales particulières, recherches où les relations entres les différentes langues nationales jouent un rôle important (chapitre XXIII).

Pendant la première moitié du XIXe siècle, la naissance et le développement de la recherche linguistique historico-comparative concernant l'Indo-européen conduit à un refoulement de la tradition, établie depuis longtemps, des études linguistiques philologico-littéraires. La création de chaires pour ce nouveau domaine de recherche contribue de manière décisive à son développement (chapitre XXIV). Cette évolution a rapidement un impact sur les 'Nouvelles Philologies', c'est-à-dire sur de nouvelles disciplines qui n'étudient plus les langues classiques grec, latin et sanskrit, mais des langues et groupes de langues plus récents. On en vient, là aussi, à une institutionnalisation et une professionnalisation, par la création de chaires et la fondation de nouvelles revues (chapitre XXV).

La 'méthode comparative' se développe, au centre de la philologie historico-comparative indo-européenne, comme un instrument de reconstruction d'états de langue antérieurs (et de la langue primitive présumée). Au cours de la seconde moitié du XIXe siècle, cette méthode est appliquée à des familles de langues non indo-européennes, comme les langues africaines, austronésiennes ou encore amérindiennes (chapitre XXVI).

Les tentatives de classification des langues adoptent au fil du temps de nouvelles formes. Les approches morphosyntaxiques dominent le début du XIXe siècle, et sont ensuite évincées entre 1850 (Steinthal) et 1921 (Sapir) par des procédés typologiques plus complexes, qui sont refoulés à leur tour par la recherche d'une unité structurelle de toutes les langues du monde où il est également question du développement d'une grammaire universelle (chapitre XXVII).

Parallèlement à cela, des méthodes de saisie de données pour les langues non fixées par écrit se développent durant le XIXe siècle, tout comme l'étude scientifique du son (linguistique) et de sa production. La phonétique prend de plus en plus d'importance grâce à ces nouvelles recherches, mais aussi dans le cadre des cours de langues étrangères. On développe des alphabets universels pour la transcription des langues non écrites et la dialectologie prend son essor (chapitre XXVIII). Les recherches sémantiques gagnent également de l'importance, depuis les propositions de Reisig, plutôt modestes, vers les années 30, et les études concernant les changements de sens de la fin du XIXe siècle, jusqu'au courant 'des mots et des choses' (Wörter und Sachen) au début du XXe siècle. Des travaux apparentés dans le domaine de la lexicographie sont également à prendre en considération (chapitre XXIX). Il faut, pour terminer, aussi mentionner les influences de la psychologie et de la physiologie sur la recherche linguistique du XIXe siècle, et tout particulièrement l'oeuvre de Wundt. C'est sous son influence que se développent des recherches sur les relations entre le langage et le cerveau, spécialement en ce qui concerne l'aphasie et l'acquisition de la langue maternelle (chapitre XXX).

Les racines de la linguistique structurale, qui, à l'occasion, ont été associées au nom de Saussure, remontent fort avant dans le XIXe siècle. On en arrive au XXe siècle à la formation de différentes écoles et orientations de recherche, avec, à leur origine, l'École de Genève. Les conceptions structuralistes deviennent par la suite également importantes pour d'autres sciences humaines comme l'anthropologie, la sociologie, la théorie littéraire et la psychologie (chapitre XXXI). Avec l'ethnolinguistique, l'Amérique du Nord choisit d'autres voies. Celle-ci trouvent aussi leurs racines au XIXe siècle, au cours duquel on a progressivement reconnu l'importance des langues amérindiennes pour la recherche linguistique. Sur ce point, les conceptions de Humboldt ont été également d'une importance décisive, tout comme les débuts d'une recherche linguistique tournée vers l'anthropologie et le développement de travaux descriptifs, menés indépendamment les uns des autres. Dans ce contexte il ne faut pas négliger la glottochronologie et la lexico-statistique, dans lesquelles on peut déceler une tentative pour donner une dimension historique aux langues sans tradition écrite (chapitre XXXII).

Entre 1940 et 1950, de nouveaux procédés de description émergent en Amérique et ailleurs; on peut les caractériser par la tentative de décrire les langues à l'aide de procédés formels, sur le modèle des mathématiques. La linguistique générative, qui apparaît plus tard, est caractéristique de ces tentatives. Les modèles mathématiques, ainsi que les travaux dans le domaine de la traduction automatique, sont d'une importance toujours croissante pour l'élaboration de théories linguistiques, qui s'articulent en un grand nombre de projets, tous plus ou moins tributaires de la grammaire générative (chapitre XXXIII).

Au XXe siècle, des études sémantiques sont menées sous de multiples formes; une petite partie seulement provient des théories de Saussure. On peut citer ici, à titre d'exemple, le contextualisme de Firth et la sémantique générative mais aussi différents modèles de lexicologie, lexicographie, onomastique, étymologie et les travaux exécutés sous l'influence de la sémiotique de Peirce (chapitre XXXIV). A partir du milieu du siècle, on en vient à une plus forte diversification de la phonologie et de la morphologie en différentes branches et courants. Le point de départ est donné par *Sound Pattern of English* de Chomsky et Halle (1968). Sont également traités des travaux allant de la 'phonologie non-linéaire' jusqu'à la 'morphologie naturelle' parmi lesquels certains trouvent leur origine dans des propositions de Chomsky et son école (chapitre XXXV).

Au cours du XXe siècle, la dialectologie, en passant par des études sur les variations linguistiques, est absorbée par la socio-linguistique. L'évolution commence avec un débat sur l'homogénéité ou l'hétérogénéité de la langue et s'achève (provisoirement) avec les études sur les contacts entre langues. Dans ce domaine, le spectre de l'intérêt de recherche s'étend des pidgins et créoles jusqu'aux questions de planification linguistique (chapitre XXXVI). Suite au 'tournant saussurien' et à l'essor des recherches synchroniques qu'il a induit, on en arrive, pendant la première moitié de notre siècle, à une stagnation relative dans le domaine des recherches sur l'histoire des langues. Sous l'influence de nouvelles hypothèses (par exemple, la théorie des laryngales et glottales), on assiste à partir du milieu de ce siècle à un regain d'intérêt significatif (chapitre XXXVII), stimulé par les résultats qu'obtiennent la créolistique et la socio-linguistique en ce qui concerne le changement linguistique. Dans les trois dernières sections sont présentées des approches alternatives ('orientées parole', si l'on peut dire) aux branches de recherches traitées jusqu'ici ('orientées langue'): il s'agit de Wittgenstein, qui met l'accent sur l'usage, de la théorie des actes illocutoires, de la pragmatique et de la linguistique textuelle, ainsi que de l'analyse de discours et de la théorie de l'énonciation (chapitre XXXVIII).

Dans le chapitre XXXIX, le chapitre le plus long de l'ouvrage, il s'agit de démontrer que la conception d'une linguistique autonome, qui a été énergiquement défendue depuis le début du XXe siècle, est aujourd'hui peu à peu délaissée au profit d'études pluridisciplinaires, qui visent l'intégration des résultats produits dans les domaines de la sémiotique, de la philosophie, de la psychologie, de la neurologie, de la biologie, de l'intelligence artificielle, de la traduction automatique, etc. Dans la mesure où la recherche linguistique se montre ouverte aux autres disciplines, des connaissances linguistiques pénètrent également ces domaines et s'avèrent fructueuses.

Dans le dernier chapitre (chapitre XL), les responsables de l'ouvrage exposent, tantôt en commun, tantôt séparément, leur conception de l'origine, de l'évolution et de l'avenir de l'histoire des sciences du langage, et exposent leur point de vue sur la méthodologie et l'épistémologie de cette discipline.

Les Editeurs

# I. The Establishment of Linguistic Traditions in the Near East
# Die Anfänge sprachwissenschaftlicher Traditionen im Nahen Osten
# La constitution des traditions linguistiques au Proche-Orient

## 1. The Sumerian and Akkadian linguistic tradition

1. Writing and languages
2. Scribal training
3. Akkadian lists
4. Linguistic consciousness
5. Bibliography

### 1. Writing and languages

Around 3000 BC in Mesopotamia – today's Iraq – the first writing system was invented. The first use of writing was for bookkeeping purposes (Nissen, Damerow & Englund 1993). The identity of the language first committed to writing – Sumerian or some substrate language that left few traces in the Sumerian vocabulary – cannot be established, since the first signs were pictograms that identified objects without being language specific. As a pictogram became simplified and stylized so that it lost its pictorial character, it became a symbol. Such a symbol is called an ideogram. An ideogram does not denote a word but a concept and can represent any word associated with that concept. Only when a particular word becomes permanently attached to the sign, does the sign become a logogram. A logogram corresponds not only to a particular word, but to a set which represents all forms of a word, the choice among which is context sensitive. Only when the choice is indicated by another sign that serves as phonetic indicator is the writing disambiguated and does the writing become language specific. In the earliest written records the order of the signs was not fixed; thus the writing did not reflect a particular language with a fixed word order, but only expressed the idea – it was ideographic; inflectional morphemes were not always written. A pictogram, which eventually evolved into a cuneiform sign, could stand not only for the name of the object it depicted but also for a homophonous word, e. g., the sign for arrow, Sumerian *ti*, for the word "life", Sumerian *ti(l)* and the sign for reed, Sumerian *gi*, for the homophonous verb "to return". On these and a few other examples is based the theory that the writing reflects the Sumerian language and not another, and that the first written texts were Sumerian.

With this application of the rebus principle, the step toward using signs to write 'empty words,' that do not represent a concrete object, was taken. As Sumerian words are preponderantly monosyllabic, the concept that a sign represents a syllable could evolve. In this sense, the invention of writing itself may well be considered testimony of linguistic analysis of the spoken language. – Sumerian being an agglutinating language, inflectional morphemes appended to a root morpheme came to be represented in the writing by a sign symbolizing a homonym; e. g., the morpheme {a} by the sign representing *a* "water". Still, writing is not purely morphemic; a sequence of morphemes can be written on a lower level as a sequence of syllables, e. g. *lugal+ak+a(k)* written as *lugal-la-ka*, while others may be written independently, as the ergative morpheme {e} when appended to the word *lugal* "king" written *lugal.e* but when appended to the (divine) name *En.lil* written *En.lil.le*. The reasons for such distinctions may be phonological, but normally cannot be ascertained. Words consisting of both root and inflectional morphemes were regarded as units; that the notion of 'word' existed can be shown by the fact that words are not divided between two lines on the tablet, and the end of the line coincides with the word boundary.

Cuneiform writing was adapted to Akkadian, a Semitic language with inner inflection, but never achieved a perfect fit. For example, there never developed a one-to-one correspondence between the number of CV signs beginning with a stop or sibilant (either voiced or voiceless), e. g., *da* and *ta*, and the number of Akkadian stops and sibilants (either voiced, voiceless, or 'emphatic'); e. g., the syllable *ṭa*, with 'emphatic' – probably glottalized – dental stop, has no separate sign but is written with either *da* or *ta*. The solutions for writing the third member of such sets were not uniform.

## 2. Scribal training

The early preoccupation of Mesopotamian scholars with linguistic matters stems no doubt from being faced with a bilingual situation, probably more prominent in the written medium, since in the Old Babylonian (OB) period (1894–1595 BC) already Sumerian was no longer a spoken language though it remained written as a literary language used in administrative, technical, and religious texts up to the first century AD. The word for "tongue, language", *eme* (Akk. *lišānu*) is applied also to dialects or trade languages; the women's dialect is called *eme.sal* "fine tongue"; others are *eme.galam* "high tongue", *eme.si.sá* "straight tongue", *eme.te.ná* "oblique[?] tongue", etc.

The necessity of training scribes gave to rise to various lists, the most basic of which is the list of signs, with glosses indicating the sign's possible pronunciations ('readings'). The earliest lists written in cuneiform, as early as the third millennium, simply catalogue objects or living beings; members belonging to a class are preceded (rarely followed) by a class mark, called 'determinative'; e. g. names of professions are preceded by the word for "man", *lú*; objects made of wood, stone, clay, reed, etc., by the word for "wood", "stone", "clay", "reed", etc. This classification while obviously semantic is also acrographic, a principle useful for mnemotechnical and didactic purposes and at the same time displaying Mesopotamian man's preoccupation with the classification of the world around him.

These Sumerian unilingual lists were eventually provided with an additional column of Akkadian translations, but their sequence still displayed the 'acrographic' principle of the Sumerian. Other bilingual lists are arranged according to (a) sign forms, (b) semantic groups, or (c) phonetic similarity (with or without etymological connection) of the Akkadian entries. As in all of Babylonian scientific literature which knows only two forms: the list and step-by-step directives, the oral instruction that must have accompanied these 'lessons' cannot be recaptured, even though we possess a humorous literary text in the form of an examination of a student by a scribe (Sjöberg 1974).

Most striking are the so-called Grammatical Texts (henceforth GT; Landsberger, Hallock & Jacobsen: 1956, 46–202), the earliest of which date to the OB period, the OBGT. They are the first example of contrastive linguistics, as they compare and contrast paradigms. Akkadian verbs, like those of other Semitic languages, express such categories as causative, passive, reflexive, etc., through stem modifications by means of infixes, consonant reduplications, and the like, and person, mood, and a direct or indirect verb object by means of prefixes and/or suffixes; by contrast, the Sumerian verb stem is invariable and the meanings corresponding to the Akkadian inflected form are expressed by affixes. The GT present in parallel columns the Akkadian inflected form and the Sumerian agglutinated form. Each category is given in the full paradigm according to person, tense, mood, etc., often resulting in compilations of several hundred lines.

OBGT III
84 *dím-ma-ab* = *e-pu-uš* /epuš/ "make!"
85 *ga-ab-dím* = *lu-pu-uš* /lūpuš/ "let me make"
86 *ab-dím-me-en* = *e-pe-eš* /eppeš/ "I shall make"
87 *nu-ub-dím-me-en* = *ú-la e-pe-eš* /ula eppeš/ "I shall not make"
88 *hé-ib-dím-me* = *li-pu-uš* /līpuš/ "let him make"
89 *na-ab-dím-me* = *la i-pe-eš* /la ippeš/ "he shall not make"

Such paradigms with imperative, cohortative, and optative forms, in this sequence, suggest that they were devised for writing letters or administrative orders.

Indicative forms follow the sequence 3rd, 1st, and 2nd persons, e. g.

OBGT VII
126 *al-sus-bi-eš* = *i-il-la-ku* "they go"
127 *al-sus-bi-en-dè-en* = *ni-il-lak* "we go"

128 *al-sus₈-bi-en-zé-en* = *ta-al-la-ka* "you [pl.] go"
129 *ì-sus₈-bi-eš* = *i-il-la-ku* "they go"
130 *ì-sus₈-bi-en-dè-en* = *ni-il-lak* "we go"
131 *ì-sus₈-bi-en-zé-en* = *ta-al-la-ka* "you [pl.] go"

Obviously, to the same Akkadian inflected form different Sumerian forms may correspond, and vice versa; what this says about the aim of the grammatical texts, whether to provide the proper Sumerian equivalent to a text composed in Akkadian or to demonstrate underlying principles of word-formation, is a still debated question. – Most completely preserved – and comprising 227 lines – are the paradigms of the verb *gar* = *šakānu* "to place" (OBGT VI, 227 lines) and *gin* = *alāku* "to go" (OBGT VII, 318 lines); other tablets list more than one verb, e. g., OBGT IX, after dealing with the compound verb *sá* ... *dug₄* = *kašādu* "to reach", ends with 27 lines listing the imperative, cohortative, and optative of each of nine common verbs, e. g.,

137 *tuš.a* = *ši-ib* "sit!"
138 *ga.tuš* = [blank]
139 *hé.tuš* = [blank]

The blanks indicate that the second and third entries have to be construed as usual in the GT, namely as *lūšib* "I will sit" and *līšib* "let him sit"; the Akkadian cohortative and optative are all replaced by blanks in the right-hand column of this tablet. Shorter, and listing less common verbs, are OBGT VIII with 65 lines with the verb *kas₄* = *lasāmu* "to run" and 26 lines with the verb *kú* = *akālu* "to eat".

Besides verb paradigms, the OBGT also compare and contrast pronouns, e. g., OBGT I 385–394 lists personal pronouns with the Akkadian emphatic ending *-ma* which has the function of a copula corresponding to the Sumerian copulative ending /am/:

OBGT I
385 *me.en.dè.àm* = *ni-i-nu-ma* "it is we"
386 *me.en.da.nam* = *ni-i-nu-ma*
387 *me.dè.en.da.nam* = *ni-i-nu-ma*
388 *me.en.za.nam* = *at-tu-nu-ma* "it is you [pl.]"
389 *za.e.me.en.za.nam* = *at-tu-nu-ma*
390 *e.ne.ne.àm* = *šu-nu-ma* "it is they"
391 *lú.ù.ne.àm* = *šu-nu-ma*
392 *lú.bi.ne.àm* = *šu-nu-ma*
393 *ur₅.meš.àm* = *šu-nu-ma*
394 *ur₅.bi.àm* = *šu-nu-ma*

The next three sections (395–400, 401–409, and 410–418) repeat the Akkadian pronouns on the right-hand column but modify the Sumerian pronouns by adding the prefixes *ì* and *in.ga* and the infix *-na-* that turn the pronoun into a nominal clause.

The OBGT list entire forms only, while the Neo-Babylonian Grammatical Texts (NBGT) also isolate morphemes. Due to the nature of the writing which can express syllables only, a consonant morpheme appears in four forms, according to all four vowels with which it combines – depending on the final vowel of the head word – in the sequence *u-a-i-e*, the same sequence which occurs in the sign lists. For example,

NBGT II 46–52:
*uš* = *a-na i-na KI.TA* "to, in, suffix"
*aš*
*iš*
*eš*
*úr*
*ar*
*ir* (there is no sign ⟨er⟩ separate from ⟨ir⟩); the /r/ morpheme is listed in a Middle Babylonian (MB) text (Civil, Gurney & Kennedy 1986: 78f., II, 35–36, 39–40, 63–64, 65–66) in the arrangement *ir* = *i-na*, *ir* = *a-na*, *úr* = *i-na*, *úr* = *a-na*, *ar* = *i-na*, *ar* = *a-na*, *ur₅* = *i-na*, *ur₅* = *a-na*.

In addition to the 'translation' of the morpheme into its Akkadian counterpart, an explanatory term is sometimes added. The meanings of some of the terms, e. g., AN.TA "prefix", KI.TA "suffix", MURUB₄.TA "infix" and MEŠ "plural", are clear, but even when the literal meaning of such others as "full" (*malû*) or "empty" (*rīqu*) is known, their relationship to the referent may be obscure. Other Akkadian terms with unclear meaning also occur. The most frequent – and most debated – of these are *hamṭu* (Sumerian LAGAB "short") and *marû* (Sumerian *gíd* "long"), which characterize two suppletive verb stems in Sumerian (cf. Civil, *forthcoming*). Several technical terms (AN.TA, KI.TA, MURUB₄, *rīqu*, *riātu*, *hamṭu*, *marû*) also appear in Sumerian-Akkadian vocabularies arranged according to the sign forms, and seven (*uhhurtu*, *atartu*, *gamirtu*, *šushurtu*, *qablītu*, *marû*, *hamṭu*) occur in the humorous examination (Sjöberg 1974).

## 3. Akkadian lists

Writing exercises: These acrographic lists of mostly verb forms replace a CVC syllable with CV-VC, e. g. *it-ta-lak*, *it-ta-la-ak* (Cavigneaux 1981), or add an enclitic particle or pronominal suffix.

Synonym lists: These cite in the left column a rare, obsolete, or foreign word and in the right column a more common word, e. g. in the list *malku* = *šarru* (Kilmer 1963: 427):

175 *abdu* (West Semitic "slave") = *ardu* "slave"
176 *rēšu* (poetic word) = ditto
177 *dušmû* "houseborn slave" = ditto.

Words of foreign – Elamite or Hurrian – origin are marked in the right column as NIM "(in) Elam(ite)" or SU.BIR$_4$ "(in) Subartu", i. e., Hurrian. Similarly marked are often foreign plant names in Akkadian plant lists.

Commentaries to scholarly texts (omina, lexical texts) or learned poetry explain rare words by synonyms, both in the two-column format and in a continuous fashion. They are often based on bilingual lexical texts but may use the Sumerian entry as tertium comparationis only. E. g., GI *ša-la-mu* GI *la-pa-tum* ... *ša-la-mu la-pa-tum ina lišāni qabi* "GI [as Sumerogram] = to be safe, GI = to be ill-portending, it is said in the synonym list [lit. "tongue"]: *šalāmu* = *lapātu* (Thureau-Dangin 1922: no. 5 rev. 39–41). Some give phonetic variants, e. g., *mi-hi-iṣ-tum* : *mi-hi-il-tum* "stroke" (Labat 1933: 124 rev. 10), or etymologies, e. g., *ri-pi-it-tum* : *ana ra-pa-du* "*ripittu* [is relevant] to [the verb] *rapādu*" (ibid. 12).

A few vocabularies translate foreign language terms (Kassite, see Balkan 1954; also Hittite) into Akkadian. Outside Mesopotamia syllabaries and vocabularies were sometimes augmented by a column in the local language (Ugaritic, Hurrian).

Literary texts often appear in bilingual form, with usually the Sumerian being the source language, as is also indicated by the layout, with the translation normally under the Sumerian and indented; that late texts were also composed in Akkadian which was then provided with a Sumerian version, is recognizable from word-for-word transpositions without regard for Sumerian syntax.

## 4. Linguistic consciousness

The variety of languages impressed and intrigued the Mesopotamians; through their contacts to the east and west they had to use interpreters (Sumerian *eme.bal* "who changes the languages" attested c. 2300 BC, Akkadian *targumannu*, "dragoman", 19th century BC); only for Lydian "among all languages from east to west that (my god) Assur had given into my hands" was no interpreter found when Gyges sent a messenger to Assurbanipal (Piepkorn 1933: 16). The sounds of foreign languages were described as birds chirping or simply as "difficult to write" (Thureau-Dangin 1912, line 364). In the second half of the first millennium Aramaic replaced Akkadian as spoken and written language; it was written in alphabetic script by special scribes (*sēpiru*). A few school texts inscribed on the obverse in cuneiform and on the reverse in the Greek alphabet are the only evidence for teaching or learning Greek under the Seleucids (Maul 1991; Geller 1997).

## 5. Bibliography

Balkan, Kemal. 1954. *Kassitenstudien*. Vol. I. *Die Sprache der Kassiten*. (= *American Oriental Series*, 37.) New Haven, CT: American Oriental Society.

Beaulieu, Paul-Alain. 1995. "An Excerpt from a Menology with Reverse Writing". *Acta Sumerologica* (Japan) 17.1–14.

Black, Jeremy A. 1984. *Sumerian Grammar in Babylonian Theory*. (= *Studia Pohl. Series Maior*, 12.) Rome: Pontifical Biblical Institute. (2nd. revised ed., 1991.)

–. 1989. "The Babylonian Grammatical Tradition: The first grammars of Sumerian". *Transactions of the Philological Society* 87: 1.75–99.

Cavigneaux, Antoine. 1981. *Textes scolaires du Temple de Nabû ša harê*. Baghdad: State Organization of Antiquities and Heritage.

–. 1983. "Lexikalische Listen". *Reallexikon der Assyriologie* VI, 609–641. Berlin: de Gruyter. [In French.]

Civil, Miguel. *Forthcoming*. "The Forerunners of *marû* and *hamṭu* in Old Babylonian".

–, O. R. Gurney & D. A. Kennedy. 1986. *Middle Babylonian Grammatical Texts*. (= *Materials for the Sumerian Lexicon, Supplementary Series*, 1., Rome: Pontifical Biblical Institute.

Edzard, Dietz. O. 1971. "Grammatik". *Reallexikon der Assyriologie*. III, 610–616. Berlin: de Gruyter.

Geller, Mark J. 1997. "The Last Wedge". *Zeitschrift für Assyriologie* 87. 43–95.

Jacobsen, Thorkild. 1974. "Very Ancient Linguistics: Babylonian grammatical texts". *Studies in the History of Linguistics* ed. by Dell Hymes, 41–62. Bloomington & London: Indiana Univ. Press.

Labat, René. 1933. *Commentaires Assyro-Babyloniens sur les Présages*. Bordeaux: Imprimeries-Librairie de l'Université.

Landsberger, Benno, Richard T. Hallock & Thorkild Jacobsen. 1956. *Materialien zum Sumerischen Lexicon*, vol. IV. Rome: Pontifical Biblical Institute.

Maul, Stefan. 1991. "Neues zu den 'Graeco-Babyloniaca'". *Zeitschrift für Assyriologie* 81.87–107.

Nissen, Hans J., Peter Damerow & Robert K. Englund. 1993. *Archaic Bookkeeping.* Chicago & London: The Univ. of Chicago Press. [Originally published as *Frühe Schrift und Techniken der Wirtschaftsverwaltung im alten Vorderen Orient: Informationsspeicherung und -verarbeitung vor 5000 Jahren.* Berlin: Becker, 1990.]

Piepkorn, Arthur C. 1933. *Historical Prism Inscriptions of Ashurbanipal.* Vol. I. (= *Assyriological Studies*, 5.) Chicago: The Univ. of Chicago Press.

Reiner, Erica, Janet H. Johnson & Miguel Civil. 1994. "Linguistics in the Ancient Near East". *History of Linguistics* ed. by Giulio Lepschy, vol. I, 61–96. London & New York: Longman.

Schmandt-Besserat, Denise. 1992. *Before Writing.* Vol. I: *From Counting to Cuneiform.* Austin: Univ. of Texas Press.

Sjöberg, Åke W. 1974. "Der Examenstext A". *Zeitschrift für Assyriologie* 64.137–176.

Thureau-Dangin, François. 1912. *Une relation de la huitième campagne de Sargon.* (= *Musée du Louvre, Textes cunéiformes,* 3.) Paris: Geuthner.

–. 1922. *Tablettes d'Uruk.* (= *Musée du Louvre, Textes cunéiformes*, 6.) Paris: Geuthner.

*Erica Reiner, Chicago (USA)*

# 2. Indigenous Egyptian grammar

1. Introductory remarks
2. Natural semantics: Paronomasia
3. Language teaching: Schooling
4. Grammatical theory
5. Indigenous linguistic terminology
6. Practical philology, diglossia
7. Lexical work
8. Foreign languages
9. The concept of language
10. Bibliography

## 1. Introductory remarks

Interest on the part of the ancient Egyptians in matters of language hardly went beyond the practical level and rarely became theoretical. In this respect their attitude was no different from that toward other branches of knowledge; its orientation was eminently empirical. Handbooks in the fields of mathematics, astronomy and astrology, medicine, calender-lore, dream-explanation, onomastics and sacred geography had no theoretical basis either, but were a systematic elaboration of practical observations and of religious speculation, the two regularly being joined as complementary. Indigenous linguistics was no different. For instance, no systematic indigenous grammatical descriptions are known from the whole Pharaonic period, nor are they likely to turn up.

However, the Egyptian interest in language gains perspective when a number of details are taken into account relating to their preoccupation with their own script and language and those they came into contact with, and put on a gradient running from the empirical to the more theoretical level. Since no consistent indigenous linguistic discipline existed, a presentation of the facts by necessity follows the outline of a modern overview, but it should do justice to the interest in certain fields displayed by the Egyptian themselves.

The indigenous writing (hieroglyphic and two cursive variants, hieratic and Demotic) is pictorial, but uses both logograms and phonograms. No vowels are written, which is a serious hampering to phonological reconstruction. Yet it is obvious that much practical knowledge of phonology is inherent to the system, and that on the graphic level phonemes are distinguished from morphemes, although nowhere any theoretical statement is made on this. In course of time, several attempts were made to adapt the writing system to the particular needs of rendering the exact phonetic constituency of a word, including its vowels: early in the Pharaonic period the so-called syllabic orthography (Schenkel 1986) was customarily employed to render foreign names, and in the Ptolemaic period occasionally Egyptian words were written with Greek letters. In due time this would lead to the replacement of the various indigenous writing systems by westernizing the script: a phonetically more adequate slightly adapted Greek system of letters, the Coptic writing system.

In a similar way as the script reveals elementary consciousness of phonetics and phonology on a non-theoretical level, so does some natural syntax emerge, from carefully composed literary (including historical and religious) texts. The single line served as the basic unit, usually combined with a following one into a couplet; triplets are also known (Burkhard 1996). The binding force between the components in such metrical arrangements is unity of thought, but its basis is natural syntax (cf. Schenkel 1972). An example is the following quotation from a Middle Kingdom story which contains two coordinated sentences: *mꜣ=sn p.t mꜣ=sn tꜣ # mkꜣ ib=sn r mꜣ(i).w* "Whether they saw the heavens, whether they saw the earth # their heart was steadier than (that of) lions" (*Sh.S.* 28–30), where the first and last words are even in alliteration, thus supporting the grammatical cohesion. In the New Kingdom such units were graphically distinguished by supralinear red dots ('verse-points').

In one of the current systems of metrical analysis, of Gerhard Fecht, an even greater analytical depth is assumed, taking as the smallest basic unit the bearer of an accent (a word or phrase), and giving it the status of a 'colon', two the three accented units or cola forming a verse line. Should this be verifiable, there would be a system of prosodic segmentation as a further testimony to a tradition of implicit linguistic analysis.

## 2. Natural semantics: Paronomasia

Paronomasia occurs in countless passages (mostly religious and literary) in texts of all periods. It served different purposes: stylistic and theological.

In literature it might be helpful as an ordering means, the occasional alliteration supporting cohesion between verse lines (cf. above, 1). Or it might call up allusions, sometimes in an ironical sense (true word play; Guglielmi 1984). Most widespread is the custom of making phonemic similarity the postulate of a historical or ritual relationship between words on theological grounds (sacral etymology). Alliteration shows that phonetic oppositions were noted, as in the following passage from the Pyramid texts: *m n=k ir.t Ḥr dꜣp(= i) ṯw im* "Take for yourself the Eye of Horus, with which I donate you" (*Pyrt.* 110), a statement which accompanies the ritual act of giving of *dꜣb 2* "two figs"; the opposition *p:b* has been exploited. Only a minority of the results of this never ending Egyptian search for meaning through etymological relationship is tenable by modern standards, e. g. when in an old text the verb *nḏr(i)* "to seize" alliterates with *ḏr.t* "hand" (*Pyrt.* 539.b, 582.b, 672.a–c, 1405.b). In most cases correspondences turn out to be unlikely, as in the following example of theologizing etymology, serving as an explanation of a particular form of the sun god: *in mi.w sw m nn irr.w=f ḫpr rn=f pw n(y) miw* "In fact, is he like (*miu*) himself in what he does? – It is the way his name 'Tomcat' (*miu*) came into being" (*Coffin Texts* IV, 288–289.a–b, version T1Cb). However false, such paronomastic elaborations, apart from having a theological value of their own, are a sure sign that on the prosodic level (for the script, cf. above, 1.) attention was given to phonemes.

## 3. Systematic formation: Schooling

Formation in schools is at the center of several forms grammatical interest could take in Ancient Egypt. Scribal training appears to have been a major component in the school curriculum (Janssen & Janssen 1990: 76–80). Although school instruction is mentioned a number of times in pre-Ramesside sources (i. e., before 1300 BCE), direct evidence is extremely scarce and consists of mere glimpses of school life. The actual products of the disciples, surviving as exercises, are best known from the New Kingdom and later. Here our main source is the village of Deir el-Medîna, a small community of workmen and their families who as decorators and sculptors worked on the tombs of royal persons and well-to-do private people in the mountains bordering the West bank of Thebes (ca. 1500–1100 BCE). The professional activities of the workmen included continuously transmitting religious texts onto the walls of tombs, and most of it was in Classical Egyptian. Hence, their métier and the administration of the workforce itself required experience in or at least an acquaintance with writing, and the degree of literacy in this village was higher here than elsewhere (Janssen 1992).

A great number of writing exercises survive. Combining this material with the sparse evidence of earlier periods and other centres, it seems likely that the young apprentices were put to copying texts right away in the cursive script (hieratic). Training meant copying entire words in the hieratic script, much of which were classical texts, in an idiom that was no longer current (Middle Egyptian). This evident interest in and respect for the cultural inheritance embodied in particular literature brought people, who otherwise spoke and wrote in the vernacular of the day, into contact with literary compositions which were several hundreds of years older. At a certain moment this became problematic: the gap between spoken and written language became unbridgeable. For coping with this linguistic problem, see below, 6.

## 4. Grammatical theory

While copying texts (classical and contemporary) was the chief part of the apprentice scribe's homework, testimony to more theoretical reflection consists of a few brief grammatical exercises, which contain the germs of theory. These and lexical work (Johnson 1994) stand central in our knowledge about the linguistic interest of the ancient Egyptians. The earliest grammatical exercises date to the Ramesside period (roughly, 1200 BCE) and are all in the vernacular, Late Egyptian; for, apart from the archaic literary component, texts in the contemporary idiom with an administrative touch were also copied; the young men were not trained as theorists or literates, but for a professional career in the administration. The grammatical notes are written in the margin of everyday notes on potsherds, the traditional writing material for all sorts of jottings. Ostracon Petrie 28, from Deir el-Medîna, contains the inflection of the particle *ỉw*, and ostracon Cairo CG 25227, from Abydos, that of the conjunctive prefix *mtw*, both carrying suffix pronouns. To form a true paradigm, the conjugation basis should be followed by a form of a lexical verb (e. g., *mtw=f sḏm* "and then he hears"), but absence of the latter in the exercises testifies to the awareness of an abstract paradigm by itself. Another such text, also from Deir el-Medîna (ostracon Turin 57118), is a fragmentary list of written out ordinal numbers.

There is a gap in our knowledge about the indigenous study of grammar for the period between the Ramesside era and the Ptolemaic period, due to the lack of well-excavated settlements where such schooling activities might have taken place. Apparently classical literary texts were being kept on the school program, as is proven by copies of the pre-Ptolemaic period (Posener 1966). Meanwhile, the Greek language was gradually finding entry into daily life and in the longer run formed a threat to the knowledge of indigenous writing systems. While Greek apprentices copied classical Greek texts as did Egyptian young scribes centuries before, those being schooled in Demotic had no such ancestral literary texts on their program (Tassier 1992: 313–314). The older texts they did learn to read and copy in a school in Karnak of Ptolemaic date, somewhere in the centre of the temple, were of a religious nature (Devauchelle 1984: 56–57). Grammatical exercises only turn up again in the abundant mass of documents written in the Demotic script (Kaplony-Heckel 1974; also, Devauchelle 1984; Tassier 1992), in the Ptolemaic period (from ca. 330 BCE on); at present a good 15 are known. They deal with the systematic inflection of verb forms (chiefly auxiliaries) and a few with that of nouns, including numerals. These texts, all of them fragmentary, are nonetheless sufficient in number to reveal a fixed order in which pronouns appear, whether after verbal elements or prepositions. Singular inflection comes first: "I", "you [masc.]", "he", "she", "you [fem.]", then the plural, where the order is different: "they", "we", "you". The Ramesside forerunners seem to separate at least singular from plural inflection, but are not informative enough to allow further comparison with the later grammatical tradition. There was standardization in other respects as well, in the ordering of the alphabet (see below, 7.).

Between the Ramesside and Ptolemaic eras, many official texts are couched in Neo-Middle Egyptian, with varying quality (Jansen-Winkeln 1996; Der Manuelian 1994: 103–294). The gap in grammatical exercise copies mentioned already leaves one to guess as to how the scribes kept up their grammatical knowledge of Classical Egyptian. Possibly this happened in the way of practical philology, by copying older texts, probably through the use of pattern books of phraseology available in temple libraries, rather than by directly taking a text from an original (Schenkel 1977: 436).

## 5. Indigenous linguistic terminology

No general equivalent of 'language' is available; rather, the terms refer to 'speech' (i. e., 'parole'), not to a system ('language'). The word *r*, lit. "mouth", by extension "spell", "text unit", also denotes "speech", e. g. "You shall hear the language (lit. speech) of Egypt" (*r n(y) Km.t*), a promise made ca. 1950 BCE (Middle Kingdom period) at a Syrian court to the Egyptian refugee Sinuhe, referring to his compatriots in residence there (*Sinuhe*/B. 31–32). That it denotes "speech', not language as a system, appears from the fact that it can be "hampered" (*swḫꜣ*), i. e., by stammering or stuttering (*Coffin Texts* V, 322.h). A New Kingdom equivalent is *mdw(.t)* "word", "speech", even "recitation".

An early New Kingdom term is *ns* "tongue", covering the notion of 'language' (more like 'langue'). According to a sun-hymn from Amarna (early New Kingdom), speaking about foreign languages, the sun god has caused that "the tongues (*ns*) are distinguished (*wp(ỉ)*) by words (*mdw.t*)" (*Texts from the Time of Akhenaten* 95.1), a concept to be dealt with later (see below, 9.). The emphasis on the phatic aspect suggests that one was well aware of differences between languages, but that they were thought to consist of the words, not properly in the system of a language. This may be another aspect of the theoretical Egyptian view on language (for this, see below, 9.). Finally, a third term is simply *ḏd* "saying", referring to words in a foreign language, e. g., "a conjuration [...] in the speech (*ḏd*) of Keftiu [Crete]" (pap. London/British Museum 10059, 11.4, New Kingdom).

In grammar again the basic unit is *mdw.t* "word", which, however, also means "matter, affair". A higher grammatical unit is *ṯs*, lit. "knot", corresponding to "utterance", "statement". It comprises *mdw.t* "words", as in "utterances of well-spoken words" (*ṯs.w n(y.w) mdw.t nfr.t*, *Instruction of Ptahhotep* 42). Here the term *ṯs* serves as a basic unit of an argumentative text. Teachings are, as are many literary texts, composed of the above mentioned thought couplets, which have a syntactic basis (see above, 1.). Thus *ṯs* has also a syntactic meaning: it can mean a "sentence" (and in another context a "verse line" or a "couplet"). Strictly morphological terms like 'noun' or 'verb' are unknown; it comes as a surprise that, following one particular proposal (Fecht 1960: 205, n. 580), the definite article seems to be referred to in one source – not by an abstract categorical term, but denominatively. One of the Middle Egyptian forms for the nascent definite article "the" is *pꜣ* (properly "this") and the reference in the source is to *pꜣw.t*, which may be rendered as "using the demonstrative pronoun/article", lit. "this-ing" or "the-ing" (stela Metropolitan Museum 12.184, 13). Although in this case the use of the article, a colloquial affair, is disapproved of, being below the norm of good speech according to this particular source, the important thing is that it is recognized as a morpheme.

To pursue the above search for terms with a grammatical touch, *mdw.t* "word", in a comparable way can also be the contents of a *ḫn* "enunciation", which may comprise more than one sentence: a *ḫn n(y) mdw.t* is a "maxim" (*Eloquent Peasant* B.1, 50 [= old, 19], Middle Kingdom), but a *ḫn* can have some length as well (perhaps in another context a distich) and amount to a "song".

Reference to lexemes is made with the word *rn* "name, denomination"; the technical term for "translate, explain" is the verb *wḥꜥ*, lit. "unwrap, unfurl" as in "he who translates (*wḥꜥ*) the word(s) (*mdw*) of all foreign countries" (stela Cairo CG 20765, a.3, Middle Kingdom).

## 6. Practical philology, diglossia

A number of examples are known of epigraphic texts having been checked by Egyptian experts for mistakes and these subsequently corrected. The majority of such modifications are graphic: signs wrongly copied from a mother text are recut in the correct manner. In general, such changes are illustrative of textual history and of philological insight. However, a minor part are grammatical changes and are therefore relevant to be discussed in this frame. Thus, in the Old Kingdom experts carefully went through the many columns of religious texts inside the Pyramid of king Unas (ca. 2340 BCE) and took care, among other things, of correcting grammatical mistakes. Thus a prospective verb form (*ḥnỉ.w=f*) was replaced by an imperfective verb form (*ḥnn=f*, Matthieu 1996: 296 = *Pyrt.* 366.a), a prepositional phrase (*m=s*) acquired its correct pronominal form (*ỉm=s*, Matthieu 1996: 296 = *Pyrt.* 139.c), an agentive particle (*ỉn* "by") was inserted which had been forgotten (Matthieu 1996: 300 = *Pyrt.* 264.c), an incorrect suffix pronoun form (*ṯ* "you") was replaced by the enclitic pronoun (*ṯm*, Matthieu 1996: 304 = *Pyrt.* 195.c), a compound negation (*n ỉs*) was removed before a particle (*ỉw*) with which it is grammatically incompatible (*Pyrt.* 392.d, differing from Matthieu 1996: 306–307), and so on. Much fewer corrections occur in the sequel to this genre, the texts on private coffins of the Middle Kingdom. Here, for instance, an emphatic particle *i̓n* was deleted from a particular focussing construction where it does not belong (*Coffin Texts* II, 334.b, version B2P). After this period the care for philological and grammatical detail of ancient texts virtually comes to a stop, the reason being given in the following.

During the early New Kingdom (18th Dynasty, ca. 1550–1300 BCE) Middle Egyptian was still the standard language of inscriptions of all genres, and command of grammar and orthography were still at a high level. However, the gap between the spoken language and language in official records had been widening and the general opinion is that knowledge of Middle Egyptian grammar was soon deteriorating in the subsequent Ramesside period, although this is also the period when canonical literary texts still belonged to the school program (see above, 3.). However, the text copies are the least trustworthy, and other school manuscripts of the New Kingdom, partly composed in Middle Egyptian but with a number of Late Egyptian influences and written by advanced students, bristle with orthographical mistakes (Erman 1925: 486). There is also considerable difference in trustworthiness between manuscript copies of the Book of the Dead of the 18th and the subsequent dynasties. In contrast, texts in unmistakable Late Egyptian, with due allowance for its more loose orthographical customs, effortlessly follow the prevailing rules of grammar. On the other hand, copying and adapting classical texts in the Saite period of cultural revival often went astray of the strict rules of orthography and morphology of the Classical idiom in details, but otherwise, independent compositions in Neo-Middle Egyptian testify to a good understanding of the rules of classical grammar (Der Manuelian 1994: 391–402, and, for an earlier period, Jansen-Winkeln 1996: 489–493, for comparative surveys).

To solve the problem of understanding the grammar and vocabulary of older texts, these were often rephrased in or even translated into the vernacular. The lightest form of this procedure is what might be called modernization: an older form is replaced by its nearest equivalent in the subsequent language stage. Already in the Middle Kingdom spells of the corpus of the Pyramid Texts, in Old Egyptian, utterances were grammatically and lexically modified so as to fit into the corpus of the so-called *Coffin Texts*, the successor to the former genre (for a recent example, see Morenz 1994). In their turn, texts in Middle Egyptian might be slightly adapted, to fit the grammar of the Late Egyptian of the day, as in the case of, for instance *di̓di̓=f sw m dꜣi̓.w n(y) s.t* "He girds himself with a woman's loincloth" (*Satire of the Trades* xix.f) which was modernized in one version into *i̓.di̓di̓=f sw*, etc. The form *i̓.di̓di̓=f* is a hybrid, but close enouth to its correct equivalent in Late Egyptian (*i̓.di̓=f*).

In cases of wide divergence, for which the term 'diglossia' has been used (Jansen-Winkeln 1995; Vernus 1996), the most thorough form became retranslation. A few 'bilingual' texts are known from the early post-Ramesside period, where an older version is provided with a sublinear rendering in the current language; in some cases the result was a reinterpretation rather than a grammatical and lexical rewriting, as in the case of *mr(i̓) bi̓k ḥꜥꜥ.wy n(y) ṯꜣ=f* "The falcon loves the joy of its fledgeling" (old version), which became *mr(i̓) Pr-ꜥꜣ pꜣ ršwy ⟨n(y)⟩ nꜣy=f ẖrd.w* "Pharaoh loves the delight of his children" (papyrus British Museum 10298, 2.9–10), apart from lexical substitution adding definite articles (*pꜣ* and *nꜣy=f*). More examples of ritual and astronomical treatises, written in classical Egyptian and provided with a targum in the later idiom, are known from the Ptolemaic period (listed in Vernus 1996: 564).

## 7. Lexical work

Lexicography in a broad sense and in an Egyptian context comprises several things. Two kinds of topic-organized reference book existed: the encyclopedia (called 'onomasticon' in the Egyptological jargon), and the dictionary, chronologically appearing in that order. Encyclopedias could be organized following two principles. The one was graphical, where a certain logogram (a determinative) served as guiding principle to put cognate words together, while the other system followed a lexical/semantic arrangement. Dictionaries were set up according to the acrophonic principle. While an onomasticon is already known from the Middle Kingdom, alphabetical dictionaries seem to be a product of the Ptolemaic period.

The principle of the onomasticon is listing by topic, a genre which doubt grew out of listing as an administrative habit. Through all times lists are known with a practical purpose for a particular occasion, inventorizing funerary offerings, linen, ointment, ritual temple property, extensive lists of royal names (Redford 1986). Equally, lists were kept up of foreign rulers and their topography for ritual (magical) purposes as well as for recording conquered territory and the tribute it had to deliver. For religious purposes the body members were catalogued (Massart 1959) as well as parts of ships and of the fishing net (*Coffin Texts spells* 389, respectively 473–481), all tabulated with the divinities responsible for their mythological aspects; divinities themselves were listed (e. g., Faulkner 1958). For some of these the rules of ordering were obvious: listing parts of the body went from top to toe, toponymical lists have a geographical orientation (from south to north), king lists follow a chronological order.

After the Old Kingdom also lists of a more abstract character appear, organizing subject-matter of great variety, truly serving as a handbook: the summit of decontextualization. The 'onomastic' tradition (Gardiner 1947) begins with the Middle Kingdom, when a single papyrus from the Ramesseum in Thebes (ca. 1700 BCE) lists all sorts of items, each time separating the lexical body of the word from the determinatives, which were set apart. This early handbook lists plants, liquids, birds, fishes, some quadrupeds, fortresses in Nubia, towns in Egypt, confectionary and so on. No explanations are offered; only at the end there is a row of abbreviated writings of bull types accompanied by brief comments. The best known and most extensive encyclopedic text is of the Ramesside age, recorded by several mss., and known as the *Onomasticon of Amenemope*. Its governing principle is not graphic, but hierarchical: it enumerates, but again does not not explain, cosmic and geographical notions, the hierarchy of gods and human ranks/occupations, anthropological notions, towns, buildings and land, and so on. This top-down list text is called a 'teaching', and perhaps it was connected with the school trade (see above, 3.). More varied onomastica appear in the early Roman period, some with explanations. They do not always exactly fit the bipartition of above; one of them is a mixture of a dictionary and a manual of sacred entities (Ray 1976; Osing 1989). The dictionary section contains verbs, neatly separated from substantives, both arranged into sections of semantic cognates (Osing 1992: 42).

The first traces of the custom of arranging words by sound correspondence are found in the New Kingdom. A few lists of Semitic names are known and in recording these names the scribes seem to have grouped some of them with the same initial consonant together (Posener 1937: 196), and such a sporadic application is also found with Egyptian names (ostracon Turin 57382). In a similar way, compound names are analyzed as core and varying satellite (ostracon Turin 57473 recto). However, true word lists organized alphabetically and dictionaries are only known from the Ptolemaic period. Thus, the sole extant full page of an alphabetic dictionary in hieratic of the 1st century CE contains words beginning with /h/ (Iversen 1958). Here contemporary phonology has got the better of historical phonetics, for words beginning with *h* and *ḥ* are put together indiscriminately. Interestingly, to judge from a sign list which had a separate entry for monoconsonantal signs, a fixed alphabetical order had been established by this time (Kahl 1991), the letters being referred to by bird-names, as appears from a papyrus from Saqqara, another Demotic word list of the 4th century BCE (Smith & Tait 1983: 198–213, no. 27), e. g., "the ibis (*hb*) was on the ebony-tree (*hbyn*)". It also appears that in those days the Egyptian order of the alphabet did not follow the north-Semitic abecedary, but that of the South Arabian alphabet (Quack 1993).

## 8. Foreign languages

Cultural contact with other languages can stir interest in linguistics in general (for whatever purposes, practical or theoretical), and may ultimately promote reflection and thus analysis of the national language. Before contacts with the western world of the Greeks became politically important, no such cultural relationship existed between the Egyptians and any of their direct neighbors. Three important areas with native language(s) surrounded Egypt: Nubia in the south, Libya in the west and Syro-Palestine in the north-east; and at times different peoples appeared on the horizon with still other languages, as in the great surge of the Sea Peoples (around 1200 BCE). In Egypt, peoples speaking foreign languages were indicated by the term *ỉʿȝw/ȝʿʿ* (Bell 1977), an unusual combination of uvulars and pharyngeals whose meaning comes close to the Greek verb *barbarízein*; the term *ȝʿʿ* "babbler" is chiefly used to refer to a dragoman. The word also served to indicate Egyptians who were able to speak or translate from a foreign language.

In the course of time the greater part of Nubia was colonized and contacts with the indigenous cultures always had imperialist overtones; at all times interest in the native culture, including the language(s), was practically nil. Throughout the Pharaonic period, if the Nubian population expressed itself in writing, it was in Egyptian (cf. Zyhlarz 1961).

Contacts with tribes living on the Libyan territory were of the same kind, except that this region was never colonized but regarded as an area where raids and outposts were the best means to guarantee peace on the border. Only the late New Kingdom saw these countries exercise influence themselves on Egyptian territory, first Libya (ca. 940–710 BDE) and then Nubia for a brief spell (ca. 710–665 BCE), including temporary occupation of the throne for a certain period (22nd Libyan Dynasty, 25th Nubian Dynasty). A few words of these languages are recorded in Egyptian texts (chiefly proper and ethnic names and a few titles), but there is no evidence of linguistic contact or interest to any depth. On the other hand, personal and topographical names were at all times carefully noted: they were the basic information for the purpose of execrative ritual and for recording conquered territories. Nubian names were already noted in the Old Kingdom (ca. 2500 BCE) and give an inkling as to how the Egyptians rendered Nubian phonology (Osing 1976).

The situation was different in regard to Syro-Palestine, which consisted politically of a number of city-states with a certain autonomy; this area was a constant battle ground of the great powers of the 2nd and 1st millennia BCE, including Egypt. In pre-New Kingdom contacts with Syro-Palestine the idea seems to have been that Egyptian was being spoken at high levels in society (as stated in the story of the fugitive Sinuhe – see above, 5.). On the other hand, names of West-Asiatic rulers and geographical names were well known and recorded in special phonetic notation (the syllabic script, see above, 1.). Semitic-speaking captives were settled in Egypt, and although leaving few traces as a language community, probably contributed to the growing number of Semitic loan-words imported into Egypt from the early New Kingdom (Hoch 1994); a great number of Semitic names are known (Schneider 1992). When the Egyptian interests established a firm footing in Western Asia and a number of local city-states became protectorates of Pharaoh, the international language was not Egyptian, but a particular brand of Akkadian. It was used in the correspondence preserved in an archive at El-Amarna (Moran 1992: xviii–xxii), a newly founded city which served as capital during the reign of King Amenophis IV or Akhenaten (ca. 1350–1310 BCE). The Akkadian used by the clerks who worked as translators of the Amarna correspondence shows the influence of Egyptian (Cochavi-Rainey 1990). Hence close contact must have existed between native speakers of Egyptian and Semitic (Artzi 1990: 140), to which also scholarly texts in Akkadian bear testimony, which even used the Egyptian system of punctuation by means of red dots (see above, 1.). It also included a much discussed bilingual vocabulary (Izre'el 1997: 77–81) which raises the question of the native language of the scribe (Meltzer 1988): Egyptian or Semitic?

Language policy with regard to foreign speakers comes to the surface several times. The official Egyptian attitude toward speakers of a foreign language was disdain. Firstly, the status of foreign names is revealing. Although a gerat number of Semitic names are known from documents in Egypt, already in the Middle Kingdom children of immigrants (mostly slaves) were given Egyptian names (Hayes 1955: 93–94), and when in the New Kingdom courtiers of Semitic provenance wished to get ahead, they adopted an Egyptian name, with the name of the ruling monarch conspicuously incorporated in it (Helck 1971: 368). In contrast, in much later times and under different socio-historical conditions, the Jewish community at Elephantine (5th and 4th centuries BCE) strictly kept to its own language. Secondly, in a few stray remarks the status of foreign languages is at issue. In the Wisdom of Ani, datable to the 18th Dynasty (around 1400 BCE), it is said (*Ani* 23.5–6): "One teaches Nubians (*nḥsy*) the speech of the Egyptian people (*md.t rmṯ n(y) Km.t*); the Syrians and any foreign country likewise". Equally, some centuries later, it was said of King Ramesses III (ca. 1180 BCE) about the Libyans and the Meshwesh, who belonged to the invading Sea Peoples, and who were among the warrior tribes pressed into Egyptian service, that "They heard the speech (*mdw.t*) of men (*rmṯ*) while accompanying the king; he let their speech (*mdw.t*) be dropped; he changed (*pnʿ*) their tongues (*ns*)" (*Ramesside Inscriptions* III,

91.6). It should be noted that the term "men" (*rmṯ*) is used for "Egyptians"; what the passage implies is that the only truly human language is Egyptian. A young scribe whose results were insufficient was scolded as "a gibbering Nubian (*nḥsy ꜣ*ˁ) who has been brought with the tribute" (papyrus Sallier I, 8.1), containing the very word that was also used for dragomans (see above, 8.). However, all this changed much later, when Egypt allowed Greek-speaking immigrants to settle in its territory; King Psamtik I (ca. 665–610 BCE) even trusted some Egyptian children to the Ionians and Carians, mercenary tribes which had settled in Egypt, in order to be taught the Greek language (Herodotus, *Hist.* II, 154). However, the linguistic interaction between Egyptians and speakers of Greek and other languages, like Carian (Kammerzell 1993) is a different topic.

## 9. The concept of language

No comprehensive Egyptian theory is known about the origin of language, although in a number of creation myths a demiurge is said to conceive an idea (*siꜣ*) in his heart, which next takes form as an authoritative word (*ḥw*) coming from his mouth, which is at the same time its material realization (Zandee 1964). On the level of everyday experience there was always interest in the first words a child might utter. A New Kingdom medical text offers a prognostic on whether a new born child will live or die. If it says *nee (ny)* it will live; if it says *embee (mbi)* it will die (papyrus Ebers 97.13). The latter word resembles the Egyptians word for "no", but the other word does not correspond to any known confirmative particle. Many centuries later the Greek writer Herodotus reported on King Psamtik I's (mentioned above, 8.) interest in linguistic universals. He tried to find out which language belonged to the first word that a child uttered for the first time after it had been withheld from contact with the speaking community from birth. In his opinion, that language would be prototypical; in the event, the outcome of the experiment was that Phrygian, not Egyptian, was the oldest language (Herodotus, *Hist.* II, 2; cf. Salmon 1956; Sulek 1982).

On many levels the thinking of the Egyptians about their culture upheld the tradition of a continuous derivation of valuable elements of all sorts from the higher levels of society, both divine and royal. The invention of the Egyptian script was attributed to Thoth, the ibis- or baboon-headed intellectual among the gods, and the sun god's own vizier in the heavenly hierarchy. Thoth, and a famous royal scribe of times immemorial, Imhotep, were the patrons of the scribe. As with writing, so with language: in the New Kingdom (cf. above, 5.) and later (Sauneron 1960), several gods might be credited with the differentiation of human languages, but, again, it was especially Thoth who was held responsible for their variety, according to a hymn in the New Kingdom: "Hail to you, Moon-Thoth, who differentiated the tongues (*ns*) from country to country" (Černý 1948). There is a socio-cultural perspective to this: such ideas are met in the early New Kingdom, when the Egyptians had for the first time to deal with foreign peoples they were ready to regard as equals, even conceding their deceased a place in the Netherworld (cf. Hornung 1989: 176; 1980: 134–137).

## 10. Bibliography

Artzi, Pinḥas. 1990. "Studies in the Library of the Amarna Archive". *Bar'Ilan Studies in Assyriology dedicated to Pinḥas Artzi*, 139–156. Ramat-Gan: Bar-Ilan Univ. Press.

Bates, Oric. 1970. *The Eastern Libyans: An essay.* London: Frank Cass.

Bell, Lanny. 1977. *Interpreters and Egyptianized Nubians in Ancient Egyptian Foreign Policy: Aspects of the history of Egypt and Nubia.* Ann Arbor: Dissertations Abstracts International 37, no. 11.

Burkard, 1996. "Metrik, Prosodie und formaler Aufbau ägyptischer literarischer Texte". *Ancient Egyptian Literature: History and forms* ed. by Antonio Loprieno, 447–463. Leiden: Brill.

Černý, Jaroslav. 1948. "Thoth as Creator of Languages". *Journal of Egyptian Archaeology* 48.121–122.

Cochavi-Rainey, Zippora. 1990. "Egyptian Influence in the Akkadian Texts Written by Egyptian Scribes in the Fourteenth and Fifteenth Centuries B.C.E.". *Journal of the Near Eastern Society* 49.57–65.

Der Manuelian, Peter. 1994. *Living in the Past: Studies in Archaism of the Egyptian twenty-sixth dynasty.* London: Kegan Paul International.

Devauchelle, Didier. 1984. "Remarques sur les méthodes d'enseignement du démotique". *Grammatika Demotika. Festschrift für Erich Lüddeckens zum 15. Juni 1983* ed. by Heinz-J. Thissen & Karl-Th. Zauzich, 47–59. Würzburg: Zauzich.

Erman, Adolf. 1925. *Die ägyptischen Schülerhandschriften.* (= *Abhandlungen der Königlich-Preußi-*

*schen Akademie der Wissenschaften zu Berlin, philosophisch-historische Klasse, Abh. 2.)* Berlin.

Faulkner, Raymond O. 1958. *An Ancient Egyptian Book of Hours (Pap. Brit. Mus. 10569).* Oxford: Oxford Univ. Press.

Fecht, Gerhard. 1960. *Wortakzent und Silbenstruktur: Untersuchungen zur Geschichte der ägyptischen Sprache.* Glückstadt: Augustin.

Gardiner, Alan H. 1947. *Ancient Egyptian Onomastica.* 3 vols. Oxford: Oxford Univ. Press.

Guglielmi, Waltraud. 1984. "Zu einigen literarischen Funktionen des Wortspiels". *Studien zu Sprache und Religion Ägyptens zu Ehren von Wolfhart Westendorf,* I, 491–506. Göttingen.

Hayes, William C. 1955. *A Papyrus of The Late Middle Kingdom (papyrus Brooklyn 35.1446).* New York: The Brooklyn Museum.

Helck, Wolfgang. 1971. *Die Beziehungen Ägyptens zu Vorderasien im 3. und 2. Jahrtausend v. Chr.* Wiesbaden: Harrassowitz.

Hoch, James. 1994. *Semitic Words in Egyptian Texts of the New Kingdom and Third Intermediate Period.* Princeton: Princeton Univ. Press.

Hornung, Erik. 1979, 1980. *Das Buch von den Pforten des Jenseits.* 2 vols. Geneva: Editions des Belles Lettres.

Iversen, Erik. 1958. *Papyrus Carlsberg Nr. VII: Fragments of a hieroglyphic dictionary.* Copenhagen: Munksgaard.

Izre'el, Shlomo. 1997. *The Amarna Scholarly Tablets.* Groningen: Styx Publications.

Jansen-Winkeln, Karl. 1995. "Diglossie und Zweisprachigkeit im alten Ägypten". *Wiener Zeitschrift zur Kunde des Morgenlandes* 85.85–115.

–. 1996. *Spätmittelägyptische Grammatik der Texte der 3. Zwischenzeit.* Wiesbaden: Harrassowitz.

Janssen, Jac[obus] J. 1992. "Literacy and Letters at Deir el-Medîna". *Village Voices. Proceedings of the Symposium 'Texts from Deir el-Medîna and their interpretation'* ed. by R[obert] J. Demarée & A. Egberts, 81–94. Leiden: Centre of Non-Western Studies.

Janssen, Jozef. 1958. "Über Hundenamen im pharaonischen Ägypten". *Mitteilungen des deutschen archäologischen Instituts, Abteilung Kairo* 16.176–182.

Janssen, Rosalind M. & Jac[obus] J. Janssen. 1990. *Growing up in Ancient Egypt.* London: Rubicon Press.

Johnson, Janet H. 1994. "Ancient Egyptian linguistics". *History of Linguistics,* vol. I: *The Eastern Traditions of Linguistics* ed. by Giulio Lepschy, 63–76. London & New York: Longman.

Junge, Friedrich. 1984. "Zur 'Sprachwissenschaft' der Ägypter". *Studien zu Sprache und Religion Ägyptens zu Ehren von Wolfhart Westendorf,* I, 257–272. Göttingen.

Kahl, Jochem. 1991. "Von h bis ḳ: Indizien für eine 'alphabetische' Reihenfolge einkonsonantiger Lautwerte in spätzeitlicher Papyri". *Göttinger Miszellen* 122.33–47.

Kammerzell, Frank. *Studien zur Sprache und Geschichte der Karer in Ägypten.* Wiesbaden: Harrassowitz.

Kaplony-Heckel, Ursula. 1974. "Schüler und Schulwesen in der ägyptischen Spätzeit". *Studien zur altägyptischen Kultur* 1.227–246.

Massart, Adhémar. 1959. "À propos des 'listes' dans les textes égyptiens funéraires et magiques". *Studia Biblica et Orientalia* 3.227–246.

Mathieu, Bernard. 1996. "Modifications de texte dans la pyramide d'Ounas". *Bulletin de l'institut Français d'Archéologie Orientale* 96.289–311.

Meltzer, Ed. 1988. "The Cuneiform List of Egyptian Words from Amarna: How useful is it really for reconstructing the vocalization of Egyptian?". *Varia Aegyptiaca* 4.55–62.

Moran, William L. 1992. *The Amarna Letters. Edited and Translated.* Baltimore & London: Johns Hopkins Press.

Morenz, Ludwig. 1994. "Zu einem Beispiel schöpferischer Vorlagenarbeiten in den Sargtexten: Ein Beitrag zur Textgeschichte". *Göttinger Miszellen* 143.109–111.

Osing, Jürgen. 1976. "Ächtungstexte aus dem Alten Reich (II)". *Mitteilungen des deutschen archäologischen Instituts, Abteilung Kairo* 32.133–185.

–. 1989. "Ein späthieratisches Onomastikon aus Tebtunis". *Akten des vierten internationalen Ägyptologen Kongresses München 1985,* III, 183–187. Hamburg: Buschke.

–. 1992. *Aspects de la culture pharaonique.* Quatre leçons au Collège de France (février–mars 1989). Paris: Boccard.

Posener, Georges. 1937. "Une liste de noms propres étrangères sur deux ostraca hiératiques du nouvel empire". *Syria* 18.183–197.

–. 1966. "Quatre tablettes scolaires de basse époque (Aménémopé et Hardjédef)". *Revue d'Egyptologie* 18.45–65.

Quack, Joachim Friedrich. 1993. "Ägyptisches und Südarabisches Alphabet". *Revue d'Egyptologie* 44.141–151.

Ray, John. 1976. "The Mountain of Lapis-lazuli". *Göttinger Miszellen* 20.49–54.

Redford, Donald. 1986. *Pharaonic King-lists, Annals and Day-books: A contribution to the study of the Egyptian sense of history.* Missisauga: Benben Publications.

Salmon, A. 1956. "L'expérience de Psammétique (Hérodote II, 11)". *Les Etudes Classiques* 24.321–329.

Sauneron, Serge. 1960. "La différentiation des langages d'après la tradition égyptienne". *Bulletin de l'Institut Français d'Archéologie Orientale* 60.31–41.

Schenkel, Wolfgang. 1972. "Zur Relevanz der ägyptischen Metrik". *Mitteilungen des deutschen archäologischen Instituts, Abteilung Kairo* 28.103–107.

–. 1977. "Zur Frage der Vorlagen Spätzeitlicher 'Kopien'". *Fragen an die altägyptische Literatur. Studien zum Gedenken an Eberhard Otto* ed. by Jan Assmann, Erika Feucht & Reinhard Grieshammer, 417–441. Wiesbaden: Reichert.

–. 1986. "Syllabische Schreibung". *Lexikon der Ägyptologie*, VI, 114–122. Wiesbaden: Harrassowitz.

Schneider, Thomas. 1992. *Asiatische Personennamen in ägyptischen Quellen des Neuen Reiches.* Freiburg/Schweiz: Universitätsverlag; Göttingen: Vandenhoeck & Ruprecht.

Sulek, Antoni. 1982. "Psammetichus, the first Experimenter: Commentary to Herodotus". *The Polish Sociological Bulletin* 1, 4.33–43.

Tassier, Emmanuel. 1992. "Greek and Demotic school-exercises". *Life in a Multi-cultural Society: Egypt from Cambyses to Constantine and beyond* ed. by Janet J. Johnson. Chicago: The Oriental Institute of the University of Chicago.

Vernus, Pascal. 1996. "Langue littéraire et diglossie". *Ancient Egyptian Literature: History and Forms* ed. by Antonio Loprieno, 555–564. Leiden: Brill.

Zandee, Jan. 1964. "Das Schöpferwort im alten Ägypten". *Verbum. Essays on some aspects of the religious function of words dedicated to Dr H. W. Obbink*, 33–66. Utrecht: Kemink en Zoon.

Zyhlarz, Ernst. 1961. "Sudan-Ägyptisch im Antiken Äthiopenreich von K'ash". *Kush* 9.226–257.

*Joris F. Borghouts, Leiden (The Netherlands)*

# 3. Die Sprachforschung in Ugarit

1. Einleitung
2. Einheimische Schriftdenkmäler im Rahmen der syllabischen Keilschrift
3. Einheimische Schriftdenkmäler im Rahmen der Keilschriftalphabete
4. Bibliographie

## 1. Einleitung

Die seit 1929 auf dem Ruinenhügel Ras Schamra ("Fenchel-Hügel") ca. 11 km nordwestlich der modernen syrischen Hafenstadt Latakya am Mittelmeer stattfindenden franko-syrischen Ausgrabungen haben die antike Stadt Ugarit ans Tageslicht gefördert, die bereits im 7. Jahrtausend v. Chr. existierte, ihre Blütezeit als Handelsmetropole und Gelehrtenzentrum aber erst im 14. und 13. Jh. v. Chr. erlebte (Yon 1997). Den Aufstieg zu einem der bedeutendsten Kulturzentren an den östlichen Gestaden des Mittelmeers verdankte Ugarit einem Herrscherhaus, das gegen Mitte des 2. Jahrtausends aus dem Südosten, möglicherweise aus der nördlichen Region des heutigen Jordanien, dorthin kam und seine neue Heimat Ende des 14. Jh. im hethitischen Großreich verankerte (Dietrich & Loretz 1988: 309–311; Dietrich 1997a: 81–85). Der Untergang der Stadt geschah Anfang des 12. Jh. und wird gemeinhin mit dem 'Seevölker'-Sturm in Verbindung gebracht, dem damals die Kulturzentren an der Levante zum Opfer fielen (Lehmann 1970, 1985). Bis zu seiner Zerstörung stellte die Hafenstadt den Endpunkt der transkontinentalen Handelsstraßen aus Kleinasien, Mesopotamien, Arabien und Syrien-Palästina und den Anfangspunkt der überseeischen Handelsrouten nach Ägypten, nach Zypern, zu den Zentren an der Südwestküste Kleinasiens, nach Kreta und in die Ägäis dar; hier wurden die Güter durch ugaritische und überseeische Händler umgesetzt. Also war die Bevölkerung Ugarits während seiner Blütezeit nicht nur gesellschaftlich vielschichtig, sondern auch ethnisch vielgesichtig. Beredte Zeugen dessen sind die bei den Ausgrabungen freigelegte Architektur und die dabei geborgenen Kleinfunde und schriftlichen Dokumente (umfassende Darstellungen: Kinet 1981; von Reden 1992).

Aus der Zeit der ugaritischen Herrscher Ammistamru I., Niqmaddu II. Arḫalba, Niqmepa, Ammistamru II., Ibirānu, Niqmaddu III. und Ḫammurapi, die das Geschehen der Stadt und deren Dependance Ras Ibn Hani im 14. und 13. Jh. bestimmten, haben sich in teilweise umfangreichen Archiven zahlreiche Staats- und Privatverträge, Briefe privater und offizieller Natur, Wirtschaftstexte für die Belieferung von Palast und Tempel sowie Zensuslisten unterschiedlicher Kategorien gefunden, die uns einen mitunter deutlichen Einblick in das offizielle, halboffizielle und häufig auch private Leben eines Herrschers, eines seiner Familienangehörigen oder Untertanen ermöglichen. Hieraus wird klar, daß Ugarit kurz vor seinem Untergang eine von allen Seiten besuchte und umworbene Handelsmetropole war: Die Namen und Taten vieler Ugariter und Nichtugariter, Gäste aus aller Herren Länder, sind für uns einsehbar – Leute des palästinischen Ortes Asdod, der Länder Amurru, Kanaan, Ägypten und Nubien stammen aus dem Süden, die aus Assur und Subartu aus dem Osten, die aus Mukiš mit dem Zentrum Alalaḫ, Ḫatti und Mitanni aus dem Norden und Nordosten sowie die von den Inseln Zypern, Kreta und Sardinien aus dem Westen, also von Übersee. Die multi-ethnische und multi-kulturelle Zusammensetzung der Einwohner Ugarits brachte es mit sich, daß die Schriftdenkmäler alle zu jener Zeit gängigen Schriften und verschriftlichten Sprachen widerspiegeln.

Das geistig-religiöse Leben der gemischten Bevölkerung von Ugarit kommt in den Texten der Tempel-, Priester- und Gelehrtenbibliotheken, die neben den Texten des täglichen Lebens (Briefe, Wirtschafts- und Rechtsurkunden) gefunden worden sind, zum Ausdruck – die Palastarchive spielen hier eine weniger wichtige Rolle. In den Tempel- und Priesterbibliotheken fanden sich Mythen und Epen, Beschwörungen, mantische Texte, Omensammlungen und Rituale, in den Gelehrtenbibliotheken Schultexte aller Art (Götterlisten, Wortlisten, Wörterbücher, Weisheitstexte), human- und veterinärmedizinische Traktate, Beschwörungen, Wahrsage- und Ritualtexte. In den Sprachen des Koine-Babylonischen und Ugaritischen ist das Gros dieser Texte verfaßt, das Hurritische, eine der traditionellen Kultsprachen in Ugarit, begegnet in den vielen Opferlisten und Ritualtexten.

Für den Sprachforscher, der sich mit den Schriftdenkmälern Ugarits beschäftigt, bedeutet dies, daß er sich einer Vielzahl heute toter Sprachen aus mindestens drei stark differierenden Sprachfamilien gegenübergestellt sieht.

## 2. Einheimische Schriftdenkmäler im Rahmen der syllabischen Keilschrift

Die politische Einbindung in das hethitische Reich öffnete für Ugarit den Weg in die Welt der Keilschrift des Koine-Babylonischen, des damals üblichen Verständigungsmittels der internationalen Diplomatie und Wirtschaft. Das bedingte, daß hier das Babylonische in seiner westlich-syrischen Ausprägung und das mit diesem verbundene Sumerische heimisch wurden (van Soldt 1995). Da, wie van Soldt (1995) ausführt, die Keilschrift unter Zuhilfenahme literarischer – hierzu gehören auch Omensammlungen – und lexikalischer Texte der mesopotamischen Tradition in babylonischer und sumerischer Sprache, bei Bedarf um eine hurritische und ugaritische Rubrik erweitert, erlernt wurde, finden sich in den Palast-, Privat- und Tempelarchiven auch zahlreiche Dokumente dieser Genres. Also haben wir es bei den sumero-babylonischen Texten mit zwei Kategorien zu tun: Eine umfaßt Schultexte, die zur Ausbildung der Schreiber nach Ugarit importiert wurden – nach J. Huehnergard (1989: 9), *canonical texts* –, und eine andere jene Texte, die in Ugarit verfaßt worden sind – nach J. Huehnergard (1989: 9) *non-canonical texts* – und eindeutige Indizien für eine Mischsprache aufweisen.

Die Schultexte literarischen und lexikalischen Inhalts spiegeln in Grammatik, Lexikon und Syllabar weitgehend zuverlässig ihre Vorlagen – ob sie nun aus Babylonien, Assyrien, Ḫattuša oder dem benachbarten Emar stammen – wider und lassen nur vereinzelt spezifisch ugaritische Züge erkennen (Huehnergard 1989: 12–14; van Soldt 1991, bes. 519–523; Kämmerer, 1998).

Dann, wenn diese ursprünglich ortsfremden Texte eine längere Tradition in Ugarit selber oder in einem syrischen Nachbarort durchlaufen haben, ist es mitunter zu sachlichen Veränderungen etwa in Lexikon und Pantheon gekommen. Solche Veränderungen fallen nicht direkt ins Auge, müssen also mit Hilfe der makro-syntaktischen Forschungsmethode erfaßt werden (Kämmerer 1998).

Eine Besonderheit stellt das in den Schulen Ugarits und anderer syrischer Zentren überlieferte Sumerisch dar. Während die lexikalischen Listen die sumerische Normalorthographie ihrer östlichen Vorlage weitgehend beibehalten haben, bieten die zusammenhängenden Texte (Sprüche, Beschwörungen, ein literarischer Brief) die im Westen beliebte unorthographische, 'syllabische' Schreibweise, die eine vielfach nicht mehr – oder noch nicht – sicher erklärbare Aussprache des dort überlieferten Sumerisch aufzeigen (Krecher 1969: 142–143).

Die *Non-canonical* (Huehnergard 1989: 9) Schriftstücke wie Wirtschafttexte, Rechtsurkunden und Briefe unterliegen den philologischen Gegebenheiten des damals in Syrien verbreiteten Koine-Babylonischen, das bis Mitte des 13. Jh. in allerlei Details einen hurro-mitannischen, danach einen assyrischen Einschlag hatte (van Soldt 1991: 521–522). Die beiden umfangreichen neueren Studien zu diesem substratbehafteten Mittelbabylonischen stammen von J. Huehnergard (1989) und W. H. van Soldt (1991); sie bieten eine umfassende Erörterung philologischer Fragestellungen und haben damit das Tor zur Einordnung des in Ugarit beheimateten Koine-Babylonischen in die weite Gruppe der Koine-Sprachen Syrien-Palästinas und Kleinasiens der Mitte des 2. Jahrtausends v. Chr. weit geöffnet.

Texte wie die *Marduk-Beschwörung* (RS 25.460: Dietrich 1994: 134–137, mit weiterführender Literatur) oder das *Gebet für den König* (RS 79.025: Dietrich 1996: 43–45, 1998: 156–171) gehören zwar zur Gruppe der literarischen Texte, stellen jedoch Dichtungen dar, die in Ugarit (und Emar) ihre uns überlieferte Gestalt angenommen haben: Sie entfalten zwar östliche Themen, tun dies aber in Wortwahl und Gottesverständnis mit einer deutlich syrischen Einstellung.

Ugaritische Wörter und Wortformen begegnen innerhalb der *non-canonical*-Texte wiederholt in koine-babylonischem Kontext oder stellen beim viersprachigen Vokabular in der rechten, d. h. letzten Rubrik die Übersetzung eines zuvor sumerisch, akkadisch und hurritisch erfaßten Wortes dar. Die Überlieferung ugaritischer Wörter in syllabischer Keilschrift ist für die Philologie von größter Wichtigkeit, weil sie die Wortformen besser zum Ausdruck bringt als die sonst für diese Wörter gebrauchte Alphabetschrift (Huenergard 1987; van Soldt 1991, 1995: 172–176).

Für die Erschließung der Aussprache von Vokalen und Konsonanten sowie für die lexikalische Erfassung von Namenselementen, die normalerweise in Alphabetschrift vorliegen, ist deren syllabische Überlieferung von größter Bedeutung. Dies gilt in gleicher Weise für Orts- (van Soldt 1996, 1998) wie für Personennamen (Gröndahl 1967; del Olmo Lete & Sanmartín 1996, *sub voces*).

Die drei- und viersprachigen lexikalischen Listen stellen sumero-babylonischen Wörtern in einer gesonderten Rubrik mitunter hurritische in syllabischer Schreibweise gegenüber. Diese Listen sind für die Erforschung des Wortschatzes der in Nordwestsyrien beheimateten Hurriter von unschätzbar hohem Wert, auch wenn sie eher in die Semantik eingebundene Wortübertragungen als Übersetzungen in unserem Sinn bieten.

## 3. Einheimische Schriftdenkmäler im Rahmen der Keilschriftalphabete

Für die Sprachforschung ist Ugarit wegen der Entwicklung einer genuinen Alphabetschrift besonders aufschlußreich: Es kamen hier Tontafeln an den Tag, die nicht mit der aus Mesopotamien importierten syllabischen und ideographischen Keilschrift beschriftet sind, sondern mit einer in Keilen ausgeführten, mit der jüngeren altphönikischen verwandten, Alphabetschrift. Da die Sprache, die dieser Schrift zugrundeliegt, kanaanäisch-südwestsemitisch-altarabische Züge aufweist, dürfte sie speziell für das in Ugarit gesprochene Idiom eingeführt worden sein, das wir vereinfachend 'Ugaritisch' nennen.

In diesem Zusammenhang ist hervorzuheben, daß auch Tontafeln gefunden wurden, die lediglich das Alphabet bieten: Also liegen uns hier die ältesten Zeugen für das Genre Alphabet vor.

Das Studium der keilschriftalphabetischen Schrift von Ugarit hat in den letzten Jahren ergeben, daß wir uns dort, wo wir meinen konnten, am Anfang der Alphabetgeschichte zu stehen, wiederum bereits an einem Endpunkt derselben befinden (Dietrich 1997b): Das ugaritische Standardalphabet umfaßt 30 rechtsläufig geschriebene Buchstaben ('Langalphabet') und ist das Produkt der Erweiterung eines levantinischen, ebenfalls in Ugarit gebrauchten Alphabets mit 22 linksläufig geschriebenen Buchstaben ('Kurzalphabet') in der *a-b-g*-Abfolge ('phönikisch-kanaanisches Alphabet') um 8 Buchstaben (Dietrich & Loretz 1988, bes. 124–143, 1989: 110–112). Diese Erweiterung wurde infolge der Zuwanderung des Herrscherhauses aus dem Südosten etwa Mitte des 2. Jahrtausends v. Chr. nötig (siehe oben 1.), das in der neuen Heimat seine Sprache einführte, deren Lautstand stärker differenziert war. Daraus folgt, daß das ugaritsche 'Langalphabet' das Produkt aus der Addition von einem nordwest- und einem südwestsemitischen Idiom war.

Die Annahme, daß das in Ugarit eingewanderte Herrscherhaus in seiner ursprünglichen Heimat eine eigene, für seine Sprache mit einem differenzierteren Lautstand besser geeignete Alphabettradition hatte, bestätigte sich jüngst: Bei den Ausgrabungen in Ugarit wurde 1988 in einem Händlerarchiv eine Tontafel entdeckt, die das südwestsemitische, 'altarabische Alphabet' mit 27 Konsonanten in der *h-l-ḥ-m*-Abfolge bietet (Bordreuil & Pardee 1995; Dietrich 1997b: 80–81).

Mithin haben wir es in Ugarit mit der Überlieferung von drei verschiedenen Alphabeten zu tun: dem 'Kurzalphabet' mit 22 linksläufig geschriebenen, dem 'Langalphabet' mit 30 rechtsläufig geschriebenen und dem 'altarabischen Alphabet' mit 27 ebenfalls rechtsläufig geschriebenen Buchstaben.

Der Begriff 'Ugaritisch' für die Sprache der zahlreichen keilschriftalphabetischen Texte aus Tempel-, Palast- und Privatarchiven, deren Zahl mit jeder Ausgrabungskampagne wächst, ist ein Notbehelf: Er soll alle jene Schriftdokumente umfassen, die während des 14. und 13. Jh. in Ugarit mit den Zeichen des 'Langalphabets' geschrieben worden sind und die für Ugarit im 2. Jahrtausend v. Chr. typische nordwestsemitische Mischsprache (Gordon 1965; Segert 1984; Sivan 1997; Tropper 1997, 2000) aufweisen. In Lexikon und Grammatik überwiegen zwar die kanaanäischen Elemente, die phönikischen, aramäischen und arabischen können aber nicht außer Betracht bleiben. Das Lexikon wird zudem von vielen Lehn- und Fremdwörtern aus kontemporären Sprachen wie dem Sumero-Babylonischen, Hurritischen – diese beiden Sprachen haben verschiedentlich auch die Grammatik des Ugaritischen beeinflußt –, Hethitischen und Ägyptischen bereichert (vgl. Watson 1995, 1996, 1998).

Aus dem Blickpunkt der Inhalte haben wir es bei den ugaritischen Texten sowohl mit religiösen Texten (Mythen, Epen, Ritualen, Beschwörungen, Omensammlungen) aus Tempel- und Privatbibliotheken, als auch mit Schultexten (Alphabeten, Schreibübungen) und administrativen Texten (Briefen, Rechts-, Wirtschaftsurkunden) aus Palast-, Tempel- und Privatarchiven zu tun (Kondordanz: Bordreuil 1989; Textedition: Dietrich, Loretz & Sanmartín 1995); wie Vertragstexte zeigen, diente das Ugaritische in begrenztem Rahmen auch internationalen Aufgaben.

Die führende Rolle der babylonischen Mantik und Beschwörungskunst hat zu einer Übersetzungsliteratur ins Ugaritische (Astrologie-, Geburts-Omina, Beschwörungen) geführt (Dietrich & Loretz 1990, 2000).

Die Sprache der Texte im 'Kurzalphabet' mit 22 linksläufig geschriebenen Buchstaben (siehe oben 2.; Dietrich & Loretz 1988: 145–204) ist, wie J. Tropper (1998) feststellt, nächstens mit dem späteren Phönikischen verwandt.

Eine umfangreiche Gruppe von Tafeln aus Priesterbibliotheken, deren etwas grobe Schrift der 'Langalphabet'-Tradition zugehört, bietet kultisch-religiöse Texte (Opferlisten, Beschwörungen, Rituale) in hurritischer Sprache. Sie weist darauf hin, daß die Hurriter eine lange Geschichte in Ugarit hatten und den offiziellen Kult nachhaltig mit ihrer Sprache und ihrem Pantheon geprägt haben (Dietrich & Mayer 1995, 1998).

Abgesehen davon, daß die Erfassung des Lexikons und der Grammatik des Hurritischen an sich noch problematisch ist, legen die hurritischen Texte in ugaritischer Alphabetschrift zusätzliche Hindernisse für ein Verständnis in den Weg: Die von ihnen angewandte Alphabetschrift verzichtet fast gänzlich auf die Darstellung von Vokalen, so daß jeder Hinweis auf Qualität oder Quantität einer Silbe fehlt, und das von ihr angewandte phonetische System wirft beim Versuch, es an das geläufige der syllabischen Keilschrift anzuschließen, viele Probleme auf (Dietrich & Mayer 1995: 32–34).

Babylonische Beschwörungen wurden, wie der Fund von vier Tafeln in einer Priesterbibliothek zeigt, auch ohne Übersetzung in Alphabetschrift überliefert: Der Text wurde, auf sein Konsonantengerippe reduziert, durch Buchstaben des Langalphabets wiedergegeben. Somit haben wir es hier mit dem philologisch höchst aufschlußreichen Phänomen einer phonetischen Gleichsetzung von Konsonanten der syllabischen und der langalphabetischen Traditionen zu tun (Segert 1988).

## 4. Bibliographie

Bordreuil, Pierre & Dennis Pardee. 1989. *La trouvaille épigraphique de l'Ougarit*, Bd. 1: *Concordance*. Paris.

–. 1995. "Un abécédaire du type sud-sémitique découvert en 1988 dans les fouilles archéologiques françaises de Ras Shamra-Ougarit". *Académie des Inscriptions & Belles-Lettres* (Paris), 855–860.

Del Olmo Lete, Gregorio & Joaquín Sanmartín. 1996. *Diccionario de la lengua ugarítica*. Bd. I. Barcelona.

Dietrich, Manfried. 1994. "Persönliches Unheil als Zeichen der Gottesferne: Das Verhältnis zwischen Schöpfer und Geschöpf nach babylonischem Verständnis". *Mitteilungen für Anthropologie und Religionsgeschichte* 8.115–141.

–. 1996. "Aspects of the Babylonian Impact on Ugaritic Literature and Religion". *Ugarit, Religion and Culture. Proceedings of the International Colloquium on Ugarit, Religion and Culture Edinburgh, July 1994. Essays presented in Honour of Professor John C. L. Gibson* hg. von N. Wyatt et al., 33–47. Münster: Ugarit-Verlag.

–. 1997a. "Die Texte aus Ugarit im Spannungsfeld zwischen Königshaus und Bevölkerung". *Religion und Gesellschaft. Studien zu ihrer Wechselbeziehung in den Kulturen des Antiken Vorderen Orients* hg. von Rainer Albertz, 75–93. Münster: Ugarit-Verlag.

–. 1997b. "Ugarit, patrie des plus anciens alphabets". *En Syrie Aux Origines de l'Écriture (Ausstellungskatalog Brüssel)*, 77–82.

–. 1998. "*buluṭ bēlī* 'Lebe mein König!': Ein Krönungshymnus aus Emar und Ugarit und sein Verhältnis zu mesopotamischen und westlichen Inthronisationsliedern". *Ugarit-Forschungen* 30. 155–200.

– & Oswald Loretz. 1988. *Die Keilalphabete. Die phönizisch-kanaanäischen und altarabischen Alphabete in Ugarit.* Münster: Ugarit-Verlag.

–. –. 1989. "The Cuneiform Alphabets of Ugarit". *Ugarit-Forschungen* 21.101–112.

–. –. 1990. *Mantik in Ugarit. Keilalphabetische Texte der Opferschau – Omensammlungen – Nekromantie.* Münster: Ugarit-Verlag.

–. –, Hg. 1995. *Ugarit – Ein ostmediterranes Kulturzentrum im Alten Orient: Ergebnisse und Perspektiven der Forschung.* Münster: Ugarit-Verlag.

–. –. 1996. *Analytic Ugaritic Bibliography 1972–1988.* Kevelaer & Neukirchen: Vluyn.

–. –. 2000. *Studien zu den ugaritischen Texten.* I. *Mythos und Ritual in KTU 1.12, 1.24, 1.96, 1.100 und 1.114.* (= *Alter Orient und Altes Testament* CCLXIX/I.) Münster: Ugarit-Verlag.

–. – & Joaquín Sanmartín. 1995. *The Cuneiform Alphabetic Texts from Ugarit, Ras Ibn Hani and Other Places.* 2. Aufl. Münster.

Dietrich, Manfried & Walter Mayer. 1995. "Sprache und Kultur der Hurriter in Ugarit". Dietrich & Loretz 1995. 7–42.

–. –. 1998. "The Pantheon of the Hurritic Sacrificial Lists from Ugarit". *Subartu* 4, 2.259–271.

Gordon, Cyrus H. 1965. *Ugaritic Textbook: Grammar, Texts in Transliteration, Cuneiform Selections, Glossary, Indices.* Rom.

Gröndahl, Frauke. 1967. *Die Personennamen der Texte aus Ugarit.* Rom.

Huehnergard, John. 1987. *Ugaritic Vocabulary in Syllabic Transcription.* Atlanta.

–. 1989. *The Akkadian of Ugarit.* Atlanta.

Kämmerer, Th. 1998. šimâ milka: *Induktion und Reception der mittelbabylonischen Dichtung von Ugarit, Emār und Tell el-ʿAmārna.* Münster: Ugarit-Verlag.

Kinet, Dirk. 1981. *Ugarit: Geschichte und Kultur einer Stadt in der Umwelt des Alten Testaments.* Stuttgart.

Krecher, Joachim. 1969. "Schreibschulung in Ugarit: Die Tradition von Listen und sumerischen Texten". *Ugarit-Forschungen* 1.131–158.

Lehmann, G. A. 1970. "Der Untergang des hethitischen Großreiches und die neuen Texte aus Ugarit". *Ugarit-Forschungen* 2.39–73.

–. 1985. *Die mykenisch-frühgriechische Welt und der östliche Mittelmeerraum in der Zeit der "Seevölker"-Invasionen um 1200.* Opladen.

Reden, Sibylle von. 1992. *Ugarit und seine Welt: Die Entdeckung einer der ältesten Handelsmetropolen am Mittelmeer.* Bergisch Gladbach.

Segert, Stanislav. 1984. *A Basic Grammar of the Ugaritic Language with Selected Texts and Glossary.* Berkeley: Univ. of California Press.

–. 1988. "Die Orthographie der alphabetischen Keilschrifttafeln in akkadischer Sprache aus Ugarit". *Cananea selecta. Festschrift für Oswald Loretz zum 60. Geburtstag* hg. von Paolo Xella. Verona.

Sivan, Daniel. 1997. *A Grammar of the Ugaritic Language.* Leiden: Brill.

Tropper, Josef. 1997. *Untersuchungen zur ugaritischen Grammatik. Schrift-, Laut- und Formenlehre.* Habilitationsschrift Berlin, ungedr.

–. 1998. "Zur Sprache der Kurzalphabettexte aus Ugarit". *Alter Orient und Altes Testament* CCL, 733–738. Münster: Ugarit-Verlag.

–. 2000. *Ugaritische Grammatik* (= *Alter Orient und Altes Testament* CCLXXIII.) Münster: Ugarit-Verlag.

Soldt, Wilfried H. van. 1991. *Studies in the Akkadian of Ugarit. Dating and grammar.* Kevelaer & Neukirchen: Vluyn.

–. 1995. "Babylonian Lexical, Religious and Literary Texts and Scribal Education at Ugarit and its Implications for the Alphabetic Literary Texts". Dietrich & Loretz 1995. 171–212.

–. 1996. "Studies in the Topography of Ugarit, (1): The Spelling of the Ugaritic Toponyms". *Ugarit-Forschungen* 28.653–692.

–. 1998. "Non-Semitic Words in the Ugaritic Lexicon (3)". *Ugarit-Forschungen* 30.751–760.

Watson, Wilfred G. E. 1995. "Non-Semitic Words in the Ugaritic Lexicon". *Ugarit-Forschungen* 27. 533–558.

–. 1996. "Non-Semitic Words in the Ugaritic Lexicon, 2". *Ugarit-Forschungen* 28.701–719.

–. 1998. "Studies in the Topography of Ugarit (3)". *Ugarit-Forschungen* 30.703–744.

Yon, Marguerite. 1997. *La cité d'Ougarit sur le tell de Ras Shamra.* Paris: Editions Recherche sur les Civilisations.


*Manfried Dietrich,*
*Münster (Deutschland)*

# II. The Establishment of the Chinese Linguistic Tradition
# Die Anfänge der Sprachwissenschaft in China
# La constitution de la tradition linguistique chinoise

## 4. Classical Chinese philosophies of language: Logic and ontology


1. Two aspects of language in early Chinese philosophy
2. Nature and function of non-substantive words in the Chinese language
3. Five positions (theories) of names and sayings in Classical Chinese philosophy
4. The Cunfucian doctrine of *zheng-ming* "rectifying names"
5. The Daoist doctrine of *wu-ming* "no names"
6. Nominalistic tendencies in Yinwenzi
7. Platonistic tendencies in Gongsun Long
8. Empirical (scientific) realism of names and language in the Neo-Moist Canons (*Jing/ Shuo*)
9. Concluding remarks
10. Bibliography


### 1. Two aspects of language in early Chinese philosophy

Classical Chinese philosophers of the period from the 6th century BC to the 3rd century BC were as a rule concerned with the problems of names (*ming*). To them names are not simple units of language but were the representations of substantive things and objects. It was not until Xunzi (ca. 300–230 BC) that names were classified into a hierarchy of categories or types and that a theory of origin and nature of names was offered. Names in general were considered identification labels which were intended to apply to and correspond with reality (*shi*). This correspondence between names and reality was conceived to be of such a nature that things in nature could be given names and the names had to identify or distinguish reality. For it was conceived that names were the products of naming (*ming*) and naming was intended to give a label to a thing, a relation, or a state of affairs, in nature, society, or in a system of values. This general assumption that all things can be named perhaps was the earliest belief held by Chinese philosophers and was not questioned until the rise of the Daoists in the 5th century BC. The Chinese term *ming* as a verb exists logically prior to its being as a norm. For until the naming of things takes place, there are no names in the world. To name is to identify and to distinguish individual things, relations, or types of individual things or relations and states of affairs. Thus *ming* is primarily explained as "naming oneself" (*zi ming ye*) in Xu Shen's *Shuo-wen* "Discourse upon language", and as the "process of illuminating" in Liu Xi's *Shi-ming* "Interpretation of names" in order to distinguish between names and actuality. But when it is found or discovered that the genuine ultimate reality need not be nameable or actually be named, and that not all names need correspond to reality and capture or represent actuality in certain aspects, various theories of the relation between names and actuality (*shi*) are proposed and various explanations of names and name-orientated language and their limited usefulness or possible misleading nature are offered, even though there are theories which propose to defend the validity of names. It might even be suggested that various ontological and logical theories in classical Chinese philosophy are responses to the nature and validity of naming and the namability of reality.

Although *ming* as a verb and a noun occupies a crucial position in philosophical issues, the classical notion of *ming* however does not lead to a definition of language in terms of *ming*. On the contrary, language is defined instead in terms of "speech" or "saying" (*yan*). Saying is considered the natural unit of expression of meaning in language unified with the intent of a speaker. In saying, naming, names, or expressions of names occur, but there would be no real need for introducing names if there is no need for saying, even though names could serve some useful purpose. In this sense saying seems to be more basic to language than names, even though naming and names were the sources of philosophical issues and disputes in classical Chinese philosophy, whereas sayings or statements (the results of saying) were not generally a genuine philosophical issue. The reason for this is not difficult to explain. Naming and names relate to and contrast with the actuality of which naming and names are made, but sayings, on the other hand, relate to a speaker and his intent. In order to make a statement, one needs to introduce names referring to characterizing the things and affairs of the world. Thus, rigorously speaking, naming and names depend on the context of saying for their introduction, whereas saying depends on our actual and possible ability to name (to identify or to characterize by using labels) for the purpose of explaining or intent or meaning. Early Chinese philosophers in general always recognized this context principle of saying and never felt seriously interested in an atomistic analysis of language in terms of names as such. Thus it is said in the *Rites of great Dai*: "To express one's intent (*zhi*) leads to saying, to speak language [i. e., to make statements] leads to names". The Song Neo-Confucianist Shao Yong in his *Huangji jingshi, guanwu neiwai pian*, says: "For the ancient people names arise from speech" (*fayan wei ming*).

To summarize, the difference between *ming* and *yan* is as follows:

(1) *Ming* must be true to reality and therefore possess an ontological significance, whereas *yan* must be true to the intent of the speaker and therefore possess an intentional significance;
(2) *Ming* must be established on the basis of human knowledge or understanding of perception, whereas *yan* must serve some practical purpose of life and action, for its truth need not always be a matter of correspondence-verification: it is also often conceived as a matter of practical or pragmatical fulfillment of expectation;
(3) The institution of *ming* and even the possibility of the institution of *ming* requires some presuppositions regarding what there is, whereas the occurrence of *yan* does not require that in its application of *ming*, *ming* has a distinctive referent. What *yan* is about need not be some distinctive object or state of affairs, but could be some implicitly intended object or state of affairs which may not have a name.

The last point about *yan* is very important, for as we shall see, in Chinese philosophy, it is generally held that unless names are specifically used to refer to things or objects, one cannot depend on *yan* for making a specific nameable reference. Often it is suggested that one can intend something without even using *yan*, not to say, using *ming*. In the context of *yan* a reference need not be mentioned by name at all. This is due to the existence of the ontological consideration of a deep structure, as well as the existence of the consideration concerning the complexity and sophistication of intent and purport of *yan* and its use.

In going through the basic classical writings of various schools, it is clear that *yan* is most frequently judged on the basis of conduct (*xing*). This is particularly true of the Confucian school of philosophy. The reason for this, of course, is that since *yan* embodies the intent and purport of a person, *yan* is to be borne out therefore by conduct which carries out the intent and purport of the person. This exhibits a pragmatic dimension of *yan*. Thus Confucius (*Analects* 13-3) says: "In saying something, what one says must be true to one's conduct". He also says (*Analects* 4-22): "In ancient time, people did not say something for having misgivings about not being able to practice it in person" and (*Analects* 4-24) "The superior man wants to be slow in saying and quick in action".

Confucius does not neglect to indicate the presence of some link between *yan* and *ming*. In his doctrine of "rectifying names" (*zhengming*), Confucius suggests that in order for sayings (language use) to be fit (*shun*), names must be rectified (*zheng*). Without elaborating at this moment on what Confucius intends by rectification of names, Confucius has made clear this: Correct names must be assumed for fit speech, where 'fit speech' means clarity and pertinence to a situation and being true to one's intent. He says (*Analects* 13-3) that "names must be sayable, and sayings must be practicable". This no doubt indicates that no name can be said to be rectified if it cannot be used in saying. Insofar as language remains a practicable human activity, names must also be created to serve human and practical purposes.

In Mencius, *yan* is also conceived as being a directive toward fulfillment in conduct. But Mencius makes it more clear than Confucius that *yan* is closely related to mind – the basis of one's intent and intentionality. He criticizes Gaozi for holding the view that if one is not satisfied with *yan*, one should not seek reasons in one's mind (*xin*); if one is not satisfied with mind, one should not seek reasons in vital feelings (*qi*). He says (*Mencius* 2a-2):

> If one is not satisfied with mind, one should not seek reason in vital feelings. This is permissible [to say]; but if one is not satisfied with *yan*, one shouldn't seek reason in mind. This is not permissible [to say].

What Mencius means by this is that one must find the source of the merit or demerit of *yan* in mind, for it is mind which gives meaning to *yan* through its intent and purposefulness. In this sense Mencius asserts that he "knows *yan*" (*zhi-yan*) because he knows the practical consequence and theoretical limit of *yan* in relation to the community good and political goals.

Our purpose in making the distinction between *ming* and *yan* in the conception of language of Chinese philosophers is to show that in a way Chinese philosophers recognize two aspects or dimensions of language – the referential-characterizing aspect or dimension and the intentional-practical aspect or dimension. The former can be conveniently identified with the informational content of reference and predication in a proposition, where the latter can be conveniently identified with the performative or illocutionary forces of speech acts. This may sound Austinian, but the important point here is that for Chinese philosophy early language (which literally may be called "name-speech" or *ming-yan*) is always a unity involving an objective side and a subjective side – a unity of naming reality and expressing intent. It may be suggested that the ideal form of language consists in expressing intent by means of using correct names or using names correctly. This means that using names is an integral part of intent expressing but not vice versa. The focus is obviously on language as a communicative medium developed for the purpose of consolidating a community or preserving its ordering. Naming is necessary and meaningful in regard to such communicative contexts. Although this may be the primary notion of language in early Chinese philosophy, the genuine distinction between *ming* and *yan* is a significant one and leads to a differentiation between modes of language use and underlies (explains) later Chinese philosophical disputes.

To sum up, we may suggest that Classical Chinese philosophy may be understood in regard to various possible theories regarding

(1) Confucius/Mencius *ming* ← *yan* ← ideal practical purpose or intent
*ming* ↕ *shi*

(2) Xunzi *shi* → *ming* → *yan* ← practical goal

(3) Laozi ontological understanding of *dao* (negation of *shi*)
↔ negation of *ming*
↔ negation of *yan*

(4) Zhuangzi, Chan Buddhists: negation of *shi* → {negation of *ming*, negation of *yan*} → {*ming*, *yan*}

(5) Gongsun Long *ming* → *shi*; *ming* ↘ *yan*; *shi* ↕ *yan*

(6) Yinwenzi *ming* ↔ *shi* (limited to shapes); *ming* ↘ *yan*; *shi* ↕ *yan*

(7) Neo-Mohists *ming* ← *shi* (unlimited to shapes); *ming* ⤡ *yan*

[Here "→" "←" and "↔" means "determine" in the direction of the arrow]

Tab. 4.1: Possible theories regarding naming and saying

the nature of naming, the nature of saying, and their relation to ontological understanding.

## 2. Nature and function of nonsubstantive words in the Chinese language

Names (*ming*) and words (*zi*) in Chinese are often classified according to the categories suggested by ontological thoughts and experiences. Three pairs of polarities of ontological import are specifically recognized. (1) Void or nonsubstantiveness (*xu*) versus substantiveness (*shi*); (2) Motion (*dong*) versus rest (*jing*); (3) Death (*si*) versus life (*sheng*). Anyone who is familiar with Chinese philosophy will recognize these three polarities as basic ontological ultimates in Confucian, Neo-Confucian, and Daoist literature. These categories are applied to classify words in language so that three pairs of words (*ming*) are generated therefrom: (1) void words (*xuci*) vs. substantive words (*shici*); (2) motion words (*dongzi*) vs. rest words (*jingzi*); (3) dead words (*sici*) vs. live words (*huoci*). I shall briefly discuss these distinctive classifications in order to explore their ontological implications.

(1) Void words vs. substantive words: Void words or terms are words or terms which do not refer to any substantive object. But to say this is to say that void words either refer to nonsubstantive things or they do not refer to anything at all. This implies that the scope of void words could be highly comprehensive: it includes all syntactically or semantically significant words, such as relations of space and time, propositions, logical operators, quantifiers, kinds of adverbs, modal words or words of modality and other syncategorematic words. It also includes words used to indicate or express emotive moods in which a sentence is introduced, ended, or related to other sentences relative to the speaker's intent. This dimension of the speech act is to suggest the mood of the speaker and his evaluation of the meaning of the sentence in use. Nobody can deny that this dimension of speech constitutes an important but hidden side of the significance of discourse. It is primarily sentence or discourse-orientated, and it can be referred to as the existential illocutionary forces of speech in use. They explain or show a certain existential relation between the speaker and the speech which may affect the existential relation between the intended listener and the speech. It may be said that void words of the later type are words standing for the existential illocutionary forces. But unlike the stressed or unstressed, they are codified and incorporated in the total written symbolism.

As void words do not say anything about the reality of the world and the reality of the speaker, but rather show or show forth the illocutionary force of some existential relation between the speaker and the speech, they can also be called words of showing, and for that matter, demonstratives are also words of showing, in distinction from words of saying or naming.

The substantive words (*shizi*) on the other hand refer to (or name) substantive things. They are words for material objects, persons, and other substantive entities or particulars, such as processes and activities. They are also words for qualities and attributes. Thus substantive words, basically speaking, include nouns, adjectives, and verbs. They form a major portion of the vocabulary of our language and carry the ontological burden of the language. They stand for objects of which names are names. Therefore they form elements for the propositional-assertive use of language.

The contrast between void words and substantive words is that, whereas substantive words generally represent and correspond to the concrete or perceivable side of reality, void words represent and correspond to the imperceivable hidden yet concrete side of reality. A whole sentence of course is a totality of two sides. It has a manifest side borne out by the substantive words and a hidden side borne out by the void words. The meaning of a sentence is a unity of the two sides and involves both the objective reference and the subjective intent. The ontological model in Chinese philosophy has clearly effected an understanding or at least a predisposition toward understanding what a whole sentence is and in what the whole meaning of a sentence consists.

On the basis of the distinction between void words and substantive words, it has also been suggested that there could be half-void words (*banxuzi*) and half-empty substantive words (*banshizi*). The intuitive grounds for such suggestion, of course, are the ontological consideration or observation of the existence of the half-void states of things, as well as the possibility of a creative context for regarding things as half-void and half-substantive. In the latter case the basis for the suggestion is, of course, the uses to which void words and substantive words are put. The following definitions are suggested by Yuan Renlin in his *Xuci Shuo* (*Dui Lei*):

Words that refer to things having forms and bodies are substantive. Words that refer to things having no forms and no bodies are void. Words that refer to things that appear to have forms and bodies, but in reality do not have them are half-void. Words which refer to things which appear to have no form and body but in reality have them are half-substantive.

In general, one can see that nouns that are used as verbs are half-void words e. g., the Chinese word for "eye", *mu*, as used in *er er mu zhi* "use ears to see" is a half-void words. For in such use, "eye" is used in the sense of seeing with the ears, which appears to have a form and in fact does not have one. Similarly, words which originally are void may be used in such a way as if some substantive object or state is referred to, then such a word would be a half-substantive word; e. g. the word *jin* "now" is a temporal adverb, but it can be used as if it is a noun referring to a state of actuality, such as *jinyu* "the present being" or *jinye* "the present moment".

The point here is that, in principle, void words can be used as if they are substantive words or used substantively and that, in principle, substantive words can be used nonsubstantively. Thus through the practical use of the words in sentences and speech the ontological nature of a name could be transformed into another. This of course illustrates the principle of the mutual transformation of *yin* and *yang* in the Great Ultimate (*daiji*) in Chinese philosophy. This also bears out the fact that *ming* receives a determinate ontological status only in the context of *yan*; *yan* being the use (*yong*) of *ming*. Many celebrated Chinese poems thrive on the use of substantive words in a non-substantive and, grammatically speaking, adverbial and modal way.

(2) Motion Words vs Rest Words: The distinction between motion words and rest words is made clear by Yuan Renlin of the Ching Period in his *Xuci Shuo* "Treatise on void words":

The same word, if used to show activity through effort, is a motion word; if used to retain its natural spontaneity, it is a rest word.

The basic rationale for the distinction is that motion words indicate motion or activity and show some effort or purpose, whereas rest words indicate a natural state of being devoid of such an effort or purpose. This distinction apparently is more functional than the distinction between void words and substantive words, for it depends on the context of *yan* "speech" for identifying the motion or rest of a state of affairs. Yuan illustrates the distinction with sentences such as:

"Respect the respectable" (*zun-zun*)
"Love [your] parents" (*qin-qin*)

By identifying the first word in the combination as a motion word and the second word as a rest word the distinction is established. But in such combinations as (cf. *Analects* 12-11):

"The ruler should be ruler-like" (*jun-jun*)
"The father should be father-like" (*fu-fu*)

We identifies the first word as a rest word and the second word as a motion word. This makes it clear that rest words and motion words are relative to each other and are mutually determined in a context of *yan*.

(3) Live Words vs Dead words: This distinction is made in the Ming text *Dui Lei* in the following way:

To say that a word is dead is to say that it refers to a state which is such and such by nature, such as the words high and low, big and small, and the like. To say that a word is live is to say that the object of its reference is made so and so, such as flying, diving, changing, and transforming and the like.

The basis for such a distinction is the presence or absence of effort and purpose in the named objects or objective state of reality.

From the above it is clear that the distinction between void words and substantive words is the basic and primary distinction. It has both a syntactic and ontological basis. The distinctions between motion words and rest words and that between live words and dead words, on the other hand, are derived from the use of void words and substantive words in the context of *yan*, and thus they reflect the various uses of the void and substantive words. The very way in which these distinctions are made suggest how the ontological understanding of reality in terms of substance (*di*) and function (*yong*) illuminate the functioning of language, and how the ontological and semantic meanings of sentences or words are mutually dependent and mutually transformable. That language can represent or show an ontology becomes quite obvious. Yuan Renlin says in his *Xuci Shuo*:

> To use words nonsubstantively or lively is not something which the rhetoricians invent and impose, it is a fact that in heaven and earth the void and the being are always mutually dependent, and that substance and function are never separate form each other, that amidst the principle of utmost tranquility there is the principle of utmost motion. All things are like this. [The deadness and the substantiveness of a word are to do with the object of its referent.] Thus the principle [of mutual transformation by using it in a non-substantive or lively way] will also naturally apply to it. As to its original meaning, it exists between its being used and its being not used.

This passage explicitly focuses on the embodiment of the ontology of *yin* and *yang* in *daiji* in the formation of language and determination of reference words in language. On the basis of this we might even say that the ontology in Chinese philosophy is the ontology of the language in Chinese philosophy.

## 3. Five positions (theories) of words and sayings in Classical Chinese philosophy

With the concept of language as sayings and names as a background, Chinese philosophers in the Classical Period developed basically five positions. These five positions were: (1) The doctrine of no names no sayings; (2) The doctrine of the rectifying of names; (3) The doctrine of nominalism; (4) The doctrine of Platonism; (5) The doctrine of empirical realism (scientific realism). The first doctrine was developed and maintained by the Daoists. The second doctrine was developed and maintained by the Confucianists. These two doctrines were initiated historically prior to the other doctrines. But between the Daoists and Confucianists, it is difficult to say which should be placed earlier in their development. Apparently, both doctrines presuppose the existence of names and can be correctly said to be developed in response to the unsatisfactory uses and abuses of names at the time of their development. For the Confucianists, the primary function of names was to serve the purpose of well regulated *yan*, which was taken to form the basis for institutionalized social order and political stability. As *yan* was conceived to be goal-orientated, the end of society and government therefore provides the ultimate context, basis, and rationale for the rectification of names and language. Insofar as social-political considerations as well as the practical significance of *yan* and *ming* have become the constant concerns of the Chinese mind from the very ancient past, one might treat the Confucian doctrine as being historically prior to any other theory.

As to the Daoist doctrine of *wu ming* and *wang yan*, it is apparent that the Daoists focus their attention on the nature of reality more than on human affairs. But then, this entire concern about ontology may merely be apparent, for they can also be said to search for a rule for solving the problems of social and political order and stability. Their solution led to their ontological insight, which they thought would lead to the solution in question. What they held is that only when we dissolve names, not rectify them, then social and political order can be restored or permanently secured. Of course, it might be the case that they first found their languageless ontology of the *dao* and then tried to apply it to life and society. It may also be true that they noticed the disruptive and destructive nature of names and consequently constructed their ontological theory. A plausible suggestion is that they wished to solve the problem of social order and political stability and they found it when they came to see the true nature of the *dao*. In this perspective, the Daoists are equally practical-minded as the Confucianists. They pay equal attention to *yan* and *ming*, where Zhuangzi's doctrine of *wang yan* as well as Confucius' doctrine of *wu yan* are mutually dependent.

Both the doctrine of nominalism and the doctrine of Platonism may appear to be far removed from practical considerations. The proponent of the former is Yinwenzi, the proponent of the latter is Gongsun Long. Both are remembered in Chinese philosophy as logicians from the School of Names. Though their doctrines appear to concentrate on the logical analysis of the origins of nature and references of *ming*, there is evidence that they are nevertheless concerned with practical problems, such as the rectification of names. Thus, their doctrines may be motivated by practical considerations, like the Confucianists, but once formulated, become more a matter of logical and ontological theory. What we wish to point out is simply that their doctrines of *ming* could be first intended ro relate to a doctrine of *yan* which is practical orientated.

The only doctrine of *ming* and *yan* which is devoid of overt practical considerations is that of empirical realism, as advanced by the Neo-Moists. Though the Neo-Moists are disciples and members of the practical-minded Schools of Moism founded by Mozi, their concentrated researches on language, logic, and science clearly provided self-sufficient and self-contained results comparable to the products of Aristotle. Their writings known as *Jing* "Canons" and *Jing Shuo* "Discourse on canons" and the *Da Ju* "The greater taking" and the *Xiao Ju* "The smaller taking" are brilliant works of their rigorous and organized research. Recent discussions of them by Needham (1954), A. C. Graham (1955, 1959, 1978, 1986), Chmielewski (1962–1966), Chung-ying Cheng (1971, 1973a, b, 1975, 1983, 1987) and Chad Hansen (1983, 1985, 1992) have made amply clear that rather than choosing to be guided by some fixed prior preoccupation or vagueness of practical values and goals the Neo-Moists are logically and scientifically disciplined thinkers who intend to establish a logical and scientific philosophy and methodology so that questions of value and norm can be adequately settled in light of them (cf. Cheng 1971). It is in this view that one can regard their work as reflecting the scientific, methodological spirit. They have developed both a logical theory of names and a logical theory of speech (*yan*).

## 4. The Confucian doctrine of *zheng-ming* "rectifying names"

As we have noted, the Confucianists regard language as a matter of sayings instituted for serving the practical purpose of stabilizing society and ordering government. Language being social in origin and used for social stability, those in a position to ensure conformity of usage and correspondence between names and what are named for the purpose of social communication and social control must see that this will happen. Names specifically must be incorporated in language (sayings) so that they will identify and characterize things correctly. This is the general basis for the Confucian doctrine of the rectifying of names.

The basic principles of this doctrine are as follows:

(1) Language is for social communication and social control, so that language must be correctly instituted and used for this purpose. Confucius says (*Analects* 20-3): "If a person does not know language, he will not know people".

(2) Names are for sayings and sayings are to ultimately serve the purpose of social ordering. Thus names must be correctly regulated and understood and not be abused lest disorder and confusion will result.

(3) All things are nameable. To name a thing is to identify it by its true characteristics. Thus names serve to provide us with knowledge of things in the world. This is the case with the names of birds, beasts, grass, and woods. Thus in speaking of the merits from learning poetry, Confucius mentions (*Analects* 17-9): "[One should] know the names of grass, wood, birds and beasts".

(4) Human relations, as well as human goals and values can also be names. As names of such, they must correspond correctly to the reality of such.

(5) To use names correctly is to rectify names. But a primary pre-condition is to have a correct understanding of reality. Since the reality of human relations, goals, and values is to be understood in terms of our experiences and visions of human nature and its relation to heaven, names resulting from such an understanding involve a correct recognition of such a reality. To correctly name is to correctly see and correctly understand the standard norm and goal of human behavior and their relation to society and government, as well as the relation of the latter to the former.

(6) Once the names of things and values are established, they should be correctly used to refer to the things which they are intended to represent, so that a blockage of social communication and social control will not take place, and confusion as to what is referred to will be avoided. Blockage of social communication and social control, and confusion of preference will lead to a breakdown of social norms, and value standards, which will in turn lead to confusion of thought and reasoning and will inevitably give rise to chaos and political instability. Therefore, in order to rectify names, one should insure not only that names correspond correctly to reality, but that in our use of sayings or languages, precaution should be taken to prevent confusion and the abuse of names.

The practical goal of rectifying names and the main tasks of rectification are suggested in Confucius' own statements (*Analects* 13-13):

If names are not rectified, sayings will not serve their purpose. If sayings do not serve their purpose, then rites and music (social mores) will not flourish. If rites and music do not flourish, then codes of punishment (laws) will not function right. If codes of punishment do not function right, then people will not know how to behave. Thus being a superior man, a ruler must make sure that names must be sayable and sayings must be practical. A superior man must be very serious and cautious with regard to his sayings.

Although Confucius does not make explicit the distinction between facts and values, it seems clear that for him there are two kinds of names: the first kind of names are natural names governed by fact and things; the second kind of names are value or norm names which govern human behavior. It might be suggested that in the realm of natural objects, names must correspond to reality, but in the realm of human values, reality must correspond to names, for it is up to man to make his reality, as a man conforms to a social standard of value so that he can be a socially cultivated entity and the larger goal of society be fulfilled. With this in view, Confucius suggests (*Analects* 12-11): "The ruler should be ruler-like, the minister minister-like; the father should be father-like; the son should be son-like". The rule of rectifying therefore is twofold: names must conform to natural objects, value names must make human persons conform to them. It is clear that Confucius' doctrine of rectifying names is developed around the latter principle. It is no wonder that he comes to formulate his well-known doctrine as answers to questions on how to conduct government. Again, although Confucius does not explicitly suggest how one may avoid confusion in the use of names once names are made to represent correct reality, yet from his various discourses we could see that he has come to adopt two basic rules of the application of names: (1) One name should apply to one type of thing; (2) A thing or a person may have many names, depending in its or his relation to other things or other persons.

In Xunzi, the basic principles of Confucius' doctrine of the rectifying of names are well elaborated and further developed. Xunzi's essay on *zhengming* "rectifying names" makes it clear that language is a social and human institution and therefore always possesses social and human significance. He further points out that a ruler, in being responsible for social ordering, must regulate language as a means of social ordering, which will contribute to the peace and well being of people, and eliminate confusion and disorder. But more than Confucius, he recognizes two more important aspects of language beside the practical-social aspect of language: Namely, language is empirically based and language is conventional. He is, furthermore, committed to demonstrating all three aspects of language by inquiring into: (1) How names are introduced (*suo-wei-you-ming*); (2) How the similarity and difference of names originate (*suo-yuan-yi-dong-yi*); and (3) How names are instituted or formulated as they are used (*zhi-ming-zhi-shu-yao*). Let us briefly describe Xunzi's theses as responses to these three questions.

(1) Xunzi points out that if there are no fixed names, our ideas of things cannot be clearly expressed and we are too confused about what objects we want to refer to. Consequently, the noble and the lowly cannot be distinguished, and the difference and the identity cannot be separated. Communication will be difficult and social action will be impossible. Thus the sage decides to institute names to refer to different things so that the noble and the lowly can be distinguished, and the difference and the identity can be separated. This means that one can distinguish between the different values which we attach to things and that we can classify and record things according to their identities and differences. Social communication and social action will result from these.

(2) The basis for instituting names of the difference and similarity of things, according to Xunzi, is our natural sense. He trusts that our natural senses share common impressions of things. Consequently, we can adopt the same names to refer to the same things and different names to refer to different things. His approach to what names stand for, therefore, is realistic yet empirical. He recognizes the different qualities of sight, sound, taste, smell, touching and feelings (desires and emotions). He recognizes that the human mind has organizing power and the power for inference. Thus he concludes that our names correspond to things in the world through our ability to know things in terms of the senses and mind. In this regard, one may say that for Xunzi, names in language are conceived to represent the objects of the

empirical worlds: language therefore has empirical origins and an empirical reference.
(3) Different things must have different names and same things must have the same name. This is the principle of correspondence. This correspondence in terms of difference and identity seems to imply that things can be recognized in terms of a hierarchy of classes. Things are the same because they belong to the same classes, and are different because they belong to different classes. The implicit criterion of identity and difference is class identity and difference. By recognizing the names of various sizes of classes or generality, Xunzi, together with the Neo-Mohists, has introduced the notion of class (*lei*) into the Chinese logical vocabulary. The purpose of naming is to identify the identical in regard to the same class (attribute) and to distinguish the different in regard to different classes (attributes). A proper name will thus distinguish one thing from all other things. A universal name (*da-gong-ming*) will identify all things in the same class. Although Xunzi is basically realistic with regard to the institution of class names, he introduces the principle of convention by saying (*Zhengming* chapter) that,

> Names have no intrinsic quality which necessitates its corresponding to a particular object. We stipulate the correspondence between one name and one object by convention (command). Once the convention is agreed upon and usage established, we will say that the name is proper. If a name is introduced (used) in disagreement with out convention, we will say this is improper.

The conventionality of names, of course, is the conventionality of the initial choice of names for a certain purpose. It does not alter the nature of correspondence or the nature of what the names correspond to. Thus Xunzi's theory does not allow us to infer that we can legislate reality to the world through the convention of names. His view of language is basically realistic and empirical. In fact, he even points out the following principle of the individuation of things: Things are to be individuated by their location and forms. When one thing changes form but does not change its nature and location, it is still to be regarded as one thing. But if two things occupy two different locations, even if they have the same form, they are to be regarded as two things.

On the basis of the above theses concerning origin, purpose, and the nature of language, Xunzi is able to reject the fallacies of sayings of the following kinds: fallacies of sayings based on using names to confuse with other names, without regard to their intended meaning and purpose; fallacies of sayings based on using objects (*shi*) to confuse with names, without regard to origins of names in difference and identity of perception; fallacies of sayings based on using names to confuse with reality without regard to goals by which institution of names or specifically class names is intended.

Two or more observations can be made about Xunzi's theory of the rectifying of names:

(1) Xunzi clearly recognizes that names are necessary for social and human life. He recognizes this on the basis of the recognition that human communication and society are based on the existence of human desires, and human desires are not eliminable. Thus language can be introduced to satisfy human needs. To avoid confusion in and by language one needs to know the truth with one's reason or with one's mind, but needs to be rid of desires and the implicit consequent thesis of no names and no language.
(2) In the beginning of his essay on rectifying names, Xunzi mentions common values, such as life (*sheng*), nature (*xing*), feeling (*qing*), deliberating (*lei*), human doing (*wei*), business (*shi*), virtuous deeds (*xing*), cognitive power (*zhi*), knowledge (*zhi*), natural capacity (*neng*), developed talent (*neng*), illness (*ping*), and accident (*ming*). If these names are considered (mentioned) as examples of names which should conform to the three conditions of names of the above, it is clear that Xunzi would recognize that the reality to which names correspond must be open to rational understanding by the mind, but is not just confined to our perceptual experience. Thus correct naming implies correct understanding of the world by the mind. In an implicit way, what an ontology is will determine what names will be introduced, just as what names are to be introduced will reflect what ontology will have to be presupposed.

## 5. The Daoist doctrine of *wu-ming* "no names"

We have discussed the doctrine of no names in Laozi and forgetting language in Zhuangzi. The obvious reason and argument for the namelessness of the *dao* in Laozi is that the *dao* as the ultimate reality is whole and indeterminate and cannot be characterized in determinations without losing sight of its totality, unlimitedness, and its source nature. Names are names of being (*you*). *Dao* is not exactly being in the ordinary sense and therefore essentially cannot have a name to identify or characterize it. That is why it is called void (*wu*) by Laozi. In fact, insofar as everything has a hidden side, the side of *yin* or *wu*, everything cannot be exactly identified and characterized by a name, for everything cannot be conceived as completely determinate. This is the true nature of things which Laozi's theory of reality envisions. In this regard, Laozi holds that basically language is superfluous and dispensable. Although it may help us to identify and characterize things in such a way that the identification and characterization may prove to be practically useful, language could be misleading and illusion-generating simply because it could prevent us from seeing the true nature of things and the totality of reality.

There is an implicit theory and argument in Laozi to the effect that things and the *dao* could remain nameless if we diminish or eliminate our need for naming them. In other words, Laozi's doctrine of the nameless of the *dao* goes hand in hand with his doctrine of desirelessness or no desires (*wu-yu*) and his doctrine of effortlessness or no action (*wu-wei*). Laozi holds that if we are devoid of desires (*yu*), we are able to see the true nature of the *dao*, whereas once possessed of desires we shall see the beginnings of things. Thus the true nature of reality is related to perception in the state of no desires, whereas the reality of differentiated things is related to perception in the state of having desires. What are desires? Although Laozi does not discuss this question in detail, his discourse provides the following indications about what desires are.

Desires are the ego-centric and selfish claims to possession and thus products of the self in opposition to the world. They are therefore exclusive of the points of view of other things. They give rise to so called knowledge which will serve private interests. They lead to actions which blind us to the true nature of things. Laozi is not opposed to natural desires, or desires which occur spontaneously, as he sees in the images of water and the uncarved block. Desires which are cultivated by cunning and promoted by intelligence are unnatural. They distort the nature of man and will not show the true nature of the *dao*. Thus having desires is to wish to do specifically something (*you-wei*). It is to possess things, control things, and divide things. To have no desires, on the contrary, is to let things happen spontaneously and to let one's creativity develop in harmony with reality without forcing or imposing. It is to create without possessiveness, to do things without arrogance, and to lead without domination.

Laozi points out that it is when the *dao* does not do anything specific that everything is done. This means that the cosmos, with its variety of life forms, involves spontaneity precisely because there is no convention nor goal for the *dao*. In this sense the *dao* can be said to have no desires and to make no effort toward a predesignated goal. Man should be guided by the image of the *dao*. In order to achieve creativity, man should remain desireless and effortless in the sense Laozi uses these terms.

This means that man should retain or cultivate a spontaneous life and a selfless attitude. To do nothing and to have no desires are therefore to have no desires and to do nothing from the point of view of oneself. It is to abandon the self (*wu-wo*), but not to abandon life or creativity. In this sense man will not only come to perceive or understand the *dao*, but he will be like the *dao*. In this sense language also becomes superfluous and dispensable, because as a vehicle for expressing desires, knowledge and guiding actions, language loses its ground of existence once desires, knowledge, and guiding actions are not needed and unnecessary. Of course, this does not mean that man will not act or know and have no life. It means that when man comes to live in harmony with other men and nature, language like weapons will not perform any useful function. Its use will not create difficulty and commotion like the uses of weapons and the use of the boat.

Laozi's vision is that in the spontaneous state of nature, living people need to have little commerce with one another, people will not war with one another and thus there is no need to use means of transportation and means of war – the weapons (*Daodejing* 80). Similarly, when no need for communication by language is necessary, language should be laid to rest and names need not be used. The true nature of things will be shown in their own light precisely because of their namelessness. We shall see the true nature of things and the totality of *dao* precisely because of their namelessness. This is the second reason why Laozi rejects names and language. He says (*Daodejing* 37): "The primal simplicity (the uncarved block) which is nameless (*wuming*) will alone do away with desires (*wuyu*)".

We may note that the Daoist doctrine of no names is the antipode to the Confucian doctrine of the rectification of names. Whereas the Confucians wish to develop language as a human institution and regulate it in serve to human goals, the Daoists wish to abolish language simply because it is a human invention and social institution on the ground of its ontological partiality and ill effects. Whereas Laozi sees desirelessness as a reason for namelessness, Xunzi responds by showing how desires cannot be dispensed with, and precisely because of this, names and language as founded on experience and reason would be preserved for guiding and yet satisfying desires.

## 6. Nominalistic tendencies in Yinwenzi

Chinese thinking is conducted in a framework of naturalistic concepts of concrete terms. But as we have argued elsewhere (cf. Cheng 1973), this does not mean that the Chinese language or Chinese philosophy does not permit or does not involve abstract theoretical thinking. What is characteristic of Chinese thinking in general, of course, is that the abstract and the theoretical are not separable from the concrete and the particular. The relation between the two is one of illumination, illustration, and symbolic embodiment, as well as ontological constitution. It would therefore be more surprising to come across Platonic views of ontology than to come across nominalistic views of ontology in Chinese philosophy.

The ontological pull toward concrete particulars is stronger than that toward an ontology of abstract universals. Even in the Neo-Confucianist philosophy of principles (*li*) advanced by Chu Xi, principles cannot be really ontologically prior to the process and power of material generation (*qi*), nor are they transcendently separable from *qi*.

On problems concerning the ontological dimensions of name, it is therefore not surprising that there are philosophers and logicians like Yinwenzi (350–270 BC) who argue that names are essentially intended for representing things on the basis of their material and observable forms (*xing*). In fact, Yinwenzi can be regarded as a typical example of the nominalistic theory or doctrine of names and language in ancient Chinese philosophy. In the remaining essays attributed to Yinwenzi, we find the following important assertions (*Yinwenzi* 1):

> The great *dao* has no forms, but to refer to concrete things (*qi*) we need names. Names are what correctly represent (*zheng*) shapes (or forms). Since shapes (forms) are to correctly represented by names, names must not be inaccurate.
> The great *dao* cannot be named. All shapes on the other hand must have names. It is because of its unameability, there is the *dao*. Because of the nameless *dao*, thus all shapes have their peculiarities (squareness, roundness). As names are born out of the peculiarities (squareness and roundness) of shapes, all names have their respective referents (*Yinwenzi* 2).

From these two passages it can be seen that Yinwenzi affirms the Daoist premise that the great *dao* has no names. But he would not draw the Daoist conclusion that we should abolish names and forget language. On the contrary he holds that names serve an important purpose. They represent reality as it is diversified into things. Since the diversification of reality into things is by way of the differentiation of shapes, names must be faithful to these shapes, in order that things can be identified or characterized.

The following two passages (*Yinwenzi* 8, 5) formulate the nominalistic requirement for the institution of names or language use by Yinwenzi.

> Names are to name shapes. Shapes are in answer to names. If shapes are not to give rise to correct names, nor to identify correct shapes, then shapes and names would remain irrelevant to each other. Though names should not be confused with shapes, they are not independent of each other either. In having no names, the great *dao* cannot be said. Having names, we use names to correctly represent shapes. Now ten thousand things exist at the same time, if we do not apply names to represent them [identify them], we will have confusion of knowledge. Ten thousand names exist at the same time, if we do not resort to shapes to answer them, we will have difficulties of thought. Therefore, shapes and names cannot but be made to correctly represent each other.

The nominalistic principle for Yinwenzi in the above is that names must answer to shapes, just as shapes must answer to names. If shapes are concrete criteria for the existence of things, then names are ontologically meaningful if and only if they correspond to some concrete features of things, such as shapes. If names do not name shapes or things with shapes (concrete particulars), names must be in error or they must have other justifications for their existence. Yinwenzi seems to favor the requirement that names would not be ontologically significant if there were no concrete objects corresponding to them. Yet he also allows that names without reference to shapes could be useful for human purposes and therefore are justifiable on pragmatic grounds. He says (*Yinwenzi* 8, 5):

All things which have shapes must have names. But we could have names which need not have shapes. Shapes that are not names do not necessarily lose the reality of their being square, round, white and black. In the case of names which do not have shapes referred to them, we must identify these names and investigate why they are different. Thus then we could use names to find out of which shapes they are true. Shapes determine names. Names determine certain states of affairs (*shi*). States of affairs will control names. When we investigate why certain names refer to shapes and certain other names to not, then we shall see that no reason is hidden from us in regard to the relation between shapes and names on the one hand between states of affairs and things on the other.

Though Yinwenzi does not specify how we justify and construe names without representing shapes, he lets it be understood that some reason must be found other than the existence of things which have no shapes. His whole essay, which is reconstructed by scholars such as Sun Yirang, indicates very clearly that he quickly moves to a doctrine of rectifying names of the Confucian persuasion, by suggesting the introduction of names as the basis of the distinction of values and in terms of the contexts of fulfillment of practical goals of society and government. This may remotely suggest the possibility of construing non-shape names in the context of practical language and thus confining ontology to names which correctly represent the shapes of things. It is noted of course that the so-called shapes (*xing*) could be interpreted to mean not just literally shapes such as squareness and roundness, but any quality of things which is open to sensory perception. Thus qualities such as white and black and the like could be the basis for the names of things (cf. Wang Dianji 1961: 70–97).

## 7. Platonistic tendencies in Gongsun Long

Although the Chinese language may appear to prohibit Platonistic thinking, the existence of the Platonistic ontology in Gongsun Long demonstrates that ordinary language or natural language does not determine the ontological picture of the world one may hold. In fact Gongsun Long's philosophy shows language is capable of receiving different local and ontological interpretations and there is no necessity for following one interpretation rather than another. The ultimate goal of Gongsun Long may still be the clarification of the relation of names to realities for social and political purposes. But his discourse and basic thesis leave no doubt that language is name-oriented and should possess ontological significance independently of and prior to its application to social and political affairs (cf. Cheng 1983).

Gongsun Long holds the celebrated thesis that "white horse is not horse" (*bei-ma-fei-ma*). It is in arguing for this thesis that he develops the Platonic theory of what reality is. Gongsun Long works out two main arguments for his thesis. First, he argues that, since the term 'horse' is a name for shape, and the term 'white' is a name for color, and the name for color is not the name for shape, therefore 'white horse' is not 'horse'. The peculiarity of this argument is that the premises of the argument do not immediately warrant the conclusion. Apparently one could only draw the conclusion that what the name 'white' stands for is not what the name 'horse' stands for. But this is what is precisely presupposed in the premises. In order to reach the conclusion that 'white horse' is not 'horse', one has to inquire into what name 'white' and what name 'horse' stand for. Apparently for Gongsun Long 'white' designates white color and 'horse' designates horse-shape form. Insofar as white color and horse shape are not particulars, they can be alternatively construed as universals, attributes, classes, or concepts.

Actually, these different construals should not make a real difference to Gongsun Long's argument. Assume that 'white' and 'horse' are universals. Then to say that 'white' is not 'horse' is to say (x) (x is white $\not\equiv$ x is horse). Since (x is horse $\equiv$ x is horse), it follows that (x) (x is white. x is horse $\not\equiv$ x is horse. x is horse). Therefore: (x) (x is white horse $\not\equiv$ x is horse). This conclusion, saying that anything is a white horse, is not equivalent to saying that anything is a horse on the grounds of the difference of truth conditions of the two sayings, which can be used to construe Gongsun Long's thesis that white horse is not horse.

Alternatively one may interpret 'white' and 'horse' as classes, namely, a class of white things [called w] and a class of horse-form things [called h]. Then the premise of the argument says:

$$\begin{array}{rl} & w \neq h \\ \text{But} & h = h \\ \text{Therefore} & w\ .\ h \neq h\ .\ h \\ \text{and} & w\ .\ h \neq h \end{array}$$

This of course says that the class of things which are white and horse is not the same as the class of horse things. Thus under extensional interpretation of 'white' and 'horse' again the conclusion of Gongsun Long's argument can be derived.

What is essential for proving the validity of Gongsun Long's argument under both interpretations is to recognize Gongsun Long's affirmation of nonequivalence of propositions or nonidentity of two classes. The paradox of this recognition is that normally one expects that white horse is horse because the class of white horse is a subclass of the horse, or alternatively because saying that anything is white horse implies that anything is horse. What Gongsun Long denies in his thesis may appear to be just the relation of class-inclusion and sentential implication. But in fact what he actually denies is the equivalence and class identity. The question is whether he is right to make such a denial. The answer is that from the use of the Chinese negation word *fei* "is not" in "white horse *fei* horse", Gongsun Long is justified in asserting identity as being denied or equivalence as being negated. In fact, Gongsun Long argues merely for the admissibility (*ke-yi*) of such an interpretation, not the necessity of such an interpretation as he makes clear in the beginning of his essay:

Q.: To say that white horse is horse, is it admissible? A.: Yes, it is admissible.

Thus we make clear that the first argument of Gongsun Long does not rule out his possible commitment to a concrete ontology. He merely indicates in his argument the possibility and acceptability of an abstract ontology because our language is capable of being construed in terms of an abstract ontology of universals or classes.

The second major argument for his thesis is that if one asks for horse, a horse of different colors will meet this request. But if one asks for white horse, only a white horse meets this request. This may appear to be an obvious pragmatic argument. But what makes this argument pragmatically valid according to Gongsun Long is some ontological fact about the qualities of white horse and horse. For Gongsun Long we would refer to horse as such as a single quality which may combine with other qualities to produce white horse, yellow horse, black horse. Thus to ask for horse is to ask for a thing identifiable by a single quality and to ask for white horse is to ask for a thing identifiable by the conjunction of two qualities. Since the identification conditions for the two requested objects are different, these two requested objects are two different objects.

The independence of different qualities, which is assumed in Gongsun Long's second argument, implies the separability of these qualities. For Gongsun Long all names are names for independent qualities. In fact, there are two kinds of names: the single names for single simple qualities, such as white, the compound names for compounds or conjunctions of single simple qualities, such as white horse. Gongsun Long's logic of inference is one of identity, according to which no simple name is equal to a compound name, or what a single name stands for is not identical with what a compound name stands for and vice versa. Gongsun Long (*Beima* chapter) says:

The 'horse' which does not fix a color is different from the 'white horse' which does fix a color. Therefore white horse is not a horse.

From the above it is clear that Gongsun Long's theory that 'white horse is not horse' leads to or presupposes the abstract ontology of qualities or universals. Once their abstract ontology is accepted, there is the question as to how we understand concrete things. Are concrete things of a different order of existence than abstract qualities? Or are they analysable into or reducible to abstract qualities? Or are they analysable into or reducible to abstract qualities? There seems to be a tendency in Gongsun Long to develop the ontology suggested in his *Bei ma lun* into a full theory which recognizes no concrete things in the world. This is seen in his work *Zhi wu lun*.

Before we discuss the complete theory and the reduction theory of Gongsun Long, we shall see another argument for the separability and independence of individual qualities in Gongsun Long's essay on hardness and whiteness, *Jien bei lun*.

In *Jien bei lun*, Gongsun Long offers a new argument for the thesis that qualities are separate and independent. His argument consists in pointing out that our different sense organs independently identify respective qualities which are different. Thus we identify the hardness of a stone by touch and identify the whiteness of a stone by sight. If we observe sight, we don't get hardness, and thus relative to sight there is no hardness. If we observe touch, we do not get whiteness, and thus relative to touch there is no whiteness. On this ground Gongsun Long concludes that whiteness and hardness are external to each other and are independent qualities. In making this argument Gongsun Long denies the relevance of our concept of a stone which possesses the qualities of white and hardness in itself. Since what we see and what we touch are not stone, Gongsun Long tends to rule out the actual existence of stone. Therefore he denies that there are three things – stone, white, and hardness – which cannot exist in some one thing of which there seems to be evidence. His argument therefore is used to establish both the separability of independent qualities and the nonexistence of things such as stone.

That qualities such as white and hard are separable and independent is also based on the fact that in verifying the existence of whiteness by sight, hardness is hidden, and in verifying the existence of hardness by touch, whiteness is hidden, so we may as well say that it does not exist in the same sense in which hardness and whiteness can be said to exist.

That Gongsun Long clearly believes that whiteness and hardness are separate universal qualities in a Platonic sense is indicated by the following statement (*Jianbei* chapter):

Things have white color, but white is not fixed and confined (*ding*) to a specific white thing. Things have hardness but hardness is not fixed and confined to a specific hard thing. What is not fixed and confined to a specific thing can characterize all things. Then how can we say that hardness and whiteness belong to a stone?

He further says:

Hardness, even not yet conjoined with stone, is hard. It is hard even not conjoined with other things. Hardness itself possesses the quality to make nonhard things hard. Thus it is hard in stone and in other things. If we find no independent hardness in the world, it is because it is hidden. If whiteness cannot make itself white, how could it make a stone and other things white? If whiteness possesses by itself the quality which makes itself white then it can remain white even not making things white. By the same token yellow and black are the same.

To generalize, Gongsun Long draws the Platonic conclusion:

All things (qualities) have independent and separate existence. Things (qualities) of independent and separate existence are normal states of being in the world.

To complete his abstract ontology, Gongsun Long finally comes to hold the Platonic reduction thesis that all things in the world are conjunctions of qualities and thus that there are no concrete things per se. What concrete things there are, are qualities manifested (*wei*) in space and time. When qualities are not manifested in space and time, they are hidden from us and are not identifiable by our senses. But this of course does not mean that they do not exist or subsist. Like Platonic forms, these qualities are not only separate from each other, they are absent from the world if they do not make themselves available to characterize things in the world.

When qualities are identified by names in the world, they are called *zhi* "objects of reference". In *Zhi wu lun*, Gongsun Long holds that nothing in the world is not *zhi* and *zhi* is not *zhi*. Again there exists many possible interpretations of this paradoxical statement of Gongsun Long. But in light of Gongsun Long's Platonistic tendencies, we may pinpoint the following two interpretations:

(1) Since all things in the world (space and time) are identifiable in terms of qualities, they are therefore compounds or conjunctions of identifiable qualities. But identifiable qualities need not themselves be identifiable in the things of the world, for they themselves may not exist in the world. Thus they are not identifiable qualities (apart from things). This interpretation makes it clear that qualities can be hidden and can be manifested and that things are manifested qualities which form objects of the reference of names, whereas qualities per se are not manifested (hidden) and thus do not form objects of reference. The abstract ontology of qualities is not only abstract but transcendent.

(2) All things are describable in terms of their qualities and there is nothing else in things aside from their qualities. But qualities per se are not further to be described or characterized by qualities, at least not by qualities of the same order. Since qualities are essen-

tially simple and separate (independent), they are not to be described by second order qualities either, for there would not be second order qualities. Therefore it is misleading and wrong to say that qualities or identifiable *zhi* are things identifiable by qualities. This is a logical interpretation of the nature of qualities. The outcome of this interpretation is that not only the abstract ontology of qualities is abstract but it cannot be describable or characterizable at all. We only come to know qualities through our names applicable to things for identification in the world. Thus one may infer that language (names) provides a means for knowing the abstract ontology of qualities.

To conclude, the moral which we can draw from Gongsun Long's Platonism is that, given a certain logic, a language can generate an ontology which differs from the normally presupposed or assumed ontology of the language. This means that ontology is a product of language under a certain interpretation or construal satisfying certain arguments in inference.

## 8. The empirical (scientific) realism of names and language in the Neo-Moist Canons (*Jing/Shuo*)

We come to the last doctrine of names in Classical Chinese Philosophy. This doctrine of names is above all, developed by logical-minded and scientific-minded followers of the Moist School. They are therefore referred to as Neo-Moists. The Neo-Moists may be motivated to develop their views of logic and language by their wish to prove the truth of their social, ethical and religious beliefs and to disprove those of their rivals. But in their rigorous collective works on logic and empirical science, such as optics and mechanics, they have achieved an objectivity of methodology and a neutrality in their investigative attitude which one does not find in other schools. Thus it is not an exaggeration to say that it is in Neo-Moist works that an objective and scientific language is developed and that the conception of language as a means to express scientific and logical truth is established. Language is not used for persuasion nor for social control. It is to indicate and formulate of reality as discovered by observation and clear thinking.

Given this conception of language, language is then seen by the Neo-Moists to involve three important aspects: It involves names, propositions, and inferences. These three aspects of language have their individual objectives. Thus the Neo-Moists say in the *Xiao Ju*:

> We use names to mention realities (things in reality) (*yin-ming ju-shi*). We use propositions (judgments) to express intention and meanings (*yi-ci shu-yi*). We use discourse or inference (agreement) to reach reasons (explanations) of things (*yi-shuo-chu-gu*).

In this manner, the Neo-Moists have paid equal attention to *ming* and *yan* in language and have linked both to the context of inference and reasoning in which their roles can be understood and their contributions recognized. *Ming* and *yan* are equally needed for reasoning, for reaching truth about the world, for settling doubt, and even for producing reason for our actions. The Neo-Moists also explicitly recognize the notion of class as a basis of inference. It is said in the *Xiaoqu*:

> We should illustrate our knowledge from taking examples from the same class of things; we should infer to unknown things by examining examples from the same class of things (*yi-lei-ju*, *yi-lei-yu*).

The notion of class plays an important role in the Neo-Moist logic although we do not have space here to elaborate upon this. It suffices to say that the Neo-Moists have developed a extentional logic in opposition to the intentional logic of abstract qualities of Gongsun Long. It is on the basis of this extentional logic founded on concrete things that the Neo-Moists advance their scientific, realistic understanding of the world. To say that the Neo-Moists view of ontology and language is realistic is to say that they are not nominalistic like Yinwenzi, nor Platonistic like Gongsun Long. To say that their views are empirical or scientific is to say that their views are not practicality-dominated like the Confucianists nor a priori-determined by a totalistic approach like the Daoists. The Neo-Moists understand language as somehow capable of presenting the true nature of the world. But this true nature of the world is subject to empirical investigations and logical clarification. Thus language can be used to define and describe reality through a process of logical analysis and clarification of the language. Reality on the other hand can be used to refine and reform language through a procedure of scientific observation and experimentation on reality. This mutual interchange and interaction between language and reality enables the Neo-Moists to produce an image of the world and language not far from what scientific philosophers or logical philosophers have strived to achieve in modern days. What the Neo-Moists strive to establish is the objectivity of truth which is their criterion for ontological understanding. They believe that language can be used to establish objective truth and they way to do this is to obey logic and argument according to logical principles. The Neo-Moists (*Mojing* Canon I-32) say:

Language is to make representation of reality possible [...] Since names are used to represent reality, *yan* is to use names to represent things for achieving objective truth by saying something about things named. Thus *yan* is to say something about names.

The importance of reasoning and argument consists in their need for establishing objective truth. The Neo-Moists believe that in argument the goal for either side of the argument is objective truth and that only the side which reaches objective truth can be said to win.

Argument: the purpose of it is to compete for the truth (*bi*) When argument is won, it is because it reaches truth (*Mojing* canon I-74).

Of course it is possible that both sides of an argument can be wrong. But it is not possible that both sides of an argument are right. The Neo-Moists are strongly opposed to the sceptical position that rejects all statements or sayings about reality as false. Such a position is held or believed to be held by Daoists. The Neo-Moists reject this position by pointing out its logical absurdity.

To regard all sayings (*yan*) as all false (self-contradictory) is self-contradictory. The explanation consists in the nature of the saying formulating this position (*Mojing* canon II-5).

The Neo-Moists have advanced many theses and views regarding many subjects bearing on problems of language and ontology. To discuss all of these or to give details on any of these will require a separate treatise. For our purpose we shall briefly mention the following highlights in addition to what we have said in the above about their general position of empirical realism.

(1) The Neo-Moists have engaged in constructing definitions of basic terms of things (or categories and concepts) for classifying purposes. These definitions also function as a basis of reasoning and scientific investigation. They are therefore terms which refer to fundamental natures of things in a logical and scientific language. For example, they have defined metalanguage terms referring to kinds of names and sayings, methodological terms of identity and difference which are distinguished by them. they even define life, time, space and important ethical terms.

(2) The Neo-Moists have engaged in empirical experimentation on optical and mechanical phenomena in order to describe them and explain them correctly. In Canon II we find highly interesting experiments made on the refraction and reflection of light. This means that the Neo-Moists permit construction of knowledge on the basis of empirical observation and scientific hypotheses. It is in this sense that they permit our understanding of the world and our formulation of our understanding in language to be guided by objective inquiry and an objective conceptional of reality. Therefore they do not favor a nominalistic approach to the description of reality.

(3) The Neo-Moists strongly reject the Platonistic theses of Gongsun Long. Their rejection of Gongsun Long's theses amounts to pointing out that Gongsun Long does not have an explicit notion of class and does not know how to classify things and therefore does not know the similarity and difference of things. For example, cow, horse, and sheep, belong to the same class (genus); they should not be treated as thoroughly different things as Gongsun Long tends to do (*Mojing* canon II-65). Without a correct notion of class one will have a false representation of things (*kuang-ju*).

Regarding Gongsun Long's thesis, 'white horse is not a horse', the Neo-Moists have this to say. First, one should distinguish the case of a disjunction (union) of two things (or qualities) from the case of a Cartesian product or conjunction of two things (or qualities). Two things A and B are disjunctively A or B, but conjunctively are neither A nor B. On the basis of this distinction and the two associated principles of inference, one can thus infer that:

Cow and horse disjunctively are cow and horse. Cow and horse conjunctively are neither cow nor horse (*Mojing* canon Ii-66).

By the same token one can say:

White and horse disjunctively is white or horse. White and horse conjunctively are neither white or horse (*Mojing* canon II-13).

In light of this clarification, Gongsun Long's thesis can be said to be misleading and not totally right if not totally wrong. Our inference to what there is depends on a clear analysis of our concepts in our language. Gongsun Long's Platonism therefore can be regarded as resulting from a confusion of or lack of reasoning.

(4) The Neo-Moists also repudiate Gongsun Long's thesis that hard and white are separate, independent qualities. According to the Neo-Moists, the error of Gongsun Long consists in not understanding or not having a proper conception of space and time as individuating principles for an individual things such as a stone. For although we could perceive hard and white successively in time and through different sense organs, what we have perceived, however, resides in one location (space) and belongs to one interval (time). Insofar as location is one and time is one, the separate impressions of white and hard cohere in one thing and therefore are not separate from each other, but rather fill each other (*xiang-yin*) because they fill each other in the same time and in the same space. It is said (*Mojing* canon II-15):

> One separates hard from white, explanation being lack of conception of interval of time and location. Hard and white are one, explanation being (that they originally belong to the same location of the same time interval).

(5) The Neo-Moists also discuss the notion of *zhi*. They differ from Gongsun Long in that they regard *zhi* as being basically acts of reference rather than objects of reference or indefinable qualities and things. They hold that we can know that something exists without being able to identify it by identifiable qualities or by pointing toward them. For example, we know that the spring has come and gone without being able to point to the spring; we know that a person has disappeared or hidden without being able to point to a person; we know that a neighbor's dog is around without knowing the dog's name; and we know that something is beyond reasonable doubt, even in the presence of *zhi* as ways of characterization, identification or as simple names. The point of the Neo-Mohists is to reject Gongsun Long's doctrine that no things are not *zhi* and *zhi* is not *zhi* as we have explained above.

## 9. Concluding remarks

In the above I have discussed the ontological import of chinese language and the conception of language in various ontological perspectives developed in Classical Chinese Philosophy. I distinguished names (*ming*) from sayings (*yan*) which are two basic aspects of chinese language. I also distinguished between ontology in and of language and ontology independent of or without language. I have shown that for the Confucianists the ontological considerations of names are subject to practical, normative considerations of *yan*. For the Daoists, both names and sayings are abolished for ontological and normative, practical reasons, and an ontology without language is tacitly suggested and presented. For Yinwenzi and Gongsun Long, the ontological import of names dominates the practical, normative ends of *yan*. Finally, for the Neo-Moists ontological considerations are to be regulated by logical and methodological considerations, and language is to be developed and refined by logic and scientific discovery into a tool for expressing objective truth and objective knowledge.

## 10. Bibliography

### 10.1. Primary sources

Confucius, *Analects*. Transl. by James Legge. Hong Kong: Univ. of Hong Kong Press, 1961.

Liang Qi-chao, *Mojing Xiaoshi* [Commentaries on the Moist Canons]. Shanghai: Commercial Press, 1922.

Laozi, *Daodejing*. Transl. by D. C. Lau. Hong Kong: Chinese Univ. Press, 1982.

*Yi ching, I Ching, Book of Changes*. Transl. into English by James Legge, *Sacred Books of the East*, XVI. Oxford, 1899. Transl. into English by Cary E. Baines, 1968. [From the German transl. by Richard Wilhelm; with a preface by Carl G. Jung.]

### 10.2. Secondary sources

Bloom, Alfred. 1981. *The Linguistic Shaping of Thought: A study in the impact of language and thinking in China and the West*. Nilsdale, N. J.: Erlbaum.

Bodde, Derk. 1939. "Chinese Categorial Thinking". *Journal of the American Oriental Society* 59.200–219.

Chao, Y. R. 1955. "Notes on Chinese Grammar and Logic". *Philosophy East and West* 5:1.31–41.

Cheng Chung-ying. 1971. "Aspects of Classical Chinese Logic". *International Journal of Philosophy*, 213–235.

–. 1973a. "A Generative Unity: Chinese philosophy and Chinese language". *Journal for the Association of Chinese Language Teaching* 3:1.90–105.

–. 1973b. "On the Problem of Subject Structure in Language, with Applications to Late Archaic Chinese". *Approaches to Natural Language: Proceedings of the 1970 Stanford Workshop on Grammar and Semantics*, 413–434.

–. 1975. "On Implication (*Tse*) and Inference (*Ku*) in Chinese Grammar and Chinese Logic". *Journal of Chinese Philosophy* 2:3.225–244.

–. 1983. "Kung-sun Lung: White horse and other issues". *Philosophy East and West* 33:4.341–354.

–. 1987. "Logic and Language in Chinese Philosophy". *Journal of Chinese Philosophy* 14:3.285–307.

– & Richard H. Swain. 1970. "Logic and Ontology in the *Chih Wu Lun* of Kung-sun Lung Tzu". *Philosophy East and West* 5:2.137–154.

Chmielewski, Janusz. 1962–66. "Notes on Early Chinese Logic". *Rocznik Orientalistyczny* 26:1 (1962) 7–22; 26:2 (1963) 91–105; 27:1 (1963) 103–121; 28:2 (1965) 87–111; 29:2 (1965) 117–138; 30:1 (1966) 31–52.

Cikoski, John S. 1970. *Classical Chinese Word-Classes*. New Haven: Yale Univ. Press.

–. 1975. "On Standards of Analogical Reasoning in the Late Chou". *Journal of Chinese Philosophy* 3:2.325–357.

–. 1978. "Three Essays on Classical Chinese Grammar". *Computational Analyses of Asian and African Languages* 8.17–152; 9.77–208.

Cua, A. A. 1985. *Ethical Argumentation: A study in Hsun Tzu's moral epistemology*. Honolulu: Univ. of Hawaii Press.

Daor, Dan. 1974. *The* Yin Wenzi *and the Renaissance of Philosophy in Wei-Jin China*. Ph. D. dissertation, University of London.

Graham, A. C. 1955. "Kung-sun Lung's 'Essay on Meaning and Things'". *Journal of Oriental Studies* 2:2.282–301.

–. 1959. "'Being' in Western Philosophy Compared with *Shih/Fei* and *Yu/Wu* in Chinese Philosophy". *Asia Major*, N. S. 7.79–112.

–. 1978. *Later Mohist Logic, Ethics and Science*. Hong Kong: Chinese Univ. Press.

–. 1986. *Yin-Yang and the Nature of Correlative Thinking*. Singapore: Institute of East Asian Philosophies.

Hansen, Chad. 1983. *Language and Logic in Ancient China*. Ann Arbor: Univ. of Michigan Press.

–. 1985. "Chinese Language, Chinese Philosophy and 'Truth'". *Journal of Asian Studies* 44.491–517.

–. 1992. *A Daoist Theory of Chinese Thought*. New York: Oxford Univ. Press.

Hu Shih. 1922. *The Development of the Logical Method in Ancient China*. Shanghai: Commercial Press.

Kaoa, Kung-yi & Diane B. Obenchain. 1975. "Kong-sun Lung's *Chih wu lun* and Semantics of Reference and Predication". *Journal of Chinese Philosophy* 2:3.285–324.

Lau, D. C. 1952–53. "Some Logical Problems in Ancient China". *Proceedings of the Aristotelian Society*, N. S. 53.189–203.

Needham, Joseph. 1954–. *Science and Civilization in China*. Cambridge: Cambridge Univ. Press.

Rubin, Vitaly A. 1982. "Wu hsing and Yin-yang". *Journal of Chinese Philosophy* 1:1.27–43.

Schwartz, Benjamin I. 1973. "On the Absence of Reductionism in Chinese Reductionism". *Journal of Chinese Philosophy* 1.24–43.

–. 1985. *The World of Thought in Ancient China*. Harvard Univ. Press.

Solomon, Bernard S. 1969. "The Assumptions of Hui Shih". *Monumenta Serica* 28.1–40.

*Chung-ying Cheng,*
*Honolulu (USA)*

# 5. The Suí-Táng tradition of *Fǎnqiè* phonology

1. Introduction
2. The origins of *Fǎnqiè*
3. Aesthetics of *Fǎnqiè* organization
4. The *Qièyùn* rime-book
5. The significance of the *Qièyùn*
6. Prosody and other linguistic ideas
7. Bibliography

## 1. Introduction

The Chinese intellectual tradition has always been profoundly literary and graphic – real, systematic phonology developed late, and then only under heavy foreign influence. Most Chinese written characters contain information about their pronunciation in the form of *xiéshēng* "sound-matching" pseudophonetic elements, but this information is haphazard and has certainly not represented any particular living form of Chinese in a systematic way since high antiquity (if even then). By late antiquity (c. AD 100), the *xiéshēng* elements were giving very misleading ideas about pronunciation, and better means of indicating pronunciation were needed. The sound of a character was often given by reference to a homophone or near-homophone:

"character X sounds like character Y" – the so-called *dúruò* method, but this too was only a partial solution.

In the late 2nd century, however, Chinese scholars developed a practical tool for describing the pronunciation of their written characters, called *fănqiè*. *Fănqiè* was not an absolute alphabetic or syllabic spelling system, but a way of analyzing the monosyllabic reading of any Chinese character into phonological elements that could be represented with other, common characters. It was a purely relative means of indicating sound. By way of illustration, consider a story told by the 6th century scholar Chinese Yán Zhītuī, thinking of his days in Shǔ, in modern Sìchuān. He was sitting with friends as the sun came out after the rain, and they saw something small glistening on the ground. They asked a boy-servant what it was, and he said, "It's just a bean-*pik*." This reply meant nothing to them, so the boy fetched it and they saw that it was a little bean sprout. But the word *pik* for something like this was still unfamiliar to them. Then Yán remembered having seen an obscure character meaning 'a little round thing' in an old dictionary, and recalled that "its sound is given as *piaŋ* plus *lik*." He adds, "Everyone was pleased and understood" (Chou Fa-kao 1960: "Miănxué" 51a).

When Yán Zhītuī says that "its sound is given as *piaŋ* plus *lik*" he is using a *fănqiè* formula. In this case, he is describing the sound of a character pronounced *pik*, and the formula he cites defines it as the combination of the first part of *piaŋ* plus the last part of *lik*:

*piaŋ* > *p-* + *-iaŋ* *lik* > *l-* + *-ik*

*p-* + *-ik* = *pik*

It must be stressed that *fănqiè* is only a relative system for showing pronunciation: Every character glossed by a *fănqiè* has its sound indicated not with any absolute or even conventionally defined phonetic symbols, but by reference to two other characters, the sounds of which are presumably known to the reader. Nowhere does the *fănqiè* tell us that *pik* begins with a *p-* and ends with an *-ik*; it only tells us that *pik* begins with the same sound as *piaŋ* and ends with the same sound as *lik*. In order to illustrate how *fănqiè* works, I have turned to a simplified formal reconstruction (designed after Martin 1953 and Stimson 1976) that is typologically close to modern varieties of Chinese. But Yán Zhītuī had no such spelling system; *fănqiè* gives only algebraic information about sound: This character has the same initial sound as that character, which has the same initial sound as a third character, and a fourth character, and so on. The same *fănqiè* gloss could be read aloud in many different varieties of Chinese, and though it might be found valid in some or all of them, it might also be invalid in some of them. *Fănqiè* are, again, only a relative system of pronunciation. Written out as above in Roman letters, the system looks perhaps a little naïve to us, but to the medieval Chinese, who had no alphabet and knew no other way to describe sound other than by reference to homophones, it was extremely powerful. The beginning of *fănqiè* was the beginning of phonological awareness in China, and they formed the basis of the whole medieval tradition of phonology.

Special terminology is associated with the *fănqiè* gloss, in both English and Chinese: the beginning of the glossed syllable is called its "initial" (*shēng*), and the end is called its final or "rime" (*yùn*); the first element of the *fănqiè* gloss, which glosses the initial, is called the "upper" (*fănqiè shàngzì*), while the second element, which glosses the final, is called the "lower" (*fănqiè xiàzì*). Here are two more examples:

| *fănqiè* | glossed word | = | upper | + | lower |
|---|---|---|---|---|---|
| 麻莫霞反 | *ma* | = | *mak* | + | *ɣa* |
| 甜徒兼反 | *dem* | = | *do* | + | *kem* |

As a general rule, we with our modern, reconstruction-aided understanding believe the *fănqiè* lower to have included all vocalic and tonal matter in the glossed syllable, though the Chinese did not at that time have terms for such things as discrete vowels or other sub-syllabic segmental elements. (J. R. Firth's conception of prosodic features is similar to what was apparently the medieval Chinese treatment of the syllable.)

*Fănqiè* were incorporated into various dictionaries, the most important of which is the *Qièyùn*, which will be discussed below. But we know of such large-scale compendia beginning only from the middle of medieval period – from around the 6th century. At first, *fănqiè* seem to have been used most often in the annotation of classical texts. These early materials are especially useful in trying to understand the principles of *fănqiè* construction. One of the best extant sources for early exegetic *fănqiè* is a book called the *Jīngdiăn shìwén*, or "Exegeses on Classical

Texts", compiled by Lù Démíng (c. 550–630). The *Shìwén* is meant to be read along with one of the standard editions of the ten classical books most revered in that day. It supplies glosses and readings for individual characters in order as they appear in the original text. Lù Démíng gathered his material from hundreds of different sources, most of which are otherwise unknown to us. Sometimes enough *fǎnqiè* from an individual scholiast appear in the *Shìwén* that we can get a working idea of the outlines of a coherent phonological system from them, but most of the time we can recover no such context.

## 2. The origins of *Fǎnqiè*

The term *fǎnqiè* dates only from the Sòng dynasty (960–1279), but it is a combination of two older terms *fǎn* 反 (also read *fān* and so written: 翻) "to turn back, overturn" and *qiè* 切 "to run together" (the reading *qiē* "to cut" for this character, commonly seen in Western works, appears to be a purely modern interpretation). One or another of these of these syllables was always used as the last part of the *fǎnqiè* formula, as you can see in Yán Zhītuī's example above: What Yán actually says is that *pik* is read as "*piaŋ lik fǎn*" – *piaŋ* and *lik* 'turned back', i. e., combined in such a way as to attach the beginning of *piaŋ* to the end of *lik*. *Fǎn* is the original term, but it also means "to rebel", and after the shattering rebellions in the middle of the 8th century, the word apparently became too sensitive to use and so *qiè* was substituted. (This explanation is due to Gù Yánwǔ 1966[1667]b.) The words *ǎn*, *fān*, and *qiè* are simply markers that identify the preceding two syllables as a *fǎnqiè* sound-gloss. It is not known how far back these terms go. Yán Zhītuī already refers to *fǎnyǔ* – "*fǎn*-expressions", and Liú Xié (c. 465–c. 532) uses *fǎn* as a verb in the sense of "to indicate pronunciation by means of *fǎnqiè*". And *fǎn* occurs in the earliest attested *fǎnqiè* formulae. Yán Zhītuī and Lù Démíng themselves attributed the invention of *fǎnqiè* to one Sūn Yán, a 3rd century follower of the eminent Confucian scholiast Zhèng Xuán (127–200), and there are a few surviving examples attributed in later works to Fú Qián and Yīng Shào, both of whom were active before AD 200.

The conceptual origins of the *fǎnqiè* system are uncertain, but it appears to be native to China. Although many scholars have sensed Indic inspiration for it (see especially Chou Fa-kao 1964), no conclusive link has ever been demonstrated, and indeed there are several reasons to think that it is an original Chinese idea. One important argument, due to Zhèng Qiáo (1104–1160), is that classical texts contain a number of examples of contractions following *fǎnqiè* principles: two characters being run together into one syllable and written as one new character. (For more on Zhèng Qiáo, see Mair 1993.) Most often this kind of contraction appears with function words. For example: the compound 如是 *njiu ʒǐ* "in this way" was often written 爾 *njǐ*, which would be a perfect example of the *fǎnqiè* running-together of *njiu* and *ʒǐ*. The common combination 之歟 *tʃi yu* "[third person pronoun as direct object] + [interrogative sentence-suffix]" was written 諸 *tʃiu*; the combination 而已 *nji ǐ* "and that is the end of it" was written 耳 *njǐ*; the combination 之矣 *tʃi ɣǐ* "[third person pronoun as direct object] + [sentence-suffix indicating completion]" was written 只 *tʃǐ*, and so on. In these examples, two syllables appear to be collapsed into one syllable in the same way that the two elements of a *fǎnqiè* gloss are run together to give the sound of a third character.

The most important reason to doubt Sanskrit influence is that *fǎnqiè* does not assign one symbol to one sound, as a syllabary- or alphabet-inspired system would – in this case, one *fǎnqiè* upper to one initial consonant. One initial, even in the same set of *fǎnqiè* material, may be represented by several different uppers, or one upper may behave in several different ways. Apparently the reason for this is that the *fǎnqiè* principle was a practical tool to show the sound of a given Chinese character and was rarely used to make general phonological statements. In Tab. 5.1. are some examples of many symbols representing one sound, all taken from a single redaction of the *Qièyùn*.

Tab. 5.1.

| *fǎnqiè* | glossed word | = | upper | + | lower |
|---|---|---|---|---|---|
| 郎魯當反 | *laŋ* | = | *lǒ* | + | *taŋ* |
| 浪郎宕反 | *làŋ* | = | *laŋ* | + | *dàŋ* |
| 苓力鼎反 | *lěŋ* | = | *liək* | + | *těŋ* |
| 靂閭激反 | *lek* | = | *liu* | + | *kek* |
| 樓落侯反 | *lou* | = | *lak* | + | *ɣou* |
| 犖呂角反 | *lak* | = | *liǔ* | + | *kak* |

Here, a single initial that we recognize as *l* -is represented by six different *fǎnqiè* uppers.

This is by no means an extreme case; in the earliest complete extant version of the *Qièyùn*, there are no fewer than 25 different *fǎnqiè* uppers representing the one initial *$k^h$-*. For this reason, we cannot reliably read off *fǎnqiè* and interpret them at sight; we need a way to show which groups of uppers and which groups of lowers constitute meaningfully contrastive groups. Such a method, called *xìliánfǎ* or "linking method" and based on algebraic principles, was eventually pioneered by the Manchu-period geographer Chén Lǐ (1810–1882), but it by no means belongs to medieval phonology. And even with this method the answers are not always clear; in the 20th century there have been serious disagreements over how many initials are actually meant to be represented in the *fǎnqiè*.

## 3. Aesthetics of *Fǎnqiè* organization

*Fǎnqiè* seem to have been composed in a fairly haphazard way, though from surviving collections we can see certain patterns that must reflect the linguistic values of the time. For instance, the uppers and lowers in the earliest *fǎnqiè* tended to be very common characters, and often characters of very few pen-strokes. *Fǎnqiè* uppers rarely end in *-m* or *-p* and most often end in open syllables or in *-ŋ* or *-k* – this must have been a question of ease of pronunciation. *Fǎnqiè* lowers are rarely aspirated. There tends to be loose agreement as to what in modern Chinese are 'medial' vowels – the semi-vowels in the *fǎnqiè* lower and following the initial of the *fǎnqiè* upper. For instance (again speaking in terms of our reconstruction), both upper and lower may share a palatalized initial and a medial or main vowel *-i-*, and the character being glossed will also have an *-i-*:

陣直刃反 *djìn* = *djiək* + *njìn*

Or both upper and lower may have a medial *-u-*, and the character being glossed will also have a medial *-u-*:

鋗火玄反 *huen* = *huǎ* + *ɣuen*

Or neither upper nor lower has a medial vowel, and the character being glossed also has no medial:

朗盧黨反 *lǎŋ* = *lo* + *tǎŋ*

Or both upper and lower have a medial main vowel *-iu* (or *-y*), as does the syllable being glossed:

月魚厥反 *ŋiuæt* = *ŋiu* + *kiuæt*

Agreement of medials – rather, what have conventionally been reconstructed as medials, for this question is by no means settled – is the general rule for *fǎnqiè* glosses, and must have been an important element of their aesthetics. In particular, what is written as a palatal medial *-i-* in the simplified system used here has an enormous effect on the construction of *fǎnqiè*. *Fǎnqiè* uppers as a group fall into two hazily distinct sets: for each recognizable initial, there is usually one set that occurs with palatalized syllables and one that occurs with unpalatalized syllables. This distinction is not rigid, as some have thought, but the tendency to make the distinction is seen almost everywhere.

For if there is any one characteristic of *fǎnqiè*, it is that only loose distinctions are made. There are many places, even in fairly consistent corpora of *fǎnqiè*, where the gloss and the glossed syllable do not quite match. For example:

役營隻反 *juæk* = *juæŋ* + *tʃiæk*

If *fǎnqiè* operated as neatly as an alphabetic system, the gloss would give a reading **jiæk*, instead of *juæk*. Another example:

生所更反 *ʃræŋ* = *ʃriŭ* + *kiæŋ*

The expected form, based on the *fǎnqiè*, would be **ʃriæŋ*. Another example:

鳳馮貢反 *biùŋ* = *biuŋ* + *kùŋ*

The expected form would be **bùŋ*. Another example:

敬居孟反 *kiæ̀ŋ* = *kiu* + *mæ̀ŋ*

The expected form would be **kæ̀ŋ*. There are even stranger cases:

芥古邁反 *kài* = *kǒ* + *mài*

夬古邁反 *kuài* = *kǒ* + *mài*

These two *fǎnqiè*, which appear in the same redaction of the *Qièyùn*, appeared in separate places in the book and so must have been considered distinct sounds, yet their *fǎnqiè* glosses are identical. Here are two more such pairs from the same source:

黠胡八反 *ɣat* = *ɣo* + *pat*
滑胡八反 *ɣuat* = *ɣo* + *pat*
行胡孟反 *ɣæ̀ŋ* = *ɣo* + *mæ̀ŋ*
蝗胡孟反 *ɣuæ̀ŋ* = *ɣo* + *mæ̀ŋ*

In these cases it is likely that the vowel of the *fǎnqiè* upper, spelled *-o* here, was ambiguous enough after a velar initial that when combined with a labial-initial *fǎnqiè* lower the presence of medial *-u-* was also ambiguously felt.

Clearly, *fǎnqiè* were composed not with rigorously distinct phonological categories in mind, but by ear (see Chao 1941 and Lù Zhìwéi 1963). They appeared very widely in medieval commentaries, and in some cases they were used in the glosses of character dictionaries such as the early *Yùpiān* of Gù Yěwáng (519−581). But as far as we know these sources never supplied a phonological framework within which to interpret them; people were evidently expected to read off *fǎnqiè* in whatever literary accents they knew, and to find the prescribed readings based on those accents.

## 4. The *Qièyùn* rime-book

The earliest surviving dictionary that does supply a kind of phonological framework for its *fǎnqiè* glosses is the *Qièyùn* of Lù Fǎyán (fl. 581−601), which exists in a number of redactions and has been far and away the most influential single source in Chinese historical phonology. The individual character-entries of the *Qièyùn* are arranged in a kind of partial phonological order by rime, which gives rise to the name "rime-books" (Chinese *yùnshū*) for all works of this kind. The *Qièyùn* was probably not the first such book − its preface names five earlier (4th?−6th century) rime-books that probably also used this format − but the *Qièyùn* is the earliest that has come down to us, and it has certainly been more authoritative than any other rime-book.

Rime-books of the *Qièyùn* type are divided into *juǎn* "volumes" by tone category: the *píng* ("level") category is represented by two *juǎn* (because it comprises so many characters), and the other tones (*shǎng* or *shàng* "rising", *qù* "departing", *rù* "entering") by one *juǎn* each. All characters in a given *juǎn* have a reading in the corresponding tone; if a character has readings in two tones, it occurs in each of the two corresponding *juǎn*.

Each tone is subdivided into several dozen rimes, each of which is named by the first word comprised in it. (It is very common in Chinese linguistics for phonological categories and features to bear exemplary names; the four tones, for instance, are named as exemplary categories.) In Tab. 6.5.2 are shown the first eleven rimes (out of some 60-odd) in all four tone categories, to which are appended simple reconstructed values.

Tab. 5.2.: Tone category

| | *píng* | *shǎng* | *qù* | *rù* |
|---|---|---|---|---|
| rime: | 東 *tuŋ* | 董 *tǔŋ* | 送 *sùŋ* | 屋 *uk* |
| | 冬 *toŋ* | ——— | 宋 *sòŋ* | 沃 *ok* |
| | 鍾 *tʃioŋ* | 腫 *tʃiǒŋ* | 用 *yiòŋ* | 燭 *tʃiok* |
| | 江 *kaŋ* | 講 *kǎŋ* | 絳 *kàŋ* | 覺 *kak* |
| | 支 *tʃi*$_1$ | 紙 *tʃĭ*$_1$ | 寘 *tʃî*$_1$ | ——— |
| | 脂 *tʃi*$_2$ | 旨 *tʃĭ*$_2$ | 至 *tʃî*$_2$ | ——— |
| | 之 *tʃi*$_3$ | 止 *tʃĭ*$_3$ | 志 *tʃî*$_3$ | ——— |
| | 微 *miəi* | 尾 *miə̆i* | 未 *miə̀i* | ——— |
| | 魚 *ŋiu* | 語 *ŋiǔ* | 御 *ŋiù* | ——— |
| | 虞 *ŋio* | 麌 *ŋiǒ* | 遇 *ŋiò* | ——— |
| | 模 *mo* | 姥 *mǒ* | 暮 *mò* | ——— |

*etc. …*

The order of the rimes within each tone is clearly purposeful. We can see this in two features: First, rimes are grouped together according to what the reconstruction shows to have been similar phonetic structure: The first three rimes have an *-ŋ* or *-k* ending and a *-u* or *-o* main vowel; the next rime has an *-ŋ* or *-k* ending and an *-a* main vowel; the next four rimes are open syllables with varieties of *-i* (distinguished formally here by numerical subscript) as the main vowel; the next three rimes are open syllables with varieties of *-u* or *-o* as the main vowel. Second, the sequence of rimes is parallel in the four tone categories. Third, the exemplary names of each of the rimes tend to have the same initial in all tones. With some exceptions, the rest of the book is organized the same way.

Each rime is subdivided into smaller units called *xiǎoyùn* "small rimes", which comprise anywhere from one to several dozens of characters, to the first of which the *fǎnqiè* for the whole group is apprended. All the characters in a given *xiǎoyùn* are homophonous, and we believe that *xiǎoyùn* within a single rime are always meant to be contrastive, although there is still much argument about the basis and nature of some of the distinctions. An important point is that the arrangement of *xiǎoyùn* within the rime seems to be generally haphazard and does not show the conscious order that the arrangement of rimes shows. Like *fǎnqiè* themselves, rime-books of the *Qièyùn* type embody a level of organization in which linguistic analysis is only partial.

The full blooming of phonology in China is not found until the rime-table traditon.

The currency of the original *Qièyùn* (which means "closely distinguished rimes") was followed by the *Tángyùn* "Rimes of the Táng dynasty" dating from the first half of the 8th century, the great Sòng dynasty *Guǎngyùn* "Expanded *Rimes*" of 1008, and the *Jíyùn* "Collected *Rimes*" of 1039. The number of entries increased from some 12,000 in the original *Qièyùn* to 26,000 in the *Guǎngyùn* to an unbelievable 53,000 in the *Jíyùn*. Part of the reason for the size of the *Jíyùn* was not more distinct characters, but great numbers of alternate readings, including much of the information in the *Jīngdiǎn shìwén* and the *Shuōwén jiězì* and countless lesser works. Both the *Guǎngyùn* and *Jíyùn* have much fuller glosses than the original *Qièyùn* did – the *Qièyùn* was really just a guide to character readings, while the later books attempted to give encyclopedic definitions and even citations to classical texts.

Later ages produced rime-books based on different principles, such as the *Zhōngyuàn yīnyùn*, which gave Northern Chinese character readings for use in colloquial drama during Mongol rule (1206–1368), and the *Hóngwǔ zhèngyùn*, which was the official rime-book of the Míng dynasty (1368–1644). The 17th and 18th centuries saw the beginning of a tradition of rime-books describing regional varieties of Southern Chinese, such as the *Qī-Lín bāyīn* of Foochow, dated 1747 but combining two earlier dictionaries. The importance of these books, particularly the *Zhōngyuán yīnyùn*, to modern linguistic research is considerable, but in their time they did not represent a radically new linguistic viewpoint. Generally speaking, these books manifest two minor innovations: they describe some form of uncanonical and often regional phonology, and make heavier use of rime-table analysis than books in the *Qièyùn* family. The *Qièyùn* tradition has remained the great tradition in China, and although some of these later works are more useful, the *Qièyùn* and *Guǎngyùn* are still the most important representatives of the whole rime-book tradition. For this reason it is worth assessing the meaning of the *Qièyùn* in its own day.

## 5. The significance of the *Qièyùn*

What actually did the *Qièyùn* represent in its time – what did Lù Fǎyán intend it to be? What kind of phonology does it embody, and how was it meant to be used? These questions, which have by no means been resolved today, are among the most important in Chinese historical linguistics – the answers to them determine, among other things, whether reconstructions of *Qièyùn* phonology are meaningful, and whether genetic interpretations of dialect affiliation can be related to known historical events and cultural relationships.

The primary source for studying these questions is the preface to the *Qièyùn*, of which an early version survives. It is written in the elegant "parallel prose" (*piántǐwén*, a highly stylized form of unrhymed prose composition in parallel couplets) of its day, and is full of polite literary expressions. In it, Lù Fǎyán describes the origins of this book at a party held at his father's home in AD 581, the first year of the Suí dynasty. At this party, some of the learnèd literary men of his father's generation – including Yàn Zhītuī – held a discussion on the correct accent to be used in reading. There are a few main points: They agree that the accents used in different time periods and different places are inconsistent, and complain that many people fail to make important phonological distinctions. They agree that a good literary accent is important for a learned person or if one wishes to experience the intimacy that comes from shared appreciation of poetry. They name five older rime-books, all of which are said to contradict each other and have errors. Rhyming practice itself is inconsistent in different parts of the country. They discuss the various features of different kinds of pronunciation, and finally appoint themselves the arbiters of correct pronunciation, concluding, "if we settle it, then settled it is." Lù Fǎyán says that he himself, only a young man at the time, took notes on this discussion. Twenty years later, in the relative isolation of retirement and having now become a tutor, he finds that exact pronunciation is important to good writing, and has gone back to those old notes and used them as the germ of his dictionary. Stripped of its elegant language, this is the gist of the preface.

Ever since serious critical study of the *Qièyùn* began in the 19th century, different ideas have vied to explain what it represented in its own time. The preface has been pored over by scholars seeking to understand Lù Fǎyán's intentions, and the discussion continues unabated today after several generations.

Below are a few common themes in this discussion.

First, it is generally agreed that the *Qièyùn* embodies a mixed phonological system; it came out of an awareness of different accents and different kinds of rhyming, ancient and modern, and representing different parts of the Suí empire. Lù Fǎyán himself says in his preface that he and the others decided that "the sounds of antiquity and of the present day have a divide between them, and what the various schools accept or reject is varied, too. [...] So I have taken from the sounds and rimes of all schools, from word-books ancient and modern, and from what I wrote down long ago, and settled this material as the *Qièyùn* in five parts." A relatively early statement of the idea of the mixed nature of the *Qièyùn* came from the philologist and anti-Esperantist Chāng Pǐng-lín (1868–1936):

[...] What the *Guǎngyùn* contains is variously the sounds of ancient and current times, of regional languages and the national language. It is not a collection of 206 weighty rime categories from one place and one time (1917–1919: 上 18b).

However, it is not agreed whether the *Qièyùn* is a disorderly heap of material or a carefully organized work. In early modern times, the original *Qièyùn* and even the *Guǎngyùn* were scarcely known at all, probably not until the beginning of the 20th century; the *Qièyùn* was known mainly in the form of the huge and chaotic *Jíyùn*. So it is not surprising to find some scholars arguing that it represents a meaningless system of hybrid and artificial origin. The philosopher and textual critic Dài Zhèn (1725–1777) wrote:

The general method of Lù Fǎyàn's *Qièyùn* is like this throughout; it deals with the reading pronunciation of its time. Based on the comparison of various differences and equivalences it prescribes specific readings, always seeking fine divisions and going too far with them; it creates distinctions that are unnatural. It even includes ancient graphs from the Xià, Shāng, and Zhōu dynasties [of high antiquity and legendary times], *jiǎjiè* loan-characters and *xiéshēng* abbreviated characters, near-rhymes and forced rhymes from the *Classic of Poetry*. To include all these for the purpose of composing songs and music was to act indiscriminately and without critical examination (Dài 1966[1775]: 6a).

The name of the book *Qièyùn* itself means "closely-distinguished rimes", and Lù Fǎyán says that his "analysis is hairsplitting, the dinstinctions manifold." This is an important element of the idea of the mixed nature of *Qièyùn* phonology. Zhōu Zǔmó (1914–1994) has shown that in organizing the *Qièyùn*, Lù Fǎyán essentially followed five earlier rime-books, making distinctions wherever any of the five made a distinction (Zhōu Zǔmó 1976[1966]). If this resulted in disorder, at least it was achieved methodically. Zhōu's view that the *Qièyùn* comprises a "maximal diasystem" (Pulleyblank 1984: 134) has been fairly widespread among 20th century scholars. Luó Chángpéi (1899–1958) had already called this system the "least common multiple of the regional languages of the whole nation" (1930: 55). Juhl (1989) has attempted to confirm that the poets of various regions of China rhymed in accordance with the phonologies of the different regional rime books on which the *Qièyùn* was based. (See also Mather 1968 for English-language discussion of some of these issues.)

There have even been those who argue that the *Qièyùn* represents a common phonological system ancestral to and underlying all modern Chinese dialects. This idea has consistently appealed to philologists and to scholars with a highly evolved appreciation of formal order. It comes up, for example, in an explication of the Western concept of historical-comparative reconstruction by the mathematician and linguistic reformer Láo Nǎixuān (1843–1921), best known in the West as Richard Wilhelm's master in the study of the *Yìjīng*:

The initials and rimes defined by ancient scholars were created after the examination of dialects spoken all over the country. And so, if one takes an interest in historical phonology, it is necessary to assemble the [ancient] features that are accurately attested in the various northern and southern dialects if one is to do a thorough job. Even if one's mouth cannot manage all the sounds, anyway one's mind can grasp the significance of each of them, and thus one will not be unnecessarily constrained by dialects (Láo 1898[1883]: 37 a).

This view appeals strongly to Chinese popular national pride, because it presents all of modern linguistic diversity as reflecting one or another aspect of an ancient unity. Luó Chángpéi wrote:

Rime-books of the *Qièyùn* system comprise regional sounds of all parts of China and from all time periods. Their goal was to find the least common multiple of the regional languages of the whole nation and use that as a unified national standard. Therefore, the sounds of any regional dialect, regardless in what part of China, can never exceed the boundaries of that system, nor can they correspond exactly to that system (Luó 1930: 55).

This particular view is now seriously disputed, though it persists as a popular and romantic myth in China. The fact that the preface explicitly mentions the "sounds of antiquity" shows that the reading of texts is meant, and not just everyday regional pronunciation.

There is another question: If the *Qièyùn* is inherently orderly, there is still the question of whether its phonology represented something authoritative in its day. Can we take it as 'standard' medieval phonology? Zhōu Zǔmó argued:

> The rime-book *Qièyùn* is extremely systematic and makes strict phonetic distinctions. Its phonological system is not based purely on the dialect of one particular place; rather, it is set up as a compromise between the different features of the North and the South, based on the 'cultured speech' and the bookish readings used by gentlemen in the South. Cultured speech and bookish readings always lean toward traditional reading pronunciation, and since the *Qièyùn* tends to be strict in the way it distinguishes rimes and prescribes readings – so that such-and-such a group of characters is not going to be confused with such-and-such a different group of characters – naturally, it preserves some of the distinctions from the language of a previous age. It was not that Yán Zhītuī [and the others] intentionally used dialect readings here and archaic readings there [...] They discussed the issues over and over again, analyzing linguistic differences, and finally decided on this system. Since it was reached through discussion among scholars and literary men from both North and South, it necessarily corresponds to the language of *both* North and South. This system can be said to be the phonological system of the literary language of the 16th century (Zhōu Zǔmó 1976[1966]: 473).

This view is now fairly widespread, in one form or another. But there have been other views of the *Qièyùn* as the representative of prestigious forms of Chinese. Bernhard Karlgren (1889–1978), who first applied rigorous Western methods of phonetic reconstruction to the study of *Qièyùn* phonology proper (Karlgren 1915–24), held that the phonology of the *Qièyùn* was that of the dialect of Changan, the first capital of the Táng dynasty, which he believed had been the basis of a *koinè* used throughout the Táng empire. He called this *koinè* "a real living and homogeneous language" (1954: 212n.), but produced no evidence to support his view; indeed, Karlgren does not seem to have analyzed the *Qièyùn* preface anywhere in his work. Karlgren's idea of a Changan-based *koinè* was long influential in the 20th century West but is now clearly defunct (see Norman & Coblin 1995). Its ghost persists, however, in the form of the 'Late Middle Chinese' (*i. e.*, post-*Qièyùn* period) reconstruction of Edwin Pulleyblank (1984: 3).

Chinese scholars after Karlgren have tended to look to Loyang as a source of *Qièyùn* phonology. Loyang, the eastern capital of many Chinese dynasties since ancient times, was the capital of the Western Qìn dynasty (AD 265–317). The eminent historian Chén Yínkè (1890–1969) argued (1949) that the prestigious accent of Western Chìn Loyang was kept as a kind of standard by aristocratic families of the Eastern Chìn and Southern Dynasties (317–589) around the southern capital of Qièkāng (modern Nanking), and that it actually influenced the language spoken by southerners and so came to be used as the basis of the *Qièyùn*. Chén Yínkè's view is contradicted by some linguistic data (Zhōu Zǔmó 1976[1966]: 472–3). Nevertheless, there have been a number of variations on this idea, and the jury is still out (see Pān Wénguó 1986).

One last question is whether the *Qièyùn* describes real spoken language or not. Although Zhōu Zǔmó and many others have mentioned that the basis of the phonology was character readings, nevertheless understanding of the distinction between character readings and spoken morphemes comes with difficulty to many Chinese scholars. Certainly, as Coblin (1996) has pointed out, Lù Fǎyán emphasizes writing and the appreciation of culture and poetry several times in the preface: "Whenever there is good writing [to be done], I require [attention to] sound and rime [...]. Desiring to broaden the road of culture, one must by all means be perfectly conversant in the 'clear' and the 'muddy'; if one would enjoy a soul-mate [with whom one can truly appreciate the verbal music of poetry], it is necessary that 'light' and 'heavy' be distinguished." ('Clear' and 'muddy', 'light' and 'heavy' are recognizable technical terms, but they are apparently used merely as tokens to give the feeling of thoroughness to what is essentially a literary composition).

There are many variations on these views, but to sum up it is generally agreed that the *Qièyùn* embodies an artificial phonological system based mainly on reading pronunciations from different traditions, not all of the same time period. This complex phonological system has been heaped with prestige since the end of the 6th century and continues to be used as the framework of general historical phonology in Chinese. Even when simpler systems of rhyming were adopted for use in the official examinations, as for instance the *Píngshuĭ* system, they were usually derived from the framework of the *Qièyùn*.

## 6. Prosody and other linguistic ideas

In early medieval times there was deep interest in phonological issues generally, and a whole technical theory of poetic prosody was developed in imitation of Sanskrit principles. (The main source we have for early medieval prosodic materials is the *Bunkyō Hifuron* of the Japanese monk Kūkai, 774–835, for which the principal Western-language study is Bodman 1978). This theory was the work of a number of 5th century poets, but it is most saliently associated with the name of Shĕn Yuē (441–513), who also gave us the names of the four canonical tone categories, *píng*, *shăng*, *qù*, and *rù*. Shĕn's prosodic rules, the so-called *sìshēng bābìng* "four tones and eight prosodic defects" emphasize arranging the syllables of a poetic couplet and quatrain so that their tones, initials and finals all contrast as much as possible. Shĕn and his followers developed the concept of contrasting the *píng* tone category with the so-called *zè* "non-level" category, embracing the *shăng*, *qù*, and *rù* tones. The terms *píng* "level" and *tsè* "non-level" for these contrasting categories survive down to the present day, but evolved out of the older names *qīng* "light" and *zhòng* "heavy", apparently themselves merely calques for the Sanskrit prosodic terms *laghu* "light" and *guru* "heavy" (Mair & Mei 1991).

Medieval prosody has left us various kinds of linguistically conscious terminology. Much of this is concerned with the details of prosody, which are not relevant here, but some of it deals with certain kinds of phonological relationships in vocabulary. For instance: Chinese poets had long used descriptive compounds composed of two syllables with the same initial or the same final, but in an early 6th century essay on literary aesthetics, the *Wénxīn diāolóng* of Liú Xié, special names were assigned to these relationships: two characters sharing the same initial are called *shuāngshēng* "doubled initials" and *diéyùn* "concatenated rimes". There was even a style of purely alliterative poetry occasionally fashionable in medieval times called the *shuāngshēng shī*. Aside from the interest of seeing the linguistic term *shēng* used in the name of a poetic form, we learn from this that Shĕn Yuē's contrastive rules were not the only kind of prosodic stricture in use.

There is one last medieval linguistic idea to mention: In their glosses on classical texts, medieval scholiasts are thought to have made conscious use of the principle of derivation by tone-change. That is, a word may exist in two forms, identical except for tone, so that the difference in tone corresponds to the difference in meaning. For example, turning again to a simple, illustrative reconstruction, *gi* (in the *píng* tone) means "to ride a horse" and *gì* (in the *qù* tone) means "a rider"; both meanings are typically represented with the same written character 騎, so that the difference in meaning and sound is not evident to the eye except in an explicit gloss. Similarly, *tom* 擔 means "to carry a burden" and *tòm* means "a burden"; *bioŋ* 縫 means "to stitch" and *biòŋ* means "a seam". This may actually have been a general principle of word-formation in classical times, and in recent decades the principle of derivation by tone-change has been incorporated into reconstructions of medieval and classical Chinese phonetics, typically by the addition of a final *-s* in *qù*-tone words. But as a feature of natural language in high antiquity it does not concern us here. It is significant that one of the preeminent phonologists of the Manchu period believed that these tone-changes were not natural at all, but were the work of ignorant commentators (Gù 1966[1667]a). Whether or not it was born of ignorance, in many early medieval exegetical texts, notably certain of those represented in the *Jīngdiăn shìwén*, there seems to be a pattern of glossing in which tone-change is used intentionally as a way of distinguishing what we would call syntactic functions or parts of speech. In most cases the derived form is in the *qù* tone, and in G. B. Downer's long list of examples from the *Shìwén* the greatest number of cases are nouns derived from verbs, although there is no simple pattern to the part of speech of derived meanings as a whole (Downer 1959). Evidently medieval exegetes used derivation by tone change as a conscious principle in glossing words.

Phonological ideas burgeoned in the early medieval period, but devoted linguistic works such as the *Qièyùn* remained in only a partial state of development. The rime-tables that developed during or before the 10th century were a far more sophisticated phonological apparatus.

## 7. Bibliography


Chao, Yuen Ren. 1941. "Distinctive Distinctions and Non-distinctive Distinctions in Ancient Chinese". [Appeared mistitled as "Distinctions within ancient Chinese" in *Harvard Journal of Asiatic Studies* 5: 3–4.203–233.]

Chén Yínkè 陳寅恪. 1949. "Cóng shǐshí lùn *Qièyùn* 從史實論切韻 [On the *Qièyùn* from the Point of View of History]". *Lǐngnán xuébào* 嶺南學報 9.1–18.

Chou Fa-kao [Zhōu Fǎgāo] 周法高, ed. 1960. *Yánshì jiāxùn huìzhù* 顏氏家訓彙注 [Collected annotations to the *Yánshì jiāxùn*.] Taipei: Academia Sinica.

–. 1964. "Fójiào dōngchuán duì Zhōngguó yīnyùnxué zhī yǐngxiǎng 佛教東傳對中國音韻學之影響 [The Influence of the Eastward Transmission of Buddhism on Chinese Classical Phonology]". Chapter 2 of *Zhōngguó yǔwén lùncóng* 中國語文論叢, 21–51. Taipei: Jíchéng túshū gōngsī 集成圖書公司.

Coblin, W. South. 1996. "Marginalia on two Translations of the *QIEYUN* Preface". *Journal of Chinese Linguistics* 24:1.85–97.

Dài Zhèn 戴震. 1775. Preface to *Liùshū yīnyùnbiǎo* 六書音韻表 by Duàn Yù-cái 段玉裁. 序 6a–7b. (Edition printed at Chéngdū by Mr. Yán of Wèinán 渭南嚴氏, n. d.; Repr. Taipei: Guǎngwén Shūjú 廣文書局, 1966.)

Downer, Gordon B. 1959. "Derivation by Tone-change in Classical Chinese". *Bulletin of the School of Oriental and African Studies* 22.258–290.

Gù Yánwǔ 顧炎武. 1667a. "Xiānrú liǎngshēng gèyì zhī shuō bújìnrán 先儒兩聲各義之說不盡然 [The Opinion of Former Scholars, that Tonal Differences had Different Meanings, is not Always True]". *Yīnlùn* 音論 [On Phonology], published in *Yīnxué Wǔshū* 音學五書, 3 [下], 2a–4b. Shānyáng 山陽, Jiāngsū. (Ed. printed at Chéngdū by Mr. Yán of Wèinán 渭南嚴氏, n. d.; Repr. Taipei: Guǎngwén Shūjú 廣文書局, 1966.)

–. 1667b. "Fǎnqiè zhī míng 反切之名 [The Name *fǎnqiè*]". *Yīnlùn* 音論 [On phonology], published in *Yīnxué Wǔshū* 音學五書, 3 [下, 9a–10a. Shānyáng 山陽, Jiāngsū. (Ed. printed at Chéngdū by Mr. Yán of Wèinán 渭南嚴氏, n. d.; Repr. Taipei: Guǎngwén Shūjú 廣文書局, 1966.)

*Guǎngyùn* 廣韻 [Expanded *Rimes*.] 1008. Compiled under the administrative supervision of Chén Péngnián 陳彭年 (961–1017). See the ed. of Zhōu Zǔmó 周祖謨 (1915–95), *Guǎngyùn jiàoběn* 廣韻校本 [A Collation of the *Guǎngyùn*] (Shanghai: Commercial Press, 1953 and many reprints.)

*Hóngwǔ zhèngyùn* 洪武正韻. 1375.

*Jíyùn* 集韻 [*Collected Rimes*.] 1039. Compiled under the administrative supervision of Dīng Dù 丁度 (990–1053). Numerous reprints and editions. For the most complete, with a thorough index, see Shanghai: Shànghǎi Gǔjí Chūbǎnshè 上海古籍出版社, 1987.

*Jīngdiǎn shìwén* 陸德明 (556–627). For an indexed ed. of the most authentic pre-modern redaction, see Wong Kuan Io [Huáng Kūnyáo] 黃坤堯 & Dèng Shìliáng 鄧仕樑, eds. *Xīnjiào suǒyǐn Jīngdiǎn shìwén* 新校索引經典釋文 (Taipei: Xuéhǎi Chūbānshè 學海出版社, 1988.)

Juhl, Robert A. 1989. "Some North-south Dialect Differences during late Six Dynasties Times". *Wen-lin: Studies in the Chinese Humanities* ed. by Tse-tsung Chow, vol. II, 277–291. Published jointly at Madison: Department of East Asian languages of the University of Wisconsin–Madison, and at N. T. T. Chinese Language Research Centre, Institute of Chinese Studies, the Chinese University of Hong Kong.

Karlgren, Bernhard. 1915–24. *Etudes sur la phonologie Chinoise*. Upsala: K. W. Appleberg. In four installments: 1915: *Archives d'Etudes Orientales*, 12; 1916: 13; 1919: 19; 1924: 24.

Láo Nǎixuān 勞乃宣. 1883. *Děngyùn yīdé* 等韻一得 [Rime Table Phonology in a Nutshell.] "Wàipiān 外篇 [Outer Chapters]". Shanghai: Tányǐnlú 蟫隱廬. (Repr. at the Government office in Wúqiáo 吳橋官廨, 1898.)

Liú Xié 劉勰. *Wénxīn diāolóng* 文心彫龍 [The Cultured Soul and the Carved Dragon.] See the edition of Fàn Wénlán 范文瀾 (1891–1969), (Shanghai: Kǎimíng Shūdiàn 凱明書店, 1947). [English translation by Vincent Shih, *The Literary mind and the carving of dragons*, New York: Columbia University Press, 1959.]

Luó Chángpéi 羅常培. 1930. *Xiàmén yīnxì* 廈門音系. Běipíng: Zhōngyāng Yánjiùyuàn Lìshǐ Yǔyán Yánjiùsuǒ 中央研究院歷史語言研究所, Dānkān jiǎ zhǒng zhī sì 單刊甲種之.

Lù Zhìwéi 陸志韋. 1963. "Gǔ fǎnqiè shì zěnyàng gòuzàode 古反切是怎樣構造的 [How were Ancient *fǎnqiè* Constructed?]. "*Zhōngguó Yǔwén* 中國語文 [Peking] 5.349–385.

Mair, Victor H. 1993. "Cheng Ch'iao's Understanding of Sanskrit: The concept of spelling in China". *A Festschrift in honour of Professor Jao Tsung-i on the occasion of his seventy-fifth anniversary* ed. by Cheng Hwei-shing, 331–341. Hong Kong: Institute of Chinese Studies, The Chinese University of Hong Kong.

–, & Tsu-lin Mei. 1991. "The Sanskrit Origins of Recent Style Prosody". *Harvard Journal of Asiatic Studies* 51: 2.375–470.

Martin, Samuel E. 1953. "The Phonemes of Ancient Chinese". Supplement to the *Journal of the American Oriental Society* 16.

Mather, Richard B. 1968. "A Note on the Dialects of Lo-yang and Nanking during the Six Dynasties". *Wen-lin: Studies in the Chinese Humanities* ed. by Chow Tse-Tsung, 247–256. Madison: Univ. of Wisconsin Press.

Norman, Jerry & W. South Coblin. 1995. "A New Approach to Chinese Historical Linguistics". *Jour-*

*nal of the American Oriental Society* 115: 4.576–584.

Pān Wénguó 潘文國. 1985. "Lùn zǒnghé tǐxì 論總和體系 [On the Idea of the Comprehensive System]". *Yánjiùshēng lùnwén xuǎnjí* 研究生論文選集, Yǔyán wénzì fēncè 語言文字分冊, 89–96. Nanking: Jiāngsū gǔjí chūbǎnshè 江蘇古籍出版社.

Pulleyblank, Edwin G. 1984. *Middle Chinese: A study in historical phonology.* Vancouver: Univ. of British Columbia Press.

*Qī-Lín bāyīn* 戚林八音. 1749.

*Qièyùn* 切韻 [*Finely Distinguished Rimes*.] 601. Compiled by Lù Fǎyán 陸法言 (fl. 581–617). Numerous redactions. For a facsimile of the earliest complete edition, of mid-Táng date, see *Tángxiěběn Wáng Rénxù Kānmiù Bǔquē Qièyùn* 唐寫本王仁昫刊謬補缺切韻 (repr. Taipei: Guǎngwén Shūjú 廣文書局, 1964). For an exhaustive collation of early fragments, see Liú Fù 劉復 (1891–1934) ed., *Shíyùn huìbiān* 十韻彙編 [*A Collection of Ten Rime Books*]. (Peking: Guólì Běijīng Dàxué 國立北京大學, 1935.)

*Shuōwén jiězì* 說文解字 [Explaining Simple and Derivative Characters.] Compiled by Xǔ Shèn 許慎 (d. c. 120). See the critical edition of Duàn Yùcái 段玉才 (1735–1815), many editions, (repr. Taipei: Límıng Wénhuà Shìyè Gǔfèn Yǒuxiàn Gōngsī 黎明文化事業股份有限公司, 1988.)

Stimson, Hugh M. 1976. *Fifty-five T'ang Poems.* New Haven: Far Eastern Publications.

*Yùnjìng* 韻鏡 [Mirror of Rimes.] See the critical edition of Lǐ Xīnkuí 李新魁 (Peking: Zhōnghuá Shūjú 中華書局, 1982.)

Zhāng Bǐnglín 章炳麟. 1917–1919. "Yīnlǐ lùn 音理論 [On the Logic of Phonology]". *Guógù lùnhéng* 國故論衡. In *Zhāngshì cóngshū* 章氏叢書, vol. I. (Repr. Shanghai: Yòuwénshè 右文社, n. d.)

*Zhōngyuán yīnyùn* 中原音韻. 1324. Compiled by Zhōu Déqīng 周德清. Numerous modern reprints. See Taipei: Yìwén Yínshūguǎn 藝文印書館, 1970.

Zhōu Zǔmó 周祖謨. 1966. "Qièyùnde xìngzhí hé tāde yīnxì jīchǔ 切韻的性質和它的音系基礎 [The Nature of the *Qièyùn* and the Basis of its Phonological System]". *Wènxué jí* 問學集, 434–473. Peking: Zhōnghuá Shūjú 中華書局. (Repr. Taipei: Zhīrén Chūbǎnshè 知仁出版社, 1976.)

*David Prager Branner,*
*New York (USA)*

# 6. The rime-table system of formal Chinese phonology

1. Introduction
2. The formal system of rime-table phonology
3. Phonological categories and their classification
4. Classification of initials
5. Classification of rimes
6. Origins
7. Higher structures of the phonological system: paired series of initials
8. Other technical terminology
9. Chinese alphabets
10. Bibliography

## 1. Introduction

Though of foreign inspiration, rime-table theory was the most influential single development in native Chinese linguistics in premodern times. It is a formal system, associated with the so-called *děngyùntú* 等韻圖, or "graded rime-tables", which appeared after the 6th and 7th century rime-books such as the *Qièyùn*. The oldest rime-tables we have date from the twelfth century, and their organizing principles have been the dominant phonological tool in Chinese up to the present day.

There are several important features that distinguish these tables from the older *fǎnqiè* 反切 tradition of rime-books (→ Art. 5). First, they are not dictionaries of the whole reading tradition, but guides to the phonological outlines of that tradition. Rime-tables are systematic syllabaries that show only one character for each sound, whereas the rime-books are more comprehensive and less methodical, listing at times dozens of homophones under a single heading, together with definitions, citations to classical texts, and miscellaneous lore. Second, rime-tables embody a formal classification scheme, under which the various phonological categories and features of Chinese are organized. Rime-books are usually more haphazard and lack explicit phonological analysis. Third, the classification scheme of the rime-tables is finely detailed and embodies significantly abstract phonological ideas, so that where *fǎnqiè* allowed readers no more than to find the pronunciation of a given character in their own accent, using rime-table phonology they could consider conceptual linguistic matters. Although rime-table phonology did not allow one to record phonetics verbatim, nevertheless one could describe the place and manner of articulation with a kind of precision that was out of the question with *fǎnqiè*. Nevertheless, from the prefaces to various rime-tables as well as from the way they are organized, it is clear that the primary purpose of early rime-table phonology was to analyze *fǎnqiè* found in books of the *Qièyùn* tradition.

It is because the rime-table movement was primarily analytical that its intellectual basis is so much easier to describe – and so much harder to learn – than that of the more impressionistic *fǎnqiè* tradition. (For more detailed studies of various aspects of rime-table phonology, see Branner, fc. 1999.)

## 2. The formal system of rime-table phonology

Fig. 6.1. shows a pair of facing pages from the earliest extant rime-table, the *Yùnjìng* 韻鏡 or "Mirror of rimes", which has come to us through Japan in an edition of the Southern Sùng (probably 12th century). It was not known to Chinese scholars during the great period of scholarship in the Manchu era (1644–1911), but in the 20th century it has come to be appreciated as the earliest surviving document of its kind, and it will serve here to illustrate many common features of rime-tables.

Classical rime-tables, like all traditional Chinese books, are read from right to left. In the right-most column is the title of this table: "inner-*zhuǎn*, Number 11, open". The words *zhuǎn* and "open" are technical terms that will be discussed below; here it is enough to say that they apply to the whole table, which is the eleventh out of a total of forty-three. The greater part of the table is taken up by a grid of twenty-three columns and sixteen rows, representing various initials and rimes of the language, respectively. As in modern syllabaries in Western linguistics, whenever a character appears at the intersection of an initial-column and a rime-row, its phonological value is defined as the combination of that initial and rime. Empty circles are used to indicate both possible syllables that happen to be unattested and also impossible syl-

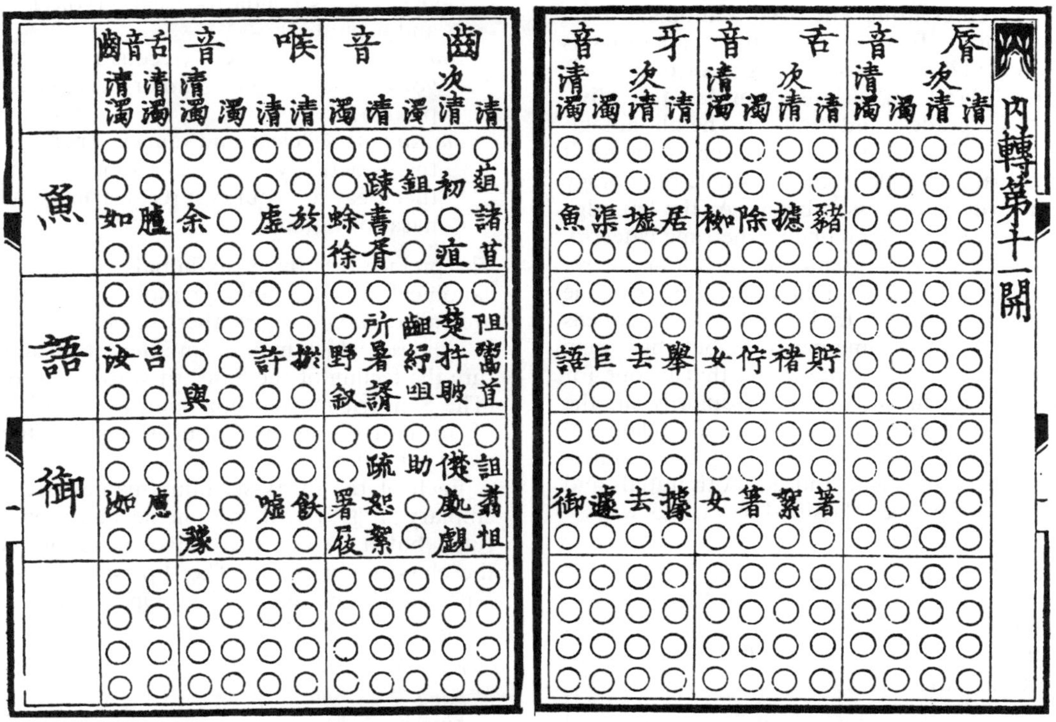


Fig. 6.1: Table 11 from the *Yùnjìng*

lables; in later rime-tables, however, it was usual to distinguish unattested from impossible syllables.

## 3. Phonological categories and their classification

Rime-tables embody a few positively epochal advances over *fǎnqiè*-phonology, and the greatest of these is to identify individual phonological categories and assign them explicit names. Tone categories and rimes already had exemplary names in the *Qièyùn* of AD 601, but rime-table phonology also identified and named initial categories, and more importantly entire classes of initials and rimes, and even different kinds of articulatory features that characterized such classes of initials and rimes. A book like the *Qièyùn* might have a dozen or more distinct *fǎnqiè* uppers corresponding to what in the rime-tables are a single, named initial category. Where *fǎnqiè* were a mere guide to pronunciation, rime-table theory was a formal system of phonological analysis; its tabular presentation implies that this analysis was felt to be complete and confident.

The rime-rows in Fig. 6.1. are divided into four groups, demarcated by horizontal lines and representing the four canonical tone categories. Each of these tone categories is subdivided into four rows, called *děng* 等 "levels" (a term variously translated as "division", "grade", and "rank"). The phonological meaning of these *děng* is one of the most important problems in rime-table phonology and will be discussed below. At the left edge of the table is the name of the rime category or categories represented in each tone, corresponding to usage in later rime-books of the *Qièyùn* tradition. In Fig. 6.1. there happens to be only one rime per tone, but there may be as many as four per tone; that is, one for each *děng* in each tone. Ordinarily all the rimes in a given table are closely related in sound, differing by tone and by the qualities that *děng* represent. Indeed, both initials and finals are further classified in various ways.

## 4. Classification of initials

The initials are arranged into six types, separated by vertical lines. Reading from right to left they are:

*chúnyīn* 脣音 "lip sounds" (reconstructed as labials);
*shéyīn* 舌音 "tongue sounds" (alveolar stops and nasals);
*yáyīn* 牙音 "fang sounds" (velar stops and nasals);
*chǐyīn* 齒音 "tooth [molar?] sounds" (sibilants);
*hóuyīn* 喉音 "throat sounds" (velar fricatives and laryngeals); and
*shéyīnchǐ* 舌音齒 "tongue-sounds-tooth" (*sic*; reconstructed as *l* and *nj2*).

If the names "fang sounds" and "tooth sounds" seem unlikely for velars and sibilants, one should be aware that the Chinese name *yá* for "fang" is an example of a velar initial (**ŋa*) and the name *chǐ* for "tooth" an example of a sibilant initial (**tʃhǐ*); the use of exemplars is very widespread in Chinese phonology.

The individual initials represented by each column also have their own exemplary names, which however are shown not on the table but in the *Yùnjìng* preface. This is an unusual arrangement; most other rime-tables have the names of the initials heading the various volumns. On *Yùnjìng* tables, however, initials are represented by the names of their four possible manners of articulation:

*qīng* 清 "clear" (voiceless and unaspirated);
*cìqīng* 次清 "secondarily clear" (voiceless and aspirated);
*zhuó* 濁 "turbid, murky" (reconstructed as voiced and by some scholars also as aspirated);
*qīngzhuó* 清濁 "clear and murky" (perhaps this is actually supposed to mean "neither clear nor murky"; reconstructed as nasal or liquid).

The preface lists thirty-six initials, which are canonical in rime-table phonology. Initials are called *zìmǔ* 字母 "mothers of characters" in Chinese, which may be an attempt to capture the feeling of the Sanskrit word *mātṛkā*. (The Sanskrit means something like "listing of formative elements" but resembles the word for "mother".)

Each of the thirty-six initial-names is exemplary: it is a real morpheme in its own right, but it begins with the same sound as the class it represents. The 'lip' sounds are represented in two series. One series is *zhòng* 重 "heavy" (bilabial):

*bāng* 幫 **p*
*pāng* 滂 **ph*
*bìng* 並 **b*
*míng* 明 **m*

The other series is *qīng* 輕 "light" (labiodental):

| | |
|---|---|
| fēi 非 | *pf > *f |
| fū 敷 | *pfh (?) > *f |
| fèng 奉 | *bv > *f or *v |
| wéi 微 | *mw > *w |

The labiodental series is interesting because (at least in this specific form) it does not seem to be attested in rime-books of the *Qièyùn* tradition, although it is known in many modern varieties of Chinese. The *Yùnjìng* shows the distinction between bilabials and labiodentals, but instead of creating a single initial category for what is now *f*, it preserves separate initials for each of the two or three *Qièyùn* tradition-initial categories to which *f* corresponds. This may be because at one time there were indeed three separate labiodental initials (as suggested in the reconstruction used here) or it may be because the anonymous compilers of the *Yùnjìng* were trying to be true to the distinctions made in the *Qièyùn*. The latter possibility would have been very characteristic of them. In any case, modern Chinese labiodentals do not always appear in precisely the same words as rime-table labiodentals.

'Tongue' sounds are also in two series. There are the *shétóu* 舌頭 "tip of tongue" (apical) sounds:

| | |
|---|---|
| duān 端 | *t |
| tòu 透 | *th |
| dìng 定 | *d |
| ní 泥 | *n |

and the *shéshàng* 舌上 "on the tongue" (dorsal) sounds:

| | |
|---|---|
| zhī 知 | *tj |
| chè 徹 | *tjh |
| chéng 澄 | *dj |
| niáng 娘 | *$nj_1$ |

'Fang' sounds are as follows, in one series:

| | |
|---|---|
| jiàn 見 | *k |
| qī 溪 | *kh |
| qún 群 | *g |
| yí 疑 | *ŋ |

'Tooth' sounds are in two series. The first is the *chǐtóu* 齒頭 "tip of the teeth" (apico-alveolar):

| | |
|---|---|
| jīng 精 | *ts |
| qīng 清 | *tsh |
| cóng 從 | *dz |
| xīn 心 | *s |
| xié 邪/斜 | *z |

The second tooth-sound series is the *zhèngchǐ* 正齒 "up against the teeth" (palato-alveolar):

| | |
|---|---|
| zhào 照 | *tʃ |
| chuān 穿 | *tʃh |
| shàn 禪 | *dʒ |
| shěn 審 | *ʃ |
| chuáng 牀 | *ʒ |

Within the tooth sounds as a whole there is a sub-distinction: between affricates, which have no special terminology and should be understood as 'plain', and fricatives, called *xì* 細 "fine".

There is one series of 'throat' sounds:

| | |
|---|---|
| yǐng 影 | *[zero initial] |
| xiǎo 曉 | *x |
| xiá 匣 | *ɣ |
| yù 喻 | *j |

Initials *xiǎo* and *xiá* are said to be "flying in pairs", while *yǐng* and *yù* "stand alone"; this may have to do with the fact that *yǐng* and *yù* are essentially vocalic while *xiǎo* and *xiá* are consonantal, but any literal meaning of the terminology is opaque.

Finally, there are two initials in the 'tongue-sounds-tooth' category:

| | |
|---|---|
| lái 來 | *l |
| rì 日 | *$nj_2$ |

## 5. Classification of rimes

Rimes are also arranged into types, called (in most tables other than the *Yùnjìng*) *shè* 攝, literally "to gather up". The nature of this category will be clear on examination of the reconstructed rimes associated with the sixteen canonical *shè* in Fig. 6.2.

It is surely significant that the *Qièyùn* itself arranges rimes very largely in keeping with *shè*-order.

Each of the forty-three tables has certain other features associated with it. One is the *zhuǎn* "cycles" – a single table may belong to either the *nèi* "inner" or *wài* "outer" cycle of tables. It is now understood that these terms refer to the height of the main vowel in the rimes on each table – low vowels were 'outer' and others were 'inner'. Another feature of tables of rimes is whether they are *hé* "closed" (i. e., generally showing lip-rounding) or *kāi* "open".

| *Name of Shè* | *Shared ending of component rimes* |
|---|---|
| *tōng* 通 | *-uŋ |
| *jiāng* 江 | *-aŋ |
| *zhǐ* 止 | *-i |
| *yù* 遇 | *-uo |
| *xiè* 蟹 | *-ai |
| *zhēn* 臻 | *-en |
| *shān* 山 | *-an |
| *xiào* 效 | *-au |
| *guǒ* 果 | *-ɑ |
| *jiǎ* 假 | *-a |
| *dàng* 宕 | *-ɑŋ |
| *gěng* 梗 | *-æŋ |
| *liú* 流 | *-u |
| *shēn* 深 | *-em |
| *xián* 咸 | *-am |
| *zēng* 曾 | *-əŋ |

Fig. 6.2: The Sixteen *Shè*

## 6. Origins

Although *fǎnqiè* are probably of native Chinese origin, there is no doubt that rime-table phonology was inspired by Indian linguistic theory (→ Art. 19), in particular by the practical systems for teaching the Sanskrit syllabary that came to be known collectively as Siddham (Chinese *xītán* 悉曇). Sanskrit Siddham was already known in China by the last decades of the 4th century, and is the subject of certain still poorly understood Chinese treatises from this time (see Ráo 1990). One of the most striking features of Siddham is the way it presents lists of initial consonants, arranged by place and manner of articulation, in tabular form. It is hard to avoid the conclusion that this was the ultimate inspiration for the Chinese rime-tables. But note that Siddham, even in Chinese, is still the study of Sanskrit phonology, not Chinese phonology. The application of its principles to Chinese must have taken place some time after the introduction of its Sanskrit form.

Rime-tables proper appear almost a millennium after the introduction of Buddhism into China, but there are other sorts of evidence suggesting that someone was already analyzing and classifying Chinese phonological categories much sooner than that. An important concept of this kind is the *niǔ* 紐 'knot, gather', a prosodic term which Roy Andrew Miller considers to be a calque of the Sanskrit term *varga* "class of consonants". A *niǔ* in Chinese was a diagram showing groups of four syllables, one in each of the four canonical tones, having in common a single initial and sometimes also a single rime. Such *niǔ* are meant to illustrate tonally different syllables sharing part or all of the rest of their phonetics. Here is an example of a *niǔ* from the *Bunkyō Hifuron* (see Bodman 1978), illustrating the principles of *tiáoshēng* 調聲 'harmonizing the tones':

| | |
|---|---|
| 尚 *ʒiàŋ* | 常 *ʒiaŋ* |
| 杓 *ʒiak* | 上 *ʒiǎŋ* |

The only differences among these four readings are their tones (there is nothing unusual in the fact that the *rùshēng* example, in the lower left corner, has a *-k* ending corresponding to *-ŋ* in the other tones). Materials like this show a kind of control of phonology that unambiguously anticipates rime-table theory, but which is absent in the rime-book tradition. *Niǔ* date from no later than the 8th and perhaps as early as the early 6th century, so we may arguably date the peculiarly Chinese transformation of Siddham into rime-table theory from this time.

Among the manuscripts rescued at Dūnhuáng 敦煌 by Paul Pelliot (1878–1945) is the precious Shǒuwēn 守溫 manuscript fragment, thought to date from the 9th century. Shǒuwēn was an ethnic Chinese bonze to whom the invention of the 36 initials had long been attributed in received sources. The Shǒuwēn fragment already mentions many of the technical terms associated with rime-table phonology, including the names of most of the initials, the four *děng*, and the solecism of *lèigé* (see below). This document is the earliest surviving record we have of rime-table phonology in its proper form, and is especially important for dating some of the reconstructed phonetic features the evidence for which comes from the rime-tables. (Important new discoveries about the Shǒuwēn fragments appear in Coblin, fc. 1999.)

As for how the actual organization of rime-table phonology developed, we have no explicit record. Nonetheless, we can tell certain things about what the compilers of this system must have had in mind. It is clear that they were trying to represent all the distinctions in some rime-book of the *Qièyùn* type (such as the *Guǎngyùn* 廣韻), even if at times they may have introduced features of their own contemporary pronunciation. In fact, there are relatively few examples of contemporary features intruding on the structure of the *Qièyùn* system – most of the time such features are indicated around the edges of the tables or in ways that do not create phonological distinctions unknown in the *Qièyùn* or eliminate known distinctions. There are important exceptions, however.

## 7. Higher structures of the phonological system: paired series of initials

So far all the features that have been discussed are either the names of simple categories or of classes of simple categories. But there was far more to rime-table phonology than just classification. One of its most important and least appreciated features is the subtle relation between the thirty-six initials and the four *děng*, truly the key to the whole system. Not all initials are actually found in combination with all rimes, so that there are patterns formed by the actual appearance of specific classes of initials in specific rimes. The *Yùnjìng* makes use of these distributional patterns to reduce the amount of space each table takes up – in most rime-tables, a single table takes up four pages, but the *Yùnjìng* uses only half that space. Whenever one of the classes of initials comprises two series, the *Yùnjìng* lists both series together, with the expectation that the reader will know which initial appears in which *děng*.

For instance, words with the 'tip of the tongue' initials (*duān* *t, etc.) appear only in the first and fourth *děng* but never in the second or third; and words with the 'on the tongue' initials (*zhī* *tj, etc.) appear only in the second and third *děng* and never in the first or fourth. In modern terminology, these two sets of initials are in complementary distribution, and although there was no comparable terminology in the 10th century, the concept was clearly understood. Some later rime-tables would nevertheless list the two sets of initials separately, using eight columns to represent them, but the *Yùnjìng* combines them into four columns. By squeezing thirty-six initials into only twenty-one columns, the *Yùnjìng* compilers produced tables that can be viewed all at once, on two facing pages. This may also be the reason that the *Yùnjìng* lists not the names but the manners of articulation of the various initials at the tops of the columns – one column often represents two initials with the same manner of articulation but slightly different places of articulation.

The fact that some series of initials are complementary illustrates something profound about the conceptual origins of the tables: the likely origin of that most puzzling single feature of the rime-tables, the *děng*. *Děng* are literally the horizontal rows of the tables into one of which each rime category is classified, but the puzzle is to understand why there are specifically four of them and what it means for a rime to be placed in a particular one of them. What do these four *děng*, these four rows, these four kinds of rime, really represent?

Als always when there is no hard evidence, speculation abounds. Since the late 19th century, scholars of many nationalities have vied to produce phonetically realistic reconstructions that would most perfectly account for these *děng*. Underlying that struggle is the assumption that the compilers of the rime-tables were practicing phonetic description; yet that is a most improbable idea, given what we know about the overwhelmingly unphonetic or indeed anti-phonetic Chinese tradition. Far more insightful is the explanation of the eminent 20th century scholar Lǐ Róng, who holds that each *děng* represents not a specific kind of sound but a specific kind of cooccurrence of initial and rime: that is, a distributional pattern of initials that occur with the rime-book rimes placed in each row of the tables. (Lǐ has apparently never published an explicit statement of this approach, though he is well known to advocate it and it is implied in his 1956: 76–79.) Since the whole inspiration of the rime-tables has to do with classification of categories, it makes good sense that the *děng* should do the same. This explanation is almost surely the right one, because it suits the profoundly analytical but only intermittently descriptive bent of the compilers of the tables.

| | Tongue-tooth | Throat | Tooth | | Fang | Tongue | | Lip |
|---|---|---|---|---|---|---|---|---|
| | | | up against teeth | tip of teeth | | on tongue | tip of tongue | |
| Type X | | | no | | | no | yes | |
| Type Y | | | yes | | | yes | no | |

Fig. 6.3: Tabulation of the Two Main Types of Rime

| | Tongue-tooth | Throat | Tooth | | Fang | Tongue | | Lip |
|---|---|---|---|---|---|---|---|---|
| | | | up against teeth | tip of teeth | | on tongue | tip of tongue | |
| Type X | | *xiá* | no | | | no | yes | *bāng* |
| Type Y1 | | *xiá* | yes (one) | | | yes | no | *bāng* |
| Type Y2 | *rì* | *yù* | yes (two) *xié* | | *qún* | yes | no | *bāng* *fēi* |

Fig. 6.4: Tabulation of the Three Main Types of Rime

In other words, the four *děng* are, in the main, part of a schematic classification of rime-categories in rime-books of the *Qièyùn* tradition. To say that there are four *děng* is to say that there are four types of correspondence between initials and rimes in the *Qièyùn*. We can derive this four-fold analysis in a few steps, as follows:

In the incidence of initials, the most significant pattern is that all rimes can be classified almost without exception into two types: those which have the 'tip of the tongue' initials but not the 'on the tongue' or 'up against the teeth' initials, and those which, conversely, can have 'on the tongue' and 'up against the teeth' initials but not 'tip of the tongue' initials. With rare exceptions, these types are in complement. They are shown in Fig. 6.3., tentatively labeled Types X and Y.

Of all the rimes in the rime-book tradition, then, the basic bifurcation is between these two types. Each of these two types of rime can be further divided in two on certain grounds. Type Y comprises one group of rimes (let us call them Y1) that can appear with only one set of the 'up against the teeth' initials, and another group ('Y2') that can appear with two contrasting sets of that series of initials. This may seem unlikely as basis for a distinction, but the split between Y1 and Y2 is certainly not haphazard because it is corroborated by several other distinctions. For example: Type Y1 can appear with only one set of the 'lip' initials (only the "heavy" *bāng* series) but Type Y2 can appear with two sets (the *bāng* series as well as the "light" *fēi* series). Type Y1 can appear with the initial *xiá* but not with *yù*; Type Y2 can appear with *yù* but not with *xiá*. And there are three other initials that appear exclusively with Type Y2 rimes: *qún*, *xié*, and *rì*. These distributions are displayed schematically in Fig. 6.4.

Note that these patterns are not merely inventions of the rime-table compilers but are actually present in rime books of the *Qièyùn* type; the three rime-types labelled here X, Y1, and Y2, are implicitly distinguished, distributionally, in the *Qièyùn*. And they correspond very closely to the first three of the four rows in the rime-tables.

The origin of the fourth row has no basis in the *Qièyùn*; almost all fourth-row rimes belong to what we have been calling Type X, together with first-row rimes. Type X rimes in the *Qièyùn* cannot be divided into two such clear groups as the first and fourth rows on purely distributional grounds. But on the basis of modern Chinese pronunciation in most dialects – and presumably in some dialects of the 10th or 12th centuries, as well – Type X can be divided into those rimes that are palatalized and those that are not. Let us call these Types X1 (plain) and X2 (palatal-

| | Tongue-tooth | Throat | Tooth | | Fang | Tongue | | Lip |
|---|---|---|---|---|---|---|---|---|
| | | | up against teeth | tip of teeth | | on tongue | tip of tongue | |
| Type X1 (unpal.) | | *xiá* | no | | | no | yes | *bāng* |
| Type Y1 | | *xiá* | yes (one) | | | yes | no | *bāng* |
| Type Y2 | *rı* | *yù* | yes (two) *xié* | | *qún* | yes | no | *bāng* *fēi* |
| Type X2 (pal.) | | *xiá* | no | | | no | yes | *bāng* |

Fig. 6.5: Tabulation of the Four Main Types of Rime

ized). And since rimes of Type Y2 are also palatalized in most attested varieties of Chinese dialects, it is natural to place the palatalized Type X2 near Type Y2. This arrangement produces a table as shown in Fig. 6.5.

And Fig. 6.5. is none other than the basic layout of the canonical rime-tables. There are complications having to do with the fact that certain words belonging to third-row rimes can actually appear in rows two and four (*i. e.*, without belonging to second- and fourth-row type rimes). But in essence it is indisputable that the four *děng* must have had their origins in the kind of analysis presented above, as Lǐ Róng has suggested. Thus, we can be sure that the *děng* of the rime-tables originated in an analysis of some book or books of the *Qièyùn* tradition, only somewhat modified by contemporary phonetic considerations.

## 8. Other technical terminology

Analysis of the *Qièyùn* tradition was the prevailing goal of early rime-table phonology. In addition to isolating phonological categories and assigning them names and classes, rime-table theorists identified certain aspects of the relation of *fǎnqiè* to rime-table categories. These features were called *mén* 門 "gateways". They were almost all mnemonic rules for figuring out how to make sense of *fǎnqiè*. The study of them was called *ménfǎ* 門法 "the method of [using] gateways". Below are discussed a few of the better-known of these *mén*.

*Yīnhé* 音和 "the sounds match" – this appears to be the name for the correct choice of *fǎnqiè* uppers and lowers to represent a given syllable.

*Lèigé* 類隔 "treating things that are distinct as belonging to the same category" – similar initials differing in some smaller aspect of articulation, *e. g.*, using the *duān* initial instead of the *zhī* initial (**t* instead of **tj*) or the *pāng*-series instead of the *fēi*-series (bilabials instead of labiodentals). *Lèigé* involving the *bāng*- and *fēi*-series was mentioned by Shǒuwēn but was assigned a separate *mén*-name in later, attested tables: *qīngzhòng jiāohù* 輕重交互 "light and heavy taking each other's place".

*Píngqiè* 憑切 "[placement of the syllable] follows the initial" – There are several subvarieties of this, all of which seem to have had to do with deciding the *děng* of the spelled syllable. In these various *mén*, the identity of the upper character in a *fǎnqiè* expression usually overrode any influence of the *fǎnqiè* lower character in deciding the *děng* of the spelled syllable. (It is clear from the great number of *mén* dealing with *děng* that they have never been an easy feature to work with.)

*Guǎngtōng* 廣通 "expanding connections". This has to do with the fact that in certain rimes, the 'lip', 'fang', and 'throat' classes of initials may have words appearing in both the third and fourth rows of the same table, yet these rimes are considered to belong inherently to the third *děng*.

## 9. Chinese alphabets

The *mén* discussed above are only a small part of the overgrowth of mnemonic tools and other arcana associated with the rime-tables. There is no question that full control of all this theory was a highly specialized branch of learning even in its own time, and there must not have been many ordinary educated people in society (*i. e.*, other than bonzes) who had such control. But if we cast aside all the elaborate formal terminology and consider only the basic ideas associated with rime-tables – the sixteen *shè*, the 'closedness' or 'openness' of syllables, and above all the thirty-six initials – then it is clear that these things rapidly achieved a permanent place in native Chinese linguistics. The thirty-six initials in particular are the first thing in attested history to have served as something like an alphabet for the Chinese themselves.

There have been other, more traditional alphabets used in Chinese in pre-modern times. The ʿPhags-pa (Chinese Bāsībā 巴思八) alphabet is always mentioned in histories of Chinese linguistics, even though it is not Chinese and does not represent an important stage in Chinese linguistic history. It was designed by the Tibetan lama ʿPhags-pa (1235–1280) based on the Tibetan alphabet, at the behest of the Mongol Qubilai Khan. Qubilai promulgated it in 1269, so that it could be used as a standard system to transcribe Mongolian and various other languages spoken within the Mongol Empire, including Chinese. (Mongolian had previously been written in the Uyghur script.) It never seems to have caught on at all among the Chinese people themselves, however, and Chinese transcriptions in ʿPhags-pa are attested today mainly by various inscriptions on steles and coins of the day and by a rime-dictionary of dubious dialectal affiliation, the *Ménggŭ zìyùn*, which is laid out like a traditional Chinese character-based rime-book but gives the sound of each homophone group in ʿPhags-pa script (see Jūnast & Yáng 1987). ʿPhags-pa consists of Tibetan-like letters with an expanded vowel set, combined to form square or rectangular shapes arranged vertically like Chinese characters. The significance of this alphabet in the history of linguistics is that it was the first attempt at a universal system of alphabetic transcription used in China; it also seems to have provided some of the inspiration for the vastly more sophisticated Korean alphabet (Ledyard 1997; → Art. 9). Other than these considerations, ʿPhags-pa is important mainly to modern research on Mongolian and Mongol-period transcriptions of Chinese.

There has not really been a true Chinese alphabet, unless one considers the set of thirty-six canonical rime-table initials to be the Chinese alphabet. Certainly rime-table phonology has accumulated enough prestige to bear this honorable name. Even in modern times, when the Mandarin Phonetic Symbols (*zhùyīn fúhào*) were devised early in the 20th century, they were arranged by phonetic classes and in an order reminiscent of the initials of the *Yùnjīng*: labials first, then apicals, then velars, then sibilants, then varieties of zero. And the rime-table tradition has provided the basic vocabulary of phonology in China ever since late Táng times; although it has evolved, it is still in use. Discussion of *Qièyùn*-tradition books since the 12th century has taken place in the main using rime-table terminology. When 16th century Jesuit missionary Nicholas Trigault (1577–1628) published his explanation of true alphabetic writing for the Chinese, he found it natural to present it in rime-table format. Manchu-era historical phonologists, grappling with the phonologies underlying ancient rhyming texts and character-formation, used rime-table language and organization as a matter of course in their discussions, and sometimes presented their conclusions in tabular form. 19th century Chinese even applied the rime-table principle to descriptive dialect studies of a kind. Rime-table categories have been the unquestioned framework used in the reconstruction of all ancient varieties Chinese ostensibly on Western comparative principles. In the 20th century, Yuen Ren Chao and later Dīng Shēngshù and Lĭ Róng developed a kind of modern rime-table for use in dialect fieldwork, which continues to be widely used. If there is any one variety of phonology that is characteristically Chinese it is rime-table science, and the irony is that it came to China from India.

## 10. Bibliography

Bodman, Richard W. 1978. *Poetics and Prosody in Early Mediaeval China: A study and translation of Kūkai's* Bunkyō Hifuron. Ph. D., Cornell University.

Branner, David Prager. Fc. 1999. *The Linguistic Philosophy of the Traditional Chinese Rime Table.* Amsterdam: Benjamins.

Coblin, W. South. Fc. 1999. "Reflections on the Shoouuen Fragments." Branner 1999.

Jūnast & Yáng Năisī 楊乃思. 1987. *Ménggŭ zìyùn jiàoběn* 蒙古字韻校本. Peking: Mínzú chūbănshè 民族出版社.

Ledyard, Gari Keith. 1997. "The International Linguistic Background of the Correct Sounds for the Instruction of the People". *The Korean Alphabet: Its history and structure*, ed. by Ioung-Key Kim-Renaud, 31–87. Honolulu: Univ. of Hawaii Press.

Lǐ Júng [Lǐ Róng] 李榮. 1956. *Qièyùn yīnxì* 切韻音系 [The Phonetic System of the *Qièyùn*.] Peking: Xīnhuá shūdiàn 新華書店. (Repr. (with some omissions) at Taipei: Dǐngwén shūjú 鼎文書局, 1973.)

Ráo Zōngyí 饒宗頤. 1990. *Zhōng-Yìn wénhuà guānxìshǐ lùnjí – yǔwénpiān: Xītánxué xùlùn* 中印文化關係史論集、語文篇: 悉曇學緒論 [Collected Essays on the History of Sino-Indian Cultural Relations – Language and Literature: Essays on Siddham studies.] Hong Kong: Chinese University of Hong Kong.

*David Prager Branner, New York (USA)*

# 7. Le rôle du savoir linguistique dans l'éducation et la société chinoise

1. Introduction
2. Avant l'instauration des examens impériaux
3. Après l'institution des examens impériaux
4. Conclusion
5. Bibliographie

## 1. Introduction

La langue, en tant que médium littéraire, mais aussi dans ses variations dialectales, a toujours joué un rôle considérable dans la société chinoise. Que savaient les Chinois anciens de leur langue, et comment ce savoir était-il transmis? Pour répondre à ces questions, il convient assurément de différencier plusieurs étapes, tant il est vrai que le savoir linguistique, qui s'est accumulé au cours des siècles, a, sinon changé de nature, du moins évolué dans ses centres d'intérêt. Deux grandes périodes doivent d'abord être distinguées, en fonction de l'existence ou non des examens impériaux, dont les épreuves testaient surtout le savoir littéraire, mais aussi philologique, des candidats. Ces examens, instaurés sous la dynastie des Sui (581–618), ont été supprimés définitivement en 1905. Ils ont servi à former une élite bureaucratique (le mandarinat), politique et culturelle, et à stratifier la société chinoise.

## 2. Avant l'instauration des examens impériaux

### 2.1. Epoque archaïque (jusqu'au III^e siècle avant J.-C.)

Le savoir linguistique semble n'avoir pas été important. Rares sont les œuvres des philosophes de la période des Royaumes-combattants (475 à 221 avant J.-C.) – qui constituent la base de ce qu'on appelle communément le chinois classique – qui traitent de questions linguistiques. On trouve, ici ou là, par exemple dans le *Xunzi*, attribué à Xunzi (ca. 313–238 avant J.-C.), ou dans le *Mozi*, attribué à Mozi (480–420 avant J.-C.), quelques considérations d'ordre sémantico-philosophique sur les dénominations, mais ces remarques sont éparses et ne constituent pas, loin s'en faut, des réflexions intégrées d'un quelconque intérêt théorique.

On est frappé du rôle tout à fait marginal que tient le savoir linguistique dans le *Lun yu* "Entretiens" de Confucius (V^e siècle avant J.-C.), qui est pourtant un recueil d'enseignements dispensés par Confucius (551–479 avant J.-C.) à ses disciples.

### 2.2. Dynastie des Han (206 avant J.-C.–220)

Une science, qu'on peut déjà qualifier de linguistique, voit le jour, en parallèle avec l'herméneutique. C'est en effet à cette époque prémédiévale qu'ont été compilés des dictionnaires qui resteront pendant longtemps la base des études classiques: le *Er ya* "Approcher la perfection", d'auteur inconnu, mais compilé vraisemblablement au I^er siècle avant J.-C. à partir de manuscrits rédigés entre le V^e et le I^er siècle avant J.-C., qui rassemble des synonymes ou quasi-synonymes et est organisé, de manière encyclopédique, en sections thématiques; le *Shuo wen jie zi* "Expliquer les figures et interpréter les caractères" (100) de Xu Shen (ca. 65–130), dictionnaire étymologique de 9353 caractères classés sous 540 clés ou éléments graphiques entrant dans la composition des caractères, et fondé indubitablement sur la pensée spéculative (théorie du *yin* et du *yang* et des cinq éléments) propre à l'époque des Han; le *Fangyan* "Expressions régionales" (I^er siècle) de Yang Xiong (53 avant J.-C. – 18), premier lexique général des différents parlers de plusieurs régions de Chine.

Le savoir linguistique commence donc à devenir important, mais il joue encore un rôle négligeable dans l'éducation et dans la société. Il concerne uniquement quelques lettrés, dont le but essentiel reste, par-delà les querelles philologiques, l'établissement d'une juste interprétation des classiques confucéens. Xu Shen, à ce sujet, est un savant typique ayant voulu fixer une fois pour toutes le sens des caractères en s'appuyant sur des graphies plus anciennes. Il n'est pas non plus impossible que ces dictionnaires aient été conçus, au départ, dans le cadre d'une politique visant à définir une norme linguistique, voulue par les empereurs ou par leurs conseillers immédiats.

### 2.3. Epoque des Wei-Jin et des dynasties Nord-Sud (220 – 589)

Elle peut être caractérisée, d'un point de vue linguistique, comme une étape transitoire, où les études phonétiques prennent quelque importance, en raison de l'expansion du bouddhisme et des traductions du sanskrit ou du pali. Une méthode est ainsi créée pour la prononciation des caractères, qui sera systématiquement utilisée jusqu'en 1918: la méthode *fanqie* "retourner et couper" (→ Art. 5). Elle consiste à transcrire le son d'un mot en le décomposant et en le glosant par deux caractères différents, le premier indiquant l'initiale, le second la finale.

## 3. Après l'institution des examens impériaux

### 3.1. Dynasties des Sui (581 – 618), des Tang (618 – 907) et des Song (960 – 1279)

Les recherches phonétiques et phonologiques sont désormais prédominantes. Deux ouvrages fondamentaux marquent le début de cette période: Le *Jingdian shiwen* "Explications des classiques" de Lu Deming (556 – 627), qui utilise la méthode *fanqie*, et surtout le *Qieyun* "Rimes standardisées" (601) de Lu Fayan (dates précises non connues), qui propose une classification d'environ 11500 caractères, selon leur prononciation et en prenant en compte trois paramètres, les tons, les rimes et les initiales.

Ce dernier Thésaurus devient très rapidement une somme indispensable à tout candidat tenu de composer des textes rimés et de connaître parfaitement les règles de prosodie, lors des examens impériaux qui viennent d'être institués. De même, le *Er ya* est désormais un ouvrage obligatoire pour les élèves du Collège impérial, dans la version du commentateur Guo Pu (276 – 324). Le *Shuo wen jie zi*, enfin, et l'étude de la phonétique ancienne, sont aussi l'objet de nombreuses recherches, surtout à partir des Song, toujours en vue de la préparation aux examens.

C'est aussi sous les Song qu'apparaît le premier recueil de particules: le *Wenzi* "Règles de composition littéraire" (1170) de Chen Kui (1128 – 1203). Il s'agit d'un petit opuscule qui discute les principales particules grammaticales (morphèmes fonctionnels) de la langue classique. L'objectif primordial de Chen Kui est d'ordre stylistique et rhétorique. Il vise à fournir une bonne maîtrise de l'emploi des particules grammaticales pour la composition littéraire.

### 3.2. Dynasties des Yuan (1279 – 1368) et des Ming (1368 – 1644)

L'invasion mongole et l'instauration de la dynastie mongole des Yuan marquent une rupture radicale avec le passé. Les points de vue sur la phonétique sont délibérément nouveaux, notamment dans le *Zhong yuan yin yun* "Rimes et sons du mandarin des plaines centrales" (1324) de Zhou Deqing (1277 – 1365), qui milite contre l'imitation des anciens, contre le respect de la tradition, et est décidé à décrire les réalités phonétiques de la langue standard de son époque.

Sous les Yuan, également, paraît le premier traité 'grammatical': le *Yuzhu* "Particules grammaticales" (1324) de Lu Yiwei (dates précises non connues). Comme celui de Chen Kui, précédemment, c'est un traité d'ordre stylistique et rhétorique. Il est néanmoins tout à fait original sur deux points cruciaux. Son auteur (un précurseur de la linguistique textuelle?) considère d'abord que les explications ne doivent pas se limiter au mot ou même à la phrase, mais tenir compte du contexte et donc se rapporter à de longs passages, voire au texte dans son entier. Ensuite, Lu Yiwei a intégré dans son recueil des particules grammaticales de la langue vernaculaire. Il donne aussi souvent les équivalents en vernaculaire, et même parfois en dialecte wu (région de Shanghai), des mots vides de la langue classique qu'il cherche à expliquer.

Ce nouveau savoir linguistique restera l'apanage d'une minorité de lettrés sous les Yuan. Il se diffusera d'autant plus mal que le système des examens est supprimé dès le début de la dynastie, et n'est restauré qu'en 1314. Lorsque les examens seront rétablis, les épreuves sur les rimes et la poésie ancienne ou moderne et régulière seront supprimées. Il faudra attendre 1757 et 1759 pour que des questions de poétique soient réintroduites dans les programmes des examens au niveau des villes et au niveau des provinces. Les recherches phonologiques ont, en conséquence, cédé le pas aux études philologiques classiques sur l'étymologie et la composition littéraire pendant toute la dynastie des Ming.

### 3.3. Dynastie des Qing (1644–1911)

L'école philologique de la dynastie mandchoue des Qing prône un retour important aux sources et aux études épigraphiques et paléographiques. Les études sur le *Shuo wen jie zi* sont ainsi relancées, notamment par Duan Yucai (1735–1815), auteur du *Shuo wen jie zi zhu* "Annotations du *Shuo wen*" (1807). Les autres dictionnaires anciens, le *Er ya* et le *Fangyan* font aussi l'objet de nombreuses recherches comparatives. L'étude de la langue archaïque est à l'honneur, et on ne compte pas le nombre des éditions critiques et révisées des textes anciens, entreprises par des lettrés célèbres comme Dai Zhen (1723–1777), Lu Wenzhao (1717–1795), Wang Niansun (1744–1832).

L'époque des Qing voit aussi le développement des études grammaticales, toujours dans une optique de retour aux sources. On peut ainsi citer: (i) le *Xuci shuo* "Traité des mots vides" (1710) de Yuan Renlin (dates exactes inconnues), qui développe le *Yuzhu* de Lu Yiwei; (ii) le *Zhuzi bianlue* "Analyse des particules" (1711) de Liu Qi (dates précises non connues), qui adopte une approche plutôt philologique que stylistique, à la différence de Yuan Renlin; le *Jingzhuan shici* "Explication des particules dans les classiques et dans les chroniques" (1798) de Wang Yinzhi (1766–1834), qu'on considère raisonnablement comme le premier essai systématique de classification et d'explication des particules pour bien comprendre les textes classiques.

Tous ces traités sont alors abondamment utilisés comme manuels dans la préparation des examens à différents niveaux. C'est aussi pour aider les candidats à la composition d'essais littéraires classiques que l'empereur Kangxi donne l'ordre en 1704 de compiler un nouvel ouvrage de référence, le *Peiwen yunfu* "Thésaurus arrangé selon les rimes", achevé et publié en 1711.

## 4. Conclusion

On l'aura compris, ce qui précède traite uniquement du savoir linguistique de l'élite, qui a toujours concerné, quelles que soient les époques, une infime minorité. Les écoles impériales ont toujours été réservées, en Chine, aux élèves parlant le mandarin et ayant déjà une très bonne connaissance du chinois classique. Et les examens, même les plus simples organisés au niveau local, théoriquement ouverts à tous, excluaient de fait plus de 90% de la population. Il est un autre savoir, le savoir populaire, pour lequel, dans la Chine ancienne et impériale, nous ne disposons d'aucun renseignement.

## 5. Bibliographie


Gong Qianyan. 1987. *Zhongguo yufaxue shigao* [Histoire de la linguistique chinoise.] Pékin: Yuwen chubanshe.

He Jiuying. 1985. *Zhongguo gudai yuyuanxue shi* [Histoire de la linguistique ancienne en Chine.] (= *Cidian yanjiu congkan* 7.) Henan: Henan renmin chubanshe.

Li Kai. 1993. *Hanyu yufa yanjiu shi* [Histoire des recherches sur la grammaire chinoise.] Nankin: Jiangsu jiaoyu chubanshe.

Lin Yushan. 1983. *Hanyu yufaxue shi* [Histoire de la grammaire du chinois.] Changsha: Hunan jiaoyu chubanshe.

Ma Jianzhong. 1898. *Ma shi wen tong* [Traité grammatical de Ma.] Réédition. Pekin: Zhonghua shuju, 1954.

Ma Songting. 1986. *Hanyu yufaxue shi* [Histoire de la grammaire de la langue chinoise.] Hefei: Anhui jiaoyu chubanshe.

Malmqvist, Göran. 1994. "Chinese Linguistics". *History of Linguistics* ed. by Giulio Lepschy. Harlow: Longman.

Pu Zhinzhen. 1990. *Zhongguo yuyanxue shi* [Histoire de la linguistique chinoise.] Taipei: Shulin chuban youxian gongsi.

Shao Jingmin. 1990. *Hanyu yufaxue shigao* [Histoire de la grammaire du chinois.] Shanghai: Jiaoyu chubanshe.

Wang Li. 1984. *Zhongguo yuyanxue shi* [Histoire de la linguistique en Chine.] Hong Kong: Joint Publishing Co.

Wang Lida. 1959. *Hanyu yanjiu xiao shi* [Petite histoire de la recherche sur le chinois.]. Shanghai: Shangwu yinshuguan.

Zheng Dian & Mai Meiqiao. 1964. *Gu hanyu yufaxue ziliao huibian* [Recueil de documents sur les études grammaticales sur le chinois ancien.] Pékin: Zhonghua shuju.


*Alain Peyraube, Paris (France)*

# 8. La tradition linguistique vietnamienne et ses contacts avec la tradition chinoise

1. La période chinoise
2. La lexicographie vietnamienne
3. L'écriture Nôm
4. La période moderne
5. Bibliographie

## 1. La période chinoise

La linguistique vietnamienne est devenue de nos jours une branche de la linguistique mondiale: les linguistes professionnels du Vietnam d'aujourd'hui sont pour la plupart formés en Occident. Ils sont en train de travailler sur une base commune avec leurs collègues étrangers, ayant les mêmes orientations théoriques, suivant les mêmes buts et adoptant les mêmes technologies.

Mais avant d'arriver à ce stade, la tradition linguistique vietnamienne a dû passer par trois étapes successives:

a) l'étape antérieure au contact avec le chinois
b) l'étape d'influence chinoise
c) l'étape d'influence française.

La première étape est encore très mal connue. Faute de recherches sérieuses sur les mythes, les prières rituelles, les interdits langagiers, les termes métalinguistiques indigènes, nous ne savons actuellement presque rien sur ce que pensaient les Proto-VietMuongs sur la nature et la fonction du langage en général, et sur leur propre langue, en particulier.

La deuxième étape est mieux documentée. C'est une étape extrêmement longue. Elle commence par dix siècles de domination chinoise, c'est-à-dire dix siècles de contact direct avec le chinois parlé (chinois archaïque, chinois moyen). Il nous reste de ces siècles, au point de vue linguistique, deux preuves sûres de l'influence chinoise: des couches successives d'emprunts de vocabulaire, et une lecture indigène des caractères chinois, appelée ordinairement 'lecture sinovietnamienne'. Cette lecture est liée à la dernière couche des emprunts (faits avant le X$^{e}$ siècle). Elle a pour source, dans l'ensemble, la pronunciation chinoise des VIII$^{e}$ et IX$^{e}$ siècles et c'est elle que les vietnamiens ont choisie pour la lecture de tous les textes écrits en caractères chinois, fussent-ils écrits par les chinois, les japonais, les coréens ou par les auteurs indigènes. Un peu plus tard cette lecture donnera, par suite de quelques évolutions ultérieures, encore une troisième lecture, celle appelée 'sinovietnamienne vietnamisée'. [Table 8.1]

La lecture sinovietnamienne se distingue non seulement par son origine, sa forme phonique et sa fonction dans la société. Sur le plan grammatical les morphosyllabèmes sinovietnamiens se distinguent aussi des anciens sinovietnamiens et des sinovietnamiens vietnamisés par leurs caractéristiques morphologiques et syntaxiques: ils n'ont plus, dans 75% de cas, le statut d'unités lexicales autonomes; ils jouent seulement le rôle de sémantèmes et de morphèmes dans des syntagmes figés, appelés ordinairement mots composés.

En dehors des couches d'emprunts et de la lecture sinovietnamienne ci-dessus citées, il est facile aussi pour les comparatistes, de voir encore une autre face de l'influence chinoise: les changements phonétiques survenus dans la langue indigène sous la pression du contact avec le chinois parlé. On voit, par exemple, la formation, avant le VI$^{e}$ siècle, d'un système

Tab. 8.1: Lectures sino-vietnamiennes

| | | ancien sino-vietnamien | sino-vietnamien | sino-vietnamien vietnamisé |
|---|---|---|---|---|
| "saison" | *wù* | *mùa* | *vụ* | |
| "chambre" | *fáng* | *buồng* | *phòng* | |
| "proche" | *jìn* | | *cận* | *gần* |
| "planche" | *păn* | | *bản* | *ván* |

de trois tonèmes, après la chute de *-ʔ, *-s, *-h; l'apparition des aspirées *ph*, *th*, *kh*; et le changement de *v- en *w-.

## 2. La lexicographie vietnamienne

Après la reconquête de l'indépendance politique au début du Xᵉ siècle, les vietnamiens continuaient de garder leur respect pour la culture chinoise, considérant le chinois comme leur langage officiel, organisant des écoles et des examens d'état d'après le modèle de leurs voisins du nord, et créant une riche littérature en *Wényán*. En même temps, la conscience nationale les poussa aussi, à partir du XIᵉ siècle, à la création d'une écriture et puis d'une littérature indigènes. Quelque temps après ils commencèrent à éditer des dictionnaires et des textes bilingues. Parmi les lexiques et dictionnaires bilingues on peut mentionner: *Thiên tự văn giải âm* (lexique chinois-nôm de 1000 caractères de date inconnue, publié en 1890); *Tam thiên tự giải âm* (lexique chinois-nôm de 3000 caractères, de date inconue, peut-être de Ngô Thời Nhậm, 1746–1803, publié en 1891); *Nhật dụng thường đàm* (dictionnaire des mots et expressions courants, de Phạm Đình Hổ, 1768–1839); *Chỉ nam ngọc âm giải nghiã* "Boussole de la langue de jade" (dictionaire chinois-nôm du XVIᵉ ou XVIIᵉ siècle, réédition de 1761); *Tự loại diễn nghiã* "Traduction des différentes catégories de caractères" (dictionnaire chinois-nôm, de date inconnue).

Il est à remarquer que le caractère syllabique, isolant du vietnamien et du chinois avait permis aux poètes indigènes non seulement d'appliquer les règles de métrique chinoise dans leur création littéraire en langue nationale: il leur avait permis également de publier de temps en temps des poèmes écrits en chinois classique, mais écrits d'après les règles de métrique vietnamienne. La composition des poèmes et des sentences parallèles suppose une connaissance plus ou moins profonde des notions de la tradition linguistique chinoise telles que la segmentation de la chaîne parlée en syllabes (vers de 7 syllabes; de 5 syllabes; de 6 et 8 syllabes; de 7, 7, 6, et 8 syllabes, etc.); l'opposition entre tons égaux et tons non égaux et parmi les tons égaux l'opposition entre le ton haut et le ton bas, etc.; la segmentation de la syllable en initiale et rime; les oppositions entre les divers types de rime, basées sur la longueur, le timbre des voyelles ou sur les différents éléments terminant les syllabes; et l'opposition entre mots pleins et mots vides.

Cependant, dans l'ensemble ce ne sont que des connaisances exclusivement pragmatiques. Les manuels de métrique, comme le *Thi thể thức, kinh nghiã thể thức* "Règles de poétique, règles de Jingyì" (de date inconnue, conservé dans une copie de 1888) nous le montrent clairement: l'enseignement de la phonétique au Vietnam n'avait presque jamais de caractère théorique. Les travaux classiques de la "science des sons et des finales" (*yinyn-xue*) n'étaient pas inconnus chez les érudits vietnamiens tels que Lê Quý Đôn (1726–1784). Cet auteur a même un chapitre consacré aux sons et aux caractères dans son œuvre encyclopédique *Vân đài loại ngữ* "Notes tirées des archives". Mais lui-même, il ne nous donne pas des théories ou des systèmes. Nous ne pouvons trouver dans son chapitre que plus d'une centaine de remarques très éparses, bien que parfois très profondes. Il parle, entre autres choses, sur l'écriture, sur la diversité des langues et écritures, sur l'importance des pictogrammes et des conglomérats sémantiques dans l'écriture chinoise, sur les caractères vulgaires créés dans différentes provinces chinoises, sur les caractères dont le sens était mal interprété. En ce qui regarde la prononciation il discute les prononciations dialectales, les mots vietnamiens mal transcrits par les chinois, les formes phoniques du mot "père" dans différentes régions, l'allongement de la particule finale *ạ* comme expression de respect, etc.

L'esprit pragmatique n'est pas un trait particulier de l'enseignement traditionnel des notions de phonétique. Nous pouvons encore le retrouver dans la lexicographie et lexicologie vietnamiennes. Dans le dictionnaire *Chỉ nam ngọc âm giải nghiã* (XVIIᵉ ou XVIᵉ siècle; cf. Stankevič 1981; Trần Xuân Ngọc Lan 1985), par exemple, bien qu'il soit précieux à plusieurs points de vue, il faut dire franchement que son auteur ne visa qu'un but purement pédagogique quand il le composa. Ceci est démontré par les points suivants. Le nombre des caractères donnés n'atteint qu'un chiffre très modeste dans le texte principal, à peu près 7000 unités; les caractères rares et difficiles sont tous donnés dans l'appendice. L'explication phonétique est très sommaire, l'auteur se contentant presque toujours d'expliquer par un homophone ou même par un quasi-homophone. Enfin, les définitions sont toutes versifiées pour que les lecteurs puissent facilement les apprendre par cœur:

*kim ô (jinwu): mặt trời sáng hồng thiềm luân (chánlún): nguyệt rạng trên không lâu làu*
"le soleil brillant, rougeâtre la lune qui luit dans le ciel, tout pur"

Il est à remarquer que l'on a versifié au Vietnam, suivant la même tradition, pour le même but, des livres entiers d'histoire, de géographie et tout récemment de longues listes de vocabulaire français et anglais, par exemple:

*bœuf: bò, sư tử: li on,*
*cheval: con ngựa, mouton: con cừu* [...].

## 3. L'écriture Nôm

L'intérêt accordé aux dictionnaires et la classification des caractères par ordre de matières montrent que la tradition linguistique vietnamienne était fortement influencée par celle des chinois. Pourtant les lexicographes indigènes avaient un esprit et un but tout différents. Il semble que dans le Vietnam d'antan tout venait de la pratique et que tout n'avait que d'utilité pratique.

La création du *Chữ Nôm* "écriture du sud, écriture du Vietnam" en est un autre exemple. Il s'agit d'une écriture du même type que celle des chinois. Elle était créée sur la base des éléments graphiques et des principes chinois, mais elle comporte aussi quelques particularités intéressantes (cf. Lê Văn Quán 1981; Nguyễn Quang Xỹ & Vũ Văn Kính 1971). Les principaux cas de l'écriture vietnamienne peuvent s'analyser de la manière suivante (Table 8.2: Ls: lecture sinovietnamienne; S: signifié; La: lecture plus ancienne; Lq: lecture quasihomophone).

Les cinq premiers cas sont des caractères pris du chinois: A, B servent à écrire les mots empruntés correspondants; C, D, E servent de transcriptions des mots indigènes. Les quatre derniers cas sont de création vietnamienne: dans F nous avons, à côté du caractère chinois, l'addition d'un petit signe annonçant aux lecteurs qu'il faut avoir une certaine modification dans la lecture; dans G, H, I nous avons des conglomérats de deux éléments chinois: deux éléments phonétiques servant à transcrire les groupes consonantiques vietnamiens dans le cas de G; deux éléments sémantiques dans le cas de H; un élément sémantique ajouté à un élément phonétique dans le cas de I.

Les caractères Nôm que nous avons actuellement ne furent pas inventés une fois pour tous. Ils sont les produits d'une création collective, englobant les apports de plusiers siècles et de plusiers régions. Enrichir le corpus des unités de l'écriture, chercher les enregistrements plus précis au point de vue phonétique et tâcher d'arriver à des caractères plus simples au point de vue graphique, voilà les principaux efforts des philologues vietnamiens de tous les temps et de tous les lieux, efforts qui étaient à l'origine de ces apports. Ayant parfaitement conscience de la distinction entre signifiant et signifié, tout comme des faits d'homonymie, ces philologues devaient aussi, dans leurs apports, s'adapter aux évolutions de la langue et s'adapter aux particularités des dialectes. Par suite de cet état de choses, l'écriture Nôm devient une riche source d'informations attirant l'attention de bon nombre de chercheurs: historiens, littérateurs, comparatistes, étymologues, dialectologues etc. Mais il en est né aussi un côté négatif: c'est une écriture extrêmement difficile à écrire, à lire, et à déchiffrer dans bien de cas litigeux.

## 4. La période moderne

Il est donc facile de comprendre pourquoi les missionnaires occidentaux venant au Vietnam au XVIIe siècle s'étaient vu obligés de créer une autre écriture, ce qu'on appelle aujourd'hui le *Quốc ngữ* dans leur apprentissage de la langue indigène et dans leurs travaux de propagande religieuse. Le premier dictionnaire alphabétique se servant de cette écriture latinisée fut publié en 1651, le dictionnaire d'A. de Rhodes. Mais l'œuvre des missionnaires restait longtemps dans l'ombre, ayant peu d'influence dans la société. Il faut attendre encore plus de deux siècles pour voir le triomphe complet de cette nouvelle écriture. C'est un triomphe acquis grâce au soutien d'une part du gouvernement colonial et de l'autre part des couches progressistes de la société vietnamienne.

Avec l'abolition graduelle de l'enseignement des caractères chinois et son remplacement par celui du français, la tradition vietnamienne entre dans la troisième étape de son histoire: l'étape de l'influence française. Le côté fort de l'ancien temps se maintient avec la publication d'un grand nombre de dictionnaires alphabétiques et de grande envergure: dictionnaires vietnamien-français (e.g., Bonet 1899–1900; Génibrel 1898), français-vietnamien, vietnamien-vietnamien (Huỳnh Tịnh Của 1895–1896), et aussi chi-

Tab. 8.2: Caractères Nôm

| Caractères Nôm | A | B | C | D | E | F | G | H | I |
|---|---|---|---|---|---|---|---|---|---|
| | 高 | 心 | 群 | 埃 | 柴 | 柴く | ⿰土弄 | 𡗶 | 種 |
| | Cao:haut /(Ls, S)/ | Tim:Cœur /(La, S)/ | Bầy:Troupe /( , S)/ | Ai:Qui? /(Ls, )/ | Thầy:Maître /(Lq, )/ | Thầy:Maître /(Lq)+(<)/ | *Klong > Trống:Tambour /(Lq)+(Lq)/ | Trời:Ciel /(S)+(S)/ | Chồng:Mari /(S)+(Lq)/ |

| Eléments chinois (Ls) | | (S) | |
|---|---|---|---|
| Cao | 高 | Haut | → A |
| Tâm | 心 | Cœur | → B |
| Quần | 群 | Troupe | → C |
| Ai | 埃 | Poussière | → D |
| Sài | 柴 | Brindille | → E |
| Sài | 柴く | Brindille | → F |
| Cổ | 古 | Ancien | → G |
| Lộng | 弄 | Jouer | → G |
| Thiên | 天 | Ciel | → H |
| Thượng | 上 | Dessus | → H |
| Phu | 夫 | Mari | → I |
| Trùng | 重 | Double | → I |

nois-vietnamien, anglais-vietnamien etc. Le point faible hérité de l'ancienne tradition chinoise – l'absence de la grammaire – se voit corrigé. Mais malheureusement, ce n'était pas un très grand bond en avant: les notions grammaticales enseignées au Vietnam avant 1945 n'étaient que des notions normatives présentées dans des manuels de lycées. La professionalisation, la modernisation et l'internationalisation de la linguistique vietnamienne, c'est l'affaire de ces quelques dernières décennies.

Il semble qu'il y déjà maintenant un certain retour aux notions traditionnelles de l'école chinoise. Poussés par leur intuition naturelle, car ils parlent tous une langue syllabique et isolante, quelques linguistes professionnels du Vietnam d'aujourd'hui commencent à réfléchir et à faire des recherches sur les caractéristiques typologiques de leur langue. Voyant qu'il y a des notions de linguistique générale qui s'étaient, en réalité, élaborées sur la base des faits indo-européens, et qui, par suite, ne concordent pas complètement avec leur langue, ils commencent à en faire des critiques sérieuses, par exemple celles de Cao Xuân Hạo (1985), de Nguyễn Quang Hồng (1994) sur l'application de la notion de phonème et celles de Nguyễn Tài Cẩn (1975, 1979, 1995; Nguyễn Tài Cẩn & Stankevitch 1985) sur l'application de la notion de mot. Dans l'analyse de la structure d'une langue comme le vietnamien, au dire de ces auteurs, une importance capitale doit être réservée au syllabème sur le plan phonologique, et au morphosyllabème, sur le plan grammatical.

## 5. Bibliographie


Bonet, J. 1899–1900. *Dictionnaire annamite-français (langue officielle et langue vulgaire)*. Paris.

Cao Xuân Hạo. 1985. *Phonologie et linéarité: Réflexions critiques sur les postulats de la phonologie contemporaine.* (= *Bulletin de la Société d'Etudes Linguistiques et Anthropologiques de France*, 18.) Paris.

Génibrel, J. F. M. 1898. *Dictionnaire annamite-français.* Saigon.

Huỳnh Tịnh Của. 1895–96. *Đại Nam quốc âm tự vị* [Dictionnaire de la langue vietnamienne.] Saigon.

Lê Qúy Đôn. 1962. *Vân đài loại ngữ* [Notes tirées des archives.] Hanoi: Văn hóa & Viện Văn học.

Lê Văn Quán. 1981. *Nghiên cứu về Chữ Nôm* [Recherches sur le Chữ Nôm.] Hanoi: Khoa học xã hội.

Nguyễn Quang Hồng. 1994. *Âm tiết và loại hình ngôn ngữ* [Syllabe et types de langues.] Hanoi: Khoa học xã hội.

Nguyễn Quang Xỹ & Vũ Văn Kính. 1971. *Tự điển Chữ Nôm* [Dictionnaire des caractères Nôm.] Saigon.

Nguyễn Tài Cẩn. 1975. *Ngữ pháp tiếng Việt* [Grammaire vietnamienne.] Hanoi: Đại học.

–. –. 1979. *Nguồn gốc và quá trình hình thành cách đọc Hán Việt* [Origine et évolution de la prononciation sinovietnamienne.] Hanoi: Khoa học xã hội.

–. –. 1995. *Giáo trình lịch sử ngữ âm tiếng Việt* [Cours de phonétique historique de la langue vietnamienne.] Hanoi: Giáo dục.

–. – & Nonna V. Stankevič. 1985. *Một số vấn đề về Chữ Nôm* [Quelques problèmes du Chữ Nôm.] Hanoi: Đại học.

Rhodes, A. de. 1991. *Từ điển Annam-Lusitan-Latinh.* Réédition du *Dictionarium* (1651) avec traduction de Thanh Lãng, Hoàng Xuãn Việt, Đỗ Quang Chính. Ho Chi Minh Ville: Khoa học xã hội & Viện Khoa học xã hội tại T. P. Hồ Chí Minh.

Stankevič, Nonna V. 1981. "*Chỉ nam ngọc âm giải nghĩa*: Pamjatnik drevnej vjetnamskoj leksikografii" [Un monument de la lexicographie vietnamienne ancienne.] *Istorija lingvističeskix učenij: Srednevekovyj Vostok* ed. by Agnija V. Desnickaja & Solomon D. Kacnel'son, 248–257. Léningrad: Nauka.

–. –. 1994. *Les interférences grammaticales entre le chinois et le vietnamien. Conférence dédiée à la mémoire de Georg von der Gabelentz.* Saint Péterbourg. [En russe.]

Schneider, P. 1992. *Dictionnaire historique des idéogrammes vietnamiens.* Nice: RIASEM.

Taberd, A. J. L. 1838. *Dictionarium Annamitico-Latinum.* Serampore.

Trần Xuân Ngọc Lan. 1985. *Chỉ nam ngọc âm, phiên âm và chú giải* [Le dictionnaire Chỉ nam ngọc âm, lecture et notes.] Hanoi: Khoa học xã hội.


*Nonna V. Stankevič, Saint Péterbourg (Russie)*

# III. The Establishment of the Korean Linguistic Tradition
# Die Anfänge der koreanischen Sprachforschung
# La constitution de la tradition linguistique coréenne

## 9. Die traditionelle Sprachforschung in Korea


1. Einleitung
2. Die Rahmenbedingungen der traditionellen koreanischen Sprachwissenschaft
3. Textsorten, Schriften, Sprachen
4. Schlussbemerkung
5. Bibliographie


### 1. Einleitung

"Die Laute der Sprache unseres Landes unterscheiden sich von denjenigen Chinas und können nicht mit [chinesischen] Schriftzeichen wiedergegeben werden, sodaß das einfache Volk sich nicht [schriftlich] artikulieren kann, auch wenn es dies tun möchte. Dies dauerte mich, und daher habe ich 28 Schriftzeichen neu geschaffen in dem Wunsche, daß jedermann sie leicht erlernen und bequem benutzen solle."

Dies ist der erste, leitmotivisch einleitende Satz aus der Präambel des 1446 veröffentlichten *Hunmin-chŏngŭm* "Das Volk die korrekten Lautungen lehren", die von König Sejong (r. 1418–1450) eigenhändig verfaßt wurde. Mit dieser Palastveröffentlichung wurde dem ganzen Volke und seinen Gelehrten die im chinesisch geprägten Kulturraum in einzigartiger Weise herausragende koreanische Buchstabenschrift bekannt gemacht, die in Silbenkomplexen geschrieben die koreanische Sprache mit einem phonetischen Alphabet wiedergibt.

In diesem Satz leuchten die wesentlichen Grundzüge auf, die die traditionelle koreanische Sprachwissenschaft mit vielen anderen Kulturentwicklungen in Korea teilt. Die vormoderne koreanische Sprachwissenschaft ging wie viele andere Bereiche der koreanischen Kultur auch den Weg von der Kopie des chinesischen Vorbildes (Imitation) über die Anpassung der hierbei gelernten Kulturtechniken und ihrer Prinzipien an koreanische Verhältnisse (Adaption) zur eigenständigen Entwicklung (Innovation). Der folgende Artikel konzentriert sich auf diesem Hintergrund daher auf die Entwicklung der traditionellen Sprachwissenschaft in Bezug auf die koreanische Sprache und vernachlässigt die rein sinologisch-philologische Forschung in Korea, da diese stets den inhaltlichen und methodischen Trends und Moden der Entwicklung in China parallel lief.

Ein weiterer die gesamte Geschichte bis in die Moderne durchziehender Faktor war, daß die Sprachwissenschaft keine eigenständige Wissenschaft war, sondern Nebenprodukt einer allgemeinen Gelehrsamkeit, die immer in enger Verknüpfung mit Politik und Verwaltungspraxis stand. Erst seit vor ca. 100 Jahren die allgemeine Gelehrsamkeit zugunsten moderner Einzelwissenschaften zurückgedrängt wurde, konnte sich die Sprachwissenschaft (zunächst in enger Verzahnung mit der Literaturwissenschaft) als eigenständige Wissenschaft etablieren. Dabei durchlief sie erneut eine ganz ähnliche Entwicklung wie die traditionelle Sprachwissenschaft, wobei das Vorbild diesmal nicht in der chinesischen Gelehrsamkeit sondern in der europäisch-amerikanischen Sprachwissenschaft gesehen wurde.

### 2. Die Rahmenbedingungen der traditionellen koreanischen Sprachwissenschaft

Die koreanische Kultur und damit die Sprachwissenschaft entwickelten sich im Spannungsfeld zwischen der – auch so ausgesprochenen – Absicht, 'Klein-China' zu werden, und der Unmöglichkeit, diese Absicht zu verwirklichen, da die kulturellen Vorgaben dieses in mehreren Wellen aus den unwirtlichen Gegenden nördlich von China eingewanderten altaischen Volkes hiermit nicht in Einklang zu bringen waren. Zu den kulturellen Widerständen gegen diese Absicht gehörte – im hiesigen Zusammenhang naturgemäß besonders gravierend –, daß das Koreanische im Gegensatz zum stark isolierenden Chinesischen eine agglutinierende Sprache ist, die neben einer extrem formenreichen und zu vielgliedrigen Endungsketten neigenden Morphologie der Verben und Nomina auch eine abweichende Syntax besitzt.

Aus dieser Tatsache ergab sich auch die wesentlichste Rahmenbedingung der Entwicklung der traditionellen koreanischen Sprachwissenschaft, die koreanisch-chinesische Zweisprachigkeit der Gelehrten. Diejenigen, die das Privileg einer Ausbildung zur Gelehrsamkeit genießen konnten, sei es als Angehörige finanziell und durch Status bevorzugter Kreise der Bevölkerung, sei es als Mitglieder einer kleinen Berufsgruppe von finanziell abhängigen Spezialisten, zu denen auch quasi-beamtete Schreiber in Amtsstuben und Übersetzer für verschiedene ostasiatische Sprachen gehörten, benutzten bis zum Ende des 19. Jh. überwiegend Chinesisch als Schriftsprache. Während hierbei aber zwar als Syntax fast unverändert die Syntax chinesischer Klassiker und Verwaltungsschriften beibehalten wurde, unterlag die Aussprache der Schriftzeichen in China einer ständigen Veränderung, die in Korea nur selten nachvollzogen wurde, und in Korea wurde sie obendrein dem koreanischen Lautsystem angepasst. Dieses 'Chinesisch' der zweisprachigen Gelehrten muss daher eigentlich als 'Korea-Chinesisch' oder 'Sino-Koreanisch' angesehen werden.

Auf dem Hintergrund dieser Zweisprachigkeit, die auch einen Gegensatz zwischen mündlicher und schriftlicher Kommunikation bedeutete, wird auch der Schwerpunkt der koreanischen traditionellen Sprachwissenschaft verständlich: eine starke Anwendungsbezogenheit und wenig Interesse an sprachtheoretischen und sprachphilosophischen Erörterungen. Im Zentrum standen, wie im folgenden dargestellt wird, ein ständiges Verfeinern der Lehrmittel zum Erlernen des Chinesischen, denen ein Hang zur Normativität anhaftete, und die pädagogisch-exegetische Analyse chinesischer philosophischer, politischer und historiographischer Texte sowie schöngeistiger Literatur, wobei in den Veröffentlichungen ein enzyklopädisches Zusammentragen sprachlicher Parallelbeispiele gegenüber einer zergliedernden Analyse vorgezogen wurde. Daneben entstand die Verschriftung des Koreanischen in amtlichen Vorgängen und Urkunden in einem stark mit chinesischen Fremdwörtern und Floskeln durchsetzten Koreanisch gleichsam 'natürlich' und theoretisch nicht untermauert aus der täglichen Verwaltungspraxis. Unter der Oberfläche der überlieferten Quellen verbirgt sich aber eine ausgeprägte und nur nicht weiter explizierte analytische sprachwissenschaftliche Forschungstätigkeit.

## 3. Textsorten, Schriften, Sprachen

Aus der voranstehenden allgemeinen Charakteristik ergibt sich, daß eine Beschreibung der traditionellen koreanischen Sprachwissenschaft nur eine Beschreibung der aus den verschiedenen Textsorten implizit erkennbaren Vorstellungen über Sprache sein kann. Diese Vorstellungen betreffen vor allem solche, die wir heute der Grammatik im engeren Sinne (Morphologie und Syntax) zuordnen würden, solche zur Phonologie und seltener solche der Etymologie und auch der Semantik.

Vor allem aber die Art der Verschriftung koreanischer Wörter und Phrasen in chinesisch-koreanischen Hybridtexten und die implizite Systematik der Anmerkungen in Ausgaben chinesischer Texte kann dem modernen Betrachter Hinweise darauf geben, wie die Koreaner Sprache analysiert haben, auch wenn die Analysemethoden und Begriffe nirgends explizit – etwa wie in einem modernen Lehrbuch der Sprachwissenschaft – beschrieben wurden. Dabei muß aufgrund der erwähnten Zweisprachigkeit eine Einteilung der Texte, die in Korea geschrieben wurden, zunächst einmal auch daran vorgenommen werden, in welcher Sprache sie (überwiegend) geschrieben wurden, d. h. Texte in Chinesisch, die den überwältigenden Teil der in Korea verfaßten Texte ausmachen, müssen von chinesisch-koreanischen Hybridtexten unterschieden werden, und diese wiederum müssen getrennt von solchen in koreanischer Sprache betrachtet werden.

Die verschiedenen entweder aus China übernommenen oder in Korea entwickelten Schriftsysteme sind als weiteres textsortenunterscheidendes Kriterien anzusehen, wobei im letzteren Falle auch noch danach zu trennen ist, ob das jeweilige in Korea entwickelte Schriftsystem auf der Basis der chinesischen Schriftzeichen entstand, oder ob es sich, wie im Falle der koreanischen Buchstabenschrift, um eine eigenständige Erfindung handelt.

Ein grober Überblick kann etwa wie folgt aussehen

I Texte in Chinesisch (ab 5. Jh.)

II chinesisch-koreanische Hybridtexte

IIa Schreibung koreanischer *nomina propria* in chinesischen Texten (ab 5. Jh.)

IIb koreanischsprachige Anmerkungen zur pädagogischen Aufbereitung chinesischer Texte (ab 9. Jh.)

IIb1 *Kugyŏl*, koreanischsprachige Lesehilfen neben den Zeilen in chinesischen Texten (ab 9. Jh.)

IIb2 *Ŏnhae*, koreanischsprachige Anmerkungen, chinesische Texte unterbrechend (in koreanischen Schriftzeichen) (ab 15. Jh.)

III Texte in Koreanisch

IIIa Die Beamtenschrift *Idu* (in chinesischen Schriftzeichen) (ab 10. Jh.)

IIIb Das koreanische Alphabet *Hunminchŏngŭm* (heute *Han'gŭl, Uri k'ŭl*) (1446)

IIIc Lehrbücher für Fremdsprachen

I Texte in Chinesisch (ab 5. Jh.)

Chinesische Texte, oder wie oben ausgeführt: 'sino-koreanische' Texte, stellen den bei weitem größten Teil der Schriftzeugnisse aus der traditionellen koreanischen Kultur. Aus Sicht der Geschichte der Sprachwissenschaften in Korea ist diese Tatsache aber wenig aufschlußreich, wenn man die evidente und banale Aussage außer Acht läßt, daß die zweisprachigen Gelehrten in dem Bewußtsein gelebt haben, daß es nicht nur eine Sprache gibt, und daß ihnen natürlich der völlig verschiedene Charakter der beiden Sprachen – isolierend vs. agglutinierend – aufgefallen sein muß. Eventuell liegt in dieser Erfahrung aber auch der Grund für ein frühes Entdekken der Funktion von Morphemen, das schon in den ganz anfänglichen Versuchen, mittels chinesischer Schriftzeichen koreanische Texte zu schreiben – *Kugyŏl* und *Idu*, s. u. –, deutlich wird.

II Chinesisch-koreanische Hybridtexte

Diese Gruppe von Textsorten ist für die Rekonstruktion der Entwicklung der traditionellen koreanischen Sprachwissenschaft die Aufschlußreichste. Zum einen sind Interferenzprobleme zu beobachten, die sich aus dem jeweils anderen Sprachbau ableiten, noch wichtiger aber ist, daß in diesen Hybridtexten der chinesische und der koreanische Textteil meist redundant aufeinander bezogen sind, sodaß man mit Vergleichstexten in zwei Sprachen arbeiten kann, d. h. der Untersuchende kann zur Lösung von Verständnisproblemen und zur Klärung verborgener sprachwissenschaftlicher Konzepte und Vorstellungen bei dem Textteil in der einen Sprache den in der jeweils anderen Sprache als Vergleichstext heranziehen.

IIa Koreanische *nomina propria* in chinesischen Texten (in chinesischen Schriftzeichen) (ab 5. Jh.)

Schon in den ältesten historiographischen und geographischen Texten, Stelen, u. ä. in China entlehnten die Schreiber unter Nichtbeachten der Bedeutung der Zeichen die Lautung einzelner Schriftzeichen, um die Silben von *nomina propria* (Ortsnamen, Personennamen, Titel) aus nichtchinesischen Sprachen darzustellen. Diese Praxis müssen koreanische Schreiber schon um 108 v. Chr. kennengelernt haben, als das chinesische Han-Reich im Norden der koreanischen Halbinsel Chaohsien (heutige koreanische Aussprache *Chosŏn*) unterwarf und eine Militärverwaltung errichtete. Die älteste erhaltene nachweislich von Koreanern in chinesischer Sprache verfaßte Steinstele (Grabstele des *Koguryŏ*-Königs Kwanggaet'o), in der diese Praxis zu finden ist, datiert allerdings erst 414 n. Chr. Immerhin kann festgehalten werden, daß die Arbitrarität von Schriftzeichen, die eine Trennung von Lautung und Bedeutung eines Zeichens und damit ihre (Teil-)Entlehnung zur Darstellung nichtchinesischer Lautkomplexe ermöglicht, den Koreanern schon in dem Moment bekannt wurde, als sie überhaupt die Kulturtechnik des Schreibens (mit chinesischen Schriftzeichen) kennenlernten.

Während zunächst fast ausschließlich die Lautungen entlehnt wurden, um die Silben koreanischer *nomina propria* phonetisch zu schreiben, kam es 757 im Zuge einer Verwaltungsreform bei den Orts- und Flurnamen zu einer umfassenden Entlehnung der Bedeutungen. Die bis dahin gelegentlich zwei-, meist aber drei- oder viergliedrigen, phonetisch geschriebenen Ortsnamen wurden nach chinesischem Vorbild zu zweigliedrigen scheinbar chinesischen Ortsnamen verändert, wobei oft auf die ursprüngliche koreanische Bedeutung rekurriert wurde: die koreanischen Ortsnamen wurden zumeist ganz oder teilweise bei der Neuverschriftung 'übersetzt'. So wurde z. B. **yasi-mai* "Wolf(?)-Fluss", "Wiesel(?)-Fluss", ursprünglich **ya-si-mai* geschrieben, und zwar mit den drei Schriftzeichen **ya* [Satzschluss-Partikel], **si* "Leichnam" und **mai* "kaufen", die Schreibung des Namens ab 757 aber geändert in zwei Zeichen, deren Bedeutung "Wiesel-Fluss" ergibt. Die sino-koreanische Lautung dieser beiden Zeichen hätte **siäng-tsän* ergeben, setzt man aber die chinesischen Zeichen **ya* + **si* "[Satzschluss-Partikel] + Leichnam" gleich altkoreanisch **yasi* "Wiesel" und chinesisch **mai* "kaufen" mit altkoreanisch **mai* "Fluss", dann wird deutlich, dass der gleiche Name lediglich von einer lautwertigen Schreibung in eine bedeutungswertige Schreibung umgewandelt wurde. Diese von nun an zweigliedrigen Ortsnamen waren aber zunächst auf den Schriftverkehr beschränkt, in der mündlichen Kommunikation wurden weiterhin die ursprünglichen koreanischen Namen 'gelesen', sodaß man sagen kann, die Schreibung durch Lautentlehnung wurde ersetzt durch Bedeutungsentlehnung. Diese Tatsache scheint sich, sicherlich mit zunehmender Verbreitung der chinesischen Bildung mündlich-schriftliche Interferenzen bildend und dadurch immer mehr abnehmend, bis gegen Ende des letzten Jahrhunderts gehalten zu haben, da diese ursprünglichen koreanischen Namen der heutigen Seniorengeneration noch immer geläufig sind.

Ausführliche Listen, in denen unter geographischer Angabe der in lautwertig zu lesenden Zeichen geschriebene 'alte' Ortsname und der in bedeutungswertig zu lesenden Zeichen geschriebene 'neue' (tatsächlich aber identische) Ortsname gegenübergestellt sind, stehen erstmals im *Samguk-sagi* "Aufzeichnungen des Historiographen zu den Drei Reichen [des Alten Korea bis 935]" aus dem Jahre 1145.

Auch im ältesten erhaltenen Kompendium koreanischer Heilpflanzen (*Hyangyak-kukŭppang*, um 1250 n. Chr.) wurden die chinesischen Zeichen promiskue mal lautentlehnend, mal bedeutungsentlehnend (teils auch als Rebus) eingesetzt.

### IIb Koreanischsprachige Anmerkungen zur pädagogischen Aufbereitung chinesischer Texte (ab 9. Jh.)

Aus zwei Gründen ergab sich in Korea die Notwendigkeit, Texte chinesischer Gelehrter mit Anmerkungen und Lesehilfen zu versehen. Zum einen brauchte man Lehrmaterial, das der Jugend ermöglichte, Chinesisch zu lernen, und das auch dem weniger Gebildeten den Zugang zu den als wesentlich angesehenen Schriften und Werken der chinesischen Kultur ermöglichte. Ein weiterer Grund ergab sich aus der Exegese, da bei schwierigen und mehrdeutigen Passagen klassischer chinesischer Texte durch grammatikbezogene Lesehilfen und Anmerkungen zur Bedeutung chinesischer Komposita bzw. Übersetzungen von Phrasen eine von einer bestimmten konfuzianischen oder buddhistischen Schule erwünschte Auslegung festgelegt und an die Anhänger weitergegeben werden konnte. Als Anmerkungen, die sich auf die Grammatik beziehen, wurden allerdings keine sprachwissenschaftlichen Erklärungen geliefert und lediglich koreanische grammatische Endungen angegeben, man kann nun aber die jeweiligen sprachwissenschaftlichen Vorstellungen und Konzepte rekonstruieren, die diesen Angaben zugrundeliegen, auch wenn nirgends eine dazugehörige Terminologie überliefert ist.

#### IIb1 *Kugyŏl*, koreanischsprachige Lesehilfen neben den Zeilen in chinesischen Texten (ab 9. Jh.)

Eine Möglichkeit, chinesische Texte im Original unangetastet zu lassen und doch Lesehilfen bereitzustellen, bestand darin, zwischen – bei der vertikalen Zeilenrichtung genauer: neben – den Zeilen die Kasusmorpheme, qualifizierenden Nominalpostpositionen ("nur", "bis hin zu", u. ä.) und Verbalendungsketten anzugeben, die die koreanische Sprache neben der syntaktischen Umordnung bei einer Übersetzung erfordert. *Kugyŏl* ist eigentlich ein chinesischer Ausdruck mit der Bedeutung "mündlich weitergegebenes Geheimnis, magische oder esoterische Formel" (*k'ou-chüeh*), hat aber im Koreanischen, ebenso wie seine Übertragung ins Koreanische *ipkyŏt*, die Bedeutung "grammatische Partikel oder Endungskette" angenommen und wird heute auch zur Bezeichnung des Schriftsystems, in dem diese geschrieben wurde, gebraucht.

Bei diesen Lesehilfen wurden alle Arten chinesischer Nominal- und Verbalphrasen wie Nominalkomposita gelesen. Stand im chinesischen Text eine Nominalphrase, wurde ein Kasusmorphem oder eine andere Nominalpostposition angegeben, bei Phrasen und Sätzen mit Nominalprädikat eine Kopula mit angefügter verbaler Neben- oder Hauptsatzendung. Handelte es sich im Chinesischen aber um eine Verbalphrase, dann wurde als denominale Verbalableitung ein Hilfsverb angefügt, das als prozessives Vollverb "tun, machen" und als qualitatives Verb dem Hilfsverb "sein" (vgl. "schön sein", "blau sein", usw.) entspricht, d. h. alle chinesischen Verbalphrasen wurden wie Nominalkomposita mittels eines angehängten Hilfsverbs in koreanische Verbalphrasen 'umgewandelt' und dadurch in die koreanische Syntax gebracht (Prädikat am Satzende). Ein dieserart entstehender Hybridtext soll im folgenden dergestalt verdeutlicht werden, dass die Übersetzung eines chinesischen Textes (hier in Majuskeln) das chinesische Original darstellen soll, in welches in kursiven Minuskeln die Entsprechungen der koreanischen Lesehilfen eingefügt sind:

EIN EHEPAAR *was dies anbetrifft* IST DIE VERBINDUNG ZWEIER FAMILIENNAMEN *ist.* HIER LIEGT DER URSPRUNG DES ENTSTEHENS EINES VOLKES *ist und* UND DER QUELL ZEHNTAUSENDFACHEN GLÜCKES *ist.* ES FINDET EINE GEGENSEITIGE VORSTELLUNG STATT UND DIE MITGIFT WIRD BESPROCHEN *tut man und* GESCHENKE WERDEN ÜBERGEBEN UND BESUCHE AUSGETAUSCHT *was dies anbetrifft* UND DAS IST EINE BETONUNG DES VERSCHIEDENSEINS *ist.* DAHER *daher* WENN MAN EINE GEMAHLIN WÄHLT *wenn man dies tut* WÄHLT MAN KEINE AUS DES GLEICHEN FAMILIENNAMENS *tut man und* UND WENN MAN EINE FAMILIE GRÜNDET *wenn man dies tut* HÄLT MAN DIE INNEREN UND DIE ÄUSSEREN ANGELEGENHEITEN AUSEINENANDER *tut man und* UND DER MANN *was diesen anbetrifft* LEBT IN DER AUSSENWELT UND REDET IN INNEREN ANGELEGENHEITEN NICHT DAZWISCHEN *tut er und* UND DIE EHEFRAU *was diese anbetrifft* LEBT IM INNEREN UND REDET IN ÄUSSEREN ANGELEGENHEITEN NICHT DAZWISCHEN tut sie. (Nach dem *Tongmong-sŏnsŭp*, "Erste Übungen für Kinder und Ungebildete", einem Lehrbuch für fünf-, sechsjährige Kinder und Ältere, o. J.)

Das verwendete Schriftsystem bildete ein geschlossenes Paradigma chinesischer Schriftzeichen, die entweder lautwertig oder bedeutungswertig entlehnt wurden, wobei die Auswahl der verwendeten Zeichen den Einfluß der Usancen, die in China zur Übertragung buddhistischer Namen und Termini aus dem Sanskrit entwickelt worden waren, überdeutlich macht. Da vom 7. bis 14. Jh. der Buddhismus offizielle Staatsreligion in Korea war, ist dieser Einfluss auch naheliegend. Schon im 10. Jh. wurden diese *Kugyŏl*-Zeichen nicht als Vollzeichen geschrieben sondern auf eine minimale Strichanzahl gekürzt, die oft auch als Ligaturen geschrieben wurden.

An diesen meist nachträglich handschriftlich angebrachten Angaben zur Grammatik der koreanischen Übersetzung wird ein hohes Analyseniveau und genaue Kenntnis der Syntax des Chinesischen und des Koreanischen und der Morphologie des Koreanischen deutlich, und es stellte sich von Anfang an eine starke Standardisierung ein. Daß diesen Lesehilfen eine genaue Analyse der Grammatik zugrundeliegt, kann z. B. daran ermessen werden, daß die im Koreanischen gleichlautenden Endungen des Nominativ und der Kopula "sein" nicht phonetisch mit dem gleichen Schriftzeichen geschrieben wurden sondern funktional getrennt mit verschiedenen Zeichen, wobei die Kopula auf die bedeutungswertige Entlehnung der chinesischen Kopula zurückgeht und das Zeichen für den Nominativ eine lautwertige Entlehnung ist.

IIb2 *Ŏnhae*, koreanischsprachige Anmerkungen zu chinesischen Texten (in koreanischen Schriftzeichen) (ab Mitte des 15. Jh.)

Nachdem 1446 das koreanische Alphabet vom Hof offiziell verkündet worden war (s. u.), wurden buddhistische und konfuzianische Schriften und auch Klassiker der chinesischen Dichtung in *Ŏnhae*-Ausgaben, "[Ausgaben mit] Erläuterungen in gewöhnlicher, gemeiner Sprache", herausgegeben. In diesen Ausgaben wurde der chinesische Originaltext an geeigneter Stelle – phrasen-, satz- oder absatzweise – von Anmerkungen in gegenüber dem Haupttext kleineren Schriftzeichen unterbrochen, gefolgt von einer Übersetzung ins Koreanische. Es handelt sich also um zweisprachige Ausgaben, Chinesisch in chinesischen Schriftzeichen und Koreanisch in koreanischen Schriftzeichen, mit grammatischen und semantischen Anmerkungen zum chinesischen Text.

Die Anmerkungen waren sehr umfangreich und verraten ein ausgeprägtes grammatisches Analysevermögen.

Zunächst wurde jedes einzelne chinesische Schriftzeichen mit sog. *saegim* "Einprägfloskeln" in Koreanisch vorgestellt, die aus einem semantischen Hinweis (eins-zu-eins Wortübersetzung des Wortfeldzentrums) und der sino-koreanischen Aussprache des Zeichens bestanden. Diese *saegim* waren nach standardisierten Formeln gebildet, je nachdem, ob es sich um die Wortarten Nomina, Verben, Adverben oder chinesische grammatische Hilfswörter handelt, wobei bei den letzteren noch die satzterminierenden Hilfswörter gesondert gekennzeichnet waren. Bestand der annotierte Textteil im chinesischen Original aus seinerseits noch weiter analysierbaren Phrasen, wurden diese in den Anmerkungen ebenfalls getrennt analysiert und ins Koreanische übertragen.

Seit dem 16. Jh. existieren auch Lehrbücher zu anderen Sprachen (Japanisch, Mandschurisch, Mongolisch), die sich der gleichen Art grammatischer Analyse bedienen, ohne daß der theoretische Rahmen für wichtig genug für eine Erörterung angesehen worden wäre (s. 3.3.).

III Koreanische Texte

Zu den ersten Versuchen, nicht nur einzelne Namen sondern ganze Texte in koreanischer Sprache zu schreiben, zählt die Gelöbnisinschrift in Stein aus dem Jahre 552 oder 612, in der zwei Mönche chinesische Zeichen in koreanischer Syntax anordneten, ohne die im koreanischen notwendigen Nominal- und Verbalendungen zu kennzeichnen. Nur eine Inschrift ist überliefert, und so muß offen bleiben, ob diese unvollkommene Art der Entlehnung chinesischer Zeichen zur schriftlichen Fixierung der koreanischen Sprache weiter verbreitet war.

IIIa Texte in *Idu* (in chinesischen Schriftzeichen) (ab 10. Jh.)

Etwa gleichzeitig mit den *Kugyŏl*-Annotationen entstand die "Beamtenschrift" *Idu*, ein Schriftsystem für Verwaltungstexte ganz in koreanischer Sprache, wenn auch durchsetzt mit sino-koreanischen fremdsprachlichen Floskeln als Terminologie des Rechtswesens. Es wurde bis in das 19. Jh. vor allem von Beamten im offiziellen Schriftverkehr benutzt und diese Textsorte besitzt daher eine starke Neigung zur juristischen und administrativen Floskelhaftigkeit. Wie bei *Kugyŏl* wurden chinesische Zeichen teils bedeutungswertig und teils lautwertig entlehnt, wobei anders als in den *Kugyŏl*-Annotationen keine abgekürzten Zeichen verwendet wurden. Auch in der *Idu*-Schreibung wird deutlich, daß, vor allem im sehr umfangreichen Paradigma der Verbalendungsketten, nicht nur phonetisch geschrieben wurde. Einige Morpheme wurden unabhängig von morpho-phonematischen Veränderungen an den Silbenfugen einheitlich funktional geschrieben, sodaß eine vorangegangene grammatische Analyse offensichtlich ist.

Koreanische Wissenschaftler weisen meist unter der Bezeichnung *Hyangch'al* "Schrift der einheimischen [Gedichte]" ein weiteres Schriftsystem getrennt aus, mit dem in zwei Quellen (10. Jh. und 13. Jh.) 25 Gedichte und Liedtexte in koreanischer Sprache überliefert sind. *Idu* und *Hyangch'al* folgen aber in den Prinzipien der Entlehnung und des Gebrauchs chinesischer Zeichen und im rekonstruierbaren Grammatikverständnis den gleichen Prinzipien und unterscheiden sich lediglich darin, daß es sich einmal um Verwaltungsprosa und einmal um Gedichte handelt.

Wie oben ausgeführt, wurden bei den *Kugyŏl*-Annotationen nur grammatische Formantien angegeben, während beim *Idu* auch die Wortstämme geschrieben wurden. Interessant für die Darstellung der Entwicklung koreanischer Sprachwissenschaft ist, daß offenbar Wortstämme und Endungen als andersartig erkannt worden sind. Erstere wurden überwiegend mit bedeutungswertig entlehnten Zeichen geschrieben, während bei den letzteren lautwertig entlehnte Zeichen den weitaus größeren Anteil ausmachen. Da inzwischen auch schon viele chinesische Wörter ins Koreanische als Lehnwörter eingedrungen waren, wurde außerdem gelegentlich durch Anfügen eines phonetisch zu lesenden Zeichens für den Auslautkonsonanten gekennzeichnet, daß das koreanische Wort und nicht das Fremd- oder Lehnwort zu lesen sei.

IIIb *Hunmin-chŏngŭm* (heute: *Han'gŭl*, *Uri k'ŭl*) (1446)

Sinologische Bildung war in Korea bis zum Ende des 19. Jh. die wichtigste Vorbedingung für die Aufnahme in den Staatsdienst, und wichtige Politiker und Staatsmänner waren stets auch hervorragende Gelehrte. Da es seit der Mitte des ersten Jahrtausends n. Chr. eine Staatsprüfung gab, die diese Vorbedingung testete, bestand seit alters her die Notwendigkeit, die Aussprache der chinesischen Zeichen zu standardisieren. Diese waren ja in einem ungesteuerten Prozess aus verschiedenen chinesischen Dialekten und zu verschiedenen Zeiten in das koreanische Gelehrtenchinesisch übernommen worden und unterlagen dann zusätzlich ebenso ungesteuert Veränderungen, die sich aus den phonologischen Systemen der koreanischen Dialekte ergaben, sodaß zu vielen Zeichen Aussprachevarianten in Gebrauch waren.

Im 15. Jh. wurden mehrere Versuche unternommen, die sino-koreanischen Lautungen auf der Basis der in China gültigen Standardlexika für Reime zu ordnen und verbindlich festzulegen. Diese Versuche waren aber zu keinem befriedigenden Ergebnis gekommen, da allein schon das Klassifizierungssystem der Aussprachen im Chinesischen in vielen Fällen nicht zum koreanischen phonologischen System paßte. Eine Kommission unter direkter Leitung und mit tätiger Mithilfe König Sejongs erarbeitete nun ein eigenes Zeichenlexikon, das unabhängig von chinesischen Standardlexia auf einer Analyse der sino-koreanischen Lautungen basierte und die Aussprachevarianten standardisierte. Das Lexikon der standardisierten sino-koreanischen Aussprache kam im Jahre 1447 unter dem Titel *Tongguk-chŏngun* "Korrekte Reime des Ostlandes [= Korea]" heraus.

Im Zuge dieser Unternehmung wurden einerseits die verschiedenen nicht-chinesischen Schriftsysteme im Umkreis der chinesischen Kultur studiert, andererseits wurde das koreanische Lautsystem genau analysiert und eine eigene phonetische Buchstabenschrift erfunden. In der chinesischen Sprachwissenschaft unterschied man bei der Silbenanalyse zwischen Anlaut (= Konsonant) und 'Reim' (= Silbengipfel und Auslautkonsonant) (→ Art. 6). Die wichtigste Entdeckung der koreanischen Kommission war nun, daß Anlaut und Auslautkonsonant gleicher Art sind, womit der Weg zur Erfindung eines Alphabetes bestehend aus Konsonantenzeichen und Vokalzeichen geebnet war. Wie stark andererseits die Prägung durch die sinologische Vorbildung und das angestrebte Ziel eines – wenn auch adaptierten – 'Klein-China' war, kann man daran ermessen, dass das Paradigma der Kennzeichnung der chinesischen Töne ('Seitenpunkte') dann auch auf die Schreibung des Koreanischen übertragen wurde. Es ist aber sehr fraglich, ob es je bedeutungsunterscheidende Töne im Koreanischen gegeben hat, oder ob nicht vielmehr eine Fehleinschätzung von Akzent- und Längungsphänomenen vorlag. Jedenfalls kamen die Seitenpunkte als Tonangaben für das Koreanische schon nach 50 Jahren ausser Gebrauch und waren ohnehin seit Anfang an unsystematisch gewesen.

Das Alphabet wurde 1446 unter dem Namen *Hunmin-chŏngŭm* "Das Volk die korrekten Lautungen lehren" bekanntgemacht. Gleichzeitig hatte man erkannt, daß mit diesem Alphabet auch die koreanische Sprache aufgezeichnet werden konnte und es setzte eine auf Volksbildung gerichtete Publikationstätigkeit ein (s. o. zu den *Ŏnhae*-Ausgaben buddhistischer Sutren und konfuzianischer Klassiker, dazu kamen Zeichenlexika und kleinere Schriften zur Einführung in die chinesische Sprache und in die sinophile Bildung).

Das neue Alphabet unterschied zwischen Vokalzeichen und Konsonantenzeichen. Die Vokalzeichen wurden nach kosmologischen Vorstellungen durch Kombinationen aus den graphischen Elementen kreisförmiger Punkt (= Himmel), Waagerechte (= Erde) und Senkrechte (= Mensch) gebildet und berücksichtigten durch spiegelverkehrende Paarung der Grapheme die Vokalharmonie des Koreanischen. Die Konsonantenzeichen dagegen ahmen in ihrer graphischen Gestalt stilisiert bei fünf Grundkonsonanten die wesentlichen Artikulationsorgane nach (Zunge, bzw. Zungenstellung für [k] und [n], Lippen für [m], Zahn für [s], Glottis für [ŋ]). Diese Einteilung in fünf Grundkonsonanten geht auf die chinesische Phonologie zurück, die Berücksichtigung der Artikulation in der graphischen Form ist aber ein einmaliger und genialer Einfall. Auch das systematisch auf einer Analyse distinktiver Merkmale beruhende Erzeugen der Grapheme weiterer Konsonantenreihen bezeugt den hohen Grad an sprachwissenschaftlicher Analysefähigkeit der damaligen Gelehrten: ein weiterer Strich kennzeichnete die Plosiven (außer bei [k]) und zwei hinzugefügte Striche der Reihe der Aspiraten; gespannte Konsonanten wurden durch Zeichenverdoppelung angezeigt.

Von Anfang an bis heute werden mit den koreanischen Buchstaben Silbenkomplexe gebildet, die ursprünglich in senkrechten Zeilen von rechts nach links aneinandergereiht wurden; heute setzt sich mehr und mehr eine Schreibung in links-rechts zu lesenden und von oben nach unten angeordneten Zeilen durch. Außerdem werden seit 1933 die Silben nicht länger an den Silbenfugen wie im mündlichen Sprachgebrauch verändert, es wird vielmehr morphemisch geschrieben. (Der alte Name *Hunmin-chŏngŭm* wurde in Südkorea ersetzt durch *Han'gŭl* "koreanische Schrift", in Nordkorea sagt man heute *Uri k'ŭl* ("unsere Schrift").

Wie oben schon erwähnt, konnte sich das koreanische Alphabet in der Gelehrtenwelt zunächst nur begrenzt durchsetzen und ist erst in der Neuzeit zum allgemeinen Schreibsystem in (heute den beiden) Korea geworden. Neben dem Wechsel von einer silbig schreibenden phonetischen Schrift zu einer morpho-phonetischen Schrift mußte auch dem sprachlichen Wandel seit dem 15. Jh. Rechnung getragen werden, vor allem der um 1800 schon erfolgten Palatalisierung und dem allmählichen Schwinden einiger Phoneme. Unter den Gelehrten seiner Zeit ragt besonders Yu Hŭi (1773–1837) hervor, der in seinem *Ŏnmun-chi* "Schrift zur gewöhnlichen [d. h. normalen koreanischen] Sprache" erneut die Sprache seiner Zeit, und zwar unter Einbeziehung der Dialekte, analysierte und notwendig gewordene Änderungen in der Orthographie vorschlug, die sich durch eine Verkleinerung des Phoneminventars als notwendig erwiesen. Er wurde damit zu einem Vorläufer der Wissenschaftler und Pädagogen, die seit Ende des letzten Jarhunderts nach Anregung der durch Japan vermittelten europäischen und später der amerikanischen Sprachwissenschaft die moderne Sprachwissenschaft aufbauten und eine Schriftreform durchführten, die u. a. das ursprünglich 28 Buchstaben umfassende Alphabet auf 24 Buchstaben verkleinerte.

### IIIc Lehrbücher für Fremdsprachen

Die traditionelle Methode für das Erlernen des Chinesischen der klassischen Schriften bestand darin, dass als Einführung in die chinesischen Schriftzeichen das *Ch'ien Tzu Wen* "Tausend-Zeichen-Klassiker" von Chou Hsing-Szu (Anfang 6. Jh.) unterrichtet wurde, und zwar anhand einer mit den erwähnten Einprägfloskeln *saegim* versehenen koreanischen Ausgabe, sodass ein gleichzeitiges Vokabellernen damit verbunden war. Auch das mit 3.350 Zeichen umfangreichere *Hunmong-chahoe* "Zeichensammlung für die Unterrichtung der Ungebildeten" (1527) von Ch'oe Sejin (1475–1542), der auch an einer Weiterentwicklung des koreanischen Alphabetes gearbeitet hat, war weit verbreitet und wurde mehrfach annotiert und neu herausgegeben. Nach dem Erlernen der Zeichen wurden Originalauszüge chinesischer Klassiker oder eigens in Chinesisch bzw. Sino-koreanisch geschriebene Lehrbücher philosophisch-moralischen und historischen Inhalts wie das erwähnte *Tongmong-sŏnsŭp* auswendig gelernt und so die Grammatik des Chinesischen intuitiv gelernt. Einige dieser Schriften wurden im 16. Jh. auch als *ŏnhae*-Ausgaben und später in Übersetzung gedruckt.

Von Ch'oe Sejin stammen auch für das Erlernen der chinesischen Umgangssprache das in der Art der *Onhae*-Ausgaben zweisprachige und annotierte *Pŏnyŏk-No-Kŏldae* "Übersetzung des *Lao Chih-Ta*" und das *Pŏnyŏk-Pak-T'ongsa* "Übersetzung des 'Übersetzers Pak' ", das später mehrfach überarbeitet und in veränderter Auflage neu herausgegeben wurde. Vor allem die Übersetzer und Dolmetscher in Regierungsdiensten und die Gelehrten einer pragmatischen Gelehrtenschule (*Shilhak*) wandten sich mehr und mehr dem kontemporären Chinesischen zu und es erschienen z. B. die Liste umgangssprachlicher Redewendungen und Ausdrücke *Ŏrokhae* "Erklärungen sprachlicher Ausdrücke" (anon., o. J.), Vokabellisten wie das *Yŏgŏ-yuhae* "Übersetzungen, klassifiziert und erläutert" (1690), und andere Hilfsmittel.

Für Japanisch, Mongolisch, Mandschurisch, Dschurdschenisch wurden ebenfalls Lehrbücher herausgegeben, und aus dem Amt für Dolmetscher und Übersetzer bei Hofe stammen mehrere mehrsprachige Wörterspiegel mit parallelen Wortlisten vor allem chinesischen, mongolischen, japanischen und mandschurischen Materials, so das *Pangŏnchipsŏk* "Sammlung zu den Randsprachen mit Erläuterungen" (1778) von einem gewissen Hong Myŏngbok, das *Samhak-yŏgŏ* "Übersetzungen zu den Drei [Fremdsprach-] Studien" von Yi Uibong (1733–1801) als Teil des *Kogŭm-sŏngnim* "Sammlung von Erklärungen zu Altem und Derzeitigem" und viele andere mehr.

## 4. Schlussbemerkung

Zweitausend Jahre sinologisch-philologische Gelehrsamkeit, sinophiles Bildungsstreben und koreanisch-chinesische mündlich-schriftliche Zweisprachigkeit haben in Korea einerseits eine traditionelle Sprachwissenschaft hervorgebracht, die der philologischen Tradition Chinas verpflichtet war und sich in Werken niederschlug, die sich nicht von solchen chinesischer Gelehrter unterscheiden. Diese zu beschreiben, hätte letztlich nur eine Wiederholung dessen ergeben, was zur traditionellen chinesischen Sprachwissenschaft zu berichten ist, und sie wurde wegen dieser Abhängigkeit hier auch nicht weiter berücksichtigt.

Auf der anderen Seite war diese sinologische Gelehrsamkeit durch die ständige Konfrontation des Sino-koreanischen mit der so völlig andersartigen koreanischen Sprache von einer überwiegend intuitiven Analyse des Koreanischen begleitet. Die Ziele und Ergebnisse dieser Analyse ergaben sich aus dem täglichen Leben in Zweisprachigkeit und sie wurde nicht als eigene Forschungsrichtung betrieben. Letztlich war hierdurch aber auch eine solide Grundlage für sprachwissenschaftliche Forschung geschaffen, und als in der Moderne durch die Einführung allgemeinbildender Schulen und Hochschulen nach westlichem Vorbild und den damit eingeführten Fächerkanon, der auch das Fach 'Koreanisch' enthielt, einsetzte, konnte darauf zurückgegriffen werden.

## 5. Bibliographie


Lee, Ki-moon. 1977. *Geschichte der koreanischen Sprache.* Dt. Übers. hg. von Bruno Lewin, Wiesbaden: Reichert.

Rutt, Richard. 1960. "The Chinese Learning and Pleasures of a Country Scholar", *Transactions of the Korea Branch of the Royal Asiatic Society* (Seoul) 36.

Sampson, Geoffrey. 1985. *Writing Systems.* Stanford, Cal.: Stanford Univ. Press.

Sasse, Werner. 1987. "Sprachreform und koreanische Kulturgeschichte". *Cahiers d'Etudes Coréennes.* V. *Twenty Papers on Korean Studies offered to Professor W. E. Skillend.* 2999–310. Paris.

–. 1988. *Studien zur Entzifferung der Schrift altkoreanischer Dichtung.* I. *Theorie und Praxis der Entzifferung.* II. *Konkordanz.* (= *Veröffentlichungen des Ostasien-Instituts der Ruhr-Universität Bochum,* 37.) Wiesbaden: Harrassowitz.

–. 1988. "Altkoreanische Dichtung: Die Silla-Hyangga". *Oriens Extremus* 32. 133–263.

–. 1991. "The Shilla Stone Inscription from Naengsu-ri, Yŏngil-gun". Korea Journal, 31:3.31–53.

–. 1996. "Choe Sejin", "Ch'ŏng Inji", "Sejong", "Yu Hŭi". *Lexicon Grammaticorum* hg. von Harro Stammerjohann, 185, 186, 849, 1035. Tübingen: Niemeyer.


*Werner Sasse, Hamburg (Deutschland)*

# IV. The Establishment of the Japanese Linguistic Tradition
# Die Anfänge der Sprachforschung in Japan
# La constitution de la tradition linguistique japonaise

## 10. The Japanese linguistic tradition and the Chinese heritage

1. The Chinese origins of Japanese linguistics
2. Phonology and the Chinese script in Japan
3. The period of 'national learning'
4. The work of Motoori Norinaga
5. The modern period
6. Bibliography

### 1. The Chinese origins of Japanese linguistics

Just as is true of so much else in the culture of Japan, so also does its linguistic tradition grow out of Chinese origins that remain strikingly evident throughout the course of its history and development. But at the same time, the considerable Japanese talent for adaptation in the course of imitation, together with the subtle shifts in emphasis and approach that inevitably are to be observed when foreign ideas and institutions are borrowed onto Japanese soil, have made themselves felt in the linguistic tradition as well. This has meant that in the final analysis, the Japenese linguistic tradition, while always in debt to its continental sources, has in sum total ended up as somewhat more than the simple imitation of Chinese ideas in a foreign, i. e. Japanese, context.

Probably the single most important difference between the two traditions has been concerned with the obvious inability of the Japanese to reproduce, or even to imitate to any significant extent, the essentially ethnocentric bias that has determined so much of the linguistic tradition in China.

By and large – and always with the exception of certain aspects of phonological study – the Chinese linguistic tradition has consistently reflected the world-view of Chinese culture and society in general; in particular, it has reflected those portions of that world-view most concerned with the socio-political orientation of man within his world, man within the universe, and man within the cosmos. To the Chinese worldview, order was everything; man, the world in which he lived, even the cosmos itself, were of interest not as subjects for intellectual speculation, or in and for themselves, but rather only in as far as they reflected, or could be reduced to, preconceived ideas of what constituted proper and rigid order – order that found its most tangible expression in the monolithic despotism of the centralized government of the classical Chinese hydraulic state.

It was only a short step to apply this normative, authoritarian, and essentially despotic world-view to the particular case of human social activity represented by language – indeed, more often than not it was no step at all, so intimately was the linguistic tradition in China consistently interrelated to the other, more comprehensive aspects of the Chinese world-view.

But the Japanese, at least in the early periods of their contacts with the rest of Asia, could not afford to indulge the Chinese delusion that theirs was the only language in the world, or that the Japanese language was the sole rational form of communication ever developed by civilized man.

From the earliest days of Japanese history, their own civilization was confronted by Chinese language and culture; and the Japanese early had to set themselves to the formidable task of grappling with the pronunciation, lexicon, and grammar of their imposing continental giant of a neighbor. Bilingual glosses, bilingual lexical sources, even a certain degree of true bilingualism, were all commonplace in early Japan, and without question did much to determine many of the original directions in which the Japanese linguistic tradition took its development, particularly when it began to depart from the rote imitation of patterns and ideas borrowed intact from China. The Japanese would not know the luxury of the splendid linguistic isolation, and the consequently arrogant linguistic ethnocentricism, of the Chinese until much later into their history, even then, they would enjoy it for brief periods only, the longest being the some three-hundred years of the Tokugawa 'closed country' isolationism.

Even while paying due respect to Chinese ethnocentricism and linguistic xenophobia, we must at the same time keep in mind that certain elements of the Indic linguistic tradition had early managed to make their way into that same tradition through Buddhist sources; this was particularly true of Chinese traditional phonological study, which was considerably in debt to Indic grammatical science in ways that are only now slowly coming to be understood. Many of these same elements of the Indic linguistic tradition that had reached China through Buddhist intermediaries were in turn also transmitted to Japan; and while there was little if any first-hand knowledge of Buddhist Sanskrit on the part of the Japenese in the pre-modern period (with the notable exception of several clerics who had studied it, along with other aspects of Buddhist learning, in T'ang China), the *siddhāṃ* script, with its implicit phonological analysis and structuring of speech sounds, was well enough known in Japan from an early period importantly to influence the local linguistic tradition.

## 2. Phonology and the Chinese script in Japan

The borrowing of a foreign writing system, that of Chinese, for the purpose of writing the Japanese language, early forced the Japenese themselves to confront the necessity of isolating the grammatical elements of their own language, mostly on the basis of the various ways in which it was observed to be either similar to or different from Chinese. The borrowed Chinese graphs ('characters') of the writing system could be used to write the uninflected forms of Japanese without much difficulty (apart of course from the difficulty of remembering which Japanese linguistic form had been assigned to go with which Chinese graph); but writing the many inflected forms of Japanese posed special orthographic problems, some of which are yet to be solved to everyone's satisfaction in the Japanese writing system even today. Most importantly, the enclitic grammatical elements of the Japanese language, including the case-suffixes, all of which were unlike anything in Chinese, required the development of special orthographic techniques if they were to be written at all.

The early degree of sophistication that the Japanese achieved in the analysis of their own language along these particular lines is well demonstrated by two famous poems in the *Man'yōshū* anthology. These are poems 4174 and 4176 in the modern numbering of the text, and are both attributed to Ōtomo Yakamochi (729–785). In them, the poet, as a conscious literary device, indulges himself in the rather spectacular feat of writing his lines without using the most common enclitic grammatical elements in the language; poem 4175 is composed without using Old Japanese *mo*, *nö*, and *Fa*, the three most common enclitic elements, resp. case-suffixes, in the language, while poem 4176 not only avoids these three grammatical elements, but also eschews *te*, *ni*, and *wo*, the next three most common such forms. And just in case any reader should not have gotten the point of the exercise involved in these two feats of grammatical juggling, each poem has a note appended, in Chinese prose, pointing out which enclitic elements have been avoided in each instance.

The same *Man'yōshū* anthology also incorporates a number of poem-texts in non-standard Old Japanese, many of which have appended notes identifying the geographical origin of their dialect materials. These non-standard dialect poems, which are written with Chingraphs used as phonograms, appear to have been prized by the compilers of the Old Japanese anthology for the exotic aesthetic effects of their phonology; but we ought not to overlook the fact that their existence and transmission also bear witness to elements of the Chinese linguistic tradition. It is hardly possible to understand how these non-standard language poems found their way into the mainstream of Japanese literary culture without reference to one of the earliest representative textual examples of the Chinese linguistic tradition, the *Fang yen* that is generally attributed (but on the basis of largely circular literary evidence) to Yang Hsiung (23 BC–18 AD). Despite the problems that complicate its authorship, there is little question that the text is an ancient one, and that it deals with non-standard forms of the Chinese language of the Han period, preserving a large number of dialect versions of central, standard-language terms. Indeed, the title *Fang yen*, literally "regional terms", has become the modern word as well as the linguistic term for 'dialect', and in this sense has also been borrowed into Japanese (*hōgen*). Without the existence of this prestigious Chinese linguistic exemplar, it is to say the least doubtful if the *Man'yōshū* anthology would have devoted the space that it does to recording poetry in regional and dialect forms of the language.

Together with Indic concepts of phonological ordering and arrangement, which reached Japan through Buddhist sources *via* China, calligraphy appears to have been another stimulus for the development of ordered sets of the Japanese syllabic inventory. These began as mnemonic devices to ensure that the student would write one example and one example only of each syllable in a fixed if arbitrary order, without repetition or omission of any syllable. The development of these syllabic inventories paralleled the development of techniques for writing Japanese entirely without, or almost without, reference to the semantic value of the Chinese morphemes associated with each graph when used to write Chinese.

The earliest of these syllabic inventories post-dates the Old Japanese eight-vowel system, but it still distinguishes two varieties of syllable-initial *e-*, this last a phonological distinction that appears to have survived up to *ca.* 950. Some of the early syllabic inventories consist of strings of semantically related words; others go together to form a meaningful text. The most famous of this latter variety is the *Iroha* inventory of the syllabary, for which the oldest surviving textual evidence is to be dated in correspondence with 1097; read as a text, the *Iroha* syllabary may be understood as a Buddhist didactic poem teaching the essential impermanence of all phenomena.

A further advance in linguistic sophistication is represented by the arrangement of the Japanese syllabic inventory into the so-called 'charts of 50 syllables'. These were phonological grids that provided spaces sufficient to accommodate all the syllables of the language; but the total of fifty such openings that these charts provide were never all necessary at any stage in the history of the Japanese language. Here again Indic phonological elements that reached Japan *via* China are surely at issue; one is reminded of the way in which the Sanskrit grammarians compulsively 'filled out" missing gaps in their phonological ordering by inventing non-existent units for this express purpose.

The earliest example of this '50 syllable' genre is to be dated to the period 1004–1028; and it is important to note that not only Indic principles of phonological analysis but also the Chinese rhyme table tradition (→ Art. 6) played a seminal role in the development of these sources. But since at the same time the Chinese rhyme table tradition was itself much in debt to Indic principles, the details of mutual influences back and forth across Asia in this segment of linguistic science is complex indeed.

As they learned more and more about the Chinese language, the Japanese were of course confronted, as are all foreign students of the language, with the Chinese tones. The Japanese early identified the tones of Chinese with the distinctive pitch-accent of their own language, and experimented with using the half-mnemonic, half-descriptive terms employed for the Chinese tones in the Chinese sources (*p'ing* "level", *shang* "rising", *ch'ü* "departing", cf. Miller 1993: 91) as a system for recording the features of the quite different Japanese pitch-accent. Some of the texts in which these notational techniques were applied to Japanese at an early period have been made to yield data for studying early periods in the history of the Japanese pitch-accent by means of written records; but certain foreign students of these problems (e. g. Martin 1987) have tended vastly to over-rate the importance of such data for the history of Japanese, focusing virtually all their attention upon these fragmentary early written-records of pitch recorded as Chinese tone, and in the process all but neglecting the history of the vowels and consonants of the language. Also misleading is the unfounded assumption that these written records dealing with the pitch-accent of rather late forms of Japanese may automatically be used to establish the pitch of Old Japanese, which is patently absurd.

## 3. The period of 'national learning'

The great revival of interest in 'national studies' that distinguished Japanese intellectual life from the mid-18th century on could not but have had important implications for the linguistic tradition also, though naturally its most striking expressions were to be found in the fields of literature, political and religious thought, and government institutions. The tremendous prestige that Chinese letters and Chinese culture had long enjoyed in Japan remained unchanged; but now new voices were raised, expressing interest and concern in purely Japanese achievements, and frequently stressing the supposed superiority of Japanese things over Chinese things more than a trifle shrilly.

Ishizuka Tatsumaro (1764–1823) sought to recover earlier orthographic princples that had been lost sight of in the spelling that had been instituted, or at least named after, the poet Fujiwara Teika (1162–1241); and in the course of his pioneering studies of the Old Japanese text-corpus was probably the first scholar to stumble upon the evidence that the early written records preserve for the Old Japanese eight-vowel system.

Another towering figure in this early stage of the linguistic tradition in Japan is the monk Keichū (1640–1701). Keichū was a member of the Shingon sect of Vajrayāna Buddhism, one of the varieties of the religion that had its roots most deeply planted in its Chinese origins; but also, and most significantly in this case, the Shingon sect always maintained a lively tradition with respect to the ultimate Indic origins of its doctrines and texts. The sect-designation Shingon, after all, is nothing but the Sino-Japanese version of the Chinese translation of *mantra*; and in stressing the didactic, mystic, and philosophical aspects of these untranslated fragments of Buddhist Hybrid Sanskrit, the Shingon clerics naturally paid attention to details of language and pronunciation, which in turn constantly kept them in touch with their Indic origins.

There can be little doubt that much of Keichū's linguistic orientation derived from the fact that, as just described, his Shingon training early put him into fairly direct contact with the Indic linguistic tradition, and that it was thanks to this that he was able to make his major contributions toward recovering the orthographic standard for Old Japanese phonology as it had predated the so-called 'Teika orthography'.

An interesting footnote to the early records of the linguistic tradition in Japan is provided by an anonymous text entitled *Kenshuku ryōkoshū*, dated in correspondence with 1695 and written by a Kyoto author of whom nothing else is known. Whoever he was, the author of this text had not only a good ear but also quite impressive training in and understanding of phonetic observation. By the time of this text Japanese *z* and *d* had fallen together as *ž* before *-i-*, but as $d^z$ before *-u-*. The author of this text lists 1,695 words known to him in which these changes had taken place, and attempts to identify their etymological origin (entirely within Japanese, of course) on the basis of other orthographic evidence.

Mention must also be made of the celebrated Tokugawa polymath Arai Hakuseki (1657–1725) and his lexicon *Tōga* (1719); again, the prestige and importance of Japan's Chinese heritage come to the fore, since both the plan of the work and its title call to mind the first Chinese lexical work *Erh ya* (→ Art. 7) (the Sino-Japanese title *Tōga* suggests that the work is an 'eastern', i. e. Japanese version of the *Erh ya*). In his *Tōga* Hakuseki demonstrated a surprising grasp of the concept of linguistic change; there too he also for the first time suggested that the Japanese language might be in some way historically related to the Korean language, commenting in detail upon similarities that he had noted in form and meaning between a total of 62 Japanese and Korean words (Lewin 1966). Even today, one frequently searches in vain for expressions in the current linguistic literature of understanding of the historical process in language, and of the possibility of non-Japanese elements in the same, equal in clarity and insight to those of Hakuseki.

## 4. The work of Motoori Norinaga

In more than one sense, the modern linguistic tradition in Japan begins with the work of the great pioneer of the 'national studies' movement Motoori Norinaga (1730–1801; → Art. 12). It is difficult to know where to begin in summarizing Motoori's achievements in Japanese linguistics, since his activities ranged over such a wide spectrum of fields. He was the first to describe the functioning of the grammatical suffixes that involve syntactic concord by means of discontinuous immediate constituents; for this phenomenon of syntactic concord he invented the term *kakari musubi*, which is still widely in use even though most modern scholarship has lost sight of the sophistication of Motoori's original description. His *Tenioha himokagami* (1771) is a study of the grammatical enclitics of the language, and the term *tenioha* which he employs for the case-suffixes is a linguistic coinage in the best manner of the Indic grammatical tradition, since the term itself embodies a listing of the morphemes thus being identified, *te*, *ni*, *o* < **wo* and *ha* < **Fa* being the principal case-suffixes. Actually, this term *tenioha* has its ultimate origins in the traditions of the schools that early developed in Japan for reading and interpreting Chinese literary texts as if they were Japanese texts. In this process, which was part paraphrase, part translation, it was of course first of all necessary to decide which Japanese grammatical elements would be fitted into what segments of the anatomy of the Chinese passage being rendered. The earliest reliable textual citation of the coinage-term *tenioha* appears to be one in the *Yakumo mishō*, a treatise on poetics written by the Emperor Juntoku (1197–1242), who was on the throne during the years 1210–21, but who of course followed his brief 'reign' with a period of activity as a 'Retired Emperor', in the customary medieval Japanese style. The term *tenioha* becomes common in the texts of the schools from 1266 on; it survives today, but now it is generally employed with no sense either of its earliest meaning or of its terminological sophistication.

Motoori was hardly a champion of Chinese importations, to say the least, and it is because of this interesting to note that even such a staunch proponent of Japenese superiority still makes two overt references to Chinese even in the title of this purely Japanese linguistic treatise. One is the word *kagami* "mirror", here to be understood as a calque upon Chin. *chien* "id.", a morpheme semantically specialized in Chinese booktitles in the sense of "survey, *speculum*". The second is *himo* "cord", which Motoori uses as his term for grammatical elements; but in this sense this Japanese lexial item too can best be understood as embracing at least a portion of the semantic content of Chin. *niu* "button, knot", which it regularly translates into Japanese, and which in Chinese is drawn from the technical language of the rhyme books and rhyme tables.

Motoori's treatise on the grammatical elements of Japanese arranges them into three major form-classes on the basis of the syntactic concord that they display; these three form-classes embrace a total of 43 sentence- and phrase-final elements with which Motoori deals. Finally, some notice must be taken of Motoori's *Mikuni kotoba katsuyō-shō* (1782), in which he classified the inflected forms of Japanese into 27 sets or inflectional categories. Again, his penchant for the alleged superiority of Japanese over Chinese was forced to give way before the reality of lexical demands, and he used the Chinese loanword *e* "meeting, assembly" for "inflectional category", rather than attempt to coin a suitable Japanese term. In this treatise, Motoori draws the bulk of his materials from the classical literary language, but he also cites valuable examples from the spoken language of his time.

## 5. The modern period

But before long, all the enormous promise of this indigenous linguistic tradition of comprehensive, rigorous grammatical analysis was totally wiped out by the impact of 'Western learning' and European – initially, Dutch – grammar. Tsurumine Shigenobu (1788–1859) published his *Gogaku shinsho* in 1833; this was the first trickle of what later became a torrent of publications that treated the Japanese language as if it were Dutch, applying to it the nine parts of speech and the nine cases of the noun that were suddenly felt to be universals, simply because they had been discovered in foreign books (→ Art. 14). Japanese scholars, needless to add, went through appalling difficulties in the course of acquiring this new information; their almost superhuman efforts to master 'European grammar' makes all the more poignant the sad truth that in the process they were in actual fact doing little but shortchanging themselves and their cultural heritage, as they traded in their own perfectly sound linguistic tradition, with its important elements inherited from the traditions of China and India, for the entirely second-hand one of the West.

Much of the important earlier work in the Japanese linguistic tradition not only grew out of Chinese origins, it also, as we have seen, served the practical concerns of those engaged in writing Japanese poetry, or in the even more demanding task of teaching others how to write it. This situation too was deeply involved with Japan's cultural inheritance from China; there too the writing of poetry was always a serious matter, and there too the requirements of the poetic schools played an important role in the development of linguistic texts and treatises, particularly of the rhyme books and tables that have yielded so much data for the modern study of Chinese historical phonology.

But as Japan moved into the modern period, and from approximately 1870 on, the elegant, courtly concern for the transmission of its antique poetic art necessarily came to an abrupt termination; soon it was replaced by 'education' as the principal stimulus not only for linguistic speculation but for grammatical analysis as well. For newly-Westernizing Japan of the Meiji period, education was seen as the one sure way in which one caught up with the West; education was the way one might prevent the social and political disasters that were overtaking the colossus of China from also swamping the tiny island nation of Japan; and teaching (and learning) one's own language through the newly discovered and supposedly rational systems of European grammars was held to be at the very heart of all education.

Paradoxically, all this went hand-in-hand with a growing sense of Japan and the Japanese language as somehow being unique expressions of the human spirit and of the human expression, first of all as something very different from anything to be found anywhere else in the world, then finally as somehow essentially superior to what might otherwise be assumed to be analogous developments in other countries and among other peoples. In the course of these changes, Japan's centuries-old cultural and intellectual linkage with the Chinese civilization was finally and completely severed.

The possibility that had earlier existed, of somehow being able to graft the fruit of Japan's indigenous linguistic accomplishments onto the once-robust root of Japan's Chinese heritage was now irretrievably lost. But one can hardly avoid speculation, more in disappointment than in surprise, about what intellectual accomplishments might have been achieved had not the 'modernizing' Japan of the 19th century and thereafter opted for the mostly bogus coin of the 'Western learning' in this field of linguistic science (→ Art. 16).

## 6. Bibliography


Lewin, Bruno. 1966. "Arai Hakuseki als Sprachgelehrter". *Oriens Extremus* 13.191–241.

Martin, Samuel E. 1987. *The Japanese Language Through Time.* New Haven: Yale Univ. Press.

Miller, Roy Andrew. 1975. "The Far East". *Current Trends in Linguistics*, vol. XIII: *Historiography of Linguistics* ed. by Thomas A Sebeok, 1213–1264. The Hague & Paris: Mouton.

–. 1993. *Die japanische Sprache, Geschichte und Struktur.* Transl. by Jürgen Stalph et al. München: judicium verlag.


*Roy Andrew Miller, Honolulu (USA)*

# 11. The First Japanese attempts at describing Chinese and Korean bilingualism


1. Background and some early developments
2. Tokugawa period (1603–1867) views on Chinese and Korean
3. The nature of comparisons and later developments
4. Bibliography


## 1. Background and some early developments

It is impossible to pinpoint when Japanese (as opposed to naturalised Koreans or Chinese, who at first were in charge of writing in Japan) first began to read and write (classical) Chinese (*kanbun*). While the import of Chinese classics and Buddhist works translated into Chinese dates back to the early 5th century, it was probably not until the 7th century that Japanese became proficient in dealing with the Chinese language, and also began to employ Chinese characters (*kanji*) to write their own language.

In the course of this, literate Japanese must have noticed various differences between Chinese and their own tongue, the most salient of which is the change necessitated in word order when 'reading' *kanbun* in Japanese; this came to be indicated by various diacritical marks including the *kaeriten* (marks showing word order). The following example illustrates this process (tones abbreviated):

Chu-jen $yu_2$ she $_{\vee}$Chiang $che_1$
SO-hito *ni* KŌ *wo* wataru hito ari

"There was a man from Chu who crossed the Yangze river"

Apart from the particles (in italics) added in the Japanese 'reading', the Chinese characters are identical, but read in either Sino-Japanese (capitals, so-called *on* readings) or as Japanese translation equivalents (so-called *kun* readings). The subscript symbols indicate the changes in word order required for the Japanese reading ($_{\vee}$ indicates that order needs to be inverted).

Japanese scholarly traditions soon emerged, and commentaries and dictionaries were produced, focusing on the readings (often including tones) and meanings of *kanji*. Clearly, this was furthered by the scholars and priests who went and studied in China as part of the official envoys that were sent there between 630 and 894.

The first comparisons of Japanese with a foreign language concerned in fact the description of Sanskrit sounds (letters) as part of the (originally Chinese) tradition of Siddham studies, in the 9th century. The arrangement of the so-called 50-sound table, which orders the 48 letters of the Japanese *kana* syllabary by initial and final, is influenced by both the Sanskrit alphabet (in the order of vowels and consonants), and by the Chinese *fan-qie* system of indicating the initial and final of an unknown character by two others (→ Art. 5). Rime tables by Japanese for composing Chinese poetry, such as the 14th century *Shūbun Inryaku* also appeared (→ Art. 6).

Medieval works on Japanese poetry contain some basic comparisons with Chinese, e. g. the *Teniha Taigaishō* (14th~15th century) says (in *kanbun*) "*Teniha* (grammatical particles) in Japanese poetry are the *okiji* [Chinese particles that are not read in Japanese] of China" (Anon., *Teniha Taigaishō* 41), and the *Anegakōjike Tenihaden* (14~15th century) comments that "in China, particles are read and understood in straight order, in Japan, in changed order; therefore, the meaning is not clear if the particles are incorrect" (Anon., *Anegakōjike Tenihaden* 63), a reference to the different basic word order of the two language (note that in the latter comment classical Chinese, not Japanese, is the standard of comparison).

## 2. Tokugawa period (1603–1867) views on Chinese and Korean

### 2.1. Confucian and Chinese scholars' views

The Confucianist scholar and politician Arai Hakuseki (1657–1725) compiled an etymological dictionary of Japanese, *Tōga* (MS about 1719, published 1903). In the introduction, the author provides the general context: He stresses (Arai, *Tōga* 6f.) that Japanese has long been influenced by Korean, Chinese and Sanskrit (more recently also by Western languages), and (ibid. 7f.) that Japanese is unrivalled in its paucity of sounds, whereas Western languages (his information is mainly based on his questioning of the Italian missionary Sidotti, who had been arrested for illegally entering the country) have a very rich inventory, followed by Chinese. Regarding Korean, he examines the theory that the Japanese 50-sound chart, which is also known by the name of *Tsushima iroha* [Tsushima *kana*], was brought to Japan by a Southern Chinese nun via the island of Tsushima [an island in the Japan Sea, positioned between Japan's southern island Kyushu and the Korean peninsula], in which case she can be assumed to have come through Korea. However, as the Korean language has sounds that Japanese lacks he finds this theory implausible (ibid. 8).

Arai considers words that appear to be native Japanese, when in fact they derive from Sino-Japanese. His examination of the examples *kure* from Sino-Japanese *go* and *aya* from *kan* gives an insight into the breadth of his scholarship and the methodology he employs: having first restated the point that there is no country with sounds as few as Japan, he quotes an analysis of the sounds of the Chinese characters according to rime tables (*go* = *jidaku* [Chinese *tz'u cho*, voiced aspirated], *kan* = *jisei* [Chinese *tz'u ch'ing*, unvoiced aspirated]), and points out that these sounds have no equivalent in Japanese, i. e., cannot be pronounced correctly. Therefore *kure* and *aya* can be seen to be Japanese approximations of the Chinese pronunciation. In the course of this argument, he gives the characters' contemporary Chinese pronunciation in *katakana* (as *wū* and *hānu*). In the case of *kan*, he assumes an intermediate stage *ana*, in support of which he points out the existence of both *ana* and *aya* in the 8th century *Nihongi* as readings of that character (ibid. 15).

Similar methods, supplemented by information on dialects, are used in his consideration of Korean-derived vocabulary. He takes up (ibid. 15) the example of *wata* "sea" that is read as *papai* in a old commentary of the *Nihongi*, by adducing a Korean dialect form *patai*. Under the entry *umi* "sea", he gives more details:

"Reading [the kanji for] *umi* as *wata* appears to be a Korean dialect. The form *hotai* for *umi* in the *Nihongi* is Paekche dialect. I understand that even now in colloquial Korean they say *patahi*" (ibid. 56).

It is a well-known characteristic of *Tōga* that many words (82, according to Ryo 1980: 8) are related to Korean, although it was not the first work to do so.

Ogyū Sorai (1666–1728), who influenced *kokugaku* "national learning" scholars such as Motoori Norinaga (→ Art. 12) through his pupil Hori Keizan, takes a new approach in his *Yakubun Sentei* (MS 1711, first 6 vols. published 1715) in that he criticises the traditional Japanese way of 'reading' Chinese texts by using Japanese translation equivalents; he points out (Ogyū, *Yakubun Sentei* 547) that "these people think that they are reading the text when in fact they are translating it". He goes on to say that Japan has its language, and China its own, both different in character. How can they be expected to match cleanly? He gives examples of Chinese characters (especially his so-called *josei*, or *teniwoha*, i. e. particles) that have no equivalent in Japanese, and stresses (ibid. 548) that words assume different meaning depending on context. Ideally he would (ibid. 549) abolish reading Chinese in Japanese order with time-honoured Japanese equivalents, especially as such established readings are often archaic and have changed their meaning, making it difficult to understand them, but as this practice is too deeply rooted, he proposes new ways of translating characters/words (ibid. 549–551). The bulk of the work in fact takes the form of a character dictionary, where the meanings of (mostly single) characters are explained in plain Japanese.

Minagawa Kien (1734–1807), scholar of Chinese and elder brother of the Japanese grammarian Fujitani Nariakira, wrote a number of works on Chinese, including *Kyoji-kai* (1783), *Jitsuji-kai* (1791) and *Joji-shōkai* (1811), reflecting his tripartite word class division into *jitsuji* "nouns", *kyoji* "verbs and adjectives", and *joji* "grammatical elements".

In the Introduction of *Joji-shōkai*, he explains *joji* as follows: "What is called *joji* should be understood as the equivalent of *teniwoha* as used in the Japanese language" (Minagawa, *Joji-shōkai* 9).

Minagawa attaches importance to what he calls *gosei*, which he defines (ibid 19ff.) as the meaning arising from a combination of characters (words) and the resulting changes in their effect on each other; the essence of it is the meaning of a character/word. However, he uses this in a different sense from the usual 'dictionary meaning', which only explains a word with reference to another, thereby obscuring the finer differences between them.

With reference to his three word classes, he points out (ibid. 20f.) that the meaning of *jitsuji* is easiest to understand, whereas *kyoji* are a little more difficult, and *joji* the most difficult.

The bulk of the work consists of a detailed account of the use of 65 *joji*, with over 4 pages on average devoted to each. In line with his way of thinking outlined above, the author refrains from giving established Japanese 'readings', explaining instead their use in colloquial Japanese, illustrating it with examples from classical Japanese poetry. To give an example of his approach, the *joji yeh*(3) is explained as follows:

This too is a word used at the end of a sentence, equivalent to the meaning of *ja* as used in *kore ha sore ja, kayafu no koto ja* "this is that, it's that kind of thing" etc. that is so commonly used in Japanese [...] *Kokinshū* [9th century anthology of poetry], Spring, Vol. 1: *Haru no yo no yami ha ayanashi ume no hana iro koso miene ka ya ha kakururu* "The darkness of a spring night is of no avail – although the colour of the plum blossoms is invisible, how could their scent be obscured?". This *ayanashi* means "useless"; after *ayanashi*, in Chinese one would use the word *yeh*(3) (Minagawa, *Joji-shōkai* 33).

After several more examples from Japanese poetry, he then gives examples from Chinese poetry and prose, with explanation of context and meaning, and partial Japanese translation.

### 2.2. Comparisons of Chinese and Japanese by *kokugaku* scholars

Scholars of National Learning (*kokugaku*) are characterised by a much more ethnocentric view. Kamo no Mabuchi (1697–1769)'s *Goikō* (first MS ca. 1760, completed 1769, published 1789) compares China, India and Japan as follows:

The land of the rising sun [Japan] is a country which forms words from 50 sounds, and communicates everything by word of mouth, whereas the land distant from the sun [China] is a country which distinguishes everything by letters, while the land of the setting sun [India] writes letters for about 50 sounds, and uses these for everything (Kamo no, *Goikō* 145).

He even links such phenomena to national character, finding a convenient way of explaining the small sound inventory of the Japanese language:

[...] because the Chinese like ingenuity, one sound contains many meanings, and things do not work without letters, but it is hard to make up letters for thousands or myriads of sounds. As the Indians enjoy passionate feelings, both things and sounds are as a consequence plentiful, and they also appear to use letters, but the reason why they devised expressing myriad things with letters that are equivalent to only 50 sounds is because they cannot suppress their passionate feelings. Because in Japan people's hearts are honest, things are few and consequently words are few, too; because things and words are few, there is no confusion and forgetting, and therefore the 50 sounds arising naturally from heaven and earth are sufficient (ibid.).

Kamo's pupil Motoori Norinaga (1730–1801) studied Chinese (*kangaku*) with Hori Keizan, and besides numerous works on Japanese produced a number of works dealing with Chinese characters, including *Mojigoe Kanazukai* (1776) and *Kanji San'onkō* (1785).

The *Mojigoe Kanazukai*, which deals with the correct use of *kana* for Sino-japanese words, has a brief introduction in 8th-century Japanese style, where Motoori comments on the object of his study as follows.

As the pronunciation of Chinese characters is an imitation of the foreign sounds of that people, not in the least similar to the refined sounds of Japan, they sound filthy when sung, and lowly when recited, for which reason they were not at all mixed [with Japanese] in old Japan. However, since Chinese books have long been transmitted to Japan, people have grown used to reading them and as time passed no longer thought of them as filthy and lowly. They have not only permeated everyday language, but even entered Japanese poetry a little, so that in the end they are now no longer felt to be foreign. As nowadays many words seem to be coined in Sino-japanese, people often don't know the right *kana* for them, but there is no work that can be consulted; as there are many easily confused instances, I have checked many sources to establish the correct usage and made a collection of examples, made some arguments about their use, and put them together in this volume (Motoori, *Mojigoe Kanazukai* 322).

Here, the empathy is very much with native Japanese, while Sino-japanese is grudgingly accepted as a necessary evil. In the *Kanji San'onkō*, a treatise on the three types of *kanji* readings, his stance has become even more radical. In the section *The regularity of Japan's sounds* he writes as follows, having first remarked that Japan is superior to all nations on account of it being the land of the sun goddess.

All things and affairs are outstandingly beautiful, but particularly the regularity and beauty of the sounds of the people's language is far superior to all other countries. Its sounds are pure and bright, as if one were looking at a cloudless sky during the day. They have no dullness, and are straight and simple without any turns and twists – truly the pure and refined sounds between heaven and earth (Motoori, *Kanji San'onkō* 381).

He goes on to support this with reference to the fact that old Japanese had no voiced sounds, and the regularity of the 50-sound table. In his thinking, any sound outside these 50 sounds is mixed and impure, and akin to the sounds of wild animals and other sounds found in nature. In the next section *On the language of Japan*, he further makes the point that although Japanese has only 50 sounds, in combination they can express everything, and are therefore neither too few nor too many in number.

In the section *The impurity of foreign sounds*, he gives concrete examples supporting the above arguments as follows (sounds transliterated from Motoori's *katakana*):

All foreign sounds are unclear, like viewing a cloudy evening sky. Therefore, *aa* also sounds like *oo* ... There are also many twisted sounds, as in the recent Chinese pronunciation for *East-West*, which sounds like *ton suwi*, where *to* is mixed up with *n*, and *su* with *wi*; furthermore, there is a twist from *to* to *n*, and from *su* to *wi* (ibid. 383).

Having given various further illustrations, including reference to the nasal sound *n* "which is totally produced from the nose, and not an oral sound at all" (ibid. 384), he concludes:

The various sounds discussed are akin to the sounds of wild animals and other natural sounds, and impure. To differing degrees this is true of all foreign contries, but as this work concerns the sounds of *kanji*, I have dealt with those (ibid.).

In the miscellany *Tamakatsuma*, Motoori discusses (classical) Chinese language, this time based on what he perceived as modifying-modified differences (section *Language use in China*).

Compared to the Japanese language, Chinese is very rough. For instance, the expression *han(3) yen(2)* is expressed in Japanese as *mare ni ifu* "rarely say", or *ifu koto mare nari* "it is rare to say", which are different in meaning. In *mare ni ifu* the main part, i. e. "say [something], which is by the way a rare thing"; in *ifu koto mare nari*, on the other hand, *mare* is the main part, i. e. "it is a rare thing to say [something]" (Motoori, *Tamakatsuma* 446).

Motoori's pupil Suzuki Akira (1764–1837) justifies his choice of topic at the beginning of *Gengyo Shishuron* "Treatise on the four classes of words", written in the 1790s, but not published until 1824):

The division into four word classes largely applies to all languages, but abroad [= China], this is a division in substance only. In Japan, there is a very clear formal division by means of *teniwoha* [i. e. inflectional endings] (Suzuki, *Gengyo Shishuron* 3f.).

He goes on to explain the differences with Chinese in more detail:

Words consisting only of content words (*shi*) without *teniwoha* attached are *tai no shi* [i. e. substance words, or nouns], those with changing *teniwoha* ending in the second rhyme [i. e. *-i*] are *arikata no shi* [i. e. words indicating shape, or adjectives], and those ending in the third rhyme [i. e. *-u*], are *shiwaza no shi* [i. e. action words, or verbs]. Because in China there are no inflectional endings, the distinction between these three classes exists only in meaning, not in the form of the word. As they are all like our nouns, their meaning can naturally get easily confused. The reason why the words in their classics are hard to understand is because all words lack the workings of *teniwoha* [here: inflection], making it often very difficult to tell whether something refers to the past, present or future, or whether it is declarative or imperative. Therefore, in the commentaries many different explanations are found, which hardly ever agree with each other. It is when we consider the detailed *teniwoha* of our inflected words that we understand that the noble and wonderful spirit of our language can never be equalled by the languages of other countries (ibid. 14ff.).

In the section *On teniwoha*, he continues his comparison with Chinese:

*Teniwoha* are equivalent to what in China are called *gosei*, *goji*, *joji*, *tanji*, *hatsugoji*, or *go no yosei* etc. *Ji* are also called *jiki*, and are the voice of the mind. Chinese particles are however very coarse, and in no way comparable to the way Japanese *teniwoha* are refined and detailed, with fine distinctions in their logic, and well-defined rules. The reason why our language is superior to that of all other countries is precisely because of the excellence of these *teniwoha* (ibid. 16f.).

## 2.3. Early accounts of *Korean*

Korean words are quoted in the 8th century *Nihongi*, at a time when Japanese-Korean comings and goings were frequent. Thereafter there is a long lapse, until Hideyoshi's invasions of Korea during the last decade of the 16th century, and the ensuing diplomatic negotiations between the two countries brought about renewed interest.

This interest was expressed in various forms. From the end of the 16th century, etymological and other dictionaries of Japanese make frequent references to Korean. We already saw an instance of this in Arai's *Tōga*, but many others, such as Keichū's *Enjuan Zakki* (MS 1699), Kaibara Ekiken's *Nihon Shakumyō* (1700), Ogyū Sorai's *Narubeshi* (MS 1736, publ. 1762) and Tanikawa Kotosuga's *Wakun no Shiori* (first instalment published 1777) contain references to Korean.

Some, like Motoori, thought that in some cases this was taken too far. In the entry *Cases where Japanese and foreign words happen to be similar or identical* in *Tamakatsuma* (136), he cautions those who want to derive everything from Korean or Chinese:

Of those words that are the same as current Korean, *tera* "temple" and *kohori* "administrative district" have in fact been adopted from Korean; as formerly, the three [ancient] Korean kingdoms were subjacent to Japan and were sending tributes, naturally words from that language may have been transmitted, and things which were not formerly known in Japan and brought here from that country may have been continued to be called by the name used there. There may also have been Japanese words that Koreans used and became part of that language and remained part of it until now, but it is a mistake to think that all these words came from there. For instance, "mother" was formerly occasionally called *omo*; the Confucianists, as usual, maintain that this came from the characters read [in Sino-Japanese] *amo*, but that is incorrect, it is an old indigenous word. In the songs from the Eastern provinces in the *Man'yōshū* it is also read *amo*, but that is not based on Chinese *amo*, but is the Eastern pronunciation of *omo*. They also claim that instances of words used in colloquial Japanese, which happen to look like words found in the Chinese classics, are taken from there, for instance recently someone said that *kaka* for "mother" came from classical Chinese, where sometimes *kaka* [Sino-Japanese] is used, but that is very far off the mark, because how could contemporary Japanese know and use a word that was only rarely used in some ancient book in China? It is a very strange thing that Confucianists these days when they come across some words that were occasionally used in some very old Chinese book seem to claim that they all hail from there.

Another area attracting scholars' interest was the Korean script, or *hankul* (at the time, *genbun* or *onmon* in Japanese; → Art. 9).

For instance, Aoki Kon'yō (1698–1769), who first studied Confucianism with Itō Tōgai before becoming a Dutch studies (*Rangaku*) scholar, introduces a table of nine basic letters and their names, and the most common combinations with their pronunciation in *katakana*: "Korean *onmon* are as shown in the following. [...] In Korea, books are translated into *onmon* for popular and easy reading" (Aoki, *Kon'yō Manroku* 40).

Yamaoka's encyclopedia *Ruiju Meibutsukō* has a section on sounds and letters; in the entry on *onmon*, the author speculates on their derivation: "The shape of the letters may be based on Sanskrit letters; they are different from Manchurian script, and in Ryukyu yet another script is used" (Yamaoka, *Ruiju Meibutsukō* VI, 35).

Only rarely are comments about similarities between Japanese and Korean found, as in the *taikō* "fundamentals" of Tanikawa Kotosuga's (1709–1776) dictionary *Wakun no Shiori*, but even they are made in connection with the writing system:

> In the Korean way of reading [*kanbun*] there are *josei* "particles", which are like our *teniwoha*. There is also something like our *iroha* [*kana*] called *onmon*, written in small size along the side of [Chinese] characters indicating their readings; the sounds of the characters are different but the way of reading is no different from ours [...] (Tanikawa, *Wakun no Shiori* 34).

These scholars clearly had an interest in the Korean language and writing system, but did not have a working knowledge of the Korean language. That was a characteristic of those concerned with intermediating and interpreting in Japanese-Korean diplomatic relations, who at the time were largely confined to the Tsushima clan.

### 2.4. Amenomori Hōshū and the study of Korean

Probably the first prominent Japanese to acquire fluent Korean, Amenomori Hōshū (1668–1755), having first studied Chinese with the Confucian scholar Kinoshita Jun'an, joined the service of the lord of the Tsushima clan as a Confucianist. He lived for most of his life on Tsushima island after settling there in 1693, but during that time also spent a number of years in Korea to learn the language. Apart from being in charge of educational matters on the island, he worked on the diplomatic relations between the two countries while passing on his Korean skills to a team of interpreters, which was to develop into a hereditary guild.

As already noted, the focus of interest in comparisons with Korean in etymological dictionaries of Japanese at the time was on vocabulary. This is also evident in the record of a conversation between Arai and Amenomori on the Korean language, as recalled by Arai:

> Amenomori Tōgorō's account of Korean.
>
> On the 18th November of Kanoe Uma [1714], Amenomori Tōgorō visited. I asked him: "It seems that the words of colloquial Korean are the same as Japanese – what do you think?" He replied: "I can think of four or five examples where they are identical. *Yanagi-gori* "willow basket" is called *kori*, written with the Chinese characters *kao-lao* but read *kori*. Also, *kama* "pot" is called *kama* in colloquial language, and *kabuto* "helmet" is called *kabuto*. There are others like that, but I have forgotten them" (Arai, *Taishiroku* 587–88).

In Amenomori's thinking, the study of Korean occupies a prominent place. He outlines his approach in the preface to the *Zen'ichi Dōjin* (MS dated 1729):

> Who in our country who is concerned with official business does not aspire to learning Korean? But as there are no books or guidance for it, one can only lament the lack of any direction. Therefore I have compiled four works; first, one reads *Inryaku Onmon* to get to know the letters and how to read them, next, *Shūsaku Gagen* to get to know the words, *Zen'ichi Dōjin* to cultivate the mind, and *Teiku Iwan* to get proficient in (language) use. [...] (Amenomori, *Zen'ichi Dōjin* 78).

Unfortunately, of the above tetralogy for learning Korean only *Zen'ichi Dōjin* survives. Judging from the above titles and description of contents, it appears to be the work least concerned with the language itself, attempting instead "to cultivate the mind". In fact, it contains a selection of moralist tales by a Ming-period Chinese playwright Wang Ting-Nei alias Chuan-yi Dao-jen (Zen'ichi Dōjin in Japanese pronunciation), probably translated from the Chinese into Korean by Amenomori.

Judging from the above quotation "first, one reads *Inryaku Onmon* to get to know the letters and how to read them", Amenomori considered the study of *hankul* to be the first step towards learning Korean. However, the format of *Zen'ichi Dōjin* does not follow that approach in that sentences are first given in Korean, transliterated in *katakana*, with *hankul* frequently given alongside it, followed by a Japanese translation.

The author himself explains this format in the introductory remarks as follows:

[...] this is merely a shortcut for guiding the student, and not the correct way of creating proficient people. The only way to do that is to select bright persons, send them from age seven or eight to Korea, and get them to learn the language using *hankul* from the start (ibid. 78).

He goes on to say that words written in *hankul* are not always pronounced as they are written, and quotes examples (e. g. *han-rim* becoming in *katakana* transliteration *harurimu*, i. e. *hal-lim*, MS: 8) after pointing out similar instances in Japanese, and notes that even Korean boys make mistakes in reading the script correctly, wherefore it is necessary to have sufficient knowledge of the phonetic rules before attempting to read texts entirely in *hankul*.

Amenomori also comments (with some irony) on phonetic differences between the two languages.

Although Koreans cannot pronounce voiced sounds, they used to be famous for being able to speak well older forms of Japanese. According to what the [Korean] interpreters say, today's young judges lack that aspiration, and say that it is funny that they pronounce even easy words such as *kosarimasu* [i. e. *gozarimasu*] as *kosarimasu*. These speakers themselves think that they are pronouncing things correctly, but to Japanese ears they all sound like *kosarimasuru*, which is funny. One must realise that the same sort of thing happens when Japanese speak Korean (ibid 14–15).

Besides being a text for familiarizing the reader with the Confucian way of thinking prevalent in Korea, *Zen'ichi Dōjin* was obviously also intended as a textbook for learning the language.

After reading *Zen'ichi Dōjin* in the *kana* version and having memorised it well, one should study it again in the *hankul* version with a Korean person; otherwise one will not master real Korean (ibid. 14–15).

The most widely used text for the study of Korean in Tokugawa/Meiji Japan is said to have been *Kōrin Shuchi* "Essential knowledge for neighbourly contacts", which is attributed to Amenomori Hōshū. Having circulated in copied manuscript form (no author given in surviving manuscripts), it was eventually printed by Japan's Foreign Ministry, which had taken over the responsibility of furthering Korean language studies, in 1881 (under Amenomori's name), and later variously in revised form.

The *Kōrin Shuchi* is organized in traditional dictionary form, arranged by subject. Entries are single or compound Chinese characters, followed by a Korean example sentence using the word, written in vertical *hankul*. To the right or left of the *hankul* is a parallel Japanese translation, in the beginning in *katakana* and *kanji* mix, later with *katakana* on the left and Chinese characters that correspond to Chinese loanwords in Korean on the right. There are no introduction or notes comparing the two languages.

Other works of a similar format include the *Ringo Taihō* "Outline of the neighbouring country", which appears to have been used for the study of Korean during the latter half of the Tokugawa period, but was also printed in Korea for the study of the Japanese language. Essentially, the format of the abovementioned works seems to be based on the 17th century Korean textbook of Japanese *Chephai Sin.e* and the dictionary *Way.e Lyuhai*.

Occasionally, Amenomori comments on differences between the languages he knows (Korean expressions given in *katakana*, and transliterated here from the same):

Spoken Japanese is long-winded and lax. For instance, *sō de gozarimasu* "that is so" is in spoken Korean, *kuritsusoi*, which is short and compressed. In spoken Chinese, it is just one character. In spoken Japanese, *sō arite kara* "thereafter" is long-winded and lax. In spoken Korean, *kurihataka* is short and compressed. In spoken Chinese, it is just one character. In this way, there are great differences between the various languages (*Hōshū Bunshû*, as quoted in Ogura 1920: 153).

## 3. The nature of comparisons and later developments

As shown above, comparisons of Japanese with Chinese were attempted by Confucian/Chinese scholars on the one hand, and *kokugaku* scholars on the other. The former concentrated on etymology and how to render grammatical elements in Japanese, but tended to compare things objectively, especially in the person of Arai Hakuseki, who often blamed opaque etymologies on the inability of Japanese to accommodate foreign sounds because of its poor sound inventory. *Kokugaku* scholars views are much more biased in favour of Japanese, accusing Chinese (and other languages) of being impure *because* of their larger sound inventory, and morphologically (and semantically) unrefined because they lack the agglutinative morphology of Japanese, an approach that echoes the arguments trying to prove the superiority of Indo-European languages over isolating and agglutinative ones by European scholars such as the Schlegel brothers and A. Schleicher in the 19th century.

Early comparisons with Korean were much more limited, which was initially due to the limited knowledge of the language, resulting in reference to the vocabulary and writing system (the emphasis of research was more on Korean institutions and customs). Later, language textbooks were compiled; some key works here were lost, so we do not really know whether there existed any structural comparison between the two languages, but from what survives it appears that the study of Korean took place in the form of side-by-side translations of text, without any grammatical explanations. This can be explained by the tradition of learning by rote without analysis (recall Amenomori's above-quoted advice "After reading *Zen'ichi Dōjin* in the *kana* version *and having memorised it well*, one should *study it again* in the *hankul* version [...]"), but also the structural similarity of the two languages, which made the side-by-side translation format possible.

Structural comparisons with Korean did not take place until well into the modern Meiji period (1868–1912), when scholars like Ōya Tōru and Kanazawa Shōzaburō began researching these aspects, using Western methodology.

## 4. Bibliography

### 4.1. Primary sources

Amenomori, Hōshū, *Zen'ichi Dōjin.* 1729. Facsimile of ms. and part-transcription *Zen'ichi Dōjin no kenkyū.* Ed. by Kyoto Daigaku Bungakubu Kokugogaku Kokubungaku Kenkyūshitsu. Kyoto: Kyoto Daigaku Kokubungakukai, 1964.

–, attr., *Kōrin Shuchi.* No date. Facsimile of ms. *Kōrin Shuchi, honbun, kaidai, sakuin.* Ed. by Kyoto Daigaku Bungakubu Kokugogaku Kokubungaku Kenkyushitsu. Kyoto: Kyoto Daigaku Kokubungakukai, 1966.

Anon., *Anegakōjike Tenihaden.* 14~15th century Transcription *Kokugogaku Taikei*, vol. VII. Tokyo: Kokusho Kankōkai, 1975.

Anon., *Teniha Taigaishō.* 14~15th century. Transcription *Kokugogaku Taikei*, vol. VII. Tokyo: Kokusho Kankōkai, 1975.

Aoki, Kon'yō, *Kon'yō Manroku.* 17th century. *Nihon Zuihitsu Taisei*, first series, vol. XX. Tokyo: Yoshikawa Kōbunkan, 1976.

Arai, Hakuseki, *Tōga.* Ms. 1719. *Arai Hakuseki*, vol. I. *Nihon kyōiku shisō taikei*, vol. X. Tokyo: Tokyō Nihon Tosho Sentā, 1979.

–, *Taishiroku.* No date. *Arai Hakuseki*, vol. II. *Nihon kyōiku shisō taikei*, vol. X. Tokyo: Tokyō Nihon Tosho Sentā, 1979.

Kamo no, Mabuchi, *Goikō.* 1789. *Zenshū* [Collected Works], vol. XIX. Tokyo: Zoku Gunsho Ruijū Kanseikai, 1980.

Minagawa, Kien, *Joji Shōkai.* 1811. Facsimile. Tokyo: Benseisha Bunko, 1978.

Motoori, Norinaga, *Mojigoe Kanazukai.* 1776. *Motoori Norinaga Zenshū* [Collected Works], vol. V. Tokyo: Chikuma Shobō, 1968.

–. *Kanji San'onkō.* 1785. *Motoori Norinaga Zenshū* [Collected Works], vol. V. Tokyo: Chikuma Shobō, 1968.

–. *Tamakatsuma.* No date. *Motoori Norinaga Zenshū* [Collected Works], vol. I. Tokyo: Chikuma Shobō, 1968.

Ogyū, Sorai, *Yakubun Sentei.* Ms. 1711. *Zenshū* [Collected Works], vol. II. Tokyo: Misuzu Shobō, 1974.

Suzuki, Akira, *Gengo Shishuron.* 1824. Facsimile *Gengo Shishuron, Gago Onjōkō, Kiga.* Tokyo: Benseisha Bunko, 1979.

Tanikawa Kotosuga, *Wakun no Shiori*, introductory volume. 1777. Facsimile Tokyo: Benseisha Bunko, 1984.

Yamaoka, Matsuake. *Ruiju Meibutsukō.* 1779. Tokyo: Kondō Kappanjo, 1904.

### 4.2. Secondary sources

Kaiser, Stefan, 1994. "Japan: History of Linguistic Thought". *Encyclopedia of Language and Linguistics* 1800–1804. Oxford: Pergamon Press.

Ogura, Shinpei. 1920. "Amenomori Hōshū no Chōsen gogaku [Amenomori Hōshū's Korean Language Studies]. (Repr. *Ogura Shinpei Hakushi Chosakushū* ed. by Kyoto Daigaku Bungakubu Kokugogaku Kokubungaku Kenkyūshitsu. Kyoto: Kyoto Daigaku Kokubungakukai, 1975.)

Ryo, Sang-hee. 1980. *Edo-jidai to Meiji-jidai no Nihon ni okeru Chōsengo no kenkyū* [Korean Language Studies in the Edo and Meiji Periods in Japan.] Tokyo: Seikō Shobō. (English summary, 314–305.)

*Stefan Kaiser, Tsukuba (Japan)*

# 12. Sprache und Denken in der japanischen Sprachforschung während der *Kokugaku*

1. Einleitung
2. Keichū (1640–1701)
3. Kamo Mabuchi (1697–1796)
4. Motoori Norinaga (1730–1801)
5. Fujitani Nariakira (1738–1779)
6. Motoori Haruniwa (1763–1828)
7. Suzuki Akira (1764–1837)
8. Tōjō Gimon (1786–1843)
9. Schluß
10. Bibliographie

## 1. Einleitung

*Kokugaku*, die sog. Nationale Wissenschaft, gilt als Höhepunkt der traditionellen japanischen Sprachwissenschaft während der Edo-Zeit (1603–1868). Die starke Reaktion auf die Überfremdung durch den Einfluß der chinesischen Kultur und Sprache auf Japan führte zu einer nationalistischen Geisteshaltung seit dem ausgehenden 17. Jh. Durch die Rückbesinnung auf die japanischen Wurzeln entstand die *Kokugaku*-Philologie als eine religiöse, poetische, philologische und historische Wiederbelebung des altjapanischen Geistes. Im 18. Jh. beschäftigten sich sehr viele Wissenschaftler mit der altjapanischen Sprache und in diesem Zusammenhang mit der Segmentierung und Erforschung der japanischen Sprache in räumlicher, zeitlicher und sozialer Hinsicht. Die frühere Blütezeit der japanischen Sprachwissenschaft ist die Heian-Zeit (794–1185), in der erst einmal die Adaption der chinesischen Schrift auf die japanische Sprache morphologisch, semantisch und grammatisch vollzogen wurde. Die höfische und klösterliche Beschäftigung mit chinesischen und japanischen Texten brachte interessante poetologische, semasiologische und orthographische Resultate mit sich. Im Mittelpunkt der Aufgaben der japanischen Philologie, die in der Heian-Zeit noch im wesentlichen nach der chinesischen Philologie ausgerichtet war, standen normative und kommentatorische Fragen.

Nach Auffassung der Vorreiter der *Kokugaku*-Philologie sollte die japanische Staatsidee durch die Erklärung der Sitten der alten Zeit und der Wörter des Altertums rekonstruiert werden, um den verlorenen Weg der Götter wiederherzustellen, der wegen des chinesischen Einflusses auf die japanische Kultur verlorengegangen sei. Dieses Unterfangen, das dadurch extrem erschwert wurde, daß das Japanische in Sprache und Schrift durch das Medium des Chinesischen überlagert und verdeckt wurde, führte durch eine intensive Beschäftigung mit den altjapanischen Texten zu einer Vervollkommnung der linguistischen Methoden und zu zahlreichen, bis heute beachteten literaturwissenschaftlichen und linguistischen Ergebnissen. Als Hauptarbeitsfelder der Philologen galten die Orthographie, die Phonologie, die Etymologie, die Lexikologie, die Morphologie, die Grammatik und die Stilistik.

## 2. Keichū (1640–1701)

Als Wegweiser für die vergleichend-historische Art des Herangehens an die Sprachanalyse gilt die Bearbeitung der Gedichtsammlung *Manyōshū* "Sammlung aus zehntausend Generationen" (8. Jh.) des buddhistischen Mönchs Keichū mit dem Titel *Waji shōranshō* "Traktat zur Richtigstellung der japanischen Schrift" (1693, gedruckt 1695). Als Fortführung der Lautforschung der japanischen Sanskritistik (*shittangaku*) und der poetischen Orthographiestudien des Mittelalters (*kanazukai* "Gebrauch der Silbenschriftzeichen") systematisierte Keichū die historische Silbenschriftorthographie auf der Basis der Fünfziglautetafel (*gojūonzu*).

Die Silbenschrift, deren vollständige Ausbildung im 9. und 10. Jh. geschah, divergierte bereits am Ende der Heian-Zeit (11.–12. Jh.) stark von der Aussprache. Die Lautveränderungen betrafen viele Lautgruppen. Zu orthographischen Problemen führten besonders der Schwund der bilabialen und palatalen Halbvokale /wo/ > /o/, /wi/ > /i/, /we/ > /e/ oder /ye/ > /e/ und die Veränderung des inlautenden /Fa/, der im Altjapanischen noch als /*pa, *pi, *pu, *pe, *po/ klang und über bilabial /Fa, Fi, Fu, Fe, Fo/ schließlich im 12. Jh. über Verstimmhaftung weiter zu /wa, wi, wu, we, wo/ geworden ist. Die Entstehung von Silbenschlußvokalen sowie langen und palatalisierten Konsonanten führte zu weiteren Abweichungen von Laut und Schriftbild.

Seit der Heian-Zeit sind mehrere Regelbücher für die Beseitigung des orthographischen Durcheinanders entstanden, die als Basis für Keichūs Studien galten. Keichū ging jedoch über die Methoden seiner Vorgänger weit hinaus, indem er die *Kana*-Orthographie auf ihre Ursprünge, auf die *Manyōgana*-Schreibung ("entlehnte Schriftzeichen des *Manyōshū*") etymologisch zurückführt. Durch die genaue Gegenüberstellung der Zeichen gelangte er zu den Schwachstellen des Systems. Die grundlegende Frage lautete für ihn jedoch nicht, welche *Kana* am besten den damaligen Lautwert wiedergeben, sondern mit welchen einzelnen Silbenzeichen die Wörter auch in der *Hiragana*-Schreibung durch das Schriftbild bedeutungsmäßig unterscheidbar sind. Seine etymologisch unantastbare Orthographie konnte die Abweichungen zwischen Schrift und Lautung zwar nicht beseitigen, dennoch blieb sie bis zum 16. November 1946, d. h. bis zum Erlaß einer neuen amtlichen Rechtschreibung als geltende Orthographie erhalten (Müller-Yokota 1987: 50).

Keichū gilt damit in Japan als Entdecker der vergleichend-historischen phonologischen Methode, da er dem Prinzip der 'Überlieferung' das Prinzip des 'Quellenvergleichs' und der 'Gesetzmäßigkeiten' gegenüberstellte (Streb 1977: 200). Durch den Umfang der herangezogenen sprachlichen Fakten und durch die Vorstellung des Vergleiches auf der Basis verschiedener Sprachstufen konnte er tiefer in den Wirkungsmechanismus der Sprache eindringen und auch die Hauptepochen der japanischen Sprache historisch umreißen. Diese neue Etappe in der Entwicklung der japanischen Sprachwissenschaft kann man als induktive, historische Sprachwissenschaft bezeichnen.

Von großer Bedeutung ist weiterhin die Tatsache, daß seine Erkenntnisse nunmehr nicht als buddhistische Geheimwissenschaft gehütet wurden, sondern daß er durch die Öffentlichkeit eine allgemeine Bereicherung der Sprachwissenschaft leistete. Ende des 17. Jhs. begann sich deutlich der wirtschaftliche Aufstieg des Landes durch die städtisch-bürgerliche Entwicklung abzuzeichnen. Von offizieller Seite gründete das Schogunat Bildungsmöglichkeiten für die Krieger- und Verwaltungsschicht. Daneben wuchsen die privaten Schulen für Medizin und chinesische und japanische Philologie, als Bildungsmöglichkeit für die Herrscherschicht und für die immer reicher werdenden Bürger.

## 3. Kamo Mabuchi (1697–1796)

Kamo Mabuchi ist neben seinen Studien der altjapanischen Dichtung und Gebete als ideologischer Begründer der *Kokugaku* bekannt geworden. Seine philologische Schule gründete er in Edo (im heutigen Tokyo). Die Konzeption der Erforschung der nationalen Kultur und Sprache legte er in fünf Abhandlungen dar: *Bunikō* "Abhandlung über die Bedeutung der Literatur" (1747), *Kokuikō* "Abhandlung über die Bedeutung des Reiches" (1767), *Shoikō* "Abhandlung über die Bedeutung der Schriften" (1767), *Goikō* "Abhandlung über die Bedeutung der Sprache", mitunter rein japanische Lesung des Titels – *Kotoba no kokoro no kōgae* (1769), *Kaikō* "Abhandlung über die Bedeutung der Dichtung" (1769).

In diesen Abhandlungen betrachtet er das Japanische als eine Sprache göttlicher Herkunft in Harmonie mit Himmel und Erde. In seiner Argumentation greift er zwei Metaphern über die japanische Sprache auf, die bis heute in der emotional-ideologischen Art der kulturtheoretischen Reflexion des Japanischen immer wieder erscheinen. Die erste Metapher bezieht sich auf die Vorstellung von der Wortseele (*kotodama*), die zweite auf das Schweigen. Da die Ahngötter von Himmel und Erde Japan die Sprache zu lehren geruhten, gibt es kein solches Beispiel in anderen Ländern. Wegen der ununterbrochenen göttlichen Tradition ist Japan das Land, das seit alters her durch die Wortseele (*kotodama*) blüht. Die andere Manifestation der Harmonie ist darin zu sehen, daß Japan das Land des Schweigens sei, denn während das alte Japan wortlos (*koto agesenu*) gewesen sei, bahnte sich China seinen Weg im Gegensatz dazu lärmend (*koto saegu*).

Das Lautsystem des Japanischen entspricht auch dem Mythos der idealen Harmonie, da die 50 Silben von Himmel und Erde selbst geschaffen (*ametsuchi no onozukara naru*) sind, daher einfach und ökonomisch geprägt wurden. Daß Phänomene schöpfungsbedingt natürlich entstanden sind, d. h. aus sich selbst hervorgetreten sind, gilt in dieser Theorie als eindeutiges Qualitätsmerkmal. Die herausragenden Vorzüge des Japanischen im Vergleich zum Chinesischen lassen sich auch an dem ursprünglichen Lautsystem erkennen. Kamo Mabuchi versucht auch die Tatsache zu deuten, daß sowohl das Chinesische als auch das Japanische einen Tonhöhenakzent besitzen, wobei er die Meinung vertritt, daß diese Distinktionen im Japanischen nicht primär seien. Weiterhin ist er der Auffassung, daß die Fünfziglautetafel etwas genuin Japanisches sei, während Keichū die Überzeugung vertrat, daß die Fünfziglautetafel auf die silbische Systematisierung der Sanskrit-Forschung zurückginge.

Die Idee, die Sprache morphologisch stärker auf die Fünfziglautetafel zu beziehen, ist zwar bereits im 13. Jh. zu erkennen, als Grundlage der Sprachbeschreibung entfaltet sich diese Idee jedoch erst zur Zeit der *Kokugaku.* So entwickelt auch Kamo Mabuchi richtungsweisend seine Theorie der Systematisierung der japanischen Konjugation, indem er die Vokale der horizontalen Stufenschemata der Fünfziglautetafel mit der Bedeutung der Wörter verbindet (Text in Fukui, *Goikō* 1975: 4).

1. a-Stufe *koto hajimuru koe* "Wortlaut des Anfangens" *yukan* (Futurum)
2. i-Stufe *koto ugokanu koe* "Wortlaut des Sich-nicht-bewegens" *yuki-* (verbales Nomen)
3. u-Stufe *koto ugoku koe* "Wortlaut des Sich-bewegens" *yuku* ('bewegliche' Finalform des Verbs)
4. e-Stufe *koto ōsuru koe* "Wortlaut des Befehlens" *yuke* (Imperativ)
5. o-Stufe *koto tasukuru koe* "Wortlaut des Helfens" (die Verbform mit postpositionellen Hilfswörtern, die häufig auf *-o* enden: *wo, to, zo, no, mo*).

Kamos Verbparadigma beschreibt noch nicht die verschiedenen Typen von Verben, sondern erst die 4-stufige Verbalflexion des klassischen Japanischen (modern 5-stufig), vermengt es jedoch in der fünften Stufe noch mit den unveränderlichen Postpositionen.

Es ist umstritten ob diese Konjugationstabelle, die sich als System im Prinzip später durchgesetzt hat, Kamo Mabuchi oder Tanigawa Kotosuga (1709–1776) zuzuschreiben ist, da sich in einer Arbeit von Tanigawa in einem Anhang zu einem Kommentar des *Nihon shoki* "Annalen Japans" (1761) das gleiche Verfahren findet.

Der Begriff des Wortwandels umfaßte nach Kamos Ansichten aus dem *Goikō* vier Arten:

1. Wortkürzung (*tsuzumegoto*), z. B. *awafumi* > *afumi;*
2. die Wortlängung (*nobegoto*), z. B. *miru* > *miraku;*
3. die Wortwendung (*utsushi-megurashi-kayou*), z. B. *mimashi* > *mimushi;*
4. die Silbenauslassung (*habukugoto*), z. B. *ihe* > *he.*

Diese Termini, die bereits in dem etymologischen Wörterbuch von Kaibara Ekiken (1630–1714) *Nihon shakumyō* "Japanische Worterklärungen" (1700) zu finden sind, wurden von Kamo und anderen *Kokugaku*-Gelehrten für die etymologische Analyse der lautlichen und silbischen Veränderungen und Worterklärungen angewandt. Eingebürgert haben sich die Termini leicht verändert als: *nobegoto, tsuzumegoto, tsūon, yakuon* und das gesamte Verfahren als *en-yaku-tsū-ryaku.* Die in der Fortführung dieser Methode praktizierte unwissenschaftliche Verbindung der einzelnen Silben mit bestimmten festen Bedeutungen im Rahmen der Wortseelenhypothese bei Hirata Atsutane (1776–1843) führte zu ideologischen Verirrungen und dazu, daß diese Art des Etymologisierens in Verruf geraten ist (Lewin 1981: 35).

Die Übernahme der chinesischen Schrift für die japanische Sprache wird von Kamo Mabuchi heftig kritisiert. Er erkennt die Ökonomie der phonetischen Wiedergabe gegenüber der ideographischen. In Indien und in Holland werden nur 50 oder 25 Buchstaben verwendet, um tausende von Büchern zu schreiben. In der chinesischen Schrift muß man zahllose Elemente behalten, die lästig seien. Weiterhin ist er der Ansicht, daß durch die Übernahme der chinesischen Schrift in der japanischen Sprache die ursprüngliche Harmonie gestört wurde. Kamos Gegenüberstellung des Chinesischen und des Japanischen, die Hypostasierung des japanischen Idealsystems führt zu einem geschlossenen Vorurteilssystem. Trotz dieses ideologischen Hintergrundes sind die Ergebnisse der philologischen Arbeit enorm. Ein ähnlicher Widerspruch zeigt sich bei seinem bedeutendsten Schüler Motoori Norinaga (vgl. 4.).

Trotz der ideologischen Widersprüche, die auf eine romantische nationale Selbstbesinnung zurückzuführen sind, ist festzustellen, daß Kamo Mabuchi einen enormen Beitrag dazu geleistet hat, die japanische Sprache zeitlich und räumlich zu charakterisieren, d. h. die Sprachwissenschaft aus einem universalistischen Verfahren hinauszuführen. Bei der Suche nach der idealen Kohärenz des Altjapanischen treten die einzelnen Entwicklungsschritte des Japanischen und deren Unterschiede im Vergleich zum Chinesischen zum Vorschein; damit wird die Differenzierung der Sprache in zeitlicher und räumlicher Hinsicht geschaffen.

## 4. Motoori Norinaga (1730–1801)

Arzt und Privatgelehrter, Begründer einer großen Privatschule für Kokugaku in Matsuzaka, war Motoori Norinaga der bedeutendste Sprachforscher des 18. Jhs., der die ganze Breite der damaligen philologischen Forschung vertrat. Seine etwa 500 Schüler übten auf die geistesgeschichtliche Entwicklung Japans eine große Wirkung aus. Seine Betätigungsfelder umfaßten die Altertumskunde, Religionswissenschaften, Philosophie, Literaturwissenschaft und Linguistik. Seine breiten historischen Kenntnisse verschafften ihm einen ungewöhnlich umfassenden Weitblick und verhalfen ihm zu scharfen Beobachtungen auf den Gebieten der Phonologie, Etymologie und Grammatik des Japanischen. Sein zentrales Werk war die Edition des *Kojiki* "Aufzeichnungen von Begebenheiten aus alter Zeit" (712) mit dem Titel *Kojiki-den* "Kojiki-Edition" (geschrieben in 35 Jahren zwischen 1764–1798, veröffentlicht 1790–1822) auf dessen Rekonstruktion alle späteren Untersuchungen dieser historischen Quelle basieren.

Bei der Ausarbeitung der Probleme der historischen Phonologie des Altjapanischen besteht das Verdienst von Motoori vor allem darin, daß er den altjapanischen Vokalbestand von 8 Vokalen anhand der in *Manyōgana* geschriebenen Texte im *Kojiki* rekonstruiert hat. In den folgenden drei Abhandlungen leistete er einen bedeutenden Beitrag zu der Weiterentwicklung von phonologischen Kategorien aus der chinesischen Phonologie und zu der Verbindung des chinesischen Lautsystems in verschiedenen zeitlichen Stadien mit dem Lautsystem des sinojapanischen Vokabulars im Japanischen. Die Erklärung von lautlichen Veränderungen beruhte auf der Konstruktion von phonologischen Oppositionen wie leicht/schwer bei den Vokalen, was etwa der westlichen phonologischen Opposition vorne/hinten entspricht. *Jion kanazukai* oder *Mojigoe kanazukai* "Orthographie der sinojapanischen Silben" (1775, gedruckt 1776) ist eine Regelung des sinojapanischen Teils der Orthographie, d. h. die Ergänzung zu Keichūs Studien. *Kanji sanonkō* "Abhandlung über die drei sinojapanischen Lautungen" (1784, gedruckt 1785) ist eine detaillierte Studie über die drei verschiedenen Formen der sinojapanischen Lesungen (*kanon*, *goon*, *tōon*) und gleichzeitig eine ideologische Streitschrift über die Richtigkeit und Überlegenheit des japanischen Lautsystems. *Chimei jimei tenyōrei* "Beispiele für den abweichenden Gebrauch sinojapanischer Lautungen in Ortsnamen" (1798, gedruckt 1800) befaßt sich mit der Laut- und Kulturgeschichte von Ortsnamen.

Sehr gute Kenntnisse des japanischen und chinesischen Lautsystems stehen bei Motoori in einem klaren Widerspruch zu seinen Vorurteilen gegen das Chinesische, die aus der Überzeugung resultieren, daß nur das vermeintlich alte japanische Lautsystem rein, richtig und elegant sei. Das Japanische sei z. B. rein, da es ursprünglich keine konsonantischen Silbenschlußlaute, lange Vokale, Diphtonge und Nasale sowie Glottisverschlußlaute besaß, während das Chinesische solche unnatürlichen Lautelemente aufwiese. Lautänderungen im Sinne von Verunreinigungen hätten aus dem Einfluß des Chinesischen resultiert, da das Japanische vor der Heian-Zeit ohne Lautgruppenänderungen korrekt war. In diesem Kontext interessierte er sich auch für das Holländische und ließ durch Schüler in Nagasaki nachprüfen, ob auch das Holländische über bilabiale Silbenlaute (*we*, *wi*) verfügen würde, die im Japanischen zu seiner Zeit bereits nicht mehr ausgesprochen wurden. Diese Frage war auch deswegen von hoher ideologischer Bedeutung, weil im Kontext von bilabialen und palatalen Halbvokalen (*yi*, *wi*), die als Kombination von zwei Vokalen zu beschreiben waren, die lautkombinatorische Richtigkeit in Harmonie mit der göttlichen japanischen Sprache geklärt werden mußte.

Die Hauptaufmerksamkeit Motooris auf dem Gebiet der Grammatik war auf die *Teniwoha* (grammatisch-morphologische Elemente des Japanischen: Postpositionen und Verbalsuffixe) und auf das Prädikat gerichtet. Unter Bezugnahme auf die poetologische Tradition in der grammatischen Erklärung untersuchte er eine Reihe von japanischen Gedichten, vor allem *Waka*, grammatisch. In den Abhandlungen *Teniowoha himokagami* "Schmuckspiegel der *Teniwoha*" (1771) und *Kotoba no tamanowo* "Perlenschnur der Wörter" (1779, gedruckt 1785) bezieht sich Motoori für die Erklärung der Wichtigkeit der *Teniwoha* auf die Schmuckmetapher. Wie in dem japanischen Altertum die Perlenketten als Schätze hochbegehrt waren, sollten auch die Partikel für die Schönheit der Sprache hochgeschätzt werden, da sie die Sätze arrangieren. Die wichtigste syntaktische und semantische Kraft der *Teniwoha* besteht in der Herstellung einer Kongruenzrelation zwischen dem Anfang und dem Ende des Satzes, die er mit *kakari-musubi* "Koordination des Nomens mit der Postposition zu der Finalform des Verbs" bezeichnet. Dieses Charakteristikum ist wiederum seit dem Götterzeitalter nur dem Japanischen eigen, so daß die chinesischen Partikel damit nicht vergleichbar wären. Chinesische Partikel stellen nämlich seiner Ansicht nach keine Harmonie zwischen Anfang und Ende einer Aussage her und überlassen alles dem impliziten Verstehen des Satzes. Motooris Entdeckung der *kakari-musubi* Relation war etwa zeitgleich mit Fujitani Nariakira. Der Begriff lebt heute in der engeren syntaktisch-morphologisch Interpretation weiter; eine breitere semantisch-textlinguistische Interpretation ist nicht mehr lebendig (Bedell 1968: 899). Nach diesem Prinzip sind im Frühmitteljapanischen bestimmte Postpositionen (*wa*, *zo*, *koso*) und die Prädikatsformen morphologisch und syntaktisch miteinander (Finalform, Attributivform, Konditionalform) verbunden. Die Korrelation der Postposition (*kakari*) mit der affizierten Flexionsform des Verbs (*musubi*) im Falle der emphatischen Postposition *zo* löst die Attributivform aus: *tada ariake no tsuki zo nokoreru* "nur Morgendämmerung [gen.] Mond wahrlich ist zurückgeblieben" = "nur eben der Mond der Morgendämmerung ist zurückgeblieben" (*-ru* Attributiv, *rentaikei*). Die Attributivform trat im Mitteljapanischen in prädikativer Stellung auf, wodurch diese Unterscheidung im modernen Japanischen nicht mehr existiert. Semantisch-argumentativ stellen Postpositionen eine bindende (*tsuzuku kaku*), etwa attributive Beziehung oder Nebensatzkonstruktion oder eine trennende (*kiruru kaku*) d. h. satzfinale Konstruktion her.

Motoori beschäftigte sich auch mit der Kategorisierung der Verbflexionsendungen. In seinem Werk *Mikuni kotoba katsuyōshō* "Traktat über die Konjugation der Wörter des erlauchten Landes" (1782, gedruckt 1886) faßte er morphologisch 27 Flexionsklassen der Verba und Qualitativa im Japanischen zusammen. Diese Klassifikation, die bei Motoori noch nicht ganz ausgereift war, wurde von seinem Sohn Motoori Haruniwa und von anderen Gelehrten wie Suzuki Akira und Tōjō Gimon weitergeführt und vervollkommnet (vgl. 6., 7., 8.).

Die Orientierung an der alten Sprache und an der Sprache der klassischen Zeit der frühmitteljapanischen Literatur konnte für den Pragmatiker Motoori Norinaga den Blick für andere Bedürfnisse seines Publikums nicht verdecken. 1888 veröffentlichte er die erste moderne und sehr freie Übersetzung des Gedichtbandes *Kokinshū* "Sammlung japanischer Gedichte einst und jetzt" (905–914) unter dem Titel *Kokinshū tōkagami* "Fernrohr zur Reflexion der Kokinshū" (1794), um seinen Schülern auch durch ihre Sprache einen emotionalen und literarischen Zugang zu der alten japanischen Poesie als Gegengewicht zu der chinesischen Literatur zu ermöglichen.

Eine der wichtigsten in der Sprachdiskussion der *Kokugaku* gewonnenen Einsichten betrifft die konstitutive Rolle der Emotionen für das Denken und die Sprache und die Einheit ihrer kognitiven Funktion. Das Ausgehen von der Behauptung, daß Bedeutungen durch die sinnlich-emotionale Erfahrung der Dinge entstehen und nur in diesem Sinne erfahrbar sind, hatte wichtige Konsequenzen für die linguistische Diskussion. Der Begriff *mono no aware* "das Bewegtsein durch die [emotionale Erfahrung] der Dinge", der von Motoori in dieser Richtung als Instrument der Erfassung von Bedeutungen vorgeschlagen wurde, führte zu einer Abkehr von der logistischen Betrachtung des Denkens.

## 5. Fujitani Nariakira (1738–1779)

Bruder des anerkannten China-Gelehrten Minagawa Kien, beschäftigte Fujitani Nariakira sich mit Geschichte, Astronomie und Dichtkunst; sein Werk ist wegen seines frühen Todes unvollendet. Fujitani gilt als der genialste Theoretiker des Japanischen, der sich von der chinesischen Tradition am stärksten losgelöst hatte (→ Art. 16). Seine eigenwillige Terminologie und Unabhängigkeit trugen dazu bei, daß er erst neuerdings volle Anerkennung erfährt (Lewin 1982: 32). In seinem frühen Werk *Kazashishō* "Traktat über die Haarpfeile" (1767) und in seinem späteren Werk *Ayuishō* "Traktat über die Saumbänder" (1773, gedruckt 1778) entwickelte er eine neue Wortklassentheorie (Lewin 1982: 33; Orig. Nakada 1960: 89):

> Mit den Namen (*na*) werden die Dinge (*mono*) verständlich gemacht, mit der Gewandung (*yosoi*) werden die Vorgänge (*koto*) bestimmt, mit den Haarpfeilen (*kazashi*) und Saumbändern (*ayui*) wird den Wörtern Hilfe geleistet, und diese vier Klassen sind anfänglich eine Wortseele (*kotodama*).

In dieser Klassifikation werden Nomina (*na*) zwar noch in der ursprünglichen Form benannt, andere Bezeichnungen weichen aber von den in dieser Zeit üblichen chinesischen Termini (*jitsuji* "nominaler Bereich", *kyoji* "verbaler Bereich", *joji* "Partikel") ab. Die Bedeutung der weiteren Bezeichnungen, die als Kleidungsstücke metaphorisch bezeichnet werden, sind: *yosoi* sind Verba und Qualitativa, *kazashi* sind Pronomina, Adverbia, Konjunktionen und Interjektionen, *ayui* bezieht sich wiederum auf Postpositionen und Suffixe. Die verschiedenen Klassen illustriert er mit klassischen und umgangssprachlichen Beispielen. Fujitanis Klassifikation ging über frühere Klassifikationsversuche hinaus, da er konsequent alle Wörter der Sprache erfaßt hat und gleichzeitig bestrebt war, eine eindeutige Zuteilung eines Wortes zu einer bestimmten Klasse vorzunehmen.

Fujitani versuchte ebenfalls, alle morphologischen Verknüpfungspunkte auszuarbeiten, und kam damit in seiner Flexionstabelle (*Yosoi no kata*) in dem Vorwort zu *Ayuishō* einen wesentlichen Schritt voran, indem er die Konjugationsformen in Stamm und Endung getrennt hat.

Fujitani führt seine Auffassung von der Sprache im Prozeß des Sprachwandels auch anhand der Kleidungsmetapher aus. Das Wesen der Sprache entspricht dem Bild eines Menschen vergangener Zeiten. Auf dem Kopf trägt er die 'Haarpfeile', auf seinem Körper die 'Kleider' und auf den Beinen die 'Saumbänder'. Die Kleidungsstücke von einst und jetzt haben sich jedoch verändert. Dieses Bild der sprachlichen Wandels folgt die Unterteilung in sechs Epochen, womit er eine genauere Bestimmung der aufgeführten Gedichtbeispiele als historische Quellen erreicht. Entsprechend dieses Prozesses fügt Fujitani den historischen Belegen umgangssprachliche Beispiele zu.

## 6. Motoori Haruniwa 1763–1828)

Sohn von Motoori Norinaga, systematisierte Motoori Haruniwa besonders den Bereich der Erforschung der Verba. Da er im Alter von 33 Jahren erblindete, mußte er mit den wissenschaftlichen Studien für seinen Vater früh aufhören.

Motoori Haruniwa führte die Lehre über die Flexionsklassen der Verba und Qualitativa weiter, indem er morphologische und semantische Unterscheidungen konsequenter aufeinander bezog. Er unterschied als erster zwischen regelmäßigen und unregelmäßigen Flexionsklassen und erkannte 7 Flexionsklassen von den heute üblichen 9. Die Endungsilbe der Verba wurde auf das Ordnungsschema der Fünfziglautetafel bezogen, indem man die Zahl der möglichen Alternationen des vokalischen Auslautes der Endungssilbe jeder Flexionsklasse auf die vertikal angeordneten Stufen (*dan*) der Tafel und die Zahl der möglichen konsonantischen Anlaute der Endungssilbe auf die horizontal angeordneten Reihen (*gyō*) bezog. In dem Werk *Kotoba no yachimata* "Acht Weggabelungen der Wörter" (1806, gedruckt 1808) hat er weitgehend die endgültige Aufstellung der Flexionsklassen geschaffen, indem er die 5 Vokalstufen der Fünfziglautetafel mit gleich auslautenden Funktionsformen kombiniert und so eine starke Reduzierung der bisherigen Klassen bewirkt. Motoori Haruniwa unterscheidet eine vierstufige (*a/i/u/e*), eine einstufige (heute obere einstufige Flexion *i*), mittlere zweistufige (heute obere zweistufige *i/u* Flexion), untere zweistufige (Alternation *u/e*) Verbalflexion sowie eine unregelmäßige *ka*-Reihe, *sa*-Reihe und *na*-Reihe. Die vierte unregelmäßige Flexionsklasse der *ra*-Reihe wurde von ihm noch nicht etabliert (Lewin 1990: 106).

Motoori Haruniwa widmet sein umfangreiches zweites Werk *Kotoba no kayoiji* "Verkehrswege der Wörter" (1828, drei Bände) der weiteren Systematisierung der Beschreibung der Verba im Japanischen. Er befaßt sich unter anderem mit den endoaktiven und exoaktiven Verba (*jidōshi* und *tadōshi*), eine Unterscheidung, die auf Fujitani Nariakira und auf dessen Werk *Ayuishō* zurückgeht (vgl. 5.).

## 7. Suzuki Akira (1764–1837)

Ursprünglich studierte Suzuki Akira Konfuzianismus und Medizin wie sein Lehrer Motoori Norinaga. Im Alter von 29 wurde er Schüler von Motoori. Suzuki konzentrierte sich besonders auf die Lehre von Wortarten und Konjugation.

Die einflußreichste Arbeit von Suzuki ist die Abhandlung *Gengyo shishuron* "Theorie über die vier Wortarten der Sprache" (1824). Er klassifiziert die japanischen Wortarten ebenso in vier Kategorien wie Fujitani, dessen Schriften er offenbar nicht kannte. Im Unterschied zu Fujitani scheint seine Kategorisierung eher von chinesischen Theorien in der Beschreibung des klassischen Chinesischen beeinflußt worden zu sein (vgl. 5.). Nach Ansicht Suzukis kann man die Wörter grundlegend in folgende Klassen trennen: in die Klasse der Nomina als Begriffswörter (*tai no kotoba*), Verbindungslemente wie Adverbien, Postpositionen, Interjektionen, Verbund Adjektivsuffixe (*teniwoha*), darüber hinaus Verba und Adjektiva (*yō no kotoba*), die wiederum in Verba, d. h. Handlungswörter (*shiwaza no kotoba*) sowie Adjektiva und Kopula d. h. Zustandswörter (*arikata no kotoba*) zu trennen sind. Die Unterscheidung in *tai* und *yō* geht auf die sinojapanische Unterteilung in unflektierbare und flektierbare Wörter zurück.

Suzuki wird mit seinem deutschen Zeitgenossen Wilhelm von Humboldt parallelisiert, besonders, was seine Auffassung über die morphologisch primitive chinesische Sprache angeht (Bedell 1968: 103). In Anlehnung an Motooris Meinung zu der Überlegenheit der morphologischen Struktur des Japanischen bemerkt er, daß das Chinesische und das Japanische zwar eine ähnliche kognitive Grundstruktur hätten, das Chinesische jedoch nicht wie das Japanische über genügend Mittel verfüge, um die Tiefenstruktur an der Oberfläche morphologisch repräsentieren zu können (vgl. 4.). Nomina, Verba und Adjektiva existieren im Chinesischen nur nach der Bedeutung und nicht nach der Form. Darüber hinaus fehlen im Chinesischen klare Tempus- und Modusformen, weswegen die Interpretation chinesischer Texte schwer sei. Solche Probleme würden seiner Ansicht nach im Japanischen nicht vorkommen. Suzuki behauptet, daß die Wortarten universal seien, wobei die Morphologie der Wortarten an der Oberfläche unterschiedlich ist. Nur das Japanische zeigt die Worarten in reinster Form.

Die Sprachentstehung steht im Mittelpunkt der Abhandlung *Gago onjōko* "Überlegungen zu den Lautungen der [klassischen japanischen] Sprache" (1816). Suzuki entwickelt hier selbständig den onomatopoetischen Ansatz der Sprachursprungstheorie. Nach seiner Auffassung kann man in der Sprache die Dinge lautlich abbilden. Er unterscheidet dabei vier Typen: Nachahmung von Tierstimmen (*karasu* "Krähe"), von menschlichen Stimmen (*kamu* "beißen"), Laute der Natur oder von Formen (*soyogu* "rauschen") Zuständen und Handlungen (*nameraka* "sanft"). Dabei ist jedoch die Beziehung zwischen Laut und Sinn teilweise nur verschwommen zu hören und zeitlich verdunkelt. Allgemein sei das Lautliche die Grundlage der Sprache und dasjenige, was die verschiedenen Sprachen verbindet. Suzuki teilt nicht mehr die Ansicht Motooris, daß das Japanische in lautlicher Beziehung alle anderen Sprachen überträfe, denn das Chinesische ist z. B. in Bezug auf die Onomatopoesie besonders stark ausgeprägt.

## 8. Tōjō Gimon (1786–1843)

Tōjō stammt aus einer Familie von buddhistischen Mönchen und Wissenschaftlern des Tempels Myōgenji in Obama (heute Fukui-Präfektur). Nach dem Tode seines Bruders 1807 übernahm er als Mönch die Leitung des Tempels. Er gilt als Motoori Schüler, ohne jedoch bei ihm persönlich studiert zu haben. Er korrespondierte mit Motooris Sohn Motoori Haruniwa. Tōjō ist weniger durch eigene Theorien bekannt, sondern als derjenige, der die Systeme anderere konsequent geordnet und vervollkommnet hat.

Auf dem Gebiet der Phonologie befaßte er sich im Werk *Namashina* "Namashina [ein Ortsname]" (geschrieben 1808, gedruckt 1837) mit den Auslauten der sinojapanischen und chinesischen Morpheme, die schon Motoori Norinaga beschäftigt hatten. In diesem Werk gelang ihm der Nachweis, daß die Auslaute *-n* auf zwei frühere Auslaute *-n* und *-m* zurückzuführen sind.

Die Studien *Tomo kagami* "Gemeinsamer Spiegel" (1823), die Konjugationstabelle *Wagosetsu ryakuzu* "Kurze Tabelle zur Erklärung japanischer Wörter" (1833) und das Kommentarwerk zu dieser Tabelle *Katsugo shinan* "Unterweisung zur Konjugation" (geschrieben 1810–1818, gedruckt 1844) bearbeiten die endgültige Systematisierung der Flexionsklassen. Von besonderer Wichtigkeit war die Eingliederung der Qualitativa in das Verbparadigma und die Analyse und Benennung der Funktionsbereiche der einzelnen Flexionsformen, die zum Teil noch in der heutigen Terminologie erhalten sind. Die Flexionsformen nannte Tōjō *gen* "Aussage(weise)":

Indefinitform *shōzengen* (= *mizenkei*),
Konjunktionalform *renyōgen* (*renyōkei*),
Finalform *setsudangen* (= *shūshikei*),
Attributivform *rentaigen* (= *rentaikei*),
Konditionalform *izengen* (= *izenkei*),
Imperativform *kegugen* (= *meireikei*).

Die Konjunktionalform fungiert im Japanischen als Prädikatsform in Vordersätzen von Satzverbindungen und als Kompositionsform des vorderen Gliedes in zusammengesetzten Verba und als Verbalnomen. Für den Begriff Flexionsform wurde von den Zeitgenossen eher die Bezeichnung *dan* "vertikale Stufen" benutzt, was später unter dem Einfluß des englischen *form* zu *kei* "Form" verändert wurde.

In der Wortarttheorie (*Katsugo shinan*) führte er die Arbeit Suzuki Akiras weiter und klassifizierte die Wörter in *taigen* "unflektierbare Wörter", *yōgen* "flektierbare Wörter" und *teniwoha* "Hilfswörter" konsequenter weiter.

## 9. Schluß

Gegenstand der japanischen Sprachwissenschaft in der Edo-Zeit war vor allem die alte und die klassische Sprache mit Vorbildcharakter. Die weltanschauliche Tragweite dieser ideologischen Position wird durch den Platz verdeutlicht, den bis heute die Stellungnahme für die Einzigartigkeit der japanischen Sprache neben der eigentlichen wissenschaftlichen Sprachwissenschaft in der öffentlichen Meinung einnimmt. Freilich ging es damals vielen vor allem darum, das Japanische von dem Chinesischen ideell weitgehend zu reinigen und die ursprüngliche, reine Form wiederherzustellen. Doch gab es nicht wenige, denen diese Konfrontation unwesentlich oder sogar schädlich erschien (z. B. Ueda Akinari, 1734–1809).

Die Leistung der *Kokugaku*-Philologie kann als zentraler Pfeiler der modernen Grammatik, Lexikologie und Syntax in Japan gelten. Auf den Gebieten der Phonologie, Orthographie, Etymologie, Grammatik und Syntax sind in der *Kokugaku*-Philologie wesentliche Leistungen erzielt worden.

Bei aller praktischen Betonung von bestimmten sprachlichen Aspekten wie Regeln, Bedeutungen und Zeichen, bleiben theoretische Voraussetzungen offen. Fujitanis und Motoori Norinagas Ausführungen zur Semantik sind zwar noch weitgehend unerforscht, dennoch kann bei diesen und anderen Autoren kaum eine kohärente Theorie für die Entstehung und das Funktionieren von Sprache vermutet werden.

Die Auseinandersetzung mit der eigenen Sprache durch historische Quellen, Literatur und Sprachwissenschaft, die vor allem von einem religiös-kulturellen Weltbild ausging, trug in dieser Zeit zur Herausbildung eines differenzierten Umgangs mit sprachlichen Fakten bei. Im gleichen Zeitraum entstanden wichtige Voraussetzungen der modernen Linguistik in Japan.

## 10. Bibliographie

### 10.1. Primärliteratur

Fukui, Kyūzō, Hg. 1938–1944. *Kokugogaku taikei.* 10 Bde. (2. Aufl., Tokyo: Hakuteisha, 1975.)

*Kokugakuin henshūbu*, Hg. 1904. *Kamo Mabuchi zenshū.* Teil II. Tokyo: Yoshikawa kōbunkan.

Motoori Norinaga, *Kojiki-den*, Bd. I. Hg. von Ann Wehmeyer, Vorwort Naoki Sakai. Ithaca: Cornell Univ. Press, 1997.

Nakada, Norio & Masao Takeoka, Hg. 1960. *Ayuishō shinchū.* Tokyo.

Ōno, Susumu, Hg. 1968–1974. *Kojiki-den. Motoori Norinaga Zenshū.* Bde. 9–12. Tokyo: Chikuma shobō.

Ueda, Mannen, Hg. 1926–1927. *Keichū zenshū.* 11 Bde. Tokyo: Asahi shinbun.

### 10.2. Sekundärliteratur

Bedell, George Dudley. 1968. *Kokugaku Grammatical Theory.* Cambridge, Mass.: MIT.

Dumoulin, Heinrich. 1955. "Zwei Texte Kamo Mabuchis zur Wortkunde". *Monumenta Nipponica* 11:3.48–63.

Eschbach-Szabo, Viktoria. 1990. "Chinesisch-Japanischer Sprachenvergleich bei Kamo Mabuchi". *Papers in Japanese Linguistics* hg. von Lone Takeuchi, 1–11. London.

Lewin, Bruno. 1982. *Sprachbetrachtung und Sprachwissenschaft im vormodernen Japan.* Opladen: Westdeutscher Verlag.

–. 1990. *Abriss der japanischen Grammatik.* 3. Aufl. Wiesbaden: Harrassowitz.

Loosli, Urs. 1981. "Sprachbeschreibung als Metapher: Fujitani Nariakira und die erste japanische Grammatik". *Referate des V. Deutschen Japanologentages vom 8. bis 9. April 1981 in Berlin* hg. von Sung-jo Park & Rainer Krempien, 130–138. Bochum: Brockmeyer.

–. 1984. *Die erste Grammatik des Fujitani Nariakira.* Diss. Universität Zürich.

Mc Ewan, J. R. 1949. "Motoori's View of Phonetics and Linguistics in his *Mojigoe no kanazukai* and *Kanji san on kō*". *Asia Major* 1.109–118.

Miller, Roy Andrew. 1993. *Die japanische Sprache: Geschichte und Struktur.* Übers. von Jürgen Stalph. München: iudicium.

Müller-Yokota, Wolfram. 1987. "Abriss der geschichtlichen Entwicklung der Schrift in Japan". *Bochumer Jahrbuch zur Ostasienforschung* 10.1–77.

Streb, Inga. 1977. *Keichūs Studien zur Entwicklung von Laut und Schrift in Japan – unter besonderer Bezugnahme auf das "Waji-shōranshō".* Diss. Universität Bochum.

Yanada, S. 1950. "Motoori Norinagas's Contribution to a Scheme of Japanese Grammar". *Bulletin of the School of Oriental and African Studies* 13.474–503.

Wenck, Günther. 1987 [1954]. "Über die Entdekkung und Systematisierung der japanischen Konjugation". Günther Wenck, *Pratum Japonisticum*, 132–143. Wiesbaden: Harrassowitz.

Winter, Prescott Bowmann. 1982. *Language, Thought and Institutions in Tokugawa Japan.* Ph. D. Stanford University.

*Viktoria Eschbach-Szabo, Tübingen (Deutschland)*

# 13. Die Frühzeit der neueren japanischen Sprachforschung: Vom *Kokugaku* zum *Kokugogaku*


1. Der Anfang der neueren japanischen Sprachforschung
2. Die linguistischen Bedingungen der Schaffung der modernen Literatur- und Umgangssprache
3. Ueda Kazutoshi (1867–1937)
4. Ōtsuki Fumihiko (1847–1928)
5. Yamada Yoshio (1873–1958)
6. Shinmura Izuru (1876–1967)
7. Matsushita Daisaburō (1878–1935)
8. Hashimoto Shinkichi (1882–1945)
9. Die Historiographie der Kokugogaku
10. Bibliographie


## 1. Der Anfang der neueren japanischen Sprachforschung

Mit der Öffnung Japans im Jahre 1868 entfaltete sich eine intensive Tätigkeit auf dem Gebiete der Sprachwissenschaft, die sich aus der ungehinderten Begegnung mit dem Westen und aus den neuen Bedingungen und Bedürfnissen der gesellschaftlichen und sprachlichen Praxis ergaben. Unter dem Terminus *Kokugogaku* "Japanische Sprachwissenschaft" oder "Wissenschaft, Philologie der Nationalsprache" (die Bezeichnung *Kokugogaku* wurde erst seit ca. 1890 gebraucht) ist die Tradition innerhalb der japanischen Sprachwissenschaft zu verstehen, die sich im wesentlichen auf die japanische Erforschung des Japanischen konzentriert. Japanisch wurde vor 1868 auch als *wago* "Sprache des Landes Wa" oder als *gengo, kotoba* "Sprache" bezeichnet, während *kokugo* "Landessprache, Nationalsprache" im Gegensatz zu fremden Sprachen als Bezeichnung der eigenen Staatssprache geprägt wurde. *Kokugogaku* geht zwar auf die traditionelle Philologie der *Kokugaku* "Nationale Wissenschaft" zurück, die sich in der Abwehrreaktion gegen die regimegeförderte Sinologie (*kangaku*) auf das ursprünglich Japanische besann, ist jedoch stark von der europäischen Sprachwissenschaft beeinflußt worden.

Die ersten systematischen westlichen Beschreibungen des Japanischen stammen von portugiesischen Missionaren, die seit Mitte des 16. Jhs. bis zu ihrer Ausweisung 1639 nach Japan kamen. Die Druckerei in Nagasaki veröffentlichte mehrere Lexika und Grammatiken des Japanischen, darunter die einmalige Grammatik von João Rodriguez (?1561–1649 *Arte da Lingoa de Iapam* 1604–1608). Rodriguez' Grammatik, die die Kategorien der lateinischen Grammatik auf das Japanische anwendet, erfaßt die Charakteristika des Japanischen über den lateinischen Rahmen hinaus sehr treffend. Die weitere europäische Beschreibung des Japanischen und die Vermittlung der westlichen grammatischen Kategorien konnten in Dejima bei Nagasaki im Zusammenhang mit derjenigen der holländischen Faktorei fortgeführt werden. Unter diesem Einfluß schrieb der *Kokugaku*-Vertreter Tsurumine Shigenobu (1788–1859) die erste Grammatik *Gogaku shinsho* "Neue Schrift zur Sprachwissenschaft" (1833), in der von einem Japaner versucht wurde, das Japanische mit den Termini aus der holländischen Grammatik wie Tempus und Modus zu beschreiben. Tsurumine stellte neun Wortklassen auf:

1. *ikotoba* "Nomen",
2. *tsukikotoba* "Qualitativa",
3. *kaekotoba* "Pronomen",
4. *tsuzukikotoba* "Attributiva",
5. *hatarakikotoba* "Verba",
6. *samakotoba* "Adverbia",
7. *tsuzukekotoba* "Konjunktionen",
8. *sashikotoba* "Präpositionen",
9. *nagekikotoba* "Interjektionen".

Mit der Öffnung Japans ging der Einfluß der *Rangaku* "Hollandwissenschaft" zurück. Für die Philologie und Sprachwissenschaft besaßen nun die ausländischen Missionare und Gastwissenschaftler eine enorme Bedeutung. In diesem Zusammenhang ist besonders das Wirken der Briten Basil Hall Chamberlain (1850–1935), William George Aston (1841–1911) – Grammatiker und Philologen – und des Amerikaners James Curtius Hepburn (1815–1911) – Lexikologe – zu erwähnen.

## 2. Die linguistischen Bedingungen der Schaffung der modernen Literatur- und Umgangssprache

In der Geschichte der Normierung der japanischen Sprache zeigt sich, daß in den grundlegenden Auffassungen über das Wesen der Sprache und besonders über die Struktur des Japanischen in den letzten Jahrzehnten des 19. Jhs. in der Zeit der Industrialisierung und

Modernisierung ein starker Wandel eingetreten ist. Dieser Wandel wurde durch die Rolle der Ausländer in der japanischen Philologie wesentlich beschleunigt. Man hat sich im großen und ganzen von dem Vorurteil befreit, daß die klassische japanische Sprache in der Form der höfischen Literatursprache des 9. und 10. Jhs. sozusagen eine ideale Urstruktur aufweist. Wesentlicher jedoch als diese Wandlung der Grundeinstellung in der Sprachwissenschaft ist die Bewegung, die von der gesamten Sprachgemeinschaft, darunter vor allem Literaten und Reformer des Schulwesens getragen wurde. "Die Gesellschaft zur Vereinheitlichung der gesprochenen und geschriebenen Sprache" (*genbun itchikai*) wurde von namhaften Politikern, Journalisten, Literaten und Linguisten im März 1900 gegründet (Maejima Hisoka, Nakai Kitarō, Ueda Kazutoshi, Ōtsuki Fumihiko, Shinmura Izuru etc.) (Twine 1991: 165).

Die wichtigsten Phasen der Entstehung der Standardsprache sind die folgenden:

1. Die sog. chaotische Phase, in der die Übersetzungstätigkeit einsetzt (1868–1885).
2. Die Zeit der Suche nach dem modernen literarischen Stil für japanische Werke (1886–1899).
3. Die Konsolidierung des einheitlichen Stils in der Schrift- und Umgangssprache (1900–1909).
4. Die Perfektionierung des umgangssprachlichen Stils (1909–1923) (Yamamoto, 1972).

Durch die eindeutige Verlegung der Hauptstadt in den Osten kam es zu der Aufwertung der gebildeten Stadtsprache von Edo. Sie zwang auch den normierenden Sprachkundler zu Zugeständnissen, zu weitgehender Berücksichtigung dessen, was tatsächlich gesprochen wurde. Der Terminus für Standardsprache *hyōjungo* "Gemeinsprache" ist als Übersetzung des Paulschen Terminus von Ueda Kazutoshi 1895 eingeführt worden. Die Vermeidung der Bezeichnung *zokugo* "vulgäre Umgangssprache", die in der bisherigen *Kokugaku*-Tradition als im wesentlichen verdorbene, von der idealen klassischen Schriftsprache abweichende Form betrachtet wurde, zeigt die geistige Einstellung Uedas. Der Terminus *hyōjungo* ist auch im Vergleich zur Bezeichnung *kōgo* "gesprochene Sprache" aufwertend gemeint. Der Terminus *hyōjungo* wurde mit der Paulschen Konzeption der Sprachnorm verbunden; so wurden auch Begriffe wie "usuelle Bedeutung" (*kanyōteki imi*), "lexikalische Bedeutung" (*goiteki imi*) und "Sprachwandel" (*gengo henka*) direkt übernommen. Der wirkliche Usus der Sprachgemeinschaft soll als Norm für die Landessprache *Kokugo* oder des Japanischen *Nihongo* gelten. Die Festlegung einer anderen als der klassischen Norm wurde bereits in der 'härtesten' Phase der Nationalen Schule im 18. Jh. vorbereitet. Motoori Norinaga, der ein glühender Vertreter der klassischen Schriftsprache gewesen war, hatte die dringliche Aufgabe erkannt und die klassische Poesie durch moderne Übersetzungen zu vermitteln versucht. Es war allerdings für die Linguisten der Meiji-Zeit nicht leicht, bei der Schaffung der neuen Norm der Umgangssprachlichkeit und den dialektalen Unterschieden Rechnung zu tragen. Der sprachhistorische Sprung in die Gegenwartssprache implizerte, daß man sich von dem etwa 900 Jahre alten Ideal der klassischen Schriftsprache und von der Verwendung des klassischen Chinesischen für viele Textgattungen trennen mußte. Ebenso große Diskussionen verursachte die Frage der Modernisierung oder aber der Abschaffung der Schrift. Vorschläge wie die Einführung des lateinischen Alphabets, der umfassenden Verwendung der Silbenschrift, die Begrenzung der Zahl der chinesischen Schriftzeichen und die Angemessenheit der historischen Silbenschriftorthographie wurden diskutiert. Mit der Reformierung der Schrift befaßten sich u. a. folgende Gesellschaften: *Kana no tomo* "Freunde der Silbenschrift" (gegründet 1882) und *Rōmaji kai* "Gesellschaft des Alphabets" (gegründet 1885) (Twine 1991: 224ff.). Die Reformierung der Schrift brachte eine neue Norm als eine leicht vereinfachte Variante der Mischschrift von Ideogrammen und Silben der traditionellen Schrift hervor.

Als Erfolg der Sprachreformbewegung ist die Entstehung einer neuen Standardsprache für die gesprochene und für die geschriebene Sprache und die stärkere Standardisierung der Schrift zu verzeichnen.

## 3. Ueda Kazutoshi (1867–1937)

Ueda Kazutoshi (Mannen) schrieb sich 1885 an der literaturwissenschaftlichen Fakultät der Kaiserlichen Universität in Tokyo ein und absolvierte bis 1888 das Fach japanische Literatur. In dem anschließenden Doktorkurs wurde er von Tsubouchi Shōyō (Literaturwissenschaftler und Sprachreformer, 1859–1935) und dem englischen Gelehrten Basil Hall Chamberlain (Englischlehrer und Linguist, der erste Ordinarius für Philologie an der Kaiserlichen Universität in Tokyo,

1850–1916) unterrichtet. Auf seiner Studienreise in Europa verbrachte er zwischen 1890–94 die überwiegende Zeit in Berlin und Leipzig und etwa ein halbes Jahr in Paris. In Berlin hatte er u. a. bei Georg von der Gabelentz gehört. In der Leipziger Zeit hatte Ueda die Gelegenheit gehabt, u. a. folgende Sprachwissenschaftler kennenzulernen: August Leskien, Karl Brugmann, Eduard Sievers, Hermann Osthoff sowie den Psychologen Wilhelm Wundt. Er knüpfte ebenfalls Beziehungen zu Hermann Paul, durch dessen Denken Ueda entscheidend geprägt wurde.

Nach seiner Rückkehr wurde er 1894 zum Professor der Philologie (*hakugengaku*) an der Kaiserlichen Universität ernannt. Ende 1895 heiratete er Murakami Tsuruko; Enchi Fumiko, eine Tochter aus dieser Ehe, wurde eine bekannte Schriftstellerin. 1898 wurde er Leiter des von ihm mitbegründeten sprachwissenschaftlichen Instituts der Universität, wo er die Gebiete japanische Sprachwissenschaft, Literatur und Geschichte betreute, die später in verschiedene Disziplinen geteilt wurden. Durch seine sprachpolitischen Petitionen an das Parlament gewann er immer größere Bedeutung und erhielt diverse Funktionen übertragen. Ebenso sichtbarer Ausdruck der Verknüpfung von Forschung und Sprachpolitik ist die auf Uedas Anregung 1900 ins Leben gerufene *Kokugo chōsa iinkai* "Kommission zur Untersuchung der Landessprache" beim Kultusministerium. Diese Kommission befaßte sich mit Untersuchungen zur Schriftreform, Sprachreform, Schulmaterialien, Umgangssprache und Dialekten. 1900 erfolgte die Umbenennung Uedas Lehrstuhls in *Gengogaku* "Sprachwissenschaft" und die Gründung der ersten fachwissenschaftlichen Zeitschrift: *Gengogaku zasshi* "Zeitschrift für Sprachwissenschaft". Im Jahr 1924 wurde er Vorstandsmitglied der *Tōyō bunko*, einer einzigartigen Asien-Bibliothek und Forschungsstelle. Mit seinem Schüler Shinmura Izuru gründete er 1926 die Japanische Gesellschaft für Phonetik (*Nihon onseigaku kyōkai*). Von der Japanischen Akademie der Wissenschaften wurde er 1926 zum Abgeordneten des Oberhauses gewählt. 1927 wurde er emeritiert und war anschließend als Leiter der Kokugakuin-Universität tätig. Ueda bildete eine ganze Generation japanischer Linguisten aus, die bis auf die Indogermanistik breit gefächert vertreten sind. Als direkte Schüler gelten Fujioka Katsuji (1872–1935), Altaische Sprachen), Shinmura Izuru (1876–1967), Lexikologe und historischer Linguist), Yuzawa Kōkichirō (1887–1963), Andō Masatsugo (1878–1952), Yoshizawa Yoshinori (1876–1954, Sprachhistoriker), Hashimoto Shinkichi (1882–1945, Grammatiktheorie), Tōjō Misao (1884–1966, Dialektologe), Ogura Shinpei (1882–1944, Koreanist), Iha Fuyū (1876–1947), Ryūkyū-Studien), Kindaichi Kyōsuke (1882–1971, Lexikologe, Ainu-Forscher), Tokieda Motoki (1900–1967, Grammatiker und Sprachtheorie), Hoshina Kōichi (1872–1955, Geschichte der Sprachwissenschaft). Eine besonders intensive Beziehung zu den Ideen der junggrammatischen Schule besteht bei Hashimoto Shinkichi und Tokieda Motoki. Mit dieser Namensliste soll gezeigt werden, daß Ueda wissenschaftspolitisch weitblickend die Disziplinenbildung und Professionalisierung der Sprachwissenschaft gefördert und somit bis in die 30iger Jahre des 20. Jhs. und in mancher Beziehung bis heute das Gesicht der japanischen Linguistik geprägt hat. Doi, der diese Zeit in seinem Werk *The Study of Language in Japan: A historical survey* (1976), sehr sorgfältig aufgearbeitet hat, behauptet, daß die neuen strukturalistischen Theorien zwar vordergründig Pauls Theorie verdrängt hätten, das ganze Gebiet aber substanziell von Pauls Prinzipien geprägt wurde und diese Ideen jetzt und in Zukunft immer wieder zurückkehren würden und die Forscher vor der Konfusion durch die Vielfältigkeit bewahren (Doi 1977: 175).

Als Sprachpolitiker kritisiert Ueda die Tendenz, sich den fremden Sprachen bedingungslos zuzuwenden (Sinologie und westliche Sprache) und ihre konfuzianische Kindespflicht (*kōkō*) gegenüber der eigenen Mutter zu vernachlässigen. Die japanische Sprache der modernen Zeit kann nicht mehr die Sprache einer gebildeten Minderheit sein, sondern die alltägliche Sprache des Volkes. Für die Entwicklung der Sprachwissenschaft seien vor allem folgende Bereiche zu bearbeiten: historische und vergleichende Grammatik, die Phonetik, die Sprachgeschichte, die Erforschung der Schriftzeichen und der Fremdwörter, der Homonyme und Synonyme, die Unterrichtsmethoden der Sprachausbildung und die Beschäftigung mit den Forschungsmethoden ausländischer Sprachen. (Diese Gedanken nimmt Ueda in seinem berühmten Vortrag *Kokugo to kokka* "Landessprache und Staat" 1894, publiziert 1895, auf).

Die für die sprachpolitische Arbeit wichtigsten Werke sind diejenigen, die konkrete

Untersuchungen auf dem Gebiet der Erforschung der modernen japanischen Sprache, Dialekte und Schrift initiierten und dann in späteren Jahren als Abschlußberichte der Kommissionsarbeit vorgelegt wurden. Der Bericht "On'in chōsa-hōkokusho "Bericht über die Aussprache in den einzelnen Landesteilen" (1905), *Kōgohō chōsa hōkokusho* "Bestandsaufnahme der Umgangssprache des Landes" (1906) konnten für die Phonologie, Orthographie und Sprachnormentwicklung benutzt werden. Die Anfangsetappen und die Entwicklung der japanischen Sprachwissenschaft wurden besonders in seiner von seinen Schülern veröffentlichten Universitätsvorlesung *Kokugogakushi* "Geschichte der Kokugaku" und in Aufsätzen wie in *Gengogakusha to shite no Arai Hakuseki* "Arai Hakuseki als Sprachwissenschaftler" (1894) und in den historischen Editionen der Philologen der nationalen Schule ermittelt. Schließlich wandte sich Ueda nach dem Vorbild Hermann Pauls dem Gebiet der Lexikologie intensiv zu und gab mehrere Lexika heraus. Seine erfolgreichsten Wörterbücher der japanischen Sprache wurden mehrfach aufgelegt und werden bis heute benutzt: das *Daijiten* "Das große Wörterbuch" (1917), das *Dai Nihon kokugo jiten* mit Matsui Kanji, das *Dai Nihon kokugo jiten* "Großes Wörterbuch der japanischen Sprache" (1915), und mit Takakusu Junjirō et al. das *Nihon gairago jiten* "Wörterbuch des japanischen Lehnwortschatzes" (1915).

Für die Schaffung der modernen Standardsprache waren bestimmte Schritte im linguistischen Denken erforderlich, die auch in der Phonologie verwirklicht werden mußten. Für den Sprachforscher war es wichtig, von den allgemeinen Gesetzen der Lautphysiologie überzeugt zu sein und sich von alten Vorurteilen über die speziellen Lauteigenschaften des Japanischen freizumachen. Die *Kokugaku*-Tradition prägte die Vorstellung, daß das japanische Lautsystem im Gegensatz zu anderen Sprachen 'gottgegeben' und deswegen 'natürlich' und 'richtig' sei. Ueda hat zu dem neuen Denken wesentlich beigetragen, wie zum Beispiel an dem konkreten Fall des altjapanischen stimmlosen Labials *p*, der später spirantisch wurde und sich über $h > f$ weiterentwickelte. Während dieses Problem in der *Kokugaku*-Philologie des 18. Jhs. Anlaß zu erbitterten Debatten bot, da man die stimmlosen Labiale nicht zu dem Phoneminventar des Altjapanischen rechnen wollte, scheint dieses Problem durch die 'Aufhellung der Gesetze und Prinzipien' der Phonologie der Neugrammatiker einfach lösbar. In dem Aufsatz *P-onkō* "Abhandlung zu dem Laut *p*" (1903) weist Ueda zwar noch kurz auf die sture Überzeugung Motoori Norinagas hin, daß die halbgetrübten Laute wie *p* keine 'richtigen' Laute des Altjapanischen seien; dennoch sprechen die Gesetzmäßigkeiten im Worzusammenhang, die Transkription der Lehnwörter aus dem Sanskrit, die Phonemstruktur der Onomatopoetika und die japanischen Lehnwörter im Ainu für die Annahme eines japanischen *p*-Phonems.

Der Einblick in den Bau jedes zu behandelnden Lautsystems konnte nach den Prinzipien der modernen Linguistik vorurteilsfrei ausgeführt werden. Die historischen Fakten wurden neu interpretiert. Ein weiterer Übelstand, nämlich die Konzentration auf die geschriebene Sprache, die durch die Übernahme der chinesischen Schrift im Japanischen die tatsächlich gesprochene Lautform noch zusätzlich verdunkelt hat, wurde unter dem Einfluß der ausländischen Philologie gänzlich aufgehoben, so daß die natürliche, unverbildete, gesprochene Sprache in den Berichten der Sprachkommissionen in den Vordergrund rücken konnte.

Da die europäische, grammatische Tradition bei der offiziellen Öffnung Japans bereits durch die Hollandwissenschaften lange bekannt war und teilweise durch die *Kokugakusha* "Nationale Schule" gedanklich vorbereitet wurde, entsteht keine offenkundige Fremdheit. Die Eingliederung des Eigenen und Fremden in ein allgemeines System wurde schon früher begonnen. Die Idee der Bestimmung der Linguistik als historische Sprachwissenschaft und Textphilologie läßt sich mit der philologischen Denkungsart der *Kokugaku*-Tradition, vor allem in der Prägung von Motoori, leicht verknüpfen. Die Erklärung empirischer Fakten und Beobachtungen durch entwicklungsgeschichtliche Zusammenhänge kann Synchronie und Diachronie verbinden; dies ist ein großer Vorteil des junggrammatischen Systems Paulscher Prägung. Die sprachlichen Erfordernisse des modernen Staates werden besonders durch die ausländische Philologie reflektiert. Die germanische Philologie als Philologie einer 'Vulgärsprache' bewirkt auch in Japan die Revolution der philologischen Denkart. Die für das Japanische so prägende chinesische und japanische klassische Schriftprache wird zugunsten der lebendigen Umgangssprache und von der neuen schriftlichen Variante des Japanischen langsam zurückgedrängt. Trotz vielfacher Beteuerung der Notwendigkeit einer kritischen Auseinandersetzung mit den sprachtheoretischen Grundlagen ist die empirische Ausprägung stärker. Die empirische Sammlung von Fakten wird historisch durchgeführt, wobei die vollständige detaillierte Erfassung intendiert wird. In den grammatischen Kategorien entsteht ein Mischsystem aus der lateinischen und der japanischen Grammatik, die viele Fragen des Japanischen, als einer nicht-indoeuropäischen Sprache, offenläßt. Die Doppelgestaltigkeit der Strukturen bleibt bis heute erhalten.

## 4. Ōtsuki Fumihiko (1847–1928)

Ōtsukis Vater war eine angesehene Autorität auf dem Gebiet der Sinologie. Er studierte selbst zuerst Sinologie, um sich später an dem Vorläufer der Kaiserlichen Universität dem Erlernen des Englischen zuzuwenden. 1872 bekam er einen Posten im Kultusministerium. Ōtsuki war Mitherausgeber des vielbändigen *Koji ruien* "Der klassifizierte Garten alter Sachen" (1879–1907), einer nach Sachgebieten geordneten Quellen-Sammlung aus der Zeit vor 1868. Ōtsuki war Mitglied der sprachpolitisch wichtigen Gesellschaft für die Silbenschriftorthographie *Kana no tomo* "Freunde der Silbenschrift" (gegründet 1882). Während die früheren Wörterbücher nach den chinesischen Schriftzeichen geordnet wurden, gab er das erste japanische Wörterbuch aus, die nach der Silbenschrift-Orthographie eingeteilt wurde, *Genkai* "Wörtermeer" (1891, mit einem neuen Grammatikentwurf). Ōtsuki definierte in dem Wörterbuch *Genkai* die Standardsprache erstmals als die gesprochene Sprache unter den gebildeten Menschen in Tokyo. Postum erschien die fünfbändige Ausgabe seines Wörterbuchs *Daigenkai* "Großes Wörtermeer" (1932–1937). Unter seiner Leitung erschienen die Forschungsresultate der Sprachkommission als die erste offizielle Grammatik der gesprochenen Sprache *Kōgohō* "Grammatik der gesprochenen Sprache" (1916 mit Supplement 1917).

Seine 1897 erschienene Grammatik *Kō Nihon bunten* "Detaillierte japanische Grammatik" wirkte nachhaltig und richtungsweisend für die Beschreibung des Japanischen, indem er die *Kokugaku*-Beschreibung mit der westlichen Art erneut zu verknüpfen versuchte. Das Buch befaßt sich mit der Orthographie, Etymologie und der Morphosyntax des Japanischen. Die Wortklassen teilt Ōtsuki in 8 Klassen ein:

1. *meishi* "Nomina",
2. *dōshi* "Verba",
3. *keiyōshi* "Qualitativa",
4. *jodōshi* "Verbalsuffixe",
5. *fukushi* "Adverbia",
6. *setsuzokushi* "Konjunktionen",
7. *teniwoha* "Postpositionen",
8. *kandōshi* "Interjektionen".

Das Weiterbestehen der eigenen Klassen der *teniwoha* (der Verbalsuffixe und der Postpositionen) aus der traditionellen Philologie führt zu der Vermischung der morphologischen und der syntaktischen Ebene der Sprachbeschreibung.

## 5. Yamada Yoshio (1873–1958)

Yamada arbeitete zuerst als Schullehrer und bildete sich autodidaktisch in der Linguistik weiter. Später wurde er als Experte von der "Sprachkommission zur Untersuchung der Landessprache" zu Rate gezogen. Ab 1928 wurde er zuerst Dozent, dann Professor an der Universität Tōhoku in Sendai. Als Mitglied der "Kommission zur Herausgabe der Landesgeschichte" mußte er wegen nationalistischer Aktivitäten 1945 zurücktreten, wurde jedoch später rehabilitiert. Sein Wirken umfaßte mehrere Disziplinen wie Linguistik, Literaturwissenschaft, Geschichtswissenschaft, Philologie. Yamada verfaßte zu der Geschichte der japanischen Sprache mehrere Werke, worunter besonders seine Beschreibung des Altjapanischen nach der Gedichtsanthologie *Manyōshū* im *Narachō bunpōshi* "Historische Grammatik der Nara-Zeit" (1913b), des frühen Mitteljapanischen *Heianchō bunpōshi* "Historische Grammatik der Heian-Zeit" (1913a) und die Aufarbeitung der historischen Orthographie *Gojūonzu no rekishi* "Geschichte der "Fünfzig-Laute-Tafel" " (1938) zu erwähnen sind.

In der Einleitung zu seinem großen Werk *Nihon bunpōron* "Theorie der japanischen Grammatik" (1902–1908), einer Schriftsprachengrammatik, die die zeitgenössischen Arbeiten weit überflügelt, befaßt er sich eingehend mit dem Verhältnis der traditionellen japanischen und der westlichen Sprachwissenschaft. Seiner Meinung nach sind Versuche, das Modell des Englischen und des Deutschen auf das Japanische anzuwenden, genauso zum Scheitern verurteilt wie die früheren Versuche mit dem Chinesischen. Für die grammatische Analyse sei zwar die äußere Form des elaborierten europäischen Systems geeignet, denn menschliche Sprachregeln sind universal, dennoch muß man in jedem Fall die Oberfläche durchdringen, um bei der Analyse nicht den Verblendungen der Elaboriertheit zu erliegen. Als theoretischen Weg, mit dem man die Basis der japanischen Grammatik aufbauen kann, bezieht er sich auf die linguistische Methoden Henry Sweet's und die psychologische Methode Wilhelm Wundts.

Yamada unterscheidet Wortlehre (*goron*) und Satzlehre (*kuron*) strikt voneinander, wodurch er zu der Herausbildung der modernen Syntax entscheidend beigetragen hat. Er ist auch einer der ersten, der eine Wortdefinition aufstellt, indem er das Wort als eine sprachlich selbständige minimale Einheit bestimmt, die irgendeinen Gedanken sprachlich ausdrückt. Die Wortkategorien entsprechen im wesentlichen den später allgemein gebräuchlichen:

die unflektierbaren Wörter (*taigen*) werden in
1. *meishi* "Nomen",
2. *daimeishi* "Pronomina",
3. *sūshi* "Numeralia" und
die flektierbaren (*yōgen*) in
4. *keiyōshi* "Adjektiva" und
5. *dōshi* "Verba" aufgeteilt.
Weitere Wortklassen sind die
6. *fukushi* "Adverbia",
7. *joshi* "Postpositionen" und
9. *setsuji* "Konjunktionen".

Yamada erkennt die eigentliche Schwäche der traditionellen japanischen Grammatik in dem fast vollständigen Fehlen der Beschäftigung mit der Syntax. In dem sehr umfangreichen syntaktischen Teil seiner Grammatik (*kuron*) basiert er seine Satzdefinition ebenfalls auf die psychologischen Funktionen und insbesondere auf die Apperzeption (*tōkaku sayō*) und die Verstandestätigkeit (*ryōkai katsudō*), indem er den Satz als Ausdruck eines apperzipierten Gedankens durch die Form der Sprache bestimmt.

Die kleinste grammatische Einheit ist das Wort (*go*, *tango*) mit Flexion (*katsuyō*), Wortendungen (*gobi*) und Affixen (*setsuji*). Wörter können semantisch Ideen (*kannen*, *kannengo* "Begriffswörter") oder Relationen (*kankei*, *kankeigo* "Bezugswörter") ausdrücken. Die Relationen unter den Wörtern werden in verschiedenen Kasusfunktionen (*ikaku*) hergestellt, die mit Partikeln oder Postpositionen (*joshi*) markiert sind. In der Syntax von Yamada ist die Phrase (*ku*) die Basiseinheit des Satzes (*bun*), die entweder als Teilsatz oder selbst als Hauptsatz gilt. Die Sätze gliedert er in zwei Hauptarten: in Ausrufesätze und Aussagesätze, während bei Wundt die diskursive Gliederung des Satzes die Dualität der Subjekt-Prädikat-Gliederung erfordert. Die Apperzeption (*tōkaku sayō*) ist zwar auch für Yamada nötig, um menschliche Gedanken zu fokussieren, dennoch ist die nach Wundt notwendige duale logische Beziehung in einem Satz nach der Meinung Yamadas im Japanischen lediglich fakultativ. Ellipsen charakterisieren die gesprochene Sprache und haben eine direkte prädikative Kraft (*chinjutsu*).

Der Begriff der prädikativen Kraft (*chinjutsu*), der nach Yamada eine eigenständige, mitunter nationalistisch geprägte Entwicklung hatte, indem die prädikative Kraft besonders dem Japanischen zugeordnet wurde, lebte in der japanischen Syntax lange weiter. Besonders schwierig wurde die Debatte dadurch, daß Yamada diesen Begriff auf mehreren Ebenen der Sprachbeschreibung angewandt hatte; so nannte er zum Beispiel auch die selbständigen, flektierbaren Wörter (Verba, Qualitativa, verbale Qualitativa, *yōgen*) selbst *chinjutsugo* "Prädikativa" im Kontrast zu den Begriffswörtern *gainengo* (*taigen* "selbständige unflektierbare Wörter").

Yamada propagierte seine Sprachtheorie in den Werken *Nihon bunpō kōgi* "Vorlesung zur japanischen Grammatik" (1992a) und *Nihon bunpōgaku yōron* "Allgemeine Theorie der japanischen Grammatik" (1931), revidierte ausführlich in *Nihon bunpōgaku gairon* "Allgemeine Lehre der japanischen Grammatik" (1936) und erweiterte das sprachliche Material mit Beispielen aus der gesprochenen Sprache *Nihon kōgohō kōgi* "Vorlesung zur japanischen gesprochenen Sprache" (1922b). Eine umfassende Analyse der Sprachtheorie Yamadas und der *Kokugaku* bietet Georg Bedell's *Kokugaku Grammatical Theory* (1968).

## 6. Shinmura Izuru (1876–1967)

Shinmura studierte Sprachwissenschaft bei Ueda an der Universität Tokyo. In den Jahren 1907–1909 hielt er sich auf einer Studienreise in England, Frankreich und Deutschland auf und nahm Kontakt zu vielen europäischen Gelehrten auf, darunter zu Henry Sweet, Antoine Meillet, Karl Brugmann und Hermann Paul. 1909 wurde er Professor an dem neu eingerichteten Lehrstuhl für Sprachwissenschaft (*gengogaku*) der Kyoto Universität, bis er 1936 die Nachfolge Uedas antrat. Shinmura ist als Lehrer bedeutend, da er für seinen anschaulichen Stil berühmt war. Auf dem Gebiet der Lexikologie war Shinmura ein wirklicher Neuerer. Seine Wörterbücher *Jien* "Wörtergarten" (1935b) und *Kōjien* "Großer Wörtergarten" (1955) gelten als Klassiker der modernen Lexikographie. Von seinen weiteren Arbeitsgebieten seien vor allem seine Editionstätigkeit und die Aufarbeitung der Geschichte *Kokugaku Tōhō gengoshi sōkō* "Essays zur Geschichte orientalischer Sprachen" (1927) und der möglichen Verwandtschaft des Japanischen *Kokugogaku keitōron* "Sprachverwandtschaftliche Beziehung des Japanischen" (1935a) genannt.

## 7. Matsushita Daisaburō (1878–1935)

Matsushita studierte an der Kokugakuin Universität in Tokyo. Er gründete ein sinojapanisches Kolleg (*Nikka gakuin*) an der Kokugakuin Universität, an der er 1926 zum Professor ernannt wurde. Ab 1931 war er bettlägerig und verstarb früh.

Matsushitas Hauptanliegen bestand darin eine eigene Grammatiktheorie für die Deskription des modernen Japanischen auszuarbeiten. Im Jahre 1901 verfaßte er die erste Grammatik des alltäglich gesprochenen japanischen *Nihon zokugo bunten* "Grammatik der japanischen Vulgärsprache". Seine weiteren grammatischen Werke tragen den Titel: *Hyōjun Nihon bunpō* "Grammatik des Standardjapanischen" (1923), *Hyōjun Nihon kōgohō* "Grammatik des gesprochenen Standardjapanischen" (1930).

In seiner Theorie der japanischen Grammatik geht Matsushita von der Annahme aus, daß es zwei Arten von Grammatik gäbe, nämlich die interne, universale und die externe, sprachspezifische Grammatik. Im Einklang mit Yamada Yoshios psychologischem Ansatz setzt er die Priorität des Gedankens vor die sekundäre Sprache. Für seine deskriptive Grammatik ist charakteristisch, daß er versucht, die verschiedenen morphologischen und syntaktischen Ebenen strikt voneinander zu trennen. Gleichsam ist er bestrebt, dem agglutinativen Charakter des Japanischen zu entsprechen, indem er die Partikeln (*teniwoha*) nicht in der Tradition der *Kokugaku* von den anderen Wortklassen isoliert.

In Matsushitas Systematik nach der "Grammatik des gesprochenen Standardjapanischen" werden die syntaktischen und morphologischen Relationen folgendermaßen konzipiert: Eine Aussage (*setsuwa*) besteht aus einem oder aus mehreren Sätzen (*danku*). Ein Satz besteht aus einem oder mehreren Wörtern (*shi*) mit oder ohne suffigierten Partikeln. Ein *shi* ist entweder ein einfaches Wort (*tanshi*) oder eine Relativphrase (*renshi*). Ein *renshi* kann aus zwei oder aus mehreren *shi* bestehen. Ein *tanshi* besteht wiederum aus einem oder mehreren elementaren Wörtern (*genji*), die wiederum als *tanji* oder als *renji* fungieren (Matsushita 1930: 15). Die syntaktischen Relationen erklärt er in Dependenzverhältnissen; er nennt das Regens (*tōritsugo*) und das Dependens (*jūzokugo*), die zusammen eine Relativphrase (*renshi*) bilden können.

Matsushitas Wortklassifikation weicht von der traditionellen Klassifizierung ab; er vereinfacht dies nach den Kriterien der Flektierbarkeit und nach der Syntax in folgende Klassen:

1. *meishi* "Nomina, Pronomina",
2. *dōshi* "Verba, Adjektiva",
3. *fukushi* "Adverbia, Konjunktionen"
4. *fukutaishi* "Adnominale",
5. *kandōshi* "Interjektionen".

Weiterhin beachtenswert sind seine Ausführungen zu Kasus und Aspekte im Japanischen.

Als Philologe ist Matsushita mit der Edition eines Zeilenindexes zur klassischen Poesie berühmt geworden, *Kokka taikan* "Großer Überblick über die Gedichte unseres Landes" (mit Watanabe, 1923).

## 8. Hashimoto Shinkichi (1882–1945)

Hashimoto studierte Sprachwissenschaft an der Universität Tokyo. Er arbeitete als Japanischlehrer für chinesische Gaststudenten, um dann in die "Kommission zur Untersuchung der Landessprache" einzutreten. 1909 wurde er Uedas Assistent an der Kaiserlichen Universität. 1929 wurde er zum Professor ernannt und 1943 emeritiert. Hashimoto befaßte sich vor allem mit den Gebieten der historischen Linguistik, der Phonologie des Altjapanischen und mit der Grammatik des modernen Japanischen.

Auf dem Gebiet der historischen Phonologie konnte Hashimoto die Hypothese Motoori Norinagas zu dem achtfachen Vokalsystem des Altjapanischen beweisen, indem er die innere lautliche Rekonstruktion des Lautsystems fortsetzte und mit vergleichend-historischen Daten aus japanischen Dialekten untermauern konnte in seinem *Jōdaigo no kenkyū* "Studien zum Altjapanischen" (1950). Hashimoto weckte als erster die Aufmerksamkeit für die portugiesischen Studien als historisches Material für das Spät-Mitteljapanische *Bunroku gannen Amakusaban Kirishitan kyōgi no kenkyū* "Das Studium der christlichen Doktrinen in der Amakusa-Edition 1592" (1928) und bearbeitete dieses Material für das Lautsystem des Mitteljapanischen.

Für die Grammatik des Japanischen ist seine Systematisierung der Klassifizierung der Wortkategorien in der *Shin bunten bekki* "Neue Grammatik" (1931–1936) von Bedeutung, womit er die Grundlage der wissenschaftlichen und der japanischen Schulgrammatik bis heute bestimmt hat, die aber auf eine längere Entwicklung im japanischen linguistischen Denken zurückgeht und an die europäische Tradition angelehnt ist.

Hashimoto teilt alle Formen in zwei Kategorien ein, nämlich in freie (*jiritsugo*) und *fuzokugo*) Formen. Selbständige Vollwörter werden in flektierbare und unflektierbare Vollwörter (*katsuyōgo*) eingeteilt und sind entweder flektierbar und prädikativ (*yōgen*) (1. *dōshi* "Verba", 2. *keiyōshi* "Qualitativa", 3. *keiyōdōshi* "verbale Qualitativa") oder unflektierbar und subjektivisch (*taigen*), adverbial, adnominal, konjunktional, isoliert. Die subjektivischen sind die folgenden: 4. *meishi* "Nomina", 5. *daimeishi* "Demonstrativa", 6. *sūshi* "Numeralia". Adverbial sind die 7. *fukushi* "Adverbia". Adnominale heißen 8. *rentaishi* "Attributiva". Konjunktional sind die 9. *setsuzokushi* "Konjunktionen". Isoliert stehen die 10. *kandōshi* "Interjektionen". Abhängige Hilfswörter werden als eigene Klasse betrachtet und in flektierbare 11. *jodōshi* "Verbalsuffixe" und unflektierbare 12. *joshi* "Postpositionen" unterschieden.

Eine sehr ausführliche Darstellung der *Kokugogaku*-Systematik der Beschreibung des Japanischen ist in dem Abriß der japanischen Grammatik von Bruno Lewin (1959) zu finden. Als Kritik an der Begriffsbildung wurde vor allem mehrfach die Frage der gelungenen oder nicht gelungenen Synthese japanischer und europäischer Systematik für die japanische Grammatik erörtert. Morphologische und syntaktische Gründe sprechen für mehrere Verschiebungen und Veränderungen, die im Rahmen der strukturalistischen Linguistik vorgenommen wurden. Am deutlichsten sind die unnötigen Komplikationen bei der Erfassung der Kopula, der Pronomina, Adjektiva, Adverbia, Verbalsuffixe und Postpositionen (siehe dazu Miller 1993: 322–326; Rickmeyer 1983).

## 9. Die Historiographie der Kokugogaku

Die Universitätsvorlesung, mit der Ueda seit 1894 eine ganze Generation von Linguisten in die Sprachwissenschaft eingeführt hatte, ist als Vorlesungsmitschrift erhalten und von Shinmura Izuru ediert worden. Der Titel lautet zwar *Kokugogakushi* "Geschichte der japanischen Sprachwissenschaft". In dieser Vorlesung bettet Ueda die Leistungen der japanischen Sprachwissenschaft in die Fortentwicklung der linguistischen Systeme der Welt ein. Die Beschäftigung mit der eigenen Geschichte setzte also parallel zu der Entstehung dieser Richtung ein (Yamagiwa 1961; Lewin 1989). Die institutionelle Etablierung der *Kokugogaku* geschah viel später während des zweiten Weltkrieges mit der Gründung einer eigenen "Gesellschaft für japanische Sprachwissenschaft". Die großen Fortschritte, die auf allen Gebieten der Linguistik erzielt wurden, um das Japanische genauer zu charakterisieren, sind in drei repräsentativen Lexika nachzuverfolgen: *Kokugogaku jiten* "Wörterbuch der Japanischen Sprachwissenschaft" (1955), *Kokugogaku daijiten* "Großes Wörterbuch der Japanischen Sprachwissenschaft" (1980) und *Kokugogaku kenkyū jiten* "Sachwörterbuch zur japanischen Sprachforschung" (1977).

## 10. Bibliographie


Bedell, George D. 1968. *Kokugaku Grammatical Theory*. Ph. D. thesis. MIT.

Doi, Toshio. 1976. *The Study of Language in Japan: A historical survey*. Tokyo: Shinozaki shorin.

Eschbach-Szabo, Viktoria. 1989. "Wilhelm Wundt und Yamada Yoshio über die Definition des Satzes". *Bruno Lewin zu Ehren* hg. von I. Hijiya-Kirschnereit & J. Stalph, 67–79. Bochum: Brockmeyer.

Hashimoto, Shinkichi. 1928. *Bunroku gannen Amakusaban Kirishitan kyōgi no kenkyū*. Tokyo: Tōyō bunko.

—. 1931–39. *Shin bunten. Shin bunten bekki*. 10 Bde. Tokyo: Fuzanbō.

—. 1946–71. *Hashimoto, Shinkichi hakushi chosakushū*. 12 Bde. Tokyo: Iwanami.

Hattori, Shirō. 1967. "Descriptive Linguistics in Japan". *Current Trends in Linguistics. Linguistics in*

*East Asia and South East Asia* hg. von Thomas A. Sebeok, 530–584. The Hague: Mouton.

Kindaichi, Haruhiko et al, Hg. 1988. *Nihongo hyakka daijiten. Tokyo.* Kokugo, Chōsa Iinkai. 1905. *On'in chōsa hōkokusho; on'in bunpuzu.* 2 Bde. Tokyo: Nihon Shoseki Kabushiki kaisha.

–. 1906. *Kōgohō chōsa hōkokusho; kōgohō bunpuzu.* 3 Bde. Tokyo: Kokutei kyōkasho kyōdō hanbaisho.

Kokugo, Gakkai, Hg. 1955. *Kokugogaku jiten.* Tokyo: Tokyodō.

–. Hg. 1980. *Kokugogaku daijiten.* Tokyo: Tokyodō.

Lewin, Bruno. 1959. *Abriss der japanischen Grammatik auf der Grundlage der klassischen Schriftsprache.* Wiesbaden: Harrassowitz. (3. verb. Auflage, 1990.)

–, et al. Hg. 1989. *Japanische Sprachwissenschaft.* Wiesbaden: Harrassowitz.

Matsushita, Daisaburō. 1901. *Nihon zokugo bunten.* Tokyo: Seibidō.

–. 1924. *Hyōjun Nihon bunpō.* Tokyo: Kigensha. (2. rev. Aufl., 1928.)

–. 1930. *Hyōjun Nihon kōgohō.* Tokyo: Chūbunkan shoten.

–. 1930. *Hyōjun kanbunpō.* Tokyo.

– & Watanabe Fumio. 1901, 1903, 1925, 1926. *Kokka taikan.* 4 Bde. Tokyo: Kigensha.

Miller, Roy A. 1993. *Die japanische Sprache: Geschichte und Struktur.* Übers. von Jürgen Stalph. München: iudicium.

Ōtsuki, Fumihiko. 1891. *Genkai.* Tokyo: Yūseidō.

–. 1897. *Kō Nihon bunten.* Tokyo: Yoshikawa.

–, Hg. 1916. *Kōgohō.* Tokyo: Kokugo Chōsa Iinkai. (Suppl. 1917.)

–. 1932–1937. *Daigenkai.* 5 Bde. Tokyo: Fuzanbō.

Paul, Hermann. 1886. *Prinzipien der Sprachgeschichte.* Halle a. S.: Max Niemeyer. (6. Aufl., Tübingen: Niemeyer, 1960.)

–. 1888. *Principles of History of the Language.* Übers. von H. A. Strong. London: Sonnenschein.

–. 1965. *Gengoshi no genri.* Übers. von Kinosuke Fukumoto. Tokyo.

Rickmeyer, Jens. 1983. *Morphosyntax der japanischen Gegenwartssprache. Heidelberg.*

Satō, Kiyoji, Hg. 1977. *Kokugogaku kenkyū jiten.* Tokyo: Meiji shoin.

Shinmura, Izuru. 1927. *Tōhō gengoshi sōkō.* Tokyo: Iwanami.

–. 1935a. *Kokugogaku keitōron.* Tokyo: Meiji shoin.

–. 1935b. *Jien.* Tokyo: Iwanami.

–. 1955. *Kōjien.* Tokyo: Iwanami.

Sugimoto, Tsutomu. 1989. *Seiyōjin no Nihongo hakken: The discovery of the Japanese language by Western people.* Tokyo: Sōtakusha.

Tsukishima, Hiroshi et al. 1982. *Bunpōshi.* (= *Kōza Kokugogakushi*, 4.) Tokyo: Taishūkan.

Tsurumine, Shigenobu. 1833. *Gogaku shinsho. Kokugogaku taikai*, hg. von Kyūzō Fukui, I, 207–318. Tokyo, 1930–1944. (2. Aufl., Tokyo: Hakuteisha, 1975.)

Twine, Nanette. 1991. *Language and the Modern State: The reform of written Japanese.* London & New York: Routledge.

Ueda, Kazutoshi. 1968. *Ueda Kazutoshi-shū. Meiji bungaku zenshū.* Hg. von Senichi Hisamatsu, XLIV. Tokyo: Chikuma shobō.

–. 1984. *Kokugogakushi.* Hg. von Izuru Shinmura & Tōsaku Furuta. Tokyo: Kyōiku shuppansha.

– & Kanji Matsui. 1939–1941. *Dai Nihon kokugo jiten.* 2. verb. Aufl. 5 Bde. Tokyo: Fuzanbō. (1. Aufl., 1915.)

–, Junjirō Takakusu et al. 1915. *Nihon gairago jiten.* Tokyo: Sanseidō.

– et al., Hg. 1917. *Daijiten.* Tokyo: Keiseisha.

Yamada, Yoshio. 1902–1908. *Nihon bunpōron.* Tokyo: Hōbunkan.

–. 1913a. *Heianchō bunpōshi.* Tokyo: Hōbunkan.

–. 1913b. *Narachō bunpōshi.* Tokyo: Hōbunkan.

–. 1922a. *Nihon bunpō kōgi.* Tokyo: Hōbunkan.

–. 1922b. *Nihon kōgohō kōgi.* Tokyo: Hōbunkan.

–. 1931. *Nihon bunpōgaku yōron.* Tokyo: Kadokawa.

–. 1936. *Nihon bunpōgaku gairon.* Tokyo: Hōbunkan.

–. 1938. *Gojūonzu no rekishi.* Tokyo: Hōbunkan.

Yamagiwa, Joseph K. 1961. Japanese Language Studies in the *Shōwa Period: A guide to Japanese reference and research materials.* Ann Arbor: Univ. of Michigan Press.

Yamamoto, Masahide. 1971. *Genbun itchi no rekishi ronkō.* Tokyo: Ōfūsha.

*Viktoria Eschbach-Szabo, Tübingen (Deutschland)*

## 14. The influence of Dutch grammar on Japanese language research

Although Japan gave up her policy of seclusion only in 1854, the country had been exposed to Western influences for three centuries.

The Portuguese had held trading rights from 1543 to 1639, the Spanish from 1592 to 1624. The first Dutch ship arrived in April 1600. On August 24, 1609, the Dutch received official permission to establish a trading post at Hirato, an island to the west of Northwest Kyushu. In 1641 the Dutch settlement was moved to Dejima, an artificial islet in the Bay of Nagasaki. Between 1639 and 1854, the Dutch were the only Europeans who were allowed to have trade relations with Japan. This exceptional position they owed to their enmity with the Portuguese and the Spaniards as well as to the fact that they were interested only in commerce and not in attempts at conversion of the Japanese to the Christian religion. They imported useful manufactured goods from Europe and the Indies and such colonial products as spices, tin and mercury. Moreover, the Japanese kept themselves informed through the Dutch of events in the rest of the world.

The isolationist policy, which had been the aim of the Japanese government for some decades before it was fully implemented in 1639, marked the end of a period of fairly intensive contact with Western culture.

Notwithstanding all the restrictions imposed during the period of seclusion, a thirst for knowledge of Western scholarship and technology continued to exist. As time went by and certain regulations were relaxed that interest grew, culminating in the second half of the 18th century in a flowering of the study of Western sciences, which were referred to collectively as *Rangaku*: Dutch learning or 'Hollandology'. The word *Rangaku* covered a wide range of disciplines including medicine, astronomy, mathematics, botany, physics, geography, geodesy, and military science. Less attention was given to European history and art. The scholars specializing in these fields, all of which had studied Dutch, were called *Rangakusha* or "Hollandologists". Japan's emergence as a major power in the second half of the 19th century is in large measure attributable to her rapid absorption and adaptation of Western knowledge; the foundations of this acculturation process were laid by the *Rangakusha*.

In the 16th and early 17th century, when Iberian missionaries and traders came to Japan, many Portuguese and a few Spanish words were assimilated into the Japanese language. In the period from 1609 until ca. 1860 a very large number of Dutch words were borrowed. Some examples are *gasu* "gas", *kōhii* (D. *koffie* "coffee"), *kokku* (D. *kok* "cook"), *masuto* "mast". More interesting in our present contect are Sino-Japanese translations of D. words (especially scientific, medical and anatomical terminology). Sino-Japanese (S.-J.) is a term applied to Chinese loan words the pronunciation of which has been adapted to the Japanese sound system. In order to designate new concepts the Japanese often coin their own S.-J. compounds in a way comparable to our combinations of words of Latin, Greek or Greek-Latin origin for new objects or ideas (e. g., automobile or television). Some examples of such loan translations are *bi-yoku* (D. *neusvleugel* "nostril", lit. nose + wing), *shi-kaku* (D. *gezichtshoek* "visual angle", lit. vision + angle), *shojo-maku* (D. *maagdevlies* "hymen", lit. maiden + membrane).

When, towards the end of the 18th century, the *Rangakusha* began to read and translate more and more Dutch scholarly books, they became acutely aware of the need to study Dutch grammar, and it was only natural that they tried to apply its concepts and rules to their own language. An exhaustive treatment of the subject being impractical here, I will confine myself to the grammatical categories.

Shizuki Tadao, *alias* Nakano Ryūho (1750–1806), Nagasaki interpreter and specialist in Western astronomy and physics, studied Sewel's *Nederduytsche Spraakkonst* (Dutch grammar) and wrote *Oranda shihinkō* "A Study of the Dutch parts of speech". Willem Sewel, a Dutchman of English descent, published his grammar in 1708; it was reprinted in 1717 and 1733. A revised and enlarged edition appeared in 1756. Shizuki's work was used for the instruction of other interpreters, but never published. His disciple Baba Sadayoshi (1787–1822) revised the text and put it into circulation on a small scale under the title *Teisei Rango kyūhinshū* "Revised collection of the nine parts of speech of the Dutch language" (1814). Baba also wrote a preface to *Orandago hōge* "Explanation of the rules of Dutch grammar" by Fujibayashi Fuzan (1781–1836). It was based on several Dutch grammars and printed in 1815.

Tsurumine Shigenobu (1788–1859) was the first to apply the methods of Dutch grammar to the Japanese language. In 1833 he published his *Gogaku shinsho* "New book on the study of language", a descriptive grammar of Japanese based on the linguistic classifications of the West.

For the understanding of Tsurumine's and others' classification it is necessary to present here a list of the parts of speech traditionally distinguished in Dutch grammar:

(1) *[zelfstandige] naamwoorden*, lit. "[independently existent] name words", i. e. nouns, substantives
(2) *bijvoeglijke naamwoorden*, lit. "attachable name words", i. e. adjectives
(3) *telwoorden*, lit. "number words", i. e. numerals
(4) *werkwoorden*, lit. "work(ing) words", i. e. verbs
(5) *lidwoorden*, lit. "member words" (translation of Latin *articuli*), i. e. articles
(6) *voornaamwoorden* (transl. of L. *pronomina*), i. e. pronouns
(7) *voorzetsels* (transl. of L. *praepositiones*), i. e. prepositions
(8) *voegwoorden* (transl. of L. *coniunctiones*), i. e. conjunctions
(9) *bijwoorden* (transl. of L. *adverbia*), i. e. adverbs
(10) *tussenwerpsels* (transl. of L. *interiectiones*), i. e. interjections

Tsurumine classified the parts of speech of the Japanese language in the following way:

(1) *[i]na-kotoba* "[existent] name words": nouns, substantives
(2) *tsuki-kotoba* "attached words": qualifiers, adjectives
(3) *kae-kotoba* "substituting words": pronouns
(4) *tsuzuki-kotoba* "continuation words": attributives
(5) *hataraki-kotoba* "working words": verbs
(6) *sama-kotoba* "condition words": adverbs
(7) *tsuzuke-kotoba* "connecting words": conjunctions
(8) *sashi-kotoba* or *sasu-kotoba* "pointing-out words": case particles
(9) *nageki-kotoba* "lamentation words": interjections

As *lidwoorden* (articles) do not exist in Japanese, this category has been omitted by Tsurumine. Some of his appellations require further explanation. The *i* of *ina-kotoba* is the *renyōkei* (continuative base) of *iru* "to exist, to be"; the Chinese characters rendering *ina* are read *jittai* "substance, entity", in S.-J. and are obviously intended to render the D. adjective *zelfstandig. Tsuzuki-kotoba* refers to the attributive base (*ren-taikei*) of the verb, *hataraki-kotoba* to its conclusive base (*shūshi-kei*). The *sama-kotoba* include the *renyōkei* of the verb.

It is not surprising that later grammarians substituted S.-J. compounds for Tsurumine's unwieldy appellations: *na-kotoba* was replaced by *meishi*, *kae-kotoba* by *daimeishi*, *hataraki-kotoba* by *dōshi*, etc. (see below).

In 1842 Mitsukuri Genpo (1799–1863) published *Oranda bunten zenpen* "Dutch grammar, part I", a reprint of *Grammatica of Nederduitsche Spraakkunst*, compiled by the Maatschappij tot Nut van 't Algemeen (Society for the Public Weal) in 1822. The parts of speech enumerated in this Dutch book, of which 5,000 copies were printed, were later rendered into Japanese by Mitsukuri and his colleagues as:

(1) *[jitsu]meishi* (*jitsu* "true"; *mei* "name"; *shi* "words") – substantives
(2) *kanshi* "capping words" – articles
(3) *keiyōshi* "form and appearance words" – adjectives
(4) *sūshi* "number words" – numerals
(5) *daimeishi* "words substituting (instead of) names" – pronouns
(6) *dōshi* "movement/action words" – verbs
(7) *fukushi* "aiding/assisting words" – adverbs
(8) *zenshi* "before words" – prepositions
(9) *setsuzokushi* "connecting words" – conjunctions
(10) *tansokushi* "lamentation words" – interjections.

In spite of its obvious shortcomings for the description of Japanese the traditional Dutch classification of the parts of speech became exemplary for later grammars of that language.

Nakagane Masahira (dates unknown) of Osaka, for instance, gives in his *Yamato gogaku tebikigusa* "Guide for the study of the Japanese language" (1871) the following eight parts of speech:

(1) *jitsu-meishi*
(2) *keiyōshi*
(3) *daimeishi*
(4) *dōshi*
(5) *bunshi* (Dutch *deelwoorden*, i. e. participles)
(6) *fukushi*
(7) *setsuzokushi*
(8) *kantanshi* ("admiration words", i. e. interjections).

When compulsory education was instituted in 1872 the teaching of grammar in primary and secondary schools became, of course, very important.

In 1897 Ōtsuki Fumihiko (1847–1928) published his *Kō Nihon bunten* "Comprehensive Japanese gammar", in which he classified the parts of speech as follows:

(1) *meishi* (nouns)
(2) *dōshi*
(3) *keiyōshi*
(4) *jodōshi* (auxiliary verbs)
(5) *fukushi*
(6) *setsuzokushi*
(7) *tenioha* (particles)
(8) *kandōshi* ("emotion words", i. e. interjections).

The first category included *daimeishi* (pronouns) and *sūshi* (numerals). *Jodōshi* is a literal translation of Dutch *hulpwerkwoorden*. *Tenioha* is the old Japanese appellation for particles and a certain number of verbal endings, but Ōtsuki used it only for morphemes indicating syntactical relationships. From his classification it becomes clear that he felt the need to emphasize certain characteristics of the Japanese language.

Ōtsuki's classification was adopted with slight modifications by Hashimoto Shinkichi (1882–1945), who was responsible for the official school reference grammar established by the Ministry of Education; it has actually remained authoritative until the present day.

Lack of space has prevented us from dealing with other subjects besides the grammatical categories, but we can certainly conclude safely that Japanese linguistic terminology in general has been strongly influenced by European examples and that its origins are to be found in the study of Dutch grammar.

## Bibliography


Fukui Kyūzō. 1953. *Nihon bunpōshi* [History of Japanese Grammar.] Tokyo: Kazama shobō.

Kindaichi Kyōsuke. 1953. *Kokugogaku nyūmon* [Introduction to Japanese Linguistics.] Tokyo: Yoshikawa kōbunkan.

Lewin, Bruno. 1959. *Abriß der japanischen Grammatik*. Wiesbaden: Harrassowitz.

–, ed. 1989. *Sprache und Schrift Japans*. Leiden Brill.

Maës, Hubert. 1975. "Un point d'histoire terminologique: *taigen* ~ *yōgen*". *Travaux du groupe de linguistique japonaise*, vol. I: *Problèmes terminologiques*, 66–760. Paris: Université de Paris VII.

–. 1975. « Un point d'histoire terminologique: *dōshi* ». *Travaux du groupe de linguistique japonaise*, vol. I: *Problèmes terminologiques*, 77–86. Paris: Université de Paris VII.

Miller, Roy Andrew. 1967. *The Japanese Language*. Chicago & London: The Univ. of Chicago Press.

Nichiran Gakkai, ed. 1984. *Yōgakushi jiten* [Dictionary of the History of "Western Learning".] Tokyo: Yūshōdō shuppan.

Numata, Jirō. "The Introduction of Dutch Language". *Acceptance of Western Cultures in Japan from the Sixteenth to the Mid-nineteenth Century*, 9–19. Tokyo: The Centre for East Asian Cultural Studies.

Saitō Makoto (Shin). 1985. *Nihon ni okeru Oranda-go kenkyū no rekishi* [A History of the Study of the Dutch Language in Japan.] Tokyo: Daigaku shorin.

Sugimoto Tsutomu. 1976–82. *Edo-jidai Rangogaku no seiritsu to sono tenkai* [The Establishment of Dutch Language Studies in the Edo Period and their Development.] 5 vols. Tokyo: Waseda daigaku shuppansha.

Vos, Frits. 1963. "Dutsch Influences on the Japanese Language (with an Appendix on Dutch Words in Korean)". *Lingua* 12:4.341–388.

Yamada Yoshi. 1936. *Nihon bunpōgaku gairon* [An Introduction to the Study of Japanese Grammar.] Tokyo & Osaka: Hōbunkan.


*Frits Vos †, Oegstgeest (The Netherlands)*

# 15. The role of linguistics in Japanese society and education

Today, just as for *ca.* the past 100 or more years, the principal role of linguistics in Japanese society and education continues to be one relatively simple to categorize, even though in actual application it inevitably displays a multifarious repertory of superficially differentiated modes. In brief, in Japan linguistics mainly serves, and has long served, as an instrument of social coercion, manipulation, and control; and it is today, just as in the past, one of the most effective means by which relatively small numbers of Japanese élite are empowered for implementing their domination and exploitation of the remaining bulk of the population, at the same time ensuring that this small élite is able to perpetuate its own socioeconomic hegemony. Thus, linguistics in Japan continues today to be what it has been throughout most of recorded Japanese history, i. e. the major effective mechanism that segments Japanese society along a rigid, self-perpetuating, vertical axis of social control; and the advent of the so-called modernization of the 19th century – in reality, little more than the entirely superficial imposition from above of an imitative pseudo-Euro-Western exploitative capitalism upon the inherited and largely unaltered feudal economic base of the society – has done little to alter the linguistic aspects of the society or those of its education in any essential particular.

The vertical imposition of an imitative version of the classical Chinese despotic hydraulic super-state bureaucracy upon Japanese agrarian society from the second half of the 7th century on led almost immediately to total atrophy in the development of genuinely indigenous Japanese institutions of social control. This entirely irrelevant pseudo-continental bureaucracy, with its music-hall *chinoiserie* trappings of hollow court ranks, resounding titles, empty enfoeffments, and numbing ceremonials was not only economically disastrous and aesthetically absurd; it also proved itself totally ineffective, and unable to provide essential services, and powerless even to collect the taxes that it so lavishly levied, leaving itself without the necessary minimum of economic resources required for its own maintenance. Thus by default the bureaucracy in short order turned the government of the country over to a variety of shadow-structures that survive in one form or another down to the present day, since these have shown themselves to be the only way out of the disaster brought about by the adoption of the Chinese-style central despotism of the 7th century.

In earlier periods these shadow-structures (hereditary landowners, beneficed clergy, monastic foundations, bands of assorted outlaws and mafiossa, etc.) were empowered as interlocking sets of horizontal despotisms; today most of these survive, but with the addition of further varieties of similar structures (e. g., in the political sphere the 'clubs' that represent the real power behind the overt political parties).

Against this historical background, it is not difficult to understand how the imported Chinese bureaucratic institutions of the abortive 7th century attempts at a continental-model centralized government were from their inception deeply embroiled in linguistic manipulation as a principal medium for societal control; and even following their early demise, this sociolinguistic component of Japanese social structure and organization has continued to flourish throughout the shadow-structures of despotic horizontal networks that have, ever since the 8th century and down to the present day, continued to dominate as well as to regulate Japanese society.

Central to the imposition of Chinese bureaucratic institutions upon Japanese society in the late 7th century was a massive linguistic onslaught. This took the form of a wholesale adoption of the Chinese language as the sole operative linguistic medium of government, administration, and social control. Henceforth all such functions were to be exercised exclusively through the agency of a foreign language accessible only to a carefully delimited and policed élite.

Overnight this astonishing *coup de langage* had the effect of rendering politically impotent the bulk of the Japanese population, and at the same time effectively isolating them from their own political institutions. At the same time it ensured that the indigenous institutions would atrophy in the bud, which to be sure they almost immediately did.

Replacing them were two structures. One was highly visible but mostly decorative and powerless, a Chinese-style charade of court and bureaucracy with their attendant satellite institutions. The other was a mostly invisible but generally effective internal-horizontal control axis of the despotic shadow institutions already mentioned. These have continued to provide the effective government of the country, just as they continue to be in the main self-perpetuating.

Both these structures from their inception managed to become empowered because of their effective monopoly upon the use of the Chinese language, and especially because of their ability to exercise strict control over the all-important paths of accessibility to that language. Today the situation remains virtually unaltered, with the minor difference that English has replaced Chinese.

This phenomenon of the elevation of a foreign language that, by definition, remains entirely beyond the grasp of all but a miniscule minority of the population is one that has been repeated time and time again throughout the history of Japanese society. In the late 7th century and immediately following, the situation with respect to this all-important control of access to the foreign language at issue, i. e., Chinese, was especially critical. Travel between Japan and the Asian mainland in the 7th century was difficult and dangerous, and long remained so; nevertheless, it was possible, and fair numbers of Japanese managed to survive the rigors of the roundtrip to China. In the main these trips tended to be little more than *grand tours*, whose survivors returned to Japan as soon as possible, having learned little or nothing of the Chinese language. But there were notable exceptions, persons who returned with considerable or in some cases even formidable linguistic skills.

These individuals provided a sudden new challenge for the system of social control based upon the élite's control of access to language-learning opportunities; and this new challenge soon generated a new and virtually unique response.

The ruling élite quickly countered the challenge to their empowerment-monopoly by replacing proper, authentic Chinese – the kind of Chinese that one might learn in China – with an altered pseudo-Chinese, a pidgin jargon that one could only learn as a participating member of the Japanese élite. So different was this artificial linguistic medium from the authentic Chinese of China that practical first-hand linguistic preparation gained through study and residence in China would be more of a drawback in mastering the new mediu than it would be an advantage. As a consequence, travel to and study in China became less and less desirable, because learning the Chinese language of China was of increasingly little utility in Japanese society. From the mid-9th century on, when official 'study missions' to China ceased, the language of the social control and despotic hegemony exercised by the Japanese élite was so far removed from authentic Chinese that the élite became almost entirely self-perpetuating: the only way to learn this new language was already to be a member of the tiny élite clique that employed it.

This extremely curious episode in linguistic history would be little more than an historical curiosity were it not for the fact that the Japanese élite has continued to implement the same gambit through subsequent centuries, down to and including the present day. Later in Japanese history the Dutch language became the sole officially sanctioned medium for intercourse with Western countries (→ Art. 14). But the Dutch that the Japanese insisted upon employing, e. g. in the negotiations with the American authorities who were determined to force open the so-called 'closed country' of the mid-19th century, was not really Dutch such as would be employed by a Dutchman, or Dutch that could be learned by a period of residence in Holland. Like the Chinese of earlier centuries, this Dutch too was an officially sanctioned artificial language, generated and manufactured by the élite for the purposes of their own élite ends and accessible only to members of that same élite. It was a language without native speakers, a special restricted medium of communication more important for its value as an agent of social control than for its ability to facilitate communication. Developed and honed by generations of Tokugawa hereditary 'Dutch interpreters' who had never been to Holland or spoken with a Dutchman, it stood in exactly the same relationship to authentic Dutch as the pseudo-Chinese of early Japanese bureaucracy did to real Chinese.

Most significantly, this same process of official élite-sanctioned 'pidginization' was in turn implemented with respect to English in the years immediately followed Japan's defeat in World War II. Long before the events of the 1940s, it had become self-evident that English would necessarily replace Dutch as the medium for Japan's intercourse with the rest of the world. Down to and including the war years, the élite were able to control access to English just as rigidly as in earlier centuries they had been able to control access to Made-in-Japan Chinese and the halting Dutch of the Tokugawa interpreters.

But after 1945, travel to English-speaking countries was no longer an activity that could be controlled effectively. Soon it became possible for virtually anyone at any level of Japanese society to go to England or the United States, live and study there, and learn something of the language there employed. When such individuals returned to Japan, they found themselves – and today still find themselves – in much the same situation encountered by the brave 8th and 9th century travellers to China. Linguistically they were well equipped, but in a manner with which Japanese society was not prepared to cope. They posed a powerful threat to the linguistic hegemony of the hereditary élite whose training in English, like the Dutch training of the Tokugawa interpreters and the pidgin-Chinese of the medieval bureaucrats, had been gained entirely in Japan. Potentially the situation was one fraught with enormous danger for the entire Japanese social structure; left unchecked, it might have led to the disempowerment of the élite and the opening of opportunities of advancement, even eventually full societal participation, by large numbers of non-élite individuals.

But as one observes so often in the course of Japanese history, in this instance too a sudden powerful stimulus was immediately countered by an equally strong repressive response. The operative agency in this case was the highly centralized Japanese state university system, established in 1886 on the model of the Prussian universities.

Few Japanese imitations of Western institutions introduced in the 19th century and following have succeeded in replicating much more than the external trappings of their originals; and this was also true of the attempt to erect a Prussian-style centralized state university system. Both *Lernfreiheit* and *Lehrfreiheit* of course ran counter to the authoritarian goals of the state, and both remain largely foreign to the Japanese universities. Instead of such factors, it was instead the demonstrated capability of the Prussian-model university to regiment the social order that most interested the Japanese; and this remains the single attribute of German higher-education that they have consistently imitated with the most remarkable success.

The Japanese élite soon realized that it would be possible to exploit the imported university system for the effective control of society by making graduation from one of these few, select institutions the *sine qua non* for meaningful participation in the social process. Without a degree from a state university, advance to positions of power in government, in business, and even in the many shadow-structures that were critically operative in Japanese society, would be impossible.

Once this system of empowerment was in place, vertical social control became a fairly simple matter, requiring only the implementation of strict controls on admissions to the universities. In turn, the university entrance examination became the major rite of passage for all Japanese society; and especially in the post-war decades, linguistic factors came to play a dominant role in these same curious rites.

This has been accomplished by requiring that all candidates for admission to a state university receive passing-grades in a series of highly involved written examinations that ostensibly test the candidate's ability in English. This requirement holds firm whether the candidate's proposed course of studies deals with English or not – nor will the successful candidate normally have occasion to hear, use, or read a word of the language during the four-year curriculum, which is conducted entirely in Japanese, down to and including classes in English.

The highly ceremonialized and entirely unrealistic nature of this entire rite of passage procedure is further highlighted by the fact that the English concerning which the candidate is examined is not even remotely connected with the employment of that language as a normal medium of communication, either oral or written. Instead, the testing is entirely devoted to intricate puzzle-solving, such as guessing what words are missing in a mutilated passage drawn from some minor British novelist of the previous century (Miller 1982: 239ff.).

The unrealistic nature of this variety of testing is best demonstrated by the fact that no one with native-speaker ability in the language can possibly pass these tests, nor can a Japanese who has spent years abroad and learned to speak and write and read English there, but has not 'studied English' in a Japanese secondary school, where years are devoted solely to preparing students to solve these pseudo-linguistic puzzles. Like the pidgin Chinese of earlier centuries, or the Made-in-Japan Dutch of the Tokugawa interpreters, the English of the Japanese university examinations is a specialized sociolect, a jargon that has no native-speakers, an idiom that may only be mastered, slowly and at great cost, within Japanese society itself. Needless to say, it consequently functions as an instrument of social control *par excellence*.

This situation is reflected in the terms used in modern Japanese to refer to English. The Sino-Japanese loan-compound *eigo* is used for the jargon that one must master in order to pass the university entrance examinations; but *eigo* has no other utility, and especially no utility outside Japan. If one wishes to communicate with Westerners one must learn another language, called *eikaiwa*. This is a low-status linguistic entity, in large measure because learning it necessarily involves one-on-one contract with foreigners, but also because it is not taught in the state universities, nor is it of utility in passing their entrance examinations. Demonstrated ability to speak and understand English, i.e. to conduct *ei-*

*kaiwa*, is a somewhat feared and mostly deprecated skill; it hints at long residence abroad, isolation if not independence from the university system; and worst of al, the possibility of intimate (perhaps even sexual) contacts with foreigners, which in turn raises the spectre of racial impurity.

Implementing this foreign-language gambit as a control-valve for admission into the dominant élite is by no means the sole role of linguistics in Japanese education. During the 1930s and 1940s, the state universities vied with one another in generating racist, jingoistic, and imperialistic propaganda involving language. They claimed to have discovered that the Japanese language was unique among human languages, and hence the outward sign of the inner superiority of the Japanese race, as well as the overt license for its imperialistic domination of the rest of Asia. These ideas found their canonical form in *Kokutai no hongi*, a notorious tract that numbered among its authors some of the bestknown professors in the state university system (Miller 1982: 92–101 and passim.). Even following Japan's defeat, many of these men continued to be influential, and their views concerning language and linguistics were in large measure uncritically taken over by much foreign Japanology, especially of the American variety. The *Kokutai no hongi*, in many respects resembled the spurious academic screeds that certain German university circles hurriedly assembled in order to bolster National Socialist racist policies. The important difference is that in Germany such voices ceased to be heard in 1945, while in Japan their language-centered racist allegations have continued to command serious attention throughout the post-war decades.

One of the corollaries of this myth of the uniqueness of the Japanese language has long been the postulate that it is now and in future will always be impossible to demonstrate a genetic relationship (*Urverwandtschaft*) between Japanese and other languages. Like all the racist postulates of the *Kokutai no hongi*, this hypothesis too survived the debacle of 1945, and continues to dominate Japanese educational circles. As a result, despite five decades of post-war activity, Japanese scholarship has yet seriously to address the question of the genetic relationship of the Japanese language. In Japan, this mostly remains a non-question: since Japanese is unique, it can be definition have no relationshps, nor any relatives.

The American structuralist Leonard Bloomfield defined language as a set of arbitrary vocal symbols by means of which a social entity cooperates. Had he known something of the role of language and linguistics in Japanese society and education, he might well have considered altering this, his typically concise and elegant statement. In Japan, he might have observed, language rather is a set of arbitrary symbols by means of which a small élite manages to exercise rigid vertical control over the rest of the population. The Japanese authorities who continue to insist upon the 'unique' nature of the Japanese language are of course not to be taken seriously. But it would also be a mistake to overlook or minimize the truly 'unique' role that linguistics, involving foreign languages as well as Japanese, has traditionally and consistently been made to play in Japanese society and education.

## Bibliography


Miller, Roy Andrew. 1977. *The Japanese Language in Contemporary Japan.* Washington, D. C.: American Enterprise Institute for Public Policy Research; Stanford: Hoover Institution on War, Revolution and Peace.

–. 1982. *Japan's Modern Myth, The Language and Beyond.* New York & Tokyo: Weatherhill.

–. 1986. *Nihongo, In Defence of Japanese.* London: The Athlone Press.


*Roy Andrew Miller, Honolulu (USA)*

# 16. Traditional linguistics and Western linguistics in Japan

The most important figure in the pre-Western Japanese linguistic tradition, and perhaps in all Japanese linguistic history, is the Kyoto scholar Fujitani Nariakira (1738–1779; → Art. 12). Fujitani's work with the analysis and description of the Japanese language was stimulated by purely practical problems confronted in providing instruction in the intricacies of composition in traditional forms of Japanese poetry. Fujitani was until very recently sadly overlooked by most Japanese scholarship. His works were not printed durig his life-time, and indeed, easily available editions of them are only recently being made available. His ideas were handed down, and understood, only by a handful of personal disciples; his terminology is always difficult, sometimes arcane; and his analysis is so extremely involved, with many different levels all inter-related to one another, that it can be made to yield up its treasures only to persistent and concentrated study. All these factors have conspired to consign Fujitani to neglect until modern times, and scholars have only now begun to assess correctly the accomplishments of this remarkable and original figure in Japanese intellectual history.

Fujitani was the second son of a physician-by-appointment to a branch of the imperial household; he was a child prodigy, and was adopted into the Fujitani line at the age of 19. His interests and talents were those of the classical polymath; his studies embraced history, astronomy, music, poetry, and linguistics. His two most important works are the *Ayuishō* (1773) and the *Kazashishō*; both appear to have been the work of students taking down and later editing their notes of his lectures, rather than original manuscripts drawn up by Fujitani himself, reminding one of the origins of de Saussure's *Cours*.

In the *Ayuishō*, Fujitani established four major form-classes for the linguistic description of Japanese (cf. Miller 1993: 319–321), employing for this purpose an elaborate terminology that had its origin in elegant metaphors relating to articles of clothing and elements of dress. Even though the essential motivation for his work was establishing data for the instruction of would-be poets seeking to write Japanese verse according to received canons of poetic aesthetics, his work nevertheless also places considerable emphasis on the colloquial language of his time (for which it thereby provides valuable documentation!); and he is careful to explain the sense and nuance of each of the literary locutions with which he is concerned in terms of the colloquial of the period. The *Ayuishō* is distinguished, above everything else, by its rigorous and comprehensive approach; and for each item of the literary language that it discusses, the text gives syntactic concords, colloquial translations, compounds, different forms observed in different times, and citations of its use in earlier poetic texts.

The *Kazashishō* limits itself to grammatical elements (isolated somewhat along the lines of the 'empty words' concept of the Chinese tradition), and deals with its materials in terms of a four-stage periodicization of Japanese linguistic history. Fujitani's understanding of the nature of historical change in language, and his attempt to divide up the history of Japanese into a number of discrete periods, count among his greatest accomplishments.

Fujitani's most difficult work is probably the *Yosoi no katagaki*, which is actually a preface to the *Ayuishō*; in this essay he sets up an elaborate system of description and terminology for the inflected forms of the language. Here his linguistic terminology has its origin in elegant metaphor involving bodily activities (e. g. *hiki* "pulling", *nabiki* "bowing", *kishikata* "coming", etc.). Everything about this system is highly original, and it repays careful consideration even today; but it also provides an excellent illustration of the way in which Fujitani's involved analysis and too often arcane terminology conspired to make much of his work almost too difficult for subsequent generations of students even to follow, much less to build upon. Here, as in so much else concerning Fujitani, one is almost tempted to risk the wrath of the Indologists and speak of the Pāṇini-like nature that distinguishes his linguistic work, at the same time that it has led to its misunderstanding and neglect.

Passed over in his own day, and largely forgotten after his death, Fujitani is now finally beginning to come into his rightful place in Japanese linguistic scholarship. It was his unfortunate fate to have his work all but swept away before the incoming flood of 'Dutch learning', which brought with it wholesale neglect of the indigenous grammatical tradition that he more-or-less single-handedly founded, in favor of the newly prestigious importations from the West. Had historical factors been more in his favor, Fujitani might well have become one of the world's best-known linguistic pioneers, and the principles of linguistic analysis in which he specialized might have been further developed and refined by subsequent generations of Japanese scholars. His achievements are particularly impressive when we contrast his work with parallel studies of Chinese in China; when we do that we immediately realize that the comprehensiveneses and rigor that characterize his work must have been reflections of his own intellectual equipment and personality, since there was nothing available to him in the way of continental models that would have encouraged him along these lines.

Suzuki Akira (1764–1837) provides a minor exception to the general statement that the work of Fujitani was by and large neglected after his death (→ Art. 12). Suzuki attempted a harmony of the work of Fujitani with that of Motoori Norinaga (1730–1801), the great pioneer in the so-called 'national studies' school. He also published a work on the classification of inflected forms based on the work of Motoori. Gimon (1786–1843) was a Buddhist cleric who coined a set of terms for certain categories of established forms established in these earlier systems; a number of these coinages, including *rentai* "adnominal", *izen* "aorist", and *ren'yō* "adverbal", have survived into modern times, though generally not in precisely the sense in which he originally employed them.

In 1833 Tsurumine Shigenobu (1788–1859) published his *Gogaku shinsho*, the first of a flood of publications presenting the linguistic analysis of Japanese in terms of Dutch (→ Art. 14); and this would be the work that was selected to serve as the basic text when teaching materials were first prepared for the presentation of Japanese grammar in the newly-established system of Japanese compulsory education promulgated in 1872. Ōtsuki Fumihiko (1847–1929), the first great lexicographer of modern Japan, published his *Kō Nihon bunten* in 1897, a work that presented Japanese grammar entirely along 'Western' lines; it marked the effective severing of the by-then already much attenuated strands that in a few areas still bound the Japanese linguistic tradition to its illustrious past.

Even those scholars who, remaining in the minority, were struggling for some revival of pre-Dutch-learning ideas of grammatical analysis, were soon nevertheless firmly caught in the grip of this same pattern of thinking. Yamada Yoshio (1873–1942) began to resurrect some of Fujitani's ideas about treating Japanese in terms of the form-classes of Japanese, rather than as a variety of Dutch. And somewhat along the same lines, Matsushita Daisaburō (1878–1935) presented original arguments in his *Hyōjun Nihon bunpō*. But these efforts to revive and render respectable the best elements of the earlier Japanese linguistic tradition went all but unnoticed in 'educational circles', and it was the 'educational circles' that mattered so far as lingustic studies were concerned, since in modern Japan education had now replaced literature, and in particular the study and composition of poetry, as the principal stimulus for linguistic scholarship.

Any account of this period in the history of the Japanese linguistic tradition would be grossly incomplete without some mention of Basil Hall Chamberlain (1850–1935), an Englishman who came to Japan in 1873, where he was at first employed as an English instructor at a military academy. He was appointed 'Professor of Japanese and Philology in the Imperial University of Japan' in 1886, a post that he held until his retirement as Professor Emeritus four years later. Even after his return to Europe, he continued his work with Japanese texts; and among the several important Japanese scholars who came under his influence during his brief academic career in Japan the names of Ueda Kazutoshi (1867–1837) and Haga Yaichi (1867–1927) stand out with particular importance.

Ueda was the first Japanese linguistic scholar to receive any formal training in the comparative method. He studied briefly in Germany, and with the grasp of the essentials of the historical method that resulted from that experience he was able to formulate the shift of pre-Old Japanese **p*- > *h*- ~ *f*- that is now accepted as an elementary given in the study of historical Japanese phonology.

Haga also studied in Germany; he was a prolific author of linguistic works, and an influential administrator in Japan's rigidly centralized, Prussian-style state university system. He is remembered in linguistic circles mainly for his codification of the form-class that he denominated *keiyō dōshi* "adjectival verb". This term had first appeared in the work of Ōtsuki, who employed it as an ad hoc device in order "to distinguish Japanese adjectives from English adjectives", when confronted with the type of dead-end that is all too common when one persists in attempting to describing one language as if it were another, particularly one of quite a different structure. The term had also been manipulated by Matsushita, but it remained for Haga to apply it rigorously to a limited form-class.

What was at issue in all this was really something quite simple. The forms called *keiyōshi* "adjectives" in the Dutch-based Japanese school-grammar actually constitute a sub-class of the verb, and are inflected for almost all the categories for which the verb is inflected. Unfortunately the entire concept of the form-class to which this term refers was established first in terms of Dutch, then later of English, grammar; and from this it follows that anything in Japanese that might be translated by a Dutch, or an English adjective, but which does not belong to this form-class in Japanese, presents a problem in analysis. As luck would have it, just such a set of forms does exist in Japanese; words like *shizuka* "quiet", *genki* "healthy", and *teinei* "polite" may be translated into Western languages by adjectives, but in Japanese they do not inflect like the 'true adjectives' already labelled *keiyōshi*, but instead appear in syntax as if they were nouns, coming directly before the copula or before the copula-alternate when modifying a noun directly following. Unable to overlook the linguistically irrelevant fact that these words are often translated into Western languages by Western adjectives, Haga identified them as *keiyō dōshi* "adjectival verbs", and for this feat he is best remembered today. One turns from the contemplation of such terminological feats of *leger de main* with added respect for the work of Fujitani and the other early scholars who were fortunate enough to be born before Japanese intellectual life turned its major attention to manufacturing a second-rate imitation of the West out of generally shoddy native materials.

Basil Hall Chamberlain was the last non-Japanese whose work and teaching in Japan would be of any significance in determining the direction of the Japanese linguistic tradition; from this point on, and well into the 1960s, the tradition would develop almost entirely as a self-contained unit, leavened only by what little the Japanese might be able to glean from foreign books, generally rare and always expensive, and from brief visits to foreign countries, the latter more often to travel and visit than to study.

Military and political circumstances conspired together and all but prevented the American descriptivist school from exercising any influence upon Japanese linguistics (Bloch 1970); and by the time these circumstances had resolved themselves, the descriptivist school itself was in shambles. A number of important studies of Japanese, ranging over both the earlier forms of the written language and the modern spoken language were published abroad in the descriptivist tradition, but they remain even now all but unknown to modern Japanese scholarship. Nor have the findings of these studies always been as widely consulted even in their own country of origin as one might hope. With more attention to this important literature, the field might for example have been spared the confusion in which, e. g., the original formulation of a basic principle in Japanese morphophonemics that goes back to Yokoyama 1950 would twenty years later be attributed to irrelevant and entirely trivial work by others, with not even a notice of Yokoyama's pioneering achievement (McCawley 1966: 173, n. 3).

Finally, when the scholars and students of a newly-affluent Japan finally began to go abroad in large numbers, and upon their return to put into the academic market-place the supposedly 'advanced Western learning' in the field of linguistics, as their Meiji grandfathers before them had done, they found that the linguistic hegemony in foreign lands had mostly fallen into the hands of the transformational-generative school of Noam Chomsky; and so they fell to imitating the approach of this school with the same enthusiasm and remarkable ability for replicating the externals of foreign fads that have always characterized Japanese cultural contacts with the outside world.

In the Meiji-period grammars of Japanese were based on the structure and analysis of Dutch and English; but then at least the subject-matter of these studies was still Japanese in large measure, even though by the time that the language had passed through the analytic mill it emerged looking rather more like a European language than it had when it went in. Now, at the hands of the transformational-generative school, even the subject-matter for their studies conducted *à la* this new fad would be foreign. Their analysis would of necessity have to be performed not directly upon Japanese texts, or upon Japanese utterances transcribed into texts, but rather upon English-language translations – often little more than pidgin renderings – of the Japanese that they were attempting to study (Inoue 1969 is a representative sample). This unfortunate paradox followed directly from the fact that the transformational-generative techniques that the Japanese encountered abroad had been developed for and through the study of English, the only language to and hence the only language studied by, the first-generation of the Chomsky school. Under these circumstances, it is hardly surprising that efforts to date at the transformational-generative study of Japanese have satisfied neither traditional-minded critics (Miller 1972), nor, for that matter, canonical transformational-generativists themselves (Kuroda 1972). And discouraging to be sure as this state of affairs is in contemporary Japan, at least it appears in a somewhat better light, because it reveals itself to be only a small part of a larger pattern, when we refer it to the overall history of traditional linguistics and Western linguistics in Japan.

## Bibliography

### 1. Primary

Matsuo Sutejirō, ed. 1932. *Ayuhishō* Tokyo: Ōokayama.

–. 1934. *Kazashishō, Yosohishō.* Tokyo: Ōokayama.

Nakada Norio & Takeoka Masao, eds. 1960. *Ayuhishō shinchū.* Tokyo: Kazama.

### Secondary

Bloch, Bernard. 1970. *Bernard Bloch on Japanese* ed. with an introduction and analytic index by Roy Andrew Miller. New Haven: Yale Univ. Press.

Inoue, Kazuko. 1969. *A Study of Japanese Syntax.* (= *Janua linguarum, Series practica*, 41.) The Hague: Mouton.

Kuroda, S. Y. 1972. Review of Inoue (1969). *Journal of the American Oriental Society* 92.353–355.

McCawley, James D. 1966. Review of *Japanese Language Studies in the Showa Period: A guide to Japanese reference and research materials* ed. by Joseph K. Yamagiwa, 1961. *Language* 42.170–175.

Miller, Roy Andrew. 1972. Review of Inoue (1969). *Language* 48.214–230.

–. 1975. "The Far East". *Current Trends in Linguistics*, vol. XIII. *Historiography of Linguistics* ed. by Thomas A. Sebeok, 1213–1264. The Hague & Paris: Mouton.

–. 1993. *Die japanische Sprache: Geschichte und Struktur.* München: judicium verlag.

Yokoyama, Masako. 1950. *The Inflections of 8th-Century Japanese.* (= *Language Dissertation*, 45.) Baltimore: Linguistic Society of America.

*Roy Andrew Miller, Honolulu (USA)*

# V. The Establishment of Sanskrit Linguistics
# Die Anfänge der Sanskritforschung
# La constitution de l'étude du sanskrit

## 17. Pāṇini


1. Introduction
2. Pāṇini's work
3. Pāṇini's derivational system
4. Operations
5. Zero
6. Bibliography


### 1. Introduction

#### 1.1. The language described

In a grammar called the *Aṣṭādhyāyī* (henceforth abbreviated **A**), Pāṇini describes a language in use at his time – at latest the 5th century BC – in the north-west of the Indian subcontinent He also accounts for features of earlier Vedic usage that differ from those of the spoken language. Pāṇini uses the locative singular forms *bhāṣāyām* and *chandasi* with reference to the spoken language and to Vedic usage, respectively. Moreover, he mentions dialectal features of easterners (*prācām*) and northerners (*udīcām*). Accordingly, it is appropriate to accept that the language described was in current use at Pāṇini's time. Nevertheless, to judge from what early commentators say in the 3rd and 2nd centuries BC, this was not the sole or even the principal medium of everyday communication. It coexisted with vernaculars that had features referred to as 'Middle Indic' features. From what Kātyāyana (3rd century BC) says, Pāṇini's grammar was intended to impart a knowledge of correct speech forms (*śabda*) and the use of such forms accompanied by a knowledge of the grammar led to religious merit (*dharma*). Patañjali (2nd century BC) also notes that a meaning is understood whether a correct speech form or an incorrect one (*apaśabda*) is uttered. A restriction is made: one should use only a correct speech form to signify a meaning; this results in felicity, prosperity (*abhyudaya*). Patañjali identifies the model speakers for such correct speech: an élite group of Brāhmaṇas, referred to as the *śiṣṭas*, who inhabit the area of north-central India called *āryāvartta* ('abode of the Ārya'). The most reasonable way to interpret all these statements is as follows. At a certain time, the high language – later called *saṁskṛta* "polished, purified" (whence 'Sanskrit', see Cardona 1997: 557–564) as opposed to *prākṛta* "belonging to the common people" (whence 'Prakrit') – could not lay claim to being the everyday medium of all communication even for Ārya Brāhmaṇas, but this language remained an élite medium, in which ritual and learned texts were preserved. The language was then accorded the same power as the rites with which it was associated.

#### 1.2. Background

Pāṇini knew the analyzed text (*padapāṭha*) that was composed by Śākalya to serve as a theoretical source for deriving the continuously recited text (*saṁhitāpāṭha*) of the earliest Vedic work available, the Ṛgveda. Pāṇini refers to Śākalya explicitly, and it is evident that his derivational system (see section 3.1.) is indebted to the procedure adopted by Śākalya. The latter posits an analyzed base text associated with the actually recited text. For example, the continuously recited text of Ṛgveda 1.1.1, transliterated with accentual marks according to traditional notations (see Cardona 1997: li–lxiv), is

(1) *a̱gnim ī̀ḷe pu̱rohìtayṁ̀ ya̱jñasyà de̱vam ṛ̱tvijàm* | *hotā̀raṁ ratna̱dhātàmam*

"I praise (*īḷe* [1sg sg. pres. indic. mid.]) Agni (*a̱gnim* [acc. sg.]), the god (*de̱vam* [acc. sg.]) of the sacrifice (*ya̱jñasyà* [gen. sg.]) set at the fore (*pu̱rohìtam* [acc. sg.]), the priest who performs the rite at the appropriate time (*ṛ̱tvijàm* [acc. sg.]), the Hotṛ officiant (*hotā̀ram* [acc.

sg.]), who best grants treasure (*ratna̱dhātà-mam* [acc. sg.])."
The padapāṭha corresponding to this is

(2) *a̱gnim* | *ī̱le̱* | *pu̱raḥ-hìtam* | *ya̱jñasyà* | *de̱vam* | *ṛ̱tvijàm* | *hotā̀raṁ* | *ra̱tna̱-dhātàmam*

Here syntactic words (*pada*) are separated by pauses (indicated by vertical lines), and pauses are made between members of unambiguously analyzable compounds like *pu̱rohìtam* as well as within words between stem forms and endings before which phonological changes apply that occur at word boundaries. The connection between the padapāṭha and the saṁhitāpāṭha assumes operations that apply to give the latter from basic forms. For example, *pu̱rohìtayṁ̐* presupposes a basic form *pu̱raḥ-hìtam*, with prepause *-aḥ* and *-m*. Phonological operations change *-aḥ* to *-o* before a voiced sound, and *-m* to a nasalized semivowel – here nasalized *y* (*yṁ̐*) – before a semivowel other than *r*; the base text has *ī̱le̱*, with two low-pitched vowels; the first of these is changed to a high-low vowel (*svarita*) – marked with a superstroke in the traditional notation – after the high-pitched vowel of the preceding word (*a̱gnim*): *ī̱le̱* → *ī̍le̱*. In addition, any basic low-pitched vowel is raised to a high – unmarked in the traditional notation – except where a high follows, in which case it is then lowered to an extra low pitch level, marked with a substroke in the traditional notation. Phonological rules of this kind are given in texts called Prātiśākhyas. Pāṇini's derivational procedure is indebted to such an earlier system but goes beyond it. For example, the padapāṭha leaves words like *a̱gnim* unanalyzed. Pāṇini posits a basic *a̱gní-am*, with the nominal base *a̱gní-* and the ending *am*, and provides for *a̱gnim* by rule (see **A** 6.1.107, section 4.1.), and a form like *pace* "I cook, am cooking" [1st sg. mid. pres. indic.] is derived from underlying *pac-a-i*, with a verbal base (*pac*), a basic ending *i* and an intervening affix *a*.

Pāṇini also assumes that a student of his grammar already knows phonetics (*śikṣā*). For example, according to **A** 1.1.9: *tulyāsya-prayatnaṁ savarṇam*, two sound are classed as *savarṇa* "homogeneous" with respect to each other if they are produced with the same (*tulya*) articulatory effort (*prayatna*) at the same place of production in the oral cavity (*āsya*). An exception in this rule (**A** 1.1.10: *nājjhalau*) provides that a vowel and a consonant (*ajjhalau*) which would qualify for being classed as *savarṇa* are not (*na*) so classed. These rules assume a knowledge of articulatory efforts (*prayatna*) and places of production (*sthāna*). They also presuppose a particular stand taken with respect to the efforts assumed for producing vowels and spirants, so that, for example, *i*-vowels and the spirant *ś*, both of which are palatal (*tālavya*), would be eligible for membership in the same class of homogeneous sounds because in producing both the articulator does not make full contact with a place of production.

## 2. Pāṇīni's work

The *Aṣṭādhyāyī* "Eight chapters" is a work of grammar (*vyākaraṇa*) divided into eight (*aṣṭan-*) chapters (*adhyāya-*), each subdivided into four quarter chapters (*pāda*). The core of this work consists of approximately 4,000 rules (*sūtra*, *śāstra*, *yoga*, *lakṣaṇa*; see Cardona 1997: 573–576). This grammar is also known as a *śabdānuśāsanam*, a means of instruction (*anuśāsanam*) whereby one learns correct speech forms (*śabda-*, see section 1.1.).

Most sūtras of the *Aṣṭādhyāyī* are operational rules. In addition, there are rules ancillaries to these: metarules (*paribhāṣā*) and rules concerning technical terms (*saṁjñāsūtra*), as well as headings (*adhikāra*) which serve to subdivide the grammar into major groups of thematically related rules. The organization of the grammar is treated in article 21.

It is plausible to assume that the *Aṣṭādhyāyī* originally was accompanied by an autocommentary, but none is extant. The earliest commentatorial work available is a series of discussions, concerning most but not all rules, by Kātyāyana (3rd century BC), whose work is preserved in the form of comments, called *vārttika*, as cited in the great commentary (*Mahābhāṣya*) of Patañjali (2nd century BC). Later commentaries explain rules and illustrate with examples and counterexamples how they work. These commentaries deal with rules in two orders: the original order of the *Aṣṭādhyāyī* and thematic rearrangements such that rules concerning technical names (*saṁjñā*), metarules (*paribhāṣā*), and sandhi are put together, as are rules concerning nominal forms and so on.

### 2.1. Ancillaries

The corpus of sūtras is accompanied by three anciliaries: Pāṇini's *dhātupāṭha*, *gaṇapāṭha* and *akṣarasamāmnāya*.

(A) The dhātupāṭha is an ordered list of primitive verbal bases (*dhātu-*, see section 3.2.) divided into ten groups (*gaṇa-*). These groups begin with the following bases: *bhū́* "be, become" (3rd sg. pres. indic. *bhav-à-ti* [← *bhó-a-ti* ← *bhū́-a-ti* ← *bhū́-ti*]), *ad**á*** "eat" (*at-tì* [← *ád-ti*]), *hu* "offer oblations" (*ju̱-ho-tì* [← … *hu-ti*]), *dív**ú*** "play, gamble" (*dīv-yà-ti* [← *dív-ya-ti* ← *dív-ti*]), *ṣu**ñ*** "press juice out of something" (*su̱-no-tì* [← *su-nú-ti* ← *sú-ti*], 3rd sg. mid. indic. *su-nu̱-te* [← *su-nu-tá* ← *su-tá*]), *tud**à*** "goad, wound" (*tu̱d-a-tì* [← *túd-ti*], *tu̱d-á-tè* [← *tud-á-ta* ← *túd-ta*]), *rudh**ìr*** "hold in, obstruct" (*ru̱ṇaddhì* [← … *ru-ná-dh-ti* ← *rúdh-ti*], *ru̱nddhé* [← … *ru-na-dh-té* ← *ru-na-dh-tá* ← *rudh-tá*), *tán**ù*** "stretch" (*ta̱n-o-tì* [← *tan-ú-ti* ← *tán-ti*], *tan-u̱-te* [← *tan-u-tá* ← *tan-tá*]), ***ḍu**krī́**ñ*** "buy" (*krī̱-ṇā-tì* [← *krī-ṇā́-ti* ← *krī́-ti*], *krī-ṇī̱-te* [← … *krī-nā-té* ← … *krī-tá*]), *cura* "steal" (*co̱r-ay-à-ti* [← *cor-é-a-ti* ← *cor-í-a-ti* ← *cor-í-ti*, *cor-í-* ← *cur-í-*], *co̱r-a-yà-te* [← … *cor-í-ta*]). As shown, bases of different groups take distinct affixes in forms with agentive verb endings. *bhav-à-ti* (← *bhó-a-ti*) has an unaccented suffix *-a-*, but *tu̱d-a-tì* (→ *túd-ti*) contains an accented suffix *-a-*, and *dīv-yà-ti* (← *dív-ya-ti*) has unaccented *-ya-*; *su̱-no-tì*, *su-nu̱-te*, *ta̱n-o-tì*, *tan-u̱-te* and *krī̱-ṇā-tì*, *krī-ṇī̱-te* contain suffixes that have alternants (*-nó-/-nu-*, *-ó-/-u-*, *-nā́-/-nī-*) before different sets of endings; and *ru̱ṇaddhì*, *ru̱nddhé* have an infix that also exhibits alternants (*-ná-/-n-*); *co̱r-ay-à-ti* has two suffixes: *-a-* as in the type *bhavàti* and accented *-í-/-é-*. As also indicated, verbs are given in the dhātupāṭha with appended markers, shown here in bold face. Such appended sounds, called *it* in Pāṇini's system are unconditionally dropped before items to which they are attached undergo operations, but they serve to show that given items undergo or condition particular operations or belong to certain grammatical classes. In addition, certain verbal bases are listed with primitive *ṣ-* and *ṇ-* – which are unconditionally replaced by *s-* and *n-* – to indicate that they are subject to particular retroflex replacements.

(B) Certain items are grouped together and listed as accompaniments to rules in which are stated classifications or operations pertinent to members of the set. For example, the set beginning with *sarva-* "whole, all" accompanies **A** 1.1.27: *sarvādīni sarvanāmāni*, which provides that members of this group (*sarvādīni*) are given the class name *sarvanāman-* "pronominal"; the group beginning with *ajā* "she goat" contains items such that the affix ***ṭāp*** follows a nominal used in the feminine (**A** 4.1.4: *ajādyataṣ ṭāp* [*striyām* 3]). Such sets of items are referred to as *gaṇas* in Pāṇini's gaṇapāṭha.

(C) The text of the *Aṣṭādhyāyī* is traditionally preceded by a catalog of sounds subdivided into fourteen groups, each closed by a consonantal marker, as follows: (1) *a i u* ***ṇ*** (2) *ṛ ḷ* ***k*** (3) *e o* ***ṅ*** (4) *ai au* ***c*** (5) *h y v r* ***ṭ*** (6) *l* ***ṇ*** (7) *ñ m ṅ ṇ n* ***m*** (8) *jh bh* ***ñ*** (9) *gh ḍh dh* ***ṣ*** (10) *j b g ḍ d* ***ś*** (11) *kh ph ch ṭh th c ṭ t* ***v*** (12) *k p* ***y*** (13) *ś ṣ s* ***r*** (14) *h* ***l***. These sounds are arranged in a manner that allows Pāṇini to refer to sets of sounds pertinent to phonological rules as stated in his grammar. A rule (**A** 1.1.71: *ādir antyena sahetā*) provides for terms of the type ***im***, that begin with an item *i* which is the first member of an ordered set or subset and end with a final marker ***m*** (shown in bold face): ***im*** denotes *i* and all intervening items up to ***m***. For example, ***ac*** names all the vowels, ***hal*** all the consonants of the list shown, and ***ik*** refers to the vowels *i u ṛ ḷ*.

## 3. Pāṇini's derivational system

### 3.1. General

(A) Pāṇini's is a derivational system which presupposes an analysis (cf. section 1.2.). Starting with bases (*prakṛti*), affixes (*pratyaya*, see section 3.3.) are introduced under meaning and cooccurrence conditions to form syntactic words (*pada*) in utterances (*vākya*), which can be simple or complex. Each such word bears a stateable relation to other words of the same utterance. The principal constituents in utterances are derivates of verbal bases, signifying actions. To these are immediately related nominal forms signifying direct participants (*kāraka*, see section 3.3.) in the accomplishment of actions. Through their direct relations with actions, kārakas are indirectly related to each other. For example,

(3a) *devadattaḥ kaṭaṅ karoti* "Devadatta is making a mat"

derives from an underlying string

(3b) (*devadatta-s*$_1$) (*kaṭa-am*$_2$) (*kṛ-ti**p***) [← *kṛ-la**ṭ***]

in which the verbal base *kṛ* "make" is followed by the ending *ti**p*** [3rd sg. act.], which replaces the L-affix *la**ṭ*** – one of ten abstract affixes replaced by endings and participial suffixes – and the nominal bases *devadatta-* "Devadatta", *kaṭa-* "mat" are respectively followed by the endings *s**u*** [nom. sg.] and *am* [acc. sg.]. The corresponding passive sentence

(4a) *devadattena kaṭaḥ kriyate* "A mat is being made by Devadatta"

is derived from a string

(4b) (*devadatta-ā*$_3$) (*kaṭa-s*$_1$) (*kṛ-ta*) [← *kṛ-la**ṭ***]

where *kṛ* is followed by *ta* [3rd sg. medio-pass.] that also replaces *la**ṭ***, but *kaṭa-* takes the ending *s**u*** and *devadatta-* is followed by the instrumental singular ending ***ṭ**ā*. Similarly,

(5a) *rājñaḥ puruṣo grāmaṅ gacchati* "The king's servant is going to the village"

is derived from

(5b) (*rājan-as*$_6$) (*puruṣa-s*$_1$) (*grāma-am*$_2$) *gam-**tip*** [← *gam-**laṭ***]

in which *gam* "go" is followed by ***tip*** replacing ***laṭ***, ***su*** and *am* respectively follow *puruṣa-* "man", *grāma-* "village", and *rājan-* "king" is followed by the ending ***ṅas*** [gen. sg.].

In (3b)–(5b) each syntactic pada is surrounded by parentheses. By definition (**A** 1.4.14: *suptiṅantam padam*) such a pada terminates in a nominal or verbal ending, respectively referred to by the abbreviatory terms ***sup***, *tiṅ* (see B, C).

(B) As shown by the subscripts, nominal endings such as *s*$_1$ (***su***), *am*$_2$, *ā*$_3$ belong to triplets of endings (*vibhakti*) which Pāṇini refers to by the traditional terms *prathamā* "first", *dvitīyā* "second", *tṛtīyā* "third", *caturthī* "fourth", *pañcamī* "fifth", *ṣaṣṭhī* "sixth", and *saptamī* "seventh". The seven triplets of basic nominal endings are: ***su*** *au **j**as*, *am au**ṭ*** *ś**as***, ***ṭ**ā bhyām bhis*, ***ṅ**e bhyām bhyas*, ***ṅ**as**i*** *bhyām bhyas*, ***ṅ**as os ām*, ***ṅ**i os su**p***. These endings are referred to by the abbreviation ***sup***, which consists of the first ending ***su*** and the final marker *p* of the last ending ***sup***, in accordance with the rule that provides for such abbreviatory terms (**A** 1.1.71, see section 2.1.C). Rules provide for introducing endings of these triplets after nominal bases (*prātipadika*) or nominals with feminine affixes, under meaning conditions. Thus, **A** 2.3.2: *karmaṇi dvitīyā* introduces endings of the second triplet (*dvitīyā*) if an object (*karman*) is to be signified, and by **A** 2.3.18: *kartṛkaraṇayos tṛtīyā* an ending of the third triplet (*tṛtīyā*) occurs if an agent (*kartṛ*) or an instrument (*karaṇa*) is to be signified. The first, second and third endings in each triplet ***su*** *au **j**as* and so on are respectively called *ekavacana*, *dvivacana*, *bahuvacana* (etymologically: "signifying one, two, many"). Their distribution is provided for in terms of semantics: bahuvacana endings occur if many entities (*bahuṣu*) are to be signified (**A** 1.4.21: *bahuṣu bahuvacanam*), dvivacana and ekavacana endings respectively if two (*dvi*) and one (*eka*) are to be designated (**A** 1.4.22: *dvyekayor dvivacanaikavacane*). Thus, in (3b) and (5b), *am*$_2$ is introduced to signify an object relative to the action in question, specifically a mat (*kaṭa-*) that Devadatta is making and a village (*grāma-*) to which the king's servant is going. In (4b), *ā*$_3$ (***ṭ**ā*) is introduced to signify an agent relative to making, specifically the person named Devadatta. Each such ending is thus treated as coreferential (*samānādhikaraṇa*) with the nominal it follows. There is a remainder of relations with respect to the possible relations between actions and kārakas as well as certain cooccurrence relations. When such a residual relation is involved (*śeṣe* "remainder"), an ending of the sixth triplet follows a nominal (**A** 2.3.50: *ṣaṣṭhī śeṣe*), as in *rājan-as*$_6$ of (5b). Endings of the first triplet, on the other hand, constitute a default set, introduced when nothing more than a base meaning (*prātipadikārtha*), gender (*liṅga*), measure (*parimāṇa*), and number (*vacana*) is to be designated (**A** 2.3.49: *prātipadikārthaliṅgaparimāṇavacanamātre prathamā*).

(C) Endings of finite verb forms are allowed to occur as replacements for abstract L-affixes, which are introduced in general if one is to signify an agent (*kartṛ*) or an object (*karman*) after verbs taking objects and an agent or the mere action (*bhāva*) after verbs not taking objects (*akarmaka*: **A** 3.4.69: *laḥ* [*kartari* 67] *karmaṇi ca bhāve cākarmakebhyaḥ*). There are ten such L-affixes, six marked with *ṭ* (***laṭ***, ***liṭ***, ***luṭ***, ***lṛṭ***, ***leṭ***, ***loṭ***), four marked with *ṅ* (***laṅ***, ***liṅ***, ***luṅ***, ***lṛṅ***). Particular L-affixes occur under conditions of time reference and modalities. For example, ***laṭ*** follows a verbal base if the action in question is spoken of as currently taking place (**A** 3.2.123: *vartamāne laṭ*). An L-affix is always replaced, by an ending or a participial affix. A set of eighteen basic verb endings replaces any L-affix (**A** 3.4.77–78: *lasya*, *tiptasjhisipthasthamibvasmastātāñjhathāsāthāndhvamiḍvahimahiṅ*). These are divided into two sets of nine endings, which in western terminology are called active and medio-passive and in Pāṇini's system belong to the classes named *parasmaipada* and *ātmanepada*: parasmaipada: ***tip*** *tas jhi*, ***sip*** *thas tha*, ***mip*** *vas mas*; ātmanepada: *ta ātām jha*, *thās āthām dhvam*, *i**ṭ*** *vahi mahi**ṅ***. These endings as a whole are referred to by the abbreviation *ti**ṅ***, made up of the first ending *ti* and the final marker of the last ending *mahi**ṅ*** (**A** 1.1.71, see section 2.1.C). As shown, each set of nine endings is subdivided into three triplets, called *prathama* "first", *madhyama* "middle", *uttama* "last", corresponding to third, second, and first person endings of western grammarians. Within each of these triplets, the endings are respectively called *ekavacana*, *dvivacana*, and *bahuvacana*, as are members of triplets of nominal endings. Restrictive rules provide for the proper distribution of parasmaipada and ātmanepada endings, for prathama, madhyama, and uttama endings, and for ekavacana, dvivacana, and bahuvacana endings. Thus, if an L-affix has been introduced when an object (*karman*) or action (*bhāva*) is to be signified, ātmanepada endings take its place (**A** 1.3.13: *bhāvakarmaṇoḥ* [*ātmanepadam* 12]). Some verbal bases are activa tantum, others media tantum, still others take either parasmaipada or ātmanepada suffixes under stateable conditions. Certain markers are used with different types of verbs. For example, a base that is marked with a svarita vowel – a vowel with a combination of high and low pitches – or with *ñ* takes ātmanepada suffixes of the result of the action in question is intended for the agent (**A** 1.3.72: *svaritañitaḥ kartrabhiprāye kriyāphale*). Once all the conditions are given for the occurrence of ātmanepada suffixes, there is a remainder (*śeṣa*) of bases and conditions such that verbs that fall into this remaining category take parasmaipada suffixes replacing an L-affix introduced to signify an agent (*kartṛ*: **A** 1.3.78: *śeṣāt kartari parasmaipadam*). The distribution of endings of the triplets named *prathama* and so on is accounted for in terms of coreference. If an L-affix is coreferential (*samānādhikaraṇe*) with a pronominal *yuṣmad* [2nd pers., loc. sg. *yuṣmadi*] that may but need not be used (*sthāniny api*) as a cooccurring term (*upapade*), then endings of the madhyama triplet occur; if the L-affix is coreferential with a potentially usable pronoun *asmad* [1st pers.], endings of the uttama triplet occur; after these and one other condition – not considered here – are accounted for, there is a remainder (*śeṣa*) such that prathama endings occur (**A** 1.4.105, 107, 108: *yuṣmady upapade samānādhikaraṇe sthāniny api madhyamaḥ, asmady uttamaḥ, śeṣe prathamaḥ*). Finally, ekavacana, dvivacana, and bahuvacana verb endings occur under the same number conditions as determine the occurrence of nominal endings. Thus, *karoti* of (3a) has the ekavacana ending ***tip*** of the prathama triplet (*tip tas jhi*) in place of the L-affix ***laṭ*** introduced to signify a single agent relative to the act of making, which is spoken of as currently taking place. In addition, the agent Devadatta is spoken of here as making a mat for someone else, so that a parasmaipada affix is used. If Devadatta were making the mat for himself, one would use *kurute*, with the ātmanepada ending *te* (← *ta*).

(D) Endings such as *tip*, *ta* belong to the class calles *sārvadhātuka*. In general, verb endings (*tiṅ*) and verb affixes marked with *ś* (*śit*) are members of the sārvadhātuka class, and the remainder (*śeṣa*) of verb affixes belong to a class called *ārdhadhātuka* (**A** 3.4.113–114: *tiṅśit sārvadhātukam, ārdhadhātukaṁ śeṣaḥ*). Verbal endings not only substitute for abstract L-affixes but also serve as contexts for introducing other affixes to verb bases. If a sārvadhātuka used to signify an object or when a mere action is signified follows a verbal base, this takes the suffix ***yak*** (**A** 3.1.67: *sārvadhātuke yak*); if the sārvadhātuka signifies an agent, verbal bases as arranged in ten groups of the dhātupāṭha (see section 2.1.) takes distinct affixes. *kri-ya-te* (← *kṛ-ya-te*) of (4a) has ***yak*** following *kṛ* used with the ending *te* signifying an object; *kar-o-ti* (← *kṛ-u-ti*) and *gacchati* (← *gam-a-ti*) in (3a) and (5a) respectively have *u* and ***śap*** following *kṛ* and *gam* used with the ending *ti* signifying an agent.

(E) (3)–(5) are simple sentences, involving only one action. Pāṇini's system also serves to derive certain complex sentences, which involve two or more related actions. For example,

(6a) *kṛṣṇaṁ namec cet sukhaṁ yāyāt* "If (*ced*) one does obeisance (*namet* [3rd sg. opt.]) to Kṛṣṇa one obtains (*yāyāt* [3rd sg. opt.] "would go to") happiness (*sukham*)"

is derived from

(6b) *kṛṣṇa-am*$_2$ *nam-**tip*** [← *nam-**liṅ***] *cet-s*$_1$ *sukha-am*$_2$ *yā-**tip*** [← *yā-**liṅ***]

This involves the acts of bowing (*nam*) to Kṛṣṇa and obtaining happiness, related as cause (*hetu*) and effect (*hetumat*). **A** 3.3.156: *hetuhetumator liṅ* provides for introducing the L-affix ***liṅ*** after verbs whose actions are said to be related as cause and effect (*hetuhetumatoḥ*), accounting for optative forms as in (6a). The following also involves two related actions:

(7a) *rājapuruṣaṁ grāmaṁ gacchantam apaśyat* "... saw (*apaśyat* [3rd sg. impfct.]) the king's servant (*rājapuruṣam*) going (*gacchantam* [acc. sg. masc.]) to the village"

This is derived from

(7b) *rājapuruṣa-am*$_2$ *grāma-am*$_2$ *gam-**laṭ*** *dṛś-**laṅ***

Ordinarily, the L-affix of *gam-**laṭ*** would be replaced by a verb ending, as in (5a). In (7b), however, ***laṭ*** introduced to signify an agent relative to the act of going is coreferential (*samānādhikaraṇa*) with *rājapuruṣa-am*$_2$, which refers to the particular agent involved in the act of going. Pāṇini operates with underlying strings like (7b) and provides for ***laṭ*** to be replaced by the participial affixes ***śatṛ***, ***śānac*** if this L-affix is coreferential with a nominal pada terminating in an ending other than one of the first triplet (**A** 3.2.124: *laṭaḥ śatṛśānacāv aprathamāsamānādhikaraṇe*). ***śatṛ***, ***śānac*** are respectively parasmaipada and ātmanepada affixes, so that they occur under the conditions that determine the use of endings like ***tip***, *ta* and so on. These affixes are also marked with *ś* to indicate that they are members of the sārvadhātuka class. Accordingly, ***śap*** is introduced after *gam* in *gam-at-*, just as it follows *gam* in *gam-ti* to derived *gacchati*. In addition, *gam-at-* is a derived nominal base and is coreferential with *rāja-puruṣa-*, both referring to an agent of going. Accordingly, the ending *-am*$_2$ is also introduced after *gam-at-*.

3.2. Units of the system

(A) As shown (section 3.1.), utterances are derived as complexes of syntactically and semantically related padas. Padas in turn contain stems (*aṅga*) with their affixes. Stems are simple or complex. For example, ((*devadatta-*)*s*$_1$) ((*kaṭa-*)*am*$_2$) consist of the simple stems *devadatta-*, *kaṭa-* and their affixes ***su***, *am*; on the other hand, (((*kṛ-*)*-u-*)*ti*) contains two stems: the complex stem *kṛ-u-* relative to *ti* and the simple stem *kṛ-* relative to *u*. The simple stems shown contain bases, which are either verbal or nominal, primitive or derived.

(B) Primitive verbal bases are given in the dhātupāṭha, an ordered set divided into ten groups (see section 2.1.A). Members of this set (*bhūvādayaḥ*) are given the class name *dhātu* 'root' (**A** 1.3.1.: *bhūvādayo dhātavaḥ*). Derived verbal bases are formed from primitive verbs or nominal forms. A primitive verbal base is followed by ***san***, ***yaṅ***, ***ṇic***, resepctively, to form desideratives, intensives, and causatives. For example, from the base ***ḍukṛñ*** "do, make" [3rd sg. pres. indic. act. *karoti*, mid. *kurute*] are derived *cikīrṣa-* (← *kṛ-san-*) "wish to do, make" (*cikīrṣati*, *cikīrṣate*), *cekrīya-* (← *kṛ-yaṅ-*) "do, make intensely, repeatedly" (*cekriyate*), *kār-i-* (← *kṛ-ṇic-*) "have ... do, make" (*kārayati*, *kārayate*). Such derivates also have the class name *dhātu* (**A** 3.1.32: *sanādyantā dhātavaḥ*) and enter into the same derivational processes as do primitive verbal bases. For example, *cikīrṣati* is equivalent to and alternates with *kartum icchati* "wishes to do, make", as in

(8) *kaṭaṅ kartum icchati* "... wishes to make a mat"

(9) *kaṭañ cikīrṣati* "... wishes to make a mat"

To a pada with a nominal ending an affix is introduced to derive an item called *dhātu*, within which nominal endings are dropped. For example,

(10a) *putram icchati* "... desires a son"

is derived from

(10b) (*putra-am*) (*iṣ-ti*) [← *iṣ-**laṭ***].

After *putra-am* of (10b), the affix ***kyac*** is optionally introduced to form the derived verbal base *putra-am-ya*, the ending within which is dropped: *putra-am-ya* → *putra-ya-* → *putrīya*. *putrīyati* is equivalent to (10a).

(C) Any meaningful element (*arthavat*) other than a verbal base (*adhātuḥ*) or an affix (*apratyayaḥ*, see below, D) is given the class name *prātipadika* "nominal base" (*A* 1.2.45: *arthavad adhātur apratyayaḥ prātipadikam*). Such bases also are either primitive or derived. Derived nominal bases are formed from verbal bases or nominal elements. Affixes called *kṛt* occur with verbal bases to form action nouns, infinitives, instrument nouns, participles; e. g., *kar-tṛ-* (← *kṛ-tṛ-*, affix *tṛc*, *tṛ**n***), *kār-aka-* ← *kṛ-aka-* (affix *aka* ← ***ṇvul***) "doer, maker", *kar-aṇa-* "doing, making", (affix *ana* ← ***lyuṭ***), *kṛ-ti-* "doing, making", *kar-tum* (← *kṛ-tum* [*tum**un***]) "to do, to make", *kar-aṇa-* "means of doing, making", *kṛ-ta-* (affix ***kta***) "done, made". Derived nominal bases are also formed from padas of syntactic strings. There are two types: compounds (*samāsa*) and derivates with affixes called *taddhita*. For example the semantically and syntactically related padas (*rājan-as*$_6$) (*puruṣa-s*$_1$) of a string such as (5b) are optionally combined to form a compound *rājan-as-puruṣa-s*, ending within which are deleted: *rājan-as-puruṣa-s* → *rājan-puruṣa* → *rājapuruṣa-*. Taddhita affixes generally follow syntactic padas, to which the derivates are equivalent. For example, the pada *putra-as*$_6$, with the nominal ending ***ṅas***, is followed optionally by *-a* (affix ***añ***) to form the derived nominal *putra-as-a-*, the ending within which is dropped *putra-as-a-* → *putra-a* → *pautra-a-* → *pautra-* "son's son". Forms of this derivate alternate with equivalent strings; e. g., *pautraḥ* [nom. sg.] is equivalent to *putrasya putraḥ*. Accordingly, Pāṇini formulates rules such as **A** 4.1.92: *tas-*

*yāpatyam*, in which a form of the pronoun *tad* "that" is used as a variable. A taddhita affix is optionally (*vā*) introduced after the first (*prathamāt*) of syntactically and semantically related (*samarthānām*) padas stated in such rules (**A** 4.1.82: *samarthānāṁ prathamād vā*). For example, *putra-as*$_6$ is a value of *tad-as*$_6$ (→ *tasya*). **A** 4.1.92 also contains another pada, *apatyam* "descendant", which designates the meaning of the affix introduced after a value of the first pada. Primitive nominal bases are those that are not treated as derived by affixation or composition, lexical items like *go* "cow, ox". There were also ancient scholars – without doubt including predecessors of Pāṇini – who considered all nominals to be derivable from verbal bases.

(D) Affixes are introduced by a large group of rules, headed by **A** 3.1.1: *pratyayaḥ* and extending through the fifth chapter. According to **A** 3.1.1, items newly introduced by subsequent rules are called *pratyaya*. In general, an affix follows (*para*: **A** 3.1.2: *paraś ca*) the unit to which it is introduced. Not all affixes, however, are suffixes. There are, for example, several infixes. These are marked with *m* and a rule (**A** 1.1.47: *mid aco' ntyāt paraḥ*) provides that an element bearing this marker (*mit*) occurs after the last (*antyāt*) vowel (*acaḥ*) of the item to which it is introduced. For example, ***śnam*** introduced to primitive verbal bases of the group beginning with *rudh**ir*** (**A** 3.1.78: *rudhyādibhyaḥ śnam*, see section 2.1.(A) is marked with *m* to show that it is an infix: *ruṇaddhi* (← *ru-na-dh-ti*). One prefix is recognized: *bahu-*, as in *bahupaṭu-* "sharpish".

(E) In addition, Pāṇini recognizes augments – called *āgama* "adventitious element" in the Pāṇinian tradition – elements that are introduced as parts of others. Augments are marked with *ṭ*, *k* (*ṭakitau*) respectively to show that they are initial and final (*ādyantau*) segments of items (**A** 1.1.46: *ādyantau ṭakitau*). For example, a form such as *abhavat* [3rd sg. impfct. act.] "was" contains a stem *abhava-* (← *abhū-a-*) with the initial augment ***aṭ*** (**A** 6.4.71: *luṅlaṅlṛṅkṣv aḍ udātta*). Endings also take augments. Thus, a parasmaipada ending like ***tip*** receives the initial augment *yā**suṭ*** if it replaces the L-affix ***liṅ***, as in (6b) (**A** 3.4.103: *yāsuṭ parasmaipadeṣūdātto ṅic ca* [*liṅaḥ* 102]): *nam-ti* → *nam-yāsti* → ... *namet*, *yā-ti* → *yā-yāsti* → *yāyāt*. A genitive plural such as *devānām* "gods" is derived from an underlying form *deva-ām*, with addition of the initial augment ***nuṭ*** to the ending *ām* (**A** 7.1.54: *hrasvanadyāpo nuṭ* [*āmi* 52]): *deva-ām* → *deva-nām* → *devānām*; and *-cit-* of *agni-cit-* "one who has set up a sacrificial fire" [acc. sg. *agnicit-am*] has the final augment ***tuk*** (**A** 6.1.71: *hrasvasya piti kṛti tuk*; see section 5). There are also augments added within items. These are marked with *m*, as are infixed affixes. For example, *iṅg* (← *ing*) "move" [3rd sg. pres. indic. *iṅgati*], *muñcati* (← *munc-a-ti*) "lets loose", *chandāṁsi* (← *chandans-i* [nom.-acc. sg. nt.]) "metres" contain the augment ***num*** (**A** 7.1.58, 59, 72: *idito nuṁ dhātoḥ, śe mucādīnām, napuṁsakasya jhalacaḥ*) introduced after the last vowels of *ig*, *muc-* in *muc-a-*, and *chandas-* in *chandas-i*.

### 3.3. Conditions for affixation

The *Aṣṭādhyāyī* is composed from a speaker's point of view, so that meanings (*artha*) are taken as conditions (*nimitta*) for introducting affixes. Pāṇini distinguishes between meanings that are understood from everyday usage and those that are not. For example, he refers to different times using *vartamāna-* "current, present" (**A** 3.2.123, see section 3.1.C) *bhūta-* "past", *bhaviṣyat-* "future", *anadyatana-* "not including today", and to numbers, using *bahu*, *eka*, *dvi* (**A** 1.4.21–22, section 3.1.B). There is evidence from commentators that some grammarians felt it necessary to specify what was meant by *adya* "today", since there were different opinions concerning just when a day was considered to begin and end. Pāṇini takes it for granted that, whatever conception one has of what stretch of time constitutes what one refers to with *adya*, this everyday knowledge suffices to account for usage in terms of his rules. On the other hand, there are terms which require particular statements. To derive utterances like (3)–(5) (section 3.1.A), Pāṇini formulates rules like **A** 2.3.2: *karmaṇi dvitīyā*, **A** 3.4.69: *laḥ* [*kartari* 67] *karmaṇi ca bhāve cākarmakebhyaḥ*, in which he uses *karman* [loc. sg. *karmaṇi*]. As used in these rules, *karman* names members of a category to which direct participants in actions (*kāraka*) are assigned under particular circumstances. According to **A** 1.4.49: *kartur īpsitatamaṁ karma*, that participant which an agent (*kartṛ*, gen. sg. *kartuḥ*) most wishes to reach (*īpsitatamam*) through an activity is given the class name *karman*. But there are also several other sūtras assigning kārakas to the karman category. For example, by **A** 1.4.46: *adhiśīṅsthāsāṁ karma* [*ādhāraḥ* 45]) that kāraka which plays the role of locus (*ādhāraḥ* "substrate") with respect to an action is classed as *karman* if the act in question is one of those denoted by *adhi-śī* "lie on", *adhi-ṣṭhā* "remain at", *adhy-ās* "be at", as in *dakṣiṇaṁ bhāgam adhiśete* "... lies on the right part". Although *dakṣiṇaṁ bhāgam* refers to a place where someone lies – this concerns a woman's lying on the right of her husband – the kāraka is classed as karman so that, by **A** 2.3.2, *dakṣiṇa-* "right" and *bhāga-* "part" are followed by the second-triplet ending *am*. *kartṛ*, *karman* and so on, referring to categories which mediate between semantics and strings, are introduced by rules that assign kārakas to different categories in the manner illustrated.

Certain affixes are also introduced under cooccurrence conditions. For example, by **A** 2.3.16: *namaḥsvastisvāhāsvadhālaṁvaṣadyogāc ca* [*caturthī* 23]), a fourth-triplet ending follows a nominal if this is syntactically connected with *namas* "obeisance, salutation" and several other terms, as in *namo devāya* "[let there be] salutation to the god", with the dative singular *devāya* (← *deva-e*4).

3.4. Meaning and form

As has been illustrated, to derive sentences Pāṇini starts from semantics. He also carefully distinguishes between meaning and form. Thus, triplets of nominal endings like ***su** au jas, am auṭ śas* are referred to simply as *prathamā, dvitīyā* and so on (section 3.1.B), not by any terms comparable to 'nominativus', 'accusativus', which have semantic content. Similarly, Pāṇini operates with verb endings ***tip** tas jhi* and so forth as well as abstract L-affixes, but he does not use terms such as *bhavantī* – comparable to 'present' – which have semantic content. There is evidence to indicate that at least some predecessors of Pāṇini did indeed use *bhavantī* and other comparable terms.

In addition, Pāṇini operates with a hierarchy with respect to utterance meanings. Rules such as **A** 2.3.2 (section 3.1.B) are headed by **A** 2.3.1: *anabhihite*. Accordingly, **A** 2.3.2 provides that a second-triplet ending is introduced if there is to be signified a karman that is not signified (*anabhihite*), and **A** 2.3.18 introduces a third-triplet ending if there is to be signified a kartṛ or karaṇa that is not signified. In deriving (3)–(5), then, the expression of karman and kartṛ by a verbal affix takes precedence over their expression by a nominal affix. Thus, in (3b) the L-affix is introduced to signify an agent, so that the third-triplet ending *ṭā* is not introduced after *devadatta-*, and in (4b) the L-affix is introduced to signify an object, so that the second-triplet ending *am* is not introduced after *kaṭa-*. On the other hand, *am* does follow *kaṭa-* in (3b), and *ṭā* follows *devadatta-* in (4b). In this way, groups of sentences of the type (3) and (4) are treated as equivalent utterances derived on the basis of a single set of relations between the same participants and a given action referred to the same time and with the same modality. Moreover, the action is treated as the principal part of the content, so that the verbal base is considered the main component of the utterance.

## 4. Operations

4.1. Pāṇini's derivational system is built around the introduction of affixes to bases (see section 3.2.). As can be seen from (3b)–(5b) in section 3.1.A, moreover, Pāṇini operates with basic forms of elements and accounts for variants through rules of substitution. To illustrate, it will suffice to show how the final utterances (3a)–(5a) are derived from the posited strings (3b)–(5b). There are substitutions that apply to particular grammatical elements in grammatical contexts. Others concern sounds in grammatical contexts, and still others are purely phonological, applying regardless of grammatical contexts. Thus, the derivation of *karoti* and *kriyate* in (3a), (4a) involve replacements for the vowel of *kṛ-* in different contexts. According to **A** 7.3.84: *sārvadhātukārdhadhātu-kayoḥ* [*guṇaḥ* 82, *aṅgasya* 6.4.1]), the final sound of a stem that ends in an *i-*, *u-*, *ṛ- or ḷ*-vowel is replaced by vowel of the guṇa class – that is, *a e o* (**A** 1.1.2: *ad eṅ guṇaḥ*) – if the stem is followed by an affix belonging to the sārvadhātuka class (see section 3.1.D) or its complement, verbal affixes called *ārdhadhātuka*. The guṇa vowel *a* thus replaces the *-ṛ* of *kṛ* before *u*, which is an ārdhadhātuka affix, and the guṇa vowel *o* substitutes for the final vowel of the stem *kṛ-u* before the sārvadhātuka affix ***tip***. In addition, a vowel substituting for *ṛ* is automatically followed by *r* (**A** 1.1.51: *ur aṇ raparaḥ*), so that the guṇa replacement for *ṛ* is *ar*. In general, guṇa substitution applying to vowels *i u ṛ ḷ* by rules where substituends are not specified is disallowed if the affix which would otherwise condition this replacement bears certain markers, among them *k* (**A** 1.1.5: *kṅiti ca* [*na* 4, *iko* *guṇavṛddhī* 3]). The suffix *yak* of *kṛ-ya-te* is marked with *k*, so that guṇa substitution does not apply before this. Instead, *-ṛ* is replaced by *-ri* (**A** 7.4.28: *riṅ śayagliṅkṣu* [*ṛtaḥ* 27]). Deriving *gacchati* of (5a) from *gam-a-ti* also involves replacing a final sound of a stem before a particular affix. The final consonants of three verbs, including *gam*, are replaced by *ch* before an affix marked with *ś* (*śiti*: **A** 7.3.77: *iṣugamiyamāṁ chaḥ* [*śiti* 75]). The affix ***śap*** in *gam-a-ti* is thus marked, so that it conditions this substitution: *gam-a-ti* → *gach-a-ti* (→ *gatch-a-ti* → *gacchati*). As shown, once the *-m* of *gam-* has been replaced by *-ch*, other operations apply. The language Pāṇini describes does not allow simple intervocalic *-ch-* preceded by a short vowel. In addition, there is an assimilatory process whereby dental stops and *s* are replaced by palatal stops and *ś* in contiguity with palatal stops and *ś* (**A** 8.4.40: *stoḥ ścunā ścuḥ*). Accordingly, Pāṇini provides for a short vowel immediately followed by *ch* to take the augment ***tuk*** (**A** 6.1.73: *che ca* [*hrasvasya tuk* 71]); this *t* is then replaced by *c* since it is immediately followed by *ch*. Deriving *rājñaḥ* in (5a) also involves several replacements: *rājan-as* → *rājn-as* → *rājñas*, *rājñas p-* → *rājñar p-* → *rājñaḥ p-*. Penultimate short *a* of a stem in *-an* is dropped if the stem is followed by a vowel-initial ending other than acc. sg., nom.-acc. du. and nom. pl. (**A** 6.4.134: *allopo'naḥ*): *rājan-as* → *rājn-as*. By the assimilation rule noted above, *n* is replaced by *ñ*: *rājnas* → *rājñas*. Since *rājñas* is a pada, its *-s* is replaced by an *-r* (*rājñas* → *rājñar*: **A** 8.2.66: *sasajuṣo ruḥ*), for which the voiceless pharyngeal spirant *-ḥ* (called *visarjanīya*) substitutes in absolute final position (*avasāna* "cessation of speech") and before voiceless stops and spirants (**A** 8.3.15: *kharavasānayoḥ visarjanīyaḥ*): *rājñar* → *rājñaḥ*. Similarly, *devadattas* → ... *devadattaḥ* and *kaṭas* → ... *kaṭaḥ* in (3a), (4a). The *-r* that substitutes for *-s* is distinguished from basic *-r* by being marked with *u* (***ru***). ***ru*** is replaced by *u* if it follows short *a* and precedes short *a* or a voiced consonant (**A** 6.1.113–114: *ato ror aplutād aplute* [*ut* 111], *haśi ca*). *puruṣa-s* of (5b) thus goes through the following replacements: *puruṣa-s* → *puruṣa-r* → *puruṣa-u*. In addition, a purely phonological rule (**A** 6.1.87: *ād guṇaḥ*) provides that a vowel of the guṇa class is the single substitute for an *a*-vowel and a following vowel. In *puruṣa-u*, the single replacement for *-a-u* is *o*: *puruṣa-u* → *puruṣo*. The same phonological rule is brought into play to derive *devadattena* of (4a) from *devadatta-ina*. For this to apply, however, a grammatical substitution must first take effect, such that *ṭā* is replaced by *ina* after a stem ending in short *a* (**A** 7.1.12: *ṭāṅasiṅasām inātsyāḥ* [*ataḥ* 9]): *devadatta-ā* → *devadatta-ina* → *devadattena*. *kaṭaṅ* as in *kaṭaṅ karoti* of (3a) also involves several replacements, one of which concerns a grammatical unit. In order to account for forms like *kaṭam*, *agnim* "fire", *vāyum* "wind" – which can occur before vowels and labials – Paṇini not only posits a basic ending *am* but also provides (**A** 6.1.107: *ami pūrvaḥ*) that the first vowel (*pūrvaḥ* "prior") of a sequence $V^1V^2$ is the single replacement for both vowels if $V^2$ is the vowel of *am*: *kaṭa-am* → *kaṭam*. In addition, word-final *-m* is replaced by the nasal offglide called *anusvāra* (*ṁ*: **A** 8.3.23: *mo' nusvāraḥ*). Moreover, word-final (*padāntasya*) *-ṁ* is optionally (*vā*) replaced by a sound homogeneous with a following stop or semivowel (*yayi parasavarṇaḥ*: **A** 8.4.58–59: *anusvārasya yayi parasavarṇaḥ, vā padāntasya*): *kaṭam k-* → *kaṭaṁ k-* → (optionally) *kaṭaṅ k-*.

Some replacements depend not on a context but on the source of an element. As noted earlier, Pāṇini posits ten abstract L-affixes, six marked with *ṭ*, four marked with *ṅ*. In the first instance, these are replaced by the basic endings shown in section 3.1.C. These endings are then subject to additional operations depending on the L-affix from which they derive. For example, that part of an ātmanepada ending which begins with its last vowel (*ṭi* [gen. sg. *ṭeḥ*]) is replaced by *e* if the ending is a substitute for an L-affix marked with *ṭ* (*ṭitaḥ*: **A** 3.4.79: *ṭita ātmanepadānāṁ ṭer e*); e. g., *ās-ta* → *āste* [3rd sg. pres. indic. mid.] "... is seated", *ās-ātām* [3rd. du.] → *āsāte* "they two are seated". The endings *ta*, *ātām* in these forms derive from the L-affix ***laṭ***. Final *-s* of first person (*uttamasya*) parasmaipada endings that replace an L-affix marked with *ṅ* (*ṅitaḥ*) is dropped (**A** 3.4.99: *nityaṁ ṅitaḥ* [*saḥ uttamasya* [98] *lopaḥ* 97]), as is final *-i* of most parasmaipada endings replacing such an L-affix (**A** 3.4.100: *itaś ca*); e. g., *kṛ-vas* → ... *akurva* [1st du. impfct. act. indic.] "we two did, made [something at sometime before today]", *kṛ-mas* → ... *akurma* [1st pl.] "we all did, made", *kṛ-ti* → ... *akarot* [3rd sg.], *kṛ-si* → ... *akaros* [2nd sg.] "... did, made". The endings of such forms replace the L=affix ***laṅ***, introduced on condition that an action is referred to past time excluding the day of reference (*anadyatane*: **A** 3.2.111: *anadyatane laṅ* [*bhūte* 84]).

4.2. As can be seen from the last examples given in section 4.1., a final form can show the absence of an element which appears at an earlier stage of derivation and is dropped. Such deletion can result in items lacking a grammatical element that appears in other comparable forms. For example, the endings of *akarot*, *akaros* lack the *-i* of *-ti*, *si* in *karoti* [3rd sg. pres. pres. act. indic.], *karoṣi* [2nd sg. ← *kar-o-si*]. These forms nevertheless contain endings. The corresponding imperfect *ahan* "... killed" [3rd sg., 2nd sg.], on the other hand, lacks any ending, though it is of the same grammatical type as *akarot*, *akaros*. To account for such a form, Pāṇini starts with *han-ti*, *han-si*, in which *-ti* and *si* are substitutes for ***laṅ***, has the *-i* of the endings dropped, then provides for dropping the remaining *-t*, *s* after a consonant. The rule in question (**A** 6.1.68: *halṅyābbhyo dīrghāt sutisy apṛktaṁ hal* [*lopaḥ* 66]) states that the endings ***su*** (nom. sg.), *ti* and *si* are replaced by zero (*lopaḥ*) after a consonant and feminine affixes referred to by ***ṅī*** and ***āp***, provided that the feminine affixes have not undergone shortening (*dīrghāt* "long vowel") and that *ti* and *si* have had their final sound dropped, so that each ending consists of a single consonant (*apṛktam*). Moreover, Pāṇini operates with abstract affixes which have no overt realization at all. For example, *brahma-han-* "one who has slain a Brāhmaṇa" is comparable to a compound such as *kumbha-kāra-* "pot maker". In the latter, *-kāra-* contains not only a form of *kṛ* "make" but also a suffix *a*, which conditions replacement of *-ṛ* by *-ār*. *brahma-han-* contains *-han-*, but there is no overt suffix. Pāṇini accounts for *-kāra-* in the type *kumbha-kāra-* by introducing an affix ***aṇ*** after a verbal base construed with a nominal term denoting an object (*karmaṇi*) of the action in question (**A** 3.2.1: *karmaṇy aṇ*). He also accounts for *brahma-han-* by introducing an affix after *han* "kill" construed with a nominal denoting an object, specifically, forms of *brahman-*, *bhrūṇa-* "foetus", *vṛtra-* "Vṛtra" (**A** 3.2.87: *brahmabhrūṇavṛtreṣu kvip* [*karmaṇi hanaḥ* 86, *bhūte* 84]). The affix introduced is ***kvip***. This affix is dropped (**A** 6.1.67: *ver apṛktasya* [*lopaḥ* 66]): *-han-v* → *-han-*.

4.3. Sanskrit is like other Indo-European languages in that it exhibits suppletion of the type seen in English *be*, *is*, *was*, German *bin*, *ist*, *war* or Latin *esse*, *est*, *fuit*. Pāṇini describes this in terms of substitution: certain verbal bases occur in place of others when one is to use affixes of the ārdhadhātuka class (see section 3.1.D). For example, Sanskrit uses *as* "be" in present and imperfect forms such as the third singular indicative *asti*, *āsīt*, (archaic *ās* [← *ās-t*]), but the corresponding future form is *bhaviṣyati* (← *bhū-isya-ti* ← *bhū-ti*), the infinitive is *bhavitum*, and the gerundive is *bhavya-* (← *bhū-ya-*). A Pāṇinian rule (**A** 2.4.52: *aster bhūḥ*) provides that *bhū* occurs instead of *as* with ārdhadhātuka affixes. Suppletion can also obtain in more limited contexts. Thus, *dṛś* "see, look" is one of a series of bases subject to replacement by other bases before an affix marked with *ś* (*śiti*: **A** 7.3.78: *pāghrā* ... *dṛśy* ... *pibajighra* ... *paśya* ... [*śiti* 75]); it is replaced by *paśya*, as *paśyati* [3rd sg. pres. indic.], *apaśyat* [3rd sg. impfct., see (5a) [section 3.1.]).

4.4. As shown in section 3.2., Pāṇinian rules serve to derive compounds from syntactic padas. There is another procedure that concerns such padas: syntactic doubling; e. g., *dive dive* "each and every day", *grāmo grāmaḥ* "each and every village". Pāṇini accounts for this type by providing that under stated conditions two (*dve*) instances of a whole (*sarvasya*) pada occur (**A** 8.1.1: *sarvasya dve*). Such doubling occurs, for example, if an activity is constantly performed (*nitya*) or one wishes to speak of a property or action as pervading something (*vīpsā*: **A** 8.1.4: *nityavīpsayoḥ*). It is noteworthy that in his padapāṭha to the Ṛgveda, Śākalya (see section 1.2.) treats such complexes as compounds. Pāṇini could not do the same for a good reason. He has of course to account for compounds like *mātāpitarau* "mother and father, parents" and does so by providing that any number of padas related to each other through addition (*cārthe* "in the meaning of *ca* ["and"]") optionally combine to form a compound of the type called *dvandva* (**A** 2.2.29: *cārthe dvandvaḥ*). Theoretically, this would allow also possibly combining homophonous padas to form compounds like **vṛkṣavṛkṣau* "two trees", **vṛkṣavṛkṣavṛkṣās* "many trees", but this has to be precluded. Accordingly, Pāṇini provides for a single remainder (*ekaśeṣaḥ*) to occur for any number of terms with the same shape (*sarūpāṇām*) to be used with a single ending (*ekavibhaktau*: **A** 1.2.64: *sarūpāṇām ekaśeṣa ekavibhaktau*). In accordance with this, Pāṇini does not treat the type *dive dive* as a compound; instead, he accounts for this type by allowing padas to be repeated (see Cardona 1995).

## 5. Zero

Pāṇini operates with zero as an unfilled slot that can also be occupied by a grammatical unit. In general, the absence (*adarśanam* "non-perception") of an item is called *lopa* (**A** 1.1.60: *adarśanaṁ lopaḥ*). In particular, however, several additional varieties of zero as a replacement for an affix (*pratyayasya*) are recognized; these are referred to by terms containing *lu* : *luk*, *ślu*, *lup* (**A** 1.1.61: *pratyayasya lukślulupaḥ*). For example, the suffix ***kvip*** introduced to form derivates like *brahmahan-* is replaced by zero (see section 4.2.). In deriving present and imperfect forms of the type *juhoti* (see section 2.1.A), the affix ***śap*** – seen in the type *bhavati* – is introduced (**A** 3.1.68: *kartari śap*). A rule (**A** 2.4.75: *juhotyādibhyaḥ śluḥ* [*śapaḥ* 72]) provides that this affix is deleted after verbs of the set beginning with *hu*: *hu-a-ti* → *hu-ø-ti*. The replacement for ***śap*** is *ślu*, which entails a particular operation. A base after which *ślu* has substituted for ***śap*** undergoes doubling (**A** 6.1.10: *ślau*): *hu-ti* → *ho-ti* → *ho-ho-ti* ... → *juhoti*.

Pāṇini states a convention whereby, in general, even in the absence of an affix (*pratyayalope*) that has been introduced and then dropped, the operation that is conditioned by that affix (*pratyayalakṣaṇam*) still takes effect (**A** 1.1.62: *pratyayalope pratyayalakṣaṇam*). To illustrate, let us consider derivates that contain the augment ***tuk***, introduced to a short vowel followed by an affix of the kṛt class – a verbal affix other than a verb ending – marked with *p* (**A** 6.1.71: *hrasvasya piti kṛti tuk*; see section 3.2.E). Sanskrit has a construction of the type

(11) *snātvā bhuṅkte* "... bathes before eating"

involving a series of actions performed by the same agent; a verbal base that refers to an action performed prior to another is then followed by *tvā* (***ktvā***) in a derivate of the type *snā-tvā* "having bathed, after bathing". In (11), bathing precedes eating (*bhuṅkte* [3rd sg. pres. indic.] "eats"). In addition, if a compound verbal derivate is involved, instead of *tvā*, a suffix *ya* (***lyap***) occurs, as in *ā-gamya* "after coming". Moreover, if this suffix follows a base that ends in a short vowel, the former ends with an augment *-t*; e.g., *upastutya* "after praising". Pāṇini accounts for the occurrence of this augment by marking the kṛt suffix *ya* with *p*, to show that it conditions the augment ***tuk***. Now, *agni-cit* "one who has set up a sacrificial fire" (see section 3.2.E) also contains this augment. The verb base in question is *ci*. If this is construed with *agni* denoting an object of the action performed in the past, the affix ***kvip*** is added to *ci* (**A** 3.2.91: *agnau ceḥ* [*kvip* 87, *bhūte* 84]). ***kvip*** is deleted (see 4.2.), but this does not mean there is no effect. *-ci-ø* is treated as though ***kvip***, which is marked with *p*, were still there to condition the introduction of the augment ***tuk***. The derivation of a nominal form like *rājā* [nom. sg.] from *rājan-s* illustrates the same convention. The ending of *rājan-s* follows a consonant, so that it is dropped (see section 4.2.): *rājan-s* → *rājan*. Now, the first five nominal endings (***su au jas am auṭ***, denoted by the abbreviation *suṭ*) used with a non-neuter base (*anapuṁsakasya*) constitute a particular group named *sarvanāmasthāna* (**A** 1.1.43: *suḍ anapuṁsakasya* [*sarvanāmasthānam* 42]). Before a sarvanāmasthāna ending except for ***su*** used in a vocative form, penultimae *-a-* of a stem in *-an* (*nopadhāyāḥ*) is replaced by the corresponding long vowel (*dīrghaḥ*) *-ā-* (**A** 6.4.8: *sarvanāmasthāne cāsambuddhau* [*nopadhāyāḥ* 7, *dīrghaḥ* 6.3.111]): *rājan-au* → *rājānau*, *rājan-as* → *rājānas*, *rājan-am* → *rājānam*. In accordance with the convention noted, the same substitution applies also to *rājan-ø*: *rājan* → *rājān*. Moreover, as *rājan-s* is a pada by virtue of terminating in a nominal ending (**A** 1.4.14 [section 3.1.A]), *rājan-ø* also is now a pada, as is *rājān*. Therefore, the rule (**A** 8.2.7: *nalopaḥ prātipadi-kāntasya*) can apply which provides for dropping *-n* in a pada which coincides with a nominal base.

The general convention established concerning zero has to be restricted. Consider some forms of the pronominal *tad* "that". The accusative singular masculine form of this base is *tam*, derived from *tad-am*, with the second-triplet ending *am*: *tad-am* → *taa-am* → *ta-am* → *tam*. Two of the operations that apply here are important for our discussion. Once a stem form *ta-* is obtained, *ta-am* is eligible for the replacement that accounts for the types *kaṭam*, *agnim*, *vāyum* (see section 4.1.). To get this, Pāṇini provides that the final sound of stems in the subgroup of pronominals that begins with *tyad* "that" (*tyadādīnām*) is replaced by *-a* before any ending (*vibhaktau*: **A** 7.2.102: *tyadādīnām aḥ* [*vibhaktau* 84]). Now, the nominative singular neuter form of the pronoun in question is *tad*, derived from *tad-s*. ***su*** is dropped after a consonant (see section 4.2.). If, however, Pāṇini let the ending of *tad-s* be replaced by simple zero, in accordance with the general convention noted above the *-d* of *tad-ø* would still be subject to replacement by *-a*, so that instead of *tad*, the grammar would allow **ta*. Morover, *tad* is also the accusative singular neuter form, to be derived from *tad-am*. Accordingly, Pāṇini lets both ***su*** and *am* be replaced by a particular zero, *luk*, after a neuter (*napuṁsakāt*) stem (**A** 7.1.23: *svamor napuṁsakāt* [*luk* 22]). He also states an exception to the general convention: an operation conditioned by the presence of an affix does not (*na*) take effect on a stem (*aṅgasya*) if the affix for that stem is replaced by a zero designated with a term containing *lu* (*lumatā*: **A** 1.1.63: *na lumatāṅgasya*).

There are also instances that involve both the general convention about zero and its exception. As shown earlier (section 3.2.C), a compound *rājapuruṣa-* is derived by combining related padas: *rājan-as-puruṣa-s*. A nominal ending (*supaḥ*) contained within a derived verbal or nominal base (*dhātuprātipadikayoḥ*) is replaced by zero (*luk*: **A** 2.4.71: *supo dhātuprātipadikayoḥ* [*luk* 58]): *rājan-as-puruṣa-s* → *rājan-puruṣa-*. As *rājan-as* is a pada, so is *rājan-ø* that results from dropping the ending within a compound. Hence, the *-n* of *rājan-* is deleted: *rājan-puruṣa-* → *rājapuruṣa-*. On the other hand, the deletion of penultimate *-a-* in *rājan-as* (→ *rājñas*, see section 4.1.) should not be allowed. It is not, since the replacement for the endings in *rājan-as-puruṣa-s* is the particular zero designated *luk*.

## 6. Bibliography

### 6.1. Primary source

Pāṇini, *Aṣṭādhyāyī*. In S. S. Pathak & S. S. Chitrao, *Word Index to Pāṇini-sūtra-pāṭha and pariśiṣṭas*, 461–648. Poona: Bhandarkar Oriental Research Institute, 1935.

### 6.2. Secondary sources

Cardona, George. 1990. "La linguistica indiana". *Storia della linguistica*, ed. by Giulio C. Lepschy, I, 51–84. Bologna: il Mulino.

–. 1994. "Indian Linguistics". *A History of Linguistics*, vol. I: *The Eastern Traditions of Linguistics* ed. by G. C. Lepschy, 25–60. London & New York: Longman.

–. 1995. "Āmreḍita Compounds?" *Studien zur Indologie und Iranistik* XX. (= *Festschrift Paul Thieme*), 67–72.

–. 1997. *Pāṇini, His Work and its Traditions*, vol. I: *General Introduction and Background.* 2nd revised ed. Delhi: Motilal Banarsidass. [1st ed., 1988.]

–. 1999. *Recent Research in Pāṇinian Studies*. Delhi: Motilal Banarsidass.

Katre, Sumitra Mangesh. 1987. *Aṣṭādhyāyī of Pāṇini*. Austin: Univ. of Texas Press. [Indian ed.: Delhi: Motilal Banarsidass, 1989.]

Scharfe, Hartmut. 1977. *Grammatical Literature* (= *A History of Indian Literature*, part II, fascicle 2). Wiesbaden: Harrassowitz.

Sharma, Rama Nath. 1987. *The Aṣṭādhyāyī of Pāṇini*, vol. I: *Introduction to the Aṣṭādhyāyī as a grammatical device.* Delhi: Munshiram Manoharlal.

–. 1990. *The* Aṣṭādhyāyī *of Pāṇini*, vol. II: *English Translation of Adhyāya One with Sanskrit Text, Transliteration, Word-Boundary, Anuvṛtti, Explanatory Notes, Derivational History of Examples, and Indices.* Delhi: Munshiram Manoharlal.

–. 1995. *The* Aṣṭādhyāyī of Pāṇini, vol. III: *English Translation of Adhyāyas Two and Three with Sanskrit Text, Transliteration, Word-Boundary, Anuvṛtti, Explanatory Notes, Derivational History of Examples, and Indices.* Delhi: Munshiram Manoharlal.

–. 1999. *The* Aṣṭādhyāyī *of Pāṇini*, vol. IV: *English Translation of Adhyāyas Four and Five with Sanskrit Text, Transliteration, Word-Boundary, Anuvṛtti, Explanatory Notes, Derivational History of Examples, and Indices.* Delhi: Munshiram Manoharlal.

[Cardona 1990, 1994 briefly consider Pāṇini in relation to predecessors and other Indian schools of thought. Scharfe 1977 is at once a more comprehensive and less detailed treatment of Indian grammar. For Pāṇini's derivational system, see Sharma 1987: 141–211, Cardona 1997: 136–400. Katre 1987 is the most recent complete translation of the *Aṣṭādhyāyī*. Sharma 1990–1999 gives not only translations but also details about how rules are understood. Most of the rules dealt with here are paraphrased and explained also in Cardona 1997.]

*George Cardona, Philadelphia (USA)*

# 18. Die Entwicklung der Sprachwissenschaft in Indien nach Pāṇini

1. Das *Mahābhāṣya*
2. Buddhistische Sanskrit Grammatiker
3. Jinistische Sanskrit Grammatiker
4. Grammatiken der mittelindischen Dialekte
5. Werke in der Tradition der Pāṇinīyas
6. Sanskrit Grammatik an den Fürstenhöfen
7. Bibliographie

## 1. Das *Mahābhāṣya*

1.1. Das bedeutendste grammatische Werk in Pāṇinis Nachfolge ist das monumentale *Mahābhāṣya* (*Mbh.*), das "Große Erklärungswerk". Es besteht eigentlich aus zwei Textschichten etwa aus dem 3. und 2. Jh. v. Chr. und hat zwei Autoren. Kātyāyana untersucht in etwa 4293 knappen Anmerkungen (*vārttika*) im *sūtra*-Stil 1245 von Pāṇinis etwa 4000 Regeln auf methodische und faktische Richtigkeit und Vollständigkeit. Patañjalis Werk ist zuerst ein Kommentar zu Kātyāyanas *vārttikas*, verfolgt dann aber die Untersuchung von Pāṇinis Regeln auch auf eigene Faust weiter. Insgesamt bespricht Patañjali 1713 Regeln Pāṇinis. Genau genommen, ist nur diese Arbeit Patañjalis das *Mahābhāṣya*; er allein wird in den Kolophonen als Autor genannt. Die *vārttikas* sind in den Text des *Mahābhāṣya* eingebettet und sonst nirgends unabhängig überliefert, obwohl Patañjali noch andere Behandlungen der *vārttikas* kannte. Die säuberliche Scheidung der beiden Autoren ist von Kielhorn (1876), weithin im Einklang mit der indischen handschriftlichen und mündlichen Tradition, herausgearbeitet und in seiner Ausgabe des *Mbh.* im Einzelnen durchgeführt worden. Selbst wenn in einigen Fällen die Zuschreibung einzelner Sätze an einen der beiden Autoren angezweifelt werden kann, sind allgemeine Zweifel an der Zuteilung nicht gerechtfertigt. — Wenn Kātyāyana mit dem Ausdruck *śāka-pārthiva* "vegetarischer König" (Pāṇini, *Aṣṭadhyāyi* = P II 1 69 värtt. 8) auf Aśoka anspielt, wäre seine Zeit etwa um 250 v. Chr. anzusetzen, während Patañjalis Hinweise auf das Ritual des Śungakönigs Puṣyamitra und die griechische Belagerung von Saketa (Ayodhyā) auf die zweite Hälfte des 2. Jh. v. Chr. für diesen Autor deuten. Kātyāyanas Heimat ist vielleicht im mittleren Gangestal nahe dem Vindhyagebirge oder im nördlichen Dekkhan zu suchen. Denn er kennt die Tradition des *Weißen Yajurveda* und ist wahrscheinlich identisch mit dem Verfasser des *Prātiśākhya* zu diesem Vedatext; außerdem postuliert er negierte Verben wie *apacasi* "Du kochst schlecht!", die möglicherweise auf dravidischen Einfluß hinweisen. Patañjali stammt eher aus der Gegend um Mathurā, einer Stadt, die in mehreren seiner Beispiele vorkommt, oder aus der Gegend nördlich oder nordöstlich davon, d. h. dem mittleren oder oberen Gangestal, weil man, wie er sagt (*Mbh.* II, 162.6f.), über Saketa nach Pāṭaliputra reist. — Beide Autoren bemühen sich in ihrer Untersuchung, in der sie Pāṇinis Regeln auf Lücken und Unstimmigkeiten abtasten, am Ende doch Pāṇinis ursprüngliche Formulierung zu retten und schlagen nur als letzten Ausweg gelegentlich Änderungen am Text vor. Der Prozeß ähnelt dem Vorgehen von Juristen, die Rechtsfälle auf der Basis viel älterer Gesetze entscheiden müssen — auch wenn der Gesetzgeber keine expliziten Provisionen für den anhängigen Fall gemacht hat. Wie im *dharma-śāstra*, wo die Interpretation eines anerkannten Kommentars den Vorrang hat vor einer unabhängigen, schlagend richtigen Neudeutung des Grundtextes, gilt in der späteren Tradition der Grundsatz *yathôttaraṃ hi muni-trayasya prāmāṇyam* "Der jeweils folgende der drei Weisen ist [höhere] Autorität" (Kaiyaṭa zu P I 1 29); gemeint sind Pāṇini, Kātyāyana und Patañjali. — Es gab offenbar einen Bruch in der mündlichen Tradition zwischen Pāṇini und Kātyāyana; denn schon Kātyāyana muß wahrscheinlich die wichtigen technischen Akzente und Nasalierungen in Pāṇinis Text mühsam erschließen. Der Hauptwert des *Mahābhāṣya* und der sich daran anschließenden Literatur liegt für uns daher nicht in ihrer (unterbrochenen) Tradition, sondern ihrer fast unglaublichen Beherrschung des Materials und ihrem tiefen Verständnis der inhärenten Probleme. Kātyāyanas Beitrag, der so eng mit dem Patañjalis verschmolzen ist, hat oft keine unabhängige Würdigung erfahren. Die kürzlichen Arbeiten von Deshpande (1980, 1985) haben seine Ansichten stärker profiliert.

Während Pāṇini gelegentlich auf abweichenden Sprachgebrauch hinweist mit Worten wie "nach Śākalya", "in Gandhāra", "nach [dem Gebrauch] der östlichen [Sprecher]", halten Kātyāyana und die ihm folgenden Grammatiker alle diese Formen für gleichberechtigt und sehen in diesen Hinweisen nur Ehrenbezeugungen. Der Grund dafür ist vermutlich, daß Sanskrit mehr und mehr von einer Umgangssprache zu einer Sondersprache gebildeter Brahmanen geworden war, im Überlebenskampf mit den verschiedenen Prakrits, die wir in staatlichen Inschriften und in den Traditionen heterodoxer Sekten finden. Die feinen Unterschiede, die Pāṇini verzeichnete, paßten nicht in dieses Bild brahmanischer Wiederbehauptung (Deshpande 1978: 102–107), und selbst wenn Patañjali gelegentlich auf dialektische Besonderheiten seiner Zeitgenossen hinweist – falsche Formen konnte es in den verehrten Texten und bei als Autorität zitierten Sprechern nicht geben, wenn die Vedas und alle Sanskritworte als ewig galten. Alle Varianten sind mit umfaßt.

1.2. Einige von Kātyāyanas Anmerkungen spiegeln deutlich sprachliche Entwicklungen im Sanskrit wider, obwohl Kātyāyana kaum historisch gedacht und diese Ausdrücke als Neuerungen angesehen hat. So lehrt Pāṇini das periphrastische Perfekt – in Übereinstimmung mit dem späteren vedischen Sprachgebrauch – allein mit Formen von *kṛ* als Hilfsverb (Typ *gamayāṃ cakāra*); Kātyāyana erkennt auch Formen von *as* und *bhū* an (P III 1 40 mit värtt. 3). Daneben gibt es viele Neuerungen im Wortschatz; häufig sind freilich die geforderten Wörter nicht anderweitig belegt, sodaß ihre Einschätzung schwierig ist. Von größerem Interesse ist Kātyāyanas verändertes Sprachgefühl; was dazu den Anstoß gegeben hat, ist bisweilen unklar. Während Pāṇini nirgends den Satz definiert, ist es für Kātyāyana (värtt. 10 bis 12 zu P II 1 1) klar, daß jeder Satz ein Verbum hat – und nur eins. Damit wird Konstruktionen wie *bhavati pacati* "Es ist wahr, er kocht" oder "Er kocht wirklich" das Recht abgesprochen als ein Satz zu gelten, und die so häufigen Nominalsätze des Sanskrit werden als Ellipsen erklärt, in denen eine Form des Verbums "sein" in der dritten Person ergänzt werden muß (värtt. 11 zu P II 3 1). Damit geht eine neue Sicht des Nominativs einher. In Pāṇinis Kasussyntax war der Nominativ sozusagen funktionslos; er diente lediglich dazu, Geschlecht und Zahl des Stammbegriffes anzuzeigen, während die anderen Kasus verschiedene Faktoren der im Satz ausgedrückten Handlung bezeichnen. Pāṇini vermied damit geschickt die Idee eines 'Subjekts', die der europäischen Grammatik mit ihrem philosophischen Ballast so viel zu schaffen gemacht hat. Denn die Funktion, die der Stammbegriff eines Wortes mit Nominativendungen im Satz haben würde, nämlich Agens in aktiven Sätzen, Objekt in passiven, ist schon durch die Endung des finiten Verbums bezeichnet: *śṛṇoti* "[er, sie, es] hört", *śrūyate* "[er, sie es] wird gehört". Aber wie steht es damit in Nominalsätzen wie *vīraḥ puruṣaḥ* "Der Mann [ist] ein Held"? Kātyāyana definiert daher den Nominativ als den Kasus, der mit dem (manchmal unausgedrückten) Verbum kongruent ist (värtt. 6 zu P II 3 1). – Das veränderte Sprachgefühl einer späteren Zeit zeigt sich auch in seiner Analyse einiger quasi-reflexiven und impersonalen Verbformen. Das indo-iranische Passiv hatte sich aus intransitiven Verbalstämmen auf *-ya-* entwikkelt wie *jāyate* "wird geboren" und *mriyate* "stirbt", die auch später weiter als Media gelten. Eine Zwitterstellung nehmen Sätze wie *odanaḥ pacyate* "Der Reis kocht" ein, wo nach Pāṇinis Regel III 1 87 der Agens der Handlung, nämlich der Reis, derselben Handlung unterliegt wie ein Objekt und daher wie ein Objekt behandelt wird: das intransitive Verbum erhält folglich die Suffixe des Passivs. Kātyāyana in seinem *Vārttika* 10 zu dieser Regel postuliert die Ellipse des Wortes *ātmanā* "durch sich selbst", wodurch der Satz *odanaḥ pacyate [ātmanā]* ein einfacher Passivsatz mit einem transitiven Verbum wird: "Der Reis wird [durch sich selbst] gekocht". Kātyāyana schafft sich damit freilich anderweitig Schwierigkeiten, z. B. bei der impersonalen Konstruktion *odanena pacyate* "Kochen durch den Reis findet statt". Diese Konstruktion – nach Patañjali (*Mbh.* II, 66.2) sprachlich korrekt – ist nämlich nur für intransitive Verben erlaubt (P III 4 69; Deshpande 1985: 8–16). – Kātyāyana macht auch sonst weiten Gebrauch von Ellipsen, z. B. in der Nominalkomposition. *śākapārthivaḥ* "Gemüsekönig" gilt als kompositionsbedingte Kontraktion von *śāka-bhojī pārthivaḥ* "Gemüse essender, d. h. vegetarischer König" (värtt. 8 zu P II 1 69), wo *bhojī* durch Schwund des hinteren Wortes (*uttara-pada-lopa*) vor dem Vollzug der Komposition abgefallen ist. Spätere Grammatiker wie Puruṣottama oder Durgasiṃha sprechen von "Schwund des mittleren Wortes" (*madhyama-pada-lopa*), d. h. im schon realisierten Kompositum **śāka-bhoji-pārthivaḥ* schwindet das mittlere Glied. Komposita wie *dadhy-odanaḥ* "Yoghurtreis" ermangeln in Kātyāyanas Meinung einer semantischen Verbindung, außer wenn ein verbindendes Wort hypostasiert wird: *dadhy [-upasikta]-odanaḥ* "mit Yoghurt vermischter Reis". *pra-parṇaḥ* "[ein Baum,] dessen Blätter dahin sind" soll elliptisch für *prapatita-parṇaḥ* "[ein Baum,] dessen Blätter dahingeflogen (oder: hingefallen) sind" stehen (värtt. 4 zu P II 1 35 und värtt. 14 zu P II 2 24). Kātyāyana (vārtt. 6f. zu P II 1 35) ist dann aber doch bereit, auf einige dieser Ellipsen zu verzichten und sich statt dessen auf eine erweiterte Semantik zu stützen, vielleicht unter dem Einfluß der Schule der Saunāgas, die nach Patañjali (*Mbh.* I, 416f.) diese Methode häufig erwähnt, Damit ist gemeint, daß der nicht direkt ausgedrückte Sinn sich aus dem Satzzusammenhang oder der Situation ergibt. Es ist ja offenbar, daß z. B. das Wort *upasikta* "vermischt" in vergleichbaren Redewendungen nicht auftritt, wenn man einfach, d. h. ohne Kompositumsbildung, sagt: *dadhnâudanaṃ buṅkte* "Er ißt Reis mit Yoghurt" (Deshpande 1985: 47–57)

Eine bemerkenswerte Neuorientierung zeigt sich in Kātyāyanas Ableitung der Desiderative. Sanskrit hat als synthetische Sprache besondere ererbte Formen wie *jigamiṣati* "[er, sie, es] will gehen", die P III 1 7 als bevorzugte Formen lehrt; daneben gibt es die analytische Ausdrucksweise *gantum icchati* "[er, sie, es] wünscht zu gehen". Pāṇini leitet das Desiderativ direkt aus der Wurzel mit einem Suffix *-sa*$^{n}$ ab, wenn gewisse Eingaben vorliegen: es soll ein Wunsch ausgedrückt werden, Wunsch und Handlung der Wurzel haben denselben Agens, und der Wunsch bezieht sich auf die Handlung der Wurzel. Kātyāyana schlägt in den *Vārttikas* 10 und 11 zu dieser Regel zwei alternative Ableitungswege vor: das Suffix *-sa*$^{n}$ tritt an den Infinitiv oder an die erste Person des Optativs, deren Endungen dann getilgt werden; Patañjali (*Mbh.* II, 14.9–12) gibt die Beispiele *kartum icchati: cikīrṣati; kuryām itîcchati: cikīrṣati.* Diese Technik, eine Form aus einer anderen durch Ellipse abzuleiten, ist eine Neuerung Kātyāyanas.

Kātyāyana hat gelegentlich versucht, in der Analyse unerklärter Wörter über Pāṇini hinauszukommen. Neben durchsichtigen Ableitungen auf *-ya* wie *vāpya* (von *vap*) und *praṇāyya* (von *nī*) hatte dieser in P III 1 129 *pāyya* "Maß" und *nikāyya* "Wohnung" als fertige Worte gelehrt, statt sie aus Elementarteilen aufzubauen. Kātyāyana schlägt vor, diese beiden Worte von den Wurzeln *mā* "messen" und *ci* "schichten" abzuleiten mit Ersetzung des anfänglichen Konsonanten: **māyya > pāyya, *[ni]cāyya > nikāyya.* Diese letztere Ableitung ließe sich durch einen Hinweis auf Perfektformen wie *cikāya* (von *ci*) stützen, wo ein solcher Wechsel /c/ > /k/ berechtigt ist. Aber es gibt keine solchen Entsprechungen zwischen /m/ und /p/. Recht mechanisch mutet Kātyāyanas Erklärung von *mātāmaha* "Großmutter" und *pitāmaha* "Großvater" an, die P IV 2 36 einfach als unregelmäßige Formen gelehrt hatte; Kātyāyana sieht hier ein Suffix $^{d}$*āmaha*$^{c}$, das an die Stämme *mātṛ* "Mutter" und *pitṛ* "Vater" angefügt ist. Dabei ist doch die Verbindung mit dem Adjektiv *mahā* "groß" ganz offensichtlich.

Andere Anmerkungen Kātyāyanas befassen sich mit methodischen oder philosophischen Fragen. Pāṇinis Grammatik ist generativ, d. h. sie führt vom Wunsch, einen Gedanken auszudrücken, zur Bildung (*vyākaraṇa*; vgl. Thieme 1982: 23–34) korrekter Worte und Satzstrukturen aus elementaren Bestandteilen. Der Aufbau der Sanskritworte aus Wurzel und Suffix, oft sogar mehreren Suffixen – der keineswegs immer auf der Hand liegt – setzt intensive Analyse des Sprachmaterials voraus, von der Pāṇini jedoch nie spricht. Kātyāyana gründet diese vorauszusetzende Analyse auf die komplementären Prinzipien von *anvaya* "Konkomitanz, Zusammenvorkommen" und *vyatireka* "Zusammen-Abwesend-Sein" (vārtt. 9 zu P I 2 45). Wenn *aśvaḥ* "[ein] Pferd" bedeutet, *aśvau* "zwei Pferde", und *vṛkṣau* "zwei Bäume", schließen wir, daß das Element *aśva* "Pferd" bedeutet, die Endung *ḥ* die Einzahl, *au* die Zweizahl, und das Element *vṛkṣa* "Baum". Eine Gegenprobe ergibt, daß Laute als solche keine Bedeutung haben (vārtt. 9–15 zu P *Śivasūtra* 5). Wie Patañjali (*Mbh.* I, 32.3–10) später zeigte, ergibt sich aus einer Reihe *kūpaḥ sūpaḥ yūpaḥ* "Brunnen, Soße, Opferpfosten" weder eine überwiegende Gemeinsamkeit auf Grund der gemeinsamen Lautgruppe /ūpa/, noch der Nachweis, daß die spezifischen Wortbedeutungen auf den Lauten /k/, /s/ und /y/ beruhen. – Folgenschwer war Kātyāyanas Ausweitung der Regel P I 4 2 *vipratiṣedhe paraṃ kāryam* "Wenn es einen Konflikt gibt, [gilt] die später [gelehrte] Operation", die ursprünglich nur bis P II 2 38 galt (in einem Abschnitt, der Definitionen gibt), auf die ganze Grammatik mit Ausnahme der drei letzten Kapitel. Damit ergab sich scheinbar ein bequemer mechanischer Weg, die Priorität verschiedener Regeln zu entscheiden; aber eine solche Regel ist nicht nur überflüssig – es ergeben sich Schwierigkeiten, und Kātyāyana führt selbst zahlreiche Fälle auf, in denen im Gegenteil die vorausgehende Regel den Vorrang hat (*pūrva-vipratiṣid-dham*). – P I 2 64 lehrt die Bildung von nominalen Dual- und Pluralformen durch einen Prozeß, den er *eka-śeṣaḥ* "nur eins bleibt übrig" nennt: für **aśvaś ca^aśvaś ca* "ein Pferd und ein Pferd" sagt man *aśvau* "zwei Pferde", für *aśvaś ca^aśvaś ca^aśvaś ca* sagt man *aśvāḥ* "Pferde". Kātyāyana widmet dieser Regel 59 Anmerkungen, in denen er u. a. der Frage nachgeht, ob man sich bei diesem Prozeß vorstellen muß, daß die einzelnen Worte ein Universale, nämlich die Form oder den Typ des Pferdes schlechthin, bezeichnen oder eher die Individuen, d. h. einzelne Pferde. Er folgt in dieser Diskussion zwei älteren Autoritäten, von denen Vājapyāyana die erstere These vertrat, Vyāḍi die letztere. Kātyāyanas Lösung (värtt. 53–59) ist ein Kompromiß: ein Wort bezeichnet das Universale, das sich in Individuen manifestiert.

1.3. Patañjalis Beitrag ist wesentlich philologischer und philosophischer Natur, obwohl auch er Entwicklungen in der Sanskritsprache verzeichnet. Die singularischen Dvandvakomposita waren ursprünglich auf Sonderfälle beschränkt wie *pāṇi-pādam* "Hand und Fuß" (P II 4 2ff.); aber nach Patañjali (I, 232.4f.) kann jedes Dvandvakompositum im Singular stehen. Sein geographischer Horizont ist erweitert: das Gebiet, dessen Sprache als maßgeblich gilt, ist jetzt der ganze zentrale Teil der nordindischen Ebene. Aber nicht alle Sprecher dieses Gebietes können als Autorität gelten, sondern nur rechtschaffene, gebildete Brahmanen (III, 174.6–15). Selbst Ehefrau oder Tochter eines Brahmanen, die üblicherweise nicht studiert haben, können durch umgangssprachliche Aussprache von der Norm abweichen (I, 19.21f.). Patañjali verweist sogar auf die Weisen (*ṛṣi*) Yarvāṇas und Tarvāṇas, so genannt, weil sie trotz ihrer großen Gelehrsamkeit und tiefen Einsicht statt *yad vā nas* und *tad vā nas* im täglichen Leben *yar vā ṇas* und *tar vā ṇas* sagten (vgl. im modernen Malayāḷam *saṃvalsalam* statt *saṃvatsaram*; *bhavel* statt *bhavet*!), aber nicht, wenn sie vedische Rituale zelebrierten (I, 11.11–14). Patañjali ist vielleicht der letzte Grammatiker, der noch mit der Autorität eines geborenen Sanskritsprechers auftritt. Sein Werk wird zu Recht für die Exaktheit seiner Argumentation und die knappe Eleganz seiner Ausdrucksweise gepriesen.

Seine Zusätze zur deskriptiven Grammatik sind wohl bescheidener als die Kātyāyanas. Er fügt in II, 157.12 das Wort *durmarṣaṇa* zu Kātyāyanas Liste hinzu, und er lehrt in II, 135.14 ein neues Suffix $^{k}$*ruka*$^{n}$, um das Wort *bhīruka* "furchtsam" von der Wurzel *bhī* ableiten zu können. In dem Satz *grāmaṃ / gramāya gantum icchati* "Er wünscht zum Dorf zu gehen" erhebt sich die Frage, wer das Objekt von wem ist. Sind "Dorf" und "gehen" beide Objekt von "wünscht"? Dann können wir P II 3 12 nicht mehr anwenden, wonach das Objekt von "gehen" die Endungen des Akkusativs oder des Dativs erhält. Ist dann "Dorf" das Objekt von "gehen" und "gehen" das Objekt von "wünscht"? Dann können wir die Passivkonstruktion nicht richtig bilden: *iṣyate grāmo gantum* "Es wird gewünscht, zum Dorf zu gehen". Die Lösung ist, daß "Dorf" das Objekt von "gehen" ist, und sowohl "Dorf" und "gehen" Objekte von "wünscht". Damit sind sowohl der Akkusativ im aktiven und der Nominativ im passiven Satz bildbar (Deshpande 1980: 81–92). In seiner Terminologie kehrt Patañjali mehrfach wieder zu Pāṇinis Ausdrücken zurück, wo Kātyāyana unter dem Einfluß der *Prātiśākhyas* davon abgewichen war: *lopa* "Schwund" gegen Kātyāyanas *apāya*, und *ādeśa* gegen sein *vikāra*. – Patañjali entwickelt Ansätze Pāṇinis zu einer Klassifizierung der Komposita weiter. P II 2 24 *anekam anekapadârthe* und 29 *cârthe dvandvaḥ* lehren, daß die Glieder eines Bahuvrīhi ein anderes Objekt bezeichnen, und daß ein Dvandva die Bedeutung "und" hat. Daraus entwickelt Patañjali eine symmetrische Klassifizierung: Avyayībhāva-Komposita haben den Schwerpunkt auf der Bedeutung des ersten Wortes, Tatpuruṣa-Komposita auf der des zweiten, Bahuvrīhi-Komposita auf der eines ganz anderen, Dvandva-Komposita auf der Bedeutung beider Worte des Kompositums (I, 378.24–379.3). Es erscheint fraglich, ob diese Definition recht auf die Avyayībhāva-Komposita (z. B. *yathā-mati* "entsprechend der Meinung") zutrifft; vielleicht floß diese Formulierung aus der Liebe zur Symmetrie.

Patañjalis stärkste Beiträge sind philologischer und philosophischer Art. Er geht von dem Prinzip aus, daß Pāṇini seine Regeln mit größter Präzision und Ökonomie verfaßt hat. Scheinbar überflüssige Ausdrücke oder Regeln sind in Wahrheit Fingerzeige (*jñāpaka*) des Meisters, die uns die Existenz einer Metaregel anzeigen sollen. Eine große Zahl solcher Metaregeln (*pari-bhāṣa*) wird postuliert, von denen ein Teil wohl Pāṇini vorgeschwebt haben mag – andere sind sekundäre Rationalisierungen. Man muß sich ja doch fragen, warum Pāṇini diese Metaregeln nicht direkt gelehrt hat, wie er es in anderen Fällen getan hat, z. B. P I 3 10 *yathā-saṃkhyaṃ anudeśaḥ samānām* "Die nachfolgenden Glieder in einer Regel, wenn sie von gleicher Anzahl mit den vorhergehenden sind, entsprechen diesen der Reihe nach." Einige dieser Metaregeln haben so viele Ausnahmen, daß man ihren Wert in Frage stellen muß. Die Metaregel (Nr. 50 im *Paribhāṣêndu-śekhara*), daß Elemente außerhalb eines Stammes (*bahir-aṅga*) keinen Einfluß auf die Bildung des Stammes selbst haben (*antar-aṅga*-Regeln), erscheint sinnvoll, stößt sich aber an einigen Fällen der bekannten Regel, daß Absolutive ohne Präfixe mit dem Suffix *-tvā* gebildet werden, die mit Präfix jedoch mit dem Suffix *-ya* (*chittvā* gegenüber *vicchidya*); denn es ergeben sich ernsthafte Schwierigkeiten, wenn das Suffix *-tvā* eine Wurzelmodifizierung verlangt, *-ya* nicht: von der Wurzel *dhā* heißt es daher (mit *dhā* > *hi*) *hitvā*, aber *pra-dhāya*. Hier hat die *bahir-aṅga* Substitution *tvā* > *ya* die Wurzelmodifizierung verhindert. Patañjali postuliert eine weitere Metaregel (Nr. 54 im *Paribhāṣêndu-śekhara*), daß ein *bahir-aṅga* Suffix *-ya* sogar *antar-aṅga*-Regeln verhindert, und er sieht einen Fingerzeig oder zwingenden Hinweis (*jñāpaka*) dafür in der Formulierung von P II 4 36. Hier lehrt Pāṇini die Wurzelsubstitution *ad* > *jagdh* (Dies ist ein Fall, wo sich zwei Wurzeln im Paradigma ergänzen wie im Deutschen *ist* und *war*) sowohl für *-ya* als auch für *-ktvā*: *jagdhvā* "gegessen habend" neben *pra-jagdhya* "aufgegessen habend"; der Hinweis auf *pra-jagdhya* ist nur sinnvoll, wenn die Metaregel 54 gilt, die an sich die Wurzelsubstitution vor *-ya* verhindern würde, und er ist deswegen gleichzeitig nicht nur sinnvoll, sondern auch notwendig, um die Substitution *ad* > *jagdh* auch vor dem Suffix *-ya* zu sichern. Ist hier ein gesundes grammatisches Prinzip mißbraucht oder ist die Metaregel 50 überhaupt ungültig, wie Kiparsky (1982: 87–102) zu beweisen sucht? Komplizierte technische Erörterungen dieser Art nehmen einen breiten Raum im *Mahābhāṣya* ein.

Andere Diskussionen sind mehr philosophischen Fragen gewidmet. Warum kann eine passive Verbform im Plural stehen, wenn mehrere Objekte betroffen sind (*pacyante odanāḥ* "Reisbreie werden gekocht"), aber nicht im unpersönlichen Passiv (*āsyate bhavadbhyām* "Sitzen von euch beiden findet statt")? Die Handlung ist nur eine, (daher der Singular des unpersönlichen Verbums), kann aber mehrere materielle Substrate (in diesem Falle Objekte, nämlich die Reisbreie) haben. Verschiedene Arten zu kochen können mit dem Substantiv *pāka* bezeichnet werden, das gegebenenfalls auch im Dual oder Plural stehen kann. Ein Substantiv, sagt Patañjali, wird wie ein Ding, dem eine Handlung inhärieren kann; es kann grammatisch gesprochen, mit einem Verbum konstruiert werden. Das ist nicht der Fall bei einer Handlung, die durch ein Verbalsuffix ausgedrückt ist; denn, wie die Philosophen sagen, kann keine Handlung einer anderen Handlung inhärieren. Grammatisch gesehen ist der Unterschied von Verbum und Nomen der, daß das erstere mit Zeit, Person und Diathese verbunden wird und einen Agens verlangt, das Nomen nicht. – Patañjali hat eine interessante Interpretation von Worten, deren Referendum (noch) nicht existiert. Jemand sagte zu einem Weber: "Webe ein Tuch aus diesem Garn!" Der Weber sperrte sich: "Wenn es ein Tuch ist, braucht es nicht erst gewebt zu werden, und wenn es erst gewebt werden muß, dann ist es kein Tuch: Die Worte 'Tuch' und 'muß gewebt werden' widersprechen sich." Patañjalis Lösung des Problems ist, daß es sich um einen potentiellen Namen (*bhāvinī saṃjñā*) handelt, d. h. der Name wird erst später realisiert: "Webe das, was, wenn es gewebt ist, 'Tuch' heißt" (I, 112.10–13). Hier bezeichnet das Wort 'Tuch' nicht ein äußeres Objekt, sondern ein geistiges Bild, dessen Realisierung auf die Zukunft wartet. – Das Verlangen etwas auszudrücken (*vivakṣā*) liegt an der Wurzel jeder grammatischen Operation. Patañjali hat diese Vorstellung, die schon in den Vārttikas angedeutet war, weiterentwickelt. P I 2 68 hatte gelehrt, daß Worte wie *bhrātṛ* "Bruder" und *svasṛ* "Schwester" so zusammengefaßt werden, daß nur das erstere übrig bleibt: *bhrātarau* "Bruder und Schwester". Kātyāyana erklärte diesen Vorgang in *Vārttika* 1 zu dieser Regel so, daß nur das Gemeinsame und nicht das Unterschiedliche ausgedrückt werden sollte (*vivakṣita*). Patañjali wendet diesen Begriff der *vivakṣā* auf viele Gebiete der Syntax an. Der Begriff "Wegnahme" (*apādāna*) wird in P I 4 24 als das definiert, was bei einem Weggang fest bleibt; er wird häufig durch ein Ablativsuffix bezeichnet. Man sagt folglich *grāmād āgacchati* "Er kommt vom Dorf". Wie steht es dann, wenn auch der Ausgangspunkt nicht wirklich fest ist, wie in dem Satz *aśvāt trastāt patitaḥ* "Er fiel von dem aufgeschreckten Pferd"? Der Ablativ ist auch hier berechtigt, denn es ist nicht beabsichtigt, die Unfestigkeit des Pferdes auszudrücken, auch wenn es als aufgeschreckt und durchgehend bezeichnet wird. Patañjali argumentiert hier erst mit einer etymologisierten Erklärung, daß es die feste Vorstellung des Pferdes (*aśva*) als schnell (*āśu*) laufendes Tier sei, die den Gebrauch des Ablativs rechtfertige. Aber diese Erklärung befriedigt nicht, denn sie kann nicht Sätze wie *dhāvataḥ patitaḥ* "Er fiel von dem Laufenden" rechtfertigen. Er kommt zu dem Schluß, daß auch hier der Sprecher nicht die Unfestigkeit ausdrücken wollte. "Es gibt Fälle, wo auch das Existierende (hyperbolisch) nicht ausgedrückt werden soll, wie *alomikâiḍakā* "die haarlose Ziege", *anudarā kanyā* "das bauchlose Mädchen"; und es gibt Fälle, wo (phantasievoll) etwas Nichtexistierendes ausgedrückt werden soll, wie *samudraḥ kuṇḍikā* "Das Meer ist ein Topf", *Vindhyo vardhitakam* "Das Vindhyagebirge ist eine Schüssel" (I, 327.10–21). Die Sprache bezieht sich hier nicht direkt auf die objektive Welt, sondern auf die Welt, wie sie dem Sprecher erscheint oder darauf, welche ihrer Aspekte er ausdrükken will.

Schon Kātyāyana (värtt. 6 zu P III 1 22) kennt den Begriff des *vigraha* für einen 'aufgelösten', analytischen Ausdruck. Einen gewundenen Gang auszudrücken, benutzt man nach (P III 1 23) stets das sogenannte Intensiv der Wurzeln für 'gehen'; Kātyāyana findet es unnötig darauf hinzuweisen, daß dies 'stets' der Fall sei, weil die einzelnen Worte nicht der Bedeutung des Intensivs gleichkommen: *na hi kuṭilaṃ kramatîti caṅkramyata iti gamyate* "Denn 'Er geht krumm, taumelt' drückt nicht genau die Bedeutung von 'Er geht nicht gerade [auf ein Ziel los], streift herum' aus" (II, 30.11f.). Patañjali kontrastiert oft einen analytischen Ausdruck wie *śastrîva śyāmā* und einen synthetischen wie *śastrī-śyāmā* "[Devadattā ist] schwarz wie ein Messer" (I, 397.13+25), *pitrā sadṛśaḥ* oder *pituḥ sadṛśaḥ* und *pitṛ-sadṛśaḥ* "dem Vater ähnlich", *aver māṃsam* und *āvikam* "Schaffleisch" (III, 124.5–7). Derartige analytische Entsprechungen gehen nach ihm den synthetischen voraus (II, 431.7f., 18), wie ja auch Pāṇini Nominalkomposita (P II 1 3 bis II 2 38) und sekundäre Nominalsuffixe (P IV 1 82 bis V 2 140) als zweiten Schritt anstelle von analytischen Ausdrücken lehrt. Für gewisse Komposita gibt es aber kein analytisches Equivalent: z. B. *brāhmaṇârtham* "zum Wohle der Brahmanen" oder *kumbha-kāra* "Töpfer"; überhaupt kann ein Suffix allein nie separat Teil eines analytischen Ausdrucks sein.

Das Problem der Zeit, besonders der Gegenwart und des grammatischen Präsens, wird von Patañjali in mehrfacher Weise erörtert. In II, 160.23–161.2 geht es um die Tempora des Verbums 'sein' bei permanenten Objekten. "Hier ist etwas Sinneswerk, etwas Vernunftwerk. Sinneswerk ist Erreichen, Vernunftwerk ist Entscheidung. So sagt ja auch einer, der nach Pāṭaliputra gehen will: 'Auf dem Weg, der bis Pāṭaliputra zurückzulegen ist, wird ein Brunnen sein'; wenn es sich nicht um Heutiges handelt (sondern um eine weitere Zukunft) '... wird ein Brunnen sein' [Futurum II]; wenn er ihn erreicht hat '... ist ein Brunnen'; wenn er ihn erreicht hat und weitergegangen ist '... war ein Brunnen' [Aorist]; wenn er ihn erreicht hat, weitergegangen ist und eine Nacht zugebracht hat '... war ein Brunnen' [Imperfekt]; wenn er ihn erreicht hat, weitergegangen ist, eine Nacht zugebracht hat und ihn vergessen hat '... ist ein Brunnen gewesen'. Wenn dieses Sinneswerk [vorliegt], dann treten diese verschiedenen Endungen ein; wenn nämlich Vernunftwerk [vorliegt], dann wird das Präsens sein." Man kann also ganz allgemein sagen: "Der Brunnen ist da."

1.3. Nur durch das *Mahābhāṣya* wissen wir von anderen Gelehrten, die in Pāṇinis Nachfolge als Grammatiker gearbeitet haben. Die Saunāgas verfaßten *vārttika*-ähnliche Anmerkungen zu seiner Grammatik (II, 105.7f. und 228.6), während die Bhāradvājīyas Kritik und Verbesserungen zu Kātyāyanas *Vārttikas* vorbrachten (z. B. I, 73.26). In mehreren Fällen beruht Patañjalis Kritik auf anonymen Anmerkungen zu Pāṇinis Grammatik in Versen (später oft *śloka-vārttika* genannt). Schließlich finden sich mehrere Zitate in *śloka*-Form, die wie Fragmente einer versifizierten Grammatik aussehen, mit deutlichen Verbindungen zu Pāṇini, aber auch mit Unterschieden: das sekundäre Nominalsuffix *-ika* (z. B. in *vārttika-sūtrika*), das Pāṇini als *ṬHa*$^k$ gelehrt hatte (wobei *ṬH* heterophonisch, d. h. als stellvertretendes Zeichen, für *ik* steht und das Determinativ $^k$ vṛddhi der ersten Stammsilbe und Akzent auf der letzten Silbe bestimmt), wird hier als *ika*$^k$ gelehrt (II, 284.1), also ohne Gebrauch des Heterophons, aber mit demselben Determinativ. Dasselbe gilt für die ähnlichen Suffixe *ika*$^n$ (Pāṇini *ṬHa*$^n$)

und $^{s}$*ika*$^{n}$ (Pāṇini $^{s}$*ṬHa*$^{n}$) in II, 284.15 und 398.13. – Auch wenn uns Patañjalis Werk als der Abschluß einer Epoche erscheinen mag, kam mit ihm die Arbeit an Pāṇinis Grammatik nicht zu einem Ende. Wir wissen aus dem Vers *Vākya-padīya* II, 484 des berühmten Bhartṛhari, daß Grammatiker wie Vaiji, Saubhava und Haryakṣa in unabhängiger Weise Änderungen zu Pāṇinis Grammatik vorgeschlagen hatten, die uns nicht erhalten sind. Es bildete sich ein Vulgatatext seiner Grammatik heraus, der weitgehend die Anregungen Kātyāyanas und Patañjalis berücksichtigte und dem mehrere Hilfstexte beigegeben wurden: die *Uṇādi-sūtras* geben etwas gezwungen wirkende Ableitungen von Worten, die sich Pāṇinis System nicht fügen wollten, das *Lingânuśāsana* und Śāntanavas *Phiṭ-sūtras* geben Faustregeln für die Bestimmung des grammatischen Geschlechts und der alten Akzente, und die *Pāṇinīya-śikṣā* orthoëpische Regeln. Einem Bhīmasena wird die Zufügung von Bedeutungen zu Pāṇinis Wurzelliste (*Dhātupāṭha*) zugeschrieben. Damit und mit der Kodifizierung von Metaregeln (*paribhāṣā*) und Wortlisten (*gaṇa*) wurde Pāṇinis Grammatik zu einem Mechanismus zur Kontrolle korrekten Sanskritgebrauchs. Erst einige Jahrhunderte später finden wir in Bhartṛhari wieder einen bedeutenden Kommentator und Philosophen, der die im *Mahābhāṣya* gegebenen Ansätze vertieft und systematisiert (→ Art. 20).

## 2. Buddhistische Sanskrit Grammatiker

2.1. Als buddhistische Schulen in den ersten Jahrhunderten n. Chr. begannen, ihre kanonischen Texte und philosophischen Erörterungen in dem wieder in höchsten Ehren stehenden Sanskrit – ein Aspekt des erstarkenden Hinduismus – zu verfassen statt in umgangssprachlichen Dialekten, entstand ein Bedürfnis nach einem praktischen Lehrbuch. Denn den Buddhisten, soweit sie nicht bekehrte Brahmanen waren, fehlte die Geläufigkeit in dieser Sprache, wie sie viele Brahmanen ihrer Zeit von Kindheit auf entwickelten. Wir haben nur Fragmente der Grammatik des Kumāralāta (nach ihm *Kaumaralāta* genannt) in Handschriften aus dem frühen 4. Jh. n. Chr., die in Turkestan gefunden worden sind. Das beliebte *Kātantra* des Śarvavarman ist wahrscheinlich eine Umarbeitung dieses Werkes. Ursprünglich ein knappes Elementarbuch, wurde es schrittweise durch Einschluß erst der primären Nominalsuffixe und dann der sekundären Nominalsuffixe, Komposition und Femininbildungen vervollständigt. Mit seiner leicht faßlichen Ordnung nach grammatischen Bereichen war das *Kātantra* das Vorbild für viele spätere Grammatiken. Pāṇinis Anordnung seiner Regeln, deren 'organisiertes Chaos' vielleicht das Gefühl eines grammatischen Mysteriums (*parokṣa*; vgl. Thieme 1982: 18) förderte, wurde nun mit einem buddhistischen Ausdruck als *akālakam* "zur Unzeit angeboten" (Candra-vṛtti zu C II 2 68) kritisiert. Von Pāṇinis generativem Prinzip ist nichts geblieben. Während Pāṇini alle Verbalendungen aus 18 Grundformen ableitete, führt das *Kātantra* alle 180 Endungen tabellenartig auf. Im Laufe von Jahrhunderten wuchs das *Kātantra* durch Anhänge und Listen zu einem vollständigen System.

2.2. Eine wissenschaftliche Leistung ist das *Cāndra-vyākaraṇa* des Candragomin (ca. 450 n. Chr.?), der unter sorgfältiger Benutzung des *Mahābhāṣya* eine Grammatik verfaßt hat, die klar und vollständig sein soll: klarer offenbar als Pāṇinis und vollständiger als Śarvavarmans Werk. Wahrscheinlich hatte sie (wie Pāṇinis Grammatik) acht Bücher zu je vier Kapiteln; aber die beiden letzten Bücher über vedische Regeln und über Akzente – wenn sie in der Tat ursprünglich existierten – sind verloren. Für die Buddhisten hatten diese Regeln kein Interesse. Die *Vṛtti* mit ihren Erläuterungen und Beispielen wurde oft als das Werk des Autors selbst angesehen. Aber nach den Arbeiten von Oberlies (1989: 2–4; 1995) und anderen muß es als wahrscheinlich gelten, daß dieser Kommentar von einem Dharmadāsa verfaßt wurde, dessen Name jetzt in den Kolophonen mehrerer Handschriften vorliegt.

Die beschriebene Sprache ist wesentlich mit der Pāṇinis identisch. Die Originalität liegt in der Beschreibung, die praktisch ohne Termini auskommt (*asaṃjñakam*: Vṛtti zu C II 2 68) und sich anstatt auf Aufzählungen und darauf basierende Kürzungen stützt, vergleichbar vielleicht mit Hans Glinz' Buch *Die innere Form des Deutschen* (1962). Pāṇini I 1 73 hatte ein Wort, dessen erste Silbe einen vṛddhi-Vokal hat, *vṛddham* genannt; Candragomin II 4 98 nennt es *ād=aij-ādy-ac* "dessen erste {a...au} {ā...ai,au} sind". In der Kasussyntax reduziert er Pāṇinis drei Stufen auf zwei: die Beschreibung der Situation (durch die Augen des Sprechers gesehen; z. B. *kri-*

*yâpya* "durch Handlung zu erreichen", d. i. Objekt: Pāṇinis erster Stufe entsprechend) oder beschreibende semantische Ausdrücke (*kartṛ* "Täter": Pāṇinis zweiter Stufe entlehnt), die dann mit den Kasussuffixen gepaart werden. Er vermeidet damit ganz die vermittelnde Kategorie der *kāraka*, die bei Pāṇini eine große Rolle spielt, obwohl er das Wort nicht konsequent meidet (C II 2 16 *kārakaṃ bahulam*). Die Sprachbeschreibung ist damit einfacher geworden, hat aber auch an Definitionsschärfe und generativer Kraft verloren. Wo P I 4 37 gelehrt hatte, daß derjenige, gegen den der Ärger bei Verben wie 'zürnen, neidisch sein' gerichtet ist, die Bezeichnung *saṃpradāna* "Übergabe" erhält, aber die Bezeichnung *karma* "Objekt", wenn das Verbum ein Präfix hat (Im ersten Fall resultiert dann ein Dativsuffix, im letzteren ein Akkusativsuffix), lehrt C II 1 76 nur *kopasthāne 'nāpye* "[Die Dativendung] für den Bereich des Zornes, wenn er kein Objekt ist". Damit soll einerseits *Devadattāye krudhyate* und andererseits *Devadattam abhikrudhyate* "Er zürnt Devadatta" erklärt werden. Pāṇini hatte genau angegeben, wenn das Verbum als transitiv zu betrachten und mit dem Akkusativ an Stelle des Dativs zu konstruieren ist; Candragomin überläßt die Entscheidung dem Sprachgefühl: der Dativ, außer wenn das Verbum transitiv ist – ohne daß er uns nun sagt, wann dies der Fall ist. Der Grund für diese Vermeidung der *kārakas* – und praktisch aller Termini überhaupt – liegt wahrscheinlich weniger in der Grammatik, obwohl ein Grammatiker wie Whitney (1893: 171) die Einführung der *kāraka* in Pāṇinis Grammatik als eine "schwierige und gefährliche Methode" bedauert hatte, als in der Philosophie. Buddhistische Philosophen lehrten, daß es z. B. keinen 'Wagen' gebe, sondern nur eine Summe von Teilen, denen man dann den Namen 'Wagen' gibt (Milindapañha II, 1.1); alle Termini sind daher in Frage gestellt. – Eine geistreiche Neuformulierung findet sich im folgenden. P VIII 4 1 f. lehrt die Ersetzung des dentalen /n/ durch das retroflexe /ṇ/ nach einem /r,ṣ/ im selben Wort, auch wenn ein Vokal, /y,v,h/, ein Guttural, ein Labial, die Präposition *ā* oder das Augment dazwischen treten (also: *karaṇaṃ*, *nṛpeṇa*, usw.). C VI 4 101 lehrt dieselbe Ersetzung, verbietet sie aber (C VI 4 132), wenn ein Palatal, Retroflex, Dental, /l,ś,ṣ,s/ dazwischen treten; d. h. er ersetzt Pāṇinis positiv einengende Zusatzregel durch eine einfachere Ausnahmeregel. Die Autoren unserer Sanskritlehrbücher folgen im allgemeinen Pāṇini, mit der Ausnahme von W. Geiger (1923: 15), der Candragomin folgt. – Oft verkürzt Candragomin den Wortlaut einer Regel gegenüber Pāṇinis Formulierung: P I 4 2 *vipratiṣedhe paraṃ kāryam* wird zu C I 1 16 *vipratiṣedhe* reduziert, und *paraḥ* gilt aus C I 1 14 weiter. Dieser Eifer, Silben zu sparen selbst auf Kosten der Deutlichkeit, ist vielen der späteren Sanskritgrammatiken eigen. Wenn Devanandins *Jainendra-vyākaraṇa* älter ist als das *Cāndra-vyākaraṇa*, ist dessen Autor dem Candragomin auch darin vorangegangen. Die Tendenz zu knappster Formulierung ist ja freilich schon in Pāṇinis eigenen Regeln inhärent, aber erst spätere Interpreten formulierten die extreme Metaregel "Grammatiker freuen sich über [die Einsparung] eine[r] halbe[n] Vokallänge wie über die Geburt eines Sohnes": Nr. 122 im *Paribhāṣênduśekhara*, wo sie schließlich jedoch abgelehnt wird. Ganz allgemein läßt sich sagen, daß Candragomin oft dem Sprecher die Wahl anheimstellt, wo Pāṇini eine direkte Anweisung gegeben hatte. – Die Vṛtti zu C I 2 99 macht den offenbar originalen Vorschlag, daß die Richtungsakkusative normalen Objektsakkusativen gleichwertig seien (Oberlies 1995: 14). Zu Candragomins Grammatik gehören außer der *Vṛtti* (und mehreren Subkommentaren) eine Wurzelliste, *Uṇādi-sūtras* für unregelmäßige Wortbildungen, *Varṇa-sūtras* über Phonetik und eine Liste von 86 Metaregeln. Die Grammatik war lange verloren geglaubt und wurde im wesentlichen erst von B. Liebich auf Grund nepalesischer Handschriften wieder zugänglich gemacht.

## 3. Jinistische Sanskrit Grammatiker

Wie bei den Buddhisten, ist auch bei den Anhängern Mahāvīras ein großer Teil des religiösen Schrifttums in den nachchristlichen Jahrhunderten in Sanskrit abgefaßt, und es ergab sich ein Bedürfnis nach eigenen Grammatiken.

3.1. Das *Jainendra-vyākaraṇa* des Deva-nandin Pūjyapāda existiert in einer älteren nördlichen Rezension mit 3063 sūtras (und dem Kommentar *Mahavṛtti* des Abhaya-nandin) und einer jüngeren südlichen Rezension mit 3708 sūtras (und dem Kommentar *Śabdârṇava-candrikā* des Somadeva). Wahrscheinlich ist das *Jainendra-vyākaraṇa* etwas älter als das *Cāndra-vyākaraṇa*, aber auf jeden Fall gehört es in den gleichen Zeitraum, die Mitte des 5. Jh. n. Chr. Devanandins größter Anspruch auf Originalität liegt in der extremen Kürze seiner Regeln und der großen Zahl technischer Sigla. Von dem Wort *vibhakti* "Kasusendung" oder vielmehr einer künstlichen Variante davon, nämlich *vibhaktī*, isoliert Devanandin die sieben Laute *v-i-bh-a-k-t-ī* und fügt /ā/ an die Konsonanten und /p/ an die Vokale als Sigla für die sieben Kasus: *vā* ist dann der Nominativ, *ip* der Akkusativ usw. (J I 2 157f.). Kātyāyanas Regel über die Kongruenz von Nominativ und Verbum *tiṅsamānâdhikaraṇe [prathamā]* (värtt. 6 zu P II 3 46) wird so reduziert zu J I 4 54 *miṅaîkârthe vāḥ*. Devanandin folgt einem Vorschlag Kātyāyanas (värtt. 29 zu P I 2 64), daß der *ekaśeṣa*-Prozeß zur Bildung der Dual- und Pluralformen der Nomina (siehe 1.2. Ende) unnötig sei, und bildet diese Formen direkt durch Anfügung der Kasusendungen an den Stamm. Unter allen Sanskritgrammatikern ist er der einzige, der die Reihenfolge der Personalendungen umtauscht: statt Pāṇinis *uttama/madhyama/prathama* (für unsere dritte/zweite/erste Person: P I 4 105–108; vgl. P III 4 78 *ti$^{p}$...mahi$^{ṅ}$*) lehrt er J I 2 152 *miṅas triśo 'smad-yuṣmad-anyāḥ* "Die Suffixe von *mi$^{p}$* bis *JHa$^{ṅ}$* [heißen] 'wir', 'ihr', [und] 'andere'." Am nächsten kommt ihm darin die Tamilgrammatik *Tolkāppiyam* (→ Art. 28), die in *Colatikāram* 203–224 zuerst die Personalendungen der ersten Person aufführt, dann die der dritten, und zuletzt die der zweiten Person. Die allererste Regel (J I 1 1 *siddhir anekāntāt* "Erreichung [der korrekten Formen] ergibt sich [auch] aus mehrdeutiger [Anweisung]") beruft sich auf den Sprachgebrauch und das Sprachverständnis der Hörer; diese Regel gilt für die ganze Grammatik. Devanandin ist damit noch radikaler als Candragomin, der sich oft auf seine Regel C I 1 103 *bahulam* "oft" verläßt, die die Gültigkeit seiner Regeln relativiert (wogegen Pāṇini den Gebrauch von *bahulam* fast ausschließlich auf die vedischen Sprachregeln beschränkt hatte).

3.2. Im 9. Jh. n. Chr. verfaßte ein Jaina Mönch Pālyakīrti das *Śākaṭāyana-vyākaraṇa* (so genannt zu Ehren des Grammatikers Śākaṭāyana, der von Pāṇini und Yāska erwähnt wird). Diese Grammatik ist eine Kompilation, die in der Anordnung nach grammatischen Gebieten Anregungen des Kātantra folgt und ihrerseits Modell für mehrere spätere Grammatiken war.

3.3. Hemacandras Grammatik (12. Jh. n. Chr.) ist sicher die beste der von Jainas geschriebenen Grammatiken. Fast ein Viertel der ca. 4500 Regeln, das ganze achte Buch, befaßt sich mit den Prakritsprachen (siehe 4.2.).

## 4. Grammatiken der mittelindischen Dialekte

4.1. Die "gewöhnlichen" (*prākṛta*) Sprachen (vgl. Pisani 1957: 185–189) waren für die orthodoxen Brahmanen nur Abweichungen (*apabhraṃśa*), ihre Formen "barbarisch" (*mleccha*), im Prinzip nicht verschieden von den grammatischen Fehlern, die in vedischen Legenden ihre Sprecher ins Verderben führten (TS II, 4.12, 1; ŚB III, 2.1.23; zitiert in *Mbh.* I, 2.7–13). Solche Fehler waren ebensowenig "permanent, ewig" (*nitya*) wie die künstlichen Termini Pāṇinis oder Pingalas (*Mbh.* I, 394.11–13; Scharfe 1971: 1–3). Damit konnte ein historisches Element in die Ableitung der Prakritsprachen aus dem Sanskrit eintreten (Deshpande 1993: 74). Für andere jedoch, u. a. die Jainas, waren *prākṛta* Formen Ableitungen von der Basis (*prakṛti*) oder gar in der Basis enthalten (Kahrs 1992: 225–249); die Basis war für einige das Sanskrit, für Namisādhu, den Jaina Kommentator von Rudraṭas *Kāvyālaṃkāra* II, 12, die "natürliche Sprache", nämlich das Prakrit (welches für ihn das Sanskrit als Sonderform einschloß). Es war daher nur natürlich, daß alle diese Grammatiker die Prakritdialekte nicht als eigene grammatische Strukturen lehrten, sondern als Übertragungen aus dem Sanskrit durch Substitutionen einzelner Elemente (*transfer grammar*). In der Tat lassen sich die mittelindischen Dialekte nicht so wie das Sanskrit aus den Elementen 'ausformen', da sie durch phonetische Entwicklungen die einzigartige Durchsichtigkeit des Sanskrit verloren hatten. Die Prakritgrammatiker unterscheiden drei Klassen von Worten: *tatsama* Worte, die den entsprechenden Worten im Sanskrit gleich sind (gegebenenfalls mit Ausnahme der Endungen), *tad-bhava* Worte, die entweder von den entsprechenden Sanskritworten abstammen (*taj-ja*) oder in ihnen enthalten sind (*tatra bhavam*) und durch Substitutionsregeln gewonnen werden, und schließlich *deśī* Worte regionalen Ursprungs, ohne deutliche Beziehung zu gleichwertigen Sanskritworten. Im Laufe der Zeit gewannen diese Dialekte ein gewisses Ansehen und ihr

Gebrauch in den klassischen Dramen ist die Regel für Personen der niederen Klassen, Frauen usw. Das Handbuch der Schauspielkunst (*Bharata-nāṭya-śāstra*, Kapitel 17; 2. Jh. n. Chr.?) gibt daher einige Faustregeln, wie ein Schauspieler einen oberflächlichen Eindruck verschiedener Dialekte hervorrufen kann.

4.2. Der dem Vararuci zugeschriebene *Prākṛta-prakāśa* beschreibt in ca. 420 sūtras (in Sanskrit) allein die Mahārāṣṭrī [*bhāṣā*], den Dialekt der Region des heutigen Maharashtra, offenbar in Anlehnung an eine Anthologie von Gedichten wie die *Sattasaï* (2. Jh. n. Chr.); später wurden Kapitel über die Paiśācī und Māgadhī hinzugefügt, schließlich auch eins über die *Śaurasenī*. Die Grundlage ist das Sanskrit im Stadium der 'Unterweisung' der technischen Regeln, d. h. vor der Ersetzung von Pāṇinis technischen Elementen durch die endgültigen Formen der Sprache: das Suffix des Nominativs Singular ist noch $s^u$, das des Genitivs noch $^{n}as$; sie werden dann bei auf *-a* auslautenden Stämmen durch *o* bzw. *ssa* ersetzt (z. B. *devo*/*devassa*). Die Substitutionen lassen sich nicht immer glatt vollziehen, was zu übermäßigem Gebrauch von Ausdrücken wie 'oft' und 'oder' führt. Spätere Prakritgrammatiker der 'östlichen Schule' sind Puruṣottama (12. Jh.), Mārkaṇḍeya (17. Jh.?) und Rāmaśarman (17. Jh.), die von den älteren Grammatikern und (oft fehlerhaften) Handschriften abhängen; sie kannten kein gesprochenes Prakrit mehr und ihr Wert für die Textkritik der alten Prakritliteratur ist recht zweifelhaft. Der Jainamönch Hemacandra (12. Jh.) lehrte die Prakritdialekte im achten und letzten Buch seiner Sanskritgrammatik. Originelle Beiträge sind seine Hinweise auf die Ardhamāgadhī (die Sprache des Jainakanons), und eine Form von Apabhraṃśa, nämlich einen Vorläufer von frühem Gujerati, mit sorgfältiger Belegung. In seinem Werk finden wir auch die erste Formulierung der offensichtlichen Regel, daß bei der Übertragung vom Sanskrit zum Prakrit ein langer Vokal vor einer Konsonantengruppe gekürzt wird (H VIII 1 84 *hrasvaḥ saṃyoge*, z. B. *sūtra* > *sutta*). Kramadīśvara mag ein Zeitgenosse Hemacandras gewesen sein oder ein Nachfolger; auch in seiner Sanskritgrammatik, dem *Saṃkṣipta-sāra*, wird Prakrit im achten Buch behandelt. Trivikrama (13. Jh.) führt in seinem *Prākṛta-śabdânuśāsana* neue technische Ausdrücke ein.

4.3. Die Buddhisten in der Tradition der Theravādin verfaßten Grammatiken der Sprache ihres Kanons, des Pāli, in eben dieser Sprache ohne Bezug auf Sanskrit. Die älteste erhaltene von diesen ist die des Kaccāyana (zwischen dem 5. und 11. Jh. verfaßt). Der Einfluß Pāṇinis und des Kātantra ist deutlich. Die Kasusendungen der verschiedenen Paradigmen werden aus einer grundlegenden Gruppe von Endungen durch Substitution gewonnen. – Wohl die beste Pāligrammatik ist die umfängliche *Saddanīti* des Aggavaṃsa aus Burma (12. Jh.), die schnell weiten Anklang fand und die Sprachform vieler der uns vorliegenden Pālihandschriften beeinflußt hat (→ Art. 25). Die moderne Pāliforschung bemüht sich über diese Normalisierung der Texte hinaus zu einem älteren Pāli vorzudringen, z. B. durch die Benutzung von Handschriften aus abgelegenen Traditionen, die dieser Normalisierung entgangen sind. Die *Saddanīti* ist vollständiger als Kaccāyanas Grammatik und besteht aus drei Teilen. Der erste Teil, genannt *Padamālā*, bietet eine Morphologie mit Paradigmen, die interessanterweise wie in Kramadīśvaras *Saṃkṣiptasāra* mit dem Verbum beginnt. Die sogenannte *Dhātumālā* gibt eine Wurzelliste mit einem Überblick über die verbalen und nominalen Ableitungen (vergleichbar mit W. D. Whitneys *Roots, Verb-forms, and Primary Derivatives of the Sanskrit Language*). Der dritte Teil schließlich, die *Suttamālā*, behandelt dasselbe Sprachmaterial noch einmal, aber diesmal mit Beschreibung der grammatischen Prozesse, Substitutionen usw. in Nachfolge Kaccāyanas. Moggalāna in seinem *Māgadham Sadda-lakkhanam* "Grammatik der Sprache von Magadha" (12. Jh.) zeigt den Einfluß von Candragomins Sanskritgrammatik z. B. in der Vermeidung mehrerer technischer Ausdrücke.

## 5. Werke in der Tradition der Pāṇinīyas

5.1. Der große zeitliche Abstand zwischen Patañjali und seinem frühesten bezeugten Kommentator Bhartṛhari (ca. 450–510 n. Chr.) zeigt keinesfalls ein mangelndes Interesse an Pāṇinis Grammatik an; denn Bhartṛhari weist sowohl in seinem Kommentar wie auch in seinem *Vākyapadīya* des öfteren auf andere Autoren hin, die sich um die Interpretation von Pāṇinis Werk bemüht haben. Aber nicht alle dieser Autoren folgten dem Pfad des *Mahābhāṣya*, dessen Tradition erst durch Candragomin wieder prominent wurde. Bhartṛharis Kommentar, die *Mahābhāṣya-ṭīkā* oder *Mahābhāṣya-dīpikā* ist nur in einer einzigen, noch dazu unvollständigen und verderbten Handschrift erhalten. Am Anfang fehlt vielleicht ein Blatt, und die Handschrift bricht mit dem Kommentar zu P I 1 55 ab, obwohl der Kommentar ursprünglich wenigstens bis zum Ende des dritten *pāda* reichte. Es ist ein sehr gelehrter Kommentar; auffallend sind die häufigen Verweise auf Handschriften und Schriftzeichen, ein Zeichen, daß das Studium der Grammatik über die rein mündliche Tradition hinaus (die gewiß weiter existierte!) auch ein Bücherstudium geworden war.

5.2. Mündlicher Unterricht, der Pāṇinis sūtras in verständliche Sätze "wendet" (*vartayati*), ist ein unabläßlicher Bestandteil der Tradition, aber keine solche alte *vṛtti* ist uns bekannt. Der älteste Text dieser Art ist die *Kāśikā Vṛtti* "*vṛtti* aus Benares"; Jayāditya gilt als der Verfasser der Bücher 1–5, und nach seinem Tode im Jahr 661 n. Chr. soll Vāmana das Werk (Bücher 6–8) vollendet haben. Diskrepanzen zwischen diesen beiden Teilen stützen diese Zuschreibungen, es finden sich aber auch solche Widersprüche innerhalb der Teile, die dem einem oder dem anderen der beiden Autoren zugeschrieben werden (Ojihara 1961–1964). Trotz des bescheidenen Titels hat die *Kāśikā* ein höheres Ziel: ein Kompendium der Grammatik in Pāṇinis Tradition zu sein, und sie hat sich als solches großer Beliebtheit erfreut. Die anscheinende Einfachheit ist oft trügerisch, indem die volle Bedeutung der Erklärungen sich nur dem erschließt, der die Diskussionen im *Mahābhāṣya* studiert hat. Die *Kāśikā* hat Candragomins Grammatik und die *Mahāvṛtti* zum *Jainendra-vyākaraṇa* benutzt, ohne sie jedoch namentlich zu erwähnen (Oberlies 1995). Die *Kāśikā* folgt dem Vulgatatext von Pāṇinis Grammatik, der sich vermutlich vor Devanandin und Candragomin herausgebildet hatte (Oberlies 1995: 47f.) und in dem viele Änderungsvorschläge des *Mahābhāṣya* akzeptiert sind. Der Kommentar *Nyāsa* dazu (8. oder 9. Jh.) versucht im Gegensatz zu zeigen, daß Katyāyanas Änderungsvorschläge unnötig seien; im 13. Jh. faßt die *Padamañjari* die Kāśikāphilologie ihrer Zeit zusammen (Sharma 1985). Die *Bhāṣāvṛtti* (12. Jh.) ist noch einfacher als die *Kāśikā* und verzichtet auf die vedischen Regeln: sie waren für den buddhistischen Autor Puruṣottama von keinem Interesse.

5.3. Die wertvollere philologische Arbeit liegt wohl in den Kommentaren und Subkommentaren zum *Mahābhāṣya*. Dem Fragment von Bhartṛharis Kommentar folgt eine ganze Kette von solchen Werken, beginnend mit dem *Mahābhāṣya-pradīpa* des Kaschmirers Kaiyaṭa (spätestens 11. Jh.), zu dem der Mahratte Nāgojībhaṭṭa (gest. 1755 in Benares) den bedeutenden *Mahābhāṣya-pradīpôddyota* verfaßte; mehrere andere Kommentare zu Kaiyaṭas Werk sind bekannt. Die Autoren streben, dem Vorbild Patañjalis folgend, nach einer widerspruchsfreien Interpretation von Pāṇinis Regeln und interpretieren Patañjalis Erklärungen mit großer philologischer Schärfe – mit gutem Verständnis für die grammatischen Probleme, aber doch nicht eigentlich als Linguisten. Ihre intime Kenntnis der Texte und ihre lebenslange Beschäftigung mit ihren Problemen machen sie auch dem modernen Interpreten wertvoll. Thieme (1980) konnte zeigen, daß Kaiyaṭas (und Bhaṭṭojidīkṣitas) Erklärung von P I 4 51 [49 *karma*] *akathitaṃ ca* "Ein Handlungsfaktor, der unberichtet bleibt, heißt ebenfalls 'Objekt' [und erhält dementsprechend eine Akkusativendung]" genau das Richtige trifft. Damit erklärt sich der Akkusativ von *gām* "Kuh" in *gāṃ dogdhi payaḥ* "Er milcht die Kuh Milch", wo die Milch das eigentliche Ziel der Handlung ist, die Kuh deren Quelle. Der Ablativ ist angezeigt, wenn diese eigentliche Rolle der Kuh als Quelle ausgedrückt werden soll: *gor dogdhi payaḥ* "Er milcht die Milch aus der Kuh"; wenn sie als unwesentlich unausgedrückt bleiben soll, ist die Kuh ein sekundäres 'Objekt' und erscheint im Akkusativ. Moderne Interpreten der letzten hundert Jahre scheiterten in ihren Versuchen, der Regel P I 4 51 einen Sinn abzugewinnen, versuchten sogar, die Regel als Einschub zu athetieren.

5.4. Auch in der Tradition der Pāṇinīyas wurde die Anordnung der Regeln zu einem Unterrichtsproblem. Es ist wohl kein Zufall, daß die erste Neufassung von Pāṇinis Grammatik von den Buddhisten ausging, die schon früher Schulgrammatiken mit thematischen Arrangements verfaßt hatten (siehe 2.1.). Dharmakīrti, ein Buddhist aus Ceylon (10. Jh. n. Chr.?) verfaßte den *Rūpâvatāra*, der Pāṇinis Regeln in einer Reihenfolge anbietet, die dem Kātantra verpflichtet ist, oft mit vollen Paradigmen illustriert. Mehrere solche Texte wurden in den folgenden Jahrhunderten in Indien verfaßt, von denen die *Siddhānta-kaumudī* von Bhaṭṭojidīkṣita (frühes 17. Jh.) den größten Einfluß hatte und oft kommentiert wurde. Obwohl dieses Schulbuch für ungezählte Studenten praktisch Pāṇinis Grammatik ersetzte, war eine genaue Interpretation seiner Regeln, z. B. Fragen der Ergänzung von Worten aus vorausgehenden Regeln, von der Kenntnis ihrer Reihenfolge in Pāṇinis Original abhängig. Diese Neufassungen unterscheiden sich von den freien Schöpfungen Devanandins und Candrogomins dadurch, daß sie keine neuen Regeln formulieren, sondern lediglich Pāṇinis Regeln, in ihrem originalen Wortlaut, in einer neuen Reihenfolge vorführen. Diese Werke belebten wieder das Studium von Pāṇinis Werk auf Kosten der verschiedenen Neuschöpfungen der vorausgegangenen Periode (siehe 6.1.).

5.5. Es gibt darüber hinaus eine Reihe von thematisch bestimmten Werken, von denen das bedeutendste, Bhartṛharis *Vākyapadīya*, gesondert gewürdigt wird (→ Art. 20). Eine Gruppe von Texten ist dem Studium der Metaregeln gewidmet. Die Vyāḍi zugeschriebene *Paribhāṣā-vṛtti* ist nach dem letzten Herausgeber (Wujastyk 1986a, 1986b) vielleicht sogar älter als Bhartṛhari; für das Alter könnte die geringere Zahl der 87 Metaregeln sprechen (Nur das *Cāndra-vyākaraṇa* hat mit 83 noch weniger) verglichen mit bis zu 140 solcher Regeln in anderen Werken. Es stimmt einen andererseits bedenklich, daß es keine sicheren alten Verweise auf diesen Text gibt. Die *Laghu-paribhāṣā-vṛtti* des Puruṣottamadeva (12. Jh.), die *Bṛhad-paribhāṣā-vṛtti* des Sīradeva (12. Jh.) und der *Paribhāṣā-bhāskara* des Haribhāskara Agnihotrin (17. Jh.) wurden von Nāgojībhaṭṭas *Paribhāṣêndu-śekhara* (18. Jh.) in den Schatten gestellt. Hierin weist der Autor viele der vorgeschlagenen Metaregeln zurück und erkennt nur diejenigen an, die im *Mahābhāṣya* gelehrt sind und entweder auf 'zwingenden Hinweisen' Pāṇinis oder allgemeinen logischen Prinzipien beruhen. Die Interpretation von Pāṇinis Werk in den letzten zwei Jahrhunderten ist wesentlich durch Nāgojībhaṭṭa geprägt. Dieser selbst steht in einer langen Traditionskette: Bhaṭṭojidīkṣita, dessen Enkel Haridīkṣita (sein direkter Lehrer) und eine lange Reihe von Schülern, die bis in die Gegenwart reicht (Abhyankar 1962: 34f.). Der *Paribhāṣêndu-śekhara* ist vermutlich eins seiner letzten Werke (Bronkhorst 1986: 173–176).

## 6. Sanskrit Grammatik an den Fürstenhöfen

6.1. Zwischen dem 11. und 13. Jh. wurden von Höflingen mehrere originelle Grammatiken verfaßt. Bhojas *Sarasvatī-kaṇṭābharaṇa* komprimiert das gesamte Material, einschließlich der Anhänge, in die über 6000 Regeln; zu Hemacandra siehe oben 3.3.; Kramadīśvaras *Saṃkṣiptasāra* behandelt ebenfalls im achten Buch die Prakritdialekte; Vopadevas *Mugdhabodha* übertrifft an algebraischer Kürze alle Vorgänger; das *Sārasvata-vyākaraṇa* war in seiner Einfachheit bei den Fürsten beliebt. Ein ungewöhnliches Werk ist Damodaras *Ukti-vyakti-prakaraṇa*, das Sanskrit durch Umsetzung aus der Umgangssprache von Benares im 12. Jh. lehrt – und uns damit unbeabsichtigt einen grammatischen Abriß der Umgangssprache seiner Zeit gibt.

Unter Akbars Regie verfaßte Kṛṣṇadāsa eine Grammatik des Persischen als *transfer grammar* auf der Basis des Sanskrit, den *Pārasī-prakāśa*; dieser folgt thematisch dem *Sārasvata-vyākaraṇa* (Slaje 1992) und bringt die Hofsprache in Beziehung zur heiligen Sprache der Hindus. – Konversationsgrammatiken wie Varada-rājas *Gīrvāṇa-pada-mañjarī* (17. Jh.) lehrten das umgangssprachliche Sanskrit ihrer Zeit (Deshpande 1993: 33–51); Wezler 1996: 327–346.

## 7. Bibliographie

### 7.1. Primärliteratur

Pāṇini, *Aṣṭādhyāyī = Pāṇini's Grammatik.* Hg. von Otto Böhtlingk. Leipzig, 1887. [Nachdr., Hildesheim: Olms, 1964.]

Patañjali, *Vyākaraṇa-Mahābhāṣya = The Vyākaraṇa-Mahābhāṣya.* Hg. von F. Kielhorn. Bombay 1880–85. (3. Aufl., K. V. Abhyankar. Poona: BORI, 1962–1972.)

Candragomin, Cāndravyākaraṇa = *Cāndravyākaraṇa of Candragomin.* Hg. von K. C. Chatterji. Poona: Deccan College, 1953–1961.

Devanandin, *Jainendravyākaraṇa.* Hg. von Śambhunāth Tripāṭhi. Benares: Bhāratīya Jñānapīṭh, 1956.

Hemacandra, *Śabdānuśāsana = Śrīsiddhahemacandra Śabdānuśāsanam.* Hg. von Vijayalāvaṇya Sūri. Bombay, 1960.

## 7.2. Sekundärliteratur

Abhyankar, K. V. 1962. *The Paribhāṣenduśekhara of Nāgojībhaṭṭa edited critically.* Poona: BORI.

Belvalkar, Shripad Krishna. 1915. *An Account of the Different Existing Systems of Sanskrit Grammar.* Poona: The Author.

Bronkhorst, Johannes. 1986. *Tradition and Argument in Classical Indian Linguistics.* Dordrecht: D. Reidel.

Deshpande, Madhav. 1978. "Pāṇinian Grammarians on Dialectal Variation". *The Adyar Library Bulletin (Brahmavidyâ)* 42.61–114.

–. 1980. *Evolution of Syntactic Theory in Sanskrit Grammar.* Ann Arbor: Karoma.

–. 1985. *Ellipsis and Syntactic Overlapping.* Poona: BORI.

–. 1993. *Sanskrit & Prakrit.* Delhi: Motilal.

Geiger, Wilhelm. 1923. *Elementarbuch des Sanskrit.* 3. Aufl. Berlin: de Gruyter.

Glinz, Hans. 1962. *Die innere Form des Deutschen.* 3. Aufl. Bern: Francke.

Kahrs, Eivind G. 1992. "What is a *tadbhava* Word?" *Indo-Iranian Journal* 35.225–249.

Kielhorn, Franz. 1876. *Kâtyâyana and Patañjali.* Bombay.

Kiparsky, Paul. 1982. *Some Theoretical Problems in Pāṇini's Grammar.* Poona: BORI.

Oberlies, Thomas. 1989. *Studie zum Cāndravyākaraṇa.* Stuttgart: Steiner.

–. 1995. "Das zeitliche und ideengeschichtliche Verhältnis der Cāndra-Vṛtti zu anderen V(ai)yākaraṇas". *Studien zur Indologie und Iranistik* 20.1–55.

Ojihara, Yutaka. 1961–64. "Causerie Vyākaraṇique (III)". *Journal of Indian and Buddhist Studies* 9:2 (1961) 753–749; 10:2 (1962) 776–766; 12:2 (1964) 847–845.

Pisani, Vittore. 1957. "On the Origin of Prākṛtam and Pāli as Language-Designations". *Felicitation Volume presented to Professor Sripad Krishna Belvalkar,* 185–191. Banaras: Motilal.

Scharfe, Hartmut. 1971. *Pāṇini's Metalanguage.* (= *Memoirs of the American Philosophical Society,* 89.) Philadelphia: American Philosophic Society.

–. 1977. *Grammatical Literature.* Wiesbaden: Harrassowitz.

Sharma, Peri Sarveswara. 1985. "Haradatta's Padamañjarī: An Analysis". *Aligarh Journal of Oriental Studies* 2.75–94.

Slaje, Walter. 1992. "Der Pārasīprakāśa". *Akten des Melzer Symposiums 1991,* 243–273. Graz: Leykam.

Thieme, Paul. 1980. "Mißverstandener Pāṇini". *Zeitschrift der deutschen morgenländischen Gesellschaft* Supplement V, 280–288.

–. 1982. "Meaning and the Form of 'Grammar' of Pāṇini". *Studien zur Indologie und Iranistik* 8/9. 3–34.

Wezler, Albrecht. 1996. "Do you speak Sanskrit?". *Ideology and Status of Sanskrit* ed. by Jan E. M. Houben, 327–346. Leiden: Brill.

Whitney, William D. 1885. *The Roots, Verb-forms and Primary Derivatives of the Sanskrit Language.* Leipzig: Breitkopf & Härtel.

–. 1893. "On Recent Studies in Hindu Grammar". *American Journal of Philology* 14.171–197.

Wujastyk, Dominik. 1986a. "An Introduction to the *Paribhāṣāvṛtti* of Vyāḍi". *Oxford University Papers on India,* vol. I, 1. Delhi: Oxford Univ. Press.

–. 1986b. *Metarules of Pāṇinian Grammar: The* Vyādīyaparibhāṣāvṛtti. Groningen: Forsten.

Yudhisthir Mīmāṃsaka. 1973. *Saṃskṛt Vyākaraṇaśāstra kā Itihās,* vol. I (3. Aufl.), vol. II (2. Aufl.). Bahālgaḍh: Ramlal Kapur Trust.

*Hartmut Scharfe, Los Angeles (USA)*

# 19. Indian theories on phonetics

1. Preformal phonetic conceptions in Vedic India
2. Possible beginnings of a Sanskrit alphabet in the *Atharvaveda*
3. Phonetic categories in the late Vedic literature
4. Beginnings of a formal tradition
5. *Prātiśākhyas* and *Śikṣās*
6. The Sanskrit alphabet
7. Articulatory processes and phonetic distinctiveness
8. Levels of distinctiveness and phonological rules
9. Other levels of distinctiveness
10. Gradual decline of the tradition of Sanskrit phonetics
11. Bibliography

## 1. Preformal phonetic conceptions in Vedic India

The formal treatment of phonetics begins in ancient India in texts called *Prātiśākhyas* and *Śikṣās*. These texts, at least in the form in which they have come down to us, belong to a post-Vedic period. In the period of the Vedic literature (1500–500 BC), the sacred scriptures of the Hindus, there was no formal treatment of phonetics, and yet one must seek the origins of the formal systems of phonetics in the preformal speculations concerning sounds in particular, and language in general, which are found throughout the Vedic period. Very few of the technical terms found in the later treatises on Sanskrit phonetics, i. e., *Prātiśākhyas* and *Śikṣās*, go back to the period represented by the *Ṛgveda*, the oldest of the Vedic texts (1500–1000 BC). Similarly, while looking at these preformal speculations, one needs to keep in mind that conceptions relating to language and linguistic units are part of a larger set of religious, magical, and philosophical conceptions.

Among these very old preformal conceptions are the notions of meters, metrical feet, words, and syllables. The *Ṛgveda* already refers to various different meters by name, e. g. *Gāyatrī*, *Bṛhatī*, and *Triṣṭubh*. The Vedic meters have two prominent features, namely a fixed number of metrical feet for a verse, and a fixed number of syllables in a metrical foot. The ancient word for a metrical foot is *pada*, which also literally means a foot. Perhaps, because a typical verse has four feet, and because the language is frequently referred to as a holy cow in the Vedas, the word for foot was naturally extended to a metrical foot. The use of the word 'foot' for a metrical foot is found in many Indo-European languages, and is, therefore, probably very old. In the Vedic language, this word, *pada*, occasionally also means a word or a name. This is, in all likelihood, a somewhat later extension of the term. However, in later Sanskrit, the word *pada* comes to refer primarily to words, and a new, though related, term, *pāda*, comes to be used for metrical foot. This change seems to have come about toward the end of the Vedic period, and is fully reflected in the formal literature on grammar, etymology and phonetics.

Another term of great importance, *akṣara* "syllable", is also found right from the oldest period of the Vedic literature. In fact, it is quite significant that the common Sanskrit term for "sound", *varṇa*, is not found until the very late Vedic period, while the term for "syllable", *akṣara*, is found from the very beginning. In the *Ṛgveda*, one finds a belief that a syllable is the very basic unit or measure of language. In terms of Vedic mysticism of language, everything ultimately rests in the divine syllable, which is in the highest heaven, or, perhaps, which is the highest heaven. *Ṛgveda* (1.164.24) is crucial to our understanding of the early notions of 'linguistic units': "With the *Gāyatrī* foot, he [i. e., the Vedic seer] measures the *Arka*; with the *Arka* the *Sāman*; with the *Triṣṭubh* foot the *Vāka*; with the two-foot and four-foot *Vāka* the recitation; with the syllable the seven voices." It seems that the attention of the ancient Vedic poet-thinkers was focused primarily on those linguistic units which were numerically fixed in some sense. Thus, the smallest countable unit is a syllable. For example, there are eight syllables in a *Gāyatrī* foot. However, these eight syllables may contain any number of individual sounds, and hence the number of sounds was not a countable number. Similarly, one should keep in mind the possibility that syllables, or rather the accoustic peaks in syllables, were noticeable and countable even to the preliterate folks, while the nature of individual sounds was not yet easily discernible, and remained subject to doubts for a long time. Meters, defined in terms of a fixed number of syllables in each foot, also probably go back to a common Indo-European period, and hence the notion of 'syllable', though not the term *akṣara*, is indeed very ancient.

## 2. Possible beginnings of a Sanskrit Alphabet in the *Atharvaveda*

An important conjecture has been advanced concerning the beginning of the tradition of Sanskrit phonetics by Paul Thieme (1985: 559). He renders the first verse of the *Śaunakīya Atharvaveda* (1.1) as: "The thrice seven that go around, wearing all the shapes – let the Lord of Speech put their powers into my body's [parts] today." What does the expression "thrice seven" (= 21) refer to? Thieme examines various interpretations offered by scholars and after a detailed argumentation concludes that these twenty-one are the twenty-one sounds of Sanskrit as conceived by the Vedic poets. He lists these as follows (1985: 563–564):

| | |
|---|---|
| *a i u ṛ e o ai au* | 8 vowels |
| *y r l v* | 4 semi-vowels |
| *k c ṭ t p* | 5 occlusives |
| *ś ṣ s h* | 4 sibilants |

Arguing for these as the earliest isolated sounds of Sanskrit, he reasons backward from the developed categories of the later phonetic treatises, where, for example, *a* stands for the whole class of *a* sounds differing in quantity, accents and nasality, and where a stop like *k*, followed by the term *varga* "class", refers to the whole class of *k*, *kh*, *g*, *gh*, and *ṅ*. Thieme (1985: 563) claims that "the sacred number 'thrice seven' could indeed be taken as the number of the abstract forms (*ākṛti-*), of the types, the kinds (*varṇa-*) of sounds of the sacred language." These sounds "wear all [possible] shapes" and thus provide the rest of the sounds of the Sanskrit language. While Thieme's conclusions are generally acceptable, with certain reservations, one could perhaps argue that this earliest phase reflects a state of knowledge where certain phonetic features were perhaps understood more than others, and that the number twenty-one, in all likelihood, is a reflection of this early non-analytical phase, rather than an allusion to 'types' found in the later developed tradition of Sanskrit phonetics. In fact, it is possible to make a reasonable case that, in this earliest phase, vowels were distinguished from consonants, though it is not clear whether semi-vowels were clearly differentiated from vowels. It seems that the phonetic feature of point of articulation was also implicitly understood. This explains the distinctions between *a*, *i*, *u* etc., or between *k*, *c*, *ṭ*, *t*, and *p*. Distinctions of voicing, aspiration etc. were probably not yet analytically understood. This may have happened at a later date.

## 3. Phonetic categories in the late Vedic literature

As we move to the later Vedic literature, i. e., *Brāhmaṇa*, *Āraṇyaka*, and *Upaniṣad* texts, we find a gradual unfolding of conceptual categories. A full spectrum of linguistic units is seen in the *Śāṃkhāyana-Brāhmaṇa* (26.5). This passage is particularly significant in our understanding of how the notion of various segments may have arisen and how it may have formed a part of the recitational and ritual practice:

"Daivodāsi Pratardana having gone to a sacrificial season of the Naimiṣīyas and having glided up asked a question on this point of doubt, 'If the priest in the Sadas should call attention to a flaw passed over or any one of the priests should note it, how would you remove the flaw?' They were silent; Alīkayu Vācaspatya was their Brahman priest; he said 'I know that not; but will ask Jātūkarṇya, the aged teacher of those formerly.' Him he asked, 'If the performer himself should note a flaw passed over or another should call attention to it, how is that flaw to be made flawless? By repetition of the Mantra or by an oblation?' 'The Mantra should be recited again,' Jātūkarṇya said. Him Alīkayu again asked, 'Should one recite in full the Śastra or recitation or Nigada or offering verse or whatever else it be?' 'So much as is erroneous only need be repeated, a verse (*ṛcam*), or half verse (*ardharcam*), or quarter verse (*pādam*), or word (*padam*), or individual sound (*varṇam*),' Jātūkarṇya replied."

This is an extremely important passage which provides a valid pre-grammatical rationale for recognizing the constituents of speech units. Not only do we find there a clear distinction between a *pāda* "metrical foot" and *pada* "word", we also find one of the early uses of the term *varṇa* to refer to "sound", in contrast with the older term *akṣara* "syllable". Thus, there is clear conceptual and terminological progress from metrical feet to words, and from syllables to individual sounds. Another interesting feature of the above passage is the order in which the successively smaller segmentations are listed: a verse (*ṛcam*), half verse (*ardharcam*), quarter verse (*pādam*), word (*padam*), individual sound (*varṇam*). This would seem to imply the sequence of segmentation into successively smaller units.

While Thieme's interpretation of the initial verse of the *Atharvaveda* will always remain conjectural, the *Śāṃkhāyana-Brāhmaṇa* clearly shows the movement of early analysis from syllables to individual sounds. It also shows the emergence of the term *varṇa* in this sense, a term which only refers to colors and social classes in the earlier literature. As we move into the late Vedic period, we see further advances into our phonetic understanding of Sanskrit sounds. The *Aitareya-Āraṇyaka* (2.2.4) says:

"Thus, this [collection of] a thousand *Bṛhatī* verses comes into existence. Of that collection, the consonants (*vyañjana*) are the body, the voice (*ghoṣa* "vowels") is its soul, and the sibilants (*ūṣman*) are its vital breath."

In *Chāndogya-Upaniṣad* (2.22.5), we have the following prescriptive passage:

"All vowels (*svara*) should be pronounced with resonance (*ghoṣa*) and force. All sibilants (*ūṣman*, lit. "aspiration-sounds") should be pronounced open, and not constricted or spitted out. All stops (*sparśa*, lit. "contact sounds") should be pronounced as slightly incomplete."

In these two important passages, one gets a reflection of the pre-systematic beginnings of the science of phonetics iin ancient India. The vowels are distinguished from consonants, and among consonants, a distinction is made between stops, i. e. 'contact' sounds, and sibilants, i. e. 'aspiration' sounds. The notions of "resonance" (*ghoṣa*), openness in the pronunciation of sibilants, and contact in the pronunciation of stops have also emerged. However, it is important to note that these passages do not mention the conception of a semi-vowel. Similarly, while the passage mentions the term *ghoṣa* "resonance", it is clearly connected exclusively with vowels, and not with consonants. Hence, the distinctions between voiced vs voiceless consonants and aspirated stops vs unaspirated stops have not yet emerged.

The *Aitareya-Āraṇyaka* (3.2.1) dating from the 7/6th century BC, provides the clearest evidence for the emergence of the notion of "semi-vowel" (*antasthā* / *antaḥsthā*), and that initially it was not universally accepted. This text quotes the opinion of a scholar named Hrasva Māṇḍūkeya:

" 'Of this self the truth is like the sibilants (*ūṣman*), the bones the mutes (*sparśa*), the marrow the vowels (*svara*), and flesh and blood, the fourth part, the semi-vowels (*antaḥsthā*),' so says Hrasva Māṇḍūkeya."

After this passage comes a quick rejection:

"We have, however, heard that the number was only three."

This passage provides the clearest evidence that it was the tradition of Hrasva Māṇḍūkeya that proposed the category of semi-vowels as an addition to the three previously accepted categories, i. e. vowels, stops and sibilants, and it is obvious that the author of the *Aitareya-Āraṇyaka* was not about to accept this new proposal. There is evidence that the Māṇḍūkeya tradition of the *Ṛgveda* came from the Northeastern region of Magadha, and represents an innovative tradition, which among other things admitted more retroflexion into the texts of the *Ṛgveda*, as compared to other more conservative traditions. A discussion found in the *Aitareya-Āraṇyaka* regarding some specific sounds in the recitation of the *Ṛgveda* among these early scholars is very instructive about the level of attention paid to phonetic details. The *Aitareya-Āraṇyanka* (3.2.6) reports:

"Now Kṛṣṇahārīta proclaims this secret doctrine, as it were, regarding speech to him. Prajāpati, the year, after creating creatures, burst. He put himself together by means of the meters, therefore it is the *saṃhitā*. Of that *saṃhitā*, the sound *ṇ* is the strength, the sound *ṣ* the breath, the self. He who knows the *saṃhitā* and the sounds *ṇ* and *ṣ*, he knows the *saṃhitā* with its breath and its strength. [...] If he is in doubt whether to say it with an *ṇ* or without an *ṇ*, let him say it with an *ṇ*. If he is in doubt whether to say it with an *ṣ* or without an *ṣ*, let him say it with an *ṣ*. Hrasva Māṇḍūkeya says: "If we repeat the verses according to the *Saṃhitā*, and if we recite according to the teaching of the Māṇḍūkeya, then the sounds *ṇ* and *ṣ* are obtained for us." Sthavira Śākalya says: "If we repeat the verses according to the *Saṃhitā*, and if we recite according to the teaching of the Māṇḍūkeya, then the sounds *ṇ* and *ṣ* are obtained for us."

## 4. Beginnings of a formal tradition

Sometime around 700 BC, it seems that there occurred a process of linguistic standardization of the orally received Vedic literature in north India. For instance, the *Ṛgveda*, which was composed in the northwestern dialect of Indo-Aryan, in which all IE **l* were reduced to *r*, was later preserved in a different dialectal region of Northeastern India, where both *r* and *l* are found. By this time, a standardized Sanskrit alphabet has come into existence and has a specific name: *akṣara-samāmnāya*. This is a very important term and it continues to be used in the later formal works like *Mahābhāṣya*, which is Patañjali's "Great Commentary" on the famous Sanskrit grammar of Pāṇini. The term *akṣara-samāmnāya* is important also because it shows a connection with the past. The term *akṣara*, which refers to syllables, has been used here to refer to individual sounds. This extension of the term *akṣara* from "syllable" to "sound" is analogous to the extension of the term *pada* from a "metrical foot" to a "word". Thus, alongside the emerging use of the term *varṇa*, extended from color and social group to sound, the old term *akṣara* is also occasionally extended to mean an individual sound. The word *samāmnāya* is used to refer to a "cumulative recitation," an oral catalogue of sounds. This is an alphabet, but not of written letters. The ordered form of this catalogue, which is known to us from the later formal texts, is indeed an effort at standardization. This standardization was necessitated, among other things, by an increasing diglossic gap between the orally preserved ancient Vedic texts and the current form of Sanskrit as well as the vernacular languages.

As the vernaculars lost ancient accents, it became increasingly difficult to properly predict accents in Sanskrit. Already in the period of late Vedic texts, this increasing loss of the ability to pronounce Sanskrit properly was becoming manifest. The following story is quoted from the *Śatapatha-Brāhmaṇa* (1.6.3.8). Tvaṣṭr wanted to have a son who would kill god Indra. For this purpose he recites a mantra: *svāhā índraśatrur vardhasva.* He wanted to say: "May you, the killer of Indra, prosper." However, he pronounced the word *índraśatru* wrongly with accent on the first syllable, and then the expression came to mean: "May you, having Indra for your killer, prosper." Had the compound been pronounced with accent on the last syllable, it would have meant "the killer of Indra". This story is later repeated by the Sanskrit grammarians and phoneticians to show the importance of learning grammar and phonetics. The *Aitareya-Āraṇyaka* (3.1.5; 3.2.6), discussed earlier, shows debates concerning sandhis in Vedic texts and whether the Vedic texts should be pronounced with or without the retroflexes *ṣ* and *ṇ*. The process of standardization was meant to put an end to such doubts. The development of the technical apparatus of Sanskrit phonetics seems to have come about to put an effective end to this perception of chaos. The Sanskrit grammarians, in fact, claim that, in the ancient golden age of Vedic studies, the priests first learned grammar, including phonetics, and then they were taught the words of the Vedic scriptures. However, in the later degenerate times, so the grammarians claimed, the priests stopped studying grammar and phonetics before studying the Vedas, and this led to a deplorable state of Vedic recitation.

## 5. *Prātiśākhyas* and *Śikṣās*

The next phase of Sanskrit phonetics is represented in formal treatises called *Prātiśākhyas* and *Śikṣās*. Of these, the *Prātiśākhyas*, as a class, are older than the *Śikṣās*. In their currently available versions, most of these texts contain late revisions, though it is safe to say that the tradition represented by the *Prātiśākhyas* is, in its essence, older than Pāṇini's grammar (±500 BC). There is also a clear linkage between the *Prātiśākhya* tradition and the authorities mentioned in late Vedic texts such as the *Aitareya-Āraṇyaka*. The *Ṛgvedaprātiśākhya* directly refers to Śākalya, the compiler of the existing version of the *Ṛgveda*, and to Hrasva Māṇḍūkeya and Śūravīra Māṇḍūkeya, who are representatives of the Māṇḍūkeya tradition of the *Ṛgveda*, which predated Śākalya's *Ṛgveda*-version. Besides the *Ṛgvedaprātiśākhya*, some of the important texts in this category are the *Taittirīyaprātiśākhya*, the *Vājasaneyiprātiśākhya*, the *Ṛktantra*, and the *Śaunakīya Caturādhyāyikā*. The *Prātiśākhyas*, as indicated by the etymology of the name from *prati* "each" + *śākhā* "branch", are sectarian texts in that each of them relates to a particular Vedic branch and is primarily concerned with describing the phonetic and euphonic peculiarities of a particular Vedic text.

The other class of phonetic treatises is referred to by the general term *Śikṣā*. The word *śikṣā* refers to training in general, and phonetic or recitational training in particular. It appears in the *Taittirīya-Upaniṣad* (1.2) which refers specifically to six types of training involved in phonetic education, i. e. *varṇa* "sounds", *svara* "accents", *mātrā* "quantity", *bala* "force", *sāma* "even articulation", and *santāna* "continuity in recitation". In later times, over a hundred texts called *Śikṣās* were produced by different authorities. Most of the surviving *Śikṣā* texts are of a relatively late period. The most well known among these *Śikṣās* is the *Pāṇinīya-śikṣā* attributed by the tradition to the famous Sanskrit grammarian Pāṇini. Other important *Śikṣās* include the *Vyāsa-śikṣā*, the *Āpiśali-śikṣā*, the *Yājñavalkya-śikṣā*, and the *Nārada-śikṣā*. A few of these *Śikṣā* texts, such as the *Pāṇinīya-śikṣā* and the *Āpiśali-śikṣā*, are non-sectarian in the sense that they do not attach themselves to a particular Vedic school, and deal with the Sanskrit language in a generic way. However, most *Śikṣā* texts are sectarian. They are attached to particular Vedic schools, and deal with the recitation of particular Vedic texts. They often provide the most minute details of the recitational practice.

## 6. The Sanskrit alphabet

However, besides such specific details which may be restricted to a particular Vedic text, the *Prātiśākhyas* and *Śikṣās* share a general description of Sanskrit sounds, the formation of a Sanskrit alphabet and details of articulatory descriptions and formation of sandhi rules. The description of articulatory features

Tab. 19.1.: Generalized Sanskrit alphabet found in the *Prātiśākhyas* and *Śikṣās*.

| | | | | | |
|---|---|---|---|---|---|
| **Vowels (*svara*)** | | | | | |
| **Simple (*samāna*)** | *a ā i ī u ū ṛ ṝ ḷ* | | | | |
| **Compound (*sandhyakṣara*)** | *e o ai au* [or *e ai o au*] | | | | |
| **Stops (*sparśa*)** | | | | | |
| | -voice -asp -nas | -voice +asp -nas | +voice -asp -nas | +voice +asp -nas | +voice -asp +nas |
| **Velar (*kaṇṭhya*)** | *k* | *kh* | *g* | *kh* | *ṅ* |
| **Palatal (*tālavya*)** | *tc* | *ch* | *j* | *jh* | *ñ* |
| **Cerebral (*mūrdhanya*)** | *ṭ* | *ṭh* | *ḍ* | *ḍh* | *ṇ* |
| **Dental (*dantya*)** | *t* | *th* | *d* | *dh* | *n* |
| **Labial (*oṣṭhya*)** | *p* | *ph* | *b* | *bh* | *m* |
| **Semi-vowels (*antaḥsthā*)** | *y r l v* [or *y v r l*] | | | | |
| **Aspirations (*ūṣman*)** | *ś ṣ s h* | | | | |

of sounds and the formation of an ordered alphabet are directly related to each other. The ordered alphabet of Sanskrit reflects the consideration of articulatory features of Sanskrit sounds. For a generalized Sanskrit alphabet found in the *Prātiśākhyas* and *Śikṣās*, without going into details of individual differences see table 19.1.

Other sounds included in the alphabetical listings, with differing placement, are *ḥ* (*visarga*), *ṃ* (*anusvāra*), *ẖ* (*jihvāmūlīya*, guttural aspiration), *ḫ* (*upadhmānīya*, labial aspiration), and *ḷ* (*duḥspṛṣṭa*, retroflex *l*). The alphabet as presented above is indeed based explicitly upon a deep understanding of the articulatory processes and features. There are several principles manifest in the order of the sounds. The sounds, in each group, such as the three pairs *a*, *ā*, *i*, *ī*, *u*, and *ū* are listed from the back of the oral cavity, i. e. the throat, to the front of the oral cavity, i. e. the lips. The same principle is seen in the ordering of the five series of stops beginning with *k*, *c*, *ṭ*, *t*, and *p*. Within each series, there is a consistent logic. The *Prātiśākhyas* and *Śikṣās* offer various theories concerning the relationships between these sounds. For instance, a theory mentioned in the *Ṛgvedaprātiśākhya* and a *Śikṣā* cited in a commentary on the *Śaunakīya Caturādhyāyikā* explains the relationship of the five stops in each series. It claims that the first stop, e. g. *k*, is the only primitive sound. The stop *kh* is derived by combining *k* with a guttural aspiration, i. e. *ẖ* (*jihvāmūlīya*). The stop *g* is derived by adding the primitive voicing (*ghoṣa*) represented by the vowel *a* to *k*. The voiced aspirate *gh* is derived by adding the voiced aspiration *h* to *k*. Finally, the nasal *ṅ* is derived by adding the primitive voiced nasal *ṃ* to *k*. The same general logic holds true in all the five series of stops.

## 7. Articulatory process and phonetic distinctiveness

The sounds which are listed in the alphabet are generally called *varṇas*. How did the Sanskrit phoneticians arrive at this listing? What is it that distinguishes one *varṇa* from another? An answer to this question is provided in the following verse from the well known *Pāṇinīyaśikṣā*:

"[The *varṇas* are distinguished from each other] on the basis of *svara* "accent", *kāla* "time, duration", *sthāna* "point of articulation", *prayatna* "manner", and *anupradāna* "phonation"."

If two sounds differ in any of these listed features, then those two sounds represent different *varṇas*. Thus, for instance, the sounds *a* and *i* differ in their point of articulation (*sthāna*) and, therefore, are two different *varṇas*. Similarly, the sounds *a* and *ā* differ in duration (*kāla*), and, therefore, are two different *varṇas*. The sounds *k* and *kh* differ in the speed of phonation (*śīghratara-anupradāna* or *mahāprāṇa*, i. e., aspiration), while the sounds *k* and *g* also differ in their phonation (*anupradāna*, i. e. voiceless breath vs. voicing). The sounds *i* and *c* differ in their manner (*prayatna*). This, in general, illustrates the principle of distinctiveness used in the formation of Sanskrit alphabet. One category not listed in this verse is that of *karaṇa* or the moving organ in the oral cavity which comes into contact with or approaches different points of articulation. These features are, in general, as follows:

*svara* "accents", i. e. different pitch-levels
*udātta* "high", *anudātta* "low", *svarita* "rising-falling"
*kāla* "vowel length", i. e. duration
*hrasva* "short", *dīrgha* "long", *pluta* "prolated"
*sthāna* "point of articulation", along the oral cavity
*kaṇṭha* "throat", *jihvāmūla* "tongue-root", *tālu* "hard-palate", *mūrdhan* "cerebrum", *dantamūla* "alveolar ridge", *danta* "teeth", *oṣṭha* "lips", *nāsikā* "nose"
*karaṇa* "moving organ", generally referring to different parts of the tongue, but sometimes to teeth, the lower lip, and the nose.
*prayatna* "manner", i. e. the way the moving organ (*karaṇa*) relates to *sthāna*
*sparśa* "contact" versus *aspṛṣṭa* "non-contact", and different degrees of contact
*upasaṃhāra* "approximation, approaching"
*vivṛta* "open", and degrees of openness such as *īṣadvivṛta* "slightly open", *vivṛtatara* "more open", and *vivṛtatama* "most open".
*saṃvṛta* "close"
*anupradāna* phonation, quality of air passing through the glottal aperture
*śvāsa* "voiceless air" with open (*vivṛta*) glottal chords (*kha*; lit. "hole or aperture of the throat")
*nāda* "resonating air" with close (*saṃvṛta*) glottal chords
*hakāra* combination of *śvāsa* and *nāda* with glottal chords partially open

There are certain ambiguities in these traditional conceptions. While *svara* "accent" is listed as a feature distinguishing one *varṇa* from another, varieties of vowels differing in accents are not generally listed in the alphabet as different *varṇas*. Similarly a feature like nasality has a certain ambiguous status. While the sounds *d* and *n*, which differ in nasality, are listed as separate *varṇas*, the sounds *a* and *ã*, which also differ in nasality, are not listed as separate *varṇas*. Generally, different *varṇas* of the Sanskrit phoneticians constitute different phonemes, i. e., we can find contrastive minimal pairs such as *kūpa* / *sūpa* / *yūpa*, where the change of one sound makes a difference in meaning. However, for several sounds listed as *varṇas* by the Sanskrit phoneticians, it is not easy to find contrastive minimal pairs. Thus, for instance, the *varṇas* *ṅ* and *ñ* cannot be demonstrated to be phonemes in Sanskrit through minimal contrastive pairs. Considering the fact that these sounds generally occur in the environment of velar and palatal consonants, respectively, they are allophones of *n* in Sanskrit. However, for the Sanskrit grammarians, they are separate *varṇas*, partly because one cannot interchange them in the recitation of the Vedas, and partly because, they complete the alphabetic matrix in a way parallel to *ṇ*, *n*, and *m*. There is also an additional likely reason for treating sounds like *ṅ* and *ñ* as separate *varṇas*. At least the *Pāṇīniya-Śikṣā* (verse 2, *prākṛte saṃskṛte cāpi*) says that the listing of sixty-three or sixty-four *varṇas* is made with reference to Prakrit and Sanskrit. If this is the case, one can find contrastive minimal pairs for these sounds in Prakrit languages.

In general, however, the determination that a sound was a distinct *varṇa* was not necessarily based on the notion of finding minimal contrastive pairs in Sanskrit, as is done in modern linguistics, but on the assumption that if one were to replace a given *varṇa*, it may either produce another word, or a totally wrong sequence in that language. The concern was with the proper pronunciation of language, and hence the modern distinction of phoneme versus allophone is quite irrelevant to this ancient concern. For instance, Patañjali says that if we mispronounce sounds, then the word *śaśa* "rabbit" might be mispronounced as *ṣaṣa*, the word *palāśa* "a specific tree" might be mispronounced as *palāṣa*, and the word *mañcaka* "couch" might be mispronounced as *mañjaka*. None of the resulting mispronunciations are lexical items of Sanskrit. Yet, Patañjali says that such mispronunciations should be avoided. The same point is illustrated with the story concerning the expression *indraśatru* discussed earlier. Such problems would be there, in the view of the Sanskrit grammarians and phoneticians, irrespective of whether a given sound was a phoneme or an allophone. This makes us aware of the fact that the ancient Indian notion of distinctiveness of *varṇas* is quite different from the notions of phonetic versus phonemic features in modern descriptive terminology.

## 8. Levels of distinctiveness and phonological rules

So far we have seen only one level of distinctiveness in Sanskrit phonetics, i. e., the notion that certain features distinguish *varṇas* from each other. However, there are several different levels of distinctiveness and non-distinctiveness in Sanskrit phonetics and grammar. To begin with, the terms *-varṇa* and

*-kāra* are affixed to individual sounds to provide a terminological difference. For instance, the term *a-varṇa* refers not just to the sound *a*, but to the whole class of *a* sounds: *a*, *ā*, *ā3*, *á*, *ā́*, *ā́3*, *à*, *ā̀*, *ā̀3*, *ã*, *ā̃*, *ā̃3*, *ã́*, *ā̃́*, *ā̃́3*, *ã̀*, *ā̃̀*, and *ā̃̀3*. Patañjali uses the term *avarṇakula* "family of *a*-sounds" to refer to this class. Generally speaking, this affixation of *-varṇa* to a simple short vowel indicates the whole class of vowels which share the same point of articulation (*sthāna*) and manner (*prayatna*), but which may differ in their accents, durations and nasality. With three possible accents, three possible durations, and nasal/non-nasal distinctions, there can be eighteen different kinds of *a* sounds included in the class represented by the term *a-varṇa*. In contrast with this *a-varṇa*, the term *a-kāra* stands for only those *a* sounds which have the same duration as the sound *a* in the term *a-kāra*, namely *a*, *á*, *à*, *ã*, *ã́*, and *ã̀*, and *ā-kāra* stands for all long *ā* varieties, namely *ā*, *ā́*, *ā̀*, *ā̃*, *ā̃́*, and *ā̃̀*. Similarly, while the term *ka-varga* stands for the whole class of velar stops and nasal, i. e., *k*, *kh*, *g*, *gh*, and *ṅ*, the terms *ka-kāra*, *kha-kāra*, *ga-kāra*, *gha-kāra*, and *ṅa-kāra* stand for just the individual sounds *k*, *kh*, *g*, *gh*, and *ṅ*. Thus, while the affixation of the terms *-varṇa* and *-varga* seems to focus exclusively on classes of sounds that share a given point of articulation and a given manner of articulation; the affixation of the term *-kāra* helps focus on a class of sounds which, in addition to the point of articulation and manner, also share the same duration, voicing, aspiration etc. It still leaves, for vowels, the differences of accents and nasality out of focus. Thus, the term *a-kāra* refers to the class of six *a* sounds which have the same duration, but which may differ in accents and nasality.

These two levels of distinctiveness addressed by the affixation of *-varṇa* and *-kāra* are again quite unlike the modern distinction of 'phonetic' versus 'phonemic'. These two levels are used in the formulation of sandhi rules in the Sanskrit phonetic and grammatical treatises. Consider, for instance, the following rules:

Rule 1: *avarṇa* + *avarṇa* ⇒ *ā*
Rule 2: *akāra*+*ḥ* ⇒ *o* / __*Voiced C*

The first rule comes to mean that any variety of *a* combined with any other variety of *a* results in a long *ā*. For the purpose of this rule, the features of point of articulation and manner remain distinctive, while the features of duration, accents and nasality remain non-distinctive. In Rule 2, on the other hand, it is necessary that the sound before *ḥ* be a short *a*. If the sound before *ḥ* were a long *ā*, this particular sandhi rule will not apply. Thus, in this particular rule, the feature of duration becomes distinctive, in addition to the features of point of articulation and manner.

## 9. Other levels of distinctiveness

At a very different level, there is another phonetic feature, i. e. the speed of delivery (*vṛtti*). We are told that there are three speeds of pronouncing the *mantras*, i. e. fast (*druta*), medium (*madhyama*), and slow (*vilambita*). Of these, the fast speed is supposed to be used when a student is reciting the *mantra*s for his own study. In the ritual use of the *mantra*s, one is supposed to use the medium speed. A teacher is supposed to use the slow speed to recite the *mantra*s while teaching his students. Using an inappropriate speed at the wrong occasion creates unacceptable situations, and in this sense, the speed is a distinctive feature at this level. However, for the purposes of euphonic and grammatical phenomena, the feature of speed is not distinctive.

In the work of Bhartṛhari, a grammarian-philosopher of ± 400 AD, there is a notion (*Vākyapadīya* I, 77–79) that there are ontologically eternal true sounds (*sphoṭa*, *varṇa*) which are manifested by the physical sounds (*dhvani*) of two kinds, original physical sounds (*prākṛta-dhvani*) and subsequent modified sounds (*vaikṛta-dhvani*). For our present purpose, it may suffice to note that the level of *sphoṭa* "true sound", in general, seems to reflect only the phonetic features of point of articulation, manner, voicing, aspiration, etc., but not duration or speed. The primary manifesting sounds have the feature of duration. The subsequent modified sounds reveal the features of speed. While Bhartṛhari's notions about the production and manifestation of sound may not be acceptable today, his diagrammatic perception of various phonetic features as concentric circles moving outwards in terms of diminishing distinctive values offers an interesting representation of the various levels of distinctiveness.

## 10. Gradual decline of the tradition of Sanskrit phonetics

In the course of time, the independent branch of Sanskrit phonetics essentially died out, and survived only as a tiny part of the widely studied tradition of Pāṇini's Sanskrit grammar (→ Art. 17, 21). In this manner, phonetic understanding of sounds was preserved more in the form of standardizing catalogues of features, rather than as a vibrant independent study of sounds. Among the different phonetic features, certain phonetic features were better preserved and understood, than others. The features of point of articulation (*sthāna*) and manner (*prayatna*) were relevant to the notion of homogeneity of sounds as defined by Pāṇini (rule 1.1.9). Similarly, the feature of point of articulation was considered to be most critical in choosing a substitute for a given sound. Thus, the feature of manner was divided between internal and external efforts, the internal being relevant for the notion of homogeneity. The features of voicing, aspiration, and accents were relegated to the category of external efforts. The understanding of some of these features finally reached almost a point of extinction, so much that we often find utterly erroneous statements in some of the recent grammatical works by Sanskrit pundits. There was also a general reluctance to actively look at the phonetics of the contemporary pronunciation of Sanskrit, let alone that of the vernaculars. The pundits would rather simply repeat the traditional classifications which they had memorized. For example, a Sanskrit pundit from Bengal would pronounce all three sibilants, i. e. *ś*, *ṣ*, and *s*, in an identical way, i. e. as *ś*. However, he would still speak of a cerebral *ś*, a palatal *ś*, and a dental *ś*. A Sanskrit pundit from Bihar was just as likely to speak of a cerebral *s*, palatal *s*, and a dental *s*. No one realized that the pronunciation of *ḥ* (*visarga*) was no longer voiceless, and that no one could distinguish between *ru* or *ri* and what was supposed to be the vowel *ṛ*. The understanding of accents was almost completely lost. The loss of this phonetic tradition, in view of the relatively continued strength of the grammatical tradition, is most intriguing.

## 11. Bibliography

### 11.1. Primary sources

*Aitareya-Āraṇyaka*, with parts of the *Śāṃkhāyana-Āraṇyaka*. Ed. and transl. by Arthur B. Keith. London: Oxford Univ. Press, 1909.

*Aṣṭadaśa-Upaniṣadaḥ*. Ed. by V. P. Limaye & R. D. Wadekar. Pune: Vaidika Saṃśodhana Maṇḍala, 1958.

*Atharva-Prātiśākhya*. Ed. and transl. by Surya Kanta. Lahore: Mehar Chand Lachman Das, 1939. (Repr., Delhi: Mehar Chand Lachman Das, 1968.)

*Atharvaveda* (*Śaunakīya*), with the *Padapāṭha* and the commentary by *Sāyaṇa*. Ed. by Vishva Banudha. 5 parts. (= *Vishveshvarananda Indological Series*, 13–17.) 1960–1964.

*Bhartṛhari, Vākyapadīya*. Ed. by Wilhelm Rau. Wiesbaden: Steiner, 1977.

*Chāndogya-Upaniṣad*. See: *Aṣṭādaśa-Upaniṣadaḥ*.

*Pāṇinīya-Śikṣā*. Critical ed. of all its five recensions by Manmohan Ghosh. Calcutta: Univ. of Calcutta, 1938.

Patañjali, *Mahābhāṣya*. Ed. by Franz Kielhorn. 3 vols. 1880–1885. (3rd revised ed. by K. V. Abhyankar. Pune: Bhandarkar Oriental Research Institute, 1962–1972.)

*Ṛgveda-Prātiśākhya*. Ed. by Mangal Deva Shastri. Vol. I. Critical text of *RPR*. Banaras: Vaidika Svadhyaya Mandira, 1959. Vol. II. *RPR* with Uvaṭa's commentary. Allahabad: The Indian Press, 1931. Vol. III. *RPR* in English transl. Lahore, 1937.

*Ṛktantra*, a *Prātiśākhya* of the *Sāmaveda*. Ed. by Surya Kanta. Lahore, 1939. (Repr., Delhi: Meherchand Lachmandas, 1971.)

*Śāṃkhāyana-Brāhmaṇa* (= *Kauṣītaki-Brāhmaṇa*). Ed. by Gulabrao Vajeshankar. 2nd ed. Pune: Anandashram.

*Śatapatha-Brāhmaṇa*. Ed. by Albrecht Weber. Berlin, 1849. (Repr., *Chowkhamba Sanskrit Series*, 96. Banaras, 1964.)

*Śaunakīyā Caturādhyāyikā*. Critical ed. with three commentaries. Ed., transl. and annot. by Madhav M. Deshpande. (= *Harvard Oriental Series*, 52.) Cambridge, Mass.: Harvard Univ. Press, 1997.

*Śikṣāsūtrāṇi* (by Āpiśali, Pāṇini, and Candragomin). Ed. by Yudhisthir Mimamsak. Ajmer, Samvat 2024.

*Taittirīya-Upaniṣad*. See: *Aṣṭādaśa-Upaniṣadaḥ*.

*Taittirīya-Prātiśākhya*, with the commentary *Tribhāṣyaratna*. Ed. and transl. by W. D. Whitney. New Haven, 1868.

*Vājasaneyi-Prātiśākhya*, with commentaries by Uvaṭa and Anantabhaṭṭa. Madras: Univ. of Madras, 1934.

Yāska, *Nirukta*, with the commentary of Durga. 2 vols. Pune: Ānandāśrama, 1921, 1926.

### 11.2. Secondary sources

Allen, W. S. 1953. *Phonetics in Ancient India*. London: Oxford Univ. Press.

Bare, James. 1976. *Phonetics and Phonology in Pāṇini*. Ann Arbor: Phonetics Library, Univ. of Michigan.

Cardona, George. 1969. *Studies in Indian Grammarians* I: *The Method of Description Reflected in the Śivasūtras*. (*Transactions of the American Philo-*

*sophical Society*, New Series) Philadelphia: American Philosophical Society.

Deshpande, Madhav M. 1975. *Critical Studies in Indian Grammarians I: The theory of homogeneity [Sāvarṇya]*. Ann Arbor: Center for South and Southeast Asian Studies, The Univ. of Michigan.

Thieme, Paul. 1985. "The First Verse of the Triṣaptīyam (AV, Ś 1.1 ≈ AV, P 1.6) and the Beginnings of Sanskrit Linguistics." *Journal of the American Oriental Society* 105.559–565.

Varma, Siddheshwar. 1929. *The Phonetic Observations of Indian Grammarians*. London, 1929. (Indian Reprint Edition, Delhi. 1961.)

*Madhav M. Deshpande, Ann Arbor (USA)*

# 20. Language and thought in the Sanskrit tradition

1. Introduction
2. Buddhist Abhidharma and Sarvāstivāda
3. Meditative experience as a source of relevant data
4. Perceptive knowledge and language
5. Bhartṛhari on language and thought
6. Diṅnāga on perception and language
7. Other reactions on Bhartṛhari
8. Mīmāṁsā: Kumārila and Maṇḍana Miśra
9. Nyāya: Jayanta Bhaṭṭa and Gaṅgeśa
10. Analysis of 'knowledge derived from words' or 'cognition based on language'
11. Further research
12. Bibliography

## 1. Introduction

According to a statement in the Upaniṣads "the one who knows the bliss of Brahman, from which words and mind revert without having reached it, does not fear anything" (*yato vāco nivartante aprāpya manasā saha* | *ānandaṁ brahmaṇo vidvān na bibheti kutaś cana* || *Taittirīya Upaniṣad* 2.9). Like several other texts and passages in Vedic literature this statement shows that an intimate relation was accepted between language (words) and thought (mind). What is remarkable, however, is that it is here at the same time recognized that there is something beyond both language and thought, and even that it is possible to know this something – the 'bliss of Brahman'. The philosophical problems involved in this statement play a role in the linguistic and philosophical literature of the Sanskrit tradition throughout its long history.

There are numerous problematic aspects to the relation between thought and language, for instance: How is language (spoken or written) perceived and understood? How is a message or idea 'encoded' in language? What truth-claims can be upheld for knowledge based on language (*vis-à-vis* knowledge based on, say, perception; cf. Matilal & Chakrabarti 1994)? What is the relation between language and the process of thinking in general, or of logical thought in particular (cf. Staal 1960 [1988: 59–79])? A basic issue relevant to all these questions is: are thought, thinking, understanding always connected with language – not just at the level of discursive thinking which seems clearly language-related, but also at the level of vaguer thoughts and ideas; or are there 'cognitive episodes' which are entirely 'free from language'? It is this basic issue which was of crucial importance in philosophical and linguistic discussions in the Sanskrit tradition. It is on this basic issue, already evoked by the cited Upaniṣadic statement, that the present article will focus.

At the background of the problems of the relation between language and thought there is a larger problematic set of notions, namely language, thought and reality. Problems concerning language and thought and their relation are always inextricably bound up with ontological questions ('what is real?'), apart from linguistic and epistemological ones. Thus, in the statement cited above, it is presupposed that the 'bliss of Brahman' is a reality – even a knowable reality, and even a reality basic to the entire universe according to Brahminical belief – although it cannot be grasped in language or thinking.

## 2. Buddhist Abhidharma and Sarvāstivāda: Language and thought, and the basic constituents of the universe

Some of the earliest traceable attempts at a systematic (rather than poetic or intuitive) treatment of the problem of language and thought are found in Buddhist Abhidharma-texts, which start to be composed in ca. the 2nd century BCE, some two centuries after the death of Gautama, the Buddha (cf. Frauwallner 1995).

The Abhidharma-texts started as lists of basic doctrinal elements (*dharmas*) in the Buddha's teaching, plus their explanations. Now, already at an early stage the followers of the Buddha, the fully 'awakened' one, considered him to be 'all-knowing': cf. the *Sutta Nipāta*, v. 1133: "they call him Buddha, the Enlightened, [...] with total vision, knowing the world to its ends" (transl. Saddhatissa 1994: 131; on the passage cf. Vetter 1990). Hence, it is not strange that the basic elements in his teaching came to be looked upon as the basic elements of reality as well (cf. further Bronkhorst 1985). A sincere concern with the ontological question 'what is real?' seems to have been common to Buddhist and Jaina thinkers, as well as to emerging Brahminical philosophies such as Sāṁkhya and Vaiśeṣika (Frauwallner 1995: 146). The Abhidharma-authors answered this question with the above mentioned lists of basic elements. These included physical elements such as earth, water, fire and air, as well as mental elements such as faith, suffering, etc. Important discussions on the elements or *dharmas* we find in the Sarvāstivāda school of Buddhism, the school according to which these *dharmas* exist in the past, present and future.

In addition to the physical and mental elements, it was at an early stage felt necessary to accept a category of elements which are neither physical nor mental. This category of *cittaviprayuktas*, as they are called, contained elements such as birth, life, old age, and death; but sometimes we find here also elements with a bearing on language as an instrument of communication: *nāmakāya* "set of names", *padakāya* "set of phrases" and *vyañjanakāya* "set of syllables". According to some, among them Vasubandhu, author of the important work *Abhidharma-Kośa-Bhāṣya* (4th or 5th century CE), these elements *nāmakāya* etc. are merely configurations of speech or sound, and cannot be accepted in the list of basic elements in the universe. Counter-arguments to the view held by Vasubandhu and a defense of the inclusion of the 'signifying units' among the basic elements were offered by Saṁghabhadra, a contemporary of Vasubandhu (Cox 1995: 160–169).

Whether or not these few problematic ones were accepted, the basic elements or *dharmas* were considered to be the only things that were *dravyasat* "substantially existent". All other things (persons, chariots, huts, etc.), whatever their tenacity in daily discourse, are composite objects which are only *prajñaptisat* "nominally or conceptually existing", and they persist on account of language (Williams 1980; Bronkhorst 1996).

## 3. Meditative experience as a source of relevant data

The sources of relevant data accepted in discussions concerning language and thought include, as may be expected in traditions centered around sacred texts, authoritative statements from these texts and from their sacred authors and propounders. Together with this, simple introspection and logical reasoning play roles which may vary in relative importance with different schools of thought. In addition, there is a source which usually plays no role in modern or classical Western traditions of linguistics and philosophy of language: the meditative experiences of ascetics, monks, holy persons etc.

Early comprehensive and well-argued discussions on this source of relevant data are again found with the Buddhists. Accounts of the Buddha's meditative experiences are important in the earliest layers of the Pali-canon (Vetter 1988). Usually, four stages are distinguished in the meditation (*dhyāna*) of the Buddha. What interests us here most is that, according to a description by Vetter (1988: XXVIf.),

> "already at the second stage of *dhyāna*, contemplation and reflection – one could also say every form of discursive reasoning – have disappeared; one is in a state of inner calm and oneness of heart".

While analysis of factors leading from states with thought (*savicāra*) to states without (*avicāra*) was of the highest relevance to practitioners trying to follow the Buddha's path, Buddhist thinkers also plunged into the numerous theoretical problems posed by the acceptance of these states. Thus, quite divergent theories were advanced to explain how thought arises again after the subject has been in a state without thought for some time. According to some, the new thought arises on account of the impressions of the last thought immediately preceding the state without thought; according to others it arises on account of corporeal factors; and according to still others thought is in fact not completely extinguished if someone is in a so-called 'state without thought' (Cox 1995: 119; cf. also Schmithausen 1987). Although these discussions do not focus on language, their relevance for, and inextricable connection with, the problem of the relation between language and thought is obvious. It is interesting to note that in some further reflections on his 1988 description of Buddhist meditation, Vetter (1991: 184f.) observed that, in order to account for the element of awareness ("Bewußtheit") which remains, one should allow for an implicit linguistic vision ("Anschauung") even in the higher meditative states – even though the early sources do not mention anything of the sort and emphasize only the absence of discursive thought.

In the Brahminical Yoga and meditation tradition – influenced by and intimately linked to the Buddhist tradition – a distinction is maintained between a "state with discursive thought" (*savitarka*) and a "state without discursive thought" (*nirvitarka*), and also between a "state with musing" (*savicāra*) and a "state without musing" (*nirvicāra*). The difference between 'discursive thought' and 'musing' is that the former has gross objects and the latter more subtle ones (*Yoga-Sūtra* 1.42–44 and *Bhāṣya* on these).

The theoretical framework of Brahminical Yoga as we find it in Patañjali's *Yoga-Sūtra* and especially in the so-called *Vyāsa-Bhāṣya* (4th century CE?) which comments on it, may be regarded as a form of Sāṁkhya which differs slightly from the classical doctrines of the *Sāṁkhya-Kārikā* (ca. 400 CE?).

Sāṁkhya is one of the six Brahminical philosophical systems which are orthodox in the sense that they accept, at least nominally, the authority of the Veda.

In its classical formulation, Sāṁkhya maintains a sharp distinction between (a) *Puruṣa*, soul or self, which is 'pure consciousness'; and (b) a universal material matrix called *Prakṛti*. In the European tradition 'dualism' stands for a philosophical position according to which all objects accessible to sense-perception, including the body, belong to the sphere of matter; and all thinking, feeling, and so on belong to the sphere of the spirit. Also Sāṁkhya is dualistic, but it accepted quite a different dividing line between spirit and matter. Matter according to Sāṁkhya comprises not just the objects perceptible to the senses but also much of what a European (Cartesian) dualist would consider part of the thinking self or 'ghost in the machine': the mental organ, the *citta* of Yoga, which corresponds to the *buddhi* "intellect", *ahaṁkāra* "ego-awareness", and *manas* "mind" of classical Sāṁkhya. In other words, with Descartes' *cogito ergo sum* "I think, therefore I am" we would still be in the sphere of materiality from a Sāṁkhya point of view. The aim of Sāṁkhya as well as of Yoga is to isolate *Puruṣa* or the soul from the entire sphere of matter, including the mental organ (or intellect, ego-awareness and mind). One may wonder what remains for the soul if we subtract the intellect, ego-awareness and mind. From the ancient Sāṁkhya and Yoga treatises it can be inferred that the soul, if it has realized its distinction from matter and the mental organ, remains a silent witness to all material processes, including processes of thinking. In accordance with this, we may interpret *Puruṣa* as 'pure consciousness (without thought)', as is sometimes done. But it is clear that we enter here a problem area which is not confined to Sāṁkhya, nor even to the Sanskrit tradition. We may well follow the advice of Wittgenstein and remain silent about this alleged consciousness beyond thinking. But the challenge to make language express – or at least approach – the inexpressible appears to be irresistible, in the Sanskrit tradition as much as in the Western tradition (cf. Katz 1978; Forman 1990).

In any case, both thought and speech will belong to the realm of 'matter' according to Sāṁkhya and Yoga. Within matter, these two are fundamentally distinct, but nevertheless commonly confused. Thus, *Yoga-Sūtra* 3.17 speaks of the 'super-imposition' of word, thing-meant and cognition: *śabda-artha-pratyayānām itaretara-adhyāsaḥ*, which the Yoga-practitioner may overcome on his way to the isolation of pure consciousness from materiality.

## 4. Perceptive knowledge and language

Apart from the somewhat extreme and theoretically highly problematic situation of a meditative 'state without thought', there is something else that is of considerable importance in South Asian philosophy and directly relevant to the problem of the relation between language and thought: the situation of "pure perception" (*pratyakṣa*). All philosophical systems accept *pratyakṣa* "perception" as a source of reliable knowledge; they only differ in their definition and in their acceptance of additional sources of reliable knowledge, such as inference and verbal testimony. Some thinkers have put forward arguments according to which perception includes both the process and the knowledge originating from it; although other thinkers did not agree and insisted on a sharp distinction between the process and the result, the two problem areas of perception and of knowledge and thought remained inseparably intertwined throughout the history of South Asian philosophical discussion. And in the usual Sanskrit philosophical terminology, the term for perception, *pratyakṣa*, includes the result of the process of perception, namely the perceptual cognition or knowledge (though the latter is properly called *pramiti*).

To illustrate the issue we may start with the uncomplicated definition of perception as it is found in an early, largely lost Sāṁkhya text, the *Ṣaṣṭitantra* (early centuries CE): "perception is the functioning of the faculty of hearing, etc." (*śrotrādivṛttiḥ pratyakṣaḥ*). The Sāṁkhya-thinker Vindhyavāsin (early 5th century), however, found it necessary, no doubt under the influence of intense philosophical discussions of his age, to explicitly exclude the thinking process, and to modify the definition to: "perception is the conceptualization-free functioning of the faculty of hearing, etc." (*śrotrādivṛttir avikalpikā pratyakṣaḥ*) (cf. Frauwallner 1958).

The philosophers of the Nyāya-system defended a different definition, formulated as follows in the *Nyāya-Sūtra* (early centuries CE?; cf. Potter 1977: 221):

"Perception is that knowledge which arises from the contact of a sense with its object, which cannot be designated, which does not go astray, and which is determinate" (*indriyārtha-saṁnikarṣotpannaṁ jñānam avyapadeśyam avyabhicāri vyavasāyātmakaṁ pratyakṣam, Nyāya-Sūtra* 1.1.4).

Apart from perception, the Nyāya-system accepts "inference" (*anumāna*), "verbal testimony" (*śabda*), and "comparison" (*upamāna*) as sources of reliable knowledge. As far as the perceptive knowledge of perception is concerned, it is the requirement that it "cannot be designated" (*avyapadeśya*) which has given rise to elaborate discussions by Nyāya-thinkers, and to polemics with thinkers of other schools on the possibility or otherwise of a cognitive episode based on perception and entirely 'free from language' (cf. Matilal 1986: 309–354).

## 5. Bhartṛhari on language and thought

Thus, in numerous philosophical schools (not only Buddhist, but also Jaina and Brahminical), problems concerning language and thought posed themselves, but the first extensive treatise in which language and its relation with thought is not a side issue but a major one, can be found not earlier than in the *Vākyapadīya*, the mature and comprehensive work on semantics, linguistics, and philosophy of language, of the Brahminical grammarian-philosopher Bhartṛhari (5th century CE).

Bhartṛhari's work can be seen as a systematic investigation of the presuppositions and basic notions and categories of the grammar composed by Pāṇini (ca. 4th century BCE) and amended and annotated by later grammarians, notably Patañjali (ca. 2nd century BCE). In his investigation, Bhartṛhari takes a grammatical category, for instance 'time', 'gender', 'number' etc., and confronts it with the diverging conceptions of time etc. in the major philosophical schools with which he was familiar. Bhartṛhari's attitude to the various views is generally non-committal: we find him often engaged in demonstrations of the compatibility of Pāṇinian notions, categories and presuppositions with those of quite diverging philosophical schools and systems. At the same time, we do see arise certain 'own' philosophical positions, or at least preferences, from Bhartṛhari's careful discussions of the views of different schools.

One of the preferences concerns the very intimate relation between language and thought and between language and knowledge:

There is no cognition in the world that does not follow language. All knowledge appears as if permeated by words.

If understanding would give up its eternal character of language, the light [of consciousness] would no longer shine. For it is that [language-character of understanding] which produces comprehension.

That [language-character of understanding] functions as the external and internal awareness of living beings. The consciousness in all forms of existence does not go beyond the dimension of that [language-character of under-standing].

(*na so 'sti pratyayo loke yaḥ śabdānugamād ṛte* |
*anuviddham iva jñānaṁ sarvaṁ śabdena bhāsate* ||
*vāgrūpatā ced utkramed avabodhasya śāśvatī* |
*na prakāśaḥ prakāśeta sā hi pratyavamarśinī* ||

*saiṣā saṁsāriṇāṁ saṁjñā bahir antaś ca vartate* |
*tanmātrām avyatikrāntaṁ caitanyaṁ sarvajātiṣu* ||
*Vākyapadīya*, ed. Rau, kā 1.131, 132, 134).

According to both his later followers and his critics, Bhartṛhari would defend here what Matilal (1990: 133ff.) has called "the strong version of Bhartṛhari's thesis":

B1: All cognitive episodes are equivalent to verbal thoughts.

If other passages in the *Vākyapadīya* are taken into account, however, Bhartṛhari seems to be willing to defend only a weaker version:

B2: Most cognitive episodes are verbal thoughts at some implicit level.

Bhartṛhari, as a sort of early 'common-language philosopher', emphasizes the intimate link between language and thought in 'normal' circumstances (cf. the verse quoted above: "There is no cognition in the world [...]"). But he also leaves open – without committing himself – the possibility of 'pure cognitions', perhaps with reference to 'non-worldly', uncommon circumstances such as the above-mentioned meditative experiences (*Vākyapadīya* 3.3.56–57; Houben 1995a: 277–282). On the other hand, Bhartṛhari leaves little room for a 'pure perception' free from language: in some profound way, perception is unavoidably shaped by language:

The difference between *ṣaḍja* [comparable to the musical note "do"] and the other [musical notes] is perceived [only] if it is explained by words; so all divisions of objects are based on the dimensions of words.
It is observed in the case of a torch-wheel etc. [ref. to the fiery circle which one perceives if a torch is turned around very fast], that the form of an object [here: a wheel] is perceived on account of words, even though the [external] basis [of the perception, *viz.* the turning torch] is entirely different.
(*ṣaḍjādibhedaḥ* [read thus instead of *śabdā-*] *śabdena vyākhyāto rūpyate yataḥ* |
*tasmād arthavidhāḥ sarvāḥ śabdamātreṣu niśritāḥ* ||
*atyantam atathābhūte nimitte śrutyupāśrayāt* |
*dṛśyate 'lātacakrādau vastvākāranirūpaṇā* ||
*Vākyapadīya*, ed. Rau, 1.123, 142).

So far we have selected passages in which Bhartṛhari presupposes or explicitly speaks of rather simple cognitions, in which a simple object expressible by a simple word is reflected. The situation becomes considerably more complex if we take into account that both verbal communication and private thinking proceed in sentences and phrases rather than in isolated words. This confronts us with a theoretical problem with far-reaching philosophical and linguistic consequences: should one see words as primary, and sentences and their meanings as based on a combination of words; or are the sentences primary, and are words and their meanings abstracted from the sentence? What is important here is that it becomes clear in Bhartṛhari's elaborate discussion of the problem (Houben 1995b) that the acceptance of the sentence as the primary unit from which words and word-meanings are analyzed, leads to a view in which the importance of external reality (especially the discrete objects corresponding to isolated words) is very much restricted. The realities corresponding to words are rather 'externalized' word-meanings, abstracted from the sentence-meaning which is not anything external but has the character of a cognition:

From the (sentence) meaning which is a cognition, the external meaning, whether or not (in fact) existing, is externalized and analyzed. As for the analysis, it is defined as an analysis of capacities.
(*saṁpratyayārthād bāhyo 'rthaḥ sann asan vā vibhajyate* |
*bāhyīkṛtya vibhāgas tu śaktyapoddhāralakṣaṇaḥ* ||
*Vākyapadīya* 2.445).

## 6. Diṅnāga on perception and language

It can be said that Bhartṛhari catalyzed a 'linguistic turn' as well as powerful counter-currents in Indian philosophy. Apart from the later grammarians who developed their own philosophical school in more definite and polemically defended terms than Bhartṛhari, the Buddhist schools show clear traces of his profound influence. One of the few thinkers who followed Bhartṛhari in his preference for the sentence as the primary unit of language is the Buddhist philosopher Diṅnāga (Hattori 1979; Hayes 1988: 215f.).

While Diṅnāga also accepted an intimate relation between language and thought, and between language and the perception of reality, he continued to defend – *contra* Bhartṛhari – earlier Buddhist ideas on a moment of 'pure perceptive cognition' before any linguistic influence has crept in. Diṅnāga considers perception to be free from conceptual construction (*kalpanā*), which means that the thing perceived is not associated with a 'name, universal, etc.' (*Pramāṇa-Samuccaya*, kārikā 3; Hattori 1968: 25). In his elaboration of this idea, however, Diṅnāga is again close to Bhartṛhari in that this conceptual construction is intertwined with language.

Largely in acordance with the grammarians, Diṅnāga distinguishes five categories of 'conceptual construction', and in each case the object perceived receives a corresponding designation or word category: if the object is associated with a 'name' it receives a proper name as designation (e. g. "John"); if with a 'universal' it receives a common noun (e. g. "cow"); if with a quality it receives a designation such as "white"; if with an action it receives a designation such as "to cook" or "a cook"; if, finally, it is conceptualized as associated with a substance it receives a designation such as "staff-bearer (a person bearing a staff)" or "horned, horn-bearer" (Hattori 1968: 83–85).

For Diṅnāga, direct perception is a very important "source of reliable knowledge" (*pramāṇa*), as he accepts only one other source, namely "inference" (*anumāna*). Language or "verbal testimony" (*śabda*), accepted in Nyāya and other systems as a separate source of knowledge, is according to him nothing but a special form of inference – though indeed a very important one, to which he devotes a separate chapter in his *Pramāṇasamuccaya*. In this chapter, Diṅnāga develops his famous theory of *anyāpoha* "exclusion of the other" (or shorter: *apoha* "exclusion"). Antecedents of *Apoha* can be found in earlier Buddhist works (Hattori 1977), as well as in theories referred to (and not rejected) by Bhartṛhari (e. g. *Vākyapadīya* 3.1.100–103). But Diṅnāga, and later on Dharmakīrti, Diṅnāga's successor and co-founder of the Buddhist logical-epistemological school, elaborated it in a unique way.

According to the *Apoha*-theory, a word such as "cow" does not lead to the cognition of an objectively given universal 'cowness', but merely to the cognition 'not-not-cow' (cf. Hattori 1968: 12). Language is here just like inference, which likewise can only give access to the cognition of a universal or class (*sāmānyalakṣaṇa*), which is not objectively given but a result of mental exclusion (*apoha*). On the basis of the perception of smoke on a hill, for instance, one may infer that there is fire, but we do not have a specific cognition of a particular fire. The object to be inferred is *not* earth, water, etc., which are known to possess no smoke: it is not anything that is not fire, or not-not-fire.

Unlike both inference and its special form, language, perception has direct access to the only things which can be considered 'real', namely the momentary particulars (*svalakṣaṇa* "proper characteristic") which are not yet subjected to conceptualization (*kalpanā*). From this angle it is quite clear how important it was to Diṅnāga to define 'perception' as something separate from anything linguistic.

## 7. Other reactions on Bhartṛhari: Mīmāṁsā, Nyāya, Kaśmir Śaivism

While Bhartṛhari's ideas on the primacy of the sentence and on the pervading influence of language on thought were critically but positively received by the Buddhist Diṅnāga, they were strongly criticized by thinkers of other Brahminical systems such as Mīmāṁsā and Nyāya (on which we will focus below; other interesting systems such as Vaiśeṣika, Vedānta and Jaina [→ Art. 18] will be largely neglected in order to keep the account surveyable). As far as the intimate relation between language and thought is concerned, however, the period of rejection is in both systems followed by a period in which one comes much closer to Bhartṛhari's position. Below we will return to these two systems.

A similar pattern we see in Kaśmir Śaivism: Bhartṛhari was initially strongly criticized by Somānanda (9th/10th century), but later on, with Utpaladeva and especially Abhinavagupta (10th and 11th century) the religious-philosophical environment of Kaśmir Śaivism gave an important place to Bhartṛhari's ideas. In the work of Utpaladeva one can observe a "glaring reversal of Somānanda's attitude towards Bhartṛhari, who, from being a punctiliously criticized and even derided opponent, becomes one of the major inspirers" (Torella 1994: XXIII).

The above-mentioned 'thesis of Bhartṛhari' was defended and elaborated in its strong version (B1): All cognitive episodes are permeated by language. Even the most abstract 'cognitive episodes' which are far removed from 'normal' linguistic expressions and discursive thinking, are considered to be of a 'linguistic' nature. The Kaśmirians distinguished four levels of speech, three of which are already mentioned in Bhartṛhari's *Vākyapadīya* and the *Vṛtti* (kārikā 1.159): these are (1) *Vaikharī*, the Elaborate Speech, which is the speech we perceive with our ears;

(2) *Madhyamā*, the Intermediate, which is sequential, mental speech; and (3) *Paśyantī*, the Seeing one, which is inner, sequenceless speech. The fourth level added by the Kaśmirians is *Parā Vāc*, the Highest Speech, which is beyond the most subtle *Paśyantī*. It is not different from ultimate reality, which in this system is called *Śiva*. The 'linguistic' character even of this ultimate reality or *Parā Vāc* is emphasized, otherwise it would not have a 'conscious' nature. However, unlike the language of the grosser levels, viz. *Madhyamā* and *Vaikharī*, language at the subtle level of *Parā Vāc* is non-conventional and free from conceptualizations (cf. Padoux 1990: 176–177). Commenting on a verse of his predecessor Utpaladeva (*Īśvarapratyabhijñā* 1.5.14), the Kaśmirian Abhinavagupta (ca. 1000 CE) quotes *Vākyapadīya* 1.131–132 (see above) to illustrate the linguistic character of awareness, which he presents as a capacity of *Parā Vāc* (*vimarśanaṁ ca parāvākśaktimayam*).

In his commentary on Bharata's *Nāṭyaśāstra*, Abhinavagupta quotes the same verse 1.131 to support his claim that even bodily gestures are 'pervaded by language': "Indeed, even bodily motions (*kāyaceṣṭā*) are pervaded by subtle motions which are mental and linguistic (*mānasībhiḥ sūkṣmābhiḥ vācikībhiś ceṣṭābhiḥ*), in accordance with the principle 'There is no cognition ...' " (Abhinavagupta, cited by Abhyankar & Limaye in their edition of the *Vākyapadīya*, 1965: 209.)

## 8. Mīmāṁsā: Kumārila (7th century) and Maṇḍana Miśra (8th century)

The system of Mīmāṁsā is rooted in the ancient ritualistic exegesis of Vedic texts. Mīmāṁsā offers rules of interpretation so that clear prescriptions can be derived from the early Vedic texts which leave so many details on the ritual practice implicit, apparently because these were considered well-known to the intended public. Although there were earlier contributions to turn the collection of 'hermeneutical' principles of the old Mīmāṁsā into a full-fledged philosophical system, Kumārila's work is, after the extensive commentary of the less philosophically inclined Śabara, the earliest comprehensive attempt to do so which is still accessible.

As a hermeneutical-philosophical system, Mīmāṁsā is mostly interested in one specific source of reliable knowledge, viz. "verbal testimony" (*śabda*). As we have seen, this was not acknowledged as a separate source of knowledge by Buddhists such as Diṅnāga, who considered it a special form of inference. For Mīmāṁsā, however, it is a separate source, and it is indispensable for knowing *dharma* – an untranslatable term, which in Brahminical works often amounts to "the entirety of religious and moral duties", and in Mīmāṁsā especially to "the entirety of ritual duties". This *dharma* or "duty" is to be understood from the Vedic texts.

While verbal testimony is the indispensable source of knowledge on *dharma*, other sources of knowledge have their validity in their own sphere. Thus, perception is authoritative with regard to objects observable by the senses. Kumārila distinguishes here between a first stage, which he calls *ālocanā* "(mere) perceiving" (a term also important in Vaiśeṣika and Nyāya), and a stage at which the object is not just perceived but also qualified through a universal, attribute, or action etc. In the first stage, the object is perceived in its entirety, in both its particular and general aspect, but the cognition is free from conceptualizations (*nirvikalpaka*), similar to that of a child or mute person (*Ślokavārttika, Pratyakṣasūtra* 112–120). Unlike the Buddhists, Kumārila includes the second stage in which the object is both perceived and conceptualized in his notion of 'perception'. But unlike Bhartṛhari and the Kaśmirians, and in accordance with the Buddhists, he strongly denies the linguistic character of the first, pure perception, which arises directly from the object:

> The cognition which arises with regard to the objects does not have a linguistic form [...]. Just as colour, [taste,] and so on, are separately cognized according to their own nature, even before [their expression in] language, like that their association with a name (*saṁjñitvam*) is only something that follows
> (*na śabdābhedarūpeṇa buddhir artheṣu jāyate* | [...]
> *yathā rūpādayo bhinnāḥ prāk śabdāt svātmanaiva tu* |
> *gamyante tadvad evaitat saṁjñitvaṁ kevalam param* ||
> *Ślokavārttika, Pratyakṣasūtra* 172ab, 175).

The Mīmāṁsā philosopher Maṇḍana Miśra considered himself a follower of Kumārila. Nevertheless, he disagreed with him on several important points; moreover, Maṇḍana's philosophical deliberations were not confined to the field of Mīmāṁsā but included that of grammar and Vedānta. An important problem area which touches the heart of both Mīmāṁsā and grammar is the perception of a special object, namely language. Bhartṛhari had presented and elaborated a theory according to which phonemes give first rise to the grasping of a unitary linguistic unit, which in turn is associated with a meaning. The term which came to be invariably associated with the notion of this unitary linguistic unit (though Bhartṛhari used also other terms) was *sphoṭa*. Now, Kumārila had criticized the notion of *sphoṭa* in strong terms (although it is fair to say that he silently also accepts much of Bhartṛhari's theory, Göhler 1995: 145). Maṇḍana Miśra, however, defended this notion in a special treatise, the *Sphoṭasiddhi* "Establishment of *Sphoṭa*". In this work he quotes profusely from both the work of Kumārila and that of Bhartṛhari. Here, it becomes clear that Maṇḍana accepts, like Bhartṛhari, not only a mental state in which the *sphoṭa* or unitary linguistic sign is clearly and distinctly apprehended, but also a preliminary stage at which the linguistic unit is still vague and undefinable (*anupākhyeya*, cf. Thrasher 1993: 16). This stage of vague perception reminds us of the first perception of Kumārila (*ālocanā*). However, this first perception was a *nirvikalpa* or "conceptualization-free" cognition for Kumārila. How did Maṇḍana think about this? Unfortunately, Maṇḍana did not write a special treatise on this interesting topic. Allan Thrasher (1993) searched for indications in other works, and found that for Maṇḍana probably even the *nirvikalpa* cognition is, in some sense, verbal (though distinct words are here utterly absent). In support he cites for instance from a treatise of Maṇḍana's called *Brahma-Siddhi* "Establishment of Brahman":

> Even the movement towards, for instance, their mother's breast, disregarding other things, that babies show could not be if they did not determine it as 'this'; unless it has been determined whether something is a post or a man there is no activity based on [its being] one or the other. Now, there is no determination without the coloration of words. Therefore even they [children], possessing the influences of words from previous births, have knowledge that is determined by being coloured by the form of speech (*Brahma-Siddhi*, 18.13–17; transl. Thrasher 1993: 88).

This would fit in with other statements of Maṇḍana according to which Brahman is *śabda* "language" (= 'linguistic in nature'?), and seems to be the 'object' of a 'non-dual' "*nirvikalpa* verbal knowledge" of an enlightened person (cf. Thrasher 1993: 98; Biardeau 1969: 91–102).

Whatever Maṇḍana Miśra's direct and indirect importance for South Asian philosophy, his role in Mīmāṁsā remained limited. The two main schools of Mīmāṁsā till the present are the schools of Kumārila Bhaṭṭa and of his earlier contemporary Prabhākara (scholars and followers of the latter have nowadays become very rare). In Vedānta, Maṇḍana Miśra was overshadowed and superseded by Śaṅkara and his mode of Advaita, which did not recognize the 'linguistic' nature of Brahman (on other doctrinal distinctions: Vetter 1969, *Einleitung*).

## 9. Nyāya: Jayanta Bhaṭṭa (9th century) and Gaṅgeśa (14th century)

That cognition would not be possible without language was entirely unacceptable to the Nyāya-philosopher Jayanta Bhaṭṭa. For him there is no basis for the distinction into three levels of speech (*Nyāya-Mañjarī*, ed. Varadacharya 1983: 183–184): The so-called Intermediate speech is not a kind of speech at all, but it is a cognition in which both the expressed and the expressor (or signified and signifier) figure (*naiṣa vācaḥ prabhedaḥ, buddhir vācyaṁ vācakaṁ ca-ullikhantī*); and the so-called Seeing one is but another name for the construction-free cognition (*paśyantīti tu nirvikalpakamater nāmāntaraṁ kalpitam*). In fact, there is only one speech which is well known, viz. the Elaborate one (*ekaiva vaikharī vāg vāg iti prasiddhā hi*).

Commenting on the Nyāya-definition of *pratyakṣa* "perception" (*Nyāya-Sūtra* 1.1.4, see above), Jayanta comes to speak of the purpose of the expression *avyapadeśya* "which cannot be designated". Jayanta discusses various possible reasons why this expression is used in the definition.

The older Nyāya-philosophers (especially Vātsyāyana in his commentary on the *Nyāya-Sūtra*) held that *avyapadeśya* was intended to exclude from perception all cognitions connected with language, so as to make it distinct from verbal testimony, a separate source of reliable knowledge. But with this interpretation too much is excluded from perception for Jayanta, who accepts, much like Kumārila whom he occasionally quotes, that there is an initial stage without conceptualizations, and a second stage in which these are present and also expressible in words. However, when the perceived object is associated with the appropriate word, no new knowledge is added. This view, then, that a perceptual cognition would originate from both sources, sense perception and language, is excluded by *avyapadeśya* (*tasmāt ubhaya-ja-jñāna-vyavacchedārtham evedaṁ padam iti, Nyāya-Mañjarī*, ed. Varadacharya 1970: 221).

The rejected view that a perceptual cognition is (partly) indebted to verbal testimony or language is illustrated with the by now well-known verse of Bhartṛhari: "There is no cognition in the world [...]" (see above). Jayanta suggests that this view of Bhartṛhari would imply that there were no such thing as perception or a perceptual cognition at all, hence there would have been no point in formulating its definition (*Nyāya-Mañjarī*, I, 290).

Radical innovations in the Nyāya-view on perception were introduced in the so-called Navya-Nyāya or New-Nyāya, which has important starting points in the work of Udayana (ca. 11th century), but which finds its first comprehensive 'classical' expression in the work of Gaṅgeśa (late 13th or early 14th century, Potter & Bhattacharya 1993: 85).

Gaṅgeśa agrees with Jayanta that perception is of two kinds, one free from conceptualizations (*nirvikalpaka*) and the other accompanied by these (*savikalpaka*) (*Tattvacintāmani* 857ff.). In the section devoted to the *nirvikalpaka*-kind, he stages a discussion with someone who doubts that there can be any awareness if conceptualizations are entirely absent: After all, we cannot prove this conceptualization-free awareness (and 'conscious' perception) by perception, since perception is what the dispute is about; and we cannot prove it by our *speaking* about perception because that necessarily has to take place on the basis of conceptualizations.

In the discussion which follows, Gaṅgeśa "revived some of the old arguments of Bhartṛhari according to whom each cognitive episode is 'inter-shot' irresistibly with concept or word or what he called *śabda-bhāvanā*" (Matilal 1986: 342). Whether Gaṅgeśa and other Navya-Nyāya thinkers are here indeed more or less directly influenced by Bhartṛhari as Matilal suggests, or whether their new position arose out of centuries of opposition to Buddhists like Diṅnāga and Dharmakīrti, it is difficult to say. As we have seen, in Diṅnāga and Dharmakīrti's system the assumption that there is a pure perception and perceptual awareness entirely free from conceptualization played a fundamental role; but when Navya-Nyāya-thinkers question the feasibility of this, they have to distance themselves also from some aspects of the old Nyāya view on conception-free awareness. A third alternative would be that their new position was a matter of maturity of insight regarding the importance of language and conceptual construction even for perceptual knowledge. In any case, in the final view as Gaṅgeśa defends it, language has encroached considerably on the domain which Jayanta and earlier Nyāya-thinkers had reserved for conceptualization-free perceptual awareness.

It is argued that if we are clearly aware of something, we are aware of it *as* something, and this presupposes a prior awareness of this qualifying something, the distinguishing attribute (*viśeṣaṇa*). A clear perception of a familiar object like a cow is therefore not entirely free from conceptualization. However, with regard to the awareness of 'cowness' as one of the preconditions for the perception of a cow, we may assume a conceptualization-free perception. It is to be noted that the Nyāya-thinkers are 'realists' in the sense that they hold (unlike 'idealists' like certain Buddhists and Vedāntists) that universals, among others, are given independently from our mind. Now Gaṅgeśa admits that even in the perception of the universal 'cowness' memory-traces may play a role. Hence, the discussion focusses on the first perception of a cow in this life (*prāthamikaṁ gaur iti pratyakṣaṁ jñānam*). Even here, perception is accompanied by conceptualization, but with regard to the 'cowness'-part of this perception-as-cognitive-episode, there is absence of conceptualization (*gaur iti savikalpakam api, gotvāṁśe nirvikalpakam, Tattvacintāmani*, 857ff.).

In the words of Matilal (1986: 348):

> The argument of Gaṅgeśa here obviously implies that we do not need to postulate a non-constructive, conception-free, perceptual awareness *always* occurring at the beginning of a constructive, conception-loaded perception. This goes against the general assumption of these philosophers that a sensory awareness in unstructured form must precede all structured, conception-loaded perceptions. Gaṅgeśa's point, if I understand it correctly, is that there is no logical necessity here. Only in some cases, (as in those already described) does such a preconceptual, unstructured perception become 'logically' and causally necessary to precede judgmental perception.

With this, Gaṅgeśa and other Navya-Nyāya-philosophers have come quite close to the 'weaker version of Bhartṛhari's thesis' (B2 above), the only one which Bhartṛhari himself was ready to fully defend even though his later followers preferred to take him as a propounder of the stronger version.

## 10. Analysis of 'knowledge derived from words' or 'cognition based on language'

With the extension of the domain of 'structured, conception-loaded' awareness, also the interest in the analysis of this awareness increased. This analysis took place through language, the unavoidable correlate of clear conceptions (and perhaps also of vague conceptions). In particular, methods were developed to analyse the cognition which arises from linguistic input in the form of, usually, sentences. This cognition is termed *śābda-bodha* "understanding from language or words". On this subject we see new controversies arise, in which Nyāya-thinkers contend with Mīmāṁsā-thinkers and grammarians (the 17th century knows some major discussants). In these controversies, the Pāṇinian system of grammatical analysis is in broad outlines accepted by all. They also adopt much of the new Nyāya-terminology. All thinkers agree that the structure of the *śābda-bodha* or cognition based on language is of the qualifier-qualificand type, but they disagree on what is the qualifier and what the qualificand. The grammarians of this period hold the sentence and sentence meaning (*vākya-sphoṭa* and *vākya-artha*) to be indivisible wholes, but they accept division on a secondary plane, for the sake of analysis. Here, the verb is the qualificand, to be qualified by all the other words of the sentence. The Mīmāṁsā-thinkers, occupied with the ritual and prescriptive part of the ancient Vedic texts, take a special interest in a special kind of sentence, viz. the injunction. For them, the qualificand is not the verb as a whole, but the verbal suffix. For Nyāya-thinkers, finally, the word in the nominative is generally speaking the main meaning-bearing element understood from a sentence, and all other words are its qualifiers (cf. Jha 1986; Matilal 1988).

## 11. Further research

This article has hopefully given an inkling of the complexity and profundity of centuries of philosophical discussions in the Sanskrit tradition which are 'novel' in their treatment of themes playing an important role in the Western tradition as well. It also may have become clear that the philosophical statements made by, for instance, the Sanskrit grammarians or the Nyāya-thinkers were not intended to apply exclusively to, say, these Sanskrit grammarians or Nyāya-thinkers, or to no-one but the South Asians, or to only Brahmins. The statements concern universals of the human condition: the perception of objects through our senses, communication through speech, the having of clear or vague cognitions, and so on. Hence, they have a claim to universal validity, even if this is usually not made explicit. It invites a comparison and confrontation with statements made in other traditions which likewise have an implicit or explicit claim to universal validity.

However, as far as the Sanskrit tradition with its extensive philosophical material is concerned, there is still no solid philological basis for such a comparison. In spite of all that has been accomplished so far, much basic work (in editing, translating, historical location etc.) remains to be done to make important Sanskrit authors such as those mentioned in this article in a satisfactory way accessible to scholars and students (let alone to a larger audience).

## 12. Bibliography

### 12.1. Primary sources

*Advaita Vedānta*. Ed. by Allen Wright Thrasher, *The Advaita Vedānta of Brahma-siddhi.* Delhi: Motilal Banarsidass, 1993.

Bhartṛhari, *Vākyapadīya.* Ed. by K. V. Abhyankar & V. P. Limaye, *Vākyapadīya of Śrī Bhartṛhari.* (= *University of Poona Sanskrit and Prakrit Series*, 2.) Poona: Univ. of Poona, 1965. Ed. by Wilhelm Rau, *Bhartṛhari's Vākyapadīya: Die Mūla-kārikās nach den Handschriften herausgegeben und mit einem Pāda-index versehen.* Wiesbaden: Franz Steiner, 1977.

Gaṅgeśa, *Tattvacintāmaṇi.* Ed. by Ramanuja Tatacharya, *Tattvacintāmani of Gaṅgeśopādhyāya, with Prakāśa of Rucidattamiśra, and Nyāya-śikhāmaṇi on Prakāśa of Rāmakṛṣṇādhvarin.* I. *Pratyakṣakhaṇḍa.* Tirupati: Kendriya Sanskrit Vidyapeetha, 1973.

Jayantabhaṭṭa, *Nyāyamañjarī.* Ed. by K. S. Varadacharya, *Nyāyamañjarī of Jayantabhaṭṭa, with Tippaṇī Nyāyasaurabha by the editor.* 2 vols. Mysore: Oriental Research Institute, 1970, 1983.

Kumārila, *Ślokavārttika.* Ed. by Ganga Sagar Rai, *Ślokavārttika of Śrī Kumārila Bhaṭṭa.. With com-*

*mentary Nyāyaratnākara of Śrī Pārthasārathi Miśra.* Varanasi: Ratna Publications, 1993.

Maṇḍana Miśra, *Brahmasiddhi.* Ed. by Kuppuswami Sastri, *Brahmasiddhi by Ācārya Maṇḍanamiśra. With commentary by Śaṅkhapāṇi.* Madras: Government of Madras, 1937. Transl. by Tilmann Vetter, *Maṇḍanamiśra's Brahmasiddhi: Brahmakāṇḍaḥ| Übersetzung, Einleitung und Anmerkungen.* (= *Sitzungsberichte der österreichischen Akademie der Wissenschaften*, phil.-hist. Klasse, 262: 2.) Wien: Böhlau, 1965.

*Sutta Nipāta.* Transl. by H. Saddhatissa, *The Sutta Nipata.* Richmond, Surrey: Curzon Press, 1994. (1st ed., 1985.)

Utpaladeva, *Īśvarapratyabhijñākārikā.* Ed. and transl. by Raffaele Torella, *The Īśvarapratyabhijñākārikā of Utpaladeva with the author's Vṛtti. Critical edition and annotated translation.* Roma: Istituto per il Medio ed Estremo Oriente, 1994.

### 11.2. Secondary sources

Biardeau, Madeleine. 1969. *La Philosophie de Maṇḍana Miśra vue à partir de la Brahmasiddhi.* Paris: École Française d'Extrême-Orient.

Bronkhorst, Johannes. 1985. "Dharma and Abhidharma". *Bulletin of the School of Oriental and African Studies* 48: 2.305–320.

–. 1996. "Sanskrit and Reality: The Buddhist contribution". *Ideology and Status of Sanskrit: Contributions to the history of the Sanskrit language* ed. by Jan E. M. Houben, 109–135. Leiden: Brill.

Cox, Collett. 1995. *Disputed Dharmas: Early Buddhist theories on existence. An Annotated Translation of the Section on Factors Dissociated from Thought from Saṅghabhadra's Nyāyānusāra.* Tokyo: International Institute for Buddhist Studies.

Forman, Robert K. C. 1990. *The Problem of Pure Consciousness: Mysticism and philosophy.* New York: Oxford Univ. Press.

Frauwallner, Erich. 1958. "Die Erkenntnislehre des klassischen Sāṁkhya-Systems". *Wiener Zeitschrift für die Kunde Süd-Asiens* 2.84–139. [= *Kleine Schriften* 223–278.]

–. 1995. *Studies in Abhidharma Literature and the Origins of Buddhist Philosophical Systems.* Transl. from the German by Sophie Francis Kidd under supervision of Ernst Steinkellner. Albany: State Univ. of New York Press.

Göhler, Lars. 1995. *Wort und Text bei Kumārila Bhaṭṭa: Studie zur mittelalterlichen indischen Sprachphilosophie und Hermeneutik.* (= *Europäische Hochschulschriften*, Reihe XX. *Philosophie*, 468). Frankfurt/M.: Lang.

Hattori, Masaaki. 1968. *Diṅnāga on Perception.* Cambridge, Mass.

–. 1977. "The Sautrāntika Background of the Apoha Theory". *Buddhist Thought and Asian Civilisation: Essays in honor of Herbert V. Guenther on his sixtieth birthday* ed. by L. S. Kawamura & K. Scott, 47–58. Emeryville, Cal.: Dharma.

–. 1979. "*Apoha* and *Pratibhā*". *Sanskrit and Indian Studies* ed. by M. Nagatomi, B. K. Matilal, J. M. Masson & E. Dimock, 61–73. Dordrecht: Reidel.

Hayes, Richard P. 1988. *Dignāga on the Interpretation of Signs.* (= *Studies of Classical India*, 9.) Dordrecht: Kluwer.

Houben, Jan E. M. 1995a. *The Saṁbandha-samuddeśa (chapter on relation) and Bhartṛhari's Philosophy of Language.* Groningen: Forsten.

–. 1995b. "Bhartṛhari's Perspectivism. 2. Bhartṛhari on the Primary Unit of Language". *History and Rationality: The Skövde Papers in the Historiography of Linguistics* ed. by Klaus D. Dutz & Kjell-Åke Forsgren, 29–62. Münster: Nodus.

Jha, V. N. 1986. "The Structure of a *śābdabodha*". *Studies in Language, Logic and Epistemology*, 70–76. Delhi: Pratibha Prakashan.

Katz, Steven T., ed. 1978. *Mysticism and Philosophical Analysis.* (= *Studies in Philosophy and Religion*, 5.) London: Sheldon Press.

Matilal, Bimal Krishna. 1986. *Perception: An essay on classical Indian theories of knowledge.* Oxford: Clarendon Press.

–. 1988. "Śābdabodha and the Problem of Knowledge-representation in Sanskrit". *Journal of Indian Philosophy* 16.107–122.

–. 1990. *The Word and the World: India's contribution to the study of language.* Delhi: Oxford Univ. Press.

– & A. Chakrabarti, eds. 1994. *Knowing from Words: Western and Indian philosophical analysis of understanding and testimony.* Dordrecht: Kluwer.

Padoux, André. 1990. *Vāc: The concept of the word in selected Hindu Tantras.* Transl. by Jacques Gontier. New York: State Univ. of New York Press.

Potter, Karl H. 1977. *The Tradition of Nyāya-Vaiśeṣika up to Gaṅgeśa.* (= *Encyclopedia of Indian Philosophies*, 2.) Delhi: Motilal Banarsidass.

– & Sibajiban Bhattacharya, eds. 1993. *Indian Philosophical Analysis: Nyāya-Vaiśeṣika from Gaṅgeśa* to Raghunātha Śiromaṇi. (= *Encyclopedia of Indian Philosophies*, 6.) Delhi: Motilal Banarsidass.

Schmithausen, Lambert. 1987. *Ālayavijñāna: On the origin and the early development of a concept of Yogācāra philosophy.* Vols. I, II. Tokyo: The International Institute for Buddhist Studies.

Staal, Frits. 1960. "Correlations between Language and Logic in Indian Thought". *Bulletin of the School of Oriental and African Studies* 23.109–122. (Repr., in Staal 1988.)

–. 1988. *Universals: Studies in Indian Logic and Linguistics.* Chicago & London: Univ. of Chicago Press.

Vetter, Tilmann. 1988. *The Ideas and Meditative Practices of Early Buddhism.* Leiden: Brill.

—. 1990. "Some Remarks on Older Parts of the Suttanipāta". *Earliest Buddhism and Madhyamaka* ed. by D. Seyfort Ruegg & Lambert Schmithausen, 36–56. Leiden: Brill.

—. 1991. "Zur religiösen Hermeneutik buddhistischer Texte". *Beiträge zur Hermeneutik indischer und abendländischer Religionstraditionen* ed. by Gerhard Oberhammer, 179–192. Wien: Verlag der Österreichischen Akademie der Wissenschaften.

Williams, Paul M. 1980. "Some Aspects of Language and Construction in the Madhyamaka". *Journal of Indian Philosophy* 8.1–45.

*Jan Houben, Leiden (The Netherlands)*

# 21. The organization of grammar in Sanskrit linguistics

1. Introduction
2. Kinds of rules
3. Organization of the *Aṣṭādhyāyī*
4. Relations among rules and operations
5. Pāṇini's commentators
6. Bibliography

## 1. Introduction

1.1. In India a grammar is conceived of as a set of rules (*śāstra*, *sūtra*, *yoga*, *lakṣaṇa*) that serves to explain (*anvākhyāna* "explanation") through derivation a system of language usage. The objects to be described – correct speech forms (*śabda*) of usage – are considered a target (*lakṣya*), and the rules that apply to derive these objects are considered means to explain (*lakṣaṇa*) the speech forms. Starting with the earliest complete grammar of Sanskrit known to us, Pāṇini's *Aṣṭādhyāyī*, such grammars are composed from a speaker's point of view, so that meaning serves from the very outset to condition the use of bases (*prakṛti*) and affixes (*pratyaya*; → Art. 17, section 3.1.A). The following is based on Pāṇini's work.

1.2. The *Aṣṭādhyāyī* represents a synthetic system: starting with bases, affixes are introduced under stated conditions to form utterances. In deriving utterances, underlying strings are posited from which actually used utterances are derived. For example, (a) in each of the following pairs is a Sanskrit utterance derived from the corresponding posited string (b) (→ Art. 17, section 3.1.A–(3ab)–(4ab)).

(1a) *devadattaḥ kaṭaṅ karoti* "Devadatta is making a mat"
(1b) (*devadatta-s*$_1$) (*kaṭa-am*$_2$) (*kṛ-tip*) [← *kṛ-laṭ*]
(2a) *devadattena kaṭaḥ kriyate* "A mat is being made by Devadatta"
(2b) (*devadatta-ā*$_3$) (*kaṭa-s*$_1$) (*kṛ-ta*) [← *kṛ-laṭ*]

Pāṇini does not have to define what particular stretch of constituents makes up an utterance (*vākya*). On the other hand, there is an interpretation system, represented by major schools of ritual exegesis (*mīmāṁsā*). One of the tasks this system assigns itself is to determine what particular stretch of Vedic material constitutes a yajus (a ritual formula) to accompany a ritual act. To this end, a definition is given of an utterance (*vākya*): A particular stretch constitutes a vākya if it has one purpose (*arthaikatvāt*) and constituents would remain in semantic expectancy (*sākāṅkṣam … syāt*) of others if one split up the unit (*ced vibhāge*). Pāṇini's derivational system, representing the speaker's viewpoint, also does not concern itself with the semantic and syntactic interpretation of utterances. The ritual exegetical system of interpretation, on the other hand, also sets forth principles for determining the relation that is to be accepted between an enjoined ritual act and something that contributes to this act in some manner. Six means of knowing such relations are given: direct statement (*śruti*), conventional capacity of reference (*liṅga*), occurring in a single utterance (*vākya*), contextual mutual expectancy (*prakaraṇa*), textual or ritual position (*sthāna*), and the use of a term in its etymological meaning (*samākhyā*) instead of its conventional meaning. These means take priority in descending order, so that direct statement takes precedence over the next five and so on.

1.3. In Pāṇini's derivational system, there is no strict demarcation between syntax and morphology as envisioned by western linguists. Inflectional endings of forms like *kaṭam* (← *kaṭa-am*), *kaṭaḥ* (← *kaṭa-s*), *karoti* (← *kṛ-u-ti* ← *kṛ-ti* ← *kṛ-l*) are introduced under meaning conditions: affix A follows base B when meaning M is to be signified. For example, any one of ten abstract affixes consisting of *l* and appended markers (***laṭ liṭ luṭ lṛṭ leṭ loṭ laṅ liṅ luṅ lṛṅ***) follows a verbal base if an agent or an object of the action in question is to be signified; a second-triplet nominal ending ('accusative ending') follows a nominal base if an object is to be signified. The distribution of particular endings is described in terms of meanings and basic forms subject to replacement. For example, ātmanepada and parasmaipada affixes – mediopassive and active affixes in western terminology – occur with certain verbal bases depending on whether or not the result of the action is intended for the agent (→ Art. 17, section 3.1.C); a basic nominal ending *ṭā* is replaced by *ina* if it follows a stem in *-a* (→ Art. 17, section 4.1.). What in western terms could be treated as derivational morphology is part of affixation that serves to form basic strings or which applies to elements in such strings. For example,

(3b) *devadatta-$s_1$ kaṭa-ām$_6$ kṛ-tṛ-$s_1$*
serves to derive
(3a) *devadattaḥ kaṭānāṅ kartā*
"Devadatta (is) a maker of mats"

The syntactic pada *kaṭa-ām* (→ *kaṭa-nām* → *kaṭānām* → … *kaṭānāṅ* [gen. pl.]) "mats" contains the genitive ending *ām* introduced to signify an object, since the base *kaṭa-* occurs in construction with a derivate *kṛ-tṛ-*, which has an affix of the kṛt class (**A.** 2.3.65: *kartṛkarmaṇoḥ kṛti* [→ Art. 17, section 3.2.C]). A kṛt affix such as *tṛc* in *kṛ-tṛ-* is generally introduced if an agent is to be signified (**A.** 3.4.67: *kartari kṛt*). Thus, (3a) and (1a) are accounted for similarly, except that in (3a) a kṛt affix instead of an L-affix is introduced to signify an agent and a genitive ending instead of an accusative is introduced to signify an object. Similarly,

(4a) *bhoktuṅ gacchati* "… is going (in order) to eat"

derives from

(4b) *bhuj-tum-s gam-ti* (← *gam-**laṭ***)

with the infinitive *bhoktum-* (← *bhuj-tum*). The affix ***tumun*** is introduced after a verbal base $V^1$ construed with another such base $V^2$, if the action denoted by $V^2$ is performed for the purpose of performing the action signified by $V^1$ (**A.** 3.3.10: *tumunṇvulau kriyāyām kriyārthāyām*). A compound such as *rājapuruṣa* is derived by optionally combining padas like *rājan-as puruṣa-s* (→ Art. 17, section 3.2.C), from which can also be derived *rājñaḥ puruṣaḥ*, with two separate related padas. Similarly, a derivate like *pautra-*, with a taddhita suffix, is formed by introducing an affix after a pada of a string (→ Art. 17, section 3.2.C).

Once underlying strings like (1b) are posited, various operations apply to result in actual utterances like (1a); → Art. 17, section 4.1.

## 2. Kinds of rules

The main type of rule is an operational rule (*vidhisūtra*), which provides for any of the different operations adopted in Pāṇini's system: affixation, replacement, augmenting, iterating, compounding (→ Art. 17, section 4.1.). Pāṇini also formulates sūtras that are ancillary to operational rules; metarules (*paribhāṣā*), rules that introduce technical terms (*saṁjñāsūtra*), and headings (*adhikāra*). There are also restrictions (*niyama*), which limit what would otherwise apply in an overbroad manner, and negations (*pratiṣedha*), which disallow something that would otherwise apply. In addition extension rules (*atideśasūtra*) extend to entities operations or properties that do not otherwise pertain to them. On this topic, see Sharma (1987: 89–120); Cardona (1997: 4–79). The following examples will serve to illustrate. As shown in section 4.1. of article 17, **A.** 7.3.84: *sārvadhātukārdhadhātukayoḥ* [*guṇaḥ* 82, *aṅgasya* 6.4.1]) states an operation. This rule is part of the section headed by **A.** 6.4.1: *aṅgasya*, so that the operation in question applies relative to a unit called *aṅga*. The classification rule **A.** 1.4.13: *yasmāt pratyayavidhis tadādi pratyaye 'ṅgam* assigns the name *aṅga* to a unit Y that begins with an element X (*tadādi*) after which (*yasmāt*) an affix A is introduced (*pratyayavidhiḥ*) and is followed by A (*pratyaye*). *aṅgasya* understood in **A.** 7.3.84 contains a genitive singular ending (*sya* ← ***ṅas***), and such an ending is used when a residual relation is to be signified (**A.** 2.3.50: → Art. 17, section 3.1.B). From the context in **A.** 7.3.84, it is not possible for a native speaker to know what relation is involved between a stem and endings of the sārvadhātuka and ārdhadhātuka classes. A metarule (**A.** 1.1.49: *ṣaṣṭhī sthāneyogā*) provides that a genitive not unambiguously interpretable in a sūtra is understood to be used in the sense of a particular relation: "in place of" (*sthāne-*). Thus, **A.** 7.3.84 is understood to state a replacement that applies to a stem followed by specified affixes. **A.** 7.3.84 also uses the term *guṇa*, which, according to **A.** 1.1.2 (→ Art. 17, section 4.1.), denotes the vowels *a e o*. In addition, **A.** 1.1.3: *iko guṇavṛddhī* provides that, if the terms *guṇa*, *vṛddhi* are used in substitution rules where the elements to be replaced are not specified, one understands the substituends to be the vowels *i u ṛ ḷ* (*ikaḥ*, gen. sg. of the abbreviation ***ik*** [→ Art. 17, section 2.1.). Since the metarule **A.** 1.1.3 applies in conjunction with the operational rule **A.** 7.3.84 which it serves to interpret, one understands *ikaḥ* in the latter. Another saṁjñāsūtra (**A.** 1.1.72: *yena vidhis tadantasya*) establishes a convention: a qualifier X by means of which (*yena*) an operation (*vidhiḥ*) is provided denotes the qualified element Y that ends in X (*tadantasya*). Another metarule (**A.** 1.1.52: *alo' ntyasya*) states that, in general, substitution applies to the last (*antyasya*) sound (*alaḥ*) of an item signified by a substituend genitive. Accordingly, **A.** 7.3.84 states that replacement by *a e o* applies to the final sound of a stem that ends with *i u ṛ ḷ* (and the corresponding long vowels). The particular replacement for each sound is specified by a restrictive metarule (**A.** 1.1.50: *sthāne' ntaratamaḥ*) according to which, if there is a choice of replacements for a substituend denoted by a genitive form the substitute most proximate (*antaratamaḥ*) to the substituend is selected. And by **A.** 1.1.50: *ur aṇ raparaḥ*, a vowel *a i u* (*aṇ*) that replaces *ṝ* (*uḥ*) is automatically followed by *r* (*raparaḥ*). Another metarule concerns contexts. If a locus is referred to using a locative form X-loc. (*tasminniti nirdiṣṭe*), the operation in question is understood to apply to what precedes X (*pūrvasya*: **A.** 1.1.66: *tasminniti nirdiṣṭe pūrvasya*). A metarule related to **A.** 1.1.3 also needs to be mentioned: **A.** 1.1.5: *kṅiti ca* [*na* 4]), whereby guṇa and vṛddhi replacements that would apply in accordance with **A.** 1.1.3 do not (*na*) apply before an element that bears a marker *g k ṅ* (*kṅiti*). In conjunction with such ancillary rules, **A.** 7.3.84 thus states that the final sound of a stem ending in *-ī̆ -ū̆ ṝ* is replaced respectively by *e o ar* before a sārvadhātuka or ārdhadhātuka affix that is not marked with *g k ṅ*. Thus, in *kṛ-u-ti*, the *-ṛ* of *kṛ* is replaced by *ar* before the ārdhadhātuka suffix *u* and the *-u* of *kṛ-u* is replaced by *-o* before the sārvadhātuka suffix *ti*. In *kṛ-ya-te*, however, guṇa substitution does not apply before the affix ***yak***: *kṛ-ya-te* → *kriyate*. A metarule parallel to **A.** 1.1.66 serves to interpret ablative forms in rules. According to **A.** 1.1.67: *tasmād ity uttarasya*, a reference made by means of an ablative (*tasmād iti* [*nirdiṣṭe* 66]) that is not otherwise interpretable in context is understood to be to an element such that an operation applies to what follows (*uttarasya*). For example, **A.** 7.1.54: *hrasvanadyāpo nuṭ* ([*āmi* 42], → Art. 17, section 3.2.E) contains the ablative *hrasvanadyāpaḥ*, interpreted by this metarule, so that the addition of the initial augment ***nuṭ*** applies to *ām* which follows a stem (*aṅgasya*: **A.** 6.4.1) that ends with a short vowel, with a vowel *ī̆ ū̆* of certain feminine stems (called *nadī*), and with feminine affixes referred to by ***āp***; e. g., *deva-ām* → *deva-nām*. Long-vowel substitution then applies: **A.** 6.4.3: *nāmi* (*dīrghaḥ* 6.3.111) provides that a long vowel (*dīrghaḥ*) replaces the final vowel of a stem before *nām*: *deva-nām* → *devānām* "gods" [gen. pl.].

As shown in section 4.3. of article 17, Pāṇini provides for certain verb bases to be replaced if they are to be used with an ārdhadhātuka affix. For example *bhū* substitutes for *as*. Now, *bhū* which is introduced as a replacement for *as* is not in the ordered list that constitutes Pāṇini's dhātupāṭha (→ Art. 17, section 2.1.A), and it is to items of this list that the class name *dhātu* is assigned by **A.** 1.3.1: *bhūvādayo dhātavaḥ* (→ Art. 17, section 3.2.). Further, if this *bhū* did not bear this name, one could not form with it derivates like *bhavitum*, *bhavya*. For the rules which introduce the affixes in question (**A.** 3.3.10 [see section 1.3.], **A.** 3.1.97: *aco yat*) are stated under the heading **A.** 3.1.92: *dhātoḥ*, so that the affixes they introduce follow items called *dhātu*. Moreover, it is not possible to introduce post-verbal affixes after *as* and then have this base replaced by *bhū*, since this procedure would not account for the proper distribution of affixes. **A.** 3.1.97 introduces ***yat*** after a verbal base that ends in a vowel (*acaḥ*); another rule (**A.** 3.1.124: *ṛhalor ṇyat*) introduces ***ṇyat*** to bases that end in *-ṝ* or a consonant (*ṛhaloḥ*). Hence, if one first allowed an affix to follow *as* and then had this base replaced by *bhū*, the affix introduced would be ***ṇyat*** instead of *yat* : *as-ya-* → *bhū-ya-*. An undesired operation would then apply. ***ṇyat*** is marked with *ṇ* to show that it conditions a particular replacement. By **A.** 7.2.115: *aco ñṇiti* (*vṛddhiḥ* 114), a vṛddhi vowel (*ā ai au*: **A.** 1.1.1: *vṛddhir ād aic*) replaces the final sound of a vowel-stem before an affix marked with *ñ* or *ṇ*; for example, the *-ū* of *bhū-i-*, with the causative suffix ***ṇic***, is replaced by *-au*: *bhū-i-* → *bhau-i-* → *bhāv-i-*

"cause to be, bring about" [3rd sg. pres. indic. *bhāvayati*]. The gerundive of *bhū* in the simple meaning "be, become" should be *bhavya-*, not *bhāvya-*, which has the added meaning "necessarily ...". The correct derivate is assured if *as* is replaced by *bhū* before the introduction of any particular ārdhadhātuka affix. Accordingly, Pāṇini provides that a replacement (*ādeśaḥ*) has the status of its substituend (*sthānivat*) except with respect to an operation that would be determined by an original sound that has been replaced (*analvidhau*: **A.** 1.1.56: *sthānivad ādeśo 'nalvidhau*). *bhū* which replaces *as* thereby bears the class name *dhātu*. It also ends in a vowel, so that the proper derivate is accounted for. In addition, a convention is adopted whereby an operation conditioned by an affix takes place even in the absence of the affix, except for an operation on a stem that would apply in the presence of an affix replaced by a zero referred to using a term with *lu*; → Art. 17, section 5.

## 3. Organization of the *Aṣṭādhyāyī*

3.1. As shown in section 2., major headings divide the *Aṣṭādhyāyī* into groups of rules. Thus, **A.** 3.1.1: *pratyayaḥ* heads a large section of rules, through the end of the fifth adhyāya, that introduce elements called *pratyaya* "affix". Within this section there are subsections. **A.** 3.1.92: *dhātoḥ* heads a group of rules, through the end of the third adhyāya, that introduce affixes to verbal bases (*dhātu*, abl. sg. *dhātoḥ*). Rules under the heading of **A.** 4.1.1: *ṅyāpprātipadikāt* introduce affixes after nominal bases (*prātipadika*) and items with feminine affixes ***ṅī***, ***āp***. Some of these rules introduce taddhita affixes (→ Art. 17, section 3.2.C), provided for by rules under the heading **A.** 4.1.76: *taddhitāḥ*. Most taddhita affixes, however, are introduced after syntactic padas. Rules which introduce these are headed by **A.** 4.1.82: *samarthānāṁ prathamād vā*. Such affixes follow the first (*prathamāt*) of syntactically-semantically related padas (*samarthānām*) referred to in sūtras, and are introduced optionally (*vā*). The heading **A.** 4.1.1 continues in force through the end of the fifth adhyāya, but within the section beginning with **A.** 4.1.82 *prātipadikāt* is construed with terms that specify particular types of nominal bases within padas after which affixes occur. For example, **A.** 4.1.95: *ata iñ* introduces ***iñ*** following a pada whose nominal base ends with (**A.** 1.1.72 [see section 2.]) *-a*. This serves to form derivates of the type *gārgi* (← ... *garga-as-i*) "son of Garga". The section headed by **A.** 6.4.1 [see section 2.), which extends through the end of the seventh adhyāya, states operations relative to stems (*aṅga*).

In addition to such major headings, there are also parts of sūtras that are understood to recur in subsequent rules. For example, it is understood that *savarṇam* of **A.** 1.1.9: *tulyāsyaprayatnaṁ savarṇam* recurs (*anuvartate*) in the next sūtra, **A.** 1.1.10: *nājjhalau*; → Art. 17, section 1.2. This is akin to natural language ellipsis: a series of utterances are related and one understands something given in one utterance to recur in a subsequent utterance. Moreover, this can require that the form of the term understood to recur be modified in accordance with the meaning of the utterance where it is understood. For example, **A.** 7.1.54: *hrasvanadyāpo nuṭ* (see section 2.) contains the ablative *hrasvanadyāpaḥ*. The genitive *aṅgasya* of the heading **A.** 6.4.1 is contextually modified to an ablative (*aṅgāt*).

3.2. Terms understood to recur in subsequent sūtras thus are incorporated into these. Traditionally, the padas thus combined are said to form a single utterance of related padas (*padaikavākyatā*). Metarules (*paribhāṣā*) and rules that introduce names (*saṁjñāsūtra*) also apply as complements to the rules they serve to interpret and as such are combined with them. Instead of being incorporated into these sūtras, however, the ancillary rules merely form a single large utterance of separate statements that apply together. Traditionally, one speaks of a single utterance made up of utterances (*vākyaikavākyatā*). For example, **A.** 7.3.84 (see section 2.) requires **A.** 1.1.2–5 in order to apply. All these sūtras and other ancillary rules mentioned in connection with **A.** 7.3.84 combine to form a single large utterance stating how the guṇa substitution provided for applies. In this connection, note that **A.** 1.1.5: *kṅiti ca* contains the locative singular *kṅiti*. Since this is an ancillary rule that does not apply independently, the locative is not immediately interpreted by means of **A.** 1.1.66 (section 2.). Instead, **A.** 1.1.5 is first brought into context with the operational rule **A.** 7.3.84, which also contains a locative, the dual *sārvadhātukārdhadhātukayoḥ*, and it is in this context that **A.** 1.1.66 comes in to interpret the locatives. Similarly, **A.** 1.1.2–5 are brought in to interpret **A.** 7.3.86: *pugantalaghūpadhasya ca*, by which guṇa replacement applies before sārvadhātuka and ārdhadhātuka affixes also for *ĭ ŭ ṝ ḷ* which are penultimate sounds in stems that end with the augment ***puk*** and for *i u ṛ ḷ* that are penultimate sounds not followed by a cluster in other verbal stems. For example, *hrīp-i-* → *hrep-i-* (*hrepayati* "causes ... to be ashamed"), *bhid-tum* → *bhed-tum* (→ *bhettum* [inf.]) "to split"). Now, if **A.** 1.1.66 applied directly with **A.** 1.1.5, the latter would disallow guṇa substitution only for vowels *i* and so on which immediately precede an element marked with *k* and so forth. Consequently, **A.** 1.1.5 would not disallow guṇa replacement in a form such as *bhid-yate* [3rd sg. pres. pass.] "is being split". Since, however, both **A.** 1.1.66 and **A.** 1.1.5 come into play together with **A.** 7.3.86, this is not the case. **A.** 1.1.5 denies guṇa replacement in a subset of instances covered by the operational rule, namely for penultimate vowels of stems before affixes with markers *k* and so on.

3.3. The *Aṣṭādhyāyī* as a whole is also divided into two major sections of unequal length, determined by **A.** 8.2.1: *pūrvatrāsiddham*. This is at once a metarule and a heading for the final three quarter chapters of the grammar, traditionally called *tripādī*. Now, it is a given that sūtras stated in the *Aṣṭādhyāyī* are established (*siddha*) with respect to each other. That is, each sūtra is 'on the books', so to speak, so that it can interact with other sūtras. For example, once **A.** 7.1.54: *hrasvanadyāpo nuṭ* ([*āmi* 52], see section 2.) has applied to give the augmented ending *-naṁ*, **A.** 6.4.3: *nāmi* (*dīrghaḥ* 6.3.111) can then apply to the result, as in the derivation of *devānām*. **A.** 8.2.1 provides that, contrariwise, a sūtra of the section headed by this rule is suspended (*asiddham*) with respect to any sūtra that precedes (*pūrvatra*). That is, unless otherwise indicated, a sūtra of the tripādī is suspended with respect to any sūtra of the preceding seven and one-quarter chapters and within the tripādī a rule R+1 is suspended with respect to a preceding rule R. That a rule is suspended means that it is treated as non-existent. Accordingly, a rule's being suspended with respect to another rule has two effects. First, if there is a context such that only one rule can apply, it of course applies; but by virtue of such a rule being suspended with respect to another rule, the results of its application are not subject to that other rule. Secondly, if a context would allow two rules possibly to apply and one is suspended with respect to the other, only the rule that is not suspended applies, since the other rule is treated as non-existent. The following examples will serve to illustrate. In

(5a) *dvau atra*

the pada *dvau* "two" [nom. du. masc.] is followed by a vowel *a-* (*atra* "here"), so that the replacement provided for by **A.** 6.1.78: *eco' yavāyāvaḥ* (*aci* 77) applies: *ay av āy āv* replace *e o ai au*, respectively, before a vowel: *dvau atra* → *dvāv atra*. According to **A.** 8.3.18–19: *vyor laghuprayatnataraḥ śākaṭāyanasya, lopaḥ śākalyasya*, prevocalic pada-final *-v, -y* are subject to two dialectal treatments. In the dialect of Śākaṭāyana, these are replaced by lightly articulated (*laghuprayatnataraḥ* "with a very light effort") glides, and in Śākalya's dialect, they are deleted (*lopaḥ*). If deletion applies to give *dvā atra*, another operation comes into consideration. A vowel of the set denoted by ***ak*** (*ă ĭ ŭ ṝ ḷ*) and a following homogeneous vowel (*savarṇe*) are both replaced by a single long vowel (*dīrghaḥ*: **A.** 6.1.101: *akaḥ savarṇe dīrghaḥ* ([*aci* 77]); e. g., *kanyā atra* → *kanyātra* "There is a girl here." The result of applying **A.** 6.1.101 would be **dvātra*. As shown, this is not the appropriate result. Instead, one has to account for

(5a) *dvā atra*/ *dvā*$^{v}$ *atra* "There are two here."

**A.** 8.3.19, which serves to delete the *-v* of *dvāv*, is suspended with respect to **A.** 6.1.101. It is treated as non-existent with respect to this rule so that **A.** 6.1.101 cannot apply to the result of applying **A.** 8.3.19. The dative singular masculine-neuter forms *tasmai, amuṣmai* "to that" are derived from *tad-e* and *adas-e*. *tad* and *adas* are pronominals, included in the subset beginning with *tyad* of the set that begins with *sarva* (**A.** 1.1.27: *sarvādīni sarvanāmāni*, → Art. 17, section 2.1.B). The derivation of *tasmai* proceeds as follows: *tad-e* → *taa-e* (**A.** 7.2.102: *tyadādīnām aḥ* [*vibhaktau* 84], → Art. 17, section 5) → *ta-e* (**A.** 6.1.97: *ato guṇe* [*pararūpam* 94]) → *tasmai* (**A.** 7.1.14: *sarvanāmaḥ smai* [*ataḥ* 9, *ṅeḥ* 13]). The final sound of pronominal stems of the set beginning with *tyad* is replaced by *-a*. In addition, *a* that is not word-final and a following guṇa vowel (*a e o*) are both replaced by the second vowel. Moreover, *smai* replaces the ending ***ṅe*** after a pronominal stem in *-a*. Similarly *adas-*

*e* → *adaa-e* → *ada-e*. At this stage, however, it is not simply **A.** 7.1.14 that has to be considered but also **A.** 8.2.80: *adaso' ser dād u do maḥ*, which provides for two simultaneous substitution concerning *adas* that no longer ends with *-s* (*aseḥ*): the sound following *d* (*dāt*) is replaced by an *u*-vowel and *d* is itself replaced by *m* (*do maḥ*). If these substitution applied in *ada-e* to give *amu-e*, the ending ***ṅe*** would not be eligible for replacement by *smai*, since the preceding pronominal stem would no longer end in *-a*. **A.** 8.2.80 is included in the tripādī, however, so that it is suspended with respect to **A.** 7.1.14. Accordingly, at the stage *ada-e*, only one of the two rules is considered to exist, so that only it can apply: *ada-e* → *ada-smai*. Moreover, **A.** 7.1.14 is not suspended with respect to **A.** 8.2.80, so that the replacements provided for by the latter can now apply to *ada-smai*: *ada-smai* → *amu-smai*. In addition, **A.** 8.2.80 is suspended with respect to preceding rules, not with respect to rules that follow. Hence, retroflex substitution applies: *amu-smai* → *amuṣmai*. **A.** 8.3.59: *ādeśapratyayayoḥ* (*apadāntasya mūrdhanyaḥ* 55, *saḥ* 56, *iṇkoḥ* 57) provides that affix-initial *s-* is replaced by the corresponding retroflex (*mūrdhanyaḥ*) *ṣ-* after a sound of the set denoted by ***iṇ*** (*i u ṛ ḷ e o ai au h y v r l*) and velar stops (*iṇkoḥ*). The past passive participle of *pac* "cook, bake" is *pakva-*, and this is derived from *pac-ta-*, with the suffix ***kta***. According to **A.** 8.2.30: *coḥ kuḥ* (*jhali* 38, *ante ca* 29), a palatal stop (*coḥ*) is replaced by a corresponding velar stop (*kuḥ*) before a nonnasal stop or a spirant (*jhali*) as well is in word-final position, and by **A.** 8.2.52: *paco vaḥ* (*niṣṭhātaḥ* 42), the *t-* of the suffixes called *niṣṭhā* (***kta*** and ***ktavatu***) is replaced by *v* after the base *pac*. This is suspended with respect to **A.** 8.2.30, so that at the stage *pac-ta-* only the latter can apply: *pac-ta-* → *pak-ta-*. But **A.** 8.2.30 is not suspended with respect to **A.** 8.2.52, so that the latter can apply to the result of applying the former: *pak-ta-* → *pak-va-*.

## 4. Relations among rules and operations

Rule suspension (see section 3.2.) as it is applied where two rules of the *Aṣṭādhyāyī* could possibly come into play in a given context obviously establishes extrinsic rule ordering: R applies before R+1. External rule ordering, as in the late phonological rules of the tripādī, is not the norm in Pāṇini's system. As far as possible, Pāṇini lets other relations among rules and the structures to which operations apply determine how rules take effect. On these relations, see Sharma (1987: 74–88); Cardona (1997: xiv–xxiii, 401–427 [623–665]; 1999: 154–161).

4.1. The most important relationship among rules is the intrinsic relation, determined by their domains (*viṣaya*) of application, between general rules (*utsarga*) and exceptions (*apavāda*) to them. This is most basically characterized in the following manner. If a rule $R^1$ has a domain such that it must apply everywhere that a rule $R^2$ can apply, then $R^2$ blocks (*bādhate*) $R^1$ within its particular domain included in the overall domain of $R^1$. For example, **A.** 6.1.77: *iko yaṇ aci* provides that semivowels *y v r l* (*yaṇ*) replace *ĭ ŭ ṝ ḷ* (*ikaḥ*), respectively, before a vowel (*aci*). This is a general phonologic rule that applies if any of the vowels in question is followed by a vowel; e. g., *dadhi atra* → *dadhy atra* "There is yoghurt (*dadhi*) here (*atra*)", *madhu atra* → *madhv atra* "There is honey (*madhu*) here." **A.** 6.4.77: *aci śnudhātubhruvāṁ yvor iyaṅ-uvaṅau*, on the other hand applies specifically to a stem (**A.** 6.4.1: *aṅgasya*, see section 2.) that ends in an *i-* or *u*-vowel which is part of the verbal suffix *śnu*, of a verbal base, or of the nominal base *bhrū* 'brow'. The final vowels of such stems are replaced by *iy* and *uv* before vowels. For example, *āp-nu-anti* → *āpnuvanti* "they reach", *kṣi-atus* → *kṣiy-atus* → ... *cikṣiyatuḥ* [3rd du. pfct.] "they two dwelt", *lū-atus* → *luv-atus* → ... *luluvatuḥ* "they two cut", *bhrū-ām* [gen. pl.] → *bhruvām*. **A.** 6.4.77 is an exception to **A.** 6.1.77, hence takes precedence: it blocks the application of the general rule in its own domain, leaving the remainder of the general domain for the general rule. Consequently, semi-vowel replacement by **A.** 6.1.77 could not apply in *i-anti*, where the verbal base *i* "go" occurs before the ending *-anti*. Yet the form to be accounted for is *yanti*, not **iyanti*, which would result from **A.** 6.4.77. Hence, Pāṇini formulates a still more specific rule (**A.** 6.4.81: *iṇo yaṇ*) as an exception to **A.** 6.4.77: the *i* of the base ***iṇ*** is replaced by *y* before a vowel. Similarly, another exception to **A.** 6.4.77 provides that *-u* in certain stems consisting of more than use syllable (*anekācaḥ*) is replaced by *-v* before a sārvadhātuka affix, namely the *-u* of *hu* "pour oblations" and of a stem with *śnu* (*huśnuvoḥ*) not preceded by a consonant cluster (*asaṁyo-*

*gapūrvasya*) (**A.** 6.4.87: *huśnuvoḥ sārvadhātuke* [*anekācaḥ asaṁyogapūrvasya* 82, *yaṇ* 81]); e. g., *hu-jhi* → ... *huhu-jhi* → *huhu-ati* → *huhv-ati* → ... *juhvati* [3rd pl. pres. indic.], *sunu-anti* → *sunvanti* "they all are pressing juice".

4.2. **A.** 6.4.77 and **A.** 6.4.81, which is an exception to it, are stated in the same section of rules. On the other hand, **A.** 6.1.77 and **A.** 6.4.77 are stated in widely separated sections. They are nevertheless brought together by virtue of their intrinsic relation. As in the case of ancillary rules (see section 3.2.), here also one traditionally speaks of rules coming together to form a single context (*ekavākyatā*).

4.3. Rules that assign class names to entities have a special status in that the blocking relation between general rules and exceptions does not normally obtain for them. For example, the nominal bases *sarva* "all, whole" are assigned the name *sarvanāman* by **A.** 1.1.27 (→ Art. 17, section 2.1.B). Accordingly, these items take part in operations stated with respect to sarvanāman elements. For example, by **A.** 7.1.14: *sarvanāmaḥ smai* [*ataḥ* 9, *ṅeḥ* 13]) *smai replaces* ***ṅe*** after a sarvanāman stem in *-a* (see section 3.3.). ***ṅe*** itself is a basic nominal ending, and such endings are introduced after items which have the class name *prātipadika* (**A.** 4.1.1: *ṅyāpprātipadikāt*, section 3.1.). Accordingly, *sarva* and so on should also belong to the more general class of prātipadikas. Pāṇini does indeed operate with such classes and subclasses involving concurrent application of class names (*saṁjñāsamāveśa*). In certain instances, however, it is required that classes be disjunct. For example, **A.** 1.1.45: *ādhāro 'dhikaraṇam* assigns the name *adhikaraṇa* to a direct participant which plays the role of a locus (*ādhāra*) with respect to an action, but **A.** 1.4.46: *adhiśīṅsthāsāṁ karma* (→ Art. 17, section 3.3.) assigns the name *karman* to direct participants that play the role of a locus in the acts of lying, sleeping and so on as denoted by particular items. These two rules are part of a group of sūtras, stated under the heading **A.** 1.4.1: *ā kaḍārād ekā saṁjñā*, introducing class names only one (*ekā saṃjñā*) of which is allowed to apply at any time to a given entity. Accordingly, **A.** 1.4.46 is now allowed to block the general rule **A.** 1.4.45, so that a locus with respect to lying as signified by *adhiśī* is assigned the name *karman* and is not simultaneously called *adhikaraṇa*. This accounts for the use of forms like *dakṣiṇam bhāgam* in construction with *adhi-śī*, as opposed to forms like *dakṣiṇe bhāge* (loc. sg.), with a seventh-triplet ending introduced to signify an adhikaraṇa (**A.** 2.3.36: *saptamy adhikaraṇe ca*). Such a locative may occur with *śī* but not with *adhi-śī*.

4.4. In Pāṇini's system, utterances are derived as strings of related padas, as in (1a, b)−(2a, b), and such padas themselves have internal structures (see section 2.1.), with stems preceding affixes. Moreover, these stems can be simple or complex, as in (((*kṛ-*) *u-*)*ti*). (((*tud-*)*a-*)*ti*), (((*kṣi-*)*a-*)*ti*) also are padas with two stems: the verbal bases *tud* and *kṣi* "dwell", the ending ***tip***, and the sārvadhātuka suffix ***śa*** that occurs with verbs of the set beginning with ***tudà*** (→ Art. 17, section 2.1.A). As can be seen, the penultimate vowel of the stem *tud-* in *tud-a-* is not replaced by the guṇa vowel *o*; contrast a form like *tottum* (inf. ← *tud-tum*), where this replacement applies, by **A.** 7.3.86 (section 3.2.). The affix ***śa*** in *tud-a-* is marked with *ś* so that it is a member of the sārvadhātuka class (**A.** 3.4.113 [→ Art. 17, section 3.1.D]). It is also not marked with *p* (*apit*), so that, by an extension rule (**A.** 1.2.4: *sārvadhātukam api* [*ṅit* 1]), it is marked with *ṅ*, thus being one of the affixes which do not condition guṇa replacement in their stems. The same suffix ***śa*** in *kṣi-a-* also does not condition guṇa substitution by **A.** 7.3.84, so that *-e* does not replace the *-i* of *kṣi-*. On the other hand, *kṣi-a-* is a stem with respect to the ending ***tip***, a sārvadhātuka affix that is marked with *p*, so that it does condition guṇa substitution in its stems, as in *karoti* ← *kar-u-ti* ← *kṛ-u-ti*. Consequently, **A.** 7.3.86 could apply to let *e* replace the penultimate *i* of the stem *kṣi-a-* followed by ***tip***. This is prevented by a bracketing convention: operations conditioned by elements within brackets take effect before operations conditioned by elements exterior to these brackets. Thus, in (((*kṣi-*)*a-*)*ti*), the substitution of *-iy* for the *-i* of the interior stem *kṣi-* (**A.** 6.4.77 [see section 4.1.]) takes precedence over the possible substitution of *e* for the *i* of the stem ((*kṣi-*)*a-*) conditioned by ***tip***: (((*kṣi-*)*a-*)*ti*) → ((*kṣiy-a*)-*ti*). Once this substitution has applied, *i* is no longer the penultimate sound of the stem *kṣiy-a-*, so that *tip* cannot condition its replacement by *e*. The same bracketing principle of course applies in respect of padas. Consider the derivation of the sentence

(6) *ayaja indram* "I venerated Indra"

At one stage, there are two padas: ((*ayaja-*)*i*) ((*indra-*)*am*). Two operations could possibly apply involving the first pada. First, by **A.** 6.1.87: *ād guṇaḥ* (→ Art. 17, section 4.1.), the guṇa vowel *e* could be the single substitute for the contiguous vowels *-a-i* of ((*ayaja-*)*i*): ((*ayaja-*)*i*) → (*ayaje*). Secondly, *-i* of the first pada and *i-* of the second pada could both replaced by a single long vowel *ī* (**A.** 6.1.101, see section 3.3.): ((*ayaja-*)*i*) ((*indra-*)*am*) → (*ayaja-*)*ī-*. Under the first alternative, the *-e* of the first pada would then be replaced by *-ay* before the vowel of the following pada (**A.** 6.1.78, see section 3.3.), then the *-y* of the pada deleted (**A.** 8.3.19, see section 3.3.): *ayaje i-* → *ayajay i-* → *ayaja i-*. Under the second alternative, the contiguous vowels *-a-ī-* would be replaced by *-e-*: ((*ayaja-*)*ī-*) → *ayaje*. As shown, the first alternative alone accounts for the desired result. This procedure is also in accord with the bracketing principle.

4.5. At the stage *kṣi-ti* in the derivation of *kṣiyati* one also has to consider two possible operations. First, the suffix *śa* is introduced after *kṣi*, since this is a base of the set beginning with *tud* (**A.** 3.1.77: *tudādibhyaḥ śaḥ*): *kṣi-ti* → *kṣi-a-ti*. Secondly, guṇa replacement could apply to the stem *kṣi-* before the sārvadhātuka affix ***tip*** (**A.** 7.3.84, see section 2.): *kṣi-ti* → *kṣe-ti*. Under the first alternative, the derivation proceeds as shown in section 4.4., resulting in the desired form *kṣiyati*. Under the second alternative, the result is *kṣayati*. *kṣi* replacing *kṣe* is a verbal base, so that the affix *śa* is introduced; then *-ay* substitutes for *-e* before *-a-*. The correct derivation is assured by another principle concerning rules $R^1$ and $R^2$ which can apply in a given context and are related as follows: If $R^2$ applies, $R^1$ can still apply, but if $R^1$ applies $R^2$ can no longer apply. Under these conditions, what is provided by $R^1$ (termed *nitya* "necessary") takes precedence over the provision in $R^2$ (termed *anitya*).

4.6. Pāṇini does not explicitly state that a rule blocks another if its domain of application is included in that of a more general rule. Nor does he explicitly formulate the bracketing principle or the principle illustrated in section 4.5. Yet he does operate with these principles, as can be seen from rules of the *Aṣṭādhyāyī*. Thus, **A.** 6.4.81: *iṇo yaṇ* (section 4.1.) is required because **A.** 6.4.77: *aci śnudhātubhruvāṁ yvor iyaṅuvaṅau* blocks the general rule **A.** 6.1.77: *iko yaṇ aci*. Since he recognizes the bracketing convention noted (section 4.4.), Pāṇini has to make particular statements concerning the verb *ṛch* "go". In accordance with bracketing, an operation that applies within (*ṛch*) takes effect before any operation that depends on an element outside the brackets. Accordingly, *ṛ* in *ṛch* immediately takes the augment *t* (**A.** 6.1.73: *che ca* [→ Art. 17, section 4.1.]): *ṛch* → *ṛtch*. Since *ṛ* in *ṛtch* is followed by a consonant cluster, it is not the penultimate sound of the base and it is classed as a heavy (*guru*) vowel. Therefore, guṇa substitution according to **A.** 7.3.86: *pugantalaghūpadhasya ca* (see section 3.2.) cannot apply to a stem *ṛtch*. In order to derive the perfect *ānarccha* [3rd sg.], then, Pāṇini has to provide specifically that guṇa replacement applies to this verb before endings that derived from the L-affix ***liṭ*** (**A.** 7.4.11: *ṛcchatyṝtām* [*liṭi* 9, *guṇaḥ* 10]). He also has to exclude this verb from the domain of an operation that applies to certain bases. Verbal bases such as *īh* "strive", *edh* "thrive", which contain initial *i- u- ṛ- e- o- ai- au-*vowels that are heavy (*guru*, **A.** 1.4.12–13: *saṁyoge guru, dīrghaṁ ca* [see section 4.7.]) form periphrastic perfects of the type *īhāñ cakre* [3rd sg.] "strove", *edhāñ cakre* "thrived", which contain forms of *kṛ* "do" and derivates with the affix *ām*. **A.** 3.1.36: *ijādeś ca gurumato' nṛcchaḥ* (*ām liṭi* 35) introduces this suffix after a base that begins with a vowel signified by *ic*, provided the vowel is heavy. The rule also specifically excludes *ṛch* (*anṛcchaḥ* "other than *ṛch*"). For, by virtue of the augment *t* that is added to this base, it contains a heavy vowel from the very beginning. Perfect forms like *ānarccha*, *cakāra* "did, made" involve iterating part of a base that is followed by an ending which derives from the L-affix ***liṭ***, as provided for by **A.** 6.1.11: *liṭi dhātor anabhyāsasya*. This is one of a series of sūtras under the heading of **A.** 6.1.1–2: *ekāco dve prathamasya, ajāder dvitīyasya*. Under conditions stated, a syllable (*ekācaḥ* [gen. sg.]) is repeated: the second (*dvitīyasya*) syllable of a vowel-initial (*ajādeḥ*) base, the first (*prathamasya*) syllable of other bases. Now, in *kṛ-atus*, *kṛ* is followed by the ending *atus* [3rd du. act.], which is a replacement of ***liṭ***, so that doubling could apply. In addition, however, *atus* begins with a vowel, so that semivowel replacement (**A.** 6.1.77, section 4.1.) can apply. Moreover, if this does apply, doubling by **A.** 6.1.11 can no longer apply. For this operation applies to an element that contains a vowel (*ekāc*), and *kr-* in *kr-atus* does not have a vowel. Further, even if doubling does apply, semivowel replacement can still take effect in *kr̥-kr̥-atus*. By the principle described in section 4.5., this takes precedence. In order to allow doubling, then, Pāṇini formulates a special extension rule (**A.** 1.1.59: *dvir-vacane' ci* [*acaḥ* 57, *sthānivat* 56]): a substitute for a vowel (*acaḥ*) has the status of its original (*sthānivat*) with respect to doubling (*dvirvacane*) if its replacement is conditioned by a following vowel (*aci*) that is part of an element before which doubling occurs (*dvirvacane*). Once semivowel replacement has applied to give *kr-atus*, then, the *-r* of *kr-* is given the status of *-r̥* with respect to doubling: *kr-atus* → *kr̥-kr-atus* → ... *cakratus* "they two made, did."

In the Pāṇinian tradition, it is noted that the principles I have described need not be explicitly formulated in the grammar, since they are well known from every day behavior. In addition, the tradition appropriately places these decision principles on a scale: nitya, internally conditioned, exception. Each successive type is more powerful than the preceding ones. Also included in this scale is the relation involving extrinsic ordering: what is subsequently stated takes precedence over something provided for earlier in the grammar. As I noted above (section 4.), extrinsic ordering is a last resort, invoked when the other principles cannot properly account for desired results.

4.7. **A.** 1.4.105, 107, 108: *yuṣmady upapade samānādhikaraṇe sthāniny api madhyamaḥ, asmady uttamaḥ, śeṣe prathamaḥ* (→ Art. 17, section 3.1.C) account for the distribution of triplets of verb endings called *prathama*, *madhyama* and *uttama*, corresponding to what western grammars call third, second, and first person endings. For example,

(7) *tvaṁ gacchasi* "You are going"
(8) *ahaṁ gacchāmi* "I am going"

respectively contain *gacchasi* [2nd sg. pres. indic.] and *gacchāmi* [1st sg.], with the madhyama ending *-sip* and the uttama ending *mip*. There are also sentences like

(9) *tvañ cāhañ ca gacchāvaḥ* "You and I are going"

in which forms of both *yuṣmad* [nom. sg. *tvam* "you"] and *asmad* [nom. sg. *aham* "I"] are involved, so that both **A.** 1.4.105 and **A.** 1.4.107 could apply. If the latter applied, however, one would derive an incorrect utterance with *gacchathaḥ* [2nd du.] instead of *gacchāvaḥ*. Moreover, none of the general principles noted can serve to determine the desired application. Hence, Pāṇini makes use of the external order of rules. **A.** 1.4.105, 107, 108 are included in the section of rules headed by **A.** 1.4.1: *ā kaḍārād ekā saṁjñā* (see section 4.3.), wherein the metarule **A.** 1.4.2: *vipratiṣedhe paraṁ kāryam* applies: in case of conflict (*vipratiṣedhe*), what is to be done (*kāryam*) as provided for by a later rule (*param*) takes precedence over what is provided by a prior rule. Rules can conflict if they are of equal strength, so that their application is not determined by any of the principles noted earlier. The same extrinsic ordering applies also with respect to rules that assign class names. For example, **A.** 1.4.10–12: *hrasvaṁ laghu, saṁyoge guru, dīrghaṁ ca* assign the names *laghu* "light" and *guru* "heavy" to particular vowels: a short vowel (*hrasvam*) is called *laghu*; a short vowel followed by a consonant cluster (*saṁyoge*) is called *guru*, as is also (*ca*) a long vowel (*dīrgham*). A vowel such as *r̥* is eligible for the class name *laghu* merely by virtue of being short. If it is followed by a cluster, as in *r̥tch* (see section 4.6.), it is also eligible for the name guru. By **A.** 1.4.2, such a vowel is now uniquely classed as guru.

## 5. Pāṇini's commentators

Pāṇinian commentators elaborated on the principles that determine how rules should apply, and discussions of these principles continue to the present. One of the major works concerning them was composed in the 18th century: Nāgeśabhaṭṭa's *Paribhāṣenduśekhara*, on which commentaries have continued to be composed up to the present. Traditional Pāṇinian scholars also not only explained rules and derivations, some reorganized rules so as to treat together rules of the *Aṣṭādhyāyī* dealing with particular themes. In such reordered treatments, the most famous of which is Bhaṭṭojidīkṣita's *Siddhāntakaumudī* (late 16th to 17th centuries), rules concerning topics like the forms of nominal stems of different genders are brought together although in the *Aṣṭādhyāyī* they may be separated physically and brought together only by virtue of their intrinsic relations.

The treatment of topics such as sandhi, nominal forms, compounds, and verbal forms in this manner is found also in earlier non-Pāṇinian grammars, for example, the

*Kātantra*. Such works, however, are properly considered reworkings of Pāṇini's *Aṣṭādhyāyī*, which remains the most important grammar of Sanskrit in India.

## 6. Bibliography

Cardona, George. 1997. *Pāṇini, his Work and its Traditions*. Part I: *General Introduction and Background*. 2nd, revised ed. Delhi: Motilal Banarsidass.

–. 1999. *Recent Research in Pāṇinian Studies* Delhi: Motilal Banarsidass.

Sharma, Rama Nath. 1987. *The* Aṣṭādhyāyī *of Pāṇini*, vol. I: *Introduction to the* Aṣṭādhyāyī *as a Grammatical Device*. Delhi: Munshiram Manoharlal.

*George Cardona, Philadelphia (USA)*

# 22. The relationship between linguistics and other sciences in India

1. Introduction
2. The origin of grammar
3. Interaction with 'etymological explanation' (*nirukta*)
4. Influence from philosophy
5. Language and philosophy
6. Bhartṛhari
7. Understanding the meaning of a sentence
8. Conclusion
9. Bibliography

## 1. Introduction

Classical India has various language sciences. Three of the six traditional auxiliary siences of the Veda (*vedāṅga*) – phonetics (*śikṣā*), etymological explanation (*nirukta*), grammar (*vyākaraṇa*) – deal with language. The various *Prātiśākhya*s – which precede the surviving treatises of *śikṣā* and are its authentic representatives according to Renou (1963: 167) – deal with Vedic phonetics. Vedic hermeneutics (*mīmāṃsā*), too, can be looked upon as a language science, and so can certain developments of Indian philosophical thought. But grammar was most widely studied. Grammar, according to the grammarian Patañjali (2nd century BCE), is the most important among the six auxiliary sciences. We will therefore confine our attention to grammar (*vyākaraṇa*) – and in particular to the oldest surviving, and most important, text of this genre: Pāṇini's *Aṣṭādhyāyī* – in its relationship to other sciences.

Grammar did not interact with mathematics and the natural sciences (astronomy and medicine), or at least not strongly. The suggestion that Pāṇini's 'linguistic zero' caused or influenced the introduction of zero in mathematics has no evidence to support it (see Ruegg 1978). Note however that the expression 'natural sciences' is apt to be misleading in the classical Indian context: physics and part of chemistry have their closest parallels in what are commonly referred to as schools of Indian philosophy. Other Indian sciences, often without parallel in the modern world, include: etymological explanation (*nirukta*); ritual science (*kalpa*), like etymological explanation one of the auxiliary sciences of the Veda (Staal [1982; 1989: 349f.] argues for the scientific status of the 'science of ritual'); Vedic hermeneutics (*mīmāṃsā*); poetic science (*kāvyaśāstra*).

Two kinds of relationship between grammar and other sciences will be primarily considered: (1) another science influenced grammar, and (2) grammar influenced another science. In reality the interaction was often less unidirectional, and in some cases the bi-directional nature of the interaction will be mentioned. For the earliest period forms of 'knowledge' that had not yet been systematised into 'sciences' will have to be taken into consideration.

## 2. The origin of grammar

Grammar arose in circles connected with Vedic ritual. Does it preserve traces of this early connection? The classical publication is Louis Renou's "Les connexions entre le rituel et la grammaire" (1941–42), which is more circumspect in its formulations than are some more recent publications. It draws attention to various parallels between the two sciences, such as the shared aphoristic (*sūtra*) style (see also Renou 1963: 175f.), the presence in both of general interpretative rules (*paribhāṣā*) – sometimes similar ones –, and the elements of vocabulary which they have in common. However, as Renou himself admits, these parallels do only in certain cases allow us to conclude that ritual influenced grammar rather than vice-versa. The influence considered is moreover limited to details, and hardly justifies the conclusion that grammar in India owes its existence, or its specific nature, to ritual science.

One of the less doubtful antecedents of grammar is the early preoccupation with the correct preservation of Vedic texts. The *Ṛgveda*, for example, has been preserved in many different forms of recitation, two of which are of particular interest here: the *padapāṭha* "word for word recitation" and the *saṃhitāpāṭha* "continuous recitation". Neither of these two (nor indeed any of the other ones) represents the original form of the *Ṛgveda*. The *padapāṭha* separates the words (and certain components of words) of the text, the *saṃhitāpāṭha* joins them in sandhi (called *saṃhitā* in Vedic literature and Pāṇini's grammar). The *padapāṭha* of the *Ṛgveda* is older than Pāṇini – he refers to it –, its *saṃhitāpāṭha* appears to be younger – it applies rules of sandhi which destroy the original meter, where Pāṇini's rules preserve it – (see Bronkhorst 1981a; 1991: 75f.). The question as to how the *saṃhitāpāṭha* is formed on the basis of the *padapāṭha* is a central concern of the *Prātiśākhyas*, and early reflections of this nature contributed no doubt to the creation of grammar. Reflections about details of sandhi also gave rise to 'mystical' speculations (e. g., *Aitareya Āraṇyaka* 3.2.6; *Śāṅkhāyana Āraṇyaka* 8.11; *Ṛgveda Prātiśākhya* 1.2f.).

Other aspects of grammar arose for different reasons. The Sanskrit term for grammar, *vyākaraṇa*, provides a clue. This means literally "separation, distinction", and this is often taken to refer to the fact that grammar distinguishes roots, suffixes, and prefixes (so e. g., Scharfe 1977: 83). Paul Thieme (1982: 11 [1178]) has however rightly pointed out that Pāṇini's grammar does not analyse. This grammar rather presupposes constituent functional elements and shows how they are to be combined. Thieme proposes "[word-]formation" for *vyākaraṇa*, which is not convincing. He overlooks the fact that grammar, though not separating the constituent elements of words, does separate words and their meanings. This, at any rate, is a theme that recurs a number of times in Vedic literature, frequently in passages that use precisely the verb *vy-ā-kṛ-*, from which *vyākaraṇa* is derived. These passages speak about the separation of name (*nāman*) and shape (*rūpa*). *Bṛhadāraṇyaka Upaniṣad* 1.4.7 – to cite but one example – states: "All this was unseparated (indistinguishable) (*avyākṛta*) [in the beginning of creation]. Then it became separated (distinguished) (*vyākriyata*) by name and shape [so it became possible to say]: 'This particular one is of the name NN and of such and such a shape'. Therefore, even to-day distinction is made (*vyākriyate*) by name and shape: 'This particular one is of the name NN [and] of such and such a shape' " [transl. Thieme]. Passages like this could be looked upon as the mythological counterpart of an important feature of Pāṇini's grammar (and for the grammars that existed before him, we may assume): meanings are its 'input', which then give rise to word-forms (Bronkhorst 1979). Early thinkers about language, we are led to believe, were interested in the details of the separation of words and things reported in their mythology.

## 3. Interaction with "etymological explanation" (*nirukta*)

The background of another aspect of grammar is elucidated by its relationship with the Vedic auxiliary science of "etymological explanation" (*nirukta*). This science is presented in a systematised form in Yāska's work called, precisely, *Nirukta* – a text which appears to belong to the period between Pāṇini (after 350 BCE; see Hinüber 1989; Falk 1993: 304) and Patañjali (around 150 BCE; see Cardona 1976: 263f.) –, but the practice of etymologizing is extremely common in the earlier Vedic Brāhmaṇas. These Vedic etymologies do not concern the histories of words – and cannot, therefore, be compared with modern linguistic etymologies –, but have altogether different aims. As a rule they reveal hidden connections with the mythological realm, which can be multiple. (In practice this means that one word can have several different 'etymologies'). Knowing them brings advantages, as does knowing other hidden truths.

The 'etymologies' in Yāska's *Nirukta* are their secularised descendants. 'Etymologizing' has here become a method for finding the meaning of unknown words. Two presuppositions underlie it: (1) The meaning of a word (primarily noun or adjective) is the result of a combination of the meanings of its parts. (2) The meanings of those parts are not assigned to them by convention, they intimately belong to them (Bronkhorst 1981b).

These same presuppositions appear to underlie Pāṇini's grammar. Here, as we have seen (§ 2), constituent functional elements of words are combined, and the meaning of the resulting word is considered to be the combination of the meanings attaching to (or, in view of the above: separated from) those elements. The complementary character of grammar and 'etymological explanation' is confirmed by Yāska, who describes 'etymological explanation' in his *Nirukta* (1.15) as the 'complement of grammar'. But whereas 'etymological explanation' concentrates on cases that resist analysis, grammar normally confines itself to words the relationship of which with other words seems obvious and regular (Bronkhorst 1984). The analytical aspect of grammar, the search for the constituents of words, we must conclude, derives from the preoccupation with 'etymological' connections characteristic of much of Vedic literature.

The interaction of grammar with 'etymological explanation' was not unidirectional. Yāska refers in his *Nirukta* to grammar, and it seems likely that Pāṇini's *Aṣṭādhyāyī* was known to him (Thieme 1935; Bronkhorst 1984: 8f.). He justifies the procedures of 'etymological explanation' – such as ignoring, modifying, or inverting sounds – by pointing at similar practices in grammar (*Nirukta* 2.1). It appears that 'etymological explanation', when it tried to attain the status of a science besides grammar, drew inspiration from the latter.

## 4. Influence from philosophy

Pāṇini's grammar shows the traces of Vedic religious thought, as we have seen. Philosophical systematic thought did not exist in India at his time, as far as we can tell. Influence from that side can be discerned in the two earliest surviving commentaries, Kātyāyana's *vārttikas* and Patañjali's *Mahābhāṣya*, especially the latter. A systematised world view was being developed at that time – for the first time in India, it seems – in the Buddhist shool called Sarvāstivāda, which was deeply interested in questions of existence. For reasons connected with the historical development of Buddhism, a list of so-called *dharmas* came to be looked upon as the complete list of all there is. These *dharmas* were considered to be the ultimate constituents of persons and things. The persons and things themselves, being collections of *dharmas*, were not believed to really exist. Sarvāstivāda introduced a number of *dharmas* whose function it was to solve certain theoretical difficulties. Most of these theoretically useful *dharmas* were given a place in the category of *dharmas* called "separated from mind" (*cittaviprayukta*). Three of these *dharmas* are of particular interest. They are *padakāya*, *nāmakāya* and *vyañjanakāya*. This could be translated as "sentence", "word" and "phoneme" respectively, where it is to be kept in mind that these linguistic units are here conceived of as *dharmas*, i. e., as partless, ultimate, really existing entities. It seems likely that originally – i. e., around the time of Patañjali – only two of these three *dharmas* were recognised, the word and the phoneme.

Most probably influenced by Sarvāstivāda, Patañjali introduces two new notions into grammatical discourse, adapting them to their new Brahmanical environment: the word and the phoneme as single, independent entities. Both are eternel, contrasting in this respect with the momentary Buddhist *dharmas*. In connection with the phoneme Patañjali introduces a term which will play an important role in later linguistic speculation: *sphoṭa*. But, as in Sarvāstivāda, the word and the phoneme are unitary, indivisible entities, different from the sound that expresses them (Bronkhorst 1987). And where for Pāṇini morphemes were the basic units of language, Patañjali assigns them a derived meaning at best (cf. Bronkhorst 1998).

## 5. Language and philosophy

The role of grammar in Indian thought has regularly been emphasised. Louis Renou (1953: 86), for example, made the often cited statement "Adhérer à la pensée indienne, c'est d'abord penser en grammairien"; and again (1941–42: 164): "La pensée indienne a pour substructure des raisonnements d'ordre grammatical". Frits Staal (1960, 1963, 1965), following D. H. H. Ingalls (1954), has made the claim that Pāṇini's grammatical method is characteristic of much of Indian philosophy, just as Euclid's mathematical method is characteristic of much of Western philosophy. This is supposed to explain that scientific developments have taken different directions in India and the West. Bimal Krishna Matilal refers to the role of grammar in Indian philosophy, e. g., in the title of his book

*Epistemology, Logic, and Grammar in Indian Philosophical Analysis* (1971).

When it comes to substantiating these claims, one is disappointed. It is true that systematic abbreviations (a characteristic of Pāṇini's grammar) occur in mathematics, astronomy, and in other grammars; that the simplicity criterion and the algebraic *sūtra* style (both also typical of Pāṇini's grammar, but perhaps first used in ritual science) are used in many philosophical works. It is also true that grammar was part of the curriculum of every educated Indian, so that grammatical discussions are to be found in practically all commentaries, whatever the nature of the text they comment upon, and elsewhere (Filliozat 1988: 19ff.). But does this touch the heart of the matter? Does this interest in grammar go beyond the correct formation of words and sentences, and affect the contents of the treatises concerned? There are some, but not so many cases where grammatical analysis is used to reach a philosophical conclusion (for some examples see Torella 1987). The situation is complicated by the fact that many Indian authors looked upon the Sanskrit language as providing preferential access to reality, quite independently of any considerations of grammar. Something must be said about this.

Two phases are to be distinguished. During the first one language came to be considered, partly no doubt under Buddhist influence, as reflecting – or even creating/organising – phenomenal reality. Such a position has philosophical consequences, which were worked out in greatest detail in the Brahmanical system of philosophhy called Vaiśeṣika. The conviction that there is a direct correspondence between words and things might be called an axiom of this system. It justifies the ontological conclusions based on verbal usage common in the writings of this school (Bronkhorst 1992, 1996a). But the influence of grammar on this school remains small. One may suspect such influence in its three main categories substance *(dravya)*, quality *(guṇa)* and movement *(karman)*, which correspond to nouns, adjectives and verbs respectively. But did the Vaiśeṣikas need grammar in order to arrive at this division of words? The triple division into nouns, adjectives and verbs is not fundamental in Pāṇini's grammar.

The second phase is characterised by what has been called the 'correspondence principle' (Bronkhorst 1996b; 1999), which can approximately be formulated as follows: 'the words of a statement correspond, one by one, to the things that constitute the situation described by that statement'. The principle is plausible in the case of many, perhaps most, statements, but leads to serious difficulties in the case of certain others. Statements of the form 'he makes a pot' become problematic, because they do not describe a situation that contains a pot; the pot is still being made. These and related difficulties have been extensively discussed in Indian philosophical literature, and various solutions have been proposed and maintained by different authors and schools. Indeed, there are reasons to think that these discussions have led to several fundamental philosophical positions (such as the *satkāryavāda*, and the theory of denotation of certain schools), which are therefore based on certain views about language, not on grammar.

The correspondence principle is visible, perhaps for the first time, in a number of the contradictions presented by the Buddhist thinker Nāgārjuna in his important *Mūlamadhyamakakārikā* (2nd century CE?). Since some of these have been claimed to be based on grammar, they deserve some attention. Nāgārjuna claims that the statement "[The road] that is being travelled is being travelled"(*gamyamānaṃ gamyate*) implies that there must be two actions of travelling in the situation described. This is a direct consequence of the correspondence principle, given that the root *gam* "to travel" is used twice over in this statement. It is also a paradox, given that the statement does not describe a situation where there are two actions of travelling. A following verse adds that if there are two actions of travelling, there must be two travellers, another conclusion that is in contradiction with the intention of the initial statement.

These arguments can be satisfactorily explained with the help of the correspondence principle. K. Bhattacharya (most recently 1995) does not agree, and has argued in a number of articles that the argument of the second verse considered ("if there are two actions of travelling, there must be two travellers") is based on grammar. It is grammar which maintains that an action resides either in an agent or in an object and that the activity of travelling, more in particular, resides in its agent. This is true, but grammar does not specify that two actions cannot reside in one and the same agent. This is Nāgārjuna's own conclusion. The link between his argument and grammar is therefore far less obvious than it is claimed to be. Indeed, the only possible influence from grammar in these arguments is that here, exceptionally, the correspondence principle is applied to verbal roots rather than to whole words.

## 6. Bhartṛhari

We turn to Bhartṛhari (5th century CE), the 'philosopher of grammar'. To what extent is his thought determined by grammar? We will not discuss the numerous passages where Bhartṛhari deals with grammatical issues, but try to determine what influence grammar has exerted on his philosophy as a whole (→ Art. 20).

This philosophy as a whole concerns the nature of reality, in which Bhartṛhari, contrary to the Buddhists, recognises the existence of composite objects. Or rather, composite objects are not really composite, they are indivisible entities that exist besides 'their' parts. More precisely again, the more encompassing a thing is, the more it is real. Highest reality, for Bhartṛhari, is the totality of all there is, has been, and will be. The words of language divide this reality into (not really existing) parts.

So far Bhartṛhari's philosophy is an interesting adaptation of the ideas described above: the objects of phenomenal reality correspond to the words of language. New is that these objects are considered to be less real than their totality. This way Bhartṛhari could do justice to some traditional Brahmanical points of view, which looked upon the absolute as being the totality of all there is. Influence from grammar is not obvious here.

It seems clear nevertheless that grammar has contributed to this vision of reality. Consider first that Bhartṛhari applies a similar reasoning to language: words are more real than the constituent morphemes (mainly stems and suffixes), sentences more real than the words they are made up of. More exactly, words are independent entities that are not constituted of morphemes, and sentences are not made up of words. It is only through artificial analysis of words that morphemes are invented by grammarians, and words on the basis of sentences.

It is clear that Bhartṛhari draws here inspiration from Patañjali's *Mahābhāṣya* which, perhaps under the influence of Sarvāstivāda, had given ontological priority to words over stems and suffixes (see above). But Bhartṛhari goes further and establishes an ontological hierarchy: words are more real than their morphemes, sentences more real than their words, and the Veda as a whole more real than its sentences. Patañjali's argument concerning the higher ontological status of words with regard to their stems and suffixes, now extended, allows in this way to climb the ontological ladder, so as to arrive at the highest insight, which is beyond words, and which concerns undivided reality. This insight brings about liberation, and in this way grammar is "the door to liberation", as Bhartṛhari puts it (Bronkhorst 1995). Grammar has thus obtained its own philosophy, including an (in the Indian context important) liberating insight. But this philosophy is not based on the analysis of language implicit in Pāṇini's grammar, but quite on the contrary on the understanding that this analysis is not ultimately 'real'.

Bhartṛhari is especially remembered for his link with the *sphoṭa*, which in his case is primarily the indivisible word, different from the manifesting sounds. Later thinkers, both inside and outside the grammatical tradition, discuss and elaborate this concept. Modern scholars – foremost among them John Brough (1951) – see in the *sphoṭa* a concept of general linguistics, "simply the linguistic sign in its aspect of meaning-bearer (*Bedeutungsträger*)". In so doing they overlook the philosophical and ontological dimension of this concept, predominant in its original context.

## 7. Understanding the meaning of a sentence

There is an area of thought where Pāṇini's analysis of the Sanskrit language has exerted a clear and unmistakable influence. It is the attempted description of the knowledge which a listener derives from hearing a sentence, the so-called verbal cognition (*śābdabodha*), which came to occupy an important place in the three schools of thought called Mīmāṃsā (Vedic hermeneutics), Navya-Nyāya (the New Logic), and Vyākaraṇa (grammar as a school of philosophy) (for a general presentation see Rao [1969], especially chap. I; Matilal [1988; 1990: 53f.]; Coward & Kunjunni Raja [1990]; → Art. 20).

The self-imposed task of Mīmāṃsā was to interpret Vedic sentences. Its thinkers had come to think that injunctions are the crucial parts of Vedic texts. These injunctions do not however express the intention of their author, for they have none (and nor do any other Vedic sentences), because the Veda was believed to have no beginning in time. How, then, do Vedic injunctions enjoin? Reflections of this kind led the Mīmāṃsakas to interpret, and paraphrase, the injunctions in ways that suited their purposes (see Frauwallner 1938). Such paraphrases are already found in Śabara's *Mīmāṃsā Bhāṣya* (5th century?), but a connection with the Pāṇinian analysis of words makes its appearance in a commentary on this work, Kumārila's *Tantravārttika* (7th century). This connection remained however incomplete, as can be seen from the following example. Śabara paraphrases the injunction *svargakāmo yajeta* "he who wishes to attain heaven should sacrifice" as *yāgena svargaṃ bhāvayet* "by means of the sacrifice he should effect [the attainment of] heaven", which deviates rather profoundly from the Pāṇinian assignment of meanings (Śabara on *Mīmāṃsā Sūtra* 2.1.1). Kumārila, presenting the position of the system (*śāstra*), assigns the general meaning "productive operation" (*bhāvanā*) to the verbal ending (*ta* in the case of *yajeta*). This deviates from the meanings assigned to the verbal ending by Pāṇini (primarily 'agent'), but takes the latter's formal analysis of the verb for granted. Pāṇini's formal analysis of the remainder of the sentence, on the other hand, does not play a role in Kumārila's discussions. It gains in importance in some of the subsequent refinements introduced in the school (cf. Bhatta 1994; Edgerton 1929). The constituent elements of a statement like *rāmaḥ odanaṃ pacati* "Rāma cooks rice" – *rāma* + *s* – *anna* + *am* – *pac* + *ti* – give rise to a paraphrase which gives each element its due, and which has the following (simplified) form:

> "The productive operation (*bhāvanā*; meaning of *ti*) happening at present, which is done through the instrumentality of cooking that has rice as its object goal, and this efficient force is qualified by Rāma as its agent."

The Mīmāṃsā points of view were subsequently taken into consideration, but combated, by Gaṅgeśa, a key figure of Navya-Nyāya (14th century). For a description of the contents of his chapter on verbal testimony see Potter & Bhattacharya (1992: 239–312; partly coinciding with Vidyabhusana [1920]). He and his followers, too, present a paraphrase of verbal cognition which remains close to the Pāṇinian analysis of the sentence. Indeed, the reality of Pāṇinian morphemes is so much taken for granted by this school, that they refer to them as "words" (*pada*). The main qualificand here is not the meaning of the verbal ending (as with the Mīmāṃsakas), but that of the word with the nominative ending. The meaning of the sentence *rāmaḥ pacati* "Rāma cooks" is here approximately paraphrased as: "Rāma who is qualified by the effort that is conducive to cooking." The verbal ending is given the meaning 'effort', which is, again, different from Pāṇini's meaning 'agent'.

Only the grammarians maintain the Pāṇinian meaning 'agent' for the (active) verbal ending. Following Bhartṛhari (*Vākyapadīya* 3.8.40ff.; transl. Bandini [1980]), they look upon the meaning of the verbal root as the main qualificand. Kauṇḍa Bhaṭṭa (17th century) – an important representative of this school – assigns the meaning 'activity conducive to the result' to verbal roots; the substratum of the activity is the agent, the substratum of the result the object. The sentence "Rāma cooks rice" (*rāmaḥ odanaṃ pacati*) is therefore to be paraphrased, in a simplified manner, as: "Present activity whose substratum is Rāma, which is conducive to the softening whose substratum is rice" (Joshi 1993; 1995, especially 22ff.).

In all these reflections and debates Pāṇini's analysis of the Sanskrit language is used as point of departure, even though the meanings assigned by him to the morphemes are only fully accepted by the grammatical philosophers.

## 8. Conclusion

The importance of grammar in Indian classical culture cannot be overestimated. The extent to which it has exerted a determining influence on the Indian sciences is less easy to estimate, and exaggerated assessments have become all too common. The search for the fundamental nature of the Indian sciences, or of Indian thought in general, as being based on the supposedly all-important influence of grammar, is not likely to lead beyond more or less attractive slogans. This does not mean that there has not been intensive interaction between grammar and the other sciences, nor that this interaction has not left its traces. Bringing those traces to light will require continued detailed philological research.

## 9. Bibliography


Bandini, Giovanni. 1980. *Die Erörterung der Wirksamkeit. Bhartṛharis Kriyāsamuddeśa und Helārājas Prakāśa zum ersten Male aus dem Sanskrit übersetzt, mit einer Einführung und einem Glossar versehen.* (= *Beiträge zur Südasienforschung*, 61.) Wiesbaden: Steiner.

Bhatta, V. P. 1994. *Maṇḍana Miśra's Distinction of the Activity: Bhāvanāviveka. With introduction, English translation with notes, and Sanskrit text.* Delhi: Eastern Book Linkers.

Bhattacharya, Kamaleswar. 1995. "Back to Nāgārjuna and Grammar". *The Brahmavidyā, Adyar Library Bulletin* 59.178–189.

Bronkhorst, Johannes. 1979 [1980]. "The Role of Meanings in Pāṇini's Grammar". *Indian Linguistics* 40:3. 146–157.

–. 1981a. "The Orthoepic Diaskeuasis of the Ṛgveda and the Date of Pāṇini". *Indo-Iranian Journal* 23.83–95.

–. 1981b. "Nirukta and Aṣṭādhyāyī: Their shared presuppositions". *Indo-Iranian Journal* 23.1–14.

–. 1984. "Nirukta, Uṇādi Sūtra, and Aṣṭādhyāyī". *Indo-Iranian Journal* 27.1–15.

–. 1987. "The Mahābhāṣya and the Development of Indian Philosophy". *Three Problems Pertaining to the Mahābhāṣya*, 43–71. Poona: Bhandarkar Oriental Research Institute.

–. 1991. "Pāṇini and the Veda reconsidered". *Pāṇinian Studies. Professor S. D. Joshi Felicitation Volume* ed. by Madhav M. Deshpande & Saroja Bhate, 75–121. Ann Arbor: Center for South and Southeast Asian Studies, Univ. of Michigan.

–. 1992. "Quelques axiomes du Vaiśeṣika". *Les Cahiers de Philosophie* 14.95–110.

–. 1995 [1996]. "Studies on Bhartṛhari. 7. Grammar as the door to liberation". *Annals of the Bhandarkar Oriental Research Institute* 76.97–106.

–. 1996a. "Sanskrit and Reality: The Buddhist contribution". *Ideology and Status of Sanskrit: Contributions to the history of the Sanskrit language* ed. by Jan E. M. Houben, 109–135. Leiden: Brill.

–. 1996b. "The Correspondence Principle and its Impact on Indian Philosophy". *Indo-Shisōshi Kenkyū/Studies in the History of Indian Thought* (Kyoto) 8.1–19.

–. 1998. "Les éléments linguistiques porteurs de sens dans la tradition grammaticale du sanscrit." *Histoire Epistémologie Langage* 20: 1.29–38.

–. 1999. *Language et réalité: Sur un épisode de la pensée indienne.* Turnhout: Brepols.

Brough, John. 1951. "Theories of General Linguistics in the Sanskrit Grammarians". *Transactions of the Philological Society* 27–46. (Repr., Staal 1972: 402–414.)

Cardona, George. 1976. *Pāṇini: A survey of research.* (Repr., Delhi: Motilal Banarsidass, 1980.)

Coward, Harold G. & K. Kunjunni Raja. 1990. "Śābdabodha". *Encyclopedia of Indian Philosophies*, vol. V: *The Philosophy of the Grammarians* ed. by Harold G. Coward & K. Kunjunni Raja, 93–97. Delhi: Motilal Banarsidass.

Edgerton, Franklin. 1929. *The Mīmāṅsā Nyāya Prakāśa or Āpadevī: A treatise on the Mīmāṅsā system by Āpadeva. Translated into English, with an introduction, transliterated Sanskrit text, and glossarial index.* (Repr., Delhi: Sri Satguru Publications, 186.)

Falk, Harry. 1993. *Schrift im alten Indien: Ein Forschungsbericht mit Anmerkungen.* Tübingen: Narr.

Filliozat, Pierre-Sylvain. 1988. *Grammaire sanskrite pāninéenne.* Paris: Picard.

Frauwallner, Erich. 1938. "Bhāvanā und Vidhiḥ bei Maṇḍanamiśra". *Wiener Zeitschrift für die Kunde des Morgenlandes* 45.212–252. (Repr. in *Kleine Schriften*, 161–201. Wiesbaden & Stuttgart.)

Hinüber, Oskar von. 1989. *Der Beginn der Schrift und frühe Schriftlichkeit in Indien.* Stuttgart: Steiner.

Ingalls, Daniel H. H. 1954. "The Comparison of Indian and Western philosophy". *Journal of Oriental Research* 22.1–11.

Joshi, Shivaram Dattatray. 1993. "Kauṇḍa Bhaṭṭa on the Meaning of Sanskrit Verbs. 1". *Nagoya Studies in Indian Culture and Buddhism, Saṃbhāṣā* 14.1–39.

–. 1995. "Kauṇḍa Bhaṭṭa on the Meaning of Sanskrit Verbs. 2". *Nagoya Studies in Indian Culture and Buddhism, Saṃbhāṣā* 16.1–66.

Matilal, Bimal Krishna. 1971. *Epistemology, Logic and Grammar in Indian Philosophical Analysis.* The Hague & Paris: Mouton.

–. 1988. "Śābdabodha and the Problem of Knowledge-Representation in Sanskrit". *Journal of Indian Philosophy* 16.107–122.

–. 1990. *The Word and the World: India's contribution to the study of language.* Delhi: Oxford Univ. Press.

Potter, Karl H. & Sibajiban Bhattacharyya, eds. 1992. *Encyclopedia of Indian Philosophies*, vol. VI: *Indian Philosophical Analysis. Nyāya-Vaiśeṣika from Gangeśa to Raghunātha Śiromaṇi.* Princeton, NJ: Princeton Univ. Press.

Rao, Veluri Subba. 1969. *The Philosophy of a Sentence and its Parts.* New Delhi: Munshiram Manoharlal.

Renou, Louis. 1941–42 [1942]. "Les connexions entre le rituel et la grammaire en sanskrit". *Journal Asiatique* 233.105–165. (Repr. in Staal 1972: 435–469.)

–. "L'érudition". *L'Inde classique*, vol. II ed. by Louis Renou & Jean Filliozat, 85–137. (Repr., Paris: Adrien-Maisonneuve. 1985.)

–. 1963. "Sur le genre du sūtra dans la littérature sanscrite". *Journal Asiatique* 251.165–216.

Ruegg, D. Seyfort. 1978. "Mathematical and Linguistic Models in Indian Thought: The case of zero and *śūnyatā*". *Wiener Zeitschrift für die Kunde Südasiens* 22.171–181.

Scharfe, Hartmut. 1977. *Grammatical Literature.* (= *A History of Indian Literature*, V: 2.) Wiesbaden: Harrassowitz.

Staal, Frits. 1960. Review of D. S. Ruegg, *Contributions à l'histoire de la philosophie linguistique indienne. Philosophy East and West* 10.53–57.

–. 1963. "Euclides en Pāṇini: Twee methodische richtlijnen voor de filosofie". Amsterdam: Polak & Van Gennep. (Repr. in Staal 1986: 77–115.)

–. 1965. "Euclid and Pāṇini". *Philosophy East and West* 15.99–116. (Repr. in Staal 1988: 143–160.)

–. ed. 1972. *A Reader on the Sanskrit Grammarians.* Cambridge, Mass.: MIT Press.

–. 1982. *The Science of Ritual.* (= *Post-graduate and Research Department Series*, 15.) Poona: Bhandarkar Oriental Research Institute.

–. 1986. *Over zin en onzin in filosofie, religie en wetenschap.* Amsterdam: Meulenhof.

–. 1988. *Universals: Studies in Indian logic and linguistics.* Chicago: Univ. of Chicago Press.

–. 1989. *Rules Without Meaning: Ritual, mantras and the human sciences.* (= *Toronto Studies in Religion*, 4.) New York: Lang.

Thieme, Paul. 1935. "Zur Datierung des Pāṇini". *Zeitschrift der Deutschen Morgenländischen Gesellschaft* 89.*21*–*24*. (Repr. in *Kleine Schriften*, 528–531. Wiesbaden, 1971.)

–. 1982. "Meaning and Form of the 'grammar' of Pāṇini." *Studien zur Indologie und Iranistik* 8–9.1–34. (Repr. in *Kleine Schriften*, vol. II, 1170–1201. Wiesbaden, 1995.)

Torella, Raffaele. 1987. "Examples of the Influence of Sanskrit Grammar on Indian Philosophy". *East and West* 37.151–164.

Vidyabhusana, Satis Chandra. 1920. *A History of Indian Logic.* (Repr., Delhi: Motilal Banarsidass, 1978.)

*Johannes Bronkhorst, Lausanne (Switzerland)*

# 23. The role of linguistics in Indian society and education

1. Need for linguistic analysis in ancient India
2. Purposes of linguistic sciences discussed by ancient linguists
3. Linguistic sciences and interpretation of texts
4. Conflicting claims about the value of linguistic sciences
5. Traditional education and the role of linguistic sciences
6. Development of Prākṛta grammars
7. Vernacular grammars under the colonial rule
8. After independence: language policies, politics, and linguistics
9. Bibliography

## 1. Need for linguistic analysis in ancient India

From the very beginning of the Vedic period (± 1500–500 BC), language used in religious texts appeared to possess a mysterious aura. Common folks were said to have access only to a quarter of the true extent of this divine language, while only the wise and thoughtful priests were said to have access to its entire mystery. It was the responsibility of these wise Brahmans to comprehend the mystery of language and explain it in appropriate ways to those who had no access to it. The linguistic sciences in ancient India originated in this religious obligation felt by the Brahman priests. There were also a number of practical considerations. The Vedic literature was produced in different geographical areas and was orally transmitted both from one generation to the next, as well as from one region to another. There were also the shifting mother tongues of the transmitters and interpreters.

The priests believed that a ritual is truly perfect in form if the recited sacred texts matched the action being carried out. Thus one had to know what these texts meant. On account of the factors described earlier, neither the understanding nor a perfect pronunciation of the sacred texts could be taken for granted. This anxiety gave rise to the early efforts by the priestly scholars to find ways to overcome these difficulties.

Besides emphasizing the moral obligation to study the sacred texts and repeating the material and spiritual rewards for doing so, the priests followed a number of explicit analytical devices. Of common occurrence in the late Vedic literature is the device of folk etymology. A typical example is: "Why is Vṛtra called Vṛtra? Since he encircled (*avṛṇot*) the heavenly waters, he is called Vṛtra." This type of etymological explanation was a prized possession of a priest, as indicated by the repeating formula: "He who knows thus, gets the reward." Further there was an explicit effort to break down larger linguistic units into smaller units. The ritual context and the need for such an analysis is explained in the following passage of the *Śāṃkhāyana-Brāhmaṇa* (26.5):

"Him [= Jātūkarṇya] he [= Alīkayu Vācaspatya] asked 'If the performer himself should note a flaw passed over or another should call attention to it, how is that flaw to be made flawless? By repetition of the Mantra or by an oblation?' 'The Mantra should be recited again,' Jātūkarṇya said. Him Alīkayu again asked 'Should one recite in full the Śastra or recitation or Nigada or offering verse or whatever else it be?' 'So much as is erroneous only need be repeated, a verse (*ṛcam*), or half verse (*ardharcam*), or quarter verse (*pādam*), or word (*padam*), or individual sound (*varṇam*),' Jātūkarṇya replied."

In the late Vedic period, we find the beginning of the formation of a Sanskrit alphabet (*akṣarasamāmnāya*), which was a part of the standardization of the orally transmitted texts. The texts had to be standardized in pronunciation and stabilized in their wording. For the second purpose, the priestly scholars like Śākalya not only produced standardized editions (*saṃhitā*) of the floating oral texts, they created word-by-word versions (*padapāṭha*) of these texts, where the received unanalyzed texts (*nirbhujapāṭha*) were broken down into their constituent words (*pratṛṇṇapāṭha*). The broken down texts were again deliberately subjected to rules of sandhi to recreate the original continuous texts (*saṃhitā*). Both of these were directly serving the needs of ritual performance through assisting the preservation and the interpretation of the sacred texts.

## 2. Purposes of linguistic sciences discussed by ancient linguists

Beginning around 500 BC, there is a great deal of scientific activity in the areas of etymology, grammar, phonetics, and metrics. These sciences, along with astronomy, geometry etc., are called the Vedāṅga literature. They are ancillary sciences serving the need of preserving, applying, and interpreting the Vedic texts. Pāṇini's grammar of Sanskrit, the *Aṣṭādhyāyī*, Yāska's treatment of etymology in his *Nirukta*, and a large number of phonetic treatises called *Śikṣās* and *Prātiśākhyas* belong to this early post-Vedic period. While Pāṇini is silent about the exact purpose of his science, the *Nirukta*, the *Prātiśākhyas*, and the *Śikṣās* explain it great detail.

Yāska's *Nirukta* says that, without etymology, one cannot understand the meaning of the Vedic expressions, and without an understanding of the meaning, a mere recitation of the texts is nothing but carrying a burden, a useless activity. We are told that a mispronounced and misapplied mantra can destroy the sacrificer and the priest. Yāska situates his science within an important perception of history, i. e. the declining abilities of the successive generations. The purposes of phonetic training explained in the *Prātiśākhyas* and *Śikṣās* are on similar lines. Both the *Nirukta* and the phonetic treatises explain their purposes strictly within the context of the Vedic tradition.

A shift is noticed when we move to grammar. While Pāṇini does not explicitly deal with purposes of studying grammar, his successors, i. e. Kātyāyana and Patañjali, carry out this task. To begin with, Pāṇini's grammar does not just deal with the language of the Vedas, but deals with Sanskrit at large (→ Art. 17). Kātyāyana explains the importance of using correct Sanskrit by elevating the whole of Sanskrit to the level of the Vedas. The Vedas display a certain dialectal diversity of Sanskrit, though it is somewhat masked by the editorial efforts at standardization. There is evidence to suggest that there were various social dialects of Vedic language, as well as the possibility that there existed Prakrit-like languages spoken by certain social strata. While it seems most likely that the Vedic seers had some form of Vedic Sanskrit as their first language, Sanskrit gradually became dissociated from the status of being a first language and was retained more as an elite variety. This may have begun by the time of Pāṇini, but is certainly in evidence in Patañjali's *Mahābhāṣya*. Patañjali describes sages named Yarvāṇatarvāṇa who were called by this name because they used the Prakritic expressions *yarvāṇa* and *tarvāṇa* for the proper Sanskrit expressions *yad vā naḥ* and *tad vā naḥ*. However, they used the proper Sanskrit expressions during the performance of ritual. Patañjali says that these sages acted properly.

Having become mostly a second language by this time (300–200 BC), Sanskrit needed to be acquired deliberately by studying grammar, extolled as the most economical means of learning Sanskrit. Besides explaining the role of grammar in relation to the preservation and interpretation of the Vedas, Patañjali says that a Brahman needs to learn Sanskrit by using grammar, so that he may not speak like a barbarian (*mleccha*). To prevent sliding into the use of *apaśabdas* "improper degenerate expressions," a term by which Patañjali often intends the Prakrit vernaculars, one must study Pāṇini's grammar. This grammar was thus promoted by the grammarians as a sure means of acquiring an elite status for the learner.

## 3. Linguistic sciences and interpretation of texts

The tradition of Sanskrit grammar began with a descriptive goal, but was soon converted into a prescriptive tool for leaning Sanskrit. While the grammarians claimed the necessity of studying grammar in order to be able to interpret the scripture, a full-scale science of interpretation of the Vedas was initiated by the tradition of *Mīmāṃsā*. This system built a whole set of guiding principles which may be said to constitute one of the oldest statements on discourse analysis. How to interpret an expression in terms of its total context? What factors constitute the context? In the face of contradictory evidence, how to evaluate alternatives? Such questions were discussed in great detail by this school (→ Art. 20). The principles which evolved out of these deliberations were of great general value, and were widely used by other systems. Such generalized rules of interpretation were eventually incorporated in the traditions of grammar, religious law, and Sanskrit poetics.

## 4. Conflicting claims about the value of linguistic sciences

It may appear, on the surface, that traditions like those of Sanskrit grammar and *Mīmāṃsā* were working hand in hand with each other. There are proverbial statements claiming that the study of Sanskrit grammar and logic (= *Nyāya*) is useful for all branches of study. Such amity was actually quite rare, since these traditions were competing with each other for clientele and patronage, and had to promote their own interests. This led them to criticize each other's claims as being extravagant. The grammarians were claiming that one could not properly interpret the ritual texts without first learning Sanskrit grammar. The Mīmāṃsakas discounted these claims, and argued that one could indeed learn Sanskrit without studying grammar, through a sort of apprenticeship. The logicians claimed that they were more concerned with the level of meaning than with the level of words. At another level, some schools pointed out that knowing the language is not the same thing as knowing the truth. In the *Upaniṣads*, a student goes to a spiritual teacher and says that he has studied all the ancillary sciences, and yet he is merely a knower of the words, and not a knower of the Self. The school of Vedānta openly pitied the adherents of Sanskrit grammar and claimed that their strange-sounding rules will not save them from the rounds of birth and death. Buddhists often argued that the Buddha deliberately used ungrammatical language in order to free people from attachment to words and focus their attention on meaning.

## 5. Traditional education and the role of linguistic sciences

On a practical level, Pāṇini's grammar was turned into a prescriptive tool to teach Sanskrit. However, as soon as this was done, it faced a great opposition from many quarters, because of the high degree of its technical metalanguage. It created a heavy overhead for the learners of Sanskrit. Eventually, grammars like *Kātantra* developed essentially to simplify the statements of grammatical rules. Many of these later grammars served specific Jain or Buddhist constituencies, and eliminated from their rules those which dealt with the Vedic texts and accents. This shows the utilitarian orientation of these grammars. The utilitarian approach of the later Pāṇinian tradition is clear from the fact that there are fewer commentaries available on those sections of grammar that deal with Vedic usage and accents. We also find a significant development of works which contained simply the nominal and verbal paradigms to be memorized (*śabdarūpāvali* and *dhāturūpāvali*), and works which attempted to teach Sanskrit through simple conversations (e. g. *Gīrvāṇapadamañjarī*). Works like the *Uktivyaktiprakarana*, in a way, taught the students how to convert their Prakritic vernacular into Sanskrit with minimal changes.

## 6. Development of Prākṛta grammars

The development of Prakrit grammars is an important chapter in the history of Indian linguistic sciences. The Prakrit grammars, in general terms, have a very different format as compared to the grammars of Sankskrit. The Prakrit grammars are all written in Sanskrit. They provide rules to derive the various Prakrits by making minimal necessary modifications in Sanskrit. There is also an order in which the different Prakrits are derived, indicating among other things, a hierarchy of prestige among the Prakrits. Deriving Prakrits by making modifications in Sanskrit, these grammars clearly situate the study of Prakrits within the sphere of Sanskrit studies. This has important implications. While the use of Prakrits in the earliest period by the Jains and the Buddhists was, in part, a linguistic revolt against the supremacy of Sanskrit claimed by the Brahmans, eventually these traditions were themselves Sanskritized. It is common to find Sanskrit commentaries on Prakrit texts, but it is uncommon to find a Prakrit commentary on a Sanskrit text. The explanation of this behavior lies in the historical fact that while Sanskrit was stabilized by the works of its grammarians at a very early date and continued to be studied in this stable form for millennia, the Prakrit vernaculars generally became archaic very fast and could not be easily understood even by the followers of the religious traditions like Jainism. The study of Sanskrit and its grammars provided an element of stability in the midst of the perpetually changing nature of vernaculars.

## 7. Vernacular grammars under the colonial rule

Coming down to the colonial period, we find some important developments. Neither the grammars of Sanskrit nor Prakrits were composed at a time when these languages were first languages of anyone. The grammars were composed only when these languages had become second languages of high religious significance. Few grammarians were interested in the description of the truly vernacular languages. A major exception to this is the southern region of India, where grammars of Tamil were composed in Tamil at a very early date (→ Art. 27). Interestingly, the early grammars of vernaculars like Kannada, Malayalam, Telugu, and even Marathi, were all composed in the southern region, and moreover, many of these were composed in Sanskrit. However, it is clear that these grammars were elite works and were hardly ever used to learn or teach these languages.

First teaching grammars of modern Indian vernaculars were composed by the Christian missionaries in different parts of India. Early grammars of Marathi and Konkani were prepared by the Jesuits in Goa. Early grammars of Tamil were also prepared by Jesuit missionaries. A massive effort to write grammars of north Indian vernaculars and to print materials in those languages was initiated by missionaries in Bengal. Besides the missionary interest in the propagation of the Bible through native vernaculars, the colonial authorities also had a great interest in starting schools for the education of the natives, so that they could be used in administrative tasks. Such Native Education and Schoolbook Committees were set up in the different provinces of British India. Through such colonial administrative efforts the tasks of preparing dictionaries, textbooks, and translations of literary and scientific works into the vernaculars were undertaken on a large scale. It is through these efforts that the standardization of vernacular languages began in the early part of the nineteenth century. For example, the name of Major Candy is important in the history of Marathi. It was through his efforts that committees of native pundits prepared textbooks for schools, and, out of a mishmash of differing dialects, he created a subset of usage for textbooks which became the core of the current standard Marathi.

At the same time, there is another impact on India from the linguistic theories developed by westerners at this time. Until this time, there was no awareness among the Indians that the northern and the southern languages came from different language families, or that they could be possibly linked to distinct racial groups, namely the Aryans and the Dravidians. Medieval grammars of south Indian languages treat them as Prakrits. It is through the works of modern linguists that the Indians were made aware of possible different historical origins. This has had major political consequences leading to the development of group politics focused on identities constructed in terms of Dravidian, Aryan, Brahman, and non-Brahman origins. This is a continuing factor in modern Indian politics.

## 8. After independence: language policies, politics, and linguistics

After independence in 1947, the question of languages became volatile in India. First, a commitment had been made to reorganize the Indian states into monolingual entities. This created major problems for all areas where there were large bilingual populations. Indian linguists took part in these political decisions as advisors and consultants. For example, the question of whether Konkani was a dialect of Marathi or an independent language was hotly debated among linguists, as among the politicians. Then the question of national language, the role of the regional languages, and the role of English were major issues, and continue to be so till today. If a language like Hindi is viewed as a national language, what sort of a language should it be? Should it be a more Sanskritized language? Should it enrich itself with vocabulary from other regional languages? What role should the national language and the state languages be given in interstate communication, education, etc.? How many languages should the students be required to learn, and at what level of education? Indian linguists have been participating in debates on all these issues (→ Art. 24).

The central as well as the state governments in India have set up institutions which promote linguistic expertise of different kinds. For instance, the central government has set up the Central Institute of English and Foreign Languages in Hyderabad, the Central Institute of Indian Languages in Mysore, and the Central Institute of Hindi in Agra. The Central Hindi Directorate and the Rāṣṭrīya Saṃskṛta Saṃsthāna (= National Institute for Sanskrit) directly work within the education ministry of the central government. The census department of the central government collects and analyses data on languages. The state governments have set up various organizations at the regional level to deal with issues relating to languages. For example, there are committees set up to create new terminologies for various fields to replace the use of English terms, committees to supervise reforms of scripts and spellings, and committees to monitor the production of translations and textbooks.

The electronic age has created its own language-related needs in India. The central department of electronics has taken the lead in setting up major institutions like the Centre for the Development of Advanced Computing in Pune. This center has taken important steps in the development of software and hardware to facilitate the use of Indian languages and scripts on the computers. Similarly, there is the Indian Typographical Research Institute in Pune devoted to the development of computer fonts and keyboard layouts for all Indian languages. All of these areas involve expertise in linguistics to different degrees. On the whole, there is enormous scope for application of linguistics to solve the language-related problems of modern India, see the bibliographic references in Khubchandani (1981).

## 9. Bibliography

### 9.1. Primary sources

Śarvavarman, *Kātantra-Vyākaraṇa.* Ed. by J. Eggeling. Calcutta, 1874–1878.

Patañjali, *Mahābhāṣya.* Ed. by Franz Kielhorn. 3 vols. 1880–1885. (3rd revised ed. by K. V. Abhyankar. Pune: Bhandarkar Oriental Research Institute, 1962–1972.)

Yāska, *Nirukta,* with the commentary of Durga. 2 vols. Pune: Ānandāśrama, 1921, 1926.

*Śāṃkhāyana-Brāhmaṇa* (= *Kauṣītaki-Brāhmaṇa*). Ed. by Gulabrao Vajeshankar. 2nd ed. Pune: Ānandāśrama, 1977.

### 9.2. Secondary sources

Das Gupta, Jyotirindra. 1970. *Language Conflict and National Development.* Berkeley & Los Angeles: Univ. of California Press.

Deshpande, Madhav M. 1993. *Sanskrit and Prakrit: Sociolinguistic issues.* Delhi: Motilal Banarsidass.

Khubchandani, Lachman M. 1981. *Language Education Social Justice.* Pune: Centre for Communication Studies.

Shapiro, Michael C. & Shiffman, Harold F. 1981. *Language and Society in South Asia.* Delhi: Motilal Banarsidass.

*Madhav M. Deshpande, Ann Arbor (USA)*

# 24. The Hindi grammatical tradition

The Hindi grammatical tradition that has evolved to the present day is a composite resulting from the fusion of several distinct grammatical traditions and methodologies. Although this tradition has at various times and in various ways shown the influence of the great Indian grammatical tradition associated with Sanskrit and Prakrit, it has not evolved directly from the older tradition. Rather, it has by and large resulted from the importation of Western approaches to grammar, themselves highly varied, and then applied in different contexts and for different purposes to New Indo-Aryan language varieties, including those that are subsumed under the general term 'Hindi'. Traditional Indian approaches to grammar, to the extent that they are reflected in linguistic accounts of Hindi, are manifest in such matters as nomenclature and particular points of grammatical analysis, but seldom in the broad organizing principles in terms of which the grammar as a whole is structured.

There are several terminological and definitional factors that complicate any discussion of the historiography of Hindi and related speech forms. One of the most important of these concerns the multiplicity of language varieties to which term the 'Hindi' applies. In one way or another the historiography of Hindi needs deal with such disparate entities as Modern Standard Hindi (*Khaṛī Bolī*), Modern Standard Urdu, regional dialects and languages sometimes subsumed under the rubric of Hindi (Bundelī, Vernacular Hindustānī, Chattisgaṛhī, the 'Bihārī' and 'Rājasthānī' languages, the so-called 'Pahāṛī' languages, the 'Dakhinī' Hindi/Urdu of Hyderabad, etc.), as well as the speech varieties associated with several premodern literary traditions (Braj, Avadhī, Sādhū Bhāṣā, Ḍingal, etc.). In addition, overseas varieties of Hindi and of related languages (known under diverse names such as Fiji Hindi, Sarnami, etc.) have been treated at various times in the Hindi grammatical tradition (Barz & Siegel 1988) and must therefore receive mention in a historiography of Hindi. Lastly, pidginized or creolized varieties of Hindi and *lingua franca* forms of Hindi in Mumbai, Calcutta and other large urban areas have been the objects of linguistic investigation (Jagannathan 1981: 413–436).

The establishment of an earliest date for the start of the Hindi grammatical tradition is controversial. In the first major study of the history of Hindi grammar, Chaudharī (1972), following Ziāddīn (1935), traces the tradition to Mirzā Khān-ibn-Fakkru-u-Dīn's Persian language grammar of Braj Bhāṣā, *Tuḥfatu-l-Hindi*, to which he ascribes a date of 1676. In the most comprehensive history of Hindi grammar to date, Bhatia (1991: 21–45) assigns a possible later date of 1711 to Mirzā Khān's grammar, and argues for the acceptance of a Dutch language grammar of Hindi and Persian by J. J. Ketelaar, which he dates to 1698, as the first grammar of Hindi.

During the centuries of colonial rule and influence in India a large number of dictionaries, grammars, primers, word lists, readers, and the like were written for a wide variety of New Indo-Aryan languages, including Hindi and Urdu in their various guises. These grammars were written primarily in English, French, Portuguese, Italian, German, Russian, and Latin. The number of such works is quite large (reaching several hundred), and it is not possible to make statements characterizing this body of literature as a whole. The reasons why these works were written are varied. Some evolve from missionary activities of one sort or another. Others are clearly ancillary to colonial administration, in particular the need for colonial powers, most particular the British, to have a cadre of officers and administrators knowledgeable in Indian vernacular languages. Such works are frequently restricted to the language of particular strata of society or vocational groups (e. g., military Hindi/Urdu or the Hindi/Urdu of ship pilots).

Grammars written during the colonial period differ also greatly among themselves in the degree of linguistic sophistication with which they were written. Many are little more than amateurish gatherings of vocabulary and impressionistically recorded grammatical patterns. Others, particularly some written in the late 19th and early 20th centuries, display sophisticated knowledge of historical and comparative linguistics, and are broadly representative of academic linguistic practice outside of the Indian sub-continent.

Among the numerous Western scholars who made substantial contributions during the colonial period to the description and analysis of Hindi grammar (see Bhatia 1991 for a lengthy description) are three worthy of note in this brief discussion. John B. Gilchrist, the author of three important works on Hindi grammar (1796, 1798, 1803), is noteworthy both for his efforts on behalf of promoting formal instruction in Hindi (he was the first head of Fort William College, opened in 1800, which greatly promoted the use of *Kharī Bolī* Hindi in educational and administrative contexts in India) and for his placing the study of Hindi grammar on solid footing. He was able to do this by viewing the grammatical categories of Hindi as being distinct from those of Latin, English, and other European languages and by basing his grammatical descriptions on wide samples of different styles of Hindi/Urdu, including much drawn from written literature (Bhatia 1991: 86–87).

A second Western scholar worthy of note here is the Reverend S. H. Kellogg, the author of what is probably the most comprehensive grammar of Hindi yet written in any European language (Kellogg 1875; second edition 1892). Kellogg's grammar was written with a particular objective in mind, namely to redress what Kellogg considered to be an unfair favoritism on the part of British colonial administrators towards a Persianized style of Urdu. He wished to further the cause of 'Hindi' by the presentation of a systematic grammar of Hindi, as written in the Devanāgarī script, based upon a detailed examination of Hindi literary texts.

Kellog's grammar far exceeds in scope even what his stated intentions were. The grammar provides a detailed description of the morphology not only in 19th century *Kharī Bolī*, grammar, but also of a wide variety of vernacular Hindi dialects (Kanaujī, Braj, Avadhī, etc.), and also several other languages (Western and Eastern Rājasthānī, Gaṛhvālī, Kumāonī, Bhojpūrī, Māgadhī, Nepālī, Maithilī, etc.). Kellogg's descriptions of Hindi constructions are considerably more detailed than those seen in earlier Hindi grammars. Kellogg also provides discussions of the historical origins of Hindi morphological constructions and grammatical markers and offers a wealth of information on such matters as Hindi meters, writing systems used for Hindi (over and beyond the expected Devanāgarī), and strata of Hindi vocabulary.

A third European scholar whose contributions to the development of Hindi grammar were particularly noteworthy was Sir George A. Grierson, the Director of the *Linguistic Survey of India* (Grierson 1903–1928). It was the *LSI* that established the first scientifically based taxonomy of the Indo-Aryan languages, within which the linguistic status of various forms of Hindi, Urdu, and other New Indo-Aryan speech forms could be based. The grammatical data which served as the basis for Grierson's assessment of the linguistic status of Hindi are contained in two separate volumes of the *LSI*. The separation of Hindi into Western and Eastern dialect zones, and the ascribing of independent linguistic status to 'Rajasthani', 'Bihari', etc. is the direct result of Grierson's classificatory efforts. Although classifications of New Indo-Aryan languages have been proposed that differ from Grierson's, taxonomy given in *LSI* has even today not been completely superseded.

In the mid-19th century a body of Hindi grammars were written in Hindi by Indian scholars, some of these grammars displaying considerable originality. Two of these worthy of mention are the *Bhāṣā-candrodya* by Paṇḍit Śrīlāl (1855) and Rājā Śivprasād's *Hindī Vyākaraṇ* (1875), the former important because of its attempt to describe Hindi grammar in terms derivative from traditional Indian (i.e., Sanskrit) grammar (Bhatia 1991: 107–109), and the latter because of its stated desire to account for the common ground between overly Perso-Arabicized Urdu and overly Sanskritized registers of Hindi (Bhatia 1991: 119–123). Two later works, Kāmtāprasād Guru's *Hindī Vyākaraṇ* (1920) and Kiśorīdās Vājapeyī's *Hindī Śabdānuśāsan* (1958) have been highly influential, and grammatical accounts appearing in these works have been appropriated or served as the starting point for discussions in many other first language Hindi grammars. Both Guru's and Vājpeyī's grammars were published by the Nāgarī Pracāriṇī Sabhā, a prominent organization founded in 1893 and dedicated to the cause of promulgating Hindi, as written in the Devanāgarī orthography, as a vehicle for national advancement and unity (see King 1994).

The grammatical cores of these grammars are essentially that of traditional Western grammar, but with grammatical terminology either loan translated from English into a neo-Sanskritic guise or adapted from Sanskrit terminology itself, albeit in an entirely non-Pāniṇian context. As examples of non-Pāninian Sanskrit terms we may quote *kṛd-*

*anta* and *tadhita*, traditionally used for specific classes of verbal derivational suffixes, but used by Vājpeyi (1958: 265–306) for many types of deverbal derivations, including those involving non-Indo-Aryan bases as suffixes. Another example is that of *sãyukt kriyā* (literally "complex verb" or "compound verb"), which is used for a multiplicity of verbal constructions formed from either the uninflected or inflected verbal stem (Guru 1920: 310–325). Neologisms are *nikaṭvartī* "proximate" and *dūrvartī* "non proximate", used with reference to the third person demonstrative pronouns *yah* and *vah*, respectively (Guru 1920: 243); and *punarukt śabd* "said again words", used for "reduplications" (Guru 1920: 413).

In the post-World War II period there has been a veritable explosion of publication of works dealing with Hindi, Urdu, and their various speech varieties. This literature can conveniently be divided into that which is primarily theoretical in nature and that which is pedagogical, although in many instances the line of separation between the two types is not sharp. For the most part, highly theoretical analyses of points of Hindi grammar have been written in European languages rather than in Hindi itself. The dominance of European languages, and English in particular, for publication by South Asian scholars of works on Hindi linguistics is no doubt a reflection of the bifurcation in South Asia of the cultures of university departments of linguistics, in which the medium of instruction is almost always English, and in which the dominant intellectual frameworks are those of linguistics outside of the Indian subcontinent, and those of departments of Hindi or Urdu, in which grammatical analysis tends to be more traditional and linked to the reading of literary texts, and in which the media of instruction are Hindi or Urdu.

In the post-independence period, linguistic analyses of Hindi have been written from the theoretical perspectives of virtually all major schools of linguistics. In the 1950s and 1960s the dominant approaches were that of American or European structuralism. Among the numerous scholars whose names can be mentioned in this regard are Henry M. Hoenigswald, Vladimír Miltner, V. P. Liperovskij, and Vincenc Pořízka. Beginning with the middle 1960s, Hindi linguistics came to be heavily dominated by insights derivative of various forms of transformational general grammar, although works written in any of several 'non-Chomskyan' forms of linguistic theory were also produced. The most well-known and productive scholar working within a generally Chomskyan framework of linguistic analysis is Yamuna Kachru, who has trained many scholars working within a broadly 'generative' approach to Hindi/Urdu grammar. During the same period of time several studies of aspects of Hindi/Urdu grammar were written from the perspective of Case Grammar, after the model of Charles Fillmore and his followers. In the 1980s and 1990s a plethora of studies of Hindi/Urdu were written from such varied theoretical models as government and binding theory, X-bar syntax, lexical morphology, and lexical phonology.

Limitations of space make it impossible to list all of the topics that have received attention over the past three decades in the theoretical literature on Hindi/Urdu grammar. It should be noted, however, that syntax has received considerably more attention than phonetics and phonology (with notable exceptions in Kelkar 1968 and Ohala 1983), historical linguistics, dialectology, and semantics. Topics that have proven to be of enduring interest and that have been discussed in subtantial numbers of publications include conjunct and compound verbs, morphologically related verb sets and causative verbs, the so-called 'ergative' construction, passives, relative clause formation, pronominalization and reflexivization, and verbal categories. Within historical linguistics, argumentation and discussion concerning the mutual relations between Hindi and Urdu (see especially Rai 1984) have continued unabated. This body of literature overlaps another dealing with such sociolinguistic concerns as the styles and registers of Hindi/Urdu, the use of distinct registers Hindi/Urdu for different purposes, and the formulation of complex linguistic repertoires in which styles of Hindi or Urdu function as components. On the pedagogical side, a vast body of teaching materials, comprising grammars, dictionaries, readers, style manuals (see particularly Jagannathan 1981), workbooks, etc. has been prepared over the past four decades. Teaching materials have been written exemplifying different approaches to language learning (e. g., reading/translation, oral/aural, pattern repetition), prepared for the benefit of different audiences (first language learners of Hindi/Urdu, speakers of Indo-Aryan languages other than Hindi/Urdu or South Asian non-Indo-Aryan languages, second language learners who are native speakers of European languages or Asian languages such as Japanese or Chinese, or members of the South Asian diaspora throughout the world). Bilingual instructional materials and dictionaries have been prepared for Hindi/Urdu through the media of English, German, French, Russian, Czech, Polish, Italian, Danish, Dutch, Japanese, Chinese, and other languages. In recent years the preparation, publication, and dissemination of pedagogical materials for Hindi/Urdu has been assisted by the development of computer software programs (including fonts for Indian scripts) and for the construction of sites and homepages on the internet.

It is beyond the scope of this paper to treat on an individual basis the hundreds of publications that constitute the raw data for the historiography of Hindi grammar. For detailed bibliographic surveys the reader is referred to Aggarwal (1978, 1982), Khan (1969), Miltner (1969), and Shapiro (1979, 1983).

## Bibliography


Aggarwal, Narindar K. 1978. *A Bibliography of Studies on Hindi Language and Linguistics.* Gurgaon: Indian Document Service. (2nd ed., 1985.)

–. 1982. "Reference Material in Hindi: State of the art." *American Institute of Indian Studies Newsletter* 9,2/3. 1968.

Barz, Richard K. & Jeff Siegel, eds. 1988. *Language Transplanted: The development of overseas Hindi.* Wiesbaden: Otto Harrassowitz.

Bhatia, Tej. K. 1991. *A History of the Hindi Grammatical Tradition.* Leiden: Brill.

Chaudharī, Ananta. 1972. *Hindī vyākaraṇ kā itihās.* Patna: Bihar Hindi Granth Academy.

Gilchrist, John B. 1796. *A Grammar of the Hindoostanee Language or Part Third of Volume First, of a System of Hindoostannee Philology.* Calcutta: The Chronicle Press. (Repr., Menston: The Scolar Press, 1970.)

–. 1798. *The Oriental Linguist.* Calcutta: Ferries & Greenway.

–. 1803. *The Strangers' East Indian Guide to the Hindoostanee.* London: Black, Pary & Kingsbury. (2nd ed., 1808.)

Grierson, George A. 1903–28. *Linguistic Survey of India.* 11 vols. Calcutta. (Repr., Delhi: Motilal Banarsidass, 1967.)

Guru, Kāmtāprasād. 1920. *Hindī Vyākaraṇ.* Vārāṇasī: Nāgarīpracāriṇī Sabhā. (Revised ed., 1962.)

Jagannathan, V. R. 1981. *Prayog aur Prayog.* Delhi: Oxford Univ. Press.

Kachru, Yamuna. 1980. *Aspects of Hindi Grammar.* New Delhi: Manohar.

Kelkar, A. R. 1968. *Studies in Hindi-Urdu,* vol. I: *Introduction and Word Phonology.* (= *Building Centenary and Silver Jubilee Series,* 35.) Poona: Deccan College.

Kellogg, S. H. 1875. *A Grammar of the Hindí Language.* London: Routledge & Kegan Paul. (2nd ed., 1893; repr., 1965.)

Khan, Masud Husain. 1969. "Urdu". *Current Trends in Linguistics,* vol. V: *Linguistics in South Asia* ed. by Thomas A. Sebeok, 277–283. The Hague: Mouton.

King, Christopher R. 1994. *One Language, Two Scripts: The Hindi movement in nineteenth century North India.* Bombay: Oxford Univ. Press.

Miltner, Vladimír. 1969. "Hindi". *Current Trends in Linguistics,* vol. V: *Linguistics in South Asia* ed. by Thomas A. Sebeok, 55–84. The Hague: Mouton.

Ohala, Manjari. 1983. *Aspects of Hindi Phonology.* Delhi: Motilal Banarsidass.

Rai, Amrit. 1984. *A House Divided: The origin and development of Hindi/Hindavi.* Delhi: Oxford Univ. Press.

Shapiro, Michael C. 1979. *Current Trends in Hindi Syntax: A bibliographic survey.* (= *Studien zur Indologie und Iranistik,* 5.) Reinbek.

–. 1983. "On Hindi Dictionaries and Related Matters". *Journal of the American Oriental Society* 103,4.749–754.

Śivaprasād. 1875. *Hindī Vyākaraṇ.* Allahabad: Government Press. (Revised ed., 1900.)

Śrīlāl. 1855. *Bhāṣā-candrodaya.* 2nd ed. Agra.

Vājpeyī, Kiśorīdās. 1958. *Hindī-śabdānuśāsan.* Kāśī: Nāgarīpracāriṇī Sabhā.

Ziāuddīn, M. 1935. *A Grammar of the Braj Bhākhā by Mirzā Khān (1676).* Calcutta: Vishva-Bharati Book Shop.


*Michael C. Shapiro, Seattle (USA)*

# 25. Indian influence on the linguistic tradition of Burma

1. Historical background
2. 'Half-indianized' Burmese phonetics
3. Burmese morphosyntax as seen through the Indian terminology
4. Bibliography

## 1. Historical background

The linguistic tradition of Burma (now referred to as Myanmar) is practically as old as its 'codified' culture as such. Along with Buddhism adopted ca. 11th century, the Kingdom of Pagan, the historical predecessor of Burma, had got access to the rich sources of Indian culture and scholarship as reflected in Buddhist treatises (according to some authorities, "the Pali books are said to have been introduced into Burmah AD [as early as] 387", Mason [1880: 177]). From that time on, Pali, the language of the Scriptures, occupied the privileged position of the idiom associated with the sacred, the lofty, to be followed as a model and imitated.

Pali linguistic works, stemming from the brilliant Sanskrit heritage, mostly followed one of the two traditions, viz. the great tradition of Kaccāyana or that of Moggalāna (cf. *Kaccāyanappakaraṇaṁ*; *Moggalāyana-Vyākaraṇa*; cf. Geiger 1916). Without attempting to analyze the differences between the two, we may state that both of them found their way into Burma, that of Kaccāyana apparently having been predominant. Actually, it was the Burmese tradition that preserved Kaccāyana's work for posterity:

"Kachchayano's Pali Grammar was supposed to be lost until its existence was reported from Burmah, where, while European and Ceylonese Pali scholars were writing it down *non est*, it was found in every library, and was being taught and had been taught from time immemorial in every monastery" (Mason 1880:197).

Very soon, Burmese Buddhist monks, who were quite naturally the first scholars to deal with the problems of language, made their first attempts at probing into the nature of language. In M. Bode's words (Bode 1909: xiv), "the technicalities of Indian grammars have attracted Burmese authors from an early period". As early as 1064, Dhammasenāpati had compiled his *Kārikā*, a concise treatise devoted to Pali prosody and metrics which touched upon some problems of grammar as well. The treatise was written on Pali and in Pali, since the vernacular Burmese was considered neither a worthy object of, nor an appropriate tool for a scholarly description: Burmese was looked upon as something profane, as opposed to the sacred Pali. There is some information about a number of other grammatical works, also on Pali and in Pali, that appeared in the 11th century, such as *Tathāgatupatti* by the Pagan monk Ñaṅa-gambhīra.

The 12th century witnesses the flourishing of *ars grammatica* in Burma. It was in the 12th century that Aggavaṁsa, preceptor and tutor to king Narapatisithu (1167–1204), compiled his famous *Saddanīti*. As its title suggests, the treatise was written in the form of *nīti*, that is of arranging its material as a collection of maxims – rules or precepts. In fact, this form of presenting a linguistic description had been practiced in India at least from the times of Pāṇini. The above treatise of Aggavaṁsa was directly concerned with the language of the Buddhist Canon, the *Tipiṭaka*. Its significance seems to have been much wider than that of a purely local event. It is reported that soon after its appearance, the treatise, thanks to the activities of Uttarājīva, was distributed among the learned monks of Mahāvihāra, Ceylon, the then center of Buddhist scholarship, who recognized the Pagan scholar's treatise as the best of its kind (Bode 1908: 88–89). Aggavaṁsa's grammar was divided into 2 parts and 25 sections (*paricchedas*), in which Pali phonetics and grammar were codified in the form of *suttas*. It is worth noting that in his treatise Aggavaṁsa showed his familiarity with Sanskrit, as he gave Sanskrit parallels to the Pali forms in the second part of the treatise (*Dhātumāla*).

Another distinguished author of grammatical treatises in medieval Burma was Chapaṭa, also known under his monastic name Saddhammajotipala. Prompted by Uttarājīva, his spiritual master, Chapaṭa went to Mahāvihāra where he was trained, among other things, in *ars grammatica*. His major works were *Suttanidesa* or *Kaccāyanasuttanidesa* and *Sankhepavaṇṇanā*. The former, as can be seen from its title, was, in fact, a commentary on Kaccāyana's *suttas*. According to some sources, however, Chapaṭa was not the real author of the two treatises traditionally ascribed to him: it is suspected that the first of them had been written by Kaccāyana himself and just transcribed by means of the Mon-Burmese alphabet in Chapaṭa's work while the second had actually been compiled by an anonymous Ceylonese author (cf. Bode 1908: 89, 90).

In some of the grammatical treatises dating back as early as the 13th/14th centuries, one can find scattered observations about the Burmese language. Thus, U Kyi Pwe, a scholar who is known to have worked at the time of the king Narathihapate (1254–1287), in his treatises used to give Burmese equivalents to Pali inflected forms. Similarly, Caturaṅgabala who flourished under the reign of Hsinbyulezishin Thihatu, also known as Kyawswange (1350–1359), is reported to have introduced certain Burmese glosses into his generally monolingual dictionary of the Pali language (Wun 1975: 1–3).

It was not until the 18th century that the first Burmese grammars concerned with the vernacular language started to appear. The very first treatises of this kind seem to have been *Kəwìlɛʔkhənā Mjāŋmā ṭədā* by Kyaw Aung San Hta Sayadaw I (1748) and *Ṭədābjūhā* by Taungdwin Sayadaw (ca. 1751). It is important to note that, actually, the texts which these grammars in question were intended to describe were not 'pure' Burmese writings (not to mention common parlance) but, rather, a so-called *nissaya* (a Pali word whose literal meaning is "dependent upon"). A Burmese *nissaya* is a text where each Pali word or phrase is supplied with its Burmese equivalent. The *nissaya* texts (that have occasionally been appearing up to these days) were originally designed to help the Burmese understand the Pali writings. It is believed by some authors (see, especially, Okell 1965) that the well-known differences between the 'formal' or 'written' and 'colloquial' or 'casual' styles in Modern Burmese grammar can be traced back to the *nissaya* texts: it is the latter that, presumably, triggered the 'written'-type innovations as a result of a regular adaptation of the original 'pre-Buddhist' Burmese to Pali.

It should be noted that for the Burmese scholars the problem of the influence of Pali on Burmese practically never arose. Since the *nissaya* texts were the first to be subjected to a grammatical analysis, the regular co-occurrence of Pali and Burmese words and phrases in such texts gave rise to a conviction that the two languages, i. e. Pali and Burmese as presented in the *nissaya*, were, 'in a higher sense', simply identical. This, in its turn, 'justified' analyzing Burmese on an equal footing with Pali. Some of the authors went so far as to insist on tracing certain original Burmese words or particles to their alleged Pali 'etyma', as when they attempted to identify *tò*, a plurality marker, with the Pali *bahu* "many" (cf. Okell 1965: 193). The combined effect of the naive identification of Burmese with Pali and of the unrivaled prestige of Indian scholarly thought naturally resulted in that the early Burmese grammarians,

> "not content with merely borrowing the grammatical nomenclature of the Pali language, attempted to assimilate the grammatical principles of the uninflected Burmese to those of the inflected Pali, so that they produced, not Burmese grammars but modified Pali grammars in Burmese dress" (Lonsdale 1899: iii–iv).

As a matter of fact, even up to this day (a few works written by European-, American- or Australian-trained linguists apart), the local tradition is crucially inspired by the ancient Indian paradigm.

## 2. 'Half-indianized' Burmese phonetics

One of the striking examples of Indian influence on Burmese linguistic thought is the traditional way of describing Burmese phonetics. As is well known, the Indian tradition analyzes consonants into 7 *vaggas* (Bu. *wɛʔgà*) organized mostly, albeit not exclusively, in terms of place of articulation, viz.: *ka-vagga* (k, kh, g, gh, ṅ), *ca-vagga* (c, ch, j, jh, ñ) and so on. The Burmese tradition faithfully reproduces the same order and the same characteristics of the sounds without paying much attention to the actual features of the Burmese consonants (or vowels). Thus, for instance, in Modern Burmese words, /c, ch, j/ (or rather, ħ, ħh, ɧ) have given way to /s, sh, z/ respectively, cf. Pali *ceto* > Bu. *seʔ* "mind" etc. Nonetheless, the latter consonants are still interpreted as palatals, not dentals (cf. Zargara 1978: 2).

In some other instances, however, the adherence to the Indian tradition seems to give Burmese grammarians (phoneticians) an advantage, compared to their Western colleagues. The phonological interpretation of the aspirates may serve as an example. In most Western works, the aspirated obstruents of Burmese (ph, th, kh etc.) are treated separately from the so-called voiceless sonorants that are transcribed, correspondingly, as /m̥, l̥/ etc. (Armstrong & Pe Maung Tin 1925; Bernot 1963 etc.). Bhaskararao & Ladefoged (1991) have shown very convincingly that these are phonetically different realizations of the above sonorants, where the 'Burmese type' is characterized, among other things, by the presence of a *voiced* portion in the sonorants in question; yet Ladefoged and his co-author retain the 'quasi-traditional' interpretation of the sonorants in question as voiceless nasal and voiceless liquid.

Apart from that, most Burmese philologists treat the aspirates and the 'voiceless sonorants' alike, using a term whose literal meaning is "chest-sounds". This is clearly reminiscent of the Indian traditional distinction between aspirates and non-aspirates as *mahā-prāṇa*, lit. "big-breath" vs. *alpha-prāṇa*, lit. "little-breath" (Allen 1953: 38). It is not just the native speaker's intuition of how the consonants are actually produced, coupled with their familiarity with the Indian tradition that led the Burmese authorities to a more profound understanding of the phonological relations in the system. Another factor of crucial importance, not duly appreciated by the Western scholars, leads one to the same conclusion: both obstruent aspirates and 'voiceless sonorants' (which are actually *pre-aspirated* sonorants) are found to function alike in causative derivation processes, cf. /kwɛ̂/ "to be divided, different" → /khwɛ̂/ "to divide" and /luʔ/ "to be free" → /hluʔ/ "to set free".

In conformity with the Indian tradition, the duration of sounds is measured in terms of *mattās*, i. e. morae. It is maintained by some authors that syllable-initial consonants are 1.5 *mattā* long, which may sound strange if we recall that, traditionally, "a short vowel = 1 *mātrā*; a long vowel = 2 *mātrā*s" (Allen 1953: 83). Yet we should remember that the Burmese use a version of syllabic alphabet where a sound-unit 'shorter' than a syllable, cannot be reduced to writing. This means that, graphically, a single consonant is 'non-existent': even devoid of any supporting graphic element, it has its own ('inherent') vowel built in. In other words, the duration of 1.5 *mattā* is that of a consonant *plus* a (short) vowel. This latter interpretation may find its justification in the same Indian tradition which assigns a value of 0.5 *mattā* to a consonant – although, strictly speaking, "the mātrā concept has no justification in connection with consonants" (Allen 1953: 84).

At the same time, Burmese scholars cannot ignore the typological specificity of their native tongue. Although, in conformity with the Indian tradition, they speak of short and long vowels that can be combined with consonants to make syllables, they do not identify syllable-initial consonants with syllable-final ones and, moreover, they classify syllables according to their tones rather than to short vs. long vowels (though tones are sometimes referred to as varieties of 'stresses'). As the tones are often indicated by super- or postscript signs, the *ṭêḍêdīŋ* (Skr. *anusvāra*) – a superscript dot indicating nasality – these are also identified as tone markers by some authors.

From the discussion in the previous paragraph one could infer a lack of discrimination between writing and phonetics, between letters and language-entities *stricto sensu*. Such an underdifferentiation is undeniable. One could admit even more than that: sound-units, graphic units (unilateral entities) *and* meaningful units (bilateral entities) are not kept apart in the traditional Burmese analysis. Thus, it is usually maintained, that a combination of a vowel and a consonant makes a meaningful unit, lit. "produces meaning" (cf. Htun Myint 1968: 209). This is not surprising when we recall that the Burmese words (or, rather, morphemes) are predominantly monosyllabic.

At the same time, the Indian tradition is not absolutely free from a similar confusion between writing and phonetics either, cf. e. g. traditional Pali expressions like *akkhara-padāni* "letters *and* words" (where the term *akkhara*, Skr. *akṣara*, originally meant "syllable" but then extended its meaning to "vowel" and thence to "letter", see Allen 1953: 80).

In spite of all that, a syllable like /ŋīŋ/ is analyzed into /ŋ/ + /īŋ/ and not into /ŋ/ + /ī/ + /ŋ/ where /-īŋ/ termed *ṭərà* (< Pali *saro* "vowel") is an 'elementary' unit in its own right (cf. the *rhyme* or *final* of the Chinese tradition, → Art. 6). Such an approach nicely agrees with that of theoretical phonology as applied to the '(mono)syllabic' languages (cf. Kasevich & Speshnev 1970; Kasevich 1975; Kasevich 1983 etc.).

## 3. Burmese morphosyntax as seen through Indian terminology

As a matter of fact, the accepted way of presenting morphosyntax in the Burmese tradition is simply by listing the 'particles', roughly classified into semantically based groups. Alongside the 'particles', the traditional approach tackles also certain 'abstract' words like *mjâmjâ* "many, much" or *nɛ̂nɛ̂* "little, few", if the latter are semantically close to some of the 'particles', in this case to those designating number.

As a rule, no theoretical principles are explicitly stated. Yet some principles, which may be traced back to the Indian grammatical theories, are discernible in the terminological system used.

The basic syntactic unit is undoubtedly the sentence (or the clause), which is termed *wɛʔhà*. The latter term is a burmanized form of the Pali *vācco* "speech" (participle of the future passive of *vatti* "to speak, say", i. e., lit. "what is to be said"), which seems to indicate that speech and sentences are practically regarded as identical. This is of course strongly reminiscent of the Indian tradition, which, especially in Bhartṛhari's treatises, emphasized the independence of sentences and the dependence, direct or indirect, of all other linguistic units on sentences (cf. e. g. Allen 1953: 9; Bhattacharya 1985; → Art. 20).

If the Indian tradition practically denies any independence to the word, the Burmese one goes even further as it does not operate at all with words as separate entities in their own right. There exists neither a technical term for the word, nor its equivalent in the common parlance. Instead, the Burmese philologists use mostly two terms: *wūŋnà* (< Pali *vaṇṇo*) "syllable" and *poʔ* (presumably a corruption of the Pali *padaṁ* "foot", "a quater of a stanza", "word").

It is important to see that, in this case, the approach adopted by the local tradition is crucially dependent upon and directly influenced by the relevant typological features of the language. Speaking of the syllable, the Burmese philologists seem to actually mean what has been dubbed elsewhere the *syllabomorpheme* (cf. e. g. Kasevich 1994: 745), i. e. a monosyllable that is grammatically 'active' irrespective of its being meaningful or meaningless (cf. the notion of *word-syllable* in Chao 1976: 260, 278).

As for the other term, *poʔ*, it is intended to designate a 'syllable' or a combination of the 'syllables' used within the syntactic framework of a sentence, with or without 'particles'. Usually, the 'particles' are the syntactic markers, hence the translation "phrase", cf. *nāŋ poʔ* "noun phrase" (*nāŋ* < Pali *nāmaṁ* "name", "noun"), *kərìjà poʔ* (*kərìjà* < Pali *kāriya*, gerund of *kāreti* "to make, perform") "verb phrase".

The syntax in this tradition is predominantly semantically oriented. Three basic syntactic functions are identified, viz.: *kaʔtâ* (< Pali *kattā* "doer", "agent"), *kāŋ* (presumably from Pali *kaṁ* "whom") and *wìḍēḍənà* (< Pali *visesanaṁ* "distinguishing"). In Pali grammars the term *kattā* is mostly used with reference to the active voice. The Burmese language, however, has no voice paradigm; so, the term *kaʔtâ* refers to the semantic role of Agent (Actor) rather than to a grammatical form or function. By extension, it denotes also any kind of grammatical subject *or* the topic. The term *kāŋ* is applied to the role of Patient and, by extension, to any kind of grammatical object or rather, complement. The term *wìḍēḍənà* is used to identify both verb and noun modifiers.

As can be seen from the above, in borrowing the Indian terminology, Burmese grammarians are usually led by the literal meanings of the terms. Their ultimate goal seems to be an analysis that establishes a correlation, as close as possible, between Pali grammatical terms and certain entities identifiable in Burmese texts.

## 4. Bibliography

### 4.1. Primary sources

[Aggavaṁsa.] *Saddanīti* [A *Nīti* for Grammar]. Ed. by H. Smith, *La grammaire palie d'Aggavaṁsa.* 4 vols. Lund, 1928–1954.

[Kaccāyana.] *Kaccāyanappakaraṇaṁ* [Kaccayana's Treatise]. Ed. by Emile Senart, *Kaccayana et la littérature du Pali.* 1re partie. *Grammaire palie de Kaccāyana. Sūtras et commentaire, publiés avec une traduction et des notes.* Paris: Imprimerie Nationale. [Extrait N 1 d'année 1871 de *Journal asiatique.*]

Kyaw Aung San Hta Sayadaw (Pahtama), *Kəwìlɛʔ-khənā mjāŋmā ṭədā* [A Burmese Grammar Systematically Arranged]. Rangoon, 1962. (1st ed. 1748.)

[Moggalāna.] *Moggalāyana-Vyākaraṇa* [Moggalāna's Grammar]. Ed. by H. Devamitta. Colombo, 1890.

Taundwin Sayadaw. *Ṭədābjūhā* [The Multitude of Words]. Rangoon, 1882. (1st ed. ca. 1751.)

### 4.2. Secondary sources

Allen, W[illiam] S[ydney]. 1953. *Phonetics in Ancient India.* London: Oxford Univ. Press.

Armstrong, Lilias E. & Pe Maung Tin. 1925. *A Burmese Phonetic Reader.* London: Univ. of London Press.

Bernot, Denise. 1963. "Une esquisse phonologique du birman". *Bulletin de la Société de linguistique de Paris.* 58.104–224.

Bhaskararao, B. & Peter Ladefoged. 1991. "Two Types of Voiceless Nasals". *Journal of the International Phonetic Association.* 21: 2.80–88.

Bhattacharya, B. 1985. *Bhartṛhari's Vakyapadiya and Linguistic Monism.* Poona: Poona Univ. Press.

Bode, Mabel Haynes. 1900. *The Pali Literature of Burma.* [London]: Royal Asiatic Society.

–. 1908. "Early Pali grammarians in Burma". *Journal of the Pali Text Society,* 81–101.

Chao, Yuen Ren. 1976. *Aspects of Chinese Sociolinguistics.* Stanford: Stanford Univ. Press.

Geiger, Wilhelm. 1916. Pali Literatur und Sprache. Straßburg.

Htun Myint, U. 1968. *Pālì ṭɛʔ wɔ̀hārà əbìdāŋ* [A Dictionary of Pali and Sanskrit]. [Rangoon].

Kasevich, V[adim] B[orisovič]. 1975. "Towards a Phonological Theory for (Mono)syllabic Languages". *Abstracts of Papers of the 8th International Congress of Phonetic Sciences.* [Leeds], 146.

–. 1983. *Fonologičeskije problemy obščego i vostočnogo jazykoznanija* [Phonological Issues in General and Oriental Linguistics]. Moscow: Izd. "Nauka".

–. 1994. "On Phonology-Morphology Interface in Sino-Tibetan Languages". *Current Issues in Sino-Tibetan Linguistics* 743–748. Osaka: Organizing Committee of the 26th International Conference on Sino-Tibetan Languages and Linguistics.

– & N[ikolaj] A[lekseevič] Speshnev. 1970. "Zero in phonological description: Chinese and Burmese". *Word* 26.362–372.

Londsdale, A. W. 1899. *Burmese Grammar and Grammatical Analysis.* Rangoon: British Burma Press.

Mason, Francis. 1880. "The Pali Language from a Burmese Point of View". Journal of the American Oriental Society. 10.177–184.

Okell, John. 1965. "Nissaya Burmese: A case of systematic adaptation to a foreign grammar and syntax". *Lingua* 15.186–227.

Wun, U. 1975. "Mjāŋmā səgâ [The Burmese Language]". *Mjāŋmāhmù* [*The Burmese Literary Arts*] [Rangoon] 1.1–28.

Zargara. 1978. "Burmese Sounds (1)." *The Working People's Daily* 25, no. 4: 2.

*Vadim B. Kasevich, St. Petersburg (Russia)*

# 26. Indian influence on the Old Javanese linguistic tradition

1. Introduction
2. 'Old Javanese'
3. The forms of Old Javanese linguistics
4. Linguistics and the composition of texts
5. Linguistics and hermeneutics
6. Religio-philosophical thought, ritual practice, and linguistic scholarship
7. Modern Javanese linguistics
8. Bibliography

## 1. Introduction

To say that the indigenous scholarly tradition concerned with the Old Javanese language was influenced by Indian linguistics is in fact an understatement. South Asia and the archipelago have been connected by cultural flows over at least the past 1600 years. There is little doubt that linguistic and language-philosophical notions developed on Indian soil encountered autochthonous ones. A process of selective and creative appropriation, analogous to that which took place in such other spheres as art, religion, mythology, and indeed language itself, must have spurred new ideas about language and discourse that were peculiar to Indonesia. Generally speaking, though, and especially if viewed out of cultural context, the thematics and modes of analysis of Old Javanese linguistics, as we know it, follow Indian models.

This is not surprising if one takes into account the objects of Old Javanese linguistic reflection. It was and is largely concerned not with morphology, syntax, and discourse structure, but with the lexicon and phonology and graphology, while a substantial part of the Old Javanese vocabulary and the entire system of its representation in writing happen to be of Indian provenance. Old Javanese linguistic thought was and remains directed above all to written genres, and the most prominent of these were originally modelled on ancient Indian forms. Examples are the *kakawin*s, narrative and expository poems whose metrical system is that of the Sanskrit *kāvya*s, the *parwa*s, prose renditions of the books of the Sanskrit *Mahābhārata*, the *mantra*s, various kinds of prayers and ritual formulas, and the *praśasti*s, charters inscribed on stone and bronze. The thematic coverage of Old Javanese linguistics, then, is not of the same breadth as that of the plethora of classical Indian grammatical schools taken as a whole – a circumstance that may itself indicate selective adoption and adaptation.

Reference was made to Old Javanese linguistics as we know it. It has been little studied and our knowledge of it is meagre. In this sketch of the state of scholarship we shall point out Indian counterparts or antecedents, but the focus is on Indonesian contexts. We conceive Old Javanese linguistics broadly, as the complex of cultural practices of analysing and reflecting upon the lingual repertoire and its use.

## 2. 'Old Javanese'

Old Javanese is an Austronesian language. First attested in a charter of 804 CE, it was pervaded by lexemes of Indian stock from the beginning of its recorded history. The source of the Indian vocabulary was Sanskrit. But while Sanskrit furnished a sizeable proportion of the lexicon – some 20 to 30 per cent of running text, depending on the genre (Gonda 1973: 197–204) – it exerted hardly any influence on morphology and syntax. (Discourse organization has not been investigated.) Even the fact that the Old Javanese phonological system, unlike that of its nearest Austronesian siblings but analogous to Sanskrit, features retroflex stops contrasting with dental ones and long vowels beside short ones, is not necessarily due to borrowing. The retroflex stops and long vowels already occurred in non-Sanskrit words in the earliest texts (Gonda 1973: 579–580; Zoetmulder 1974: 57–59).

The label 'Old Javanese' is not without problems. The first concerns the association with Java and the Javanese that it suggests. Several of the lingual varieties that the term covers were used in original writing in Bali from around 1000 CE and later also in Lombok, by people who by all accounts did not consider themselves Javanese. Yet, linguistically Old Javanese is an ancestor of contemporary Javanese and not of Balinese. The second and more substantial problem relates to the adjective and is one of identification in time and space. There was no neat succession 'Old'-'Middle'-'Modern' Javanese. The genealogy and distribution of varieties remain so opaque that Zoetmulder, in his study of *kakawin*s and *parwa*s, felt compelled to lump together as Old Javanese all texts in Javanese lacking Arabic loans or Islamic influence (1974: 35–36), a definition that yields a vast corpus of great internal heterogeneity, produced on several islands over twelve centuries. The term also easily obscures that some varieties are still alive. This is so in Bali more than in Java.

Used in scholarship, ritual, and narrative, Old Javanese is not spoken extempore save in certain dramatic genres in Bali. Its strong association with authoritative learning and inspired creativity is exemplified by the Balinese and Javanese terms that name it: *basa kawi* "kawi idiom" and *tĕmbuṅ kawi* "kawi words", in which the noun *kawi* (a Sanskrit loan) is the appellation of the eminent poets of ancient times. These terms also reveal a deep-rooted metalinguistic tendency. Language – Old Javanese or otherwise – is spoken of principally as vocabulary and its use.

## 3. The forms of Old Javanese linguistics

We know the traditional study of Old Javanese from manuscripts written in Bali, Lombok, and Java, and from present-day folk linguistics in these islands. The surviving texts are about grammar, lexicography, and phonology and pertain to Sanskrit, Old Javanese, and their interrelations and commonalities. As noted above, their prime object is written language. Though Old Javanese and Sanskrit texts were read as song or chant, even the sound system is largely conceptualized in respect of writing. *Mantra*s, for instance, are an oral genre, but they are highly text-oriented; witness the ritual importance of special symbols for vocables such as *oṃ* (Zurbuchen 1987: 56–58; cf. Weck 1986: 79) and the fact that graphemic oppositions such as *s-ṣ-ś*, not phonemic today, remain significant in Balinese *mantra*s (Staal 1995: 10).

The *Kārakasaṅgraha* is "[t]he only text so far published which answers the idea of a 'grammar' at least to some degree" (Schoterman 1981: 433; see also Gonda 1973: 183–184; Radicchi 1996). Composed in Sanskrit *śloka*s with Old Javanese translation and commentary, its topic is Sanskrit. It has three chapters. The first, the *Kārakasaṅgraha* proper, discusses the case endings, the second and third the compounds. Radicchi has argued that the Sanskrit text of the first chapter, which belongs to the grammatical school of

Kātantra, was compiled around the 10th century in northern India and may have entered Java shortly afterwards. The other chapters were presumably added to it in Java, before it reached Bali, where all known manuscripts are from. The second chapter seems to be of Indian origin, the third not (Radicchi 1996). Beside the *Kārakasaṅgraha*, a few brief treatments of the declension of Sanskrit nouns and pronouns and fragments of verb paradigms have been found (Schoterman 1981: 436–437).

The lexicon features in a wide range of works. The main type is called *kṛtabhāṣā*. Apparently short for *Saṃskṛtabhāṣā* "the Sanskrit language", this is the generic name for dictionary-like texts that are mostly concerned with nouns and the proper names and epithets of deities and other classes of mythological beings (Juynboll 1911: 207–215; Gonda 1973: 184–185; Schoterman 1981: 424–430; cf. Zurbuchen 1987: 102–103). Each 'entry' is usually a list of synonymous words or alternative names in Sanskrit or Old Javanese (which, of course, often amounts to the same) followed by a definition in (Old) Javanese or Balinese. As in the Sanskrit *kośa*s and modern thesauri, the entries tend to be grouped by cultural category: deities, dignitaries, animals, parts of the body, etc. Provided the reader knows his way around the text, he may use it to trace either the synonyms or their definitions. Some *kṛtabhāṣā*s also list the meanings of homonymic or polysemous words – again a pattern with Indian parallels. A special kind of *kṛtabhāṣā* is called *Bhāṣā Ekalawya* after its opening section, which presents a set of eleven triads of words with the same consonants but varying vowels, such as *gara-giri-garu* and *sara-sari-saru*. Each word is glossed (Juynboll 1911: 206; Schoterman 1981: 430–431; Zurbuchen 1987: 102). The purpose of this section is unknown.

Relatively much scholarly attention has gone to two compendia of linguistic and poetical texts. The *Caṇḍakiraṇa*, a copy of which was found in West Java, and the *Caṇṭakaparwa*, represented in manuscripts from Bali and Lombok, include *kṛtabhāṣā* sections, some of which they share in common (Juynboll 1907: 170–172; Juynboll 1911: 219–222; Gonda 1973: 185; Ensink 1967; Schoterman 1981: 421–427). The *Caṇṭakaparwa* also gives interpretive definitions that have somewhat misleadingly been described as etymologies. A word is dissected into segments, usually syllables, that are each identified as segments of other words, which serve to characterize and enhance the original word's meaning. This approach to lexical semantics, also exemplified in other texts, has Indian roots. It is found, *inter alia*, in Vedic texts.

The main treatise on phonology, graphology, and orthography is the *Swarawyañjana* "Vowels and consonants". It is devoted to the topics in its title and the rules of sandhi (Juynboll 1911: 216–219; Gonda 1973: 181–183; Schoterman 1981: 431–433). Its terminology and order of treatment accord basically with Sanskrit theory, but Old Javanese examples are also given. Gonda judged that "the author has tried to explain Sanskrit by pointing to parallels in his own language and even to interpret the latter as if it were Sanskrit, to apply the Sanskrit rules to Javanese" (1973: 183), but the *Swarawyañjana* is not focused on either language. It calls itself a discussion of the "arrangement" or "life" of the characters of the syllabary (*tiṅkahniṅ akṣara* or *huripniṅ akṣara*) – a syllabary that suits both languages.

These branches of Old Javanese linguistics played a role in several related domains of cultural theory and practice: composition, hermeneutics, and religio-philosophical speculation and ritual.

## 4. Linguistics and the composition of texts

Knowledge of Sanskrit was of practical value to early writers, not only because of the origins of part of the Old Javanese lexicon, but even more because they quoted and paraphrased Sanskrit works in their prose narratives and treatises, and because they composed Sanskrit texts themselves. In some cases it has been possible to trace the Sanskrit quotations back to Indian exemplars, but the problem of the precise purposes of their inclusion in Old Javanese texts remains unsolved (Gonda 1973: 194–196; Zoetmulder 1974: 89–92). Sanskrit was occasionally used for inscriptions up to the 14th century CE (Gonda 1973: 180), and later, too, texts were written in a form of the language that has been labelled 'archipelago Sanskrit' and is often characterized as simplified or defective (Schoterman 1979). It is likely that authors used the linguistic treatises mentioned above, and others that have since been lost, as textbooks or reference works for writing Sanskrit.

The same applies to Old Javanese. The lexicons, the *Swarawyañjana*, and parts of the *Kārakasaṅgraha* must have been useful to authors of Old Javanese texts, the metrically and poetically exacting *kakawin*s in particular (Gonda 1973: 185; Schoterman 1981: 435, 438; Radicchi 1996: 290; Creese 1998: 46–47). This is even more likely if one does not assume that Old Javanese linguistics was primarily concerned with Sanskrit. Save the pieces on case and inflection, the linguistic texts were relevant to Old Javanese as well. Treatises on poetics and prosody existed as further aids to composition (for introductions see Gonda 1973: 185–187 and Zoetmulder 1974: 104–109 on prosody; Creese 1998: 46–49 on poetics).

## 5. Linguistics and hermeneutics

The linguistic treatises seem also to have supported the interpretation of Old Javanese texts, rarely an easy undertaking due to their specialized format, uncommon idiom, and profound subject matter. This has been demonstrated for at least the *kṛtabhāṣā*s. They were still used for the interpretation of *kakawin*s in Bali in the 1970s (Schoterman 1981: 439). Schoterman has argued that some texts in the *kṛtabhāṣā* category must have been glossaries on particular works (1981: 428), and indeed Kuntara has identified a *kṛtabhāṣā* from Java which contains glosses on the *Arjunawiwāha*, an early-11th-century *kakawin* (1990: 206, 216). The interpretive freedom that the author allowed the users of his glossary is remarkable. He usually noted several lexical meanings for each word, like in the synonym lists from which he probably quoted, and not just the one meaning that he may have considered most appropriate.

## 6. Religio-philosophical thought, ritual practice, and linguistic scholarship

Textual exegesis shades into the broader field of religio-philosophical thought on language and discourse. Interpretation was often metaphorical, as illustrated by a work titled *Sukṣmabasa* "The essence of idiom". Applying the syllabic dissection technique found in the *Canṭakaparwa*, it expounds the covert philosophical meanings of words and names in two Old Javanese poems from Bali (Juynboll 1911: 216). Linguistic speculation infused ritual practice, too. Like in Indian Śivaism and Tantric Buddhism, the elements of the syllabary were *mantra*s associated with the limbs and other parts of the human body (e. g. Kats 1910: 53–55, 102–104). In Bali the imposition of the vowels and consonants on the body continues to be part of a Brahmin priest's daily worship and other rituals (Hooykaas 1973: 122–123; cf. Weck 1986: 67–80; Zurbuchen 1987: 55–56).

Perhaps due in part to an *a priori* assumption, there is a consensus among most contemporary scholars that the Old Javanese linguistic texts were practical manuals that served composition and interpretation, and as has become apparent, ritual too. No doubt they were, but there are indications that their study was also an end in itself. They were part of the scholarly heritage. Awareness of their contents contributed to personal enlightenment and could be displayed in various interactional contexts. For instance, Balinese puppeteers open a shadow play by reciting an exordium in which the Sanskrit/Old Javanese vowels and consonants are mentioned, as well as a number of phonological terms and the textual source of this information, the *Caṇḍakiraṇa* (Hooykaas 1973: 112–117; Zurbuchen 1987: ix–x, 267–268). Though in 19th century Java Old Javanese works were no longer composed and rarely studied, versions of the *Swarawyañjana* continued to be copied (Juynboll 1911: 218) and one was incorporated into the *Cĕnṭini*, the famous compendium of "all Javanese knowledge" (Wirawangsa with Ardja widjaja 1915: 85–89). As a final example, the syllabic dissection approach to lexical signification endures as a rhetorical device. In modern Java it is called *keratabasa*, a term that may derive from *kṛtabhāṣā*.

## 7. Modern Javanese linguistics

Some Old Javanese linguistic thought, then, survived in Java. It mingled with notions from Arabic linguistics (→ Art. 50), which was studied in Islamic schools and could in part be projected onto Javanese. In the mid-19th century, European scholars, probably working with Javanese colleagues, devised a new terminology for use in language textbooks. It featured Sanskrit-derived and Sanskritized terms: *wyakarana* "grammar", *paramasastra* "grammar", *dwilinga* "duplicated", etc. (Arps 1997). These European scholars knew about Sanskrit studies and, moreover, coined novel Javanese terms that were made to sound scholarly by being based on archaic words and morphemes, often of Sanskrit provenance. There was in most cases no direct line of transmission from Old Javanese linguistics.

## 8. Bibliography

Arps, Bernard. 1997. "Koning Salomo en het dwerghertje: Taalpolitiek, taalonderwijs en de eerste grammatica's in het Javaans" [King Solomon and the Mouse Deer: Language policy, language teaching, and the first grammars in Javanese.] *Koloniale taalpolitiek in Oost en West: Nederlands-Indië, Suriname, Nederlandse Antillen en Aruba* ed. by Kees Groeneboer, 85–105. Amsterdam: Amsterdam Univ. Press.

Creese, Helen. 1998. Pārthāyaṇa: *The Journeying of Pārtha: An eighteenth-century Balinese kakawin.* Leiden: KITLV Press.

Ensink, Jaco. 1967. *On the Old-Javanese Cantakaparwa and its Tale of Sutasoma.* The Hague: Martinus Nijhoff.

Gonda, Jan. 1973. *Sanskrit in Indonesia.* 2nd edition. New Delhi: International Academy of Indian Culture.

Hooykaas, Christiaan. 1973. *Kama and Kala: Materials for the study of shadow theatre in Bali.* Amsterdam & London: North-Holland.

Juynboll, Hendrik Herman. 1907. *Supplement op den catalogus van de Javaansche en Madoereesche handschriften der Leidsche universiteits-bibliotheek*, vol. I: *Madoereesche handschriften, Oudjavaansche inscripties en Oud- en Middeljavaansche gedichten.* Leiden: Brill.

–. 1911. *Supplement op den catalogus van de Javaansche en Madoereesche handschriften der Leidsche universiteits-bibliotheek*, vol. II: *Nieuwjavaansche gedichten en Oud-, Middel- en Nieuwjavaansche prozageschriften.* Leiden: Brill.

Kats, J. 1910. Sang hyang Kamahâyânikan: *Oud-Javaansche tekst met inleiding, vertaling en aanteekeningen.* The Hague: Martinus Nijhoff.

Kuntara Wiryamartana, I. 1990. Arjunawiwāha: *Transformasi teks Jawa Kuna lewat tanggapan dan penciptaan di lingkungan sastra Jawa* [Arjunawiwāha: The Transformation of the Old Javanese Text through Response and Creation in Javanese Literary Circles.] Yogyakarta: Duta Wacana Univ. Press.

Radicchi, Anna. 1996. "More on the *Kārakasaṃgraha*, a Sanskrit Grammatical Text from Bali". *Ideology and Status of Sanskrit: Contributions to the history of the Sanskrit language* ed. by Jan E. M. Houben, 289–306. Leiden: Brill.

Schoterman, Jan Anthony. 1979. "A Note on Balinese Sanskrit". *Bijdragen tot de Taal-, Land- en Volkenkunde* 135.323–346.

–. 1981. "An Introduction to Old Javanese Sanskrit Dictionaries and Grammars". *Bijdragen tot de Taal-, Land- en Volkenkunde* 137.419–442.

Staal, Frits. 1995. *Mantras between Fire and Water: Reflections on a Balinese rite.* With an appendix by Dick van der Meij. Amsterdam: North-Holland.

Weck, Wolfgang. 1986 [1937]. *Heilkunde und Volkstum auf Bali.* N. p.: Bap Bali & Intermasa.

Wirawangsa & Ardja widjaja, eds. 1915. Serat Tjeṇṭini: *Babon asli saking kiṭa Leiden ing negari Nederland* [Cĕṇṭini: The exemplar from Leiden, the Netherlands.] Vols. VII–VIII. Betawi: Ruygrok.

Zoetmulder, Petrus Josephus. 1974. Kalangwan: *A survey of Old Javanese literature.* The Hague: Martinus Nijhoff.

Zurbuchen, Mary Sabina. 1987. *The Language of Balinese Shadow Theater.* Princeton: Princeton Univ. Press.

*Bernard Arps, Leiden (The Netherlands)*

# VI. The Establishment of Dravidian Linguistics
# Die Anfänge der dravidischen Sprachforschung
# La constitution de la linguistique dravidienne

## 27. Les débuts de la tradition linguistique tamoule


1. Les plus anciens témoignages
2. Le plus ancien texte: le *Tolkāppiyam*
3. Les académies
4. Le *Tolkāppiyam* et ses prédécesseurs
5. Bibliographie


### 1. Les plus anciens témoignages

La tradition linguistique tamoule est sans doute née au début de notre ère. Son véhicule était le tamoul classique et son objet privilégié l'activité poétique. Il nous reste de cette entreprise un corpus de textes, les uns littéraires et les autres théoriques, dont la chronologie est difficile à établir car nous n'avons aucun manuscrit ancien, les feuilles de palmier ne résistant pas plus de 400 ans. De plus nous sommes lourdement tributaires pour les comprendre des commentateurs de l'époque médiévale, lesquels vivaient dans un univers culturel et religieux très différent de celui dans lequel les premières œuvres ont été composées: ils avaient donc, tout comme nous, un problème d'interprétation. Un locuteur tamoul d'aujourd'hui (ils sont environ 60 millions à parler cette langue qui est l'une des quatre principales langues dravidiennes du Sud de l'Inde), s'il veut accéder au tamoul classique, doit passer par deux intermédiaires: le tamoul médiéval des commentateurs et le tamoul formel contemporain, utilisé aujourd'hui à l'écrit (v. Asher 1985: ix; Britto 1986). Les dates ici données dans cette courte présentation sont généralement reprises du livre *The Smile of Murugan*, dû à K. V. Zvelebil (1973), qui est l'auteur de plusieurs ouvrages de référence.

Les témoignages les plus anciens sur le pays tamoul, hormis les sources externes, notamment grecques et romaines, sont ceux que nous donne l'épigraphie, à partir du III^e^ siècle avant notre ère. Ils semblent recouper le témoignage des poèmes de la partie la plus ancienne du corpus, puisque des noms de rois qui y figurent ont été retrouvés dans des inscriptions (v. Gros 1983: 84). Cette culture connaissait l'écriture, mais nous ne savons pas si son rôle était important. L'anthologie *Akam* contient des descriptions de "pierres plantées" (*naṭu kal*) à la mémoire de guerriers morts au combat sur lesquelles on peut voir, "des lettres qu'a gravées le ciseau pointu et dont les traits s'effacent" (*kūr uḷi kuyiṉṟa kōṭu māy eḻuttu, Akam* 343–347). La valeur guerrière et la férocité étaient admirées. Deux des anthologies sont consacrées, partiellement (*Puṟam*) ou totalement (*Patiṟṟuppattu*) à louer des rois ou des chefs de clan. Cet éloge était le fait de poètes, parfois richement récompensés, dont le répertoire comportait aussi les thèmes de la poésie amoureuse, objet de six autres anthologies. A côté de ces poètes qui composaient, il y avait place pour des interprètes: chanteurs, musiciens, et même danseurs, que nous voyons apparaître par moments dans les poèmes (v. Hart 1975).

### 2. Le plus ancien texte: le *Tolkāppiyam*

Si l'on s'en tient aux textes qui nous sont parvenus, par copies successives, l'histoire substantielle de la tradition linguistique tamoule ne peut concrètement commencer qu'avec le *Tolkāppiyam* (T) (→ Art. 28) qui pourrait dans son état actuel dater du 5ème siècle (v. S. Vaiyapuri Pillai 1988: 48 et Zvelebil 1973: 146). Aucun texte théorique antérieur au T ne semble en effet avoir été conservé. Cependant, il est tentant de parler d'une préhistoire de la tradition. En effet, le texte du T fait explicitement référence à des ouvrages de prédécesseurs, même s'il ne nous donne pas leurs noms. Il se réfère en outre constamment au savoir collectif des *pulavar*-s "lettrés, poètes" tamouls, qu'il a pour ambition de présenter de façon abrégée: il est donc vraisemblable qu'une partie de son contenu est un remaniement de traités antérieurs, tout comme nous voyons certaines grammaires médiévales reprendre, éventuellement en les adaptant, des *sūtra*-s du T. D'autre part, certains textes postérieurs au T font référence à des ouvrages plus anciens que lui, dont le plus fameux est *Akattiyam* (A, v. infra), attribué au rishi védique Agastya. Enfin des éléments du savoir que le T codifie, et notamment la poétique, se laissent entrevoir à travers le corpus poétique classique tamoul, dont la composition remonte sans doute pour partie aux premiers siècles de notre ère. Celui-ci consiste en deux ensembles: huit anthologies (*Akam*, *Kuṟuntokai*, *Naṟṟiṇai*, *Puṟam*, *Aiṅkuṟunūṟu*, *Patiṟṟuppattu*, *Kali*, et *Paripāṭal*) qui rassemblent environ 2300 poèmes courts pour un total d'environ 29300 lignes; dix longs poèmes, totalisant environ 3500 lignes. Il faut noter que ce corpus n'est pas homogène chronologiquement. L'édition de référence est celle de Murray S. Rajam (1957).

## 3. Les académies

L'ensemble de poèmes qui vient d'être énuméré est parfois désigné par l'expression "Littérature du Sangam (*caṅkam*)". Celle-ci fait référence à un récit, de nature semi-légendaire, qui cristallise un certain nombre d'informations sur les débuts de la tradition savante tamoule. Ce récit se trouve dans le commentaire sur le *Iṟaiyaṉār Akapporuḷ*, qui date peut-être du VIIIe siècle (v. Buck & Paramasivan 1997). Il raconte qu'il y eut successivement au pays tamoul, dans le royaume Pāṇḍiya, trois académies (*caṅkam*) sous patronage royal, les césures entre elles étant liées à des catastrophes naturelles. Les durées mentionnées pour chacune (4440, 3700 et 1850 ans) semblent de nature symbolique, peut-être à diviser par 37, dont elles sont toutes multiples. Un autre élément non-réaliste, mais significatif, est la participation du panthéon shivaïte à la première académie. Le lien entre les humains et les dieux est effectué par le rishi védique Agastya qui siège à la première académie et auquel le récit attribue une grammaire, l'*Akattiyam* (A), qui en est l'ouvrage de référence. L'académie pour laquelle nous avons les éléments les plus réalistes dans le récit est la troisième: le nombre de poètes (449) ayant présenté leurs œuvres est proche de celui que l'on constate dans le corpus classique effectivement conservé. On peut penser que le rédacteur du récit faisait référence à un triple passé: un passé proche, celui de la troisième académie, défini par un corpus de textes disponibles; un passé lointain, celui de la deuxième académie, caractérisé par des œuvres dont on ne possédait plus que les titres ou des fragments conservés comme citations; un passé mythique, fondant une origine divine de la grammaire, rapportée à Śiva, dont le culte était devenu hégémonique, puisque la forme dominante de l'hindouisme est alors le shivaïsme. On observe d'ailleurs un cheminement semblable dans la tradition paninéenne puisque c'est progressivement que les trois grammairiens fondateurs Pāṇini, Kātyāyana et Patañjali sont transformés par leurs successeurs en *muni*-s, que l'*Aṣṭādhyāyī* acquiert le statut de Véda, les 14 premiers *sūtra*-s étant supposés reçus directement de Śiva (v. Deshpande 1998; → Art. 18).

## 4. Le *Tolkāppiyam* et ses prédécesseurs

Un point qui a souvent été discuté est celui de la relation entre T et A, la grammaire perdue attribuée à Agastya. Celle-ci est citée dans le récit déjà mentionné comme ayant eu rang de manuel de référence pour les trois académies successives, alors que le T ne l'aurait été que pour les deuxième et troisième académies. Trois autres traités, eux aussi perdus, sont d'ailleurs mentionnés pour la seconde académie: *Māpurāṇam*, *Icainuṇukkam* et *Pūtapurāṇam*. Par ailleurs, des commentateurs postérieurs expliquent que l'auteur du T était l'un des douze disciples de Agastya, maître avec lequel il se serait brouillé, des malédictions réciproques étant échangées. Les douze disciples sont crédités de la composition des douze chapitres d'un ouvrage collectif également perdu, le *paṉṉiru paṭalam* (v. Meenakshisundaran 1974: 2). Cependant, les faits sont: premièrement, que ni le T ni sa préface ne font référence au A; au contraire, on trouve une référence à un traité (ou système) intitulé *Aintiram*; deuxièmement, que le A est un ouvrage dont nous ne possédons aujourd'hui que le titre et 18 citations, le texte qui en contient le plus étant le commentaire de Mayilainātar sur le *Naṉṉūl* (→ Art. 29). Si un tel texte a existé, il n'a pas suffi de l'attribuer à un rishi védique et d'en faire l'ouvrage de référence d'une académie ou siégeait Śiva pour le faire survivre à travers des siècles où le shivaïsme était dominant, alors que le T, œuvre d'un auteur qui était probablement de religion jain, selon certains indices (v. Zvelebil 1973: 137) a été conservé précieusement, avec six commentaires. On est donc tenté de penser que dans l'esprit de ceux qui ont associé T et A, ce dernier, réduit à quelques citations et exemples, jouait, malgré l'antagonisme supposé, un rôle symbolique de caution par rapport à une orthodoxie dominante qui n'en demandait pas plus. La question vraiment sérieuse était de préserver le traité le meilleur.

Du point de vue de la chronologie, il a été défendu (v. Zvelebil 1973: 137–147) que plusieurs niveaux coexistent dans le T tel que nous l'avons et que certaines parties peuvent être très anciennes (avant notre ère) tandis que d'autres, principalement dans TP, seraient récentes. Il est clair que le texte tel que nous l'avons n'a pas surgi *ex nihilo*. Quant à sa relation avec le corpus littéraire, elle est complexe: d'une part, le T semble généralement forger ou cristalliser des emplois techniques de termes qui se rencontraient déjà à l'intérieur du corpus littéraire dans des emplois mondains (ou ordinaires), lesquels sont parfois attestés dans le T lui-même. Mais il arrive qu'un emploi technique soit déjà attesté dans des textes plus anciens que le T. On peut prendre l'exemple d'un terme caractéristique, le mot *tiṇai*, dont les sens mondains sont "lignée, noblesse" (*Puṟam* 159) et "condition (sociale), caste?" (*Kuṟuntokai* 45). Ce deuxième sens est même attesté dans le T (TC5–11), mais il passe presque inaperçu à côté de deux emplois techniques massifs: l'un pour désigner les deux *tiṇai* "classes" (*uyar-tiṇai* "classe supérieure" vs. *al-tiṇai* "hors-classe") dans la bi-partition des êtres (rationnels vs. non-rationnels) et par conséquent des mots par laquelle s'ouvre le TC, bi-partition qui est le prélude à une division en cinq genres grammaticaux (*pāl*) dont une manifestation visible est l'accord en genre entre un sujet et son prédicat; l'autre pour désigner les cinq *tiṇai* "régions", qui associent de façon détaillée un stade d'une relation amoureuse à un paysage conventionnel (*kuṟiñci*, *neytal*, *pālai*, *mullai* et *marutam*) que A. K. Ramanujan (1967) a éloquemment traduit par "interior landscape". Mais il est important de noter que ce second emploi, technique par excellence, semble déjà attesté dans l'un des dix longs poèmes (*Maturaik Kāñci* 326), qui pourrait dater du début du IIIe siècle, et dont un passage contient des descriptions des cinq régions. Le poète suivait une norme, dont le T n'est que la plus ancienne présentation préservée.

Le préface du T cite le nom d'une autorité, *Aintiram*, par rapport à laquelle l'ouvrage serait en relation d'allégeance. Le terme serait dérivé du nom de Indra, en tant que fondateur d'un système. Dans son ouvrage de 1875, A.C. Burnell a essayé de montrer que le T est le représentant pour le tamoul d'une école grammaticale à laquelle il faudrait aussi rattacher les *Prātiśākhya*-s, le *Nirukta* et le *Kātantra*. Cette école, antérieure à la tradition paninéenne, serait la plus ancienne des huit écoles de grammaire mentionnées par la tradition de grammaire sanskrite. Pour s'en tenir ici au corpus tamoul, Aṭiyārkku Nallār, le commentateur médiéval du *Cilappatikāram* (V[e]–VIe siècle) mentionne lui aussi plusieurs fois (chap. XI, 98–99; 152–164) l'existence d'un *Aintira Viyākaraṇam*, c'est à dire *Aindra Vyākaraṇam* "Grammaire de Indra". Dans le passage source qu'il commente, cet ouvrage (ou ce système) est tout d'abord présenté par un brahmane comme l'œuvre du roi des dieux (Indra), puis mentionné par une ascète jain qui dit qu'il fait partie de leurs écritures.

En ce qui concerne la filiation du T par rapport aux systèmes de grammaire sanskrite, il faut sans doute aussi considérer comme significatif le renvoi fait dans le chapitre de phonétique [TE3, 20; 21] aux écritures (litt. "secrets") des brahmanes (*antaṇar maṟai*).

## 5. Bibliographie

### 5.1. Sources primaires

*Akanāṉūṟu, Aiṅkuṟunrūṟu, Kalit Tokai, Kuṟuntokai, Naṟṟiṇai, Paripāṭal, Pattup Pāṭṭu, Pattiṟṟup Pattu, Puṟanāṉūṟu, Tolkāppiyam.* Ed. par Murray S. Rajam. 10 volumes. 2e éd. Madras: New Century Book House, Madras, 1981. (1e éd., 1957.)

Iḷaṅkō Aṭikaḷ [V[e] siècle?], *Cilappatikāram.* Commentaire de Aṭiyārkku Nallār [XII[e] siècle?], *Cilappatikāra Mūlamum Arumpatavuraiyum Aṭiyārkkunallāruraiyum* ed. par U. Ve. Cāminātaiyar [1855–1942]. Tanjore: Tamil University, 1985. (Réimpr. de la 3e éd., 1927.]


### 5.2. Sources secondaires

Asher, Ronald E. 1985. *Tamil.* London: Croom Helm.

Britto, Francis. 1986. *Diglossia: A study of the theory with application to Tamil.* Washington, D.C.: Georgetown Univ. Press.

Buck, David C. & K. Paramasivam. 1997. *The Study of Stolen Love: A translation of Kaḷaviyal eṉṟa Iṟaiyaṉār Akapporuḷ with commentary by Nakkīraṉār.* Atlanta, Georgia: Scholars Press.

Burnell, Arthur C. 1986. *On the Aindra School of Sanskrit Grammarians: Their place in the Sanskrit and subordinate literature.* Madras: Pioneer Book Services Reprint. (1e éd., Tanjore, 1875.)

Deshpande, Madhav. 1998. "Evolution of the Notion of Authority of the Pāṇinian Tradition". *Histoire Epistémologie Langage* 20:1.5–28.

Gros, François. 1983. "La littérature du Sangam et son public». *Puruṣārtha* 7, *Inde et Littératures* éd. par Marie-Claude Porcher, 77–107. Paris: Ecole des Hautes Etudes en Sciences Sociales.

Hart, III, George Luzerne. 1975. *The Poems of Ancient Tamil, Their Milieu and their Sanskrit Counterparts.* Berkeley: Univ. of California Press.

Marr, John Ralston. 1985. *The Eight Anthologies.* Madras: Institute of Asian Studies. (Ph. D., University of London, 1958.)

Meenakshisundaran, T. P. 1974. *Foreign Models in Tamil Grammar.* (= *Dravidian Linguistics Association Publication*, 15). Trivandrum: University of Kerala.

Ramanujan, A. K. 1967. *The Interior Landscape: Love poems from a classical Tamil anthology.* Bloomington & London: Indiana Univ. Press.

Zvelebil, Kamil V. 1973. *The Smile of Murugan: On Tamil literature of South India.* Leiden: Brill.

Vaiyapuri Pillai, S. 1988. *History of Tamil Language and Literature (From the Beginning to 1000 AD.)* Madras: New Century Book House. (1e éd., 1956.)

*Jean-Luc Chevillard, Paris (France)*

# 28. Le *Tolkāppiyam* et le développement de la tradition linguistique tamoule

1. Structure du *Tolkāppiyam*
2. Le "Livre des Lettres"
3. Le "Livre des Mots"
4. Le "Livre des Matières"
5. Bibliographie

## 2. Structure du *Tolkāppiyam*

Le *Tolkāppiyam* (T; → Art. 27) se compose de 3 livres (TE, TC, TP) possédant chacun 9 chapitres (TE1 à TP9) qui traitent respectivement "Des Lettres" (*Eḻuttatikāram*, TE), "Des Mots" (*Collatikāram*, TC) et "Des Matières [Poétiques]" (*Poruḷatikāram*, TP). Les références données ici renvoient à l'édition Rajam (1957) sans commentaire. Les trois livres font respectivement environ 1000, 1050 et 2000 lignes réparties en environ 480, 460 et 660 strophes ou *cūttiram* (sanskrit *sūtra*), le nombre de ces dernières pouvant varier du fait d'un découpage variable selon les commentateurs qui nous ont préservé le texte et son interprétation. Seul l'un d'entre eux, Iḷampūraṇar, qui est du Xe ou XIe siècle pour Meenakshisundaram (1974: 4), et du XIe ou XIIe siècle pour Zvelebil (1973: 134), commente la totalité du T. Les autres n'en commentent qu'une partie: ce sont Cēṉāvaraiyar (XIIIe–XIVe siècle) pour TC, Pērāciriyar (XIIIe siècle) pour une partie de TP (de TP6 à TP9), Nacciṉārkkiṉiyar (XIVe siècle) pour TE, TC et une partie de TP (de TP1 à TP5, plus TP8), Teyvaccilaiyār (XVIe siècle?) pour TC, Kallāṭaṉār (XVe–XVIIe siècle?) pour une partie de TC (jusqu'au milieu de TC7) et un anonyme plus tardif, dont le commentaire est fragmentaire (de TC1 à TC3 presque complet).

Le livre les plus commenté est donc TC, le *Livre des Mots*, dont l'objet est d'introduire des éléments de description à la frontière de la syntaxe et de la morphologie, le sujet qui reçoit le traitement le plus détaillé étant celui des cas. Avant lui, le *Livre des Lettres* (TE) se sera situé dans une problématique à la fois phonologique, phonétique, et même morphophonologique, sans exclure des considérations graphiques pertinentes par rapport au système d'écriture. Enfin, le dernier livre, TP, expose les différents éléments de la poétique tamoule, métrique comprise. Le T n'est donc pas une grammaire au sens strict. Pris dans son ensemble, on peut le caractériser comme la synthèse de différents savoirs, comme une encyclopédie condensée, comme une grammaire au sens large, dont le couronnement est probablement la poétique, comme l'atteste une anecdote contenue dans le commentaire déjà cité (→ Art. 27) pour la légende des trois académies, où nous voyons un roi faire rechercher des lettrés compétents dans les trois branches du savoir que représentent TE, TC et TP, et se montrer très désappointé parce que sa quête n'a fourni de résultat que pour les deux premières branches, aucun lettré compétent en TP n'ayant été trouvé.

## 2. Le "Livre des Lettres"

TE1, le premier chapitre du T, donne une présentation des unités élémentaires, qui sont appelées *eḻuttu* "lettres, phonèmes". Celles-ci, énonce le premier *sūtra*, sont 30, auxquelles s'ajoutent 3 éléments auxiliaires. Suit le détail des 12 voyelles (*uyir*) et des 18 consonnes (*mey*). Il faut tout de suite noter que nous sommes ici dans une abstraction par rapport au système d'écriture. Le tamoul s'écrivait (et s'écrit encore) avec un syllabaire, où les éléments les plus fréquents sont de type "consonne vocalisée" (*uyirmey*), comme par exemple les signes *ka*, *ki* et *ku*. Le nombre théorique des éléments syllabiques est 216 (i. e. 12 fois 18). Par ailleurs, des signes spéciaux sont utilisés à l'initiale des mots commençant par des voyelles. En un sens élémentaire, le mot *uyir* peut renvoyer aux douze voyelles en tant qu'elles sont visualisables grâce à ces signes spéciaux: les cinq 'brèves' (*a*, *i*, *u*, *e*, *o*), qui ne font qu'une 'mesure'; les sept 'longues' (*ā*, *ī*, *ū*, *ē*, *ai*, *ō*, *au*) qui en font deux. En un sens plus général et plus courant, mais que les commentateurs prennent soin d'expliciter, il renvoie aux éléments abstraits sous-jacents au système d'écriture. C'est ainsi par exemple que le *sūtra* TE1-10, "même si elle est combinée avec une consonne, la voyelle ne change pas de nature" est interprété par les commentateurs comme signifiant que les attributs 'long' et 'bref' sont aussi applicables aux consonnes vocalisées. Et c'est aussi pour cette raison que TE1-18 précise que "la voyelle suit la consonne" (à l'intérieur d'une consonne vocalisée, selon l'explicitation de I), et que TE4-4 explique qu'un mot se terminant par une consonne vocalisée est à considérer comme un mot à finale vocalique.

Le caractère concret des remarques élémentaires permet d'ailleurs d'effectuer un ancrage temporel du texte: les épigraphes distinguent en effet trois systèmes successifs dans les inscriptions en écriture brāhmī tamoule qui ont été découvertes pour la période allant du III^e siècle avant notre ère au II^e siècle de notre ère (v. Siromoney 1990). Dans le premier système, le symbole de base est *k* et possède une première forme modifiée qui se lit *ka* ou *kā* (les autres voyelles correspondent à d'autres modifications). Dans le second système, la forme de base peut représenter *k* ou *ka*, la première forme modifiée correspondant à *kā*. Enfin, dans le troisième système, la forme de base représente *ka*, et *k* s'obtient en lui ajoutant un point, ce qui est une innovation (la technique pour représenter *kā* et les autres consonnes vocalisées ne change pas dans le principe). Or c'est ce troisième système qui concorde avec celui que décrit TE: il est expliqué en TE1-15 que "la nature de la consonne est de résider avec un point", ce que Ilampūranar caractérise comme l'explication de la différence graphique entre une consonne vocalisée et une consonne isolée; de plus il est expliqué en TE1−17 qu'une consonne sans point a deux possibilités de vocalisation, ou bien se vocaliser avec *a* et garder sa forme (graphique), ou bien se vocaliser avec une autre voyelle et avoir sa forme métamorphosée.

Parmi les notions de base mises en place au premier chapitre, on note aussi une division des 18 consonnes en trois groupes: 'fortes' (*k*, *c*, *ṭ*, *t*, *p*, *ṟ*), 'douces' (*ṅ*, *ñ*, *ṇ*, *n*, *m*, *ṉ*), 'intermédiaires' (*y*, *r*, *l*, *v*, *ḻ*, *ḷ*) un couplage étant d'ailleurs établi entre les deux premiers groupes (*k* et *ṅ*, *c* et *ñ*, *ṭ* et *ṇ*, etc.) en terme de point d'articulation, ce qui anticipe un peu sur TE3, mais permet de présenter plus efficacement le point suivant qui est l'énumération des séquences possibles de deux consonnes.

Ces premiers éléments mis en place, TE2 aborde la question de la distribution des phonèmes dans le "mot" (*moḻi*), terme primitif dont aucune définition explicite n'est proposé mais dont les contours se précisent au fur et à mesure que sont énoncées des règles dont il est le domaine. Un des éléments importants qui sont discutés dans ce chapitre est le '*u* ultra-bref' (d'une demi-mesure, selon TE1-12), l'un des trois éléments auxiliaires que le premier *sūtra* de TE mentionnait comme s'ajoutant aux 30 lettres et qui est une réalisation particulière de la voyelle brève *u* dans un certain nombre de contextes qui sont ici précisés. Sont aussi passées en revue les initiales et les finales possibles: quelles voyelles? quelles consonnes suivies de quelles voyelles? La description est parfois effectuée en termes négatifs: quelles sont les lettres que l'on ne rencontre pas dans certains contextes?

Puis TE3 aborde des considérations de phonétique articulatoire: sont présentés les lieux d'articulation des différentes phonèmes (*eḻuttu*) ainsi que les organes qui sont en jeu et les actions dans lesquelles ils sont impliqués.

Après cet intermède phonétique, les six derniers chapitres à partir du chapitre TE4 sont consacrés à des questions de morphophonologie. Il s'agit en effet de présenter les phénomènes de sandhi (ou rencontre), c'est-à-dire les modifications qui se produisent lorsque deux mots ou expressions, A et B, se suivent en une séquence A–B. Ce qui est ici noté A est appelé "mot-pilier" (*niṟutta col*); quant à B, il est désigné comme "expression qui vient intentionellement" (*kuṟittu varu kiḷavi*), c'est-à-dire avec une visée tournée vers A: il y a donc, pour le dire anachroniquement, une relation syntaxique entre A et B et non pas une simple juxtaposition. Le découpage en chapitres est justifié par le fait qu'il faut d'abord présenter les principes généraux et les outils théoriques avant d'énoncer ensuite les premières règles, générales, et de traiter enfin dans le détail les différents cas particuliers répartis en fonction de critères comme la nature de la finale de A: voyelle (TE7), consonne (TE8) ou bien *u* ultra-bref (TE9).

C'est dans TE4 que sont répertoriées les différentes possibilités. Les finales et initiales de A et B peuvent être vocaliques ou consonantiques: cela fournit quatre combinaisons. En termes de parties du discours, il y également quatre possibilités, puisque tous deux peuvent être noms (*peyar*) ou verbes (*toḻil*). Quant aux événements phonétiques qui ont lieu à la rencontre de A et B, ils tombent aussi sous le coup d'une division en quatre, où un cas d'invariance s'oppose à trois cas de modification, puisque toute chaîne de 'lettres' peut être transformée en une autre par une succession d'opérations élémentaires (apparition d'une lettre, disparition d'une lettre et transformation d'une lettre en une autre). Enfin, en ce qui concerne la relation entre A et B, deux grands types sont posés: elle peut être casuelle (*vēṟṟumai*); elle peut être non-casuelle (*al-vaḻi*). Par ailleurs, même si le nom et le verbe ont été mis en avant, il est en pratique fréquemment question d'une autre partie du discours: les particules. D'une part, le sandhi applicable à plusieurs d'entre elles quand elles sont en position A est présenté. D'autre part, le chapitre TE6 traite principalement de situations où A est un nom et B appartient à une catégorie spéciale de particule: les "morphèmes casuels" (*vēṟṟumai urupu*), qui sont au nombre de six (*ai, oṭu, ku, iṉ, atu, kaṇ*). Enfin tout au long des six chapitres qui traitent du sandhi, une autre catégorie spéciale de particules joue un rôle instrumental: il s'agit des incréments (*cāriyai*). A vrai dire, nous ne savons pas exactement comment l'auteur du T voyait le fonctionnement de ces deux catégories d'éléments puisque c'est chez les commentateurs que nous avons des exemples concrets. En première approximation, les incréments sont le résidu de l'analyse grammaticale une fois qu'on a enlevé le radical/lexème et le suffixe casuel. Quant à leur fonction, les commentateurs se sont efforçés de montrer que certains d'entre eux permettent parfois d'effectuer des distinctions sémantiques. Bien que cela ne valût pas pour tous les incréments, cela leur suffisait pour satisfaire au principe du T selon lequel "Tous les mots visent une valeur" (TC5-1). A titre d'exemple, Iḷampūraṇar analyse la forme *marattoṭu* "avec (un) arbre" comme le résultat de la combinaison de *maram* "arbre" avec le morphème casuel *oṭu* (3e cas), cette combinaison ayant entraîné l'apparition non-optionnelle ici de l'incrément *attu*. Une liste non-exhaustive de neuf incréments (*iṉ, vaṟṟu, attu, am, oṉ, āṉ, akku, ikku, aṉ*) est donnée au *sūtra* TE4-17. Le choix de l'incrément dépend des caractéristiques phonologiques du lexème et certains sont optionnels.

## 3. Le "Livre des Mots"

Dans le "Livre Des Mots", qui suit, le premier chapitre, TC1, est consacré à poser un certain nombre de notions qui seront opératoires par rapport aux présentations contenues dans des chapitres ultérieurs. Les plus visibles sont certainement celle des "classe" (*tiṇai*) (→ Art. 27), et celle de "genre" (*pāl*), qui la prolonge, puisque la 'classe supérieure' est subdivisée en trois 'genres' (masculin, féminin et pluriel épicène) tandis que la 'hors-classe' se subdivise en deux (neutre singulier et neutre pluriel). L'une des problématiques mise en jeu en TC1 est celle de la phrase ou de l'énoncé, même s'il n'y a pas dans le T de terme technique qui désigne univoquement ce niveau linguistique, le terme *kiḷavi* étant ce qui s'en rapproche le plus (il peut désigner un schéma de phrase), mais renvoyant aussi le plus souvent à un simple mot ou à un syntagme. En effet, l'un des *sūtra*-s (TC1-11) énonce qu'il n'y a pas désaccord en genre entre le nom et le verbe, les exemples et anti-exemples donnés par les commentateurs montrant qu'il est bien ici question de la phrase. C'est d'ailleurs le verbe qui permet dans certains cas de connaître le genre d'un nom avec lequel il s'est accordé puisque celui-ci n'est pas toujours en évidence.

Les trois chapitres suivants, de TC2 à TC4, sont consacrés à la question des "cas" (*vēṟṟumai*). Ceux-ci ont déjà été traités d'un point de vue phonologique dans TE, mais il est question ici principalement de leurs valeurs. Une liste de huit termes reprend les six morphèmes mentionnés en TE4-11, y ajoutant un nominatif (ou cas 'nom') en tête et un vocatif (ou cas 'appel') en fin. Ce dernier et huitième cas (*viḷi*), présenté en TC2-2 comme surnuméraire, fait l'objet d'un chapitre à part (TC4), où sa morphologie est présentée, selon des critères principalement phonologiques. Quant au premier cas, aussi qualifié de "cas origine" (*eḻuvāy vēṟṟumai*), sa forme est présentée comme celle du "nom apparaissant seul", le vocabulaire grammatical tamoul ne connaissant pas les morphèmes zéros. Pour ce qui est des six autres cas, il y est fait référence tantôt au moyen de numéros (allant du deuxième au septième) et tantôt au moyen des morphèmes, déjà cités, qui les caractérisent: *ai, oṭu, ku, iṉ, atu, kaṇ*. Pour chaque cas, une caractérisation large de ses emplois est d'abord proposée, suivie d'une caractérisation détaillée. La première, tout en faisant appel à un vocabulaire tamoul, semble souvent inspirée d'une forme de la théorie des *kāraka*-s que l'on rencontre en grammaire paninéenne. Quant à la caractérisation détaillée, elle est ce que le style des *sūtra*-s utilisés dans le T permet comme approchant le plus des exemples concrets, ces derniers étant fournis par les commentateurs. Ainsi, à titre d'exemple, pour le 'deuxième cas', dont le suffixe est *ai*, et qui pourrait se laisser traduire par accusatif, une liste non-limitative de 28 noms verbaux est donnée en TC2-11: garder, ressembler, chevaucher, construire, etc., que les commentateurs illustreront par des exemples du type: "il garde le village-ACCUSATIF", "il ressemble [à] son père-ACCUSATIF", etc. Quant à la caractérisation générale en terme de *kāraka*, elle est ici très allusive, TC employant le terme de *mutal* "cause première", ce qui permet aux commentateurs d'affiner l'explication: Iḷampūraṇar se contente de le remplacer par le terme *nimittam* "facteur causal", emprunté au sanskrit; Cēṉavaraiyar le remplace par le terme *viṉai-mutal* "antécédent(s) [d'un acte]", et renvoie au *sūtra* TC3-29 où ce terme figure et où son propre commentaire l'identifie au sanskrit *kāraka* (v. Chevillard 1996: 155, 219) et où une liste canonique de huit 'antécédents' est donnée. Cependant, il est important de noter qu'il n'y a pas concordance avec le canon paninéen (*Aṣṭādhyāyī* I, 4.24–55). Celui-ci ne connaît que six *kāraka*-s: K1 = *apādāna* "ablation"; K2 = *saṃpradāna* "dation"; K3 = *karaṇa* "instrument"; K4 = *adhikaraṇa* "location"; K5 = *karman* "objet"; K6 = *kartṛ* "agent" (v. Renou 1966: 66–73; → Art. 21). Parmi ceux-ci, cinq seulement coïncident avec des éléments de la liste des huit *mutaṉilai*-s "antécédents": *viṉai* "action" (M1); *ceyvatu* "agent" (M2 = K6), *ceyappaṭu poruḷ* "objet" (M3 = K5); *nilaṉ* "lieu" (M4 = K4); *kālam* "temps" (M5); *karuvi* "instrument" (M6 = K3); *iṉṉataṟku* "destinataire" (M7 = K2), *itu payaṉ āka* "but" (M8). Il faut aussi noter que l'énumération met à part les deux derniers (M7 + M8), et que les six premiers réapparaissent seuls au *sutra* TC6-37, où sont énumérées les relations (syntaxiques) possibles entre un participe adnominal et le nom avec lequel il se construit dans ce qui est l'équivalent tamoul des relatives (v. Chevillard 1966: 363).

Après la présentation des sept cas et de leurs valeurs, le chapitre suivant TC3 est principalement consacré à l'examen de tout ce qui ne rentre pas dans la cadre théorique qui vient d'être défini, c'est-à-dire notamment aux situations où deux cas sont en concurrence.

La présentation des cas s'étant achevée par une discussion du vocatif (en TC4), les quatre chapitres suivants sont consacrés respectivement aux quatre parties du discours: les noms (TC5), les verbes (TC6), les particules (TC7) et les 'mots propres' (TC8), avec à chaque fois une présentation différente. Ainsi les noms sont divisés en trois grands groupes: les noms de la classe supérieure, les noms de la hors-classe et les noms mixtes, dont le référent peut aussi bien être de la classe supérieure que de la hors-classe. Pour chaque groupe, il y a plusieurs énumérations dont les termes sont tantôt des noms particuliers (ce qui inclut les pronoms personnels, comme par exemple *yāṉ* "je") et tantôt des catégories particulières de noms: on rencontre ainsi les *tiṇai-nilaip peyar* "noms selon le statut de caste", pour lesquels les commentateurs fourniront les illustrations ultimes, comme par exemple *pārppār* "brahmanes", *āyar* "bergers", etc. En ce qui concerne les noms mixtes, un cas important est celui des noms propres, comme *Cāttaṉ*, dont le référent peut être aussi bien un humain qu'un animal.

La disposition du chapitre des verbes (TC6) est en apparence semblable à celle du chapitre précédent, puisqu'elle fait elle aussi intervenir trois groupes, selon le même principe. Cependant, là où les énumérations de TC5 mettaient en jeu des lexèmes, ou groupes de lexèmes, à chaque fois différents, les énumérations de TC6 mettent en jeu les différents constituants du paradigme commun à tous les verbes, généralement illustrés au moyen de la conjugaison du verbe 'faire'. On trouvera ainsi: parmi les formes verbales de la classe supérieure les premières personnes (du singulier et du pluriel: inclusif et exclusif); parmi les formes de la hors-classe les formes verbales neutre (singulier et pluriel) de la 3$^{e}$ personne; parmi les formes mixtes, la 2$^{e}$ personne (parce que, disent les commentateurs, on peut dire "tu" à certains animaux tout comme aux humains) et toutes les formes non-personnelles (les différents modèles de participes). Au delà de cette présentation, un point retient particulièrement l'attention, c'est l'affirmation qu'il existe deux types de verbes, entre lesquels la différence réside dans l'expression du temps: les verbes ordinaires, que les commentateurs appellent *teri-nilai viṉai* "verbes explicites" et dont la morphologie permet (théoriquement) de distinguer des paradigmes de passé, de présent et de futur; les *kuṟippu viṉai* "verbes idéels", qui ne possèdent qu'un paradigme, mais qui sont supposés exprimer quand même le temps, parce que telle est la caractérisation des verbes (TC6-1). A titre d'exemple de 'verbes idéels' on peut citer, suivant les commentateurs, des verbes (-adjectifs) comme "être-noir" (*kariyaṉ* "il-est-noir", *karitu* "cela-est-noir", v. Chevillard 1992: 45–46) ou bien les verbes (défectifs) comme "ne-pas-avoir" (*ilaṉ* "il n'a pas", etc.) ou "ne-pas-être" (*alaṉ* "il n'est pas" etc.).

Le chapitre suivant, TC7, est consacré aux "particules" (*iṭaic col*), dont le statut est, selon son premier *sūtra*, subalterne par rapport aux noms et aux verbes. Suit une énumération des différents types de particules, sept en tout, parmi lesquelles on reconnaît: les incréments (type 1), déjà traités en TE4; les morphèmes casuels (type 3), déjà traités, notamment en TE4, TE6, TC2 et TC3; les infixes temporels (type 2), qui auraient dû être traités en TC6 ou dans TE, mais qui ne le sont pas parce que, selon Cēṉāvaraiyar, le T ne traite pas du sandhi interne (*oru-moḻip puṇarcci*, litt. "le sandhi d'un seul mot"). Parmi les quatre restants, le type 7 (les particules de comparaison) est renvoyé au chapitre TP7. Quant aux types 4, 5 et 6, qui sont des explétifs de deux espèces (les "appoints syllabiques" et les "compléments métriques") et les particules modales (litt. "celles qui produisent un effet de sens grâce à leur visée"), ils sont effectivement traités dans ce chapitre qui s'achève comme un dictionnaire des particules, chaque particule examinée donnant lieu à une liste de valeurs, que les commentateurs illustreront. Il n'y a d'ailleurs pas forcément séparation stricte entre les types puisqu'un certain nombre de particules modales peuvent être explétives. D'un point de vue syntaxique, mais cette question ne reçoit pas d'attention particulière dans TC, un certain nombre de ces particules sont des clitiques. Plusieurs d'entre elles ont déjà été traitées en TE.

Le chapitre TC8 est sans doute le plus déroutant. Il concerne en effet une partie du discours, les "mots propres" (*uric col*) dont la caractérisation est assez obscure, les commentateurs n'étant d'ailleurs pas tous d'accord entre eux sur l'interprétation exacte. Des auteurs modernes ont d'ailleurs soutenu que le T reconnaissait ainsi l'existence de l'adjectif comme une partie du discours en tamoul, mais cette opinion semble difficilement défendable (v. Chevillard 1992). L'une des sources de la difficulté est l'écart entre la présentation générale par laquelle commence le chapitre et son contenu effectif. A titre d'exemple, le *sūtra* TC8-4 contient l'assertion *purai uyarpu ākum* (*purai* est "élévation"). Celle-ci explique, très allusivement, au moyen du mot *uyarpu* "élévation" la valeur du 'mot propre' *purai*, que les commentateurs illustreront par une forme du verbe *puraital* "émuler, être digne de, ressembler à". De même, le *sutra* TC8-5, *kuruvum keḻuvum niṟaṉ ākummē* (*kuru* et *keḻu* sont "couleur") explique la valeur des deux mots *kuru* et *keḻu* au moyen du mot *niṟañ* "couleur". Le chapitre TC8 ressemble de fait à un fragment de lexique qui donne les sens de mots poétiques rares, souvent regroupés selon des critères phonétiques (par assonance) ou sémantiques (par synonymie). Il essaie par ailleurs de répondre à la question: "comment expliquer le sens des mots?", la position qu'il défend étant qu'on ne peut en fait pas expliquer le sens des mots courants et qu'on explique les mots rares aux étudiants au moyen des mots courants. En ce qui concerne la forme de citation, la démarche suivie se situe en deçà de la notion de partie du discours. Les 'mots propres' expliqués sont plus souvent cités sous une forme syntaxiquement neutre (nom verbal, nom de qualité) et plus rarement sous une forme syntaxiquement marquée (comme le participe). Selon la formulation de TC8-1, ils "se confondent concrètement avec les noms et les verbes", ce que Cēṉāvaraiyar explique en disant qu'ils en sont le radical (*mutaṉilai*), terme qu'ailleurs il rapprochera du sanskrit *dhātu* "racine". Selon cette position, les 'mots propres' ne constituent pas une partie du discours à part, ils sont, de façon complémentaire par rapport aux particules, l'un des termes de l'analyse des mots, faisant peut-être apparaître le propre des mots. Lorsque l'auteur du T, après avoir dit en TC5-4 qu'il y a deux parties du discours, noms et verbes, en mentionnait en TC5-5 deux autres, particules et mots propres, il ne faisait pas une addition, même si les commentateurs parlent des quatre espèces de mots, additionnant 2 et 2, tout en notant la différence de statut. Cela étant, la caractérisation générale des mots propres ne peut être sémantiquement effectuée que de façon minimale, TC8-1 disant qu'ils "se manifestent à propos d'un son, d'une idée ou d'une qualité".

Enfin le dernier chapitre, TC9, aborde un certain nombre de sujets qui n'ont pu être traitées dans les chapitres précédents et parmi lesquelles on peut citer la typologie des mots utilisables en poésie (avec notamment le sort à réserver aux mots sanskrits), la classification et la caractérisation des composés (casuels, comparatifs, verbaux, qualitatifs, copulatifs et exocentriques), et enfin des considérations sur la notion d'incomplétion (qui sert notamment à expliquer la syntaxe des formes participiales).

## 4. Le "Livre des Matières"

Il resterait à présenter le contenu du troisième livre, TP, celui qui traite "Des Matières [Poétiques]", qui est le couronnement de l'ouvrage mais qui nous ferait sortir de la grammaire au sens strict. On se contentera donc de dire ici de façon brève qu'il a pour objets: les conventions de la poésie amoureuse (TP1, TP3, TP4 et TP5); celles de la poésie guerrière (TP2); un traité des sentiments (TP6); la comparaison (TP7); la métrique (TP8); des conventions diverses (TP9).

## 5. Bibliographie

### 5.1. Sources primaires

[Note: La plupart des commentaires ont été édités (et très souvent réimprimés) par la *Caiva Cittānta Nūṟpatippuk Kaḻakam*, habituellement désignée comme l'édition *kaḻakam*. Cependant, pour beaucoup d'entre eux, il est très difficile d'avoir des données bibliographiques précises pour cette série bon marché très répandue et destinée aux étudiants. On ne trouvera donc ici que les données concernant d'autres éditions.]

*Tolkāppiyam*. Ed. par Murray S. Rajam. Madras: New Century Book House 1981. (1e éd., 1957.)

*Tolkāppiyam Eḻuttatikāram*. Commentaire de Iḷampūraṇar [XIe siècle?]. Ed. par Ku. Cuntaramūrtti. Annamalai Nagar: Annamalai University, 1979.

*Tolkāppiyam Eḻuttatikāram*. Commentaire de Nacciṉārkkiṉiyar [XIVe siècle]. Ed. par Ci. Kaṇēcaiyar. Ceylan: Cuṉṉākam, 1937.

*Tolkāppiyam Collatikāram*. Commentaire de Iḷampūraṇar [XIe siècle?]. Ed. par Aṭikaḷāciriyar. Tanjore: Tamil University, 1988.

*Tolkāppiyam Collatikāram*. Commentaire de Cēṉāvaraiyar [XIIIe–XIVe siècle]. Ed. par Āṟumuka Nāvalar. Chidambaram (Tamil Nadu): Citampara Caivap Pirakāca Vittiyā Cālai, 1934. (1e éd., 1886.)

*Tolkāppiyam Collatikāram*. Commentaire de Kallāṭaṉar [XVe–XVIIe siècle?]. Ed. par Te. Po. Mīṉāṭcicuntaraṉār. Madras: Tamil Nadu Government Oriental Series, 1971.

*Tolkāppiyam Collatikāram*. Commentaire de Nacciṉārkkiṉiyar [XIVe siècle]. Ed. par Mē. Vī. Vēṇukopālap Piḷḷai. Madras: Pavāṉantar Kaḻakam, 1941.-

*Tolkāppiyam Collatikāram*. Commentaire de Teyvaccilaiyār [XVIe siècle?]. Ed. par R. Vēṅkaṭācalam. (= *Tamil University Publication*, 5.) Tanjore: Tamil University, 1984. (1e éd., 1929.)

### 5.2. Sources secondaires

Chevillard, Jean-Luc. 1992, "Sur l'adjectif dans la tradition grammaticale tamoule". *Histoire Epistémologie Langage* 14:1.37–58.

–. 1996. *Le commentaire de Cēṉāvaraiyar sur le Collatikāram du Tolkāppiyam*. Pondicherry: Institut Français de Pondichéry.

Renou, Louis. 1966. *La grammaire de Pāṇini: Texte sanskrit, traduction française avec extraits des commentaires*. Paris: Ecole Française d'Extrême-Orient.

Siromoney, Gift. 1990. "An Outline of Tamil Orthography". *Encyclopedia of Tamil Literature* éd. par G. John Samuel, I, 105–122. Madras: Thiruvanmiyur.

Subrahmany Sastri, P. S. 1930. *Tolkāppiyam, The Earliest Extant Tamil Grammar, with a short commentary in English*. I: *Eluttatikāram*. (= *Madras Oriental Series*, 3.) Madras.

–. 1979. *Tolka:ppiyam Collatika:ram.* Annamalai Nagar: Annamalai University. (1e éd., 1945.)

Zvelebil, Kamil V. 1972–75. "Tolkāppiyam Eḻuttatikāram". *Journal of Tamil Studies* 1.43–60 [TE1–TE3]; 2.13–29 [TE4–TE6]; 3.17–27 [TE7]; 4.13–23 [TE8]; 5.34–36 [TE9: 407–420]; 7.62–66 [TE9: 421–462]; 8.8–11 [TE9: 463–483]; Madras: International Institute of Tamil Studies. [Traduction anglaise annotée de TE.]

–. 1978–85. "Talkāppiyam Collatikāram". *Journal of Tamil Studies* 13.79–86 [TC1: 1–30]; 20.5–14 [TC1: 31–61]; 21.9–19 [TC2]; 28.67–80 [TC3]. Madras: International Institute of Tamil Studies. [Traduction anglaise annotée des 3 premiers chapitres de TC.]

*Jean-Luc Chevillard, Paris (France)*

# 29. Les successeurs du *Tolkāppiyam*: le *Naṉṉūl*, le *Vīracōḻiyam* et les autres écoles

1. La grammaire après le *Tolkāppiyam*
2. L'organisation de la grammaire
3. La terminologie
4. Le *Naṉṉūl*
5. Bibliographie

## 2. La grammaire après le *Tolkāppiyam*

Si le *Tolkāppiyam* (T; → Art. 28) est l'origine, de nature encyclopédique, que la tradition linguistique tamoule s'est choisie, oubliant de préserver les ouvrages qui l'ont précédé, quitte à leur donner statut divin, après lui commence l'histoire proprement dite, avec ses commentateurs, dont ceux du T, avec ses grammairiens nouveaux, le plus influent étant l'auteur du *Naṉṉūl*, écrit au début du XIIIe siècle par Pavaṇanti Muṉivar. Et cette histoire, en tant qu'histoire autonome, s'achève sans doute au XVIIIe siècle, alors que les occidentaux sont déjà actifs en Inde du Sud depuis deux siècles, que leurs missionnaires ont imprimé dès le XVIe siècle des livres en tamoul et qu'ils ont écrit en latin des grammaires du tamoul, la première étant celle de Anriquez vers 1552 (v. Zvelebil 1990: xvii). Cependant, l'impression, qu'ils ont introduite pour leur usage, ne sera utilisée pour la première fois qu'au XIXe siècle par les lettrés qui sont les descendants des *pulavar*.

Des siècles qui suivent le T nous restent un certain nombre de textes dévotionnels, littéraires et grammaticaux, la distinction entre les genres n'étant pas toujours claire, puisque plusieurs recueils d'hymnes religieux sont considérés comme des chefs-d'œuvre littéraires. Quant aux ouvrages grammaticaux, l'appartenance religieuse de leurs auteurs possède une importance: d'une part les instances religieuses ont joué un rôle pour la préservation du savoir (par exemple, les monastères hindous, ou *maṭam*, entretenaient des lettrés); d'autre part, l'allégeance religieuse supposée des œuvres n'était pas toujours sans incidence sur leur rayonnement. A cet égard, si l'on observe l'évolution sur le long terme de ce que l'on peut peut-être appeler des écoles, on voit au cours des siècles des lettrés hindous reprendre à plusieurs reprises le flambeau grammatical des mains des jain. Quant aux bouddhistes, leurs contributions semblent rester plus isolées, quels que puissent en être les mérites ou le caractère innovant, comme dans le cas du *Vīracōḻiyam*. Enfin, la fin de cette période voit même un auteur chrétien écrire une grammaire tamoule en tamoul: il s'agit du jésuite Beschi, qui sous le nom de Vīramāmuṉivar écrira au 18e siècle le *Toṉṉūl Viḷakkam*.

## 2. L'organisation de la grammaire

Une autre caractéristique des textes de la période historique est leur plus grande spécialisation et le redécoupage qu'ils effectuent sur le champ du savoir. Alors que le T, avec ses trois livres, était un ouvrage à visée globale, les textes qui suivent ont généralement un objet plus spécialisé. Ainsi le *Naṉṉūl*, ouvrage de grand rayonnement, ne comporte pas de poétique pour prolonger ses deux parties, *Eḻuttatikāram* "Chapitre des Lettres" et *Collatikāram* "Chapitre des Mots", dont les objets sont identiques à ceux des deux premiers livres du T (TE et TC). Il en est de même pour *Nēminātam*, composé par Kuṉavīrapaṇṭitar (XIIIe siècle). De manière encore plus spécialisée, au XVIIe siècle, le *Pirayōkavivēkam* composé par Cuppiramaṇiya Tīṭcitar et l'*Ilakkaṇak Kottu* dû à Cuvāmināta Tēcikar ne traitent, au sens traditionnel, que du 'mot', ce qui inclut des questions de syntaxe.

Les sujets qui étaient traités dans TP, le 3e livre du T, font à plusieurs reprises l'objet d'ouvrages nouveaux, mais l'ensemble des savoirs traditionnels sera souvent présenté comme faisant cinq branches, et non plus trois, la nouvelle liste étant: I. *Eḻuttu* "lettres"; II. *Col* "mots"; III. *Poruḷ* "matières [poétiques]"; IV. *Yāppu* "métrique"; V. *Aṇi* "ornement", ces deux derniers sujets ayant été extraits de *Poruḷ* et ayant pris leur autonomie (ils étaient respectivement traités en TP8 et TP7). Comme ouvrage à visée spécialisée pour le *poruḷ* au sens restreint (c'est-à-dire la thématique et les conventions), on peut citer, concernant respectivement les poésies amoureuses et guerrières: le *Akapporuḷ Viḷakkam* de Nāṟkavirāca Nampi (XIIIe siècle), qui se situe dans la lignée du *Iṟaiyaṉār Akapporuḷ* (VIIIe siècle, → Art. 27); le *Pūrapporuḷ Veṇpāmalai* de Aiyaṉāritaṉār (IXe siècle). Pour la métrique, les ouvrages importants sont *Yāpparuṅkalam* et *Yāpparuṅkalak Kārikai*, dus à Amitacākarar (XIe siècle). Pour les "Ornements" (*Aṇi*) enfin, ou rhétorique, on peut citer le *Taṇṭi Alaṅkāram* (XIIe siècle).

Des ouvrages cependant tentent d'émuler le point de vue global sur le savoir des lettrés que représentait le T. Ainsi, le *Vīracōḻiyam*, écrit par Puttamittiraṉār (XIe siècle), comporte 10 chapitres (ou *paṭalam*), qui couvrent les cinq branches déjà mentionnées. Précisément, on a: I. *cantip paṭalam* "chapitre du sandhi"; II. *vēṟṟumaip paṭalam* "chapitre des cas", *upakārakap paṭalam* "chapitre des auxiliaires", *tokaip paṭalam* "chapitre des composés", *tattitap paṭalam* "chapitre des suffixes secondaires», *tātup paṭalam* "chapitre des racines" et *kiriyā patap paṭalam* "chapitre des verbes"; III. *poruṭ paṭalam* "chapitre des matières poétiques"; IV. *yāppup paṭalam* "chapitre de la métrique"; V. *alaṅkārap paṭalam* "chapitre des ornements". Quantitativement, ce sont les branches V., IV. et II. (cette dernière tous chapitres confondus) qui reçoivent le traitement le plus détaillé, la branche I. étant traitée le plus rapidement. Six siècles plus tard, l'*Ilakkaṇa Viḷakkam* (XVIIe siècle) proposera aussi un ouvrage global, mais avec une terminologie et une optique plus traditionnelles. Enfin, au XVIIIe siècle, le *Toṉṉūl Viḷakkam* de Beschi couvre lui aussi les cinq branches.

## 3. La terminologie linguistique

Si le T fait parfois allégeance à des ouvrages de la tradition sanskrite (la 'langue du Nord'), et si l'on peut tenter de déterminer ses sources, comme le fait P. S. Subrahmanya Sastri (1934), sa terminologie est dans une large mesure purement tamoule: il préférait le calque à l'emprunt. Au contraire, parmi les ouvrages qui viennent d'être cités, deux font appel de façon assez massive à un vocabulaire sanskrit: ce sont le *Vīracōḻiyam* (V) et le *Prayōka Vivēkam* (PV). C'est le cas par exemple de six titres de chapitres sur dix dans V: *canti*, *upakārakam*, *tattitam*, *tātu*, *kiriyā patam* et *alaṅkāram* sont en effet les adaptations à la phonologie du tamoul des termes *sandhi*, *upakāraka*, *taddhita*, *dhātu*, *kriyā pada* et *alaṃkāra*. Quant au PV, les titres de ses quatre chapitres présentent le même caractère: *kārakap paṭalam* "chapitre des facteurs", *camācap paṭalam* "chapitre des composés", *tattitap paṭalam* "chapitre des suffixes secondaires" et *tiṅṅup paṭalam* "chapitre des désinences verbales" contiennent les formes tamoulisées de *kāraka*, *samāsa*, *taddhita* et *tiṅ*, ce dernier n'étant pas un mot courant mais un élément du métalangage paninéen.

Des grammaires comme le V et le PV n'ont en fait jamais vraiment eu de réel succès au pays tamoul. Elles ont pu avoir une influence indirecte à travers des grammairiens ultérieures capables de tamouliser leur apport. Mais leur public ne pouvait être qu'un public venant à la grammaire tamoule en ayant déjà maitrisé l'une des formes de la grammaire sanskrite, tant ils sont pleins de termes techniques: l'éditeur moderne de PV donne une liste de plus de 400 expressions sanskrites.

## 4. Le *Naṉṉūl*

Sur toute la période historique, l'ouvrage qui a le retentissement le plus fort est le *Naṉṉūl* (N). On lui compte environ 10 commentateurs jusqu'au XIXe siècle, les plus connus étant ceux dûs à Mayilainātar (XIVe siècle), à Caṅkaranamaccivāyar (*Puttamputturai*, XVIIe siècle) et à Civañāṉa Muṉivar (*Viruttiyurai*, XVIIIe siècle). L'émulation principale se joue entre T et ses commentateurs d'une part, N et ses commentateurs d'autre part. Iḷampūraṇar, l'un des commentateurs du T, est d'ailleurs considéré comme l'une des sources d'inspiration du N, l'une des autres sources supposées étant l'œuvre, aujourd'hui perdue sauf pour quelques fragments, du grammairien Aviṉāyaṉar (v. Vijayavenugopal 1968), autre disciple supposé de Akattiyar (→ Art. 27). Comme témoignage extérieur sur le rayonnement de ces grammaires au XVIIIe siècle, on peut citer celui de Beschi, qui écrit dans la préface de sa grammaire du *Centamiḻ*, datée de 1730 (v. 1917: xi–xii):

Les règles en ayant été consignées dans un premier traité [composé par lui] on dit que l'autorité pour le dialecte [tamoul] châtié est un ascète de nom de Akattiyaṉ [...] mais les livres qu'il a écrits, nous ne pouvons plus les trouver nulle part [...]. Par contre ceux qu'a écrits sur cette langue quelqu'un du nom de Tolkāppiyaṉār, [...] j'ai encore été en mesure de les trouver; mais par sa concision il est si obscur qu'un autre ascète, du nom de Pavaṇanti, a jugé utile de composer un livre qu'il a appelé *Naṉṉūl* [...]. Le nom de cet ouvrage est dans la bouche de tous; pourtant, seuls quelques-uns à peine ont payé leur hommage à l'œuvre à partir de son seuil [en en lisant la préface] (*Primo arte conscriptis regulis hujus elegantioris linguae auctorem dicunt monachum quemdam Agattien [...] sed quos ipse scripsit libros nullibi invenire jam possumus. [...] Quae autem de hac lingua scripsit quidam nomine* tolkāppiyaṉār *[...] alicubi adhuc inveni; adeo tamen brevitate obscurus est ut operae pretium duxerit monachus alter, cui nomen* pavaṇanti *librum edere, quem* naṉṉūl *inscripsit [...] Hujus operis nomen omnium versatur ore, cum vix aliqui opus ipsum e limine salutaverint*)

Ce témoignage est bien sûr celui d'un étranger, venu évangéliser le pays tamoul, qui n'a pas forcément rencontré les meilleurs lettrés, sans doute concentrés dans les monastères shivaïtes. Cependant, si on le compare avec ce que U. Vē. Cāminātaiyar (UVS), grand lettré né en 1855, racontera dans son autobiographie de la difficulté de sa quête des manuscrits pour sauver de la disparition toute une littérature ancienne, il apparaît prémonitoire. Un âge est en train de s'achever au XVIIIe siècle. Une renaissance va commencer au XIXe siècle. Et ses artisans, Āṟumuka Nāvalar, Ci. Vai. Tāmōtaram Piḷḷai, UVS, etc. ne seront plus seulement des commentateurs. Ils devront être des éditeurs, pour pouvoir franchir à leur tour, et faire franchir à d'autres, le seuil des textes anciens.

## 5. Bibliographie

### 5.1. Sources primaires


Cāmināta Tēcikar [XVIIe siècle], *Ilakkaṇak Kottu, Mūlamum Uraiyum.* Ed. par Ti. Vē. Kōpālaiyar. (= *Tañcai Caracuvati Makāl Veḷiyīṭu*, 146.) [Tanjore], 1973.

Cuppiramaṇiya Tīṭcitar [XVIIe siècle], *Prayōka Vivēkam, Mūlamum Uraiyum.* Ed. par Ti. Vē. Kōpālaiyar. (= *Tañcai Caracuvati Makāl Veḷiyīṭu*, 147.) [Tanjore], 1973.

Kuṇavīrapaṇṭitar [XIIIe siècle], *Nemiṉātam.* Ed. par Ra. Irākavaiyaṅkār. Madurai: The Mandura Tamil Sangam, 1923.

Puttamittiraṉār [XIe siècle], *Vīracōḻiyam.* Commentaire de Peruntēvaṉār [11e–12e siècle]. Ed. par K. R. Kōvintarāca Mutaliyār. Madras: Kaḻakam [Pavāṉantar Kaḻakam], 1970. (1e èd., 1942.)

Pavaṇanti Muṉivar [XIIIe siècle], *Naṉṉūl Mūlamum Mayilai Nātar Uraiyum.* Commentaire de Mayilai Nātar [XIVe siècle]. Ed. par U. Vē. Cāminātaiyar. 2e èd. Madras, 1946.

Pavaṇanti Muṉivar [XIIIe siècle], *Naṉṉūl Mūlamum Caṅkara Namaccivāyar Uraiyum.* Commentaire de Caṅkara Namaccivāyar [XVIIe siècle]. Ed. par U. Vē. Cāminātaiyar. Madras, 1935.

Pavaṇanti Munivar [XIIIe siècle], *Naṉṉūl Viruttiyurai.* Commentaire de Civañāṉa Muṉivar [XVIIIe siècle]. Ed. par. Ca. Taṇṭapāṇi Tēcikar.

Tiruvāvaṭuturai Ātīṉam, 1957. Vīramāmuṉivar [XVIIIe siècle], alias Constantius Josephus Beschi, *Aintilakkaṇat Toṉṉūl Viḷakkam.* Madras: Kaḻakam, 1984.


### 5.2. Sources secondaires


Beschi, Constantius Josephus, s. j. 1917. *A Grammar of High Tamil, Latin text published for the first time, with the English translation by B. B. Babington.* Ed. par L. Besse, s. j. Trichinopoly: St Joseph Industrial School Press. (Ms. de 1730.)

Nachimuthu, K. 1998. "A Critical Edition of Vīracōḻiyam". *Kōlam* 2 [Electronic Journal.] Cologne: Institute of Indology and Tamil Studies.

Subrahmanya Sastri, P. S. 1934. *History of Grammatical Theories in Tamil and Their Relation to the Grammatical Literature in Sanskrit.* Madras: Journal of Oriental Research. [Thèse de doctorat, Madras University, 1930.]

Vijayavenugopal, G. 1968. *A Modern Evaluation of* Naṉṉūl (Eḻuttatikāram). Annamalai Nagar: Annamalai University.

Zvelebil, Kamil V. 1990. *Dravidian Linguistics: An introduction.* Pondicherry: Pondicherry Institute of Linguistics and Culture.


*Jean-Luc Chevillard, Paris (France)*

# VII. The Establishment of Tibetan Linguistics
# Die Anfänge der Sprachforschung in Tibet
# La constitution de la linguistique tibétaine

## 30. The early Tibetan grammatical treatises and Thon-mi Sambhoṭa


1. Date and authorship of the treatises
2. The text of the treatises
3. The contents of the treatises
4. Conclusion
5. Bibliography


### 1. Date and authorship of the treatises

Traditionally the work of the Tibetan grammarians has almost entirely been conducted in the form of commentaries upon, expansions of, and discussions pro and con concerning two short texts, the *Sum-cu-pa* (*SCP*) and the *Rtags-kyi-ḥjug-pa* (*TKJ*). These the Tibetan historical tradition has dated in the third or fourth decade of the 7th century, attributing them to a Thon-mi Sambhoṭa, who was believed to have been dispatched to India by the Tibetan king Sroṅ bstan sgam po "along with sixteen companions in order to study writing; he studied with a *paṇḍita* named Lha-rig pai seṅ-ge, created the Tibetan alphabet based on a Kashmiri prototype, and composed eight works on writing and grammar" (Beyer 1992: 40). Six of these eight texts are traditionally held to have been lost at an early date, with only the *SCP* and *TKJ* surviving.

Modern critical study of the various stages attested in the growth of the tradition concerning the dates and authorship of these two texts has shown that it can no longer seriously be maintained (Miller 1976). Instead of two 7th century works from the pen of Thonmi Sambhoṭa, what we have instead are two indubitably early grammatical treatises, the *SCP* and *TKJ*; but these are surely not from the same hand nor does either date from the reign of Sroṅ bstan sgam po; and no authentic, respectively documentary link can be established between these texts and the historical figure of Thon-mi Sambhoṭa, an early translator of Buddhist texts. Both these two early treatises preserve internal evidence for multiple authorship; text-critical study has further revealed that both are conflated composite redactions that incorporate fragments drawn from a number of other, still earlier Tibetan grammatical texts now surviving only in these first two treatises (Miller 1993).

It is not presently possible to propose a secure terminus for the redaction of our received text of either the *SCP* or the *TKJ*. The first commentary that testifies to the existence of both *qua* texts, and that also for the first time cites them by their present received titles, is that of Dbus-pa-blo-gsal-byaṅ-chub-ye-šes (first half of the 14th century) (Mimaki 1992). But both texts were either in part or in whole known to the Sa-skya paṇḍita Kun-dgaḥ-rgyal-mtshan (1182–1251), even though, significantly for the history of these texts, he does not identify them by their present titles, nor does he attribute them to Thonmi Sambhoṭa (Miller 1993: § 6).

The *SCP* is demonstrably older than the *TKJ*, and the earliest materials that entered into its redaction incorporated a substantial number of specifically Old Tibetan linguistic materials. This is in sharp contrast to the later Classical Tibetan that is the concern of the *TKJ*. Both texts are obviously in debt to Indic linguistic science, but they also show significant traces of Chinese influence that is more difficult to document and to explain. E. g., while in these two treatises the distinction between free lexical word-forms and bound syntactic word-forms appears at first glance to be of entirely Indic origin, and to correspond to Sanskrit *prātipadika* "free, lexical word form" or *nāman* "bound syntactic word form" as opposed to Sanskrit *pada*, respectively, it is curious in the extreme that Tibetan *miṅ* and *tshig*, the two technical terms used for these major linguistic-analytic categories, are both transparent loans from Chinese, identified long ago by Simon (1930) but subsequently scarcely mentioned in the literature. Adding to this problem is the fact that the phonology of the Chinese original underlying Tibetan *miṅ* is suspiciously recent, even modern, while that of Tibetan *tshig* is startlingly old, the *-g* of this word implying at the latest that very early stage in Chinese historical phonology which Karlgren denominated "Archaic" (1940: *miṅ*, no. 826a, *tshig*, no. 972j).

## 2. The text of the treatises

The Chinese etymological origins of these basic technical terms in the first two treatises show us that not only is it impossible to follow the Tibetan tradition in ascribing the starting point of the grammatical tradition to the *SCP* and *TKJ*, much less to their putative author Thon-mi Sambhoṭa, but also that these two treatises are the result of later redactions and editorial pastiches that drew upon a large repertoire of now otherwise lost early experiments in and attempts at grammatical description. Much of this grew out of more-or-less easily identifiable Indic materials, but much of it also originated in now less readily recognized Chinese sources, the latter in particular covering a considerable time-span. In this connection, we can scarcely overlook the activities of such figures as the Tibetan-Chinese bilingual erudite Chos-grub, alias Fa-ch'eng (fl. 9th century), author of an early sketch of Tibetan and Chinese case-grammar that in turn drew upon Indic sources (Verhagen 1992). Non-Tibetans from China and Central Asia, with backgrounds and skills similar to those of Chos grub, no doubt played important roles in the genesis of our received texts of both these two early treatises. Ruegg has argued convincingly (1992: 241) for "the simultaneous presence in eighth-century Tibet of both Chinese and Indian Buddhist masters and the resulting encounter and confrontation between their doctrines"; internal linguistic evidence of the first two grammatical treatises also bears testimony to the same variety of Tibetan-Chinese contact that otherwise resulted in the "Great Debate of Bsam yas", the famous encounter towards the end of the 8th century that brought together Chinese, Indian, and Tibetan advocates of different approaches to far-reaching questions of Mahāyāna doctrine and practice (Ruegg 1992).

The received text of the *SCP* incorporates three major textual strata or segments, each marked by overt internal syntactic indicators (Miller 1993: § 2,3). The first is a fairly simple phonological component; the second (which accounts for the bulk of the treatise) describes the morphophonemics of the principal enclitics including the case-suffixes; the third discusses the nature of the relationship between the phonological configuration of a morpheme and its semantic component. Most important for dating the earlier materials now incorporated into the received text of the *SCP* are its morphophonemic prescriptions for the case-suffixes. Confrontation of the statements in the text with manuscripts and other documentary evidence now available from Central Asian finds makes it clear that these statements were originally written to describe not the Classical Tibetan of the Buddhist canonical translations but rather the Old Tibetan of the Yar-luṅ dynasty

> "from the seventh to the ninth centuries – the era of Tibet's greatest military expansion and the time when the foundations of Tibetan culture were laid [...] the time when terrifying Tibetan hordes, with their faces painted red, conquered and occupied the strategic oases of Central Asia" (Beyer 1992: 29).

In this limited sense only, then, do certain portions of the *SCP* actually bear witness to very early stages in the history of written Tibetan, but emphatically not in the full sense of the later Thon-mi Sam-bhoṭa myth. In preparing the received text of the *SCP* a not completely succesful attempt had to be made to rework these Old Tibetan morphophonemic statements in order to make them conform to the somewhat different case-suffix morphophonemics of the language of the later authorized-version canonical Buddhist translations ('Classical Tibetan'). The task of this editorial reworking was moreover rendered even more difficult by considerations of rule-ordering and descriptive economy, the effects of which may today be traced in the received text, where at the same time they preserve important evidence for the multifarious origins of the text as we now have it.

The received text of the *TKJ* is concerned with inventories of a number of the different sets into which it is possible to arrange the consonants of the later Classical Tibetan of the canonical Buddhist translations on the basis of their mutual co-occurrence and simultaneous phonological restrictions to specific positions within the morpheme. Each of these sets, whose phonemic inventory is non-exclusive and frequently shifting according to its rule-ordered location within the description, is labelled with a metalinguistic designation (Tib. *rtags*, Skt. *liṅga*) drawn from a tantristic vocabulary ("male", "female", "neuter", "very female", etc.) that displays obvious connections with the sexual metaphors of the Vajra-yāna schools; the text also attempts certain rudimentary phonetic, i. e. non-morphophonemic description.

The present received text of the *TKJ* shows traces of editorial harmonization carried out upon three earlier now-lost sources. These are $Q_1$, a relatively short and concise spelling-book or orthographic manual that epitomized the essential conventions necessary to observe in order to write texts in conformity with the then-new canonical norms of the authorized Buddhist translations; $Q_2$, a pronunciation manual for the same written language that was the concern of $Q_1$; and $Q_3$, an early linguistic-speculative treatise dealing with Buddhist theories of language and grammar that was originally composed in some language other than Tibetan, and that also originally had immediate reference not to Tibetan but instead to some variety of Indic employed in the Buddhist schools of Central Asia (Miller 1993: § 4).

## 3. The contents of the treatises

Despite obvious differences in the textual genesis and subject-matter of the *SCP* on the one hand and the *TKJ* on the other, and also despite the striking absence of genuinely old linguistic materials in the *TKJ* in contrast to the clearly surviving traces of Old Tibetan in the *SCP*, both texts show a significant inventory of common features and treatments. Both devote considerable space to negative prescriptive statements, a somewhat redundant descriptive technique that makes sense only in terms of the well-known predilection of the Buddhist logicians for distinguishing different varieties of negation. Neither text identifies or assigns overt semantic values to specific Tibetan morphemes. This is especially striking in the case of the frequently shifting metalinguistic terminology of the *TKJ*; these are exhaustively listed and inventoried, and their occurrence-patterns stipulated in both positive and negative prescriptive statements, but they are never 'explained' semantically or specifically illustrated with lexical examples. Misunderstanding of this peculiarity of the *TKJ* has led to elaborate but mostly unrewarding attempts to 'solve' the semantic components of the morphophonemic statements of the *TKJ* both in traditional Tibet and now also in the West (e. g. Tillemans & Herforth 1989, cf. Miller 1992), and in the process to establish 'what was in the mind of Thon-mi Sambhoṭa when he wrote the text'.

Most significant of the elements common to both texts is their frequent evocation of fairly recondite tantristic, respectively Vajrayāna concepts; these include the *āli* "vowel" and *kāli* "consonant" terminology, and especially the strikingly tantristic structural penchant for arranging linguistic data and its related descriptive statements into symmetrical sets of fours, conforming to the Vajrayāna postulate *evaṃ sarve catvāraḥ* "everything goes by fours" (Miller 1994). This last feature incidentally offers another valuable criterion for the late dating of both treatises, but especially of the *TKJ*, since the comparatively late tantristic postulate implicit in this structural device can scarcely revert to the earliest stages either of Tibetan literary culture or of Tibetan Buddhism.

Neither the *SCP* nor the *TKJ* cites illustrative examples in support of its statements, whether descriptive or prescriptive. This technique has left open the door for the exercise of virtually unbridled imagination on the part of later commentators, both Tibetan and foreign. Particularly instructive examples of this problem are to be observed in the secondary literature that has grown up on the slender foundation of *SCP* 8.9–10, where the absence of specific illustrative examples in the text itself has led to an enormous but in the main self-contradictory literature of sheer speculation (e. g. Yamaguchi 1985). Similarly *TKJ* 11–15, where generations of Tibetan scholastics and now Western students of Tibetan as well have engaged in similarly baseless speculation about what 'Thon-mi-Sambhoṭa meant', all to little or no avail (Miller 1992).

## 4. Conclusion

In the future study of these and many other mostly moot passages in the first two treatises, the task remains of first reading the texts as we have them, and only then turning to the speculations of the later grammarians. The essential monolithic unity of the Tibetan grammatical tradition superficially appears to be broken by the wide divergence of these later speculations, but that diversity is only apparent, not real; in fact, it too derives only from the absence of illustrative examples in the texts themselves. This in turn means that we actually have to reckon with only a single Tibetan grammatical tradition, the essential unity of which becomes easier to recognize once we understand the nature of the two early treatises out of which it grew.

From their inception (Laufer 1898), Western studies of the *SCP* and *TKJ* have had a disappointing and mostly unproductive history (Miller 1993: § 1). The pioneering translation and study of Bacot (1928) deserve great credit; but they also obscured the descriptive statements and techniques of the texts by attempting to read them in terms of irrelevant preconceptions of Latinate grammar, and also virtually without reference to their proximate Indic models.

The earlier European studies also led to false expectations, especially because they mostly perpetuated (and still perpetuate) the myth of the authorship of Thon-mi Sambhoṭa, and promised unwarrantedly that the study of the *SCP* and *TKJ* would somehow unlock the morphological and semantic 'secrets' of the Tibetan language. Since it almost immediately became apparent that this was not true, the consequent disillusionment (e. g. Wolfenden 1929: 23–24 and passim.) have tended to discourage further serious attempts to utilize the *SCP* and *TKJ* for scientific-linguistic ends.

## 5. Bibliography

Bacot, Jacques. 1928. *Une grammaire tibétaine classique, Les ślokas grammaticaux de Thonmi Sambhoṭa avec leurs commentaires, traduits du tibétain et annotés.* (= *Annales du Musée Guimet, Bibliothèque d'études*, 37.) Paris: Musée Guimet.

Beyer, Stephen V. 1992. *The Classical Tibetan Language.* Albany: State Univ. of New York Press.

Karlgren, Bernhard. 1940. *Grammata Serica: Script and phonetics in Chinese and Sino-Japanese.* Stockholm: Museum of Far Eastern Antiquities.

Laufer, Bertold. 1898. "Studien zur Sprachwissenschaft der Tibeter: Zamatog". *Sitzungsberichte der philos.-philolog. u. histor. Classe der kgl. bayer. Akademie der Wissenschaften zu München*, Heft III, 519–594.

Mimaki, Katsumi. 1992. "Two Minor Works Ascribed to dBus pa blo gsal". *Tibetan Studies, Proceedings of the 5th Seminar of the IATS*, vol. II: *Language, History and Culture* ed. by Ihara Shōren & Yamaguchi Zuihō, 591–598. Narita: Naritasan Shinshoji.

Miller, Roy Andrew. 1976. *Studies in the Grammatical Tradition in Tibet.* (= *Amsterdam Studies in the Theory and History of Linguistic Science*, III: *Studies in the History of Linguistics*, 6.) Amsterdam: Benjamins.

—. 1992. "Indic Models in Tibetan Grammars". *Journal of the American Oriental Society* 112: 1.103–109.

—. 1993. *Prolegomena to the First Two Tibetan Grammatical Treatises.* (= *Wiener Studien zur Tibetologie und Buddhismuskunde*, 30.) Wien: Arbeitskreis für Tibetische und Buddhistische Studien.

—. 1994. "Evam sarve catvāraḥ". *Proceedings of the 6th Seminar of the IATS*, vol. II ed. by Per Kvaerne, 558–569. Oslo: Instituttet for Sammenlignende Kulturforskning.

Ruegg, D. Seyfort. 1992. "On the Tibetan Historiography and Doxography of the 'Great Debate of bSam yas". *Tibetan Studies, Proceedings of the 5th Seminar of the IATS*, vol. I: *Buddhist Philosophy and Literature* ed. by Ihara Shōren & Yamaguchi Zuihō, 237–244. Narita: Naritasan Shinshoji.

Simon, Walter. 1930. *Tibetisch-Chinesische Wortgleichungen: Ein Versuch.* Berlin: de Gruyter.

Tillemans, Tom J. F. & Derek D. Herforth. 1989. *Agents and Actions in Classical Tibetan: The indigenous grammarians on* bdag *and* gźan *and* bya byed las gsum. (= *Wiener Studien zur Tibetologie und Buddhismuskunde*, 21.) Wien: Arbeitskreis für Tibetische und Buddhistische Studien.

Verhagen, Pieter Cornelis. 1992. "A Ninth-Century Tibetan Summary of the Indo-Tibetan Model of Case Semantics". *Tibetan Studies, Proceedings of the 5th Seminar of the IATS*, vol. II: *Language, History and Culture* ed. by Ihara Shōren & Yamaguchi Zuihō, 833–844. Narita: Naritasan Shinshoji.

Wolfenden, St. N. 1929. *Outlines of Tibeto-Burman Linguistic Morphology.* London: Royal Asiatic Society.

Yamaguchi Zuihō. 1985. "'*La*-gi shichiji' no yōhō bunrui to *de nyid* no kaishaku – Chibettogo bunten no fubi, II". *Tōkyō daigaku bungakubu, Bunka kōryū shisetsu kenkyū kiŷo* 7.1–29.

*Roy Andrew Miller, Honolulu (USA)*

# 31. The classical Tibetan grammarians

1. Historical introduction
2. Smṛtijñānakīrti and Roṅ-zom Chos-kyi-bzaṅ-po
3. Bsod-nams-rtse-mo
4. Sa-skya Paṇḍita Kun-dga'-rgyal-mtshan
5. Źa-lu-lo-tsā-ba Chos-skyoṅ-bzaṅ-po
6. Si-tu Paṇ-chen Chos-kyi-'byuṅ-gnas
7. Dṅul-chu Dharmabhadra and Dṅul-chu Dbyaṅs-can-grub-pa'i-rdo-rje
8. Minor authors
9. Bibliography

## 1. Historical introduction

For the moment setting aside the two seminal treatises *Sum-cu-pa* (*SCP*) and *Rtags-kyi-'jug-pa* (*TKJ*) (→ Art. 30), the dating and authorship of which are problematic, the earliest period in the history of indigenous Tibetan grammar (11th–13th centuries) has seen the production of creative, original works, such as *Smra-sgo* (second section), *Byis-'jug* and *Yi-ge'i-sbyor-ba*, to be discussed infra. Particularly the first two are independent works dealing (partly) with subject matter treated, often in different terms, in *SCP* or *TKJ*, but containing no evidence of an intertextual relationship with either. In later periods, roughly from the 14th century onwards, Tibetan grammatical literature tends to consist almost exclusively of commentaries on *SCP* and/or *TKJ*. The traditional grammatical commentary centers around the paraphrase of the rule, adding the elements which are left implicit in the basic text, and examples of the application of the rule. The more elaborate commentaries can contain a further discussion of the rule and its applications, commonly in the traditional Indic commentary format of an exchange where questions and objections are raised and sub-sequently answered, often introducing counter-examples. The main grammatical topics discussed in the commentatorial literature are naturally the same as those in the basic texts: phonology, morphology pertaining to syllable-structure, morphophonemics and semantics of the enclitic particles (part of which is the case-grammar), verbal morphology and the verb-centered syntactic model of *bdag/gźan* (→ Art. 30 and 32).

It is patently incorrect to speak of <u>the</u> Tibetan indigenous grammatical tradition. It is no uniform, homogeneous tradition; we find that grammarians have expressed divergent views on many issues, some of minor relevance, others however lying at the very core of their interpretation and their scholastic agenda (e. g. Tillemans & Herforth 1989: 8ff.). This diversity of interpretations, even at crucial points, has been taken as evidence for an interruption in the transmission of the grammatical lore between the composition, c. q. final redaction of *SCP* and *TKJ* and the inception of the commentarial traditions that have come down to us (Miller 1993: 34–35). Many of the early texts have been lost, but evidence of some of these early grammarians' views can be gleaned from quotations in later literature. In the 18th century Si-tu's commentary constitutes an attempt at unifying and standardizing the tradition. In his extensive commentary he refutes many conflicting views and interpretations, in most cases setting forth one authoritative reading of the rule. Although Si-tu's work was of major importance, and of unprecedented authority, even after him we find no universal consensus on the interpretation of *SCP* and *TKJ* in all details.

## 2. Smṛtijñānakīrti and Roṅ-zom Chos-kyi-bzaṅ-po

The *Smra-sgo* (*-mtshon-cha*) "Introduction to Speech, which is like a Weapon" is in fact the earliest reliably datable treatise devoted (for an important part) to Tibetan grammar, which is available to us now. This particular text, together with a commentary, was incorporated into the Tibetan Buddhist canon. Most probably the basic text was written by the Indian Buddhist scholar Smṛti(jñānakīrti), who was active in the transmission of mystical traditions as well as the schools of theoretical speculation on metaphysics, Abhidharma, in Tibet in the 11th century. The commentary may be the work of Smṛti himself, or of the Tibetan Roṅ-zom Chos-kyi-bzaṅ-po, a personal disciple of Smṛti, and a well-known scholar in the Rñiṅ-ma-pa tradition in his own right. The text (total of 495 verse-lines) consists of two major segments: the first a theoretical exposé on the three linguistic *kāyas* (l. 1–319; → Art. 32) and the second a description of a number of Tibetan enclitic particles (l. 320–464). The first segment is clearly based on Indic models, the tripartite system stemming from the tradition of Abhidharma, and when an identification is possible, the object-language is Sanskrit. The second segment is dealing specifically, and in a far more practical, descriptive style, with Tibetan grammar. The first segment appears to be a translation from a Sanskrit original, while the second is an original composition in Tibetan. The segment on the Tibetan enclitics describes some thirty grammatical elements, mostly particles, but also some pronouns and adverbial groups; in addition some aspects of the formation of composite particles are discussed. Seventeen of the thirty items described here are also dealt with in *SCP*, in a different order, and, more importantly, frequently in different semantic terms.

## 3. Bsod-nams-rtse-mo

In Tibet we find a genre of scholastic texts, known as *klog-thabs* "pronunciation-manual", instruction manuals for the recitation of the Sanskrit esoteric formulas (*mantras*) that play a central role in many branches of Tibetan Buddhism, particularly in the mystical traditions of Tantrism. Usually these texts focus on the pronunciation of Sanskrit. The earliest example that has come down to us is *Byis-'jug* (*Byis-pa-bde-blag-tu-'jug-pa* "Easy Access for the Beginners") by the famous scholar and hierarch of the Sa-skya-pa sect, Bsod-nams-rtse-mo (1142–1182). This particular work is extremely important, not only on account of its attestable early date, but also in that it describes the phonology of both Sanskrit and Tibetan. *Byis-'jug* occasionally touches on articulatory phonetics, e. g. when describing dialectal variations in pronunciation for the Central Tibetan provinces of Dbus and Gtsaṅ (Verhagen 1995: 963–965). Both this text and Smṛti's *Smra-sgo* have remained extremely influential throughout the history of Tibetan linguistics, being cited and referred to by authors in this field in all periods.

## 4. Sa-skya Paṇḍita Kun-dga'-rgyal-mtshan

Indubitably one of the pre-eminent Tibetan scholars of his day, considered by many as one of the true founders of Tibetan scholastics, Sa-skya Paṇḍita (1182–1251) wrote extensively on linguistics. His major works in this field are *Yi-ge'i-sbyor-ba* "Application of the Phonemes" (3 fol.), which is a synthetic compilation of materials now contained in *SCP* and *TKJ* (Miller 1993: 130–153), a commentary on *Byis-'jug* (13 fol.), a topical outline of Smṛti's *Smra-sgo* (2 fol.), and a youth-work entitled *Sgra-la-'jug-pa* "Access to Language" (10 fol.), attempting a synthesis of Sanskrit and Tibetan grammar. Moreover we have a grammatical treatise *Mkhas-pa'i-kha-rgyan* "Head-ornament of the Wise" (4 fol.) which is traditionally attributed to him, the authorship of which is uncertain however (→ Art. 32.3.). One of his major general scholastic works, *Mkhas-pa-'jug-pa'i-sgo* "Entrance Gate for the Wise", a manual on exegetical and expositional techniques for the Buddhist scholar, moreover, contains so many elements of a linguistical nature that it is traditionally classified as a work on linguistics. In his works he does not mention *SCP* or *TKJ* by name, although he did know most of the materials now constituting the received versions of *SCP* and *TKJ*, as he integrated these materials into his *Yi-ge'i-sbyor-ba*. A feature particularly prominent in Sa-skya Paṇḍita's language-oriented work, yet to some extent evident in all Tibetan scholastics, is the tendency to consider the linguistic and grammatical analysis that the Tibetans encountered in the Sanskrit traditions to be valid as universals, and therefore to attempt to describe the Tibetan language and discourse conventions as much as possible in the terms and schemata handed down to them from the extraordinarily rich background of Sanskrit linguistics.

## 5. Źa-lu-lo-tsā-ba Chos-skyoṅ-bzaṅ-po

This scholar (1441–1528), who played a central role in the transmission of grammatical traditions, both Sanskrit and Tibetan, in his time, wrote commentaries on *SCP* (14 fol.) and *TKJ* (18 fol.), but arguably his most important work is *Za-ma-tog-bkod-pa* "Array of Baskets" (first made accessible to the Western world by Laufer 1898). This particular text, written in the standard Tibetan scholastic verse form, is primarily devoted to orthography and lexicography, listing frequent Tibetan lexemes systematically arranged according to initial consonant cluster, with semantic glosses to some entries, and adding Sanskrit equivalents to many entries in infralinear notes. Purely grammatical description is also found, in sections on the phonological categories, both in *SCP* and *TKJ* (gender) terms, and a section on the morphophonemics of eleven enclitic particles. At the very end of the text a most interesting brief sketch of the history of grammatical studies in Tibet is included.

## 6. Si-tu Paṇ-chen Chos-kyi-'byuṅ-gnas

By far the most significant and pivotal work in this literature is the extensive commentary by the "great scholar" (*paṇ-chen*) Si-tu (1699?–1774), one of the major intellectual figures of his time, entitled *Mkhas-pa'i-mgul-rgyan Mu-tig-phreṅ-mdzes* "Necklace of the Wise, Beautiful String of Pearls" (86 fol.). This commentary, one of the most voluminous and certainly the most authoritative in this literature, sets out to formulate definitive interpretations of the rule systems of *SCP* and *TKJ*. Fequently Si-tu cites views of earlier and contemporaneous grammarians on specific topics, without however, stating their names. A later sub-commentary on Si-tu identifies at least seven scholars whose opinions are cited, yet often refuted, in Si-tu, among whom we find Dbus-pa Blo-gsal and Źa-lu (Tillemans & Herforth 1989: 9). The crucial position of Si-tu justifies a division of Tibetan grammatical literature into a pre-Si-tu period, of a more tentative, formative nature, and a post-Si-tu literature, generally characterized by a more rigid scholastic attitude, and dominated by the views of Si-tu, which, if not followed literally, in any case could not be disregarded by any subsequent grammarian (Tillemans & Herforth 1989: 2ff.). The style and language of the work is often abstruse, strewn with numerous longwinding excursus, making it very hard reading by any standard, which is no doubt the main reason why, despite its tremendous importance, it still awaits an exhaustive investigation in Tibetology (partial studies: Durr 1950: 51–95; Miller 1976: 19–31; Tillemans & Herforth 1989: 2–8, 19–23, 62–73).

## 7. Dṅul-chu Dharmabhadra and Dṅul-chu Dbyaṅs-can-grub-pa'i-rdo-rje

Two influential grammarians in the most recent history of classical Tibetan culture are the two scholars from Dṅul-chu in western Gtsaṅ province, Dharmabhadra (1722–1851) and his nephew and intellectual heir Dbyaṅs-can-grub-pa'i-rdo-rje (1809–1887). The elder's major work on grammar is his epitome of Si-tu's commentary entitled *Si-tu'i-żal-luṅ* "Oral instruction on Si-tu['s commentary]" (26 fol., edited by Inaba 1986: 392–461), one of the most popular accesses to the often abstruse and prolix comments by Si-tu. He also authored another work on *SCP* and *TKJ*, of less importance, in the format of replies to objections regarding specific points, under the title *Nor-bu-ke-ta-ka'i-do-śal* "Shoulder Pendant of Ketaka Jewels" (8 fol.), as well as two *klog-thabs* treatises. The major of his nephew's works in the field of grammar are *Legs-bśad-ljon-dbaṅ* "Miraculous Tree of Aphorisms" on *SCP*, consisting of a verse synopsis (1 fol.) and commentary (10 fol.), and *Dka'-gnad-gsal-ba'i-me-loṅ* "Lamp Clarifying Difficult Crucial Points" (5 fol.), elucidating the more problematic sections in *TKJ*.

## 8. Minor authors

Dbus-pa Blo-gsal (Byaṅ-chub-ye-śes) (first half 14th century): The two commentaries that this author, one of the compilers of the first redaction of the Tibetan Buddhist canon, wrote on *SCP* and *TKJ* respectively, are among the earliest that have been preserved, i. c. in manuscript form. They are at the same time the earliest grammatical texts that mention the titles of the two seminal treatises. The latter commentary, the only one made partly accessible thus far, contains variant readings that are most important for establishing the text of *TKJ* (Mimaki 1992: 595ff.).

– Go-bo rab-'byams-pa Bsod-nams-seṅ-ge (1429–1489): His commentary on *TKJ* is a work which represents some remarkable views on the *bdag/gżan* schema, involving what appears to be a curious lack of distinction between, or rather confusion of, linguistical primes such as a simple noun and a verb-expressed action (Tillemans & Herforth 1989: 11, 30).
– Skyogs-ston Ṅag-dbaṅ Rin-chen-bkra-śis (ca. 1495–after 1577), one of the chief disciples of Źa-lu-lo-tsā-ba, was active in several linguistic disciplines, notably Sanskrit and Tibetan grammar and lexicography.
– Lcaṅ-skya Rol-pa'i-rdo-rje (1717–1786) was a prominent scholar and religious master at the court of the Chinese emperor Qianlong (1736–1795), spiritual preceptor to the em-

peror, whose many activities at the court included teaching Sanskrit and Tibetan to the emperor's fourth son, Hongli. His commentary claims to set forth the interpretation of *SCP* and *TKJ* of Ża-lu-lo-tsā-ba in synoptic form (edited and translated by Schubert 1937).

– Gser-tog Blo-bzaṅ-tshul-khrims-rgya-mtsho (1845–1915) was an ecclesiastic hierarch from A-mdo, eastern Tibet, whose voluminous commentary incorporates the views of the two Dṅul-chu grammarians and several other writers. (Miller 1976: 71–84; Tillemans & Herforth 1989: 16; Tillemans 1991: 488–496).

## 9. Bibliography


Durr, Jacques A. 1950. *Deux Traités Grammaticaux Tibétains. Commentaire dévollopé des çlokas du Sum rTags admirable collier de perles des Savants par SITU (çlokas 12, 13, 14, 15 et 25 du rTags 'ajug) et Examen définitif ou Commentaire élucidant les notions difficiles du rTags 'ajug appelé Miroir de Pur Cristal (Dvangs Shel Me Long) par Don 'agrub.* (= *Bibliothek der Allgemeinen Sprachwissenschaft*, 3. Reihe: *Darstellungen und Untersuchungen aus einzelnen Sprachen.*) Heidelberg: Winter.

Inaba, Shōju. 1986 [1954]. *Chibettogo Koten Bunpōgaku. Zōhohan.* Kyōto: Hōzōkan.

Laufer, Berthold. 1898. "Studien zur Sprachwissenschaft der Tibeter, Zamatog". *Sitzungsberichte der philosophisch-philologischen und der historischen Klasse der k. b. Akademie der Wissenschaften zu München* 1.519–594.

Miller, Roy Andrew. 1976. *Studies in the Grammatical Tradition in Tibet.* (= *Amsterdam Studies in the Theory and History of Linguistic Science*, Series III: *Studies in the History of Linguistics*, 6.) Amsterdam: Benjamins.

–. 1993. *Prolegomena to the First Two Tibetan Grammatical Treatises.* (= *Wiener Studien zur Tibetologie und Buddhismuskunde*, 30.) Wien: Arbeitskreis für Tibetische und Buddhistische Studien.

Mimaki, Katsumi. 1992. "Two Minor Works Ascribed to dBus pa blo gsal". *Tibetan Studies, Proceedings of the 5th Seminar of the International Association of Tibetan Studies, Narita 1989*, vol. 2, 591–598. Narita: Naritasan Shinshoji.

Schubert, Johannes. 1937. *Tibetische Nationalgrammatik: Das Sum.cu.pa und Rtags.kyi.'ajug.pa des Grosslamas von Peking Rol.pai.rdo.rje, ein Kommentar zu den gleichnamigen Schriften Thon.mi Sambhoṭa's auf Grund der Erklärung des Lamas Chos.skyoṅ.bzaṅ.po, Lo.tsa.ba von Zha.lu.* Leipzig: Verlag der Offizin Richard Hadl.

Tillemans, Tom J. F. 1991. "gSer tog Blo bzaṅ tshul khrims rgya mtsho on Tibetan Verb Tenses". *Tibetan History and Language. Studies dedicated to Uray Géza on his seventieth birthday*, 487–496. (= *Wiener Studien zur Tibetologie und Buddhismuskunde*, 26.) Wien: Arbeitskreis für Tibetische und Buddhistische Studien.

– & Derek D. Herforth. 1989. *Agents and Actions in Classical Tibetan. The indigenous grammarians on Bdag and Gźan and Bya byed las gsum.* (= *Wiener Studien zur Tibetologie und Buddhismuskunde*, 21.) Wien: Arbeitskreis für Tibetische und Buddhistische Studien.

Verhagen, Pieter Cornelis. 1995. "Studies in Tibetan Indigenous Grammar. 2. Tibetan phonology and phonetics in the *Byis-pa-bde-blag-tu-'jug-pa* by Bsod-nams-rtse-mo (1142–1182)". *Études Asiatiques/Asiatische Studien* 49.943–968.


*Peter Verhagen, Leiden (The Netherlands)*

# 32. The influence of the Sanskrit tradition on Tibetan indigenous grammar


1. Historical introduction
2. The basic treatises
3. Subsidiary literature
4. Conclusions
5. Bibliography


## 1. Historical introduction

The adoption of Buddhism in Tibet (first dissemination mid 7th to mid 9th century CE, the second starting from the 11th century) entailed the production of an extraordinary quantity of usually sound, reliable Tibetan translations of Indic, predominantly Sanskrit, texts in the period between roughly the 7th and the 15th centuries CE. Naturally, for the craft of the translator, so brilliantly developed in the Tibetan traditions, it was essential to be well versed in Sanskrit grammar. The natural access to this discipline for the Tibetans of course lay in the Indic indigenous schools of grammar, in particular the *Cāndra* and *Kātantra* grammars that were the most popular in the Buddhist circles in Northern

India, and translations of the major texts of which were incorporated into the Tibetan Buddhist canon (Verhagen 1994: 50ff.).

Tibetan Buddhist literature in general is characterized by extensive adoption and emulation of models from the enormous Indic Buddhist literature. Particularly the immensely rich exegetical and scholastic literature produced by Tibetan authors throughout the centuries is truly permeated by Indic conventions and features. Not surprisingly, therefore, Tibetan indigenous grammar shows evidence of considerable influence from the Sanskrit indigenous grammar, indubitably one of the most sophisticated and highly developed sciences in the Indic culture. Two basic questions will be discussed here: (a) Which elements in Tibetan indigenous grammar are of Indic origin? and (b) From what Indic source do these elements stem?

The earliest grammarians in Tibet for whom historical sources provide solid evidence were generally active in the fields of Sanskrit and Tibetan grammar, and many of the early grammatical writings in Tibet in some way deal with grammatical issues pertaining to both languages (→ Art. 31. 2.−4.). The oldest datable Tibetan documents (8th−9th century) found in Dunhuang, containing some form of grammatical description either deal with Sanskrit, as part of the translation effort, or they do not explicate the object-language, e. g. the summary of the cases (presumably) by the Tibeto-Chinese bilingual scholar Chos-grub (9th century), which could apply to Sanskrit and Tibetan (Verhagen 1992: 833ff.). The interaction between the disciplines of Sanskrit indigenous grammar, with an ancient tradition centered around Pāṇini (5th century BC) and Tibetan indigenous grammar, then a budding discipline, may have been the most intensive in the period of the second dissemination of Buddhism culminating in the establishment of the two Tibetan Buddhist canons (mid 14th century), but the interest in Sanskrit studies remained alive in the Tibetan scholarly world also in the following centuries. This is highlighted by the production of the first Tibetan translation of the basic text of Pāṇini's grammar and the *Prakriyā-kaumudī* commentary, as late as the 17th century CE, under the auspices of the fifth Dalai Lama (Verhagen 1994: 154ff.).

## 2. The basic treatises

Let us now consider the extent of the Indic influences evident in the seminal treatises *Sum-cu-pa* (*SCP*) and *Rtags-kyi-'jug-pa* (*TKJ*). First and foremost characteristic of the *sūtra*-style of the Sanskrit grammarians is brevity. The individual rules (Skt. *sūtra*) usually consist of nominal phrases formulated with the utmost economy of words. This economy is achieved by a number of techniques and conventions, such as ellipsis, the use of technical terms and markers, the specific technical use of certain cases, etc. Some of these techniques are found in *SCP* and *TKJ* as well, but not all, and when they are applied they are not stretched to the limits of their possible applicability as one tends to see in Pāṇini. In general one should not expect to find in Tibetan grammar the degree of sophistication and elegance of description that Pāṇini and his tradition offer.

Two techniques characteristic for the *sūtra*-style are the grouping and ordering of rules describing similar elements or grammatical operations applying under similar conditions, and the use of *anuvṛtti*, i. e. ellipsis of recurring phrases and terms. The grouping principle is exemplified by the interpolation of *SCP* 12, describing the concessive particle *-kyaṅ* and its alternants, in the section on the case-particles (*SCP* 8−11 and 15−17), thus avoiding the repetition of the initial morphophonemics that *-kyaṅ* has in common with genitive and instrumental particles (*SCP* 9−11) (Miller 1993: 87). An example of *anuvṛtti* is the zero-form in *SCP* 11−14, ellipsis of *sa* (*SCP* 10) or *sgra* (*SCP* 8) (Miller 1993: 85−86).

Moreover, evidently of Indic origin are the linguistical primes "phoneme" (Skt. *varṇa*, Tib. *yi-ge*), distinguishing between vowels and consonants, "free, lexical word form" (Skt. *prātipadika* or *nāman*, Tib. *miṅ*) and "bound syntactic word form" (Skt. *pada*, Tib. *tshig*), and grammatical concepts such as the phonological classes (Skt. *varga*, Tib. *sde*) or the group of case functions (to a large extent corresponding to the Sanskrit syntacto-semantic functions termed *kāraka*). Both *SCP* and *TKJ* commence with a presentation of the phoneme inventory and functional subsets within these phonemes, which has an evident parallel to the phonological statements at the beginning of the basic texts of Sanskrit grammar, in particular the form of presentation in *SCP* being similar to that in *Kātantra*. A further instance of the close correspondence between Tibetan grammar and *Kātantra* is their common predilection for a proximate of the item-and-arrangement descriptive model, while the other schools of Sanskrit grammar generally favour item-and-process types of description. The source of the descriptive techniques and terminology discussed thus far clearly lies in the indigenous Sanskrit grammatical traditions (Verhagen 1995: 423–427).

However, we also find the admixture of elements stemming from the broader context of Buddhist literature. *TKJ* 32, for instance, formulates a derivational model 'phoneme' > 'free lexical word form' > 'bound syntactical word form', which clearly echoes an ontological schema of language in the Buddhist Abhidharma tradition of metaphysical speculation, consisting of the triad 'corpus of phonemes' (or 'syllables'), 'of words' and 'of phrases' (Skt. *vyañjana-*, *nāma-* and *pada-kāya*, Simonsson 1982: 537ff.), the Abhidharma schema itself of course ultimately based on the analysis by the Sanskrit grammarians. The phonological description in the two basic treatises displays striking correspondences with, and would therefore seem to be structurally related to, the descriptive conventions in the exegesis of *mantras* in the esoteric Tantric forms of Buddhism, in particular as laid down in the *klog-thabs* "manuals of pronunciation". The phonological terms *āli*, the '*a*-series', and *kāli*, the '*k*-series', for vowels and consonants respectively (*SCP*, Miller 1976: 33–55), and the reference to specific sets of phonemes by means of covert labels in casu gender terms ('masculine' for consonants, 'feminine' for vowels, and other more complex subdivisions involving 'neuter', 'very feminine' and 'barren feminine' categories, specific for *TKJ*, Verhagen 1993: 332ff.) have their origin in this Tantric phonology. Parenthetically, one should mention comparable covert terminology in morphophonemic description in the *klog-thabs* literature, occasionally recurring in later subsidiary grammatical texts also. There, in the description of the syllable structure, the terms "father" and "mother" designate the consonants and the vowels, respectively (with the term "son" for the resulting syllable), in their turn related to the 'body' graphs of the consonants, in particular the initial consonant (cluster), and the 'limb' graphs of the vowels. The former terminology can conceptually be related to the gender terms mentioned above, the latter is primarily based on the visual aspect of Tibetan orthography, where the vowel graphs are indeed appended as 'limbs' above or below the 'body' of the consonant graphs. Note that most of the phonology in *SCP*, in terms of the 'classes' based on the analysis of points and process of articulation, and the method of reference to phonemes by place-number within the classes as reflected in the traditional alphabet arrangement, seems to be based on Indic grammatical models, although these do occur in the Tantric context as well. Another instance where two possible sources of derivation present themselves could be seen in the set of syntactic arguments 'subject', 'direct object', 'instrument' and (verb-expressed) 'action', that of course ultimately stem from Sanskrit grammar, but could also have reached Tibetan scholastics via the Buddhist philosophical traditions that frequently employ these same categories.

The limited repertoire of Tibetan verbal morphology contrasts sharply with the proliferation of morphological and semantic variation in the Sanskrit verbal system. Therefore, very few terms on verb grammar are derived from the Sanskrit traditions: this appears to be restricted to the termini for the four tense c. q. modal forms, scil. present, perfect, future and imperative. Significantly, the concept of the "verbal root" (Sanskrit *dhātu*), the isolation of which is arguably one of the major achievements of Sanskrit grammar, and the derivation of nominal lexemes from these roots through a complex system of affixation, have not found their way into the Tibetan description.

What, then, can be deemed original in Tibetan indigenous grammar? Which elements cannot be traced to an Indic antecedent? As main items one should mention the concepts and the relevant terminology for the enclitic particle, and the consonantal constituents in the syllable-structure: radical, pre-, super-, sub-radical, and final consonants. An example of the maximal expansion of a Tibetan syllable in which all positions in the syllable structure are occupied is the form *bsgrubs* "established". A Tibetan innovation in descriptive technique is the morphological derivation of one particle from another unrelated particle (as in the case particle *-su* > semifinal particle *-ste*, *SCP* 13). A special case is formed by the *bdag/gźan* dichotomy. In syntactic analysis of transitive phrases the label *bdag* "self" is applied to the present tense verb form and the nominal syntactic arguments 'agent' and 'instrument', while *gźan* "other" applies to the future tense verb form and 'direct object' (Tillemans & Herforth 1989; Tillemans 1988). The categories as such and the terms chosen for them appear to be original. The notion, set forth in some secondary literature, that these could be equalled to the *parasmaipada* "active mood" and *ātmanepada* "medium mood" of the Sanskrit verb is untenable, considering the fundamental differences between the two pairs. In one salient respect the *bdag/gźan* system does have a parallel in Indic grammar (and it could conceivably be inspired on this aspect of the model), viz. the application of identical labels to verbal and nominal syntactic arguments, which we also find in the Indic *kāraka* analysis (Verhagen 1995: 427–431).

## 3. Subsidiary literature

As mentioned above (→ Art. 31.1.), one of the tasks of the commentary consists in supplying in its paraphrase of the rule the elements left implicit in the basic text. As a result the commentaries at times use terms that are not found in the root-text, not only in the passus they are commenting on, but in the text as a whole as well. For example, the phonological terms for the points of articulation (usually: throat, palate, tongue, nose, top of the palate, teeth and lips) are not explicitly mentioned in *SCP* or *TKJ*, but we do find them supplied in most commentaries on the phonological sections. This whole analysis in terms of "point" (Skt. *sthāna*, Tib. *'byuṅ-gnas*) and "process" (Skt. *prayatna*, Tib. *rtsol-ba*) of articulation is modelled on Indic grammar, of course with additions and adaptations specific for Tibetan (Miller 1976: 19–31).

Some works in this literature could not properly be called commentaries, but they do constitute treatises supplementary to the seminal texts. The *Za-ma-tog-bkod-pa* (→ Art. 31.5.) and *Mkhas-pa'i-kha-rgyan* (→ Art. 31.4.) could be reckoned among these. The latter is particularly interesting in the present context as it emulates the Indic *sūtra* style to a higher degree than *SCP* or *TKJ* proper: the metrical form of the Tibetan scholastic stanza is abandoned, and techniques such as ellipsis of recurring phrases, and specific technical functions of cases, are used more abundantly. Dealing with much of the subject-matter covered in *SCP* (morphophonemic constituents of the syllable, and the grammar of the enclitic particles) and some from *TKJ* (notably the verb-centered syntactic schemata of *bdag/gźan* and agent, direct object and action), it appears to be a reworking of these materials in a much more strictly Indic format.

## 4. Conclusions

The primary models that the Tibetan grammarians have followed in the description of their own language, were the Buddhist traditions of Sanskrit grammar of *Cāndra* and *Kātantra*, both more or less distant derivatives of Pāṇini's grammar. In addition, there is ample evidence of elements from specific, language-oriented genres of Buddhist literature having found their way into the Tibetan grammatical description as well, notably stemming from the Abhidharma and other traditions of philosophical speculation, and from the *mantra*-exegesis in esoteric Buddhism. The result of this amalgam of influences is, however, by no means a carbon copy, or a slavish following of the Indic models. How could it be when the language described is so fundamentally different from any Indic language? Here, as was the case in the entire process of the transcultural reception of Buddhism in Tibet, translating, in the sense of making applicable to the own culture, was the key word.

## 5. Bibliography


Miller, Roy Andrew. 1976. *Studies in the Grammatical Tradition in Tibet.* (= *Amsterdam Studies in the Theory and History of Linguistic Science*, series III: *Studies in the History of Linguistics*, 6.) Amsterdam: Benjamins.

–. 1993. *Prolegomena to the First Two Tibetan Grammatical Treatises.* (= *Wiener Studien zur Tibetologie und Buddhismuskunde*, 30.) Wien: Arbeitskreis für Tibetische und Buddhistische Studien.

Simonsson, Nils. 1982. "Reflections on the Grammatical Tradition in Tibet". *Indological and Buddhist Studies. Volume in Honour of Prof. J. W. de Jong on his Sixtieth Birthday*, 531–544. Canberra.

Tillemans, Tom J. F. 1988. "On *bdag*, *gzan* and related notions of Tibetan grammar". *Tibetan Studies. Proceedings of the 4th Seminar of the International Association for Tibetan Studies, Schloss Hohenkammer, Munich 1985* ed. by H. Uebach & J. L. Panglung, 491–502. (= *Studia Tibetica. Quellen und Studien zur tibetischen Lexikographie*, 2.) München.

– & Derek D. Herforth. 1989. *Agents and Actions in Classical Tibetan. The indigenous grammarians on Bdag and Gźan and Bya byed las gsum.* (= *Wiener Studien zur Tibetologie und Buddhismuskunde*,

21.) Wien: Arbeitskreis für Tibetische und Buddhistische Studien.

Verhagen, Pieter Cornelis. 1992. "A Ninth-Century Tibetan Summary of the Indo-Tibetan Model of Case-semantics". *Tibetan Studies. Proceedings of the 5th Seminar of the International Association for Tibetan Studies NARITA 1989*, vol. II, 833–844. Narita: Naritasan Shinshoji.

–. 1993. "*Mantra*s and Grammar. Observations on the study of the linguistical aspects of Buddhist 'esoteric formulas' in Tibet". *Aspects of Buddhist Sanskrit. (Proceedings of the International Symposium on the Language of Sanskrit Buddhist Texts', Oct. 1–5, 1991)*, 320–346. Sarnath: Central Institute of Higher Tibetan Studies.

–. 1994. *A History of Sanskrit Grammatical Literature in Tibet.* Vol. I: *Transmission of the Canonical Literature.* (= *Handbuch der Orientalistik*, Abt. 2, Bd. 8.) Leiden: Brill.

–. 1995. "Influence of Indic *vyākaraṇa* on Tibetan indigenous grammar". *Tibetan Literature. Studies in Genre: Essays in honor of Geshe Lhundup Sopa*, 422–437. Ithaca, N. Y.: Snow Lion Press.

*Peter Verhagen, Leiden (The Netherlands)*

# VIII. The Establishment of Hebrew Linguistics
# Die Anfänge der hebräischen Sprachforschung
# La constitution de la linguistique de l'hébreu

## 33. The origins of Hebrew linguistics and the exegetic tradition


1. Exegesis
2. Masora
3. Grammar
4. Saadia Gaon
5. Conclusion
6. Bibliography


### 1. Exegesis

The seeds of language study in Hebrew lie in the interpretation of the Holy Scriptures. The holy text of the Hebrew Bible evoked constant exegetic attempts dating back almost to the time of the creation of the text. The Oral Law was considered to be the legitimate and binding interpretation of the Written Law, accompanying it constantly and emanating, according to Jewish Rabbanite tradition, from the same divine source. Similarly, traditional exegesis accompanied the text, supplying the foundation for religious law and for accepted interpretation. The Karaites, however, a religious community which arose in the 8th century and denied the legitimacy of the Oral Law, felt themselves bound to practice independent study and exegesis of the Scriptures.

#### 1.1. Talmudic Exegesis

The seeds of exegesis are found in all the components of the Oral Law literature: *Mishna*, *Talmud* and *Midrash* (Berliner 1878–1879). The various types of interpretation called for a profound understanding of the structure of the Hebrew language, but contained nothing resembling a grammatical discipline. The very common homiletical interpretation, the *dĕrāš*, is often founded on a basic recognition of morphological and syntactic structure, without reaching any degree of systematic grammatical analysis. This first approach to language produced basic terms that later served also in grammatical description, such as *yāḥid* "singular", *rabbim* "plural", *zāḵār* "masculine", *nĕqevā* "feminine", *ʿāvār* "past", *ʿātid* "future", *ʾot* "letter", *tevā* "word", etc. (Bacher 1895: 3–7).

It is hard to draw the line between tendentious homiletical strategies aimed at proving an exegetic thesis even at the price of inaccuracies, on the one hand, and sound linguistic knowledge, on the other hand. The many homiletical exercises contain some grammatical distinctions, albeit without technical terminology, e. g., between active and passive voice: *yoḵal* "he will eat" vs. *ye ʾāḵel* "he will be eaten", or between a noun-adjective structure and a construct genitive structure *ʿęvęd ʿivri* "a Hebrew slave" vs. "a Hebrew's slave". Sometimes they arrived at quasi-grammatical formulations, like the rule defining the function of the locative *-āh* for direction (replacing the prefixed preposition *lĕ-*) (Babylonian Talmud, *Yevamot* 13b et al.).

Sometimes Hebrew scholars resorted to other languages in order to explain words of obscure meaning, e. g. Greek, Arabic and African languages. Their contact with other languages also made them imitate practices of study common in other cultures, mainly in Greek. They took advantage of methods prevailing in Greek and applied them to Hebrew homiletic interpretation. Thus when searching for etymologically obscure Hebrew words they sometimes resorted to the Greek custom of dividing words. For instance, *ḥašmal* "amber" (in Bible translations; Ez. 1:27) was explained as *ḤAyyot ʾeŠ mĕMALlĕlot* "fire animals talking" (Babylonian Talmud, *Ḥagiga* 13a–b), or the etymologically obscure *karpas* "fine cloth" (in Bible translations [Est. 1:6] "green"; perhaps from Persian *karpās* "fine cloth"), was explained as *KARim šęl PASsim* "pillows of stripes", "striped pillows" (Babylonian Talmud, *Megilla* 12a). Moreover, they sometimes borrowed etymologies from other languages. Thus, to understand *hādār* (Lev. 23:40), applied in the text to a fruit plant, the sages of the Talmud referred to Greek ὕδωρ "water" to explain it as "that [plant] which grows on water" (Babylonian Talmud, *Succa* 35a).

The method of searching for the etymology by mechanical division of words may be traced back to Greek writers (Arens 1969: 8ff.; → Art. 53). In the *Cratylus* Plato quotes Socrates explaining ἀήρ "air" as emanating from αἴρει "it raises" (because air is capable of raising things like leaves and smoke from the ground), or from ἀεὶ ῥεῖ "always flows" (Waterman 1963: 6–10).

Homiletics was a tool of the oral sermon, aimed at being practiced on liturgical occasions in sermons and speeches to larger publics. The festive occasion determined the section of the biblical text to be interpreted, for instance the relevant weekly portion of the Pentateuch to be read on a certain Sabbatical or Holiday synagogue service. This homiletic interpretation was intended to be a means for transmitting values, ideology and especially the Oral Law through the biblical text. From the outset, exegesis was in the service of homiletics and was shaped according to its needs. Some of the midrashic compilations known to us are basically collections of auxiliary midrashic material arranged according to the needs of homiletic preachers. This was a sophisticated indirect way of exegesis with perhaps the best chance to reach the respective audience.

It can be summarized that in the Talmudic era (200–500 CE) scholars made use of language and language forms for their exegetical purposes, sometimes using formal tools that were to be used later also by grammarians. But their aim remained exegetical, never reaching a degree of language study *per se*. All pre-grammatical knowledge was based on native intuition, but did not and could not constitute a systematic set of rules, let alone a grammatical description.

### 1.2. Karaite Exegesis

Karaite biblical interpretation was not much different from the Rabbanite one, inasmuch as the underlying pre-grammatical knowledge was concerned. In order to justify their separation from the Rabbanites, the Karaites had an even greater incentive to establish an independent exegesis, and to build it on sound rules, hence the tendency to arrive at systematic formulations. Although one might have expected Karaite commentaries on the Bible at an earlier period, the first comprehensive biblical commentator remains Saadia Gaon (cf. below 4.1.). The main Karaite commentators known to have preceded him are Benjamin an-Nahawandī (9th century) of whom nothing has come down to us, and Daniel al-Qūmisī (second half of the 9th century) of whose commentaries only some parts are extant. Their commentaries, as well as those of the Rabbanites, abound in observations concerning the language aspect of the text.

## 2. Masora

### 2.1. Masora

However, the main approach to language involved the aim to preserve the holy text of the Hebrew Bible, a task undertaken by the *Masora* practiced by both Karaites and Rabbanites. In its broader sense Masora encompasses everything that is transmitted together with the holy text in terms of graphemes, auxiliary graphic signs, as well as instructions for the reader and for the scribe. Such instructions, it may be assumed, were being transmitted alongside the written text, since the time of its inception, first orally, but in the course of time they came to be committed to writing (Dotan 1971: 1409ff.).

The marking of graphemes and instructions, i. e. *Masora*, was not possible while the holy text was being copied on scrolls, since the written scroll preserved the sanctity endowed to it by the Oral Law, the *Halakha*. However, due to the introduction of the Roman writing customs, assumedly in the 5th or 6th century, Scripture started gradually to be copied in the form of a 'codex', i. e. a number of leaves bound by two wooden plates. The new mode of writing made the text halakhically unfit for public reading as part of a religious ritual. The reduced holiness of the codex made it possible to add various kinds of graphic signs, something that had not been possible before, since these signs would have desecrated the text on the scroll.

Although the first explicit mention of a codex in Hebrew (*miṣḥaf*, borrowed from Arabic *muṣḥaf* "volume") is found in a source assumed to be not earlier than the 8th century, there is sound ground to believe that the holy text was copied in the form of codices as early as the 6th or, at the latest, the 7th century.

What had been transmitted from time immemorial, orally and, during public ritual recitation, with the help of manual signs (cheiromantics), was reduced at this stage to two sets of graphic signs: graphemes denoting vowels and other phonetic or phonemic features (e. g. *dāgeš* denoting consonantal nature or gemination), named *niqqud* "pointing", "vocalization", and graphemes denoting the musical recitation, named *ṭĕʿāmim* "accents", "accentuation". The accentuation was basically a set of graphemes marking (musical) pauses, thus conveying both the music for cantilation and the logical pauses necessary to convey the meaning of the text (Yeivin 1980). The two sets of graphemes, vocalization and accentuation, seem to have been the first signs added to the consonantal text. Presumably (cf. Dotan 1981, 1987) the marking of accentuation preceded the marking of vocalization.

Gradually, notes concerning the reading of the Bible were added in the margins of the text. These were instructions for proper pronunciation and for exact copying of the text, instructions which used to be handed down orally from generation to generation and finally were set down in writing. Although the term Masora (Hebrew *māsar* "to transmit") encompasses all that was transmitted in conjunction with the consonantal text, and originally included therefore marginal notes as well as the two sets of graphemes, the term is usually applied in its narrower sense to denote basically the marginal notes.

The Masora notes were copied in different graphic shapes and according to different kinds of elaboration (the longer Masora *magna* and the concise Masora *parva*). It seems that the most important type and perhaps the earliest to be noted, were the indispensable *qĕre* (Aramaic passive participle) "is being read" notations, indicating a different phonetic realization of certain consonantal structures. In this manner the consonantal text was sometimes corrected for various reasons, e. g., to avoid euphemisms (instead of the letters YŠGLNH [Deut. 28:30]: YŠKVNH = *yiškavẹnnā* "he shall lie with her" is to be read), to replace archaic forms (instead of BNYKY [II Kings 4:7]: BNYK = *bānayiḵ* "your sons" is to be read); or to correct apparent errors (instead of the letters WYʿŚ [I Sam. 14:32]: WYʿṬ = *wayyaʿaṭ* "he flew upon").

Other masoretic notes deal with word or form counts, and all kinds of unique phenomena in orthography, vocalization or accentuation. Some of these notes also serve as an auxiliary tool for biblical exegesis. It has been demonstrated (e. g., Fernández Tejero 1996) that some masoretic notations could occasionally throw light on the interpretation of obscure passages of the Old Testament.

### 2.2. Transition to grammar

Apart from their importance as far as preservation is concerned, and apart from their exegetical value, the masoretic notations also constituted a great contribution towards what was later to become 'grammar'.

Already the masoretes themselves gathered the notes, counted them and compiled them into full lists, arranged according to a common structural or numerical denominator. These compilations — the most famous one is the *'Oḵlā wĕ-'Oḵlā* — paved the way for grammatical generalizations and formulation of rules, for observing the underlying rules appertaining to orthography and graphic notation or to pronunciation and to meaning. These first rules constituted the nucleus that contained the linguistic materials from which Hebrew grammar was to grow.

In order to understand the transition from Masora to grammar, it is essential to mark the difference between the two in their approach to text and language, since these are sometimes completely opposed. In spite of the fact that both of them, Masora and Hebrew grammar, had originally one and the same purpose — the preservation of the holy text and its language with the utmost precision — their roads towards the realization of this goal were very different.

Grammar observes the text as a whole, and seeks for the regular phenomena common to all its parts in order to record, describe and formulate them in a series of generalizing rules and present the minority as an exception, sometimes abstaining from it or at least putting it in a lower degree than the rule; whereas the Masora is centered around the exceptional details and seeks in them the peculiar and the extraordinary, the irregular and the rare, and since these details cannot be generalized in rules, the Masora counts them, sums them up and records the number of occurrences, lest the exceptional minority fall into oblivion. The grammarian sees the whole forest, the Masorete looks for the individual trees. Grammar books are sets of rules describing linguistic phenomena with the exceptions dragging behind as neglected details, as a nuisance upsetting the regularity of the rule and the peace of mind of the grammarian. The Masora, on the contrary, is the celebration of the minority, the feast of the irregular forms, making them the center of interest and granting them specific importance, precisely because they are different and contradict the regularity of the majority.

It is evident that, in order to discern the irregular minority forms, the regularity of the majority must be conceived clearly. In other words, the recording of exceptions and minority forms implies a comprehensive acquaintance with what is regular and of common use, otherwise the determination of exceptions and minority forms would be impossible. Consequently, it is inconceivable that grammatical thinking did not exist during the activity of the Masora. On the contrary, only fundamental grammatical knowledge might have produced certain distinctions scattered in masoretic notes, if not in all, certainly in some of them.

Of these two principal methods to preserve the biblical text, the Masora must have been practiced earlier, because it did not require theoretical tools for generalization. These were necessary for grammar and it took some time and perhaps foreign influence before such tools were available. The early grammatical distinctions in Hebrew originated then in the vast undertaking of text preservation and gradually developed through Masora into what we know as grammar.

While the first traces of quasi-grammatical distinctions, aimed at preserving the text, can be detected already in the Talmud (cf. 1.1.), the earliest ones dating back to the time of Rabbi Akiva (mid 2nd century), and perhaps even earlier, the phenomenon continued and spread and became quite common in the masoretic literature. Many examples can be adduced to illustrate the existence of a linguistic intuition, semantic and lexical distinctions, awareness of idiomatic usage and the like, all in all strengthening the impression that a grammatical understanding must have been in the background of the Masora (Dotan 1990: 22–23). This understanding, although it did not yet reach a concrete formulation in regular grammatical terms, was nevertheless simmering under the surface, lying in wait for the formal linguistic tools that were going to redeem it from its primordiality, and breathed into it the spirit of a living grammar.

The turning point came with the encounter with the Arabs and Arabic culture, especially with the fruitful contact with Arabic grammar. It is usually assumed that the beginning of Arabic grammar did not precede the end of the 8th century, and some time afterwards, not more than a century later, its influence started to show its marks in Hebrew.

Linguistic consciousness took shape in two main directions: a) a practical approach, a kind of applied linguistics, interested mainly in the normativity of the biblical text, its correct reading, chanting and copying. This can be regarded as a quasi-linguistic trend for which some (Eldar 1992) have suggested the name of 'orthoepy' (= the art of correct reading). b) a formal grammatical approach aimed at a systematical arrangement of the facts of language, the outcome being a linguistic description of a kind.

Although these two co-existed and developed in a parallel way, the first started earlier as an answer to a practical need, while the other developed mainly as a result of the contact with Arabic language study. We shall treat them separately.

## 3. Grammar

### 3.1. Masoretic grammar

The constant preoccupation with correct reading brought about the invention of vowel and accent marks as well as some of the masoretic notations (cf. above 2.1.). However, at a later stage, perhaps around the 8th century, 9th at the latest, lists of masoretic peculiarities started to be formalized and expressed in rules binding together many of the details. Thus, rules were being circulated regarding certain details of reading, as for instance, rules about the pronunciation of the *šĕwā* in particular positions, e. g. after initial *ham-* or in verbs of the root *b.r.k.* Some of these rules are relatively ancient and were formulated either in Aramaic or in Hebrew rhymed prose (resembling the then current Arabic *sağʿ* style).

These rules constituted autonomous chapters and were copied independently, mostly in Bible codices and sometimes separately (Baer & Strack 1879: x-xviii). The choice of chapters was sporadic and varied from scribe to scribe. Only at the beginning of the 10th century was the first compilation of such masoretic chapters made by the master masorete Aaron ben Asher, and named *Diqduqe ha-Ṭĕʿāmim* "Accuracies of the accents". This compilation did not amount to a systematic set of rules for reading, but rather a selection aimed at teaching some important aspects of the biblical accents (*ṭĕʿāmim*), stressing their affiliation to the vocalization system, especially to the problematic entity *šĕwā*.

Ben Asher's compilation, which included also some original chapters authored by himself, such as the important chapter on the rules of *pāseq*, was the first organized manual of directives for the correct reading of the Bible.

Thus a special literary genre came into being, a genre which initially consisted of scattered isolated masoretic chapters, which through the initiative of relatively late authors were assembled into compilations and transmitted as anonymous masoretic treatises. This development started in the East, mainly in Tiberias, but later spread out all over the Jewish Diaspora. This is evidenced by manuscript remnants of such compilations, which have come down to us from many Jewish communities, such as Palestine, Egypt, Yemen, Babylon, Persia, Spain, Portugal, Turkey, Greece, Italy and Germany. In the course of time such anonymous treatises and semi-treatises were sometimes translated in Arabic-speaking communities from their original Hebrew or Aramaic into Arabic (Dotan 1992: 40–43).

The transmission of texts of the orthoepic genre became quite common, and many anonymous works, mostly in Arabic, have come down to us, albeit in a fragmentary shape (e. g., Levy 1936). In the 11th century this culminated in an Arabic treatise with a systematic set of rules entitled *Hidāyat al-qāriʾ* "Instruction of the reader", attributed until recently to an anonymous author from the East, presumably from Palestine. It has been suggested recently (Eldar 1994: 40–42) that the author was the Karaite grammarian from Jerusalem ʾAbū l-Farağ Hārūn who flourished in the first half of the 11th century. It so happens that he is the first scholar, and as far as we know, the only one to write books in both genres, the one under discussion and the grammatical one (cf. 3.3.).

### 3.2. Grammar

The grammatical development is linked with two historic events: the expansion of Islam on the one hand and the rise of Karaism on the other hand. The Arabic influence is certainly due to the rich cultural environment, which opened before the Jews in the East the gates of sciences, of systematic philosophical inquiry, as well as the methodology of linguistic analysis. The contribution of the Karaites may lie in the greater centrality and uniqueness which they attributed to the Hebrew Bible, the Written Law, and perhaps also in their more direct access to Arabic sources, which enabled them to serve frequently as mediators.

### 3.3. Karaites

The importance of the Karaite contribution is discernible quite clearly in comparing the Karaite literary activity with the Rabbanite one. As mentioned above (1.2.), Rabbanite biblical exegesis was, at the beginning, mainly part of homiletical interpretation.

For the Karaites who denied the Oral Law and adhered strictly to the Hebrew Scripture alone, the cultivation and preservation of the Hebrew Bible was not only of greater importance, but essentially the center of their religious conviction. This brought them very close to the Hebrew language, and their exegetical activity became one of their main learned occupations. Thus, both the Masora and the systematic knowledge of the language were in the line of their common practice.

The desire to achieve distinction in the cultivation and knowledge of the language became a matter of rivalry between the two communities. Both practiced Masora and were equally attracted to grammatical study, though it was a Rabbanite scholar, Rav Saadia Gaon (882–942), who won recognition as the first Hebrew grammarian. Extensive grammatical works by Karaite scholars became known only relatively late, the most outstanding of them being ʾAbū l-Farağ Hārūn, in the first half of the 11th century (cf. above 3.1.). Recently, fragments of a grammatical work by his teacher ʾAbū Yaʿqūb Yūsuf ibn Nūḥ and of others have been discovered (Khan 1998).

## 4. Saadia Gaon

### 4.1. Saadia Gaon

As has been pointed out, the Masora was a completely Jewish enterprise, under the aegis of which linguistic knowledge had developed. It needed just an outside trigger, in the form of Arabic systematic language study, to develop from observations scattered all over the literary sources (Talmud, Midrashic exegetic literature, Masora) into practical grammatical study. This happened at the hands of Saadia Gaon, an outstanding scholar in all branches of Judaic studies (Malter 1921).

Saadia is considered the greatest Jewish scholar in the gaonic period. Born in Egypt where he spent his youth, he migrated to Palestine where he lived for several years, presumably in Tiberias, the foremost community of the time, and finally (in 922) settled in Babylonia, Irak, where he became a leading figure in the Jewish community. He excelled in all fields of learning and became the foremost scholar in every field he engaged in. A very lively community activist, he played an active role in internal Jewish conflicts, e. g. the calendar dispute with Ben-Meir, the gaonate dispute with Ben-Zakkai, and his ongoing major controversy with the Karaites and heretics. Besides, he showed no less and perhaps even more activity as an innovative author.

In Halakha he composed monographs on halakhic decisions covering many fields of the Jewish religious code of law. In composing halakhic monographs he was undoubtedly a pioneer introducing a revolution in Rabbinic literature. In philosophy, too, a pioneer, he is the first known to have composed a major philosophic work (*Kitāb al-'amānāt wa-l-i'tiqādāt*), and the first Jewish philosopher attempting reconciliation between biblical revelation and philosophical thought. Although he generally followed in the footsteps of the Arab Mu'tazilites (→ Art. 43) he found a way to integrate other schools of thought as well. In biblical exegesis, too, Saadia was an innovator. He may not have been the first translator of the Bible into Arabic, but, by composing commentaries in addition to his translation of many biblical books, he was the first to establish a standard Arabic translation (*Tafsīr*), sometimes annotated and expanded, accepted by some Arabophone Jewish communities over the generations. In liturgy he compiled the first methodically arranged Prayer-Book, and incorporated in it liturgical poems (*piyyuṭim*) of his own pen, intending them to be recited during services. All this shows the centrality of Saadia in Jewish learning on the one hand, and on the other hand, his creative innovation and pioneering in almost every field he touched.

It is not surprising at all to find him in that same role in the field of language: outstanding scholarship and pioneering innovation. He created the new subject of Hebrew lexicography and grammar.

Questions of language interpretation, and consequently of structure, turned out to be crucial in biblical exegesis, especially in the bitter ideological and theological debate with the Karaites on the interpretation of theologically critical passages. This made it necessary to base philological interpretation on systematic grounds and create a special methodology for the purpose. In so doing Saadia did for language what he did also for all other fields of his research, especially Halakha and philosophy, namely, to introduce systematic structure, methodology and logical order in the discipline. He also used the Arabic language as a literary tool (instead of Aramaic and Hebrew) in most fields of learning, even in Halakha and in the Prayer-Book, where this was indeed a revolution.

As regards language study, after its tendentious beginnings, it turned into a systematic discipline only upon encounter with the Arab culture, in particular with Arabic language study. Being a scholar of wide interests, well versed in all fields of learning, among which, of course, also Arabic grammar, Saadia paved the way and initiated the study of the Hebrew language along the tracks of his Arab predecessors and contemporaries. Using formal elements from Arabic grammar, he built something entirely new. He borrowed from the Arabs a great part of his grammatical concepts, methodology and terminology – his grammar too, it should be remembered, was written in Arabic – applying them with the necessary changes to Hebrew, thus creating a new discipline known as 'Hebrew grammar'.

### 4.2. Saadia's linguistic enterprise

Saadia's two main linguistic works are the *Sefẹr hā-'Ẹgron* "Book of Collection" and the *Kitāb faṣīḥ luġat al-'ibrāniyyīn* "Book of Elegance of the Language of the Hebrews". From some other works, too, his linguistic theories can be gleaned. The most important of these are: *Kitāb as-sab'īn lafẓa al-mufrada* "Book of the Seventy Isolated (Hapax) Words", in which he supports the affinity of the Oral Law literature to the Bible by proving the lexical affinity of the two; and his Arabic commentary on *Sefẹr Yĕṣirā* "Book of Creation" (an ancient cosmogonic-mystic treatise), a commentary which contains some lengthy linguistic digressions and discussions of pronunciation and phonology.

The *'Ęgron*, which he wrote at the age of twenty, is the first Hebrew dictionary, or rather a word-list in two parts arranged alphabetically: one by the first letters as a dictionary and one by the last letters of the words, intended as an auxiliary for poets to help them choose proper acrostics and rhymes. In the introduction, written in ornate Hebrew style, after describing, inter alia, the history of the Hebrew language, he gives a functional division of the twenty-two letters (lacking the concept of 'consonant') of Hebrew, dividing the eleven servile letters still further into seven particles and four verbal prefixes. He also suggests a very concise analytical classification of the noun and its ramification into other derivations (Goldenberg 1973−1974). The introduction is fragmentary, but these topics are further developed in his other main grammatical work (cf. below 4.3.2., 4.3.3.). Subsequently he translated the *'Ęgron* into Arabic, turning it thus into a bilingual dictionary, intended for a very specific public, as indicated by the additional Arabic introduction and by the new Arabic title, *Kitāb 'uṣūl aš-ši'r al-'ibrānī* "The Book of the Principles of Hebrew Poetry".

Besides being the first Hebrew lexicographical undertaking, this work is of less linguistic importance than Saadia's main grammatical work, *Kitāb faṣīḥ luġat al-'ibrāniyyīn* (henceforth: *KFL*) mentioned above, the importance of which cannot be exaggerated (Skoss 1955), because, even in its fragmentary form (only about two thirds of the original work are extant) it comprises a lengthy dissertation of Saadia's linguistic thought and practice. *KFL*, now published in a comprehensive critical edition by Dotan (1997), is the source of most of his grammatical theories; some of them are elaborated on below (4.2.1.−4.3.4.).

It must be emphasized that it was not only the urge to write a grammatical description of Hebrew that Saadia acquired from the Arabs. He was also completely familiar with their doctrines of language and with their grammatical tenets, both of practical grammar and of theoretical linguistic thinking, philosophy of language, and axiomatic questions concerning the origin of language − all these he absorbed and passed on in his book, to the great benefit of the study of the Hebrew language.

### 4.2.1. Language comparison

It is nowadays generally accepted that Jews were the initiators of linguistic comparison, since the educated among them were polyglots, familiar with a minimum of three languages: they spoke Arabic as did any civilized person, and Hebrew and Aramaic fell to their lot as a private heritage. In this field, too, Saadia was the pioneer of language comparison, to be followed by Judah ben Qurayš (beginning of 10th century), Dunaš ben Labraṭ (middle of 10th century), Jonah Ibn Ğanāḥ (first half of 11th century), and others (→ Art. 36).

It should be remembered that in ancient times comparing languages was not just a new angle of interest in language, but indeed a revolution. Linguistic treatment used to be focused around the national language, the language of prominence, which was the only one that merited study and research. This language was not only preferred to all other languages but also given exclusive status. Other languages did not count and deserved neglect. Such was the status of Greek in Greece, against which every other language was βάρβαρος "un-Greek, savage, grotesque". Such was the status of Arabic in the Arab world, against which every other language was *'ağamī* "un-Arabic, savage, [Persian]". In such a cultural situation, even after the boundaries between the 'matron' tongues and the 'slave' tongues faded out, the raising of the other languages to the status of languages comparable to the 'matron' language, in our case Hebrew which retained its priority at all times, this alone constituted a radical change of values in the world of language study. This may certainly be regarded as a notable open-minded revolution in the development of linguistic thought.

### 4.2.2. General outlook on language

While the Hebrew language was studied in detail by Saadia, he was able, at the same time, to see the Hebrew language in the broad context of human language in general, not just in the context of the languages with which he compared Hebrew directly. So beyond language comparison Saadia took an additional step, in that he perceived not only the elements common to the languages he compared, but also those that were universal. He ascribed to the generality of human language certain properties the languages he compared had in common, and he made inferences from these findings about the universality of language. He was not only the first of the Hebrew grammarians to do so, but practically the only one. It is clear from his writings that the general phenomenon of human language as such interested him no less than the grammar of a specific language.

This strong desire to uncover the elements common to all languages and to examine the special mechanism of language, of every language, as man's vehicle of expression, is evidenced at the outset of each discussion Saadia devotes to a fresh grammatical topic.

Thus, for example, in the Hebrew introduction to the *Sefęr hā-'Ęgron* he speaks explicitly about his fundamental attitude: "When I decided to write this book to teach all who have chosen the language of the holy angels, I thought about the speech of man and all the pronunciation of their lips and uttering of their mouths, found in all the languages of the nations". It is clear that he gave careful consideration to human speech (*parole*) in general, as embodied in every language. Thus in his Arabic commentary of *Sefęr Yĕṣirā* mentioned above (4.2.), Saadia gives a phonetic description of the Arabic sounds *ḍād, ẓā', ǧīm, lām* ('thickened' as in the Arabic word *Allāh*), the Persian *šin*, the special *pe* (presumably emphatic), and in fact relies, for matters of Arabic, on "one of the books written by the Arabs".

It is, however, in the beginning of the various chapters of *KFL* that Saadia's insights are especially noteworthy. These opening sections sometimes appear to be a theoretical introduction to the matters discussed in the body of the chapter. In the beginning of the chapter on inflection, for instance, he writes: "The rules and fundamentals of this chapter are not just relevant to the Hebrew language, but to all the languages known to us [...]. This chapter is devoted entirely to facilitating the study of any known language, and only very little of it applies to Hebrew alone." In this way Saadia introduces the five principles that are fundamental to every language (known to him). One of these principles is the division of words into the three categories: nouns, verbs, particles – a division originating in ancient Greek thinking and a basic precept of Arabic grammar (Versteegh 1977).

Or, for example, introducing the chapter on the vowels, he says: "And before we mention what of this perception of the vowels is special to the Hebrew language, we shall refer to that side in the perception of vowels which is common to all languages." He then goes on formulating four principles applying to all languages and concludes: "And since we have already mentioned these four general principles, it is now time to present that which is special to the Hebrew language." These general principles deal with the universal question of the definition of the various types of a syllable – clearly a matter of general linguistics and relevant to languages in general. The examples of the different types of syllable are taken not from Hebrew but from Arabic, as for example *muṣḥaf, 'arḍ, samā'*.

In this endeavour, Saadia went beyond the conceptual framework of his Arab teachers and, in doing so, laid the foundations for the first steps of general linguistics.

4.2.3. Origin of language

A cardinal question in linguistic thinking throughout the Middle Ages is the question of the origin of human language; this question, too, is treated by Saadia Gaon, as well as the related question of the correspondence of words to ideas signified by them, a question which had been transferred from Greek philosophy to Islamic scholarship (→ Art. 43). The ancient disputes, which had died down after more than a millennium (from the time of Plato and Aristotle in the 5th and 4th centuries BCE; → Art. 53), recurred in full force in the 9th century CE and occupied an important place in the world of Arabic science, not only among scholars of language but also, and to an even greater degree, among theologians and philosophers (Kopf 1956: 55–56; Loucel 1963–1964: 188–208; Mahdi 1970: 51ff.; Weiss 1974; Goldziher 1994: 38–44).

Saadia, steeped in Arabic culture and in the questions with which it was concerned, preoccupied himself with the same questions and sought solutions for them. In two places in his linguistic work *KFL* he raises the question of the origin of language. He disputes the view that nouns (names of substantives) are determined by nature, and reveals his firm opinion that they were determined by convention (*iṣṭilāḥ*) among people. The speakers of the language have received language forms as they are, as a result of this consensus, and not as a matter of choice. Indeed, the choice (*iḫtiyār*) lay in the hands of the "institutor of the language" (*wāḍiʿ al-luġa*). This concept of *wāḍiʿ al-luġa*, which to most Moslems refers to Almighty God, is used by Saadia to clarify the concept of 'convention', which cannot be conceived of as a one time event. Convention, too, started from some point in the distant past, and is the work of the anonymous 'institutor of language'. It was he who chose the words and fixed their form, and from him they were accepted by convention for use by speakers. They agreed to accept what had been determined.

The name is not, therefore, an inevitable outcome of the meaning of the object, for if the meaning of the object were to demand a specific name, there could be no difference between the languages of mankind, nor could an object be called by different names in different languages. Thus, for example, it would be necessary for *'ẹvẹn* "stone" (in Hebrew) to be called not *ḥağar* "stone" (in Arabic) but *'ẹvẹn* in Arabic too. Since every object has a different name in each language, there is proof that the names are not determined by any intrinsic meaning of the physical object, but are rather the result of consensus among people, which led to the adoption of different names in every language. Not only the words but also their specific consonants and vowels were the outcome of convention among people.

Saadia also makes a point of warning against anarchy in language. Convention is not in the hands of just anyone, and certainly not of the current speaker of the language, but has been handed down from earliest antiquity. The 'institutor of language', who determined the names, is certainly not a deity, but an anonymous being (a man or a group of men) from the time of the origin of the language. Although he expresses his mind about the identity of this being elsewhere (*Commentary on Genesis* 65–67 where he mentions Adam) he does not mention it here, thus leaving the question open in order to maintain the universal character of his theory and make it possible to fit any other language beside Hebrew. Islamic scholars were interested mainly in the Arabic language and adhered to the *Qur'ān*, wheras the writings of Saadia are formulated as generalizations applying to all languages, or to human language in general, and not to the Hebrew language in particular, although he saw in Hebrew the first language.

It was the institutor of language who chose the names for the objects in an arbitrary manner, about which consensus among people was achieved, and this consensus was transmitted from generation to generation. From here it is a natural progression to the concept of the arbitrariness of the linguistic sign, although of course we should not expect to find in his writings actual Saussurean terminology of this nature.

Not only do universal linguistic considerations figure prominently in Saadia's thinking, but he also succeeded in assigning them a diachronic dimension, as a process in which the transmission from generation to generation has a part to play. It is tradition that preserves the purity of the language. In this respect he goes further and to a greater depth than the Arab school of *iṣṭilāḥ* which was bound by the dogmas of Islam. He added his own input, both in terminology and in original thinking, and he was able to do so since he was not limited by the shackles of Islamic religious beliefs and thus could follow paths which Arab scholars could not.

The concept of tradition is vitally important for Saadia's theories, because without it language as consensus between people would amount to anarchy, and people could agree to one thing today and another tomorrow. That, in fact, is the primary weakness in the arguments of those who support 'convention', as opposed to those who favour "divine determination" (*tawqīf*) or "divine inspiration" (*'ilhām*) (Arnaldez 1956: 39ff.). For the latter the words of God suffice: It is impossible and inadmissible to alter them (and from this point of view they are no different from those who held the Greek concept that language is by nature); but what are the former to do? It fell to Saadia to add the dimension of 'tradition', revered by all, certainly by the Jews, and, moreover, this dimension is compatible with the Masora that is linked with the biblical text, from which it receives and to which it in turn lends support. With the help of the notion of tradition (*intiqāl*), Saadia redeemed the notion of convention in language from the realm of the present and enhanced it with the splendour of ancient times, in order to preserve the language from possible harm at the hands of its speakers.

### 4.3. Saadia as grammarian

In the common descriptions of the development of Hebrew linguistic thought in the Middle Ages, it is customary to belittle all that preceded Judah Ḥayyūğ (beginning of 11th century) as beginners' endeavours, and regard all preceding grammarians as forerunners that announced the appearance of the real grammar. Ḥayyūğ is considered as the one who established the foundations of 'scientific' Hebrew grammar, and he is the source and origin of everything grammatical that developed since, even to the present day. The predecessors of Ḥayyūğ, Judah ben

Qurayš (beginning of 10th century), Menaḥem ben Sarūq, Dunaš ben Labraṭ (both middle of 10th century) and their disciples (Bacher 1892, 1895), also the Karaite David ben Abraham al-Fāsī (first half of 10th century), whom Ḥayyūǧ may not have known at all. They all merit the credit of preparing the ground with their preliminary conceptions and their efforts to understand the construction of words, paving the way by trial and error. Ḥayyūǧ accepted from them what was acceptable and rejected what seemed to him useless. He established linguistic rules of phonology and morpho-phonology that have been part and parcel of conventional Hebrew grammar since.

This still common attitude may have been valid when Saadia's grammatical work was unknown to scholars, but now that his major work (*KFL*) has been published, it becomes clear that Saadia's work was not a hesitant and uncertain attempt, but that he was an independent thinker. Ḥayyūǧ is not a continuation of Saadia; he has a completely different way. Saadia's ideas are not foundations carried out by his followers. In many respects Saadia has a completely independent approach which has not been continued by those who came after him, perhaps because these ideas, as also all grammatical works of Saadia, were not known to them. It is difficult to speculate today what turn Hebrew grammar would have taken had Ḥayyūǧ and Jonah Ibn Ǧanāḥ seen Saadia's grammar, and how this would have affected the development of Hebrew grammar since.

### 4.3.1. The root

The concept of the root can serve as a good demonstration. At the heart of his morphological discussion, Saadia chose to place a concrete concept, an existing entity phonetically realizable, unlike the common abstract concept of 'root'. He borrowed the Arab concept *'aṣl* "root, ground form of a word", a definite structure of consonants and vowels as it practically exists, evidently in the form of a noun, without being augmented by all kinds of affixes. This is the original concept common among the early Arab grammarians and lexicographers such as al-Ḫalīl and Sībawayhi (Troupeau 1984; Baalbaki 1988), and Saadia follows in their footsteps. Since 'root' has a different connotation in modern grammatical use, the term 'base' will be used in what follows, to translate *'aṣl*, as well as all its Saadianic synonyms such as *ǧawhar*, *'unṣur*, *'uss*, *ṭabī'a*, *ṭab'*, *ḏāt*.

According to Saadia, the 'base' is the nominal minimal unit serving as basis for derivation. In Hebrew this is not necessarily the *maṣdar*, as in Arabic grammar (especially the Basran school) but any nominal form expressing action. Thus, for Saadia, while *'aṣl* can denote regular infinitives or verbal nouns like *něśi'ā* "carrying", *nětiqā* "disconnecting", it can also denote a type of nomen actionis in a wider sense, e. g., the substantives *'omẹr* "utterance", *ḥefẹṣ* "wish", *hešẹq* "desire". All other forms are derived from the 'base' by affixation (through prefixes, suffixes and infixes), namely, forms of plural, construct and inflections, and the whole verbal system. The derived forms are called *'araḍ* "accident" or *far'* "branch". The 'base' may also alternate morphologically in other ways without change of meaning, by analogy, augmentation or contraction (cf. 4.3.3.).

The idea of 'root' as the consonantal skeleton bearing a certain basic meaning further defined by vowels and affixes is as alien to Saadia as to his Arab predecessors and contemporaries and seems to be the product of relatively modern, perhaps 19th century thinking. Medievalist grammarians, Arabs and Jews alike, clung to a necessary classification of words according to the number of stable consonants that could not be omitted (Goldenberg 1980).

The outcome of such a division are 'roots', vowelless abstract groupings of 'letters' that may carry each more than one basic meaning. Thus we find that Saadia's successors, David ben Abraham al-Fāsī and Menaḥem ben Sarūq, recognized roots of even one letter, while every root, whether of one or more letters, may hold more than one meaning, belong to more than one semantic or etymological group. The revolutionary approach of Judah Ḥayyūǧ brought with it the recognition of the constant triliterality of the 'root' and the alternation of its components with quiescent elements, but it did not change the essential concept of the 'root' (→ Art. 34). This can be seen in the structure of his two grammars *Kitāb al-'af'āl ḏawāt ḥurūf al-līn* "Book of Verbs Containing Feeble Letters", and *Kitāb al-'af'āl ḏawāt al-miṯlayn* "Book of Verbs Containing Double Letters", and of the dictionary of his successor, Jonah ibn Ǧanāḥ, *Kitāb al-'uṣūl* "Book of Roots". This concept of 'root' was held by Hebrew grammarians throughout the Middle Ages, and has been retained to some extent to the present day.

Saadia abstained from such abstract entities and adhered to essentially extant forms as base forms for grammatical treatment. Saadia's linguistic works, for reasons that have still not been explained satisfactorily, were unavailable to his successors. It is hard to guess what shape Hebrew grammar would have taken if Saadia's 'base' concept would have gained control.

### 4.3.2. Affixation

Another example of Saadia's originality is his broad concept of affixation. In his division of the twenty-two letters into eleven 'radicals' and eleven 'serviles', the former may occur as components of 'bases' alone, while the latter may occur both in this function and as affixes. This idea, with minor variations in detail regarding the number of letters in each group, is maintained in the Middle Ages by Saadia's successors.

What remains unique to Saadia and has no continuation after him is his approach to the 'serviles'. He did not distinguish between what we call derivational affixes and prefixed particles. When discussing the functions of *zawā'id* "appendages" he groups them together, as for example when he describes the functions of the letter *he* which carries four functions: 1) definite article, 2) interrogative particle, 3) infinitive prefix (in *nif'al* and *hif'il* conjugations), 4) causative verbal prefix (in *hif'il* conjugations). Or, for example, the letter *mem* having two functions: 1) preposition, 2) participle prefix (in all conjugations except *qal*).

### 4.3.3. Morphological ramification

This grouping of the letters made it possible or perhaps necessary for Saadia to describe the ramification of the 'base' accordingly. This ramification, namely the change of the 'base' into derived forms, is not merely the result of common morphological changes (plural, construct and inflexions, verb by involving tense), but is achieved also by annexation of particles, such as prepositions, definite article etc. The terms *'araḍ* and *far'* denote, therefore, not only forms derived morphologically from the 'base' but also 'base' forms with prefixed particles. Saadia, in principle, makes no differentiation between the two types; they are both considered derivations of equal level. He only marks a structural difference between the two: those affixes that change the shape, the vowel theme, of the 'base', and those that do not. The former are the inflexional affixes, morphological derivations, while the latter are the prefixed particles.

New forms, derivations of the 'base', emerge, but they in turn may serve as 'base' for further derivations. Thus the 'base' *dẹrẹḵ* "way" has the plural derivation *dĕrāḵim*, which in turn is the 'base' of its construct *darḵe*, and this is the 'base' of the inflected *dĕrāḵẹḵā* "your ways". In all these cases Saadia uses the same term *'aṣl*, which therefore is a relative concept. *'Aṣl* is certainly the first 'base', but it denotes also each stage of derivation which is the point of departure for the next stage.

While the 'base' constitutes the naked noun in its primary form, the regular derivations may be formed by affixation of both kinds mentioned. However, 'base' forms can develop in two more ways, either by alternation or by analogy.

The 'base' may alternate into a morphologically variant form equal in meaning with the 'base'. This may occur either by augmentation (*tafḫīm*) of letters or by contraction (*iḫtiṣār*) of letters. For instance, augmentation with *h* as in *'oro* (Is. 13:10) "his light" which becomes *'orehu* (Job 25:3) with the same meaning; or by repetition of a letter, as in *'āqim* (Am. 9:11) "I will raise up" which becomes with repeated *m*: *'ăqomem* (Is. 44:26). Examples for contraction of letters may be, for instance, when the 'base' forms *'oḵẹl* "food", *hāloḵ* "walking" in turning into verbs (by introducing a tense) lose the first letter ', *h* respectively and become: *'oḵal*, *toḵal* "I, you will eat", *'eleḵ*, *teleḵ* "I, you will go"; or the 'base' *ma'ăśẹh* "action, deed" when turning into a verb loses its first and last letters, *m* and *h*: *ya'aś* "he will make"; similarly ' may be omitted as in *šĕ'eriṯ* (Gen. 45:7) "remnant" which becomes *šeriṯ* (1 Chr. 12:39).

Analogy, too, is a method of derivation, and new forms may be constructed according to given patterns. Thus from the verb *pāṣaḥ* (Is. 14:7) "break forth" a new noun *peṣaḥ* can be coined according to the pattern of an existing form *šema'* (Ex. 23:1) "report, fame" which is the noun behind the verb *šāma'* "hear".

### 4.3.4. Analysis

This approach of pursuing the 'base' along its progressing derivations gave Saadia the option of analysis in the opposite direction, from fully developed forms into their smallest components. Thus he analyses a complex form in search of its 'base': *wĕhammiṯnaśśe'* "and the exalted [literally: the one who exalts himself]" (1 Chr. 29:11) is analysed into the 'base' *śe'* and the ramification *wĕhammiṯna-*. The latter in turn falls apart into its components: *w* (*wĕ-*) conjunction, *h* (*ha-*) definite article, *t* (*-t-*) reflexive, *m* (*mi-*) nominal (participle), *n* omitted on affixation of preformatives (which is the case here). It should be noted that he terms the whole augmented form *ʿaraḍ*, and also the augmented part alone (*wĕhammiṭna-*) is so termed. Similarly he analyses forms like *uḵṯoʿăvoṯęhęn* (Ez. 16:47), *umimmoʿăṣoṯehęm* (Prv. 1:31), where the *ʿaraḍ* is *-oṯehęn*, *-oṯehęm* (respectively), which, after neglecting the obvious particles *uḵ-*, *umi-*, leaves the 'base' (*ǧawhar*) to be either *-toʿăv-*, *-moʿăṣ-* or the consonantal skeleton *tʿb*, *mʿṣ* (respectively).

In the latter case this would mean a step towards the 'root' concept of his successors. Another step towards this concept is Saadia's assertion that in consonantal homographic pairs the difference in meaning is caused by the vocalic difference.

## 5. Conclusion

To sum up: Saadia's performance as a linguist was that of an enlightened thinker, innovative and well versed in current disciplines, who in his *KFL* confirmed the accepted ideas of contemporary Arab linguistic scholars, adapted them with creative originality to the particular needs of the Hebrew language, and developed them further to set up a new discipline in Hebrew.

Saadia's linguistic works and many of his theories, as some of his other literary creations, were doomed to oblivion. His personality, and consequently his works, attracted opposition and controversy, mostly from his Karaite opponents, but also on the part of his fellow Rabbanites. This was perhaps one of the reasons for the decline of some of his works.

Those who came after him did not follow in his footsteps. In many respects they can be regarded as a regression. The concept of the 'base' as an existing (nominal) entity was abandoned, or rather never adopted, and instead they all preferred to adhere to the abstract skeleton of letters, even of a single letter. This concept was to remain the leading practice in Hebrew grammar, to be improved only by the theory of triliterality of the root introduced from Arabic by Judah Ḥayyūǧ at the beginning of the 11th century in Spain. Ḥayyūǧ's innovation was the turning point in medieval Hebrew linguistics and the beginning of the era of what is generally regarded as 'scientific grammar'.

## 6. Bibliography

### 6.1. Primary sources

*Diqduqe haṭ-Ṭĕʿāmim.* Ed. by Aron Dotan, *The Diqduqé Haṭṭĕʿāmim of Ahăron ben Moše ben Ašér.* (= *The Academy of the Hebrew Language, Texts and Studies*, 7.) Jerusalem: Academy of the Hebrew Language, 1967. [In Hebrew.]

Ḥayyūǧ, *Kitāb al-ʾafʿāl ḏawāt ḥurūf al-līn; Kitāb al-ʾafʿāl ḏawāt al-miṯlayn.* Ed. by John William Nutt, *Two Treatises on Verbs Containing Feeble and Double Letters by R. Jehuda Hayug of Fez, Translated into Hebrew [...] by R. Moses Gikatilia of Cordova; to which is added the Treatise on Punctuating by the same author, translated by Aben Ezra.* London & Berlin: Asher, 1870.

Ibn Ǧanāḥ, *Kitāb al-ʾuṣūl* = ʾAbū l-Walīd Marwān ibn Ǧanāḥ, *Kitāb al-ʾuṣūl.* Ed. by Adolf Neubauer, *The Book of Hebrew Roots by Abuʾl-Walīd Marwān Ibn Janāh called Rabbi Jōnāh.* With an appendix by Wilhelm Bacher. Oxford, 1875. (Repr., Amsterdam: Philo Press, 1968.)

Saadia Gaon, *Commentary on the Sefęr Yeṣirā*. Ed. by Mayer Lambert, *Commentaire sur le* Séfer Yesira *ou livre de la création par le gaon Saadya de Fayyoum.* Paris, 1891.

Saadia Gaon, *Commentary on Genesis.* Ed. by Moshe Zucker, *Saadya's Commentary on Genesis.* New York: The Jewish Theological Seminary of America, 1984. [In Hebrew.]

Saadia Gaon, *Ha-ʾĘgron – Kitāb ʾuṣūl aš-šiʿr al-ʿibrānī.* Ed. by Nehemiah Allony. Jerusalem: Academy of the Hebrew Language, 1969. [In Hebrew.]

Saadia Gaon, *Kitāb al-ʾamānāt wa-l-iʿtiqādāt.* Ed. by Samuel Landauer. Leiden: E. J. Brill, 1880.

Saadia Gaon, *KFL* = Saadia Gaon, *Kitāb faṣīḥ luġat al-ʿibrāniyyīn.* Ed. by Aron Dotan, *The Dawn of Hebrew Linguistics: The Book of Elegance of the Language of the Hebrews by Saadia Gaon*, vol. I: *Introduction*, vol. II: *Text and Translation.* Jerusalem: World Union of Jewish Studies, 1997. [In Hebrew.]

Saadia Gaon, *Kitāb as-sabʿīn lafẓa.* Ed. by Nehemiah Allony. *Ignace Goldziher Memorial Volume*, vol. II ed. by Samuel Löwinger, Alexander Scheiber & Joseph Somogyi, Hebrew section 1–48. Jerusalem, 1958.

*Sefęr ʾOḵlā wĕ-ʾOḵlā.* Ed. by Solomon Frensdorff. Hannover, 1864. Ed. by Fernando Díaz Esteban.

Madrid, 1975. Ed. by Bruno Ognibeni, *La seconda parte del Sefer 'oklah we'oklah: Edizione del ms. Halle: Universitätsbibliothek Y b 4° 10, ff. 68–124.* Madrid & Freiburg, 1995.

## 6.2. Secondary sources

Arens, Hans. 1969. *Sprachwissenschaft.* 2nd ed. Freiburg & München.

Arnaldez, Roger. 1956. *Grammaire et théologie chez Ibn Ḥazm de Cordoue.* Paris: Vrin.

Baalbaki, Ramzi. 1988. "A Contribution to the Study of Technical Terms in Early Arabic Grammar: The term *aṣl* in Sībawayhi's *Kitāb*". *A Miscellany of Middle Eastern Articles in Memoriam Thomas Muir Johnstone 1924–1983* ed. by A. K. Irvine, R. B. Serjeant & G. Rex Smith, 163–177 Harlow: Longman.

Bacher, Wilhelm. 1882. *Die grammatische Terminologie des Jehūdā b. Dāwīd Ḥajjūǧ.* Wien: C. Gerold.

—. 1892. *Die hebräische Sprachwissenschaft vom 10. bis zum 16. Jahrhundert. Mit einem einleitenden Abschnitte über die Massora.* Trier: S. Mayer. (Repr., Amsterdam: Benjamins, 1974.)

—. 1895. "Die Anfänge der hebräischen Grammatik". *Zeitschrift der deutschen morgenländischen Gesellschaft* 49.1–62, 335–392. (Repr., Amsterdam: Benjamins, 1974.)

Baer, Seligman Isaac & Hermann Leberecht Strack. 1879. *Die* Dikduke Ha-Tĕamim *des Ahron ben Moscheh ben Ascher und andere alte grammatisch-massoretische Lehrstücke zur Feststellung eines richtigen Textes der hebräischen Bibel.* Leipzig.

Berliner, Abraham. 1878–79. "Beiträge zur hebräischen Grammatik im Talmud und Midrasch". *Jahresbericht des Rabbiner-Seminars für das orthodoxe Judentum pro 5639*, 3–59.

Blanc, Haim. 1975. "Linguistics among the Arabs". *Current Trends in Linguistics*, vol. XIII: *Historiography of Linguistics* ed. by Thomas A. Sebeok, 1265–1283. The Hague & Paris: Mouton.

Dotan, Aron. 1971. "Masorah". *Encyclopaedia Judaica* XVI. 1401–1482. Jerusalem: Keter.

—. 1981. "The Relative Chronology of the Hebrew Vocalization and Accentuation". *Proceedings of the American Academy for Jewish Research* 48.87–99.

—. 1987. "The Relative Chronology of the Accentuation System". *Meḥqarim Ballašon* 2–3.355–365. [In Hebrew.]

—. 1990. "De la Massora à la grammaire: Les débuts de la pensée grammaticale dans l'hébreu". *Journal Asiatique* 278.13–30.

—. 1992. "Masora in Arabic Translation". *Balšanut ʿivrit. Studies on the Hebrew Language Throughout its History, Dedicated to Gad B. Sarfatti on his 75th Anniversary* ed. by Menaḥem Zevi Kaddari & Shimon Sharvit, 179–183 Ramat-Gan: Bar-Ilan Univ. Press. [In Hebrew.]

Elamrani-Jamal, Abdelali. 1983. *Logique aristotélicienne et grammaire arabe.* Paris: Vrin.

Eldar, Ilan. 1992. "The Art of Correct Reading of the Bible". *Masoretic Studies* 7.33–42.

—. 1994. *The Study of the Art of Correct Reading as Reflected in the Medieval Treatise* Hidāyat al-qāri. (= *Guidance of the Reader*). Jerusalem. [In Hebrew.]

—. 1996. "The Beginning of Hebrew Language Science: R. Saadia Gaon between theory and practice". *Evolution and Renewal: Trends in the Development of the Hebrew Language*, 102–126. Jerusalem: The Israel Academy of Sciences and Humanities. [In Hebrew.]

Fernández Tejero, Emilia. 1996. "Masora or Grammar revisited". *Masoretic Studies* 8.11–23.

Fischer, J. B. 1962–63. "The Origin of Tripartite Division of Speech in Semitic Grammar". *Jewish Quarterly Review* N. S. 53.1–21.

Ginsburg, Christian David. 1880–1905. *The Massorah Compiled from Manuscripts.* With a Prolegomenon, Analytical Table of Contents and Lists of Identified Sources and Parallels by Aron Dotan. 4 vols. London. (Repr., New York, 1975.)

Goldenberg, Esther. 1973–74. "ʿIyyunim bā'Ęgron lĕ-rav Sĕʿadyā Gā'on [Studies in the *'Ęgron* of Rav Saadia Gaon]". *Leshonenu* 37.117–136, 275–290; 38.78–90.

Goldenberg, Gideon. 1980. "ʿAl ha-šoḵen hęḥālāq wĕ-ha-šoręš ha-ʿivri [On the quiescent letter and the Hebrew root]". *Leshonenu* 44.281–292.

Goldziher, Ignaz. 1994. *On the History of Grammar Among the Arabs: An essay in literary history* transl. and ed. by Kinga Dévényi & Tamás Iványi. Amsterdam & Philadelphia: Benjamins.

Goodman, L. E. 1992. "Jewish and Islamic Philosophy of Language". *Philosophy of Language, An International Handbook of Contemporary Research* ed. by Marcelo Dascal, Dietfried Gerhardus, Kuno Lorenz & Georg Meggle, vol. I,1,34–55. Berlin & New York: de Gruyter.

Hirschfeld, Hartwig. 1926. *Literary History of Hebrew Grammarians and Lexicographers.* London: Oxford Univ. Press.

Khan, Geoffrey. 1998. "The Book of Hebrew Grammar by the Karaite Joseph ben Noaḥ". *Journal of Semitic Studies* 43.265–286.

Kopf, Lothar. 1956. "Religious Influences on Medieval Arabic Philology". *Studia Islamica* 5.33–59.

Levy, Kurt. 1936. *Zur masoretischen Grammatik: Texte und Untersuchungen.* Stuttgart: Kohlhammer.

Loucel, Henri. 1963–64. « L'origine du langage d'après les grammairiens arabes ». *Arabica* 10.188–208, 253–281; 11.57–72, 151–187.

Mahdi, Muhsin. 1970. "Language and Logic in Classical Islam". *Logic in Classical Islamic Culture* ed. by Gustav E. von Grunebaum, 51–83. Wiesbaden: Harrassowitz.

Malter, Henry. 1921. *Saadia Gaon: His life and works.* Philadelphia.

Peters, Johannes R. T. M. 1976. *God's Created Speech: A study in the speculative theology of the Mu'tazilī Qāḍī l-Quḍāt Abū l-Ḥasan 'Abd al-Jabbār bn Aḥmad al-Hamaḏānī.* Leiden: Brill.

Poznanski, Samuel A. 1925–26. "New Material on the History of Hebrew and Hebrew-Arabic Philology During the X–XII Centuries". *Jewish Quarterly Review* N. S. 16.237–266.

Skoss, Solomon L. 1955. *Saadia Gaon, the Earliest Hebrew Grammarian.* Philadelphia: Dropsie College.

Steinschneider, Moritz. 1900. "Saadia Gaon's arabische Schriften". *Gedenkbuch zur Erinnerung an David Kaufmann*, 144–168. Breslau.

Troupeau, Gérard. 1962. "La grammaire à Baġdād du IXe au XIIIe siècle". *Arabica* 9.397–405.

—. 1984. "La notion de 'racine' chez les grammairiens arabes anciens". *Matériaux pour une histoire des théories linguistiques* ed. by Sylvain Auroux, Michel Glatigny, André Joly, Anne Nicolas & Irène Rosier, vol. I, 239–246. Lille.

Versteegh, Kees H. M. 1977. *Greek Elements in Arabic Linguistic Thinking.* Leiden: Brill.

—. 1993. *Arabic Grammar and Qur'ānic Exegesis in Early Islam.* Leiden: Brill.

Waterman, John T. 1963. *Perspectives in Linguistics.* Chicago.

Weiss, Bernard G. 1974. "Medieval Muslim Discussions of the Origin of Language". *Zeitschrift der deutschen morgenländischen Gesellschaft* 124.33–41.

Yeivin, Israel. 1980. *Introduction to the Tiberian Masorah.* (= *Masoretic Studies*, 5.) Transl. by Ernest John Revell. Missoula: Scholars' Press.

*Aron Dotan, Tel Aviv (Israel)*

# 34. Die Entwicklung der hebräischen Sprachwissenschaft während des Mittelalters

1. Quellen und Anregungen
2. Inhalt
3. Methode
4. Bibliographie

## 1. Quellen und Anregungen

"*Diqduq* oder Grammatik", erklärte 'Abū l-Walīd Marwān (Rabbi Yonah) ibn Ǧanāḥ in seinem Hauptwerk *Sefer ha-Diqduq* (Das Buch des genauen Untersuchens, arab. Titel *Kitāb at-Tanqīḥ*, vor 1050), "bedeutet im Grunde *ha-ḥaqirah we-ha-ḥippus*, das Suchen und Forschen" (*Riqmah* 29). Objekt dieser Forschung waren die Struktur und die Bedeutung des *lešon ha-qodeš*, der "heiligen Sprache", bzw. der Sprachgebrauch (*minhag*) der alten Hebräer, wie er in den vierundzwanzig Büchern der hebräischen Bibel festgelegt war. Ibn Ǧanāḥs Versuch, seine orthodoxen Gegner von dem Nutzen dieser Disziplin zu überzeugen, indem er sich mehrmals auf talmudische Vorgänger bezog (*Riqmah* 8–19), war reine Geschichtsfälschung: die Rabbiner der Spätantike haben zwar ein ständiges Interesse an Hermeneutik gezeigt, jedoch niemals systematische Sprachforschung betrieben.

Dennoch gab es am Ende des ersten Millenniums innerhalb der jüdischen Tradition Ansätze, die den Anfang der Grammatik vorbereitet haben. Die phonetische Klassifizierung der Konsonanten entnahmen die Gelehrten fast ausnahmslos den mystischen Interpretationen des Alphabets in dem spättalmudischen Buch der Schöpfung (*Sefer Yeṣirah* III.3, wo die fünf *moṣa'e ha-dibbur* Kehle, Gaumen, Zunge, Zähne und Lippen zum erstenmal aufgezählt werden). Von grundlegender Bedeutung war auch die Kodifizierung der Masorah, das ursprünglich oral überlieferte, anonyme System der Vokalzeichen und Akzente, das die Orthographie des Bibeltextes gewähren sollte. Ergänzt wurde die Masorah von einer Reihe Traktaten der tiberiensischen Ben Ašer Dynastie, wie Aharon ben Ašers *Diqduqe ha-Ṭe'amim* (Dotan 1967), deren phonetisch-morphologische Betrachtungen laut Abraham ibn Ezra (1089–1164) neben der Grammatik "die erste Säule der hebräischen Sprache" bildeten (*Moznayyim*, fol. 196a–b).

Doch erst die Auseinandersetzung mit der arabischen Sprachwissenschaft hat es diesen Ansätzen erlaubt, sich zu einer einheitlichen Disziplin zu entwickeln, wie aus dem Reimwörterbuch *Egron* hervorgeht, das um 920 von Sa'adya Gaon (882–942), dem Urheber der hebräischen Linguistik, in Bagdad verfaßt wurde (→ Art. 33). In der arabischen

Einleitung zu seinem Lexikon setzt sich der Gaon als "Retter der heiligen Sprache" dem legendären Grundleger der arabischen Linguistik 'Abū l-'Aswad ad-Du'alī gleich, der, so lautete eine Abbasidische Tradition, schon am Ende des 7. Jhs. die Kunst der Grammatik erfand, um die Sprache des Korans vor weiteren Verstümmelungen durch die neu unterworfenen Völker zu bewahren (*Egron* 150–153).

Doch nicht nur die Motivation zur hebräischen Grammatikschreibung, auch ihre Themen wurden weitgehend von Saʿadyas arabischen Vorbildern geprägt. Die Wahl des biblischen Dialekts als Objekt der Forschung zum Beispiel reflektiert die Verherrlichung des klassischen Koranarabischen – schon die masoretische Terminologie weist auf Einfluß koranischer Textarbeiten hin.

Das arabische Erbe bestimmte auch die Position der *ars grammatica* innerhalb des wissenschaftlichen Curriculums und sogar in der Gesellschaft. Wie ihre islamischen Zeitgenossen haben die jüdischen Dichter der Goldenen Ära in Spanien (950–1050) den *artes* des traditionellen Triviums, darunter die oft als *ṣaḥot ha-lašon* "korrekte Sprache" (Jesaia 32:4) angedeutete Grammatik, ein hohes soziales Prestige beigemessen.

Doch auch das Lehrprogramm, in dem die meist als *ḥokmat ha-lašon*, d. h. Sprachwissenschaft, aufgeführte Grammatik einen eher niedrigen Rang besetzte, war nach griechisch-arabisch ausgerichteten philosophischen Einsichten formuliert. Der wissenschaftliche Status der Sprachwissenschaft als eine rein propädeutische Disziplin entsprach der ursprünglich aristotelischen Auffassung der individuellen Sprachen (cf. *De Interpretatione* 16a3–8 und 16a26–28) als Konventionen, deren Relevanz jeweils auf einzelne Nationen beschränkt war. Diese Theorie der Sprache als willkürliches Symbol der *intellegibilia* – mit Ausnahme der heiligen, hebräischen Sprache, deren Natur der Essenz der realen Wirklichkeit entsprach – wurde während des Mittelalters von fast allen jüdischen Gelehrten akzeptiert. Auf Grund dessen konnte sich die Linguistik wohl kaum einem unvorteilhaften Vergleich mit der universalen Kunst der Logik entziehen.

Die Anfänge der hebräischen Grammatik wurden aber auch von innerjüdischen, religiösen Motiven inspiriert. Noch bevor er in Bagdad den *Egron* vollendete, bediente sich Saʿadya der Lexikographie in seinem Kampf gegen den Karaismus, eine jüdische Strömung, die die Autorität des Talmuds ablehnte und die Bibel als einzige Quelle ihrer Religionsgesetze anerkannte. Als manche Karaiten nicht nur die religiöse, sondern auch die sprachliche Relevanz der rabbinischen Werke zu leugnen wagten, kompilierte der Gaon den *Kitāb as-Sabʿīn Lafẓa* "Das Buch der siebzig Wörter", eine Liste von sechsundneunzig (!) biblischen *hapax legomena*, die die Unentbehrlichkeit der nach-biblischen Sprache bei der Interpretation seltener biblischer Ausdrücke beweisen sollte. Der *Kitāb as-Sabʿīn* war ein Versuch, die Sektierer mit eigenen Waffen zu schlagen: Schon im 7. oder 8. Jh. hatten karaitische Gelehrte die Sprachforschung zu einer festen Komponente ihrer Bibelauslegung gemacht – das Gebot "die Sprache in ihren Einzelheiten zu kennen" wurde einer ihrer zehn Glaubenspunkte (Hadassi, *Eškol ha-Kofer*, fol. 21b). Die karaitischen Sprachanalysen waren dennoch mehr als nur ein Anstoß zum rabbanitischen Sprachstudium: Sie haben Inhalt und Methode dieses Studiums in hohem Maße bestimmt.

## 2. Inhalt

Die hebräische Grammatik des 10. und 11. Jhs. zeichnet sich aus durch eine minutiöse und zugleich oberflächliche Beschreibung sprachlicher Einzelheiten aller Art. Diesen diffusen Charakter verdankte sie nicht zuletzt ihrem exegetischen Ursprung, der bis in das 7. oder 8. Jh. zurückverfolgt werden kann, als das *Sefer ha-Diqduqim* verfaßt wurde. In diesem exegetischen Handbuch präsentierte ein unbekannter karaitischer Redaktor eine Reihe linguistischer Disziplinen – darunter neben der morphologisch-semantischen Analyse der Sprache (v. i.) auch masoretische Kategorien, Phonologie, eine rudimentäre Form der vergleichenden Sprachwissenschaft, bei der neben Aramäisch und Arabisch auch die griechische Sprache erwähnt wurde, stilistische Notizen und sogar rabbinische Hermeneutik – als "den rechten Weg der Bibelinterpretation" (Mann 1926; Allony 1964).

Um 950 wurde dieser Ansatz von Dunaš (Adonim ha-Levi) ben Labrāṭ, Schreiber, Dichter und Grammatiker am Hofe des ʿAbd ar-Raḥmān III in Cordoba, zu einem definitiven Programm umgearbeitet. Der ehemalige Student Saʿadyas formulierte dreizehn masoretische, grammatikalische und stilistische Kategorien, nach denen "alle *ḥuqqim* und *mišpaṭim* [der Sprache] gemessen werden sollen" (Einleitung zu *Tešuvot le-Maḥberet Menaḥem* 6a). In dieser Beschäftigung mit den 'Gesetzen' der Sprache macht sich die präskriptive Einstellung zur Grammatik der Schule von Cordoba, deren Forschung sich auf den *mišqal ha-lašon*, die normative Struktur der Sprache (*Tešuvot* 74) konzentrierte, bemerkbar. Die grammatikalischen Einheiten entnahm Ben Labrāṭ, wie schon sein Lehrer Saʿadya, der arabischen Grammatik, wo ihm die drei Kategorien *šem* "Nomen", *poʿal* "Verb" und *millah* "Partikel", zur Verfügung standen (*Tešuvot* 5b).

Die dreizehn *middot* des Dunaš ben Labrāṭ lagen, wenn auch nur implizit, dem Inhalt des *Kitāb at-Tanqīḥ*, die originellste Schöpfung der mittelalterlichen jüdischen Sprachwissenschaft, zugrunde. Dennoch übersteigt Ibn Ǧanāḥs *magnum opus* in seinem Umfang sowie im Detail die Werke aller seiner Vorgänger. Neben einer erschöpfenden Darstellung morphologischer Themen enthält das Werk zahlreiche Stellen, die die noch immer enge Beziehung der Grammatik zur Exegese verraten. Nicht weniger als zehn der fünfundvierzig Kapitel sind der Bibelauslegung gewidmet und enthalten eine Fülle an Beobachtungen zu Syntax, Rhetorik und Stil der hebräischen Schrift. Bemerkenswert ist vor allem die Liste der sogenannten Tropen (Bibelstellen in denen Ibn Ǧanāḥ problematische Ausdrücke durch andere Worte ersetzte) im 28. Kapitel des Buches.

Die andalusische Hebraistik wurde im Jahre 1140 in Rom von Abraham ibn Ezra, der es zu seiner Aufgabe gemacht hatte, sie unter der jüdischen Bevölkerung des christlichen Abendlandes zu verbreiten, in dem *Moznayyim* "[Die] Waage" auf eine Liste von neunundfünfzig Termini reduziert (fol. 196b–197a). Der Katalog, der sich ausschließlich auf orthographische, phonetische und morphologische Grundkenntnisse beschränkte, fand bald seinen Weg zurück in die karaitische Sprachwissenschaft: Schon 1148/49 wurde er in Konstantinopel von dem byzantinischen Karaiten Judah Hadassi als "die sechzig Könige der Wörter" (cf. Hohelied 6:8) in die halachische Enzyklopädie *Eškol ha-Kofer* aufgenommen (fol. 60b).

Die endgültige Systematisierung der mittelalterlichen hebräischen Linguistik folgte allerdings erst im späten 12. Jh., als die jüdische Teilnahme an den Wissenschaften einen bedeutenden Aufschwung erlebte. Auch die Sprachwissenschaft erfreute sich eines erhöhten Interesses, fiel aber inhaltlich einem gewissen Stillstand zum Opfer. In der Provence wurden die arabisch verfaßten Werke der sogenannten "kreativen Periode" (Tene 1971, 1355) ins Hebräische übertragen und von der sephardischen Exilantenfamilie Qimḥi in ein System einfacher Paradigmen umgearbeitet. Während Judah ibn Tibbon (ca. 1120–ca. 1190) in Lunel die hebräische Übersetzung zu Ibn Ǧanāḥs *Tanqīḥ* abschloß (1171), kompilierte Josef Qimḥi in Narbonne im Stile Ibn Ezras das *Sefer ha-Zikkaron* "Das Buch des Gedenkens". Kurz darauf faßte sein Sohn Moses die Sprachstudien seines Vaters in dem *Mahalak Ševile ha-Daʿat* "Der Gang über die Wege der Weisheit" zusammen. Die Systematisierung des Materials führte in manchen Fällen zu wichtigen Erneuerungen: Josef Qimḥi führte nicht nur die maßgebende Einteilung der hebräischen Stammformen in acht aktive bzw. passive *binyanim* ein, sondern ordnete auch als erster rabbanitischer Grammatiker die traditionellen sieben Vokale ('Könige') der Masorah ihrer Länge bzw. Kürze nach in zwei Gruppen von je fünf Lauten ein.

Der Wunsch, die hebräische Sprache in ihren Grundprinzipien darzustellen, verrät ein didaktisches Anliegen, wie vielleicht am besten aus der Struktur des *Sefer ha-Miklol* hervorgeht, das um 1200 von dem jüngsten Sproß der Qimḥi-Dynastie, David ben Josef, aufgezeichnet wurde. Indem er die traditionelle, logische Priorität des Nomens überging – "obwohl das Nomen dem Verb vorangeht und sich zu ihm verhält wie eine Substanz zu ihrem Akzident" (*Miklol*, fol. 1b) – erklärte Qimḥi das Studium des Verbs auf Grund seiner "Häufigkeit und Bedeutung" zum Ausgangspunkt der ganzen morphologischen Beschreibung.

Erst die Gelehrten des 14./15. Jhs. erstellten eine – durchaus fruchtbare – Synthese aus Grammatik und Logik, eine Disziplin die in der christlichen scholastischen Sprachforschung wie in der jüdisch-christlichen philosophischen Polemik eine große Rolle spielte. Aus dem *ars recte scribendi* wurde ein wichtiges Instrument der Philosophie.

In einer Reihe exegetischer Traktate entwickelte Josef ben Abba Mari ibn Kaspi aus Argentière (1279–ca. 1340) sein eigenes Konzept des *higgayon* (wörtlich: "Logik"), das es ihm ermöglichte, der heiligen Sprache die vollständige Lehre der Physik und Metaphysik zu entnehmen. Die *meyasde ha-lašon ha-ʿivrit* "Grundleger der [konventionellen] hebräischen Sprache" hatten, laut Ibn Kaspi, über ein phenomenales Wissen des aristotelischen Universums verfügt und diese Weisheit ungekürzt in dem biblischen Idiom festgelegt (*Retuqot Kesef*; Übersetzung Mesch 1975: 31 ff.). Die älteren Grammatiker, "allen voran Ibn Ǧanāḥ und Ibn [*sic*] Qimḥi" (Last 1907: 656), hätten die fundamentelle Bedeutung der *ars logica* für die Lexikographie nicht erkannt.

In den ersten Kapiteln des *Maʿaseh Efod* (1403), im Grunde eine Rehabilitation des kreativen Genius des Ibn Ǧanāḥ, analysierte der Polemiker Profiat Duran (st. ca. 1410) die *causae* der Sprache im Rahmen der aristotelischen Aetiologie. Auch seine Definition der einzelnen Sprachen als Sammlungen "aller menschlichen Laute, die sich auf Grund einer Konvention auf eine Nation und auf die realen Objekte beziehen" (*Efod* 27), sowie die Verifikation dieser Definition, verraten ein starkes Interesse an den Kategorien und Kriterien der Logik. Letzter Exponent dieser spätmittelalterlichen aristotelischen Tradition war Abraham de Balmes, der seine bilinguische Grammatik *Miqneh Abram/Peculium Abrae* für christliche Schüler in Italien schrieb (Klijnsmit 1992).

## 3. Methode

Auf Grund ihres exegetischen Ursprungs kannte die früheste Hebraistik keinen formalen Unterschied zwischen 'Grammatik' und 'Lexikographie'. Die Identifizierung eines biblischen Lemmas wurde erzielt durch die Kombination von morphologischen und semantischen Äquivalenten. "*Torah* (das biblische Lemma) wird erklärt durch den *peruš* (die Auslegung). Diese Auslegung beruht auf einem *domeh*, d. h. einem morphologischen Äquivalenten und auf einem *ʿinyan davar*, einem Äquivalenten, der die Bedeutung des Wortes reflektieren soll. Ein *peruš*, der nicht auf einem *domeh* sowie auf einem *ʿinyan* beruht, ist falsch," warnte schon der Autor des *Sefer ha-Diqduqim* (Mann 1926: 442).

Die Schule von Cordoba dokumentierte die zweifache Suche nach dem *šoreš* "Wurzel" und seinem *pittaron* "Bedeutung" in alphabetisch geordneten Wörterbüchern und deren kritischen Rezensionen (v. i.). Erst Ibn Ǧanāḥ führte in dem *Tanqīḥ* die (arabische) Dichotomie in *naḥw* und *luġa* ein. Die Inflexionen und Konjugationen wurden in dem ersten Teil, dem *Kitāb al-Lumaʿ* (hebr. *Sefer ha-Riqmah*) analysiert; die Bedeutung der Wurzeln behandelte er im *Kitāb al-ʾUṣūl* (*Sefer ha-Šorašim*), wobei er für die morphologische Begründung seiner Etymologien systematisch auf den *Lumaʿ* (*Šorašim* 2) zurückgriff. Spätere Gelehrte wie Jacob ben Elazar ha-Levi von Toledo (*Kitāb al-Kāmil*) und David Qimḥi in dem *Sefer ha-Miklol* folgten diesem Beispiel.

Da die frühesten Grammatiker aber noch nicht mit der dreiradikaligen Struktur der hebräischen Wurzel vertraut waren, war die Identifizierung des richtigen *domehs* anfangs oftmals zweifelhaft. Um die Suche nach dem Wortstamm zu vereinfachen hatte schon Saʿadya in seiner nur fragmentarisch erhaltenen Grammatik *Kutub al-Luġa* (Skoss 1955: 5−7) die Buchstaben des hebräischen Alphabets in zwei Kategorien eingeteilt. Er zählte elf Radikalen und ebenso viele Servilbuchstaben, d. h. die Stammbuchstaben *ṭḥ sfr gzʿ ṣdq* und die übrigen, 'dienenden' Konsonanten, welche entweder als Prä- oder Suffix dazu dienten, die verschiedenen grammatischen Funktionen des Stammes zu verwirklichen.

Die Tatsache, daß Saʿadyas Einteilung dennoch keinen absoluten Erfolg versprach, ist lediglich auf die phonologischen Eigenschaften mancher Konsonanten zurückzuführen. In Konjugationen, in denen die sogenannten 'Dehnungsbuchstaben' *alef*, *wav* und *yod* assimilierten und *nun* (in Initialposition) oder identische Konsonanten (in zweiter und dritter Position) elidiert wurden, blieb dem Grammatiker eine monosyllabische Form, die in keinerlei Weise das Prinzip der Triliteralität nahelegte.

Die Unvertrautheit mit dem dreiradikaligen Radix hatte nicht selten dramatische Folgen. In den ersten Lexika erscheinen die morphologischen Äquivalenten nicht selten von einer verblüffenden Willkür: Während Menaḥem ben Saruq von Cordoba (fl. ca. 950) in seiner *Maḥberet* bestimmte Formen des Verbs *ntn* "geben" der Wurzel *tn* (*Maḥberet* 185a), andere aber dem Stamm *t* (*Maḥberet* 186b) unterordnete, präsentierte David al-Fāsī, ein zeitgenössischer Karait aus Palestina, in dem *Ǧāmiʿ al-ʾAlfāẓ* sogar eine Liste von vierzehn 'monokonsonantischen' Stämmen (Skoss 1939: 5−9).

Die *Maḥberet* des Menaḥem gab bald Anlaß zu einer Polemik, deren scharfer Ton nicht zuletzt von dem theologischen Verantwortungsbewußtsein der andalusischen Hofgrammatiker bestimmt wurde. Mit dem *Sefer*

*Tešuvot*, eine Responsensammlung, in der er Menaḥems puristische Methodologie und zahlreiche seiner Etymologien kritisierte, eröffnete Ben Labrāṭ, wie er sagte, "den heiligen Krieg". In späteren *Tešuvot* versuchten die Schüler Menaḥems und Ben Labrāṭs jeweils ihren Lehrer zu rehabilitieren. Die Polemik wurde auf Hebräisch geführt und war deshalb den Juden in Aschkenaz, die sonst von den arabischen Wissenschaften so gut wie ausgeschlossen waren, bekannt. Noch 1150 verteidigte Jacob ben Meir "Rabbenu Tam" aus Ramerupt in Nordfrankreich die Philologie Menaḥems in seinem "Buch der Entscheidungen". Zwanzig Jahre später wurde die Diskussion jedoch von Josef Qimḥi in dem *Sefer ha-Galuy* (cf. Jer. 32:14) aufgrund des neuen Forschungsstandes beendet.

Die Lexikographie Qimḥis reflektiert die im 12. Jh. in Südeuropa schon längst weit verbreitete Vertrautheit mit dem Prinzip der hebräischen Triliteralität, das in der rabbanitischen judaeo-arabischen Linguistik entwikkelt worden war und deshalb dem Aschkenasischen Judentum entgangen war. Schon während der zweiten Hälfte des 10. Jhs. war es Judah ben David al-Fāsī "Ḥayyūǧ", wahrscheinlich einer der drei *Talmide Menaḥem*, gelungen, dieses "Prinzip der hebräischen Sprache, welches in der Diaspora verloren gegangen war, wieder herzustellen", wie es der Philosoph Abraham ibn Dā'ūd in seinem *Sefer ha-Qabbalah* (1160/61) formulierte (Cohen 1967: 73 [hebräisch], 101–102 [Übersetzung]). Arabische Theorien bezüglich der *ḥurūf al-līn wa-l-miṯlayn*, die Dehnungs- und Doppelbuchstaben, standen Ḥayyūǧ dabei zur Verfügung (Kaplan 1994). In zwei Monographien sammelte er die Verben, die solche Buchstaben enthielten, diagnostizierte ihre "Krankheit" (*i'tilāl*) und klassifizierte auf Grund biblischer Analogie (*qiyās*) die grammatikalischen Eigenschaften, die zu der Assimilation bzw. Elision ihrer Radikalen geführt hatten. Mit Hilfe dieser Klassifizierung konnte jede Form auf eine drei-radikalige Wurzel zurückgeführt werden.

Doch Ḥayyūǧs Analysen waren keineswegs erschöpfend gewesen und führten deshalb zu einer Reihe von Diskussionen zwischen Ibn Ǧanāḥ, der im Jahre 1012 in dem *Kitāb al-Mustalḥiq* "Das Buch der Kritik" (Derenbourg 1880) die Lehre Ḥayyūǧs ergänzt und korrigiert hatte und dem gelehrten Staatsmann Samuel ibn Nagrela (ha-Nagid, "dem Fürsten") von Granada. In ihren *Risālāt* "Sendschreiben" widmeten sie sich der Erweiterung und Präzisierung der neuen Theorien.

Die Kontroverse bestätigte letztendlich die Autorität des Ibn Ǧanāḥ. Während uns von den grammatikalischen Schriften des Nagid nur das Lemma *alef* des Lexikons *Kitāb al-Istiġnā'* "Das Buch der Vollständigkeit" geblieben ist, wurden die Werke Ibn Ǧanāḥs von Epigonen überall in der jüdischen Diaspora nachgeahmt. Die wichtigste Überarbeitung wurde wohl in Italien von Ibn Ezras Schüler Salomon ibn Parḥon hergestellt, dessen *Maḥberet he-'Aruk* (Salerno 1160) nicht nur dem "Buch des Onyx" (*Sefer ha-Šoham*) des englischen Grammatikers Moses ben Isaac ha-Nesi'ah zugrunde lag, sondern auch lange Zeit als einzige Quelle diente für die Einleitung zum *'Anaq* "Die Halskette", der poetischen Zusammenfassung der andalusisch-jüdischen Linguistik des Philosophen und Dichters Salomon ibn Gabirol (Sáenz-Badillos 1980).

Ab dem 11. Jh. erschienen, zum ersten Mal seit Sa'adyas *Egron*, wieder spezialisierte Wörterbücher wie das Homonymenlexikon *Kitāb at-Taǧnīs* des Judah ben Bal'am (Abramson 1975) und Nathan ben Jeḥiels talmudisches (aramäisches) Wörterbuch *'Aruk* (Kohut 1878). Ein Unikum in der hebräischen Sprachwissenschaft des Mittelalters bildet der *Muršid al-Kāfī* des Jerusalemer Exegeten Tanḥum Yerušalmi (13. Jh.). Der "Zureichende Führer" war das erste Wörterbuch zu dem Werk eines zeitgenössischen Autors, nämlich zu dem Gesetzeskompendium *Mišneh Torah*, das der Philosoph Moses Maimonides (1135/8–1204), wie Tanḥum Yerušalmi bestätigte, "in der Sprache der Mišnah geschrieben hatte" (Toledano 1961: 24).

Noch während der ersten Hälfte des 15. Jhs. verfaßte Isaac ben Nathan Kalonymos *Me'ir Nativ*, eine biblische Konkordanz, die seinen Glaubensgenossen in ihren Disputationen mit christlichen Opponenten als Quelle biblischen Beweismaterials dienen sollte. Doch als im Laufe des 16. Jhs. die christlichen Gelehrten Europas ein ständig wachsendes Interesse an der biblischen Sprache zeigten, fiel manchem jüdischen Grammatiker die Rolle des Vermittlers zu: Wie Abraham de Balmes in Italien, veröffentlichte der Aschkenazische Linguist Eliah Levita (Baḥur; 1468/9–1549) seine Werke – das biblische Lexikon *Harkavah*, das aramäische *Meturgeman* und das mišnäische Wörterbuch *Tišbi* – oft in enger Zusammenarbeit mit christlichen Hebraisten wie dem Basler Humanisten Paul Fagius und dem Kardinal Egidio da Viterbo, in dessen Palast Levita 1517 sein *Sefer ha-Baḥur* schrieb.

## 4. Bibliographie

### 4.1. Primärliteratur

Ben Ašer, *Diqduqe ha-Ṭeʿamim* = Aharon ben Moses ben Ašer, *Sefer Diqduqe ha-Ṭeʿamim le-R. Aharon ben Mošeh ben Ašer.* Hg. von Aharon Dotan. 3 Bde. Jerusalem: Ha-Aqademiah la-Lašon ha-ʿIvrit, 1967.

Ben Balʿam, *Kitāb at-Tağnīs* = Judah ben Balʿam, *Šelošah sefarim šel rav Yehudah ben Balʿam: I. Ha-Ṣimmud, Kitāb at-Ṭağnīs.* Hg. von Shraga Abramson. Jerusalem: Kiryat-Sefer, 1975.

Ben Elʿazar, *Kitāb al-Kāmil* = Jakob ben Elʿazar [Yaʿaqov ben Elʿazar], *Kitāb al-Kāmil.* Hg. von Neḥemya Allony. (= *The American Academy for Jewish Research Monograph Series,* 1.) Jerusalem: Central Press, 1977.

David al-Fāsī, *Ğāmiʿ al-ʾAlfāẓ* = David ben Abraham al-Fāsī, *The Hebrew-Arabic Dictionary of the Bible known as Kitāb Jāmiʿ al-Alfāẓ (Agrōn) of David ben Abraham Al-Fāsī the Karaite (Tenth Century).* Hg. von S. L. Skoss. (= *Yale Oriental Series Researches,* 20, 21.) 2 Bde. New Haven, 1936–45.

De Balmes, *Miqneh Abraham* = Abraham ben Meir de Balmes, *Miqneh Abraham. Peculium Abrae. Grammatica hebraea una cum Latino nuper edita.* Venedig: Daniel Bomberg, 1523.

Dunaš ben Labrāṭ, *Tešuvot* = Dunaš Adonim ha-Levi ben Labrāṭ, *Tešuḇot de Dunaš Ben Labrat.* Hg. von Angel Sáenz-Badillos. Granada: Universidad de Granada, 1980.

Hadassi, Judah. 1836. *Eškol ha-Kofer.* Eupatoria.

Ḥayyūğ, *Ḥurūf al-līn wa-l-miṯlayn* = Judah ben David Ḥayyūğ, *The Weak and Geminative Verbs in Hebrew. By Abû Zakariyya Yaḥyâ ibn Dâwud of Fez known as Ḥayyūg.* Hg. von Morris Jastrow. Leiden: Brill, 1897.

Ibn Daud, *Sefer ha-Qabbalah* = Abraham ibn Daud, *A Critical Edition with a Translation and Notes of The Book of Tradition (Sefer ha-Qabbalah) by Abraham ibn Daud.* Hg. von Gershon D. Cohen. (= *Judaica Texts and Translation, First Series,* 3.) Philadelphia: The Jewish Publication Society, 1967/5728.

Ibn Ezra, *Moznayyim* = Abraham ben Meʾir ibn Ezra, *Diqduqim: Moznayyim.* Hg. von Eliah Levita. Venedig: Daniel Bomberg, 1545.

Ibn Gabirol, *ʿAnaq* = Salomo ibn Gabirol, *ʿAnaq.* Hg. von Angel Sáenz-Badillos, "El ʿAnaq, poema linguístico de Šelomoh ibn Gabirol", *Miscelánea de Estudios Árabes y Hebraicos* 29 (1981) 5–30.

Ibn Ğanāḥ, *Kitāb al-Mustalḥiq* = ʾAbū l-Walīd Marwān ibn Ğanāḥ, *Opuscules et traités d'Abou 'l-Walid Merwan ibn Djanah de Cordoue.* Hg. von Joseph & Hartwig Derenbourg. Paris: Imprimerie Nationale, 1880.

Ibn Ğanāḥ, *Riqmah* = ʾAbū l-Walīd Marwān ibn Ğanāḥ, *Sefer ha-Riqmah (Kitāb al-Lumaʿ) le-R. Yonah ibn Ğanāḥ be-targumo šel R. Yehuda ibn Tibbon.* Hg. von David Tene. 2 Bde. 2. Aufl. Jerusalem: Ha-Aqademiah la-Lašon ha-ʿIvrit, 1964. [Erstausgabe Michael Wilenski, Berlin: Ha-Aqademiah le-Maddaʿe ha-Yahadut, 1928/29.]

Ibn Ğanāḥ, *Sefer ha-Šorašim* = ʾAbū l-Walīd Marwān ibn Ğanāḥ, *Sepher Haschoraschim. Wurzelwörterbuch der hebräischen Sprache von Abulwalîd Mervān Ibn Ganâḥ (R. Jonah) aus dem Arabischen ins Hebräische Übersetzt von Jehuda Ibn Tibbon.* Hg. von Wilhem Bacher. Berlin: M'kize Nirdamim, 1896.

Ibn Kaspi, *Šaršot Kesef* = Josef ben Abba Mari ibn Kaspi, *Šaršot Kesef.* Hg. von Isac Last, "Sharshot Kesef. The Hebrew Dictionary of Roots, by Joseph Ibn Kaspi". *Jewish Quarterly Review* 19 (1907) 651–688.

Ibn Parḥon, *Maḥberet he-ʿAruk* = Solomon ibn Parḥon, *Maḥberet he-ʿAruk.* Hg. von Salomo G. Stern. Preßburg, 1844.

Levita, Eliah (Baḥur), 1517. *Sefer ha-Baḥur.* Rom.

—. 1518. *Sefer ha-Harkavah.* Rom.

—. 1541. *Tišbi.* Isny.

—. 1541. *Meturgeman.* Isny.

Menaḥem, *Maḥberet* = Menaḥem ben Saruq, *Maḥberet Menaḥem.* Hg. von Angel Sáenz-Badillos. Granada: Universidad de Granada, 1986.

Moses ben Isaac ha-Nesiʾah, *Sefer ha-Šoham* = Moses ben Isaac ha-Nesiʾah, *The Sepher haShoham (The Onyx Book) by Moses ben Isaac haNessiah.* Hg. von Benjamin Klar & Cecil Roth. London & Jerusalem: Mekize Nirdamim, 1947.

Nathan ben Jeḥiel, *ʿAruk* = Nathan ben Jeḥiel, *Aruch Completum sive Lexicon (...) auctore Nathane filio Jechielis.* Hg. von Alexander Kohut. Vienna: Georg Brög, 1878.

Profiat Duran, *Efod* = Isaac ben Moses ha-Levi Profiat Duran, *Maase Efod, Einleitung in das Studium und Grammatik der Hebräischen Sprache von Profiat Duran.* Hg. von Jonathan Friedländer & Jakob Kohn. Wien: J. Holzwarth, 1865.

Qimḥi, David, *Miklol* = David ben Josef Qimḥi, *Sefer Miklol še-ḥibber (...) R. David Qimḥi.* Hg. von I. Rittenberg. Lüttig, 1862.

Qimḥi, David, *Sefer ha-Šorašim* = David ben Josef Qimḥi, *Sefer ha-Šorašim. Rabbi Davidis Kimchi Radicum Liber sive Hebraeum Bibliorum Lexicon cum Animadversionibus Eliae Levita.* Hg. von J. H. R. Biesenthal & F. Lebrecht. Berlin, 1847.

Qimḥi, Josef, *Sefer ha-Galuy* = Josef Qimḥi, *Sefer ha-Galuy.* Hg. von H. J. Matthews. Berlin, 1887.

Qimḥi, Josef, *Sefer Zikkaron* = Josef Qimḥi, *Sefer Zikkaron. Grammatik der hebräischen Sprache.* Hg. von Wilhelm Bacher. Berlin, 1888.

Qimḥi, Moses, *Mahalak* = Moses ben Josef Qimḥi, *Mahalak Ševile ha-Da'at.* Hg. von Sebastian Münster. Basel: Froben, 1531.

Sa'adya Gaon, *Egron* = Sa'adya ben Josef al-Fayyūmī Gaon, *Ha'Egron. Kitāb 'Uṣūl al-Shi'r al-'Ibrānī by Rav Se'adya Ga'on.* Hg. von Neḥemya Allony. Jerusalem: Ha-Aqademiah la-Lašon ha-'Ivrit, 1969.

Sa'adya Gaon, *Kitāb as-Sab'īn* = Sa'adya ben Josef al-Fayyūmī Gaon, *Kitāb as-sab'īn lafẓa.* Hg. von Neḥemya Allony, "Haqdamat Rav Sa'adya Gaon le-sifro 'Šiv'im ha-Millim ha-Bodedot'", *Sefer Zeidel*, 233–252. Jersualem, 1962.

*Še'elot 'Atiqot* = *Še'elot 'Atiqot.* Hg. von Neḥemya Allony, "Ha-millim ha-bodedot bi-'Še'elot 'Atiqot'". *Hebrew Union College Annual* 28 (1957) 1–14 (Hebrew Section).

*Sefer ha-Diqduqim* = *Sefer ha-Diqduqim.* Hg. von Neḥemya Allony, "Rešimat munaḥim kara'it me-ha-me'ah ha-šeminit". *Sefer ha-Zikkaron le-Korngreen*, 324–364. Tel Aviv, 1964.

*Sefer Yeṣirah* = *Sefer Yeṣirah. Das Buch der Schöpfung.* Hg. von L. Goldschmidt. Frankfurt/M. 1894. [Nachdr. Darmstadt: Wissenschaftliche Buchgesellschaft, 1969.]

Talmide Menaḥem, *Tešuvot* = Talmide Menaḥem, *Sefer Tešuvot. I. Tešuvot Talmide Menaḥem ben Jacob ibn Saruq. II. Tešuvot (...) Yehudi ibn Šešet.* Hg. von Salomo G. Stern. Wien, 1870.

Tanḥum Yerušalmi, *al-Muršid al-Kāfī* = Tanḥum ben Josef ha-Yerušalmi, *Sefer al-Muršid al-Kāfī [ha-Madrik ha-Maspiq] le-R. Tanḥum ben Josef ha-Yerušalmi (lamed–šin).* Hg. von Hadassah Shay. 2 Bde. Jerusalem: Ha-Aqademiah la-Lašon ha-'Ivrit, 1975.

Tanḥum Yerušalmi, *al-Muršid al-Kāfī* = Tanḥum ben Josef ha-Yerušalmi, *Sefer al-Muršid al-Kāfī [ha-Madrik ha-Maspiq] me-ha-paršan ha-yadu'a we-ha-medaqdeq ha-gadol Rabbi Tanḥum b. Josef ha-Yerušalmi* I (*alef–kaf*). Hg. von B. Toledano. Tel Aviv, 1961.

Yehudi ben Šešet, *Tešuvot* = Yehudi ben Šešet, *Tešubot de Yehudi ben Šešet.* Hg. von Encarnación Varela Moreno. Granada: Universidad de Granada, 1981.

### 4.2. Sekundärliteratur

Kaplan, Roger J. 1994. *A Critical Study of the Philological Methods of Yehuda ben David (Hayyuj).* Ph. D. University of Ann Arbor.

Klijnsmit, Anthony J. 1992. *Balmesian Linguistics: A Chapter in the History of Pre-Rationalist Thought.* (= *Cahiers voor de Taalkunde*, 7.) Amsterdam: Stichting Neerlandistiek VU.

Mann, Jacob. 1926. "On the Terminology of the early Massorites and Grammarians". *Oriental Studies published in Commemoration of the 40th Anniversary (...) of Paul Haupt (...)*, 436–447. Baltimore: Hopkins Press.

Mesch, Barry. 1975. *Studies in Joseph ibn Caspi, Fourteenth-Century Philosopher and Exegete.* (= *Études sur le judaisme médiéval*, 8.) Leiden: Brill.

Skoss, S. L. 1955. *Saadia Gaon. The Earliest Hebrew Grammarian.* Philadelphia: Dropsie College Press.

Tene, David. 1971. "Hebrew Linguistic Literature". *Encyclopaedia Judaica* XVI, 1352–1401.

*Irene E. Zwiep, Amsterdam (Niederlande)*

# 35. Hebrew linguistics in Arabic

1. Massoretic grammar
2. Saadya Gaon
3. Ḥayyūǧ
4. Ibn Ǧanāḥ
5. Later grammarians
6. Bibliography

## 1. Massoretic grammar

Hebrew grammar emerged as a natural corollary of the activity of the Massoretes (Klar 1954; → Art. 33). Given the extent to which the Massoretes paid attention to the biblical Hebrew text, the meticulousness with which they counted the words and the verses of the Hebrew bible, and the detailed quality of their lists of every anomaly and curiosity in the biblical Hebrew text, they are clearly steeped in the languages of their documents, and thereby acquired a basic understanding of the grammar of Hebrew. They articulated this understanding in rules or principles which were then handed on orally from generation to generation. The *Diqduqe ha-ṭĕ'amim* of Aaron ben Ašer (10th century) is one of the first compilations of the grammatical rules or principles of the Massoretes (Levy 1936; Dotan 1990, 1977–78). Consequently, the first oral formulation of Hebrew grammar was in all probability done in Hebrew.

The written formulation of that grammar was done both in Arabic and in Hebrew, and it seems that the Arabic formulation preceded the Hebrew one. It is good to keep in mind the Arabic was the language that people understood and that was used to express the full range of human ideas, feelings and experiences.

In any case we must note that the origins of Hebrew grammar until the time of Saadya Gaon (882–942) are still enveloped in obscurity. Extant documents are generally fragmentary, and often quite difficult to identify and date. In the future we expect the situation to get better with the growing study of many Arabic fragments from the Cairo Geniza and from Russian libraries.

The first center for the study of the Hebrew grammar arose in Tiberias (Allony 1995), in conjunction with the work of the Massoretes. The Tiberian massoretic system would serve as the foundation for all grammatical theorizing, although Sephardic grammarians would pursue their task with the modifications introduced by Sephardic pronunciation (Morag 1986, 1992, 1962). One of the first Hebrew grammatical treatises in Arabic, the *Kitāb al-Muṣawwitāt* "Book of the Vowels" of Moše ben Ašer (9th century), was written in Tiberias. The attribution of this work to Moše ben Ašer has some difficulties but it seems a reasonable hypothesis (Allony 1965, 1983a, 1995; Morag 1979). This quite ancient work already reveals the influence of Arabic on vowel terminology. Equally of interest is the author's recourse to Mishnaic Hebrew because, he says, it was the language of Israel "when they did not use other languages".

The so-called *Seder ha-Simanim* "The Order of the [vowel] Signs" is a work similar to the *Kitāb al-Muṣawwitāt*. It was also written in Arabic probably in the middle of the 10th century by an anonymous author. The original title has been lost. The author deals with the topic of vowels and their changes. He makes reference to Aramaic in order to explain Hebrew "because it has a pronunciation similar to the Hebrew" (Allony 1964; Del Valle 1981a).

The mid 10th century treatise about the *šĕva* – absence of a vowel or sign of a reduced vowel – written in Arabic in Palestine deals with the Tiberian pronunciation of the *šĕva* (Levy 1936; Morag 1996). It equally belongs to Massoretic grammar just as the previously mentioned works; that is, it is focused essentially on correct pronunciation, on the letters, vowels and their changes, but it reveals a higher level of theorizing.

A new dimension in the study of grammar was introduced by the work of ʿEli ben Juda ha-Nazir, the teacher of Saadya Gaon in Tiberias, who wrote a work with the probable title of *Kitāb ʾuṣūl al-luġa al-ʿibrāniyya* "Book of the principles of the Hebrew language". But the attribution is not sure. What is noteworthy in this fragmentarily preserved treatise is its methodology. The author analyses the Hebrew biblical text, deduces from it grammatical rules and then verifies the rules by comparison with the popular Hebrew pronunciation of the uneducated people of Tiberias. In the process he either corrects the rules, sets them aside or confirms them (Allony 1970b).

Massoretic grammar is still extant with a number of Sephardic communities even after Ḥayyūǧ's discovery of the triliteral root structure of weak and geminate verbs. An example is the 11th century anonymous Arabic work, *Hidāyat al-qāriʾ* "Reader's Guide", which some scholars still attribute to Juda ibn Balaʿam (Allony 1983b); or to ʾAbū l-Faraǧ (Eldar 1994, 1985). It is an abridgement of a work originally written in Arabic dealing with the rules governing letters, vowels and accents. The work has been preserved in two versions, one longer (Eldar 1981) and the other shorter (with Hebrew translation: Busi 1983, 1984; Eldar 1986, 1992, 1994). Dating to the 13th century, there is an other Hebrew grammar in Arabic that follows the interest of the Massoretes, the *Maḥberet ha-tigan* (Neubauer 1891; Eldar 1986; for the Hebrew version see Derenbourg 1870).

From the viewpoint of method, there is the remarkable work of Juda ibn Qurayš (10th century), the *Risāla* to the Community of Fez, in which he establishes the foundations of the comparative study of Hebrew, Arabic and Aramaic (→ Art. 36). Becker (1984) published a critical edition of the work. There is also a Hebrew translation of the whole treatise (Becker 1984).

## 2. Saadya Gaon

The first complete Hebrew grammar appears with Saadya Gaon (d. 942; → Art. 34). Aside from his Arabic prologue to the *ʾEgron* (Allony 1969) and the grammatical tracts in his commentary on the *Sefer ha-Yĕṣira* (Lambert 1891; Kafih 1972), Saadya is the author of a wide ranging grammatical work, the *Kitāb faṣīḥ luġat al-ʿibrāniyyīn* (*Kĕtab ṣaḥot lĕšon ha-qodeš*) "The Book of the correctness of the language of the Hebrews", a work consisting of twelve books – therefore also widely known as *Kutub al-luġa* "Books of language". The work covered all aspects of Hebrew language, phonology, morphology, and syntax. Until now only a few fragments of the work have been published (Skoss 1933, 1951/52, 1955). However recently some new fragments have been discovered, which will be incorporated in Dotan's new edition. Of this work eight parts have been preserved (complete or defective) of the original twelve, i. e. two-thirds of the work. A perusal of the work reveals Saadya as a true linguist who studies the phenomena of language with a view to making generalizations. Thus he discovers a fixed component and a variable or functional one in every language, arriving near in this way at the modern concepts of *lexeme* and *morpheme*. All languages evidence three features of discourse: noun, verb, particle; all languages have sounds that cannot be combined in one root; with regard to vowels he discovered four principles that were valid for all languages.

Saadya's treatment of Hebrew vowels also demonstrates his ability as a linguist. As far as pronunciation is concerned, every vowel, like every consonant, takes on a specific configuration in the mouth. The deepest vowel is *al-ḥolem*, pronounced deep in the mouth at the opening of the throat. From there, in an ascending direction, the rest of the vowels have their respective locations: passing over the upper palate (*al-qameṣ*), over the upper part of the tongue (*al-pataḥ*), past the lower sides of the mouth (*al-sĕgol*), over the front of the tongue with teeth uncovered (*al-ṣere*) or with teeth covered (*al-ḥireq*), and through teeth and lips (*al-šureq*). Changes in vocalization always occur in an ascending or descending direction depending on the position of the vowel in the mouth, in quite regular fashion. Saadya produced an analysis of all vocalic combinations produced in pronouncing Hebrew, seeking thereby a criterion for the punctuation of doubtful words (Skoss 1951–52).

The various compendia of Saadya's grammar demonstrate its impact on other scholars of the time. One of these at least was written in Arabic, the *Kitāb naḥw al-ʿibrānī* "The Book of Hebrew grammar" (edited by both Eldar 1981b and Allony 1982). In his famous list of the first Hebrew grammarians, *Sefer ha-Moznayim*, Abraham ibn ʿEzra gives Saadya the honorary title of *roš ha-mĕdabbĕrim bĕ-kol maqom* "the first of the speakers/grammarians in every place". In fact he begins his list of Hebrew grammarians with Saadya. Yet the important grammatical work of Saadya scarcely survived his time. For only a few decades after Saadya's death, Ibn Ǧanāḥ (11th century) confessed that he did not know the *Kitāb faṣīḥ luġat al-ʿibrāniyyīn*.

## 3. Ḥayyūǧ

Juda ibn Daud, called Ḥayyūǧ (Fez/Córdoba, second half of the 10th century), hailed by ancient grammarians as the 'first grammarian', is regarded by modern scholars as the father of scientific Hebrew grammar because of his discovery of the triliteral root structure of weak and geminate verbs. In this way he set the proper foundation for a correct morphology of Hebrew. Details of Ḥayyūǧ's biography are lacking, hence the problem of the historical understanding of his work. Of Ḥayyūǧ's four grammatical works (*Kitāb al-ʾafʿāl ḏawāt ḥurūf al-līn*, *Kitāb al-ʾafʿāl ḏawāt al-miṯlayn*, *Kitāb at-Tanqīṭ* and *Kitāb an-Nutaf*), the first three were published in the 19th century, in the original Arabic (Jastrow 1897; Nutt 1870) as well as in the Hebrew version of Moše ha-Cohen ibn Chiquitilla (Nutt 1870) and of Abraham ibn ʿEzra (Dukes 1844; Nutt 1870; Tene 1972). Our knowledge of the *Kitāb an-Nutaf*, a philological commentary on the Former Prophets, has been advanced thanks to the publication of new fragments from the Cairo Geniza (Allony 1970a; Abramson 1977–78; 1978–79; Eldar 1978–79). The most problematic feature of Ḥayyūǧ's grammar is that of *as-sākin al-līn* (*naḥ neʿelam*, the silent letter that sometimes follows a vowel), which constituted the basis for his theory of the triliteral roots of verbs (Eldar 1984; Sivan 1989). Specifically, what is problematic is the pronunciation of the *naḥ neʿelam* (as a long vowel; cf. Del Valle 1981b), and the question of its immediate antecedents (for a discussion about Hebrew meter see Del Valle 1981; the terminology appears already in the commentary of Dunaš ben Tamim on the *Sefer Yĕṣira*, cf. Eldar 1984).

Ḥayyūǧ understood that language is a relatively fixed system that undergoes modifications by deletion (*ḥaḏf*), change (*inqilāb*), assimilation (*iddiġām*), addition (*ziyāda*) [Eldar 1989–90]. Kinberg (1986–88) has demonstrated the great influence of Arabic on Ḥayyūǧ's syntax and terminology. His grammatical terminology has recently been analyzed by Watad (1994), who has also provided Ḥayyūǧ's work with a concordance. As of now there is still no solution to the problem of whether Dunaš ben Labrat preceded Ḥayyūǧ in the discovery of the triliteral root structure of weak and geminate Hebrew verbs. The reasons for this are, first of all, that the authenticity of *Sefer tiqqum ha-sĕgagot* has been questioned and secondly, that there is no certainty about when the works of Dunaš and Ḥayyūǧ were written (Del Valle 1980).

## 4. Ibn Ǧanāḥ

The work of Ḥayyūǧ was continued by R. Yona ('Abū l-Walīd Marwān ibn Ǧanāḥ; first half of the 11th century). In his five minor works (*Kitāb al-Mustalḥaq*, *Risālat at-Tanbīh*, *Kitāb at-Taqrīb wa-t-Tashīl*, *Kitāb at-Taswiya*, *Kitāb at-Taśwīr*) [Derenbourg 1880] he completed Ḥayyūǧ's linguistic analysis of weak verbs in biblical Hebrew, and in his major work (*Kitāb at-Tanqīḥ*, in two parts, *Kitāb al-luma'* [Derenbourg 1886] and *Kitāb al-'uṣūl*) he applied Ḥayyūǧ's discovery to the whole of Hebrew grammar, thereby offering a much more complete overview of Hebrew grammar. Becker (1992, 1995) has shown that Ibn Ǧanāḥ depends on the Arabic grammarians more than anyone hitherto imagined. He demonstrated that in some cases Ibn Ǧanāḥ copied Arabic grammarians almost verbatim. This is the case, for example, in his chapter on numerals where he copies the work of Muḥammad ibn Yazīd al-Mubarrad (826–898). Of Ibn Ǧanāḥ's polemic with some of his contemporaries, especially with Samuel ha-Nagid (d. 1056), to whom are attributed three grammatical works (*Rasā'il ar-Rifāq*, *Kitāb al-Ḥuǧǧa*, *Kitāb al-istiġnā'*), we have no more knowledge than can be derived from the small fragments published by Derenbourg (1880) and Kokovzov (1916).

In the East, Ḥayyūǧ's doctrine about the triliteral root structure of the Hebrew verb was slow in being introduced, especially in Karaite circles. A typical example of this is the work of the Jerusalemite Karaite, 'Abū l-Faraǧ Hārūn (11th century). His two Hebrew grammars in Arabic (*Kitāb al-Kāfī fī l-luġa al-'ibrāniyya* and *Kitāb al-Muštamil*) were recently studied by Zislin (1962) and Maman (1996a, b), who published some fragments and are preparing a definitive edition. Poznanski (1896) published a long fragment of the *Muštamil*. The work of 'Abū l-Faraǧ not only lacks the Western Sephardic systematization of Hebrew morphology, but also bespeaks a different philosophical conception of language. There is an abridged edition of the *Kitāb al-Kāfī*, entitled *Kitāb al-'uqūd fī taṣārīf al-luġa al-'ibrāniyya*, a selection of which has been published by Hirschfeld (1892).

## 5. Later grammarians

After Ibn Ǧanāḥ's rather wide-ranging work, his immediate successors devoted their attention to monographic themes of Hebrew grammar. In the 11th century, there are three Sephardic grammarians who stand out: Moses ha-Cohen ibn Chiquitilla, Juda ben Samuel ibn Bala'am and 'Abū 'Ibrāhīm 'Isḥāq ibn Barūn. Ibn Chiquitilla is the author of *Kitāb fī t-taḏkīr wa-t-ta'nīṯ* about masculine and feminine gender. The work is known only through some citations and a few fragments collected by Poznanski (1895), and Kokovzov (1916). Ibn Bala'am is the author of three minor works (*Kitāb at-taǧnīs*, *Kitāb ḥurūf al-ma'ānī* and *Kitāb al-'af'āl al-muštaqqa min al-'asmā'*) published by Kokovzov (1916) and Abramson (1963, 1975). The *Hidāyat al-qāri'*, attributed by some scholars to Ibn Bala'am (Allony 1983b), was also written in the 11th century, not in Spain but in Palestine (Eldar 1986; Busi 1983, 1984). Ibn Barūn wrote the *Kitāb al-Muwāzana bayna l-luġa al-'ibrāniyya wa-l-'arabiyya* "Book of comparison between the Hebrew and the Arabic language", in which he takes up a subject of special interest to Hebrew grammarians from the very beginning: comparative linguistics. Kokovzov (1893, 1916) published the Arabic text, and Wechter (1964) an English version. Becker made known several more fragments of the work by means of his study of ancient citations of it (Becker 1979–80).

Of the other Sephardic Hebrew grammarian of the 11th century, 'Isḥāq ibn Yašūš, we know only a few fragments of his *Kitāb at-Taṣārīf*, published by Derenbourg (1880) and Kokovzov (1916).

The philosopher and poet, Juda ha-Levi (d. 1141), made at least two important contributions to the field of the Hebrew grammar. He distinguished three linguistic levels in the analysis of Hebrew; in the process he found an explanation for the most difficult problem in the Hebrew morphology, that of vowel changes. And, secondly, he wrote the first treatise about Hebrew meter (Brody 1930; Schirmann 1964; Del Valle 1988), which from the time of Abraham ibn ʿEzra's *Sefer Ṣaḥot* became a significant chapter of Hebrew grammar. Ha-Levi's treatises of Hebrew are basically contained in *Kuzari* (vol. II, 66–81; Del Valle 1988); the most important study of his linguistic perspectives continues to be that of Bacher (1881).

At the close of the 12th and the beginning of the 13th century, Jacob ben Eleazar (Toledo, ca. 1116–1240) wrote his *Kitāb al-Kāmil*, a summa of Hebrew grammar, of which only fragments have been preserved (Allony 1977). The author showed interest in the reduction of noun types into much smaller groups. Allony thought the *Kitāb al-Kāmil* served as the pattern which David Qimḥi would follow in his *Miklol*. According to Allony, the *Pĕtaḥ dĕbaray* is a condensed translation of the *Kitāb al-kāmil*, but this is denied by Serfaty (1978).

From the 13th century onwards, aside from some of the previously mentioned grammars of the Masoretic sort, no other significant works in Arabic on Hebrew linguistics were produced until the middle of the 15th century. Saadya ibn Danan (d. 1497) of Granada wrote *aḍ-Ḍarūrī fī l-luġa al-ʿibrāniyya*, still unedited (Ms. 1492 of the Bodleian Library of Oxford). The work offers a compendium of the grammatical doctrine of the Andalusian school. Its most notable feature is its chapter on Hebrew meter in which sixteen types of meter are described, and where the author utilizes a set of terms for feet and meter type for the first time. Heavy Arabic influence is recognizable in the work (Neubauer 1865; Del Valle 1988).

## 6. Bibliography


Abramson, Shraga. 1963. "Sefer ha-Tağnīs (ha-Simmud) lĕ-Rav Yĕhuda ben Balaʿam". *Henoch Yalom Jubilee Volume on the Occasion of his Seventy-fifth Birthday* ed. by Saul Lieberman, 51–149. Jerusalem: Kiryat Sepher.

–. 1975. *Šĕloša sĕfarim šel rab Yĕhuda ben Balaʿam*. Jerusalem.

–. 1977–78. "Min Kitāb al-Nutaf lĕ-Rab Yĕhuda Ḥayyūğ li-Šĕmu'el. 2". *Lešonenu* 42.203–236.

–. 1978–79. "Pĕraqim še-nogĕʿim lĕ-Rab Yĕhuda Ḥayyūğ u-lĕ-Rab Yona ben Ğanāḥ". *Lešonenu* 43.260–270.

Allony, Nehemya. 1950. "Yĕhuda ben Dawid wi-Yĕhuda Ḥayyūğ". *Minḥa li-Yĕhuda muggaš lĕ-Rab Yĕhuda Leb Zalotniq*, 67–83. Jerusalem.

–. 1964. "Seder ha-Simanim". *Hebrew Union College Annual* 35.1–35. [In Hebrew.]

–. 1965. "Sefer ha-qolot. Kitāb al-Muṣawwitāt lĕ-Moše ben Ašer (ha-maqor wĕ-ha-targum)". *Lešonenu* 29.9–47.

–. 1969. *R. Sĕʿadya ben Yosef al-Fayyūmi ha-'Egron. Kitāb 'uṣūl aš-šiʿr al-ʿibrānī.* Jerusalem: The Academy of the Hebrew Language.

–. 1970a. *Mi-Sifre ha-Balšanut ha-ʿIbrit bime ha-Bĕnayim.* Jerusalem.

–. 1970b. "ʿEli ben Yĕhuda ha-Nazir wĕ-ḥibburo yĕsodot ha-lašon ha-ʿibrit". *Lešonenu* 34.75–102, 187–209.

–. 1977. *Yaʿaqob ben Elʿazar Kitāb al-Kāmil.* Jerusalem.

–. 1982. "Kitāb naḥw al-ʿibrānī. Diqduq ha-lašon ha-ʿibrit". *Sinai* 90.101–127.

–. 1983a. "Sefer ha-qolot (Kitāb al-Muṣawwitāt) lĕ-Moše ben Ašer (qeṭaʿ ḥadaš mi-gĕnizat Qahir, Ky"b)". *Lešonenu* 47.85–124.

–. 1983b. "El prefacio del libro 'horaiat hakore' de Ibn Balʿam". *Estudios Masoréticos* ed. by E. Fernández Tejero, 185–203. Madrid: CSIC.

–. 1986. *Pirqe R. Seʿadyah Gaʾon. Meḥqare lašon wĕ-sifrut*, vol. I, 205–232. Jerusalem.

–. 1995. *Ha-balšanut ha-ʿibrit bĕ-Ṭiberia.* Jerusalem.

Bacher, Wilhelm. 1891. "Jehuda Halevi Concerning the Hebrew Language". *Hebraica* 8.136–149.

Becker, Dan. 1979–80. "Hašlamot lĕ-Kitāb al-Muwāzana (Sefer ha-Hašwa'a) lĕ-Yiṣḥaq ibn Barūn". *Lešonenu* 44.293–298.

–. 1984. *The* Risāla *of Juda ben Qurayš.* Tel Aviv. [In Hebrew.]

–. 1991. "Šittat ha-simanim šel Darke ha-poʿal ha-ʿibri lĕfi ha-mĕdaqdĕqim ha-qara'im 'Abū l-Farağ Hārūn u-baʿal 'Me'or ha-ʿayin'". *Tĕʿuda. Meḥqarim bĕ-Maddaʿe ha-Yahadut* ed. by Mordekay A. Friedman, 249–275. Tel Aviv.

–. 1992. "Yona ibn Ğanāḥ u-tĕluto bi-mĕdaqdĕqim ha-ʿarabiyyim". *Lešonenu* 57.137–145.

–. 1995. "Li-mĕqorotaw ha-ʿarabiyyim šel R. Yona ibn Ğanāḥ". *Tĕʿuda. Meḥqarim ha-lašon ha-ʿibrit. Sefer Zikkaron lĕ-Eliezer Rubinstein* ed. by Aron Dotan & Abraham Tal, vol. IX, 143–168. Tel Aviv.

Busi, Giulio. 1983. "Sulla versione breve (araba ed ebraica) della Hidāyat al-Qāri". *Henoch* 5.371–395.

–. 1984. *Horayat ha-Qore: Una grammatica ebraica del secolo XI.* Frankfurt.

Del Valle, Carlos. 1980. *La Escuela hebrea de Córdoba.* Madrid: Editora Nacional.

—. 1981a. "El llamado Seder ha-simanim: En los orígenes de la gramática hebrea". *Estudios Bíblicos* 39.339–376.

—. 1981b. "La Cantidad vocálica y la Masora". *Boletín de la Asociación Española de Orientalistas* 17.137–146.

—. 1988. *El diván poético de Dunash ben Labrat.* Madrid: CSIC.

Derenbourg, Joseph. 1870. "Manuel du lecteur d'un auteur inconnu". *Journal Asiatique*, 109–550.

—. 1886. *Le livre des parterres fleuris: Grammaire hébraïque en arabe d'Abou 'l Walid.* Paris.

— & Hartwig Derenbourg. 1880. *Opuscules et Traités d'Abou 'l-Walīd Merwān Ibn Djanāh (Rabbi Jōnāh) de Cordoba.* Paris. (Repr., Amsterdam, 1969.)

Dotan, Aron. 1977–78. "Min ha-massora 'el diqduq". *Lešonenu* 42.155–168.

—. 1990. "De la massora à la grammaire: Les débuts de la pensée grammaticale dans l'hébreu". *Journal Asiatique* 278.13–30.

—. 1995. "Particularism and Universalism in the Linguistic Theory of Saadya Gaon". *Sefarad* 55.61–76.

—. 1996. "Saadya Gaon on the Origins of language". *Tarbiz* 65.237–249. [In Hebrew.]

Dukes, Leopold. 1844. "Sifre Diqduq me-roš ha-mĕdaqdĕqim Rav Yĕhuda Ḥayyūğ: Grammatische Werke des R. Jehuda Chajjug aus Fetz". *Beiträge zur Geschichte der ältesten Auslegung und Spracherklärung des Alten Testaments* ed. by H. Ewald & Leopold Dukes, vol. III. Frankfurt/M.

Eldar, Ilan. 1977–78. "Mišnato ha-diqduqit šel R. Yĕhuda Ḥayyūğ ha-Sĕfardi". *Lešonenu* 42.169–181.

—. 1978–79. "Qeṭa' min kitāb an-Nutaf lĕ-R. Yĕhuda Ḥayyūğ li-tĕre 'asar". *Lešonenu* 43.254–259.

—. 1981. "Hidāyat al-qāri (The longer Arabic Version): A specimen text, critically edited, with Hebrew translation, commentary and introduction". *Lešonenu* 45.233–259. [In Hebrew.]

—. 1981b. "Kitāb Naḥw al-'ibrānī: Taqṣir mi-diqduqo šel rab Sĕ'adya Ga'on". *Lešonenu* 44.105–132.

—. 1984. "Gilgulo šel mussag as-sākin al-līn (hanaḥ ha-rafe) mi-Sĕfarad lĕ-'ereṣ Yisra'el". *Miscelánea de Estudios Árabes y Hebraicos* 33.1–9. [In Hebrew.]

—. 1985. "È davvero Yehudah ibn Bal'am l'autore della *Hidāyat al-Qāri?*". *Henoch* 7.301–324.

—. 1986. "Muḫtaṣar Hidāyat al-qāri". *Lešonenu* 50.214–230; 51–52.3–41.

—. 1989–90. "Ḥayyūğ's Grammatical Analysis". *Lešonenu* 54.169–181. [In Hebrew.]

—. 1992. "Mukhtasar (an abridgement of) Hidāyat al-Qāri: A grammatical treatise discovered in the Geniza". *Genizah Research after Ninety Years: The case of Judaeo-Arabic* ed. by Joshua Blau & S. C. Reif, 66–73. Cambridge: Cambridge Univ. Press.

—. 1994. *Torat ha-qĕri'a ba-Miqra: Sefer Horayyat ha-qore u-mišnato ha-lĕšonit.* Jerusalem.

Jastrow, Morris. 1897. *The Weak and Geminative Verbs in Hebrew by Abū Zakariyyā Yaḥyā Ibn Dāwud of Fez known as Ḥayyūğ: The Arabic text now published for the first time.* Leiden: E. J. Brill.

Hirschfeld, Hartwig. 1892. *Arabic Chrestomathy in Hebrew Characters.* London.

Kafih, Joseph. 1972. *Peruš Sĕ'adya Ga'on lĕ-Sefer Yĕṣira.* Jerusalem.

Kinberg, Naphtali. 1986–88. "Tĕfisato ha-taḥbirit šel R. Yĕhuda Ḥayyūğ". *Lešonenu* 51–52.144ff.

Klar, Benjamin. 1954. "Me-rešito šel ha-diqduq ha-'ibri". *Meḥqarim wĕ-'iyyunim bĕ-lašon, bĕ-šira u-bĕ-sifrut.* Tel Aviv: Maḥberot la-Sifrut.

Kokovzov, Paul. 1893. *Kniga svravneniya evrejskogo jazyka s arabskim Abu Ibrahima ibn Baruna* [...]. St. Petersburg.

—. 1916. *Novye Materialy dlja charakteristiki Iechudy Chajjudza Samuejla Nagida* [...]. St. Petersburg. (Repr. in *Mi-Sifre Ha-Balšanut ha-'Ibrit bime ha-Benayim* ed. by Nehemiah Allony. Jerusalem, 1970.)

Lambert, Mayer. 1891. *Commentaire sur le Sefer Yĕṣira ou Livre de la Création par Saadya de Fayyoum.* Paris.

Levy, Kurt. 1936. *Zur masoretischen Grammatik: Texte und Untersuchungen.* Stuttgart: Kohlhammer.

Maman, Aharon. 1996. "Ha-Maḥašaba ha-diqduqit bime ha-benayim: Ben ha-qara'im lĕ-rabbanim". *Meḥqarim ba-Lašon*, vol. VII, 79–96.

—. 1996b. "Ha-Maqor wĕ-šem ha-pĕ'ula bi-Tĕfisat 'Abū l-Farağ Hārūn". *Meḥqarim ba-lašon ha-'ibrit u-bi-lĕšonot ha-Yĕhudim muggašim li-Šĕlomo Morag.* Jerusalem.

Metzger, M. 1889. *Le Livre des parterres fleuris.* Paris.

Morag, Shelomo. 1986. "The Pronunciation of Hebrew in Medieval Spain: Some notes on its early history". *Salvación en la palabra. En memoria del Prof. Alejandro Díez Macho*, 749–757. Madrid.

—. 1992. "The Jewish Communities of Spain and the Living Traditions of the Hebrew language". *Morešet Sepharad: The Sephardi Legacy* ed. by H. Beinart, 103–114. Jerusalem.

Neubauer, Adolf. 1891. *Petite grammaire hébraïque provenant de Yemen: Texte arabe publié d'après les manuscrits connus.* Leipzig.

Nutt, Johan W. 1870. *Šĕloša sifre diqduq, halo hemma Sefer 'otiyyot ha-noaḥ wĕ-ha-mešek, Sefer po'ole ka-kefel, Sefer ha-Niqqud, 'ašer ḥibbĕram bĕ-lašon 'arabi roš ha mĕdaqdĕqim R. Yĕhuda ha-niqra Ḥayyūğ wĕ-targemam li-lĕšon ha-qodeš R. Moše ha-Kohen ha-mĕkunne ben Chiquitilla wĕ-yas'u la-'or ba-pa'am ha-rišona 'im ha'taqětam lě-lašon angli.* London.

Poznanski, Samuel. 1895. *Mose b. Samuel Hakkohen Ibn Chiquitilla nebst den Fragmenten seiner Schriften: Ein Beitrag zur Geschichte der Bibelexegese und der hebräischen Sprachwissenschaft im Mittelalter.* Leipzig.

—. 1896. "Aboul-Faradj Haroun ben Al-Faradj: Le grammairien de Jérusalem et son Mouschtamil". *Revue d'Etudes Juives* 33.24.

—. 1909. "Les ouvrages linguistiques de Samuel Hannaguid". *Revue d'Etudes Juives* 57.253–257.

Skoss, Solomon L. 1933. *Fragments of Unpublished Philological Works of Saadya Gaon.* Philadelphia.

—. 1951–52. "A Study of Hebrew Vowels from Saadya Gaon's Grammatical Work 'Kutub allugha' ". *Jewish Quarterly Review* 42.283–317.

—. 1955. *Saadya Gaon: The Earliest Hebrew Grammarian.* (= *Proceedings of the American Academy for Jewish Research* 21 (1952). 75–100; 22 (1953). 65–90; 23 (1954). 59–73.) Philadelphia.

Sivan, Daniel. 1989. "Biblical Hebrew Roots and Quiescents according to Judah Hajjuj's Grammatical Works". *Hebrew Union College Annual* 60.115–127.

Tene, David. 1972. "Linguistic (Hebrew) Literature". *Encyclopaedia Judaica*, vol. XVI, 1352–1390. Jerusalem.

Watad, Eli. 1994. *Mišnato ha-lěšonit šel R. Y. Ḥayyūğ mi-bě'ad li-munahaw bi-měqoram ha-'arabi u-bě-targumam ha-'ibri (kolel millon qonqordanṣiyyoni).* Haifa.

Wechter, Pinchas. 1964. *Ibn Barun's Arabic Works on Hebrew Grammar and Lexicography.* Philadelphia: The Dropsie College.

Zislin, M. N. 1962. "A Chapter from the Grammatical Work of Abu-l-Faraj Harūn ibn al-Faraj, al Kāfī". *Palestinskij Sbornik* 70.179ff. [In Russian.]

*Carlos del Valle, Madrid (Spain)*

# 36. Hebrew linguistics and comparative Semitic grammar

1. The beginnings of Hebrew linguistics in the Middle Ages: Saadia Gaon
2. Yehuda ibn Qurayš
3. The Karaites: David al-Fāsī
4. 'Isḥāq ibn Barūn
5. The end of Hebrew comparative linguistics in the Middle Ages
6. Bibliography

## 1. The beginnings of Hebrew linguistics in the Middle Ages: Saadia Gaon

With the Arab conquests following the rise of Islam in the 7th century all the countries between Spain and Persia were converted into a single territory dominated by the new religion. The majority of the Jewish people came under Muslim rule and this generally meant for the Jews a great improvement in their situation. A long period started in which Jews became part of a new and original civilisation which developed under the aegis of Arabic conquerors and kings.

A conspicuous feature of Muslim culture was its medium of expression, the Arabic language. Arabic is one of the Semitic languages, and there can be little doubt that this language offered a rich source of linguistic and lexicographic information for medieval Hebraists and Semitists alike. Already in pre-Islamic time tribes on the Arabic peninsula had developed a strong tradition of poetry which was to set an example for most later Arabic poetical activity. The conquests made Arabic an imperial language, soon also the language of a great and diverse culture. During the first centuries of Islam Arabic developed into the chief idiom of everyday use and remained the sole instrument of literature and science, superseding old culture languages like Coptic, Aramaic, Greek and Latin.

Jews belonged to the very early speakers of Arabic, although the triumphal march of Arabic was not completed in one day. In smaller Jewish communities of Babylonia, for instance, Aramaic remained the spoken language for a long time. Elsewhere, however, there was in fact much readiness to turn to Arabic in both speech and writing. The reasons for this phenomenon have been thoroughly discussed by Joshua Blau (1981: 20–22). Aramaic, the second holy language of Jewry after Hebrew, was spoken throughout Palestine, Syria, and Babylonia by both Jews and Gentiles. When Aramaic began to give way to Arabic, the Jews did not feel that they were exchanging their own language for a foreign one. The same process of Aramaic losing ground and Arabic making headway took place also among their Gentile neighbours. Therefore, the use of Arabic instead of Aramaic seemed to many of them not the abandonment of a special Jewish idiom for a foreign language, but a natural process affecting everyone, irrespective of religion or nationality.

Aramaic had been for a long time the linguistic medium of Jewish religious literature in which the most sacred matters of Judaism were discussed. The superseding of this medium almost automatically led to the penetration of Arabic into both everyday vernacular and religious writings. Arabic was unhesitatingly used by Jews within the context of their spiritual life, encroaching to a high extent upon the sacred sphere of religious literature. This development represented a revolutionary change. The acquisition of the Arabic language by the Jews led to their adoption of Arab ways of thinking and forms of literature, as well as religious notions of Islam. Thus, Arabic could be employed for all kinds of literary activities, not only for secular or scientific purposes, but just as much for expounding and translating the Bible and rabbinic treatises, for discussing Jewish law and ritual, and even for the study of Hebrew grammar and lexicography (Goitein 1955: 131–140).

From the beginning of the 10th century Jewish scholars who lived in the cultural environment of the Arabs started to realize that the comparison of Hebrew with other related languages, specifically Arabic and also Aramaic, could assist in the understanding of the more obscure passages of the Hebrew Bible. The first grammarian who used the methodology of the Arab linguists was Saadia Gaon (882–942; → Art. 33). Throughout his life Saadia wrote extensively on religious thought, exegesis, philosophy, poetry and grammar. As a rabbinically educated Jew within the Islamic orbit, fluent in Hebrew, Aramaic and Arabic, it was quite natural for him to engage in comparative Semitics. In his commentaries as well as in his Bible translations Saadia allowed himself to understand the difficulties of the biblical text in a philologically grounded way. His comparative work was mainly intended to elucidate biblical, and to a lesser extent rabbinic, terminology. This lexicographic approach is best illustrated by his concern with the rare words of the Bible, the *hapax legomena*. In his *Kitāb as-sab'īn lafẓa l-mufrada* "Book of the Seventy Isolated Words", Saadia explained obscure biblical words on the basis of post-biblical Hebrew or the language of the *Mishna*, the standard rabbinic study book on Jewish law and practice. The language of the *Mishna* is Hebrew as it developed in late Second Temple times and afterwards (200 BCE–200 CE). In vocabulary and syntax, it has an affinity to the younger books of the Hebrew Bible, but its fairly large accretion of words from Aramaic, Greek and Latin makes it quite distinct from biblical Hebrew. Saadia employed this distinctiveness of biblical and mishnaic Hebrew for the explanation of the *hapax legomena* in a clear exegetical perspective. Only occasionally he enters into a discussion of permutation of consonants in Hebrew and Aramaic (Allony 1958: 1–47; Dotan 1989: 1–14).

## 2. Yehuda ibn Qurayš

Although biblical Hebrew was the focus of Saadia's study, (Judeo-)Arabic, mostly in Hebrew script, was the language in which he wrote his grammatical works, Bible translations and commentaries. Saadia's linguistic views and his attempts to promote a better knowledge of Hebrew were able to exercise much influence on other Jewish grammarians who did the actual work of comparison and mutual explanation, thus laying the foundations for scientific comparative linguistics. About the same time as Saadia, we find Yehuda ibn Qurayš, born at Tahort in the province of Qayrawan, North Africa. When he learned that the tradition of reading the Aramaic Bible translation of the weekly Hebrew Bible portion (*Targūm*) had been abandoned in the synagogues of Fes and its surroundings, he addressed the Jewish community in a "Letter" (*Risāla*) (cf. van Bekkum 1983). In his epistle Ibn Qurayš admonished the community's elders to withdraw their decision, because reciting the Aramaic *Targūm* was extremely helpful in finding explanations for difficult biblical words and passages (Becker 1984: 116–119).

To clarify the need for the Aramaic reading, Ibn Qurayš divided his *Letter* into three separate sections, each systematically dealing with lexical comparisons. In the first section he compared the vocabulary of the Hebrew Bible with Aramaic cognates. The second section is devoted to mishnaic Hebrew. The alphabetical list of comparisons almost exclusively consists of biblical *hapax legomena* followed by explanations on the basis of words found in *Mishna* and *Talmud*. The number of the words discussed is seventy-two, and this suggests a relation with the previously mentioned "Book of the Seventy Isolated Words" by Saadia Gaon (Allony 1970: 409–425). The central theme of the third section is the comparison between Hebrew and Arabic words, including some Berber expressions. The majority of these comparisons is restricted to the treatment of phonological similarities; only in a few instances do we find semantic explanations of cognate words and there is a short description of verbal afformatives in Hebrew, Arabic, and Aramaic, illustrating the rules of inflexion. Internal morphological structures remained hidden to Ibn Qurayš. The important principle of the three root-consonants in the Hebrew verbal stem was unknown to him.

Both in his introduction and in the actual comparisons Ibn Qurayš took the genetic relationship of Hebrew, Aramaic and Arabic as a basic assumption. In the preface of his epistle he even argues that Biblical Hebrew cannot be regarded as a holy tongue in isolation, since it contains scattered Aramaic words and is mixed with Arabic expressions. This idea was the consequence of Ibn Qurayš's comparative analysis of the three languages in contact. At the same time he acknowledged the dangers of his point of view with regard to the established authority of the Hebrew Bible and its tradition of rabbinic exegesis which were at stake in the fierce polemics between defendants of rabbinic Judaism and their Karaite opponents (Zwiep 1997: 203–207).

## 3. The Karaites: David al-Fāsī

Yehuda ibn Qurayš represented an early comparativist position, but few were to build on his foundation. For most Jewish grammarians and lexicographers the very use of (Judeo-)Arabic included a comparative element in the explanation of certain linguistic phenomena of Hebrew. The best example for this situation is the grammatical and exegetical activity of the Karaites. The Karaites (whose name presumably means "those who read and study Scripture") distinguished themselves from rabbinic Judaism by their rejection of traditional rabbinic-talmudic authority and turned to a strong biblicism and literalism in their teachings. Karaite scholars of the 10th and 11th centuries emphasized the study of the Bible by producing a series of Arabic Bible translations, exegetical commentaries, and grammatical compositions. The importance of these words lies in the insight they offer us into the Karaite theories and practices of dealing with the biblical text by a general use of Arabic language and script (Khan 1990).

The 10th-century lexicographer and grammarian David ben Abraham al-Fāsī became an adherent of the Karaite community after moving from Fes to Jerusalem. Between the years 930–950 he composed a comprehensive dictionary dealing with the Hebrew and Aramaic of the Bible. This *Kitāb Ǧāmiʿ al-ʾAlfāẓ* "Book of the Collection of Words" contains many comparisons between Hebrew and Aramaic and between Hebrew and Arabic. Some of his comparative observations seem to have been taken directly from the *Letter* of Ibn Qurayš. The dictionary gives a good impression of al-Fāsī's linguistic ideas. On the one hand, he reveals a strong consciousness of comparative linguistics, and his methodology leads to many exegetical clarifications. On the other hand, his classification of Hebrew words in four groups according to the number of root letters, starting with one up to four, is hindered by his failure to recognize and formulate the Hebrew root system and the difference between radicals and afformatives. The unsatisfactory degree of clarity about the triliteral root even affected the understanding of phonological correspondences and interchanges of consonants (Skoss 1936–1945).

## 4. ʾIsḥāq Ibn Barūn

Like Ibn Qurayš and al-Fāsī, a third North African Jewish grammarian known by name, Dunaš ibn Tamīm (c. 890–c. 955), wrote a comparative lexicographic study of Hebrew and Arabic in which he tried to prove the antiquity of Hebrew. His work did not survive, but quotations are found in the books of other linguists and in a unique book on Hebrew poetics composed by the renowned poet and grammarian Moses ibn ʿEzra (c. 1055–after 1135). It is unclear from these few remarks whether Ibn Tamīm is making a conscious use of a comparative method or merely detecting parallels between Hebrew and Arabic without discerning a general line. An uncomplete copy of his Judeo-Arabic written exegetical treatise on the mystical *Sēfer ha-Yĕẓīrāh* "Book of Creation" leaves no doubt about his equal familiarity with the currents of Jewish and Muslim culture and his personal command of both Hebrew and Arabic (Bacher 1907: 700–704; Fenton 1988: 45–55).

At the end of the 11th century comparative Hebrew linguistics was enriched by a valuable writing entitled *Kitāb al-Muwāzana bayna l-luġa l-ʿIbrāniyya wa-l-ʿArabiyya* "Book of Comparison between the Hebrew and Arabic Languages". This work was written in Arabic around the year 1100 by 'Isḥāq 'Abū 'Ibrāhīm ibn Barūn, a grammarian who was born in Saragossa in the middle of the 11th century and died ca. 1128 in Malaga (Kokovcov 1893; Wechter 1964). The 11th century was notable for an improved knowledge of Hebrew linguistics, which is reflected in the division of the *Book of Comparison*. The first section is devoted to a comparative grammar in which Ibn Barūn offers a wide-ranging analysis and classification of the noun and the verb in both Hebrew and Arabic. A few comparisons include Aramaic, and another language designated by Ibn Barūn as 'foreign', possibly Spanish or Latin. Of Arabic dialects he mentions explicitly those of *Ḥiǧāz* and *Ḥimyar*.

His grammar is supplemented with a second section, an alphabetically arranged lexicon, which includes all biblical Hebrew roots having Arabic equivalents. In the introduction to the lexicon Ibn Barūn explains his comparative method by informing the reader that, while the first part of the book was devoted to a discussion of the degree of relationship between both languages with respect to grammar, conjugation of verbs and other related phenomena, the second part will consist of a lexicon comprising all roots in whose pronunciation and meaning both languages agree. The detailed analysis of these roots is preceded by a general statement in which seven closely related categories and similar aspects of individual words in both languages are summarized: (1) similarity in orthography, pronunciation and meaning; (2) similarity resulting from the interchanging of phonologically corresponding letters, like Hebrew *sīn* and Arabic *sīn*, Hebrew *zāyin* and Arabic *ḏāl*, etc.; (3) similarity resulting from the interchange of letters contiguous in the alphabet, like Hebrew *nūn* and Arabic *mīm*; (4) similarity due to metathesis; (5) similarity due to erroneous orthography, e. g., in Ezechiel 1:14 the word *bāzāq* "lightning", is similar to Arabic *bārāq*; (6) similarity of words with opposite meanings; (7) similarity in meaning but not in pronunciation.

Having enumerated the various possibilities of his comparative lexicon, Ibn Barūn touches upon semantic aspects of the Hebrew roots and their Arabic equivalents, recommending the reader to prefer the literal meaning of the word to any other interpretation, whether it be figurative or metaphorical. Here he clarifies his intentions with regard to lexical material common to both languages: the comparative method is suitable for establishing the appropriate meaning of individual roots and their derivatives for the benefit of biblical exegesis.

Having formulated his comparative methodology and his views on the most preferable ways of biblical interpretation in the introduction, Ibn Barūn exhibits many other ways of comparison in the lexicon together with a great number of quotations from the works of many important Hebrew and Arab linguistis and poets.

## 5. The end of Hebrew comparative linguistics in the Middle Ages

The *Book of Comparison* was described by Moses ibn ʿEzra in laudatory terms as a unique and important contribution, but the poet also mentions that Ibn Barūn's comparative approach met with resistance. Jewish grammarians like Ibn Barūn and his predecessors were suspect for their rationalist bias and their comparative method. Their activities were felt as part of a conflict of values in the intellectual life of Jews who struggled for their orientation between Hebrew tradition and Arabic acculturation. Most grammarians introduced their works with apologies for Hebrew linguistic science and argued that it was a valuable tool in the service of Hebrew Bible exegesis. The comparative approach, however, seemed to imply an unacceptable equivalence of the Hebrew and Arabic languages, which left the legitimacy of Hebrew comparative grammar and lexicography questionable. Ibn Barūn's work and the comparative writings of his predecessors fell into oblivion. Medieval Hebrew comparative study was largely lost, only to be resumed again in the humanistic pursuit of Hebrew by Christian scholarship.

## 6. Bibliography

Allony, Nehemya. 1958. "The Book of Seventy Words by Rav Saadia Ga'on". *Ignaz Goldziher Memorial Volume*, ed. by Samuel Löwinger, Alexander Scheiber & Joseph Somogyi II, 1–47. Jerusalem: Rubin Mass.

–. 1970. "Seventy Unique Words in the Risāla of Yehuda ibn Quraysh". *Shmuel Yeivin Jubilee Volume*, ed. by Samuel Abramsky 409–425. Jerusalem: Qiryat Sefer.

Bacher, Wilhelm. 1907. "Aus einem alten Werke hebräisch-arabischer Sprachvergleichung". *Zeitschrift der deutschen morgenländischen Gesellschaft* 61.700–704.

Becker, Dan. 1984. *The* Risāla *of Judah ben Quraysh: A Critical Edition.* Tel Aviv: Tel Aviv University.

Bekkum, Wout Jac. van. 1983. "The 'Risāla' of Yehuda ibn Quraysh and its Place in Hebrew Linguistics". *The History of Linguistics in the Near East*, ed. by Kees Versteegh, Konrad Koerner & Hans-Josef Niederehe, 71–91. Amsterdam: J. Benjamins.

Blau, Joshua. 1981. *The Emergence and Linguistic Background of Judaeo-Arabic.* Jerusalem: Ben-Zvi Institute for the Study of Jewish Communities in the East.

Dotan, Aharon. 1989. "A New Fragment of Saadiah's 'Sab'īn Lafẓah'". *Jewish Quarterly Review* 80.1–14.

Fenton, Paul. 1988. "New Fragments from the Arabic Original of Dunash b. Tamim's Commentary to Sēfer Yĕẓīrāh". *Alei Sefer* 15.45–55.

Goitein, S. D. 1955. *Jews and Arabs, their Contacts through the Ages*, New York: Schocken Books. (3rd ed., New York: Schocken Books, 1974.)

Khan, Geoffrey. 1990. *Karaite Bible Manuscripts from the Cairo Genizah.* Cambridge: Cambridge Univ. Press.

Kokovcov, Pavel K. 1893. *Kniga sravnenija evrejskogo jazyka s arabskim Abu Ibragima (Isaaka) Ibn Baruna ispanskogo evreja konca XI i načala XII veka: K istorii srednevekovoj evreiskoj filologii i evrejskoi-arabskoj literaturi*, I. St. Petersburg: Imperatorskaja Akademija Nauk. (2nd ed., Jerusalem: Qedem, 1971.)

Skoss, Solomon L. 1936–1945. *The Hebrew-Arabic Dictionary of the Bible known as Kitāb Jāmi' Al-Alfāẓ (Agrōn) of Dawid ben Abraham Al-Fāsī the Karaite (Tenth Cent.).* New Haven: Yale Univ. Press.

Wechter, Pinchas. 1964. *Ibn Barūn's Arabic Works on Hebrew Grammar and Lexicography.* Philadelphia: The Dropsie College for Hebrew and Cognate Learning.

Zwiep, Irene. 1997. *Mother of Reason and Revelation: A short history of Medieval Jewish linguistic thought.* Amsterdam: Gieben.

*Wout Jac. van Bekkum, Groningen (The Netherlands)*

# IX. The Establishment of Arabic Linguistics
# Die Anfänge der arabischen Sprachforschung
# La constitution de la linguistique arabe

## 37. The first beginnings of Arabic linguistics: The era of the Old Iraqi School

1. Methodological and textual problems
2. The Old Iraqi School: Outline of a tentative hypothesis
3. The Old Iraqi School: Further observations about its teaching
4. Bibliography

### 1. Methodological and textual problems

Students of the early history of Arabic grammar face a paradoxical situation in which the earliest extant grammatical treatises date back to the end of the 2nd/8th century and are mature products of comprehensive and sophisticated observations on the structure of Arabic. In contrast, information about the first beginnings of this scholarly branch (reportedly 130 years earlier) are documented in later works, both biographical and literary, which hardly throw any light on the formation of Arabic linguistic thinking but are characteristically abundant with personal details about alleged pioneers in the field. The first examples of this literature hark back to the beginning of the 3rd/9th century and the latest works were written in the 10th/17th century. Since it is typical of this literature to reproduce (both literally and paraphrastically) earlier accounts, it is not uncommon to find in the later treatises unique accounts which survived from earlier lost compositions.

Throughout the centuries one version of the history of the discipline of grammar, which evolved originally in the city of Baṣra in southern Iraq, took the status of an official history of early Arabic grammar. Subsequently, other early versions, such as a Ḥiǧāzi tradition, were modified in accordance with the dominant line (Talmon 1985a, 1986a). The Baṣran version refers to a statesman named 'Abū l-'Aswad (d. 69/785) as the first Arab grammarian, whose teaching was inspired by the fourth Caliph, ʿAli ibn 'Abī Ṭālib (Talmon 1985b). A series of students is then mentioned leading up to the first extant book of grammar, namely Sībawayhi's *al-Kitāb*, including, among other Baṣran figures, ʿAbdallāh ibn 'Abī 'Isḥāq (d. 117/735), ʿĪsā ibn ʿUmar (d. 149/766), 'Abū ʿAmr ibn al-ʿAlā' (d. 154/771), Yūnus (d. 183/798), and Sībawayhi's teacher, Ḫalīl ibn 'Aḥmad (d. 175/791). The writers, who deserve the title of cultural historians, often indicate a socio-linguistic situation in the first decades of Islam which enhanced the formation of interest in grammar: the decay of 'correct' Arabic, mainly in the use of case- and mood-inflexion (both called *'iʿrāb*), due to the strong influence of the 'incorrect' language of the newly Islamicized non-Arabs. A largely accepted modern view of the historical development of Arabic confirms this description of the socio-linguistic situation. The official description of the early growth of Arabic grammar presents a series of early scholars, most of whom are Arabs. Although the historians never discuss the issue of the origins of grammatical thinking, it is understood that they conceived of its formation as purely Arabic. A major development in the field, according to their description, was the introduction into Kūfa (north-west of Baṣra) of language studies, grammar and lexicography, by students of the Baṣran masters, sometime in the second half of the 2nd/8th century. Ru'āsī (d. ca. 193/809), Kisā'ī (d. 189/805) and Farrā' (d. 207/823) are the most prominent scholars of that city, whose role in the creation of a local center was decisive enough to change the course of the history of Arabic grammar by presenting a rival school to the older Baṣran center. Later development in the heart of the Islamic empire shifted the cultural center to Baghdad and brought together scholars of the two schools to create a 'mixed school' (Troupeau 1962). Again, the historians' description of the characteristics of each school is deficient; however, in addition to the demonstrated difference of terminology, they consider the Baṣran analogical reasoning (*qiyās*) more coherent than the Kūfan.

We have referred above to problems concerning the reliability of the official, pro-Baṣran version in its description of the early development of the field. Another factor which determined the emphasis chosen by early transmitters of relevant information was the polemical dialogue of various sectors of the Islamic elite which continuously attempted to reconstruct the glory of the early Islamic era according to their interests. Such attempts yielded contradictory reports about the early grammarians' creed, which were invented by both Rationalists (Muʿtazilites, Qadarites) and their Orthodox opponents (Talmon, 1988a), or about their racial origin according to the pro-Arabs and, on the opposite side, members of the anti-Arab Šuʿūbite movement. Not less significant were the efforts made by scholars from the 3rd/9th century onward to illuminate the dark age by meticulous interpretation of the earliest extant grammatical treatises. They read especially carefully the relatively few details about scholars, their views, debates and anecdotes concerning their social conduct. It was not long before an attractive literary genre of grammatical debates was invented, which included a grain of grammatical material extracted from the early texts embellished with dramatic elements and modified accordingly. The most outstanding case is the "Hornet's Controversy" (*al-masʾala az-zunbūriyya*), which describes how Sībawayhi was defeated by his Kūfan rival Kisāʾī in their public debate over the analysis of a certain syntactic structure and how he subsequently abandoned his position in Baṣra, went back to Persia and died there tragically. The authentic information was collected carefully by comparison of the syntactic teaching of Sībawayhi's *al-Kitāb* and of Farrāʾ's voluminous *Maʿānī l-Qurʾān* (Talmon 1986a, 1988b), a Qurʾānic exegesis with emphasis on grammatical analysis. Reports which seem to refer to identification of the two as rivals are first documented already in the middle of the 3rd/9th century.

Modern Western scholarship has been suspicious about essential parts of the official version for almost a hundred years and has ever since examined alternative sketches of the early history of Arabic grammar. The story about ʾAbū l-ʾAswad as the early inventor of Arabic grammar has been described as a legend; several attempts were made to prove the existence of foreign influence on its creation (notably Guidi, Merx, Praetorius, Rundgren and Versteegh) and a long prevailing critical thesis was developed by Weil (1913), which maintained that a Kūfan school never existed, that Sībawayhi's book marks the real beginning of Arabic grammar and that Mubarrad (d. 285/898), who desired to establish a continuous history of a Baṣran school, introduced a fictitious chain of scholars from ʾAbū l-ʾAswad to the historical figures, Ḫalīl and Sībawayhi. As a reaction, Weil maintained, Mubarrad's contemporary, Ṯaʿlab, who admired the Kūfan Farrāʾ, invented a parallel Kūfan chain. In a way, these modern theses constitute renewed attempts at interpretation of the scant information provided by the early extant grammatical texts from the end of the 2nd/8th century and the beginning of the next century. For a long time, these modern attempts were in an inferior position to those made by their medieval predecessors because the available (mainly published) early works were few indeed. As a result, publication of additional texts during the last decades (e.g. Farrāʾ, *Maʿānī l-Qurʾān*; Mubarrad, *Muqtaḍab* and Ibn Sikkīt, *ʾIṣlāḥ al-Manṭiq*) enabled Baalbaki (1981) to prove that Weil's thesis is incorrect as far as pre-Mubarrad evidence about the Kūfan-Baṣran linguistic dichotomy is concerned. However, scholars are now content that advancement of our understanding of the early development of Arabic grammar should be based first and foremost on a comparative study of the information provided by the earliest extant treatises of Arabic grammar and that a special effort should be made in this study to interpret the historical significance of the difference between the various grammatical descriptions provided in these early texts. In addition to Sībawayhi's *al-Kitāb*, this corpus now includes three *Qurʾān* commentaries written by the grammarians Farrāʾ, ʾAbū ʿUbayda and ʾAḫfaš, two morphological treatises written by Farrāʾ, and several other minor, partly related short treatises, such as ʾAḫfaš's two works on prosody and Kisāʾī's epistle on common mistakes and another, on similar (*mutašābih*) Qurʾānic verses. Even more promising is a series of texts whose provenance is either unknown, debatable or late, but which presumably include material and grammatical concepts harking back to a period preceding Sībawayhi's and Ḫalīl's teaching. This corpus includes, among others, the grammatical passages of the first comprehensive dictionary in Arabic, which is rightly attributed to Ḫalīl (for analysis and summary of the grammatical material in it, see Talmon 1997a), a passage in Ḫwarizmī's encyclopaedia about Ḫalīl's (presumably early) terminology of vocalic system, a short treatise attributed to Sībawayhi's contemporary, Ḫalaf al-ʾAḥmar, and several 10th century books, including Muzanī's *Ḥurūf*, Ibn Šuqayr's *Ǧumal* and a grammatical chapter in Ibn Farīʿūn's compendium of sciences. Last we mention the significant early treatise of logic written by Ibn Muqaffaʿ, either the famous statesman and translator (d. 139/756) or his son (?) Muḥammad (d. ca. 215/830). In addition to its value as evidence of the early state of understanding of logic in Islam and its significance as a predecessor to the writings of later logicians, such as Kindī, ʾIḫwān aṣ-Ṣafāʾ and others, it provides several details which create a breakthrough for attempts to uncover the role played by Greek grammatical and philosophical theorems in the early formation of Arabic grammar.

## 2. The Old Iraqi School: Outline of a tentative thesis

A turning point in the study of the pre-Sībawayhian era was reached with the analysis of the term *naḥwiyyūn* in *al-Kitāb*. Its twenty-one occurrences there are characterized by polemical argumentation which Sībawayhi levels against this group. Carter (1972a) was convinced that the group was anonymous, that the term had not yet come to mean 'grammarians', which is commonplace in (later) Arabic literature, and that members of this group were amateurs whose linguistic interest belonged to a pre-grammar era. Carter concluded that Sībawayhi, rather than Ḫalīl, was the founder of Arabic grammar. While we agree basically that Sībawayhi engaged in polemics with his predecessors, we have shown elsewhere (Talmon 1982) that their teaching is highly sophisticated and that the term *naḥwiyyūn* refers to such grammarians as ʿĪsā and Yūnus, not to an anonymous group. Our conclusion is that Sībawayhi (following his teacher Ḫalīl) had fundamental reservations about the teaching of his predecessors, mainly about their inconsistent use of analogy (*qiyās*), but considered himself their follower in many respects.

This thesis is supported by later findings and further study of Sībawayhi's criticism of the *naḥwiyyūn*. (Talmon 1993a; 1993b) It turns out that in several cases their teaching, to which our Baṣran grammarian objected so firmly, is clearly part of Farrāʾ's and Kisāʾī's teaching. We have now come to the conclusion that these late 2nd/8th century Kūfans were following an established framework of grammatical theory and detailed description held previously by Baṣran and Kūfan scholars. Their teaching reflects a stage which preceded Ḫalīl's and Sībawayhi's cardinal modifications. Whereas Baṣran scholars, beginning with ʾAḫfaš, tended to adopt many of these modifications, the prominent Kūfans stuck to the old teaching. Later generations projected the differences between Sībawayhi's and Farrāʾ's texts onto earlier generations and considered Sībawayhi a follower of an earlier local Baṣran school. It is our conviction that while Sībawayhi was an innovator and revolutionary, Farrāʾ was faithful to the teaching of Ḫalīl's and Sībawayhi's predecessors in both Baṣra and Kūfa. In contrast to Sībawayhi's teaching, which was followed first only by Baṣrans, we call this earlier stage, tentatively, "the era of the Old Iraqi School".

Another direction in which progress has been attained is the study of the relations between Ibn Muqaffaʿ's treatise and early Arabic grammar. It has often been noted that Kūfan grammarians did not use the Baṣran term *ẓarf* "container" to denote locatives. Instead they used *ṣifa*, which in both schools was known as a synonym of *naʿt* in the sense of attribute as well as adjective. The origins of the adverbial-locative *ṣifa* are traceable to Ibn Muqaffaʿ's summary of Aristotle's *De Interpretatione*, in which he unexpectedly gives the famous eight-part division of the parts of speech, known from Greek grammar and its Syriac translation (for an incomplete analysis see Talmon 1991). However, the list is a modified version whose two final items, *lāṣiqa* and *ġāya*, are unknown in any previous treatment. While *lāṣiqa* is identifiable as adjective/attribute and renders the Greek ἐπίθετον, the origin of *ġāya* is far from being clear. Later in this treatise, we learn that the two terms are useful categories with which Ibn Muqaffaʿ discussed various sentence-types of logical teaching. One particular type is called *al-kalām al-wāṣif*. It includes a member termed *ṣifa*, which amplifies the predicate and is originally, according to various indications, the adverb. These indications are provided mainly by that text and by previous Syriac accounts of the same Aristotelian treatise, in which the old term *znā* (later: *aynayūtā*; the third category "quality") was employed. According to our study (yet unpublished) there is evidence to support the view that in other instances too, a connection can be demonstrated between the logical and the Old School's (later identified as Kūfan) tradition. The body of early scholars of the Old School seem to have chosen the relevant categories and terminology for their description of the structure of Arabic. In the case of *lāṣiqa*, *ġāya* and *ṣifa*, their choice did not survive for long. In fact, there is no single instance of *lāṣiqa* left in the early grammatical writings, whereas vestiges of the other two terms have survived. *Naʿt*, another term from the sphere of logic (roughly, it means the predicate and it is used as an umbrella term for the nine categories which are predicated of the subject), replaced *lāṣiqa*; *ġāya* hardly presevered; its vestiges in the extant texts vaguely reflects the original sense. When the concept of 'adverb' was rejected, soon *ṣifa* degenerated into a preposition (for details about the situation in Farrā''s *Maʿānī* see Kinberg 1996), a prepositional phrase and otherwise into a synonym of *naʿt*. The particular *ẓarf* category of locatives, borrowed literally from logic (Aristotle's ἀγγεῖον), survived.

To conclude, comparison of the grammatical material in three types of texts – the earliest extant treatises, allegedly early grammatical works (e.g. Ibn Šuqayr's *Ǧumal* attributed to Ḫalīl) as well as early material preserved in later texts, and Ibn Muqaffaʿ's *Introduction to Logic* – has made possible the penetration of the pre-Sībawayhian era of Arabic grammar, an era which seems to be characterized, in contrast to the next stage, by a united Kūfan-Baṣran theoretical model of grammatical analysis and which may be called, for the moment, "The Old Iraqi School" (first formulation in Talmon 1993a: 74). Our findings are still rather sporadic (see Section 3); caution calls for constant examination of their relations with Sībawayhi's teaching to review our thesis that differences had resulted from his (and Ḫalīl's) deliberate modifications of the Old School's teaching.

## 3. The Old Iraqi School: Further observations about its teaching

### 3.1. Part of speech division

It will now be assumed that early Arabic grammar made use of the two main divisions of the parts of speech of the Greek tradition, the Dionysian system mentioned above, and the Aristotelian tri-partite division of ὄνομα, ῥῆμα and σύνδεσμος. The term *ṣila* makes a fine illustration of this situation. On the one hand, it may have rendered in an early stage the third and last Aristotelian part, σύνδεσμος (Syr. *esārā*, lit. "bond, tie", see Talmon 1997c). On the other hand, it denotes and reflects various classes and sub-classes of the Dionysian system, including the prepositions (see 3.2.), the article (hence its transformation into the relative pronoun or its complement, according to Farrā', Sībawayhi and later grammarians), and even a sub-class of redundant (Gr. παραπληρωματικός) words. The relations of Sībawayhi's identification of the third (and last) part of speech *mā ǧāʾa li-maʿnan* and its Aristotelian definition as ἄσημος, which have baffled scholars ever since Silvestre de Sacy, seem to be best interpreted as Sībawayhi's own modification of the original. It is uncertain if *ʾadā* reflects an original denotation of the third part of speech better than *ḥarf*.

### 3.2. The study of *ʾiʿrāb*

Interest in the changeable endings of nouns and verbs characterizes the Greek and Arabic grammatical traditions. After all, the structure of the two languages with case and mood inflection calls for special attention. The assumption that both grammatical traditions focused on the affinity of the verb's mood system with the noun's cases impelled Guidi (1877: 433) to suggest Greek influence on the Arabic concept of *muḍāraʿa*. In what follows we shall discuss various facets of the Old School's analysis of case and mood inflection.

Despite the basic similarity in structure, the two languages part on the distribution over which their prepositions range. The Arabic preposition group is restricted to the genitive relations. By contrast, their large distribution with genitive, dative and accusative in Greek has determined the prepositions' status as 'relation-words' more dramatically – so much so that the Syrian grammarians, who borrowed many central observations from their Greek predecessors, assigned to the Syriac *B*, *D*, (*W*), *L* letters – roughly the equivalents of the Greek prepositions – the function of 'relation-word'. These play a central role in the description of intricacies within their national grammar even though Syriac does not possess a similar case structure (→ Art. 51). The appellation *ḥurūf al-ʾiḍafa* and *zāʾid*s, as its multi-sided synonym given by the early Arab grammarians (including Sībawayhi) to the prepositions, reflects borrowing of the concept from their Syrian colleagues.

With the restriction of prepositions (with their early epithet: *ḥurūf al-ʾiḍāfa*) to genitival relations, the Old School grammarians exercised their talents regarding the question of how to effectively account for the *naṣb*-accusative case. Prominent among the early general concepts of *naṣb* is the one formulated as "Deviation from the Category/Predicate of [...]" (*al-ḫurūǧ min an-naʿt*). We have collected evidence in favor of its derivation from a logico-grammatical scheme whose vestiges are documented in Apollonius Dyscolus' grammar (cf., at the moment, Kemp [1978: 116] and to some extent Blank [1982: 487]). This concept may be sketched as follows: Subject-Predicate relations syntactically reflect identity relations of two grammatical categories with respect to one and the same referent; e. g., "Zayd is human" is a sentence in which the attribute 'human' is predicated on the specific noun 'Zayd' and is considered its 'category'. But in "Zayd is behind you" (*Zayd^un ḫalf-A-ka*), the last constituent is alien to the referent of the subject term and is defined therefore as 'deviating from Zayd's category (or predicate)'. The Old School grammarians believed that the case markers reflect these relations: The *rafʿ*-nominative /u/ marks the identity between subject and predicate, whereas *naṣb*-accusative /a/ (cf. *ḫalf-A-ka*) indicates non-identity and deviation from a state of identity, the normal purport of sentences according to these scholars. Interestingly, Sībawayhi's revolution against this theory was not radical. His analysis of *naṣb*, known since Carter's study (1972b) under the title of *ʿišrūna dirham^an*, is basically similar to the above *ḫurūǧ min an-naʿt*. The following generations of grammarians neglected this theory entirely and dwelt instead on the characteristics of each individual function. The linkage between these functions now focused on formal aspects based on *ʿamal* theory. Because of problems imposed by the source situation, it seems impossible to trace the whole historical process which led eventually to this neglect of a borrowed theorem. However, a break in tradition is already observable in Sībawayhi's account of this theorem.

It was Sībawayhi who first drew up a distinction between noun- and verb-opening sentences. In fact, he was the first to use the term *mubtadaʾ* in the sense of what we would call 'the subject of a noun-opening sentence'. Until then, variants of the Greek ὄνομα–ῥῆμα pair, *ism-ḫabar* and *ism-fiʿl*, were the standard corresponding categories known in Arabic grammar (Talmon 1990, then only for Farrāʾ; further progress was achieved in Talmon 1993c). Whenever identity of reference of the subject and predicate exists, it was used by the early grammarians as an explanation of the *rafʿ* mark, as explained above.

Before Sībawayhi, grammarians used to identify *naṣb* marked nominals in such structures as *li-llāhi darruhu fāris^an* as *ḫabar al-maʿrifa*, using the term which normally denotes the predicate. It was Sībawayhi's modification which separated the two by classifying this type of *manṣūb* as a member of the category of circumstantial expressions (*ḥāl*). This is an extreme example of Sībawayhi's surrender to the coherence of analogy, which ignored the temporal character of *ḥāl* and the fact that *ḫabar al-maʿrifa* may include definite forms which *ḥāl* never does.

The early texts tell how the Old School grammarians employed modal and aspectual categories in their study of the imperfect verb and its three-mark endings. Ḫalīl was the first to introduce a systematic formal concept whereby all *naṣb* cases in the imperfect verb are interpretable as due to the operation (*ʿamal*) of the either overt or covert particle *ʾan*. The process, which eventually ended with the almost complete disappearance of syntactic analysis of modal and aspectual categories from Arabic grammar, was quite rapid. While Sībawayhi did not neglect the old teaching totally, he did give prominence to Ḫalil's teaching and seems to have extended and elaborated the implication of this theorem beyond his teacher's vision.

### 3.3. Phonetics

The basic division of articulated sounds in Greek grammar includes: (a) vowels which are termed φωνήεντα "voiced"; (b) the group of liquids and other related consonants which are called "half-voiced" (ἡμίφωνα); (c) the mute, "voiceless" consonants (ἄφωνα). In spite of their wish to adopt the Greek phonetic categories, the Old Syrian grammarians could not help modifying them. The fact that the Semitic script demotes short vowels from the status of major articulated sounds seems to have influenced the two-part division of sounds into *qalaniyātā* "voiced", which are the *matres lectionis*, and *lā qalaniyātā* "voiceless", namely all the consonants. In an early Arabic theory, which the 4th/10th century Sīrāfī attributed to Farrā' (Sīrāfī, *Mā ḏakarahu l-Kūfiyyūn* 59), the two terms "voiced" (*muṣawwit*) and "voiceless" (*'aḫras*) occur in what seems to be a comprehensive division of consonants, probably into fricatives and stops, respectively. There are several vestiges of early phonetic description attributed in *Kitāb al-ʿAyn* to Ḫalīl which, in addition to the above, enhance the plausibility of a hypothesis that the early development of an Arabic indigenous consonantal division created several significant modifications in the original Greek model of a tripartite division of articulated sounds. These are as follows: (a) The long vowels followed their short cognates and were excluded from the paradigm owing to morpho-phonetic considerations involving their instability in the inflection of 'weak' verbs and nouns. (b) The bipartite division of consonants reflects various aspects of interpretation and modification of the original 'half-voiced" and 'voiceless" groups. The division attributed to Farrā' keeps close to the Greek terminology but seems to interpret the dichotomy in terms of stop vs. fricative. In Ḫalīl's teaching in *Kitāb al-ʿAyn*, the terminological clue is less revealing, but the function of the Greek 'half-voiced' as "stable" (ἀμετάβολα) in morphological inflection is roughly reflected in the description of the equivalent group (namely, the six *ḏulq+šafawiyya* letters). (c) Sībawayhi's dichotomy of *riḫwa* vs. *šadīda* takes us a step further from the original Greek system. We are unable to judge at present where the famous *mağhūra-mahmūsa* pair enters the scene (cf. Blanc [1967] and the bibliography mentioned there; Talmon 1997b).

So far, our reconstruction of the early, pre-Sībawayhian growth of Arabic grammar has claimed influence by two Greek linguistic traditions, mainly *via* a Syriac medium. The present paragraph, which treats the origin of vowel names, argues that it was Syriac Masora. Two rather strictly distinct terminological sets are used in the earliest extant grammatical works. In Versteegh's exposition of the situation in early exegetical texts (1993: 125ff.), the material is too sporadic to draw conclusions. According to Sībawayhi's scheme, discussed in Chapter 2 of his *al-Kitāb*, the *rafʿ-naṣb-ğarr-ğazm* set functions as terms of *'iʿrāb* marking, whereas the *ḍamm-fatḥ-kasr-sukūn/waqf* counterpart marks vowels in all other positions (i. e. inner and non-*'iʿrāb* endings). While this scheme was adopted by all the later grammarians, it was not strictly followed in the corpus of early grammatical treatises, not even by Sībawayhi himself! The less binding restriction observed in Farrā''s *Maʿānī l-Qur'ān*, according to which the *rafʿ* etc. set may occur in non- *'iʿrāb* positions while its counterpart never takes its place in *'iʿrāb* positions is not strictly observed in either Ibn Kalbī's exegesis or in *Kitāb al-ʿAyn*. This 'chaotic' situation suggests that the two sets reflect borrowing from the Syriac stock, which includes *ʿeṣāṣā-petāḥā-ḥebāṣā* (suggested cognates of the non-*'iʿrāb* set) and *esāqā-zeqāpā-rebāṣā* (which correspond to the *'iʿrāb* set; *rebāṣā* is a cognate of *ḫafḍ*, a common synonym of *ğarr*). While evidence for the existence of these Syriac terms before the 9th century is not certain, the terms *gārōrā* and *pāsōqā*, from which *ğarr* and *ğazm* originated, according to Talmon (unpublished) are well attested already in the 6th century. The former renders Greek παροξύτονος and means "to draw out or prolong in recitation", similar to the function of *ğarr* with /-*i*/ in Ḫalīl's example *lam yaḏhab-**i** r-rağul*, documented in Ḫwārizmī (44f.). It is not out of place to mention that the two systems of vocalization in Arabic, the earlier of which used dots and the later, small *'alif-wāw-yā'*, take after Syriac models. The idea of using small Greek letters was first realized by Jacob of Edessa (d. 708). The Arabic parallel is sometimes attributed to the much later Ḫalīl (Abbott [1972: 7] in reference to Dānī).

### 3.4. Morphology

At the moment no comprehensive study has been made of the vestiges of the Old School's theory in the field of morphology. It stands to reason that much of the morphological teaching preserved in the early extant works reflects the grammarians' interest in this field previous to Sībawayhi. Two unique passages in *al-Kitāb* refer to a large disagreement between Ḫalīl and anonymous Kūfan grammarians on a highly theoretical matter, concerning the abstract pattern of such forms as *mayyit* and *sayyid*. In *Kitāb al-ʿAyn* (cf. Talmon 1997a: 167 f.), a sophisticated methodology is used in the analysis of verbs and nouns with 'weak' roots. According to this method, each root member of a word consists of three elements, the consonantal body, its potential inflectibility and its sound value (*ḥarf wa-ṣarf wa-ṣawt*). It is far from clear if this brilliant element of morphological teaching is attributable to Ḫalīl and whether it was the author's invention. In the Hebrew *Sefer Yeṣīra*, whose date is debated among scholars (between the 3rd and 8th century) we encounter, within the description of consonants, the triad "sound, stream and thing" (*qōl ve-rūḥ ve-dābār*; *qōl* = *ṣawt*, *rūḥ* = *ṣarf* [the abstract notion], *dābār* = *ḥarf* [the substantive element]), which might be an allusion to the theoretical model observed above in *Kitāb al-ʿAyn*.

## 4. Bibliography

### 4.1. Primary sources

Farrāʾ, *Maʿānī* = ʾAbū Zakariyyāʾ Yaḥyā ibn Ziyād al-Farrāʾ, *Maʿānī l-Qurʾān*. Ed. by Muḥammad ʿAlī an-Naǧǧār. 3 vols. Cairo: ad-Dār al-Miṣriyya, 1955–1972.

Ḫalīl, *ʿAyn* = ʾAbū ʿAbd ar-Raḥmān al-Ḫalīl ibn ʾAḥmad al-Farāhīdī, *Kitāb al-ʿayn*. Ed. by Mahdī al-Maḫzūmī & ʾIbrāhīm as-Sāmarrāʾī. 8 vols. Beirut: Muʾassasat al-ʾAʿlamī li-l-Maṭbūʿāt, 1988.

Ḫwārizmī, *Mafātīḥ* = ʾAbū ʿAbdallāh Muḥammad ibn ʾAḥmad al-Ḫwārizmī, *Kitāb mafātīḥ al-ʿulūm*. Ed. by Gerlof van Vloten. Leiden: E. J. Brill, 1895.

Ibn as-Sikkīt, *ʾIṣlāḥ* = ʾAbū Yūsuf Yaʿqūb Ibn as-Sikkīt, *ʾIṣlāḥ al-manṭiq*. Ed. by A. M. Šākir. Cairo, 1949.

Ibn Šuqayr, *Muḥallā* = ʾAbū Bakr ʾAḥmad ibn al-Ḥasan Ibn Šuqayr, *al-Muḥallā, wuǧūh an-naṣb*. Ed. by Fāʾiz Fāris. Beirut & Irbid: Muʾassasat ad-Dirāsa & Dār al-ʾAmal, 1987.

Mubarrad, *Muqtaḍab* = ʾAbū l-ʿAbbās Muḥammad ibn Yazīd al-Mubarrad, *al-Muqtaḍab*. Ed. by Muḥammad ʿAbd al-Ḫāliq ʿUḍayma. 4 vols. Cairo: Dār at-Taḥrīr, 1965–1968.

Muzanī, *Ḥurūf* = ʾAbū l-Ḥusayn al-Muzanī, *Kitāb al-ḥurūf*. Ed. by M. H. Maḥmūd & M. Ḥ. ʿAwwād. Amman, 1983.

Sīrāfī, *Mā ḏakarahu* = ʾAbū Saʿīd al-Ḥasan ibn ʿAbdallāh as-Sīrāfī, *Ma ḏakarahu l-Kūfiyyūn min al-ʾidġām*. Ed. by Ṣ. at-Tamīmī. Jedda, 1985.

### 4.2. Secondary sources

Abbott, Nabia. 1972. *Studies in Arabic Literary Papyri*, III. Chicago & London: Univ. of Chicago Press.

Baalbaki, Ramzi. 1981. "Arab Grammatical Controversies and the Extant Sources of the Second and Third Centuries A. H.". *Studia Arabica et Islamica. Festschrift for Ihsan Abbas*, ed. by Wadād al-Qadi, 1–26. Beirut: American Univ.

Blanc, H. 1967. "The 'Sonorous' vs. 'Muffled' Distinction in Old Arabic Phonology". *To Honor Roman Jakobson*, I, 295–308. The Hague: Mouton.

Blank, David L. 1982. *Ancient Philosophy and Grammar.* Chico, Cal.: Scholars Press.

Carter, Michael G. 1972a. « Les origines de la grammaire arabe ». *Revue des Etudes Islamiques* 40.69–97.

–. 1972b. "Twenty Dirhams in the *Kitāb* of Sībawaihi". *Bulletin of the School of Oriental and African Studies* 35.485–496.

Guidi, Ignazio. 1877. "Sull' origine delle masore semitiche". *Boletino Italiano degli Studi Orientali* 1.430–434.

Kemp, Alan. 1978. "Apollonius Dyscolus: A pioneer of Western grammar". *Work in Progress.* (Dept. of Linguistics, Edinburgh Univ.) 2.107–119.

Kinberg, Naphtali. 1996. *A Lexicon of al-Farrāʾ's Terminology in his Qurʾānic Commentary.* Leiden: E. J. Brill.

Merx, A. 1889. *Historia artis grammaticae apud Syros.* Leipzig. [Repr., Nendeln: Kraus, 1966.]

Praetorius, Franz. 1909a. "Die grammatische Rektion bei den Arabern". *Zeitschrift der deutschen morgenländischen Gesellschaft* 63.495–503.

–. 1909b. "Ḥarf = Terminus". *Zeitschrift der deutschen morgenländischen Gesellschaft* 63.504–505; 857–858.

Rundgren, Frithiof. 1976. "Über den griechischen Einfluß auf die arabische Nationalgrammatik". *Acta Societatis Linguisticae Upsaliensis.* Nova Series 2:5.119–144.

Talmon. 1985a. "An Eighth-Century Grammatical School in Medina". *Bulletin of the School of Oriental and African Studies* 48.224–236.

–. 1985b. "Who Was the First Arab Grammarian". *Zeitschrift für arabische Linguistik* 15.128–145.

–. 1986a. "Schacht's Theory in the Light of Recent Discoveries". *Studia Islamica* 65.31–50.

–. 1986b. "*Al-masʾala az-zunbūriyya*". *al-Karmil* 7.131–163.

–. 1988a. Review of G. H. A. Juynboll, *Muslim Tradition.* Cambridge: Cambridge Univ. Press, 1983. *Jerusalem Studies in Arabic and Islam* 11.248–257.

–. 1988b. "*ʿAlā hāmiš al-baḥṯ fī l-masʾala az-zunbūriyya*". *Al-Karmil* 9.75–86.

—. 1990. "The Philosophizing Farrā'". *Studies in the History of Arabic Grammar* II, ed. by Michael G. Carter & Kees Versteegh, 265–279. Amsterdam: J. Benjamins.

—. 1991. "*Naẓra ǧadīda fī qaḍiyyat 'aqsām al-kalām*". *Al-Karmil* 12.43–67.

—. 1993a. "The Term *Qalb*". *Zeitschrift für die Geschichte der arabisch-islamischen Wissenschaften* 8.71–113.

—. 1993b. "*Ḥattā* + Imperfect and Chapter 239 in Sībawayhī's *Kitāb*". *Journal of Semitic Studies* 38.71–95.

—. 1993c. "Two Early 'non-Sībawaihian' Views of *'amal* in Kernel-Sentences". *Zeitschrift für arabische Linguistik* 25.278–288.

—. 1997a. *Arabic Grammar in its Formative Age:* Kitāb al-'Ayn *and its attribution to Ḫalīl b. Aḥmad.* Leiden: E. J. Brill.

—. 1997b. "A Study of the Early History of the Term *muṣawwit* and Related Terms in Arabic Linguistic Literature." *Massorot: Studies in Language Traditions and Jewish Languages* 9–10–11: 209–224. [In Hebrew.]

—. 1997c. "Ṣila". *Encyclopaedia of Islam.* 2nd ed. IX, 603a. Leiden: E. J. Brill.

Troupeau, Gérard. 1962. "La grammaire à Baġdād du IXe au XIIIe siècle". *Arabica* 9.397–405.

Versteegh, Kees. 1977. *Greek Elements in Arab Linguistic Thinking.* Leiden: E. J. Brill.

—. 1993. *Arabic Grammar and Qur'ānic Exegesis in Early Islam.* Leiden: E. J. Brill.

Weil, Gotthold. 1913. *Die grammatischen Fragen der Basrer und Kufer.* Leiden: E. J. Brill.

*Rafael Talmon, Haifa (Israel)*

# 38. Sībawayhi

1. Sībawayhi's biography
2. The *Kitāb*
3. Some of the grammatical theories and notions in the *Kitāb*
4. Sībawayhi's phonetic description
5. Bibliography

## 1. Sībawayhi's biography

Sībawayhi is the nickname of 'Abū Bišr 'Amr ibn 'Uṯmān, the leading figure in the field of Arabic linguistics and grammar, and the author of *al-Kitāb*,the first extant source on Arabic grammar. Not much is known about his life: he was a Persian, born in the village of al-Bayḍā', which is situated in the environment of Shiraz in Southern Iran. He lived in the second half of the 8th century AD, but the exact years of his birth and death are unknown, although it is usually said that he died in 180/796. According to tradition, he started studying Arabic at the age of thirty-two in the city of al-Baṣra in Southern Iraq (Goldziher 1952: 54–55). This city, which in that time was one of the most important cultural centres of Moslem civilization, was the stage of his scientific work. In al-Baṣra he also composed his very important treatise, *al-Kitāb*.

It may be inferred from the text of the *Kitāb* that Sībawayhi was mainly influenced by his teacher al-Ḫalīl ibn 'Aḥmad al-Farāhīdī, who died between the years 170/786–175/791. His other teachers were 'Abū 'Amr ibn al-'Alā' (d. 154/770), 'Abū l-Ḫaṭṭāb al-'Aḫfaš (d. 177/793), Yūnus ibn Ḥabīb (d. 182/798?) and 'Īsā ibn 'Umar aṯ-Ṯaqafī (d. 149/766).

According to tradition, Sībawayhi participated in a competition about difficult grammatical problems, which took place in the palace of the vizier Yaḥyā ibn Ḫālid al-Barmakī in Baghdad. His rival was the famous Kūfī grammarian al-Kisā'ī (d. 183/799), who won this competition. It is said that Sībawayhi lost, because al-Kisā'ī bribed some Beduin informants who claimed that the answers given by him were the correct ones (Ibn al-'Anbārī, *'Inṣāf* 292–295). Sībawayhi was so frustrated that he did not go back to al-Baṣra. Instead, he went back to his birthplace, the village of al-Bayḍā', where he died (Goldziher 1952: 55). According to other traditions, he died in al-Baṣra or in Shiraz (Ibn al-'Anbārī, *Nuzha* 42).

Sībawayhi's admiration for his teachers, especially for al-Ḫalīl, is indicated by the text of the *Kitāb*, where they are frequently quoted (cf. Humbert 1995: 8–14): al-Ḫalīl 608 times (Troupeau 1976: 228–230); Yūnus 217 times (Troupeau 1976: 230–231); 'Abū 'Amr 53 times (Troupeau 1976: 227–228); 'Abū l-Ḫaṭṭāb al-'Aḫfaš 58 times (Troupeau 1976: 227) and 'Īsā 20 times (Troupeau 1976: 230).

Sībawayhi often mentions linguistic information which he heard from his teachers, as well as their grammatical notions and analysis. He also mentions some of his discussions with al-Ḫalīl, which were based on questions asked by Sībawayhi. When Sībawayhi finds that the views of some of his teachers differ on a certain point, he usually accepts those of al-Ḫalīl.

It should be emphasized that Sībawayhi's pupil, 'Abū l-Ḥasan al-'Aḫfaš (d. 215/830 or 221/835), does not mention Sībawayhi's name in his famous book, *Ma'ānī l-Qur'ān*. According to tradition, al-'Aḫfaš even intended to claim the *Kitāb* as his own (Ibn al-'Anbārī, *Nuzha* 42).

Sībawayhi's relations with the grammarians of the Kūfa school of grammar, Ḫalaf al-'Aḥmar (d. ±180/796), al-Farrā' (d. 207/822) and al-Kisā'ī were tense (Ibn al-'Anbārī, *'Inṣāf* 293). Irrespective of that, it is said that al-Kisā'ī studied the *Kitāb*, and that al-Farrā' kept a copy of it under his pillow (Derenbourg in the introduction to his edition of the *Kitāb* I, xxiv).

## 2. *The Kitāb*

### 2.1. The contents of the *Kitāb*

As mentioned above, Sībawayhi is the author of *al-Kitāb* "The Book", the first Arabic grammar known to us. It consists, in Derenbourg's edition, of 571 chapters, published in two volumes (vol. I 441 pp., vol. II 481 pp.; on the manuscripts and editions of the *Kitāb* see Humbert 1995). The *Kitāb* contains a description and analysis of the Old Arabic language, as well as some linguistic theories and notions.

The discussions in the *Kitāb* are divided into three main parts: syntax (vol. I), morphology and phonetics (vol. II). The book also includes some introductions, dealing with the following topics: (1) the division of words into three parts of speech (*Kitāb* I, 1); (2) the declinable and indeclinable endings of words (*Kitāb* I, 1–6); (3) the relation between form and meaning: (i) the difference in meaning between different forms; (ii) the phenomenon of synonymity; (iii) the phenomenon of polysemy (*Kitāb* I, 6–7); (4) phenomena deviating from the norm (*Kitāb* I, 7); (5) correct and incorrect utterances, according to logical and formal criteria (*Kitāb* I, 7); (6) the differences between the poetical language and the spoken language (*Kitāb* I, 7–10).

The following is a small selection of topics discussed in the *Kitāb*:

I Syntax
1. the two indispensable parts of the sentence (*Kitāb* I, 3)
2. sentences beginning with intransitive and transitive verbs (verbal sentences) (*Kitāb* I, 10–21)
3. sentences beginning with a noun (nominal sentences) (*Kitāb* I, 239)
4. interrogative sentences (*Kitāb* I, 39–56)
5. sentences expressing command or prohibition (*Kitāb* I, 58–61)
6. negative sentences (*Kitāb* I, 61–63)
7. conditional sentences (*Kitāb* I, 384–401)
8. elliptic sentences (*Kitāb* I, 116–125; 126–137; 140–151)
9. the vocative and other exclamations (*Kitāb* I, 262–300)

II Morphology
1. diptote and triptote nouns (*Kitāb* II, 1–40; 44–56)
2. indeclinable nouns (*Kitāb* II, 40–44)
3. the formation of relative adjectives by adding the ending *-iyy* (called by Sībawayhi *'iḍāfa*, rarely *nisba*) (*Kitāb* II, 65–88)
4. the formation of diminutives (*Kitāb* II, 104–146)
5. the broken plural (*Kitāb* II, 181–188; 190–194; 196–209; 211–224)
6. verb forms and classes (*Kitāb* II, 224–240; 243–263; 270–277; 391–401; 416–425; 429–436; 446–447)

III Phonetics
1. the consonants and the long vowels (*ḥurūf*) (*Kitāb* II, 452–455)
2. the assimilation of consonants (*Kitāb* II, 455–481)
3. the *'imāla* (see below 4.2.) (*Kitāb* II, 279–294)
4. pausal forms (*Kitāb* II, 306–320).

### 2.2. Sībawayhi's method and sources

The text of the *Kitāb* makes clear that Sībawayhi's method is mainly descriptive, although some prescriptive remarks can also be found. His description and analysis of Arabic is based on three main sources: (1) the text of the *Qur'ān*; (2) ancient Arabic poetry; (3) the speech of some native speakers whom he calls *al-'Arab*. The data in the *Kitāb* indicate that the language spoken by the *'Arab* is the main source of the description (Levin 1994: 204–214). These *'Arab* appear to have been Beduins belonging to the various tribes living in the environment of al-Baṣra.

Sībawayhi was aware of the fact that the Beduins who supplied him with his linguistic information spoke various dialects. Hence his description of their language deals in detail with many dialectal features and differences typical of their language. The dialects Sībawayhi described were of the Old Arabic type, differing in their phonological, morphological and syntactic structure from Modern Arabic dialects. Nevertheless, some of the dialectal phenomena described by Sībawayhi still exist in the contemporary modern dialects. A comparison between some of these modern dialectal phenomena and their corresponding phenomena, as described in the *Kitāb*, proves that Sībawayhi's linguistic description is reliable and accurate (Levin 1994: 217–236).

Sībawayhi does not consistently give the distribution of the dialectal phenomena he describes. He quite often ascribes such phenomena either to the dialects of the Tamīm tribe, or to those of al-Ḥiǧāz (see the references in Troupeau 1976: 244–245). Apart from these he occasionally mentions features from some fourteen other dialects. However, the quantity of dialectal features discussed in the *Kitāb* without tribal or geographical ascription is much larger than those explicitly assigned to a certain dialect or dialects. Sībawayhi was aware of the frequency of occurrence of the various phenomena in the speech of the Beduins (see, for example, *Kitāb* I, 11; 89; 90; 127; 336; 356; II, 149).

2.3. Sībawayhi's evaluation of his sources

In Sībawayhi's period, the language of the urban population of Iraq differed from that of the Beduins: while the former spoke dialects of the Modern Arabic type, some of the latter still spoke dialects of the Old Arabic type (Blau 1997: 17–18), and some of them spoke transitional dialects, of a stage between Old and Modern Arabic.

Sībawayhi believed that the speech of those Beduins who spoke dialects of the old type was a model to be imitated by anyone who wanted to speak good Arabic (Levin 1994: 217). Hence he offered prescriptive remarks inferred from his description of their speech. His aim in including such comments was to instruct educated people who used the urban modern dialects how to speak good Arabic, i. e., how to speak in an Old Arabic dialect, or in a mixture of more than one. It is clear that Sībawayhi's prescriptive remarks do not form any deviation from his descriptive method, since they were made for the sake of people interested in learning the language of the *ʿArab*, either as a foreign dialect or even as a foreign language.

To Sībawayhi, the status of the speech of the Beduins as a source of linguistic information is the same as that of the *Qurʾān*, and higher than that of ancient poetry (Levin 1994: 215). Linguistic forms and syntactic constructions heard from the Beduins are accepted by Sībawayhi even if they differ from those found in the *Qurʾān* (Levin 1994: 215). Sometimes, he even holds that grammatically, a given syntactic construction in the dialect of certain Beduins is preferable to a corresponding construction found in the *Qurʾān*. The most salient example is that of nominal sentences negated by *mā*. In the dialects of al-Ḥiǧāz, the predicate of such sentences takes the accusative, as in *mā ʿabdu llāhi ʾaḫaka* "ʿAbdallah is not your brother" (*Kitāb* I, 21), but in the dialects of the Banū Tamīm, the predicate in the corresponding construction takes the nominative, as in *mā ʿabdu llāhi ʾaḫūka*. Sībawayhi prefers the Banū Tamīm construction, although the Ḥiǧāzī construction is the one found in the *Qurʾān* in the example *mā hāḏā bašaran* "This is not a human being" (Q. 12/31; Levin 1994: 215).

Sībawayhi accepts given syntactic constructions used by certain Beduins, although these constructions do not agree with his grammatical theories, and he tries hard to solve the theoretical problems thus created (Levin 1994: 234–235). He does not show any preference for any one dialect. In most of his linguistic discussions he does not say that a certain dialectal feature is preferable to a corresponding one in another dialect. In some of his discussions he says that certain dialectal features occurring in the dialects of Tamīm are preferable to the corresponding features in the dialects of al-Ḥiǧāz (*Kitāb* I, 21–22; 317; 356–357), and vice versa (*Kitāb* II, 474; 479).

Since the speech of the Beduins is, in Sībawayhi's view, the highest linguistic authority, his main criterion for accepting or rejecting a given syntactic construction is its occurrence or non-occurrence in the speech of the Beduins. As he observed that certain syntactic constructions used by the Beduins are restricted to given expressions, he declares that one should use these specific constructions only with the expressions articulated by the Beduins in these constructions (see, for example, *Kitāb* I, 69; 166; 173; 174–175).

The above principle led Sībawayhi to reject syntactic structures inferred by the grammarians, since they did not exist in the spoken language of the Beduins (Levin 1994: 235–236; cf. Talmon 1982: 22–24). He was very critical in this respect, especially as regards the view of his teacher, Yūnus, according to whom one can use in speech morphological forms and syntactic constructions not occurring in Beduin speech, since they can be inferred from it by analogy (*Kitāb* I, 335–336; 355; II, 160).

The *Kitāb* text shows that the status of the early poetical language, as a source for Sībawayhi's linguistic description, is inferior to that of the spoken language of the *ʿArab*. Sībawayhi explicitly says that the poetical language differs in certain respects from the spoken language of the Beduins and he mentions some of the typical phenomena occurring in it because of poetic licence (*Kitāb* I, 7–10; 41). Apart from this he holds that some of the syntactic constructions occurring in the ancient poetry are inappropriate in speech (*Kitāb* I, 18; 33; 83). Thus it is clear that Sībawayhi does not consider the poetical language of the *ʿArab* as a model to be imitated by anyone wishing to speak good Arabic.

### 2.4. Evaluation of the *Kitāb*

The *Kitāb*, apart from being the first Arabic grammar that we have, is also the most important work and the most reliable source in this field. Sībawayhi's main achievement is his accurate and detailed description of the Old Arabic language. There can be no doubt that this description is the result of his original study and research, irrespective of the fact that only part of the linguistic information on which it is based was collected by the author himself from the speech of the Beduins, while the rest was gathered by his teachers.

Sībawayhi's description is authentic and reliable, as attested by the fact that some of the dialectal phenomena he describes still exist in the contemporary modern dialects (Levin 1994: 217–234). The way Sībawayhi dealt with the old Beduin dialects show that he was a great descriptive linguist who was mainly interested in the field of the old Arabic dialects.

The numerous citations of the views of Sībawayhi's teacher, al-Ḫalīl, indicate that many of the latter's linguistic theories and notions are incorporated in the *Kitāb*, most of al-Ḫalīl's views being explicitly accepted by Sībawayhi (cf. Blanc 1975: 1268).

The impact of the *Kitāb* on the grammatical literature is extraordinary (→ Art. 39): the later grammarians of the 9th and 10th centuries, like al-Mubarrad (d. 285/898), Ibn as-Sarrāǧ (d. 316/928), ʾAbū ʿAlī al-Fārisī (d. 377/987), Ibn Ǧinnī (d. 392/1002) and others admired Sībawayhi and regarded the *Kitāb* as the best grammatical authority. They adopted Sībawayhi's description of Old Arabic, as well as most of the grammatical theories and notions he expressed in the *Kitāb*. They differ from him only in part of their terminology, and in minor topics. The later grammarians, following those of the 9th and 10th centuries, also accepted Sībawayhi's description, as well as his grammatical theories. These grammarians were influenced by Sībawayhi, either directly, by studying the *Kitāb*, or indirectly, by studying the works of the 9th and 10th century authors.

Since it is evident that Sībawayhi's description and analysis of Arabic is mainly based on the spoken dialects of the Beduins, and since all the grammatical treatises written after him rely on his description, it is clear that traditional Arabic grammar is mainly based on the spoken dialects of the Beduins, and not on written texts. It should be emphasized that the description and analysis of so-called classical Arabic texts started only later in Europe in the 16th century (→ Art. 100).

### 2.5. Commentaries, translations and indexes of the *Kitāb*

Since the *Kitāb* is one of the most difficult texts in Arabic literature, it frequently needs interpretation. Unfortunately, we do not have a complete satisfactory commentary of this book. The only complete commentary of the *Kitāb*, as far as it is known, is that of ʾAbū Saʿīd as-Sīrāfī (d. 368/979). Although as-Sīrāfī's commentary is very helpful in many respects, it should be emphasized that frequently he expresses his own views, instead of referring to Sībawayhi's text. Thus, he does not always deal with difficult passages in the *Kitāb*. Sometimes his interpretation is incorrect or unsatisfactory (on al-Fārisī's criticism of as-Sīrāfī's scholarship see al-Fārisī, *Masāʾil* 159–176). Most of as-Sīrāfī's commentary is still unpublished (cf. Masʿad, n. d.; for a list of manuscripts of his work see Hegazi 1971: 10–16).

Another famous incomplete commentary is that of ʿAlī ibn ʿĪsā ar-Rummānī (d. 384/994). Most of its text is unpublished (for a study on this commentary see Mubārak [1974: 161–194] which includes a description of this work and its manuscripts). Part of ar-Rummānī's text has been published in Mubārak (1974: 345–457), and by ad-Damīri.

The work of ʾAbū ʿAlī al-Fārisī (d. 377/987), *at-Taʿlīqa ʿalā Kitāb Sībawayhi*, is an excellent commentary on selected problems in the text of the *Kitāb*. Another commentary on selected problems in Sībawayhi's text is *an-Nukat fī Šarḥ Kitāb Sībawayhi* by al-ʾAʿlam aš-Šantamarī (d. 1083). For other commentaries of Sībawayhi see Hegazi (1971: 1–3).

The *Kitāb* was translated into German by Jahn (1895–1900). This translation was criticized by many scholars because of the errors and the misinterpretations occurring in it (see, e. g., Praetorius 1894). However, it should be emphasized that Jahn's translation is a pioneer work which is still very important and useful for the understanding of Sībawayhi's text. This work includes a good selection of numerous citations from as-Sīrāfī's commentary.

The following indexes of the *Kitāb* may be mentioned: (1) Troupeau (1976), which is arranged according to Derenbourg's edition of Sībawayhi; (2) ʿUḏayma (1975), arranged according to the Būlāq edition; this index is not arranged alphabetically (!); (3) the index volume (volume 5) of Hārūn's edition; (4) an-Naffāḫ (1970), arranged according to the Būlāq edition; this is only an index to verses and to examples from the *Qurʾān* and *Ḥadīṯ*.

## 3. Some of the grammatical theories and notions in the *Kitāb*

### 3.1. The theory of *ʿamal*

The notion called here the 'theory of *ʿamal*' is one of the main theories of Arabic grammar. It was invented by the early grammarians preceding Sībawayhi to explain the phenomenon of the declension of the case endings of the noun and the mood endings of the imperfect verb, known as the phenomenon of *ʾiʿrāb*. According to this theory, the case and mood endings change because of certain factors which are called *ʿawāmil*, singular *ʿāmil* "something which affects". The sense of *ʿāmil* as a technical term is "a factor affecting and determining the case ending of the noun and the mood ending of the imperfect verb" (Levin 1995a: 218). The effect of the *ʿāmil* is called *ʿamal*. The grammarians believe that most of the *ʿawāmil* are words included in the sentence expressed by the speaker. For example: in the utterance *yaḏhabu zaydun* "Zayd is going away", the verb *yaḏhabu* is the *ʿāmil* affecting the subject *zaydun* in such a way that it takes the nominative ending *-u* (Levin 1995a: 219–220).

According to Sībawayhi, some of the *ʿawāmil* are not words, but abstract notions. For example, the *ʿāmil* called *ibtidāʾ*, which affects the subject of the nominal sentence in such a way that it takes the nominative, is the aggregate of two qualities of the subject: the fact that its case ending is not affected by any word occurring in the sentence and the fact that it takes a predicate. In the utterance *ʿabdu llāhi munṭaliqun* "ʿAbdallah is leaving", for instance, the subject *ʿabdu llāhi* takes the nominative because its case ending is not affected by any word occurring in the sentence and because it takes the predicate *munṭaliqun* (*Kitāb* I, 239). Similarly, Sībawayhi holds that the *ʿāmil* producing the indicative endings in the imperfect verb is also an abstract notion. According to him, this verb takes the indicative whenever it occurs in the sentence in a position where it is possible for a noun to occur, as in the example *yaqūlu zaydun ḏā* "Zayd says this". In this example, the verb *yaqūlu* takes the indicative ending *-u* since it occurs in a position where the subject of a nominal sentence can occur (*Kitāb* I, 363–364).

It should be emphasized that according to this theory, the effect (*ʿamal*) of a certain *ʿāmil* is produced only when the noun or the imperfect verb affected by it occur in a given sentence or in a given clause. Hence, an isolated noun or an isolated imperfect verb, not part of a sentence or a clause, cannot be affected by any *ʿāmil* (Ǧurǧānī, *Muqtaṣid* I, 214; Zamaḫšarī, *Mufaṣṣal* 12).

### 3.2. The theory of *taqdīr*

The theory called here the 'theory of *taqdīr*' is also one of the main theories of the early grammarians. This theory is based on the notion of al-Ḫalīl, Sībawayhi's teacher, that when pronouncing given utterances, the speaker intends it to be as if he were expressing another utterance, differing in construction, but not in its intended meaning from his literal utterance (*Kitāb* II, 137). Thus, when the speaker expresses a given literal utterance, a corresponding imaginary utterance exists in his mind. If we mark the literal utterance by X and its corresponding imaginary utterance by Y, we can say that the main notion of the theory of *taqdīr* is that the speaker intends, or imagines, that when he says X it is as if he were saying Y. For example: Sībawayhi believes that when saying *zaydan ḍarabtuhu* (= X) "Zayd [acc.], I hit him", the speaker intends that it is as if he were saying *ḍarabtu zaydan ḍarabtuhu* (= Y) lit. "I hit Zayd, I hit him". The imaginary utterance *ḍarabtu zaydan ḍarabtuhu* is called by the later grammarians *taqdīr* (Levin 1997: 142–145). The definition of *taqdīr* in this case is "the imaginary utterance which the speaker intends as if he were saying it, when expressing a given literal utterance" (Levin 1997: 151–157).

Sībawayhi's terminology referring to the *taqdīr* theory mainly consists of terms and phrases derived from the roots *n-w-y*, *r-w-d*, *m-ṯ-l* and *ḍ-m-r*. The term *taqdīr*, referring to the imaginary utterance intended by the speaker, occurs in the *Kitāb* only once (I, 259). Sībawayhi usually uses instead of *taqdīr* the phrase *ka'annahu qāla* "It is as if he [i. e. the speaker] were saying" (*Kitāb* I, 30; Levin 1997: 151–152), as well as the term *tamṯīl* "an utterance which the speaker imagines as if he were saying it" (*Kitāb* I, 28; 32; 42; 65; see the references in Troupeau 1976: 193–194; Levin 1997: 160–161, and see Ayoub 1991). In this section the term *taqdīr* will be used for the sake of convenience since it has become the standard term in later grammar.

The theory of *taqdīr* was invented by the grammarians in order to solve a theoretical difficulty, and they apply it whenever they find that the literal construction of a certain utterance does not accord with one of their grammatical theories. Hence, even an ordinary utterance such as *zaydan ḍarabtuhu* is held to have a corresponding *taqdīr* construction, since its literal construction does not accord with the principles of the theory of *ʿamal*: the form *ḍarabtuhu*, occurring in the beginning of the *taqdīr* construction, is unnecessary for understanding the literal utterance *zaydan ḍarabtuhu*. Grammatically, however, it is indispensable, since it is considered the *ʿāmil* producing the accusative in *zaydan*: according to the theory a verb cannot be simultaneously the *ʿāmil* of a noun and a pronoun referring to the same noun (Levin 1985a: 122–123). In the utterance *zaydan ḍarabtuhu*, the verb included in the form *ḍarabtuhu* is the *ʿāmil* affecting the pronoun *-hu* in such a way that it takes the accusative form. Since this pronoun refers to its antecedent *zaydan* in *zaydan ḍarabtuhu*, the verb included in *ḍarabtuhu* cannot be the *ʿāmil* of *zaydan*. To create the *ʿāmil* producing the accusative in *zaydan*, Sībawayhi and other grammarians contend that the *taqdīr* construction of *zaydan ḍarabtuhu* is *ḍarabtu zaydan ḍarabtuhu* (Levin 1997: 144–145; 151–152). In the *taqdīr* construction, the verb *ḍarabtu* preceding *zaydan* is the *ʿāmil* producing the accusative in *zaydan*. Thus, the construction of the imaginary utterance called *taqdīr* is brought into line with the principles of the theory of *ʿamal*.

It may be inferred from the sources that, in the grammarians' view, the relevant construction as far as grammatical analysis is concerned, is that of the imaginary utterance (*taqdīr*), and not that of the literal one (*lafẓ*), since it is the construction of the former which exists in the speaker's mind. This notion led the grammarians to believe that a *taqdīr* construction, according with their theories, enables the occurrence of a corresponding literal utterance which does not comply with them.

Sībawayhi assumes the *taqdīr* to exist in the speaker's mind in the following four cases:

(1) When he holds that a given part of the sentence is unexpressed by the speaker since it is concealed in his mind. The unexpressed part is usually called by him *muḍmar* "concealed [in the mind]" (*Kitāb* I, 32; 42), or *muḍmar fī n-niyya* "concealed in the mind [of the speaker]" (*Kitāb* I, 106). The considerations leading Sībawayhi to hold that a given part of the sentence is concealed in the speaker's mind are usually grammatical, but sometimes they are both grammatical and semantic. Frequently, he believes that a given part of the sentence is unexpressed in the literal construction since the latter does not include a word which can serve as an *ʿāmil*, producing the case ending of a given noun, or the mood ending of a given imperfect verb. Thus, he holds that when the speaker says *zaydan ḍarabtuhu* "Zayd [acc.], I hit him", he intends it to be as if he were saying *ḍarabtu zaydan ḍarabtuhu* "I hit Zayd, I hit him" (*Kitāb* I, 31–32) (see above).
(2) Sībawayhi believes that there are given utterances which include a 'superfluous' part. In this case he assumes that a corresponding imaginary utterance, which does not include this 'superfluous' part exists in the speaker's mind. For example, Sībawayhi says that when pronouncing the utterance *mā 'atānī 'aḥadun 'illā zaydun* "Nobody came to me except Zayd", the speaker intends it to be as if he were saying *mā 'atānī 'illā zaydun* (*Kitāb* I, 315; for the theoretical considerations leading Sībawayhi to hold this view see Levin 1997: 146–148). Note that the *taqdīr* construction in this case is shorter than the literal one.
(3) Sībawayhi believes that in given syntactic constructions the literal word order of the sentence differs from that intended by the speaker. For example, when the speaker says *ḍarabanī wa-ḍarabtuhum qawmuka* "Your people hit me and I hit them", the speaker intends it to be as if he were saying *ḍarabanī qawmuka wa-ḍarabtuhum* (*Kitāb* I, 30).

(4) Sībawayhi also believes that when pronouncing given utterances, the speaker intends to express another utterance, corresponding in sense to his literal one. For example, when saying *mā 'aḥsana zaydan* "How good is Zayd!", the speaker imagines that it is as if he were saying *šay'un 'aḥsana zaydan*, lit. "Something made Zayd good" (for the theoretical considerations leading Sībawayhi to hold this view see Levin 1997: 148–149).

### 3.3. The division of sentences according to their structure

It can be inferred from Sībawayhi's discussions that he distinguishes, syntactically, between two types of sentences: sentences beginning with a verb, later called *ǧumla fi'liyya* "verbal sentence", and sentences beginning with a noun, or a preposition + genitive, later called *ǧumla ismiyya* "nominal sentence" (*Kitāb* I, 20–21; 239).

The nominal sentence is called by Sībawayhi *ibtidā'*. The subject of this type of sentence is called by him *mubtada'* or *ibtidā'*, and the predicate is usually called *mabniyy 'alā l-mubtada'* or *mabniyy 'alayhi* (*Kitāb* I, 239). Sometimes it is called by him *ḫabar* (*Kitāb* I, 238). The verbal sentence has no specific term in the *Kitāb*. Its subject is called *fā'il* "agent", and its predicate is sometimes referred to as *fi'l al-fā'il* "verb of the *fā'il*".

Sībawayhi's distinction between nominal and verbal sentences seems to derive from the theory of *'amal*: when the subject takes the nominative because of the effect of the abstract *'āmil* called *ibtidā'*, the sentence is classified as a nominal sentence. But when the subject takes the nominative because of the effect of the verbal predicate the sentence is classified as a verbal sentence. Sentences beginning with *'inna wa-'aḫawātuhā* are neither nominal nor verbal since their subject takes the accusative because of the effect of the particle, as in the example *'inna zaydan munṭaliqun* "Verily Zayd is leaving".

### 3.4. The division of sentences according to their content

Sībawayhi divides sentences, according to their content, into three main types:

(i) *ḫabar* "declarative sentence". This category includes both affirmative and negative sentences, as well as conditional sentences (*Kitāb* I, 49; 61)
(ii) *istifhām* "interrogative sentence" (*Kitāb* I, 45; 49)
(iii) *al-'amr wa-n-nahy* "sentences expressing a command or a prohibition" (*Kitāb* I, 58)

### 3.5. The sentence and its parts

The sentence is called by Sībawayhi *kalām* (*Kitāb* I, 50; 223). It should be emphasized that the same form usually denotes in the *Kitāb* an utterance which is not a complete sentence (*Kitāb* I, 239).

The parts of the sentence are divided into two main groups: indispensable parts, and dispensable parts. Every sentence includes two indispensable parts: the first, which is either the subject or the predicate, is called *musnad*; and the second, which is also either the subject or the predicate, is called *musnad 'ilayhi*. The literal sense of *musnad* is "that [part of the sentence] upon which the [*musnad 'ilayhi*] leans", while the literal sense of *musnad 'ilayhi* is "that [part of the sentence] which leans upon it [i. e., upon the *musnad*]" (Levin 1981: 150–151).

For example, in the nominal sentence *'abdu llāhi 'aḫūka* "'Abdallah is your brother", the subject *'abdu llāhi* is the *musnad* and the predicate *'aḫūka* is the *musnad 'ilayhi*, while in the verbal sentence *yaḏhabu zaydun* "Zayd will go away", the predicate *yaḏhabu* is the *musnad* and the subject *zaydun* is the *musnad 'ilayhi* (Levin 1981: 145–151; 162–163).

In Sībawayhi's view, the status of the direct object is a special one: it is inferred on the one hand that Sībawayhi holds that a verbal sentence beginning with a transitive verb is complete even if it does not take a direct object (*Kitāb* I, 223; Levin 1995b: 196). However, we find elsewhere in the *Kitāb* that Sībawayhi feels that the information supplied by such a sentence is incomplete because of the absence of an object (*Kitāb* I, 11; Levin 1995b: 196). Although Sībawayhi believes that the direct object is not, formally, an indispensable part of the sentence, he holds that it is the part which makes it complete semantically, because of the essentiality of the information supplied by it. Hence, the position of the direct object in the hierarchy of the parts of the sentence is lower than that of the indispensable parts – the subject and the predicate – but its position is higher than that of all the other dispensable parts of the sentence.

### 3.6. The part which makes the sentence complete

The second indispensable part of the sentence is frequently called by Sībawayhi *mabniyy 'alayhi* "the part which makes the sentence complete" (Levin 1985b: 302; 334–342).

Thus, the predicate of the nominal sentence is called *mabniyy ʿalā l-mubtadaʾ* "the part which makes the sentence complete, when occurring as the predicate of the *mubtadaʾ*" (Levin 1985b: 308–311). The term *mabniyy ʿalā l-fiʿl* denotes "the part which makes the verbal sentence complete when joined to the verb". According to Sībawayhi, the *mabniyy ʿalā l-fiʿl* is one of the following parts of the verbal sentence: the subject (*fāʿil*); the direct object (*mafʿūl bihi*); a combination of a preposition + indirect object (Levin 1985b: 315–318).

It should be emphasized that most parts of the sentence called *mabniyy ʿalayhi* are indispensable parts of the sentence. The only parts which seem to form an exception to this rule occur in the verbal sentence as a direct object or as a combination of a preposition + indirect object, which according to Sībawayhi is equivalent in its syntactic function to that of a direct object (Levin 1985b: 316–317). The direct object is called *mabniyy ʿalayhi* since it is the part which makes the sentence complete semantically, although formally the sentence is considered complete even without it (Levin 1985b: 342–345).

### 3.7. The logical relation between certain parts of the sentence

Sībawayhi sometimes refers to the logical relation existing between certain parts of the sentence. He holds that in nominal sentences where the predicate is a noun, an adjective or a participle, the predicate is logically identical to the subject. For example, in the sentence *ʿabdu llāhi munṭaliqun* "ʿAbdallah is leaving", the subject *ʿabdu llāhi* is identical to the predicate *munṭaliqun*, since both of them denote the same entity: ʿAbdallah is the one who is leaving, and the one who is leaving is ʿAbdallah (*Kitāb* I,239; Levin 1979a: 199–202).

In contrast, the predicate is not identical to the subject when the predicate in the nominal sentence is an expression denoting place or time (*Kitāb* I, 239), as in the examples *zaydun fī d-dāri* "Zayd is in the house" and *al-qitālu ġadan* "The battle will take place tomorrow".

Sībawayhi states that in verbal sentences the subject is not identical to the predicate. For example, in the sentence *ḏahaba zaydun* "Zayd went away", the subject *zaydun* is not identical to the verb *ḏahaba* (*Kitāb* I, 10).

### 3.8. The underlying and primary structure of given sentences

The underlying and primary construction of given sentences beginning with a verb or with a particle, is according to Sībawayhi a nominal sentence, to which a verb, or a verb + preposition, or a particle is preposed. For example, the nominal sentence *ʿabdu llāhi munṭaliqun* "ʿAbdallah is leaving" is the underlying and primary structure of the following types of sentences:

(i) sentences beginning with a verb followed by two accusatives, as in the example *raʾaytu ʿabda llāhi munṭaliqan* "I saw ʿAbdallah leaving" or "I knew that ʿAbdallah was leaving".
(ii) sentences beginning with *kāna* or one of its 'sisters', as in the example *kāna ʿabdu llāhi munṭaliqan* "ʿAbdallah was leaving"
(iii) sentences beginning with a verb which is connected with its object by means of a preposition: *marartu bi-ʿabdi llāhi munṭaliqan* "I passed by ʿAbdallah when he was leaving"
(iv) sentences beginning with one of the particles belonging to the category of *ʾinna wa-ʾaḫawātuhā*, as in the example *layta zaydan munṭaliqun* "I wish Zayd would leave" (*Kitāb* I, 6; Levin 1979a: 196–198).

### 3.9. Transitive and intransitive verbs

Sībawayhi's distinction between transitive and intransitive verbs derives from the notion of *ʿamal*. In his view, the essential quality of the transitive verb is that its effect (*ʿamal*), and not its act, passes over from its subject (*fāʿil*) to a direct object (*mafʿūl bihi* or *mafʿūl*). For example, in the sentence *ḍaraba ʿabdu llāhi zaydan* "ʿAbdallah hit Zayd", the *ʿamal* of the transitive verb *ḍaraba* affects its subject *ʿabdu llāhi* in such a way that it takes the nominative, then the *ʿamal* of the verb passes over to the direct object *zaydan*, affecting it in such a way that it takes the accusative. To Sībawayhi, it is irrelevant whether the act expressed in the verb passes over or does not pass over from a certain subject to a certain object (Levin 1979b: 193–199). Hence, even a verb like *kāna* "he was", which in his view does not express an act, is classified by him as a transitive verb, since he believes that its *ʿamal* passes over from its subject to an object, as in the example *kāna ʿabdu llāhi ʾaḫāka* "ʿAbdallah was your brother" (Levin 1979a: 186–191; Levin 1979b: 198–199).

In contrast to the transitive verb, the main feature of the intransitive verb is that its *ʿamal* does not pass over from its *fāʿil* to a direct object, as in *ḏahaba zaydun* "Zayd went away".

The transitive verb is twice called by Sībawayhi *al-fiʿl al-mutaʿaddī ʾilā mafʿūl* "the verb whose *ʿamal* passes over [from its subject] to an object" (*Kitāb* I, 10). Usually,

Sībawayhi uses the expression *ta'addā 'ilā* (also *ta'addāhu 'ilā*) in phrases referring to the transitive and intransitive verb (Levin 1979b: 193–194).

3.10. The parts of speech

Words are divided by Sībawayhi into three main categories: *ism* "noun", *fi'l* "verb" and *ḥarf* "particle" (*Kitāb* I, 1).

3.11. *Kalima* in the sense of "morpheme"

The form *kalima* (plural *kalim*), commonly translated as "a word", sometimes occurs in the *Kitāb* as a grammatical term corresponding in sense to the modern linguistic term 'morpheme' (*Kitāb* II, 330–339; Levin 1986: 423–431; 443–445). For example: the first person singular nominative pronoun suffix *-tu*, as in *ḏahabtu* "I went away", is a *kalima*. However, *kalima* is not always identical with morpheme, since Sībawayhi does not conceive of certain linguistic units which in modern usage would be morphemes, as *kalim*. For example, the prefixes of the imperfect *'a*, *ta-*, *ya-* and *na-*, are not conceived of as *kalim*, although Sībawayhi conceives of them as elements denoting a given meaning (Levin 1986: 431–445).

## 4. Sībawayhi's phonetic description

### 4.1. The consonants and the long vowels (*ḥurūf*)

Sībawayhi's phonetic description is one of his greatest achievements. It is based on data gathered from those Beduin dialects which were regarded by him as 'good' dialects. His description and analysis of the phonetic system of Old Arabic include all the sounds existing in these dialects, irrespective of whether they were accepted or rejected in the recitation of the *Qur'ān* and in poetry.

The sounds, like the letters of the alphabet, are called by Sībawayhi *ḥurūf* (singular *ḥarf*). As a phonetic term, the form *ḥarf* denotes a sound which is represented in Arabic orthography by a letter. Irrespective of this sense of *ḥarf*, it is attested by the text of the *Kitāb* that the distinction between a sound, as a phonetic unit, and a letter of the alphabet, was clear to Sībawayhi (*Kitāb* II, 56–57).

Sībawayhi mentions in his description 35 *ḥurūf*. Seven of them are not accepted in the recitation of the *Qur'ān* and in poetry (*Kitāb* II, 452–455). The *ḥurūf* described by him include all the consonants, the semi-vowels *w* and *y*, and the long vowels *ū*, *ā*, *ī*. The short vowels *u*, *a*, *i* are called *ḥarakāt* (singular *ḥaraka*), and they are not classified as *ḥurūf*, since they are not represented by a letter in the Arabic alphabet. Sībawayhi holds that the short vowels form a part of their long equivalents (*Kitāb* II, 342; 384; Blanc 1967: 297). In referring to Sībawayhi's description of the consonants, Blanc (1967: 297) says:

> The consonants are described by point of articulation and manner of articulation, on the whole with admirable clarity and precision.

Sībawayhi divides the sounds into *mağhūra*, lit. "sonorous", and *mahmūsa*, lit. "muffled". The *mağhūra* are the consonants *'*, *ġ*, *ğ*, *ḍ*, *z*, *d*, *ḏ*, *ḏ̣*, *b*, *l*, *m*, *n*, *r*, *'*, *q*, *ṭ*, the semi-vowels *y* and *w*, and the long vowel *ā*. The *mahmūsa* are the consonants *h*, *ḥ*, *ḫ*, *k*, *š*, *s*, *ṣ*, *t*, *ṯ* and *f* (Blanc 1967: 296). Blanc notes that all the *mahmūsa* are voiceless consonants, while most of the *mağhūra* are voiced sounds, except *hamza* (= glottal stop), *q* and *ṭ*, which are voiceless (Blanc 1967: 298; for an alternative analysis that posits a voiced realisation of *q* and *ṭ* in Classical Arabic see Cantineau 1960: 31–32, 67–71). In his conclusion Blanc accepts Garbell's view that the *mahmūsa* are 'breathed' sounds and all the *mağhūra* are 'non-breathed' (Garbell 1958: 307; Blanc 1967: 306–307). In referring to Sībawayhi's distinction between *t* and *d*, which is not based on the absence vs. the presence of voice, but on the presence vs. the absence of (pure) breath, Blanc (1967: 303–304) says:

> This would imply, inter alia, the existence of phonological thinking more than a millenium before the formulation of the distinctive feature principle [...].

### 4.2. The *'imāla*

Sībawayhi's discussion of the phenomenon known as *'imāla* is the best evidence of the authenticity and accuracy of his linguistic description. *'Imāla* is a term used by Sībawayhi and the later grammarians to denote the fronting and raising of old Arabic *ā* towards *ī*, and of the old short *a* towards *i* (Levin 1978: 174; 1992: 74). Sībawayhi, who was the first to describe the *'imāla*, says that it occurred in some old Beduin dialects (*Kitāb* II, 284). The phenomenon is also known from some medieval Arabic dialects (Levin 1978: 261–265), and from many modern dialects (Levin 1971: 79–412).

According to Sībawayhi's description, the *'imāla* was not a general phenomenon in Old

Arabic, as it occurred only in some of the ancient dialects (*Kitāb* II, 284). These sometimes also differed from each other with respect to the *'imāla*, since the *ā* shift was not homogeneous in all of them (ibid.). Sībawayhi does not say anything about the quality of the *'imāla* vowel. Thus, it is not possible to get a precise idea of the nature of this quality in the 8th century, and one cannot judge whether the *'imāla* vowel was closer to *ē* or to *ī*. As-Sīrāfī and Ibn Ǧinnī (d. 392/1002) say that the vowel of the *'imāla* was pronounced somewhere between *ā* and *ī* (Levin 1992: 76). This suggests that the vowel of the *'imāla*, at least in most dialects, was *ē*.

The *'imāla* occurred in both medial and final position (Levin 1978: 176–179). Sībawayhi mentions three types of medial *'imāla*. The main type is conditioned, he says, by the vocalic environment of the medial *ā*. This *'imāla* occurs when the vowel of the syllable adjacent to the *ā* is *i* or *ī*, as in *kilāb* "dogs"; *šimlāl* "brisk camel"; *'ābid* "worshippper"; *mafātīḥ* "keys" (*Kitāb* II, 279). This type of *'imāla*, conditioned by the occurrence of *i* or *ī* in the syllable adjacent to the *ā*, does not occur when one of the emphatic consonants *ṣ*, *ḍ*, *ṭ*, *ḏ*, or the back consonants *q*, *ġ*, *ḫ*, is placed next to the *ā*: *qā'id* "sitting"; *ġā'ib* "absent"; *'āṭis* "sneezing" (*Kitāb* II, 285–286). However, Sībawayhi gives us to understand that the *'imāla* does occur in the immediate proximity of these consonants in the speech of people "from whose dialect no example can be taken" (*Kitāb* II, 286).

Blanc was the first to notice that in the modern *qəltu* dialects of Iraq and Anatolia and in the modern dialect of Aleppo, the factors conditioning the medial *'imāla* correspond to those described by Sībawayhi in the 8th century. The medial *'imāla* in these modern dialects is conditioned by the historical vocalic environment: the *'imāla* usually occurs when the historical vowel of the historical syllable adjacent to the *ā* was *i* or *ī*. For example: *klīb* "dogs" in Judaeo Baghdadi, *klēb* in Christian Baghdadi, and in Mosul, Anatolia and Aleppo; *ǧīmə'* "mosque" in Judaeo Baghdadi, *ǧēmə'* in Christian Baghdadi, and in Mosul and Anatolia; *mafētīḥ* "keys" in the Jewish dialect of Mosul, *mfētīḥ* in Aleppo (Levin 1994: 219). In these modern dialects, the medial *'imāla* thus occurs in the proximity of old *i*, even if this *i* has dropped out or been changed.

In comparing the factors conditioning the medial *'imāla* as described by Sībawayhi with those prevailing in the above-mentioned dialects, it can be inferred that the main conditioning factors in some 8th century Iraqi dialects resemble those found today in the *qəltu* dialects of Iraq and Anatolia, and in the modern dialect of Aleppo.

The resemblance between the main factors conditioning the medial *'imāla* in old and in modern dialects shows that Sībawayhi's description of the *'imāla* is authentic and accurate. This inference is supported by his remark that some people pronounce the form *an-nās* "the people" with *'imāla*, as an exception to the usual conditioning factors. The same exception is found today in some of the *qəltu* dialects: the form *nēs* "people" occurs in Christian Baghdadi and in the dialects of Northern Iraq and Anatolia (Levin 1994: 220). The existence of this common exception in both the old and the modern dialects offers important evidence for the authenticity and accuracy of Sībawayhi's description of the *'imāla*.

## 5. Bibliography

### 5.1. Primary sources

Fārisī, *Masā'il* = 'Abū 'Alī al-Ḥasan ibn 'Aḥmad al-Fārisī, *al-Masā'il al-Ḥalabiyyāt*. Ed. by Ḥ. Hindāwī. Damascus & Beirut, 1987.

Fārisī, *Ta'līqa* = 'Abū 'Alī al-Ḥasan ibn 'Aḥmad al-Fārisī, *at-Ta'līqa 'alā Kitāb Sībawayhi*. Ed. by 'Iwaḍ Bin Ḥamad al-Qūzī. 6 vols. Cairo, 1990–96.

Ǧurǧānī, *Muqtaṣid* = 'Abū Bakr 'Abd al-Qāhir ibn 'Abd ar-Raḥmān al-Ǧurǧānī, *Kitāb al-Muqtaṣid fī Šarḥ al-'Īḍāḥ*. Ed. by Kāẓim Baḥr al-Marǧān. 2 vols. Baghdad: Wizārat aṯ-Ṯaqāfa wa-l-'I'lām, 1982.

Ibn al-'Anbārī, *'Inṣāf* = Kamāl ad-Dīn 'Abū l-Barakāt 'Abd ar-Raḥmān ibn Muḥammad Ibn al-'Anbārī, *Kitāb al-'Inṣāf fī masā'il al-ḫilāf bayna n-naḥwiyyīna l-Baṣriyyīna wa-l-Kūfiyyīn*. Ed. by Gotthold Weil. Leiden: E. J. Brill, 1913.

Ibn al-'Anbārī, *Nuzha* = Kamāl ad-Dīn 'Abū l-Barakāt 'Abd ar-Raḥmān ibn Muḥammad Ibn al-'Anbārī, *Nuzhat al-'alibbā' fī ṭabaqāt al-'udabā'*. Ed. by 'Ibrāhīm as-Sāmarrā'ī. Baghdad, 1959.

Rummānī, *Šarḥ* = 'Abū l-Ḥasan 'Alī ibn 'Īsā ar-Rummānī, *Šarḥ Kitāb Sībawayhi*. Ed. by al-Mutawallī Ramaḍān 'Aḥmad ad-Damīrī. I. *Qism aṣ-ṣarf*. II. *ad-Dirāsa*. Cairo, 1988.

Šantamarī, *Nukat* = al-'A'lam aš-Šantamarī, *an-Nukat fī Tafsīr Kitāb Sībawayhi*. 2 vols. Kuweit, 1987.

Sībawayhi, *Kitāb* = 'Abū Bišr 'Amr ibn 'Uṯmān Sībawayhi, *al-Kitāb*. Ed. by Hartwig Derenbourg, *Le Livre de Sībawaihi. Traité de grammaire arabe.* 2 vols. Paris, 1881–1889. [Other editions: ed. Būlāq, 2 vols., 1316–1317 AH; ed. by 'Abd as-Salām Hārūn, 5 vols., Cairo, 1966–1977.]

Sīrāfī, *Šarḥ* = 'Abū Sa'īd al-Ḥasan ibn 'Abdallāh as-Sīrāfī, *Šarḥ Kitāb Sībawayhi*. Ed. by Ramaḍān 'Abd at-Tawwāb a. o. Cairo, 1986, 1990. [Only two parts published so far.]

Zamaḫšarī, *Mufaṣṣal* = 'Abū l-Qāsim Maḥmūd ibn 'Umar az-Zamaḫšarī, *al-Mufaṣṣal*. Ed. by Jens Peter Broch. 2nd ed. Christiania: Libraria P. T. Mallingii, 1879.

## 5.2. Secondary sources

Ayoub, Georgine. 1991. "La forme du sens: Le cas du nom et le mode du verbe". *Proceedings of the Colloquium on Arabic Grammar* ed. by Kinga Dévényi & Tamás Iványi, 37–87. Budapest: Eötvös Loránd University & Csoma de Kőrös Society.

Baalbaki, Ramzi. 1979. "Some Aspects of Harmony and Hierarchy in Sībawayhi's Grammatical Analysis". *Zeitschrift für arabische Linguistik* 2.7–22.

—. 1988. "A Contribution to the Study of Technical Terms in early Arabic Grammar: The term *'aṣl* in Sībawayhi's *Kitāb*". *A Miscellany of Middle Eastern Articles in Memoriam Thomas Muir Johnstone, 1924–1983* ed. by A. K. Irvine et al., 153–167. Essex.

Blanc, Haim. 1967. "The Sonorous vs. Muffled Distinction in Old Arabic Phonology". *To Honor Roman Jakobson. Essays on the Occasion of his Seventieth Birthday*, 295–308. The Hague & Paris: Mouton.

—. 1975. "Linguistics among the Arabs". *Current Trends in Linguistics*, vol. XIII: *Historiography of Linguistics* ed. by Thomas A. Sebeok, 1265–1283. The Hague & Paris: Mouton.

Blau, Joshua. 1977. *The Beginnings of the Arabic Diglossia: A study of the origins of Neo-Arabic.* Malibu: Undena.

Cantineau, Jean. 1960. *Etudes de linguistique arabe: Cours de phonétique arabe suivi de Notions générales de phonétique et de phonologie.* Paris: Klincksieck.

Carter, Michael G. 1972. "Twenty Dirhams in the *Kitāb* of Sībawayhi". *Bulletin of the School of Oriental and African Studies* 35.485–496.

—. 1973. "An Arab Grammarian of the Eighth Century AD: A contribution to the history of linguistics". *Journal of the American Oriental Society* 93.146–157.

Garbell, Irene. 1958. "Remarks on the Historical Phonology of an East Mediterranean Arabic Dialect". *Word* 14.303–337.

Goldziher, Ignaz. 1952. *A Short History of Arabic Literature.* Jerusalem. [In Hebrew.]

Hegazi, Mahmoud M. F. 1971. *'Abū Sa'īd al-Sīrāfī, der Sībawaih-Kommentator als Grammatiker.* Diss. Universität München.

Humbert, Geneviève. 1995. *Les voies de la transmission du* Kitāb *de Sībawayhi.* Leiden: Brill.

Levin, Aryeh. 1971. *The* 'Imāla *in the Arabic Dialects.* Ph. D. Hebrew University, Jerusalem. [In Hebrew, English summary pp. xiii–liv.]

—. 1978. "The *'imāla* of *'alif fā'il* in Old Arabic". *Israel Oriental Studies* 8.174–203.

—. 1979a. "Sībawayhi's View of the Syntactical Structure of *kāna wa'axawātuhā*". *Jerusalem Studies in Arabic and Islam* 1.185–211.

—. 1979b. "The Meaning of *ta'addā al-fi'l ilā* in Sībawayhi's *al-Kitāb*". *Studia Orientalia Memoriae D. H. Baneth Dedicata*, 193–210. Jerusalem: Magnes Press.

—. 1981. "The Grammatical Terms *al-musnad, al-musnad 'ilayhi* and *al-'isnād*". *Journal of the American Oriental Society* 101.145–165.

—. 1985a. "The Distinction Between Nominal and Verbal Sentences According to the Arab *Grammarians". Zeitschrift für arabische Linguistik* 15.118–127.

—. 1985b. "The Syntactic Technical Term *al-mabniyy 'alayhi*". *Jerusalem Studies in Arabic and Islam* 6.299–352.

—. 1986. "The Medieval Arabic Term *kalima* and the Modern Linguistic Term Morpheme: Similarities and differences". *Studies in Islamic History and Civilization in Honor of Professor David Ayalon* ed. by M. Sharon, 423–446. Jerusalem.

—. 1992. "The Authenticity of Sībawayhi's Description of the *'imāla*". *Jerusalem Studies in Arabic and Islam* 15.74–93.

—. 1994. "Sībawayhi's Attitude to the Spoken Language". *Jerusalem Studies in Arabic and Islam* 17.204–243.

—. 1995a. "The Fundamental Principles of the Arab Grammarians' Theory of *'amal*". *Jerusalem Studies in Arabic and Islam* 19.214–232.

—. 1995b. "The Status of the Direct Object in Early Arabic Grammar". *Proceedings of the Colloquium on Arabic Linguistics, Bucharest, August 29–September 2, 1994* ed. by Nadia Anghelescu & Andrei A. Avram, 195–199. Bucharest: Univ. of Bucharest.

—. 1997. "The Theory of *al-taqdīr* and its Terminology". *Jerusalem Studies in Arabic and Islam* 21.142–166.

Mas'ad, 'Abd al-Mun'im Fā'iz. n. d. *as-Sīrāfī an-Naḥwī fī ḍaw' šarḥihi li-Kitāb Sībawayhi.* n. p. [This book includes an edition of as-Sīrāfī's commentary on chapters 432–512 of the *Kitāb*.]

Mubārak, Māzin al-. 1974. *ar-Rummānī an-Naḥwī fī ḍaw' šarḥihi li-Kitāb Sībawayhi.* Damascus: Maṭba'a Ǧāmi'a Dimašq.

Naffāḫ, 'Aḥmad Rātib. 1970. *Fihris šawāhid Sībawayhi.* Beirut.

Praetorius, Franz. 1894. "Sībawaihi's Buch über die Grammatik übersetzt und erklärt von Jahn". *Göttingische gelehrte Anzeigen*, 9.

Talmon, Rafael. 1982. "*Naḥwiyyūn* in Sībawayhi's *Kitāb*". *Zeitschrift für arabische Linguistik* 8.12–38.

Troupeau, Gérard. 1976. *Lexique-Index du* Kitāb *de Sībawayhi.* Paris: Klincksieck.

ʿUḍayma, ʿAbd al-Ḫāliq. 1975. *Fahāris Kitāb Sībawayhi wa-dirāsa lahu.* Cairo.

*Aryeh Levin, Jerusalem (Israel)*

# 39. The development of Arabic linguistics after Sībawayhi: Baṣra, Kūfa and Baghdad

1. Introduction
2. Sources
3. Traditional accounts of the schools
4. Characteristics
5. Reality of the schools
6. The schools in context
7. Conclusion
8. Bibliography

## 1. Introduction

Sībawayhi's early death (ca. 180/796) prevented him not only from producing a definitive version of his famous *Kitāb* (which was achieved posthumously by his pupil al-ʾAḫfaš, d. 215/830) but also from establishing any kind of school (→ Art. 38). In fact, his work passed into a temporary eclipse from which it was only rescued by the efforts of al-Mubarrad (d. 285/898), who elevated the *Kitāb* to its position as the supreme authority for all grammatical speculation (Bernards 1993: 94–96, 1997: 92–93).

At the time when Sībawayhi was formulating his ideas in Baṣra, in the second half of the 2nd/8th century, the city of Kūfa was an equally vigorous centre of activity for the evolving Arab sciences, and in both places we can be sure there were sophisticated minds at work on problems of exegesis, law, grammar and theology. There was considerable rivalry between the two, both being new foundations created out of the Islamic conquests (Baṣra conventionally in 17/638, Kūfa perhaps a year or two later), and when Baghdad, the new capital of the Islamic empire, was founded in 145/762, this rivalry came out into the open: the ʿAbbāsid court became an arena in which prestige and patronage were to be acquired by such profitable occupations as tutoring the sons of the caliphs and, on a more humble level, ensuring the stability of the classical language in all the administrative, religious and cultural contexts where Arabic now functioned as the exclusive medium.

The biographical literature has retrospectively schematized this state of affairs into three grammatical 'schools', Baṣran, Kūfan and a mixed Baghdad school, which we shall now examine. From the outset it must be observed that there is disagreement about the reality of the so-called 'schools', both as to their origins and history, and their technical differences. The Arabic sources are consistent in assigning grammarians to one or another of the schools, but they are rather vague about their distinctive grammatical features, while Western scholarship tends to be more informative on the linguistic peculiarities associated with each school but is less able to demonstrate why a given grammarian should be categorized as a member of a particular school other than on biographical or educational grounds. For this reason a brief review of the sources is necessary.

## 2. Sources

### 2.1. Biographical literature

With one exception, the earliest complete, surviving biographical works date mostly from the 4th/10th century, by which time the division into Baṣran and Kūfan schools was already established. The exception is a short and curious treatise by ʾAbū Ḥāmid (d. ca. 250/864, cf. Versteegh 1995: 172f.) which strongly inclines towards the Kūfans. The introductory portions of al-Ǧumaḥī (d. 231/845), *Ṭabaqāt fuḥūl aš-šuʿarāʾ* are of special interest because al-Ǧumaḥī was not only an acquaintance of Sībawayhi but was also credited with a history of the grammarians, unfortunately lost (for possible quotations see Sezgin 1984: 13). This article relies mostly on 4th/10th century works (reviewed by Sezgin

1984: 11–27; Bernards 1993: 14f., 1997: 12–14), principally the *Marātib an-naḥwiyyīn* of 'Abū ṭ-Ṭayyib al-Luġawī (d. 351/962), the *'Aḫbār an-naḥwiyyīn* of as-Sīrāfī (d. 368/979), the *Ṭabaqāt an-naḥwiyyīn* of az-Zubaydī (d. 379/989) and the *Fihrist* of Ibn an-Nadīm (d. 385/995). Later works are largely derivative but may preserve fragments of lost material, e. g. a work on grammatical disagreements ascribed to Ṯa'lab (d. 291/904; Sezgin 1984: 23; 141) and a biographical treatise by al-Mubarrad (d. 285/898; ib. 14).

2.2. Controversial literature

Disagreements between grammarians are often recorded anecdotally in the biographies and grammatical texts, and more systematically in a small group of works entitled *Maǧālis* "sessions", notably (of those surviving) by Ṯa'lab and az-Zaǧǧaǧī (d. 337/949), or *'Amālī* "dictations", e. g. of az-Zaǧǧāǧī and Ibn aš-Šaǧarī (d. 542/1148). The most important collection of grammatical disputes between Baṣrans and Kūfans is the *'Inṣāf* of Ibn al-'Anbārī (d. 577/1181), the earliest of its type to survive (Sezgin 1984: 23f.). The *Tabyīn* of al-'Ukbarī (d. 616/1219) closely resembles Ibn al-'Anbārī's *'Inṣāf* (though is seemingly independent of it, see 4.3.) but the same author's *Masā'il ḫilāfiyya fī n-naḥw* does not belong to this group, as it deals with grammatical issues on a higher and more scholastic level detached from the Schools. All these sources are vulnerable to the criticism of anachronism and over-simplification: az-Zaǧǧāǧī's accusation of *muġālaṭa* "sophism" (*Maǧālis* 292; *'Amālī* 62) directed at grammarians of a previous generation is clearly a back-projection of the practice of disputation in az-Zaǧǧāǧī's own time.

2.3. Substantive texts

No full-scale works overtly stating and systematically defending an exclusively Kūfan position are known to survive, assuming that the *Muqaddima* attributed to Ḫalaf al-'Aḥmar (d. ca. 180/796) is in fact spurious (Sezgin [1984: 126] sees no reason why it cannot be accepted as authentic). This is to be expected since 'Kūfan' grammar at least from Ṯa'lab onwards is always reactive to Baṣran grammar and the latter had been presented in a fully systematized form by Sībawayhi in the *Kitāb* and subsequently elaborated and refined by the later grammarians, most effectively in the *Muqtaḍab* of al-Mubarrad (see below, 3.). The nearest we have to a purely Kūfan source, apart from the *Ma'ānī* of al-Farrā' and Ṯa'lab's *Maǧālis* (see below, 3.) is the *Ǧumal* of Ibn Šuqayr (d. 315/927 or 317/929), wrongly attributed to al-Ḫalīl, and which does indeed abound in terms usually regarded as Kūfan. Regrettably the ideas of a far more radically committed Kūfan grammarian, 'Abū Bakr Muḥammad Ibn al-'Anbārī (d. 327/939 or 328/940, not to be confused with the later Ibn al-'Anbārī, author of the *'Inṣāf* etc.) are only accessible through occasional references in later sources.

2.4. Secondary literature

The principal resource is Sezgin (1984). Several recent works, e. g. Bernards (1993, 1997), Dīra (1991), 'Alāma (1993), Goldziher (1994), Maḥmūd (1986), summarize the field and offer more recent bibliographical information. Although first published in 1862, Flügel's *Die grammatischen Schulen der Araber* still provides a mass of biographical and bibliographical information, drawn largely from later sources. It is probably Flügel who is responsible for the term *madrasa* "school" which occurs so frequently in the Arabic secondary literature, displacing the indigenous word *maḏhab* (cf. Bernards 1993: 104, n. 21, 1997: 11).

## 3. Traditional accounts of the schools

Conventional narratives trace the division between Baṣrans and Kūfans to the origins of grammar itself, and substantial differences of opinion are reported by the time of Sībawayhi in Baṣra and his Kūfan rivals ar-Ru'āsī (d. in the reign of ar-Rašīd, 170–193/786–809 approx.) and al-Kisā'ī (d. 189/805). The acknowledged historical reality is that Baṣra has a chronological "precedence in grammar" (*qudma bi-n-naḥw*, al-Ǧumaḥī, *Ṭabaqāt* 5), but a tenuous Kūfan link with the legendary founder of all grammar, the Baṣran 'Abū l-'Aswad ad-Du'alī (d. 69/688), is asserted through the figure of al-Furqubī, said to be a Kūfan pupil of 'Abū l-'Aswad and master of ar-Ru'āsī (Sezgin 1984: 125). Somewhat questionably ar-Ru'āsī is also said to have supplied the prototype for the first Arabic dictionary, the *Kitāb al-'Ayn* by the Baṣran al-Ḫalīl ibn 'Aḥmad (d. 160/776 or 175/791) or possibly for the *Kitāb* of Sībawayhi itself (Baalbaki 1981b).

With the foundation of Baghdad the conflict moved to the capital, where it was initially represented by a kind of shadow boxing between Sībawayhi and al-Farrā' (d. 207/822). Subsequently the battle was fought in a historically more authentic way between two commanding figures who consciously championed the rival schools, viz. the Baṣran al-Mubarrad (d. 285/898) and the Kūfan Ṯaʿlab (d. 291/904). The surviving works of both authors confirm that there was by their time a fully developed polemical opposition, but it was largely inspired by personal and professional jealousy (see below, 6.) and did not correspond to a codified or mutually exclusive concept of grammar. To be sure, the *Muqtaḍab* of al-Mubarrad is a complete reworking of the contents of Sībawayhi's *Kitāb*, overtly critical not only of 'Kūfans' but even of 'non-Baṣrans', whoever they may be (II.85), and does present a mature and evolved Baṣran grammar, but the only comparable Kūfan response, the *Maǧālis* of Ṯaʿlab, is an anthology of miscellaneous grammatical, lexical and poetic observations which is certainly conscious of its 'Kūfan' role but is neither systematic nor exhaustive enough to count as a definitive statement of a Kūfan type of grammar.

As other developments took place in grammar (see below, 6.) the Sībawayhian model, under al-Mubarrad's promotion, eventually dominated the whole system. For a time in the 4th/10th century there were grammarians and linguistic scholars who, at least according to the biographies, had studied 'eclectically' under both Baṣran and Kūfan masters, e. g. az-Zaǧǧāǧ (d. 311/923), Ibn Kaysān (d. 299/912 or 320/932), Ibn Durustawayhi (d. 347/938), Ibn Qutayba, d. 276/889, al-Kirmānī, d. 329/941), 'Abū Ḥanīfa ad-Dīnawarī (d. 282/895), al-'Aḫfaš al-'Aṣġar (d. 315/927), Ibn Ḫālawayhi (d. 370/980) etc., but the distinction soon ceased to matter and, by the 6th/12th century, had become a purely antiquarian concern. The last important grammarian to be regarded as a genuine Kūfan, and whose work survives, for example, is Ibn Fāris, d. 395/1005.

There is much less certainty about the historical reality of a 'Baghdad' school, and the biographical notices seldom go further than stating that a certain grammarian 'mixed the two schools', scil. the Baṣran and Kūfan (see below, 5.). Even if individual Baġdād grammarians are credited with creating a unique theoretical position out of the Baṣran and Kūfan models, such as ar-Rummānī's theory of the operators in nominal sentences, in practice grammar remains generally Baṣran and any peculiarities may be ascribed to the individuality of the grammarian rather than a real systematic difference. There is an interesting speculation by Maḥmūd (1986: 153 ff.) that *Baġdādī* was originally used to refer to Kūfan grammarians who had moved to Baghdad or who sympathised with Kūfan views (cf. also Flügel 1862: 152). It is true that in 4th/10th century Baghdad a grammarian might be labelled as a Kūfan (e. g. Ibn Šuqayr, d. 315–7/927–9 or Ibn al-'Anbārī, d. 329/939) or Baṣran (e. g. Ibn as-Sarrāǧ, d. 316/928, 'Abū ʿAlī al-Fārisī, d. 377/987), but other grammarians from the same period studied under both Baṣran and Kūfan masters (see below, 3.). In any case it did not prevent a grammarian who was attached to one system from taking positions in keeping with the other, exactly as Ibn as-Sarrāǧ is said to have done, favouring the Kūfans occasionally while nevertheless being the favourite pupil of the arch-Baṣran al-Mubarrad.

## 4. Characteristics of the schools

### 4.1. Closed corpus vs. open corpus

The fundamental quality of Baṣran grammar is its tendency to discount anomalous data in the interests of greater systematic regularity, while the Kūfans are correspondingly known for their willingness to acknowledge isolated linguistic facts as a potential basis for analogical extension or to support as theory. The two attitudes are summed up in the words *qiyās* "analogy" and *samāʿ* "orally recorded data" representing the Baṣran and Kūfan preoccupations respectively (though not exclusively, see below, 7.). Weil's comparison with the classical dispute between Analogists and Anomalists (Ibn al-ʿAnbārī, *'Inṣāf*, introduction 44 ff.) is superficially attractive but not well founded: there is no demonstrable connection between the two, and furthermore the Analogist v. Anomalist debate as such did not take place in Islam, the nearest discussion being that initiated by Ibn Ǧinnī (→ Art. 40) as to whether linguistic rules are closer to those of revealed law (i. e. essentially irrational) or those of theology (i. e. essentially rational). The recently published *Intiṣār* of Ibn Wallād (d. 332/943; see Bernards 1997, especially Arabic text pp. 74–76) reveals that the root of the dispute lay in the conscious Baṣran decision to close the corpus and thus put an end to the inductive reasoning on which grammar had hitherto been based, substituting for induction a set of general principles (*'uṣūl*), which could henceforth be applied deductively and account for all linguistic phenomena (Carter 1999). This closure in effect elevated the *Kitāb* of Sībawayhi to the status of a definitive corpus (see below, 6.). A late formulation by as-Suyūṭī (d. 911/1505; *al-Iqtirāḥ* 84) often quoted in the secondary literature gives a succinct definition of Kūfan principles: "if they hear a single verse authorizing something against the rules they make it a general principle and the basis for a whole category" (*law samiʿū baytan wāḥidan fīhi ǧawāz šay' muḫālif li-l-'uṣūl ǧaʿalūhu 'aṣlan wa-bawwabū ʿalayhi*). As-Suyūṭī is of course over-simplifying, but there was certainly a disagreement in attitude between certain early grammarians which could have hardened into the position described by as-Suyūṭī: an important criticism of Sībawayhi by Ṯaʿlab (Zubaydī, *Ṭabaqāt* 123–124) centres on al-Farrā''s concern that statements about language should conform closely to the spirit or nature of that language, and elsewhere (Zaǧǧāǧi, *Maǧālis* 121) al-Mubarrad scornfully accuses Ṯaʿlab of abandoning Qur'ānic and majority usage in favour of the word of "some stupid old bedouin woman"! Even if inauthentic, the anecdotal evidence gives a good picture of what it was the Baṣrans found so objectionable about Kūfan attitudes.

4.2. Terminology

Certain items and concepts are denoted differently, and the following is merely a list of terms extracted from the secondary sources and generally regarded as reflecting a Baṣran (B) or Kūfan (K) allegiance. The approximate literal translations are provided to give some idea of the nature of the terminological distinctions:

*ǧarr* (B) "oblique form" ("genitive"), lit. "dragging" = *ḫafḍ* (K), lit. "lowering"
*ḥarf* (B) "particle" = *'adā* (K), lit. "instrument"
*ḍamīr al-faṣl* (B) "separating pronoun" = *ʿimād* (K), lit. "prop, support"
*ṣarf* (B) "divergence" (impeding concord) = *ḫilāf* (K), lit. "difference"
*ʿaṭf* (B) "coordination", lit. "bringing together" = *nasaq* (K), lit. "stringing together"
*badal* (B) "substitution" = *tarǧama, tabyīn* (K), lit. "glossing, clarifying"
*tamyīz* "distinguishing" (B) = *tafsīr* (K), lit. "explaining"
*maṣdar* (B) "verbal noun", lit. "source" = *ism al-fiʿl* (K), lit. "noun of the verb" (not to be confused with the Baṣran use of the term *ism al-fiʿl* to denote various kinds of interjections!)
*ḥurūf ziyāda* (B) "redundant elements" = *ḥurūf aṣ-ṣila* or *ḥurūf al-ḥašw* (K), lit. "particles of attachment or padding"
*ḍamīr aš-ša'n* (B) "anticipatory pronoun", lit. "pronoun of the matter" = *ḍamīr al-maǧhūl* (K), "pronoun of the unknown"
*ḍamīr* (B) "pronoun", lit. "kept in mind" = *maknī* or *kināya* (K), lit. "alluded to indirectly"
*ẓarf* (B) "space/time qualifier", lit. "container" = *ṣifa* (K), lit. "quality" or *maḥall* "place"
*nafy* (B) "negation" = *ǧaḥd* (K), lit. "denying"
*ṣifa* (B) "adjective", lit. "attribute" = *naʿt* (K), lit. "characterizing"
*lā li-nafy al-ǧins* (B) "categorical negative", lit. "*no* for negating the genus" = *lām at-tabri'a* (K), "*no* of quittance"

It will be seen that some differences are merely taxonomic, there being no new categories involved, e. g. *ʿaṭf/nasaq*, *ḍamīr/kināya*, *nafy/ǧaḥd*, and some seem to reflect a genuinely different conception of the item, e. g. *badal/tarǧama*, *tabyīn*, *ẓarf/ṣifa*. In the latter group we should include the alleged Kūfan practice of using the same terminology for the names of the vowels as for the inflections (*rafʿ*, *naṣb* etc. instead of *ḍamma/rafʿ*, *fatḥa/naṣb* etc.), though the theoretical implications of this are by no means clear. The Kūfans also stood alone in identifying a third tense, which they called *al-fiʿl ad-dā'im* lit. "enduring, lasting action", corresponding to what the Baṣrans treated as a present participle. See below, 4.4. on the diagnostic vagueness of terminology as evidence of Baṣran or Kūfan allegiance.

4.3. Systematic differences

The *'Inṣāf* of Ibn al-'Anbārī contains no fewer than 121 topics on which Baṣrans and Kūfans disagree, and clearly it would be impossible to discuss them all here. They cover the full linguistic range from syntax to morphology, but even Ibn al-'Anbārī's list is not complete: a later work, the *Tabyīn* of al-ʿUkbarī comprises 85 topics of which a quarter are not found in the *'Inṣāf*. Most of these extra cases, however, do not involve specifically Baṣran and Kūfan disputes, which reminds us that not all disagreements could be fitted into this rigid scheme.

It will be more instructive to give examples of a few problems which are identified as Baṣran and Kūfan issues much earlier than Ibn al-'Anbārī's time, which makes them less likely to be tainted by anachronism or over-systematization. The *'Īḍāḥ* of az-Zaǧǧāǧī is a good source, as he is one of the first to formulate the disputes in terms of schools. Among the disputed issues we find the priority of nominal inflection over verbal, (Versteegh 1995: 121ff.), the priority of the verbal noun over the verb (ib. 72ff.), the notion of the verb as fundamentally predicative (ib. 67), the nature of dual and sound masculine plural inflection (ib. 231ff.), and the syntax of *kāna* (ib. 250, n. 8). Curiously it was never disputed that nouns are logically prior to verbs (ib. 135ff.), nor, again, is every controversy in the *'Īḍāḥ* presented as an argument between Baṣrans and Kūfans.

While the issues are often real enough, particularly at the syntactic level, it is not always easy to see any coherent theoretical background for a given position, since neither side can leave a phenomenon unexplained (below, 7.), no matter how far fetched the explanation may be. In this the Kūfans reveal themselves as no less pedantic and complex than their Baṣran rivals, or at least as their disputes are reworded in the late sources. Moreover in earlier records the disagreements are often more laconic and the principles left implicit. Thus in Ibn Šuqayr's version (*Ǧumal* 49–50) of the case of the *fi'l at-ta'aǧǧub* "verb of surprise" the Kūfans reject the paraphrase of *mā 'a'ẓama llāha* "how great God is!" as **šay'un 'aẓẓama llāha* "something has made God great" as heretical and "not to be used for analogy" (*lā yuqāsu 'alayhi*), and the Baṣrans respond that "an analogical argument cannot be based on a single instance" (*lā yaḏhab al-qiyās bi-ḥarf wāḥid*), but by Ibn al-'Anbārī's time the discussion has grown to many pages and the potential blasphemy in **šay'un 'aẓẓama llāha* is deeply buried among a mass of intricate pleadings as if the Kūfans were aware that the original basis of their objection was not linguistic but theological and needed a stronger logical justification (*'Inṣāf* 57–68).

### 4.4. The problem of identification

In spite of the various terminological and methodological differences it is still not possible to identify a grammarian as Baṣran or Kūfan merely on technical criteria: there are no shibboleths which will betray a grammarian's school unequivocally. A good example is the term *ḫafḍ*, commonly taken to be typically Kūfan, in contrast with the Baṣran *ǧarr*, but in fact used by more than one Baṣran, among them al-Mubarrad, perhaps the most aggressively Baṣran grammarian of them all (e.g. *Muqtaḍab* II,155). The sources are obviously uneasy about this, and an anecdote in which al-Ḫalīl questions al-'Aṣma'ī about the two terms (az-Zaǧǧāǧī, *Maǧālis* 253) is clearly designed to support the view that at this stage *ḫafḍ* had not become exclusively Kūfan. That is certainly why az-Zaǧǧāǧī himself uses it regularly, for example in his famous pedagogical text *al-Ǧumal* (*pace* Versteegh 1995: 205). The allegedly Kūfan term *na't* likewise is used just as often by both sides (including Sībawayhi), so as to be wholly inconclusive. There is sufficient irregularity in the distribution of the technical terms generally for them to be most unreliable indicators of a grammarian's allegiance.

At the systemic level likewise the two schools may be difficult to tell apart. Some terms, as already mentioned above, do not in any case imply any difference of methodology, only of nomenclature: for example, the principle that dependent (*naṣb*) forms may be selected for elements which are syntactically excluded from their antecedents is the same whether it is called *ṣarf* or *ḫilāf* (Carter 1973). An impressive example of methodological congruence is the formulation of al-Farrā' (*Ma'ānī* I,389) defining a correct utterance as *muktafin yaṣluḥ as-sukūt 'alayhi*, i.e. "self-sufficient and proper for silence to follow", which corresponds exactly to Sībawayhi's criteria of "self-sufficient" and "correct for silence" but which he happens to express through the terms *mustaǧnin* and *yaḥsun as-sukūt 'alayhi* (e.g. *Kitāb* I,122, where both notions occur in the same context), synonymous with those of al-Farrā'.

Whether one follows the schematicized presentation of Ibn al-'Anbārī or the less formal evidence of earlier sources, it remains true that no grammarian can be classified as exclusively Kūfan or Baṣran if judged solely by opinions expressed or attributed. In the Baṣran camp, Sībawayhi disagrees with both al-Ḫalīl and Yūnus, al-Mubarrad disagrees with Sībawayhi, Ibn Wallād disagrees with al-Mubarrad, and so on, and among the Kūfans, al-Farrā' disagrees with al-Kisā'ī, and Ṯa'lab with al-Farrā'. Some strange alliances are formed: al-Kisā'ī and al Farra' together reject a Kūfan position, Sībawayhi sides with al-Farrā' against al-Ḫalīl and al-Kisā'ī, and in another case al-Farrā' joins a group of early Baṣrans who happen to disagree with another group of early Baṣrans. The *'Inṣāf* of Ibn al-'Anbārī supplies abundant evidence of this ideological chaos: on one issue the Kūfans are united but the Baṣrans offer four different theories (prob. 84, p. 250), on another there is utter disarray, with al-Mubarrad and az-Zaǧǧāǧ siding with the Kūfans (id. prob. 34, p. 118ff.). Ibn al-'Anbārī, himself a consciously thoroughbred Baṣran (see below, 7.) still prefers the Kūfans in seven issues in his *'Inṣāf* (Qāsim ND:28f.: problems no. 10, 18, 26, 70, 97, 101, 106). In other words the schools are very ill-defined: even az-Zaǧǧāǧī does not seem to know where to put Ibn Šuqayr (whom he knew personally!), calling him a Kūfan and a Baṣran within two pages (Versteegh 1995: 122; 124). But the same az-Zaǧǧāǧī (*Ǧumal* 77) also hedges his bets when he refers to *at-tamyīz wa-t-tafsīr* (cf. 4.2.) thus using the Baṣran and Kūfan terms in the same breath!

## 5. The reality of the schools

Although there is little doubt that in the Arab tradition the Baṣran and Kūfan schools and the school of Baghdad (the last with some reservations) are accepted as historically authentic, there is less unanimity in western scholarship (see summary in Bernards 1993: 6ff., 1997: 93–97). The following points seem fairly firmly established.

Whatever differences of opinion existed in the 2nd/8th century were informal and even largely impersonal: although the anecdotal literature brings face to face such rivals as al-Kisā'ī and Sībawayhi there is no reflection of this in their actual writings. A western tendency to oppose Sībawayhi and al-Farrā' in literary terms on the basis of their two most famous works, the *Kitāb* and *Ma'ānī l-Qur'ān* respectively, is perhaps artificial, since these works are fundamentally different in character, purpose, size, technical comprehensiveness and date of composition (Carter 1994: 395). Sībawayhi in any case is so careful to balance *qiyās* and *samā'* that he could hardly be said to belong to either camp, while al-Farrā' stubbornly remains an individual in spite of attempts to make him into a founder of Kūfan grammar.

By the 3rd/9th century a sense of personal rivalry is unmistakable and, since our most detailed record of it was composed by one who knew the major participants, namely az-Zaǧǧāǧī, it has to be accepted that the hostility between al-Mubarrad and Ṯa'lab was real and expressed itself through a genuine disagreement over grammatical issues, published in their respective works, the *Muqtaḍab* and the *Maǧālis* (see above, 3.). "Like Mu'āwiya and 'Alī", is al-Mubarrad's answer when a patron asks him how he and the Kūfans get on with each other (Zaǧǧāǧī, *Maǧālis* 123). This animosity is corroborated by several sources, the most striking being the person of Ṯa'lab's most extreme partisan, 'Abū Mūsā al-Ḥāmid (d. 305/918), whose by-name is aptly rendered "Sourpuss" (Bernards 1993: 19; cf. Versteegh 1995: 123). He is portrayed as so heavily prejudiced in favour of Kūfans and critical of Baṣrans that he flatly accused Sībawayhi of being unable to speak correct Arabic (Yāqūt, *Mu'ǧam al-'udabā'* I,51), not to mention being diabolically inspired, a slander which was even too extreme for Ṯa'lab ('Abū ṭ-Ṭayyib, *Marātib* 88).

It is, however, too early for 'schools'. Although all parties were well aware of the growing formalization of their differences of opinion, everything remains on a personal level. Thus both al-Mubarrad and Ṯa'lab (who can rightly be considered as self-conscious antagonists, unlike Sībawayhi and al-Farrā') refer to their opponents occasionally by the generic names of 'Baṣrans' and 'Kūfans', but we must take it that this denotes a civic origin rather than allegiance to a rigorous theoretical position. Consider Ṯa'lab's comment on a construction which the Kūfans labelled as *taqrīb* (e. g. *hāḏā l-'asadu maḫūfan* lit. "this is the lion, to be feared!", cf. the modern phenomenon of 'presentative'): he remarks somewhat dismissively (*Maǧālis*, 43) that "Sībawayhi knew nothing about *taqrīb*", thus keeping the issue on a personal level, and we must agree with Baalbaki (1985: 16f.) that it is a mistake to generalize such early differences into disputes between schools.

Quṭrub (d. 206/821) stands completely outside the system and no biographer seriously considers him (except in birth and education) a genuine Baṣran, though in fact he studied with Sībawayhi. But his notion that inflections have no meaning in themselves but are merely euphonic phenomena totally isolated him from the tradition (Versteegh 1983).

By the 4th/10th century the schools have emerged as the retrospective creation of the biographers of this period, clearly perceived and delineated, with every grammarian now allotted to the Baṣrans or Kūfans either on the basis of birth or for having studied with a member of a school. Much of the anecdotal material of this period is clearly designed to reinterpret individual differences as general differences between schools, e. g. the account of al-Farrā''s views on inflection (az-Zubaydī, *Ṭabaqāt* 143 ff.), the acrimonious debates between Ṯa'lab and al-Mubarrad (cf. 4.1.), a discussion between al-'Aḫfaš and al-Māzinī on the nature of *qiyās* (az-Zaǧǧāǧī, *Maǧālis* 313–315), a long conversation between Ibn Kaysān and al-Mubarrad on the nature of inflection which looks very much like a contrived apologia for the Baṣran position (az-Zaǧǧāǧī, *Maǧālis* 218–226), to mention a few instances of conspicuous reconstruction.

For the first time it becomes possible to speak of a grammarian as 'mixing the two schools', meaning that he studied under both Baṣran and Kūfan masters: the earliest such references are in Ibn an-Nadīm (d. ca. 385/995, *Fihrist* 121) and by a certain al-Kāššī who died in the first half of the 4th/10th century (Sezgin 1984: 190). Important grammarians who are said to have merged the schools are listed above, 3.: the resulting amalgam was somewhat unbalanced, however, as the type of grammar which evolved in Baghdad was essentially Baṣran adapted to the major changes in intellectual and social life which were by then in progress (see below 6.).

This is probably why the Baghdad school is so ill-defined. There is no explicit category of 'Baghdad' grammarians in the biographical literature as there is for Baṣrans and Kūfans, and furthermore there is no distinctive terminological or methodological character for a school of Baghdad: although some features are occasionally identified as typical of 'Baghdad' grammar (above, 3.), it hardly makes a school. The biographers, in fact, seem unwilling to admit the existence of a school. Ibn an-Nadīm, writing in the late 4th/10th century, after dealing with the Baṣrans and Kūfans, and briefly those who mixed the schools, simply gives up and announces that the rest of the grammarians are too vaguely known to be properly classified. Even more interesting is az-Zubaydī (d. 379/989), who carefully separates Baṣrans and Kūfans but has no category for Baghdad grammarians at all, although he does have a classification for grammarians from Egypt and Qayrawān, with no hint that these constitute any kind of school.

It has been speculated that there were even schools in Mecca and Medina, which would therefore antedate the developments in Baṣra and Kūfa (Talmon 1985). Whatever discussions about grammar may have occurred in these cities, there is very little evidence that anyone was conscious of representing an organized and comprehensive view of language in competition with some other such as would merit the title of 'school'.

## 6. The schools in context

The schools evolved within a powerful stream of broader developments in the history of the Arab sciences and their role in the new Arab-Islamic civilization. It hardly needs emphasizing that the language sciences played a more important part in this process than would be expected in the contemporary world, where the relationship between language and power is diffuse and veiled. The secondary literature has already considered the possible links between grammatical schools and Qur'ānic textual studies (e. g. Maḫzūmī 1958: 14; Versteegh 1995: 174 ff.) and even social and intellectual differences between the two towns have been invoked. (Zakī 1961: 95–117). The main factors may be considered under the following headings:

(a) Personal. It has already been argued (3.) that the original disputes were mainly personal. The partisan Baṣran litterateur al-Ǧāḥiẓ (d. 255/868–9) maliciously points out how embarrassing it must have been for the Kūfan al-Kisā'ī to have to rely on the Baṣran al-'Aḫfaš to teach him Sībawayhi's *Kitāb* and moreover to tutor his children! (al-Qifṭī, *'Inbāh* II,350). It was even possible for members of the same family to belong to different schools, such as the Baṣran 'Abū Muḥammad al-Yazīdī (d. 202/818, Sezgin 1984: 63), whose son Ibn al-Yazīdī was a pupil of the Kūfan al-Farrā' (Sezgin 1984: 135). The intensity of 'Abū Ḥāmid's hostility towards Sībawayhi is notorious (5.2.) and the *Maǧālis* literature abounds in episodes in which one grammarian humiliates another in the presence of some dignitary. The grammarian might even find himself behaving like a courtier, as in the anecdote in which a governor makes a mistake and finds a convenient grammarian to explain that it was not a mistake at all! (Zaǧǧāǧī, *Maǧālis* 54, and cf. Versteegh 1995: 173 for more).

(b) Professional. Closely allied with the personal aspect is the professional. As early as the turn of the 3rd/9th century it is apparent that teaching Arabic, especially to the children of the nobility, was a lucrative and prestigious occupation. A growing bureaucracy also had need of Arabic, and the religious and legal sciences were in their turn beginning to evolve, with increasing dependence on a standard Arabic both for the textual sources and the discourse in which they were discussed. Of the many achievements of al-Mubarrad the creation of a pedagogical system out of Sībawayhi's descriptive grammar is the most lasting: it had as an unforeseen consequences the almost total obliteration of two great intermediaries between him and Sībawayhi, his masters al-Ǧarmī (d. 225/839) and al-Māzinī (d. 248–9/862–3), neither of whose works survive except in quotation or radical rewriting.

(c) Intellectual. The discovery of Greek logic which had begun at least by the 2nd/8th century (→ Art. 43) led to the birth of an Islamic philosophy and, in parallel to this, to the creation of scholastic theology and organized legal theory. The sources tell us that from the earliest days there were contacts between grammarians and philosophers: the names of both al-Kisā'ī and Sībawayhi are biographically linked to that of an-Naẓẓām (d. 221/836 or 231/846), and al-Farrā' is connected with philosophical tendencies (Talmon 1990), though in neither case is there much direct evidence of the consequences. Mu'tazilite links can be suspected between al-'Aḫfaš and 'Abū Šammār (Sezgin 1984: 86) and certainly the notion of *i'tizāl* "withdrawing [from dogmatic certainty and taking a middle position]" surfaces explicitly in a debate between al-'Aṣma'ī and al-Māzinī (Zaǧǧāǧī, *Maǧālis* 294). Slight but unmistakeable traces of logical influence are discernible in al-Mubarrad, and by the next century there can be no doubt, with the coupling of the names of al-Fārābī and Ibn as-Sarrāǧ, after which grammar always has a rationalist tinge, treating language now as thought rather than as behaviour as Sībawayhi had done. This growing systematization tended to make Baṣran triumph more or less inevitable: not only did the Baṣrans have a complete and exhaustive treatise already available in the *Kitāb*, but the classic Baṣran approach was inherently more appropriate to the general need for a comprehensive and systematic method of dealing with the language (Carter 1999).

(d) Among the grammarians who profited from the new intellectual climate in Baghdad is Ibn as-Sarrāǧ, d. 316/928, pupil of al-Mubarrad and az-Zaǧǧāǧ and associate of al-Fārābī, and best known for his *Kitāb 'uṣūl an-naḥw* "The principles of grammar" (cf. Baalbaki 1988: 173; Bohas et al. 1990: 10–11), in which a theory of grammar is exhaustively presented for the first time on a purely rational foundation, i. e. independent of descriptive, pedagogical or religious considerations. In this Ibn as-Sarrāǧ slightly anticipated a trend which was already under way in legal reasoning, developments being inspired by the preoccupation of the Mu'tazila with demonstrating the ultimate rationality of Islamic thinking. Ibn as-Sarrāǧ represents a major step in the evolution of grammar: even his pedagogical text *al-Mūǧaz* is conspicuous for its use of *taqsīm* or dichotomous classification, an important new technique which is totally absent from Sībawayhi's *Kitāb* and the *Muqtaḍab* of al-Mubarrad.

The most influential pupil of Ibn as-Sarrāǧ was az-Zaǧǧāǧī, whose *'Īḍāḥ* is a radical examination of the basic presuppositions of grammar, in particular the notion of grammatical causality. One purpose of the work is to demarcate the now rationalized science of grammar from that of logic, reflecting a well-documented rivalry between grammarians and philosophers in competition for the right to control the interpretation of the sacred text. In common with most grammarians az-Zaǧǧāǧī also composed a teaching grammar, *al-Ǧumal* ("comprehensive general statements", not "sentences") which has always enjoyed a high reputation and inspired a huge number of commentaries (see Sezgin 1984: 88–94).

The interaction between grammar, law, theology and philosophy continued, however, and one of Ibn as-Sarrāǧ's pupils, ar-Rummānī (d. 384/994), has the distinction of having sailed too close to the philosophers. His works do support this reputation, though like many Mu'tazilites he was respected for his contributions to theory (especially in the relatively new field of rhetoric) even if some of his comments on divine speech bordered on heresy. Among other grammarians of this lively and stimulating century 'Abū 'Alī al-Fārisī (d. 377/987) and 'Aḥmad ibn Fāris (d. 395/1005) certainly deserve more consideration than can be given here: the former is known for his deep interest in the manuscripts of Sībawayhi's *Kitāb* and for being a teacher of Ibn Ǧinnī, while Ibn Fāris is one of the first to recognize the basic interdependence of the legal and grammatical sciences, with both disciplines being essentially the rationalization of transmitted data. As with the other religious sciences, grammar depended for its authority on a closed corpus, and the establishment of the definitive Qur'ānic text and body of Traditions from which the law was derived, is essentially the same process which led to the emergence of the Baṣran and Kūfan schools.

(e) Institutional. The late 4th/10th century is also the period in which the characteristic Muslim method of higher education, the *Madrasa*, makes its first appearance. By the end of the next century such institutions were spread throughout the Islamic world, each with its endowment, its complement of teachers and staff, and above all, its syllabus, supported by the relatively new genre, the textbook. Since each *Madrasa* was associated with a particular legal school the parallelism with the developments in grammar, both substantively and retrospectively reconstructed, cannot be overlooked. The schools of law and grammar are both called *madhab* "way of proceeding", i. e. "school" (cf. Bernards 1993: 6ff., 21ff., 1997: 11–14; Bohas et al. 1990: 7) and there is an evident similarity in the manner by which Islamic law formalized itself into schools which accommodated a wide range of relative strictness and flexibility, and grammar (admittedly with less sublety, or rather, more individualism) still managed to stretch over the spectrum from total rigour to complete anarchy, with every grammarian from the 4th/10th century being free to make his own choice. The fact that the choice was nearly always for the Baṣran position simply reflects a predominant taste for order and predictability. The *Madrasa* was, after all, an instrument for producing orthodox Muslims.

There may even have been a correlation between a scholar's grammatical and legal school, though research still remains to be done on this. Certain it is that grammatical and legal theory were formally equated by the time of Ibn al-'Anbārī (cf. Goldziher 1994: 50–53), and it is noticeable that Ibn al-'Anbārī, himself a Šāfi'ī in legal terms, maintains the Šāfi'ī position regarding the linguistic principle (borrowed in fact from law) of *istiḥsān*, discretionary choice among legitimate possibilities presented by ambiguous data, which as a Šāfi'ī Ibn al-'Anbārī regards as weak, while the Ẓāhirī grammarian Ibn Ḥazm (d. 456/1064) explicitly rejects such a process out of hand in keeping with his Ẓāhirī point of view.

## 7. Conclusion

The schools of Baṣra and Kūfa, whatever we may think about their historical reality, represent an important phase in the evolution of what has been called "canonical grammar" (Bohas et al. 1990: 49), i. e. the essentially scholastic grammar which was taught throughout the Islamic world and within which the various disagreements have become more or less ritualized by the 6th/12th century. The traces of the schools have never been eradicated: as long as any mention of them is made in an earlier work, all subsequent commentaries continue to discuss them. Probably as a result of having been organized and elaborated by the later sources, the argumentation on both sides often appears to be equally abstruse and unrealistic: just because they were opposed to an over-rigid application of analogy, *qiyās*, it does not mean that the Kūfans could not deploy all the complexity and misplaced subtlety of true scholastic dialectic, e. g. *'Inṣāf* problems 23, 24, 25. Ibn al-'Anbārī's *'Inṣāf* is itself quite rightly seen as an attempt to produce some order out of the chaos of conflicting opinions (cf. Bernards 1993: 98f.).

In the end the goal of the debates was to secure the authority to control language, and all the detailed argumentation was designed to test and demonstrate the exhaustiveness of the system on which that authority depended. There was never any doubt that control of language meant control of people, and the polemical jousting was intended to assert a systematic dominance by propounding irrefutable, though often entirely artificial arguments, in which the Kūfans were always a match for the Baṣrans in technique at least. To lose the argument was to admit the inadequacy of the system.

But the Baṣrans were always going to win because they started with the winning hand, a complete system supplied by Sībawayhi, and the presumption of the ultimate rationality of language. If they could not defeat the Kūfans by dialectic they could (and did, e. g. al-Qāsim n.d.: 14) simply deny the validity of the evidence: the Kūfan tendency to accept dialectal and isolated expressions made them especially vulnerable to this weapon. Organized and institutionalized Islam needed explanations: al-Kisā'ī's *kadā ḫuliqat* "that's just how it was created" (Dīra 1991: 297) was not enough to satisfy this need for intellectual certainty.

It is fitting to conclude with another reference to Ibn al-'Anbārī, because he was the first grammarian to form a comprehensive view of the history of grammar not only in its biographical but in its theoretical aspects and especially its true place in the Islamic sciences. We therefore must be struck by the arrangement of his own biographical dictionary, the *Nuzhat al-'alibbā'* which begins with the legendary founder of all grammar, the Baṣran 'Abū l-'Aswad and ends with Ibn al-'Anbārī's own teacher Ibn aš-Šağarī (d. 542/1147), whose academic pedigree is set out on the very last page of the work and connects him (and thus Ibn al-'Anbārī as well) directly to 'Abū al-'Aswad by an unbroken chain of Baṣran grammarians (Bernards 1997: 9).

## 8. Bibliography

### 8.1. Primary sources

All the grammatical and biographical works referred to above are detailed in Sezgin (1984), and most are mentioned in Bernards (1993, 1997) and Versteegh (1995); therefore only published works dealing exclusively with grammatical disputes are listed here:

Ibn al-ʿAnbārī, *'Inṣāf* = Ibn al-'Anbārī, 'Abū l-Barakāt, *Kitāb al-'Inṣāf fī masā'il al-ḫilāf, Die grammatischen Streitfragen der Basrer und Kufer.* Ed. by Gotthold Weil. Leiden: Brill 1913. [Other editions in Sezgin 1984: 24.]

ʿUkbarī, *Tabyīn* = al-ʿUkbarī, 'Abū l-Baqā', *At-Tabyīn ʿan maḏāhib an-naḥwiyyīn al-Baṣriyyīn wa-l-Kūfiyyīn.* Ed. by ʿAbd ar-Raḥmān ibn Sulaymān al-ʿUṯaymīn. Beirut: Dār al-ʿArab al-'Islāmī, 1986.

ʿUkbarī, *Masā'il* = al-ʿUkbarī, 'Abū l-Baqā', *Masā'il ḫilāfiyya fī n-naḥw.* Ed. by Muḥammad Ḫayr al-Ḥulwānī. Aleppo: Maktabat aš-Šahbā', n. d.

Sezgin (1984: 24–25 also lists works known only by title or the occasional quotation, and two unpublished manuscripts:

Anon, *Masā'il al-ḫilāf bayn al-Baṣriyyīn wa-l-Kūfiyyīn*, Ẓāhiriyya, ʿāmm 6867, fol. 53a–60b.

Anon, *I'tilāf an-nuṣra fī ḫtilāf nuḥāt al-Kūfa wa-l-Baṣra*, Şehid Ali Paşa 2348, 90ff. [See A. S. Furat, *Zeitschrift für arabische Linguistik* 1 (1978) 8–23.]

## 8.2. Secondary sources

ʿAlāma, Ṭalāl. 1993. *Taṭawwur an-naḥw al-ʿarabī fī madrasatay al-Baṣra wa-l-Kūfa.* Beirut: Dār al-Fikr al-Lubnānī.

Baalbaki, Ramzi. 1981a. "Arabic Grammatical Controversies and the Extant Sources of the Second and Third Centuries AH". *Studia Arabica et Islamica, Festschrift for Iḥsān ʿAbbās* ed. by Wadād al-Qadi, 1–26. Beirut: American Univ. of Beirut.

–. 1981b. "A Possible Early Reference to Sībawayhi's *Kitāb*?". *Zeitschrift der deutschen morgenländischen Gesellschaft* 131.114–118.

–. 1983. "A Difficult Passage in Farrā''s *Ma'ānī l-Qur'ān*". *Bulletin d'Etudes Orientales* 35.13–18.

–. 1989. "A Contribution to the Study of Technical Terms in Early Arabic Grammar: The term *aṣl* in Sībawayhi's *Kitāb*". *A Miscellany of Middle Eastern Articles, in Memoriam Thomas Muir Johnstone 1924–1983* ed. by A. K. Irvine et al., 163–177. Harlow: Longman.

Bernards, Monique. 1993. *Establishing a Reputation: The reception of Sibawayh's Book.* Ph. D., Univ. of Nijmegen.

–. 1997. *Changing Traditions: Al-Mubarrad's refutation of Sībawayh and the subsequent reception of the Kitāb.* Leiden: Brill.

Bohas, Georges, Jean-Patrick Guillaume & Djamel Eddine Kouloughli. 1990. *The Arabic Linguistic Tradition.* London & New York: Routledge.

Carter, Michael George. 1973. "*Ṣarf* et *ḫilāf*: Contribution à l'histoire de la grammaire arabe". *Arabica* 20.292–304.

–. 1994. "Writing the History of Arabic Grammar". *Historiographia linguistica* 21.387–416.

–. 1999. "The Struggle for Authority: A re-examination of the Baṣran and Kūfan debate". *Tradition and Innovation: Norm and deviation in Arabic and Semitic linguistics* ed. by Lutz Edzard & Mohammed Nekroumi, 55–70. Wiesbaden: Harrassowitz.

Ḍayf, Šawqī. 1968. *Al-madāris an-naḥwiyya.* Cairo: no publisher given.

Dīra, al-Muḫtār 'Aḥmad. 1991. *Dirāsa fī n-naḥw al-Kūfī min ḫilāl Ma'ānī l-Qur'ān li-l-Farrā'.* Beirut: no publisher given.

Flügel, Gustav. 1862. *Die grammatischen Schulen der Araber.* Leipzig: F. A. Brockhaus. (Repr. Nendeln: Kraus, 1966.)

Goldziher, Ignaz. 1994. *On the History of Grammar among the Arabs.* Transl. by Kinga Dévényi and Tamás Iványi. Amsterdam: Benjamins. [Originally published in Hungarian, "A nyelvtudomány története az araboknál", *Nyelvtudományi Közlemenyék* 14 (1878) 309–375, and issued separately, Budapest: Franklin.]

Maḫzūmī, Mahdī al-. 1958. *Madrasat al-Kūfa.* Cairo: Muṣṭafā l-Bābī l-Ḥalabī.

–. 1963. *Ar-Rummānī an-naḥwī fī ḍaw' šarḥihi li-Kitāb Sībawayhi.* Damascus: Maṭbaʿat Ǧāmiʿat Dimašq.

Maḥmūd, Muḥammad Ḥusaynī. 1986. *Al-Madrasa al-Baġdādiyya fī ta'riḫ an-naḥw al-ʿarabī.* Beirut: no publisher given.

Owens, Jonathan. 1990. *Early Arabic Grammatical Theory: Heterogeneity and standardization.* Amsterdam: Benjamins.

Qāsim, 'Aḥmad Muḥammad. n. d. *an-Naḥw al-Baġdādī wa-nawāṣib al-muḍāriʿ.* Cairo: Dār aṭ-Ṭibāʿa al-Muḥammadiyya.

Sezgin, Fuat. 1984. *Geschichte des arabischen Schrifttums.* IX. Leiden: Brill.

Talmon, Rafael. 1985. "An eighth-century Grammatical School in Medina: The collection and evaluation of the available material". *Bulletin of the School of Oriental and African Studies* 48.224–236.

–. 1987. "Schacht's Theory in the Light of Recent Discoveries Concerning and [sic] the Origins of Arabic Grammar". *Studia Islamica* 65.31–50.

–. 1990. "The Philosophizing Farrā': An interpretation of an obscure saying attributed to the grammarian Ṯaʿlab". *Studies in the History of Arabic Grammar* II ed. by Kees Versteegh & Michael Carter, 265–279. Amsterdam: Benjamins.

Versteegh, Cornelis [Kees] H. M. 1983. "A Dissenting Grammarian: Quṭrub on declension". *The History of Linguistics in the Near East* ed. by Kees Versteegh et al., 167–193. Amsterdam: Benjamins.

–. 1993. *Arabic Grammar and Qur'ānic Exegesis in Early Islam.* Leiden: Brill.

–. 1995. *The Explanation of Linguistic Causes: Az-Zaǧǧāǧī's theory of grammar.* Amsterdam: Benjamins.

–. 1997. *The Arabic Linguistic Tradition.* London: Routledge.

Zakī, 'Aḥmad Kamāl. 1961. *Al-ḥayāt al-'adabiyya fī l-Baṣra 'ilā nihāyat al-qarn aṯ-ṯānī l-hiǧrī.* Damascus: Dār al-Fikr.

*Michael G. Carter, Oslo (Norway)*

# 40. La nouvelle approche de la grammaire au IVe–Xe siècle: Ibn Ǧinnī (320/932–392/1002)

1. Préliminaires
2. Ibn Ǧinnī et la morpho-phonologie: Le *Sirr ṣināʿat al-ʾiʿrāb*
3. La réflexion d'Ibn Ǧinnī sur la relation entre langue et grammaire: le *Ḫaṣāʾiṣ*
4. L'héritage d'Ibn Ǧinnī
5. Bibliographie

## 1. Préliminaires

### 1.1. La grammaire au IVe/Xe siècle: vue d'ensemble

Le IVe/Xe siècle constitue une période cruciale dans le développement de la tradition grammaticale arabe: alors que, dans les siècles précédents, l'élaboration de la pensée grammaticale restait dominée par une grande hétérogénéité apparaissant à tous les niveaux, l'époque qui nous intéresse se caractérise par une volonté clairement assumée de réorganisation et de refondation du savoir grammatical traditionnel sur des bases plus systématiques et plus explicites. Ce mouvement prend deux grandes directions. La première est orientée vers l'élaboration de traités à visée didactique, s'attachant à présenter, de façon plus structurée et, partant, plus accessible, l'essentiel des acquis de la tradition grammaticale. Ces tentatives restent encore très diverses dans leur conception et leur organisation; cependant, elles ont toutes en commun un certain nombre de préoccupations qui les distinguent, collectivement, des écrits datant de la période précédente: le souci de donner des définitions claires et précises des termes techniques de base, et, plus généralement, de distinguer l'usage métalinguistique de ces termes (ce qu'on appelle à l'époque les *iṣṭilāḥāt an-naḥwiyyīn*, les "conventions [terminologiques] des grammairiens") de leur usage ordinaire; le souci, également, de présenter les faits et les règles d'une façon plus pédagogique, en distinguant plus nettement leur niveau de généralité ou de représentativité. On peut citer, parmi les ouvrages de ce type, le *Kitāb al-Ǧumal* d'az-Zaǧǧāǧī (mort vers 340/950), qui connut une grande vogue en Egypte et en Afrique du Nord jusqu'au VIe/XIIIe siècle, mais aussi le *Šarḥ al-Kitāb* d'ar-Rummānī (mort en 384/994) qui, en dépit de ce que laisse entendre son titre n'est pas tant un commentaire qu'une refonte de l'ouvrage de Sībawayhi, la matière de chaque chapitre étant réorganisée selon une grille standard (Mubārak 1974); contrairement à la précédente, cette tentative n'eut guère de succès. Toutefois, la réalisation la plus significative en ce domaine reste incontestablement le *Kitāb al-ʾUṣūl* d'Ibn as-Sarrāǧ (mort en 316/928), l'un des plus jeunes disciples d'al-Mubarrad: organisant pour la première fois la matière grammaticale selon un ordre rigoureusement systématique fondé sur des principles explicites et clairement définis, il offre un modèle totalement reproductible, où la place de chaque question, de chaque classe de données et de chaque discussion est déterminée, de façon univoque, par son statut dans l'organisation générale de la théorie. Il s'agit là d'une véritable révolution scientifique, en ce qu'elle permet aux grammairiens de dépasser le stade de l'improvisation individuelle et d'installer leur discipline dans une perspective réellement cumulative. De fait, l'ordre d'exposition de la matière grammaticale élaboré par Ibn as-Sarrāǧ devait progressivement s'imposer comme le 'modèle canonique', repris, avec des variantes mineures, par la quasi-totalité des traités grammaticaux depuis le VIe/XIIe siècle.

Parallèlement à cette refonte de la doctrine, l'effort des grammairiens s'oriente également vers une tentative globale pour définir et expliciter le statut de leur discipline, pour en fonder rationnellement les concepts et les catégories, et pour en justifier les méthodes. Cette réflexion, qui semble propre aux grammairiens du IVe/Xe siècle, s'inscrit dans une perspective polémique et apologétique, implicitement ou explicitement dirigée contre certaines idées véhiculées par la *falsafa*, la tradition philosophique d'inspiration aristotélicienne, qui atteint alors sa plus grande diffusion dans le monde musulman et vise à peu près ouvertement à l'hégémonie culturelle. Son attitude tend à réduire la grammaire au rang d'une discipline auxiliaire, cantonnée à l'étude de la "forme" (*lafẓ*) extérieure et inessentielle des énoncés dans tel ou tel idiome particulier, la logique étant seule habilitée à en analyser le sens (*maʿnā*) au moyen de procédures universelles (Elamrani-Jamal 1983). A l'inverse, les grammairiens s'attachent, souvent en empruntant des armes à l'adversaire, à établir et à consolider deux propositions fondamentales: (a) la radicale spécificité et la supériorité de la langue arabe relativement aux autres idiomes, supériorité que seul le grammairien, muni des outils de sa discipline, est en mesure de percevoir et de mettre au jour; et (b) l'autonomie de la grammaire, capable de fonder et de légitimer elle-même sa démarche et ses concepts opératoires, sans faire appel aux 'sciences importées' (i. e. l'héritage philosophique et scientifique grec) non plus qu'à toute discipline extérieure. Ces deux propositions, avec des inflexions et des illustrations très diverses, sont au cœur de deux ouvrages particulièrement représentatifs de cette période, le *Kitāb al-'Īḍāḥ fī 'ilal an-naḥw* d'az-Zaǧǧāǧī, (Versteegh 1995), et le *Ḫaṣā'iṣ* d'Ibn Ǧinnī (voir 3.). Mort en 392/1002, ce dernier appartient à la dernière génération des grammairiens du IV^e^/X^e^ siècle. Sa pensée, brillante, originale et très personnelle, en fait d'un certain point de vue le meilleur représentant d'une époque marquée par une créativité vigoureuse, où la normalisation de la doctrine, quoique déjà bien entamée, n'impose pas encore un modèle unique et rigide à son expression, et où de vastes espaces de liberté restent ouverts à la réflexion et à l'expérimentation individuelles.

### 1.2. Aperçu de la carrière et de l'œuvre d'Ibn Ǧinnī

Au-delà de ses aspects anecdotiques, la trajectoire d'Ibn Ǧinnī (étudiée avec plus de détail dans Mehiri 1973: 19–87) apparaît assez caractéristique du type de carrière que pouvaient mener les grammairiens, et plus généralement les lettrés, à cette époque: en l'absence d'institutions d'enseignement susceptibles de leur fournir les moyens d'une existence indépendantes (elles n'apparaîtront, progressivement, qu'à partir du milieu du V^e^/XI^e^ siècle, sous la forme des *madrasas*), leur principale source de revenus, mais aussi de prestige social, était la protection de quelque grand personnage. Simultanément, le morcellement de l'empire abbaside et l'émergence de principautés semi-indépendantes multiplient les occasions de mécénat, les chefs de ces nouvelles puissances ayant à cœur de s'attacher les savants et les lettrés les plus prestigieux. Ces derniers bénéficient par conséquent d'un 'marché' particulièrement favorable, dès lors qu'ils possèdent les qualités sociales nécessaires pour s'imposer dans une société brillante, mais traversée d'âpres rivalités, et où aucune position n'est jamais acquise. Le type le plus achevé de ces 'grammairiens de cour', s'il faut du moins en juger par l'image qu'en donnent les sources biographiques arabes, est 'Abū 'Alī al-Fārisī (mort en 377/986), le maître d'Ibn Ǧinnī. Outre le rôle qu'il joua dans la formation et la carrière de notre grammairien, al-Fārisī occupe une place de première importance dans l'élaboration de la tradition grammaticale arabe. Particulièrement célèbre, en son temps, pour l'étendue et la sûreté de sa connaissance du corpus grammatical (rappelons que celui-ci, constitué à partir de la vieille poésie tribale, est beaucoup plus diversifié et hétérogène que l'usage courant de l'arabe classique), il est aussi et surtout le principal disciple d'Ibn as-Sarrāǧ (voir 1.1.) dont il contribua à diffuser l'enseignement dans le *Kitāb al-'Īḍāḥ*: cet ouvrage reproduit, avec des variantes mineures, le système d'exposition du *Kitāb al-'Uṣūl*. Contrairement à son modèle, qui eut, semble-t-il, une diffusion assez restreinte, l'*Īḍāḥ* connut un important succès, s'il faut en juger par le nombre de commentaires et de 'dérivés' (abrégés, commentaires des vers-témoins ...) auquel il donna lieu: Sezgin (1984: 103–107) en dénombre 47, dont 13 commentaires propres. Né à Mossoul vers 320/932 dans un milieu très modeste (son père était un affranchi d'origine byzantine) Ibn Ǧinnī s'attacha très tôt à 'Abū 'Alī, qu'il rencontra à l'occasion d'un voyage de celui-ci dans sa ville natale, et dont il partagea la carrière brillante, auprès de l'émir ḥamdanite d'Alep, Sayf ad-Dawla, puis des émirs buwayhides de Šīrāz et de Bagdad, 'Aḍud ad-Dawla et son fils Bahā' ad-Dawla, auquel Ibn Ginnī devait dédier le *Ḫaṣā'iṣ*. Grâce à l'appui de son maître, mais aussi à ses qualités personnelles, il acquit une grande renommée, connut d'importants succès mondains, et se lia avec certains des esprits les plus distingués de son époque, notamment le poète al-Mutanabbī, avec lequel il devait entretenir une relation suivie, ainsi que le poète et philologue aš-Šarīf ar-Raḍī, l'éditeur du *Nahǧ al-Balāġa*. Contrairement à al-Fārisī, dont l'enseignement oral était fort recherché et constituait une partie importante de l'activité, Ibn Ǧinnī ne semble être intervenu que de façon secondaire dans ce domaine, ce qui explique sans doute qu'il n'ait guère eu de disciples importants. En revanche, il consacra l'essentiel de ses efforts à l'écriture, et laissa une production abondante (détaillée dans Sezgin 1984: 173–182). Les ouvrages grammaticaux et philologiques y occupent une place de choix; outre ceux qui seront abordés plus en détail en 2. et en 3., on peut y relever plusieurs commentaires de recueils poétiques (notamment celui d'al-Mutanabbī), ainsi qu'un précis grammatical, le *Kitāb al-Luma'*, reprenant sous une forme abrégée le contenu et le plan de l'*Īḍāḥ* d'al-Fārisī; rédigé en 369, c'est-à-dire assez tôt dans la carrière du grammairien, l'ouvrage connut une incontestable notoriété, puisqu'il donna lieu à 23 commentaires (Sezgin 1984: 174–176), rédigés pour la plupart aux V^e/XI^e et au VI^e/XII^e siècles. Cependant, selon le jugement unanime de la postérité, c'est essentiellement dans le domaine de la morpho-phonologie (*taṣrīf*) qu'Ibn Ǧinnī devait apporter sa contribution la plus abondante, la plus significative et la plus originale (sur l'organisation générale de cette discipline, voir Auroux et al. 1989: 272–278, ou Bohas, Guillaume & Kouloughli 1990: 73–99). Elle comprend notamment des traités 'classiques' dans leur conception et leur contenu, comme le *Munṣif*, lui-même un commentaire particulièrement développé du *Kitāb at-Taṣrīf* d'al-Māzinī, l'un des grands maîtres de Baṣra (mort vers 248/860), et le *Mulūkī*, abrégé très succinct qui fut notamment commenté par Ibn Ya'īš (mort en 643/1245). Hormis l'acuité et la précision de certaines analyses, ces ouvrages (dont plusieurs aspects sont discutés dans Bohas & Guillaume 1984) ne s'écartent guère du modèle courant. Tel n'est pas le cas, en revanche, du *Sirr Ṣinā'at al-'i'rāb* et du *Ḫaṣā'iṣ*, les deux œuvres majeures du grammairien, rédigées l'une et l'autre vers la fin de sa vie, dans les années 380/990. Par la puissance et l'ampleur de la réflexion qu'ils enregistrent, ces deux textes occupent une place à part dans l'histoire de la tradition grammaticale arabe; on consacrera les pages qui suivent à en exposer brièvement quelques idées-forces.

## 2. Le *Sirr Ṣinā'at al-'i'rāb*

### 2.1. Organisation générale

Contrairement à ce que pourrait laisser penser le titre de cet ouvrage, il n'est pas consacré à la syntaxe, mais à la phonétique et à la morpho-phonologie: *'i'rāb*, ici, n'est pas à entendre dans son acception technique de "marquage casuel / modal" (d'où "analyse syntaxique"), mais au sens plus général de "expression claire et élégante, conforme à l'usage des anciens Arabes". Cet emploi, assez peu fréquent chez les grammairiens de l'époque, de même que le titre 'racoleur' (il pourrait se traduire par "Le secret de l'art de l'expression" et présente une connotation nettement ésotérique: *ṣinā'a*, surtout accolé à *sirr*, évoque le 'grand-œuvre' des alchimistes) semble indiquer que l'ouvrage s'adresse à un public plus vaste que les seuls spécialistes, et qu'il s'inscrit dans cette perspective d'apologie et d'auto-promotion de la grammaire que l'on a relevée plus haut (1.1.). Son organisation, elle aussi, reflète le souci de présenter le savoir grammatical sous une forme plus homogène, basée sur un classement formellement rigoureux. Une introduction générale, manifestement destinée à piquer la curiosité du lecteur, problématise d'emblée la variété des sons de la langue et introduit, de façon encore très globale, certaines notions de base de la phonétique, notamment celle de point d'articulation (*maḫraǧ*); elle contient également d'intéressantes considérations sur les glides (*ḥurūf al-līn wa-l-madd*), et leur réalisation contextuelle comme voyelles longues, ainsi que sur le statut des voyelles brèves. Ces discussions, d'une grande subtilité, manifestent une tension certaine entre la position 'canonique' de la tradition arabe, selon laquelle les voyelles brèves (*ḥarakāt*, littéralement "motions") ne sont pas à proprement parler des segments phonétiques (*ḥurūf*), mais plutôt des 'accidents' du segment (consonne ou glide) qui les précède, et l'évidence d'une étroite parenté entre les glides dans leur réalisation comme voyelles longues, et les voyelles brèves correspondantes. Après cette introduction, un premier chapitre présente un inventaire des segments phonétiques, met en évidence les divers points d'articulation, et expose et discute leurs variantes de réalisation, contextuelles ou non (Fleisch 1958), puis développe une classification des segments selon une série d'oppositions binaires. Les unes, purement phonétiques, concernent les 'modes' d'articulation, comme *maǧhūr* vs. *mahmūs* ("criée" vs. "murmurée"), qui correspond approximativement à l'opposition sonore/sourde; d'autres ont trait au statut phonologique de certains segments, comme *ṣaḥīḥ* vs. *mu'tall* ("sain" vs. "malade"), le second terme désignant les glides soumis à des processus spécifiques (effacement, assimilation ...); d'autres encore se réfèrent au statut morphologique, comme *'aṣlī* vs. *zā'id* ("segment radical" vs. "augment"). Le reste (plus des 9/10) de l'ouvrage, traite, dans l'ordre alphabétique, de chaque segment phonétique pris individuellement, selon un plan invariable. Après un bref développement consacré au segment concerné dans son statut 'basique' (i. e. lorsqu'il fait partie de la racine et n'est pas le résultat d'un processus de substitution), sont abordés les cas où le segment concerné est produit d'une substitution (*badal*), c'est-à-dire, en gros, d'un processus d'assimilation, puis les cas où il est augment (*zā'ida*) introduit dans la racine par les règles de la morphologie lexicale. Ainsi, pour prendre un exemple, le segment /m/ est basique dans *tamr* "dattes", il est substitué dans *'ambar* "ambre" dont la forme sous-jacente (reproduite par la graphie) est *'anbar*, et il est augment dans *miftāḥ* "clé" dérivé nominal du verbe *fataḥa* "ouvrir".

### 2.2. Originalité du *Sirr ṣinā'at al-'i'rāb*

L'originalité de l'ouvrage provient, pour une bonne part, du regroupement qu'elle opère entre la phonétique et la morpho-phonologie; d'une manière générale, en effet, les traités de *taṣrīf* classiques n'abordent pas la phonétique proprement dite. Celle-ci, au demeurant, apparaît déjà constituée de façon à peu près définitive dès le *Kitāb* de Sībawayhi et ne connut guère de développements ultérieurs. On notera, dans le même ordre d'idées, que l'organisation suivie ne permet pas de maintenir la distinction entre les deux parties canoniques du *taṣrīf*, la première correspondant à la morphologie (dont relève notamment l'opposition segment basique vs. augment) et la seconde à la phonologie (opposition basique vs. substitué). En fait, la lecture de l'ouvrage apparaît quelque peu déroutante à un lecteur plus familier des traités canoniques (y compris ceux d'Ibn Ǧinnī lui-même); cela tient, pour une part, au contraste entre l'organisation très structurée de chaque développement, et l'hétérogénéité des critères qui déterminent cette organisation. Ce à quoi s'ajoute, pour une bonne part, l'hétérogénéité de la matière traitée: bien que l'objet de l'ouvrage soit en principe la morpho-phonologie, on y trouve d'abondants développements concernant des points de syntaxe. Ainsi, dans le chapitre sur le segment /b/, Ibn Ǧinnī traite longuement du statut des prépositions clitiques *bi-* "à, par" *li-* "à, pour" et *ka-* "comme", la question étant de savoir s'il faut les analyser comme des augments (*zawā'id*), ainsi que l'affirment certains grammairiens, ou comme des éléments lexicaux autonomes. Ce genre de discussions, menées le plus souvent avec un grand luxe de détails et d'arguments, peuvent apparaître comme autant de digressions sans rapport avec le sujet principal; il importe toutefois de comprendre qu'elles s'inscrivent dans un mode particulier d'organisation du discours scientifique de l'époque, le *taḥqīq* "examen approfondi". Cette pratique, qu'al-Fārisī, dit-on, maniait avec une maîtrise redoutable, consiste à étudier une question dans tous ses aspects, et surtout à discuter toutes les affirmations antérieures la concernant de près ou de loin, si naïves ou marginales qu'elles puissent apparaître, en examinant tous les arguments pour et contre. Dans le cas que l'on vient de citer en exemple, le seul fait que certains grammairiens aient catalogué les propositions monolittères comme *bi-* en tant qu'"augments" (ou, plus précisément, qu'ils aient confondu en une seule appellation, *zā'ida*, ce que nous distinguons soit comme augments soit comme clitiques) impose à Ibn Ǧinnī de statuer sur la question, lors même que l'opinion discutée, d'après ce que l'on peut inférer de la discussion elle-même, apparaît ultra-minoritaire et de surcroît tombée de l'usage des grammairiens contemporains: l'omettre purement et simplement serait interprété comme une preuve d'ignorance, exposant l'auteur au blâme de ses pairs. Un ouvrage composé selon cette méthode n'est pas toujours, cela va sans dire, d'une extrême simplicité; il n'en reste pas moins, dans le cas qui nous occupe, que la façon qu'a Ibn Ǧinnī de subvertir les divisions habituelles de la matière grammaticale, et de rapprocher des données ou des analyses que d'autres ouvrages maintiennent séparées, le met en mesure de présenter de nombreux aperçus originaux et éclairants.

## 3. Le *Ḫaṣā'iṣ*

### 3.1. Conception et visée générale

Composé entre 379/967 et 384/972, le *Ḫaṣā'iṣ* (titre que l'on pourrait traduire par "Questions particulières", ou encore par "Particularités remarquables", i. e. de la langue arabe), est incontestablement l'ouvrage le plus célèbre et le plus original d'Ibn Ǧinnī; comme on l'a dit plus haut, il s'inscrit dans une perspective de 'défense et illustration' de la langue arabe et, simultanément, de la grammaire. Tout comme le *Sirr Ṣinā'at al-'i'rāb*, et de façon plus marquée encore, il s'adresse non aux seuls grammairiens mais au public lettré du temps, dont il s'attache à piquer la curiosité et à flatter les goûts: par sa structure comme par son style, le *Ḫaṣā'iṣ* s'apparente étroitement aux ouvrages des prosateurs humanistes de l'époque classique, dont il partage la rhétorique subtile et recherchée (en contraste très net avec la prose simple normalement utilisée dans les traités didactiques, grammaticaux ou autres) et le refus de tout didactisme et de tout esprit de système, au profit d'une approche privilégiant la variété et l'imprédictibilité. L'ouvrage se constitue ainsi d'un ensemble de chapitres largement autonomes, chacun étant consacré à une question d'ordre général relevant de l'épistémologie ou de la méthodologie de la grammaire; le traitement de chaque question met en jeu un ensemble de faits et de discussions relevant de domaines tout à fait distincts dans le découpage traditionnel de la grammaire; tout l'art d'Ibn Ǧinnī consistant à mettre en lumière les rapports 'subtils et mystérieux' qu'ils entretiennent les uns avec les autres dans l'économie générale de la langue, et de montrer la pertinence de chacun à la discussion principale. Cette écriture, que l'on pourrait qualifier de baroque, jointe à l'extrême subtilité de la dialectique mise en œuvre, rend parfois la pensée d'Ibn Ǧinnī difficile à suivre: on est plus d'une fois amené à se demander si telle de ses affirmations représente simplement une manœuvre tactique dans le cadre d'une discussion locale, ou reflète une position d'ordre général. Mais il faut souligner que cet art d'écrire correspond très précisément à l'intention globale qui anime le *Ḫaṣā'iṣ*: montrer que la grammaire n'a pas seulement une portée utilitaire (apprendre à parler correctement l'arabe), mais qu'elle constitue une science valide et légitime, et qu'elle est susceptible, pour peu qu'on en approfondisse les démarches et les concepts, d'ouvrir un champ quasi-illimité à une réflexion et à une spéculation désintéressées; qu'elle fait, en d'autres termes, partie intégrante de cet humanisme aristocratique qui, à l'époque, caractérise l'élite intellectuelle arabo-musulmane.

3.2. Quelques idées-forces du *Ḫaṣā'iṣ*

Parmi les nombreux thèmes abordés dans cet ouvrage, deux ont tout particulièrement retenu l'attention des arabisants: la question de l'origine du langage et celle de la "dérivation élargie" (*al-ištiqāq al-'akbar*). Sur le premier point, Ibn Ǧinnī développe une argumentation serrée, sans pour autant arriver à des positions radicalement nouvelles ou originales par rapport aux discussions antérieures et postérieures (résumées dans Loucel 1963–64): le rejet implicite de la thèse naturaliste (déjà acquis par les théologiens du siècle précédent, voir Weiss 1974; → Art. 43) l'amène à poser la question de l'origine du langage en termes d'"instauration" (*waḍ'*, équivalent et probablement calque du grec *thésis*), la seule incertitude portant sur la nature précise de cette instauration: fixation (*tawqīf*) divine ou convention (*iṣṭilāḥ*) humaine? Comme la plupart des penseurs musulmans qui ont abordé la question, Ibn Ǧinnī conclut finalement à une suspension du jugement entre les deux thèses. En fait, le choix de l'une ou de l'autre n'a guère d'incidence théorique ou pratique sur son propos, l'important pour lui étant de souligner l'harmonie qui existe, à tous les niveaux, dans le système de la langue; cette harmonie étant, pour lui comme pour d'autres grammairiens de son temps, le reflet de la "sagesse" (*ḥikma*) admirable, avec laquelle le ou les instaurateurs de la langue arabe en ont prévu et planifié les moindres détails. En fait, la principale contribution d'Ibn Ǧinnī au débat (mais il n'est pas le seul dans ce cas, ni le premier) est de déplacer la problématique d'une approche purement lexicale, dominante chez les juristes vers une approche plus grammaticale: ce qui est en jeu n'est plus le simple rapport du nom à son dénominé, mais l'organisation générale de la langue. Or, dire que celle-ci est "instaurée", i. e. fixée par une décision souveraine, quelle qu'en soit l'origine, n'implique aucunement qu'elle soit arbitraire: au contraire, rien n'interdit de prêter à l'instaurateur des choix conscients et volontaires, des "intentions" (*'aġrāḍ*) qu'il convient au grammairien de tenter de découvrir en dégageant, à travers l'hétérogénéité et le désordre apparent des faits, l'ordre caché qui les organise. En ce qui concerne la 'dérivation étendue', elle consiste dans l'hypothèse, partiellement fondée sur des faits empiriques, que les racines trilittères dont les deux premiers éléments sont identiques présentent des valeurs sémantiques voisines (e. g. *laṭaḥa* "frapper légèrement de la main", *laṭafa* "caresser", *laṭaḫa* "donner une gifle"); il en irait de même des racines trilittères composées des mêmes éléments, mais dans un ordre différent (e. g. *qawl* "dire", *qilw* "âne sauvage, onagre", *waqala* "escalader une montagne", *walaqa* "se hâter" ... contiennent tous, selon Ibn Ǧinnī, l'idée de vitesse et de légèreté). Ces spéculations, présentées par Ibn Ǧinnī comme un 'secret' particulièrement important de la langue arabe, ont suscité l'intérêt de nombreux philologues anciens et modernes.

D'une portée plus universelle apparaissent, en revanche les discussions portant sur le statut des explications, ou des "causes" (*'illa*, plur. *'ilal*) en grammaire. Ibn Ǧinnī, qui consacre à la question l'un des plus longs chapitres de son ouvrage, insiste sur le fait que celles-ci sont de nature non seulement à décrire les faits de façon adéquate, mais aussi à en rendre compte, à en dégager la raison d'être. A ce titre, les explications grammaticales, selon lui, se rapprochent davantage de celles des théologiens que de celles des juristes: là où ceux-ci se limitent à édicter des règles normatives dont la raison d'être profonde leur échappe, ceux-là, s'attachant à donner un fondement rationnel aux vérités révélées, sont au contraire tenus de se fonder sur l'intuition commune, sensible ou rationnelle. Or, c'est précisément, affirme Ibn Ǧinnī, ce que font les grammairiens, puisque l'ensemble des règles qu'ils élaborent repose en fin de compte sur la notion de "lourdeur" (*istiṯqāl*), qui relève de l'intuition sensible. Cette notion, abondamment sollicitée dans l'ensemble de l'ouvrage, représente assurément une tentative de grande ampleur pour ramener, sinon toute la grammaire (les applications de la notion de 'lourdeur' en syntaxe sont moins systématiques), du moins la morpho-phonologie, au jeu d'une contrainte unique, et à la fonder sur les propriétés sensibles des sons de la langue. La 'lourdeur', telle que l'entend Ibn Ǧinnī, peut s'interpréter comme la quantité d'énergie nécessaire pour produire un son, ou une séquence de sons; chaque élément phonétique est associé à un certain degré de lourdeur, selon une échelle qui présente d'étroites affinités avec l'échelle de sonorité: en gros, un élément est d'autant plus lourd qu'il est moins sonore (Bohas 1981). Ainsi, les voyelles sont plus légères que les glides, eux-mêmes plus légers que les consonnes; à l'intérieur des deux premières catégories, le /a/ et son homologue, le glide abstrait *'alif* sont légers, le /i/ et le /y/ sont moyennement lourds et le /u/ et le /w/ sont absolument lourds. La lourdeur globale d'une forme, cependant, n'est pas définie simplement par la lourdeur de tous les éléments qui la constituent, mais aussi par la position réciproque des éléments lourds. Ainsi, une séquence iCu (C étant pour 'consonne'), passant du lourd (le /i/) au plus lourd (le /u/) est-elle plus lourde qu'une séquence inverse uCi: on en tire argument pour rendre compte du fait que la première n'est jamais attestée dans les schèmes verbaux et nominaux (il n'y a pas de forme *fi'ul*), alors que la seconde n'est attestée que dans les schèmes verbaux, où elle sert à former le passif. Autrement dit, la lourdeur extrême de la première l'empêche d'être attestée dans la langue, tandis que la lourdeur relative de la seconde la cantonne dans un emploi spécifique, la charge de sens supplémentaire qu'elle assume étant censée compenser la quantité d'énergie nécessaire à sa réalisation. De même, une séquence VGV (V étant pour 'voyelle' et G pour 'glide') est lourde par définition, puisqu'elle juxtapose des éléments de nature semblable, tout comme une séquence $C_iVC_i$ représentant des consonnes identiques); lorsqu'une telle séquence est réalisée par le jeu de la morphologie dérivationnelle, les processus morphologiques voulus entrent en jeu pour l'alléger. Parallèlement à la notion de lourdeur ainsi esquissée, Ibn Ǧinnī fait appel à une autre contrainte globale opérant en sens inverse, le "blocage de l'ambiguïte" (*man' al-iltibās*), qui a pour effet d'empêcher l'application de processus morphologiques lorsque ceux-ci auraient pour effet de faire disparaître des informations cruciales pour l'identification morphologique d'une forme. Il s'agit là assurément d'une tentative du plus haut intérêt et d'une vaste portée; il faut cependant souligner qu'elle reste encore dans une large mesure intuitive et marquée par de nombreuses décisions ad hoc, et que toutes les tentatives anciennes ou récentes pour en fournir une modélisation cohérente ont achoppé sur ce point.

Corollaire du point précédent, l'un des thèmes les plus abondamment développés dans le *Ḫaṣā'iṣ* est celui de la réalité psychologique des règles grammaticales: celles-ci, selon Ibn Ǧinnī, reproduisent bien, encore que de façon artificielle, l'intuition des locuteurs 'authentiques', les Arabes bédouins. Ici encore, il s'agit d'une idée déjà présente dans les écrits de certains grammairiens antérieurs, mais qui prend ici un tour nouveau. Un demi-siècle environ avant Ibn Ǧinnī, az-Zaǧǧāǧī dans son *Kitāb al-'Īḍāḥ*, attribue à al-Ḫalīl un propos affirmant en substance que le but de la grammaire est bien de retrouver les causes ou les motivations qui ont amené les Arabes à parler comme ils parlent, mais qu'elle ne saurait aboutir, en ce domaine, qu'à des conclusions hypothétiques et provisoires (Versteegh 1995: 89 sqq). Pour Ibn Ǧinnī, au contraire, il est possible, du moins dans certains cas, de démontrer que les explications élaborées par les grammairiens ne font que reproduire, dans un langage plus technique et sophistiqué, celles que fournissent les Bédouins eux-mêmes en se fondant simplement sur leur intuition de locuteurs, et malgré leur ignorance totale des 'conventions' des grammairiens. Il mentionne à ce sujet de nombreuses anecdotes, dont l'une est particulièrement significative (I, 249): interrogé à propos de sa récitation de Coran 36/40 *wa-lā l-laylu sābiqu an-nahāri* "ni la nuit précédant le jour-génitif", un Bédouin répond que cela est identique à *wa-lā l-laylu sābiqun an-nahāra* (avec l'accusatif), mais que la construction au génitif est moins 'pesante'. Selon Ibn Ǧinnī, trois conclusions sont à tirer de cela: (a) la notion de 'forme sous-jacente' (ici, la construction à l'accusatif par rapport à la construction au génitif) qui occupe une place centrale dans la technique d'analyse grammaticale correspond bien à l'intuition des locuteurs; (b) il en va de même des explications fondées sur la notion de lourdeur; (c) la notion d'allègement, corollaire de la précédente, est bien un procédé général, explicitement recherché par les locuteurs.

## 4. L'héritage d'Ibn Ǧinnī

En dépit de la notoriété et du prestige dont il n'a pas cessé de jouir dans la tradition arabe, Ibn Ǧinnī n'a pas réellement fait école, du moins en ce qui concerne ses idées les plus novatrices: de ce point de vue, il est certain qu'Ibn as-Sarrāǧ, à travers son *Kitāb al-'Uṣūl*, a exercé une influence beaucoup plus décisive et profonde sur le développement ultérieur de la tradition. Plus encore, certaines des orientations privilégiées de la réflexion d'Ibn Ǧinnī ont été l'objet de critiques implicites ou explicites de la part de grammairiens postérieurs, souvent sceptiques devant l'utilité et la plausibilité d'une recherche orientée vers les 'motivations de l'instaurateur de la langue'. Si le plus virulent d'entres eux, le polémiste almohade Ibn Maḍā' al-Qurṭubī (mort en 606/1208), n'a joué qu'un rôle secondaire et si son *Radd ʿalā n-nuḥāt* "Réfutation des grammairiens" relève plus de la déclamation incantatoire que d'une véritable tentative pour refonder la grammaire, d'autres, tels ʿAbd al-Qāhir al-Ǧurǧānī (mort en 472/1078) et, après lui, az-Zamaḫšarī (mort en 539/1143), poursuivant l'effort lancé par Ibn as-Sarrāǧ, s'attacheront à mettre au premier plan l'aspect sémantico-syntaxique de l'analyse linguistique (Kouloughli 1985), le premier à travers son œuvre majeure, le *Dalā'il al-'Iʿǧāz* "Preuves de l'inimitabilité du Coran", mais aussi son grand commentaire de l'*Īḍāḥ* d'al-Fārisī, le *Muqtaṣad*, le second à travers son commentaire du Coran, le *Kaššāf* (qui reprend une bonne part des idées lancées par le *Dalā'il al-'Iʿǧāz*), mais aussi et surtout dans son précis grammatical, le *Mufaṣṣal*, qui devait s'imposer comme l'un des manuels de base pour l'enseignement de la grammaire dans tout l'Orient musulman, au moins jusqu'à la fin du VIIe/XIII[e] siècle.

## 5. Bibliographie

### 5.1. Sources primaires (principaux textes d'Ibn Ǧinnī)

*Ḫaṣā'iṣ (al-)*. Ed. par M. ʿA. an-Najjār. 3 vols. Le Caire, 1952. (Réimpr., Beyrouth, s. d.)

*Lumaʿ (al-) fī l-ʿArabiyya*. Ed. par. H. al-Mu' min. Beyrouth, 1985.

*Munṣif (al-)*. Ed. par I. Muṣṭafā & ʿA. 'Amīn. 3 vols. Le Caire, 1954. (Réimpr., Beyrouth, s. d.)

*Sirr Ṣināʿat al-'Iʿrāb*. Ed. par M. as-Saqqā et al. Le Caire, 1954. (Réimpr., Beyrouth, s. d.)

*Taṣrīf (al-) al-Mulūkī*. In: Ibn Yaʿīš, *Šarḥ al-Mulūkī*, éd. par F. D. Qabāwah. Alep, 1973.

### 5.2. Sources secondaires

Auroux, Sylvain et al. 1989. *Histoire des idées linguistiques*. I. *La naissance des Métalangages*. Bruxelles & Paris: J. Mardaga.

Bohas, Georges. 1981. "Quelques aspects de l'argumentation et de l'explication chez les grammairiens arabes". *Arabica* 28.204–221.

–. & Guillaume, Jean-Patrick. 1984. *Etudes des théories des grammairiens arabes*. I. *Morphologie et phonologie*. Damas: Institut Français d'Etudes Arabes.

–. –. & Kouloughli, Djamel Eddine. 1990. *The Arabic Linguistic Tradition*. London: Routledge.

Elamrani-Jamal, Abdelali. 1983. *Logique aristotélicienne et grammaire arabe*. Paris: Vrin.

Fleisch, Henri. 1958. "La conception phonétique des Arabes d'après le *Sirr Ṣināʿat al-Iʿrāb* d'Ibn Ǧinnī". *Zeitschrift der deutschen morgenländischen Gesellschaft* 108.74–105.

Kouloughli, Djamel Eddine. 1985. "À propos de *lafẓ* et *maʿnā*". *Bulletin d'Etudes Orientales* 35.43–63.

Loucel, Henri. 1963–64. "L'origine du langage d'après les grammairiens arabes". *Arabica* 10.188–208, 253–281; 11.57–72, 151–187.

Mehiri, Abdelkader. 1973. *Les théories grammaticales d'Ibn Jinnī*. Tunis: Publications de l'Université de Tunis.

Mubārak, Māzin. 1974. *Ar-Rummānī an-naḥwī fī ḍaw' šarḥihi li-Kitāb Sībawayhi.* Beyrouth: Dār al-Kitāb al-Lubnānī.

Owens, Jonathan. 1990. *Early Arabic Grammatical Theory: Heterogeneity and standardization.* Amsterdam & Philadelphia: Benjamins.

Sezgin, Fuat. 1984. *Geschichte des Arabischen Schrifttums.* IX. *Grammatik.* Leiden: Brill.

Versteegh, Kees. 1995. *The Explanation of Grammatical Causes: Az-Zaǧǧāǧī's theory of grammar.* Amsterdam & Philadelphia: Benjamins.

Weiss, Bernard. 1974. "Medieval Muslim Discussions on the Origin of Language". *Zeitschrift der deutschen morgenländischen Gesellschaft* 125.33–41.

*Jean-Patrick Guillaume, Paris (France)*

# 41. La période post-classique de la linguistique arabe: d'Ibn Ǧinnī à al-'Astarābāḏī

1. Les grands centres d'étude
2. Les principales œuvres
3. Bibliographie

## 1. Les grands centres d'étude

Durant la période classique, les études grammaticales, qui étaient nées dans les deux métropoles du sud de l'Irak: Baṣra et Kūfa, s'épanouirent principalement dans la capitale de l'empire abbasside, Bagdad, où une pléiade de grands grammairiens enseignèrent. En revanche, pendant la période post-classique, ces études se développèrent dans toutes les provinces de l'empire, où s'étaient multipliés les centres d'enseignement de la grammaire. Dans cette première partie, nous présenterons les notices biographiques des principaux grammairiens de cette époque, dans l'ordre chronologique et à l'intérieur de chacune des grandes provinces de l'empire musulman.

### 1.1. En Irak

Après avoir connu leur apogée au Xe siècle, les études grammaticales à Bagdad subirent une certaine éclipse au début du XIe siècle, mais elles reprirent avec la fondation de la madrasa Niẓāmiyya, inaugurée en 459/1067 par le vizir saljoukide Niẓām al-Mulk. Cette madrasa devint un centre de diffusion du sunnisme, possédant une chaire pour l'enseignement de la grammaire, dans laquelle se succédèrent cinq grands grammairiens jusqu'au début du XIIIe siècle: at-Tibrīzī (m. 502/1109), originaire de Tabriz, se rendit en Syrie où il étudia auprès d'al-Ma'arrī et, après avoir enseigné un certain temps en Egypte, il alla se fixer à Bagdad, où il devint bibliothécaire et professeur à la madrasa Niẓāmiyya; al-Faṣīḥī (m. 516/1123), natif de 'Astarābāḏ, où il fut l'élève d'al-Ǧurǧānī, succéda à at-Tibrīzī, mais il fut accusé de chi'isme et destitué; al-Ǧawāliqī (m. 539/1144), bagdadien, élève d'at-Tibrīzī et calligraphe renommé, fut appelé à succéder à al-Faṣīḥī; Ibn al-'Anbārī (m. 577/1181), natif d'al-'Anbār, élève d'al-Ǧurǧānī et d'Ibn aš-Šaǧarī, enseigna un temps, puis se retira pour se consacrer à la dévotion; al-'Ukbarī (m. 616/1219), bagdadien, élève d'Ibn al-Ḫaššāb, composa de nombreux ouvrages, bien qu'il fût aveugle. Mais à côté de ces enseignants à la madrasa Niẓāmiyya, les grammairiens sont particulièrement nombreux en Irak, durant tout le XIIe siècle. A la première moitié de ce siècle, appartiennent trois grammairiens: al-Ḥarīrī (m. 516/1122), auteur des fameuses "séances" (*maqāmāt*), résidant à Baṣra, où il possédait de vastes propriétés qu'il gérait lui-même; aṣ-Ṣaymarī (m. 541/1146), originaire des environs de Baṣra, se rendit en Egypte, où il composa un manuel très prisé des gens du Maghreb; Ibn aš-Šaǧarī (m. 542/1148), élève d'at-Tibrīzī et contemporain d'al-Ǧawāliqī, était *naqīb* des chi'ites d'al-Karḫ à Bagdad, où il enseigna la grammaire durant 70 ans. Dans la seconde moitié du XIIe siècle, nous trouvons trois grammairiens bagdadiens, exactement contemporains; Ibn al-Ḫaššāb (m. 567/1172), élève d'al-Ǧawāliqī et d'Ibn aš-Šaǧarī, était également versé dans les sciences philosophiques et mathématiques; Ibn Ṣāfī (m. 568/1173), élève d'al-Faṣīḥī, après avoir séjourné dans plusieurs villes d'Iran, revint se fixer à Damas, où il se faisait appeler "Roi des grammairiens" (*malik an-nuḥāt*); Ibn ad-Dahhān (m. 569/1174), quitta son pays natal pour aller résider à Mossoul, auprès du vizir de l'Atabeg de cette ville, en laissant à Bagdad sa bibliothèque qui fut anéantie par une crue du Tigre. Au XIIIe siècle, nous n'avons que trois grammairiens à mentionner: az-Zanǧānī, qui acheva son célèbre manuel en 654/1257, et Ibn 'Ayāz (m. 681/1282), qui enseigna à la madrasa Mustanṣiriyya, inaugurée en 631/1234 par le calife al-Mustanṣir.

### 1.2. En Iran

A la suite des grands lexicographes qui ont illustré les études grammaticales en Iran au Xe siècle: al-'Azharī, al-Ǧawharī et Ibn Fāris, le premier grammairien persan de la période post-classique est encore un lexicographe originaire de Nisabur: aṯ-Ṯaʿālibī (m. 429/1038), par ailleurs auteur d'une anthologie poétique réputée. Elève d'un neveu d'al-Fārisī, l'un des principaux grammairiens de Bagdad au siècle précédent, al-Ǧurǧānī (m. 471/1078) ne quitta pas sa ville natale, Ǧurǧān, où l'on venait de l'Irak suivre son enseignement. Connu surtout pour son recueil de proverbes, al-Maydānī (m. 518/1124), qui vécut toute sa vie à Nisabur, fut aussi un grammairien fécond. Originaire du Ḫwārizm, az-Zamaḫšarī (m. 538/1144) est le plus célèbre grammairien persan de cette période; ayant accompli le pèlerinage à la Mekke, il y séjourna si longtemps qu'il fut surnommé "le Voisin de Dieu" (*ǧār Allāh*); adepte de la doctrine muʿtazilite, il est l'auteur d'un grand commentaire du *Coran*, aussi connu et commenté que son ouvrage grammatical. Né l'année même de la mort d'az-Zamaḫšarī, al-Muṭarrizī (m. 610/1213) était, comme lui, originaire du Ḫwārizm et muʿtazilite, si bien qu'on disait de lui qu'il était son successeur (*ḫalīfa*); au cours de son pèlerinage à la Mekke en 601/1024, il passa par Bagdad, où il eut des discussions au sujet de la doctrine muʿtazilite. Un autre savant, originaire du Ḫwārizm, est as-Sakkākī (m. 626/1229), spécialiste reconnu de rhétorique, mais aussi grammairien original. Des deux derniers grammairiens du XIIIe siècle: al-'Isfarā'inī (m. 684/1285) et al-'Astarābāḏī (m. 688/1289), nous ne savons presque rien.

### 1.3. En Syrie

Les études grammaticales en Syrie, à l'époque post-classique, sont représentées par des grammairiens peu nombreux, mais fort célèbres. Le plus ancien est le grand poète et prosateur aveugle, al-Maʿarrī (m. 449/1057) qui, au cours du bref séjour qu'il fit à Bagdad en 399/1008, connut les élèves des derniers grands grammairiens du Xe siècle. L'alépin Ibn Yaʿīš (m. 643/1245) faisait route vers Bagdad afin de rencontrer Ibn al-'Anbārī, lorsqu'il apprit la mort de celui-ci à Mossoul; il se rendit alors à Damas, puis revint à Alep, où il vécut très vieux et eut de nombreux élèves, parmi lesquels on compte les auteurs de deux dictionnaires biographiques célèbres: Ibn Ḫallikān et Yāqūt. Un autre alépin, al-Ǧabrānī (m. 668/1269), qui ne semble pas avoir été l'élève d'Ibn Yaʿīš, devint professeur à la grande mosquée d'Alep. Natif de Jaén, en al-Andalus, Ibn Mālik (m. 672/1274) quitta son pays très jeune pour aller résider en Syrie; après avoir étudié auprès d'Ibn Yaʿīš à Alep, il se fixa à Damas, où il se consacra à l'enseignement de la grammaire.

### 1.4. En Egypte

L'école grammaticale égyptienne, illustrée au Xe siècle par Ibn Wallād et son contemporain an-Naḥḥās, a fourni quelques grammairiens importants durant la période post-classique. Descendant d'une famille d'origine irakienne installée en Egypte, Ibn Bābāšāḏ (m. 469/1077) fut professeur à la mosquée de ʿAmr au Caire, en même temps que rédacteur des lettres officielles au *Dīwān al-'inšā'* de la cour fatimide; devenu ascète à la fin de sa vie, il se tua en tombant du minaret de la mosquée où il logeait. Elève d'Ibn Barakāt, le successeur d'Ibn Bābāšāḏ, Ibn Barrī (m. 582/1187) devint lui aussi professeur à la mosquée de ʿAmr et réviseur de la correspondance officielle. D'origine maghrébine, Ibn Muʿṭī (m. 628/1231), après avoir étudié auprès d'al-Ǧuzūlī, se rendit en Orient où il enseigna la grammaire, d'abord à Damas, puis au Caire. Né de parents kurdes à Esné, en Haute-Egypte, Ibn al-Ḥāǧib (m. 644/1249) étudia au Caire, où il commença à enseigner, puis en 617/1220 il se rendit à Damas où il devint professeur à la grande mosquée; mais à la suite d'un différend qu'il eut avec le prince ayyoubide, il fut chassé de la ville en 639/1241; revenu au Caire, il alla se fixer ensuite à Alexandrie.

### 1.5. Au Maghreb

Pour la période post-classique, nous n'avons que trois grammairiens à mentionner au Maghreb. Si nous disposons de peu d'informations sur les deux premiers: al-Laḫmī (m. 557/1162) et Ibn al-'Aǧdabī (m. ca. 600/1203), dont nous savons seulement qu'ils étaient originaires, le premier de Ceuta et le second de Tripoli, nous sommes mieux renseignés sur le troisième et le plus célèbre, al-Ǧuzūlī (m. 607/1210); d'origine berbère, né à Marrakech, il accomplit le pèlerinage à la Mekke et, à son retour, il s'arrêta au Caire, où il étudia auprès d'Ibn Barrī; après avoir enseigné longtemps à Bougie, puis à Alméria, où il eut pour élèves aš-Šalawbīn et Ibn Muʿṭī, il devint prédicateur dans sa ville natale.

1.6. Dans al-Andalus

Les études grammaticales, introduites dans al-Andalus au X^e^ siècle par le bagdadien al-Qālī venu enseigner à Cordoue en 330/941, furent poursuivies par son élève az-Zubaydī. Durant la période post-classique, ces études se développèrent grâce à plusieurs grammairiens, dont certains manifestèrent des idées originales dans leur discipline. Le lexicographe aveugle Ibn Sīdah (m. 458/1066), natif de Murcie, alla vivre sous la protection du prince de Dénia; à la mort de son protecteur, il fut obligé de quitter cette ville, mais il put y revenir peu après. Originaire de Santarem, Ibn as-Sarrāǧ (m. ca. 549/1154) quitta son pays en 515/1121 pour se rendre en Egypte et au Yémen; devenu professeur à la grande mosquée du Caire, il y eut pour élève Ibn Barrī. Natif de Cordoue, Ibn Maḍā' (m. 592/1195) alla étudier à Séville auprès d'Ibn ar-Rammāk; adepte de la doctrine ẓāhirite, il fut cadi à Fès et à Bougie et, après avoir été grand cadi de l'état almohade, il retourna à Séville. C'est de cette ville que sont originaires les trois derniers grammairiens du XIII^e^ siècle: aš-Šalawbīn (m. 645/1248) et ses deux élèves: Ibn ʿUṣfūr (m. 669/1271) et Ibn'Abī r-Rabīʿ (m. 688/1289); à la suite d'une brouille avec son maître, Ibn ʿUṣfūr quitta sa ville natale, parcourut al-Andalus, puis se rendit dans plusieurs villes d'Ifriqiyya et du Maghreb, pour se fixer finalement à Tunis.

## 2. Les principales œuvres

La production des 37 grammairiens que nous venons de présenter est extrêmement abondante. Dans cette seconde partie, nous en ferons l'inventaire, en répartissant les ouvrages dans les neuf genres principaux que l'on peut distinguer dans la littérature grammaticale de cette époque.

2.1. Le commentaire (*šarḥ*)

Le commentaire destiné à expliquer l'œuvre d'un auteur antérieur, souvent dicté par le professeur à ses élèves, était un procédé très utilisé dans l'enseignement de la grammaire, comme d'ailleurs dans les autres disciplines. Durant la période post-classique, ce genre d'ouvrages est bien représenté, puisque l'on en dénombre une trentaine. Les grammairiens de cette période ont d'abord commenté des œuvres d'auteurs anciens, et c'est le *K. al-'Īḍāḥ* d'al-Fārisī qui vient en tête, avec cinq commentaires par Ibn ad-Dahhān, al-ʿUkbarī, al-Ǧurǧānī, Ibn ʿUṣfūr et Ibn'Abī r-Rabīʿ. Viennent ensuite le *K. al-Lumaʿ* d'Ibn Ǧinnī, avec quatre commentaires par Ibn aš-Šaǧarī, Ibn al-Ḫaššāb, Ibn ad-Dahhān et al-ʿUkbarī; le *Kitāb* de Sībawayhi, avec deux commentaires par al-Maʿarrī et Ibn ʿUṣfūr; le *K. al-Ǧumal* d'az-Zaǧǧāǧī, avec deux commentaires par Ibn Bābāšāḏ et Ibn ʿUṣfūr; le *K. at-Taṣrīf* d'Ibn Ǧinnī, avec deux commentaires par Ibn aš-Šaǧarī et Ibn Yaʿīš; enfin, le *K. al-'Uṣūl* d'Ibn as-Sarrāǧ, avec le commentaire d'Ibn Bābāšāḏ. Cette liste est intéressante, car elle nous fait connaître les auteurs anciens qui étaient les plus étudiés dans les centres d'enseignement à cette époque et, inversement, ceux qui étaient tombés dans l'oubli. Mais les grammairiens ne se se bornèrent pas à commenter les ouvrages des auteurs anciens, ils expliquèrent aussi les œuvres d'auteurs récents, voire contemporains. C'est ainsi que furent commentés: la *Muqaddima* d'Ibn Bābāšāḏ par Ibn ʿUṣfūr; le *K. al-Mufaṣṣal* d'az-Zamaḫšarī par al-ʿUkbarī, Ibn Yaʿīš et Ibn al-Ḥāǧib; la *Muqaddima* d'al-Ǧuzūlī par Ibn al-Ḥāǧib, aš-Šalawbīn et Ibn ʿUṣfūr; le *K. al-Miṣbāḥ* d'al-Muṭarrizī par al-'Isfarā'inī; la *Kāfiya* et la *Šāfiya* d'Ibn al-Ḥāǧib par al-'Astarābāḏī. Il arrivait aussi que l'auteur lui-même commentât son propre ouvrage, comme al-Ǧurǧānī qui composa deux commentaires de son *K. al-ʿAwāmil al-mi'a*, dont l'un fut, à son tour, commenté par Ibn al-Ḫaššāb, ou comme Ibn Bābāšāḏ, qui dicta à ses élèves deux commentaires sur sa *Muqaddima*, ou encore az-Zanǧānī, qui commenta son *K. al-Hādī*.

2.2. Les fondements (*'uṣūl*)

On peut diviser les ouvrages de ce genre en deux catégories: les traités complets, qui présentent les faits grammaticaux d'une manière détaillée et exhaustive, et les manuels abrégés, qui les résument d'une manière succinte et rudimentaire.

2.2.1. Les traités complets

A la suite du *Kitāb* de Sībawayhi et des œuvres des grands grammairiens de l'époque classique, comme le *K. al-'Uṣūl* d'Ibn as-Sarrāǧ, les ouvrages qui traitent des fondements de la grammaire sont divisés en deux grandes parties, à peu près égales. La première partie, appelée *naḥw* ou *'iʿrāb*, est consacrée à l'étude des comportements (*maǧārī*) de la finale des mots dans l'énoncé (*kalām*). Elle comprend généralement neuf divisions dans lesquelles les finales (*'awāḫir*) des trois sortes de mots: noms, verbes et particules, sont successivement examinées du point de vue de leur flexion (*'iʿrāb*) ou de leur fixité (*binā'*). La seconde partie, appelée *taṣrīf*, est réservée à l'étude de la transformation des formes (*'abniya*) des mots en eux-mêmes, dans le lexique (*luġa*). Cette partie comprend généralement trois sections qui traitent des points suivants: les transformations qui portent sur les schèmes des mots et produisent un changement de sens; les transformations qui affectent les radicales des mots et ne produisent pas de changement de sens; les transformations purement phonétiques. C'est cette division bipartite que nous retrouvons dans les traités complets de la période post-classique, qui semblent avoir été nombreux, puisque les sources attribuent un ouvrage de ce genre à une dizaine de grammairiens de cette époque. Mais nous ne connaissons que le titre des œuvres de six d'entre eux: al-Maʿarrī, Ibn Ṣāfī, Ibn ad-Dahhān, al-ʿUkbarī, Ibn Muʿṭī et Ibn Maḍā'. Seuls, nous sont parvenus: la seconde partie du *K. at-Tabṣira* d'aṣ-Ṣaymarī, le *K. al-Mufaṣṣal* d'az-Zamaḫšarī, le *K. Tashīl al-fawā'id* d'Ibn Mālik et et le *K. al-Muqarrib* d'Ibn ʿUṣfūr. Mais alors qu'aṣ-Ṣaymarī, Ibn Mālik et Ibn ʿUṣfūr suivent le plan bipartite traditionnel, az-Zamaḫšarī innove en divisant son ouvrage en quatre sections dans lesquelles il décrit successivement les phénomènes syntaxiques et morphologiques propres à chacune des trois parties du discours: le nom, le verbe et la particule, puis les phénomènes communs (*muštarak*) à ces trois sortes de mots. Enfin, il faut faire une mention spéciale de la partie grammaticale du *K. Miftāḥ al-ʿulūm* d'as-Sakkākī, dont les deux premières sections sont consacrées à la morphologie (*ṣarf*) et à la syntaxe (*naḥw*). Dans sa présentation des faits grammaticaux, as-Sakkākī s'écarte de la méthode traditionnelle en utilisant des termes techniques qui lui sont propres, comme *hay'a* "forme" au lieu de *binā'*, *qābil* "réceptif" au lieu de *muʿrab*, *fāʿil* "régissant" au lieu de *ʿāmil* et *'aṯar* "marque" au lieu de *'iʿrāb*.

2.2.2. Les manuels abrégés

Comme à l'époque classique, les grammairiens de la période suivante ont été conduits, pour des raisons didactiques, à composer des abrégés, afin de faciliter l'apprentissage de la grammaire aux étudiants, rebutés par la prolixité des traités complets. C'est ainsi que les sources attribuent des résumés intitulés: *muḫtaṣar*, *muntaḫab*, *talḫīṣ*, à plusieurs grammairiens du XIIe siècle: al-Ǧawālīqī, Ibn Ṣāfī, al-ʿUkbarī, mais un seul nous est parvenu, le *K. al-'Unmūḏaǧ*, dans lequel az-Zamaḫšarī résume son *K. al-Mufaṣṣal*. Au XIIIe siècle, apparaissent deux abrégés grammaticaux d'un genre nouveau, composés sous forme de poèmes de mille vers: le *K. ad-Durra al-'alfiyya* d'Ibn Muʿṭī et le *K. al-Ḫulāṣa al-'alfiyya* d'Ibn Mālik, qui consacre plus de la moitié de son précis à l'étude détaillée de la syntaxe, au détriment de la morphologie, traitée de façon fort succinte. Quant au *K. al-Mulaḫḫaṣ* d'Ibn 'Abī r-Rabīʿ, il est inédit.

2.3. La syntaxe (*'iʿrāb*)

C'est au début du XIe siècle que les grammairiens entreprirent de composer des ouvrages exclusivement consacrés à la première partie de la grammaire qui, comme nous l'avons vu, étudie le comportement de la finale des mots dans l'énoncé, selon qu'ils sont fléchis (*muʿrabāt*) ou fixes (*mabniyyāt*). Les ouvrages de ce genre apparaissent avec le *K. Mulḥat al-'iʿrāb* d'al-Ḥarīrī, petit poème de 370 vers groupés en 55 chapitres, et la *Muqaddima al-Muḥsiba* d'Ibn Bābāšāḏ divisée en 10 sections. Dans ces deux traités, les auteurs suivent le plan traditionnel en étudiant d'abord les mots dont la finale est fléchie, puis ceux dont la finale est fixe. En revanche, dans le *K. al-ʿAwāmil al-mi'a*, al-Ǧurǧānī étudie le comportement de la finale des mots selon un plan original, non plus en fonction des mots régis (*maʿmūlāt*), mais en fonction des cent mots régissants (*ʿawāmil*) qu'il dénombre et qu'il classe en trois groupes: 91 régissants élocutifs (*lafẓī*) qui sont de 13 sortes, 7 régissants analogiques (*qiyāsī*) et 2 régissants sémantiques (*maʿnawī*). Au XIIe siècle, c'est le plan d'al-Ǧurǧānī que suivra al-Muṭarrizī dans le *K. al-Miṣbāḥ* divisé en 5 chapitres, et il est probable que c'est ce plan, qu'à la même époque, aš-Šantarīnī a suivi dans le *K. Talqīḥ al-'albāb* qui est inédit. Au siècle suivant, Ibn al-Ḥāǧib, dans le *K. al-Kāfiya*, revient au plan traditionnel, en fonction des mots régis, mais en ajoutant, à la fin de son ouvrage, plusieurs chapitres qui ne font pas partie de la syntaxe, mais appartiennent à la morphologie. Les ouvrages de deux autres grammairiens du XIIIe siècle, le *K. al-Hādī* d'az-Zanǧānī et le *K. al-Lubab* d'al-'Isfarā'inī, étant inédits, nous ignorons le plan suivi par leurs auteurs.

2.4. La morphologie (*taṣrīf*)

Contrairement à la syntaxe, dès le IXe siècle, la morphologie a fait l'objet d'ouvrages qui lui étaient exclusivement consacrés. Le premier traité de ce genre est le *K. at-Taṣrīf* d'al-Māzinī, dont Ibn Ǧinnī fit un volumineux commentaire, le *K. al-Munṣif*, avant de composer lui-même un petit ouvrage intitulé *K. at-Taṣrīf al-mulūkī*, dans lequel il étudie les cinq transformations qui affectent les radicales des mots. Les plus anciens traités de ce genre dans la période post-classique, sont le *K. Nuzhat aṭ-ṭarf* d'al-Maydānī, le *K. al-Muqtaṣid* d'Ibn Ṣāfī et le *K. at-Taṣrīf* d'al-ʿUkbarī, tous inédits. Des quatre traités que les grammairiens du XIIIe siècle ont consacrés à la morphologie, trois sont édités: le *K. at-Taṣrīf al-ʿizzī* d'az-Zanǧānī, le *K. aš-Šāfiya* d'Ibn al-Ḥāǧib, le *K. al-Mumtiʿ* d'Ibn ʿUṣfūr, le quatrième, le *K. 'Īǧāz at-taʿrīf* d'Ibn Mālik, étant inédit. Aux cinq transformations qui affectent les radicales des mots, décrites par Ibn Ǧinnī, les auteurs de ces trois traités ajoutent certaines transformations qui portent sur les schèmes des mots, et certaines transformations purement phonétiques.

2.5. Les causes (*ʿilal*)

Les grammairiens ne se contentèrent pas d'énumérer et de décrire, de manière empirique, les phénomènes grammaticaux qu'ils observaient dans leur langue. Ils essayèrent de classer et d'expliquer ces phénomènes d'une manière rationnelle, au moyen de la recherche des causes (*taʿlīl*). Le premier ouvrage consacré à cette recherche est le *K. al-'Īḍāḥ fī ʿilal an-naḥw* d'az-Zaǧǧāǧī. Au XIIe siècle, la théorie de la recherche des causes, élaborée par az-Zaǧǧāǧī, reçut une application parfaite avec le livre intitulé *K. 'Asrār al-ʿarabiyya* d'Ibn al-'Anbārī. Dans cet ouvrage, comme son titre le suggère, tous les 'secrets' de la langue arabe sont dévoilés, c'est-à-dire que tous les phénomènes grammaticaux, qu'ils soient d'ordre syntaxique, morphologique ou phonétique, reçoivent une explication logique et une justification rationnelle, au moyen de la recherche des causes. Cette recherche se fait au moyen de questions que pose l'élève sur la cause de tel ou tel fait de grammaire, et de réponses que fournit le maître. Dans ses réponses, le maître utilise un raisonnement de type syllogistique, qui n'est pas toujours exempt de sophismes. A la même époque, un autre grammairien de Bagdad, al-ʿUkbarī, composa, sur le même sujet, un ouvrage intitulé *K. al-Lubab*, encore inédit. Mais alors qu'en Orient, la recherche des causes se développait, en Occident, cette théorie était violemment contestée. En effet, sous l'influence de la doctrine ẓāhirite, illustrée par le célèbre théologien et juriste Ibn Ḥazm (m. 456/1064), le grammairien de Cordoue Ibn Maḍā', critiqua, au nom de cette doctrine, la théorie des causes grammaticales. Dans sa fameuse réfutation des grammairiens, intitulée *K. ar-Radd ʿalā n-nuḥāt*, il rejeta non seulement la notion de régissant et le raisonnement par analogie, mais aussi les causes des deuxième et troisième degrés, en ne retenant que les causes du premier degré, c'est-à-dire la simple constatation des phénomènes grammaticaux.

2.6. Les divergences (*ḫilāf*)

Le premier ouvrage portant sur les divergences qui ont existé entre les grammairiens de Baṣra et ceux de Kūfa, est le *K. Iḫtilāf an-naḥwiyyīn* du kūfien Ṯaʿlab. La disparition de cet ouvrage et de sa réfutation par Ibn Durustawayhi, rend d'autant plus considérable l'intérêt du *K. al-'Inṣāf fī masā'il al-ḫilāf* qu'Ibn al-'Anbārī a consacré à cette question. Dans sa préface, Ibn al-'Anbārī déclare que c'est à la demande de ses collègues enseignants à la madrasa Niẓāmiyya de Bagdad, qu'il a composé un livre sur les divergences entre les grammairiens de Baṣra et ceux de Kūfa, à la manière des ouvrages qui traitent des divergences entre les juristes chafiʿites et les juristes hanafites, et qu'il a présenté les opinions des uns et des autres avec équité (*'inṣāf*) et sans parti pris (*taʿaṣṣub*). De fait, Ibn al-'Anbārī expose les questions sur lesquelles les grammairiens des deux écoles étaient en désaccord, en fournissant les arguments des uns et des autres, avec une grande objectivité. Au nombre de 122, la moitié de ces questions sont relatives à la rection (*ʿamal*) et au régissant (*ʿāmil*) qui, effectivement, posaient de délicats problèmes aux grammairiens des deux écoles. Ibn al-'Anbārī rapportant les arguments des grammairiens de Kūfa en utilisant leur propres termes, il nous permet de connaître, dans une certaine mesure, la méthode de ces grammairiens dont les œuvres semblent perdues. Quant au *K. al-Masā'il al-ḫilāfiyya* d'al-ʿUkbarī, il a été édité; en revanche on ne sait rien du *K. al-'Isʿāf fī l-ḫilāf* d'Ibn 'Ayāz.

2.7. Les fautes (*laḥn*)

Les ouvrages des grammairiens destinés à corriger les fautes de langage commises par les gens du commun (*ʿāmma*) par rapport à la norme linguistique, furent particulièrement nombreux durant la période classique, mais bien peu nous sont parvenus. L'un des rares traités de ce genre que nous possédions est le *K. Laḥn al-ʿawāmm* de l'andalou az-Zubaydī. Pour la période post-classique, l'ouvrage le plus célèbre dans ce domaine est le *K. Durrat al-ġawwāṣ fī ʾawhām al-ḫawāṣṣ* d'al-Ḥarīrī qui, par le titre qu'il a donné à son livre, nous apprend que les gens de l'élite (*ḫāṣṣa*), comme les gens du commun, commettaient des fautes de langage. L'ouvrage d'al-Ḥarīrī fut complété par al-Ǧawālīqī dans un livre intitulé *K. at-Takmila*, de même qu'il fit l'objet de gloses (*ḥawāšī*) de la part d'Ibn Barrī qui, par ailleurs, releva les fautes commises par les juristes dans son *K. Ġalaṭ aḍ-ḍuʿafāʾ min ʾahl al-fiqh*. Enfin, le *K. al-Mudḫal ʾilā taqwīm al-lisān* d'al-Laḫmī est une réfutation du *K. Laḥn al-ʿawāmm* d'az-Zubaydī et du *K. Taṯqīf al-lisān* du sicilien Ibn Makkī (m. 501/1108).

2.8. La lexicographie (*luġa*)

Dans les trois grands dictionnaires composés au X^e siècle: le *K. Tahḏīb al-luġa* d'al-ʾAzharī, le *K. Ṣiḥāḥ al-ʿarabiyya* d'al-Ǧawharī et le *K. Muǧmal al-luġa* d'Ibn Fāris, les mots étaient classés selon l'ordre alphabétique de leur première ou de leur dernière radicale. Or c'est un classement différent qu'Ibn Sīdah adopta pour son *K. al-Muḫaṣṣaṣ*, dans lequel les mots sont groupés non pas sous des lettres, mais autour de notions appartenant à quatre grands champs sémantiques: l'homme, les animaux, la nature et les plantes, l'homme dans la société. L'abondance des synonymes dans la langue arabe a conduit plusieurs grammairiens de l'époque post-classique à composer des lexiques spécialisés dans ce domaine, comme le *K. Fiqh al-luġa* d'aṯ-Ṯaʿālibī, le *K. al-ʾIqnāʿ* d'al-Muṭarrizī, le *K. al-ʾAlfāẓ al-muḫtalifa* d'Ibn Mālik et le *K. Kifāyat al-mutaḥaffiẓ* d'Ibn al-ʾAǧdabī. Dans un domaine voisin, Ibn aš-Šaǧarī fut amené à composer un lexique des homonymes, le *K. mā ttafaqa lafẓuhu wa-ḫtalafa maʿnāhu*. Par ailleurs, al-Muṭarrizī a consacré au vocabulaire du droit le *K. al-Muġrib*, et al-Ǧabrānī nous a laissé un petit lexique de la terminologie grammaticale. Quant à l'étymologie, l'un des premiers ouvrages traitant de cette discipline est le *K. al-Muʿarrab*, dans lequel al-Ǧawālīqī dresse l'inventaire des mots qu'il considère comme étrangers et arabisés, parmi lesquels on relève un grand nombre de toponymes et d'anthroponymes. Pour chaque mot, al-Ǧawālīqī fournit sa signification et indique sa langue d'origine: persan, hébreu, nabatéen, syriaque, éthiopien. Le *K. al-Muʿarrab* a fait l'objet de gloses de la part d'Ibn Barrī.

2.9. Les biographies (*ṭabaqāt*)

Ce dernier genre, illustré au X^e siècle par le *K. ʾAḫbār an-naḥwiyyīn al-baṣriyyīn* d'al-Sīrāfī et le *K. Ṭabaqāt an-naḥwiyyīn wa-l-luġawiyyīn* d'az-Zubaydī, est représenté durant la période post-classique par un seul ouvrage, le *K. Nuzhat al-ʾalibbāʾ fī ṭabaqāt al-ʾudabāʾ* d'Ibn al-ʾAnbārī. Dans son livre, l'auteur fournit les biographies de 181 grammairiens, classées selon l'ordre chronologique, depuis ʾAbū l-ʾAswad ad-Duʾalī (m. 67/686) jusqu'à Ibn aš-Šaǧarī. A la suite de la biographie d'Ibn aš-Šaǧarī, qui fut son maître, Ibn al-ʾAnbārī donne la liste des 14 grammairiens qui, depuis ʾAbū l-ʾAswad, se sont transmis la science de la grammaire jusqu'à lui.

## 3. Bibliographie

### 3.1. Sources primaires

ʾAstarābāḏī, al-. *Šarḥ Kāfiyat Ibn al-Ḥāǧib.* Ed. Istanbul, 1892.

—. *Šarḥ Šāfiyat Ibn al-Ḥāǧib.* Ed. par M. Nūr al-Ḥasan. Le Caire, 1939.

Ǧawālīqī, al-. *K. al-muʿarrab.* Ed. par A. M. Šākir. Le Caire, 1969.

—. —. *K. at-Takmila.* Ed. par Hartwig Derenbourg. Leipzig, 1875.

Ǧurǧānī, al-. *K. al-ʿAwāmil al-miʾa.* Ed. par Thomas Erpenius. Leiden, 1617. Ed. par J. Baillie. Calcutta, 1802. Ed. par A. Lockett. Calcutta, 1814.

—. —. *K. al-Muqtaṣid.* Ed. par K. B. al-Marǧān. Bagdad, 1982.

Ḥarīrī, al-. *K. Durrat al-ġawwāṣ.* Ed. par H. Thorbecke. Leipzig, 1871.

—. —. *K. Mulḥat al-ʾiʿrāb.* Ed. par L. Pinto. Paris, s. d.

Ibn al-ʾAnbārī. *K. ʾAsrār al-ʿarabiyya.* Ed. par Christian F. Seybold. Leiden, 1886.

—. —. *K. al-ʾInṣāf fī masāʾil al-ḫilāf bayna n-naḥwiyyīna l-baṣriyyīn wa-l-kūfiyyīn.* Ed. par Gotthold Weil. Leiden, 1913.

—. —. *K. Nuzhat al-ʾalibbāʾ fī ṭabaqāt al-ʾudabāʾ.* Ed. par Attia Amer. Stockholm, 1962.

Ibn al-Ḥāǧib. *K. al-Kāfiya.* Ed. Rome, 1592. Ed. par J. Baillie. Calcutta, 1805.

Ibn Maḍāʾ. *K. ar-Radd ʿalā n-nuḥāt.* Ed. par Šawqī Ḍayf. Le Caire, 1947.

Ibn Mālik. *K. al-Ḫulāṣa al-'alfiyya.* Ed. par Antoine Isaac Silvestre de Sacy. Paris & Londres, 1883. Ed. par L. Pinto. Constantinople, 1887. Ed. par Antonin Goguyer. Beyrouth, 1888.

—. —. *K. Tashīl al-fawā'id.* Ed. par M. R. Barakāt. Le Caire, 1967.

Ibn Mu'ṭī. *K. ad-Durra al-'alfiyya.* Ed. par K. V. Zetterstéen. Leipzig, 1900.

Ibn Sīdah. *K. al-Muḫaṣṣaṣ.* Ed. Bulaq. Le Caire, 1898–1903.

Ibn 'Uṣfūr. *K. al-Muqarrib.* Ed. par A. al-Ǧawārī. Bagdad, 1971.

—. —. *K. al-Mumti'.* Ed. par F. Qabāwa. Beyrouth, 1970.

Ibn Ya'īš. *Šarḥ al-Mufaṣṣal.* Ed. par Gustav Jahn. Leipzig, 1882–1886.

—. —. *Šarḥ al-Mulūkī.* Ed. Alep, 1973.

Muṭarrizī, al-. *K. al-Miṣbāḥ* Ed. par J. Baillie. Calcutta, 1802.

Qifṭī, al-. *K. 'Inbāh ar-ruwāt.* Ed. par M. A. 'Ibrāhīm. Le Caire, 1950–1955.

Sakkākī, as-. *K. Miftāḥ al-'ulūm.* Ed. Le Caire, 1938.

Suyūṭī, as-. *K. Buġyat al-wu'āt fī ṭabaqāt al-luġawiyyīn wa-n-nuḥāt.* Ed. Le Caire, 1908.

Ṯa'ālibī, aṯ-. *K. Fiqh al-luġa.* Ed. par R. Daḥdāḥ Paris, 1861.

'Ukbarī, al-. *Masā'il ḫilāfiyya fī n-naḥw.* Ed. par M. Ḥ. al-Ḥalwānī. Alep, s. d.

Zamaḫšarī, az-. *K. al-Mufaṣṣal.* Ed. par Jens Peter Broch. Christiania, 1879.

Zanǧānī, az-. *K. at-Taṣrīf al-'izzī.* Ed. par J. B. Raimond. Rome, 1610.

### 3.2. Sources secondaires

Brockelmann, Carl. 1943, 1937. *Geschichte der arabischen Literatur.* I, 330–382. *Supplementband.* I, 491–547. Leiden: Brill.

Baillie, J. 1802–1895. *The Five Books upon Arabic Grammar.* 3 vols. Calcutta.

Bohas, Georges & Jean-Patrick Guillaume. 1984. *Etude des théories des grammairiens arabes.* I. *Morphologie et phonologie.* Damas: Institut Français d'Etudes Arabes.

Fleisch, Henri. 1957. "Esquisse d'un historique de la grammaire arabe". *Arabica* 4.1–22.

Goguyer, Antonin. 1888. *Manuel pour l'étude des grammairiens arabes.* Beyrouth.

Lockett, A. 1814. *Two Elementary Treatises on Arabic Syntax.* Calcutta.

Pellat, Charles. 1986. "Laḥn al-'āmma". *Encyclopaedia of Islam*, V, 609–614. Leiden: Brill.

Silvestre de Sacy, Antoine Isaac. 1829. *Anthologie grammaticale.* Paris.

Troupeau, Gérard. 1962. "La grammaire à Bagdad du IXe au XIIIe siècle". *Arabica* 9.397–405.

—. 1963. "Deux traités grammaticaux arabes traduits en latin". *Arabica* 10.225–236.

—. 1993. "Naḥw". *Encyclopaedia of Islam*, VII, 913–915. Leiden: Brill.

Versteegh, Kees. 1982. "Arabische Sprachwissenschaft". *Grundriß der arabischen Philologie*, II, éd. par Helmut Gätje, 148–176. Wiesbaden: Reichert.

*Gérard Troupeau, Argenteuil (France)*

# 42. The structure of Arabic grammatical theory

1. Introduction
2. A standard grammar
3. Syntax and morphology
4. Syntax (*naḥw*)
5. Morphology (*ṣarf*)
6. Markedness (*'aṣl* and *far'*)
7. Bibliography

## 1. Introduction

Arabic grammatical theory (*naḥw*) is a structuralist edifice *par excellence* in the sense that it consists of a finite number of positions each serving as a locus where further elements occur. Every position is characterized by inherent defining properties, which circumscribe the elements that can occur at that position. This characterization applies at both the morphological and syntactic levels.

There are a number of corollaries which the Arabic grammarians linked to this conception of structure. First, there must be minimal elements which can be distributed into the positions. In the simplest case there are typical elements which fall into each position. Secondly, the properties that define the positions are not univocal. The total set of characteristics which define a position entail different criteria, which frequently allows a range of elements beyond the simplest one to occur at a position. The entire class of elements can be quite large and heterogeneous. This property, as will be seen below, allows the total number of positions to be kept to a manageable minimum. Thirdly, the properties defining a position, and the elements occurring at them may be characterized in hierarchical terms according to the principle that some elements are more typical representatives of a position than are others, or that some positions are in some sense more basic than others. The notion of hierarchy, though dependent on the definition of syntactic and morphological components and hence logically adventitious upon it, is so central to Arabic linguistic thinking that section 6. will be devoted to its description.

Arabic grammatical theory is structuralist in the sense that it consists of well-defined positions whose place is filled by a defined set of elements. The term structuralist is not used in the sense of structural linguists from a specific modern era, nor is it chosen to suggest that Arabic theory is based on form rather than content. Arabic theory is strongly form-orientated, though, as will be seen, the shape of the form is dictated by formal, functional, semantic, pragmatic and various other factors. Inevitably, many parallels will be discernible with modern linguistic models, though the properties which define Arabic theory are, in their mode of combination, at times in the choice of components, quite *sui generis*.

Before introducing Arabic theory, it should be noted that despite the centrality of the notion of position, there is no single term which encodes it at all levels of grammatical analysis, even if at any given level there are terms which can be invoked to represent it. It is not unusual, however, for the Arabic grammarians to leave key terms and ideas undefined. Their audience, it should be recalled, was not the general public or general linguists, but rather those versed in, or becoming versed in, the Arabic language.

## 2. A Standard Grammar, Ibn as-Sarrāǧ's *'Uṣūl*

The bulk of this exposition will be orientated around Arabic grammatical theory as expounded by the 10th century grammarian Ibn as-Sarrāǧ. Though he did not write the longest grammar – that honor might go to Ibn Yaʿīš's *Šarḥ* (1514 dense pages) – Ibn as-Sarrāǧ is a seminal figure in that it is in his three volume *al-'Uṣūl fī n-Naḥw* "The Foundations of Grammar", that pedagogical grammars assumed a fairly tightly organized form, such as will be sketched below. (References to Ibn as-Sarrāǧ are to his *'Uṣūl.*) Whether or not Ibn as-Sarrāǧ was actually the model for successor grammarians, the fact is that all later grammarians use either a very similar organization, or an organization which can be understood relative to his. Thus, although this chapter is largely a-historical, what is described in it pertains in a general way to the entire grammatical tradition. Most ideas in the *'Uṣūl* can be traced back to earlier grammariens, Sībawayhi in particular (→ Art. 38). However, there are, on the one hand, many ideas more compactly, sometimes differently, formulated by Ibn as-Sarrāǧ, on the other some ideas of Sībawayhi and other earlier grammarians not developed at all, or totally neglected (see Bernards 1997).

## 3. Syntax and Morphology

The comprehensive Arabic grammar is divided into two main parts which may be roughly translated *naḥw* "syntax" and *ṣarf* "morphology", the latter including morphophonology. The two are roughly given equal space, as the following list (1) from three comprehensive grammars indicates, though in later treatments syntax may take up a slightly larger proportion. The figures can only be approximate, since the assignment of certain topics (like diptotes) is ambiguous.

| (1) | *naḥw* | *ṣarf* |
|---|---|---|
| Sībawayhi | vol. 1, pp. 1–441 | vol. 2, pp. 1–481 |
| Ibn as-Sarrāǧ (*'Uṣūl*) | vol. 1 1–440, vol. 2 1–76, 222–318 | rest of vol. 2, vol. 3 1–481 |
| Ibn ʿAqīl | vol. 1 1–673, vol. 2 1–319 | vol. 2 320–659 |

Among the more specialized works, however, it would appear that at least among books readily available in bookstores in the Arabic world today, works on syntax predominate. (Ibn al-) 'Anbārī's *'Asrār*, Astarābāḏī's *Šarḥ*, and Ibn Ǧinnī's *Lumaʿ*, for example, are concerned wholly or chiefly with syntactic issues. One touchstone to gauge the relative weight of the two domains is 'Anbārī's *'Inṣāf*. Admittedly, in many problems discussed in the *'Inṣāf* evidence is adduced from both the syntactic and morphological realms, and a finer classification should take into account the relative emphasis of each domain in the different chapters. A better unit of counting would probably be the individual arguments (*ḥuǧǧa*) advanced rather than the chapter as a whole. Nonetheless, in most questions a primary emphasis is evident. Questions relating to word order (*taqdīm*) or governance (*ʿamal*) are syntactic, for example, whereas establishing a basic form (*binā'* or *wazn*) of a certain word is morphological. This classification yields a count of 63 of the 121 chapters devoted to syntactic topics, 42 to morphology, and 16 either undecidable, or being predominantly of semantic nature. Given the integrative and broadly summarizing nature of 'Anbārī's work, I think it is a good measure of where, generally, the main foci of the grammarians lay. Furthermore, it can be noted that the term *naḥw* can mean both syntax in a narrow sense and grammar in a general sense, including both syntax and morphology, suggesting that syntax had an eponymic symbolism by which grammarians understood their craft. It would thus appear that *naḥw* has a slightly more central role than does *ṣarf* in the overall Arabic grammatical *œuvre*.

It should not be forgotten, however, that there are important works devoted solely to morphology, e. g. Ibn ʿUṣfūr's two volume *Mumtiʿ*, 'Abū Ḥayyān's *Mubdaʿ* and most notably, Ibn Ǧinnī's three volume *Munṣif*. In addition, morphological problems figure prominently in Ibn Ǧinnī's metatheoretical *Ḫaṣā'iṣ*.

## 4. Syntax (*naḥw*)

### 4.1. Word classes (*kalim, kalimāt* or *kalām*)

The general grammar begins with syntax, so in this chapter too syntax will be the first aspect of grammar that is treated (see Owens 1993). First the basic elements which occur at the syntactic positions are defined, namely the word classes (depending on author and context = *kalim, kalimāt, kalām*, see 5.3. for some differentiating discussion) classes, of which there are three, nouns, verbs and particles. Nouns (*ism*, including nouns, adjectives, pronouns and demonstratives) and verbs (*fiʿl*) are defined by specific sets of features. Nouns, for example, are marked by an indefinite *-n* (*tanwīn*) suffix, can occur as agent, do not contain an inherent time element, and are marked for case. Verbs take person prefixes, occur as predicates and do contain an inherent time component. Various characterizing criteria are introduced by different grammarians, drawn from all levels of grammatical analysis, from phonology to semantics. It turns out, however, that not all criteria sufficiently cover the class they are meant to characterize. There is, for instance, a class of nouns (diptotes) which lack the indefinite *-n* (even if indefinite in meaning, e. g. *makātibu* "desks") and another class invariably ending in *-ā*, undifferentiated for case (e. g. *raḥā* "mill"). Close inspection of the criteria leads to the conclusion that distributional criteria are always those which are most general, indeed, the only generally sufficient criteria for assigning words to one class or another. That is, it is the syntactic positions which ultimately justify the simple tripartite division of the word classes (Owens 1989, 4.3. below). The third class of elements is that of the particles, including negative, question and vocative particles, prepositions, verbal determiners, and many other subclasses (at one point Ibn as-Sarrāǧ identifies 8 sub-classes, I, 42). Even if well-rounded characterizations of some sub-classes of particles can be given, particles are ultimately defined negatively as a class, as what is neither noun or verb.

### 4.2. Case (*'iʿrāb*)

Before moving to a characterization of the syntactic positions, the grammars usually treat nominal case inflection. Case form plays an important role in the treatment of the syntactic positions, so it is appropriate to consider them early. A fundamental distinction is drawn between inflectable nouns (*'asmā' muʿraba* or *mutamakkina*) and non-inflectable ones (*'asmā' mabniyya*). The former have three case endings, typically (see Versteegh 1985 for more abstract definitions) *-u* "u-infl(ection)" = *rafʿ*, *-a* "a-infl(ection)" = *naṣb*, *-i* "i-infl(ection)" = *ǧarr*, whereas the latter always end in the same invariable vowel or consonant. It is important to bear in mind that the case endings are not introduced in the exposition of syntax (*naḥw*) simply for the sake of the reader's convenience; they are conceptually a part of syntax in the Arabic thinking, as will be discussed in 4.4. As a terminological note, the endings are here termed inflectional endings rather than the more familiar nominative (*-u*), accusative (*-a*) and genitive (*-i*) (see Versteegh 1995: xiv). The reason for this is that in Arabic grammar the 'same' endings appear on verbs as modal markers (see (15) below), and the verbal endings are given the same names, e. g. *ya-ḍrib-u* "he-hits-indic", where the *-u* is also termed *rafʿ*, in the present terminology, u-infl.

4.3. Syntactic positions

Broadly speaking, there are three u-infl-marked positions, topic (*mubtadaʾ*) and comment (*ḫabar*) of a nominal sentence, and agent (*fāʿil*) of a verbal one. Formally, a nominal sentence is one which begins with a u-infl topic, a verbal one with a verb (e. g. (4), (5) below). For present expository purposes, the last position, agent, covers a range of sub-types, including agent of a passive verb, agent-like complements of participles, and agent-like complements of verbal nouns. Describing the first of these three positions in some detail will give the reader an idea about what sort of information can be 'stored' in a syntactic position. Examples of the topic are given in (2). The topic position is underlined.

(2a) *allāh-u rabb-u-nā*
God-u Lord-u-our
"God is our Lord".

(2b) *ar-rağul-u ya-nṭaliq-u*
def-man-nom 3msg-leaving-u
"The man is leaving"

(2c) (*)*rağul-u-n qāʿid-u-n*
man-u-indef sitting-u-indef
"(It is) a man sitting"

(2d) *marar-tu bi-rağul-i-n qāʾim-i-n ʾabū-hu*
passed-I by-man-i-indef standing-i-indef father/u-his
"I passed a man whose father was standing"

According to Ibn as-Sarrāğ (I, 58–62), the topic is u-infl marked, it occurs first in the sentence, is not governed by an overt governor (see ʾAnbārī, *ʾInṣāf* 46), must be followed by a comment (*ḫabar*) in order to produce a complete sentence (*kalām tāmm*), represents what is spoken about (*muḥaddaṯ ʿanhu*), and is definite. Typical examples are (2a) and (2b). The underlined word is the topic, the following word in (2a–c) the comment. Clearly the definition of 'topic' entails criteria of different types including case form, word order, governance relations, syntagmatic obligatoriness, text or context-related given-new information, and the pragmatic prominence of the position. Co-occurrence restrictions with predicates based on semantic components are added when the predicative positions (verb/topic, see below) are considered.

The first two examples meet all the typical criteria of a normal topic. The second two do not, though this does not necessarily make them incorrect or exclude them from topichood. (2c) is indefinite, violating the definiteness constraint for topics. As it stands, Ibn as-Sarrāğ would say that it is wrong (hence the "*" in brackets). However, if it were an answer to the question "Is it a man sitting there or a woman?" Ibn as-Sarrāğ allows it. In (2d) the topic occurs after the comment *qāʾimin*, violating the sequence rule. This is allowable in this particular case however, due to the peculiar syntax of the entire sentence. *ʾabū-hu* is topic of a dependent sentence whose comment is *qāʾimin*. The inversion of topic and comment that occurs is here determined by a further rule: *qāʾimin* is a participial adjective modifying *rağulin*, and an adjective must directly follow the noun it qualifies (Ibn as-Sarrāğ II, 222). In fact, inversion of topic and comment occurs in other contexts as well, which Ibn as-Sarrāğ (I, 60) generalizes by saying that where the comment can be 'supported' by something, inversion is permissible. In (2d) the support comes from the preceding noun (*rağulin*); in other cases it can come from a negative particle or a question particle.

Ibn as-Sarrāğ discusses other special properties of the topic position, which I will not go into here since I believe this brief summary gives a representative idea about how the different syntactic positions are described. First their salient properties are described, along with the elements which typically occur in them. Thereafter follows a more detailed discussion of cases which deviate from the general rules, but which usually can be explained by appeal to a subsidiary principle.

There is, however, one important principle which does not come to the fore in Ibn as-Sarrāğ's summary of topic, and this is the notion of paradigmatic equivalence. It can be illustrated with the following example (I, 65), which should be contrasted with (2a) or (2b) above.

ment position. The compactness of the Arabic syntactic system derives from the ability to establish equivalences of items of different internal structure — a single noun vs. a whole sentence (in (2a) vs. (3) for instance). A further dimension, then, in the definition of the syntactic positions is the delimitation of the total range of structures — single words, prepositional phrases, sentences, etc. — which can occur at them.

(3)     ₁[*zayd-u-n*     ₂[*'abū-hu*     *munṭaliq-u-n*]₂]₁
         Zayd-u-indef    father/u-his    leaving-u-indef
                         S2   topic      comment
         S1  topic                       comment
         "As for Zayd, his father is leaving".

(3) contains one nominal sentence (S2) inside another one (S1), the sentence enclosed by the brackets labeled "2" (= "his father is leaving") within a larger sentence, labeled "1". Both sentences have the same structure, topic + comment, but note that the comment of sentence 1 is not a single word, a single noun or verb, but rather is itself a sentence, namely sentence 2. There are various conditions associated with structures of this sort, for instance that the embedded sentence, S2, must have a pronoun referring to the topic of S1 (in (3), -*hu* to *zaydun*). What is crucial for Arabic theory, however, is that the embedded sentence takes over the position filled by a single noun or verb, the items which normally occur in comment position (see (2a, b)). This allows the grammarians to generalize the scope of the comment position to include elements of different size and structure. Note that this solution is not self-evident. A feasible alternative would have been to define (3) as a completely different type of structure from the basic topic-comment one. There is, in fact, at least one early grammar, *Kitāb al-Ǧumal* "The Book of Collections" (attributed to Ibn aš-Šuqayr or al-Ḫalīl, Owens 1990: 180, 189) which summarizes in listwise fashion all classes of items which fill positions, without, however, generalizing properties of the positions themselves. Such an approach, however, expands the total number of positions considerably, obscuring any idea of overall coherency. The solution chosen by Ibn as-Sarrāğ and Arabic grammar generally, on the other hand, keeps the number of positions to a minimum, while increasing the complexity of the internal structure of the position. This is evident in the present example, where a range of items can occur at com-

This point is an essential one, because ultimately what establishes the status of an item occurring at a position is not its case form or some other simple formal property, but rather, whether or not it can plausibly be understood as fulfilling the necessary criteria for occurrence at a position. In (3) an entire dependent sentence functions as comment. In Ibn as-Sarrāğ, the topic can be realized by a single word marked by u-infl, the normal case, a sentence, a prepositional phrase, or a locative noun marked by a-infl. Functional, and therefore categorical equivalences via substitution can be established at the morphological level as well. *niʿma* in *niʿma ar-raǧul-u zayd-un* "how good a man Zayd is!" (Ibn as-Sarrāğ I, 112), has many morphological resemblances to a noun. In fact, the form *niʿma* has a purely nominal meaning as well, namely "bounty, benefit". Nonetheless, because it can be interpreted as having a verbal meaning, and as behaving like a verb in governing (see below) nominal complements (*ar-raǧulu* is agent, *zaydun* a modifier of *ar-raǧulu*, under one interpretation), it is interpreted as being a special type of verb (*fiʿl*). The Kufans are reputed to have argued for a nominal interpretation of *niʿma* (*'Inṣāf* I, 97), and 'Anbārī's summary of their arguments seems to me to be cogent. The standard (= Basran) interpretation as just sketched, however, also follows the logic of Arabic grammatical practice, which leaves the ultimate definition of what a particular element is to how appropriately it fits at a given place in structure.

Counting only the major syntactic positions, 3 are u-infl marked (*mubtada'* "topic", *ḫabar* "comment", *fāʿil* "agent", 8 are a-infl (*mafʿūl muṭlaq* "absolute object", *mafʿūl bihi* "direct object", *mafʿūl fīhi* "locative object", *maf'ūl ma'ahu* "accompaniment object" *maf'ūl lahu* "reason object", *ḥāl* "circumstance", *tamyīz* "specifier", *'istiṯnā'* "exception"), 2 i-infl (*muḍāf 'ilayhi* "possessor", *mağrūr* "object of preposition"), 5 are agreeing categories (*ṣifa* "attribute", *tawkīd* "emphasizer", *badal* "substitute", *'aṭf* "conjunct", *'aṭf al-bayān* "qualifying conjunct"), and there is a verbal predicate (*fi'l* "verb"). In addition, there are positions not necessarily marked by a case-marked noun (i. e. invariable), e. g. vocative (*nidā'*), and elegiac (*nudba*), as well as a few positions, like the sentential complement of a relative pronoun (*ṣilat al-mawṣūl*) which are outside the realm of case-markable positions. The above count is a minimal one, though even a more liberal recognition of positions would increase the overall count mainly via a more detailed subdivision of the positions listed above. The total of 19 gives a rough, if conservative, idea about how many distinct syntactic positions are found in a typical syntactic treatise. Each position is described in detail and numerous sub-classes may be established on the basis of different sorts of criteria.

Later grammars continued in the same vein as Ibn as-Sarrāğ, and in fact the reification of syntactic positions as embodying sets of fixed properties became more pronounced in later times. Ibn 'Uṣfūr's *Šarḥ* for example, explicitly lists ways in which one syntactic position, such as the adjective (*ṣifa*), differs from another, like the emphasis (*tawkīd*), while works such as 'Astarābāḏī's *Šarḥ* carefully define each position, and often explain that a certain term of a definition is introduced in order that the position be distinguished from another.

Before turning to the next subject, I would note that there is no fixed Arabic term for syntactic position. Two which sometimes occur are *mawḍi'* "position, function", and *mawqi'* "place" (Versteegh 1978), though when the distribution of items is discussed, they are generally simply said to assume the identity of a given position. In (2a), for instance, *ar-rağulu* can be said to be the topic. Topic (and any other position) can be ambiguously understood as signifying the position, or the item representing that position.

### 4.4. Dependency (*'amal*)

The various positions need a formal link between them. What is *ar-rağulu* in (2b) a topic of? It is not, it should be noted, said to be topic of the sentence (*kalām* or *ğumla*), which might be expected from a modern functional perspective. It is noteworthy that Ibn as-Sarrāğ gives no definition of sentence, as if it can be dispensed with as a theoretical concept. He does recognize that a N + N may form a sentence (*kalām*), though in the context of defining the topic, not giving a general account of sentence structure. It also appears that Sībawayhi did not work with an explicit term for 'sentence' (Talmon 1988). Later grammarians (e. g. Zamaḫšarī *Mufaṣṣal* 5) do explicitly define a sentence-like term (*kalām* or *ğumla*) at the beginning of their grammars, developing the notion of "predication" (*'isnād*) as a defining feature of the core elements (Levin 1981, 1985; Goldenberg 1988; Versteegh 1995: 214). However, this notion pertained only to subject (*musnad 'ilayhi*) and predicate (*musnad*), and did not encompass others sentential elements except to the extent that other elements might be related to the *'isnād* by implication. Moreover, the relatively late appearance of 'sentence' as an explicitly-defined category does suggest that other syntactic relations, in particular those defining pairwise relations between words, are more central, with sentence or predication becoming important only after Ibn as-Sarrāğ.

What binds the syntactic positions together in Arabic theory, more precisely the elements occurring at them, is the dependency relation. In the Arabic terminology, one item, the governor (*'āmil*) is said to govern (*'amila*) another (the *ma'mūl*) in a particular case form. A standard example is the verb governing agent and direct object.

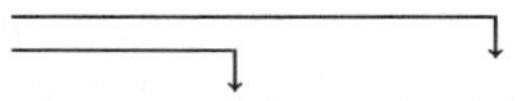

(4) *kataba* *r-ragul-u* *r-risālat-a*
Verb Agent Direct Object
wrote the-man-u the-letter-a
"The man wrote the letter"

The verb requires that the agent be in the u-infl case, the object in the a-infl. The terms dependency and govern are deliberately chosen, as there are fundamental formal identities between the Arabic notion of *'amal* and the modern western idea of dependency (e. g. as practised by Tesnière [1959], see Owens [1988] chapter 2).

As noted, the dependency relation is the crucial link between syntactic positions, and the formal mark of the dependency relation is the case inflection. In (4) agent and object are distinguished by the inflections *-u* vs. *-a*.

The Arabic conception of governance is causal: the verb brings about the different inflectional forms in the nouns. It follows from this that case inflections are a part of syntax, since their function is preeminently syntactic.

### 4.5. An example

Before proceeding it is appropriate to give a sample sentence, analyzed in terms of its syntactic positions and governance relations. The example follows a pedagogically-inspired sentence from Ibn as-Sarrāğ (I, 202).

| | | | | | | |
|---|---|---|---|---|---|---|
| (5) | *ʾaddaba* | *r-rağul-u* | *walad-a-hu* | *taʾdīb-a-n* | *šadīd-a-n* | *al-yawm-a* |
| | verb | agent | direct object | absolute object | | loc object |
| | | | pssd pssr | noun | adjective | |
| | disciplined | def-man-u | son-a-his | disciplining-a-indef | hard-a-indef | def-day-a |

"The man disciplined his son very hard today".

This is a verbal sentence whose verb is *ʾaddaba*, u-infl marked agent *ar-rağul-u*. It has an a-infl marked direct object (*mafʿūl bihi*), *walada*, an a-infl marked absolute object (*mafʿūl muṭlaq*) *taʾdīban* and an a-infl marked (temporal) locative object (*mafʿūl fīhi*) *al-yawma*. The object noun *walada* is possessed (*muḍāf*) by the pronominal suffix *-hu* (*muḍāf ʾilayhi*), and the absolute object *taʾdīban* is qualified by the adjective (*ṣifa*) *šadīdan*, agreeing with the noun in terms of gender and case. In terms of governance relations, the verb governs both the u-infl agent, and all of the a-infl marked complements directly, including, it should be pointed out, the adjective *šadīdan* (Owens 1995). In addition, the possessor complement *-hu* may be said to be governed by the possessor *walad*, though the question of what the governor of the possessor noun is, is not completely straightforward. Note that the direct object is *walada*, not *waladahu*. Arabic grammar as a dependency-based one generally does not recognize a larger constituent-based unit as the basis for contracting grammatical relations.

### 4.6. Adjunct theories

While syntactic positions bound by governance relations define the core of syntactic theory, there are numerous sub-components which partly intertwine with these two elements, and partly define their own domains. These sub-components may be termed adjunct theories, or simply adjuncts. On the one hand, they describe a relatively discrete grammatical sub-component and are characterized by a typical, sometimes even unique, vocabulary. On the other hand, they rarely command separate attention in their own right. There are no books devoted solely to transitivity, for instance, in the way there are books only on morphology or only on syntax. Rather, transitivity is always introduced as one aspect of the characteristics of objects (*mafāʿīl*). Pronominalization, passivization, word order, relativization, the definiteness hierarchy, and transitivity are examples of adjunct theories. They are not limited to syntax. Phonetic classification itself, briefly described in the next section, is an adjunct to morphology. It is relevant to sketch one of these domains in order to give the reader a better idea about the detail of Arabic theory. Transitivity (*taʿdiya*) describes the valency of verbs in terms of intransitive (no direct object), transitive, bi- and tritransitive. *ʾaddaba* in (4), for instance is transitive. Within the last two classes a distinction is made between those where the two (or three) direct objects are obligatory (6a) vs. those where only one is (6b). In the obligatory type, the second object always stands in a predicative relation to the first object (a fact duly noted by the grammarians). The structure in (6) is V-Agent-$Obj_1$-$Obj_2$

| | | | | |
|---|---|---|---|---|
| (6a) | *ẓanna* | *zayd-u-n* | *ṣāḥib-a-hu* | *ḏakiyy-a-n* |
| | thought | Zayd-u | friend-a-his | smart-a-indef |

"Zayd considered his friend smart".

| | | | | |
|---|---|---|---|---|
| (6b) | *ʾaʿṭā* | *zayd-u-n* | *ṣāḥib-a-hu* | *(dirham-a-n)* |
| | gave | Zayd-u | friend-a-his | dirham-a-indef |

"Zayd gave his friend (a dirham)".

Furthermore, systematic diathetic relations, like causativization and passivization, implying either an increase or a decrease in the number of objects, were integrated into the descriptions. Tritransitive verbs, for instance, are noted always to be the causative of a bitransitive, e. g. *ʾaʿlama* "cause x to know y to be z" < *ʿalima* "know y to be z".

Transitivity implies more than the relation of verb to direct object. There are in total five types of objects. The basis for designating two of them as object (*mafʿūl maʿahu, mafʿūl lahu*) remains obscure. The other three, the direct object, absolute object (*mafʿūl muṭlaq*) and locative object (*mafʿūl fīhi*) (see (5)) share the property of being able to become agents of passive verbs, but in a hierarchical order: if a direct object is present, it must assume the agent role (7a); if not, one of the other ones can (7b, c) (Ibn as-Sarrāǧ I, 202).

(7a) *ʾuddiba walad-u-hu taʾdīb-a-n šadīd-a-n al-yawm-a*
disciplined son-u-his disciplining-a-indef hard-a-indef today-a
"His son was disciplined hard today"

(7b) *ʾuddiba taʾdīb-u-n šadīd-u-n al-yawm-a*
disciplined disciplining-u-indef hard-u-indef today-a
"It was hard disciplined today".

(7c) *ʾuddiba al-yawm-u taʾdīb-a-n šadīd-a-n*
disciplined today-u disciplining-a-indef hard-a-indef
"Today it was hard-disciplined".

kākī's (*Miftāḥ al-ʿUlūm*) work in relating propositional types to grammatical structures, and the explicitly semantic orientation of the *waḍʿ al-luġa* (Weiss 1966). Anticipating the next section, Ibn Sīnā similarly set out a physiological basis for a theory of phonetics.

### 4.7. The development of syntactic thinking

As mentioned already, later grammarians operate essentially with the same categories as did Ibn as-Sarrāǧ. Where significant development took place was not in the core area of syntax (or morphology), but rather in the areas of pragmatics and the organization of information in texts. Ǧurǧānī (*Dalāʾil* 95), for example, argued that the difference between (8a) and (8b)

(8a) *ʾa zayd-an ta-ḍrib-u*
Q Zayd-a you-hit-u
"Is it Zayd you are hitting"?

(8b) *ʾa ta-ḍrib-u zayd-an*
Q you-hit-u Zayd-a
"Are you hitting Zayd"?

lay in the thematic organization of the texts. Both describe the same action, and in both there is a verb governing a direct object in the a-infl case. The syntax is nearly the same (both are verbal sentences). According to Ǧurǧānī, (8a) would be appropriate, if the focus is on "Zayd", (8b) if the focus lies on the action of hitting. Prior to Ǧurǧānī differences between (8a) and (8b) had been faithfully catalogued under the general rubric of word order (*taqdīm wa-taʾḫīr*, Ibn as-Sarrāǧ II, 222ff.), an example of what in 4.6 was termed an adjunct theory. Though the adjunct theory of word order probably prepared the way for Ǧurǧānī's work, until him no systematic explanation had been given for when either variant in (8) would be appropriate.

Further extensions of Arabic linguistic thinking are found in the speech-act orientation of ʾAstarābāḏī (see Larcher 1992), Sak-

What all of these later developments had in common, however, was their acceptance of the basic grammatical categories, as exemplified above, as the starting point of their own work. Thinking in terms of concentric circles, the important later developments in Arabic linguistic thought may be represented as adding new conceptual circles around the relatively fixed core of morphology and syntax.

In passing it can be noted that throughout the Arabic tradition lexicography (*luġa*) was a discipline parallel to grammar.

## 5. Morphology (*ṣarf*)

Ibn Ǧinnī delineated the boundary between syntax (*naḥw*) and morphology (*ṣarf*) in the following way: morphology describes the 'essences' of words, whereas syntax describes the change in the case ending (*ḥarakāt ḥurūf al-ʾiʿrāb*) in the context of different governors (*Munṣif* I, 4, see Owens, to appear). In a later treatment ʾAbū Ḥayyān (*Mubdaʿ* 49) basically follows this formulation, though he speaks of *ṣarf* as describing words in isolation, *naḥw* words joined to other words (in *tarkīb*, see 5.1 below for Ibn ʿUṣfūr's more explicit characterization of *ṣarf*.) Ibn Ǧinnī's interest is to show that no matter which case ending a word takes, its (lexical) meaning remains unchanged. Both writers remark that logically the study of Arabic should start with *ṣarf*, since the knowledge of what words are precedes their study in context. However, one writer, Ibn ʿUṣfūr notes that the study of grammar customarily begins with syntax because of the "fineness" (*diqqa*) of morphology. This explanation is perhaps a *post hoc* justification of the traditional pedagogical sequence (Mubarrad's *Muqtaḍab* is a notable exception), though if 'fineness' is understood as 'difficulty' (or perhaps 'dryness'), it may give a clue as to why Arabic grammars traditionally do not begin with morphology.

## 5.1. The morphological template (*fʿl*)

A highly formalistic positional template underlies the representation of Arabic morphological structure in much the same way it does syntactic analysis, and as with the syntactic analysis each position is characterized by special properties and by a set of elements, in this case consonants, which can occur at them. In this context it is appropriate to point out, however, that the concept joining the positions syntagmatically is not a dependency one, but rather one of inclusion, inclusion in the morphologically given notion of 'word'.

The template used to represent morphological structure is composed of the *ḥurūf* (*sg. ḥarf*) "letters" or "sounds" *f-ʿ -l* (< *f ʿl* "do, make"). These represent the positions of the tri-radical root, which constitutes the basic morphological unit, the *'aṣl*. The root *ktb* "relating to writing" would be said to have a *k* occurring at the "f" position, *t* at "ʿ" and *b* at "l". The basic template is expanded upon in various ways, as will be now summarized.

A fundamental division, explicitly formulated by later morphologists like Ibn ʿUṣfūr (*Mumtiʿ* I, 30, 31, see Bohas & Guillaume 1984: 17ff.), divided morphology into two parts, one the definition of the total range of morphological patterns which exist, the second a description of the morphophonological processes which sounds undergo. These two aspects will be discussed in turn.

Arabic morphology is characterized by a consonantal root (*'aṣl*) from which is derived a functional morphological form by the addition of short vowels and possibly the addition of consonantal prefixes, suffixes and infixes. The basic root consonants, as just noted, are represented by the *f-ʿ-l* template. There can be up to 5 basic root consonants, additional roots being represented by repetitions of the root consonants, e.g. *tarǧama* "translate" = *f-ʿ-l-l*. The affixes are known as added consonants (*ḥurūf zā'ida*) and they are represented by themselves in the templates. A writer, for instance, is a *kātib*, based on the root consonants *ktb* but with the infix *ā*, hence its representation *fāʿil*. The past participle, *maktūb* (*ma-ktuwb*) "written" = *mfʿwl* shows that a form can have both prefixal (*m-*) and infixal (*w*) added consonants. Root + added consonants will be termed here the extended root. The status of the short vowels is somewhat inexplicit. These are not usually represented in the Arabic orthography, and they do not enter into the basic dichotomy between basic and added sounds. They are, however, essential in the formation of what is sometimes (though not consistently) distinguished as a "stem" (*bunya*/*binya* or *binā'* or *wazn*), consisting of the root consonants (basic or extended) plus attached short vowel pattern. The stems of *kataba* and *maktūb* are thus represented as follows with the added consonants underlined:

(9) *kataba* *m̲a-ktu-w̲-b*
fa'ala m̲a-f'u-w̲-l

Note that the case endings are not part of the stem representation. All Arabic morphological forms are represented by the following formula:

(10) basic consonants
(+ added consonants) + short vowels

The cataloguing of the total range of morphological forms in terms of their basic and added consonants is known as *taṣrīf*. Alternatively, if one is asked to '*ṣarrafa*' a basic root, one is asked to define all the possible morphological forms, basic and derived, which a root or stem can be distributed into.

In most instances the division of the consonants of a given form into basic and added ones is a straightforward exercise. Nonetheless, there are problematic cases. In fact, in the detailed treatment of the Arabic grammarians many words of rare usage and problematic structure are discussed, as if a challenge to their theoretical apparatus. Various criteria are developed to diagnose the status of the consonants, including discrete meaning, behavior of the root in other morphological structures (*Munṣif* I, 35), and morphotactic constraints (e. g. *Munṣif* I, 110), the discussion becoming quite detailed in many instances. Inversely, the added consonants are defined according to their function. The addition of a certain meaning is probably the statistically most common function, though one classification ('Abū Ḥayyān, *Mubdaʿ* 118) lists 7 in all, including meaning and phonological necessity (Guillaume & Bohas 1984: 173ff.). Generally speaking, the grammarians had an ingrained suspicion against considering the semi-vowel consonants *w* and *y* as basic consonants, and part of their morphological theory was formulated towards excluding these from basic structures (cf. the notion of *'ilḥāq*, Owens 1988: 116). Note that the 'consonantal long vowel' *ā* was by definition considered to be an added consonant, i. e. never to occur at "f", "ʿ" or "l".

5.2. Morphophonology

The second part of morphology, the second aspect of *taṣrīf*, according to Ibn ʿUṣfūr's conception, is morphophonology. Its treatment is quite detailed. The last 240 pages of the third volume of Ibn as-Sarrāǧ's *'Uṣūl*, for instance, is devoted to this topic, something like 40% of all morphological topics. Just over half of the 300 pages of 'Abū Ḥayyān's *Mubdaʿ* are about morphophonology.

The morphological structure, the *binā'* of a particular word does not necessarily reflect its final form, though in many cases it will. The morphological structure of *kataba* = *faʿala*, the pattern of the perfect verb, is also its final surface form. The identical morphological structure of *qawala* = *faʿala*, however, surfaces as *qāla* "he said" = *fāla*. It is the function of the morphophonological rules to account for the discrepancy between 'underlying' and 'surface' forms. This is done by a series of rules, which make use of familiar (*ḥaḏf* "deletion", *'idġām* "assimilation", *qalb* "assimilation [of semi-vowels]") and not-so-familiar (*'ibdāl li-ġayr 'idġām* "substitution", *naql* "transference") phonological processes to arrive at a surface form. Generally speaking, the not-so-familiar rules define lexically exceptional rules while the others usually are interpretable in terms of natural and/or general phonological processes. The form *qāla* is derived from *qawala* by a general rule deleting a semivowel between a short *a* and another short vowel:

(11) *f-aw/yV-l* → *fāl*
*a-w/y-V* → *ā, qa-w-ala* → *qāla*
(Guillaume & Bohas 1984: 242)

The same rule is also operative in *ḫawifa* → *ḫāfa* "fear" *bayaʿa* → *bāʿa* "sell", *banaya* → *banā* "he built", and *bawab* → *bāb* "door" (Mubarrad I, 110). Arabic morphological practice links an underlying stem U to a surface one S, via a set of morphophonological rules. If no rules apply, U and S will be identical. In (12b) no morphophonological rules are needed to get from U to S. In (12a) one rule is. In other cases chains of 5 or 6 rules are needed.

These rules have been termed morphophonological because nearly every one is morphologically or morpholexically restricted. In the present case, there are a small number of verbs, like *ḥawila* "be cross-eyed" where the *awV* sequence is maintained. Such cases were recognized as exceptions, and various explanations offered (Guillaume & Bohas 1984: 250). Whatever the value of such explanations, however, the fact is that nearly all phonologically-formulated rules, like (11), are morphologically restricted, hence morphophonological in character. Two short examples can be cited, the first one illustrating the derivation from a categorical base form, the second the constraining effects of ambiguity. Perfect verbs like *'aṭāla* "he made tall" are said to surface as follows.

(13) *'a-ṭwala*
↓ transference of *a* to *ṭ* (*naql*)
*'aṭaw(a)la*
↓ via (11), (interpreting an understood *a*, the *a* of the base form, after *w*)
*'aṭāla*

The comparative adjective form, however, which is formally identical to the first stage of (13), *'a-ṭwal* "taller", is prevented from undergoing (13) lest it ambiguously have the same form as the verb (*Mumtiʿ* II, 480, 465, (also *Munṣif* I, 192).

Mubarrad (*Muqtaḍab* I, 108) says that *maryam* "Maryam", would be expected to undergo (13), just as *maqām* "residence" < *maqwam* does. That it does not is due to the fact, according to Mubarrad, that *maqām* is derived from a verb stem (*qwam* "stand") and hence eligible for (13), whereas *maryam* is derived directly from a noun, and so is not.

Other general principles which are invoked at one place or another include the nature of the sound which does/does not undergo a morphophonological rule, the effect of neighboring sounds and the position of the sound in the word (at "f", "ʿ" or "l"). Furthermore, a range of principles are developed which explain more or less general phenomena, including high frequency of use (*Munṣif* I, 61, 63), and paradigmatic regularity (Mubarrad *Muqtaḍab* I, 88, 'Anbārī, *'Inṣāf* 542, 785). The range of interlocking rules and principles operating within *ṣarf* is quite large, and the extent of their systematicity remains to be defined.

| (12) | | (a) | (b) |
|---|---|---|---|
| | underlying stem | *bayaʿa* | *kataba* |
| | ↓ morphophonological rules | ↓ *ayV* → *ā* | ↓ |
| | surface stem | *bāʿa* | *kataba* |

It may be noted that phonetics itself belongs to these principles. Though the phonetic categories themselves are articulatorily or perceptually based, phonetics itself is not introduced as an independent component of grammar parallel to syntax and morphology, but rather in conjunction with one aspect of morphophonology, namely assimilation (*'idġām*, e. g. Sībawayhi, *Kitāb* II, 460). Assimilation rules, like the voicing of *t* in *iḍḍaraba* "be confused" (< *iḍtaraba* = *ift'ala*), or the emphaticization of *t* in the same example, are specifiable only with a precise phonetic description of the sounds involved, for assimilation can be due to various phonetic factors: in the example just cited two independent assimilation processes are operative, one voicing (*taǧhīr*), the other emphasis (*'iṭbāq*).

5.3. The morphology-syntax boundary

The boundary between morphology (*ṣarf*) and syntax (*naḥw*) as defined by Ibn Ǧinnī and his successors is conceptually clear. The logic of Arabic grammar, however, does lead to cases where similar, if not identical, morphosemantic elements fall into different domains. The perfect verb suffixes, for instance the *-tu* in *ḍarab-tu* "hit-I", are considered agents in the syntactic construction verb + agent, of a syntactic class with *ar-raǧulu* in (5) and are classified as a discrete sub-class of nouns, namely pronouns (*ḍamā'ir*), "affixed" or "connected" pronouns (*ḍamīr muttaṣil*) to be precise. The personal verb prefixes in the imperfect like *'a-* "lsg", *'a-ḍribu* "I-hit", on the other hand, are treated as added morphological elements (*ḥurūf zā'ida*) with no independent syntactic standing and as a consequence having no nominal status as pronouns. The different classification of the elements *-tu*, *'a-* follows, perhaps, from the definition of verbal and nominal sentences. Verbal sentences have the basic sequence V + agent, nominal sentences on the other hand topic (= noun) + comment. Were the imperfect prefixes considered pronouns, it would follow that all imperfect verbs occur in nominal sentences (topic = pronoun) whereas all perfect verbs occur in verbal ones. Rather than split the verb-initial sentences into two syntactic types, the imperfect person prefixes were classified differently, as non-nominal. Should this explanation be the correct one (Owens 1988: 83) it would indicate yet again (see *ni'ma* above) that the syntactic component of Arabic theory took precedence over the morphological in that the categories of verbal morphology are adapted in this case to the sentential syntax.

The example in the previous paragraph, *ḍarab-tu* vs. *'a-ḍribu* implies another contrast operative in Arabic theory, namely that between discrete morpheme segments as the basis of morphological analysis vs. the entire stem as the basic unit. As noted, the syntactic relation of *ḍarab-* to *-tu* is that of verb to agent. A verb-agent relation implies a relation between two discrete elements, and this indeed is what *ḍarab-* and *-tu* are conceived of, each as a *kalima* "morpheme, word" (Levin 1986). The relation between *'a-* and *-ḍrib*, on the other hand, is that of added consonant (*'-*) to basic stem (*-ḍrib*), the whole forming what above was termed an extended stem with the stem structure (*binā'*) of *'a-f'il*. The entire pattern, *'af'il* consisting of added consonant + basic consonant, is identified as being a typical structure of the imperfect verb. *Ḍarab-tu*, on the other hand, is interpreted as representing a discrete sequence of two morphemes (*kalima* = "morpheme" in this context), *ḍarab-* + *-tu*. It is noteworthy that at least one Arabic grammarian, 'Astarābāḏī (*Šarḥ* I, 5–6), did envisage extending the notion of a discrete morphemic analysis (*kalima* = "morpheme") to entire patterns. He asked, for instance, whether it wouldn't be possible to say that *'aḍrib* consisted of a morpheme (*kalima*) signifying the action of hitting (= the root consonants *ḍrb*) plus another morpheme (*kalima*) signifying imperfect, indicated by the sequence of consonants + vowels (Ø + *-i-*, *-ḍØrib*). He rejected such an analysis on psychological grounds (the component meanings of the imperfect verb are understood as a whole), though the thrust of 'Astarābāḏī's comments indicate that the conceptual contours of Arabic grammatical structures were, in many cases, consciously and explicitly marked.

## 6. Unmarked and marked (*'aṣl, far'*)

A fundamental aspect of Arabic grammatical theory cross-cuts morphology and syntax. Within a standard grammatical treatise it does not form an independent component of its own, though there are books devoted mainly to its principles (e. g. Zaǧǧāǧī's *'Īḍāḥ*, Suyūṭī's *Iqtirāḥ*), but rather is present implicitly at every grammatical juncture. The Arabic vocabulary used to describe it appears as a series of binary oppositional terms, *'aṣl/far'* "basic/secondary", *'aḫaff/'aṯ-*

*qal* "lighter/heavier", *'aqwā/'aḍ'af* "stronger/weaker", *qabl/ba'd* "before/after". Very frequently one of these terms will be used to describe a particular phenomenon in one context or will be used by one author, another term in another context or by another author, or two terms will come together to describe the same phenomenon. Ṣaymarī (98), for instance, says that a single noun (*mufrad*) is "before" (*qabl*) a possessed + possessor (*'iḍāfa*) combination and is basic (*'aṣl*) to it. The fundamental presupposition behind this idea is that different realizations of the same grammatical category manifest the prototypical properties of the category to a greater or lesser extent. The realizations can be ranked relative to each other in a hierarchy (Baalbaki 1979), one member being more basic, or the metaphor I use, unmarked, than another. Always linked to the ranking, however, is a reason or cause (*'illa*, Versteegh 1995: 90–91 for etymological discussion of this term) for arranging the hierarchy as it is. 'Anbārī (*Luma'* 93) schematizes the ranking as follows. His schema applies explicitly only to the *'aṣl/far'* dyad, though the motivation, in terms of a reason, is nearly always discernible when items are classified by any binary pair listed above.

(14) *'aṣl* ----------- *'illa* ⟶ *far'*
unmarked reason marked

The schema is applied in two complementary ways:

(15) a category acquires a marked attribute, for a particular reason, or
(16) a category is marked and therefore behaves differently or is treated differently from the unmarked, for a particular reason.

The first perspective is processual, while the second works in terms of given categories which are ordered in terms of markedness according to the properties each has.

As mentioned, the markedness hierarchy pervades all aspects of Arabic grammar. For one, markedness governs the organization of the standard syntactic and morphological works. As seen above, in syntax, categories are introduced in the order u-infl, a-infl, agreeing categories, uninflected categories. That u-infl is the least marked, the reason in sense (16) above, is that the obligatory parts of the sentence are in u-infl. Without a u-infl, either as topic + comment or as agent of verb, there can be no sentence. In later treatments (e. g. Ibn Ya'īš, *Šarḥ* I, 74) these parts of the sentence were given a special name, *'umda* "support". A-infl and i-infl, on the other hand, are optional (and are sometimes collectively termed *faḍalāt* "leftovers, optional complements", Ibn Ya'īš, *Šarḥ* I, 73, 'Astarābāḏī, *Šarḥ* II, 19). The adjective position is more marked than that of the noun it qualifies because it follows it sequentially, and agrees with it in terms of case and gender. It is clear that the pairwise determination of markedness leads to markedness hierarchies, for example, moving from least to most marked, u-infl positions > a-infl/i-infl positions > adjective (and other agreeing positions).

Markedness further determines sub-orders within the introduction of elements in a grammar. The nominal sentence is introduced before the verbal, for instance (see section 2). The nominal sentence is the unmarked category here (again in sense (16)) because a sentence can consist entirely of nouns (see (2a)), whereas a verb always requires an agent (2b). This observation is linked to a further markedness assumption saying that nouns are unmarked relative to verbs (Zaǧǧāǧī, *'Īḍāḥ* 83, 100). Markedness also coincides with the dependency nature of syntactic relations (see (4)). Dependency relations presume relations between single items, between words, and it is held that a single word (*mufrad*) is unmarked relative to a larger unit (see Ṣaymarī's example above). From this it follows that the way to establish paradigmatic equivalences as in (3) is to define the behavior of the single unit, the word, and to gauge the status of the larger unit relative to the smaller one.

Similarly in morphology. Very cursorily, in 'Abū Ḥayyān's *Mubda'* first nouns consisting only of the basic (*'aṣl*) sounds are introduced, then those with the added ones (*zawā'id*). Within each of these two categories, first forms with 3 consonantal roots are introduced, because this is considered the most unmarked form, then those with 4 or 5. 'Abū Ḥayyān then follows the same procedure with verbs. Furthermore, the notion of markedness is implicit in the basis of morphophonological rules. In (11) the stem (*'aṣl*) *qawala* is said, for a reason (*'illa*) to undergo the given change. The resulting form is not usually termed *far'*, though its derived status is evident.

A commonly cited example for the first interpretation (15) of markedness is the explanation for the modal inflectional endings on imperfect verbs. Within the Arabic dependency practice words are divided into two classes, inherent governors = verbs and particles and inherently governed = nouns (Zağğāğī, *'Īḍāḥ* 77). As a rule, the former are not governed, and the latter are not governors. There are exceptions, however, the most important being the imperfect verb, which does have three modal suffixes, *-u* (u-infl, indicative), *-a* (a-infl, subjunctive), *-Ø* (Ø-infl, jussive), their appearance being governed by various particles. *lan*, for instance, requires that the verb stem end in *-a, lan yaḍrib-a* "he will not hit". The governing particles are not the reason for the imperfect verb being modally inflectable, however. Rather, the causal chain is explained as follows:

| (17) | *'aṣl* ——— | *('illa)* ———→ | *far'* |
|---|---|---|---|
| | uninflected verb | resemblance to noun | becomes inflectable |
| | *'a-ktub* | *(kātib-u)* | *'aktub-u* "I write" |

The verb is inherently uninflected. Because, however, the imperfect verb resembles the noun in certain respects, it acquires a fundamental nominal property, namely the ability to be modally inflected. To name only one resemblance, the sequences of consonants and vowels in the imperfect verb and in certain nouns, as well as their structure in terms of added and based letters may be identical. *'aktubu* "I hit" for instance, has the same structure, CVCCVCV as the noun *kātibu* "writer-nom", at least in the Arabic system of orthographic representation where a long *ā* is represented as a sequence of short *a-* + consonant, hence CVCCVCV (see Zağğāğī, *'Īḍāḥ* 107ff., 'Anbārī, *'Asrār* 24; Goldenberg 1989: 110). Note that the name of the imperfect verb, *al-fi'l al-muḍāri'* "the resembling verb" probably derives from this analogy.

It would seem that the basis of the decision what is unmarked, what is marked is common sense, observation of statistical frequency and, above all, the desire to normalize the structure of the language, if not at the 'surface level', at least at a (in some sense) deeper one. The assumption, for instance, that verbs are inherent governors, nouns inherently governed would appear to rest on the observation that virtually all nouns vary for three cases, while only the imperfect verb varies for mode. The perfect verb does not.

The theory of markedness highlights the structural basis of Arabic grammatical practice. The ranking of items as unmarked and marked is as much a part of the definition of what a grammatical (in the broadest sense) position is as are the explicitly listed formal properties of that position. Indeed, the theory of the *'uṣūl* may be said to be the (synchronic) means by which Arabic grammatical theory achieved the comprehensiveness and compactness which it did. As seen above, every category of Arabic theory is defined by a set of properties; elements which do not wholly conform to these properties may, through the theory of markedness, nonetheless realize the category and be included in it, if an appropriate reason can be found explaining its special behavior. A wide (in fact, potentially infinite) range of similar phenomena can thus be accommodated under a finite set of grammatical categories.

## 7. Bibliography

### 7.1. Primary sources


'Abū Ḥayyān, *Mubdi'* = 'Abū Ḥayyān Muḥammad ibn Yūsuf al-Ġarnāṭī al-'Andalusī, *al-Mubdi' fī t-taṣrīf*. Ed. by 'Abd al-Ḥamīd Ṭalab. Beirut: Maktaba Dār al-'Urūba.

'Anbārī, *'Inṣāf* = 'Abū l-Barakāt 'Abd ar-Raḥmān ibn Muḥammad al-'Anbārī, *Kitāb al-'inṣāf fī masā'il al-ḫilāf bayna n-naḥwiyyīna l-baṣriyyīn wa-l-kūfiyyīn*. Ed. by Muḥammad 'Abd al-Ḥamīd. 2 vols. Beirut: Dār al-Fikr, n. d.

'Anbārī, *Luma'* = 'Abū l-Barakāt 'Abd ar-Raḥmān ibn Muḥammad al-'Anbārī, *al-'Iġrāb fī ğadal al-'i'rāb wa-luma' al-'adilla fī 'uṣūl an-naḥw*. Ed. by Sa'īd al-'Afġānī. Beirut: Dār al-Fikr, 1971.

'Anbārī, *'Asrār* = 'Abū l-Barakāt 'Abd ar-Raḥmān ibn Muḥammad al-'Anbārī, *'Asrār al-'arabiyya*. Ed. by Muḥammad al-Bīṭār. Damascus: al-Mağma' al-'Ilmī al-'Arabī, 1957.

'Astarābāḏī, *Šarḥ* = Raḍī d-Dīn Muḥammad ibn Ḥasan al-'Astarābāḏī, *Šarḥ Kāfiyat Ibn al-Ḥāğib*. 2 vols. Beirut: Dār al-Kutub al-'Ilmiyya, 1969.

Farrā', *Muḏakkar* = 'Abū Zakariyyā' Yaḥyā ibn Ziyād al-Farrā', *Kitāb al-muḏakkar wa-l-mu'annaṯ*. Ed. by Ramaḍān 'Abd at-Tawwāb. Cairo: Dār at-Turāṯ, 1975.

*Ğumal* = *Kitāb al-ğumal fī n-naḥw*. Ed. by Faḫr ad-Dīn Qabāwa. Beirut, 1985.

Ğurğānī, *Dalā'il* = 'Abū Bakr 'Abd al-Qāhir ibn 'Abd ar-Raḥmān al-Ğurğānī, *Dalā'il al-'i'ğāz*. Ed. by Muḥammad Riḍā. Beirut: Dār al-Ma'rifa, 1978.

Ibn 'Aqīl, *Šarḥ* = Bahā' ad-Dīn 'Abdallāh Ibn 'Aqīl, *Šarḥ al-'Alfiyya*. Ed. by Muḥammad Muḥyī d-Dīn 'Abd al-Ḥamīd. 14th ed. 2 vols. Beirut: Dār al-Fikr, 1972.

Ibn Ğinnī, *Ḫaṣā'iṣ* = 'Abū l-Fatḥ 'Uṯmān Ibn Ğinnī, *al-Ḫaṣā'iṣ*. Ed. by Muḥammad 'Alī an-Nağğār. Cairo, 1952–56. (Repr., Beirut: Dār al-Hudā, n. d.)

Ibn Ǧinnī, *Luma'* = 'Abū l-Fatḥ 'Uṯmān Ibn Ǧinnī, *Kitāb al-luma' fī n-naḥw.* Ed. by Ḥusayn Šaraf. Beirut: 'Ālam al-Kutub, 1979.

Ibn Ǧinnī, *Munṣif* = 'Abū l-Fatḥ 'Uṯmān Ibn Ǧinnī, *al-Munṣif, šarḥ li-Kitāb at-taṣrīf li-l-Māzinī.* Ed. by 'Ibrāhīm Muṣṭafā & 'Abdallāh 'Amīn. 3 vols. Cairo: 'Idāra 'Iḥyā' at-Turāṯ al-Qadīm, 1954.

Ibn as-Sarrāǧ, *'Uṣūl* = 'Abū Bakr ibn as-Sarī Ibn as-Sarrāǧ, *Kitāb al-'uṣūl fī n-naḥw.* Ed. by 'Abd al-Ḥusayn al-Fatlī. Beirut: Mu'assasat ar-Risāla, 1985.

Ibn Sīnā, *'Asbāb* = 'Abū 'Alī al-Ḥusayn ibn 'Abdallāh Ibn Sīnā, *'Asbāb ḥudūṯ al-ḥurūf.* Ed. by Muḥammad aṭ-Ṭayyān & Yaḥyā 'Alam. Damascus: Maǧma' al-Luġa al-'Arabiyya bi-Dimašq, 1983.

Ibn 'Uṣfūr, *Mumti'* = 'Abū l-Ḥasan 'Alī ibn Mu'min Ibn 'Uṣfūr al-'Išbīlī, *al-Mumti' fī t-taṣrīf.* Ed. by Muḥammad 'Abd al-Ḥamīd. 2 vols. Beirut: Dār al-Kitāb al-'Arabī, 1955.

Ibn 'Uṣfūr, *Šarḥ* = 'Abū l-Ḥasan 'Alī ibn Mu'min Ibn 'Uṣfūr al-'Išbīlī, *Šarḥ Ǧumal az-Zaǧǧāǧī.* Ed. by Ṣāḥib 'Abū Ǧanāḥ. 2 vols. Baghdad: Dār al-Kutub li-ṭ-Ṭibā'a wa-n-Našr, 1980.

Ibn Ya'īš, *Šarḥ* = Muwaffaq ad-Dīn Ya'īš Ibn Ya'īš, *Šarḥ al-Mufaṣṣal.* 10 vols. Beirut & Cairo: 'Ālam al-Kutub & Maktabat al-Mutanabbī, n. d.

Mubarrad, *Muqtaḍab* = 'Abū l-'Abbās Muḥammad ibn Yazīd al-Mubarrad, *al-Muqtaḍab.* Ed. by Muḥammad 'Abd al-Ḫāliq 'Uḍayma. 4 vols. Cairo: Dār at-Taḥrīr, 1965–68. (Repr., Beirut: 'Ālam al-Kutub, n. d.).

Sakkākī, *Miftāḥ* = 'Abū Ya'qūb Yūsuf ibn 'Abī Bakr Muḥammad ibn 'Alī as-Sakkākī, *Miftāḥ al-'ulūm.* Ed. by Na'īm Zarzūr. Beirut: Dār al-Kutub al-'Ilmiyya, 1984.

Ṣaymarī, *Tabṣira* = 'Abū Muḥammad aṣ-Ṣaymarī, *at-Tabṣira wa-t-taḏkira.* Ed. by F. 'Alā' ad-Dīn. Mecca: 'Umm al-Qurā University, 1982.

Sībawayhi, *Kitāb* = 'Abū Bišr 'Amr ibn 'Uṯmān Sībawayhi, *al-Kitāb.* Ed. by Hartwig Derenbourg. 2 vols. Paris: Imprimerie Nationale, 1881–1889. (Repr., Hildesheim: Olms, 1970.)

Suyūṭī, *Iqtirāḥ* = Ǧalāl ad-Dīn 'Abū l-Faḍl 'Abd ar-Raḥmān ibn 'Abī Bakr as-Suyūṭī, *al-Iqtirāḥ fī 'ilm 'uṣūl an-naḥw.* Ed. by 'Aḥmad Qāsim. Cairo: Maṭba'a as-Sa'āda, 1976.

Zaǧǧāǧ, *Yanṣarif* = 'Abū 'Isḥāq 'Ibrāhīm ibn as-Sarī az-Zaǧǧāǧ, *Mā yanṣarif wa-mā lā yanṣarif.* Cairo: Laǧna 'Iḥyā' at-Turāṯ al-'Islāmī, 1970.

Zaǧǧāǧī, *'Īḍāḥ* = 'Abū l-Qāsim 'Abd ar-Raḥmān ibn 'Isḥāq az-Zaǧǧāǧī, *al-'Īḍāḥ fī 'ilal an-naḥw.* Ed. by Māzin al-Mubārak. Cairo: Dār an-Nafā'is, 1979.

Zamaḫšarī, *Mufaṣṣal* = 'Abū l-Qāsim Maḥmūd ibn 'Umar az-Zamaḫšarī, *Kitāb al-Mufaṣṣal fī n-naḥw.* Beirut: Dār al-Ǧīl, n. d.

### 7.2. Secondary sources

Baalbaki, Ramzi. 1979. "Some Aspects of Harmony and Hierarchy in Sībawayhi's grammatical analysis". *Zeitschrift für arabische Linguistik* 2.7–22.

Bernards, Monique. 1997. *Changing Traditions: Al-Mubarrad's refutation of Sībawayh and the subsequent reception of the* Kitāb. Leiden: Brill.

Bohas, Georges & Jean-Patrick Guillaume. 1984. *Etude des théories des grammairiens arabes,* vol. I: *Morphologie et phonologie.* Damascus: Institut Français de Damas.

Goldenberg, Gideon. 1988. "Subject and Predicate in Arab Grammatical Tradition". *Zeitschrift der deutschen morgenländischen Gesellschaft* 138.39–73.

—. 1989. "The Contribution of Semitic Languages to Linguistic Thinking". *Ex Oriente Lux* 30.107–115.

Larcher, Pierre. 1992. "La particule *lākinna* vue par un grammairien arabe du XXIII$^{e}$ siècle, ou comment une description de détail s'inscrit dans une 'théorie pragmatique'". *Historiographia Linguistica* 19.1–24.

Levin, Aryeh. 1981. "The Grammatical Terms *al-musnad, al-musnad ilayhi* and *al-isnād*". *Journal of the American Oriental Society* 101.145–165.

—. 1985. "The Syntactic Technical Term *al-mabniyy 'alayhi*". *Jerusalem Studies in Arabic and Islam* 6.299–352.

—. 1986. "The Mediaeval Arabic Term *kalima* and the Modern Linguistic Term Morpheme: Similarities and differences". *Jerusalem Studies in Arabic and Islam* 7.423–446.

Owens, Jonathan. 1988. *The Foundations of Grammar: An introduction to Medieval Arabic grammatical theory.* Amsterdam & Philadelphia: Benjamins.

—. 1989. "The Syntactic Basis of Arabic Word Classification". *Arabica* 36.211–234.

—. 1990. *Early Arabic Grammatical Theory: Heterogeneity and standardization.* Amsterdam: Benjamins.

—. 1993. "The Arabic Syntactic Tradition". *Syntax. An international handbook of contemporary research* ed. by Joachim Jacobs, Wolfgang Sternfeld, Theo Vennemann & Arnim von Stechow, 208–215. Berlin: de Gruyter.

—. 1995. "A mollusc replies to A. E. Houseman, Jr.". *Historiographia Linguistica* 22.425–440.

—. To appear. "The Arabic Morphological Tradition".

Talmon, Rafael. 1988b. "*'Al-kalām mā kāna muktafiyan bi-nafsihi wa-huwa ǧumla'*: A study in the history of sentence concept and the Sībawaihian legacy in Arabic grammar". *Zeitshrift der deutschen morgenländischen Gesellschaft* 138.74–98.

Tesnière, Lucien. 1959. *Eléments de syntaxe structurelle.* Paris: Klincksieck.

Versteegh, Kees. 1978. "The Arabic Terminology of Syntactic Position". *Arabica* 25.261–281.

–. 1985. "The Development of Argumentation in Arabic Grammar: The declension of the dual and the plural". *Studies in the History of Arabic Grammar*, II ed. by Michael G. Carter & Kees Versteegh, 152–173. Amsterdam: Benjamins.

–. 1995. *The Explanation of Linguistic Causes: Az-Zağğāğī's theory of grammar.* Amsterdam & Philadelphia: Benjamins.

Weiss, Bernard G. 1966. *Language in Orthodox Muslim Thought: A study of* waḍʿ al-lughah *and its development.* Ph. D. Princeton Univ.

*Jonathan Owens, Bayreuth (Germany)*

# 43. Grammar and logic in the Arabic grammatical tradition

1. Introduction
2. The debate between logicians and grammarians
3. The role of the Muʿtazila and the theories on the origin of speech
4. Logic and grammar in al-Fārābī
5. Conclusion
6. Bibliography

## 1. Introduction

The Islamic empire that was founded in the course of the Arabs' large-scale conquests in the 7th century CE was to a large degree multilingual. Both during and after the period of the conquests speakers of many different languages (Coptic, Syriac, Berber, Persian and others) were incorporated in this empire. Nevertheless, the Arabic linguistic tradition that originated during the first centuries of the Islamic empire remained, just like many other linguistic traditions, monolingual in the sense that the grammarians' sole aim was the codification, description, and analysis of the Arabic language. Naturally, they regarded this language as superior to all other languages, be it only because it was the language of the *Qur'ān*, the language God had chosen for his last message to mankind.

The grammarians were, of course, aware of the fact that there were other languages. The point is that they did not regard these languages as worthy of linguistic study. The first Arab grammarian who wrote a complete analysis of the language, Sībawayhi (d. 177/793?), was a Persian, but nowhere in his *Kitāb* does he make any effort to compare the Arabic and the Persian language, and there is no indication at all that he was interested in the analysis of languages other than Arabic. At a later period the grammarian Ibn Ǧinnī (d. 392/1002) mentions in his *Ḫaṣā'iṣ* (I, 243) that he asked his teacher al-Fārisī (d. 377/987) and other scholars whose mother tongue was Persian, what they thought about the Persian language: they were unanimous in upholding the superiority of the Arabic language (*luṭf al-ʿarabiyya*).

This general disinterest in languages other than Arabic remained an essential trait of the entire Arabic grammatical tradition. It was at least partly responsible for the fact that the relationship between speaking and thinking, between language and thought, fell outside the frame of reference of the grammarians. In the 9th century CE, however, the introduction of Greek logical and philosophical ideas forced them to consider the issue of the relationship between language and thought. During this period logicians, who were influenced by Greek thought, claimed that thought processes were universal, but that the linguistic expression of these processes was accidental. This claim forced the grammarians to deal with problems they had until then ignored.

Greek influence may have been present from the start in the Islamic empire. In the beginning of the Arab grammatical tradition some elements from the surrounding Hellenistic culture may have filtered through in the concepts the Arabs used to describe their own language (cf. Versteegh 1993: 22–28). Older theories (cf. Merx 1884) assigned traces of Greek influence in Arabic grammar to the influence of Peripatetic logic; recently Talmon (→ Art. 37) has claimed that Greek logical and philosophical influence was particularly intense in what he calls the Old ʿIrāqī School. But whatever the Greek contribution to the origins of Arabic grammar might have been, its influence was shortlived and did affect neither the elaboration of the grammatical tradition nor its theoretical presuppositions.

During the Umayyad caliphate (661–750 CE) there were isolated attempts to translate Greek writings, mainly on medicine and astrology. In the 9th century, however, the interest in Greek scholarship and Greek science reached its apogee when the ʿAbbāsid caliph al-Maʾmūn ordered the translation of Greek treatises on logic, philosophy, medicine, pharmacology and astronomy on a massive scale in the so-called *Bayt al-Ḥikma* "House of Wisdom" in Baghdad, in which dozens of professional translators strove to translate as much as possible from the Greek heritage, first from Greek into Syriac and then from Syriac into Arabic (for a critical appraisal of the traditional account of the translation movement, see van Koningsveld 1998). At first the majority of the translators were Syriac-speaking Christian scholars, but later, Arabic speakers too became involved in the translation and adaptation of Greek works into Islamic culture.

The incorporation of the Greek heritage, particularly in the field of logic and philosophy had a profound influence on the general culture of Islam. In theology the school of the Muʿtazila attempted to bring about a synthesis of Greek logic and Islamic religion by accepting the primacy of the *ratio* and using reason as the basis for their theological speculations. In their theology they adhered to a strict monotheism, firmly rejecting any anthropomorphic interpretation of the *Qurʾān*. This also implied that they could not accept the common belief in the eternal nature of the Revelation; rather, they established that the revealed Holy Book was created (cf. Peters 1976). The second principle of their theology was the firm belief in God's justice, which in their view meant that man has to have a free will: otherwise, God's punishment of man for his sins would be injust.

Both the Muʿtazilites' investigation into the nature of God's speech and their preoccupation with mental processes such as willing and thinking induced them to develop an interest in the nature of language and the relationship between language and thought. This remained a lasting characteristic of their school and even affected the development of Islamic theology at large (on Greek logical influence in Islamic theology, see van Ess 1970).

The doctrine of the Muʿtazila, in particular their belief in the createdness of the *Qurʾān*, was established by al-Maʾmūn as state doctrine, but after 232/847 his decrees were rescinded by the caliph al-Mutawakkil, and the Muʿtazila was banned from theological universities. After the official fall of the Muʿtazila, the Muʿtazilites shifted their activities to other fields (cf. Makdisi 1984), chief among them linguistics (cf. Versteegh 1996a). They managed to infiltrate the discipline both with their methods and their favourite topics such as their views on *ʾiʿǧāz*, the createdness of the *Qurʾān* and the free will (→ Art. 44 and cf. below, section 3.).

## 2. The debate between logicians and grammarians

The introduction of Greek logic into Islam did not take place without serious resistance. When Islamic philosophers such as al-Kindī (d. middle of the 3rd/9th century) and al-Fārābī (d. 339/950) started to deal with philosophical issues, they could not avoid the animosity of the orthodox theologians who vehemently defended the primacy of the revealed Book.

In linguistics the introduction of logic was marked by a debate that touched on the relationship between language and thought. For the logicians it was obvious that Greeks and Arabs meant the same things when they expressed a judgment on the exterior world, but the way they expressed these judgments differed according to the language they used. Since they regarded mental processes as independent from the language in which they were expressed, some logicians drew the conclusion that they should occupy themselves with these mental processes and not bother with the different languages people used. This was the topic of a famous debate that took place in Baghdad in 320/932 at the court of the vizier. The two opponents were the Syrian Christian Mattā ibn Yūnus (d. 328/940) and the grammarian ʾAbū Saʿīd as-Sīrāfī (d. 368/979), who later became famous through his commentary on the *Kitāb Sībawayhi*. The positions the two opponents took in this debate are exemplary for the conflict between logic and grammar in this period (for an analysis of the debate, see Mahdi 1970, Endress 1986). According to the logician Mattā logic is an instrument to distinguish between correct and incorrect utterances, since it occupies itself with the truth value of speech. The form of speech differs according to the nation, but the meaning (*maʿnā*) is universal. According to him, the logician is competent for the study of the meanings (*ma'ānī*), whereas the task of the grammarian is confined to the study of the forms (*'alfāẓ*), which is arbitrary (on the dichotomy 'meaning'/'form' in the Arabic tradition, cf. Versteegh 1997b: 227–233; 251–258). This means that the logician does not need grammar, whereas the grammarian needs the help of logic, because he would never be able to analyse speech without knowing its meaning.

In this debate as Sīrāfī retorts that meaning is intimately related to the convention of a specific language. He expresses his surprise that someone like Mattā (a Syrian Christian) who does not know Arabic very well, and who does not know Greek either, because it is a dead language, dares to pose as a connoisseur of meaning. Since Arabic was indeed the second language for most of the Syrian translators, it was relatively easy for someone like as-Sīrāfī to demonstrate Mattā's incompetence in Arabic. When he asks him about the "meanings" (*ma'ānī*) of the preposition *fī* "in", Mattā does not know what to say. Obviously, we are dealing here with a different use of the term 'meaning': for Mattā *ma'ānī* are the universal meanings of the speech utterances, akin to Plato's ideas, whereas for the grammarians *ma'ānī* are the grammatical functions for which a word can be used according to the rules of the language. Thus, a preposition can be said to have certain grammatical functions; unfortunately, as a non-native speaker, Mattā does not know these.

The defeat of the logician Mattā at the hands of the grammarian as-Sīrāfī was symptomatic for the relationship between the two disciplines. In the following centuries logic as well as the other imported sciences were relegated to the position of *'ulūm yūnāniyya* "Greek sciences" that did not find a place within the Islamic curriculum. Grammar, on the other hand, remained an entirely Islamic doctrine, although even the most traditional grammarians could not avoid being affected by the import of Greek logic. Thus, for instance, the grammarian az-Zaǧǧāǧī (d. 337/949) devotes an entire chapter to the definition of 'definition', in which he gives as an example the various definitions that philosophers have given to the notion of 'philosophy' (*'Īḍāḥ* 6–47; Versteegh 1997a: 43–48). When it comes to purely grammatical notions, however, he mentions the Aristotelian definition of the noun, which had been borrowed by some grammarians, and then states in the same passage:

> According to logical requirements and logical theory, it is correct, indeed, but their objective is not the same as ours, nor do we have the same purpose. Therefore, according to our linguistic standard, this definition is incorrect.

Notwithstanding his rejection of logical influence, in his work he often deals with issues that clearly belong to the domain of logic (e. g., the status of the nominatum, *musammā*, cf. Versteegh 1997a: 37, n. 21, and the discussion of the priority of noun or verb, cf. Versteegh 1997a: 135–138).

Even after the confrontation with logic Arabic grammarians continued to occupy themselves exclusively with the Arabic language, which was assumed implicitly – and sometimes even explicitly – to represent the ideal structure of a human language. The need to study foreign languages was obviated by the fact that Arabic had been elected by God for His last revelation.

## 3. The role of the Mu'tazila and the theories on the origin of speech

After the public disgrace of the Mu'tazila their influence in Arabic grammar became increasingly important. Because the Mu'tazilite creed pervaded grammar, many of the issues that had been discussed by Mu'tazilite theologians were now transmuted into linguistic issues. Thus we find in Ibn Ǧinnī, a Mu'tazilite himself, statements to the effect that the study of grammar is necessary because it helps people to avoid the kind of blasphemous mistakes some people make when they interpret verses from the *Qur'ān* that refer to God's hand or body and believe that these are physical attributes (*Ḫaṣā'iṣ* III, 245–246).

But the influence of Mu'tazilite theology and logic also meant that new issues were dealt with in grammar that had never been discussed before. One of the topics the Mu'tazilites introduced into the discipline of linguistics is that of the origin of speech. In the Islamic tradition the traditional Biblical division of languages/peoples into the descendants of the three sons of Noah was taken over without questioning. But naturally, the classification of languages immediately led to the question of the cause of this diversity. The discussion about the origin of speech in Islam was of course severely constrained, as it was in the Christian and the Jewish tradition, by the existence of the Revelation, which stated clearly (*Qur'ān* 2/31): *wa-'allama 'Ādama l-'asmā'a kullahā* "and He taught Adam all the names [or: all the words]", which was traditionally interpreted to mean that God had revealed to Adam all the words of the language. Later, different interpretations of the Qur'ānic verse gained currency; cf. Suyūṭī, *Muzhir* I, 28–30; Loucel 1963–64; Weiss 1974; Versteegh 1996b).

In linguistics proper the discussion about the origin of speech never gained hold. The question was raised only during the period in which the Mu'tazila was dominant, and then only by some grammarians – almost all of whom were Mu'tazilites anyway. The Mu'tazilite dogma of the createdness of the *Qur'ān* was closely connected with a theory on the human origin of language. Language in their view is a human phenomenon and a human invention; it does not contain any pre-established meaning, since that would endanger human free will.

The best summary of the discussion is given by Ibn Ǧinnī (d. 392/1002) in his book *al-Ḫaṣā'iṣ* (I, 40–47). After having reviewed the textual arguments from the *Qur'ān* in favour of divine intervention in the creation of speech (*waḥy, 'ilhām, tawqīf*) and the logical arguments in favour of human convention (*iṣṭilāḥ, waḍ', tawāḍu'*), he admits his inability to decide on the matter (*Ḫaṣā'iṣ* I, 47). On the one hand, he is persuaded by the rational arguments, in favour of human convention, but on the other, the superiority of Arabic and its excellence make him doubt the truth of this rational argument.

Most grammarians agreed with this summing up of the issue. Only a few grammarians took the trouble to find independent arguments for or against the divine origin of speech. Ibn Fāris (d. 395/1004), for instance, gives an elaborate defense of the traditional, orthodox position in his *Kitāb as-Ṣāḥibī* (5–11) stating right from the start that "the language of the Arabs is revelation (*tawqīf*), and the proof of that is in God's words 'He taught Adam all the words' ".

Later grammarians either do not mention the topic at all or simply refer to the existing arguments without taking a position themselves. Not even the question of the language of paradise was able to raise much interest: most scholars assumed more or less implicitly that this language was Arabic, and only a literalist such as Ibn Ḥazm (d. 456/1064) could argue that in the absence of scriptural evidence on this matter, it could just as well be Hebrew or Greek (cf. Arnaldez 1956: 45).

The general disinterest in the origin of language issue on the part of linguists corresponds to the usual position in theology and other disciplines, where it was held that the debate was fruitless, the only really important point being the "givenness of language" (*waḍ' al-luġa*), i. e., the fact that in contemporary language the meaning is conventional, arbitrary, and institutionalised. This became the starting point for the extensive literature on the semantic/pragmatic value of the religious texts (for instance, those of al-Ġazzālī, d. 402/1111, cf. Gätje 1974). Eventually, this resulted in a special genre of treatises on *waḍ'* (cf. Weiss 1966), in which all linguistic elements are categorised and analysed according to their legal implications (e. g., in terms of their general or particular application in legal texts). In the narrow sense of grammar as it was practised by the Arabic grammarians these treatises did not belong to the discipline of grammar (*naḥw*). In their classificatory scheme of the sciences the studies of *waḍ' al-luġa* belonged to the science of the *'uṣūl al-fiqh*, the fundamental principles of legal science.

## 4. Logic and grammar in al-Fārābī

In logic the approach to language, including the topic of the origin of speech, was quite different from that of linguistics. The fame of the 'second Aristotle', the logician 'Abū Naṣr al-Fārābī (d. 339/950), even in Medieval Western Europe, stems from his commentaries on Aristotle's writings, particularly in logic and syllogistics (on his logical writings, see Lameer 1994). But he also wrote original treatises on various subjects, some of which are of considerable interest for the topic at hand (cf. Haddad 1969). We know that he was interested in grammar: one of his teachers was the grammarian Ibn as-Sarrāǧ (d. 316/928), who in his turn learned from al-Fārābī logic (and music).

Fārābī's contribution to the study of language took place outside the heated atmosphere of the discussion reported on above. It is an analysis of the nature of language according to Aristotelian categories. It is not known with certainty what his native tongue was – probably some Turkic language – but we know for a fact that his approach to other languages, even apart from the understandable interest in Greek, was refreshingly new. In the *Kitāb al-ḥurūf* "Book of Letters" he states (111–112) that all languages except Arabic possess a word functioning as the copula in equative sentences, such as Persian *hast* and Greek *estin*. He then says:

When philosophy was transmitted to the Arabs and those philosophers who used Arabic and talked about the meanings of philosophy and logic in Arabic felt the need [for such a word], they found that since its earliest origin Arabic had lacked an expression to translate those constructions in which Greek *estin* and Persian *hast* are used (*Ḥurūf* 112.4–7).

He then describes the ways philosophers attempted to find equivalent means of expressing the notion of the copula in Arabic. This open admission of a lacuna in Arabic compared to all other languages is quite unusual in Arabic writings; it would certainly be unthinkable in a grammatical treatise.

In the *Kitāb al-ḥurūf* al-Fārābī also dealt with other topics such as the cause of the difference between languages and the origin of speech, which he analyses in a strictly conventionalist framework (*Ḥurūf* 131–142): just like law, religion(!), and writing, languages (i. e., collections of words as denominations of things) originate as a result of the collective acceptance by the community of something invented by an individual. He then goes on to describe in minute detail the rest of the process of 'constructing' the language.

Fārābī's views on the relationship between grammar and logic are treated in his catalogue of the sciences (*'Iḥṣā' al-'ulūm*), where he defines the task of the two disciplines as follows. Grammar consists of two parts, the first of which deals with the "preservation of the meaningful utterances in a community" (*ḥifẓ al-'alfāẓ ad-dālla 'inda 'umma mā; 'Iḥṣā'* 9.11–12), the second with the rules of these utterances (*qawānīn tilka l-'alfāẓ; 'Iḥṣā'* 10.1). This brings him to the following comparison between grammar and logic:

This discipline [i. e., logic] is related to the discipline of grammar since the relation of the discipline of logic to the mind and the intelligibles is the same as that between the discipline of grammar to language and the utterances; the rules that the discipline of grammar gives us for the utterances have their equivalent in the rules that the discipline of logic gives us for the intelligibles (*'Iḥṣā'* 23.1–5).

This division of tasks differs from the one used by the logician Mattā ibn Yūnus, who did not acknowledge the linguistically relevant study of meanings of utterances, whereas al-Fārābī fully recognises the expertise of grammarians in this respect.

One of al-Fārābī's pupils, Yaḥyā ibn 'Adī (d. 363/974), who was a Christian, wrote a *Maqāla fī tabyīn al-faṣl bayna ṣinā'atay al-manṭiq al-falsafī wa-n-naḥw al-'arabī* "Treatise on the clarification of the difference between the two disciplines: philosophical logic and Arabic grammar". Basically, he defended the same position as Mattā ibn Yūnus had done – he may even have attended the debate although he does not say so – but in more prudent terms. According to Yaḥyā (*Risāla* 189.5–9) the task of the grammarian is to provide the correct case-endings to words. It is true, he argues, that grammarians assign "meanings" (*ma'ānī*) to these endings, but these do not belong to his domain: when speakers utter expressions without case-endings or with the wrong ones, they may still have a clear intended meaning, which is therefore independent of the grammarian's expertise. Logic, on the other hand, deals with the "expressions that signify universal things" (*al-'alfāẓ ad-dālla 'alā l-'umūr al-kulliyya; Risāla* 182.19–20).

In spite of his logical background, al-Fārābī did not shy away from purely linguistic issues (cf. Elamrani-Jamal 1983). In his *Kitāb al-'alfāẓ al-musta'mala fī l-manṭiq* he gives us an idea of the scope of linguistic work done by logicians. His Aristotelian version of the definition of the noun (*Šarḥ* 29.1–2 *lafẓa dālla bi-tawāṭu' muǧarrada min az-zamān wa-laysa wāḥid min 'aǧzā'ihā dāll 'alā nfirādihi* "an expression that signifies by convention, not determined by time, none of whose parts signifies on its own") and of the verb (*Šarḥ 33.1–2 al-kalima [...] mā tadullu ma'a mā tadullu 'alayhi 'alā zamān wa-laysa wāḥid min 'aǧzā'ihi yadullu 'alā nfirādihi* "the verb is [...] what cosignifies time with its signification and none of its parts signifies on its own") were well-known in grammatical circles. Even though he uses a terminology that differs from that of the grammarians (cf. Zimmermann 1972), e. g., by using *kalima* for "verb" (Greek *rhēma*; instead of *fi'l*) and *rābiṭ* for "particle" (Greek *súndesmos*; instead of *ḥarf*), he is clearly well aware of the grammatical doctrine of his contemporaries. When he deals with the third part of speech, the particle, he brings the terminology of the Greek grammarians to the attention of the Arabic grammarians:

Another class of meaningful expressions is the one called by the grammarians *ḥurūf* "particles", which signify a meaning. There are many categories of these particles, but up till our time it has not been customary for the scholars of Arabic grammar to give each category its own name. Therefore, in enumerating these categories we shall have to use the names that have come down to us from the scholars of Greek grammar (*'Alfāẓ* 42.7–11).

He then lists the names of these classes, such as *ḫawālif* (Greek *antōnumíai* "pronouns"), *wāṣilāt* (Greek *árthra* "articles"), which correspond to the classification of the parts of speech in Dionysios Thrax' *Tékhnē* (cf. Gätje 1971). His interest in Greek grammatical doctrine and practice is also reflected by his use of the word *qawānīn* for "linguistic rules", which refers to the Greek *kanónes*, general rules that regulate the behaviour of linguistic forms.

## 5. Conclusion

The Arab grammatical tradition is a typically monolingual tradition that was developed solely for the study of one language, Arabic. The Arabic grammarians exhibit no interest at all in the structure of other languages, not even in those languages that were related to Arabic, such as Hebrew and Syriac (unlike the Hebrew grammarians, → Art. 36). Only very sporadically do grammarians refer to other languages at all, usually either to stress the fact that all languages have the same structure, or to emphasise the superiority of Arabic (they claim, for instance, that it is the only language with a declensional system of *'i'rāb*; Ibn Fāris, *Ṣāḥibi* 42).

There are only very few exceptions to this rule: one of these is the grammarian 'Abū Ḥayyān (d. 745/1344) who not only wrote on Arabic, but also on Turkic, Berber, Mongolian and Ethiopian (→ Art. 48). In other grammatical traditions, such as Persian (→ Art. 49) and Coptic (→ Art. 47) indigenous grammarians used the Arabic model for the analysis of their own language, since it was the only one available to them.

Within the Arabic tradition there was not much (linguistic) interest in the relationship between language and thought. Since linguistic and mental processes belonged to different disciplines, the question of the relationship between the two was never raised, except in the confrontation with hard-liners amongst the logicians in the 4th/10th century. In the aftermath of this confrontation the grammarians became even more fixed on their own language, although the contact with logical ideas may have made them more receptive to another development in Arabic grammar, the interest in semantics which had been almost completely absent in the preceding period. With the efforts of linguistically oriented rhetoricians such as al-Ǧurǧānī (d. 471/1078) and as-Sakkākī (d. 626/1229) semantics became an integral part of the discipline (→ Art. 45).

The only noticeable effect of the confrontation between logic and grammar in purely grammatical treatises was the form of presentation: from the 4th/10th century onwards, for instance, Arab grammarians showed an intense interest in definitions, which had been absent almost completely before that time. Even those grammarians who rejected logical influence, such as az-Zaǧǧāǧī and as-Sīrāfī, freely used logical methods in their linguistic analysis. Some grammarians from this period were accused of 'mixing logic and grammar', such as ar-Rummānī (cf. Carter 1984), but in their grammatical writings they exhibit a remarkably conventional approach to grammar, and only very occasionally does one find any direct traces of logical influence in these writings.

## 6. Bibliography

### 6.1. Primary sources

Fārābī, *'Alfāẓ* = 'Abū Naṣr Muḥammad ibn Muḥammad al-Fārābī, *Kitāb al-'alfāẓ al-musta'mala fī l-manṭiq*. Ed. by Muḥsin Mahdī. Beirut: Dār al-Mašriq, 1968.

Fārābī, *Ḥurūf* = 'Abū Naṣr Muḥammad ibn Muḥammad al-Fārābī, *Kitāb al-ḥurūf*. Ed. by Muḥsin Mahdī. Beirut: Dār al-Mašriq, 1970.

Fārābī, *'Iḥṣā'* = 'Abū Naṣr Muḥammad ibn Muḥammad al-Fārābī, *'Iḥṣā' al-'ulūm*. Ed. and transl. by Ángel Gonzalez Palencia. 2nd ed. Madrid & Granada: Consejo Superior de Investigaciones Científicas, 1953.

Fārābī, *Šarḥ* = 'Abū Naṣr Muḥammad ibn Muḥammad al-Fārābī, *Šarḥ Kitāb 'Arisṭūṭālīs fī l-'Ibāra*. Ed. by William Kutsch & Stanley Marrow. Beirut: Imprimerie Catholique, 1960.

Ibn Fāris, *Ṣāḥibī* = 'Abū l-Ḥusayn 'Aḥmad Ibn Fāris, *aṣ-Ṣāḥibī fī fiqh al-luġa*. Ed. by Moustafa Chouémi [Muṣṭafā aš-Šu'aymī]. Beirut: Badran, 1964.

Ibn Ǧinnī, *Ḫaṣā'is* = 'Abū l-Fatḥ 'Uṯmān Ibn Ǧinnī, *al-Ḫaṣā'iṣ*. Ed. by Muḥammad 'Alī an-Naǧǧār. 3 vols. Cairo, 1952–56. (Repr., Beirut: Dār al-Hudā, n. d.).

Suyuṭī, *Muzhir* = Ǧalāl ad-Dīn ʾAbū l-Faḍl ʿAbd ar-Raḥmān ibn ʾAbī Bakr as-Suyūṭī, *al-Muzhir fī ʿulūm al-luġa*. Ed. by Muḥammad ʿAḥmad Ǧār al-Mawlā, ʿAlī Muḥammad al-Baǧāwī & Muḥammad ʾAbū l-Faḍl ʾIbrāhīm. 2 vols. Cairo: Maṭbaʿa ʿĪsā al-Ḥalabī, n. d.

Tawḥīdī, *ʾImtāʿ* = ʾAbū Ḥayyān ʿAlī ibn Muḥammad at-Tawḥīdī, *Kitāb al-ʾimtāʿ wa-l-muʾānasa*. Ed. by ʾAḥmad ʾAmīn & ʾAḥmad az-Zayn. Beirut & Saida: al-Maktaba al-ʿAṣriyya, 1953. [Arabic text of the debate between as-Sīrāfī and Mattā ibn Yūnus 108.5–128.19; French transl. by Elamrani-Jamal 1983:149–163; German transl. by Endress 1986:238–270.].

Yaḥya ibn ʿAdī, *Risālā* = Yaḥyā ibn ʿAdī, *Maqāla fī tabyīn al-faṣl bayna ṣināʿatay al-manṭiq al-falsafī wa-n-naḥw al-ʿarabī*. Ed. by Gerhard Endress, *Journal for the History of Arabic Science* 2 (1978) 181–193. [German transl. by Endress 1986:272–296; French transl. by Elamrani-Jamal 1983:187–197.]

Zaǧǧāǧī, *ʾĪḍāḥ* = ʾAbū l-Qāsim ʿAbd ar-Raḥmān ibn ʾIsḥāq az-Zaǧǧāǧī, *al-ʾĪḍāḥ fī ʿilal an-naḥw*. Ed. by Māzin al-Mubārak. Cairo: Dār al-ʿUrūba, 1959.

## 6.2. Secondary sources

Arnaldez, Roger. 1956. *Grammaire et théologie chez Ibn Hazm de Cordoue: Essai sur la structure et les conditions de la pensée musulmane*. Paris: Vrin.

Carter, Michael G. 1984. "Linguistic Science and Orthodoxy in Conflict: The case of al-Rummānī". *Zeitschrift für Geschichte der arabisch-islamischen Wissenschaften* 1.212–232.

Elamrani-Jamal, Abdelali. 1983. *Logique aristotélicienne et grammaire arabe: Etude et documents*. Paris: Vrin.

Endress, Gerhard. 1977. "al-Munāẓara bayna l-manṭiq al-falsafī wa-n-naḥw al-ʿarabī fī ʿuṣūr al-ḫulafāʾ". *Journal for the History of Arabic Science* 1.339–351.

–. 1986. "Grammatik und Logik: Arabische Philologie und griechische Philosophie im Widerstreit". *Sprachphilosophie in Antike und Mittelalter* ed. by Burkhard Mojsisch, 163–299. Amsterdam: Grüner.

Ess, Josef van. 1970. "The Logical Structure of Islamic Theology". *Logic in Classical Islamic Culture* ed. by Gustav E. von Grunebaum, 21–50. Wiesbaden: Harrassowitz.

Gätje, Helmut. 1971. "Die Gliederung der sprachlichen Zeichen nach al-Fārābī". *Der Islam* 47.1–24.

–. 1974. "Logisch-semasiologische Theorien bei al-Ġazzālī". *Arabica* 21.151–182.

Haddad, Fuad. 1969. "Alfārābīs Views on Logic and its Relation to Grammar". *Islamic Quarterly* 13.192–207.

Koningsveld, Pieter Sjoerd van. 1998. "Greek Manuscripts in the Early Abbasid Empire: Fiction and facts about their origin, translation and destruction". *Bibliotheca Orientalis* 55.345–372.

Lameer, Joep. 1994. *Al-Fārābī and Aristotelian Syllogistics: Greek theory and Islamic practice*. Leiden: Brill.

Loucel, Henri. 1963–64. "L'origine du language d'après les grammairiens arabes". *Arabica* 10.188–208, 253–281; 11.57–72, 151–187.

Mahdi, Muhsin. 1970. "Language and Logic in Classical Islam". *Logic in Classical Islamic Culture* ed. by Gustav E. von Grunebaum, 51–83. Wiesbaden: Harrassowitz.

Makdisi, George. 1984. "The Juridical Theology of Shāfiʿī: Origins and significance of the *uṣūl al-fiqh*". *Studia Islamica* 59.5–47.

Merx, Adalbert. 1889. *Historia artis grammaticae apud Syros*. Leipzig. (Repr., Nendeln: Kraus, 1966.)

Peters, Jan R. T. M. 1976. *God's Created Speech: A study in the speculative theology of the Muʿtazilī Qāḍī l-Quḍāt Abū l-Ḥasan ʿAbd al-Jabbār bn. Aḥmad al-Hamaḏānī*. Leiden: Brill.

Versteegh, Kees. 1993. *Arabic Grammar and Qurʾānic Exegesis in Early Islam*. Leiden: Brill.

–. 1996a. "The Linguistic Introduction to Rāzī's *Tafsīr*". *Studies in Near Eastern Languages and Literatures: Memorial volume of Karel Petráček* ed. by Petr Zemánek, 589–603. Prague: Academy of Sciences of the Czech Republic.

–. 1996b. "Linguistic Attitudes and the Origin of Speech in the Arab World". *Understanding Arabic: Essays in contemporary Arabic linguistics in honor of El-Said Badawi* ed. by Alaa El-Gibali, 15–31. Cairo: American University in Cairo Press.

–. 1997a. *The Explanation of Linguistic Causes: Az-Zaǧǧāǧī's theory of grammar*. Amsterdam & Philadelphia: Benjamins.

–. 1997b. "The Arabic Tradition". *The Emergence of Semantics in Four Linguistic Traditions: Hebrew, Sanskrit, Greek, Arabic* ed. by Wout van Bekkum, Jan Houben, Ineke Sluiter & Kees Versteegh, 227–284. Amsterdam & Philadelphia: Benjamins.

Weiss, Bernard G. 1966. *Language in Orthodox Muslim Thought: A study of* waḍʿ al-lughah *and its development*. Ph. D. dissertation, Princeton Univ.

–. 1974. "The Medieval Discussions of the Origin of Language". *Zeitschrift der deutschen morgenländischen Gesellschaft* 125.33–41.

Zimmermann, F. W. 1972. "Some Observations on al-Fārābī and Logical Tradition". *Islamic Philosophy and the Classical Tradition: Essays presented by his friends and pupils to Richard Walzer on his seventieth birthday* ed. by Samuel M. Stern, Albert Hourani & Vivian Brown, 517–546. Oxford: Cassirer.

*Kees Versteegh, Nijmegen (The Netherlands)*

# 44. Language and revelation in Islamic society

1. Introduction
2. Language as a component of the Revelation
3. Language as proof of the Revelation
4. The obligation to preserve the text and the language
5. Bibliography

## 1. Introduction

"By the Clear Book, behold, We have made it an Arabic Koran". This verse from the *Qur'ān* (43/2–3) indicates a strong and vital link between the text of the Revelation and the language in which it was transmitted. And, in fact, both the more formal summaries of Islamic creed and the daily practice of Muslim believers show that the Arabic language is far more than the simple vessel of Revelation; the language is believed to be an integral part of it.

The story of Muḥammad's vocation as a prophet portrays the angel Gabriel ordering Muḥammad to 'recite' a text, and as Muḥammad complained that he did not know what to recite, the angel pronounced a few sentences – in Arabic – that are considered to be the beginning of the Revelation (96/1–5). The prophet repeated this text and by doing so he started its *Qur'ān*, its recitation or reading.

In modern studies, the term *Qur'ān* is generally said to be derived from an old Christian term in Syriac (*qeryānā*) indicating the ceremonial and liturgical reading from Jewish and Christian Scriptures. In a similar way later in his life, Muḥammad ordered to write down this first revealed text together with other holy texts that were transmitted to him by the angel, and to 'recite' parts of them during the congregational ceremonies of his new community. This oral recitation of the revealed text in its original Arabic form has remained a central feature in Islamic religious practice, both public and private; it forms part of the official prayers in the mosque, and is daily practice in traditional Qur'ānic schools, where young children are memorizing the entire text of the *Qur'ān*. The reciting of this Arabic text of the *Qur'ān* has become a special form of art with its own rules and traditions, even in those countries where Arabic is not used or even understood in daily life.

Notwithstanding this cardinal function of 'recitation', the written text too is considered to be God's holy word to the prophet and to all mankind. This text really is God's Revelation, not just a support for the memory of those who recite it or a guarantee for an exact transmission to a new generation of believers. The example of the Jewish and Christian Scriptures was predominant in the early years of Islam. Muḥammad's followers were asking for a written book with God's revelation just like the Jews and the Christians had. The Revelation itself mentions Jews and Christians with respect and calls them "the people of the Book" (*'ahl al-Kitāb*), and in a similar way the *Qur'ān* too is called "the Book" (*al-Kitāb*). Even in the story of Muḥammad's vocation and the first revelation, mention is already made of a written text: the angel is said to have enveloped the prophet in a cloth of brocade in which a text was woven, in this way squeezing these words into his heart.

Maybe even more than the recited *Qur'ān*, the written text plays an important role in Islamic society. The high esteem for the Book is visible when it is displayed in a ceremonial place in the house of Muslims, but also by the way in which calligraphic verses are attached to the walls. In Islamic art, Qur'ānic texts are frequently used as a means of decoration in mosques and other public and private architecture. In popular Islam we meet with a use of the written text which recalls its function in the story of Muḥammad's vocation: people look for means to really interiorize the holy words of the Revelation. The original Arabic text of the *Qur'ān* is believed to possess a special *baraka* "power or blessing", and people try – literally – to swallow this *baraka*. Thus the ink of a written text is washed away with some water, and the water is drunk or rubbed into the skin, or the text is burned on charcoal and the smoke inhaled. And always, and throughout the Islamic World, it is the original text in Arabic language and Arabic writing that is copied, used as a decoration, venerated or used for its *baraka*; Revelation, Arabic language and Arabic script are firmly linked together.

Religious reasons – the veneration for the word of God and the *baraka* attributed to the text – have been important to secure the central role of the *Qur'ān* and its language in

Islamic history and Islamic society, but there were also strong reasons of a more sociological nature. The *Qur'ān* was, and still is, the most important – according to some, the only – really uniting power in Islamic society. Christianity is build around the person of a Messenger, who is believed to be living in the religious community and keeping it together; Muḥammad does not have a similar function in Islam. Nor does the Islamic community have the kind of hierarchy that could guarantee its coherence (with the exception of the Shīʿī minority, which does have its own forms of religious leadership). The experience of unity, of belonging to a community of believers, the world-wide *'umma*, is based upon a shared belief in the Word of God in the *Qur'ān*, and is expressed in the fulfilment of the pillars of Islam, five rituals which strengthen the sense of coherence among Muslims all over the world.

It was shortly after the death of Muḥammad in 632 AD that his successors already realized the importance of the Book as the main uniting factor in the fast expanding state. They needed a unique text that could be distributed all over the empire. Revealed texts that were recited by Muḥammad and often already written down at his command, were collected and spread over the newly conquered and converted regions. According to the Islamic tradition, it was because of the differences in the texts used in various places – differences that caused dissent among the believers – that the caliph ʿUṯmān was asked to provide a canonical text. And thus, some twenty years after Muḥammad's death, an authorized consonantal text was established and promulgated. This text was enforced and other readings were officially banned, but since the text was not vocalized, variant readings remained possible. It was only when a *scriptio plena* was developed, that the canonical text really could be fixed in all detail.

Together with the text of the Revelation, the Arabic language became in the first century of Islam an instrument of unification in the new and expanding state. Arabic was the language of the conquerors, it was the language of the powerful, and this surely has provoked its acceptance in the new provinces. But it was also the language of the word of God, the language of the Book around which the new community was built. Where the *Qur'ān* was a strong uniting force in the Islamic *'umma*, the Arabic language became a solid vessel for the religious, cultural and social unification of the new Islamic society. In this way, Revelation and Arabic language went hand in hand in building the structures of the new Islamic society and civilization.

Since God's Revelation and its language are so intrinsically interwoven, a translation of the *Qur'ān* can never truly and fully render the message that God has conveyed. God's word is the Arabic text of the *Qur'ān*. But since in many Islamic countries the great majority of the Muslims no longer understands Arabic, as is the case in modern Turkey or Indonesia, the need to render the text of the divine Revelation understandable for all believers aroused a discussion about whether a translation of the Qur'ānic text would be allowed or even possible. Notwithstanding a sometimes fierce opposition from traditional circles, it became an accepted custom to print a 'rendering' of the Arabic text into the local language in the margin of the original text or on the page opposite to it. This is the way in which commentaries on the *Qur'ān* were usually printed, and by choosing this kind of presentation it was emphasized that the translation does not take the place of the true revealed text, but that it constitutes rather a kind of description or commentary, and that the Arabic language remains the one and only vessel of God's Revelation.

We will explore this vital link between Revelation and its language in three paragraphs: language as an essential component of Revelation, language as proof of the divine character of Revelation, and the obligation to keep inviolate both Revelation and its language.

## 2. Language as a component of Revelation

"Nay, but it is a glorious Koran, in a guarded tablet" (85/21–22). According to the traditional Islamic interpretation of this verse, there exists with God a heavenly book or tablet, which is also called the "Mother of the Book" (*'umm al-Kitāb*, 43/4). This book should contain the entire text of the Revelation, every word that God would reveal to Muḥammad and to the prophets who lived before him. The angel Gabriel brought sections from this heavenly book to the prophet at any moment that God deemed it appropriate in the given circumstances to communicate a specific part of his message to mankind. Consequently, every *sūra* and every verse of the *Qur'ān* is a copy, word for word, from the original text as it is kept in heaven on the tablet or in the book.

According to this interpretation of the nature of revelation and according to traditional forms of Islamic faith, this heavenly tablet or book is a concrete text that consequently must have been composed in a certain language. Since the *Qur'ān* is the final revelation, preserved against any form of mutilation or addition, and since it is a faithful copy from the heavenly original text, this text must be in Arabic too. This conviction that God's word to mankind is formulated in Arabic, gives way to stories in which God is speaking in Arabic to the angels and the demons even before the creation of mankind. This implies that the Arabic language is not an artefact of man, like other languages, but God's personal creation.

Elaborating the theological reflection about the nature of the heavenly Book of revelation, traditionist thinkers stated that this text was eternal, co-eternal with God, and as a consequence not created by God. This could even imply that the Arabic language too is eternal and uncreated.

More rationalist theologians in the early centuries of Islam, especially from the school of the Muʿtazila, rejected this interpretation leading to an eternal language. For them language is a vessel of speech, and speech consists of sounds which must convey a meaning to be really speech and not just sounds. A written text is just a reference to real speech, which is the oral form by which a listener is addressed. This essentially communicative character of speech makes it impossible, even for God, to speak or to create speech as long as there is no creature, be it angel, demon or man, who can listen to the words spoken. This implies that speech, and language, cannot be eternal, but that it is produced at the moment of communication.

For the Muʿtazilita the heavenly Book is a metaphor for God's knowledge and His will. The revelation is God's word, which he creates at the moment that the angel communicates it to the prophet; it is called a representation (*ḥikāya*) of the heavenly book. The language that is chosen, the exact formulations, the grammatical forms are all adapted to the period and the circumstances in which the text is communicated. More traditionalist theologians also use the term *ḥikāya* for the actual revealed text, but they stress the complete identity of the revealed verses with the heavenly original. In this opinion, both texts are identical, and the aspects of communication are additional to the nature of the text. The moment chosen by God for the transmission of a passage from His heavenly book can convey a more specific meaning to the words concerned; their function in the actual circumstances of the transmission is determined by God. Besides its general message for all mankind of all times and all places, a revealed verse can in this way convey a special message when and where it is communicated.

In the debate about the eternal or created nature of God's speech and the *Qur'ān*, more specifically theological questions are at stake. The existence of an eternal *Qur'ān* endangers the belief in the uniqueness of God; does this not imply the existence of something outside of God from all eternity, a second divine substance? And when it is stated, that this *Qur'ān* does exist as part of the divine nature, does this not lead to a vision of God's nature that has some resemblance with the Christian faith in an eternal Word of God? In order to stress the unity and uniqueness of God, the Muʿtazila rejected the existence of anything besides God before the beginning of His creation, as they rejected any division within God's nature.

A second theological question which played an important role in the debate about the nature of the heavenly *Qur'ān* was concerned with the freedom of human beings to act and, consequently, their responsibility for their acts. The revealed texts stress this responsibility and announce punishment and reward at the end of times. But if, according to a widespread interpretation of the belief in the eternal heavenly Book, everything that will happen in the course of history is already written down before the creation of the world, man has no choice whatsoever and cannot be held responsible for his deeds. Even when the contents of the heavenly book are restricted to the actual text of the *Qur'ān* as we know it in this world, the above said holds true for the persons whose acts have been described in this text. It would conflict with God's justice if He would nevertheless reward or punish these persons for what they have done or neglected.

During the first half of the 9th century AD, the discussion about the *Qur'ān* acquired a strong political dimension and the words "createdness of the *Qur'ān*" (*ḫalq al-Qur'ān*) even became a shibboleth. The statement of the Muʿtazila that the *Qur'ān* was created, produced by God at the moment that He decided to communicate His message, could have serious political and social consequences in a society that – as we have seen – was built upon the text of this book. The thesis of the Muʿtazila gave the *Qur'ān* a kind of contiguity and dependence upon the time and the place when and where God created it. Moreover: it is His created word, He could have said other things and He still can do so. This intellectual approach could consequently endanger the unity of the state and Islamic society as a whole, for this unity was based upon the firm belief in the once and forever revealed text of God's eternal will. In this way, the continuity of the state was based upon the uncreatedness of the *Qur'ān*.

After a short period, in which the doctrine of the Muʿtazila gained the upper hand and the createdness of the *Qur'ān* was used by the caliph al-Ma'mūn as a shibboleth to distinguish between good and evil (833–849 AD) – probably because this doctrine could be used as an instrument to strengthen the power of the civil servants against that of the religious leaders – it was rejected by his successors. The belief that the *Qur'ān* is God's uncreated Word, part of His eternal essence, forms the basis for a fundamentalistic interpretation of the text as God's eternal message, directed to all people of all times, and consequently to be followed and observed in our days as it was in those of Muḥammad. By virtue of this belief, the *Qur'ān* still is the major uniting force in modern Islam.

## 3. Language as proof of the Revelation

"Say: if men and jinn banded together to produce the like of this Koran, they would never produce its like, not though they backed one another!" (17/88). The divine origin of the texts that Muḥammad pronounced and about which he said that they were revealed to him by the angel was not generally accepted during the first period of his public activities. People suggested that they were communicated to him by some spirit or demon, just as it was the case with poets or soothsayers; they asked Muḥammad for proof of the alleged heavenly origin of the texts.

Muḥammad did not authenticate his mission by doing miracles; stories about miraculous events during his life all date from a later period, after his death. According to Muḥammad, the proof of his being a prophet was the text of the *Qur'ān* and the proof of its divine origin could only be given by the text itself. For the *Qur'ān* is the Word of God, in every phrase and in every expression; every verse points to its creator. The term used in traditional and modern vocabulary to indicate a verse from the *Qur'ān*, the Arabic word *'āya*, is used in the older *sūra*s of the *Qur'ān* to indicate the 'signs' of God's presence and work in nature; the use of this term in later *sūra*s to indicate revealed texts corroborates Muḥammad's conviction that the revealed texts themselves are the true and only proof of their divine origin. This is expressed in the verse quoted above: nobody can produce a text like that of the *Qur'ān*, even when demons and men work together. No one can really imitate the creation of God. This principle is known as the *'iʿǧāz al-Qur'ān*, generally translated as "the inimitability of the *Qur'ān*". Literally it means: "the *Qur'ān* renders everyone incapable", *viz.* to produce the like of this book.

First of all, it were the contents of the *Qur'ān*, the stories told, the truth revealed, that should confirm its origin. Muḥammad pronounced things that he could not have known before. He did not know the stories about the Jewish prophets or about Jesus; he was illiterate and could not have read the old texts.

But since the *Qur'ān* was created by God himself, not only its contents but also its language and style should be of the level of God's creation and constitute a proof for its origin. In this way, the expression *'iʿǧāz al-Qur'ān* is taken as a reference to the highest possible quality of style. This interpretation has led to a number of studies in which the stylistic qualities of the *Qur'ān* were analysed and confronted with those of other old Arabic texts. Comparisons were made with texts uttered by the soothsayers in the time of Muḥammad: the older texts from the *Qur'ān* resemble the style and rhyme of these utterances, and Muḥammad himself was reproached to be no more than a simple soothsayer. But also the old pre-Islamic poetry, the most precious element of Arab legacy, had to be compared with the style of the *Qur'ān*.

A problem arose when some authors did try to imitate or even surpass the style of the *Qur'ān* and challenged their opponents to demonstrate the inferior quality of their texts.

This proved to be a very difficult discussion and consequently some authors adhered to the thesis that to imitate the style of the revealed text is not impossible in itself, but that God had prevented people in Muḥammad's days to produce something like the *Qur'ān*. Thus the real miracle was, that nobody did produce the like of it.

In popular belief, the style of the *Qur'ān* remains far above all other texts written by men; and since this unsurpassed and unsurpassable chef d'œuvre has been composed in Arabic, the Arabic language must surpass all other languages. This kind of statements about the Arabic language have, throughout the history of Islam, given rise to fierce debates about the linguistic or stylistic qualities of other languages, starting with a comparison between Arabic and Persian in the 9th and 10th centuries AD and culminating in comparisons between Arabic and French or English in our days.

The firm belief in this *'i'ǧāz* of the *Qur'ān* – as to its contents and to its language – is a major argument in the defence of the traditional Qur'ānic schools, where young children in the course of several years learn to read the *Qur'ān*, memorize the entire text, and after several years start to study its language and finally its contents. The text of the *Qur'ān* is believed to contain every form of knowledge that a child can need, and even memorizing an Arabic text that the child does not (yet) understand is important for his education, because it makes him familiar with God's word and with the Arabic language.

## 4. The obligation to preserve the text and the language

"Recite what has been revealed to thee of the Book of thy Lord; no man can change His words" (18/27). This and similar verses from the *Qur'ān* are used to underline the universal meaning of the text. Every passage has been revealed at the most appropriate moment and had a function in its geographical and chronological context; but at the same time it is God's message for all people of all nations and all times. Therefore, the text itself must be kept unchanged and be transmitted to all people in this world.

This conviction that the text must be transmitted unchanged in its original form and must be understood by people of different nations and cultures, has led to the study of Arabic grammar and language on the one hand, and to a tradition of *tafsīr*, exegesis of the *Qur'ān*, on the other. Modern methods of exegesis as applied to biblical texts – study of historical sources, of older texts from the same background, of the development of the text – are virtually excluded. The study, however, of variant readings, of the circumstances of the revelation, and of pre-Islamic texts that can clarify the meaning of obscure words or expressions has produced in the first centuries of the Islamic era some very important works on various aspects of Qur'ānic exegesis.

The concern for a correct transmission of the divine text has had great influence upon the fixation and the development of the Arabic language and also upon the conservation of the traditional Arabic script. It has led to a codification of the structure of the language of the *Qur'ān* and to continuous efforts to keep it pure and to conserve this language in its original form. The reasons for these efforts can be found in our paragraphs above: reverence for the text and its language, concern for a correct understanding, a guarantee for the unity of the Islamic *'umma*. In some traditional circles the conviction that the Arabic language should not change was converted into the conviction that up to our days this language has not changed at all.

When in the early seventies of our century the Lebanese ministry of Education initiated a project to modernize the teaching of Arabic throughout the entire educational system, a study was started to analyse the modern Arabic language as it is used today in literature, in the press and in official addresses. It became evident, that not only the vocabulary but also the use of linguistic structures was different from the classical handbooks and from the grammars and text-books used in primary and secondary education. This analysis was confronted by statements that the Arabic language had not changed at all till our days, but that this project to modernize the teaching of Arabic would in fact endanger the integrity of the language.

In recent discussions about a possible modernization of the Arabic script, a similar sensitiveness could be distinguished. During the fifties of the 20th century, the Arab League started a contest in order to redesign the traditional form of the script. Several efforts were made, proposals subjected to a jury, not all of them very convincing. But it became evident that traditionists considered it to be part of the Islamic heritage and even part of the revealed text, not to be changed, as the Qur'ānic text quoted above could suggest.

Revelation and language, indissolubly linked together, both created by God, for the benefit of mankind, to teach and to be taught, to be transmitted till the end of time: they remain at the heart of the Islamic faith.

## 5. Bibliography

Audebert, Claude-Franc. 1982. *Al-Ḫattābī et l'inimitabilité du Coran: Traduction et introduction du* Bayān iʿǧāz al-Qur'ān. Damascus: Institut Français de Damas.

Boullata, Issa J. 1988. "The Rhetorical Interpretation of the *Qur'ān*: *iʿǧāz* and related topics". *Approaches to the History of the Interpretation of the Qur'ān* ed. by Andrew Rippin, 139–157. Oxford: Clarendon Press.

Ess, Josef van. 1996. "Verbal Inspiration? Language and revelation in classical Islamic theology". *The Qur'an as Text* ed. by Stefan Wild, 177–194. Leiden: Brill.

Neuwirth, Angelika. 1983. "Das islamische Dogma der 'Unnachahmlichkeit des Korans' in literaturwissenschaftlicher Sicht". *Der Islam* 60.166–183.

Poonawala, Ismail K. 1988. "An Ismāʿīlī Treatise of the iʿjāz al-Qur'ān". *Journal of the American Oriental Society* 108.379–385.

—. 1994. "Al-Sulṭān al-Ḫaṭṭāb's Treatise on the iʿǧāz al-Qur'ān". *Arabica* 41.84–126.

Radscheit, Matthias. 1996. "*Iʿǧāz al-Qur'ān* im Koran?". *The Qur'an as Text* ed. by Stefan Wild, 113–124. Leiden: Brill.

Rahman, Yusuf. 1996. "The Miraculous Nature of Muslim Scripture: A study of ʿAbd al-Jabbār's *Iʿjāz al-Qur'ān*". *Islamic studies* 35.409–424.

*Jan Peters, Nijmegen (The Netherlands)*

# 45. Les relations entre la linguistique et les autres sciences dans la société arabo-islamique

1. Introduction
2. Grammaire et rhétorique
3. Rhétorique et *'uṣūl al-fiqh*
4. *'Uṣūl al-fiqh* et logique
5. *'Uṣūl al-fiqh* et *fiqh*
6. *Fiqh, 'uṣūl al-fiqh* et grammaire
7. Conclusion
8. Bibliographie

## 1. Introduction

Par 'linguistique arabe' on entend ici l'ensemble des disciplines traditionnelles qui, en islam, traitent, en arabe, de l'arabe. Un tel rassemblement n'est pas sans précédent dans la tradition arabo-musulmane elle-même. On peut citer le *Miftāḥ al-ʿulūm* (*MU*) de Sakkākī (m. 626/1229), véritable encyclopédie des sciences du langage conjoignant grammaire, rhétorique, logique et poétique, que l'auteur présente (p. 2) comme "différentes espèces de belles-lettres formant un tout cohérent" (*ʿidda 'anwāʿ 'adab muta'āḫida*). On peut également citer la *Muqaddima* de Ibn Ḫaldūn (m. 808/1406) qui consacre un chapitre (I, 1055–1070) aux "sciences de la langue arabe" (*ʿulūm al-lisān al-ʿarabī*), au nombre de quatre: lexique, grammaire, rhétorique et littérature. La comparaison des deux ouvrages montre que le noyau dur de la linguistique arabe est constitué de la grammaire et de la rhétorique. Par ailleurs, aucune de ces disciplines n'est par avance 'donnée'. Toutes au contraire sont le produit d'une histoire longue et complexe, qui n'est achevée qu'à l'époque postclassique (i. e. postérieurement à la lère moitié du Ve/XIe siècle et parfois bien après). L'objet du présent article est de traiter des relations que ces deux disciplines proprement linguistiques entretiennent entre elles d'une part, avec d'autres disciplines non proprement linguistiques d'autre part et, ce, dans la synchronie de l'époque postclassique, sauf dans le dernier alinéa, où nous donnerons un aperçu diachronique, et le contexte de la société arabo-musulmane.

## 2. Grammaire et rhétorique

### 2.1. *naḥw/ṣarf/luġa*

La grammaire (*naḥw*) se décompose en deux parties: l'une, syntaxique, est homonyme du tout, ce qui révèle sa primauté sur l'autre, morphophonologique (*ṣarf* ou *taṣrīf*). Cette dernière ne nous intéresse que sur un point.

Il ressort clairement du *Šarḥ al-Kāfiya* (*ŠK* I, 5) de ʾAstarābāḏī (m. après 688/1289) que *naḥw* et *taṣrīf* ont en commun le caractère "régulier" (*qiyāsī*) des "expressions linguistiques" (*ʾalfāẓ* pl. de *lafẓ*) dont ils s'occupent, même s'ils ont pour différence le rang de ces unités ('complexe' pour la première, 'simple' – formellement ou fonctionnellement – pour la seconde). En revanche, *taṣrīf* et lexique (*luġa*) ont en commun le rang de l'expression ('simple') dont ils s'occupent, mais pour différence le caractère 'régulier', pour le premier, ou "irrégulier" (*samāʿī*), pour le second, de celle-ci. C'est certainement parce que le *taṣrīf* comprend la morphologie lexicale que Sakkākī tout en reconnaissant la *luġa* comme "une espèce de *ʾadab*" l'exclut de sa construction, la composante lexicale ne traitant plus que de la part irrégulière du lexique. On n'en mentionnera pas moins, pour mémoire, l'existence d'une lexicographie/logie remarquable qui culmine, à l'époque post-classique, avec les deux grands dictionnaires que sont le *Lisān al-ʿArab* de Ibn Manẓūr (m. 711/1311) et le *Qāmūs*/*Tāǧ al-ʿarūs* de Fīrūzābādī (m. 817/1415)/Zabīdī (m. 1205/1791) et la somme lexicologique *al-Muzhir fī ʿulūm al-luġa* de Suyūṭī (m. 911/1505).

2.2. *maʿānī/bayān/badīʿ*

La rhétorique (*balāġa*) est aussi une construction essentiellement bipartite comme le montre le nom même de la partie rhétorique du *MU*, *ʿilmā l-maʿānī wa-l-bayān* "les deux sciences des significations et de l'expression", tout à la fois synthèse de l'œuvre de ʿAbd al-Qāhir al-Ǧurǧānī (m. 471/1078) et base, via le *Talḫīṣ* (= *T*) de Qazwīnī (m. 739/1338), de toute la rhétorique ultérieure (*Šurūḥ at-Talḫīṣ* = *ŠT*). La troisième composante (*badīʿ*) qu'y ajoute Qazwīnī, tout en venant de très loin (du *Kitāb al-badīʿ* "Livre du nouveau style" de Ibn al-Muʿtazz, m. 296/908), n'est que le produit d'une assomption, due à Badr ad-dīn Ibn Mālik (m. 686/1287), de ce qui chez Sakkākī est un simple appendice tropologique (*MU* 179 sq.). Nous n'en traiterons pas ici. Autant les relations entre les deux composantes de la grammaire sont claires, autant celles entre les deux composantes de la rhétorique d'une part, la rhétorique et la grammaire d'autre part, sont complexes (Baalbaki 1983).

2.3. *naḥw/maʿānī*

En ce dernier cas, elles sont d'ailleurs compliquées par l'apparition dans les textes rhétoriques (e. g. Qazwīnī, *ʾĪḍāḥ*, in *ŠT* I, 132) de l'expression *maʿānī n-naḥw* qui fait interpréter le *ʿilm al-maʿānī* comme une "sémantique de la syntaxe" (*EI2*, art. AL-MAʿĀNĪ WA-L-BAYĀN). Il suffit pourtant d'observer que ce qui structure au premier chef l'exposé du *maʿānī*, c'est la classification des "énoncés" (*kalām*) en *ḫabar* "affirmation" et *ṭalab* "jussion" ou *ʾinšāʾ* "performatif", au sens de tout ce qui n'est pas affirmation) pour comprendre que le *ʿilm al-maʿānī* récupère aussi, comme le reconnaît d'ailleurs le même article de *EI2*, la vieille tradition des *maʿānī l-kalām*. La lecture des chapitres consacrés au *ḫabar* et au *ʾinšāʾ* confirme d'ailleurs le caractère réducteur de l'interprétation de *EI2*. Sous le nom de *fāʾidat al-ḫabar* "information apportée par l'affirmation" et *lāzim fāʾidat al-ḫabar* "ce qu'elle implique", Sakkākī (*MU* 72) et ses successeurs (*ŠT* I, 194 sq.) distinguent entre deux fonctions d'une même affirmation *p*, faire savoir ou faire savoir que l'on sait, selon que l'allocuté ne sait pas ou sait *p*. En outre, il est possible de faire comme si ce dernier, sachant et *p* et que le locuteur sait *p*, l'ignorait, l'énonciation de *p* ayant alors une troisième fonction, de rappel et même de rappel à l'ordre. Et sous le nom de *ḫabar ibtidāʾī* "initial", *ṭalabī* "jussif" et *ʾinkārī* "dénégatoire", les mêmes (*MU* 74 et *ŠT* I, 203 sq.) distinguent entre trois types d'affirmations, s'adressant respectivement à quelqu'un "sans idée" (*ḫālī ḏ-ḏihn*) sur *p* ou, au contraire, ayant une attitude d'interrogation ou de dénégation à l'égard de *p*. Là encore, il est possible de faire comme si l'allocuté avait une telle attitude, c'est-à-dire d'anticiper sa réaction et partant de se régler sur la situation, non pas explicite, mais implicite. Autrement dit, dans les deux cas, les rhétoriciens se livrent à ce que l'on peut appeler, pour la forme, un calcul du sens de l'énoncé, dans la mesure où il affecte la forme d'une suite, et, pour le fond, de nature pragmatique, dans la mesure où il met en jeu, avec l'énoncé, ses interprètes. Mais c'est seulement dans le cas 2 que ce calcul repose sur des marques facultatives ou obligatoires dans l'énoncé: le renforcement *ʾinna* peut apparaître devant *p* en 2b et doit apparaître en 2c; le renforcement *la-* peut apparaître devant le prédicat en 2c. C'est encore un calcul pragmatique que l'on trouve au chapitre du *ṭalab*/*ʾinšāʾ*: Sakkākī (*MU* 132 sq.) et ses successeurs (*ŠT* II, 234 sq.) y montrent comment à partir des cinq valeurs "primaires" (*ʾaṣliyya*), elles-mêmes dérivées du *ṭalab*, que sont *tamannī* "souhait", *istifhām* "interrogation", *ʾamr* "ordre", *nahy* "défense" et *nidā'* "interpellation" et pour lesquelles sont 'instituées' certaines expressions, "s'engendrent" (*tawallada*), situationnellement, un certain nombre de valeurs "secondaires" (*far'iyya*), pour lesquelles ces expressions se trouvent "employées". On a aucun mal à reconnaître ici une "dérivation illocutoire" (Moutaouakil 1982) et une "sémantique en Y" (Larcher 1992), dans la mesure où le sens est le résultat, symbolisé par le pied du Y, de deux composants respectivement linguistique ("institution" *waḍ'*) et rhétorique ("emploi" *isti'māl*), symbolisés par les deux branches du Y. Pour autant le *ma'ānī* ne se réduit pas à une sémantique de l'énoncé, auquel ne sont consacrés que 2 des 8 chapitres du *Talḫīṣ* (le I et le VI). Son concept central est en fait celui de "phrase" (*ǧumla*). C'est elle, comme résultat d'une "prédication" (*'isnād*), qui fait le lien entre les deux classes d'énoncés (tout *kalām* est une *ǧumla*); elle qui se décompose, directement ou indirectement, en constituants: *musnad 'ilay-hi* "support" et *musnad* "apport" et, via ce dernier, *muta'alliqāt al-fi'l* "compléments du verbe" (II, III et IV); elle enfin qui se compose, de manière asyndétique ou non, avec une autre phrase pour constituer un énoncé complexe (VII). Mais si elle n'est ni exclusivement de la syntaxe ni exclusivement de l'énoncé, cette sémantique est partout une pragmatique, dans la mesure où pour rendre compte des variations de forme, de place, de sens d'une expression, qu'elle qu'en soit le rang, elle prend partout en considération la situation d'énonciation.

2.4. *ma'ānī/bayān*

Si le *ma'ānī* se désigne par son nom même comme une sémantique, le *bayān* se désigne comme une stylistique. Le premier traite de la signification de l'expression, le second de l'"expression propre" (*ḥaqīqa*) ou "figurée" (*maǧāz*), de la signification. Autrement dit, ce qui paraît différencier au premier chef *ma'ānī* et *bayān*, c'est le point de vue: sémasiologique pour le premier (i. e. du *lafẓ* vers le *ma'nā*) et onomasiologique pour le second (i. e. du *ma'nā* vers le *lafẓ*). Il suffit pourtant d'observer que le *maǧāz* dit *'aqlī* "logique" par opposition à *luġawī* "lexical" et qui concerne la phrase, alors que le second concerne le mot, est traité dans le *bayān* par Sakkākī (*MU* 166 sq.) mais dans le *ma'ānī* par Qazwīnī (*T* 44 sq.) pour conclure que le rang de l'unité linguistique a fini par l'emporter sur le point de vue. En fin de course, la *balāġa* apparaît comme une seule et même sémantique contextuelle: de la phrase (comme unité nodale) dans le contexte du discours pour le *'ilm al-ma'ānī*, du mot dans le contexte de la phrase pour le *'ilm al-bayān*.

2.5. *balāġa/ḫaṭāba*

La traduction de *balāġa* par "rhétorique" ne doit donc pas en masquer la double différence par rapport à la rhétorique aristotélicienne. Celle-ci, sous le nom de *ḫaṭāba* "art oratoire", connaît un prolongement et une réduction en islam dans le cadre de la philosophie hellénisante (*falsafa*): c'est une partie de la *Logique* (*manṭiq*) s'intéressant exclusivement à l'aspect argumentatif de la *Rhétorique* d'Aristote (pour une vue d'ensemble, cf. Black 1990). La première différence entre les deux est que la *balāġa* transcende les genres, étant tout autant une poétique: comme vient le rappeler son nom (*'ilmā l-'arūḍ wa-l-qawāfī* "sciences de la prosodie et des rimes"), la partie poétique du *MU* ne traite en effet que des aspects techniques, mètre et rime, de la poésie. La seconde différence est qu'elle met en son centre une activité illocutoire, plus que perlocutoire, même si elle n'ignore pas cette dernière, dont elle fournit au passage un critère: les actes de ce type sont systématiquement dénommés par des verbes factitifs (e. g. *tandīm* "faire regretter", *taškīk* "faire douter", *tabkiya* "faire pleurer" etc.) qui permettent de la définir comme l'acte de faire faire quelque chose à quelqu'un par le fait de dire. En revanche, la rhétorique aristotélicienne et à sa suite la *ḫaṭāba* mettent en leur centre l'acte perlocutoire type, celui de "persuader" (*'iqnā'*, litt. "rendre convaincu"). Cette double différence tient elle-même à deux faits. Le premier est que la seule forme d'éloquence institutionnalisée en islam est celle de la chaire: la *ḫuṭba* "sermon, prône" est un discours d'autorité, ne s'inscrivant en rien dans un débat contradictoire. Le second, comme vient le rappeler le prolongement dogmatique du [*'ilm al-*]*balāġa*, le *'i'ǧāz al-Qur'ān* "inimitabilité du Coran", où *'i'ǧāz* est défini comme le plus haut degré de la *balāġa* "efficience", est qu'elle met une 'parole' au dessus de tous les autres, dont le destinataire n'est ni juge ni spectateur, comme dans les trois genres, délibératif, judiciaire et épidictique, de la *Rhétorique* d'Aristote, mais, déjà convaincu, interprète (sur la 'littérature du *'i'ǧāz*', cf., outre l'article 'I'DJĀZ de *EI2*, Audebert 1982).

## 3. Rhétorique et *'uṣūl al-fiqh*

C'est en effet 'rhétorique', au sens qui vient d'être défini, qu'apparaît le mécanisme d'interprétation juridique du *Coran* et de la *Sunna*, les deux premières "sources" (*'uṣūl*) de la "jurisprudence" (*fiqh*) en islam, comprises comme étant respectivement les paroles, en totalité pour la première et en presque totalité pour la seconde, d'Allāh et de Mahomet: le terme de *ḥadīṯ* a d'ailleurs les deux sens de 'tradition' (ce que l'on rapporte que Mahomet a dit ou fait) et de 'dit' de Mahomet. Là où les rhétoriciens divisent le *kalām* en *ḫabar* et non-*ḫabar*, les *'uṣūliyyūn*, dans la ligne du *Maḥṣūl* (I: 1, 317–318) de Faḫr ad-dīn ar-Rāzī (m. 606/1209), divisent l'"adresse" (*ḫiṭāb*), définie par l'encyclopédiste Kaffawī (m. 1094/1683), comme l'"énoncé orienté vers l'autre à fin de faire entendre" (*al-kalām al-muwağğah naḥwa l-ġayr li-l-'ifhām*) en *ṭalab* et non-*ṭalab* (*Kulliyyāt*, art. *ḫiṭāb*). D'après 'Āmidī, m. 631/1233 (*'Iḥkām* I, 91 sq.), le *ṭalab*, selon qu'il "impose" (*iqtiḍā'*) de "faire" (*fi'l*) ou "ne pas faire" (*tark*), de manière "catégorique" (*ğāzim*) ou non, se réalise en "obligation" (*'īğāb*) et "prohibition" (*taḥrīm*), "recommandation" (*nadb*) et "répréhension" (*karāh(iy)a*); le non-*ṭalab* ou "donne le choix" (*taḫyīr*) entre les deux (c'est une "permission" *'ibāḥa*), ou "asserte" (*'iḫbār*) que telle chose est valide ou non, cause, empêchement ou condition de telle autre, "devoir rigoureux" (*'azīma*) ou "tolérance" (*ruḫṣa*) (Weiss 1992; Larcher 1992). Ces six actes législatifs (*šar'*) constituent les *'aḥkām šar'iyya* "qualifications légales" (i. e. le droit), "prescriptifs" (*taklīfiyya*) pour les cinq premiers et "ascriptifs" (*waḍ'iyya*) pour le sixième (Kaffawī, *Kulliyyāt*, art. *ḫiṭāb*).

## 4. *'Uṣūl al-fiqh* et logique

Des normes primaires, pragmatiquement dérivées, on peut en dériver des secondaires, logiquement, i. e. par raisonnement (*qiyās*), autre source de la jurisprudence. On a souvent distingué la logique juridique de celle des logiciens par le type de raisonnement (analogie vs syllogisme), au centre de chacune d'elles, mais en oubliant qu'ils étaient homonymes. A l'époque postclassique, les *'uṣūl al-fiqh* ont récupéré la syllogistique, mais l'ont pervertie, comme le montre le célèbrissime exemple de *an-nabīḏ muskir* "le vin est une boisson enivrante", *kull muskir ḥarām* "toute boisson enivrante est interdite", *an-nabīḏ ḥarām* "le vin est interdit". Ce qui fait la spécificité de ce syllogisme, ce n'est pas sa forme. Si l'on se reporte à la partie logique du *MU* de Sakkākī, qui sous le nom de *'ilmā l-ḥadd wa-l-istidlāl* "sciences de la définition et de l'argumentation" présente une logique parfaitement classique, on vérifiera que c'est un syllogisme de la première figure, d'un des deux modes affirmatifs, l'analogue de notre *Darii* (sauf que la mineure est énoncée avant la majeure). Ce qui fait sa spécificité, c'est qu'il enchaîne énoncés descriptifs et prescriptifs: le caractère de norme de la majeure (qui est un 'dit' de Mahomet) et de la conclusion est attesté par le fait qu'on peut remplacer "x est *ḥarām*" par le performatif "*ḥarramtu* x" ("j'interdis x") ('Āmidī, *'Iḥkām* I, 12 et IV, 48; sur la logique juridique, cf., outre article MANṬIQ de *EI2*, Brunschvig 1970 [1976]; Larcher 1992; Weiss 1992; Hallaq 1994).

## 5. *'Uṣūl al-fiqh* et *fiqh*

Le concept de *'inšā'* nous amène ainsi au *fiqh*, d'où il est issu. Nous avons là-dessus le témoignage éloquent de Kaffawī (*Kulliyāt* 5, 314): "l'acte de la langue, c'est dire (*'iḫbār*) et non faire (*'inšā'*), et, de même, celui de tous les autres organes, c'est faire et non dire; mais le droit a fait de l'acte de la langue un faire sur le plan légal, qui est ainsi devenu semblable aux actes de tous les autres organes". Dans la partie de leurs traités consacrée aux "transactions" (*mu'āmalāt*), les juristes (*fuqahā'*), e. g. Kāsānī, m. 587/1189 (*Badā'i'*), ne font rien d'autre que dériver, sous ce nom, l'efficacité juridique de la parole, selon les principes de la sémantique contextuelle posés par la *balāġa*: ainsi *bi'tu* ne devient un performatif de vente ("je vends") ou, plus exactement, d'"acceptation" (*qabūl*) de vente qu'en réponse à un autre énoncé valant "proposition" (*'īğāb*) tel que *hal tabī'u lī hāḏā bi-kaḏā* "Me vendrais-tu telle chose à telle prix?", qui en bloque l'interprétation comme affirmation passée ("j'ai vendu"), les deux énoncés constituant le "contrat" (*'aqd*). La forme *fa'altu* y apparaît comme la forme "opérative" (*'īqā'*) par excellence. La récupération de ce concept et de cette forme par les *'uṣūliyyūn* revient à mettre en parallèle création du contrat et création de la norme et permet ainsi une caractérisation nouvelle de ces deux disciplines et de leur articulation: elles sont pour des parties essentielles d'elles-mêmes des pragmatiques respectivement appliquées à la parole du législataire et à celle du législateur.

## 6. *Fiqh, 'uṣūl al-fiqh* et grammaire

On a souvent signalé l'influence des sciences juridiques sur la constitution des sciences linguistiques, moins souvent que cette influence n'était pas unilatérale et qu'elle s'était exercée tout au long de leur développement. On en a une bonne illustration avec les aspects sémantico-pragmatiques de la grammaire. Si certains auteurs proposent de lire Sībawayhi (m. 177/793?) en termes d'énonciation et d'actes de langage (Buburuzan 1993), on n'en noterait pas moins que cette lecture est particulièrement justifiée là où les actes de langage ont en même temps une valeur juridique. Ainsi, décrivant le nom d'action (*maṣdar*), à l'accusatif, *ʿurfan* "reconnaissance" dans la phrase *lahu ʿalayya 'alfu dirhamin ʿurfan* "je lui dois mille dirhams, je le reconnais", Sībawayhi (*Kitāb* I, 380) note qu'"il est devenu une corroboration de lui-même, seulement parce qu'en disant 'je lui dois' l'énonciateur a fait acte d'aveu et de reconnaissance". Autrement dit, le *maṣdar*, redondant, désigne explicitement l'acte de reconnaissance de dette implicitement performé par l'énonciation de la phrase qui précède (Larcher 1992). Ultérieurement, Mubarrad (m. 286/900), pour rendre compte de l'accusatif du nom, premier terme d'une annexion, apparaissant dans la structure vocative *yā ʿAbda llāhi* "ô Abdallah" supposera un verbe *'adʿū* "j'appelle" ou *'urīdu* "je vise", dont ce nom est le complément d'objet et auquel la particule *yā* se substitue (*Muqtaḍab* IV, 202). Mais il ajoute aussitôt: "non pas que tu assertes que tu fais, mais, par contre, cette particule a pour effet que tu as accompli un acte (*qad 'awqaʿta fiʿlan*)". Autrement dit, le verbe supposé pour des raisons syntaxiques est purement virtuel et ne peut être réalisé pour des raisons sémantiques. Ce qui est remarquable ici et ne peut passer pour une coïncidence, c'est l'emploi, par un grammairien, avec dans son champ *fiʿl*, du verbe *'awqaʿa*, dont *'īqāʿ* est le nom d'action et que les juristes utilisaient depuis longtemps avant celui de *'inšā'* (cf., par exemple, *al-Ǧāmiʿ al-kabīr* de Šaybānī, m. 189/805) pour désigner l'activité illocutoire. Le caractère paradoxal de la structure vocative, qui ne peut être représentée que par elle-même, a en fait servi de porte d'entrée à la dimension pragmatique en grammaire, si l'on en croit cette curieuse déclaration de Ibn as-Sarrāǧ (m. 316/929), selon laquelle "dire *yā*, c'est l'acte même, en quoi le vocatif se distingue de tout le reste du discours, car celui-ci est une énonciation dispensant de faire, alors que faire, dans le cas du vocatif, c'est énoncer" (*'Uṣūl* I, 333). Mais il faut néanmoins attendre Ibn al-Ḥāǧib (m. 646/1249), qui était tout à la fois grammairien et *'uṣūlī*, pour voir la grammaire faire un large usage de la catégorie de *'inšā'* et son principal commentateur, 'Astarābāḏī, pour la voir en faire un usage systématique. On peut abstraire du traité de ce dernier une véritable 'théorie' pragmatique, se présentant comme un diptyque, dont la catégorie de *'inšā'* constitue le volet conceptuel et *faʿaltu* le volet formel. Est *kalām* tout ce dont l'énonciation constitue un "acte de l'énonciateur" (*fiʿl al-mutakallim*). La priorité donnée au critère sémantico-pragmatique sur le critère formel (*ǧumla*) lui permet d'abord d'étendre la catégorie de *'inšā'* à l'ensemble des énoncés. 'Astarābāḏī divise certes le *kalām* tantôt (*ŠK* I, 8) en *ḫabar, ṭalab* et *'inšā'* et tantôt (*ŠK* II, 221) en *ḫabar* et *'inšā'*, en le subdivisant en *ṭalabī* et *'īqāʿī* (double classification qui confirme que la catégorie de *'inšā'* est bien le produit d'une généralisation à partir des performatifs tout à la fois explicites et juridiques). Mais, prolongeant une réflexion commencée par Ibn al-Ḥāǧib sur les énoncés mixtes, de type exclamatif, "susceptibles d'être tout à la fois assertifs et performatifs" (*'Amālī* IV, 149–150), puis poursuivie par Ibn Mālik, m. 672/1274, sous le nom de *ḫabar 'inšā'ī* (*Šarḥ at-Tashīl* III, 33), 'Astarābāḏī les regroupe sous le nom générique de *'inšā' ǧuz'u-hu l-ḫabar* (*ŠK* II, 93 et 311). Il ouvre ainsi la porte à l'interprétation de l'"élément" (*ǧuz'*) *ḫabar*, non comme posé, mais comme présupposé, ce que fait explicitement, en marge même du *ŠK*, sous le nom de *lāzim ʿurfī* "implication empirique", son propre commentateur, ʿAlī ibn Muḥammad al-Ǧurǧānī (m. 816/1413), par exemple l'élément *Zaydun ḥasanun* "Zaydun est bon" par rapport au performatif d'"admiration" (*taʿaǧǧub*) *mā 'aḥsana Zaydan* "que Zayd est bon!". De là, il passe aux affirmations ascriptives, type *Zaydun 'afḍalu min ʿAmrin* "Zayd est supérieur à Amr", dont il dit que son énonciation performe un acte de *tafḍīl*, que son propre commentateur définit, non comme "faire supérieur", mais comme "dire supérieur", puis purement descriptives, type *Zaydun qā'imun* "Zayd est debout", dont il dit que son énonciation performe un acte d'"assertion" (*'iḫbār*). Le même critère lui permet d'étendre les catégories de *'inšā'* et de *kalām* en deçà et au delà de l'énoncé classique: en deçà comme dans le cas des *'asmā' al-'af'āl* "interjections" *'uff* "fi!" et *'awwah* "hélas!", qui "ont le sens de *taḍaǧǧartu* et *tawaǧǧa'tu* performatifs" (*ŠK* II, 65); au delà comme dans le cas des connecteurs pragmatiques *p lākinna* ("mais") *q*, accomplissant un acte de "rectification préventive" (*istidrāk*), par *q*, de la fausse conclusion *r* risquant d'être tirée de *p* par l'interlocuteur, ou *p 'inna* ("car") *q*, présentant une "justification" (*'illa*) de *p* par *q* (*ŠK* II, 348–349). Cet 'acte de l'énonciateur' est représentable par un performatif *fa'altu*. Celui-ci est certes, formellement, une *ǧumla*, mais si l'on adopte le formalisme des philosophes du langage (F(*p*)) et des logiciens (f(*x*)), il apparaît comme une force illocutoire (F), non comme une proposition (*p*), un modus, non un dictum. Cette force est d'ailleurs assimilable à une fonction (f) que ne vient saturer aucun argument (cas des interjections, propos sur un thème implicite), ou ayant pour argument un terme *n* (cas du vocatif), une proposition *p* (cas de l'énoncé classique), un terme *n* d'une proposition incomplète (cas des exclamatifs), un ou plusieurs énoncés explicites ou implicites (cas des connecteurs pragmatiques). Cette représentation est purement sémantique ou syntaxico-sémantique, selon qu'elle ne joue pas ou joue un rôle dans la dérivation même des phrases, comme dans le cas du vocatif *yā Zaydu* (< *nādaytu/da'awtu Zaydan* "j'appelle Zayd", *ŠK* II, 132) ou de *ḥaqqan* dans la phrase *Zaydun qā'imun ḥaqqan* "Zayd est debout, en vérité" (< *qultu Zaydun qā'imun qawlan ḥaqqan* "je dis 'Zayd est debout' d'un dire véridique", *ŠK* II, 124). Enfin, elle est abstraite, en ce sens qu'il n'existe pas nécessairement de performatif explicite correspondant à l'acte illocutoire ou que, s'il existe, il n'a pas nécessairement la forme *fa'altu*, uniquement préférée par 'Astarābāḏī pour son pouvoir expressif, comme il le note à propos du vocatif, et équivalant ainsi à une véritable formalisation. On a ici une bonne illustration de l'ambivalence d'un savoir médiéval, la même forme *fa'altu* se rattachant aussi bien à l'univers de l'herméneutique qu'anticipant sur les théories linguistiques modernes.

## 7. Conclusion

A l'époque classique, les différentes disciplines, à partir d'une situation de large indistinction, se constituent progressivement avec leur objet propre. A l'époque postclassique, ces disciplines constituées ne sont pas pour autant indépendantes: on a voulu suggérer ici qu'une commune dimension énonciativo-pragmatique constituait un lien fort et original entre elles.

## 8. Bibliographie

### 8.1. Sources primaires

'Āmidī, *'Iḥkām* = Sayf ad-dīn 'Abū l-Ḥasan 'Alī ibn 'Alī al-'Āmidī, *al-'Iḥkām fī 'uṣūl al-'aḥkām*. Le Caire, 1487/1967.

'Astarābāḏī, *ŠK* = Raḍī d-dīn Muḥammad ibn Ḥasan al-'Astarābāḏī, *Šarḥ Kāfiyat Ibn al-Ḥāǧib*. Istanbul, 1310H.

Fīrūzābādī, *Qāmūs* = al-Fīrūzābādī, *al-Qāmūs*. Le Caire, 1357/1938.

Ǧurǧānī, *Ḥāšiya* = 'Alī ibn Muḥammad al-Ǧurǧānī, *al-Ḥāšiya 'alā šarḥ al-Kāfiya*. Cf. 'Astarābāḏī, *ŠK*.

Kaffawī, *Kulliyyāt* = al-Kaffawī, *Kulliyyāt al-'ulūm*. Ed. par 'Adnān Darwīš & Muḥammad al-Maṣrī. Damas, 1981.

Ibn al-Ḥāǧib, *Kāfiya* = 'Abū 'Amr 'Uṯmān Ibn al-Ḥāǧib, *al-Kāfiya fī n-naḥw*. Cf. 'Astarābāḏī, *ŠK*.

Ibn al-Ḥāǧib, *'Amālī* = 'Abū 'Amr 'Uṯmān Ibn al-Ḥāǧib, *al-'Amālī an-naḥwiyya*. Beyrouth: 'Ālam al-kutub, 1405/1985.

Ibn Ḫaldūn, *Muqaddima* = Walī d-dīn 'Abd ar-Raḥmān ibn Muḥammad Ibn Ḫaldūn, *al-Muqaddima*. (= T. I du *Kitāb al-'ibar*.) Beyrouth, 1967.

Ibn Mālik, *Šarḥ* = Ǧamāl ad-dīn 'Abū 'Abdallāh Muḥammad ibn 'Abdallāh Ibn Mālik, *Šarḥ at-Tashīl*. Ed. par 'Abd ar-Raḥmān as-Sayyid & Muḥammad al-Maḫtūn. Le Caire: Haǧr, 1410/1990.

Ibn Manẓūr, *Lisān* = Ibn Manẓūr, *Lisān al-'Arab*. Būlāq, 1300–1307H.

Ibn al-Mu'tazz, *Badī'* = Ibn al-Mu'tazz, *Kitāb al-badī'*. Ed. par Ignatius Kratchkovsky. (= *E. J. W. Gibb Memorial*, New Series, 10.) 1935.

Ibn as-Sarrāǧ, *'Uṣūl* = 'Abū Bakr ibn as-Sarī Ibn as-Sarrāǧ, *al-'Uṣūl fī n-naḥw*. Ed. par 'Abd al-Ḥusayn al-Fatlī. Beyrouth: Mu'assasat ar-Risāla, 1405/1985.

Kāsānī, *Badā'i'* = al-Kāsānī, *Kitāb badā'i' aṣ-ṣanā'i' fī tartīb aš-šarā'i'*. Le Caire, 1327H.

Mubarrad, *Muqtaḍab* = 'Abū l-'Abbās Muḥammad ibn Yazīd al-Mubarrad, *al-Muqtaḍab*. Ed. par Muḥammad 'Abd al-Ḫāliq 'Uḍayma. Beyrouth: 'Ālam al-kutub, s. d.

Qazwīnī, *'Īḍāḥ* = Al-Qazwīnī, *al-'Īḍāḥ fī šarḥ Talḫīṣ al-Miftāḥ* Cf. *ŠT*

Qazwīnī, *Talḫīṣ* = al-Qazwīnī, *Talḫīṣ al-Miftāḥ* Ed. par 'A. al-Barqūqī. Le Caire, s. d.

Rāzī, *Maḥṣūl* = Faḫr ad-dīn Muḥammad ibn 'Umar ar-Rāzī, *al-Maḥṣūl fī 'ulūm 'uṣūl al-fiqh*. Ed.

par Ṭāhā Ǧābir Fayyād al-ʿUlwānī. Riyad: Imām Muḥammad b. Saʿūd University, 1399/1979.

Sakkākī, *MU* = ʾAbū Yaʿqūb Yūsuf ibn ʾAbī Bakr Muḥammad ibn ʿAlī as-Sakkākī, *Miftāḥ al-ʿulūm*. Le Caire, 1348 H.

*ŠT* = *Šurūḥ at-Talḫīṣ*. Le Caire, 1937.

Šaybānī, *Ǧāmiʿ* = aš-Šaybānī, *al-Ǧāmiʿ al-Kabīr*. Ed. par Riḍwān Muḥammad Riḍwān. Le Caire: Maktabat al-Istiqāma, 1356 H.

Sībawayhi, *Kitāb* = ʾAbū Bišr ʿAmr ibn ʿUṯmān Sībawayhi, *al-Kitāb*. Ed. par ʿAbd as-Salām Muḥammad Hārūn. Beyrouth: ʿĀlam al-kutub, s. d.

Suyūṭī, *Muzhir* = Ǧalāl ad-dīn ʾAbū l-Faḍl ʿAbd ar-Raḥmān ibn ʾAbī Bakr as-Suyūṭī, *al-Muzhir fī ʿulūm al-luġa*. Le Caire, s. d.

Zabīdī, *Tāǧ* = az-Zabīdī, *Tāǧ al-ʿarūs*. Le Caire, 1306–1307 H.

### 8.2. Sources secondaires

Audebert, Claude-France. 1982. *Al-Ḫaṭṭābī et l'inimitabilité du Coran. Traduction et introduction au* Bayān Iʿǧāz al-Qurʾān. Damas: Institut Français.

Baalbaki, Ramzi. 1983. "The Relation between *naḥw* and *balāġa*: A Comparative Study of the Methods of Sībawayhi and Ǧurǧānī". *Zeitschrift für arabische Linguistik* 11.7–23.

Black, Deborah L. 1990. *Logic and Aristotle's Rhetoric and Poetics in Medieval Arabic Philosophy*. Leiden: Brill.

Brunschvig, Robert. 1970 [1976]. "Logic and Law in Classical Islam". *Logic in Classical Islamic Culture* éd. par Gustav E. von Grunebaum, 9–20. Wiesbaden: Harrassowitz. [Trad. fr. "Logique et droit dans l'Islam classique". *Etudes d'islamologie*, II, 347–361. Paris: Maisonneuve et Larose, 1976.]

Buburuzan, Rodica. 1993. "Exclamation et actes de langage chez Sībawayhi". *Revue Roumaine de Linguistique* 38: 5.421–437.

EI2 = *Encyclopédie de l'Islam*, nouvelle édition, 1960 –. Leiden: E. J. Brill.

Heinrichs, Wolfhart. 1987. "Poetik, Rhetorik, Literaturkritik, Metrik und Reimlehre". *Grundriss der arabischen Philologie*, vol. II: *Literaturwissenschaft* éd. par Helmut Gätje, 177–207. Wiesbaden: Ludwig Reichert.

Hallaq, Wael B. 1994. *Law and Legal Theory in Classical and Medieval Islam*. Aldershot: Variorum.

Larcher, Pierre. 1988, 1991, 1992. "Quand, en arabe, on parlait de l'arabe ... I. Essai sur la méthodologie de l'histoire des métalangages arabes. II. Essai sur la catégorie de *ʾinšāʾ* (vs. *ḫabar*). III. Grammaire, logique, rhétorique dans l'islam postclassique". *Arabica* 35.117–142; 38.246–273; 39.358–384.

Moutaouakil, Ahmed. 1982. *Réflexions sur la théorie de la signification dans la pensée linguistique arabe*. Rabat: Publications de la Faculté des Lettres et des Sciences Humaines.

Simon, Udo Gerald. 1993. *Mittelalterliche arabische Sprachbetrachtung zwischen Grammatik und Rhetorik: ʿilm al-maʿānī bei as-Sakkākī*. Heidelberg: Heidelberger Orientverlag.

Weiss, Bernard. 1992. *The Search for God's Law: Islamic Jurisprudence in the Writings of Sayf al-Dīn al-Āmidī*. Salt Lake City: Univ. of Utah Press.

*Pierre Larcher, Aix-en-Provence (France)*

# 46. Traditional linguistics and Western linguistics in the Arab world

1. Traditional linguistics
2. Western linguistics
3. Bibliography

## 1. Traditional linguistics

Insofar as traditional linguistic research is concerned in the contemporary Arab world, one can reasonably claim that such investigation tends to be a continuation of the classical period tradition that started in the 8th century AD. This practice had peak periods between the 9th and 13th centuries, and low points at other times. Early stages of linguistic investigation emphasized the codification of the Arabic language, including the collection of lexicon, grammar (syntax), and morphology. Other facets of the language were also recorded, for example *laḥn* "speech errors" and *al-muʿarrab* "loan words" into Arabic from other languages, mainly Persian.

In the 19th century the period of the Arab *Nahḍa* "Renaissance" witnessed renewed activities in the field of lexicography and description of the Arabic language. Scholars such as Buṭrus al-Bustānī (1819–1883), (ʾAḥmad) Fāris aš-Šidyāq (1804?–1887; cf. Sawaie 1990) and Ǧurǧī Zaydān (1861–1914; cf. Sawaie 1987), among many others, were ardent advocates for the rejuvenation of the Arabic language to express the rising needs of their society. To this end, for example, al-Bustānī compiled the famous dictionary *Muḥīṭ al-Muḥīṭ* in an attempt to bring works in Arabic lexicography to the level of Western standards; aš-Šidyāq wrote several treatises on Arabic, manuals on teaching Arabic to foreigners and a major lexicographic work, *al-Ǧāsūs ʿalā l-Qāmūs*; and Ǧurǧī Zaydān wrote two analytical accounts on the origin and evolution of language, *al-Falsafa al-Luġawiyya* and *al-Luġa al-ʿArabiyya Kā'in Ḥayy*, thus subjecting Arabic to new ways of scrutiny.

Traditional linguistic research currently practiced in the Arab world emulates to some extent the classical linguistic studies. Since classical grammarians prolifically produced authentic treatises on grammar (syntax) and morphology, little was left for contemporary traditional scholars. However, in addition linguistic investigation currently places significant importance and a considerable amount of energy on lexicographic materials. Because the Arab world faces fundamental changes due to the advent of technology and the hegemony of Western culture(s), there is an urgent need for specialized dictionaries comprising terminologies for new sciences, imported technological objects, and cultural items. New terminologies still need to be established for computers, economics, trade, social sciences, psychology (as a branch of a new science), petroleum and oil, science and technology, engineering, and electronics, etc. Because of this urgent need, a plethora of such dictionaries has appeared in the last two decades.

The various Arabic language academies are fairly active in these endeavors, and devote specialized treatises to coinage(s) or 'arabicized' terms. Specialized scholars in the sciences, or committees of specialists, are assigned the task of locating proper terminologies in classical Arabic for the new sciences introduced into universities, or for the cultural objects that have become an integral part of the fabric of the 'new' emerging Arab society. In the absence of such terminologies, these scholars are expected to coin neologisms. At this writing there are six Arabic language academies in the following countries: Syria (established in 1919), Egypt (established in 1931/32?), Iraq (established in 1947), Jordan (established in 1976), Libya (established in 1994), and Palestine (established in 1995). (For information about the Libyan Arabic Language Academy see *Maǧalla Maǧmaʿ al-Luġa al-ʿArabiyya al-'Urdunnī* [Journal of the Arabic Language Academy in Jordan] 46 [1994] 244–245; for information about the Palestine Language Academy see *'Aḫbār at-Turāṯ al-ʿArabī* [Arab Heritage Newsletter] no. 67, vol. 6 [1995] 17).

In addition to the aforementioned Arabic language academies, it is worth mentioning that there are other organizations of other types elsewhere in other Arab countries that are engaged in issues of arabicization. The fate of such organizations is typically uncertain, and information about them is sometimes not available.

As many early known major grammatical works (from the 8th to 13th centuries AD) have been published in book form, traditional linguistic analysis currently practiced in the Arab world emphasizes the preparation of critical, annotated editions of grammatical treatises and biographical information about early Arab grammarians and language sciences. These editions often make available works that have not been accorded adequate attention previously. An example of this is Ibn Kamāl Pāšā Zādeh's (d. 1533/34 AD) *'Asrār an-Naḥw* "The Mysteries of Grammar", that has recently been published. One must add here that practitioners of traditional Arabic linguistics often train in linguistic sciences, grammar and philology, at traditional institutions such as the Azhar University in Cairo or the Dār al-ʿUlūm College (now a college of Cairo University oriented toward traditional Arabic language sciences and literature, whose primary goal was, at one time, to train teachers of the humanities in Arabic with some reference to Western scholarship).

## 2. Western linguistics

A survey of the linguistic scholarship in the first half of the 20th century indicates that most works tended to focus on description of various Arabic dialects, phonetic and phonological investigations, prosodic analysis, and biographical-*cum* analytical works on Classical Arabic grammarians and the study of the phenomenon of loan words into Arabic. Such linguistic investigation by Arabic-speaking scholars returning from Western universities to the Arab world tends to reflect the prevalent schools of linguistics that they were exposed to and in which they received training.

However, the rise of Chomskyan linguistics and its dominance in many circles, and the establishment of linguistics as an independent discipline following the publishing of Chomsky's *Aspects of the Theory of Syntax* in 1965 reverberated throughout the Arab world. As a result of the proliferation of universities in many Arab countries during this period, a number of students were dispatched to various Western universities (mainly North American and some European) for training in linguistics. Upon the return of these scholars to their home institutions they introduced the various prevalent schools of linguistics: Friesian, Firthian, Hallidayian, Chomskyan, Labovian, and others. Some universities established linguistic institutes (e. g. the Institut de Linguistique et de Phonétique, Université d'Alger, which was established in 1966 and publishes *al-Lisāniyyāt, Revue Algérienne de Linguistique*, a journal devoted to linguistic investigation). Other universities established phonetics laboratories (e. g. at King Saud University, Riyadh; cf. Bakalla 1983: xxxviii). Such linguistically-oriented establishments have probably been instrumental in introducing 'modern' linguistics as a discipline in the university curriculum.

Different schools and orientations color current linguistic scholarship in the Arab world, not only in terms of research, but also in the diversification of the linguistic subdisciplines under investigation. In addition to the 'core' fields of syntax and semantics, morphology, and lexicography, more research in new subfields of linguistics may be observed: experimental phonetics (acoustics and auditory), phonology, discourse analysis, psycholinguistics (language acquisition and second language learning), applied linguistics, stylistics, comparative/contrastive linguistics, computational linguistics and sociolinguistics.

Whereas the study of dialects in traditional Arabic linguistics was ignored, Arab linguistic practitioners returning from the West after the mid-1960s did not avoid, in most cases, subjecting their dialects to scholarly investigation. Thus we observe a significant increase of literature on Arabic dialectology, focusing either on single dialects, or on comparative dialect studies.

Because of the prominent role gained by some oil-rich Arab countries in the mid-1970s, Westerners as well as Easterners showed an increased interest in learning Arabic. Additionally, a rekindled interest in Islam during this period and the following years has encouraged the study of Arabic by Muslims from oil-rich Asian and African countries. This sudden increase in enrollment in Arabic in foreign language classes has prompted the establishment of specialized institutes for the teaching of the language. Examples include the Arabic Language Institute (ALI) at the American University of Cairo (AUC), the Arabic Language Institute at the Kind Saud University in Riyadh, the Institut Bourguiba in Tunis, and many other similarly oriented institutes at universities in several Arab countries.

To meet the increasing demand for qualified teachers of Arabic as a foreign language, the Arab League Educational and Scientific Organization (ALECSO) established the Khartoum International Institute of Arabic for the purpose of training teachers of Arabic as a foreign language in the mid-1970s. This institute and similar ones contribute, directly or indirectly, to linguistic investigation, both theoretical and applied. A respectable number of teachers at AUC's ALI has been visible of late in the organization of linguistic panels at national and international conferences (such as the Middle East Studies Association [MESA], always held in North America). King Saud University organized a conference in 1978 on applied linguistics. In 1982 the Khartoum Institute started publishing *al-Maǧalla al-ʿArabiyya li-d-Dirāsāt al-Luġawiyya* [Arab Journal of Linguistic Studies], which has become a forum for linguistic practitioners Arab world-wide. However, a word of caution is in order. The fluctuating financial and political support for some of these establishments has either slowed down, or impeded, their activities. One notices, for example, that the activities of the Khartoum International Institute of Arabic have diminished (as evidenced by a decrease in the number of the trained teachers graduating from this Institute). Also, the appearance of its specialized linguistic journal has been affected. This is undoubtedly linked to financial and political problems that have plagued the Arab League and the Sudan in the past ten to fifteen years. The futures of these organizations remain unpredictable.

Western-style linguistics practiced in the Arab world is gaining support – albeit in limited ways – through institutional channels. This is evidenced by the rise of local and regional conferences, either wholly dedicated to linguistic investigation, or held in conjunction with conferences on literary and other topics. Examples at the time of this writing include a bi-annual conference organized at the Yarmouk University in Jordan; a bi-annual conference at the Azhar University in

Cairo with a focus on the problem of the scientific Arabic terminology, and arabicization of the sciences, i. e., the use of Arabic in teaching sciences and technological subjects at the university level; and occasional conferences on translation and its linguistic ramifications, e. g., the issue of lexicon and scientific idioms (at Yarmouk University, Jordan, and King Fahd School of Translation in Tangiers, Morocco). There are other occasional linguistic conferences, e. g., the one that was held at AUC in December 1994, which was co-sponsored by the United States-based Arabic Linguistic Society.

Important outlets for the publication of Western linguistic investigation by Arab scholars include the *Ḥawliyyāt* "Annual Journals" published by a large number of Arab universities and periodic publications by other organizations. These *Ḥawliyyāt* tend to be limited in distribution or circulation, thus depriving scholars outside the local institution from keeping pace with current linguistic research. In addition to the *Ḥawliyyāt*, there are other journals (cited earlier in this article) with a focus on linguistics, and specialized lexicographic volumes by the Arabic language academies. Mention should also be made of other periodic publications, for example the *Maǧallat al-Muʿǧamiyya* [Journal of Arabic Lexicology], a specialized journal established by the Association de Lexicologie Arabe in Tunis in 1985. This annual publishes articles, reviews, and conference and book news relevant to Arabic lexicography and lexicology. Similarly, the *Maǧalla Maʿhad al-Maḫṭūṭāt al-ʿArabiyya* [Journal of the Institute of Arabic Manuscripts] in Cairo publishes, among other materials, articles pertaining to Arabic linguistic topics.

## 3. Bibliography


Badra, M. Kh. & Thurayya Kurd Ali. 1982. *Dalīl al-Bāḥiṯ al-Luġawī fī d-Dawriyyāt al-ʿArabiyya* [Guide of the Linguistic Researcher in Arab Periodicals]. Vol. I. Beirut: Mu'assasat ar-Risāla.

Bakalla, Mohammed H. 1975. *Bibliography of Arabic Linguistics*. London: Mansell.

—. 1983. *Arabic Linguistics: An introduction and bibliography*. London: Mansell.

Sawaie, Mohammed. 1987. "Jurji Zaydan (1861–1914): A modernist in Arabic linguistics". *Historiographia Linguistica* 14.283–304.

—. 1990. "An Aspect of 19th Century Arabic Lexicography: The modernizing role and contribution of (Ahmad) Faris al-Shidyaq (1804?–1887)". *History and Historiography of Linguistics: Proceedings of the fourth international conference on the history of the language sciences* ed. by Hans-Josef Niederehe & Konrad Koerner, 157–171. Amsterdam & Philadelphia: Benjamins.

—. 1996. Eight short encyclopedic articles on: 'Aḥmad Fāris aš-Šidyāq (pp. 859–860); 'Ibrāhīm al-Yāziǧī (pp. 1034–1035); Nāṣif al-Yāziǧī (p. 1035); Buṭrus al-Bustānī (pp. 151–152); Rifāʿa aṭ-Ṭahṭāwī (pp. 904–905); Ḥafnī Nāṣif (pp. 668–669); Ḥusayn al-Marṣafī (pp. 607–608); and Ǧurǧī Zaydān (p. 1040). *Lexicon Grammaticorum* ed. by Harro Stammerjohann. Tübingen: Niemeyer.

UNESCO. 1991. *Taqaddum al-Lisāniyyāt fī l-'Aqṭār al-ʿArabiyya* [Development of Linguistics in the Arab World. Proceedings of a conference held in Rabat, Morocco, 1987.] Beirut: Dār al-Ġarb al-'Islāmī.


*Mohammed Sawaie, Charlottesville, VA (USA)*

# 47. L'influence arabe sur la linguistique copte

1. Introduction
2. La grammaire
3. Terminologie grammaticale
4. La lexicographie
5. Bibliographie

## 1. Introduction

Au courant du XIII$^{e}$ siècle (VII$^{e}$ de l'hégire), les Coptes connurent une Renaissance intellectuelle et littéraire sous le signe de la langue et culture arabes (Graf 1947: 344–444; Sidarus 1993). Dans ce cadre, l'étude intensive et systématique de leur langue nationale et religieuse, qui se voyait disparaître dans l'usage courant, du moins au Caire et dans le Delta, méritât une attention particulière.

Si la lexicographie pouvait se prévaloir d'une tradition nationale plusieurs fois millénaire, la grammaire, jusque là inexistante, ne pouvait se développer que dans le giron de la linguistique arabe, dont les principaux mentors se trouvaient alors en Egypte. C'est ainsi que, parmi les grammaires nationales qui surgirent au Moyen Age dans la dépendance de cette vigoureuse tradition, la grammaire copte (qui se prolonge à nos jours en milieu égyptien) mérite à un triple titre une attention particulière: (a) elle est rédigée entièrement en langue arabe; (b) elle n'a eu recours à aucune autre tradition autochtone antérieure; (c) elle décrit une langue non-sémitique. Par ailleurs, cette production copto-arabe a exercé un rôle déterminant dans la naissance de la tradition nationale de philologie éthiopienne (Moreno 1949; Cohen 1963).

La grammaire copte de langue arabe est appelée *muqaddima* "préface, introduction, avant-propos, prolégomènes". Sans exclure l'influence qu'a pu avoir exercée le fait que dans la littérature arabe le terme entre dans la composition de plusieurs titres de traités grammaticaux, il nous semble qu'il s'est imposé historiquement à ce domaine de la philologie copte à cause de la première de toutes les grammaires, à savoir la *Muqaddima samannūdiyya*. Non seulement elle se présente, du point de vue de la forme et du contenu, comme une véritable 'introduction' grammaticale au *Sullam kanā'isī* "Scala ecclesiastica" de l'évêque Jean de Samannud (Yūḥannā as-Samannūdī, *fl.* 1230–1260), mais c'est sous l'impulsion directe de cette première ébauche que trois, au moins, des autres grammaires ont vu le jour.

Mais as-Samannūdī lui-même aurait pu s'être inspiré de l'ancien vocabulaire gréco-copto-arabe intitulé Βιβλίον τῶν Βαθμῶν / *Kitāb Daraǧ as-sullam* "Livre des degrés de l'échelle", lequel semble avoir été à l'origine de la dénomination arabe *sullam* "scala, échelle" donnée aux lexiques copto-arabes et, par extension, aux codex de miscellanées philologiques coptes (Sidarus 2000: 4–5). En effet, le premier chapitre de ce vocabulaire fonctionne un peu comme 'avant-propos' lexico-grammatical, sous forme de séries paradigmatiques, par rapport à la partie onomasiologique proprement dite (ch. 2–19) et est considéré comme véritable *Muqaddima* dans l'une des deux versions principales (Sidarus 1997: 316; 1978b: 135; Mallon 1910: 58).

## 2. La grammaire

S'avançant sur un terrain encore vierge, le pionnier de la grammaire copte, Yūḥannā as-Samannūdī se contente essentiellement de dresser un tableau des éléments morphologiques qui s'affixent au mot copte: articles divers, préfixes, suffixes pronominaux et autres particules de liaison. Dans une sorte d'appendice très disparate et peu savant, l'auteur passe en revue une série de 'particularités' de la langue copte, qu'il n'est pas en mesure de classer systématiquement: elles sont d'ordre orthographique, morphologique, syntaxique, idiomatique et même lexical.

A vrai dire, l'évêque de Sammanūd ne prétendait aucunément rédiger une grammaire, mais offrir tout simplement au lecteur de son *sullam*, sous la forme d'une "introduction abrégée des parties du discours copte" (*muqaddima muḫtaṣara li-'aqsām al-kalām al-qibṭī*), les éléments de base qui lui permettront de "déduire le féminin à partir du masculin, le pluriel à partir du singulier, le passé du futur, la première ou deuxième personne de la troisième [...], en fonction du contexte" (Mallon 1906: 121; Van Lantschoot 1948: 4–6). Son lexique, de fait, constituant un glossaire de textes bibliques et liturgiques, enregistre les mots ou unités lexicales dans la forme où ils se présentent dans le premier passage du corpus dépouillé, omettant – du moins en principe – "de répéter les formes analogues".

Ce n'est que plus tard que les sucesseurs d'as-Samannūdī chercheront à composer de véritables grammaires. Ibn Kātib Qayṣar, le grand bibliste de son temps (m. 1266/67), reprend dans sa *Tabṣira* (Kircher 1643: 20v–37) la matière de la *Muqaddima samannūdiyya*, l'étoffe considérablement et l'articule en un 'discours' linguistique continu, dans lequel les divers éléments de la morphologie (*al-'alfāẓ al-mufrada*) se trouvent magistralement intégrés. Le style même du traité rappelle singulièrement la *Kāfiya* d'Ibn al-Ḥāǧib – cette grammaire arabe qui eut un grand succès en Egypte, dès sa parution dans la première moitié du XIII^e^ siècle. Suivant la division devenue classique ches les Arabes et qui s'imposera désormais dans les grammaires coptes, la *Tabṣira* traite successivement du nom (pronoms et articles inclus), du verbe et du *ḥarf* (particules, prépositions et conjonctions diverses). Ce qui est tout à fait nouveau, c'est la partie sur la syntaxe (*al-ǧumla al-kalāmiyya al-murakkaba*), avec ses propositions verbales, nominales et attributives (l'adjectif copte construit sous la forme d'une proposition relative: *al-ǧumla an-na'tiyya*).

Néanmoins, cette intéressante grammaire copte a le défaut d'être trop dépendante de la structure idiomatique de la langue arabe. On a l'impression, des fois, de se trouver devant un manuel de traduction arabe-copte. C'est l'opposé extrême de la grammaire de son prédécesseur, que tempèreront bientôt d'autres auteurs.

La perspective qui poussera al-Wağīh al-Qalyūbī (m. ap. 1271) à poursuivre, dans sa *Kifāya* (inédite), le travail de mise au point d'une bonne grammaire de la langue copte, se révèle être d'une grande rigueur scientifique. C'est à peu près dans ces termes qu'il s'explique là-dessus: pour traduire correctement il faut respecter le génie propre à chaque langue, en se gardant bien de traiter l'une d'après les règles ou la structure de l'autre (cf. Mallon 1906: 127; Van Lantschoot 1948: 76–77). Cette mise en garde prend en considération le fait que, chez les Coptes de l'époque, l'usage de l'arabe prédominait de loin sur celui du copte: il leur fallait donc assimiler laborieusement les règles grammaticales et les constructions idiomatiques propres à cette dernière langue.

At-Tiqa Ibn ad-Duhayrī trouvera, pour sa part (cf. Mallon 1906: 130–131), que la *Kifāya* tout comme la *Tabṣira* sont restées trop dépendantes de la *Muqaddima samannūdiyya*, somme toute bien élémentaire; elles s'avèrent, partant, incomplètes, en même temps qu'elles comportent plusieurs erreurs et certains points de divergences qu'il convient de discuter. Composée certainement après 1266–1267, sa grammaire (inédite) n'a pas de titre et se divise dans les trois parties traditonnelles, réparties en dix chapitres, les huit premiers pour le 'nom' tout seul (!).

Malgré la valeur de cette dernière *muqaddima*, à laquelle s'apparentent celles (de même inédites) de 'Abū l-Farağ Ibn al-ʿAssāl (m. av. 1266–1267) et de 'Abū Šākir Ibn ar-Rāhib (vers 1210–1290), il faudra attendre la deuxième moitié du XIVe siècle pour avoir, avec la *Qilādat at-taḥrīr fī ʿilm at-tafsīr* "Le collier assemblé concernant la science de l'interprétation" de l'évêque Athanase de Qūṣ (*fl.* 1360–1380), en Haute-Égypte, la grammaire la plus complète, la plus pertinente et la mieux structurée de l'idiome copte, sahidique et bohaïrique tout à la fois. Dans son édition de cette grammaire bi-dialectale, Bauer (1972: 61–70) entreprend une analyse détaillée de son contenu avec références constantes aux chapitres correspondants de quelques-unes des autres *muqaddimāt*.

Mais Athanase, le dernier grand écrivain copto-arabe du Moyen Age (Sidarus 1977), a rédigé aussi un long commentaire (*Šarḥ*) à sa propre grammaire, qui constitue un considérable développement de la matière grammaticale: exemples et tableaux paradigmatiques supplémentaires, nouvelles règles et considérations grammaticales. Les longs fragments conservés dans le manuscrit de la Vaticane, Borgia copte 133, ont constitué la source première de l'intrigante et première grammaire copte européenne (Tuki 1778), comme démontré par Petersen (1913), dans une thèse de doctorat offrant l'édition d'environ un cinquième des fragments et demeurée ignorée jusqu'à peu (Sidarus 1977: 28b; 2000: 14, M 13; 23, T 22).

## 3. Terminologie grammaticale

L'étude, tant systématique qu'historique, de la terminologie proprement grammaticale des *muqaddimāt* coptes est encore à faire. Une série de questions, en effet, se posent à l'historien de la linguistique. Quels ont été les termes ou expressions techniques arabes qui ont servi à décrire la langue copte? De quelles écoles ou manuels philologiques proviennent-ils? Forgés qu'ils étaient pour rendre compte d'une langue sémitique, ces termes ont-ils été appliqués à l'idiome copte d'une manière satisfaisante? (On notera à ce propos que, bien que le copte, en tant que dernier représentant de l'ancien égyptien, appartienne au groupe linguistique chamito-sémitique ou afro-asiatique, sa structure morphologique présente, d'un point de vue synchronique, une tendance à l'*agglutination* qui l'éloigne encore plus du rameau sémitique; cf. Sidarus 1978a: 268). Par ailleurs, quel a été le sens nouveau que certains termes arabes ont dû acquérir? Quels néologismes ou locutions néologiques ont dû être créés? Existent-ils des parallèles dans les autres traditions grammaticales dépendantes de la linguistique arabe? Dans quelle mesure, enfin, les grammairiens coptes de cette basse-époque connaissaient-ils leur langue d'origine et avaient l'intelligence correcte de ses règles et de sa structure?

L'entreprise a été inaugurée par Bauer (1972: 71–150), qui a procédé à une analyse critique du vocabulaire technique d'Athanase de Qūṣ à partir de la *Qilāda*. Il faudra aujourd'hui étendre cette étude à son *Šarḥ*. D'autre part, on manifestera une grande réserve devant plusieurs cas considérés, trop facilement, comme néologismes: non seulement Bauer a consulté relativement peu de sources originales, mais elle a négligé la masse de traités philologiques arabes d'époque tardive, surtout de tradition égyptienne, ceux-là précisement qui avaient dû inspirer, en premier lieu, les grammairiens coptes (on note, par exemple, que certaines des expressions jugées nouvelles dans l'analyse en question se trouvent être d'usage courant dans l'enseignement indigène de nos jours ...).

Pour les autres grammairiens, il faut attendre encore l'édition critique de leurs œuvres — à commencer par la première de toutes, *al-Muqaddima as-samannūdiyya*, qui fut jusqu'Athanase lui-même le modèle de toutes les autres.

Ceci dit, l'analyse circonscrite de Bauer se trouve largement corroborée par la lecture des prédécesseurs d'Athanase, comme le montre, par exemple, l'étude de Sidarus (sous-presse) portant sur quelques cas de terminologie ayant trait au système d'écriture, à la phonologie ou à la morphologie. D'une manière générale, on peut dire que les philologues coptes du Moyen Age ont bien mené leur tâche. Non sans les ajustements nécessaires: extensions ou restrictions de sens, dérivations ou compositions, analogies ou néologismes —, les catégories grammaticales arabes se sont révélées aptes à décrire la langue des anciens Egyptiens dans sa dernière phase.

## 4. La lexicographie

Quand l'influence arabe s'est fait ressentir dans la recherche philologique copte, la lexicographie se situait dans la ligne de la tradition locale antérieure, qui avait fondu ensemble l'héritage pharaonique ancien et la culture hellénique (Sidarus 1990b; 1990c; 2000). Le nouvel impact suscita de nouvelles formes de vocabulaire, notamment le genre "rimé" (*muqaffā*) et le poème didactique (*'urǧūza*), mais aussi une nouvelle méthode de travail, qui faisait prévaloir la systématisation et le recours à la compilation littéraire (Sidarus 1990).

C'est ainsi, par exemple, que le genre onomasiologique ancien a connu alors les meilleures productions: la dernière édition du "Livre des Degrés" trilingue déjà mentionné (éd. Munier 1930: 61—249) et la "Scala magna" (*as-Sullam al-kabīr*) bilingue de l'encyclopédiste 'Abū l-Barakāt Ibn Kabar (m. 1324; éd. Kircher 1643: 39—272). De même pour les lexiques du type 'glossaire de textes': c'est la "Scala ecclesiastica" d'as-Samannūdī (éd. Munier 1930: 1—43), qui en est le meilleur représentant.

Quant aux lexiques alphabétiques rimés à la manière arabe, on les doit aux deux polygraphes du XIIIe siècle: 'Abū Šākir Ibn ar-Rāhib et 'Abū 'Isḥāq Ibn al-'Assāl (Sidarus 1978a: 271—272; 1978b: 129—131). Le premier ne nous est pas parvenu, mais on en connaît la méthode savante grâce au prologue conservé avec la grammaire qui lui servait de *muqaddima*: manifestement, il doit avoir été supérieur à la "Scala rimata" (*as-Sullam al-muqaffā*) d'Ibn al-'Assāl, éditée dans le recueil de Kircher (1643: 273—495).

Le seul spécimen d'*'urǧūza* lexicographique copte dont on connaît l'existence est celle d'Athanase de Qūṣ, au titre de *Bulġat aṭ-ṭālibī ... fī taǧānus al-'alfāẓ al-qibṭiyya wa-šarḥ tafsīrihā bi-l-'arabiyya* "Satisfaction du chercheur en matière de mots coptes homonymes et de leur explication en arabe". Là aussi, nous n'en possédons que l'avant-propos méthodologique (Bauer 1972: 244—246), où est exposé, entre autres, la forme strophique (*al-muṯallaṯ*) dans laquelle le vocabulaire a été 'versé' (Sidarus 1977: 25b—26a). Cet ouvrage traitant de vocables sahidiques, fait suite aux travaux antérieurs portant sur les homonymes bohaïriques, lesquels comprennent en général, tant des homographes que des homophones et même des paronymes (Sidarus 1978b: 136—137). Au contraire de ce que nous avons pu dire (ib.: 137), l'influence de la lexicographie arabe relative aux *muštabihāt/mutašābihāt* "mots ambigus/similaires" a dû avoir joué un rôle dans la naissance du genre chez les Coptes, non seulement parce qu'en définitive nous ne connaissons pas de témoins comparables pour l'époque grécocopte, mais c'est grâce au passage par les équivalents arabes que la distinction des vocables s'est fait possible.

## 5. Bibliographie

Bauer, Gertrud. 1972. *Athanasius von Qūṣ* Qilādat at-taḥrīr fī 'ilm at-tafsīr: *Eine koptische Grammatik in arabischer Sprache aus dem 13./14. Jahrhundert.* Freiburg i. Br.: Schwarz.

Cahen, M. 1963. "Sur les lexiques éthiopiens et en particulier leurs origines coptes. (Séance du 22 mai 1963)". *GLECS* 9.99—101.

Graf, Georg. 1947. *Geschichte der christlichen arabischen Literatur*, vol. II. Città del Vaticano: Biblioteca Apostolica Vaticana.

Kircher, Athanase. 1643. *Lingua aegyptiaca restitua.* Roma: apud Ludouicum Grignanum. [Edition défectueuse de quelques textes.]

Mallon, A. 1906/1907. "Une école de savants égyptiens [coptes] au Moyen Age". *Mélanges de la Faculté Orientale [de l'Université Saint-Joseph]* 1.109–131, 2.213–264.

–. 1910. "Catalogue des scalae coptes de la Bibliothèque Nationale [de Paris]". *Mélanges de la Faculté Orientale [de l'Université Saint-Joseph]* 4.57–90.

Moreno, M. M. 1949. "Struttura e terminologia del *Sawāsĕw*". *Rassegna di Studi Etiopici* 8.12–62.

Munier, Henri. 1930. *La scala copte 44 de la Bibliothèque Nationale de Paris*, vol. I: *Transcription*. (= *Bibliothèque d'Etudes Coptes*, 2.) Le Caire: I.F.A.O. [Seule partie parue.]

Petersen, Theodore Christian. 1913. *An Unknown Copto-Arabic Grammar by Athanasius Bishop of Kūs or the Source of Tukhi's* Rudimenta linguae coptae sive aegyptiacae. Ph. D. Thesis, Catholic University of America.

Sidarus, Adel. 1977. "Athanasius von Qūṣ und die arabisch-koptische Sprachwissenschaft des Mittelalters". *Bibliotheca Orientalis* 34:22b–35a.

–. 1978a. "La philologie copte arabe au Moyen Age". *La signification du Bas Moyen Age dans l'histoire et la Culture du Monde Musulman* (Actes du 8e Congrès de l.'U.E.A.I.), 267–281. Aix-en-Provence: Edisud.

–. 1978b. "Coptic Lexicography in the Middle Ages: The Coptic Arabic Scalae". *The Future of Coptic Studies* éd. par R. McL. Wilson, 125–142. Leiden: Brill.

–. 1990a. "Bibliographical Introduction to Medieval Coptic Linguistics". *Bulletin de la Société d'Archéologie Copte* 29.83–85.

–. 1990b. "Les lexiques onomasiologiques gréco-copto-arabes du Moyen Age et leurs origines anciennes". *Lingua restituta orientalis. Festgabe für Julius Aßfalg* éd. par R. Schulz & M. Görg, 348–359. (= *Ägypten und Altes Testament*, 20.) Wiesbaden: Harrassowitz.

–. 1990c. "Onomastica aegyptiaca: La tradition des lexiques thématiques en Égypte à travers les âges et les langues". *Histoire Epistémologie Langage* 12. 1.7–19.

–. 1993. "Essai sur l'âge d'or de la littérature copte arabe (XIIIe–XIVe siècles)". *Acts of the Fifth International Congress of Coptic Studies* (Washington, August 1992) II, éd. par D. Johnson, 443–462. Rome: Centro Internazionale di Microfichas.

–. 1997. "Un recueil original de philologie gréco-copto-arabe: La *scala* copte 43 de la Bibliothèque nationale de France". *Scribes et manuscrits du Moyen-Orient: Actes des Journées de codicologie et de paléographie des manuscrits du Moyen-Orient* (Paris, juin 1994) éd. par F. Déroche & F. Richard, 293–326. Paris: Bibliothèque nationale de France.

–. 1998. "*Sullam* (Vocabulaire copto-arabe / Coptic Arabic Vocbulary)". *Encyclopédie de l'Islam / The Encyclopaedia of Islam* X, 883–884 / 879–880. Leiden: E. J. Brill.

–. 2000. "La tradition sahidique de philologie gréco-copto-arabe (manuscrits des XIIIe–XVe siècles)". *Actes des 9èmes Journées d'études coptes* (Montpellier, juin 1999) éd. par N. Bosson. Bruxelles: Peeters.

– (sous presse). "Le modèle arabe en grammaire copte: Une approche des *muqaddimât* copto-arabes médiévales". *Le voyage et la langue: Hommage à André Roman et Anouar Louca* éd. par J. Dichy & H. Hamzé. Damas: Institut Français d'Études Arabes.

– (sous presse). "Medieval Coptic Grammars: The Arabic *Muqaddimāt*". *Journal of Coptic Studies* 3.

Tuki, Raphael. 1778. *Rudimenta linguae coptae sive aegyptiacae*. Rome: Typis Sacrae Congregationis.

Van Lantschoot, Arnold. 1948. *Un précurseur d'Athanase Kircher. Thomas Obicini et la scala Vat. copte 71*. Louvain: Institut Orientaliste. [Edition de quelques textes].

*Adel Sidarus, Évora (Portugal)*

# 48. The description of Turkic with the Arabic linguistic model



## 1. Arabic treatises of Turkic

Arabic scholars were hardly ever profoundly interested in other languages than Arabic. One of the main reasons for this was the close association of the study of language with Qur'ānic studies. No language on earth could have the same status as Arabic. Nevertheless, some scholars did take the trouble to describe other languages using the model and the conventions which had been developed for describing Arabic. The Arabic linguistic system served as a model for the description of a number of Oriental languages, such as Persian (→ Art. 49), Mongolian, Coptic (→ Art. 47) and several variants of Turkic.

The earliest known example of the description of a Turkic language with the Arabic model is (a) al-Kāšġarī's *Dīwān Luġāt at-Turk* (464–469/1072–1077). *Dīwān* is set up according to the principles of Arabic lexicography (*ʿilm al-luġa*); it was arranged in the same way as al-Fārābī's (d. 381/961) *Dīwān al-ʾAdab* (cf. Bergsträsser 1921; Kelly 1971, 1976 and 1980; Dankoff & Kelly 1982–85; Clauson 1972). In *Dīwān* grammatical information is given only occasionally. The linguistic terminology in *Dīwān* reflects the early Arabic grammatical tradition and at a first glance shows some Kufan influence (cf. Ermers 1999: 50, n. 89). Most grammars of Turkic, however, were compiled in Mamlūk-ruled Egypt in the 14th century. The most important of these are the following (cf. Pritsak 1959; Flemming 1977; Ermers 1999): (b) *Kitāb al-ʾidrāk li-lisān al-ʾatrāk*, (1313) by ʾAbū Ḥayyān al-ʾAndalusī (d. 745/1345); (c) *al-Qawānīn al-kulliyya li-ḍabṭ al-luġa at-turkiyya*, anonymous, 14th century; (d) *at-Tuḥfa aḏ-ḏakiyya fī l-luġa at-turkiyya*, anonymous, 14th century; (e) *Tarǧumān turkī wa-ʿarabī wa-muġalī*, anonymous, 1343 (for the date see Flemming 1968); (f) an unpublished anonymous text in the margins of the Istanbul Veli ed-Dīn 2896 manuscript (henceforth MG), which can be best described as a compilation of fragments from both known and unknown sources (cf. Ermers 1999: 41). Two grammars that were not compiled under Mamlūk rule: (g) *Ḥilyat al-ʾinsān wa-ḥalabat al-lisān*, Ibn Muhannā, 14th century; (h) a grammar in Arabic of Ottoman Turkish: aš-*Suḏūr aḏ-ḏahabiyya fī l-luġa at-turkiyya* (1619) by Ibn Muḥammad Ṣāliḥ. Finally, some Ottoman grammatical treatises, two of which are described by Kerslake (1994). In turcological accounts of 'grammars' two other 14th century sources are added to this listing, (i) *Bulġat al-muštāq fī luġat at-turk wa-l-qifžāq* and (j) *ad-Durra al-muḍīʿa fī l-luġa at-turkiyya*. For the study of the linguistic model, however, their importance is limited, as they consist of word lists only. These and other sources were edited and studied by turcologists whose interest, however, was focused on the collection of the Turkic language material in the sources rather than the way in which they were arranged. Some aspects of the application of the Arabic model on linguistic and phonological features of Turkic were only recently presented by Ermers (1999).

The Turkic language described in *Dīwān* belongs to the branch of **ʾadaq** languages within the Turkic language family, whereas the Turkic language in all other sources belongs to the **ʾayaq**-branch. The language material of the Mamlūk-texts has been roughly defined as "Qipčaq" (cf. Pritsak 1959) with varying degrees of Oġuz influence. New research on the grammatical structure of the languages in these texts, with a serious interpretation of the grammarians' remarks, might shed some more light on the provenance of their speakers and the relations with modern Turkic languages.

The arrangement of the material in the sources allows us to make some suggestions as to possible relations between the sources. A first distinction one can make is that between *Dīwān* and the other sources. *Dīwān* forms part of the lexicographical branch of Arabic linguistics, whereas the others belong to the grammatical tradition (*ʿilm an-naḥw*). The grammatical treatises belonging to the second category can be subdivided in two groups, based on their internal arrangement. The first group comprises those works that are arranged according to word type. In Arabic grammar a word is either *ism* (noun), *fiʿl* (verb), or *ḥarf* (particle). Traditional grammars of Arabic, such as az-Zamaḫšarī's (d. 538/1144) *Mufaṣṣal*, maintain this division in their overall structure, dealing subsequently with each linguistic category. The second group includes *Tuḥfa* and *ʾIdrāk*, which show a different, more analytic division. Both are divided into three parts: lexicography, morphology and syntax. The latter division resembles very much ʾAbū Ḥayyān's division in his *Irtišāf* and appears to be based on Sībawayhi's arrangement of *al-Kitāb*.

Although the importance of *Dīwān* for Turkic and Arabic linguistics is undoubtedly immense, there is nevertheless no evidence for the assumption that it served as a source for the 14th century Mamlūk-sources: the only source which can be related to it is MG. It is suggested in various studies that in particular ʾAbū Ḥayyān must have known *Dīwān* and used it as a source for his *ʾIdrāk*. However, the two works show many differences in approach, structure, terminology and variety of Turkic language and seem to stand more or less independent of each other. The anonymous *Qawānīn*, too, has often been associated with ʾAbū Ḥayyān. The internal arrangement of *Qawānīn*, however, shows an approach so different from that of ʾAbū Ḥayyān's works, that he is very unlikely to have been its author. In two instances, i. e.

*Tuḥfa* and *Šuḏūr*, 'Abū Ḥayyān's name is mentioned in the text. In the case of *Tuḥfa* the dependence on *'Idrāk* is further evidenced by a similar internal arrangement; in the case of *Šuḏūr* the relation with 'Abū Ḥayyān is less obvious, since the author claims to have used his *Durra*. For 'Abū Ḥayyān's authorship of *Durra* there is, however, no real evidence.

## 2. Arabic linguistic concepts applied to Turkic

The Arabic sociolinguistic concept of language was, of course, determined by the Arabic linguistic situation: one prestigious variant existed side-by-side with non-prestigious city dialects. This concept is to some extent reflected in the grammars of Turkic too. All authors claim to describe the pure *turkiyya* positing it against less pure variants. Kāšġarī, for instance, puts the dialect of the Čigil tribe against that of the *Turkmān* or *Ġuziyya* (often including *Qifǧāq*) (cf. Dankoff & Kelly 1982–85: I, 4f.), apparently giving equal weight to both. Some political awareness may have underlain this approach, since the Selǧuq sultan in Baghdad at that time was of Oġuz descent. In the 14th-century sources *turkiyya* is usually contrasted with *turkmāniyya*, probably to be understood as Oġuz in a broad sense, and, occasionally, *qibǧāqiyya*. They use qualifications as *wa-l-'afṣaḥ* and *wa-l-'aḥsan* "the purest" and "the best", respectively. The author of *Qawānīn* warns severely against the use of *turkmāniyya* "The language of the *turkmān* is not *turkiyya* [...] it is held in contempt by them and whoever speaks it is despised by them" (*Qawānīn* 7.15). This and other, less strongly formulated statements to the same effect in the sources suggest that *turkiyya* is a rigidly defined language and, perhaps, close to or even altogether identical with *qibǧāqiyya*. In practice, however, this claim for purety does not hold, since all sources occasionally accept forms in *turkiyya* and words that only occur in Oġuz languages, e. g., **ḍuḍaq** "lip" (*Qawānīn*).

Grammatical concepts, too, were based on features of classical Arabic. The hierarchical relations between the syntactic elements as posited in Arabic grammar can be understood in terms of syntactic versus semantic case in Generative Grammar (e. g., Babby & Freidin 1984; Babby 1986). Syntactic cases can be explained in terms of governance, are therefore predictable, and may be omitted from surface structure. Semantic cases, on the other hand, contribute to the meaning of the phrase, are not predictable, and cannot be omitted. In this analysis Arabic cases could best be defined as "syntactic". Indeed, the Arabic grammarians explain their concept of case (*'i'rāb*) in terms that strongly remind of syntactic case. Apart from some clearly semantic cases, such as the genitive, locative and ablative, Turkic languages possess one case which can be classified as typically syntactic: the accusative. Its occurrence is quite predictable in terms of governance, for it occurs only when the noun is governed by a transitive verb.

The Arabic grammarians describe the Turkic accusative case ending **nī** in terms that are very similar to that of the Arabic accusative case ending *a*. For instance, in **'aġaš-ni al-ḍu-m** /stick-ACC/ "I took the stick" (*Qawānīn* 31.6), the terms "marker of objectivity" (*'alāmat al-maf'ūliyya*) and *'alāmat an-naṣb* "marker of the accusative" are used (compare: Širbīnī, *Nūr* 60; Zamaḫšarī, *Mufaṣṣal* 11.4). From these parallels it is evident that **nī** is regarded as a type of *'i'rāb*. The distribution of **nī** is not fully similar to that of *a* in Arabic. In the first place, of course, **nī** never occurs on verbs, unlike *a*. Further, *a* is also used for other objects such as the objects of time, place and circumstance, whereas **nī** is only used with the direct object.

The description of the Turkic dative case ending **gā/ġā** seems more problematic. In some instances **gā/ġā** is assigned the status of a particle, equivalent to *'ilā* "to", which governs the genitive case, e. g. **kant kā kat-tu-m** /town DAT go-PAST-1sg/ "I went to the town" *ḏahabtu 'ilā l-baladi* (*Qawānīn* 42.7). Other occurrences of **gā/ġā** cannot be solved in this way. The Turkic dative also serves to mark the indirect object, even when the verb is a passive form, e. g. **bir-il-dī sanǧar-ġā bir-aqǧā** /give-PASS-PAST sanǧar-DAT one-coin/ "A coin was given to Sanǧar". In Arabic the indirect and direct objects are not distinguished in form, and perhaps for this reason Arabic theory lacks the means to distinguish between indirect and direct objects. In the Arabic version of the Turkic sentence, *sanǧar* has the nominative case, viz., *'u'ṭiya sanǧar-u dirham-a-n* /give-PASS-PAST sanǧar-NOM dirham-ACC-INDEF/ "Sanǧar was given a dirham". The grammarians note that in Turkic the verb governs **sanǧar** through a particle, whereas in Arabic this particle is absent. The occurrence of a particle, however, can be accounted for within the framework of Arabic theory.

In Arabic grammar the term *muta'addin 'ilā talātati mafā'īl* "transitive to three objects" indicates a verb governing three objects in the accusative case, e. g., *'a'lamtu l-'amīr-a l-faras-a musarraǧ-a-n* /I made known the chief-ACC the horse-ACC saddled-ACC-INDEF/ "I told the chief that the horse is saddled". The tritransitive verb **bil-dur-dum** is the pendant of Arabic *'a'lamtu*, in **bī-gā bil-dur-dum 'āṭ 'ayarla-n-ubtur** /chief-DAT know-CAUS-PAST-1sg horse saddle-PASS-PAST/ "I informed the chief 'the horse has been saddled' ". Here **gā/ġā** is considered a "marker of the non-pure object" (*'alāmat al-maf'ūl ġayr aṣ-ṣarīḥ, 'Idrāk* 129.5–8). A non-pure object is a type of object which can also be expressed by means of a particle, as opposed to the pure object (*al-maf'ūl aṣ-ṣarīḥ*). The importance of this analysis resides in the fact that here **gā/ġā** does not have the status of a particle (*ḥarf*), but rather that of a marker (*'alāma*), thus being incorporated in the concept of *'i'rāb*. Simultaneously, **gā/ġā** is an independent syntactic element, *ḥarf ǧarr* "particle of the genitive". In this way the description of the new language appears to have influenced the grammarians' concept of the object.

## 3. Bibliography

### 3.1. Primary sources


*Dīwān* = Maḥmūd ibn al-Ḥusayn ibn Muḥammad al-Kāšġarī, *Dīwān luġāt at-turk.* Facsimile edition of the MS by the Turkish Ministry of Culture. Ankara, 1990.

*Ḥilya* = Ǧamāl ad-Dīn ibn al-Muhannā, *Kitāb ḥilyat al-'insān wa-ḥalabat al-lisān.* Ed. by Kilisli Mu'allim Rif'at (Bilge). Istanbul, 1921.

'Abū Ḥayyān, *'Idrāk* = 'Abū Ḥayyān Muḥammad ibn Yūsuf ibn 'Alī al-'Andalusī, *Kitāb al-'Idrāk li-lisān al-'atrāk.* Ed. and transl. into Turkish by A. Caferoğlu. Istanbul: Evkaf, 1931.

'Abū Ḥayyān, *Irtišāf* = 'Abū Ḥayyān Muḥammad ibn Yūsuf ibn 'Alī al-'Andalusī, *Irtišāf aḍ-ḍarab min lisān al-'arab.* Ed. by Muṣṭafā 'Aḥmad an-Nammās. 3 vols. I. Cairo: Maṭba'a an-Našr aḏ-Ḏahabī, 184; II and III Cairo: Maṭba'a al-Madanī, 1987–1989.

*Qawānīn* = *al-Qawānīn al-kulliya li-ḍabṭ al-luġa at-turkiyya.* Ed. by M. Rif'at. Istanbul: Evkaf, 1928.

Širbīnī, *Nūr* = as-Sayyid Muḥammad aš-Širbīnī, *Kitāb nūr as-sağiyya fī ḥall 'alfāẓ al-'Āǧūrrumiyya.* Ed. and transl. in Carter (1981.)

*Šuḏūr* = Mollā Ibn 'Aḥmad Ṣāliḥ, *aš-Šuḏūr aḏ-ḏahabiyya wa-l-qiṭa' al-'aḥmadiyya fī l-luġa at-turkiyya.* MS Bibliothèque Nationale, Paris, Supplément Arabe No. 4333.

*Tarǧumān* = *Tarǧumān turkī wa-'arabī wa-muġalī.* Ed. and comm. in Houtsma (1889.)

*Tuḥfa* = *at-Tuḥfa aḏ-ḏakiyya fī l-luġa at-turkiyya.* Facsimile edition of MS 3092 Veli Eddin, by T. Halasi Kun, *La langue des Kiptchaks d'après un manuscrit arabe d'Istanboul.* Budapest: Société Körösi Csoma, 1942.

Zamaḫšarī, *Mufaṣṣal* = 'Abū l-Qāsim Maḥmūd ibn 'Umar az-Zamaḫšarī, *Kitāb al-Mufaṣṣal fī n-naḥw.* Ed. J. P. Broch. Christiania: Libraria P. T. Malingii, 1879.


### 3.2. Secondary sources


Babby, Leonard. 1986. "The Locus of Case Assignment and the Direction of Percolation". *Case in Slavic* ed. by Brecht & Levine, 170–219. Columbus, Ohio: Slavica Publishers.

– & R. Freidin. 1984. "On the Interaction of Lexical and Syntactic Properties: Case structure in Russian". *Cornell Working Papers in Linguistics* 6.71–103.

Bergsträsser, Gotthelf. 1921. "Das Vorbild von Kāšġarī's *Dīwān luġāt at-Turk*". *Orientalistische Literaturzeitung* 21.154–155.

Carter, Michael. 1981. *Arab Linguistics: An introductory classical text with translation and notes.* Amsterdam: Benjamins.

Clauson, Gerard. 1972. *An Etymological Dictionary of pre-Thirteenth Century Turkish.* Oxford: Clarendon Press.

Dankoff, Robert & James Kelly. 1982–85. *Compendium of Turkic Dialects.* Harvard: Harvard Univ. Press. [Translation of Maḥmūd al-Kāšġarī's *Dīwān luġāt at-Turk.*]

Ermers, Robert. 1999. *Arabic Grammars of Turkic: The Arabic linguistic model applied to foreign languages and translation of 'Abū Ḥayyān al-'Andalusī's* Kitāb al-'Idrāk li-Lisān al-'Atrāk. Leiden: Brill.

Flemming, Barbara. 1968. "Ein alter Irrtum bei der chronologischen Einordnung des *Tarǧumān Turkī wa-'Arabī wa-Muġalī*". *Der Islam* 44.226–229.

–. 1977. "Zum Stand der mamlūk-türkischen Forschung". *Vorträge des XIX. Deutschen Orientalistentages in Freiburg (Breisgau) 1975. Zeitschrift der deutschen morgenländischen Gesellschaft* Suppl. III: 2.1155–64.

Halasi Kun, Tibor. 1942. *La Langue des Kiptchaks d'après un manuscrit arabe d'Istanbul.* Budapest: Société Körösi Csoma.

Houtsma, Martinus. 1889. *Tarǧumān Turkī wa-'Arabī wa-Muġulī: Ein türkisch-arabisches Glossar nach einer leidener Handschrift.* Leiden: E. J. Brill.

Kelly, James. 1971. "On defining Dhū ath-Thalāthah and Dhū al-'Arba'ah". *Journal of the American Oriental Society* 91.132–136.

Kerslake, Celia. 1994. "Two Ottoman Turkish Grammars of the Tanẓīmāt Period". *Proceedings of CIEPO VII, Pécs 1986*, 133–168. Ankara: Türk Tarih Kurumu.

Owens, Jonathan. 1988. *The Foundations of Grammar.* Amsterdam: Benjamins.

–. 1990. *Early Arabic Grammatical Theory: Heterogeneity and standardization.* Amsterdam: Benjamins.

Pritsak, Omeljan. 1959. "Das Kipčakische". *Philologica Turcicae Fundamenta* ed by L. Bazin, 79–85. Wiesbaden: Steiner.

Telegdi, Szigmund. 1983. "Eine türkische Grammatik in arabischer Sprache aus dem XV. Jhdt.". *Körösi Csoma Archivum*, Ergänzungsband H 3, 282–326. Budapest.

Versteegh, Kees. 1993. *Arabic Grammar* and *Qur'ānic Exegesis in Early Islam.* Leiden: Brill.

–. 1995. *The Explanation of Linguistic Causes: az-Zaǧǧāǧī's theory of grammar. Introduction, translation, commentary.* Amsterdam & Philadelphia: Benjamins.

Zajączkowski, Ananiasz. 1954. *Vocabulaire Arabe-Kiptchak de l'époque de l'État Mamelouk* Bulġat al-Muštāq fī luġat at-Turk wa-l-qifžāq, vol. II: *Verba.* Warszawa.

–. 1958. *Slownik Arabsko Kipczaki z okresu Panstwa Mameluckiego* Bulġat al-Muštāq fī luġat at-Turk wa-l-qifžāq, vol. I: *Le Nom.* Warszawa.

–. 1965a. "Chapitres choisis du vocabulaire arabe kiptchak *ad-Durra al-muḍī'a fī l-luġa t-turkiyya* I". *Rocznik Orientalistyczny* 29.39–98.

–. 1965b. "Chapitres choisis du vocabulaire arabe kiptchak *ad-Durra al-Muḍī'a fī l-luġa t-turkiyya* II". *Rocznik Orientalistyczny* 29.67–116.

–. 1968. "Material kolokwialny arabsko-kipczacki w Słowniku 'ad-Durra al-muḍī'a fī l-luġa t-turkiyya'" *Rocznik Orientalistyczny* 31.71 ff.

–. 1969. "Chapitres choisis du vocabulaire arabe kiptchak *ad-Durra al-muḍī'a fī l-luġa t-turkiyya* III". *Rocznik Orientalistyczny* 32.

*Robert Ermers, 's-Hertogenbosch (The Netherlands)*

# 49. Arabic influence on Persian linguistics

1. Introduction
2. Sources of linguistic ideas: lexicography and prosody
3. Basic concepts
4. Changes in the meaning and usage of Arabic terms
5. Summary
6. Bibliography

## 1. Introduction

New Persian as a relatively unified form of the written literary language appeared in the 10th century. Despite the dominance of the Classical Persian language and literature, especially poetry in the larger Persian-speaking areas from Anatolia to India in the Islamic period, the grammar of Persian in its own terms was not studied until the last century. The reasons are manifold: in the multilingual (Arabic, Persian, Turkish and Hindi) area the superiority of Arabic as the language of science was unquestionable, although scholars of Persian origin contributed significantly to Islamic sciences, especially linguistics. In Iran, however, there was no linguistic tradition, *ars grammatica* as a linguistic science was completely missing. Iranians did not deal with grammatical problems of their own mother tongue in an explicit way. This means that they did not write grammars, did not treat any practical or theoretical problems of Persian. One of the possible reasons for this situation was the lack of a firmly established literary norm or a highly respected canon like the *Qur'ān*, on the basis of which the grammar of the language could have been worked out. This point was put by Šams-i Qays (*ŠQ*) in his book on prosody in the early 13th century most clearly: "There is no exact norm (*miqyās*) of the rules of Persian, on the basis of which the correct and corrupt usage could be defined" (*Mu'ǧam* 174–175). The literary language, far from being uniform in the first period (9th–11th centuries), was based mainly on texts by highly respected poets, who occasionally represented different dialectal usage, both in their vocabulary and grammar. Therefore the main task of the men of letters was to hand down the text, to collect and interpret the rare and strange lexical and grammatical forms only because they were in the text. Consequently, in the absence of a tradition of textual criticism and exegetical literature, anything that could have been called a technical or pedagogical grammar was missing. According to modern Iranian sources, the first grammar was published in 1846 in Tabriz (Jeremiás 1993).

## 2. Sources of linguistic ideas: Lexicography and prosody

There are sources, however, from which one can infer the state of grammatical thinking in the classical period. From the oldest period poetry itself testifies that the poets who were able to write correct Persian verse with rhyme (*qāfiyat*) and quantitative metre (*ʿarūḍ* or *vazn*), features shared by Arabic and Persian poetry (de Blois 1992: 42), must have had a knowledge of Persian grammar. This intuitive knowledge was put to use by them when they adapted Arabic prosody, including rhyme-science, to Persian. Therefore, the history of Persian grammatical literature from the beginning until the last century is to be conceived as a process of translation, adaptation or restructuring of the Arabic model. Translation played an unimportant role because most of the scholars concerned wrote and worked in both languages. Adaptation always involved some degree of restructuring of the original description in most cases, even if in different degrees. The main question here is how a Semitic model was adapted to Persian, an Indo-European language with a different structure, in which the consonants (*ḥarf*) and the vowels (*ḥaraka*) of the word are of equal value, whereas in Arabic the semantic load of the words is represented in particular by the consonants.

Another group of sources touching upon questions of language was lexicography. The first dictionaries of Persian in the 11th–12th centuries, the classical poetic dictionaries called *farhang* (e. g., ʾAsadī's *Luġat-i furs* ca. 1058–1068) or the Arabic-Persian dictionaries (e. g., Zawzanī d. 1093, Zamaḫšarī d. 1144, Ḥubayš Tiflīsī ca. 1156; cf. Storey 1984) were compiled to serve first and foremost literary and exegetic purposes. Nevertheless, they also contained important grammatical information. Ǧawharī's *Ṣiḥāḥ* was wellknown in Iran, and the 'rhyme-order', that is, the alphabetical arrangement of words according to the last letter, then the first, was dominant. The difference, however, was enormous: there was no trace of the three root-consonant representation of Arabic in Persian, no attempt to derive verbal and nominal forms from the same "base" (*ʾaṣl*). On the other hand, the principle of the arrangement of words in the dictionaries was independent of their derivational history. This clearly shows that the Iranians were aware of the fact that their language was basically different from those of their neighbours, Arabic, Turkish or Hindi. This must have been common knowledge since the 8th century, when the first steps to adapt Persian words to the Arabic writing were made by Sībawayhi or Ḥamza al-ʾIṣfahānī (Meier 1981: 71; Ḫānlarī 1975: 117).

## 3. Basic concepts

The universality of certain basic concepts such as the three parts of speech (*ism*, *fiʿl*, *ḥarf*; cf. Versteegh 1995: 26) and morphological procedure (*ḥarf*-method; cf. Elwell-Sutton 1986: 671) of Arabic grammar, however, was generally accepted. Through the adaptation of these some properties of Persian as opposed to Arabic were occasionally formulated. While treating the equivalents of the three parts of speech, for instance, the lexicographer Ḥubayš Tiflīsī recognized that some Persian words inherently contained the possibility to figure as either nouns (singular or plural), verbs or particles, a phenomenon absolutely impossible in Arabic: "There are many words which appear to be both a noun and a verb and there are many words which are both a [singular] noun and a plural and it is possible that a noun, a verb and a plural [simultaneously] are all implied in the same word. [...] It is also possible that a noun, a verb and a particle are all contained in the same word" (*Qānūn-i ʾadab*, preface 23).

But most of the dictionaries deal with practical problems of arrangement, that is, how to define the last *ḥarf*, and consequently, the base form (*ʾaṣl*) and the elements attached to it (*zāʾid*). When defining these terms, lexicography could rely on another science, prosody. The model is that of Arabic prosody, but the adaptation reveals originality. The oldest compendium of Persian prosody, including a treatment of rhyme, was written by Šams-i Qays in the early 13th century, itself already a summary of some previous *ʾadab*-literature. The theory and practice of this science, however, must have been known much earlier in Iran, as Classical Persian poetry testifies. This is true even if the earliest records often fail to meet the strict rules of rhyme (Jeremiás 1997). This rhyme-science provides an important source of grammatical analysis. Rhyme in Persian means that each verse-line has an identical part, which is exactly alike in spelling, but not in meaning.

The main task was to define the *ravī*, the last *ḥarf* of a word in its basic form, which may be preceded by two letters and followed by six others (called *zā'id*), whereas only two are allowed in Arabic as a maximum. The technique of defining the terms *ravī*, *'aṣl* and *zā'id* in Persian was to satisfy two conditions. The base word was to have a "full meaning" (*kalimat tāmm al-ma'nā*), while the *zā'id* element attached to it was to have a clearly definable "meaning and cause" (*ma'nā u 'illat-i 'ilḥāq*, *ŠQ* 175). In Persian all the morphems of inflection and derivation were regarded as *zā'id* elements. The sequence of *'aṣl* and *zā'id* was to produce a "transparent compound" (*ẓāhir at-tarkīb* or *mašhūr at-tarkīb*). Consequently, a finite verb (*guft-am* "I spoke"), a plural noun (*'asb-hā* "horses") or a deverbal noun (*guft-ār* "speech") were analysed as compounds. The condition of meaningfulness was met only if the first constituent of the word was a 'word with a full meaning'.

A second condition was that the base word was to consist of a minimum of two letters (*du ḥarfī*). One *ḥarf* with its vowel (*mutaḥarrik*) could not form a word. This was a basic rule taken over from Arabic. In Persian this was mainly an orthographical rule, but it had grammatical implications when *'aṣl* or *tarkīb* were to be defined. The final short vowels (*a, i, u*) of one-syllable words (CV) were written with the letters *hā'* or *wāw* (*dalālat-i ḥarakat*), e. g., *gufta* [gfth] "spoken", *ci* [ch] "what" with the letter *hā'-i sakt* ("silent *h*", *ŠQ* 216), or *tu* [tw] "you [nom.]" with the letter *vāv-i bayān-i ḍamma* ("representing ḍamma", *ŠQ* 213). These words were conceived as true words consisting of two *ḥarfs* as the rule required. But if a *zā'id* (a morpheme of whatever kind) was attached to a one-syllable word the second *ḥarf* denoting the final short vowel was omitted in writing, although the vowel was pronounced (i. e., the first *ḥarf* became *mutaḥarrik*). Therefore the syntagm ceased to be a 'transparent compound' and was analysed as *'aṣl* rather than *tarkīb*, e. g., *tu-rā* [tr'] "you + object suffix". As a consequence of this rule, another rule was also formulated in the oldest literature and continued to be maintained until the last century ('Iravānī 1846: 5 r), scil. that all Persian words end in a final *sukūn*, i. e., vowelless consonant (*ŠQ* 178). This was true only in an orthographical sense.

A consistent observation of the two conditions yielded different results. The first condition helped Šams define several elements of Persian morphology by listing nearly all the inflectional and derivational morphemes (*ḥurūf-i taṣrīf* and *kalimāt-i 'adavāt*, *ŠQ* 175). The technique of dividing the word into the base and supplementary elements proved to be a practical solution through which a morphological analysis of the Persian word was carried out on an elementary level, although no grammatical unit below the word-level was recognized. So Šams succeeded in analyzing the constituent structure of finite verbs by separating a form, the stem in modern terminology, which practically coincided with finite forms (the imperative for the present stem and the 3rd person singular of the Past Tense for the past stem, both of them with a zero morph) and the personal affixes. The three usages of pronominal clitics were also clearly distinguished. But the second condition (*du ḥarfī*), that is, the adaptation of a basic rule of the Arabic syllable structure to Persian, caused confusion, for instance in the analysis of 'compounds' (Jeremiás 1999).

## 4. Changes in the meaning and usage of Arabic terms

Lexicography and prosody as sources for the grammatical analysis of Persian used exclusively Arabic terms. The system, however, in which they were used, was partly or fully different from the Arabic system and also showed some alteration through the centuries. Similarly, the Arabic terms still appear in more recent literature, but occasionally with a different denotation. The following list and commentary is mainly based on three sources: Šams-i Qays' prosody (*ŠQ*), the *Burhān-i qāṭi'* (*BQ*), a Persian-Persian vocabulary by Muḥammad Ḥusayn Tabrīzī from 1652, and 'Iravānī's grammar from 1846. Identifing "meaningful letters" (*ḥurūf-i ma'ānī*) representing either consonant or vowel at the end of the word was the oldest way to specify certain grammatical functions when *zā'id* was to be defined. From the 14th century onwards such lists of 'meaningful *ḥarfs*' got to be included in lexicographical works, first scattered under different headings, then more systematically. The *Ṣiḥāḥ al-*

*ʿağamiyya* by Hindūšāh Naḫcivānī (ca. 1328 Tabriz; cf. Storey 1984: 6) contains three chapters on the verb, on the noun and on the rules. The last chapter shows mainly how to derive the present forms from the past. Later these rules, together with the list of *ḥarfs* classified under different headings, were put at the beginning of the vocabulary as an introductory chapter on the "rules" (*qavāʿid*) of Persian.

From the 16th century onwards all the dictionaries were supplied with such 'grammatical rules', including the most popular one, the *Burhān-i qāṭiʿ*. In this kind of introductory chapter increasingly more grammatical information was piled up, but the originally consistent system began to disintegrate. The list of *ḥarfs*, previously called *zāʾid* was enlarged gradually and extended to the items appearing at the beginning (e. g., verbal prefixes) and in the middle of the word. Although this extension was not unknown in Arabic (Versteegh 1977: 25), the term *zāʾid* lost its original meaning in Persian. The list of these *ḥarfs* contained all the elements, either letters, words or word-like segments, which were considered to have a lexical, grammatical or 'aesthetic' meaning. The classical term *zāʾid* or *zāʾida* came to be used to denote only those items which were considered to be redundant and employed simply as "embellishment" (*zīnat*). This group consisted of archaic pre- and postpositions, verbal prefixes, which had been used in the earlier periods of Persian, but later became obsolete or had their meanings changed. But they were all preserved in the texts of classical literature which served as corpus for the lexicographers, and they had to be accounted for.

The other basic term *ʾaṣl* also changed its meaning. In Šams' prosody this term referred to an underived 'naked' base form, although there were exceptions. But in the subsequent lexicographic tradition *ʾaṣl* was used mostly in a non-technical way denoting the base form from which the other forms were to be deduced. In theory this form was the *maṣdar*, i. e. the infinitive, in most cases. The infinitive, in fact, is a derivative in Persian as in most Indo-European languages as opposed to the Arabic *maṣdar*, therefore the members of the paradigm were derived intuitively from the two simplest forms, the 3rd person sing. Past Tense and the imperative. This is one of the few theoretical problems ʾIravānī dealt with for the first time in his grammar in 1846:

"As the Arabs chose *maṣdar* as the source of derivation, it would be convenient to do the same in Persian [...] if someone has an objection to how a *maṣdar* can serve as a source of derivation having more letters, my reply is that scholars do not decide on the basis of the number of letters in judging the derivation [...] and there is no doubt that in all languages *maṣdar* is the best known" (8 v).

## 5. Summary

During the last millennium of New Persian investigated here, the grammar of Arabic was the model to be followed. The Arabic terms, in fact, were taken over selectively (e. g., there is no mention of the *ʾiʿrāb* in the sense of "declension") and with certain modifications. There was, however, a practical recognition, even if the relevant theory remained to be formulated, that the difference between Arabic and Persian was not restricted to surface differences between words and *ḥarfs*, but meant essential structural differences. Surprisingly, some basic rules of the Arabic model, e. g., the *ḥarf*-method, were never challenged and, as a consequence, this type of grammatical analysis came to a deadlock by the middle of the 19th century.

## 6. Bibliography

### 6.1. Primary sources

Ḥubayš Tiflīsī. *Qānūn-i adab.* 2 vols. Ed. by Ghulāmriḍā Ṭāhir. Teheran, 1972.

ʾIravānī, ʿAbd al-Karīm. *Qavāʿid-i fārsiyyat.* Tabriz (lithograph), 1846.

Muḥammad Ḥusayn Tabrīzī. *Burhān-i Qāṭiʿ.* Ed. by Muḥammad Muʿīn. Teheran: ʾAmīr Kabīr, 1963.

Šams-i Qays. *al-Muʿğam fī maʿāyīr ʾašʿār al-ʿağam.* Ed. by M. Qazwini & E. G. Browne. Leiden & London: Brill, 1909.

### 6.2. Secondary sources

Blois, François de. 1992. *Persian Literature: A Bio-bibliographical survey.* Begun by the late C. A. Storey. Vol. V, Part 1. London: The Royal Asiatic Society.

Elwell-Sutton, L. P. 1976. *The Persian Metres.* Cambridge: Cambridge Univ. Press.

—. 1986. "ʿArūż". *Encyclopaedia Iranica* ed. by Ehsan Yarshater, II, 670–679, London: Routledge & Kegan Paul.

Jeremiás, Éva M. 1993. "Tradition and Innovation in the Native Grammatical Literature of Persian". *Histoire Epistémologie Langage* 15: 2.51–68.

–. 1997. "*Zā'id* and *aṣl* in Early Persian Prosody". *Jerusalem Studies in Arabic and Islam* 21.167–186.

–. 1999. "Grammar and Linguistic Consciousness in Persian". *Proceedings of the Third European Conference of Iranian Studies, Held in Cambridge, 11th to 15th September 1995*, 19–31. Wiesbaden: Reichert.

Ḫānlarī, Parvīz Nāṭil. 1975. *Vazn-i šiʿr-i fārsī*. Teheran.

Meier, Fritz. 1981. "Aussprachefragen des älteren Neupersisch". *Oriens* 27–28.70–176.

Storey, C. A. 1984. *Persian Literature: A Bio-bibliographical survey*. Vol. III, Part I. Leiden: Brill.

Versteegh, Kees. 1977. *Greek Elements in Arabic Linguistic Thinking*. Leiden: Brill.

–. 1995. *The Explanation of Linguistic Causes: Az-Zağğāğī's theory of grammar.* Introduction, translation, commentary. Amsterdam: Benjamins.

*Éva M. Jeremiás, Budapest (Hungary)*

# 50. Arabic influence on Malay linguistics

1. Introduction
2. The knowledge of Arabic in the Malayo-Indonesian Archipelago
3. Arabic influence on Malay
4. Arabic influence on Malay linguistics
5. Bibliography

## 1. Introduction

As no comprehensive or systematic research has been done about this topic, the information given here should be regarded as preliminary. First some information will be given about the knowledge of Arabic in the Malay world, which consists of present-day Malaysia, Singapore, Brunei, Southern Thailand, and large parts of Indonesia; in the last country Malay is indeed the native language in some of the Western provinces, but nowadays a modern off-shoot of Malay, Bahasa Indonesia, is the national language, which is more and more gaining ground at the expense of regional languages, like Javanese, Sundanese, and Acehnese. For the sake of convenience, this entire region will be called the Malayo-Indonesian Archipelago. After this, I will deal with the influence of Arabic on the Malay language, before finally reaching the actual topic of this contribution: the Arabic influence on Malay linguistics.

## 2. The knowledge of Arabic in the Malayo-Indonesian Archipelago

Since the coming of Islam to this part of the world, assumedly at the end of the 13th century, the Arabic language, as the liturgical language of Islam, has been held in high esteem. In a traditional setting there were two different ways of studying Arabic. In the first place, there was the 'native' method in which the teacher, without any introduction to Arabic grammar, started to translate a simple Arabic work into Malay. The students, who wrote this translation between the lines, in this way learned to render the contents of an Arabic text, albeit without mastering the basic principles of Arabic grammar, like flection and syntax. The second method, called the 'Meccan' method, which was occasionally used in the Malayo-Indonesian Archipelago, started with progressive instruction in Arabic grammar. After mastering a booklet on spelling, the students were taught the most elementary grammatical terms in Arabic, followed by the rules of flection (*taṣrīf*). Having completed this, the student continued by studying entire sentences in an Arabic grammar. Only after all this had been accomplished did the study of Arabic grammar really begin, with the teacher using Malay to explain this grammar (Drewes 1971: 63–65). Many different Arabic grammars were in circulation in the Malayo-Indonesian Archipelago, and of these the most popular were the *'Alfiyya*, a didactic poem comprising some 1000 verses, written by Ibn Mālik aṭ-Ṭā'ī (d. 1274), and the *'Āğurrūmiyya* by Ibn 'Āğurrūm (d. 1323) (Drewes 1971: 68–69).

In present-day Indonesia the study of Arabic forms part of the curriculum of the traditional Islamic boarding schools, the *pesantren*, where in some places the old Arabic grammars like that of Ibn Mālik and the *'Āğurrūmiyya* are still in use. Arabic is also taught in several institutes for higher education (Meuleman 1994: 25–27). In other parts of the Malayo-Indonesian Archipelago knowledge of Arabic is also substantial, in particular among the Muslim scholars of the region.

## 3. Arabic influence on Malay

The influence of Arabic on the Malay language is considerable, but has not yet been studied very thoroughly. The most salient point is that the Malay language adopted the Arabic script. This script has been modified slightly to make it appropriate for the reproduction of the Malay language; this adapted form is called Jawi script. The oldest known use of Jawi script is the so-called Trengganu inscription, dating from the 14th century. At the beginning of the present century this script gradually fell into abeyance, although in some parts of Malaysia it is still in use (Meuleman 1994: 14–15).

Another clear proof of the influence of Arabic on Malay is the vocabulary. In a preliminary inventory of loanwords from Arabic made by the Indonesian Etymological Project in 1978, 2750 of these words from sources in Bahasa Indonesia and traditional Malay were listed. This list not only includes words related to Islam, but encompasses borrowings from several other fields, such as philosophy, botany, medicine, science, and even linguistics, like *huruf* "letter" (Arab. *ḥarf*), *jamak* "plural" (Arab. *ğamʿ*), *saraf* "inflection" (Arab. *ṣarf*) and *nahu* "grammar" (Arab. *naḥw*) (Jones 1978). So far, research into the transformations these loanwords underwent as they were absorbed into the Malay language has been minimal. This holds equally true for the related question of whether a certain word of Arabic origin came into Malay directly from Arabic, or indirectly, through the intermediary of other languages such as Persian (Campbell 1996).

At the syntactic level it is also possible to detect the influence of Arabic on Malay. This field of study tends to concentrate on what is sometimes called Kitab-Malay. This term has not yet been standardized, but is generally used to denote the language of those Malay Islamic texts that are based on an Arabic original, often taking the form of a literal translation. It is evident that this type of Malay is well-suited to study syntax, if the Arabic original is known. The study of Kitab-Malay is still in its infancy and only a few scholars have devoted separate publications to it.

A fundamental study in this field was written by the Dutchman Ph. S. van Ronkel (1870–1954) in 1899. In this publication van Ronkel reports on his research into the way in which all sorts of Arabic expressions had been rendered in Malay, presenting these findings systematically under the headings: verbs, cases, prepositions, and conjunctions. In his conclusion van Ronkel argues that many expressions in Malay are based on Arabic, as far as word order and thought (in Dutch *gedachte*) are concerned, and that this influence was due to the great familiarity of the Malay authors with translations of Arabic writings (van Ronkel 1899).

The pioneering article by van Ronkel received a follow-up in P. Riddell's (1990) study on the *Tarğumān al-mustafīd* by the 17th century scholar ʿAbd ar-Raʾūf as-Singkilī. This work is the oldest commentary preserved in Malay on the *Qurʾān* as a whole; it consists of a rendering of the *Qurʾān* into Malay, supplemented by clarifications on this translation, mainly derived from the Arabic *Tafsīr al-Ğalālayn* (Riddell 1990: 38–69). Riddell pays ample attention to the linguistic aspects of the Malay rendition. He compares in detail the Malay of part of the *Tarğumān al-mustafīd* with a body of 17th century Malay works from a comparable setting, thereby establishing widespread influence in word order as well as verbal and prepositional usage of Arabic in the Malay of the *Tarğumān al-mustafīd*, for instance in the increased frequency of verb-initial clauses (Riddell 1990: 70–113). Whether or not and, if answered in the affirmative, how these particular features of Kitab-Malay have entered classical and other forms of Malay is another issue which has barely been touched upon by scholars.

## 4. Arabic influence on Malay linguistics

Although the influence of Arabic on Malay is considerable, the Arabic influence on Malay linguistics is virtually non-existent. One important reason for this is that the tradition of Malay linguistics was set into motion by Western scholars. As a matter of course these Western scholars did not fall back on Arabic to describe and explain the linguistic phenomena they came across in Malay, but used instead the linguistic principles which they had become acquainted with during their own education. One author who seems to have had an open mind about the feasibility of using Arabic examples for Malay is the reverend Joh. Roman, who wrote one of the oldest publications on Malay grammar in 1653. In his introduction, Roman expressed his regret that he had not been able to write a better book because he could not find a well-educated Arabic informer with knowledge of Malay (Gonda 1936: 868). Unfortunately, we will never know what Roman wished to ask of this informant, and consequently what his grammar would have looked like, had he been able to find one, but Roman's remark shows at least an appreciation for the importance of Arabic for understanding Malay.

Another reason for the very limited influence of Arabic on Malay linguistics is that the Malays themselves seem to have had a rather low opinion about their own language. Many educated Malays were well-versed in Arabic grammar and thus would have been capable of writing about the Malay language in categories borrowed from Arabic grammar. However, the low esteem in which they held their native language prevented any such enterprise. Illustrative of this is an often quoted saying by the early 19th century Malay writer Abdullah Munshi, who is regarded as the first modern Malay writer. Abdullah claims that in writing the Malays preferred Arabic to Malay expressions, even when it was perfectly possible to express the same idea in pure Malay. Also the renowned Raja Ali Haji (ca. 1809–ca. 1872) from Riau (East Sumatra) mentions that many Malays who were able to write showed indifference (*kelelayan*) to and even disrespect for the Malay language (Raja Ali Haji 1310 [1892]: 10–11). It is understandable that in such an atmosphere Malay scholars were loath to squander their efforts in a systematic treatment of their own language. Actually, we see that until the end of the 19th century scholars from the Malayo-Indonesian Archipelago did not write about Malay grammar, but put their efforts into Arabic grammar. Examples of such scholars are Nawawi Bantan (d. 1897) (Drewes 1971: 69) and Daud Patani, who died in the middle of the 19th century (Matheson & Hooker 1988: 65–66). This was done, of course, to teach their Malay countrymen the language of Islam *par excellence*, Arabic.

From the period in which Malay became a systematic object of study, there is one fairly isolated example of an author who used Arabic grammatical terms to describe the Malay language. This author is Raja Ali Haji who has been referred to above. His works reveal that he had various Arabic grammars at his disposal, including the *'Āğurrūmiyya*, the *'Alfiyya* by Ibn Mālik, the *'Awāmil al-mi'a* by al-Ǧurǧānī (d. 1078), and commentaries on the *Kāfiya* by Ibn Ḥāgib (d. 1248). In 1851 Raja Ali Haji finished a Malay book, according to the conventions of the period using the Jawi script. This Malay book bears the Arabic title *Bustān al-kātibīn li-ṣ-ṣubyān al-muta'allimīn* "The garden of the writers meant for the boys who wish to study" and deals systematically with the Malay language. The introduction makes it plain that the book is intended for those who wish to write the Malay language correctly, both with regard to spelling and to syntax. Paragraphs 1–10 deal with the spelling of Malay. This was done with Arabic letters to which five new letters had been added, /c/, /g/, /ng/, /ny/ and /p/. Furthermore, the vowel signs are treated. These signs are called *'i'rāb*, and are simply equated with the /a/, /i/, /u/ sounds, thus using the term *'i'rāb* in a sense different to that in Arabic. Paragraphs 11–14 deal with word classes. According to Raja Ali Haji there are three type of words in Malay: *ism* "noun", *fi'l* "verb", and *ḥarf* "particle". These concepts are also subdivided according to the rules of Arabic grammar. For instance, *ism* is divided into *ism nakiratin* "indefinite noun" and *ism ma'rifatin* "definite noun", which in turn is again divided into 5 other types of *ism*. The concept of *fi'l* is subdivided into *fi'lun māḍin* "past", *fi'lun muḍāri'un* "non-past", and *fi'lu 'amrin* "imperative". Paragraphs 15–31 treat Malay syntax. In these sections a large number of Arabic grammatical terms are also treated and illustrated with Malay expressions, e. g. in section 19 the term *maf'ūl bihi* "object" is explained as "someone to whom something is done" (Malay: *yang diperbuat akan dia*) and, amongst other examples, is illustrated with the phrase *aku pukul akan si Zayd* "I beat Zayd". Later, Raja Ali Haji presented the same linguistic ideas in the introduction to his *Kitab Pengetahuan Bahasa*, which he started compiling in 1858. This work is an incomplete encyclopaedic dictionary, in which the author provides all kinds of opinions and data under the words he claims to define (Raja Ali Haji 1986–1987).

Unfortunately, it is not possible to determine which Arabic grammar Raja Ali Haji used as his model for the *Bustān al-kātibīn* and the *Kitab Pengetahuan Bahasa*: we know that he had several Arabic grammars at his disposal, which were rather similar as far as organization of the subject material and the borrowing of examples were concerned (e. g., by using the names *Zayd* and *ʿAmr* as subject and/or object); finally, Raja Ali Haji mentions that he omitted a great deal for the sake of brevity. It seems probable that he made use of his general knowledge of Arabic grammar.

The Indonesian linguist Harimurti Kridalaksana, who has made a critical evaluation of both works by Raja Ali Haji, has pointed out that in a number of cases the models followed are less than useful. For instance, the use of the concept of *ism ʾiḍāfa* is explained with the following examples: *budak Si Zayd* "the slave of Zayd", and *budakku* "my slave" and *budaknya* "his slave", in which *Si Zayd*, and the possessive pronouns *-ku* and *-nya* are termed the *ism ʾiḍāfa*. In this case the application of Arabic grammatical models is certainly not suitable for describing the linguistic phenomena in Malay. The same holds true for the division of the verb into *fiʿlun māḍin*, *fiʿlun muḍāriʿun* and *fiʿluʾamrin*, because in Malay the verb is not conjugated, while the tense can be indicated by a special marker (Harimurti 1991: 354–355).

On the whole the efforts made by Raja Ali Haji do not seem to have won many disciples in the field of Malay linguistics. The only example of which I know is a little book by the son of Abdullah Munshi, Muhammad Ibrahim Munshi, entitled *Pemimpin Johor* "The Guide to Johor [Malay]" (1878), which seems to have been influenced by the *Bustān al-kātibīn* (Basri 1981: 56). Perhaps, future research will come across other as yet unknown, indigenous Malay grammars which will reveal more influence of Arabic. Those indigenous authors who wrote in Malay about Malay grammar followed the tradition of Malay linguistics which had been set into motion by Western-educated scholars. An example of this is the influential Malay grammar by K. Sasrasoegonda entitled *Kitab jang menjatakan djalannja bahasa Melajoe* (published for the first time in 1910). This book leaned heavily on the 1889 grammar by the Dutch scholar D. Gerth van Wijk (Teeuw 1961: 23).

## 5. Bibliography


Basri, M. A. Fawzi Mohd. 1981. "Kitab Pemimpin Johor: Suatu Pengenalan". *Jurnal Persatuan Sejarah Malaysia* 10. 47–57.

Campbell, Stuart. 1996. "The Distribution of *-at* and *-ah* Endings in Malay Loanwords from Arabic". *Bijdragen tot de Taal-, Land- en Volkenkunde* 152: 1.23–44.

Drewes, G. W. J. 1971. "The Study of Arabic Grammar in Indonesia". *Acta Orientalia Neerlandica. Proceedings of the Congress of the Dutch Oriental Society, held in Leiden [...], 8th–9th May 1970* ed. by P. W. Pestman 61–70. Leiden: Brill.

Gonda, J. 1936. "Over oude grammatika's en ouds in de grammatika". *Indische Gids* 58: 2.865–878.

Harimurti Kridalaksana. 1991. "Bustanulkatibin dan Kitab Pengetahuan Bahasa: Sumbangan Raja Ali Haji dalam ilmu bahasa Melayu". *Masa lampau bahasa Indonesia: sebuah bunga rampai* ed. by Harimurti Kridalaksana, 349–361 (= *Seri ILDEP*, 43.) Yogyakarta: Kanisius.

Jones, Russel. 1978. *Arabic Loan-words in Indonesian: A checklist of words of Arabic and Persian origin in Bahasa Indonesia and Traditional Malay, in the Reformed Spellling.* London: SOAS.

Matheson, V. & M. B. Hooker. 1988. "Jawi Literature in Patani: The maintenance of an Islamic tradition". *Journal of the Malayan Branch of the Royal Asiatic Society* 60: 1.1–86.

Meuleman, Johan H. 1994. "Arabic in Indonesia". *Indian Journal of Applied Linguistics* 20.11–34.

Raja Ali Haji. 1310 [1892]. *Bustān al-kātibīn li-ṣ-ṣubyān al-mutaʿallimīn.* Singapore. [Dutch transl. by Ph. S. van Ronkel, "De Maleische schriftleer en spraakkunst getiteld Boestānoe'l kātibīna". *Tijdschrift voor Indische Taal-, Land- en Volkenkunde* 44 (1901) 512–581.]

–. 1986–1987. *Kitab Pengetahuan Bahasa: Kamus Logat Melayu Johor, Pahang, Riau dan Lingga.* Pekanbaru: Departemen Pendidikan dan Kebudayaan.

Riddell, Peter. 1990. *Transferring a Tradition; ʿAbd Al-Raʾūf Al-Singkilī's Rendering into Malay of the Jalālayn Commentary.* Berkeley: Centres for South and Southeast Asian Studies.

Ronkel, Ph. S. van. 1899. "Over de invloed der Arabische syntaxis op de Maleische". *Tijdschrift voor Indische Taal-, Land- en Volkenkunde* 41.498–528.

Teeuw, A. 1961. *A Critical Survey of Studies on Malay and Bahasa Indonesia.* The Hague: Nijhoff.



*Nico Kaptein, Leiden (The Netherlands)*

# X. The Establishment of Syriac Linguistics
# Die Anfänge der syrischen Sprachforschung
# La constitution de la linguistique syriaque

## 51. Foreign influence in the Syriac grammatical tradition


1. Introductory remark
2. Greek influence in Syriac grammar
3. Arabic influence on Syriac grammar
4. Bibliography


### 1. Introductory remark

Although Syriac linguistics underwent the influence of Greek linguistic studies throughout its history, the extent of this influence is clearly divided between two periods. During the first period (6th–10th century) no other culture could compete with this influence, whereas in the second period (11th–13th century) the Arabic grammatical tradition played a decisive role in the formulation of the linguistic principles of Syriac grammar. Other characteristics of the Syriac linguistic tradition are its preoccupation with two different domains of interest, namely pure grammar and masoretic studies, and the development of two distinct traditions, a Jacobite western and a Nestorian eastern tradition. Since the educational background of the Syriac grammarians included the basic principles of Aristotelian logic, the linguistic categories inherent in the Aristotelian system were familiar to them and these were occasionally introduced into their writings.

### 2. Greek influence in Syriac grammar

During the earliest period of Syriac grammar difficulties in reading correctly the basically consonantal Syriac script prompted students of the masora to attempt to create systems of diacritics in order to distinguish between homographs, as well as other notational devices – conventionally termed 'accents' – to indicate sentences, their partition and the identification of their different notional types (cf. Segal 1953). Manuscripts attest to these attempts already from the 5th century onwards. The earliest extant document by Thomas the Deacon, which lists and names thirteen accents is dated to the beginning of the 7th century. He relates this study to Aristotle's division of sentence types, with clear reference to the role of the accents in indicating the resulting senses of various sentence types. An early named grammarian is the Jacobite Aḥudemmeh (d. 575). A short passage of his teaching cited in a later treatise (cf. Merx 1889: 33) indicates the strong influence of Greek grammar in his classification of 'schemes' of participles.

The first known grammar of the 6th century is Huzaya's translation of Dionysios Thrax' *Tékhnē grammatikḗ* (Merx 1889: 9–28). It contains the section about the parts of speech of the original and a paradigm of the verb *túptō* "to hit". The following points deserve notice.

(a) Many of the terms used in his translation have not been taken over by later grammarians, such as the names of the nominal cases, the term *mṣa'yutā* (*mesótēs*) "middle voice of the verb", or the term *kpurā* for the negated element for which later grammarians use *marimānā*. Another example is his use of *mēmrā* "verb" (*rhē̃ma*), where all later grammarians use *melltā*.
(b) Other grammatical notions are indicated by slightly different names, e. g., his *mqadmut syāmā* (*próthesis*), which in later grammatical writings is *qdimut syāmā*.
(c) Many terms, however, have remained in use in later treatises, e. g., *adšā* (*eĩdos*), *eskimā* (*skhē̃ma*), *gensā* (*génos*) or the term *ḥšā* (*páthos*), which is used for the passive of verbal and nominal forms. Especially noteworthy are such cases as *kunāšāyā* (*epirrhḗmata athroíseōs dēlotiká*), which is used by Barhebraeus for "adjoining words" and which seems to be an imitation of the terminology in the translation of Dionysios Thrax's *Tékhnē*.

(d) As a rule, Huzaya presents Syriac calques for the Greek terminology, *ginsānaʾit* (*genikḕ ptõsis*) "genitive case" being one of the exceptions; such a modification of Greek terms might indicate the existence of a genuine Syriac tradition of language studies.

(e) An important modification in the Greek model is the presentation of the fourth part of speech, the article (*šritā* [*árthron*], which later grammarians render by *artron*). Since the Syriac language lacks this category (as well as the category of case), Huzaya emphasizes its inflectional behavior by introducing a series of prepositions consisting of one consonant, *B-D-L*, as representatives of the oblique cases dative, genitive and accusative, respectively. This interesting adaptation of an essential category of a foreign grammatical tradition continued to occupy the interest of later grammarians, who considered it a Syriac equivalent of the Greek and Arabic case systems.

Early Syriac translations (e. g. Proba, 6th century) and compendia of Aristotelian logic (e. g., Paulus Persa, second half of the 6th century) contributed to the development of Syriac grammar already in its formative stage by introducing linguistic terminology and concepts of the Peripatetic school. Some of the nine attributive categories are frequently used by grammarians, notably *lwāt medem* (*prós ti*) "relation" and *znā*, later *aynyūtā* (*poiótēs*) "quality". The notions of "speech" (*lógos*), "subject" (*tò hupokeímenon*) and "predicate" (derivatives of *katēgoreîn*) are commonly translated as *melltā*, *haw d-sim* and *qaṭreg*, respectively. In later grammatical works we find early logical terminology for sentence types, such as *qaṭapisā* (*kataphẽsai*) and the use of the eighth category *qanyutā* (*héxis, eĩdos poiótētos*) as an attribute of temporary character. The Aristotelian division of parts of speech into three typically distinguishes the logical tradition from the grammatical scheme, yet it is partly used in the Syriac grammatical literature.

Although only a few fragments survive of his writings on linguistic matters, Jacob of Edessa (d. 708) is unanimously acclaimed as the greatest Syriac grammarian. Since he was a Jacobite his teaching was followed by later scholars of this creed, but he was highly esteemed by the East Syriac grammarians as well. Of his main grammatical book, *Turaṣ mamllā nahrāyā* "Grammar of the Syriac Language", only a few exerpts survive, which contain parts of his nominal paradigms in morphology. We also possess an essay about vowels and accents, titled *On persons and tenses*, a translation of Aristotle's *Categoriae* and a few smaller writings which include incidental linguistic observations. Later scholars, notably Barhebraeus (d. 1286), contribute to our reconstruction of Jacob of Edessa's achievements by quotations from his teachings.

The extant evidence of Jacob's teaching in the field of phonology includes observations about the vowel system, a revolutionary attempt to introduce a new orthographical system of vowels written on the line and a classification of the features of consonants which explain certain phonetic shifts. Jacob's vowel system consisted of eight vowels. It is different from the five vowel system which was adopted by the Jacobites and which is wrongly attributed to him. In general it seems to correspond with most of Barhebraeus' observations about four groups of *A-E-I-U* vowel qualities. We are not sure if this system expresses the later well documented split of the western /o/ vs. the eastern /a/ value of the vowel called *zqāpā* (cf. Voigt 1997).

Notwithstanding the all too fragmentary character of Jacob of Edessa's extant phonetic teaching, it is significant that no traces are left to warrant the assumption that Jacob used any of the terminological systems known in the Syriac tradition for vowel names, nor that he was engaged in the study of the phonetic rules governing the pronunciation of the *bgd-kpt* group of consonants.

Within his morphological discussion Jacob incorporates the description of the syllabic structure of nouns and identifies three types of syllables, the simple CV, the compound CCV, and the doubly compound CCCV. Later grammarians neglected the use of the notion of 'syllable'.

In morphology, Jacob faithfully followed the Greek model of the canons, in the systematic organization of the noun types. In addition, some ideas about derivation are also recorded in his *Turaṣ*, again with a strong influence of Greek teaching, which manifests itself in his use of the dichotomy *prōtótupon – parágōgon* (*qaḏmāyā/ʿellṯā – trayyānā/ʿellṯānāyā*) to indicate the relation between 'primitive' and 'secondary' nouns. This notion is taken from Dionysios Thrax' *Tékhnē*.

A single passage in his short epistle on accents discloses a brief reflexion about parts of speech. In this passage nouns and verbs seem to be conceived as the main parts of speech, with one (*hadmā*) or more (*hadme*) additional parts completing the system.

In the domain of syntax we know through Barhebraeus that Jacob's scheme of sentence types comprised five types.

Jacob's importance as a linguist can be appreciated also by his contribution to the study of accents, which includes modification and closer definition of the system of accents, including the introduction of several new ones.

As noted above, several phonetic topics which are particularly prominent in Syriac grammatical literature are absent in the extant writings of Jacob of Edessa. To this we should add that there are no traces either of the study of the *atwātā bdulitā* (the *B-D-W-L* consonants) in the extant documentation of his teaching.

The total number of vestiges of Jacob's grammatical vocabulary amounts to some 60 terms.

Very few works have survived from the last part of this first era of Syriac grammar. The names of ʿAnānišoʿ (7th century) and David bar Paul (8th century) are mentioned. The former was a Nestorian who compiled a book on homographs, a typical masoretic study, which was later edited with annotations by Ḥunayn ibn ʾIsḥāq (d. 876), the famous scholar from Baghdad, who was an official translator at the caliphal court. David's short studies in phonetics and the functions of particles have also reached us. Ḥunayn's independent contributions are lost, but according to the reported titles of two such works he wrote a book on diacritical points and accents and interestingly, a book size comparison (*Kitāb ʾaḥkām al-ʾiʿrāb ʿalā maḏhab al-Yūnāniyyīn*; cf. Merx 1889: 105–106) of the Greek and Arabic systems of *ʾiʿrāb*, an Arabic term which describes the changeable case and mood endings of nouns and imperfect verbs in the Arabic grammatical tradition.

The fact that Syriac grammar developed in the two centuries before Islam makes it a likely candidate as a source of influence on the developing language studies among the Arabs. So far, however, the actual effect Syriac masora, grammar and philosophical studies exercised in the Arabic grammatical tradition is not clearly understood. Arabic grammar soon took an independent course, which was especially corroborated when Sībawayhi wrote his comprehensive book of grammar, *al-Kitāb* (for traces of Syriac influence in the field of phonetics, morphology and especially syntax → Art. 37).

## 3. Arabic influence on Syriac grammar

Both grammar and masoretic studies seem to have produced hardly any original thinking after the works of Jacob of Edessa and until Barhebraeus. Greek patterns of linguistic thinking continued to direct the orientation of all grammarians, mostly transmitted through the works of their predecessors, far less so from circulation of any original Greek or Byzantine writings. In this period the work of Arabic grammarians played an increasingly important role in the production of the later Syriac scholars, who were acquainted with their writings, admired the impressive precision with which they created comprehensive grammars, and imported topics, concepts, categories and terms from the Arabic grammatical tradition into their own field.

Masoretic studies maintained their traditional patterns and were not exposed to the influence of Arabic grammar, in part probably because no equivalent field of continuous masoretic interest developed in Islam along similar lines of orthoepy mixed with grammatical studies. The close study of Syriac vowels, developed in a masterly fashion by Barhebraeus along the lines of a long tradition, is after all part of the interest in the *puḥāme* (diacritic and vowel points) and is closely related to masoretic interest.

A study of some sixty terms listed in the terminological index in Moberg's edition of Barhebraeus' *Book of Rays* as calques together with their Arabic equivalents indicates that over forty terms occur in Barhebraeus's major grammar (see below) alone. Among the remaining twenty, *šalyutā* and *zoʿā*, rendering the Arabic *sukūn* "vowelless (consonant)" and *ḥaraka* "vowel" are considered to be the earliest loans.

It should be noted that several points of similarity with the Arabic equivalents may have an intricate history. Some terms may have been inspired by parallels in Jacob of Edessa's grammar: *ḥuššabā*, for instance, may represent Arabic *ḍamīr* "pronoun", but it could also be the equivalent of a Greek term, and so may *atwātā mettawspanitā* in relation to Arabic *ḥurūf az-zawāʾid* "letters added [to the 'basic' ones in word derivation]", even though Jacob used the same term in his *Turaṣ*.

Influence in the field of phonetics mainly concerned the Arabic distinction of various classes of consonants, whereas borrowing in the domain of morphology and syntax was more complex. The former involved terms of noun classification, noun derivation and other terms concerning the pronouns and particles, while the latter included sentence functions and sentence types.

Six grammarians have left writings in this field. Elias of Ṣoba (d. 1025) wrote his short *Toraṣ mamllā suryāyā*, which concentrates mainly on phonetic matters and includes our first record of the intricate conditions regulating the pronunciation of the *B-D-W-L* and *bgd-kpt* 'letters'.

Elias of Ṭirhān's (d. 1049) book with the same name is a short manual which probably served students with a background in Arabic grammar. In a catechetic style he attempts to prove the advantages of Syriac language and grammar over their Arabic equivalents, in a style which very much resembles the polemic work of his contemporary Jacob of Nisibis (cf. Samir 1991–92); nevertheless, his book is still a grammatical treatise. His emphasis on the role of the *B-D-L* letters as the Syriac analogue of the Arabic (and Greek) case marks is typical of the attempts made in this tradition to compete with the strongest points of the prestigious rival science.

Bar Zoʿbi, Severus bar Šakko (also known as Jacob of Tagrit) and Joseph Bar Malkon are Nestorians of the 12–13th century. The first is the most famous grammarian of his community. His work was hardly influenced by Arabic and had a strong hold in Greek grammar and rhetorics. Nothing is original in the work of the other two. Severus' *Memrā ʿal gramaṭiqitā* or *Ktabā da-dyalogo*, another catechetic manual, opens with a detailed description of the seven parts of speech and continues with the traditional stock of phonetic matters and the study of the accents, followed by a prosodic description.

Gregorius Barhebraeus (d. 1286) is the only Syriac scholar whose grammatical studies, expressed in his exegetical studies but mainly in his great grammar *Ktabā d-ṣemḥe* "Book of Rays [i. e., Sections]", constituted an original contribution to the discipline of Syriac grammar. His detailed book constitutes a comprehensive description of Syriac and is of the highest scholarly quality. It is distinct from the earlier treatises described so far, probably with the exception of that of Jacob of Edessa, in its systematic presentation of the grammatical facts and in its precise observations, which are greatly influenced by the accuracy of the terminology of the Arabic grammarians on the one hand and by his sensitivity to the Syriac idiom, on the other. This combination of Syriac tradition and Arabic grammatical categories created a synthesis between the two concepts of the parts of speech. The tripartite division is expressed in the main division of the book according to nouns, verbs, and particles, while the study of the traditional seven parts is maintained in accordance with the Syriac adoption of the Greek grammatical model.

## 4. Bibliography

### 4.1. Primary sources

Barhebraeus, *Buch der Strahlen: Die grössere Grammatik des Barhebräus.* Ed. by Axel Moberg. 2 vols. Leipzig: Harrassowitz, 1907, 1913.

Elias of Soba, *A Treatise on Syriac Grammar by Mār Eliā of Ṣobʰā.* Ed. and transl. by Richard James Horatio Gottheil. Leipzig, 1886.

Elias of Tirhan, Turaṣ Mamlelā Suryāyā oder *Syrische Grammatik des Mar Elias von Tirhan.* Ed. by Friedrich Baethgen. Leipzig, 1880.

Jacob of Edessa, *A Letter by Mār Jacob, Bishop of Edessa, on Syriac Orthography* [...]. Ed. by G. Phillips. London, 1869.

–. *Fragments of the* Turrāṣ mamllā nahrāyā *or Syriac Grammar of Jacob of Edessa* [...]. Ed. by William Wright. London, 1871.

### 4.2. Secondary sources

Baumstark, Anton. 1922. *Geschichte der syrischen Literatur mit Ausschluß der christlich-palästinenischen Texte.* Bonn: A. Marcus & E. Weber.

Contini, Ricardo. 1998. "Considerazioni interlinguistische sull' adattamento siriaco della ΤΕΧΝΗ ΓΡΑΜΜΑΤΙΚΗ di Dionisio Trace". *La diffusione dell' eredità classica nell' età tardoantica e medievale: Il 'Romanzo di Alessandro' ed altri scritti* ed. by R. B. Finazzi & A. Valvo, 95–111. Alexandria: Edizioni dell' Orso.

Duval, Rubens. 1907. *La littérature syriaque des origines jusqu'à la fin de cette littérature après la conquête par les Arabes au XIII siècle* [...]. Paris: Lecoffre. (Repr., Amsterdam: Philo Press, 1970.)

Hoffmann, G. 1873. *De Hermeneuticis apud Syros Aristotelicis.* Leipzig.

–. 1880. *Opuscula Nestoriana.* Kiel & Paris.

Land, Jan Pieter Nicolaas. 1875. *Anecdota Syriaca*, IV. Leiden: E. J. Brill. (Repr., Jerusalem: Raritas, 1971.)

Merx, Adalbertus. 1889. *Historia artis grammaticae apud Syros.* Leipzig. (Repr., Nendeln: Kraus, 1966.)

Samir, Khalil Samir. 1991–92. "Langue arabe, logique et théologie chez Elie de Nisibe". *Mélanges de l'Université Saint-Joseph* 52.229–367.

Segal, J. B. 1953. *The Diacritical Points and the accents in Syriac.* London.

Talmon, Rafael (forthcoming). "Jacob of Edessa the Grammarian". *Proceedings of the Seminar 'Jacob of Edessa (c. 640) and the Syriac Culture of his Day.* Leiden, April 1997.

Voigt, Rainer. 1997. "Das Vokalsystem des Syrischen nach Barhebraeus". *Oriens Christianus* 81.36–72.

*Rafael Talmon, Haifa (Israel)*

# 52. The role of linguistics in Syrian society

As was the case with many other linguistic traditions, the origin of the Syriac language sciences was inextricably linked with the preservation of their literary heritage, primarily the corpus of sacred texts represented by the Old and New Testaments, translated from Hebrew and Greek respectively. The translational nature of their Scriptures certainly sharpened the awareness of linguistic problems in the minds of learned Syrians of Late Antiquity, to a large extent bilingual in Aramaic and Greek. Not surprisingly, in a society whose educational system was for a long time shaped according to the classical ideal of *enkýklios paideía* (Watt 1993), the reflection of Syriac scholars on their own language, and on language generally, was subjected to the influence of Greek linguistic thought. This, exerted through the twofold channel of Aristotelian logic and Hellenistic school grammar, was however grafted on to a pre-existing indigenous tradition of orthoepic notations designed to ensure a correct 'oral performance' of the sacred texts in the liturgical usage (Segal 1953).

The only 'professional' linguistic scholars known from the sources in Syrian culture are two figures of teachers in the East Syrian School of Nisibis between the 5th and the 7th centuries, whose curriculum and teaching organization may be supposed to have been shared by most Syriac-language schools of Late Antiquity (cf. Vööbus 1965, especially 100ff. and 160ff.): the *maqrəyānā* "teacher of reading" was charged with imparting to his pupils philological, lexical, and particularly grammatical notions (besides liturgical recitation and chanting); the *məhaggəyānā*, possibly "teacher of spelling", probably taught reading at an elementary level, no mean task considering that the Syriac consonantal script was at the time still devoid of organic vocalization systems. He has also been conjectured by an eminent modern Syrian scholar to have illustrated the lexical differences between Syriac vernaculars and the literary language (Scher 1907: 399). Both *maqrəyānā* and *məhaggəyānā* were subordinated to the *məpaššəqānā* "interpreter", the professor of biblical exegesis, who was generally at the same time the head of the school: the relatively low rank of these instructors in linguistic subjects – which reflects the ancillarity of the language sciences to *philologia sacra* in Syriac culture – is confirmed also by the severe disciplinary measures to which they were liable, according to the statutes of the school, if they neglected their duties (Vööbus 1961: 83f.).

Not much is known about the established curriculum of grammar in the schools, but a 6th century *maqrəyānā* of the School of Nisibis, Yāwsep Huzāyā, is credited by the East Syrian tradition with the authorship of the Syriac adaptation – rather than simple translation – of Dionysius Thrax's *Tékhnē grammatikḗ*, the standard grammatical textbook of Byzantine schools (Robins 1993: 28, 41ff.), adjusted at about the same time also to the description of Armenian and later of Georgian (Versteegh 1990: 199f.; → Art. 64, 63).

Apart from the teaching of *maqrəyānē* and *məhaggəyānē*, however, an active interest in the language sciences was evinced, as a subsidiary but by no means insignificant part of their literary output, by several distinguished Syriac authors. The most original linguistic scholar in the Syriac tradition, the philhellenic Syrian Orthodox bishop Jacob of Edessa (d. 708), was actuated in his grammatical concern not only by his paramount preoccupation with biblical philology and exegesis, but also by the necessity of preserving literary Syriac in its time-honoured purity before the increasing diffusion of Arabic: to this end

Jacob composed the first complete grammar of the language (unfortunately preserved only in scanty fragments, edited by Merx 1889: 73*–84*), that cleverly adapted Greek linguistic notions to a phonological description of Syriac morphology (Revell 1972), and introduced a new set of vocalic signs, not intended as a general script reform, but rather as didactic aids to the correct pronunciation of words which were ambiguous in the consonantal writing.

Later native grammars of Syriac, both short teaching handbooks and massive treatises, were produced in an Arabic-speaking environment by bilingual authors for the use of adherents of the Syrian Churches, following two rival linguistic schools, viz. the traditional Greek-modelled Syriac approach introduced by Jacob of Edessa (e. g. the very popular handbook by the East Syrian metropolite Elias of Nisibis [d. 1046] and the vast compilation – still in its main part unpublished – by the early 13th century East Syrian monk John bar Zōʿbī), on the one hand, and the admirers of Arab linguistic science who endeavored to introduce its methods into the description of Syriac, on the other. Representatives of the latter were the first experiment by the 11th century East Syrian Elias of Ṭirhān and the more successful grammatical compendium *Kṯāḇā d-ṣemḥē* "Book of the rays" by the Syrian Orthodox polyhistor Barhebraeus (d. 1286) (cf. the outline of the history of Syriac indigenous grammar in Merx 1889 and → Art. 51).

No less than grammar, Syriac indigenous lexicography was conceived essentially as an aid to philology, that is, to the disambiguation of homographs or to the elucidation of rare terms, e. g. technical loanwords from Greek. The second need was evidently an offshoot of the intensive activity of translation from Greek into Syriac of a great variety of theological, philosophical and scientific writings from the 5th century onwards (excellent survey in Brock 1982). Accordingly, the prince of East Syrian translators, Ḥunayn ibn ʾIsḥāq (d. 873), who played a leading role in the celebrated *Bayt al-ḥikma* in Baghdad, where a prodigious number of Greek secular works were translated into Syriac on their way to Arabic under official Abbasid patronage, is considered to be the author of the first comprehensive Syriac dictionary, evolved from a previous compilation of glosses on Greek loanwords (Macomber 1974).

While orthoepic tradition and grammar appear closely linked to the schools, and therefore basically to sacred philology, Syriac lexical science seems to have been moreover partly dependent on the practice of lay professional translators, although lexical questions were also the object of another discipline of the Greek curriculum taught in Syrian institutions of learning, namely rhetoric, as can be seen in the lexicological section of the first book of the important treatise by the (probably) 9th century Syrian Orthodox monk Antony of Tagrīt (cf. Duval 1906: 484, awaiting the critical edition of Book I announced by P. E. Eskenasy and J. W. Watt).

A striking *unicum* in Syriac lexicography is the Syriac-Arabic dictionary *Kitāb at-tarǧumān* "Book of the translator" by Elias of Nisibis, whose lexical material is organized according to what modern linguistics would label 'semantic fields' (God, man, man's immediate environment, the animal world, etc.). Keen upholder though he was of Syriac traditional grammar against the newly introduced competing 'arabizing' school, the metropolite of Nisibis was ready to adopt an Arabic technical model (i. e. the specific onomasiological *genre* instanced in Arab lexicography by *al-Ġarīb al-muṣannaf* by ʾAbū ʿUbayd ibn Sallām [d. 838]) with the view of teaching literary Syriac to the Arabic-speaking Christians of Mesopotamia (Weninger 1994). Elias's linguistic ideology is well expressed in the linguistic section of his famous dialogic apology of Christianity, the *Maǧālis* "Sessions" with the Muslim vizir ʾAbū l-Qāsim al-Maġribī (who, however cultivated, was no grammarian). In the 6th *maǧlis*, which took place at Nisibis on July 27th, 1027, the East Syrian divine displays his expertise in Arabic grammar, as well as in Aristotelian logic (taught in the Syrian schools since the 6th century as a tool for the interpretation of biblical and patristic texts), in order to assert the superiority of Syriac over Arabic, against the prevalent Arab view, as regards morpho-syntax, lexicon, and even writing (Samir 1977: 5–76, 1995: 1–92).

This nationalistic attitude towards their literary language must have been shared by most Syrian intellectuals, witness the widespread belief in the status of Syriac as the primordial language of humanity (an idea apparently originated by the Syrian-born 5th century Greek Father Theodoret of Cyrrhus) which we find expressed not only in Syriac commentaries to the episod of the Tower of

Babel in *Genesis* 11, but also in chronographical and theological works (cf. the representative précis in Borst 1957: 258ff.), most frequently after the Islamic conquest of Syria and Mesopotamia had drastically reduced the domain of Syriac as well as the number of its speakers and writers.

The strong attachment to Classical Syriac as a symbol of cultural – when not declaredly national – identity on the part of Syrian Christian minorities in Islamic countries explains the concern with linguistic matters on the part of Syriac authors of almost every description. A rich repository of linguistic remarks, particularly of semantic and etymological import, which still needs to be scrutinized systematically, are the extensive Syrian Orthodox and East Syrian traditions of biblical exegesis (cf. lately Van Rompay 1995). Altogether, from a socio-cultural perspective, the situation of Syriac indigenous linguistic scholars between the 5th and the 13th centuries seems much more similar to that of grammarians in the theocratical society of Byzantium (described by Robins 1993: 1–39) than, for instance, to the pattern of professional activities of grammarians in the Arab tradition (illustrated by Versteegh 1989). Like their Byzantine counterparts, Syrian linguistic scholars were first and foremost teachers who conceived their activity as directed towards the preservation of their specific Christian Oriental cultural legacy: linguistic – particularly grammatical – study and teaching were a vital means of securing the survival of that inheritance and, as such, deemed to be worthy of the attention of prominent Syriac writers in different fields, mainly of course biblical scholars and theologians, and of high dignitaries of the Syrian Churches. Not unlike Michael Syncellus and Maximus Planudes, some of the leading native Syriac grammarians played a significant part in public life or Church affairs: e. g. the East Syrian Patriarch Elias of Ṭirhān, his coreligionist but adversary in grammatical theory Elias, metropolite of Nisibis, and the polymathic Syrian Orthodox maphryan of the East, Barhebraeus. In accordance with this socio-scientific context, a future Patriarch of the Maronites, Ǧirǧis ʿAmīra (d. 1644) was to produce, in his *Grammatica syriaca* (Rome 1596), the synthesis of native Syrian linguistic lore and Latin grammatical technique which triggered the scientific codification of Syriac in Renaissance Europe (Contini 1996: 493f.).

## Bibliography


Borst, Arno. 1957–1963. *Der Turmbau von Babel: Geschichte der Meinungen über Ursprung und Vielfalt der Sprachen und Völker.* 4 vols. Stuttgart: Hiersemann.

Brock, Sebastian P. 1982. "From Antagonism to Assimilation: Syriac attitudes to Greek learning". *East of Byzantium* ed. by Nina Garsoïan et al., 17–39. Washington, D. C.: Dumbarton Oaks Press.

Contini, Riccardo. 1996. "Gli inizi della linguistica siriaca nell'Europa rinascimentale". *Italia ed Europa nella linguistica del Rinascimento* ed. by Mirko Tavoni, II, 483–502. Modena: Panini.

Duval, Rubens. 1906. "Notice sur la Rhétorique d'Antoine de Tagrit". *Orientalische Studien Theodor Nöldeke* ed. by Carl Bezold, I, 479–486. Giessen: Töpelmann.

Macomber, William F. 1974. "The Literary Activity of Ḥunain b. Isḥaq in Syriac". *Ephrem-Ḥunayn Festival*, 545–575. Baghdad.

Merx, Adalbert. 1889. *Historia artis grammaticae apud Syros.* Leipzig.

Revell, E. John. 1972. "The Grammar of Jacob of Edessa and the other Near Eastern Grammatical Traditions". *Parole de l'Orient* 3.365–374.

Robins, Robert Henry. 1993. *The Byzantine Grammarians: Their place in history.* (= *Trends in Linguistics, Studies and Monographs*, 70.) Berlin & New York: Mouton de Gruyter.

Rompay, Lucas van. 1995. "La littérature exégétique syriaque et le rapprochement des traditions syrienne-orientale et syrienne-occidentale". *Parole de l'Orient* 20.221–235.

Samir, Khalil. 1975–76. "Deux cultures qui s'affrontent: Une controverse sur l'*iʿrāb* au XI. siècle entre Elie de Nisibe et le vizir Abū l-Qāsim". *Mélanges de l'Université Saint-Joseph* 49.619–649.

–. 1991–92. "Langue arabe, logique et théologie chez Élie de Nisibe". *Mélanges de l'Université Saint-Joseph* 52.229–367.

Scher, Addaï, ed. 1907. *Mar Barhadbšabba ʿArbaya, Cause de la fondation des écoles.* (= *Patrologia Orientalis*, vol. IV, 4.) Paris.

Segal, Judah B. 1953. *The Diacritical Point and the Accents in Syriac.* (= *London Oriental Series*, 2.) Oxford: Oxford Univ. Press.

Versteegh, Cornelis H. M. [= Kees]. 1989. "A Sociological View of the Arabic Grammatical Tradition: Grammarians and their professions". *Studia linguistica et orientalia memoriae Haim Blanc dedicata* ed. by Paul Wexler et al., 289–302. Wiesbaden: Harrassowitz.

–. 1990. "Borrowing and Influence: Greek grammar as a model". *Le langage dans l'antiquité* ed. by Pierre Swiggers & Alfons Wouters, 197–212. Leuven: Peeters.

Vööbus, Arthur. 1961. *The Statutes of the School of Nisibis.* Stockholm. ETSE.

—. 1965. *History of the School of Nisibis.* (= *Corpus Scriptorum Christianorum Orientalium*, 266.) Leuven: Peeters.

Watt, John W. 1993. "Grammar, Rhetoric, and the *enkyklios paideia* in Syriac". *Zeitschrift der deutschen morgenländischen Gesellschaft* 143.45–71.

Weninger, Stefan. 1994. "Das 'Übersetzungsbuch' des Elias von Nisibis (10./11. Jh.) im Zusammenhang der syrischen und arabischen Lexikographie". *The world in a list of words* ed. by Werner Hüllen, 55–66. Tübingen: Niemeyer.

*Riccardo Contini, Naples (Italy)*

# XI. The Establishment of Linguistics in Greece
# Die Anfänge der griechischen Sprachforschung
# La constitution de la linguistique en Grèce

## 53. Sprachbezogene Reflexionen im frühen Griechenland


1. (Früh)antike Sprachbetrachtung
2. Das frühgriechische Epos und die Lehrgedichte Hesiods
3. Die Vorsokratiker
4. Die Sophistik
5. Platon
6. Bibliographie


### 1. (Früh)antike Sprachbetrachtung

Wie bei zahlreichen anderen Bereichen westlicher Kultur und Geisteswelt liegen auch die Ursprünge der europäischen Sprachreflexion in Griechenland, genauer gesagt, in der griechischen Antike. Dank der guten Quellenlage lassen sich diese Ursprünge sogar erstaunlich weit zurückverfolgen, und zwar bis in die Zeit des 8. vorchristlichen Jhs., in dem mit der Verbreitung des (aus dem phönizischen Schriftsystem entwickelten) griechischen Alphabets allererst die Möglichkeit gegeben war, Gedanken schriftlich zu fixieren. Freilich muß man sich hierbei zugleich der Tatsache bewußt sein, daß der wirkliche Beginn der abendländischen Sprachreflexion selbst bei einem Rückgang auf diese frühesten Quellen noch nicht in den Blick kommt. Denn der mit der schriftlichen Fixierung einsetzenden Überlieferung geht notwendigerweise eine Phase bloß mündlich formulierter und tradierter Reflexion voraus. Und insofern repräsentieren auch die Quellen des 8. Jhs. v. Chr. nicht den Anfang griechischer Sprachreflexion, sondern einen Punkt, der bereits die Summe eines langwierigen Prozesses geistiger Auseinandersetzung mit sprachlichen Phänomenen darstellt.

Gegenstand dieses Kapitels ist jedoch nicht nur diese früheste greifbare Phase abendländischer Sprachreflexion, sondern der gesamte Zeitraum, der dem Werk des Aristoteles (384−322) vorausliegt (→ Art. 54). Dementsprechend ist hier auf eine Periode einzugehen, die etwa vier Jahrhunderte umfaßt und deren Bogen sich, um nur die wichtigsten literarischen und geistesgeschichtlichen Quellen dieser Zeit zu nennen, von den dem 8. Jh. angehörenden Epen des Homer über die Lehrgedichte Hesiods (um 700), die Schriften der Vorsokratiker (7.−5. Jh.) und der Sophisten (5./4. Jh.) bis zum Œuvre Platons spannt, der von 428/7 bis 349/8 lebte.

Diese vier Jahrhunderte bilden jedoch keine homogene Einheit. Die Sprachreflexion dieser Zeit ist zwar einerseits durch eine gewisse Kontinuität geprägt, und zwar insofern bestimmte Themen wie die Frage nach dem Verhältnis von Sprache, Denken und Wirklichkeit und die damit verbundene *phúsei-thései*-Problematik durchgängig behandelt werden, ja sogar im Mittelpunkt der Diskussion zu stehen scheinen. Neben dieser Kontinuität auf der Ebene der Problemgeschichte sind aber auch gravierende Diskontinuitäten zu verzeichnen, und diese betreffen dann in erster Linie die epistemologische Basis, auf deren Hintergrund die aufgeworfenen Probleme behandelt werden und in deren Konsequenz man zu unterschiedlichen Lösungen für dieselben Fragen kommt.

Die Brüche in den Denk- und Erklärungsmustern jener Zeit scheinen so offensichtlich, daß sie sowohl von der antiken Reflexion als auch von der späteren Historiographie immer wieder angesprochen wurden und zu einer weithin akzeptierten Phasendifferenzierung führten. So wird schon in der *Metaphysik* des Aristoteles, deren erstes Buch den frühesten umfangreicheren Abriß der abendländischen Philosophiegeschichte enthält, eine scharfe Trennungslinie zwischen der Vorsokratie und der vorausliegenden Phase der Dichtung gezogen, wobei Aristoteles die Vorsokratiker als erste 'echte' Philosophen den als "Philomythen" charakterisierten Dichtern gegenüberstellt (vgl. Aristoteles, *Met.* 982b7−

993a27, 1000a9–20). Heutzutage wird dieser Übergang in Anlehnung an Nestle (1941) gerne als Weg "vom Mythos zum Logos" beschrieben, doch dürfte auch diese Formulierung bereits ihre Vorläufer in der Antike haben, wo wohl erstmals Pindar (ca. 522–nach 446; 1. *Olymp.* Ode 28–29) das Begriffspaar 'Mythos' und 'Logos' verwendet hat, um damit den Gegensatz von nichtrationalen und rationalen Denkansätzen zu bezeichnen. Zudem setzt die Philosophiegeschichte bekanntlich auch die Vorsokratiker und die Sophisten – wenn auch aus verschiedenem Grund – von Sokrates bzw. Platon ab, womit eine weitere Phasendifferenzierung vorliegt und der von uns behandelte Zeitraum insgesamt wie folgt zergliedert wird, wobei freilich zu beachten ist, daß es bei den Phasen 2 und 3 zu einer chronologischen Überschneidung kommt, da verschiedene Sophisten nicht nur Zeitgenossen des Sokrates (470–399), sondern auch Platons (428/7–349/8) sind:

Phase 1 (8./7. Jh.):
Dichtung (Homer + Hesiod) Mythos

Phase 2 (7.–4. Jh.):
Vorsokratiker + Sophisten
} Logos
Phase 3 (5./4. Jh.):
Sokrates/Platon

Obwohl *opinio communis*, blieb diese Differenzierung und insbesondere die der Gegenüberstellung von Mythos und Logos zugrundeliegende Qualifikation der mythischen Dichtung als nichtrational nicht gänzlich unbestritten (vgl. z. B. Gatzemeier 1992: 12; Laspia 1996). Wir werden daher diesen Punkt im folgenden (cf. 2. u. 3.) noch eingehender zu diskutieren haben.

Mit dem Problem der Kontrastierung von mythischem und rationalem Denken ist auch schon die Frage angesprochen, welche Merkmale überhaupt für die Sprachreflexion des 8. bis 4. vorchristlichen Jhs. charakteristisch sind. Ohne dabei näher auf die historischen Bezüge zwischen damaliger und moderner Sprachbetrachtung eingehen zu wollen, scheint mir hier – sozusagen auf der Ebene der ahistorisch operierenden Forschungslogik Poppers (1935) – ein Vergleich der epistemologischen Prinzipien beider Arten von Sprachbetrachtung sehr erhellend. In einem einzigen Satz und daher notgedrungen stark verkürzend formuliert, könnte man die moderne Sprachwissenschaft, wie sie sich seit dem 19. Jh. etabliert hat, als 'rationale, systematische, theoriebasierte und methodenbewußte institutionalisierte Auseinandersetzung mit dem fokussierten Untersuchungsobjekt Sprache' definieren. Von diesen sechs Definitionsmomenten – der Rationalität, Systematizität, Theoriebezogenheit, Methodizität und Institutionalisierung der Sprachforschung sowie der Fokussierung ihres Untersuchungsgegenstands – entfällt das wissenschaftsorganisatorische Moment der Institutionalisierung für den hier behandelten Zeitraum der Antike schon von vornherein, da man von einer solchen Institutionalisierung sprachbezogener Forschung allenfalls von der Alexandrinischen Philologie an (3./2. Jh. v. Chr.) sprechen kann.

Aber nicht nur das formalorganisatorische Kriterium der Institutionalisierung ist hier nicht erfüllt, vielmehr sind auch im Bereich der materialen Definitionsmerkmale wesentliche Differenzen feststellbar. So gilt *erstens* generell für die von uns behandelten Quellen, daß Sprache hier noch nicht – wie etwa in der späteren Alexandrinischen Philologie oder in der Grammatikographie des Dionysios Thrax (ca. 160–90) und Apollonios Dyskolos (2. Jh. n. Chr.) – als eigenständiger Untersuchungsgegenstand erscheint. Zudem basiert die hier beobachtbare Reflexion auf Sprache keineswegs auf einem genuinen Interesse an der Sprache selbst, sondern erfüllt lediglich die subsidiäre Hilfsfunktion, zur Klärung von Fragen beizutragen, die einerseits die Erkenntnis der Welt und andererseits das menschliche Handeln betreffen.

*Zweitens* gelten auch die Kriterien der Rationalität, Systematizität, Methodizität und Theoriebezogenheit nicht in demselben Maß für unsere (früh)antiken Quellen wie für die Moderne. Inwieweit diese Kriterien für die Texte unseres Untersuchungszeitraums Geltung haben, ist freilich nicht immer leicht bestimmbar. Denn in diesem Fall haben wir es nicht mehr mit der einfachen Opposition von Erfüllung oder Nichterfüllung eines Kriteriums zu tun, sondern mit dem Faktum, daß sich unsere Texte sowohl von der modernen Sprachwissenschaft als auch voneinander weniger durch An- bzw. Abwesenheit eines dieser Definitionsmerkmale unterscheiden als durch den jeweiligen Grad, in dem sie diesen vier Kriterien Genüge tun. Hinzu kommt noch als weitere Schwierigkeit, daß die sprachbezogenen Ausführungen innerhalb ein und desselben Textes bisweilen in bezug auf ihre eigenen konzeptionellen Grundlagen unterschiedliche Reflexionsniveaus aufweisen und solche Texte daher nicht pauschal einem bestimmten Entwicklungsstand zuzuordnen sind. Wie sich im folgenden Paragraphen zeigen wird, ist in diesem letztgenannten Punkt wohl auch die Lösung für die vorhin erwähnte Kontroverse um die Einschätzung der frühantiken Dichtung als nichtrational zu suchen.

## 2. Das frühgriechische Epos und die Lehrgedichte Hesiods

Wenden wir uns nun den vorhin unterschiedenen einzelnen Phasen zu, so ist zunächst, wie in 1. schon angedeutet, zu beachten, daß die Auseinandersetzung mit sprachlichen Phänomenen keineswegs aus einem Interesse an der Sprache selbst entsteht. Sie hat sich unseren ältesten Zeugnissen, den Homerischen Epen *Ilias* und *Odyssee* sowie den rhapsodischen Werken Hesiods, zufolge vielmehr aus einer, wie man heute sagen würde, 'sprachphilosophischen' Problemstellung heraus entwickelt. Diese Problemstellung wird freilich bei Homer und Hesiod noch nicht theoretisch formuliert, doch läßt sie sich vor dem Hintergrund der späteren Diskussion zweifelsfrei aus den Homerischen und Hesiodeischen Betrachtungen über verschiedene Eigennamen aus der Götter- und Heroenwelt rekonstruieren. Zudem erlaubt der Vorgriff auf die spätere Diskussion zugleich, die Position, die Homer und Hesiod innerhalb dieser Problemstellung vertreten, präzise zu bestimmen und in eine Entwicklungslinie einzuordnen.

Am deutlichsten greifbar ist das Problem, um das es hier geht, in Platons *Kratylos*. Es wird dort als bereits länger etablierte Frage nach der "Richtigkeit der Namen" (ὀρθότης τῶν ὀνομάτων, Platon, *Krat.* 383a/384ab) vorgestellt und näherhin als Diskussion um den kontroversen Punkt beschrieben, ob ein sprachlicher Ausdruck, kurz: Name, "von Natur aus" (φύσει, 383a) richtig ist oder seine Richtigkeit auf "Vertrag und Übereinkunft" (συνθήκη καὶ ὁμολογία, 384d) respektive "Konvention" (νόμῳ καὶ ἔθει, ebd.) beruht (cf. 5.). Dahinter steht der Streit um die Gültigkeit der These, daß die Namen das Wesen der von ihnen denotierten Sachen und Personen widerspiegeln und somit das wahre Sein der Namenträger offenbaren (cf. z. B. 393d, 433d). Folgt man dieser These, dann könnte man, wie es in einem spätantiken Platonkommentar des Proklos (412–485) heißt, "durch die Namen zur Erkenntnis des Seienden" (διὰ τῶν ὀνομάτων ἐπὶ τὴν τῶν ὄντων γνῶσιν, Proklos, *Parmenides* 623,35–624,1) gelangen. Und genau dies ist der sprach- und erkenntnistheoretische Ansatz, der den eben erwähnten Betrachtungen über Eigennamen bei Homer und Hesiod zugrunde liegt.

Damit man das wahre Sein der Dinge aus ihren Benennungen erschließen kann, bedarf es freilich einer Interpretationsmethode, genauer, eines formanalytischen und semantischen Verfahrens, das es nicht nur erlaubt, Simplizia semantisch zu interpretieren, sondern auch komplexe Wörter in semantisch deutbare Komponenten zu zerlegen. Doch auch dieses methodologische Problem wird erst relativ spät explizit und systematisch reflektiert, denn wieder ist der Platonische *Kratylos* die älteste Quelle, in der solche ahistorisch operierenden Verfahren detailliert beschrieben und exemplarisch angewendet werden. Und noch später, nämlich erst in der Schule der älteren Stoa (3. Jh. v. Chr.), wird dann als Terminus technicus für diese wortanalytischen Interpretationsverfahren der Begriff "Etymologie" (ἐτυμολογία) geprägt, den ein Scholion zur Grammatik des Dionysios Thrax – im Gegensatz zu manchen modernen Autoren (z. B. Erbse 1970: 101; Wartburg 1977: 135; Schmitt 1977b: 1) – zutreffend als "Entflechtung der Wörter, durch die das Wahre offenkundig wird" (ἀνάπτυξις τῶν λέξεων, δι' ἧς τὸ ἀληθὲς σαφηνίζεται, *Scholia D. T.* 14–15), definiert und den wir näherungsweise mit "Lehre von den Benennungsmotiven" (Herbermann 1996: 358) wiedergeben können (zu den Differenzen zwischen antiker und moderner Etymologie sowie zu deren historischer Entwicklung vgl. etwa Leroy 1968; Herbermann 1981; Swiggers 1996).

Es bleibt somit festzuhalten, daß weder die sprach- und erkenntnistheoretischen Prämissen noch die Methode der Namendeutung bei Homer und Hesiod thematisch werden und beides nur aus ihrem Umgang mit der Sprache erschlossen werden kann. Daher ist Sprache hier nicht nur, wie eingangs dieses Paragraphen ausgeführt, kein fokussierter eigenständiger Gegenstand der Reflexion, vielmehr sind auch die in 1. genannten Kriterien der Methodizität und der Theoriebezogenheit der Auseinandersetzung mit sprachlichen Phänomenen lediglich insofern erfüllt, als bestimmte – weder begründete, noch auch nur explizit gemachte – Vorannahmen die Voraussetzung für die Homerische und Hesiodeische Namendeutung sind. Zudem werden nur verschiedene ausgewählte Eigennamen interpretiert, so daß von einer systematischen Vorgehensweise nicht die Rede sein kann. Diesen Status der Reflexion pflegen wir heute als 'vortheoretisch' und 'vorwissenschaftlich' zu bezeichnen. Nichtsdestotrotz werden diese Namendeutungen nicht nur bis hin zu Platon, sondern auch noch darüber hinaus immer wieder aufgegriffen und stellen damit auch unter rezeptionsgeschichtlichem Aspekt den entscheidenden Ausgangspunkt der abendländischen Sprachreflexion dar.

Wenden wir uns diesen Namendeutungen nun im einzelnen zu (cf. Kamptz 1982; Kraus 1987; Leclerc 1993; Liebermann 1971, 1996; Lingohr 1954; Mühlestein 1987; Peradotto 1990; Rank 1951; Risch 1947; Schmitter 1990), so stoßen wir auf zwei Klassen von Fällen, wobei die zweite Klasse noch einmal in verschiedene Subklassen zerfällt. Die *erste Klasse* wird repräsentiert von denjenigen Etymologien, in denen dem Benannten ein einziger Name zugeordnet ist und dieser Name so gedeutet wird, daß er das wahre Sein des Namenträgers zu erkennen gibt, indem er ein grundlegendes Merkmal dieses Namenträgers offenbart. Hierher gehören etwa die Hesiodeischen Explikationen des Namens der Kyklopen (sie werden Κύκλωπες genannt, weil sich ein kreisförmiges Auge [κυκλοτερὴς ὀφθαλμός] auf ihrer Stirn befindet; Hesiod, *Theogonie* 144–145), des mythischen Pferds Pegasus (es erhielt den Namen Πήγασος, weil es an den Quellen [πηγαί] des Okeanos geboren ist; ebd. 281ff.) oder auch der Pandora (Hephaistos gab ihr den Namen Πανδώρη, weil ihr alle [πάντες] Olympischen Götter eine Gabe (δῶρον] mitgegeben haben; Hesiod, *Erga* 80ff.).

Doch während hier das Wesen des Benannten in einem einzigen charakteristischen Punkt gebündelt wird, ist die *zweite Klasse* der Etymologien dadurch definiert, daß das Wesen des Benannten dort in divergierenden Erscheinungsformen in den Blick gerät. Statt einer Einszueins-Relation zwischen Namen und Benanntem, wie sie für die erste Gruppe der Etymologien gilt, ist dort eine Relation gegeben, bei der das 'wahre Sein' des Denotats durch verschiedene – in den Namen abgebildete – Merkmale repräsentiert wird und gleichsam eine sprecherbezogene Perspektivierung an die Stelle einer einheitlichen, für alle Sprecher gleichen Sehweise getreten ist. Dennoch wird auf dieser Ebene der Sprachreflexion nicht daran gezweifelt, daß auch die perspektivisch differierenden Namen ein Abbild des wahren Wesens des Benannten sind.

Die diese zweite Klasse kennzeichnende Perspektivität wird nun in verschiedenen Formen greifbar. Eine erste Form begegnet in dem Fall, wo der Name Odysseus im freien Assoziationsspiel sowohl mit dem Zorn des Zeus (ὠδύσαο, *Od.* 1, 62) als auch mit der für Odysseus charakteristischen Eigenschaft (cf. z. B. *Od.* 5, 160; 9, 13; 11, 214), über sein und seiner Familie Schicksal zu klagen (ὀδυρόμενος, *Od.* 1, 55), in Verbindung gebracht und so unter zweifachem Aspekt gedeutet wird. Wird hier der Aspektreichtum der Wirklichkeit von ein und demselben Namen umfaßt, so kommt die Perspektivität der Wesensbestimmung des Benannten in einer zweiten Form darin zum Ausdruck, daß dort demselben Denotat verschiedene Namen zugeordnet sind. Hierher gehören beispielsweise die Doppelbenennungen bei Homer, die zudem die interessante Besonderheit aufweisen, daß die mit ihnen verbundene Perspektivität auf gruppenspezifische Sehweisen (Götter vs. Menschen [z. B. *Ilias* 1, 402ff.: *Aigaion/Briareos*], aber auch verschiedene Gruppen innerhalb der Menschen selbst [z. B. *Ilias* 6, 402ff. u. 22, 506–507: *Skamandrios/Astyanax*; *Odyssee* 18, 5ff.: *Arnaios/Iros*]) zurückgeführt wird.

In Form einer Synopse dargestellt, lassen sich somit bei Homer und Hesiod folgende Typen von Benennungsrelationen unterscheiden (s. Abb. 53.1).

Die Methode dieser Etymologisierungen wird bei Homer und Hesiod zwar noch nicht thematisiert, doch können ihre Grundprinzipien leicht aus den Beispielen erschlossen werden. Danach handelt es sich um ein Verfahren, nach dem man (a) diejenigen Wortstrukturen, die für komplex erachtet werden, in kleinere Bestandteile zerlegt, wobei es darauf anzukommen scheint, Formstrukturen zu gewinnen, die entweder direkt einem im Griechischen vorhandenen Lexem oder Morphem entsprechen und daher semantisch interpretierbar sind oder doch zumindest aufgrund ihres Lautbestandes einem solchen Lexem bzw. Morphem ähnlich sehen. Die von vornherein gegebenen oder mittels Analyse gewonnenen 'einfachen' Strukturen werden dann (b), sofern sie nicht von sich aus dem lexematischen und morphologischen Inventar des Griechischen entsprechen, lautlich derart uminterpretiert, daß sie daran anschließbar erscheinen.

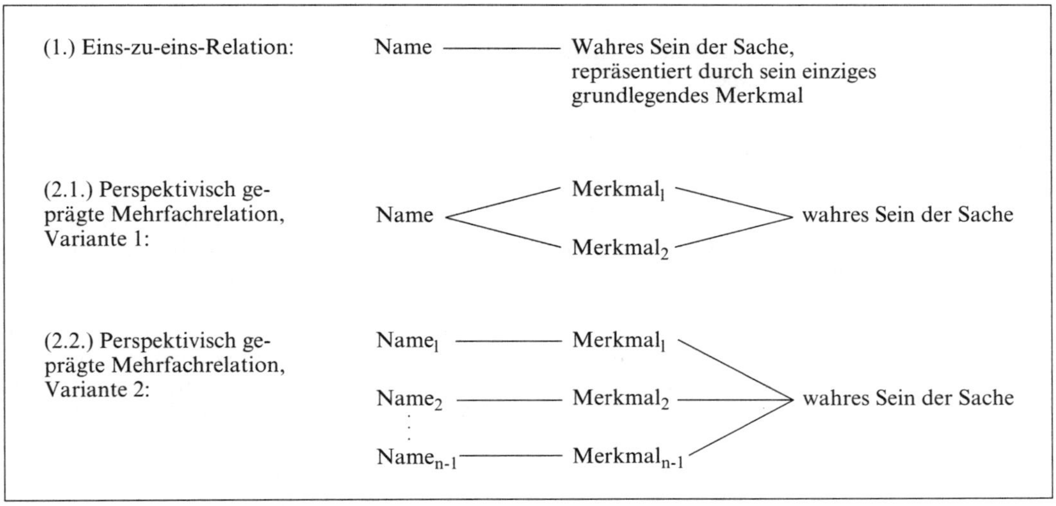


Abb. 53.1: Benennungsrelationen bei Homer und Hesiod.

Ist diese Methode, die übrigens in ihrem Kern für die gesamte antike Etymologie gilt (cf. Herbermann 1996), auch im einzelnen anfechtbar, so setzt ihre Anwendung doch bestimmte grundlegende rationale Reflexionen über die morphologische Struktur des Griechischen voraus. Den eingehenden Untersuchungen von Laspia (1996) zufolge lassen sich derartige rationale Reflexionen über Sprache ebenfalls für den Bereich der Phonation und Audition erschließen. Denn wie die in *Ilias*, *Odyssee* und den Homerischen *Hymnen* beobachtbare systematische Verwendung bestimmter nominaler, verbaler und adjektivischer Ausdrücke für den Bereich 'Laut, Stimme und Sprache' (φθόγγος/φθέγγομαι, φωνή/φωνέω, αὐδή/αὐδήεις/αὐδάω, *ὄψ etc.) nahelegt, liegen Homers Sprachgebrauch verschiedene konzeptionelle Differenzierungen (etwa in bezug auf biologisch-physiologische, artikulatorische und semantische Aspekte der Äußerung von Lauten durch Mensch und Tier) zugrunde, die dann in der späteren griechischen Medizin (Hippokrates; cf. Laspia 1996: 710) und bei Aristoteles (cf. Ax 1978, 1986; Sinnott 1989) explizit erörtert werden.

Infolgedessen muß auf der einen Seite festgehalten werden, daß das frühgriechische Epos und die Lehrgedichte Hesiods durchaus verschiedene Elemente einer Sprachreflexion widerspiegeln, die als 'rational' bezeichnet werden kann und somit dem Kriterium der Rationalität partiell genüge tut. Auf der anderen Seite basieren die Homerischen und Hesiodeischen Namendeutungen jedoch auf einem mythischen Denkmodell. Gegenüber der Frühform des mythischen Denkens, für die – entsprechend der vorphilosophischen "Situationsbefangenheit" (Hülser 1997: 848) menschlicher Welterfahrung – die Vorstellung einer noch ungeschiedenen Einheit von real gegebener, konzeptualisierter und bezeichneter Wirklichkeit gilt (cf. u. a. Calogero 1967; Coseriu 1975: 27–28; Di Cesare 1980: 9–10; Schmitter 1990: 12–13), stellen die verschiedenen Positionen Homers und Hesiods (vgl. Abb. 53.1.) zwar einen Fortschritt im Hinblick auf eine zunehmende Differenzierung dar. Denn erkennendes und benennendes Subjekt sind dort bereits generell vom benannten Objekt unterschieden. Doch selbst wenn wir mit der Perspektivität der Namen, die im raffinierteren Modell der Mehrfachrelationen zwischen Name(n) und Benanntem greifbar wurde (vgl. Abb. 53.1., Punkt 2), auf eine gewisse subjektive Komponente der Nomination gestoßen sind, bleibt das Denkmodell Homers und Hesiods im Prinzip der mythischen Vorstellung verhaftet. Und zwar erstens, weil auch auf dieser avancierten Stufe, wo verschiedene sprecherspezifische Weisen des Benennens unterschieden werden, noch nicht zwischen der gedanklichen Vorstellung von einer Sache und deren sprachlicher Benennung differenziert wird. Und zweitens, weil hier ungeachtet der entdeckten Perspektivität einzelner Nominationen von der vorrationalen Ansicht ausgegangen wird, daß der (noch undifferenzierte) Komplex Vorstellung/Benennung ein unmittelbar von der Sache selbst hervorgerufenes Abbild eben dieser Sache ist und der Grund für die 'Richtigkeit der Namen' folglich in der benannten Sache selber liegt und nicht in der Erkenntnis- und Benennungsleistung des erkennenden und benennenden Subjekts (vgl. auch Kraus 1990: 263). Wollte man diese Position im Vorgriff auf die Terminologie der späteren *phúsei-thései*-Diskussion (cf. dazu insbes. Coseriu 1996) als *phúsei*-Position bezeichnen, dann wäre hier unter *phúsei* zu verstehen, daß die Namen insofern 'von Natur aus' sind, als sie (a) von den benannten Sachen her determiniert und (b) ein wahres Abbild dieser Sachen sind.

Schematisch ließe sich die bisherige Entwicklung etwa wie folgt darstellen:

(φύσις τῶν ὄντων, Arist. *Met.* 982b7ff.) dann auch, wie eingangs schon erwähnt, die abendländische Philosophie beginnt und eine neue Stufe der Reflexion erreicht wird.

## 3. Die Vorsokratiker

Auch die Sprachbetrachtungen der Vorsokratiker stehen in einem erkenntnistheoretischen Kontext. Nur hat sich jetzt, Hand in Hand mit tiefgreifenden ökonomischen Veränderungen (Übergang vom Grundbesitz zur Handelswirtschaft), die Vorstellung von dem, was Wissen ist und wie man zu gesicherter Erkenntnis kommt, gewandelt, und infolgedessen wird auch die Rolle, die der Sprache bzw. den Benennungen im Erkenntnisprozeß

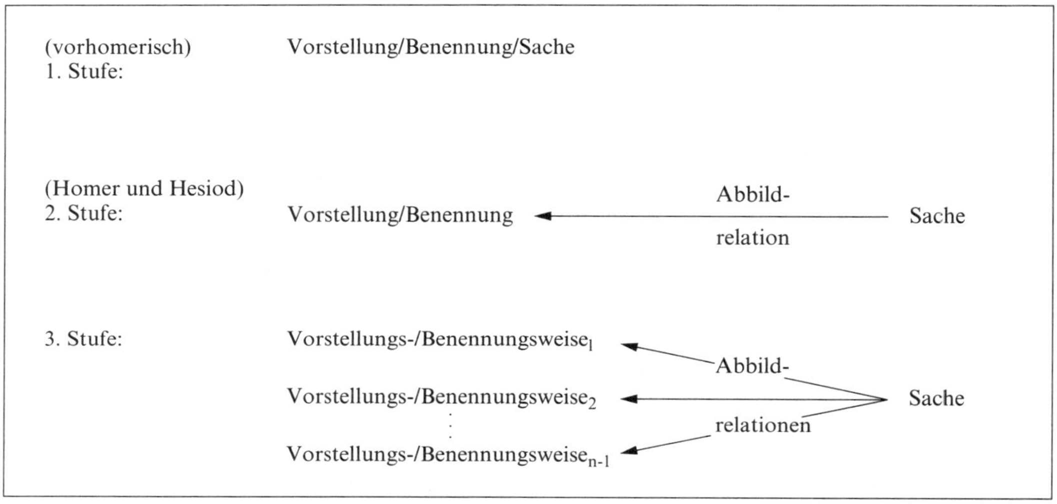


Abb. 53.2: Fortschreitende Differenzierung des Erkenntnisaktes im Rahmen 'mythischer' Sprachreflexion.

In Anbetracht dieses Befunds erscheint nur eine differenzierte Antwort auf die in 1. aufgeworfene Frage nach der Zuordnung der Homerischen und Hesiodeischen Sprachreflexion zu Mythos oder Logos angemessen: Der eher technische Bereich der 'Sprachanalyse' ist stark von *rationalen* Überlegungen bestimmt, während das 'sprachphilosophische' Denkmodell Homers und Hesiods noch weitgehend auf *mythischen* Annahmen basiert. Mit dem Konzept der Perspektivität gerät jedoch das erkennende und benennende Subjekt stärker in den Blick. Und damit scheint bereits der Keim für die weitere Destruktion des mythischen Modells gelegt, wie sie dann einige Zeit später von den Vorsokratikern betrieben wird, mit deren neuartiger Antwort auf die Frage nach dem Wesen allen Seins

zugebilligt wird, anders defniert. Wie diese Rolle im einzelnen bestimmt wird, hängt freilich von den spezifischen epistemologischen Positionen des jeweiligen Autors ab. Gemeinsam ist den Vorsokratikern jedoch zunächst einmal der durch die Zunahme empirischer Kenntnisse bedingte neue Wissensbegriff, der von den ionischen Naturphilosophen Thales (geb. um 625 v. Chr.), Anaximander (geb. um 610) und Anaximenes (geb. um 585) grundgelegt wird. Im Gegensatz zur mythisch-religiösen Weltdeutung Homers und Hesiods, die Entstehung, Entwicklung und Ordnung des Kosmos als Geschichte des Werdens personaler Götter und als Produkt der schaffenden und ordnenden Tätigkeit dieser göttlichen Wesen begreift, wird der Kosmos nunmehr als ein *Naturphänomen* aufgefaßt, dessen Entwicklung und Ordnung der personalen Götter nicht bedarf, weil beides auf einem natürlichen Prozeß beruht, der *aus sich selbst* heraus erklärbar ist, "*autonom fortschreitet* und sich *gesetzmäßig* vollzieht" (Mansfeld 1987: 16; zur ionischen Naturphilosophie im einzelnen Röd 1976; Kirk, Raven & Schofield 1983; Guthrie 1988). Damit tritt an die Stelle einer als 'Wissen' aufgefaßten *mythologischen* Interpretation der Welt ein rationales, d. h. vernunftbasiertes, *theoretisches* Wissen, das einerseits auf Spekulation und andererseits auf Empirie basiert. Wie Krings & Baumgartner (1972: 643) mit Recht bemerken, setzt sich dieser neue Ansatz aber nicht nur von der mythischen "Erzählung eines Uranfanges" ab, sondern auch von der Annahme eines "unmittelbaren Erkennen[s] der Dinge oder Geschehnisse", wie sie den oben diskutierten Benennungsmodellen des Homer und Hesiod zugrunde liegt, in denen Erkenntnis als ein passiv-rezeptiver Vorgang angesehen wird. Demgegenüber wird Erkennen jetzt als aktive Leistung des um Erkenntnis ringenden Subjekts gesehen, wie es dann auch explizit bei Xenophanes (ca. 570–ca. 475) zum Ausdruck kommt, wenn dieser in polemischer Wendung gegen die traditionelle These, die Götter hätten den Menschen das Wissen gebracht, schreibt: "Keineswegs haben die Götter [...] alles den Sterblichen aufgezeigt, vielmehr finden sie mit der Zeit suchend (ζητοῦντες) Besseres vor" (*DK* 21 B 18).

Mit diesem neuen Wissens- und Erkenntnisbegriff ist nun nicht nur die entscheidende Differenz benannt, die die in 1. beschriebene Trennung des frühgriechischen Epos von der Vorsokratie gerechtfertigt erscheinen läßt, vielmehr gewinnen vor dem Hintergrund dieser neuen Wissenskonzeption und der mit ihr aufgeworfenen Fragen auch erst die relativ wenigen sprachbezogenen Fragmente an Kontur, die aus der Zeit der Vorsokratie überliefert sind und isoliert kaum deutbar wären. Dann wird nämlich deutlich, daß es gerade dieser neue Wissensbegriff ist, der zur Kritik an der traditionellen, aber erst später so benannten *phúsei*-These führt, und zwar einer Kritik, die von punktuellen Korrekturen bis zu tiefgreifenden Modifikationen dieser These reicht oder aber sogar nach sich zieht, daß die *phúsei*-These in gewissem Sinne gänzlich aufgegeben wird.

Als Beispiel für eine punktuelle Kritik an der These der naturgegebenen Richtigkeit der Namen kann erneut Xenophanes herangezogen werden. Denn in dem einzigen sprachbezogenen Fragment, das von ihm überliefert ist, weist er die herkömmliche Nomination des Regenbogens als "Iris" und die damit verbundene mythische Deutung dieses Phänomens als Erscheinung der Götterbotin zurück, weil dieses Phänomen "seiner Natur nach" eine "Wolke" sei (*DK* 21 B 32). Zu einer prinzipiellen kritischen Auseinandersetzung mit der *phúsei*-These führt der Widerspruch zwischen den Erkenntnissen des rationalen Denkens und den in den sprachlichen Bezeichnungen greifbaren Auffassungen von den Dingen aber erst bei Heraklit (ca. 550/530–ca. 480) und bei Parmenides (ca. 515–ca. 445), die das Verhältnis von Name und Benanntem systematisch reflektieren und im Falle des Parmenides auch diskursiv zur Sprache bringen (nicht überzeugend ist hier Coseriu [1996: 883], der die Behandlung dieser Problematik bei Parmenides und Heraklit für nicht gegeben hält).

### 3.1. Heraklit und Parmenides

Für beide Philosophen ist zunächst charakteristisch, daß sie die methodologischen Fragen, die der Theoriebildung der Milesier zugrunde lagen, aber von diesen noch nicht explizit erörtert worden sind, direkt thematisieren und dabei zu dem Ergebnis kommen, daß nur das reine Denken, nicht aber die Empirie zu verläßlicher Erkenntnis führt. Dabei wird die Empirie jedoch als Erkenntnismittel nicht restlos verworfen. Ihr wird vielmehr nur eine begrenzte Leistungsfähigkeit zuerkannt, und zwar deshalb, weil sie der Ansicht Heraklits und Parmenides' zufolge bei dem unmittelbar wahrnehmbaren Erscheinungsbild der Dinge stehen bleibt und so das hinter den Erscheinungen "verborgene Wesen der Dinge" (cf. Heraklit, *DK* 22 B 123: φύσις κρύπτεσθαι φιλεῖ) nicht erkennt. Während die Empirie somit nur zu einer unzuverlässigen Doxa führt, vermag das spekulative Denken die vor Augen liegenden Erscheinungen zu transzendieren und die wahre Ordnung der Welt zu entdecken. Dementsprechend setzen beide Autoren zwei Ebenen des Denkens an, eine 'doxastische' (z. B. Heraklit, *DK* 22 B 17, 70; Parmenides, *DK* 28 B 1.30, 8.51, 19), die dem Augenscheinlichen verhaftet bleibt, und eine 'noetische' (Heraklit, *DK* 22 B 40, 104, 114; Parmenides, *DK* 28 B 6, 8.36 u. ö.; cf. Fritz 1968: 292–315; Kraus 1987: 74–77), die diese Begrenztheit überwindet. Hintergrund für diese methodologischen Erörterungen ist die damals heftig diskutierte Frage, ob sich die Welt, wie es den Sinnen scheint, im Zustand stetiger Veränderung befindet und den Dingen infolgedessen kein festes, unveränderliches 'Sein' zugesprochen werden kann, was dann letztlich zum Agnostizismus führt, oder ob der wahrgenommene Wandel im Grunde eine Täuschung ist und den Dingen in Wirklichkeit doch ein bestimmtes 'Sein' zukommt, so daß die Dinge trotz ihrer offenkundigen Veränderung erkennbar sind.

Doch welche Rolle ordnen Parmenides und Heraklit der Sprache bzw. den Benennungen in Rahmen ihrer epistemologischen Ansätze zu? Kurz zusammengefaßt (ausführlicher Schmitter 1984, 1987b, 1990, 1996b: 68–75; cf. insbes. auch Di Cesare 1980, 1986; Gatzemeier 1992; Heitsch 1974, 1979; Held 1980; Jantzen 1976; Karakulakow 1970; Kélessidou 1986; Kraus 1987; Liebermann 1971; Rehn 1986; Sluiter 1997), folgende: Wenn man Heraklit nicht, wie das häufiger geschieht, von den spätantiken Scholiasten Proklos und Ammonios sowie den Aussagen des Platonischen *Kratylos* über die Herakliteer her interpretiert, sondern von den Heraklitischen Fragmenten selber ausgeht und dabei zugleich in Rechnung stellt, daß nach Heraklit das wahre Sein der Dinge nicht deren jeweilige gegensätzliche Erscheinung als 'Tag' oder 'Nacht', 'Krieg' oder 'Frieden' (DK 22 B 67) usw. ist, sondern im Zusammenfall der Gegensätze – in der *concordia discors* oder *coincidentia oppositorum*, wie man auch sagt – beruht (cf. u. a. Di Cesare 1980: 15ff.; Pleger 1987), dann sind die 'Namen' für die Dinge zumeist irreführend. Denn in der Regel erfassen sie, wie aus den Fragmenten *DK* 22 B 23 (Dike-Fragment), 32 (Zeus-Fragment) und 67 (Tag/Nacht-Fragment) erschlossen werden kann, nur *eine* Seite der dialektischen Einheit der Gegensätze und gehören damit der Ebene des bloßen Wahrnehmungswissens, d. h. der Doxa, an (cf. Schmitter 1987b, 1996b: 70ff.). Lediglich in einem Ausnahmefall, wie ihn das vieldiskutierte Bogen-Fragment (*DK* 22 B 48) vor Augen führt, in dem das griechische βιος einerseits als "Bogenwaffe" (*biós*) und damit als Tod und andererseits als "Leben" (*bíos*) gedeutet wird, weist ein Name für den, der ihn in diesem Doppelsinn zu verstehen weiß, auf den Zusammenfall der polaren Gegensätze hin, den das noetische Denken als Grundprinzip des Seins erkannt hat. Nimmt man diese vier Zeugnisse – und dies sind die einzigen Stellen, an denen Heraklit die Relation von Name und Benanntem explizit thematisiert – zusammen, dann hat sich die Sprache auf der Ebene der Benennungen als unzuverlässiger Indikator für die Grundordnung des Kosmos und damit für das wahre Sein erwiesen, weshalb sie nur in einem *stark modifizierten* Sinn als 'richtig' im Sinne der *phúsei*-These gelten kann (zur abweichenden Rekonstruktion von Di Cesare 1986: 9 und Kraus 1987: 108–109, die für Heraklit eine ungebrochene *phúsei*-Konzeption ansetzen; vgl. Schmitter 1996b: 72 mit Anm. 55).

Die gegenüber Homer und Hesiod vorliegende Modifikation betrifft aber nicht nur den Umstand, daß die Nominationen lediglich in dem eben beschriebenen restriktiven Sinn als zutreffend betrachtet werden können, sondern auch die folgenden drei Punkte, die den Heraklitischen Namendeutungen als Voraussetzung zugrunde liegen, teilweise aber auch explizit in den erkenntnistheoretischen Fragmenten angesprochen sind. Nämlich erstens, daß in bezug auf die Dinge selbst zwischen deren wahrem Sein und ihrem Erscheinungsbild zu unterscheiden ist; zweitens die Benennungen kein unmittelbar von der Sache selbst hervorgerufenes Abbild der benannten Sachen sind, sondern die Erkenntnisleistung des erkennenden Subjekts repräsentieren; und drittens zwischen konzeptueller Vorstellung von einer Sache und deren sprachlicher Benennung – und innerhalb der Vorstellung wiederum zwischen einer Vorstellung, die auf reinem Denken, und einer, die auf bloßer Wahrnehmung beruht – zu differenzieren ist, womit dann nicht nur die noch ungeschiedene mythische Einheit von Vorstellung und Benennung aufgelöst ist, sondern auch noch eine Binnendifferenzierung innerhalb der Größe 'Vorstellung' vorgenommen worden ist. Letzteres ergibt sich notwendig daraus, daß die Nominationen kritisch reflektiert und ihre Bedeutung mit dem doxastischen und dem noetischen Wissen, das man von einer Sache hat, verglichen wird.

Während die drei letztgenannten Punkte für Parmenides genauso gelten wie für Heraklit, divergieren die Theorien dieser beiden Philosophen in bezug auf die Beurteilung der Sprache insofern, als Parmenides im Gegensatz zu Heraklit nicht von einem Gesamtkomplex von Benennungen ausgeht, dessen einzelne Elemente dann Ausdruck unterschiedlicher Erkenntnisleistung sind, sondern strikt zwischen doxastischem "Benennen" (ὀνομάζειν) und noetischem "Sprechen" (λέγειν, φάσθαι, φράζειν etc.) unterscheidet (cf. auch Di Cesare 1986: 31–32). Dem noetischen Denken entspricht das noetische Sprechen, dem doxastischen das doxastische Benennen (cf. Parmenides, *DK* 28 B 6.1, 7, 8.7ff., 8.16ff., 8.38ff., 8.53ff.). Grundlage dieser Aufspaltung ist die explizit formulierte These, daß es zwei Wege der Erkenntnis gibt, einen verläßlichen, der zu "überzeugender Wahrheit" führt, und einen trügerischen, auf dem nur "Meinungen" gewonnen werden können, die "keine wahre Verläßlichkeit besitzen" (28 B 1.29–30). Der erstgenannte Weg führt zur Erkenntnis der Grundordnung des Kosmos, die nach Parmenides in einem ewigen und unveränderlichen Sein besteht und der entsprechend auch nur die Ausdrükke "es ist" (ἔστι) und "das Seiende" (τὸ ἐόν) ausgesagt werden können. Alle sonstigen Aussagen wie "es ist nicht" oder die Nominationen, die eine Veränderung oder Bewegung, ja überhaupt irgendein bestimmtes Sosein zum Ausdruck bringen, sind dagegen aus noetischer Sicht falsch. 'Werden', 'Vergehen', 'Sein', 'Nichtsein' usw. sind, wie es bei Parmenides (*DK* 28 B 8.38ff.) heißt, "so benannt, wie die Sterblichen es angesetzt haben", und zwar im irrigen "Vertrauen darauf, daß an der gerade zitierten Stelle *DK* 28 B 8.39 – ebenso wie B 19.3 – erstmals eine begriffliche Fixierung der Gegenposition zur *phúsei*-Auffassung erscheint und diese mittels der Qualifikation des 'Benennens' als eines bloßen 'Setzens' (κατέθεντο "sie haben angesetzt") formuliert wird. Möglicherweise hat hier der später verwendete Terminus θέσει (erst für die nacharistotelische Zeit sicher belegt) seinen letztlichen Ausgangspunkt. Darüber hinaus wird in *DK* B 19.3: τοῖς δ' ὄνομ' ἄνθρωποι κατέθεντ' ἐπίσημον ἑκάστῳ "Für diese Dinge aber haben die Menschen einen Namen angesetzt, für jedes einen kennzeichnenden" die Relation zwischen Name und Benanntem als Kennzeichnung bestimmt, so daß die doxastischen Benennungen schließlich als 'angesetzte Kennzeichen' definiert sind, denen aufgrund ihres semantischen Gehalts nur eine sehr beschränkte Richtigkeit zugesprochen werden kann.

Fassen wir den jetzt erreichten Diskussionsstand wiederum in einer schematischen Übersicht zusammen, ergibt sich folgendes Bild:

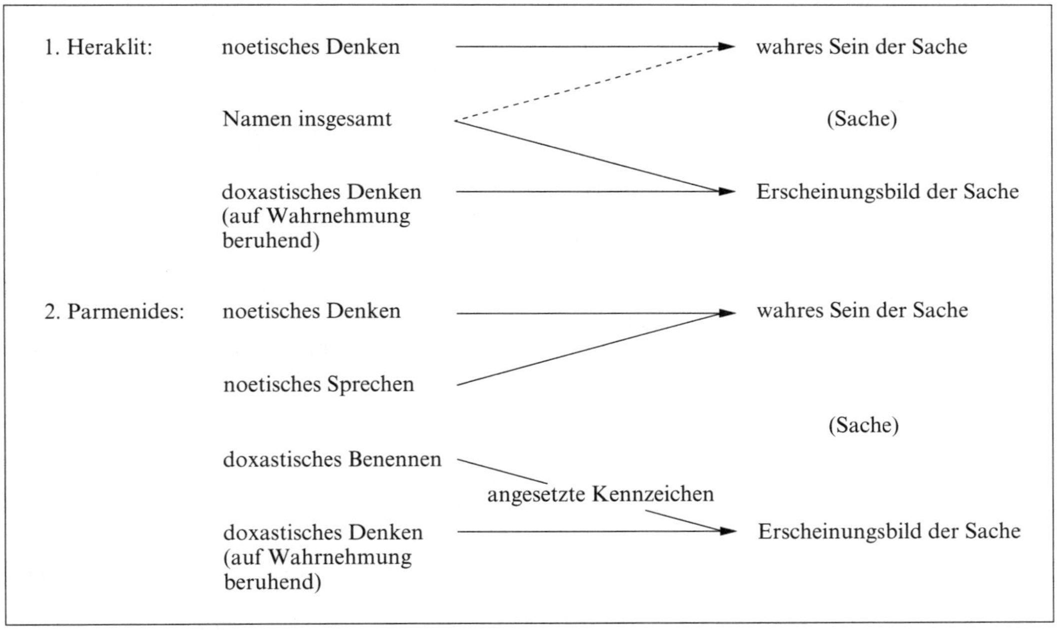


Abb. 53.3: Name, Sache und Erkenntnis bei Heraklit und Parmenides.

daß es wahr sei". Freilich werden auch diese Benennungen nicht restlos verworfen, denn wenn sie auch nicht das 'wahre Sein' erfassen, stellen sie doch die Summe der Erfahrung dar (cf. auch Gatzemeier 1992: 9). Bemerkenswert ist übrigens in diesem Zusammenhang, Trotz aller tiefgreifender Modifikationen ist bei Parmenides und Heraklit die überkommene *phúsei*-Konzeption nicht restlos aufgegeben. Bei beiden gelten die Benennungen zwar *nicht* mehr als unmittelbar von der Sache her determiniert und daher als 'naturgegeben' richtig, doch beurteilen sie die Richtigkeit der Namen nach dem Grad der Übereinstimmung zwischen der erkannten Sache und der semantischen Information, die der jeweilige Name über die benannte Sache gibt. Auch wenn die Namen jetzt als Produkt des erkennenden Subjekts betrachtet werden, wird also die Hypothese beibehalten, daß die Namen nicht beliebig sind, sondern in einer Beziehung zu den Sachen stehen, die man als 'Aussage über die Sache' charakterisieren kann. Und das gilt selbst für den Fall, wo, wie bei Parmenides, die doxastischen Namen explizit als 'angesetzte Kennzeichen' bezeichnet werden. Unter Benutzung der späteren *phúsei-thései*-Terminologie könnte man daher sagen, daß hier die Benennungen in bezug auf ihre Entstehung (Setzung durch den Menschen) *thései*, in bezug auf ihre Funktion (Sachbezug) jedoch *phúsei* sind, wobei freilich jetzt, anders als in 2., unter *phúsei* nur die sachbezogene Richtigkeit, auch die bloß doxastische, zu verstehen wäre.

3.2. Demokrit

Die nächste Stufe der Modifikation ist dann bei Demokrit gegeben (geb. um 460 v. Chr.), für den die Namen, der Terminologie nach, prinzipiell nicht *phúsei*, sondern *nómōi* sind. Grundlage dieser Entwicklung ist ein weiterer Zuwachs an Erfahrungswissen und, im Vergleich zu Parmenides und Heraklit, eine stärkere Stützung auf die Empirie als Ausgangspunkt der Erkenntnis. Erste Ansätze zu einer Sprachkritik, die durch das neugewonnene empirische Wissen von den Dingen motiviert war, sind uns schon bei Xenophanes begegnet. Diese Linie wird jetzt über Anaxagoras (ca. 500–428) und Empedokles (etwa 492–432), von denen je zwei Fragmente überliefert sind (*DK* 59 B 17, 19; 31 B 8, 9), wo sie verschiedene ihrer Ansicht nach unzutreffende Benennungen "durch eine wissenschaftlich fundiertere Terminologie zu ersetzen" trachten (Kraus 1990: 264), fortgesetzt bis zu Demokrit, der diese Sprachkritik dann radikalisiert. Festzuhalten ist hier aber zunächst einmal, daß Empedokles (*DK* 31 B 9) und Demokrit (*DK* 68 B 9, 125) die Existenz der sachlich inadäquaten Namen ausdrücklich der Konvention zuschreiben, die hier als νόμος "Brauch" bezeichnet wird. Denn damit tritt neben dem von Parmenides verwendeten Begriff der 'Setzung' als weiterer Gegenbegriff zur *phúsei*-Konzeption der Terminus νόμος auf, der für die erste, bis Platon reichende Phase des sogenannten *phúsei-thései*-Streits (cf. Coseriu 1996: 881–882) charakteristisch ist und in unserem speziellen Fall zum Ausdruck bringt, daß die fraglichen Benennungen keine naturgegebenen und wahren Abbilder der Dinge, sondern lediglich (a) auf Brauch beruhende und dazu noch (b) unzureichende Namen sind, weil sie nicht das wahre Sein der Dinge, sondern nur deren oberflächliches Erscheinungsbild repräsentieren.

Die Radikalisierung der Sprachkritik durch Demokrit besteht nun darin, daß dieser, wie der spätantike Scholiast Proklos (412–485) in seinem Kommentar zum Platonischen *Kratylos* (6, 20ff. = *DK* 68 B 26) berichtet, die Namen prinzipiell als auf "Setzung" (θέσει) beruhend angesehen und seine Auffassung mit vier sprachanalytischen Argumenten untermauert hat. Seit Steinthal (1863: 173ff.) wurde dieses Proklos-Zeugnis zwar immer wieder angezweifelt und für eine anachronistische Rückprojektion späterer Thesen auf Demokrit erklärt, doch sind diese Zweifel nur teilweise berechtigt (cf. auch Di Cesare 1980: 33ff.). Sie gelten sicherlich für den Anfangsteil, in dem Proklos Demokrit die Verwendung des nacharistotelischen Begriffes θέσει zuschreibt und in dem der Scholiast die an Aristoteles' Kategorienschrift (cf. Brancacci 1986: 18–19) erinnernden Termini 'Homonymie' und 'Polyonymie' benutzt. Sie gelten aber nicht für den Schluß des Proklos-Zeugnisses, in dem es heißt, daß Demokrit selbst für die von ihm zum Beweis für seine These herangezogenen Sprachphänomene die Begriffe πολύσημον ('Polysemie', heute: Homonymie), ἰσόρροπον ('Isorropie', Gleichgewichtigkeit, heute: Synonymie), νώνυμον ('Nonymie', Namenlosigkeit, d. h. Fehlen bestimmter vom Sprachsystem her möglicher Wortbildungsformen) und – wie Diels/Kranz ergänzen – μετώνυμον ('Metonymie', d. h. Umbenennung eines Denotats) verwendet hat. Mit diesen genuin Demokritischen Begriffen sind einige semantische Erscheinungen benannt, die eindeutig beweisen sollen, daß zwischen Namen und benannten Sachen keine durchgängige Einszueins-Entsprechung vorliegt; und anders als dies in vergleichbaren Fällen bei Homer und Hesiod gegeben war (cf. Abb. 53.1. u. 53.2.), wird dieses Faktum nun, wie Proklos schreibt, als Gegenargument gegen die *phúsei*-Konzeption gewertet. Daß dieser Interpretation des Proklos zuzustimmen ist und Demokrit die Namen der normalen Alltagssprache in der Tat als konventionell betrachtet hat, ergibt sich dann aus den bereits vorhin erwähnten Fragmenten *DK* 68 B 9 und B 125, wo die sachlich inadäquaten Namen dem νόμος zugeschrieben sind (cf. auch Di Cesare 1980: 33–34). Somit wäre Proklos wohl lediglich insofern zu korrigieren, als Demokrit noch nicht den *thései*-Begriff, sondern den zu seiner Zeit üblich werdenden Ausdruck νόμος verwendet.

Zu dieser aus der synchronen Sprachbeobachtung erwachsenen Konventionalismusthese würde es gut passen, wenn Demokrit, wie Diodoros Siculus (1. Jh. v. Chr.) berichtet, ebenfalls einen konventionalistischen Sprachursprung angenommen hätte. Doch ob der von Diodor überlieferte Text wirklich auf Demokrit zurückgeht, ist sehr stark umstritten (cf. Kraus 1987: 156, Anm. 8 u. 9), und infolgedessen will ich mich hier darauf beschränken, lediglich die wichtigsten inhaltlichen Parallelen zur benennungsbezogenen *nómōi*-These anzuführen (mehr dazu bei Di Cesare 1980: 45ff.; Gatzemeier 1992: 12). Diodor (I 8,1 (3)f. = *DK* 68 B 5) zufolge hat also Demokrit – ähnlich wie gut hundert Jahre später Epikur (ca. 341–271; zu seiner Sprachursprungstheorie cf. Hossenfelder 1996: 218ff.) – die Entstehung der Sprache(n) aus den praktischen Interessen und Bedürfnissen des Menschen abgeleitet und in diesem Zusammenhang u. a. gesagt, die Menschen hätten "untereinander Zeichen (σύμβολα) für jedes einzelne Ding, das ihnen zu Gesicht kam, festgesetzt (τιθέντας), damit sie für alles ein Verständigungsmittel (ἑρμηνείαν) hatten". Darüber hinaus wird in diesem Text auch die Sprachverschiedenheit damit erklärt, daß die auf der Erde verstreut lebenden Menschengruppen die Wörter (λέξεις) so gebildet hätten, wie der Zufall es gerade wollte.

Während Demokrit die allgemein gebräuchlichen Namen als unzureichend kritisiert, ist er, wie schon angedeutet, selbst darum bemüht, Benennungen zu schaffen, die seiner naturphilosophischen Erkenntnis Rechnung tragen und die Dinge so bezeichnen, wie sie 'wirklich' sind. Auch diese Benennungen sind als menschliche Sprachschöpfungen selbstverständlich *nómōi*, doch unterscheiden sie sich von den üblichen konventionellen Namen eben dadurch, daß sie aufgrund ihrer Bedeutung 'richtig' sind. Damit liegt hier eine Konzeption vor, nach der die Benennungen zwar generell als *nómōi* angesehen werden, der *nómos*-Begriff aber ebenso wie der Parmenideische Begriff des 'angesetzten Kennzeichens' einen Faktor, der einer modifizierten *phúsei*-Konzeption entspricht, enthält, nämlich die Komponente 'sachbezogene Aussage', die dann entsprechend der Demokritischen Differenzierung von Wissenschafts- und Alltagssprache in bezug auf die wissenschaftlichen Benennungen als zutreffend und in bezug auf die alltagssprachlichen als unzureichend (weil nur am Erscheinungsbild der Dinge orientiert) qualifiziert wird.

Auch Demokrits 'Sprachtheorie' ist Teil seiner Erkenntnistheorie. Ohne hierauf näher einzugehen, sei lediglich gesagt, daß Demokrit als Urprinzip des Seins von ewigen und unveränderlichen Atomen (dem "Ichts" [τὸ δέν, als Gegenbegriff zu "Nichts", τὸ ουδέν, gebildet], "Festen" oder "Seienden"; *DK* 68 A 37) und deren ebenfalls ewigem und unveränderlichem Bewegungsraum (der "Leere", dem "Nichts" oder dem "Unbeschränkten") ausgeht und die konkreten seienden Dinge als eine bestimmte Kombination und Verteilung von Atomen im Raum beschreibt. Diese konkreten Dinge sind aber nicht direkt erkennbar; erkennbares Wahrnehmungsobjekt ist nur ihr Bild, das aus einem interaktiven Prozeß zwischen Ding und menschlicher Wahrnehmung entsteht. Während nun die bloße 'Wahrnehmung', auch "dunkle Vernunft" (γνώμη σκοτίη) genannt, lediglich sogenannte "Vorstellungen" (φαντασίαι) entwickelt, die nur das oberflächliche Erscheinungsbild erfassen, vermag der 'Verstand', die "echte Vernunft" (γνώμη γνησίη), die wahre "Gestalt" (μορφή) zu erkennen, d. h. die spezifische 'Form', 'Anordnung' und 'Lage' der Atome, die das konkrete Ding ausmachen, zu erschließen (cf. 67 A 6; 68 A 135, B 9, 10, 11b). Diesen beiden Größen scheinen nun die verschiedenen Typen von Benennungen zugeordnet zu sein: den 'Gestalten' die wissenschaftlichen und zutreffenden Namen, den 'Vorstellungen' die alltagssprachlichen Namen, die in bezug auf das wahre Sein der Dinge unzureichend sind. Damit ergibt sich etwa folgendes (stark vereinfachende) Bild (s. nächste Seite).

Schließlich ist noch zu erwähnen, daß die 'sprachwissenschaftlichen' Fragestellungen, denen Demokrit im Kontext 'sprachphilosophischer' Erörterungen nachgegangen ist, ein größeres Eigengewicht zu haben scheinen und bei Demokrit bereits eine Tendenz zur Verselbständigung sprachbezogener Forschungen feststellbar ist. Zumindest gilt das dann, wenn die Titel, die Thrasyllos unter den musischen Schriften Demokrits nennt (cf. die Abt. μουσικά bei Mansfeld 1987: 586), von denen aber nichts erhalten ist,

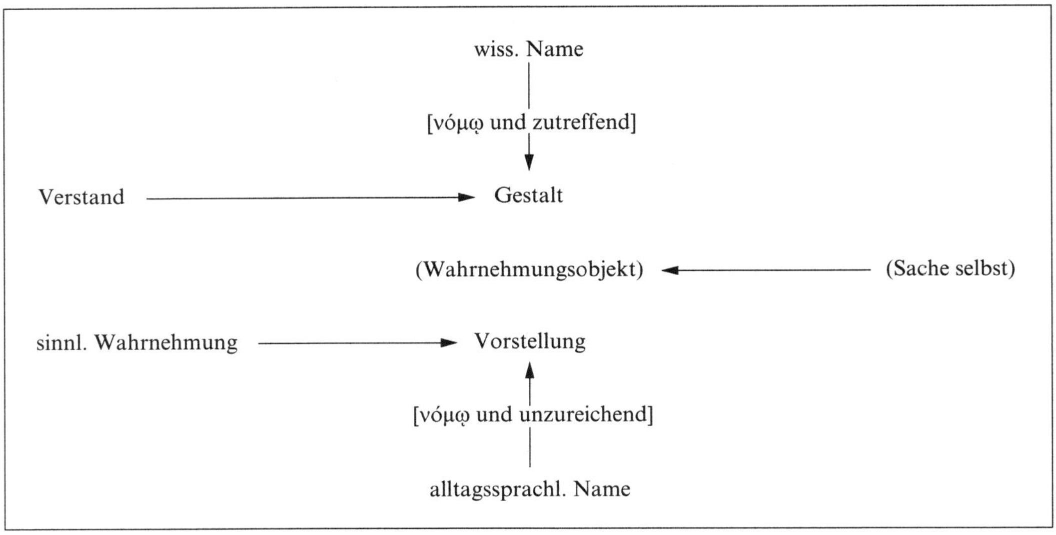


Abb. 53.4: Name, Sache und Erkenntnis bei Demokrit.

wirklich Demokrit zuzuschreiben sind. Denn darunter finden sich u. a. Werke über Orthoepie, Onomastik und Rhemata (Verben?).

Greifen wir zuletzt noch einmal die in 1. eingeführte Liste der Kriterien für (sprach)-wissenschaftliches Handeln auf, so scheint das Kriterium der Rationalität bei den Vorsokratikern grundsätzlich erfüllt zu sein. Außerdem ist festzustellen, daß – soweit die Quellen dazu Aufschluß geben – von Anaximander an eine Kosmogonie bzw. Kosmologie entwickelt wird, die sowohl systematisch als auch theoriebezogen ist, und daß dann bei Heraklit und noch deutlicher bei Parmenides und Demokrit außer den erkenntnistheoretischen auch die methodologischen Grundlagen ihrer kosmologischen Konzeptionen *explizit* offengelegt werden. Und insofern deren sprachphilosophische Reflexionen integrativer Bestandteil ihrer Kosmologien sind, gilt das gleichermaßen auch für sie. In bezug auf die 'etymologische' Analyse ist jedoch keine Progression feststellbar. Denn diese bewegt sich auf denselben Bahnen wie bei Homer und Hesiod (cf. z. B. die dem Heraklitischen Fragment *DK* 22 B 32 zugrunde liegende Verknüpfung von Ζηνὸς ὄνομα "Name des Zeus" mit ζῆν "leben") und wird, soweit ersichtlich, auch an keiner Stelle explizit thematisiert.

## 4. Die Sophistik

Zeitgleich mit den jüngeren Vorsokratikern ist im gesamten griechischen Sprachbereich, vor allem aber in Athen, eine Bewegung beobachtbar, die für die 2. Hälfte des 5. Jhs. als charakteristisch gilt: die sogenannte Sophistik. Auf die verwickelte Begriffsgeschichte des Terminus σοφιστής "Sophist", die wechselvolle rezeptionsgeschichtliche Bewertung der Sophistik und die genaueren historischen Bedingungen sowie das breite Spektrum sophistischer Tätigkeit kann hier freilich nicht näher eingegangen werden (vgl. dazu etwa Guthrie 1971; Kerferd 1981; Di Cesare 1991). An dieser Stelle muß vielmehr der pauschale Hinweis reichen, daß die sophistische Bewegung aus den Erfordernissen entstand, die der für verschiedene griechische Stadtstaaten, und hier wieder insbesondere für Athen, kennzeichnende Übergang von aristokratischen zu demokratischen Strukturen und die (z. T. hiermit verknüpfte) Infragestellung traditioneller Werte, Normen und Institutionen mit sich brachten. Als professionelle Lehrer, die von Stadt zu Stadt zogen und Unterricht gegen Entgelt erteilten, boten die Sophisten den daran interessierten freien Bürgern die Vermittlung von Kenntnissen und Fertigkeiten an, die ihrer Ansicht nach besonders hilfreich waren, um im privaten und politischen Bereich erfolgreich zu agieren.

Eine herausragende Bedeutung kam hierbei selbstverständlich dem effizienten Umgang mit der Sprache zu, was nicht nur zur Entwicklung der Rhetorik und ihrer speziellen Form des eristischen Streitgespräches führte, sondern auch zu weiteren Reflexionen über das Verhältnis von Wort und Sache und den Wahrheitsgehalt der Benennungen Anlaß gab. Kurzum, die *nómos-phúsis*-Diskussion wird auch in der Sophistik fortgeführt, doch ist hierbei zugleich hervorzuheben, daß die Frage, ob *nómōi* oder *phúsei*, in dieser Zeit gesellschaftlichen Wandels nicht nur im sprachtheoretischen Kontext virulent war, sondern zum beherrschenden Tagesthema wurde und als wichtiges Kriterium für die Beurteilung des gesamten überkommenen Wissens und aller tradierter Institutionen – Gesetze, politische Einrichtungen, anthropologische Fragen, ethische Normen usw. – diente (cf. Guthrie 1971: 55ff.; zur Begriffsgeschichte Heinimann 1945; Pohlenz 1953).

### 4.1. Prodikos

Versucht man aus der Vielzahl der Sophisten einige herauszugreifen, die unter sprachtheoretischem Aspekt besonders interessant erscheinen, so stößt man u. a. auf Prodikos von Keos (5./4. Jh. v. Chr.), der allgemein als Begründer der wissenschaftlichen Synonymik gilt, dessen Position im *nómos-phúsis*-Streit aber nicht eindeutig bestimmbar zu sein scheint. Prodikos ist nach Platons Zeugnis (*Laches* 197d; vgl. auch *Euthydemos* 277e) der renommierteste Experte in einer Kunst gewesen, die unter den Sophisten sehr verbreitet war. Dies war die Kunst des Wörterunterscheidens, des ὀνόματα διαιρεῖν, d. h. die Kunst der Synonymendifferenzierung. Das Phänomen der Synonymie selbst war zwar auch vorher schon, so etwa von Simonides (ca. 557–468/67; cf. Di Cesare 1991: 104) und von Demokrit (3.2.), gesehen worden, doch scheint Prodikos das Verdienst zuzukommen, als erster eine ausgearbeitete Methodik für die Synonymendifferenzierung entwickelt zu haben (grundlegend zur Synonymik des Prodikos: Mayer 1913; vgl. auch Gentinetta 1961: 39–44).

Aristoteles (*Topik* 112b22) zufolge bestand diese Methode darin, verschiedene (Quasi)-Synonyme miteinander zu vergleichen und – modern gesprochen – auf ihre invariante Kernbedeutung und ihre semantischen Differenzen hin zu untersuchen. Dabei geht Prodikos zugleich kontextuell vor, indem er die spezifische Bedeutung der Quasisynonyme an deren unterschiedlicher Verwendungsweise illustriert (vgl. Platon, *Protagoras* 337ab). Als Exempel solcher Analysen werden u. a. die Abgrenzung von χαρά, τέρψις und εὐφροσύνη, d. h. von Wörtern aus dem lexikalischen Feld 'Freude', genannt (Aristoteles, *Topik* 112b22) oder auch die Differenzierung von Verben wie 'streiten/zanken', 'achten/loben', die Prodikos von Platon (*Protagoras* 337ab) in den Mund gelegt wird (Weiteres z. B. bei Rijlaarsdam 1978: 194–206).

Kann damit eine, wenn auch nur vage, Vorstellung von der analytischen Vorgehensweise des Prodikos gewonnen werden, so bleibt der sprachtheoretische Hintergrund der Analysen doch weitgehend im Dunkeln. Angesichts der mageren Quellenlage bleibt man hier auf Spekulationen angewiesen, und so ist es nicht verwunderlich, daß die moderne Forschung verschiedene Erklärungen offeriert. So wird bisweilen als Motiv für diese Synonymendifferenzierung die Erhöhung der "Leistungsfähigkeit der Sprache" (Gatzemeier 1992: 15) angesetzt und damit ein sprachverbesserischer Impetus, der einerseits von der Konventionalität der Sprache (*nómōi*-These) ausgeht, und zwar insofern die Benennungen als menschliche Sprachschöpfungen angesehen werden, andererseits aber zugleich das Ziel verfolgt, eine sachliche Adäquatheit der Benennungen herbeizuführen und damit eine gewisse *phúsei*-Relation zwischen Namen und Benanntem zu konstituieren (so auch Di Cesare 1980: 79). Eine solche Zielvorstellung dürfte wohl in etwa der Forderung entsprechen, die Demokrit an *wissenschaftliche* Nominationen stellt, so daß in diesem Fall die Position, die Prodikos innerhalb der *nómos-phúsis*-Diskussion einnimmt, nicht wesentlich von der des Demokrit abweichen würde.

Demgegenüber findet sich in der zeitgenössischen Literatur jedoch ebenfalls die Auffassung (z. B. Sluiter 1997: 176), die von Prodikos vorgenommenen semantischen Analysen seien als ein Versuch zu deuten, die Demokritische These von der Konventionalität der Sprache, die von Demokrit ja u. a. mit dem Hinweis auf das Phänomen der Synonymik begründet worden war, auf empirischem Weg zu widerlegen und zu zeigen, daß es in Wirklichkeit gar keine echten Synonyme gibt und die feinen semantischen Differenzen subtile Unterschiede in den Sachen widerspiegeln. Das sprachtheoretisch-sprachphilosophische Ziel der Dihairesen, die übrigens nach allgemeinem Urteil auch für die Entwicklung der Platonischen Methode der Dihairesis bedeutsam waren (vgl. auch Platons Selbstzeugnis, *Protagoras* 341a), bestünde in diesem Fall darin, im Gegenzug zu Demokrit die traditionelle *phúsei*-Auffassung zu rehabilitieren.

Da keine dieser beiden Interpretationen abwegig erscheint, die Quellen aber auch, wie schon gesagt, keinen konkreten Hinweis in die eine oder andere Richtung geben, muß die Frage, welcher Deutung man den Vorzug geben soll, wohl offen bleiben.

4.2. Protagoras

Eindeutiger Anhänger der Konventionalismusthese ist dagegen der Sophist Protagoras (ca. 485–415). In Platons gleichnamigem Dialog erscheint er als Vertreter einer, freilich nicht näher erläuterten, konventionalistischen Sprachursprungshypothese (Platon, *Protagoras* 322a), d. h. der Hypothese, daß die Sprache nicht unmittelbar göttlichen Ursprungs sei, sondern eine kunstvolle Erfindung des Menschen, zu der der Mensch aufgrund seiner Teilhabe an göttlichen Vorzügen fähig war. Daß die Sprache Menschenwerk und kein Geschenk der Götter sei, versuchte man zu dieser Zeit, nebenbei gesagt, auch experimentell nachzuweisen, und zwar mit einem Experiment, das klären sollte, ob dem Menschen jeweils eine ganz bestimmte Einzelsprache angeboren – und damit von Gott geschenkt – ist oder ob er, unabhängig davon, wo er geboren ist, je nach der Umgebung, in der er aufwächst, eine jeweils andere Sprache erlernt, was für die Konventionalität der Sprache sprechen würde (vgl. die der Schule des Protagoras zugeschriebenen *Dissoi Logoi* [cf. Di Cesare 1980: 86, 1996: 92]).

Grundlage ist die Konventionalismusthese auch für ein anderes Projekt, als dessen herausragender Vertreter Protagoras gilt: das Projekt der Orthoepeia (ὀρθοέπεια), d. h. der Rederichtigkeit bzw. des korrekten Sprachgebrauchs (vgl. hierzu Fehling 1965; Siebenborn 1976). Wie es Demokrit bereits für den engeren Bereich der Wissenschaftssprache fordert, ist es Ziel dieses Projekts, die Sprache überhaupt so zu gestalten, daß die verwendeten sprachlichen Mittel der benannten Sache angemessen sind. Auch hier führt die *nómos*-These also nicht dazu, die Forderung nach einer sachgemäßen Übereinstimmung von Name und Sache aufzugeben, vielmehr wird – unter Beibehaltung des (modifizierten!) *phúsei*-Ideals der Sachgemäßheit sprachlicher Bezeichnungsmittel – aus der *nómos*-These die Notwendigkeit abgeleitet, die gegebene Sprache kritisch zu sichten und gegebenenfalls so zu reformieren, daß sie dem genannten Ideal entspricht. Die Zwittergestalt solcher Konzeptionen ist übrigens auch schon den antiken Kommentatoren nicht entgangen, was z. B. bei dem Neuplatoniker Ammonios (um 500 n. Chr.) dazu führt, daß er Theorien, nach denen Namen "zwar von den Menschen gebildet [sind], jedoch der Natur der Sache gemäß", sowohl als Variante der *phúsei*-These als auch als Variante der *thései*-These verzeichnet (zit. n. Coseriu 1996: 882). – Neben der Herstellung der Sachgemäßheit der Bezeichnungen lag dann ein zweiter Schwerpunkt der Orthoepie auf der Beseitigung morphologischer Anomalien.

Wie die Kritik des Protagoras am Sprachgebrauch der homerischen Epen deutlich macht (vgl. *DK* 80 A 28 und A 29), rückt bei dessen orthoepischen Bestrebungen zugleich etwas Neues in den Blick, nämlich die Genera der Nomen und die Modi des Verbs. Was die Nomina betrifft, soll Protagoras als erster die drei Genera ἄρρενα "männlich", θήλεα "weiblich" und σκεύη "sächlich" unterschieden haben (vgl. *DK* 80 A 27). Diese Genera werden von Protagoras als semantisch-biologische Kategorien interpretiert, und so kritisiert er denn Homer auch, wenn die von diesem für bestimmte Nomen angesetzten Genera (die Protagoras bei artikellos gebrauchten Nomen anhand der beigegebenen Adjektive identifiziert) nicht dem Charakter der bezeichneten Dinge entsprechen. Ein von Aristoteles überliefertes Beispiel hierfür ist die Kritik an Vers 1 und 2 der *Ilias*, wo μῆνις "Zorn" ein feminines Genus hat, aber der Auffassung des Protagoras zufolge maskulin sein müßte, weil der Zorn als etwas Männliches zu betrachten sei (vgl. *DK* 80 A 28). Daß diese Art von Orthoepie einerseits wohl sehr verbreitet war, andererseits aber keineswegs auf ungeteilten Beifall stieß, zeigen die *Wolken* (658ff.) des Aristophanes (5./4. Jh. v. Chr.), wo sich eine köstliche Persiflage auf solche Reformbestrebungen, die dort allerdings der Person des Sokrates zugeschrieben werden, findet.

Eine weitere Kritik erfahren die Einleitungsverse der *Ilias*, weil dort eine Aufforderung an eine Göttin (μῆνιν ἄειδε, θεά "Singe, Göttin, den Zorn") imperativisch formuliert sei, während es sich nach der Sprecherintention nur um eine Bitte handeln könne, die im Griechischen als Optativ zu realisieren sei (vgl. *DK* 80 A 29). Auch dieser Kritik liegt die sprachphilosophische Forderung zugrunde, daß die Sprache mit der bezeichneten Wirklichkeit übereinzustimmen habe; und unter linguistischem Aspekt ist hier bemerkenswert, daß Protagoras, wie Diogenes Laertios berichtet (*DK* 80 A 1), nicht nur als erster die für das Griechische typischen vier Verbalmodi (Optativ, Konjunktiv, Indikativ und Imperativ) unterschieden haben soll, sondern auch die vier damit zusammenhängenden Satzarten oder "types of discourse" (Sluiter 1997: 175) Bitte, Frage, Antwort und Befehl.

4.3. Gorgias

Gingen Prodikos und Protagoras – wenn auch möglicherweise in verschiedener Hinsicht – vom Postulat der Sachgemäßheit der Bezeichnungen aus, so vertritt der als maßgeblicher Begründer, größter Theoretiker und auch größter Praktiker der Rhetorik geltende Sophist Gorgias (ca. 480–380) die gegenteilige These. Seiner Ansicht nach gibt es nämlich weder eine unmittelbar von den Dingen selbst hervorgerufene Sachgemäßheit der Bezeichnungen (ursprüngliche *phúsei*-These) noch eine Sachgemäßheit, die in der menschlichen Erkenntnis gründet und in den menschlichen Sprachschöpfungen ihren Niederschlag gefunden hat (*nómos*-These mit *phúsei*-Komponente). Damit ist der Sprache jede erkenntnistheoretische Relevanz entzogen, was dann auch für die Beurteilung des Zwecks sprachlicher Äußerungen bestimmte Folgen hat (s. u.).

Begründet wird diese Auffassung von Gorgias im Rahmen einer Fundamentalkritik an den Thesen des Parmenides, einer Kritik, die Gorgias in der verloren gegangenen, aber in Auszügen bei Sextus Empiricus, *Adversus mathematicos* VII, Kap. 65–87, und in dem pseudoaristotelischen Werk *De Melisso Xenophane Gorgia* 979a11–980b21 referierten Schrift *Über das Nichtseiende oder Über die Natur* (Περὶ τοῦ μὴ ὄντος ἢ Περὶ φύσεως) niedergelegt hat (zur unterschiedlichen Zuverlässigkeit der beiden Quellen vgl. insbes. Newiger 1973). War Parmenides davon ausgegangen, daß allein dem "es ist" Wahrheit und Sein zukommt und auch nur dieses "es ist" erkannt und ausgesagt werden kann (vgl. 3.1 und Schmitter 1996b: 73–74), so stellt Gorgias dem die Thesen entgegen: (a) "es gibt nichts"; (b) "wenn es etwas gäbe, wäre es nicht erkennbar"; (c) "wenn es etwas gäbe und dies erkennbar wäre, wäre es anderen nicht mitteilbar" (*De Melisso* [...] 979a12–13). Während nun die Thesen (a) und (b) ausschließlich apriorisch begründet werden, und zwar durch den Nachweis, daß die Annahme des Gegenteils zu logischen Widersprüchen und semantischen Inkonsistenzen führt (cf. Newiger 1973), benutzt Gorgias für den Beweis der These (c) weitgehend empirische Argumente, wobei er sich vor allem mit dem Problem der Aussagbarkeit und Mitteilbarkeit der Dinge auseinandersetzt. Im Rahmen dieser Argumentation versucht er dann zweierlei nachzuweisen, nämlich erstens, daß die grundsätzliche Heterogenität von Sprache und Wirklichkeit eine Aussage über die Wirklichkeit unmöglich macht, und zweitens, daß zwei Subjekte, selbst wenn sie etwas über die Wirklichkeit aussagen könnten, sich dennoch nicht verstünden (cf. *De Melisso* [...] 979a–980b).

Ohne hier näher auf weitere Details der Argumentation und deren z. T. stark umstrittene Deutung eingehen zu können (vgl. aber z. B. die näheren Hinweise bei Adrados 1981; Di Cesare 1980: 68ff., 1996:95ff.; Gatzemeier 1992: 14; Guthrie 1971: 193ff.; Kraus 1990: 265ff.; Newiger 1973), scheint sich nach dem heutigen Stand der Forschung jedoch folgendes Gesamtbild zu ergeben: Dem Einen Sein des Parmenides stellt Gorgias die Vielfalt der Dinge (πράγματα) gegenüber. Dabei leugnet er weder die Existenz der Dinge noch deren sinnliche Wahrnehmbarkeit, sondern nur die Möglichkeit der Erkenntnis eines 'wahren Wesens' der Dinge. Da die subjektive Wahrnehmung nach Gorgias "la única vía de conocimiento" (Adrados 1981: 13) ist, treten an die Stelle 'wahren' Wissens Denkinhalte (φρονούμενα), die lediglich einer relativistischen Meinung entsprechen. Die Rede, den λόγος, scheint Georgias nun als erster der griechischen Denker als ein bilaterales Zeichen (σημεῖον) aufzufassen, das aus einer lautlichen Ebene und einer Bedeutungsebene besteht (cf. Newiger 1973: 154; Adrados 1981: bes. 15–16; Kraus 1990: 267) und dessen Bedeutung zwar nicht mit den Denkinhalten identisch ist, diesen aber äquivalent zu sein scheint. Daher können die relativistischen Denkinhalte zumindest in gewisser Weise übermittelt werden, doch sind sie für den Hörer, der übrigens hier auch wohl erstmals explizit in sprachtheoretische Überlegungen einbezogen wird, nur insoweit verstehbar, als sich seine eigene sinnliche Erfahrung mit der des Sprechers deckt.

Die zentralen erkenntnistheoretischen Elemente dieser Konzeption könnte man – in Ergänzung und leichter Modifikation eines Modells von Kraus (1990: 268) – wie folgt schematisch darstellen (s. Abb. 53.5):

Wie schon angedeutet, hat diese erkenntniskritische Konzeption weitreichende Folgen für die Einschätzung des Zwecks der Rede. Statt der bislang angesetzten kognitiven Funktion spricht Gorgias ihr nunmehr eine neue Aufgabe zu, nämlich die psychologische

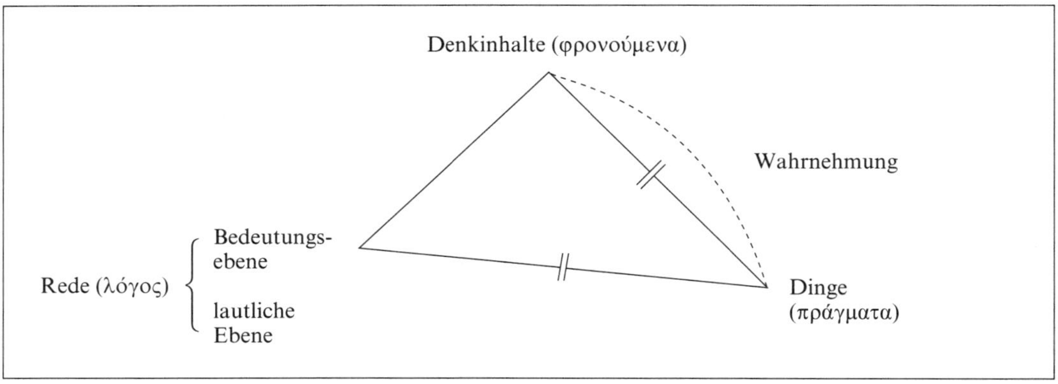


Abb. 53.5: Rede, Dinge und Erkenntnis bei Gorgias.

Beeinflussung des Hörers. Die Rede wird als ein μέγας δυνάστης "ein großer Potentat" (*DK* 82 B 11, § 8) betrachtet, der Emotionen wecken und abklingen lassen kann (ebd. §§ 810) und dazu in der Lage ist, z. B. vor Gericht und in jeder anderen Versammlung die Meinungen der Hörer in seinem Sinne zu manipulieren und die Hörer auf diese Weise zu beherrschen (vgl. ebd. §§ 1014 sowie Platon, *Gorgias* 452e). Dies führt zur Ausarbeitung einer kunstvollen Rhetorik, von der die beiden erhaltenen Reden, das *Lob der Helena* (DK 82 B 11) und die *Verteidigungsrede für Palamedes* (*DK* 82 B 11a) ein anschauliches Beispiel geben.

## 5. Platon

Wie im bisherigen Überblick über die Sprachreflexion des frühgriechischen Epos, der Vorsokratiker und der Sophisten deutlich wurde und auch in der gegenwärtigen Literatur ausdrücklich konstatiert wird (cf. z. B. Kraus 1996: 18–19; Sluiter 1997: 178), waren deren zentrale Themen die Beziehung von Name/Sprache und Sache, das Verhältnis von Sprache, Denken und Wirklichkeit und die Frage der Wahrheit der Benennungen und Aussagen. Dabei ließ sich eine Entwicklung beobachten, die einerseits in einer Zunahme an Rationalität, Systematizität, Methodenbewußtsein und Differenziertheit bei der Analyse der drei Größen Name/Sprache, Vorstellung/Denkinhalt und Ding bestand und andererseits von einem blinden Vertrauen in die Richtigkeit der Namen zu einer wachsenden Skepsis gegenüber der Erkenntnisleistung der Sprache führte.

Dies bildet den Hintergrund für die Reflexionen Platons (428/27–348/47), der als

> "Verfechter einer Philosophie, zu deren vitalen Grundlagen die Gewinnung und Vermittlung wahrer Erkenntnis im ernsthaften philosophischen Dialog gehörte, [...] die Bestreitung der Möglichkeit intersubjektiver Kommunikation ebensowenig akzeptieren [konnte] wie die Aufhebung jedes sprachlichen Wahrheitskriteriums" (Kraus 1990: 271).

Obwohl sprachbezogene Reflexionen das gesamte Platonische Werk durchziehen – angefangen von den Frühdialogen, wo die geradezu stereotype Frage "Du nennst doch etwas X?" als Ausgangspunkt der Bestimmung des Definiendums erscheint, bis hin zum späten 7. Brief –, können doch einige wenige Schriften als besonders relevant hervorgehoben werden. Und das sind die Dialoge *Kratylos, Theaitetos* und *Sophistes.* Die exegetisch-historiographische Literatur hierzu ist Legion, und daher sei hier nur (in subjektiver Auswahl) auf folgende neuere Arbeiten verwiesen: Adrados 1977; Baxter 1992; Borsche 1996; Coseriu 1996; Di Cesare 1980: 89–155, 1989; Derbolav 1972; Detel 1972; Gaiser 1974; Heitsch 1985; Hülser 1997: 850–852; Ildefonse 1997: 53–72; Kraus 1987, 1990, 1996; Pagliaro 1956; Palmer 1988; Rehn 1982, 1986; Rijlaarsdam 1978; Schmitter 1975 = 1987c; Sluiter 1997: 177–188; White 1992.

Der *Kratylos*, die älteste vollständig erhaltene sprachtheoretische Schrift des Abendlandes, greift unmittelbar die zeitgenössische Kontroverse um die "Richtigkeit der Namen" (ὀρθότης τῶν ὀνομάτων) auf und läßt in der Gestalt des Kratylos einen Vertreter der *phúsei*-These und in der Gestalt des Hermogenes einen Verfechter der *nómos*-These aufeinander prallen. Da sich beide nicht einigen können, wird Sokrates herangezogen, um die Frage zu klären. Zu Beginn vertritt der als Herakliteer eingeführte Kratylos die Auffassung, "es gebe für jedes Ding eine Richtigkeit des Namens, die ihm aufgrund seiner Natur (φύσει) zugewachsen ist, [...] und diese sei für Griechen und Barbaren dieselbe" (383a4–b2), während Hermogenes sich nicht davon überzeugen läßt, "daß es eine andere Richtigkeit des Namens gibt als Vereinbarung und Übereinkunft (συνθήκη καὶ ὁμολογία) [...], denn nicht aufgrund seiner Natur sei jedem Ding ein Name zugewachsen, sondern aufgrund von Brauch und Gewohnheit (νόμῳ καὶ ἔθει)" (384c10–d8). Da in diesen Thesen aber überhaupt nicht expliziert wird, worin denn nun die jeweils angenommene Richtigkeit genau besteht, untersucht Sokrates im Verlauf des weiteren Dialogs eben diese Frage und veranlaßt dabei zugleich die beiden Kontrahenten, ihre Ausgangsbehauptungen zu radikalisieren. So sieht sich Kratylos gezwungen, die verschärfte These zu vertreten, daß es überhaupt keine besseren und weniger guten, sondern nur richtige Namen gibt (429b7–11), und Hermogenes zu der Behauptung gedrängt, daß sogar jeder einzelne für sich die Namen willkürlich festlegen könne und sie trotzdem richtig seien (385a1–b1, d2–9).

Das hat zur Konsequenz, daß es nach beiden Thesen ausschließlich richtige Namen gibt und in bezug auf die mittels sprachlicher Benennungen vollzogenen Aussagen über die Dinge nicht zwischen wahr und falsch unterschieden werden kann. Erforderlich ist jedoch eine Theorie, die gerade eine solche Differenzierung erlaubt und ein Kriterium an die Hand gibt, um wahre, d. h. sachlich adäquate, von sachlich falschen Benennungen zu unterscheiden.

Die Grundlagen für eine solche Theorie entwickelt Sokrates in seiner Diskussion mit Hermogenes, dessen radikale *nómos*-These es zu widerlegen gilt, anhand einer systematisch durchgeführten Analogie zwischen der Tätigkeit des Webens und der des Benennens (387b8–391b3). Dabei wird, um nur die wichtigsten Punkte hervorzuheben, das Benennen (ὀνομάζειν) bestimmt als eine Handlung (πρᾶξις), zu der man ein spezielles Werkzeug braucht, das wiederum einem ganz bestimmten Zweck dient. Das Werkzeug (ὄργανον) des Benennens ist der Name (388a8), sein Zweck, zu lehren und das Sein zu unterscheiden. Der "Name ist", wie es wörtlich bei Platon (388b13–c1) heißt, "ein belehrendes und wesensunterscheidendes Werkzeug" (Ὄνομα ἄρα διδασκαλικόν τί ἐστιν ὄργανον καὶ διακριτικὸν τῆς οὐσίας [...]).

Schon in dieser Definition klingt an, daß Platon eine Position vertritt, die der in 4.3. behandelten Auffassung des Gorgias in zentralen Punkten widerspricht. Denn während die Dinge nach Gorgias weder sprachlich erfaßt noch mitgeteilt werden können, wird dort dem Namen sowohl eine kommunikativ-didaktische Funktion zugesprochen als auch die Funktion, die Dinge ihrem Wesen nach zu unterscheiden. Wie dies Letztere geschehen kann, wird dann in Fortführung der Analogie zwischen Weben und Benennen in dem (häufig mißverstandenen) Werkzeug- oder Organonmodell des Namens – Karl Bühlers späteres Organonmodell (Bühler 1934) hat hier seine Quelle – ausgeführt (insbes. 388c–390a). Dieses Modell liefert, wie Di Cesare (1980: 103) sehr treffend formuliert, "una vera e propria *stratificazione del nome*" und gibt eine Beschreibung des Verhältnisses von Name und Sache, die auf folgenden Annahmen basiert: (a) der Annahme einer allgemeinen Idee des Namens, d. h. dessen, was einen Namen als Namen konstituiert (αὐτὸ ἐκεῖνο ὃ ἔστιν ὄνομα, 389d6–7); (b) der Annahme einer spezifischen Idee, die jedem einzelnen Namen im Hinblick auf den zu benennenden Gegenstand zukommt (τὸ ἑκάστῳ φύσει πεφυκὸς ὄνομα, 398d4–5; τὸ τοῦ ὀνόματος εἶδος [...] τὸ προσῆκον ἑκάστῳ, 390a5–6); (c) der Annahme von lautlichem und silbischem Material (φθόγγοι καὶ συλλαβαί), in das die spezifische Namensidee hineingelegt wird (τιθέναι εἰς, 389d5–6); (d) der Annahme einer Differenz von konkretem Erscheinungsbild und Wesen oder Idee (εἶδος) einer Sache (389b–d).

Platons Auffassung zufolge sähe nun das Modell eines idealen Namens so aus, daß die spezifische Idee des Namens, man könnte auch sagen: die Bedeutung, die in die materielle Namenskomponente hineingelegt ist, der Idee oder dem Wesen der benannten Sache entspricht. Deshalb wird auch die Relation, die zwischen diesen beiden Einheiten besteht, als *phúsei*-Relation betrachtet. Die Beziehung zwischen der spezifischen Idee des Namens und dem materiellen Namenselement ist dagegen konventionell festgelegt; sie ist eine Setzung. Unter Einbeziehung der konkreten benannten Sache selbst, die ihrerseits – wie im *Kratylos* (389b8–10) freilich nur angedeutet und erst im *Timaios* ausführlich erörtert wird – zur Idee der Sache in einer Teilhabebeziehung (μέθεξις) steht, ergibt sich damit für Platons Theorie des idealen Namens folgendes tetradische Zeichenmodell (cf. Schmitter 1975: 54 = 1987c: 28 und Kraus 1990: 276–277):

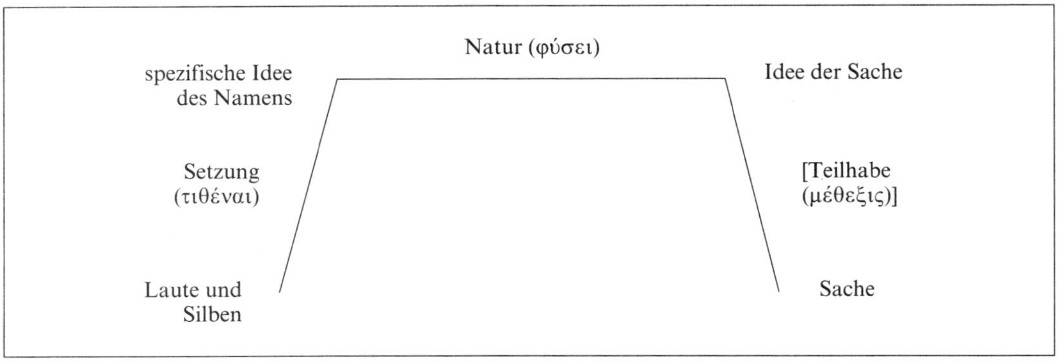


Abb. 53.6: Name, Sache und Erkenntnis in Platons *Kratylos*.

In diesem Idealmodell eines zutreffenden Namens erscheint die *nómos-phúsis*-Kontroverse gelöst, da sich die Namen hier auf einer höheren Betrachtungsstufe in bestimmter Hinsicht als *nómōi* und in einer anderen Hinsicht als *phúsei* erweisen. Damit ist einerseits der Seinsbezug der Benennungen gewahrt und andererseits auch deren kommunikative und didaktische Funktion gesichert. Zudem haben im Theorem der μέθεξις auch die kritischen Einwände gegen die Erkennbarkeit eines wahren Wesen der Dinge Berücksichtigung gefunden, die Gorgias daraus abgeleitet hatte, daß nur die Vielfalt der Dinge empirisch zugänglich sei.

Dennoch wird nach einer längeren etymologischen Erörterung im Schlußteil des Dialogs (437d–440e) auf die Unmöglichkeit einer Erkenntnis des wahren Wesens der Dinge mittels der Namen hingewiesen. Und der Grund dafür liegt darin, daß man die Idee der benannten Sache bereits kennen muß, um zur spezifischen Idee ihres Namens zu gelangen (vgl. ebenfalls *Theaitetos* 147b2). Infolgedessen kann die Erkenntnis des wahren Wesens der Dinge nur unmittelbar durch die Vernunft (νοῦς) und nicht über die Betrachtung der Namen gewonnen werden (440c3–5), womit die Frage nach der erkenntnisvermittelnden Funktion der Benennungen letztlich doch eine negative Antwort erfährt. – Nebenbei sei an dieser Stelle darauf hingewiesen, daß dieses hochdifferenzierte Platonische Modell von der Rezeption kaum aufgegriffen wurde. Statt dessen griff man auf das einfachere dreigliedrige Modell des Aristoteles (cf. Lieb 1981; Weidemann 1996: 182–183) zurück, das dann insbesondere über Porphyrius (234–ca. 304) und Boethius (ca. 480–524) an die Sprachtheorie des Mittelalters und der Neuzeit weitervermittelt wurde.

Im umfangreichen etymologischen Teil des Dialogs (397a–437d; vgl. hierzu insbes. Gaiser 1974: 45ff.; Rijlaarsdam 1978: 121ff.; Di Cesare 1980: 109ff.), bei dem auch Kratylos in die Diskussion miteinbezogen wird, wird die Relation zwischen der Idee der Sache und der materiellen Seite eines Namens untersucht und die Frage gestellt, ob die lautliche Form eines Namens das Wesen des benannten Dings erkennen läßt. Dabei geht Platon im Prinzip methodisch auf zweierlei Art vor. Einerseits werden, wie schon bei Homer und Hesiod (vgl. 2.), komplexe Wortstrukturen als Kombination aus einfachen Lexemen aufgefaßt und im Rückgriff auf die Bedeutung dieser Lexeme gedeutet. Zum anderen aber legt er eine mehrstufige Analyse komplexer Ausdrücke (ὕστερα ὀνόματα) in "primäre Namen" (πρῶτα ὀνόματα) und der primären Namen in kleinste Elemente (στοιχεῖα) vor, wobei er diese kleinsten Elemente dann im Rückgriff auf die "Bewegung der Sprechorgane" (Gaiser 1974: 62–63) lautsymbolisch interpretiert. Das Ergebnis dieser Analysen ist letztendlich negativ, da sie zu einer widersprüchlichen Interpretation des Seins (ist das Wesen der Dinge feststehend und gleichbleibend oder veränderlich?) führen. – Abgesehen von seinem sprachphilosophischen Inhalt ist dieser etymologische Teil auch in linguistischer Hinsicht interessant. Denn neben dem Versuch, die Benennungen auf eine mögliche

Lautsymbolik hin zu untersuchen, werden diachrone Lautwandelprozesse ebenso einkalkuliert wie dialektale Unterschiede und der Einfluß fremder Sprachen.

Insgesamt gesehen ist damit in diesem Dialog zugleich deutlich geworden, daß sich die ursprüngliche Annahme, der Name sei der Ort der Wahrheit in der Rede und deshalb sei 'wahr reden' gleichbedeutend mit 'richtig benennen', nicht aufrechterhalten läßt. Vielmehr sind die Fragen nach der Richtigkeit der Benennung und der Wahrheit der Rede als zwei unterschiedliche Fragestellungen zu betrachten, womit – wie Borsche (1996: 151) in diesem Zusammenhang bemerkt – "der Grundstein für die spätere Trennung von Erkenntnistheorie und Sprachtheorie gelegt" ist.

Die Frage nach den Bedingungen der Wahrheit der Rede wird dann in den Dialogen *Theaitetos* und *Sophistes* behandelt. Unter sprachwissenschaftlichem Aspekt ist hier besonders interessant, daß neben dem Seinsbezug der Namen ein weiteres Thema verstärkt in den Blick rückt, nämlich die Struktur des λόγος. Auch dieses Thema klingt im *Kratylos* schon an einer Stelle an, an der der Logos als eine Zusammensetzung (σύνθεσις) von ὀνόματα und ῥήματα betrachtet wird (431b5–c1). Doch was genau darunter zu verstehen ist, wird dort im Unklaren gelassen. Im *Theaitetos* wird dann deutlich, daß dem Logos eine hervorragende Rolle bei der Definition des wahren Wissens zukommt. Denn von den drei Hypothesen, die dort auf die Frage "Was ist Wissen (ἐπιστήμη)?" diskutiert werden, nämlich den Hypothesen 'Wissen ist Wahrnehmung' (αἴσθησις; 160d5–6), 'Wissen ist wahre Meinung' (ἀληθὴς δόξα; 187b5–6) und 'Wissen ist wahre Meinung mit Erklärung' (μετὰ λόγου ἀληθὴς δόξα; 201c9–d1), scheint Sokrates die letztgenannte die vielversprechendste zu sein. Doch wenn es dann darum geht, den in dieser Definition enthaltenen Logosbegriff näher zu bestimmen, beläßt es der *Theaitetos* bei der Diskussion verschiedener Thesen, die allesamt von Sokrates als unbefriedigend empfunden werden und das Thema der Verknüpfung von ὀνόματα und ῥήματα zudem auch nur in Form der Aussage berühren, daß man seine Gedanken durch die Stimme mittels ὀνόματα und ῥήματα zum Ausdruck bringt (206d1–2; zum gesamten Argumentationsverlauf des Dialogs und seinen zahlreichen sprachtheoretischen Implikationen vgl. bes. Hardy 1998).

Eine nähere Explikation der Begriffe ὄνομα und ῥῆμα und eine Antwort auf die Frage, unter welchen Bedingungen ein λόγος wahr ist, gibt erst der *Sophistes*. Hier wird in einer kurzen Passage (260a–264b) die Frage, was denn überhaupt ein λόγος, eine Rede, sei, behandelt, und dabei wird zunächst festgehalten, daß nicht jede beliebige Zusammenfügung von Wörtern einen Logos ergibt, sondern nur die Zusammenfügung von solchen, die in ihrer Zusammenstellung etwas über das Sein offenbarmachen (δήλωμα, δηλοῦν; 261e5, 262d2). Von solchen Wörtern werden nun zwei Arten unterschieden: die ῥήματα, die etwas über Handlungen (πράξεις) kundtun, und die ὀνόματα, die Zeichen (σημεῖον) für diejenigen sind, die die Handlungen verrichten (262a1–7). Eine bloße Aneinanderreihung von mehreren ὀνόματα (wie etwa *Löwe Hirsch Pferd*) oder mehreren ῥήματα (wie etwa *geht läuft schläft*) allein macht noch keinen Logos aus, da diese nichts über das Sein aussagen würde. Ein Logos wäre erst die Verknüpfung von einem ὄνομα und einem ῥῆμα, wie sie etwa in der Rede ἄνθρωπος μανθάνει "der Mensch lernt" vorliegt (262bc). Etwas später (263a4) scheint das ὄνομα als das spezifiziert zu werden, worüber etwas anderes ausgesagt wird, und ῥῆμα als das, was über das erstgenannte etwas aussagt. Solcherlei Formulierungen rücken die beiden Begriffe zwar in die Nähe der späteren grammatischen Termini Nomen und Verb und der urteilslogischen Begriffe Argument und Prädikat, doch ist Borsche (1996: 154) sicher zuzustimmen, wenn er sagt, daß die Platonische Unterscheidung von ὄνομα und ῥῆμα noch *nicht* deren formalgrammatische und formallogische Bestimmtheit erreicht hat.

Die Frage der Wahrheit einer Rede wird schließlich an den Beispielen "Theaitet sitzt" und "Theaitet fliegt" erörtert. Und hier dürfte ein Kriterium für die Beurteilung der Wahrheit oder Falschheit der Rede deren Übereinstimmung mit der Wahrnehmung sein, während ein anderes möglicherweise in der Verträglichkeit bzw. Unverträglichkeit der Ideen beruht, die mittels der sie bezeichnenden Wörter im Logos verbunden werden (vgl. dazu etwa die Diskussion in Rehm 1982: 138ff.).

Insgesamt ist damit eine Position erreicht, nach der die Sprache zwar nicht mehr als direkter Weg zur Erkenntnis angesehen werden kann, aber auf allen Stufen der Erkenntnisgewinnung eine Rolle spielt. Zudem wurde im

Laufe der Entwicklung von Homer zu Platon nicht nur eine sehr differenzierte Sicht bezüglich der Relationen von Sprache, Denken und Wirklichkeit gewonnen, vielmehr wurden auch etliche linguistische Probleme und Einsichten formuliert, an die die weitere Sprachreflexion anknüpfen konnte.

## 6. Bibliographie

### 6.1. Primärliteratur

*DK* = *Die Fragmente der Vorsokratiker. Griechisch und Deutsch* von Hermann Diels. 6., verb. Aufl. Hg. von Walther Kranz. 3. Bde. Berlin: Weidmann, 1951–52.

Parmenides = *Parmenides. Die Anfänge der Ontologie, Logik und Naturwissenschaft. Die Fragmente.* Hg., übers. und erl. von Ernst Heitsch. München: Heimeran, 1974.

Proklos, *Kratylos* = *Procli Diadochi in Platonis Cratylum commentaria* edidit Georgius Pasquali. Leipzig: B. G. Teubner, 1908. (Nachdr., Stuttgart & Leipzig, 1994.)

Proklos, *Parmenides* = *Procli philosophi Platonici opera inedita* emendavit et auxit V[ictor] Cousin. Pars tertia continens *Procli commentarium in Platonis Parmenidem.* Paris, 1864. (Nachdr., Hildesheim: Olms 1961.)

*Scholia D. T.* = *Scholia in Dionysii Thracis artem grammaticam* (= *Grammatici Graeci* I, 3). Hg. von Alfred Hilgard. Leipzig: Teubner, 1901.

Xenophanes = *Xenophanes. Die Fragmente.* Hg., übers. und erl. von Ernst Heitsch. München & Zürich: Artemis, 1983.

### 6.2. Sekundärliteratur

Adrados, Francisco Rodríguez. 1977. "Sprache, Ontologie und Logik bei Platon und den Sophisten". *Sprache und Bedeutung* hg. von Francisco Rodrígues Adrados, 141–171. München: Fink.

—. 1981. "La teoría del signo en Gorgias de Leontinos". *Logos Semantikos. Studia linguistica in honorem Eugenio Coseriu 1921–1981*, Bd. I: *Geschichte der Sprachphilosophie und der Sprachwissenschaft* hg. von Jürgen Trabant, 9–19. Berlin & New York: de Gruyter; Madrid: Gredos.

Ax, Wolfram. 1978. "ψόφος, φωνή und διάλεκτος als Grundbegriffe aristotelischer Sprachreflexion". *Glotta* 56.245–271.

—. 1986. *Laut, Stimme und Sprache: Studien zu drei Grundbegriffen der antiken Sprachtheorie.* Göttingen: Vandenhoeck & Ruprecht.

Baxter, T. M. S. 1992. *The Cratylus: Plato's Critique of Naming.* Leiden: Brill.

Borsche, Tilman. 1996. "Platon". Schmitter 1996a.140–169.

Brancacci, Aldo. 1986. "Les mots et les choses: La philosophie du langage chez Démocrite". *Philosophie du langage et grammaire dans l'antiquité* hg. von Henry Joly, 9–28. Bruxelles: Editions Ousia; Grenoble: Université des Sciences Sociales de Grenoble.

Bühler, Karl. 1934. *Sprachtheorie: Die Darstellungsfunktion der Sprache.* Jena: Fischer.

Calogero, Guido. 1967. *Storia della logica antica.* Bari: Laterza.

Coseriu, Eugenio. 1975. *Die Geschichte der Sprachphilosophie von der Antike bis zur Gegenwart: Eine Übersicht*, Bd. I: *Von der Antike bis Leibniz.* 2., überarb. Aufl. Tübingen: Narr.

—. 1996. "Der φύσει-θέσει-Streit". *Sprachphilosophie / Philosophy of Language / La philosophie du langage* hg. von Marcelo Dascal, Dietfried Gerhardus, Kuno Lorenz & Georg Meggle, II, 880–898. Berlin & New York: de Gruyter.

Derbolav, Josef. 1972. *Platons Sprachphilosophie im Kratylos und in den späteren Schriften.* Darmstadt: Wissenschaftliche Buchgesellschaft.

Detel, Wolfgang. 1972. *Platons Beschreibung des falschen Satzes im Theätet und Sophistes.* Göttingen: Vandenhoeck & Ruprecht.

Di Cesare, Donatella. 1980. *La semantica nella filosofia greca.* Roma: Bulzoni.

—. 1986. "Heraklit und die Sprache". Mojsisch 1986.1–16.

—. 1989. "Language and Dialectics in Plato: Reflections on the linguistic foundation of philosophical enquiry". *Kodikas/Code* 12.3–19.

—. 1996. "Die Geschmeidigkeit der Sprache: Zur Sprachauffassung und Sprachbetrachtung der Sophistik". Schmitter 1996a.87–118.

Erbse, Hartmut. 1970. "Etymologika". *dtvLexikon der Antike. Philosophie, Literatur, Wissenschaft*, II, 101–103. 2. Aufl. München: Deutscher Taschenbuch Verlag.

Fehling, Detlev. 1965. "Zwei Untersuchungen zur griechischen Sprachphilosophie. 1. Protagoras und die ὀρθοέπεια. 2. φύσις und θέσις". *Rheinisches Museum* 108.212–229.

Fritz, Kurt von. 1968. "Die Rolle des ΝΟΥΣ". *Um die Begriffswelt der Vorsokratiker* hg. von Hans-Georg Gadamer, 246–363. Darmstadt:Wissenschaftliche Buchgesellschaft.

Gaiser, Konrad. 1974. *Name und Sache in Platons 'Kratylos'.* Heidelberg: Winter.

Gatzemeier, Matthias. 1992. "Sprachphilosophische Anfänge". *Sprachphilosophie / Philosophy of Language / La philosophie du langage* hg. von Marcelo Dascal, Dietfried Gerhardus, Kuno Lorenz & Georg Meggle, I, 1–17. Berlin & New York: de Gruyter.

Gentinetta, Peter M. 1961. *Zur Sprachbetrachtung bei den Sophisten und in der stoisch-hellenistischen Zeit.* Winterthur: Keller.

Guthrie, William K. C. 1971. *The Sophists.* Cambridge: Cambridge Univ. Press. (Erstveröffentlichung 1969 als Teil 1 von *A History of Greek Philosophy*, III.)

–. 1988. *A History of Greek Philosophy*, XII. Cambridge: Cambridge Univ. Press. (Erstveröffentlichung 1962.)

Hardy, Jörg. 1998. *Epistemologie und Sprachphilosophie in Platons Dialog 'Theaitetos'*. Diss. Universität Münster, Philosophische Fakultät.

Heinimann, Friedrich. 1945. Νόμος und Φύσις: *Herkunft und Bedeutung einer Antithese im griechischen Denken des 5. Jahrhunderts.* Basel: Reinhardt. (Nachdr., Darmstadt: Wissenschaftliche Buchgesellschaft, 1965.)

Heitsch, Ernst. 1974. *Parmenides. Die Anfänge der Ontologie, Logik und Naturwissenschaft. Die Fragmente.* München: Heimeran.

–. 1979. *Parmenides und die Anfänge der Erkenntniskritik und Logik.* Donauwörth: Auer.

–. 1983. *Xenophanes. Die Fragmente.* München & Zürich: Artemis, 1983.

–. 1985. "Platons Sprachphilosophie im 'Kratylos': Überlegungen zu 383a4–b2 und 387d10–390a8". *Hermes* 113.44–62.

Held, Klaus. 1980. *Heraklit, Parmenides und der Anfang von Philosophie und Wissenschaft: Eine phänomenologische Besinnung.* Berlin & New York: de Gruyter.

Herbermann, Clemens-Peter. 1981. "Moderne und antike Etymologie". *Zeitschrift für Vergleichende Sprachforschung* 95.22–48.

–. 1996. "Antike Etymologie". Schmitter 1996a.353–376.

Hossenfelder, Malte. 1996. "Epikureer". Schmitter 1996a.217–237.

Hülser, Karlheinz. 1997. "Zeichenkonzeptionen in der Philosophie der griechischen und römischen Antike". *Semiotik / Semiotics* hg. von Roland Posner, Klaus Robering & Thomas A. Sebeok, I, 837–861. Berlin & New York: de Gruyter.

Ildefonse, Frédérique. 1997. *La naissance de la grammaire dans l'antiquité grecque.* Paris: Vrin.

Jantzen, Jörg. 1976. *Parmenides zum Verhältnis von Sprache und Wirklichkeit.* München: Beck.

Kamptz, Hans von. 1982. *Homerische Personennamen: Sprachwissenschaftliche und historische Klassifikation.* Göttingen: Vandenhoeck & Ruprecht.

Karakulakow, Wladimir W. 1970. "Die ersten griechischen Philosophen über die Rolle der Sprache in der Erkenntnis". *Das Altertum* 16.204–215.

Kélessidou, Anna. 1986. "Dire et savoir (*legein eidenai*) chez Xénophane et Parménide". *Philosophie du langage et grammaire dans l'antiquité* hg. von Henry Joly, 29–45. Bruxelles: Editions Ousia; Grenoble: Université des Sciences Sociales de Grenoble.

Kerferd, George Briscoe. 1981. *The Sophistic Movement.* Cambridge: Cambridge Univ. Press.

Kirk, G. S., J. E. Raven & M. Schofield. 1983. *The Presocratic Philosophers: A critical history with a selection of texts.* 2nd ed. Cambridge: Cambridge Univ. Press.

Kraus, Manfred. 1987. *Name und Sache: Ein Problem im frühgriechischen Denken.* Amsterdam: Grüner.

–. 1990. "Platon und das semiotische Dreieck". *Poetica* 22.241–281.

–. 1996. "Platon (428/27–348/47 v. Chr.)". *Klassiker der Sprachphilosophie: Von Platon bis Noam Chomsky* hg. von Tilman Borsche, 15–32, 449–452. München: Beck.

Krings, H. & H. M. Baumgartner. 1972. "Erkennen, Erkenntnis". *Historisches Wörterbuch der Philosophie*, Bd. II hg. von Joachim Ritter, Sp. 643–662. Basel & Stuttgart: Schwabe.

Laspia, Patrizia. 1996. *Omero linguista: Voce e voce articolata nell' enciclopedia omerica.* Palermo: Novecento.

Leclerc, Marie-Christine. 1993. *La parole chez Hésiode: A la recherche de l'harmonie perdue.* Paris: Les Belles Lettres.

Leroy, Maurice. 1968. "Etymologie et linguistique chez Platon". *Bulletin de la Classe des Lettres et des Sciences Morales et Politiques (Académie Royale de Belgique*). 5. Serie. 54.121–152.

Lieb, Hans-Heinrich. 1981. "Das 'semiotische Dreieck' bei Ogden und Richards: Eine Neuformulierung des Zeichenmodells von Aristoteles". *Logos Semantikos. Studia linguistica in honorem Eugenio Coseriu 1921–1981*, Bd. I: *Geschichte der Sprachphilosophie und der Sprachwissenschaft* hg. von Jürgen Trabant, 137–156. Berlin & New York: de Gruyter; Madrid: Gredos.

Liebermann, Wolf-Lüder. 1971. "Voraussetzungen antiker Sprachbetrachtung: Zur Erkenntnisfunktion der Sprache im frühen Griechenland". *Donum Indogermanicum. Festgabe für Anton Scherer zum 70. Geburtstag* hg. von R. Schmitt-Brandt, 130–154. Heidelberg: Winter.

–. 1996. "Sprachauffassungen im frühgriechischen Epos und in der griechischen Mythologie". Schmitter 1996a.26–53.

Lingohr, Hans-Jörg. 1954. *Die Bedeutung der etymologischen Namenserklärungen in den Gedichten Homers und Hesiods und in den homerischen Hymnen.* Diss. Berlin (Freie Universität.)

Mansfeld, Jaap. 1987. *Die Vorsokratiker. Griechisch/Deutsch. Auswahl der Fragmente, Übersetzung und Erläuterung.* Stuttgart: Reclam.

Mayer, Hermann. 1913. *Prodikos von Keos und die Anfänge der Synonymik bei den Griechen.* Paderborn: Schöningh.

Mojsisch, Burkhard, Hg. 1986. *Sprachphilosophie in Antike und Mittelalter.* Amsterdam: Grüner.

Mühlestein, Hugo. 1987. *Homerische Namenstudien.* Frankfurt/M.: Athenäum.

Newiger, Hans-Joachim. 1973. *Untersuchungen zu Gorgias' Schrift 'Über das Nichtseiende'.* Berlin & New York: de Gruyter.

Nestle, Wilhelm. 1941. *Vom Mythos zum Logos: Die Selbstentfaltung des griechischen Denkens von Homer bis auf die Sophistik und Sokrates.* 2. Aufl. (1. Aufl., 1940; Nachdr., Stuttgart: Kröner, 1975.) Antonio Pagliaro, *Nuovi saggi di critica semantica,* 47–76. Messina & Firenze: D'Anna. (Erstveröffentlichung 1952.)

Palmer, M. D. 1988. *Names, Reference and Correctness in Plato's Cratylus.* New York.

Peradotto, John. 1990. *Man in the Middle Voice: Name and Narration in the Odyssey.* Princeton: Princeton Univ. Press.

Pleger, Wolfgang H. 1987. *Der Logos der Dinge: Eine Studie zu Heraklit.* Frankfurt/M.: Lang.

Pohlenz, Max. 1953. "Νόμος und φύσις". *Hermes* 81.418–438.

Popper, Karl Raimund. 1935. *Logik der Forschung.* Wien. (5. Aufl., Tübingen: Mohr, 1973.)

Rank, Louis Philippe. 1951. Etymologiseering en verwante verschijnselen bij Homerus. Assen: Hak & Prakke.

Rehn, Rudolf. 1982. *Der logos der Seele: Wesen, Aufgabe und Bedeutung der Sprache in der platonischen Philosophie.* Hamburg: Meiner.

–. 1986. "Zur Theorie des Onoma in der griechischen Philosophie". Mojsisch 1986.63–119.

Rijlaarsdam, Jetske C. 1978. *Platon über die Sprache: Ein Kommentar zum Kratylos.* Utrecht: Bohn, Scheltema & Holkema.

Risch, Ernst. 1981. "Namensdeutungen und Worterklärungen bei den ältesten griechischen Dichtern". Ernst Risch, *Kleine Schriften* hg. von A. Etter & M. Looser, 294–313. Berlin & New York: de Gruyter. (Erstveröffentlichung 1947.)

Röd, Wolfgang. 1976. *Die Philosophie der Antike,* Bd. I: *Von Thales bis Demokrit.* München: Beck.

Schmitt, Rüdiger, Hg. 1977a. *Etymologie.* Darmstadt: Wissenschaftliche Buchgesellschaft.

–. 1977b. "Einleitung". Schmitt 1977a.16.

Schmitter, Peter. 1975. "Das Wort als sprachliches Zeichen bei Platon und de Saussure". *Gedenkschrift für Jost Trier* hg. von Hartmut Beckers & Hans Schwarz, 45–62. Köln & Wien: Böhlau.

–. 1984. "Zum Heraklitverständnis in der gegenwärtigen Geschichtsschreibung der Linguistik". *Matériaux pour une histoire des théories linguistiques* hg. von Sylvain Auroux et al., 57–68. Lille: Université de Lille III.

–. 1987a. *Das sprachliche Zeichen: Studien zur Zeichen und Bedeutungstheorie in der griechischen Antike sowie im 19. und 20. Jahrhundert.* Münster: Institut für Allgemeine Sprachwissenschaft der Westfälischen Wilhelms-Universität.

–. 1987b. "Heraklit und die Physei-These". Schmitter (1987a: 1–18). (Erstveröffentlichung 1985.)

–. 1987c. "Das Wort als sprachliches Zeichen bei Platon und de Saussure". Schmitter (1987a: 19–42). [Überarb. Fassung von Schmitter 1975.]

–. 1990. "From Homer to Plato: Language, thought, and reality in Ancient Greece". *Essays towards a History of Semantics* hg. von Peter Schmitter, 11–31. Münster: Nodus Publikationen.

–, Hg. 1996a. *Geschichte der Sprachtheorie,* Bd. II: *Sprachtheorien der abendländischen Antike.* 2., verb. Aufl. Tübingen: Narr.

–. 1996b. "Vom 'Mythos' zum 'Logos': Erkenntniskritik und Sprachreflexion bei den Vorsokratikern". Schmitter 1996a.57–86.

–, Hg. 1996c. *Geschichte der Sprachtheorie,* Bd. V: *Sprachtheorien der Neuzeit II: Von der Grammaire de PortRoyal (1660) zur Konstitution moderner linguistischer Disziplinen.* Tübingen: Narr.

Siebenborn, Elmar. 1976. *Die Lehre von der Sprachrichtigkeit und ihren Kriterien.* Amsterdam: Grüner.

Sinnott, A. Eduardo. 1989. *Untersuchungen zu Kommunikation und Bedeutung bei Aristoteles.* Münster: Nodus Publikationen.

Sluiter, Ineke. 1997. "The Greek Tradition". *The Emergence of Semantics in Four Linguistic Traditions: Hebrew, Sanskrit, Greek, Arabic* hg. von Wout van Bekkum, Jan Houben, Ineke Sluiter & Kees Versteegh, 147–224. Amsterdam & Philadelphia. Benjamins.

Steinthal, Heymann. 1863. *Geschichte der Sprachwissenschaft bei den Griechen und Römern mit besonderer Rücksicht auf die Logik.* Berlin: Dümmler.

Swiggers, Pierre. 1996. "L'étymologie: Les transformations de l'étude historique du vocabulaire aux Temps Modernes". Schmitter 1996c.352–385.

Wartburg, Walther von. 1977. "Grundfragen der etymologischen Forschung". Schmitt 1977a.135–155. (Erstveröffentlichung 1931.)

Weidemann, Hermann. 1996. "Grundzüge der Aristotelischen Sprachtheorie". Schmitter 1996a.170–192.

White, Nicholas P. 1992. "Plato (427–347)". *Sprachphilosophie / Philosophy of Language / La philosophie du langage* hg. von Marcelo Dascal, Dietfried Gerhardus, Kuno Lorenz & Georg Meggle, I, 234–244. Berlin & New York: de Gruyter.

*Peter Schmitter, Münster/Seoul (Deutschland/Südkorea)*

# 54. Sprache und Denken bei Aristoteles

1. Data
2. Logische Grundbegriffe
3. *Perì hermēneías* und *Perì psukhē̃s*
4. Sprachliche Elemente
5. Satz
6. Sprechen
7. Kritische Betrachtung
8. Konsequenzen
9. Bibliographie

## 1. Data

Aristoteles hat sich niemals mit der Sprache um ihrer selbst willen befaßt, sie niemals zum Gegenstand seines Nachdenkens gemacht, weder in seiner *Logik* (*Organon*) noch in seiner *Poetik* noch in *Perì psukhē̃s* (*De anima*) und den *Problemata physica*; in letzterem selbst im Abschnitt über die Stimme nicht. In der Poetik werden die Teile der Sprache aufgezählt, in *De anima* wird sie indirekt behandelt, in *De interpretatione* (*Perì hermēneías*), dem 2. Teil des *Organon*, wird sie nur im Hinblick auf die Logik betrachtet. Doch auch hier ist sie nicht sein Gegenstand. Aristoteles hat – Jahrhunderte nach den größten Schöpfungen in seiner Sprache – noch nicht einmal ein feststehendes Wort für 'Sprache'. Er trifft jedoch grundlegende Feststellungen, die mehr gegebene Tatsachen als Ergebnisse seines Nachdenkens zu sein scheinen und über die Jahrhunderte in Geltung blieben wie die Lehren seiner kurzen *Poetik*.

## 2. Logische Grundbegriffe

In seiner Lehre vom Aussagesatz (*Perì hermēneías*) geht Aristoteles von dessen ihm selbstverständlichen Teilen, Subjekt und Prädikat, aus, d. h. von *ónoma* und *rhē̃ma*; *ónoma* aber bedeutet "Name", "Wort", "Nomen" (einschließlich Adjektiv), "Subjekt", meint also hier speziell "Nomen im Nominativ", *rhē̃ma* aber ist alles Ausgesprochene: "Wort" (also darin mit *ónoma* übereinstimmend), "Prädikat", grammatisch "Verb"; es muß als Prädikat nicht éin Wort sein, sondern kann aus "ist" + Adjektiv oder + Partizip Präsens bestehen. Die Reihenfolge der beiden Satzglieder muß auch nicht die angegebene sein; wenn sie ihre Plätze vertauschen, bleibt die Bedeutung dieselbe. Abgesehen von den verschiedenen Stellungen der Verneinungspartikel ist dies die einzige Angabe zur Syntax.

Es ist also klar, daß Aristoteles von der Logik ausgeht: der Aussagesatz muß demzufolge bestehen aus einem Gegenstand und der Aussage über ihn. Er erwähnt nicht, daß in seiner Sprache, wie auch im Lateinischen, ein Wort genügt: *légō* "ich sage", *badízei* "er wandert" sind auch Aussagesätze, und außerdem gibt es subjektlose Aussagen, bloße Vorgänge bezeichnend wie *húei* "es regnet". Beide Grundbegriffe werden, auffallenderweise, weder hier noch in der *Poetik* noch in *De anima* definiert, vielmehr werden sie nur unterschieden von einander als *ónoma* = Begriff ohne Zeitangabe und *rhē̃ma* als Begriff + Zeitangabe. Während vom *ónoma* nur noch gesagt wird, daß es im Nominativ stehen müsse, also nur formal bestimmt wird, heißt es vom *rhē̃ma* immerhin, daß es immer das Zeichen sei für etwas, das von einem andern gesagt wird (Aussage, Prädikat), was es also auf die 3. Person einschränkt; und nicht nur das: das eigentliche *rhē̃ma* steht im Präsens, die andern Tempora sind *ptṓseis* "Flexionsformen". Ferner wird im 4. Kapitel der *Kategorien* seine Aussage in zehn verschiedenen Arten, also inhaltlich erfaßt, nämlich als eine Substanz, eine Quantität, eine Qualität, eine Relation, ein Wo, ein Wann, eine Lage, ein Haben, ein Wirken oder ein Leiden. Diese Kategorien, die sich nur auf das reale Sein beziehen, werden nicht deduziert, sondern nur behauptet und in ihrer Wort*form* nicht bestimmt. Beim Subjekt wird hingegen nicht einmal Konkretheit und Abstraktheit unterschieden, und man muß annehmen, erstere sei immer gemeint. Dies alles hat mit wirklichem Sprachdenken oder gar mit Grammatik nichts zu tun.

Vom *ónoma* und vom *rhē̃ma*, sofern letzteres eine Verbform ist, gilt, daß sie nicht in kleinere Bedeutungsträger geteilt werden können, also die kleinsten semantischen Einheiten sind, und diese éine Bedeutung haben sie nicht "von Natur" (*phúsei*) oder einem ersten Namengeber, der das Wesen des Gegenstandes erkannte und ihn danach benannte, sondern *katà sunthḗkēn*, durch Übereinkunft (konventionell). Diese überraschende Feststellung klingt aber, als ob Aristoteles gegen die Annahme einer natürlichen oder übernatürlichen Entstehung der Namen die rein menschliche setze: "kein Wort ist von Natur, sondern [erst], wenn es zum Zeichen gesetzt wird" – das ist in dieser Form ein logischer

Widerspruch, denn das *ónoma ist* ja ein Zeichen, kann nicht erst dazu werden; es müßte von *phōnḗ* "Stimme, Lautgebilde" gesagt sein: "erst, wenn ein Lautgebilde zum Zeichen wird"; was allerdings voraussetzt, daß der Mensch einen Vorrat an bloßen Lautgebilden hat oder jeweils ein neues erfindet: Diese beiden Feststellungen, die Aristoteles macht, als ob sie sich von selbst verständen, verwerfen gängige Lehren von der Sprache, die sein Lehrer Platon im *Kratylos* behandelt hat, nämlich 1. die Namen der Dinge bezeichnen ursprünglich ihre Natur; 2. diese *étuma* "Grundbedeutungen" konnten durch Zerlegung in ursprüngliche semantische Einheiten erkannt werden (was eigentlich nicht eine Wendung zur Sprach*geschichte* war, sondern nur Ausdruck der Überzeugung von der 'Richtigkeit' der Namen) d. h. von der Übereinstimmung von Zeichen und Bedeutung; 3. überhaupt die Idee eines solchen ersten Namengebers. An seine Stelle trat der Konsens der Menge (den man sich natürlich auch der primären Schöpfung folgend denken konnte), die Sprache also eine gesellschaftliche Erscheinung, ein soziales Phänomen. Aristoteles scheint also der Meinung des Hermogenes im *Kratylos* zu sein, der von der Beliebigkeit der Bezeichnungen überzeugt war. Er hat so die unter Intellektuellen aktuelle Frage, ob die Wörter *phúsei* oder *thései* "naturgemäß oder willkürlich" seien, entschieden, die Suche nach der Richtigkeit der Wörter erledigt. Er hat die Sprache des Mythos entkleidet, sie zu einem potentiellen Gegenstand der Wissenschaft gemacht.

## 3. *Perì hermēneías* und *Perì psukhē̃s*

In *Perì hermēneías* gibt Aristoteles zuerst einen Überblick: "Zuerst muß festgesetzt werden [*thésthai*, also nicht: definiert], was *ónoma* und was *rhē̃ma* ist [...]" Die Hauptbegriffe leitet er folgendermaßen her: *tà en tē̃i phōnē̃i* (*phōnḗ* = Stimmlaut, Stimme, Laut, Wort, Wortverbindung, Sprache), also: die stimmlichen oder sprachlichen Gebilde – aber natürlich meint er nicht sämtliche, sondern keine Geräusche und keine Partikeln – also alle Bedeutungsträger, und das sind für Aristoteles nur die onomata und rhemata – sind *tō̃n en tē̃i psukhē̃i pathēmátōn súmbola*: der vage Ausdruck *pathḗmata* "Widerfahrnisse" in der Seele meint offenbar Eindrücke der äußeren Dinge, deren *homoiṓmata* "Abbilder". Und diese Wahrnehmungen werden durch die Wörter bezeichnet. Aristoteles denkt natürlich nicht an flüchtige Impressionen, und für diese sind auch die Wörter nicht da, sondern ihm geht es um Aussage oder Behauptungssätze, demgemäß sind unter den *pathḗmata* Begriffe zu verstehen: Das Wort *psukhḗ* ruft eine unzulängliche Vorstellung hervor: sie ist laut Aristoteles ohne bestimmten Ort im Körper, aber in Teilseelen überall in ihm wirkend; sie ist nicht nur die Wahrnehmungsfähigkeit, sondern auch *noũs*, Erkenntnis und Denkvermögen. Sie entspricht also mit ihren 'Ablegern' oder Nebenseelen dem Gehirn als Zentrum des Nervensystems, ohne das es kein lebendes Wesen gibt. Aristoteles spricht von der "wissenden Seele" und sagt, "daß sich die Wahrnehmung [...] auf das einzelne, das Wissen aber auf das Allgemeine [d. h. den Begriff] richtet. Dieses aber befindet sich in gewisser Weise in der Seele selbst". Das Denken sei gewollt, das Wahrnehmen nicht. Aber das sagt er nicht in *Perì hermēneías*, sondern in *De anima* (430a4). Er fügt hinzu, daß die Seele "gewissermaßen die Gesamtheit der Dinge ist" (431b21) und: "Das wahrnehmende und wissende Vermögen der Seele ist der Möglichkeit nach gleich den Dingen, dem Wißbaren auf der einen, dem Wahrnehmbaren auf der andern Seite". Es ist also auffallend, daß bezüglich des Denkens nicht von einem Werden oder menschlichen Gestalten die Rede ist, sondern von einem Sein und einem seelischen Vorgang. Alles Wahrnehmbare und Denkbare *ist* in der Seele statt: sie *schafft* alle Bilder und Gedanken. Wie beide sich zueinander verhalten, wird nicht einmal angedeutet, alles ist sozusagen eine bestehende Ordnung. Dieser Auffassung entspricht die scholastische eines *modus essendi activus* und *passivus* in doppelter Form: das Wahrnehmbare der konkreten Formen und das Wißbare der Begriffe. Ebenda sagt er, daß in den wahrnehmbaren Formen die denkbaren enthalten seien, "sowohl die sogenannten abstrakten als auch die des Sinnlichen". Das ist eine weitere Umgehung des eigentlichen Erkenntnis- und Denkprozesses. Er fügt hinzu: "Wenn man etwas erfaßt, muß man es zugleich mit einem Vorstellungsbild erfassen"; es steht demnach zwischen Wahrnehmung und Begriff. Er zeigt seine eigene innere Unsicherheit (oder erweckt jedenfalls den Anschein), wenn er mit der Frage fortfährt: "Aber die ersten Begriffe, inwiefern sollten sich diese von Vorstellungsbildern unterscheiden? Oder es sind auch die übrigen Begriffe keine Vorstellungsbilder, aber nicht ohne sie" (432a12). Das alles wird in *De anima* entwickelt und in *Perì hermēneías* als bekannt vorausgesetzt. Man erschließt also aus dieser definitionslosen Darstellung die *pathḗmata* als ein Wandlungsphänomen: Wahrnehmung – Vorstellungsbild – Begriff, ohne daß die beiden Grundfunktionen, Abstraktion und Analyse, genannt werden. Diese Begriffe seien bei allen Menschen dieselben, wie die Dinge (also Konkreta?), deren Abbilder sie primär sind. Hierzu ist zu bemerken: zwar wird jedes Menschenauge Erscheinungen wie Mensch, Tier, Berg, Fluß, Wald als solche sehen und unterscheiden, aber für alle Dinge gilt das nicht und somit nicht für alle Begriffe. Diese, betont Aristoteles, sind einzeln weder wahr noch falsch (denn wahr oder falsch könne etwas nur in Beziehung zu etwas sein, nicht für sich). Also liege nur in der Verbindung von Begriffen in Bejahung oder Verneinung, Wahres oder Falsches. Nun gebe es in der *phōnḗ* wie in der *psukhḗ* (also sprachlich und begrifflich) beide: die einzelnen Begriffe und die, die durch ihre Verbindung wahr oder falsch sein müssen. Wie aber aus den Abbildern (*homoiṓmata*) oder Vorstellungsbildern der objektiven Dinge sich falsche Urteile ergeben sollen, ist unklar. Liegt es an einer unrichtigen Wahrnehmung (kann es sie geben?) oder an der falschen Interpretation einer richtigen? Aristoteles sagt nur, daß *ónoma* und *rhē̃ma* allein nichts Wahres oder Falsches besagen, nicht einmal das eigene Sein, und zwar ganz unabhängig davon, ob das Nomen etwas Konkretes oder Abstraktes *bezeichne*. Er führt als Beispiel *ánthrōpos* "Mensch" an, vermutlich als Verwerfung der Suche (in Platons *Kratylos*) nach einer ursprünglichen Zusammensetzung des Wortes. Sowenig ein Teil des Wortes eigene Bedeutung habe, habe es für sich allein eine (im Sinne des Urteils); nur wenn "(et)-was" hinzugefügt werde, werde es zu einer Bejahung oder Verneinung; *ti* als "etwas" ist zu allgemein, *tí*? "was?" würde zum Nomen wie zum Verb die passende Ergänzung meinen. Das allein genannte Verb (also ein Infinitiv) befriedige zwar den Hörer und bezeichne etwas, jedoch kein Sein, vermutlich weil das Verb nur in der 3. Person die Affirmation eines Attributs bedeutet.

## 4. Sprachliche Elemente

Wenn man die Lehre vom Aussagesatz des Aristoteles genauer allgemein formuliert, heißt das: Wenn man die Sinnträger allein ausspricht, bedeuten oder besser: besagen sie nichts. Ein Wort hat immer nur Bedeutung in bezug auf etwas: entweder auf andere Wörter oder auf eine sinnlich wahrnehmbare, aber nicht bezeichnete Gegebenheit wie die Luft, ein Bild, Töne, kurz: kontextuell oder situativ. Nomen und Verbum sind also insofern nicht verschieden von den Wörtern, die Aristoteles als bezeichnende und nur in Verbindung mit bezeichnenden einen Sinn erhaltende oder verleihende einstuft (*Poetik* Kap. XX); m. a. W.: die Wort*bedeutung* ist nur aus dem jeweiligen Zusammenhang zu erschließen. Eine der wesentlichsten Erkenntnisse des Logikers ist die, daß das einzelne Wort keine Bedeutung hat. Das gilt für diejenigen, die nach seiner Meinung allein Bedeutungsträger sind, d. h. *ónoma* und *rhē̃ma*: nur in Verbindung mit, in bezug auf etwas anderes *besagen* sie etwas, das wahr oder falsch ist; was nicht gilt von allen andern 'Wortarten', z. B. "unter", "aber". Ein Wort allein existiert nicht, es ist nur denkbar; wie es praktisch nicht einen einzelnen Menschen gibt oder gegeben hat, sondern nur theoretisch, als Denkform. Alles lebt nur in Gemeinschaft; die Sprache selbst ist, wie Aristoteles sieht, ein Produkt einer Gemeinschaft, eine unter vielen. Da alles Einzelne nur gedacht, d. h. durch Abstraktion oder Analyse gewonnen ist, weist er der 'Seele' alle Begriffe als Inhalt zu, statt daß er sie sie erzeugen läßt. Die in Beziehung zueinander gesetzten und so ein Urteil bildenden *onómata* und *rhē̃mata* müßten, gemäß der in *Perì hermēneías* (16f.) von Aristoteles gebotenen Lehre, eigentlich immer Richtiges oder Wahres aussagen; das Falsche oder Unwahre könnte seinen Ursprung nur in der denkenden 'Seele' haben. Aber was ist denn das Denken? Er sagt es nicht, definiert es sowenig wie seine andern Hauptbegriffe. Leider bietet er auch keine Beispiele für falsche Aussagesätze. Denn die Wörter sind ja die Zeichen (*súmbola*) der gedachten Begriffe, die aus den Wahrnehmungen hervorgehen. Ihre Lautungen sind national verschieden, sie selbst nicht. Obwohl die Begründung des Vokabulars durch Übereinkunft einen sehr großen zeitlichen Abstand voraussetzt, werden die Kategorien Zeit und Entwicklung – im Gegensatz zu Platon – nicht beachtet. Die Sprache ist ihm, wie es scheint, ein zeitloses fertiges Gebilde, nicht ein Gewordenes, sondern ein Gegebenes. Das ist insofern ganz natürlich, als niemand sich in seinem kurzen Leben an irgendeine Veränderung in seiner Sprache erinnern kann, noch auch an die Kunde von einer solchen; die Sprache war etwas Selbstverständliches und Unveränderliches wie der Körperbau. Das war die natürliche Einstellung zu ihr, die die scholastische Philosophie der Grammatik mit der Sprachlogik des Aristoteles verband. Eine Ahnung von Veränderung der Wortform und -bedeutung konnten nur etwa die Homer-Philologen gewinnen.

Die Wörter also sind Zeichen der Begriffe, und alles Denken geschieht mit den gedachten oder gesprochenen Zeichen: die Wörter *sind* die Begriffe. Aristoteles sagt das nicht explizit, es versteht sich von seiner Darstellung, die sich nur auf Konkreta zu beziehen scheint und da in ihrer Entsprechung DING – Vorstellungsbild – BEGRIFF – WORT klar ist.

In Kap. XX der *Poetik* zählt Aristoteles "die Teile des sprachlichen Ausdrucks in seiner Gesamtheit" auf, nämlich: Buchstabe (*grámma*, nicht unterschieden vom artikulierten Laut bis ins 19. Jh.), Silbe (als nächstgrößere, aber noch bedeutungslose Sprecheinheit aus Konsonant(en) + Vokal, über die er in der *Metaphysica* VI,17 ausführt, daß sie mehr sei als die Summe ihrer Elemente, aber nicht, warum); sodann 'bedeutungslose' Wörter, die er *súndesmos* und *árthron* nennt (*súndesmos* ist "Verbindung", in der Grammatik "Konjunktion"; *árthron* ist "Bindeglied", in der Grammatik "Artikel"). Wenn er beide *ásēmos* nennt, so heißt das nicht "bedeutungslos", sondern "nicht bezeichnend", nämlich weder ein Ding noch einen Begriff; als wirklich bedeutungslos pflegte man hingegen *blíturi* und *skindapsós*, onomatopoetische Bildungen, anzuführen. Wie hätte Aristoteles z. B. ein so bedeutungsschweres, ja entscheidendes Wort wie *ou(k)* "nicht" bedeutungslos nennen können? Ihnen entsprach nichts in der Dingwelt, sie hatten nur eine Bedeutung in der Gedankenwelt, und wenn die Fülle der Partikeln semantisch schwer zu bestimmen war, ihre sprachliche Funktion war dennoch klar.

Es folgen die eigentlichen Wortarten Nomen und Verbum, dann Flexion (*ptō̃sis* "Fall", grammatikalisch "Kasus", meist der eines Substantivs, aber auch alle Formen, in denen Nomen und Verb 'vorfallen' können, d. h. alle Formen der Deklination, Konjugation, Adjektivsteigerung und Adverbableitung vom Adjektiv) und schließlich: Satz (*lógos*). *Ptō̃sis* meint natürlich das ganze Wort, nicht nur die Endung. "Die Teile des sprachlichen Ausdrucks" scheinen nach Größe und Bedeutung geordnet zu sein, jedoch mit der Silbe als reiner Sprecheinheit und der *ptō̃sis* als Akzidens von Nomen und Verbum. Die Ordnung ist also uneinheitlich, teils formal, teils funktional. Der Abstand von der ersten Grammatik (Dionysios Thrax, vermutlich 2. Jahrhundert vor Chr., *Tékhnē grammatikḗ/ Ars grammatica*) ist beträchtlich: sie fängt zwar auch mit Buchstabe und Silbe an, nennt dann aber acht Redeteile oder Wortarten, einschließlich Präsenspartizip, aber ohne Numerale; beim Adverb, das für Aristoteles nicht erwähnenswert zu sein scheint, unterscheidet sie 25 Arten. Die unbezeichnenden Wortarten, die Aristoteles *súndesmos* und *árthron* nennt, sind nicht als grammatische Termini aufzufassen, über die dann Unverständliches ausgesagt wird, so daß diese Stelle in *Poetik* XX als verderbt gilt, sondern sie scheinen etwa die Grundbedeutungen 'Bindeglied' und damit Partikeln zu meinen, die sich mit Substantiven und Verben zusammensetzen und so die Bedeutung modifizieren (Präpositionen und Adverbien oder Konjunktionen, die Sätze und Begriffe zueinander in Beziehung setzen). Unter den Begriffen Nomen und Verbum sind wahrscheinlich noch mitverstanden einerseits Personalpronomen und Numerale und vielleicht das deskriptive Adverb als eine *ptō̃sis* des Adjektivs, anderseits ist zum Verb hinzuzurechnen das Partizip Präsens. Während Aristoteles in Kap. XX nur die in *Perì hermēneías* vom Standpunkt der Logik gemachten Angaben wiederholt, bietet er im folgenden eine Ergänzung zur *Poetik* des Nomens.

Er unterscheidet allgemein- und sondersprachliche Wörter, Metaphern und Neubildungen etc. und endet mit der Nennung der Genera und ihrer Wortausgänge, was doch nach Aristoteles' eigenen strengen Fachabgrenzungen nichts mit der Poetik zu tun hat. Er bietet jedoch Beispiele zu allen von ihm unterschiedenen Arten des Substantivs.

## 5. Satz

Die 'Definition' des Satzes (*lógos*, ein vieldeutiges Wort wie *ónoma* und *rhē̃ma*) ist einerseits gleich der in *Perì hermēneías* gegebenen ("ein zusammengesetztes Lautgebilde mit Bedeutung, von dem Teile auch Bedeutung haben"), dem aber hinzugefügt wird "denn nicht jedes Wortgefüge besteht aus Verben und Substantiven". Das heißt wohl: nicht jeder *lógos* ist ein Aussagesatz. Die Beispiele zeigen, daß er jedes Wortgefüge, vom kleinsten (im Gehen; Kleon, der Sohn des Kleon) bis zum größten meint. Es kann also auch ohne Verb, also ohne formale Aussage sein, wie etwa die Definition des Menschen: "Ein auf dem Lande lebendes, zweifüßiges, vernunftbegabtes Wesen". *Lógos* ist also nicht = Satz, sondern etwa "Wortgefüge" oder "Rede". Eine Einheit könne es auf zweierlei Art sein: entweder indem es ein Einziges bezeichne wie die Definition oder aus der Verknüpfung von mehrerem bestehe: eine solche Einheit sei die *Ilias*. Von einer grammatischen oder psychologischen Definition ist also keine Rede, während sie in der ersten Grammatik lautet: "eine Verbindung von Wörtern, welche einen in sich vollendeten Sinn darstellt". Auch *lógos* macht also deutlich, daß jede Wiedergabe der Hauptbegriffe durch je ein einziges Wort unmöglich ist. Im übrigen hat aber Aristoteles selbst zuvor verschiedene Satzarten in unserem Sinne angeführt und deren spezielle Kenntnis einem andern Fach(-mann) zugewiesen: "Was Befehl ist und was Wunsch oder Erzählung oder Drohung oder Frage oder Antwort". Das ist also eine gemischt inhaltliche und formale Sonderung, die keiner 'Fachkenntnisse' bedarf.

## 6. Sprechen

Das Sprechen als die Hervorbringung von bedeutungsvollen Zeichen vermittels der Stimme hat mit der Lehre vom Aussagesatz nichts zu tun und wird darum in *Perì hermēneías* nicht behandelt, sondern in *De anima* im Zusammenhang mit dem Wahrnehmungsvermögen (420b). "Die Stimme ist etwas wie der Schall eines beseelten Wesens". Unbeseeltes – ein Tier oder ein Musikinstrument – hat keine Stimme (ersteres erzeugt nur Geräusche, die Flöte ein Stimmähnliches). Die Stimme ist also etwas spezifisch Menschliches; sie habe "Tonspannung, Melodie, Sprechklang" wie ein Instrument. Die Natur mache, wie auch in manchen anderen Fälle, doppelten Gebrauch von der eingeatmeten Luft: zur inneren Erwärmung und zum Sprechen. "Organ für das Atmen ist der Kehlkopf", der um der Lunge willen vorhanden sei. Die Stimme wird daher (ausnahmsweise) definiert als "das von der in diesen Körperteilen wohnenden Seele bewirkte Anschlagen der eingeatmeten Luft an die sogenannte Luftröhre. Denn nicht jeder Ton des Lebewesens ist Stimme [...], sondern das Anschlagende muß beseelt sein und eine bestimmte Vorstellung (*phantasía*) haben, ist doch die Stimme ein Ton, der etwas bedeutet, und nicht der Ton der eingeatmeten Luft" (*De anima* 420b). Das Sprechen kommt also zustande durch ein bewußtes Zusammenwirken der Organe. Es ist dies der Versuch, das Sprechen zu erklären durch Einsetzung aller Denknotwendigkeiten als Fakten. Die 'beseelte' Tätigkeit von Lunge und Kehlkopf ist also eine bewußte, weil vom Gehirn gesteuerte zum Zwecke der Erzeugung von Lautgebilden, die Träger einer bestimmten Bedeutung sind und als solche von den andern Gliedern der Sprachgruppe natürlich verstanden werden. Sprechen könne man nur beim Anhalten des Atems. "Denn wer den Atem anhält, bringt mit der eingeatmeten Luft die (Stimm-)bewegung hervor". Damit ist also lediglich erst eine Voraussetzung für die Verlautbarung einer vom Gehirn intendierten Mitteilung geschaffen. Für diese steht ein Lautvorrat zur Verfügung: die Buchstaben oder artikulierten Laute (*grámmata*); das sind unteilbare und mit anderen zusammensetzbare im Gegensatz zu den von Tieren erzeugten, nämlich stimmhafte, halbstimmhafte und stimmlose (*phōnḗenta*, *hemíphōna*, *áphōna*). Die Stimme bildet die Vokale allein mit dem Kehlkopf, der halbstimmhafte ist ein zusätzlich mit Anlegung der Zunge geformter hörbarer Laut, wie *s* und *r*, der stimmlose oder Konsonant aber ist selbst mit ihrer Anlegung ein nicht hörbarer Laut, den man nur vor einem Vokal vernimmt, z. B. *g* und *d* (die stimmhaften Verschlußlaute werden also von den stimmlosen nicht geschieden) (*Poetik* Kap. XX). Diese Darstellung ist noch sehr oberflächlich im Vergleich mit der von Dionysios Thrax gegebenen, die zwar auch nicht nach stimmhaft und stimmlos unterscheidet, aber doch schon Zischlaute und Aspiraten kennt. Man erfährt tatsächlich nicht, wo und wie die Laute gebildet werden und sich dadurch wesensmäßig unterscheiden, obwohl Aristoteles durch Selbstbeobachtung die Bildung hätte ermitteln können, z. B. der Bilabialen und Dentalen. Er fügt nur summarisch hinzu, daß die Laute sich ferner unterscheiden durch Mundstellung, Mundstelle (des Anlegens der Zunge), Rauheit oder Glattheit (d. i. Behauchung oder Nichtbehauchung, d. h. entweder *ph th kh* gegen *p b, t d, k g* oder *spiritus asper* und *lenis*, ferner Länge und Kürze, Tonhöhe, Tontiefe oder Mittellage (die aber semantisch i. a. bedeutungslos ist). Die genauere Behandlung dieser Dinge komme der Metrik zu. Offenbar ist er an der Phonetik ebensowenig interessiert wie an der

Grammatik. Das geregelte Zusammenwirken von Lunge, Kehlkopf (die Stimmbänder sind ihm noch nicht bekannt), Luftröhre, Mundraum, Zunge, Lippen, kombiniert mit Laut- und Sinnvorstellung – eine komplizierte Kooperation – bringt also die artikulierten und zusammensetzbaren, immer in gleicher Form wiederholbaren Elemente der Sprache hervor, während die Tiere mit der bloßen Stimme – nicht anders als der Mensch – nur Empfindungen und Triebe ausdrücken können, nicht aber durch Buchstaben repräsentierbare Laute und ihre Zusammensetzung zu bestimmten Gebilden. So in der *Poetik* XX. Auch in seinen Gedanken über die 'Stimme' (*Problemata* XI) gelangt er keinen Schritt darüber hinaus. Der Mensch habe "nur eine Stimme, aber viele Sprachen"; diese Tatsache führt er zurück auf die große Zahl der artikulierten Laute, speziell der Konsonanten, von denen die Tiere fast keine haben (*Problemata* XI,57).

## 7. Kritische Betrachtung

Die entschiedene Feststellung in *Perì hermēneías* daß das Wort kein Naturprodukt wie die tierische Lautäußerung sei, sondern vom Menschen in der angegebenen Weise bewußt hervorgebracht mit einer auf Übereinkunft beruhenden Bedeutung, ergänzt durch die Setzung, daß kein Teil von ihm gesonderte Bedeutung habe, was er sogar vom Kompositum behauptet, ist nicht als das Ergebnis eines intensiven Sprachstudiums anzusehen, sondern als eine unerläßliche Bedingung für seine Lehre vom Urteil und vom Beweis: jedes Wort mußte eine klare Bedeutung haben, die nicht durch 'etymologische' Ableitung oder Zerlegung in bedeutungsvolle Wortbestandteile in Frage gestellt und sophistisch verdreht werden konnte. Aber was für ein Simplex klar ist, kann nicht ohne weiteres auch für alle Komposita gelten. Hier ist die Unstimmigkeit zu bemerken, daß er nicht, seinen Worten gemäß, von einem Simplex zu einem Kompositum übergeht, sondern mit letzterem beginnt, und zwar einem Eigennamen, der ja nichts Reales bedeutet, sondern Ausdruck eines elterlichen Wunsches zu sein pflegt, und erst im 4. Kap. einen Einsilber anführt. In dem Namen *Kallippos* habe im Gegensatz zu dem *lógos* '*kalòs híppos*' "ein schönes Pferd" *híppos* keine Bedeutung (*kalós* auch nicht? ebensowenig wie in seinem eignen Namen *áristos* "der Beste"?) Sein Simplex-Beispiel wird dann *mũs* "Maus", in dem *(h)ũs* "Schwein" nichts bedeute (wie *aus* in *Maus*) Zu beiden Fällen ist zu bemerken, daß der *spiritus asper* nicht beachtet wird, weil er kein Buchstabe ist, *ippos* und *us* aber gibt es gar nicht. Das Beispiel ist also nicht nur falsch gewählt, sondern steht auch am falschen Platz, da, wo *mũs* stehen müßte. Dann erst kommt das eigentliche Beispiel (im Sinne des Aristoteles) für Kompositum: *epaktrokélēs* "leichtes Piratenschiff" = *epaktrón* "leichtes Schiff" + *kélēs* "Reit-, Rennpferd, schnelle Jacht", von dem er behauptet, daß es darin nichts bedeute, was nur möglich ist, wenn er an 'Reitpferd' denkt. Auch hier wird das erste Glied übergangen. In beiden Kompositionsfällen erbringt er keinen schlüssigen Beweis.

Vielleicht meint er nur, daß das Zusammengesetzte für den Sprecher eine Einheit ist, deren Bestandteile er i. a. nicht realisiert, und sagt vermittelnd, daß die Glieder der Komposita zwar einzeln etwas bedeuten oder bezeichnen *wollen*, es aber nicht tun. An *tragélaphos* "Bockhirsch" ist es aber gerade die semantische Unvereinbarkeit der Glieder, die ihn veranlaßt, der Erfindung des Aristophanes die Bezeichnung von etwas Unwirklichem zuzusprechen (später wurde es sogar zur Dingbezeichnung). Anscheinend versteht er unter Zusammensetzung nur eine von Nomina, nicht ein mit Präposition oder Adverb wie *eũ* "gut", das doch immer ein die Bedeutung bestimmender Bestandteil ist. Er gibt leider Erklärungen nur, wenn sie für die *hermēneía* erforderlich sind. So gibt er auch keine zu *katà sunthḗkēn* – das ist eine bequeme Umgehung des Problems Ursprung der Sprache. Was er mit der Konvention verneinte, war klar, doch nicht, wie er sie verstand; das hätte er vielleicht selbst nicht darlegen können; aber er hatte die Sprache zum sozialen Phänomen erklärt, das war entscheidend. Daß der Ausdruck hier nicht "gemäß Zusammensetzung" bedeutet, ist klar: zwar ist das Wort aus einzelnen Lauten zusammengesetzt, doch entsteht die Bedeutung nicht aus der Zusammensetzung (*sunthḗkē*).

Die am Anfang von *Perì hermēneías* gebotene lakonische Entwicklung vom Ding zum Wort mit Hilfe der *pathḗmata* erklärt sich leicht aus der Tatsache, daß sprachlich die Wahrnehmung, das Wahrgenommene und der Begriff *eins* sind: *nóēma*. Die Sprache legt also zumindest die Sicht der Dinge nahe, bzw. die noch herrschende Unschärfe der Begriffsbildung zeitigt diese Darstellung, ohne daß der Denker selber sich eines solchen Einflusses bewußt sein könnte, ja überhaupt der Möglichkeit eines solchen. Die Sprache ist vom Denken abhängig – also kann es nicht umgekehrt sein. Er sagt nichts über die Kommunikationsbedürftigkeit des Menschen, deutet sie nur an, indem er bemerkt, die *hermēneía*, d. h. hier: "die Selbstäußerung, Mitteilung" diene dem Wohlsein des Menschen. (*De anima* 420b, 19). Daß er über den Zwang des *zōon politikón* zur gegenseitigen Verständigung kein Wort verliert, ist auffallend.

Es ergibt sich also aufgrund der Gleichheit der Menschen und ihrer Gehirnstruktur (‚Seele'): Ding = Begriff = Bezeichnung. Die Gleichheit ganz verschiedener Seinsarten wie konkret und abstrakt, Ding und Name, die uns unmöglich scheint und durch 'Entsprechung' ersetzt werden müßte, war aber des Aristoteles Vorstellung. Er hat übrigens in *Sophistici elenchi.* Kap. 1 bemerkt, daß die Zahl der Dinge unendlich, die der Wörter aber begrenzt sei. Darum müsse dieselbe Rede, dasselbe Wort mehreres bedeuten. Diese Erkenntnis läßt sich aber kaum in seine Logik einbauen. Seine simplifizierende Darstellung macht den Eindruck, nur auf Konkreta bezogen zu sein, als handle der Aussagesatz, das Urteil nur von ihnen. Er gibt keinen Hinweis, wie die so zahlreichen *nomina abstracta* in seine Sprache kommen. Da seine Lebens- und Arbeitswelt die der *psukhḗ*, d. h. des Denkens ist, ist sie völlig abstrakt, fast mathematisch, und da die Begriffe, mit denen er in seiner Wissenschaft von der Beweisführung arbeitet, real sein müssen, hat er sie als von der Dingwelt unmittelbar gegeben dargestellt, aber tatsächlich wird die Gedankenwelt zu einem selbständigen Bereich, der unabhängig von der Dingwelt und der Sprache ist und wo sich ständig neue Begriffe erzeugen. Sie existieren zwar nur in sprachlicher Form, weil sie eine andre gar nicht annehmen können, aber diese selbstverständliche Tatsache tendiert zur Unsichtbarkeit. Aristoteles war sich zweifellos ihrer nicht bewußt. Er glaubte an das absolute Denken, über das er sich nicht hinausschwingen konnte zu einer Betrachtung des Denkens selbst: Ebensowenig vermochte er seine Sprache in ihrem Wesen und ihrer Struktur, ihrer Grammatik zumindest, zu erkennen. Daß er in *Perì hermēneías* alles von der Logik her betrachtet und behandelt, zeigt sich auch darin, daß er sprachlich Unsinniges nennt, um es dann vom Aussagesatz auszuschließen, z. B. Genitiv, Dativ und Akkusativ oder ein verneintes Nomen wie "Nichtmensch" als Subjekt, ein verneintes Verb wie "nicht-arbeitet" als Prädikat, weil beide nichts bezeichnen. Aber beide Bildungen sind reine Denkfiguren. Hingegen sagt er nichts über die innere Beziehung zwischen *ónoma* und *rhē̃ma*, ausgedrückt durch des letzteren Flexion: 3. Pers. im selben Numerus wie ersteres. Und da das *rhē̃ma* als Begriff + Zeitbezeichnung definiert ist, kann man das verbale Prädikat durch "ist" + Partizip Präsens ersetzen: "Sokrates schläft" = "Sokrates ist schlafend" (wie: "Sokrates ist weise"), so daß der Aussagesatz auf eine Grundform reduziert ist. Die Tatsache, daß "sein" in der Form "ist" ein wesentlicher Bestandteil des Aussagesatzes ist, veranlaßt ihn, das Wort an sich als bedeutungslos, nur als Copula zu bestimmen und seine Bedeutung "existiert, ist Realität" zu übergehen, obwohl z. B. "Gott ist" doch ein Aussagesatz ist. Ja er präzisiert, daß "sein" nicht Zeichen der Wirklichkeit sei, selbst "das Seiende" für sich allein nicht. Im Grunde kann er sich bezüglich des 'Seins' nicht entscheiden. Er gerät vielmehr in Verwirrung und Widerspruch mit sich selbst. Da "sein", "ist", "seiend" weder etwas Wirkliches bezeichnet noch die Wirklichkeit selbst, kann es auch nichts zusätzlich bezeichnen (*prossēmaínein*), wie das *rhē̃ma* zum Begriff die Zeit, also als reine Copula die Synthesis. Die Vieldeutigkeit oder wechselnde Funktionalität des *verbum substantivum* hat ihn erklärlicherweise verwirrt, aber er untersucht nicht das Problem des indefiniblen Wortes im Aussagesatz, der richtig oder falsch sein muß. Dies linguistische und logische Problem führt ihn ebenfalls nicht zu einer Bewußtmachung des eigenen Sprechens und Denkens, die ihm möglicherweise die Fragen gelöst hätte. Und ebenso wie er die Abstraktionskraft der 'Seele' nicht ausspricht, sondern nur mitdenkt, nennt er auch ihre Tendenz zur Analyse der Wahrnehmung nicht, d. h. die Zerlegung des Wahrgenommenen in lauter Einzelheiten, die in der Sprache Form gewinnen und in dem Maße, wie diese an die Stelle des Denkens tritt, die Auffassung der Wirklichkeit zu beeinflussen vermag. Ein Gedanke, der Aristoteles gar nicht in den Sinn kam. Für ihn war es klar, daß die Erscheinung 'Baum' eine Einheit aus Größe, Umriß, Gestalt, Farbe etc. nur zu sehen und abzubilden war, nicht aber sagbar, außer durch das Wort für die Art oder das Genus oder die Aufzählung seiner Eigenschaften in einer Beschreibung, die notwendig hinter der vielseitigen Wirklichkeit zurückbleiben muß. Wie genaue Selbstkontrolle ihm die Artikulation der Konsonanten seiner Sprache gezeigt hätte, hätte sie ihn vermutlich auch belehrt, daß alles Denken sich nur in sprachlichen Formen vollzieht. Aber Aristoteles ist kein Mann der Selbstbeobachtung, er glaubt an die Möglichkeit des 'reinen' Denkens, das an keine sprachlichen Formen gebunden ist, wenn er denkt, ohne zu sprechen; denn nur das Sprechen ist ihm Sprache. Daß er ohne ihre Prägungen keinen Begriff zur Verfügung hätte, ist ihm nicht bewußt. Man kann ohne Übertreibung sein Verhältnis zur Sprache naiv nennen.

Er zeigt sich in dem, was er über sie sagt, unbeeinflußt von Vorgängern, vor allem von Platon. Er ist über das anfängliche Staunen des Menschen über die ihm zur Verfügung stehende Sprache hinaus oder hat es gar nicht geteilt: Er sieht sie primär im Dienste und unter den Gesetzen der Logik. Da diese sich in sprachlicher Form präsentieren bzw. sich aus einfachen sprachlichen Gebilden ableiten läßt, ist ihre innere Beziehung erwiesen, die Wortarten sind Begriffssymbole, d. h. nur Nomen und Verbum, die man als das Seiende und das Sein definieren könnte, was Aristoteles aber unterläßt; die innere Beziehung zur Logik ist in der griechischen Sprache gegeben, wo das Zentralwort *lógos* – "Begriff" kann man wegen seiner enormen Vielseitigkeit kaum sagen – den rein sprachlichen (Rede, Geschichte, Debatte, Satz etc.) Bereich und den gedanklichen (Relation, Proportion, Rechnung, Grund) umfaßt, was sich in der Ableitung beschränkt wiederholt: *logikós* "das Sprechen betreffend, intellektuell, dialektisch, logisch". Der inneren Beziehung zur Logik ist für über zwei Jahrtausende die Beschäftigung mit der Sprache nicht mehr frei geworden. Für Platon hatte es noch eine Vergangenheit der gegenwärtigen Sprachformen, die Kategorie der Entwicklung gegeben, für ihn gab es sie nicht mehr: er kannte nur *seine* Sprache als festgefügtes Zeichensystem, wenn auch ohne Grammatik. Erst mehr als zwei Jahrhunderte später, nach einer Zeit, in der seine Werke verschwunden waren, erschien die *Tékhnē grammatikḗ* des Dionysios Thrax, kamen die Werke durch Andronikos von Rhodos wieder ans Licht. Man kann sagen, daß sie zusammen ein neues Zeitalter eröffneten: das der Auswirkung der Lehre des Aristoteles.

## 8. Konsequenzen

So stellt sich die 'Lehre' des Aristoteles von der Sprache auf grund der vorhandenen Texte dar. Man muß sich jedoch bewußt sein, daß er nicht lehrt, wie sie aufzufassen, was von ihr zu denken sei, sondern nur, insofern sein eigentlicher Gegenstand es erfordert, von ihr spricht. Denn die Sprache als solche, als selbstverständliche Lebensäußerung des Menschen bedurfte keiner Erforschung und Erkenntnis. Darum ist die Linguistik ein später Nachkomme der Wissenschaften, von ihrer Terminologie existiert noch nichts. Und nicht, was er wirklich gedacht hat, sondern wie man die überlieferten Texte in den folgenden Jahrhunderten interpretierte, offenbart ihre Wirkung, erweist ihre Bedeutung. Im Rahmen der Logik nur nahm man zur Kenntnis, was der unbestrittene Lehrer der Menschheit von der Sprache dachte, d. h. im Anfang von *Perì hermēneías*. Doch nicht eigentlich die Lückenhaftigkeit dieser Aussagen, sondern die Lehre von der Beweisführung bedurfte der klaren Wiedergabe. Die ersten uns überlieferten Kommentare erschienen um rund 500, d. h. über 800 Jahre nach des Aristoteles Tode. Der griechische Kommentar des Ammonios Hermeiu und der lateinische des Boethius, dessen Übersetzung später allgemein als Originaltext diente, der in der Zeit von 800 bis 1500 in 194 Handschriften erhalten ist. Die Tatsache, daß die Sprachauffassung nicht nur im Werk über die Logik, sondern auch in enger Verbindung zur Logik als Wissenschaft stand, bestimmte die Entwicklung der Sprachwissenschaft als Sprachlogik für Jahrhunderte (vgl. Arens 1984: 6–15). Diese Entwicklung war nur möglich, weil Aristoteles als *der* Lehrer der Wahrheit galt wie nach ihm keiner mehr. Es ist ein absonderlicher Fall, daß ein Mann, der Für 'Wort' und 'Sprache' noch über keine eindeutigen Bezeichnungen verfügte, ja überhaupt kein Sprach*wissen* besaß, wie es dann Dionysios Thrax in seiner ersten Grammatik zeigte, einen solchen bestimmenden Einfluß jahrhundertelang auf die Sprachauffassung haben sollte; das ist z. T. auf das Einleuchtende der Aussage des Aristoteles, z. T. auf die Tendenz zur immateriellen Betrachtung anhand *einer* Sprache (das Griechische, dann das Lateinische) und auf die Schwierigkeit des Gegenstands Sprache und die mangelnde Sachkenntnis über ihn zurückzuführen. Da man *wußte*, daß es verschiedene Sprachen gab, und überzeugt war von der *einen* Logik, ergab sich das Bemühen, dies zu erweisen. Wie für Aristoteles das Griechische so war für die Späteren das Lateinische *die* Sprache schlechthin, und die Sprachen Europas schienen das zu bestätigen. Wenn man die *pathḗma-*

*ta tēs psukhēs* ganz selbstverständlich als Begriffe auffaßte, eigentlich Abstraktionen von den Abbildern der Einzeldinge, und diese *pathēmata* bei allen Menschen dieselben sind, wie Aristoteles sagt, sind sie psychophysisch bedingt und also natürlich und müssen in den von Menschen geschaffenen Sprachen vorhanden sein. Diese Denkformen sind als Wortarten oder -klassen (obenhin 'Redeteile') bekannt. Wenn man das Seiende und das Sein, Nomen und Verbum, und ihre Qualifikanten als die Hauptklassen ansieht, kommt man etwa auf des Aristoteles Standpunkt, der, wie man aus der *Poetik* erschließen kann, selbst- und mitbezeichnende Wörter unterschied wie andererseits Selbst- und Mitlauter in der Phonetik. Man hielt sich jedoch an die vom Grammatiker Dionysios Thrax überlieferte Achtzahl, die ja auch das Latein aufwies. Man hat sich jahrhundertelang um die Definition dieser zugleich grammatischen und sprachlogischen Elemente bemüht. So entstand aus der von Aristoteles geschaffenen Grundlage die Allgemeine Grammatik.

## 9. Bibliographie

### 9.1. Primärliteratur

Aristoteles, *Organon*. Übers. und erläutert von Eugen Rolfes. 2 Bde. Leipzig: Felix Meiner, 1948. (Abdruck der 2. Auflage, 1925.)

–. *Organon Graece*. Hg. von Theodor Waitz. Leipzig: Hahn, 1844. (Repr., Aalen: Scientia Verlag, 1965.)

–. *Categoriae et Liber de interpretatione recognovit brevique adnotatione instruxit* L(orenzo) Minio-Paluello. Oxonii e Typographeo Clarendoniano, 1949.

–. *Über die Dichtkunst*. Neu übers. u. m. Einleitung u. einem erklärenden Namen- u. Sachverzeichnis versehen von Alfred Gudeman. (= *Philosophische Bibliothek*, 1.) Leipzig: Felix Meiner, 1921.

–. *Poetik*. Übers., Einleitung u. Anmerkungen von Olof Gigon. (= *UB* 2337.) Stuttgart: Reclam, 1961.

–. *Über die Seele*. Übers. u. m. Erläuterungen, Gliederung u. Literaturhinweisen hg. von Willy Theiler. (= *Rowohlts Klassiker, Griechische Philosophie*, 22.) o. O., 1968.

–. *Problemata physica*. Bd. 19 der Werke in deutscher Übersetzung hg. von Ernst Grumach. Berlin: Akademie-Verlag, 1962.

Dionysios Thrax, *Ars grammatica*. Hg. von Gustav Uhlig. Leipzig, 1883.

### 9.2. Sekundärliteratur

Arens, Hans. 1984. *Aristotle's Theory of Language and its Tradition: Selection, translation and commentary Texts from 500 to 1750.* (= *Studies in the History of Linguistics*, 29.) Amsterdam & Philadelphia: Benjamins.

Bareto, Manuel Saraiva. 1970. "A convencionalidade do signo linguistico em Aristoteles." *Revista de ciências do homem* 3.

Isaac, J. 1953. *Le Peri Hermeneias en occident de Boèce à Saint Thomas: Histoire littéraire d'un traité d'Aristote.* Paris: Vrin.

Pinborg, Jan. 1967. *Die Entwicklung der Sprachtheorie im Mittelalter.* (= *Beiträge zur Geschichte der Philosophie des Mittelalters* 42, 2.) Münster: Aschendorff.

Steinthal, Heyman. 1890–91. *Geschichte der Sprachwissenschaft bei den Griechen und Römern mit besonderer Rücksicht auf die Logik.* 1. Bd. Zweite vermehrte und verbesserte Auflage. Berlin: Dümmler.

*Hans Arens, Bad Hersfeld (Deutschland)*

# 55. Language and thought in Stoic philosophy

1. Introduction: the importance of the study of thought and language to the Stoa
2. Mentally processing the world
3. Language
3.1. Sound and meaning
3.2. The concept of λεκτόν
4. Transferring thought to language and vice versa
4.1. Thought to language: the speaker
4.2. Language to thought: the hearer
5. Conclusion
6. Bibliography

## 1. Introduction: the importance of the study of thought and language in the Stoa

The Stoa prided itself on the unity and coherence of its philosophical system. Its three parts, logic (or dialectic), physics and ethics are intimately bound up with each other. In particular, this means that their ethics was grounded on a scientific basis.

The ultimate goal of human existence was to become a 'wise man', someone who lived 'in accordance with nature', because of his capacity correctly to assess the world around him und his own place in it. The wise man realizes that there is only one essential 'good', namely virtue, and only one essentially bad thing, namely vice. Virtue can theoretically be attained by any human being, and its pursuit – and the avoidance of its opposite – is therefore worthwhile and rewarding. Everything other than virtue and vice is strictly speaking indifferent if one strives for a state of freedom from emotional disturbances (ἀπάθεια): being rich or poor, sick or healthy, and even alive or dead is ultimately irrelevant for the state of one's soul.

The correct assessment and evaluation of situations and events is instrumental to the wise man's happiness. These assessments are the result of thought-processes and take the form of judgements or propositions, the bearers of truth and falsity. Propositions are expressed in language. Therefore, ultimately a correct understanding of thought and language is intimately connected to one's capacity to secure happiness.

In the same vein, ambiguity is a fundamental threat because it may deceive one into assenting to a false proposition or withholding assent from a true one, thus endangering one's success as a moral agent (Atherton 1993: 53). For Stoic ethics, see Forschner (1981).

## 2. Mentally processing the world

### 2.1. The processing of sense perception

What happens in our minds when we confront the world according to the Stoa? In our material souls a "presentation" or "impression" (φαντασία) is formed, defined as "an impression in the commanding-part [of the soul]" (τύπωσις ἐν ἡγεμονικῷ, S. E. *M.* 8.400), or "an impression in the soul, i. e. a change" (ἀλλοίωσις; Chrysippus ap. D. L. 7.50; S. E. *M.* 7.228). Many of these impressions or presentations will arise through sense-perception (αἴσθησις).

The occurrence of such impressions is not subject to our control, but the next step is: we may either give or withhold assent (συγκατάθεσις) to the impression (S. E. *M.* 8.397 = FdS 257). If the impression originates from something 'real', and if it is strikingly clear and precise, it is called a καταληπτικὴ φαντασία "a cognitive impression", i. e., an impression capable of grasping (its object) (LS 1987: 1.250). "Comprehension" or "cognition" (κατάληψις) is the assent to a cognitive impression (ibid.). The cognitive impression itself is a criterion of truth (Diocles ap. D. L. 7.49; cf. LS 40).

So far, sense-perception, assent and cognition are individual and particular events; as such they are steps in the process of forming knowledge open to anyone, but the last step to true knowledge is reserved for the wise man. It is the acquisition of a body of knowledge, i. e. a collection of invariably correct individual acts of cognition. (Cf. Zeno's visual illustration of these four steps in FdS 369, Cic. Ac. 2.144f.)

### 2.2. Rational impressions

Impressions can be categorized in different ways. Some of them are the result of sense-perception, some arise through the activities of the mind (D. L. 7.51) – I will return to this in 4.2. Another division is that into "rational" (λογικαί) and "irrational" (ἄλογοι) ones. 'Rational' impressions are the impressions of rational – including human – beings. A rational impression may also be called νόησις "a thought-process" (D. L. 7.51; FdS 271 = [Gal.] *Def. medicae* 126, 19.381 K.), although it seems more accurate to say that νόησις cannot take place without φαντασία: impression is a necessary condition for the theory about assent, cognition and thought:

> "For impression comes first; then thought, which is capable of expressing itself, puts into the form of discourse what it experiences through the impression" (προηγεῖται γὰρ ἡ φαντασία, εἶθ' ἡ διάνοια ἐκλαλητικὴ ὑπάρχουσα, ὃ πάσχει ὑπὸ τῆς φαντασίας, τοῦτο ἐκφέρει λόγῳ, D. L. 7.49).

This is where we enter the area of the relationship between thought and language.

### 2.3. 'Internal' and 'uttered' discourse

The Stoa distinguished between "internal discourse" (λόγος ἐνδιάθετος) and "uttered discourse" (λόγος προφορικός). The idea that thought is internal speech was first developed in Plato's *Sophist* 263e: thought (διάνοια) and λόγος are essentially similar, but διάνοια is the dialogue within the soul of the soul with itself without sound, while λόγος is what streams forth from the soul through the mouth with sound.

Chrysippus describes the same connection when he claims that speech, speaking in oneself, thought, internal production of the sounds and sending them forth all come from διάνοια: (Gal. *PHP* III, 7,42–4, p. 220 De Lacy = FdS 451; see further FdS 512; 528ff. for the distinction between λόγος προφορικός and ἐνδιάθετος; Chiesa [1992]).

The main question that will concern us hereafter is how thought comes to be 'translated' into language, one of the main obstacles being the role of linguistic meaning as an intermediary between thoughts, things and expressions. Thought, i.e. physical or material impressions affecting a rational material mind, is a corporeal phenomenon according to the Stoics. It is material mind in a certain disposition. On the other hand, linguistic meaning is one of the few items in the Stoic world-view that are incorporeal. Before dealing with the problem of the transfer between thought and language, we must look more precisely at Stoic views about language.

## 3. Language

### 3.1. Sound and meaning

Stoic ideas of language are discussed under two headings, one dealing with language's formal aspects ("sound", φωνή), the other with meanings (σημαινόμενα) (D. L. 7.43). In any given meaningful utterance three elements are combined, the signifier (σημαῖνον), the extra-linguistic referent (τυγχάνον) and the meaning (σημαινόμενον) (S. E. *M.* 8.11f.). Seneca puts it as follows:

*'sunt' inquit 'naturae corporum, tamquam hic homo est, hic equus; has deinde sequuntur motus animorum enuntiativi corporum. hi habent proprium quiddam et a corporibus seductum, tamquam video Catonem ambulantem: hoc sensus ostendit, animus credidit. corpus est quod video, cui et oculos intendi et animum. dico deinde: "Cato ambulat". non corpus' inquit 'est quod nunc loquor, sed enuntiativum quiddam de corpore, quod alii effatum vocant, alii enuntiatum, alii edictum. sic cum dicimus "sapientiam", corporale quiddam intellegimus; dum dicimus "sapit", de corpore loquimur. plurimum autem interest utrum illud dicas an de illo'* (Seneca *Ep.* 117.13 = LS 33E = FdS 892).

Signifier and referent are corporeal, for they can act or be acted upon and this capacity for ποιεῖν and πάσχειν characterizes a σῶμα (e.g. a word can travel from speaker to listener; cf. Aetius *Plac.* IV 20.2 = SVF II 387). Meaning is incorporeal, and remains unaffected by whatever happens to either the signifier or the referent. The sentence 'Cato walks' is a corporeal signifier, the person Cato is the equally corporeal referent who gets to be named in a linguistic form (hence τυγχάνον "receiver", cf. LS 30A + comm.). The walking Cato, i.e. Cato in a certain physical disposition, is an object of sense-perception in the world out there, and the source of an impression. The mind believes the impression; it assents and undergoes "movements of predication" (*motus enuntiativi*), i.e. it exerts a predicating activity and accordingly it predicates something *about* the corporeal material. The meaning 'that Cato walks' is incorporeal, it predicates something *about* Cato and is very different from, yet somehow related to the (material) thoughts (and hence, the presentations or impressions) of the speaker. The importance of predication in this process also explains why the Stoics focused so much on the predicate part of the proposition (see 3.2. and 3.2.1.).

### 3.2. The concept of λεκτόν

The term σημαινόμενον is general; in their dialectic, the Stoa preferred the more specific concept of the λεκτόν or "sayable", as it has come to be translated, the bearer of truth and falsity, and therefore an essential concept in both Stoic dialectic and Stoic ethics. Despite recent disclaimers (Barnes 1993; Schubert 1994), there can be no doubt that the Stoic λεκτόν is not independent from thought or the rational impression. It is defined in the following terms:

The Stoics claimed in general that the true and the false reside in the sayable. They say that 'sayable' is what subsists in accordance with a rational impression. An impression is rational if what is presented can be rendered in discourse (ἠξίουν οἱ Στωικοὶ κοινῶς ἐν λεκτῷ τὸ ἀληθὲς εἶναι καὶ τὸ ψεῦδος. λεκτὸν δὲ ὑπάρχειν φασὶ τὸ κατὰ λογικὴν φαντασίαν ὑφιστάμενον, λογικὴν δὲ εἶναι φαντασίαν καθ' ἣν τὸ φαντασθὲν ἔστι λόγῳ παραστῆσαι. τῶν δὲ λεκτῶν τὰ μὲν ἐλλιπῆ καλοῦσι, τὰ δὲ αὐτοτελῆ, S. E. *M.* 8.70 = FdS 699; cf. D. L. 7.63 = FdS 696).

Λεκτόν, λογικός and λόγος are closely related. Λόγος is "reason, discourse, speech", but also the ultimate divinity permeating the Stoics' world in the form of a very fine substance called πνεῦμα. I take Sextus' statement to mean the following: there are impressions which are characterized by the fact that their contents (τὸ φαντασθέν) can be expressed in discourse: such an impression is called a λογικὴ φαντασία, one that can be expressed in λόγος. Λογικαὶ φαντασίαι are thought-processes (νοήσεις, cf. above 2.2.), perceived and described from their linguistic aspect: by definition they allow of linguistic expression. A λεκτόν seems to be the semantic content of this linguistic expression, incorporeal, hence not existing, but rather subsisting in accordance with the impression itself.

Like time, place, and the void, the λεκτόν is not endowed with corporeal 'being' (it is not an ὄν), but it is a "something" (τι) according to Stoic ontology (cf. LS 27). It is distinct from the source of the impression, and also from the (rational) impression, i. e. the thought, itself. On the other hand, it is dependent on the existence of a rational impression.

The close relationship between the impression (and hence, thought) and the λεκτόν is confirmed by Diogenes Laertius (7.43) in the division of the topics to be dealt with in dialectic: τὸν περὶ τῶν φαντασιῶν τόπον καὶ τῶν ἐκ τούτων ὑφισταμένων λεκτῶν "the chapter on impressions and the sayables subsisting in dependence on them".

Λεκτά can be complete or incomplete, depending on the completeness of the linguistic expression (ἐκφορά) of which they are the semantic content (D. L. 7.63, FdS 696). This illustrates the other side of their double determination: on the one hand, their connection to the λογικὴ φαντασία ties them up to a *mental* (corporeal) input – and through that eventually to facts and things in the world. On the other hand, they are linked to the eventual *linguistic output* (λόγος, ἐκφορά) resulting from the processing of that input.

### 3.2.1. The section on meanings

The section of Stoic dialectics dealing with meanings (cf. D. L. 7.63ff.) contains discussions of a number of topics that I can only touch upon briefly here.

The heart of the λεκτόν is the predicate (κατηγόρημα). This is the part of a proposition that does not actually 'designate' anything in the world – and in fact this characteristic may well have put the Stoics on the track of the existence of incorporeal meanings in the first place (cf. 4.2.3. on μετάβασις). The possibility of making a true κατηγορία "predication" about it characterizes the true φαντασία, and equally a false φαντασία can lead to a false predication (S. E. *M.* 7.244). Here, κατηγορία is almost indistinguishable from ἀξίωμα, which shows the central role of predication in the formation of a proposition. Impressions, thought and language are defined in each other's terms, impressions being regarded as the potential source for the semantic content of a proposition.

The predicate was called an 'incomplete λεκτόν', with a number of slots that need filling in order to produce a complete λεκτόν (λεκτὸν αὐτοτελές). If the predicate is formed by what we would call a one-place verb, all that is required is a nominative case (ὀρθὴ πτῶσις) to form a complete proposition. The 'nominative case' itself is never called an incomplete λεκτόν, presumably precisely because, unlike the predicate, it does designate. Seneca's explanation is again instructive (cf. above 3.1.):

*sic cum dicimus "sapientiam", corporale quiddam intellegimus; dum dicimus "sapit", de corpore loquimur. plurimum autem interest utrum illud dicas an de illo* (Seneca *Ep.* 117.13 = LS 33E = FdS 892). (For a recent discussion of the concept of πτῶσις, see Frede [1994].)

The Stoics draw an interesting distinction between universal concepts (which they regarded as non-entities, figments of the mind) and general terms, like man, or horse. Things in the world can be mentally arranged under universal concepts, and they get a name in order to allow them to be linguistically expressed: either a common name (noun), προσηγορία, expressing a common property, or a proper name, expressing the individual essence of the designated individual (cf. LS 30 with comm.).

First among the complete λεκτά is the standard form of a proposition, the axiom, bearer of truth and falsity. Besides the axiom, there are several non-axiomatic complete λεκτά, like questions, oaths, commands etc. (see Schenkeveld [1984] for a complete discussion and parallels with modern speech-act theories). In this chapter of their dialectics, the Stoics also discussed complex propositions expressing different connections between states of affairs (D. L. 7.68ff.). Some of them were probably introduced to facilitate the discussion of ethical problems (cf. Sluiter 1988).

Finally, the larger unit of the argument (λόγος) belongs under this heading (D. L. 7.76ff.).

## 4. Transferring thought to language and vice versa

### 4.1. Thought to language: the speaker

Now it is time to return to the question of how the translation of a corporeal state of mind into incorporeal meaning is supposed to take place (cf. Atherton 1993: 255ff.). Galen informs us that Diogenes of Babylon identified the heart as the locus for λόγος, διάνοια and φωνή. In the course of his argument he informs us about his views on the close relationship between language and thought:

But that too is certainly true, viz. that language is sent forth from thought; for some people actually define language as meaningful utterance sent out from thought. And it is probable in any case that language is sent out imprinted, and stamped as it were, by the conceptions present in thought, and that it is temporally coextensive with both the act of thinking and the activity of speaking (ἀλλὰ μὴν γε κἀκεῖνο ἀληθές, τὸ τὸν λόγον ἐκ τῆς διανοίας ἐκπέμπεσθαι. ἔνιοι γοῦν καὶ ὁριζόμενοι αὐτόν φασιν εἶναι φωνὴν σημαίνουσαν ἀπὸ διανοίας ἐκπεμπομένην. καὶ ἄλλως δὲ πιθανὸν ὑπὸ τῶν ἐννοιῶν ἐνσεσημασμένον τῶν ἐν τῇ διανοίᾳ καὶ οἷον ἐκτετυπωμένον ἐκπέμπεσθαι τὸν λόγον καὶ παρεκτείνεσθαι τῷ χρόνῳ κατά τε τὸ διανενοῆσθαι καὶ τὴν κατὰ τὸ λέγειν ἐνέργειαν, Gal. *PHP* 2.5, 11f., [p. 130.12ff. De Lacy] = FdS 450 = LS 53U [transl. LS adapted]).

Once again, this text supports the view that to the Stoics meaningful language (λόγος) is dependent on thought and related to the actual process of forming discourse, or producing speech. These same two elements were stressed in the description of the λεκτόν, as connected both to the mental input and the linguistic output. Here, however, it is λόγος, the signifier originating in thought that is said to be coextensive in time with both these processes, and that does not therefore have an independent existence.

The text also shows the obvious difficulty of describing how language acquires its incorporeal meaning. It focuses on the relation between corporeal thought and corporeal signifier and therefore does not directly address the problematic relation to either of the incorporeal meaning. The verbs used here suggest a process analogous to that by which impressions influence the mind. However, language's being 'stamped' by the concepts in the mind is qualified by an 'as it were', to indicate that strictly speaking this word is inappropriate precisely because no direct physical imprint is involved. After all, there is the intermediary function of the λεκτόν, which cannot be an 'imprint', but subsists on the signifier – this, however, is left implicit. The other verb used, ἐνσημαίνω, 'to endow with a sign, imprint', is not so qualified, maybe because it is felt to be able to convey the precise technical meaning of endowing a signifier with meaning (σημαινόμενον). In Gal. *PHP* 2.5,20 (p. 130,33ff. De Lacy) = FdS 450, a Chrysippean passage, the same verb is used for 'conveying the meaning of what is said to the mind':

And it is likely anyway that what is said also gets its meaning from the place to which it conveys its meaning, and that the sounds originate from that place in the manner mentioned (πιθανὸν δὲ καὶ ἄλλως, εἰς ὃ ἐνσημαίνεται τὰ λεγόμενα, καὶ σημαίνεσθαι ἐκεῖθεν καὶ τὰς φωνὰς ἀπ' ἐκείνου γίγνεσθαι κατὰ τὸν προειρημένον τρόπον).

Like λόγος, τὰ λεγόμενα can refer to language as signifier, i. e. the corporeal aspect with a semantic component. This explains *that* it can be affected (endowed with meaning, made meaningful, σημαίνεσθαι) or can itself affect something else (transfer the meaning to the mind), but *how* this process takes place remains unclear.

### 4.2. Language to thought: the hearer

Even if we simply accept the transfer from a corporeal thought-process to the subsistence of a λεκτόν, we should still explain how an incorporeal λεκτόν can affect, or even reach, the hearer, if only bodies can act or be acted upon in Stoic physics. An awareness of this problem can be detected in the refinements of the theory of the impression. Thus, we hear that some impressions arise as a result of sense-perception, but some do not:

Non-perceptible ones come through thought, for instance impressions of incorporeals and of whatever else is taken in through reason (οὐκ αἰσθητικαὶ δ' αἱ διὰ τῆς διανοίας καθάπερ τῶν ἀσωμάτων καὶ τῶν ἄλλων τῶν λόγῳ λαμβανομένων, D. L. 7.51).

The distinction seems to be made with the express purpose of accommodating the impact of λεκτά on the mind: Apart from the fact that it subsists on a rational impression, presumably in the mind of the speaker, it can in its turn somehow initiate an impression in a hearer's mind. Again the precise nature of the transfer is left unclear, but the problem as such was recognized. It is relevant in the Stoic theory of the proof, the sign and the cause.

#### 4.2.1. The λεκτόν as (part of) a proof

How can a "proof" (ἀπόδειξις), basically a system of (incorporeal) propositions, have the impact of an impression? This is a critical question raised by Sextus Empiricus (*M.* 8.403). Apparently, the Stoics suggested that strictly speaking it does not, but that an impression comes about through our own mental activities which are somehow related to the ἀσώματα involved:

The incorporeals do not act nor do they make an impression on us, but we are the ones who are affected by an impression in connection with them (τὰ ἀσώματα οὐ ποιεῖ τι οὐδὲ φαντασιοῖ ἡμᾶς, ἀλλ' ἡμεῖς ἐσμὲν οἱ ἐπ' ἐκείνοις φαντασιούμενοι, S. E. *M.* 8.406).

The expression ἐπ' ἐκείνοις recalls the phrase λεκτὸν δὲ ὑπάρχειν φασὶ τὸ κατὰ λογικὴν φαντασίαν ὑφιστάμενον (cf. 3.2.). Just as λεκτά "subsist in accordance with a rational impression", a formulation that avoids postulating a direct causal relationship between the corporeal and the incorporeal, so are we not directly affected by incorporeals, but "in relation to them". The Stoics tried to illuminate this by the following comparison:

For they [the Stoics] say, just as the trainer or drill-sergeant sometimes takes hold of the boy's hands to drill him and to teach him to make certain motions, but sometimes stands at a distance and moves to a certain drill, to provide himself as a model for the boy – so too some impressors touch, as it were, and make contact with the commanding-faculty to make their printing in it, as do white and black, and body in general; whereas others have a nature like that of the incorporeal sayable, and the commanding-faculty is impressed in relation to them, not by them (ὥσπερ γάρ, φασίν, ὁ παιδοτρίβης καὶ ὁπλομάχος ἔσθ' ὅτε μὲν λαβόμενος τῶν χειρῶν τοῦ παιδὸς ῥυθμίζει καὶ διδάσκει τινὰς κινεῖσθαι κινήσεις, ἔσθ' ὅτε δὲ ἄπωθεν ἑστὼς καί πως κινούμενος ἐν ῥυθμῷ παρέχει ἑαυτὸν ἐκείνῳ πρὸς μίμησιν, οὕτω καὶ τῶν φανταστῶν ἔνια μὲν οἱονεὶ ψαύοντα καὶ θιγγάνοντα τοῦ ἡγεμονικοῦ ποιεῖται τὴν ἐν τούτῳ τύπωσιν, ὁποῖόν ἐστι τὸ λευκὸν καὶ μέλαν καὶ κοινῶς τὸ σῶμα, ἔνια δὲ ⟨οὐ⟩ τοιαύτην ἔχει τὴν φύσιν, τοῦ ἡγεμονικοῦ ἐπ' αὐτοῖς φαντασιουμένου καὶ οὐχ ὑπ' αὐτῶν, ὁποῖά ἐστι τὰ ἀσώματα λεκτά, S. E. *M.* 8.409 = FdS 272 = LS 27E; transl. LS).

Again, the solution pivots on the postulated existence of different types of impressions, some originating from physical contact (αἰσθητικαί), some not. The boy in the example is compared to the commanding-faculty, so that in the case of 'long-distance transfer' no actual physical impression is made – or so it is claimed. Sextus is not convinced by this argument, because the trainer is corporeal either way. According to him this comparison does not show that a proof or demonstration (ἀπόδειξις) can in fact 'make the impression of a presentation (or impression) on the commanding-faculty' (φανταστικῶς τυποῦν τὸ ἡγεμονικόν, ibid.) – which strictly speaking is not what the Stoics claimed. In fact, they carefully avoided postulating any such direct causal relationship (cf. τοῦ ἡγεμονικοῦ ἐπ' αὐτοῖς φαντασιουμένου καὶ οὐχ ὑπ' αὐτῶν). Sextus is not altogether fair here. However, it must be admitted that the nature of the process described is again left unclear.

The Stoic system is consistent in so far as it avoids any terminology that suggests a direct relation of cause and effect. The bipartition provided by Diogenes Laertius (7.52) gives two propositions (λεκτά) as examples of objects of κατάληψις resulting from reasoning, not from sense-perception:

According to them, cognition originates from perception on the one hand (of white and black, rough and smooth), from reasoning on the other (of conclusions reached by demonstration), e. g. that gods exist, and that they exert providence (ἡ δὲ κατάληψις γίνεται κατ' αὐτοὺς αἰσθήσει μὲν λευκῶν καὶ μελάνων καὶ τραχέων καὶ λείων, λόγῳ δὲ τῶν δι' ἀποδείξεως συυαγομένων, ὥσπερ τοῦ δεοὺς εἶναι, καὶ προνοεῖν τούτους)

Once it is accepted – on faith! – that an impression (i. e. a material affection of the soul) can arise in relation to an incorporeal λεκτόν, there is a starting-point for the cognitive process. In this way the Stoics explain both how an incorporeal λεκτόν can perform the function of a 'sign' in a logical demonstration, and how it can be a 'cause'.

### 4.2.2. The λεκτόν as a 'sign'

It is Sextus again who formulates the general objection that a λεκτόν cannot function as a sign on the grounds that it cannot indicate or clarify anything without being corporeal (*M.* 8.262ff. = FdS 700). Long (1971) rightly points out that signs (σημεῖα) should not be confused with signifiers (σημαίνοντα): a sign is actually a proposition, i. e. a λεκτόν, that can function as the protasis of a conditional complex axiom (of the form 'if the first, the second'; the sign is 'if the first'). Its definition makes this clear:

A sign is an indicative axiom, serving as the protasis in a valid conditional complex proposition, that reveals the conclusion (σημεῖόν ἐστι ἐνδεικτικὸν ἀξίωμα ἐν ὑγιεῖ συνημμένῳ προκαθηγούμενον , ἐκκαλυπτικὸν τοῦ λήγοντος, S. E. *M.* 8.245 = FdS 1029 [cf. FdS 1026ff.]).

If a sign is an axiom, it is a λεκτόν and therefore incorporeal. Sextus' objection should therefore be met, and indeed, in the context of the sign we get some more information about how a λεκτόν can come to be the source of a φαντασία (cf. 4.2. above).

Human beings do not just receive simple impressions, like animals, but they can also process "an impression based on inference (transition) and combination" (φαντασία μεταβατική καὶ συνθετική, S. E. *M.* 8.276):

They [the doctrinaire philosophers] say that it is not uttered speech but internal speech by which man differs from non-rational animals; for crows and parrots and jays utter articulate sounds. Nor is it by the merely simple impression that he differs (for they too receive impressions), but by impressions based on inference (transition) and combination. Therefore, because he has the conception of 'following' he immediately also gets the idea of sign because of the (concept of) following. For sign is itself of the kind 'If this, then that'. Therefore, the existence of signs follows from man's nature and constitution' (ἄνθρωπος οὐχὶ τῷ προφορικῷ λόγῳ διαφέρει τῶν ἀλόγων ζῴων (καὶ γὰρ κόρακες καὶ ψιττακοὶ καὶ κίτται ἐνάρθρους προφέρονται φωνάς), ἀλλὰ τῷ ἐνδιαθέτῳ, οὐδὲ τῇ ἁπλῇ μόνον φαντασίᾳ (ἐφαντασιοῦτο γὰρ κἀκεῖνα), ἀλλὰ τῇ μεταβατικῇ καὶ συνθετικῇ. διόπερ ἀκολουθίας ἔννοιαν ἔχων εὐθὺς καὶ σημείου νόησιν λαμβάνει διὰ τὴν ἀκολουθίαν· καὶ γὰρ αὐτὸ τὸ σημεῖόν ἐστι τοιοῦτον· εἰ τόδε, τόδε. ἕπεται ἄρα τῇ φύσει καὶ κατασκευῇ τἀνθρώπου τὸ καὶ σημεῖον ὑπάρχειν, S. E., *M.* 8.275f. = FdS 1031 = LS 53T).

A φαντασία μεταβατική καὶ συνθετική 'transcends' the data of strict sense-perception (in an as yet unexplained way). This enables it to handle λεκτά, and makes it possible to grasp logical connections by combining propositions and processing the resulting complex proposition.

This text links three things: the natural constitution of man, his having the conception of 'following', and the φαντασία μεταβατική καὶ συνθετική. The natural constitution of man is such that he has this type of φαντασία, which is equivalent to his having the notion of following (for ἀκολουθία, cf. Long 1971: 95f.). Ἀκολουθία is said to be an ἔννοια. This means that it is part of our permanent mental furniture as a result of numerous experiences (cf. LS 39E-F). Its presence has a direct causal link (διά) to our getting a rational impression of a sign, the sort of impression that can be linguistically expressed (for νόησις = φαντασία λογική, cf. 2.2.). In fact, a sign functions precisely as the conditional protasis in a complex conditional in which one element 'follows from' the other (cf. D. L. 7.71); therefore, signs have to do with the mental input and the linguistic output (the complex axiom) of ἀκολουθία. Their status as an impression means that they are available as the starting-point of the cognitive process.

### 4.2.3. The concept of μετάβασις

Sextus Empiricus gives us more information about the process through which those impressions come about that do not originate in sense-perception, but in reasoning; this process is called ἀναλογιστικὴ μετάβασις, and it takes sense-data as its point of departure (*M.* 11.250). Similarly, in *M.* 7.25 processing "evident things" (τὰ ἐναργῆ) is differentiated from processing "non-evident things" (ἄδηλα):

They think that things evident come to be known directly through a criterion and that things non-evident are discovered through signs and proofs, in a process of inference (transition, transcendence) from the evident (τὰ μὲν ἐναργῆ διὰ κριτηρίου τινὸς αὐτόθεν γνωρίζεσθαι δοκεῖ, τὰ δὲ ἄδηλα διὰ σημείων καὶ ἀποδείξεων κατὰ τὴν ἀπὸ τῶν ἐναργῶν μετάβασιν ἐξιχνεύεσθαι, S. E. *M.* 7.25).

In Diogenes Laertius (7.53) μετάβασις is less wide-ranging: it does not cover all methods of cognition that are based on the non-evident, but forms one such species only. Things thought (τὰ νοούμενα) can be arrived at through direct physical contact (κατὰ περίπτωσιν), but also e. g. through resemblance (thinking of Socrates when seeing his portrait), or analogy (thinking of a Cyclops or a Pygmy when seeing a human being by mentally increasing or diminishing its size). After a whole list, Diogenes Laertius adds three forms of thought-processing that he had not announced in his initial division in 7.52 – possibly this is an indication of conflated sources:

Some things [or: 'somethings', the items belonging in the ontological category τι] are thought in a process of transcendence (1), like the sayables and space. A concept of just and good arises by nature (2). And by privation (3), e. g. handless (νοεῖται δὲ καὶ κατὰ μετάβασίν τινα (1), ὡς τὰ λεκτὰ καὶ ὁ τόπος. φυσικῶς (2) δὲ νοεῖται δίκαιόν τι καὶ ἀγαθόν· καὶ κατὰ στέρησιν (3), οἷον ἄχειρ, D. L. 7.53).

Unfortunately, these passages do not explain how μετάβασις is supposed to work. It is clear that μετάβασις is the way one can get a φαντασία through λόγος, not αἴσθησις (D. L. 7.52), and that it covers φαντασίαι produced by proofs and signs (i. e. forms of λεκτά) (D. L. 7.52; S. E. *M.* 7.25). It starts from sense-data (S. E. *M.* 7.25), as is also suggested by comparing Sextus Empiricus' ἀναλογιστικὴ μετάβασις (*M.* 11.250) with Diogenes Laertius' method κατ' ἀναλογίαν (7.53).

There is a certain ambiguity in Diogenes Laertius: does the 'metabatic' method provide insight in the *concept* of the λεκτόν, or does it make *particular* λεκτά accessible for thought-processing (cf. Schubert 1994: 131 ff.)? If the former, the word τινα may refer to the ontological category of the τι. But even if the λεκτόν itself is the object of μετάβασις, individual λεκτά are also part of the method, for they constitute signs and proofs.

However that may be – and our sources seem to be inconclusive – in both cases it is possible to see how one could arrive at an impression of a λεκτόν (either the concept, or a particular one) while starting from sense-data. First the concept: As the concept of 'place' is arrived at by inference from the perceptible things occupying it (cf. LS 49), so can perceptible utterances bring the observer to the inference that there must be such a thing as the incorporeal λεκτόν. This inference is brought about by the observable fact that Greeks and barbarians alike are able to perceive a certain utterance, but that the barbarians miss the message that the Greeks do pick up. Therefore such a thing as 'meaning' must exist. This argument was first made explicit in Plato's *Theaetetus* (163b1 ff.), and the Stoics availed themselves of it precisely in distinguishing the σημαινόμενον from the φωνή of an utterance.

Meaning is the thing itself that is indicated by it (the sound), and that we perceive as it subsists on our understanding, but barbarians do not understand it although they hear the sound (σημαινόμενον δὲ αὐτὸ τὸ πρᾶγμα τὸ ὑπ' αὐτῆς [sc. τῆς φωνῆς] δηλούμενον καὶ οὗ ἡμεῖς μὲν ἀντιλαμβανόμεθα τῇ ἡμετέρᾳ παρυφισταμένου διανοίᾳ, οἱ δὲ βάρβαροι οὐκ ἐπαίουσι καίπερ τῆς φωνῆς ἀκούοντες, S. E. *M.* 8.12; cf. 8.134; 1.155; 1.37f., cf. *P.* 2.214; 3.267)

When taken as a method to grasp the content of particular λεκτά and make them available as impressions, μετάβασις also departs from observable entities, e. g. the walking Cato, or burning wood. These are bodies, and starting from them we can predicate something *about* them, that is related to the sense-data, but does not itself correspond to anything in the material world, e. g. the proposition: 'Cato is walking' (cf. 3.1. above, Seneca *Ep.* 117.13 = LS 33E = FdS 892).

#### 4.2.4. The λεκτόν as a 'cause'

The last context in which the incorporeal nature of the λεκτά clashes with their alleged functioning, is their role in a chain of causation (cf. Atherton 1993: 255 ff.). Again, the Stoic solution preserves the internal consistency of the theory, this time by allowing some stretching in the use of the word 'cause'. However, no real explanation is found. A preliminary problem that must be dealt with is that the role of λεκτά in the Stoic theory of causation has been taken as a counter-argument to the thought-related nature of the λεκτόν: in this one context λεκτά seem to be something like objective facts.

The usual theory is that causes are corporeal, and that they are a cause *for* another corporeal entity (i. e. they work on bodies), but that they can be the cause *of* an incorporeal predicate.

The Stoics say that every cause is a body which becomes the cause to a body of something incorporeal. For instance the scalpel, a body, becomes the cause to the flesh, a body, of the incorporeal predicate 'being cut'. And again, the fire, a body, becomes the cause to the wood, a body, of the incorporeal predicate 'being burnt' (οἱ Στωικοὶ μὲν πᾶν αἴτιον σῶμά φασι σώματι ἀσωμάτου τινὸς αἴτιον γίνεσθαι, οἷον σῶμα μὲν τὸ σμιλίον, σώματι δὲ τῇ σαρκί, ἀσωμάτου δὲ τοῦ τέμνεσθαι κατηγορήματος, καὶ πάλιν σῶμα μὲν τὸ πῦρ, σώματι δὲ τῷ ξύλῳ, ἀσωμάτου δὲ τοῦ καίεσθαι κατηγορήματος, S. E. *M.* 9.211 = FdS 765 = LS 55B [transl. LS]; cf. LS 55D; 55N).

In this same context belongs the difference between 'wisdom' – a corporeal state of mind, and 'being wise' – an incorporeal predicate caused by the former (Stob. Ecl. I 13,1 = FdS 762); and between truth – again a material state, namely πνεῦμα in a certain disposition or quality –, and the true: an incorporeal λεκτόν of the most basic form, namely an axiom ('this is true') (cf. S. E. *P.* 2.80 ff. = FdS 322).

In a chain of causation, we should probably imagine a body (e. g. fire) being a cause for a body (e. g. wood) of an incorporeal predicate 'burning'. In a next step, a body ('burning wood') may be a cause for a body (e. g. a man) of the incorporeal predicate 'getting warm' etc. It is undoubtedly true that causal relationships are somehow 'real' to the Stoics (De Lacy 1945: 255; Frede 1978: 64), and that they can be reflected in language. It does not necessarily follow, however, that in the context of causation the λεκτόν (caused by a body to another body) is an objective state of affairs, independent from thought or rational presentation, as "facts or putative facts ... available to be thought and expressed whether anyone is thinking about them or not" (cf. LS 1987: 1.201 f.). The λεκτόν is not identical to the causal relationship, but presupposes some form of logical processing of sequences of corporeal states (wood, fire, burning wood).

First of all, the succession of bodies and material circumstances linked up in a chain of causation (e. g. match, burning match, burning house, LS [1987: 1.343]) does not require the independent existence of the fact 'that the match is burning'. The material bodies in their several dispositions will form φαντασίαι for animals, but only rational beings will perceive that a state of affairs is actually caused by (and thus follows) the interaction of two bodies, one being responsible for the effect occurring in the other (responsibility is part of the Stoic concept of 'cause', cf. LS [1987: 1.340]).

Secondly, cause itself, as the active organizing principle that structures matter, is identified with reason (λόγος) (Seneca *Ep.* 65.2 = LS 55E), and reason is equivalent to god (SVF I 160ff.):

*Apud vestros quoque sapientes λόγον, id est sermonem atque rationem, constat artificem videri universitatis. Hunc enim Zeno determinat factitatorem, qui cuncta in dispositione formaverit, eundem et fatum vocari et deum et animum Iovis et necessitatem omnium rerum* (Tertull. *Apol.* 21 = SVF I 160).

God is a rational animal permeating the universe (cf. D. L. 7.147); Zeus' λόγος is equivalent to fate (εἱμαρμένη) (Plut. *St. rep.* 1056C = LS 55R), which in turn is defined as αἰτία τῶν ὄντων εἰρομένη "an endless chain of causation". This means that in a large sense, there is always a λόγος to process the λογικαὶ φαντασίαι to do with causation and that there is no reason to assert the independent existence of λεκτά. In the last resort, they will subsist on the λογικὴ φαντασία of god.

The second problem announced above is the following: if a λεκτόν is used as part of a proof, or as a sign, or even as part of an unphilosophical communication, it seems to function as a cause itself, instead of just being the incorporeal effect of the interaction of two bodies. If we give an order, there is an imperative λεκτόν that should cause the addressee to obey us.

The available 'solutions' again do not address the core of the problem, but they preserve the internal consistency of the theory. Starting-point is the now familiar postulate that any λεκτόν can form the basis of a φαντασία οὐκ αἰσθητική. Further, the Stoics admit that a λεκτόν can be called a 'cause', but they allow that usage only for lack of a better alternative, in the context of the linguistic expression of causal relationships:

Others call bodies 'cause' in the strict sense of the word, but incorporeals in an improper sense, as it were quasi-causally (οἱ δὲ τὸ μὲν σῶμα κυρίως αἴτιόν φασι, τὸ δὲ ἀσώματον καταχρηστικῶς, καὶ οἷον αἰτιωδῶς, Clemens Al., *Strom.* VIII 9 § 26,1–5, p. 96 sq. Fr. = FdS 763).

A similar loose usage is adduced to explain the (internal linguistic) relationship between the two propositions in the complex causal axiom (of the form 'because the first, the second'):

For the first clause is, *as it were*, the cause of the second (*οἱονεὶ* γὰρ αἴτιόν ἐστι τὸ πρῶτον τοῦ δευτέρου, D. L. 7.72).

With this we may compare the explicit distinction between a cause (αἴτιον) and the linguistic expression of a causal relationship (αἰτία) attributed to Chrysippus:

[Chrysippus says] that the cause is 'because', while that of which it is the cause is 'why?'. He says that an explanation is the statement of a cause, or statement concerning the cause *qua* cause ([Χρύσιππος ... λέγει] ... αἴτιον μὲν ὅτι, οὗ δὲ αἴτιον διὰ τί. αἰτίαν δ' εἶναι λόγον αἰτίον, ἢ λόγον τὸν περὶ τοῦ αἰτίου ὡς αἰτίου, LS 55A).

## 5. Conclusion

The nodal point of Stoic theories of language and thought is the λεκτόν. Subsisting on a rational impression, the λεκτόν constitutes an incorporeal locus of linguistic meaning as well as the bearer of truth and falsity. Since the other elements in the cognitive process are material and consist in various physical affections of the (material) mind, the problem of the transfer between matter and the incorporeal λεκτόν arises. This problem is especially acute in the theory of the sign, proof and causation, because in all three contexts the incorporeal λεκτόν seems to act or to be acted upon – something of which only bodies are capable.

The Stoics betray a definite awareness of the problematic role of the λεκτόν in these contexts. They postulate that a φαντασία (the beginning of every cognitive process) does not necessarily originate in sense-perception only, but also in reasoning. The procedure involved is that of μετάβασις, a form of inference starting from sense-data. Further, they carefully avoid any formulation that would put λεκτά in the position of immediate agents. Instead they describe interaction of bodies as occurring 'in relation to' λεκτά (ἐπί + dat., e. g. S. E. *M.* 8.406; cf. 4.2.1.), while λεκτά are somehow dependent on, but not directly caused by thought-processes (κατά + acc., e. g. D. L. 7.63, cf. 3.2; ἐκ + gen., e. g. D. L. 7.43, cf. 3.2). For the rest they make an appeal to the inadequacy of language to express the precise nature of the transfer, thus making their theory at least consistent, even if its explanatory power may be felt to be deficient.

## 6. Bibliography

### 6.1. Primary sources

FDS [quoted according to number of fragment] = Karlheinz Hülser. *Die Fragmente zur Dialektik der Stoiker.* (4 vols.). Stuttgart-Bad Cannstatt: Frommann-Holzboog, 1987.

LS [quoted by volume and page, or by number of fragment] = Anthony A. Long & David N. Sedley, *The Hellenistic Philosophers.* I. *Translations of the principal sources, with philosophical commentary*; II. *Greek and Latin texts with notes and bibliography.* Cambridge: Cambridge Univ. Press, 1987.

SVF [quoted by volume and number of fragment] = Johannes von Arnim, *Stoicorum veterum fragmenta.* 4 vols. Leipzig: Teubner, 1905–1924.

### 6.2. Secondary sources

Atherton, Catherine. 1993. *The Stoics on Ambiguity.* Cambridge: Cambridge Univ. Press.

Baratin, Marc. 1991. "Aperçu de la linguistique stoïcienne". *Sprachtheorien der abendländischen Antike* ed. by Peter Schmitter, 193–216. Tübingen.

Barnes, Jonathan. 1993. "Meaning, Saying and Thinking". *Dialektiker und Stoiker. Zur Logik der Stoa und ihrer Vorläufer* ed. by Klaus Döring & Theodor Ebert, 47–61. Stuttgart.

Chiesa, C. 1992. "Le problème du langage intérieur dans la philosophie antique de Platon à Porphyre". *Histoire Epistémologie Langage* 14.15–30.

Cortasso, G. 1978. "Pensiero e linguaggio nella teoria stoica del ΛΕΚΤΟΝ." *Rivista di Filologia e di Istruzione Classica* 106.385–394.

De Lacy, Phillip. 1945. "The Stoic Categories as Methodological Principles". *Transactions of the American Philological Association* 76.246–263.

Dinneen, F. P. 1985. "On Stoic Grammatical Theory". *Historiographia Linguistica* 12.149–164.

Egli, Urs. 1978. "Stoic Syntax and Semantics". *Les Stoiciens et leur logique, actes du colloque de Chantilly* ed. by Jacques Brunschwig, 135–54. Paris.

Forschner, Maximilian. 1981. *Die Stoische Ethik.* Stuttgart: Klett-Cotta.

Frede, Michael. 1978. "Principles of Stoic Grammar". *The Stoics* ed. by John M. Rist 27–75. Berkeley: Univ. of California Press.

–. 1994. "The Stoic Notion of a Grammatical Case". *Bulletin of the Institute of Classical Studies* 39.13–24.

Lloyd, A. C. 1971. "Grammar and metaphysics in the Stoa". *Problems in Stoicism* ed. by Anthony A. Long, 58–74. London: Athlone Press.

Long, Anthony A. 1971. "Language and Thought in Stoicism". *Problems in Stoicism* ed. by Anthony A. Long, 75–113. London: Athlone Press.

Schenkeveld, Dirk M. 1984. "Studies in the History of Ancient Linguistics. II. Stoic and Peripatetic kinds of speech act and the distinction of grammatical moods". *Mnemosyne* 37.291–353.

Schubert, Andreas. 1994. *Untersuchungen zur Stoischen Bedeutungslehre.* Göttingen: Vandenhoeck & Rupprecht.

Sluiter, Ineke. 1988. "On Ἠ διασαφητικός and propositions containing ΜΑΛΛΟΝ/ΗΤΤΟΝ". *Mnemosyne* 41.46–66.

–. 1990. *Ancient Grammar in Context: Contributions to the study of ancient linguistic thought.* Amsterdam: VU Univ. Press.

*Ineke Sluiter, Leiden (The Netherlands)*

# 56. La linguistique grecque chez les alexandrins: Aristophane de Byzance et Aristarque

1. Repères historiques et sources
2. Sources inférentielles des théories grammaticales d'Aristophane et d'Aristarque
3. Place de l'analogie dans la philologie alexandrine
4. La question de l'autonomisation de la grammaire
5. La base normative de la philologie alexandrine
6. Conclusion
7. Bibliographie

## Repères historiques et sources

### 1.1. Introduction

Traiter des conceptions linguistiques de ces deux grands philologues d'Alexandrie que furent Aristophane de Byzance et Aristarque représente un peu une gageure, pour une raison qui tient précisément à la philologie. En effet, bien peu de fragments de leurs œuvres nous sont parvenus directement. Ce fait est d'autant plus surprenant que, d'une part, ces deux philologues doivent principalement leur notoriété à la publication des grands textes de la littérature grecque, et que, d'autre part, leur autorité dans le domaine grammatico-philologique ne semble pas faire de doute. En particulier, dès le milieu du premier siècle avant notre ère, dans les livres VIII à X du *De lingua Latina*, de Varron, Aristophane de Byzance, et surtout Aristarque, sont présentés comme les chefs de file du courant analogiste dans la prétendue querelle entre les tenants de la régularité (analogie) et les tenants de l'irrégularité (anomalie) dans la langue. Quoi qu'il en soit, force est de constater que l'absence presque totale de sources fiables et authentiques ne peut que nous inciter à la plus extrême prudence dans la représentation que nous pouvons donner des conceptions linguistiques de nos deux philologues. Tout ce qui a été dit (à commencer par Varron lui-même) et tout ce que je dirai ici doit donc être considéré comme fortement conjectural.

### 1.2. Eléments biographiques

Rappelons d'abord quelques maigres repères chronologiques et biographiques. Aristophane, originaire de Byzance, a vécu à Alexandrie semble-t-il entre 257 et 180 avant notre ère. A partir de 194, il devient responsable de la Bibliothèque royale. Cette fonction impliquait qu'il soit à la fois éditeur et conservateur des grands textes de la littérature grecque ainsi que précepteur des enfants du prince. Soupçonné d'avoir été sollicité par Eumène II de Pergame (l'autre grande bibliothèque du monde hellénique), il est emprisonné puis congédié. Plutarque raconte qu'il eut pour rival auprès d'une marchande de fleurs ... un éléphant. On lui doit des éditions de l'*Iliade* et de l'*Odyssée*, de poètes lyriques comme Pindare, de poètes dramatiques comme Euripide. Il a contribué à l'établissement d'une liste des meilleurs poètes. Poète lui-même, il semble avoir abordé les problèmes de langue essentiellement sous l'angle du lexique: il aurait rédigé des traités sur les mots désignant les âges de la vie des hommes et des animaux, sur les noms de parenté et sur les mots dialectaux (attiques, laconiens). L'existence de son traité sur l'analogie (*Perì analogías*) paraît tout à fait douteuse.

On ne sait pas non plus grand chose de la vie d'Aristarque. Originaire de Samothrace, il a vécu entre 217 et 145 environ. Disciple d'Aristophane à Alexandrie, il prend la tête de la Bibliothèque vers 153. A l'avènement de Ptolémée VIII Physcon, en 145, il est exilé à Chypre, où celui qu'Athénée surnomma "l'éruditissime" (*ho grammatikṓtatos*) meurt. La tradition lui attribue trois types de textes: des éditions critiques (*diorthṓseis*) des poètes, et surtout d'Homère, caractérisées par un grand respect de la tradition manuscrite; des commentaires (*hupomnḗmata*) sur les œuvres littéraires; enfin différents traités (*sungrámmata*) sur des questions philologiques.

### 1.3. Etat des sources et conséquences pour l'interprétation

Malheureusement pour nous, il reste fort peu de choses des œuvres de nos deux érudits. Aristophane est connu essentiellement par quelques fragments, quelques citations et quelques gloses rédigées en marge d'éditions tardives des poèmes homériques et mentionnant son nom (scholies). L'ensemble occupe un faible volume. En ce qui concerne Aristarque, on dispose d'un nombre assez important de scholies homériques et de quelques citations d'Apollonios Dyscole. En revanche, rien ne permet d'assurer l'existence des commentaires ou des traités d'Aristarque. Le nom d'Aristarque apparaît beaucoup plus fréquemment dans les scholies d'Homère que celui d'Aristophane de Byzance, ce qui montre évidemment son importance dans la tradition manuscrite des poèmes homériques. Mais la lecture de ces scholies est assez frustrante pour un historien de la linguistique. En effet, il n'y est en général question que des 'leçons' d'Aristophane ou d'Aristarque, invoqués (et surtout le second) comme des autorités en ce qui concerne l'édition des textes. Comme le faisait déjà remarquer Steinthal, les raisons de ces 'leçons' ne sont presque jamais fournies. Quand elles le sont, elles ne peuvent jamais être considérées comme totalement sûres, soit parce que les explications rapportées sont des connaissances indirectes, souvent introduites par un "on dit que" (*phasí*) — c'est le cas en particulier des conceptions d'Aristarque rapportées par Apollonios Dyscole —, soit parce que les explications sont très difficiles à démêler des conceptions de l'auteur de la référence, dont on ignore même s'il ne cherche pas simplement à justifier l'autorité qu'il invoque. Bref, l'étude des conceptions linguistiques d'Aristophane et d'Aristarque repose sur une base philologique très lacunaire. Dès lors, la méthode généralement suivie pour reconstruire ces conceptions consiste à procéder à des recoupements de textes de différentes époques de la tradition grammaticale antique, pour permettre au moins de situer nos auteurs dans l'ensemble de l'évolution des idées linguistiques.

## 2. Sources inférentielles des théories grammaticales d'Aristophane et d'Aristarque

### 2.1. Incidence du débat sur l'authenticité de la *Tékhnē*

Deux débats ont été à cet égard essentiels. Le premier concerne l'authenticité de la *Tékhnē grammatikḗ* de Denys le Thrace (→ 57). En effet, si le texte de Denys s'avère intégralement authentique, il paraît difficile qu'un élève d'Aristarque en soit très éloigné sur le plan des conceptions grammaticales. Or le traité de Denys suppose un degré assez avancé des connaissances grammaticales, tant sur le plan de la flexion et de la morphologie que sur le plan syntaxique ou même surtout celui du métalangage. Il faudrait alors supposer chez les prédécesseurs immédiats de Denys un niveau de connaissance relativement équivalent. En revanche, si la *Tékhnē* est pour l'essentiel un traité largement postérieur, faussement attribué à Denys, rien n'oblige à le rapprocher des conceptions linguistiques d'Aristophane et Aristarque. Compte tenu de la minceur de nos sources directes, la question de l'authenticité de la *Tékhnē* est donc lourde de conséquences dans la représentation que nous pouvons nous faire des théories linguistiques des philologues alexandrins.

Sans reprendre ce débat qu'il ne m'appartient pas de trancher ici, je voudrais présenter quelques arguments qui ne me semblent pas avoir été utilisés. D'abord l'absence de témoignage direct émanant des alexandrins eux-mêmes sur leurs propres conceptions grammaticales s'accorderait mieux avec un état de développement modéré des théories linguistiques et de leur autonomisation (cet argument va dans le même sens, mais ne doit pas être confondu avec l'absence de papyrus de la *Tékhnē* avant le III^e^ ou IV^e^ siècle, argument *e silentio* de Di Benedetto 1990). Ensuite il semble que l'autonomisation du métalangage soit très différente entre les textes qui évoquent les théories des alexandrins et ceux de la *Tékhnē*. Selon Apollonios Dyscole, dans un des rarissimes textes de témoignage direct, "Aristarque appelait les pronoms des mots conjoints en fonction des personnes" (*Pron.* 3,12). Quelle que soit l'interprétation que l'on donne (morphologique ou syntaxique) de ce qui n'est pas censé être une définition mais une appellation, la terminologie d'Aristarque paraît nettement différente de celle d'Apollonios et de celle de Denys, non seulement parce que le terme et la notion sont radicalement différents, mais aussi parce que formellement l'appellation est moins spécifique et dispose donc d'un statut moins fortement métalinguistique. Enfin je ne crois pas qu'on ait jamais fait remarquer qu'Apollonios Dyscole revendiquait l'originalité et la nouveauté de son projet, au début de son traité *Sur la syntaxe*. Or la *Tékhnē* présuppose souvent des analyses syntaxiques. Je serais donc plus enclin à me rallier aux thèses de Di Benedetto, qui voit dans la *Tékhnē* un manuel du IV^e^ siècle de notre ère. Les trois philologues alexandrins (Aristophane, Aristarque et Denys) seraient ainsi réunis par le caractère précisément philologique de leur 'programme de recherche', dont la grammaire ne serait que l'auxiliaire encore assez mal autonomisée.

### 2.2. Incidence de la querelle entre analogistes et anomalistes

Le second débat censé permettre d'attribuer leur place à Aristophane et Aristarque est celui qui a été présenté par Varron comme une querelle entre analogistes et anomalistes. Là aussi selon la position adoptée à l'égard de cette querelle, la conception que nous aurons de l'apport des philologues alexandrins sera radicalement différente. Il s'agit toujours, soit de faire des Alexandrins les artisans d'un système grammatical achevé, soit de nier l'existence à ce stade d'une méthode descriptive systématique.

Pour Varron, selon un schéma qui est bien rappelé par F. Douay et J.-J. Pinto (1991), il y aurait eu une véritable querelle d'écoles entre les Alexandrins, partisans de la conception analogiste, et les sectateurs du premier responsable de la Bibliothèque de Pergame, le stoïcien Cratès de Mallos. Le problème qui se pose à propos de cette querelle, c'est que Varron en est pratiquement l'unique témoin dont nous disposions. Par exemple, dans l'édition d'Aristophane par Slater, le chapitre sur le douteux traité de l'analogie ne comporte pratiquement que des citations de Varron. C'est pourquoi le soupçon pèse depuis très longtemps sur la participation de nos philologues à une querelle opposant analogistes et anomalistes. Et ce soupçon en entraîne souvent un second concernant la conscience claire d'une méthode analogique chez les philologues d'Alexandrie.

Ce double soupçon se trouve déjà chez Steinthal (1891), pour qui l'analogie et l'anomalie ne sont pas des concepts chez Aristophane, ni même chez Aristarque, bien que certains textes semblent reposer sur une méthode analogique. Mais selon Steinthal il s'agit plutôt de balbutiements, aucun projet proprement grammatical n'étant véritablement envisagé par les philologues. Evidemment la démarche de Steinthal peut nous paraître datée dans la mesure où elle se fonde sur une confiance glorieuse dans le science grammaticale et philologique de son époque, conçue comme l'aboutissement de plusieurs siècles d'études.

La contestation de l'existence de la querelle a pris une forme particulièrement radicale chez D. Fehling (1956–57), qui fait de Varron l'inventeur pur et simple de la querelle. Il associe à nouveau à cette contestation celle de la méthode analogique. Mais cette fois, il considère la théorie de la flexion comme achevée à l'époque d'Aristarque. La méthode analogique se serait développée plus tard pour servir d'argument à la théorie flexionnelle. Il y a là une inversion originale (mais à vrai dire un peu surprenante) par rapport aux conceptions habituelles qui considèrent que la méthode analogique a préparé la théorie de la flexion.

En tout cas, cette position a paru très extrémiste à E. Siebenborn (1976), qui considère que la remise en cause du témoignage varronien par Fehling est excessive. Il se montre très prudent sur la querelle elle-même, rappelant notamment l'absence de toute référence à cette querelle chez Sextus Empiricus (fin du II^e^ siècle de notre ère), néanmoins pourfendeur de la position analogiste. En revanche, il propose une vision plus historique du concept d'analogie. Chez les alexandrins, l'analogie aurait eu une fonction essentiellement philologique, permettant d'établir et de justifier le bon texte. Ce n'est que plus tard, avec le développement de la perspective grammaticale que l'analogie aurait trouvé son terrain grammatical, ce qui aurait débouché notamment sur la théorie flexionnelle. Dans cette perspective, il paraît tout de même difficile qu'il y ait eu une véritable querelle de grammairiens sur la nature des règles linguistiques à l'époque alexandrine.

Le doute à l'égard d'une querelle entre analogistes et anomalistes est plus net chez J. Pinborg (1975), pour qui la principale activité des philologues alexandrins est la critique des textes, la grammaire étant pour eux une simple pratique (*empeiría*) que Pinborg assimile à l'adéquation observationnelle, qui est le premier niveau dans la hiérarchie chomskyenne auquel il est fait référence. Le manuel de Denys, quelle que soit l'époque de sa composition (mais en tout état de cause *après* Aristarque) représente au contraire un stade plus autonome de la grammaire, et surtout plus scientifique, comme l'illustre le terme même de *tékhnē*, qui sert à le désigner et sur lequel nous reviendrons. Mais pour Pinborg (1975: 110) le développement du caractère scientifique de la grammaire, sans être exempt de tensions, s'est fait dans le cadre d'une discipline unique:

> "nous trouvons une seule science grammaticale avec des méthodes uniformes et une approche uniforme du langage, qui est fondamentalement différente de la grammaire philosophique".

Autrement dit, pour Pinborg, il ne saurait y avoir eu dans l'Antiquité deux traditions grammaticales concurrentes et radicalement différentes, sources de querelles renouvelées. Cette position est évidemment reliée à la question de l'authenticité de la *Tékhnē*. En effet, dans l'hypothèse où, comme le suppose Di Benedetto, il s'agit d'un traité de la fin de l'Antiquité, le manuel de Denys serait précisément la synthèse de ce grand courant grammatical unitaire envisagé par Pinborg. Dans le cas inverse où le manuel serait bien de Denys, on pourrait davantage le considérer comme une grande synthèse analogiste.

C'est d'ailleurs dans ce sens qu'ont œuvré les travaux de l'auteur de l'édition des scholies de l'*Iliade*, H. Erbse. En effet, dans son article sur la grammaire normative chez les Alexandrins (1980), il tente de démontrer simultanément l'authenticité de la *Tékhnē*, l'importance de l'usage que fait Aristarque de la méthode analogique et son désir de trouver une réponse aux irrégularités constatées dans la langue homérique. En somme, l'état d'avancement des connaissances grammaticales chez Aristarque lui paraît tel que le manuel de Denys dans son intégralité en serait l'aboutissement logique.

Quant à Aristophane de Byzance, c'est sur l'analyse minutieuse du témoignage de Varron que s'appuie W. Ax (1990) pour établir l'authenticité de sa position analogiste. Là aussi, l'attitude à l'égard de la 'querelle' entre analogistes et anomalistes reste prudente, mais il est clair qu'en donnant aux conceptions linguistiques d'Aristophane un caractère nettement analogiste, Ax rend possible une véritable *position* analogiste.

Pour s'en tenir à l'essentiel en ce qui concerne ce second débat, sans vouloir trancher sur l'authenticité de la 'querelle', il est clair que, ne pouvant rien assurer en ce qui concerne la querelle elle-même, les chercheurs qui se sont penchés sur cette question ont déplacé le débat sur ses conditions de possibilité et en particulier sur celle-ci: Aristophane de Byzance et Aristarque pouvaient-ils être analogistes? Et cela revient à répondre à la question: à quel degré de développement et de consolidation Aristophane et Aristarque ont-ils porté le concept d'analogie en grammaire? C'est donc plutôt en fonction de l'état d'avancement de ce concept que s'organise le débat: Steinthal, Pinborg et Siebenborg sont très réservés sur l'existence d'un concept clair d'analogie grammaticale chez les Alexandrins, au contraire Erbse et Ax donnent des arguments en sa faveur. Quant à Fehling, dont on a vu la position originale, dans son compte-rendu de l'ouvrage de Siebenborn, il retire aux Alexandrins la théorie de la flexion qu'il situe plutôt à l'époque de Varron. Il se dégage ainsi une certaine unanimité pour faire de l'analogie la base de la théorie flexionnelle, le problème étant bien celui de l'émergence de ce concept.

## 3. Place de l'analogie dans la philologie alexandrine

### 3.1. Histoire de l'analogie: des mathématiques à la grammaire

Il est temps maintenant de définir ce qu'entendaient les Grecs par analogie. L'histoire de ce terme a été remarquablement décrite par E. Siebenborn (1976). Le mot *analogía* se trouve d'abord dans le domaine mathématique, où il désigne un rapport proportionnel, soit arithmétique (il y a autant entre 9 et 6 qu'entre 6 et 3) soit géométrique (le rapport entre 1 et 2 est le même qu'entre 2 et 4). Ce rapport proportionnel est ensuite envisagé métaphoriquement chez les philosophes: pour Platon, si les quatre éléments ont permis au Dieu de créer l'Univers, c'est grâce à l'harmonie du rapport proportionnel: "ce que le feu est à l'air, l'air l'est à l'eau, et ce que l'air est à l'eau, l'eau l'est à la terre" (*Timée* 32b). Siebenborn montre également que les analogies à deux éléments reposent sur une part d'implicite. Quand Aristote établit une analogie entre la bouche et les racines, il s'agit en fait de montrer une identité fonctionelle: la bouche est à l'homme ce que les racines sont à la plante, un moyen de s'alimenter. On voit que l'analogie devient ainsi un procédé heuristique. Et Siebenborn suggère que la médecine empirique aurait pu constituer le chaînon entre les domaines mathématique et philosophique d'une part et le domaine grammatical d'autre part: l'inférence par analogie (*metábasis kat' analogían*) permet en effet d'appliquer des remèdes utilisés pour des maladies connues au traitement de maladies inconnues. De même en grammaire, l'analogie est une méthode de résolution des incertitudes ou d'extension des connaissances.

### 3.2. Analogie et philologie

Mais c'est ici qu'il convient d'être très prudent: il ne s'agit pas pour les philologues d'Alexandrie de découvrir les règles de la compétence linguistique. Leur but est tout à fait pratique, comme d'ailleurs celui de la médecine. C'est d'ailleurs la perspective de Denys dans sa définition de la grammaire, généralement considérée comme authentique: "La grammaire est l'expérience (*empeiría*) des façons de parler courantes des poètes et des prosateurs". On pourrait dire que, de même que la médecine cherche à guérir les maladies, de même la grammaire telle que la conçoivent les Alexandrins cherche à corriger les grands textes littéraires. C'est ce qu'ils appellent la diorthose (*diórthōsis*). L'analogie serait donc l'un des moyens pratiques pour établir le bon texte. Par exemple, il s'agit pour Aristarque d'établir si le participe *peirōn* (*Iliade* 24, 8) porte le ton sur la première ou la deuxième syllabe. Il propose de l'accentuer sur la première, à partir du raisonnement suivant: on sait que le participe *keírōn*, ainsi que l'imparfait *ékeire* qui lui correspond, s'accentuent sur la première syllabe; or l'imparfait correspondant à *peirōn* est *épeire* accentué sur la première syllabe; par conséquent *peírōn* s'accentue comme *keírōn* sur la première syllabe. Il s'agit clairement d'un exemple d'application de la quatrième proportionnelle.

3.3. De l'analogie comme concept à l'analogie comme préfiguration de la règle

Mais il faut faire ici quelques remarques. D'abord je ne suis pas sûr que les textes qui, comme celui-ci, illustrent la méthode analogique des Alexandrins soient absolument authentiques: en effet, les scholiastes qui citent Aristarque ou Aristophane ne différencient pas très bien le point de vue de l'auteur cité du leur. Ensuite, si cette méthode était strictement fondée sur la quadruple proportion, on s'attendrait à en trouver beaucoup plus d'exemples qu'il n'y en a en réalité. En fait on trouve plutôt des rapprochements entre deux termes: l'un des deux est considéré comme sûr, le second est en question. Et même dans ces cas-là on n'est pas sûr que le rapprochement ne soit pas, surtout sous une forme abstraite et grammaticale, une simple référence à des cas connus à l'époque du scholiaste. En revanche il paraît beaucoup plus vraisemblable qu'une méthode de *type* analogique ait été mise en place par les philologues alexandrins, fondée précisément sur l'expérience (*empeiría*) des textes. Pfeiffer (1968: 226) cite un passage de Porphyre (III^e^ siècle) évoquant le principe interprétatif général d'Aristarque:

"Prétendant expliquer Homère à partir d'Homère (*Hómēron ex Homḗrou saphēnízein*), je montrais comment il s'interpréte lui-même, tantôt dans le contexte immédiat, tantôt ailleurs".

On peut considérer (et il faut reconnaître que les scholies elles-mêmes y invitent) que ce qui vaut pour l'interprétation du texte vaut aussi pour l'aspect linguistique et grammatical de l'établissement du texte. On peut donc supposer que les Alexandrins, et tout particulièrement Aristarque, appuyaient leurs choix grammaticaux sur une pratique approfondie de l'usage homérique. On en arrive ainsi à l'essentiel de leur méthode, et qui rejoint l'inspiration analogique. Les rapprochements entre différentes parties du texte homérique ne débouche généralement pas sur des règles. Il s'agirait plutôt d'une sorte de préfiguration des règles sous la forme d'un morceau de paradigme. On pense ici à ce que dit R. W. Langacker (1987) des règles linguistiques, qui peuvent selon lui être apprises soit 'par le haut', c'est-à-dire comme de véritables règles générales, ou 'par le bas' c'est-à-dire comme des listes. On pense aussi à l'usage des incipit pour intituler une œuvre littéraire. Et je citerai enfin la relation associative chez Saussure. Ces références, qu'on ne s'y trompe pas, ne sont pas proposées ici pour faire des Alexandrins des 'précurseurs' de la linguistique actuelle. Il s'agit de faire comprendre comment, *avant* de disposer d'un concept de règle de grammaire bien consolidé, rien n'empêche d'avoir recours à des formes de règles qu'on peut appeler 'primitives' (sans mettre dans ce terme de jugement de valeur). En ce sens, l'écart entre l'analogie reposant sur la quatrième proportionnelle et la prise en compte de simples ressemblances est peut-être moins important et moins pertinent qu'on ne l'a dit parfois. Par exemple, Erbse (1980) tente de démontrer que chez Aristarque, contrairement à ce que dit Siebenborn, la correction des textes ne reposait pas sur de simples rapprochements mais sur une véritable méthode analogique à quatre termes. Il prétend en même temps qu'une méthode analogique présuppose obligatoirement la connaissance des régularités grammaticales. Je crois qu'il y a là une méconnaissance du fonctionnement de l'analogie. Comme nous l'avons dit, l'analogie c'est la règle avant la règle, l'amorce du paradigme. La présentation de l'analogie par Saussure (*CLG* 228) va, à mon avis, tout à fait dans ce sens:

"Pour former *indécorable*, nul besoin d'en extraire les éléments (*in-décorable*); il suffit de prendre l'ensemble et de le placer dans l'équation:
*pardonner : impardonnable*, etc.,
= *décorer : x*.
*x = indécorable*.
De la sorte on ne suppose pas chez le sujet une opération compliquée, trop semblable à l'analyse consciente du grammairien".

L'analogie se trouve ainsi assimilée à une approche spontanée de la régularité et bien sûr il faut que la langue (ou le texte) en fournisse le support. Mais précisément la conscience de règles abstraites n'est absolument pas nécessaire à la conscience de cette forme déjà sophistiquée de régularité qu'est l'analogie. Si Saussure a raison, le caractère spontané de l'analogie peut expliquer par ailleurs pourquoi les scholies se contentent le plus souvent d'appuyer les choix de texte en notant une simple ressemblance entre deux termes. C'est que l'analogie à quatre termes est simplement plus explicite mais c'est la même opération.

En fait je crois qu'il faut distinguer là-dessus deux questions. La première est celle de cette attention à la régularité qui se manifeste dans la méthode alexandrine, telle que nous pouvons la connaître. Il y a bien un présupposé de régularité à la fois dans l'usage des auteurs et dans la langue. Mais d'autre part cette attention à la régularité pose la question du caractère plus ou moins technique de la méthode, de ses concepts et de sa terminologie. Il me semble que, pour cette deuxième question, on doit être beaucoup plus prudent: l'état d'autonomie et d'avancement de la description linguistique et de son métalangage chez les Alexandrins paraît beaucoup plus douteux. Et je crois que c'est un peu le fond du débat entre les philologues contemporains depuis Steinthal: la grammaire a-t-elle été constituée en discipline autonome par les philologues alexandrins?

## 4. La question de l'autonomisation de la grammaire

### 4.1. Problème général

Cette question de l'autonomie du champ grammatical est tout à fait cruciale pour deux raisons. La première c'est qu'elle interfère avec l'interprétation du témoignage de Varron. En effet, il est généralement admis que l'autonomisation du champ grammatical était beaucoup plus avancée à l'époque de Varron. Dès lors la visée rétrospective qu'il a pu avoir de la période alexandrine risque d'avoir été influencée par cette évolution épistémique. La seconde raison tient à notre propre position d'historiens de la grammaire. Car ce qui est vrai pour Varron l'est a fortiori pour nous: le champ de la linguistique actuelle étant nettement autonome, nous risquons soit de 'grammaticaliser' des théories qui ne sont pas strictement grammaticales, en confondant par exemple des remarques sur la langue avec des remarques grammaticales, soit de séparer ce qui relève de la grammaire parce que cela nous paraît naturel.

### 4.2. Le métalangage

De ce point de vue, le critère d'autonomisation le plus utilisable pour l'Antiquité me paraît être le degré de consolidation du métalangage, dans la mesure où l'usage métalinguistique d'un terme suppose un passage du signe-occurrence au signe-type. Or précisément nous avons quelques rares témoignages qui semblent montrer une évolution entre Aristophane et Aristarque. Le terme le plus révélateur est cité par Apollonios Dyscole (*Pron.* 62,17): selon lui, Aristarque appelait le pronom *autós* "appositif" (*epitagmatikḗ*) parce qu'il accompagne notamment un pronom personnel tonique. De même, on a évoqué plus haut la terminologie utilisée par Aristarque pour désigner le pronom. On trouve aussi dans les scholies un assez grand nombre de termes grammaticaux, par exemple celui qui désigne le participe (*metokhḗ*). Il faut ajouter à cela la différence de statut entre Aristophane de Byzance et Aristarque chez Varron: le premier serait simplement à l'origine de la méthode analogique, alors que le second serait le véritable chef de file de l'école alexandrine dans la querelle grammaticale avec Cratès. De même Varron, qui n'a pas grande estime pour Aristophane, évoque les manipulations très pragmatiques, simples commutations de lettres qui lui tiennent lieu de théorie flexionnelle (*De Ling. Lat.* 6,2). Il est donc probable que le métalangage chez Aristophane était nettement moins fixé que chez Aristarque, même si rien n'est absolument sûr en ce qui concerne le métalangage d'Aristarque. Mais il paraît raisonnable de supposer que l'émergence d'un métalangage spécifique révèle l'autonomisation d'un champ de réflexion. De ce point de vue, il est exact, pour paraphraser la remarque de Erbse (1980) concernant l'ensemble du manuel de Denys de Thrace (ce qui me semble aller beaucoup trop loin), que l'existence d'une définition précise de la grammaire (*grammatikḗ*) est tout à fait à sa place chez un disciple d'Aristarque.

### 4.3. *Empeiría* et *tékhnē*

Cette progression semble corroborée par ailleurs à un autre niveau, celui du passage de l'*empeiría* à la *tékhnē*. On trouve déjà chez Platon et Aristote une opposition entre ces deux modes de connaissance. L'*empeiría* est une sorte de connaissance artisanale sans composante théorique ou logique, une sorte de synthèse de l'expérience d'un domaine. Au contraire la *tékhnē* correspond à une connaissance reliée à une théorie explicative. C'est ce dernier type de connaissance qui se trouve évidemment valorisé par les philosophes. Le médecin qui soigne des maladies en utilisant son expérience antérieure a recours à une connaissance empirique; celui qui réinterprète son expérience dans une perspective étiologique et rationnelle, amenée parfois à contredire les données observables, fait bénéficier sa pratique d'une connaissance technique. Si l'on se place maintenant sur le terrain de la grammaire, on ne peut qu'être frappé, comme l'étaient déjà les commentateurs des scholies de Denys, par la contradiction entre le titre du manuel de Denys et la définition 'authentique' de la grammaire. Le manuel est intitulé *tékhnē* alors que la grammaire est définie comme une *empeiría*. C'est évidemment un argument pour intercaler plusieurs siècles entre les deux mots. Mais il faut ajouter que l'approche de la langue que nous pouvons constater chez les philologues alexandrins relève davantage, comme nous l'avons dit, de l'*empeiría* que de la *tékhnē*. Ce qui a fait l'autorité d'Aristarque c'est notamment sa connaissance de la langue et des textes homériques, ce que Steinthal appelle son *Sprachgefühl*. Il y a là avant tout une expérience qui conditionne une pratique, en l'occurrence la diorthôse, qui préside à l'établissement du texte. Cela correspond assez bien en somme à la définition de la grammaire par Denys. Mais l'emploi de *tékhnē* dans le titre n'est pas forcément contradictoire avec cette conception. C'est à l'intérieur du mot *tékhnē* que se situerait la contradiction. En effet la rencontre entre la grammaire et l'idée de scientificité semble ne s'être faite que bien après Aristarque, notamment au premier siècle avant notre ère, chez Asclépiade de Myrléa, cité notamment par Sextus Empiricus (*M.* 1,72). On se retrouve alors face au problème déjà évoqué: une fois l'autonomisation scientifique d'un domaine réalisée, le regard rétrospectif est très difficile. Les progrès dans la scientificité accomplis depuis Aristarque ne l'ont évidemment pas empêché (et *a fortiori* son disciple) de considérer son activité comme une *tékhnē*. Simplement, l'emploi du mot *empeiría* dans la définition de Denys implique que la pratique à laquelle il renvoie ne soit pas contradictoire avec le statut accordé à la *tékhnē*. Cela cadrerait à la fois avec le caractère apparemment très empirique (ce qui ne veut pas dire inorganisé) de la pratique grammaticale des Alexandrins, et avec l'idée d'une radicalisation ultérieure de l'opposition *tékhnē/empeiría* en grammaire.

### 4.4. L'analogie entre *tékhnē* et *empeiría*

Si l'on revient maintenant à la question de la méthode analogique, il est frappant de constater que la présentation que nous avons proposée plus haut semble tout à fait parallèle à celle de l'évolution du concept de *tékhnē*. D'abord une pratique empirique reposant sur les ressemblances et la comparaison, puis une systématisation des procédures comparatives recourant à la proportionnalité à quatre termes et débouchant sur des paradigmes, enfin, certainement plus tard, des 'règles' instituant les paradigmes en modèles de flexion représentant des classes. Siebenborn (1976) a bien montré que la pratique analogique des Alexandrins, malgré son présupposé de régularité linguistique, devait être rapprochée de la médecine empirique (→ Art. 60). Plutôt que de soutenir que le concept d'*analogía* est passé de l'*empeiría* à la *tékhnē*, je ferais l'hypothèse que c'est la radicalisation de l'opposition *tékhnē/empeiría* qui a d'abord conduit à systématiser le concept d'*analogía* avant de l'intégrer dans le dispositif technique comme un héritage de l'empirisme. Mais l'empirisme de l'*analogía* aurait été relu comme une technique scientifique permettant d'établir les paradigmes et les règles flexionnelles.

## 5. La base normative de la philologie alexandrine

### 5.1. La norme morale

En réalité, comme on l'a vu, l'objectif des Alexandrins semble avoir été beaucoup plus pratique: établir le texte des grands auteurs. C'est ce qui a débouché sur la méthode d'Aristarque consistant à 'expliquer Homère à partir d'Homère'. A ce stade, Steinthal avait déjà fait remarquer qu'intervenait chez Aristarque une certaine naïveté sur le plan de l'interprétation. Il rejette certains vers d'Homère sous prétexte qu'ils ne sont pas conformes à ses préjugés moraux: Alkinoos ne peut pas souhaiter avoir pour gendre un inconnu (= Ulysse), Phoenix ne peut pas préméditer le meurtre de son père. Contrairement au principe de l'objectivité philologique, Aristarque recourt à une certaine normativité morale qui, à défaut d'être un critère philologiquement recevable, permet de choisir un 'bon' texte.

### 5.2. De la norme textuelle à la norme linguistique

Or on retrouve cette méthode normative au plan de la langue elle-même. La première norme c'est l'usage homérique. On choisira la leçon la plus conforme à cet usage. C'est alors l'expérience des textes homériques qui permet de faire un choix. Dans ce cas, on peut dire que la norme fonctionne comme une exigence de cohérence. Mais si cette méthode n'est pas concluante, il faut faire appel à la connaissance générale de la langue. C'est là que se produit un phénomène intéressant et peut-être capital: cherchant à établir le 'bon' texte, le philologue est amené à trouver les critères de la langue correcte. En ce sens, l'exigence de correction serait au départ une exigence philologique, contre-coup de la nécessité de justifier un choix éditorial. La méthode analogique (quel que soit son degré de dévelopement chez les Alexandrins) constitue alors une forme de rationalisation de la norme linguistique censée justifier un choix textuel. Ainsi, la base grammaticale de la philologie alexandrine n'est normative que par souci de rigueur philologique. Il faut ajouter que, en sens inverse, postuler une norme dans l'usage autorise une rationalisation de l'analyse linguistique, de même que postuler une cohérence dans l'usage homérique autorise une rationalisation du choix philologique. La valorisation normative de la "grécité" (*hellēnismós*) a donc peut-être été à l'origine de l'approche rationnelle du langage, dans la mesure où, présupposant un principe d'organisation interne, elle conduit à proposer une description de l'usage qui repose sur une régularité immanente.

Une référence intéressante, de ce point de vue, se trouve dans le traité *Du pronom* d'Apollonios (71,22). R. Schneider, l'éditeur de ce texte, y voit une citation d'Aristarque, qu'il met entre guillemets. Celui-ci aurait di qu'Homère était "un modèle de grécité" et on trouve à la suite la présentation d'une régularité d'usage homérique concernant les pronoms réfléchis. Cela signifierait que, pour Aristarque, les régularités mises au jour par des méthodes philologiques pour l'établissement du texte homérique pouvaient servir de modèles pour fixer la norme linguistique. Je crois qu'il y a là l'amorce d'une généralisation du principe d'immanence. En expliquant Homère à partir d'Homère, on met à jour des régularités d'usage qui permettent d'établir le bon texte. Mais si on applique le même principe au niveau de la langue elle-même, on en vient à expliquer la langue à partir d'elle-même, ce qui permet d'établir le bon usage. En ce sens, on pourrait dire que le point de vue normatif a bien été une condition de possibilité de développement de la description linguistique. Evidemment il faut peut-être attendre Apollonios lui-même pour que se trouve explicité le principe d'explication rationnelle de l'usage (*lógos*). Mais c'est le rôle de la norme dans la philologie alexandrine qui avait préparé le terrain.

### 5.3. Le problème de l'histoire de la langue

Il est tout de même surprenant pour nous que les Alexandrins aient pu considérer Homère comme un "modèle de grécité" dans la mesure où ils avaient conscience que sa langue était très éloignée de l'attique classique et encore plus de la *koinè* hellénistique. Mais ce n'est pas un problème isolé: c'est toute la représentation de l'histoire de la langue qui est ici en cause. En fait, il est possible de rendre compte de ce paradoxe à partir d'un ensemble de déplacements.

D'abord le rôle normatif de la langue et des textes littéraires tendait probablement à restreindre la légitimité de l'évolution linguistique. On trouve, en particulier chez Aristophane de Byzance, une opposition entre l'usage des anciens poètes et celui des nouveaux poètes. Mais, outre que cela ne fait que maintenir l'autorité des poètes sur les usages légitimes, cela n'implique nullement que l'usage des anciens poètes puisse être contesté dans son authenticité normative: les nouveaux usages ne se substituent pas totalement aux anciens. De ce point de vue, les commentateurs n'ont peut-être pas toujours été assez prudents en confondant l'usage des poètes et l'usage tout court. Pfeiffer (1968) crédite Aristophane d'un intérêt pour la langue de son époque un peu trop rapidement à mon sens. On n'est pas sûr que les usages 'récents' auxquels réfère Aristophane ne sont pas tout simplement les usages littéraires récents (ce qui ne veut pas forcément dire contemporains). Mais, même si on peut supposer que le fait que certains usages soient qualifiés de récents correspond à un changement dans la langue, ce qui importe aux Alexandrins c'est l'établissement du texte. L'évolution linguistique se trouverait ainsi conçue comme un changement de style littéraire.

Par ailleurs, si les Alexandrins ont une conscience claire des phénomènes dialectaux, on peut se demander s'ils ne constituent pas pour eux un modèle de représentation de l'histoire de la langue. En effet, les variations dialectales sont des différences nettes mais que l'on peut réduire à des variations superficielles reposant sur un substrat commun. De la même manière, prendre acte d'un changement linguistique ne signifierait pas accepter l'idée d'une évolution spontanée de la langue. Les poètes récents ne s'expriment pas comme les poètes anciens. Il faut en tenir compte pour établir le texte et pour l'interpréter. Mais cela n'implique nullement un concept d'évolution linguistique. C'est toujours la même langue sous des formes différentes. On pourrait même dire que le rôle normatif dévolu aux œuvres littéraires dans la grammaire alexandrine (telle que nous pouvons nous la représenter) permet d'assurer une mainmise sur l'évolution de la langue. En ce sens l'histoire de la langue se trouve à la fois niée et refusée.

Enfin un certain nombre de procédés explicatifs qui apparaissent dans les textes évoquant les conceptions des Alexandrins peuvent être considérés comme des moyens détournés de rendre compte de l'évolution linguistique sans la reconnaître véritablement. On trouve ainsi des particularités concernant l'usage homérique, qui sont décrites en faisant appel soit au pléonasme soit à l'ellipse (que ce soit sur le plan syntaxique, sur le plan morphologique, ou même sur le plan phonétique). Encore retrouve-t-on là la base contrôlée et littéraire du fonctionnement linguistique, puisque ces écarts par rapport à l'usage courant sont rattachés aux habitudes du poète (cf. Ap. Dysc. *Synt.* 107,8). On en arrive ainsi au concept de *skhẽma* (figure syntaxique) qui correspond à des tours spécifiques du poète. Ces procédés continuent à être utilisés par Apollonios Dyscole et permettent de rendre compte du changement linguistique en le niant totalement, puisque l'ellipse et le pléonasme supposent qu'en profondeur la langue n'a pas changé.

On retrouve la même dénégation de l'histoire dans la partie de la grammaire dont on pourrait croire qu'elle est essentiellement historique, l'étymologie. En réalité, l'étymologie telle qu'elle apparaît chez les Alexandrins (et sans doute aussi plus tard) consiste à justifier la forme d'un mot par son appartenance à une famille lexicale. C'est au fond une sorte de mise en évidence d'une chaîne de ressemblance analogique qui sous-tend une dérivation. On donne ainsi un sens à la forme du mot. Les étymologies prétendent donc proposer une origine aux dénominations, alors qu'elles ne sont que des hypothèses sur les structures dérivationnelles. Quant à la question de l'origine, on sait qu'elle est éminemment une dénégation de l'histoire.

## 6. Conclusion

Si l'on essaye, pour conclure, de résumer l'apport de la grammaire alexandrine dans l'histoire de la linguistique grecque, on peut dire qu'elle a été la première tentative pour appliquer à la langue les méthodes philologiques. La langue se trouve ainsi définie comme un texte cohérent dont les parties se tiennent. La décrire c'est faire apparaître cette cohérence, c'est mettre en relation la langue avec elle-même, et on aura noté tout au long de notre présentation que pour les alexandrins seule la langue peut expliquer la langue. Il y a là une attitude spontanément synchronique d'autant plus étonnante que, comme on l'a vu, il y a chance que la grammaire alexandrine n'ait pas été un domaine autonome.

## 7. Bibliographie

### 7.1. Sources primaires

*Aristophanis Byzantii Fragmenta.* Ed. par W. J. Slater. Berlin: de Gruyter, 1986.

*Grammatici Graeci* (I–II). Ed. par A. Hilgard. Leipzig: Teubner, 1867–1910. (Réimpr., Hildesheim: Olms, 1965.)

*Scholia Graeca in Homeri Iliadem*, (I–VI). Ed. par H. Erbse. Berlin: de Gruyter, 1969–1977.

Sextus Empiricus, *Contra mathematicos.* Ed. par R. G. Bury. Londres: Loeb, 1949.

Varron, *De lingua latina quae supersunt.* Ed. par G. Goetz & F. Schoell. Leipzig: Teubner, 1910. (Réimpr., Amsterdam: Hakkert, 1964.)

### 7.2. Sources secondaires

Ax, Wolfram. 1982. "Aristarch und die 'Grammatik'". *Glotta* 60.96–109.

–. 1990. "Aristophanes von Byzanz als Analogist: Zu Fragment 374 Slater (= Varro, *de lingua Latina* 9,12)". *Glotta* 68.4–18.

Baratin, Marc. 1989. "La constitution de la grammaire et de la dialectique". *Histoire des idées linguistiques*, I éd. par Sylvain Auroux, 186–206. Liège: Mardaga.

–. 1989. "La maturation des analyses grammaticales et dialectiques". *Histoire des idées linguistiques* I éd. par Sylvain Auroux, 207–242. Liège: Mardaga.

Baratin, Marc & Françoise Desbordes. 1981. *L'analyse linguistique dans l'Antiquité classique.* Paris: Klincksieck.

Callanan, Ch. K. 1987. *Die Sprachbeschreibung bei Aristophanes von Byzanz.* (= *Hypomnèmata*, 88.) Göttingen.

Di Benedetto, Vincenzo. 1990. "At the Origins of Greek Grammar". *Glotta* 68.19–39.

Douay, Françoise & Jean-Jacques Pinto. 1991. "Analogie/anomalie: Reflet de nos querelles dans un miroir antique". *Communications* 53.7–16.

Erbse, Hartmut. 1980. "Zur normativen Grammatik der Alexandriner". *Glotta* 58.236–258.

Fehling, Detlev. 1956. "Varro und die grammatische Lehre von der Analogie und der Flexion". *Glotta* 35.214–270.

–. 1957. "Varro und die grammatische Lehre von der Analogie und der Flexion". *Glotta* 36.48–100.

–. 1979. Compte-rendu de Siebenborn (1976). *Gnomon* 51.488–490.

Ildefonse, Frédérique. 1997. *La naissance de la grammaire dans l'antiquité grecque*. Paris: Vrin.

Lallot, Jean. 1985. "Denys le Thrace, *Technè grammatikè*". *Archives et Documents de la SHESL*, 6. Paris.

Langacker, Ronald W. 1987. *Foundations of Cognitive Grammar*, I. Stanford: Stanford Univ. Press.

Ludwich, Arthur. 1884–1885, *Aristarchs homerische Textkritik nach den Fragmenten des Didymos.* 2 vol. Leipzig: Teubner.

Matthaios, Stephanos. 1999. *Untersuchungen zur Grammatik Aristarchs: Texte und Interpretation zur Wortartenlehre.* Göttingen: Vandenhoek & Ruprecht.

Pfeiffer, Rudolf. 1968. *History of Classical Scholarship.* Oxford: Clarendon Press.

Pinborg, Jan. 1975. "Classical Antiquity: Greece". *Current Trends in Linguistics*, XIII. *Historiography of Linguistics* éd. par Thomas A. Sebeok, 69–126. The Hague: Mouton.

Saussure, Ferdinand de. 1916. *Cours de Linguistique Générale*. Lausanne & Paris: Payot.

Siebenborn, Elmar. 1976. *Die Lehre von der Sprachrichtigkeit und ihren Kriterien: Studien zur antiken normativen Grammatik*. Amsterdam: Grüner.

Steinthal, Heyman. 1891. *Geschichte der Sprachwissenschaft bei den Griechen und Römern*, II. Berlin: Dümmler's. (Réimpr., Hildesheim, 1961.)

*Frédéric Lambert, Bordeaux (France)*

# 57. Dionysius Thrax and the *Tékhnē Grammatikḗ*

1. Introduction: Dionysius Thrax
2. The definition of grammar and its partition
3. The *Tékhnē* and its authorship
4. Conclusion
5. Bibliography

## 1. Introduction: Dionysius Thrax

Dionysius Thrax was an Alexandrian grammarian: the name Thrax probably derived from his father's country of origin. He lived approximately between 170 and 90 BC, was a pupil of Aristarchus of Alexandria and later taught in Rhodos.

The lexicon of Suidas informs us that he composed πλεῖστα γραμματικά τε καὶ συνταγματικὰ καὶ ὑπομνήματα: his works, therefore, included commentaries and treatises. We know some of the titles, which possibly refer only to sections from individual works: Περὶ ποσοτήτων (Schol. *Il.* II, 111 b [Did.]), Περὶ τῆς ἐμφάσεως (Clem. Alex. *Strom.* V, 8.45.4), Μελέται (Schol. *Od.* XXII, 9), Παραγγέλματα (Sext. *Adv. Gramm.* 57), Πρὸς Κράτητα (Schol. *Il.* IX, 464 b [Did.]), Περὶ Ῥόδου (Steph. Byz. *Ethn.* 605.5).

The fragments of Dionysius Thrax have recently been edited by K. Linke (1977). This edition is not without defects (see also Fehling [1979: 488, n. 1]). The testimony of Sextus concerning Παραγγέλματα is not included, nor is that of Apollonius Dyscolus *Pron.* GG II, 1.1.5.18–19 (the testimony of Schol. Dion. Thr. GG I, 3.160.26 [fr. 54] does not cover all the facts). The fr. 35 and the fr. 50 should have been included among the dubious fragments. Occasionally, the commentary is inadequate.

As far as we can gather from the fragments, Dionysius Thrax's grammatical interests were – particularly with regard to Homeric criticism – varied: diacritical signs, questions of spelling, breathings and – with particular emphasis – accents, evaluation of vowel length, metrical questions, evaluation of variant readings, interpunction, rejection or defence of the transmitted text, explanation of syntactical peculiarities, etymology, semantic value of single words or phrases, seeming incongruities and other particularities of the text, including the content.

In the extant fragments disagreements with Aristarchus are much more frequent than agreements. Obviously an opinion of Dionysius that disagreed with Aristarchus was more likely to be preserved in the erudite and scholiastic tradition. But the amount of disagreement that is found in the fragments warrants the conclusion that his standing as a scholar showed a certain independence from his teacher: fragments 4, 5, 6, and 24 are particularly significant in this respect. As far as Zenodotus is concerned only critical statements are known (cf. fr. 14 and 18; in the latter he refuses Zenodotus' opinion with scorn). It is noteworthy that Dionysius accepted an opinion that was already supported by the Stoic Chrysippus (cf. fr. 3).

Fr. 52 (Clem. Alex. *Strom.* VIII 45.4–6) demonstrates a remarkable ability for theorizing. Dionysius notices a correlation between certain sentences and certain particular objects, in the sense that in both cases a prescription is expressed: if only in the well-limited realm of cult and religion Dionysius is able to perceive a link between two different aspects of reality.

## 2. The definition of grammar and its partition

In the definition of grammar and in its partition Dionysius shows a remarkable ability for theoretical systematization.

Sextus Empiricus (*Adv. gramm.* 57) states that the Dionysian definition of grammar (and obviously this applies to its partition as well) was mentioned ἐν τοῖς παραγγέλμασι. It is unknown what the size of these Παραγγέλματα was. Concerning the title one could speculate that this was Παραγγέλματα ⟨γραμματικά⟩ (thus Fraser 1972: II, 680) or Παραγγέλματα ⟨γραμματικῆς⟩ (thus Di Benedetto 1958: 182, on the basis of a comparison with the Παραγγέλματα ῥητορικῆς of Theophrastus: the argument is repeated by Schenkeveld [1995: 42]).

In the Παραγγέλματα Dionysius defines grammar in the following way: "Grammar is the maximally extensive experience of what is said by poets and prose writers" (γραμματική ἐστιν ἐμπειρία ὡς ἐπὶ τὸ πλεῖστον τῶν παρὰ ποιηταῖς τε καὶ συγγραφεῦσι λεγομένων). In other words, the specific field of grammar is constituted by written texts, and it is of these texts that the grammarian acquires the maximally extensive experience.

A different formulation of this definition is the one at the beginning of the *Tékhnē grammatikḗ* attributed to Dionysius Thrax (henceforth *Tékhnē*): γραμματική ἐστιν ἐμπειρία τῶν παρὰ ποιηταῖς τε καὶ συγγραφεῦσιν ὡς ἐπὶ τὸ πολὺ λεγομένων (GG I, 1.5.2–3). However according to this formulation one would have to exclude from the field of grammatical research those words and expressions that are attested infrequently or only once in the authors (this interpretation, necessitated by the position of ὡς ἐπὶ τὸ πολύ in the sentence, is also found in Schol. Dion. Thr. GG I, 3.11.12ff.; 301.10ff.; 452.15ff.) and this is contradicted by the practice of grammar in the Alexandrian-Aristarchean tradition as well as by the fact that Dionysius mentions the explanation of 'glosses' in his partition of grammar. Furthermore, the criticism of Asclepiades of Myrlea (*fl.* 1st century BC) which is reported by Sextus Empiricus (Adv. *gramm.* 72ff.) presupposes the formulation given by Sextus rather than the one in the *Tékhnē*. It is inconceivable that Asclepiades would have been mistaken. Lallot's attempt (1989: 69) to minimize the differences between the two formulations is not convincing; and the passage of Schol. Dion. Thr. GG I, 3.301.16ff. is irrelevant, since it refers to the problem of whether history and philosophy should be involved in the study of grammar.

According to Dionysius there are six parts of grammar. In this respect Sextus Empiricus (*Adv. gramm.* 250) is on the whole correct, even if his version is shorter than the one in the *Tékhnē* (GG I, 1.5.4–6.3). The version of the *Tékhnē* is as follows: μέρη δὲ αὐτῆς ἐστιν ἕξ· πρῶτον ἀνάγνωσις ἐντριβὴς κατὰ προσῳδίαν, δεύτερον ἐξήγησις κατὰ τοὺς ἐνυπάρχοντας ποιητικοὺς τρόπους, τρίτον γλωσσῶν τε καὶ ἱστοριῶν πρόχειρος ἀπόδοσις, τέταρτον ἐτυμολογίας εὕρεσις, πέμπτον ἀναλογίας ἐκλογισμός, ἕκτον κρίσις ποιημάτων, ὃ δὴ κάλλιστόν ἐστι πάντων τῶν ἐν τῇ τέχνῃ.

These are, therefore, the six parts of grammar: expert 'reading' concerning the accents, interpretation according to the poetical 'tropes', explanation of 'glosses' and 'stories', finding of etymology, setting out of analogy, judgement of poems (κρίσις ποιημάτων). The result is an articulated and complete framework that corresponds substantially with the philological-exegetical activity of Aristarchus, and also with that of Dionysius Thrax himself, inasmuch as we can reconstruct it through the fragments.

Pfeiffer (1968: 269 and n. 2) mistakenly interprets κρίσις ποιημάτων as "literary criticism" with the exclusion of "textual criticism": cf. Di Benedetto 1973: 807, n. 1 and

1990: 37, n. 32 (with reference to Sext. *Adv. gramm.* 93: the same argument is repeated by Schenkeveld 1995: 47, n. 9). In fr. 13 of Dionysius Thrax the expression κρίσις ποιημάτων is used in connection with the analysis of a metrical anomaly in Homer.

The notion of ἀνάγνωσις (the 'reading' in the first element of the Dionysian partition) needs some explanation. The formulation of this notion in the Dionysian partition is confirmed by his fr. 4. From this fragment we can reconstruct Dionysius' own words: concerning the accentuation of αἰδω and ἠω and of Πυθω and Ληθω he asserts κακῶς ἀνεγνωκέναι τὸν Ἀρίσταρχον κατὰ τὸν περισπώμενον τόνον (note the construction with κατά). The notion of ἀναγινώσκειν was in fact used in Alexandrian grammar in connection with the determination of what was the correct reading according to the grammarian. Specifically, ἀνάγνωσις ἐντριβὴς κατὰ προσῳδίαν refers to the determination of the correct accent of a word. In Dionysius' fragments this is found not only in fr. 4, but also in fr. 5 (ἀναγινώσκει), fr. 6, Fr. 7 (ἀνέγνωσαν), fr. 8 and fr. 9 (as far as Aristarchus is concerned, it may suffice to refer to the literal quotation in Schol. *Il.* I, 396 b[1] [Herod.] ἐὰν ... κατ᾽ὀρθὸν τόνον ἀναγνῶμεν). Furthermore in *Adv. gramm.* 59 Sextus Empiricus in connection with the Dionysian definition mentions the problem of how to "read" (ἀναγνωστέον) in Plato the sequence η δ ος, i. e. whether η and ος had to be read with rough breathing (this operation was connected with the problem of determining the accent, as Herod. *Pros. cath.* GG III, 1.1.7.2–5 shows; besides, with regard to η δ ος not only the breathing was at issue, but also the problem of accentuation: cf. Schol. *Il.* I, 219 a).

In conclusion we may say that the usual interpretation of Dionysian ἀνάγνωσις, according to which this notion meant for Dionysius the act of reading by the use of one's own voice (thus also Pfeiffer 1968: 268 f.), is mistaken.

The ἀνάγνωσις is the first part of grammar and, as we said, all of them together give us a complete picture of the activity of Alexandrian grammarians. But a technical treatment of linguistic material (letters, syllables, parts of speech) is foreign to the Dionysian conception of grammar, which results from his definition and partition of grammar. This is also confirmed by Sextus Empiricus, who follows (*Adv. gramm.* 91 ff.) the partition of grammar proposed by Asclepiades of Myrlea (→ Art. 58), who divided grammar into the τεχνικόν (the technical-grammatical part of grammar, comprising the treatment of letters, syllables, parts of speech, etc.), the ἱστορικόν, and the ἰδιαίτερον (the part more specifically concerned with the interpretation of literary texts). Among the six parts of Dionysius' partition Sextus (*Adv. gramm.* 250–251) has only the part dealing with etymology and the part dealing with analogy corresponding to the τεχνικόν of Asclepiades of Myrlea. In other words Sextus could not find in the Dionysian partition any element corresponding to the technical-grammatical treatment of letters, syllables and parts of speech.

It is inconceivable that a topic as important as the specific treatment of technical grammar was included in the Παραγγέλματα of Dionysius Thrax without being mentioned in the parts of grammar. Schenkeveld (1995: 51) asserts that the Παραγγέλματα contained a systematic discussion of linguistic matters and that this belonged to the treatment of the second part of grammar. But this is a mere speculation, not supported by any evidence. It is, moreover, a poor conjecture. If the study of poetical modes of expression were to presuppose a technical-formal knowledge of the language, this would also apply to the other parts of grammar (F. Montanari's assertion *apud* Schenkeveld [1994: 303] that Sextus Empiricus warrants the authenticity of the §§ 1–4 of the *Tékhnē*, i. e. not only of § 1, but also of §§ 2–4, is based on a manifestly inadequate knowledge of the facts).

There is something else to be considered. To presuppose technical-grammatical notions does not mean that these were dealt with *ex professo*. In Aristarchus' case, too, it is possible to reconstruct many technical-grammatical elements (cf. Erbse 1980; Ax 1982), but this does not warrant the attribution to Aristarchus of a specific technical-grammatical treatment of the language; on the contrary such statements were remarks that came up in the course of his critical-grammatical analysis of the Homeric text (→ Art. 56). Leaving aside the *Tékhnē*, technical-grammatical statements have also been transmitted from Dionysius Thrax (cf. T. 2, and fr. 54 and 55), but we have no reason to suppose that on this matter Dionysius' case is to be considered differently from Aristarchus' (in fr. 11, concerning *Il.* XV, 571 Dionysius uses the notions of εὐκτικόν and προστατικόν, which shows that he had reflected on the normal use of these verbal moods in everyday speech). With regard to the names of the accents (T. 2 = [Sergii] *Explan. in Donat.* I, GL IV, 529.7–10) we should keep in mind that Varro's source for the information was Tyrannion the Elder, a pupil of Dionysius Thrax, and this explains the emphasis on Dionysius for the issue.

## 3. The *Tékhnē* and its authorship

Nevertheless, an elementary grammatical treatise, usually called *Tékhnē*, which has had an enormous influence in Western linguistics, has been attributed to Dionysius Thrax. A critical edition was published by Gustav Uhlig in 1883 (GG I,1); a translation and – for the first time – a good commentary was provided by Lallot (1989).

The attribution of the *Tékhnē* to Dionysius Thrax was rejected already in Antiquity; cf. Prol. A, Schol. Dion. Thr. GG I, 3, 124.7–14 and Prol. B, Schol. Dion. Thr. GG I, 3, 160.24–161.8. Both Prol. A and Prol. B exhibit a high level of erudition and Prol. B is connected with David the Armenian and his school (cf. Di Benedetto 1958: 171–178). The denial of the authenticity was not an *ad hoc* conjecture, but was based on facts.

In the first half of the 19th century the authenticity of the *Tékhnē* was denied by C. G. Goettling and K. Lehrs, but since the work of M. Schmidt (1852–53) its authenticity was generally regarded as an established fact, until it was called into question by Di Benedetto (1958, 1959). Let us now summarise the arguments against the authenticity of the *Tékhnē*.

In the first place, there is a striking discrepancy between § 1 (definition and partition of grammar, in accordance with Dionysius Thrax) and the rest of the work (§§ 2–20): § 1 deals with the philological-grammatical approach to literary texts, while §§ 2–20 deal with elementary notions which are of a completely different level and cover a domain that is not included in the six parts of grammar enumerated in § 1. According to Erbse (1980: 245 ff.) the author of the *Tékhnē* may have had in mind readers who practised the exegesis of classic authors (cf. § 1) and who in order to accomplish this activity needed "eine handliche Zusammenstellung der grammatisch-normativen Grundbegriffe" (cf. §§ 2–20). But whoever practised "Klassikerexegese" was familiar with these elementary notions, and therefore the junction of § 1 and §§ 2–20 does not cease to be surprising.

§§ 6–20 deal with letters (§ 6), syllables (§§ 7–10), parts of speech (§§ 11–20: § 11 λέξις, § 12 noun, § 13 verb, § 14 conjugations of the verb, § 15 participle, § 16 article, § 17 pronoun, § 18 preposition, § 19 adverb, § 20 conjunction: the number of the parts of speech is eight); but already in the §§ 2–5 the discrepancy with § 1 is manifest.

Whereas in § 1 the ἀνάγνωσις ἐντριβὴς κατὰ προσῳδίαν refers to the procedure of establishing the correct accentuation of the words in a text, the ἀνάγνωσις which is mentioned in § 2 is a radically different notion and a very elementary one. In § 2 the point at issue is the manner in which written texts are to be read by the use of one's own voice, with due attention to accents, interpunction and literary genre. Notwithstanding some superficial points of contact, the difference between the two paragraphs is enormous and cannot be bridged (a different point of view was expressed by Di Benedetto 1990: 38–39). Moreover, προσῳδία in § 1 is a fact to be defined by the grammarian, whereas in § 2 it is a fact already present, which is to be reproduced in the oral presentation of the text. There are therefore two different kinds of ἀνάγνωσις and already Sextus was aware of it, as the comparison of *Adv. gramm.* 49 and 59 demonstrates: the grammatical-philological ἀναγνωστέον of § 59 is radically different from the ἀναγινώσκειν of § 49, which concerns people who learn the basic elements of writing and reading.

Connected with the ἀνάγνωσις of § 2 are also the §§ 3, 4, and 5. Since boys learning to read need to observe the accents and the interpunction, it is not surprising that § 2 is followed by § 3, dealing with the accents, and by § 4, dealing with interpunction (since the division of accents into three kinds was a very simple and generally accepted principle – as is confirmed by Herod. *Pros. cath.* GG III, 1.1.5–11 and also by GL IV, 529.9 *quibus nunc omnes utuntur* – the parallel with GL IV, 529.7–10 does not prove that § 3 derives from Dionysius Thrax). Furthermore, since pupils who practised reading used especially the Homeric poems, it is not surprising that a paragraph (§ 5) deals with the definition of ῥαψῳδία, in the sense of a part of a poem and hence a book of the *Iliad* or the *Odyssey* (the connection appears already in Schol. Dion. Thr. GG I, 3.28.11 ff.).

What, then, is the *Tékhnē*? It is an elementary grammatical treatise, composed around the 4th century AD, that opens with the famous definition (and partition) of grammar by Dionysius Thrax (the celebrity of his definition and partition is proved by Sextus Empiricus). Because of their reputation the Dionysian definition and partition of grammar were placed at the head of the treatise, in spite of the fact that the grammar of which Dionysius spoke is radically different from the technical-grammatical contents of §§ 2–20 of the *Tékhnē* (we need also to keep in mind that the habit of introducing the systematic treatment of grammar with a part of text dedicated to the definition of grammar is found in the Latin grammarians of the 4th century AD, such as Charisius, Diomedes and Victorinus).

A link between § 1 and the §§ 2–20 was provided by the notion of ἀνάγνωσις, and even though the meaning of ἀνάγνωσις was different in § 1 from § 2, the compiler of the *Tékhnē* certainly intended to make this link visible; note also that ποιημάτων ἢ συγγραμμάτων in § 2 corresponds with ποιηταῖς τε καὶ συγγραφεῦσιν in § 1. On the other hand, the Dionysian definition in § 1 appeared radically modified (and falsified) through the substitution of ὡς ἐπὶ τὸ πολύ for ὡς ἐπὶ τὸ πλεῖστον and its placement before λεγομένων. This modification caused a shift from the critical-philological activity to the everyday language, which was the basis for the technical-grammatical part of the *Tékhnē*.

It is not even certain whether the compiler of the *Tékhnē* directly knew the Παραγγέλματα of Dionysius Thrax, and it is not certain, either, that the attribution of the *Tékhnē* to Dionysius Thrax was made by the compiler himself. In any case, note that Pap. Lit. Lond. 182 – written about 300 AD – has the *subscriptio* Τρύφωνος τέχνη γραμματικοί (*scil.* γραμματική), although it is certainly not a work by Tryphon (cf. Di Benedetto 1958: 191–196).

In fact, apart from the discrepancy between § 1 and §§ 2–20 there are other arguments against the authenticity of the *Tékhnē*.

Prol. B refers to the authority of the τεχνικοί, i. e. to Apollonius Dyscolus, in connection with two items: the fact that Dionysius distinguished between ὄνομα and προσηγορία, and that he combined the pronoun and the article (for the second item we have an exact confirmation in Apoll. Dysc. *Pron.* 5.18–19; cf. Di Benedetto 1990: 20–26). Furthermore, for a third item, namely the definition of the verb, Prol. B refers to Apollonius Dyscolus' Ῥηματικόν. All three instances concern views and formulations that are different and even contradict the *Tékhnē*. Pfeiffer (1968: 271) speaks of them as of "three small items " but I do not believe this is correct. The issue is about arguments that are not at all trivial: the systematization of the parts of speech, and the nature and definition of the noun, the article, the pronoun and the verb (against the point of view that the definition of the verb mentioned in the Ῥηματικόν is compatible with the one in the *Tékhnē* cf. Di Benedetto 1990: 27–28). Concerning the first two items Pfeiffer asserts that Dionysius "may well have changed his mind". This is of course possible, but it means superimposing a hypothesis on real facts (and in *Pron.* 5.18–19 Apollonius simply mentions Dionysius Thrax, without specifying whether he is referring to Dionysius Thrax no. 1 or to Dionysius Thrax no. 2).

There is another aspect to this matter which needs to be taken into consideration. Among the 23 technical-grammatical papyri (cf. Wouters 1995: 97) there is none reporting any part of the *Tékhnē* before the 4th century AD. So much for the direct tradition; and the indirect tradition does not give us attestations of the *Tékhnē* as a work of Dionysius Thrax until the 5th/6th centuries AD: Timotheus of Gaza, Ammonius and Priscian.

This coincidence between the direct and the indirect tradition cannot be dismissed simply by calling it an *argumentum ex silentio* (thus Pfeiffer 1968: 270). It should be noted that between the time when Dionysius Thrax lived and the 4th century AD there is a series of authors, many of whose works have come to us and which we can still read: Apollonius Dyscolus, Herodianus, Sextus Empiricus and Quintilian. How could it be possible that they all joined in a conspiracy, in a pact never to speak of this work of Dionysius Thrax (which would have been the earliest technical-grammatical codification in Greek culture)?

The evidence from Apollonius Dyscolus can certainly not be considered an *argumentum ex silentio.* Not only does he not mention Dionysius Thrax's *Tékhnē*, not only does he supply information about Dionysius Thrax which contrasts with the *Tékhnē*, but Apollonius even gives us positive indications about the origins of Greek grammar which scarcely fit in with the *Tékhnē* as written by Dionysius Thrax. From Tryphon (the grammarian active in the 2nd half of the 1st century BC) Apollonius has handed down to us

52 pieces of evidence, which concern an area covered also by the *Tékhnē* (and titles such as Περὶ ἄρθρων, Περὶ προσώπων, Περὶ προθέσεων, Περὶ συνδέσμων, Περὶ ἐπιρρημάτων). On the contrary, we know in Apollonius of only two pieces of evidence for Dionysius Thrax (to which one more can be added by conjecture). To Apollonius Dionysius Thrax was a grammarian of relatively minor importance, who in some points had accepted the doctrine of the Stoics; Thryphon on the contrary was a grammarian who was highly esteemed for a long series of technical-grammatical works.

## 4. Conclusion

The origins of Greek grammar as far as its specifically technical-grammatical aspect is concerned are to be placed in the 1st century BC, after Dionysius Thrax. There is another grammarian in the 1st century BC, Tyrannion the Elder, who reportedly wrote a work with the title Περὶ μερισμοῦ τῶν τοῦ λόγου μερῶν, and likewise we know the titles of technical-grammatical works by Habron, a pupil of Tryphon. But not even for any of the grammarians of the 1st century BC is there any handbook attested of the type of the *Tékhnē*. These are the facts, and on this basis Pinborg (1975) has given a well-documented and insightful account of the origins and development of Greek grammar, which is more exact than Pfeiffer's, and which has not yet been superseded; useful and exact information was given also by Fraser (1972).

The new definition of grammar given by Asclepiades of Myrlea in explicit polemic with Dionysius Thrax, and the definitions given by Chares and Demetrius Chlorus reflect the turning-point in the 1st century BC. The information contained in the grammatical papyri is very useful, too: it is not until the 1st century AD that we find papyri containing (parts of) technical-grammatical treatises. Elsewhere (Di Benedetto 1958) I have examined the papyri that were known at that time and noted the divergences and convergences with the *Tékhnē*. The investigation can be usefully continued with the study of the papyri that have become available in the meantime, and with new insights (in 1979 an edition of the available grammatical papyri was published by Wouters).

Another promising field of research is the comparison between the *Tékhnē* and the works of Apollonius Dyscolus and the Latin grammarians. The analysis of Di Benedetto (1959) shows that more than once a formulation in the *Tékhnē* presupposes a more exact and more articulated formulation, and this fact suggests a process of atrophy and trivialization, in accordance with the mediocre level of the *Tékhnē*. The *Tékhnē* does not mark the beginning, but the end of a long development.

## 5. Bibliography

### 5.1. Primary sources

Apoll. Dysc. *Pron.* = Apollonius Dyscolus, *De pronomine.* Ed. by Richard Schneider. Leipzig: Teubner, 1878.

Clem. Alex. *Strom.* = Clemens Alexandrinus, *Stromata.* Ed. by Otto Stählin. Leipzig: Hinrichs, 1906–1909.

GG = *Grammatici Graeci.* 6 vols. Leipzig: Teubner, 1878–1910.

GL = *Grammatici Latini.* 7 vols. Ed. by Heinrich Keil. Leipzig: Teubner, 1857–1880.

Herod. *Pros. cath.* = Herodianus, *Prosodia catholica.* Ed. by August Lentz. Leipzig: Teubner, 1867–1870.

[Sergii] *Explan. in Donat.* I = [Sergii] *Explanationum in Artem Donati liber I.* Ed. by Heinrich Keil. Leipzig: Teubner.

Sext. *Adv. gramm.* = Sextus Empiricus, *Adversus grammaticos.* Ed. by Jürgen Mau. Leipzig: Teubner, 1950–1984.

Schol. Dion. Thr. = Scholia in Dionysii Thracis *Artem grammaticam.* Ed. by Alfred Hilgard. Leipzig: Teubner, 1901.

Schol. *Il.* = Scholia in Homeri *Iliadem.* Ed. by Hartmut Erbse. Berlin de Gruyter, 1969–1988.

Schol. *Od.* = Scholia in Homeri *Odysseam.* Ed. by Wilhelm Dindorf. Oxford: Typographeo Academico, 1855.

Steph. Byz. *Ethn.* = Stephanus Byzantius, *Ethnica.* Ed. by August Meineke. Berlin: Reimer, 1849.

### 5.2. Secondary sources

Ax, Wolfram. 1982. "Aristarch und die 'Grammatik' ". *Glotta* 60.96–109.

Di Benedetto, Vincenzo. 1958–59. "Dionisio Trace e la *Techne* a lui attribuita". *Annali della Scuola Normale Superiore di Pisa*, Serie II, 27.169–210; 28.87–118.

–. 1966. "Demetrio Cloro e Aristone di Alessandria". *Annali della Scuola Normale Superiore di Pisa*, Serie II, 35.321–324.

–. 1973. "La *Techne* spuria". *Annali della Scuola Normale Superiore di Pisa*, Serie III, 3.797–814.

–. 1990. "At the Origins of Greek Grammar". *Glotta* 68.19–39.

–. 1995. "Afterword". Law & Sluiter (1995: 151–152).

Erbse, Hartmut. 1980 "Zur normativen Grammatik der Alexandriner". *Glotta* 58.236–258.

Fehling, Detlev. 1979. Review of Elmar Siebenborn, *Die Lehre von der Sprachrichtigkeit und ihren Kriterien*, Amsterdam, 1976. *Gnomon* 51.488–490.

Fraser, P. M. 1972. *Ptolemaic Alexandria*. 2 vols. Oxford.

Lallot, Jean. 1989. *La grammaire de Denys le Thrace*. Paris.

Law, Vivien & Ineke Sluiter, eds. 1995. *Dionysius Thrax and the* Technē Grammatikē. Münster: Nodus.

Linke, Konstanze. 1977. *Die Fragmente des Grammatikers Dionysius Thrax*. Berlin & New York.

Pfeiffer, Rudolf. 1968. *History of Classical Scholarship from the Beginnings to the Hellenistic Age*. Oxford: Clarendon Press.

Pinborg, Jan. 1975. "Classical Antiquity: Greece". *Current Trends in Linguistics*, vol. XIII. The Hague: Mouton.

Schenkeveld, Dirk Marie. 1994. "Scholarship and Grammar". *Entretiens sur l'Antiquité Classique* 40.263–306.

–. 1995. "The Linguistic Contents of Dionysius' Παραγγέλματα". Law & Sluiter (1995: 41–53).

Schmidt, Moriz. 1852–53. "Dionys der Thraker". *Philologus* 7.360–382; 8.231–253, 510–520.

Wouters, Alfons. 1979. *The Grammatical Papyri from Graeco-Roman Egypt: Contribution to the study of the* Ars Grammatica *in Antiquity*. Brussels: Paleis der Academiën.

–. 1995. "The Grammatical Papyri and the *Technē Grammatikē* of Dionysius Thrax". Law & Sluiter (1995: 95–109).

*Vincenzo Di Benedetto, Pisa (Italy)*

# 58. The organization of grammar in ancient Greece

1. Introduction
2. The beginnings of 'grammar'
3. Stoic 'grammar'
4. 'Grammar' in the students of Diogenes
5. Dionysius Thrax and Asclepiades of Myrlea
6. Apollonius Dyscolus
7. Bibliography

## 1. Introduction

It is not possible to write a brief, but comprehensive study of the organization of Greek 'Grammar' before the later Roman Empire. In one sense, it is not possible to write any sort of study of it at all. For if we take 'grammar' as the observation of and the formulation of rules for correct expression in speech and writing, we find that this was not an independent discipline in our period. Linguistic study in Greece was always part of some larger enterprise. Often it was taught in order to help one understand how to compose well, as in poetics or rhetoric. It was also part of the study of logic or dialectic, where a knowledge of how language worked was necessary in order to formulate and analyze propositions and arguments. It was also part of the discipline called "philology" (*philología*), "criticism" (*kritikḗ*), or "grammar' (*grammatikḗ*), which was devoted to the study of literature. Even in this last guise there are grave difficulties in dealing with organization. None of the works written about this subject before those of Apollonius Dyscolus in the 2nd century CE has come down to us. Further, although it appears that general handbooks on the subject as a whole propounded and followed an organizational framework or division of the expertise, its practitioners wrote numerous works on individual themes, and it is not at all clear that they always thought of these works as occupying a particular place, let alone the same place, in an organizational framework. The present article will therefore of necessity be very incomplete. It will begin with a few historical points and then concentrate on the contexts in which there was demonstrably a treatment of much of what we think of as 'grammar' and about whose organization we can say something; and it will use material from other ancient 'expertises', above all medicine, to throw light on the innumerable disputes about the character, structure, and purpose of grammar. Our programme will cover, first, Stoic dialectic, followed by three early general works on 'criticism' or 'grammar', those of Tauriscus the Cratetean, Dionysius the Thracian, and Asclepiades of Myrlea, known to us in part only indirectly. The survey will conclude with Apollonius Dyscolus, some of whose works actually survive.

## 2. The beginnings of 'grammar'

In classical Greece on learned to read and write – if at all – from the teacher of general competence to whom one was entrusted as a child or in some cases from a specialized tutor, called a *grammatistḗs*. This tutor taught the forms and sounds of letters and their possible combinations, and also introduced his charges to the reading and memorization of poetry, which was regarded as a repository of fine thoughts and deeds. We can scarcely specify the exact limits of what such a tutor might teach, but it is unlikely that he will have covered more than a small part of what we think of as 'grammar'. Indeed, Plato has his character Protagoras (325D–326E), in a context where he can be expected to be reflecting received values, intimate that the main purpose of education was to inculcate morality in the young: as soon as children could understand speech, they were told what to do and what not to do; as soon as they were taught to read, they were given the works of poets who would tell them and show by example what was fine and what was base.

Some studies pertinent to 'grammar' in our sense were made by others in the classical period, but hardly by *grammatistaí*. Thus, we hear of those who explicated rare words in Homer (*glōssográphoi*) and of 'sophists', such as Prodicus or Protagoras, whose interest in *orthoépeia* "correct speech" or *orthótēs onomátōn* "correctness of names" regarded the distinction of parasynonyms and the invention of words or forms of words which might correspond better to what they designate (→ Art. 53). The study of the 'correctness of names' could be useful in philosophy, as it allowed one to make certain distinctions among related concepts; more surprisingly, to a modern audience, it had the advantage of allowing one to confuse one's opponents in argument (Aristotle, *Sophistic Refutations* 173b17ff.).

As these beginnings indicate, then, what we would consider 'grammatical' studies were conducted in classical Greece in the name of other activities or even disciplines. In his *Cratylus*, Plato's Socrates analyzes and then criticizes the tendency of some thinkers of his day to claim that the study of names will reveal much to us about the nature of things: far better to study the things themselves, in so far as we can. The study of language was certainly given high status within those disciplines which relied on it for their effect. Thus, Aristotle's works on *Poetics* and *Rhetoric* contain some detailed work on language, especially on diction (→ Art. 54). But here, while conscious of a larger context of studies related to language, Aristotle is careful to confine himself to what is most relevant to the expertise at hand. Thus, the study of arguments made with language is said to be more relevant to rhetoric than to poetics (*Poetics* 1456a33ff.), the distinction of various "forms of diction" (*skhḗmata léxeōs*) rather to the expertise of acting than to poetics (1456b8–19). At 1456b20ff. Aristotle begins with what is genuinely the concern of poetics, the "parts of diction" (*mérē léxeōs*: element, syllable, conjunction, name, verb, article, case, sentence), and their sub-classifications. Finally (1458a18ff.), he discusses the consequences of the fact that it is the virtue of diction to be clear (*saphḗs*), but not plain (*tapeinḗ*), so that the poet must, in accordance with a particular genre and metre, mix the use of the "proper" or "appropriate" (*kúria*) words for things, which ensure clarity, with the use of "individual" (*idiōtikón*) and "foreign" (*xenikón*) expressions, which ensure loftiness, often at the expense of clarity. This last theme, the 'virtues of diction', was developed by Aristotle's pupil Theophrastus in a treatise, *On Diction*, which seems to have belonged to the sphere of rhetoric (cf. Rabe 1890; Stroux 1912).

On another front, the analysis of language necessary to understand assertions and contradictions was carried out by Aristotle in the work which has come down to us under the title *On Interpretation*. The understanding of contradictory assertions was a necessary preliminary to dialectic, in which a respondent chooses one of a contradictory pair of assertions, and it is the task of a questioner to force the respondent to assert the contradictory of the assertion chosen (cf. Whitaker 1997). The *lógos* or complete sentence comprises, basically, a noun/subject (*ónoma*) and a verb/predicate (*rhē̂ma*), and Aristotle is clearly concerned with these only in so far as they contribute to the truth-value, as we would say, of the *lógos*. It was also in service of their 'dialectic' that the Stoics carried on much of their own work on language, as we shall now see.

## 3. Stoic 'grammar'

We may let Philo of Alexandria remind us of what a thinker of the 1st century CE thought of as grammar:

Reading and writing is the promise of the more unrefined (*atelestéra*) kind of grammar, which some call with a slight alteration 'grammatistic', while the unfolding of what is in poets and prose-writers is the promise of the more perfect sort. Now, when they [i.e., grammarians] explicate the parts of speech, do they not push aside and steal the discoveries of philosophy? For it is her proper job to investigate what a conjunction is, or a name, or verb, or a common versus a proper name, or what is defective in discourse, or complete, or declarative, or a question, inquiry, imperative ['comprehensive', Mss.], prayer, or imprecation. For she is the one who has composed the courses on complete [sc. *lektá*], propositions, and predicates. Is it not by philosophy that one has worked on and achieved the possibility of grasping vocalic, semivocalic, and wholly nonvocal elements and how each of these is called, along with the entire theory of voice, elements, and the parts of the sentence? Squeezing drops as from a cascade and squeezing them into their rather small souls, the thieves do not blush to give out their theft as their own (*On Intercourse for the Sake of Education* 148–150).

As we shall see, the place from which these materials were 'stolen' by the grammarians was Stoic dialectic (→ Art. 55).

According to the report in Diogenes Laertius (*DL* 7.41–42), some Stoics divided the 'logical part' of philosophy – that concerned with *lógos* in all its guises – into rhetoric, the science of speaking well concerning continuous discourses, and dialectic, the science of conversing correctly concerning discourses consisting in question and answer, while others added to these the 'definitional part', concerned with truth. Dialectic, in turn, was divided (7.43) into two *tópoi* "areas", one concerning "things meant" (*sēmainómena*) and one concerning "voice" (*phōnḗ*). The first of these was further divided into 'areas' about impressions and the "sayables" (*lektá*) subsisting on these – roughly, the contents of thoughts and the meanings communicable via language – including propositions, predicates of various sorts, syllogisms, and sophisms. The area concerning 'voice' dealt with (7.44): voice as it is divided into letters (the phoneme, of course, plays no part in ancient speech-analysis); the parts of the sentence (*mérē lógou*, usually known as the 'parts of speech'); solecism, barbarism, poems, and ambiguities; melodic voice; music; and (according to some Stoics) definitions, divisions, and 'expressions'. This division of the area concerning 'voice' is the result of the analysis of DL 7.44 by Schenkeveld (1990: 91; Schenkeveld then goes on [92–93] to correlate his analysis of this passage with the more extended discussion in 7.55–62, and arrives at a tripartite division of this area: definitions of voice, speech, sentence [or discourse], the elements or letters, the differences between speech and sentence, the parts of the sentence; the virtues and vices of discourse, the definitions of poem, poetry, and ambiguities; definition, genus, concept, species, division, distribution; on this organization see the presentation below).

It is evident that, while some of these topics fit easily into our conception of what a 'grammar' should cover, others do not, and the overall intention of the study in which they are imbedded is quite different from what we think of as the point of 'grammar' (on the relation of Stoic philosophy to grammar, see Frede 1977, 1978). The Stoics believed that the world was suffused with and controlled by reason (*lógos*), and that the human soul was a part of that rational world. The sage, who lived in complete accord with the universal reason, was infallible, and thus was always master of what was the right thing to think and to say in every situation – what was true or corresponded to the way the world was – and how to say it, and this was the subject of the 'logical part' of Stoic philosophy (for a discussion of the sage's need for logic see Atherton 1993, ch. 2). If speech expresses thought, then first one must know what to say, then how to express it in speech, hence the order of these parts of Stoic dialectic in the bibliography of Chrysippus (ca. 281–208 BCE) in DL VII, 190–192: the first concerned with the incorporeal, intelligible content, the *prágmata* or *lektá*, and the second with the corporeal voice or expression of that content (when Diogenes Laertius's longer account of Stoic dialectic [VII, 55ff.] begins with the assertion that the theory of dialectic is agreed by most to begin with the area concerning voice, this order is perhaps a result of the priority of active to passive: "Dialectic is, as Posidonius says, a science of what is true, false, and neither; it is, as Chrysippus says, about signifiers and what is signified (*sēmaínonta kaì sēmainómena*)" [DL VII, 62]). The structure of the content of sentences, whether individually or related to each other logically, was supposed by the Stoics to mirror the structure of the world. In our spoken or written language, these structures are expressed by the parts of the sentence and by sentences related to one another by certain conjunctions which express the logical relations of the content of sentences.

Thus, the Stoic study of language would be centred on the understanding, in the realms of the intelligible content and of the corporeal expression, of the parts or elements of the sentence and then on their combination. Thus, among the books of Chrysippus listed in the second part of the logical area (according to a different division than the one given in Diogenes Laertius' exposition in VII, 44 and VII, 55ff., which may have come from Chrysippus' student Diogenes of Babylon), that on "words and the *lógos* relating to them" (compare Antipater's work *On léxis and what is said*, cited at DL VII, 57), the second group contains the following works (DL VII, 192–3): *On the elements of lógos and of what is said* (5 books); *On the syntax of what is said* (4 books); *On the syntax and elements of what is said, against Philippos* (3 books); *On the elements of lógos against Nicias* (1 book); *On what is said in relation to other things* (1 book).

One would need to know how each of the elements was to be used to contribute to the formation of a complete sentence (or also, in the case of conjunctions, of a structure of sentences) and of its content, and therefore how each part of the sentence and each of its types was to be defined. Spoken language only begins to be significant, for the Stoics, at the level of parts of speech; *léxis* is articulate, but not yet meaningful, and its 'elements' are letters, not words. Yet the capacity of any word to perform its function as a part of the sentence depends on its form and on its capacity to be understood as the word it is, often in a particular form. In order to be correct about these matters, the Stoic needed to study the way in which the voice is divided into different sounds, what are called 'elements' or 'letters', how these sounds are combined into syllables and words, and how these words can be formed with variable elements to allow particular relations to other words in the sentence, expressing particular structures of the intelligible content of the sentence. The sage would also need to know everything about the relation between content and its linguistic expression, including the problems which arise in that relation – solecism, in which the structure of the expression fails to be consistent with itself and with that of the content; barbarism, where the correct or accepted form of a word is not used; and ambiguity, in which the expression fails to correspond to one and only one content – and also about alternative modes of expression, such as poetry.

Stoic dialectic, then, presents many elements which will be essential to later 'grammatical expertise'. These elements, however, belong to one large part of Stoic philosophy and are made to serve purposes peculiar to it. The information we have on the organization of these parts of Stoic philosophy comes largely from the structure of Chrysippus' bibliography (recorded by the doxographer Diogenes Laertius) and from Diogenes' lengthy report on the area of dialectic concerned with the voice, which is based on Chrysippus' student Diogenes of Babylon's (late 3rd to early 2nd century BCE) *Tékhnē (Technical Handbook) on Voice*, along with Diogenes Laertius' account of the area of dialectic concerned with meanings. The organization of these materials is of indeterminate origin. It is unclear which Stoic arranged Chrysippus' bibliography, and the organization of Diogenes of Babylon's 'expertise concerning voice' may have been the compiler's own invention, abstracted from what he learned from Chrysippus, for whom a work of this title is not attested, or have been based on Chrysippus' own *Dialectical Tékhnē, against Aristagoras* (1 book) (DL VII, 190).

In any event, the organization of each of the two areas in Diogenes Laertius' report follows the basic principle of building up from the less to the more complex, and from the general to the specific. The area concerning voice (DL VII, 55–62) moves from voice, to the voice which animals emit from impulse, to articulate voice, *léxis*, to significant articulate voice, *lógos*, which only rational creatures possess, and to *diálektos*, 'language' (for an analysis and history of these elements see Ax 1986; Schenkeveld 1990). *Léxis* has 'elements' (*stoikheĩa*), the 24 'letters' (*grámmata*) which are divided into vowels, unvoiced, semivoiced, etc. The difference between *lógos*, which is always meaningful, and *léxis*, which is not, is paralleled by a distinction between "saying" (*légein*) things or *lektá* and "uttering" (*prophéresthai*) sounds. There follows the list and definitions of the 'parts of *lógos*'. Next come the 'virtues of *lógos*' and the definitions of *poíēma* and *poíēsis*, the metrical parallels to *léxis* and *lógos* in that *poíē-*

*ma* is metrical or rhythmical *léxis* with arrangement, going beyond the prosaic (*logoeidḗs*), while *poíēsis* is a meaningful *poíēma* containing representation of divine and human matters. The definition of 'definition' is included presumably because this is a special, and especially important, kind of *lógos*, one necessary for conceptual analysis, and this will account too for the presence of the definitions of related concepts, i. e. genus, concept, species, division, distribution. Finally, there is the kind of *léxis* which, while it is meaningful, signifies more than one thing, ambiguity.

The area concerning "things and what is meant" proceeds (DL VII, 63–83) in an analogous way, beginning with the definition of the *lektón* and its division into incomplete and complete *lektá*; the account proceeds again from the simple to the complex, but here the importance of logic, in the sense of the systematic study of inference, makes itself felt more clearly. Incomplete *lektá* are "predicates" (*katēgorḗmata*), of which there are various types; complete ones are: *axiṓmata* or propositions, which are bearers of truth-values; non-propositional *lektá* such as questions, inquiries, commands, and oaths (cf. Schenkeveld 1984); and combinations of simple propositions into complex propositions and arguments, especially syllogisms. The account of the proposition has explained this division of *axiṓmata* into 'simple' and 'non-simple', and then listed the types of both of these by way of internal structure and of the logical connective used respectively, the types of non-simple proposition being followed by an analysis of their truth conditions. Significantly, the culmination of this section is the classification of types of *lógos* in the sense of "argument".

Besides the analysis in the area concerning voice of the notions of *poíēma* and *poíēsis* as rhythmical *léxis* and *lógos* respectively, the Stoics were intensely interested in poetry as a part of their ethical theory. Besides a work of unknown content about *léxis*, Zeno wrote (DL VII, 4), a treatise on listening to poetry. The fifth section of the part of Chrysippus' bibliography concerning "ethical discourse and the articulation of ethical concepts" contains a treatise on proverbs, one on poems, one called *How to listen to poetry*, and one *Against the critics*. From Plutarch's own *How the young should listen to poetry*, a principal source for which was Chrysippus, we can get a good idea of the content of Zeno's and Chrysippus' treatises: how should one show a young person the way to understand the good moral precepts contained in poetry, while avoiding the trap of thinking that good poets are actually commending the bad precepts sometimes found in their poems. Zeno also wrote five books of 'Homeric Problems' (DL VII, 4); the contents may have resembled those of Aristotle's 'Homeric Puzzles', detailed studies of passages in Homer whose interpretation has caused problems for critics, especially for those trying to show that Homer contains good moral precepts.

## 4. 'Grammar' in the students of Diogenes

We know of no place in the works of the early Stoa in which work on language was fused with the interpretation of poetry. Of the students of Diogenes of Babylon, however, Crates of Mallos (mid-2nd century BCE) founded a school of literary interpretation and Apollodorus of Athens (mid-2nd century BCE) brought his knowledge of Stoic dialectic to Aristarchus' (ca. 216–144 BCE) school of philology in Alexandria. Crates and Aristarchus, the two leaders (*koruphaĩoi*) of the science of the grammarians (Strabo, *Geography* I, 2.24), along with the latter's predecessor Aristophanes of Byzantium, were said to have 'perfected' grammar (Sextus Empiricus, *M* I, 44; → Art. 56). The commentaries on Dionysius Thrax (*Scholia D. T.*) report a very different interpretation of the history of grammar, in which the discipline was invented by the 6th century BCE allegorist Theagenes of Rhegium and then 'perfected' by the Peripatetics Praxiphanes and Aristotle (*Scholia D. T.* [Vat.] 164.24). Despite his many contributions to the study of language, we know that Aristotle did not do 'grammar' in the sense which interests us, nor is it likely that the other persons named by this interpretation did.

Crates is known to have assigned the 'grammarian' a very limited role:

> Crates said that the 'critic' was better than the grammarian and that while the critic was experienced in all of logical science, the grammarian was simply an interpreter of rare words (*glõssai*), establisher of accents and knower of things like these; hence the critic was like an architect and the grammarian like his servant (Sextus Empiricus, *M* I, 79).

In thus subordinating the 'grammarian' to the 'critic' (a term revived by him which had first been used by the 'scholar-poet' Philetas of Cos, cf. Pfeiffer 1968: 89, 157–159, 238), Crates was taking aim at the Alexandrians, who called themselves 'grammarians': a Cratetean 'grammarian' could never accede to the highest task involved in the study of literature, the 'criticism' of poems, which for Crates was a judgement based on its sound (for the Alexandrians cf. Sextus Empiricus, *M* I, 93 and *Scholia D. T.* 170.2–5; 303.28–304.5; 471.30–472.18; for Crates cf. Philodemus, *On Poems* V). This task may have been quite different from what the Alexandrians thought the grammarian should do: judge the condition of a work's textual transmission and its authenticity. Further, Crates' claim that the critic was experienced in all of 'logical science', which may include either all of the Stoic 'logical part' of philosophy or even all of philosophy, implies a much vaster sphere of knowledge than that of the grammarian. But, since his discipline of "criticism" (*kritikḗ*) seemed essentially co-extensive with the Alexandrians' 'grammar', it was usually taken as its equivalent. Indeed, Crates was said to have introduced 'the study of grammar' into Rome, when, having been sent to Rome as an ambassador of King Attalus of Pergamum in 168 or early 167 BCE (cf. Kaster 1995: 59–60) and having fallen into a drain on the Palatine, thus breaking his leg, he used the forced extension of his stay as the occasion for a number of lectures which inspired various locals to imitate him by editing and commenting on poems hitherto little known (Suetonius, *De Gramm. et Rhet.* 2).

While Crates wrote about numerous topics in grammar and literary criticism, we have no indication that he ever wrote a general work on *kritikḗ*. However, one of his students did write such a work, and we know something of its general organization. We owe this knowledge to the treatise attacking the grammarians written by the skeptical philosopher Sextus Empiricus (2nd or 3rd century CE). In this treatise, which follows the structure of a *tékhnē grammatikḗ*, Sextus gives summaries of the grammatical doctrines which make up the entire expertise. I have argued that his principal source for these doctrines was an Epicurean treatise which took the *Perì grammatikẽs* of Asclepiades of Myrlea and polemized against its utility and that of each of its tenets (Blank 1998: xliv–l). Asclepiades was active in the last quarter of the second and the first quarter of the 2nd century BCE. He may have studied in Alexandria with Dionysius Thrax, but there is no hard evidence for this, and he may have taught in Rome in the 1st century. He certainly taught in Turdetania in Southern Spain. He wrote on Homer and perhaps other poets, as well, on Nestor's cup in the *Iliad*, on astronomy, the myths and legends of Bithynia and Turdetania, about grammarians and about grammar (for details see Blank 1998: xlv–xlvi).

Sextus repeats many of the Epicurean arguments against grammatical expertise, adding to them arguments of a Pyrrhonian skeptical character. When he comes to show that 'the historical part of grammar' is impossible or incoherent, Sextus says (*M* I, 248–249):

That this is considered in general to be a part of grammar is clear. Certainly Tauriscus the pupil of Crates, who like the other 'critics' subordinated grammar to criticism, says that the parts of criticism are the rational, the empirical and the historical. The rational part is concerned with diction and the grammatical figures, the empirical is the part about the dialects and the different forms or types of style, while the historical part is about the preexisting unordered raw material.

Sextus treats this division of *kritikḗ* as the equivalent of a division of grammar. The tasks which Crates was earlier (I, 79) said to have assigned to the 'grammarian', i. e. being an interpreter of rare words (*glõssai*), establisher of accents and knower of things like these, would be covered by these three parts. The critic must use these parts of *kritikḗ* as preliminaries to the activity of 'judgement' itself, which will subject their results to further analysis using 'all of logical science'. He is the 'master craftsman', an image which goes back to Aristotle, who said that the 'master craftsman' knows the reasons for his creations, while the subordinate craftsmen do not (*Metaphysics* 981a30ff.), and who also made political science into the 'architectonic' or master science relating to human activity (*Nicomachean Ethics* I, 1; note that at *Scholia D. T.* [Melampus] 12.12ff. the critic is compared to the politician, and cf. Dihle [1986]). As a master craftsman, Crates' critic is constantly served in his exercise of judgement by the subordinate disciplines, rather than needing a separate part of his science in which he goes about judging literary works. This is one way, as we shall see, in which Crates differs from another of our authorities, Dionysius Thrax.

Sextus' account brings in the important topic of the 'parts' of an expertise. We know of comparable distinctions among 'parts', 'duties', etc. in other fields, e. g., in philosophy and medicine. Indeed, the prologues of technical works tended to mention a standard group of topics, and after the treatment of definition and subject matter of the expertise, and the fact that its study is useful, the topics of the expertise's "parts" (*mérē*), "functions" (*érga*), and "tools" (*órgana*) were usually considered. The distinctions among these last three categories, however, were never very clear, and at least part of the urge to distinguish them at all came from the dispute over the parts of philosophy, which involved divisions according to subject matter (e. g., logic, physics, ethics; cf., e. g., Sextus Empiricus, *M* VII, 16) and functions (e. g., productive, practical, theoretical; cf., e. g., Aristotle, *Metaphysics* 5.1, 1025b1–1026a32; Cicero is said to have wanted to be called a philosopher, rather than an orator, since he had chosen philosophy as his *érgon* [here meaning "job"], but used rhetoric as a tool, Plutarch, *Cicero* 32), as well as problems over whether, for example, logic was a 'part' or a 'tool' of philosophy (cf. Alexander of Aphrodisias *in An* 1.3–4.29 Wallies: this passage clearly shows that not all parties to the debate agreed on the meanings and distinctions of the terms involved). In the debate on the parts of philosophy, 'part' usually referred to a single area of knowledge. In references to the parts of technical disciplines, 'part' may refer to an area of knowledge, to a task – sometimes called a 'duty' – which the expert must be able to perform, or to the result of the application of some activity. What precisely was meant, however, was rarely made plain. When 'parts', 'functions', and 'tools' were distinguished, the situation was sometimes, but not always, more clear. And in some cases, careful writers made helpful distinctions. Thus, the empiricist physician Theodas distinguished "constituent" (*sustatiká*) parts of medicine – the methodological tools of the expertise, i. e., autopsy, history, analogy – from "final" (*teliká*) parts – the resultant areas of the expertise, i. e., diagnostic, therapeutic, hygienic. The therapeutic branch was then divided into pharmacy, surgery and regimen (Galen, *subf. emp.* 52.13; cf. Deichgräber 1930: 288f.), and it appears to be this subdivision to which Sextus (95) compares the three parts of grammar which structure his treatise, saying that each part is necessary for the others. Galen mentions the three parts as surgery, pharmacy, regimen (*comp. med. per gen.* XIII, 604.7–10) and he too says that each of them needs the others.

The salient feature of Tauriscus' catalogue of the 'parts' subservient to *kritikḗ* is their division according to epistemological factors: each 'part' must have included or comprised rules belonging to one of these three modes of understanding or inquiry, 'rational, empirical, historical', which the critic must apply in order to 'judge' literary works. Each of the three labels, 'rational', 'empirical', 'historical', is familiar from the debates surrounding medical empiricism. In empiricist medicine *logikós* is of course the name given to the opposition 'rationalists', while "practice" (*tribḗ*) is the "practical exercise of experience" (Galen, *subf. emp.* 48.25). 'Practiced (*tribikḗ*) experience' is that which results from the use of 'transition to the similar' or analogy; it is so called because it takes much practice and cannot be used by just anybody (Galen, *On sects for beginners* I, 69.1; cf. *subf. emp.* 45.20; 49.17). Finally, "history" (*historía*) was the second pillar of empirical medicine, comprising the detailed record of the personal experience (*autopsía*) of other physicians (cf. Galen, *subf. emp.* 67.4 with Deichgräber 1030: 298–301 and Slater 1972: 327–328). As Sextus' account indicates, grammatical *historía* works on the 'unordered', 'unmethodical' material of myths, historical facts, persons, places, etc., from which the poet can choose for his or her poems. This material can be organized into various kinds of files, e. g. geographically or genealogically, but it can not be described by rules.

How does the parallel with empiricist medicine help us with the Cratetean taxonomy? It is difficult to say exactly why Tauriscus attributed the study of diction and grammatical figures to reason (*logikón*) while assigning the dialects and styles to skill or experience (*tribikón*). Possibly, Tauriscus wanted to distinguish the choice of a framework of diction, which is defined by a model – either the usage of speakers of a particular dialect, or writers who used a particular style – and to which one adheres by imitation, from the language as described by rational rules such as we see in treatises on Hellenism, or 'pure Greek'. Thus, the study of the items in the first part of *kritikḗ* will involve the elaboration of rational rules of combination, inflection, derivation, and syntax; the styles and dialects will be studied by reading and by observation of local patterns of expression; the study of personages, topographical allusions, plots, etc., will proceed by the systematic study and collection of items from among the 'unordered' mass of things mentioned in literature, historical accounts, etc.

## 5. Dionysius Thrax and Asclepiades of Myrlea

The next system of grammar we are in any position to discuss is that of Dionysius the Thracian. A famous Alexandrian grammarian of the late 2nd century BCE, Dionysius was a pupil of the great Aristarchus, and his is the first name associated with the writing of a treatise called *Tékhnē grammatikḗ*. Sextus (57) seems to call this work *Precepts* (*parangélmata*). At one point (Proll. Voss. in *Scholia D. T.* 4.13) a commentator seems to be under the impression that the extant treatise, on which he is commentating, is entitled *On the eight parts of the sentence* (*perì oktṑ merō̃n lógou*). The work entitled *Tékhnē grammatikḗ* which has been transmitted to us under Dionysius' name is, in my opinion, not identical with the work Dionysius wrote (→ Art. 57). Some of its opening sentences are quoted by Sextus in virtually the same form as in the surviving treatise, but this does not guarantee the authenticity of the rest. In fact, even the early chapters from which these sentences were drawn by Sextus' source may well have been much longer and more discursive than those now in the treatise. Given the immediate, massive, argumentative response touched off by Dionysius' *Tékhnē* and reported to us by Sextus and by the later commentators, it is difficult to believe that Dionysius' work did not explain itself any more than does the treatise we now possess. The loss of Dionysius' original treatise makes the reconstruction of early grammars difficult, as we have no complete specimen earlier than the Roman school grammars. But Dionysius did write a *Tékhnē grammatikḗ* which was very widely read and criticized, and it presumably corresponded to the statement given by him of the definition and the parts of grammar:

Grammar is an experience (*empeiría*) for the most part of what is said in poets and writers. [...] The parts of grammar are practiced reading aloud with attention to prosody, interpretation according to the poetic figures present ⟨in the text⟩, explication of words and histories [i. e. problematic allusions to persons and places, etc.], discovery of etymology, calculation of analogy, judgement of poems (Sextus Empiricus, *M* I, 57 + 250; cf. Dionysius Thrax, *Tékhnē* 5.2–6.3).

The six parts into which Dionysius divided grammar are listed almost identically in Sextus and in the beginning of the extant treatise. The only significant omission is in the third part, which the treatise lists as the "ready (*prókheiros*) explication of glosses (*glō̃ssai*) and histories". *Prókheiros* may have been omitted by Sextus because it had just been used in the description of Tauriscus' 'historical' part. This coincidence calls our attention to another, i. e. that reading aloud is characterized as "practiced" or "empirical" (*entribḗs*), recalling the second of Tauriscus' parts. On the other hand, where Tauriscus' 'parts' could be understood as divisions of the rules needed by the practitioner according to their epistemological status, Dionysius' 'parts' are the tasks which must be undertaken by the interpreter of a work of literature.

The extant treatise goes on (6.4 ff.) immediately to define reading aloud; a good reading must respect delivery, from which we grasp the excellence of the poem; prosody, from which we grasp its expertise or artistry; and segmentation by pauses, from which we grasp its sense; and the differences between the appropriate qualities of readings of different genres of poetry – tragedy, comedy, elegy, epic, lyric, and oiktos – are cited. Failure in the observation (*paratḗrēsis*) of these differences spoils the poets' excellences and makes the reader ridiculous. Three brief sections on related items follow: tonal accent (*tónos*), pause (*stigmḗ*), and rhapsody (*rhapsōidía*, defined as the part of a poem containing a plot-summary), which would hardly have amounted to a treatment of reading aloud commensurate with the manner in which the topic was introduced. After that, the extant treatise begins the standard – or what has become or was to become the standard – description of the structure of speech, going from elements and syllables to the word (*léxis*), and thence to the parts of the sentence.

It appears from its definition, from the listing of its parts, and from what remains of the section on reading aloud that Dionysius' *Tékhnē grammatikḗ* was primarily a work on how to deal with poetry and prose, rather than one on the elements of language. Yet it seems likely that he covered these elements – at least the nature of the vowels, consonants, etc., the ways in which syllables are formed, the word-classes – since Sextus, dependent on Asclepiades, treats him as having done so. We can learn something of the content of Dionysius' divisions of grammar from Sextus' criticisms of them. Sextus does not criticize or report criticisms of Tauriscus' division of the parts of *kritikḗ*, and his only reason for mentioning it is its recognition of an 'historical part of grammar'. It is clear, however, from the way in which he has centred the discussion of the definition of grammar around the criticism of Dionysius' definition (I, 57–90: the critics cited are: Ptolemy the Peripatetic, Asclepiades, Chaeris, Demetrius Chlorus; for an analysis of the various positions see Blank 1998 *ad locum*) that Sextus – following Asclepiades – considered it necessary to deal with his disagreements with Dionysius. After reporting Dionysius' division of grammatical expertise, Sextus gives two critiques of it (250–251): first, that Dionysius 'may have' mistakenly made some of grammar's "results" (*apotelésmata*) and "subparts" (*mória*) into "parts" (*mérē*); second, that he "agreedly" (*homologouménōs*) – i. e., obviously – derived his six parts from the three parts assumed by Sextus.

The first critique is related to one which appears in much fuller form in the later, Byzantine commentaries on the treatise that goes under the name of Dionysius. Their general line is that Dionysius' six parts are chosen for didactic reasons, having been derived from what they refer to as an 'old' systematization of four parts – textual criticism (*diorthōtikón*, lit. "corrective"), reading aloud, exegetical, critical – all of which, in the original Greek, have the *-ikón* suffix. We do not know just how old this quadripartite system was. It was analysed by Usener (1892: 304f.) and attributed by him to Tyrannio, a 1st century BCE grammarian working in Rome (cf. Marrou 1950: 250f.; *contra* Haas 1970: 171f.). I do not believe that Usener (1913: 270, 272, 303ff.) was justified in assuming that the four-part system must have been an attempt to go one better than the three-part system of Asclepiades. Varro had the same division in a different form, and he (in his *Disciplinarum libri* of ca. 33 BCE) provides a clear *terminus ante quem* (Usener 1913: 279). On the basis of the four-part structure of Varro's *Antiquitates*, Usener made the beginning of that work (ca. 55 BCE) the *terminus ante quem* for the grammatical system (1913: 287).

The four parts in this system defined the things a grammarian must do, and they were often taken to be the parts of a classroom hour, so that the teacher would first make corrections to the text from which the student would read the assigned passage aloud, then offer an explication of each word in the text and of the passage as a whole, and finally, using the results of the previous operations produce the judgement or critique of the passage (see e. g. Melampus in *Scholia D. T.* 12.3ff.). But there is some dispute in the commentaries over the nature of these 'parts', nor are they the only divisions envisioned in the commentaries. Besides the four 'parts', there were also four "tools" (*órgana*), representing the kinds of knowledge the grammarian needed to be able to apply (for this term see *Scholia D. T.* [Prol. Voss.] 10.8ff.; Stephanus in *Scholia D. T.* [Vat.] 170.19f.; [Vat.] 123.13ff.; see Aristotle, *Politics* 1.4, 1253b25 for 'tool' vs. 'function'): glossematical (*glōssēmatikón*), historical (*historikón*), metrical (*metrikón*), technical (*tekhnikón*); and there were also sub-parts (*mória*; the term is used by, e. g., *Scholia D. T.* 10.12, Stephanus in *Scholia D. T.* [Marc.] 302.7, as well as Sextus, probably following Asclepiades). Varro, in the 1st century BCE, is said to have distinguished the same four items as we have seen in the commentators' 'parts', ascribing them to the grammarian as four 'duties' (*lectio, enarratio, emendatio, iudicium*; fr. 236 = Diomedes, *GL* I, 426.21ff.; on this text see Usener 1913: 278ff.). In Roman grammarians we usually encounter a dichotomy of grammar into 'methodical' and 'historical' parts (Quintilian I, 9.1), which are said to correspond to Quintilian's 'correct speech' and 'explanation of poets' (I, 4.2). On this dichotomy, which probably goes back to Varro and was transmitted to Quintilian by Q. Remmius Palaemon, see Glück (1967: 21). Quintilian also seems to have known the fourfold division, however, as he says that corrected reading precedes exegesis and judgement is mixed with all of these (I, 4.3; cf. Usener 1913: 277). Seneca (*Ep.* 88.3) cites a threefold division like that of Asclepiades: care for language first, then histories, and finally poetry.

The scholiasts' report of the critique of Dionysius is highly complex, and reflects a long history of critique and riposte; unfortunately, only the first stages of this debate were based on Dionysius' original treatise, while much is predicated on the extant treatise and its uneasy relation to the preserved original partition. Thus Heliodorus (*Scholia D. T.* [Lond.] 452.34ff.) says that Dionysius is not strictly accurate about the parts of grammar, and asks whether indeed they are 'tools', in the usage of the younger commentators. Perhaps, he says, they are rather the goals which the grammarian must pursue. Tools, according to the commentator Stephanus, differed from parts and sub-parts in that, while a part is related only to that of which it is a part, a tool can be used by more than one expertise, as, for example, a knife can be used by more than one kind of artisan: so, the study of glosses can be used not only by the grammarian, but by the rhetorician or physician as well. He claimed that of Dionysius' six 'parts' only the first two (reading aloud and explication according to poetic tropes) were actually parts, while the rest were tools (*Scholia D. T.* [Vat.] 168.25ff.; cf. 164.9ff., Proll. Voss. in *Scholia D. T.* 10.10ff.). According to some commentators, Dionysius' 'discovery of etymology' was not a part on its own, but rather a subpart of the quadripartite system's exegetical part (*Scholia D. T.* [Marc.] 303.10ff.; [Lond.] 471.8f.). According to Heliodorus (*Scholia D. T.* [Lond.] 453.15ff.; cf. Melampus at *Scholia D. T.* 13.7ff.), textual criticism, the first of the four parts, was divided into its sub-parts – glosses and histories, etymology, analogy – and these were substituted for it in the list. Note that these three 'sub-parts' correspond to three of the 'tools', as well: glosses and histories to the glossematic and historical tools, etymology and analogy to the technical tool. This move derives Dionysius' six parts from the quadripartite system attributed (by Usener) to Tyrannio, but in order to reach the tripartite system adopted by Sextus, one must add to it the second move in Sextus' first critique: that Dionysius has included a 'result' of grammar as one of its parts, which can refer only to reading aloud, the result of understanding the prosodies and word-division of a text. That leaves three parts: textual criticism, exegetical, and critical, which could be made to correspond to Sextus' expert, historical, and special (the part about poets and prose-writers) respectively.

Sextus' second critique gives a direct derivation of Dionysius' six parts from Sextus' three, which are thus treated as the real parts underlying the false division of Dionysius. The part about poets and prose-writers supplied Dionysius with his practiced reading aloud, exegesis (of poetical tropes, i. e., of poetical expressions taken quite generally; cf. Schenkeveld 1991: 153–156) and judgement of poems, while etymology and analogy came from the expert part, and contrasting with them is the historical part, which consists in the explanation of historia and (unusual) words. The author of the second critique is obviously Asclepiades, since it assumes his system. If the common assumption that Asclepiades was an ultimate source of the commentaries on the treatise attributed to Dionysius (cf. Kaibel 1898: 25f.) is correct, then Asclepiades is probably the source of the first critique as well. This seems quite likely, and Sextus will have taken over the whole section 248–253 from his source, an Epicurean demolition of Asclepiades.

When Sextus came to say what 'the parts of grammar' were, he refused to go into the many controversies in this area (91–93):

> It will suffice to say without adornment that one part of grammar is expert, another historical, and another special, by which things concerning poets and writers are treated. Of these the expert part is that in which they make arrangements concerning the elements, the parts of a sentence, orthography and Hellenism, and what follows from these. The historical part is where they teach about persons, for example divine, human, and heroic, or explain about places such as mountains or rivers, or transmit traditions about fictions and myths or anything else of this kind. The special part is the one through which they examine what concerns poets and writers, where the grammarians explain what is unclearly said, judge the sound and the unsound, and sort the genuine from the spurious.

When he comes to deal with the third part (270), he calls it "the part of grammar dealing with poets and prose-writers". From Sextus' description of Asclepiades' system, it is plain that the system he has adopted is that of Asclepiades (252):

> Asclepiades in his *On Grammar* said the first parts of grammar were three: the expert, the historical, and the grammatical, which touches on both, that is on the expert and historical, and then he divided the historical part in three.

Evidently, Sextus' "proper" or "special" (*idiaíteron*) part is another way of referring to Asclepiades' 'grammatical' part, the one specifically dedicated to the interpretation of what is in poets and prose-writers. The other two parts of Asclepiades' system are evidently related to those postulated by Tauriscus. Both systems name their parts according to the kind of knowledge they require: both have an 'historical' part, while to Tauriscus' 'rational' part will correspond Asclepiades' "technical" or "expert" (*tekhnikón*) part; it is not clear where Asclepiades placed the study of dialects and styles, which constituted Tauriscus' 'empirical' part, but probably these were in Asclepiades' 'grammatical' part, since they were not in the technical or historical parts and they concerned individual poetic genres.

Asclepiades does not complain that Dionysius ignored much of what grammar should treat (the complaint was made by others, however: cf. Proll. Voss. in *Scholia D. T.* 4.20ff.) and he states specifically that both Dionysius and Asclepiades included the study of glosses under 'history', so we should assume that most, if not all, of what was included in Asclepiades' 'expert' part was also in Dionysius' 'discovery of etymology' and 'calculation of analogy', and that what was in Asclepiades' 'grammatical' part was in Dionysius' 'reading aloud', 'interpretation according to the poetic figures present', and 'judgement of poems'. What, then, do we know of the contents of Asclepiades' *On Grammar*?

I have argued (Blank 1998: xlix, 116ff., 124, 126ff.) that large parts of Sextus' opening sections were taken from Asclepiades: 45–49 on the name 'grammar' and the distinction between 'higher' and 'lower' grammar, the latter sometimes being called 'grammatistic', and the derivation of the name of the lower grammar from "letter" (*grámma*), that of the higher grammar from "written work" (*grámma*); 57–90 on the definition of 'grammar'; 91–94 on the parts of grammar. And when Sextus comes to the detailed confutation of the grammarians' doctrines, his exposition follows that of Asclepiades. Sextus divides the 'expert' part of grammar into the following topics: elements (99–119); Syllables (120–130); expression (*léxis*) and the parts of the sentence (*tà toũ lógou mérē* [131–158]; distribution (*merismós* [158–168]; presumably this regarded the distribution of words in a sentence to the different word-classes, although this is not what Sextus argues against); orthography (169–174); and Hellenism (175–247). Under his first or 'methodical' part, Quintilian, who was also clearly influenced by Asclepiades' grammar, treats: elements (I, 4.6–17); the parts of speech (*partes orationis*) and their accidents (I, 4.18–29); the three virtues of speech (I, 5.1–4); the vices of speech (I, 5.5–72); *latinitas* or propriety in speech (I, 6.1–45); orthography or propriety in writing (I, 7.1–35); and reading aloud (I, 8.1–17). Most telling for Quintilian's dependence on Asclepiades is his adoption of Asclepiades' tripartite division of plots (II, 4.2 with Sextus I, 252, 263ff.; cf. Müller 1903: 29; Heinicke 1904). Another author influenced by Asclepiades, Dionysius of Halicarnassus, has: voice (14); letters or elements (14); syllables (15); words (15); and *lógos* (16).

Can we sketch, at least, what Dionysius Thrax' original *Tékhnē* contained? The material in Asclepiades' 'expert part' may have overlapped with Dionysius' 'discovery of etymology' and 'calculation of analogy' by way of Hellenism. Quintilian (I, 6.1) gives a fourfold list of the 'criteria of analogy': reason, antiquity, authority, usage. Reason, he adds, consists mostly in analogy, but sometimes in etymology; he then goes on to discuss how to apply these criteria to determine the word-forms one ought to use (I, 6.4–27 on analogy, 28–38 on etymology; cf. Siebenborn 1976). Sextus treats analogy (176ff.) and etymology (241ff.) as the 'technical' bases for a *tékhnē*, a principled, rule-governed, rule-prescribing expertise of Hellenism, as opposed to the non-technical criterion of the observation of usage (see Blank 1998: 205f.; Sextus is forced by his recommendation of usage as a criterion to treat antiquity and authority under the heading of analogy). It is possible, then, that Dionysius considered etymology and analogy as the bases of Hellenism or correct Greek. He may have put etymology before analogy out of a conviction that the demonstration of a word(-form)'s correctness on the basis of its etymology was more direct and more reliable than one on the basis of analogy, about the criteria and certainty of which there was a considerable amount of debate. Treating etymology and analogy as fundamental for Hellenism would certainly have allowed Dionysius to treat the parts of speech, with their various types, inflections, etc., under the rubric of 'calculation of analogy'. Orthography, which Sextus treats before Hellenism, could easily have been considered a part of it, and their criteria were the same. We cannot know for certain whether Dionysius treated the structure of speech at the levels below that of significant *lógos*, i. e. the elements, syllables, and *léxis*. He might have been able to do so under the heading of analogy, since the entire linguistic system was considered to be ordered by *lógos*, which is the foundation of analogy. Alternatively, he could have treated at least the elements and syllables in his section on 'reading aloud', since the kinds of sounds made in pronouncing the letters and the lengths of syllables would have been necessary for anyone who was to perform poetry. Dionysius' 'reading aloud', however was connected by Asclepiades with his own 'grammatical part', so that we would have to assume that the placement of this material was not considered important enough to block the connection of etymology and analogy with Asclepiades' 'expert part'.

There seems to be little difficulty about the general content of Dionysius' third part, that devoted to 'the ready explication of glosses and histories'. Asclepiades, who seems to have made it a specialty, gave a complex subdivision of histories (Sextus, *M* I, 252ff.):

He says that under history one type is true, one is false, and one is as if true, where the actual history is true, that about myths is false, and that about fictions and such genres as comedy and mime is as if true [reading *pseudē̃ dè tḕn perì {plásmata kaì} múthous, hōs alethē̃ dè ⟨tḕn perì plásmata⟩ hoĩa*, with Kaibel]. And of true history there are again three parts: one is about the persons of gods, heroes and famous men, another about places and times, and the third about actions. Of false history, that is mythical history, he says there is only one kind, genealogy. And he says, as Dionysius does too, that the part concerning 'glosses' is generally placed under the historical part, since it finds by research [*historeĩ*] that *krē̃guon* [*Ilias* I, 106] means "true" or "good"; and similarly with the part concerning proverbs and definitions.

We have no evidence about Dionysius' own divisions of histories, but there is little reason to doubt that he dealt on the whole with persons divine and human, places, and deeds which appeared in various kinds of poetry. It is worth noting that Asclepiades' reason for including histories and glosses under the 'historical part', that they both proceed by means of research in books or *historía*, may have applied to Dionysius as well. Finally, there is a good possibility that proverbs and definitions were also included in Dionysius' section on history.

In his demolition of the third part of Asclepiades' grammar, Sextus cites only the claims made by grammarians for the usefulness of their expertise in the interpretation of poetry, the source of many fine maxims and precepts, "starting points toward wisdom and a happy life" (270). This claim, which conflicts with the primacy of philosophy and was therefore a prime target for the Epicurean critique cited by Sextus, need not have exhausted Asclepiades' grammatical part, however. The fact that Asclepiades' 'grammatical' part corresponded to Dionysius' 'reading aloud', 'interpretation according to the poetic figures present', and 'judgement of poems', allows the supposition that Asclepiades also talked about these matters. That would mean that he dealt with the different kinds of poetry and the kind of performance appropriate to each, something we see in the extant treatise attributed to Dionysius. Another likely section of this part of Asclepiades' grammar is the theory of poetic (and possibly also rhetorical) styles, characters, or *plásmata*, something we know of from Tauriscus. Then there would have been the discussion of poetic forms of expression or *trópoi*. Finally, there might have been a section on judgement, which might have centred on making aesthetically and technically grounded decisions about the worthiness and therefore about the authenticity of poems or their parts. The correspondence with Asclepiades also makes it possible that Dionysius' section on judgement included, at least as an introductory explanation of why grammar was useful and why judgement was the 'finest' part of the expertise, a discussion of the moral and philosophical value of poetry and the sentiments it housed.

The following tables will summarize and perhaps make more clear the results of the preceding discussion of Asclepiades, Tauriscus, and Dionysius: (See Tab. 58.1.–58.4.)

## 6. Apollonius Dyscolus

Thus far we have been working on schemata and reflections of works which do not survive. With Apollonius Dyscolus (early 2nd century CE) we have our first opportunity to examine an intact (or in some cases, nearly intact) work by one of the great Greek grammarians, and we see how rich and full of controversy the field really was.

Apollonius' treatises are the masterpieces of 'analogical' grammar (on Apollonius see Thierfelder 1935; Blank 1982, 1993; van Ophuijsen 1993; Sluiter 1990; Ildefonse 1997). They are built around the thesis that language is an ordered, rule-following system and that all apparent violations of these rules can and should be explained as the result of regular and codifiable corruptions. By the tool of 'pathology' the grammarian traced the *páthē* or corruptions by which 'original', 'complete', or 'healthy' word – forms or syn-

Tab. 58.1.: Asclepiades' Grammatical Expertise
The constituents of *grammatike*
(source: Sextus Empiricus, *M* I, 91–96, 252–253 and passim)

| *tekhnikón* "expert" | *historikón* "historical" | *grammatikón* "grammatical" |
|---|---|---|
| letters, syllables, *léxis*, parts of the sentence, distribution, (syntax of the parts of the sentence) | glosses | benefits of knowledge of poetry (and prose) |
| orthography | histories: true, false, as if true | (dialects and styles) |
| Hellenism: analogy, etymology, virtues of speech, vices of speech | proverbs and definitions | (reading aloud of different literary genres) |
| | | (poetic figures) |
| | | (judgement: appropriateness, beauty, authenticity) |

Tab. 58.2.: Tauriscus' Critical Expertise
The tools of *kritikḗ*
(source: Sextus Empiricus, *M* I, 79, 248–249)

| *logikón* "rational" | *tribikón* "empirical" | *historikón* "historical" |
|---|---|---|
| (letters, syllables,) *léxis*, parts of the sentence, (distribution, syntax of the parts of the sentence) | dialects | histories |
| (orthography) | | |
| (Hellenism) | | |
| grammatical figures | styles: *kharaktēres, plásmata* | (glosses) |

Tab. 58.3.: The quadripartite system
(sources: *Scholia D. T.* 10.8ff., 12.3ff., 13.7ff., 115.8ff., 168.19ff., 170.17ff., 452.34ff., 471.8ff.)

(1) Parts of *grammatikḗ*

| *diorthōtikón* "textual criticism" | *anagnōstikón* "reading aloud" | *exhēgētikón* "interpretation" | *kritikón* "criticism" |
|---|---|---|---|
| glosses and histories | | (etymology) | judgement: appropriateness, beauty, authenticity |
| etymology | | | |
| analogy | | | |

(2) Tools of *grammatikḗ*

| *glōssēmatikón* "glossematical" | *historikón* "historical" | *metrikón* "metrical" | *tekhnikón* "technical, expert" |
|---|---|---|---|

Tab. 58.4.: Dionysius Thrax' Grammatical Expertise
The constituents of *grammatikḗ*
(sources: Sextus Empiricus, *M* I, 250 and Dionysius Thrax, *Tékhnē* 5.2–6.3; the two rows immediately under the names of the parts indicate the provenance assigned to those parts in the first and second critique given by Sextus Empiricus, *M* I, 250f.; for the first critique, cf. Heliodorus in *Scholia D. T.* 435.15ff. and Melampus in *Scholia D. T.* 14.21–15.25; the third row indicates whether the item was considered a part or a tool by Stephanus in *Scholia D. T.* 168.25ff.)

| *anágnōsis* "reading aloud according to prosody | *exhḗgēsis* "exegesis according to poetic figures present | *glō̃ssai kaì historíai* "explication of words and histories" | *etumología* "discovery of etymology" | *analogía* "calculation of analogy" | *krísis* "judgement of poems" |
|---|---|---|---|---|---|
| [actually a result] | | [sub-part of textual criticism] | [sub-part of textual criticism] | [sub-part of textual criticism] | |
| [> Ascl. grammatical part] | [> Ascl. grammatical part] | [> Ascl. historical part] | [> Ascl. expert part] | [> Ascl. expert part] | [> Ascl. grammatical part] |
| [part] | [part] | [tool] | [tool] | [tool] | [tool] |
| (genres and styles of poetry) | poetic figures | glosses | (Hellenism) | (Hellenism: [letters, syllables, *léxis*, parts of speech, distribution, syntax of the parts of speech, orthography]) | (judgement: appropriateness, beauty, authenticity) |
| accents, breathing | | histories | | | (benefits of knowledge of poetry and prose) |
| (pauses) | | (proverbs and definitions) | | | |
| (letters, syllables) | | | | | |
| (metres) | | | | | |

tactic constructions degenerated to become the forms encountered in ordinary language, the various dialects, and in poetry (cf. Wackernagel 1876).

Apollonius shows in the beginning of his *Syntax* that the fundamental order governs all levels of language, letters, syllables, words, and sentences, and it must also be present in the metalanguage with which we talk about the linguistic system, i. e., in the order of the alphabet, the parts of speech, the cases, etc. (3.3–12.7 = I, 3–11; e. g., *Syntax* 16.12ff. = I, 14; cf. Blank 1982: 12f.; Lallot 1986). The aim of Apollonius' treatments of irregularities is always to "derive" (*kathistánein*) the corrupted form from its orignal, showing the ultimate place of the corrupted form within the linguistic system (e. g., *Conjunctions* 232.15; *Syntax* 228.2; see Thierfelder 1935: 81).

Apollonius determined what the original form or construction was by recourse to a number of heuristic schemes, such as that the more frequent phenomenon is the rule for the less frequent, so that the latter must be derived by corruption from the former (e. g., *Pronouns* 72.6; see Thierfelder 1935: 28ff.).

The rule of frequency points to the importance of analogy: those forms which can be paralleled and put into orderly schemata are the original ones. "Analogy" (*analogía*), in turn, points to the importance of *lógos*: the order of reason is the same as the order of the sentence and of the linguistic system as a whole. We are told that corruptions affect the form, but not the sense of an utterance (e. g., *Conjunctions* 224.11; *Adverbs* 136.32). Thus, the sense is assumed always to be in order, and the derivation of an expression from its original form demonstrates the form which originally corresponded to and properly expressed the sense. The 'sense' which plays this role for Apollonius is the Stoic *lektón* and its parts (cf. Blank 1982, ch. III). We have seen that this distinction between the intelligible and corporeal components of *lógos*, between *lektón* and expression, formed the basic dichotomy of Stoic dialectic. Now it will condition the structure of Apollonius' works on the parts of speech, as well.

Apollonius is said to have written many works on all aspects of language. His bibliography as given in the *Suda* (α 3422) comprises: *On distribution of the Parts of the Sentence* (four books), *On Syntax of the Parts of the Sentence* (four books), *On the Verb or 'Verbal'* (five books), *On the Derivatives of Verbs ending in -mi* (one book), *On Names or 'Nominal'* (one book) *On Names by Dialect, On the Nominative in feminine Names* (one book), *On Paronyms* (one book), *On Comparatives, On Dialects, Doric, Ionic, Aeolic, Attic, On Homeric Schemata, On False History, On Pathe, On Forced Accents* (two books), *On Crooked Accents* (one book), *On Prosodic Markings* (five books), *On Elements, On Prepositions, On Didymus' Persuasive points, On Composition, On Words with Two Forms, On* Tís, *On Genders, On Breathings, On Possessives, On Syzygy.* To these must be added at least *On Pronouns, On Adverbs*, and *On Conjunctions*, which survive for the most part. Many of these works could be put together to build up a systematic treatment of the materials covered in, say, Asclepiades' technical part of grammar, covering: elements, prosodic markings, schemata, names, verbs, pronouns, adverbs, prepositions, conjunctions, syntax, distribution of the parts of the sentence; the works on false history, breathings, dialects, and Homeric schemata would then represent the second two parts of an Asclepiadean *tékhnē*. The 19th century saw a debate over whether or not Apollonius, or indeed a later editor, had in fact arranged his works in such a sequence to form a *Tékhnē Grammatikḗ*. The evidence is not conclusive either way, but I tend to doubt whether he did so (cf. Cohn 1895: 137f.).

Although we have no Apollonian *tékhnē* whose structure we can study, we do have the works *On Pronouns, On Adverbs,* and *On Conjunctions*, as well as the great *Syntax*. The works on individual parts of the sentence (usually referred to as the *'scripta minora'*) each fall into two parts: the discussion of the *énnoia* "sense" and the discussion of the *skhē̂ma tē̂s phōnē̂s*, the "word-form". The sense is treated first, and this section begins with the discussion of the names (*klḗseis*) of the part of the sentence (frequently there was debate about its proper name: cf. *Pronouns* 3.9), and continued with its definitions (*hóroi*; see the discussion in Thierfelder 1935: 1–19; Maas 1936: 288): both topics belong under the 'sense' because the name must suit the *ousía*, and the *lógos* of that is the definition (e. g., *Conjunctions* 215.14). Then, according to the things this part of the sentence is used to indicate, Apollonius distinguishes its various kinds (*génē*; e. g., *Conjunctions* 219.12). The treatment of 'sense' continues with the syntax of this part of the sentence, since every part is used because of its particular *énnoia* (cf. *Syntax* 35.10 = I, 39). The first main part of each treatise then concludes with discussions of words which may or may not be properly assigned to this part of the sentence, because Apollonius insists that such assignment (*merismós*) must be made on the basis of *énnoia*. The second part, about the word-form, deals with the forms and prosody of the individual words assigned to this part of the sentence, especially noting their dialect forms and the *páthē* by which they were corrupted.

In the course of each of these books, Apollonius finds ample opportunity to referee the opinions of others on questions of name, definition, membership of the word-class, etc. Thus, his *scripta minora*, each dealing with one part of the sentence, may perhaps give us an idea of the way in which earlier writers too dealt with the parts of speech. These writers, as Apollonius himself did, may have written generally about a particular part of the sentence or about one of its classes or features in particular; they may also have written generally about all the parts of the sentence, either in a treatise of that title or even in the context of a *Grammatikḕ Tékhnē*. If this was the case, then we can see how the doctrine of the parts of the sentence came to be the center of ancient treatments of the technical part of grammar.

The parts of the sentence also provide the framework for Apollonius' *Syntax*. As we have seen, the Stoics had a 'syntax of the things said' in which they dealt with the composition of *lektá* and the combination of complete *lektá* to produce arguments (cf. Egli 1986, with further references). For Apollonius too, syntax is a matter of combining 'the intelligibles subsistent upon the words' in order to form the complete *lógos* (*Syntax* 1.3–3.2 = I, 1–2; see the analyses of Camerer 1965; Frede 1977: 353ff.; Baratin & Desbordes 1981: 60ff.; Blank 1982, chs. III, IV). Parts of the sentence can only be uttered together in a sentence if the intelligibles which subsist on them, and which we combine when we combine the words, are compatible or congruent (*katállēla*): thus the second-person subsistent on the pronoun-form *sú* conflicts with the first-person subsistent on the verb-form *paideúō*. An uttered sentence requires the addition of another word or words if the *lektón* subsistent on it requires completion in order to form a complete sentence (*autotelês lógos*). Although the intelligible content of a sentence is always well-ordered, its expression is subject to *páthē*, which occur on all levels of the linguistic system, and it is the job of the syntactician to discover what the intelligible structure was and establish the pathology by which the expression came to be corrupted: thus there is a rational rule dictating the protaxis of modifiers, so that *xanthòs Atreídēs* will be more 'regular' (*katallēlóteron*) than *Atreídēs xanthós*, which will be explained as the result of the '*páthos* of transposition' Blank 1982: 47f.). Consequently, Apollonius says that "the present investigation of *katallēlótēs* will correct what has suffered in any way whatsoever in *lógos*" (*Syntax* 51.11f. = I, 60).

From these principles is derived the structure of Apollonius' *Syntax*. An introductory section defines the task and justifies the possibility of the expert study of syntax. This justification is based on an analogy with the possibility of the detailed study of orthography: since the study of corruptions and their restitution to the rational rule allows such detailed treatment of the makeup of words, it will allow the same kind of treatment of the makeup of the sentence. The parallel drawn by Apollonius allows us, I think, to infer something else about the study of syntax: as orthographical treatises dealt with individual questions about the correct spelling of words whose alternative forms could not be distinguished aurally, syntax will deal with selected problems of syntactical construction in which one might not see the way in which *páthē* have disturbed the original, rational construction. Apollonius states that the purpose of his work on syntax is to show that even the unnoticed transpositions in ordinary language adhere to the rule of reason, and that one ought not just to take what is in poets as exceptions (*Syntax* 183.14ff. = II, 77; cf. Blank 1982: 9–10).

Apollonius then outlines the plan of the particular discussions which make up the work: since the other parts of the sentence are referred to the syntax of the verb and name, he will treat the constructions of each part of speech which can be used with, or substituted for and also used with, the name or the verb, as pronouns can be used instead of or in combination with names, and participles both instead of and along with verbs, and so on for the other parts of the sentence in order (*Syntax* 33.9–34.2 = I, 36). The ensuing discussions deal with questions about the article (I, 37–157) and the pronoun (II). The third book begins with a discussion of correct construction or *katallēlótēs* and its opposite, solecism (III, 1–53). Then there is a treatment of the general syntax of the verb (III, 54–190), followed in book IV by the syntax of prepositions. This will have been followed in the lost portions of the fourth book by questions in the syntax of adverbs (of which part is preserved with the treatise *On Adverbs*, pages 201–210) and conjunctions.

In Apollonius' *Syntax* and works on the parts of the sentence, we see clear and well motivated structures. They are the work of a creative grammarian who builds on and engages in controversies with his predecessors. As these are the first works of any Greek grammarian to survive, we should be alive to the help that they can give us in the understanding of previous grammarians' works, whose skeletons are all that remain for us to examine.

## 7. Bibliography

### 7.1. Primary sources

Apollonius Dyscolus, *Fragmenta*. Ed. by Richard Schneider, *Librorum Apollonii Deperditorum Fragmenta* (= *Grammatici Graeci* II/3). Leipzig: B. G. Teubner, 1910.

–, *Pronouns*. Ed. by Richard Schneider, *Apollonii Dyscoli de pronominibus* (= *Grammatici Graeci* II/1.2.1–116). Leipzig: B. G. Teubner, 1878. [For the first part of *Pronouns* see: *Apollonii Dyscoli De pronominibus pars generalis*, ed. by Paul Maas (= *Kleine Texte für Vorlesungen und Übungen*, 82), Bonn, 1911.]

–, *Scripta minora*. Ed. by Richard Schneider, *Grammatici Graeci* II/1.1. Leipzig: B. G. Teubner, 1878.

–, *Syntax*. Ed. by Gustav Uhlig, *Apollonii Dyscoli de constructione libri quattuor* (= *Grammatici Graeci* II/2). Leipzig: B. G. Teubner, 1910. [Annotated transl. by Fred Householder, *The Syntax of Apollonius Dyscolus*, Amsterdam: Benjamins, 1981; and by Jean Lallot, *La syntaxe d'Apollonius Dyscole*, Paris: Vrin, 1997.]

Diogenes Laertius (DL) = *Diogenis Laertii Vitae Philosophorum*. Ed. by H. S. Long. 2nd ed. Oxford: Clarendon Press, 1966.

Dionysius Thrax, *Tékhnē grammatikḗ*. Ed. by Gustav Uhlig, *Grammatici Graeci* II/1. Leipzig: B. G. Teubner, 1883.
*Scholia D. T.* = *Scholia in Dionysii Thracis Artem Grammaticam*. Ed. by Alfred Hilgard, *Grammatici Graeci* I/3, 1–586. Leipzig: B. G. Teubner, 1901.

Sextus Empiricus, *M.* = Sextus Empiricus, *Adversus mathematicos, libri i-vi*. Ed. by Jürgen Mau. 2nd ed. Leipzig: B. G. Teubner, 1961.

## 7.2. Secondary sources

Atherton, Catherine. 1993. *The Stoics on Ambiguity*. Cambridge.

Ax, Wolfram. 1986. *Laut, Stimme, Sprache: Studien zu drei Grundbegriffen der antiken Sprachtheorie*. Göttingen.

Baratin, Marc & Françoise Desbordes. 1981. *L'analyse linguistique dans l'antiquité classique*, vol. I: *Les théories*. Paris.

Blank, David L. 1982. *Ancient Philosophy and Grammar. The syntax of Apollonius Dyscolus*. Chico, Cal.

–. 1993. "Apollonius Dyscolus". *Aufstieg und Niedergang der römischen Welt* 34, 1.708–720.

–. 1998. *Sextus Empiricus Against the Grammarians*. Oxford.

Camerer, R. 1965. "Die Behandlung der Partikel *an* in den Schriften des Apollonios Dyskolos". *Hermes* 93.168–204.

Cohn, Leopold. 1895. "Apollonios (81)". *Realenzyklopädie* II, 1.136–139.

Deichgräber, Karl. 1930. *Die griechische Empirikerschule: Sammlung der Fragmente und Darstellung der Lehre*. Berlin: Weidmannsche Verlagsbuchhandlung. (Repr., Berlin & Zürich, 1965.)

Dihle, Albrecht. 1986. "Philosophie – Fachwissenschaft – Allgemeine Bildung". *Aspects de la philosophie hellénistique* ed. by Helmut Flashar & Olaf Gigon, 185–231. Geneva: Fondation Hardt.

Egli, Urs. 1986. "Stoic Syntax and Semantics". *Historiographia Linguistica* 13.281–306.

Frede, Michael. 1977. "The Origin of Traditional Grammar". *Historical and Philosophical Dimensions of Logic, Methodology, and Philosophy of Science* ed. by Robert E. Butts & Jaakko Hintikka, 51–97. Dordrecht: Reidel. (Repr., Michael Frede, *Essays in Ancient Philosophy*, 338–359. Oxford & Madison, 1987.)

–. 1978. "Principles of Stoic Grammar". *The Stoics* ed. by John M. Rist, 27–75. Berkeley: Univ. of California Press. (Repr., Michael Frede, *Essays in Ancient Philosophy*, 301–337. Oxford & Madison, 1987.)

Glück, Manfred. 1967. *Priscians Partitiones und ihre Stellung in der spätantiken Schule*. Hildesheim: Olms.

Haas, Walter. 1977. *Die Fragmente der Grammatiker Tyrannion und Diokles*. (= *Sammlung griechischer und lateinischer Grammatiker*, 3.) Berlin & New York: de Gruyter.

Heinicke, Balduin. 1904. *De Quintiliani Sexti Asclepiadis Arte Grammatica*. Diss. Universität Straßburg.

Ildefonse, Frédérique. 1997. *La naissance de la grammaire*. Paris: Vrin.

Kaibel, Georg. 1898. Die Prolegomena *Perì Komoidias*. *Abhandlungen der Göttingischen Gesellschaft der Wissenschaften* N. F. 2.4.

Kaster, Robert A. 1995. *Suetonius. De Grammaticis et Rhetoribus*. Oxford: Clarendon Press.

Lallot, Jean. 1986. "L'ordre de la langue: Observations sur la théorie grammaticale d'Apollonius Dyscole". *Philosophie du langage et Grammaire dans l'Antiquité*. 413–426 (= *Cahiers de Philosophie Ancienne*, 5.), Bruxelles.

Maas, Paul. 1936. Review of Thierfelder (1935). *Gnomon* 12.287–288.

Marrou, Henri-Irénée. 1950. *Histoire de l'éducation dans l'Antiquité*. Paris: Editions du Seuil.

Müller, Bruno Albinus. 1903. *De Asclepiade Myrleano*. Diss. Universität Leipzig.

Ophuijsen, Jan M. van. 1993. "The Semantics of a Syntactician: Things meant by verbs according to Apollonius Dyscolus *Peri suntaxeos*". *Aufstieg und Niedergang der römischen Welt* 34, 1.731–770.

Pfeiffer, Rudolf. 1968. *History of Classical Scholarship*, vol. I: *From the Beginnings to the Hellenistic Age*. Oxford: Clarendon Press.

Rabe, Hans. 1890. *De Theophrasti Libris PERI LEXEOS*. Diss. Universität Bonn.

Schenkeveld, Dirk M. 1984. "Studies in the History of Ancient Linguistics. II. Stoic and Peripatetic kinds of speech act and the distinction of grammatical moods". *Mnemosyne* 37.291–353.

–. 1990a. "Studies in the History of Ancient Linguistics. III. The Stoic TEKHNE PERI PHONES". *Mnemosyne* 43.86–108.

–. 1990b. "Studies in the History of Ancient Linguistics. IV. Developments in the study of ancient linguistics". *Mnemosyne* 43.290–306.

–. 1991. "Figures and Tropes: A border-case between grammar and rhetoric". *Rhetorik zwischen den Wissenschaften.* ed. by G. Ueding, 149–157. (= *Rhetorik-Forschungen*, 1) Tübingen.

Siebenborn, Elmar. 1976. *Die Lehre von der Sprachrichtigkeit und ihren Kriterien: Studien zur antiken normativen Grammatik.* Amsterdam: Grüner.

Slater, William J. 1972. "Asklepiades and Historia". *Greek, Roman and Byzantine Studies* 13.317–333.

Sluiter, Ineke. 1990. *Ancient Grammar in Context: Contributions to the study of ancient linguistic thought.* Amsterdam: VU Univ. Press.

Stroux, Johannes. 1912. *De Theophrasti Virtutibus Dicendi*, I. Diss. Universität Straßburg, 1912.

Thierfelder, Andreas. 1935. *Beiträge zur Kritik und Erklärung des Apollonios Dyskolos.* (= *Abhandlungen der Sächsischen Akademie der Wissenschaften*, philol.-hist. Kl. 43, 2.) Leipzig: Hirzel.

Usener, Hermann. 1913. "Ein altes Lehrgebäude der Philologie". *Kleine Schriften* II. 265–314. Berlin & Leipzig: Teubner. (Originally published in *Sitzungsberichte der philosophischen, philologischen und historischen Klasse der Bayerischen Akademie der Wissenschaften* 4 [1892]. 582–648.)

Wackernagel, Jacob. 1876. *De pathologiae veterum initiis.* Diss. Universität Basel. (Repr., Jacob Wackernagel, *Kleine Schriften* III ed. by B. Forsmann, 1445–1496, Göttingen.)

Whitaker, Charles W. A. 1997. *Aristotle De Interpretatione. Contradiction and Dialectic.* Oxford: Clarendon Press.

*David Blank, Los Angeles (USA)*

# 59. Greek linguistics in the Byzantine Period

1. Introduction
2. Works
3. State of the texts
4. Byzantine sources
5. Byzantine developments
6. Standards
7. Methods
8. Conclusion
9. Bibliography

## 1. Introduction

Linguistics, like other aspects of learning in the Byzantine age, was in the main part the continuation of work undertaken in the Hellenistic period, and later in the period of Roman rule. After the Alexandrian conquests of the later 4th century BC, the rulers of the successor states took on, for whatever reasons, the imposition of the Greek language and Greek literature on the territories that they controlled. This process was known as Hellenizing, and the years following 300 BC were known in Asia Minor and Egypt as the Hellenistic age.

Culturally little was changed when from c. 200 BC. the Romans incorporated by stages the Hellenistic states into the Roman Empire, as it came to be known. Though governed by Latin officials and guarded by Roman soldiers, these countries continued to have Greek as the language of education and of social advancement, and most Latin speakers sent out to the eastern provinces had learned Greek or set themselves to learn both the language and its literature.

As with other attempts at historical dating, the start of the Byzantine age must be arbitrarily decided in relation to some historical event. A convenient point is the inauguration of Byzantium as the 'New Rome', Constantine's city, Constantinople, in 330 AD, by the Emperor, completing the separation of the Western Latin Empire and the Greek Eastern Empire that had begun in the preceding century through the policies of Diocletian.

Constantine intended that his 'New Rome' should be governed along the lines of the former unitary Empire, and for the first few centuries officials in the Eastern Empire bore Latin titles such as *praetor* and *consul.* Priscian's large Latin grammar, the *Institutiones grammaticae* (*GL* II; III, 3–377) and his much shorter *Institutio de nomine pronomine et verbo* (*GL* III, 443–456), both written c. 500 AD, were clearly intended as part of the resources for teaching Latin in a Greek speaking community. But these intentions never penetrated very deeply nor spread very widely, and it has been calculated that by 800 Latin was known and read only as a second language by scholars (cf. Runciman 1933: 232).

Increasingly as the Western Empire collapsed under Germanic pressures and invasions, and the attempt by Justinian (527–565), one of the last Latin speaking Emperors, to reconquer the whole of the old Empire had failed, the Eastern Empire, with Constantinople as its capital, maintained and even intensified the Hellenizing policies of earlier centuries.

In the 12th century the famous Byzantine historian Anna Comnena, in her account of the reign of her father Alexius I, describes the teaching being carried on in the orphan school that he had set up (Reifferscheid 1884: 293–294): pupils were being taught Greek grammar and were writing grammatical exercises, some Latin speakers and Scythians were learning Greek from the start, and illiterate Greek speakers were being introduced to the classical language and to classical Greek literature. Greek language studies in the Byzantine world were deliberately and self-consciously aimed at preserving the standards of the ancient classical world. The citizens of Constantinople called themselves *Rōmaĩoi* "Romans", and the word *Romaic* has persisted into modern times as a term for the current Greek language; *Héllēnes* meant something else, specialists in the Greek of the classical age and students of Greek Antiquity.

## 2. Works

The principal types of writing within the language sciences in the East were the following:
(1) *Skhólia* "commentaries", on previously established grammatical texts, dating from Antiquity or from earlier Byzantine scholarship.
(2) Lexicons listing words of scholarly or literary importance and those liable to be misunderstood. To some extent these matched the *Etymologies* of Isidore of Seville in the West, and their entries varied between the purely lexicographical and the often longer encyclopaedic articles.
(3) Extensive tabulated lists of the inflectional paradigms of nouns (which included today's adjectives) and verbs. The best known of these were the *Kanónes* of Theodosius (4th century) with the commentaries of Choeroboscus (c. 750–825; cf. Bühler & Theodoridis 1976) and Sophronius (9th century) (*GG* IV 2, 1–371; 372–434).
(4) Systematic and relatively concise expositions of the structure of classical Greek, containing orthographic phonetics, 'the pronunciation of the letters', morphology, and syntax, together with the semantic distinctions carried by the various categories and syntactic constructions.

## 3. State of the texts

A good deal of the linguistic work of the Byzantine age remains unedited and in manuscript form. The best conspectus of the available gramatical corpus is still to be found in Krumbacher (1897: 579–593.)

Edited texts in printed form include the following:
(1) Priscian's *Institutiones* (*GL* II; III, 3–377), which remained an important authority for those grammarians who could still read Latin.
(2) Volumes I: 1 and I: 3 of *Grammatici Graeci* contain the text of the *Tékhnē grammatikḗ* "The science of grammar" attributed to Dionysius Thrax (c. 100 BC; → Art. 57), and the later scholia on it (*GG* I: 1, 3–100; I: 3, 1–586). The text of the *Tékhnē* as we now have it may well be a Byzantine revised reedition of an earlier original.
(3) Etymological information given by commentators and in the entries of lexicologists. These reflect the etymological theory of the Ancient and Mediaeval World, in which the meaning of more complex and derived words was to be explained ('unfolded') by reference to parts of more primitive words. This conception of etymology, synchronic rather than historical in the modern sense, goes back to Plato. One of the best known Byzantine lexicons is the *Etumologikòn méga* (c. 12th century.)
(4) The *Tabulations* (*Kanónes*) serve exhaustively to expand the elementary lists of word classes and grammatical inflections given in the *Tékhnē*. The *Kanónes* of Theodosius (late 4th century) list in order the entire inflectional corpus of Greek nouns and verbs; most famous is the totality of the possible inflections of the verb *túptō* "strike", assuming that every derivational and inflexional formation could be exploited in full (*GG* IV: 1). Commentators point out that a good number of these forms are not actually used in classical literature, but it was found useful to see how the full range of possible formations would look on one lexical base. In this connection it has been pointed out that the Byzantine grammarians followed the descriptive pattern

of their classical predecessors in setting out morphology on a 'word-and-paradigm' basis (Hockett 1954: 210); the concept of the independent morpheme was not developed: one form (e. g., the nominative singular of nouns and the first person present indicative active of verbs) was taken as basic and the other forms were described in terms of changes and additions made to them.

So far the following Greek grammar books of the Byzantine period have been individually edited and printed, with modern commentary:

Michael Syncellus (9th century), *Méthodos perì tē̃s toũ lógou suntáxeōs* "The syntactic structure of the sentence" (Donnet 1982).

Gregory of Corinth (12th century), *Perì toũ lógou ḗtoi perì toũ mḗ soloikízein* "On the sentence: the avoidance of syntactic errors" (Donnet 1967a).

John Glykys (14th century), *Perì orthótētos suntáxeōs* "On correct syntax" (Jahn 1839).

Perhaps the most theoretically insightful of the grammarians was Maximus Planudes (c. 1300), a scholar well versed in Latin as well as in classical Greek and one responsible for the Greek translation of several classical and mediaeval texts into Greek. He wrote two works on grammar, the *Diálogos perì grammatikē̃s* "Dialogue on grammar", in style similar to a Platonic dialogue, and a textbook *Perì suntáxeōs* "On syntax" (Bachmann 1828).

Among the later Byzantine grammarians, who spent much of their lives in Italy teaching Greek grammar were Chrysoloras (c. 1353–1415), Lascaris (15th century), and Theodore of Gaza (15th century). They were the authors of the principal grammar books that brought the classical Greek language back into Italy and thence to the rest of Europe. Chrysoloras's *Erōtḗmata* "Questions" was a brief Greek grammar book comparable to the two short Latin grammars of Donatus (4th century), set in question-and-answer form. It was probably first made public in 1397 and printed in Italy about a century later (1471).

By this time the influence of the Latin grammarians was again making itself felt. Chrysoloras's noun inflections are ordered into ten declensions, on similar lines to the five Latin declensions established in late Antiquity, and better organized than the much more numerous separate lists of forms in Theodosisus's *Kanónes*.

## 4. Byzantine sources

The authorities on which the Byzantine grammarians essentially relied were three in number: the *Tékhnē grammatikḗ* attributed to Dionysius (*GG* I: 1), the immensely long syntactic books of Apollonius Dyscolus (2nd century AD), only some of which survive, and for those who could read Latin the *Institutio* and the *Institutiones* of Priscian.

The *Tékhnē* in the form that the Byzantines had was treated as wholly authoritative; one commentator referred to the author as "Dionysius Thrax who taught us the eight word classes": noun (including adjectives), verb, participle, article, pronoun, preposition, adverb, and conjunction (*GG* I: 3, 27–28, 128). These word classes and the grammatical categories associated with them, case, tense, number, etc., were used by Apollonius and all the Byzantines. The commentators' *skhólia* were mostly explanatory, though they are occasionally critical of the actual wording of the *Tékhnē*.

The author of the *Tékhnē* mentioned the term 'syntax' but did not deal further with it. After a definition of 'grammar' he set out the orthographic phonetics of Greek and then concerned himself primarily with each word class in turn and its categories and subclassifications. Single concise grammar books of Greek, covering morphology and syntax together in textbook form would appear to have been a creation of the Byzantine scholars.

## 5. Byzantine developments

### 5.1. Phonetics

Little was said by the Byzantines on phonetics beyond what had already been said in the *Tékhnē*. The misdiagnosis of the voiced plosives as *mésa grámmata* "middle letters", lying somehow articulatorily between the aspirated and the unaspirated plosives, continued; but commentators took note of the fact that the distinction between aspirated and unaspirated plosives, like that between initial aspirated and unaspirated vowels, was a feature of classical Greek (cf. *GG* I: 3, 33, 14, 20–21). By Byzantine times the former aspirated plosives had come to be pronounced as voiceless fricatives in the way they are pronounced in Modern Greek (cf. Allen 1974: 23). On the loss of distinctive aspiration in initial vowels it was also noted that this had already been a dialectal feature (*psílōsis*) in classical times (cf. Buck 1927: 49–51).

### 5.2. Grammar

#### 5.2.1. Nominal case

Much attention was paid to the syntax and semantics of case. Efforts were made to identify, not always successfully, a basic meaning or *Grundbedeutung* for each particular case and for the category of case itself. One such attempt to define the meanings of the three oblique cases was made by Maximus Planudes, linking the genitive with motion from, the dative with place at or in, and the accusative with motion to (the vocative case, though morphologically distinct in some nouns, was recognized as ungoverned and on its own, unlike the others). Planudes's system fits in very well with the separate meanings of the tricasual prepositions such as *prós*, with the genitive "from the vicinity of", with the dative "near", with the accusative "towards"; and it also coincides with the meanings of several unicasual prepositions: *ek* "out of" and *apó* "from" take the genitive, *en* "in" constructs with the dative, and *eis* "into" takes the accusative; and each of these three cases can be used alone with the same local meanings (cf. *AG* 121–123).

Some linguists, notably Hjelmslev (1935: 10–12), have seen Planudes as the first expositor of a full localist theory of case, such as was taken up in the 19th century by Bopp and others (Bopp 1833: 136), to the effect that all the case meanings in languages can be shown to be taken originally from locative meanings.

Since Hjelmslev's (1935) statement considerable controversy has continued on the legitimacy of the localist theory of case meanings. The question in its starkest form is whether a plausible localist origin can be identified in case functions such as subject and object marking by nominative and accusative case forms in the classical languages of the Indo-European family (to go no further). Hjelmslev takes up Bopp's assertion of case localism at the hands of later grammarians, distinguishing 'localists', 'antilocalists', and 'demilocalists' (1935: 33–61).

More specifically on Planudes himself, two questions may be asked: Was he in fact expounding a localist case theory as such, and, if he was, how far was he original in what he said?

He set out his analysis of basic case meanings both in his *Dialogue* and his *Syntax*. In both these books he gave detailed attention to the locational meanings of the oblique cases, used alone or governed by prepositions, aligning the genitive with place from (and time past), the dative with place in or at (and time present) and the accusative with place (in)to (and time to come; *AG*, 121–123). As has been seen above, his theory applies particularly well to classical Greek, though some attested occurrences require some explanation. But he was writing systematically about Greek, not setting out universal grammar like his Western contemporaries, the scholastic grammarians; nor was he laying down the basic case meanings in other languages, in the manner of Bopp.

In the debate on the ('alleged') localist theory of case attention is focussed on Planudes's statement (*AG*, 122): *katá tina physikḕn akolouthían hai treĩs haũtai erōtḗseis, tò póthen kaì poũ kaì pẽ, tàs treĩs plagías eklērṓsanto ptṓseis: tò mèn póthen tḕn genikḗn, tò dè poũ tḗn dotikḗn, tò dè pẽ tḕn aitiatikḗn* "by some sort of natural agreement the three questions, *whence, where*, and *whither*, have had assigned to them the three oblique cases, *whence* having the genitive *where* the dative, and *whither* the accusative".

In the opinion of the present writer this passage does constitute a concise statement of a localist theory of the Greek oblique cases. But it must be said that others have taken a different and less exciting interpretation of Planudes's text. Certainly the Byzantine commentators on the *Tékhnē* refer to the locative associations of the three cases (*GG* I: 3, 549), and such interpretations are found in some of the earlier Byzantine grammarians such as Heliodorus (7th century) and Syncellus (9th century), but if a localist interpretation of case is accepted, Planudes's account represents a far more systematic exposition of it. A gradual realization of the localism inherent in the meanings of the three cases is entirely plausible except to those who persistently deny the Byzantine grammarians any original thinking at all.

The question must remain undecided so far, with leading specialists taking their different stances. For a summary of the discussion so far the reader may consult Robins (1993, chapter 11) and the references up to 1992 there cited.

5.2.2. Verbal tense

Verbal tense inflections were much discussed in their relations to real time, along with the philosophical problem of an actual present moment in the continuous passage of time (cf. *GG* I: 3, 248.13–27, 250.1–25). It is interesting to notice that Sophronius points out that, whatever the philosophers may argue, the present tense form must be regarded as basis for the verbal paradigm in view of homophonous future forms of different verbs: *leípō* "I leave" and *leíbō* "I make a libation" have identical future forms *leípsō* (*GG* IV: 2, 414).

In the classical period the Stoics had shown how a two-dimensional frame of time, past, present, and future, and of aspect, complete and incomplete, made for a more coherent statement of the semantics of the Greek verbal tenses, and, as Varro was to show, of the Latin verbal tense forms (*De Lingua Latina* IX, 96–97; X, 48). This however was not preserved in the mainline tradition, and the Byzantines followed the *Tékhnē* in grouping the four tenses, imperfect, perfect, aorist, and pluperfect, as representing four sorts of past time, distinguished where necessary by temporal adverbs such as *árti* "recently", *pálai* "a long time ago", and *propálai* "an even longer time ago". This unidimensional analysis of the Greek tense system goes back to Aristotle, who had defined one of the distinctive features of the verb, that it consignified time.

Planudes, however, did succeed in incorporating aspectual distinctions into the semantic analysis of the Greek tenses in his *Dialogue* (*AG*, 6–7), by introducing temporal reference points other than the speaker's present: for example a pluperfect form 'I had been writing' could be explained by saying "If you had asked me yesterday 'What have you done?', I would have said 'I have been writing'.

5.2.3. Verbal voice

In the *Dialogue* Planudes also sets out a discussion of the differences of meaning of the three Greek voices, active, passive and middle, although the middle voice is only distinctively marked in the future and aorist tense forms. The semantics of the middle voice are notoriously complex. Planudes concentrates on one of the central meanings, reflexivity; he compares the aorist forms *élousa* "I washed (something)", *eloúthēn* "It was washed (by someone else)", and *elousámēn* "I washed myself". After a discussion he concludes that the three voices are distinct, but that the middle voice is nearer to the active voice since both involve the subject doing something himself (*AG*, 7–11).

5.2.4. Syntax

Discussions and analyses such as those that have been noticed here, and others, whether or not one agrees with their conclusions, go some way to refute the too frequent assertion that originality is neither to be expected nor found in the work of the Byzantine grammarians.

Of the grammarians whose works are currently in printed form, Syncellus, Gregory, John Glykys, and Planudes all have the word 'syntax' in the titles of their books, so that the term might seem almost synonymous with 'grammar' itself, as it is in many writings of the generative grammarians today. Indeed, much attention was paid to syntax, defined as the arrangement of words in sentences and their interpretation, both in later Antiquity and in the Byzantine Age. But it was a syntax based on a prior morphology; that is to say that it was primarily concerned with the syntactic relations of concord and government between nouns, verbs, and prepositions, and with the categories of case, gender, number, tense, and voice, all of which had been established by their categorial meanings and their morphological marks. This is not surprising when it is recalled that the word classes and their morphological categories had been established in Alexandrian times and had been accepted by the beginning of the Christian era. It was two centuries later that Apollonius wrote his pioneering books on syntax, openly based on the morphological classes and categories that he had before him. He introduced his subject by writing (*GG* II: 2, 1.1–2.2):

> "In our previous publications we have discussed the theory of word forms in a way that the subject required. The present work will deal with the syntax of these in the correct construction of independent sentences" (Uhlig 1910: 1,1–2,2).

This same order was followed by Priscian three centuries on, in what amounts to a Latin translation of the passage quoted from Apollonius (*GL* III, 108.5–7).

In an important article Donnet (1967b) points out that specifically syntactic concepts such as subject, object, and complement, which came into being in western grammatical theory, do not appear in Byzantine syntax. *Hupokeímenon* "subject" remained as a wholly logical item. Concordial and governmental relationships were between the morphologically established categories of the earlier tradition.

## 6. Standards

In their syntactic studies, as elsewhere in linguistics, the Byzantines were especially concerned about what they considered to have been a decline in standards of correctness and elegance even in the writings of even the most esteemed current and recent authors, as compared to the 'pure' form of the Greek language found in classical authors such as Plato and Thucydides. This was part of the strongly held belief that the Eastern Empire had the duty of preserving all that it could of the standards of the classical age.

Some Greek transitive verbs and some prepositions constructed with more than one case, carrying different meanings within one semantic field. Such distinctions were being lost or confused. One writer, John Glykys, likened the situation to a river which had overrun its former banks and was obliterating its former tributaries and distinct channels (*Perì orthótētos* 4). Objection was also taken to the modern tendency of linking clauses in a sentence by a succession of *nominativi pendentes*, allegedly in the interests of vividness (*Perì orthótētos* 53–54).

Glykys provides a list of bicasual transitive verbs and tricasual prepositions, with their exact and correct meanings, even though his explanation of these would not be acceptable today: *krateîn* with an accusative means "to hold physically", for example a spear; with a genitive it means "to take or hold power" over a person or a people (*Perì orthótētos* 11–12). Gregory of Corinth gives examples of the different uses of prepositions within an overall semantic field of relations when constructed with different cases: for example, *pará* with the genitive means "from the side of", as in *hē boḗtheiá mou parà Kuríou* "my help comes from the Lord God"; with the accusative it means "to the side of, into the presence of", as in *parà sè ē̃lthon* "I came into your presence"; and with the dative "at the side of", *parà soi hē elpís mou* "with you rests my hope" (Donnet 1967a: 199–201). A similar distinction of the different meanings of the tricasual preposition *prós* by Maximus Planudes has already been noticed (5.2.1.).

## 7. Methods: *schédē*

The Byzantine grammarians were by no means uninterested in theoretical linguistic questions, as is sometimes stated. But necessarily within the context of their times and their appreciation of their own culture, their main efforts were directed to the teaching of 'correct' Greek and to the proper understanding of classical Greek literature.

A didactic device that was in regular use was the *skhédos* "lesson"; *skhedographía* meant "the writing of *skhédē*". This Byzantine word may derive from the physical meaning "board", comparable to the schoolchild's slate in quite recent times. It sprang from the classical practice *merismós* or *epimerismós* "parsing", the division of the sentence into its component words and the allocation of these to their respective word classes and subclasses. This could readily be incorporated into grammar lessons, and in later years it was enriched with further items of information that could be attached to the word. This sort of practice would result in gobbets of school learning that could be memorized by the pupils; and it became an essential teaching method. Some people disliked it, including Anna Comnena (1, above), finding it banal and philistine, rather as today some language scholars dislike the excessive formalism of the generativists' parsing grammar (cf. Reifferscheid 1884: 293–294). But Krumbacher (1897: 592) compared it favourably with some parts of the Prussian school practice of the later 19th century as a mark of approval.

The Latin term for *epimerismós* or *skhédos* was *partitio*, and a book of *Partitiones* based on the initial lines of each book of Vergil's *Aeneid* was written by Priscian as part of his educational publications (*GL* III, 459–515; more generally cf. Glück 1967). Each word in the first line of each book was made the peg on which to hang a whole set of notes, often in question-and-answer form, which could be learned and used in a single lesson. The first word of line 1 in Book 2 of the *Aeneid*, *conticuere* "they fell silent", provides an example of a *partitio* (*GL* III, 469.14–470.3):

"What part of speech? Verb. What sort? Perfect tense. What mood? Indicative., second conjugation [...] Give the first person singular, present indicative. Conticeo [...]".

It may be noted that the Byzantine Greek grammarians drew their words from both Christian and classical (pagan) literature, and freely mingled such texts in a single note or lesson. In his *skhédos* on the first line of *Psalm 1*, "Blessed is the man who [...]", Choeroboscus takes the word *anḗr* "man" and sets out information that includes its class, noun, its status, as a common noun, its declension, genitive *andrós* etc., its different meanings "male adult", "husband", and "courageous man", these differences exemplified with quotations from the Homeric poems. The whole *skhédos* is quite long, covering three printed pages. Some were much shorter, and information given in previous *skhédē* was not repeated (Gaisford 1842: 6–8).

## 8. Conclusion

The sort of information provided in the *skhédē*, the glosses of the commentators on classical texts of all sorts, the grammar books of the Byzantines, and the Byzantine grammarians themselves who in the last decades of the Eastern Empire came to teach and to write in Italy, were the instruments and the agents of the recovery and restitution of the learning of the Greek language and of Greek literature in the Italian and then in the whole Western European Renaissance. It is hard to see how all this could have come about so quickly and have established so firm a hold on Western European education and scholarship without the material and intellectual achievements of the Byzantine linguistic scholars over a period of more than a thousand years, while the Eastern Empire endured.

## 9. Bibliography

### 9.1. Further reading

For a concise introduction to Byzantine history and culture Runciman (1933) is still a standard book. Wilson (1983) provides a general coverage of Byzantine literature; and a brief summary of the whole known *œuvre* of the Byzantine linguists is to be found in Krumbacher (1893: 579–593).

In Robins (1993) an attempt is made to set out a general account and evaluation of the Byzantine linguistic achievement, with extensive quoted passages from eight grammatical texts.

### 9.2. Primary sources

*AG* = *Anecdota Graeca*, vol. II. Ed. by Ludwig Bachmann. Leipzig: Hinrichs, 1828.

Apollonius Dyscolus, *Syntax* = *Apollonii Dyscoli de Constructione libri quattuor.* Ed. by Gustav Uhlig. (= *GG* II: 2.) Leipzig: B. G. Teubner, 1910. (Repr., Hildesheim: Olms, 1965.) [English transl. by Fred W. Householder. Amsterdam: Benjamins, 1981.]

Choeroboscus, *Epimerismoí* = *Georgii Choerobosci Epimerismoi in Psalmos.* Ed. by Thomas Gaisford. Oxford: Oxford Univ. Press, 1842.

Chrysolaras, Manuel. *Erotemata.* Venice: Adam von Ambergau, 1471.

*GG* = *Grammatici Graeci.* 6 vols. Leipzig: B. G. Teubner, 1883–1901. (Repr., Hildesheim: Olms, 1965.)

*GL* = *Grammatici Latini.* Ed. by Heinrich Keil. Leipzig: B. G. Teubner, 1855–1880. (Repr., Hildesheim: Olms, 1961.)

Glykys, *Perì orthótetos syntaxeos* = *Joannis Glycae Patriarchae Constantinopoli opus de vera syntaxeos ratione.* Ed. by Albert Jahn. Bern: Jenn, 1839.

Varro, *De lingua latina* = Marcus Terentius Varro, *De lingua latina.* Ed. and transl. by Roland G. Kent. 3rd. ed. 2 vols. Cambridge, Mass. & London: Loeb Classical Library.

### 9.3. Secondary sources

Allen, W. Sidney. 1974. *Vox Graeca.* Cambridge: Cambridge Univ. Press.

Bopp, Franz. 1833. *Vergleichende Grammatik des Sanskritischen, Lateinischen, Litauischen, Gotischen und Deutschen.* Berlin: Dümmler.

Buck, Charles D. 1927. *Greek Dialects.* Boston: Athenaeum Press.

Bühler, Winfred & Christos Theodoridis. 1976. "Johannes von Damaskos, Terminus post quem für Choeroboskos". *Byzantinische Zeitschrift* 69.397–401.

Donnet, Daniel. 1967a. *Le traité* Peri syntaxeōs tou logou *de Gregoire de Corinthe.* Rome: Institut historique belge.

–. 1967b. "La place de la syntaxe dans les traités de grammaire grecque des origines au XII^e siècle". *Antiquité Classique* 36.122–146.

–. 1982. *Le traité de la construction de la phrase de Michel le Syncelle.* Rome: Institut historique belge.

Glück, Manfred. 1967. *Priscians* Partitiones *und ihre Stellung in der spätantiken Schule.* Hildesheim: Olms.

Hjelmslev, Louis. 1935. *La catégorie des cas.* Aarhus: Universitetsforlaget.

Hockett, Charles F. 1954. "Two models of grammatical description". *Word* 10.210–224.

Krumbacher, Karl. 1897. *Geschichte der byzantinischen Litteratur.* Munich: Beck.

Reifferscheid, Augustus, ed. 1884. *Annae Comnenae* Alexias. Leipzig: B. G. Teubner.

Robins, Robert H. 1993. *The Byzantine Grammarians; Their place in history.* Berlin: Mouton de Gruyter.

Runciman, Sir Steven. 1933. *Byzantine Civilization.* London: Arnold.

Wilson, Nigel G. 1983. *Scholars of Byzantium.* London: Duckworth.

*Robert H. Robins †, London (Great Britain)*

# 60. Die Beziehungen der griechischen Sprachforschung zu anderen Disziplinen

1. Überblick
2. Frühe Beziehungen zur Musik, Poesie und Rhetorik
3. Beziehungen zur Philosophie
4. Beziehungen zur Medizin
5. Ausblick
6. Bibliographie

## 1. Überblick

Der Einfluß anderer Disziplinen auf die griechische Sprachforschung ist außerordentlich weitreichend und tiefgreifend. Dafür gibt es zunächst einen historischen Grund. Von systematischer und eigenständiger Sprachforschung kann man erst zu einem späten Zeitpunkt des griechischen Geisteslebens sprechen. Wie in anderen Kulturen entwickelte sich ein grammatisches Bewußtsein offensichtlich erst, als drei Voraussetzungen gegeben waren: (1) die hohe Literatur war zum Abschluß gekommen; sie sollte ediert und gedeutet werden; (2) man empfand einen Unterschied zwischen literarischer Sprache, gebildeter Umgangssprache und Volkssprache; hieraus erwuchs das Bestreben, die reine und richtige Sprache zu bewahren oder wiederherzustellen; (3) sprachlich genial begabte Persönlichkeiten, deren Sprachbewußtsein durch die Kenntnis strukturell verschiedenartiger Sprachen zusätzlich geschult war, nahmen sich des Gegenstandes an. Unter solchen Bedingungen entstand das grammatische Lehrbuch, die τέχνη γραμματική. Ihr voraus liegen unsystematische nicht fachspezifische und dennoch sehr reichhaltige sprachliche Untersuchungen historisch vorgeordneter Wissenschaften, deren Gegenstandsbereiche eine Beschäftigung mit der Sprache erforderten: der Poetik, der Rhetorik, der Musik, der Tanzkunst, der Philosophie. Im Unterschied zur Grammatik galt der Blick weniger der Binnenstruktur als den Außenbeziehungen der Sprache. Das Verhältnis zur Welt der Dinge und Ideen, zur Wahrheit und zum Adressaten, die Ziele der Wahrheitsfindung, des künstlerischen Ausdrucks und der persuasiven Beeinflussung standen im Vordergrund. Dennoch führten solche Untersuchungen oft weit in das Gebiet der Grammatik im heutigen Sinn. Ihr Einfluß auf die hellenistische τέχνη γραμματική reicht vom wissenschaftlichen Problemhorizont über die methodischen Prinzipien bis hin zur Terminologie.

Neben der historischen hat die Beeinflussung durch andere Disziplinen eine weitere Wurzel. Generell wird in der antiken Literatur die enge Verwandtschaft aller Disziplinen betont (vgl. bes. Cicero, *Arch.* 2). Sie sind alle einem gemeinsamen Ziel, der Bildung, verpflichtet, bedienen sich vergleichbarer Arbeitstechniken und benutzen, was vor allem augenfällig ist, in ihren schriftlich kodifizierten Regelwerken (τέχναι) die gleichen Darstellungsmethoden des Abstrahierens, Klassifizierens und Subsumierens. Von daher liegt auch eine Beeinflussung durch nicht unmittelbar benachbarte Disziplinen nahe. Einige Disziplinen werden in eine besondere Nähe zueinander gerückt. Bekanntermaßen gilt das vor allem für die Malerei (γραφική) und die Dichtung (ποιητική). Charakteristisch dafür sind die Aussagen bei Horaz (*ars* 361 *ut pictura poesis*) und vor allem Plutarch (*de gloria Atheniensium* 347 a: "Die Malerei ist schweigende Dichtung, die Dichtung sprechende Malerei"). Ebenso scheint auch bei den Grammatikern und Rhetoren die Vorstellung einer besonderen Nähe zu bestimmten Disziplinen des Wissenschaftskosmos ausgeprägt gewesen zu sein. Die rhetorische Begriffsbildung wurde, zumindest zu bestimmten Zeiten, vor allem durch die Musik und die Tanzkunst beeinflußt (s. Koller 1958: 5–40). Die Grammatiker ihrerseits betonen in alexandrinischer Zeit die besondere Nähe ihres Fachs zur Medizin. In einem Scholion zur τέχνη des Dionysius Thrax (158.3) heißt die Grammatik eine "Schwester der Medizin". So kommt es, daß die antiken Sprachtheoretiker ihre Beispiele zwar den unterschiedlichsten Seinsbereichen entnehmen: bei Varro findet man Vergleiche aus den Bereichen der Landwirtschaft, der Musik, der Architektur und des Rechtswesens (vgl. Siebenborn 1976: 116ff.). Am weitesten und tiefsten jedoch gehen die Beziehungen zur Medizin. Die besondere Nähe der Grammatik zur Medizin dokumentiert sich nicht nur in einer Vielzahl von Vergleichen, sondern vor allem in der Entlehnung von Begriffen, dihaeretischen Kategorien und Erkenntnismethoden (s. u.).

## 2. Frühe Beziehungen zur Musik, Poesie und Rhetorik

Die ersten linguistischen Erkenntnisse stehen in engem Zusammenhang mit der sophistischen Rhetorik. Die Sophisten Gorgias und Thrasymachos empfanden ein Ungenügen an der kunstlosen Ausdrucksweise der Redner ihrer Zeit. In dem Bestreben, dem gesprochenen Wort vor Gericht und in politischen Versammlungen größere Wirkung und Durchschlagskraft zu verleihen, einem Grundmotiv sophistischen Wirkens überhaupt, stellten sie neben die bestehende Sprachgestaltungskunst, die Poesie, eine neue Disziplin: die Rhetorik als die Kunst des Überredens; als Mittel zu diesem Ziel lehrten sie die kunstvolle Durchgestaltung der Prosasprache. Insbesondere entdeckten sie die Wirkung des rhythmischen Sprechens (des Prosarhythmus), der Stilfiguren und der im Unterschied zum kunstlosen umgangssprachlichen Satz kunstvoll durchgestalteten Periode. In den Begriffen, die sie zur Erschließung dieses Aufgabenfeldes bildeten, lehnten sie sich an die Poesie und an die Musik an. Das läßt sich vor allem an dem wichtigsten von ihnen geprägten Begriff, περίοδος, zeigen: er ist ursprünglich der Tanzkunst entlehnt: er bezeichnet dort den tanzenden Umgang eines Chores um den Altar und (metonymisch) das Chorlied bzw. den Chorliedteil, der während des Umgangs gesungen wurde. Die ähnliche künstlerische Durchformung, die vergleichbare durchgehende rhythmische Gestaltung und die Kreisbewegung, die viele Perioden mit ihrem Aufbau in einen spannungserzeugenden und einen spannungslösenden Teil beschreiben, führte zur Übernahme des Begriffes in die Rhetorik (vgl. Siebenborn 1987: 229ff.). Daß auch andere sprachtheoretische Gedankengänge und Begriffe der Sophisten im Zusammenhang mit der Musik (μουσική) und der Tanzkunst (ὀρχηστική) stehen, zeigt Koller (1958: 5ff.). Insbesondere gehört dazu die Lehre von den σχήματα. Ursprünglich sind damit die Tanzfiguren gemeint, in denen der Sänger und Tänzer von der reinen Mitteilung abweicht und Gefühlsbewegungen ausdrückt. Die frühen Sprachtheoretiker übertrugen die Unterscheidung von reiner Mitteilung und Gefühlsausdruck auf die Sprache. Sie unterschieden zwischen den sachlich zutreffenden Benennungen und den (Gefühle zum Ausdruck bringenden, einen bewegten Vortrag bewirkenden) Stilfiguren, die sie mit demselben Begriff wie die Tanzfiguren bezeichneten: σχήματα.

## 3. Beziehungen zur Philosophie

Den größten Einfluß auf die Entwicklung der Sprachwissenschaft hat die Philosophie. Schon die vorsokratischen Philosophen erforschten die Sprache, und zwar als Ausdruck des Denkens, als Instrument zur Bezeichnung der Dinge und als Mittel der Wahrheitsfindung (→ Art. 53). Insbesondere bewegte sie eine erkenntnistheoretische Frage: Stehen die Wörter in einem logischen Zusammenhang mit den Dingen, die sie bezeichnen, sind sie den Dingen gleichsam naturhaft zugewachsen, enthalten sie geradezu die Definitionen der Dinge, oder ist die Beziehung zwischen Worten und Dingen zufällig und bar jeglicher inneren Logik? Im ersten Fall könnte man durch Untersuchung des Wortlauts zum Wesen der Dinge und zur wahren Erkenntnis gelangen, im zweiten Fall wäre dem Philosophen diese Möglichkeit versagt. Die beiden Positionen werden mit den Begriffen φύσει und νόμῳ (bzw. θέσει) belegt, einem Gegensatzpaar, das auch in anderen philosophischen Fragestellungen eine Rolle spielte (so in der Frage der Geltung der Gesetze, des Wesens der Sittlichkeit, des Wesens der Götter) und die wie keine andere das frühe Denken prägte (vgl. Steinthal 1890: 44ff.; Heinimann 1965).

Bedeutendster Niederschlag des Streites um die Geltung der Namen für die Dinge ist der platonische Dialog Kratylos. Die Methode, die darin zur Wortdeutung und Wesenserfassung benutzt wird, ist die Etymologie. Scherzhaft oder im Ernst, die Forscher sind sich in dieser Frage nicht einig, werden zahllose Etymologien durchgespielt: θεός "Gott" soll mit θεῖν "laufen", οὐσία "Sein" mit ὠθέω/ὤσω "stoßen" zusammenhängen, Ἀπόλλων aus ἀεὶ βάλλων "ständig werfend" zusammengesetzt sein. Durch die Etymologie gelangt man zu den Urworten und zu dem semantischen Wert der Einzellaute, die ursprünglich, wie man glaubt, onomatopoetischen Charakter haben: so drückte der Laut *r* das Bewegte aus, *i* das Dünne, *l* das Glatte, *n* das Innere. Als Nebenprodukt zur Untersuchung der στοιχεῖα, der Urlaute, ergibt sich die Klassifizierung der Laute in Vokale, Mutae und sog. 'mittlere Laute', worunter die Liquidae zu verstehen sind.

Die Etymologien spiegeln das heraklitische Weltbild wider (vgl. die Etymologie von οὐσία, s. o.), und es scheint, als ob Heraklit oder einer seiner Schüler sie in den Dienst der Bestätigung seiner Weltauffassung gestellt habe. Sokrates/Platon distanziert sich zum

Ende des Dialogs von dieser Art der Sprachbetrachtung, die er zuvor selbst durchexerziert hat: Dem Namensgeber seien gute und treffende Bezeichnungen gelungen, in anderen Fällen habe er versagt, weil er keinen Einblick in das Reich der Ideen gehabt habe und deshalb das eigentliche Wesen der Dinge nicht habe erfassen können. Die Wahrheit sei also nicht durch Wortuntersuchungen zu finden, sie liege nicht im Einzelwort (ὄνομα), sondern im Satz (λόγος), bzw. im Urteil, d. h. in der richtigen Verbindung der Begriffe miteinander.

Die sprachlichen Forschungen der frühen Philosophen, wie sie sich vor allem im platonischen *Kratylos* niederschlagen, haben die Sprachtheorie späterer Zeiten tiefgreifend beeinflußt. Die Etymologie ist ein wichtiger Grundbestandteil der antiken Sprachtheorie geblieben. Wie im *Kratylos* spielte darin die Zusammensetzung eine größere Rolle als die Ableitung; man wird kritisch einwenden müssen, daß durch die Betrachtungsweise des *Kratylos* die Erkenntnis von Wortverwandtschaften, Wortfamilien, zusammengehörigen Flexionsformen und von Derivationsregeln eher erschwert als gefördert wurde. Die Frage der Beziehung zwischen bezeichnetem Gegenstand und bezeichnendem Wortlaut ist ein Grundproblem der antiken (und der heutigen) Sprachforschung geblieben. Das Gegensatzpaar νόμῳ (θέσει) – φύσει hat in der hellenistischen Sprachtheorie, übertragen auf das Problem der Sprachentstehung, eine große Dynamik entfaltet. Zudem ist die Onomatopoietik als Weg zur Erklärung der Sprachentstehung, des ursprünglichen Verhältnisses von Gegenstand und Wortlaut und als stilistische Erscheinung weiterhin (bis heute) von größter Bedeutung.

Nach Platon bleiben die denkbar engen Beziehungen der Sprachforschung zur Philosophie bestehen. Auch Aristoteles untersucht die Sprache, wie die Vorsokratiker, Sokrates und Platon, vor allem unter philosophischen (und zusätzlich rhetorischen und poetologischen) Fragestellungen; ebenso wie die sprachtheoretischen Texte Platons wirken sich jedoch gerade auch seine Untersuchungen auf die Grammatik im engeren Sinn der Erforschung der Binnenstruktur von Sprache aus. Wenn man von der voraristotelischen Sprachforschung sagen kann, daß sie vor allem der Lautlehre und der Semantik bleibende Anstöße gab, so führen die Gedanken des Aristoteles vor allem in den Bereich der Syntax. Auch Aristoteles geht es um die Frage, auf welcher Ebene des Sprechens und Denkens die Wahrheit anzusiedeln sei. Ebenso wie Platon sieht er sie nicht in den Begriffen liegen, sondern in deren Verbindung miteinander. Diese muß die richtige Beziehung der Dinge zueinander zum Ausdruck bringen. Dabei unterscheidet Aristoteles wenig zwischen Wörtern, Vorstellungen und Außendingen: er stellt sich deren Verhältnis zueinander, im Unterschied zur stoischen Sprachtheorie, sehr einfach vor: Sprache ist eine Spiegelung oder eine unmittelbare Akolouthie des Denkens. Die Untersuchung des richtigen Denkens kann also über die Erforschung der Sprache erfolgen. In der aristotelischen Lehre von den Urteilen und Schlüssen wird demzufolge die richtige Beziehung zweier bzw. dreier Begriffe (ὅροι) zueinander erforscht. Die πρότασις, der Satz als Teil des Schlusses, gibt das Verhältnis zweier Dinge und, als dessen Spiegelung, zweier Begriffe wider. Sie besteht aus zwei Teilen: dem, worüber etwas ausgesagt ist (καθ' οὗ κατηγορεῖται, in späterer Terminologie ὄνομα), und dem Ausgesagten (καθηγορούμενον, später ῥῆμα). In der Lehre von den Schlüssen ihrerseits geht es um das richtige Verhältnis von drei Dingen oder Sachverhalten (Sokrates, Mensch, sterblich) zueinander. Man sieht, wie diese Untersuchungen, die zunächst die logische Richtigkeit intendieren, tief in die Lehre vom Satz, ja in die Textgrammatik als der Lehre von der Kohärenz von Sätzen, hineinreichen. Bisher wurde von den Forschern manchmal übersehen, daß bei Aristoteles rudimentär auch bereits die Lehre von den semantischen Merkmalen angelegt ist. Aristoteles faßt die Worte 'fliegen', 'schwimmen', 'gehen', 'kriechen' zusammen, weil sie alle eine πορεία, eine Fortbewegung, bezeichnen – heute würden wir sagen: alle ein gemeinsames semantisches Merkmal haben (*part. animal.* 1,1 639a19).

Richtungsweisend für spätere sprachtheoretische Forschungen ist auch die Poetik des Aristoteles (→ Art. 54). Die Kapitel 20 und 21 berühren unmittelbar grammatische Gegenstände. Im 20. Kapitel behandelt Aristoteles die μέρη τῆς λέξεως, im Kapitel 21 schließt sich eine Gliederung des Wortschatzes nach morphologischen (einfache und zusammengesetzte Wörter) und stilistischen Kriterien an. In stilistischer Hinsicht unterscheidet Aristoteles zwischen dem ὄνομα κύριον (dem eigentlich zutreffenden Begriff) und dem ὄνομα ξενικόν (dem uneigentlichen, fremdartigen statt des passenden Wortes). Die ξενικά gliedert er, wie Ax (1987: 25ff.) zeigt, nach den vier Änderungskategorien, die später in unterschiedliche Bereiche der Grammatik und Rhetorik Eingang gefunden haben: die Figurenlehre, die Lehre von den barbarismi und solecismi, die Etymologie, die Flexionslehre, die Orthographie und die Dialektologie. Sie bezeichnen dort jeweils die Abweichung vom Richtigen und von der sprachlichen Norm (in lateinischen Begriffen: *adiectio*, *detractio*, *immutatio*, *transmutatio*) – ein besonders eindrucksvolles Beispiel für den Sachverhalt, daß sich die antiken τέχναι gegenseitig befruchten und daß grammatische Kategoriensysteme aus anderen Disziplinen übernommen wurden.

Auch als die Grammatik in hellenistischer Zeit der Philosophie zu entwachsen und sich zu verselbständigen beginnt, bleiben die Beziehungen zur Philosophie denkbar eng. Gerade der bedeutendste Zweig der hellenistischen Philosophie, die Stoa, interessiert sich weiterhin, und zwar in besonderem Maße, für die Sprache. Die Logik, die Lehre vom richtigen Denken und Sprechen, ist neben der Physik (Naturphilosophie) und der Ethik integrierender Bestandteil der Philosophie. Hauptgliederungspunkte des logischen Teiles (λογικὸν μέρος) der Philosophie sind die Rhetorik und die Dialektik, wobei diese hinwiederum in die Lehre von den σημαινόμενα (den Begriffsinhalten der Wörter) und die Darstellung der σημαίνοντα (der Lautgestalt der Wörter) aufgegliedert ist (s. u.).

Im Vergleich mit den sprachlichen Untersuchungen der früheren Philosophie fallen in der Stoa, bei aller Übernahme früherer Probleme und Fragestellungen, umfangreichere gedankliche und begriffliche Differenzierungen und ein deutlicheres Interesse für innersprachliche (also im eigentlichen Sinn grammatikalische) Fragestellungen auf (→ Art. 55).

Die größere Differenzierung zeigt sich zunächst und vor allem in der Frage des Verhältnisses von Wort und Ding. Aristoteles und Platon kannten hier drei Faktoren, die allerdings in einem ganz unmittelbaren, unabgrenzbaren, Zusammenhang standen (Akolouthie): Dinge, Seeleneindrücke und deren unmittelbaren Ausdruck, das Wort. Die Stoiker unterscheiden (1) das zugrundeliegende Ding (ὑπάρχον), (2) die Vorstellung (ἔννοια), (3) die Vorstellung, insofern sie in einem Wort sprachlich ausgedrückt wird (σημαινόμενον) und (4) die reine Lautgestalt der sprachlich in einem Wort ausgedrückten Vorstellung (σημαῖνον, φωνή).

Ein weiteres Beispiel für die größeren Differenzierungsanstrengungen der Stoiker ist auf dem Gebiet der Etymologie zu erkennen. Die stoische Etymologie verfährt im allgemeinen durchaus noch im kratyleischen Sinn, geht jedoch insofern weiter, als sie die Bedeutungsübertragungskategorien systematisiert und klassifiziert.

Noch wichtiger ist der zweite o. g. Unterschied zu vorhergehenden Sprachforschungen. In der Entdeckung der φωνή, der Lautgestalt, bringen die Stoiker die Grammatik einen entscheidenden Schritt weiter. Jetzt geht der Blick nicht mehr nur auf die Außenbeziehungen, sondern auf die Binnenstruktur der Sprache. Der Gesamtaufbau der Sprache wird systematisch erforscht. Das ist ein Ansatz, der im περὶ φωνῆς τόπος bzw. in der περὶ φωνῆς τέχνη zu vielfältigen grammatischen Kategorien im eigentlichen Sinn führt: zur Beachtung der Redeteile (Wortarten), der Kasus, der transitiven und intransitiven, der persönlichen und unpersönlichen Verben, der Tempora und der Genera verbi sowie der Satzarten (zum Inhalt des stoischen περὶ φωνῆς τόπος s. neuerdings vor allem Schenkeveld 1990: 86ff.). Vom stoischen περὶ φωνῆς τόπος ist es nur noch ein kleiner Schritt zur τέχνη γραμματική mit ihren noch weitergehenden Differenzierungen und Klassifizierungen. Wie Pohlenz (1939: 190) feststellt, ist die neue Perspektive der stoischen und der späteren Sprachforscher der Zweisprachigkeit Zenons und Chrysipps zu verdanken. Der Gegensatz zur Struktur ihrer Muttersprache, des Semitischen, führte zu einem besonderen Interesse am Gesamtaufbau der Sprache und an einzelnen charakteristischen Erscheinungen (wie insbesondere dem griechischen Tempussystem).

Wie in der hellenistischen Sprachtheorie generell stehen zudem auch in der Stoa die Fragen der Sprachentstehung (φύσει oder θέσει, in Übertragung früherer Kategorien auf ein neues Thema) und der Kriterien der Sprachrichtigkeit (s. u.) im Vordergrund. Hierin unterscheidet sich der περὶ φωνῆς τόπος wenig von den späteren grammatischen Handbüchern.

Ein besonderes Wort ist zur Syntax der Stoa zu sagen. Frühere Forschungen erkennen hier den gleichen Mangel wie in der gesamten antiken Sprachtheorie, daß nämlich die antiken Grammatiker sich nicht aus den Fesseln einer rhetorischen und logisch-philosophischen Satzbetrachtung befreien konnten. Die Schrift Chrysipps περὶ συντάξεως stelle, wie man glaubte, ebenfalls überwiegend einen dialektischen, keinen grammatischen Traktat dar. Neuere Forschungen weisen auf Ansätze einer stoischen Syntax hin, die, in der Nachfolge der aristotelischen Lehre von den Schlüssen, an moderne Syntaxtheorien erinnert (s. Egli 1987: 107ff.).

## 4. Beziehungen zur Medizin

Wissenschaftstheoretisch nahm die Medizin im dritten Jahrhundert v. Chr. eine führende Position ein. Zwei medizinische Richtungen, die in ihrem Denken ihrerseits vielfältig durch die klassische und zeitgenössische Philosophie beeinflußt waren, standen sich gegenüber: die logische und die empirische Schule. Sie unterschieden sich in der Wissenschaftsauffassung und in der Frage der Erkenntnismethoden. Die logische Schule ging in der Frage der zu wählenden Heilverfahren deduktiv vor: die angemessene Therapie sei aus der Physiologie und aus der Humoralpathologie, der Lehre von den vier Körpersäften, herzuleiten. Die empirische Schule gewann ihre Grundsätze aus der Erfahrung. Sie entwickelte als methodisches Instrumentarium den sog. empirischen Dreifuß, der aus der Autopsie, dem literarischen Erfahrungsschatz (ἱστορία) und der Schlußfolgerung vom Bekannten zum ähnlichen Unbekannten (μετάβασις καθ'ὁμοιότητα) bestand.

Die Grammatiker der Zeit verstanden die wichtigsten Zweige ihrer Wissenschaft, die Diorthose (Herstellung des richtigen Wortlauts eines Autors) und den Hellenismos (Ermittlung der richtigen Sprechweise), als Heilverfahren. Der Begriff Diorthose für die Textherstellung ist eine medizinische Metapher. Er bezeichnet dort die Heilung eines beschädigten Körperteils durch Reposition (Einrenkung, Einrichtung). Es ist deshalb naheliegend, daß die Grammatiker ihre Erkenntnismethoden der Medizin entlehnten. Tatsächlich läßt sich auch in der Grammatik ein Streit zweier Schulen nachweisen, der krateteischen (stoischen) und der alexandrinischen Richtung. Der Richtungstreit der Grammatiker ist ein Abbild der Auseinandersetzungen innerhalb der Medizin. Krates lehnte sich an die logische Schule an: er versuchte, das deduktive Verfahren der logischen Ärzte auf die Homerdiorthose anzuwenden. Einzelne Entscheidungen zur Frage des richtigen homerischen Wortgebrauchs leitete er aus philosophischen Grundsätzen ab (s. Siebenborn 1976: 130; anders Mette 1952: 45ff.). Anders die Alexandriner: sie übernahmen die induktiven Erkenntnismethoden des empirischen Dreifußes und wandten sie zunächst auf die Diorthose an. Der medizinischen Autopsie entspricht dabei die Beobachtung des homerischen Sprachgebrauchs, der medizinischen ἱστορία die diorthotische ἱστορία (bzw. παράδοσις), d. h. die Anlehnung an die Textveränderungsvorschläge früherer Fachgelehrter, der medizinischen μετάβασις, d. h. dem Analogieschluß vom Bekannten zum ähnlichen Unbekannten, die grammatische Analogie (ἀναλογία). Ihr entsprechend lasse sich z. B. die unbekannte Prosodie von πηλός aus der Analogie zu πηρός erschließen.

Eben dieselben Methoden, die zur Herstellung des richtigen Dichtertextes führen, lassen sich auch in der Frage des ἑλληνισμός, der richtigen Lautgestalt der Worte des aktuellen Sprachgebrauchs, anwenden. Diese ist wie die Diorthose der vielfältig durch die mündliche Tradition veränderten Dichtertexte zu einem Hauptanliegen der hellenistischen Grammatiker geworden. Sie sind bestrebt, die Sprache zu normieren und bei mehreren miteinander konkurrierenden Varianten der Umgangssprache eine als die richtige auszuwählen, die anderen zu verwerfen. Als Kriterien bieten sich die Prinzipien an, in denen man ohne weiteres eine Übertragung des empirischen Dreifußes erkennen kann: die Analogie (ἀναλογία), die gebildete Umgangssprache (συνήθεια) und der frühere (literarische) Sprachgebrauch anerkannter Autoren (ἱστορία, παράδοσις). Erweitert wird dieser Katalog um die Etymologie. Ebenso wie für den ἑλληνισμός, das richtige Sprechen, gilt der Kanon auch für die ὀρθογραφία. Dort ist allerdings die συνήθεια, die zur Ermittlung der richtigen Schreibweise nicht herangezogen werden kann, durch die διάλεκτος ersetzt: Dialektformen können in manchen Fällen Aufschluß über die Orthographie eines Wortes geben, besonders in den Fällen zweifelhafter ι- oder ει-Schreibung: daß εἶναι in der ersten Silbe digraphisch geschrieben werden muß, läßt sich z. B. aus der äolischen Form ἔμμεναι erschließen. Der so entstandene viergliedrige Kriterienkanon ist in unterschiedlicher Terminologie bis zum Ausgang der Antike vielfach überliefert.

## 5. Ausblick

Der ursprünglich enge Zusammenhang der griechischen Sprachtheorie mit anderen Disziplinen hat aller Sprachforschung zunächst eine große Weite und Tiefe verliehen. Die Anlehnung an weiter fortgeschrittene Wissenschaftszweige brachte es mit sich, daß Sprache in wechselnden Aspekten als künstlerisches Ausdrucksmittel, als Instrument der persuasiven Beeinflussung, als Mittel der Wahrheitsfindung und der Seinserfassung und als historisch gewordenes und aktuell funktionierendes Verständigungsmittel betrachtet werden konnte. Dabei standen die Außenbeziehungen der Sprache und der sprachlichen Zeichen im Vordergrund des Interesses. Die Besinnung auf die Binnenstruktur der Sprache, wie sie sich im Hellenismus im Rahmen des grammatischen Lehrbuchs durchsetzte und zu einer neuen Disziplin, eben der τέχνη γραμματική, führte, war notwendig und sinnvoll: sie führte zu einer systematischen Erforschung und Erfassung sprachlicher Gegebenheiten und entfaltete den Grundbestand der auch heute noch weitgehend benutzten grammatikalischen Kategorien; andererseits jedoch bedeutete sie eine Verarmung: in der Trennung von der Rhetorik und der Philosophie ging im Verlauf der Grammatikgeschichte der ursprünglich weite Sprachbegriff verloren. Das wird im Vergleich der antiken Grammatiken und selbst des tiefsten römischen sprachtheoretischen Denkers, Varros, mit den tiefschürfenden Sprachreflexionen des Aristoteles und der Stoa (die leider nur sehr fragmentarisch erhalten sind) unmittelbar ersichtlich. In Abgrenzung von Rhetorik und Philosophie haben sich die antiken Grammatiker seit der alexandrinischen Zeit im wesentlichen auf die Lehre vom einzelnen sprachlichen Zeichen und dessen Veränderungen sowie auf die Untersuchung der Wortverbindungen (Junkturen) beschränkt. Die Lehre vom Satz überließen sie der Philosophie und der Rhetorik (s. o.). Das hatte die bekannten Auswirkungen: die Frage der Binnenstruktur des Satzes, der Zusammensetzung aus Satzgliedern und deren hierarchischer Ordnung, konnte in der Antike niemals befriedigend gelöst werden. Auch Ansätze zur Erfassung der Struktur satzübergreifender sprachlicher Gebilde konnten keineswegs in der antiken Grammatik, wohl aber in der Rhetorik entwickelt werden. Die Lehre von der Funktionalität des sprachlichen Zeichens entstand ebenfalls in der Rhetorik, nicht in der antiken Grammatik. Erst die sprachtheoretischen Neueinsätze dieses Jahrhunderts, die unterschiedlichen Satzgrammatiken (vor allem zu nennen: die generative Transformationsgrammatik und die Valenz- bzw. Dependenzgrammatik), die Textgrammatik, die Textlinguistik und die Textpragmatik, konnten den ursprünglich weiten Sprachbegriff (zumindest teilweise) wieder einholen.

## 6. Bibliographie


Ax, Wolfram. 1984. *Laut, Stimme und Sprache. Studien zu drei Grundbegriffen der antiken Sprachtheorie.* Göttingen: Vandenhoeck & Ruprecht.

—. 1987. "Quadripertita ratio: Bemerkungen zur Geschichte eines aktuellen Kategoriensystems (adiectio – detractio – transmutatio – immutatio)". Taylor (1987: 17–40).

Derbolav, Josef. 1972. *Platons Sprachphilosophie im Kratylos und in den späteren Schriften.* Darmstadt: Wissenschaftliche Buchgesellschaft.

Egli, Urs. 1987. "Stoic Syntacs and Semantics". Taylor (1987: 107–232).

Gentinetta, Peter. 1961. *Zur Sprachbetrachtung bei den Sophisten und in stoisch-hellenistischer Zeit.* Winterthur: Keller.

Heinimann, Felix. 1965. *Nomos und Physis: Herkunft und Bedeutung einer Antithese im griechischen Denken des 5. Jahrhunderts.* Darmstadt: Wissenschaftliche Buchgesellschaft.

Pohlenz, Max. 1939. *Die Begründung der abendländischen Sprachlehre durch die Stoa.* Göttingen: Vandenhoeck & Ruprecht.

Mette, Hans Joachim. 1952. *Parateresis: Untersuchungen zur Sprachtheorie des Krates von Pergamon.* Halle: Niemeyer.

Schenkeveld, Dirk Marie. 1990. "Studies in the History of Ancient Lingistics. III. The Stoic τέχνη περὶ φωνῆς". *Mnemosyne* 53.86–108.

Siebenborn, Elmar. 1987. "Herkunft und Entwicklung des terminus technicus περίοδος". Taylor (1987: 229–249).

—. 1976. *Die Lehre von der Sprachrichtigkeit und ihren Kriterien.* Amsterdam: Gruener.

Steinthal, Heymann. 1890. *Geschichte der Sprachwissenschaft bei den Griechen und Römern.* Berlin: Dümmler. (Nachdruck der 2. Auflage, Hildesheim: Olms, 1971.)

Taylor, Daniel J., ed. 1987. *The History of Linguistics in the Classical Period.* Amsterdam & Philadelphia: Benjamins.


*Elmar Siebenborn, Essen (Deutschland)*

# 61. The impact of language studies on Greek society and education

1. Archaic and Classical Period (800–300 BC)
2. Hellenistic Period (300–30 BC) and Imperial Age (30 BC – end of Antiquity)
3. Bibliography

## 1. Archaic and Classical Period (800–300 BC)

### 1.1. Society

The origins of a systematic theory about Greek language are found in the efforts of philosophers and sophists to understand language and in the attempts of sophists and other teachers to explain poetical texts, specifically those of Homer, and to shape their findings into some teachable form. A similar concern can be detected among rhetoricians when they start to describe the language means by which a speaker will persuade his audience. These efforts contribute towards the gradual emergence of language research as a separate discipline but this does not come about before the end of the Hellenistic period. To describe the impact of language theory on Greek society of the Classical period is, therefore, almost equivalent to giving a survey of the role of philosophers, sophists and rhetoricians have in Greek society as far as aspects of language research are concerned. Such a survey is, in view of the sources, limited to Athenian society, with a few glances at other communities. The same restriction holds for Greek education. Finally, though philosophers, to take one instance, are part of society and for this reason their discussions on matters of language might be mentioned here, this will not be done. In this section attention will be paid to glimpses of language research detectable outside professional circles of rhetoricians, philosophers and sophists. Thus, not Protagoras' views on 'rightness of words' concern us here, but Aristophanes' use of these in his comedies. Interest in language is already manifest in the Homeric epics where the poet often explains the names and words he uses. Thus the very name *Odusseús* is thought to reflect both *odússomai* "to hate", and *odúromai* "to lament" (*Odyssee* 1.55; 62). The epics are an integral ingredient of Greek life but later more and more words need to be explained. Collections of 'glosses' are being made, in which etymology plays a big role (Herbermann 1991). In Aristophanes' earliest comedy, the *Banqueters*, an old father asks his son to explain Homeric glosses and the boy tests his father for his knowledge of legal terms (fr. 222 K.). The fact that in the theatre a discussion of Homeric glosses can be used to raise laughter not only shows education to be a perennial object to poke fun at but also betrays an important trait of Greek culture, the spirit of interpretation. At various levels Greeks like other people have to interpret texts and phenomena but in this society the outstanding position of the Homeric epics (Verdenius 1970) compels them, as it were, to pay more attention to interpreting, one of its consequences being a desire to understand language. At symposia friends are entertained by Homeric problems, at festivals professional reciters declaim parts of these texts and give an interpretation (Plato, *Ion*), political issues can be discussed in terms of what Homeric heroes did (Aeschines 3.185). Interpretation is also necessary in the case of oracles, a recurrent phenomenon in Greek society (Herodotus 7.140f.). These are put in epic language, a fact which makes the right interpretation more difficult. It should be said, however, that in contrast to the Romans with their strict formulas the Greeks are free in their use of language in hymns and prayers, and accordingly, they have no need for interpretation of formulaic prayers in an antiquated language, for these do not exist. Different, of course, is the interpretation of an Orphic Theogony found in a very early papyrus of the 4th century BC (the Derveni papyrus, *ZPE* 47, 1982). Here a religious text is being commented upon and one finds examples of paraphrasis, explanation of single words and even a grammatical term, *huperbatón*, used in order to clarify a specific line. Another field of interpretation are the laws of Solon and other ancient law-givers. These laws are written in Old Attic and many terms have later become unknown or got a different meaning. In the context of a case on slander Lysias (*Or.* 10) explains some such old words, thereby touching on the problem of intent and letter of the law but also expressing the otherwise important view that notions remain the same whereas words can change. Of course, the need for interpretation is not dependent on the existence of written texts, for orally transmitted epics already elicit a similar response and even when literacy in Athens has become more widespread oral transmission and explanation are still strong (Thomas 1989). However, to the degree that written records and texts become more common, the greater the impulse to use tools of interpretation will have been. Written texts in ancient Greece stimulate this tendency also by their form because on stones and in papyri Greek is always written without blanks between words and without accents. Also after introduction of a new alphabet, the Ionic one, in 403/2 the usage continues. This unbroken writing generates questions how to distinguish between words and one understands that e. g. Aristotle (*Poetics* 25) has a category of Homeric problems which are due to accentuation. Concern for language *per se* is manifest in the efforts of the sophists and philosophers. Their studies are multifarious and cause much discussion in Athens (Sluiter 1990: 1–13). One indication is Herodotus' report on a language experiment by an Egyptian pharaoh who wishes to determine which people are the older one, Egyptians or Phrygians and settles the matter by a language test (*Hist.* 2.2). In the *Clouds* 658ff. (423 BC) Aristophanes exploits Protagoras' research into the connection between meaning and grammatical gender. The sophist looks for correctness of diction in form (*orthoépeia*) and criticizes (playfully or not) Homer for combining words like *mē̃nis* "wrath" and *pḗlēx* "helmet", notwithstanding their typically masculine sense, with feminine adjectival forms. In this comedy Socrates, introduced here as a true sophist, instructs a pupil not to use any longer the common word *alektruṓn* for both "cock" and "hen" but to use for "cock" *aléktōr* (a poetical word) and to introduce the neologism *alektrúaina* for the female species. Another sophist, Prodicus, is very much concerned with the "correctness of words" (*orthótēs onomátōn*) as to their meaning and differentiates between apparent synonyms. Aristophanes uses this method in his *Frogs* (1181ff.). The famous passage in Thucydides' *Histories* on changes in verbal evaluation produced by the internal troubles on Corcyra and by which e. g. prudent delay became to be considered specious cowardice (*Hist.* 3.82.4, see Wilson 1982), can be seen as due to philosophical concern with the contrast between conventional meaning and the true nature of things. This conflict, shortly indicated by the couple *ónoma/prã̄gma* "word/thing" and closely related with that of *dóxa/alḗtheia* "appearance/true nature", is found in tragedy too. Europides has many allusions to it in his *Helen* (42–43; 66–67 etc., cf. Kannicht 1969: 57ff.) when he is exploiting the dramatic possibilities of a real Helen and her phantom. Related to this couple is that of "convention/nature" (*nómos/phúsis*). The question whether language is a product of human convention or a natural growth, is part of the bigger question about human culture versus nature. It is being hotly debated in professional circles of the 5th and 4th century (Di Cesare 1991) and we hear echoes hereof in several writings of the Hippocratic corpus (Heinimann 1945: 86ff., 157ff.), e. g. when the author of *The Art* (of Medicine, 2) asserts that this art is existing because it is based on a real essence, not because it has a name, "for it is absurd – nay impossible – to hold that real essences spring from names. For names are conventions and real essences are not conventions, but the offspring of nature".

### 1.2. Education

Our knowledge about the educational system in the Classical period and the role of language training therein is rather scanty. We know that in Classical Athens children go to some school though private teaching is still very common (some vase paintings have interesting scenes from schools, e. g. in Schubart 1961: 135–137). At school pupils learn from their master (*grammatistḗs*) to write and read, they can recite poems and at a later stage some exegesis is taught. When about fifteen years old, the boys may go to a sophist for further education (Marrou 1945: 68–98). This training is very much focused on listening to and preparing model speeches, such as Gorgias' *Palamedes* and Antiphon's *Tetralogies*, by which the pupils are also trained in using types of argument. In the 4th century more systematization enters the system. The first handbooks by sophists on rhetoric are now written and one can have an impression of what these are like from Anaximenes' *Rhetorica ad Alexandrum.* In the schools of Isocrates, Plato (Academy) and Aristotle (Lyceum) attention to formal aspects of language is very much present, both in preparing speeches and when studying logic (Kennedy 1994).

### 1.3. Oratory and dialectics

Orators in courtroom, assembly and festive gatherings are exploiting the possibilities of Greek language and their art of persuasion illustrates the awareness of the Greeks of what they can do with language. Thus the use of prose rhythm (alternation of combinations of long and short syllables at the end of a colon and period), the construction of periods, Demosthenes' avoidance of collocation of more than three short syllables, avoidance of poetical words in prose speech, or, inversely, its deliberate application in order to have a certain effect, the extensive usage of Gorgianic *schēmata* like *isókōlon* and *homoeotéleuton*, as well as the warnings against an excessive use of them, all these data should be mentioned as indicative of language awareness (Kennedy 1994). Influence from linguistic views in a more restricted sense can be found in the use of grammatical terms such as *súndesmos* "conjunction", in both *Rhet. ad Alexandrum* (25) and Aristotle's *Rhetoric* (3.6). This research is explicitly manifest in dialectics, Though dialectics are discussed elsewhere, here specific attention may be drawn to one off-shoot of dialectics, the public debating contests. There the danger of fallacious arguments and paralogisms is always present. Plato's *Euthydemus* gives an example of the kind of false argumentation used by two sophists and Aristotle devotes a separate treatise to methods of refuting these apparent but not real proofs. Having discussed in his *Topics* right ways of argumentation he then switches to fallacious arguments in his *On Sophistical Refutations*. Here a main distinction is that between fallacies due to language and those independent of language. Those dependent on language are subdivided into six types (165b23ff.) such as homonymy, amphiboly and the form of expression type. This kind of treatment of fallacies will have a long tradition, is found again in the Stoic theory of ambiguity and the usage of grammatical distinctions is apparent everywhere (Atherton 1993).

### 1.4. The social status of the language researcher

To the Greeks of the Classical Period to spend time as a citizen on language research is quite different from earning money by teaching Greek. On the whole, the upper class Athenians think to be active in the *epistēmai eleuthérioi* (liberal arts, Aristotle, *Pol.* 1137b15) as a professional is banausic, not worthy of a free citizen. The latter will spend attention on these fields of knowledge in so far as he has free time from his social-political activities. This attitude does not hinder a rich Athenian to invite a famous sophist into his home and to pay sometimes heavy sums for his teaching. But these sophists are non-Athenians and cannot participate in the political life of the city. A genuine Athenian will therefore not consider the possibility to be a sophist himself (Christes 1975: 25ff.). About the status of a *grammatistḗs*, a man lower in the hierarchy of education, we have no explicit testimonies but it must have been low.

## 2. Hellenistic Period (300–30 BC) and Imperial Age (30 BC–end of Antiquity)

### 2.1. General background

The situation for language research about 300 BC is different from that in 300 AD and both in education and in society its role has changed, but not so fundamentally that the Hellenistic period should have a discussion separate from the Imperial age. The enormous new territories conquered by Alexander the Great and his successors are administrated by Greek speaking people, who keep to their language even under the Roman emperors. One consequence is a growing awareness of being Greek and another one the wish of having a Greek education, which implies reading and knowing the Classics (Said 1991). For the cultured Romans of the first centuries BC and AD, too, knowing Greek language and literature is a requisite.

### 2.2. Education

The prevalent outline of education (Marrou 1960: 218ff.; 389ff.) distinguishes several successive stages: first comes the elementary school (*grammatodidaskaleîon*), where the teacher (*grammatistḗs*) instructs his pupils in writing, reading and some arithmetic. When about twelve years old, the pupils go to secondary school. Here the *grammatikós* teaches grammar and literature, especially poetry; finally comes the *rhḗtōr* (also called *sophistḗs*), whose instruction is in public speech and the study of the classic orators. This third stage may also include attendance at schools of philosophers or further instruction in arithmetic and geometry. This picture is in general acceptable but runs the risk of being built too much on modern parallels. There are enough indications that e. g. boys of rich parents often skip the first stage, go to the *grammatikós* and learn from him the elementary subjects also, and it seems that children of the lower classes attend the *grammatodidaskaleĩon* and stop then (Kaster 1983; for a scene in relief from Neumagen see Schubart 1961: 143). In this contribution the tripartite division will be kept for reasons of a simple arrangement (more information and modern discussion in Schneider 1967: 135ff.; Pleket 1981 and Kaster 1988: 32ff.). Inevitably this contribution focuses on language instruction in schools but a large part of the time there is given to training in music and athletics. For instance, more prizes awarded in competitions for the latter subjects are known than for reading or recital of epic texts (Nilsson 1955: 42ff.). Nevertheless, the part reserved for literary education is considerable.

2.2.1. Instruction in reading and writing starts with single letters, then continues with all possible combinations of consonants and vowels and by way of syllables and single words ends with sentences. The pupil is finally able to read some texts, much of which he has to know by heart. The part of grammar at this stage is not well-known. If we follow Dionysius of Halicarnassus (*On Demosthenes* 52, cf. *On composition* 25), pupils first learn a complete grammar, containing all the parts of speech with all their attributes before they start reading and writing. This description looks implausible and papyri containing children's school exercises give a different picture with grammar coming later (Ziebarth 1914: 124ff.; Marrou 1960: 200ff.). One should not think light of the pupil's performances because of the difficulties inherent to *scriptio continua* with no accents and some punctuation only, while to him the Greek of the text is both poetical and antiquated and the further away he is in time from the originals the more changes in pronunciation occur (e. g. iotacism by which *ē*, *u*, *ei* and *oi* sound like an *i*). For this reason one can understand that among the 'parts of *grammatikḗ*' distinguished by Dionysius Thrax the very first one concerns "skill in reading with due attention to prosodic features" (*GG* I: 1, 3). The historian Polybius rightly draws attention to the admiration of an illiterate man for a boy reading a book (10.47.8).

2.2.2. The explanation of poetical texts, which comes at the next stage of schooling, concerns the meaning of individual words and their etymology; information on characters, places, histories etc. is given and moral interpretation is not being neglected. The part of linguistic instruction is important. Here belongs the second part of the list given by Dionysius of Halicarnassus and mentioned above:

"[When we learn grammar properly, we begin by learning by heart the names of the elements of sound, which we call *letters*. Then we learn how they are written and what they sound like. When we have discovered this, we learn how they combine to form syllables, and how these behave]. Having mastered this, we learn about the parts of speech – I means nouns, verbs, conjunctions, and their properties, the shortening and lengthening of syllables and the high and low pitch of accents; genders, cases, numbers, moods, and countless other related things." (*On Demosthenes* 52, tr. Usher).

The reason why this elementary instruction in language theory is given in the context of poetical exegesis is first a matter of priority: poetry comes in the curriculum before prose, which is studied under the *rhḗtōr*. Behind this fact lies a cultural condition: poetry, especially that of Homer, dominates the Greek culture of the Classical and Hellenistic period and this kind of literature is therefore the first to be taught at school, which tradition is being maintained in later times. The connection between exegesis of poetry and knowledge of language theory is apparent from the first rough sketch of a grammar in Aristotle's *Poetics* (20–21), and also from the *Téchnē grammatikḗ* of Dionysius Thrax (1–6). There the second part of grammar is called "interpretation, taking note of the *poiētikoì trópoi* found in the text" (*GG* I: 1, 1). These *trópoi* are called by Tauriscus *grammatikoì trópoi* (S. E. *Adv. Math.* 1.249) and appear to be 'poetical manners of expression' in a very wide sense, not the literary tropes only (see Schenkeveld 1991). A later development is the distinction between tropes and figures. This segment of literary expression is usually seen as part of rhetorical instruction and indeed it is found there also, but one should not forget that the handbooks on tropes and figures as published in Spengel's *Rhetores graeci* III, e. g. Tryphon, *De tropis*, first and foremost belong to the domain of the *grammatikós*.

2.2.3. At the end of his stay at the grammarian's the pupil is introduced to the production of *progumnásmata*, elementary exercises of composition. In principle these fall under the teaching of the rhetorician (thus Quintilian 1.9) but at some time in the Hellenistic period grammarians encroach on the domain of their successors. Here the pupil learns an active use of language. Later he goes to the *rhḗtōr*, who reads with him the orators and teaches rhetoric. As far as language theory is concerned, here explicit instruction seems absent but implicit application of grammatifal rules is present everywhere. Thus when dealing with types of style (*aretaì léxeōs*, Latin *virtutes dicendi*) the teacher will discuss tropes and figures and come across metaphors, synecdoche and similar tropes but also those figures which involve principles of grammatical composition, such as *huperbatón*, *asúndeton* and *élleipsis*, and when instructing his pupils in the *status* theory he will come across one subtype concerning the difference between intent and letter of the law (see also section 1.1.)

2.2.4. Thus the pupils — a small segment of the male Greek youth only —, have the possibility of obtaining a thorough knowledge of Greek literature and language when they stay all the courses, for they read epic (parts of Homer), tragedy (Euripides), comedy (Menander), fables (Aesop), history (Herodotus, Thucydides), oratory (Demosthenes and other orators), make exercises and are trained in public speech. However, their knowledge of the Greek language system is still elementary: sets of rules are given in the handbooks (*téchnai, artes*), which the pupils have to know by heart. The structure of these books is mostly uniform: letter, syllable, word and sentence are shortly mentioned, defined and some examples are given. The number of parts of speech is referred to and all parts get a definition and examples. Their *parepómena* (*accidentia*) are summed up and illustrated, and sometimes quotations from Homer or another author are given (Wouters 1979: 33ff.). Exercises go through all possible (and impossible) forms of verbs and nouns, e. g. the words *ho philósophos Puthagóras* are declined in all cases and numbers, the dual included (Nilsson 1955: 14) and the verb *túptō* is conjugated for all tenses, moods, persons, numbers and diatheses, here again non-existent forms included (*GG* I: 1, 125). Having painstakingly assembled from their texts all kinds of grammatical forms grammarians try to formulate general rules of declension and conjugation (*kanónes*). Their number continuously increases because the level of generality is still too specific — a Varronian approach of the verb (Hovdhaugen 1982: 68ff.) is lacking on the Greek side. Another matter is the neglect of syntax in the handbooks; it is often dealt with in rhetorical context but then as a facet of literary composition. If syntactic matters are discussed, they concern question like: "With which case is this verb construed?" (thus e. g. Moeris Atticista). From the so-called *Epimerismoí* (*Partitiones*) we get an idea of how pupils are taught to apply their grammatical knowledge to a poetical text. When reading a Greek text written in *scriptio continua*, a pupil should first apply the method of partition (*merismós*) and so separate the individual words with the correct accents and punctuation. Partition is used at a higher level of grammatical knowledge also and is now the classification of parts of speech with their accidents. This method of instruction is known from the attack of Sextus Empiricus (2nd century AD) on the grammarians (*M.* I, 159ff.), from which it appears that pupils first read the words and analyze the metre, then partition the text into the separate parts of speech ('parsing'). This procedure is also called *epimerismós*. The form of these *epimerismoí* often is that of question and answer (*erōtapókrisis*) and follows the lines of the text (*Epimerismoì tē̃s Álpha Homḗrou Iliádos* in *An. Par.* III, 294ff.) or are arranged alphabetically (*Homḗrou Merismoí* in *An. Ox.* 1). A common structure is that of "part of speech, etymology, flexion/conjugation with reference to the *kanṓn* the word belongs to, and meaning" (Glück 1967: 23ff.; 31ff.). The existing *Epimerismoí* are all of a late date (5th century AD and later) but they reflect a much earlier didactic method as we can see from Epictetus (50—130 AD), *Diss.* 2.19.7.

2.2.5. As self-appointed guardians of language (*custodes Latini sermonis*, Seneca *Ep.* 95.65) the grammarians protect the language against corruption (Kaster 1988: 11ff.). A grammarian is, by nature or profession, inclined to make observations and to put these into rules, a procedure which inevitably runs the danger of maintaining the *status quo.* But anxiety about correct Greek is already apparent at the time of sophists (see section 1.), is also found in Aristotle's discussion of *hellēnismós* (*Rhet.* 3.5) and Theophrastus makes this aspect the first *aretḗ léxeōs* (virtue of style), a requirement to which all speakers and writers should comply (Kennedy 1994: 85). Among the figures of style grammarians and rhetoricians separate one group of *figurae grammaticae* (Quintilian 9.3.2ff.), those collocations of words which infringe upon rules of ordinary syntax but are accepted because of the authority of their author, their old date or some other reason. Quintilian compares these to faulty expression (*vitia*) and Dionysius of Halicarnassus speaks of *soloikophaneĩs schẽmatismoí* (constructions bordering on solecisms, *On Dinarchus* 8). Mistakes against the Greek are usually classified as *barbarismós* and *soloikismós* according to the criterium whether the fault involves one word or more (S. E. *M.* 1.210, see Siebenborn 1976: 35f.; Sluiter 1990: 23n.). Sometimes inexact language (*akurología*) is also mentioned as a fault but mostly in the context of a discussion on lucidity (*saphẽneia*, *perspicuitas*) (D. H. *On Lysias* 4, cf. Quintilian 8.2.3f.). Sextus (*M.* I, 169ff.) attacks orthographic studies of grammarians and gives an impression of which problems they discuss: should one write *euchálinon* with an *iõta* only or with the diphthong *ei* and does the *bẽta* in the word *óbrimos* belong to the first or to the second syllable (Siebenborn 1976: 38ff.). Later on Sextus also discusses what are to him inanities of grammarians in the field of barbarism and solecism (1.209ff.). Criteria of *hellẽnismós* are *analogía* (a set of acknowledged grammatical rules), *sunẽtheia* (ordinary usage) and *parádosis* (literary tradition, particularly as evident in the works of the great writers of the past). Especially the third criterion shows the conservative character of many linguistic studies: if one can point out a parallel in an ancient writer one's usage of a particular form or construction may be excused. This tendency can lead to heated exchanges as Aulus Gellius' *Noctes Atticae* many times show (Kaster 1988: 50ff.).

This concern for pure Greek should be kept apart, at least for its beginnings, from the classicistic return to Classical Attic, the Atticism, which comes up in the 1st century BC and is very much alive in the following centuries (Gelzer 1978; Schenkeveld 1994: 202f.). Then the anxiety for pure Greek comes together with that for Attic Greek. Hence e. g. the distinction between 'Attic' and 'Hellenic' in the list of words discussed by Moeris (see 2.1.4.), and one may compare Lucian's parody *The Solecist* (2nd century AD)., but this concern is not general for a work like Ammonius' *On differences between related words* (1st century BC or AD) rather discusses exact meanings of words.

2.2.6. Not connected with the regular curriculum but in some sense still a part of education is the language instruction at the *Mouseĩon* and similar foundations for scholarship in the Greco-Roman world. Instituted by Ptolemy I (about 300 BC) the Museum at Alexandria brings together men of letters and many scientists, who are devoted to the cult of the Muses and live in the precincts of the royal palace. The Museum is first maintained by the Ptolemies and later by the Roman emperors. Among its members are famous grammarians such as Aristarchus and Dionysius Thrax. At the end of the 4th century AD this foundation is abolished (Gross 1969). We do not hear of any obligation to lecture but in the biographies of many scholars 'teachers' as well as 'pupils' are mentioned; therefore, we may assume the existence of some fellowship of masters and disciples. Dionysius Thrax is one of Aristarchus' pupils and again Dionysius is the teacher of other famous grammarians such as Tyrannion and Asclepiades of Myrlea (Pfeiffer 1968: 98, 266, 272). The Museum has been of great importance to the research of Greek language and although the contents of this research is being treated elsewhere, it is right to mention this establishment in the part on education. Other Hellenistic centres of scholarship are found in Pergamum, where the Attalids (3rd/2nd century BC) promoted scholarly research, at Rhodes – Dionysius Thrax is teaching there after leaving Alexandria – and Athens. In the Imperial era Alexandria and Athens keep their fame, and Rome, Constantinople, Antioch and other cities have rival foundations.

2.3. The social status of the grammarian

From the start of the Hellenistic period onwards one can discern a growing respect among the cultured people and the authorities for the grammarian and his activities, though he will never reach the level of respectability the rhetor/sophist reaches. In this period cities and countries may well send a rhetor or a philosopher to Rome to plead their cause before the Senate, but we do not hear that a grammarian is chosen for this task. In later Antiquity, however, grammarians will occasionally serve as public spokesmen or conduits of patronage, as is the case with a certain Nicocles of Sparta, who is active in Constantinople and enjoys much influence under the reign of Julian (Kaster 1988: 203ff.). The status of the professional is still thought to be impaired because he works for money (Christes 1975: 114ff.). But on the whole this fact is not held against the *grammatikoí*, who at least have the distinction of belonging to the cultured people and being therefore separate from the big masses (Olympiodorus, *Comm. Alcib.* 1.95.17ff. West.). Thus grammarians, like other professionals, may get immunities from taxation as a token of the emperor's goodwill (*Dig.* 50.4.11 and Kaster 1988: 223ff.) – but not the *grammatodidáskalos* (Dig. 50.5.2) – and many of them carry titles of respectability. A list of grammarians known from the period between 250 and 560 AD is to be found in Kaster (198: 233ff.).

2.4. Influence on society

2.4.1. The years a pupil spends with grammatical studies, which merge into those at the rhetorician's, cannot but shape his mind and impart him an approach he will apply in other fields of knowledge and activity. The result of all these studies is "an essentially language-oriented scientific paradigm", also called "philological paradigm" (Sluiter 1995: 522, 533–534). This bookish attitude is manifest as a rhetorical strategy in studies on medicine and on the Bible and in juridical works. When, for instance, Galen takes an inaccurate use of nouns and verbs in an aphorism of Hippocrates as an argument against its authenticity (*In Hipp. Aphorismos comm* 7.69, 18A.183f. K.) he is of the opinion that the language of the great physician is in principle faultless. This does not mean that his usage recommended as a model to be followed. It is not that of a purist for Hippocrates' indifferent use of the feminine or masculine gender for the word *líthos* "stone" proves otherwise but this use is perfectly understandable (*De simpl. med. temp.* 9.2., 12.193 K.). Hippocrates is not fussy and an occasional solecism may occur but is waved aside by Galen. Thus literary tradition may be in conflict with current usage or even battle against analogy but it can still stand. These and other remarks clearly show that Galen cannot but approach Hippocratic works in the mood of a scholar. In general, in this approach one defends the text to be discussed and therefore has to explain away grammatical mistakes, if present, unclear expressions and/or a style which is not sophisticated at all. The latter two deficiencies are related rather to rhetorical training but lack of clarity (or even obscurity) can be caused by using e.g. *zeũgma* (*epízeuxis*) too much (Arist. *Rhet.* 3.5), an item also falling under the grammarian's jurisdiction. A common line of defence is that the philosophers cannot be bothered with minute linguistic distinctions and that as long as they succeed in making themselves understood, linguistic criticism is uncalled for (Sluiter 1995: 527). At other times these faults heavily count against someone. Thus Epictetus' solecisms and barbarisms are the reason why someone in his audience thinks him worth of no attention (Epict. *Diat.* 3.9.13–14). Chrysippus is more than once charged with having solecisms everywhere in his texts (Galen, *Plac. Hipp. et Plat.* 2.5 5.23 K.) and Porphyry admits that Plotinus did not pay attention to orthography and similar matters but in defence of the master he points out that he was concerned with the contents only (*Vita Plotini* 8; 13). In the case of the very simple style of the Bible, which offends cultivated readers from the very start, an apology is found in the argument that the *lingua piscatoria* "the language of the fishermen" is superior to the embellishments of rhetoric. The clarity of the Scripture is paramount and its truth cannot be bothered with the straight-jacket of 'the rules of Donatus' (Sluiter 1995: 526). The same approach is evident in the introductions to later commentaries on Aristotle and other texts (Mansfeld 1994).

2.4.2. The impact of language research on literature, apart from the etymologizing tendency, is manifest only where the subject or literary genre permits explicit or implicit references. Thus, in so far as poetry is concerned, Lucretius' *De rerum natura*, an epic poem about the structure of the cosmos and its inhabitants along the lines of Epicurean philosophy, has a part on language in the context of the genesis of culture (5.1028–90) but such a parallel is understandably absent from Vergil's *Aeneis*. In many epigrams the habits and circumstances of grammarians are ridiculed. Just like other schoolmasters they are criticized for their untidiness, sexuality, cruelty and poverty but the most characteristic trait of this profession is the pedantry of the grammarian. This is perceptible in their love of obsolete words, obscure references and enthusiasm for monosyllabic words, a category which defies rules of analogy. The mockery is sometimes rather subtle and asks for a thorough knowledge of grammatical oddities. Thus in *AP* 11.335 a Kunegeiros known from Herodotus (6.114) as having died after losing an arm, is now pitied because a grammarian has posthumously deprived him of a foot, i. e. has called him "Kunegeir", for which procedure Herodian (*GG* III: 1, 49) has parallels (Sluiter 1988: 49f.). The penchant for etymologizing, already evident in Homer's epics, continues in epics and other types of poetry, e. g. in the *Argonautica* of Apollonius of Rhodes (3rd century BC) or the *Dionysiaca* of Nonnus of Panopolis (4th/5th century AD), but of greater importance is the way Apollonius and other Hellenistic poets, like Callimachus and Theocritus, use the traditional epic language in their own way. Their usage betrays a thorough knowledge of this kind of language and an expertise in developing its possibilities. In prose the repercussions of language research are more evident. Thus Lucian (2nd century AD) chooses at least three times grammarians as a target of his satirical writings. In his *Lexiphanes* hyperatticism is ridiculed and Lucian plays on the differences between obsolete and current uses of words, in *Soloecista* a sophist prides himself on his ability to avoid grammatical blunders but fails to notice the series of deliberate errors concealed in the words of his interlocutor. Professional incompetence is also examined and censured in *Pseudologista*. In other works also Lucian exposes language errors of speakers and shows his keen awareness of language discussions in his time. Plutarch (ca. 45–ca. 125) is a man of wide-ranging knowledge, who can also handle grammatical problems. He is acquainted with these from his education and immense reading and among his many friends are also several grammarians and sophists. In his *Platonic Questions* X he discusses the problem (*zḗtēma*) "What was Plato's reason for saying [*Sophist* 262c2–7] that speech is a blend of nouns and verbs?" (and not of the well-known eight parts of speech). The solution is that Plato realized that the verb and the noun produce the first combination admitting of truth and falsity and that the remaining parts render some service only – this argument recurs in the late commentaries on Aristotle's *De interpretatione* (e. g. in that of Ammonius, *CAG* IV, 12.27–30). Plutarch's treatise is full of grammatical points of view and of great interest. In *Table Talk* (5.4) the meaning of a Homeric line is being discussed and one of the speakers can point out without further explanation that Homer is apt to use the comparative interchangeably with the positive (677D) and book 9 of this collection contains other talks on (semi-)grammatical matters. A collection particularly directed towards subjects concerning the *grammatikós* is the *Deipnosophistae* of Athenaeus of Naucratis (2nd/3rd century AD). Some thirty learned people, among whom are several grammarians and sophists, have dinner and discuss antiquarian, grammatical and literary items, thereby producing hundreds of quotes from classical writers and drawing attention to obscure words.

## 3. Bibliography

### 3.1. Primary sources


Ammonius, *De adfinium vocabulorum differentia.* Ed. by Klaus Nickau. Leipzig: Teubner, 1966.

*AP* = *Anthologia Palatina.* Ed. by H. Beckby. 4 vols. 2nd ed. Munich: Heimeran (Tusculum), 1967–1968.

*An. Ox.* = *Anecdota Oxoniensia.* Ed. by J. A. Cramer. Oxford, 1835–1837. (Repr., Amsterdam, 1963.)

*An. Par.* = *Anecdota Parisiensia.* Ed. by J. A. Cramer. Oxford, 1839–1841.

*CAG* = *Commentaria in Aristotelem Graeca.* Berlin 1882ff.

*Dig.* = *Digesta Justiniani, Corpus iuris civilis*, I. Ed. by P. Krüger a. o. 14th ed. Berlin, 1956.

Dionysius of Halicarnassus, *Critical Essays.* Ed. and transl. by Stephen Ussher. *LCL*, 1974–1985.

Galen, *Opera.* Ed. by C. G. Kühn. Leipzig, 1821–1833.

GG = *Grammatici Graeci.* Ed. by Gustav Uhlig a. o. Leipzig, 1883–1901. (Repr., Hildesheim: Olms, 1965.)

Hippocrates, *The Art.* Ed. and transl. by W. H. S. Jones, Hippocrates, *Writings*, III. London & Cambridge, Mass.: Loeb Classical Library, 1923.

Moeris Atticista, *Lexicon.* Ed. by I. Bekker. Berlin, 1833.

Olympiodorus, *On the Alcibiades.* Ed. by L. G. Westerink. Amsterdam, 1956.

Plutarch, *Platonic Questions.* Ed. and transl. by Harold Cherniss, Plutarch's *Moralia*, XIII:1. London & Cambridge, Mass.: Loeb Classical Library, 1976.

Porphyry, *Vita Plotini.* Ed. and transl. by A. H. Armstrong, Plotinus, *Enneads*, I. London & Cambridge, Mass.: Loeb Classical Library, 1969.

*Rhet. gr.* = *Rhetores graeci.* Ed. by L. Spengel. Leipzig, 1853–1856. (Repr., Frankfurt a. M., 1966.)

S. E., *M* = Sextus Empiricus, *Adversus Mathematicos.* Ed. and transl. by R. G. Bury. London & Cambridge, Mass.: Loeb Classical Library, 1933–1949.

### 3.2. Secondary sources


Atherton, Catherine. 1993. *The Stoics on Ambiguity.* Cambridge: Cambridge Univ. Press.

Christes, J. 1975. *Bildung und Gesellschaft: Die Einschätzung der Bildung und ihrer Vermittler in der griechisch-römischen Antike.* Darmstadt: Wissenschaftliche Buchgesellschaft.

Di Cesare, Donatella. 1991. "Die Geschmeidigkeit der Sprache: Zur Sprachauffassung und Sprachbetrachtung der Sophistik". Schmitter 1991.87–118.

Dihle, Albrecht. 1986. "Philosophie – Fachwissenschaft – Allgemeinwissenschaft". *Aspects de la philosophie hellénistique* ed. by Helmut Flashar & Olof Gigon, 185–223. Genève: Fondation Hardt.

Gelzer, Thomas. 1978. "Klassizismus, Attizismus und Asianismus". *Le Classicisme à Rome* ed. by Helmut Flashar, 1–41. Genève: Fondation Hardt.

Glück, Manfred. 1967. *Priscians Partitiones and ihre Stellung in der spätantiken Schule.* Hildesheim: Olms.

Gross, Walter H. 1969. "Museion". *Der kleine Pauly*, vol. III, 1482–1485.

Heinimann, Felix. 1945. *Nomos und Physis.* Basel: Reinhardt.

Herbermann, Clemens-Peter. 1991. "Antike Etymologie". Schmitter 1991.353–376.

Hovdhaugen, Even. 1982. *Foundations of Western Linguistics.* Oslo: Universitetsforlaget.

Kannicht, Richard. 1969. *Euripides Helen*, vol. I: *Einleitung und Text.* Heidelberg: Winter.

Kaster, Robert A. 1983. "Notes on 'primary' and 'secondary' schools in Late Antiquity". *Transactions of the American Philological Association* 113.323–346.

–. 1988. *Guardians of Language: The grammarians and society in Late Antiquity.* Berkeley, Los Angeles: Univ. of California Press.

Kennedy, George A. 1994. *A New History of Classical Rhetoric.* Princeton, N.J.: Princeton Univ. Press.

Mansfeld, Jaap. 1994. *Prolegomena.* Leiden: Brill.

Marrou, Henri-Irenée. 1960 [1948]. *Histoire de l'Education dans l'Antiquité.* 5th ed. Paris: Editions du Seuil.

Morgan, Teresa. 1998. *Literate Education in the Hellenistic and Roman Worlds.* Cambridge: Cambridge Univ. Press. [This important study appeared too late to be used here.]

Nilsson, M[artin] P. 1955. *Die hellenistische Schule.* München: Beck.

Pfeiffer, Rudolf. 1968. *History of Classical Scholarship.* Oxford: Oxford Univ. Press.

Pleket, H[arry] W. 1981. "Opvoeding in de Grieks-romeinse wereld: Een inleiding". *Lampas* 14.147–154.

Said, S[uzanne], ed. 1991. ΕΛΛΗΝΙΣΜΟΣ: Quelques jalons pour une histoire de l'identité grecque. Leiden: Brill.

Schenkeveld, Dirk Marie. 1991. "Figures and Tropes: A border-case between grammar and rhetoric". *Rhetorik zwischen den Wissenschaften* ed. by G. Ueding, 149–157. Tübingen: Niemeyer.

–. 1994. "Scholarship and Grammar". *La philologie grecque à l'époque hellenistique et romaine* ed. by F. Montanari, 263–301. Genève: Fondation Hardt.

Schmitter, Peter, ed. 1991. *Geschichte der Sprachtheorie*, vol. II: *Sprachtheorien der abendländischen Antike.* Tübingen: Narr.

Schneider, Carl. 1967–69. *Kulturgeschichte des Hellenismus.* 2 vols. München: Beck.

Schubart, Wilhelm. 1961. *Das Buch bei den Griechen und Römern.* 3rd ed. by Eberhard Paul. Leipzig: Koehler & Amelang.

Siebenborn, Elmar. 1976. *Die Lehre von der Sprachrichtigkeit und ihren Kriterien.* Amsterdam: Grüner.

Sluiter, Ineke. 1988. "Perversa subtilitas: De kwade roep van de grammaticus". *Lampas* 21.41–65.

–. 1990. *Ancient Grammar in Context.* Amsterdam: VU Univ. Press.

–. 1995. "The Embarassment of Imperfection: Galen's assessment of Hippocrates' linguistic merits". *Ancient Medicine in its Socio-cultural Context* ed. by Philip J. van der Eijk a.o., 519–535. 2 vols. Leiden: Brill.

Thomas, Rosalind. 1989. *Oral Tradition and Written Record in Classical Athens.* Cambridge: Cambridge Univ. Press.

Verdenius, W[illem] J. 1970. *Homer the Educator of the Greeks. Mededelingen koninklijke Nederlandse Akademie* NR 33:5.

Wilson, John. 1982. "The Customary Meanings of Words Were changed – or Were They?: A note on Thucydides 3.82.4". *Classical Quarterly* 32.18–20.

Wouters, Alfons. 1979. *The Grammatical Papyri from Graeco-Roman Egypt.* Brussel: Paleis der Academiën.

Ziebarth, Erich. 1914. *Aus dem griechischen Schulwesen: Eudemos von Milet und Verwandtes.* 2nd ed. Leipzig: Teubner.


*Dirk M. Schenkeveld, Heemstede (The Netherlands)*

# 62. Variety of speech in Greek linguistics: The dialects and the *koinè*

1. The Greek language community and its dialects
2. Dialect levelling and the rise of Great Attic
3. The rise of Hellenistic *koinè* and its expansion
4. Interdialectal formations in Doric territories
5. Atticism
6. Bibliography

## 1. The Greek language community and its dialects

Before the times of the national unity installed by the Macedonians around the middle of the 4th century BC Greece was composed of many regions or city states, where various literary standards and grammatically different regional dialects were found. The ancient grammarians spoke of the four literary dialects (Attic, Ionic, Aeolic and Doric), to which the *koinè* was added as a fifth. But the awareness of the ethnolinguistic diversity is found already in Homer and Herodotus. Homer (N 685) speaks of the "Ionians, trailing the tunic" as of the neighbours of Boeotians, Locrians and Phthians. Athens was considered a cradle of the ancestors of the aristocratic families in the twelve Ionian cities in Asia Minor, and Herodotus, a Dorian from Halicarnassus, in a celebrated passage (1.146) scoffs at the claims of their pure-blooded ancestry:

> Even those who started from the Government House in Athens and believe themselves to be of the purest Ionian blood, took no women with them but married Carian girls, whose parents they had killed.

While the linguistic affinity of Ionic and Attic was beyond any doubt, the extent of the former Ionic territory was somewhat uncertain. According to various accounts of questionable value the Ionians once lived in the northern Peloponnese, the latter Achaea (Hdt. 1.145–46), Megara (Strabo 9.392), Epidauros (Paus. 2.26.2), and Cynuria (Hdt. 8.73). Modern scholarship projects the formation of Proto-Ionic in Attica and adjacent regions to the period following the collapse of Mycenaean political power (ca. 1200 BC).

The ethnolinguistic affinities of the Aeolians were less clear to the ancients. In Herodotus (7.176) we find the tradition that the historical Thessalians were invaders from the coastal Thesprotia (in Epirus), and indeed there are certain West Greek features in Thessalian (stronger in Thessaliotis than in more distant Pelasgiotis). The Boeotians are called Aeolians by Thucydides (7.57), and their dialect displays even stronger West Greek characteristics than Thessalian. Another passage in Thucydides (1.12) allows us to conclude that the ancestors of the historical Boeotians were a tribe of West Greek invaders from Epirus (cf. Mt. Boeon). The Aeolic element may be ascribed to the earlier substrate (e. g. the Minyans of Orchomenus). In Boeotia their language came into close contact with the Ionic of Attica and Euboea. About 1000 BC a part of the Aeolian population of Thessaly moved to Lesbos and the adjacent coast of Asia Minor, where their language came under the strong influence of Ionic. Some of the isoglosses linking these three dialects are: Proto-Greek labiovelars $*k^w$ and $*g^w$ became labials /p/ and /b/ in all environments (contrast Lesbian πέσσυρες, Boeotian πέτταρες "four" with Attic τέτταρες) and /o/ instead of /a/ before or after liquids (contrast Lesbian στρότος "army" and Thessalian βροχυς "short" with Attic-Ionic στρατός and βραχύς).

The most fundamental division of the Greek dialects is that into the West and the East dialects, to be understood as referring to their location prior to the great migrations. To the latter group belong the Ionic and Aeolic, while the Doric belong to the West dialects. Modern scholarship refers to the West dialects as *ti*-dialects, while the former are classified as *si*-dialects (contrast Doric φέροντι with Ionic φέρουσι). Due to their later arrival into the historical lands the Doric are most conservative among the ancient Greek dialects (e. g. they preserved PIE $*\bar{a}$ and $*w$ until Hellenistic times). That they were related to the North-West dialects (of Phocis, Locris, Aetolia, Acarnania and Epirus) was not perceived clearly by the ancients. For instance, Herodotus (8.73.1) reported that among the seven distinct "peoples" (ἔθνη) in the Peloponnese there were four "immigrants" (ἐπήλυδα): Dorians, Aetolians, Dryopes and Lemnians. While the Dorian communities were well known and numerous, the Aetolians had only one, Elis. And indeed the Elean dialect displays certain features which appear in Aetolia and Locris (the open pronunciation of *e* before *r*, φάρω, and the Aetolian Dat Pl φερόντοις or the Aeolic φερόντεσσι).

A considerable later intermingling of Doric and Aeolic elements led the geographer Strabo (Augustus' times) to proclaim their affinity by the following 'analogical' statement: "We may say that the Ionic is the same as the ancient Attic, and [...] the Doric dialect is the same as the Aeolic" (8.I.2). Another unwarranted statement appears to be Strabo's overextension of the ethnonym Aeolic: "all the Greeks outside the Isthmus, except the Athenians and the Megarians and the Dorians who live about Parnassus, are to this day still called Aeolians" (8.I.2). However, the perusal of the earlier writers reveals that the historical Phocians, Locrians, Aetolians, Acarnanians were not called Aeolic. Strabo's inaccuracy was corrected by some of his successors, who characterized the dialects spoken north of the Corinthian gulf as Doric (e. g. Stephanus of Byzantium regarding the dialect of Aetolia). In modern scholarship inspired by the inscriptional evidence they are recognized as a North-West subgroup of the West dialects (cf. Thumb-Kieckers 1932; Bartoněk 1972).

On the whole one has to keep in mind that a very important criterion in the works of ancient authors which determined the classification of Greek dialects was the correlation of the dialects with literary genres. Thus undoubtedly Attic was classified as an independent dialect separate from the Ionic of Asia Minor on the basis of different literary activities (Attic drama vs. Ionic epic poetry).

The lack of linguistic uniformity which was so typical of the Greek speech community in the 5th century continued to prevail until the period of Macedonian domination produced a thorough-going change in the functional structure of Greek. However, it is worth mentioning that even during the period of Macedonian domination the old practice prevailed in various centres — most notably in Delphi under the protection of the Aetolians, who tried to make Delphi an Aetolian counterpart of Macedonian Athens (Rostovtzeff 1953: 219). Here we witness the usage of regional Phocian variants in public and private documents — as opposed to the supraregional Hellenistic *koinè* of Macedonian invaders — by the community whose cultural prestige remained undisputed in the three pre-Christian centuries. The overall situation, however, is quite complex because certain public documents (most notably proxeny decrees) make dialectal concessions to foreign honorands (e. g. if the recipient is an Athenian magistrate the Attic-Ionic form ἱερομνήμονι "to the sacred recorder", not the local Phocian ἱερομνάμονι will be used.

## 2. Dialect levelling and the rise of Great Attic

Before the Persian wars (490—479), Ionic enjoyed the highest status among the Greek dialects. Ionic writers developed the first Greek literary prose. It is somewhat paradoxical that its two main representants, Herodotus and Hippocrates, were probably native speakers of Doric since they came from the Doric speaking areas of Halicarnassus and Cos. East Ionic was used as an administrative language even in neighbouring non-Ionic communities and Ionic influence is apparent in contemporary Attic inscriptions of that time.

After the Persian wars, Attic gradually replaced Ionic in its position of the most prestigious among the Greek dialects. The reasons have to do with the increasing political power Athens exerted in the First Maritime League (the confederacy of Delos) which dominated the Ionic insular world from 478/7. In the following years the city of Athens became the centre of a commercial and cultural empire. This development gradually changed the direction of linguistic influence. It was now the westernmost Ionic dialect, i. e. the Attic idiom of the Greek mainland which was imitated by other Greeks, especially by Ionians.

During these two centuries we witness a mutual influence of Attic on Ionic and of Ionic on Attic. Some traces of Attic influence can already be seen in Ionic inscriptions of the 5th century from the Cycladic islands. In the 4th century 38% of Ionic inscriptions show an admixture of Attic forms and approximately 28% are substantially Attic. In the following century the process of contamination has almost been completed (80% of all inscriptions are now in Hellenistic *koinè*, 16% percent in koineized Ionic and only approximately 4% in pure Ionic, cf. Debrunner & Scherer 1969: 36). At the same time the Attic dialect, as spoken in Attica, lagged considerably in its development behind 'Great' Attic, i. e. the administrative language of the Athenian empire in the 5th to 4th century used in Euboia, Ionic Cyclades and the littoral of Asia Minor.

The roots of Hellenistic koinè lie precisely in this variety, the Great Attic, which in linguistic terms may be viewed as a 'de-Atticized Ionized' Attic. It has been suggested (Hock 1986: 486) that the ultimate origin of a de-Atticized version may have lain in the variety which developed in one of the most important harbours of Ancient Greece, Peiraieus. Here the Attic dialect came into daily contact with 'mild' Doric dialects spoken across the Saronic gulf in Megaris, Corinthia and Eastern Argolis, and with the Western Ionic dialects spoken in Euboia and the adjacent Cycladic islands. Thus it is quite conceivable that here the interdialectal variety based on Attic, West Ionic and 'mild' Doric dialects developed.

## 3. The rise of Hellenistic *koinè* and its expansion

Attic was probably adopted as an official administrative language at the Macedonian court under Philip II, Alexander's father. This is obviously the most illustrative example of the increasing prestige of this high-status dialect in the 4th century – despite the decline of Athenian political power. It is of fundamental importance for the determination of the development of *koinè* that the Attic of the Macedonian inscriptions of that time is almost identical with the language found in contemporary Athenian official inscriptions. In other words, Macedonian adopted the practical, matter-of-fact form of Attic used by the middle class (such as administrators, politicians and merchants) in daily life.

The final and decisive factor to guarantee the Attic-Ionic *koinè* an entirely unchallenged position as the Greek official language was the political and economic expansion under Alexander and the establishment of new states through his successors, with this dialect as the official language of an autocratic administration. In the new Greek communities made up of a mixed immigrant population of different dialectal origins, there was no alternative to the official language of the authorities; the roots of the other dialects had been torn off by the emigration of their users. The non-Attic dialects were doomed to die out rapidly in the overseas communities.

It is important to realize that the ancient grammarians originally considered *koinè* as the abstract notion of Greek as the common language of all Greeks (somewhat like nowadays all the Arabs claim that they speak one 'common' (*'āmmiyya*) language in spite of the geographic varieties found in Syria, Egypt, etc.). During the Hellenistic era this common language became identical with the colloquial Hellenistic Greek. Who among the grammarians added *koinè* as the fifth dialect to the above two pairs of the Greek dialects (Ias and Atthis, Doris and Aiolis) is unknown. *Koinè* as the fifth dialect is mentioned by Clemens Alexandrinus (150–215 AD) in *Stromata* I 21, 142, and in the Scholia on Dionysius Thrax (in 14.14 and four other passages). The ancient grammarians differed considerably in their understanding of the relationship of *koinè* to the other four dialectal groups. For instance the Grammaticus Meermannianus (ed. Schaeffer 642) derived the dialects from *koinè* (ἐκ ταύτης ἄρχονται πᾶσαι); similarly, the scholiast on Dionysius Thrax (496.6) considered *koinè* to be a 'mother' of all dialects. It was the other way around for the Grammaticus Leidensis who stated that *koinè* arose from the four dialects. That one could establish 'derivational histories' from one to another variety was known to the son of Apollonios Dyskolos, Herodianus, who treated the relationship between the *koinè* and dialectal forms as that between "original" (πρωτότυπα) and "derived" (παράγωγα) in I, 401.15–16.

From the preceding it is obvious that the concept of *koinè* by the ancient grammarians differed considerably from that of modern sociolinguistic theories. While the modern theoreticians emphasize the dialect mixing (cf. Siegel's 1985 definition: "a *koinè* is the stabilized result of mixing of linguistic subsystems such as regional or literary dialects. It usually serves as a lingua franca among speakers of the different contributing varieties ..."), ancient Greek grammatical literature dealt with the problem rather philosophically and ahistorically: the *koinè* as the common language was seen as the 'genus' and the four dialects as the 'species' to be necessarily included in the common language (cf. Versteegh 1986: 433.

## 4. Interdialectal formations in Doric territories

During the three pre-Christian centuries there evolved several regional interdialectal formations in Doric-speaking territories (called usually Doric *koinès*): South-East Aegean Doric *koinè* (centred around the island of Rhodes), North-West Doric *koinè* (centred in Aetolia) and Achaean Doric *koinè* (in Peloponnesian Achaea). As we saw in § 1 above the linguistic situation in the latter two regions prompted Strabo to declare that the "Doric dialect is the same as the Aeolic".

The Aegean Doric *koinè* – as we know it from the inscriptions – is based on the local 'middle' Doric dialects with some of the local peculiarities eliminated, and showing a strong admixture of forms from the advancing Hellenistic *koinè*. Its geographic focus was the biggest island in that area, Rhodes, which asserted itself as a major power in the East Aegean corner of the Hellenistic world. One of the phonological features of this variety is the height dissimilation affecting the sequence of the two mid vowels: *eo* becomes here *eu*, whereas in the Ionic dialects these two vowels contract into *ǭ*; hence the forms such as the South-East Aegean ποιεύμενος "being made" vs. Ionic ποιούμενος (both from ποιεόμενος). In Rhodes these forms lost their ground to the advancing Hellenistic *koinè* ποιούμενος (= the Ionic form with rasing *ǭ* > *ū*) in the 1st century BC, whereas in neighbouring Cos they survived until the 1st century AD. A distinct Rhodianism is the infinitive in -μειν, which survived at least until the 1st century AD. On the other islands we find the common West Greek forms with -μεν (Anaphe, Telos, Cnidos, Calymna, Cos) or with -εν (Anaphe, Nisyros, Cnidos). As far as our evidence goes, Rhodian -μειν diffused to Telos and Carpathos. In all these places the local West Greek forms competed with Hellenistic -ειν.

The North West Doric *koinè* is essentially a 'mild' Doric based *koinè*, showing an admixture of Hellenistic forms. It was employed, from the 3rd century BC onwards, in all the decrees of the Aetolian league (Aetolia, Acarnania, Western Locris, Phocis, Aenis, Malis and Phthiotis). The two most salient of its morphological features come from the North West Greek dialects:

(i) The preposition ἐν "in" can also be used in the meaning of "to" if combined with the accusative, while in Hellenistic *koinè* this function is fulfilled by a different preposition, εἰς.

(ii) The Dat Pl of athematic nouns and participles takes the thematic suffix -οις, e. g. φερόντοις "to the carrying (ones)" (vs. Ionic and Hellenistic φέρουσι).

The Achaean Doric *koinè* did not develop the extreme features that are typical of the Aegean Doric *koinè* (such as the height dissimilation *eo* > *eu*) or of the North West Doric *koinè* (such as the two above). This variant is therefore essentially an unmarked Doric *koinè* (with features of 'mild' Doric dialects, such as those of neighbouring Corinthia and Sicyonia). In Achaea itself, this general Doric *koinè* held ground until the 1st century BC. The first Hellenistic inscriptions appeared here as late as the second half of the 1st century BC.

## 5. Atticism

In § 3 above we stopped short of considering the 'nativized' *koinè* which brings us now to the analysis of the writings of Polyb, Diodorus Siculus, Plutarch and Josephus Flavius. Polyb's language (ca. 201–120 BC) is structurally still very close to the later Attic in his use of tenses and moods. But his lexicon and phraseology are Hellenistic; it has been pointed out that there are certain similarities in his diction with that of contemporary public inscriptions (according to Debrunner & Scherer [1969: 20] both had a common basis, the 'elevated style of the public chancellery'). As an example of his non-Attic phraseology we may mention various prepositional periphrases of the genitive (e. g. τὸ κατὰ τοὺς πεζοὺς ἐλάττωμα "the defeat of the pedestrians" (5, 69, 11); ὁ παρ' ἡμῶν πατήρ "our father" (22, 3, 6); ἀπείρων ὄντων τῆς περὶ τὰς πεντήρεις ναυπηγίας "because they were inexperienced in the building of battleships" (1, 20, 10)). Similarly, in the following century, Diodorus Siculus displays a strong taste for Atticism in his use of the optative (esp. in its aspectual function of the iterative); but, on the other hand, he replaces the synthetic genitive by prepositional phrases as Polybius does (e. g. ἡ κατὰ τὴν ἀρχὴν ἀπόθεσις "the surrender of the rule" (1, 65, 5) instead of ἡ τῆς ἀρχῆς ἀπόθεσις). Similar observations could be made about later post-Christian authors, Plutarch of Chaeroneia (ca. 46–120 AD) and his contemporary Josephus Flavius. The latter composed his celebrated history of the Jewish wars in his native Aramaic and only later on, with the help of native speakers of Greek, prepared a Greek translation of the work. The Greek version displays several features of increasing Atticism; e. g. there are grammatical forms such as ἐτετάχατο "they were arranged" (the synthetic mediopassive pluperfect) instead of the analytic Hellenistic τεταγμένοι ἦσαν; the preposition περὶ is used with the dative; and the dual reappears (after it has disappeared from the Attic inscriptions during the 4th century BC).

During its later period the rise of this classizing tendency is linked with authoritative statements on grammar and rhetoric by the rhetoricians such as Dionysius of Halicarnasus, an admirerer of Demosthenes and Thucydides. Subsequently, Atticism spread through the literary education of the social elite throughout the Roman empire. Its heyday was during the 2nd century AD when its protagonists – famous rhetoricians and philosophers – advised a return to the manner of Lysias and Demosthenes. Aelius Aristeides (ca. 129–189), a defender of rhetoric against Plato, composed his (55 preserved) speeches in pure Attic. In his opinion the "optatives express [the Attic] simplicity" (τὰ εὐκτικὰ τῆς ἀφελείας) and "clarify the sentence" (καθαρὸν ποιεῖ τον λόγον). By contrast, not a single optative is documented in Epictetus's diatribes or *Encheiridion* (1st/2nd century AD) or in the New Testament. The analysis of the use of tenses in the latter document (vs. the 'correct' Attic uses) cannot be undertaken here. Suffice it to mention that the NT heralds the analytic future (μέλλω + Infinitive) and the pluperfect (γεγραμμένον ἦν – ἐγέγραπτο, also in Polybius; γεγραμμένον ἐστίν – γέγραπται) of later Greek.

As far as education is concerned, the pupils in contemporary gymnasia were exposed to a rigorous linguistic purism buttressed by lists of linguistic prescriptions. The Atticist lexica of Aelius Dionysius, Pausanias, Moeris and Phrynichus listed both the current Hellenistic words and forms to be avoided and what they thought to be their Attic equivalents. For instance, Moeris rejects the perfect form ἀπέκταγκεν "he has killed" in favour of ἀπέκτονεν (with ablaut); the analytic mediopassive pluperfect τεταγμένοι ἦσαν "they were arranged" (found in Polybius, NT, Josephus Flavius) in favour of ἐτετάχατο (by analogy with the rest of the paradigm); the 2nd Sg Impf ἦς "you were" in favour of ἦσθα (with the suffix -θα limited to two other verbs: ἔφησθα "you said", οἶσθα "you know" and (Plqpf) ᾔδησθα "you knew"); θάρσος "audacity" in favour of assimilated θάρρος; analogical οἴδασι "they know" in favour of ἴσασι; analogical παῖξαι "to play" in favour of παῖσαι; αὐτοί "they" in favour of σφεῖς, etc. It is important to realize that Atticism, unlike modern linguistic purism, was concerned only with certain stylistic levels of language, namely public speaking and 'high' literature; technical writers and the Christian community composed their books in Hellenistic *koinè*. We may conclude that educated people of those days ended up with a 'double' standard (to use Blanc's term, 1968: 248). At the center of the continuum ranging from the most localized epichoric dialect to the ever-distant model of 'pure Attic', there were the average 'informal' and 'formal levels': Hellenistic *koinè* and Atticizing *Hochsprache*.

## 6. Bibliography

### 6.1. Primary sources


*Grammatici Graeci.* Ed. by Richard Schneider et al. Leipzig: B. G. Teubner, 1878–1910. (Repr., Hildesheim: G. Olms, 1965.)

Gregory of Corinth, *Le traité* ΠΕΡΙ ΣΥΝΤΑΞΕΟΣ ΛΟΓΟΥ *de Grégoire de Corinthe.* Ed. by Daniel Donnet. (= *Etudes de Philologie, d'Archéologie et d'Histoire anciennes*, 10.) Brussels & Rome: Institut Historique Belge de Rome, 1967.

Gregory of Corinth, *Gregorii Corinthii et aliorum grammaticorum libri de dialectis linguae.* Ed. by Gottfried H. Schaeffer. Leipzig: Weigel, 1811. [Contains the *Perì dialéktōn* and the texts of the Grammaticus Meermannianus, Grammaticus Leidensis and Grammaticus Parisinus.]

Herodian, *Herodiani technici reliquiae collegit disposuit emendavit explicavit praefatus est.* Ed. by August Lenz. (= *Grammatici Graeci* III/1–2.) Leipzig: B. G. Teubner, 1867–1870.

Moeris, *Moeridis Atticistae Lexicon Atticum.* Ed. by Johannes Pierson. Leiden: P. van der Eyk & C. de Pecker, 1759.

*Scholia in Dionysii Thracis Artem Grammaticam.* Ed. by Alfred Hilgard. (= *Grammatici Graeci* I/3.) Leipzig: B. G. Teubner, 1901.


### 6.2. Secondary sources


Bartoněk, Antonín. 1972. *Classification of the West Greek Dialects at the Time about 350 BC.* Prague: Academia.

Blanc, Haim. 1968. "The Israeli Koine as an emergent national standard". *Language Problems of Developing Nations* ed. by Joshua Fishman et al., 237–252. New York: Wiley.

Bubenik, Vit. 1989. *Hellenistic and Roman Greece as a Sociolinguistic Area.* Amsterdam: Benjamins.

Buck, Carl D. 1955. *The Greek Dialects.* Chicago: Univ. of Chicago Press.

Debrunner, Albert & A. Scherer. 1969. *Geschichte der griechischen Sprache.* Vol. II. *Grundfragen und*

*Grundzüge des nachklassischen Griechisch.* Berlin: de Gruyter.

Hock, Hans H. 1986. *Principles of Historical Linguistics.* Berlin: Mouton de Gruyter.

Rostovtzeff, Michael I. 1953–59. *The Social and Economic History of the Hellenistic World.* 3 vols. Oxford: Clarendon.

Schwyzer, Edward. 1923. *Dialectorum Graecarum Exempla Epigraphica Potiora.* Leipzig: Hirzel.

Siegel, Jeff. 1985. "Koines and Koineization". *Language in Society* 14.353–378.

Threatte, Leslie. 1980. *The Grammar of Attic Inscriptions.* Berlin: de Gruyter.

Thumb, Albert & Eduard Kieckers. 1932. *Handbuch der griechischen Dialekte.* Heidelberg: Winter.

Versteegh, Kees. 1986. "*Latinitas, Hellènismós, ʿArabiyya*". *Historiographia Linguistica* 13.425–448.

*Vit Bubenik, St. John's (Canada)*

# 63. Greek influence in Georgian linguistics

The history of grammatical thought in Georgia has its beginnings in ancient times. Written Georgian goes back to the 5th century (the first dated inscription is attested in the year 493) and it is in the script itself that the results of linguistic study of the Georgian language are observable. Moreover, analysis of the Old Georgian script leads us to assume that Greek grammatical theory was known to the creator of *mrgvlovani* "rounded", the oldest form of the Georgian script. Georgian tradition ascribes the invention of script to king Parnavaz (3rd century BC). There have been attempts to link it with Semitic prototypes, but recent research has shown with reasonable certainty that Old Georgian script was modelled on Greek. This conclusion is reached not merely on the basis of external manifestations, i. e., the patterns of graphic signs, but on that of internal evidence. The script which is nearly perfect as a phonological system, includes vowels; the general paradigmatic structure displays alphabetic sequence (indicated by the numerical values of the letters) following the main features of the Greek script; graphic symbols for specific Georgian consonants make up an additional group, after the alphabetic sequence arranged in accordance with the Greek one; to avoid violation of the Greek system of numerical values a letter designating *ey* (← *ei*) takes the eighth place in Georgian as does η in Greek, despite the fact that other vowel combinations have no special graphic symbols. There is also a letter corresponding to ω, though there are no long vowels in Old Georgian. *u* is designated by a digraph, as in Greek; this is the only exception, all other phonemes having one graphic sign each. These are the main facts which point to the Greek script as the archetype for the Old Georgian (Gamkrelidze 1994). Moreover, the distribution of symbols for specific Georgian consonants – the last twelve – in the alphabet, being phonetically conceptualised, favours the assumption that the creator of the Old Georgian script was familiar with the phonetic principles of the classification of sounds laid down by Dionysius Thrax (Boeder 1975). Visually graphemes of *mrgvlovani* "rounded" script are for the most part unlike any other script, a straight line and a semicircle within a square being the graphic elements forming the letters (Mač'avariani 1982). However, the possibility of deliberate transformation of some Greek models in order to create an original writing should also be considered (Gamkrelidze 1994: 66).

In the period following the conversion of Georgia to Christianity the task of translating the Bible and the works of the Church Fathers inevitably led to speculation in linguistic problems. Traces of the problems the translators had to face are represented in the form of glosses, either marginal or inserted in the text. Loanwords and proper names are often explained. There are many examples in the Sinai Homiliary (864 AD). After having translated from his original that *keleliel* is *stepanos* (στέφανος) in Greek, the translator adds that the 'Assyrian' word is *gwrgwni* "crown" [sic!] in Georgian. In the Athos Bible (978 AD) *iliktrioni* (ἤλεκτρον Ez. 1,4) is explained (in the text) as being an alloy of gold, silver and copper!

Direct evidence of the fact that knowledge of 'philological grammar' was acquired by

Georgians at an early period is to be found in a Ms. copied in the 10th century. It is here that we find an excerpt from a commentary on Dionysius Thrax by Diomedes concerning the history of the Greek script, followed by a fragment of Epiphanius' treatise *On Weights and Measures* in which Hebrew alphabet is discussed (Q'auxčišvili 1923: 179ff.).

The foundation of the Iviron Monastery on Mt. Athos marks a turning-point in the history of Georgian scholarship. Closer contact with the Hellenic world brought on creative assimilation of Byzantine speculative thought. With foundations for linguistic research already laid down, the influence of Byzantine scholarship resulted in much original thinking on lexical and grammatical problems. The famous Hagiorites, Euthymios (d. 1028) and George (d. 1066) translated exclusively from Greek; in their works frequent references to the problems of translation are to be found; Greek loanwords in the text are often followed by notes defining their meaning.

Numerous original and translated works of Eprem Mcire (Ephraim the Little, second half of the 11th century) clearly reveal the attention the great scholar paid to linguistic problems. He defines grammar as being the first of 12 Greek 'arts', the following two being philosophy and rhetoric, i. e. the Trivium. *Gramatikosi* "grammarian" is "one who melts writing". This definition indicates his knowledge of some commentaries on Dionysius. He deals with several linguistic features of both languages. Eprem notes the importance of stress for distinguishing the meaning of words, illustrating this with suitable examples. He mentions the existence of different genders in Greek, and names the articles used with different nouns; he comments on plural forms of some Greek words and explains *pluralia tantum* as the result of the influence of the Attic dialect. In Georgian, he notices the change of meaning when different preverbs are used and demonstrates forms of compound nouns and describes their formal charcteristics. He also speaks of the difference between literary and colloquial language; the former is *c'ignuri* "of the books", the latter *sopluri* "that of the world" or *ušueri* "rough". But his interest is mainly in what would be called nowadays semantics and lexicology. When discussing these problems, Eprem shows considerable linguistic insight. He explains the words he uses (both Greek and Georgian), defining the subtle shades of their meaning with surprising accuracy and states that the same Greek works have been differently translated by his predecessors as well as by himself because of their different meanings. He translates γνώμη, which, according to him, has 28 [sic!] meanings, by four different words.

On the other hand, he sometimes complains that Georgian has only one equivalent for two or more Greek words, as in the case of πνεῦμα and ψυχή which are both translated as *suli* "soul, spirit etc.". Eprem is extremely fond of using Greek words in his works, because, as he says, there are no words having exactly the same meaning in Georgian. Here again he points out that he is following the example of the Greeks, who do the same when speaking of exotic plants, objects etc. (Sarǯevelaʒe 1984: 204). He explains *krist'e* "Christ" as "anointed" in Greek, and mentions *mesia* as having the same meaning in Hebrew. In Greek, he says, there are many Hebrew words, but in Georgian they are only present when they have been borrowed by the Greeks. He concludes the passage by sayiong that Georgians use *krist'e* "in honour of the Greeks" (Šaniʒ 1968: 92).

In his original lengthy "Introduction" to the Commentary on the Psalter Eprem gave a detailed account of the form and use of the Greek 'Lexicons'. He himself compiled a glossary for his own work (ms. copied in 1091). He explains that "the Greeks" arrange words "which are difficult and have a deep meaning" according to the alphabet and that he himself has done the same. The glossary comprises about 200 words taken from the Psalter and arranged in alphabetical order with suitable theological definitions. Eprem's work therefore may rank as the first original Georgian Glossary (Šaniʒe 1968: 77ff.). Eprem also devised a system of punctuation following the Greek practice. One task that Eprem assumed was the mistaken one of attempting to introduce the feminine gender into the Georgian language, coining artificial forms to distinguish male and female human beings. Grammatical questions are often discussed in the works of Eprem's pupils and followers – representatives of the 'Philhellene school'. Arseni Iq'altoeli and the anonymous translator of Ammonius' works created or borrowed many new grammatical terms. Ioane Pet'ric'i has the credit of being the creator of Georgian philosophical terminology.

The first original Georgian work dealing exclusively with grammar is a treatise written in the 11th century, bearing the title *Discourse on Articles* (Shanidze 1984: 54ff.; Šanize 1988: 224ff.). The work was written to clarify a passage in one of John Chrysostom's homilies, which the translator found difficult to translate owing to the absence of articles in Georgian.

The anonymous author makes an attempt to demonstrate the forms and usage of the Greek articles. The structure of the work, as well as the grammatical terms employed by him, reveal his knowledge not only of the grammar of Dionysius, but of his commentators as well. The declension of the words θεός, τριάς, πνεῦμα is demonstrated both with and without articled. Greek words and articles are transliterated, as usual, in Georgian. Stress and breathing are sometimes indicated. Grammatical terms are mostly literal renderings of the respective Greek ones. *Artroni* "article" and *leksi* "word" are loanwords. Declension is *dreka* "bending", cf. κλίσις; gender is *natesavi* "kin, genus", cf. γένος; noun is *saxeli* "name", cf. ὄνομα. Masculine gender is *mamali* "male", feminine gender *dedali* "female", neuter gender *šua* "the middle one". The names of numbers and cases are formed with the suffix *-it* (as in modern Georgian). Three numbers are indicated: singular (*ertobiti*, a term derived from *erti* "one"), dual (*orobiti*, from *ori* "two") and plural (*ganmravlebiti* from *ganmravleba* "multiplying"). Nominative is *advilobiti* (from *advili* "easy, not difficult"). Genitive is usually *natesavobiti*, derived from *natesavi* "kin, genus". *Šobilobiti*, derived from *šobili* "born", also denotes the genitive. Both terms, of which the former is the one now generally in use, are translations of γενική. Dative is *micemiti*, from *micema* "giving"; also a term in use today, cf. δοτική. The name for accusative is *mizezobiti*, from *mizezi* "cause", cf. αἰτιατική. Vocative is *c'odebiti*, from *c'odeba* "calling", cf. κλητική. Paradigms of Greek declension are followed by the Georgian ones, the chosen examples having the same meaning: *γmerti* "God", *sameba* "Trinity", *suli* "soul, spirit". In order to prove the absence of articles in Georgian, the author puts Greek articles before the Georgian words, remarking at the same time that it is impossible to use such forms in Georgian. The only exception is the vocative, for which he uses *ō* (which is an interjection in Georgian, as it is in Greek). The author also calls the attention of the readers to other differences between the two languages. He declares that it is difficult to explain the dual number, as it does not exist in Georgian. Adopting the Greek case system as adequate for Georgian, the author gets himself into a difficulty, as the forms which are differentiated in Greek as dative and accusative are unavoidably presented in Georgian (in the examples cited) in dative. He stresses the fact that contrary to Greek the two cases are expressed by one form, though it has two meanings. The fact that relative pronouns are classified as subjective articles is another significant proof of the influence of Greek theory. Their name is *artroni damorčilebiti*, a literal translation of ἄρθρον ὑποτακτικόν.

The significance of the treatise for the history of Georgian grammatical ideas is undeniable. It is the first concrete evidence of the fact that grammatical research started in Georgia as a part of scholarly studies as early as the 11th/12th centuries. Grammatical works written later, such as the monumental *Grammar* of Catholicos Anthony (first version, 1753; second 1767), were based on a continuity of tradition going back to a source which was greatly influenced by the Greek cultural environment.

## Bibliography


Boeder, Winfried. 1975. "Zur Analyse des altgeorgischen Alphabets". *Forschung und Lehre: Festgruß Joh. Schröpfer*, 17–34. Hamburg: Slavisches Seminar.

Gamkrelidze, Thomas V. 1994. *Alphabetic Writing and the Old Georgian Script: A Typology and Provenience of Alphabetic Systems.* New York: Delmar.

Mač'avariani, Elene. 1982. *Kartuli anbanis grapik'uli sapuzvlebi* [The Graphic Base of the Georgian Alphabet.] Tbilisi: Xelovneba.

Sarzvelaze, Zurab. 1984. *Kartuli salit'erat'uro enis ist'oriis šesavali* [Introduction to the History of the Georgian Literary Language.] Tbilisi: Ganatleba.

Q'auxčišvili, Simon. 1923. "Šat'berdis k'rebulis sasc'avlo c'igni" [Manuel d'enseignement du manuscrit de Chatberd.] *Bulletin de l'Université de Tiflis*, 3.178–185.

Shanidze, Mzekala [= Šanize, Mzekala]. 1968. *Šesavali Eprem Mciris psalmunta targmanebisa* [Introduction to the Commentary on the Psalter by Ephraim the Little.] (= *Saiubileo, zveli kartuli enis katedris šromebi*, 11.) Tbilisi: Universit'et'is Gamomcemloba.

–. 1984. "An Old Georgian Grammatical Treatise in a Collection of Homilies attributed to John Chrysostom". *Bedi Kartlisa, Revue de Kartvélologie* 42.53–68.

–. 1990. *Sit'q'uay artrontatws. ʒveli kartuli grama-t'ikuli t'rakt'at'i.* [Discourse on Articles. An Old Georgian Grammatical Treatise.] Tbilisi: Universi-t'et'is Gamomcemloba. [English summary 224–243.]

*Mzekala Shanidze, Tbilisi (Republic of Georgia)*

# 64. Greek influence in early Armenian linguistics

1. Introduction
2. Background
3. The contents of the Armenian version of the *Grammar*
4. Chronology and translation technique
5. The aftermath
6. Bibliography

## 1. Introduction

Medieval Armenian linguistics is uniquely connected with the *Grammar* of Dionysius Thrax. The Armenian version of this work influenced Armenian grammatical writing down to the 17th century. The most important issues around the Armenian version are: the adaptation of the Greek model to the linguistic structure of Armenian and the date of the translation, around the 6th or 7th century. As no conclusive external evidence for dating is available, the chronology of the translation is intimately linked with an analysis of the translation technique applied by the translator. This technique, the so-called 'philhellene' style, provided the elements of Armenian scientific expression down to modern times.

## 2. Background

Armenian written literature originates in the 5th century AD with the translation of the Bible and other Christian Greek and Syriac texts. Armenian literature originates as a translation literature, and early Armenian linguistic thought addressed translation exigencies. The 5th century Armenian linguistic paradigm follows the thoughts expressed by Eusebius of Emesa (ca. 300–360) in the introduction to his *Commentary in Genesis*; in this introduction (surviving only in a 5th-century Armenian translation) Eusebius defends the principles of a translation *ad sensum*, i. e., of a paradigm which, following the classification proposed for Old Syriac by Brock (1983), was sentence-orientated (as against atomistic), dynamic (as against formal), respecting the syntax of the target language. The translation of the *Grammar*, together with other Greek secular philosophical texts, into Armenian marks a new translation paradigm, aimed at precise mirroring of the source, and introduces theoretical linguistic thought in Armenia. The change of paradigm may reflect a change in exegetical outlook from factual Antiochene to allegorical Alexandrian, the latter requiring the availability of precise textual renderings (Mahé 1988). This Alexandrian influence in turn is chronologically related to the religious disputes leading to the final rejection of the doctrine of Chalcedon by the Armenian Church on the second Council of Dvin in 555. Mahé's perspective is culturally well embedded and therefore preferable to the alternative view, according to which the new paradigm rather originated in Constantinople around 570 (Terian 1982: 183).

The exact place of the Armenian version of the *Grammar* in this process is not clear, but for many scholars (Manandean 1928: 115–124; Terian 1982: 177) the translation of the *Grammar* itself marks the beginning of the new paradigm. Absolute dates proposed for the Armenian version vary from the middle 5th century (J̌ahukyan 1954: 52–53), which certainly is too early, to the 7th century (Adontz 1970 [1915]: clxxix).

## 3. The contents of the Armenian version of the *Grammar*

The Armenian version aims at retaining the categorization and structures of the Greek text very precisely, while at the same time making an effort to present the subject-matter in conformity with the structure of the Armenian language. The translator very well understood the grammatical theory of the

Greek text and had a good command of Armenian; modern scholarship has a favourable opinion of his translation (Ervine 1988: 45; Sgarbi 1991: 625).

In a number of cases, the Armenian version introduces adaptations to do justice to specific Armenian linguistic features (J̌ahukyan 1954: 61–76; Ervine 1988: 31–45; Sgarbi 1991). Important differences occur in the sections on the alphabet which copes with the 36 signs of the Armenian; on the phonological classification, where Armenian phonemes not present in the Greek are incorporated; on conjugation, where 17 stem-classes are distinguished against eight in the Greek in an effort to account for Armenian stems ending in a fricative; on adverbs where 35 semantic classes are distinguished, against 26 in the Greek; on prepositions which mentions fifty units against 18 in the Greek.

An example in the realm of phonetics will illustrate the translator's activity: in the Armenian version, the following phonemes are stated to be aspirates: *pʿ, kʿ, x, tʿ, cʿ, l, ǰ, čʿ, ṙ*. From a structural point of view Armenian *pʿ, kʿ, tʿ* are equivalent to the Greek aspirated stops (φ, χ, θ); being aspirated fricatives, Armenian *cʿ* and *čʿ* are correctly assigned to this series; the translator's own adaptation is visible in the inclusion of the remaining sounds (Ervine 1988: 34–37; Sgarbi 1991: 550–558).

In all major issues, the Armenian version follows the categorization of the Greek. As a result, categories are assigned to Armenian even when the language does not posses them. The most obvious instances are the treatment of vowel length, absent in Armenian (Ervine 1988: 45; Sgarbi 538–544), the nominal gender and the dual. Following the Greek text it is stated that Armenian, a strictly genderless language, possesses three grammatical genders; later Armenian commentators have expanded this notion and have assigned grammatical gender (understood as a semantic category) on the basis of word ending (Ervine 1995: 156). In a similar way, contrary to the synchronic situation, Armenian is stated to possess a dual; the forms presented in the version, (*Petru* "two Peters", *monkʿ* "the two of us", *ganom* "the two of us hit") show artificial endings (e. g. taken from Armenian *erku* "two"; Schmitt 1991) or possibly assign non-standard forms to this postulated category (Sgarbi 1991: 572–573).

In a few instances, however, new descriptional features are introduced: this is the case in the section on prepositions where the category of postpositions is added. An instrumental case, called "narrativus" (*aṙakʿakan*) lacking in Greek, is added to the cases mentioned in the sections on nominal and pronominal inflection (Adontz 1970 [1915]: clv; Ervine 1988: 38–39).

## 4. Chronology and translation technique

Tradition ascribes the translation of the *Grammar* to a certain Dawitʿ; this Dawitʿ "the Translator" possibly is the same as Dawitʿ "the Commentator", the author of one of the earliest extant Armenian commentaries on the *Grammar* (Ervine 1988: 46–53). The name Dawitʿ is a source of chronological confusion because much of the scholarly and translation activity in 6th–7th century Armenia is centered around person(s) with that name (Mahé 1990). According to Adontz, the various prosopographical indications can be reconciled by dating the translation of *Grammar* to the (early) 7th century; Ervine (1988: 53) cautiously proposes a late 6th century date.

Another approach to the chronology of the Armenian version has been made by exploring the translation technique applied. The translation of the *Grammar* renders an image of the Greek text in Armenian. In the 6th–8th centuries more of such translations have been produced, mainly introductions to Greek secular learning, including works of Philo, rhetorical and philosophical (Aristotelian) writings; such translations are termed 'philhellene' (Terian 1982; Calzolari 1989). Translations classified as 'philhellene' show two main characteristics: they mirror Greek syntax by maintaining Greek word-order and sentence constructions regardless of Armenian syntactic restraints. Secondly, in rendering Greek technical terms they make a systematic use of calques containing newly developed lexical elements: e. g. Greek *epírrhēma* "adverb" is calqued with *mak-bay*, like English *ad-verb* (cf. German *übertragen* next to *metaphoric*); the element *mak-* is unknown in this function in earlier Armenian texts. The system of hellenophile calquing and syntax is conveniently summarized by Mercier (1978–1979) and extensively discussed by Sgarbi (1990).

As a group, the philhellene texts can only be dated approximately within the limits of the 6th–8th century. However, following Manandean (1928) one may arrange individual philhellene translations on a scale of increasing complexity and tentatively date them relative to each other. According to Manandean the translation of the *Grammar* belongs to the first group of philhellene translations, together with a rhetorical compendium, the Book of *Chreiai*, and works of Philo Alexandrinus; in fact, Manandean (1928: 115–124) considers the *Grammar* as the very first philhellene translation. He argues that the grammatical terminology, which is common to all of these texts, must first have been created by the translator of the *Grammar*. In this perspective the *Grammar* forms the starting point of a concerted effort (a 'Philhellene School') to open Armenia to Greek learning, starting with the grammar as part of the *trivium*. In addition, Manandean argued, by its inconsistent renderings of Greek words, the *Grammar* shows itself to reflect the initial stage of the new translation movement; an often debated instance being Greek *sullabḗ*, rendered with the calques *šal-a-šar* "together-arranging", *p'al-aṙut'iwn* "with-taking", and the native *vang* (cf. from different perspectives Manandean 1928: 119; Adontz 1970 [1915]: cxlvii–cxlviii; Ervine 1988: 68–69; Clackson 1995: 127–130 with additional references).

The dates proposed by Ervine and Manandean for the translation of the *Grammar* are difficult to reconcile for those who date the beginnings of the philhellene translation to the middle of the 6th century. However, Manandean's argumentation for an early translation of the *Grammar* is not cogent; the underlying assumption, that philhellene style involves an increasingly uniform rendering of the Greek, reflects a too rigid conception of the 'Philhellene School'.

The internal dynamics of philhellene translations are better approached by applying the parameters which Brock (1983) established (see above, section 2). Armenian philhellene word formation addresses the bound morpheme. The method entails that words are analyzed in prepositional prefix and root; the prepositional element is translated using specific lexical elements which it is possible to systematize (Manandean 1928; Muradyan 1971). By contrast, as Clackson (1995) points out, word final elements do not enter into a very elaborate system of Armenian-Greek correspondences. Also, the morphemic analysis does not involve roots (of the type *lógos: léxis*; Clackson 1995: 127). In fact, the synchronic limits of morpheme analysis may be deduced from the teaching of the *Grammar* itself: whereas the Armenian version counts more than fifty prepositional elements, only three postpositions are distinguished.

Within the perspective offered by Brock, there is a great discrepancy between the *Grammar* and the works which Manandean groups together with it: the *Chreiai* and Philonic treatises. The Armenian version of the *Grammar* is very proficient in its analysis at morpheme level; by contrast, no translation of an individual Philonic text reaches a similar density of philhellene compounds. In this perspective, the translation of the *Grammar* does not belong to the early period of philhellene translation. In chronological terms this means that the results of the biographical approach are compatible with the internal dating method and that the translation might well have been executed around the later 6th century date which Ervine proposes.

## 5. The aftermath

Subsequent linguistic activity in Armenia found its expression in commentaries on the *Grammar* (Ervine 1988; 1995). Two of these stand out as comprehensive repositories of earlier generations: the commentaries by Grigor Magistros (10th century) and by Yovhannēs Erznkac'i (13th century). Their contents gradually move away from the *Grammar* itself towards integration in philosophical thought. For Erznkac'i in particular musical and number theory linked the study of grammar to the study of the human soul and body (Ervine 1995).

The commentary tradition ended in the 16th century with the work of Dawit' Zeyt'unc'i. But the new 17th century Armenian prescriptive grammar relied on the *Grammar* for its forms and paradigms. The philhellene translation technique stopped to be used in the 8th century. The terminology it created and the lexical procedures it developed, however, still are the building bricks of Armenian scientific terminology. The influence of 'the grammarian' on Armenian linguistic thought cannot easily be overrated.

## 6. Bibliography

Adontz, Nicolas. 1970 [1915]. *Denys de Thrace et les commentateurs arméniens.* Louvain: Imprimerie Orientaliste. (Transl. from by R. Hotterbeex from the original Russian edition, St. Peterburg 1915.)

Brock, Sebastian. 1983. "Towards a History of Syriac Translation Technique". III Symposium Syriacum ed. by René Lavenant, 1–14. (= *Orientalia Christiana Analecta*, 221.) Rome.

Calzolari, Valentina. 1989. "L'école hellénisante". *Âges et usages de la langue arménienne* ed. by M. Nichanian, 110–130. Paris: Editions Entente.

Clackson, James Peter. 1995. "The *Technē* in Armenian". *Dionysius Thrax and the Technē Grammatikē* ed. by Vivien Law & Ineke Sluiter, 121–133. (= *The Henry Sweet Society Studies in the History of Linguistics*, 1.). Münster: Nodus Publikationen.

Ervine, Roberta Ruth. 1988. *Yovhannes Erznkac'i Pluz's 'Compilation of commentary on Grammar'*. Ph. D. Columbia Univ., New York.

–. 1995. "Yovhannēs Erznkac'i Pluz's *Compilation of Commentary on Grammar* as a Starting Point for the Study of Medieval Grammars". *New Approaches to Medieval Armenian Language and Literature* ed. by Jos J. S. Weitenberg, 149–165. (= *Dutch studies in Armenian Languages and Literature*, 3.) Amsterdam & Atlanta, GA: Rodopi.

J̌ahukyan, Gevorg. 1954. *K'erkanakan ew ułłagrakan ašxatut'yunnerə hin ew miǰnadaryan Hayastanum* [Grammatical and Orthographic Works in Old and Medieval Armenia.] Erevan: Erevan Univ. Press.

Mahé, Jean-Pierre. 1988. "Traduction et exégèse: Réflexions sur l'exemple arménien". *Mélanges Antoine Guillaumont. Contributions à l'étude des christianismes orientaux* ed. by R.-G. Coquin, 243–255. (= *Cahiers d'orientalisme*, 20.) Geneva: Cramer.

–. 1990. "David l'Invincible dans la tradition arménienne". *Simplicius Commentaire sur les Catégories.* Fasc. I. *Introduction* by Irène Hadot, première partie, 189–207. (= *Philosophia Antiqua*, 50/1). Leiden: Brill.

Manandean, Yakob. 1928. *Yunaban dproc'ə ew nra zargac'man šrjannerə: K'nnakan usumnasirut'iwn* [The Philhellene School and the Periodization of its Development.] (= *Azgayin Matenadaran*, 119.) Vienna: Mechitarists.

Mercier, Charles. 1978–79. "L'école hellénistique dans la littérature arménienne." *Revue des Etudes Arméniennes* NS 13.59–75.

Muradyan, Arusyak Nersisi. 1971. *Hunaban dproc'ə ew nra derə hayereni k'erakanakan terminabanut'yan stełcman gorcum* [The Philhellene School and its Role in the Formation of Armenian Grammatical Terminology.] Erevan: Academy.

Schmitt, Rüdiger. 1991. "Osservazioni sull'adattamento Armeno del sistema grammaticale dei Greci". *Rendiconti dell' Istituto Lombardo. Classe di Lettere* 125.215–219.

Sgarbi, Romano. 1990. "Tecnica dei calchi nella versione Armenia della *grammatikē téchnē* attribuita a Dionisio Trace". *Memorie dell' Istituto Lombardo – Accademia di Scienze e Lettere. Classe di Lettere, Scienze Morali e Storiche* 39, 4.233–369.

–. 1991. "Studio contrastivo sull' adattamento strutturale Armeno della *'Téxnē'* Dionisiana". *Memorie dell' Istituto Lombardo – Accademia di Scienze e Lettere. Classe di Lettere, Scienze Morali e Storiche* 39, 7.535–632.

Terian, Abraham. 1982. "The Hellenizing School: Its time, place, and scope of activities reconsidered". *East of Byzantium: Syria and Armenia in the Formative Period* ed. by Nina G. Garsoïan, Thomas F. Mathews & Robert W. Thomson, 175–186. Washington DC: Dumbarton Oaks.

*Jos Weitenberg, Leiden (The Netherlands)*

# 65. Greek influence in the grammatical theory of Church Slavonic

1. The path to the grammatical codification of Church Slavonic
2. Models of Graeco-Slavic linguistic dualism
3. Bibliography

## 1. The path to the grammatical codification of Church Slavonic

The first full-fledged grammar of Church Slavonic appeared in 1619; it was preceded by several other grammatical treatises, the most important of which are listed below (for detailed overviews, see Worth 1983; Mečkovskaja 1984; Nimčuk 1985; Mečkovskaja & Suprun 1991; Kolesov 1991; Archaimbault 1992; Toscano 1998):

(a) *Osm' čestii slova* "The Eight Parts of Speech". This short, incomplete compilation of several Byzantine sources (Jagić 1896: 56ff.) originated in the 14th century in a Serbian environment, but circulated chiefly among the Eastern Slavs (ed. by Jagić 1896: 40–54; Weiher 1977: 386–417, with German translation). Of the eight parts of speech, only the first four (noun, verb, participle and article) are discussed (the remaining four receive a brief treatment in a manuscript edited by Žukovskaja 1982: 39–42). The discussion concentrates on the grammatical categories (*poslědujušta, parhepómena*) of each part of speech, which are taken over from Greek but exemplified with Slavic forms.

(b) *Adelphótēs. Gramatika dobroglagolivago ellinoslovenskago jazyka* (ed. by Horbatsch 1973). The curious title of this grammar is not easy to translate; Toscano (1998: 139) suggests: "Adelphotes, grammar for the correct use of the Helleno-Slavonic tongue". In reality, this is not a grammar of the "Helleno-Slavonic tongue" (*pace* Uspenskij 1987: 34), but a grammar of Greek, compiled from various sources (C. Lascaris, M. Crusius, Ph. Melanchthon and N. Clenard, see Horbatsch 1973: iiif.) and published by the Orthodox brotherhood of L'viv in 1591. The *Adelphotes* owes its place in the history of Church Slavonic grammar to the fact that it was accompanied by a translation, which includes not only rules but also paradigms and produces therefore the erroneous impression that it can serve as a description of Slavic morphology. It is doubtful, however, whether the translation was meant to be anything more than a practical aid to the student of the original text (for typological parallels to this kind of bilingual grammar, see Ising 1970: 29f.). The bulk of the *Adelphotes* deals with the morphology of the eight parts of speech; there is also a short dictionary of irregular verbs and a final section on 'prosody' (accentuation).

(c) The *Grammatika slovenska* "Slavonic Grammar" (Vilnius, 1596) by Lavrentij Zyzanij is the first attempt to arrive at a description of Church Slavonic that is comprehensive and methodical enough to be used in class (ed. by Freidhof 1972; Nimčuk 1980). As in the previous grammars, most space is occupied by etymology, i. e. morphology, followed by two short sections on orthographical rules and versification.

(d) The codification of Church Slavonic grammar culminates in Meletij Smotryc'kyj's *Hrammatiki Slavenskija pravilnoe Sintagma* "Collection of Rules of Slavonic Grammar", which was printed in the vicinity of Vilnius in 1619 (ed. by Horbatsch 1974; Nimčuk 1979). This grammar consists of four parts: orthography, etymology, syntax (included for the first time into Church Slavonic grammar), and prosody (i. e. versification). Smotryc'kyj's work very quickly came to enjoy authoritative status, as attested by numerous copies and several reprints; a revised edition appeared in Moscow in 1648 (Horbatsch 1964: 37ff.; Horbatsch 1974: viiiff.).

There is a significant degree of terminological overlap between these grammars and, in some areas, a genuine progress towards the establishment of the grammatical categories of Slavic: the *Eight Parts of Speech* and, obviously, the *Adelphotes* know only the five (four) cases of Greek; Zyzanij adds the Instrumental, and Smotryc'kyj the Prepositive (Locative) case, called by him *skazatel'nyj* "Narrativus" (cf. Keipert 1991: 281f.). Less progress was made in verbal morphology, where a multiplicity of largely artificial tense forms obscured the fundamental opposition of aspect (Daiber 1992: 168ff.; Mečkovskaja 1984: 90f.). The Greek influence is visible throughout, but (with the exception of the *Eight parts of speech*) never exclusive; in fact, Smotryc'kyj's grammatical systematization would hardly have been possible without his thorough familiarity with Renaissance Latin grammar (Kociuba 1975: 520ff.).

Leaving aside the Serbian prelude of the 14th century, all our grammars were written among the Orthodox population of Poland-Lithuania, which during the last decades of the 16th century became gradually acquainted with the new ideological currents of Western Europe (Zaxar'in 1995: 31ff.; to be used with caution, cf. Tomelleri 1996). The chief contribution of Russia to grammatical theory also has a Western European background: it is a translation of Aelius Donatus' *Ars minor*, carried out by Dmitrij Gerasimov at the end of the 15th century (→ Art. 86). This translation represents the same typological stage as the *Adelphotes*; however, no Zyzanij or Smotryc'kyj came forth to make the step towards an autonomous, comprehensive codification of Church Slavonic. For a long time, the highest authority in matters of grammar that the Russians knew of was Maksim Grek, a Greek monk who was sent to Moscow as a translator of religious works in 1516. Maksim stressed the importance of grammatical analysis, especially as a prerequisite for successful translation (Bulanin 1995: 32–34; Živov & Uspenskij 1986: 260), but was concerned exclusively with Greek grammar; in his grammatical works, the exact number of which remains still to be established (Jagić 1896: 294–345), he mentions briefly some features of Slavic that would help his readers understand better the grammatical distinctions of Greek (Worth 1983: 65–75, but cf. the criticism of Živov 1986: 76ff.). A systematic study of Greek did not begin in Russia until the 1680s, when the Slavo-Graeco-Latin Academy was founded; the first teachers of this Academy, the brothers Ioannikios and Sophronios Leikhoudes, taught not only scholarly, but also 'common', 'simple' Greek, which was perceived as the counterpart of such linguistic phenomena as the *prosta mova* of the Polish-Lithuanian commonwealth and the Russian *prostorečie* (Strakhov 1998: 68ff.; Yalamas 1993: 1ff.).

## 2. Models of Graeco-Slavic linguistic dualism

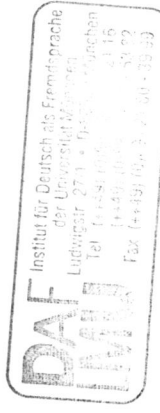

As we have seen, the Slavs borrowed the first tools of linguistic analysis from the grammatical tradition of Greek. But the Greek influence on the grammatical theory of Church Slavonic operated also on another level: no serious reflection on Church Slavonic could leave out the fact that this language was patterned to a large extent after Greek models. One of the earliest works of Church Slavonic literature, Xrabr's treatise *O pismenex* "On the letters", is an attempt to justify the creation of a new literary tradition (ed. by Džambeluka-Kosova 1980; a critical edition by G. Ziffer is in preparation). Most of Xrabr's arguments were taken over from Greek sources (Jagić 1896: 22–37; Ziffer 1995), which he used to show that Greek had undergone a phase of initial development comparable to that of Slavic and in some respects even inferior to it.

Translation theory was, of course, an area where the most interesting comparisons between Greek and Slavic were made. Let us mention only two of them – one from the beginnings and one from the last period of the development of Church Slavonic literature. John the Exarch declared in the 10th century that one should not try to preserve the linguistic structure (*slovo, glagol*) of the original text, but only its semantic contents (*razum*); as any other language, Greek should not be imitated mechanically (*ravně polagati sja*) in translation (Sadnik 1967: 18ff.); similar positions are defended in another text of the time, the *Macedonian Folio* (cf. Bulanin 1995: 27ff.). More than six centuries later, Zaxarija Kopystens'kyj takes the opposite stance: for him, the dignity of Church Slavonic lies precisely in its alleged capacity to render even the minutest details of the linguistic structure of Greek (Titov 1924: 74).

Another occasion for unfavorable comparisons was the relative stability of the Greek liturgical books and the constant deterioration of the Church Slavonic ones. This is the subject of a lengthy treatise written at the beginning of the 15th century by Konstantin Kostenečki, a Bulgarian refugee to the court of the Serbian despot Stefan Lazarević: the *Skazanie iz'javljenno o pismenex* "Elucidating treatise on the letters" (ed. by Jagić 1896: 95–199; Kuev & Petkov 1986: 82–224). Konstantin correctly identified the two main sources of textual instability: the absence of a codified norm and the bad training of the scribes. In his reform proposals, which have both a linguistic and a pedagogical side, he places great emphasis on the *antístoikha* – homophonous letters that could be used to differentiate between nonsynonymous words, as *světь* "light" vs. *svetь* "holy" (Jagić 1896: 114; Kuev & Petkov 1986: 109). It must have been Konstantin's attempts to learn Greek that taught him the importance of the *antístoikha*; indeed, some translation mistakes in the *Skazanie* bear witness to his inability to keep apart the many homophones of this language (*énklisis* = *zvanie*, i. e. *énklēsis*; *etumología* = *gotovoslovie*, i. e. *(h)etoimología*; for a different appreciation of Konstantin's abilities as a translator, see Goldblatt 1987: 321ff.). Carried to the extreme, Konstantin's program of orthographic reform would lead to a complete parallelism between form and meaning in written language and thus abolish, to a certain extent, the arbitrariness of its signs. All this fits well into the framework of the medieval philosophy of the sign with its well-known predilection for iconicity: Konstantin's linguistic views are hardly comparable to those of the Italian Humanists (*pace* Picchio 1975: 167ff.); neither is there a need to see in them a particular reflection of Orthodox monastic spirituality (Hesychasm) or the doctrinal positions of Gregory Palamas, the Byzantine theologian of the 14th century (*pace* Goldblatt 1984: 73ff.; cf. Živov 1986: 107f.).

## 3. Bibliography

### 3.1. Primary sources

*Adelphotes. Die erste gedruckte griechisch-kirchenslavische Grammatik. L'viv-Lemberg 1591.* Ed. by Olexa Horbatsch. München: Sagner, 1973. (2., um das Faksimile erweiterte Auflage 1988.)

Kostenečki, Konstantin = *Săbrani săčinenija na Konstantin Kostenečki* [Collected works of Konstantin Kostenečki.] Ed. by Kujo Kuev & Georgi Petkov. Sofia: Izdatelstvo na Bălgarskata Akademija na Naukite, 1986.

Smotryćkyj, Meletij, *Hrammatiki slavenskija pravilnoe syntagma.* Ed. by Olexa Horbatsch. Frankfurt/M.: Kubon & Sagner, 1974.

–. *Hramatyka.* Ed. by Vasylyj Vasyl'evyč Nimčuk. Kiev: Naukova dumka, 1979.

Xrabăr, Černorizec, *O pismenex* [On the letters.] Ed. by Alda Džambeluka-Kossova. Sofija: Izdatelstvo na Bălgarskata Akademija na Naukite, 1980.

Zyzanij, Lavrentij, *Hrammatika slovenska.* Ed. by Gerd Freidhof. Frankfurt/M.: Kubon & Sagner, 1972.

–. *Hramatyka Slovens'ka.* Ed. by Vasylyj Vasyl'evyč Nimčuk. Kiev: Naukova dumka, 1980.

### 3.2. Secondary sources


Archaimbault, Sylvie. 1992. "Les premières grammaires du slavon". *Histoire des idées linguistiques*, vol. II: *Le développement de la grammaire occidentale* ed. by Sylvain Auroux, 239–250. Liège: Mardaga.

Bulanin, Dmitrij M. 1995. "Drevnjaja Rus'" [Old Russia.] *Istorija russkoj perevodnoj xudožestvennoj literatury. Drevnjaja Rus'. XVIII vek* [History of Russian Literary Translations. Old Russia. 18th century.] Vol. I: *Proza* ed. by Ju. D. Levin, 17–73. Köln, Weimar & Wien: Böhlau; Saint-Petersburg: Dmitrij Bulaniu.

Daiber, Thomas. 1992. *Die Darstellung des Zeitworts in ostslavischen Grammatiken von den Anfängen bis zum ausgehenden 18. Jahrhundert.* Freiburg/Br.: Weiher.

Goldblatt, Harvey. 1984. "The Church Slavonic Language Question in the Fourteenth and Fifteenth Centuries: Constantine Kostenečki's *Skazanie iz'javljenno o pismenex*". *Aspects of the Slavic Language Question*, vol. I: *Church Slavonic – South Slavic – West Slavic*, 67–98. New Haven: Yale Concilium on International and Area Studies.

–. 1987. *Orthography and Orthodoxy: Constantine Kostenečki's Treatise on the Letters* (Skazanie iz'javljenno o pismenex.) Firenze: Le lettere.

Horbatsch, Olexa. 1964. *Die vier Ausgaben der kirchenslavischen Grammatik von M. Smotryćkyj.* Wiesbaden: Harrassowitz.

–, ed. 1973. *Adelphotes. Die erste gedruckte griechisch-kirchenslavische Grammatik. L'viv-Lemberg 1591.* München: Sagner. (2. ed., with facsimile, 1980.)

–, ed. 1974. *Meletyj Smotryćkyj. Hrammatiki slavenskija pravilnoe syntagma.* Frankfurt a. M.: Kubon & Sagner.

Ising, Erika. 1970. *Die Herausbildung der Grammatik der Volkssprachen in Mittel- und Osteuropa.* Berlin: Akademie der Wissenschaften.

Jagić, V[atroslav]. 1896. *Codex slovenicus rerum grammaticarum.* Berlin. (Repr. of separate ed., München: Fink, 1968.)

Keipert, Helmut. 1991. "Bezeichnungsmotive für den Präpositiv im Slavischen". *Natalicia Johanni Schröpfer octogenario a discipulis amicisque oblata*, 277–290. München: Kovač.

Kociuba, Ostap. 1975. *The Grammatical Sources of Meletij Smotryc'kyj's Church Slavonic Grammar of 1619.* Ph. D., Columbia University.

Kolesov, V[ladimir] V[iktorovič]. 1991. "Razvitie lingvističeskix idej u vostočnyx slavjan ėpoxi srednevekov'ja" [The Development of Linguistic Ideas among the Eastern Slavs in the Middle Ages.] *Istorija lingvističeskix učenij: Pozdnee srednevekov'e* [History of Linguistics: Late Middle Ages], 208–254. Saint-Petersburg: Nauka.

Kuev, Kujo & Georgi Petkov, eds. 1986. *Săbrani săčinenija na Konstantin Kostenečki* [Collected Works of Konstantin Kostenečki.] Sofia: Izdatelstvo na Bălgarskata Akademija na Naukite.

Mečkovskaja, Nina Borisovna. 1984. *Rannie vostočnoslavjanskie grammatiki* [The Early Grammars of the Eastern Slavs.] Minsk: Izdatel'stvo "Universitetskoe".

–. & A[dam] E[vgen'evič] Suprun. 1991. "Znanija o jazyke v srednevekovoj kul'ture južnyx i zapadnyx slavjan" [Linguistic Knowledge in the Medieval Culture of the Southern and Western Slavs.] *Istorija lingvističeskix učenij: Pozdnee srednevekov'e* [History of Linguistics: Late Middle Ages], 125–181. Saint-Petersburg: Nauka.

Nimčuk, Vasylyj Vasyl'evyč. 1985. *Movoznavstvo na Ukrajini v XIV–XVII st.* [Linguistics in the Ukraine in the 14th–17th Centuries.] Kiev: Naukova dumka.

Picchio, Riccardo. 1975. "On Russian Humanism: The philological revival". *Slavia* 44.161–171.

Sadnik, Linda, ed. 1967. *Des Hl. Johannes von Damaskus* Ékthesis akribẽs tẽs orthodóxou písteōs *in der Übersetzung des Exarchen Johannes.* Wiesbaden: Harrassowitz.

Strakhov, Olga B. 1998. *The Byzantine Culture in Muscovite Rus': The case of Evfimii Chudovskii (1620–1705).* Köln, Weimar & Wien: Böhlau.

Titov, Xv[edor]. 1924. *Materijaly dlja istoriji knyžnoji spravy na Vkrajini v XVI–XVIII v. v.* Kiev. (Facsimile repr., *Materialien zur Geschichte des Buchwesens in der Ukraine im 16. bis 18. Jahrhundert.* Köln & Wien: Böhlau, 1982.)

Tomelleri, Vittorio Springfield. 1996. Review of Zaxar'in (1995). *Ricerche Slavistiche* 43.589–596.

Toscano, Silvia. 1998. "Orthodox Slavdom". *History of Linguistics*, vol. III: *Renaissance and Early Modern Linguistics* ed. by Giulio Lepschy, 123–148. London & New York: Longman.

Uspenskij, Boris Andreevič. 1987. *Istorija russkogo literaturnogo jazyka (XI–XVII vv.)* [History of the Russian Literary Language (11th–17th centuries).] München: Sagner.

Weiher, Eckhard. 1977. "Die älteste Handschrift des grammatischen Traktats 'Über die acht Redeteile'". *Anzeiger für slavische Philologie* 9.367–427.

Worth, Dean S. 1983. *The Origins of Russian Grammar: Notes on the state of Russian philology before the advent of printed grammars.* Columbus, Ohio: Slavica Publishers.

Yalamas, Dimitris A. 1993. "The Significance of Standard Greek for the History of the Russian Literary Language and Culture in the Sixteenth-Eighteenth Centuries: The linguistic views of the Leikhoudis Brothers". *Modern Greek Studies Yearbook* 9.1–49.

Zaxar'in, Dmitrij Borisovič. 1995. *Evropejskie naučnye metody v tradicii starinnyx russkix grammatik (XV–ser. XVIII v.)* [The Methods of European Science in the Grammatical Tradition of Old Russia (15th–mid-18th century).] München: Sagner.

Ziffer, Giorgio. 1995. "Le fonti greche del monaco Chrabr". *Byzantinoslavica* 55.561–570.

Živov, V[iktor Markovič]. 1986. "Slavjanskie grammatičeskie sočinenija kak lingvističeskij istočnik" [Slavic Grammatical Works as a Linguistic Source.] *Russian Linguistics* 10.73–113.

–. & B[oris Andreevič] Uspenskij. 1986. "Grammatica sub specie theologiae". *Russian Linguistics* 10.259–279.

Žukovskaja, L[idija] P[etrovna]. 1982. "Barsovskij spisok grammatičeskogo sočinenija 'O vos'mi častjax slova' " [The Barsov Copy of the Grammatical Treatise 'On the Eight Parts of Speech'.] *Sxidnoslov'jans'ki hramatyky XVI–XVIII st.,* 29–51. Kiev: Naukova dumka.

*Yannis Kakridis, Thessaloniki (Greece)*

# XII. The Establishment of Linguistics in Rome
# Die Anfänge der Sprachforschung
# La constitution de la linguistique à Rome

## 66. Varro and the origin of Roman linguistic theory and practice


1. Introduction
2. Language and literature in early Rome
3. Varro's careers and works
4. The *De Lingua Latina*
5. Varro's language science
6. Conclusion
7. Bibliography (selected)


### 1. Introduction

Roman linguistics and Latin literature share a common origin in the latter half of the 3rd century BC: Livius Andronicus translates Homer's *Odyssey* into Latin around 240, and later Ennius (239–169 BC), the father of Latin literature, proudly boasts of his trilingualism (Latin, Greek, Oscan). This intellectual symbiosis continues throughout both the Roman republic and the empire, for the formal study of language and literature is from the outset the keystone of Roman education. So when St. Augustine establishes the word as the semiotic sign *par excellence* near the close of classical antiquity in the 4th century AD, he is merely putting his ecclesiastical *imprimatur* on what had long been the case in both pagan and Christian Rome. Language, literature, and education are intimately connected from start to finish in the Roman world, and the Roman *ars grammatica* becomes one of Rome's most significant contributions to Western intellectual history. Roman grammatical doctrine dominates the mediaeval world, and an enhanced understanding of ancient Roman linguistic and literary principles is crucial to the origin and development of Renaissance humanism, and thus of the modern intellect as well. Roman language science may be humble in origin and slow to develop, as Suetonius' late 1st century AD account of it makes clear, but it becomes a monumental intellectual and cultural achievement that even today garners the utmost respect and admiration.

### 2. Language and literature in early Rome

As Ennius and other early Roman poets strive for improved metrical and linguistic expression, they stretch both the Latin language and their audiences' understanding of that language. Plautus' comedies abound with *figurae etymologicae*, puns, and word play of all sorts, and since Plautus is Rome's most popular playwright, the degree to which he sportingly manipulates the Latin language suggests that his audiences were perhaps not quite as linguistically unsophisticated as usually supposed. His language is exceptional when compared with contemporary documents in prose, e. g., the *Senatus Consultum de Bacchanalibus*, and its virtues are later extolled as being worthy of the Muses, who would use Plautine diction were they to speak Latin. In 168 BC or so the Stoic philosopher Crates of Mallos comes to Rome on a diplomatic mission, breaks a leg (apparently by stumbling into one of Rome's famous sewers), and discourses upon grammatical subjects while recuperating. This event signals the beginning of a more formal and more intense interest in linguistic matters on the Romans' part. Poets such as Lucilius (180?–102) and Accius (170–90) actually argue over Latin orthography and even suggest reforms in spelling, thereby witnessing to another distinguishing feature of Roman language science, namely, its eminently practical bent. The so-called Scipionic circle consciously seeks a more elegant Latinity: Lucilius' satires criticize poor expression and prove that the quality of a man's speech is of importance in Roman society, and Terence, a non-native speaker of Latin who is destined to become early Rome's most quoted literary figure, writes a Latin that is so exquisite it provokes contemporary charges of plagiarism but later engenders extravagant praise from the likes of Cicero and Julius Caesar.

A generation later Lucius Aelius Stilo (late 2nd century), who can claim both Cicero and Varro as students, becomes Rome's first scholar of note. Though a Stoic, he introduces Romans to Alexandrian or Hellenistic language science, which privileges literary criticism as the noblest part of grammar and emphasizes philological activity. Stilo therefore edits and critiques poetic texts, interprets and comments on extant early Latin hymns and legal documents, and employs his keen sense of etymology in all his endeavors; he initiates the complicated process, completed ultimately by Varro, of separating genuine Plautine plays from the many spurious ones circulating in Rome at the end of the 2nd century. The first grammar mentioned in a Latin text dates to the early 1st century BC, but it is probably never completed and surely never published. In the course of that historic century Cicero and Caesar both achieve unparalleled political success due partly to their ability to use the Latin language with force and vigor. Rome had never before heard or read anything quite like Ciceronian orations or Caesar's commentaries on his Gallic campaigns. Though politically divided, together they raise Latin prose to unprecedented heights, and they do so consciously, as witness the many linguistic topics in Cicero's correspondence and Caesar's treatise on analogy. In poetry Lucretius imports the Epicurean theory on the origin of language to Rome, and Catullus makes fun of Romans who ignorantly mimic a fake Greek accent. Nigidius Figulus' recondite Pythagorean commentaries on literature indirectly suggest that some intellectuals are by now writing primarily for their peers. As for Greeks, both the rhetorician Dionysius of Halicarnassus and the grammarian Tryphon come to Rome to ply their crafts, and Didymus learns enough about Latin linguistics to author a treatise on analogy among the Romans. Far and away the most important figure in the intellectual life of Rome in the 1st century BC, or of any century for that matter, is Marcus Terentius Varro (116–27), and the subject that is dearest to his heart is the Latin language.

## 3. Varro's careers and works

Varro's lengthy lifetime spanned one of the most volatile and violent periods in Roman history, and for slightly more than half his life Varro actively pursued a not undistinguished military career, in the course of which he earned decoration and honor, traveled widely, amassed great wealth, and acquired vast knowledge. He then commenced his scholarly career, which was interrupted by the great civil war. In the ugly aftermath to the Ides of March, which saw Cicero murdered ignominiously, Varro too was proscribed, went into hiding, and escaped death only through the intervention of highly placed friends. He died in the year which traditionally marks the beginning of the Roman empire, having authored at least 74 scholarly works consisting of 620 books or chapters, a prodigious output by any standard. Some of his works were authored during his military career, but most must have been written later in life, some presumably at his luxurious villa south of Rome at Casinum which contained an extensive library, unfortunately destroyed by Mark Antony. Varro's immense productivity has amazed everyone from St. Jerome, who transmits an incomplete catalogue of his works, to modern scholars interested in his scholarly methods. Varro's interests were as wide as learning itself, and he habitually dictated notes on what he observed, excerpts from the many books he read, and voluminous comments of his own; he then compiled the notes, excerpts, and comments into learned tomes, which as a result were often less than well organized, and he added little or no literary polish to his prose, which from the outset has been repeatedly criticized. Nonetheless Varro's scholarship brought him an unparalleled reputation which began during his lifetime and which has been continuously reaffirmed throughout the centuries by scholars equally distinguished, e. g., Quintilian, St. Augustine, Petrarch, Montaigne, and today he is uniformly acknowledged as ancient Rome's most productive and most outstanding scholar.

Varro's corpus is remarkable for both breadth and depth, for he is an intellectually curious observer of Roman life and letters and a prolific chronicler of Roman cultural history. His major works include, *inter alia*, the *Antiquitates*, a veritable encyclopedia of Roman religious and cultural institutions; the *Imagines*, an illustrated biographical dictionary, presumably the first work of its kind; the *Disciplinae*, an account of the nine *artes liberales* (the usual seven plus medicine and architecture); the *Logistorici*, miscellaneous dialogues named after famous persons; the

*De Re Rustica*, a set of discursive but genial conversations on farming; several works on the Roman stage and Plautus; and literary satires, especially of the Menippean variety, in which he pokes fun at himself and his peers. Yet it is as a linguist that Varro is known best, for perhaps as many as ten of his treatises deal with grammatical topics. Unfortunately, most of Varro's immense corpus is no longer extant, and only three works have survived in a readable form. The *De Re Rustica* is complete in three books and shows that even in a work on agriculture Varro's interest in language never lags far behind the main topic; the 600 or so lines of his Menippean satires attest amply to his wit, patriotism, and, on occasion, felicity of expression; and six books of his *magnum opus*, the *De Lingua Latina*, provide us with the greatest insights into his linguistic theory and practice. The *De Lingua Latina* originally consisted of an introductory book followed by six books on etymological theory (2–4) and practice (5–7), six books on morphological theory (8–10, usually misread as an account of a putative analogy/anomaly quarrel) and practice (11–13), and then twelve books (14–25) on syntax, which were probably as logical as they were linguistic. Only books 5–10 survive, however, and it is on these that Varro's longstanding scholarly reputation is based.

## 4. The *De Lingua Latina*

Though Varro inherits much from Greek language science, most notably its elaborate taxonomy and developed nomenclature, he nonetheless consistently charts his own independent course in the *De Lingua Latina*. Thus he both borrows (*analogia*) and calques (*tempus, casus*) as well as invents (*casus sextus*) technical terms, although he often employs the vocabulary of everyday intellectual discourse in Latin as a technical metalanguage. He eschews entirely the semantic-based Hellenistic definitions of the canonical parts of speech, preferring to define his *partes orationis* on a strictly morphological basis, the presence or absence of case and tense, and therefore to enumerate only four: words with case, with tense, with both case and tense, with neither; this system based on binary distinctive morphological features is unique to Varro. Varro distinguishes, for the first time in the history of linguistics, between derivational and inflectional morphology and as a result has a much clearer view of both nominal and verbal morphology, to which he applies abstract mathematical models, another first. These models in turn allow him to identify some entirely novel grammatical constructs, namely, five declensions and three conjugations. By adapting a Stoic account of verbal aspect and applying his arithmetical model Varro also identifies the future perfect indicative, an entity otherwise completely absent from Latin grammar for the next 15 centuries, at which time the *De Lingua Latina* is edited for the first time in its present castrated form. Varro even advances the cause of etymology by deriving Latin words from other Latin words and privileging Latin semantics rather than positing Greek origins and relations. He regularly cites obsolete words attested in archaic documents as evidence for otherwise inexplicable contemporary forms and sometimes reconstructs unattested forms to explain aberrant synchronic forms. He uses *radix* "root" in a quasi-modern sense and does not indulge in etymologies *ex contrariis* "on the basis of antonyms", thereby departing from standard Roman practice in two significant ways. The *De Lingua Latina*, especially book ten, the contents of which are almost completely unprecedented and wholly Varronian, is therefore a seminal text in the history of linguistics, and Varro's version of language science is both independent and innovative.

## 5. Varro's language science

For Varro *declinatio* "morphological variation" is a universal linguistic process; *declinatio voluntaria* is derivational morphology, and *declinatio naturalis* is inflectional morphology. As the Latin adjectives denote, the former is arbitrary and human, the latter is systematic and natural, and so, although the former is for the most part subject to etymological analysis, the latter is the proper domain of linguistic inquiry. The grammarian therefore seeks to determine, define, and delimit morphological regularity, i. e., establish paradigms, by comparing words, which are the atomic primes of language. (Varro does employ *exitus* as "ending, desinence" and does isolate morphemes, but his is a word-based theory nonetheless.) Such comparison must be conducted properly: only words in the same part of speech can be compared with one another. The basis of the comparison is twofold: sound and grammatical meaning; semantics are not at issue, and the lexicon is not involved. Words manifesting a linguistic *analogia* "proportion" as rigorous as an arithmetical *analogia* may be classified together. Nominal inflection is like a disjoined proportion (1:2::10:20). Aspect is fundamental to the character of the Latin verb, and therefore imperfective verbs must be compared only with other imperfective verbs, and perfective verbs only with other perfectives. The verbal model is conjoined (1:2::2:4) because the past is to the present as the present is to the future. When properly compared on the basis of phonological form and morphological substance, Latin nouns can be classified into five sets, most easily identified by the vowel (*a, e, i, o*, or *u*) ending the ablative case, the case-form unique to Latin. Verb conjugations are three in number, as witness the vowels (*a, e, i*) before the *-s* in the second person singular active indicative present form. As is obvious, Varro ignores vocalic length, and so his declensions and conjugations are not quite exact. They are all there in theory, however, and only need to be fleshed out in practice, and he has identified them by means of orderly and principled heuristic procedures, which together constitute a rather sophisticated methodology for the 1st century BC. Varro's approach is rigorously formal, for linguistic questions are asked for their own sake and require linguistic, and only linguistic, answers. It is in such a way that Varro makes of language science an autonomous endeavor.

## 6. Conclusion

In time Varro becomes far and away the most frequently cited linguist in the monumental Roman grammatical tradition, and in that sense he is its most authoritative figure. He is also a founding figure. He commences the important process of importing, Latinizing, and thereby rendering permanent the technical vocabulary of Greek language science. He accords such a respect to etymological analysis and practices it with such expertise that despite its critics etymology remains a commonplace intellectual and academic endeavor throughout Roman (and most subsequent) history. He succeeds in distancing Roman language science from the subtle semantic distinctions ubiquitous in Greek grammar and in predicating Latin grammar on a more formal, morphological foundation, which makes Latin language science both more practical and therefore more characteristically Roman. And perhaps most important, he discovers the declensions and conjugations of Latin, which become the centerpiece of all subsequent Latin grammatical theory and practice. Varro's numerous linguistic texts do not survive primarily because they never became a part of the Roman educational system. Varro's successors, however, revise many of his specific analyses (e. g., his declensions and conjugations), rename others (the *regula Varronis* becomes the *regula ablativi*: the ending in the ablative singular predicts the entire plural inflection), and dispense with others (e. g., his four *partes orationis*); they also amass a wealth of citations from Latin literature to serve as evidence for the many grammatical rules and regulations they propose, and, of course, they do to the entire apparatus of Latin grammar what Romans do best – they organize it into the monumental *ars grammatica* (→ Art. 68, 69). *In fine*, Varro originates and bequeathes to posterity a fully autonomous and distinctly Roman language science that becomes the first of the liberal arts and one of ancient Rome's most longlasting contributions to intellectual history.

## 7. Bibliography (selected)

Collart, Jean. 1954. *Varron grammairien latin*. Paris: Les Belles Lettres.

Dahlmann, Hellfried. 1932. *Varro und die hellenistische Sprachtheorie*. Berlin & Zürich: Weidman. (Repr., 1964.)

Kaster, Robert A. 1995. *Suetonius: De grammaticis et rhetoribus*. Oxford: Clarendon; New York: Oxford Univ. Press.

Pfaffel, Wilhelm. 1981. *Quartus Gradus Etymologiae: Untersuchungen zur Etymologie Varros in De Lingua Latina*. Königstein/Ts.: Hain.

Rawson, Elizabeth. 1985. *Intellectual Life in the Late Roman Republic*. Baltimore: John Hopkins Univ. Press.

Taylor, Daniel J. 1996. *Varro: De Lingua Latina X*. Amsterdam & Philadelphia: Benjamins.

*Daniel J. Taylor, Appleton, WI (USA)*

# 67. A l'origine de la tradition artigraphique latine, entre mythe et réalité

1. Introduction
2. Palémon et son *ars* d'après les textes anciens
3. La reconstruction de Barwick et ses faiblesses
4. Palémon et l'hellénisation de la grammaire à Rome
5. Un témoin de la structure originelle de l'*ars* latine: Quintilien
6. Bibliographie

## 1. Introduction

La première allusion qui soit faite dans les textes latins à une *ars grammatica* remonte à la *Rhétorique à Hérennius*, dans les années 80 a.C. Le contexte est celui du développement sur l'élocution, dont l'auteur anonyme dit qu'elle a trois qualités, *elegantia* "élégance", *compositio* "arrangement harmonieux des mots" et *dignitas* "ornementation"; l'*elegantia* à son tour a deux subdivisions, *latinitas* "latinité" et *explanatio* "clarté", et l'auteur commente ainsi la *latinitas* (4, 17):

La latinité est ce qui garde sa pureté au langage en le mettant à l'abri de tout défaut. Les défauts du langage, qui l'empêchent d'être vraiment latin, peuvent être de deux sortes: le solécisme et le barbarisme. Il y a solécisme lorsque, dans un groupe de mots, le mot qui vient après ne se combine pas avec le mot qui vient avant; il y a barbarisme quand il y a une prononciation fautive dans les mots. Comment éviter cela, nous le montrerons dans une *ars grammatica* "une grammaire".

Cette indication ne garantit nullement qu'il y ait eu à Rome à l'époque de ce texte une grammaire latine du genre des *artes* tardives. L'auteur de la *Rhétorique à Hérennius*, qui suivait selon toute vraisemblance un modèle grec, peut s'être ici simplement conformé aux indications de ce modèle sur la répartition des tâches entre rhétorique et grammaire, et avoir transposé littéralement en latin le projet purement grec de rédiger une *tékhnē grammatikḗ* – tout comme il expose par ailleurs (3, 3) son projet d'écrire un traité sur l'art militaire et un autre sur l'art politique. En tout état de cause, quand bien même l'auteur anonyme aurait réalisé ce projet, il n'en reste aucune trace. Il ne paraît donc pas raisonnable de placer si haut l'origine de la tradition artigraphique latine.

En fait, il n'y a pas d'attestation sûre d'une *ars grammatica* à Rome avant celle de Palémon, au début du Ier siècle de notre ère. Cet auteur occupe ainsi le point d'origine de la tradition artigraphique, au moins d'après les attestations dont nous disposons. Cette particularité l'a placé au centre d'un débat historiographique important, qui met en jeu la vision d'ensemble que l'on peut avoir de la tradition grammaticale romaine. Ce débat culmine avec l'ouvrage de K. Barwick (1922), *Remmius Palaemon und die römische ars grammatica.* Le problème historiographique qui est ici en question a pris une telle importance qu'il convient de l'exposer lui-même, pour saisir les enjeux de toute interprétation sur Palémon.

## 2. Palémon et son *ars* d'après les textes anciens

Mais d'abord, de quels éléments dispose-t-on à propos de Palémon? A vrai dire, on sait beaucoup de choses sur ce personnage, grâce à la notice de Suétone dans le *De grammaticis et rhetoribus* (XXIII). Esclave de naissance, ayant "appris les lettres en accompagnant à l'école le fils de sa maîtresse", il enseigna à Rome, une fois affranchi, avec beaucoup de succès, malgré la mauvaise réputation attachée à ses mœurs, et qui était telle que Tibère, puis Claude, affirmaient qu'il était le dernier à qui confier ses enfants. Suétone insiste sur quelques particularités de ce personnage: ses talents de versificateur, "dans des mètres variés et peu communs"; sa superbe, qui l'avait conduit notamment à proclamer "que les lettres étaient nées et mourraient avec lui", et à traiter Varron de porc; ses rapports avec l'argent et les femmes, sa prodigalité et ses débauches; il était en tout cas fort riche, devant sa fortune à la fois à son école, à ses fabriques de confection et à ses vignes, si célèbres que Pline lui-même s'en fait l'écho (*Nat. hist.* 14, 49–51).

Pour des raisons discutées, Suétone ne dit rien de l'*Ars grammatica* qui a assuré le succès posthume de Palémon. Ce texte est pourtant régulièrement associé dans l'Antiquité à Palémon, ainsi chez Pline, dans le passage déjà cité ([...] *Remmio Palaemoni, alias grammatica arte celebri* [...]), ou chez Juvénal, qui pour évoquer une pédante lui met entre les mains l'*Ars* de Palémon (6, 451–453). Le même Juvénal fait de Palémon le représentant de toute la profession, l'archétype du grammairien, mais en tant que tel il le présente comme pauvre, alors qu'il était au contraire fort riche: dans l'esprit de Juvénal il ne s'agissait pas d'évoquer l'individu Palémon, mais les grammariens en général. Pourquoi est-ce Palémon plutôt qu'un autre grammairien qui a été choisi pour désigner génériquement toute la profession? Il semble bien qu'il doive ce succès à cette fameuse *Ars*.

La tradition nous a transmis quelques fragments de ce texte. Quatre passages sont en effet rapportés nommément à Palémon chez les artigraphes. Charisius en présente trois, qui chacun sont des chapitres consacrés à une catégorie de mots particulière, la conjonction (*GL* I, 225.5–226.10), la préposition (231.1–236.15), et l'interjection (238.23–25). Consentius présente un quatrième passage, qui est une brève notice sur la répartition des formes de l'optatif et du subjonctif (*GL* V, 375.7–8). A ces quatre passages on doit ajouter une citation de Priscien, qui évoque le nom de Palémon à propos de la traduction latine de la notion grecque d'esprit doux (*GL* II, 35.27).

A l'époque moderne, il est apparu très tôt que ces rares témoignages ne représentaient certainement qu'une partie de l'héritage palémonien dans les textes grammaticaux latins qui nous sont parvenus. C'est la composition même de certains chapitres de Charisius qui a fait naître cette idée. Dans les exposés qu'il consacre à la conjonction, à la préposition et à l'interjection, où il cite nommément Palémon, Charisius procède toujours de la même façon. Il superpose en effet trois textes d'origine différente, chaque fois dans le même ordre: un court paragraphe de Cominianus comporte la doctrine grammaticale sous sa forme la plus scolaire, puis vient le chapitre de Palémon, et enfin Charisius cite des extraits, parfois très longs, d'un traité de Julius Romanus, les *Aphormai*, où les termes analysés sont cités par ordre alphabétique.

Or cette même composition se retrouve dans le chapitre consacré à l'adverbe (180.27–224.22). Là aussi Charisius procède par superposition, en commençant par Cominianus et en terminant par Romanus. Entre eux, Charisius cite deux textes, mais anonymes. Il est évidemment tout à fait vraisemblable que l'un des deux remonte à Palémon, comme dans les chapitres sur la conjonction, la préposition et l'interjection. Précisément, le second de ces textes s'ouvre par l'exemple *Palaemon docet* (187.1). Dès 1857, H. Keil, dans la préface de son édition de Charisius, soulignait fortement ce point (*GL* I, xlix). C'est l'amorce de l'extension des attributions à Palémon: dès lors que Charisius, qui cite plusieurs chapitres de Palémon, ne se prive pas à l'occasion d'utiliser son texte sans référence explicite, il est légitime de considérer que l'*Ars* de Palémon a été beaucoup plus exploitée que Charisius ou sa source ne veut l'avouer. H. Keil note ainsi que l'ensemble du livre III de Charisius, consacré à des remarques annexes sur le verbe, a toute chance de remonter à Palémon.

On le voit, l'idée de faire de Palémon l'une des sources essentielles du texte de Charisius est ancienne.

Par ailleurs, il était également admis avant les travaux de K. Barwick que Palémon avait composé une *ars* grammaticale fortement marquée par la grammaire alexandrine. Sur de nombreux points en effet la comparaison entre les textes explicitement attribués à Palémon chez Charisius et les passages correspondants de la *Tékhnē* qui nous a été transmise sous le nom de Denys le Thrace montre une identité de doctrine et parfois même de formulation. Déjà G. Uhlig (*GG* I, 1, vi) insistait sur cette parenté dans son édition de la *Tékhnē*. Ces rapprochements ont leurs limites, mais sont fondés: quelle que soit la date de composition de la *Tékhnē* attribuée à Denys, ce texte comporte des éléments anciens de la grammaire alexandrine, et il est légitime, lorsqu'on repère des parallélismes entre ce texte et ce qui nous reste de Palémon, de considérer que cet auteur a pu introduire lui-même dans la grammaire romaine ces éléments de la grammaire alexandrine.

Ainsi, à la fin du XIXe siècle, les témoignages de l'*Ars* de Palémon étaient considérés comme étant en principe extensibles: le texte d'origine avait dû peser sur la tradition artigraphique bien au-delà des passages nommément rapportés à Palémon, et l'analyse de ce texte appelait a priori de nouvelles attributions.

## 3. La reconstruction de Barwick et ses faiblesses

Karl Barwick a enrichi et complété cette doctrine en l'insérant dans une vision d'ensemble. Si l'on résume la thèse qu'il développe dans son *Remmius Palaemon*, tout part selon lui de l'un des points traités par l'Ancien stoïcisme dans le cadre de sa dialectique, le *tópos perì phōnḗs*, dont on a une idée précise grâce au résumé de dialectique stoïcienne raporté par Diogène Laërce (*Vie des Philosophes*, VII, 43–83), et dont on sait qu'il a été à l'occasion isolé sous forme de *Tekhnē perì phōnḗs* "traité de la voix". De ce traité stoïcien auraient découlé d'une part une *Tékhnē* stoico-pergaménienne, très proche dans sa conception de son modèle stoïcien, et d'autre part la *Tékhnē* de Denys le Thrace, marquée quant à elle par la science alexandrine. Le texte le plus proche de l'origine stoïcienne, la *Tékhnē* stoico-pergaménienne, serait passée très tôt à Rome sous la forme d'une *ars* scolaire, fondant ainsi à Rome la *Schulgrammatik* qui va se maintenir jusqu'à la fin de l'Antiquité. Par ailleurs, la *Tékhnē* de Denys le Thrace aurait inspiré plus tard, au I^er^ siècle de notre ère, une autre *ars*, celle de Palémon. Ce texte, qui introduit à Rome les innovations de la science alexandrine, aurait entraîné des modifications dans la *Schulgrammatik*, et suscité un écho profond chez les artigraphes postérieurs. Dans cette perspective, l'*Ars* de Palémon occuperait un rôle central dans l'histoire de la grammaire latine. Dans l'espèce de triangle dont les trois sommets seraient d'une part l'origine stoïcienne, d'autre part le traité de Denys, enfin les *artes* latines tardives, le texte de Palémon occuperait en quelque sorte le centre, la place de pivot: c'est lui qui assurerait l'unité de l'ensemble, qui garantirait la cohérence de l'histoire de la grammaire latine antique. D'autres textes grammaticaux seraient assurément présents dans la tradition latine, mais leur influence n'aurait qu'un caractère marginal: ce serait le cas par exemple des études de Pansa sur la *latinitas*. Quant au texte de Quintilien sur la grammaire, au livre I de l'*Institution oratoire*, ce serait un montage, sans véritable unité organique.

La conception développée par Karl Barwick appelle de profondes critiques.

Sur le fond, son interprétation est caractérisée par le fixisme historique qu'elle tend à instaurer dans la grammaire ancienne. Selon Karl Barwick, l'*ars grammatica* romaine est bâtie sur un schéma qui remonte à la *Tékhnē perì phōnḗs* des stoïciens, c'est-à-dire qu'il n'y aurait, de Chrysippe à Donat, que des évolutions marginales: "des éléments à l'énoncé, la progression est la même" (1922: 92). Cette affirmation est erronée.

Dans la théorie dialectique qui nous est rapportée par Diogène Laërce, l'analyse du signifiant, qui constitue la première partie de cette théorie, est présentée selon les trois réalisations possibles de ce signifiant: la *phōnḗ*, la *léxis*, le *lógos*. La *phōnḗ*, ou "voix", n'est a priori ni articulée ni porteuse de signification, et comprend donc aussi bien la voix animale que la voix humaine: c'est simplement le son vocal; la *léxis* est caractérisée par le fait qu'elle est articulée, et donc susceptible d'être présentée sous forme écrite, mais elle n'est pas a priori porteuse de signification: c'est du son vocal articulé; enfin, le *lógos* est doublement caractérisé par le fait qu'il est articulé et porteur de signification: c'est le signifiant en tant qu'énoncé. On peut considérer ce découpage comme une hiérarchie en pyramide, où la *phōnḗ* est l'ensemble du son qui peut être émis par un organe vocal, la *léxis* l'ensemble plus restreint du son vocal qui peut être articulé, et le *lógos* l'ensemble encore plus restreint du son vocal articulé qui est porteur d'une signification. La *phōnḗ* n'a pas elle-même de souscatégories dans la mesure où elle n'est pas susceptible de découpages; en revanche, la *léxis* se décompose en éléments, les sons élémentaires qu'on articule dans une langue; quant au *lógos*, l'énoncé, sa description est triple: il est d'abord décomposé en constituants (les 'parties du discours' ou constituants de l'énoncé), puis sont présentés ses qualités et ses défauts (*aretaí* et *kakíai*), enfin sont distinguées ses diverses formes.

Tout différemment, la progression que l'on trouve dans les grammaires (lettre/syllabe/mot/énoncé) remonte à la pratique de la lecture: dans la succession de lettres que constitue la ligne d'écriture, l'apprentissage de la lecture devait procéder par découpages successifs, c'est-à-dire par découpage de la syllabe où se réalise le son, puis découpage d'une unité plus étendue où se réalise un sens partiel, puis découpage d'une grande unité où se réalise un sens complet. Ce qui suffit à montrer la très profonde différence des deux analyses, celle des stoïciens et celle des grammaires, c'est que l'une des unités sur laquelle se fondent les grammaires, la syllabe, fondamentale puisqu'elle est le découpage de base dans la progression qui conduit des lettres à l'énoncé, est entièrement absente de l'analyse stoïcienne, qui n'en a que faire étant donné sa propre perspective. Etablir un lien de filiation entre ces deux types de description n'a aucune pertinence.

Par ailleurs, la place accordée à la *Tékhnē* de Denys le Thrace dans l'analyse de Karl Barwick suppose non seulement son authenticité, remise en cause depuis et qui constitue un débat sur lequel on ne s'aventurera pas ici (→ Art. 57), mais surtout son unité, sur laquelle Karl Barwick s'appuie pour établir un paralléliseme entre ce texte et la *Tékhnē perì phōnē̃s* stoïcienne ou les *artes* latines tardives. Or quoi qu'on pense du problème de l'authenticité, l'unité même du texte, constitué d'une part d'une introduction sur les différentes parties de la grammaire, d'autre part d'une analyse des 'parties du discours', est tout à fait improbable.

Enfin, et toujours dans cette même perspective d'un fixisme historique, Karl Barwick postule une stabilité du plan des *artes* romaines qui est tout à fait illusoire. Ce qui est présenté comme le plan de base est celui de l'*Ars maior* de Donat, subdivisée en trois parties: la première consacrée à la voix, la lettre, la syllabe, les pieds, l'accentuation et la ponctuation; la deuxième aux catégories de mots; la troisième aux défauts de l'énoncé (solécisme, barbarismes et 'autres défauts') et à ses qualités (métaplasmes, figures et tropes). Le texte de Donat a la réputation d'être le modèle le plus achevé de ce type de traités. C'est affaire d'appréciation, mais on ne peut pas dire qu'il représente l'unique modèle du schéma artigraphique. Si l'on examine en effet les autres grandes *artes* du III$^{e}$ et du IV$^{e}$ siècles qui nous sont parvenues, celles de Sacerdos, de Charisius et de Diomède, on se trouve en présence de plans tout à fait différents, comme cela sera exposé dans le chapitre suivant (→ Art. 68).

Sans doute Karl Barwick tient-il compte de ces divergences, mais il les présente comme des phénomènes secondaires: tandis qu'il affirme dès les premières lignes de son ouvrage que le plan d'ensemble des grammaires romaines est stable (1922: 1), il cite les divergences incontestables que nous venons d'évoquer aux pages 245 à 248, et les présente comme résultant de modifications du plan originel, dues à des raisons pédagogiques et à des confusions entre le domaine des *artes* et celui des traités sur la *latinitas*. Cette interprétation revient à retrouver le plan de Donat dans toutes les autres *artes*, et à interpréter celles-ci comme de simples variantes, affectées d'un plus ou moins haut degré de déviance, par rapport à ce schéma donatien érigé en plan type. C'est reconnaître assurément la diversité du plan des *artes*, mais pour y distinguer une preuve supplémentaire, et paradoxale, de la stabilité de ce plan.

Ce fixisme historique a conduit Karl Barwick à élaborer l'hypothèse de la *Schulgrammatik*, pièce essentielle dans ce dispositif et qui n'est en fait qu'une abstraction. A partir de premiers rapprochements entre Donat et Charisius, Karl Barwick, à la suite de Jeep et de Bölte, établit, pour chaque point de doctrine, une sorte de faisceau de points d'accord entre les grammairiens. L'ensemble de ces faisceaux, Karl Barwick lui donne une consistance, un véritable caractère concret: c'est la *Schulgrammatik*, l'enseignement scolaire de base, la vulgate par rapport à laquelle certaines doctrines se démarquent, mais qui sert, dans le dispositif mis en place, à établir une continuité, une permanence doctrinale. En fait, Karl Barwick transforme une abstraction, en l'occurrence le plus petit dénominateur commun d'un ensemble de textes, en un texte particulier, et mieux en une série de textes particuliers, qui se reproduiraient de siècle en siècle, avec même des évolutions, dues à l'influence des recherches savantes. C'est une pure hypothèse, qui renforce le fixisme historique de l'ensemble en faisant remonter certains points de doctrine à l'origine de la grammaire à Rome, sous prétexte qu'ils apparaissent à la fois chez plusieurs grammairiens des III$^{e}$ et IV$^{e}$ siècles.

Dans le détail enfin les reconstructions auxquelles se livre Karl Barwick, et les arguments qu'il apporte à l'appui de sa thèse, tiennent souvent le succès qu'ils ont rencontré de leur enchevêtrement, qui décourage la vérification. En fait, si on démêle patiemment l'écheveau des hypothèses ainsi formé, on s'aperçoit que la multiplication des conjectures ne les renforce pas, mais les affaiblit. Un bon exemple de ce phénomène est apporté par l'analyse de la 'troisième partie' de l'*ars* latine. Cette troisième partie, consacrée aux *uitia uirtutesque orationis*, porterait tout particulièrement la marque de l'origine stoïcienne de la grammaire, dans la mesure où la dialectique stoïcienne comporte elle-même une présentation des *aretaì lógou* "qualités de l'énoncé" et des *kakíai lógou* "défauts de l'énoncé", dans la partie qui porte sur la description du signifiant, après la liste des différentes catégories de mots. En fait, la perspective n'est pas la même: chez les artigraphes latins l'analyse porte sur les écarts par rapport à la norme, ces écarts étant situés symétriquement par rapport à cette norme, avec trois écarts négatifs d'un côté (barbarisme, solécisme, autres défauts), et trois écarts positifs de l'autre (métaplasme, figure, trope); dans la perspective adoptée par les stoïciens en revanche, l'étude des *aretaì lógou* et des *kakíai* repose sur une opposition entre la norme, définie par cinq qualités (grécité, clarté, concision, justesse, élégance), et les fautes, divisées en barbarisme et solécisme. Il n'y a rien de commun entre ces deux constructions. En plus, cette recherche d'une source stoïcienne présuppose que la présentation des qualités et des défauts de l'énoncé est une donnée constante, homogène et stable de l'*ars* latine, sa 'troisième partie', mais ce n'est même pas le cas, comme le montre la diversité des plans des *artes*. Ce que l'on voit simplement à l'œuvre dans toute cette recherche d'une source stoïcienne, c'est cette audace de méthode si fréquente en matière de *Quellenforschung*, qui consiste à reconstituer la source d'après le descendant qu'on lui suppose. On peut faire de semblables remarques à propos de la définition et des classifications des catégories de mots, et de place en place à propos de la plupart des reconstructions qui tendent à confirmer par des analyses de détail la vision d'ensemble initialement affirmée. Le fameux argument de Schottmüller (1858), ce *wahrer Talisman* comme on a dit à l'époque (Palémon introduirait systématiquement ses exemples par le terme *uelut*) ne convainc pas davantage: considéré isolément, dans les passages explicitement attribués à Palémon, il ne paraît pas suffisamment pertinent, et au-delà de ces limites, même combiné avec d'autres 'indices', notamment terminologiques, il devient trop conjectural pour être valablement retenu.

Il paraît donc indispensable de renoncer à la conception d'ensemble de Karl Barwick, où la dialectique stoïcienne jouait le rôle de matrice, la *Tékhnē* de Denys le rôle de relais enrichi par la science alexandrine, et Palémon celui d'introducteur à Rome du schéma mis au point par Denys, au détriment de la grammaire scolaire simplement marquée par son origine purement stoïcienne. Comment dès lors aborder le problème posé par Palémon?

## 4. Palémon et l'hellénisation de la grammaire à Rome

Il serait inutile et stérile de partir des mêmes bases que Karl Barwick. En d'autres termes, l'objectif ne doit pas être de partir d'un nom, celui de Palémon en l'occurrence, et d'y raccrocher par approximations successives le maximum d'éléments en espérant parvenir à une certaine masse critique qui permette de créer un effet de consistance doctrinale. Quelle que soit la vraisemblance à laquelle on peut parvenir, le résultat ne serait pas différent dans son principe de celui auquel Karl Barwick est parvenu, et reposerait de la même façon sur une somme de détails dont chacun est en fait contestable. Plutôt que de chercher à accumuler des hypothèses, il paraît préférable de se limiter au principe historique auquel Palémon peut être rattaché, et qui permette d'interpréter le rôle et la fonction de ce grammairien dans l'histoire.

Quand on examine dans le détail les textes qui nous ont été transmis sous le nom de Palémon, on constate, comme on l'a fait depuis plus d'un siècle, une parenté avec la doctrine grammaticale telle qu'elle est attestée dans la *Tékhnē* qui nous est parvenue sous le nom de Denys. C'est par exemple le cas pour le texte sur la conjonction: la classification proposée par Palémon s'inspire des conceptions alexandrines, fondées sur des catégories essentiellement sémantiques, et sur leur multiplication. En revanche, il existait auparavant à Rome une classification en cinq catégories, qui s'est d'ailleurs maintenue par la suite au détriment des innovations de Palémon, et qui n'était pas déterminée par des critères sémantiques, mais fondée sur le modèle classique d'analyse des relations entre éléments dans un ensemble complexe, par addition, soustraction, permutation ou substitution, que les Anciens appliquent aux phénomènes les plus divers. L'application de ce modèle aux conjonctions est une spécificité romaine, et aboutit par exemple à ce que des conjonctions comme *aut* ou *neque* soient associées dans une seule et même catégorie (parce qu'elles marquent toutes deux une relation de soustraction), alors que leurs correspondants sont toujours distingués chez les grammairiens grecs, et répartis entre deux catégories différentes. Contre l'application de ce modèle et la classification en cinq catégories à laquelle elle aboutissait, Palémon est l'auteur d'une classification plus riche, mais dans le fond moins réfléchie, constituée sur la base des catégories sémantiques élaborées par la grammaire alexandrine et dont on retrouve encore la trace dans la *Tékhnē* attribuée à Denys.

Il en va de même pour les modes. On trouve chez Varron (*De Lingua Latina* X, 31) une quadripartition des formes modales qui montre que l'objectif de cet auteur était de parvenir à une coïncidence rigoureuse entre d'une part des séries morphologiques et d'autre part des catégories d'énonciation (interrogation, réponse, souhait, ordre). Varron donne ainsi une expression systématique au recouvrement de la morphologie verbale et des catégories de l'énonciation, alors que ce recouvrement n'apparaissait que de façon partielle et empirique chez les grammairiens alexandrins. Ce type de découpage aboutit à reconnaître un optatif, mais pas de subjonctif: la notion de subjonctif n'a rien à voir avec des catégories de l'énonciation. C'est une analyse linguistique originale, restée sans postérité. Contre cette analyse, Palémon a épousé étroitement le point de vue de la grammaire alexandrine, et admis parmi les modes latins à la fois un optatif et un subjonctif.

Le principe auquel le nom de Palémon s'est attaché, c'est celui de l'hellénisation de la grammaire romaine. Contre un courant de recherche marqué par une grande liberté vis-à-vis des modèles d'origine, et illustré avant tout par Varron, Palémon paraît avoir voulu montrer que le caractère systématique et global de la description grecque, sous forme de *tékhnē*, était applicable à la langue latine. Loin des tâtonnements, des hésitations et des innovations guidées par la spécificité du latin, le nom de Palémon est lié à une démarche d'apparence simple, méthodique et exhaustive, permise par la relative proximité de la structure des deux langues.

Ce que l'on peut dire de Palémon tient ainsi à des détails, et à un principe: les détails, issus de l'analyse des textes qui lui sont nommément attribués, ou qu'on peut raisonnablement lui attribuer, font apparaître des liens incontestables avec la tradition grammaticale alexandrine (→ Art. 56), et le principe est celui de l'hellénisation de la grammaire romaine. En revanche, il paraît beaucoup plus aventureux de se risquer à esquisser la structure de l'*Ars* de Palémon: ce qui vaut pour la correspondance entre quelques détails avec la *Tékhnē* attribuée à Denys ne vaut pas forcément pour la structure d'ensemble. Il est inutile, parce qu'excessivement conjectural, d'essayer de reconstituer un archétype de l'*Ars* de Palémon, qui ne serait en fait que le reflet anticipé d'une *ars* tardive, ou de la *Tékhnē* attribuée à Denys, ce qui revient sans doute au même.

## 5. Un témoin de la structure originelle de l'*ars* latine: Quintilien

Faut-il pour autant renoncer à reconstituer la structure de l'*ars* latine originelle? En fait, non, mais pour y parvenir il faut renoncer à s'attacher à un nom, en l'occurrence à Palémon, fût-il le premier auteur auquel soit attribuée une *ars*. Il est préférable de se reporter tout d'abord brièvement aux conditions générales qui ont vu apparaître ce type de description linguistique, dans le domaine grec.

Lors de la période charnière de la fin du II$^{e}$ siècle a.C. et du début du I$^{er}$, on est passé progressivement d'une conception de la grammaire comme *compétence en matière de textes* à une conception de la grammaire comme *système de la langue*: face aux observations accumulées par les philologues alexandrins, l'idée s'est en effet dégagée à cette époque de mettre au point des règles générales, indépendantes des emplois particuliers à tel ou tel auteur, mais qui pouvaient, éventuellement, expliquer ou justifier ces emplois particuliers. Cette analyse a eu ainsi pour objet de mettre au jour les propriétés communes et invariables de la langue, en un mot ses aspects systématiques. C'est tout le sens de la conception de la grammaire comme *tékhnē*, comme *système*, telle qu'elle apparaît au tournant des II$^{e}$–I$^{er}$ siècles avant notre ère. Une opposition devient ainsi fondamentale à cette époque dans la démarche grammaticale, entre une partie dite *historikón*, où l'analyse procède cas par cas, au fil du texte à expliquer, et une partie dite *tekhnikón*, où il s'agit de dégager des règles générales de fonctionnement (→ Art. 58).

Cette démarche s'inscrit dans une analyse plus large, celle de l'une des 'qualités du discours', la correction. Cette notion de 'qualités du discours' remonte à la rhétorique, depuis Aristote et Théophraste au moins. Ces 'qualités' sont par exemple celles que cite Théophraste: correction, clarté, convenance, ornement. Mais il y a deux façons de concevoir la 'qualité'. Ce peut être d'abord ce qui se distingue, en mieux, de l'ordinaire; c'est le cas de l'ornement, par exemple, qui est en principe une amélioration. Toutes les qualités ne peuvent cependant être considérées comme des améliorations par rapport à une norme: la correction notamment ne peut guère se concevoir comme autre chose qu'une norme. L'étude de la correction conduisait ainsi à un type d'analyse spécifique par rapport à la perspective rhétorique; la correction dépend en effet de règles qu'on peut appliquer indistinctement à tout discours, sans se soucier de son contenu ou de ses intentions, c'est-à-dire sans se soucier de ce qui est l'essence même de la perspective rhétorique. S'intéresser à la correction, c'est s'intéresser à ce qui, dans un énoncé, est indépendant des circonstances où il est émis ou de la personne qui l'emploie. La correction est affaire de langue, non de discours. L'étude de cette qualité qu'est la correction s'est donc ainsi dissociée résolument de l'analyse rhétorique, et a constitué le cœur d'une discipline spécifique, la grammaire.

La grammaire s'est ainsi donné pour objet la systématisation des problèmes de correction. Or il est possible de se faire une idée de la structure générale de ce type de description à ses débuts grâce aux indications concordantes de Quintilien (*Institution oratoire* I, IV–IX) et de Sextus Empiricus (*Contre les grammairiens* 91–93). Pour pouvoir traiter valablement des problèmes de correction, et s'en donner les moyens, la grammaire procède d'abord à une analyse qui dégage les éléments qui constituent la langue, et leurs variations formelles. D'où, comme plan: une première partie sur les éléments (lettres, syllabes, catégories de mots), et une deuxième sur la correction, c'est-à-dire sur les manquements dont elle peut faire l'objet et sur les critères qui permettent de l'établir.

Le texte de Quintilien s'organise selon ce schéma, avec des divisions et des subdivisions multiples, dont on n'indiquera ici que les principales. Quintilien distingue tout d'abord deux parties fondamentales dans l'enseignement grammatical: la *recte loquendi scientia*, ou étude de la correction, et la *poetarum enarratio*, ou explication des poètes. C'est la reprise de l'opposition entre le *tekhnikón* et l'*historikón*. Dans le cadre de l'analyse systématique (I, IV–VII), Quintilien distingue:

1. éléments
   1.1. lettres
   1.2. syllabes (renvoyé à 2.1.2.2.)
   1.3. catégories de mots
2. qualités du langage
   2.1. correction
      2.1.1. lieux de la correction et types de fautes
      2.1.2. règles de la correction
         2.1.2.1. correction orale (orthoépie)
         2.1.2.2. correction graphique (orthographe)
   [2.2. clarté (renvoyé à la rhétorique)]
   [2.3. ornementation (renvoyé à la rhétorique)]

Quintilien passe ensuite, au chapitre VIII, à la lecture et à l'explication de textes, et évoque, dans le très bref chapitre IX, les exercices.

Il n'y a aucune raison de penser que cet exposé de Quintilien résulte d'un montage. N'étant pas grammairien lui-même, Quintilien n'avait aucun motif de chercher particulièrement à être original dans sa conception d'ensemble de la présentation de la grammaire. Le plus simple est de penser qu'il a emprunté le plan considéré comme 'reçu' à son époque, quitte à donner un avis personnel sur tel ou tel point de détail. Au demeurant, la similitude entre le plan proposé par Quintilien et celui qui ressort du *Contre les grammairiens* de Sextus Empiricus montre bien que la part d'originalité de Quintilien à ce niveau est très faible, ou nulle. Si nous pouvons avoir une trace de l'*ars* latine originelle, c'est ainsi dans l'*Institution oratoire*.

Cela étant, est-il possible de faire coïncider les deux points d'origine dont nous disposons, et attribuer ainsi à Palémon, auteur de la première grammaire latine *attestée*, la première grammaire latine *conservée*, dont on retrouve les axes principaux dans l'*Institution oratoire*? Il est vrai que Quintilien cite Palémon, à propos du nombre des catégories de mots (I, IV, 20), et la tradition veut qu'il ait été son élève. Mais l'unique citation de Quintilien est insuffisante pour établir un lien d'élève à maître. Surtout, le texte de Quintilien révèle l'état de l'analyse grammaticale à la fin du 1$^{er}$ siècle, alors que les passages attribués à Palémon chez un auteur comme Charisius rapportent sans doute la doctrine de Palémon, mais sous une forme qui a quelque chance d'être propre aux artigraphes tardifs. Par exemple, lorsque Charisius indique (*GL* I, 227.4–11) que Palémon retenait parmi sa liste de conjonctions, des *finitiuae*, des *optatiuae* et des *subiunctiuae*, avec pour chacune de ces catégories une liste de conjonctions, cela signifie incontestablement que Palémon distinguait les conjonctions selon le mode avec lequel elles se construisaient, mais le fait de présenter ce point d'analyse sous la forme d'une simple catégorie de conjonctions, avec un nom et une liste, sans plus, cela remonte-t-il à l'*Ars* de Palémon, ou est-ce un effet de réécriture des artigraphes postérieurs, et des progressives simplifications pédagogiques?

En l'absence d'une impossible réponse sûre à cette question, et les textes attribués à Palémon ne touchant que des points de détail, la trace la plus ancienne de la structure originelle de l'*ars* latine reste décidément le texte du livre I de l'*Institution oratoire*.

## 6. Bibliographie

### 6.1. Sources primaires

*GG* = *Grammatici Graeci*. 6 vols. Leipzig: B. G. Teubner, 1883–01. (Réimpr., Hildesheim: Olms, 1965.)

*GL* = *Grammatici latini*. Ed. par Heinrich Keil. Leipzig: B. G. Teubner, 1855–80. (Réimpr., Hildesheim: Olms, 1981.)

### 6.2. Sources sceondaires

Ax, Wolfram. 1986. *Laut, Stimme und Sprache: Studien zu drei Grundbegriffen der antiken Sprachtheorie.* Göttingen: Vandenhoeck & Ruprecht.

Baratin, Marc. 1989. *La naissance de la syntaxe à Rome.* Paris: Editions de Minuit.

– & Françoise Desbordes. 1986. "La 'troisième partie' de l'*Ars grammatica*". *Historiographia Linguistica* 13.215–240.

Barwick, Karl. 1922. *Remmius Palaemon und die römische Ars grammatica.* Leipzig: Dieterich'sche Verlagsbuchhandlung. (Réimpr., Hildesheim: Olms, 1967).

–. 1957. *Probleme der stoischen Sprachlehre und Rhetorik.* Berlin: Akademie-Verlag.

Collart, Jean. 1938. "Palémon et l'Ars grammatica", *Revue de Philologie* 64.228–238.

Colson, Francis H. 1914. "The Grammatical Chapters in Quintilian I, 4–8". *Classical Quarterly* 8.33–47.

–. 1916. "Some Problems in the Grammatical Chapters of Quintilian". *Classical Quarterly* 10.17–31.

–. 1924. *M. Quintiliani Institutionis oratoriae, liber I.* Cambridge.

Desbordes, Françoise. 1990. *Idées romaines sur l'écriture.* Lille.

Fuhrmann, Manfred. 1960. *Das systematische Lehrbuch: Ein Beitrag zur Geschichte der Wissenschaften in der Antike.* Göttingen: Vandenhoeck & Ruprecht.

Heinicke, Balduin. 1904. *De Quintiliani, Sexti, Asclepiadis arte grammatica.* Strasbourg.

Marschall, Carolus. 1888. *De Q. Remmii Palaemonis libris grammaticis.* Diss. Université de Leipzig.

Nettleship, Henry. 1886. "The Study of Latin Grammar Among the Romans in the First Century A.D.". *Journal of Philology* 15.189–214.

Schottmüller, Alfred. 1858. *De C. Plinii libris grammaticis.* Bonn.

*Marc Baratin, Paris (France)*

# 68. L'ars grammatica dans la période post-classique: le *Corpus grammaticorum latinorum*

1. Le *corpus* de Keil
2. L'effet de *corpus*
3. Diversité réelle et évolution
4. Bibliographie

## 1. Le *corpus* de Keil

### 1.1. Description sommaire

L'édition des *Grammatici latini*, procurée par H. Keil et ses collaborateurs au siècle dernier, est toujours le point de départ de toute recherche sur les grammairiens latins de la période post-classique. Les sept volumes, publiés entre 1855 et 1880, rassemblent en effet l'essentiel de la production grammaticale latine à partir du II^e siècle de notre ère. À la différence de ce qui se passe pour la période précédente, il s'agit ici de textes intégraux, non de fragments issus de citations ultérieures. Leur nombre, tout à fait impressionnant, contraste aussi avec la situation du domaine grec où règnent presque sans partage Denys le Thrace (avec ses commentateurs) et Apollonios Dyscole.

Le contenu de cette édition peut être sommairement décrit de la façon suivante:

| | |
|---|---|
| I | Charisius, Diomède, *Anonymus Bobiensis* |
| II, III | Priscien |
| IV | 'Probus', Donat, Servius |
| V | commentateurs de Donat: Clédonius, Pompéius; textes courts: Consentius, Phocas, Eutyches, 'Augustin', 'Palémon', Asper, Macrobe |
| VI | métrique: Asmonius (soudé au début de l'*Ars* de Victorinus), Bassus, Fortunatianus, Terentianus Maurus, Sacerdos, Mallius Theodorus |
| VII | orthographe: Scaurus, Longus, Caper, Agroecius, Cassiodore, Papirius, Beda, Albinus; textes courts: Audax, Dosithée, Arusianus, 'Fronton' |

À cet ensemble s'ajoute un huitième volume, *supplementum*, qui reprend l'édition des *Anecdota Helvetica* par H. Hagen en 1870, édition de textes grammaticaux généralement plus tardifs (après le VI^e siècle).

### 1.2. Principes de sélection et textes absents

Dans la perspective de l'opposition entre *ars* et *historia*, les deux aspects de l'activité du *grammaticus* posés par Varron et repris par Quintilien, cette édition a sélectionné les textes 'techniques' et a laissé de côté d'autres textes grammaticaux reflétant l'aspect 'historique' de la grammaire ancienne. On pense en particulier aux travaux de lexicographie (de Festus et de Nonius Marcellus, par exemple), mais surtout aux nombreux commentaires de Virgile, de Térence, d'Horace, le commentaire de texte classique étant longuement considéré comme l'aboutissement pratique de l'activité grammaticale. En revanche, l'édition de Keil a retenu les nombreux traités d'orthographe de la période, une matière qui appartient de droit à la grammaire technique, mais qui n'est que très rarement intégrée dans les *artes* proprement dites. Elle a aussi retenu les traités de métrique, une discipline qui est en principe distincte et indépendante de la grammaire, mais à laquelle la grammaire technique fait des emprunts, limités le plus souvent à ce qui peut être utile à la scansion des classiques, parfois plus ambitieux dans une perspective d'étude complète de la langue.

L'édition de Keil n'a laissé de côté que quelques textes de grammaire technique qui auraient pu y trouver place: l'*Ars breviata* d''Augustin', la grammaire de 'Sergius' transmise avec l'œuvre de Cassiodore. Pour avoir une vue complète des textes grammaticaux de ce période, on se réportera aussi aux encyclopédistes, à Martianus Capella en particulier dont le livre grammatical est d'une grande richesse, mais aussi à Cassiodore (dans les *Institutions*) et à Isidore de Séville (dont le résumé de grammaire, dans les *Etymologies*, a eu un grand succès). Depuis l'edition de Keil, l'inventaire des textes grammaticaux ne s'est enrichi que de la découverte de quelques fragments de Sacerdos (De Nonno 1983: 401–409) et d'une *ars* qui peut être de Scaurus ou dérivée de Scaurus (Law 1987). En tenant compte de ces quelques ajouts, on fait le tour de la littérature grammaticale latine tardive.

### 1.3. Problèmes d'identification et d'attribution

Le rassemblement de presque tous ces textes en un même *corpus* a mis en évidence de nombreuses ressemblances. Quand on feuillette ces gros volumes, on est en effet frappé par l'identité visible de pages entières: sous des noms d'auteurs différents, on retrouve un contenu invariable. De ce fait, une grande partie du travail des philologues modernes a consisté et consiste toujours à essayer de retracer les filiations et les emprunts, non sans difficulté, car au phénomène de la copie viennent s'ajouter des questions d'anonymat et de pseudonymat. En face de quelques cas bien clairs, comme celui de Donat ou celui de Priscien, on rencontre une multitude de problèmes d'identification et d'attribution, dont on se contentera ici de donner quelques exemples caractéristiques.

Il faut ainsi distinguer au moins deux Probus, dont un Valérius Probus de Beyrouth (Ier siècle de notre ère), connu par une notice de Suétone et peut-être représenté dans le *Corpus* par les recueils d'abbréviations publiés par Mommsen au tome IV; il ne s'agit certainement pas du 'Probus' dont le nom figure en tête de cinq ouvrages du même tome IV et qui reste un personnage entièrement hypothétique, d'autant plus hypothétique qu'on constate que ses *Catholica* sont en fait identiques au livre II de Sacerdos, et que ses *Instituta artium* doivent être une version d'un ouvrage perdu de Palladius, connu par les extraits qu'en a faits Audax (le *De Scauri et Palladi libris excerpta* d'Audax additionne un résumé de Scaurus, *GL* VII, 315–349.8, qui est très semblable à l'*Ars* de Victorinus et à divers passages de Diomède citant Scaurus, et des extraits de Palladius, *GL* VII, 349–362).

Autre exemple, pour lequel la recherche moderne n'est pas encore parvenue à un consensus des spécialistes: les noms de Victorinus, Marius Victorinus, Maximus Victorinus correspondent-ils à un, deux ou trois auteurs différents? Un point est sûr: Marius Victorinus, le célèbre grammairien et rhéteur converti au christianisme, est bien l'auteur d'un début d'*ars grammatica* (*GL* VI, 3.6–31.12, où le développement sur les syllabes a été soudé au traité de métrique d'Aphthonius (= Aelius Festus Asmonius). On est ainsi tenté de lui attribuer une *ars* complète associée à un appendice *De metrica institutione* (*GL* VI, 187–215) qui sont transmis ensemble ou séparément sous le nom de Victorinus ou sous le nom de Palémon. On est plus embarrassé d'un *De ratione metrorum* (*GL* VI, 216–228) attribué à Maximus Victorinus, et d'un *De finalibus metrorum* (*GL* VI, 229–242), qu'on pourrait peut-être attribuer à un Metrorius (lire *De finalibus Metrorii*?).

On pourrait encore parler des doutes sur les deux ouvrages attribués à Augustin (*Ars breuiata* et *Regulae*) ou sur l'identité problématique d'un ou deux Sergius. À cela s'ajoutent les problèmes de filiation, en particulier avec des auteurs qu'on ne connaît plus que par des citations, éventuellement abondantes (Scaurus, Palémon, Romanus, Palladius, Cominianus etc.). Ces auteurs, dont les textes ont disparu en tant que tels, ont certainement été très importants, mais il est très difficile et à vrai dire souvent arbitraire de les reconstituer en partant des textes que nous avons conservés.

## 2. L'effet de *corpus*

### 2.1. L'unité de la grammaire

Tout en s'efforçant d'identifier les auteurs, la *Quellenforschung* qui s'est exercée et s'exerce toujours sur cet ensemble a pourtant longtemps abouti, paradoxalement, à donner le sentiment que les 'grammairiens' sont une entité dont on peut parler sans faire de distinctions. Il est vrai que d'un texte à l'autre, d'un volume à l'autre, reviennent les mêmes doctrines (souvent dans les mêmes termes) et les mêmes exemples sous la plume d'auteurs qui ont les mêmes sources ou se copient les uns les autres "imposing a deadly uniformity to their material" (Kaster 1986: 324).

Un premier point commun frappant de tous ces textes est leur intérêt exclusif pour la langue classique écrite: ils ne tirent leurs exemples que des grands auteurs et n'ont rien à dire sur la langue parlée de leur temps. Cela correspond au rôle conservateur assumé par l'école antique: des maîtres dont la position sociale est assurée à un niveau modeste (par rapport aux rhéteurs) enseignent aux fils de leurs patrons la 'culture générale' qui cimente les classes dirigeantes de l'Empire (Kaster 1988). La grammaire semble donc affaire atemporelle: de génération en génération, on se transmet les textes à connaître avec la manière de les analyser.

La critique moderne en est même venue à projeter dans le passé plus lointain le contenu des textes techniques existants et à considérer la grammaire ancienne comme une donnée unique et non soumise à évolution chronologique. Les auteurs du IV^e^ et V^e^ siècles dont nous possédons les textes tenaient leur savoir d'auteurs antérieurs qui disaient déjà la même chose. Le contenu commun est donc reporté à la date la plus haute à laquelle on puisse parvenir: les premières œuvres grammaticales contenaient ce que contiennent les dernières, la grammaire était achevée dès ses commencements. Ainsi remonte-t-on de Donat à l'hypothétique *Schulgrammatik* du II^e^ siècle avant notre ère et de là à la tout aussi hypothétique grammaire des Stoïciens (Barwick 1922). Le plan de l'*Ars maior* de Donat passe donc pour le schéma ordinaire de la grammaire latine censée être restée plus fidèle à l'original stoïcien que la *Tékhnē* de Denys, qui n'a pas de 'troisième partie':

première partie
- de uoce
- de littera
- de syllaba
- de pedibus
- de tonis
- de posituris

deuxième partie (de partibus orationis)
- de nomine
- de pronomine
- de uerbo
- de aduerbio
- de participio
- de coniunctione
- de praepositione
- de interiectione

troisème partie
- de barbarismo
- de soloecismo
- de ceteris uitiis
- de metaplasmo
- de schematibus
- de tropis

À l'examen de ce plan et des textes qui y correspondent, on conclut que la grammaire des Latins comportait des éléments de phonétique, une importante étude de morphologie, pas de syntaxe (avant Priscien), mais une ébauche de stylistique.

### 2.2. Phonétique

La 'phonétique' est très succincte: le chapitre *De littera* contient généralement un classement en voyelles, semi-voyelles, muettes, avec des remarques sur les lettres à problème (*H, K, Q, X, I, V*) et sur les trois accidents, *nomen, figura, potestas*, le tout envisagé de façon très abstraite: ce n'est pas la qualité phonique du son qui intéresse les grammairiens, dans la notion de *potestas* en particulier, mais la possibilité pour une lettre de se différencier des autres (et aussi de faire ou de ne pais faire 'position' dans un vers). De même, chez les grammairiens, l'étude de la syllabe est limitée à la détermination de la quantité, toujours dans une perspective de scansion des vers — alors qu'il y a des traces (Varron, Martianus Capella, Priscien) d'une autre conception de la syllabe, comme combinaison de lettres dans laquelle se réalisent les trois 'dimensions' de la voix considérée comme un corps (hauteur, largeur, longueur), sous les espèces d'accent, aspiration, quantité.

C'est presque en vain qu'on chercherait dans les *artes* un chapitre de phonétique articulatoire décrivant la position des organes phonateurs dans l'émission du son correspondant à chaque lettre. Che chapitre existe pourtant, mais c'est chez les métriciens qu'on le trouve (le seul texte grammatical où on le rencontre est celui de Martianus Capella, au livre III du *De nuptiis*, texte à tous égards très singulier). L'étude de la parenté articulatoire des lettres (*cognatio litterarum*) conduisant à un classement du type labiales, dentales, etc., n'est pas non plus un sujet systématiquement traité par les *artes*. C'est encore dans la métrique qu'on le trouvera, ou, parfois dans les traités d'orthographe. Cette *cognatio* sert surtout à justifier la *mutatio litterarum*, le passage d'une lettre à une autre. Cela se voit occasionnellement chez les *grammatici*, Charisius, par exemple: *b littera (...) propinqua p litterae, quae saepe mutatur, ut supponunt* (*GL* I, 19.18). Mais un traitement systématique de la *mutatio* est fort rare. Quintilien (qui témoignait, au I^er^ siècle, d'une orientation de la grammaire assez différente de celle des grammairiens tardifs) reste seul à distinguer *mutatio* diachronique et *mutatio* synchronique. Martianus Capella et Priscien sont les seuls à examiner toutes les lettres, une par une, sous cet angle, et encore s'en tiennent-ils surtout à la *mutatio* synchronique. L'ébauche de phonétique historique qu'on trouvait chez Quintilien n'a pas de suite dans les *artes*.

Le peu d'intérêt pour la phonétique se marque dans l'attachement au terme *littera*, même après l'introduction du terme *elementum* (censé représenter l'unité orale, distincte de la graphie), qui reste très rare: les grammairiens ont une vue abstraite de la langue où ce sont les différences qui comptent et non la substance des réalisations. Ils se sont ainsi placés, même inconsciemment, même maladroitement, sur le terrain de la phonologie, et leur *littera* préfigure le phonème.

### 2.3. Morphologie

Le même caractère abstrait se retrouve dans l'étude de la morphologie ou plus exactement des *partes orationis*. Cette étude très développée (elle occupe une grande place dans les textes), a trouvé son expression achevée dans la forme *ars*, dont elle est en retour la meilleure illustration. L'*ars* se caractérise en effet par un type d'exposé méthodique dont Fuhrmann (1960) a montré l'importance dans toutes les disciplines anciennes, et que Holtz (1981) a bien mis en lumière dans son étude de Donat. L'*ars* apparaît lorsqu'une discipline quelconque arrive à un état de maturité où les éléments s'organisent en système et peuvent être dès lors l'objet de divisions et de dénombrements exacts et finis. L'*ars*, en effet, c'est le système, à la fois en tant que principe d'organisation de la matière et, indissolublement, en tant que méthode d'exposé: c'est parce que la matière est organisée systématiquement qu'on peut la présenter systématiquement. De ce fait, le cœur de l'*ars grammatica*, c'est l'étude des *partes orationis* dont on peut produire un dénombrement exact et auxquelles on peut appliquer un système de subdivisions fondées sur les catégories générales telles que *genus*, *numerus*, *figura*, *casus*, *tempus*, etc.

La liste des *partes orationis* est à peu près constante et calquée sur la liste grecque, avec remplacement de l'article par l'interjection: nom, pronom, verbe, adverbe, participe, conjonction, préposition, interjection. Pour une *pars* généralement très détaillée, le verbe, par exemple, on a plus souvent sept accidents: *qualitas* (qui se subdivise en deux, le mode: indicatif, impératif, optatif, conjonctif, infinitif, impersonnel; et la forme: parfaite, 'méditative' [type *lecturio*], fréquentative, inchoative); genre: actif, passif, neutre, déponent, commun; nombre: singulier, pluriel; figure: simple, composé; temps: présent, passé (*praeteritum perfectum*, *imperfectum*, *plus quam perfectum*), futur; personne (*prima*, *secunda*, *tertia*).

Chez Donat et ceux qui sont les plus proches de lui, il est clair que l'application de ces catégories sert surtout à montrer les caractères du langage en général à travers l'exemple du latin – ou plutôt à vérifier la pertinence du concept d'*utraque lingua* qui constate la parenté du latin et du grec et autorise qu'on utilise les mêmes instruments d'analyse pour ces deux langues (à l'exclusion des autres): en quoi on peut dire que si les grammairiens grec 'faisaient' du grec, les grammairiens latins 'font' de la linguistique. On s'en convaincra en voyant par exemple comment Donat traite le nom, en soumettant la notion à une analyse minutieuse de ses propriétés: qualité (le nom est propre ou commun), genre (masculin, féminin, neutre, commun, épicène), nombre, cas, figure (simple ou composée), propriétés qui, avec leurs subdivisions, sont plus importantes que des traits formels comme déclinaisons et désinences; c'est ainsi que Donat décline non point un exemple de chaque paradigme formel, mais un représentant de chaque genre (*magister, musa, scamnum, sacerdos, felix* (*Ars minor, GL* IV, 355.28–356.30). De même, la volonté d'aligner le latin sur le grec peut contraîner les grammairiens à des contorsions pour retrouver l'article en latin, ou l'optatif; on peut aussi les voir faire du futur antérieur un futur du subjonctif (Serbat 1978), etc.

### 2.4. Syntaxe et stylistique

Le développement de la morphologie a pour corollaire l'absence de ce que nous entendons par syntaxe. Cette absence (avant Priscien, qui s'inspire du grec Apollonios Dyscole pour composer ses livres XVII et XVIII *De constructione*) a longtemps paru choquante aux linguistes modernes: "C'est peu de dire qu'elle est traitée par eux [les grammairiens] en parenté pauvre, elle est traitée en quantité négligeable" (Collart 1978: 195). Mais la grammaire ne s'occupe que des mots, laissant l'étude de l'énoncé à la dialectique ou à la rhétorique et présupposant que l'addition du sens de chaque mot donnera le sens de l'énoncé, si elle a été faite correctement (sans solécisme, seul point où la grammaire donne des règles d'assemblages ou plutôt un signalement des fautes d'assemblage).

Au lieu d'une syntaxe proprement dite, c'est une étude des qualités et défauts de l'énoncé que l'on trouve en troisième partie de l'*ars*. Dans cette troisième partie, la méthode artigraphique par divisions et subdivisions retrouve du reste ses droits, même si elle plaque des systèmes artificiels sur sa matière; ainsi on distinguera les barbarismes par "addition, soustraction, mutation, métathèse" (*adiectio, detractio, immutatio, transmutatio*), mais on classera les métaplasmes, formellement identiques (ce sont les barbarismes autorisés des poètes, et souvent les mêmes exemples sont cités à titre de qualités et de défauts), en utilisant une terminologie entièrement grecque, empruntée à la pathologie (discipline grecque qui nomme les variations affectant une forme première intacte): *relliquias* est ainsi cité chez Donat comme barbarisme *per adiectionem* (*GL* IV, 392.11) et comme métaplasme de type *epénthesis* (*GL* IV, 396.4). On a longtemps voulu voir dans cette trosième partie une survivance de l'orientation stoïcienne qu'on postulait à l'origine de la grammaire antique. Mais il s'agit plus probablement d'une extension secondaire de la grammaire technique, de son domaine d'origine, la correction (barbarisme, solécisme), à une autre qualité du discours, l'ornementation, sous la double influence de la rhétorique et de la lecture expliquée, fin pratique de l'activité grammaticale (Baratin & Desbordes 1986).

## 3. Diversité réelle et évolution

### 3.1. Diversité des textes

Parmi les textes de Keil, cependant, plusieurs se signalent par quelque singularité qui suffirait à ruiner l'idée que les *grammatici* sont identiques. Ainsi, la verbosité de l'abondant commentaire de Donat que donne Pompeius s'explique si l'on suppose qu'il s'agit en fait de l'enregistrement d'un entretien oral et même, comme Kaster (1986: 330) semble bien l'avoir démontré, des conseils qu'un grammairien émérite donne à un collègue sur l'art et la manière d'interpréter Donat. Autre enregistrement d'oral, des plus étranges, dans le morceau subsistant de l'*ars* authentiquement attribuable à Marius Victorinus: le chapitre d'orthographe théorique, unique dans ce type de grammaire, se trouve en outre entrelardé de conseils à des élèves qui s'entraînent à la copie, font des fautes et récidivent. La grammaire de Dosithée, unique en son genre, était conçue comme un texte latin donné avec sa traduction en grec (soit ligne par ligne, soit dans une colonne parallèle), traduction inachevée qui s'effrite peu à peu (mots isolés traduits sporadiquement, puis abandon). Le traité de Macrobe comparant le verbe grec et le verbe latin, dont nous sont parvenus des extraits, devait être un ouvrage unique, écrit dans un esprit de 'science désintéressée', ce pourquoi il n'a pas eu de succès; mais il a éte dépecé à toutes fins utiles: dans l'entourage de Priscien, on en a utilisé des morceaux pour composer un *De uerbo* (*GL* V, 634–654) destiné à apprendre le latin à un grec; inversement, les Carolingiens y chercheront avant tout des renseignements sur le grec (De Paolis 1990).

Ce sont là des cas exceptionnels sans doute, mais l'uniformité du corpus de Keil est de toute façon plus illusoire que réelle. On doit distinguer les *artes* proprement dites (Charisius, Diomède, Priscien, Donat, Victorinus, etc.), les commentaires de Donat (Servius, Sergius, Cledonius, Pompeius etc.), les traités de métrique du tome VI et les traités d'orthographe du tome VII; à quoi on pourrait ajouter quelques textes singuliers, comme les *Partitiones* de Priscien, qui relèvent de la grammaire en action (commentaire de tous les mots de chaque premier vers de chaque chant de l'*Enéide*) ou les *Differentiae* attribuées à Fronton. Du côté des *artes*, c'est-à-dire de la grammaire technique, on distinguera encore entre l'*ars* proprement dite, exposé de type général, et ce qu'on appelle *regulae*, textes qui donnent le détail des déclinaisons et conjugaisons (Phocas, Priscien dans l'*Institutio de nomine et pronomine et uerbo*, les *Regulae* d''Augustin', le livre II de Sacerdos, copié aussi comme *Catholica Probi*, etc.). On pourrait encore s'arrêter à distinguer les *artes* brèves en un volume, grammaires scolaires de Scaurus, Sacerdos (I), Marius Victorinus, *Ars* de Donat, et les textes plus complexes, nourris d'emprunts à des sources diverses et ajoutant des développements érudits (Sacerdos pris dans son ensemble, Charisius, Diomède [...], sans parler de Priscien).

3.2. Plans variables

En outre le plan type de Donat (phonétique, morphologie, stylistique) n'est pas toujours observé, au contraire. On peut même avoir un agencement très différent, par exemple chez Diomède dont la dédicace évoque la nécessité d'une progression pédagogique: le livre I se consacre aux *partes*, bases de la connaissance de la langue; le livre II réunit des éléments de 'phonétique' et de 'stylistique', qui sont en fait un ensemble de notions nécessaires à la lecture; le livre III est une esquisse de poétique et une métrique détaillée.

Le noyau des *partes orationis*, reconnu comme le propre de la grammaire, est certes toujours présent, soit sous la forme théorique des catégories de l'*ars*, soit sous la forme pratique des déclinaisons et conjugaisons des *regulae*. Mais l'étude des qualités et des défauts est souvent absente, éventuellement remplacée par autre chose, de la métrique par autre chose, de la métrique par exemple.

La 'première partie' n'est pas non plus uniforme, les auteurs se demandant souvent ce que doit être le début de l'*ars*. Par quoi faut-il commencer? par la définition d'*ars*, d'*ars grammatica*, de la définition elle-même, par la voix, par les lettres, par le nom?

Certains ont commencé par la notion même de système, d'autres par les éléments ou lettres, beaucoup par les cas, un très grand nombre par les catégories de mots, quelques-uns par le son, un petit nombre par la flexion des noms; moi, je commencerai par l'énoncé (Diomède, *GL* I, 300.4).

Les textes eux-mêmes portent témoignage de plusieurs façons de commencer et enchaînent de façon variable des développements en nombre variable. Autour d'un noyau de *uoce, de littera, de syllaba*, les *artes* combinent diversement des questions qui relèvent des préliminaires théoriques (par quoi commencer?, *de arte, de grammatica, de definitione, de latinitate, de dictione, de oratione*), de la lecture et du traitement des lettres (*de lectione, de tonis, de positluris, de pronuntiatione, de modulatione*), de la métrique *stricto sensu* (*de pedibus, de metro, de hexametro*); Marius Victorinus intercale même un *de orthographia* entre le *de littera* et le *de syllaba*, peut-être sur le modèle d'Apollonios Dyscole.

3.3. Analyses variables

En termes de contenu, on peut aussi montrer que les grammairiens ne disent pas toujours la même chose. Il leur arrive même de se contredire explicitement. Pompeius estime ainsi que Sacerdos se trompe (sur le génitif pluriel, *GL* V, 190.24–26), Consentius s'en prend à ceux qui confondent barbarismes et métaplasmes (*GL* V, 391.25), Charisius signale que si certains grammairiens assignent les noms du type *dies* à la deuxième déclinaison, d'autres estiment qu'il faut créer une cinquième déclinaison pour ces noms (Taylor 1991: 345). On discute toujours de terminologie, de la possibilité de distinguer ou non *nomen, uocabulum, appellatio*, de la liste des accidents du verbe, etc.

D'autre part, si conservateurs que soient les grammairiens, l'évolution de la langue s'insinue tout de même dans la perception de certains, et partant dans leurs textes. Servius (*GL* IV, 522.24) reconnaît: *syllabas natura longas difficile est scire. Sed hanc ambiguitatem sola probant auctoritatis exempla, cum uersus poetae scandere coeperis* – paradoxalement, c'est donc désormais le texte écrit qui préserve l'opposition orale longue/brève, disparue de la langue parlée. À propos de [i] Pompeius (*GL* V, 104.6) remarque: *si dicas Titius, pinguius sonat et perdit sonum suum et accipit sibilum* – ce qui doit correspondre à l'évolution réelle du groupe [ti]. On trouverait aussi mainte remarque sur l'accent, qui indique un abandon de la doctrine traditionnelle (aigu, grave, circonflexe) au profit d'une simplification ("l'accent est dans la syllabe qui sonne le plus", Servius, *GL* IV, 426.16). Consentius (*GL* V, 391.25), surtout, tire de la langue de son temps (et non des poètes) ses exemples de barbarismes: *pīper* pour *piper* (faute des Africains), *salmentum* pour *salsamentum, bobis* pour *uobis, stetim* pour *statim* (*quod uitium plebem Romanam quadam deliciosa nouitatis affectione corrumpit*). Son texte sur le iotacisme (*GL* V, 394.11) mérite citation intégrale, comme observation de phénomènes phonétiques, probable mais surdéterminée par un présupposé idéologique (juste milieu romain entre la lourdeur gauloise et légèreté grecque):

*Galli pinguius hanc utuntur, ut cum dicunt ite, non expresse ipsam proferentes, sed inter e et i pinguiorem sonum nescio quem ponentes, Graeci exilius hanc proferunt, adeo expressioni eius tenui studentes, ut, si dicant ius, aliquantulum de priore littera sic proferant, ut uideas disyllabum esse factum. Romanae linguae in hoc erit moderatio, ut exilis eius sonus sit, ubi ab ea uerbum incipit, ut ite, aut pinguior, ubi in ea desinit uerbum, ut habui, tenui.*

Parallèlement, l'écart qui se creuse entre la langue écrite des classiques et la langue orale contemporaine entraîne une multiplication des traités d'orthographe en même temps qu'un changement de leur orientation. Les traités du II^e^ siècle, de Scaurus et de Longus, sont soucieux de déterminer et justifier la correction graphique à l'aide d'une analyse de l'énonciation orale, alors que les auteurs tardifs enseignent dogmatiquement qu'il faut écrire comme on a écrit, remplaçant l'idée de l'orthographe représentation correcte de l'oral par celle de l'orthographe reproduction d'une graphie.

On voit un certain nombre d'analyses se préciser et se perfectionner d'un auteur à l'autre. Ainsi les genres du verbe qui sont neuf dans la première *ars* conservée, celle de Sacerdos (*GL* VI, 429: actif, passif, déponent, neutre, commun, inchoatif, défectif, fréquentatif, impersonnel), sont réduits aux cinq premiers par distinction entre flexion et dérivation (Hovdhaugen 1986: 319). L'impersonnel, catégorie propre au latin qui regroupe le passif impersonnel et les verbes que nous appelons encore 'impersonnels', cause de nombreuses perplexités et se trouve catégorisé tantôt comme mode (parce qu'il se forme à partir de la première personne du singulier de l'indicatif présent), tantôt comme genre (parce qu'il n'est pas un mode, se conjugant dans tous les modes), parfois comme figure (Asper, avec simple, composé, inchoatif, fréquentatif, désidératif, dérivé), parfois avec les irrégularités. L'analyse traditionnelle aboutit à 'rétablir' un pronom pour compléter le verbe:

[la signification impersonnelle des verbes] n'est pas énoncée avec les personnes propres, mais on doit nécessairement lui joindre, de l'extérieur, des pronoms, sans lesquels les verbes de cette sorte ne peuvent rien signifier. (Diomède, *GL* I, 338.2).

Mais une autre analyse apparaît d'abord succinctement, y compris chez les grammairiens qui exposent la première, comme Charisius ("on montre non qui fait, mais ce qui est fait"), puis de façon un peu plus développée chez 'Augustin', qui explique que *taedet* équivaut à *taedium est, piget* à *pigritia est* (avec l'exemple *piget me fecisse — non surgit meus animus probare quod fecit*), et plus en details encore chez Macrobe qui estime que *legitur, curritur, agitur* se contentent d'exprimer le fait en laissant de côté les personnes auxquelles revient l'office de lecture, de course ou d'action. Mais Macrobe avait certainement lu le traité du verbe d'Apollonios Dyscole — qui est aussi la source des célèbres analyses de Priscien entendant *curritur cursus* dans *curritur*.

### 3.4. Priscien

La considérable originalité de Priscien, dans le *corpus* de Keil, est en effet sans doute moins le résultat d'une évolution de la doctrine latine que de la volonté de revenir aux sources grecques, en particulier Apollonios et Hérodien, en passant par dessus la tradition latine, que Priscien juge avec sévérité (cf. *GL* II, 195.7). Cette originalité se voit dans maint détail; par exemple, alors que la tradition latine reconnaît l'équivalence de la voix articulée et de la voix scriptible (scriptible précisément parce qu'elle est articulée), Priscien (*GL* II, 5.5) oppose la *uox articulata (quae coartata est, hoc est copulata cum aliquo sensu mentis eius qui loquitur*) et la *uox literata* qui peut être écrite (les sifflements et gémissements humains sont 'articulés' puisqu'on en comprend le sens, mais ne peuvent être écrits). De façon plus large, Priscien entreprend de distinguer plus soigneusement écrit et oral, *littera* et *elementum*, et introduit une dose non négligeable de 'phonétique' dans l'examen des lettres. Mais c'est surtout l'apparition de la syntaxe aux livres XVII et XVIII qui fait la singularité de Priscien.

Dans cette *Constructio*, Priscien s'inspire de la *Syntaxe* d'Apollonios Dyscole qu'il traduit souvent littéralement et que, de toute façon, il suit de très près, car cela lui permet de dépasser les 'anciens grammariens latins' qui sont restés au niveau du mot sans passer à celui de l'énoncé. Sur les traces de son modèle, il montre que les formes indiquent généralement les significations qui déterminent une construction (*Priscianus*, nominatif singulier masculin implique forcément certaines formes du verbe ou de l'adjectif), qui sera conforme à la rationalité de la cohérence (*consequentia*). Certaines catégories de mots, cependant, les conjonctions et prépositions, n'ont qu'une propriété de cosignification (considéré seul *in* peut se construire avec l'ablatif ou avec l'accusatif, mais se trouve déterminé dans l'expression *in urbem*).

Mais Priscien va au-delà des acquis d'Apollonios. Constatant que les propriétés dynamiques de la construction permettent de désambiguiser l'énoncé, il élabore une théorie et une pratique des 'figures', variations possibles ou non des formes au regard de l'intelligibilité. Ainsi dans le célèbre exemple d'Enéide I, 212, *pars in frusta secant, pars* est porteur d'une signification plurielle opposée au singulier qui indique la matérialité de la forme. C'est la construction qui révèle la valeur plurielle implicite dans *pars* — ce qui ne veut pas dire qu'on peut construire n'importe quoi avec n'importe quoi: encore faut-il que les termes mis en présence aient quelque signification compatible: personne ne dit *ego facis, tu facio*! Opposant grammaticalité stricte et intelligibilité, et reprenant en quelque sorte les recherches des poètes et des rhéteurs sur la *iunctura*, Priscien met en évidence une logique du sens (Baratin & Desbordes 1981: 62–65; Baratin 1989).

### 3.5. Nouvelle approche

Ces différences et évolutions sont déjà visibles dans le recueil de Keil, mais elles le sont plus encore aujourd'hui où (depuis une vingtaine d'années, surtout) l'on a porté un œil neuf sur ces vieux textes. Ce nouveau regard a amené à reprendre l'étude des manuscrits et a bénéficié en retour de l'édition sur nouveaux frais de très nombreux textes (entre autres, Charisius, Donat, Consentius, Phocas, Macrobe, Marius Victorinus). Ces éditions indépendantes les unes des autres (même si elles abondent en références les unes aux autres!) ont donné une relative indépendance à chaque texte, dont on essaie maintenant de préciser l'histoire. On s'attache à l'histoire de la diffusion, en essayant de voir ce que signifiaient les transformations d'un texte remis à jour ou adapté pour un public particulier (Law 1986). On s'attache aussi à restituer le profit des premiers destinataires de chaque texte et à faire l'histoire des conditions de production.

Ces conditions ont en effet changé entre le III$^{e}$ siècle (date de la plus ancienne *ars* conservée, celle de Sacerdos) et le VI$^{e}$ siècle: il ne s'agit plus de donner aux élèves latinophones du *grammaticus* les instruments utiles pour bien lire les grands classiques, mais bel et bien d'apprendre le latin à des gens dont ce n'est pas la langue maternelle. Les grammariens qui, avec les rhéteurs, étaient les garants de la continuité idéologique et, partant, de la stabilité sociale, ont rencontré des problèmes nouveaux avec l'importance prise par la capitale d'Orient, Constantinople, et avec le développement de l'Eglise et la diffusion des Ecritures. Il faut apprendre le latin à des parleurs de langues germaniques ou celtiques, principalement pour donner accès aux textes sacrés. Il faut aussi l'apprendre aux habitants de l'Est qui peuvent savoir affaire avec l'administration ou la loi de l'Empire latin (cf. Dionisotti 1984). Ces conditions nouvelles expliquent la multiplication des textes de type *regulae*, qui donnent les déclinaisons et conjugaisons sans se soucier de la catégorisation des *artes*. Elles attirent aussi l'attention sur le fait que parmi ces *grammatici* beaucoup sont des Grecs, écrivant pour des Grecs (en particulier, tout le groupe Charisius, Diomède, Dosithée, *Anonymus Bobiensis*), et il semble désormais intéressant de réévaluer ces textes à la lumière de ce fait.

## 4. Bibliographie

### 4.1. Sources primaires


Charisius = *Flauii Sosipatri Charisii Artis grammaticae libri V.* Ed. par Karl Barwick. Leipzig: Teubner, 1925. (Réimpr., 1964.)

Consentius = *Consentii Ars de barbarismis et metaplasmis. Victorini fragmentum de soloecismo et barbarismo.* Ed. par Max Niedermann. Neuchâtel, 1937.

Donat = *Ars Donati.* Ed. par Louis Holtz (1981).

*GL* = *Grammatici Latini.* Ed. par Heinrich Keil. 8 tomes. Leipzig: Teubner, 1855–1880. (Réimpr., Hildesheim: Olms, 1965.)

Macrobe = *Macrobii Theodosii De uerborum Graeci et Latini differentiis uel societatibus excerpta.* Ed. par Paolo De Paolis. Urbino: QuatroVenti, 1990.

Marius Victorinus = *Marius Victorionus Ars Grammatica.* Ed. par Italo Mariotti. Florence: Le Monnier, 1967.

Phocas = *Phocas Ars de nomine et uerbo.* Ed. par F. Casacelli. Naples: Libreria Scientifica, 1974.


### 4.2. Sources secondaires


Baratin, Marc. 1989. *La naissance de la syntaxe à Rome.* Paris: Editions de Minuit.

— & François Desbordes. 1981. *L'analyse linguistique dans l'Antiquité classique,* vol. I: *Les théories.* Paris: Klincksieck.

–. –. 1986. "La 'troisième partie' de l'*Ars grammatica*". *Historiographia Linguistica* 13.215–240.

Barwick, Karl. 1922. *Remmius Palaemon und die römische* Ars grammatica. Leipzig: Dieterici. (Réimpr., Hildesheim: Olms, 1967.)

Collart, Jean. 1978. "À propos des études syntaxiques chez les grammairiens latins". *Varron, grammaire antique et stylistique latine* éd. par Jean Collart et al., 195–204. Paris: Belles Lettres.

De Nonno, Mario. 1983. "Frammenti misconosciuti di Plozio Sacerdote con osservazioni sul testo del *Catholica Probi*". *Rivista di Filologia e d'Istruzione Classica* 111.385–421.

Dionisotti, A. C. 1984. "Latin grammar for Greeks and Goths". *Journal of Roman Studies* 74.202–208.

Fuhrmann, Manfred. 1960. *Das systematische Lehrbuch: Ein Beitrag zur Geschichte der Wissenschaften in der Antike.* Göttingen: Vandenhoeck & Ruprecht.

Holtz, Louis. 1981. *Donat et la tradition de l'enseignement grammatical: Etude sur l'Ars Donati et sa diffusion (IV^e^–IX^e^ siècle) et édition critique.* Paris: Editions du CNRS.

Hovdhaugen, Even. 1986. "*Genera verborum quot sunt?* Observations on the Roman grammatical tradition". *Historiographia Linguistica* 13.307–321.

Kaster, Robert A. 1986. "Islands in the Stream: The grammarians of Late Antiquity". *Historiographia Linguistica* 13.323–342.

–. 1988. *Guardians of Language: The grammarian and society in Late Antiquity.* Berkeley: Univ. of California Press.

Law, Vivien. 1986. "When is Donatus not Donatus: Versions, variants and new texts". *Peritia* 5.235–261.

–. 1987. "An Unnoticed Late Latin Grammar: The *Ars minor* of Scaurus?". *Rheinisches Museum* 130.67–89.

Serbat, Guy. 1978. "Le 'futur antérieur' chez les grammairiens latins". *Varron, grammaire antique et stylistique latine* éd. par Jean Collart et al., 263–272. Paris: Belles Lettres.

Taylor, Daniel J. 1991. "Roman language science". *Geschichte der Sprachtheorie*, vol. II: *Sprachtheorien der abendländischen Antike* éd. par Peter Schmitter, 334–352. Tübingen: Narr.

*Françoise Desbordes †, Toulouse (France)*

# 69. L'organisation de la grammaire dans la tradition latine

1. Introduction
2. L'établissement du corpus
3. Les préliminaires et les parties du discours
4. *Vitia et virtutes orationis*
5. Conclusion
6. Bibliographie

## 1. Introduction

Notre étude vise à analyser les dispositions accordées par les grammairiens latins à des matériaux grammaticaux communs hypothétiques, tout en reconnaissant qu'un quelconque étude de ce genre est tributaire de quelques travaux de la fin du XIX^e^ et du début du XX^e^ siècle (Jeep 1893; Barwick 1922). Il faut établir une série de prémisses qui rendent plus facile le cadrage de notre objet d'étude. Tout d'abord, les matériaux à analyser seront ceux de l'*ars grammatica* en tant que manuel. Il est intéressant de préciser que, même si l'on admet la double acception de la *grammatica* que les grammairiens latins donnent souvent, *ars recte loquendi et enarratio poetarum*, ceux dont nous nous occupons s'en tiennent en général davantage à la première fonction. Malgré cela, il ne faut pas perdre de vue la séparation subtile qui existe entre une préparation pour la correction dans l'expression et l'habilité qui en dérive pour faire une lecture critique des auteurs classiques.

Nous mettons aussi à l'écart ce que l'on pourrait appeler des traités grammaticaux monographiques et les ouvrages fragmentaires. Il est assez absurde, par exemple, d'avoir recours, comme le fait Della Casa (1978: 218), à l'analyse des fragments de Nigidius Figulus, César ou Pline l'Ancien pour en conclure qu'on n'y conserve point de traces de l'ordre traditionnel, étant donné qu'il s'agit de fragments qui, en outre, procèdent de traités monographiques et non pas de manuels. En second lieu, nous ne nous occuperons pas non plus directement du problème des modèles, bien que l'on puisse tirer des conclusions à ce propos à partir de notre analyse. En effet, nous partons de l'idée que chaque grammaire, qu'elle soit issue du traitement d'une seule source, ou qu'elle soit le résultat de la compilation de plusieurs de ces sources – c'est le cas de Charisius – a reçu une disposition de matériaux qui est le fruit de la volonté de son 'auteur' dans le processus de création ou d'adoption des modèles. S'il est ainsi par rapport aux sources immédiates, nous le constaterons à plus forte raison si l'on augmente la référence à des modèles plus lointains du point de vue linguistique ainsi que dans l'espace; c'est le cas des grammaires grecques. En somme, les matériaux sur lesquels nous nous appuyons, consultés parfois dans d'autres éditions, et à la réserve des remarques mentionnées ci-dessus, sont contenus dans les volumes du corpus des *Grammatici Latini*.

## 2. L'établissement du corpus

Il n'y a pas d'accord définitif en ce qui concerne la date où se 'fixe' le patron de *ars grammatica* diffusé, avec des variantes plus ou moins accusées, jusqu'au Moyen Age et la Renaissance. D'après Barwick, c'est Remmius Palaemon, au I^er^ siècle apr. J.-C. qui fournit le modèle suivi plus tard (Collart 1938; Dunlap 1940; → Art. 67), quoique les restes de la première grammaire conservée datent du III^e^ siècle: Sacerdos. D'une manière plutôt imprécise, Della Casa (1978: 224) situe la date de diffusion des *artes grammaticales* durant le III^e^ siècle, parallèlement aux nouveaux besoins de l'ensemble des élèves de plus en plus éloignés de la langue classique, ce qui exige l'adoption d'instruments théoriques simples et normatifs.

Même si effectivement nous ne disposons pas de grammaires antérieures au II^e^ siècle, il est aussi vrai que nous trouvons une référence à un *ars grammatica* dans la *Rhetorica ad Herennium* (4, 2, 17), dénomination générique qui nous fait penser à une sorte de manuel qui, d'après la citation, devait inclure un chapitre ou section sur le barbarisme/solécisme: *Latinitas est [...] Soloecismus est [...] Barbarismus est [...] Haec quae ratione uitare possumus, in arte grammatica dilucide dicemus.* D'ailleurs, le recours au traité de Varron *De Lingua Latina*, même s'il est incomplet, peut nous fournir quelques renseignements, de la même façon que nous pourrons employer postérieurement Quintilien pour nous faire une idée sommaire des tendances des arts grammaticaux de la fin du I^er^ siècle apr. J.-C.

### 2.1. Varron

La façon dont nous nous servirons de Varron (→ Art. 66) ne cherche pas à trouver dans la disposition du traité les traces d'un possible schéma; il s'agit tout simplement d'observer s'il y a des coïncidences entre cet auteur et quelques chapitres communs habituels dans les manuels. En effet, Varron s'occupe à plusieurs reprises des parties du discours dans le traitement de l'analogie, lorsqu'il cherche des points d'appui pour les différentes opinions qu'il maintient. Cela arrive surtout dans le livre VII et d'une façon plus nuancée dans le livre X.

Mais sa double façon de classifier les parties du discours ne nous intéresse tant que les remarques que cette classification suscite. Les parties du discours dans VIII, 9 s'accordent avec l'existence de deux *genera*: *fecundum et sterile*. Ce sont, en fait, (VIII, 12) les deux parties aristotéliques du discours, *uocabula et uerba*, dans sa double catégorie de *priora et posteriora*. Il y a des *uocabula priora* comme *homo*, des *posteriora* comme *doctus*; des *uerba priora* comme *scribit*, et des *posteriora* comme *docte*, c'est à dire un adverbe dérivé, car les simples comme *cras* sont compris dans le genre *sterile*. C'est une classification qui n'apparaît plus dans les grammairiens postérieurs. Il cite tout de suite un groupement en trois parties atribué à Dion: [...] *quae adsignificat casus, alteram quae tempora, tertia⟨m⟩ quae neutrum*.

Une autre sorte de classification est mise en œuvre dans VIII, 44. Le discours admet quatre parties: celle qui a des cas, celle qui a des temps, celle qui a tous les deux et celle qui n'a ni l'un ni l'autre. Le groupement en parties qui en résulte est le suivant: *appellandi* (*Nestor, homo*), *dicendi* (*scribit*), *adminiculandi* (*docte*) et *iungendi* (*scribens*). C'est justement cette dernière classification qui va être développée. En commençant par *appellandi* (§ 45), Varron reconnaît deux groupes: *finitum* (*pronomina*: *hic haec*) et *infinitum* (*prouocabula*: *quis quae*), auxquels correspondent *quasi finitum* (*nomina: Romulus*) et *quasi infinitum* (*uocabula: scutum*). L'utilisation de *hic* comme modèle, au lieu des pronoms personnels *ego/tu*, peut être due à son emploi comme article dans les paradigmes du *nomen*. Il reprend ainsi des substantifs propres et des communs, en scindant aussi les pronoms en définis et indéfinis. La même classification de § 44, maintenant sans les designations d'*appellandi, dicendi*, etc., se répète dans X, 17, à propos des mots *declinata natura*. Ceux qui ont un cas se divisent en *nominatus* et *articuli*, qui sont finis et infinis (§ 18), de même que les *nominatus* (§ 20) comprennent le *uocabulum* et le *nomen*.

Jusqu'à présent nous avons deux classifications qui reconnaissent d'un côté deux parties du discours scindées en quatre: substantif – adjectif, verbe – adverbe. Et une seconde (reprise dans les livres VIII et X) qui comprend quatre parties fondamentales, dont nous pouvons obtenir sept par abstraction: *nomen, uocabulum, pronomen, prouocabulum, uerbum, participium, aduerbium.* Mais cette classification est d'autant plus intéressante à partir du moment où, en faisant l'étude de chacune des parties du point de vue de l'analogie, elle suit très étroitement les accidents de chacune d'elles: genre, nombre, cas (VIII, 46–52; X, 21), dérivation (VIII, 53), composition (VIII, 61), comparaison (VIII, 75), formation des diminutifs (VIII, 79). Dans le cas du verbe, qui n'était pas développé dans le huitième livre, c'est dans le livre X, 31–33 qu'il s'occupe du temps, de la personne, des modes, de l'aspect, de la voix et du nombre. Autant dans le cas du livre VIII que dans celui du livre X, la perte de plusieurs feuilles dans le manuscrit produit l'interruption de l'exposé. Indépendemment du fait que le modèle que nous appelons traditionnel eût déjà été fixé au moment où Varron écrit le *De lingua Latina*, ce qu'il y a de certain c'est que les définitions des parties du discours s'accompagnent de leurs accidents, un schéma auquel Varron s'ajustera pour échafauder ses remarques sur l'analogie. Il faut souligner, à cause de son influence sur les grammaires futures, le choix de l'ablatif singulier comme critère de caractérisation des différentes declinaisons (X, 62), et de la deuxième personne pour les verbes (IX, 109).

Un fragment de Varron, conservé par Diomède (*GL* I, 426), où il parle des *litterae* regroupées dans des *syllabae*, celles-ci dans la *dictio* et les *dictiones* se groupant par des *partes orationis*, qui se rassemblent dans l'*oratio*, montre une classification qui rappelle un type de commencement des manuels traditionnels. Collart (1978: 10) considère cette affirmation plus orientée vers une philosophie du langage que vers une grammaire pratique. D'ailleurs, le fragment pourrait appartenir aux *Disciplinarum libri IX*, pourvu que l'on accepte l'existence d'un livre consacré à la grammaire (Hadot 1984).

## 2.2. Quintilien

Sous une perspective différente, celle de cet auteur qui aborde les tâches d'un maître, nous possédons plusieurs chapitres de Quintilien qui peuvent nous aider à reconstruire ce qui put être une grammaire à cette époque, même si l'on a dit qu'elle ne semble pas avoir eu devant elle "tratatti esposti con un ordine sistematico" (Della Casa 1978). Comme nous le voyions dans le fragment cité de Varron, la doctrine transmise commence par *littera*, la distinction entre voyelles et consonnes, l'étude de celles-ci isolées ou en groupe, les changements etc. Puis il passe à la syllabe, dont l'étude est l'objet de l'ortographe. Puis il s'introduit dans les *partes orationis*, en évitant le problème de la *dictio*, comme s'il le considérait inclu dans les parties du discours, qui n'est qu'un groupement des *dictiones* dans des classes différentes. Il accorde une importance spéciale aux différents groupements en parties (§§ 18–20). La division en huit parties acceptée par Quintilien, en accord avec Aristarque (II$^{e}$ siècle av. J.-C.) et Remmius Palaemon, ne les mentionne pas explicitement. En même temps les digressions préalables qui établissent les fondements des groupements chez Varron disparaissent, ce qui est logique si nous pensons au caractère appliqué des normes enregistrées par Quintilien. La division choisie apparemment par Quintilien (il faut tenir compte du fait qu'il ne les mentionne pas, il n'en donne que le nombre), a des racines stoïciennes. Nous ne traiterons pas le problème intéressant des raisons qui mènent aux différents groupements des parties du discours; actuellement on a tendance à nier la validité d'un simple processus d'accumulation à partir d'Aristote (Taylor 1986).

Ensuite, conformément au but de ces chapitres, Quintilien fait remarquer la nécessité de maîtriser la déclinaison et la conjugaison (§ 22). En étroit rapport avec cela, il insiste sur le besoin de connaître les accidents: genre, cas dans les *nomina; genus, qualitas* et *persona, numerus* dans les verbes. Il continue avec les emplois du passif et avec une longue série d'anomalies. Il n'aborde pas de façon detaillée chaque partie du discours parce que ce sont les parties déclinables qui présentent une problématique plus grande, et parmi celles-ci il considère paradigmatiques le substantif et le verbe. On traite les cas particuliers plus ou moins profondément d'après leur longueur.

La section consacrée au barbarisme et au solécisme – et non pas aux *uirtutes* correspondantes, citées dans la *praelectio* (I, 8.16) et développées dans les livres VIII et IX consacrés à la rhétorique – est traîtée assez longuement (6,1 sqq.) comme tâche propre au grammairien en accordant également une attention particulière à la classification des mots. Il convient de souligner le fait que Quintilien ne suit pas le schéma que l'on considère caractéristique de la grammaire dès le début: *uitia* et *uirtutes orationis* (Baratin & Desbordes 1986).

Après le barbarisme et le solécisme, il fait un exposé des critères qui doivent guider l'application de la norme: *ratio (analogia/etymologia), uetustas, auctoritas, consuetudo*, un chapitre essentiellement théorique. Il finit par l'ortographe (*scribendi scientia*). C'est à ce moment seulement qu'il considère accomplie la tâche du grammairien qui fait référence aux *loquendi scribendique partes*. Si l'on tient compte du fait que la grammaire est définie dans la première partie surtout comme art du *recte loquendi*, il est possible qu'une interprétation stricte ait exclu des arts une section consacrée à l'*ars scribendi*, qui n'est d'ailleurs pas soumise à des règles fixes. Quant au chapitre consacré aux critères fondamentaux sur lesquels s'appuie la grammaire, son caractère théorique, peu applicable dans les niveaux élémentaux de l'enseignement, semble recevoir l'attention de Quintilien comme substrat indispensable pour le grammairien, mais non pas pour être transmis. Il faut se rendre compte que Quintilien écrit expressément pour les maîtres et non pas pour les élèves. Cela expliquerait aussi les avertissements qu'il donne au grammairien (I, 8.16) sur la *praelectio* qu'il doit faire du texte, où il lui conseille de se concentrer sur les *uirtutes orationis*: *tropi* et *schemata*, sans les reprendre dans les parties de l'enseignement grammatical qu'il doit donner, et où il parle seulement de la connaissance des *uitia* (barbarisme et solécisme) comme fondement indispensable pour la correction linguistique (Baratin & Desbordes 1986).

On aurait, donc, un enseignement, pour ne pas parler d'un *ars*, qui comprendrait trois sections différentes: un premier exposé des préliminaires, complément du travail du *grammatista*, dont la fonction est simplement d'apprendre à lire et à écrire; c'est à dire, le *grammaticus*, pour commencer, qui fournit un fondement théorique-analytique à la fonction exclusivement pratique du *grammatista*. Ensuite apparaissent les normes qui guident l'emploi correct du langage et qui divisées en deux parties coïncident avec la deuxième et la troisième partie des grammaires: normes et infractions de la norme. Les premières sont disposées selon les parties du discours et leurs accidents – un aspect peu formalisé chez Quintilien – et les secondes (barbarisme et solécisme) en fonction de leur rapport avec un seul élément de la phrase ou bien avec plusieurs, un chapitre qui semble avoir été présent dans les grammaires du I^er^ siècle av. J.-C. (cf. *Rhetorica ad Herennium* 4, 2, 17). Quintilien ajoute à tout cela un chapitre théorique (*Latinitas*) et un autre exclusivement pratique (*orthographia*), tous deux non susceptibles d'être reduits à des normes. Les normes qui touchent le *significanter ornateque loquendi* les sépare et les destine au travail du *rhetor* (VII, 32). Nous nous trouvons, comme dans le cas de Varron, bien que d'une façon plus nuancée, face à un schéma grammatical. Chez Varron ce schéma était employé pour soutenir les réfléxions sur le problème de l'analogie; chez Quintilien, le schéma vise à l'application d'un *ars grammatica* à l'enseignement (→ Art. 70).

## 3. Les préliminaires et les parties du discours

Pour en revenir à ce que nous disions au début, nous avons choisi les grammariens qui offrent, ou ont l'intention d'offrir, un *ars grammatica* qui comprend au moins deux des trois parties traditionnelles: préliminaires, *de partibus orationis* et *uitia* et *uirtutes orationis*. Nous laissons donc en dehors les œuvres grammaticales qui abordent seulement des domaines particuliers et aussi les parties des œuvres qui ne s'accordent pas au schéma traditionnel, par exemple, les traités de métrique qui accompagnent parfois l'*ars grammatica* ainsi délimitée.

Ainsi donc, nous avons choisi le plus ancien des grammairiens dont l'œuvre nous est parvenu: Marius Plotius Sacerdos (III^e^ siècle). De sa production en trois livres, nous prenons le livre 1 qui s'accorde au schéma du manuel traditionnel (*GL* VI, 427–546). Des deux œuvres de Probus Iunior, grammairien du IV^e^ siècle, peut-être un peu antérieur à Donat (Holtz 1981: 99, n. 12), nous avons considéré les *Instituta artium* (*GL* IV, 47–192). De Donat l'*ars minor* – consacré seulement aux parties du discours – et l'*ars maior*. Ce dernier sera appelé Donat I, II ou III d'après la partie correspondante: préliminaires, parties du discours, 'barbarisme'. Puis, Flavius Sosipater Charisius, du IV^e^ siècle, dont le manuel peut être considéré en quelque sorte l'antithèse de celui de Donat; même si les modèles où il s'est inspiré sont en partie des grammaires scolaires, la technique d'accumulation de sources prédomine, à partir de grammaires brèves aussi bien que de longues. Ce manuel compte quatre livres (Holtz 1978). Le premier livre est consacré au *nomen*, le deuxième aux parties du discours, le troisième au verbe et le quatrième aux *uitia et uirtutes orationis.* Comme dans le cas de Donat, nous les citerons selon la numération I II III IV. Ensuite, Diomède, à la seconde moitié du IV siècle (*GL* I, 300–529); parmi les trois livres, nous avons étudié les deux premiers; le premier contient les *partes orationis*, le deuxième est consacré aux *uitia* et *uirtutes*. Finalement Priscien, déjà dans le IVe siècle, auteur d'une grammaire latine composée dans le territoire grec. Ce sont 18 livres dont les 16 premiers nous intéressent spécialement parce que le livre XVII et le livre XVIII sont consacrés à la 'syntaxe' (*GL* II, 1–597; III, 1–377). Cette grammaire n'est pas conçue en parties ou en livres à entité indépendante, mais en sections ou sous-sections qui se succèdent en une séquence continuelle, interrompue seulement par le besoin d'offrir une distribution par livres.

3.1. Préliminaires

Nous aborderons d'abord le problème des préliminaires qui n'ont pas souvent que la valeur d'une simple introduction. Par contre dans d'autres occasions comme Donat I, Diomède II ou Priscien, ils atteignent un développement relatif et ils constituent même dans le cas de Donat une première partie du traité scolaire. Pour Sacerdos, nous ne conservons pas la partie initiale; seulement l'allusion à la fin du livre II (II, 492) au chapitre *de pedibus* nous rapproche du modèle de Donat, comme nous le verrons plus tard.

Cela se présente seulement dans deux cas sous une orientation éminemment phonique: Donat I et Diomède II. La séquence complète chez Donat est: *de uoce, de litteris, de syllabis, de pedibus, de tonis, de posituris.* Il ne faut pas oublier que sous la 'lettre' se cache le concept de 'son'. D'ailleurs, la sous-section *de pedibus* ne donne pas d'information sur la versification, mais elle semble annoncer le prochain traitement des périodes en prose (Holtz 1981: 63). Ce même trait est offert par Diomède II, mais avec une configuration différente: *de uoce, de definitione, de littera, de grammatica, de syllaba, de accentibus, de dictione, de pronuntiatione, de modulatione, de Latinitate,* etc.; sur le fondement de 'voix', 'lettre' et 'syllabe', il a introduit une série d'épigraphes nouveaux. Il faut ajouter que chez Diomède cette somme de sous-sections précède les *uitia* et *uirtutes orationis* et non pas les parties du discours comme cela arrive plus souvent. Le dessein d'intégration de Diomède II se manifeste par la présence d'un *de Latinitate* plus proche de la critique proprement dite.

Chez Charisius I, malgré la répétition du noyau commun avec Donat I et Diomède II: *de uoce, de litteris, de syllabis*, comme antécédent dans ce cas d'un exposé sur le *nomen*, la série se complète avec un *de grammatica* qui est en tête et un *de dictione* qui sert de conclusion. La présence de ces deux chapitres, contrairement à la place qu'ils occupent, est un trait commun avec Diomède. Outre ceci, il faut remarquer la présence d'un *de Latinitate* et *de analogia* plus tard, dans la section consacrée au *nomen*.

Charisius semble avoir cherché l'énumération des éléments qui conduisent au *nomen*, dans un ordre de complexité progressive. Cela nous éloigne du problème de la *lectio*, perceptible chez Donat et Diomède II, pour le premier dans les *de tonis* et *de posituris* et pour le second dans la série *de accentibus, de pronuntiatione* et *de modulatione*.

Un schéma reduit entre Charisius I/Donat I et Diomède II peut être trouvé dans Probus: *de uoce, de grammatica (= de Latinitate), de litteris* et *de syllabis*.

En revanche, les préliminaires aux *partes orationis* dans Charisius II et Diomède I semblent avoir une autre fonction: Chez *Charisius* un *de definitione, de genere, de specie,* suivi d'un *de oratione* donne lieu au *de partibus orationis*, aussi que Diomède I qui met devant cette section un *de arte grammatica* suivi du *de oratione*. Ce sont des prolégomènes très brefs en guise de présentation de la section centrale – *de partibus orationis* –, un rôle très différent des longs préliminaires aux parties du discours dans Donat I – et même Probus – et des autres sections dans Charisius I et Diomède II. Finalement, chez Priscien il y a un schéma cohérent, dont nous venons de voir quelques indices légers dans Charisius I: chacun des éléments cités est à l'origine du suivant par addition: l'union des lettres donne lieu à la syllabe, les syllabes à la *dictio* et ces *dictiones* à l'*oratio*. Grâce à l'insertion succéssive de deux sections: '*dictio*' et '*oratio*', on obtient une optique grammaticale au sens large du terme, même si les sections consacrées à la 'lettre' ou à la 'syllabe' continuent à avoir un contenu phonique.

En somme, il y aurait deux types d'introduction: une simple présentation de la section correspondante et une autre qui joue le rôle de véritables préliminaires. Dans ces derniers, la section phonique représentée par Donat I et partiellement par Diomède II se mêle ou alterne avec une autre sorte de préliminaires, plus liés a la section grammaticale qui est exposée tout de suite: les parties du discours. Il est intéressant dans les deux cas de remarquer la présence sporadique de sections mineures consacrées au *de Latinitate*, qui nous mènent à celle qui est considérée la fonction principale du grammairien à l'époque hellénistique: la critique du texte, qui aurait pu avoir plus tard une fonction normative.

3.2. *De partibus orationis*

La grande section suivante est celle *de partibus orationis*, pour les grammairiens la partie fondamentale (Servius, *GL* IV, 405.4). Elle comprend nécessairement une énumération des parties du discours, suivie d'un exposé individuel sur chacune d'elles. L'ordre dans lequel se succèdent les *partes* est symptomatique de la perspective prise dans chaque occasion par rapport à leurs fonctions.

Comme l'on vient de dire pour la section antérieure, chez Sacerdos, à cause des accidents de la transmission, il nous manque les deux quaternions initiaux du manuscrit (Naples, Bibl. Naz., lat. 2 — *olim* Vindob. lat. 16), ce qui fait que l'*ars grammatica* commence *in medias res*, avec quelques remarques sur les terminaisons du génitif et de l'ablatif pluriels selon la terminaison de l'ablatif singulier des *nomina, pronomina* et *participia*. Quoi qu'il en soit, nous pouvons en déduire à partir de l'ordre de chacune d'elles dans l'exposé sous-séquent quel était l'ordre de l'énumeration des *partes orationis*.

3.2.1. Le *nomen*

Si l'on exclut Priscien, qui suit très étroitement le modèle grec, il y a un trait commun pour les autres: dans Donat II, Charisius II et Diomède I le *nomen*, interrompu par l'insertion de la partie la plus voisine, le *pronomen*, est suivi de l'autre partie fondamentale dans la phrase: le *uerbum*. À partir de ce moment les coïncidences entre ces trois auteurs ne se maintiennent pas: Donat et Charisius placent l'adverbe juste à côté du verbe comme modificateur, tandis que Diomède préfère accorder cette place au *participium*, qui partage des traits avec le *nomen* et le *pronomen* et qui est placé chez Donat et Charisius après l'adverbe. L'ordre du reste est commun pour tous les trois: *coniunctio, praepositio, interiectio.*

Cependant, la *praepositio* suit chez Sacerdos le *pronomen*, probablement parce que cette catégorie est réduite à la préposition sans le préfixe et, de cette manière, s'attache aux deux parties déclinables antérieures: le *nomen* et le *pronomen*; dans le reste des grammairiens, la préposition comprend le préfixe. L'ordre le plus rare est celui de Probus qui met le *nomen* et le *pronomen* en tête, insère ensuite les quatre parties invariables avec l'ordre habituel et finit par le *participium* et le *uerbum*.

Cette énumération des parties du discours est suivie du traitement de chacune d'elles dans ce même ordre, à l'exception de Probus, qui situe le *participium* dans l'énumération qui suit le *pronomen* dans une nouvelle position: après l'interjection et avant le *uerbum*, à l'avant-dernière place. Dans le traitement de toutes ces parties se trouve inclue une définition et les accidents de chacune d'elles. La seule exception est une fois encore Probus qui passe souvent sous silence la définition.

Nous commençons par le *nomen*. Les accidents qui sont communs à tous les auteurs sont les suivants: *qualitas, genus, numerus, figura, casus*. Cela ne veut pas dire que le contenu soit le même dans tous les cas. Par exemple, la *qualitas* chez Probus se réduit à *nomina propria* et *appellatiua*, de même que dans Charisius II. Et pourtant, dans Donat II et Diomède I, la *qualitas*, organisée d'abord dans *propria* et *appellatiua* devient dans cette dernière section une catégorie où l'on admet toutes les classifications du nom: d'après les critères sémantiques et grammaticaux (morphologiques surtout), etc. L'absence de développement de cette section chez quelques auteurs provoque après l'explication des accidents l'apparition d'une grande section, intégrée parfois formellement dans un *de ablatiuo casu*, où est inséré toute une sorte de classifications nominales existentes en vertu de la *qualitas*. Naît ainsi chez Donat et Diomèdes une apparence d'organisation parfaite, apparente dans la mesure où l'une des sections mineures, celle qui correspond aux *nomina appellatiua*, est une somme hétérogène de différentes types difficilement susceptibles d'être réduits à quelques traits communs. Quoi qu'il en soit, l'existence d'une sous-section consacrée à la *qualitas* n'exclut pas la présence, une fois les accidents traités, de quelques remarques destinées à enregistrer les anomalies, un *de ablatiuo casu* ou une petite section de régimes de quelques *nomina*.

La *comparatio*, présente chez Probus et Donat II comme accident autonome, passe à la *qualitas* chez Diomède I, et à la partie finale hétérogène de Charisius II. Quant aux phénomènes traités dans l'*ordo* (*positio, deriuatio et deminutio*) de Probus, ils sont compris aussi dans la *qualitas* de Donat II et de Diomède I ou bien dans la section finale de Charisius II. On a un traitement différent du *nomen* dans Charisius I; on ne s'occupe que du genre, du nombre et du cas et l'on passe ensuite aux déclinaisons et à une série de problèmes concernant le *nomen*: *singularia* et *pluralia tantum*, les diminutifs, les caractéristiques des déclinaisons, le genre, *de Latinitate*, le comparatif, *de analogia, de ablatiuo casu [...]*.

Priscien reprend les cinq accidents communs, *species* (= *qualitas*), *genus, numerus, figura, casus*, et développe la première d'une façon différente. À la division de *species* en *propria* et *appellatiua*, il ajoute la scission de chacune d'elles en *principalia* et *deriuatiua*. Il s'occupe d'abord des *propria*, pour passer ensuite aux *appellatiua* dont il présente des classifications interminables. En rapport avec l'accident *species*, il consacre des sous-sections au comparatif, superlatif, diminutif et dénominatif, en classifiant ces derniers d'après leurs terminaisons, comme il l'avait déjà fait avec les patronimiques dans la section correspondante. Quant au reste des accidents, il énonce les genres d'après leurs terminaisons et il parle de *singularia* et *pluralia tantum* seulement dans le *de numeris*. Le *de casibus*, organisé soit par terminaisons soit par déclinaisons, reçoit un traitement considérable. La *figura* ne change pas. On en distingue toujours deux sortes, *simplex* et *composita*, suivies presque toujours des règles pour la formation de noms composés.

### 3.2.2. Le *pronomen*

En ce qui concerne le *pronomen*, le trait commun est toujours la présence dans l'énumération de *qualitas/species, genus, numerus, figura, persona et casus*, même s'ils n'apparaissent pas dans cet ordre. La *qualitas* est placée d'habitude en tête, à l'exception de Probus qui la place à la fin suivie du *de accentu* caractéristique, ce qui montre une fois encore son penchant pour la métrique et la musique.

Diomède, lui aussi, ajoute un accident: l'*ordo*, qui lui sert de point d'appui pour la tâche difficile de classifier les pronoms. En effet, contrairement à ce qui arrivait dans le cas du *nomen*, Diomède s'éloigne de Donat sur ce point. Celui-ci emploie la *qualitas* comme réceptacle de toute sorte de classifications: *finita, infinita, minus quam finita; demonstratiua/relatiua*; d'après la signification: *gentis, ordinis, numeri*, etc.; d'après l'emplacement: *praepositiua (quis), subiunctiua (is)*. De cette manière, une fois finis les accidents avec le traitement du cas, il suffit de faire deux remarques pour établir une vision relativement complète: absence de comparatif et différence entre *pronomen* et *articulus*. Donat, à la différence du reste, n'a même pas besoin de s'occuper des déclinaisons; il consacre l'*ars minor* à ce travail. Diomède distribue entre la *qualitas* et l'*ordo*, et spécialement dans ce dernier, les classifications du 'pronom', et laisse pour la *qualitas* la distribution générale entre *finita, infinita, minus quam finita*. La *qualitas* chez Probus est à la base d'une classification fondamentale: *finita, minus quam finita, infinita et possessiua*, ce qui donne lieu aux déclinaisons correspondantes.

Dans Charisius II, le traitement systématique de définition et d'accidents n'apparaît que dans la version initiale; à l'intérieur de la *qualitas* on fait la distinction de *finita* et *infinita*, même si dans le déroulement nous trouvons aussi les *possessiua*. Dans le développement de la deuxième et de la troisième version, on inclut également des catégories comme *minus quam finita, pronomina ad aliquid* ou *praepositiua* et *subiunctiua*, sans les attribuer spécifiquement à la *qualitas*. Tout cela est acompagné des déclinaisons (qui se répètent parfois) et des singularités de la déclinaison. Chez Priscien nous retrouvons en partie le schéma de Donat, mais celui-ci est distribué d'une façon différente qui rappelle celle du *nomen*. La classification dominante dans la *species* (= *qualitas*) est celle des *nomina primitiua*: les pronoms personnels: *hic ipse iste*, et les *deriuatiua*: les possessifs. Malgré tout, après le dernier accident, *de casibus*, on insiste sur la valeur des pronoms: *substantiua, loco propriorum, demonstratiua, relatiua*, etc. L'impossibilité de distribuer toute l'information dans le chapitre des accidents rend inévitable l'existence de cette section finale dépourvue de titre.

On a tendance à inclure dans les accidents toute sorte de groupements qui sont augmentés afin de pouvoir recevoir le plus grand nombre de catégories pronominales; cela n'empêche pas parfois la présence, à la fin du chapitre, de types pronominaux qui n'ont pas de place ailleurs.

### 3.2.3. Le *uerbum*

La coïncidence des accidents enregistrés est assez fréquente; cependant l'ordre dans lequel on en fait mention ne l'est point. Il y a seulement une coïncidence dans l'ordre d'énumération entre Sacerdos et Charisius.

Les accidents communs à tous sont: *genus, figura, numerus, modus* (sauf Diomède), *tempus, persona et coniugatio*. Nous donnons l'ordre de Sacerdos parce qu'il est plus ancien. On doit y ajouter la *forma* pour Sacerdos, la *qualitas* pour Sacerdos et Donat II, Charisius II et Diomède I et la *species* pour Probus et Priscien. Cela mène à la variation du nombre d'accidents: 9 pour Sacerdos, 7 pour Donat et 8 pour le reste. Mais si l'on réfléchit à ce sujet, on s'aperçoit que Donat est d'accord avec Sacerdos sur la matière traitée, puisque les accidents *forma* et *modus* – le premier exclusif de Sacerdos – sont à l'origine du contenu de la *qualitas*. Quant à Probus et Priscien, le nombre de 8 est la conséquence de l'omission de la *qualitas*, présente chez Charisius et Diomède et de l'addition de la *species*. D'autre part, la *qualitas* semble être implicite à Probus – ainsi considéré, le nombre passerait à 9 –, étant donné que dans la section consacrée au *genus*, qui porte le titre alternatif de *qualitas*, sont compris quelques phénomènes appartenant au *genus* et a la *qualitas* respectivement.

Probus et Priscien sont d'accord sur les accidents et le nombre, mais pas pour l'ordre: *tempus, modus, numerus, persona, figura, genus, coniugatio, figura, species* (ordre de Probus) face à *genus, tempus, modus, species, figura, coniugatio, persona* (ordre de Priscien); Charisius donne: *qualitas, genus, figura, numerus, modus, tempus, persona,* face à Diomède: *tempus, persona, numerus, figura, qualitas, genus, modus.* Diomède change l'ordre des trois derniers dans l'énumération: *genus, modus, qualitas*. Il y a coïncidence totale entre Sacerdos et Charisius si l'on exclut la présence de *forma* chez Sacerdos placée en tête: *qualitas, genus, figura, numerus, modus, persona, coniugatio*.

Il n'y a pas de différences fondamentales dans le contenu de *figura (simplex/composita), numerus, tempus* et *persona*, même si tous les auteurs trouvent des nuances intéressantes. Il y a en revanche des différences accusées entre *qualitas, genus, modus* et *coniugatio*.

Chez Sacerdos et Charisius la *qualitas* des verbes est *finita* et *infinita* (équivalente aux formes personnelles et non personnelles). *Qualitas* apparaît chez Probus comme dénomination alternative de *genus* et possède des traits qui sont parfois inclus sous les concepts de *genus* et *qualitas* respectivement: *actiuum, passiuum, neutrale*, etc. et *inchoatiuum, frequentatiuum*, etc. Chez Diomède la *qualitas* englobe les aspects verbaux, *absoluta, inchoatiua, iteratiua*, ainsi que les autres catégories morphologiques (défectifs et *transgressiua* – *audeo, ausus sum* –) ou sémantiques (*ambigua*). Comme nous l'avons dit antérieurement, la *qualitas* de Donat comprend la *in formis*, équivalente à la *qualitas* de Diomède, c'est à dire, les catégories aspectuelles du verbe: *perfecta, meditatiua, frequentatiua*, et celle *in modis*, correspondant à l'accident 'mode'. Nous observons donc qu'il s'agit d'un accident sans entité propre car c'est le résultat d'une fusion de deux accidents qui chez Sacerdos par exemple apparaissent séparés.

Un autre accident où se mèlent des catégories qui ne sont pas homogènes est le *genus* (Hovdhaugen 1986). À la base de la classification des *genera* se trouve le concept de 'voix': active, neutre, commune et déponente. Nous trouvons cette réduction chez Donat II, Charisius II (troisième version) et Priscien. Le même contenu lié à *impersonale* chez Diomède I, Priscien et dans la première version de Charisius. À la sous-section, résultat de l'addition des deux, s'ajoute une série de catégories verbales aspectuelles chez Sacerdos, Probus et dans la quatrième version de Charisius. L'oscillation dans la catégorisation des aspects verbaux est évidente: ils aparaissent parfois sous *qualitas*, parfois sous *genus*. On pourrait dire exactement la même chose de 'l'impersonnel' qui apparaît parfois entre les 'modes' (Probus, Donat), parfois entre les *genera* et les *modi* en même temps: Charisius et Diomède; la *species* chez Priscien coïncide à peu près avec la *qualitas* de Diomède; sous la seconde sous-division générique, *primitiua* et *deriuatiua*, il mentionne *inchoatiua, frequentatiua*, mais aussi *impersonalia*.

En ce qui concerne la conjugaison, en dehors de l'inclusion ou de l'exclusion des paradigmes verbaux (tous les citent sous la dénomination *declinatio* à l'exception de Donat et Priscien), la différence la plus accusée est la considération de trois ou quatre conjugaisons. Seulement Charisius II et Priscien en offrent quatre, les autres en admettent trois et présentent deux variantes pour la troisième d'après la voyelle brève ou longue.

### 3.2.4. L'*aduerbium*

Le traitement de l'adverbe est relativement semblable; à l'exception de Priscien, tous les autres offrent les mêmes accidents: *significa-*

*tio, comparatio* et *figura*, en développant spécialement le 'signifié', comme système de classification des adverbes, si l'on exclut l'ordre alphabétique suivie par Charisius II dans la dernière partie aussi qu'une classification selon les terminaisons chez Charisius et Priscien. Dans Donat II et Charisius II cette dernière classification est liée à un chapitre qui précède souvent les accidents et qui tient compte de deux catégories d'adverbes, primitifs et dérivés, c'est à dire, ceux qui dérivent d'autres parties du discours. Cette classification des adverbes est précisément marginale aux accidents chez tous les grammairiens choisis, sauf dans Priscien qui, en éliminant la *comparatio* et en la remplaçant par la *species*, lui donne le contenu des *primitiua* et *deriuatiua* ordonnés d'après les terminaisons. Nous trouvons, donc, trois critères de présentation des adverbes: celui purement morphologique – les terminaisons –, le sémantique et l'alphabétique, bien que ce dernier soit le moins repandu.

Chez tous les auteurs, une dernière partie reprend les traits qui ne puissent pas être insérés dans la simplicité du schéma imposé: confusion de l'adverbe avec d'autres parties du discours, refus de l'union préposition-adverbe, exceptions ou remarques d'emploi etc.

#### 3.2.5. La *praepositio* et l'*interiectio*

Nous laissons de côté la préposition dont seulement Diomède fait mention des accidents – il parle seulement de 'cas' –, et qui est présentée sous les régimes d'accusatif, ablatif ou tous deux. Même situation pour l'interjection.

#### 3.2.6. La *coniunctio*

La conjonction reçoit un traitement uniforme par rapport aux accidents, même chez Priscien. Les accidents sont: *potestas, figura, ordo*; chez Priscien cela change à *figura* et *species/potestas*. L'*ordo* fait référence à sa place relative dans le discours: *praepositiuae et subiunctiuae*; le contenu de *potestas* est toujours le même, sauf dans une des versions de Charisius II et Priscien. Le critère appliqué dans cette classification est de toute façon sémantique, de même que dans la version la plus employée: *copulatiuae, disiunctiuae, expletiuae, causales, rationales*, comme dans la plus complète de Charisius et Priscien, qui ajoutent encore douze types de conjonctions: *effectiuae, approbatiuae, subdisiunctiuae*, etc. Il est intéressant de trouver chez Donat, à la fin de la conjonction, une référence à la confusion entre conjonctions et adverbes (Baratin 1988).

## 4. *Vitia et uirtutes orationis*

La section consacrée aux *uitia et uirtutes orationis* manque dans deux des grammairiens étudiés, Probus et Priscien. Aucun des autres ne coïncide avec le reste dans l'ordre d'énumeration des sous-sections et il y a même des différences dans le nombre de sous-sections qui font partie de ce chapitre (Baratin & Desbordes 1986). D'après la définition des différents défauts et vertus de la phrase, ceux-ci se correspondent deux à deux: barbarisme/métaplasme et solécisme/*schemata*. La différence de considération entre défaut ou 'vertu' se trouve dans l'accomplissement involontaire (barbarisme et solécisme) ou volontaire à cause du mètre ou de l'ornement (métaplasme, *schema*). Donat groupe d'un côté barbarisme et solécisme et d'un autre métaplasme et *schemata*. Ils sont separés par un *de ceteris uitiis* et se terminent par les 'tropes' ou *dictio translata*, employés comme ornement par nécessité. Cet ordre semble viser à une certaine symétrie: des défauts concrets qui se complètent avec un chapitre où sont inclus le reste des *uitia* et *uirtutes* correspondants aux défauts concrets, auxquels sont ajoutés, parallèlement au de *ceteris uitiis*, les tropes. Le barbarisme et le solécisme s'accompagnent d'une définition et de l'énoncé correspondant à leur façon de se produire. La sous-section *de ceteris uitiis* n'est qu'une énumeration de défauts et une explication de leur nature. Dans le reste des cas la définition est suivie de l'énumération et de la nature des vertus qui répondent à la dénomination de métaplasme, *schema* et trope.

Cet ordre ne se répète dans nos auteurs ni avant ni après Charisius. De toute façon, Sacerdos le conserve, sauf dans l'inversion de la place de métaplasme et *de ceteris uitiis*. Cela pourrait faire penser à un faux placement du *metaplasmus* dû aux déficiences de la transmission manuscrite. Charisius II change cet ordre et place le 'trope' en tête des *uirtutes*, à l'intérieur desquelles il fait la distinction entre métaplasme, *schemata lexeos* et *schemata dianoeas*. Une présentation tout à fait différente qui s'accorde parfaitement à son traitement des préliminaires est celle de Diomède I. Il fait attention surtout aux 'vertus': métaplasme, *schemata* et *uirtutes orationis*. C'est une vision qui penche plus du côté de la critique (*enarratio poetarum*) et de la création, en accord avec tout le reste de sa grammaire. En effet, l'*obscuritas*, le manque d'ornement et l'absence de *Latinitas* (*barbarismus*) sont considérés des défauts du discours qui supposent l'apparition de barbarismes et de solécismes. La *proprietas* et l'*ornatus* sont également des *uirtutes orationis* qui s'obtiennent grâce aux tropes. Il est évident que l'on met beaucoup plus en valeur la partie positive, comme conséquence de l'*ornate et proprie loqui*, que la partie négative.

## 5. Conclusions

Même s'il existe d'une façon générale une affinité évidente dans la disposition et le développement des grammaires latines depuis les premières références, il n'est pas moins vrai que cette affinité ne parvient jamais à l'extrême de la coïncidence. Les fluctuations qui existent même dans l'ordre des parties du discours – objet d'étude principal de la grammaire – et surtout dans le traitement des accidents du *nomen* et du *uerbum* accordent à la tradition grammaticale une vivacité inattendue. Il y a paralysie si l'on considère que les données employées ne changent pas, mais les auteurs apportent leurs traits personnels lorsqu'ils les organisent dans l'ensemble de la grammaire. Dans le cas des pronoms, par exemple, la présence d'un nouvel accident, l'*ordo*, est bien l'indice de l'intérêt pour essayer une classification plus adéquate. Nous venons de voir que l'immobilité de la dernière section sur les *uitia* et *uirtutes* était seulement apparente: le simple déplacement d'une section par rapport aux autres, la subordination chez Diomède à des concepts préalables propres à la *Latinitas* sont des symptomes d'une tentative de renovation. L'inclusion chez Diomède d'un *de uerborum consensu cum casibus* et d'un *de coniunctione temporum* d'une orientation clairement syntaxique nous mène aux mêmes conclusions (Charpin 1978). Ajoutons à tout cela la présence de la 'syntaxe' chez Priscien, innovation de grande portée en latin.

Chaque grammairien introduit des variantes plus ou moins importantes, parfois à peine perceptibles, mais qui nous orientent dans la direction de l'insatisfaction par rapport aux modèles reçus. C'est en ce sens que toute modification, si petite soit-elle, doit être objet d'étude, puisqu'elle est le reflet d'un changement, d'un mouvement. Seule la forte présence de Donat, s'imposant au reste des manuels, peut avoir donné un sentiment qui pèse sur nos jugements actuels, celui d'une conformité totale entre les grammaires.

## 6. Bibliographie

### 6.1. Sources primaires


Charisius, *Ars Grammatica*. Éd. par Karl Barwick. Leipzig: Teubner, 1964.

*Grammatici Latini*. Éd. par Heinrich Keil. 7 vols. Leipzig: Teubner. (Réimpr., Hildesheim: G. Olms)


### 5.2. Sources secondaires


Baratin, Marc. 1988. "Les limites de l'analyse de l'énoncé chez les grammairiens latins". *L'héritage des grammairiens latins de l'Antiquité aux Lumières. Actes du Colloque de Chantilly 2–4 septembre 1987* éd. par Irène Rosier, 69–80. Paris: Peeters.

– & Françoise Desbordes. 1986. "La troisième partie de l'*ars grammatica*". *Historiographia Linguistica* 13.215–240.

Barwick, Karl. 1922. *Remmius Palaemon und die römische* Ars Grammatica. Leipzig: Teubner.

Charpin, François. 1978. "La notion de solécisme chez les grammairiens latins". *Varron, Grammaire antique et Stylistique latine* éd. par Jean Collart, 211–216. Paris: Les Belles Lettres.

Collart, Jean. 1938. "Palémon et l'*ars grammatica*". *Revue de Philologie* 12.228–238.

–. 1978. "L'œuvre grammaticale de Varron". *Varron, Grammaire antique et Stylistique latine* éd. par Jean Collart, 3–21. Paris: Les Belles Lettres.

Della Casa, Adriana. 1978. "Giulio Romano nella storia della grammatica latina". *Varron, Grammaire antique et Stylistique latine* éd. par Jean Collart, 217–224. Paris: Les Belles Lettres.

Dunlap, J. 1940. "Fragments of a Latin grammar from Egypt". *American Journal of Philology* 61.330–344.

Fuhrmann, Manfred. 1960. *Das systematische Lehrbuch*. Göttingen: Vandenhoeck & Ruprecht.

Hadot, Ilsetraut. 1984. *Ars libéraux et philosophie dans la pensée antique*. Paris: Etudes Augustiniennes.

Holtz, Louis. 1978. "Sur les traces de Charisius". *Varron, Grammaire antique et Stylistique latine* éd. par Jean Collart, 225–233. Paris: Les Belles Lettres.

–. 1981. *Donat et la tradition de l'enseignement grammatical: Etude et édition critique*. Paris: CNRS.

Hovdhaugen, Even. 1986. "*Genera verborum quot sunt*? Observations on the Roman grammatical tradition". *Historiographia Linguistica* 13.307–321.

Jeep, Ludwig. 1893. *Zur Geschichte von den Redetheilen bei den lateinischen Grammatikern*. Leipzig: Teubner.

Taylor, Daniel J. 1986. "Rethinking the history of language science in classical Antiquity". *Historiographia Linguistica* 13.175–190.


*Carmen Codoñer, Salamanca (Espagne)*

# 70. Grammar and rhetoric in Roman schools

1. Preface
2. The Roman school system
3. Grammatical doctrines in the schools
4. Rhetorical doctrines in the schools
5. Conclusion
6. Bibliography

## 1. Preface

Perhaps the most important single statement to be made about grammar and rhetoric in Roman schools is that grammatical concepts were only gradually stabilized over several centuries, while Romans as early as the time of Cicero (BCE 106–43) had inherited a completely developed system of rhetorical concepts refined from Hellenistic sources.

A striking example of this disparity may be found in the *Institutio oratoria* (CE 95) of Marcus Fabius Quintilianus, which provides the best single description of the Roman school system. While Quintilian is able to devote nine of his twelve books to a detailed discussion of rhetorical doctrines which had been well accepted for nearly two centuries, he is able to spend only half of his first book (I.iv–vii) on grammar, and here he must explain such rudimentary matters as accent, etymology, conjugation, orthography, and usage.

For rhetoric he can cite acknowledged authorities like Cicero and Aristotle; for grammar he has mainly his own wits and references to 'the Greeks' or 'scholars'. It seems clear that at the end of the 1st century CE there was still no standard grammatical authority to whom Quintilian could refer his students.

If he had been writing three centuries later, of course, he could have referenced Aelius Donatus, whose *Ars minor* and *Ars maior* (ca. CE 350) were to become so dominant that the term 'Donat' later was to become a synonym for 'primer' or first book in any subject. Or, a century and a half after Donatus, he could have cited the extensive *Institutiones grammaticae* of Priscianus Caesariensis (fl. CE 500), which comprised eighteen books.

In any case it is clear that both grammar and rhetoric played significant roles in Roman schools. It is the schools, however, which were the arenas for these two arts, and so it may be useful first to consider the nature of those schools before turning to the arts themselves.

## 2. The Roman school system

It seems fair to say that by the end of the 1st century CE Roman education had begun to evolve into a 'system', with a recognizable *curriculum* or course of studies. This system persisted throughout Roman antiquity, and in some places at least survived the barbarian invasions and influenced medieval education. Renaissance humanists revived it in the 15th century, and under both Catholic and Protestant auspices it prospered in Europe and later was exported to the New World first by Spanish and then by English colonists. The basic system persisted into the 19th century, though some educational programs (e. g. the Jesuits) still follow its main principles today.

It is important to note that the concept of 'school' as we know it was essentially a Roman invention. Greek education, and early Roman education under the Republic, was delivered by individual teachers who attracted students by their skill or fame; consequently there was a wide range of subject matters and teaching methods. In some cases teaching was done by an individual tutor, often a family slave or a freedman, who had only the family child as pupil.

The genius of the later Roman systematization, on the other hand, was the creation of the 'public' school – i. e. one with many students – which followed a generally accepted sequence of studies and exercises to achieve rhetorical facility by about the age of sixteen or seventeen.

There were three stages: the *litterator* taught basic reading and writing, sometimes at home, sometimes in the school; the *grammaticus* taught grammar, including what we would call literature, especially the poets; the *rhetor* taught the principles of rhetoric and had the older students engage in *declamationes*, or fictitious debates, in front of their classmates.

'Habit' was the organizing principle of Roman schools. Quintilian for example makes a clear distinction between Precept – that is, principles which can be told to a student – and the development of a Facility which lies within the student himself.

But these precepts of being eloquent, though necessary to be known, are not sufficient to produce the full power of eloquence unless there be united to them a certain Facility, which among the Greeks is called *hexis* "habit" (*Institutio oratoria* X.1.1).

After all, the ultimate objective of the Roman school was to take a boy of six or seven and over a dozen years mold him into an orator capable of speaking effectively on any subject in any time or place. This required what Quintilian calls *facilitas*, or the capacity for intelligent improvisation based on the circumstances.

"One great quality in an orator", he says, "is discretion, because he must turn his thoughts in various directions, according to the various bearings of his subject" (II.13.1–2)

To accomplish this goal the Roman schools strove to equip the student with an arsenal of linguistic possibilities – not just sets of memorized precepts but habits instilled by detailed exercises practiced over many years. These years of habituation would later make it almost instinctive to find the right words for any occasion. This habituation was true of grammar, and it was true of rhetoric.

The remarkable continuity of teaching methods over several centuries makes it possible to analyze the basic elements of the program. Quintilian is the best guide (Russell 1981: 119; Bonner 1977: 165–327). What he describes at the end of the first Christian century is still true centuries later; in the 6th century, for example, teachers were still listed in the public budget by 'barbarians' like Theodoric and his successor Athlaric, and their methods remained unchanged (Riché 1976: 40).

As Quintilian points out, the program depends on the interrelation of four activities: reading, writing, speaking, and listening. No one was more important than the others. Reading and listening accustomed the student to both the shape and sound of words used by others, while writing and speaking taught him to use his own talents to shape new word combinations. In these circumstances grammatical and rhetorical knowledge was absorbed in practice as much as it was taught as precept. Consequently it is critical to understand the nature of Roman teaching methods in order to comprehend the role played by grammar and rhetoric.

### 2.1. Roman teaching methods as described by Quintilian

The cultural impact of Roman schools and their teaching methods can only be described as enormous. The elements of the Roman teaching system were inherited from the Greeks, but it was the Romans who made them into a 'system' and spread that system over Europe and into Africa and the Middle East. Behind the conquering soldiers came the civilians, and the schools for their children. As Pattison (1982: 67) has pointed out,

"The soldier and the grammarian proceeded in lockstep to spread the Roman way, one by conquering the world, the other by providing it with correct Latin as a medium of organization".

By the time of the Emperor Vespasian the schools had become an agent of public policy, a means to Latinize the world.

Government, both imperial and local, supported schools in various ways: an edict of Diocletian, for example, set monthly fees for teachers, and in 362 Julian required that masters be publicly licensed to teach (Dionisotti 1982: 122). One consequence of public involvement was the proliferation of records for teachers; one modern study (Kaster 1988) is able to provide biographical details on 281 Roman teachers. For the conquered people, on the other hand, the schools often became a means of social mobility, a way to elevate themselves in the Roman world. Rhetoric and its supporting art of grammar were thus an integral part of Empire.

Romans were social engineers as well as structural engineers. Five means of instruction were employed to bring correctness and facility to the young. Naturally there were variations from teacher to teacher, but the evidence for the overall pattern is overwhelming. These five categories, and their relation to each other, can best be seen in tabular form:

(A) Precept: a set of rules that provide a definite method and system of speaking or writing. Grammar as precept occupies part of one book of Quintilian's work. Rhetoric as precept, occupying most of the work, is itself divided into the five parts of Invention, Arrangement, Style, Memory, and Delivery.
(B) Imitation: the use of model texts, both oral and written, to learn how others have used language. A specific sequence has six steps: reading aloud (*lectio*); master's detailed analysis of the text (*praelectio*); memorization of models; paraphrase of models; transliteration (verse to prose, or Latin to Greek, and the reverse); recitation of paraphrase or transliteration; master's correction of the recitation.
(C) *Progymnasmata*: graded composition exercises in writing and/or speaking. Each succeeding exercise is more difficult, and incorporates what is learned in the preceding one. The following twelve

were common by Cicero's time and recur thereafter: a) Retelling a fable; b) Retelling an episode from a poet or a historian; c) *Chreia*, or amplification of a moral theme; d) Amplification of an aphorism (*sententia*) or proverb; e) Refutation or confirmation of an allegation; f) Commonplace, or confirmation of a thing admitted; g) *Encomium*, or eulogy (or dispraise) of a person or thing; h) Comparison of things or persons; i) Impersonation, or speaking or writing in the character of a given person; j) Description, or vivid presentation of details; k) Thesis, or argument for/against an answer to a general question not involving individuals; and l) Arguments for or against a specific law.
(D) Declamation: assigned fictitious speeches, in two types: *suasoria*, or deliberative (political) speech arguing that a certain action should or should not be taken, and *controversia*, or forensic (legal) speech prosecuting or defending a fictitious or historical person in a law case.
(E) Sequencing: the systematic ordering of classroom activities to accomplish two goals: moving from the simple to the complex, and reinforcement by constant reiteration of the elements of the classroom exercises.

Ideally these learning activities should continue throughout the boy's schooling. For example the process of Imitation under the rhetorician looks to orations for models rather than the poems of the grammarian; in fact a contemporary of Quintilian, Asconius Pedianus, prepared a set of commentaries on Cicero's speeches using this method (Asconius, *Commentarii in orationes Ciceronis*). It is clear enough that some teaching tasks belong to one or the other teacher: basic grammar, interpretation of poets, the most elementary *progymnasmata*, to the grammarian; at the other end of the scale the rhetorician consistently claims the right to handle Declamation. Nevertheless there were gray areas in between.

In a system based on boys being passed at some point from *grammaticus* to *rhetor*, it was perhaps inevitable that there should be not only overlap but actual rivalry between the two types of teachers. Quintilian in fact opens Book Two (II.1.1–6) with the complaint that boys come to the teachers or rhetoric later than they should, both because the grammarians encroach on the rhetoricians' sphere and because rhetoricians themselves do not deign to teach the elementary parts of their subject. "The two professions", he declares, "must be assigned their proper sphere". He adds that grammar, "not content with the theory of correct speech, no inconsiderable subject, has usurped the study of practically all the highest departments of knowledge". The historian Suetonius, writing at almost the same time, confirms Quintilian's judgment when he says that rhetoricians tend to abandon the *progymnasmata* and want to teach only Declamation (Suetonius, *De grammaticis* 25.4).

This inter-art rivalry poses an important question for the history of grammar and rhetoric. What are the boundaries between grammar and rhetoric, if indeed there are boundaries? Chronologically the study of grammar comes first for Roman students, but does that mean that the later teacher of rhetoric can ignore it? In practical terms, throughout the Empire the teacher of grammar had lower social status and a lower salary than the rhetorician; often his school was physically separate from that of the rhetorician (Kaster 1988: 50ff.). Yet this social situation does not provide a complete answer to the intellectual question posed here – it merely tells us which art won greater approval at a certain time.

Under these circumstances it will be useful to turn for answers to a more detailed description of Roman teaching. Quintilian's description of the Roman school system is a useful one, both because it is clear and because his account is confirmed generally by other writers up to the time of Saint Augustine in the 5th century.

Language acquisition, for Quintilian, begins in the cradle; proper pronunciation and usage are so important that even the child's nurse should be chosen with that in mind. Writing begins with letters of the alphabet carved into a board so that the child's tracing of the inscribed letters with a stylus will quickly result in kinesthetic reinforcement of the shapes seen by his eyes. Then the child learns syllables, then makes words from them, then makes sentences from the words. Reading – i.e. reading aloud – begins as soon as the child is capable, not at a certain arbitrary age. Quintilian prefers that formal writing and reading instruction begin with Greek, on the grounds that Latin will come to the child easily from his surroundings; most later teachers do not agree with him, though Greek and Latin are used interchangeably throughout the formal exercises of both the *grammaticus* and the *rhetor*.

As soon as the child can read and write both Greek and Latin he is turned over to the *grammaticus*, or teacher of grammar. Quintilian defines grammar as "the art of speaking and writing correctly, and the interpretation of the poets" (I.4.1). But it should be remembered that in the Roman 'public' school context, speaking entails listening, and writing entails reading.

It is difficult to determine exactly how much direct 'precept' transmission is involved – that is, transmission of grammatical principles by what we would call a subject lecture. Certainly Quintilian declares that students must learn how to conjugate verbs and decline nouns and notes that memorization is necessary to learn certain syllables. Nevertheless the main thrust of the Roman teaching program is to inculcate both grammatical and rhetorical knowledge through a process of gradual absorption based on the reception and criticism of texts – both written and oral.

After declaring that grammar is the foundation of oratory, Quintilian begins his discussion of it by treating barbarisms and solecisms, then schemes or figures (promising fuller details later when he discusses 'rhetorical' figures in Books Eight and Nine). Rules of language for both speakers and writers, he says, are based on reason, including analogy and etymology, on antiquity (i. e. archaic words), on authority, and on usage ("the agreed practice of educated men"). Orthography and reading (i. e. reading aloud) are both described as servants of usage, in that correct writing and pronunciation depend on a knowledge of the accepted. At every stage he compares Greek and Latin in detail.

Quintilian does not discuss syntax. This is perfectly reasonable within the Roman system, since the students learn word patterns and word order through the guided study of texts, particularly in the complex exercise known as Imitation (*imitatio*). There was no ancient equivalent of what today we call 'composition' (Scaglione 1972: 3).

It is interesting to note that he feels it necessary to defend the study of grammar. Some readers, he fears, might feel such matters to be "trivial details which are likely to prove a hindrance to those who are intent upon a greater task" (I.7.33). But Quintilian points out that even Cicero demanded correct speech from his own son and declares that it is only excessive quibbling about minor grammatical points that does any harm. As for what we would call 'literature', he is rhapsodic in his praise.

> The study of literature is a necessity for boys and the delight of old age, the sweet companion of our privacy, and the sole branch of study which has more solid substance than display (I.4.5).

When he turns to reading he makes it clear that the master's criticism of the student's oral reading is a means to inculcate both grammatical and rhetorical principles. The reader must know how to distinguish prose patterns from meter, how to modulate his voice to convey meaning, how to use pausation to indicate clauses and sentences, and how to pronounce words according to good usage. While Quintilian does not say so, because it would be obvious in his culture, the student also might have to distinguish between the words themselves if the scribe of the text had not added punctuation marks separating them: Latin monumental inscription normally had no word separations but of course would not be used for classroom reading.

The master's own reading (aloud), like his speaking, is intended as a model. But the master's reading of a text is described as a far more complex matter than simply the recitation of a text. Since Quintilian treats the master's reading in the context of the exercise known as *imitatio*, it may be useful here to discuss that major teaching device.

### 2.2. Teaching grammar and rhetoric in *imitatio*

Quintilian constantly urges the grammarian (as well as the rhetorician later) to pay attention to minute details in a text, for they are the building blocks from which the student will make his own compositions. The text thus becomes the arena in which grammar or rhetoric is discussed. At the elementary level, after a text is read aloud – and here the master's voice and demeanor are to be models for the students even beyond the value of the written text – the grammarian is to analyse its grammatical features. In the next stage of *imitatio* the student is asked to write his own version of the same text, and the master repeats the analytic process of criticism aloud for the benefit of the student and the rest of the class. For verse, the parts of speech are noted, the types of feet, different meanings of words, solecisms or barbarisms, etymologies of words, cases, and the like. In other words, the master first uses an existing text to delineate what needs to be known, then tests the student's ability to remember and use those knowledges in his own writing. The same procedure applies in the other stages of *imitatio*. In the transliteration step, moving from verse to prose or Latin to Greek, attention to detail is especially keen as the use of either two modes or two languages requires not only knowledge of each but comparisons of each. For instance, Quintilian points out, the student has to remember how accent is rendered in each language.

We do not have a sample grammatical *praelectio* or critical analysis from Quintilian, though one could be adduced from his several scattered allusions to the process. We do have one, however, from a later period; it is so similar to descriptions by Suetonius, Quintilian, Ausonius and others that it may serve as a good example. The author is the grammarian Priscianus Caesariensis, writing in Constantinople in the 6th century; the work is an analysis of the first line in each of the twelve books of Virgil's *Aeneid*. The following excerpt from the first book may indicate the manner in which the *praelectio* dissects a text.

Scan the line, *Arma virumque cano Troiae qui primus ab oris*. How many caesuras are there? Two. What are they? The penthemimera and the hepthemimera. Which is which? The penthemimera is *Arma virumque cano*, and the hepthemimera *Arma virumque cano Troiae*. How many 'figures' has it? Ten. Why has it got ten? Because it is made up of three dactyls and two spondees. [Priscian takes no notice of the final spondee.] How many words ["parts of speech"] are there? Nine. How many nouns? Six – *arma, virum, Troiae, qui* [sic!], *primus, oris*. How many verbs? One – *cano*. How many prepositions? One – *ab*. How many conjunctions? One – *que*. Study each word in turn. Let us begin with *arma*. What part of speech is it? A noun. What is its quality? Appellative. What kind is it? General. What gender? Neuter. Now do you know? All nouns ending in –*a* in the plural are neuter. Why is *arma* not used in the singular? Because it means many different things (Marrou 1956: 279–280).

This meticulous attention to detail, applied to thousands of texts over the ten or twelve years of schooling, is calculated to produce a linguistic sensitivity in which every word and every sound is critical to the future orator. Moreover, since it is a written text analyzed orally, the exercise also begins to prepare the ear of the student to recognize the subtleties of language he is to hear later in orations studied under the rhetorician. Grammar is absorbed over time, through repetition of analyses.

Exactly the same process is used for the rhetorical analysis of an oration. Quintilian has a clear description. There is an oral reading by master or student.

Then, after explaining the cause for which an oration was composed (so that what is said will be better understood), he should leave nothing unnoticed which is important to be remarked, either in the thought or the language: he should observe what method is adopted in the *exordium* for conciliating the judge; what clearness, brevity, and sincerity is displayed in the statement of facts; what design there is in certain passages, and what well-concealed artifice (for that is the only true art in pleading, which cannot be perceived except by a skilful pleader); what judgment appears in the division of the matter; how subtle and urgent is the argumentation; with what force the speaker excites, with what amenity he soothes; what severity he shows in his invectives, what urbanity in his jests; how he commands the feelings, forces a way into the understanding, and makes the opinions of the judges coincide with what he asserts. In regard to his style, too, he should notice any expression that is particularly appropriate, elegant, or sublime; when the amplification deserves praise, what quality is opposed to it; what phrases are happily metaphorical, what figures of speech are used; what part of the composition is smooth and polished, yet manly and vigorous (II.5.6–9).

There is a panoply of rhetorical principles laid out in his choice of items to consider, just as the grammarian's choice of items to discuss is an indicator to the student of what is important.

It is important to repeat here that the basic pedagogical principle is that any text – whether it be by Virgil, Cicero, the master, or the student – becomes the object of public classroom analysis to point out the correct and the good. When the student is asked to paraphrase, say, a poem by Ovid or an oration by Cicero, his own product becomes the next text for study in the classroom. His grammatical felicities, or errors, become teaching devices when identified by his fellows or by the master. Purposeful use of faulty texts can be useful too, so that "it should be shown how many expressions in them are inappropriate, obscure, timid, low, mean, affected, or effeminate" (II.5.10).

Under these circumstances, some modern critics maintain, the Roman school becomes a place to chastise errors rather than a site for positive learning. This view, however, overlooks the deliberately staged grammatical and rhetorical criticism which brings textual values to the student's attention. In Quintilian's case, he also points to the moral values absorbed from taking in the content as well as the form of well-chosen models.

In sum, the Roman school system aims to habituate the student into a capacity for ready language use in any circumstances (*facilitas*) through a process not only of precept but of absorption through textual criticism and imitation. In this system grammar prepares the way for rhetoric. But methods are the same for both; only the subject matters differ.

## 3. Grammatical doctrines in the schools

The technical details of grammatical doctrine under the Empire are discussed elsewhere in this volume (→ Art. 68), but one observation is worth making at this point. It is a reinforcement of the opening statement in this article about the irresolute nature of Latin grammar at the end of the first Christian century. Quintilian's treatment of the subject reveals that he has few accepted set of principles on which to rely. For example he is not sure how many parts of speech there are, and he concludes by saying "it is a matter of no importance" (I.4.21). While any brief summary of his treatment may make it appear that he is systematic, he is far less systematic with grammar than he is with rhetoric. The very brevity of his account – one half of one book out of twelve books – may demonstrate how little he had to work with compared to rhetoric. It is not for lack of interest, because he is passionately concerned for the linguistic welfare of the students; for him grammar is the "foundation of oratory". In this connection he is as likely to cite the orations of Cicero for grammatical examples as he is to look to the few technical writers he knows. In fact he is concerned that the analysis of grammatical principles is so little advanced: at one point he gives up on a discussion of cases and tenses: "Why should I mention other words when it is even doubtful whether the genitive of *senatus* is *senatus* or *senati*?" (I.6.27). He follows this with the famous remark that "it is one thing to speak Latin and another to speak grammar". He has two solutions to many grammatical questions: either he expresses his own opinion, or, as he concludes in respect to orthography, "the teacher must use his own judgment" (I.7.30). All this of course is in marked contrast to the later concretizations of Donatus and Priscian – "grammars that are representative of the pedagogic tradition" (Matthews 1994: 68). The self-assurance of Priscian's *praelectio* on Virgil would have been impossible in Quintilian's day.

In the sense that ancient grammar books are for teachers rather than students – the 'textbook' for students as we know it is a product of the printing age – the gradual acceptance of a standardized Latin grammar by the time of Donatus should have made later Roman teachers of grammar feel more assured as they sat in front of their students to lay out the virtues and vices of their familiar texts. The students should have benefited from a consistency beyond the master's personal opinions. Whatever the actual result, though, the methods remained the same.

## 4. Rhetorical doctrines in the schools

The schools inherited an accepted five-part rhetorical system which had emerged at Rome nearly a century before Christ. The system, apparently crystallized from unknown Hellenic sources, is first described in two Latin treatises written almost simultaneously by Marcus Tullius Cicero and an anonymous author now thought to be one Cornificius.

Cicero, then 19 years old, wrote his *De inventione* about BCE 89. He declares that rhetoric is divided into the five parts of Invention, Arrangement, Style, Memory, and Delivery; he treats only the first part but promises to treat the others at a later time. The promise was never fulfilled. At almost the same time an anonymous author published a work about BCE 86 which did cover all five parts. Since it is addressed to a Gaius Herennius, it has traditionally been titled *Rhetorica ad Herennium*. This first complete Latin rhetorical manual, like Cicero's, is earnestly practical.

> The task of the public speaker is to discuss capably those matters which law and custom have fixed for the uses of citizenship, and to secure as far as possible the agreement of his hearers (I.2.2).

The two works are so similar that for centuries Cicero's *De inventione* was known as his "First Rhetoric" and the *Rhetorica ad Herennium* was called Cicero's "Second Rhetoric" or "New Rhetoric". The humanist Rafael Regio, writing in 1493, was the first to question Cicero's authorship. This similarity is important since it indicates the Roman acceptance of a standardized system at some time around BCE 100 or perhaps earlier. And the young Cicero was certainly writing from what he had been taught, not from his own experience.

The two authors' definitions of the five parts are almost identical. Thus the *Rhetorica ad Herennium*: "Invention is the devising of matter, true or plausible, that would make the case convincing"; and Cicero's *De inventione*: "Invention is the discovery of valid or seemingly valid arguments to render one's cause plausible".

They agree that Arrangement is the ordering and distribution of matter; Style is the fitting of proper language to the matter; Memory is the firm mental retention of matter, words, and arrangement; and Delivery is control of body, voice, and facial expression appropriate to the speech and occasion. They agree with Aristotle's identification of three types of orations: Forensic, dealing with court cases; Deliberative, dealing with public policy; and Epideictic, dealing with praise or blame.

Invention, or the finding of arguments, proceeds either through the use of 'status' or 'issue' questions about fact, definition, nature of an act, or legal process; or through 'topics', such lines of argument as Definition, Cause and Effect, or Division. Arrangement lays out six parts of an oration: *Exordium* or introduction; Narration or statement of facts; Division or the outline to be followed; Confirmation or proof; Refutation or attack on the opponent's arguments; and Peroration or conclusion. Style is described as being of three levels: Plain, Middle, or Grand; it gains Distinction from 'figures of speech' and 'figures of thought' (64 of which are treated for the first time in the *Rhetorica ad Herennium*). Memory is either natural or 'artificial' (i. e. artistic); the artificial memory system in the *Rhetorica ad Herennium* uses a mnemonic process of backgrounds and images; Delivery involves control of vocal tones, facial expressions, and movement.

It is fair to call this a 'Roman' rhetoric. Its longevity over many centuries is probably due to its practicality – that is, it is a system which works.

The author of the *Rhetorica ad Herennium* (I.2.3) states early in the book that "all these faculties [the five parts] we can acquire by three means: Theory, Imitation, and Practice" – a recognition of the educational principles long assumed but not fully described until the time of Quintilian, almost two centuries later. The principles can be traced back in part to ancient Greece in the writings of Protagoras, Plato, and especially Isocrates, but here is a direct attachment of rhetoric to them.

It should not be surprising then to find that Quintilian takes the five-part system for granted (after his usual practice of discussing alternative views), and the bulk of his *Institutio oratoria* is built around it. He devotes five books to Invention and Arrangement, two to Style, and one to Memory and Delivery; the remaining books deal with the schools, with adult self-education, and the moral virtues required in the orator. The homogeneity and continuity of the five-part system is also demonstrated by the 4th and 5th century texts edited by Charles Halm in his *Latini rhetores minores* (1863).

How was rhetoric taught in Roman schools? There seem to be three modes: first, the constant interjection of rhetorical principles as the occasion permits, whether in a formal *praelectio* or in other comments (I.Pref.23–24); second, composition exercises in the higher levels of the *progymnasmata*, beginning with amplifications for which the teacher provides a model or even an outline (I.7.2); and the final, most difficult exercise of Declamation (*declamatio*).

This last, the hallmark of the Roman rhetorician, enables the master to require from the student full-fledged orations on forensic and deliberative themes. The progymnasmatic exercise known as *Encomium* would already have prepared the student for epideictic speaking. The declamation known as *controversia* uses subjects from forensic oratory, while the *suasoria* uses deliberative themes. The student is posed a problem in the form of a hypothetical situation – e. g. "Alexander considers whether to cross the ocean" – and is asked to prepare and deliver a speech advocating an answer. Again, it should be remembered that this speech occurs in a public classroom before his peers, with master and other students prepared to treat his speech as the subject of criticism just as they would any other 'text'.

Declamation had many critics in ancient times (Bonner 1949: 71–83), but Quintilian and many others point out that the fictitious battles of the classroom prepare the young men for the real contests of courtroom and Senate. What is certain is that the practice persisted in the schools for centuries. Some of the criticisms, too, stem from public declamations outside the schoolroom, displays by orators striving to show their prowess as a means of popular entertainment. The historian Eunapius reports that when the orator Prohaeresius spoke at Antioch about 350 the crowds were so great that soldiers had to be called in to control them (*Lives of the Sophists*, 495–497).

In any case the declamation was the culmination of the long training which had begun about the age of six or seven and lasted into adulthood at sixteen or seventeen. It was the most purely rhetorical exercise, demanding mastery of every element of the teaching system, and command of all of the five parts of rhetoric. If grammar supplies the elementary 'bricks' in the Roman school, it is rhetoric which supplies the 'architecture' to make those elements into purposeful, structured writing and speech.

There is one important area of the grammar-rhetoric relationship which remains to be considered, the 'figures'. In his first book (I.8.13–17) Quintilian urges the master to acquaint his students with 'faults' that are given other names when they occur in poetry, namely metaplasms and schemata, with their two divisions of 'figures of speech' and 'figures of thought'. Tropes, he says, are used for ornament in both poetry and oratory. Then he says he will postpone his discussion until later when he treats ornaments of oratory. He actually devotes two full books, Eight and Nine, to Style, including the figures and tropes. His sophisticated treatment is both lengthy and complex, beyond summary here. But the fact that he speaks of the figures both under grammar and under rhetoric points to an issue which even today has achieved no satisfactory resolution. There is no standard history of figures and tropes, though many attempts have been made (cf. Vickers 1988: 294–339).

The basic issue seems to be that the whole theory of figures (of which tropes are a subset) depends on a principle of deviation from a norm. Now, if grammar teaches 'correctness', what is one to make of a purposeful incorrectness? One solution has been the 'permitted fault', with special privilege for 'poetic license' (as in Quintilian's case). But the matter has been complicated by territorial disputes – Donatus says figures of speech belong to grammarians, figures of thought to orators (*Ars maior* III.5) – and classification problems, for example where Donatus has 13 tropes and the *Rhetorica ad Herennium* ten. Numbers of figures identified also vary from writer to writer, and Quintilian himself devotes part of Book Nine (e. g. IX.3.ff.) to choosing which figures should be identified as such. However, this issue may be of more interest to us today as observers than it was to the student in the Roman school, for he learned figures from both the grammarian and the rhetorician and undoubtedly acquired from all his studies the sense that language effectiveness was more important to him than any controversy about abstract theories.

## 5. Conclusion

It seems clear that both grammar and rhetoric, in their different ways, played key roles in the Roman schools over many centuries. Yet it is also clear that they were embedded in a text-based teaching system which was in a sense just as important as the subjects they inculcated. The aim, after all, was to attain the capacity for adaptive language use – the *facilitas* necessary to choose the best language for any time and place. This linguistic 'habit' – to use Quintilian's term – derived from years of interrelated reading, writing, speaking, and listening. It is probably true that the successful lawyer or administrator in, say, 4th century Bordeaux did not much care what his teachers had been called, or what their subjects had been called. He had their results: his ability, his career. No doubt he was willing to pay to send his own children to one of the 21 teachers who have been identified in 4th century Bordeaux (Kaster 1988: 459). And he probably would not have realized that his child would be partaking of a 'system' already centuries old.

## 6. Bibliography

### 6.1. Primary sources

Asconius, *Commentarii* = Asconius Pedianus, *Commentarii in orationes Ciceronis*. Venice: Johannes de Colonia & Johannes Manthen, [1477.]

Cicero, *De inventione* = Marcus Tullius. Cicero, *De inventione. De optimo genere oratorum. Topica.* Ed. and transl. by H. M. Hubbell. Cambridge, Mass.: Harvard Univ. Press. 1949.

Donatus, *Ars maior* = Aelius Donatus, *Ars maior*. Ed. by Heinrich Keil, *Grammatici latini*, IV, 367–402. Leipzig: Teubner, 1864.

Eunapius, *Lives of the Sophists* = Philostratus and Eunapius, *Lives of the Sophists*. Ed. and transl. by Wilmer C. Wright. Cambridge, Mass.: Harvard Univ. Press, 1922.

Priscianus, *Partitiones* = Priscianus Caesariensis, *Partitiones duodecim versum eneides principalium*.

Ed. by Heinrich Keil, *Grammatici latini*, III, 459–515. Leipzig: Teubner, 1864.

Quintilianus, *Institutio oratoria* = Marcus Fabius Quintilianus, *Institutio oratoria.* Ed. and transl. by E. Butler. Cambridge, Mass.: Harvard Univ. Press, 1921–1922.

*Rhetores latini minores*, Ed. by Charles Halm. Leipzig: Teubner, 1863.

*Rhetorica ad Herennium* = [Cicero], *Ad C. Herennium: De ratione dicendi (Rhetorica ad Herennium)*. Ed. and transl. by Harry Caplan. Cambridge, Mass.: Harvard Univ. Press, 1954.

Suetonius, *De grammaticis* = C. Suetonius Tranquillus, *De grammaticis et rhetoribus.* Ed. and transl. by Robert A. Kaster. Oxford: Oxford Univ. Press, 1995.

### 6.2. Secondary sources

Bonner, Stanley F. 1949. *Roman Declamation in the Late Republic and Early Empire.* Liverpool: Univ. Press of Liverpool.

–. 1977. *Education in Ancient Rome from the Elder Cato to the Younger Pliny.* Berkeley: Univ. of California Press.

Dionissotti, Carlotta. 1982. "From Ausonius' Schooldays? A schoolbook and its relations". *Journal of Roman Studies* 72. 83–125.

Kaster, Robert A. 1988. *Guardians of Language: The grammarian and society in Late Antiquity.* Berkeley: Univ. California Press.

Marrou, Henri I. 1956. *A History of Education in Antiquity.* Transl. by George Lamb. New York: Sheed & Ward.

Matthews, Peter. 1994. "Grammars under the Empire". *History of Linguistics* ed. by Giulio Lepschy, II, 67–133. London: Longman.

Pattison, Robert. 1982. *On Literacy: The politics of the word from Homer to the age of Rock.* Oxford: Oxford Univ. Press.

Riché, Pierre. 1976. *Education and Culture in the Barbarian West, Sixth through Eighth Centuries.* Transl. by John Contreni. Columbia, SC: Univ. of South Carolina Press.

Russell, D. A. 1981. *Criticism in Antiquity.* Berkeley: Univ. of California Press.

Scaglione, Aldo. 1972. *The Classical Theory of Composition from its Origins to the Present: A historical survey.* (= *University of North Carolina Studies in Comparative Literature*, 53.) Durham, NC: Univ. of North Carolina Press.

Vickers, Brian. 1991. *In Defence of Rhetoric.* Oxford: Oxford Univ. Press.

*James J. Murphy, Davis, CA. (USA)*

# 71. Augustin und die Sprache

1. Wie lernt man die Sprache
2. Augustins Theorie des Sprechens
3. Eine Aporie?
4. Bibliographie

## 1. Wie lernt man die Sprache?

An zwei Stellen seiner zwischen etwa 395 und 400 n. Chr. geschriebenen *Confessiones* behandelt Augustin die praktische Sprachfunktion und die konkrete Weise, wie das Kind seine Muttersprache erlernt. In *Conf.* 1, 6, 8 meditiert er über die Frage, wie ein *infans* die Kenntnis und den Gebrauch der Sprache entbehrt und durch andere Sachen ersetzen und kompensieren muß. In diesem Passus stellt Augustin fest, daß ein Kind, das noch nicht reden kann (*infans*) – das gilt aber auch jeder Person, die wohl oder gerade nicht sprechen kann – Wünsche, *voluntates*, hat, die er anderen Menschen zeigen (*ostendere*) will. Diese *voluntates* befinden sich innerhalb des Menschen, in der Seele (*intus [...] in anima*).

Das Problem ist nun, wie man diese 'Wünsche' oder Gedanken den 'Außenstehenden' (*foris autem illi*) ohne die Hilfe, ohne die Kenntnis der Sprache kenntlich machen kann. Das macht man mit Bewegungen der Glieder oder durch 'Klänge' und 'Laute', *voces*, das heißt mit Zeichen, *signa*, welche den Gedanken, den Wünschen entsprechen: *signa similia voluntatibus*. Und auf der Stelle zeigt sich die Ohnmacht der nicht-verbalen Zeichen: sie sind der Wahrheit nicht ähnlich, *non enim erant veri similia*.

Aber wie entwickelt sich ein *infans* zu einem *puer loquens*? (In *Conf.* 1, 8, 13 beschreibt Augustin diesen Werdegang. Auch in diesem Lebensabschnitt bleibt der Grund, warum der Mensch die Sprache lernt: der Wunsch, die Gefühle des Herzens zu äußern (*edere velle sensa cordis*), welche er bis soweit nur mit Klängen (*vocibus*) und Bewegungen der verschiedenen Glieder (*membrorum motibus*) kenntlich zu machen versucht hat.

Das Erlernen der Sprache geschieht mit Hilfe der von Gott geschenkten *mens* (Intelligenz oder Geist): man prägt sich (*prensabam*) als Kind nämlich den Klang (*vox*), das heißt den Wortlaut, mit dem die Älteren und die Eltern eine Sache benennen (*ipsi appellabant rem aliquam*), die darauf zur Begleitung dieses Klanges (*secundum eam vocem*) ihre Körper zu der betreffenden Sache bewegen, ins Gedächtnis (*memoria*) ein. Das Kind sieht und versucht im Gedächtnis zu behalten, welcher Klang nun der Sache entspricht, die von den Erwachsenen gezeigt worden ist. Die Älteren helfen ihm dabei mit ihren Bewegungen des Körpers (*motus corporis*), die gleichsam die natürlichen Wörter aller Völker sind (*verba naturalia omnium gentium*): diese *verba naturalia* werden durch das Mienen- und Augenspiel, die Tätigkeit anderer Glieder und durch den Klang der Stimme (*vultu et nutu oculorum ceterorumque membrorum actu et sonitu vocis*) hervorgebracht und deuten die Stimmung und Wünsche der Seele an (*affectio animi*). Und diese Wörter, *verba*, hört das Kind dann in verschiedenen Sätzen und Wortfügungen und versteht allmählich aus dem ganzen Kontext (*colligebam*), von welchen Sachen sie die Zeichen seien (*quarum rerum signa essent*). Die Wörter definiert Augustin hier denn auch als "die Zeichen der Willensäußerungen" (*voluntatum enuntiandarum signa*) (Für die Kritik von Wittgenstein an dieser Sprachtheorie Augustins: Wittgenstein 1953: 1; Simone 1972: 30–31; Ayers 1976: 4–5).

## 2. Augustins Theorie des Sprechens

### 2.1. Was machen wir eigentlich, wenn wir reden?

Ganz so wie vor ihm Platon im *Kratylos* (383a4–384d8) beginnt Augustin die Erörterung im Dialog *De magistro* nicht mit der Definition sprachtheoretischer Grundbegriffe wie 'Zeichen', 'Name' oder 'Satz', sondern fragt nach der Praxis des 'Redens' (*loqui*). Die Schrift beginnt mit der Frage Augustins, was wir mit dem Sprechen (*loqui*) bewirken wollen: *Quid tibi videmur efficere velle, cum loquimur?* (*Mag.* 11, 1). Der Gegenstand der Frage ist also nicht *lingua*, die Sprache, in dem uns geläufigen Sinn von 'la langue' (nach De Saussure), sondern *loqui*, das Reden (Borsche 1986: 124).

Auf die Frage seines Vaters antwortet Adeodatus: "Wie es mir jetzt vorkommt: entweder lehren oder lernen" (*Quantum quidem mihi nunc occurrit, aut docere aut discere, Mag.* 1, 1). Im Laufe der Auseinandersetzung wird diese Definition jedoch reduziert auf 'lehren', 'mitteilen' (*docere*), zunächst in einem sehr weiten Sinn aufgefaßt, der alle Arten von Mitteilung einschließt. Eine der wichtigsten 'Unterrichtsarten' ist die *commemoratio*, das Vergegenwärtigen und Mitteilen von Dingen, die wir bereits wissen (*At ego puto esse quoddam genus docendi per commemorationem, magnum sane, Mag.* 1, 2). Die Schlußfolgerung Augustins ist denn auch, daß die Sprache nur dem *docere* und *commemorare* zuliebe eingerichtet worden ist (*Mag.* 1, 2). Auch wenn wir in der Stille, im Geist beten, sprechen wir (*dum oramus, utique loquimur*). Obgleich wir, während eines Gebets, keine Worte herausbringen, denken wir an die Worte selbst und sprechen wir auf diese Weise in unserem Geist (*quia verba cogitamus, nos intus apud animum loqui, Mag.* 1, 2). Wenn wir also denken, denken wir Wörter: und dies ist inneres Sprechen, im Geist.

Wir lehren folglich, wenn wir sprechen. Während Augustin in seinem *De magistro* unmittelbar nach dieser Definition (sprechen = lehren) und nach dem Fallen des Ausdrucks *verba*, "Wörter, Worte" auf die Frage übergeht, was nun 'Wörter' sind, definiert er in seinem *De doctrina christiana*, in dem er von dem Kern seiner in *De magistro* entwickelten Zeichenlehre nicht abweicht (Mayer 1974: 100–101), zunächst den Gegenstand dieses 'Unterrichts', dieser 'Lehre' (*doctrina*).

Augustin fängt in seinem *De doctrina christiana* also nicht mit der Frage an, was wir machen, wenn wir sprechen – denn diese Frage ist schon in seinem früheren Dialog *De magistro* beantwortet worden –, sondern was der Gegenstand dieses 'Unterrichts' sei.

"Der ganze 'Unterricht' hat die Sachen oder die Zeichen zum Gegenstand, aber die Sachen lernt man mittels der Zeichen. Die Sachen im eigentlichen Sinne des Wortes werden nicht benutzt um etwas zu 'bezeichnen', wie etwa 'Baum', 'Stein' usw. Es handelt sich hier nicht um den Baum, den Moses ins bittere Wasser warf, um dessen Bitterkeit zu tilgen [*Exod.* 15, 25. Augustin läßt hier also die figurativen Ausdrücke, Metaphern und Symbole in der Heiligen Schrift außer Betracht; vgl. auch Ayers 1976: 8] [...] Denn diese Gegenstände sind auf jene Weise Sachen, indem sie auch Zeichen anderer Sachen sind. Es gibt jedoch andere Zeichen, die einzig und allein um etwas zu 'bezeichnen' (*significare*) verwendet werden, wie etwa die Wörter. Keiner verwendet ja Wörter, ohne etwas andeuten, 'bezeichnen' (*significare*) zu wollen. Von daher versteht man, was ich 'Zeichen' nenne: die Sachen (*res*), welche benutzt werden um etwas anzudeuten. Deshalb ist jedes Zeichen auch eine Sache (*res*); denn wenn es keine Sache ist, ist es absolut nichts. Nicht ist jedoch jede Sache auch ein Zeichen [...] Wir dürfen nicht vergessen, daß wir jetzt in den Sachen dasjenige betrachten müssen, was sie sind, und nicht was die Sachen außer ihrer eigentlichen Bedeutung noch weiter bezeichnen" (*Doctr. chr.* 1, 2, 2).

Nach Simone (1972: 11) und Jackson (1969: 35, 45–49; 1972: 92–147) wird der Ausdruck und der Begriff 'Zeichen' von Augustin in Übereinstimmung mit der stoischen Tradition verwendet, und Augustins Originalität bestehe darin, daß er diese traditionelle 'Zeichen'-Theorie adaptiert und mit einer neuen Aufgabe zur Interpretation der Heiligen Schrift versehen hat.

Wir fassen diese Theorie Augustins zusammen: 1) Der Unterricht (*doctrina*) hat zum Objekt die *res* und die *signa*; 2) Eine Sache, *res*, wie etwa Baum und Stein, ist kein Zeichen (*signum*) von etwas Anderem. Nur im biblischen und figurativen Sprachgebrauch können die Sachen (*res*) Zeichen (*signa*) anderer Sachen sein; 3) Es gibt jedoch Zeichen, die qualitate qua nur um etwas zu bezeichnen benutzt werden: die Wörter; 4) Da alle 'Zeichen' etwas darstellen, sind sie auch *res*; aber nicht alle *res* sind auch 'Zeichen'.

Im Kontext der Sprache interessiert Augustin sich natürlich nicht für das Wesen einer Sache, einer *res* (wie etwa Baum, Stein usw.), sondern nur für die Zeichen, die *signa*, und zwar für die Zeichen, welche qualitate qua einzig und allein um etwas zu bedeuten gebraucht werden: die Wörter. Aber bevor er die *signa* auf 'Wörter' beschränkt, gibt er in seinem *De doctrina christiana* eine Definition des Begriffs *signum*: "Ein Zeichen (*signum*) ist eine Sache (*res*), die – außer dem Anblick (*speciem*), den es in die Sinnesorgane hineinführt – aus sich selbst noch etwas anderes denken läßt" (*Doctr. chr.* 2, 1, 1).

Aus dieser Definition ergibt sich, daß es zwei Arten von 'Zeichen' gibt, die sogenannten natürlichen Zeichen, *signa naturalia*, und die künstlichen Zeichen, *signa data* (vgl. auch Ayers 1976: 6). Die *signa naturalia* definiert Augustin folgenderweise:

"Es gibt zwei Arten von Zeichen: die natürlichen und die 'gegebenen' (d. h. konventionellen oder künstlichen) Zeichen. Die natürlichen Zeichen sind die Zeichen, welche, unbeabsichtigt und ohne irgendeinen Wunsch etwas zu bezeichnen, aus sich selbst etwas anderes außer sich selbst zeigen, wie etwa der Rauch Feuer andeutet und voraussetzt. Der Rauch macht dies ja unbeabsichtigt, aber wir wissen, aus Erfahrung – indem wir die Sachen beobachten und wahrnehmen –, daß ein Feuer vorhanden ist, obwohl nur der Rauch sichtbar ist" (*Doctr. chr.* 2, 1, 2).

Die *signa data*, d. h. die konventionellen oder künstlichen Zeichen, sind Zeichen, die alle lebendigen Wesen (die Menschen, die Tiere, aber auch Gott) aneinander geben, um ihre *motus animi*, ihre Gemütsbewegungen zu zeigen.

Für Augustins Theorie über die menschliche Sprache sind die *signa naturalia* irrelevant, und von den *signa data* nur 'die Zeichen der Menschen' interessant. Die Zeichen der Menschen unterscheidet er in zwei Kategorien, die sichtbaren und die hörbaren Zeichen.

Die bedeutendste Einschränkung und Schlußfolgerung am Ende der Argumentation Augustins in *De doctrina christiana* ist, daß, um die Gedanken auszudrücken, unter den menschlichen Zeichen die Wörter die wichtigste Stelle bekommen haben und daß die Menge von Zeichen, mit denen die Menschen ihre Gedanken (*cogitationes*) entfalten, in den Wörtern festliegt. Und diese Wörter sind sofort verschwunden, sobald sie ausgesprochen sind. Deshalb haben die Menschen allmählich angefangen, visuelle Zeichen zu benutzen, welche die Klänge und die Wörter, die *voces*, festlegen sollten.

### 2.2. Die Wörter sind Zeichen: Die Ohnmacht der nicht-verbalen Zeichen

Daß Augustin in seinem *De doctrina christiana* so rasch auf seine Folgerung zugeht, liegt in der Tatsache, daß er dabei tatsächlich an den Folgerungen seines *De magistro* weiterspinnt. Wir kehren jetzt denn auch wieder zu *De magistro* zurück. Das Letzte, das wir soeben in *De magistro* festgestellt haben, war, daß Augustin zwei Arten von 'sprechen' unterscheidet: sprechen = *docere* oder *commemorare*, das heißt das äußere Wort, und das *cogitare verba* = *intus apud animum loqui* (*Mag.* 1, 2), das heißt das innere Wort. Augustin konstatiert dies zwar an dieser Stelle, aber über das Wesen und die Beziehung des inneren Wortes = dem Gedanken zu dem äußeren Wort spricht er weiter nur kurz im vorletzten Kapitel (Kap. 13) seines *De magistro*, wohl aber später in seinem *De trinitate*.

In seinem *De trinitate* nennt Augustin das Wort, "das wir im Herzen sprechen: Denken, das von der Sache, die wir wissen, geformt ist" (*formata quippe cogitatio ab ea re quam scimus, verbum est quod in corde dicimus,*

*Trin.* 15, 10, 19). Da das Herz Zentrum metaphysischen, das heißt auf den absoluten Grund hin sich sammelnden Denkens ist, ist es auch Ursprung für das Medium dieses Aufstiegs: des Wortes (Beierwaltes 1971: 183). Augustinisch gesprochen eruiert also die Antwort das innere Wort (*verbum interius*) oder das Wort des Herzens (*verbum cordis*) als Wesen der Sprache. Das innere Wort ist so ermöglichendes Prinzip des äußeren Wortes, logisch und ontologisch eher als dieses (Beierwaltes 1971: 183): *tamquam in cardine cordis mei, tamquam in secretario mentis meae praecessit verbum vocem meam* (*Sermo* 288, 3). Das innere Wort oder *verbum cordis* wurde Prinzip des äußeren, der *vox verbi*, genannt. Es ist weder griechisch noch lateinisch (*Trin.* 15, 10, 19). Das äußere Wort dagegen ist bedingtes Bild oder Zeichen des inneren: *verbum quod foris sonat, signum est verbi quod intus lucet* (*Trin.* 15, 10, 20). Sprechen und Denken ist für Augustin ein simultaner Akt (siehe unser letztes Kapitel).

Das menschliche Sprechen geschieht durch Wörter. Die Wörter sind in der Erinnerung, im Gedächtnis aufbewahrt (vgl. auch oben *Conf.* 1, 8, 12). Die Worte üben keine andere Funktion aus als die, die Sachen selbst vor den Geist zu rufen durch die Erinnerung, die sie als Zeichen für die Sachen darstellen (Kuypers 1934: 18). Ein Zeichen deutet immer etwas an, sonst ist es kein Zeichen. Daher stellt Augustin sich die Frage: "Kann ein Zeichen Zeichen sein, wenn es nichts bezeichnet? Nein" (*Signum, nisi aliquid significet, potest esse signum? Non potest, Mag.* 2, 3). Augustin betrachtet also die Wörter als Zeichen par excellence und versucht die Zeichentheorie von den Sprachzeichen her zu begründen (Markus 1957: 65; Borsche 1986: 130; Simone 1972: 11).

Nach der einleitenden Feststellung der beiden Grundvoraussetzungen der antiken Sprachbetrachtung, a) daß die Rede aus Wörtern besteht und b) daß die Wörter Zeichen sind, formuliert Augustin die Hauptfrage der Semantik (Borsche 1986: 131). Die – stoische? (Ruef 1981: 82ff.) – Äquivalenz zwischen *verbum* und *signum* führt sofort zu einem Problem bei Wörtern wie *si, ex, nihil.* Bei diesen Wörtern kann man nicht von einem Zeichen sprechen, das etwas Konkretes andeutet. Diese Ausdrücke deuten denn auch keine äußere Sache an, sondern die Disposition des Geistes (*affectio animi*). Das Problem verlegt sich besonders auf die 'abstrakten' Wörter wie *si, nihil* und *ex*. Sie müssen also Zeichen sein: aber wovon? 'Nichts' bezeichnet etwas, was nicht existiert (*'Nihil' quid aliud significat, nisi id quod non est?, Mag.* 2, 3). *Si* kann man nicht mit einem anderen Wort erklären, und *ex* ist ungefähr dasselbe wie *de*. Mit dem Wort *nihil* wird irgendein 'Zustand des Geistes', der eine Sache sucht, aber findet, daß sie nicht existiert (Duchrow 1965: 89), das heißt eine *affectio animi* bezeichnet, "eher als die Sache selbst, welche nicht besteht" (*potius quam rem ipsam quae nulla est, Mag.* 2, 3). Es ist also möglich – meistens sogar ganz einfach –, Wörter mit Wörtern, das heißt Zeichen mit Zeichen (*verbis verba id est signis signa*), etwas Bekanntes mit etwas anderem auszulegen, aber damit ist das Wesen von demjenigen, was durch das verbale Zeichen angedeutet ist, noch nicht erklärt worden (*Mag.* 2, 4).

Die nächste Frage, welche von Augustin denn auch gestellt wird, ist: Wenn das Wesen der Sachen, von denen die Wörter die Zeichen sind, offenbar mit verbalen Zeichen nicht oder kaum zu benennen ist, gibt es dann vielleicht Sachen, die durch sich selbst, das heißt ohne verbale Zeichen, angedeutet werden? Was die drei Silben des Wortes *paries* (Mauer) bezeichnen, kann man ohne Worte mit dem Finger anzeigen, so daß man die Sache selbst, *res ipsa*, sieht, deren Zeichen dieses Wort von drei Silben ist (*Mag.* 3, 5).

Während Adeodatus anfangs die Möglichkeit, Sachen ohne Worte (beispielsweise durch einen Fingerzeig) anzudeuten, auf alle sichtbaren Sachen, *omnia visibilia*, beschränkt – also nicht auf alle körperlichen Sachen, *omnia corporalia*, da *sonus, odor, sapor, gravitas, calor* und dergl. nicht ohne Körper gefühlt werden können (*sentiri sine corporibus nequeant, Mag.* 3, 5) –, muß er seine Meinung ändern, wenn Augustin ihm vorhält, daß die Tauben in ihrer Gebärdensprache, also ohne Worte, nicht nur die sichtbaren Sachen, sondern auch Klänge, Geschmäcke und dergl. zeigen und die Pantomimespieler ganze Theaterstücke ohne Worte, nur mittels Bewegungen vorführen (*Mag.* 3, 5). Der Fingerzeig nach einer Mauer ist jedoch keine Mauer, sondern nur ein Zeichen, mit dem man auf eine Mauer zeigt. Diese *signa visibilia* stellen an dieser Stelle also ein ganz anderes – primitiveres – Niveau dar als jene in Augustins *De doctrina christiana* (wie etwa 'ein Kopfnicken'). Die Folgerung von Adeodatus lautet mithin, daß es nichts gibt, was ohne Zeichen gezeigt werden kann (*Mag.* 3, 6).

Es gibt aber Handlungen wie *ambulare, edere, bibere, sedere, stare, clamare* und dergl., die auf den ersten Blick besser *per se* als *per signa* gezeigt werden können (*Mag.* 3, 6). Aber selbst wenn die wörtliche Handlung 'laufen' (*ambulare*) gemeint wird, gibt es noch einen Unterschied zwischen *ambulare* und *festinare* (sich beeilen), und man spricht auch von Eile (*festinatio*) beim Schreiben, beim Lesen und zahlreichen anderen Sachen (*in scribendo et in legendo aliisque innumerabilibus rebus, Mag.* 3, 6). Also können Begriffe wie 'laufen', 'trinken', 'sitzen', 'stehen', 'rufen' und dergl. nicht durch sich selbst – ohne ein Zeichen – benannt werden. Die Folgerung von Adeodatus kann denn auch nur sein: eine Sache können wir nicht ohne ein Zeichen andeuten (*Fateor rem non posse nos monstrare sine signo, Mag.* 3, 6).

### 2.3. Die verbalen Zeichen

Das wichtigste Zeichen, mit dem man etwas bezeichnet, ist die Sprache (*Cum enim loquimur, signa facimus, de quo dictum est significare, Mag.* 4, 7). In dieser zweiten 'Sitzung' des Dialogs sprechen Augustin und Adeodatus denn auch nicht mehr über 'Zeichen' im allgemeinen, sondern nur über 'die Wörter' und denken über die Macht (und die Ohnmacht) der verbalen Zeichen nach. "Das, was beim Reden aus deinem Munde kommt, sind Wörter. Nun ist Löwe ein Wort. Also kommt, wenn du Löwe sagst, ein Löwe aus deinem Munde gesprungen". Durch dieses Sophisma will Augustin darauf hinweisen, daß man jedes Wort sowohl direkt auf den Gegenstand, den es bezeichnet, als auch indirekt auf das Wort selbst als Gegenstand beziehen kann (Borsche 1986: 136). Es ist zwar richtig, daß man im Prinzip jedes beliebige Wort in direkter oder indirekter Bedeutung gebrauchen kann. Aber "ein Gespräch zwischen uns ist ganz unmöglich, wenn nicht der Geist, indem er die Wörter hört, zu den Dingen geführt wird, deren Zeichen die Wörter sind" (*sermocinari nos omnino non posse, nisi auditis verbis ad ea feratur animus, quorum ista sunt signa, Mag.* 8, 22). Sie stellen fest, daß der Ausdruck *homo* ein *nomen* ist (*Mag.* 8, 24). Aber wenn ich 'dich' sehe, dann sehe ich doch nicht ein 'nomen'? (*Cum te video, num nomen video?, Mag.* 8, 24). Wenn man jedoch fragen würde, was der Mensch sei (*quid esset homo*), dann könnte man antworten: *animal.* Ein *homo* ist also sowohl ein 'nomen' als ein 'animal', und zwar ein 'nomen', insofern es ein Zeichen ist (*ex ea parte qua signum est*), und ein 'animal', insofern es eine Sache bezeichnet (*ex parte rei quam significat*). Es liegt in der Natur des Sprechens, daß sich, sobald irgendwelche Laute als Wörter wahrgenommen werden, die Aufmerksamkeit den durch sie bezeichneten Dingen zuwendet (*ut auditis signis ad res significatas feratur intentio, Mag.* 8, 24).

Die Frage, die sich weiter aufdrängt, ist: Was ist wichtiger, die bezeichnete Sache oder das Zeichen? Die Antwort lautet schließlich: "Ferner möchte ich, daß du einsiehst, daß die bezeichneten Sachen höher einzuschätzen sind als die Zeichen" (*Proinde intelligas volo, res quae significantur, pluris quam signa esse pendendas*). Denn dasjenige, was für etwas anderes steht (*propter aliud est*), ist notwendigerweise niedriger (*vilius*) als dasjenige, dessen Vertreter es ist (*quam id propter quod est, Mag.* 9, 25). Die Gleichsetzung der Bedeutung eines Wortes mit der Erkenntnis einer Sache bildet den Angelpunkt der augustinischen Argumentation in *De magistro*. Es setzt die *cognitio rerum* bzw. die *significatio verborum* als schon bekannt voraus (Borsche 1986: 143). Augustin fragt daher weiter, ob und wie man durch nicht-sprachliche Zeichen, die unmittelbar auf die durch sie bezeichneten Sachen verweisen, oder durch die Sachen selbst ohne Zeichen lernen könne, was die Sache ist (*quid sit res*).

## 3. Eine Aporie?

Durch Zeichen, ob sie nun verbal oder nichtverbal sind, können wir also nichts Unbekanntes lehren oder lernen. Sie können nur an schon Bekanntes erinnern oder uns nur auffordern, die Sachen, die sie bezeichnen, zu suchen. Augustin schließt doch mit einigem Optimismus. Die (verbalen) Zeichen können aber noch eine dritte Funktion haben. Ein Mensch, der die Dinge in ihrer Gesamtheit verstehen will und die durch bestimmte Wörter bezeichneten Sachen sucht, kann aus eigener Kraft nur eine subjektive Kenntnis der Wahrheit erlangen. Daher müssen wir über die intelligiblen Dinge nicht einen außen (*foris*) Redenden, sondern innen die Wahrheit befragen. Im inneren Menschen wohnt ja die unserem Geist vorstehende Wahrheit, Christus, die ewige Weisheit, und diese 'Kraft Gottes' befragen wir, durch Worte dazu angeleitet, über die Dinge in ihrer Gesamtheit. Wie wir bei der Wahrnehmung der *sensibilia* für die Farben das Licht usw. und unsere Sinne, deren sich der Geist als Werkzeuge bedient, befragten, so befragen wir bei der Erkenntnis der *intelligibilia* – das heißt der Sachen, die wir mit dem Geist betrachten (*quae mente conspicimus*) – mit der Vernunft das innere Licht der Wahrheit (*interiore luce veritatis*): *ratio* und *intellectus* sind ja die 'Sehkraft' (Duchrow 1965: 67) der *mens* (*Mag.* 12, 40). Der Hörer wird belehrt, ob etwas wahr sei, nicht durch die Worte des Sprechers, sondern kraft göttlicher Erleuchtung durch die offenbare Gegenwart der geistigen Dinge selbst (*Mag.* 12, 40). Wer nun die Wahrheit sieht, ist, innen, der Schüler der Wahrheit, und, äußerlich, der Richter des Sprechenden oder vielmehr dessen Sprache (*quisquis autem cernere potest, intus est discipulus veritatis, foris iudex loquentis, vel potius ipsius locutionis, Mag.* 13, 41).

Die Wörter, welche ein Mensch äußert, vertreten die Sachen, welche man 'gedacht' hat (*earum rerum quae cogitantur, verba proferri*), auch bei den Lügen, jedoch mit Ausnahme des *lapsus linguae* (*Mag.* 13, 42). Derjenige also, der die Wörter hört und empfängt, darf davon ausgehen, daß der Sprecher dieser Wörter über die Sachen, welche durch diese Wörter angedeutet werden, nachgedacht hat (*Mag.* 13, 45). Aber der Einzige, der innen lehrt, ist der Herr im Himmel, der einzige Lehrer (*Mag.* 14, 46; vgl. *Mt.* 23, 8–10).

Diese Theorie, daß Christus der innere Lehrer der Menschen ist, stellt eine christliche Modifikation der platonischen Anamnesis dar (Beierwaltes 1971: 179–195; Madec 1975: 25). Christus ist also der Lehrer, und das Wort gibt nur eine äußere Warnung und Mahnung. Christus wird uns lehren, durch den wir von Menschen durch Zeichen aufmerksam gemacht werden, damit wir so als innerlich ihm Zugewandte (von ihm selbst) geistig emporgeführt werden (*Mag.* 14, 46). Dies also ist auch in der intelligiblen Ebene der 'Nutzen' der Worte: *admonitio* "Aufforderung", daß wir uns innerlich der Sache selbst zuwenden (Duchrow 1965: 69).

Die Zeichen stellen für uns also zwar keine hinreichende, aber doch eine notwendige Voraussetzung des Lernens dar. Auch die Bemerkungen über den Spracherwerb des Kindes im ersten Buch der *Confessiones* geben einen Hinweis darauf, wo Augustin eine Lösung für das Problem des Lernens sucht: "Woher ich sprechen gelernt habe?". "Nicht die Großen lehrten es mich [...], sondern ich selbst, vermöge meines Geistes, den Du, mein Gott, mir gegeben hast" (*Conf.* 1, 8, 13). Das eigentliche Lernen vollzieht sich im Innern der Seele durch den Geist (*mente*).

Wie dieser Prozeß des Lernens sich im Innern des Geistes oder der Seele vollzieht, wird im *De magistro* nicht mehr behandelt. Dafür müssen wir einen späteren Traktat Augustins (von 397 bis nach 420) befragen: *De trinitate* (für folgendes, siehe vor allem Borsche 1990: 157–58). Was der Geist dort innen sieht, ist ein inneres, unsinnliches, eben intelligibles 'Bild' (*Trin.* 15, 10,17–16,26). Das innere Wort des Geistes, das keiner besonderen Sprache angehört und lautlos bleibt, erscheint als das eigentliche Wort, dem "der Name des Wortes eher gebührt" (*Proinde verbum quod foris sonat signum est verbi quod intus lucet, cui magis verbi competit nomen, Trin.* 15, 11, 20) als den in Laute gekleideten Wörtern der menschlichen Rede. Dieses innere Wort ist ein unmittelbares Abbild (*imago*; *simillimum rei*), das seinen Gegenstand auf natürliche Weise und vollständig darstellt; es ist "aus dem Wissen geboren" (*verbum simillimum rei notae, de qua gignitur et imago eius, [...] quod est verbum linguae nullius, verbum verum de re vera, nihil de suo habens, sed totum de illa scientia de qua nascitur, Trin.* 15, 12, 22). Im Verhältnis zum äußeren Wort betrachtet, ist das innere Wort der Gedanke (Borsche 1990: 164). Und dieser Gedanke (Verbeke 1962: 58–60) ist ein Sehen des Geistes, *cogitatio visio est animi*: und dieses 'Sehen des Geistes' ist nicht abhängig von der Tatsache, ob die 'körperlichen Augen' (*oculi corporales*) oder die anderen Sinnesorgane etwas sehen bzw. fühlen (*Trin.* 15, 9, 16).

Dieses Denken gilt den *nota*, den Dingen, die uns schon bekannt sind, wenn wir an sie denken, und die in unserem Wissensschatz (*in notitia*) verbleiben; auch wenn wir nicht an sie denken, mögen sie zur beschaulichen Wissenschaft (*contemplativa scientia*), das heißt der *sapientia*, oder mögen sie zur tätigen Wissenschaft (*activa scientia*) gehören, das heißt der *scientia* im wahrsten Sinn des Wortes (*Trin.* 15, 10, 17). Wir denken 'Dinge, die uns schon bekannt sind' (*nota*), und auch wenn sie von uns nicht gedacht werden, sind sie doch bekannt. Wollen wir freilich diese Dinge aussprechen, dann können wir das nur, wenn wir an sie denken (*si ea dicere velimus, nisi cogitata non possumus*). Wenn auch keine Worte ertönen, so spricht doch, wer denkt, in seinem Herzen (*Trin.* 15, 10, 17).

Sprechen und Denken ist für Augustin also ein simultaner Akt: Sprache ist der Modus, in dem das Denken sich vollzieht; andererseits ist das Denken ein Prinzip der Sprache, da Ungedachtem kein Wort entspricht und es deshalb nicht ausgesprochen werden kann. Diese 'Urkenntnis', die *nota* des Menschen, nennt Augustin weiter auch *scientia* (*Trin.* 15, 12, 21) oder *intima scientia* (ibidem): aus dieser (*intima*) *scientia* wird unser wahrheitsgetreuer Gedanke gebildet, wenn wir nämlich dasjenige sagen, was wir (von dieser 'Urkenntnis' her) wissen, – dies im Gegensatz zu den 'Gedanken', die dem Geist durch die körperlichen Sinnesorgane vermittelt werden und öfter anders sind als die Wirklichkeit (*Trin.* 15, 12, 21).

Die *intima scientia* ist dasjenige, wodurch wir wissen, daß wir leben (*intima scientia est qua nos vivere scimus, Trin.* 15, 12, 21). Wer aber nicht nur das noch nicht ausgesprochene Wort, sondern sogar die noch nicht gedachten Bilder der Laute von Wörtern versteht, ist imstande, in diesem Spiegel und in diesem Rätselbilde (*aenigma*) (I *Cor.* 13, 12) die *similitudo* des (göttlichen) Wortes zu sehen, über das gesagt wurde (*Joh.* 1, 1): Im Anfange war das Wort, und das Wort war bei Gott, und Gott war das Wort (*Trin.* 15, 10, 19). Wenn wir die Wahrheit sprechen, das heißt: wenn wir sprechen, was wir wissen, dann muß aus dem Wissen, welches unser Gedächtnis enthält, ein Wort geboren werden; es ist durchaus von der Art, von der das Wissen ist, von dem es geboren wird. Der von dem gewußten Gegenstand geformte Gedanke ist nämlich das Wort, das wir im Herzen aussprechen. Es ist nicht griechisch, nicht lateinisch, noch einer sonstigen Sprache zugehörig (*Trin.* 15, 10, 19). Wenn es aber denen, mit denen wir sprechen, zur Kenntnis gebracht werden soll, dann nimmt es ein Zeichen an, um durch dieses selbst bezeichnet zu werden. Mit Hilfe der visuellen und auditiven Zeichen können wir also mit den (unmittelbar) Anwesenden kommunizieren.

Danach wurden die Buchstaben erfunden, damit wir auch mit den Abwesenden sprechen können. Sie sind Zeichen der Laute, während die Laute in unserer Sprache selbst Zeichen der Dinge sind, die wir denken (*Trin.* 15, 10, 19; vgl. Jackson 1969: 27).

Das Wort, das draußen erklingt, ist also Zeichen des Wortes, das drinnen leuchtet; diesem kommt mit größerem Rechte die Bezeichnung 'Wort' (*Proinde verbum quod foris sonat signum est verbi quod intus lucet, cui magis verbi competit nomen, Trin.* 15, 11, 20). Unser Wort, d. h. das äußere Wort, wird gewissermaßen körperlicher Laut (*ita enim verbum nostrum vox quodam modo corporis fit, Trin.* 15, 11, 20), indem es diesen annimmt, um so für die Sinne wahrnehmbar zu werden, wie das Wort Gottes Fleisch wurde, indem es dies annahm, um sich so auch den Sinnen der Menschen zu offenbaren. Wie unser Wort ein Laut wird und sich nicht in den Laut verwandelt, so ist das Wort Gottes zwar Fleisch geworden; aber fern sei uns der Gedanke, daß es in das Fleisch verwandelt wurde (*Et sicut verbum nostrum fit vox nec mutatur in vocem, ita verbum dei caro quidem factum est, sed absit ut mutaretur in carnem, Trin.* 15, 11, 20).

Dies beinhaltet, daß die auditive oder visuelle Äußerung des inneren Wortes beschränkt-subjektiv ist. Wenn nämlich das Wissen in einem Klanglaut oder durch ein sonstiges körperliches Zeichen ausgesprochen wird, dann wird es nicht ausgesprochen, wie es ist, sondern wie es durch das Sinnesorgan gesehen oder gehört (vgl. Jackson 1969: 26) werden kann (*Trin.* 15, 11, 20). Nur wenn im Worte ist, was im Wissen ist, dann ist es ein wahres Wort und die Wahrheit, die man vom Menschen erwartet.

Aber dennoch können wir der Auskünfte der *sensus corporis* nicht entbehren (*Trin.* 15, 12, 21); durch die Sinnesorgane haben wir ja den Himmel und die Erde und alles, was der Schöpfer uns darin bekannt machen wollte, gelernt. Zu dieser Kategorie von 'Auskünften' rechnet Augustin auch das Zeugnis anderer Menschen (einschließlich der *historica lectio*), denn ohne dieses *testimonium aliorum* würden wir nicht wissen, daß es andere Länder und den Ozean gibt, und wir würden sogar bekannte Städte nicht kennen. Dies ist nun die eine Gattung der von uns gekannten Sachen; die andere Gattung betrifft jene Sachen, die der Geist durch sich selbst (*per se*) kennt. Und der Geist hält alles, was es durch sich selbst (*per se*) oder durch die Sinnesorgane oder durch das Zeugnis anderer sich angeeignet hat und weiß, in der Schatzkammer des Gedächtnisses geborgen (*thesauro memoriae condita*). Daraus wird das wahre Wort gezeugt, wenn wir aussprechen, was wir wissen (*quando quod scimus loquimur*), das Wort, das jeglichem Klanglaut, ja jeglichem Denken des Klanglautes vorangeht.

Aus dem Schauen der Kenntnis, *visio scientiae*, entsteht das Schauen des Gedankens, *visio cogitationis*, was ein Wort ist, das an keine einzige Sprache gebunden ist: das wahre Wort aus der wahren Sache (*verbum verum de re vera, Trin.* 15, 12, 22). Unser Wort, das keinen Laut (*sonus*) und keinen

Gedanken des Lautes (*cogitatio soni*) hat, sondern nur den Gedanken jener Sache, die wir innen sehen und sagen, ist *in hoc aenigmate*, in diesem Rätselbilde dem Wort Gottes ähnlich: dieses unser Wort ist aus unserer *scientia* geboren, Gottes Wort (= Christus) aus der *scientia patris* (*Trin.* 15, 14, 24).

Dieses Ding, dieses 'innere Urwort', das erst Wort sein kann und deshalb schon die Bezeichnung Wort verdient, ist etwas *formabile nondumque formatum*; und dieses Formbare und noch nicht Geformte ist nichts anderes als eine Realität in unserem Geiste (*quiddam mentis nostrae*), die wir in einer Art kreisender Bewegung (*volubilis quaedam motio*) dahin und dorthin wenden, da von uns bald dies, bald jenes gedacht wird, wie es uns eben gerade in den Sinn kommt und es sich gerade trifft. Dann entsteht ein wahres Wort (*verum verbum*), wenn der Vorgang, den wir eben ein Wenden in einer kreisenden Bewegung nannten, zu einem Gegenstand gelangt, den wir wissen (*ad id quod scimus pervenit*), und wenn es von dorther geformt wird und so die volle Ähnlichkeit mit dem Gewußten annimmt, so daß, wie ein Ding gewußt wird, es auch gedacht wird (*ut quomodo res quaeque scitur sic etiam cogitetur*), das heißt: daß es so ohne Klanglaut (*sine voce*), ohne das Denken eines Klanglautes (*sine cogitatione vocis*), die auch noch einer Sprache angehört, im Herzen gesprochen wird.

Kurzum: 'Wort' darf man jenes Etwas des menschlichen Geistes nennen, das aus unserem Wissen gestaltet werden kann, noch bevor es gestaltet ist, eben weil es sozusagen gestaltbar ist (*Trin.* 15, 15, 25). Es gehört nicht nur keiner gesprochenen Sprache an, sondern geht sogar noch seiner Vorstellung in Lauten, dem stummen Gespräch der Seele mit sich selbst, voraus (*verbum ante omnem sonum, ante omnem cogitationem soni, Trin.* 15, 12, 22). Das Wissen, das verborgen und unzugänglich in der Seele ruht, offenbart sich der Seele durch das Wort des Geistes in der Zeit. Dieses Wort wird "aus dem Wissen gezeugt" (*gignit de scientia, Trin.* 15, 11, 20). Das innere Wort des Geistes (der Gedanke) ist kein Zeichen (*signum*) des Wissens, denn es ist nicht körperlich. Es ist ein Bild (*imago*) des Wissens im Denken (*Trin.* 15, 12, 22).

## 4. Bibliographie

### 4.1. Primärliteratur

Augustin, *Conf.* = Augustinus, *Confessionum libri XIII.* Ed. by Martinus Skutella. Leipzig, 1934.

Augustin, *Doctr. chr.* = Augustinus, *De doctrina christiana libri IV.* Ed. by Joseph Martin. *Corpus Christianorum* XXXII, 1–167. Turnhout: Brepols, 1962.

Augustin, *Mag.* = Augustinus, *De magistro.* Ed. by Klaus-Detlef Daur. *Corpus Christianorum* XXIX, 157–203. Turnhout: Brepols, 1970.

Augustin, *Sermo* = Augustinus, *Sermones* 225, 288. *Patrologia Latina* XXXVIII, 332–1484. Paris: J.-P. Migne.

Augustin, *Trin.* = Augustinus, *De trinitate libri XV.* Ed. by William J. Mountain. *Corpus Christianorum* L-L A. Turnhout: Brepols, 1968.

### 4.2. Sekundärliteratur

Allard, Jean Bernard. 1976. "L'articulation du sens et du signe dans le *De doctrina christiana* de S. Augustin". *Studia Patristica* 14.377–88.

Ayers, Robert H. 1976. "Language theory and analysis in Augustine". *Scottish Journal of Theology* 29.1–12.

–. 1979. *Language, Logic and Reason in the Church Fathers: A study of Tertullian, Augustine and Aquinas.* (= *Altertumswissenschaftliche Texte und Studien*, 6). Hildesheim: Olms.

Bachmann, O. o. J. *Die Bekenntnisse des heiligen Augustinus.* Köln: Atlas Verlag.

Baratin, Marc & François Desbordes. 1982. "Sémiologie et métalinguistique chez saint Augustin". *Langages* 16.75–89.

Beierwaltes, Werner. 1971. "Zu Augustins Metaphysik der Sprache". *Augustinian Studies* 2.179–195.

Borsche, Tilman. 1990. *Was etwas ist: Fragen nach der Wahrheit der Bedeutung bei Platon, Augustin, Nikolaus von Kues und Nietzsche.* München.

–. 1985. "Macht und Ohnmacht der Wörter: Bemerkungen zu Augustins *De magistro*". *Kodikas/Code. Ars Semeiotica* 8.231–252.

–. 1986. "Macht und Ohnmacht der Wörter: Bemerkungen zu Augustins *De magistro*". *Sprachphilosophie in Antike und Mittelalter*, hg. von Burkhard Mojsisch, 121–161. Amsterdam: Grüner.

Brasa Díez, M. 1976. "El contenido del 'cogito' augustiniano". *Augustinus* 21.277–85.

Cerqueira Gonçalves, J. 1978–79. "Pedagogia e linguagem na obra de Santo Agostinho". *Euphrosyne* 9.187–191.

Colish, Marcia L. 1968. *The Mirror of Language: A study in the medieval theory of knowledge.* New Haven: Yale Univ. Press.

Coseriu, Eugenio. 1967. "L'arbitraire du signe: Zur Spätgeschichte eines aristotelischen Begriffes". *Archiv für das Studium der neueren Sprachen und Literaturen* 119.81–112.

Duchrow, Ulrich. 1961. "*Signum* und *superbia* beim jungen Augustin (386–390)". *Revue des études Augustiniennes* 7.369–372.

–. 1963. "Zum Prolog von Augustins *De doctrina christiana*". *Vigiliae Christianae* 17.165–172.

–. 1965. *Sprachverständnis und biblisches Hören bei Augustin.* Tübingen: Mohr.

Engels, Joseph. 1962. "La doctrine du signe chez saint Augustin". *Studia Patristica*, 6.366–373.

Flores, Ralph. 1975. "Reading and Speech in St. Augustine's *Confessiones*". *Augustinian Studies* 6.1–13.

Heinimann, Felix. 1945. *Nomos und Physis: Herkunft und Bedeutung einer Antithese im griechischen Denken des 5. Jahrhunderts.* Basel: Reinhardt.

Jackson, Belford Darrell. 1969. "The Theory of Signs in St. Augustine's *De doctrina christiana*". *Revue des études Augustiniennes* 15.9–49.

–. 1972. "The Theory of Signs in De doctrina christiana". Markus 1972.92–147.

Johnson, Douglas W. 1972. "*Verbum* in the early Augustine (386–397)". *Recherches Augustiniennes* 8.25–53.

Kelly, Louis G. 1975. "Saint Augustine and Saussurean Linguistics". *Augustinian Studies* 6.45–64.

Körner, Franz. 1956. "*Deus in homine videt:* Das Subjekt des menschlichen Erkennens nach der Lehre Augustins". *Philosophisches Jahrbuch der Görres-Gesellschaft* 64.166–217.

Kuypers, Karel. 1934. *Der Zeichen- und Wortbegriff im Denken Augustins.* Amsterdam: Swets & Zeitlinger.

Madec, Goulven. 1975. "Analyse du *De magistro*". *Revue des études Augustiniennes* 21.63–71.

Mandouze, André. 1975. "Quelques principes de 'linguistique augustinienne' dans le *De magistro*". *Forma Futuri. Studi in onore di Michele Pellegrino*, 789–795. Torino: Bottega d'Erasmo.

Markus, Robert Austin. 1957. "St. Augustine on signs". *Phronesis* 2.60–83.

–. 1964. "*Imago* and *similitudo* in Augustine". *Revue des études Augustiniennes* 10.125–143.

–. 1972. *Augustine, a collection of criticial essays.* Garden City, N. Y.: Anchor Books.

–. 1996. *Signs and Meanings: World and text in ancient Christianity.* Liverpool: Liverpool Univ. Press.

Maxsein, Anton. 1966. *Philosophia cordis: Das Wesen der Personalität bei Augustinus.* Salzburg: Mueller.

Mayer, Cornelius. 1969. *Die Zeichen in der geistigen Entwicklung in der Theologie jungen Augustins.* Diss., Universität Würzburg.

–. 1974. "*Res per signa:* Der Grundgedanke des Prologs in Augustins Schrift *De doctrina christiana* und das Problem seiner Datierung". *Revue des études Augustiniennes* 20.100–112.

Morán, José. 1968. "La teoría de la 'admonición' en los Diálogos de san Augustín". *Augustinus* 13.257–271.

–. 1968. "La teoría de la 'admonición' en las Confessiones de san Augustín". *Augustinianum* 8.147–154.

Rodríguez Neira, T. 1973. "Intellección y lenguaje en san Augustín". *Augustinus* 18.145–156.

Ruef, Hans. 1981. *Augustin über Semiotik und Sprache. Sprachtheoretische Analysen zu Augustins Schrift De dialectica, mit einer deutschen Übersetzung.* Bern: Wyss Erben.

Schindler, Alfred. 1965. *Wort und Analogie in Augustins Trinitätslehre.* Tübingen: Mohr.

Schmaus, Michael. 1951. *Aurelius Augustinus, Über den dreieinigen Gott. Ausgewählt und übertragen von Michael Schmaus.* Zweiter Druck. München.

Schulte-Herbrüggen, Heinrich. 1976. "Die Mehrschichtigkeit des sprachlichen Zeichens". *Scritti in onore di Giuliano Bonfante*, II, 979–1001. Brescia: Paideia.

Simone, Raffaele. 1972. "Sémiologie augustinienne". *Semiotica* 6.1–31.

Verbeke, Gerard. 1962. "Pensée et discernement chez saint Augustin: Quelques réflexions sur le sens du terme 'cogitare'". *Recherches Augustiniennes* 2.58–80.

Watson, Garard. 1982. "St. Augustine's Theory of Language". *Maynooth Review* 6.4–20.

Wittgenstein, Ludwig. 1953. *Philosophische Untersuchungen.* 2. Bd. Oxford.

*Arpád Orbán, Utrecht/Nijmegen (Niederlande)*

# XIII. The Cultivation of Latin Grammar in the Early Middle Ages
# Die Pflege der lateinischen Grammatik im frühen Mittelalter
# La culture de la grammaire latine dans le Haut Moyen-Age

## 72. The study of Latin as a foreign language in the Early Middle Ages

1. Latin in the Roman empire
2. Latin and Greek-speakers
3. The role of Aelius Donatus
4. Speech and writing before the Carolingians
5. Latin in the British Isles
6. The process of standardization
7. The conceptual separation of Latin from Romance
8. Bibliography

### 1. Latin in the Roman empire

Latin was originally the native language of the inhabitants of the area of Latium (modern Lazio), around the city of Rome. By the end of the Middle Ages, it was taught and learnt as a foreign language even by those who spoke as their native language one of the Romance languages that had developed out of spoken Latin. The process by which this language became foreign even to those who spoke evolved versions of it is a complex one and not yet entirely understood by the historical linguists, although many details in the process have become clearer in recent years.

From the earliest stages of the spread of Roman political and military influence outside their home territory they came into contact with speakers of related Italic languages, such as Oscan, more distantly related Indo-European languages, such as Celtic, and languages of other families entirely, such as Etruscan. In order to prosper or even survive in the expanding Roman state, native speakers of these other languages had to learn Latin. By the height of the Roman Empire, Etruscan and Oscan and other languages once spoken on the Italian Peninsula seem to have been spoken no more; the Latinization process seems to have been so successful as to lead to a largely monolingual peninsula (ignoring, for the moment, Greek-speaking communities in the south and in Sicily). But we have no record of any pedagogical method that was then used to teach, learn and study Latin as a foreign language. Probably the language was learnt in living circumstances rather than at school or in night classes; traders in the markets, soldiers in the armies, slaves in Roman households and others needed a knowledge of spoken Latin and acquired it informally in situ. The Romans probably had no coherent plan to stamp out the languages they met, but of these only Greek had any prestige at all, and it is unlikely that outside special circumstances a native Latin-speaker would have learnt any other language than Greek. In all newly-conquered areas we can surmise the existence of bilingual communities for many decades, but in most places, after the initial contact period, subsequent generations increasingly learnt Latin as a first language, or as one of two first languages, in a native manner. For the evidence that we have suggests that the teaching of Latin in schools and academies was designed to increase the literary skills of those who already spoke Latin, rather than teach Latin to those who did not yet know it (see Balsdon 1979).

### 2. Latin and Greek-speakers

As the Roman State expanded out of the Italian Peninsula it encountered and dominated speakers of many other languages, including Phoenician, Berber languages, Iberian, Celtic, Germanic, Greek, Aramaic, Syriac and Coptic. But although we know of the existence of schools, the only documentary clues that survive for us concerning the practice of teaching and learning Latin as a foreign language during these centuries come from the Greek-speaking areas at a somewhat later time, and even that evidence is hard to assess. In some areas, such as the British Isles, knowledge of Latin seems rarely to have been monolingual, with the result that the pre-existing Celtic continued to flourish, although a knowledge of spoken Latin may well not have died out entirely, as used to be thought; Harvey (1992) argues convincingly for its survival to some extent not only in Britain but also in Ireland, which was never part of the empire. St. Patrick wrote in Latin there in the late 5th century, and a knowledge of Latin literacy can be seen behind the elaboration of Ogam as the written form of Irish. In other areas, such as Gaul, the hold of Latin became stronger, and eventually (in the Early Middle Ages) may have ousted Celtic; but although Latin must have been learnt at some time by hundreds of thousands of people in these areas who already spoke some other language, we cannot say to what extent it was taught to them in any formal sense as an object of study.

Some surviving bilingual Latin-Greek papyri found in the sands of North Africa seem to attest to linguistic school exercises, probably, at least in some cases, designed for Greek-speakers learning Latin, although not necessarily in a formal classroom setting (Wouters 1979). In his study of the Bu Njem tablets of the 250s, Adams (1994) argues that Phoenician-speaking soldiers learnt colloquial Latin in the army in an unstructured manner; we have there rare examples of first-generation Latin-learners who have been taught to write, largely with the help of whole model words and phrases, but who display unusual mistakes characteristic of second language learners. The graffiti of the orginally Celtic-speaking potters of La Graufesenque are another case (see Flobert 1992). The bilingual Greek-Latin word-lists known as *Hermeneumata* are often ancient in origin and pre-Christian in content, and may have had a similar function to the papyri; but their most recent assessment (Dionisotti 1982, 1984) sees them as largely a Western phenomenon, that is, mostly destined for Latin-speaking Greek-learners (about whom we know rather more). There is a late 4th-century grammarian called Dositheus whose *Ars Grammatica*, in Latin, seems to have been prepared, perhaps from the start, with a companion translation in Greek (Keil 1855–1880: VII, 376–436); presumably the translation was made to aid Greek-speaking Latin students, but we need not assume that that was Dositheus's original intention. There undoubtedly were students of this type at the time, such as those attending the law schools in Beirut once Greeks were declared to be subject to Roman Law in 212, but even in the Eastern end of the Empire the main reasons for learning Latin were the simple practicalities of international life, such as the need to survive in the army, or the desire to gain employment elsewhere, perhaps in Rome itself. Even in the Greek-speaking area there seems not to be anything we could call a pedagogical or intellectual tradition of 'Latin as a foreign language'; when Priscian, in the early 6th century (between 512 and 528), turned his attention to an attempt to explain Latin syntax to the predominantly Greek speakers of Byzantium, his intellectual inspiration and written sources were to be found in the local grammars of Greek, since the study of Latin syntax (as opposed to morphology) had not yet been broached but Greek syntax had been being analysed since the 2nd century. It looks as if on the whole even educated speakers of Greek saw no particular reason to learn Latin before the general adoption of Christianity. Greek culture could satisfy most literary tastes. Even Plutarch had claimed to have learnt only a little Latin, in an informal manner, and was probably told of material in his Latin sources by his colleagues. But in the 4th century the Church hierarchy in Constantinople, Antioch, Alexandria and elsewhere needed translators for practical purposes, such as ensuring they had accurate records of Councils, and many Greek speakers may have been eager to learn Latin (Fisher 1982: 175). The 4th-century Greek Claudian wrote in Latin; this is also the date of most of the bilingual papyri. Yet even Jerome and the other Biblical translators of the 4th century (translating from Greek into Latin) seem not to have established a continuing tradition of Latin being taught in a regular pedagogical manner to native speakers of Greek; conversely, we also know of Latin texts that were then translated into Greek (including Saints' Lives by Jerome himself).

## 3. The role of Aelius Donatus

The reasons for this apparent lacuna are not hard to appreciate; in general there can be no effective tradition of the study of a foreign language until there already exists a native monolingual tradition of what we would now call 'descriptive linguistics'. It takes linguists of genius to perceive the organizational principles of their native language in such an objective way that they can be presented as objects of study to others, and a tradition of analysis of the nature of Latin linguistics took a long time to be established even in the native-speaker intellectual context. Varro, Quintilian and others were mines of ideas and information for advanced study, but the basics of the language did not really begin to be codified into a coherent form suitable for elementary study until the work of Aelius Donatus in the 4th century AD (although he may have drawn on some previous work now unknown to us). Donatus (Jerome's teacher) compiled a short *Ars Grammatica*, usually known as the *Ars Minor*, and a longer one known as the *Ars Maior*. The *Ars Minor* seems unsatisfactorily uncomprehensive to us now (lacking, for example, reference to what have come to be called the fourth and fifth declensions, or to exceptions to the main paradigms), but it included a great deal of basic morphological information in a moderately accessible structure; gaps were progressively filled by the many commentators in subsequent centuries who used the *Ars Minor* as the starting point for their own further elucubrations, and collectively their analyses formed the basis of the educational tradition of Latin language-study that has lasted in many respects to the present day (Pinkster [1990] is the first serious attempt to start again for over sixteen centuries). The *Ars Maior* was longer than the *Ars Minor* because it contained extra material that would be classified now as literary rather than linguistic; thus it was the *Ars Minor* that came to be the basis for all subsequent linguistic education in Latin. (Louis Holtz's monumental study [1981] has made the development of this tradition much easier to trace, but the outstanding modern study of the grammatical work of the Early Middle Ages is the remarkable book by Irvine [1994]).

Donatus, however, was writing for the benefit of those who knew the language already, and his focus was directly on written language alone (which is what *Grammatica* originally meant). That is, Donatus saw his brief as being to help his students to write, and understand the written form of, the language which they already spoke. The ability to write 'correctly' at that time (understandably, although to the eternal disappointment of all subsequent philologists) did not rest on the ability to provide a phonetic transcription of vernacular morphosyntax, but to spell words as the ancients did, using the morphology and syntax which they had used in earlier texts. This seems to have seemed to Donatus and his colleagues to imply a need above all for long lists of morphological paradigms, particularly of nouns and pronouns. This concentration in turn appears to imply that not all the nominal endings lovingly illustrated could be trusted to come naturally to the mind of the contemporary native speaker; a deduction which fits the conclusion, reached by the Romance philologists who aim to reconstruct the nature of spoken Latin at this time, that nominal morphology was simplifying in the speech of all. An ability to recognize the separate paradigms and inflectional morphemes was taken to be essential for the correct writing and understanding of texts; and it is probably here that we find the origin of the Early Medieval grammatical habit of regarding the nominal word endings (such as *-m*) as forming part of the study of orthography, rather than of syntax or of pronunciation.

No Latin grammarian before Priscian had much to say about syntax, and since Donatus was writing for the native speaker alone, he included no instructions on pronunciation either, and very few on vocabulary. Not many of his predecessors or contemporaries mentioned pronunciation at all either, and there is no documentary evidence for the belief of some modern Romance philologists working in the Reconstruction tradition – that is, reconstructing Proto-Romance from the evidence of the several subsequently-attested Romance languages – that there existed a separate educated 'Latin' pronunciation at that time, consciously differentiated from the normal Early Romance pronunciations that were beginning to be part of everybody's speech throughout the late Empire. That is, the balance of probability now seems to be that in essence many of the reconstructed pronunciations did indeed exist then, such as a vocalic system based on quality rather than length, but that archaic alternatives were not also in use at the same time (until they were reinvented much later by the Carolingians, when they established Medieval Latin *grammatica* as a consciously distinct international clerical standard: see below). Those who read Donatus, taught classes with his help, or learnt from him in such classes, continued to speak with their existing Early Romance pronunciation, but were in addition studying to read and write their own language with greater certainty of being 'correct'.

## 4. Speech and writing before the Carolingians

Since instruction concerning vocabulary and pronunciation is of immediate importance and relevance to the learner of a foreign language, Donatus's work cannot have been easy to use by a non-Latin speaker. As Servius, Pompeius (both well studied in Kaster 1988), Isidore of Seville (Díaz y Díaz 1982) and others eclectically elaborated and expanded the tradition set by Donatus, grammatical studies became more comprehensive, more discursive and more closely entwined with the analysis of prestigious texts; but these developments in themselves would not have assisted the foreign learner. Previous grammars largely disappeared from view; there was, for example, apparently no Medieval circulation of Varro's *De Lingua Latina*. Outside Byzantium, the Early Romance-speaking community, including within it the Latin-studying community, remained essentially monolingual for centuries yet; but the influence of Donatus came to be unavoidable. As Irvine phrases it (1994: 194), "to escape Donatan or late Imperial *latinitas*, Gregory would have had to stop writing" (that is, Gregory the Great, Pope from 590 to 604). In the wide Early Romance speaking area there were naturally sociolinguistic, stylistic and geographical variations and complexities, but their study of *Grammatica* remained throughout the Early Middle Ages the study of the elevated and educated registers of their own language. The arrival of Priscian's *Institutiones Grammaticae* onto the European higher education curriculum, from the early 9th century onwards, as the standard textbook for higher education, to be studied subsequent to the study of Donatus and his commentators as the standard textbooks at a simpler level, and the adoption of the Anglo-Saxons' practice of pronouncing the texts with a sound for each written letter of standard spellings, together provided the inspiration needed to establish the process that was to turn the study of Latin into a foreign-language study for speakers of Romance languages as well.

This analysis of the pre-Carolingian Romance-speaking communities as being complex but monolingual is still in some respects controversial, despite fitting what evidence there is (Wright 1995a); the earlier view, which sees a clear distinction even at that early time between 'Romance' and 'Latin' as conceptually separate language systems, still has many adherents. Kaster (1988: 38) is particularly pessimistic about the abilities of the unlettered, but the studies in McKitterick (1990) suggest we can be more bullish. The monolingual view does not imply a lack of linguistic evolution in these communities; in particular, most of the phonetic developments which are generally declared by modern philologists to be characteristic of Romance rather than of Latin were well under way even by the end of the Roman Empire. The traditional spellings of words continued to be taught as correct, naturally, for phonetic script had not been invented yet, and would not have been thought desirable if it had; but the gradually increasing divergences, between correct orthography and any intuitions which we can envisage them as having had concerning phonetic details, do not seem to have worried Romance speakers. In practice, it may be reasonable for us to suggest that the teaching of spelling was done on an increasingly logographic basis – that is, word by word (as in Modern Britain) rather than merely sound by sound; in the same way, the ubiquitously employed abbreviations, and the 'Tyronian' shorthand as used in particular by notaries, naturally referred to the lexical word rather than to its phonetic constituents. Thus there were details of writing that did not apply to speech, but there always are, in any community. We can deduce, for example, from the phrasing of the orthographical instructions that Cassiodorus gave to his monks in 6th-century Italy, that the addition of a final *-m* to a noun was seen as a matter of written correctness alone.

Written language had variations in style too, of course. By the mid-8th century, at least, several writers had the sophistication to adjust the register level of their compositions to suit the intended audience (for example, in the preparation of those Saints' Lives that were intended for recitation to the congregation rather than for private monastic study). In a series of remarkable studies (e. g. Banniard 1993), stemming from his thesis and then book entitled *Viva Voce* (1992), Michel Banniard has established beyond much reasonable doubt that even writers of such intellectual standing as Augustine, Gregory, Isidore and the 8th-century hagiographers expected their texts to be generally intelligible when read aloud; and most texts were read aloud. The implications we can draw from this are that not only did the *lectores* deliver phonetically evolved forms of words that were easily recognizable by an unlettered Romance audience, but that the traditional morphology and syntax used in the texts were not yet baffling to the general public. That is, the morphological and syntactic changes which we identify now as taking place from 'Latin' to 'Romance' took much longer to complete than the phonetic changes, because the older usages often remained in general passive comprehension competence for centuries after the arrival of the newer alternatives that seem in retrospect to have neatly taken their place (Green 1991). And such a complex yet monolingual situation could have continued to be the case for a long time yet but for the advent of what has come to be known as the Carolingian 'Renaissance'.

## 5. Latin in the British Isles

Some of the expertise acquired by bilingual Latin-Greek speakers, and some of the texts prepared on the basis of their experience, seem to have survived in the Western Empire, as Dionisotti's (1982, 1982a, 1984) acute studies of the *Hermeneumata* and glossaries suggest, where they would not have been used directly to teach Latin as a foreign language. Sometimes we can glimpse Romance-speaking commentators on Donatus using Eastern expertise (indeed, the manuscripts of these Latin-for-Greeks works tend to survive in the West rather than the East; all three surviving manuscripts of Dositheus are 10th-century copies from St. Gall; see Dionisotti 1982: 84). And Greek-based expertise did contribute to the initial stage of the general transformation of the study of Latin in the West from the textual study of a known language to the learning of an unknown and foreign one, when the revival of Latin study began to take place in the British Isles. Vivien Law's masterly book on the Insular Latin Grammarians (1982) has made the process easier to follow; and although details of the way in which Irish writers learnt to use Latin remain unclear, it was certainly based on textual traditions rather than native contacts in Ireland itself, such that their usage seemed archaic in vocabulary and style when Irish scholars moved to the Continent (see Herren 1981). The most productive intellectual impulse in the Anglo-Saxon area seems to have come in the 7th century, at least partly from the Greek-speaking Eastern Mediterranean, rather than from the Augustinian mission in the 6th century. The credit for the growth of interest in Latin study in Britain can be allotted to two emissaries from the Papacy who travelled to the Isles in 669 AD: Theodore, a Greek scholar who had worked and studied and learnt Latin in Greece, initially as a foreign language, and Hadrian, a colleague of the Pope's (Pope Vitalian). It is possible to reconstruct that some general expertise in the practice of teaching and learning Latin as a foreign language was provided at that point by Theodore; even though he did not bring with him all of Priscian's *Institutiones*, which were at a higher intellectual level than was needed at that time, practical advice was clearly forthcoming, and books came with him – not necessarily all the way from the East –, probably including some of the more elementary Latin grammatical works compiled for Greeks, such as the briefer Priscian extract known as the *Institutio de nomine et pronomine et verbo*. We can also glimpse a habit of textual analysis from surviving Latin-Anglo-Saxon glosses from 7th-century Canterbury. Thus from the start the type of Latinity that educated Anglo-Saxons began to have contact with came from Italy rather than from Gaul; Aldhelm of Malmesbury, for example, was a personal pupil of Theodore's; even so, despite the initial impulse from these personal contacts, Insular studies of Latin were to be primarily text-based rather than supplied by native-speaker expertise. Meanwhile, Irish latinity at this time continued, as it had been hitherto, to be essentially based on the Bible, and despite the renewal of contacts the teaching of Latin to both Celtic and Germanic speakers was more directly related to the study of texts than to a need for colloquial intercourse. Richter's recent study of Irish culture at this time (1994), indeed, stresses the vital nature of the native oral traditions in comparison to the stilted Latin texts.

The linguistic works that survive from the pen of Insular scholars attest to a pedagogical and scholarly tradition that began with Bede (673–735). Bede kept what seems to be a teacher's notebook, in which he progressively noted down all kinds of useful details valuable to the teacher of Latin; unfortunately this work has been given the title of *De Orthographia*, but in effect it covers all linguistic levels (Irvine 1994: 288–290; Dionisotti 1982a). Subsequent Insular grammarians that we know of include Tatwine, Boniface, and the authors of the anonymous grammars named after the libraries where their manuscripts are preserved (Berne and Amiens). This last has some Biblical quotations from the *Vetus Latina* rather than the Vulgate, which suggests ancient source material, probably from Gaul (Irvine 1994: 114). Even so, they can all be seen to belong in Bede's educational tradition, although Boniface, who exported Insular expertise to the Germanic-speaking continent, seems to have been more influenced in his own Latinity by Aldhelm. Irish grammars, probably including the impressive one now known as *Anonymus ad Cuimnanum* which contrasts ancient and standard Latin and also manifests a knowledge of Greek, continued to have a partly separate tradition (→ Art. 82). The preferred vocabulary of Insular Latin-speakers was that of the Bible, whether or not it sounded archaic in the Romance world. For they spoke and recited Latin; Bede even seems to have expected his *Historia* to be read aloud; but they met it in written form from the start. They therefore encountered the registers and styles of the language in a most non-native order. On the Western Romance-speaking Continent, native speakers acquired colloquial styles first, naturally, as children, and only learnt to read and write later, if at all; in the British Isles, those who learnt this language met the written registers from the start, and colloquial styles probably never, unless they crossed the Channel. The result was the acquisition of a stilted level of Latinity which at times was unrecognizable on the Continent, as Boniface was apparently incomprehensible to the Pope. In particular, they developed the practice of pronouncing Latin words in the way that we all do now, that is, on the basis of giving a specified sound to each already written letter (or digraph) of the standard spelling of the words. This probably explains why the Anglo-Saxons called Grammar *staefcraeft* "lettercraft". This strange and unnatural practice led to great differences between the way they pronounced Latin, in effect reading texts aloud as if they were in phonetic script, and the pronunciations that had become normal in the native Romance-speaking world, where many spellings were learnt and taught logographically rather than phonographically. In particular, the Anglo-Saxons' near neighbours in Gaul had by then come to employ varieties of speech which had undergone many sound changes, often dropping whole syllables from the phonetic form that had orignally inspired the orthographic shape of the words a millennium earlier.

By the 7th and 8th century the motives for learning to understand and compose texts in Latin were more likely to be religious than literary (cf. Riché 1962). The Insular teachers, and others, felt a need to Christianize their didactic material. Vivien Law (1982), for example, has studied a variant of Donatus, used, and even perhaps prepared, by Paul the Deacon in Italy, in which the text is slightly Christianized, in that the morphologically paradigmatic examples of feminine, neuter and common gender nouns have been changed to *ecclesia* (from *musa*), *templum* (from *scamnum*) and *fidelis* (rather than *sacerdos*, which to the pagans had indeed been a common gender noun, whereas Christian priests had to be male). Isidore, Bishop of Seville, in early 7th-century Spain, seems to have begun his academic life with a priestly distrust of pagan literature that came to be increasingly diluted as he developed his career as polymath and gradually appreciated its fascination. The Christianized Donatus tradition seems also to have been known in the British Isles.

## 6. The process of standardization

Donatus did his best, as did his commentators, to work out what actually happened in the language of the Latin texts they admired and respected. Priscian did his best to adapt the conceptual techniques he found in his Greek sources to the study of Latin; sometimes this had misleading results, as when he declared that the use of reflexive syntax in Latin (that is, with *se*) necessarily implied a reflexive meaning in which the grammatical subject was the agent of the action (*actio*: Keil III, 14), an analysis which worked for Greek, where *heautón* was always tonic, but not for Latin, in which (as in many Romance languages still) an apparently reflexive construction with an atonic *se* could be used quite literally for agentless passive meaning (Wright 1995b). But on the whole Priscian's analyses of Latin syntax are impressive and often convincing; and both Donatus and Priscian were essentially descriptive in motivation, trying to establish what actually happened. Unfortunately, as the centuries went by, and the grammatical details found in ancient texts and in these grammarians' analyses began to correspond to only a few of the available variants in the morphology and syntax of Romance speech, the descriptive came to be seen as prescriptive; that is, teachers assumed that what Donatus and Priscian had said was the case was what they themselves ought to be doing, and, more significantly, that any variant which Donatus and Priscian had not mentioned was one which teachers ought not to be recommending, using or writing; and by taking this extra step, they were introducing the moral dimension into grammar which has been so destructive and still tends to dominate linguistic teaching. Thus 'correct' Latin slowly came to be uniquely defined by this combined tradition, and the books of Donatus, his commentators, and Priscian were appealed to in order to instruct even the native-speakers about what they ought now to be doing themselves, rather than merely about what others before them had, as a matter of fact, been doing when preparing texts.

Written Latin was thus already by the time of the so-called Carolingian 'Renaissance' – their own word was *renovatio*; see Contreni (1995) – in danger of becoming a foreign language for its supposed native-speakers; but this dissociation was not inevitable, and with a little flexibility the old monolingualism could probably have carried on for centuries (as it has in China, and as it still is, if precariously, in the English-speaking world now; cf. McKitterick 1989). The decisive catalyst in the long process can be seen at the moment when the two systems clashed, the Insular and the native Romance. More precisely, the key moment can be seen in retrospect to have been the appointment by Charlemagne of an Englishman, Alcuin of York, who had been schooled in the Bede inheritance, to reform the Carolingian education system (→ Art. 74). Several Insular grammarians were already known on the Continent, and Alcuin inherited their prestige. He first arrived in 782, but his linguistic studies seem to have extended in the 790s, when he was working at Tours on his standard Biblical text, his grammar, and the *De Orthographia* which aimed to establish correctness in both speaking and writing (Irvine 1994: 313–333); and Alcuin, unlike his other compatriots, also studied there Priscian's *Institutiones*. Alcuin had no interest in any vernacular, not even his own. Among many other aspects of the educational reforms he inspired there seems to have been a desire to encourage all those in the church to pronounce Latin words in the stilted Anglo-Saxon way, a sound for each letter, rather than in the normal local evolved manner as the clergy had used naturally hitherto. This would have made the language seem foreign indeed; Banniard (1992) even suggests that Alcuin wanted to insist that all parishioners spoke the Anglo-Saxon way when confessing to their priests, but since it proved difficult to do, and difficult to understand if done correctly, that plan lapsed. If Banniard is right in this, it is easy to envisage the annoyance caused there by the arrival of a foreigner telling them that they did not know their own language (as when German-speaking editors now try to correct the English of native-speaking writers). In 813, after Alcuin's death, the Carolingian church also decided that the formal pronunciation need not apply to sermons, whose function lay in their very intelligibility. But in the long run, this reform took root with all the other aspects of Alcuinian *grammatica* that laid the foundations for later Medieval culture. At first maybe it was normal practice only at Alcuin's home base of Tours, and centres influenced by Tours; for theirs was not in practice a centralized state, and cultural variations continued; but subsequently Alcuin's star pupil, Hrabanus Maurus (c. 784–856), Abbot of Fulda and eventually Bishop of Mainz, who was the centre of a huge web of intellectual contacts, seems to have been a key figure in promoting the general use of the newly standardized *grammatica*, conceptually separate from Romance, within the clerical education system. In the Romance world, other centres managed to continue the new system, including Fleury, where the Visigoth Theodulf (abbot from 798 to 818) had established the Alcuinian model, Odo of Cluny had revived it (abbot from 937) and the library maintained an excellent grammatical collection throughout. When the educational world began to expand again with the 12th-century Renaissance, the reformed non-vernacular pronunciations, at least in their essential requirement that every letter deserved to be given some sound – even if that sound was sometimes going to vary from place to place as the Romance phonetics varied – survived together with the requirements of 'correct' morphology, syntax and vocabulary usage, as an essential part of the *Grammatica* that was generally taught and learnt as the basis of all education, in Romance areas as well as non-Romance. The study of *Grammatica* as a wholly separate language spread then to Romance-speaking areas that were not in the Carolingian realms (in the Iberian Peninsula; Sardinia; Southern Italy; not, it seems, Romania), such that by the height of the 12th-century Renaissance Latin had come to be studied generally as a foreign language wherever the classes were. The new Universities of the 13th century then developed the tradition to a higher intellectual level, but it had been Alcuin and his colleagues who brought the study of Latin to a sufficiently objective level for the new Universities to exploit.

## 7. The conceptual separation of Latin from Romance

The establishment in this way of Medieval Latin as a conceptually separate language from everyone's vernacular meant, in addition, that it became in due course necessary to invent new written systems for non-reformed Romance; texts in experimental Romance orthographies, in which the letter-sound correspondences of the new system were employed to represent spoken morphology, syntax, word order and vocabulary, turn up in all Romance areas as a direct consequence of the adoption of the reformed Latin system, because the educational reform meant that texts written in the old style could no longer necessarily, as before, be read aloud easily in the vernacular intelligible manner, particularly by native Germanic speakers. The metalinguistic context, consequent on the conscious categorization of the stylistic differences into two languages in the same geographical area rather than just one, changed with the advent of the two 'Renaissances', the Carolingian and the 12th-century.

Renaissances often run the risk of destroying by fossilization what they claim to want to preserve, or at the least confining it to a small élite; cf. Contreni's question (1995: 714), "who would train the rural clergy?"; in the event the consequences of Alcuin's prejudices were largely pernicious in the Romance-speaking lands, since the Reform not only drove wedges between those who did and those who did not master the new system, it led, as a necessary consequence of their exclusively phonographic obsession, to the need to elaborate different new spelling systems in different kingdoms, which in turn abetted the growing poison of divisive nationalism within what had once been an international Romance-speaking whole. The new Romance spellings were not elaborated for the illiterate, of course, who could no more cope with the new spelling than with any other; all the earliest written Romance texts come from centres of expert Latinity. For a long time anyone literate in the new Romance written systems would have been trained first in reading (and perhaps also writing) Latin, so at first written Romance might well have been harder for many of them to operate than the traditional Latin; but once there was a sizeable group of people literate in their new local written Romance form but not in Latin – which happened in the 13th century – old-style written Latin forms could start to seem foreign even to the literate, and the change was for practical purposes complete (see Herman 1990; Selig et al. 1993).

The Anglo-Saxon tradition had inspired the transformation of the study of *Grammatica* from instruction in how to write the language of Early Romance speakers into a guide to the learning of a foreign language, separate from the vernacular of all, and through the 9th century scholars from the British Isles (including Ireland) still had the authority to go to the Continent and give advice on how to proceed with their linguistic reforms. But the developing continental tradition, with its input from Priscian, was coming to be more sophisticated than the British one already by the time when the Scandinavian invasions of the 9th century disrupted the Insular traditions. In the following century, we find that the Continental scholars now had the authority to come to the Isles and tell aspiring scholars what to do. Abbo of Fleury, for example, went to Ramsey in 985–987, at a time when Fleury was a renowned centre of intellectual and linguistic expertise, welcoming scholarly visitors from every direction; Abbo wrote his *Quaestiones Grammaticales* as an answer to questions posed to him by his Anglo-Saxon speaking students (and as a result the work is informative about Anglo-Saxon, as well as about differences in the Latinity of the two communities; see Guerreau-Jalabert 1982). The questions answered tend to cover matters not dealt with in the Alcuinian rules, such as the positioning of stress in polysyllables. Germanic-speaking scholars on the Continent continued to be influential after the Carolingian age, however, and since they naturally saw all forms of Latin and Romance as foreign, and often learnt how to read reformed Latin without learning to speak Romance, they helped the dissociation process to continue. (This seems the best explanation in context for the elaboration of a Latin-based Romance spelling in the late 9th-century *Cantilena Eulaliae* from St. Amand during Hucbald's abbacy, at least: see Wright 1982: 128–135). However, Richter has argued that literacy was not an important feature of Germanic society until after the 12th century. In Moslem Spain there are many written Latin texts from the 9th century, but hardly any thereafter; it looks as though the Christians there, in view of the increasing dissimilarity between the Visigothic linguistic traditions that they inherited and the manner of their Romance speech, decided, possibly even consciously, to reserve their literacy for the Arabic they needed to know anyway in their society, despite continuing to be bilingual Arabic-Romance in speech. The Arabic-speakers usually knew Romance, but it is unlikely they studied Latin (cf. Wasserstein 1991; Wright 1998).

All periodizations are, of course, administrative fantasies; but if we are searching for a means of distinguishing chronologically the Early Middle Ages from the High Middle Ages, the point at which Latin became in effect a foreign language for everybody is as distinctive a turning point as any other.

## 8. Bibliography


Adams, J. N. 1994. "Latin and Punic in Contact? The case of the Bu Njem Ostraca". *Journal of Roman Studies* 84.87–112.

Balsdon, J. P. V. D. 1979. *Romans and Aliens.* London: Duckworth.

Banniard, Michel. 1992. *Viva Voce: Communication écrite et communication orale du IV^e au IX^e siècle en Occident latin.* Paris: Institut des Études Augustiniennes.

–. 1993. "Latin tardif et français prélitteraire". *Bulletin de la Société de Linguistique de Paris* 88.139–162.

Contreni, John J. 1995. "The Carolingian Renaissance: Education and literary culture". *The New Cambridge Medieval History, II: c.700–c.900* ed. by Rosamond McKitterick, 709–757. Cambridge: Cambridge Univ. Press.

Díaz y Díaz, Manuel C. 1982. "Introducción general". *San Isidoro de Sevilla: Etimologías* ed. by José Oroz Reta, 1–260. Madrid: Biblioteca de Autores Cristianos.

Dionisotti, A. C. 1982. "From Ausonius' Schooldays? A schoolbook and its relatives". *Journal of Roman Studies* 72.83–125.

–. 1982a. "On Bede, Grammars and Greek". *Revue Bénédictine* 92.111–141.

–. 1984. "Latin grammar for Greeks and Goths". *Journal of Roman Studies* 74.202–208.

Fisher, Elizabeth A. 1982. "Greek Translations of Latin Literature in the Fourth Century A.D.". *Yale Classical Studies* 27.173–215.

Flobert, Pierre. 1992. "Les graffites de la Graufesenque: Un témoignage sur le Gallo-latin sous Néron". *Latin vulgaire – latin tardif* III ed. by Maria Iliescu & W. Marxgut, 103–114. Tübingen: Niemeyer.

Fontaine, Jacques & J. N. Hillgarth, eds. 1992. *Le Septième siècle: changements et continuités.* London: The Warburg Institute.

Green, John N. 1991. "The Collapse and Replacement of Verbal Inflection in Late Latin / Early Romance: how would one know?". *Latin and the Romance Languages in the Early Middle Ages* ed. by Roger Wright, 83–99. London: Routledge. [Repr., Pennsylvania: Penn State Press, 1996.]

Guerreau-Jalabert, Anita, ed. 1982. *Abbo Floriacensis: Quaestiones Grammaticales.* Paris: Les Belles Lettres.

Harvey, Anthony. 1992. "Latin, Literacy and the Celtic Vernaculars around the Year A.D. 500". *Celtic Languages and Celtic Peoples,* 11–26. Halifax: St. Mary's University.

Herman, József. 1990. *Du Latin aux langues romanes.* Tübingen: Niemeyer.

Herren, Michael W. 1981. "Hiberno-Latin Philology: the state of the question". *Insular Latin Studies,* 1–22. Toronto: Pontifical University.

Holtz, Louis. 1981. *Donat et la tradition de l'enseignement grammatical: étude sur l'Ars Donati et sa diffusion (IV^e–IX^e siècle) et édition critique.* Paris: CNRS.

Irvine, Martin. 1994. *The Making of Textual Culture: "Grammatica" and literary theory, 350–1100.* Cambridge: Cambridge Univ. Press.

Kaster, Robert A. 1988. *Guardians of Language: The grammarian and society in Late Antiquity.* Berkeley: California Univ. Press.

Keil, Heinrich. 1855–80. *Grammatici Latini.* 7 vols. Leipzig: Teubner.

Law, Vivien. 1982. *The Insular Latin Grammarians.* Woodbridge: Boydell Press.

Law, Vivien, ed. 1993. *History of Linguistic Thought in the Early Middle Ages.* Amsterdam: John Benjamins.

McKitterick, Rosamond. 1989. *The Carolingians and the Written Word.* Cambridge: Cambridge Univ. Press.

–, ed. 1990. *The Uses of Literacy in Early Medieval Europe.* Cambridge: Cambridge Univ. Press.

Pinkster, Harm. 1990. *Latin Syntax and Semantics.* London: Routledge.

Riché, Pierre. 1962. *Éducation et culture dans l'occident barbare, VI^e – VII^e siècles.* Paris: Du Seuil.

Richter, Michael. 1994. *The Formation of the Medieval West: Studies in the oral culture of the Barbarians.* Dublin: Four Courts Press.

Selig, Maria, Barbara Frank & Jörg Hartmann, eds. 1993. *Le passage à l'écrit des langues romanes.* Tübingen: Narr.

Wasserstein, David J. 1991. "The language situation in Al-Andalus". *Studies in the Muwaššaḥ and the Kharja*, ed. by Alan Jones & Richard Hitchcock, 1–15. Oxford: Oxford Univ. Press.

Wouters, Alfons. 1979. *The Grammatical Papyri from Graeco-Roman Egypt: Contributions to the study of 'Ars Grammatica' in Antiquity.* Brussels: Koninklijke Academie.

Wright, Roger. 1982. *Late Latin and Early Romance (in Spain and Carolingian France).* Liverpool: Francis Cairns.

–. 1995a. *Early Ibero-Romance.* Newark, Delaware: Juan de la Cuesta Monographs.

–. 1995b. "La sintaxis reflexiva con semántica no agentiva". *Actas del I Congreso Nacional de Latín Medieval*, 415–432. León: Universidad de León.

–. 1998. "The End of Written Ladino in al-Andalus". *The Formation of al-Andalus, Part 2: Language, Religion, Culture and the Sciences* ed. by Maribel Fierro & Julio Samsó, 19–35. Aldershot: Variorum.

*Roger Wright, Liverpool (Great Britain)*

# 73. Linguistics and theology in the Early Medieval West

1. Introduction
2. Christian grammar
3. Exegesis
4. Allegory
5. Truth and authority
6. Virgilius Maro Grammaticus
7. The Carolingian Renaissance and the Seven Liberal Arts
8. Smaragdus
9. Godescalc of Orbais
10. Eriugena
11. The St. Gall Tractate: An interdisciplinary approach
12. Bibliography

## 1. Introduction

Early medieval grammarians inherited from Antiquity a large number of textbooks, of which the two works of Donatus became universally known. The *Ars minor* provided the model for elementary language teaching, while the *Ars maior* established itself as the principal object of commentary at a more advanced level. These were the two genres within which early medieval teachers developed their ideas on language. In the ancient curriculum, grammar was intimately associated with the study of literature, being defined as the art of correct speech (*recte loquendi*) and explication of poets (*enarratio poetarum*). This traditional definition goes back to Quintilian, who had, moreover, depicted the art of grammar as the foundation (*fundamentum*) of the study of rhetoric. These ideas of the nature and position of grammar continued to be relevant throughout the Early Middle Ages, during which grammar lent its method to the service of Christian culture. The main intellectual efforts of Pre-Carolingian scholars were devoted to Bible study, and it was grammar that provided the basic skills to penetrate its literal and allegorical meaning. While the technical tool itself came to be transferred to the service of Bible study in a somewhat straightforward manner, new questions arose as inspired by the new ideological context of language study. Such questions, which concerned for instance the adequacy of human language to express the eternal truths of Christian faith, remained on the grammarian's agenda throughout the Middle Ages.

The fact that grammar had been intimately associated with the study of pagan literature in ancient schools continued to preoccupy early medieval teachers, although the conflict between classical and Christian education had been resolved in late Antiquity. In the writings of the early Church Fathers, all the arts of discourse – grammar, dialectic and rhetoric – had come under attack because of the danger that their study was felt to represent for the Christian's spiritual life. Augustine was a central figure in the process of legitimizing the secular arts to the service of Christian learning (→ Art. 71). Throughout the early Middle Ages, the concept of Christian grammar was justified over and over again in the works of authoritative figures, such as Cassiodorus, Gregory the Great, and Isidore of Seville. In their defense of grammar they resorted to the traditional polemic of the early Church Fathers, questioning the 'truth' and authority of grammar. The 'truth' of grammar involved dissociating it completely from the study of pagan authors, whose works were permeated with lies and fictive tales (*mendacium, figmenta, fabulae poetarum*). The authority of the Bible over the rules of Donatus seems to have been unanimously accepted by the early medieval teachers, who rejected the idea that the divinely inspired text could contain errors. They thus warned against emending the text of the *Vulgate*. Whenever the sacred text appeared to contain something obscure or contradictory, it was not to be understood literally, but as expressing its meaning in a figurative way, through enigmas.

That the Bible speaks of spiritual issues obliquely, through enigmas, was commonplace in medieval exegesis. The sacred text thus has a semantics of its own which requires special tools of interpretation. In addition to the immediate, literal sense of the text, a deeper meaning must be sought in the Bible. Since Patristic times, a fourfold method of interpretation was applied in biblical exegesis which made use of three kinds of figurative senses. Grammar and biblical exegesis developed in parallel in the early Middle Ages, and many features of biblical exegesis came to be transferred to grammatical commentaries. The grammarians not only adopted many features of exegetical techniques, but they occasionally approached their grammatical text as if it had a deeper meaning, comparable to the figurative sense of the sacred text.

While grammar was the principal technical aid in the study of Scripture during the first Christian centuries, from the Carolingian renaissance on it was more often dialectic that lent its method to the study of other disciplines. The study of dialectic was revived by Charlemagne's teacher Alcuin, and it began to assume an increasingly important role as an art relevant to all learning. The Seven Liberal Arts came to be regarded as the ideal form of secular learning, grammar being defined as their origin and foundation (*origo et fundamentum liberalium litterarum*). Alcuin's identification of the Seven Liberal Arts with the seven pillars of Solomon's temple became a popular image of Christian learning in the 9th century. However, the strongest claims as to the importance of the Liberal Arts in Christian education were made by Eriugena, according to whom the arts make the soul immortal. He developed his ideas within the Neoplatonic theory of recollection, claiming that the arts are innate in man. In this scheme, according to which the arts are a constituent part of human nature, grammar is regarded, together with rhetoric, as subdivisions of dialectic, the mother of all arts.

## 2. Christian grammar

In what way can a grammatical textbook, with its apparently neutral definitions and lists of morphological paradigms, be Christian or non-Christian? The most obvious way that an early medieval master would have answered this question is: When a grammar draws its examples from pagan texts. In justifying the concept of Christian grammar, he would resort to the language of traditional polemic associating it with truth as opposed to the pagan art which is throughout permeated with the lies of the pagans. He would probably also appeal to the authority of Jerome or Augustine in justifying the Christian use of grammar. Such a view is expressed for instance by the Christian grammarian Smaragdus at the beginning of the 9th century:

> Far from basing my book on Vergil's or Cicero's authority, or that of any other pagan, I have adorned its pages with verses from the Holy Scriptures, with the intention of pouring out for my reader a pleasant draught of the Liberal Arts and the Scriptures, so that he may come to grasp the discipline of grammar and the sense of the Holy Scriptures side by side (*In partibus Donati* lf.; quoted and translated by Law 1994: 100).

Although early medieval grammarians rarely make such ideas as explicit as Smaragdus, many of them seem to have tacitly followed a similar approach. A number of grammatical texts from the first medieval centuries witness to efforts to christianize grammar by replacing the traditional examples in Donatus' grammar with Christian ones. It is believed that a Christian *Ars maior* was widely known in the pre-Carolingian era although no copy of this work has survived. Many grammatical compilations seem to have exploited its Christian examples. The earliest surviving example of this practice can be found in the *Ars Asporii* (or *Asperi*), dating possibly from late 6th-century Gaul (Law 1982: 40ff.). In his *Ars minor* the author has largely replaced Donatus' examples with Christian ones. Thus, instead of the traditional examples of proper nouns *Roma* and *Tiber* we find *Hierusalem, Iordanis, Sion, Michael, Petrus, Stephanus, Esaias, Aaron*, and *Ezechiel.* Common nouns are represented by *angelus, apostolus, martyr, propheta, sacerdos*, and *rex* (*Ars* 39.6–8). The superlative is exemplified by *pereminentissimus prophetarum Helias* "Elias, the most eminent of prophets", and *sapientissimus regum Salomon* "Solomon, the wisest of kings" (*Ars* 40.7–8).

Meanwhile, many grammarians retained the Classical examples with their references to mythological figures and pagan deities. Thus Tatwine and Boniface, for instance, quote *Hector fortissimus Troianorum* "Hector, the strongest of the Troians" as an example of the superlative (Tatwine, *Ars* 24, 701; Boniface, *Ars* 19, 130). Iuppiter stands as an example of nouns which have only two cases (Tatwine, *Ars* 14.322), while Floralia, Bachanalia and Saturnalia represent *pluralia tantum* (Tatwine, *Ars* 19, 488; Boniface, *Ars* 30, 422). The names of the days of the weeks as deriving from pagan gods are discussed in several 9th century works without any comment (*dies Iovis a Iove, dies Veneris a Veneri, dies Saturni a Saturno, quem sabbatum dicimus*, Sedulius Scottus, *In Donatum maiorem* 131.32–37). *Aeneas filius Veneris* together with *Maria virgo* serve to exemplify the usage of pronouns (Murethach, *In Donatum maiorem* 119.18–a23).

Christian thought has penetrated into the structure of grammar much more profoundly in the works of Julian of Toledo from the middle of the 7th century, permitting the modification of grammatical categories accordingly. In his discussion of the noun he is concerned to show that the word *Deus* "God" does not properly admit number. Within the category of quality in the noun, it is customary to distinguish between proper (*proprium*) and common (*appellativum*), the former being the name of one thing (*unius nomen*) and the latter of many (*multorum*). Julian gives as an example of proper quality three words: *sol* "sun", *luna* "moon", and *deus* "god", which though "names of one thing only" can nevertheless be used even in the plural. Julian explains away their use in the plural in each case as instances of figurative speech. When we say *soles ire et redire possunt* "the suns can go away and return" (Catullus 5.4), we actually mean "days". When people talk about first, second and third moons (*luna prima, secunda, tertia*), they are referring to feasts. The expression *deus deorum* "God of Gods" is used merely as pertaining to human rulers. That which belongs to one thing only, as he concludes, is a proper noun, e. g. *Deus* "God"; that which belongs to many, is common, e. g. *dies* "day" (*Ars* 14.114–129).

Angels are taken into account in the discussion of the traditional definition of man by Julian: *animal rationale mortale risus capax* "man is a rational, mortal animal capable of laughter". He first distinguishes men and angels from animals, the former being rational. He then proceeds to distinguish men from angels, the latter being immortal. Finally, the ability to laugh distinguishes men from angels and animals, because only human beings are able to laugh (*Ars* 11.51–62). Julian develops his views on word formation, leaning on biblical authority. According to him, the pronouns *meus* and *tuus* are composite by figure, because in the Bible *-us* is said to be a noun: *Vir erat in terra Us pro nomine Iob* [Iob 1,1] "there was a man in the land of Uz, whose name was Job".

## 3. Exegesis

Grammar, originally a tool for the exegesis of literary texts, became itself an object of commentary, providing a platform for the higher level of linguistic speculation which inquired into the foundations of the grammatical doctrine itself. Such speculation often drew inspiration from Christian doctrine, being influenced, from the 9th century onwards, by dialectic as well. The technique which early medieval teachers employed in grammatical and biblical exegesis was similar: focussing on one word or phrase at a time, they separated a lemma, and provided a commentary which explained the word, its historical context, the persons involved in an event and so forth.

The biblical and grammatical exegete's primary question is: What does the text really mean? Indeed, the commentator's technique involved asking innumerable questions: Why were there, for instance, twelve apostles, five loaves, two fishes? (e. g. Law 1997: 80–81). Similar questions were asked concerning grammatical doctrine: Why are there three persons in the verb? Why are there eight parts of speech? Smaragdus found several scriptural examples of the significance of the number eight, such as the eight passengers on the Ark, the eight Beatitudes, the eight cubits of the porch of the gate, David, the eighth son of Jesse, and the circumcision on the eighth day (*In partibus Donati* 6.16–7.33). "No doubt this is divinely inspired", as he claims. An anonymous author from the 9th century draws a parallel between the three persons of the verb and the three persons of the Trinity. "This, I think, is divinely inspired (*divinitus esse inspiratum*)", he concludes, "as that which we believe in the faith of Trinity, is seen to manifest itself in speech" (Thurot 1868: 65). Such examples show how the grammarian came to approach the grammatical text much in the same way as the Scripture, seeking for a deeper significance in its technical details (cf. Holtz 1977: xxix–xxxiii). The exegetical method permitted the grammarians to point out conflicting views in their textbooks, whereby they did not hesitate to criticize their grammatical authority. Terms used of Donatus include *vituperatur, mentitur, mendax, fallax* (Law 1982: 83). The text of the Bible was not criticized in a similar manner. When the rules of grammar were incompatible with the text of the *Vulgate*, its authority was subjected to that of the divinely inspired Word.

Because of the parallel development of the exegetical method in the two fields, grammatical and biblical commentaries show similar features. The metalanguage of the two disciplines shows overlapping, when, for instance, both make a distinction between the external and internal aspects of words. Gregory the Great sees the literal meaning of the word as a surface (*superficies*) only, or as a plain with the higher senses stretching up like a mountain (*In Regum* I, prologue 49.13). Similarly the grammarian came to talk about the surface of the word (*superficies or sonus*), as opposed to its meaning (*sensus, intellectus*). A commonplace shared by Insular (and particularly by Irish) exegetes and grammarians was a concern with the *tres linguae sacrae* "three sacred languages" of the Church, Latin, Greek and Hebrew (see e. g. McNally 1958; Bischoff 1966–67b: 248–250). These three languages were sacred, according to Isidore, for it is in these three languages that Pilate wrote above the cross of the Lord the charge against him (*Et.* 9.1–3). It was customary to list the Greek and Hebrew equivalents for certain basic concepts, such as the persons of the Trinity; in grammar, the equivalents for noun, letter, syllable and so forth were also given in the three languages.

Similar features also occur in the *accessus* to biblical and grammatical commentaries, in which the work under study is introduced. Both the biblical and grammatical exegete would introduce their authority in terms of a series of questions concerning the *locus* "setting", *tempus* "date" and *persona* "person" of the author, and sometimes the *causa scribendi* "reason for writing" (Bischoff 1966b: 84). From the 9th century on, this *accessus* formula was occasionally replaced by one based on the so-called seven circumstances: 'who', 'what', 'where', 'when', 'why', 'how', and 'by what means'.

## 4. Allegory

The study of Scripture was the ultimate goal of Christian education, constituting the higher knowledge, by means of which one rises to the understanding of spiritual issues. It was commonplace throughout the Middle Ages to think that the sacred text has a particular mode of signifying, different from all other texts. In addition to the literal (or historical) meaning (*sensus litteralis* or *historicus*), the text of the Bible was thought to carry a more profound signification. While it talked about historical events, these events as such had a deeper meaning, as signs of transcendental realities or even as referring forwards in time. Bible study thus required specific tools of interpretation. Since Patristic times, it became usual to analyze biblical texts in terms of four senses: the literal (or historical), and three figurative senses: allegorical (or spiritual), anagogical (or prophetic) and tropological (or moral) (Evans 1984: 114ff.). Allegorical interpretation remained the primary mode of biblical exegesis in the early medieval West. This method, introduced by Clement of Alexandria and Origen, and further developed by Ambrose (c. 340–397), Jerome (c. 326–420) and Augustine (354–430), found continuity in the works of several early medieval teachers.

It was commonplace in early medieval exegesis to think that God had ceased to speak to man directly, after the communication between man and God had broken down in the Fall. According to Augustine, God continued to speak to man, but he had adapted his Word to man's imperfect understanding. He met man on man's terms, speaking to him, no longer directly, but obliquely. Following the Patristic tradition, Gregory the Great explained in the 6th century that man became blind in his spiritual understanding, as he began his exile in this present life in the world. The divine method of speaking obliquely, through enigmas and allegory is, as he explains, God's way of lifting man's soul from its place at a great distance below God, bringing it towards him (*In Cant.* 3.5–15). Thus, if we laugh at certain passages in the Bible for their apparent banality, we are failing to see the great mercy of God in speaking to us in a way we can understand (*In Cant.* 4.27–30) (quoted and translated by Evans 1984: 1–2). The principle that God speaks to man figuratively in Scripture was developed by Augustine within a traditional theory of meaning, to which he introduced the idea that things themselves can be signs (*De doct. christ.* 1.2.2; → Art. 71).

Bede (ca. 700) was heavily influenced by Augustine in his work *De schematibus et tropis.* According to Bede, the Scripture surpasses all other texts not only by its divine authority, or by its utility, as leading to eternal life, but even by its antiquity. By showing that examples of all rhetorical figures of speech can be found in the Scripture, Bede wants to prove that their Christian use is prior to their use by the Greeks, who unjustly pride themselves of having invented them (*De schem.* 142.11 – 143.19). In his employment of Christian examples, he is believed to depend upon a work of an anonymous master from the late 5th or early 6th century, also used by Isidore of Seville and Julian of Toledo (Schindel 1975: 95).

Bede defines the trope as "a word which has been transferred from its proper sense to some similitude which is not proper, for the sake of decoration or for necessity" (*De schem.* 151, 160–161; cf. *Et.* I.37.1). Not surprisingly, allegory is treated in great detail, being defined as a trope by means of which one thing is said and another is meant (161, 177). In his treatment of allegory, Bede followed consistently the Augustinian distinction between those allegories that are based on words (*verba*), and those that are based on things (*res*). Bede explains that allegory has necessarily one of the following senses: historical, figurative, tropological or anagogical, and it often happens that all four senses coexist in one and the same word or thing. For instance, the Lord's temple is historically a house built by Solomon. According to the allegorical interpretation, it is the body of Christ of which he himself has said: "Destroy this temple and in three days I will raise it up" (John 2,19). Or else, the temple refers to the church, of which it is said: "[...] the temple of God is holy, which temple you are" (I Cor. 3,17). According to the tropological interpretation, the temple refers to the faithful: "Know ye not that ye are the temple of God, and that the Spirit of God dwelleth in you?" (I Cor. 3,16). According to the anagogical interpretation, the temple points to future joys: "Blessed are they that dwell in thy house: they will be still praising thee" (Psalm 85,5, according to the *Vulgate*).

It became customary to refer to the use of tropes by the term *translatio*. However, the term *translative* "metaphorically" frequently occurs in medieval exegesis with a slightly different meaning. It is used in connection with the discussion about the inadequacy of human language to describe the Divine Essence. This topic was developed in the Early Middle Ages particularly by Eriugena.

## 5. Truth and authority

The conversion of grammar did not go beyond a partial substitution of the traditional examples for Christian ones. Isidore and Julian of Toledo, for instance, who introduced some Christian examples into their grammars, left many Classical ones untouched. Many early medieval grammarians felt no need to employ Christian examples at all, which suggests that the threat was not felt to be very real. All the same, polemic against the pagan association of grammar continued to be expressed throughout the Early Middle Ages. Such polemic often focussed on the question of truth and authority of grammar, and drew heavily upon statements by such authoritative figures as Augustine, Jerome, Isidore of Seville, and Gregory the Great.

The topic of truth had been introduced into the polemic against pagan classics by such early exegetes as Clement of Alexandria (fl. 200) and Origen (ca. 185–254). Augustine, the most authoritative Christian writer in the Early Middle Ages, upheld the association between grammar and truth in several of his early works, which were concerned with education and the use of the ancient disciplines in Christian education. In the *Soliloquia*, grammar is defined as "the guardian of articulate speech", which necessarily deals with everything that has been written down, thus even with fictive tales. But the role of grammar is not to make falsehoods but to teach truth according to rational principles (2.11.9). In the *De ordine*, too, he claims that the task of grammar is to study things which are untrue. This is burdensome (*laboriosa*) to grammar, threatening its rationality. But Augustine maintains that the untrue is not in the grammar as such (cf. *Soliloquia* 2.11.19). But where does the truth of grammar lie? He finally asks, suggesting that it lies in its association with dialectic. By contrast, dialectic is true in itself.

Cassiodorus was influenced by Augustine's *De doctrina christiana* in compiling his guide for exegesis, which combines Christian and secular traditions of learning. In the *Institutiones divinarum et humanarum litterarum* he defends the use of the Seven Liberal Arts, by claiming that they have their origin in the Scriptures, from where they were later transferred to secular use (*Inst.* I *praef.* 6). The task of grammar as the first liberal art is "correct speaking" (*recte loquendi*) but this does not mean that the grammarians are allowed to correct the divine authority (1.15.16), as he maintains. When the biblical usage of nominal case and gender or tense does not accord with human rules, the text of the Scripture has to be left untouched (1.15.5–6). Bishop Gregory the Great also famously defended the biblical authority over that of Donatus in the preface to the *Moralia*: "I consider it quite improper to subject the words of the celestial oracle to the rules of Donatus" (7, 220–221). But learning in secular letters is nevertheless useful, when directed towards the correct interpretation of the Scripture. Indeed, it is solely to this end that the liberal arts are supposed to be studied (471, 2072–2074). God placed secular knowledge on earth so that we could ascend by steps, like those of Jacobs's ladder (cf. Cassiodorus, *Inst.* I, *praef.* 2) to the heights of Scripture (Irvine 1994: 192ff.).

Isidore of Seville warns against reading the figments of the poets (*figmenta poetarum*), with their empty tales which are merely entertaining. The eloquent words of the gentiles possess external splendour, while remaining devoid of moral wisdom (*Sent.* 3.13.1–3). God's speech has a hidden splendour of wisdom and truth, as contained in the cheapest vessels of words. The style of the Scriptures is humble so that men would not be led to faith by means of words but rather by means of spirit. God has made foolish the wisdom of this world, as St. Paul writes (I Cor. 1,19). Earthly wisdom, while serving to exalt man, is conducive to perilous arrogance. Thus the pretense of grammar must not be preferred to the humble style of the Scripture. But it is nevertheless better to be grammarians than heretics, Isidore declares, for the grammarian's teaching benefits the Christians when it has been put to a better use (*Sent.* 3.13.10–11). In spite of his harsh words, Isidore placed an immense importance on grammar as the foundation of the Liberal Arts. Thus Isidore's position concerning secular learning remains ambivalent as was customary throughout the Early Middle Ages.

Many traditional topics of Christian apology are repeated in the prologue to an anonymous Donatus-commentary known as *Anonymus ad Cuimnanum* from the 7th or 8th century. The author discusses the sacred origins of wisdom in Adam associating them with secular learning. According to the author of this text, all arts, sciences and languages were invented by Adam, who possessed the spirit of wisdom (2.42–44; 3.74–78). The division of the languages took place after the building of the Tower of Babel, and the number of languages amounts to that of the daughters of Adam, that is, seventy-two. The various arts, which were contained in Adam undivided (*originaliter, causaliter*), were later divided in different ways. These secular divisions are not, as he asserts, incongruent with those originally placed in Adam, which became manifest through the wisdom of Solomon, and which the Greek scholars claimed to be their own inventions later on (3.74–93) (see also Bischoff 1966–1967a: I, 282–288). The author proceeds to justify the study of the arts by quoting various statements by Christian authors. Augustine had recommended the use of the gold and silver spoils from Egypt to be used in the building of God's temple. Jerome praised the truth of the art of grammar in some people, and the

Saviour himself has said: "If you continue in my word, you shall know the truth, and the truth shall make you free' (John 8,31–32).

Grammar is true, as the anonymous author explains, when it pertains to "emendation of speech" (*emendatio loquendi*). Christian authors use this art in explaining the mysteries of the sacred Scriptures, whereas secular philosophers employ the same art to tell tales permeated throughout with lies. For knowledge is external as a vessel prepared for one who wants to drink. Consentius says: "The grammarian merely has to follow the rules of external speech (*vocum tantum regulas*)". Origen says: "Instead of words, we want to focus on things". Instead of blaming grammar, he shows a timorous attitude towards it so as not to commit an error in speaking. St. Jerome admits that Victorinus and Donatus were his teachers in Rome, and it is here that Donatus' authority is proven. What Augustine says does not destroy the rules of grammar: "Let us not be afraid of the rods of the grammarians in order to arrive at a fuller understanding of the Scripture". The prologue ends with a eulogy of the importance of grammar for various ecclesiastical functions: "Let not grammar be despised by anyone who wants wisdom, which cannot be gained without grammar" (17, 551–552).

## 6. Virgilius Maro Grammaticus

Grammar, wisdom and the Liberal Arts are important themes in the two most enigmatic 'grammars' of the Middle Ages – the *Epistolae* and *Epitomae* by Virgilius Maro Grammaticus. Wisdom, as Virgilius declares in the opening section of the *Epitomae*, is twofold: heavenly and earthly, that is, humble and sublime (*Epit.* I, 2.3–13). The former deals with the laws of the Hebrews (i. e. the Scripture), and the latter with the arts of philosophy (i. e. the Liberal Arts). It is customary, as Virgilius states, to start the process of learning from the lowest things and rise gradually to a higher level. Thus the humble earthly wisdom has to be put in the service of the celestial things, just like the human body has to be put in the service of the spirit. He declares that he has devoted a great deal of energy to the pursuit of the earthly kind of wisdom, but he nevertheless has not the courage to subject the celestial order to earthly wisdom (*Epit.* I, 2.14–4.25).

We have to do here with yet another defense of secular learning, but rather a puzzling one. References to such authorities as Jerome, Augustine and Gregory the Great are strikingly absent. The cast of Virgilius' dramatic exposition is quite different, consisting of Romans, Greeks, biblical characters and barbarians. Moreover, Virgilius seems to have had more sympathy with the humble, earthly kind of learning, that is the study of natural phenomena, than was generally current in monastic culture. As has recently been suggested by Law (1995), Virgilius has probably veiled in his works a challenge to the strict limits imposed on secular learning by several authoritative figures, each of which in turn had condemned the study of the secular arts for their own sake.

The two works of Donatus form the basis of Virgilius' two grammars and the author calls himself a grammarian. But these works leave their readers somewhat puzzled as to the author's actual intentions. While his contemporary grammarians exposed their doctrine in a dry matter-of-fact style, convinced of the usefulness of their teaching, Virgilius delights in linguistic oddities, which are hardly of educational value. He is extremely creative in his own use of language at a time when one exegete after the other recommended the strict observance of biblical authority (*auctoritas vetustatis*), and warned against *novitates vocum*. Modern scholars have regarded Virgilius' two works as a parody of the pompous style of the grammarians of the later Empire. Recently, the deeper religious intentions of these works have been unravelled in an exciting book by Law (1995). While admitting that parody plays an important part in Virgilius' writing, it is not, according to her, the solution to the problem of his intentions. In his grammars Virgilius, "by turns grammarian, etymologist, parodist, tease, heretic, pupil and guardian of the mysteries" (1995: 197), has veiled a plea for the recognition of plural routes to Wisdom. My presentation follows closely Law's novel analysis.

Virgilius is concerned with multiplicity in a number of phenomena. From biblical exegesis he was familiar with the idea that the sacred text bears several meanings simultaneously – a principle that Virgilius thought of as working in non-biblical texts too. Even the subject matter of grammar, latinity (*latinitas*), is multiple, as he claimed. He actually posited as many as twelve kinds of latinity, only one of which is in current use (*usitata*). He illustrates this multiplicity by means of the word "fire" (*ignis*), describing the various aspects in which it can be viewed.

Virgilius is a creative user of language, whose innovations occasionally correspond to the needs of contemporary religious discourse. It was Patristic commonplace to distinguish between the "physical eyes" (*oculi carnis*), clouded by impurity, and "the eyes of the mind" (*oculi mentis* or *cordis*), in terms of which it was possible to understand spiritual realities. Virgilius creates a new verb, *vidare*, to mean "seeing with the eyes of the mind", reserving the traditional Latin verb *videre* for the corporeal type of seeing (*Epit.* VIII, 18–19; Law 1995: 18). The corporeal/incorporeal distinction has also inspired a couple of interesting innovations concerning grammatical metalanguage. The biblical exegete, in search of a higher meaning of a biblical text, resorts to the distinction between the external, physical aspect of words and their various deeper meanings. Virgilius introduces a new term – *fonum* – to account for the physical aspect of the word, reserving the original word *verbum* for the semantic aspect. He also feels the need to differentiate his vocabulary concerning words signifying 'sentence'. Of the two current terms *oratio* and *sententia*, the former was polysemous, meaning, for instance, "speech, prayer, word", while the latter had distinctly semantic connotations. Associating *oratio* with *latinitas*, and *sententia* with the meaningful aspects of the utterance, Virgilius introduced two more words into this semantic field, both accounting for the formal aspect of the utterance: *testimonium* and *quassum* (Law 1995: 19–20).

"Virgilius's creative use of language finds its natural counterpart in his numerous allusions to Creation", as Law concludes. "Grammar, the key to the scriptures, parallels natural philosophy, the key to God's Creation" (1995: 107). Virgilius is certainly one of those grammarians who looked upon the grammatical text as a bearer of a deeper meaning, parallel to the sacred texts. But his method is less explicit than that of Smaragdus, for instance, who wrote about these issues without any obscurity. Virgilius intended to be far less educational, hiding his meaning in the alluring complexities of his texts. Virgilius is concerned about explaining his reasons for concealing mysteries in twisted language:

> My son, words are scrambled for three reasons: first, so that we may test the ingenuity of our students in searching out and identifying obscure points; secondly, for the ornamentation and reinforcement of speech, thirdly, lest mystical matters which should only be revealed to the initiated be discovered easily by base and stupid people (*Epit.* X, 128.3–9, translated by Law 1995: 83).

Virgilius' concern with multiplicity in various phenomena involved thinking that there were multiple ways to divine wisdom. Thus Virgilius was probably a dissident, whose ideas would not have appealed to Isidore of Seville and the author of *Anonymus ad Cuimnanum.* But the works of these authors have points in common. Among pre-Carolingian grammarians, the works of these three authors stand out as remarkably self-conscious in their efforts to relate grammar to a wider context of study, by introducing discussion of the Liberal Arts into the prologues of their works. This habit of reflecting upon the role of grammar in secular and religious education became commonplace in the Carolingian period, when Isidore's definition of grammar as the foundation of the Liberal Arts became the standard one. But Virgilius' idea of humble and sublime wisdom also found its way into at least one Carolingian grammar, the one by pseudo-Clemens Scottus.

## 7. The Carolingian Renaissance and the Seven Liberal Arts

Two famous documents are associated with the revival of learning under Charlemagne (→ Art. 74): *Admonitio generalis* (789) and *Epistola de litteris colendis* (ca. 790). In the preface to the *Admonitio*, which contains Charlemagne's proposals for the reform of the Church and its ministers and on the education of the people, it is stated that the ruler's fundamental responsibility is the salvation of the people. In order to be well educated in Christian doctrine, the clergy must have proper copies of the vital Christian texts available, as well as the level of literacy to study and correct them. "For often, although people wish to pray to God in the proper fashion, they yet pray improperly because of uncorrected books" (clause 72, translated by Brown). Both monasteries and cathedral churches should therefore set up schools to teach the psalms, musical notation, singing, computation and grammar (Brown 1994: 17, 19). Although the primary interest of this reform was to promote Christian learning, an important role in man's salvation was even assigned to the secular arts. The Seven Liberal Arts were the most usual form of secular learning, of which only the three arts of the trivium were studied in practice.

The role of the Arts in Christian education was discussed in Alcuin's treatise *De vera philosophia* which is heavily influenced by Augustine's *De ordine*. Augustine discusses the process of learning within the Neoplatonic framework of ascent, as applied to the study of the Seven Liberal Arts. The seven disciplines – described as steps (*gradus*) – represent rationality, in terms of which the mind is able to rise from the level of material perceptions to immaterial realities which are understood only by the mind (see e. g. Hadot 1984: 101–117). In *De vera philosophia*, these steps are associated with the Seven Pillars of the Temple of Wisdom (*Prov.* 9,1; cf. Cassiodorus, *Inst.* II, *praef.* 2), as well as the seven gifts of the Holy Spirit. Thus Alcuin assigns Augustine's argument a thoroughly Christian interpretation, the Liberal Arts reflecting the underlying structure of true knowledge, which can be gained through the study of Scripture (Marenbon 1994: 173).

Eriugena developed this theme in his various works claiming that the arts are innate in man, but knowledge of them has been clouded by the Fall. The study of the arts can help to restore man to his pristine state, and their cultivation constitutes the link with the Divine. According to him, no one enters heaven except through philosophy (Lutz 1939: 64; Mathon 1969: 58–64). In the *Periphyseon*, Eriugena elaborates on the role of the Liberal Arts within the Neoplatonic theory of recollection. While arguing that the Liberal Arts return to their particular principles, he notes that grammar and rhetoric are different from the other arts. They do not concern natural order, but rather the rules of the human voice which are determined not by nature, but by custom. They are counted among the arts because they are joined to dialectic, the mother of the arts, and flow from it like the branches of a river (Contreni 1981: 26–27). In maintaining an association between dialectic and grammar, Eriugena is not simply repeating Augustine's argument in *De ordine*, but following a more general Carolingian approach to the study of the arts.

In the 9th century, reflection upon the role of the Liberal Arts began to gain ground in prologues to grammatical works – a practice pioneered in a couple of pre-Carolingian grammars. In the prologue to his newly discovered commentary on Priscian's *Institutiones grammaticae*, Eriugena claims that the Seven Liberal Arts "shine with the light of wisdom", illuminating the minds of the wise with the knowledge of God just as corporeal light illuminates their bodies (27; 86). He further remarks that the arts are learned for their own sake (cf. *Annotationes* 86.25–26) – a view also echoed in the work of his compatriot Sedulius Scottus. Sedulius' position concerning the role of the arts remains ambivalent. On the one hand, *liberales* implies that "because of the truth of their rules and the speculation of wisdom, these arts are loved for their own sake" (58.3). On the other hand, they are *serviles* when their study aims at higher things, for instance, when somebody studies grammar and dialectic in order to gain spiritual knowledge (58.5–59.10) (see also Luhtala 1995: 119–123).

At the beginning of his *Ars*, Hilderic of Monte Cassino discusses the sacred origins of wisdom, which was bestowed on the first man in order that he should excel by his intellect all his fellow creatures except the angels. This wisdom, being subsequently lost in the Fall, could be restored to him in three ways: by divine inspiration, through the Scripture, and by means of reflection. The latter is the preoccupation of the philosophers, the representatives of secular wisdom, whose origin is in Aristotle, divine wisdom having been first revealed to Moses (*Ars* 11.1–12.2). (Pseudo-)Clemens Scottus discusses at great length the various divisions of knowledge raising the question of whether the teachers of the sacred texts can be called philosophers. Yes they can, it is claimed, for whosoever learns and teaches divine and human letters with all his heart, can be called a philosopher, i. e., a lover of wisdom. It is further asked, whether the traditional division of philosophy into natural, moral and logical can be found in Scripture. This is indeed the case, the author asserts; the books of *Genesis* and *Ecclesiastes* deal with natural philosophy; moral philosophy is present throughout Scripture and particularly in the *Proverbs*; logic is taught in the *Song of Solomon* and in the *Gospels* (*Ars* 5.1–19).

Thus the Carolingian grammarians show their increasing self-consciousness of the position of the art of grammar by reflecting upon its role within various schemes of secular learning. Many authors are content to quote the definition of grammar as the art of correct speaking and the foundation of the Liberal Arts in the footsteps of Isidore. The Carolingians did not hesitate to quote the definition in full, maintaining the ancient association between the study of grammar and classical literature (*enarratio poetarum*), which had been suppressed by Isidore (Fontaine 1983: 53). Hraban Maur, Alcuin's most influential pupil, went so far as to assert that the study of secular literature is useful insofar as the reader converts it to Christian usage (*PL* CVII, 395–404). There was certainly some degree of interest in pagan Roman texts among the learned elite in the Carolingian period, although their study continued to be condemned in accordance with the Patristic tradition. As a result of this renewed interest, a substantial part of the classical heritage was preserved and transmitted to medieval Europe (Brown 1994: 38–39).

The teaching of grammar was at the heart of the Carolingian reform, and its usefulness for the study and emendation of Christian texts was constantly asserted. However, Christian elements are mostly absent from the grammars compiled by Charlemagne's teachers, Alcuin, Peter of Pisa and Paul the Deacon. In his grammar, Alcuin was concerned about inspiring a philosophical inquiry into the foundations of grammatical doctrine (Luhtala 1993: 148ff., 1996: 284–286). However, this does not mean that the Christian topics ceased to figure on the grammarian's agenda. On the contrary, the early 9th century saw the emergence of the most Christian grammar compiled in the Early Middle Ages, the one by Smaragdus.

## 8. Smaragdus

Smaragdus' grammar combines many elements existing in the Christian polemic during the preceding centuries. However, his grammar is unique in at least two respects. His use of biblical examples is quite unparalleled in our sources, their number amounting to ca. 750 (Holtz 1986: xlvii). Moreover, his search for a deeper meaning in the grammatical doctrine itself surpassed the efforts of his predecessors such as Julian of Toledo and Virgilius, whose works were known to him. Adopting the principle that the facts of grammar are divinely inspired, thus reflecting a transcendental order of things, he has modified the contents of a number of grammatical categories.

The nature of the Trinity continued to exercise the minds of 9th-century scholars, who tackled the issue in strictly linguistic terms. Smaragdus, after he had become abbot of Saint-Mihiel-sur-Meuse (ca. 810), was invited to attend a conference at Aix-la-Chapelle as an expert on the famous debate known as *filioque*. The notion of the Trinity had preoccupied him even when he taught grammar in his earlier career. According to Smaragdus, the grammatical feature of number can be based on three things: on nature, on usage, and on mystery. It is based on nature, when we say, for instance, *sol* "sun", *luna* "moon" and *mundus* "world", because these things were created as unique things. Examples of singular number as established by usage are for instance *sanguis* "blood", *pulvis* "dust", *vinum* "wine". The singular number is based on mystery, when the Apostle says: *una fides, unum babtisma, unus spiritus, unum corpus, cor unum et anima una* "there is one faith, one baptism, one spirit, one body, one heart, one soul" (Eph. 4,4–5). "No other faith must be confessed, alongside ours, by which we believe and confess that God is one in Trinity", Smaragdus declares solemnly (*In partibus Donati* 65.11–66.33).

The discussion of the noun contains many elements capable of inspiring religious commentary, the noun being the part of speech most intimately associated with name-giving. While it was customary to distinguish between proper and common quality in the noun, the former being 'the name of one thing' and the latter 'the name of many things'. Smaragdus wants to introduce the distinction between Creator and the created things into this discussion. According to him, the true distinction within this category is into proper and common, so that the proper noun pertains solely to the Creator, as it is said in the Psalm that "he spake, and it was done; he commanded, and it stood fast" (Psalm 33,9). A created thing (*creatura*) is represented by a common noun (*appellativum*), as, according to the Bible, everything that has weight, number and measure has been created (Sap. 11,21). The traditional division of proper nouns into *nomen, praenomen, cognomen* and *agnomen* (exemplified by Publius Cornelius Scipio Africanus) is found to be outdated by Smaragdus. This was common practice, he admits, with the Romans, but is no longer observed in our days. Who introduces himself by saying: "My *cognomen* is ...?" he asks, particularly when this is not customary in the Gospel, where it is simply said: *Iohannes est nomen eius* "His name is John" (Luke 1,63). He quotes several examples of the plain use of personal names in the Scriptures.

Like Virgilius, Smaragdus is interested in polysemy, focussing on biblical examples in his discussion on homonyms and synonyms. For instance, *vas* has several meanings in the Bible. It stands for the sun (Sir. 43,2), the moon (Sir. 43,6,9), for cities (I Macc. 14,10), for people (Prov. 20,15), for swords (Ezech. 9,2) and for vases (I Ezra 1,10) (*In partibus Donati* 20.210−21.225).

## 9. Godescalc of Orbais

Godescalc of Orbais (ca. 803−867) never wrote a grammar, but his theological argumentation is heavily influenced by grammar. His name is associated with a famous controversy on the nature of the Trinity in the mid-9th century, in which his main opponent was Hincmar, Archbishop of Reims. The debate focussed on the expression *trina deitas*, involving the question of its plural versus singular reference. Godescalc is confident that grammatical features as such provide a guide to reality, and even to the mysteries of faith. Bishop Hincmar directed his attack on Godescalc in a work entitled *De una et non trina deitate*, in which he accused Godescalc not only of heresy but even of not knowing the grammar of Donatus (540D−541B). This accusation was hardly justified. In addition to the works of Donatus, Charisius, and Pompeius, he even knew Priscian's massive *Institutiones grammaticae* (Jolivet 1977: 24).

The debate had its origin in Bishop Hincmar's suggestion of replacing the expression *deitas trina* by *deitas sancta* in the opening phrase of a hymn *Te trina deitas unaque poscimus*. He thus wanted to avoid Arian heresy, which acknowledges three distinct deities. According to Godescalc, the fact that the expression *trina* is singular is proof enough of the orthodoxy of this phrase. Surely the Arians would wish to turn this phrase into the plural, he argues: *Vos tres deitates poscimus*. According to Godescalc, the formula *trina deitas* does perfect justice to the orthodox faith in revealing at once the unity and trinity of the Christian deity, the adjective *trina* pointing to trinity, and the singular number to the unity of God (22.2−4). Unless the grammarians want to be heretical, he declares, they had better admit that the expression *trina deitas* is in the singular, as is known by everyone who knows the rudiments of grammar (23.10−15).

Hincmar provides a counterargument which is similarly based on the knowledge of grammar. In claiming that singular number as such implies non-plurality of reference Godescalc shows ignorance of grammar. Donatus quotes examples of words which are singular in form (*sono*), and yet have a plural meaning (*intellectu*). But unlike Godescalc, Hincmar leans heavily on philosophical argumentation, namely on the difference between the ways in which the nouns *deitas* and *trinitas* signify. *Deitas* is what Hincmar calls a substantial notion, meaning, as he explains, roughly the same as nature, substance, divinity, and essence. But trinity is a relational notion. The nature of deity is not divided, and therefore it is not orthodox, according to Hincmar, to say *trina deitas*, as if introducing number to the description of deity. However, he accepts the expressions *trinus Deus* and *trina trinitas*, as referring to the persons of trinity (484C−D; 518A).

Elsewhere, too, Godescalc is preoccupied with the plural versus singular number of expressions referring to divinity. In such issues, as he points out, the Scripture must be our guide, and indeed he finds out that in every case the orthodox faith is confirmed by the biblical authority. In *Genesis*, the plural *faciamus* is used of the Creator, which is fully acceptable as the expression refers to all the three persons: *Faciamus hominem ad imaginem et similitudinem nostram* "Let us make man in our image, after our likeness" (Gen. 1,26) (31.14−17). However, the singulars *imaginem* et *similitudinem nostram* correctly imply the unity of the deity. The Sabellinian heresy posits the singular *faciam* here, while the Arians would probably wish to change *imaginem* and *similitudinem* into the plural. Godescalc also discusses the orthodox way of addressing the persons of the Trinity in prayer. While addressing only one person, we are supposed to use the singular, e. g. *tibi deo gratias*, whereas when we address all persons, we use the plural of the pronoun (*vobis*) but a singular number of God (*deo*): *vobis deo gratias* (31.9−14.23). But whosoever uses the plural *Vobis diis gratias* is either pagan or Arian (33.15−23).

In a longish tract dedicated to linguistic issues, *Opuscula de rebus grammaticis,* Godescalc raises a comparable question concerning the duality of human nature. Flesh and spirit are two distinct substances in every human being, representing the corporeal and incorporeal, visible and invisible, mortal and immortal aspects respectively. When they are distinguished by special names, the plural is used in the Scripture: *Haec invicem adversantur* "these are contrary the one to the other" (Gal. 5,17). But when they are referred to by a common name, the singular must be used in accordance with the blessed Athanasius and Augustine, and what is more, in accordance with the pronouncement of the Lord himself (cf. John 7,23). The external and the internal man are not two distinct human beings but one, for even 'body' as such is occasionally referred to as 'man', for instance: *quidam sepelientes hominem* "they were burying a man" (II Kings 13,21). Again, the 'spirit' as such is called 'man': *si exterior homo noster corrumpitur tamen interior renovatur* "though our outward man perish, yet the inward man is renewed day by day" (II Cor. 4,16, cf. also II Cor. 12,2). Now the outward man Paul rests in a grave in Rome, and the inward Paul is triumphant in heaven with the Lord, Godescalc argues, concluding that the outward or inward persons are not two distinct persons but make up one man. Similarly the Father, Son and Holy Spirit, though referred to in the plural by means of relative nouns, yet are referred to by the singular common nouns such as God, the Lord, the Spirit. There can be no kind of diversity, inequality or dissimilitude whatsoever in the persons of Trinity (468.8–469.4).

## 10. Eriugena

The name of the most eminent early medieval philosopher, John Scot Eriugena, is first mentioned in association with a Carolingian theological controversy concerning predestination, during which he was invited by Hincmar of Reims and Pardulus of Laon to write against the views of Godescalc of Orbais. In 849 Godescalc's teachings were condemned and he was forced to withdraw into a monastery. At the time Eriugena was engaged in teaching the Liberal Arts at the court of Charles the Bald. Among his works on the various arts, two commentaries have survived, one on Martianus Capella's *De Nuptiis Mercuri et Philologiae* and another one on Priscian's *Institutiones grammaticae*. He touched upon many linguistic issues in his theological works, the most prominent theme being the applicability of Aristotelian categories to Divine Essence.

In the prologue to the Homilies of St. John's Gospel, Eriugena discusses the nature of the verb "was" *(erat)*, claiming that it is without a temporal signification in the opening phrase of St. John's Gospel (226.3–11): "In the beginning was the Word". In this case the verb signifies merely the subsistence of something, without any temporal signification, and the biblical phrase amounts to saying: "the Son subsists in the Father". Elsewhere this verb does signify temporal motions in analogy with other verbs, as he points out. In his Priscian commentary he is preoccupied with the same question. He argues that the verb *sum* has a twofold signification; just like the Divine Nature, it expresses immutable essence which can be neither diminished nor augmented. But it also signifies the essence of particular creatures which are involved in action, hence indicating temporal motions (Barcelona, Archivo de la Corona de Aragón, ms. Ripoll 59, f. 283v–284r).

The most prominent linguistic theme in Eriugena's theological works is the applicability of Aristotle's categories to the Holy Trinity, which is discussed in the first book of the *Periphyseon*. The question concerning the inadequacy of the human language to express the eternal and unchangeable facts of Christian faith had first been raised by Clement of Alexandria, and this Patristic theme was repeated and reworked in Marius Victorinus' *Adversus Arium* and *Ad Candidum*, as well as in Augustine's *De Trinitate*. The issue continued to fascinate many early medieval authors, such as Claudianus Mamertus in the 6th century, and the anonymous authors of such early Carolingian works as *Dicta Albini* and *Dicta Candidi*. Augustine, who tackled the problem in terms of the Aristotelian categories, concluded that only the category of substance can be applied to God in a proper sense, while the others are applicable only metaphorically *(translative)*. Eriugena extends this ineffability even to the first category, substance, describing God as beyond human understanding to the extent of being indescribable in terms of any of the Aristotelian categories, even substance. Nothing can be said properly about God, since He surpasses every intellect and all sensible and intelligible meanings. I will discuss in some detail Eriugena's treatment of the categories of *agere* and *pati*, which has bearing on the question whether God can be said to love people and to have created all things.

In this dialogue acting and undergoing action are first related to the Aristotelian concept of motion, and then to the grammarian's active and passive verbs. "Tell me, pray, how does it seem to you? Are not moving and being moved an acting and suffering?". This is indeed said to be the case. "That these verbs and their like are actives and passives no one instructed in the Liberal Arts is ignorant of". (176.22–27; Sheldon-Williams' translation will be used throughout the following account). "If then these verbs, whether they are active or passive in meaning, are no longer properly predicated of God, but metaphorically, and if nothing that is predicated metaphorically is said of Him in very truth but after a certain manner, then in very truth God neither acts nor is acted upon, neither moves nor is moved, neither loves nor is loved", as he argues.

Eriugena then repeats the commonplace about God's condescending to speak to man in terms of metaphors in order to meet man on his own terms.

It is not to be believed that the Holy Scripture is a book which always uses verbs and nouns in their proper sense when it teaches us about the Divine Nature, but it employs certain allegories and transfers in various ways the meanings of the verbs or nouns out of condescension towards our weakness and to encourage by uncomplicated doctrine our senses which are still untrained and childish (189.10–19). If God is called Love by metaphor although He is More-than-love and surpasses all love, why should He not in the same way be said to love although He surpasses every motion of loving (197.17–20).

He argues that while action is motion, and motion has a beginning and an end, God is without beginning, because nothing precedes Him or makes Him to be; nor does He have an end because He is infinite (204.6–10). The question is further raised whether God existed before he created all things (208.3). No, he did not, for if He did, the making of all things would be an accident to Him, and if the making of all things were an accident to Him, it would mean that motion and time were in Him. But God's making is co-essential and co-eternal. Are God and His making, that is, His action, two things, or one simple and indivisible thing? (208.10–11). They are said to be one: for God does not admit number in Himself, since He alone is innumerable and Number without number and the Cause of all numbers which surpasses every number (208.12–14). So when we hear that God makes all things we ought to understand nothing else than that God is in all things, that is, that He is the Essence of all things (208.18–20). Do you see, then, how true reason completely excludes the category of making from the Divine Nature, so as to conclude that nothing else is signified by them but the Divine Essence and More-than-essence itself, which is simple and immutable and cannot be grasped by any intellect or signification? For instance: when we hear that God wills and loves or desires, sees, hears, and the other verbs which can be predicated of Him, we should simply understand that we are being told of His ineffable Essence and Power in terms which are adapted to our nature, lest the true and holy Christian religion should be so silent about the Creator of all things that it dare not say anything for the instruction of simple minds (208.35–210.4).

## 11. The St. Gall Tractate: An interdisciplinary approach

Godescalc and Eriugena are prime examples of the manner in which the Carolingian scholars engaged in the study of the various arts and theology, frequently transgressing the traditional disciplinary boundaries. There was thus a lively interaction between the various disciplines. While grammar offered its tools of analysis for Godescalc's theological argumentation, dialectical method was applied to theology and grammar by Eriugena. I will conclude by introducing a poorly known text from St. Gall, dating from the late 9th or 10th century, entitled *How the Seven Circumstances of Things are to be ordered in Reading.* This treatise attests to the penetration of all the arts of the trivium into linguistic description, the highly advanced tools of analysis being applied to the very central concepts of Christian faith such as the creed and the beginning of St. John's Gospel.

In this pedagogical text, which is designed to help pupils in construing continuous periodical style, pride of place is given to the rhetorician's argumentative loci, the so-called Seven Circumstances ('who', 'what', 'where', 'when', 'why', 'how', and 'by what means'), which are thus put into a completely new usage. They serve to identify the various semantic constituents of the sentence. The main preoccupation of the author is with the ordering of the text so as to make it more accessible to readers, the basic tenet being the so-called natural order. According to the natural word order, adopted from Priscian's grammar, and based ultimately on philosophical doctrine, the noun must be placed before the verb. These are the two basic constituents of the sentence, which are identified with the rhetorician's first two circumstances, 'who' and 'what', and the dialectician's subject and predicate. The author is quick to point out that the biblical texts frequently exhibit divergencies from this natural Subject-Verb word order, which is based on logic and ontology. "In Scripture we find with no difference in meaning *Dominus dixit* and *Dixit dominus* 'The Lord spoke' " (translated by Grotans 1995: 46–47). The inverted word order involves no difference in meaning in this case, as the author remarks, but examples can be found where a careful grammatical analysis is crucial for an orthodox interpretation of a biblical passage. For "it confuses readers considerably to not know these things [i. e. concerning natural word order], to the point that they begin to be heretical when they follow the inverted word order in the Gospel, where it is said: 'And the word was God' (*Et deus erat verbum*)". They ought to recognize the subject and predicate, and say, according to a natural word order: *Et verbum deus erat.* It is not permitted by Reason (*ratio*) to set God (*deus*) in first place as the subject and to predicate of him the "word" (*verbum*). The case is similar in the creed where we confess our faith by saying "God the father, God the son, God the Holy Spirit" (*Ita deus pater, deus filius, deus spiritus sanctus*). The formula must be analyzed in terms of three propositions as predicated subsequently from the three persons as subjects, in the following manner: "The father is God; the son is God; the Holy Spirit is God" (*Ita pater deus est, ita filius deus est, ita spiritus sanctus deus est*) (Grotans 1995: 46–49).

The author shows a remarkable skill in analyzing Latin construction. Being fully versed in the methods of the inherited disciplines, he does not hesitate to rely upon his own linguistic observations. This is the case when he notes that a writer can actually organize the structure of a text at his own will, placing whichever of the seven circumstances first and so forth. The major part of this long text is dedicated to providing evidence of a whole variety of word orders manifest in predominantly Christian texts. The natural word order nevertheless remains a convenient method in classroom teaching.

## 12. Bibliography

### 12.1. Primary sources


Alcuin, *De vera philosophia. PL* CI, 854–902.

Anonymus ad Cuimnanum, *Expositio Latinitatis.* Ed. by Bernhard Bischoff & Bengt Löfstedt. *CCSL* CXXXIII D. Turnhout: Brepols, 1992.

Asporius/Asper, *Ars. GL* VIII, 39–61.

Augustine, *De doct. christ.* = Augustinus, *De doctrina christiana.* Ed. by Joseph Martin. *CCSL* XXXII. Turnhout: Brepols, 1962.

Augustine, *De mag.* = Augustinus, *De magistro.* Ed. by K.-D. Daur. *CCSL* XXIX. Turnhout: Brepols, 1970.

Augustine, *De ord.* = Augustinus, *De ordine.* Ed. by W. M. Green. *CCSL* XXIX. Turnhout: Brepols, 1970.

Augustine, *Sol.* = Augustinus, *Soliloquia. PL* XXXII, 869–904.

Bede, *De schematibus et tropis.* Ed. by C. B. Kendall. *CCSL* CXXIII A. Turnhout: Brepols, 1975.

Boniface, *Ars* = *Bonifatii (Vinfreth), Ars grammatica.* Ed. by George John Gebauer & Bengt Löfstedt. *CCSL* CXXXIII B. Turnhout: Brepols, 1980.

Cassiodorus, *Inst.* = Cassiodorus, *Institutiones.* Ed. by R. A. B. Mynors. Oxford: Clarendon Press, 1937.

*CCCM/SL* = *Corpus christianorum continuatio medievalis/series latina.* Turnhout: Brepols.

Clemens Scottus, *Ars* = *Clementis Ars grammatica.* Ed. by J. Tolkiehn. Leipzig: Dieterich'sche Verlagsbuchhandlung, 1928.

Diomedes, *Ars* = Diomedes, *Ars grammatica. GL* I, 299–529.

Donatus, *Ars* = Donatus, *Ars minor* and *Ars maior.* Ed. by Holtz, 1981: 585–674.

*GL* = *Grammatici latini.* Ed. by Heinrich Keil. 8 vols. Leipzig: Teubner, 1857–80.

Godescalc, *Œuvres* = Godescalc of Orbais, *Œuvres théologiques et grammaticales de Godescalc d'Orbais.* Ed. by D. C. Lambot. (= *Spicilegium Sacrum Lovaniense*, 20.). Louvain: Université Catholique, 1945.

Gregory the Great, *Moralia in Job.* Ed. by M. Adriaen. 3 vols. *CCSL* CXLIII–CXLIIIB. Turnhout: Brepols, 1979–85.

–. *In canticum canticorum* and *In librum primum regum.* Ed. by P. Verbraken. *CCSL* CXLIV. Turnhout: Brepols, 1963.

Hilderic of Monte Cassino, *Ars grammatica* (excerpts). Ed. by Anselmo Lentini. Montecassino, 1975.

Hincmar of Reims, *De una et non trina deitate* III. *PL* CXXV, 473–620.

Hraban Maur, *De clericorum institutionibus libri tres. PL* CVII, 293–420.

Isidore of Seville, *Et.* = Isidorus, *Etymologiae.* Ed. by W. M. Lindsay. Oxford: Oxford Univ. Press, 1911.

–. *Sent.* = Isidorus, *Sententiae. PL* LXXXIII, 537–738.

John Scottus (Eriugena), *Periphyseon I–III.* Ed. by I. P. Sheldon-Williams. Dublin: Institute for Advanced Studies, 1968–81.

–. *Homélie sur le Prologue de Jean.* Ed. by Edouard Jeaneau. (= *Sources Chrétiennes*, 151.) Paris: Editions du Cerf, 1969.

–. *Iohannis Scotti Annotationes in Martianum.* Ed. by Cora Lutz. Cambridge, Mass.: Mediaeval Academy of America, 1939.

John Scottus (Eriugena)?, *Glosa in Priscianum.* Barcelona, Archivo de la Corona de Aragón, ms. Ripoll 59,ff. 257v–288v. [See Dutton & Luhtala 1994.]

Julian of Toledo, *Ars* = *Ars Iuliani Toletani episcopi.* Ed. by M. A. H. Maestre Yenes. Toledo: Instituto Provincial de Investigaciones y Estudios Toledanos, 1973.

Murethach, *In Donati Artem maiorem.* Ed. by Louis Holtz. *CCCM* XL. Turnhout: Brepols, 1977.

*PL* = *Patrologiae (latinae) cursus completus.* 221 vols. Paris: J.-P. Migne 1844–64.

Priscian, *Institutiones grammaticae. GL* II, 1–597; III, 1–377.

Sedulius Scottus, *In Donati Artem maiorem.* Ed. by Bengt Löfstedt. (= *Grammatici hibernici carolini aevi.* Pars III,1–2). *CCCM* LX B–C. Turnhout: Brepols, 1977.

Smaragdus, *Liber in partibus Donati.* Ed. by Bengt Löfstedt, Louis Holtz & Adele Kibre. *CCCM* LXVIII. Turnhout: Brepols, 1986.

*The St. Gall Tractate: A medieval guide to rhetorical syntax.* Ed. by Anna A. Grotans & David W. Porter. Columbia: Camden House, 1995.

Tatwine, *Ars* = *Ars Tatuini de partibus orationis.* Ed. by Maria de Marco & F. Glorie. *CCSL* CXXXIII. Turnhout: Brepols, 1968.

Virgilius Maro Grammaticus, *Epitomi ed Epistole.* Ed. by Giovanni Polara. Naples: Liguori, 1979.

## 12.2. Secondary sources

Bischoff, Bernhard. 1966–67a. "Eine verschollene Einteilung der Wissenschaften". *Mittelalterliche Studien* 1.273–288.

–. 1966–67b. "Wendepunkte in der Geschichte der lateinischen Exegese im Frühmittelalter". *Mittelalterliche Studien* 1.205–272.

Brown, Giles. 1994. "Introduction: The Carolingian Renaissance". *Carolingian Culture: Emulation and Innovation* ed. by Rosamond McKitterick, 1–51. Cambridge: Cambridge Univ. Press.

Contreni, John. 1981. "John Scottus, Martin Hiberniensis, the Liberal Arts, and Teaching". *Insular Latin Studies* ed. by Michael Herren, 23–44. Toronto: Pontifical Institute of Mediaeval Studies.

Dutton, Paul Edward & Anneli Luhtala. 1994. "Eriugena in Priscianum". *Mediaeval Studies* 56.151–161.

Evans, G. R. 1984. *The Language and Logic of the Bible: The earlier Middle Ages.* Cambridge: Cambridge Univ. Press.

Fontaine, Jacques. 1983. *Isidore de Séville et la culture classique dans l'Espagne wisigothique.* Vol. I. 2nd ed. Paris: Etudes Augustiniennes.

Hadot, Ilsetraut. 1984. *Arts libéraux et philosophie dans la pensée antique.* Paris: Etudes Augustiniennes.

Holtz, Louis. 1977. Introduction to edition of Murethac, *In Donati Artem Maiorem.*

–. 1981. *Donat et la tradition de l'enseignement grammatical: Etude sur l'Ars* Donati *et sa diffusion (IVe–IXe siècle) et édition critique.* Paris: CNRS.

–. 1986. Introduction to edition of Smaragdus, *Liber in partibus Donati.*

Irvine, Martin. 1994. *The Making of Textual Culture: 'Grammatica' and literary theory, 350–1100.* Cambridge: Cambridge Univ. Press.

Jolivet, Jean. 1977. *Godescalc d'Orbais et la trinité.* Paris: J. Vrin.

Law, Vivien. 1982. *The Insular Latin Grammarians.* Woodbridge: Boydell.

–. 1994. "The Study of Grammar". *Carolingian Culture: Emulation and innovation* ed. by Rosamond McKitterick, 88–110. Cambridge: Cambridge Univ. Press.

–. 1995. *Wisdom, Authority and Grammar in the Seventh Century: Decoding Virgilius Maro Grammaticus.* Cambridge: Cambridge Univ. Press.

–. 1997. "Linguistics in the earlier Middle Ages: The Insular and Carolingian grammarians". *Grammar and Grammarians in the Early Middle Ages* ed. by Vivien Law, 70–90. London & New York: Longman (Originally published in *Transactions of the Philological Society* 83 [1985] 171–193.)

Luhtala, Anneli. 1993. "Syntax and Dialectic in Carolingian Commentaries on Priscian's *Institutiones grammaticae*" *Historiographia Linguistica* 20.151–197.

–. 1995. "On the Grammarian's Self-image in the Early Middle Ages". *History of Linguistics 1993* ed. by Kurt R. Jankowsky, 115–126. Amsterdam & Philadelphia: Benjamins.

–. 1996. "Grammar and Dialectic: A topical issue in the ninth century". *Johannes Scottus Eriugena.*

*The Bible and Hermeneutics. Proceedings of the Ninth International Colloquium of the Society for the Promotion of Eriugenian Studies* ed. by Gerd van Riel, Carlos Steel & James McEvoy, 279–301. Leuven: Leuven Univ. Press.

Marenbon, John. 1994. "Carolingian Thought". *Carolingian Culture: Emulation and innovation* ed. by Rosamond McKitterick, 171–193. Cambridge: Cambridge Univ. Press.

Mathon, Gérard. 1969. "Les formes et la signification de la pédagogie des arts libéraux au milieu du IXe siècle: L'enseignement palatin de Jean Scot Erigène". *Arts Libéraux et philosophie au Moyen Age. Actes du quatrième congrès international de philosophie médiévale*, 47–64. Paris: J. Vrin & Montréal: Institut d'Etudes Médiévales.

McNally, R. E. 1958. "The 'tres linguae sacrae' in early Irish Bible Exegesis". *Theological studies* 19.395–403.

Schindel, Ulrich. 1975. *Die lateinischen Figurenlehren des 5. bis 7. Jahrhunderts und Donats Vergilkommentar.* Göttingen: Vandenhoeck & Ruprecht.

Thurot, Charles. 1868. *Extraits de divers manuscrits latins pour servir à l'histoire des doctrines grammaticales au moyen âge.* Paris: Bibliothèque Nationale.

Vineis, Edoardo. 1988. "Grammatica e filosofia del linguaggio in Alcuino". *Studi e Saggi Linguistici* 28.403–429.

*Anneli Luhtala, Helsinki (Finland)*

# 74. Alcuin et la redécouverte de Priscien à l'époque carolingienne

1. La réception de l'œuvre de priscien
2. La tradition insulaire
3. Alcuin et la réforme carolingienne
4. L'héritage d'Alcuin
5. Bibliographie

## 1. La réception de l'œuvre de Priscien

L'œuvre monumentale de Priscien est née à Constantinople dans le premier quart du VIe siècle, à une époque où à Rome les élites, pourtant favorables à la royauté ostrogothique, militaient, sous la conduite de Boèce et de Symmaque, en faveur d'un renouveau de l'hellénisme dans la péninsule italique. Priscien est au service de cette cause, qui, du moins à l'origine, était dépourvue chez ses promoteurs d'arrière-pensées politiques: c'est ainsi que les *Institutions grammaticales* ont été composées sur la demande du consul et patrice Julianus auxquelles elles sont dédiées. De même Priscien offre à Symmaque, au cours d'un séjour de celui-ci dans la capitale impériale, les trois opuscules qu'il lui avait commandés et qui présentent, en trois disciplines, signes numériques, métrique, rhétorique, un enseignement rénové et fondé sur l'exemple des Grecs (sur les liens entre Priscien et l'aristocratie romaine du temps, voir Courcelle 1948: 307–312).

Du renouvellement qu'il apportait, Priscien avait parfaitement conscience, c'est du moins l'impression que donne la lecture de ses préfaces. À l'entendre, le zèle des grammairiens latins d'autrefois pour marcher sur les traces de leurs modèles grecs a été si grand qu'ils ont même imité leurs erreurs (*Institutions* II, 1, 4, 2, 10). En adaptant à la grammaire latine les principes établis au IIe siècle par Hérodien et Apollonius, Priscien se propose donc de corriger ces erreurs. Et pour la rhétorique, le modèle choisi par lui est le traité d'Hermogène, ce qui tranchait avec la pédagogie du temps.

Cette œuvre qui, en ses divers aspects, exploite des sources plus récentes s'adresse autant aux élèves hellénophones ou bilingues qui suivaient les cours de Priscien à Constantinople qu'à ses correspondants de l'aristocratie romaine et à leur clientèle. Mais vis à vis des maîtres qui enseignaient la grammaire à Rome ou en Italie, elle avait un côté provocateur et même polémique.

Ces circonstances dans leur ensemble ne sont pas étrangères à la fortune de l'œuvre et à l'histoire singulière de sa tradition. La rupture entre l'aristocratie romaine et le royaume ostrogothique, la guerre acharnée qui s'en suivit entre Byzance et les Goths étaient peu propices à la diffusion des conceptions nouvelles que contenait l'œuvre de Priscien. Elle arrivait à l'époque même où s'effondrait en Occident le système scolaire traditionnel, fondé sur le cycle de la grammaire et de la rhétorique: car, si Byzance l'avait finalement emporté sur les Goths, la guerre était passée par là, balayant à la fois les hommes et leurs rêves de réformes, maîtres comme élèves, et en somme annihilant dans une Italie exsangue toute véritable vie intellectuelle.

Au lendemain de la guerre ostrogothique, le programme de Boèce et de Symmaque n'était plus de saison: l'époque n'était pas faite pour les renouvellements, mais pour la conservation d'un héritage ressenti à juste titre comme menacé. Voilà pourquoi l'œuvre grammaticale de Priscien, la plus importante que nous ait livrée le monde romain, a mis du temps à s'imposer et n'a d'abord connu qu'une diffusion limitée, et cela en raison même du souffle nouveau qu'elle apportait.

Les seules attestations de son existence dans l'Italie du VI<sup>e</sup> siècle sont fournies par Cassiodore. Et encore est-ce tardivement que le fondateur de Vivarium réussit à se procurer le texte des *Institutions grammaticales*. Dans le chapitre liminaire (*De grammatica*) du livre des *Institutions humaines*, Cassiodore prend Priscien pour un auteur grec (Courcelle 1948: 326sq.), bévue corrigée dans la version définitive parce qu'entre temps Cassiodore s'était procuré le grand ouvrage de Priscien et l'avait utilisé dans son *De orthographia*. Mais la lecture même qu'il en fait montre qu'il n'a pas attaché une importance particulière aux *Institutions grammaticales* dont il n'a recueilli que quelques données orthographiques éparses. Le chapitre XII du *De orthographia* où Cassiodore regroupe ces emprunts est intitulé: *Ex Prisciano grammatico, qui nostro tempore Constantinopoli doctor fuit de libro primo ipsius ista collecta sunt.* S'agissant d'orthographe, il était normal que Cassiodore puisât dans le chapitre *De littera* de Priscien. Mais peut-être aussi n'a-t-il pas dépassé le premier ou à la rigueur le second livre des Institutions grammaticales (*GL* VII, 207–209).

Et comme on sait, ce n'est pas dans les traités de Priscien que Cassiodore conseille à ses moines de Vivarium d'apprendre la grammaire, mais dans ceux de Donat et de ses commentateurs. Effaçant du même coup, par une sorte de réaction, tout souvenir de l'effervescence intellectuelle qui avait marqué le règne de Théodoric, Cassiodore prône les bons vieux auteurs qu'il avait lui-même fréquentés au temps de ses études romaines. L'enseignement de la grammaire, là où il se maintient dans l'occident du Haut Moyen Age, gardera cette forme traditionnelle pendant plus de deux siècles encore. Priscien lui-même avait du reste dû composer avec la tradition de la grammaire occidentale. Il se réfère plusieurs fois à Donat (cf. Holtz 1981: 242–244) et aux autres auteurs anciens, et même consent, en écrivant l'*Institutio de nomine pronomine et uerbo*, à se mettre à la portée du niveau élémentaire. C'est par le biais de cette 'petite institution', composée postérieurement aux *Institutions grammaticales*, que l'enseignement du maître de Constantinople commencera à se répandre dans le Haut Moyen Age.

## 2. La tradition insulaire

Mais le cas de Cassiodore montre que dès la seconde moitié du VI<sup>e</sup> siècle il existait en Italie au moins un manuscrit des *Institutions grammaticales*. Car c'est bien à Vivarium et non lors de son long séjour à Constantinople de 541 à 550 que Cassiodore en prit connaissance. Les dédicataires romains des œuvres de Priscien avaient sans doute reçu de leur côté un exemplaire des ouvrages qui leur étaient dédicacés. Et pourtant, pour entendre à nouveau parler de Priscien, il faudra attendre la fin du VII<sup>e</sup> siècle et l'œuvre d'Aldhelm de Malmesbury. A notre connaissance, il n'y a pas de trace de Priscien dans l'Espagne du VII<sup>e</sup> siècle, ni dans la Gaule mérovingienne.

Dans son traité intitulé *De metris et enigmatibus et pedum regulis*, Aldhelm, faisant l'étude d'un certain nombre de types métriques, recherche la caution des grammairiens sur la quantité de telle ou telle syllabe. Nous sommes donc en mesure de reconstituer en partie un rayon de sa bibliothèque. Il a en mains les *Institutions grammaticales*, du moins les seize premiers livres, et sans doute aussi l'*Institutio de nomine et pronomine et uerbo*. Il se réfère nommément à Priscien dont il cite quelques uns des livres (*De metris* 181.6: le livre III; *De metris* 156.5: le livre VI), ce qui laisse supposer que son exemplaire était antique et reproduisait la numérotation des livres par des titres courants. Sa lecture est fort attentive, mais ne s'attache qu'à des détails: comme Cassiodore, il ne recherche dans l'œuvre de Priscien que des attestations ponctuelles, sans prendre en compte l'orientation générale de l'œuvre ni les nouveautés qu'elle apporte.

C'est bien, croyons-nous, dans les Iles Britanniques, que Priscien commença pour la première fois en Occident à être lu et utilisé à des fins scolaires. Plusieurs ouvrages grammaticaux du VIII<sup>e</sup> siècle utilisent la petite institution sans en nommer l'auteur: l'*Anonymus ad Cuimnanum*, la grammaire de Tatwine, la grammaire de Boniface organisent l'étude des déclinaisons nominales sur le schéma de l'opuscule de Priscien. Quand on essaie de démêler les écheveaux de la tradition, on est gêné à la fois par la difficulté d'assigner à telle ou telle œuvre une date précise, et par le problème que posent les échanges constants, dès cette haute époque, entre les Iles Britanniques et les centres continentaux. En ce qui concerne les Anglo-Saxons, la tradition Aldhelm – Tatwine – Boniface est la plus claire. Elle atteste que dans les écoles anglo-saxonnes du VIIIe siècle la doctrine de Priscien sur les déclinaisons, qui classe celles-ci selon la voyelle terminale du génétif singulier, s'est imposée.

Les traités hibernolatins, l'*Ars Ambrosiana*, l'*Anonymus ad Cuimnanum*, et l'*Ars Bernensis* (ce traité grammatical porte le nom de la bibliothèque où est conservé le manuscrit principal qui le transmet, originaire de Fleury; cf. Holtz 1994) sont bien moins datés et renvoient l'image d'un échange régulier entre Bobbio et l'Irlande ou la Northumbrie. Il semble avéré aujourd'hui qu'ils ont été écrits tous les trois à Bobbio, puisqu'ils sont les seuls à citer des textes qui ne nous ont été transmis que par Bobbio. Des trois traités, c'est l'*Ars Ambrosiana*, dont il faut placer la rédaction autour de l'an 700, qui est le plus ancien (voir Loefstedt 1980: 301sq.). Il est le seul à ne pas utiliser Priscien directement, sans pour autant ignorer totalement le grammairien de Constantinople. Si Cuimnanus, le dédicataire du second traité, est bien le personnage qui termine sa vie comme abbé de Bobbio et meurt à l'âge de 94 ans sous le règne de Luitprand, ce commentaire ample et riche de l'*Ars maior* de Donat doit avoir été composé non pas vers la fin du VIIe siècle, comme la chose était plausible, mais autour des années 730 (voir la préface de l'éditeur, p. xxii). Quant à l'*Ars Bernensis*, ce traité est sans doute le plus récent, mais ne présente aucune trace d'une influence quelconque en provenance de la cour franque, et nous semble donc antérieur aux années 780 (voir Holtz 1995).

Au VIIIe siècle donc les maîtres de grammaire insulaires découvrent la doctrine et l'œuvre de Priscien, sans doute par des voies différentes. On sait d'où les Anglo-Saxons du Haut Moyen Age se procurent les livres: en général, ils puisent directement dans les bibliothèques romaines. Quant à la tradition hibernolatine, elle est en relations étroites avec le centre de Bobbio, fondation de saint Colomban, dont les livres conservés attestent que des maîtres irlandais s'y occupaient de grammaire dès la fin du VIIe siècle (le manuscrit unique de l'*Anonymus ad Cuimnanum* est originaire de Northumbrie et porte un traité rédigé à Bobbio). Il est vraisemblable que les deux traditions, anglo-saxonne et irlandaise, se sont inextricablement mêlées. Aldhelm le premier reconnaît sa dette envers ses maîtres irlandais, ce qui ne signifie pas forcément qu'il a reçu d'eux le texte de Priscien.

Pourtant, même si Priscien est entré en scène au cours du VIIIe siècle parmi les grammairiens latins de l'Antiquité utilisés dans les écoles insulaires, ce n'est pas pour autant que son œuvre immense s'est trouvée du jour au lendemain assimilée. Certes, la petite institution n'est pas, dès cette époque, le seul texte à être mis à profit. Et du reste ce traité, que Priscien avait écrit à l'intention des débutants, renvoie lui-même aux *Institutions grammaticales*. Dans l'*Ars* de Tatwine par exemple, plusieurs passages supposent l'utilisation des chapitres consacrés dans le grand ouvrage aux terminaisons nominales.

Tout cela s'explique facilement par le profil de la tradition de Priscien: l'œuvre n'est pas parvenue en Occident par petits morceaux, mais organisée selon un corpus dont la tradition ultérieure nous renvoie l'image: deux tomes contenant l'un les seize premiers livres des *Institutions grammaticales*, l'autre les livres XVII et XVIII suivis des opuscules, dont l'*Institutio de nomine, et pronomine et uerbo* (sur l'inventaire des manuscrits voir Gibson 1972; Passalacqua 1978; Ballaira 1982; Jeudy 1982, 1984a, 1984b). Certes, à l'époque carolingienne, on voit assez souvent ce traité élémentaire transmis à part, détaché du corpus des œuvres de Priscien, et rapproché des grammaires de Donat. Mais cette tradition-là ne peut avoir été qu'une tradition secondaire, qui s'explique par un long usage pédagogique faisant du traité élémentaire de Priscien un complément nécessaire de la grammaire de Donat. Le rapport des deux traités de Priscien, le grand et le petit, est alors fixé de façon claire dans la terminologie: la petite institution est le *Priscianus minor*, les *Institutions grammaticales* le *Priscianus maior*. Plus tard, à parir du XIe siècle, quand l'Occident aura pleinement reconnu l'originalité des livres XVII et XVIII des *Institutions grammaticales*, qui alors seront volontiers copiés dans des manuscrits séparés, la mention *Priscianus maior* désignera les livres I à XVI et *Priscianus minor* les seuls livres XVII et XVIII.

## 3. Alcuin et la réforme carolingienne

Telle était la situation dans le monde insulaire à la veille de la réforme carolingienne et de l'arrivée d'Alcuin à la cour du roi des Francs. Comme on le voit, la renommée de Priscien, son utilisation à des fins pédagogiques, la perception aussi d'une certaine spécificité par rapport à l'enseignement traditionnel symbolisé par Donat – par exemple en ce qui concerne le pronom, dont la définition par Priscien est beaucoup plus étroite que dans la théorie traditionnelle – sont des faits acquis dès le VIII^e^ siècle outre Manche.

Alcuin avait eu la chance de faire ses études dans un centre particulièrement riche, puisque ce centre avait hérité de la bibliothèque de Bède. Cette bibliothèque d'York, Alcuin lui-même, dans son poème sur les évêques, les rois, les Saints d'York, nous donne une idée de son contenu. Parmi les auteurs de la culture classique qu'elle s'enorgueillit de réunir, Alcuin cite les grammairiens:

*Artis gramaticae uel quid scripsere magistri*
*Quid Probus atque Focas, Donatus Priscianusue*
*Servius, Euticius, Pompeius, Cominianus.*
*Inuenies alios perplures, lector, ibidem*
*Egregios studiis, arte et sermone magistros.*
(Les écrits laissés par les maîtres de la discipline grammaticale, ceux de Probus et de Phocas, de Donat et Priscien, de Servius, d'Eutycius [= Eutychès], de Pompée, de Cominianus [= de Charisius]. Tu en trouveras là bien d'autres encore, lecteur, de ces maîtres éminents par leurs études, leur science et leur style; v. 1555–1559).

Dans cette énumération non limitative, l'ordre est poétique plus que chronologique. On remarque particulièrement la place faite à Priscien: Donat et Priscien semblent désormais inséparables. Ils sont à mon avis, dans l'esprit d'Alcuin écrivant ces vers, liés moins par le voisinage dans les manuscrits, que par leur fonction d'auteurs fondamentaux de la science grammaticale. Cela signifie une remise en cause du canon traditionnel: Donat n'existe désormais que complété par Priscien. Le fait est acquis dans l'esprit d'Alcuin antérieurement à son entrée à la Cour, car ce poème, en dépit des réserves de son dernier éditeur, ne s'adresse qu'à ses élèves d'York et reflète la culture et la pédagogie de l'école d'York: c'est sans doute l'un des seuls écrits de Priscien apportés par lui sur le continent. Mais il apportait aussi des livres, et spécialement des livres de sa bibliothèque d'York.

La bibliothèque de la Cour palatine s'enrichit de livres en provenance de tout l'Occident, et tout particulièrement en provenance des Iles Britanniques. Alcuin a dû emporter avec lui son Priscien, un Priscien qu'il avait lu jusqu'au bout. Car s'il vient à la Cour, c'est officiellement avec le titre de *magister*, qui lui sera toujours reconnu par le Roi et par les Grands. Dans la correspondance d'Alcuin on trouve, par exemple, l'adresse de la lettre 144 (*Epistulae* p. 228): *Carolus [...] dilectissimo magistro*, celle de la lettre 195 envoyée par la princesse Gisèle, fille de Charles (ibid. p. 323): *Venerando patri nobisque cum summo honore amplectando Albino magistro* (cf. lettre 247, ibid., p. 399) ou encore la dédicace de Joseph Scot à Alcuin: *Care magister aue, Dominus te saluet ubique* (ibid., p. 483). Certes, il sera bien plus qu'un simple professeur, mais aussi un conseiller, un maître spirituel, un secrétaire, un rédacteur, un homme que sa science rend souvent providentiel, un ami. Mais à l'époque, le premier rôle d'un *magister* est d'enseigner les arts libéraux, et d'abord la grammaire. Ce rôle est également tenu par Pierre de Pise et par Paul Diacre, plus tard par Clément Scot.

Enseigner, cela signifie transmettre des connaissances acquises, et trouver la bonne méthode pour que le message soit adapté à l'auditoire du moment. Le maître commente les livres de référence traditionnels, il en écrit de nouveaux, susceptibles de mieux répondre à la situation de ses élèves. Le rapport de maître à élève crée un lien pour toujours. Les écrits pédagogiques d'Alcuin reflètent cette activité, et ce souci. Ceux d'entre eux qui relèvent de la science grammaticale montrent quelle place les traités de Priscien tiennent dans l'enseignement d'Alcuin.

En fait nous avons conservé de lui deux écrits pédagogiques destinés à l'enseignement de la grammaire. L'un, bien connu, est son *De grammatica*, sur lequel nous allons revenir, l'autre, trop peu exploité, est constitué par l'abrégé qu'il avait tiré lui-même des *Institutions grammaticales*.

Ces extraits se rencontrent dans quatre manuscrits, dont trois font partie de l'ancien fonds de Saint-Amand, déposé à la bibliothèque de Valenciennes. L'un de ceux-ci (Valenciennes BM 393) est un manuscrit composite, contenant de nombreux textes hibernolatins et datant des toutes premières années du IX^e^ siècle. Un quatrième exemplaire est le MS Paris, BnF lat. 7502, copié à Tours vers l'an 820. Plusieurs cahiers sont palimpsestes et l'écriture inférieure portait nos extraits. Le dernier folio d'un cahier n'a pas été effacé, et le texte d'un chapitre s'y lit en clair. Lors d'un colloque sur les grammairiens et leur tradition médiévale tenu à Erice en 1997 nous avons démontré l'authenticité de ces extraits, dont la présence dans des manuscrits de Saint-Amand doit être mise en relation avec le fait que le meilleur élève d'Alcuin et sans doute son préféré, Arn, ait longtemps cumulé les fonctions d'abbé de Saint-Amand et d'archevêque de Salzbourg. L'origine tourangelle du palimpseste confirme l'authenticité, qui se marque encore par certains détails de rédaction.

Il ne s'agissait pas d'extraits informes, mais d'une sorte de manuel, organisé en deux livres comprenant le premier 98 et le second 93 chapitres pourvus chacun d'un titre. Ces extraits sont particulièrement intéressants, parce qu'ils nous apprennent dans quel esprit Alcuin lisait les *Institutions grammaticales* de Priscien. Il les lisait d'un bout à l'autre, mais dans la perspective que Priscien met bien en lumière, particulièrement dans la préface des deux derniers livres qui portent le sous-titre commun *De constructione* "De la construction de la phrase": tout l'exposé analytique concernant les parties du discours, qui occupe les seize premiers livres, n'a de sens qu'en vue de la construction de la phrase, cet aspect primordial de l'énoncé, dont la tradition grammaticale depuis des siècles évite de parler. Toutes ces études des parties du discours, ces *De partibus orationis* en quoi se résument les traités antérieurs, ne prennent en compte que l'analyse des catégories de mots l'une après l'autre. Mais le couronnement de l'enseignement grammatical, ce n'est pas la partie du discours, mais c'est le discours, *oratio*, la phrase pourvue d'un sens complet; bref, Priscien, dans le sillage de ses sources grecques, apporte la syntaxe.

Le signe que l'auteur des extraits a bien eu en ligne de mire cet objectif, c'est l'agencement même des extraits, qui par un passage incessant d'un point de vue à l'autre mêlent en une synthèse harmonieuse les observations ponctuelles contenues dans les seize premiers livres, et le point de vue de la syntaxe exprimé dans les deux derniers.

Mais ces textes font aussi toucher du doigt la méthode pédagogique du maître: ce qu'il retient de l'œuvre de Priscien, ce qu'il élimine. Pour les jeunes Francs élèves d'Alcuin, toute une part de l'œuvre du grammairien de Constantinople, celle écrite pour des Grecs et émaillée de citations des classiques grecs, était absolument illisible. Toutes les comparaisons que Priscien multipliait entre faits de langue latins et grecs sont donc systématiquement retranchées, et il en est de même pour les nombreuses références des citations latines. Cette méthode de résorption des exemples et des faits grecs est commune à tous les excerpteurs latins de Priscien, qui sous la masse des exemples produits, s'emploient, dans l'exposé touffu du maître, à retrouver les notions fondamentales. De plus, les excerpteurs sont rarement hellénistes, et quant aux exemples extraits des *auctores*, il est tentant, comme ils sont coupés de leur contexte, de les éliminer ou d'en réduire le nombre. Les citations sont d'une part réduites en nombre ou en importance et d'autre part laissées le plus souvent dans l'anonymat. Les archaïsmes sont éliminés, de même que les explications de type métrique. Le latin des classiques de jadis devient donc une référence linguistique anonyme, une sorte de miroir de la correction.

A quelle date ces extraits ont-ils été agencés? Est-ce du temps où le maître séjournait encore dans son île? Le problème se pose de leur position chronologique par rapport au *De grammatica*. Sont-ils même la source du *De grammatica*? En fait, plusieurs faits donnent l'impression qu'Alcuin est revenu plusieurs fois sur le texte de Priscien, ce qui est à tout prendre la démarche normale d'un pédagogue. Pourtant l'antériorité des *Excerpta* sur le *De grammatica* ne fait guère de doute. Logiquement, on voit mal le maître recommencer à tirer des extraits littéraux d'un texte après s'en être une première fois inspiré pour un ouvrage aussi personnel que le *De grammatica*. Pour y voir clair, des analyses précises s'imposent qui en particulier ne peuvent être menées en l'absence d'une bonne édition critique du dialogue entre Franco et Saxo.

Ce *De grammatica* d'Alcuin sous forme dialoguée est une vraie création originale, qui n'a pas son pareil dans la tradition grammaticale. Certes, cette forme est courante dans les traités de pédagogie grammaticale depuis l'*Ars minor* de Donat et particulièrement dans le domaine insulaire. Mais ici il ne s'agit pas d'un dialogue entre le maître et l'élève, mais entre deux élèves en présence du maître, appelé à intervenir de temps en temps et chaque fois pour élever le débat. Les noms ne sont pas choisis au hasard, et chacun des interlocuteurs a sa personnalité. C'est Saxo qui est l'aîné, mais de peu: la distance qui les sépare symbolise celle qui, à la même époque, sépare les Saxons des Francs en matière de culture. Les premiers n'ont qu'une courte longueur d'avance sur les seconds.

Le traité est un vrai compromis entre Donat et Priscien: Donat fournit le moule en ce qu'il s'agit d'un traité *de partibus orationis* introduit, comme l'*Ars maior*, par une partie plus courte consacrée aux éléments constitutifs des mots, lettres, syllabes, et aux définitions générales, inspirées pour une part des *Etymologies* d'Isidore de Séville. L'ordre de traitement des *partes orationis* est celui de Donat. Mais la matière elle-même est pour la plus grande partie empruntée aux *Institutions grammaticales*, y compris les exemples. Toutefois, c'est un peu comme si seuls existaient les livres I à XVI des *Institutions grammaticales* ou encore comme si Alcuin n'avait disposé que du premier tome des œuvres de Priscien. Car le traité ne se termine en rien par l'amorce d'un *De constructione*. Est-ce par renonciation, comme si le maître avait jugé qu'il suffisait pour les bons élèves de bien connaître les parties du discours, les études syntaxiques étant pour l'instant hors de leur portée?

Priscien est qualifié de *Latinae eloquentiae decus* "la gloire de l'éloquence latine" (Alcuin, *De grammatica*, PL 101, col. 873 C), mais Donat est toujours le "magister" par excellence: "Que veux-tu, maître, demande Saxo à Alcuin, devons-nous poser des questions au sujet des accents et des pieds, en suivant le plan du maître Donat?" (*quid vis, magister, an de pedibus et accentibus ordinem Donati magistri sequentes interrogemus, De grammatica* 857 D). Il est des points sur lesquels les deux auteurs antiques sont en désaccord, notamment sur le pronom; d'autres sur lesquels le maître choisit de passer, parce qu'ils sont encore, comme la métrique, hors du programme de Franco et de Saxo: *Sed has rationes metricae subtilitatis esse reor, in quibus necdum eruditi sumus* "Mais ce sont là des questions qui, je pense, relèvent des arcanes de la métrique, discipline en laquelle nous n'avons pas encore été initiés" (*De grammatica* 856 B). On voit bien ici la distance qui sépare les personnages cultivés de la Cour, capables de s'adonner eux-mêmes à la création poétique, et leurs élèves, tenus à distance du monde poétique par des règles dont ils n'ont même pas connaissance. Bref, les considérations pédagogiques l'emportent et le rôle de cette grammaire dialoguée et en acte est de présenter les connaissances grammaticales de base qu'un élève de la Cour devait assimiler avant d'aller plus loin. Il ne fait pas de doute qu'Alcuin, comme tout bon pédagogue, s'est sans cesse posé la question des niveaux de connaissance. Nous avons par le *De grammatica* le reflet, l'écho d'un enseignement vivant, qui laisse entrevoir au-delà du contenu intellectuel, un lien réel entre des personnes, lien de camaraderie entre les élèves, lien de respect mêlé d'affection entre les élèves et le maître, qui joue à leur égard le rôle d'un véritable père.

## 4. L'heritage d'Alcuin

Le maître de l'école palatine a vu passer bien des élèves, issus de la meilleure aristocratie, devenus rapidement des administrateurs, comtes, abbés, évêques. Ce sont eux les agents de la politique du roi, en toute matière, pour la paix comme pour la guerre, y compris dans le domaine religieux, dans celui de la culture et de l'enseignement. Ils ont tous été fortement marqués par la forte personnalité d'Alcuin et par ses méthodes. C'est eux, quand ils étaient à la tête d'un évêché ou d'un monastère, qui ont organisé l'enseignement et présidé à la rénovation des bibliothèques. Par eux a passé la diffusion de l'œuvre de Priscien fin VIII début IX siècle. Nous avons évoqué la personnalité d'Arn de Salzbourg. Pareillement un homme comme Raban Maur, l'un des meilleurs élèves d'Alcuin et qui a présidé de façon brillante à la destinée du monastère de Fulda, a recueilli dans son enseignement l'exemple et la méthode de son maître. Nous devinons que le *De grammatica* d'Alcuin, précédé de son prologue de nature à la fois théologique et philosophique sur les sept disciplines, a été entre les mains de Loup de Ferrières, quand il a séjourné à Fulda vers l'an 830. Raban avait pour son propre compte tiré d'Alcuin une grammaire que nous avons encore, et qui, comme le *De grammatica* de son propre maître, est fondée spécialement sur les livres I à XVI des *Institutions grammaticales*.

À la Cour palatine l'un des successeurs d'Alcuin, le Scot Clément, nous a laissé lui aussi un manuel. Certes, l'*Ars* de Clément s'inspire de sources diverses, en particulier irlandaises. Mais Clément connaissait le *De grammatica* d'Alcuin, dont il recopie, sans le nommer, de nombreux passages. Clément avait aussi entre les mains son propre Priscien. Certains paragraphes de Clément s'inspirent à la fois de Priscien et d'Alcuin, comme si Clément avait contrôlé ou voulu infléchir les emprunts qu'Alcuin avait faits à Priscien. Semblablement, un autre grammairien qui avait lui aussi dans son jeune âge séjourné à la Cour, Smaragde de S. Mihiel, de culture septimanienne, a de son côté lu Priscien et en a tiré des paraphrases insérées dans son propre traité.

On a l'impression que désormais tout enseignement de la grammaire se doit d'insérer la doctrine ou la formulation de Priscien contenue dans les *Institutions grammaticales*. Mais, nous l'avons vu, à date ancienne déjà, une tradition irlandaise liée à Bobbio, dont la bibliothèque possédait plusieurs exemplaires de Priscien, utilise elle aussi le grammairien de Césarée. Cette tradition se retrouve dans les grammaires hibernolatines du IXe siècle qui, Clément excepté, ne sont pas, semble-t-il, redevables directement à Alcuin. Parmi elles, l'anonyme *Donatus ortigraphus*, véritable chaîne grammaticale, offre la particularité de présenter non des paraphrases mais d'exactes citations de Priscien, comme si le texte dépendait directement d'un recueil d'extraits. Les autres traités, écrits par des Irlandais enseignant sur le continent, se contentent d'une paraphrase, tel l'Irlandais Murethac, le maître d'Auxerre, ou encore l'Anonyme auteur de l'*Ars Laureshamensis* (ainsi désignée du nom du plus ancien manuscrit qui nous en transmet le texte); et il en est de même pour le grand commentaire de Sédulius Scottus à l'*Ars Maior* de Donat. Mais dans le cas de ces trois commentaires, il est vraisemblable que l'utilisation de Priscien n'est pas directe, mais dépend d'une source commune perdue qui disposait elle-même d'un recueil d'extraits assez voisin à celui qu'utilise *Donatus Ortigraphus*. D'après les sondages que nous avons faits, ce recueil ne doit rien à Alcuin et émane d'un lecteur qui peut-être résidait dans le domaine insulaire.

En fait sous des formes variables, c'est toujours désormais la même synthèse qui s'opère entre Donat et Priscien, le premier fournissant le cadre, le second la matière enseignée: cette synthèse, n'en doutons pas, est insulaire et précarolingienne: entre l'an 700 et l'an 850 on voit la part de Priscien s'accroître dans tous les traités. Dans cette transformation progressive de l'enseignement de la grammaire, le rôle d'Alcuin a, il est vrai, été prépondérant, puisque c'est lui qui, par l'influence qu'il a exercée sur de nombreux élèves, est responsable de la diffusion rapide de Priscien dans l'Empire franc et sur l'ensemble du continent. Vers 850 les *Institutions grammaticales* étaient dans toutes les bibliothèques. Et les maîtres d'alors, même s'ils lisaient Priscien sans recourir à la version ou aux extraits d'Alcuin, bénéficiaient à leur insu de l'élan qu'avait donné le conseiller de Charlemagne en faveur du grammairien de Constantinople. Mais tout cela n'avait été possible que parce que tant les Anglo-Saxons que les grammairiens irlandais avaient appris bien avant l'époque de Charlemagne à lire cette œuvre touffue et à en extraire des lignes de force pour enseigner le latin à leurs élèves.

En effet, le succès de Priscien chez les peuples insulaires tient à ce que le grammairien présente à l'appui de son enseignement un luxe d'exemples et, à profusion, un vocabulaire d'une richesse sans commune mesure avec la sécheresse calculée des traités de Donat: il fallait apprendre le latin, donc acquérir du vocabulaire et pas seulement répéter des règles de grammaire. Au début les maîtres, par habitude, ont eu recours à la petite institution; puis, avec de plus en plus d'audace, se sont mis à lire les *Institutions grammaticales*. Mais ils lisaient l'ouvrage moins pour dépasser Donat que pour le nourrir. Aucun ne l'utilise encore pour son apport original, celui de la syntaxe.

Seul Alcuin, avec sa perspicacité et l'acuité de son intelligence, a perçu la nouveauté de Priscien. En avance sur son siècle, qui s'est contenté des seize premiers livres des *Institutions grammaticales*, il a apprécié l'apport du *De constructione* et dirigé en ce sens la lecture d'un petit nombre d'élèves choisis, mais en sachant bien que les esprits n'étaient pas mûrs pour tirer vraiment profit de cette lecture. L'objectif des maîtres du temps n'était pas de faire progresser la linguistique, mais de retrouver la norme de la langue écrite (→ Art. 72).

Comme on le sait, dans les traités de grammaire antiques et médiévaux, les exemples sont rarement innocents. Lorsque Priscien, au livre des *Institutions grammaticales*, propose comme exemple la phrase *Aristophanes Aristarchum docuit* "Aristophane [de Byzance] a été le maître d'Aristarque", ce qui, vu la chronologie des deux personnages, est la simple vérité historique, Alcuin, recopiant ce passage pour l'inclure dans ses extraits, change les noms et en lieu et place propose la phrase *Priscianus Donatum docuit* "Priscien a été le maître de Donat". Quoi donc? Alcuin ignorait que Priscien avait vécu près de deux siècles après Donat? Non bien sûr, mais ce qu'il veut dire par là, c'est qu'à ses yeux Priscien en sait plus que Donat. Cette phrase nous donne peut-être à comprendre ce qu'entendait Alcuin quand il écrivait dans son poème les simples mots *Donatus Priscianusue*.

## 5. Bibliographie

### 5.1. Sources primaires


Alcuin, *The Bishops, Kings and Saints of York*. Éd. par Peter Godman. (= *Oxford Medieval Texts*). Oxford: Clarendon Press, 1982.

Alcuin, *Epistulae*. Éd. par E. Dümmler. *Monumenta Germaniae Historica, Epistulae* IV, *Epistulae Karolini Aevi* II. Berlin: Weidmann.

Aldhelm, *De metris et enigmatibus et pedum regulis*. Éd. par R. Ehwald. *Monumenta Germaniae Historica*, ant. XV. Berlin: Weidmann, 1919.

*Anonymus ad Cuimnanum*. Éd. par Bernard Bishoff & Bengt Loefstedt. (= *Corpus Christianorum Series Latina* CXXXIII D.) Turnhout, 1992.

*Ars Ambrosiana (Commentum anonymum in Donati partes maiores)*. Éd. par Bengt Loefstedt. (= *Corpus Christianorum Series Latina* CXXXIII C.) Turnhout, 1982.

*Ars Bernensis*. Éd. par H. Hagen. *Grammatici Latini* VIII, 62–142.

*Ars Laureshamensis, Expositio in Donatum maiorem*. Éd. par Bengt Loefstedt. (= *Corpus Christianorum Continuation Mediaevalis* XL A.) Turnhout, 1977.

Bonifatius, *Ars grammatica* = *Bonifatii (Vinfreth) Ars grammatica*. Éd. par George John Gebauer & Bengt Loefstedt. (= *Corpus Christianorum Series Latina* CXXXIII B.) Turnhout, 1980.

Clemens, *Ars grammatica* = *Clementis Ars grammatica*. Éd. par Joannes Tolkiehn. (= *Philologi Supplement*. XX, fasc. III.) Lipsiae, 1928. [Une nouvelle édition est annoncée au *Corpus Christianorum*.]

Donatus Ortigraphus, *Ars grammatica*. Éd. par John Chittenden. (= *Corpus Christianorum Continuation Mediaevalis* XL D.) Turnhout, 1982.

Murethac (Muridac), *In Donati artem maiorem*. Ed. par Louis Holtz (= *Corpus Christianorum Continuatio Mediaevalis* XL.) Turnhout, 1977.

Sédulius Scottus, *In Donati artem maiorem*. Éd. par Bengt Loefstedt. (= *Corpus Christianorum Continuatio Mediaevalis* XL B.) Turnhout, 1977.

Smaragde, *Liber in partibus Donati*. Éd. par Bengt Loefstedt, Louis Holtz & Adele Kibre. (= *Corpus Christianorum Continuatio Mediaevalis* LXVIII.) Turnhout, 1986.

Tatuinus, *Ars* = *Ars Tatuini de partibus orationis*. Éd. par Maria de Marco. (= *Corpus Christianorum Series Latina* CXXXIII.) Turnhout, 1968.


### 5.2. Sources secondaires


Ballaira, Guglielmo. 1982. *Per il catalogo dei codici di Prisciano*. Turin: Giappichelli.

Courcelle, Pierre. 1948. *Les lettres grecques en Occident de Macrobe à Cassiodore*. Paris.

Gibson, Margaret. 1972. "Priscian *Institutiones Grammaticae*, a handlist of manuscripts". *Scriptorium* 26.105–124.

Holtz, Louis. 1981. *Donat et la tradition de l'enseignement grammatical*. Paris: CNRS.

–. 1994. "Una nuova fonte manoscritta dell'Arte Bernese (con edizione critica parziale del testo)". *Problemi di edizione e di interpretazione nei testi grammaticali latini*, 5–29. Rome.

–. 1995. "L'*Ars Bernensis*, essai de localisation et de datation". *Aquitaine and Ireland in the Middle Ages* éd. par Jean-Michel Picard, 111–126. Dublin: Four Courts Press.

Jeudy, Colette. 1982. "Complément à un catalogue récent des manuscrits de Priscien". *Scriptorium* 36.313–325.

–. 1984a. "Nouveaux compléments à un catalogue récent des manuscrits de Priscien". *Scriptorium* 38.140–150.

–. 1984b. "Nouveaux fragments de textes grammaticaux". *Revue d'Histoire des Textes* 14.131–141.

Passalacqua, Marina. 1978. *I codici di Prisciano*. (= *Sussidi Eruditi*, 29.) Rome: Storia e letteratura.


*Louis Holtz, Paris (France)*

# 75. The role of linguistics in early medieval education


1. Introduction
2. Grammar meets Christianity
3. Latin variations
4. Monastic literacy
5. Commentaries on Donatus and Priscian
6. Christianized grammar
7. Grammar and multilingualism
8. Conclusion
9. Bibliography


## 1. Introduction

In the Early Middle Ages (from the death of St. Augustine [430 CE] to the Norman Conquest [1066 CE]), the study of language and the teaching of literacy were developed primarily in the monastic schools and centers of learning. The principal object of language study was Latin. In addition to teaching basic literacy, language study influenced other areas of early medieval society and discourse, including textual interpretation, the status of the vernaculars, and ideas about cultural and regional differences.

## 2. Grammar meets Christianity

The Christian grammarians and teachers of the Early Middle Ages continued many of the traditional Hellenic and Roman concepts and descriptions of grammar. Grammar was the art of speaking correctly (*recte loquendi scientia*) and the knowledge of how to interpret the poets (*interpretatio poetarum*). The study of Latin word classes formed the basis for Latin literacy and for all higher studies of the Bible, literature, logic, and the other arts. During the patristic period, Christian and secular schools often coexisted in western Europe. Cassiodorus (d. 583), a member of a prominent Roman senatorial family, converted to Christianity and retired in 537 CE to found a monastery at Vivarium and establish a Christian school modeled in part on the Roman secular schools. At Vivarium, the study of the Psalms was at least as important as the study of the trivial arts (grammar, rhetoric, and dialectic). But the community at Vivarium promoted a culture of literacy that used the Roman grammatical tradition to establish written Latin correctness and clarity in the service of scriptural study. Less concerned than Cassiodorus with Latin correctness, Augustine (d. 430) in an earlier period nonetheless called upon Christians to take whatever was useful from classical learning to nourish their spiritual understanding (→ Art. 71). In *De doctrina christiana*, Augustine argued that classical culture (especially grammar and rhetoric) is indispensable to the baptized in that it enables readers to derive meaning from Biblical texts and commentaries and to communicate that knowledge to others. Rather than shrug them off, Christians should convert their studies of language and classical texts to better understand complex scriptural texts, just as the Israelites had taken Egyptian gold to use for their own religious purposes (*De doct. christ.* 2.40; cf. Hovdhaugen 1982: 105–111; Amsler 1989: 82–118; Irvine 1994).

However, the changing linguistic situation of Europe and the expectations of Christian literacy prompted grammarians to expand the traditional Latin *ars grammatica* to include the description of new linguistic features, contrastive analyses of Latin, Greek, and vernaculars, more specifically grammatical interpretation of sacred and secular texts, and a broader introduction to the liberal arts, especially rhetoric and dialectic. Increasingly, grammarians emphasized teaching Latin grammar, reading, and scriptural interpretation to non-native speakers, glossing texts for new Christian readers and producing new glossaries and grammars for monastic readers in both Latin and the vernaculars such as English, High German, Icelandic and Irish. During the early Middle Ages, the role of the grammarian, and hence linguistics, expanded considerably to embrace a wider educational program.

Despite the adaptation of secular schooling by Christian communities, patristic and early medieval education and language study were often at odds with the normative tradition of Roman grammar. Scriptural reading demanded attention to more than Latin. Augustine writes

> Knowledge of languages is the great remedy against unknown particular words. And people of the Latin language whom I now have taken upon me to instruct, need two other languages to understand the Holy Scriptures, namely Hebrew and Greek, so they can turn to the originals if the infinite variety of Latin translators gives them doubt (*De doct. christ.* 2.2).

Grammar unlocked textual meanings, so the grammarian stood at the doorway to knowledge by providing readers with the description of and access to the Latin language and the languages of Scripture. Moreover, forms of scriptural or later Latin did not always conform to the Roman grammarians' descriptions of Latin morphology or syntax. Smaragdus (9th century), for example, argues that

> Concerning *scala* and *scopa* and *quadriga*, we do not follow Donatus and those who have said that these words are always plural, because we know they have been specified (*dictata*) as singular by the Holy Spirit [i. e., in scriptural Latin] (*Liber in partibus Donati* 68: 67).

## 3. Latin variations

The recognition among Christian grammarians of the differences between Roman and scriptural Latin illustrates a much deeper linguistic awareness of the changing nature of Latin in the early Middle Ages. Changes in late Latin phonology and morphology prompted Christian grammarians to revise some classical grammatical rules and descriptions. Augustine differed from more conservative grammarians when he noted spelling-sound variations and observed that Latin was not always pronounced in his time as it had been. He asked rhetorically whether barbarism was

> [...] anything else than to pronounce a word with other letters and sounds than they used to do who spoke Latin before us? (*De doct. christ.* 2.13).

Rather than regard changing pronunciation as a corruption of language standards by inferior or non-native speakers, Augustine acknowledged sound changes as part of the historical condition of language. Augustine and others also noted, and then emphasized, morphological changes, such as the cases with prepositions: "Whether we say *inter homines* or *inter hominibus* has no influence on him who wants to know the facts" (*De doct. christ.* 2.13). Pope Gregory the Great (d. 604) also resisted the pull of normative Roman grammar and, in the name of a prior Christian truth, privileged the scriptural Latin which differed phonologically, syntactically, and semantically (to varying degrees) from Classical Latin:

> I have refused to pay attention to the art of speaking which the instructors of outward instruction insist on [...] I do not shun frequent use of the letter *m* before words beginning with vowels, I do not avoid the mingling of barbarisms, I disdain to pay attention to hiatus and tropes and the cases governed by prepositions, because I strongly find it unbecoming to restrain the words of the celestial oracle through the rules of Donatus (*Moralia in Iob*, Pref. 143: 7).

Although Gregory's own Latin writings conformed closely to the standards of classical Latin, his attitude toward traditional Latin *grammatica* (the 'rules of Donatus') in relation to Christian literacy had a marked effect on the new directions of early medieval grammarians. The course of early medieval grammar was set by these teachers' and grammarians' ongoing dialogue with traditional Roman grammar and their uses of grammar as the foundation for Christian monastic literacy.

## 4. Monastic literacy

By 700 CE, monastic and cathedral schools had replaced the Roman secular schools as the centers of learning and intellectual culture in Europe. Monastic Latin literacy included reciting prayers and the Psalter, reading and interpreting the Latin Bible, and assimilating the wealth of commentaries and exegesis which traveled with the sacred texts (→ Art. 72, 73). Monastic education deployed the grammar curriculum as a framework for general education, especially the verbal arts (grammar, rhetoric, dialectic), principally because they served sacred reading. Rather than replacing the secular liberal arts with a rigorously Christian curriculum, most monastic and cathedral schools adopted a streamlined study of the secular arts as necessary background for religious study and scriptural exegesis (Riché 1976: 100–135; 307–446).

Using this pedagogy of guided reading, early medieval grammarians produced a complex body of work which adapted Roman grammarians' description and analysis of Latin for new readers and different linguistic situations. Donatus' *Ars minor* (focusing on word classes) and *Ars maior* (including sounds, solecisms, barbarisms, and figures of speech) remained the reference texts for early medieval grammar. Typically, an early medieval linguistic text was a commentary on one of Donatus' grammars, arranged as a series of glosses and notes on individual terms and lemmas from Donatus' text. The commentary format derived from grammarians' classroom practice, whose primary goal was to teach students to read aloud and comprehend Latin texts, especially the Bible. The teacher listened as pupils recited Donatus' descriptions of word classes and responded to the grammarian's questions:

> On the noun. What is a noun? A part of speech with case indicating a body or a thing specifically or generally. How many attributes has a noun? Six [...] (IV, 355).

The teacher might then produce an extended gloss or explanation of a word or reference in Donatus' grammar, or elaborate on the morphological, syntactic, or semantic properties of an exemplary word. For example, after the Q and A on the noun, Donatus's text includes a morphosyntactic discourse on the word *magister*:

> *Magister* is an appellative noun of the masculine gender, singular number, simplex figure and nominative and vocative case and is inflected as follows: in the nominative *hic magister*, in the genitive *huius magistri* [...].

4th- and 5th-century Roman grammarians such as Servius, Pompeius, and Cledonius followed the format of Donatus' grammar in their commentaries, sometimes amplifying Donatus' text and elaborating or clarifying his explanations, other times disagreeing with Donatus' descriptions in light of contemporary Latin usage.

Early medieval grammarians adapted the Roman grammatical tradition to the needs of contemporary readers in several ways: 1) commentaries on Donatus and Priscian which explained grammatical doctrine for non-native speakers and sought to provide a more philosophical framework for linguistics, 2) commentaries which Christianized Roman grammar and textual interpretation and substituted the Bible for the classical poets as the exemplars of Latin, and 3) grammatical discourses which responded to the multilingualism of early medieval Europe and the changes in Latin usage.

## 5. Commentaries on Donatus and Priscian

Early medieval grammarians framed Donatus' grammars with elaborate commentary, which in effect 'taught' the metalanguage of grammatical analysis and Latin morphology to beginning and advanced readers. In addition, the grammarians provided interpretation of and commentary on particular textual or linguistic references found in Donatus' grammatical examples or in the canon of elementary Latin texts in the grammar curriculum. Incorporating and framing key passages from Roman grammatical discourse (especially Pompeius), these commentaries by 6th- through 9th-century Gallic, Germanic, Anglo-Saxon, and Irish grammarians probably served as teaching aids for countless other grammar teachers in early medieval schools.

The monastic grammatical commentaries initially emphasized descriptions of the eight Latin word classes and morphology, barbarisms (nonstandard pronunciation as well as speech errors) and solecisms (ungrammatical constructions), and to a lesser extent, explanations of poetic schemes and tropes and the description of syntax (cf. Irvine 1994; Law 1982, 1990). By the 9th century, Alcuin and other Carolingian grammarians supplemented their commentaries on Donatus' grammars with more philosophical and detailed linguistic analyses, drawing on Boethius and Priscian's *Institutiones grammaticae* (early 6th century) or, more commonly, on the classroom-friendly condensation of Priscian's grammar, entitled *Institutio de nomine et pronomine et verbo*, especially popular among Irish and Anglo-Saxon grammarians and in the monastic schools of northern France (cf. Bayless 1993; Luhtala 1993; Amsler 1989: 207–250; → Art. 74).

Carolingian grammarians such as Alcuin and the Irish grammarians increasingly turned to Priscian's texts as the basis for Latin grammatical descriptions and for analyses of particular elements of language. While Priscian continued much of the late Roman grammatical discourse, he abandoned Donatus' question and answer format, included more syntactic analysis in his Latin grammars, and connected grammatical discourse with rhetoric and logic. Carolingian grammarians often used Priscian as a linguistic authority to rival Donatus. Priscian's grammar provided 9th-century grammarians with more philosophical foundations for linguistic ideas and prompted grammarians to apply logical notions to syntactic analysis in their commentaries. For example, following an idea in Priscian, Sedulius (Irish, 9th century) and other grammarians considered whether the verb also signifies substance. A 10th-century gloss on Priscian states:

> The verb has in it the absolute force of the nominative, that is, of the nominative inhering in the verb even if concealed. Principally, the verb signifies action and undergoing action, but latently substance (Paris, BN, MS lat. 7501, 141v, cited by Luhtala 1993: 166; cf. Sedulius, *In Priscianum* 76).

Such explanations increased the intellectual prestige of *grammatica* by linking linguistic analysis with philosophical or theological questions and thus identifying the grammarian as more than a teacher of basic literacy to nonnative speakers.

## 6. Christianized grammar

A second way early medieval grammarians adapted Roman linguistics was to Christianize the framework for linguistic description and grammatical explanations or to expand individual grammatical glosses on Donatus' grammars with encyclopedic material (history, philosophy, mythology, geography) which would aid monastic readers. Many early medieval grammars often included specific grammatical examples from Biblical texts as well as examples from contemporary social circumstances. Sometimes, Biblical examples and names were substituted for the traditional Greco-Roman ones in Donatus' grammar. The Irish grammarian Malsachanus (8th century) simply added numerous Biblical and Christian examples to Donatus' illustrations. In his *Ars grammatica* (late 6th century), Asporius adapted Donatus' elementary grammar to a nonnative audience and illustrated grammatical forms with examples from Hebrew and Biblical names and words specific to the monastic world (*ecclesia* "church", *ieiunium* "fast"). Smaragdus (9th century) and other grammarians expanded the number of endings for each noun declension to include Hebrew names and other biblical names within a Latin grammatical framework. For example, the writer of the *Beatus quid est* grammar (early 11th century) gave the endings of the first noun declension as: *-a* (*Maria*), *-as* (*Andreas*), *-es* (*Agnes*), and *-am* (*Abraham*). However, other grammarians preferred to leave Hebrew names undeclined, thus marking them as unassimilated sacred vocabulary on the margins of Latin morphology.

The most famous example of Christianizing earlier Roman grammar is Bede's revision of Donatus' *Ars maior*, Part 3 on schemes and tropes, based in part on earlier Christianized grammars by Isidore and Julian of Toledo (cf. Holtz 1981). Bede thoroughly appropriated Donatus' description of *enarratio* "interpretation" by substituting examples of tropes from the Bible and Christian writers such as Venantius Fortunatus for those from classical texts. The Psalter replaces the classical *Disticha Catonis* as the morally appropriate text for beginning readers and as the example of artful uses of language. But while the grammatical structure and pronunciation of 8th-century Latin differed somewhat from those of the 4th century, Bede's account of figurative language framed the language of the Bible within the classical description of the schemes and tropes. The scriptures exemplified and added further authority to, rather than revised, the classical schemes and tropes.

Because the *ars grammatica* was intended to teach students how to understand figurative language and to interpret texts and metrics, early medieval grammatical discourse, as linguistic description and educational practice, established the norms for textual exegesis and Biblical reading. Literal and allegorical commentaries on scripture appropriated the strategy of lemmas, glosses, and interpretation found in the commentaries on Donatus' grammars and in secular commentaries on the *Aeneid* by Servius (4th century) and dramatized in Macrobius' *Saturnalia* (5th century). Linguistic analysis, especially etymology and analysis of compound words, provided the skilled reader with the interpretive strategies to explain or construe the sacred text. The grammarian as exegete unlocked the signification of the sacred text by dividing and then analyzing keywords or using words' origins to explain the text's larger meaning. In his influential *Exposition of the Psalms*, Cassiodorus parsed the text of Psalm 9 with detailed semantic and etymological analysis:

> The words *in infernum* follow, lest they believe they are to be sent anywhere else. *Infernum* "hell" is so called because souls are continually being carried into [*in+fero*] that place, or, as some believe, [*infernum* is so called because it is derived] from *inferior* "lesser part". But here *infernum* seems to mean the eternal death to which those who hold God's law in contempt will doubtless come.

Most grammatical exegetes interpreted names and words in a more direct 'read-off' manner. In his *Commentary on the Book of Jonah*, Haymo of Auxerre (d. 853), a student of the Irish grammarian Muredach, writes:

> For this reason, Jonah was called 'son of Amittai'. 'Amittai' means 'truth', and because Elijah spoke truth, Jonah was called 'son of truth' ... The Lord himself is the 'son of Amittai', that is, of God, because God is truth (Prologue, chap. 1; cf. Amsler 1989: 118–132).

These grammatical modes of interpretation, derived from classical and Patristic commentaries (especially Jerome's glosses on Biblical names), dominated monastic reading. Some textual commentaries emphasized the literal, grammatical, and historical levels of the text, while others derived allegorical or spiritual meanings based on linguistic explanations. In his *Commentary on the Book of Jonah*, Haymo of Auxerre glossed Hebrew and Latin words to link the literal and spiritual senses of the text:

> And he said to them, 'I am a Hebrew, and I fear the Lord God of heaven who made the sea and the dry land' [Jonah 1: 9]. 'Hebrew' (*Hebraeus*) means 'one who crosses over'. He did not say 'Judean', by which name they began to be called when the ten tribes were divided from the two, but he said, 'I am a Hebrew', a pilgrim and a stranger, according to the Psalmist, who says concerning the same people, 'They passed from nation to nation' [Psalm 104: 13] (chap. 1).

and

In the Psalm which is inscribed, 'For the beginning of the day' [21: 1], the Lord called Himself a worm (*vermis*), saying, 'But I am a worm, and not a man' [21: 7]. For indeed the worm rises from the ground without seed; humble, it creeps, and it moves without a sound, and Christ was born from the earth, from a virgin, humble among reproaches, not crying out against the Passion (chap. 3).

Haymo's work illustrates the rich texture of Carolingian scriptural commentaries in which the grammarian as exegete weaves together lexical glossing and intertextual interpretation to produce multiple meanings for the Christian reader.

Early medieval grammar produced not only specific models for scriptural exegesis but also the framework for systematizing knowledge in encyclopedias and compendia. Isidore of Seville's (d. 636) *Etymologiae* is the most influential early medieval grammatical encyclopedia and served as the model for later compendia such as Hrabanus Maurus' *On the Nature of Things* (9th century). Grammar, according to Isidore, is the master discipline of the schools, and the grammatical analysis of etymologies, derivations, and compounds forms the basis for his wide-ranging encyclopedia of human knowledge organized alphabetically and by subject or topic. Isidore writes:

Every inquiry into a thing [or subject] is clearer when the etymology is known (*Etymologiae* 1.29).

Isidore's text deliberately institutionalizes the grammarian as the purveyor of encyclopedic knowledge. As a master discipline, grammar becomes the doorway to other subjects, including rhetoric, logic, poetry, music, peoples of the world, arithmetic, astronomy, and so on. For example, Isidore defines *historia* as the genre which tells what actually occurred, usually in prose, and is sometimes referred to as *monumentum* because it allows for remembering military campaigns. To help explain the subject, Isidore also provides a Greek etymology of the Latin word "*apo tou istorein*, that is, from seeing or learning" (1.41). Of course, Isidore's encyclopedia only covers the basic terminology for each subject area. But the grammatically based *Etymologiae* transmitted to the early Middle Ages a reference text which integrated the ancient world's official knowledge with the broader Latin literacy curriculum of grammar, rhetoric, logic, sacred names, poetic interpretation, and an anthropology of languages and peoples. Despite its highly derivative composition, Isidore's *Etymologiae* established the grammatical curriculum as the foundation of learning and the grammarian as the purveyor of encyclopedic knowledge. The world was organized as a book (cf. Amsler 1989: 133–172).

## 7. Grammar and multilingualism

Early medieval grammarians also adapted Roman grammar and language study to the changing bilingual situation of Latin literacy in several ways. Earlier, Latin had existed in a bilingual situation with Greek, and some Roman grammarians wrote grammars for Greeks who wanted to learn Latin. By the Carolingian era, there were no native speakers of Latin, and there had been no Roman speakers of Latin in Europe for many centuries. The deep importance of this rather obvious linguistic fact has yet to be fully thought through in the history of early medieval linguistics. Latin was taught throughout Europe, always as a second language, sometimes only to be read, most often to be both spoken and read (→ Art. 72). There is clear evidence that grammarians taught Latin using the students' vernacular in the classroom. Grammarians provided vernacular glosses for teaching grammars, sometimes composed grammars in a vernacular, and began to describe other European languages using the structural framework of the Latin *ars grammatica* (cf. Page 1982). At the same time, the analysis of linguistic differences, when combined with the description of regional and religious differences, began to shape a more complex anthropology of human societies in the early Middle Ages (cf. Wright 1982; Bischoff 1961).

While Roman grammarians had noted differences between ancient and contemporary usage, Christian grammarians such as Isidore of Seville described the historical development of Latin in the wider context of the diversity of languages caused by God's destruction of the Tower of Babel to punish the Israelites' pride. "Originally, in the Garden of Eden and then before the Flood, all nations had one language called Hebrew" (*Etymologiae* 9.1), but Isidore is ambivalent as to whether God's own generated speech in Genesis 1: 1 was Hebrew or some Ur language. While recognizing there are many languages in the world, Isidore emphasizes the three sacred languages for Christian literacy and textuality: Hebrew, Greek, and Latin. Isidore's description of Latin's historicity is what most concerns us in terms of the history of early medieval linguistics.

Some have said there are four Latin languages, namely, Ancient, Latin, Roman, and Mixed (9.1).

While he does not provide much detailed phonetic, morphological, or syntactic analysis of these four types of Latin, Isidore seems to recognize that as Latin came to be spoken or written by more and more diverse peoples, the language itself changed.

The earliest inhabitants of Italy spoke the 'rude' Ancient Latin (*prisca*); the original Etruscans and inhabitants of Latium spoken Latin; Roman is the language which the Roman people after the banishment of the kings started to use [...] and which Virgil and Cicero made dominant; Mixed is the language which, after the empire had been enlarged to a rather wide extent, burst into the Roman state together with customs and nations and corrupted the integrity of the world through barbarisms and solecisms (9.1; cf. Wright 1982; Amsler 1993).

Isidore's characterization of his own 7th-century Latin as *mixta* reveals the conflict over multilingualism in early medieval linguistic thought. On the one hand, Latin is said to be corrupted by non-native, non-Roman speakers who were swept into the dominant speech community by Roman imperialism and colonialism and then stigmatized as corrupting the integrity of the world through nonstandard pronunciations (barbarisms) and usage (solecisms). On the other hand, Isidore regards a distinct language to be a principal feature of a people's collective identity, so contemporary mixed versions of Latin would constitute new regional identities.

Accordingly, we have first treated languages and then nations because nations have originated from languages, and not languages from nations (9.1).

As one of the most learned Christian writers of the 7th century, Isidore seems to have regarded contemporary Latin as comprised of different levels of usage, some more consistent with classical Latin as described in the Roman Imperial grammars and others more representative of the Latin used by non-Romans in early medieval Europe.

Other grammarians responded to the multilingualism of the early Middle Ages by adapting traditional grammar to the teaching of Latin and vernacular literacy for non-Latin speakers. In some cases, these pedagogical situations prompted a deeper contrastive analysis of Latin and the vernaculars. Ælfric (d. 1036) composed a Latin grammar in Old English, a Latin-Old English glossary, and a set of Latin dialogues (*Colloquy*) for use in the classroom. The *Colloquy* gives a running dialogue in Latin on various topics in everyday life, with an interlinear Old English translation (→ Art. 85). Like other Carolingian grammarians, Ælfric based his teaching grammar on Priscian. Ælfric translates all Latin terms, examples, and explanations into Old English and also invents some Old English grammatical terms not found in Latin. Ælfric's grammatical description depends on showing students how English works and then comparing English grammatical structures with Latin ones. For example, he defines the pronoun as a grammatical category in much the same way Roman grammarians had done.

The pronoun is the noun's replacement which replaces the noun so that you do not need to name it twice.

Ælfric then compares English and Latin pronouns.

If we say now, *hwa lærde ðe?* "who taught you?", then I would say, *dunstan* "Dunstan". *hwa hadode ðe?* "Who ordained you?". *He me hadode* "he ordained me". Then the *he* stands in the noun's place and replaces it. Then, if you ask, *quis hoc fecit?/ hwa dyde ðis* "who did this?", when you say, *ego hoc feci/ic dyde ðis* "I did this", then the *ego/ic* "I" is in the noun's place. [And so] *tu/ðu* "you", *ille/ se* "that"

With these bilingual examples, Ælfric's comparative analysis of pronouns implies that Latin pronouns function much the same as English pronouns.

However, when Latin and Old English grammar differ, Ælfric treats each language separately so that students learning to read both Latin and English will have the knowledge they need to parse sentences. For example, he describes Latin nouns as divided into five declensions, but when he describes English nouns he emphasizes Latin and Old English cases, not declensions. After giving Latin examples with Old English translations of each of the cases, he concludes

These six cases include and enclose whatever people speak about, if there are words for saying it to do so

While Ælfric provides clear examples of Latin declensions and cases, he gives only the structural framework of the students' native language, presumably because the teacher and the students would fill in the examples for themselves. Although Old English grammar does not fit neatly within a Latin grammatical system, Ælfric's grammar shows the discursive power of Latin grammatical discourse to set the framework for the description of the vernaculars. At the same time, his written version of vernacular grammar teaching suggests the more widespread use of the vernacular to teach Latin as a second language among the clergy and the elite.

Some early medieval grammarians modified or expanded the traditional grammatical metalanguage and looked for the underlying structure of the vernaculars themselves. The bilingual contact between Latin and the vernaculars prompted some early medieval grammarians to explore the contrasts between Latin and other languages and to expand or revise some traditional categories for language analysis. Although some Irish grammarians revised the Latin grammatical terms, for example, substituting *accusatio* for *accusativus*, to suggest a different theoretical approach to cases as expressing action, Ælfric's grammar suggests how early medieval grammarians also substituted vernacular terms for the traditional Latin metalanguage. Such vernacularization of grammar made it easier to describe a language in its own right rather than as a subtype of Latin. The Irish *Auraicept na nÉces* "Instructions of Poets" (composed around 650 with glosses and elaborations through 1000) was written for the *filid* "learned poets" and presents a contrastive analysis of Old Irish by expanding the six cases in Latin to describe twenty-six cases in Old Irish. The grammar also recognizes the social variation of five stylistic registers (colloquial to formal) within Old Irish vocabulary (→ Art. 82).

Around 1150, the author of the *First Icelandic Grammatical Treatise* compared, quite successfully and with sophisticated analysis, Latin and Icelandic phonology and writing (→ Art. 84). The grammarian analyzes the pronunciation of Old Icelandic and then proposes an orthographic reform.

> I have used all the Latin letters that seemed to fit our language well and could be rightly pronounced, as well as some letters that seemed needful to me, while those were taken out that did not suit the sounds of our language. Some of the consonants of the Latin alphabet were rejected, and some new ones added. No vowels were rejected, but a good many were added, since our language has the greatest number of vowel sounds (13).

The Icelandic grammarian notes the distinctions between nasalized and oral vowels, short and long vowels, and so forth. In short, the Icelandic grammarian's careful analysis of Old Icelandic pronunciation reshapes the framework for describing speech given through the traditional Roman grammatical discourse.

Numerous manuscripts of elementary texts and Latin poetry (e. g., Horace) show evidence of the construe marks and marginal notations used by teachers and readers to parse Latin sentences and indicate parallel constructions, phrase structures, and word order. Some construal systems focused on reading Latin texts in themselves while others used the reader's native language to help bridge the gap between vernacular and Latin syntax (cf. Draak 1967; Page 1982; Wieland 1985; Reynolds 1996).

## 8. Conclusion

In the early Middle Ages, the role of linguistics shifted to accommodate the new Christian educational program of the monasteries and the changing forms of Latin in a multilingual society. Grammarians not only instructed students in basic Latin literacy but also produced the hyperliterate texts which traveled with scripture and poetry as part of monastic reading: exegesis, glossaries (of Latin, Hebrew, and other languages), encyclopedias, comparative analyses of Latin and the vernaculars, and linguistically oriented discussions of logic and theology. Grammar became the master discipline of early medieval learning. In addition, the forms of late imperial and early medieval Latin did not always conform to the descriptions in Roman grammars, so early medieval grammarians supplemented the received grammatical discourse by rethinking the description of morphology, spelling-sound correlations, and syntax and by describing the Latin as well as the vernaculars they and their students actually used (cf. Page 1982). Many early medieval grammarians, rather than presenting themselves as guardians of an ancient linguistic past (cf. Kaster 1988), reshaped the Latin grammatical categories to account for the varieties of Latin and vernaculars spoken and written in Europe.

## 9. Bibliography

### 9.1. Primary sources

Ælfric. Ed. by Julius Zupitza, *Ælfrics Grammatik und Glossar.* 2 vols. Berlin: Weidmann, 1880.

Augustine, *De doctrina christiana.* Ed. by Joseph Martin. (= *Corpus Christianorum, Series Latina,* 32.) Turnhout: Brepols, 1962.

*Auraicept na nÉces.* Ed. by Anders Ahlqvist, *The Early Irish Linguist: An edition of the canonical part of the* Auraicept na nÉces. Helsinki: Societas Scientiarum Fennica.

*Beatus quid est.* Ed. by Martha Bayless, "*Beatus quid est* and the Study of Grammar in Late Anglo-Saxon England". *History of Linguistic Thought in the Early Middle Ages* ed. by Vivien Law, 85–110. Amsterdam: Benjamins, 1993.

Bede, *Opera.* Pars I. *Opera Didascalica.* Ed. by C. W. Jones & C. B. Kendall. (= *Corpus Christianorum, Series Latina,* 123A). Turnhout: Brepols, 1975.

Cassiodorus, *Expositio Psalmorum.* Ed. by M. Adriaen. (= *Corpus Christianorum, Series Latina,* 97–98.) Turnhout: Brepols, 1958.

Donatus, *Ars maior.* Ed. by Louis Holtz, *Donat et la tradition de l'enseignement grammatical,* 603–674. Paris: CNRS, 1981.

Donatus, *Ars minor.* Ed. by Louis Holtz, *Donat et la Tradition de l'enseignement grammatical,* 585–602. Paris: CNRS, 1981.

*First Grammatical Treatise.* Ed. by Einar Haugen. 2nd rev. ed. London: Longman, 1972.

Gregory the Great, *Moralia in Iob.* Ed. by M. Adriaen. (= *Corpus Christianorum, Series Latina,* 143–143A–143B.) Turnhout: Brepols, 1979.

Haymo of Auxerre, *Enarratio in Jonam Prophetam. Patrologiae Cursus Completus [...] Series Latina* 117, 127–142.

Isidore of Seville, *Etymologiae sive origines.* Ed. by W. M. Lindsay. Oxford: Clarendon Press, 1911.

Sedulius Scottus, *Commentarii in Donati Artem Minorem, In Priscianum, In Eutychem.* Ed. by Bengt Löfstedt. (= *Corpus Christianorum, Continuatio Mediaevalis,* 40C.) Turnhout: Brepols, 1977.

Smaragdus, *Liber in partibus Donati.* Ed. by Bengt Löfstedt, Louis Holtz & Adèle Kibre. (= *Corpus Christianorum, Continuatio Mediaevalis,* 68.) Turnhout: Brepols, 1986.

## 9.2. Secondary sources

Amsler, Mark. 1989. *Etymology and Grammatical Discourse in Late Antiquity and the Early Middle Ages.* Amsterdam: Benjamins.

–. 1993. "History of Linguistics, 'Standard Latin', and Pedagogy". *History of Linguistic Thought in the Early Middle Ages* ed. by Vivien Law, 49–66. Amsterdam: Benjamins.

Bayless, Martha. 1993. "*Beatus quid est* and the Study of Grammar in Late Anglo-Saxon England". *History of Linguistic Thought in the Early Middle Ages* ed. by Vivien Law, 67–82. Amsterdam: Benjamins.

Bischoff, Bernard. 1961. "The Study of Foreign Languages in the Middle Ages". *Speculum* 36.209–224.

Draak, Maartje. 1967. "The Higher Teaching of Latin Grammar in Ireland during the Ninth Century". *Mededelingen der Koninklijke Nederlandse Akademie van Wetenschappen* afd. Letterkunde, N.S. 30.109–144.

Holtz, Louis. 1981. *Donat et la tradition de l'Enseignement grammatical.* Paris: CNRS.

Hovdhaugen, Even. 1982. *Foundations of Western Linguistics: From the beginning to the end of the first millenium A.D.* Oslo: Universitetsforlaget.

Irvine, Martin. 1994. *The Making of Textual Culture: 'Grammatica' and literary theory 350–1100.* Cambridge: Cambridge Univ. Press.

Kaster, Robert. 1988. *Guardians of Language: The grammarian and society in Late Antiquity.* Berkeley: Univ. of California Press.

Law Vivien. 1982. *The Insular Latin Grammarians.* Woodbridge: Boydell.

–. 1990. "The History of Morphology: Expression of a change in consciousness". *Understanding the Historiography of Linguistics: Problems and projects* ed. by Werner Hüllen, 61–74. Münster: Nodus.

Luhtala, Anneli. 1993. "Syntax and Dialectic in Carolingian Commentaries on Priscian's *Institutiones Grammaticae*". *History of Linguistic Thought in the Early Middle Ages* ed. by Vivien Law, 145–191. Amsterdam: Benjamins.

Page, R. I. 1982. "The Study of Latin Texts in Late Anglo-Saxon England. 2: The evidence of English glosses". *Latin and the Vernacular Languages in Early Modern Britain* ed. by Nicholas Brooks, 141–165. Leicester: Univ. Press.

Reynolds, Suzanne. 1996. *Medieval Reading: Grammar, Rhetoric and the Classical Text.* Cambridge: Cambridge Univ. Press.

Riché, Pierre. 1976. *Education and Culture in the Barbarian West.* Transl. by John J. Contreni. Columbia: Univ. of South Carolina Press. [Transl. from the French ed., 1962.]

Vineis, Edoardo. 1994 [1990]. "Linguistics and Grammar". *History of Linguistics: Classical and Medieval Linguistics* ed. by Giulio Lepschy, 136–272. Harlow, England: Longman. [Transl. by Emma Sansone from the original ed., 1990.]

Wieland, Gernot. 1985. "The Glossed Manuscript: Classbook or library book?" *Anglo-Saxon England* 14.153–173.

Wright, Roger. 1982. *Late Latin and Early Romance in Spain and Carolingian France.* Liverpool: Francis Cairns.

*Mark Amsler, Ypsilanti, MI (USA)*

# XIV. Linguistic Theory in the Late Middle Ages
# Sprachtheorien des späten Mittelalters
# La théorie linguistique au Bas Moyen-Age

## 76. La grammaire spéculative du Bas Moyen-Age

1. Introduction
2. La grammaire comme science
3. La théorie des modes de signifier
4. La syntaxe
5. L'approche intentionaliste
6. Conclusion
7. Bibliographie

### 1. Introduction

Le début du XIII^e siècle marque un changement très sensible dans les réflexions sur le langage, et tout particulièrement dans la discipline grammaticale, changement auquel on peut attribuer deux causes, intimement liées. La première est d'ordre institutionnel. Si le XII^e siècle était celui des écoles urbaines, des 'sectes' organisées autour d'un maître, le XIII^e siècle est le siècle des universités. Or l'Université inaugure un mode nouveau de production et de transmission du savoir. Elle instaure d'une part des méthodes d'enseignement, le commentaire par questions et la dispute, d'autre part un cursus, un programme, identifié à un certain nombre de textes à lire (Weijers 1995; 1996). Le cursus des arts comprend la grammaire, la logique et la philosophie. La seconde cause tient à l'arrivée d'un corpus de textes, les textes philosophiques d'Aristote, accompagnés de commentaires arabes. La grammaire, conçue comme discipline universitaire, va profondément se modifier. Sur le plan épistémologique, la grammaire se définit maintenant comme une science, fondée sur des principes premiers, possédant un sujet universel et intelligible. Par ailleurs, l'interaction entre les disciplines enseignées à la faculté des arts a des conséquences importantes pour la grammaire universitaire: si le lien avec la logique se maintient, en prenant de nouvelles formes, des liens nouveaux se tissent avec plusieurs textes du nouveau corpus aristotélicien, et notamment avec la *Physique* d'un côté, le *Traité de l'âme* et la *Métaphysique* de l'autre. La *Physique*, nous le verrons, permet une redéfinition totale des notions grammaticales et syntaxiques essentielles. Le *Traité de l'âme* et la *Métaphysique* conduisent les grammairiens à ne plus simplement considérer en elles-mêmes les catégories linguistiques, mais à s'interroger sur les relations entre les unités linguistiques et les éléments de la pensée et du réel.

La production grammaticale universitaire se développe dans des genres divers: (1) des commentaires, sur les *Institutiones Grammaticae* de Priscien (sur Priscien majeur: livres I–XVI, et sur Priscien Mineur: livres XVII–XVIII) (Kneepkens 1995), sur la troisième partie de l'*Ars Maior* de Donat ou *Barbarismus*, sur le *Doctrinale* d'Alexandre de Villedieu; (2) des sophismes, énoncés difficiles qui sont le point de départ de discussions argumentées, ces sophismes étant parfois regroupés en recueils ou 'sommes' (Rosier 1991), comme la *Summa grammatica* de Roger Bacon; (3) des traités indépendants, tel le *Tractatus de constructione* de Gosvin de Marbais ou les *Modi significandi* de Martin de Dacie. Les auteurs des traités sur les 'modes de signifier' ou Modistes, représentent un courant important dans l'ensemble de la grammaire spéculative, qui se développe sur une période assez brève, à Paris tout du moins, entre 1270 et 1320 environ (Pinborg 1967; Marmo 1994), mais voit également des développements ailleurs notamment en Italie ou dans les universités d'Europe centrale (Pinborg 1967). Mais la production de la première moitié du XIII^e siècle doit être considérée pour elle-même, et pas seulement comme annonciatrice des développements ultérieurs, ce que résume l'épithète de 'prémodiste' qui lui est trop souvent accolée. Trois points sont à souligner: (1) certaines caractéristiques sont communes à l'ensemble de la grammaire universitaire et apparaissent dès la première moitié du XIII$^{e}$ siècle; (2) les traités de cette première période élaborent une analyse des constructions non-standard à laquelle s'opposeront les Modistes, et que l'on peut caractériser comme une approche 'intentionaliste', à cause de l'importance accordée à la notion d'intention de signifier; (3) les Modistes développent une philosophie du langage qui est tout à fait originale et sera contestée, sur ce même terrain, au XIV$^{e}$ siècle (Rosier, 1999).

## 2. La grammaire comme science

Comme les autres disciplines enseignées à l'Université, la grammaire doit se définir comme une science, au sens très précis qu'Aristote donne à ce terme dans les *Seconds Analytiques* (Sirridge 1988). Pour cette raison, les commentaires grammaticaux, dès la première moitié du XIII$^{e}$ siècle, posent en guise de préambule des questions très générales: peut-il y avoir une science du langage, y a-t-il une science unique du langage, la grammaire est-elle une science, est-elle une science nécessaire, etc. Les grammairiens se doivent d'introduire une distinction entre ce qui, dans le langage, se prête à une analyse scientifique, et ce qui est de l'ordre du variable et du contingent. Par opposition à la *grammatica positiva* ou *impositiva*, qui s'intéresse aux usages particuliers, la *grammatica regularis* peut être scientifique car elle s'occupe d'événements susceptibles de se laisser décrire au moyen de règles générales et c'est elle qui est appelée *grammatica speculativa*:

La grammaire régulière est celle qui enseigne, au moyen de règles précises, à exprimer correctement les idées qu'on a dans l'esprit; et on la désigne autrement sous le nom de grammaire spéculative parce qu'elle spécule sur les principes, règles et conclusions de la science grammaticale (*Commentaire sur les Flores grammatice* de Ludulphus de Luco).

La grammaire est spéculative "car elle enseigne à spéculer sur [c'est-à-dire à donner les raisons de] ce qui est correct, incorrect et figuré, dans le discours" (Pseudo-Kilwardby, *Super Priscianum maiorem* 31). Les classifications des sciences divisent fréquemment les sciences spéculatives en deux groupes, celles qui traitent des signes et celles qui traitent des choses, et rangent sous les premières les trois disciplines du *trivium* (grammaire, logique, rhétorique), même si elles ne leur reconnaissent parfois que le statut de 'sciences spéculatives auxiliaires' (Jean de Dacie, *Divisio scientie* 41).

Pour être science, la grammaire doit d'abord procéder par voie démonstrative à partir de principes propres et indémontrables. Ces principes sont les modes de signifier. Elle doit avoir un sujet connaissable et universel, distinct de celui des autres sciences. Alors que chez Aristote (*Peri Hermeneias*, c. 1), c'étaient les *passiones animae* qui étaient "identiques chez tous", la grammaire revendique maintenant que quelque chose dans le langage lui-même soit universel. Dès la première moitié du XIII$^{e}$ siècle, l'on dira souvent que ce sont les règles de formation des énoncés qui sont universelles (*Guide de l'étudient* § 162). Les modes de signifier sont partout ce qui permet de constituer les unités linguistiques comme constructibles et d'expliquer leurs constructions.

## 3. La théorie des modes de signifier

Il importe de distinguer l'utilisation grammaticale de la notion de mode de signifier, des élaborations théoriques auxquelles elle a donné lieu.

### 3.1. L'utilisation grammaticale de la notion de mode de signifier

La notion de mode de signifier remonte au XII$^{e}$ siècle (→ Art. 79). Elle a pour origine l'idée, développée par Priscien, selon laquelle les parties du discours doivent être distinguées selon "les propriétés de signification" de chacune d'elles (*Institutiones Grammaticae*, II, 55.4–5), et non pas à partir de la considération de caractéristiques morphologiques comme la déclinaison (*ibid.*, II, 55.20–21). Pierre Hélie commente ce passage en précisant que ce sont les modes de signifier qui permettent de caractériser une partie du discours comme telle, par exemple, pour le nom, le fait de signifier la substance et la qualité (*Summa super Priscianum*, I, 181–182). Tous les noms, quelle que soit leur signification lexicale, se caractérisent par ce mode de signifier, que l'on appellera *mode de signifier essentiel.* Par ailleurs, les grammairiens du XII$^{e}$ siècle reprennent à Aristote, via Boèce, l'idée que le verbe consignifie le temps (*Perì Hermēneías* 16 b), et étendent cette notion de consignification à d'autres accidents grammaticaux, mais également à toute signification secondaire ou oblique: on dit alors que le nom et le verbe correspondant signifient la même chose, mais sur des modes différents (*alio modo, aliter et aliter*) (Pinborg 1967:

30sq.; Fredborg 1973: 28sq. et 1988). Ces significations secondes, qui coïncident en partie avec les accidents, seront appelées *consignificata* puis *modes de signifier accidentels*. On distinguera ensuite ceux qui sont *relatifs* (*respectivi*) (ex. le *cas*, le *nombre*, etc.), et ceux qui sont *absolus* (ex. la *figure*, pour le nom), selon qu'ils jouent ou non un rôle dans la construction.

Vers le milieu du XIII^e^ siècle, les auteurs parisiens opposent la *signification spéciale*, qui correspond au signifié lexical, à la *signification générale*, qui correspond à la propriété caractéristique d'une partie du discours. A la même époque, les auteurs anglais, notamment Robert Kilwardby et Roger Bacon, élaborent un système plus complexe qui permet d'unifier sous la notion de mode de signifier toutes les propriétés grammaticales d'un constructible. Il sera repris par les Modistes (Bursill-Hall 1971). Prenons le mot *homo*, par exemple, en plus de son signifié lexical il comporte (1) un mode de signifier essentiel général qui le situe dans le genre des noms, (2) un mode de signifier essentiel spécifique qui, à l'intérieur de ce genre, le place dans l'espèce des substantifs, (3) des modes de signifier accidentels, qui déterminent ses accidents (masculin, singulier, nominatif), etc. Dès le XII^e^ siècle, les grammairiens insistent sur l'idée que ces propriétés grammaticales sont indépendantes de la signification lexicale: un nom qui signifie un non-être (*chimère, rien*) peut très bien être signifié comme substantif. Robert Kilwardby le dira très clairement au XIII^e^ siècle: la catégorie logique dont relève la chose signifiée ne détermine en rien la catégorie grammaticale dont relève le nom qui la signifie:

Puisque les parties du discours ne se distinguent pas en fonction de distinctions relevant des choses, mais en fonction de distinctions relevant des modes de signifier, toutes les choses peuvent être signifiées sur le même mode, à savoir le mode de la disposition [*modus habitus*, qui caractérise le nom]; par conséquent, quelle que soit la catégorie dont elles relèvent, la quantité, la qualité, etc. les choses peuvent toutes être signifiées par des noms. Et c'est pour cette raison qu'il n'y a pas dix parties du discours, comme il y a dix catégories générales de choses (Robert Kilwardby, *Super Priscianum minorem*, texte cit. par Pinborg 1967: 48).

La construction va être redéfinie à partir de la notion de mode de signifier:

Une construction est une union correcte de constructibles, qui a pour cause leurs modes de signifier, et est inventée dans le but d'indiquer un concept de l'esprit (par exemple, *Glosa Admirantes* sur le *Doctrinale* d'Alexandre de Villedieu 219).

Cette définition est généralement acceptée, mise à part une controverse sur le point de savoir si elle doit ou non comporter l'épithète 'correct'. Contrairement à leurs prédécesseurs, les Modistes pensent généralement que la définition doit pouvoir convenir à toutes les constructions, le fait d'être correct ou incorrect étant un mode d'être accidentel de celles-ci, et non un trait essentiel. La définition s'explicite à partir des quatre causes aristotéliciennes: 'constructibles' dit la cause matérielle, 'union' la cause formelle, 'modes de signifier' la cause efficiente, 'pour indiquer etc.' la cause finale (*Glosa Admirantes*, *ibid.*). Les discussions sur les 'causes de la construction' sont présentes dès la première moitié du XIII^e^ siècle. On cherche à expliquer que chacun des constituants grammaticaux du mot, à l'exclusion de son signifié lexical, a un rôle à jouer dans la construction. L'argumentation se fonde sur le principe simple que les mêmes causes produisent les mêmes effets. Par conséquent, si l'on constate qu'en faisant varier un élément, la construction diffère (devient par exemple incorrecte) on pourra en conclure que cet élément est 'principe de construction'. Puisque *homme blanche* (vs. *homme blanc*) et *Socrate (accusatif) court* (vs. *Socrate court*) sont incorrects, le mode de signifier accidentel est principe de construction. Puisque *blanc court* (vs. *l'homme court*) est incorrect, c'est que le mode de signifier essentiel spécifique (permettant de distinguer adjectif et substantif) l'est également. Le raisonnement vaut dans les deux sens: pour démontrer que le signifié lexical n'est pas principe de construction on peut soit dire que l'on trouve la même construction avec des constructibles de sens différents (*le cheval de Socrate, le chapeau de Socrate*) soit que deux constructibles de même sens (par ex. *une leçon* [*lectio*], *il lit* [*legit*]) ont des constructions différentes. On ne peut pas conclure de la différence d'acceptabilité entre *l'âne rationnel* et *l'homme rationnel* au rôle que pourrait avoir le signifié lexical: en effet, cette différence relève de la "propriété" sémantique (*proprietas*), et non de la "congruité" grammaticale (*congruitas*). Or cette "propriété" (*proprietas*) ou acceptabilité, qui se fonde sur la compatibilité sémantique des constituants, et dépend donc de leur signification lexicale, est par définition hors du champ de la grammaire. Elle est par contre du ressort de la logique, puisqu'elle permet de déterminer si un énoncé est vrai ou faux: en effet, *l'âne est rationnel* est faux, alors que *l'homme est rationnel* est vrai (voir par ex. *Glosa Admirantes* 220–221; Martin de Dacie, *Modi significandi* 94–100; Mathieu de Bologne, *Quaestiones* 83–88 et 115–126).

### 3.2. Les discussions philosophiques sur la notion de mode de signifier

C'est essentiellement dans les traités *Sur les modes de signifier*, que l'on rencontre des discussions philosophiques sur la notion de mode de signifier. La triade aristotélicienne (cf. Aristote, *Peri Hermeneias*, c. 1), mot, concept, chose se voit ainsi redoublée en une seconde triade, mode de signifier, mode d'intelliger, mode d'être. Une même 'chose', par exemple la souffrance, peut avoir différents modes d'être, peut être au repos ou en mouvement, et donc être conçue et signifiée comme associée à l'un ou l'autre de ces modes d'être: associée au premier elle deviendra un nom (*souffrance*), au second un verbe (*souffrir*):

Les parties du discours se distinguent par leurs modes de signifier, par lesquelles elles se distinguent spécifiquement, et ne se distinguent pas par leurs signifiés, puisque l'on peut avoir un signifié un et identique pour toutes les parties du discours, ou du moins pour plusieurs parties du discours, ce qui apparaît bien dans les mots *dolor* [douleur, nom], *doleo* [verbe], *dolens* [participe], *dolenter* [adverbe], *heu* [interjection], qui signifient une et même chose selon le signifié spécial (Michel de Marbais, *Summa de modis significandi* 13).

Au départ, les deux triades sont comprises de manière parallèle: de même que le mot est signe du concept qui est signe de la chose, de même le mode de signifier est signe du mode d'intelliger qui est signe du mode d'être. Mais l'on réinterprète très tôt les deux triades dans un sens différent: de même qu'il s'agit de la même chose qui existe, qui est pensée, et qui est signifiée, il s'agit de la même propriété qui existe, est pensée et est signifiée. Mode d'être, mode d'intelliger et mode de signifier sont trois modes d'existence de la même réalité (Martin de Dacie, *Modi significandi* 6–7). Ces deux conceptions vont être articulées grâce à l'introduction de la distinction entre modes de signifier et d'intelliger passifs et actifs, chez les Modistes de la seconde génération. L'identité réelle concerne les modes passifs: la propriété peut exister réellement (mode d'être), ou être conçue (mode d'intelliger passif), ou encore être signifiée (mode d'intelliger actif). La relation de signe vaut pour les modes de signifier actifs: le mode de signifier actif est le signe du mode d'intelliger actif et du mode d'être (*Quaestiones super Sophisticos Elenchos* 122–123; Michel de Marbais 16–17; voir Marmo 1994: 151–158). La constitution d'une unité linguistique complète dépend d'une double imposition (ou articulation), qui consiste en l'adjonction successive de deux formes à une matière qui est le son vocal (*vox*): l'adjonction d'une *ratio significandi* transforme ce son en signe d'une chose, ou *dictio*. L'adjonction d'une *ratio consignificandi* ou mode de signifier actif transforme le son vocal en 'con-signe' qui est formellement une partie du discours: en plus de la chose, un mot comme *souffrance* renvoie à plusieurs de ses propriétés réelles, qu'elle 'consignifie' (Jean de Dacie, *Summa grammatica* 213–214; cf. aussi p. 105).

Les modes de signifier actifs vont être, en tant que propriétés du son vocal signifiant, ce qui détermine les constructions possibles dans lesquelles il peut entrer. L'on repensera également en termes nouveaux la question de l'équivocité d'un nom comme *canis* (chien de terre, chien de mer, constellation) et on s'interrogera pour déterminer quel est le mode d'existence de ses trois signifiés, s'il s'agit d'un nom unique ou de trois noms distincts, ou encore si le verbe dont il est sujet doit être au singulier ou au pluriel (Ebbesen 1980; Marmo 1994: chap. 5.1). Les réflexions sur la signification et les modes de signifier doivent autant aux discussions grammaticales inspirées par les *Institutiones* de Priscien, qu'aux débats sur l'équivocité, prenant leur source dans les *Réfutations Sophistiques* d'Aristote.

Ces élaborations théoriques permettent de renforcer la démonstration, menée sur le plan grammatical (cf. *supra* 3.1.), de l'indépendance de principe entre les modes de signifier et le signifié lexical, qui fonde l'autonomie de la grammaire et délimite le champ de problèmes qui est de son ressort. En effet, les modes d'être des choses sont indépendants de leur être même. Toute chose peut donc être conçue et signifiée sur n'importe quel mode. Ceci confirme le caractère *ad placitum* du langage. Celui qui a institué les mots a pu très bien choisir de désigner une réalité n'ayant pas d'existence réelle comme si elle était subsistante, d'où le substantif *nihil*, ou une chose en mouvement comme si elle était au repos, d'où le nom *motus*. En fait, cette indépendance de principe des modes de signifier fait l'objet de discussions et de désaccords. Certains remarquent que le nom *homme* est au masculin, parce qu'il renvoie à une personne de sexe mâle, ou que *Socrate* est un nom propre au singulier, parce qu'il désigne un individu: dans de tels cas le premier instituteur, qui était à la fois grammairien (pour connaître les propriétés des noms) et métaphysicien (pour connaître les propriétés des choses), a été contraint de faire coïncider l'imposition seconde (celle des modes de signifier) avec l'imposition première (celle qui lie un signifié à un son vocal). Ce fonctionnement semble nécessaire à la démonstration du caractère 'scientifique' de la grammaire, car il montre que les modes de signifier ont bien une origine réelle et ne sont pas de pures "fictions" (*figmenta*). Raoul le Breton en conclut que le langage n'est pas *totaliter ad placitum* "totalement arbitraire": si l'imposition du signifié l'est, ce n'est pas le cas de l'imposition des modes de signifier ou propriétés grammaticales, qui doivent être non contradictoires avec la chose signifiée et entre eux (Lambertini 1989; Rosier 1992; 1994a).

C'est cette philosophie du langage des Modistes qui va être critiquée au XIV<sup>e</sup> siècle, dans des milieux différents (Pinborg 1967: chap. II.3; Kaczmarek 1994, 1985; Rosier 1996). Cependant, l'acception grammaticale de la notion de mode de signifier, séparée de ses implications ontologiques, va subsister, même dans des traités plus élémentaires.

## 4. La syntaxe

Un trait qui distingue de manière particulièrement claire la grammaire spéculative du XIIIe siècle est l'utilisation de la *Physique* d'Aristote. C'est un point historiquement intéressant, car on sait que la *Physique* a fait l'objet d'interdictions officielles à plusieurs reprises, dans la première moitié du XIIIe siècle. Or il est à noter que cette physicisation de la grammaire apparaît chez deux maîtres anglais, Robert Kilwardby et Roger Bacon, alors que les maîtres parisiens de la première moitié du XIIIe siècle n'y ont pas particulièrement recours. Dans la seconde moitié du XIIIe siècle, elle semble se répandre de manière très générale, aussi bien dans des ouvrages non modistes (cf. le *Tractatus de constructione* de Gosvin de Marbais) que dans les traités *Sur les modes de signifier.*

La *Physique* permet d'abord de redéfinir les catégories grammaticales. Le nom est dit, selon Priscien, signifier la substance et la qualité, le verbe, l'agir et le pâtir. Un auteur parisien comme Jean le Page, dans les années 1250, utilise exclusivement cette terminologie, qui sera qualifiée de *dicta antiquorum* dans les années 1260. Kilwardby introduit, à côté des définitions traditionnelles, des formulations nouvelles à partir de l'opposition physique entre repos ou disposition stable (*quies, habitus*) et mouvement, devenir (*motus, fieri*). Cette opposition sera utilisée par les Modistes de la première génération, avant qu'on ne lui substitue la distinction entre *modus entis* et *modus esse.*

La lecture de la *Physique* conditionne également, de manière très caractéristique, la modification des définitions des différents cas. Pierre Hélie, au XIIe siècle, avait déjà introduit, à côté de la définition du cas comme 'inflexion' ou déclinaison, une caractéristique fonctionnelle, en disant que le cas est la marque des différentes manières dont on peut parler d'une chose, en tant qu'elle agit ou pâtit, en tant qu'on agit sur elle, etc. (*Summa super Priscianum* I, 386). Avec la *Physique*, ce trait fonctionnel va être repris différemment. On décrit en effet la phrase comme un mouvement, se déroulant entre un *terminus a quo* (ou *principium*) et un *terminus ad quem* (Kelly 1977). Le cas devient alors le mode de signifier conférant au constructible la propriété d'occuper l'une de ces deux fonctions, ou éventuellement les deux, comme dans le cas de l'ablatif. Un nom à l'ablatif peut en effet être terme d'un verbe transitif actif, ou principe d'un verbe impersonnel passif.

La *Physique* permet également de repenser les catégories traditionnelles de transitivité et d'intransitivité, à partir de la distinction entre action transitive, qui se réalise dans une chose extérieure à l'agent (l'action de bâtir est dans ce qui est bâti), et action immanente, qui n'a pas d'autre fin qu'elle-même, et qui est totalement en son agent (voir Aristote, *Métaphysique* Θ 8):

> Un est l'acte dont la nature est telle qu'il ne lui suffit pas d'avoir un agent, et qui n'est pas en son agent comme dans un sujet, mais qui requiert une matière extrinsèque à l'agent. Un tel acte transite en une matière extrinsèque, et c'est un acte transitif, comme *je frappe Socrate.* Autre est l'acte qui ne transite pas dans une matière extrinsèque, mais qui est en son agent, et ne requiert pas une matière extrinsèque en laquelle il transite, c'est un acte absolu, qui apparaît bien dans cet acte *je cours*; la course en effet est dans celui qui court (Boèce de Dacie, *Modi significandi* 188–189)

Le principe organisateur de la construction est la notion de *dépendance*, qui se substitue à celle de régime (*regimen*) introduite précédemment:

Toute combinaison de mots est une relation naturelle de dépendance (Roger Bacon, *Summa grammatica* 42).

Robertus Anglicus explicite, dans ses *Sophismata Grammaticalia*, les différents modèles qui ont permis de mettre en place cette relation. La relation du *dépendant* (*dependens*) au *terminant* (*terminans* = le mot qui termine la relation de dépendance ouverte par le *dépendant*) est analogue à la relation de l'accident par rapport à la substance, de la forme par rapport à la matière, de la puissance par rapport à l'acte. Puisque, en effet, selon la *Physique*, toute génération se fait à partir de termes opposés, il importe que les deux constituants d'une combinaison soient d'une nature telle qu'elle leur permette de se combiner. La relation accident-substance devient le paradigme de toute construction, le *dépendant* signifiant sur le mode de l'adjacence, le *terminant* sur le mode de la substance ou de l'indépendance (*modus per se stantis*). On retrouve cette relation dans la construction adjectif-substantif, mais également dans la relation verbe-substantif, par exemple.

Cette théorie de la dépendance a une autre origine, à savoir l'analyse de la détermination telle qu'elle intervient dans le cadre des *Réfutations Sophistiques*, et plus précisément à propos de la *fallacia compositionis et divisionis*, qui décrit la polysémie potentielle au niveau de la phrase. Dans une proposition comme *Deus desinit nunc esse* l'ambigüité vient de ce que l'adverbe *nunc* peut déterminer soit le verbe principal (sens: Dieu maintenant commence à être), soit l'infinitif (sens: Dieu commence à être-maintenant). L'on cherche à établir des règles régissant ces processus de détermination, qui permettent de décrire comme sens composé l'interprétation jugée la plus naturelle, comme sens divisé l'autre. Plusieurs critères sont discutés, qui reposent sur la nature grammaticale du déterminant (l'adverbe de négation est plus apte à déterminer un verbe à l'indicatif), des déterminables (par exemple leur degré d'autonomie: l'infinitif étant plus autonome, il est plus apte à être déterminé par l'adverbe dans l'exemple ci-dessus; le substantif est plus apte à terminer une dépendance qu'un adjectif, *je vois un homme-bon musicien* sera donc composé, *je vois un homme bon-musicien*, divisé) ou encore l'ordre des constituants (le déterminant doit précéder le déterminable) (de Libera 1984; 1990).

L'on a ainsi, avec la notion de *dépendance*, un principe général qui permet de décrire toutes les constructions comme des relations asymétriques à deux termes, l'un qui ouvre la dépendance, l'autre qui la termine. Ces deux fonctions dans la relation dépendent des propriétés des constituants, les modes de signifier. L'on voit ainsi que l'ensemble du système fonctionne à partir d'une dialectique entre puissance et acte. Les modes de signifier sont des traits syntaxico-sémantiques qui confèrent au constructible une aptitude à occuper telle ou telle fonction dans une construction. Chaque type de construction (transitive, intransitive, des actes, des personnes) est décrite en énumérant les propriétés que doivent posséder le *terminant* et le *dépendant*.

Tab. 76.1: Les types de constructions

| | | | |
|---|---|---|---|
| intransitive des actes ⟨1⟩ | *terminant*<br>Socrate | ⇐ | *dépendant*<br>court |
| intransitive des personnes ⟨2⟩ | *déterminable*<br>cheval | ⇐ | *déterminant*<br>blanc |
| transitive des actes ⟨3⟩ | *dépendant*<br>il-lit | ⇒ | *terminant*<br>un livre |
| transitive des personnes ⟨4⟩ | *déterminant*<br>le fils | ⇒ | *déterminable*<br>de-Socrate |

Les différentes relations de construction s'imbriquent entre elles pour former une phrase:

| | | | | |
|---|---|---|---|---|
| *video*<br>dépendant | ⇒ | *legentem*<br>terminant | | |
| | | *legentem*<br>dépendant | ⇒ | *librum*<br>terminant |
| *video*<br>je-vois | | *legentem*<br>celui-qui-lit | | *librum*<br>un-livre |

On voit dans cet exemple que la fonction se définit par rapport à une construction donnée, et non au niveau de la phrase: le participe *legentem* a plusieurs modes de signifier, qui lui permettent aussi bien d'occuper une fonction de *terminant* (dans la première construction) que de *dépendant* (dans la seconde). Ce type de modèle, cependant, rencontre des difficultés, (1) lorsque les constructions semblent impliquer plus de deux constructibles, comme c'est le cas avec la préposition (verbe+prép.+nom) ou la conjonction (ex nom+*et*+nom), (2) lorsqu'elles concernent, en surface du moins, un seul constructible (ex. *currit*, il-court), (3) lorsqu'il s'agit de constructions dont les constituants sont des propositions (non dotées en principe de modes de signifier) et non des mots simples (ex. *l'homme court, donc l'animal court*). L'on peut y ajouter le cas des constructions dites absolues (*magistro legente, pueri proficiunt* "le maître lisant [= pendant que le maître lit], les élèves profitent") qui ne semblent dépendre, ni syntactiquement, ni pour l'assignation de leur cas, d'autres éléments de l'énoncé (Rosier 1983: chap. 4; Covington 1984; Pinborg 1984: VII et IX; Marmo 1994: chap. 6).

## 5. L'approche intentionaliste

Les éléments du système que nous avons décrit dans les paragraphes 3.1, et 4. se mettent en place dès la première moitié du XIII^e^ siècle, notamment dans les traités d'origine anglaise, mais sont élaborés en un système cohérent par les Modistes, chaque génération apportant des raffinements et réélaborations originales, en fonction des difficultés rencontrées. Dès la première moitié du XIII^e^ siècle, cependant, on voit discuter d'autres questions, liées au problème des énoncés figurés ou déviants, et de leur acceptabilité. L'idée générale est que de tels énoncés, bien que grammaticalement incorrects, peuvent cependant être acceptables, en raison de l'intention de signifier particulière du locuteur. Cette idée sera explicitement critiquée par les Modistes, pour des raisons de nature épistémologique: la grammaire devant procéder par causes, pour déterminer des règles de fonctionnement universelles, ne peut considérer tel ou tel énoncé dans sa singularité. Seul un énoncé construit selon règles définies par la grammaire peut être jugé acceptable. En d'autres termes, la grammaticalité gouverne strictement l'acceptabilité. Tout en reconnaissant ces objections, les tenants de l'approche 'intentionaliste', Robert Kilwardby, Roger Bacon, et de nombreux auteurs anonymes, tout au long du XIII^e^ siècle, développent un modèle qui ne prend pas simplement en compte les propriétés des constituants et leurs combinaisons, mais également les relations dynamiques entre locuteur et auditeur:

[...] L'énoncé le plus correct est celui qui représente le plus correctement l'intention du locuteur (*intentio proferentis*), qu'on le prenne en lui-même ou qu'on le considère par rapport à l'intention du locuteur; il n'est pas cependant toujours correct pris absolument, et il arrive souvent qu'il soit incorrect selon les règles de la grammaire (Robert Kilwardby, *Commentum super Priscianum minorem*, éd. dans Kneepkens 1985: 138 = Roger Bacon, *Summa grammatica* 15–16; cf. Rosier 1994b: 42).

Ces auteurs distinguent en effet, pour un énoncé, deux types de complétude. La première est *ad sensum*: les constituants présentent 'aux sens' tout ce qui est nécessaire à l'interprétation de l'énoncé. La seconde est *ad intellectum*: les données offertes aux sens sont insuffisantes, mais l'auditeur peut, par un effort intellectuel, reconstruire la forme correcte, et comprendre le sens visé par le locuteur. C'est le cas, de manière très simple, avec les constructions figurées. Une construction de ce type, par exemple *turba ruunt* "la foule se précipitent" est grammaticalement incorrecte. Cependant elle possède une *ratio excusans*: d'un côté une raison qui a rendu cette infraction aux règles possible (ici le fait que *la foule* a un sens pluriel), de l'autre une raison qui l'a rendue nécessaire (l'intention de l'auteur d'insister, précisément, sur cette pluralité). En reconnaissant ces deux *rationes*, l'auditeur peut à la fois reconstruire l'énoncé grammatical de même sens, et comprendre le sens particulier voulu par l'auteur (Rosier 1988; Kneepkens 1985; Sirridge 1990).

Certains auteurs laissent entrevoir la source de ce type d'analyse, à savoir la lecture des textes sacrés. Lorsqu'un passage lu ne se laisse pas interpréter au plan de l'intellection première (*intellectus primus*), c'est-à-dire en se reportant simplement aux règles du langage ordinaire, il importe pour l'interprète de passer à un second plan, celui de l'intellection seconde (*intellectus secundus*). Comme le dit l'un des auteurs, à partir d'un adage emprunté au *De Trinitate* d'Hilaire de Poitiers, et souvent utilisé par les théologiens, ce n'est pas la chose qui doit se soumettre au discours, mais le discours à la chose (*verba subserviunt intellectum et* ⟨*sermo*⟩ *subiectus est rei*). Il invoque explicitement Augustin pour justifier que, comme c'est le cas pour l'Ecriture Sainte, l'on doive parfois s'écarter des règles du discours commun. Cette inspiration augustinienne coïncide bien avec la prise en compte des relations entre locuteur et auditeur.

Ce modèle de description est très puissant et permet d'expliquer le caractère acceptable d'énoncés non canoniques. Parmi ces énoncés se trouvent:

(1) des énoncés incomplets tels que le constructible manquant puisse être automatiquement restitué en fonction de ses proprié-

tés grammaticales intrinsèques (*de virtute sermonis*), c'est le cas de *curro* "je-cours": en effet, s'il n'y a pas un sujet exprimé, on retrouve celui-ci automatiquement, puisqu'il est "(sous-)entendu" (*intelligitur*) dans le verbe de première personne. Pour donner un autre exemple, souvent repris, on peut citer celui que donne Priscien: — *Quel est le bien suprême dans la vie?* — *L'honnêteté. L'honnêteté* est à lui seul une phrase, mais une phrase incomplète, sans verbe. Or du fait qu'il s'agit d'une réponse, on peut, en se reportant à la question, rétablir la phrase complète, de manière automatique: *L'honnêteté est le bien suprême dans la vie.*

(2) des énoncés incorrects qui doivent être interprétés en faisant recours à l'*intentio proferentis*: c'est le cas pour les constructions figurées, que nous avons déjà mentionné.

(3) des énoncés incomplets où ce qui manque peut être restitué, avec un certain choix de la part de l'interprète, *ex discretione lectoris* ou *auditoris*. C'est un cas intéressant où l'auditeur se trouve face à un énoncé incomplet, et où il a donc à restituer une forme canonique correspondante, mais où, contrairement aux cas précédents, plusieurs restitutions sont possibles. Rober Bacon prend l'exemple *ite, missa est*. Il explique que l'auditeur peut comprendre différents verbes sous-entendus (la messe est chantée, dite, etc.). Le caractère elliptique de l'énoncé lui confère une richesse sémantique supérieure à celle qu'il aurait si un seul verbe était exprimé. Le sens de l'énoncé est pour ainsi dire la résultante de tout ce qui peut être sous-entendu. L'auditeur peut alors sélectionner, selon son choix propre, celui qui lui paraît le plus adéquat dans une situation donnée. Il y a donc ici un choix pour l'auditeur (*discretio auditoris*).

(4) des énoncés où le constructible qui fait formellement défaut peut être retrouvé par recours à la situation ou au contexte linguistique, notamment ceux qui comportent un acte exercé (*actus exercitus*). Les auteurs développent ici une conception que l'on pourrait appeler pragmatique du langage. On peut l'illustrer au moyen de quelques exemples. L'un, souvent utilisé, est celui de la séquence *Aqua aqua*! "De l'eau, de l'eau!". Sur le plan grammatical, il s'agit de la répétition de deux substantifs, qui normalement ne constituent pas un énoncé complet. Mais si elle est utilisée dans une situation particulière où il y a un feu, tout le monde comprend qu'elle équivaut à dire que l'on veut qu'on aille chercher de l'eau; cette séquence est alors totalement adéquate l'intention de signifier du locuteur (*intentio proferentis*), au sens visé (*intellectus intentus*). Un autre exemple est celui de la phrase constituée par la simple prononciation de l'adverbe *bene*! "bien". Il lui manque un sujet et un verbe. Mais, expliquent nos grammairiens, le verbe, qui correspond à un acte signifié (*actus significatus*), n'a pas à être exprimé car il est *exercé* dans la situation de discours. En effet, si je dis *bene* à un maître en train de frapper un élève, tout le monde comprend que je veux l'encourager à le frapper. L'acte de frapper *verberare*, réellement exercé, dispense de l'expression correspondante, qui produirait une répétition inutile (ex. *bene verbera*). Un autre exemple fait partie d'un corpus d'énoncés liturgiques: *In nomine patris, filii et spiritus sancti* "Au nom du Père, du Fils et du Saint-Esprit". Cet énoncé ne comporte pas de verbe. Cependant ce dernier n'a pas besoin d'être exprimé, c'est-à-dire d'exister comme un acte signifié, du fait que l'acte est exercé. Le prêtre ne veut pas signifier la bénédiction, mais l'effectuer: il s'agit donc d'un énoncé particulier qui n'est pas simplement fait pour signifier quelque chose, mais pour faire quelque chose, ce qui est la définition moderne d'un énoncé performatif (sur ces exemples, voir Rosier 1994b: chap. 1 et 5).

## 6. Conclusion

La grammaire spéculative, telle qu'elle se développe avec la naissance de l'université, n'est pas monolithique. Elle subit des évolutions, tout au long du XIII$^{e}$ siècle et au-delà, et des variations très sensibles lorsqu'on considère des textes contemporains. Ces évolutions ne peuvent se laisser décrire linéairement et en bloc, pour tous les aspects de l'analyse du langage. Dans l'état actuel de la recherche, il semble plus fructueux — et plus prudent — de considérer de manière dissociée chacun de ces aspects (les discussions de nature épistémologique sur la scientificité de la grammaire, l'utilisation et la justification philosophique de la notion de mode de signifier, les notions intervenant dans les analyses syntaxiques, comme celle de dépendance, l'approche intentionaliste pour l'analyse des énoncés déviants, la prise en considération des actes de langage), quitte à voir ensuite comment ils s'articulent entre eux. L'on comprendra mieux ainsi que certains traits de ces analyses se développent très tôt et dans des milieux donnés ou que d'autres se combinent en un système visant davantage la cohérence théorique que l'adéquation empirique, que certains éléments font l'objet de critiques de nature philosophique, au XIVe siècle, tandis que d'autres peuvent se maintenir jusque dans des traités plus élémentaires.

## 7. Bibliographie

### 7.1. Sources primaires


An., *Destructiones modorum significandi.* Ed. par Kaczmarek (1994).

Boèce de Dacie, *Modi significandi* = Boethius Dacus, *Modi significandi.* Ed. par Jan Pinborg & Heinrich Roos. La Haye: Mouton, 1969.

*Glosa Admirantes* = An., *Glosa Admirantes super Doctrinali Alexandri de Villadei.* Ed. d'extraits dans Thurot (1869).

Gosvin de Marbais, *Tractatus de constructione.* Ed. par Rosier (1998).

*Guide de l'étudiant.* Ed. par Claude Lafleur, *Le 'Guide de l'étudiant' d'un maître anonyme de la Faculté des Arts de Paris au XIIIe Siècle.* Laval: Faculté de Philosophie, 1992.

Jean de Dacie, *Divisio scientie* = Johannes Dacus, *Divisio scientie.* Ed. par Otto (1955).

Jean de Dacie, *Summa grammatica* = Johannes Dacus, *Summa grammatica.* Ed. par Otto (1955).

Ludofus de Luco, commentaire sur les *Flores Grammatice* = Ludolfus de Luco (ca. 1489–1494), *Flores grammatice sive Florista cum Commento.* Basel: Johannes Amerbach. [Bibl. Nat. lat. 4° Rés. X 781 (1).]

Martin de Dacie, *Modi significandi* = Martinus Dacus, *Modi significandi.* Ed. par Heinrich Roos. Copenhague: Gad, 1961.

Mathieu de Bologne, *Quaestiones* = Matheus Bononiensis, *Quaestiones super modos significandi.* Ed. par Rosier (1992).

Michel de Marbais, *Summa de modis significandi* = Michael de Marbasio, *Summa de modis significandi.* Ed. par Kelly (1995).

Pierre Hélie, *Summa super Priscianum* = Petrus Helias, *Summa super Priscianum.* Ed. par Leo Reilly. Toronto: Pontifical Institute of Medieval Studies, 1993.

Ps-Kilwardby, *Super Priscianum maiorem.* Ed. par Karen Margaretha Fredborg, Niels Jorgen Green-Pedersen, Lauge Nielsen, Jan Pinborg, "The Commentary on 'Priscianus Maior' ascribed to Robert Kilwardby". *Cahiers de l'Institut du Moyen Age Grec et Latin* 15. (1975).

Priscien, *Institutiones Grammaticae.* Ed. par Martin Hertz. (= *Grammatici Latini*, II–III). 1855–1859. (Réimpr. Hildesheim: Olms, 1981.)

*Quaestiones super Sophisticos Elenchos* = An., *Quaestiones super Sophisticos Elenchos.* Ed. par Ebbesen (1977).

Roger Bacon, *Summa grammatica* = Rogerius Baco, *Summa grammatica.* Ed. par Robert Steele, *Opera hactenus inedita Rogeri Baconi*, fasc. XV. Oxford: Clarendon Press, 1940.


### 7.2. Sources secondaires


Bursill-Hall, Geoffrey L. 1971. *Speculative Grammars of the Middle Ages: The doctrine of* partes orationis *of the modistae.* La Haye: Mouton.

Covington, Michael A. 1984. *Syntactic theory in the High Middle Ages: Modistic models of sentence structure.* Cambridge: Cambridge Univ. Press.

Ebbesen, Sten. 1977. *Incertorum Auctorum, Quaestiones super sophisticos elenchos.* Hauniae: Gad.

–. 1980. "Is 'canis currit' Ungrammatical?: Grammar in Elenchi commentaries". *Studies in Medieval Linguistic Thought Dedicated to Geoffrey L. Bursill-Hall* éd. par Konrad Koerner et al., 53–68. Amsterdam: Benjamins.

Fredborg, Karen Margareta. 1973. "The Dependence of Petrus Helias' *Summa super Priscianum* on William of Conches' *Glose super Priscianum*". *Cahiers de l'Institut du Moyen Age Grec et Latin* 11.1–57.

–. 1988. "Speculative grammar". *A History of Twelfth-Century Western Philosophy* éd. par P. Dronke, 176–195. Cambridge: Cambridge Univ. Press.

Kaczmarek, Ludger. 1985. "*Modi significandi* and their Destructions: A 14th century controversy about methodological issues in the science and theory of language". *Fallstudien zur Historiographie der Linguistik: Heraklit, d'Ailly und Leibniz* éd. par Klaus Dutz & Peter Schmitter, 21–33. Münster: Nodus.

–. 1994. *Destructiones modorum significandi.* Amsterdam: Grüner.

Kelly, Louis Gerard. 1977. "La *Physique* d'Aristote et la phrase simple dans les traités de grammaire spéculative". *La grammaire spéculative, des Modistes aux Idéologues* éd. par André Joly & Jean Stefanini, 105–124. Lille: Presses Universitaires.

–. 1995. *Michael de Marbasio*, Summa de modis significandi: Critical edition with an introduction. Stuttgart–Bad Cannstatt: Frommann-Holzboog.

Kneepkens, Cornelis H. M. 1985. "Roger Bacon on the Double Intellectus: A note on the Development of the Theory of *Congruitas* and *Perfectio* in the first half of the thirteenth century". *The Rise of British Logic: Acts of the Sixth European Symposium on Medieval Logic and Semantics* éd. par P. O. Lewry, 115–143. Toronto: Pontifical Institute.

–. 1995. "The Priscianic Tradition". *Sprachtheorien in Spätantike und Mittelalter* éd. par Sten Ebbesen, 239–264. Tübingen: Narr.

Lambertini, Roberto. 1989. "*Sicut tabernarius vinum significat per circulum*: Directions in contemporary interpretations of the Modistae". *On the Medieval Theory of Signs* éd. par Umberto Eco & Costantino Marmo, 107–142. Amsterdam: Benjamins.

Libera, Alain de. 1984. "Référence et champ: Genèse et structure des théories médiévales de l'ambiguité (XII$^{e}$–XIII$^{e}$ siècles)". *Medioevo* 10.155–208.

–. 1990. "De la logique à la grammaire: Remarques sur la théorie de la *determinatio* chez Roger Bacon et Lambert d'Auxerre (Lambert de Lagny)". *Studies in Medieval Grammar and Linguistic Theory in Memory of Jan Pinborg* éd. par Geoffrey Bursill-Hall, Sten Ebbesen & Konrad Koerner, 209–226. Amsterdam: Benjamins.

–, & Irène Rosier. 1992. "La pensée linguistique médievale". *Histoire des Idées Linguistiques*, vol. II, éd. par Sylvain Auroux, 115–186. Liège: Mardaga.

Maierù, Alfonso. 1990. "La linguistica medioevale: Filosofia del linguaggio". *Storia della linguistica* éd. par Giulio Lepschy, vol. II, 101–168. Bologna: Il Mulino.

Marmo, Costantino. 1994. *Semiotica e linguaggio nella scolastica: Parigi, Bologna, Erfurt 1270–1330. La semiotica dei Modisti.* Rome: Istituto Storico Italiano per il Medioevo.

–. 1995. "A Pragmatic Approach to Language in Modism". *Sprachtheorien in Spätantike und Mittelalter* éd. par Sten Ebbesen, 169–183. Tübingen: Narr.

Otto, Alfredus. 1955. *Johannis Daci Opera.* Hauniae: Gad.

Pinborg, Jan. 1967. *Die Entwicklung der Sprachtheorie im Mittelalter.* Münster: Aschendorff.

–. 1994. *Medieval Semantics: Selected studies on Medieval logic and grammar* éd. par Sten Ebbesen. Londres: Variorum Reprints.

Rosier, Irène. 1988. "Le traitement spéculatif des constructions figurées au XIII$^{e}$ siècle". *L'héritage des grammairiens latins, de l'Antiquité aux Lumières*, éd. par Irène Rosier, 181–204. Louvain: Peeters.

–. 1991. "Les sophismes grammaticaux au XIII$^{e}$ siècle". *Medioevo* 17.175–230.

–. 1992. "Mathieu de Bologne et les divers aspects du pré-modisme". *L'insegnamento della logica a Bologna nel XIV secolo* éd. par D. Buzzetti et al., 73–164. Bologna: Presso l'Istituto per la storia dell'Università.

–. 1994a. "*Res significata* et *modus significandi*: Les enjeux linguistiques et théologiques d'une distinction médiévale". *Sprachtheorien in Spätantike und Mittelalter* éd. par Sten Ebbesen, 135–168. Tübingen: Narr.

–. 1994b. *La parole comme acte: Recherches sur la grammaire et la sémantique au XIII$^{e}$ siècle.* Paris: Vrin.

–. 1996. "Quelques controverses mediévales sur le conventionnalisme, la signification et la force du langage". *Philosophies and Language Sciences: An historical perspective in honour of Lia Formigari* éd. par Daniele Gambarara, S. Gensini & A. Pennisi, 69–84. Münster: Nodus.

–. 1998. *Le Tractatus de constructione de Gosvin de Marbais.* Nijmegen: Artistarium.

–. 1999. "Modisme, pré-modisme, proto-modisme: Pour une définition modulaire". *Medieval Analyses in Language and Cognition* éd. par Sten Ebbesen & Russ Friedman, 45–81. Copenhague.

Sirridge, Mary. 1988. "Robert Kilwardby as 'scientific Grammarian'". *Histoire, Epistémologie, Langage* 10: 1.7–28.

–. 1990. "Robert Kilwardby: Figurative constructions and the limits of grammar". *Studies in Medieval Grammar and Linguistic Theory in Memory of Jan Pinborg* éd. par Geoffrey Bursill-Hall, Sten Ebbesen & Konrad Koerner, 221–237. Amsterdam: Benjamins.

Thurot, Charles. 1869. *Extraits de divers manuscrits latins, pour servir à l'histoire des doctrines grammaticales au Moyen Age.* Paris: Bibliothèque Impériale (Réimpr., Frankfurt a. M.: Minerva, 1964).

Weijers, Olga. 1995. *La 'disputatio' à la Faculté des Arts de Paris (1200–1350 environ).* Turnhout: Brepols.

–. 1996. *Le maniement du savoir: Pratiques intellectuelles à l'époque des premières universités (XIII$^{e}$–XIV$^{e}$ siècles).* Turnhout: Brepols.

*Irène Rosier-Catach, Paris (France)*

# 77. Linguistic description and analysis in the Late Middle Ages

1. Introduction: The sources
2. The 12th century: The period of systematization and innovation
3. The end of the 12th and the first decades of the 13th century: The period of transition and the division of grammar
4. The influence of new learning
5. The second part of the 13th century and the 14th century
6. Epilogue
7. Bibliography

## 1. Introduction: The sources

The implicit model for linguistic description in Ancient grammar was the 'word and paradigm'. Through the works of the Latin grammarians Donatus (4th century) and Priscian (6th century) in particular, this model also became the framework for language description in the Middle Ages (Hockett 1954: 210; Robins 1990: 29). The 'word and paradigm' model is based on (1) the identification of the word as an isolable, significative linguistic entity (cf. also Auroux 1994: 174–175); (2) the establishing of word classes to distinguish and classify the words in a language; (3) the introduction and definition of adequate grammatical categories to describe and analyse (a) the flection of the words, which are classified according to paradigms of related forms (Lyons 1981: 100, n. 1; Auroux 1994: 174); and (b) the syntactic relations between the words in the construction of phrases or sentences.

Two levels of description are clearly distinguished in this model; they have remained the most important parts in which the subject matter of traditional school grammar is divided: (1) the level of flection or morphology; and (2) the level of syntax, which – and this should be borne in mind – is mainly focused on the relationship between words and does not exceed the domain of the sentence (Robins 1960: 122; Auroux 1994: 174).

In the works of the Ancient grammarians the medieval scholars found the most important ingredients for the identification of the parts of speech, for establishing the grammatical categories by means of definitions and descriptions, and for a systematical arrangement of them. These constituted the source and the point of departure for further discussion. In Ancient grammar, the *dictio* was considered to be the smallest isolable independent unit of an *oratio*. It contrasted with the linguistically inferior level, the syllable, by the fact that it has a meaning of its own. The *dictiones* were classified into the parts of speech according to semantic-morphological-syntactic criteria.

In the linguistic theories of the 13th and 14th centuries, however, the distinction between *dictio* and *pars orationis* was theoretically underpinned and became of paramount importance (Pinborg 1967: 43–44: a *dictio* is a word that does not yet have a *modus significandi*, and is therefore not yet part of the actual language; Rosier 1983: 52ff.). The grammatical secondary categories, especially flection, were transmitted in the most important sources in a clear and coherent manner. What was lacking was a uniform linguistic theory and a coherent explanation of the terminology with which the language was described. Moreover, syntactic doctrine had been developed only rudimentally in Antiquity; this situation was to continue up till the beginning of the 12th century.

Basically, both in Antiquity and during the Middle Ages grammar was semantically oriented. Though language was not considered to be a blueprint of reality, isomorphy between language, thought and reality was commonly accepted (Priscian, *IG* XI, 7; de Rijk 1977: 233); and together with thought, or rather as an extension of thought, language was the very tool to get a grip on reality. It was the task of grammar to describe and establish language. This was done with the help of a set of semantic instruments that was based on the difference between the *prima impositio* (the first name imposition which concerns the names of things, events, qualities etc., e. g. "horse" or "to walk") and the *secunda impositio*, which concerns the names of names such as *nominativus*, *genus* (Pinborg 1967: 37–38). This dichotomy has deep epistemological and metaphysical roots. The grammatical categories were primarily described in terms of their correlates in the non-linguistic reality, with which they show a certain similarity (Bursill-Hall 1972: 23; cf. also Pinborg 1967: 82).

The significatory aspect had always been central in the descriptions and definitions on the word level and on the sentence level. Priscian indicates this very clearly by starting his section on the parts of speech with a discussion of the characteristic features of their respective structures of meaning (*proprietates significationum*, *IG* II, 17ff.). The definition of the sentence (*oratio*) also has a strongly significatory character: a correctly construed series of words which conveys a perfect (or complete) meaning (*perfecta sententia*; Rosier 1988a: 357–358). Furthermore, one has to bear in mind that the metaphysical set of concepts 'substance' and 'accident' is at the basis of Priscian's view of the composition of the sentence: the noun or pronoun and the verb have a mutual relationship that is similar to that between substance and accident, since a (pro)noun signifies a substance and a verb the accident (*IG* XVII, 105–106). Another aspect which contributed to a more or less philosophical approach was the translation of the Alexandrian-Greek term *parhepómena* into Latin *accidentia*, which was also the Latin term for the Aristotelian *sumbebēkóta* (Robins 1990: 39).

The only set of syntactic notions of some importance transmitted by Priscian was concentrated on the concept of *transitio*, which was used, however, only intuitively and epitechnically.

## 2. The 12th century: The period of systematization and innovation

This situation of considerable dependence on the Ancient sources continued till the early 12th century. In the first decades of that century, the key notion became the *causa inventionis*: the investigation of the significatory rationale and structure – the raison d'être – of the word (Fredborg 1973: 12ff.). An important innovation was the introduction of the distinction in the nominal signification between *significatio/significatum*, the meaning of a noun, i.e., its intension, the unique result of one imposition or name giving; and the *nominatio/nominatum* (in the 12th century also called *appellatio/appellatum*), the extension of a term, i.e., its referential aspect (de Rijk 1967: I, 194, 228, 525ff.; Fredborg 1988: 181–185). In the middle of the century a distinction was made between those secondary grammatical categories which are co-significatory, such as number, case and tense, the so-called *significationes secundariae*, and those categories which are not co-significatory but are, in fact, common properties, such as *species* (being a principal or a derivative word) or *figura* (being uncomposed, composed derived from a composed word). These are the so-called 'common properties', which are of marginal importance (Hunt 1950: 34; Fredborg 1973: 32ff.).

From a grammarian's point of view, the most important activity of the second half of the 12th century may have been the systematization of syntax. Notions such as *regere/regimen*, *exigere*, *transitio* and related concepts, *suppositum/appositum*, *a parte ante/a parte post* (i.e. the division of the sentence in a part before and a part after the finite verb), and *constructio* were defined and, step by step, brought together in a manageable and more or less coherent system (Hunt 1950: 35–36; Kneepkens 1978, 1990a, 1990b). Important discoveries were, *inter alia*, the identification of the notion of 'grammatical subject' (*suppositum/supponere verbo*), and the operationalization of the distinction between the binary construction and the sentence construction. But notwithstanding these new developments, it was the Aristotelian-Boethian dialectica model as it was found in the writings of the *Logica Vetus* which constituted the underlying theoretical framework, and Priscian's model of description remained the manifestly present point of departure.

## 3. The end of the 12th and the first decades of the 13th century: The period of transition and the division of grammar

Near the end of the 12th century we are confronted with two competing divisions of grammar. One was based on the *Ars maior* of Donatus; it comprised normative grammar (*grammatica preceptiva*: books I–II), prohibitory grammar (*grammatica prohibitiva*, also called *De barbarismo*: the first part of book III) and the grammar of figurative speech (*grammatica permissiva*: the rest of book III). In fact, only book III would play a serious role in grammatical thinking in the later Middle Ages.

The other division was founded on Priscian's works: (1) orthography (*orthographia*: the rules were found, for the most part, in the first two books of the *Institutiones grammaticae*); (2) morphology (called *etymologia*: the discussion of the eight parts of speech, preserved in book II–XVI; books I–XVI were known under the name of the *Priscianus maior*); (3) syntax (*dyasynthetica*: transmitted in books XVII and XVIII; also called the *Prisci-*

*anus minor*); and (4) prosody (*de accentu*, mainly based on the Ps.-Priscian, *De accentu*, 12th century).

Though both divisions interfered, the latter division, Priscian's, was dominant. On the other hand, especially the 13th century grammarians – who have recently been called the 'Intentionists' – paid particular attention to the domain of figurative speech (Rosier 1988b: 57–58, 1994).

## 4. The influence of new learning

The effects of the influx of new learning occasioned by the translation of Aristotle's *Analytica Posteriora*, a work fundamental to his scientific methodology, and by the rediscovery in the last decades of the 12th and the early 13th centuries of the Stagirite's works on psychology, physics, metaphysics and ethics, together with the Arabic commentaries on these works, were crucial for the development of knowledge in the Latin West. These works produced a new scientific paradigm and created new theoretical frameworks for grammatical description (Pinborg 1982: 255). Many achievements of the late 12th century were, however, impossible to delete, as for instance the reception of Petrus Helias' *Summa* and the anonymous *Summa* on the *Priscianus minor*, the so-called *Absoluta cuiuslibet* show. A highly important factor was also that Priscian's *Institutiones* and Donatus' *De barbarismo* were part of the curriculum of the arts faculties and were regularly read at the newly founded universities. This resulted in a new scholarly genre, university grammar. The grammarians were not focused any longer on teaching Latin grammar and language, but on teaching grammar as such – a trend which in our modern academic system would be called 'general linguistics'. This development, however, which had already started in an embryonic stage in the 12th century (Fredborg 1980), had a drastic influence on the intellectual framework in which the texts were commented on, and on the conceptual instruments used for language description (Rosier 1995: 135–136; Kneepkens 1995: 248–249). The teaching of grammar, logic, physics, metaphysics and ethics was thrown together in a more or less uniform fashion; the commentaries, questions, and procedures were remarkably similar in all disciplines, which also led to the adoption of similar doctrinal views.

This development can already be observed clearly in the first decades of the 13th century. In the *quaestiones* commentary by Nicholas of Paris on Priscian's book XVII, the first grammatical commentary of this type known to us, one meets as central notions the *significatio generalis* (and the corresponding *significata generalia*) and the *significatio specialis* (and the *significata specialia*), which are respectively (a) the general meaning, which is common to every word belonging to a specific part of speech and is therefore constitutive of the part of speech; and (b) the lexical meaning, which is different for every word. The *significatio generalis* belongs to the domain of the grammarian, who is interested in well-formedness or grammatical congruity (*congruitas*). It is the principle of construction (*principium construendi*), as is emphasized in a commentary on Aristotle's *De interpretatione*, attributed to Nicholas.

The signification of the noun is twofold, sc. the general signification by which every noun is said to be a noun, i. e. since it signifies substance with quality. And this general signification is the principle of construction. Therefore the grammarian uses it for his definition the noun (*Duplex est significatio nominis scilicet generalis qua nomen omne dicitur esse nomen, idest quia significat substantiam cum qualitate. Et hec significatio generalis est principium construendi. Ideo hanc ponit gramaticus in diffinitione nominis*; cf. Ms München clm 14460, 65[ra]).

In combination with the co-significatory *accidentia* – these are based on the common properties of the things – this 'principle of construction' is the cause of the well-formedness of the phrase or sentence.

The *significatio specialis*, for which the noun was invented *ad placitum*, is the 'chasse gardée' of the logician, since here truth and falsity, sc. of the proposition, are at stake. But the *significatio specialis* cannot be part of the definition of the noun, since it varies for every noun.

There is also a special signification for which a noun has been imposed arbitrarily. And this signification is considered by the logician, since it is relevant for truth and falsity. But he could not put it in the definition of the noun, since it is not one and the same, but varies according to the nouns (*Est etiam significatio specialis ad quam impositum est nomen ad placitum. Et hanc considerat logicus, quia penes hanc consistit ueritas et falsitas. Sed hanc non potuit ponere in diffinitione nominis, quia non est una sed diuersa in diuersis nominibus*; cf. Ms München clm 14460, 65[ra]).

This discussion and the subsequent creation of a theory of signification is a result of the attention paid by the Parisian academics in the 1230s to the *syncategoremata* (Braakhuis 1979, 1997) and of the semantic difficulties with which these scholars were confronted when dealing with the definitions of the noun and of the verb in Aristotle's *De interpretatione* (Kneepkens 1999: 36−37), in particular with regard to the infinite noun (*non-homo*) and verb (*non-currit*), in other words when the scope of the negation was at stake. However, in the end it turned out not to be the current track.

On the other hand, the commentaries on Aristotle's definitions of the noun and of the verb in his *De interpretatione* show that the university teachers of this period were well aware of the existence of two different approaches. Nicholas of Paris argued in his *De interpretatione* commentary that the grammarians had put case in the definition of the noun (cf. Donatus in his *Ars maior* and in his *Ars minor*: *nomen est pars orationis cum casu corpus aut rem proprie communiterve significans* "a noun is a part of speech with case signifying a body or a thing properly or commonly"), since case is that accident which most pertains to substance and is syntactically the most important.

The grammarian defines the noun by means of case, since of all the accidents case most pertains to substance and most contributes to its position in a sentence; according to Petrus Helias case is the principle on which the relation of substance to act is based. Since it is the grammarian's task to pay attention to the congruent and incongruent arrangement of the constructions, he correctly defines the noun by means of case, since case is more important to arrangement [than tense/time] (*Dicendum quod propterea gramaticus diffinit nomen per casum, quia casus inter omnia accidentia magis est apprehendens substantiam et etiam plus faciens ad ordinationem, ut dicit Petrus Helyas: Casus est principium ordinandi ad actum substantiam. Vnde cum ipse gramaticus plus intendat ordinem constructionum congruum et incongruum, conuenienter diffiniuit per casum, quia plus operatur ad ordinem*; cf. Ms Vat. lat. 3011,f. 23[ra]).

The logician is more interested in tense/time, since the truth and falsity of a proposition can change in accordance with time.

The logician considers, however, the noun inasmuch as it effects truth or falsity, and therefore he is obliged to insert the aspect of time into the definition [Aristotle, *De interpretatione* c. 2: "a noun is a spoken sound significant by convention, without time, none of whose parts is significant in separation"], since by its change time changes truth or falsity (*Loycus autem cum consideret nomen inquantum operatur uerum et falsum, debuit diffinire per tempus, quia tempus per sui mutacionem mutat ueritatem et falsitatem*, Nicholas, ib.).

In discussions on medieval language description, the term *modus significandi* nearly always has a central role. For the development of the notion of *modus significandi* the period at issue was of paramount importance (→ Art. 76). Although the term *modus significandi* had already been regularly used in a grammatical context as early as the 12th century (Fredborg 1973: 28; Rosier 1995: 138−139), we find in the logical writings of Nicholas of Paris for the first time a technical use of the terms *modus significandi substantialis* (later to be called *essentialis*), which is constitutive of the part of speech, and the *modus significandi accidentalis* or *modus consignificandi*, which corresponds with the co-significatory accidents (*consignificata*) and is, together with the *modus significandi substantialis*, regarded as the cause of the well-formed construction (Kneepkens 1999: 18−19).

Evidently, this change is connected with contemporary developments in the field of logic: the *logica moderna* with its focus on the context and the properties of the terms (de Rijk 1967: I). Of course, the interaction between grammar and logic is a frequent phenomenon, but, apart from the doctrinal aspects, this approach is in so far new that it tackles a semantico-logical problem with a grammatico-semantic instrument which, afterwards, was applied to grammar itself. Moreover, it is obvious that the masters of the faculty of arts, who were teaching grammar/linguistics and logic at the same time, looked for a coherent doctrine of signification.

An entirely different contribution to linguistic description came from Aristotle's *Physics* (Kelly 1977). In his *quaestiones* commentary on the *Priscianus minor* (Ms Oxford, Bodl. Lat. misc.f. 34), Nicholas of Paris had already based his analysis of the constructions on the notions of Aristotle's *Physics*, books III and VIII, 8. The constructions, which traditionally had been defined and classified with the help of *transitio* and related notions (*intransitio*/*reciprocatio*/*retransitio*), were reconceptualized with the *motus* concept: every construction is with motion or without motion (*omnis constructio aut est sine motu aut cum motu*). The traditional terminology, however, is maintained in the description: the intransitive construction corresponds to the construction without movement (*sine motu = quies*), the transitive construction to the construction with direct movement (*cum motu directo*), the reciprocal construction to the construction with circular movement (*cum motu circulari*), and finally the retransitive construction to the construction with bended back movement (*cum motu reflexo*).

A confusion of the complex of the notions of *actus/passio* and the *motus* concept is also found in Nicholas' *De interpretatione* commentary (Vat. lat. 3011,f. 24[ra]):

"The substance from which the act comes forth/the indicative verbs are, in comparison with the substance, in flux and movement" (*substantia a qua egreditur actus/verba indicativa comparata ad istam substantiam sunt in fluxu et in motu*).

A similar situation is found in the commentary on the *Priscianus minor* by Robert Kilwardby and in the *Summa gramatica* of his pupil, Roger Bacon, who were both active in the 1240s in Paris. *Substantia, actio/passio* and *transitio* remained the central notions, but the attention for the *modus significandi* was increasing. Kilwardby and Bacon systematically used the difference between the *modus significandi essentialis* and *accidentalis*. The verb was said to signify a movement or with the mode of movement and, linked to the notion of movement, the terms of the movement were also introduced into grammar: the *terminus a quo* and the *terminus ad quem*. The *terminus a quo* is only found before the verb, and must be a nominative case (cf. *Summa gramatica* 78.242–5; 79.9–14; 85.24–26), the *terminus ad quem* is *a parte post*: the object term.

Another innovation regarding syntax in particular, was the introduction of the dependence model, although in the field of syntax, too, continuity remained. The *regimen* model elaborated in the early 12th century was to remain operational during the entire Middle Ages, especially, but not exclusively, in elementary grammar. The dependence model rooted in the binary construction (*constructio dictionis cum dictione*), which had been elaborated theoretically in particular by Robert Blund (ca. 1180; Fredborg 1988: 193–194; Kneepkens 1990a: 175). In Nicholas of Paris' *quaestiones* commentary the verb is said to depend on (*dependens*) the nominative case (*casus rectus*), which is independent (*per se stans*) and represents the agent; Nicholas speaks of *dependere a*. In Kilwardby's commentary the term has already become more current, and the combination *dependere ad* is applied to the difference between the nominative case (*casus rectus*) and the oblique cases: the *casus rectus* is based on the mode of independence (*modus per se stantis*), the *obliqui* signify with dependence on something else.

The nominative case has been placed before the oblique cases, since these are derived from the nominative and signify with dependence, whereas the nominative case has independence (*Rectus est ante obliquos, quia cadunt ab ipso et quia significant cum dependentia ad aliud, cum rectus fit per modum stantis*; Vat. Chigi, L.V-159,f. 5[rb-va]).

The semantically incomplete substantive verb, sc. "to be", or a pronoun which, by its nature, is not qualified, depend when used in a sentence, on a following part of the proposition, which acts as its determinative.

'I am that': the substance signified by the substantive verb, is not yet qualified; therefore it is still depending on the following word, looking for it as its determinative (*'ego sum ille': nondum qualificata est substantia significata per verbum substantivum; quare adhuc ad subsequens dependet expectans ipsum tamquam sui determinativum*; Vat. Chigi, L.V-159,f. 13[vb]).

The combination *dependentiam determinare* is also found in Bacon's *Summa*. He even argues that dependence is the principle of every construction (Kneepkens 1990b: 164). Remarkably, we do not meet the term "terminate" (*terminare*), which the next generation of grammarians connected with dependence, in a *dependentia* context in Bacon's writings. *Terminare* appears to be part entirely of the *motus/fluxus* complex.

The infinitive verb has another nature, sc. the mode of signifying its contents, sc. by the mode of standing upright, of nominative and of fixed; and as far as this nature is concerned it [the infinitive verb] is able to terminate the fluens, at least that which is not truly a movement, but something which behaves by the mode of fluens, which is the significate of this verb 'is' (*Alia natura est in illo, scilicet modus significandi suam rem, scilicet per modum stantis et recti et fixi, et quantum est de natura hac potest terminare fluens, adminus illud quod non est vere motus, set aliquid se habens per modum fluentis, quod est significatum hujus verbi 'est'*; Bacon, *Summa gramatica* 131).

In fact we are confronted with a deepening of linguistic thinking, which took place gradually. Up till the first decades of the 13th century the traditional Priscianic scheme of definitions and descriptions was operational, which had a firm semantic-morphological-syntactic basis. A noun was described semantically as signifying substance or in the way of a substance (*substantia* or *modo substantiae*), which was translated, however, morphosyntactically: without tense and with case inflection (*sine tempore et in casuali inflectione*; Petrus Helias 196). On the elementary level this system was found throughout the Middle Ages.

On the level of advanced linguistic instruction it was replaced by a system of description in which the conceptualization of reality became central: the parts of speech and the grammatical categories were reformulated within the framework of the *modi significandi*. The Ancients said that every noun signifies substance with quality; this must be understood, however, in a modal way (Martinus of Dacia, *Summa* 11.9–10: *modaliter intelligendum est*; cf. Pinborg 1967: 47–49). The first signs of a new, complete system of language decription is found in Kilwardby's commentary. He states explicitly that the parts of speech are not distinguished according to the distinction of the things (*res*) in the outer world, but that they are differentiated according to the difference of mode of signifying. He argues that the *res* of all the *praedicamenta* can be signified in the same way, e. g. by the mode of habit (*non distinguuntur partes orationis secundum distinctiones rerum, sed secundum distinctionem modorum. Possunt autem omnes res eodem modo significari, scilicet per modum habitus*; Ms Vat. Chigi, L.V-159, f. $8^{rb}$).

He also presents a general framework for the description of the parts of speech which, except for some minor points, was to remain valid in the 14th and 15th centuries. First, he uses the distinction between signifying an affect of the mind (*mentis affectus*) and signifying a concept of the mind (*mentis conceptus*) in order to separate the interjection from the other parts of speech (*Pars orationis aut significat mentis conceptum aut mentis affectum. Si mentis affectum, sic est interiectio*) – as we shall see below, this separation was cancelled in the 14th century.

The Priscianic distinction between the declinable and indeclinable parts was founded by Kilwardby on signifying a thing, a *res* or signifying a disposition or circumstance (*Si mentis conceptum, aut significat rem aut habitudinem siue dispositionem aut circumstanciam rei*). The noun, pronoun and participle signify the thing (*res*) they signify, by the mode of standing independently and of whether or not (the pronoun) qualified substance; the verb signifies its *res* by the mode of being and becoming (*Si significet rem, aut ergo se habentem per modum stantis et substantie aut per modum esse et fieri. Si secundo modo, sic est uerbum. Si primo modo, aut significat substantiam puram et sic est pronomen aut substantiam perfectam siue completam per qualitatem*). The difference between the noun and the participle is that both signify a qualified substance, but the noun signifies it without action or being acted upon, whereas the participle signifies it with action and being acted upon (*Et hoc dupliciter. Aut enim significat substantiam qualificatam sine actione et passione et sic est nomen, uel cum actione uel passione et sic* ⟨*est*⟩ *participium*). In this point the grammarians of the second part of the 13th century would also make a correction. The verbal character of the participle was more stressed, and together with the verb it received the same *modus significandi essentialis generalis*. The three indeclinable parts left signify a habitude or disposition: the preposition signifies the habitude of the substance to the act (*significat habitudinem substantie ad actum, et sic est prepositio*), the adverb the habitude of the act to the substance (*aut actus ad substantiam, et sic est aduerbium*), and the conjunction the habitude of substances to each other or the habitude of acts to each other (*indifferenter habitudinem substantiarum ad inuicem et actum ad inuicem, et sic est coniuncio*).

## 5. The second part of the 13th century and the 14th century

### 5.1. The intentionists and the modists

Although apparently the Priscianic model remained in force (Robins 1990: 90), and the traces of Kilwardby's commentary, which was used as the university textbook for centuries, turned out to be ineradicable, within the new model increasingly a more evident arrangement was made, regardless of whether one is dealing with treatises of the so-called intentionists (Rosier 1994) or of the stricter and more fundamentally directed Modistae.

The *modi essentiales generales* became the point of departure of language description: the *modi* which are assigned to a *dictio* by our mind through which the *dictio* is a certain part of speech. Thus for instance, the *modus significandi per modum habitus et quietis et per modum determinatae apprehensionis* is the *modus significandi essentialis generalis* of the noun. Without this mode a *dictio* is not a noun.

Martinus of Dacia (ca. 1260) adduced the Aristotelian *materialforma* dichotomy, and called the *modus habitus et quietis* the material part, the *modus determinatae apprehensionis* the formal part. The traditional signifying by the mode of substance, which was commonly found in the writings of the grammarians of the middle of the century was reformulated into *significare per modum habitus et quietis*.

The next level of Martinus' modal hierarchy are the special modes of signifying (*modi significandi speciales*), the modes which are constitutive of the distinction between the proper noun and the appellative noun. These modes are, in their turn, subdivided into other modes so that finally all the items of the Priscianic model are covered.

At the bottom of the modal hierarchy, after all the *modi essentiales*, we find the accidental modes of signifying (*modi significandi accidentales*), which are constitutive of the *accidentia*, which according to Martinus of Dacia are the principles of construction (*principia constructionis*). It is important to stress that these always presuppose the essential modes. The distinction between the respective accidental modes (*modus significandi accidentalis respectivus*), which are constitutive of the constructional *accidentia* like case and number, and the absolute accidental modes (*modus significandi accidentalis absolutus*, which are constitutive of the other *accidentia* like *species*, *figura* and so on, is not yet found in Martinus' treatise (Pinborg 1967: 73; we must bear in mind that this distinction covers the distinction between the *proprietates communes* and the *significationes secundariae* [see above] only partially).

Boethius of Dacia (ca. 1270) replaced the term *pars formalis* of Martinus' *modus significandi essentialis generalis* with the term *specificus*. The specific mode of signifying demarcates one part of speech from another. The *modus significandi per modum habitus et quietis*, for instance, is the *modus essentialis generalis* of the noun, but this mode is also the general mode of the pronoun. Therefore Boethius adduced the *modus significandi per modum determinatae apprehensionis* as the *modus significandi specificus* which separates the noun from the pronoun. The *modi accidentales respectivi* are explicitly called the *principium constructionis* (Boethius 103.42–43), the *modus absolutus* is not involved in syntax (cf. Michael of Marbais 27.23 ff.).

The next generation of modistic grammarians such as Ralph Brito (ca. 1300) and Siger of Courtrai (Kortrijk; ca. 1300) introduced the distinction between the active and passive *modi significandi*: the active *modus significandi* is a property of the sound (*vox*) given by the intellect to the sound, which enables the sound to signify the mode of being; the passive mode of signifying is the property or mode of being in as far as it is signified by an active mode of signifying. This innovation was of paramount importance for the modistic 'Sprachlogik', but did not affect the model of linguistic description seriously.

The *modi significandi essentiales* of the declinable parts were divided by the majority of the grammarians of this period in a material part and a formal part. We have met this division already in Martinus of Dacia's work (see above). To subsume all the parts of speech under the Aristotelian scheme of matter and form and not only the declinable parts, it was necessary to adapt the indeclinable parts, which thus far had only had a simple essential mode of signifying. This shortcoming of the system was remedied in the beginning of the 14th century. Their *modus significandi essentialis generalis*, which is the material part, becomes, for all the indeclinable parts, the *modus significandi per modum disponentis*. Siger of Courtrai subsumes noun and pronoun together under the *modus significandi (essentialis generalis) substantiae, permanentis habitus seu entis* (Siger 3), the *modus significandi essentialis generalis* of the verb and of the participle is, in his system, the mode of signifying by the mode of *fluxus*, becoming or motion, or being (*per modum fluxus, fieri seu motus, seu esse*; Siger 16). It is remarkable that Siger explicitly mentions that the *modus significandi essentialis generalis* of the noun is the principle of the construction of the *suppositum* with the *appositum* (Siger 3–4). In his system all the indeclinable parts, the interjection included, have the *modus disponentis* as the *modus significandi essentialis generalis* (Siger 55–66).

This model, in the form in which it is found at the beginning of the 14th century (Simon, Siger of Courtrai and others; cf. Pinborg 1967: 126), remains the standard and is still met in the Donatus commentary by Erhard Knab (1458 at Heidelberg; *Commentarius in Donatum*, Ms Pal. Lat. 1589, f. 299[ra]).

### 5.2. Syntax

The most important syntactic concepts were developed during the early 13th century (dependence, terminance) and were gradually refined. There is a manifest tendency for syntax to concentrate on binary combinations (see also above). This can be observed in the grammar by Gosvain of Marbais (Gosvain 7.22–26) and in the modistic grammarians. The Modists arranged their syntax in three stages in ascending line. The first stage is that of construction: the combination of constructibles, i. e. of words, not of phrases. A construction is only possible when both dependence and terminance are involved. At this level the intransitive and transitive constructions were distinguished. The Modists spoke of an intransitive construction when the dependence is directed immediately or mediately to the – ideal – *primum constructibile*, the subject term, and there is no mode of terminating in another than the prime constructible (*modus terminantis in alio a primo constructibili*), as in *Socrates currit bene* "Socrates runs well". The finite verb *currit* is dependent on *Socrates*, the adverb *bene* is dependent on *currit*, and so mediately depending on *Socrates*.

A construction is transitive, when we are confronted with a dependence *a parte post*, which is directed to another constructible than the first constructible, e. g. in the sentence *Socrates percutit Platonem* "Socrates strikes Plato"; Here the finite verb *percutit* depends on the subject term, but also on the direct object term. This implies that in the proposition *Socrates percutit Platonem*, *percutit* has a double dependence: one on the first constructible, *Socrates*, and one on the accusative, *Platonem*, and that there are two constructions, an intransitive and a transitive one (cf. Martinus of Dacia 90–94; Thomas of Erfurt 282–284). It is obvious that in this model there is no room left for reciprocal or reflexive constructions: they are all transitive.

The next stage is that of well-formedness (*congruitas*). *Congruitas* is based on the conformity of the *modi significandi*. At this level incongruent combinations such as *Socrates Plato* or *albus currit* were removed from acceptable language use. Which modes were required, however, depended on the construction: *homo albus* is correct, but *albus currit* is not, for *albus* signifies *per modum significandi adiacentis* and cannot, for that reason, function as a *supposium*, subject term.

Finally, we find the perfection. The modistic grammarians spoke only of a perfect sentence when the requirements of the earlier stages were correctly met, a *suppositum* and its *appositum* were present and all the present dependencies were terminated; the latter requirement served to exclude only subordinate clauses.

## 6. Epilogue: The struggle about the modi *significandi* in the 14th and 15th centuries

The discussions about the non-existence of the *modi significandi* which arose in the 1330s and continued till the end of the Middle Ages affected the underlying theory fundamentally, but generally speaking they left the model of language description intact (Pinborg 1967: 195–197, 1982: 268). It must be remarked, however, that those grammarians who had anti-modistic feelings were more inclined to have recourse to *regimen* grammar.

Finally, we must bear in mind that the medieval grammarians tried to incorporate the Priscianic model into the theoretical developments with which they were confronted. They also attempted to explain it from new theoretical insights which arose. This was a challenge to their inventivity and creativity, but, on the other hand, ist also had, sometimes, the disadvantage of acting as a straitjacket.

## 7. Bibliography

### 7.1. Primary sources

Boethius of Dacia, *Modi significandi sive quaestiones super Priscianum maiorem*. Ed. by Jan Pinborg & Henricus Roos. Copenhagen: Gad, 1969.

Gosvin of Marbais, *Tractatus de constructione*. Ed. by Irène Rosier-Catach. Nijmegen: Ingenium Publishers, 1998.

Martinus of Dacia, *Opera*. Ed. by Henricus Roos. Copenhagen: Gad, 1961.

Michael of Marbais, *Summa de modis significandi*. Ed. by Louis G. Kelly. Stuttgart-Bad Cannstatt: Frommann-Holzboog, 1995.

Nicholas of Paris, *Quaestiones super primum librum Prisciani minoris*. Ms Oxford, Bodl., Lat. misc. f. 34.

Nicholas of Paris, *Commentarius in Aristotelis De interpretatione*. Ms Vat. lat. 3011.

Nicholas of Paris, *Commentarius in Aristotelis De interpretatione*. Ms München, CLM 14460 (Attributed to Nicholas.)

Petrus Helias, *Summa super Priscianum*. 2 vols. Ed. by Leo Reilly. Toronto: Pontifical Institute of Mediaeval Studies, 1993.

Priscianus, *IG* = Priscianus, *Institutionum grammaticarum libri XVIII*. 2 vols. Ed. by M. Hertz. Leipzig: Teubner, 1855–1859. (Anast. repr., Hildesheim: Olms, 1961.)

Ralph Brito, *Quaestiones super Priscianum minorem*. 2 vols. Ed. by Heinz W. Enders & Jan Pinborg. Stuttgart-Bad Cannstatt: Frommann-Holzboog, 1980.

Robert Kilwardby, *Commentarius in Priscianum minorem*. Ms Vat. Chigi, L.V-159.

Roger Bacon, *Summa gramatica magistri Rogeri Bacon*. Ed. by Robert Steele. Oxford: Clarendon Press, 1940.

Siger of Kortrijk/Courtrai, *Summa modorum significandi. Sophismata*. Ed. by Jan Pinborg. Amsterdam: Benjamins, 1977.

Thomas of Erfurt, *De modis significandi sive grammatica speculativa*. Ed. by Geoffrey L. Bursill-Hall. London: Longman, 1972.

## 8.2. Secondary sources

Auroux, Sylvain. 1994. *La révolution technologique de la grammatisation: Introduction à l'histoire des sciences du langage*. Liège: Mardaga.

Braakhuis, Henricus A. G. 1979. *De 13de eeuwse tractaten over syncategorematische termen: Inleidende studie en uitgave van Nicolaas van Parijs' Sincategoreumata*. 2 vols. Ph. D., University of Leiden.

–. 1997. "The Chapter on the *Liber Peryarmenias* of the Ripoll "*Student's Guide*": A comparison with contemporary commentaries". *L'enseignement de la philosophie au XIII^e siècle: Autour de « Guide de l'étudiant » du ms. Ripoll 109* ed. by Claude Lafleur, 297–323. Turnhout: Brepols.

Bursill-Hall, Geoffrey L. 1972. *Thomas of Erfurt, Grammatica speculativa*. An edition with translation and commentary. London: Longman.

Fredborg, Karin Margareta. 1973. "The Dependence of Petrus Helias' *Summa super Priscianum* on William of Conches' *Glose super Priscianum*". *Cahiers de l'Institut du Moyen-Âge grec et latin, Université de Copenhague* 11.1–57.

–. 1980. "Universal Grammar According to Some 12th-century Grammarians". *Historiographia Linguistica* 7.69–84.

–. 1988. "Speculative Grammar". *A History of Twelfth-century Western Philosophy* ed. by Peter Dronke, 177–195. Cambridge: Cambridge Univ. Press.

Hockett, Charles F. 1954. "Two Models of Grammatical Description". *Word* 10.210–231.

Hunt, Richard W. 1950. "Studies on Priscian in the Twelfth Century. II. The School of Ralph of Beauvais". *Mediaeval and Renaissance Studies* 2.1–56. (Repr., *The History of Grammar in the Middle Ages*. Collected Papers. Edited with an introduction, a select bibliography and indices by Geoffrey L. Bursill-Hall, Amsterdam: Benjamins, 1980.)

Kelly, Louis G. 1997. « La *Physique* d'Aristote et la phrase simple dans les ouvrages de grammaire spéculative ». *La grammaire générale des Modistes aux Idéologues* ed. by André Joly & Jean Stéfanini, 107–124. Lille: Publications de l'Université de Lille III.

Kneepkens, C. H. 1978. "Master Guido and his View on Government: On twelfth century linguistic thought". *Vivarium* 16.108–141.

–. 1990a. "Transitivity, Intransitivity and Related Concepts in 12th Century Grammar: An explorative study". *De Ortu Grammaticae. Studies in Medieval Grammar and Linguistic Theory in Memory of Jan Pinborg* ed. by Geoffrey L. Bursill-Hall, Sten Ebbesen & Konrad Koerner, 161–189. Amsterdam & Philadelphia: Benjamins.

–. 1990b. "On Medieval Syntactic Thought with Special Reference to the Notion of Construction". *Histoire Epistémologie Langage* 12:2.139–176.

–. 1995. "The Priscianic Tradition". *Sprachtheorien in Spätantike und Mittelalter* ed. by Sten Ebbesen, 239–264. Tübingen: Narr.

–. 1999. "*Significatio generalis* and *significatio specialis*: Notes on Nicholas of Paris' contribution to early thirteenth-century linguistic thought". *Medieval Analyses in Language and Cognition. Acts of the symposium. The Copenhagen School of Medieval Philosophy, January 10–13, 1996* ed. by Sten Ebbesen & R. L. Friedman, 17–43. Copenhagen: The Royal Danish Academy of Sciences and Letters, and the Institute for Greek and Latin, University of Copenhagen.

Lyons, John. 1977. *Semantics*. 2 vols. Cambridge: Cambridge Univ. Press. (Repr., 1978.)

–. 1981. *Language and Linguistics: An introduction*. Cambridge: Cambridge Univ. Press.

Pinborg, Jan. 1967. *Die Entwicklung der Sprachtheorie im Mittelalter*. Münster (Westfalen): Aschendorffsche Verlagsbuchhandlung & Copenhagen: Verlag Arne Frost-Hansen.

–. 1982. "Speculative Grammar". *The Cambridge History of Later Medieval Philosophy from the Rediscovery of Aristotle to the Disintegration of Scholasticism, 1100–1600* ed. by Norman Kretzmann, Anthony Kenny & Jan Pinborg, 254–269. Cambridge: Cambridge Univ. Press.

Rijk, L. M. de 1967. *Logica modernorum: A contribution to the history of early terminist logic*, vol. II/1: *The Origin and Early Development of the Theory of Supposition*. Assen: Van Gorcum.

–. 1977. *Middeleeuwse wijsbegeerte: Traditie en vernieuwing*. Assen & Amsterdam: Van Gorcum.

Robins, R. H. 1960. "In Defence of WP". *Transactions of the Philological Society* (1959) 116–144.

–. 1990. *A Short History of Linguistics.* 3rd ed. London & New York: Longman.

Rosier, Irène. 1983. *La grammaire spéculative des Modistes.* Lille: Presses Universitaires de Lille.

–. 1988a. « La définition de Priscien de l'énoncé: Les enjeux théoriques d'une variante, selon les commentateurs médiévaux ». *Grammaire et histoire de la grammaire. Hommage à la mémoire de Jean Stéfanini* ed. by Claire Blanche-Benveniste, André Chervel & Maurice Gross, 353–373. Aix-en-Provence: Université de Provence.

–. 1988b. « *O Magister* ...: Grammaticalité et intelligibilité selon un sophisme du XIIIe siècle ». *Cahiers de l'Institut du Moyen-Âge grec et latin, Université de Copenhague* 56.1–102.

–. 1994. *La parole comme acte: Sur la grammaire et la sémantique au XIII^e siècle.* Paris: Vrin.

–. 1995. « *Res significata* et *modus significandi*: Les implications d'une distinction médiévale ». *Sprachtheorien in Spätantike und Mittelalter* ed. by Sten Ebbesen, 135–168. Tübingen: Narr.

*Corneille H. Kneepkens, Groningen (The Netherlands)*

# 78. Linguistique et logique durant le Bas Moyen-Age

1. Introduction
2. L'étude de la signification
3. Analyse de la référence
4. Langage, pensée, raisonnement
5. Conclusion
6. Bibliographie

## 1. Introduction

La logique joue un rôle décisif dans l'élaboration de la pensée linguistique au Moyen-Age. Certes, cela se fait en interaction constante avec les autres sciences du langage, et en relation avec d'autres champs disciplinaires. Les premières réflexions proprement médiévales sur la signification des termes se situent au recoupement de la grammaire et de la théologie, mais la grammaire est alors elle-même fortement pénétrée de réflexions logiques et philosophiques. En logique, les premiers manuels de dialectique se prolongent dans les traités sur les propriétés des termes qui, au XIII^e siècle, s'organisent en véritables sommes, au moment où la théorie modiste traduit l'aspiration de la grammaire à une scientificité autonome. Mais la prépondérance de la logique sur les autres arts du langage se confirme au XIV^e siècle et ne se démentira plus jusqu'à la fin du Moyen-Age.

La logique se définit d'abord comme un art ou une science du langage, étudiant le langage en tant qu'il est susceptible de vérité et de fausseté. Mais cette caractérisation n'est pas pleinement adéquate. En premier lieu, la logique s'étend d'un côté à l'analyse de la signification, de l'autre à la validité des raisonnements. En second lieu, à partir d'Albert le Grand, sous l'influence d'al-Fārābī (→ Art. 43) et d'Ibn Sīnā (Avicenne), la logique est aussi définie comme une discipline rationnelle et non plus seulement langagière. Au XIV^e siècle toutefois, la pensée se trouvera elle-même définie comme un langage mental. Logique et analyse du langage resserrent à nouveau leurs liens, et c'est dans le cadre de la logique que se déploie l'analyse de la signification, de la référence, de l'ambiguïté des énoncés.

Ces différents moments de l'analyse logique du langage sont liés aux textes disponibles. Il est usuel de distinguer trois stades. La *logica vetus*, désignant le corpus disponible jusque vers le milieu du XII^e siècle, comprend les *Catégories* et le traité *De l'interprétation* d'Aristote, l'*Isagoge* de Porphyre, et un certain nombre de commentaires ou traités de Boèce. La *logica nova* résulte de la redécouverte au XII^e siècle du reste du corpus logique d'Aristote. Elle est complétée par quelques textes d'origine arabe. Le *De scientiis* (*'Iḥṣā' al-'ulūm*) d'al-Fārābī fournit des éléments de réflexion sur le statut de la logique et sur ses subdivisions. Au milieu du XIII^e siècle, les maîtres disposent de la quasi totalité de la logique du *Šifā'* d'Ibn Sīnā, ainsi que de la logique d'al-Ġazzālī. La *logica moderna* y ajoute un certain nombre de traités, en particulier sur les propriétés des termes, qui, dans leur forme comme dans leur contenu, sont irréductibles au corpus aristotélicien (voir Kretzmann et al. 1981: 45–79, 161–173).

Une évolution aussi complexe est loin de se réduire à l'accumulation de nouveaux matériaux textuels. Elle se fonde en vérité sur la découverte de diverses difficultés logico-linguistiques dans la sémantique des noms divins, dans l'analyse des propositions sacramentelles, dans l'unité de signification d'un énoncé. Ici se croisent logique et grammaire d'une part, ontologie et théologie de l'autre. Ce sont ces exigences théoriques qui stimulent à la fois la redécouverte de nouveaux matériaux et l'invention de traités originaux.

## 2. L'étude de la signification

Le cœur de la réflexion logique médiévale sur le langage est formé par l'interrogation sur la signification, entendue en un sens large. Il s'agit de savoir ce qui fait qu'un terme, un son ou une inscription renvoient à d'autres réalités selon des modalités à définir. Cette réflexion sur la signification trouve ses matériaux textuels à la fois dans la sémiologie augustinienne, dans la grammaire et dans le corpus logique aristotélico-boécien.

### 2.1. Logique, linguistique et théologie

Aux XI^e^ et XII^e^ siècles, l'analyse sémantique se déploie aux confins de la logique, de la grammaire et de la théologie. Un rôle décisif revient à Anselme de Cantorbéry qui, dans son *De grammatico* (ca. 1080), pose les fondements de la distinction entre signification et référence. Il s'interroge sur la signification du terme *grammaticus* (le lettré, celui qui possède la science de lire et d'érire). Il se demande comment *grammaticus* peut être à la fois une substance et une qualité (Henry 1964). Son analyse recoupe la définition que le grammairien Priscien avait donnée du nom: le propre du nom est de signifier une substance avec une qualité (Priscien, *Institutiones* 55). Anselme est conduit à distinguer entre deux sortes de renvois signifiants: *grammaticus* signifie une qualité *per se*, mais signifie une substance *per aliud.* On a ainsi les prémices de toutes les analyses ultérieures de la signification en signification première et signification seconde, ou en signification et connotation. On peut encore dire qu'un tel terme signifie une qualité mais appelle une substance. Et l'on voit alors émerger une notion qui sera cruciale au XIII^e^ siècle, celle d'*appellatio*.

Au XII^e^ siècle, de telles considérations linguistiques se répandent dans les textes théologiques. Dans ses commentaires sur les *Opuscula sacra* de Boèce, Gilbert de la Porrée articule la réflexion sur les éléments de la signification d'un nom avec la distinction, inspirée de Boèce, entre le *quod est* et le *quo est*, le sujet-substance et la forme qui confère l'être (Jolivet & Libera 1987). La relation logico-grammaticale de paronymie, par exemple le rapport entre *albus*, *albedo* et le verbe *albet*, fournit le cadre conceptuel où penser le rapport entre un subsistant, une nature, et l'être conféré par le créateur. Ainsi, pour Gilbert, tout nom a de lui-même une double signification, mais, une fois employé dans une proposition, il 'propose' l'une ou l'autre des réalités qu'il signifie (Nielsen 1976). Cette démarche se poursuit dans l'ensemble de la théologie 'porrétano-boécienne', en des développements qui anticipent souvent sur l'analyse ultérieure des modes de référence des termes. Alain de Lille, en particulier, réfléchissant sur le transfert des catégories du naturel au divin, est conduit à distinguer entre emploi propre et impropre en relation avec ce à partir de quoi un terme est donné (l'humanité pour 'homme') et à quoi il est donné (l'homme individuel) (de Libera 1987).

Pierre Abélard, théologien et logicien, également formé à la grammaire par son maître Guillaume de Champeaux, est l'autre figure marquante du XII^e^ siècle (Jolivet 1969). Dans ses commentaires d'Aristote ou de Boèce, comme dans sa *Dialectique*, il multiplie les analyses sur la nature et les formes de la signification: invention des mots, signification de mots et signification de choses, rôle de *l'intellectus*. Il développe aussi des considérations sur l'univocité et de l'équivocité, il s'attache aux emplois dérivés ou impropres, aux phénomènes de *translatio*, et même à l'influence du contexte.

### 2.2. Problèmes linguistiques transmis par les textes de base de la logique

Tous ces développements sont nourris des textes de la *logica vetus*, qui soulèvent de nombreux problèmes linguistiques se retrouvant tout au long du Moyen-Age. Ainsi, les définitions du début du *Traité de l'interprétation*, avec les commentaires de Boèce, ont fourni le cadre d'une discussion récurrente sur la nature et la convention. Cette discussion prend la forme d'une réflexion sur l'imposition des noms, acte mythique par lequel un sens est attribué à un son vocal. Évoquée comme schème global, l'imposition est simplement destinée à rendre compte du caractère conventionnel des signes vocaux. Mais elle se trouve également investie, à travers l'idée de cause de l'invention (motif initialement grammatical, mais repris par exemple dans l'école porrétaine), dans certaines analyses de la signification.

Plusieurs éléments viennent toutefois nuancer ou complexifier ce thème de la conventionnalité du langage humain. La distinction augustinienne entre les signes naturels et les signes que l'âme se donne (*signa data*), recouvrant des phénomènes plus larges que le seul son vocal institué arbitrairement, vient croiser la référence boècienne. La coupure devient parfois moins nette entre nature et convention, comme dans le cas des interjections, qui conduisent à réfléchir sur le rapport entre la dimension affective et la dimension intellectuelle de l'acte de parole (Rosier 1994: 85ff.). On s'interroge aussi sur l'existence d'un langage chez les animaux, en se référant au commentaire d'Avicenne au *Traité de l'âme*. Celui-ci, en effet, s'appuyant sur la place conféré à l'imagination parmi les facultés de l'âme, estime que les animaux peuvent produire des sons afin de manifester des affects ou de susciter des réactions chez leurs congénères. Ces thèmes sont repris par Albert le Grand (Rosier 1994: 303–315).

Enfin, l'opposition de la nature et de la convention sera réinvestie dans la théorie du langage mental. Ainsi, Guillaume d'Ockham présentera le signe conceptuel, élément du langage mental, comme un signe naturel par opposition aux signes écrits et parlés, conventionnels, qui lui sont subordonnés (*Summa logicae* 7–9, 41–44).

Le début des *Catégories*, quant à lui, lègue aux Médiévaux la question de la synonymie, de l'univocité et de l'équivocité, de la paronymie. Si la synonymie ne soulève guère que quelques questions sur l'équivalence des formules sacramentelles, ou dans un autre registre, sur la présence de synonymes dans le langage mental, l'univocité occupe davantage de place. Originellement, l'*univocatio* désigne le fait que des termes soient subordonnés à un même concept. C'est pourquoi l'homme en tant qu'individu et l'homme en tant qu'espèce étaient considérés comme des univoques, par opposition à l'équivocité de l'homme réel et de l'homme peint, par exemple. En conséquence, l'univocité, désignant l'identité de la 'raison' qui préside à plusieurs usages d'un nom, sert au XII$^{e}$ siècle à thématiser divers phénomènes sémantiques qui seront ultérieurement pensés à travers l'opposition de la signification et de la référence (*suppositio*).

La question connexe de la signification des termes universels revêt de multiples déterminations, métaphysiques et noétiques autant que logiques, c'est pourquoi elle ne saurait être traitée ici dans toute son ampleur (on se reportera à de Libera 1996). On doit cependant la mentionner comme l'un des lieux et moyens de l'analyse de la signification des termes. Pour Abélard, la controverse sur l'universel, qui a pour point de départ la différence entre nom propre et nom commun, est avant tout un problème de langage (*Logica 'ingredientibus'* 9–32). Deux siècles plus tard, d'autres auteurs, au lieu de déployer l'analyse de l'universel dans des études à la frontière du métaphysique et du noétique comme l'avaient fait Albert le Grand ou Duns Scot, chercheront à nouveau à en faire une question purement logico-linguistique. Tel est le cas de Guillaume d'Ockham, tenant l'universel pour un signe mental signifiant en un seul acte (confusément) une pluralité d'individus (*Summa logicae* 47–54; sur les différentes positions concernant l'universel au Moyen-Age tardif, voir l'exposé qu'en fait Jean Sharpe [1990: 50–80]).

2.3. Théories du signe

Ces analyses de la signification recoupent à plusieurs reprises une réflexion générale sur les signes. En ce domaine, l'héritage augustinien est omniprésent, dans les textes théologiques comme dans les productions de la faculté des arts. De la sémiologie augustinienne, les Médiévaux ne retiennent toutefois que quelques éléments: la distinction générale des signes et des choses, l'opposition des signes naturels et des signes que l'âme se donne (*signa data*), et surtout la définition générale: *Signum est res praeter speciem quam ingerit sensibus, aliud aliquid ex se faciens in cognitionem venire* "Le signe est une chose qui, outre l'impression qu'elle produit sur les sens, fait venir, d'elle-même, quelque chose d'autre à la connaissance" (Augustin, *De doctrina christiana* 239; → Art. 71).

La sémiologie d'Augustin se diffuse dans les textes théologiques principalement à l'occasion de l'étude des sacrements. Pierre Lombard a en effet repris au début du livre IV de ses *Sentences* la définition augustinienne du sacrement comme signe sacré. Dès lors, l'étude des sacrements est l'occasion de rappeler ce qu'est un signe et, plus encore, un des lieux d'approfondissement de plusieurs questions sémiologiques ou linguistiques, telles que le rapport entre signe et cause, la synonymie des formules ou le rôle de l'intention du locuteur (Rosier 1994: 112–122, 198–206).

Un exemple de cette démarche se trouve dans le *Commentaire des Sentences* (vers 1235–1245) de Richard Fishacre. La question sur les sacrements y est l'occasion d'une interrogation sur le signe et sur la relation du sensible à l'intelligible. C'est également là que, comme le reprendra ensuite Bonaventure (*Commentaire des Sentences* en 1250–1252), est mise en évidence une double relation constitutive du signe: une relation à quelque chose (ce que le signe signifie) et une relation à celui pour qui il signifie, la seconde étant requise pour que quelque chose fasse vraiment signe.

Roger Bacon va reprendre tous ces éléments pour en faire la synthèse. Il présente dans le *De signis*, en 1267, puis dans le *Compendium studii theologiae*, en 1292, toute une typologie qui permet de réinscrire le signe linguistique dans une théorie générale des signes. Cette classification assez complexe aboutit à une tripartition: signes naturels (tels que la relation de la fumée au feu), signes signifiant naturellement (c'est-à-dire produits sur un mode naturel, soit par l'âme sensitive des animaux, soit par l'âme rationnelle humaine, tels que les cris et les gémissements), et signes signifiant par convention (qu'ils soient linguistiques ou relèvent d'autres systèmes sémiotiques).

Bacon souligne que la définition uselle reçue d'Augustin est insuffisante car elle suppose que le point de départ de la relation signifiante soit sensible et s'ordonne à l'intelligible alors que pour lui, d'une part, la signification est une relation qu s'applique aux choses elles-mêmes, d'autre part, certains intelligibles, tels que les concepts, sont aussi des signes. Il est ainsi conduit à amender la définition augustinienne et propose: *Signum [...] est illud quod oblatum sensui vel intellectui aliquid designat ipsi intellectui* "Le signe est ce qui, offert au sens ou à l'intellect, désigne quelque chose pour cet intellect" (*De signis* 82).

Enfin, il reprend la distinction entre deux relations constitutives du signe, mais en accentuant pour sa part la relation à l'intellect pour lequel il signifie. Le fondement de cette inflexion réside dans la thèse selon laquelle le locuteur rénove l'imposition à chaque acte de langage, conférant à nouveau au mot son sens ou bien le modifiant. Par là, Roger Bacon représente l'un des points culminants d'une tendance à accentuer l'importance de l'intention de signifier dans les phénomènes sémantiques.

Roger Bacon contribue de manière décisive à intégrer la sémiologie à la logique. En prolongeant certaines analyses baconiennes, Guillaume d'Ockham fonde sa doctrine des termes sur une brève théorie des signes (Biard 1989: 52–73; 1997: 15–54). Le concept est un signe naturel, auquel le signe parlé ou le signe écrit sont subordonnés, et qui constitue le principal domaine d'étude de la logique. Cette signification naturelle du concept est fondée sur une relation causale qui, du point de vue de la théorie de la connaissance, conduit du contact intuitif avec la chose à l'élaboration de concepts, propres et communs, qui en retour sont à considérer non pas selon un quelconque être objectif ou intentionnel, non pas comme des objets de signification, mais bien comme des signes, assimilés aux actes mêmes d'intellection. Le signe proprement logico-linguistique se distingue des autres signes qui peuvent signifier par ressemblance (images) ou par causalité (vestiges), en ce que ces derniers impliquent un caractère remémoratif qui n'est pas nécessairement requis par le signe linguistique, et en ce qu'il est destiné à être utilisé dans une proposition. Sur cette base sémiologique sont redéfinis tous les principaux éléments de la logique: la différence de l'abstrait et du concret, la division catégorielle, la signification de l'universel (Biard 1989: 97–126).

## 3. Analyse de la référence

À travers les multiples écoles qui constituent le milieu intellectuel du XII^e^ siècle, se met en place le cadre original, non réductible au corpus aristotélico-boécien, de la sémantique jusqu'à la fin du Moyen-Age: l'études des 'propriétés des termes', qui va se déployer dans des traités sur la *suppositio*, l'*appellatio*, la *copulatio*, l'*ampliatio* ou la *restrictio*, sur les syncatégorèmes ou dans des recueils de sophismes (de Rijk 1962, 1967, 1982; Kretzmann 1982; Spade 1982a).

### 3.1. Émergence de la *logica modernorum*

On a beaucoup débattu de l'origine de terme *suppositio* (de Rijk 1962: 20–22; 1967: 513–528; 1982; Ebbesen 1981b: 35–48). L'usage grammatical du terme, opposant le *suppositum* (sujet) à l'*appositum* (l'attribut), remonte à Priscien et se perpétue jusque dans la grammaire spéculative. En même temps, le *suppositum* peut désigner aussi bien le sujet d'un énoncé que son substrat ontologique, selon une double détermination héritée d'Aristote et de ses commentateurs grecs.

Lorsque la supposition devient le principal concept sémantique et qu'elle est prise comme objet spécifique, elle associe (d'abord pour le sujet, puis plus généralement), une fonction référentielle à une fonction syntaxique. Elle en vient à désigner la propriété qu'a un terme de se référer, en situation contextuelle (et généralement propositionnelle), à une ou à plusieurs choses (de Rijk 1967: II/2, 325, 371, etc.). De ce fait, une relation directe entre le mot et la chose vient au premier plan de l'analyse sémantique. D'abord exprimé à travers les idées de nomination ou d'appellation, ce rapport se condense dans la supposition, entendue comme usage pour quelque chose.

Comparé aux concepts antérieurement mis en œuvre, celui de supposition permet une généralisation. Ainsi, l'appellation, dérivée du modèle de la nomination, ne s'appliquait qu'à des usages 'significatifs' du nom, c'est-à-dire ceux par lesquels les individus sont désignés sur fond de signification d'une nature ou d'une forme commune. La supposition va inclure des usages 'non-significatifs' tels que *homo est nomen* ou *homo est species*. Corrélativement, la supposition n'est plus attachée exclusivement au terme sujet mais devient une propriété du terme, défini comme partie ou extrême de la proposition, donc aussi bien du prédicat que du sujet (de Rijk 1967: II/2, 371).

A côté de l'idée traditionnelle de signification, s'est donc imposée celle de référence des termes, et l'exigence d'étudier les variations de cette référence en fonction de l'usage et du contexte. Il en résulte bouleversement dans la manière d'aborder les questions sémantiques.

Dans les grands traités terministes du XIIIe siècle, la supposition se subordonne tous les autres concepts par lesquels on avait antérieurement cherché à penser les phénomènes de référence, mais la signification reste indépendante de la supposition et antérieure à celle. C'est particulièrement net dans les textes de la 'tradition parisienne' (de Libera 1982b), dont le point culminant est représenté par les *Traités* de Pierre d'Espagne et par la *Somme* de Lambert de Lagny (ou Lambert d'Auxerre). Chez Pierre d'Espagne, le passage consacré à la signification (début du VIe *Traité*) est très bref; en vérité, le lieu d'élection de l'idée de signification est le premier traité, où les sons vocaux, sont, suivant le *Perì hermēneías* d'Aristote, distingués en signifiants et non signifiants. Est significatif, comme l'a établi Boèce, un son vocal qui représente quelque chose à l'esprit de l'auditeur (Pierre d'Espagne, *Tractatus* 80).

La signification entendue en ce sens est donc présupposée par la supposition. Cependant, un terme peut supposer pour des choses qu'il ne signifie pas. Car il signifie strictement ce pour quoi il a été inventé et, dans le cas d'un terme signifiant une nature comme (ce qui est largement admis au XIIIe siècle), la signification ne s'étend pas aux individus qui sont contenus sous elle (Lambert d'Auxerre, *Logica* 206). La priorité de la signification sur la supposition est donc à entendre globalement: seul un terme déjà signifiant est susceptible d'avoir une supposition.

Les textes d'Oxford adoptent pour leur part une présentation un peu différente. Allant moins loin dans l'universalisation de la supposition, la logique *Cum sit nostra* en propose une définition centrée autour de la désignation et limitée aux termes substantifs en position de sujet. De là découle la différence entre signification et supposition: supposer, c'est placer sous un *appositum*, signifier c'est désigner la chose selon la principale raison de son institution (de Rijk 1967: II/2, 446).

En dépit de leurs différences, tous ces textes font de la signification un préalable et pour cela ils ne la placent pas sur le même plan que les autres propriétés des termes. Un tel schéma se retrouve pour l'essentiel dans les textes du XIVe siècle, qu'il s'agisse par exemple de Guillaume d'Ockham à Oxford ou de Jean Buridan à Paris. Cependant, Guillaume d'Ockham fonde l'ensemble sur une théorie du signe où le signe logico-linguistique est caractérisé par son aptitude à supposer pour une ou plusieurs choses dans une proposition, et il analyse de façon plus fine les relations entre les actes de signifier et de supposer pour quelque chose, en diversifiant les sens de signifier, et en traitant de fait la signification comme supposition potentielle (Biard 1989: 74–96). Par la suite, les auteurs s'intéressent essentiellement à l'analyse des variations de la référence en acte, et c'est la supposition, avec ses subdivisions, qui s'impose comme le principal concept opératoire.

L'autre concept qui continue à jouer un rôle crucial au cours du XIIIe siècle est celui d'appellation. À l'origine, l'idée était liée à celle du nom appellatif (ou commun), mais elle a connu une évolution diversifiée. De façon largement dominante, l'appellation est une relation entre un terme et des individus présents. Une fois subordonnée à la supposition, elle devient donc une forme particulière de référence, la dénotation d'étants présents. Les débats portent sur la question de savoir si une telle dénotation est le point de départ d'une *ampliatio* ou le résultat d'une *restrictio*. Les logiciens d'Oxford ont tendance à estimer que les termes signifient d'abord les étants présents, cette capacité référentielle étant ensuite étendue en raison du temps du verbe dans la proposition. Tel est le cas aussi bien de Guillaume de Sherwood (*Introductiones* 128, 274) que de Roger Bacon (*Summulae dialectices* 276–287). Les principaux logiciens parisiens, en revanche (Jean Lepage, Pierre d'Espagne, Nicolas de Paris, Lambert de Lagny), posent que le terme suppose naturellement sans détermination de temps, et que cette supposition naturelle est ensuite restreinte en fonction du temps co-signifié par la copule de la proposition (voir de Libera 1982a).

Au siècle suivant, le sens de ces notions se transforme. L'idée d'appellation perd de son importance: c'est une propriété du prédicat, subordonnée à la supposition (Guillaume d'Ockham, Gauthier Burley). Pour presque tous les auteurs, la supposition naturelle disparaît. Seul Jean Buridan (*Summulae de suppositionibus* 45–49) conserve la supposition naturelle, mais il la redéfinit comme la supposition qui a cours dans certaines propositions, telles que les propositions scientifiques, au sein desquelles le présent ne renvoie pas à un moment déterminé mais revêt une valeur omnitemporelle.

### 3.2. Divisions de la supposition

L'usage d'un terme dans un contexte propositionnel se diversifie en raison de contraintes linguistiques ou d'intentions de signification. Trois siècles de logique terministe ont permis la mise au point d'un outil précis et efficace, aboutissant chez chaque auteur à une division détaillée des modes de supposition.

Une division de base est celle de la supposition personnelle, de la supposition simple et de la supposition matérielle. La supposition matérielle est l'usage auto-référentiel, comme celle du terme parlé "homme" dans "'homme' est un nom". Cette notion provient d'une attention ancienne (déjà fortement présente chez Abélard), aux usages métalinguistiques des termes. La supposition personnelle par contre (comme dans "Socrate est un *homme*") est d'abord la relation privilégiée du terme aux choses singulières. Alors que pour Pierre d'Espagne, Guillaume de Sherwood ou Gauthier Burley, il s'agit de la relation aux individus subsumés sous la nature qui est signifiée par un terme commun, pour Guillaume d'Ockham, il s'agit de la relation du terme aux choses qu'il signifie. Ce déplacement, qui découle à la fois de son ontologie et de sa théorie de la signification, permet de généraliser l'idée de supposition personnelle à des phrases où le signifié n'est pas une chose extra-linguistique ("tout nom vocal est une partie du discours"). La supposition simple, enfin, dont l'exemple canonique est "[l'] homme est une espèce", suscite davantage de débats. Pour un auteur comme Gauthier Burley, prolongeant le réalisme qui était dominant au XIII^e^ siècle, le terme "homme" suppose alors pour ce qu'il signifie, à savoir une nature commune (*De puritate artis logicae* 11–19). Pour Guillaume d'Ockham, en revanche, seul un signe peut être universel, de sorte que l'espèce n'est qu'un concept spécifique. Dans la proposition parlée "[l'] homme est une espèce", le terme "homme" renvoie ainsi au concept auquel le terme parlé est subordonné. Jean Buridan, quelques décennies plus tard, récusera l'idée même de supposition simple comme vestige de l'ancien réalisme, et l'assimilera à une forme de supposition matérielle, accentuant la bipartition entre usage significatif et usage autonyme ou autoréférentiel d'un terme (*Summulae de suppositionibus* 38–44).

C'est la signification du prédicat qui permet de savoir si un terme est employé en supposition simple ou en supposition matérielle et non en supposition personnelle. La subdivision de la supposition personnelle, en revanche, se reconnaît par les inférences que celle-ci permet, en termes médiévaux la "descente" (*descensus*). Les divisions peuvent varier (Maierù 1972: 306–318), mais on peut prendre comme exemple celle qui est proposée par Guillaume d'Ockham, assez classique (*Summa logicae* 209–230).

La supposition discrète est celle d'un nom propre ou d'un démonstratif pris significativement; la supposition commune est celle d'un terme commun. Le critère reste ici purement morphologique.

La supposition commune est déterminée quand on peut descendre aux singuliers par une proposition disjonctive, par exemple *homo* dans *homo currit* "un homme court" (à entendre de façon indéfinie) parce que l'on peut dire "un homme court, donc cet homme-ci court, ou cet homme-là court, etc.", et que de n'importe quelle singulière correspondante, on peut inférer la proposition initiale. Ce mode de supposition concerne autant le prédicat que le sujet.

On appelle 'supposition confuse' toutes les suppositions d'un terme commun autres que la supposition déterminée. La supposition seulement confuse est définie par le fait qu'on ne peut pas descendre aux singuliers par une proposition disjonctive sans modification de l'autre extrême, mais seulement par une proposition dont le prédicat est disjoint, et qu'on pourrait l'inférer de n'importe quelle singulière correspondante. Par exemple "animal" dans "tout homme est un animal", parce que l'on peut en inférer seulement "tout homme est cet animal-ci ou cet animal-là, etc.", et qu'on peut l'inférer de "tout homme est cet animal-ci".

La supposition est confuse et distributive lorsqu'il est possible de descendre d'une certaine manière à une conjonction de propositions, et que la proposition initiale ne peut être formellement inférée d'aucun élément de cette conjonction. Par exemple de "tout homme est un animal" on peut inférer "donc cet homme-ci est un animal, et cet homme-là est un animal, et ainsi de suite". Mais de "cet homme-ci est un animal", on ne peut pas inférer "tout homme est un animal".

Cette descente ne se fait pas toujours de la même manière, puisque parfois elle est possible sans variation à l'intérieur des propositions, excepté la transformation du terme commun en terme singulier – la supposition est alors dite mobile –, parfois elle ne peut se faire que moyennant quelque variation, comme dans "toute homme sauf Socrate court", où le signe syncatégorématique disparaît lorsque j'infère "donc Platon court, et Cicéron court, etc." – et la supposition est alors dite immobile.

### 3.3. Analyse de l'ambiguïté

La théorie de la référence se nourrit de l'étude de toutes les formes d'ambiguïté syntaxico-sémantiques (Rosier 1983, 1988). Les traités du XIIe siècle sur les *Fallacie* reprennent les classifications d'Aristote (de Rijk 1962; Ebbesen 1979, 1981a sur la tradition des *Réfutations sophistiques*). Les paralogismes y sont divisés en fallacies *extra dictionem* et *in dictione*. Ces dernières comprennent six modes: équivocité, amphibolie, composition, division, accent et figure du discours.

Parmi les formes de *multiplicitas in oratione*, la distinction entre sens composé et sens divisé devient un instrument omniprésent dans l'analyse du langage, jusqu'à la fin du Moyen-Age, au point de déboucher au XIVe siècle sur des traités *de sensu composito et diviso* (Maierù 1972: 499–600). Elle conduit dès le XIIe siècle à introduire une distinction entre structure syntaxique immédiate et structure sémantique interprétative.

Cette démarche s'applique à toute forme de composition d'un terme avec un autre, mais elle est surtout mise en œuvre pour résoudre divers problèmes logiques. L'un de ses aboutissements se trouvera dans les traités sur les *Exponibilia*, c'est-à-dire des termes qui exigent que la proposition soit développée ('exposée') en plusieurs phrases sous-jacentes: tel est le cas des verbes "commence" ou "finit", ou d'expressions comme "en tant que", "excepté", etc.

La distinction du sens composé et du sens divisé est aussi appliquée à l'analyse des modalités. Elle sert à marquer la différence entre une proposition où un mode (en particulier: possible, impossible, nécessaire, contingent) porte sur ce que dit la proposition, comme dans *Sortem currere est possibile* et celle où il porte seulement sur la copule, comme dans *homo necessario est animal*. Si les logiciens s'intéressent surtout à différencier les conditions de vérité des modales, et cherchent quelles inférences de l'une à l'autre sont légitimes, ce domaine recoupe d'autres problèmes sémantiques, comme la question du statut du *dictum propositionis* exprimé par la proposition infinitive correspondante (Kretzmann 1970).

À partir du dernier quart du XIIe siècle, ces phénomènes sont étudiés dans la cadre de traités originaux. Ainsi, les *Syncategoremata* examinent des termes qui n'ont pas par eux-mêmes de signification fixe et déterminée. On dira qu'ils 'co-signifient', ou qu'ils modifient la signification des autres termes, dits quant à eux 'catégorématiques' (Kretzmann, 1982: 211–245; Braakhuis 1979). Les *Syncategoremata* traitent de la conjonction, de la disjonction, de la négation, de l'exclusion, de l'exception, de la condition, de la relation, de la distribution, de la modalisation. Lorsque les traités consacrés aux syncatégorèmes tendent à disparaître à la fin du XIIIe et au XIVe siècle, leur matière se trouve répartie dans d'autres genres: les sommes de logique pour les phénomènes de quantification, les modalités, la condition (avec les traités sur les conséquences), les exponibles pour l'exception, l'exclusion et la reduplication, ou encore les recueils de sophismes.

Pourtant l'attention aux syncatégorèmes a été un moment fort de l'analyse médiévale du langage. On est passé d'une recension de termes à l'analyse de fonctions syntaxiques ou sémantiques, avec l'idée qu'un même terme peut faire l'objet d'un usage catégorématique ou d'un usage syncatégorématique. De même, l'étude des syncatégorèmes a conduit à analyser les phénomènes d'inclusion dans la portée d'un terme, donc la question de la subordination logique impliquée par l'ordre de la phrase, à travers des phrases types comme *Omne animal est rationale vel irrationale*. Les variations sémantiques dues à l'ordre des termes seront appliquées à des termes comme 'infini' (Guillaume Heytesbury, *Tractatus de sensu composito et diviso*), et les idées d'inclusion et de portée utilisées plus largement pour analyser les verbes signifiant des actes de l'esprit ("promettre", "devoir") (par exemple Jean Buridan *Sophismata*).

Comme ces derniers exemples l'indiquent, l'étude des syncatégorèmes recouvre largement celle des sophismes, c'est-à-dire de propositions ambiguës, au premier abord déroutantes, susceptibles d'être vraies et fausses selon tel ou tel point de vue.

Les sophismes sont un des lieux majeurs des innovations médiévales en matière de logique et de théorie du langage (Read 1993). Ils servent à traiter des questions de grammaire ou de logique, mais aussi parfois de physique, voire de métaphysique. Au XIIIe siècle, les sophismes sont parfois des œuvres de grande ampleur, destinées à exposer toute une confrontation doctrinale. Au siècle suivant, le genre se maintient surtout à Oxford, avec Guillaume Heytesbury ou Richard Kilvington (*Sophismata*). À Paris, les *Sophismes* d'Albert de Saxe (1502) sont encore classés par syncatégorèmes, tandis que ceux de Jean Buridan sont organisés par chapitres consacrés aux propriétés sémantiques.

Parmi les sophismes, une espèce particulière, les insolubles, revêt une importance croissante. Il sont essentiellement consacrés à l'examen des paradoxes sémantiques du type du 'Menteur' ("je dis faux"). Tous les grands logiciens du XIVe siècle leur consacrent un chapitre (Jean Buridan dans ses *Sophismes*) ou un traité (Gauthier Burley, Guillaume Heytesbury, Pierre d'Ailly ...). Plusieurs types de solution s'affrontent, parmi lesquelles on mentionnera la *cassatio*, qui revient à estimer que de telles propositions n'ont pas de sens, la *restrictio*, qui exclut la proposition elle-même du champ de signification de ses termes, la *transcasus*, qui joue sur le moment de l'énonciation, etc.

## 4. Langage, pensée, raisonnement

### 4.1. Argumentation

La place privilégiée des arts du langage dans la formation, les exigences herméneutiques, tant en philosophie qu'en théologie, l'omniprésence de la *disputatio* comme mode d'exposition et de confrontation de thèses, tout cela invite à réfléchir sur les différentes formes de l'argumentation (Jacobi 1993).

L'argumentation est examinée d'abord dans les *Topiques*, ou théorie des lieux (Green-Pedersen 1984). Les lieux sont d'abord des types d'arguments; en conséquence, ils fournissent des stratégies d'argumentation. Boèce avait commenté les *Topiques* de Cicéron et rédigé un *De differentiis topicis*. Utilisés dans les écoles dès Gerbert d'Aurillac, ces textes font l'objet de nombreux commentaires au XIIe siècle, avant de s'effacer progressivement devant les *Topiques* d'Aristote, introduits dans l'enseignement peu avant 1150, et devenus dominants au XIIe siècle.

Dans la tradition boécienne, le lieu est défini comme le "siège de l'argument"; il sert à caractériser les termes ou les choses auxquels ces termes renvoient (tout, partie, genre, définition, etc.), et il permet d'énoncer des règles (*maxima propositio*), connues par soi, régissant les inférences entre propositions sur la base de tels lieux. La *differentia*, caractérisant les relations entre types de termes (par exemple entre tout et partie), permet de différencier et classer les maximes.

Aristote, quant à lui, distinguait l'argumentation dialectique, formant le champ propre des topiques, de l'argumentation démonstrative et de l'argumentation sophistique. Un argument dialectique repose sur des prémisses probables, caractère qui se transmet à la conclusion quelle que soit la rigueur de l'inférence. Pierre d'Espagne traite les topiques comme une forme incomplète de syllogisme, dont la validité est exhibée grâce à une 'différence' et une 'maxime'. Un argument topique peut donc être reconduit à un syllogisme dialectique.

Mais dès le XIIe siècle, certains auteurs tendent à traiter les arguments topiques comme des syllogismes conditionnels. Pour Garland le Computiste (*Dialectica*), les règles topiques fournissent la prémisse conditionnelle d'un syllogisme conditionnel simple (c'est-à-dire avec une prémisse conditionnelle et une catégorique). Certains passages de la *Dialectique* d'Abélard vont dans le même sens. Sur cette base, les topiques vont recouper l'intérêt pour les inférences, qui va croissant à la fin du XIII$^{e}$ siècle.

Les *Consequentie* traitent des inférences valides entre deux propositions, nommées l'antécédent et le conséquent, et reliées par le mot "si" ou "donc". Leur point de départ se trouve dans les traités de Boèce sur les syllogismes hypothétiques, mais la réflexion sur les conséquences s'est aussi nourrie des chapitres sur le connecteur propositionnel "si" dans les *Syncategoremata*, de l'étude du paralogisme du conséquent dans les *Fallacie*, de l'étude de la conversion entre propositions dans les commentaires sur les *Premiers Analytiques*. Les Médiévaux traitent généralement les conséquences comme des propositions conditionnelles, mais à travers elles se dégagent les formes valides ou non valides de l'argumentation. Chez Gauthier Burley, les syllogismes sont traités comme un cas particulier de conséquences (*De puritate artis logicae*).

On trouve diverses définitions de la conséquence. Abélard définissait l'*inferentia* comme la nécessité de la connexion, d'après laquelle du sens de l'antécédent surgit la pensée du conséquent (Abélard, *Scritti filosofici* 253). D'autres définitions cherchent à formuler la validité de la conséquence sur la base de la signification, ou encore de la vérité des propositions. D'autres encore estiment que l'opposé du conséquent doit être incompatible avec l'antécédent. Mais on en revient généralement à une description purement formelle afin de se consacrer aux règles valides de l'inférence et à la distinction des divers types de conséquences.

Gauthier Burley distingue les conséquences valides *simpliciter*, absolument, de celles qui le sont seulement *ut nunc*, pour maintenant. Parmi les premières, certaines sont naturelles, qui tiennent par un lieu intrinsèque; d'autres accidentelles, qui tiennent par un lieu extrinsèque. Les conséquences *ut nunc*, quant à elles, dépendent de la vérité factuelle d'une proposition (*De puritate artis logicae* 199).

Les traités sur les conséquences aboutissent à des exposés très élaborés des règles de déduction (Jean Buridan, *Sophismata*; Albert de Saxe, *Perutilis logica*). Les Médiévaux, c'est bien connu, formulent les lois de De Morgan. Ils discutent aussi des principes contre-intuitifs tels que *ex impossibili sequitur quodlibet* et *necessarium sequitur ex quolibet* (Jacobi 1993: 101–212). Les *Consequentie* sont ainsi l'un des domaines où la formalisation du langage atteint son plus haut point (Boh 1982; Schupp 1988).

Un autre champ de la logique médiévale tardive, tout en atteignant également un haut point de formalisation, privilégie le dialogue entre interlocuteurs. Les *obligationes* codifient un type particulier de débat. Dans le cadre d'une situation hypothétique (un *casus*), définissant un univers de discours tenu pour réel le temps de la dispute, sont mis en scène deux interlocuteurs. L'*opponens* soumet une série de propositions et le *respondens* doit répondre à chaque étape par *concedo*, *nego* ou *dubito*. Le jeu consiste, de la part de l'*opponens*, à amener le *respondens* à se contredire. Les traités énoncent les règles selon lesquelles on doit accepter ou refuser ce qui est proposé, en fonction de ce qui a été initialement (et conventionnellement) posé, et des propositions qui ont été entre temps admises ou refusées. On peut donc considérer que ces traités définissent des règles spécifiques d'inférence dans un contexte disputationnel, qui induit certaines différences d'évaluation par rapport aux règles habituelles des conséquences. Une place importante (notamment chez Gauthier Burley) est accordée aux paradoxes qui résultent de la référence, dans une prémisse, à l'acte même d'évaluation de cette prémisse. D'autres difficultés résultent de changements au cours du temps de la dispute.

La terminologie des obligations émerge dans certains textes du XII$^{e}$ siècles. Les premiers traités datent de la seconde moitié du XIII$^{e}$ siècle (voir de Rijk 1974–1976; Stump 1982; Spade 1982). La théorie standard est représentée par le traité de Gauthier Burley, datant de 1302. Tous les grands logiciens du Moyen-Age tardif composent encore des traités sur les obligations (Ashworth 1994), et des controverses se développent à la suite du traité de Roger Swineshead (Ashworth 1996). La théorie des obligations conduit à une complexification, voire à une modification, des règles classiques de l'inférence, en faisant intervenir des facteurs pragmatiques.

### 4.2. Le langage mental

Durant toute une partie du Moyen-Age, l'objet des disciplines du *trivium* est le langage humain parlé (secondairement écrit), abordé sous les trois aspects de la congruence, de la vérité et de l'ornement. Le domaine des affections psychiques n'intervient qu'à titre d'objet de signification, requérant une étude de type noétique. La tendance à faire de la logique une science rationnelle conduit à déplacer vers la pensée l'objet de la logique et à redéfinir les rapports entre pensée et langage. Au Moyen-Age tardif, on assiste ainsi à un double mouvement: la mise au premier plan d'un langage conceptuel, et la dévalorisation de la grammaire au profit de la logique. D'une certaine manière, l'idée de langage mental est fort ancienne. On peut la faire remonter à la philosophie grecque, avec la notion de *lógos* mêlant étroitement langage et raison, et avec la distinction entre langage intérieur et langage extérieur ou proféré. Mais malgré quelques passages de Boèce ou d'Augustin, l'idée de langage mental est peu intégrée à la réflexion latine sur le langage avant le XIVe siècle. C'est Guillaume d'Ockham qui la met au centre de l'analyse logico-linguistique (Panaccio 1999).

Pour Guillaume d'Ockham, c'est le signe conceptuel qui est le premier porteur des propriétés sémantiques. Ce langage mental se voit doté d'une véritable structuration linguistique. Il comprend des catégorèmes et des syncatégorèmes. On y retrouve la plupart des parties du discours définies par Priscien: des noms, des verbes, des pronoms, des adverbes, des conjonctions, des prépositions. On y retrouve même certains accidents de ces parties du discours. Pourtant, quelques parties du discours, telles que le participe, ou quelques accidents, comme le genre pour les noms, ou la conjugaison pour les verbes, n'existent pas dans le langage mental, parce que ces traits n'ont pas de pertinence pour déterminer la signification des termes et la vérité des propositions. Le domaine de la pensée, structuré par une syntaxe logiquement pertinente, peut alors être soumis à toute la technique d'analyse des propriétés des termes. Très vite, cette démarche se répand dans les *Commentaires des Sentences*, tant à Oxford qu'à Paris (Panaccio 1996), comme dans les productions de la faculté des arts. Jean Buridan utilise l'idée de proposition mentale pour exhiber la signification et la vérité des propositions parlées, renvoyées à un arbitraire radical (Jean Buridan, *Sophismata*). Mais c'est dans les textes de Pierre d'Ailly que s'épanouit l'assimilation du langage et de la pensée. Dans les *Destructiones modorum significandi*, même des notions typiquement grammaticales comme la congruence, le régime ou la construction concernent d'abord et à titre premier le langage mental. C'est le domaine de la pensée, par son dynamisme propre, qui régit la construction du langage parlé, qui préside à la formation des signes, et qui détermine leurs combinaisons. Mais ce domaine est lui-même un langage: le *Conceptus* de Pierre d'Ailly assimile signifier, concevoir et représenter. Cette tendance se prolongera jusqu'au début du XVIe siècle.

Qu'est-ce qu'une telle promotion du langage mental implique quant à la conception du langage en général? Elle met au premier plan un langage dont la signification est naturelle, et qui par conséquent prétend à l'universalité. L'universalité linguistique a hanté les Médiévaux. Si un Roger Bacon, au milieu du XIIIe siècle, prenait acte de la pluralité des langues pour en conclure à la nécessité d'apprendre les langues étrangères, les grammairiens modistes, quant à eux, mettaient au premier plan la recherche de structures universelles du langage. La critique logicienne de la grammaire spéculative tend à renvoyer la grammaire à l'étude positive des langues et déplace vers le langage mental le requisit d'universalité.

Ce langage peut servir de critère pour évaleur telle ou telle séquence linguistique prise comme objet d'analyse. Il ne s'agit pas d'élaborer de toutes pièces un langage idéal, mais de restituer à partir d'une langue donnée, déjà dotée d'un statut de langue de communication élargie par rapport aux langues vernaculaires et largement pénétrée de termes et de procédés techniques, un langage épuré des traits jugés non pertinents. Partant d'exigences théoriques – le besoin de composer les signes conceptuels en un véritable langage –, déduisant ce qui paraît nécessaire pour exprimer la signification et la référence des termes, la vérité des propositions, la validité des raisonnements, on reconstruit par idéalisation un langage qui en retour sert à évaluer des séquences linguistiques particulières, tant pour résoudre les problèmes logiques que pour clarifier le sens des énoncés en philosophie naturelle ou en théologie.

Les relations qui se nouent ainsi entre le langage et la pensée forment une configuration originale qui se dissoudra à l'âge classique au profit d'une analyse de la représentation d'une part, d'une approche du langage qui fait des idées le signifié des mots d'autre part. L'idée d'un langage mental se maintiendra toutefois chez Locke, Hobbes ou les Encyclopédistes, en de nouvelles dialectiques entre représentation intuitive et discursivité.

## 5. Conclusion

La logique est l'un des domaines où la pensée médiévale s'est montrée la plus inventive. Elle comporte des parties qui s'éloignent de considérations proprement linguistiques, au sens d'une étude du langage et des langues, au bénéfice d'études plus ou moins formelles du raisonnement. Mais même dans ce cas, elle ne perd pas de vue le langage, que l'on prête attention à son fonctionnement effectif ou que l'on exhibe sa structure sémantique.

De la sémantique des termes à l'étude des formes d'argumentation, la pensée médiévale multiplie les analyses de la signification et de la référence, s'intéresse au rôle du locuteur relativement aux contraintes syntaxico-sémantiques, élucide les diverses formes de l'ambiguïté et les phénomènes de champ, étudie l'impact des quantificateurs et des connecteurs propositionnels, invente la logique du changement (avec la théorie des verbes aspectuels tels que *incipit* ou *desinit*), esquisse des 'logiques régionales' (logique épistémique ou logique déontique) avec les verbes d'attitude propositionnelle. Certains de ces domaines ont été récemment mis en valeur parce que leur importance a été soulignée par la logique contemporaine. Mais c'est l'ensemble de ces dimensions qu'il faut prendre en compte pour la théorie médiévale du langage, y compris les relations complexes entre langage et pensée, aboutissant au XIV$^{e}$ siècle à l'idée de langage mental. La logique médiévale constitue ainsi un chapitre irremplaçable de l'histoire de la pensée linguistique, en raison de la place de la logique dans la formation des maîtres et dans la pratique de la philosophie, et parce que, fondamentalement, pour des raisons à la fois institutionnelles, philosophiques et théologiques, une extrême attention est portée au langage.

## 6. Bibliographie

### 6.1. Sources primaires


Abelard, *Logica "ingredientibus"*. Éd. par Bernhardt Geyer, *Peter Abaelards philosophische Schriften*. (= *BGPM*, 21/1–3.) Münster: Aschendorff, 1919–1927.

Abelard, *Logica "Nostrorum petitioni sociorum"*. Éd. par Bernhardt Geyer, *Peter Abaelards philosophische Schriften*. (= *BGPM*, 21/4.) Münster: Aschendorff, 1933.

Abélard, *Scritti filosofici*. Éd. par Mario dal Pra. Roma, 1954: Fratelli Bocca Editori, 1954. (Rééd., Firenze 1969.)

Abélard, *Dialectica*. Éd. par Lambert-Marie de Rijk. Assen: van Gorcum, 1956.

Albert de Saxe, *Sophismata*. Paris, 1502. (Reprod., Hildesheim: G. Olms, 1975.)

Albert de Saxe, *Perutilis logica*. Venise, 1522. (Reprod., Hildesheim: G. Olms, 1974.)

Anselme de Cantorbéry. Éd. par Michel Corbin, *L'œuvre de s. Anselme de Cantorbéry*, II. Paris: Éditions du Cerf, 1986.

Augustin, *De doctrina christiana. Bibliothèque augustinienne*, XI. *La Doctrine Chrétienne*. Paris: Desclée de Brouwer, 1997.

Avicenne (Ibn Sīnā), *Liber de anima sive Sextus de naturalibus*. Éd. par Simone Van Riet, *Avicenna latinus*. 2 tomes. Louvain: Peeters, 1968–1972.

Boèce, *Commentarii in librum Aristotelis Peri hermeneias*. Éd. par Carolus Meiser. Editio prima et editio secunda. 2 tomes. Lipsiae, 1877, 1880.

Boèce, *In categorias Aristotelis. Migne Patrologia latina*, LXIV. Paris, 1847.

Garland le Computiste, *Dialectica*. Éd. par Lambert-Marie de Rijk. Assen: van Gorcum, 1959.

Gauthier Burley, *De puritate artis logicae, Tractatus longior*. Éd. par Philotheus Boehner. St. Bonaventure, NY: The Franciscan Institute, 1955. (With a revised ed. of *Tractatus brevior*.)

Gilbert de la Porrée, *Commentarii*. Éd. par Nicolas K. Häring, *The Commentaries on Boethius by Gilbert of Poitiers*. Toronto: Pontifical Institute of Medieval Studies, 1966.

Guillaume d'Ockham, *Summa logicae*. Éd. par Philotheus Boehner, Gedeon Gal & Stephen Brown, *Opera philosophica*, I. St. Bonaventure, NY: The Franciscan Institute, 1974.

Guillaume de Sherwood, *Introductiones in logicam*. Éd. par Charles Lohr, Peter Kunze & B. Mussler, *Traditio* 39 (1983) 209–299.

Guillaume Heytesbury, *Tractatus de sensu composito et diviso. Regulae eiusdem cum Sophismatibus* [...]. Venise, 1494.

Jean Buridan, *Tractatus de suppositionibus*. Éd. par Maria Elena Reina, *Rivista critica di storia della filosofia* 12 (1957) 175–208, 323–352.

Jean Buridan, *Summulae de Suppositionibus*. Éd. par Ria van der Lecq. Nimègue: Nijmegen Ingenium Publishers, 1998.

Jean Buridan, *Sophismata*. Éd. par Theodor K. Scot. Stuttgart: Frommann-Holzboog, 1977.

Jean Sharpe, *Questio super universalia*. Éd. par Alessandro D. Conti. Firenze: Olschki, 1990.

Lambert d'Auxerre, *Logica (Summa Lamberti)*. Éd. par Franco Alessio. Milano: La nuova Italia, 1971.

Lambert de Lagny (= Lambert d'Auxerre), *Tractatus De appellatione*. Voir de Libera (1982a).

Pierre d'Ailly, *Conceptus*. Éd. par Ludger Kaczmarek, *Modi significandi und ihre Destruktionen: Zwei Texte zur scholastischen Sprachtheorie im 14. Jahrhuneert*. Münster: Nodus, 1980.

Pierre d'Ailly (?), *Destructiones modorum significandi*. Éd. par Ludger Kaczmarek. Amsterdam: B. Grüner, 1994.

Pierre d'Espagne, *Tractatus called afterwards Summulae logicales.* Éd. par Lambert-Marie de Rijk. Assen: van Gorcum, 1972.

Priscien, *Institutiones grammaticae.* Éd. par Martin Hertz, *Grammatici latini*, II–III. Leipzig: Teubner, 1855, 1859.

Richard Kilvington, *Sophismata.* Éd. par Norman Kretzmann & Barbara Ensign Kretzmann, *The Sophismata of Richard Kilvington.* Cambridge: Cambridge Univ. Press, 1990.

Roger Bacon, *De signis.* Éd. par Karen Margareta Fredborg, Lauge Nielsen & Jan Pinborg, "An inedited part of *Opus maius*: *De signis*". *Traditio* 34 (1978) 176–195.

Roger Bacon, *Summulae dialectices.* I. *De termino.* II. *De enuntiatione.* Éd. par Alain de Libera. *Archives d'histoire doctrinale et littéraire du Moyen Age* 53 (1986) 139–289.

Roger Bacon, *The Compendium of the Study of Theology.* Éd. et trad. par Thomas S. Maloney. Leiden: E. J. Brill, 1988.

### 6.2. Sources secondaires

Ashworth, E. Jennifer. 1994. "*Obligationes* Treatises: A catalogue of manuscripts, editions and studies". *Bulletin de philosophie médiévale* 36.118–147.

–. 1996. "Autour des *obligationes* de Roger Swineshead: La *nova responsio*". *Les Etudes Philosophiques* 3.341–360.

Biard, Joël. 1989. *Logique et théorie du signe au XIV$^{e}$ siècle.* Paris: Vrin.

–. 1997. *Guillaume d'Ockham: Logique et philosophie.* Paris: Presses Universitaires de France.

Boh, Ivan. 1982. "Conséquences". Kretzmann et al. (1982: 300–314).

Braakhuis, Henk A. G. 1979. *De 13de eeuwse Tractaten over syncategorematische termen: Inleidende studie en uitgave van Nicolaas van Parijs'* Sincategoreumata. 2 tomes. Leiden: Brill.

De Rijk, Lambert-Marie. 1962, 1967. *Logica modernorum, A Contribution to the History of Early Terminist Logic.* Vol. I: *On the twelfth century theories of fallacies.* Vol. II/1: *The origins and early development of the theory of supposition.* Vol. II/2: *Texts and indices.* Assen: van Gorcum.

–. 1974–1976. "Some Thirteenth Century Tracts on the Game of Obligations". *Vivarium* 12.94–123; 13.22–54; 14.26–49.

–. 1982. "The Origins of the Theory of the Properties of Terms". Kretzmann et al. (1982: 161–173).

Ebbesen, Sten. 1979. "The Dead Man is Alive". *Synthese* 40.43–70.

–. 1981a. *Commentators and Commentaries on Aristotle's Sophistici Elenchi.* 3 tomes. Leiden: Brill.

–. 1981b. "Early Supposition-Theory, 12th–13th century". *Histoire, Epistémologie, Langage* 3:1.35–48.

Green Pedersen, N. J. 1984. *The Tradition of the Topics.* Munich: Philosophia Verlag.

Henry, Desmond Paul. 1964. *The* De grammatico *of St. Anselm: Theory of Paronymy.* Notre-Dame: Univ. of Notre-Dame Press.

Jacobi, Klaus. 1993. *Argumentationstheorie: Scholastische Forschungen zu den logischen und semantischen Regeln korrektes Folgerns.* Leiden: Brill.

Jolivet, Jean. 1969. *Arts du langage et théologie chez Abélard.* paris: Vrin.

– & Alain de Libera, éds. 1987. *Gilbert de Poitiers et ses contemporains: Aux origines de la logica modernorum.* Napoli: Bibliopolis.

Kretzmann, Norman. 1970. "Medieval Logicians on the Meaning of the *Propositio*". *Journal of Philosophy* 67.767–787.

–. 1982. "*Syncategoremata, exponibilia, sophismata*". Kretzmann et al. (1982: 211–245).

–, Anthony Kenny & Jan Pinborg, éds. 1982. *The Cambridge History of Later Medieval Philosophy.* Cambridge: Cambridge Univ. Press.

Libera, Alain de. 1982a. "Le traité *de appellatione* de Lambert de Lagny (Lambert d'Auxerre)". *Archives d'histoire doctrinale et littéraire du Moyen Age*, année 1881, 227–285.

–. 1982b. "The Oxford and Paris traditions in logic". Kretzmann et al. (1982: 174–187).

–. 1987. "Logique et théologie dans la *Summa quoniam homines* d'Alain de Lille". Jolivet & de Libera (1987: 437–469).

–. 1996. *La Querelle des universaux de Platon à la fin du Moyen Age.* Paris: Seuil.

– & Irène Rosier. 1989. "La pensée linguistique médiévale". *Histoire des idées linguistiques* éd. par Sylvain Auroux, vol. I, 115–186. Liège & Bruxelles: Mardaga.

Maierù, Alfonso. 1972. *Terminologia logica della tarde scolastica.* Rome: Edizioni dell'Ateneo.

Nielsen, Lauge. 1976. "On the Doctrine of Logic and Language of Gilbert Porreta and his Followers". *Cahiers de l'Institut du Moyen Age grec et latin* 17.40–69.

Panaccio, Claude. 1991. *Les Mots, les Concepts et les Choses: La sémantique de Guillaume d'Ockham et le nominalisme d'aujourd'hui.* Montréal & Paris: Bellarmin-Vrin.

–. 1996. "Le Langage Mental en Discussion: 1320–1335". *Les Etudes philosophiques* 3.323–338.

–. 1999. *Le Discours intérieur de Platon à Guillaume d'Ockham.* Paris: Seuil.

Pinborg, Jan. 1972. *Logik und Semantik im Mittelalter: Ein Überblick.* Stuttgart-Bad Cannstatt: Frommann-Holzboog.

Read, Stephen, ed. 1993. *Sophisms in Medieval Logic and Grammar.* Dordrecht: Kluwer.

Rosier, Irène. 1983. "L'un et le multiple: Problèmes sémantiques de la tradition médiévale des commentaires sur les *Réfutations sophistiques* d'Aristote". *Modèles linguistiques* 5:2.39–68.

—. 1988. *L'Ambiguïté: Cinq études historiques.* Lille: Presses Universitaires.

—. 1994. *La Parole comme acte.* Paris: Vrin.

Schupp, Franz. 1988. *Logical Problems of the Medieval Theory of Consequences, with an Edition of the Liber consequentiarum.* Napoli: Bibliopolis.

Spade, Paul Vincent. 1982a. "The semantics of terms". Kretzmann et al. (1982: 188–197).

—. 1982b. "Obligations. B. Developments in the fourteenth century". Kretzmann et al. (1982: 335–341).

Stump, Eleonor. 1982. "Obligations. A. From the beginning to the early fourteenth century". Kretzmann et al. (1982: 315–334).

*Joël Biard, Tours (France)*

# 79. Language study and theology in the Late Middle Ages

1. Introduction
2. Models of language
3. Grammar as semantics
4. Tools of grammar
5. God and parts of speech
6. Terminology and models
7. Conclusion
8. Bibliography

## 1. Introduction

In the Early Middle Ages theologian and grammarian took their cue from St Augustine *De doctrina christiana* I.ii.2: any science deals with things (*res*) and the signs (*signa*) which express them. This applied with special force to the embryonic science of theology, which was bounded by Scripture and its interpretation. The 4th century cast theology in a rhetorical mould. It remained so until Carolingian theologians sought their tools of interpretation in grammar. From the late 11th century theology, as did all the other sciences, came under the sway of dialectic (Chenu 1957: 33; Colish 1968: 92). It then bifurcated into the traditional 'monastic theology' based on Biblical exegesis, and 'academic theology', which Albertus Magnus terms *ratio vel sermo de Deo* "accounting of God or speech about him". This describes God not only according to his being and substance, but also according as he is the principle and end of everything in existence (*Summa theologiae* I.ii ad 3). This sophisticated *theologia speculativa* was concerned with the processes of God's being, for example the generation of the Trinity, his acts of creation, and the relation of humanity to him. Aquinas on Book I.xxii of Peter Lombard's *Liber sententiarum* (Sentences) on naming God shows that a scientific interest in *res* necessarily includes *nomina* because the right name is essential to a proper statement of belief (cited McInerny 1961: 50).

Grammar has a similar history. The discipline in the Classical world is epitomised in an illuminating sentence from Cicero *De oratore* I.xlii.187: *In grammaticis poetarum pertractatio, historiarum cognitio, verborum interpretatio, pronuntiandi quidam sonus...* "In grammarians we find analysis of the poets, the knowledge of history, interpretation of words, and a certain character in the pronunciation [...]". It is this prescriptive and literary grammar that was transmitted to the schools of later times by Donatus. But as did academic theology, academic grammar, more properly *grammatica speculativa*, developed as a fully-fledged science under the impulse of dialectic. As such, it was science of becoming: it sought to establish the causes and purpose of language, it accounted for the operations by which language reached its perfection, and it revealed the system of universals underlying language processes.

Grammatical and literary approaches to Biblical criticism were developed in the early 3rd century by Origen (ca. 185–251). He was one of the first to use grammar to find the 'literal', 'allegorical' and 'moral' senses of Scripture. In the Latin West Origen's influence was passed through artefacts of Roman education. In the light of the above definition from Cicero, the school exercise of *enarratio* became the major exegetic tool. Augustine used it to great effect in his *Enarrationes in psalmos* (396–ca. 426), a series of sermons on the psalms. The displacement of rhetoric by grammar between the 7th and the 12th centuries was due to two factors: the barbarian invasions of the Roman world, and the spread of the Benedictine Rule (Colish 1968: 3–94). As a result of the invasions the social systems of Roman Europe, particularly education, collapsed. Yet Latin culture spread into northern Europe, so that Latin was taught as a foreign language. The Benedictine Rule enjoins academic work on the monks. In both cases grammar was necessary: it was an essential part of Latin teaching, and for the Benedictine, the ancient *enarratio*, which constantly absorbed new approaches to grammar, was a tool necessary for his academic and religious duties. The drill is assumed in medieval works on transferred senses, like Bede's *De schematibus et tropis* (730?), which deal with Biblical interpretation. They left in their wake the medieval *integumentum*, "envelope" of commentary around a text.

In terms of Michel Foucault's philosophy of science, the 'archive' of the medieval theologian bridged theology and grammar. Its grammatical part stemmed from Donatus, Priscian and their medieval disciples. The Latin Bible and Augustine and the extant parts of Plato, Aristotle and their followers were the basis of the theological and philosophical part of the archive. A century after Augustine came Boethius (480–524/26), whose legacy included his Aristotle translations and commentaries and the *Opuscula sacra* which applied the insights of Aristotle's *Organon* to theology. Two centuries later Joannes Scotus Eriugena (ca. 810–877) translated the Pseudo-Dionysian *De divinis nominibus* and *De caelesti hierarchia* into Latin. Theologians with a taste for dialectic worried this early part of the tradition like dogs at a bone, and were added to the archive: the most important names for our purposes are Anselm of Canterbury (ca. 1033–1109), Peter Abelard (1079–1142) and Gilbert of Poitiers (ca. 1985–1154). Their work was consolidated during the 12th century by such authors as Alain de Lille (d. 1203) and William of Auxerre (1140–1231), and during the 13th century by Alexander of Hales (ca. 1185–1245), Roger Bacon (ca. 1214–1292/94), Albertus Magnus (ca. 1200–1280) and Thomas Aquinas (ca. 1225–1274). Then came changes in direction from John Duns Scotus (ca. 1265–1308) and William of Ockham (1285–1347/49).

The questions asked about the *res et signa* of theology fell under two heads. The first of these heads was God. The major issues here were God's nature, his acts, and the relationships between him and humankind. The second set of issues related to the nature of theology itself. While beginning as an interpretative science dealing with a text, by the 13th century it has taken on the trappings of a speculative science. These developments had a radical effect on speculative grammar. For even if some believed that theological language was beyond grammatical rules, others thought that with patience and common sense Scriptural language could be explained within the bounds of grammar.

## 2. Models of language

Biblical exegesis assumed an 'intentionalist' view of language: at the centre of the theory of the four senses of Scripture lies the assumption that God communicates with Man on his own terms (Colish 1968: 2). Dialectic brought with it a formalist view of how a text signified. The task of grammar is laid out by Bonaventure in the fourth sermon of his *Hexaemeron* (1273): grammar has the expression of the concept as its task, and nobody can be a good grammarian unless he knows the reality language is a sign of. Three basic sets of concepts inextricably link theology and grammar. The first is the *signum*, the second the model of word generation posited by Boethius, and the third Aristotle's model of cognition in *De anima*.

### 2.1. The linguistic sign

In essence the primary object of linguistic analysis was the word, its genesis and its sign functions. Augustine gives us a typical Roman definition of the *signum* in *De dialectica* (5): *Signum est et quod seipsum sensui et praeter se aliquid animo ostendit* "A sign is something that shows itself to the senses and at the same time something else to the mind". This definition is wide enough to cover all the senses of *signum* in both the Bible and Classical literature. *Signum* means any evidence from which a conclusion may be drawn, for example weather signs, symptoms of a disease, traces left by a person or animal, evidence of divine favour or disfavour. In classical rhetoric *signum* also meant the evidence for a criminal charge: the definition given by Cicero in *De inventione* (I.48) adds that a *signum* requires confirmation by other evidence. The forensic tradition colours Augustine's discussion of *signum* in the *De dialectica* (387) as it relates to truth in dialogue and argument. Two years later Augustine deepened his ideas on the teaching function of language in *De magistro* (389) and in *De doctrina christiana*, begun in 397 and not completed until 427. These two works laid the foundation for the sign-theories of the next fifteen centuries (→ Art. 71). He distinguishes between natural and conventional signs, characterising the word as a conventional sign designed for the ear (*De magistro* x.34). It is a combination of *sonus* and *significatio*, a binary model familiar from the similar and more complicated discussions by Saussure. The *sonus* (*signifiant*) is the sounds we speak, the *significatio* (*signifié*) is a mental image of the thing signified and not the thing itself. A word functions as a sign only if both speaker and hearer share the knowledge on which it is based. Augustine (*De catechizandis rudibus* II.3) hints that the *sonus* is both the physical sound of speech and our mental image of it (Kelly 1975: 51). Near the end of his life Augustine developed his original pedagogical model into a Platonist theory of language and divine inspiration: *De trinitate* distinguishes between the *verbum intus* (the result of divine illumination) and the *verbum quod foras sonat*, (speech) (see Markus 1957; Kelly 1975). The most persuasive attempt to see into Augustine's thought is Amsler (1989: 102–105). Augustine grounds the teaching function of language in the divine origin of cognition. The *verbum quod foras sonat* (what we say) reflects the *verbum intus* (the inner word based on a Platonist innate form); this in turn takes us back to immanent knowledge and the divine λόγος. Thus he passed on the view that language has two levels, a set of conventions by which sound is used to communicate, and cognition through divine illumination.

Like Augustine the 11th and the 12th centuries took for granted Platonist views of cognition, the realist view of the necessary relationship between sign and object, and the presence of speaker and hearer. It was a period of doctrinal controversy fought with grammatical weapons. The towering figure of the period is Anselm of Canterbury, who underpinned his religious faith through a logician's view of the linguistic sign (*fides quaerens intellectum*). His famous ontological proof for the existence of God depends on his sign theory: in stating that it depends on *rationes necessariae* he assumes the Platonist idea of a necessary connection between *sonus* and *significatio*. The validity of a sign depends on its *rectitudo*. As Augustine had said, a word of itself does not bring knowledge, it merely points to knowledge shared by speaker and hearer. Language users judge the rectitude of a word by comparing word and object. *Rectitudo* of a word or any other sign depends on interpretation. Thus a sense impression that seems erroneous, like a straight stick which seems to be bent when seen through water, is automatically corrected by experience or by prior knowledge (Colish 1968: 113–114). Words and utterances are subject to the same type of interpretation and correction. The rectitude of the word is one of the factors essential to the truth of an utterance. Augustine remains a presence in the 13th century, but his sign theory is not usually cited *in extenso*. One author who does is Henry of Ghent whose article on naming God (*Summa* XXIII) amplifies both Augustine and Boethius by analysing the *modi significandi* of signs. Duns Scotus modifies the almost universal consensus that the word signified the mental image. He takes it to be the immediate significate of the word. But the *species in animo* is a sign for the mediate or ultimate significate, which is the *res*. He thus develops Augustine's implication that the verbal sign is the sign of a sign – the *species in animo* stands in a sign relationship to the thing understood (see Perler 1993).

### 2.2. The triad of Boethius

Medieval grammatical theory begins from Boethius's triad, *Res*, *Intellectus*, *verbum*, developed in the commentaries on Aristotle's *De interpretatione*. In the *Opuscula sacra* this triad becomes an important method of analysing both thought and language about God. Boethius, it seems, wished to bring some rigour into contemporary debate on the nature of Christ by a good dose of logic. His attitude was that of Augustine: sound knowledge of the *res* will follow proper definition of the *signa*. Gibson (1981) traces the fortunes of the *Opuscula* during the Middle Ages. They played a role as school texts from the Carolingian period. Their method had particular influence on Eriugena. In particular he analysed relationships between God and universal nature in terms of Aristotle's categories. The ancient metalanguage having used categorial terms, this was to have an immediate effect on grammar (see Luhtala 1993). A couple of centuries after Eriugena's work, Peter Lombard, Thierry of Chartres, Abelard and Gilbert of Poitiers came under the influence of the *Opuscula*. Then after the founding of the universities it became normal for a Bachelor of Theology to begin his professional career with a commentary on Peter Lombard's *Liber sententiarum* (Sentences), a task demanding sophisticated grammatical scholarship, even as the interests of the Paris Faculty of Arts were moving towards philosophy to the neglect of grammar. But such commentaries would not have been possible if Boethius had not shown that one can elucidate theological questions by standard logical methods.

### 2.3. The soul and language

Naming something depended on knowing its nature. The psychological model of language transmitted to the early 13th century through Augustine rose out of knowledge of the natures of things through divine illumination. Boethius too was strongly Platonist, even though he adopted the Aristotelian overlay normal in neo-Platonism. However, in the late 13th century the model of intellection and expression proposed in Aristotle's *De anima* III was to predominate. The *intellectus possibilis* was passive before the object in act and the *intellectus agens* produced the verbal sign from the *species impressa* in the intellect. This left no room for Augustine's illumination. The major line of transmission of the *De anima* was through theology. When the Council of Paris (1215) banned Aristotle's natural science, the Paris Faculty of Theology was not covered. Thus, while the Arts people were silenced until the ban on Aristotle was lifted in 1231, theologians were not prevented from paying attention to the *De anima* (Steenberghen 1970: 66–88). The *De anima* of Guillaume d'Auvergne (1230) rejected Avicenna's reworking of Aristotle on the intellect in favour of the Augustinian tradition. A couple of years later Philip the Chancellor (d. 1236) incorporated Aristotelian models of intellection into the traditional theology of the soul, and Jean de la Rochelle's *Summa de anima* completed the task by adding Aristotle's teaching that the soul was the seat of intellection to Augustine's view that it was a spiritual substance. From this point Aristotle's model of intellection became part of both theology and grammar, and indeed it is quoted in many *modistae*, e. g. Michel de Marbais (ca. 1270).

## 3. Grammar as semantics

The grammar of the early 1270s makes no secret of its ancestry: terminology from the *De doctrina christiana* is a frame in which to mature 13th century research on the soul and language in Aristotle. But the model of the sign used in theology had to contend with a long tradition beginning with Plato, leading through Philo and Plotinus and culminating in Pseudo-Dionysius as presented to the Latin world by Eriugena. But this did not rule out fruitful speculation on the sign as modelled by Augustine. 12th century exegetes begin to enrich commentary on the Scriptures by systematic reflection on theological doctrine shaped by the sciences of grammar, logic and rhetoric (Valente 1995b: 34); and one must add Canon Law to the list. But the major sources for the new formalist grammar are the commentaries on Peter Lombard's *Liber sententiarum* and the many *Summae* of theology.

### 3.1. Rhetoric to logic to grammar

The *De divinis nominibus* of Pseudo-Dionysius discusses the paradox that we speak of God even though God could not be named because the human being is not capable of knowing his essence. The solution man adopts is the *translatio in divinis*. Following the example of Augustine and Jerome we can find the origin of this *translatio in divinis* in classical rhetorics like those of Cicero and Quintillian. Bede's *De schematibus et tropis* is a lineal descendant of this tradition, as is Peter the Chanter's *De tropis loquendi*. Peter the Chanter (1120/30–1197), a famous Biblical scholar skilled in the *artes*, had a relaxed attitude to the Dionysian paradox precisely because he could defend the use of the *artes* in interpreting Scripture by his own example (Evans 1983: 25–27). Valente (1990) discusses how *De tropis loquendi* exploits the tradition of the logical *Fallaciae* in Biblical interpretation. Peter organises his *De tropis loquendi* along the lines of a manual of *Fallaciae*, each section being exemplified copiously from the Biblical text (Valente 1990: 74–76). This strictly verbal approach is unlike the classical attempts to apply logic to rhetoric. Peter filters traditional rhetorical doctrine through the latest treatments of dialectic, including the *Sophistici elenchi* – Valente (1990: 74) sees close resemblances between *De tropis loquendi* and the *Fallaciae Parvipontani* and the *F. Londinenses*. One could say that appeals to rhetoric such as Peter's were old-fashioned: grammatical argumentation had been developed in 11th century theology, particularly in the circle of Lanfranc, his pupil, Anselm, and Anselm's adversary, Berengarius. It is clear from Colish (1968) and Marenbon (1988) that Anselm benefited from the Carolingians and left a legacy of grammatical doctrine that was exploited in several ways during the centuries which followed him. The strong conviction that the Word of God was not subject to grammar gave rise to several *Regulae theologiae* which benefited from Anselm's work. The most significant of these rule-books is that of Alain de Lille (ca. 1125–1203). He begins by emphasising that obscurity of Scripture demands special rules for its *enarratio*. These rules had to reconcile philosophical statements about God with traditional doctrines about language (see Valente 1995b). Many of them go back to Boethius's *Opuscula sacra*, but they show some influence from Anselm and his pupils. The major problem was the unity and simplicity of God – God was not made up of matter and form, therefore what was said of him belonged to his essence. In consequence nouns used of God became the equivalent of pronouns as they signified *meram substantiam* (cf. Fredborg 1990: 63–65); in relation to God *esse* is not a copula but an existential verb; all nouns (including adjectives) applied to God are descriptions of essence. The theologian inferred much about the nature of God from his actions, and therefore reaffirmed certain aspects of traditional sign theory: Gregory the Great (590–604), for example, had noted that the noun, *angelus*, is not a *nomen naturae* but a *nomen officii*. Guillaume d'Auxerre *In I Sentences* (3) rereads this principle in more formal terms: the adjective, *iustus*, applied to God signifies the divine essence *in habitudine ad actum*, i. e. disposed to act.

### 3.2. *Vox* and *Impositio*

The essential result of such rules was to clarify modes of imposition by emphasising the creativity and adaptability of modes of understanding. The issue of *dictio* and *res significata* (thing signified) is fully discussed by Rosier (1995). Meaning was not a contextual affair: Abelard had affirmed that signification was prior to construction. At least since the Roman grammarian, Varro, *impositio* had been the term for the process by which a *vox*, Augustine's *sonus*, becomes a sign, or in more formal terms, how its potency towards meaning is realised. In the 5th century Augustine was amplified by Boethius, but from Aristotle's logical works. In contrast the tools for amplifying Boethius during the 12th century came from the Latin translations of Aristotle's *De anima*, supplemented by commentaries like that of Ammonius, translated into Latin by William of Moerbeke. As a material thing with matter and form the *vox* enjoyed a natural ordering towards its proper end, signification (*De anima* II.8 420a–420b) Therefore meaning is imposed on a word by an act of the will (Aquinas, *Quaestio disputata de veritate* 4 ad 1; cf. McInerny 1961: 51). In this way it becomes *dictio*, an act of signification and the sign of the definition of its object. Aquinas (*Summa theol.* I.85.2 ad 3) states that the *dictio* does not signify the *species intelligibilis*, but what the intellect makes of it in order to come to judgements about things outside the mind (McInerny 1961: 52).

*Dictio* and *res significata* are in relation to each other as *subiectum* and *terminus*. Such *relationes* being arbitrary, the issue of just what was imposed on the *vox* was hotly debated during the 12th century. There was agreement that the *significatum* of a noun was the general substance of something. *Significatum* was distinguished from *nominatum*, about which there was considerable disagreement. The *Glosulae*, an 11th-century commentary on Priscian, had the *nominatum* refer to the substance of individuals; a slightly later commentary on Priscian referred it to the special form of an individual (humanity is the form of Man), while William of Conches saw the *nominatum* as referring to individuals only (Fredborg 1988: 183–185). *Nominatio* was distinguished from *significatio* as it excluded universals (Kneepkens 1992: 47). This distinction seems to disappear during the 13th century, but leaves behind a distinction between signifying and naming. Henry of Ghent (ca. 1217–1293) (*Summa* LXXIII.ii ad 1) says of the names Father, Son and Holy Spirit, that they are *nomina naturae*. Albertus Magnus *Postilla super Isaiam* VII.14 commenting on the name, "Emmanuel", given to Christ in the Christian tradition, distinguishes between *nomen naturae* and *nomen impositionis*: as nature gives the form to something, it also gives a name. Thus "Emmanuel" (God with us) rises from Christ's participation in divine and human natures. The *nomen impositionis* is arbitrary: as an example Albertus cites "Jesus" and "Christus" as "names given to the Lord".

### 3.3. The consequences of naming God

One of the many 12th century writers on the problem of naming God was Thierry of Chartres (fl. 1100–1150), who left behind him commentaries on Cicero's *De inventione*, on *Ad Herennium* ascribed to Cicero, and on Boethius's *Opuscula sacra*. There are some fragments of Biblical commentaries, and, most important for us, the Heptateuchon, or "volume of the seven liberal arts". Thierry was a fervent Platonist. He taught that all knowledge was one: the seven liberal arts were in the service of *philosophia* and their final goal was *sapientia* "wisdom". He accepted that one can not speak properly of God, because one can not understand him (Dronke 1988: 366). However he resolved the issue by a copybook piece of Platonist doctrine. First, one can speak of God and the universe through metaphor: like metaphor itself the world is only a similitude and image of something perfect. Second, both understanding and naming come about because the soul is 'proportioned' to the world: while the divine mind is the *forma formarum*, the human soul is the form of artistic forms. Commenting on Boethius *De trinitate* II Thierry writes that forms can not exist without names, and names give things their being. Therefore naming is a well-directed penetration into the divine mind to the essence of a thing as shown by its name (Dronke 1988: 370–373). Metaphor becomes a tool of this penetration. Thierry adduces a long line of authorities for his teaching. The most powerful is the account of Creation in Genesis I: as Philo Iudaeus had argued in his *Life of Moses* (20 AD), God made the world by speaking, and God's words are deeds. Nobody else among the Latin medievals ever went as far as this, even though he seems to have furnished a precedent for Albertus Magnus's *Postilla super Isaiam* VII.14 on "Emmanuel".

One of the most extensive 13th century discussions of whether God can be signified by linguistic signs is that by Henry of Ghent (ca. 1217–1293). His discussion in his commentary on the *Sentences* (1280?) bridges sign theory from Augustine to Aquinas. He begins from the sign definitions in *De dialectica* and *De doctrina christiana* showing that applying signs to the task of speaking about God is possible because one does not have to understand fully the nature of what one imposes the sign on. A sign has arbitrary *modi significandi* based on a perceived similitude between the object designated and a concept. Thus the designated object is proportioned to the understanding of the person speaking about it (see Marenbon 1991: 144–153).

## 4. Tools of grammar

### 4.1. Updating Boethius's triad

Boethius's triad left a number of problems revolving around the *relatio* between the physical *vox* and the immaterial mental image. Its full development depended on the crucial relationship between grammar and ontology (Ashworth 1991: 50–51). The 13th century triad, *modus essendi*, *modus intelligendi*, and *modus significandi*, though derived from Boethius's progression *res*, *intellectus*, *significatio*, is a typically medieval attempt to account for 'causes' and mechanisms through their version of Aristotle. Yet it seems that all three terms began as non-technical expressions outside grammar. As far as theologians are concerned they seem to have remained transparent and flexible, for example Aquinas (*Quodlibet* 4.9.2 resp.) treats the gerund as a transitive verb: *modus intelligendi unam et eandem rem*. By Abelard's time *modus essendi* and *modus significandi* were well established. In earlier usage, *modus essendi* and its synonym, *modus se habendi*, seem to cover concepts like dependent and independent existence. It seems too simple to need definition. In the usage of Aquinas *modus essendi* still has this air about it, but he allows for several modes of being for the same object: in his discussion of whether the name of God is communicable (*Summa theologiae* I.xiii.9 ad 2), he argues that the name of God is communicable *per similitudinem* but not *in re* because nouns do not follow the mode of being in the real thing, but the mode of being according to which the thing is known by us.

*Modus intelligendi* is less well attested before the 13th century. The 11th and 12th centuries show widespread experimentation with terms like *modus concipiendi*, which is common in Abelard and remains as a non-technical word in the 13th century. When *modus intelligendi* finally became standard, it seems that our theologians did not distinguish between *modi intelligendi* and *rationes intelligendi*. Before the rise of Nominalism there seem to be two layers in understanding of the term: especially in the theology of God, *modi intelligendi* are *ad placitum*; but there is a Platonist tinge to the understanding: a *modus intelligendi* must have some similitude of the thing understood. We see this in Henry of Ghent's discussion of the sign. Abelard's *Logica ingredientibus* warns that existence is one thing, understanding another. Ebbesen (1987: 427–428) ascribes to Stephen Langton (ca. 1150–

1228) the view that a word could signify an understanding (*significare intellectum*) without passing through the normal triad of *vox*, *intellectus* and *res*. Scotus on the same problem concentrates on the problems of understanding something in its absence. In his view the act of understanding God is *abstractivus*, because it abstracts its object from its existence or non-existence, and from its presence and absence. After Ockham, *modi intelligendi* are an interior language that can be erroneous (see Panaccio 1995).

*Modus significandi* comes from Guillaume de Conches (Rosier 1995: 138), though Ashworth (1991: 54) points out that the concept has its roots in Boethius. It is first used extensively in a system involving *significatum* and *res significata* in theology by Abelard and his contemporaries. *Modus significandi* is often replaced at this time by *modus nominandi*, just as *significatum* commuted with *nominatum*. In the light of Kneepkens (1992) I would suspect that *modus significandi* has a nominalist tinge to it: in a fully realist world of language, one would not have to make allowance for a range of different ways of signifying dependent on the arbitrariness of the human will. Gilbert of Poitiers saw this as a semantic problem: words, he remarks constantly in his commentary on Boethius *De trinitate*, are like images in a mirror. Some of his ideas and usage were picked up by Peter Lombard in the *Sentences* (Colish 1987). As yet *modus significandi* pertains mainly to semantics: one signified a *res significata* by one of its qualities, or through a transferred sense of a word. And only nouns are involved. Fredborg distinguishes two uses for the term in those early days: it replaces *officium* (function) and designates the properties of a quality (Fredborg 1973: 28–32). Even into the 13th century many theologians' use of *modus significandi* conforms largely to the older usage Fredborg describes. Jean Quidort on *I Sentences* VIII.1 (1292) reminds his readers that the *modus significandi* follows the *modus intelligendi*. Therefore in the case of God defects in the *modus significandi* are due to our defective understanding of God. Guillaume d'Auxerre's argumentation in his *Summa aurea* about the *modus praedicandi* of adjectives like *bonus*, *iustus* etc. in denoting God has undertones of a *modus significandi*: for they signify God as being *in habitudine ad actum* through representing him by, as it were, a *modus bonitatis* or *modus iustitiae*. This developed into general semiotics: in the beginning of his *Summa* (ca. 1245) Alexander of Hales remarks that theology differs from the sciences in general in that both things and words have *modi significandi*. Valente (1995a) shows how this developed from Augustine's view that in Scripture both things and words had meaning. It would seem that this view had considerable influence on sacramental theology, as a sacrament is a *signum efficiens* which produced the effect it signifies. By the early 13th century it is clear that all three, *modi essendi*, *intelligendi*, *significandi* are technical terms. The technical language of these theologians accorded the *dictio* its *significatum* and took *modi significandi* to be properties of the *dictio*. 'Part of speech' therefore was a functional label rather than an actual analytical category having to do with the generation of language. The final stage of modistic terminology distinguishing the *modi intelligendi et significandi activi* from *modi passivi*, seems to have developed independently in grammar (→ Art. 76).

The moderate realist view of *modus significandi* was attacked by William of Ockham. The implications are fully discussed by Biard (1989: 52–126) and Panaccio (1995). Ockham took the linguistic sign as arbitrary in that its *modi significandi* are derived from our understanding of the thing signified; and that the linguistic sign stands for (*supponit*) its referent, and is not materially identical with it. Though Ockham fully works out the theory in his *Summa logicae*, it is seen at its best in his commentary on *1 Sentences* 22 with its careful discussion of theory and refutation of the oldfashioned, like Thomas Aquinas. There Ockham makes the following points: the word signifies according to the intention of the user; it signifies a thing, not one's concept of it. Thus even if, as Aristotle states, a word does signify the essence of a thing, the person who imposes the word does not have to know or understand this essence, he merely has to use a word whose reference is clear.

### 4.2. *Consignificatio*

Lambert of Auxerre states the general principle: the noun *consignificat illud quod ei accidit ultra principale significatum* (cited Ashworth 1991: 55). William of Conches gives three meanings for *consignificare*: *secondario significare* "to have secondary meanings", *denominare* "to imply or entail", and *cum alio significare*. From the discussion in Rosier (1995: 144–146), it seems that these three meanings of *consignificare* cross in 12th- and

13th-century theological discussion, and even run into each other. In the beginning *consignificatio* is semantic. The simplest use is the first one, to be capable of signifying different things. For example, Valente (1990: 82–83) compares Peter the Chanter's discussion of the preposition *de* with that in the *Fallaciae parvipontanae*. Both authors demonstrate that the meaning of the preposition varies according to context. But where the logician sees this *equivocatio ex varia consignificatione* as a logical vice, the theologian takes such logical concepts as tools to refine his *enarratio*. Much of Peter's argumentation on the meaning of prepositions in context remains unchanged in Peter Hispanus's *Syncategoreumata*, before being reused by Albertus Magnus and Aquinas in their theological works and further discussed by grammarians.

Many theologians lean towards William's second sense, implication or connotation, as the technical sense of *consignificatio*. The 12th-century theologian, Simon of Tournai, discussing the Trinity takes *persona*, which being *per se una* denotes individuality, as consignifying diversity (*Disputatio LXXXIII*). About a century later Guillaume d'Auxerre's discussion of the same question links *consignificare* with logical composition: masculine pronouns differ from neuter in consignifying rationality and distinctness. Albertus Magnus accords *consignificare* several layers of composition. While quoting Simon of Tournai on *persona* (*1 Sentences* XXIII 2 ad 6), he notes that *persona* signifies substance and consignifies a certain individualising property (*1 Sentences* XXIIIB 2). *Consignificatio* is for him a matter of intent to use the linguistic sign in a certain signification, be it semantic or grammatical (cf. *1 Sentences* XXIII.vii.2 arg. 2). Aquinas in his commentary on the *Sentences*, an early work, takes *consignificatio* to be semantic, thus 'master' implies (*consignificat*) 'slave' and 'slave', 'master'. And this is the meaning of *consignificatio* we find in William of Ockham on the *Sentences*.

After Boethius some of these subsidiary meanings had clearly been taken to be grammatical. As early as Abelard *Dialectica*, *consignificare* had the sense of signifying a semantic prime through one of Aristotle's categories: a verb measured its signification according to time, and this definition remains constant (cf. Aquinas, *Perihermeneias* I.iii.5.7). Given the technical sense of *mensurare*, *consignificare* becomes *unius rationis* with the property it signifies, a very standard piece of metaphysics. The word, *consignifcare*, came into grammar relatively late: where later works would read *consignificare*, the 12 century *Notae Dunelmenses* have *significare alio modo* (Kneepkens 1992: 39). Yet John of Salisbury says that Bernard of Chartres held that *albedo*, *album*, *albet* all signify the same thing but differ in consignification (Kneepkens 1992: 36). In *albedo* the semantic prime, 'white', is being expressed through the consignification of independent existence, in *album* through that of an inherent quality, and in *albet*, through the consignification of time. It was probably at about this time that *modus significandi* and *modus consignificandi* became almost synonymous. Aquinas (*Quodlibeta* 4.9.2 resp.), for example, traces diversity in consignification to diversity in *modus significandi*. But this was not entirely arbitrary. Because these *consignificationes* reflect a measure and a real mode of being, 'God', a word signifying the most unique of beings, can not rightly have a plural (for a full discussion see Kelly 1988: 206). A temporal expression, particularly the present, used of God does not measure (*mensurare*) his existence, but it *consignificat nunc aeternitatis*, i. e. measures his existence as eternal and permanent (Duns Scotus, *1 Sentences* xl.1).

### 4.3. Active and passive

No speculative grammarian after the 1270s does more than hint at the philosophical precedents for the terms, *modus significandi activus* and *modus significandi passivus*. By 1215 collocations of the adverbs, *active* or *passive* and verb, seem to have been well established in philosophy and theology: *...cum dicitur praedestinatio aut reprobatio, potest intelligi active vel passive...* "When we say 'predestination' or 'blame', it can be understood as active or passive" (Alexander of Hales, *1 Sentences* 40). Collocation of *active* and *passive* with gerundival forms, as in *modus dicendi active vel passive*, is a mid-13th-century mannerism whose grammatical basis Aquinas remarks on many times. The gerund is morphologically ambiguous: it can be either active or passive. Similarly postverbals of transitive verbs, e. g. *creatio*, *nocumentum*, can be either active and passive in force: certain nouns, like *origo*, *unio*, can signify either the action or its result. Scholastics habitually defined the 'voice' of such nouns by the phrase, *active et passive sumpta*. The source of this scientific model was Aristotle's *Physics*: natural processes depend on the reaction between active and passive potencies if they are to reach their perfection. This model is all-pervasive in the theologians: in the discussions of creation and generation, in discussions of the reactions between matter and form, and in descriptions of knowledge and cognition. Interaction between active and passive depends on the Aristotelian category, *relatio*. Active principles are in the *subiectum*, and the passive in the *terminus*. Passive and active potencies being in proportion to each other, a *terminus* receives the action of a *subiectum* according to its own modalities. It is probably from here that the dichotomy between *actio* and *passio* comes into grammar. After the 1260s it is exploited at all levels of grammatical theory from imposition to syntax. To express what they want to, which is the final perfection of language, speakers set in motion the active and passive potencies of *res*, *dictio* and *pars*. The model of linguistic processes became a recursive one accounting for every language process from imposition to syntax by the same mechanism. Thus in the formation of the *dictio* the passive potency of an object, *res significanda*, becomes the *significatum* by receiving the active potency of a *vox*, *modus significandi*, to signify it because of the material principle in it. Because passive and active modes of signifying are in proportion to each other, a thing receives the signifying action of a word according to its own modalities. Likewise words enter into construction through respective modes of signifying, like case and number, which operate according to fulfilment of potency: e. g. a noun as a *suppositum* has a passive potency which can only be fulfilled by the act brought by a finite verb.

## 5. God and parts of speech

Even if God was not subject to grammar, his lack of subjection had to be discussed in grammatical terms. Priscian became an oft-quoted authority. When the Carolingians had begun interpreting his terminology strictly, they led back to Aristotle and Boethius. Apart from relatively anodyne statements about the *oratio*, medieval theologians say little about syntax. Morphology offered richer prospects: *rationes consignificandi* pertain to the properties, both essential and accidental, of things signified. The essential properties, the *modi rei*, give rise to the essential differences between parts of speech, while the accidents of the thing signified gave rise to the accidents of the parts of speech. The question put from the late 12th century onwards is what part of speech can be fittingly used to denote God. And this question prepares the way for argumentation about what light the accidents of parts of speech cast on his nature. The ranking of parts of speech according to their suitability is a topos associated with *1 Sentences* 22. All of them are unsuitable, but the noun is the least unsuitable, because it does not consignify time, as the verb and participle do, and it signifies a substance as defined, unlike the pronoun.

Discussions of the noun revolve around endless interpretations of Priscian's *substantia cum qualitate*. Gilbert of Poitiers interpreted Priscian's definition of the noun through the Neoplatonist readings of Aristotle found in Boethius's *Opuscula sacra*. He picked up Boethius's distinction between the Neoplatonist terms, *id quod* and *id quo*. *Id quod*, defined as *subsistens in quo est subsistentia*, is the object itself, the *ens*; *id quo*, defined as *subsistentia quae est in subsistente*, is the form or *species* of the object, the *esse* of the *ens*, the form which gives rise to the accidents by which we come to know a thing (de Rijk 1988–89). De Rijk disagrees with Nielsen (1982), who sees the *id quo* as a cause, a very literal reading of "that which makes the object to be". Gilbert left his make. Alexander of Hales (*Summa* II.i.1.1) and Bonaventure (*1 Sentences* XXII.i.1) take *substantia* as the *significatum* itself and *qualitas* as that same substance insofar as it can be known. But Bonaventure then goes on *et hoc per modum quietis*: *quies* is a state of equilibrium proper to the noun and eminently proper to God (see also Albertus Magnus *Summa theologiae* I.xiv.58 solutio). Thus *qualitas* is not merely something imposed by the mind, but the form as it lets itself be known to the intellect. Hence Aquinas's distinction between *id ad quod nomen imponitur* and *id a quo nomen imponitur*. The first is the object signified: *lapis* "stone" for instance, is a certain physical thing (Aquinas, *Summa theologiae* I.1.13. 2 ad 2). *Id a quo* is the aspect (*qualitas*) by which we can know it, e. g. as the accepted etymology implied, the object against which one stubs one's toe. But as the will chooses the mode of signifying, we can denote a stone by its appearance, its purpose, or its relations with other things (McInerny 1961: 54–55; Rosier 1995: 141 ff.). Given the peculiarities of Latin grammar, *id cui nomen imponitur* is a common variant for *ad id quod* (e. g. *3 Sentences* VI.1. ad 3). Both can be read as purpose constructions. Hence *id cui* is that for which a noun stands (*supponit*). This principle Aquinas traces back to Priscian (Ashworth 1991: 47). *Suppositio* seems more congenial to theologians than the grammarians (see Brown 1993).

As the verb was measured by time and signified *per modum adiacentis*, it could not be a name for God. Yet in *Exodus* 3.14 God says his name is "Qui est". Gilbert of Poitiers quotes Priscian to show that the *verbum substantivum* denotes essence and existence and does not denote change or instability. And in any case, *est* can denote the eternal present (Kelly 1979: 172, Kelly 1988: 207). The major discussions of the pronouns fall within the theology of the Mass. In the formula, *Hoc est corpus meum*, the consensus was that the pronoun did not refer to the substance of bread, which was obvious to the senses, but to the Body of Christ, which was not: it brought *demonstratio*, but to the intellect and not to the senses (Rosier 1990: 417). For the grammarian the lesson was that the pronoun did not signify undefined substance, but a defined substance *per modum indeterminatae apprehensionis*.

The theology of God's names tended towards the formalist, while sacramental theology was intentionalist. The combination of word and act in a sacrament is directed towards producing the effect it is the sign of (Rosier 1990: 396). Discussions of sacramental theology all have a tone of pragmatics as befits a use of language that was communicative to both God and Man. In *Summa theologiae* 3 Aquinas takes the sense of words and actions, the letters of the words, and the intention of the minister as parts of a whole. This needed saying: in the Latin Rite many parish clergy were not good Latinists and they often mangled the sacramental formulas; so there was some doubt among the scrupulous about validity which could only be solved by a pragmatic approach like that of Robert Kilwardby. Second, the Byzantine Church, whose orders and sacraments were recognised, worshipped in Greek. Rosier (1990: 399) cites Bonaventure *4 Sentences* III.i.3: although the priests of the two churches spoke in different languages, they met in their understanding and in the *modi intelligendi* of the words. Therefore meaning and *modus significandi* of the sacramental formulas were equally valid.

As was often noted, flexions express *consignificationes* (Aquinas, *1 Sentences* 41.1.5.ad 4). For Lambert of Auxerre (1240?), nominative, masculine and singular are all consignifications of *homo*. Because *substantia*, *persona*, and *tempus*, are the grammatical consignifcations directly relevant to theology, theological argument influences the grammarians' concept of them. Where aspects of flexion were used by the late 13th-century theologians, the grammatical tradition was comprehensive enough not to require modification.

## 6. Terminology and models

With the assistance of philosophy, theology influenced grammar in two respects: terminology and actual modelling of language behaviour. The 13th-century formalisation of grammar was driven by the habitual medieval misreading and appropriation of their classical authorities. The 13th century assumed that ancient grammarians had used Aristotelian philosophical terminology in the rigorous 13th-century manner. What puzzled them was that Donatus and Priscian seemed to be so careless. The Carolingians began correcting this situation, by seeking a simple and coherent terminology through a return to Aristotelian sources. Their basic motivation was an attitudinal one: a simple and coherent terminology is not a mere nomenclature – it is a structure whose linguistic basis reflects the shape of the theory. And it is this which evolves from the Carolingian readings of Priscian's discussions of the *proprium* of a given part of speech, and reaches its final form in Radulphus Brito. After 1270 the technical terms of grammar unmistakeably indicate that the underlying model of *grammatica speculativa* is a physical theory of process.

By a 'simple and coherent' terminology I mean first that the 13th-century terminology falls into a paradigmatic structure marked by proportional oppositions between words; second, that these proportional oppositions are semantically and morphologically precise and regular. Third, the semantics of the terms are as precise in grammatical contexts as in philosophical, with the minimum of change for grammatical purposes. It is probable that this is a case where a theory was developed to fit an existing terminology. Aristotle's *Categoriae* was taken as an account of the properties of terms, and then as an account of the properties of things. As theology was a science describing God through his acts, it exploited paradigmatic oppositions, e. g. within the categories, between subject and terminus, *suppositum* and *appositum*. Adaptation to language through dialectic begins in the Carolingian period. The result was that the classical grammatical terms, a large number of them Aristotelian, were interpreted in the strictest possible light by the 12th- and 13th-century dialecticians and built into a paradigmatic structure marked largely by binary opposition. Apart from semantic oppositions, e. g. *esse*, *intelligere*, *significare*, the cohesion of this structure depends largely on systematic exploitation of the flexional possibilities of Latin. Rhetoricians and philosophers since Cicero had been taking advantage of the flexional and derivational morphology of Latin. To take active and passive as an example, regular oppositions from philosophy and theology. e. g. *determinatum* ≠ *determinabile*, *determinatum* ≠ *indeterminatum*, *determinabile* ≠ *indeterminabile*, become essential to the intellectual structure of grammar.

Apart from specialising Aristotle's sign-model to the word, Augustine's major legacy was his emphasis on the arbitrariness inherent in the sign-function of language, an element further developed through the doctrine of free will. The Carolingians laid the foundation for the later recursive model of language, developed and exploited by the dialecticians. 12th-century theologians, particularly Gilbert of Poitiers, eased the rigour of the dialectician's model of grammar. Because a rigidly realist model of grammar could not stand up under the strain put on it by God and the Scriptures, it was made flexible enough to handle these extreme problems and the day-to-day used of language which defy logical modelling. 13th-century theologians had the sense to balance intentionalist against formal.

## 7. Conclusion

From Origen until the end of the Middle Ages philosophy, theology and grammar lived in a mutually beneficial symbiosis. In measuring language against God, its most difficult test, theologians materially altered the direction of grammar. For Latin Europe the tone was set by Augustine: Aristotle is embedded in Plato, and the neoplatonist Aristotelianism of Boethius did not change matters. The balance between Augustine and Aristotle in medieval language theory still has to be assessed: despite the ostensible domination of Aristotelian doctrine, there is an ambiguity underlying medieval ideas on the relationship between language, the soul and reality. We have shown that the traffic between theology and grammar was reciprocal. Theology made such a fruitful use of grammar because language was considered a natural process, and as such it was amenable to scientific analysis. It could therefore fittingly contribute to modelling other sciences. Theology contributed to grammar because its problems put grammatical principles and methods under severe enough tests to cause them to be modified.

To sum up. Grammar gave theology a number of tools, the first of them being *enarratio*: it is not difficult to see parallels between Book III of the Donatus *Ars maior* and the Patristic Biblical commentaries. This was an intentionalist grammar which led easily into rhetoric. The advent of Priscian under the Carolingians paved the way for a more formalist use of grammar in theology. For Priscian gave some grammatical teeth to the *Logica vetus*, thus contributing greatly to the development of *theologia speculativa* in the 12th century. The result was a generative model of language which owed much to Aristotle's categories. As we have seen the meaning, semantic and grammatical, of words was as far as possible coterminous with the essence and properties of the thing signified, and Augustinian illuminism leavens Aristotelian arbitrariness. In recent years major attention has been given to Thomas Aquinas's skilled use of grammatical argumentation. However Albertus Magnus and a large number of theologians up to the end of the 13th century provide pickings as rich. In the theologians there is a complementary relationship between intentionalist and formalist language analysis. This reflection of a division among the grammarians is in the nature of theology itself. Where theology analyses a religious act, as in the theology of prayer, worship and the sacraments, it is the pragmatics of language that must predominate. Where the theologian is modelling the objects of belief, like God, Creation, it is the content of language that predominates. Where one can safely say that theology had a credit balance in the exchange with grammar during the 12th century, in the 13th, honours were even.

## 8. Bibliography


Amsler, Mark. 1989. *Etymology and Grammatical Discourse in Late Antiquity and the Early Middle Ages.* Amsterdam & Philadelphia: Benjamins.

Ashworth, E[arline) J[ennifer]. 1991. "Signification and Modes of Signifying in Thirteenth-century Logic: A preface to Aquinas on Analogy". *Medieval Philosophy and Theology* I.39–67.

Biard, Joël. 1989. *Logique et théorie du signe au XIV$^{e}$ siècle.* Paris: Vrin.

Brown, Stephen F[rancis]. 1993. "Medieval Supposition Theory in its Theological Context". *Medieval Philosophy and Theology* 3.121–157.

Chenu, Marie-Dominique, OP. 1957. *La théologie comme science au XII$^{e}$ siècle.* Paris: Vrin.

Colish, Marcia L[illian]. 1968. *The Mirror of Language.* Newhaven: Yale Univ. Press.

–. 1987. "Gilbert, the Early Porretans, and Peter Lombard: Semantics and theology". Jolivet & Libera (1987: 229–250).

Dronke, Peter. 1988. "Thierry of Chartres". *A History of Twelfth-century Philosophy* ed. by Peter Dronke, 358–385. Cambridge: Cambridge Univ. Press.

Ebbesen, Sten. 1987. "The Semantics of the Trinity according to Stephen Langton and Andrew Sunesen". Jolivet & Libera (1987: 401–436).

–, ed. 1995. *Sprachtheorien in Spätantike und Mittelalter.* Tübingen: Narr.

Evans, G[illian] R[osemary]. 1983. *Alan of Lille: The Frontiers of theology in the Later Twelfth century.* Cambridge: Cambridge Univ. Press.

Fredborg, K[arin] M[argareta]. 1973. "The Dependence of Petrus Helias' Summa super Priscianum on William of Conches' Glose Super Priscianum". *Cahiers de l'Institute du Moyen Âge Grec and Latin* 11.1–57.

–. 1988. "Speculative Grammar". Dronke (1988: 177–195).

Gibson, Margaret. 1981. "The *Opuscula sacra* in the Middle Ages". *Boethius, His Life, Thought and Influence* ed. by Margaret Gibson, 214–234. Oxford: Blackwell.

Jolivet, Jean. 1969. *Arts du langage et théologie chez Abélard.* Paris: Vrin.

– & Alain de Libera, eds. 1987. *Gilbert de Poitiers et ses contemporains.* Naples: Bibliopolis.

Kelly, L[ouis] G[erard]. 1975. "Saint Augustine and Saussurean Linguistics". *Augustinian Studies* 6.45–64.

–. 1979. "*Modus significandi*: An interdisciplinary concept". *Historiographia Linguistia* 6.159–180.

–. 1990. "God and Speculative Grammar". *L'héritage des grammariens latins, Actes du colloque de Chantilly, 2–4 September, 1987*, 205–213. Louvain: Peeters.

Kneepkens, C[orneille] H[enri]. 1992. "Nominalism and Grammatical Theory in the Late Eleventh and Early Twelfth Centuries: An explorative study". *Vivarium* 30.34–50.

Luhtala, Anneli. 1993. "Syntax and Dialectic in Carolingian Commentaries on Priscian's *Institutiones grammaticae*". *Historiographia Linguistica* 20.145–191.

Marenbon, John. 1988. *Early Medieval Philosophy (480–1150).* London: Routledge.

–. 1991. *Later Medieval Philosophy.* London: Routledge.

Markus, R[obert] A[ustin]. 1957. "St Augustine on Signs". *Phronesis* 2.60–83.

McInerny, Ralph M[atthwe]. 1961. *The Logic of Analogy: An interpretation of St Thomas.* The Hague: Nijhoff. (Repr., 1971.)

Nielsen, Lauge Olaf. 1982. *Theology and Philosophy in the Twelfth Century.* (= *Acta theologica Danica*, 150). Leiden: Brill.

Pannacio, Claude. 1995. "La philosophie du langage de Guillaume d'Occam". Ebbesen (1995: 184–206).

Perler, Dominik. 1993. "Duns Scotus on Signification". *Medieval Philosophy and Theology* 3.97–120.

Rijk, L[ambertus] M[aria] de. 1988–1989. "Semantics and Metaphysics in Gilbert of Poitiers: A chapter on twelfth-century Platonism." *Vivarium* 26.73–112; 27.1–35.

Rosier, Irène. 1990. "Signes et sacrements: Thomas d'Aquin et la grammaire spéculative". *Revue des Sciences Philosophiques et Théologiques* 74.392–436.

–. 1995. "Res significata et modus significandi: Les implications d'une distinction médiévale". Ebbesen (1995: 135–168).

Steenberghen, Fernand van. 1970. *Aristotle in the West: The Origins of Latin Aristotelianism.* Transl. by Leonard Johnston. 2nd ed. Louvain: Nauwelaerts.

Valente, Luisa. 1990. "Arts du discours et *'sacra pagina'* dans le *'De tropis loquendi'* de Pierre le Chantre". *Histoire Epistémologie Langage* 12:2.69–102.

–. 1995a. "Une sémantique particulière: La pluralité des sens dans les Saintes Écritures". Ebbesen (1995: 12–32).

–. 1995b. "Langage et théologie pendant la seconde moitié du XII$^{e}$ siècle". Ebbesen (1995: 33–54).


*Louis G. Kelly, Ottawa (Canada)*

# 80. Die Beziehungen der spätmittelalterlichen Sprachforschung zu anderen Disziplinen

1. Wege der Naturerkenntnis und Naturbeherrschung im Mittelalter
2. Naturphilosophie im Mittelalter
3. Einige Aspekte der Wissenschaftstheorie und Physik Wilhelms von Ockham
4. Metalinguistische Physik im 14. Jahrhundert
5. Magie, Divination und Prohibitive Wissenschaften im Spätmittelalter
6. Sprache, Gedächtnis, Mnemotechnik: Thomas Bradwardine
7. Bibliographie

## 1. Wege der Naturerkenntnis und Naturbeherrschung im Mittelalter

In seiner im Mittelalter stark rezipierten Schrift *De doctrina christiana* legt der Kirchenvater Aurelius Augustinus (354–430) seinem Wissenschaftsschema eine primäre Einteilung in *scientia realis* oder Sachwissenschaft und *scientia sermocinalis* oder Sprachwissenschaft zugrunde: *omnis doctrina est de rebus vel de signis* (I,2). Diese basale Unterscheidung nach 'Modi von Wirklichkeitserkenntnis' (dazu Schneider 1992) hat im Verein mit der augustinischen Einbindung des Begriffs vom sprachlichen Zeichen in eine einflußreiche allgemeine Zeichentheorie (Meier-Oeser 1997: 1–34; Maierù 1981) für lange Zeit zu einer Dominanz pansemiotischer Betrachtungen in der Naturkunde geführt und dort symbolistische und allegoreseorientierte Deutungen unterstützt (Brinkmann 1980; vgl. Kap. 49–61 in Posner et al. 1997: 984–1198). Mittelalterliche Sprachforschung (zum mittelalterlichen Sprachbegriff im allgemeinen vgl. Schneider 1995a) ist in erster Linie Sprachzeichenwissenschaft im Sinne einer linguistischen Semiotik (Semiologie). Bereits der elementare Grammatikunterricht als strukturvermittelnde, propädeutische Basis des Triviums (zu dem noch Dialektik/Logik und Rhetorik gehören) vermittelt die elementarsten Kenntnisse von der Natur aus der Sicht einer Wörter-und-Sachen-Perspektive (Freyer & Keil 1997: 12).

Die wechselseitigen Beziehungen zwischen der auf der Logik basierenden theoretischen Sprachbetrachtung einerseits (wie sie im Trivium erfolgte) und den die Sachaspekte der Natur erforschenden Disziplinen des Quadriviums (zunächst Arithmetik, Geometrie, Astronomie und Musik, später dann die (spät-)mittelalterlichen Entsprechungen von Physik, Mathematik, Biologie und Chemie) andererseits werden sich erst dann hinreichend deutlich beschreiben lassen, wenn für diese einzelnen Disziplinen der Naturwissenschaft auch ihre jeweiligen Geschichten geschrieben worden sein werden. In diesem Kontext ist auch die Medizin zu nennen, die sich als *potissima pars* (Vincent von Beauvais) der Naturphilosophie erst spät als eigene Wissenschaft aus diesem Kanon ausgliedert.

Zu bedenken ist, daß curriculare Erfordernisse der als besonders wichtig erachteten Unterrichtspraxis selten oder nie den jeweiligen theoretischen Vorgaben der Wissenschaftsklassifikationen (Weisheipl 1965; Schneider 1995b) folgen, so daß *ordo inventionis*, *ordo naturae* und *ordo doctrinae* stark divergieren, wie besonders deutlich in den großen mittelalterlichen enzyklopädischen Darlegungen zum Ausdruck kommt. Auch liegt eine Vielzahl von modernen Studien zum Problemkreis vor, diese behandeln jedoch – wie nicht anders zu erwarten – immer nur einzelne Aspekte mittelalterlicher Wissenschaft und Spezialprobleme der Technik (vgl. die Bibliographie von Kren 1985). Eine umfassende Geschichte der mittelalterlichen Kosmologie hat neuerdings Grant (1994; vgl. auch 1996) veröffentlicht. Eine Gesamtsynthese ist aber seit Sartons *Introduction* (1927–1948) nicht wieder versucht worden und kann wohl auch nicht mehr in einem überschaubaren Rahmen geleistet werden.

## 2. Naturphilosophie im Mittelalter

Die Naturphilosophie des Mittelalters untersucht Auslegung ihrer allgemeinen Definition durch Aristoteles im II. Buch der Physikvorlesung (*De physico auditu* 192b 20–23) Körper, die Bewegungen, Veränderungen, Wechseln oder Übergängen unterworfen sind bzw. diese vollziehen. Dabei versucht sie die Gründe (*causae*) zu ermitteln, nach denen die Natur sich verändert, und sie will ganz allgemein beschreiben, was Bewegung und Veränderung überhaupt sind. Im großen Maßstab sind dabei insbesondere die Bewegungen der Himmelskörper von großem Interesse, im kleinen die Bewegungen und der Wandel der vier Elemente (Feuer, Wasser, Luft und Erde). Das Entstehen und Vergehen aller Dinge und Lebewesen ist ebenfalls Gegenstand der Naturphilosophie. Die sogenannten okkulten Wissenschaften, insbesondere die Magie, die in ihrem Erkenntnisinteresse über weite Passagen mit der Naturphilosophie konform gehen, jedoch im Unterschied zu letzterer die Naturphänomene nicht allein erkennen und beschreiben, sondern auch konkret beeinflussen und beherrschen wollen, werden an den mittelalterlichen Universitäten nicht gelehrt. Sie haben aber – wie Astrologie und Alchemie – durchaus Berührungspunkte mit dem Hochschulunterricht. Man kann die Unterscheidung in magische und nicht-magische Wissenschaften als grundlegend für die Auseinandersetzung des Menschen mit der Natur betrachten.

In der Liste der Verständnisweisen von Natur, die Vincent von Beauvais (c. 1187–1264) in seiner Enzyklopädie *Speculum maius* der aristotelischen Definition folgen läßt (*Natura est principium motus & quietis, eius in quo est, per se, & non per viam accidentis,* [*Speculum* 1373]; in einigen Aspekten präzisierend so noch Ockham, *Expositio* I, 215), findet im übrigen auch der magische Naturbegriff seinen Platz. Vincent (*Speculum* 1373) nennt vier Auffassungen von *natura*:

(1) *vis insita rebus, ex similibus similia procreans,* worunter auch das magische Verständnis mitsamt seinem – von der späteren medizinischen Homöopathie aufgegriffenen – Simile-Prinzip und der Kraft-aus-Sympathie-Lehre zu ordnen wäre;
(2) *principium motus et quietis,* die physikalische Standarddefinition von Natur;
(3) *communis vel usitatus naturae cursus mortalibus notus* oder das biologische Prinzip, das Naturvorgänge von Wundern und Übernatürlichem (*mirabilia*) trennt;
(4) *possibilitas creaturae,* das finalistisch-teleologische Naturprinzip, wie es von Gott (als *natura naturans*) eingegeben wird.

Der rhetorische Charakter der natürlichen Ordnung kommt in der mächtigen Metapher vom 'Buch der Natur' zum Ausdruck (Ohly 1995), in dem die rationale Ordnung der Welt, die erst durch Sprache semantisch gefaßt und ausgedrückt werden kann, aufgeschrieben steht und vom Kundigen gelesen werden kann. Denn Unterscheiden und Benennen und Bezeichnen, jene elementaren kognitiven Auseinandersetzungen des Menschen mit der ihn umgebenden Natur, sind ohne Sprache gar nicht denkbar. Historisch interessant ist dabei die Verschiebung von der auf neoplatonischer Logos-Tradition und christlicher Verbum-Lehre beruhenden moralisch-spirituellen Allegorese, die die semiotisch-linguistische repräsentationale Einheit des Wortes in den Mittelpunkt stellt, hin zu einer Propositionalisierung des Wissens – auch im Sinne geordneter Ansammlungen von Aussagen, innerhalb einer sprachpragmatischen Argumentationstheorie, die sich am Begriff des Satzes orientiert (zu den Satzlehren des 14. Jhs. vgl. Perler 1990; 1992). Diese Entwicklung beginnt im 12. Jh. (Wilhelm von Conches; vgl. Cadden 1995) und erreicht ihren Höhepunkt in den philosophisch ausgerichteten Wissenschaften des 14. Jhs., die einer allgemeinen Sophismatisierung unterzogen werden (s. u.).

Die mittelalterliche Naturphilosophie läßt sich hinsichtlich des Grades ihrer Mathematisierung in ein Kontinuum einteilen, an dessen einem Rand die Hochschulphysik steht, die mit den Mitteln der verstandesmäßigen Analyse und der Metaphysik *mutatio* und *motus* untersucht, und an dessen anderem Rand die Mathematik angesiedelt ist, die die meß- und quantifizierbaren Aspekte von Körpern herausarbeitet. Dazwischen sind "mittlere Wissenschaften" (*scientiae mediae*) angesiedelt, wie Optik, Astronomie und Statik, bei denen mathematische und physikalische Aspekte gleichermaßen wichtig sind. Insbesondere die mittelalterliche Optik und Theorie des Sehens und des Lichts hat in letzter Zeit viel Aufmerksamkeit seitens der Forschung erfahren. Man hat erkannt, daß die naturphilosophischen Theorien des Sehens mit ihren Berührungspunkten zur Physiologie, zur Wahrnehmungstheorie, zu mathematisch-physikalischen Fragen des Bildaufbaus und der Fortbewegung des Lichtes für die geschichtliche Entwicklung der Ansichten über Erkenntnis, Kognition und Semantik von erheblicher Wichtigkeit sind (Tachau 1988; Lindberg 1976 [dt. 1987]; 1996).

## 3. Einige Aspekte der Wissenschaftstheorie und Physik Wilhelms von Ockham

Die in neueren Arbeiten unterstrichene Semiotisierung der Naturphilosophie ("sémiophysique", de Libera 1990: 162) im 14. Jh. hängt aufs engste mit der Ockhamschen Wissenschaftstheorie und mit seiner Hermeneutik der logischen Sprachanalyse (Schepers

1981) zusammen. Wissenschaft handelt nach Ockham nicht von extramentalen Dingen (*non est de rebus*), sondern ausschließlich von Notwendigem und Allgemeinem, von Universalem, d. h. von unseren Begriffen oder Intentionen, die für die Dinge stehen ('supponieren'), und zwar in sprachlich-begrifflichen Kontexten von Sätzen (*propositiones*), denn Wissenschaft kann es auch nur von Zusammengesetztem, Verknüpftem geben (*omnis scientia est respectu complexi vel complexorum*; Ockham, *Expositio* I, 11). Eine zentrale Forderung Ockhams lautet, daß kontingente Aussagen oder Sätze über Kontingentes, wie sie Tatsachenurteile enthalten, in Möglichkeitsaussagen oder hypothetische Urteile umgeformt werden. Realwissenschaften und Rationalwissenschaften unterscheiden sich dahingehend, daß die Begriffe der *scientia realis* für Dinge stehen, die Begriffe der *scientia rationalis* dagegen für Begriffliches, für andere Begriffe. Auch für die Wissenschaft von der Natur wie die Physik (zu Ockhams Physik umfassend Goddu 1984; Brown 1981) gilt, daß sie nicht – wie man annehmen könnte, aber das ist nur uneigentlicher, metaphorischer Sprachgebrauch – von natürlichen, vergänglichen und beweglichen Dingen handelt. Vielmehr beschäftigt sie sich mit den zweiten Intentionen, die für diese Dinge in Aussagen stehen (*scientia naturalis est de intentionibus animae communibus talibus rebus et supponentibus praecise pro talibus rebus in multis propositionibus, Expositio* I, 11; *scientia realis non est de rebus, sed est de intentionibus supponentibus pro rebus, quia termini propositionum scitarum supponunt pro rebus, Expositio* I, 12). Entsprechend müssen nach Ockhams Ansicht auch die wissenschaftlichen Autoritäten erläutert (*glossari*) werden, die sagen, eine bestimmte Wissenschaft beschäftige sich mit bestimmten Dingen. Sie meinen nämlich eigentlich die Termini, die für jene Dinge stehen (Ockham, *Expositio* I, 12; die entsprechenden Stellen aus dem Prolog zu Ockhams Physik-Kommentar dt. von R. Imbach [Ockham, *Texte* 186–215]).

Ockhams Ansatz, der die semantische Struktur der lateinischen Wissenschaftssprache(n) seiner Zeit untersucht, enthält auch eine Kritik an der überkommenen aristotelischen Wissenschaftssprache, die er als philologisches Argument einsetzt: Alle Wörter sind in gewisser Hinsicht mehrdeutig (polysem): *cum omnia vocabula quasi sint aequivoca* (Ockham *Expositio* I, 19). Da Aristoteles und sein Kommentator Averroes recht sorglos mit den Nomina umgegangen seien, hätten sie viele Wörter an diversen Stellen ihrer Werke in unterschiedlicher Bedeutung verwendet und damit Mißverständnisse durch spätere Interpreten geradezu provoziert, weil diese oft eine eindeutige Bedeutung unterstellten. Streben nach "Kürze im sprachlichen Ausdruck" (*causa brevitatis, brevitas sermonis*) und "rhetorischer Redeschmuck" (*ornatus locutionis*) sind die Ockhamschen Standardbegründungen, um die zahlreichen Vorkommen von Simplicia in wissenschaftlichen Terminologien zu erklären. Da dabei allerdings nur strukturelle Kompliziertheit durch semantische Komplexität ersetzt wird (*aequivalent complexis in significando*), muß die Bedeutung derartiger Kürzel in paraphrastische Langformen (*oratio longa, propositiones exponentes*) zergliedert werden. Auch dürfe nicht der *actus signatus*, bei dem metasprachlich über Prädikationen gesprochen wird, mit dem *actus exercitus* verwechselt werden, bei dem tatsächlich eine Prädikation vollzogen wird, mithin dann nicht *propositiones*, sondern die Dinge selbst gemeint sind. Diese Verwechslung komme bei den Interpreten des Aristoteles allerdings häufig vor.

Konnotative Ausdrücke (in der Physik sind das Nomina wie *mutatio*, *motus*, *tempus*, *instans*, *privatio*, *actio*, *passio*, *calefactio* usw.) dürfen nicht als absolute Ausdrücke mißverstanden und somit nicht reifiziert werden, da auf diesem Wege nur fiktive Realitäten behauptet werden (Brown 1981: 122ff.). Solche Konnotativa täuschen uns durch ihre Oberflächenform, die sie wie absolute Termini erscheinen läßt, doch haben sie tatsächlich komplexe Bedeutungen, die aufzudecken Aufgabe des Physikers ist – so wie Ockham ihn versteht. Referenzbasis bleibt immer die *res permanens*. Derartige Wörter setzen uns immer der Gefahr aus, fiktive Realitäten zu erzeugen; die Präger und Nutzer terminologischer Neuerungen – und das gilt wohl für jeden Wissenschaftler – laufen ständig Gefahr, in die Reifikationsfalle ("reification trap", Brown 1981: 124) der Wissenschaftssprachen zu geraten. Auch Naturwissenschaftler entgehen nicht der sozialen Systematizität von Sprache, denn sie sind immer einem Vermittlungs- und Glaubwürdigkeitsproblem ausgesetzt, wenn ihre Forschungen kommunizierbar bleiben sollen. Darum, meint Ockham, darf die *suppositio impropria* der Umgangssprache (Metaphern, figurative Bildsprache, idiomatische Ausdrücke und Redewendungen) bei allem Streben nach Exaktheit, das sich in einem steten Mangel an Wörtern und Termini (*penuria nominum*) in den Fachsprachen zeige, nicht außer Acht gelassen werden: *loquendum est ut plures* (Ockham, *Expositio* II, 199; Quelle dieses Florilegia-Ausspruchs ist Aristoteles, *Topica* II,2, 110a15–21).

An anderer Stelle (*Expositio* I, 425f.) zeigt Ockham, wie die Klasse der Verbalnomen oder -substantive (*nomina verbalia*; er nennt als Beispiele: *negatio*, *contradictio*, *privatio*, *perseitas*, *contingentia*, *universalitas*, *quantitas*, *actio*, *passio*, *calefactio*, *frigefactio*, *mutatio*), die ihre deverbale Herkunft in den prädikamentalen Klassen 'Handeln' und 'Erleiden' haben, hinsichtlich ihrer Bedeutung komplexen Sätzen entsprechen und bei der Analyse in solche umgewandelt werden müssen. Da diese Wörter suppositionell immer in ihrem konkreten Verwendungskontext gesehen werden müssen, erhalten wir hier wieder die Ockhamsche paraphrastische Expansion von Relationen zwischen Sätzen. Ein Beispiel bietet die elementar und klar klingende Aussage *motus est in tempore*. Um seine Semantik deutlicher werden zu lassen, muß dieser Satz aber expandiert werden zu dem komplizierten Bedingungsgefüge: *quando aliquid movetur, non adquirit vel deperdit omnia quae adquirit vel deperdit simul, sed unum post aliud* (*Expositio* I, 435).

Auf die Frage *quid est mutatio* darf keinesfalls geantwortet werden, *mutatio* sei eine *res* oder eine *qualitas*. Vielmehr muß der Charakter dieses Wortes als Nomen verbale verdeutlicht werden: *mutatio est adquisitio vel deperditio alicuius*. Diese Aussage wird expandiert zum konditional-temporalen Satzgefüge: *quando aliquid mutatur, adquirit vel deperdit aliquid*. Eine Explikation von *mutatio* hat daher zu beginnen mit konjunktionsinitialisierten Formulierungen wie *quando aliquid mutatur [...]*, *quod mutatur [...]*, oder *si mutatur [...]*. Andererseits darf natürlich der Ausdruck *mutatio [est] subita* nicht aufgelöst werden zu *quod mutatur, est subitum*. Es muß statt dessen nämlich heißen: *quod mutatur, adquirit vel deperdit illud quod adquiritur vel deperditur, totum simul et non partem post partem* (Ockham, *Expositio* 429).

Wie Ockhams Beispielanalysen deutlich werden lassen, stehen lexikalisierte fachsprachliche Ausdrücke trotz ihres formalen Charakters als Simplizia semantisch für theoriegebundene komplexe Wissenskontexte, die syntaktisch in komplizierte Gebilde zergliedert werden müssen. Allerdings, so vergißt Ockham nicht hinzuzufügen, ist es schwierig, eine einheitliche Regel (*unum modum generalem*) für die Expositionsprozedur(en) zu finden.

Nötig und zugelassen sind für seine Analyse des Bewegungsbegriffs und dessen Bezeichnungen nur *res permanentes*, die sich dadurch auszeichnen, daß für sie gilt: *non sunt simul*. Die Annahme von *res successivae* ist dagegen unnötig. Das – in den zeitgenössischen Wissenschaftssprachen (*in modernis temporibus*, wie Ockham klagt) durchaus übliche – Bilden von Abstrakta liefert nur Pseudoanalysen. Mit absurden Konsequenzen könnte man dann aus den vorhandenen Konjunktionen abstrakte Substantive bilden (*et-itas* oder *et-eitas*, *si-itas*, *vel-itas*, *dum-itas*; *Expositio* I, 434; 547) und hätte dann z. B. in dem Satz *a et b* drei *res*: a, b und die Etitas. Um solche unsinnigen Ergebnisse zu vermeiden, sollte die Wissenschaftssprache keine Abstrakta verwenden, sondern nur Verben, Adverbien, Präpositionen, Konjunktionen und synkategorematische Ausdrücke (z. B. Quantoren), und zwar in ihren ursprünglichen Bedeutungen: *sicut primario fuerunt instituta*. Dann erledigten sich bereits viele Schwierigkeiten in der Physik.

Die spezifische Auflösung des Terminus "Bewegung" (*motus*) lautet bei Ockham nun wie folgt: Ein *motus* besteht aus verneinenden und bejahenden Aussagen, d. h. damit eine Bewegung vorliegt, genügt es, daß es Teile (*partes*) der Bewegung und *res permanentes* gibt, die aber nicht gleichzeitig (*simul*) vorkommen dürfen. Um die Aussage *motus est* wahr zu machen, genügen gewisse affirmative und negative Sätze. Durch diese Sätze werden keine anderen als *res permanentes* eingeführt oder denotiert. Beim "Wechsel" (*motus alterationis*) genügt es z. B., daß es zuerst eine *res* gibt (und keine andere) und anschließend eine andere *res* (und sonst nichts). Und so braucht man nichts außer der *res permanens* (*Expositio* I, 434f.; dt. Übers. von Buch III, Kap. 2, §§ 6–8, S. 430–449 des Physikkommentars Ockhams auch in Wöhler 1994: 96–114).

Eine Aufarbeitung der Beziehungen zwischen der naturphilosophisch-physikalischen Bewegungstheorie und der modistischen Sprach- und Grammatiktheorie sowie der sie bekämpfenden nominalistisch-logischen nebst ihrer Terminologie(n) bleibt erst noch zu leisten. Das gilt insbesondere im Zusammenhang mit Überlegungen zur psychophysischen *immutatio*-Lehre der Spätscholastik und deren Auswirkungen auf die semiotisierte Sprachtheorie (vgl. Kaczmarek 1990; neue Quellen bei Bakker 1996) sowie auch auf die magische Sprachtheorie (s. u.), wobei zu beachten bleibt, daß die mittelalterlichen Autoren wissenschaftsklassifikatorisch gesehen ihre psychologischen Traktate *De anima* ebenfalls der Naturphilosophie zurechnen. Deshalb finden sich in Auseinandersetzungen mit der modistischen Sprach- und Grammatiktheorien, z. B. in den *Destructiones modorum significandi* (anon.), immer wieder Argumentationen, die den Gebieten Psychologie und Naturphilosophie oder Physik entnommen sind.

## 4. Metalinguistische Physik im 14. Jahrhundert

Die spezifisch Ockhamsche Lösung semantischer Probleme durch seine besondere Suppositionstheorie und mittels der speziellen Technik der Paraphrasenexpansion sowie sein besonderer ontologischer Denotationspartikularismus (*nihil est extra animam nisi particulare*; Ockham, *Expositio* I, 87) können sich nicht auf allen Gebieten durchsetzen. Durch die Arbeiten der sogenannten Oxforder Calculatores (dazu Sylla 1982; 1991a [1970]) erfährt die Naturphilosophie des 14. Jhs. eine explizite Hinwendung zu Fragen der logisch-linguistischen Pragmatik (zu nennen sind hier Thomas Bradwardine (c. 1290–1349), *Incipit*; William Heytesbury (c. 1312–1372/3) *On "insoluble" sentences* und *On maxima and minima* [Wilson 1960]; Richard Swineshead (*fl.* 1340–1355) [Sylla 1987]; Richard Kilvington (1302/05–1362), *Sophismata*; Walter Burley (Burleigh, c. 1275–1344/5), *De primo et ultimo instanti*; Richard Billingham (*fl.* 1344–61) [Knuuttila & Lehtinen 1979] und John Dumbleton (c. 1310–c. 1349) [Sylla 1991b]). Diese Engländer entwickeln eine bis nach Italien rezipierte spezifische Variante der Disputationskunst – ein Hauptstück der scholastischen Hochschulpädagogik – anhand der Obligationslehre und mittels Analyse spezieller Sophismen weiter. Sophismen (es werden *sophismata grammaticalia, logicalia* und *physicalia* [Nef 1983; de Libera 1989] unterschieden) sind für die Entwicklung der komplexen Argumentationsspiele besonders wichtig und werden sowohl in der konkreten Unterrichtspraxis geübt als auch als literarische Form gepflegt. Zwischen dem 13. und 14. Jh. läßt sich eine deutliche Entwicklung in Auffassung und Strukturierung dieser Sophismen, die materiell oft unverändert bleiben, feststellen.

Innerhalb des Kontextes dieser besonderen pragmatischen Vermittlungs- und Einübungsformen von Problemen logischer, naturphilosophischer und wissenschaftstheoretischer Art entwickelt sich im 14. Jh. eine besondere Klasse von analytischen 'Sprachen', die zum Zwecke der begrifflichen Analyse und bei Gedankenexperimenten als Werkzeuge innerhalb der Naturphilosophie und -wissenschaft eingesetzt werden (Murdoch 1974; 1975; 1978; 1979; 1981; 1982a,b,c; 1989; de Libera 1990; Caroti 1992; Caroti & Souffrin 1997). Diese Begriffssprachen sind

(1) proto-mathematische Sprachen, die mittels besonderer Meßverfahren semantische Probleme lösen, die insbesondere zum Typ der Situationssemantik gehören oder bei der Bestimmung von Phasen und Grenzen auftreten. Diese Begriffssprachen werden nach ihren lateinischen Codewörtern bezeichnet, und zwar (a) *intensio/remissio formarum*, (b) *De 'incipit' et 'desinit'*, (c) *De maximo et minimo* und (d) der Proportionenkalkül (*De proportionibus*).

(2) Es werden logische Sprachen eingesetzt wie die in verschiedenen Spielarten auftretende Suppositionstheorie und die Metalinguistik der zweiten Intentionen (*intentiones secundae*), die eine Theorie der mentalen Sprache zur Voraussetzung hat (Panaccio 1992; Normore 1992).

Für die Sprachwissenschaft besonders aufschlußreich sind – um nur diese hier zu nennen – die semantischen Analysen und Phasenbeschreibungen von Situationen bzw. Szenen, die sich aus der Verwendung bestimmter Verben wie *incipit* "fängt an, beginnt" oder *desinit* "hört auf, endet" ergeben. Dabei geht es z. B. um die Bestimmung von Grenzen, um Beginn (Anfänge, Eingänge) und um Ende (Schlüsse, Ausgänge) von Vorgängen, Ereignissen, Prozessen, Situationen, Tätigkeiten und Handlungen. Wann beginnt ein Vorgang? Wann ist er noch nicht angefangen? Wann ist der Anfang eingetreten? Wann endet ein Ereignis? Wie unterscheiden sich die Beschreibungen von Anfängen und Endausgängen? Sind sie etwa einfach Umkehrungen voneinander? Gibt es Regelhaftigkeiten? Lassen sich Klassifikationen der Thematik entwickeln? Um bei der Entscheidung solch diffiziler Probleme Entscheidungskriterien an die Hand zu bekommen, werden die genannten analytischen Begriffssprachen entwickelt und die Physik der Ereignisse und Situationen als Metalinguistik (*mediantibus vocibus*) betrieben.

Ein Sophisma ist, wie Kretzmann (1977: 6) definiert hat, "ein Satz, der für sich oder auf der Basis gewisser Annahmen verblüfft und der gebildet wird, um ein abstraktes Problem schärfer zu fassen". Als Beispiele für Sophismen seien hier aus Kilvingtons Sammlung angeführt: *Socrates est albior quam Plato incipit esse albus* (Nr. 1); *Socrates erit ita albus praecise sicut Plato erit albus in aliquo istorum* (Nr. 8). Albert von Sachsen (1502), der Kilvingtons Sophisma Nr. 1 (mit der Verbform *incipiat* statt *incipit*) stolz *magis lucide si possim* abzuhandeln verspricht (Nr. 2.138a), analysiert im selben Problemkreis die Aussagen: *Sortes est albior quam Plato immediate post hoc erit albus* (Nr. 2.318b) und *Sortes incipit esse albior quam Plato incipit esse albus* (Nr. 2.139).

Im 14. Jh. entbrennt ein Kampf um die Definitionen naturphilosophischer und mathematischer Begriffe und Ordnungsrelationen ('Punkt', 'Linie', 'Fläche', 'Zeitpunkt', 'Grad', 'Teil/Ganzes', 'größer/kleiner als'), bei dem die syntaktosemantische Struktur des Satzes, in dem der jeweilige Begriff zum Ausdruck kommt, zum Kriterium der Definitionslehre wird. Dieses Vorgehen bedeutet eine wesentliche Abkehr von der wortbasierten synchronischen Definitionslehre, die noch Vincent von Beauvais unter der Bezeichnung Etymologie propagiert hatte (*expositio alicuius vocabuli per aliud vocabulum*, *Speculum* 83). Ockham hatte die Existenz der Denotate fiktiver Elemente wie *punctus* und *instans* oder auch konnotativer Termini wie *motus* und *tempus* bestritten und derartige Ausdrükke durch eine propositionale Analyse ersetzt. Die semantische Beschreibung von Grenzen und die Analyse von Vagheit als semantischer Modalität ist dabei ein Erbe der terministischen Logik, wie sich etwa in der Suppositionslehre an der Beziehung zwischen der *suppositio confusa tantum* und dem Phänomen der linguistischen Vagheit zeigen läßt.

Durch sein spezifisches Vorgehen *secundum imaginationem* (Hugonnard-Roche 1989) gelangt das spätscholastische Nachdenken über die Natur nicht etwa vom 'Gedankenexperiment' zur experimentellen Überprüfung von Hypothesen an den Gegebenheiten *in rebus*. Vielmehr wird der Bereich des logisch Möglichen ausgelotet und semantische Problemräume erkundet. Dabei wird der Begriff der göttlichen Allmacht, der *potentia Dei absoluta*, vorausgesetzt, derzufolge Gottes Handeln allein dem logischen Kontradiktionsprinzip zu gehorchen hat: *Deus potest facere omne quod fieri non includit contradictionem.*

## 5. Magie, Divination und Prohibitive Wissenschaften im Spätmittelalter

Das andere Ende der großen Bifurkation in der theoretischen Auseinandersetzung des Menschen mit der Natur wird von ihrer magischen Betrachtung besetzt. Magie läßt sich mit Biedermann (1973: 211) und Rothschuh (1978: 7) verstehen als "die Umsetzung eines auf Entsprechungen und Sympathien gegründeten Weltbildes in die Praxis". Für die Sprachforschung aufschlußreich ist an der Magie (*magia*, gr. *mageia* "Gelehrsamkeit", "Gottesdienst bei den Persern") die Theorie ritueller Sprechakte, die diesen elementaren und wesentlichen Zugriff auf die Welt kennzeichnet und von Wissenschaft (*scientia*) unterscheidet (vgl. Thorndike 1915; Cardini 1979: 107–111 [Lit. u. Quellentexte]; Kieckhefer 1989). Das besondere Interesse heilender, an "Erhaltung, Wiedererlangung und Stärkung der Gesundheit" ausgerichteter mittelalterlicher Medizin (Keil 1987) und verwandter Iatrowissenschaften (Iatroastrologie, -chemie, -mathematik, -physik, -theologie und eben -magie [vgl. auch Biedermann 1978]) an der Incantatio (Harmening 1979: 221ff.), der "Macht" (*vis*, *virtus*) des geschriebenen und gesprochenen Wortes, an dem geheimnisvollen und oft auch geheim gehaltenen *Wirkungszusammenhang* der Kommunikation zwischen hierarchisierten und miteinander verketteten kosmischen Ordnungen ("a series of structure-preserving mappings", Molland 1988: 214) aufgrund von als verborgen begriffenen Harmonien, Zuneigungen (*inclinationes*), Sympathien (*vinculum naturae*) und auch Antipathien, von Entsprechungen, Äquivalenzen, Nachahmungen, Einflüssen, Assoziationen und symbolisch-zeichenhaften Beziehungen zwischen den Dingen, aber auch zwischen Sprache, Denken und Wirklichkeit, ist seit der Antike (Luck 1985) bekannt und von der Wissenschaftsgeschichtsschreibung berücksichtigt und dokumentiert worden. Magisches Wort und Ritual, mit denen Wirkungen in der Natur hervorgerufen werden können, gelten als sprachliche Reaktion auf eine besondere, sinnheischende Interpretation von 'Zufall', der "als determiniertes Moment eines umfassenden

Zusammenhangs beeinflußbar ist" und gesehen wird als "Zeichen einer Koinzidenz oder einer Synchronizität, in der alle Ereignisse sinngemäß verbunden sind, wenngleich nicht unbedingt 'kausal'" (Geier 1982: 379).

Nach Nikolaus Oresme (1320/22–1382) – um nur einen prominenten und originellen Kopf des 14. Jhs. zu nennen – weist die magische *incantatio* strukturell gesehen zwei Bestandteile auf (*De configurationibus qualitatum et motuum*, *Tractatus* 368; vgl. Paschetto 1981):
(a) *vis significationis*, als bedeutungs- bzw. auch bezeichnungstheoretische Komponente ein wichtiger Aspekt jeder Sprach- und Zeichentheorie, wie spätestens seit Ockham immer wieder unterstrichen wird: der Zusammenhang zwischen Lautung und Bedeutung ist im Sprachzeichen zwar grundsätzlich arbiträr, im sozialen Zusammenhang aber, in dem Sprache nun einmal verwendet wird, ganz und gar nicht beliebig. Bedeutungen müssen in korrekten Verwendungskontexten erlernt werden und binden ihren Nutzer;
(b) *virtus formationis et figurationis sonorum*, die – beeinflußt durch Platons *Timaeus* – gestalthafte, phonetisch-musikalische Komponente, die den Ton (*sonus*) innerhalb der Reihung *verba*, *cantus*, *soni* im Stufenaufbau der Natur betrifft: *Inde est quod artes magicae fundantur pro parte in quorundam sonorum certe configurationis potentia et virtute tam in melodia quam in verbis* (*Tractatus* 334; speziell zum magischen Gesang anhand literarischer Beispiele vgl. Groupe de recherches 1997).

So, wie die Erfahrungswissenschaft der Alchemie (Haage 1996; zu ihrer fachsprachlichen Lexik im 16. Jh. Barke 1991) – oft auch in Union mit der Magie, wie etwa prominent bei Roger Bacon (c. 1219–c. 1292/94) – die verborgenen Ordnungen der dinglichen Welt in ausgeklügelten Verfahren experimentell zu beeinflussen sucht, will die magische Kunst in ritueller Praxis eine zwar arkane, aber für den Eingeweihten trotzdem erkennbare Ordnungsstrukturen (Sympathien und Antipathien) aufweisende Semantik mit Mitteln der Sprache beherrschen. Dabei gelangt sie zu einer Systematik der Heilwirkungen (vgl. Rothschuh 1978: 14f.), die ihre Mittel entweder nach Ähnlichkeiten (Simile-Prinzip) oder aber nach überraschend Andersartigem gruppiert.

In der bekannten Wissenschaftsklassifikation *De ortu scientiarum* I,2 (um 1250) des Robert Kilwardby (gest. 1279) ist die Magie noch einfach schlechte, schädliche Philosophie (*scientia vituperabilis, quae communiter dicitur magica*), weder notwendig noch irgendwie nützlich, sondern im Gegenteil *superstitiosa, nociva et vitanda* (*De ortu scientiarum* 9). Auch Vincent von Beauvais (*Speculum* 851–854), der Isidor von Sevillas Definition und Genealogie der Magier aus dem 8. Buch der *Etymologiae* anbietet, dann auf jene Aspekte der Magie hinweist, die sie mit der Medizin verwandt erscheinen läßt, und der anschließend eine Klassifikation versucht, nennt die Magier betrügerisch und infam. Schließlich plädiert er für deren Exkommunikation. Ihre Riten und Gesänge werden eigens erwähnt, ohne daß aber Beispiele folgen.

Im 15. Jh. mehren sich die Auseinandersetzungen mit den 'verbotenen' divinatorischen ('prognostischen' und 'weissagenden') Wissenschaften, zu denen die verschiedenen Typen der Magie vornehmlich gerechnet werden. Das auf deutsch verfaßte *Buch aller verbotenen Künste* des Münchener Arztes Johannes Hartlieb (c. 1400–1468), das aus christlicher Mystik und hebräischer Kabbalistik ebenso schöpft wie aus Werken der arabischen Astrologie und Magie, verdeutlicht die Gefahren der Zauberei einem größeren Publikum und macht den neuen Leserkreis zugleich auch mit den lateinischen Fachtermini vertraut. Hartlieb nennt: Nigromantia, die 'Schwarze Kunst', sowie Geomantia, Hydromantia, Aeromantia und Pyromantia, die sich auf die Elemente Erde, Wasser, Luft und Feuer beziehen, desweiteren Chiromantia, die Handlesekunst, und Spatulamantia, die Kunst, Tierknochen zu deuten.

Im 16. Jh. versucht dann Cornelius Agrippa von Nettesheim (1486–1533), Theologe und Mediziner und, wie Paracelsus (1493–1541), Schüler des humanistisch gesinnten, an Sprachtheorie und Steganographie/Kryptographie (Shumaker 1982; Eco 1997: 135–137) interessierten Benediktinerabts Johannes Trithemius (1462–1516), in seinem Buch *De occulta philosophia* (1533 [Ms. 1510]) die Magie auf eine rationale, theologisch unbedenkliche Grundlage zu stellen. Dabei treten die semiotischen und sprechakttheoretisch interessanten Verfahren dieser okkulten Kunst deutlich hervor und werden von Agrippa auch entsprechend thematisiert.

Auffällig ist nun, wenn im späten 15. Jh. Florentius Diel (gest. nach 1518), Protagonist der Mainzer Nominalisten, in seinem umfangreichen ernsthaften Grammatiktraktat *Etymologia praeclara Donati* (1490 [dazu

Kaczmarek 1995; Puff 1995: 177–193]) gleich in der ersten *quaestio* (f.b2r), die danach fragt, ob die Grammatik eine Sermozinalwissenschaft sei, für den modernen Leser recht unvermittelt auf die Unterscheidung zwischen verbotenen und erlaubten Wissenschaften und Künsten eingeht, um sodann die einzelnen Typen der Magie abzuhandeln, allerdings ohne dabei einen sprachtheoretisch interessierenden Zusammenhang zum eigentlichen Thema seines Buches herzustellen. Die Aufzählung der Bereiche magischer Divinationskünste, die sich weitgehend an Vincent anlehnt, ohne ihn zu nennen, umfaßt bei Diel: *pyromantia*, *aeromantia*, *hydromantia*, *geomantia*, *necromantia*, *haruspicina*, *auspicium* und *chyromancia*. Daneben nennt er noch einige spezielle Arten von "üblen" Zauberern (*malefici*), die mittels spezieller Techniken, eigentümlicher Geräte und Verfahrensweisen – fehlerhafte – Aussagen über die Zukunft von Menschen treffen und mit der Macht ihrer Worte Schaden anrichten können. Solche Spezialzauberer sind: *specularii*, die Spiegel und ähnliche Gerätschaften benutzen, *phytonici*, die vom Teufel angetrieben sind, *prestygiatores*, die die menschlichen Sinne verdunkeln und verwirren, *geneathliaci*, die aus den Geburtsdaten die Zukunft lesen, *'mathematici'*, die keine Mathematiker sind, sondern bloß abergläubische Astrologen. Weiter kennt Diel noch die *sortilegi*, die Losstäbchen legen, sowie die *prodigiatores*, die Wunderzeichen deuten, aber tatsächlich deren Bedeutungen beeinflussen und steuern (*dirigunt significationem*). Alle diese hermeneutisch-semiotischen Künste sind manipulativ, täuschend und verfälschend, weil sie vom Teufel eingegeben werden. Hier hilft nur Vertrauen auf die wahre Religion und auf Gott. Das ist dann genau der Ort, an dem Agrippa seinen berühmten magischen Traktat aufbaut und sich bemüht, Magie als strenge Wissenschaft mit starker sprachtheoretischer Komponente zu fassen.

Auch der vielseitig interessierte Leonardo da Vinci spricht um das Jahr 1500 Geistern die Fähigkeit zur Stimm- und Lauterzeugung als ein spezifisches Humanum schlichtweg ab und rechnet anderslautende Annahmen der schwarzen Magie und dem Volksglauben zu (nach Panconcelli-Calzia [1961: 126; vgl. 1943], dessen Quellenbasis für das Mittelalter allerdings sehr dürftig ist).

Was nun Agrippas magische Sprachtheorie (vgl. dazu Klein 1992: 147–154) und seine Ansichten über die perlokutive Wirkung magischer Sprechakte im einzelnen betrifft, so schreibt er zu diesem Thema ohne explizite Nennung seiner Quellen längere Passagen aus *De harmonia mundi* (1525) des venezianischen Ficino-Kenners Georgius Franciscus (Francesco Giorgi[o] oder Zorzi OFM, c. 1460/1–1540; cf. Klein 1992: 191) aus. Weiter bedient er sich des 6. und umfangreichsten Kapitels (*De virtute verborum*) von al-Kindīs (c. 800–870) einflußreichstem Traktat *De radiis* [*stellicis* bzw. *stellarum*] (lat. ed. 1975; dazu Thorndike 1923–58: I, 644–646; vgl. Burnett 1996; Klein 1992 erwähnt diese Quelle nicht). Al-Kindīs Schrift war im Mittelalter bezeichnenderweise auch als *Theorica artium magicarum* bekannt. In ihr wird der Zusammenhang zwischen 'richtigen' magischen Sprechhandlungen – fernab von Volksaberglauben – und 'wissenschaftlicher', experimenteller Methode bestätigt – wie sie später dann Roger Bacon übernimmt (Molland 1974; 1993: 154–158; 1997: 72f.; Lindberg 1983: xliv–xlv; liv). Drei Hauptbedingungen formuliert al-Kindī für die Sprachmagie: Die magischen Namen, Wörter und Wendungen müssen geäußert werden: (a) am richtigen Ort und zur richtigen Zeit (*debitis locis et temporibus*); (b) mit einer genauen, zielgerichteten Absicht (*cum intentione exacta*, die später dann zum 'festen Glauben' an die Perlokution wird) und (c) mit der angemessenen Feierlichkeit vorgetragen (*cum sollempnitate prolata*). Sind diese Bedingungen erfüllt, können apotropäische Abwendungs- und Fürbitten (*deprecativa*), Beschwörungen und Anrufungen (*obsecrativa*), Verwünschungen und Flüche (*exsecrativa*) ihre gewünschten Wirkungen bzw. Hemmungen – immer gesehen als "Bewegungen", *motus* – bei Menschen, Tieren und in den Dingen hervorrufen (*faciunt motus et impedimenta motuum in materia convenienti*).

Gelegentlich greift Agrippa auch auf Reuchlins (1455–1522) religionsphilosophische Abhandlung über die Kabbala, *De verbo mirifico* (1494; zum Inhalt Zika 1976), zurück. Diesen drei genannten Quellen Agrippas (al-Kindī, Georgius, Reuchlin) ist gemeinsam, daß sie zwischen Naturwissenschaft und falscher Magie, Astrologie (North 1986) und Volkszauber zu unterscheiden wissen, ohne der Magie, insbesondere der Sprachmagie mit ihrem instrumentalen Zeichenbegriff, unter bestimmten, angebbaren Bedingungen und bei Beachtung gewisser Ordnungsfaktoren Wirksamkeit und pragmatische Brauchbarkeit abzusprechen.

Agrippa (*De occulta philosophia* 230) zufolge besitzen sprachmagische Wendungen und Aussprüche die Kraft, etwas zu verändern, anzuziehen, zu verhindern und zu binden oder zu verpflichten (*virtus immutandi, attrahendi, impediendi et ligandi*). Wenige Seiten weiter (*De occulta philosophia* 235) spricht er von *vis imprimendi, immutandi, ligandi et stabiliendi*. Georgius Franciscus (*De harmonia mundi totius* fol. 36v), den er hier wörtlich ausschreibt, ist sein Zeuge:

*Sunt itaque verba aptissimum medium inter loquentem et audientem* [ein geläufiger Topos], *deferentia secum non tantum conceptum, sed et virtutem loquentis energia quadam transfundentia in audientes et suscipientes, tanta saepe potentia, ut non immutent solummodo audientes, sed etiam alia quaedam corpora et res inanimatas.*

Festzuhalten ist, daß an dieser Stelle die tatsächliche Wirkkraft nicht den einfachen Wörtern (*verba simplicia*) zugeschrieben wird, sondern eine solche in propositionalen, wahrheitswertfähigen Aussagen angenommen wird (*in enunciationibus quibus aliquid affirmatur aut negatur*; Agrippa, *De occulta philosophia* 235).

Derartige Aussagen finden sich auch in den verschiedenen Vertextungsformen und Sprechaktsorten der Magie, die Agrippa anzubieten hat. Er zählt dazu *carmina*, *incantamenta*, *imprecationes*, *deprecationes*, *orationes* [hier natürlich nicht als einfache 'Rede' zu verstehen, sondern im Sinne von 'Gebet'], *invocationes*, *obtestationes*, *adiurationes*, *exorcismata* und andere, über die er allerdings den Leser mit der Wendung *et huiusmodi* im Ungewissen läßt. Bereits Marsilio Ficino (1433–1499) hatte Wert auf die Feststellung gelegt, daß es bei derartigen 'Gebeten' nicht etwa um Anbetung anderer Götter gehe – das verbietet ja die Heilige Schrift –, sondern vielmehr um Versuche, Kraft und Einfluß höherer, himmlischer Mächte (z. B. der Gestirne) nachzuahmen oder wenigstens zu beeinflussen. Zu der *invocatio* weiß Agrippa an anderer Stelle noch zu sagen – und das wohl auch stellvertretend für die anderen Vertreter seiner Klassifikation –, daß sie nach genauen, von Eingeweihten überlieferten Regeln und Verfahren, die erst erlernt und beherrscht werden müssen, konstruiert und gebraucht werden muß: *quae et ipsa fabricanda est debito numero, pondere et mensura iuxta regulas traditas* (*De occulta philosophia* 584). Der Magus, der *verbis mysteriosis et locutione quadam ingeniosa* (*De occulta philosophia* 394) spricht, ist über das Wort in einer Repräsentationskette mit Gott verbunden:

*Verbum igitur id est simulacrum Dei, intellectus agens est simulacrum Verbi, anima est simulacrum intellectus, verbum autem nostrum est simulacrum animae, per quod agit in res naturales naturaliter, quoniam natura opus illius est* (*De occulta philosophia* 395).

Es fällt auf, daß die Klassifikation der magischen Sprechakte bei Agrippa genauso eigentümlich leer bleibt wie bei den anderen Autoren des Spätmittelalters und des Humanismus, die über Magie schreiben. Dies mag sich mit dem Hinweis auf den Ehrenkodex zur Geheimhaltung dieser Kunst begründen lassen, doch ist weiter zu bemerken, daß die angebotenen Gliederungs- und Ordnungsversuche selten stabil sind und schon terminologisch zwischen Synonymie, Polysemie und Vagheit schillern. Auch muß der wichtige Aspekt der Namenmagie berücksichtigt werden. Diese übt über die Auffindung, Kenntnis, Chiffrierung und Dechiffrierung sowie den richtigen – und dann erst wirksamen – Gebrauch von (geheimen bzw. verhüllenden) *Namen* und *Nomenklaturen* – insbesondere der Namen Gottes, der Gestirne und Planeten – Kommunikations- und Herrschaftswissen aus. Diese Magie der (Eigen-)Namen ist eng verknüpft mit der spezifischen Zahlen- und Buchstabenmagie Agrippas, die erheblichen Raum in seinem Werk beansprucht. Die speziell magische, neoplatonistisch und kabbalistisch beeinflußte Auffassung von der Zahl und ihrer Diskretheit im Übergang vom Mittelalter zur Renaissance und frühen Neuzeit eröffnet auch der Geschichte der Zeichen- und Sprachtheorie ein eigenes interessantes Gebiet (Molland 1988; zu historischen Grundlagen des mittelalterlichen Zahlverständnisses Knapp 1988).

## 6. Sprache, Gedächtnis, Mnemotechnik: Thomas Bradwardine

Zwei Bereiche, die neben dem Wissens*erwerb* und der *Mehrung* des Wissens spezifisch scholastische Ausformungen erhalten haben und an denen Sprache – nicht zuletzt über die pädagogisch ausgerichtete Zeichentheorie in Augustins *De magistro* vermittelt (→ Art. 71) – einen wesentlichen Anteil hat, sind der Wissens*erhalt* und auch die Wissens*vermittlung*, die primär mündlich erfolgt. Beide sind über eine repräsentationale Gedächtnistheorie und besondere Techniken des Memorierens ineinander verschränkt.

Die Kunst der Mnemotechnik nutzt die Tendenz des menschlichen Gedächtnisses und des kognitiven Apparats, zeitlich aufeinanderfolgende Ereignisse psychisch als gleichzeitig darzustellen (Vincent von Beauvais, *Speculum* 1385) und damit einen zeitlichen *ordo* der Ereignisfolgen durch einen räumlichen, bildhaften *ordo* zu repräsentieren. Das Erinnern als einer der drei das Zeitkontinuum *in animo* gliedernden Aktionsmodi (*expectare*, *attendere*, *meminisse*), von denen noch Vincent spricht, und als unmittelbar wichtige Fähigkeit zur Teilnahme an den scholastischen Lehr- und Lernprozessen, wird zu einer eigenen *Ars memorandi* ausgebaut. Im 14. Jh. entwickelt diese Kunst Bischof Thomas Bradwardine in seiner Abhandlung *De memoria artificiali* zu einem alltagstauglichen technischen Memorierprogramm. Seine Anleitung arbeitet mit semantischen Rollen, Körperschemata und Wahrnehmungsrichtungen, und sie läßt den verblüfften modernen Leser in ihrer Verwendung sprachbasierter repräsentationaler Loci an kognitionspsychologische Überlegungen zu imaginären Museen, Szenarien, semantischen Tableaus bis hin zur Skripttheorie der Künstlichen Intelligenz denken. Und sie kann durchaus mit neuesten Vorschlägen zur Mnemotechnik konkurrieren.

## 7. Bibliographie

### 7.1. Primärliteratur

Agrippa, *De occulta philosophia* = [Heinrich] Cornelius Agrippa [von Nettesheim], *De occulta philosophia libri tres*. Hg. von V[ittoria] Perrone Compagni. Leiden: Brill, 1992.

Albert von Sachsen, *Sophismata* = Albertus de Saxonia, *Sophismata*. Paris, 1502. (Nachdr., Hildesheim: Olms, 1975.)

[anon.], *Destructiones modorum significandi*. Hg. u. mit Einl. u. Reg. versehen von Ludger Kaczmarek. (= *Bochumer Studien zur Philosophie*, 9.) Amsterdam & Philadelphia: Grüner, 1994.

Diel, Florentius, *Modernorum de collegio maiori moguntino etymologia praeclara donati nouiter exarata: et in duas primo minorem et secundo maiorem editiones partita: ad discipulorum diversorum capacitatem successiuam*. Spire [Speyer], 1490. (Ex. Trier, Stadtbibl., Inc. 1774 8⁰.)

Georgius Franciscus [Giorgi[o], Francesco], *De harmonia mundi totius cantica tria*. Venetiis: B. De Vitalibus, 1525.

Hartlieb, Johannes, *Das Buch aller verbotenen Künste*. Hg. u. ins Neuhochdeutsche übertr. von Frank Fürneth. Mit einer Einf., einem Nachw. u. zeitgenöss. Holzschnitten. Frankfurt/M.: Insel, 1989.

al-Kindī, *De radiis*. Hg. von Marie-Thérèse d'Alverny & Françoise Hudry. *Archives d'histoire doctrinale et littéraire du Moyen Age* 49 (1975). 139–260.

Nikolaus von Oresme, *Tractatus* = Nikolaus von Oresme, *Tractatus de configurationibus qualitatum et motuum secundum doctorem et magistrum Nych. Orem*. Hg. von Marshall Clagett, (1968: 157–517).

Ockham s. Wilhelm von Ockham

Reuchlin, *De verbo mirifico* = Johannes Reuchlin, *De verbo mirifico*. Basel, 1494. Hg. von Widu-Wolfgang Ehlers, Lothar Mundt, Hans G. Roloff & Peter Schäfer u. Mitwirkung v. Benedikt Sommer, *Das wundertätige Wort*. (= *Sämtliche Werke*, 1,1.). Stuttgart–Bad Cannstatt: Frommann-Holzboog.

Richard Kilvington, *Sophismata* = *The Sophismata of Richard Kilvington*. Text by Norman Kretzmann & Barbara Ensign Kretzmann. (= *Auctores Britannici Medii Aevi*, 12.) Oxford: Published for the British Academy by Oxford Univ. Press, 1990. [Enthält nur lat. Text.]

–. *The Sophismata of Richard Kilvington*. Introduction, Translation and Commentary by Norman Kretzmann & Barbara Ensign Kretzmann. New York etc.: Cambridge Univ. Press, 1990. [Enthält nur engl. Übersetzung.]

Robert Kilwardy, *De ortu scientiarum*. Hg. von Albert G. Judy. (= *Auctores Britannici Medii Aevi*, 4.) [o. O.]: The British Academy; Toronto: The Pontifical Institute of Medieaeval Studies, 1976.

Thomas Bradwardine, *Treatise on 'incipit' and 'desinit'*. Hg. mit einer Einleitung von Lauge Olaf Nielsen. *Cahiers de l'Institut du Moyen-Age Grec et Latin* 42 (1982). 1–83.

–. *De memoria artificiali*. [Ms. Cambridge, Fitzwilliam Museum, MS. McClean 169.] Engl. Übers. in Carruthers, 1990: App. C. 281–288.

Vincent von Beauvais, *Speculum* = Vincent von Beauvais, *Speculum quadruplex sive Speculum maius*, vol. II: *Speculum doctrinale*. Duaci [Douai]: Ex Off. Typ. B. Belieri, 1624. (Photomech. Nachdr., Graz: Akad. Druck- u. Verlagsanstalt, 1965.)

Walter Burley, *De primo et ultimo instanti*. Hg. von Herman Shapiro & Charlotte Shapiro. *Archiv für Geschichte der Philosophie* 47 (1965) 157–173.

Wilhelm von Ockham, *Texte* = Wilhelm von Ockham, *Texte zur Theorie der Erkenntnis und der Wissenschaft*. Lateinisch/deutsch. Hg., übers. u. komm. von Ruedi Imbach. (= *Universal-Bibliothek*, 8239.) Stuttgart: Reclam, 1984.

–. *Expositio* I = Wilhelm von Ockham, *Expositio in libros Physicorum Aristotelis*. [Vol. I:] *Prologus et Libri I–III*. Hg. von Vladimirus Richter & Gerhardus Leibold. (= *Guillelmi de Ockham Opera philosophica*, 4.) St. Bonaventure, N. Y.: St. Bonaventure University, 1985.

–. *Expositio* II = Wilhelm von Ockham, *Expositio in libros Physicorum Aristotelis*. [Vol. II:] *Libri IV–*

*VIII.* Hg. von R. Wood, R. Green, G. Gál, J. Giermek, F. Kelley, G. Leibold & G. Etzkorn. (= *Guillelmi de Ockham Opera philosophica*, 5.) St. Bonaventure, N. Y.: St. Bonaventure University, 1985.

William Heytesbury, *On "Insoluble" Sentences. Chapter One of His "Rules for Solving Sophisms"*. Transl. with an Introd. and Study by Paul Vincent Spade. (= *Medieval Sources in Translation*, 21.) Toronto: Pontifical Institute of Mediaeval Studies, 1979.

–, *On Maxima and Minima. Chapter 5 of Rules for Solving Sophismata, with an Anonymous Fourteenth-Century Discussion.* Transl., with an Introd. and Study, by John Longeway. (= *Synthese Historical Library*, 26.) Dordrecht, Boston & Lancaster: Reidel, 1984.

## 7.2. Sekundärliteratur

Bakker, Paul J. J. M. 1996. "Syncatégorèmes, concepts, équivocité: Deux questions anonymes, conservées dans le ms. Paris, B. N., lat. 16.401, liées à la sémantique de Pierre d'Ailly (c. 1350–1420)". *Vivarium* 34.76–131.

Barke, Jörg. 1991. *Die Sprache der Chymie. Am Beispiel von vier Drucken aus der Zeit zwischen 1574–1761.* Tübingen: Niemeyer.

Biedermann, Hans. 1973. *Handlexikon der magischen Künste von der Spätantike bis zum 19. Jahrhundert.* 2., verb. u. wesentl. verm. Aufl. Graz: Akad. Druck- u. Verlagsanstalt.

–. 1978. *Medicina magica: Metaphysische Heilmethoden in spätantiken und mittelalterlichen Handschriften.* 2. Aufl. Graz: Akad. Druck- u. Verlagsanstalt.

Brinkmann, Hennig. 1980. *Mittelalterliche Hermeneutik.* Tübingen: Niemeyer.

Brown, Stephen F. 1981. "A Modern Prologue to Ockham's Natural Philosophy". Kluxen et al. (1981: I, 107–129).

Burnett, Charles. 1996. *Magic and Divination in the Middle Ages: Texts and techniques in the Islamic and Christian worlds.* Aldershot & Brookfield, Vt.: Variorum.

Cadden, Joan. 1995. "Science and Rhetoric in the Middle Ages: The natural philosophy of William of Conches". *Journal of the History of Ideas* 56.1–24.

Cardini, Franco. 1979. *Magia, stregoneria, superstizioni nell'Occidente medievale.* Firenze: La Nuova Italia.

Caroti, Stefano, Hg. 1989. *Studies in Medieval Natural Philosophy.* Firenze: Olschki.

–. 1992. "Nuove prospettive della storiografia di storia della scienza medievale: Le proposte di John E. Murdoch". *Nuncius* 7.231–252.

– & Pierre Souffrin, Hg. 1997. *La nouvelle physique du XIV^e^ siècle.* Firenze: Olschki.

Carruthers, Mary J. 1990. *The Book of Memory: A study of memory in Medieval culture.* Cambridge: Cambridge Univ. Press.

Clagett, Marshall, Hg. 1968. *Nicole Oresme and the Medieval Geometry of Qualities and Motions: A treatise on the uniformity and difformity of intensities known as* Tractatus de configurationibus qualitatum et motuum. Ed. with an introduction, English translation and commentary. Madison, Milwaukee: Univ. of Wisconsin Press.

Eco, Umberto. 1997. *Die Suche nach der vollkommenen Sprache.* Aus dem It. v. Burkhart Kroeber. München: Deutscher Taschenbuch Verlag. (It. Orig. 1993.)

Freyer, Michael & Gundolf Keil. 1997. *Geschichte des medizinisch-naturkundlichen Unterrichts: Einführung in Grundlagen und Verlauf der Entwicklung eines neuen Lehrgebiets.* Fürth: Filander Verlag.

Geier, Manfred, 1982. "Die magische Kraft der Poesie: Zur Geschichte, Struktur und Funktion des Zauberspruchs". *Deutsche Vierteljahrsschrift für Literaturwissenschaft und Geistesgeschichte* 56.359–385.

Goddu, André. 1984. *The Physics of William of Ockham.* Leiden: Brill.

Grant, Edward. 1994. *Planets, Stars, and Orbs: The Medieval cosmos, 1200–1687.* Cambridge: Cambridge Univ. Press.

–. 1996. *The Foundations of Modern Science in the Middle Ages: Their religious, institutional, and intellectual contexts.* Cambridge: Cambridge Univ. Press.

Groupe de recherches "Lectures médiévales", Université de Toulouse-Le Mirail. 1997. *Chant et enchantement au Moyen Age.* Toulouse: Editions Universitaires du Sud.

Haage, Bernhard Dietrich. 1996. *Alchemie im Mittelalter: Ideen und Bilder – von Zosimos bis Paracelsus.* Zürich & Düsseldorf: Artemis & Winkler.

Harmening, Dieter. 1979. *Superstitio: Überlieferungs- und theoriegeschichtliche Untersuchungen zur kirchlich-theologischen Aberglaubenliteratur des Mittelalters.* Berlin. Schmidt.

Hugonnard-Roche, Henri. 1989. "Analyse sémantique et analyse 'secundum ymaginationem' dans la physique parisienne au XIV^e^ siècle". Caroti (1989: 133–153).

Kaczmarek, Ludger. 1990. "*Vitalis immutatio*: Erkundungen zur erkenntnispsychologischen Terminologie der Spätscholastik". *Mathesis rationis. Festschrift für Heinrich Schepers* hg. von Albert Heinekamp, Wolfgang Lenzen & Martin Schneider, 189–206. Münster: Nodus.

–. 1995. "Sprach- und Zeichentheorie in der deutschen Spätscholastik: Gabriel Biel, 'Ultimus scholasticorum', Florentius Diel, 'Primus modernorum', und die Grammatiker des 15. Jahrhunderts". *Sprachtheorien in Spätantike und Mittelalter* hg. von Sten Ebbesen, 207–236. Tübingen: Narr.

Keil, Gundolf. 1987. "Organisationsformen medizinischen Wissens". *Wissensorganisierende und wissensvermittelnde Literatur im Mittelalter: Perspek-*

*tiven ihrer Erforschung. Kolloquium 5.–7. Dezember 1995* hg. von Norbert Richard Wolff, 221–245. Wiesbaden: Reichert.

Kieckhefer, Richard. 1989. *Magic in the Middle Ages.* Cambridge: Cambridge Univ. Press.

Klein, Wolf Peter. 1992. *Am Anfang war das Wort: Theorie- und wissenschaftsgeschichtliche Elemente frühneuzeitlichen Sprachbewußtseins.* Berlin: Akademie-Verlag.

Kluxen, Wolfgang [Leitung], Jan P. Beckmann, Ludger Honnefelder, Gabriel Jüssen, Barbara Münxelhaus, Gangolf Schrimpf & Georg Wieland, Hg. 1981. *Sprache und Erkenntnis im Mittelalter. Akten des VI. Internationalen Kongresses für mittelalterliche Philosophie der Société internationale pour l'Étude de la Philosophie médiévale, 29. August–3. September 1977 in Bonn.* 2 Halbbde. (= *Miscellanea Mediaevalia*, 13,I–II.) Berlin & New York: de Gruyter.

Knapp, Georg. 1988. "Zahl als Zeichen: Zur 'Technisierung' der Arithmetik im Mittelalter". *Historia Mathematica* 15.114–134.

Knuuttila, Simo & Anja Inkeri Lehtinen. 1979. "*'Plato in infinitum remisse incipit esse albus'*: New texts on the Late Medieval discussion on the concept of infinity in Sophismata literature". *Essays in Honour of Jaakko Hintikka on the Occasion of his Fiftieth Birthday* hg. von Esa Saarinen, Risto Hilpinen, Ilkka Niiniluoto & Merrill Provence Hintikka, 309–329. Dordrecht & Boston: Reidel 1979.

Kren, Claudia. 1985. *Medieval Science and Technology: A selected annotated bibliography.* New York & London: Garland.

Kretzmann, Norman. 1977. "Socrates is Whiter than Plato Begins to Be White". *Noûs* 11.3–15.

–, Anthony Kenny, Jan Pinborg & Eleonore Stump, Hg. 1982. *The Cambridge History of Later Medieval Philosophy: From the rediscovery of Aristotle to the disintegration of scholasticism, 1100–1600.* Cambridge: Cambridge Univ. Press.

Libera, Alain de. 1989: "La problématique de 'l'instant du changement' au XIIIe siècle: Contribution à l'histoire des 'sophismata physicalia'". Caroti 1989.43–93.

–. 1990. "Le développement de nouveaux instruments conceptuels et leur utilisation dans la philosophie de la nature au XIVe siècle". *Knowledge and the Sciences in Medieval Philosophy. Proceedings of the Eighth International Congress of Medieval Philosophy (S.I.E.P.M.), Helsinki 1987,* hg. von Monika Asztalos, John E. Murdoch & Ilkka Niiniluoto, I, 159–197. Helsinki: Societas Philosophica Fennica.

Lindberg, David C. 1976. *Theories of Vision from Al-Kindi to Kepler.* Chicago: Univ. of Chicago Press. (Deutsche Übers. *Auge und Licht im Mittelalter: Die Entwicklung der Optik von Alkindi bis Kepler.* Frankfurt/M.: Suhrkamp, 1987.)

–. 1983. *Roger Bacon's Philosophy of Nature: A critical edition, with English translation, introduction, and notes, of* De multiplicatione specierum *and* De speculis comburentibus. Oxford: Clarendon Press.

–. 1996. *Roger Bacon and the Origins of Perspectiva in the Middle Ages. A critical edition and English translation of Bacon's* Perspectiva *with introduction and notes.* Oxford: Clarendon Press.

Luck, Georg. 1985. *Arcana mundi, Magic and the Occult in the Greek and Roman Worlds: A collection of ancient texts.* Baltimore: The Johns Hopkins Press. (Nachdr., o. O.: Crucible, 1987.)

Maierù, Alfonso. 1981b. "'Signum' dans la culture médiévale". Kluxen et al. (1981: I,51–72).

Meier-Oeser, Stephan. 1997. *Die Spur des Zeichens: Das Zeichen und seine Funktion in der Philosophie des Mittelalters und der frühen Neuzeit.* Berlin & New York: de Gruyter.

Molland, A. G[eorge]. 1974. "Roger Bacon as Magician". *Traditio* 30.445–460.

–. 1988. "Cornelius Agrippas's Mathematical Magic". *Mathematics from Manuscript to Print, 1300–1600* hg. von C. Hay, 209–219. Oxford: Clarendon Press. (Nachdr., G. Molland, *Mathematics and the Medieval Ancestry of Physics*, Aldershot: Variorum.)

–. 1993. "Roger Bacon and the Hermetic Tradition in Medieval Science". *Vivarium* 31.140–160.

–. 1997. "Roger Bacon's *De laudibus mathematicae*: A preliminary study". Sylla & McVaugh (1997: 68–83).

Murdoch, John E[mery]. 1974. "Philosophy and the Enterprise of Science in the Later Middle Ages". *The Interaction between Science and Philosophy* hg. von Yehuda Elkana, 51–74. Atlantic Highlands, N. J.: Humanities Press.

–. 1975. "From Social into Intellectual Factors: On aspects of the unitary character of Late Medieval learning". *The Cultural Context of Medieval Learning* hg. von John E. Murdoch & Edith Dudley Sylla, 271–348. Dordrecht: Reidel.

–. 1978. "The Development of a Critical Temper: New approaches and modes of analysis in fourteenth-century philosophy, science, and theology". *Medieval and Renaissance Studies* 7.51–79.

–. 1979. "Propositional Analysis in Fourteenth-century Natural Philosophy: A case study". *Synthese* 40.117–146.

–. 1981. "*Scientia mediantibus vocibus*: Metalinguistic analysis in Late Medieval natural philosophy". Kluxen et al. (1981: I,73–106).

–. 1982a. "The Analytic Character of Late Medieval Learning: Natural philosophy without nature". *Approaches to Nature in the Middle Ages* hg. v. Lawrence D. Roberts, 172–213. Binghamton, N. Y.: Center for Medieval and Early Renaissance Studies. [Mit Kommentar v. Norman Kretzmann, a. O. 214–220.]

–. 1982b. "Infinity and Continuity". Kretzmann et al. (1982: 564–591).

–. 1982c. "William of Ockham and the Logic of Infinity and Continuity". *Infinity and Continuity in Ancient and Medieval Thought* hg. von Norman Kretzmann, 165–206. Ithaca & London: Cornell Univ. Press.

–. 1989. "The Involvement of Logic in Late Medieval Natural Philosophy". Caroti (1989: 3–28).

Nef, Frédéric. 1983. "Présentation des *sophismata physicalia*: Contribution à l'étude du chiasme sémantique/physique". *Archéologie du signe* hg. von Lucie Brind'Amour & Eugene Vance, 287–304. Toronto: Institut Pontifical d'Études Médiévales.

Normore, Calvin. 1990. "Ockham on Mental Language". *Historical Foundations of Cognitive Science* hg. von J[ohn]-C[hristian] Smith, 53–70. Dordrecht, Boston & London: Kluwer.

North, John D. 1986. "Celestial Influence: The major premiss of astrology". *'Astrologi hallucinati': Stars and the end of the world in Luther's time* hg. von Paola Zambelli, 45–100. Berlin & New York: de Gruyter.

Ohly, Friedrich. 1995. "Zum Buch der Natur". Friedrich Ohly, *Ausgewählte und neue Schriften zur Literaturgeschichte und zur Bedeutungsforschung* hg. von Uwe Ruberg & Dietmar Peil, 727–843. Stuttgart & Leipzig: Hirzel.

Panaccio, Claude. 1992. "From Mental Word to Mental Language". *Philosophical Topics* 20.125–147.

Panconcelli-Calzia, Giulio. 1943. *Leonardo als Phonetiker.* Hamburg-Wandsbek: Hansischer Gildenverlag.

–. 1961. *3000 Jahre Stimmforschung: Die Wiederkehr des Gleichen.* Marburg: Elwert.

Paschetto, Eugenia. 1981. "Linguaggio e magia nel 'De configurationibus' di N. Oresme". Kluxen et al. (1981: II, 648–656).

Perler, Dominik, Hg. 1990. *Satztheorien: Texte zur Sprachphilosophie und Wissenschaftstheorie im 14. Jahrhundert. Lateinisch-Deutsch.* Darmstadt: Wiss. Buchgesellschaft.

–. 1992. *Der propositionale Wahrheitsbegriff im 14. Jahrhundert.* Berlin & New York: de Gruyter.

Posner, Roland, Klaus Robering & Thomas A[lbert] Sebeok, Hg. 1997. *Semiotik. Ein Handbuch zu den zeichentheoretischen Grundlagen von Natur und Kultur.* 1. Teilbd. (= *Handbücher zur Sprach- und Kommunikationswissenschaft*, 13/I.) Berlin & New York: de Gruyter.

Puff, Helmut. 1995. "*Von dem schlüssel aller Künsten / nemblich der Grammatica": Deutsch im lateinischen Grammatikunterricht 1480–1560.* Tübingen & Basel: Francke.

Rothschuh, Karl Ed[uard]. 1978. *Iatromagie: Begriff, Merkmale, Motive, Systematik.* Opladen: Westdeutscher Verlag.

Sarton, George. 1927–48. *Introduction to the History of Science.* 3 Teile in 5. Baltimore: Published for the Carnegie Institution of Washington by Williams & Wilkins.

Schepers, Heinrich. 1981. "Verifikation durch Reduktion: Zur Diskussion des Verhältnisses von Sprache und Wissenschaft im Spätmittelalter". Kluxen et al. (1981: I, 130–133).

Schneider, Jakob Hans Josef. 1992. "*Scientia sermocinalis/realis*: Anmerkungen zum Wissenschaftsbegriff im Mittelalter und in der Neuzeit". *Archiv für Begriffsgeschichte* 34.54–92.

–. 1995a. "Der Begriff der Sprache im Mittelalter, im Humanismus und in der Renaissance". *Archiv für Begriffsgeschichte* 38.66–149.

–. 1995b. "Wissenschaftseinteilung und institutionelle Folgen". *Philosophy and Learning. Universities in the Middle Ages* hg. von Maarten J. F. M. Hoenen, J. H. Josef Schneider & Georg Wieland, 64–121. Leiden: Brill.

Shumaker, Wayne. 1982. "Johannes Trithemius and Cryptography". *Renaissance Curiosa: John Dee's Conversation with Angels, Girolamo Cardano's Horoscope of Christ, Johannes Trithemius and Cryptography, George Dalgarno's Universal Language* hg. von Wayne Shumaker, 91–131. Binghamton, N. Y.: Center for Medieval and Early Renaissance Studies.

Sylla, Edith [D]udley. 1982. "The Oxford Calculatores". Kretzmann et al. (1982: 540–563).

–. 1987. "Mathematical Physics and Imagination in the Work of the Oxford Calculators: Richard Swineshead's *On Natural Motion*". *Mathematics and its Applications to Science and Natural Philosophy in the Middle Ages. Essays in Honor of Marshall Clagett* hg. von Edward Grant & John E. Murdoch, 69–101. Cambridge & London: Cambridge Univ. Press.

–. 1991a. *The Oxford Calculators and the Mathematics of Motion, 1320–1350: Physics and measurement by latitudes.* New York: Garland. [Ph. D. Univ. of Harvard, 1970.]

–. 1991b. "The Oxford Calculators and Mathematical Physics: John Dumbleton's *Summa logicae et philosophiae naturalis*, Part II and III". *Physics, Cosmology and Astronomy, 1300–1700: Tension and accomodation* hg. von Sabetai Unguru, 129–161. Dordrecht, Boston & London: Kluwer.

–, & Michael McVaugh, Hg. 1997. *Texts and Contexts in Ancient and Medieval Science: Studies on the occasion of John E. Murdoch's seventieth birthday.* Leiden: Brill.

Tachau, Katherine H. 1988. *Vision and Certitude in the Age of Ockham: Optics, epistemology and the foundations of semantics.* Leiden: Brill.

Thorndike, Lynn. 1915. "Some Medieval Conceptions of Magic". *The Monist* 25.107–139.

–. 1923–58. *A History of Magic and Experimental Science.* 8 Bde. New York: Columbia Univ. Press.

Weisheipl, James A[thanasius]. 1965. "Classification of the sciences in Medieval thought". *Mediae-*

*val Studies* 27.54–90. (Nachdr., James A. Weisheipl, *Nature and Motion in the Middle Ages* hg. von William E. Carroll, 207–237. Washington, D. C.: The Catholic Univ. of America Press, 1985.)

Wilson, Curtis. 1960. *William Heytesbury: Medieval logic and the rise of mathematical physics.* Madison: The Univ. of Wisconsin Press.

Wöhler, Hans-Ulrich, Hg. 1994. *Texte zum Universalienstreit.* II. *Hoch- und spätmittelalterliche Scholastik: Lateinische Texte des 13.–15. Jahrhunderts.* Berlin: Akademie Verlag.

Zika, Charles. 1976. "Reuchlin's *De verbo mirifico* and the magic debate of the late fifteenth century". *Journal of the Warburg and Courtauld Institutes* 39.104–138.

*Ludger Kaczmarek, Borgholzhausen (Deutschland)*

# XV. The Cultivation of Latin Grammar in the Late Middle Ages
# Die Pflege der lateinischen Grammatik im Spätmittelalter
# La culture de la grammaire latine dans le Bas Moyen-Age

## 81. La *Grammatica positiva* dans le Bas Moyen-Age


1. Introduction
2. Les développements au XIII^e^ siècle
3. Grammaire et lexicographie
4. Grammaire et rhétorique
5. La syntaxe
6. Les commentaires grammaticaux
7. Niveaux d'enseignement et grammaire normative
8. Les œuvres de moindre diffusion
9. Conclusion
10. Bibliographie


### 1. Introduction

C'est seulement vers le milieu de notre période, vers la mi-XIII$^{e}$ siècle, qu'apparaît l'expression de *grammatica positiva*, pour désigner ce qu'on nommait auparavant simplement *grammatica*, par opposition aux nouvelles tendances de la réflexion grammaticale, désignées par l'expression de *grammatica speculativa*, et ce couple s'identifie également sous les appellations de *grammatica practica/theorica* ou *grammatica usualis/regularis*. La *grammatica positiva* se définit donc moins par un contenu précis que par rapport à ce qui constitue la pointe de la recherche dans ce domaine. Nous sommes de fait les héritiers de cette situation, puisque l'expression de *grammatica positiva* recouvre d'une façon encore imprécise tout ce qui n'a pas trait au domaine le mieux étudié de la réflexion grammaticale médiévale, les analyses spéculatives du langage, qu'on a pu qualifier de marginales dans l'histoire de la grammaire, tant du point de vue de la durée que par leur rattachement à la tradition logique (Law 1986: 125). La *grammatica positiva* reste pourtant le secteur le moins connu: si les deux manuels les plus populaires, le *Doctrinale* et le *Graecismus*, sont accessibles dans des éditions modernes, bien des textes sont inédits, comme les traités d'Alexandre Neckam, Bene da Firenze, Jean de Garlande, Jean de Génes, Papias ou encore Hugutio de Pise, voire à identifier parmi la masse de textes encore anonymes. Cette tradition est d'autant plus inexplorée, que comme ce sont des textes scolaires, l'enseignement auquel ils servent de point d'appui passe par le biais de gloses, textes aujourd'hui encore plus inédits si possible que les traités attribués des auteurs identifiés, à l'exception des extraits du commentaire du *Doctrinale* connu sous le nom de *glosa Admirantes* publiés il y a plus d'un siècle par Thurot.

Au début de la période qui nous occupe, la *grammatica positiva* présente un certain nombre de caractéristiques qui vont demeurer celles de toute la période suivante: la définition que donne Isidore de Séville de la grammaire (*ars artium*, *scientia scientiarum*, *origo*) continue à circuler, comme l'énumération des buts qu'il lui assigne (*ars recte scribendi recteque loquendi*), et elle apparaît toujours, au moins pour ceux qui l'enseignent, comme le fondement de toutes les sciences. La base de son enseignement est constituée par les manuels antiques de Donat et de Priscien, qui restent les autorités de l'enseignement grammatical. En suivant ces deux auteurs, les divisions des sciences proposent généralement deux divisions de la grammaire, tripartite avec Donat (préceptive, permissive, prohibitive), quadripartite avec Priscien (orthographe, prosodie, étymologie, syntaxe, division qui reflète l'articulation lettre, syllabe, mot, phrase). Cette quadripartition figure dans le *Liber excerptionum* de Richard de Saint-Victor (*grammatica dividitur in litteram, sillabam, dictionem et orationem*, I, 22; p. 111), chez Gundissalvi (*primo occurrit tractatus de littera, postea de sillaba, tercio loco de dictione, ad ultimum de oracione*, cité par Hunt 1980: 122), et dans la *Summa* de Pierre Hélie (p. 65, cité ibid. n. 3).

Au delà de ces constantes existe un matériel scolaire hétérogène et encore mal connu, bien que les études de V. Law aient fait progresser notre connaissance de la tradition de l'*Ars minor* de Donat dans cette période. L'instruction élémentaire se fait à partir de cet *Ars minor*, dont le Moyen Age entier fournit beaucoup de témoins, alors que les copies de l'*Ars maior* se raréfient parallèlement (Holtz 1981: 507–508). Cet *Ars* peut être soit interpolé, comme cela se fait depuis le VII^e^ siècle au moins, soit commenté, ces commentaires connaissant une diffusion réelle à partir du XI^e^ siècle pour devenir très nombreux au XIII^e^ siècle. Tous ces remaniements partent de défauts ressentis dans l'œuvre de Donat, forme prosaïque (et les enseignants du XIII^e^ siècle se féliciteront de la forme versifiée des traités postérieurs), trop grande concision dans l'expression, lacunes, que les commentaires tentent de combler en transformant le traité donatien en un manuel complet de morphologie latine, par rétablissement des paradigmes manquants et par addition de verbes de toutes conjugaisons. Trois types de dérivés se dégagent donc à ce moment: les versions plus ou moins interpolées, les versions avec paraphrase en forme de commentaire, et les versions en vers (Law 1986: 138). Cet inventaire peut être complété pour la période suivante par la *Grammatica* d'Hugues de Saint-Victor, qui fournit, en suivant Donat et Isidore de Séville, un examen traditionnel des huit parties du discours et des figures.

À cette classification des dérivés du *Donat mineur*, il faut ajouter pour avoir une idée un peu plus complète du matériel scolaire grammatical en circulation beaucoup de textes épars: des *Artes legendi* comme ceux de Tebaldus (auteur au X^e^ ou XI^e^ siècle d'un *De primis syllabis* versifié), Siguinus, dont l'*Ars lectoria* datée de 1088 ne donne pas lieu à beaucoup de copies mais connût une grande influence au Moyen Age en étant reprise un peu plus tard, avec le traité de Tebaldus, dans l'*Ars* d'Aimericus, le *Barbarismus* de Donat, le *De accentu* du Ps.-Priscien et beaucoup de traités encore anonymes, soit en vers, soit en prose, comme le *Scalprum Prisciani*, florilège des seize premiers livres des *Institutiones Grammaticae* de Priscien, dont le plus ancien témoin connu remonte à la mi-XI^e^ siècle. Les compilations réalisées à la fin du XII^e^ siècle par Évrard de Béthune et Alexandre de Villedieu jettent aussi un éclairage sur ce qui constituait une sorte de fonds commun à la disposition des maîtres de la fin du XII^e^ siècle: on voit ainsi le *Graecismus* emprunter à Pierre Hélie (Lohmeyer 1901: 420, n. 1), utiliser en une version remainiée le *De ornamentis verborum* de Marbode de Rennes (PL 171 col. 1687–92), liste versifiée de *colores rhetorici* (Thurot 1869: 101, n. 1; Faral 1971: 50), reprendre un traité anonyme versifié lui aussi, dérivé de Priscien *Institutiones Grammaticae* I, pour traiter de l'orthographe et des *commutationes litterarum* (Kneepkens 1981), lui assortir un recueil d'étymologies grecques voisin des *Differentie* de Guillaume de Corbeil (Williams 1972), et emprunter au *Liber Pauperum* de Jean de Beauvais (Sivo 1996). Il en va de même pour le *Doctrinale*, pour lequel Alexandre de Villedieu reconnaît dès le deuxième vers de son introduction avoir beaucoup emprunté à ses maîtres (*Pluraque doctorum sociabo scripta meorum*, cité par Hurlbut 1933: 258); Reichling (1893) avait déjà établi que les deux sections monumentales consacrées à l'étymologie et à la syntaxe ne remontaient pas à Priscien mais plutôt à des prédécesseurs inconnus du XII^e^ siècle, tandis que la section traitant des figures faisait la majorité de ses emprunts au *Barbarisme* de Donat (1893: XXXI), et Hurlbut (1933) a complété cette analyse en montrant que la section X, 1703–2101 sur la quantité des premières syllabes remontait à l'*Ars lectoria* d'Aimericus. Le *Graecismus* et le *Doctrinale* ont d'ailleurs une dizaine de passages en commun (Reichling 1893: LXXX, n. 1), et chacun d'eux partage des vers avec Osbern de Gloucester (Reichling 1893: 32, n. 446; Williams 1972: 299, n. 31), Alain de Lille et Alexandre Neckam (Williams 1972: 300): le fait que ces deux manuels, *Graecismus* et *Doctrinale*, soient des compilations d'éléments qui ne sont pas tous identifiés aujourd'hui atteste que notre connaissance du matériel scolaire des XI^e^ et XII^e^ siècle est encore très parcellaire.

Apprentissage de la fonction de compréhension d'un texte, apprentissage par l'imitation des auteurs ou mise en pratique des règles enseignées par la grammaire normative, la lecture active des auteurs tient une place importante dans l'enseignement de la discipline. Elle se fait parallèlement à l'étude du *Donat mineur* par la lecture commentée de textes standard, les *Libri Catoniani*, combinaisons variables des *Distiques* de Caton, de l'*Ecloga* de Theodolus, des *Fabulae* d'Avianus, des *Elegiae* de Maximianus, parfois remplacée par les *Remedia Amoris* d'Ovide, du *De raptu Proserpinae* de Claudianus, de l'*Achilleis* de Statius minor, auxquels viennent s'ajouter l'*Ilias latina*, plus rarement, le *Tobias* de Matthieu de Vendôme presque dès sa mise en circulation, le *De Contemptu mundi* et le *Facetus* (Boas 1914; Bonaventure 1961: 7–11). Ces *Libri Catoniani* sont en contexte scolaire expliqués dans des analyses qui suivent la méthode des *Partitiones versuum XII Aeneidos* de Priscien, souvent désignées par l'appellation de *Priscianellus*, analyse mot à mot des vers initiaux des douze livres de l'*Énéide* également utilisé en contexte scolaire (Law 1986: 138). À un niveau supérieur, lecture et commentaire des Auteurs sont encore représentés par l'école d'Orléans, où les deux ennemis prestigieux que sont Matthieu de Vendôme, dont l'*Ars versificatoria* continue d'avoir une certaine influence au XIIIe siècle, et Arnoul d'Orléans, auteur de commentaires originaux et abondants sur l'œuvre d'Ovide, sur la *Pharsale* de Lucain et peut-être sur les *Odes* d'Horace, veulent encore einseigner la grammaire par l'imitation des Auteurs. Raoul de Beauvais et son *Liber Tytan* illustrent également la survivance de ces commentaires des auteurs anciens.

Le XIIe siècle voit donc se dessiner les tendances de la *grammatica positiva* qui vont triompher au siècle suivant: le changement plus visible du point de vue de la forme extérieure est l'introduction de la versification, dont nous avons vu qu'elle commence très tôt à s'exercer sur les dérivés du *Donat mineur*. Un corpus d'éditions plus fourni permettrait d'ailleurs probablement de mieux évaluer la part croissante de ce mode d'expression dans les traités didactiques.

On assiste parallèlement à un début d'intégration de la syntaxe dans le cursus élémentaire avec la floraison de nombreux traités anonymes, qui fondent dès la mi-IX[e] siècle le type nouveau des grammaires à analyse. Omniprésentes dans les manuscrits, constituées de quelques feuillets anonymes, elles commencent toujours par *X quae pars?*, X étant un nom, et se complètent au fil du temps de questions de plus en plus élaborées, comme *Nominativus unde regitur?* (évolution décrite par Law 1986: 139–140). Ce nouveau type de grammaires fait donc entrer dans la discipline ce qui manquait dans l'*Ars minor*, la syntaxe, que Priscien était le seul, parmi les grammairiens légués par la Rome antique au Moyen Age, à traiter. Ces nouveaux textes sont encore séparés des traités classiques de morphologie, comme le sont aussi les traités de syntaxe indépendants de Robertus (vers 1160) et de Robert Blund (vers 1180).

Les divisions des sciences qui se multiplient se font l'écho de discussions sur la place de la grammaire: dans la première moitié du XIIe siècle, le *Didascalicon* d'Hugues de Saint-Victor, qui divise la logique en *grammatica* et *ratio disserendi* (6, 14; p. 131, 25; notons qu'à la même époque, mais pour la logique, Ablard reprend dans ses gloses sur Porphyre cette discussion inspirée par Boèce, voir Dahan 1990: 21), mentionne une position qui réduit la grammaire à être un instrument de la philosophie et non une de ses parties (*quidam dicunt grammaticam non esse partem philosophie, sed quasi quoddam appendicium et instrumentum ad philosophiam*, 2, 27; p. 45, 3). Plus habituellement, les divisions des sciences assignent à la grammaire sa place dans l'espace communément défini par le *trivium*, au sein duquel elle sert à préférer le congru à l'incongru, parallèlement à la logique qui enseigne à distinguer le vrai du faux, et à la rhétorique qui distingue l'orné du non-orné, comme le rappelle au XIIe siècle le *Liber excerptionum* de Richard de Saint-Victor:

> *Novissima autem inventa est logica, causa eloquentie, ut sapientes qui predictas principales disciplinas investigarent et invenirent, rectius, veracius, honestius illas tractare, de illis disserere scirent: rectius per grammaticam, veracius per dialecticam, honestius per rethoricam* (I, 5; p. 106) *Grammatica est scientia recte loquendi. Dialectica disputatio acuta, verum a falso distinguens. Rethorica est disciplina ad persuadendum queque idonea* (1, 22; p. 111).

On voit qu'on se situe là dans la perspective de la production d'un discours grammaticalement correct, vrai sur le plan de la logique, agréable à entendre du point de vue de son expression, ce qui est caractéristique d'une *grammatica positiva* déjà bien distincte des premiers traitements spéculatifs du XIIe siècle retracés par K. M. Fredborg (1988), et bien éloignée de la différenciation pourtant contemporaine entre *grammatica*, entendue au sens de grammaire universelle, et *species grammaticae*, grammaires individuelles des langues vernaculaires (Fredborg 1980), comme de la précision comparable que donne Gundissalvi, dans sa description du *trivium*, à la séparation entre logique et grammaire, en réservant l'étude du fonctionnement du langage en général à la logique:

*Quamvis enim grammatica et logica in hoc conveniant, quod utraque dat regulas de dictionibus, differunt tamen in hoc, quod grammatica non dat regulas nisi de dictionibus unius gentis tantum* (*De scientiis* 2; p. 69) *Scientia grammatice in omni lingua non attendit nisi in quantum est proprium illius lingue* (2; p. 70).

## 2. Les développements au XIIIe siècle

Même si les termes ne sont pas employés, la distinction entre grammaire normative et grammaire spéculative est donc présente dès le XIIe siècle, et les deux genres sont déjà aussi séparés que dans le XIIIe siècle que nous allons voir maintenant, où ils sont dus à des auteurs bien distincts, logiciens comme Robert Kilwardby, Martin de Dacie ou Siger de Courtrai pour la grammaire spéculative, pour la grammaire normative grammairiens au sens strict comme Jean de Garlande, dont le corpus d'œuvres pourtant considérable ne comprend pas de traité de logique, et contenus dans des manuscrits très différents, tant par l'allure générale que par le contenu (les collections de *sophismata* et de *quaestiones* sont rarement associées à des textes à caractère normatif) (Law 1986: 126ff.). Dans cette *grammatica positiva*, naît vers 1200 un courant majoritaire qui cristallise beaucoup des nouvelles tendances de la grammaire, et se reconnaît à quelques caractéristiques majeures: il s'exprime sous forme de sommes théoriques, qui vont au delà des frontières habituelles de la grammaire, sont rédigées en vers, et donnent naissance à des commentaires scolaires et à un niveau intermédiaire de grammaire. Les deux piliers de l'enseignement de cette *grammatica positiva* dans la seconde partie du Bas Moyen Age sont Alexandre de Villedieu et Évrard de Béthune, dont le *Doctrinale* et le *Graecismus* incarnent, ne serait-ce que par le nombre de témoins subsistants, une tradition majoritaire, le *Doctrinale* étant représenté par plus de 400 manuscrits et plus de 300 éditions étalées entre 1470 et 1520, et le *Graecismus* par plus de 200 manuscrits mais une vingtaine seulement d'éditions. Ces sommes théoriques ont probablement été rédigées ou compilées (voir pour les problèmes de composition du *Graecismus* Lohmeyer 1901 à compléter par Thurot 1869: 100–101) à une dizaine d'années d'intervalle (on situe en général la composition du *Doctrinale* vers 1199, celle du *Graecismus* entre 1180 et 1200, question qui a donné lieu à beaucoup de discussions rappelées par Williams [1972]), et elles exposent de façon très concise la matière grammaticale contemporaine, en réduisant considérablement les références aux auteurs: alors que le *Barbarisme* de Donat illustrait chaque figure d'au moins un exemple pris à un auteur, Évrard de Béthune traite une centaine de figures en ne mentionnant au total qu'une trentaine de citations, dont la moitié seulement est empruntée à des auteurs classiques.

Leur tendance encyclopédique se lit dès leurs plans: le *Doctrinale* d'Alexandre de Villedieu se divise en trois, puis en quatre parties avec le dédoublement de la dernière, pour aboutir au découpage suivant: étymologie (chap. I à VII, soit les vers 1–1073, traitant des paradigmes nominaux et verbaux), syntaxe (chap. VIII et IX, 1074–1549), prosodie et orthographe (chap. X, 1550–2281), accentuation et figures (chap. XI et XII, 2282–2645). Le *Graecismus*, dans la version sous laquelle nous le connaissons ajourd'hui, traite des figures et couleurs de rhétorique (chap. I–II–III), de prosodie (chap. IV), d'orthographe (chap. V), d'étymologie (chap. VI–XXIV) et de syntaxe (chap. XXV–XXVII). Les deux manuels connaissent un succès immédiat, et sont cités (et associés) pour la première fois semble-t-il par Jean de Garlande dans son *Compendium Gramatice* rédigé entre 1234 et 1236 (Haye 1995), et on a d'ailleurs soupçonné le *Graecismus* de devoir son succès à sa proximité avec le *Doctrinale* (Murphy 1974: 151). Ces plans extensifs et en apparence semblables cachent quelques différences de contenu et d'approche de la discipline, comme la place que tiennent les règles de l'accentuation dans le *Doctrinale* alors qu'elles manquent dans le *Graecismus*, sur lesquelles nous aurons l'occasion de revenir.

## 3. Grammaire et lexicographie

La grammaire tend donc à s'annexer soit des domaines nouveaux soit des secteurs marginaux d'autres disciplines, et l'exemple le plus significatif est probablement celui de la lexicographie. Les deux matières ont toujours été fortement liées: quand les glossaires ne puisaient pas dans les grammaires, ils les alimentaient, et il a toujours été établi que les grammairiens étaient les glosateurs par excellence (voir à ce sujet le rappel de A. Della Casa 1981: 36–39). Le Bas Moyen Age resserre encore ce lien, et la *grammatica positiva* est dès sa naissance ancrée dans une tradition lexicographique, d'abord par l'identité même de ses auteurs: Papias est à la fois l'auteur à la mi-XI[e] siècle de l'*Elementarium* et d'une *Grammatica* des huit parties du discours compilée de Priscien et encore majoritairement inédite en dehors des extraits publiés par Hagen (*Anecd. Helvet.* 1870, CLXXIX–CLXXXIV; cf. de Angelis 1977: VI), Hugutio de Pise a composé outre ses *Derivationes* à la fin du XIIe siècle une grammaire élémentaire, le *Rosarius*, Alexandre Nequam a produit le *De nominibus utensilium* et les *Corrogationes Promothei*. De même, au XIIIe siècle, Jean de Garlande est à la fois grammairien et auteur de *Synonyma*, d'*Aequivoca* et d'un *Dictionarius*, comme Jean Balbi dont l'œuvre achevée en 1286 porte le titre sans équivoque de *Summa grammaticalis que vocatur Catholicon*. Le phénomène d'emprunt et d'échange entre les deux courants est maintenu: Priscien est présent dans l'*Elementarium* de Papias, dans la *Panormia* d'Osbern de Gloucester, et via celui-ci dans les *Derivationes* d'Hugutio de Pise, et Guillaume Brito emprunte pour sa *Summa*, composée à la mi-XIII[e] siècle beaucoup de ses citations à des grammairiens de la génération précédente, Alexandre de Villedieu, Évrard de Béthune et Magister Bene.

Le lien entre les deux disciplines est d'autant plus affirmé que dans les manuscrits, on voit souvent les textes de grammaire normative voisiner avec des glossaires, mais très rarement avec des textes de grammaire spéculative ou de logique, et l'aboutissement de ce voisinage est la fusion des deux disciplines dans des textes communs, le *Catholicon*, mais aussi avant le *Graecismus*, dont les chapitres consacrés aux parties du discours, en particulier ceux qui traitent des substantifs et des verbes, sont en fait en grande partie des suites de vers différentiels, au point que Lohmeyer (1901: 419) a pu parler de "Synonymik" pour désigner ces chapitres et que A. della Casa (1981: 44, n. 27) voit dans ce manuel le point de fusion de ces deux traditions si proches, grammaire et lexicographie. On retrouve la même tendance englobante dans la *Summa* de Bene da Firenze, vaste synthèse rassemblant morphologie, orthographe et lexicographie, composée presque en même temps que le *Doctrinale* et le *Graecismus*.

Cette intégration des connaissances lexicographiques va de pair avec le développement exponentiel du nouvel outil au service de la grammaire et de la compréhension de la langue qu'est l'étymologie, et cette connaissance se traduit par la technique d'exposition des mots, qui se fait par recours à des mots de la même langue ou à des mots étrangers, grecs le plus souvent; là encore, le *Graecismus* sert de relais avec son chapitre VIII exclusivement consacré aux mots à racine grecque. Ces listes de racines et dérivés qui circulent (voir encore une fois celle de Guillaume de Corbeil, Williams 1972) ne masquent cependant pas une connaissance très superficielle des autres langues, et quand Évrard de Béthune tente d'expliquer par recours au grec pourquoi la forme *sui* n'a pas de nominatif (XIV, 31 f.), sa solution lui vaut le jugement cinglant (*non valet unam fabam*) d'un commentateur des premières années du XIVe siècle (Paris BNF lat. 14746, f. 136va). La connaissance de l'étymologie fonde pourtant la supériorité du grammairien-lexicographe, technicien de la langue par excellence, qui connaît les véritables noms des choses par leur origine, comme en témoignait déjà Jean de Saint-Bertin dans son récit des mirables de Bernard le Pénitent, en signalant que les 'grammairiens' appellent le pou du mouton *usia quasi ab urendo* (*pediculus ovinus, quem grammatici usiam quasi ab urendo vocant*, BHL 1203, AASS Apr. II, 8; p. 680C).

La *grammatica positiva* du Bas Moyen Age présente donc une facette non négligeable d'apprentissage du vocabulaire. En s'interrogeant sur le rôle de cet aspect nouveau de la grammaire, on retrouve des préoccupations proches de celles de la rhétorique. C. Codoñer a rappelé récemment (1996: 64) la double orientation de ces listes de mots, *differentiae* d'origine rhétorico-dialectique qui recherchent la précision dans le vocabulaire, et *synonyma* qui visent à la maîtrise de la *copia vocabulorum* de la rhétorique. Sur un même groupe de mots (*gladius*, *ensis* et *mucro*), la première tendance est représentée dans le *Graecismus* par les vers IX 304–305, qui enseignent à les distinguer strictement (*mucro pedem, medium gladius, totum tenet ensis / mulcet hic, iste secat, dividit ille gulam*), la seconde, effet d'une compilation un peu désordonnée, par le vers XXV 6, qui les dépeint explicitement comme des synonymes (*gladius ensis mucro synonymantur*).

## 4. Grammaire et rhétorique

La connexion entre grammaire, lexique et rhétorique se fait plus étroite encore avec l'insertion des figures et couleurs de rhétorique. La tradition d'intégration dans les grammaires de ces termes techniques, dont la classification commence avec la *Rhetorica ad Herennium*, remonte aux artigraphes antiques, et ces termes sont repris dans les encyclopédies, celles de Martianus Capella, Isidore de Séville, Cassiodore (Murphy 1990: 241), si bien que l'on ne sait plus très bien si ces termes relèvent du rhéteur ou du grammairien. On a également signalé la tendance de ces listes à exister parallèlement aux traités de rhétorique complets (Murphy 1974: 183), comme c'est le cas des *Rhetorici colores* composées par Onulf de Spire au XI$^e$ siècle: dès lors que ces listes sont détachées des traités complets, elles deviennent autant d'éléments susceptibles d'être récupérés par une discipline voisine. L'exemple typique de cette évolution est fourni par Marbode, dont le *De ornamentis verborum* vient prendre place dans le *Graecismus*, à la suite d'emprunts au *Barbarisme* de Donat. Cette tradition ancienne est en outre reprise au Moyen Age dans une perspective presque lexicographique de catalogage méthodique de ces termes; le *Graecismus* et dans une moindre mesure le *Doctrinale* reprennent en la modifiant la liste fournie par le *Barbarismus*: si Alexandre se contente de la compléter par quelques couleurs de rhétorique ajoutées en fin d'ouvrage, le reclassement opéré par le *Graecismus*, qui ajoute d'ailleurs beaucoup plus de termes au point d'y mêler ce que l'on classera bientôt parmi les figures de construction, l'*evocatio* ou l'*antiptosis*, est différent puisque, tout en conservant la lettre du cadre traditionnel (métaplasme, schema, trope), il procède à des regroupements originaux selon que telle figure ne doit pas être confondue avec telle autre dont le nom lui ressemble: on voit qu'on est ici loin de l'apprentissage raisonné des couleurs de rhétorique, mais par contre en pleine lexicographie.

Cette part faite à la rhétorique, par le biais de son vocabulaire, dans les grammaires didactiques évoque aussi le lien très fort qui existe entre grammaire et *dictamen*: beaucoup d'*artes dictaminis* incluent du matériel grammatical, pour la bonne raison que la prose ne doit pas seulement être elégante mais aussi correcte (Camargo 1991: 26), et Paul Camaldule joint ainsi dès la fin du XII$^e$ siècle une grammaire et un *Ars dictaminis* (Thurot 1869: 91). Le maître de grammaire a en effet l'habitude de regrouper toutes les formes d'expressions, écrite et orale, sous son enseignement (Murphy 1961: 197), et ceci se vérifie particulièrement dans la partie nord de l'Europe, où l'enseignement du *dictamen* semble se délivrer dans les écoles de grammaire, donc avant l'entrée à l'Université (Camargo 1991: 56).

## 5. La syntaxe

La syntaxe confirme d'autre part son entrée dans la *grammatica positiva*, hors de l'étude et du commentaire des œuvres de Priscien, ce dont témoigne la structure des deux sommes que nous avons détaillées plus haut. Le *Doctrinale* y consacre deux chapitres; le traité initial d'Évrard de Béthune a été complété, en plus des huit chapitres initiaux, par trois chapitres finaux consacrés à cette spécialité, qui pallient de façon assez particulière l'absence de la syntaxe dans la tradition antérieure: le chapitre consacré au nom chez Donat, qui a été remplacé par les séries de vers différentiels évoquées plus haut, revient ici sous une forme dérivée avec le titre *De speciebus nominum*, auquel s'ajoutent un *De accidentibus verborum* et un *De syntactica*. Cette intégration de la syntaxe dans le cursus de la *grammatica positiva* se fait cependant dans la continuité de Priscien, par l'analyse de constructions individuelles plutôt que par l'élaboration d'une réflexion sur la théorie de la phrase en général qui est l'œuvre de la *grammatica speculativa* (Robins 1980). Cette tendance est particulièrement illustrée par les figures de construction, qui apparaissent à des degrés divers dans les grammaires du tournant XII$^e$–XIII$^e$ siècle: systématisées dans de petits traités anonymes comme ceux que rassemble le manuscrit Paris BNF lat. 2774 (ff. 56v–59v, 59v–63v et 76v–78v), les cinq puis bientôt huit figures de construction (*prolepsis*, *syllepsis*, *antiptosis*, *synthesis*, *zeugma* et *evocatio*, *appositio*, *synecdoca*; v. Colombat 1989) résument en partie les analyses de contruction. Le *Doctrinale* en réunit quatre (prolepse, syllepse, zeugme et synecdoque) dans la section consacrée à la syntaxe, et les retraite comme figures de style dans son dernier chapitre (Rosier 1988); elles sont dans le *Graecismus*, quand elles sont traitées, éparpillées dans la section proprement dévolue aux figures, à l'exception de la synecdoque, notion utilisée déjà par Pierre Hélie (*Summa*

p. 462, 52–59 et p. 1027, 90–98) pour décrire l'accusatif de relation, alors que le commentaire du *Barbarisme* attribué à Robert Kilwardby (vers 1240) développe la distinction entre une 'synecdoque de construction' (le phénomène syntaxique) et une 'synecdoque de locution' (le trope).

À côté de ces innovations, et d'autres comme l'introduction de la notion d'adjectif (voir aussi celles que signale Thurot 1869: 147–148), une des caractéristiques de la *grammatica positiva* réside alors dans sa forme versifiée: on pense bien sûr aux deux sommes que nous avons déjà évoquées, mais aussi aux œuvres de Jean de Garlande (*Compendium*, *Aequivoca*, *Synonyma*, etc.), au *Donatus metrificatus* d'Henri d'Avranches, ainsi qu'à ses plus amples *Comoda gramatice* (premières décennies du XIIIe siècle; Heironimus & Russell 1929). Les commentateurs, en particulier du *Graecismus* et du *Doctrinale* utilisent d'ailleurs le fait que ces textes soient versifiés pour montrer leur supériorité sur les manuels anciens de Donat et surtout de Priscien; les gloses du *Doctrinale* et du *Graecismus* traitent ce thème dans des termes identiques, en s'appuyant sur une citation identique aussi de Matthieu de Vendôme, *Ars versificatoria* (*glosa Admirantes* citée par Thurot 1869: 101, commentaire du *Graecismus* de Paris BNF lat. 14746f. 4rb).

## 5. Les commentaires grammaticaux

La versification des manuels de grammaire de la seconde partie du Moyen Age, liée au fait que ce sont des textes d'enseignement, a favorisé la naissance de commentaires: un texte possédant cette double caractéristique, versification et visée pédagogique, doit être un instrument de mémorisation, non de lui-même, mais de l'arrière-plan plus large dont il est issu, et il n'est que l'instrument mnémotechnique d'une culture moins elliptique que son résumé en vers. La voie pour retrouver derrière ce texte concis sa source théorique est ouverte par le cours oral transcrit dans les manuscrits par les gloses, si uniformes d'ailleurs qu'elles semblent dériver d'une seule source, comme le remarque Thurot pour le *Doctrinale* (1850b: 50). Ces gloses, dont la mieux connue est la *glosa Admirantes* sur la *Doctrinale* (le plus ancien témoin daté, Orléans 252, est de 1284) sont typiques de l'enseignement dans la seconde moitié du XIIIe siècle, et on les voit s'élaborer progressivement en des combinaisons variées de gloses interlinéaires (qui ne donnent que des synonymes de mots d'interprétation difficile) avec des gloses marginales ou un commentaire à lemme. Ces gloses obéissent à différents mobiles: élucidation du texte, ce qui permet dans les cas extrêmes de le corriger sans contredire ouvertement l'*auctoritas* du maître, résolution des contradictions avec d'autres autorités, et par là défense de l'auteur contre des accusations d'insuffisance ou d'erreur, amélioration du commentaire précédent par correction d'interprétations erronées et par addition de données nouvelles, dont des prologues successifs où s'introduisent des divisions des sciences de plus en plus élaborées; on voit qu'au fur et à mesure qu'elles se développent, les gloses agissent à deux niveaux différents, s'exerçant à la fois sur le texte et sur les générations précédentes de gloses, qui ne sont pas éliminées. Ces commentaires sont en général anonymes ou dus à des inconnus comme Jean de Vignay (HLF 30: 280–293) ou Pierre de Herunco (Morand 1863), mais de grands noms se sont également prêtés à cet exercice, comme Jean de Garlande (Colker 1974) ou Pierre d'Auvergne, qui ont tous deux commenté le *Doctrinale*, et il devait être courant qu'un même auteur glose les deux sommes: Jean de Garlande avait annoncé son intention de commenter le *Graecismus* (Bursill-Hall 1976: 157–158), et l'anonyme du Paris B. N. F. lat. 8427 (XIIIe siècle) évoque au f. 9v de son commentaire du *Graecismus* les *Notule* qu'il a rédigées sur le *Doctrinale* (HLF 30: 295–302). Ces textes, destinés à rester anonymes ou susceptibles d'attributions seulement partielles à cause de la stratification qui leur est propre, n'ont pas encore fait l'objet de toutes les études qui permettraient d'y voir plus clair dans une tradition complexe, mais les relevés par T. Hunt (1979, 1991) de quantités de gloses bilingues (voir aussi celles que donnait Thurot 1869: 527–528) ont au moins attiré l'attention sur la présence de nombreuses traductions vernaculaires et la qualité de leur apport à la connaissance de la langue vernaculaire.

## 6. Niveaux d'enseignement et grammaire normative

Ces gloses destinées à faciliter le cours d'un maître attirent l'attention sur le fait que la mise en circulation du *Doctrinale* et du *Graecismus* marque la naissance d'un niveau intermédiaire dans l'enseignement de la grammaire, puisque ces deux manuels prennent directement la suite de l'*Ars minor* de Donat: tandis que la grammaire élémentaire continue de s'enseigner avec Donat, la tranche d'âge suivante reçoit un enseignement fondé sur le *Doctrinale* et le *Graecismus*; un peu plus tard, on verra même l'Université de Freiburg i. B. imposer l'étude du *Donat mineur* en même temps que celle du *Doctrinale* et du *Graecismus* (Ott & Fletcher 1964: 55, 67). Les mentions de l'âge du public visé que fournissent les auteurs ne sont cependant pas très explicites, Évrard déclarant dans son prologue s'adresser "aussi bien aux débutants qu'aux plus avancés" (*tam rudibus quam provectis*, Wrobel, 1887: 2, 8–9), mais déclarant suivre l'ordre de Donat à cause de sa volonté "éduquer les plus jeunes" (*doctrinare minores*) en tête de son chapitre sur les pronoms (Wrobel 1887: XIV, 4; Law [1986: 130] voit dans ce passage la preuve que le *Gracecismus* s'adresse à des élèves déjà familiers du manuel de Donat), tandis qu'Alexandre de Villedieu parle dans son introduction de *pueri*. Malgré ce flou, on voit que se dégage au XIII$^{e}$ siècle une grammaire à trois niveaux, normative avec son niveau élémentaire fondé sur Donat pour les débutants, complété de ce niveau intermédiaire apparu au début du siècle, et spéculative, stade le plus élevé fondé sur Priscien (Law 1986: 130).

C'est, semble-t-il, à la mi-XIII$^{e}$ siècle qu'on signale les premières apparitions de l'appellation *grammatica positiva*; Thurot la relève en opposition à *grammatica regularis* dans le manuscrit de la *glosa Admirantes* de 1284 (1869: 214); elle figure aussi dans un prologue à la glose du *Graecismus* dans le manuscrit Paris BNF lat. 15133 (ff. 2va–b) daté de 1270, et le développement qui y est inclus montre la scission profonde qui existe entre *grammatica speculativa* et *grammatica positiva*, cette dernière n'étant pas considérée comme une science (la question est: *utrum gramatica sit scientia sive ars*):

> *[...] Ad idem omnis sciencia est de eis que impossibile est se aliter habere. Gramatica est ex permutabilibus. ⟨Ergo grammatica non est sciencia. Quod sit ex permutabilibus⟩, patet quoniam gramatica est de vocabulis (var. lect. vocibus) significantibus ad placitum non a natura. Solutio: duplex est gramatica, regularis et positiva. Unde dicendum est quod gramatica regularis est de impermutabilibus (var. lect. impermutabilis) et talis est sciencia, sed positiva est permutabilis et talis non est sciencia.*

## 8. Les œuvres de moindre diffusion

À côté des grandes sommes qui donnent le ton de la *grammatica positiva*, que trouve-t-on? Différents types de traités, dont certains présentent des caractéristiques communes avec la tradition majoritaire évoquée ci-dessus, comme le fait d'être versifiés, qu'il s'agisse de textes inspirés par les grandes sommes, comme les *Comoda gramatice* d'Henry d'Avranches (voir la section consacrée aux *Aequivoca* éd. par Heironimus & Russell 1929: 16–26; Law 1986: 133) qui n'ont connu aucun succès, ou comme le *Graecismus Novus* du chantre de Zurich Conrad de Mure, composé en 1244, qui n'a connu qu'une diffusion très réduite, ou d'œuvres de portée plus limitée que les grandes sommes et qui connaissent une diffusion moyenne, comme les *Flores* de Ludolphe de Lucho, qui ne traitent que de syntaxe (57 manuscrits), ou le *Deponentiale* de Nicolas de Brakendale, autre exemple de diffusion essentiellement nationale. Mais l'essentiel de la production réside probablement dans les très nombreuses œuvres (traités de grammaire spécialisés, commentaires, dictionnaire) de Jean de Garlande qui sont encore trop mal connues et pour la plupart inédites (Faral 1971: 40–41; Bursill-Hall 1976, qui rassemble un nombre très élevé de manuscrits): on sait du moins qu'il se pose en opposant résolu ou en concurrent des deux grandes sommes versifiés, et qu'il consacre le chapitre III de son *Compendium grammatice* à redresser les erreurs du *Doctrinale* et sourtout du *Graecismus*: les huit manuscrits subsistants de ce *Compendium* attestent cependant une influence peu marquée. Cette présentation de la *grammatica positiva* serait à compléter par l'étude des traditions nationales: ainsi, la péninsule italienne offre cette particularité que, comme dans la zone ibérique, le *Catholicon* y concurrence le *Doctrinale* (Della Casa 1981: 40). Si la somme de Jean Balbi, compilation des plus grandes autorités antiques et contemporaines (Donat, Isidore, Papias, Hugutio, Évrard de Béthune, Raban Maur, Alexandre de Villedieu, Pierre Riga) (Sivo 1989: 113), ne bénéficie pas encore d'une édition à la taille de sa diffusion ni de la complexité de sa tradition, on sait du moins qu'elle est à mettre en relation avec la *Summa grammaticae* composée vers 1250 par Petrus de Isolella (éd. par Ch. Fierville 1886), car la section *De generibus nominum* de la troisième partie (*De etymologia*) du *Catholicon* présente de fortes analogies avec la section correspondante de la *Summa grammaticae* (Sivo 1989: 114). Aujourd'hui représentée par 46 témoins subsistants, dont quelques-uns en domaine anglais, cette *Summa*, ensemble de lęcons sur des sujets aussi divers que la phonétique, la syntaxe, la poésie rhythmique ou le *dictamen*, a aussi été étudiée dans ses rapports avec l'œuvre de Bene da Firenze (Alessio 1983: LXXIV–LXXVII). La tradition anglaise est tout aussi spécifique, avec l'existence, à Oxford, d'une faculté de grammaire séparée de la faculté des arts, qui soumet au XIV^e^ siècle ses futurs maîtres à des épreuves de versification (Thompson 1983: 304). La diffusion des sommes versifiées a connu aussi ses particularités: on recense aujourd'hui dans les bibliothèques relativement peu de manuscrits du *Graecismus*, l'Angleterre semblant lui avoir préféré le *Doctrinale*, qui circule accompagné du commentaire de Jean de Garlande.

## 9. Conclusion

Essayons en conclusion de définir ce que l'on appelle *grammatica positiva* au XIII^e^ siècle. L'élargissement de la discipline se reflète dans de nouvelles divisions de la grammaire, où Gundissalvi insérait dès le XII^e^ siècle la Poétique: le XIII^e^ siècle et ses introductions à la philosophie contribuent à mettre en circulation des définitions extensives de la grammaire, dont la première tendance est de réinsérer la fonction de compréhension des textes. Les deux conceptions de la grammaire ont toujours coexisté: si l'*ars grammatica* de Diomède la décrit à la fin du IV^e^ siècle comme la science de l'explication des auteurs (*grammatica est specialiter scientia exercitata lectionis et expositionis eorum que apud poetas et scriptores dicuntur*, I, 426.13), la définition d'Isidore (*scientia recte loquendi, etym.* I, 5) reflète en revanche une grammaire orientée vers la production d'un discours conforme à un ensemble de règles. C'est cette définition que reprend le XII^e^ siècle, pour qui la grammaire est la *scientia loquendi sine vicio* (Hugues de Saint-Victor, *Didascalicon* 2, 30; p. 47, 23), la *scientia recte loquendi* (Richard de Saint-Victor, *Liber excerptionum* I, 22; p. 111), la *scientia gnara recte scribendi et recte loquendi* (Pierre Hélie, *Summa* p. 61, 6), définition dont R. W. Hunt (1980: 120) a souligné la proximité avec celle de Gundissalvi. Pierre Hélie précise plus loin (p. 63, 41): *finis ergo huius artis est recte scribere et recte loqui, sive in scribendo et loquendo soloecismi et barbarismi vitatio*. La première tendance subsiste cependant chez Alexandre Neckam, pour qui la grammaire est avant tout un *ars intelligendi*, ceux qui la décrivent comme un *ars recte scribendi et recte proferendi* étant dans l'erreur. Ces deux conceptions opposées fusionnent dans certaines définitions du XIII^e^ siècle, et l'on trouve ainsi vers 1250 dans la *Divisio scientiarum* d'Arnoul de Provence la définition de la grammaire comme science du bien parler, du bien écrire et du bien comprendre (*gramatica est scientia gnara recte loquenci, recte scribendi recteque intelligendi*, 586–588, éd. par Lafleur 1971: 295–335). Ce type de définition composite est particulièrement apprécié des commentateurs de manuels comme le *Doctrinale* ou le *Graecismus*: le prologue *Sicut dicit philosophus* (vers 1300) définit ainsi la discipline comme la science de bien écrire, de bien comprendre ce qui est écrit, de bien énoncer ce qui est compris (*gramatica est sciencia recte scribendi, recte scripta intelligendi (cod.: intellecta pronunciandi), recte intellecta proferendi*, Paris BNF lat. 14746f. 3vb–4ra), tandis que le prologue *Quemadmodum* l'introduisait déjà entre 1260 et 1270 comme la science qui enseigne à bien écrire, bien comprendre, bien construire et bien prononcer (*grammatica est ars que docet recte scribere, recte intelligere, recte ordinare et recte pronunciare*, Paris BNF lat. 15133f. 2rb).

Ce *recte ordinare* rapproche aussi la définition de la seconde tendance, qui rappelle dans les définitions de la grammaire l'importance de la syntaxe. Cette tendance était déjà présente chez Pierre Hélie qui insistait sur la construction et la prononciation (*[grammatica] est litteralis scientia, eo quod litteratum efficit. Litteratum vero dicimus illum qui litteras in sillabis, sillabas in dictionibus, dictiones congrue ordinare scit in orationibus, et ordinatas compententer novit pronunciare*, p. 61, 14–62, 17), et elle se confirme à la mi-XIII^e^ siècle, dans des définitions composites qui circulent dans les accessus au *Graecismus* par exemple: *gramatica est sciencia recte loquendi, recte scribendi, recte pronunciandi, recte construendi sine barbarismo et soloecismo* (Paris BNF lat. 15133f. 1va).

Au XIII^e^ siècle, à l'Université de Paris, seuls sont mentionnés par les statuts Priscien majeur et mineur, et Donat pour son *Barbarisme* (Thurot 1850a: 51; CUP I, 20; p. 78 et I, 246; p. 278). La situation de la *grammatica positiva* est donc profondément modifiée par l'inscription au programme des Universités du *Doctrinale* et du *Graecismus*, qui incarnent cette branche de la grammaire pour une bonne part de l'Europe médiévale. Après avoir été lus dans les écoles (une glose du XIII^e^ siècle atteste l'usage du *Doctrinale* à Paris: *opus fuit receptum et explicatum Parisius*, Morand 1863, cité par Reichling 1893: XIII n. 7) et dans les collèges, les deux manuels sont recommandés par les statuts universitaires, et cette prise en compte des nouvelles exigences de la pédagogie se fait d'abord à Toulouse, dont les statuts préconisent l'emploi du *Graecismus* et du *Doctrinale* dès 1328. Il est vrai que Toulouse, où Jean de Garlande a enseigné, bénéficie très tôt d'un enseignement de la grammaire plus structuré qu'ailleurs: on y trouve dès 1229 une distinction faite entre *magistri artium* et *magistri artis grammatice*, et une Faculté de grammaire séparée y est mentionnée en 1329 (Gabriel 1969: 100). Cette université est suivie en 1366 par Paris, en 1386 par Heidelberg, en 1389 par Vienne (Reichling 1893: XLIX).

Un demi-siècle plus tard environ s'esquisse un tri très progressif dans la tradition, dans ce legs des années 1200 à la fin du Moyen Age, en ce sens qu'avant même la fin du XIV^e^ siècle, les statuts universitaires ne prescrivent plus que des parties du *Doctrinale* et du *Graecismus*, sans que l'on puisse savoir si cette précision entérine un usage général, ou si la suppression des chapitres en question doit être tenue pour une innovation pédagogique contemporaine. Les statuts semblent en effet souvent préconiser, outre le *Donat mineur*, l'enseignement des deux ou des trois premières parties du *Doctrinale* et de la *secunda pars Grecismi*, et non plus des manuels dans leur ensemble. Le phénomène est attesté à Vienne en 1389 où les statuts précisent que l'aspirant au grade de bachelier ès-arts doit avoir entendu la première (I–VII, étymologie) et la seconde partie (VIII–IX, syntaxe) du *Doctrinale*, la seconde partie du *Graecismus*, plus un livre de rhétorique (Thurot 1869: 103). Les statuts de l'université de Paris de 1366 ne donnaient aucune précision similaire, mais le phénomène est aussi attesté à Freibourg i. B. en 1460–1490, avec cette différence que seule la quatrième partie du *Doctrinale* y est éliminée (Ott & Fletcher 1964: 40). Cette précision pédagogique est peut-être à rapprocher de certaines particularités des manuscrits du *Doctrinale* et du *Graecismus* copiés au XV^e^ siècle: alors que les utilisateurs des XIII^e^–XIV^e^ siècle n'en retouchaient pas l'organisation, le XV^e^ siècle ne se prive pas de retrancher des deux manuels ce qui lui apparaît désormais superflu. Pour le *Doctrinale*, Reichling (1893: 140–141) relève ainsi parmi les mss. du XV^e^ siècle une énorme majorité de témoins incomplets. Pour le *Graecismus*, des exemples sont fournis par certains manuscrits (recensés à l'incipit *Est pater hic cura* par Bursill-Hall 1981), qui ne contiennent que la seconde partie du *Graecismus* (chap. IX–XXVII), excluant donc, outre le *prohemium* en prose, les huit premiers chapitres consacrés entre autres aux figures et à la prosodie.

Ceci tend donc à réduire l'utilisation des sommes de *grammatica positiva* à des frontières plus strictes, description des parties du discours et syntaxe, même si les longs passages à caractère lexicographique du *Graecismus* sont pour le moment conservés. Le tri dans la tradition se poursuit cependant dans la seconde moitié du XV^e^ siècle avec la différenciation des destins des deux sommes, le *Doctrinale* réussissant mieux son passage à l'imprimé de 300 éditions entre 1470 et 1520) que le *Graecismus* (une vingtaine d'éditions, dont la dernière datée de 1500).

Parallèlement, la frontière entre grammaire normative et grammaire spéculative se fait moins nette: V. Law remarque à ce propos qu'au XIV^e^ siècle, les concepts modistes se sont tellement diffusés qu'ils ont pénétré les grammaires scolaires au point qu'on ne peut faire de séparation nette entre les deux genres (1986: 128); le *Speculum grammaticale* de Jean de Cornouailles (1346), qui utilise concepts modistes et terminologie des *modi significandi* est caractéristique à cet égard. D'autre part, les commentateurs de textes de logique et de textes normatifs ne sont plus aussi séparés, puisque l'on voit déjà Pierre d'Auvergne, mort en 1304, commenter Aristote et Alexandre de Villedieu; enfin, par le biais des gloses, les innovations contemporaines se glissent, avec un petit temps de retard parfois, dans l'enseignement: le traitement spéculatif des constructions figurées, avec recherche de l'impropriété et de la double cause excusante, systématisé dans le commentaire du *Barbarisme* attribué à Robert Kilwardby, apparaît dans un manuscrit de 1263 autour du texte normatif du *Graecismus* (Wien S. N. 2692) et est signalé en 1284 dans la *glosa Admirantes* (Thurot 1869: 475); on voit un peu plus tard, vers 1300, un commentaire du *Graecismus* utiliser des *sophismata* célèbres à propos des pronoms (*nominativo hic dominus et in pace inidipsum dormiam et requiescam*, dans Paris BNF lat. 14746f. 140ra). L'insertion de ces nouveautés en même temps que le décalage qui l'accompagne peuvent être dus au fait que les maîtres qui complètent ces commentaires sont souvent issus de la Faculté des Arts, et utilisent des connaissances professées par la génération qui les précède.

La production de textes de grammaire normative ne se fait plus sous forme de sommes complètes mais dans des traités plus ciblés et plus nombreux, comme ceux de John Leland, maître de grammaire à Oxford au début du XV$^{e}$ siècle, auteur de traités sur des sujets réduits comme les déclinaisons, les genres, les cas, et d'une courte grammaire élémentaire, compilée à partir de matériaux disparates, Priscien, Donat, Papias, Pierre Hélie, Alexandre de Villedieu (Sivo 1989: 115). On trouve cette tendance à un certain éparpillement, du moins par rapport au siècle précédent, dès Giovanni del Virgilio (premier quart du XIV$^{e}$ siècle), auteur d'un *Ars dictaminis*, et entre autres de quatre traités de grammaire consacrés aux verbes impersonnels, aux figures de syntaxe, aux comparatifs et superlatifs, et aux conjonctions, inspirés de façon mixte de traités modistes comme ceux de Martin de Dacie ou Simon de Dacie, comme de textes de grammaire normative, *Doctrinale* et *Graecismus*.

La fin du Moyen Age voit aussi l'introduction de la langue vernaculaire dans l'enseignement de la grammaire normative latine, dès le *Speculum grammaticale* de Jean de Cornouailles, qui complète son étude des huit parties du discours et de leur syntaxe par des séries de constructions latines traduites pour certaines en moyen anglais. Cette spécificité de la tradition oxonienne connaît son prolongement avec John Leland, auteur probable de grammaires du latin composées en moyen anglais.

"Ce *Graecismus* m'appartient à moi, Pierre de Pontèves, licencié en droit, de Saint-Maximin, habitant à Aix; je l'ai acheté à trois florins à Jean Curet en 1481, et je l'ai prêté à Jacques de Pontèves, fils d'André, mon neveu, avec l'intention de la récupérer quand je le voudrai" (*Iste liber Grecismus appellatus pertinet michi Petro de Ponteves iurium licenciato, de Sancto Maximino, habitatori Aquensi, quem emi a magnifico domino Io. Cureti precio florenorum trium, MIIIICLXXXI primo; et accomodavi Iacobo de Ponteves, filio Andree, nepoti meo, animo recuperandi, dum et quando videbitur michi* etc., Marseille, Bibl. Mun. 1016,f. 130v, note du début du XVI$^{e}$ siècle).

Pierre de Pontèves a acquis vers la fin du XV$^{e}$ siècle, probablement pour ses études, un *Graecismus* glosé contenu dans un manuscrit du XIV$^{e}$ siècle; vingt ou trente ans plus tard, il le prête à son neveu, probablement encore pour les études de celui-ci, avec la ferme intention de la récupérer quand il en aura besoin. Cette utilisation d'un manuel des années 1200 en plein humanisme invite à faire le bilan des acquis d'une évolution: qu'est-ce que les trois siècles que nous avons parcourus ont apporté à la *grammatica positiva*? Il existe manifestament des éléments permanents, et le moindre n'est probablement pas le rôle de la grammaire dans la transmission de la culture puisque le seul contact avec les poètes classiques est assuré par le biais des exemples grammaticaux, qui constituent le bagage de citations communes (Della Casa 1981: 35; Munk-Olsen 1994: 67), mais l'acquis le plus important est sans doute l'entrée définitive dans les manuels de grammaire de la syntaxe, qui est conservée dans le tri qui s'opère à partir de la fin du XIV$^{e}$ siècle. Le second acquis de cette évolution est le fait que la *grammatica positiva* est maintenant enseignée dans les facultés des arts, et qu'il s'agit d'une grammaire en général épurée, débarrassée des emprunts à d'autres disciplines, recentrée sur l'étude des huit parties du discours et de leurs accidents, et de la syntaxe.

## 10. Bibliographie

### 10.1. Sources primaires

*Bene Florentini Candelabrum.* Éd. par G. C. Alessio. Padova: Antenore, 1983.

Dominique Gundissalvi, *De scientiis.* Éd. par P. Manuel Alonso Alonso. Madrid & Granada, 1954.

Guillaume Brito, *Summa.* Éd. par L. W. Daly & B. A. Daly. Padova: Antenore, 1975.

Hugues de Saint-Victor, *Didascalicon.* Éd. par C. Buttimer. (= *Studies in Mediaeval and Renaissance Latin*, 10.) Washington, 1939.

Onulf de Spire, *Rhetorici colores.* Éd. par W. Wattenbach. *Sitzungsberichte der Akademie zu Berlin* 1 (1894) 369–386.

*Papiae Elementarium. Littera A*, vol. I–III. Éd. par V. de Angelis. Milano: Cisalpino-Goliardica, 1977–80.

Pierre Hélie, *Summa super Priscianum.* Éd. par L. Reilly. Toronto: Pontifical Institute of Mediaeval Studies, 1993.

Alexandre de Villedieu, *Doctrinale.* Éd. par D. Reichling. Berlin: A. Hofmann, 1893.

Richard de Saint-Victor, *Liber exceptionum.* Éd. par J. Châtillon. Paris, 1958.

Évrard de Béthune, *Graecismus*. Éd. par J. Wrobel. Breslau: Koebner, 1887. (Réimpr., Hildesheim: Olms 1987.)

## 10.2. Sources secondaires

Boas, M. 1914. "De librorum Catonianorum historia atque compositione". *Mnemosyne* 42.17–46.

Bonaventure, Brother, F. S. C. 1961. "The Teaching of Latin in Later Medieval England". *Medieval Studies* 23.1–20.

Bursill-Hall, Geoffrey Leslie. 1981. *A Census of Medieval Latin Grammatical Manuscripts.* Stuttgart: Frommann-Holzboog.

–. 1976. "Johannes de Garlandia: Forgotten grammarian and the manuscript tradition". *Historiographia Linguistica* 3.155–177.

Camargo, Martin. 1988. "Toward a Comprehensive Art of Written Discourse: Geoffrey of Vinsauf and the *Ars dictaminis*". *Rhetorica* 6:2.167–194.

–. 1991. *Ars dictaminis-Ars dictandi.* (= *Typologie des Sources du Moyen Age Occidental*, 60.) Turnhout: Brepols.

Codoñer, Carmen. 1996. "Isidore de Séville: Différences et vocabulaires". *Les manuscrits des lexiques et glossaires de l'Antiquité tardive à la fin de Moyen Age* éd. par J. Hamesse, 57–77. Louvain-la-Neuve: FIDEM-Brepols.

Colker, Marvin L. 1974. "New Evidence that John of Garland revised the Doctrinale of Alexander de Villa-Dei". *Scriptorium* 28.68–71.

Colombat, Bernard. 1989. "Le vocabulaire des figures de construction à la Renaissance". *Rhétorique et discours critiques. Actes du Colloque tenu à l'École Normale Supérieure les 13 et 14 mars 1987*, 41–58. Paris: Presses de l'École Normale Supérieure.

Denifle, Henri & Émile Chatelain. 1889. *Chartularium universitatis parisiensis.* Paris.

Dahan, Gilbert. 1990. "Les classifications du savoir aux XII^e^ et XIII^e^ siècles". *L'Enseignement philosophique* 40:4.5–27.

Della Casa, Adriana. 1981. "Les glossaires et les traités de grammaire du Moyen Age". *La lexicographie du latin médiéval et ses rapports avec les recherches actuelles sur la civilisation du Moyen Age*, 35–46. Paris: CNRS.

Faral, Edmond. 1971. *Les arts poétiques du XII^e^ et du XIII^e^ siècles.* Paris: Vrin.

Fredborg, Karin Margareta. 1980. "Universal Grammar According to Some 12th-Century Grammarians". *Studies in Medieval Linguistic Thought* éd. par Konrad Koerner et al., 69–84. Amsterdam: Benjamins.

–. 1988. "Speculative Grammar". *A History of Twelfth-Century Philosophy* éd. par P. Dronke, 177–195. Cambridge: Cambridge Univ. Press.

Gabriel, Astrik L. 1969. *Garlandia, Studies in the History of the Mediaeval Universities.* Notre Dame (Ind.): The Medieval Institute, Univ. of Notre Dame.

Haye, Thomas, ed. 1995. *Johannes de Garlandia, Compendium gramatice.* Köln: Böhlau.

Heironimus, John Paul & Josiah Cox Russell. 1929. "Two Types of Thirteenth Century Grammatical Poems". *Colorado College Publication, General Series* 158.3–27.

Holtz, Louis. 1981. *Donat et la tradition de l'enseignement grammatical.* Paris: CNRS.

Hunt, Richard William. 1980. "The Introductions to the 'Artes' in the Twelfth Century". *The History of Grammar in the Middle Ages. Collected papers* éd. par Geoffrey L. Bursill-Hall, 117–144. Amsterdam: Benjamins.

Hunt, Tony. 1979. "Vernacular Glosses in Medieval Manuscripts". *Cultura Neolatina* 39.9–37.

–. 1991. *Teaching and Learning Latin in XIIIth Century England.* Cambridge: Brewer.

Hurlbut, Stephen A. 1933. "A Forerunner of Alexander de Villa Dei". *Speculum* 8.258–263.

Kneepkens, Corneille Henri. 1981. "*Ecce quod usus habet*: Eine Quelle von Eberhard von Béthunes *Graecismus*, cap. V". *Mittellateinisches Jahrbuch* 16.212–216.

Lafleur, Claude. 1988. *Quatre introductions à la philosophie au XIII^e^ siècle: Textes critiques et étude historique.* Paris & Montréal: Vrin.

Law, Vivien. 1986. "Panorama della grammatica normativa nel tredicesimo secolo". *Aspetti della letteratura latina nel secolo XIII* éd. par C. Leonardi & G. Orlandi, 125–147. Perugia & Firenze: La Nuova Italia.

Lohmeyer, Karl. 1901. "Ebrard von Béthune: Eine Untersuchung über den Verfasser des *Graecismus* und *Laborintus*". *Romanische Forschungen* 11.412–430.

Morand, François. 1863. "Questions d'histoire littéraire: Au sujet du *Doctrinale Metricum* d'Alexandre de Villedieu". *Revue des Sociétés savantes des départements*, 3^e^ série, 2.50–59.

Munk-Olsen, Birger. 1994. *L'attegiamento medievale di fronte alla cultura classica.* Roma: Unione Internazionale degli Istituti di Archeologia, Storia e Storia dell'Arte in Roma.

Murphy, James J. 1974. *Rhetoric in the Middle Ages: A history of rhetorical theory from St. Augustine to the Renaissance.* Berkeley: Univ. of California Press.

–. 1990. "*Topos* and *Figura*: Historical cause and effect?". *De Ortu Grammaticae* éd. par Geoffrey L. Bursill-Hall, Sten Ebbesen & Konrad Koerner, 239–253. Amsterdam & Philadelphia: Benjamins.

–. 1961. "The Arts of Discourse, 1050–1400". *Medieval Studies* 23.194–205.

Ott, H. & J. M. Fletcher. 1964. *The Mediaeval Statutes of the Faculty of Arts of the University of Freiburg im Breisgau.* Notre-Dame (Ind.).

Robins, Robert H. 1980. "Functional Syntax in Medieval Europe". *Studies in Medieval Linguistic Thought* éd. par Konrad Koerner et al., 231–240. Amsterdam: Benjamins.

Rosier, Irène. 1988. "Le traitement spéculatif des constructions figurées". *L'héritage des grammairiens latins* éd. par Irène Rosier, 181–204. Louvain: BIG-Peeters.

Sivo, Vito. 1989. "Ricerche sulla tradizione grammaticale mediolatina". *Annali della Facoltà di lettere e filosofia dell'Università di Bari* 32.111–50.

–. 1996. "Una fonte del *Graecismus* di Eberardo di Béthune: Il *Liber Pauperum* di Giovanni di Beauvais". *Studi Umanistici Piceni* 16.109–121.

Thomson, David. 1983. "The Oxford Grammar Masters Revisited". *Mediaeval Studies* 45.298–310.

Thurot, Charles. 1850a. *De l'organisation de l'enseignement dans l'Université de Paris au Moyen Age.* Paris. (Réimpr., Minerva 1967.)

–. 1850b. *De Alexandri de Ville-Dei Doctrinali ejusque fortuna.* Paris.

–. 1868. *Notices et extraits de divers manuscrits latins pour servir à l'histoire des doctrines grammaticales au Moyen Age.* Paris: Imprimerie Impériale. (Réimpr., Minerva 1964.)

Williams, John R. 1972. "The *De differentiis et derivationibus grecorum* attributed to William of Corbeil". *Viator, Medieval and Renaissance studies* 3.298–301.

*Anne Grondeux, Paris (France)*

# 82. The Latin tradition and the Irish language

The first known manifestation of Latin learning being adapted to thinking on linguistic lines in Ireland is the Ogam alphabet, which was used mainly for funerary inscriptions dating from at least the 4th century AD onwards. It consists of four groups of five characters that together form a systematic linear code for the sounds of Irish. Of these, one group contains the vowels and the three others the consonants. Although certain details (see Ahlqvist 1992: 119 for some of them) concerning the invention of the invention of the Ogam alphabet still require further elucidation, there is no doubt but that it is ultimately based upon the Latin grammarians' classification of the letters of the alphabet, into vowels, semi-vowels, mutes and Greek letters.

The rationale behind the invention of this mode of writing was a linguistic one and the independence of mind shown by its creator(s?) is an important feature of its history (McManus 1990: 30–31). So, moreover, is the fact that Latin grammar was so well known in Ireland at the time that the possibility arose that one of its doctrines might be used as basis for the Ogam alphabet.

*Auraicept na nÉces* "The Scholars' Primer" is an Old Irish text that deals with language: see Calder 1917 (for an edition that includes a sizeable quantity of later mediaeval commentary) and Ahlqvist 1982 (for an edition of the early canonical text only). The early text includes topics such as: the origin of the Irish language; the classification of letters of the alphabet in Latin and Irish; grammatical gender; an analysis of linguistic oppositions such as those between active and passive verbs as well as the elements of rime.

The section (see Ahlqvist 1982: 47 for an edition of it) that deals with the origin of the Irish language is not, strictly speaking, based on linguistic ideas. However, it reveals certain rather striking ideas about the relative status of languages, maintaining, as it does, that Irish was a language deliberately formed out of all the seventy-two languages that came out of the tower of Babel, and, therefore, superior to the other ones.

Furthermore (see Ahlqvist 1982: 48), the Latin division of the consonants into semi-vowels and mutes is rejected for Irish. The category of semi-vowels is considered redundant. The argumentation for this is based on the names of the letters and does therefore not follow much of a linguistic train of thought, but the independence of mind as regards Latin grammar most certainly deserves some attention from historians of linguistics.

Terminological originality is shown in the way a special term was devised to denote pronouns when used to refer to the gender of a nouns, as in the passage dealing with gender (Ahlqvist 1982: 49) where the question *catte dechor eturru?* "what is the nature of the difference between then [the three genders]?" is given the answer *Ni ansae: nos·dechrigetar a tri airlainn insce .i. 'is é in fer'* "Not difficult: their three markers of gender keep them distinct, that is: 'he's the man' ". Latin seems to have no term corresponding exactly to *airlann*. The original concrete lexical meaning of this word appears to have been something like "pre-mentioning", even if it clearly means "marker" in the *Auraicept*. In other respects, it seems likely (Ahlqvist 1989: 2–4) that this passage was modelled on the discussion of grammatical gender in some Latin source, like Diomedes (Keil 1857: 301): *Genera nominum sunt principalia tria, masculinum femininum neutrum, masculinum est cui numero singulari casu nominativo pronomen praeponitur 'hic', ut 'hic Cato'.*

It also contains an appendix of nominal paradigms, based on the six cases of the Latin declensional pattern, but much extended, so as to cover most (over 20) cases of Irish nouns preceded by prepositions and other proclitics, including the copula *is* "is".

As Hovdhaugen (1982: 130) has put matters, "this illustrates clearly the strange mixture of the classical tradition and Irish originality concerning linguistic terminology and analysis". This table of paradigms is reproduced in table 82.1., with some adaptations, from the latest available edition (Ahlqvist 1982: 52–53).

The names of the Irish cases have been translated into English, using the terms found to name cases in Finnish and Hungarian, whenever possible. This is due to the fact that most modern accounts of those two languages involve a number of grammatical cases that is fairly close (see Ahlqvist 1985: 251) to that found in the *Auraicept*.

It is very likely that the above table did not actually exist in the exact form given to it here, in any single mediaeval manuscript. In its printed form, the table has been collated from a fairly large (see Ahlqvist 1982: 22–35) number of different manuscripts. Also, even in its present form, the table is manifestly incomplete, lacking as it does feminine and neuter equivalents of quite a few of the masculine examples. However, the fact that the archaic (see Ahlqvist 1982: 62) accusative singular *bein* (instead of later *mnaí*) of *ben* "woman" is found in one part of the para-

Tab. 82.1.: The nominal paradigms

| | "case" | m.sg. | m.pl. | f.sg. | f.pl. | n.sg. | n.pl. |
|---|---|---|---|---|---|---|---|
| 1 | aainmniugud | *fer* | *fir* | *ben* | *mná* | *nem* | *nime* |
| | aṡelbad | *fir* | *nafer* | *mná* | *namban* | *nime* | *nanime* |
| | arath | *dofiur* | *doḟeraib* | *domnaí* | *domnáib* | *donim* | *donimil* |
| | ainchosc | *infer* | *innafiru* | *inmbein* | *innamná* | *annem* | *innanin* |
| 5 | athogairm | *afir* | *afiru* | *aben* | *amná* | | |
| | aḟochsal | *ófiur* | *óferaib* | *ómnaí* | *ómnáib* | *ónim* | *ónimib* |
| | aḟuirmiud | *ocfiur* | *ocferaib* | *ocmnaí* | *ocmnáib* | *ocnim* | *ocnimil* |
| | aascnam | *cofer* | *cofiru* | *comnaí* | *comna* | *conem* | *conime* |
| | aṡechmall | *sechfer* | *sechfiru* | *sechmnai* | *sechmná* | *sechnem* | *sechnin* |
| 10 | athregtad | *trėfer* | *trefiru* | *tremnaí* | *tremná* | *trenem* | *trenime* |
| | ainotacht | *ifer* | *ifiru* | *immnaí* | *immná* | *innem* | *innime* |
| | aaittreb | *ifiur* | *iferaib* | *immnaí* | *immnáib* | *innim* | *innimib* |
| | aḟortud | *forfer* | *forfiru* | *formnaí* | *formná* | *fornem* | *fornime* |
| | aḟothad | *fofiur* | *foferaib* | *fomnaí* | *fomnáib* | *fonim* | *fonimib* |
| 15 | athairsce | *tarfer* | *tarfiru* | *tarmnaí* | *tarmná* | *tarnem* | *tarnime* |
| | aḟresgabál | *arfiur* | *arfiru uel arferaib* | | | | |
| | aairchellad | *arfer* | *arferaib* | | | | |
| | aḟrecmarc | *cíafer* | | | | | |
| | aimthimchell | *imfer* | *imferaib* | *immnaí* | *immnáib* | | |
| 20 | adígbál | *defiur* | *deferaib* | *demnaí* | *demnáib* | | |
| | aasgabál | *afiur* | | | | | |
| | athúarascbáil | *isfer* | *itfir* | *asben* | *asmná* | | |
| | aḟreslige | *frifer* | *frifiru* | | | | |
| | athíarmóracht | *íarfiur* | *íarferaib* | *íarmnaí* | *íarmnáib* | | |
| 25 | atháebtu | *lafer* | *laferaib* | *lamnaí* | *lamnáib* | | |
| | aremiud | *ríafiur* | *ríaferaib* | | | | |
| | athórmach | *frisinfer* | *frisnaferaib* | *frisanmnaí* | *frisnamnáib* | | |
| | athuistide | *indfir* | | | | | |

| | | **m sg.** | **m.pl.** | **f.sg.** | **f.pl.** | **n.sg.** | **n.pl.** |
|---|---|---|---|---|---|---|---|
| 1 | its nominative: | *uir* | *uiri* | *femina* | *feminae* | *caelum* | *caela* |
| | its genitive: | *uiri* | *uirorum* | *feminae* | *feminarum* | *caeli* | *caelorum* |
| | its dative: | *uiro* | *uiris* | *feminae* | *feminis* | *caelo* | *caelis* |
| | its accusative: | *uirum* | *uiros* | *feminam* | *feminas* | *caelum* | *caela* |
| 5 | its vocative: | *o uir* | *o uiri* | *o femina* | *o feminae* | | |
| | its ablative: | *(a) uiro* | *(a) uiris* | *(a) femina* | *(a) feminis* | *(a) caelo* | *(a) caelis* |
| | its adessive: | *apud uirum* | *apud uiros* | *apud feminam* | *apud feminas* | *apud caelum* | *apud caela* |
| | its allative: | *ad uirum* | *ad uiros* | *ad feminam* | *ad feminas* | *ad caelum* | *ad caela* |
| | its praeterlative: | *praeter uirum* | *praeter uiros* | *praeter feminam* | *praeter feminas* | *praeter caelum* | *praeter caela* |
| 10 | its perlative: | *per uirum* | *per uiros* | *per feminam* | *per feminas* | *per caelum* | *per caela* |
| | its illative: | *in uirum* | *in uiros* | *in feminam* | *in feminas* | *in caelum* | *in caela* |
| | its inessive: | *in uiro* | *in uiris* | *in femina* | *in feminis* | *in caelo* | *in caelis* |
| | its super-lative: | *super uirum* | *super uiros* | *super feminem* | *super feminas* | *super caelum* | *super caela* |
| | its subsessive: | *sub uiro* | *sub uiris* | *sub femina* | *sub feminis* | *sub caelo* | *sub caelis* |
| 15 | its translative: | *trans uirum* | *trans uiros* | *trans feminam* | *trans feminas* | *trans caelum* | *trans caela* |
| | its prae-essive: | (rest) *prae uiro* | *prae uitis* | | | | |
| | its praelative: | (motion) *prae uiro* | *prae uiris* | | | | |
| | its interrogative: | *quis uir?* | *qui uiri?* | | | | |
| | its circumdative: | *circum uitum* | *circum uiros* | | | | |
| 20 | its delative: | *de uiro* | *de uiris* | *de femina* | *de feminis* | | |
| | its descriptive: | *est uir* | *sunt uiri* | *est femina* | *sunt feminae* | | |
| | its elative: | *ex uiro* | | | | | |
| | its adversative: | *contra uirum* | | | | | |
| | its postlative: | *post uirum* | *post uiros* | *post feminam* | *post feminas* | | |
| 25 | its comitative: | *cum uiro* | *cum uiris* | *cum femina* | *cum feminas* | | |
| | its antelative: | *ante uirum* | *ante uiros* | *ante feminam* | *ante feminas* | | |
| | its augmentative: | *contra uirum* | *contra uiros* | *contra feminam* | *contra feminas* | | |
| | its possessive: | *uiri* | | | | | |

digms shows that at least some of the passages describing feminines must be rather early. In any case, ist is clear that the origin of these paradigms lies in a table giving the six cases of Latin, in which the ablative even in the Latin may have been listed together with a preposition, as for instance in the following one, supplied by Diomedes (Keil 1857: 242):

*Cato nomen appellativum [...] declinabitur sic: nominativo 'hic Cato', genetivo 'huius Catonis', dativo 'hic Catoni', accusativo 'hunc Catonem', vocativo 'o Cato', ablativo 'ab hoc Catone'.*

Once one case involving a preposition had been included on the list, it would have seemed logical to add the remaining ones. The use of extremely literal Latin, rather than English glosses, in the edition given here, is designed to make this part of the process quite clear.

Linguistically speaking, this is by far the most interesting part of the text, for several reasons. Firstly, it must be noted that the view of language that underlies these paradigms is entirely consistent with Old Irish scribal practices in respect of word separation. These provide for spaces to be written, not between words as we know them nowadays, but between stress-groups that correspond fairly well to the major constituents in a sentence. Thus, in the case of the 'ablative' *ófiur*, modern practice (cf. Thurneysen 1946: 24–25) would be to write the preposition *ó* "from" separate from the dative singular form *fiur* "man", as follows: *ó fiur*. Likewise, in the 'illative' *ifer*, the preposition *i* (with the accusative it means "into" and with the dative "in") is nowadays usually written separate from the accusative singular *fer*, as follows: *i fer*. However, in the case of an edition of the *Auraicept* paradigms, even a modern editor must follow the early scribal practice, given the fact that it is part of an integrated framework for describing and writing the language.

Also, there are some interesting parallels of this way of treating Old Irish, making it into a mildly polysynthetic language, in the work of at least one modern scholar (cf. Borgstrøm 1968 and the comments in Ahlqvist 1974: 181, 185). In most modern grammars of Irish, on the other hand, numbers of cases (and the terminology) are based closely on Greek and Latin models. Thus Thurneysen (1946: 155) distinguishes five cases in Old Irish: nominative, vocative, accusative, genitive and dative.

The *Auraicept* may have been written by an historical person, Cenn Fáelad, as early as the second half of the 7th century. Its textual transmission during the Middle Ages has a complex history, involving a notably large number of manuscripts and much glossatorial and commentatorial activity, on the same scale as for the early Irish law manuscripts. The sheer magnitude of its textual history proves that it was taken very seriously indeed in the Middle Ages, something that rather stands in contrast with the treatment it has received from some later scholars. Thus, one must, to some not inconsiderable extent, question Bergin's (1938: 205, 207) often quoted statements according to which the "ancient Irish knew nothing about grammar", an argument based, amongst other things, on the notion that the *Auraicept* was a mere "confused mixture of fabulous tales [...]". For one thing, one may compare the in itself theoretically consistent method of analysing the Irish nominal system presented in the *Auraicept* with the entirely Latin-based six-case one often found even much later, for instance, in the first known grammar of Finnish (Petræus 1649: 12).

Priscian was much studied in mediaeval Ireland, and there is an extensive body of glosses on his grammar, in a number of mainly 9th century manuscripts. Even though very many of these glosses had been written in Old Irish and thus constitute a valuable source for our knowledge of the language itself, as far as their content is concerned, it is clear that they deal with Latin materials only, and much more from a pedagogical than from a linguistic point of view (cf. Hofman 1993).

In the history of linguistics the St. Gall glosses are nevertheless noteworthy. This is due to the fact that, together with the *Auraicept*, they have provided the Irish language with the foundations for its present-day grammatical terminology (see further Ó Cuív 1966). For instances, the Modern Irish term meaning "accusative" is *áinsí*, which derives directly from the Old Irish *áinsid*, which itself is a calque on Latin *accusatiuus*, based as it is on the verb *ad·nessa*, literally "accuses".

During the earlier part of the Modern Irish period (cf. Thurneysen (1946: 1, 673) for the periodization of Irish), a rich grammatical literature (see Ó Cuív 1973 for further details) was created for Irish. It is often called Bardic grammar, because its main purpose was to codify the language for the use of poets, i. e. bards. Claims have been made to regard its teaching as being totally independent from any Latin influence. Thus, Bergin (1938: 209) states that "here we find a complete break with the Latin system, and a fresh start", when dealing with the three parts of speech of Bardic grammar. These he describes as follows: "The native grammarians of the time reckon three parts of speech: *focal* concrete noun, including the adjective and the stressed pronoun; *pearsa* verbal noun, or verb in general, since verbal forms are always classified under the verbal noun; and *iarmbéarla* particle, including the definite article, the preposition, the various preverbs, the infixed pronoun, and the copula, in short, all proclitics." However, it can quite easily be demonstrated (O'Rahilly 1946: 87, n. 2; Ó Cuív 1966: 152 and Ahlqvist 1980) that they derive from a Latin source, very possibly Isidore, which in turn was, ultimately, based on Aristotle's (see for instance Kassel 1965: 1465$^{b}$21) tripartite division of the parts of the parts of speech into ῥῆμα "verb", ὄνομα, "noun" and σύνδεσμος "conjunction".

During the latter part of the Modern Irish period, after the invention of printing, Latin was again adopted as a model for the description of Irish. Thus, a grammar written in 1634 states that Irish has seven parts of speech. Somehow, and rather surprisingly, its author, Bonaventura Ó hEodhasa, failed to mention either the partiple or the interjection commonly used to bring the canonical number of eight parts of speech into lists of this sort: "Partes orationis Hybernis sunt septem, videlicet, *airteagal* .i. articulus; *ainm* .i. nomen; *insgne* .i. pronomen; *briathar* uel *pearsa*.i. verbum; *reimhbhriathar* .i. adverbium; *coimcheangal* .i. conjunctio; *iarmbéarla* .i. praepositio" (Mac Aogáin 1968: 15). These terms are a mixture of straight loans, like *airteagal*, translation loans, like *ainm*, and indigenous creations, like *iarmbéarla*, literally "after-speech".

## Bibliography

Ahlqvist Anders. 1974. "Notes on 'Case' and Word-Boundaries'. *Ériu* 25.181–189.

–. 1980. "The Three Parts of Speech of Bardic Grammar". *Studia Celtica* (= *Fs. Kenneth Jackson.*) 14/15:12–17.

–. 1983. *The Early Irish Linguist: An Edition of the Canonical Part of the Auraicept na nÉces.* (= *Commentationes Humanarum Litterarum*, 73.) Helsinki-Helsingfors: Societas Scientiarum Fennica.

–. 1985. "The Study of Language in Early Ireland". *Neuphilologische Mitteilungen* 86:246–257.

–. 1989. "Latin Grammar and Native Learning". *Sages, Saints and Storytellers: Celtic Studies in Honour of Professor James Carney*, 1–6. Maynooth: An Sagart.

–. 1992. Review of McManus (1990). *Cambridge Medieval Celtic Studies* 23.118–119.

Bergin, Osborn. 1938. "The Native Irish Grammarian". *Proceedings of the British Academy* 24.205–235.

Borgstrøm, Carl Hj[almar]. 1968. "Notes on Gaelic Grammar". *Celtic Studies: Essays in memory of Angus Matheson* ed. by James Carney & David Greene 12–21. London: Routledge & Kegan Paul.

Calder, George. 1917. *Auraicept na nÉces.* Edinburgh: John Grant.

Hofman, Rijcklof. 1993. "The linguistic preoccupations of the glossators of the St Gall Glosses". *Historiographia Linguistica* 20.111–126.

Hovdhaugen, Even. 1982. *Foundations of Western Linguistics.* Oslo: Universitetsforlaget.

Kassel, Rudolf, ed. 1965. *Aristotelis de arte poetica liber.* Oxford: Oxford Univ. Press.

Keil, Heinrich. 1857. "Diomedis artis grammaticae libri III". *Grammatici Latini* I, 297–429. Leipzig: Teubner.

Mac Aogáin, Parthalán, ed. 1968. *Graiméir Ghaeilge na mBráthar Mionúr.* [The Irish Grammars of the Friars Minor.] Dublin: Institute for Advanced Studies.

McManus, Damian. 1990. *A Guide to Ogam.* Maynooth: An Sagart.

Ó Cuív, Brian. 1966. "Linguistic terminology in the mediaeval bardic tracts". *Transactions of the Philological Society* 1965: 141–164.

–. 1973. "The Linguistic Training of the Mediaeval Irish Poet". *Celtica* 10.114–140.

O'Rahilly, T[homas] F[rancis]. 1946. *Early Irish History and Mythology.* Dublin: Institute for Advanced Studies.

Petræus, Eskil. 1649. *Linguæ Finnicæ brevis institutio.* Aboae: Wald.

Thurneysen, Rudolf. 1946. *A Grammar of Old Irish.* Dublin: Institute for Advanced Studies.

*Anders Ahlqvist, Galway (Ireland)*

# 83. The Latin tradition and Welsh

1. The Middle Welsh grammars
2. Contents of the grammars
3. Bibliography

## 1. The Middle Welsh grammars

Although unknown, a Latin source lies behind the lost Welsh ancestor from which three extant Middle Welsh grammars descend. The texts appear in *Peniarth* 20 (c. 1325–40), *Llyfr Coch Hergest* (*LCH*, c. 1382–1400), and *Llanestephan* 3 (c. 1400–1410). The three texts were edited in a volume entitled *Gramadegau'r Penceirddiaid* "Grammars of the Chief Bards" because their editors believed them to "contain a compendium of information received by pupils in the bardic schools" (Williams & Jones 1934: v). This appraisal of their function continues to be accepted although in 1961 T. Parry (1961: 177–195) challenged their bardic authority, arguing that (i) training in a Latin-based grammatical system would not have promoted mastery of Welsh poetic usage, and that (ii) the treatment of features of versification does not reflect 14th-century bardic practice. Whether or not they may claim bardic authority, were it not for the compiler's desire to codify the essential elements of the verse, we would not have this account of the non-universal features of Welsh at so early a date.

The grammars have been attributed variously to Einion Offeiriad (fl. c. 1314–1355) and Dafydd Ddu (c. 1330–1380), both of them clerics and minor bards. (See: I. Williams 1913–14; Smith 1962–64; Lewis 1967; Daniel 1985; Gruffydd 1995).

Modeled on a Latin source, the Welsh texts ignore prominent features of Welsh (e. g., mutations), and adopt inapplicable letters, descriptions and subcategories often incompatible with Welsh (e. g., concord). Yet the compiler was resourceful and intelligent in his account of the syllables and diphthongs, which were critical in prosody. The grammar provides the earliest examples of a linguistic terminology now discarded. Among the early texts, *Peniarth* 20 is notable in creating Welsh equivalents for Latin terms, *LCH* and *Llanstephan* 3 generally retaining the Latin. The term "grammar" (*gramadeg*) nowhere appears, nor does the common Middle Welsh noun *dwned* < *Donatus*. Of note is the sense of language as both oral and written but this may derive from the Latin model.

Most studies have focused on problems of attribution (I. Williams 1913–14; Smith 1962–64; Daniel 1985; Gruffydd 1995), a few on bardic issues (Parry 1961; Bromwich 1977). S. Lewis placed *Peniarth* 20 in the tradition of speculative grammar, which he took to explain the deviations from the linguistic system of Welsh (S. Lewis 1967). A. Matonis queried this claim noting the lack of interest in signification, modes of meaning and understanding, and the absence of the distinctions central to speculative grammatical theory; rather, the Welsh text inherited semantic, morphological and syntactic criteria from its Latin source. She reviews the treatment of letters, syllables, vowels and diphthongs and the noun and verb against Middle Welsh and the matter derived from a Latin source (Matonis 1981; 1989). The Welsh texts ignore etymology, lack semantic criteria and the ties to logic and dialectics that characterize speculative grammar. C. Lewis (1979) and Matonis (1990) review problems of authority, date, and the circumstances of the grammar's composition.

## 2. Contents of the grammars

The grammar divides into two major units: the first and shortest comprises grammar (letters, syllables and diphthongs, parts of speech, syntax, and sentence construction). The second is prescriptive/proscriptive instruction on native metrics, panegyric, poetics, the bardic orders, their function and the verse forms appropriate to each rank.

The grammar begins with the alphabet, incorrectly claims 24 letters for Welsh, and closely follows Latin texts although it lacks the broader comments on words (*a voce*) and letters (*de litera*) and omits certain elementary definitions (e. g., *Littera est pars minima vocis articulatae*). *Peniarth* 20 uniquely includes the graph *q*; all correctly exclude *x* and *z*, identifying the latter as a Greek letter (as do Probus, Donatus, and Priscian). All add *ll* to indicate the voiceless lateral spirant represented orthographically by ligatured *l*. While a Latin source is behind the description of *h* as a spirant, the Welsh text adds that "there is no *h* as regards meter [...] yet it is necessary in Welsh." The compiler modifies the Latin vocalic system, which had too few vowels for Welsh, adding *w* and *y* to the Latin five. The account of the consonants relies heavily on Latin and thus is somewhat flawed. Adopting the Latin categories, the Welsh groups the consonants into liquids, which except for *d* correspond to the Latin semi-vowels (*d* [ð], *f*, *l*, *m*, *n*, *r*, *s*) and mutes (*b*, *c*, *g*, *k*, *p*, *q*, *t*), but drops *d* and *h*, which are fricatives in Welsh. The calque *tawdd* "melting" describes the liquids which "dissolve in poetry." The Latin *mutae* (W. *mud*) is retained, adding that "their sound is very slight compared with the sound of the vowels," an explanation found neither in Donatus nor Priscian. While the alphabet inadequately reflects the orthographic and phonetic realities of Welsh, it does accommodate both rather satisfactorily.

The Welsh grammars expand the classification and discussion of the syllable although they omit a description such as we find in Priscian (i. e., a sound that can be written and uttered in one breath and bearing one accent (*Inst. Gram.* 2.1). Later, in a mnemonic list of 'the threes of poetry', a syllable is said to have letter(s), tense, and accent. The grammar proper states that a syllable ranges in size from one letter to six (as in Priscian), noting that some monosyllables of six letters may include a seventh as a "sign of aspiration".

The unit on the syllable and diphthong represents a notable, independent contribution to descriptive linguistics. The compiler identifies three major classes of syllables (with sub-groups) and attempts a phonetic description of each. In the classification of syllables the Welsh diphthongs are described in notable detail, albeit the examples are chosen to reflect bardic usage. In selecting complex features of Welsh verse for description, the compiler has provided a rare phonetic account of a medieval vernacular, distinguishing between minimal pairs in the syllable and supplying a distinctive feature classification of the diphthongs. While limited to aspects of language bearing on bardic composition, the compiler's efforts to explain what he perceived as inconsistencies between bardic composition and what he as a Welsh speaker heard suggest that he was aware that neither bardic practice nor the written form consistently represented spoken practice.

The Welsh grammars over-rely on Latin in the unit on parts of speech, beginning with the definition of the word, said to be composed of syllables, some of which are parts of speech. The compiler was no doubt distinguishing between derivational suffixes and base forms, but even this is an imprecise simplification as applied to the nominal and verbal systems. The division of parts of speech into substantives and verbs follows the familiar division found in Dionysius Thrax and later Latin grammars. Like the Latin grammars, the Welsh fuses semantic and logical criteria in the description and classification of the noun. The division of nouns into noun-substantives and noun-adjectives was easily maintained in Welsh.

The division of the substantive into physical and abstract retains both the Latin categories and the terminology. The defintion of the adjective, called a weak noun, also derives from Latin as does the account of adjectival comparison, adopting the Latin for *possyeit* "positive" and *superleit* "superlative" but creating a calque, *cymhariaeth*, for the comparative. The Welsh uncritically copies the Latin and claims three genders despite there being but two in Welsh. Masculine and feminine are said to be naturally inherent; neuter (common) gender applies to both. Since Welsh lacked a declensional system, case is omitted. Included are perfunctory remarks on noncompound and compound words (a word is noncompound before compounding). The weaknesses in the analysis of the noun are many and not all due to its Latin source (e. g., the failure to note any of the distinctive methods of forming the plural). The account of the nouns is little more than a classification of types of nouns drawn from the semantically referential classes located in Latin.

The verb follows Donatus' criterion of meaning in its reference to voice (active and passive), retains two of the formal criteria (tense and person), but omits reference to number. While the review of the verb is neither comprehensive nor systematic and is heavily indebted to Latin notions and categories, the classification is on the whole accurate though superficial. It excludes formal criteria, drops inapplicable categories (neuter and substantive verbs), but includes erroneous statements on tense, mood, and voice.

Similarities between Latin and Welsh tenses facilitated the adoption of the three primary tenses: present, past, and future. Also copied from Latin are the three past forms: preterite (*perffeith*), imperfect (*amherfeith*) and pluperfect (*mwy no pherfeith* "more than perfect"). The Welsh keeps the five moods of Latin instead of omitting the optative and infinitive, both absent in Welsh, which has a verbal noun whose constructions are those of the noun. It is likely that the Welsh compiler, given to meaning-based classification, was misled into accepting the optative and infinitive as necessary and existing moods. His example of a verb in the optative is inflected for the imperfect (an inflection shared by the indicative and subjunctive first person singular).

As regards voice, the Welsh grammars accept three of the five Latin genera: active ('doing'), passive ('suffering to be done'), and common ('common to both') although Welsh had only active and passive. The compiler had difficulty with verbs such as "I live", in which the issue of having or not having an object is irrelevant. The review of transitive and intransitive verbs fuses semantic and syntactic criteria in an attempt to differentiate the two. Throughout the units on the verb, the Welsh compiler ignores morphological suffixes and fails to distinguish between formal and semantic criteria. Like many medieval grammarians, the Welsh compiler saw mood mainly as a statement of attidude and tense as a temporal category only.

Like Priscian, the Welsh compiler places the pronoun after the verb and not after the noun, as do Probus and Donatus. The threefold classification (personal, possessive, and interrogative) and the itemization of twenty-four pronouns, which are incorrectly claimed for Welsh, is entirely derivative. The treatment of pronouns is seriously incomplete and flawed in some of its misclassifications.

In the unit on proper and improper constructions a sentence is said to be correct if it contains a noun and verb; improper if made up of a series of nouns without a verb or *vice versa*. Dependence on a Latin model allowed the compiler to ignore Welsh nonfinite sentences. The grammar proper concludes with a brief comment on rhetorical *schemas*, here identified as figures, colors of diction, and permissible faults. The divisions and terms reflect the conflation of classical and medieval treatises on grammar, rhetoric, and poetic. "Figures" (W. *figur*) here must refer to tropes; the calque *lliw* "colors" to *colores rhetorici*, and "permissible faults" (W. *esgus dros gam ymadrawd*) to solecisms.

There follows a lengthy treatment of the classical meters of Welsh poetry, the major function of which is said to be praise and satire. In the grammatical and metrical units, poetry is defined as a composition of grammatically correct constructions expressed in ornamented words. This description and the orientation of the text documents the intersection of poetics with grammar, metrics, and rhetoric, identifies the Welsh grammar as a conservative tract, and places it firmly within the late Latin tradition.

## 3. Bibliography


Bromwich, Rachel. 1977. "Gwaith Einion Offeiriad a Barddoniaeth Dafydd ap Gwilym". *Ysgrifau Beirniadol* 10.157–180.

Daniel, Iestyn. 1985. "Awduriaeth y Gramadeg a Briodolir i Einion Offeiriad a Dafydd Ddu o Hiraddug". *Ysgrifau Beirniadol* 13.178–208.

Gruffydd, R. Geraint. 1995. "Dafydd Ddu o Hiraddug". *Llên Cymru* 18.205–220.

Lewis, Ceri. 1979. "Einion Offeiriad and the Bardic Grammar". *A Guide to Welsh Literature* II ed. by A. O. H. Jarman & G. Hughes, 58–87. Llandybie, Dyfed: Davies.

Lewis, Saunders. 1967. *Gramadegau'r Penceirddiaid*, G. J. Williams *Memorial Lecture*. Cardiff: Gwasg Prifysgol Cymru.

Matonis, Ann T. E. 1981. "The Welsh Bardic Grammars and the Western grammatical tradition". *Modern Philology* 79.121–145.

–. 1989. "The Concept of Poetry in the Middle Ages: The Welsh evidence from the Bardic Grammars". *Bulletin of the Board of Celtic Studies* 36.1–12.

–. 1990. "Problems Relating to the Composition of the Welsh Bardic Grammars". *Celtic Language, Celtic Culture: A Festschrift for Eric P. Hamp* ed. by Ann T. E. Matonis & Daniel Melia, 273–291. Van Nuys, Cal.: Ford and Bailie.

Parry, Thomas. 1961. "The Welsh Metrical Treatise Attributed to Einion Offeiriad". *Proceedings of the British Academy* 47.177–195.

Smith, J. Beverly. 1962–1964. "Einion Offeiriad". *Bulletin of the Board of Celtic Studies* 20.339–347.

Williams, G. J. & E. J. Jones, eds. 1934. *Gramadegau'r Penceirddiaid.* Cardiff: Gwasg Prifysgol Cymru.


*Ann T. E. Matonis, Philadelphia (USA)*

# 84. The Latin tradition and Icelandic


1. Introduction
2. The Latin tradition in Iceland
3. The study of language in medieval Iceland
4. The Icelandic Grammatical Treatises
5. The intellectual background
6. Bibliography


## 1. Introduction

Evidence for linguistic speculation in medieval Iceland is provided mainly by a small but remarkable corpus of writings, consisting in four treatises and some fragments, spreading over a period of two centuries, approximately from the middle of the 12th century to the middle of the 14th century. They represent in many ways an exceptional event in medieval grammatical writing, because their object of study is not the Latin language, but the vernacular, i. e., the Old Norse-Icelandic language. These treatises are usually cited as *First*, *Second*, *Third* and *Fourth Grammatical Treatise* (in the following, *FGT*, *SGT*, *ThGT*, *FoGT*) according to their consecutive order in the manuscript which contains them all, the Còdex Wormianus. This sequence has long been considered as corresponding to their succession in time, although recently doubt has been cast on this assumption. The term 'grammatical' which has become canonical to refer to such texts, is actually unsatisfactory as pertains to their subject matter, since neither the ancient nor the modern meaning of the word describes precisely the heterogeneous contents of the treatises.

## 2. The Latin tradition in Iceland

The study of language in Iceland is connected with the introduction of Latin, which, however, probably stimulated an inborn interest in language, its different forms and use. The prolonged familiarity with runic epigraphy and with the strict rules of eddic and skaldic poetry must have aroused an early awareness of the formal and structural side of language. Grammatical writing undoubtedly started in connection with the establishment of local schools, which began to appear around 1100, also as a consequence of the widespread habit for the higher clergy and members of outstanding families to study abroad, particularly in Germany, England, France. Some of them, such as the first Icelandic Bishop, Ísleifr Gizurarson, are known to have established their own schools in Iceland (Walter 1971). Evidence from the available sources suggests that tutorial activity in Iceland was much the same as in the rest of Europe (Tómasson 1988a: 15–35). The instruction imparted seems to have been based on *grammatica* until well into the 13th century, in contrast with most other European centres, where by that time this subject had been superseded by *dialectica*. It appears that most of the texts which were fundamental to Continental culture were also known in medieval Iceland (Lehmann 1937; Walter 1971; Tómasson 1988a: 15–35; Collings 1967: 29–42). Book inventories from the 14th and the 15th centuries refer to Priscian's *Institutiones grammaticae*, Isidore's *Etymologiae*, Alexander of Villadei's *Doctrinale*, Ebrard of Béthune's *Graecismus*, and Cato's *Disticha* (*skólabœkr* "school-books"; Olmer 1902: 11, 16, 21–22, 53, 73).

## 3. The study of language in medieval Iceland

It is symptomatic of the prestige granted to the native tongue that, in spite of the growing importance of Latin and of the development of an influential Christian-Latin literature, a rich grammatical-rhetorical tradition appeared, focussing upon the Old Norse-Icelandic language and literature. A stimulus to this was the search for answers to the specific needs of Icelandic in relation to the new Latin alphabet, which was introduced in Iceland during the 11th century and was first used in vernacular texts from the early 12th century (Benediktsson 1965: 26, 40). The first attempts at writing reflect the problems arising in the process of adaptation of the Latin alphabet to the native tongue. Adjustments were modelled on the example of non-Latin speaking peoples who had been using the Latin alphabet for a long time, in particular the English people, as stated clearly in the *FGT* (84.9–16). Theoretical-epistemological questions related to the criteria to be adopted are discussed especially in the *FGT* and the *SGT*. An early interest in topics associated with the study of language such as rhetoric and stylistics is to be assumed, also due to a long-standing familiarity with skaldship. It is noteworthy that all known witnesses of the Icelandic grammatical treatises are handed down in manuscripts including also parts of Snorri Sturluson's *Edda*, which may have been intended as a sort of 'handbook' for apprentice skalds, and of which the grammatical treatises have long been considered an appendix. The incorporation of grammatical texts in manuscripts containing Snorri's work was obviously based on their handling the 'same' subject matter – i. e., the rules required for correct versification, but such relationship is unlikely to be indigenous and is rather to be regarded as a later development reflecting Latin patterns. The original intention underlying the composition of the four grammatical treatises undoubtedly is primarily a practical, didactic one, i. e., they were to provide a guide to the correct use of the native language in written, mainly literary texts. The public addressed seems to be that of the advanced students, as in all these writings the basic graphic, phonological and morphological notions are taken for granted.

## 4. The Icelandic Grammatical Treatises

The *FGT* is witnessed only in the Codex Wormianus (MS Copenhagen, AM 242, fol., second half of the 14th century), which includes Snorri's *Edda* and all the four grammatical treatises, here introduced by a *Prologue*. The *SGT* is handed down in the Codex Wormianus and in the Codex Upsaliensis (MS Uppsala, University Library, De La Gardie 11, early 14th century) (cf. Raschellà 1982). The *ThGT* is the only one to have three main witnesses, whose reciprocal relationship is not completely clear as yet, that is, the Codex Wormianus, the MS Reykjavík,

AM 748 I b, 4° (early 14th century) and the MS Reykjavík, AM 757 a, 4° (late 14th century) (cf. Ólsen 1884). The *FoGT* is only found in the Codex Wormianus, like the *FGT* and the *Prologue*.

4.1. The *First Grammatical Treatise*

The *FGT*, which is supposed to have been written around 1150 (possibly a little earlier: Benediktsson 1972: 31–33), contains a suggestion for a reform of the Latin alphabet to make it fit the Icelandic language. The establishment of a graphic norm is felt necessary, according to the First Grammarian (henceforth FG), "because languages differ from each other [...] different letters are needed in each, and not the same in all" (84.3–5, tr. Benediktsson 1972). The explicit purpose of the *FGT* is to make it easier to write and read all kinds of texts (84.12–15). The author states that he will follow the English example, thus showing his familiarity with the situation among the Anglo-Saxons, and this agrees well with what we know about the role played by England in the process of adaptation of the Latin alphabet to vernacular writing (Benediktsson 1965: 18 ff.).

The treatise consists of an introduction, a discussion of vowels and consonants, and a concluding chapter. The description of vowels is organized according to a strictly systematic principle, by which the different sounds are described, illustrated by means of examples and critically discussed. The FG suggests the introduction of four new letters, *ǫ ę ø y*, to represent new vocalic sounds produced by the action of umlaut and argues for the necessity to introduce diacritics, i. e., an apex and a dot, to mark distinctions of quantity and of nasality, respectively. In this way the FG describes a vowel system consisting of 36 vowel units, each being short or long, nasal(ized) or non-nasal(ized), thus providing the most complete and to a great extent reliable account of the vocalic inventory for 12th century Icelandic. The FG's analysing and verification procedure is striking. The need for the new orthographic signs is demonstrated by means of word pairs, in which the substitution of one letter for another brings about a change in the meaning (*sur* "sour"/ *syr* "sow"; *har* "hair"/*hár* "shark"). The FG's description and analysis of consonants are vaguer and less orderly arranged than those of vowels. The main points made by the FG are the exclusion of a few redundant letters such as *x*, *z*, *&*, the introduction of the runic sign *þ* for expressing the interdental spirant and a suggestion for using small capital letters (*hǫfuðstafir*) instead of geminates. Here the FG's main concern seems to be the question of the relationship between a letter and its name. Apparently the graphic innovations for both vowels and consonants advocated in the *FGT*, which are not invented by the author but occur sporadically in earlier and contemporary writing, were not as successful as we might expect, since they are only rarely witnessed in manuscripts.

However, the value of the *FGT* in relation to the history of linguistic studies lies undoubtedly not so much in its more or less appreciated orthographic reforms, as in its systematic descriptive and analytic method and in its clear and efficacious way of argumentation. According to some scholars, the FG's approach and procedure bear remarkable resemblance with methods and concepts of modern structural linguistics, in particular with the technique of the 'minimal oppositional pairs' (Hjelmslev's 'commutation') and with concepts like 'phoneme' and 'distinctive opposition'. The point was first made by Bergsveinsson (1942) and Christiansen (1946), then independently by Haugen (1950 and 1972), followed by Benediktsson's (1972) detailed and thorough analysis.

It has been argued that the letter (*stafr*, corresponding to the Latin *littera*) is meant by the FG as an abstract entity endowed with three concrete attributes, name, shape and power (*nafn*, *líkneski*, *jartein*, corresponding to Latin *nomen*, *figura*, *potestas*), thus providing "an early form of the modern phoneme" (Haugen 1972: 53). This view emerges also in handbooks on the history of linguistics such as Robins (1979: 66–93). Other scholars, in particular Albano Leoni (1975, 1977) and Ulvestad (1976) have rejected such an interpretation, emphasizing the dependence of the FG's idea of *stafr* on the Latin *littera* as defined especially in Priscian, of which it shares several theoretical inconsistencies. It has been maintained that not only the *FGT*'s contents but even its methodology (word pairs, Albano Leoni 1975: 28) is likely to build to a great extent upon late antique and medieval learning and practice. More recently the 'pre-structuralist' view, which according to Widding (1965: 32) rests fundamentally upon the fact that the treatise is studied in a modern linguistic perspective rather than within the general frame of medieval learning, has been held by Braunmüller

(1986) and Kusmenko (1993). Ulvestad (1995) is a reply to the latter, while a recent criticism, in particular of Haugen's position, is in Koerner (1997).

The FG undoubtedly has a good knowledge of Classical grammatical and rhetorical lore and of the phonological doctrine expounded in canonical grammatical texts (Donatus' *Ars maior*, Priscian's *Institutiones grammaticae*). This can be seen in his familiarity with the notion of *littera* and its three attributes, in the classification of letters into vowels and consonants, in the implicit distinction of the latter into *semivocales* and *mutae*, in the possibility for vowels to take consonantal value, and in various other cases (Holtsmark 1936; Benediktsson 1972; Albano Leoni 1975). However, such acquaintance usually results from more or less vague echoes rather than from direct parallels.

At least part of the material, as well as its peculiar treatment, seem undeniably to point to a long-standing, not necessarily written, native tradition. Ólsen (1883: 46–89; 1884: xxiii–xxv) argued that the *FGT* builds on a piece of such indigenous tradition, i. e., an alleged treatise on the reform of the runic alphabet by Þóroddr Gamlason rúnameistari (b. ca. 1100), a fragment of which is still extant, according to Ólsen, in the *ThGT* (chapts. 3–4). However, this view has been challenged (see below). Analogies can be found with the *SGT*, whose author either used the *FGT* or shared one of the *FGT*'s sources.

4.2. The *Second Grammatical Treatise*

The *SGT*'s date of composition is a matter of dispute among scholars, who in the course of time have variously placed it between the end of the 12th century and the last three decades of the 13th century. F. Albano Leoni (1975: 40–42) first questioned the reciprocal relationship between the *FGT* and the *SGT*. Recent scholarship (Raschellà 1982: 126–132) suggests that it may belong to the second half of the 13th century, i. e., that it may be later than the *ThGT*. The anonymous Second Grammarian (henceforth SG) appears to share fundamentally the same normative-didactic intention of the *FGT*, suggesting some modifications of the graphic rules and a better distribution of the signs. The opinion has been held (Mogk 1889) that the *SGT* was meant essentially as a linguistic introduction to Snorri's *Háttatal*. This view is shared by Braunmüller (1983, 1984), who regards the treatise as an attempt at a theory of syllabic structure, in particular of the rhyming syllable (*hending*), in relation to its use in versification. According to Braunmüller (1986), the SG, like the FG, adopts analytic and descriptive methods similar to those of structural linguistics and develops concepts such as 'complementary distribution', 'allophone', maybe even "eine Art Morphembegriff" (Braunmüller 1986: 62). On the other hand Raschellà (1982, 1983), following a suggestion by Finnur Jónsson (1898), believes that the *SGT* was conceived independently of *Háttatal*, in order to organize according to a more rational pattern the orthographic practice. This view is in accordance with a later date for the *SGT*, after the Latin alphabet had been in use for some time, which is supported by the graphic-phonological analysis (Raschellà 1982: 84–91, 126–132).

The Latin tradition apparently has little, if any, part in the composition of the *SGT*. Apart from the well known question-and-answer pattern in the opening, and from the general division of letters into vowels and consonants, scholars have failed to find precise parallels in Classical tradition (see Melazzo 1985). The introductory passage, involving considerations on the typology of natural sounds, seems to result from an original reworking of materials connected with the rediscovery of Aristotle's theories in the 12th and 13th centuries and exhibits a vague similarity with passages in the *Summulae logicales*, or *Tractatus*, by Petrus Hispanus (probably written in the 1230s) and the *Summulae dialectices* by Roger Bacon (ca. 1250) (Raschellà 1982: 108 ff.).

The section dealing with the description and classification of letters also seems to be independent of Latin sources, especially in the use of a circular scheme, in which five concentric rings include all possible sounds subdivided according to type, and of a rectangular drawing comparing the phonation process with the mechanism of the hurdy-gurdy. The SG's sound classification into two main groups, according to their occurrence at the beginning or at the end of a syllable, is also peculiar.

It seems likely that the SG is acquainted with the *FGT* (or at least with one of its sources), as shown by the discernment of quantity distinctions in both vowels and consonants, by the suggestion to mark long vowels through a superscript stroke and geminate consonants through capital letters, and by the use of a loop in writing 'ligatures' (ę ǫ instead of *æ ꜵ*). According to Raschellà (1982: 114–122), the *SGT* exhibits a basically independent, original technical terminology, which in part at least may be connected with runic epigraphy of a pre-Christian phase.

4.3. The *Third Grammatical Treatise*

In contrast with the other treatises, the *ThGT* is not anonymous. Its authorship has been ascribed to Snorri's nephew, Óláfr Þórðarson hvítaskald (ca. 1212–1259), according to evidence from various sources (*ESS* II, 62, n., 76, n.; III, 378 ff.; Ólsen 1883: 63–66, 1884: xxxii ff.; F. Jónsson 1927: 3–10). He held a school at Stafaholt, and presumably wrote his treatise in connection with his tutorial activity in the years 1242/5–1252. It is often said that the *ThGT* is the only one of the four tracts to be rightly entitled to the appellative 'grammatical', being more complete in its contents in comparison with the others, but this is merely because it conforms better to the typology of the Latin *artes grammaticae*. Early editors regarded it as being divided into two parts, i. e. the *Málfræðinnar grundvöllr* "Foundations of the language science" and the *Málskrúðsfræði* "Science of the ornament of language", which are joined by a short prologue. The *Málfræðinnar grundvöllr* consists in an introduction on sound typology and a description of the various elements of language (letter, syllable, parts of speech), including also an extensive comparison between the runic row and the Latin alphabet. The *Málskrúðsfræði* incorporates a survey of language faults such as barbarism and solecism and a catalogue of rhetorical figures, with examples taken from skaldic poetry. The public addressed is that of advanced students, who already know the rules for writing correctly and wish to proceed to learning how to use their language for literary, especially poetic, purposes. This is also evident in the author's neglect of a detailed account of aspects such as morphology, the parts of speech, etc. and in his dwelling at length on theoretical considerations instead.

The *ThGT* shows an explicit link with Latin tradition. The two sections of the *ThGT* reproduce in broad lines its two main models, i. e. Books I and II of Priscian's *Institutiones grammaticae* and Book III of Donatus' *Ars maior*, although Óláfr may have used Donatus' *Ars minor*, too, in the description of the parts of speech. The introductory passage describes the different types of sound according to sources which cannot be traced precisely. Comparisons have been drawn with several Classical and medieval authors, e. g., Probus, Audax, various commentaries (Micillo 1993), and with the opening of the *SGT*, which shows some points of contact, especially in the examples provided (ibid.). It appears, however, that Óláfr's complicated typology of sound results from the combination of different sources, shared in part by the *SGT*. The first section is an elaboration, applied to sound, of the *arbor porphyriana*. The next part relies explicitly on Priscian and on the definition of *vox* as found in the *Summulae dialectices* by Roger Bacon. The closing part is a reworking of Petrus' and Bacon's sound classifications, ultimately depending upon Boethius' translations and commentaries to Aristotle's *Perì hermēneías*. Attention to Petrus' and Roger Bacon's texts had been already drawn by Raschellà (1982: 110, n.; 1983: 303). Parallels between the *ThGT*'s introductory section and passages in the two logical treatises are in some cases really striking and include precise correspondence in the wording. Petrus' text, in particular, exhibits the closest similarity and may represent a direct source.

The *Málskrúðsfræði*, in spite of all evidence, may not, or not only, rely on Donatus' work, but rather on one or more later commentaries with lemmas from Donatus. This is evident from the comparison with a closely related group of commentaries written by Irish grammarians from the 9th century, connected with Carolingian centres on the Continent, i. e., the commentaries on the *Ars maior* by Sedulius Scottus and by Murethac, and the so-called *Ars Laureshamensis* (→ Art. 73). Many specific analogies can be shown to exist between the *ThGT* and the Irish tradition represented by these three works (Micillo 1999), which borrow from the same Irish source. Ælfric's *Grammar* (end of the 10th century; → Art. 85) seems to provide a few analogies with the *ThGT* (Ólsen 1884: xxxviii–xxxix), although in some cases it is just one of the possible sources.

The superimposing of Latin grammatical and rhetorical structures to the Old Icelandic tradition and their illustration by means of vernacular examples respond to an underlying aim, revealed by Óláfr in the prologue joining the two sections – to put the vernacular poetry on equal footing with the Latin poetic tradition, and thus to show that skaldic poetry still retained its value and importance, even in comparison with the new Christian-Latin models (see Albano Leoni 1985).

4.4. The *Fourth Grammatical Treatise*

The *FoGT*, written around the middle of the 14th century (after 1319: Ólsen 1884: xliii), follows in the Codex Wormianus immediately after the *ThGT*, of which it represents a continuation, and to which it adds a number of new rhetorical figures, alongside with a new definition of some figures already in the *ThGT*. The author of the *FoGT*, whom B. M. Ólsen (1883: 44–60; 1884: xxxviii) recognized in the writer of the *Prologue* to the four grammatical treatises, probably also compiler and editor of the Codex Wormianus, adopts the same procedure as Óláfr, whose authority is explicitly cited. A series of rhetorical figures are described and illustrated by means of skaldic examples, then there follows a commentary. The main sources are two verse treatises belonging to the 12th century, i.e., Alexander de Villadei's *Doctrinale* and Ebrard of Béthune's *Graecismus* (→ Art. 81). The last section of chapter XII of Alexander's treatise forms the *FoGT*'s framework. Materials are presented in the same order as in the *Doctrinale*, while Ebrard's text provides the definition of some figures which are not dealt with by Alexander. The Fourth Grammarian may be the author of much of the commentary illustrating the examples quoted. However, in other cases he seems to refer back to other sources, probably to commentaries of the same kind as those (anyway later!) quoted by Ólsen (1884). One vernacular source, explicitly mentioned twice, is Óláfr Þórðarson's treatise (chapts. 9 and 11; Ólsen 1884: 131 and 133).

4.5. The Prologue to the Four Grammatical Treatises

The *Prologue* to the four grammatical treatises (Ólsen 1884: 152–155) contained in the Codex Wormianus has been the object of speculation since B. M. Ólsen's work from 1883. He believed that this was originally an introduction to the first part of the *ThGT* (parallel to the prologue to the second part, see above), which had been used by the editor of the Codex Wormianus as an introduction to the whole group of grammatical works (Ólsen 1883: 51 ff.; 1884: xxiii–xxv). Its function and significance have been discussed recently by Tómasson (1993), according to whom the *Prologue* contains valuable information on the very first attempts at employing the Latin alphabet for writing Icelandic and was written by the editor of the Wormianus compilation, who meant it as a defense for the use of the vernacular in poetry.

Evidence of a continuing activity in grammatical study is provided by fragments from grammatical works of various kinds. MS AM 748 I b, 4° contains the closing part of a treatise (ca. second half of 13th century) dealing with rhetorical figures which appear to belong to a native rhetorical tradition and, like in Óláfr's *Málskrúðsfræði*, are illustrated by skaldic examples (Ólsen 1884: 159, xlvii). One more grammatical piece in MS Reykjavík, AM 921 III, 4° (ca. 1400; Ólsen 1884: 156–158), obviously for use in the school, records the conjugation of the Lat. verb *amo* according to Donatus (*Ars minor*, Ólsen 1884: xliv) with the Icelandic translation of each form, in a manner which resembles Ælfric's *Grammar*.

## 5. The intellectual background

The question of the relationship between the Icelandic and the Continental grammatical tradition is a much debated one. On the evidence available it seems obvious that the Old Icelandic tradition shared much of the intellectual background of medieval Europe. The very existence in Old Icelandic of a technical vocabulary clearly showing either its direct Latin origin or the influence of the Latin tradition is one proof of this. Basic concepts such as, e. g., 'vowel', 'consonant', 'pronunciation', are expressed by means of loan translations (*raddarstafr*, *samhljóðandi*, *framfæring*), like many others, e. g., the names of the parts of speech (*fornafn*, *viðorð*, *samtenging*, corresponding to the Latin terms *pronomen*, *adverbium*, *coniunctio*). The designation of the 'verb', *orð*, literally "word", is a semantic borrowing of Lat. *verbum*, while a number of other technical terms (e. g., *persóna*, *figúra*, *partr*), are borrowed from Latin. Thus, familiarity with the canonical grammatical texts and with late antique and medieval learning in general is displayed in varying degrees by the Icelandic treatises. However, a direct knowledge of individual texts is not always easy to demonstrate. Then in many cases, even when specific sources can be located, the materials look very different from the original texts. This may sometimes be the consequence of a conscious activity of rearrangement and reworking of sources, sometimes it results from the mediation of other texts, e. g. commentaries. Generally speaking, the readings of the Icelandic grammarians appear to fall into the following types: (1) Classical grammatical tradition, (2) native grammatical and historical lore, (3) vernacular (skaldic) verse, (4) medieval commentaries, especially of Insular origin, mediated by Carolingian centres, (5) contemporary philosophical writings and, probably, (6) English grammatical tradition. As regards native grammatical sources, the hypothesis has often been made of an Icelandic grammatical 'school', supported, on the one hand, by the very existence of a flourishing vernacular tradition, and on the other, by the circumstance that in several cases the Icelandic treatises seem to refer to sources unknown to us, which show a peculiar 'flavour' and diverge sensibly from those of Latin origin. A local tradition has been postulated also on the basis of a number of linguistic terms, which may be the reflex of a native, pre-Christian tradition (Raschellà 1982: 114–122). As regards Classical grammatical tradition in general, explicit reference to authors and texts is scanty and in practice it is limited to the *ThGT*. However, the case of the *ThGT* shows very clearly that if our knowledge of medieval texts is implemented, the dependence of Icelandic grammatical writing on the commentary tradition will become much clearer than it is now.

## 6. Bibliography

### 6.1. Primary sources

#### 6.1.1. Editions

Albano Leoni, Federico. 1975. *Il primo trattato grammaticale islandese. Introduzione, testo, traduzione e commento.* Bologna: Il Mulino. [*FGT*, with an Italian transl.]

Benediktsson, Hreinn. 1972. *The First Grammatical Treatise. Introduction, text, notes, translation, vocabulary, facsimiles.* (= *University of Iceland Publications in Linguistics*, 1.) Reykjavík: Institute of Nordic Linguistics. [*FGT*, with an English transl.]

*ESS* = *Edda Snorra Sturlusonar. Edda Snorronis Sturlæi.* 3 vols. 1848–87. Hafniæ: Sumptibus legati Arnamagnæani. [The four grammatical treatises according to the Codex Wormianus, with a Latin transl.]

Haugen, Einar. 1972. *First Grammatical Treatise: The earliest Germanic phonology. An edition, translation and commentary.* 2nd. rev. ed. London: Longman. (1st. ed., 1950.) [*FGT*, with an English transl.]

Jónsson, Finnur. 1927. *Óláfr Þórðarson. Málhljóða- og málskrúðsrit: Grammatisk-retorisk afhandling.* (= *Det Kgl. Danske Videnskabernes Selskab, Hist.-filolog. Meddelelser*, 13, 2.) Copenhagen. [*ThGT*; normalized ed.]

Mogk, Eugen. 1889. "Untersuchungen zur Snorra-Edda. I. Der sogenannte [sic] zweite grammatische traktat der Snorra-Edda". *Zeitschrift für deutsche Philologie* 22, 3.129–167. [*SGT*, with a German transl.]

Ólsen, Björn Magnússon. 1884. *Den tredje og fjærðe grammatiske afhandling i Snorres Edda, tilligemed de grammatiske afhandlingers prolog og to andre tillæg.* (= *Samfund til udgivelse af gammel nordisk literatur*, vol. XII: *Islands gramm. lit. i middelald.*, 1.) Copenhagen. [*ThGT*, *FoGT*, *Prologue*, other fragments.]

Raschellà, Fabrizio D. 1982. *The So-Called Second Grammatical Treatise. Edition, translation and commentary.* Firenze: Le Monnier. [*SGT*, with an English transl.]

#### 6.2.1. Translations

Collings, Lucy G. 1967. *The 'Málskrúðsfræði' and the Latin Tradition in Iceland.* Unpubl. MA thesis. Cornell University. Ithaca, NY. [Engl. transl. of the second part of *ThGT*.]

Krömmelbein, Thomas. 1998. *Óláfr Þórðarson Hvitaskáld. Dritte Grammatische Abhandlung. Der isländische Text nach den Handschriften AM 748 I, 4° und Codex Wormianus, herausgegeben von Björn Magnus* [sic for Magnússon] *Ólsen*. Oslo: Novus Forlag [Germ. transl. of Ólsen's edition.]

### 6.2. Secondary sources

Albano Leoni, Federico. 1977. "Beiträge zur Deutung des isländischen 'Ersten grammatischen Abhandlung'". *Arkiv för nordisk filologi* 92.70–91.

–. 1985. "Donato in Thule: Kenningar e tropi nel terzo trattato grammaticale islandese". *Cultura classica e cultura germanica settentrionale. Atti del Convegno Internazionale di Studi – Macerata-S. Severino Marche, 2–4 maggio 1985* ed. by Pietro Janni et al., 385–498. Macerata: Università di Macerata. (Repr., *Annali dell'Istituto Universitario Orientale – Filologia germanica* 28–29 [1985–86] 1–15.)

–. 1988. "La tradizione grammaticale latina nell'Islanda medievale". *L'héritage des grammairiens latins de l'antiquitè aux lumières. Actes du Colloque de Chantilly 2–4 sept. 1987* ed. by Irène Rosier, 233–244. Paris: Société pour l'information grammaticale.

–. 1996. "Icelandic grammars". *Lexicon Grammaticorum. Who's Who in the History of World Linguistics* ed. by Harro Stammerjohann et al., 456–457. Tübingen: Niemeyer.

Árnason, Kristján. 1993. "Málfræðihugmyndir Sturlunga". *Íslenskt mál og almenn málfræði* 15. 173–206.

Benediktsson, Hreinn. 1965. *Early Icelandic Script as Illustrated in Vernacular Texts from the Twelfth and Thirteenth Centuries.* Reykjavík: The Manuscript Institute of Iceland.

Bergsveinsson, Sveinn. 1942. "Wie alt ist die 'phonologische Opposition'?". *Archiv für vergleichende Phonetik* 6.59–64.

Braunmüller, Kurt. 1983. "Der sog. Zweite Grammatische Traktat: Ein verkanntes Zeugnis altisländischer Sprachanalyse". *Akten der Fünften Arbeitstagung der Skandinavisten des deutschen Sprachgebiets* ed. by Heiko Uecker, 45–56. St. Augustin: Kretschmer. (Repr., Kurt Braunmüller, *Beiträge zur skandinavistischen Linguistik*, 210–226. Oslo: Novus Forlag 1995.)

–. 1984. "Fandtes der en fonotaktisk analyse i middelalderen?". *The Nordic Languages and Modern Linguistics* V ed. by Kristian Ringgaard & Viggo Sørensen, 221–229. Århus: Nordisk Institut, Århus Universitet.

–. 1986. "Mittelalterliche Sprachanalysen: Einige Anmerkungen aus heutiger Sicht". *Germanic Dialects: Linguistic and philological investigations* ed. by Bela Brogyanyi & Thomas Krömmelbein, 43–79. Amsterdam & Philadelphia: Benjamins.

Christiansen, Hallfrid. 1946. "Verdens første fonolog". Unpubl. paper. Oslo Videnskaps-Akademi.

Foote, Peter. 1984. "Latin Rhetoric and Icelandic Poetry: Some Contacts". *Aurvandilstá. Norse Studies* ed. by Michael Barnes et al., 249–270. Odense: Odense Univ. Press. (Originally published, *Saga och sed* [1982] 107–127.)

Hagland, Jan Ragnar. 1993. "Møte mellom to skriftspråkskulturar? Til spørsmålet om runeskrift har noko å seia for lingvistisk analyse i Første grammatiske avhandling". *Íslenskt mál og almenn málfræði* 15.159–171.

Helgason, Jón. 1970. "Þriðji íhaldskarl". *Fróðskaparrit. Annales Societatis Scientiarum Færoensis* 18.206–226.

Holtsmark, Anne. 1936. *En islandsk scholasticus fra det 12. århundre.* (= *Skrifter utgitt av Det Norske Videnskaps-Akademi i Oslo*, vol. II: *Hist.-Filos. Klasse*, 3.) Oslo.

–. 1960. "Grammatisk litteratur om modersmålet". *Kulturhistorisk Leksikon for Nordisk Middelalder*, V, 414–419. Copenhagen: Gyldendal.

Jónsson, Finnur. 1898. "Edda Snorra Sturlusonar: dens oprindelige form og sammensætning". *Aarbøger for Nordisk Oldkyndighed og Historie*, 2. rk., 13.283–357.

Koerner, E. F. K[onrad]. 1997. "Einar Haugen as a historian of linguistics". *American Journal of Germanic Linguistics and Literatures* 9:2.221–238.

Kusmenko, Jurij K. 1993. "Einige Bemerkungen zu den altisländischen grammatischen Abhandlungen". *skandinavistik* 23:2.85–95.

Lehmann, Paul. 1937. *Skandinaviens Anteil an der lateinischen Literatur und Wissenschaft des Mittelalters.* 2. Stück. München: Bayerische Akademie der Wissenschaften. (Repr., Paul Lehmann, *Erforschung des Mittelalters*, V, 331–429. Stuttgart: Anton Hiersemann, 1962.)

Malm, Mats. 1990. "Sannkenningars egentliga egenskaper". *Arkiv för nordisk filologi* 105.111–130.

Melazzo, Lucio. 1985. "The Opening of the so called Second Grammatical Treatise: In search of the sources". *Cultura classica e cultura germanica settentrionale. Atti del Convegno Internazionale di Studi – Macerata-S. Severino Marche, 2–4 maggio 1985* ed. by Pietro Janni et al., 399–424. Macerata: Università di Macerata.

Micillo, Valeria. 1993. "Classical Tradition and Norse Tradition in the 'Third Grammatical Treatise'". *Arkiv för nordisk filologi* 108.68–79.

–. 1994. "La terminologia tecnica nel *Terzo trattato grammaticale islandese*". *Annali dell'Istituto Universitario Orientale* – sezione germanica, N. S. 4:1–2.125–142.

–. 1995. "Motivi letterari medievali nel prologo del *Terzo trattato grammaticale islandese*". *Annali dell'Istituto Universitario Orientale* – sezione germanica, N. S. 5:1–2.65–81.

–. 1999. "Die grammatische Tradition des insularen Mittelalters in Island: Spuren insularer Einflüsse im *Dritten Grammatischen Traktat*". *Übersetzung, Adaptation und Akkulturation im Insularen Mittelalter* ed. by Erich Poppe & Hildegard L. C. Tristram, 215–229. Münster: Nodus Publikationen.

Olmer, Emil. 1902. *Boksamlingar på Island 1179–1490.* (= *Göteborgs högskolas årsskrift* VIII, 2.) Göteborg: Wettergren & Kerber.

Ólsen, Björn Magnússon. 1883. *Runerne i den oldislandske litteratur.* Copenhagen: Gyldendal.

Pálsson, Hermann. 1965. "Fyrsta málfræðiritgerðin og upphaf íslenzkrar sagnaritunar". *Skírnir* 139.159–177.

–. 1982. "'Malum non vitatur, nisi cognitum'". *Gripla* 5.115–126.

Perridon, Harry. 1985. "Neutralization, Archiphonemes and the *First grammatical treatise*". *Amsterdamer Beiträge zur älteren Germanistik* 23.71–96.

Raschellà, Fabrizio D. 1983. "Die altisländische grammatische Literatur: Forschungsstand und Perspektiven zukünftiger Untersuchungen". *Göttingische Gelehrte Anzeigen* 235:3–4.271–315.

–. 1993. "Grammatical Treatises". *Medieval Scandinavia. An Encyclopedia* ed. by Phillip Pulsiano, 235–237. New York & London: Garland.

–. 1994. "Rune e alfabeto latino nel trattato grammaticale di Óláfr Þórðarson". *Sagnaþing helgað Jónasi Kristjánssyni sjötugum (10. Apríl 1994)* ed. by Gísli Sigurðsson et al., 679–690. Reykjavík: Hið íslenska bokmenntafélag.

Robins, Robert H. 1979. *A Short History of Linguistics.* 2nd. ed. London: Longman. (1st. ed., 1967.)

Santini, Carlo. 1994. "'Kenningar Donati': An investigation of the classical models in the *Third Icelandic Grammatical Treatise*". *International Journal of the Classical Tradition* 2:1.37–44.

Tómasson, Sverrir. 1988a. *Formálar íslenskra sagnaritara à miðöldum.* Reykjavík: Stofnun Árna Magnússonar.

–. 1988b. "Fyrsta málfræðiritgerðin og íslensk menntun á 12. öld". *Tímarit Háskola Íslands* 3.71–78.

–. 1993. "Formáli málfræðiritgerðanna fjögurra í Wormsbók". *Íslenskt mál og almenn málfræði* 15.221–240.

Ulvestad, Bjarne. 1976. "Grein sú er máli skiptir: Tools and traditions in the *First Grammatical Treatise*". *Historiographia Linguistica* 3:2.203–223.

–. 1995. "Noch einmal: *Die erste grammatische Abhandlung*". *skandinavistik* 25:1.51–59.

Walter, Ernst. 1971. "Die lateinische Sprache und Literatur auf Island und in Norwegen bis zum Beginn des 13. Jahrhunderts: Ein Orientierungsversuch". *Nordeuropa. Studien* 4.195–230.

Widding, Ole. 1965. "Skriften". *Norrøn Fortællekunst: Kapitler af den norsk-islandske middelalderlitteraturs historie* ed. by Hans Bekker-Nielsen et al., 27–34. Copenhagen: Akademisk Forlag.

*Valeria Micillo, Naples (Italy)*

# 85. Ælfric and his relation to the Latin tradition

1. Introduction
2. Background
3. The *Grammar*
4. The *Colloquy* and *Glossary*
5. Conclusion
6. Bibliography

## 1. Introduction

In the history of linguistic scholarsphip, the Anglo-Saxons have played an important role as catalystic agents in the transformation of *grammatica* – the science of interpreting the poets and other writers and the systematic principles for speaking and writing correctly (Irvine 1994: xiii) – from a discipline concerning the mother tongue to the study of a second language. Broadly speaking, this process covered two periods separated by the devastating Viking attacks in the 9th century. The earlier period witnessed the tradition of Insular, i. e. Irish and Anglo-Saxon, grammatical scholarship, while the second period saw the rise of a vernacular Anglo-Saxon culture which adopted the textual values of Latin grammatical culture, as well as various literary genres (Irvine 1994: 405). The Anglo-Saxon Abbot Ælfric (955–1020/25), also known as *Ælfric Grammaticus*, provided the culmination of this vernacularisation of linguistic scholarship by compiling a grammar of Latin in Old English – the first ever written in a European vernacular – for students in a monastic school (Law 1993: vii). Although Ælfric's preoccupation with teaching Latin also resulted in a glossary and a colloquy, this grammar has given him pride of place among Anglo-Saxon language scholars in the 10th and 11th centuries.

## 2. Background

To understand the tradition of Anglo-Saxon scholarship in which Ælfric worked, it is imperative that we briefly go back some 300 years in Anglo-Saxon history, to the arrival of Archbishop Theodore of Tarsus in May 669, and his companion, the North-African Abbot Hadrian. In their Canterbury school they studied Biblical exegesis, chronology, metrics, Roman law, and, above all, Latin and Greek (Lapidge 1986: 45–72); and attracted students from far and wide. Their most illustrious pupil was Aldhelm of Malmesbury, whose learning was based not only on the Canterbury School but also on the Irish tradition of scholarship that he had picked up at Malmesbury Abbey, founded by the Irish Saint Maeldubh. Aldhelm, in turn, influenced the Venerable Bede (673–735), whose scholarship also reached back to the school of Theodore and Hadrian via his teacher, the Northumbrian Benedict Bishop. Bede's learning was prodigal, and his writings concerned not only history and liturgy but also Latin. The main reason for Aldhelm, Bede, and others to write about Latin was the need to teach Anglo-Saxon priests the doctrines of the Church. Their efforts form part of an Insular tradition of grammar writing, which ultimately had its roots in the rich heritage of Classical and Late Latin grammarians.

With the missionary activities of English and Irish monks, Insular manuscripts, including grammars and glossaries, were transferred to the continent where they were studied and multiplied. The scholarship derived from them formed a major contribution to the Carolingian Renaissance, which, in turn, instigated a renewed interest in Classical learning. It was the Anglo-Saxon scholar Alcuin (735–804) whose work on grammar initiated a return to the Roman and Late Latin grammarians (Law 1987: 103; → Art. 74).

Alcuin was still alive when the first Vikings attacks devastated the abbey of Lindisfarne, in 793. Less than a century later, in 877, the sole remaining English king, Alfred of Wessex, was forced to take refuge in the marshes of Somerset, and the tradition of Anglo-Saxon learning had all but disappeared. After he restored the West-Saxon Kingdom, Alfred set out to rebuild the State and Church by means of an educational program that focused on the diffusion of important historical and ecclesiastical works. In his famous preface to the Old English translation of Gregory the Great's *Cura Pastoralis*, the King expressed his concern at the state of learning in his kingdom and complained that there was hardly a priest in England who could translate English into Latin. Alfred stressed the need for teachers and set the example by translating some important books into Latin and ordering the translation of several others. His actions had far-reaching consequences: the study of both English and Latin became the pivot of a campaign for literacy, and more than ever before, the vernacular started to play a role in domains hitherto reserved for Latin. The basis of this entire "hybrid Latin and English grammatical culture" lay in the role of *grammatica* in European scholarship (Irvine 1994: 406).

King Alfred's campaign to restore the state of learning in England contributed indirectly to Ælfric's education, since the emphasis on the vernacular continued to exist after Alfred's death in 899 (Smyth 1995: 565–566). Little more than half a century later, the efforts of St. Dunstan, Archbishop of Canterbury from 960 to 988, and his famous pupil Æthelwold, who was appointed Bishop of Winchester in 963, occasioned a monastic revival in England, inspired by the Benedictine reform of Cluny. Ancient monasteries were re-founded or reformed and, in them, schools were set up to teach the regular as well as the secular clergy. Dunstan's *Class-book*, which contains grammatical texts as well as Classical and medieval fragments (Irvine 1994: 407–411), is evidence of his promoting grammatical studies, which lay at the heart of Benedictine tuition.

Even though Ælfric had received some prior Latin instruction, his principal education took place at Æthelwold's school in Winchester, where his ideas about Latin and the vernacular took shape. After he finished his schooling around 987, he was sent to the recently established abbey of Cerne Abbas in Dorset where he was responsible for the monastic school. In 1005 Ælfric became Abbot of the newly founded abbey of Eynsham near Oxford, where he spent the final years of his life. In the Winchester tradition, Ælfric's main activities concentrated on teaching, writing and translating, which resulted in numerous works of great interest. His Old English writings include two sets of sermons known as his *Catholic Homilies*, a series of *Saints' Lives*, pastoral letters, translations of various books of the Bible and of Bede's *De Temporibus Anni*. However, his most important works for our purposes are his Latin *Grammar*, his *Glossary* and his *Colloquy*; three works specifically aimed at the teaching of Latin to young monks, and written, according to Clemoes (1959: 244), between 992 and 1002 when he was teaching at Cerne Abbas. The *Grammar*, *Glossary* and *Colloquy* together fit in what Law (1987: 51) described as the main aim of Ælfric's work: "to provide a body of literature through which the monk or nun with only a scanty knowledge of Latin could nonetheless come to understand the Christian faith".

## 3. The *Grammar*

Ælfric's *Grammar* is unique for being in English, but it is not the only 10th-century grammar intended specifically as an introduction to Latin. One such work, a parsing grammar entitled *Beatus Quid Est*, has been preserved in a collection of educational texts that also includes Ælfric's *Grammar*. Both works rely on Classical and Late Latin grammars for their material, but, unlike Ælfric's *Grammar*, *Beatus quid est* was written in question-and-answer form and was probably designed to be learnt by heart. That *Beatus Quid Est* was not the only parsing grammar around is demonstrated by a list of books owned by a grammarian named Athelstan, which dates from the second half of the 10th century. It includes a grammar book entitled *Terra quae pars*, of which a copy has been found in Bern (Lapidge 1985: 53–54). Another parsing grammar, beginning *Iustus quae pars*, has been discovered in an English manuscript. However, whereas other contemporary elementary grammars were written in Latin, Ælfric deliberately chose to present his work in the vernacular, an approach that set him apart from both contemporaneous and preceding scholars.

In his Old English preface, Ælfric reveals why he chose the vernacular as his medium. Indirectly, he referred back to King Alfred's introduction to Gregory's *Cura Pastoralis* by warning monks and priests that knowledge of the holy doctrines should never more be allowed to decline or cease to exist as it had done previously. A vernacular grammar provided an extra assurance that, in the case of a similar disaster, knowledge of Latin could easily be picked up (Law 1987: 56). Another reason is presumably that the initial stage of teaching Latin took place in English, and that the use of that language therefore corresponded to class-room practice (Riché 1981: 115). To underline the elementary level of his work, Ælfric stressed that the book was designed for "young children" until they had reached a more advanced level. The vernacular served as a temporary didactic instrument.

The vernacular as a medium presented Ælfric with the problem of finding clear and unambiguous renderings of Latin grammatical terms and devising a suitable metalanguage. Each Latin term is translated or explained at least once in the *Grammar*, although the frequency with which these translations return varies. In general, Ælfric prefers the Latin terms to the English; in a table of occurrences of Latin and English, Williams (1958: 461–462) shows that Latin is used almost to the exclusion of English in instances such as *diptongus*, *conjunctivus*, *infinitivus*, *optativus*, *neutrum*, *supinum*, and the names of the cases. Variations in the nature of Ælfric's English terminology suggest an existing tradition of discussing Latin grammar in English. Several terms indicating basic concepts like *nama*, *nomen*; *word*, *verbum*; *dæl*, *pars*; *stæf*, *littera*; etc., were used commonly without their Latin counterparts (Williams 1958: 461–462; Law 1987: 62–63). They are logical translations of the Latin terms and consist of words also otherwise applied in Old English. Most other English terms consist of literal translations of the Latin originals. Law (1987: 63) indicates that "their formation is reminiscent of the lexical glossing commonplace in late Anglo-Saxon manuscripts", and distinguishes between loan translation, e. g. *prae-positio* > *fore-set-nys*; loan rendition, e. g. *pro-nomen* > *naman spel-iend*; loan words, e. g. *declinung*; and paraphrases, e. g. *denominativum* > *eal þæt of naman cymð*. It is evident that Ælfric, a gifted translator, was concerned with principles of translation. In the introduction to his translation of Genesis, he professed that "whoever teaches or translates from Latin to English must always arrange it according to the structure of the English language, otherwise any reader unacquainted with the structure of Latin will be misled". However, he explained in the Latin preface to the *Grammar* that for didactic reasons he "followed a simple translation, so as to avoid putting off the reader". He continues by exclaiming that he is "content to express it just as we mastered it in the school of the venerable prelate Æthelwold, who inspired many to good". Besides a formal apology for his style of translation, this last remark can be seen as further evidence of an existing tradition of discussing Latin grammar in English.

Ælfric's reference to the "school of Æthelwold" also indicates that the immediate sources of his grammatical knowledge have to be looked for in the Benedictine movement. Presumably, the school of Æthelwold offered a considerable variety of works on grammar. Concrete evidence of books used by a 10th-century grammarian can be found in the aforementioned list of books owned by the grammarian Athelstan, which includes *De Arte Metrica*, presumably by Bede; Donatus's *Ars Minor*; Donatus's *Ars Major*; a work by Alcuin, presumably *De orthographia* or *De grammatica*; the aforementioned *Terra quae pars*; and a *Glossa super Donatum*, which Lapidge considers to be one of the Late Latin commentaries on Donatus (Lapidge 1985: 50–52). Other books on grammar found in Anglo-Saxon booklists from the 10th–12th centuries include anonymous treatises entitled *Tractatus grammatice artis*; *Liber magnus de grammatica arte*; Sedulius Scottus's *Ars grammatica*; and Sergius's *De voce et littera* (Lapidge 1985: 82–89). The materials used by the Benedictine movement did not directly derive from an English or Insular tradition of grammatical scholarship, but, just like the reform itself, originated mostly from elsewhere.

After the demise of the English scholarly tradition at the hands of the Vikings, the instruments of learning were imported from the Continent. However, Law (1982: 98–108) describes how Continental grammatical scholarship was mostly based on both Insular and Classical grammars transferred by Anglo-Saxon and Irish missionaries to newly founded abbeys on the Continent in the 7th and 8th centuries, where the study of these grammars was continued (→ Art. 72). From the 9th century onwards, Carolingian scholars turned back to Classical authors like Donatus and Priscian; they reworked Insular texts, abridged and abbreviated Classical works and compiled collections of excerpts from various grammars. Out of these adaptations new grammars were compiled, which were often shorter and easier to understand than their Classical predecessors (Law 1982: 103–104).

Although it was formerly believed that Ælfric used a selection of original works to compile his own grammar (e. g. Bolognesi 1965), in fact he selected one of these adaptations as a basis for his Old English translation. The German philologist Max Förster pointed out in 1917 that Ælfric's exemplar was a 10th-century compilation entitled *Excerptiones de Prisciano*, a copy of which Förster had inspected in the library of the Museum Plantin Moretus, in Antwerp. Although this manuscript (now Antwerp, Museum Plantin Moretus MS 16.2) originates from England and contains Old English marginal glosses which are related to glosses found at the end of extant copies of Ælfric's *Grammar*, Förster concluded on the grounds of textual discrepancies that the Antwerp copy could not have been Ælfric's exemplar. Law (1987: 51–54), who described this as yet unedited text, identified several other manuscripts, and signals that the method of compilation is typical of Ælfric:

"This procedure would parallel exactly his method of compiling his homilies, where he first prepared a Latin version of the text he proposed to use as his basis, rearranging its content and interpolating material from other sources" (Law 1987: 66).

In her analysis of the *Excerptiones*, Law (1987: 51–54) describes it as "a fairly lengthy work" in which the compiler attempted to fit Priscian's *Institutiones grammaticae* into the framework of Donatus's *Ars maior*. He left out those aspects from Priscian which were not touched upon by Donatus, and wished to make Priscian's grammatical scholarship accessible with the help of Donatus's more familiar paradigm. Moreover, the compiler condensed Priscian's material, leaving out lengthy Latin quotations. Where Priscian relied on the Greek tradition – he worked at Constantinople at the turn of the 5th century (Law 1982: 20–21) – the compiler of the *Excerptiones* adapted it to the Late Latin paradigm. As a result, the order of the parts of speech was altered, and Priscian's Greek examples were all changed into Latin words and phrases. With regard to the resulting structure of the work, Law signals a typological correspondence to 8th-century *Declinationes nominum* tracts, which were made up of paradigms introduced by short comments, followed by long lists of examples (Law 1987: 53; 1982: 56–64). However, the compiler of the *Excerptiones* kept the number of examples limited and did not systematize the various cases into paradigms. Examples reminiscent of Classical pagan culture were replaced by words of a Christian nature, something Christian grammarians had been doing since the 5th century (Law 1982: 30–31). Following the information from Priscian's *Institutiones grammaticae*, there are further excerpts from Priscian's *De figuris numerorum* and a section, headed *Triginta diuisiones grammaticae artis*, which derives mainly from the first book of Isidore's *Etymologiae*, but which also contains parts of Bede's *De arte metrica* and *De schematibus et tropis* (Law 1987: 54). Ælfric's *Grammar* is a yet abbreviated Old English rendering of this text.

Bearing this in mind, together with the fact that Ælfric followed the text of his exemplar quite closely (Law 1987: 59), the question remains to what extent Ælfric himself might have been involved in the compilation of the *Excerptiones in Prisciano*. Although Law remains undecided, Lapidge (1991: cxlix–cl) holds that it "is arguably the work of Ælfric, for it served as the basis for his grammar". Lapidge based his assumption about Ælfric's authorship of the *Excerptiones* on Ælfric's modus operandi, and stated that "Ælfric was by nature an abbreviator". He illustrates this by means of an early 11th-century commonplace-book in Ælfric's own hand, found in Boulogne-sur-mer, and a copy of a hagiographical commonplace-book found in Paris, which both contain abbreviated excerpts from various Latin works that were used by Ælfric for the compilation of several homilies, saint's lives and pastoral letters. The manuscripts show that Ælfric first collected excerpts from Latin works he was interested in, and subsequently compiled a new text out of these excerpts (Lapidge 1991: cxlviii). The aim of this procedure was to achieve clarity and conciseness in his work. His much quoted remark from the introduction to the Lives of Saints demonstrates that he applied brevity for stylistic as well as didactic purposes:

"It is further to be noted that I abridge the more extensive lives, not in sense but in wording, so that boredom will not be inflicted on weary readers if the vernacular version should end up as lengthy as the Latin original: brevity does not always disfigure speech but very frequently renders it more attractive" (text and translation from Lapidge 1991: cl).

Although the question as to Ælfric's involvement with the compilation of the *Excerptiones* remains unsolved, many characteristics of Ælfric's method and principles can be recognized in the *Excerptiones* as well as in its Old English rendering.

The importance of Ælfric's *Grammar* in the 11th and 12th centuries is reflected by its popularity and the degree of its institutionalisation. Gneuss's "preliminary list of manuscripts written or owned in England up to 1100" lists 24 manuscripts or fragments of manuscripts containing grammatical texts, of which no fewer than 13 contain Ælfric's *Grammar*, whereas relatively few other grammars are found in 11th-century manuscripts (Law 1987: 63–64). Therefore, the degree to which Ælfric's *Grammar* derived its information from Classical and/or Insular predecessors is largely indicative of the influence of these earlier grammarians on grammatical education in 11th-century England. Unaware of the relation between Ælfric's Old English *Grammar* and the *Excerptiones*, Teresa Pàroli (1967–1968) made a detailed analysis of it, starting from the assumption that Ælfric compiled his *Grammar* directly from Classical sources. Although her work has lost some of its relevance, it still gives a good overview of the influences present in Ælfric's work, and of the sources of the *Excerptiones*.

Besides excerpts from Donatus and Priscian, material from various other authors occurs in Ælfric's work, both grammatical definitions and examples. Even if Ælfric were not the original compiler, it is quite likely that he knew its components from the school of Æthelwold in Winchester. In the section *De littera* (Zupitza 1880: 4–7), Pàroli (1967: 12–13) recognized elements from a Donatus commentary by Sergius, presumably – although she does not make it clear – the commentary on the *Ars maior* I (Law 1982: 17). This same section as well as the one on *De diptongis* (Zupitza 1880: 7–8) also show traces of comments attributed to Servius (Pàroli 1967: 14), a North African grammarian who commented on Donatus and Virgil (Amsler 1993: 54–55). Both Servius and Sergius are also named as possible sources for parts of the *Praefatio de partibus orationis* (Zupitza 1880: 8–18; Pàroli 1967: 14–21). In the section on the five declensions of nouns (Zupitza 1880: 21–32), Ælfric's *Grammar* depended on one of Priscian's minor works, *Institutio de nomine, pronomine et verbo*, which contains a short exposition on the inflecting parts of speech and was a very popular grammatical work in the 7th and 8th centuries (Pàroli 1967: 22; Law 1982: 21). Another minor work by Priscian, *Partitiones duodecim versuum Aenidos principalium*, was also used repeatedly (Pàroli 1968a: 128). The definition of the pronoun was supplied by Isidore's *Etymologiae* I, viii, 1, which was also used in other places (Pàroli 1967: 15), not only for grammatical definitions but also for examples. Further sources of examples distinguished by Pàroli (1967: 35–36; 1968a: 83) include Probus's *Catholica*, *Appendix Probi* and *Instituta artium*, works which were relatively little known during the Middle Ages (Law 1982: 26–27), and a treatise entitled *De Accentibus*, once attributed to Priscian, but probably from a later date (Pàroli 1967: 35). The sources discovered by Pàroli demonstrate that the Insular tradition played little – or no role in Ælfric's Old English *Grammar*, and presumably this also holds good for the *Excerptiones in Prisciano*. Only Law's suggestion (1987: 54) that some of Ælfric's additional examples may derive from a *Declinationes Nominum* text may suggest Insular influence.

By replacing and adding examples, Ælfric deliberately gave the *Grammar* a local Anglo-Saxon as well as a Christian character. Replacing traditional words referring to Classical literature by words from the Christian tradition had been characteristic of early Medieval grammars, not least of the Insular grammarians (Law 1982: 30–41; → Art. 73). Although the full extent of Ælfric's changes is yet to be determined – the *Excerptiones* may well derive from a Christianised *Institutiones grammaticae* – he still saw further need to purge his texts from pagan reminiscences. Examples listed by Law (1987: 58) include the change of *pius et fortis fuit Aeneas* to *pius et fortis fuit David rex* (Zupitza 1880: 258), and the addition of Biblical verses to the discussion of impersonal verbs and conjunctions (Zupitza 1880: 206–207, 261). The examples from local contemporaneous Anglo-Saxon life are more typical (Law 1987: 56–58). The names of *Æthelwold*, *Edgar* and *Dunstan* occur; patronyms include *Penda* and *Pendingas*; *Beda* occurs among the first-declension masculines. Other words, like *cantor*, *sangere*; *cantrix*, *sangestre* recur in the *Glossary*, while yet other words and sentences resemble lines and topics in the *Colloquy*, reinforcing the relation between these three works.

These typically Anglo-Saxon examples indicate that Ælfric was more than just a translator, even if we leave his role in the compilation of the *Excerptiones* out of account. His personal contribution appears not only in his selection of material but also in his elaborations on various subjects where he considered the information in his exemplars insufficient, including Latin morphology, the function of the cases and possessive pronouns (Law 1987: 59–60). In several of his explanations, Ælfric draws comparisons or indicates contrasts between Latin and Old English, such as his observations on words with a different gender in the two languages, his statement that all six Latin copulative conjunctions were to be translated by English "and", and the conclusion that each language had different interjections which could not easily be translated (Zupitza 1880: 18–19, 259, 279–280). Such observations have given rise to questions about the contrastive nature of Ælfric's *Grammar*. After all, he based his ideas and principles on Æthelwold's school at Winchester, where education centred around the study of language, English as well as Latin, and which has been considered instrumental in the development and spreading of a standard form of Old English (Gneuss 1972: 63–83). Law (1987: 60) disclaims that the *Grammar* shows how Ælfric perveived the structure of English, but Derolez (1989: 472–474, 476) argues that "Ælfric was well aware of the fact that each language had its individual character and structure" and that, consequently, the "*Latin Grammar* should be studied not only for its sources but also as a contrastive grammar *avant la lettre*". Although further study may bring more examples to light – for instance, the observation that patronyms did not occur in Latin, but were nevertheless found in English (Zupitza 1880: 14–15) – the amount of evidence in the *Grammar* for a deliberate contrastive approach seems rather small.

The most apparent purpose of Ælfric's English *Grammar* was its function as a didactic instrument to teach the rudiments of Latin to Anglo-Saxon pupils. Law (1987: 55) considers Ælfric's *Grammar* typical of a recurring phenomenon in language studies: "the filtering-down of doctrine originally at the forefront of research to the most elementary pedagogical levels". This skillful didactic approach would then prepare them for the study of unabridged Latin grammars. Another, but no less important aim of the *Grammar* is the teaching of vocabulary, which was essential if students wished to attain the level of knowledge required to understand the documents setting out the doctrines of the Christian Church. The great store of examples together with English translations makes the *Grammar* an extensive Latin-English vocabulary, an aspect which is borne out by its relation to two other didactic tools employed by Ælfric: a colloquy between a master and his pupils and a Latin-Old English glossary.

## 4. The *Colloquy* and *Glossary*

The *Colloquy* has been regarded as a companion piece to the *Grammar* because the latter work occasionally features fragments of similar dialogues, describing scenes of everyday life, and ostentatiously listing the tools of the trade (Law 1987: 57; Lendinara 1983: 187). Questions like *Quales pisces capis?* (Garmonsway 1966: 27), moreover, gave rise to small word lists, in this case types of fish, and this links the *Grammar* to the *Glossary* as well. The aim of the *Colloquy*, as that of its companion pieces, is clearly didactic: Porter (1994: 464, 469) claims that the dialogue was meant to train pupils to speak Latin properly – the *recta locutio* – but above all, to teach Latin vocabulary; Irvine (1994: 414) considers reading to be Ælfric's main aim. The interlinear Old English glosses, in London, British Library MS Cotton Tiberius A. iii, are presumably not by Ælfric but by a later revisor.

Although the use of dialogues for the diffusion of knowledge can be traced back to Antiquity, Plato being perhaps the best example, the origin of the dialogue as a tool in language education is traditionally attributed to the 4th-century Roman grammarian Dositheus, whose *Ars Grammatica Dosithei Magistri* was designed for teaching Greek to Romans or vice versa. An unknown later revisor added to this grammar exercises for students to memorise or translate, as well as lists of conjugated verbs, nouns grouped according to their declensions, and words according their meanings (Garmonsway 1959: 249–254). This collection, known as the *Hermeneumata Pseudo-Dositheana*, became an important tool in monastic schools for teaching Latin and Greek, traditionally referred to as *Uterque Lingua*, a term first used in this context by Horace (Bullough 1972: 460). It is indicative of the Anglo-Saxon attitude to languages in the 10th and 11th centuries that King Alfred's biographer, Bishop Asser of Sherborne, refers to Latin and English by means of this very term (Keynes & Lapidge 1983: 90), something Ælfric repeated in the Latin preface to his *Grammar* (Bullough 1972: 460; Zupitza 1880: 1). These parallels at least suggest that the traditional method of teaching Greek to Latin students may have formed a source of inspiration for Ælfric's methodology; perhaps even his own experience of mastering Greek, of which he knew only little.

Ælfric's *Colloquy* surpasses traditional colloquies in that the dialogues between the master and his pupils touch on various contemporary occupations and afford a view of the Anglo-Saxon world rarely found anywhere else (Lendinara 1983: 186–187). Its imaginative and clear dialogue has delighted students of Anglo-Saxon so much that they have been inclined to attribute it to genuine class room situations (Garmonsway 1966: 8; Porter 1994: 469). This also holds true for the colloquies by one of his pupils, Ælfric Bata, who expanded his master's work into vivid descriptions of monastic life (Lendinara 1993: 272). In the work of Ælfric Bata, the didactic approach taken by his master and himself becomes even clearer. He listed series of grammatically different examples expressing the same meaning, thus showing their awareness of the difference between meaning and structure, and their preference of a communicative approach (Porter 1994: 467–469). Just like Ælfric, Ælfric Bata's main aim was teaching vocabulary, and he filled his lines with synonyms, intrusive glosses and lists of related words, part of which he derived from Ælfric's Latin-Old English *Glossary* (Porter 1994: 469–473).

This *Glossary* is a class glossary, and it follows the *Grammar* in seven of the eleven manuscripts (Derolez 1992: 20; Law 1987: 59). Unlike the *Glossae collectae*, which derived from attempts to clarify difficult Latin texts, class glossaries listed words in categories according to their meaning, and had a didactic purpose. Thomson (1981: 155–157) described Ælfric's *Glossary* as "the first attempt at a bilingual dictionary of English", and showed that its contents derived mainly from the Christian ecclesiastical tradition, although several forms are listed which occur only in Classical sources such as Ovid and Horace. The practical nature of the glossary is also underlined by Lendinara (1992: 238), who states that "it is a clear attempt to fuse the old glossographical tradition with a new strain of ecclesiastical vocabulary and new *lemmata* drawn from Christian authors". Ultimately, many Old English glossaries can be partly traced back to the *Hermeneumata Pseudo-Dositheana*; the Latin interpretation of the Greek lemma was converted into the lemma proper, to which an Old English gloss was then added (Lendinara 1992: 216). Instances such as *lapis* and *petra*, which occur in the *Hermeneumata*, but in no other Old English glossaries (Lendinara 1992: 226, 231) raise the question whether Ælfric resorted to this type of glossary for his material. Moreover, Ælfric's *Glossary* bears a strong resemblance to another class glossary in Antwerp, Plantin Moretus Museum MS 16, 2 and London, British Library MS Add. 32246, the very manuscript that also contains the *Excerptiones in Prisciano* and a version of the *Colloquy*. This glossary has been explained both as a later version of Ælfric's *Glossary* and as one deriving from the same exemplar (Lendinara 1992: 233–234; Gillingham 1981: 38–71). A comprehensive edition of Anglo-Saxon glosses – as yet a desideratum – would provide an important instrument for further research in this field.

## 5. Conclusion

The purpose of Ælfric's language studies, then, was not the continued development of linguistic scholarship. Instead, he adopted a utilitarian stance towards linguistics with the ultimate aim to secure the dissemination of Christian doctrines by effectively teaching Latin and by reworking and translating a selection of ecclesiastical works into a corpus of vernacular texts. Undeniably, he relied on the Benedictine school of Æthelwold of Winchester, where he was grounded in the Continental tradition of linguistic scholarship. The emphasis on translation, which originated in the days of King Alfred, made the Winchester Benedictines the first English philologists, and Ælfric their paragon. He stood at the heart of this hey-day of Latin and vernacular scholarship which was, at the time, unprecedented in Medieval Europe. However, it did not last. Although his *Grammar* superseded similar Latin works in the 11th and 12th centuries, surviving for a while the Norman Conquest, the latest copy dates from the first half of the 13th century, when the scribe of the "Worcester Tremulous Hand" adapted it to Early Middle English standards (Law 1987: 64). The demise of the Old English vernacular tradition rendered such bilingual didactic instruments superfluous. The late Anglo-Saxon tradition of linguistic scholarship proved a dead end.

Ælfric's *Grammar* and *Glossary*, however, saw a rebirth in the 16th and 17th centuries, as they were among the first Old English texts to re-emerge when antiquarian scholars went in search of the rudiments of the English history and language. John Leland and Laurence Nowell studied manuscripts of the *Grammar* and *Glossary* to learn the then obscure Old English language with the help of the Latin translations, turning Ælfric's works into grammar and vocabulary of Old English (Buckalew 1982; → Art. 106). Soon afterwards, manuscripts and transcripts found their way to the Continent, where scholars became increasingly interested in Old English, from the late 16th century onwards (Dekker 1997: 20, 134–136). In 1659 William Somner published Ælfric's *Grammar*, and the above mentioned Antwerp–London *Glossary* as additions to his *Dictionarium Saxonico-Latino-Anglicum*, the first dictionary of Old English ever printed. The English vernacular which Ælfric had incorporated in the study of Latin in the Middle Ages became the prime focus of interest in his works, during the Renaissance.

## 6. Bibliography


Amsler, Mark. 1993. "History of Linguistics, 'Standard Latin' and Pedagogy". *History of Linguistic Thought in the Early Middle Ages* ed. by Vivien Law, 50–66. Amsterdam & Philadelphia: Benjamins.

Bayless, Martha. 1993. "*Beatus Quid Est* and the Study of Grammar in Late Anglo-Saxon England". *History of Linguistic Thought in the Early Middle Ages* ed. by Vivien Law, 67–110. Amsterdam & Philadelphia: Benjamins.

Bender Davis, Jeannine-M. 1988. *Aelfric's Techniques of Translation and Adaptation as Seen in the Composition of His Old English Latin Grammar.* Ph. D. Pennsylvania State University.

Bolognesi, Giancarlo. 1967. *La grammatica latina di Ælfric: Parte prima, studio delle fonti.* Brescia: Paideia.

Buckalew, Ronald E. 1982. "Nowell, Lambarde, and Leland: The significance of Laurence Nowell's transcript of Aelfric's *grammar* and *glossary*". *Anglo-Saxon Scholarship: The first three centuries* ed. by Carl T. Berkhout & Milton McC. Gatch, 19–50. Boston: Hall.

Bullough, Donald A. 1972. "The Educational Tradition in England from Alfred to Ælfric: Teaching *Utriusque Linguae*". *Settimane di studio del Centro Italiano di Studi sull'Alto Medioevo* 19.453–494.

Clemoes, Peter A. M. 1959. "The Chronology of Ælfric's Works". *The Anglo-Saxons: Studies in some aspects of their history and culture presented to Bruce Dickins* ed. by Peter Clemoes, 212–247. London: Bowes & Bowes.

Dekker, Kees. 1997. *"The Light under the Bushel": Old Germanic Studies in the Low Countries and the Motivation and Methods of Jan van Vliet (1622–1666).* Ph. D., University of Leiden.

Derolez, Rene. 1989. "Those Things are Difficult to Express in English ...". *English Studies* 70.469–476.

–. 1992. "Anglo-Saxon Glossography: A brief introduction". *Anglo-Saxon Glossography: Papers read at the International Conference Brussels, 8 and 9 September 1986* ed. by Rene Derolez, 9–42. Brussels: Paleis der Academiën & Brepols.

Förster, Max. 1917. "Die altenglische Glossenhandschrift Plantinus 32 (Antwerpen) und Additional 32246 (London)". *Anglia* 61.94–161.

Garmonsway, George Norman. 1959. "The Development of the Colloquy". *The Anglo-Saxons: Studies in some aspects of their history and culture presented to Bruce Dickins* ed. by Peter Clemoes, 248–261. London: Bowes & Bowes.

–. 1966. *Ælfric's Colloquy*. New York: Appleton-Century-Crofts.

Gneuss, Helmut. 1972. "The Origin of Standard Old English". *Anglo-Saxon England* 1.63–83.

–. 1994. "A Grammarian's Greek-Latin Glossary in Anglo-Saxon England". *From Anglo-Saxon to Early Middle English: Studies presented to Eric Gerald Stanley* ed. by Malcolm Godden & Douglas Gray, 60–89. Oxford: Clarendon.

Irvine, Martin. 1994. *The Making of Textual Culture: 'Grammatica' and literary theory, 350–1100*. Cambridge: Cambridge Univ. Press.

Keynes, Simon & Michael Lapidge. 1983. *Alfred the Great: Asser's life of King Alfred and other contemporary sources*. Harmondsworth: Penguin.

Lapidge, Michael. 1985. "Surviving Booklists from Anglo-Saxon England". *Learning and Literature in Anglo-Saxon England: Studies presented to Peter Clemoes on his sixty-fifth birthday* ed. by Michael Lapidge & Helmut Gneuss, 33–89. Cambridge: Cambridge Univ. Press.

–. 1986. "On the School of Theodore and Hadrian". *Anglo-Saxon England* 15.43–71.

– & Michael Winterbottom. 1991. *Wulfstan of Winchester: The life of St Æthelwold*. Oxford: Clarendon Press.

Law, Vivien. 1982. *The Insular Latin Grammarians*. Woodbridge: The Boydell Press.

–. 1987. « Anglo-Saxon England: Ælfric's *Excerptiones de Arte Grammatica Anglice* » *Histoire Epistémologie Langage* 9:1.47–71.

–. 1993. "The Historiography of Grammar in the Early Middle Ages". *History of Linguistic Thought in the Early Middle Ages* ed. by Vivien Law, 1–23. Amsterdam & Philadelphia: Benjamins.

–. 1997. *Grammar and Grammarians in the Early Middle Ages*. London & New York: Longman.

Lendinara, Patrizia. 1983. "Il colloquio di Ælfric e il colloquio di Ælfric Bata". *Feor ond neah: Scritti di filologia Germanica in memoria di Augusto Scaffidi Abbate* ed. by Patrizia Lendinara & Lucio Melazzo, 173–249. Palermo: Università di Palermo.

–. 1991. "The World of Anglo-Saxon Learning". *The Cambridge Companion to Old English Literature* ed. by Malcolm Godden & Michael Lapidge, 264–281. Cambridge: Cambridge Univ. Press. (Repr. 1992, 1993.)

–. 1992. "Glosses and Glossaries". *Anglo-Saxon Glossography: Papers read at the International Conference Brussels, 8 and 9 September 1986* ed. by Rene Derolez, 209–243. Brussels: Paleis der Academiën & Brepols.

Pàroli, Teresa. 1967–68. "Le opere grammaticali di Ælfric ". *Annali dell'Istituto Orientale di Napoli*, sezione Germanica 10.5–43; 11.35–133.

Porter, David W. 1994. "The Latin Syllabus in the Anglo-Saxon Monastic Schools". *Neophilologus* 78:3.463–482.

Rees Williams, Edna. 1958. "Ælfric's Grammatical Terminology". *Publications of the Modern Language Society of America* 73:5.453–462.

Reinsma, Luke M. 1987. *Ælfric: An annotated bibliography*. New York & London: Garland.

Riché, Pierre. 1981. « L'étude du vocabulaire latin dans les écoles anglo-saxonnes au début du X$^{e}$ siècle ». *La lexicographie du latin médiéval et ses rapports avec les recherches actuelles sur la civilisation du Moyen-Age* ed. by Yves Lefevre, 115–124. Paris: Editions du Centre National de Recherches.

Smyth, Alfred P. 1995. *King Alfred the Great*. Oxford: Oxford Univ. Press.

Stevenson, William Henry & Wallace Martin Lindsay. 1929. *Early Scholastic Colloquies*. Oxford: Clarendon Press. (Repr., New York: AMS Press, 1989.)

Thomson, R. L. 1981. "Ælfric's Latin Vocabulary". *Leeds Studies in English* 12.155–161.

White, C. L. 1974. *Ælfric: A new study of his life and his writings* with a supplementary classified bibliography prepared by Malcolm R. Godden. Hamden, Conn.: Archon Books. (Originally published London: Lamson & Wolffe, 1898.)

Wilcox, Jonathan. 1994. *Ælfric's Prefaces*. Durham: Durham Medieval Texts.

Zupitza, Julius. 1880. *Ælfrics Grammatik and Glossar*. Berlin: Weidmannsche Buchhandlung. (2nd edition with introduction and bibliography by Helmut Gneuss, Berlin: Niehans, 1966.)

*Kees Dekker, Leiden/Groningen (The Netherlands)*

# 86. La tradition latine et les langues slaves dans le Bas Moyen-Age

1. Introduction
2. Slavia romana
3. Slavia orthodoxa
4. Bibliographie

## 1. Introduction

Les langues slaves sont généralement réparties en trois groupes, répondant à des critères linguistiques et géographiques: les langues slaves orientales, dont le russe et l'ukrainien, les langues slaves occidentales, dont le tchèque et le polonais, les langues slaves méridionales, dont le serbe et le croate. Cependant, à la suite des travaux de Ricardo Picchio (1972, 1984), les historiens de la linguistique (cf. Lepschy 1991) s'accordent aujourd'hui à distinguer deux grandes familles culturelles, selon la sphère d'influence religieuse: la Slavia romana et la Slavia orthodoxa. Cette perspective nous paraît s'imposer au sujet ici traité, à savoir l'influence de la tradition grammaticale latine.

On rappellera que la rencontre des peuples slaves et de la chrétienté latine a eu lieu tard. Mises à part les provinces illyriques et la Dalmatie, les pays slaves ne connurent en effet le latin que comme langue littéraire et religieuse. Le Bas Moyen-Age, période de fondation des universités, s'étend jusqu'aux années 1348 pour Prague, 1364 pour Cracovie, les premières universités fondées dans les pays slaves. Quant à la Russie, l'influence latine s'y fait sentir certes dès les prémisses de la description grammaticale, mais au début du XVIe siècle.

## 2. La grammaire latine en Slavia romana

Le latin joue le rôle de langue supranationale que joue le slavon d'église dans la Slavia orthodoxa, mais avec des différences linguistiques telles que les langues locales et le latin n'entraient pas en concurrence. Les premières et la seconde avaient leur sphère d'influence respective.

C'est par le biais des ordres religieux mendiants que la grammaire latine s'est introduite en Bohème et en Pologne (Kloczowski 1993). Dès la seconde moitié du XIIIe siècle, la province franciscaine de la Saxe embrassait une part importante de la Silésie, tandis que la province bavaroise des Augustins s'étendait à la Bohème et à la quasi-totalité de la Pologne. Dans le courant du XIVe siècle, c'est l'ordre des Carmes qui s'établit durablement, tandis que les Dominicains sont suffisamment implantés pour créer une province autonome de Bohème et Hongrie. Dans les écoles conventuelles, les élèves apprenaient la grammaire chez Donat et Priscien, ce dont témoigne le nombre relativement important de manuscrits conservés dans les archives de Prague et de Cracovie. Dans les recensements des commentaires médiévaux du Donat en Europe (Bursill-Hall 1981), on dénombre dix manuscrits à Prague, dix à Cracovie. Ceux-ci se présentent comme des commentaires anonymes: *Circa initium Donati Parisiensis incipit editio primare ... Circa initium Donati (minoris) quaeritur (primo) utrum tantum sint septem artes liberales ...*, certains faisant référence à une méthode d'enseignement grammatical associant Donat et son complément naturel Priscien, ainsi *Circa initium Donati secundum Priscianum qui fuit optimus grammaticorum [...].*

Si les études concordent pour dire que l'enseignement du latin se fait à travers Donat (Vidmanová 1973), il apparaît aussi que les commentaires ont nourri les premières grammaires vernaculaires commises et publiées par les milieux humanistes. Avant d'en venir à ce point, nous mentionnerons le traité d'orthographe attribué à Jean Hus *De orthographia Bohemica* (1406?) dans lequel l'alphabet latin est adapté aux propriétés phonétiques du tchèque, grâce à l'ajout de différents signes diacritiques (la *gracilis virgula* ajoutée aux voyelles, qui deviendra l'accent de longueur, le *punctus rotundus* ajouté aux consonnes qui distingue les palatales et la vélaire l·, et qui deviendra le háček). C'est selon toute vraisemblance une adaptation tchèque de la grammaire de Donat qui servit de base à la première grammaire tchèque de Optát, Gzel et Philomates, publiée en 1533. Cette *Grammatyka česka*, qui connut plusieurs rééditions (1548, 1588 et 1643) est divisée en deux parties, Orthographe et Étymologie (Freidhof 1974). La grammaire est rédigée en tchèque et les faits de langue décrits sont manifestement tchèques; toutefois, le métalangage grammatical utilisé est prioritairement le latin et les traductions visant à la création d' un métalangage autonome restent modestes.

L'influence de Donat sur cette grammaire est manifeste, tant en ce qui concerne l'ordre de présentation des parties du discours que les noms des cas ou bien des temps. En revanche, les commentaires sont un tissu de citations latines d'Erasme accompagnées de leur traduction tchèque.

Les années 1530–1540 voient l'intérêt pour les pays slaves, notamment la Bohème, grandir en Occident. C'est en 1537 que paraît à Bâle le glossaire en quatre langues de l'humaniste Sigismond Gelenius *Lexicum Symphonum, Quo quator lingvarum Evropae familiarum, Graecae scilicet, Latinae, Germanicae ac Sclauinicae concordia consonantiaque indicatur*. Et vers les années 1540, Johannes Gunther installe à Olomouc une imprimerie où seront éditées grammaires et méthodes d'enseignement de la langue tchèque.

A cette époque, sont introduits en Bohème des *Elementa Donati* latins-tchèques-allemands (Ising 1970); sont connus également des Eléments en latin et tchèque dits *Donat exponovaný*, qui connaitront par la suite plusieurs éditions: *Donat exponowaný, Donati elementa de etymologia partium oratione, cum interpretatione Boemica ad collectionem &c...* (1567, 1638, 1647). Le texte est en latin, avec une traduction tchèque interlinéaire; le frontispice représente la grammaire sous les traits d'une femme enseignant aux enfants. La grammaire est par ailleurs définie comme l'un des sept gradins permettant l'accès au savoir, schéma bien connu des Donat en Occident.

Entre 1559 et 1604, l'humaniste Leonhard Culmann assurera la publication de nombreuses éditions de la Méthode de Donat en Bohème, dont *Aelii Donati viri clarissimi, de octo partibus orationis Methodus, quaestiumculis puerilibus undique collectis illustrata* (Prague, 1562), qui présente un texte rédigé entièrement en latin et des gloses tchèques en marge faisant ressortir un métalangage grammatical autonome. Notons également *Donati Methodvs de etymologia partium orationis cum interpretatione Boiemica...* de Matouš Kolín (1564) et de Martin Bachaček *Donat declinationum paradigmata* (1591).

En Pologne, la grammaire spéculative s'implante profondément et Donat et Priscien seront complétés, puis remplacés par de nouveaux textes grammaticaux, notamment Pierre d'Espagne ou Alexandre Villedieu. L'*ars lectoria*, liée à la récitation liturgique et en réfectoire, a favorisé la rédaction d'ouvrages de métrique, comme le *Metrificale* de Marc d'Opatowiec (1ère moitié du XVe siècle), fortement influencé par le *Doctrinale* d'Alexandre de Villedieu, qui servait à Cracovie de manuel d'enseignement (Gansiniec 1960: 44 sq). On peut voir une autre trace de l'influence de la grammaire spéculative en Pologne dans le manuel grammatical versifié, *Fundamenta Puerorum* (~ 1470), conservé à la bibliothèque Jagellonne de Cracovie.

En Pologne, les versions bilingues seront cependant nombreuses, et les parutions s'étaleront jusqu'à la fin du XVIIIe siècle: paraissent en 1523 les *Barbarismes* de Donat, puis en 1524 des commentaires, dits *Pseudo-Remigius*. Les *Éléments* paraîtront en 1583 *Aelii Donati vetustissimi Grammatici Elementa una cum traductione polonica*, puis en 1639, *Aelii Donati vetustissimi Grammatici Elementa una cum traductione polonica*, cette dernière version, comportant le texte latin avec traduction intégrale interlinéaire, sera souvent rééditée par la suite (une édition en 1786).

Les premières tentatives d'élaboration d'une terminologie autonome apparaissent dans les *Regulae grammaticales, regimina et constructiones* (1542) et dans la traduction du Donat (1583). La comparaison des termes grammaticaux laisse apparaître de profondes convergences (Koronczewski 1961: 13 sq), les termes sont dans les deux cas des calques des termes latins (*verbum: slowo*; *adverbium: pryslowie*; *praepositio: przelozenie*). Cette terminologie sera modifiée par J. J. Moravus dans ses *Questiones de primis grammatices rudimentis* (1592), qui y intègre des emprunts tels que *diphtongus: dyftong*; *declinatio: declinacyja*; *coniugatio: coniugacija*. C'est également par emprunts que J. Januszowski enrichira le lexique lié à la phonétique et l'orthographe (*Nowy karakter polski*, 1594), intégrant les termes *konsonans*, *syllaba*, *akcent*.

## 3. La grammaire latine en Slavia orthodoxa

La première tentative connue de présentation systématique de la morphologie du slavon d'église consiste en le traité grammatical *Des huit parties du discours* (XIVe siècle), compilation serbe de sources byzantines longtemps attribuée à Jean Damascène, d'où son nom, *Damaskin*. La terminologie créée à cette occasion pour nommer les parties du discours, adaptation des termes et de l'ordre de Denys le Thrace, ouvrira la voie à un cadre majoritairement grec.

Sur ce fond grec se détache l'adaptation slavonne de Donat (1522), dont la paternité est attribuée au traducteur Dmitrij Gerasimov, ambassadeur du Grand Prince Basile III. Le manuscrit originel est perdu, il en subsiste deux copies de la fin du XVIe siècle, l'une à Saint-Pétersbourg, l'autre à Kazan. L'adaptation fut réalisée à Novgorod, ville ouverte sur la Hanse. Il s'agit tout à la fois d'une confrontation intéressante à une tradition grammaticale inconnue, d'une tentative d'adapter une méthode d'enseignement de la grammaire éprouvée, et d'assurer la promotion du latin au même titre que le grec et le slavon.

L'idée de *catéchisme grammatical* à laquelle recourt Holtz (1981) pour qualifier l'*Ars minor* s'applique ici parfaitement. En tête de la grammaire, le copiste a noté le résumé suivant: "Ce livre est appelé le mineur de Donat (*Donatus menšoj*), on y parle des huit parties d'oration ou de discours (*časti veščanija ili reči*), c'est-à-dire du nom, du pronom, du verbe, de l'adverbe, du verbe et du nom participe, de la conjonction, de la préposition et de l'interjection. Les élèves débutants l'étudient après l'alphabet".

Bien qu'il s'intitule *Ars minor*, l'opuscule contient une grande quantité d'exemples tirés de l'*Ars major*, ce qui en fait une adaptation des deux livres de Donat (Archaimbault 1995). La forme dialoguée, qui a permis de revivifier la tradition donatienne, est ici reprise, ainsi que des conseils pédagogiques adressés au maître pour lui permettre d'enchaîner les différents exercices.

La terminologie, ainsi que l'ordre des parties du discours, sont repris au Donat. Ils accusent des différences sensibles avec la présentation du pseudo-Damascène dont il a été question plus haut. Ils ne connaitront pas une grande fortune dans l'histoire de la tradition grammaticale en Russie, où la greffe grecque a pris durablement, pour des raisons autant linguistiques que religieuses et culturelles (→ Art. 65). Il n'empêche que cette tentative isolée d'intégration de la tradition latine laissera quelques traces profondes, que nous verrons maintenant.

Les faits de langue décrits sont à la fois représentatifs du slavon et du russe. Il s'agit de la première attestation de formes russes dans une grammaire. Le mélange des formes peut apparaître jusqu'au sein d'un même paradigme.

Dans le domaine de la description du verbe, la reprise au Donat des quatre formes du verbe (perfecta *obraz soveršennyj*, meditativa *blagoizvol'nyj*, frequentativa *učaščaemyj* et inchoativa *načinatel'nyj*), chacune associant à une marque suffixale une valeur sémantique particulière, aboutira, pour la description du russe, à la mise en valeur de deux suffixes à valeur fréquentative et inchoative. Le problème de la dérivation suffixale se trouvant au centre du traitement morphologique des aspects du verbe, il y a là un legs important de Donat à la tradition grammaticale russe.

Certaines caractéristiques linguistiques rapprochent le russe du latin davantage que du grec. C'est le cas du rôle marginal, voire inexistant, de l'article. La traduction slavonne du Donat répercute l'absence d'article latin. Elle renvoie *različie* (litt. "la distinction", l'article dans le *Damaskin*) à l'interjection, conservant ainsi une entrée existant dans le traité *Des huit parties du discours*, mais lui assignant un contenu différent. Les exemples suivant la présentation des parties du discours sont assez fournis et servent de support à des exercices de reconnaissance des formes, sur le type d'une analyse grammaticale.

Véritable méthode d'entraînement au maniement du métalangage slavon et à la reconnaissance morphologique, le manuscrit reste en même temps une description des faits de langue latine. A cette contradiction, les copies répondent de façon différente. Préservant la présentation de la langue latine grâce à un métalangage adapté, le manuscrit de Pétersbourg transcrit les exemples latins en alphabet cyrillique. Le manuscrit de Kazan, à l'inverse, les traduit, la littéralité des traductions rendant par moments le texte incompréhensible. Cette confusion entre langue décrite et métalangue, entre original et traduction, crée une coupure entre la règle énoncée et le fait de langue décrit. Le texte anticipe lui-même parfois sur les confusions que peuvent commettre des élèves russes et rétablit *in fine* la norme slavonne (Worth 1985).

Si Horbatsch (1973) a montré les points de convergence entre la grammaire de Lascaris et Ἀδελφότης, grammaire gréco-slavonne rédigée en 1591 par les confréries laïques orthodoxes de Lviv, l'introduction de cette grammaire contient une allusion au Donat à travers "la tour du savoir, avec l'alphabet comme clé, la grammaire comme gradin inférieur et au sommet la théologie" (Ďurovič 1995: 23).

On trouve une première synthèse des traditions grecque et latine dans la grammaire de Laurent Zizanius (1596). La forme dialoguée adoptée dans un premier temps est par la suite abandonnée, mais l'auteur prend acte des 'formes du verbe' de Donat, et présente en doublons les noms des modes, calquant le terme grec, puis le terme latin (*obraz izjavitel'nyj ili ukazatel'nyj*; *želatel'nyi imeti ili molitvennyj, nepredel'nyj ili neobavnyj*).

Dans sa grammaire de 1619, *Grammatiki Slavenskija pravilnoe Syntagma* (Jevje, près Vilnius) Meletij Smotrickij consolidera les suffixes itératifs et inchoatifs hérités de Donat, tout en consacrant pour l'essentiel la terminologie grecque. Principal manuel d'enseignement dans les pays slaves orthodoxes, palliant l'absence de description des langues vernaculaires, en même temps qu'elle en retardait l'émergence, cette grammaire contribuera à asseoir le cadre terminologique grec.

## 4. Bibliographie

### 4.1. Sources primaires

'Αδελφότης. 1591. *Grammatika Dobroglagolivavo Ellinoslovenskavo Iazyka...* L'vov. Ed. par Olexa Horbatsch. (= *Specimina Philologiae Slavicae*.) München: Kubon & Sagner, 1973.

Donat = *Donatus sireč grammatika...* Ed. par Vatroslav Jagic. (= *Codex Slavonicum Rerum Grammaticarum*, 25.) München: Slävische Propyläen, 1885–1895. (Réimpr., 1968.)

*Metryficale Marka z Opatowca i traktaty gramatyczne XIV i XV wieku* [Le Metrificale de Marc d'Opatowiec et les traités grammaticaux des XIVe et XVe siècle]. Ed. par R. Gansiniec. Wroclaw, 1960.

Optát Beneš, Petr Gzel & Václav Philomates. *Grammatyka česka: die Ausgaben von 1533 und 1588.* [Grammaire tchèque]. Ed. par Gerd Freidhof. (= *Specimina Philologiae Slavicae*, 7, 1–2.) Frankfurt/M. & München: Kubon & Sagner, 1974.

Smotrickij, Meletij. 1618–1619. *Grammatiki Slavenskija...* Ed. par Olexa Horbatsch & Gerd Freidhof (= *Specimina Philologiae Slavicae*, 4.) Frankfurt/M. & München: Kubon & Sagner, 1974.

Zizanij, Lavrentij. 1596. *Hrammatika slovenska...* Ed. par Gerd Freidhof. (= *Specimina Philologiae Slavicae*, 1.) Frankfurt/M. & München: Kubon & Sagner, 1972.

### 4.2. Sources secondaires

Archaimbault, Sylvie. 1995. *L'émergence de la notion d'aspect dans les grammaires russes.* Thèse de Doctorat, Univ. Denis Diderot, Paris.

Bursill-Hall Geoffrey L. 1981. "Medieval Donatus Commentaries". *Historiographica Linguistica* 8.69–97.

Ďurovič, L'ubomir. 1995. "Emergence de la pensée grammaticale en Russie ancienne et formation de la grammaire du russe normatif". *Histoire Epistémologie Langage* 17.17–32.

Holtz, Louis. 1981. *Donat et la tradition de l'enseignement grammatical.* Paris: CNRS.

Ising, E. 1970. *Die Herausbildung der Grammatik der Volkssprachen in Mittel- und Osteuropa.* Berlin.

Kloczowski, Jerzy. 1993. "Panorama geografico, cronologico e statistico sulla distribuzione degli *Studia* degli ordini mendicanti". *La Pologne dans l'Église médiévale* (= *Collected Studies series*, 417.) Aldershot: Variorum.

Koronczewski, Andrzej. 1961. *Polska Terminologia Gramatyczna.* Wroclaw: Zaklad Narodowy Imienia Ossolinskich Wydawnictwo Polskiej Akademii Nauk.

Lepschy, Giulio C. 1991. *Storia della linguistica*, II, 245–275. Bologna: Il Mulino.

Mareš, Franz W. 1973. "Die Kyrillo-Methodianischen Wurzeln der tschechischen diakritischen Orthographie". Sonderabdruck aus dem *Anzeiger der phil.-hist. Klasse der Österreichischen Akademie der Wissenschaften*, 110, So. 3. Wien.

Picchio, Ricardo. 1984. "Guidelines for a Comparative Study of the Language Question amongs the Slavs". *Aspects of the Slavic Language Question* éd. par Ricardo Picchio & Harvey Goldblatt, I, 1–42.

Vidmanová, Anežka. 1973. "Ze středověké školy". *Laborintus, Latinska literatura středověkých Čech* (1994), Praha: KLP.

Worth, Dean S. 1983. *The Origins of Russian Grammar: Notes on the state of Russian philology before the advent of printed grammars.* (= *UCLA Slavic Studies*, 5.) Columbus, Ohio: Slavica Publishers.

*Sylvie Archaimbault, Paris (France)*

# 87. Sprachstudium und literarische Traditionen: Das Okzitanisch

1. Sprachstudium und Volkssprachen
2. Raimon Vidal, *Razós de trobar* (1190–1213, Katalonien)
3. Uc Faidit, *Donatz Proenzals* (ca. 1240, Norditalien)
4. Jofre de Foixà, *Regles de trobar* (1282–1296, Sizilien)
5. Terramagnino da Pisa, *Doctrina d'Acort* (ca. 1282–1296, Sardinien)
6. Sprachwissenschaft des Okzitanischen im 14. Jahrhundert
7. Das *Consistori del Gai Saber* von Toulouse (1323)
8. Das *Consistori* von Barcelona
9. Die Wiederentdeckung der okzitanischen Grammatik
10. Bibliographie

## 1. Sprachstudium und Volkssprachen

### 1.1. Sprachen und Grammatikographie im romanischen Mittelalter

Im Hohen Mittelalter ist *grammatica* Synonym für Latein. Nur die lateinische Sprache wird analysiert, beschrieben und in Regeln gefaßt. Zwar behauptet Petrus Helias (?–1140–1166–?) aus universalgrammatischer Perspektive, "Sunt [...] species artis grammaticæ genera linguarum in quibus ars grammatica tractata est", und zwar "in lingua Græca et Latina, Hebraea et Chaldaica", und er nimmt sogar an, man könne die *species* der Grammatik durch Studien etwa zur "lingua Gallica" erweitern (Petrus Helias, in Fredborg 1980: 79), aber dies bleibt weitgehend Lippenbekenntnis (Robins 1976: 96; Dahan, Rosier & Valente 1995).

Das vorherrschende Interesse am Lateinischen erhält in der 2. Hälfte des 12. Jh. eine neue Qualität durch die nunmehr einsetzende, radikale Kritik am Studium literarischer Texte. Die philosophisch-logisch orientierte Sprachbetrachtung wird nun zur dominierenden Forschungsrichtung (Kap. XIV). Dieser Interessenwandel wird, namentlich im nordfranzösischen Raum, durch heftige Polemiken gegen die 'lügnerische' Literatur zusätzlich gefördert (Niederehe 1993).

In einem geistigen Klima, welches keinerlei sprachforscherisches Interesse an den 'Volkssprachen' Französisch, Spanisch oder Italienisch bekundet und sich zudem immer literaturfeindlicher gebärdet, entstehen die ersten Beschreibungen des Okzitanischen, der Sprache der Trobadors.

### 1.2. Die Bedeutung des Okzitanischen im Mittelalter

Die Trobadorlyrik war zu Beginn des 12. Jh. im Süden des heutigen Frankreich entstanden und hatte rasch Anhänger im In- und Ausland gefunden. Namentlich Katalonien und (Nord-)Italien sind hier zu nennen, wo man sich sogar darum bemüht, es den Trobadors auf Okzitanisch (auch: 'Provenzalisch', 'Limousinisch') gleichzutun.

In anderen Ländern findet die Trobadorlyrik Nachahmer in der jeweiligen Landessprache, in Nordfrankreich (die Trouvères), auf der Iberischen Halbinsel in Galicien (Alfons X., der Weise), und im deutschen Sprachraum (die Minnesänger).

Es ist bezeichnend, daß die okzitanische Kultur sich nicht im Umfeld der ganz auf das Lateinische fixierten Universitäten und ihrer aliterarischen Sprachforschungen entwickelt, sondern im höfischen, später auch im bürgerlichen Umfeld.

### 1.3. Vorläufer und Vorbilder der okzitanischen Grammatikographie

Die Grammatiken der Trobadorsprache stellen in den romanischen Ländern eine Neuerung dar, aber es sind nicht die ersten Grammatiken einer Volkssprache überhaupt (→ Art. 82–86); die isländischen usw. Grammatiken kommen als Vorbilder der okzitanischen Grammatikographie jedoch wegen fehlender Berühungspunkte nicht in Betracht.

Vorbilder können daher nur im Bereich der lateinischen Grammatikographie gesucht werden, aber wegen des vorrangigen Interesses der okzitanischen Grammatiker an der Literatursprache ist dabei allerdings eher von einer Affinität zur 'traditionnellen' lateinischen Grammatikographie eines Donat oder Priscian als zur philosophisch-logisch orientierten Sprachforschung der Universitäten auszugehen.

## 2. Raimon Vidal, *Razós de trobar* (1190–1213, Katalonien)

Die erste Grammatik der okzitanischen Sprache, die *Razós de trobar*, entsteht zu Beginn des 13. Jahrhunderts, wohl zwischen 1190–1213 (Marshall 1972: LXIX–LXX, LXX; Heinimann 1963: 28). Ihr Autor ist der

Katalane Ra(i)mon Vidal (?–?) 'aus Besalú' (Prov. Girona).

Vermutungen, vor den *Razós* habe es bereits ähnliche (volkssprachliche) Traktate gegeben (Anglade 1971: IV. 93), haben sich bislang nicht bestätigt.

Seine 'Abhandlungen über das Dichten' wenden sich an "Totz hom que vol trabar ni entendre" ('alle, die dichten bzw. [die Dichtung] verstehen wollen'; Ms. B, ed. Marshall 1972, Z. 59) und zeigen eine gute Vertrautheit mit der überlieferten Trobador-Lyrik. Seine Kenntnisse der lateinischen Grammatiktradition müssen dagegen eher als bescheiden bezeichnet werden (Schlieben-Lange 1991: 106).

### 2.1. Dichtersprachen und Sprachnorm

Für Raimon Vidal ist das 'Limousinische' die Sprache der Dichtung *par excellence* (Ms. B, ed. Marshall 1972, Z. 74–76). Das Französische eigne sich dagegen eher für "romanz et pasturellas" (Ms. B., ed. Marshall 1972, Z. 72–73). Das Lateinische bleibt als mögliche Dichtersprache unerwähnt.

Das Modell guter Sprache findet man nach Raimon Vidal beim *native speaker*: (Ms. B, ed. Marshall 1972, Z. 64–65). Seine Sprache ist Richtschnur, gleichzeitig aber auch die der "bon trobador", der guten Dichter (Ms. B, ed. Marshall 1972, Z. 431). Diese Normvorstellungen legt er allerdings recht eng aus (Marshall 1972: LXXXV).

Ziel der *Razós de trobar* ist es, allen, die auf Okzitanisch dichten wollen, den korrekten Gebrauch der Trobadorsprache zu vermitteln. Das Publikum der *Razós* sucht man also mit Marshall zu Recht bei "Vidal's Catalan compatriots", genauer bei "the aristocratic public of the Catalan courts" (1972: LXX).

Raimon Vidal geht von der Feststellung aus, daß viele seiner Landsleute daß Okzitanische nicht fehlerfrei handhabten, besonders was das Zwei-Kasus-System des Okzitanischen (die morphologische Unterscheidung von Nominativ [Rektus] und Akkusativ [Obliquus] der Maskulina), die Verwechslung von offenem und geschlossenem *e*, *o* im Reim und die 2. Person Plural auf *-etz*, ("graficamente" mit *-ets* verwechselt) anbelangt. (Ruffinatto 1968: 33).

### 2.2. Die Grammatik in den *Razós*

Die lateinische Grammatik und ihre Schemata spielen demgegenüber eine untergeordnete Rolle. Nur einmal findet sich ein Hinweis auf einen Genusunterschied zwischen Latein (*gramatica*) und Volkssprache (*romanz*) (Ms. B, ed. Marshall, 1972, Z. 144–149). Ohne sonderliche Konsequenzen für die Darstellung des Stoffes bleibt auch der Hinweis auf die 'acht Redeteile' ["nom, pronom, verb, averbi, particip, coniunctio, prepositio, interiectio"; abweichende Reihenfolge in Ms. H.], welche 'in allen Sprachen der Welt' zu finden seien (Hs. B, ed. Marshall 1972, Z. 90–93), der sogleich eine neue Einteilung nach "adiectivas, sustantivas" und "ni l'un ni l'autre" folgt.

Diese Unterteilung wird dann zur Gliederung des sprachlichen Materials benutzt, wobei es ihm namentlich um die Deklination und die Genera geht (mask., fem., neutr., commune und 'omne'; Ms. B Z. 138–139). Durch die Unterscheidung von Rektus und Obliquus ergeben sich im Okzitanischen, nach Raimon Vidal, sechs Kasus, bei denen das Nomen masculinum 'verlängert' wird ["s'alonga"], gegenüber 6 weiteren, bei denen 'die Wörter sich verkürzen' ["s'abreuion"] (Hs. B, Z. 157–160). Dies wird mit Beispielen aus der Trobador-Lyrik illustriert.

Es folgen kurze Ausführungen zu den Pronomina, dann zu den Adverbien, bei denen man ebenfalls 'Verlängerungen bzw. Verkürzungen' registrieren könne (Ms. B Z. 336). Auf wenigen Seiten behandelt er dann das Verb, immer wieder mit Beispielen aus den 'bons trobadors' illustriert, um abschließend erneut die intensive Einübung der 'parladura natural e drecha' zu empfehlen.

Insgesamt gesehen sind seine Ausführungen nicht dazu geeignet, Okzitanisch *ab ovo* zu erlernen, sondern allenfalls, bereits vorhandene Kenntnisse zu verbessern (der Abstand zwischen Okzitanisch und Katalanisch ist damals nicht sehr groß).

## 3. Uc Faidit, *Donatz Proenzals* (ca. 1240, Norditalien)

Die zweite okzitanische Grammatik, der *Donatz Proenzals*, entsteht um 1240 (evtl. auch zwischen 1225–1245) in der Provinz Treviso, in Norditalien. Die Grammatikographie des Okzitanischen folgt somit den Trobadors, welche in der Folge der Albigenserkriege (1209–1229) ihr Heimatland hatten verlassen müssen (Ruffinatto 1968: 16; Nadal & Prats 1982: 200)

Autor des *Donatz* ist ein gewisser Uc 'Faiditius', den Janzarik (1989) mit Uc de St. Circ identifiziert. Über Uc Faidit ist praktisch nichts bekannt (zu Uc de St. Circ vgl.

Janzarik 1989). Bestimmte sprachliche Eigentümlichkeiten deuten allerdings auf seine Herkunft aus dem Languedoc bzw. dem Rouergue hin (Marshall 1969: 73–75)

Der *Donatz* wurde, wie bereits Gröber (1884: 290–193) gezeigt hatte, auf Bitten zweier Adeliger aus dem Umfeld Friedrichs II. verfaßt (Marshall 1969: 64), von denen zumindest einer, Giacomo di Mora, im Jahre 1239 *podestà* von Treviso war (Marshall 1996: 62; Janzarik 1989: 273) und wohl auch für die Verbreitung der Trobador-Dichtung in Sizilien maßgeblich wurde, deren Vorbild ab ca. 1230 zur Gründung der *scuola poetica siciliana* führte (Migliorini 1975: 7; *Dizionario Critico*, sv. *Siciliani* [390 b; 391 b]) (s.unten, § 4, Jofre de Foixà).

Der *Donatz proenzals*, zu dem auch, anders als bei der lateinischen *Ars grammatica* des Aelius Donatus (c.310–380), ein umfangreiches okzitanisch-lateinisches Reimwörterbuch gehört (ed. Marshall 1969: 186–255), ist zusammen mit einer (nachträglich hinzugefügten und möglicherweise nicht von Uc Faidit angefertigten [Marshall 1969: 18–19]) lateinischen Interlinearversion überliefert, welche wohl dazu diente, den Italienern, deren Sprache sich deutlich vom Okzitanischen unterscheidet, den Text der Grammatik näher zu erschließen.

### 3.1. Uc Faidit als Grammatiker

Uc Faidit geht es primär nicht um die Einübung in eine, wie auch immer definierte Sprachnorm, sondern, so möchte man eher vermuten, um die Vermittlung von Lese- und Interpretationsfähigkeiten (Marshall 1969: 78). Mit seinen Beispielen erläutert er vor allem grammatische Fragen, nicht aber, wie bei Raimon Vidal, den Sprachgebrauch der Trobadors. Das beigefügte Reimwörterbuch scheint allerdings eher für die Absicht zu sprechen, er habe auch aktive Sprachkenntnisse vermitteln wollen.

Zur Beschreibung des Okzitanischen bedient er sich des traditionnellen Rahmens von Donats *Ars maior* II [*De partibus orationis*] (und nicht des Frage- und Antwortespiels der *Ars minor*) (Anders Marshall 1969: 259.1–3).

Er beginnt mit den acht Redeteilen, die in derselben Reihenfolge wie bei Raimon Vidal präsentiert werden (Ms. A, ed. Marshall 1969: 88; in anderen Hss. in anderer Reihenfolge). Diese werden ausführlich und systematisch erklärt. Dabei lassen seine Definitionen von *nomen*, *pronomen* und Verb erkennen, daß er auch mit Priscians *Institutiones grammaticae*, welche ab dem 11. Jahrhundert höher als die *Ars* des Donat eingeschätzt wurde, vertraut war. Theoretische Erwägungen, wie sie an der Universität üblich waren, sind ihm dabei allerdings fremd (Marshall 1969: 66).

Wie Raimon Vidal unterscheidet er fünf Genera (maskulinum, femininum, neutrum, 'communis', 'omnis'; ed. Marshall 1969: 88), also weniger als Donat oder Priscian (Marshall 1969: 259.12–13). Aber ansonsten bemüht er sich darum, die bei Donat vorgegebenen Kategorien auch "en vulgar provençhal" (ed. Marshall 1969: 88) nachzuweisen.

Das macht namentlich Schwierigkeiten beim Optativ, der von den lateinischen Grammatikern aus der griechischen Grammatikographie übernommen worden war.

Bei den Tempora des Subjunktivs fragt er zudem nach Übersetzungsäquivalenzen, was zur Identifikation des lateinischen Imperfekt Subj. mit dem okzitanischen Imperfekt Ind. führt.

### 3.2. Die Rezeption des *Donatz proenzals*

Direkte Nachwirkungen des *Donatz proensals* sind bis ins frühe 14. Jahrhundert nachweisbar, nach Marshall (1969: 63) allerdings nur in Italien.

In Italien wurde er jedenfalls von dem anonymen Autor eines provenzalisch-italienischen Glossars vom Anfang des 14. Jh. benutzt (ed. Castellani 1958: 1–43).

Er wird allerdings später auch in Spanien von Enrique de Villena (1384?–1434) zitiert, nach der Erwähnung von Raimon Vidal und vor "las leyes del Consistorio de la gaya dotrina que por luengos tiempos se tovo en el collegio de Tolosa" [‚den Gesetzen des *Consistori* der Fröhlichen Wissenschaft, welches während langer Zeit in Toulouse stattfand'] (vgl. Zamora 1993: 27; s. dazu § 6).

Um die Mitte des 16. Jahrhunderts wird Uc Faidit von italienischen Humanisten dann wieder neu entdeckt, die sich mit der Trobadordichtung beschäftigten (Marshall 1969: 79).

## 4. Jofre de Foixà, *Regles de trobar*, 1285–1291, Sizilien

### 4.1 Katalanische Expansion

Der Autor des *Donatz Proenzals* war Okzitane, der nach den Albigenserkriegen sein Land verlassen hatte und nach (Nord-)Italien gekommen war. Nun kommen auch Katalanen nach Italien. Sizilien wird zum wichtigen Handelsplatz, mit katalanischen Konsulaten in Palermo und Messina (Nadal & Prats 1982: 268) und *En Jaume* ("Herr J.") von Sizilien (1285–1291) sammelt viele Trobadors um sich (Nadal & Prats 1982: 386–387; Ruffinatto 1968: 24).

Das Katalanische wird im 14. Jahrhundert zu einer der wichtigsten Sprachen des Mittelmeerraumes. Ihr Verbreitungsbereich reicht von Katalonien (und Teilen Aragóns) bis zu den Balearen und "totes les illes del mar llatí" ['allen Inseln des lateinischen Meeres'], Sizilien, Neapel und sogar bis zum Papsthof in Avignon (vgl. Nadal & Prats 1982: 36, 367).

Mit den Katalanen kommt auch der Franziskanerbruder und spätere Benediktinermönch Jofre de Foixà nach Sizilien (vgl. Marshall 1972: LXXII sq.; Nadal & Prats 1982: 387)

In seinem Hauptwerk, den *Regles de trobar* (V, 10–11) nennt der Verfasser sich selbst mit Namen und gibt an, den Traktat auf Geheiß von "En Iacme [...] rey de Sicilia" ['Herrn Jaume, König von Sizilien'] verfaßt zu haben. Verschiedene Indizien legen es nahe, dieses Werk auf 1289–1291 zu datieren (Marshall 1972: LXXIII; Kukenheim 1932: 95).

### 4.2. Charakteristik der *Regles de trobar*

Zu Beginn der *Regles de trobar* erklärt Jofre de Foixà, er strebe an, sich von "En Ramon Vidals de Besuldu" dadurch unterscheiden zu wollen, daß er seine *Regles* für Leute schreibe, die die lateinische Grammatik nicht beherrschten ("[que] no sabon gramatica"), nämlich Adelige und Bürger (Marshall 1972: 56). Er vermeidet daher auch durchgängig Termini der Latein-Grammatik und verwendet statt dessen volkssprachliche Wendungen wie *esdevenidor* "futurum", *maneyra* "modus", *linyatge* "genus", ferner: *seguir aquesta maneyra, alongar, abreuiar, mudament* "deklinieren, Deklination".

Raimon Vidal ist ausgiebig herangezogen worden. Wie die *Razós* sind die *Regles* in drei Teile gegliedert. Der zentrale morphologische Teil ist eingerahmt von zwei weniger systematisch aufgebauten Teilen, von denen der erste jene Punkte behandelt, bei denen der zukünftige Dichter leicht Fehler machen könne, wogegen der letzte Teil verschiedene alternative (stilistische) Möglichkeiten bespricht und Reimproben behandelt (vgl. Marshall 1972: xc).

Dennoch hält sich Jofre nicht sklavisch an seine Quelle, sondern benutzt sie vornehmlich als Anlaß für eigene, meist sehr intelligente Kommentare. Marshall (1972: xc) erläutert eingehend eine Reihe konkreter Beispiele.

Seine Kenntnisse des Okzitanischen sind hervorragend. Katalanismen sind außerordentlich selten (Marshall 1972: xcii).

Bemerkenswert ist auch sein Interesse an syntaktischen Fragen. Marshall (1972: xciii) sieht hier, unter Hinweis auf Robins (1951), sicherlich zu Recht Parallelen zur (lateinischen) Grammatiktheorie des 13. Jahrhunderts in Frankreich. Jofre de Foixà ist auch der erste Grammatiker einer Volkssprache, der den bestimmten Artikel (*article*) als eigenständiges Phänomen behandelt.

## 5. Terramagnino da Pisa, *Doctrina d'Acort*, ca. 1282–1296, Sardinien

Die in Sardinien entstandene *Doctrina d'Acort* (etwa: "Lehre von der Übereinstimmung") des Terramagnino da Pisa ist nach Meyer als "la mise en vers des *Razos de trobar* de Raimon Vidal" anzusehen; nur in der Wahl der Beispiele zeige er Originalität (Meyer 1879: 182; vgl. auch Swiggers 1988: 11).

Diese Auffassung bedarf jedoch einiger Nuancierungen. Terramagnino geht es darum, die *Razós de trobar* zu einer Versgrammatik [vgl. Alexander von Villadei (1160/1170–1240/1250), Eberhard von Béthune (?–c.1212)] umzuschreiben. Dabei wird namentlich das, was nicht direkt zur Grammatik gehört, stark gekürzt bzw. ganz ausgelassen.

Eine Neuerung gegenüber den *Razós* stellt auch der Hinweis auf zu vermeidende Barbarismen und Solözismen dar (vv. 763–772), und die, sehr knappe, Behandlung der Position von *accens agutz* "Akut" und *greus* "Gravis" im *chantars* "Lied" (vv. 773–776), womit die betonte bzw. unbetonte Silbe gemeint ist. Das Ziel Terramagninos ist also vor allem didaktischer Natur (vgl. Ruffinatto 1968: 56), genau wie das der Lateingrammatiken von Alexander von Villadei und Eberhard von Béthune.

Im Sinne dieser Didaktisierung orientiert er sich oft stur an den Schemata der lateinischen Grammatik. So werden etwa die indeklinablen Formen *cors* (*corpus*) und *chantairitz* "Sängerin" zwölfmal unverändert wiederholt, um der Deklination des Lateinischen gerecht zu werden. M.a.W., die *Doctrina d'Acort* markiert die Annäherung der volkssprachlichen Grammatik an die Lateingrammatik, eine Entwicklung, die in den folgenden Jahren noch deutlicher wird.

## 6. Sprachwissenschaft des Okzitanischen im 14. Jahrhundert

Vom Anfang des 14. Jahrhunderts stammt ein kleines anonymes provenzalisch-italienisches Glossar, welches zeigt, daß in Italien das Interesse an der provenzalischen Lyrik immer noch fortbesteht. (Ms. in Florenz, vgl. Castellani 1958: 1). Es stammt aller Wahrscheinlichkeit nach aus Norditalien. Zu seinen Quellen gehört der *Donatz proenzals* (Castellani 1958: 10). Die wichtigeren Entwicklungen vollziehen sich von nun an aber außerhalb Italiens, nämlich wieder im Heimatland der Trobadors, in Okzitanien.

## 7. Das *Consistori del Gai Saber* von Toulouse (1323)

Hier kommt es in der 1. Hälfte des 14. Jahrhunderts zu einer Wiederbelebung der Trobadordichtung. Träger dieser 'Renaissance' ist jetzt aber nicht mehr der Adel, sondern das okzitanische Bürgertum, welches im Jahre 1324 in Toulouse eine Dichterschule gründet, welche die erloschene Tradition des Minnesangs wieder beleben soll. Das Organisationskommitee nennt sich *Consistori del Gai Saber* "Kommitee der Fröhlichen Wissenschaft", gelegentlich auch *Sobregaya* (die "höchst Fröhliche") (Einzelheiten vgl. Anglade 1971: I.13, II.26–27).

Die Struktur des *Consistori* ist der Universitätsstruktur nachempfunden (genaueres bei Anglade 1971: IV.33–39). Die 'Meistersinger' erhalten Diplome, die ihnen das Recht einräumen

> d'argumenter, interroger, reciter et lire nos Lois ... pour semer le Gai Savoir. (Anglade 1971: IV.27)

Es gibt auch ein Doktorat in der (ziemlich ernst gemeinten) 'Fröhlichen Wissenschaft' (vgl. Anglade 1971: I.23), welches aber erst nach dem Erwerb des Grades des *Bachelier en Gai Savoir* erworben werden kann. Der 'Doktorand' muß folgende Bedingungen erfüllen:

> [il doit être] savant et entendu dans la science primordiale de grammaire; et il doit être examiné rigoureusement, de manière à pouvoir répondre sur tout point douteux de la Gaie Science. (Anglade 1971: IV.28)

Erst der *docteur en Gai Savoir* hat das Recht, in der Versammlung mit Argumenten einzugreifen und zu diskutieren (*determenar*; Terminus der Universität, vgl. Anglade 1971: IV.27).

Um eine exakte Richtschnur beim Urteil über das beste Preislied zu haben, gibt das *Consistori* Lehrbücher in Auftrag, welche die grammatischen Regeln der okzitanischen Sprache und die rhetorischen Figuren der Trobadordichtung genauestens darlegen und für den Unterricht vorstellen sollten. Der Verfasser eines dieser Lehrbücher ist Guilhem Molinier (Ruffinatto 1968: 27; Nadal & Prats 1982: 386).

### 7.1. Guilhem Molinier

Guilhem Molinier trägt zu diesem Zweck viele bekannte sprachliche (und poetologische) Regeln zusammen und kompiliert daraus die *Leys d'Amor* "Gesetze der Liebe[sdichtung]" (und die *Flors del Gay saber* "Blumen der Fröhlichen Wissenschaft" (s. u.). Diese Bücher tragen entschieden zur weiteren Verbreitung des *Gai saber* bei.

#### 7.1.1. Die Handschriften

Von den *Leys d'Amors* existieren zwei sehr unterschiedliche handschriftliche Versionen, eine, von Gatien-Arnoult (1977 [= 1849]) herausgegebene Version in 5 Büchern (von 1341) und eine andere, von Anglade (1971) in den Druck gegebene Version in 3 Büchern (von 1356). Zu diesen Versionen ist noch eine weitere zu rechnen (von 1343), welche in Versform vorliegt und üblicherweise als *Flors del gay saber* bezeichnet wird (Zamora 1993: 27; anders Ruffinatto 1968: 28). "La rédaction des *Leys* se fit donc en plusieurs fois et nous en avons plusieurs 'états'." (Anglade 1971: IV. 26).

Im Unterschied zur Redaktion von 1341 (vgl. dazu Anglade 1971: I.82) verzichtet Molinier in der späteren Fassung auf die Behandlung der Rhetorik, erweitert das Werk jedoch um eine Geschichte des Konsistoriums.

#### 7.1.2. Sprachkonzeption

Da es sich bei den *Leys d'Amor* um eine Einführung in die Sprache *und* Dichtungslehre der Trobadors handelt, ist hier festzuhalten, daß sprachwissenschaftliche Fragen zunächst einmal in Buch I und II (in der Version von

1341) bzw. in Buch II der Version von 1356 behandelt werden. Hier geht es, neben einem Überblick über diverse Probleme der provenzalischen Metrik (Vers, Reim, Strophe) ausführlicher um Fragen der Orthographie (und Prosodie). Noch wichtiger ist Buch III, welches in beiden Versionen die Grammatik des Okzitanischen darlegt, wobei dieser Teil in der Version von 1356 detaillierter und umfangreicher ausfällt.

Dabei beruft Guilhem Molinier sich immer wieder auf den *bon usage*, den *us acostumat* (Anglade 1971: III.79, 98, 102) bzw. den *lonc usatge acostumat* (vgl. Anglade 1971: VI.87)

Dieser 'lonx uzatges' ist ihm das oberste Kriterium in grammatischen Fragen und wird häufig verwendet [...]. Nur wo dieses Hilfsmittel, die Befragung der alten Gedichte im Stich lasse, solle man seine Zuflucht nehmen zum "us acostumat", d. h. zu dem Sprachgebrauch, wie er mindestens in einer ganzen bischöflichen Diöcese des "romanischen" Sprachgebiets geübt werde [...]. Das dritte Kriterium "segon art" d.i. das kunstgemäße Latein der grammatischen Überlieferung spielt zwar eine große Rolle in den Leys, ist aber das schwächste von den dreien [...]. (Lienig 1890: 4)

Bemerkenswert ist auch die Tatsache, daß Guilhem Molinier Dialekte unterscheidet und zwar nach Diözesen (Anglade 1971: IV.87; vgl. III.112, 113, besonders III.164). Die beste Sprachform ist für ihn in Toulouse zu finden.

#### 7.1.2.1. Allgemeine Verdienste

Heinimann resumiert die Verdienste Guilhem Moliniers wie folgt:

Der Mitte des 14. Jhs. gehört der Grammatiker an, der zum erstenmal mit bemerkenswertem Erfolg den Versuch unternimmt, außer dem Formenbestand auch syntaktische Erscheinungen seiner Muttersprache darzustellen. Es ist Guilhem Molinier, der im Auftrag des Konsistoriums von Toulouse zusammen mit seinen Helfern und Beratern die *Leys d'amors* verfaßte. Das 3. Buch seines Werkes widmet er ganz der Grammatik. In herkömmlicher Weise wird der Stoff nach den acht Wortarten gegliedert. Den breitesten Raum nehmen auch bei ihm Nomen und Verbum ein. Anstatt sich aber wie seine provenzalischen Vorläufer im wesentlichen auf die elementare *Ars minor* des Donat zu stützen, baut Guilhem Molinier vorwiegend auf dem viel ausführlicheren, auch syntaktische Erscheinungen behandelnden Priscian auf. Ihm folgt er meist in der Gliederung des Stoffes und in den Definitionen. Natürlich ist ihm Donat ebenfalls vertraut. Überdies benützt er Isidor von Sevilla und an mittelalterlichen Werken das *Doctrinale* des Alexander de Villedieu, das *Catholicon* von Johannes von Genua, das *Elementarium doctrinae rudimentum* von Papias und den Prisciankommentar von Petrus Helias. In der längeren Fassung beruft er sich überdies auf den *Graecismus* von Évrard de Béthune und auf 'andere Grammatiker', deren Namen er allerdings nicht nennt (Heinimann 1987: 24)

Guilhem Molinier kommt überdies der Verdienst zu, "als erster den Versuch [unternommen zu haben], das Wesen des romanischen Artikels zu ergründen ..." (Heinimann 1987: 35)

#### 7.1.2.2. *Ethimologia*

Er ist aber auch vertraut mit der zeitgenössischen, in Latein geführten wissenschaftlichen Diskussion zur 'Lexikologie', was u. a. hervorgeht aus seiner Auffassung zur *Ethimologia* (damals zur Wortbildungslehre (*derivatio*) gerechnet); hierbei verwendet er Formulierungen, welche so bereits bei Johannes von Genua (?–1298? O. P.) zu finden ist (vgl. Niederehe 1975).

Ethimologia de letras non es veraya derivatio, quar non es motz qu'om no·l pogues ethimologizar per letras o per sillabas; et enayssi tug serian derivatiu. ... ['Ableitungen nach Buchstaben' sind keine wahren Ableitungen, gibt es doch kein Wort, welches man nicht hinsichtlich seiner Buchstaben bzw. seiner Silben 'etymologisieren' könnte, es folglich also als 'abgeleitet' angesehen werden könnte'] (Anglade 1971: III.21)

#### 7.1.2.3. Latein

Angesichts seiner Vertrautheit mit dem Lateinischen (bzw. der lateinsprachigen Sprachwissenschaft) verwundert es nicht, daß er trotz seines Interesses für das Okzitanische das Latein als 'vollkommenste aller Sprachen' ansieht ("es lengatges mays perfieytz e mays aproatz que degus dels altres a nos conogutz") (vgl. Anglade 1971: III,114).

#### 7.1.3. Die grammatischen Quellen

Für die Schule von Toulouse waren laut Massó Torrents (1932), außer einer Reihe von poetologischen Traktaten, folgende traditionelle Grammatiken des Okzitanischen von Wichtigkeit:

1. *Las Razós de Trobar*, von Raimon Vidal de Besalú
3. *Doctrina d'Acort,* von Terramagnino da Pisa
4. *Regles de trobar*, von Jofre de Foixà

Es sind dies praktisch alle okzitanischen Grammatiktraktate, welche aus Katalonien und Sizilien angeführt werden konnten. Ob Guilhem Molinier auch Uc Faidits *Donatz Proenzals* gekannt hat, ist dagegen unsicher.

Parmi les provençalistes, Galvani et Stengel croient que G. Molinier n'a pas connu le *Donat Proensal*, ou que, du moins, il n'est pas possible de démontrer qu'il l'ait connu. Diez était d'un avis contraire; Lienig, *Op. laud.*, p. 14 (Anglade 1971: IV.98)

Anglade selbst neigt der Diezschen (und Lienigschen) Auffassung zu; er schreibt:

L'ouvrage d'Uc Faidit ne paraît pas avoir eu de notorité dans le pays de langue d'Oc. Cependant on verra qu'il était connu des rédacteurs des *Leys* (Anglade 1971: IV.95)

Marshall (1969: 63) ist dagegen der Überzeugung, der *Donatz* sei ausschließlich in Italien bekannt gewesen; Guilhem Molinier könne ihn daher nicht gekannt haben.

### 7.2. Raimon de Cornet (1324)

Raimon de Cornet, eine etwas zwielichtige Gestalt, gehörte dem Konsistorium nur mittelbar an. Er war verantwortlich für alles, was grammatischen Fragen anbelangte.

Si Raimon de Cornet acceptait la direction grammaticale du Consistoire, il paraît avoir voulu conserver son indépendance de poète (Anglade 1971: IV.101 n.)

Er ist Verfasser eines *Doctrinal de trobar*, (Toulouse?, 1324), welches einen "rapide aperçu des principales formes grammaticales (noms, pronoms, verbes) en se référant aux usages des meilleurs Trobadors du temps passé [...]" bietet (Anglade 1971: IV.100). Es ist auf das Jahr 1324 zu datieren und besteht aus 543 sechssilbigen Versen, die Peter von Aragón gewidmet sind.

Das *Doctrinal* enthält einen Abriß der wichtigsten grammatischen Formen (Nomen, Pronomen, Verb), die durch den 'Usus der besten Trobadors' illustriert werden, genauso wie in den späteren *Leys d'Amors* (Anglade 1971: IV.100).

Teil 2 (v. 245–408; Anglade 1971: IV.99 sq.) behandelt den Akzent und die am Häufigsten vorkommenden rhetorischen Figuren. Teil 3 (v. 341–408) ist dem Reim gewidmet und gibt zudem eine knappe Definition der lyrischen Genera. Teil 4 (ab v. 409) bietet einen Diskurs über die "Trobadors ançiens".

### 7.3. Joan de Castelnou, *Glosari*, 1341

Der aus dem Roussillon stammende Joan de Castelnou kritisiert in seinem *Glosari* (1341) das *Doctrinal* des Raimon de Cornet (vgl. Anglade 1971: IV.101).

Das Werk ist dem Infanten Peter, Graf von Ampurias und Ribagorza gewidmet, dem auch Raimon de Cornet sein Werk gewidmet hatte. Wahrscheinlich laufen über ihn die Kontakte, die später zu einer Wiederbelebung der Trobadordichtung in Katalonien (s. u.) führten (Nadal & Prats 1982: 387).

Im *Glosari* ist erstmals die Rede von den *Leys d'Amors* (Anglade 1971: IV.100).

La "glose" de Joan de Castelnou témoigne d'une connaissance plus complète et plus judicieuse des lois de la grammaire et de la métrique "romanes"; il reconnaît la nécessité d'avoir recours au latin en matière de grammaire, mais il s'en refère au "romans" en dernier ressort pour toutes les difficultés, invoquant le bon usage et les habitudes, suivant la doctrine des *Leys* (Anglade 1971: IV.102).

## 8. Das *Consistori* von Barcelona (1393)

### 8.1 Entstehungsgeschichte

Das Toulouser Beispiel findet Nachahmer in Katalonien, ungefähr 15 Jahre nach der Gründung des *Consistori.* Auch hier beginnt man zunächst mit einem Dichterwettbewerb, der am 31. Mai 1338 in Lleida stattfindet. In Anwesenheit von Peter IV., genannt der 'Förmliche' (*el Ceremoniòs*), wird der erste Preisträger ermittelt. Er erhält eine goldene Rose und ein prächtiges, golddurchwirktes Tuch, genannt *diasprell.*

Die eigentliche Meistersingerschule wird aber erst 1393 in Barcelona von König Joan I (1350; 1387–1395), Sohn Peters des 'Förmlichen', durch eine offizielle Eröffnung der 'Festspiele der Fröhlichen Wissenschaft' begründet, welche von nun an jährlich am Fest Mariä Verkündigung durchgeführt werden (Anglade 1971: IV.106; Ruffinatto 1968: 29).

### 8.2. Die offizielle Gründung des *Consistori*

Im Jahr der Festspiele von 1393 – später werden sie *Jocs Florals* "Blumenspiele" genannt werden – beauftragt Juan I. von Aragon und Katalonien den 'Ritter' Jaume March und einen Bürger von Barcelona, Lluis d'Averçò, mit der Bildung eines katalanischen Konsistoriums nach dem Vorbild von Toulouse (s. Anglade 1971: IV.106). Jaume March und Lluis d'Averçò waren aber bereits deutlich vor dem hier genannten Datum für das *Consistori* aktiv, so daß ihre Nominierung lediglich als öffentliche Anerkennung einer bis dahin inoffiziellen Vorbereitungsphase angesehen werden kann (s. u.).

Wie in Toulouse gilt auch das *Consistori* von Barcelona "com una autèntica escola o facultad universitària" ['als echte Schule bzw. als universitäre Fakultät'] (Nadal & Prats 1982: 486). Manche inhaltlichen und organisatorischen Details sind uns dadurch überliefert, daß der spanische Dichter Enrique de Villena (1384?–1434) in seiner 'Dichtungslehre', dem *Arte de trobar*, der im übrigen auch 'sprachwissenschaftliche' Kommentare enthält, ausführlicher über das *Consistori* berichtet (Casas Homs 1956: I. XCV).

In Folge dieser Gründung entsteht auch eine katalanische Adaptation der Prosafassung der *Leys d'Amors* (kurze Beschreibung des Ms. bei Anglade 1971: IV.106) und ebenfalls eine Fassung der *Leys* in Reimen, die *Flors del Gay Saber* (Anglade 1971: IV.106 n).

Zu den in Katalonien entstandenen Versionen der *Leys* und den *Flors* lassen sich nach Anglade folgende Informationen zusammenstellen:

[...] d'abord une traduction catalanisée de l'une des rédactions en prose des *Leys d'Amors note*: Conservée aux Archives de la Couronne d'Aragon, à Barcelone. Ms. en papier, de la fin du quatorzième siècle. [...], puis et surtout la rédaction en vers des *Flors del Gai Saber*, dont c'est le seul manuscrit qui se soit conservé.

La rédaction en vers, appelée *Flors del Gai Saber note*: [...] Le ms. est à Barcelone, *Biblioteca de Catalunya*, n° 239. 7.500 vers environ de huit syllabes, paraît se rattacher à la rédaction en six livres en l'abrégeant. Dans la quatrième partie, la morphologie des verbes est exposée en une trentaine de vers seulement. La cinquième est consacrée aux *vices et figures* (livre IV de la rédaction G. A.). La sixième est très brève. Le *rimario* manque ainsi que la chanson à Notre-Dame [...] (Anglade 1971: IV:106 sq.)

### 8.3. Die Vorbereitung der Gründung

1372 hatte König Peter von Aragón (1335–1387) "protecteur de la poésie et poète lui-même" bereits Jaume March beauftragt, einen *Livre de Concordances* bzw. einen *Dictionnaire de rimes* zu erstellen (vgl. Anglade 1971: IV.105 n).

Eine weitere 'vorbereitende' Schrift ist aber noch wichtiger, der im letzten Viertel des 14. Jahrhunderts entstandene *Torcimany* "Dolmetscher" des Lluis d'Averçò.

Tra il primo tentativo di Lleida e l'istaurazione del "Concistori" di Barcellona, e sicuramente per fini simili a quelli delle *Leys d'amors* tolosane, furono composti in Catalogna due trattati poetico-grammaticali: il *Diccionario* di Jacme March ed il *Torcimany* di Luys d'Averçò. ['Zwischen den ersten Anfängen von Lleida und der Gründung des *Consistori* von Barcelona wurden, sicherlich aus ähnlichen Gründen wie bei den *Leys*, in Katalonien zwei poetisch-grammatische Traktate verfaßt, der *Diccionario* von Jaume March und der *Torcimany* des Lluis d'Averçò'] (Ruffinatto 1968: 29).

Der *Torcimany*, dessen genaues Entstehungsdatum nicht bekannt ist, ist jedenfalls nach den *Flors del Gay Saber* verfaßt worden, werden sie hierin doch regelmäßig zitiert (Casas Homs 1956: I. xxiv; vgl. auch BOCT 1985: 518).

### 8.4. Jaume March, *Diccionari* (1371)

Der *Libre de concordances appellat diccionari* von Jaume Marche ist 1371 fertiggestellt worden. Die Handschrift findet sich in Barcelona, in der Biblioteca de Catalunya, unter der Signatur 239. Es handelt sich dabei um "un'ampia raccolta di vocaboli, disposti secondo la consonanza ad uso del poeta che cerca rime per le sue liriche. [Ed. Griera 1921.]" ['eine umfangreiche Wortsammlung, nach Wortausgängen gegliedert, welche dem Dichter bei der Suche nach geeigneten Reimen helfen sollte'] (Ruffinatto 1968: 30).

Laut Prolog ist das Werk auf Bitten von König Peter von Aragon im Jahre 1371 angefertigt worden. Es heißt da: "Presentacio del prolech del libre de concordances appellat diccionari ordenat per en Jacme March a istancia del molt alt e poderos senyor en Pere per la gracia de deu Rey d'Arago e fou fet en l'any .M. CCC. LXXI." ['Präsentation des Prologs des Buchs über die Reimausgänge, genannt *Diccionari* und herausgegeben von Jaume March auf Bitten des sehr hohen und mächtigen Herrn Peter, durch die Gnade Gottes König von Aragon, und abgefaßt im Jahre 1371'] (Incipit, zit. nach Griera 1921: 23; vgl. Nadal & Prats 1982: 492).

Es ist bezeichnend, daß man auch noch im 14. Jahrhundert ein Lehrbuch einer Fremdsprache nicht in der Sprache des Sprachstudenten, sondern in der Zielsprache abfaßte, also genau so wie man beim Lateinischen vorging. Im Falle des *Diccionari* handelt es sich dabei um "un occità absolutament convencional, cada cop més catalanitzat" ['ein gänzlich konventionelles Okzitanisch, welches aber zunehmend katalanische Einflüsse erkennen läßt'] (Nadal & Prats 1982: 493).

### 8.5. Lluis d'Averçò, *Torcimany* (1380?)

Lluis d'Averçò ist vor 1350 geboren (Casas Homs 1956: I. xx); er stirbt zwischen 1412 und 1415 (Casas Homs 1956: I. xxiii). Möglicherweise hat er den oben erwähnten spanischen Dichter Enrique de Villena gekannt, dem wir manche Informationen über das *Consisori* verdanken.

Sein *Torcimany* weist ihn als jemanden aus, der solide Kenntnisse in lateinischer Grammatik und Rhetorik besaß (Casas Homs 1956: I. x). Aus zeitgenössischen Dokumenten erfahren wir zudem, daß er direkt mit dem politischen Leben Barcelonas verbunden war. Er ist Ratsherr, leitet Delegationen des katalanischen Parlaments und genießt das Vertrauen des Königs (Nadal & Prats 1982: 493).

Nach Casas Homs ist sein *Torcimany* als neuer, ausführlicher grammatisch-rhetorischer Traktat nach Art der Abhandlungen von Guilhem Molinier anzusehen ["[c]onstituye el *Torcimany*, en realidad, un extenso y nuevo tratado gramatica-retórico-poético a la manera de los de Molinier." (Casas Homs 1956: I. xlviii)].

Das Werk ist zweigeteilt; Teil I enthält Poetik und Grammatik, Teil II einen Traktat über Reime sowie ein Reimwörterbuch, wie bei Jaume March *Diccionari* genannt (Nadal & Prats 1982: 494).

Teil I gliedert sich in drei *partidas*, wobei zunächst einmal die Lautlehre (Alphabete, Vokale vs. Konsonanten, Diphthonge, Silben, Akzent), dann das Wort, der Satz, etc. behandelt werden. Die zweite *partida* geht zunächst darauf ein "Que vol dir trobar" ('was Dichten bedeutet'), dann auf Formen, Stilfiguren, Stilmängel, etc. Es folgt eine sehr detaillierte Behandlung von Kasus, Deklination, Numerus, *vós* ("vox"), Tempus, Genus, Person und schließlich, in der 3. *partida*, eine Definition der Grammatik (*Fi de la sciencia de gramatica*) und ihrer Teile (*Divisió de gramatica"* und schließlich eine Wiederholung des Ganzen (*Recogitació*), dann Redefiguren (*figura de locució*), ein Abriß der Rhetorik sowie ihre Unterscheidung von der Grammatik, und schließlich (nach der Behandlung von Barbarismus etc.) die *colores rhetorici*.

Seine Grammatikdefinition läßt seine Vertrautheit mit der lateinischen Grammatik des Mittelalters erkennen, so etwa sein Hinweis auf die Lehre von der *congruitas*. ["Gramatica es sciencia de dretament parlar e de dretament escriure, e las cosas escritas dretament pronunciar. Lo dretament parlar está en congruitat de parlar" 'Die Grammatik ist die Wissenschaft vom richtigen Sprechen und vom richtigen Schreiben und von der richtigen Aussprache des Geschriebenen. Das richtige Sprechen beruht auf der *congruitas*'] (Averçó in Casas Homs 1956: I.233).

Es folgt eine Unterteilung der Grammatik in *gramatica preceptiva o mandativa*, *gramatica permissiva o licenciativa* und *gramatica prohibitiva y contrastiva*, welche nach Casas Homs (Anm. ibid.) auf Donat zurückgehen könnte, aber wahrscheinlich doch eher einem 'comentarista' zuzuschreiben ist. Dabei geht es vor allem um "las dretas locucions figurativas" ['die korrekten figurativen Redewendungen'] (Averçó in Casas Homs 1956: I.237).

In der Definition der *Veu* ("vox") folgt er Priscian (Casas Homs 1956: I.32). Die *letra* "es veu qui divisir no·s pot" ['ist ein Lautzeichen, welches nicht weiter unterteilt werden kann'] und 'das schreibt auch Guilhem Molinier in den *Flors del gay saber*, im Kapitel xxvi' ["E axí ho posa mosen Guilhem Moliner en las *Flors del gay saber* [...], en lo capitol xxvi,"] (Averçó in Casas Homs 1956: I.43).

Auch die *dicció* und die *oració* werden unter ausdrücklicher Anlehung an die *Flors del gai saber* definiert. (Averçó in Casas Homs 1956: I.45–46), ebenso die *silaba* (Averçó in Casas Homs 1956: I.60) und der *accent* (*ibid.* 64–68).

Dasselbe gilt auch für seine ausführliche Abhandlung *Dels cases* (Averçó in Casas Homs 1956: I.176) und der *Senyals dels cases* [Nom. mask.: *le*, fem. *la*, Genitiv *de*, *del* ...] (*ibid.* 178).

Hierbei bedient er sich eines, aus dem Lateinunterricht bekannten didaktischen Verfahrens, der 'erotematischen' Präsentation des behandelten Stoffes ('in Fragen und Antworten'; vgl. etwa Averçó in Casas Homs 1956: I.183). Ja, manchmal setzt er geradezu Lateinkenntnisse voraus, denn er übersetzt ein Beipiel "der größeren Klarheit wegen" ins Lateinische (*ibid.* 188; 190).

8.5.1. Sprachenwahl

Im Mittelalter ist es üblich, Grammatiken des Lateinischen auch auf Latein abzufassen, und dem entsprechend auch Grammatiken des Okzitanischen auf Okzitanisch. Erst Lluís d'Averçò weicht als erster von dieser Praxis mit der folgenden Begründung ab:

> Jo no·m servesch en la prezent obra, per duas raons, dels lenguatges que los trobadors en lurs obras se servexen; la primera és com prosaichament lo present libre jo pos, e en lo posar prosaich no ha necesitat a servir-se dels lenguatges ja ditz, per tal és que si jo·m servia d'altre lenguatge sinó del català, que és món lenguatge propi, he dupte que no·m fos notat a ultracuydament, car pus jo

son català, no·m dech servir d'altre lenguathe sinó del meu. ['Aus zwei Gründen bediene ich mich in dem vorliegenden Werk nicht der Sprache der Trobadors, und zwar weil ich in Prosa schreibe und es deswegen keine Notwendigkeit gibt, mich besagter Sprache zu bedienen und, wenn ich mich einer anderen Sprache als meiner eigenen, dem Katalanischen, bediente, man mir dies als Überspanntheit anrechnen würde, denn da ich Katalane bin darf ich mich keiner anderen Sprache als meiner eigenen bedienen'] (Averçó in Casas Homs 1956: I.17; vgl. Nadal & Prats 1982: 494).

### 8.5.2 Luis d'Averçò, *Diccionari*

Obwohl es mehr als wahrscheinlich ist, daß Lluis d'Averçò das Reimlexikon seines Mitkonsistorialen Jaume March gekannt hat, ist sein eigenes Reimlexikon, der *Diccionari,* unabhängig davon entstanden (vgl. Casas Homs 1956: I. LXIV, LXVII). Jedenfalls ist bislang keine Quelle hierfür nachweisbar. Der aufgenommene Wortschatz selbst enthält eine große Zahl von Katalanismen, so daß Nadal & Prats (vgl. 1982: 497–498) mit einigem Recht von einem "recull de lèxic català" ('eine katalanische Wortschatzsammlung') sprechen kann.

### 8.5.3 Die Nachwirkung des *Diccionari*

Allerdings ist der *Diccionari* nur in einer Handschrift überliefert, gegenüber drei von Jaume March. Casas Homs vermutet daher, er habe so gut wie keine Nachwirkungen gehabt, wofür auch der fragmentarische Charakter des *Diccionari* spräche (vgl. Casas Homs 1956: I. xcv).

### 8.6. Das rhetorische Handbuch des *Consistori* (1393?)

Nach dem Vorbild von Toulouse und dem dort beheimateten Guilhem Molinier scheint auch das *Consistori* von Barcelona ein 'rhetorisches Handbuch' des Meistersanges vorbereitet zu haben, welches uns wohl in Ms. 239 (2. Hälfte 14. Jahrhunderts) der Biblioteca de Catalunya, Barcelona, vorliegt.

En el mismo manuscrito, [...] se ha transmitido una colección de tratados gramaticales y de preceptiva literaria (aparte de los de J. de Foixà y de B. de Noya, hallamos los de Raimón Vidal de Besalú, de Joan de Castellnou, de Terramagnino de Pisa, de Guilhem Molinier y otros anónimos), lo que permite suponer que pertenecía a los jueces del Consistorio de Barcelona y justifica, a la vez, el hecho de que nos hayan llegado a través de la misma tradición manuscrita. ['Im gleichen Manuskript finden sich eine Sammlung grammatikalischer Traktate und literarischer Vorschriften (von J. de Foixà und B. de Noya, Raimón Vidal de Besalú, Joan de Castellnou, Terramagnino de Pisa, Guilhem Molinier sowie weitere anonyme Werke), was vermuten läßt, das es den Preisrichtern des Konsistoriums von Barcelona gehörte und gleichzeitig erklärt, warum sie zur selben Manuskripttradition gehören.'] (Comas 1955: 368–369)

Ambas ediciones [Li Gotti, Jofre de Foixà, 1952 & Palumbo, Berenguer de Noya, 1955] están basadas en la lectura del ms. 239 de la Biblioteca Central de Barcelona [...] ['Beide Ausgaben basieren auf ms. 239 der Biblioteca de Cataluny, Barcelona'] (Comas 1955: 368).

Anglade (1971: IV.106) sieht eine Art von Kausalzusammenhang zwischen dem Gründungsauftrag von 1393 und der Entstehung des Handbuchs. Da aber spätestens seit 1338 (Lleida) Aktivitäten des Meistersinger bezeugt sind, könnte auch an eine deutlich früher in Angriff genommene Sammlung der einschlägigen Texte gedacht werden.

## 9. Die Wiederentdeckung der okzitanischen Grammatik

Nach dem *Consistori* von Toulouse und der gleichnamigen Institution aus Barcelona, beide Gründungen des 14. Jahrhunderts, gerät die Lehre von der Trobador-Dichtung inklusiv ihrer Grammatik mehr und mehr in Vergessenheit. Erst im Zuge der Romantik, im 19. Jahrhundert, besinnt man sich wieder der alten Lehren. So kann Guessard im Jahre 1857 schreiben:

Les deux grammaires que je publie de nouveau [Raimon Vidal & Uc Faidit] sont restées inédites jusqu'en 1840, bien qu'on connût l'existence. M. Raynouard [1761–1836] lui-même ne leur a consacré qu'une courte notice (*Choix* T. II, p. CL). (Guessard 1857: xvii)

Guessard selbst steht aber erneut 'an den Anfängen' des Studiums der Sprache der Trobadors und ihrer Grammatik. Er versteht beispielsweise die (im Großen und Ganzen korrekt formulierte) Zweikasusregel bei den beiden Grammatikern völlig falsch, wenn er schreibt: "Je ne vois dans la théorie de nos deux grammairiens qu'une application maladroite et forcée du principe latin de la distinction des cas par la terminaison." (Guessard 1973 [= 1857]: xxvi). "Les deux dialectes romans du midi et du nord de la France ont été longuement embarrassés de ces superfluités et c'est celui qui le premier paraît s'en être déchargée, qui a etouffé l'autre, en passant rapidement de l'enfance à la virilité" (Guessard 1973 [= 1857]: xxvii).

Nach einer langen Zeit der Unterbrechung kann man offensichtlich nicht dort wieder einsetzen und einfach weiter machen, wo man vor langer Zeit einmal die Forschung früherer Zeiten gestanden hat. Für das Vergessen alter Traditionen hat man seinen Preis zu zahlen.

Aber das 19. Jahrhundert tut dies, und zwar unter Einsatz aller Kräfte. Die damals entstehende Romanische Philologie steht, zumindesten in ihren Anfängen bei Friedrich Diez (1794–1876), ganz im Zeichen der Trobadors und ihrer Sprache.

## 10. Bibliographie

Anglade, Joseph, Hg. 1926. *Las Flors del Gay Saber.* (= *Memòries: Secció Filològica*, I–1.) Barcelona: Institut d'Estudis Catalans.

–, Hg. 1971 [= 1919–1920]. *Las Leys d'Amors.* Manuscrit de l'Académie des Jeux Floraux. 4 tomes. New York & London: Johnson Reprint Corporation. (Toulouse: Édouard Privat & Paris: Auguste Picard.)

BOCT = Jorgensen Concheff, Beatrice. 1985. *Bibliography of Old Catalan Texts.* Madison: The Seminary of Hispanic Studies.

Casas Homs, José María, Hg.; Luis de Averçó. 1956. *Torcimany.* Tratado retórico gramatical y diccionario de rimas Siglos XIV–XV. Bd. I, II. Barcelona: Consejo Superior de Investigaciones Científicas.

Castellani, Arrigo. 1958. "Le glossaire provençal-italien de la Laurentienne (Ms. Plut. 41, 42)". *Lebendiges Mittelalter. Festgabe für Wolfgang Stammler* hg. von der Philosophischen Fakultät der Universität Freiburg Schweiz, 1–43. Freiburg, Schweiz: Universitätsverlag. [Mit Ausgabe des Glossars ab S. 17].

Comas, Antonio. 1955. Rezension von Li Gotti (1952) und Palumbo (1955). *Revista de Filología Española* 39.368–371.

Dahan, Gilbert, Irène Rosier & Luisa Valente. 1995. "L'arabe, le grec, l'hébreu et les vernaculaires". *Sprachtheorien in Spätantike und Mittelalter*, hg. von Sten Ebbesen, 265–321. (= *Geschichte der Sprachtheorie*, 3.). Tübingen: Gunter Narr.

*Dizionario critico della letteratura italiana* diretto da Vittore Branca. Vol. I–III. Torino: Unione Tipografica–Editrice Torinese, 1973.

Field, Hugh, Hg.; Ramon Vidal de Besalú. 1991. *Obra poètica. Introducció i edició.* (= *Autors Catalans Antics*, 7–8.) Barcelona: Curial 1.

Fredborg, Maria Margareta. 1980. "Universal Grammar According to Some 12th Century Grammarians". *Festschrift für G. Bursill-Hall* hg. von Konrad Koerner et al., 69–84. Amsterdam: J. Benjamins.

Gatien-Arnoult, Adolphe-Frédéric, Hg. 1977 [= 1841–1843]. *Monumens de la littérature romane depuis le quatorzième siècle I–III: Las Flors del Gay Saber estier dichas Las Leys d'Amors.* Genève: Slatkine. [Paris: Silvestre & Toulouse: Bon et Privat. Es handelt sich hierbei nach heutiger Terminologie um die *Leys,* nicht die *Flors.*]

Gonfroy, Gérard. 1981. *La rédaction catalane en prose des Leys d'amors.* Édition critique des trois premières parties. 2 Bde. Poitiers: Thèse. [Vgl. Schlieben-Lange 1991, *Revue de Linguistique Romane* 5.125.]

González Hurtubise, E. 1913. "Jofre de Foixá (...1267–1295...) – nota biográfica". *Congrès d'historia de la Corona d'Aragò*, II, 521–535; 1171–1172. Barcelona.

Griera, Antoni. 1921. *Diccionari de rims de Jaume Marche* editat per Antonio Griera. (= *Biblioteca Filològica de l'Institut de la Llengua Catalana*, VIII.) Barcelona: Institut d'Estudis Catalans.

Gröber, Gustav. 1884. "Der Verfasser des Donat proensal". *Zeitschrift für romanische Philologie* 8. 112–117.

–. "Gaucelm Faidit o Uc de Sant Circ?" *Giornale storico della letteratura italiana* 4. 203–208.

–. 1884. "Zur Widmung des Donat proensal". *Zeitschrift für romanische Philologie* 8. 290–293.

Gubern, R. 1957. "Els primers jocs florals a Catalunya: Lleida, 31 de maig 1338". *Bulletin of Hispanic Studies* 34.95–6.

Guessard, F. 1973 [= 1858]. *Grammaires provençales de Hugues Faidit et de Raymond Vidal de Besaudun (XIIIe siècle).* 2 e éd., revue, corrigée et considérablement augmentée. Genève: Slatkine.

Heinimann, Siegfried. 1963. "Zur Geschichte der grammatischen Terminologie im Mittelalter". *Zeitschrift für romanische Philologie* 79.23–37.

–. 1965. "Die Lehre vom Artikel in den romanischen Sprachen von der mittelalterlichen Grammatik zur modernen Sprachwissenschaft: Ein Beitrag der Geschichte der grammatischen Begriffsbildung". *Vox Romanica* 24.23–43.

Holtz, Louis. 1981. *Donat et la tradition de l'enseignement grammatical. Étude sur l'Ars Donati et sa diffusion (IVe–IXe siècle) et édition critique.* Paris: Centre National de la Recherche Scientifique.

Janzarik, Diether. 1989. "Uc de St. Circ – auteur du *Donatz Proensals?*" *Zeitschrift für romanische Philologie* 105.264–275.

Li Gotti, Ettore. 1955. "Jofre de Foixà". *VII Congreso Internacional de lingüística románica*, II (*Actas y Memorias*), 297–301. Barcelona.

–, Hg. 1952. *Jofre de Foixà. Vers e regles de trobar.* (= *Istituto di Filologia Romanza dell'Università di Roma. Testi e Manuali*, 37.) Modena: Società tipográfica Modenese.

Lienig, Paul. 1890. *Die Grammatik der provenzalischen Leys d'amors verglichen mit der Sprache der Troubadours.* 1: *Phonetik*. Breslau: Koebner.

Llabrès, G. 1909. *Poéticas catalanas de Berenguer de Noya y Francesch de Oleza.* Barcelona & Palma de Mallorca.

Marshall, John Henry, Hg. 1969. *The "Donatz Proensals" of Uc Faidit.* London: Oxford Univ. Press.

–, Hg. 1972. *The "Razos de Trobar" of Raimon Vidal. Raimon Vidal, "Razos de trobar". Terramagnino da Pisa, "Doctrina d'Acort". Jofre de Foixà, "Regles de trobar". "Doctrina de compondre dictats". Two anonymous treatises from MS. Ripoll 129.* London: Oxford Univ. Press.

Mas i Usó, Pasqual. 1995. "La mètrica catalana en les acadèmies i certàmens valencians del barroc". *Zeitschrift für Katalanistik* 8.63–73.

Massó Torrents, Jaume. 1922. *L'antiga escola poètica de Barcelona.* Lliçons donades en els cursos monogràfics d'alts estudis i d'intercanvi els dies 29 i 30 d'abril, 1, 2, 6, 7 i 9 de maig de 1921. Barcelona: Caritat.

–. 1932. *Repertori de l'antiga literatura catalana.* Vol. I: La Poesia. Barcelona: Editorial Alpha. [Mehr nicht erschienen.]

Meyer, Paul. 1877–1879. "Traités catalans de grammaire et poétique". *Romania* 6.341–358; 8.181–210; 9.51–70.

–. 1879. "Über Terramagnino". *Romania* 8.181–210.

Migliorini, Bruno. 1975. *Cronologia della lingua italiana.* Firenze: Le Monnier.

Nadal, Josep M. & Modest Prats. 1982. *Història de la llengua catalana.* I: *Dels inicis fins al segle XV.* Barcelona: Edicions 62.

Nicolau d'Olwer, L. 1907. "Notes sobre les "Regles de trobar" de Jofre de Foixà y sobre les poesíes que li han atribuit". *Estudis Universitaris Catalans* 1.234–256.

Niederehe, Hans-Josef. 1975. *Die Sprachauffassung Alfons' des Weisen.* Studien zur Sprach- und Wissenschaftsgeschichte. Tübingen: Niemeyer.

–. 1975. "Derivatio. Zur linguistischen Terminologie des ausgehenden Mittelalters". *Filología y didáctica hispánica. Homenaje al Profesor Hans-Karl Schneider*, 243–254 (= *Romanistik in Geschichte und Gegenwart*, 1.). Hamburg: Buske.

–. 1978. "Okzitanien: Wiederbelebung einer Sprache". *Dokumente* 34: 1.39–45.

–. 1993. "Dichtung oder Wahrheit. Einige Anmerkungen zur Entstehung der französischen Prosa". *Literarhistorische Begegnungen. Festschrift zum sechzigsten Geburtstag von Bernhard König* hg. von Andreas Kablitz & Ulrich Schulz-Buschhaus, 279–291. Tübingen: Gunter Narr.

Roncaglia, Aurelio. 1992. *La lingua dei trovatori: profilo di grammatica storica del provenzale antico.* 2ª ed. Roma: Ateneo.

Ruffinatto, Aldo. 1968. *Terramagnino da Pisa. Doctrina d'Acort.* Edizione critica, introduzione e note a cura di Aldo Ruffinatto. Roma: Ateneo.

Palumbo, P. 1955. *Berenguer de Noya. Mirall de trobar.* Palermo: Università di Palermo.

Rafanell, Agustí, Hg. 1991. *Un nom per a la llengua. El concepte de llemosí en la historia del català.* Barcelona: Eumo / Estudi General de Girona / Estudis Universitaris de Vic.

Riquer, Martín de. 1975. *Los trovadores, historia literaria y textos.* 3 Bde. Barcelona: Planeta.

Robins, Robert H. 1967. *A Short History of Linguistics.* London: Longman

Sánchez Cantón, F. J., Hg. 1923. *Enrique de Villena*, Arte de trovar. Madrid: Victoriano Suárez.

Schlieben-Lange, Brigitte. 1991. "Okzitanisch: Grammatikographie und Lexikographie". *Lexikon der romanistischen Linguistik* hg. von Günter Holtus, Michael Metzeltin & Christian Schmitt, V/2, 105–126. Tübingen: Niemeyer.

–. 1996. ""abitut". Zur Verwendung eines modistischen Terminus in den "Leys d'amors" ". *Language Philosophies and the Language Sciences. A Historical Perspective in Honour of Lia Formigari* hg. von Daniele Gambarara, Stefano Gensini & A. Pennisi. 49–68. Münster: Nodus.

Stengel, Edmund. 1971. *Die beiden ältesten provenzalischen Grammatiken "Lo Donatz Proensals" und "Las Razos de Trobar" nebst einem provenzalisch-italienischen Glossar von neuem getreu nach den Hss. hrsg.* Niederwalluf: Sändig. (Unveränderter Nachdr. der Ausgabe Marburg: Elwert, 1878.)

Swiggers, Pierre. 1989. "Les premières grammaires occitanes: les *Razos de trobar* de Raimon Vidal et le *Donatz proensals* d'Uc (Faidit)". *Zeitschrift für romanische Philologie* 105.134–147.

–. 1991. "La méthode grammaticale d'Uc Faidit dans le *Donatz proensals*". *Revue des Langues Romanes* 95.343–350.

–. 1992 "Les plus anciennes grammaires occitanes: Tradition, variation et insertion culturelle". *Contacts de langues, de civilisations et intertextualité. IIIème congrès international de l'Assotiation internationale d'études occitanes, Montpelier, 20–26 sep. 1990*, I, hg. von Gérard Gouiran, 131–148. Montpellier: Centre d'Études Occitanes de l'Université.

Zamora Munné, Juan Clemente. 1993. *Historia lingüística. Edad Media y Renacimiento.* Salamanca: Ediciones Colegio de España.

*Hans-J. Niederehe, Trier (Deutschland)*

# XVI. The Classical Languages in the Age of Humanism
# Die klassischen Sprachen im Zeitalter des Humanismus
# Les langues classiques à l'époque de l'humanisme

## 88. The traditional study of Latin at the university in the age of Humanism


1. Defining the boundaries of the theme
2. The concepts of 'latin', 'grammar' and 'the vernacular' from the Middle Ages to Humanism
3. The liberal arts and the teaching of Latin in the universities
4. Teaching Latin in Italian universities in the fourteenth century: Padua and Bologna
5. The *Studia humanitatis*, the figure of the humanist and the dispute over the arts in the fourteenth century
6. Teaching Latin in the universities in the fifteenth century
7. Bibliography


### 1. Defining the boundaries of the theme

The plan of this work is so extraordinarily comprehensive that it is indeed an arduous task to deal with the theme assigned to this article without repeating or anticipating contents belonging properly to bordering articles. What should be understood by the phrase "the traditional study of Latin in the university in the age of Humanism" is the continuation of the study and teaching of Latin employing the methods established in the late Middle Ages. These methods may be divided into two main strands: on the one hand positive grammar, represented by Donatus and Priscian with their commentaries and by the grammars in verse such as the *Doctrinale* by Alexandre de Villedieu (1199) and the *Grecismus* by Eberard de Béthune (1212?); on the other hand, the speculative grammar of the *modistae*, who were based at the University of Paris, and who, from the middle of the thirteenth century on, spread a new philosophy of language of a 'radical' Aristotelian brand. Both of these schools of grammatical studies should be conceived of as 'traditional' compared to the innovations brought about by humanism, as is shown by the fact that both schools were the object of bitter humanist polemics. Since both schools have been dealt with in article 81 (and more generally in the course of Chapter XV) and in article 76 (and more generally in Chapter XIV), a treatment of the "traditional study of Latin in the university in the age of Humanism" in terms of the "internal history of linguistics", that is in terms of the analysis of theories and methods specific to linguistics, would inevitably lead to repetitiveness. On the other hand, a review or a mere erudite map highlighting those areas where the traditional methods of studying Latin in the universities persisted, that is a purely "external" history of the study of Latin, would not really be appropriate to the aims of this work. Hence, in order to adhere to and further the general plan of the work, I interpret the theme assigned to the present article as representing the bridge between "traditional" theories and methods of teaching Latin (extensively dealt with in Chapters XIV and XV), and "innovative" theories and methods (which will be treated in article 90). I will therefore deal with the "institutional space" which the teaching of Latin occupied in the universities in the Middle Ages, and with its "remodelling" in the age of humanism. In fact, the changes in theoretical approach, in the cultural and scientific paradigm that humanism introduces, have important institutional implications. The humanists were professional figures trained outside the university system. Their objective was to conquer positions in a university system which initially excluded them. They carried on their battle aggressively, finally succeeding in restructuring the system to their favour, in overturning the hierarchy between the disciplines (a war which was reflected in the so-called "dispute of the arts", which was waged throughout the fifteenth century), in gaining hegemony in the educational system, in reserving to themselves the fundamental role in training the new ruling classes. Latin – the universal language of culture and science, the privileged, if not the sole, model of grammatical speculation, a cult object of humanist renovation – found itself at the centre of this momentous conflict. As the subject being scrutinised is the institutional space occupied by the teaching of Latin in the university, reference will have to be made to humanist innovation as well as to traditional forms of study.

## 2. The concepts of 'latin', 'grammar' and 'the vernacular' from the Middle Ages to Humanism

The reader's attention must be briefly called to the categorial opposition between Latin and vernacular languages, a constitutive trait of the entire system of medieval knowledge which determines the concept of grammar typical of this age and which survives well into the age of humanism. The teaching of Latin plays a crucial role in this knowledge system, a fact which may be accounted for by the conceptual categorisation referred to in the previous sentence, or, to phrase it differently, this conceptual categorisation is the ideological mirror reflection of that order. Thus, throughout the late Middle Ages and right up until well into the fifteenth century and beyond, namely when humanism was at its height, linguistic 'common sense' shared by the majority of educated men, and implicitly or explicitly handed down by the educational system, stated that Latin was not a natural, historical language on a par with the vernaculars. Rather, it was a language which was intrinsically, qualitatively and ontologically different. Latin was regarded as an artificial language, created by the universal consensus of the learned as the international language of knowledge, the fruit of creation and learning which were wholly reflective, that is, the product of *ars* founded on *ratio*. On the contrary, vernacular languages were seen as natural, spontaneous creations of the human language faculty, the fruit (we would say today) of the language "instinct", that is, the product of *natura* founded on *usus*. This dual conceptual opposition – *natura* vs. *ars* and *usus* vs. *ratio* – may be seen as the theorisation of the situation of diglossia characterising medieval culture in Western Europe, which viewed Latin as the universal language of education and the vernaculars as local, natural languages limited to domestic and practical uses. Thus Latin was no man's mother tongue, and vernacular languages were both rigorously excluded from the educational system, and foreign and extraneous to the activity of scientific observation carried out by the learned. This view of things may be found in the writings of numerous philosophers, grammarians and scholars from various parts of Western Europe (see Thurot, 1869, *passim*). The most complete statement of this position occurs in Dante Alighieri's work *De vulgari eloquentia* (first decade of the XIV century). Thus, Latin is identified with grammar. The word *grammar* is synonymous with "the Latin language" both in medieval Latin and in various modern European languages, a meaning it retains up until the XVI century. This 'short circuit' between lexical meanings is a signal which reveals much about the linguistic and cultural system which produced it: Latin was regarded as the *only* grammatical language, and vernacular languages were *by definition* ungrammatical, that is, not in the empirical and banal sense that written grammars had not (yet) been written of the vernacular languages, but in the much stronger sense of the term that they were intrinsically devoid of grammaticality. That grammaticality is an inherent component of every natural language is, in fact, a modern concept; the medieval system, instead, conceived of grammaticality as a rational, reflexive product, and attributed this feature to the sole universal educational language, conceived of, as I was saying, as an artificial product. The obviously logical consequence of this mental scheme – however paradoxical it might appear to we modern linguists – was that Latin, or *grammar*, had never been a natural language, learnt from one's mother or wet nurse, not even in Ancient Rome. It was precisely this debate on what language the ancient Romans spoke (Tavoni 1984), a debate which involved all the major Italian humanists between 1435 and the end of the century, which offered the opportunity to bring into sharp focus for the first time, and in opposition to the traditional position, the view of Latin as a historical, natural language, hence a language which was infinitely richer and better structured than vernacular languages, but not ontologically different from the latter. This conceptual framework is consistent with and strongly supportive of the fact that Latin constituted the basis of knowledge and of the educational system in the whole of Western Europe, and that no vernacular language was the object of grammatical attention, nor of teaching, not even at the primary school level, throughout Europe.

## 3. The liberal arts and the teaching of Latin in the universities

### 3.1. The study of Latin and the liberal arts

To situate Latin as the foundation stone for the building of knowledge and as the basis of university teaching, we must start from the seven liberal arts (see Abelson 1906; *Arts liberaux* 1969; Wagner, Ed. 1983): the verbal arts, or *artes sermocinales*, of the *trivium* (grammar, rhetoric, dialectic) and the mathematical arts of the *quadrivium* (arithmetic, music, geometry, astronomy). The system of the seven liberal arts represented the model of secondary education in the Latin-Christian world from late Antiquity (from Martianus Capella and Cassiodorus, V-VI century) to the advent of Scholasticism and beyond. This system clearly sanctions the basic role played by the study of Latin: grammar (that is, the Latin language and its grammar, as we have already seen) constitutes the primary and indispensable subject, the door through which one enters the building of knowledge (*ianua* will be the *incipit* of a highly successful short elementary grammar book used both in Italy and in Northern Europe in late medieval times: see Black 1996). But grammar is only the first of the three *artes sermocinales*: the *trivium* as a whole represents the complete training course in the adept use of the word. Grammar is to be integrated first by rhetoric and then by dialectic. It may be anticipated that the fundamental feature discriminating tradition from innovation in the study of Latin in the age of humanism may be summarised as follows: while traditional university pedagogy conceives of grammar as functional to dialectic, humanist pedagogy views grammar as functional to rhetoric (cfr. Grafton & Jardine 1986). Clearly, the nature of grammar changes radically depending on which perspective is adopted. The entire conflict between traditionalists and humanists may be summed up as a conflict seeking to overturn the hierarchy of importance amongst the disciplines of the *trivium*, so as to affirm the superiority of rhetoric over dialectic, in order, thereby, to destroy the basis of logicising grammar, founded on *ratio* and functional to dialectic, and to impose a grammar based on *usus* and functional to rhetoric.

### 3.2. The grammatical study of Latin as a preparatory discipline in the university system

But we must first see how the system of liberal arts which emerged in the late ancient world, was integrated into the universities when the latter were founded and achieved a solid position in Europe in the course of the XIII and XIV centuries, and in particular what place Latin found and what status it attained in the universities. The universities were born to furnish more specialised and more professionally-oriented knowledge compared to the humanist-encyclopaedic knowledge represented by the liberal arts, a knowledge which was mainly orientated towards philosophy, theology, law and medicine. In the new order of high-level training brought into being by the introduction of the universities, the seven liberal arts found their place in the Faculty of Arts, of course, that is, of the liberal arts. The seven liberal arts were institutionalised within the university system by becoming a specific faculty whose name was taken from those arts themselves. But the seven arts did not occupy all the space available in the faculty which took its name from them. Rather they represented a large proportion of the introductory stage. The Faculty of Arts was actually oriented towards the teaching of philosophy as its final stage, and philosophy represented the real goal of the curriculum. Indeed, emphasis was increasingly laid on the importance of philosophy as a specific subject distinct from the liberal arts. Thus Hugh of St. Victor (first half of the XII century) held that *secreta philosophiae* coincided with the *trivium* and the *quadrivium*; and when, between the XII and XIII centuries, Étienne de Tournai referred to the University of Paris, he made no distinction between *artes liberales* and *philosophia*; on the contrary, shortly after the middle of the XIII century, Saint Thomas affirmed that "the seven arts do not represent a complete sub-division of theoretical philosophy" (Roos 1969: 193). As a result of the increasing specialisation in philosophy which characterised the Faculty of Arts, between the XIII and XIV centuries "the seven liberal arts at Oxford as at Paris were considered not as ends in themselves, but as *opera propaedeutica* to the study of the three philosophies", that is, of natural philosophy, moral philosophy and metaphysics (Weisheipl 1969: 209–210). At the same time, throughout the XIV century, the entire *facultas septem artium liberalium* was conceived of and defined as the *fundamentum omnium aliarum facultatum,* ('foundation of all the other faculties') or, *fundamentum, origo et principium omnium aliarum scientiarum, sine qua nulla alia scientia haberi potest perfecte, commode nec complete* (ibidem) ('foundation, origin, and principle of all the other sciences, without which no other science can be attained perfectly, easily and completely'). Thus the function of the study of Latin as preparatory to the university system of knowledge is repeatedly stressed: first of all, the *artes sermocinales* prepared one for the scientific subjects of the *quadrivium*; secondly, within the Faculty of Arts itself, the seven liberal arts together prepare the student for the study of the three philosophies; thirdly, the entire Faculty of Arts prepares students for the more specialised faculties. This markedly preparatory pedagogic function could be read as a sign of the importance of the *artes sermocinales* and in particular of the study of Latin grammar (the word *fundamentum* seems to allude to this importance); however, several facts induce one into giving the opposite interpretation: in concrete terms, since the study of Latin grammar was a preliminary to the study of all other subjects, it must have been perceived as an elementary stage, and, consequently, it must have been seen as less prestigious compared to the other, more advanced subjects ("the average 'artist' heartily despised the mere grammarian or schoolmaster": Rashdall 1958: III, 344). It must therefore be concluded that the study of positive grammar in the context of high level education oriented to specialist knowledge was reduced to a mere completion of an elementary knowledge of grammar acquired before entering university, not a particularly prestigious business. It was only those who worked along the lines of speculative grammar, culminating in the modists, that the 'common' and 'introductory' nature of grammar acquired epistemological value: this form of grammar was conceived of as an 'introductory science' in the strong sense of the term, as speculation concerning the linguistic bases of philosophy and the other sciences.

### 3.3. Grammar as a pre-university discipline

It must also be remembered that Latin is essentially a pre-university subject. The label "grammar school", which is still used in the Anglo-Saxon world, reflects the continued existence of this type of school, with its medieval origins and its objective to furnish a basic education: in the Middle Ages, such schools were run by the clergy, and were closely connected to the cathedral, or to simple parish churches, which were far more widely scattered over the country than were the universities. In the university towns, it sometimes happened that the grammar schools came under the jurisdiction of the universities, as was the case with Oxford (Rashdall 1958: III, 345–352). This phenomenon only underlined the introductory nature of the teaching of grammar in the university curriculum. Confirmation of the low sociocultural status of the teaching of grammar comes from an in-depth study on a non-university town which was to become an important centre of humanism: Florence: "The grammar master *was* an humble figure. Often he had no university training himself, and yet one part of his job was to prepare students for the university" (Gehl 1993: 3). Gehl's book shows that the basic cultural function of the grammar school was conservative, more moral than linguistic: to keep alive the knowledge of a traditional corpus of moral Latin texts, which had proven their worth over the centuries and which were inspired by universalistic Christian values, thereby forming a bastion both against the emerging literatures written in the vernacular languages and against the humanist avant-garde.

## 4. Teaching Latin in Italian universities in the fourteenth century: Padua and Bologna

We saw towards the end of § 3.2 that speculative grammar, which flourished in Paris in the middle of the XIII century, gave distinction to the study of grammar compared to its normally low sociocultural status, by elevating the study of the subject to the domains of logic and philosophy. In the Italian universities in the course of the XIV century, the status of grammar is further enhanced, this time by being extended to the study of rhetoric (see Kristeller 1953 and 1984), and most notably so in the two great Italian universities, Padua and Bologna. Padua is the main centre of so-called 'pre-humanism', before Petrarch. In actual fact, the pre-humanist renewal of the study of Latin came about outside the university itself – the leading light in the process being the poet laureate and historian Albertino Mussato (1261–1329). Nevertheless, the movement exerted great influence over the Latin of eminent university teachers such as the natural philosopher Pietro d'Abano and the political philosopher Marsilio da Padova (Billanovich 1978, Kristeller 1985). Developments in the study of grammar and rhetoric were particularly significant at the University of Bologna (Raimondi 1956; Avellini Ed. 1990; Cristiani Ed. 1990), a university prevalently concerned with law, and therefore interested in cultivating the rhetoric required by notaries, judges and administrative personnel in general. The type of rhetoric particularly required by these sectors were formulae and rules for the drawing up of letters and other official, administrative and political texts. This sub-field was known as *ars dictaminis*. The practical, that is civil, political and legal, nature of the Faculty of Law was functional to the civilisation of the Bolognese and Italian Communes. This requirement therefore contributed to the renovation of the study of grammar and rhetoric. Although these subjects had been fostered informally within the Law School from the XII century on, they also gained ground in the Faculty of Arts, increasingly becoming an introduction to the direct reading of the Latin classics, to the cost of the logicising grammar which prevailed in the Northern European universities. While the low prestige label "grammar" characterised the elementary, pre-university stage of the curriculum, university teachers of *oratoria* such as Giovanni del Virgilio enjoyed great prestige.

## 5. The *Studia humanitatis*, the figure of the humanist and the dispute over the arts in the fourteenth century

*Studia humanitatis* – a term already used informally by Cicero and by Gellius – became the official name of chairs of grammar, rhetoric, history, poetry and moral philosophy whose teaching method was based on the reading of Latin classics on which such subjects were founded. This set of disciplines did not correspond to the verbal arts of the *trivium*: dialectic was excluded, while other disciplines which were included were poetics (an extension not only of rhetoric, but also of history and of moral philosophy, given the frequent connotation of poetry as being related to wisdom), history (connected to rhetoric right from Antiquity) and a part of philosophy – while the other parts of this subject were excluded, namely natural philosophy and metaphysics. The effect of including certain disciplines and excluding others (dialectic, natural philosophy and metaphysics) produced a restructuring of the system of knowledge which was radically different from that which had dominated the universities in the Middle Ages. It was almost the foundation of a dichotomy, one which was to lead, in the Modern Age, to the dichotomy between the "two cultures": on the one hand, that culture which will be generically classified as 'humanist', and on the other hand scientific culture, which in modern times would be labelled "the exact sciences". With regard to the study of Latin in the universities, this new "modelling" of knowledge supported by the humanists attributed the subject great value, freeing it from the narrow spaces of the mere teaching of grammar, relating it to the study of authorial style, historicizing it in the rediscovery of the differences between classical Latin and the Latin of modern usage.

The term *humanista* recurs – in an extremely limited number of occurrences – from the end of the XV century on, in the technical sense of a teacher of *humanitas*, which is precisely the set of subjects described above (Campana 1946; Kristeller 1961, p. 160 n. 61; Grendler 1967 and 1971; Giustiniani 1985). This word – destined to broaden its semantic scope quite significantly over the centuries in all European languages – is initially only a university jargon word to indicate a teacher who is specialised in a certain field of teaching.

The humanists wanted to conquer new territories for their subjects – grammar, rhetoric, poetics, history, moral philosophy – in the universities too, as well as in the chancelleries and in the princely courts, those centres where they had first laid their roots; and they did so in an aggressive fashion, with attacks in their writings on the medieval teaching of grammar – both positive grammar and speculative grammar – of dialectic and of natural philosophy which were quite violent. This obviously created tension and conflict. The "dispute of the arts" is the mirror of these conflicts (Garin 1947; Avellini, Ed., 1990; Cristiani, Ed., 1990). The canonical dispute is that which sets law in opposition to medicine, the two basic liberal professions. While medicine may be considered to be the representative of the whole of natural philosophy, it cannot be said that law is equally representative of the entire gamut of 'humanist' knowledge. The arguments advanced are manifold, complex and intertwined. Underlying them is an extremely strong and pervasive humanist drive to achieve a radical reform and revaluation of the study of Latin as the foundation of a new edifice of knowledge in all its manifestations.

## 6. Teaching Latin in the universities in the fifteenth century

Throughout the XV century, all the universities in Western Europe are the theatre of bitter battles between traditionalists and humanists for domination in the methods of teaching Latin. A few partial maps of the entire war have been drawn at the national and local level. In Italy studies have concentrated for many decades on the pedagogic-linguistic innovations introduced by the humanists (see the recent work by Rizzo 1996), from Gasparino Barzizza to Guarino of Verona, Leonardo Bruni, Poggio Bracciolini, Francesco Filelfo, right up to Lorenzo Valla, Pomponio Leto and so forth. (The innovative reforms of these scholars will be examined in article 90.) The resistance put up by the traditionalists in the field of teaching Latin have not been subjected to systematic investigation in any way. There are good reasons for this. First and foremost, the different stature of the players in the game: on the one side, a significant number of highly eminent humanists who influenced the study of Latin in the whole of Renaissance Europe, confronted, on the other side, only by obscure schoolteachers. On this matter, it should not be forgotten that the Italian disciples of speculative grammar, the only strand which offered an autonomous alternative of any weight and which could claim scientific status, were indeed weak. It could almost be asserted that in Italy the space devoted to the higher level teaching of Latin, that is at a university or comparable level, was entirely occupied by humanists, and that the battle was between more radical and less radical innovators – the most radical and consistent being Lorenzo Valla, while the least innovative included Antonio da Rho, Bartolomeo Facio, Poggio Bracciolini. Valla carried on a bitter polemic with these scholars, despite their belonging to the school of humanism. Then, because the tradition of literature in the vernacular was particularly strong and more illustrious in Italy than in any other country, a polar conflict developed between the supporters of Latin and the supporters of the vernacular which left no room for conservative resistance within the Latin camp. As Gehl convincingly demonstrates in his book (1993), such resistance was put up in a town like Florence in the XIV century and not in the XV century, and in the primary grammar schools and not in the universities. The situation is different in other countries, where the humanist movement was weaker and could count less on local forces, forcing it to depend heavily on Italian sources. With regard to German-speaking countries, the works by Heath 1971 and by Jensen 1996 (see also Overfield 1984) provide a wealth of information. They show a university map which is like a leopard's skin, on which areas of humanist innovation alternate with areas of traditionalist resistance and reaction, fed by modist grammar. Such resistance was therefore able to counter the humanist approach with its own autonomous, philosophical, rationalist foundation. That speculative grammar retained its vitality is demonstrated by the fact that it re-emerged in France and Spain in the XVI century in the works of Scaliger (Jensen 1990) and Sanctius. Between the XV and XVI centuries, Spain is extremely backward with regard to the higher level teaching of Latin. Resistance was purely passive, and incapable of producing culturally significant counterattacks against the "Italianising" humanist campaign launched by Nebrija against the "inauspicious grammarians" of the medieval tradition (Rico 1978).

## 7. Bibliography

Abelson, Paul. 1906. *The Seven Liberal Arts. A Study in Medieval Culture.* New York: Teachers College Columbia University.

*Arts libéraux et philosophie au Moyen Âge. Actes du quatrième Congrès international de philosophie médiévale. Université de Montréal, Canada, 27 août – 2 septembre 1967.* Montréal-Paris: Institut d'études médiévales – Librairie philosophique J. Vrin, 1969.

Avellini, Luisa, ed. 1990. *Sapere elè potere. Discipline, Dispute e Professioni nell'Università Medievale e Moderna. Il caso bolognese a confronto. Atti del 4° convegno, Bologna, 13–15 aprile 1989. Vol. I. Forme e oggetti della disputa delle arti.* Bologna: Comune di Bologna – Istituto per la Storia di Bologna.

Billanovich, Giuseppe. 1978. "L'insegnamento della grammatica e della retorica nelle università italiane tra Petrarca e Guarino". In Ijsewijn – Paquet, Ed., 365–380.

Black, Robert. 1996. "*Ianua* and elementary education in Italy and Northern Europe in the Later Middle Ages". In Tavoni, Mirko *et alii*, Ed. 1996, II, pp. 5–22.

Campana, Augusto. 1946. "The origin of the word *humanist*", *Journal of the Warburg and Courtauld Institute* 9, 60–73.

Cristiani, Andrea, ed. 1990. *Sapere elè potere. Discipline, Dispute e Professioni nell'Università Medievale e Moderna. Il caso bolognese a confronto. Atti del 4° convegno, Bologna, 13–15 aprile 1989. Vol. I. Verso un nuovo sistema del sapere.* Bologna: Comune di Bologna – Istituto per la Storia di Bologna.

Garin, Eugenio, ed. 1947. *La disputa delle arti nel Quattrocento.* Firenze: Vallecchi (II ed. con nuova introduzione Roma: Ist. Poligrafico e Zecca dello Stato, 1982.

Gehl, Paul F. 1993. *A Moral Art. Grammar, Society and Culture in Trecento Florence*, Ithaca and London: Cornell University Press.

Grafton, Anthony & Jardine, Lisa. 1982. "Humanism and the School of Guarino: A Problem of Evaluation", *Past and Present* (?), 16, 51–80.

Grafton, Anthony & Jardine, Lisa. 1986. *From Humanism to the Humanities. Education and the Liberal Arts in the Fifteenth- and Sixteenth-Century Europe.* London: Duckworth.

Grendler, Paul F. 1967. "Five Italian occurrences of *umanista*, 1540–1574". *Renaissance Quarterly* 20, 317–325.

–. 1971. "The concept of humanist in Cinquecento Italy". *Renaissance Studies in Honor of Hans Baron*, Firenze: Sansoni, 445–463.

Heath, Terrence 1971. "Logical Grammar, Grammatical Logic and Humanism in Three German Universities". *Studies in the Renaissance*, 18, 9–64.

Ijsewijn, Josef & Paquet, Jacques, eds. *The Universities in the Late Middle Ages.* Leuven: Univ. Press.

Jensen, Kristian. 1990. *Rhetorical Philosophy and Philosophical Grammar. Julius Caesar Scaliger's Theory of Language.* München: Wilhelm Fink Verlag.

–. 1996. "Humanist Latin grammars in Germany and their Italian background". In Tavoni *et alii*, Ed., II, 23–41.

Kristeller, Paul Oskar. 1953. *Die italienischen Universitäten der Renaissance.* Krefeld: Scherpe ("Schriften und Vorträge des Petrarca-Institut Köln" I).

–. 1961. *Renaissance Thought: the Classic, Scholastic and Humanistic Strains*, New York.

–. 1984. "The Curriculum of the Italian Universities from the Middle Ages to the Renaissance". *Proceedings of the Patristic, Mediaeval and Renaissance Conference.* Villanova, Pa.: Augustinian Historical Institute of Villanova Univ., 9, 1–15.

–. 1985. *Umanesimo e scolastica a Padova fino al Petrarca.* Padova: Antenore.

Overfield. James. 1984. *Humanism and Scholasticism in Late Medieval Germany.* Princeton: Princeton University Press.

Raimondi, Enzo. 1956. "Quattrocento bolognese: università e umanesimo". *Studi e memorie per la storia dell'Università di Bologna*, n.s., I- 325–356, rist. in: Idem, *I sentieri del lettore*. Vol. I: *Da Dante a Tasso*, Bologna: Il Mulino, 1994, 205–241.

Rashdall, Hastings. 1958. *The Universities of Europe in the Middle Ages. A new edition in three volumes.* London: Oxford University Press.

Rico, Francisco. 1978. *Nebrija frente a los bárbaros. El canon de gramáticos nefastos en las polémicas del humanismo*, Salamanca: Universidad de Salamanca.

Rizzo, Silvia. 1996. "L'insegnamento del latino nelle scuole umanistiche". In Tavoni *et alii*, Ed., I, 3–29.

Roos, Heinrich. 1969. "Le *Trivium* à l'Université au XIIIe siècle". In *Arts libéraux et philosophie au Moyen Âge*, 193–197.

Tavoni, Mirko. 1984. *Latino, grammatica, volgare. Storia di una questione umanistica.* Padova: Antenore.

Tavoni, Mirko *et alii*, Ed. 1996. *Italy and Europe in Renaissance Linguistics: Comparisons and Relations. Proceedings of the International Conference. Ferrara, Istituto di Studi Rinascimentali, 20–24 March 1991. Vol. I: Italy and the Romance World. Vol. II. Italy and the non-Romance World. The Oriental Languages.* Modena: F. C. Panini.

Thurot, Charles. 1869. *Extraits de divers manuscrits latins pour servir à l'histoire des doctrines grammaticales au moyen âge*, Paris (photographic reproduction Frankfurt am Main, 1964).

Vasoli, Cesare. 1990. "Le discipline e il sistema del sapere". In Cristiani, Ed. 1990: 11–36.

Wagner, David L., Ed. 1983. *The Seven Liberal Arts in the Middle Ages.* Bloomington: Indiana University Press.

Weisheipl, James A. 1969. "The Place of the Liberal Arts in the University Curriculum during the XIVth and XVth Centuries". In *Arts libéraux et philosophie au Moyen Âge*, 209–213.

*Mirko Tavoni, Pisa (Italy)*

# 89. The rediscovery of the classics in the age of Humanism

1. Rediscovery and reception of the classics
2. The Paduan pre-humanists, Petrarch and Boccaccio
3. The first half of the 15th century
4. The linguistic and philological implications of the discoveries
5. Bibliography

## 1. Rediscovery and reception of the classics

There exists an abundant bibliography on the "rediscovery" of the classics in the age of Humanism. This bibliography was initiated by Sandys' (1908) review at the beginning of this century and was enriched by the works of Remigio Sabbadini. The latter made available an exceptional amount of erudite, first-hand information, on which the basic framework of our knowledge concerning this topic continues to depend. Sabbadini's *Le scoperte dei codici latini e greci ne' secoli XIV e XV* ('The Discoveries of the Latin and Greek Codexes in the 14th and 15th centuries') (2 vols., 1905–1914, 2nd ed. 1967) recounts the glorious epoch of the humanist discoveries in chronological order, and *Storia e critica dei testi latini* ('The History and Criticism of Latin Texts') (1914, 2nd ed. 1971) reorders these discoveries by author (Cicero, Donatus, Tacitus, etc.), providing for each one the framework of the textual tradition as it was created and amplified in the age of Humanism. Two works are fundamental in up-dating the picture: Reynolds-Wilson (1968) (chapter IV is especially pertinent to our present concerns), which reproduces the structure of the first of the two works I have quoted by Sabbadini, and Reynolds ed. (1983), which duplicates the structure of the second of Sabbadini's works, that is, by author. Another work that must be mentioned is that by Leonardi & Olsen, eds. (1995).

The discovery or rediscovery of "lost" Latin classics, that is of texts which had fallen into disuse during the Middle Ages and thus no longer formed part of common knowledge, and of which only the titles and some "indirect" information was then available, nevertheless constitutes only the most obvious aspect of the re-appropriation of the classical heritage in this period. Each newly re-found text appeared to the humanists like a battle won in the war to re-conquer the lost patrimony. In the wake of Sabbadini's studies, 20th century humanist philologists who have reconstructed the history of this centuries-long war, shared the ethos of their humanist colleagues and they modelled their historical account on this ethos. But it must be remembered that the rediscovery of a text is only the first, albeit fundamental, act in the re-appropriation of that text. Equally important stages are the production and diffusion of copies of the newly-found text; the study of the text employing the philological approach (which includes comparing the various witnesses of the text available over time and developing a method regulating how such collations should be carried out); the study of the contens of the text, the encyclopaedia of knowledge concerning Antiquity which was thus becoming gradually enriched; and, above all, with regard to the history of linguistics, the study of the variety of Latin employed by the various authors in the various epochs which became possible as a consequence; finally, the stimulus the discoveries provided for the production of new literature, both at the level of content and at the level of stylistic models. In conclusion, the account of the discoveries cannot be divorced from the account of how those texts were received, and from the multiform immediate effects which those discoveries produced on the living culture of their times: see Fera (1989) and Schmidt (1995).

## 2. The Paduan pre-humanists, Petrarch and Boccaccio

The most important phenomenon with regard to our topic in the age of Humanism was the enthusiastic, almost feverish hunt for manuscripts containing "lost" Latin classics. This search reached its apex in the first half of the 15th century, but its beginnings may be traced back to as early as the second half of the 13th century. It was in Padua in those decades that the first "pre-humanists" brought back to light some extremely important Latin poetical texts. Padua was the seat of a great university (the oldest in Italy, together with Bologna), but the movement which was to rediscover the classics was initiated outside the university, almost as if to mark from the very outset that dualism between Humanism and university culture which was to characterise the entire rise of the humanist movement.

The two standard-bearers of the movement were the magistrate Lovato Lovati (1241–1309) and the notary Albertino Mussato (1261–1329). Lovato Lovati demonstrates an incredibly precocious acquaintance with a formidable set of Latin poetical texts: "one generation in advance of his contemporaries, Lovato shows he knew Lucretius, Catullus, the *Odes* by Horace, the whole of Tibullus, Propertius, Martial, the *Silvae* by Statius, Valerius Flaccus and little known works such as Ovid's *Ibis*. The chronology of Humanism needs to be thoroughly revised. Petrarch was not the first humanist to know the works of Propertius, nor was Salutati the first to possess the complete works of Tibullus; Lovato was acquainted with Lucretius and Valerius Flaccus a century and a half before they were discovered by Poggio and used Catullus at least fifty years before the date traditionally assigned to its resurrection in Padua" (Reynolds-Wilson $^{3}$1987: 132). We know where Lovato obtained his most precious works: that is, from the library of the abbey of Pomposa, on the Po delta. The other library that abetted the rediscoveries of the Paduan pre-humanists was the Chapter Library in Verona.

During the centuries in which the transmission of literary culture had been greatly reduced, the Latin classic had been conserved in monastic and ecclesiastic libraries. Albertino Mussato studied in depth Seneca's tragedies (contained in a venerable manuscript in Pomposa) and gave a new lease of life to modern tragedy by writing the *Ecerinis*, which brought him great renown and caused him to become a poet laureate. This example demonstrates that the rediscovery of the classics was not simply a phenomenon of erudition, but one which nourished the lively literature in Latin produced by the humanists. The enthusiasm which animated this season of research and discovery was the enthusiasm of literary militancy, of men committed to producing their own literature in *Latin*; the newly re-discovered texts were immediately studied and stimulated the production of modern literature. Pliny's *Epistles* were also discovered in the Chapter Library in Verona, as was a text which was destined to exert enormous influence over Renaissance historiography: the *Historia Augusta*.

No matter how important the contribution of the Paduan precursors was, the importance of Francesco Petrarca (1304–1374), the recognised founder of the Humanist movement, towers over all others for his capital contribution to the rediscovery of the classics. Petrarch took the fullest advantage possible of his position with the Papal court at Avignon (where the Papacy was housed from 1309–1377). The Holy See was in fact the place where all the learned men of Europe converged, and it played a unique role as go-between linking Northern Europe and Italy. In Avignon Petrarch found a lively interest in the search after and discovery of ancient literary texts, an interest which had been created by the preceding generation of scholars. A cogent instantiation of Petrarch's contribution is his recovery of Livy. During the Middle Ages each decade had had its own distinct tradition. The Harley 2493 manuscript in the British Library was assembled by Petrarch who reunited the first and fourth decades (the latter then being extremely rare) around a nucleus represented by the third decade. He thus constructed the most complete Livy of the period, enriching it by adding variants to it himself taken from other authoritative witnesses. Petrarch's Livy is based on a manuscript found in Chartres cathedral and taken to Avignon by Landolfo Colonna.

Petrarch's Livy later came into the possession of Lorenzo Valla (1407–1457), who enriched it further with amendments by his own hand. This manuscript thus typifies to perfection the role played by Avignon as the centre of mediation between Northern Europe and Italy, and by Petrarch as the key person in the reconstruction of ancient Latin literature.

Petrarch was also an untiring investigator of the works of Cicero, to the point that he became the possessor of the most complete collection of his time. This included almost all the philosophical works, most of the rhetorical works, many speeches (the *Philippics*, the *Catilinarians*, the *Verrins*, the *Caesarians*). In 1345 he discovered the *Epistulae ad Atticum*, which, together with those by Seneca – immediately became a vital font of the stile of his own *Epistles*. The margins of Petrarch's Vergil manuscript (Ambrosian Library, manuscript S. P. 10/27, formerly A.79 inf.) conserve the philological work Petrarch carried out on the poet he loved most.

After having devoted the first part of his life to writing narrative prose in the vernacular, Giovanni Boccaccio (1313–1375) became a convert to the cult of Petrarch and of Latin literature in the second part of his life, and, with the help of the humanist Zanobi da Strada, had transferred to Florence some of the treasures stored in the Montecassino abbey library: the *Annales* and the *Historiae* of Tacitus, the *Metamorphoses* by Apuleius and the *De lingua latina* by Varro.

## 3. The first half of the 15th century

Coluccio Salutati (1331–1406), a notary and the chancellor of the Florentine Republic, played a fundamental role in importing the humanist movement founded by Petrarch into Florence, and contributed to the rediscovery of the classics by publicising Cicero's *Epistulae ad Familiares* discovered by the Milan chancellor Pasquino Cappelli in the Chapter Library in Vercelli. Coluccio was thus the first to collect the complete letters of Cicero (from which he derived a model for the integration of intellectual activity and of political activity which contributed to the establishing of what was defined as Florentine "civil humanism"). Salutati is also to be commended for having invited Manuel Chrysoloras to come and teach in Florence, thereby introducing the study of Greek into Italy (see article 91). This was destined to become the second language of Humanism and was to modify its structure.

The greatest discoverer of manuscripts in the Italian humanist movement was Poggio Baccolini (1380–1459). In his position as apostolic writer, he followed the Holy See of the Anti-pope John XXIII at the Council of Constance (1414–1417). He took advantage of his stay to explore thoroughly the libraries of the monasteries of Northern France, Germany and Switzerland, making monumental discoveries. In Cluny in 1415 he found a manuscript of the orations of Cicero containing two hitherto unknown works (the *Pro Roscio Amerino* and the *Pro Murena*); in St. Gall in 1416 he discovered the first complete witness of Quintilian's *Institutio oratoria* (a text which was destined to exert a crucial influence over Valla's conception of Latin), the *Commentary* by Asconius on five of Cicero's orations, and the *Argonautica* by Valerius Flaccus. 1417 in St. Gall saw the discovery of Lucretius' *De rerum natura*, Silius Italicus' *Punica* and Manilius's *Astronomica*. In the same year, he brought back from Fulda a manuscript of the *Res gestae* by Ammianus Marcellinus, and from Langres and probably from Cologne eight new orations by Cicero (*Pro Caecina*, *Pro Roscio comoedo*, *De lege agraria* I–III, *Pro Rabirio perduellionis reo*, *In Pisonem*, *Pro Rabirio Postumo*), as well as *Silvae* by Statius. On his return from England in 1423, he discovered in Cologne the *Coena Trimalchionis* by Apuleius, a text of great linguistic importance, because it is a rare example of spoken Latin. Most of the manuscripts discovered by Poggio have been lost, but the copies he made have survived. For many of the above-mentioned texts, these copies constitute the sole or fundamental witness. In Lodi cathedral in 1421, Gerardo Landriani discovered a collection of rhetorical works by Cicero, including the complete text of the *De oratore* and of the *Orator*, previously mutilated works, and *Brutus*, a previously unknown work. As a result Cicero's rhetoric underwent a profound change. The following year, Biondo Flavio carried out a transcription of *Brutus* at the behest of Guarino of Verona (the present manuscript Vatican Ottob. Lat. 1592): the great familiarity that Biondo Flavio acquired of this text is crucial, as we shall see shortly, in accounting for his having focussed on the vernacular as deriving from Latin.

In 1429 Nicholas of Cues brought to Rome a German manuscript of Plautus containing his twelve hitherto unknown comedies, another vital find in the process of integrating our knowledge of archaic and spoken Latin.

## 4. The linguistic and philological implications of the discoveries

These discoveries of new manuscripts and of lost texts did not lead simply to an increase in the amount of knowledge available, but brought about fundamental qualitative improvements in the comprehension of the textual heritage of the classics, in the view of Latin, and in the understanding of linguistic phenomena in general.

We owe to the discovery of the rhetorical works of Cicero, as we have already mentioned, the humanist Biondo Flavio's theory that the vernacular derives from Latin, through its contamination by barbarian languages which began in the late Empire and which ended with the lasting invasion of the Longobards. Up to that time, the medieval view had held sway that the vernacular was the low variety of literary Latin, and had coexisted with Latin right from Antiquity, a stance which was still held by the great humanist Leonardo Bruni (circa 1370–1444). In a polemic with Bruni, Biondo Flavio wrote an ample treatise entitled *De verbis romanae locutionis* in 1435, in which he developed – based on the *Orator* and above all on *Brutus* – the idea that Latin was the only language in use through Ancient Roman society, even though it was stratified into three (we would say diaphasic) levels: spoken vernacular, the language of oratory, and the language of poetry (see Tavoni 1984: 3–41, especially 19–24).

Nor would the colossal work on Latin accomplished by Lorenzo Valla, the most penetrating analyst of Latin in the 15th century, have been possible without the discovery of Latin texts which took place during the first two decades of that century. His *Elegantie latine lingue* is based on a systematic cataloguing of the development of Latin literature from its beginnings to the late Empire and beyond. An investigator of even the smallest detail of Latin usage in all its diachronic and diaphasic varieties, we would put it in modern terms, Valla bequeathed to Europe an imposing summa which was also a highly sophisticated analysis of the morphosyntactic structures of Latin. This analysis is founded on the availability of both Plautus and Apuleius, as well as of archaic Latin, legal Latin and Christian Latin. Ancient *latinitas*, whose original and authentic nature was identified, was separated from the debased variety that had come into use in the Middle Ages; nevertheless, its historical development was also traced. Valla's anti-Ciceronian stance, which also constitutes the basis of Erasmus's thought, rejects the fetishism of a single model of language, and offers the varied resources of a composite tradition which was recognised as such as the object of scholarly study and as a stimulus to the unchained freedom to produce of the moderns. And it is precisely due to its legitimate internal variation that Latin could rightly claim to be a living language, the language of a militant culture which can speak about every aspect which modern culture must be able to speak about. This would not have been possible had the set of texts and manuscripts we have talked of not been discovered. Nor would this have been possible if, on a different level, one single text, a text of capital theoretical importance with regard to Valla's linguistic thought, had not been discovered: Quintilian's *Institutio oratoria*. Valla's theory of usus necessarily presupposes Quintilian's moderately anomalist theory, namely his distinction between *grammatice loqui* and *latine loqui*; and Valla's Quintilian (Latin manuscript 7723 in Paris Bibliothèque Nationale, with Valla's corrections and notes) provides us with the material evidence of the intensive use he made of the text.

Humanist linguistics and philology are both closely connected with the rediscovery of the classics. The acquaintance with the newly discovered texts, the opportunity to compare various manuscripts of the same text, created in the humanists an increasing awareness of the procedures required to evaluate the quality of textual evidence, of the procedures to be adopted in order to recognise or reconstruct the lesson which most closely corresponded to the original lesson the author wished to impart, starting from the various readings offered by the extant tradition. It is only in the second half of the 15th century that we encounter a philological approach which is close to our own: the masterwork in this field may be identified as Politian's (1454–1494) *Miscellanea* which begins to judge the reliability of manuscripts not on the basis of what appears to be the quality of the lessons they impart, but on the basis of their genealogical position, that is on whether they occupy a relatively "high" or "low" position in the chain of transcriptions of the text. Valla's philology, on the contrary, is essentially linguistic. His capital and courageous contributions to philology – let us at least recall the demonstration of the falsity of the *Constitutum Constantini*, the *Collatio Novi Testmenti* and the *Emendationes in Novum Testamentum* – criticise the reliability of traditional texts and lessons not by contesting their philological authenticity, but by demonstrating the inconsistency with linguistic usage of their times or, in the case of translations from Greek, an imprecise understanding or rendering of the meaning of the original text. It is the sophisticated ability to detect each shade of meaning of the *latinitas*, and not special philological expertise in preparing critical editions, which allows Valla to evaluate the quality of the lessons offered by the text.

On a more general plane, all the polemic levelled at "inauspicious grammarians" (Rico 1978), that is against the perversions of logicising medieval grammar, presuppose that humanists are highly familiar with the habits of classical authors, and that this familiarity could only have been acquired through the discovery of texts and manuscripts. The mature stage of humanist linguistics and philology presupposes the heroic stage of the exploration of the libraries in the hunt for manuscripts. This preparatory stage constitutes the foundation stone of the very culture of Humanism.

## 5. Bibliography

Fera, Vincenzo. 1989. "Problemi e percorsi della ricezione umanistica". In *Lo spazio letterario di Roma antica.* Ed. Guglielmo Cavallo, Paolo Fedeli, Andrea Giardina. *Vol. III. La ricezione del testo.* Roma: Salerno Editrice, 513–543.

Grafton, Anthony. 1983. *Joseph Scaliger. A Study in the History of Classical Scholarship. I. Textual Criticism and Exegesis.* Oxford: Clarendon Press.

Leonardi, Claudio & Olsen, Birger Munk, eds. 1995. *The Classical Tradition in the Middle Ages and the Renaissance. Proceedings of the first European Science Foundation Workshop on the "Reception of Classical Texts". Florence, Certosa del Galluzzo, 26–27 June 1992.* Spoleto: Centro Italiano di Studi sull'Alto Medioevo.

Reynolds, Leighton D. & Wilson, Nigel Guy. 1968. *Scribes and Scholars: A Guide to the Transmission of Greek and Latin Literature.* Oxford: Oxford University Press. (Italian translation *Copisti e filologi. La tradizione dei classici dall'antichità ai tempi moderni.* Terza edizione riveduta e ampliata. Padova: Antenore, 1987; French translation *D'Homère à Érasme. La trasmission des classiques grecs et latins.* Paris: Editions du Centre national de la recherche scientifique, 1984.)

Reynolds, Leighton D., ed. 1983. *Texts and Transmission. A Survey of the Latin Classics.* Oxford: Clarendon Press.

Rico, Francisco. 1978. *Nebrija frente a los bárbaros. El canon de los gramáticos nefastos en las polémicas del humanismo*, Salamanca: Universidad de Salamanca.

Sabbadini, Remigio. 1967². *Le scoperte dei codici latini e greci ne' secoli XIV e XV.* Edizione anastatica con nuove aggiunte e correzioni dell'autore a cura di Eugenio Garin. 2 voll. Firenze: Sansoni (I ed. Firenze 1905–1914).

–. 1971². *Storia e critica di testi latini.* Padova: Antenore (I ed. Catania 1914).

Sandys, John Edwin. 1908. *A History of Classical Scholarship. Vol. II. From the Revival of Learning to the End of the Eighteenth Century (in Italy, France, England, and the Netherlands).* Cambridge: Cambridge University Press.

Schmidt, Peter Lebrecht. 1995. "Rezeptionsgeschichte und Überlieferungsgeschichte der klassischen lateinischen Literatur", in Leonardi & Olsen, Eds. 1995, pp. 3–21.

Tavoni, Mirko. 1984. *Latino, grammatica, volgare. Storia di una questione umanistica.* Padova: Antenore.

*Mirko Tavoni, Pisa (Italy)*

# 90. La réforme de l'étude du latin à l'époque de l'humanisme

1. Les grammaires élémentaires italiennes du XVᵉ siècle
2. Les sommes grammaticales
3. Les réformateurs du XVIᵉ siècle
4. Manuels d'apprentissage et travaux lexicographiques
5. Bibliographie

A l'époque de l'humanisme, l'étude du latin fait l'objet d'une intense activité. Les ouvrages se multiplient et, qu'il s'agisse de grammaires, de dictionnaires ou de méthodes d'apprentissage, leur forme change. Néanmoins, sur le plan des fondements théoriques de la description, la rupture avec le Moyen Âge n'a pas été aussi forte qu'on l'a cru longtemps, sur la foi même de certains humanistes. Ce qui se modifie d'abord, c'est l'attitude à l'égard de la langue latine, certes toujours considérée comme le fondement du système éducatif et le support de la production et de la circulation d'une culture commune (Tavoni 1990: 170–171), mais également envisagée comme objet d'étude en elle-même et pour elle-même. La redécouverte de nombreux textes antiques perdus ou oubliés fait prendre conscience à la fois du riche passé de cette langue et de son altération récente, et impose le désir d'en restaurer la pureté.

## 1. Les grammaires élémentaires italiennes du XVᵉ siècle

A la Renaissance, deux ouvrages médiévaux (→ Art. 82) sont toujours largement utilisés pour l'apprentissage du latin. Le premier, la

*Ianua*, ainsi appelée à cause de son *incipit* (*Janua sum rudibus*..., "Je suis la porte pour les ignorants..."), est une adaptation de l'*Ars minor* de Donat datant de la fin du Moyen Âge (Grendler 1989). Le second est le *Doctrinale* d'Alexandre de Villedieu, composé ca. 1200 et encore régulièrement édité (297 éd. entre 1470 et 1588). La présentation versifiée (2645 hexamètres) sert de support mnémotechnique, mais l'ouvrage fait, comme au Moyen Âge, l'objet de nombreux commentaires, nécessaires pour en expliciter le sens. Néanmoins les humanistes italiens du XV$^{e}$ siècle composent également des grammaires de leur cru, dont la taille s'étoffe progressivement. Parmi les plus diffusées figurent les *Regulae grammaticales* de Guarino Veronese (composées ca. 1418), les *Rudimenta grammatices* (1463) de Niccolò Perotti (1429–1480), la grammaire latine de Giovanni Sulpizio (composée ca. 1470) et celle d'Aldo Manuzio (1$^{re}$ éd., 1493). La première partie de ces ouvrages traite des parties du discours et de leurs 'accidents' (les catégories qui les affectent), souvent sous forme de questions *vs* réponses, en suivant de préférence l'ordre d'exposition et les définitions données par Priscien. La morphologie est essentiellement présentée sous la forme de règles de formation (certaines en vers) pour l'apprentissage du genre et des déclinaisons du nom et la formation des prétérits et supins des verbes. La syntaxe, fondée sur l'opposition entre accord et régime, est pour la plus grande part consacrée à la construction des verbes (Colombat 1999). Elle est complétée par un exposé sur les huit figures de construction qui traitent principalement des accords complexes (Colombat 1993). Bien que les auteurs condamnent la grammaire médiévale et revendiquent l'autorité de l'Antiquité, leurs analyses restent le plus souvent inscrites dans le moule traditionnel (Percival 1976).

## 2. Les sommes grammaticales

A côté de ces grammaires élémentaires, il existe des ouvrages beaucoup plus volumineux, comme les *Elegantiae linguae Latinae* (composées entre 1430 et 1449) de Lorenzo Valla (1406–1457). Persuadé qu'on peut à la fois restaurer le latin classique et s'en servir comme d'une langue vivante (Regoliosi 1995), Valla entend donner du latin une description aussi précise que possible, à la fois pour l'emploi des formes et leur construction. L'ouvrage développe donc une série d'observations et d'analyses sur des points de vocabulaire, d'étymologie et de syntaxe du latin classique. Donnant lieu à de nombreuses adaptations, il est à l'origine de toute une tradition de manuels à vocation stylistique et traitant des élégances latines. Fortement influencé par les humanistes italiens, mais prenant plus en compte qu'eux la tradition issue de Donat, l'Espagnol Antonio de Nebrija (1441/1444–1522) donne dans ses *Introductiones Latinae*, enrichies par des gloses à partir de 1495, une somme grammaticale en cinq gros livres où il fait une large place aux auteurs antiques. Encore plus importants en volume sont les *Commentarii Grammatici* du Flamand Johannes Despauterius (ca. 1460–1520), qui résultent de la réunion de sept traités composés entre 1506 et 1519: *Rudimenta*, *Prima pars* (morphologie), *Syntaxis*, *Ars versificatoria*, *De figuris*, *Ars epistolica*, *Orthographia*. L'auteur veut rendre l'enseignement du latin plus accessible qu'il ne l'est par le *Doctrinale*, dont il reprend en grande partie l'organisation, en estimant qu'il faut en amender le contenu. Aussi associe-t-il des règles en vers et un commentaire en prose où l'influence des humanistes italiens est sensible, mais sa syntaxe est fragmentée en une multitude de règles contextuelles. Par l'intermédiaire de ses nombreux adaptateurs, l'ouvrage a exercé une profonde influence sur l'enseignement de la grammaire latine dans l'Europe du Nord et en France.

## 3. Les réformateurs du XVI$^{e}$ siècle

Certains ouvrages produits au XVI$^{e}$ siècle marquent une nouvelle approche de la langue, en particulier dans le domaine de la syntaxe. Le *Libellus de constructione octo partium orationis* (1513, 1515) est un petit ouvrage initialement rédigé par William Lily (1468?–1523?), mais très remanié par Érasme. Les auteurs ont pour but de fournir un précis clair, pratique et pédagogiquement facile de la syntaxe latine, présentée sous la forme de règles très brèves. Renonçant au système fonctionnel médiéval, mais s'écartant également des grammaires humanistes, le *Libellus* annonce l'entreprise de réorganisation simplificatrice de Ramus. Plus important encore pour la tradition grammaticale latine est le *De emendata structura Latini sermonis* (1524) de l'Anglais Thomas Linacre (1465–1524). L'auteur entend construire une grammaire raisonnée de la langue latine classique qui présente deux points spécialement originaux. D'une part la syntaxe est construite, non sur l'opposition concordance *vs* régime, mais sur la notion de transition ou non transition de la personne, Linacre appelant 'personne de la construction' une entité abstraite rendant compte de la rection verbale, des relations casuelles et de la concordance. D'autre part une syntaxe 'juste' est opposée à une syntaxe 'figurée' qui permet de réduire à la première pratiquement toutes les constructions par le biais de l'ellipse et de l'énallage (ou recatégorisation des parties du discours). Le *De emendata* influence Philipp Melanchthon (1497–1560) dont la grammaire et la syntaxe latines (1526–1546), claires et accessibles, resteront les manuels de référence (248 éd.) dans les pays luthériens jusqu'au XVIIe siècle.

Le *De causis linguae Latinae* de Julius Cæsar Scaliger (1540) obéit à un projet complètement différent. Le but de l'auteur est d'aborder la langue latine en philosophe, et non en grammairien, c'est-à-dire en l'analysant à la lumière des quatre causes aristotéliciennes et en proposant une analyse critique de toute la tradition antérieure. Sous un volume relativement important, le *De causis* consacre, après un index des 627 erreurs relevées par Scaliger chez ses prédécesseurs et un préambule sur le but et la méthode du grammairien, deux livres aux éléments phonétiques, neuf livres au mot (*dictio*) et à ses différentes classes, les deux derniers traitant de la figure, de l'étymologie et de l'analogie. La référence des éléments constitutifs du langage aux causes d'Aristote permet à Scaliger de poser le principe de la rationalité linguistique, parfois perturbée par la tyrannie de l'usage (Lardet 1988). L'auteur est soucieux de chercher le fondement profond des entités linguistiques en s'abstrayant des marques morphologiques, comme le montre la recherche de définitions très générales (par ex. le nom est le signe d'une réalité durable, le verbe le signe d'une réalité en devenir). Si l'on a pu juger que la démonstration scaligérienne relevait trop souvent d'une rhétorique un peu artificielle (Jensen 1990), le *De causis* n'en a pas moins exercé une influence sensible jusqu'au XVIIIe siècle. La grammaire latine de Petrus Ramus (1564) est un manuel court et à fonction pédagogique, mais construit à partir d'option théoriques contraignantes qui en font une grammaire formelle, 'structurale' avant la lettre. Refusant souvent la terminologie et les concepts traditionnels (ainsi les termes *partes orationis* et *accidentia*, le mode verbal, les figures de construction), l'auteur limite le nombre des classes de mots à quatre catégories principales (nom et verbe, adverbe et conjonction), qu'il différencie au moyen de distinctions binaires et de critères essentiellement morphologiques. L'originalité de l'ouvrage a laissé des traces chez Sanctius et Schoppe.

Le *De institutione grammatica* (1572) du Portugais Manuel Álvares (1526–1583) a atteint une très forte diffusion internationale (530 éd. recensées), plus grâce à ses qualités pédagogiques et à la position institutionnelle de son auteur que par les innovations de son contenu. Il s'agit d'une grammaire didactique, partiellement en vers, avec des commentaires, dont l'auteur veut qu'elle soit utilisable par les Jésuites dans le monde entier. Elle se caractérise par une présentation très claire de la morphologie et une syntaxe très inspirée de Linacre. Plus importante sur le plan théorique est la *Minerua* (1587) de l'Espagnol Franciscus Sanctius (1523–1601). S'appuyant sur un corpus important d'exemples, l'auteur veut donner des structures du latin une vision claire grâce à quelques règles et principes fondamentaux qui lui permettent de réduire la variété des usages. Posant le principe de la monocatégorisation des mots et des morphèmes, il attribue à chaque lexème et à chaque outil grammatical une valeur fondamentale et utilise l'ellipse pour réduire les écarts par rapport à quelques structures jugées canoniques. L'ouvrage exercera une forte influence sur les grammaires latines ultérieures, puis sur la grammaire générale. La *Grammatica philosophica* (1628) de Caspar Schoppe (1576–1649) systématise sous la forme de règles brèves le contenu de la *Minerua*, tandis que l'énorme *Aristarchus* (1662 [1[re] éd., sous un autre titre, 1635]) de Gerardus Joannes Vossius (1577–1649) étudie systématiquement ce qui, dans la langue latine, relève de l'analogie et de l'anomalie, en résumant la position des grammairiens antérieurs depuis l'Antiquité. La *Nouvelle Méthode Latine* de Claude Lancelot (ca. 1616–1695), d'abord inspirée de Despautère (1re éd. 1644), intègre à partir de 1650 de très nombreuses remarques inspirées de Sanctius, et constitue la grammaire latine de référence pendant un siècle et demi.

## 4. Manuels d'apprentissage et travaux lexicographiques

A côté des grammaires coexistent des ouvrages spécifiques utilisés pour les débuts de l'apprentissage. Des textes courts et faciles, comme les *Disticha Catonis* (III<sup>e</sup> siècle p. C.), servent encore à la Renaissance, mais d'autres sont composés *ad hoc*, comme les *colloquia*, ou méthodes de conversation, qui ont pour but de mettre l'enfant directement dans une situation de communication. Parmi les 'colloques' les plus connus, ceux de Petrus Mosellanus (= Peter Schade (1493–1524; 1519), d'Érasme (1518–22), de Juan Luis Vivès (1538–39) et de Mathurin Cordier (1479–1564). Dans cette lignée s'inscrivent les manuels nommés "portes des langues", comme la *Ianua linguarum* (1611) de William Bathe (1564–1614) et la *Ianua linguarum reserata* (1631) de Jan Amos Comenius (1592–1670) qui proposent une progression soigneusement calculée dans l'apprentissage de la syntaxe et du vocabulaire latin. D'autres ouvrages répondent à des besoins précis: ainsi les traités de composition épistolaire (comme le *De componendis epistolis* que Perotti adjoint à sa grammaire, ou le *De conscribendis epistolis* (1521–22) d'Érasme), ou encore les traités des particules, comme ceux de Godescalc Steewech (1580) ou de Orazio Torsellini (1598), qui enseignent l'usage subtil des 'petits mots' latins (pronoms, adverbes, conjonctions).

Dans le domaine lexicographique, Perotti rédige un gros commentaire philologique et encyclopédique de Martial, le *Cornu Copiae*, publié en 1489, qui peut être considéré comme le pendant lexical d'une œuvre unique dont les *Rudimenta grammatices* seraient le correspondant grammatical (Furno 1995). Malgré sa réputation, le *Dictionarium linguae Latinae* d'Ambrogio Calepino (très nombreuses éd. à partir de 1502), n'est pas un multilingue au sens moderne du terme: dictionnaire encyclopédique de consultation, il sert essentiellement à décrire le monde en latin, mais apporte quelques brèves informations sur les autres langues grâce à la traduction de ses entrées dans des idiomes de plus en plus nombreux. Par ailleurs les vrais dictionnaires bilingues (latin-vernaculaire et inversement) se multiplient dans toute l'Europe, et pour pratiquement toutes les langues (y compris celles des Amériques), dès la fin du XV<sup>e</sup> siècle. Parmi les plus précoces, les dictionnaires latin-espagnol (1492), puis espagnol-latin (ca. 1495) de Nebrija, et les *Dictionarium latinogallicum* (1538) et *Dictionaire françois-latin* (1539) de Robert Estienne (1503–1559), qui a produit aussi un monolingue, le *Thesaurus linguae Latinae* (1531), somme lexicographique à l'influence durable. Mentionnons enfin l'*Etymologicon linguae Latinae* de Vossius (1662).

L'Humanisme traduit une mutation dans l'approche de la langue latine. Celle-ci apparaît d'abord comme un corpus fermé de textes hiérarchisés à imiter, avec pour référence les grands textes de l'Antiquité. De là l'importance donnée aux *testimonia*, et la question du respect à accorder à l'usage antique, dont un révélateur est le débat sur le cicéronianisme (dans la production du latin moderne, faut-il, ou non, se restreindre à l'ensemble des expressions utilisées par Cicéron?). Mais la confrontation du latin avec les vernaculaires devient inévitable et se manifeste par la traduction, au moins partielle, des ouvrages grammaticaux et des dictionnaires, de plus en plus présentés sous forme bilingue. Support de la description de quasiment toutes les langues du monde (d'où le concept de 'grammaire latine étendue'; Auroux 1994), le latin devient aussi l'objet de théories qui, plus ou moins explicitement, le décrivent en contraste avec les langues modernes. Ainsi l'ellipse, développée par Linacre et surtout Sanctius, permet de rapprocher le système des cas latins et les syntagmes prépositionnels des vernaculaires (pour Sanctius, une préposition est à sous-entendre devant tout ablatif latin). Dans ces conditions, l'analyse du latin suppose nécessairement une approche différentielle dans laquelle les structures des vernaculaires jouent un rôle de plus en plus important.

## 5. Bibliographie

### 5.1. Sources primaires

La première date donnée est celle de l'édition utilisée; date entre [ ] = date de la 1<sup>re</sup> éd.; date entre ⟨ ⟩ = date de composition.

Álvares, Manuel. 1596 [1572]. *De institutione grammatica libri tres.* Köln: A. Mylius.

Despauterius, Johannis. 1537. *Commentarii Grammatici.* Paris: R. Estienne.

Erasmus, Desiderius [Érasme] & William Lily. 1973 [1513]. *Absolutissimus de octo partium orationis constructione libellus.* Éd. par M. Cytowska. *Erasmi opera omnia*, I.4. Amsterdam: North-Holland Publishing Company.

Guarino Veronese [Guarinus Veronensis]. 1497 ⟨ca. 1418⟩. *Grammaticales Regulae.* Venezia: P. Jo. de Quarengiis.

Lancelot, Claude. 1653 [1644]. *Nouvelle méthode pour apprendre facilement [...] la langue latine.* 3<sup>e</sup> éd. Paris: A. Vitré.

Linacre, Thomas. 1524. *De emendata structura Latini sermonis libri sex.* London: R. Pynson.

Manuzio, Aldo [Alde Manuce]. 1508 [1493]. *Institutionum grammaticarum libri quatuor.* Venezia: A. Manuzio.

Melanchthon, Philipp [Schwarzerd]. 1854 [1526]. *Grammatica latina. Opera quae supersunt omnia.* Éd. par H. E. Bindseil. Vol. 20: *Reliqua scripta philologica*, cols 245–336. Brunswick & Halle/S.: C. A. Schwetschke & Söhne.

–. 1854 [1529]. *Syntaxis. Opera quae supersunt omnia.* Éd. par H. E. Bindseil. Vol. 20: *Reliqua scripta philologica*, cols 347–374. Brunswick & Halle/S.: C. A. Schwetschke & Söhne.

Nebrija, Antonio de [Aelius Antonius Nebrissensis]. 1510 [1481]. *Introductiones in Latinam grammaticén cum longioribus glossematis* [*Introductiones Latinae*]. Logroño: Arnao Guillén de Brocar.

Perotti, Niccolò. 1473 ⟨1463⟩. *Rudimenta grammatices.* Roma: C. Sweynheym & A. Pannartz.

–. 1526 [1489] ⟨1477–1479⟩. *Cornu Copiae.* Venezia: A Manuzio.

Ramus, Petrus [Pierre de la Ramée]. 1564 [1559]. *Grammatica [latina].* Paris: A. Wechel.

Sanctius, Franciscus [Francisco Sánchez de las Brozas]. 1587. *Minerua, seu de causis linguae Latinae.* Salamanca: J. & A. Renaut.

Scaliger, Julius Caesar. 1540. *De causis linguae Latinae libri tredecim.* Lyon: S. Gryphius.

Schoppe, Caspar [Scioppius]. 1664 [1628]. *Grammatica philosophica.* Amsterdam: J. Pluymer.

Sulpizio Verulano, Giovanni [Johannes Sulpitius Verulanus]. ca. 1490 ⟨ca. 1470⟩. *[Grammatica].* Napoli: F. del Tuppo.

Valla, Laurenzo. 1540 [1471] ⟨1449⟩. *Elegantiarum linguae Latinae libri VI.* In: *Opera.* Bâle: H. Petrus. (Reprod. in: Laurentius Valla, *Opera omnia*, Torino: Bottega d'Erasmo. 1962. I.)

Vossius, Gerardus Joannes. 1662 [1635]. *Aristarchus, siue de arte grammatica libri septem.* Amsterdam: I. Blaeu.

## 5.2. Sources secondaires

Auroux, Sylvain. 1994. *La révolution technologique de la grammatisation.* Liège: Mardaga.

Breva-Claramonte, Manuel. 1983. *Sanctius' Theory of Language: A contribution to the history of Renaissance linguistics.* Amsterdam & Philadelphia: Benjamins.

Caravolas, Jean-Antoine. 1994. *La didactique des langues, Précis d'histoire I (1450–1700).* Montréal & Tübingen: Presses de l'Université de Montréal & Narr.

Chomarat, Jacques. 1981. *Grammaire et rhétorique chez Erasme.* 2 vols. Paris: Les Belles Lettres.

Clerico, Geneviève. 1982. *Sanctius, Minerve, ou les causes de la langue latine.* Introduction, traduction et notes. Lille: Presses universitaires de Lille.

Codoñer, Carmen & Juan Antonio González Iglesias, éds. 1994. *Antonio de Nebrija: Edad Media y Renacimiento.* Salamanca: Universidad.

Colombat, Bernard. 1993. *Les figures de construction dans la syntaxe latine (1500–1780).* Louvain & Paris: Peeters & Bibliothèque de l'information grammaticale.

–. 1999. *La grammaire latine en France à la Renaissance et à l'Âge classique. Théories et pédagogie.* Grenoble: ELLUG, Université Stendhal.

Furno, Martine. 1995. *Le 'Cornu Copiae' de Niccolò Perotti: Culture et méthode d'un humaniste qui aimait les mots.* Genève: Droz.

Grendler, Paul F. 1989. *Schooling in Renaissance Italy: Literacy and learning, 1300–1600.* Baltimore & London: The Johns Hopkins Univ. Press.

Jensen, Kristian. 1990. *Rhetorical Philosophy and Philosophical Grammar: Julius Caesar Scaliger's theory of language.* München: Fink.

Lardet, Pierre. 1988. "Scaliger lecteur de Linacre". *L'héritage des grammairiens latins, de l'Antiquité aux Lumières (Actes du colloque de Chantilly, 2–4 septembre 1987)* éd. par Irène Rosier, 303–323. Louvain & Paris: Peeters & Bibliothèque de l'information grammaticale.

Padley, G[eorge] A[rthur]. 1976. *Grammatical Theory in Western Europe, 1500–1700: The Latin tradition.* Cambridge: Cambridge Univ. Press.

Percival, W[alter] Keith. 1976. "Renaissance Grammar: Rebellion or evolution?" *Interrogativi dell'Umanesimo* éd. par Giovannangiola Secchi Tarugi, 2, 73–90. Firenze: Leo S. Olschki.

Regoliosi, Mariangela. 1995. "La concezione del latino di Lorenzo Valla: radici medioevali e novità umanistiche". *Mediaevalia Lovaniensia*, Series I/ Studia XXIV, 145–157. Leuven Univ. Press.

Tavoni, Mirko. 1990. "La linguistica rinascimentale". *Storia della linguistica* a cura di Giulio C. Lepschy, 2, 169–312. Bologna: il Mulino.

*Bernard Colombat, Grenoble (France)*

# 91. L'étude du grec à l'époque de l'humanisme

1. Le premier humanisme italien et le grec
2. Le grec dans l'Europe de la Renaissance
3. Bibiographie

## 1. Le premier humanisme italien et le grec

### 1.1. Le grec dans le Moyen Age occidental

#### 1.1.1. Mise en perspective

Alors que le Moyen Age occidental a très largement ignoré le grec, les XVe et XVIe siècles sont marqués par une renaissance des études grecques en Occident. A partir de 1397, année où débute l'enseignement de Manuel Chrysoloras (v. 1350–1415) à Florence, la connaissance du grec est réintroduite en Occident et se développe d'abord en Italie, puis, essentiellement au XVIe siècle, dans les autres pays européens. L'essor des études grecques est alors indissociable du développement du mouvement humaniste: dans l'Europe de la Renaissance, la connaissance du grec fait partie intégrante de la culture humaniste et ce trait persistera bien au-delà du XVIe siècle (Berschin 1989; Wilson 1992).

Le renouveau du grec en Occident est rapidement salué comme un événement majeur par les humanistes. Dans son *Rerum suo tempore gestarum commentarius*, Leonardo Bruni (v. 1370–1444), un des premiers Italiens à apprendre le grec, délivre un jugment devenu rapidement un lieu commun de l'historiographie humaniste:

> Depuis sept cents ans, personne en Italie ne s'est occupé de lettres grecques; et nous savons pourtant que celles-ci ont donné naissance à l'ensemble les disciplines (Bruni 1926: 431).

Le nouvel intérêt que portent les premiers humanistes italiens à la littérature et à la civilisation antiques les conduit rapidement à rechercher une connaissance directe de la langue grecque. Or leur aspiration se heurte à un obstacle fondamental: la grande indigence des études grecques dans les pays latins.

Très peu de centres réussissent, en effet, à maintenir au Moyen Age une certaine connaissance de la langue grecque. Celle-ci n'était pas totalement ignorée, tant s'en faut, mais malgré les initiatives des Irlandais de l'epoque carolingienne et des Anglais de l'école d'Oxford au XIIIe siècle, le grec resta cantonné dans quelques foyers périphériques de la chrétienté occidentale, l'Espagne et la Sicile principalement.

La grammaire grecque de Roger Bacon (v. 1220–après 1292), composée en 1268, constitue un document exceptionnel, peu représentatif de l'état des études grecques de son époque: "je décrirai surtout ce que les Latins ignorent le plus" (Bacon 1902: 126), dit l'auteur, qui tient ses connaissances en la matière de professeurs grecs et semble se fonder sur un manuel érotématique d'origine byzantine. Mais le peu de succès que connut l'œuvre, conservée dans un seul manuscrit, confirme l'inadaptation des écoles à un enseignement méthodique de la langue grecque (Weiss 1975b: 83–89).

#### 1.1.2. Pétrarque et Leonzio Pilato: l'apport italo-grec

Les choses changent à l'époque de Pétrarque (1304–1374). La correspondance de Pétrarque montre qu'il est obsédé par le désir d'accéder directement aux grands auteurs grecs (v. Petrarca 1975, ad indices). Ce désir est suscité chez lui par la lecture de Cicéron, auteur dont il est profondément imprégné. Cicéron n'est non seulement l'adaptateur de la pensée grecque dans ses écrits philosophiques, il a aussi très largement recours aux citations grecques dans sa correspondance, dont Pétrarque a précisément redécouvert une partie, les *Lettres à Atticus* (Mann 1989: 35 et passim).

C'est sous l'égide de Pétrarque et de Boccace que Leonzio Pilato († 1367/68), un Calabrais, traduit et commente Homère et vient enseigner le grec à Florence. Mais cet enseignement est resté sans résultat apparent: Boccace, qui est le seul bénéficiaire connu de ces cours, ne parvient jamais à vraiment maîtriser le grec (Pertusi 1964). L'épisode a néanmoins fait naître dans l'historiographie moderne l'hypothèse d'un apport spécifique des italo-grecs à la renaissance des études grecs en Occident: pour A. Pertusi (1963 et 1981), il existait en Calabre et en Sicile une tradition propre d'enseignement du grec classique, qui, notamment par le biais de Pilato, aurait à son tour influencé les premiers humanistes de l'Italie du Nord. Alimentée notamment par des attributions hâtives de nombreux manuscrits grecs aux régions méridionales de l'Italie (Cavallo 1980), cette hypothèse ne tient pas suffisamment compte du contenu des textes. Les écrits de Pilato lui-même lèvent toute ambiguïté: ses gloses sur le texte de l'Iliade et de l'Odyssée (voir les extraits édités par Pertusi (1964: 261–380)) proviennent directement des grands commentateurs alexandrins qui étaient couramment utilisés dans les écoles byzantines.

### 1.2. Le renouveau des études grecques en Italie à partir de 1397

#### 1.2.1. L'apport byzantin

Ce n'est pas l'Italie du Sud, mais bel et bien Constantinople elle-même qui a exercé une influence directe et déterminante: l'enseignement qui débute à Florence en 1397 a lieu grâce à des contacts directs entre les élèves de Pétrarque et les cercles intellectuels de la capitale de l'empire. Manuel Chrysoloras est un proche de l'empereur, il est issu d'une ancienne famille constantinopolitaine (Cammelli 1941).

La *translatio litterarum graecarum* saluée par les humanistes ne peut se faire sans l'apport de Byzance, seule dépositaire de la culture grecque. C'est cet apport qui conditionne durablement et profondément l'étude du grec en Occident. Les intellectuels byzantins étaient des intermédiaires obligés dans la transmission de la connaissance linguistique. Leur emprise sur les études grecques en Occident est déterminante pendant presque tout le XV^e^ siècle. Ce rôle, ils ne le jouent pas sans une motivation extrêmement forte. L'enseignement du grec, la diffusion de l'hellénisme fait partie d'une stratégie politique visant à sauver l'Empire byzantin (Thomson 1966). Chrysoloras et plus tard Bessarion (1408–1472), Théodore Gaza (v. 1400–v. 1476) et Constantin Lascaris (1434–1501) ont une conscience aigüe de la menace qui pèse sur Constantinople et donc sur la civilisation grecque tout entière. Leur rôle d'enseignants s'inscrit dans la même perspective que leur activité d'ambassadeurs.

#### 1.2.2. Les enseignants

Le rapprochement politique et religieux entre Constantinople et les pays latins dans la deuxième moitié du XIV^e^ siècle (Nicol 1980) a ouvert la voie à un rapprochement entre les cercles savants de Constantinople et les humanistes florentins. A l'extrême fin du XIV^e^ siècle, le mépris de Pétrarque pour les 'graeculi' censés tout ignorer de la culture grecque (Petrarca 1975: 826–827) a cédé la place à une admiration durable. Invité à Florence pour enseigner publiquement le grec, Manuel Chrysoloras est le premier d'une série de maîtres byzantins à diffuser la connaissance du grec en Italie: lui-même enseigne d'abord à Florence, puis avec des interruptions, à Pavie et à Rome. Parmi ses successeurs on peut nommer Démétrios Chalcondyle (1424–1511), Théodore Gaza, Jean Argyropoulos (v. 1415–1487), Constantin Lascaris (Martínez Manzano 1994). Mais l'enseignement du grec n'est pas l'apanage de ces savants byzantins, leurs élèves italiens assument également cette tâche: dans la première moitié du siècle, deux élèves de Chrysoloras, Guarino de Vérone (1374–1460) et Palla Strozzi (v. 1373–1462), jouent notamment un rôle important.

#### 1.2.3. Les méthodes de l'enseignement du grec

L'enseignement ainsi dispensé se déroule en trois phases: dans un premier temps, le maître enseigne la grammaire élémentaire, c'est-à-dire essentiellement l'écriture, la phonétique et la morphologie: c'est sans doute à cet usage que Chrysoloras rédigea ses *Erotemata*, manuel grammatical très fortement imprégné de la tradition alexandrine, mais qui innove par une nouvelle présentation des déclinaisons nominales (Pertusi 1963; Förstel 1992; Robins 1993: 247–252). Adapté et traduit par Guarino de Vérone, l'ouvrage est le modèle de tous les manuels ultérieurs au moins jusqu'à la fin du XV^e^ siècle. L'abondance des témoins manuscrits, leur présence parmi les premiers ouvrages grecs imprimés prouve que ces grammaires avaient leur place dans les tout premiers pas de l'apprentissage du grec. Les manuels s'ouvrent sur l'alphabet grec: l'apprentissage de l'écriture grecque n'est pas alors une simple formalité, rapidement maîtrisée par l'élève; bien au contraire, cet apprentissage doit conduire l'élève à copier très rapidement des textes et à pallier ainsi à la rareté des livres grecs.

La deuxième étape de l'enseignement était le commentaire d'un texte grec: le maître commençait par donner une traduction mot à mot du texte qui permettait aux élèves de disposer d'un calque précis, donnant à la fois la signification de chaque mot et calquant ses caractéristiques morphologiques. Le texte grec devenu ainsi compréhensible pour l'élève fait l'objet d'un commentaire grammatical qui correspond à la pratique byzantine du μερισμός. Le maître identifie la catégorie grammaticale, la partie du discours, à laquelle appartient chaque mot ou au moins les mots qui n'ont pas d'équivalent grammatical exact en latin et explique ses particularités. Le procédé est celui de la schédographie byzantine (Hunger 1978: 2.23–29), il permet, à propos d'un mot concret, de redéployer le contenu du manuel de grammaire. Vient enfin le commentaire sémantique, explication approfondie par le maître du sens d'un mot ou d'une expression que le calque littéral ne saurait rendre. Ces diverses phases de l'enseignement sur un auteur se retrouvent dans les rares documents conservés. Un élève anonyme a ainsi transcrit les cours de Chrysoloras sur le Charon de Lucien: son exemplaire du texte grec, une copie du manuscrit de Chrysoloras, est doté d'une traduction interlinéaire partielle accompagnée occasionellement d'une note grammaticale. En marge figurent des explications plus longues sur la signification de certains mots (Berti 1985, 1987a, 1987b).

Ces deux premières phases de l'enseignement du grec sont directement inspirées des méthodes de l'enseignement à Byzance. A l'époque des Paléologues, un des buts essentiels de l'éducation est la maîtrise de la langue savante grecque, une Hochsprache totalement artificielle qui n'a plus rien à voir avec la langue populaire (Mango 1980: 147–148). L'enseignement a par conséquent pour base la grammaire, "l'art qui nous apprend à bien écrire et à bien lire" (Hilgard 1979: 300) comme le dit une scholie de la grammaire du pseudo-Denys qui est l'archétype de tous les manuels byzantins (Lallot 1989). La grammaire elle-même définit le cadre dans lequel se situe toute étude du grec: lecture, explication et critique des textes anciens (Lallot 1989: 40–41, 69–81); et ce cadre est encore celui de l'enseignement du grec au XV$^{e}$ siècle. Résolument conservateur, l'enseignement linguistique byzantin a pour seul objet le grec: cet hellénocentrisme, qui a au demeurant contribué à l'isolement de la linguistique byzantine et au caractère tardif de son adaptation en Occident, est évidemment partiellement abandonné lorsque les maîtres byzantins enseignent le grec en Italie. Le monolinguisme byzantin est alors remplacé par un bilinguisme grec-latin: dorénavant l'étude du grec en Occident se fait en latin, les langues vernaculaires étant exclues pour longtemps de cet enseignement.

L'adaptation de l'étude du grec à l'Occident impose une troisième étape de l'enseignement, la traduction: celle-ci ne constitue pas seulement un moyen de diffuser un texte grec dans un milieu non helléniste, elle est aussi une étape dans l'apprentissage du grec. La première traduction latine du Charon de Lucien (Berti 1987b), celle de l'éloge de Dionysos d'Aelius Aristide par Cencio dei Rustici (Förstel 1994: 114 et n. 7) sont ainsi directement liées à l'enseignement de Chrysoloras. L'importance de la traduction comme méthode d'apprentissage (Berti 1988) est illustrée par les exposés théoriques de Chrysoloras et de Leonardo Bruni (Thiermann 1993: 151–196).

## 2. Le grec dans l'Europe de la Renaissance

### 2.1. Genèse de la philologie classique

#### 2.1.1. La disponibilité des textes

Les méthodes de l'enseignement du grec ne connaissent pas de changement notable jusqu'au XVI$^{e}$ siècle. Cependant, peu à peu, cet enseignement bénéficie d'un environnement culturel plus favorable: au début du XV$^{e}$ siècle, les textes grecs sont encore extrêmement rares, et les premiers cours de grec se fondent sur les manuscrits rapportés de Constantinople par Chrysoloras. Progressivement, toutefois, ses élèves constituent des collections, soit en copiant eux-mêmes des textes, soit en rapportant des manuscrits d'Orient. Le mouvement prend de l'ampleur avec les premières collections princières de livres grecs. Au milieu du XV$^{e}$ siècle, les bibliothèques grecques les plus importantes se trouvent à Rome: la collection de Bessarion compte environ 800 manuscrits (Labowski 1979), la bibliothèque pontificale environ 400 (Devreesse 1965).

Ces collections s'enrichissent dans le troisième quart du siècle des premiers livres imprimés en grec: les grammaires élémentaires du grec en présentation bilingue sont ainsi largement diffusées (Förstel 1992: 109–110). A partir de la fin du siècle, les textes classiques grecs bénéficient d'une diffusion imprimée grâce notamment à l'imprimerie d'Alde Manuce (Lowry 1978).

Dans l'Italie de la deuxième moitié du XV$^{e}$ siècle, la plupart des auteurs grecs sont ainsi accessibles sous forme manuscrite ou imprimée. L'enseignement du grec peut par ailleurs s'appuyer sur les grammaires et les lexiques, ces derniers de diffusion récente.

#### 2.1.2. La conception du langage

Ces conditions éminemment favorables conduisent à un changement profond dans l'étude du grec: la disponibilité de la plupart des textes et la présence de nouveaux instruments de travail permettent de se passer de la médiation byzantine. Malgré des exceptions notables, les Grecs venus en Occident à la fin du siècle ne jouent plus un rôle déterminant dans les études grecques: leur enseignement ne jouit plus du même prestige qu'au début du siècle. Georges Hermonyme de Sparte, pourtant le premier à enseigner le grec en France, à partir de 1476, est ainsi présenté par Erasme et Budé, ses élèves à Paris, comme un très médiocre helléniste (Irigoin 1977; Chomarat 1981: 1.303).

Cette perte d'influence des maîtres byzantins entraîne une évolution importante dans l'hellénisme occidental. Séjournant à Constantinople au début du XV^e^ siècle, Guarino de Vérone admire la langue parlée par le peuple de la capitale (Cammelli 1941: 139 n. 2). Pour lui, cette langue est le grec ancien. En fait, les Byzantins parlaient depuis longtemps un idiome beaucoup plus proche du grec moderne que du grec classique. Mais dans son jugement, Guarino partage la conception linguistique de Chrysoloras. Aux yeux des Byzantins, la langue grecque est en effet une entité non soumise à des inflexions historiques, leur vision de la langue est résolument synchronique. Les seules variations admises par la linguistique byzantine sont de nature dialectale.

La vision linguistique byzantine et la tradition pédagogique qui en résulte sont peu à peu battues en brèche par un nouvel esprit historique symbolisé par l'œuvre de Lorenzo Valla (v. 1405–1457). Ce renouveau se traduit par un intérêt accru pour les historiens grecs – Valla a traduit Thucydide (Wilson 1992: 68–75) – et, plus généralement, par une prise de conscience de l'évolution qu'ont connue les lettres grecques d'Homère au XV^e^ siècle. Le rôle des maîtres byzantins s'en trouve tout naturellement dévalué.

### 2.1.3. Linguistique et philologie

L'irruption de l'histoire dans le domaine linguistique conduit à un affinement de la méthode philologique et celui-ci est perceptible jusque dans les manuels de grammaire élémentaire. La grammaire grecque de Mélanchthon (1497–1560), parue en 1518 (éd. 1854; Förstel 1997), recourt fréquemment à des comparaisons avec la langue latine, qui lui permettent de faire ressortir les particularités du grec. Dans son ensemble, le manuel est toujours très proche de ses modèles byzantins du XV^e^ siècle, mais ce qui est nouveau, c'est qu'au lieu de s'inspirer étroitement d'un des manuels précédents, il s'appuie sur l'ensemble de la littérature grammaticale du XV^e^ siècle pour choisir comme modèle tantôt l'un tantôt l'autre. La méthode sous-jacente à la rédaction du manuel est, on le voit, la confrontation des sources.

Cette méthode apparaît plus ouvertement quand on analyse les études grammaticales de Jean Cuno (1462/63–1513) à l'extrême fin du siècle (Sicherl 1985: 142–143; Förstel 1993): dans un cahier conservé à la Bibliothèque de Sélestat, Cuno a sonsigné ce qui, à première vue, apparaît comme un simple condensé de la grammaire élémentaire grecque. A y regarder de plus près, toutefois, on s'aperçoit que Cuno a réuni et confronté le contenu de presque toutes les grammaires grecques du XV^e^ siècle et il ne s'est pas contenté d'étudier les différents ouvrages, il a également confronté les différentes éditions d'une même auteur. Des excerpta grammaticaux d'Ange Politien (Cesarini Martinelli 1992), légèrement antérieurs, trahissent le même procédé appliqué cette fois aux sources alexandrines elles-mêmes. Dès lors, on comprend mieux pourquoi beaucoup de manuscrits et certaines éditions de la fin du siècle renferment en un seul volume plusieurs ouvrages de grammaire élémentaire.

Les notes grammaticales de Cuno révèlent un autre aspect important de l'étude du grec à la fin du XV^e^ siècle et au début du XVI^e^ siècle: le lieu où Cuno a rédigé ces notes n'est pas une salle de cours, mais une bibliothèque, sans doute celle de Reuchlin (Förstel 1993: 304–305; 1999). L'étude du grec se fait de plus en plus par le recours direct au livre. Les éditions incunables des manuels élémentaires sont ainsi le plus souvent accompagnées d'une traduction qui porte sur l'ensemble du texte: au texte grec originel de la grammaire, fait face la version latine qui traduit même les paradigmes. La traduction intégrale du texte grammatical a le mérite de permettre à l'autodidacte d'en appréhender le contenu. Avec les premières grammaires rédigées par des occidentaux, la présentation prend une forme plus moderne, proche des manuels scolaires modernes.

A la fin du XV^e^ siècle, l'apprentissage du grec se caractérise, on le voit, par un usage plus intensif du livre. Fidèle reflet de l'enseignement élémentaire, le manuel de grammaire multiplie les références aux textes grecs: alors que les grammaires de Chrysoloras et de Théodore Gaza ne contiennent pratiquement aucune référence à la littérature grecque, l'ouvrage de Mélanchthon en est rempli. L'éventail des citations qu'il contient est révélateur de la nouvelle approche philologique qui caractérise l'enseignement du grec au XVI$^{e}$ siècle.

### 2.2. Le grec et les courants religieux et politiques

#### 2.2.1. Le retour à l'évangile

L'ampleur du champ couvert par la philologie grecque des débuts de la Renaissance peut surprendre; l'essor que connaît alors l'hellénisme peut s'expliquer si l'on tient compte du puissant mouvement religieux dont la réforme est un des aboutissements. Le courant de la *devotio moderna* dans les Pays-Bas et en Allemagne, une forme plus générale de rejet de la théologie scolastique telle qu'elle était enseignée dans les universités, fondent l'aspiration à une vie religieuse plus proche de l'évangile. Ce mouvement profond suscite un intérêt renouvelé pour le texte du Nouveau Testament: formé par les Frères de la Vie commune aux Pays-Bas, Erasme consacre une partie importante de son activité à l'établissement du texte grec des évangiles: il publie ainsi en 1505 les *Adnotationes in Novum Testamentum*, où le Nouveau Testament fait l'objet d'une étude philologique, et en 1516 l'édition princeps du texte grec (Chomarat 1981: 1.467–470). Avec Erasme, l'Ecriture est devenue un objet de critique philologique qui va au-delà de la traduction canonique de saint Jérôme. L'attitude des réformateurs se situe dans le prolongement de cette approche philologique: la traduction allemande du Nouveau Testament par Luther s'appuie ainsi sur l'édition d'Erasme et donc sur le texte grec des évangiles.

#### 2.2.2. La *prisca theologia*

Les humanistes acquièrent ainsi la possibilité de lire dans le texte d'origine le Nouveau Testament. De même, pour l'Ancien Testament, certains humanistes comme Jean Pic de la Mirandole (1463–1494) et Jean Reuchlin (1456–1522) apprennent l'hébreu et étudient les traditions cabalistiques. Reuchlin écrit même une première grammaire hébraïque occidentale, le *De rudimentis hebraicis* publié en 1506. Mais cet intérêt pour les livres sacrés juifs a aussi une incidence sur l'étude du grec: pour les humanistes de la fin du XV$^{e}$ siècle et du début du XVI$^{e}$ siècle, l'Ancien Testament est une des sources de la *prisca theologia*, cette théologie ou philosophie qui naît des révélations faites directement par Dieu à Moïse. L'autre source, ce sont les philosophes grecs de Pythagore à Platon. Dans sa *Theologia platonica*, Marsile Ficin élabore une synthèse de la philosophie platonicienne, dans une perspective néoplatonicienne et chrétienne. Pour Ficin, Platon est le dernier et le plus grand représentant de l'ancienne philosophie, qui descend de Moïse en passant par Pythagore, Hermès Trismégiste, Zoroastre et Orphée (Kristeller 1972: 15; Kraye 1988: 356–357; Hankins 1990: 1.266–366). On comprend aisément les conséquences pour l'étude du grec de cette *pia philosophia*: la plupart des textes envisagés sont grecs et Marsile Ficin est le premier à avoir traduit l'ensemble du corpus platonicien en latin. Dernier représentant de l'ancienne philosophie, Platon est aussi l'inspirateur majeur de la nouvelle philosophie, celle des néoplatoniciens: Plotin, Porphyre, Proclus, Denys l'Aréopagite en constituent les représentants majeurs et Ficin s'en inspire directement. Fondé sur un prétendu accord avec la tradition de l'ancien christianisme, le retour de Platon et des Néo-Platoniciens constitue un apport majeur pour les études grecques: l'entreprise ficinienne établit un lien fort entre la philosophie grecque et la plus ancienne tradition chrétienne (Vasoli 1988: 68). L'étude du grec, au même titre que celle de l'hébreu, trouve là une justification définitive.

#### 2.2.3. Les pouvoirs monarchiques et le grec

Les courants philosophiques et religieux de la fin du XV$^{e}$ siècle et du début du XVI$^{e}$ siècle placent le grec au cœur des *studia humanitatis*. A un moment où les pouvoirs monarchiques cherchent à prendre le contrôle du mouvement humaniste, l'étude du grec devient aussi un enjeu politique. En Italie, cette tendance est perceptible dès le milieu du XV$^{e}$ siècle: le pontificat de Nicolas V est ainsi marqué à Rome par une vaste campagne de traduction d'auteurs grecs à laquelle participent les plus éminents humanistes sous l'égide de Bessarion (Hankins 1990: 1.180–190); la bibliothèque pontificale et celle de Bessarion fournissent alors les sources de l'entreprise. Un demi-siècle plus tard, alors que la bibliothèque pontificale s'est enrichie un peu plus en manuscrits grecs, la fondation envisagée du Collège du Quirinal qui prévoit surtout un enseignement du grec, ainsi que l'édition, à Rome et sous l'autorité du pontife, de classiques grecs montrent l'emprise croissante du pouvoir politique sur l'hellénisme occidental.

L'aboutissement de cette évolution se produit dans le deuxième quart du XVI^e^ siècle en France: sous François Ier, la royauté parvient à contrôler presque entièrement l'étude du grec. l'institution du collège des lecteurs royaux en 1529, le futur Collège de France, accorde une place éminente à l'enseignement du grec. Quelques années plus tard, le roi constitue à Fontainebleau une bibliothèque presque exclusivement composée de livres grecs (Balayé 1989: 78–80; Förstel 1998). La création des imprimeurs du roi, dont un est spécialement chargé des éditions grecques, intervient sensiblement en même temps. L'enseignement, la bibliothèque et l'édition constituent les trois volets d'une politique qui permet à la royauté d'imposer une mainmise presque totale sur les études grecques en France. Dans cette entreprise le roi est très fortement influencé par les idées ficiniennes d'une part, et par le mouvement de retour à l'évangile symbolisé par l'œuvre philologique d'Erasme d'autre part: le premier ouvrage imprimé par l'imprimeur du roi pour le grec est l'édition princeps de l'Histoire ecclésiastique d'Eusèbe de Césarée qui relate l'histoire de l'Eglise paléochrétienne.

Ces éditions rattachent l'hellénisme royal à l'œuvre de Ficin et d'Erasme, mais les humanistes s'efforcent de donner à l'étude du grec en France une orientation plus nationale. Le rôle de Georges Hermonyme qui a assuré le premier enseignement du grec à Paris après avoir été un des membres du cercle de Bessarion, est dénigré puis passé sous silence. Avec lui, c'est l'influence italienne dans les études grecques en France que l'entourage du roi cherche à masquer. Ce n'est donc pas par référence à l'Italie, mais par un lien direct à l'antiquité grecque que se définit l'hellénisme de François Ier: le personnage central de cette filiation est Denys l'Aréopagite, dont un éloge byzantin est publié par les presses royales en 1547 (Martin 1982). Athénien, compagnon de saint Paul, évêque et martyr de Paris, Denys concilie dans ses œuvres philosophie platonicienne et christianisme. Il fait le lien entre le premier christianisme et la France, entre Athènes et Paris. Budé le cite comme le grand Denys et aucun des humanistes de l'entourage du roi ne se permet de douter de l'authenticité d'une légende dont la critique avait pourtant déjà été faite par Lorenzo Valla au XV^e^ siècle.

Exemplaire à bien des égards, le développement des études grecques en France dans la première moitié du XVI^e^ siècle n'est pas sans parallèle dans les autres pays européens: en Allemagne, sous l'impulsion de Reuchlin, le grec devient une composante importante de la philologie classique. Reuchlin lui-même traduit directement en allemand des discours de Démosthène (Sicherl 1966: 278–287). Les traductions en langues vernaculaires d'œuvres grecques se multiplient dès lors en Europe: l'étude du grec n'est pas sans incidence sur les littératures nationales. En France, les poètes de la Pléiade s'inspirent ainsi directement de la poésie grecque.

### 2.3. Epilogue: grec classique et grec moderne

Prenant définitivement sa place parmi les disciplines enseignées dans les écoles et les universités, le grec est devenu au XVI^e^ siècle un élément distinctif de l'humanisme occidental. Dissociée de la civilisation byzantine et de sa conception unitaire du langage, l'étude du grec prend alors des caractéristiques plus proches de la philologie moderne. L'introduction de critères historiques conduit à la sélection pour l'enseignement d'auteurs classiques et à la mise à l'écart de la littérature grecque médiévale et contemporaine. Celle-ci devient affaire de spécialistes: la rédaction de la première grammaire du grec moderne par Nicolas Sophianos (v. 1500–v. 1550) vers le milieu du XVI^e^ siècle s'inscrit dans cette perspective. Dans la deuxième moitié du siècle, l'helléniste Martin Crusius (1526–1607) maîtrise couramment le grec ancien et le grec moderne: il traduit notamment en grec la *Batrachomyomachia* attribuée à Homère (Kresten 1970: 13–37). Même s'il reste exceptionnel, cet intérêt pour le grec moderne constitue l'aboutissement d'une évolution qui mène du premier enseignement du grec en Occident à l'affirmation d'un hellénisme occidental.

## 3. Bibliographie

Bacon, Roger. 1902. *The Greek Grammar of Roger Bacon, and a Fragment of His Hebrew Grammar* éd. par Edward Nolan & S. A. Hirsch. Cambridge: The Univ. Press.

Balayé, Simone. 1989. "La naissance de la Bibliothèque du Roi". *Histoire des Bibliothèques françaises* 2.77–84. Paris: Promodis.

Berschin, Walter. 1989 [1980]. *Medioevo greco-latino: Da Gerolamo a Niccolo Cusano.* Traduzione italiana a cura di E. Livrea. (= *Nuovo Medioevo*, 33.) Napoli: Liguori editore.

Berti, Ernesto. 1985. "Uno scriba greco-latino: il codice Vat. Urb. gr. 121 e la prima versione del Caronte di Luciano". *Rivista di Filologia e di Istruzione Classica* 113.416–443.

–. 1987a. "Alla Scuola di Manuele Crisolora. Lettura e commento di Luciano". *Rinascimento* 27.3–73.

–. 1987b. "Alle origini della fortuna di Luciano nell'Europa occidentale". *Studi Classici e Orientali* 37.303–351.

–. 1988. "Traduzioni oratorie fedeli". *Medioevo e Rinascimento* 2.245–266.

Bruni, Leonardo. 1926. *Rerum suo tempore gestarum Commentarius.* A cura di Carmine di Pierro. (= *Rerum Italicarum Scriptores*, 19.3.) Bologna: Zanichelli.

Cammelli, Giuseppe. 1941. *I Dotti bizantini e le origini dell'Umanesimo.* Firenze: Vallecchi.

Cavallo, Guglielmo. 1980. "La Trasmissione scritta della cultura greca antica in Calabria e in Sicilia tra i secoli X–XV. Consistenza, tipologia, fruizione". *Scrittura e Civiltà* 4.157–145.

Cesarini Martinelli, Lucia. 1992. "Grammatiche greche nello scrittoio del Poliziano". *Dotti bizantini e libri greci nell'Italia del secolo XV. Atti del Convegno internazionale: Trento, 22–23 ottobre 1990.* (= *Collectanea*, 6), 257–290. Napoli: M. D'Auria Editore.

Chomarat, Jacques. 1981. *Grammaire et rhétorique chez Erasme.* (= *Les Classiques de l'Humanisme. Etudes*, 10.) Paris: Belles Lettres.

Devreesse, Robert. 1965. *Le Fonds grec de la Bibliothèque Vaticane des origines à Paul V.* (= *Studi e Testi*, 244.) Città del Vaticano: Biblioteca Apostolica Vaticana.

Förstel, Christian. 1992. "Les grammaires grecques du XVe siècle. Etude sur les ouvrages de Manuel Chrysoloras, Théodore Gaza et Constantin Lascaris". *Ecole Nationale des Chartes: Positions des Thèses* 105–110.

–. 1993. "Jean Cuno et la grammaire grecque". *Bibliothèque de l'Ecole des Chartes* 151.289–305.

–. 1994. "Bartolomeo Aragazzi et Manuel Chrysoloras: le codex Vratislav. Akc. 1949 Kn. 60". *Scriptorium* 48.111–121.

–. 1997. "Die griechische Grammatik Melanchthons". *Melanchthon und das Lehrbuch des 16. Jahrhunderts: Begleitband zur Ausstellung im Kulturhistorischen Museum Rostock 25. April–13. Juli 1997* (= Rostocker Studien, 1.), 35–56. Rostock: Universität Rostock, Philosophische Fakultät.

–. 1998. "Les manuscrits grecs dans les collections royales sous François Ier". *Revue française d'histoire du livre* 98–99.71–88.

–. 1999. "Die griechische Grammatik im Umkreis Reuchlins: Untersuchungen zur 'Wanderung' der griechischen Studien von Italien nach Deutschland". *Reuchlin und Italien*, herausgegeben von Gerald Dörner (= *Pforzheimer Reuchlinschriften*, 7.), 45–56. Stuttgart: Jan Thorbecke Verlag.

Hankins, James. 1990. *Plato in the Italian Renaissance.* (= *Columbia Studies in the Classical Tradition*, 17.) Leiden & New York: Brill.

Hilgard, Alfred, éd. 1979 [1901]. *Scholia in Dionysii Thracis artem grammaticam.* (= *Grammatici Graeci*, 1.3.) Hildesheim & New York: Olms.

Hunger, Herbert. 1978. *Die hochsprachliche profane Literatur der Byzantiner.* (= *Handbuch der Altertumswissenschaft*, 12.5.) München: Beck.

Irigoin, Jean. 1977. "Georges Hermonyme de Sparte: ses manuscrits, son enseignement à Paris". *Bulletin de l'Association Guillaume Budé* 1.22–27.

Kraye, Jill. 1988. "Moral Philosophy". *The Cambridge History of Renaissance Philosophy* éd. par Charles B. Schmitt et al. Cambridge: Univ. Press. 301–386.

Kresten, Otto. 1970. *Das Patriarchat von Konstantinopel im ausgehenden 16. Jahrhundert: Der Bericht des Leontios Eustratios im Cod. Tyb. Mb 10: Einleitung, Text, Übersetzung, Kommentar.* (= Österreichische Akademie der Wissenschaften, Philosophisch-Historische Klasse. *Sitzungsberichte*, 266. Band, 5. Abhandlung.) Wien, Köln & Graz: Hermann Böhlaus Nachf.

Kristeller, Paul Oskar. 1972. *Die Philosophie des Marsilio Ficino.* Frankfurt a. M.: Klostermann.

Labowsky, Lotte. 1979. *Bessarion's Library and the Biblioteca Marciana: Six early inventories.* Roma: Edizioni di Storia e Letteratura.

Lallot, Jean. 1989. *La grammaire de Denys le Thrace.* (= *Sciences du Langage.*) Paris: Editions du CNRS.

Lowry, Martin. 1979. *The World of Aldus Manutius: Business and scholarship in Renaissance Venice.* Oxford: Blackwell.

Mann, Nicholas. 1989 [1984]. *Pétrarque. Essai*, traduit de l'anglais par Edith McMorran. Arles: Actes Sud.

Mango, Cyril. 1994 [1980]. *Bynzantium. The Empire of the New Rome.* London: Phoenix.

Martin, Henri-Jean. 1982. *Histoire de l'édition française* 1.231–237. Paris: Promodis.

Martinez Manzano, Teresa. 1994. *Konstantinos Laskaris, Humanist, Philologe, Lehrer, Kopist.* (= *Meletemata. Beiträge zur Byzantinistik und Neugriechischen Philologie*, 4.) Hamburg: Institut für Griechische und Lateinische Philologie der Universität Hamburg.

Melanchthon, Philipp. 1854 [1518]. *Grammatica graeca integra* éd. par C. G. Bretschneider & H. E. Bindseil. (= *Corpus Reformatorum*, 20.) Braunschweig: Schwetschke.

Monfasani, John. 1976. *George of Trebizond: A biography and a study of his rhetoric and logic.* (= *Co-*

*lumbia Studies in the Classical Tradition*, 1.) Leiden & New York: Brill.

Nicol, Donald M. 1993 [1972]. *The Last Centuries of Byzantium: 1261–1453.* Cambridge: Cambridge Univ. Press.

Pertusi, Agostino. 1962. "ΕΡΩΤΗΜΑΤΑ. Per la storia e le fonti delle prime grammatiche greche a stampa". *Italia Medioevale e Umanistica* 5.321–351.

–. 1964. *Leonzio Pilato fra Petrarca e Boccaccio. Le sue versioni omeriche negli autografi di Venezia e la cultura greca del primo Umanesimo.* Venezia–Roma: Istituto per la Collaborazione Culturale.

–. 1980. "L'Umanesimo greco dalla fine del secolo XIV agli inizi del secolo XVI". *Storia della Cultura Veneta* 3:2.177–264. Vicenza: Neri Pozza Editore.

Petrarca, Francesco. 1975. *Opere: Epistolae de rebus familiaribus* [éd. par Giuseppe Fracassetti]. Firenze: Sansoni.

Robins, Robert H. 1993. *The Byzantine Grammarians: Their place in history.* (= Trends in Linguistics. Studies and Monographs, 70.) Berlin & New York: Mouton de Gruyter.

Sicherl, Martin. 1966. "Los Comienzos del humanismo griego en Alemania". *Estudios clasicos* 10. 273–299.

–. 1985. "Neue Handschriften Johannes Cunos und seiner Schüler". *Les Amis de la Bibliothèque humaniste de Sélestat* 35.141–148.

Thiermann, Peter, 1993. *Die "Orationes Homeri" des Leonardo Bruni Aretino: Kritische Edition der lateinischen und kastilianischen Übersetzung mit Prolegomena und Kommentar.* (= *Supplements to Mnemosyne.*) Leiden & New York: Brill.

Thomson, J. 1966. "Manuel Chrysoloras and the Early Italian Renaissance". *Greek, Roman and Byzantine Studies* 7.63–82.

Vasoli, Cesare. 1988. "The Renaissance Concept of Philosophy". *The Cambridge History of Renaissance Philosophy* éd. par Charles B. Schmitt et al., 55–74. Cambridge: Cambridge Univ. Press.

Weiss, Roberto. 1975a [1951]. "The Study of Greek in England during the fourteenth Century". *Medieval and Humanist Greek. Collected Essays* by Roberto Weiss, 80–107. Padova: Antenore.

–. 1975b [1952–1952]. "Petrarca e il mondo greco". *Medieval and Humanist Greek. Collected Essays* by Roberto Weiss, 166–192. Padova: Antenore.

Wilson, Nigel G. 1992. *From Byzantium to Italy. Greek studies in the Italian Renaissance.* Baltimore: Johns Hopkins Univ. Press.

*Christian Förstel, Amiens (France)*

# 92. L'etude de l'hébreu et des autres langues orientales a l'epoque de l'humanisme

1. Les humanistes et l'hébreu
2. Des juifs aux chrétiens
3. Un public multiple
4. Lieux d'enseignement
5. Outils de travail
6. Conclusion
7. Bibliographie

## 1. Les humanistes et l'hébreu

Il a suffi d'une petite cinquantaine d'années pour que l'étude de l'hébreu se répande dans toute l'Europe humaniste. Lorsqu'en 1498 Conrad Pellikan veut apprendre la langue sainte, il a toutes les peines du monde à se procurer, non pas une grammaire ou un dictionnaire – il n'en existe pas encore – mais un simple manuscrit en caractères hébraïques. En 1550, en revanche, l'hebraïsant débutant ou confirmé avait le choix entre diverses institutions universitaires partout en Europe, de Paris à Padoue, de Bâle à Louvain, de Heidelberg à Salamanque. S'il préférait lire l'Ancien Testament en autodidacte, il avait à sa disposition plusieurs éditions de la Bible et de nombreux manuels de différents niveaux. Cette transformation de l'offre et de la demande en matière d'hébraïsme chrétien, que Friedman (1983: 13) a qualifiée de "révolution intellectuelle", est la conséquence de plusieurs facteurs, aussi bien intellectuels en effet que matériels et psychologiques; nous en rappellerons les trois principaux.

Tout d'abord, la Bible est l'instrument privilégié d'une sensibilité humaniste désireuse de revenir aux sources, attachée à l'étude philologique et à la pédagogie, nostalgique d'une antiquité idéalisée. Le développement des études hébraïques est indissociable de cette suprématie de l'Ecriture dans la société. Deuxièmement, les controverses religieuses du début du XVIe siècle donnent à la Bible une place centrale: les éditions de textes et de travaux bibliques (commentaires, traductions en langues vernaculaires etc.) se multiplient entre 1530 et 1600, au fur et à mesure que s'accentuent les différences confessionnelles, comme l'a montré Roussel (1989: 125–197). Enfin, l'accès aux textes est facilité par le développement de l'imprimerie. Daniel Bomberg (mort en 1549) publie dès 1518 à Venise une Bible rabbinique dont la seconde édition, parue en 1525, sera corrigée et supervisée par des savants juifs comme Elie Lévita (1469–1549). Il en est de même dans les autres pays d'Europe: une quarantaine de grammaires hébraïques furent par exemple imprimées ou rééditées en France entre 1521 et 1569. Mais, au-delà du texte original de la Bible, des versions anciennes, des commentaires rabbiniques et des outils de travail, l'imprimerie mettait également à la portée des chrétiens les textes ésotériques de la tradition juive, leur ouvrant par là 'un nouveau monde', comme le dit Secret 1985, auquel on se reportera pour tout ce qui touche à la kabbale chrétienne, dont nous nous contenterons de souligner ici que, contemporaine des Bibles polyglottes et des collèges trilingues, elle a contribué à susciter des vocations d'hébraïsants.

## 2. Des juifs aux chrétiens

Les cinquante premières années du XVI^e^ siècle voient donc changer les motivations des hébraïsants (pour le détail, voir Kessler-Mesguich 1996: 88–97); parallèlement, elles correspondent à un transfert de connaissances entre juifs et chrétiens. En effet, les premiers hébraïsants avaient recours à des enseignants juifs ou convertis: Johannes Reuchlin (1455–1522) fut par exemple l'élève d'Ovadia Sforno (*ca.* 1470–*ca.* 1550), philosophe juif renommé pour son commentaire de la Bible, et W. F. Capiton (1478–1541) – qui sera critiqué par Pellican pour ses interprétations par trop "judaïsantes" (voir Hobbs 1980) – suivit les leçons du converti Matthieu Adrianus. De même, les premiers grammairiens citent comme sources les ouvrages hébraïques du moyen-âge (voir Dahan 1989: 421–423 pour un aperçu des nombreuses publications et traductions au XVI^e^ siècle de commentaires rabbiniques médiévaux), tandis que ceux qui écrivent après 1550 s'inspirent des écrits de la génération d'hébraïsants chrétiens qui les a précédés. Ces 'échanges' amènent les humanistes à entrer occasionnellement en contact avec leurs contemporains juifs ou avec des ouvrages rédigés par des juifs, mais la méfiance demeure profonde vis-à-vis des uns comme des autres. Concernant leurs contemporains, les hébraïsants chrétiens ne comprennent pas pourquoi ils persistent dans leur 'aveuglement' et refusent de se convertir: c'est un lieu commun que l'on retrouve dans de nombreuses préfaces de grammaires. Ce mépris rejaillit parfois sur l'attitude des hébraïsants, les amenant par exemple à dénier aux juifs la qualité d'informateurs en matière linguistique: ainsi, Pagninus explique que les exils successifs leur ont fait oublier la langue de leurs ancêtres, et qu'il est donc inutile de s'adresser à eux pour en connaître la prononciation exacte (ce qu'ont cependant fait d'autres hébraïsants chrétiens, puisque les variations d'une communauté à l'autre sont mentionnées par plusieurs auteurs); cette décadence touche la langue elle-même, initialement parfaite puisque d'origine divine, mais devenue "la plus pauvre de toutes, en raison de l'impiété et des innombrables crimes de ce peuple". Il est intéressant de constater que Pagninus reprend en fait ici, en termes péjoratifs, une argumentation de Profiat Duran, philosophe et grammairien juif du début du XV^e^ siècle. Quant à l'ambivalence par rapport aux sources rabbiniques et kabbalistiques, elle est clairement illustrée par la controverse Reuchlin/Pfefferkorn (1510–1514) et se reflète dans les précautions prises par la plupart des grammairiens et des exégètes qui puisent dans les ouvrages en hébreu tout en affirmant haut et fort qu'ils ont su se garder de 'judaïser'.

## 3. Un public multiple

Qui apprend l'hébreu au XVI^e^ siècle? Et que signifie 'apprendre l'hébreu'? Les données fournies par l'histoire du livre sont précieuses, mais difficiles à interpréter car incomplètes. On constate par exemple, en ce qui concerne la France, un nombre élevé de rééditions pour certains ouvrages: mais comme il n'est pas toujours possible de connaître le nombre de tirages par édition (Febvre & Martin 1958: 327–330 avancent un chiffre moyen de 1000 à 1500 exemplaires), il est délicat d'en tirer des conclusions précises. Les inventaires après décès et des catalogues des bibliothèques ayant appartenu à des particuliers ou des institutions semblent quant à eux indiquer que le 'grand public' chrétien lettré n'achetait guère de livres en hébreu, et que la possession d'une Bible ou d'un outil de travail en cette langue n'était le fait que de membres du clergé (voir Rothschild 1992). Cependant, il faut se garder des erreurs d'optique que risque d'entraîner le caractère partiel de ce type de sources: les inventaires après décès concernent le plus souvent des groupes professionnels (secrétaires du roi, avocats, magistrats) qui n'ont pas de raison particulière de posséder de grammaires hébraïques. Or, parmi ces dernières, si certaines ont eu des difficultés à trouver leur public (la grammaire de Reuchlin s'est par exemple fort mal vendue), d'autres en revanche ont été rééditées plusieurs fois en l'escape de quelques années: ainsi, la *Tabula in grammaticen hebraeam* de Nicolas Clénard, qui connut un réel succès éditorial (vingt-trois éditions de 1529 à 1589) et dont les bibliographes, Bakelants et Hoven 1981, ont retrouvé trois cent soixante-huit exemplaires dans dix-neuf pays. Les imprimeurs parisiens comme Etienne ou Martin Lejeune, pour ne citer qu'eux, se seraient-ils lancés dans des éditions et rééditions souvent coûteuses s'ils n'avaient été sûrs d'en écouler au moins une partie importante? En fait, les inventaires de bibliothèque confirment le sentiment que coexistent, dans un siècle marqué par le désir du 'retour aux sources', des niveaux variés de sensibilité et de connaissances. A côté d'hébraïsants 'amateurs', qui se contentent des connaissances rudimentaires que leur apporte l'*Alphabetum hebraicum*, certains biblistes possèdent et utilisent des Bibles hébraïques et des instruments de travail élaborés (concordances, dictionnaires, grammaires); d'autres tiennent compte de ce renouveau exégétique, mais, ne maîtrisant pas l'hébreu, font appel à des aides extérieures; on ne trouve sur leurs étagères qu'une Bible hébraïque, parfois un dictionnaire bilingue, et pas de grammaires.

## 4. Lieux d'enseignement

### 4.1. Universités et collèges

4.1.1. A la diversité des publics et des manuels correspond celle des lieux d'enseignement. La traduction pédagogique de l'idéal érasmien est le collège trilingue, d'abord à Alcala (voir Hall 1969), ensuite à Louvain (voir De Vocht 1951–55), enfin à Paris (voir Lefranc 1893). Dans les deux derniers cas, les collèges trilingues permettent d'introduire un renouveau dans l'enseignement de l'Ecriture, jusqu'alors domaine exclusif des Facultés de théologie, ce qui ne se passe pas sans heurts (voir Farge 1992). A Paris, deux des premiers lecteurs royaux d'hébreu (A. Guidacerius, P. Paradis) viennent d'Italie; le troisième, F. Vatable (*ca.* 1493–1547), est originaire de Picardie mais est l'élève d'un hébraïsant italien, J. Aléxandre. Une ou deux fois par semaine, le lecteur royal, "regius interpres", lisait et traduisait le texte biblique (avec une préférence pour les Prophètes et les Hagiographes, en particulier les Psaumes et les Proverbes), en y ajoutant un commentaire grammatical ou exégétique. Le placard de 1534 mentionne deux grammaires de référence: celle de Sanctes Pagninus (Lyon, A. du Ry, 1526) et celle de Moïse Qimḥi, publiée à Paris en 1520. Le rôle des "interprètes royaux" est donc de 'lire' le texte biblique en hébreu et d'en faire surgir, grâce à l'utilisation de la grammaire et de la traduction araméenne, le sens littéral (sur l'enseignement de ces premiers lecteurs parisiens, voir Kessler-Mesguich 1998).

4.1.2. Même lorsque les collèges trilingues finissent par s'essouffler, l'exigence humaniste d'une interprétation fondée sur le meilleur texte possible a pour conséquence l'entrée de l'hébreu dans le cursus des études supérieures, aussi bien chez les catholiques (en particulier les jésuites) que chez les protestants. Pour les Réformateurs, le recours aux textes originaux est lié à la volonté de garantir l'authenticité du texte et d'écarter les interprétations théologiques basées sur des traductions erronées. L'hébreu figure donc au programme des collèges de Lausanne (fondé en 1540) et de Genève (1541, réorganisé par Calvin en 1559). Mais la difficulté de trouver des professeurs compétents – ce qui prouve au passage qu'en se généralisant les études d'hébreu ne se sont guère approfondies – fait que l'hébreu demeure, dans l'ensemble, une matière de l'enseignement supérieur. Ainsi, les statuts de l'académie de Genève, qui serviront de modèle à ses homologues françaises, fixaient l'existence de cinq chaires, dont une d'hébreu; le premier titulaire en fut A. R. Chevalier (1523–1572). Les huit académies protestantes de France comportent un enseignement obligatoire de l'hébreu, et l'examen donnant accès aux fonctions de ministre comprend l'explication d'un passage de l'Ancien Testament dans sa langue d'origine. Les programmes, parfois ambitieux mais pas toujours appliqués, privilégient, comme ceux des lecteurs royaux, les Prophètes et les Hagiographes: on y trouve également le Pentateuque (en particulier la Genèse). Les professeurs d'hébreu exerçaient souvent les fonctions de pasteur dans les villes académiques où ils résidaient; à quelques exceptions près (l'école de Saumur), le niveau moyen de l'enseignement semble avoir été peu élevé.

4.1.3. Quant aux catholiques, ils ne rejettent pas tout recours aux 'originaux' grecs et hébreux, mais refusent l'idée que ceux-ci offriraient une version plus parfaite de l'Ecriture. Dès les premières sessions (1546) du concile de Trente, la Bible est considérée comme un 'fondement nécessaire' des travaux à accomplir; et la commission qui révisa la Vulgate à l'initiative de Sixte Quint comportait plusieurs hébraïsants, dont le jésuite Robert Bellarmin (1542–1612). Etudiant les sources de la pédagogie des jésuites, G. Codina Mir (1968) a mis en lumière la place de l'influence humaniste et réformée dans l'élaboration des programmes d'étude de la Compagnie. Sur le plan pédagogique, la réponse aux protestants sera la leçon d'Ecriture sainte, qui se fait devant tous les fidèles en langue vulgaire. Jérôme Nadal (1507–1582), qui organisa le premier collège de l'ordre (Messine 1548), était lui-même passionné de langues anciennes et avait appris l'hébreu en Avignon auprès de maîtres juifs. On n'est donc pas surpris de le voir souligner l'importance des langues pour la compréhension de l'Ecriture et inscrire l'hébreu parmi les matières enseignées à Messine, qui servira de modèle aux autres collèges jésuites. Mais, comme pour l'enseignement en milieu protestant, il faut distinguer entre les déclarations d'intentions des programmes, pénétrées de phraséologie humaniste, et la réalité des contenus. Tout texte pédagogique du XVIe siècle se doit de comporter une référence aux langues bibliques: en ce sens, le texte-programme de *Pantagruel* ("J'entends et veulx que tu aprenes les langues parfaictement [...] premierement en Grec le Nouveau Testament, et Epistres des apostres, et puis en Hebrieu le Vieulx Testament") a parfaitement capté 'l'air du temps': mais, si l'hébreu est entré dans les programmes d'études et dans les mœurs intellectuelles, s'il devient une référence obligée, il a cependant du mal à s'affirmer en tant que science indépendante par rapport à la théologie.

4.2. A côté de cet enseignement 'institutionnel' existaient d'autres circuits pour apprendre l'hébreu. La grande mobilité des professeurs (liée aux nécessités de leur formation, aux épidémies, aux péripéties des querelles religieuses) favorisait le développement de ces cours: s'ils avaient quelque réputation, ils étaient immédiatement sollicités, lorsqu'ils s'établissaient dans une ville, pour des leçons d'hébreu. Parfois, c'est le public qui venait à eux: ainsi, pendant plusieurs années, des universitaires de Grande-Bretagne sont allés suivre des cours à Strasbourg, Zurich, Bâle et Genève; inversement, J. Drusius (1550–1616) fuyant les persécutions aux Pays-Bas, vint étudier les langues orientales à Cambridge avant de les enseigner à Oxford (voir Jones 1983: 201–203).

4.3. Enfin, une foule d'autodidactes, multiforme, difficile à cerner, se découvre au hasard des correspondances et des annotations manuscrites. Si certains d'entre eux – G. Postel, J. J. Scaliger par exemple – sont parvenus à maîtriser plusieurs langues orientales, d'autres ne dépassent pas l'étude de l'alphabet. Bien que le nombre de ces hébraïsants 'occasionnels' ait considérablement augmenté par rapport aux dernières années du XVe siècle, il semble bien qu'ils appartiennent presque tous aux milieux lettrés. Là encore, il y a un décalage entre la Bible – qui grâce aux nombreuses traductions pénètre toutes les couches de la société – et l'hébreu, qui reste malgré tout une affaire d'érudition.

## 5. Outils de travail

### 5.1. L'hébreu

5.1.1. Le modèle de description de l'hébreu biblique qui se met en place dans les trente premières années du siècle repose sur la tradition grammaticale hébraïque, synthétisée dans deux ouvrages, le *Mahălâḵ šəḇîlêy hadda'aṯ* (= "les chemins de la connaissance") de Moïse Qimḥi (mort *ca.* 1190) et le *Miḵlol* (= "Somme") de son frère David (1160–1235) dont le rôle de textes fondateurs est bien marqué par Münster, pour qui David et Moïse Qimḥi sont les Priscien et Donat de la grammaire hébraïque. Le *Mahălâḵ*, beaucoup plus élémentaire, a surtout inspiré les premiers hébraïsants: Reuchlin, auteur en 1506 du *De Rudimentis Hebraicis*, la première grammaire hébraïque due à un chrétien (décrite en détail par Greive 1978), et Clénard, qui s'en inspire pour sa présentation des paradigmes. Mais, par l'intermédiaire d'Elie Lévita (relayé par les nombreuses traductions de S. Münster et du néerlandais J. Campensis, 1491–1538) et de Pagninus, c'est la grammaire de David Qimḥi qui devient rapidement 'la' référence des grammairiens chrétiens.

5.1.2. Ceux-ci, qui doivent opérer une synthèse entre la tradition gréco-latine et la tradition hébraïque, concentrent leurs efforts sur deux chapitres: la phonétique et la morphologie. La syntaxe, presque totalement absente des sources juives, n'est abordée que de manière indirecte. En effect, la classification traditionnelle des parties du discours en nom, verbe et particule, empruntée par les grammairiens juifs aux grammairiens arabes et généralement conservée dans les ouvrages des humanistes, aboutit à une présentation essentiellement morphologique des deux premières catégories (nom et verbe); la troisième consiste surtout en des listes de mots invariables (appelés *dictiones* ou *consignificativa*). Les questions de syntaxe sont donc abordées au fur et à mesure, selon les éléments auxquels elles se rattachent: par exemple, l'état construit est abordé dans le chapitre sur la morphologie nominale; les prépositions sont à la fois traitées dans la partie phonétique (étant monoconsonantiques, elles sont classées parmi les 'lettres') et avec les particules si elles sont composées de plusieurs lettres. Cependant, deux auteurs se démarquent de leurs contemporains dans le traitement de la syntaxe: Abraham de Balmes (1440–1523) et Pierre Martin (mort en 1594). De Balmes, juif italien, est l'auteur de la première grammaire bilingue hébreu/latin, le *Miqnêh ʿAḇram* (Venise 1523: décrite et analysée par Klijnsmit 1992). Fortement marqué par l'influence aristotélicienne, il y propose de nombreuses observations syntaxiques originales. Quant au réformé Pierre Martin, disciple de Ramus, sa *Grammatica hebraea* de 1590, dont le second livre est intitulé *De Syntaxi*, influencera Buxtorf.

5.1.3. Dans la mesure où les dictionnaires sont organisés par racines, les grammairiens doivent donner à leurs lecteurs les moyens d'identifier celles-ci. C'est le but de la partie morphologique, essentiellement descriptive et relativement peu propice aux innovations autres que pédagogiques (détails dans Kukenheim 1951: 106–110). A leurs prédécesseurs juifs, qui donnent à la morphologie une place prépondérante, les grammairiens occidentaux empruntent en les simplifiant plus ou moins des listes de substantifs et d'adjectifs classés par schèmes; quant au verbe, sa description (nombre et répartition des conjugaisons, présentation des paradigmes) varie d'un auteur à l'autre, mais tous essaient plus ou moins de concilier la tradition hébraïque avec les catégories latines de temps, de mode et de voix.

5.1.4. Incontestablement, c'est dans le domaine de la description phonétique que les grammairiens humanistes innovent le plus, par rapport à la tradition hébraïque comme par rapport à la tradition occidentale. Leurs prédécesseurs juifs, qui écrivent pour un public connaissant l'hébreu, se soucient assez peu de prononciation (dans le *Miḵlol*, un bref chapitre sur les voyelles se trouve au beau milieu de la partie consacrée au nom): aussi les grammairiens du XVI$^{e}$ siècle sont-ils amenés à des développements phonétiques nouveaux pour caractériser les différents sons, en précisant le rôle des organes phonatoires et en affinant leur terminologie (voir par exemple l'emploi métalinguistique du terme *quiescens*, calqué sur l'hébreu ou de *blaesus* pour qualifier la prononciation de la chuintante). Surtout, les ouvrages reprennent presque tous (y compris les plus médiocres, comme ces rudiments de lecture et de prononciation que sont les modestes livrets intitulés *alphabetum hebraicum*), le classement des consonnes en cinq groupes selon le point d'articulation: labiales, dentales, linguales, palatales et gutturales. Cette classification provient du *Sêfer Yəṣîrâ*, ouvrage mystique qui fut composé entre le III$^{e}$ et le VI$^{e}$ siècle. La tradition humaniste d'étude de l'hébreu a ici joué un rôle d'une grande importance (mis en lumière par Percival 1986), en familiarisant la pensée linguistique occidentale avec des notions de phonétique absentes de la tradition gréco-latine.

5.1.5. A côté de la grammaire, on trouve sur la table de travail des hébraïsants le dictionnaire hébreu/latin. Là encore, les auteurs traduisent et adaptent David Qimḥi, dont le *Sêfer haššorâšîm* (= "Livre des Racines") fait autorité depuis sa publication à Naples en 1490. Chez Reuchlin, le lexique est encore intégré à la grammaire, dont il constitue d'ailleurs plus des neuf dixièmes. Münster publie plusieurs dictionnaires, deux bilingues (hébreu/latin, Bâle 1523 et araméen/latin, Bâle 1525) et un trilingue (latin/grec/hébreu, Bâle 1530), tous trois réédités plusieurs fois. Quant au *Thesaurus linguae sanctae* de Pagninus, imprimé à Lyon en 1529 et réédité plusieurs fois au cours du siècle à Paris et Genève, c'est un outil pédagogique que l'auteur a voulu accessible même aux débutants: le dictionnaire commence par des listes permettant d'identifier les substantifs basés sur des racines "faibles" ou des schèmes difficiles à analyser. Comme dans l'original hébreu, les entrées sont classées par racines; souvent, Pagninus 'étoffe' l'article de Qimḥi en ajoutant des explications prises dans ses commentaires, des remarques grammaticales ou des interprétations chrétiennes de passages bibliques controversés. Une version abrégée, l'*Epitome Thesauri linguae sanctae*, connaîtra de nombreuses rééditions dont l'une en appendice à la Polyglotte d'Anvers (1568–73).

### 5.2. L'araméen

Dans la préface de sa *Chaldaica grammatica* de 1527, Münster souligne l'importance de l'araméen, que l'on nomme alors "chaldéen": (i) c'est une langue biblique; (ii) il permet de lire le Targum; (iii) il donne l'accès aux commentaires rabbiniques. Sa proximité (*cognatio*) avec l'hébreu en fait une langue facile à maîtriser. En 1549 le grammairien français Jean Mercier (mort en 1570) ira dans le même sens: "la langue chaldaïque est éminemment utile et d'un grand intérêt pour toute la religion chrétienne", sans compter que c'est aussi la langue vernaculaire du Christ. Enfin, certains auteurs considèrent l'araméen comme un meilleur prétendant que l'hébreu au titre de langue primitive. Même si l'on peut considérer Mercier comme un précurseur des exégètes critiques du siècle suivant, il est visible que, pour lui comme pour Münster, l'étude de la langue araméenne est au service de l'exégèse biblique et doit permettre une meilleure compréhension du sens littéral. Le XVI$^{e}$ siècle s'est donné pour tâche de retrouver et de comprendre le texte massorétique: il n'est pas encore question de le confronter aux autres versions dans une perspective critique.

### 5.3. L'arabe

L'arabe, qui reste longtemps considéré comme un outil au service d'une 'croisade pacifique', destiné à combattre les infidèles avec leurs propres armes, est encore peu étudié dans l'Europe du XVI$^{e}$ siècle (voir Dannenfeldt 1954). Le cas de N. Clénard demeura exceptionnel, et son désir de connaître cette langue se heurta à des difficultés matérielles qui rappellent celles de l'hébreu à la fin du XV$^{e}$ siècle: pas de professeurs (il devra aller jusqu'au Portugal pour en trouver un), pas de manuels: c'est du *Psalterium octaplum* de Justiniani (Gênes 1516) que Clénard tira son premier alphabet, et, pour l'alphabet arabe de Postel (1538) on dut, faute de caractères, utiliser des planches de bois gravées (voir Secret 1962). Jusqu'à la publication de la *Grammatica arabica* de Postel, non datée (1538 ou 1540), il n'existait qu'une seule grammaire imprimée, rudimentaire, celle de Pedro de Alcalá (1506), que Clénard parvint à se procurer à Salamanque; le premier dictionnaire ne verra le jour qu'en 1613 [...] Langue non biblique, l'arabe devra donc attendre le siècle suivant pour être sérieusement étudié (voir Fück 1955): lorsque les grammairiens humanistes de l'hébreu citent des exemples en arabe, c'est toujours de seconde main.

### 5.4. Grammaire comparée: premières tentatives

Les premiers hébraïsants étaient aussi des hellénistes (Reuchlin, Tissard, Vatable), ce qui se comprend dans la perspective des études bibliques (grec et hébreu étant tous deux liés à la Révélation). Mais, dans le deuxième tiers du siècle, l'hébreu est associé à l'arabe, à l'araméen et à l'éthiopien, regroupés sous l'appellation de 'langues orientales' comme en témoigne le titre d'un chapitre de la *Linguarum duodecim characteribus differentium introductio* de Postel (1538): "De lingua Hebraica caeterarum omnium orientalium parente" (fol. B, v°). Dans cet ouvrage, remarquable surtout par la prouesse typographique qu'il représente, Postel oppose, en un développement où Percival 1986 voit l'embryon d'une approche typologique des langues, les caractéristiques morphologiques du latin et du grec avec celles des langues orientales. Seize ans plus tard, l'italien A. Caninius (1521–1557) publie des *Instituiones linguae Syriacae, Assyriacae atque Thalmudicae, una cum Aethiopicae atque Arabica collatione* (Paris 1554). Les conjugaisons arabes y sont notées en caractères hébraïques (voir ci-dessus le § 5.3.). Il serait abusif de qualifier de 'grammaire comparée' ce traité, qui accorde une place prépondérante à l'araméen; cependant, de par sa vision juste de l'histoire de la langue (l'araméen ancien est distingué de l'araméen d'empire) et de la parenté entre les diverses langues orientales, on peut voir en lui un précurseur des études philologiques du XVII$^{e}$ siècle.

## 6. Conclusion

En l'espace de quelques décennies, on voit se mettre en place les bases d'un outillage destiné, au départ, à l'interprétation exacte du texte biblique dans sa langue d'origine. Dans le premier tiers du siècle, c'est le temps de la découverte: on traduit et on adapte pour des lecteurs latins les grammaires et les dictionnaires élaborés au moyen-âge en hébreu. Il se forme ainsi un modèle de description grammaticale de l'hébreu biblique, exposé dans des ouvrages fondateurs (ceux de Reuchlin, Münster, Panginus et Clénard) puis repris dans des manuels plus scolaires, des éditions abrégées et/ou annotées. Au cours de cette seconde étape, celle de la diffusion, les données nouvelles pénètrent les différentes couches qui composent le public des hébraïsants par le biais d'ouvrages de vulgarisation parfois médiocres, qui donnent l'impression d'une relative stagnation. Les historiens de la grammaire hébraïque se sont montrés sévères pour ces 'manuels d'épigones' (Kukenheim 1951). Certes, les hébraïsants de l'époque humaniste n'ont guère innové (sinon sur le plan de la pédagogie) par rapport aux connaissances accumulées entre le X^e^ et le XV^e^ siècle, mais ils ont joué un rôle essentiel de relais. La grammaire de Reuchlin, encore très proche de Priscien, témoigne de l'effort qu'ont dû faire les hébraïsants chrétiens pour intégrer des notions telles que la non-notation des voyelles ou l'absence des cas, qui ont pu apparaître à la longue comme familières, mais qui sont au départ déroutantes pour des savants formés en latin. Il fallait sans doute cette répétition parfois fastidieuse d'un ouvrage à l'autre, cet apparent 'rabâchage', pour que se réalise l'imprégnation nécessaire: lorsque les notions de 'lettres quiescentes' ou d''affixes' seront devenues familières (et elles ne le deviennent que lorsqu'elles sortent des ouvrages spécialisés pour aller traîner dans des manuels scolaires), les hébraïsants pourront aborder d'autres points: l'évolution de la langue, avec l'apparition vers la fin du siècle de travaux prenant en compte l'hébreu rabbinique, ses rapports avec les autres langues sémitiques, qui commencent à intéresser les grammairiens vers 1550, et finalement le statut de texte massorétique. Alors, la langue hébraïque ne sera plus seulement celle, prestigieuse, de la Bible; alors, on constatera qu'elle fait partie d'une famille dont elle n'est pas l'ancêtre mais l'un des membres: les mentalités seront prêtes à une approche critique de la langue et du texte. Ainsi, à l'époque humaniste, la connaissance de l'hébreu fait partie de ces nouveaux savoirs qui, sous l'impulsion érasmienne, contribuent à modifier en profondeur les relations entre philologie et théologie; mais la rencontre des deux traditions grammaticales, hébraïque et occidentale, se répercute bien au-delà des nécessités de l'exégèse biblique puisqu'elle offre des moyens nouveaux d'analyse, tant du point de vue de la description des langues que de leur comparaison. Langue biblique, l'hébreu s'inscrit profondément dans la culture humaniste; langue orientale, son étude ouvre des horizons nouveaux à la pensée linguistique européenne.

## 7. Bibliographie


Bakelants, Louis & René Hoven. 1981. *Bibliographie des œuvres de Nicolas Clénard 1529–1700*, vol. I et II. Verviers: Gason.

Burmeister, Karl Heinz. 1964. *Sebastian Münster, eine Bibliographie mit 22 Abbildungen.* Wiesbaden: Pressler.

Codina Mir, Gabriel. 1968. *Aux sources de la pédagogie des jésuites, le "modus parisiensis".* Rome: Institutum Historicum S. I.

Dahan, Gilbert. 1989. "L'exégèse juive de la Bible". *Le temps des Réformes et la Bible* éd. par Guy Bedouelle & Bernard Roussel, 401–426. Paris: Beauchesne.

Dannefeldt, Karl H. 1954. "The Renaissance Humanists and the Knowledge of Arabic". *Studies in the Renaissance* 2. 96–114.

De Vocht, Henry. 1951–55. *History of the Foundation and Rise of the Collegium Trilingue Lovaniense.* 4 tomes. Louvain.

Farge, James Knox. 1992. *Le parti conservateur au XVI^e^ siècle: Université et Parlement de Paris à l'époque de la Renaissance et de la Réforme.* Paris: Collège de France (Documents et Inédits), diff. Les Belles-Lettres.

Febvre, Lucien & Henri-Jean Martin. 1958. *L'apparition du livre.* Paris: Albin Michel. (Rééd. 1971.)

Friedman, Jerome. 1983. *The Most Ancient Testimony, Sixteenth Century Christian-Hebraica in the Age of Renaissance Nostalgia.* Athens, Ohio.

Fück, Johannes. 1955. *Die arabischen Studien in Europa bis in den Anfang des 20. Jahrhunderts.* Leipzig: Harrassowitz.

Greive, Hermann. 1978. "Die hebräische Grammatik Johannes Reuchlins". *Zeitschrift für alttestamentliche Wissenschaft* 90:3. 395–409.

Hall, Basil. 1969. "The Trilingual College of San Ildefonso and the Making of the Complutensian Polyglot Bible". *Studies in Church History*, 5, éd. par G. J. Cuming, 114–146. Leyde.

Hobbs, R. Gérald. 1980. "Monitio amica: Pellican à Capiton sur le danger des lectures rabbiniques". *Horizons européens de la Réforme en Alsace, Mélanges J. Rott* éd. par Marijn de Kroon & Marc Lienhard, 81–93. Strasbourg: Librairie Istra.

Kessler-Mesguich, Sophie. 1996. "Hébraïsants du XVIe et du XVIIe siècle". *La linguistique de l'hébreu et des langues juives*, *HEL* 18:1. 87–108.

–. 1998. "L'enseignement de l'hébreu et de l'araméen à Paris (1530–1560) d'après les œuvres grammaticales des lecteurs royaux". *Les origines du Collège de France* éd. par Marc Fumaroli, 349–366. Paris: Klincksieck.

Klijnsmit, Anthony J. 1992. *Balmesian Linguistics. A chapter in the history of pre-rationalist thought.* (= *Cahiers voor Taalkunde*, 7.) Amsterdam: Stichting Neerlandistiek VU.

Kukenheim, Louis. 1951. *Contributions à l'histoire de la grammaire grecque, latine et hébraïque à l'époque de la Renaissance.* Leiden: Brill.

Lefranc, Abel. 1893. *Histoire du Collège de France, depuis ses origines jusqu'à la fin du premier Empire.* Paris: Hachette.

Jones, Gareth Lloyd. 1983. *The Discovery of Hebrew in Tudor England: A third language.* Manchester Univ. Press.

Percival, W. Keith, 1986. "The Reception of Hebrew in Sixteenth-century Europe: the impact of the Cabala". *The History of Linguistics in Spain* éd. par A. Quilis & H. J. Niederehe. *Amsterdam Studies in the Theory and History of Linguistic Science*, Series 3. (= *Studies in the History of Linguistics*, 34). 21–38. Amsterdam & Philadelphia: Benjamins.

Rothschild, Jean-Pierre. 1992. "Quelles notions le 'grand public' des lettrés chrétiens dans la France du XVIe siècle eut-il de l'hébreu? Enquête parmi les inventaires de bibliothèques". *L'hébreu au temps de la Renaissance* éd. par Ilana Zinguer, 172–196. Leiden & New York: Brill.

Roussel, Bernard. 1989. "La Bible de 1530 à 1600". *Le temps des Réformes et la Bible* éd. par Guy Bedouelle & Bernard Roussel, 125–305. Paris: Beauchesne.

Secret, François. 1962. "Guillaume Postel et les études arabes à la Renaissance". *Arabica* 9. 21–36. Leiden: Brill.

–. 1985. *Les Kabbalistes Chrétiens de la Renaissance.* Nouvelle éd. mise à jour et augmentée. Milan: Archè.

*Sophie Kessler-Mesguich, Paris (France)*

# XVII. The Teaching of Languages in the 15th Through the 18th Centuries in Europe
# Der Fremdsprachenunterricht in Europa (15.–18. Jahrhundert)
# L'enseignement des langues du XV$^{e}$ au XVIII$^{e}$ siècle en Europe

## 93. Kommerzielle und kulturelle Interessen am Unterricht der Volkssprachen im 15. und 16. Jahrhundert


1. Zwei unterschiedliche Motivationen
2. Wirtschaftliche Interessen
3. Kulturelles Interesse
4. Fremdsprachenpolitische und fremdsprachendidaktische Konsequenzen
5. Bibliographie


### 1. Zwei unterschiedliche Motivationen

Der Erwerb einer modernen Fremdsprache kann aufgrund von Wirtschaftsbeziehungen erfolgen oder aber auch kulturell motiviert sein (Interesse an der Literatur, Kultur und Geschichte des betreffenden Sprachraumes). Häufig spielen beide Komponenten in unterschiedlicher Gewichtung eine Rolle. Ein primär wirtschaftlich ausgerichteter Fremdsprachenunterricht verfolgt partiell andere Zielsetzungen und Inhalte als ein auf kulturellen 'Bildungserwerb' bezogener (etwa: Entwicklung einer fachlich akzentuierten kommunikativen Kompetenz, Ausbildung einer fachsprachlichen Komponente, Befähigung zur Abwicklung der Handelskorrespondenz und des Rechnungswesens auch in der Fremdsprache, Heranbildung einer Übersetzungsfertigkeit bezogen auf Fachtexte). Kulturelle Interessen beim Fremdsprachenerwerb implizieren neben der Ausbildung einer nicht-spezialisierten allgemeinsprachlichen Kompetenz eine Hör-, Lese- und Übersetzungsfertigkeit, bezogen auf fiktionale und expositorische Texte. Wirtschaftlich orientierter Fremdsprachenerwerb ist auch anders organisiert (ausgedehnte Praktika, in der Moderne: Besuch anderer Schulformen). – Bildungsideologen neuhumanistisch-idealistischer Prägung haben seit dem ausgehenden 18. Jh. den 'utilitaristisch' ausgerichteten Fremdsprachenunterricht (kommerzielles bzw. technisches Interesse) gegenüber dem kulturell motivierten, auf 'Bildungserwerb' abzielenden, literarisch oder aber 'kulturkundlich' ausgerichteten abqualifiziert. Letzterer galt als gymnasial adäquat, zu Abitur und Hochschulreife führend, ersterer als minder bildend, den nicht-gymnasialen Schulformen und -typen vorbehalten und daher als minder wertvoll. Erst in jüngster Zeit wurden Versuche unternommen, den ideologischen Graben zwischen berufsorientierter und allgemeiner Fremdsprachenbildung vor dem Hintergrund einer modernen Arbeits- und Freizeitwelt zu überwinden (berufspropädeutische, nicht-literarische Komponenten in der gymnasialen Bildung, Rekurs auf interkulturelles Lernen in der Berufsbildung, vgl. hierzu Blättner 1960, Schröder 1975, Meyer 1987).

Für die früheste Zeit spielt angesichts geringerer Spezialisierungsgrade und des Fehlens expliziter Bildungstheorien und nationalliterarischer Traditionen die hier skizzierte Problematik bestenfalls eine marginale Rolle: Sinnvoll ist im Bereich der Ausbildung, was der eigenen Person, der Familie, der *natio* – in welcher Weise auch immer – nutzt. Auch die Frage, was älter sei, das kommerzielle oder aber das kulturelle Interesse am Erwerb der Volkssprachen, ist müßig: Beide Interessen gehen bis ins Hochmittelalter zurück und sind miteinander verwoben.

## 2. Wirtschaftliche Interessen

Das ausgehende Mittelalter kennt in Europa zwei internationale Handelssprachen, nachklassisches Latein, teilweise in pidginisierter Form, auf dem Kontinent und den britischen Inseln, sowie Sabir als Anrainer-Mischsprache in den Mittelmeerländern. Daneben spielt in hansischen Kreisen Niederdeutsch eine Zeitlang eine gewisse Rolle. Das Lateinische reicht im Prinzip so weit, wie der Arm der römischen Kirche reicht, und dies bedeutet, daß beispielsweise der hansische Rußlandhandel nicht mit Hilfe dieser internationalen Sprache abgewickelt werden kann. Gleiches gilt in späterer Zeit für die politischen und wirtschaftlichen Kontakte zum ottomanischen Reich.

### 2.1. Die hansisch-russischen Handelsbeziehungen als Beispiel

Im hansischen Kontor zu Nowgorod, dem Petershof, werden bereits im 13. und 14. Jh. junge hansische Kaufleute und Kaufmannslehrlinge ermutigt, sich Russischkenntnisse anzueignen. Ansonsten läuft der internationale Geschäftsverkehr über Dolmetscher, sogenannte Tolke ab, doch sie sind selten und teuer. Eine Satzung der deutschen Kaufleute zu Nowgorod aus dem Jahre 1346 (Stieda 1884: 159) bestimmt, daß nur junge Leute unter 20 Jahren Russisch lernen mögen: Offenbar wird die Sprache angesichts des Fehlens von adäquaten Unterrichtsmaterialien als extrem schwierig angesehen, so daß sie im höheren Alter nicht mehr erlernbar ist. Die Nowgoroder Schra, das innerdeutsche Hausgesetz des Hansekontors, wiederholt im 15. Jh. die Festlegung mit der Begründung, daß sonst der Kaufmann wegen zu alter Sprachschüler Geringschätzung erleiden müsse (Raab 1955/56: 343 – hier auch die folgenden Belege). Im Jahre 1423 führen Vertreter der Hanse Klage darüber, daß zwei junge hanseatische Kaufleute, die der Sprachstudien wegen außerhalb des Petershofes zu Nowgorod leben mußten, von einem Russen so geschlagen worden seien, daß der eine daran gestorben sei, während der andere sich in ärztliche Behandlung habe begeben müssen. Eine ähnliche Klage führt die Hanse im Jahre 1436. Ebenfalls 1423 verbietet der Hansetag zu Lübeck, daß man junge Holländer "auf die [russische] Sprache bringe". Spätere Hansetage, so der von 1434 zu Wolmar, der von 1442 zu Stralsund und der von 1443 zu Lübeck (Stieda 1884: 160), bringen weitere diesbezügliche Entschließungen. 1434 wird gefordert, daß niemand in Livland die russische Sprache lernen solle, es sei denn, er sei Hanseat. 1442 werden die nötigen Schritte unternommen, um nach der Aufnahme der Stadt Kampen in die Hanse den Kampenern die Entsendung von Nicht-Hanseaten zu Sprachstudien in Rußland unmöglich zu machen. Im gleichen Jahr geraten bei der Schließung des deutschen Hofes zu Nowgorod durch die Russen auch hansische Sprachschüler in Gefangenschaft. Als 1494 das Nowgoroder Handelskontor endgültig geschlossen wird, werden abermals hansische Sprachschüler gefangen gesetzt. "Das Bewußtsein der privilegierten Stellung der Sprachkundigen und Sprachlernenden war bei den Hanseaten so tief verwurzelt, daß solche Vorkommnisse besonders unerhört gefunden wurden." (Raab 1955/56: 343f.) In der Folgezeit wird ein umfangreicher Schriftwechsel geführt, um die Freilassung der Gefangenen beim Moskauer Großfürsten Iwan III. zu erwirken. In einem Schreiben Revals an Lübeck vom 5. 1. 1495 heißt es in diesem Zusammenhang, "daß unerhört ist, daß Sprachlerner gefangen seien". Tatsächlich gibt Iwan III. als erstes die 11 Sprachschüler frei, während die übrigen Gefangenen noch länger zurückgehalten werden.

Das Interesse an der Handelssprache Russisch hält das 16. und 17. Jh. hindurch unvermindert an. Ein erstes handschriftliches russisch-deutsches Gesprächsbuch von Thomas Schrowe aus Dorpat datiert von 1546. Die Handschrift, früher in der Staatsbibliothek Berlin aufbewahrt, ist verschollen. Ein weiteres Gesprächsbuch wird von Tönnies Fenne 1607 in Pskov (Pleskau) zusammengestellt. (Hammerich 1961–86, als Überblicksdarstellung vgl. Schröder 1987–99, besonders Bd. 5 [1997]: 316–318). Die ursprünglich 566 Seiten umfassende Arbeit ist von erheblichem kulturhistorischem und fremdsprachendidaktischem Interesse. Fenne ist norddeutscher Herkunft; der Text des Gesprächsbuchs legt enge Kontakte zu hanseatischen Kaufleuten nahe. Dabei zeigt der Text deutlich, daß es gerade nicht die kulturellen Kontakte sind, die das Interesse am Russischen ausmachen: Der Autor empfielt dem deutschen Reisenden und Sprachlerner, in Rußland strikt seinen eigenen, mitteleuropäischen Lebensstil zu wahren: Er soll die Russen behandeln, wie ein Adliger mit seinen Knechten verfährt, minderwertiges russisches Essen zurückweisen und, wenn er mit Worten nicht weiterkommt, die Teller tanzen lassen. Herrenvolk-Ideologie ist bei Fenne allgegenwärtig; einer der Dialoge enthält die Anregung, einen Russen im Walde aufzuhängen.

2.2. Italienisch und Französisch

Trotz der bis ins 17. Jh. greifbaren Rolle des Lateinischen als internationale Handelssprache setzt das Bestreben, die Sprachen der Handelspartner zu erwerben, auch jenseits des Rußlandhandels früh ein. Das Diktum, daß die beste Sprache des Handels die des Kunden sei, wird einem Fugger zugeschrieben. In dem Versroman *Der gute Gerhard* des Rudolf von Ems aus dem 13. Jh. kommt ein Kaufmann vor, der Französischkenntnisse besitzt (Kuhfuß 1976: 325), und in der Konungskuggsja aus dem gleichen Jahrhundert mahnt der Vater den Sohn für den Fall, daß dieser Kaufmann werden wolle, mit folgenden Worten: "Wenn du vollkommen an Kenntnissen werden willst, so lerne alle Mundarten, aber ganz besonders Lateinisch und Welsch [in diesem Falle ist Französisch gemeint], denn die Zungen reichen am weitesten." (Stieda 1884: 157). Im 14. und 15. Jh. lernen die Söhne der kaufmännischen Patrizier die mittlerweile komplex gewordenen Abläufe des internationalen Handels zunächst im väterlichen Hause, dann aber, 13- bis 20jährig, in befreundeten ausländischen Handelshäusern oder aber in den Auslandsniederlassungen der eigenen Firma. So hält sich beispielsweise der Nürnberger Patrizier Hilpolt Kress im Jahre 1389 als 18jähriger Jüngling in Venedig auf, um ortsspezifische Fachkenntnisse zu gewinnen, politische und geschäftliche Kontakte zu knüpfen, aber besonders auch, um Italienisch zu lernen. Später werden Pisa, Siena, Mailand, Genua, Aquileja und sogar Neapel und Bari im Zusammenhang mit entsprechenden Auslandsaufenthalten aufgesucht (Beck 1914: 385). In Venedig besteht bereits im Jahre 1308 eine Privatschule für deutsche Scholaren (Pausch 1972: 49). 1342 hält sich ein Verwandter des Kaufmanns Georg von Regensburg in Venedig auf, "causa addiscendae linguam" (Pausch, a. a. O.). Die aus dem Jahre 1356 stammende, möglicherweise früheste Handschrift eines polyglotten Gesprächsbuches, ursprünglich in der Bibliotheca Palatina zu Heidelberg aufbewahrt und inzwischen im Besitz der Vatikanischen Bibliothek, ist für Handeltreibende gedacht und hat die Sprachen Latein, Italienisch, Tschechisch und Deutsch zum Gegenstand (Bischoff 1961: 221). Im Jahre 1424 entstehen in der Offizin eines venezianischen Berufsschreibers zwei Handschriften jenes italienisch-deutschen Sprachbuches, das dann der Ausgangspunkt ist für eine weitverzweigte Genealogie von polyglotten Gesprächsbüchern und Glossaren, die bis ins frühe 18. Jh. hineinreicht. Autor ist Meister Georg von Nürnberg, offenbar ein Sprachmeister aus der Nachbarschaft des *Fondaco dei Tedeschi* zu Venedig und, wie er am Ende der Handschrift von sich selbst sagt, "ein züchtiger Mann; [...] er hat einen klugen Sinn, zu lehren". Das 3. Hauptstück seines Werkes enthält zwei Handelsdialoge, die in ihrer Lebensnähe und Frische noch heute einen faszinierenden Einblick in die damalige Welt des Handels vermitteln, und die sich wohltuend von Lehrwerk-Texten späterer Zeiten, besonders aber denen des 19. Jhs., unterscheiden. Die nachfolgende Zusammenfassung des 1. Dialogs folgt Pausch (a. a. O.):

> Ein deutscher Kaufmann kommt am Morgen in den Kleiderladen eines ihm bekannten Venezianers [...]. Nur der Sohn Bartolamio ist anwesend, sein Vater weilt auf einer Geschäftsreise in Cremona. Der Deutsche möchte gerne 25 Stück Barchent haben und fragt nach dem Preis [...]. Ein Stück Barchent kostet 4½ Dukaten, ein Stück Boccaccino 6½. Dies erscheint dem Käufer zu teuer, er will für den Barchent höchstens 4 Dukaten geben [...]. Nach einem Streitgespräch, das mit einem gemeinsamen Erfrischungstrunk endet, beschließt der Deutsche, nach dem Frühstück im Deutschen Haus [dem Fondaco] mit einem Makler wiederzukommen. [...] Bartolamio will ihnen 30 Stück minderen Barchents um 112 Dukaten verkaufen, was einen Stückpreis von 3,7 Dukaten ergibt. [...] Der Deutsche bietet für eine bessere Qualität 100 Dukaten für 25 Stück. Zum gleichen Preis will er Valescio erstehen, und zwar 50 Stück. Bartolamio wendet ein, daß diese Stoffsorte schon im Einkauf zu Cremona 3½ Dukaten koste [...] und macht dem Makler Vorwürfe, weil er den Preis drücken wolle. Der Deutsche wiederum ist mißtrauisch, weil der Makler und Bartolamio einander kennen. Schließlich scheint es zu einer Einigung bei 4½ Dukaten pro Stück Barchent zu kommen, doch bis zum endgültigen Abschluß [...] gibt es noch einige Spiegelfechtereien. Der Deutsche leistet 10 Dukaten Anzahlung [...], worauf Bartolamio Träger aus dem *Fondaco dei Tedeschi* bestellt. In der Zwischenzeit werden Geld und Ware gewogen. Als der Deutsche eine Zugabe fordert, beginnt der venezianische Verkäufer ein Lamento. [...] Mit Hilfe des Maklers einigt man sich bei 6 Dukaten [...] und trinkt den Leitkauf. Dabei versucht Bartolamio, dem Deutschen auch noch Boccaccino zu verkaufen. (Pausch 1972: 37)

Trotz ihres inhaltlichen Reizes ist die Arbeit in vieler Hinsicht unausgewogen und unbeholfen. Da finden sich beispielsweise, nur teilweise systematisch geordnet, Wortgruppen, eingestreute Sentenzen, Redensarten und eine nicht konsequent aufgebaute Sammlung von Verben. Die Systematik beginnt mit Gott und der Schöpfung, dem Wetter und Wasser. Es folgen Zeiteinteilungen und Feiertage. Ein neuer Abschnitt beschäftigt sich mit dem menschlichen Körper, seiner Bekleidung und Pflege. Dann folgen das Haus und seine Einrichtung sowie die Zahlwörter. Ein weiteres Kapitel befaßt sich mit Lebensmitteln und Speisen, mit Metallen, Edelsteinen sowie Geld und Gewichten. Sodann werden Ausdrücke der Erziehung und Schule geboten sowie Wortgruppen, die mit Arzt und Apotheker zusammenhängen. Danach geht der Autor auf Burg, Stadt und Beruf über. Hier sind besonders die gerichtlichen und musikalischen Termini von Interesse. Dann wird die Steigerung der Adjektive vorgeführt. Es folgt eine facettenreiche Aufzählung von Tieren und Pflanzen. Nach der Behandlung der Verwandtschaftsgrade sowie der geistlichen und weltlichen Hierarchie, gefolgt von Orts- und Ländernamen, kommt der Verfasser auf den kirchlichen Bereich zurück, zu den Sünden und guten Eigenschaften. – Die Manuskripte sind im weiteren Verlauf des 15. Jhs. mehrfach abgeschrieben worden, und sie sind eingegangen in das 1477 in Venedig erschienene italienisch-deutsche Sprachbuch des Adam von Rottweil (vgl. Schröder 1987–99, besonders Bd. 5 [1997]: 3–5) mit dem Titel *Introito e porta di quelli che vogliono imparare e comprendere tedesco e latino cioè italiano, il quale è utilissimo per quelli che vanno a praticando per il mondo, sia tedesco o italiano*, besser bekannt vielleicht unter dem Titel des 2. Drukkes von 1479: *Solennissimo vochabuolista [vocabolista] e utilissimo a imparare leggere per quelli che desiderassero senza andare a scuolo como artigiani e donne; ancora può imparare tedesco l'Italiano, ed il Tedesco può imparare italiano perchè in questo libro se si contiene tutti i nomi, vocaboli e parole che si possono dire in più modi* (Bologna: Domenico de Lapi). (Vgl. dazu Rossebastiano Bart 1984.)

Der flämisch-französische Raum bietet zwei Parallelen, das von einem unbekannten Sprachmeister aus Brügge in der ersten Hälfte des Jhs. verfaßte *Livre des Mestiers, Dialogues français-flamands* (Michelant 1875) und die wahrscheinlich 1417 niedergeschriebene, 1483 von William Caxton in Brügge gedruckte Sammlung *Dialogues in French and English* (Bradley 1900). Das *Livre des Mestiers* war für Sprecher beider Sprachen gedacht, die *Dialogues* wandten sich in erster Linie an ein englisches Publikum, konnten aber auch in umgekehrter Richtung benutzt werden, was sie zum frühesten Lehrmaterial für neuzeitliches Englisch als Fremdsprache macht. Beide Werke sind einander gegenübergestellt bei Kelz (1994).

Im Verlauf des 16. und 17. Jhs. wird die wirtschaftsbezogene Dimension des Erwerbs moderner Fremdsprachen in erster Linie von den polyglotten Lehr- und Lernmaterialien, gewissermaßen nebenbei, transportiert (vgl. hierzu besonders Kapitel XVII, → Art. 94 und 101). Allerdings ist für den deutschsprachigen Raum und Französisch als Zielsprache zumindest eine Arbeit von Interesse, die auf den Sprachmeister Gérard du Vivier (de Viure) aus Gent zurückgeht, der seit etwa 1557 in Köln ansässig ist und dort seit 1563 mit Zustimmung des Stadtrates eine eigene Schule betreibt (Schröder 1987–99, Bd. 2 [1989]: 30). Seine *Deux livres de l'utilité du train de marchandise, entremêlés de lettres missives, à ce même effet* erscheinen erstmals 1575 und werden in mehreren Ausgaben neu verlegt (Rotterdam: Waesberghe 1588, Köln: Grevenbruch 1597 und 1628, die letztgenannten beiden Ausgaben bearbeitet von dem Kölner Sprachmeister Abraham des Mans). Du Viviers Dialoge haben nicht die Leuchtkraft derer des Georg von Nürnberg, und sie sind enzyklopädischer gehalten, doch auch sie geben lebensechte Einblicke in zeitgenössische Handelstransaktionen, wobei eine Orientierung in den flämischen Raum hinein und nach Antwerpen gegeben ist.

## 3. Kulturelles Interesse

Im Bereich der kulturellen Motivationen lassen sich drei Ansatzpunkte ausmachen, die das Interesse an den Volkssprachen, damit notwendigerweise aber auch an den modernen Fremdsprachen erklären: die aus dem Hochmittelalter herrührende höfische Tradition des Französischen, das in der Renaissance erstarkende nationalstaatliche Denken und das Bestreben der Reformation, die Bibel in der Sprache des Gläubigen zugänglich zu machen.

### 3.1. Die höfische Tradition des Französischen

Die Tradition des Französischen als sprachlicher Inkarnation einer verfeinerten Kultur geht auf die Troubadour- und Trouvère-Bewegung des 13. Jhs. zurück (zum Okzitanischen → Art. 87). Gerade der deutschsprachige Raum spiegelt die Einwirkung der französisch-ritterlichen Kultur des Hochmittelalters durch die Aufnahme französischer Begrifflichkeit in die mittelhochdeutsche Literatursprache, aber auch durch zahlreiche Anspielungen in der zeitgenössischen Dichtung. In dem Versroman *Der gute Gerhard* des Rudolf von Ems aus der ersten Hälfte des 13. Jhs. heißt es beispielsweise: "Dô sprach der fürste kurtoys/'sagent an, verstât ir franzoys?'/'jâ, herre, mir ist wol erkant/beidiu sprâch und ouch daz lant' " (zitiert nach Kelz 1994: 6). In seinem Lehrgedicht *Der Renner* stellt Hugo von Trimberg um das Jahr 1290 fest: "manger hin ze paris vert, /d'wenig lernet und vil verzert" (zitiert nach Boerner & Stiehler 1906: 336). In England ist Französisch bis in die 60er Jahre des 14. Jhs. hinein Sprache des Adels, der Kirche und der Verwaltung. Einige der bedeutendsten altfranzösischen Dichterpersönlichkeiten leben zeitweilig am königlichen Hofe zu London. Zwar geht der französische Einfluß in Europa im 14. und 15. Jh., bedingt durch den Hundertjährigen Krieg sowie durch Seuchen und soziale Unruhen, zurück, doch es ist leicht, ihn im 16. Jh. wiederzubeleben: Spätestens mit König Franz I. betritt Frankreich 1515 als innerlich geeinter, zunehmend zentralistisch organisierter Nationalstaat die europäische Bühne; die Dichter der Pléiade verhelfen Frankreich zu literarischem Ruhm und befassen sich zugleich, wie du Bellay in seinem 1549 erschienenen berühmten Traktat, mit der *Défense et illustration de la langue française*. Darüber hinaus ist das Französische die Sprache Calvins, eine Sprache, die die Hugenotten nach 1572 in der gesamten protestantischen Welt verbreiten werden. Worauf Hugo von Trimberg schon hinweist, wird später Standardprogramm: Zur Bildungsreise (*iter litterarius*) der Prinzen, Patrizier und auch der meisten Studierenden gehört der Frankreichaufenthalt, nicht zuletzt der Sprache wegen. Im 16. Jh. leben in häufig besuchten Städten wie Paris, Blois und Orléans Sprachlehrer, die ihren Lebensunterhalt mit Unterricht in Französisch als Fremdsprache für durchreisende Adlige und Jungakademiker verdienen. Einige von ihnen haben in ganz Europa einen guten Ruf. Zu diesen gehört offenbar auch der gelehrte Humanist Jean Pillot, der Verfasser der frühesten für deutsche Lernende ausgelegten, 1550 in Paris erschienenen *Gallicae linguae institutio latino sermone conscripta* (spätere Auflagen und Ausgaben: Paris 1555, 1561, 1563, 1581, Orléans 1560, 1571, Douai 1575). Die Arbeit ist dem Pfalzgrafen Wolfgang, Herzog von Bayern und Zweibrücken, gewidmet. Dessen Vetter und Pflegekind, Georg Johann Graf zu Lützelstein, ist Pillots Schüler im Französischen; die Berufung des Präzeptors hat allem Anschein nach Wolfgang selbst ausgesprochen. Pillot hält sich, von Paris kommend, seit etwa 1550 in der Pfalz auf. Den Druck der Grammatik überwacht sein Pariser Freund, der Humanist Claude Colet. Der 1571 an die Universität Wittenberg berufene früheste Lektor der französischen Sprache an einer deutschen Hochschule, Guillaume Rabot, erwähnt in seiner 1562 erschienenen Schrift *Scriptum publice propositum, quo significatum est de lingua gallica doctrina* Pillots Arbeit als Grundlage für das grammatische Sprachstudium.

### 3.2. Der Einfluß der Renaissance

Das oft apostrophierte neue Lebensgefühl der Renaissance ist die Frucht einer Loslösung von mittelalterlichem religiösem Denken, eines Zeitalters der Entdeckungen, eines umfassenden Neuansatzes in den Wissenschaften und Künsten, aber auch größerer sozialer Sicherheit und einer (zumindest für die männliche Bevölkerung) steigenden Lebenserwartung. An die Stelle mittelalterlicher politischer Gliederungen tritt der Nationalstaat, der von seinen Einwohnern als Vaterland identifiziert werden kann und damit auch Kristallisationspunkt für neue kollektive emotionale Bindungen wird. Der Nationalstaat impliziert die Nationalsprache. Die Ausgestaltung dieser Sprache, mehr oder minder deutlich am Vorbild des Lateinischen, ist Gradmesser nationalen Fortschritts. Das – in moderner Terminologie – klassische Zeitalter der modernen Literaturen (Shakespeare, Milton, Corneille, Racine, Molière, Cervantes usw.) ist auch Ausfluß einer politischen Entwicklung sowie Manifestation eines politischen Willens. Die Nationalsprachen und Nationalliteraturen verkörpern einen Machtanspruch; sie implizieren die Zurückdrängung neutraler, überstaatlicher Verständigungsmittel wie etwa des Lateins. Zumindest wird man das Lateinische nun so aussprechen, als sei es der Phonetik der jeweiligen Nationalsprache unterworfen: Der *Great Vowel Shift* des Englischen verändert die Aussprache des Lateins auf den britischen Inseln ebenso sehr wie die Aussprache des Englischen selbst. Und natürlich bedingen die konkurrierenden Nationalsprachen Fremdsprachenlerner, Fremdsprachenlehrer, Übersetzer und Dolmetscher. (Zu den sprachenpolitischen Hintergründen der Entwicklung des Fremdsprachenunterrichts vgl. Schröder

1993, für die hier interessierende Zeit besonders 43–50.) Wo der Nationalstaat fehlt, da bleibt allerdings auch die Ausbildung der Nationalsprache zurück: Für die Deutschen, die Tschechen, die Österreicher und die Ungarn findet das klassische Zeitalter erst im späten 18. und im 19. Jh. statt. Daran ändern auch die auf dem Territorium des Heiligen Römischen Reiches deutscher Nation vergleichsweise zahlreichen frühen Bibelübersetzungen nichts.

### 3.3. Der Einfluß der Reformation

Die von den Reformatoren propagierte Freiheit des Christenmenschen gegenüber der Amtskirche ist nur möglich auf der Basis eines unmittelbaren Kontaktes zwischen dem Gläubigen und seinem Gott, gegründet der Heiligen Schrift. Der Ansatz kann nur greifen, wenn zwei Voraussetzungen erfüllt sind: Der Christenmensch muß lesen können, und die Bibel muß in der jeweiligen Volkssprache vorhanden sein. Ersteres impliziert eine allgemeine Elementarschulpflicht bzw. entsprechende Unterweisung in Sonntagsschulen, besonders auch für das weibliche Geschlecht, letzteres impliziert die Übersetzung der Bibel, wobei gleichzeitig die Volkssprache gehoben werden muß, um adäquates Ausdrucksmittel des Wortes Gottes zu werden. Die Reformation hat ein theologisches Interesse an den Volkssprachen, gleichzeitig wird für den protestantischen Theologen die internationale Sprache und Kirchensprache Latein zur Sprache des Papismus, damit aber des konfessionellen Gegners. Konsequenz ist, daß auch die theologische Fachliteratur in der Volkssprache abgefaßt wird. Wer aber als Theologiestudent, als Prediger oder aber nur als akademisch gebildeter, gläubiger Laie diese Literatur nutzen will, der muß zumindest die Fähigkeit erwerben, die betreffenden Fremdsprachen lesend zu verstehen. Tatsächlich ist theologisches Fachinteresse das Hauptmotiv für englische Sprachstudien im protestantischen Europa des 17. und frühen 18. Jhs., man vergleiche hierzu beispielsweise Christian Andreas Teubers *Tractatus philologico-exegeticus de utilitate linguae anglicanae in explicatione Sanctae Scripturae* (Leipzig: Förster 1733).

## 4. Fremdsprachenpolitische und fremdsprachendidaktische Konsequenzen

Obwohl die Renaissance eine *ad fontes*-Bewegung ist und der Humanismus die klassische Latinität wiederentdeckt, legen beide Strömungen den Keim zum Niedergang des Lateinischen als internationaler Sprache. Die Renaissance wertet die Volkssprachen staatspolitisch auf, die Reformation macht sie zum Ausdrucksmittel des göttlichen Wortes. Konsequenterweise werden die jungen Nationalsprachen zum Medium nationaler Literaturen und dann in zunehmendem Maße auch zum Medium der Gelehrsamkeit, nicht nur im Bereich protestantischer Theologie. Für die Reformation sind alle Sprachen vor Gott gleich, so wie alle Menschen (in der Theorie) gleich sind. Nicht so für die Politik. Schon 1492 führt Antonio de Nebrija im Widmungsbrief seiner *Grammatica castellana* an Königin Isabella aus, "que siempre la lengua fue companera del imperio". Spätestens seit dem ausgehenden 16. Jh. – die Antrittsvorlesungen früher Französisch-Professoren an deutschen Universitäten beweisen es – werden die modernen Sprachen als Mittel der Außen- und der Machtpolitik eingesetzt. Seit der Renaissance und bis zum heutigen Tage ist Fremdsprachenunterricht damit immer auch ein eminent politisches Unterfangen. Seit Kardinal Richelieu betreibt Frankreich nach innen und nach außen eine konsequente Politik zugunsten seiner Sprache, nach innen als Mittel der Zentralisierung, nach außen als Vehikel einer expansiven Politik. Der Dreißigjährige Krieg wird um Monate verlängert, weil die französischen Unterhändler keine lateinischen Dokumente der kaiserlichen Gesandten annehmen (Moser 1750: 50ff., 149ff.); im 18. Jh. ist Französisch unumstrittene internationale Sprache, bis nach 1813 ein jäher Absturz erfolgt (vgl. dazu – exemplarisch – Arndt 1813). Doch erst der Versailler Vertrag des Jahres 1919 höhlt die Hegemonialstellung des Französischen als Diplomatensprache aus: Es gibt eine gleichberechtigte englische Version. Der Fremdsprachenunterricht und Fremdsprachenerwerb folgt seit der zweiten Hälfte des 16. Jhs. der außen-, kultur- und wirtschaftspolitischen Rangfolge der Staaten und Sprachen. Dabei lösen wirtschaftlicher Erfolg bzw. Mißerfolg und militärische Erfolge bzw. Niederlagen mitunter erdrutschartige Verschiebungen aus (für die Zeit nach 1815 vgl. u. a. Schröder 1989). Gleichzeitig kommt es zu bestimmten klischeehaften Zuordnungen von Sprachen und Lebensbereichen: Französisch wird gesehen als Sprache des Theaters und des Rationalismus, Italienisch als Sprache der Oper, Englisch als Sprache der Theologie und der Naturwissenschaften. Früh entwickeln sich stereotype Charakterisierungen von Sprache, wie sie bereits für die erste Hälfte des 17. Jhs. in pädagogischer Fachliteratur und auch in Lehrwerken bezeugt sind: gravitätisches Spanisch, italienischer Belcanto, perfekte Schönheit des Französischen. Oder, wie ein im 18. Jh. im deutschsprachigen Raum weit verbreitetes Lehrwerk des Französischen, die *Nouvelle et parfaite grammaire royale* des Des Pepliers es ausdrückt (zitiert nach der Ausgabe Berlin 1716: 394): "Der Franzose singt, der Deutsche röchelt, der Italiener zischt, der Spanier redet im Gewicht, der Engländer heult." – Der Umgang mit den Volkssprachen im 15. und 16. Jh., ob politisch oder pädagogisch gefaßt, determiniert die weiteren sprachenpolitischen und sprachpädagogischen Entwicklungen. Insofern ist auch eine Analyse der gegenwärtigen europäischen Sprachenpolitik nur möglich vor dem Hintergrund einer Kenntnis des hier interessierenden Zeitalters.

## 5. Bibliographie

Arndt, Ernst Moritz. 1813. *Über Volkshaß und über den Gebrauch einer fremden Sprache.* Leipzig: Johann Benjamin Georg Fleischer.

Beck, Christoph. 1914. "Die neueren Sprachen in der Reichsstadt Nürnberg". *Zeitschrift für neusprachlichen Unterricht* 13.385–393.

Bischoff, Bernhard. 1961. "The Study of Foreign Languages in the Middle Ages." *Speculum* 36. 209–224.

Blättner, Fritz. 1960. *Das Gymnasium. Aufgaben der höheren Schule in Geschichte und Gegenwart.* Heidelberg: Quelle & Meyer.

Boerner, O. & E. Stiehler. 1906. "Zur Geschichte der neueren Sprachen". *Neue Jahrbücher für Pädagogik* 6.392–412.

Bradley, Henry. 1900. *William Caxton. Dialogues in French and English. Adapted from a fourteenth-century book of dialogues in French and Flemish. Edited from Caxton's printed text (about 1483), with introduction, notes, and wordlists.* (= *Early English Text Society, Extra Series* 79.) London.

Hammerich, Louis L. et al., Hg. 1961–86. *Tönnies Fenne's Low German Manual of Spoken Russian, Pskov 1607.* 4 Bde. Kopenhagen: Munksgaard.

Kelz, Irene. 1994. *Das Französische als Handels- und Geschäftssprache vom Ausgang des Mittelalters bis zum 19. Jahrhundert. Eine Untersuchung an Lehrwerken für den berufsbezogenen Französischunterricht.* (= *Augsburger I&I-Schriften* 69.) Augsburg: Universität.

Kuhfuß, Walter. 1976. "Frühformen des Französischunterrichts in Deutschland. Beiträge zur ersten Ausweitungsphase organisierter französischer Sprachunterweisung, 1554–1618". *Sprachen und Staaten. Festschrift Heinz Kloss*, Teil 1: *Der politische und soziale Status der Sprachen in den Staaten der Europäischen Gemeinschaft* hg. von Harald Haarmann & Anna-Liisa Värri-Haarmann, 323–341. Hamburg: Stiftung Europa-Kolleg, Selbstverlag.

Meyer, Meinert A. 1986. *Shakespeare oder Fremdsprachenkorrespondenz? Zur Reform des Fremdsprachenunterrichts in der Sekundarstufe II.* Wetzlar: Büchse der Pandora.

Michelant, Henry-Victor, Hg. 1875. *Le Livre des Mestiers, Dialogues français-flamands composés au XIV$^{e}$ siècle par un maître d'école de la ville de Bruges.* Paris: Tross.

Moser, Friedrich Carl. 1750. *Abhandlung von den europäischen Hof- und Staats-Sprachen, nach deren Gebrauch im Reden und Schreiben.* Frankfurt/M.: Johann Benjamin Andreae.

Raab, H. 1955–56. "Die Anfänge der slawistischen Studien im deutschen Ostseeraum unter besonderer Berücksichtigung von Mecklenburg und Vorpommern". *Wissenschaftliche Zeitschrift der Ernst-Moritz-Arndt-Universität Greifswald. Gesellschafts- und Sprachwissenschaftliche Reihe* 5.341–402.

Pausch, Oskar 1972. *Das älteste italienisch-deutsche Sprachbuch. Eine Überlieferung aus dem Jahre 1424. Nach Georg von Nürnberg.* (= *Österreichische Akademie der Wissenschaften, Philosophisch-historische Klasse, Denkschriften* 111, *Veröffentlichungen der historischen Kommission* 1.) Köln: Böhlau.

Rossebastiano Bart, Alda. 1984. *Antichi vocabolari plurilingui d'uso popolare: La tradizione del 'Solenissimo Vochabuolista'.* Alessandria: Edizioni dell'Orso.

Schröder, Konrad. 1975. *Fremdsprachenunterricht in der Sekundarstufe II.* (= *Deutscher Bildungsrat, Gutachten und Studien der Bildungskommission* 41.) Stuttgart: Klett.

–. 1987–99. *Biographisches und bibliographisches Lexikon der Fremsprachenlehrer des deutschsprachigen Raumes, Spätmittelalter bis 1800.* 6 Bde. (= *Augsburger I&I-Schriften* 40, 51, 63, 68, 73, 74.) Augsburg: Universität.

–. 1989. "Über Volkshaß und über den Gebrauch einer fremden Sprache. Zur historischen Dimension des Schulsprachenstreites Englisch–Französisch, unter besonderer Berücksichtigung der nach-Napoleonischen Zeit". *Fremdsprachenunterricht zwischen Sprachenpolitik und Praxis, Festschrift für Herbert Christ zum 60. Geburtstag* hg. von Eberhard Kleinschmidt. Tübingen: Narr.

–. 1993. "Languages". *What is Europe?*, Book 2: *Aspects of European Cultural Diversity* hg. von Monica Shelley & Margaret Winck, 13–64. Milton Keynes: The Open University.

Stieda, Wilhelm. 1884. "Zur Sprachenkenntnis der Hanseaten". *Hansische Geschichtsblätter* (erschienen: 1885). 157–161.

*Konrad Schröder, Augsburg (Deutschland)*

# 94. La tradition des manuels polyglottes dans l'enseignement des langues

1. Généralités
2. Les notes des voyageurs
3. Venise et l'Orient: les méthodes pratiques entre école et voyage
4. Venise et l'Europe du Nord: Georg von Nürnberg et le "Solenissimo Vochabuolista"
5. Anvers: école et marché
6. Anvers: les *Colloquia* de Noël de Berlaimont
7. Divers
8. Bibliographie

## 1. Généralités

Les manuels polyglottes pour l'enseignement des langues étrangères sont particulièrement nombreux pour la période du XV^e siècle, qui répond de cette façon aussi bien au vide résultant de la perte de l'ancienne 'lingua franca', le latin, qu'à la curiosité naturelle pour l'exotique, mis en évidence par les nouvelles découvertes géographiques.

Les auteurs sont souvent des maîtres d'école, bons connaisseurs des méthodes pratiques directement appliquées sur leurs élèves, mais parfois ce sont des professeurs improvisés, quittant pour l'occasion leur poste de lecteurs, pour celui de réalisateurs d'œuvres nouvelles, enrichies selon leur expérience personnelle.

Les destinataires se divisent en principe en deux catégories: les marchands (déjà en activité ou *in fieri*, élèves des écoles créées à leur intention) et les voyageurs; les uns et les autres sont souvent désireux de communiquer les résultats de leur expérience linguistique, acquise à la suite des contacts avec un monde différent. Parmi eux, on cite aussi parfois, et explicitement, des femmes.

La tendance à comparer une langue avec une autre à l'aide de listes parallèles de mots est très ancienne: on peut la faire remonter au moins au deuxième millénaire a. C., mais c'est au cours du Moyen Age européen que l'on rencontre des racines plus au moins directes des œuvres destinées à un bon succès à l'aube de l'époque moderne.

## 2. Les notes des voyageurs

Les *Glosses de Kassel*, IX^e siècle, roman-bavarois, sont une première ébauche de manuels pratiques pour les voyageurs de l'Europe centrale, due probablement à une expérience directe.

Il s'agit d'une liste de mots en langue romane, traduits en langue germanique, se rapportants aux parties du corps humain, aux animaux, à la maison, etc., précédant une série de phrases analogues à celles que l'on trouve aujourd'hui dans les guides pour touristes.

En revanche, le corpus du *Glossaire de Monza*, italien-grec, X^e siècle, est plus sobre: la liste comprenant peu de mots (corps humain, vêtements, ustensiles, éléments de l'univers, animaux, jours) est suivie d'une seule phrase: "clamat homo – grasi andropus" (Bischoff 1961: 218 sq.).

Un recueil de mots et de phrases hébreu-latin, probable témoignage d'un pèlerinage à Jérusalem, date de la même période. En dépit des propos pieux, la conversation est strictement d'ordre pratique, du genre: "Tenli chos echad iain", c'est à dire: "Donne-moi une coupe de vin" (Bischoff 1961: 218).

C'est au siècle suivant que se situe une petite œuvre du même type, dans laquelle le latin fait face au grec vulgaire, avec des exemples de conversation centrés sur les nécessités quotidiennes: "Da mihi panem – DOS ME PSOMI" (Bischoff 1961: 219).

Les Croisés étaient des voyageurs un peu particuliers: à eux était destiné un petit manuel grec vulgaire-latin, probablement du XII^e siècle: suivant les intérêts des destinataires, on quitte les thèmes quotidiens pour aborder des sujets plus 'hauts', comme la situation politique de l'empire byzantin ou la recherche d'armes. Cependant la liste de mots se rapportants aux thèmes usuels n'est pas absente; là aussi on trouve: animaux, jours de la semaine, parties du corps humain (Bischoff 1961: 219).

On voit des notes analogues dans le journal de William Wey du *Royal College* d'Eton, pèlerin à Jérusalem et à Saint Jacques de Compostelle vers le milieu du XV^e siècle, qui ajute à la relation de ses voyages un précis anglais-grec moderne, où l'on peut lire des phrases d'usage commun, utiles aux touristes de tout temps et de tout lieux: "Tel me the way", "Bring heder wyne", etc. Suivent les numéraux et un répertoire lexical, par ordre alphabétique, gréco-latin, avec des insertions, non conscientes, d'hébreu (Banfi 1985: 28–51).

Le recueil du noble allemand Arnold von Harff (fin du XVe siècle), inséré dans son récit sur ses pérégrinations à Jérusalem, à Saint Jacques de Compostelle et au Mont Saint Michel (éd. Groote 1860), n'est le fruit d'une expérience pénitentielle qu'en apparence. Les langues intéressées sont nombreuses: croate, albanais, grec, arabe, hébreu, turc, hongrois, basque, breton; la matière, comme d'habitude, est tout à fait pratique, subdivisée en listes de mots, phrases, numéraux. La phraséologie présente un air galant, convenant mieux à un chevalier en quête d'aventures qu'à un pèlerin en marche pour le salut de son âme. Voici quelques exemples: "Où est la taverne?", "Bonne femme, laissez-moi dormir avec vous!" (Bischoff 1961: 219–220; Banfi 1985: 53–54).

Citons encore une liste de mots français traduits en turc, qui trouve place en appendice de *Le grant voyage de Jérusalem*, imprimé à Paris en 1517 (Madrid, BN R 9353).

Au début du siècle suivant, les limites de la terre deviennent bien plus amples, à la suite des nombreuses découvertes, tant dans l'ancien comme dans le nouveau monde. A cette époque, l'attrait pour l'exotique, libre de la tendance vers le merveilleux, se renforce grâce à des séduisantes perspectives commerciales.

La nécessité de pénétrer, y compris linguistiquement, dans un univers inviolé est bien comprise par un navigateur comme Antonio Pigafetta, le 'chevalier errant', qui, rentré chez lui après sa circumnavigation de la terre, compose le récit de son voyage, serti de quatre petits 'vocabulaires', c'est à dire de listes de mots et de brèves phrases en langages indigènes du Brésil, de la Patagonie, des îles Philippines, des Moluques. L'œuvre parut entre 1526 et 1536, d'abord en français (*Le voyage et navigation faict par les espaignolz es isles de Mollucques*), puis en italien comme *Il viaggio fatto dagli spagnoli intorno al mondo* (Pozzi 1994: 115, 122–124, 149–151, 176–181). Voici quelques exemples de la dernière série: "Como se chiama questo? / apenamaito?", "Bon giorno / salam alichum. Al rispondere, alichum salam [...]".

On trouve des exemples du langage des indigènes de l'actuel Canada dans le *Bref récit, et succinte narration de la navigation faicte en ysles de Canada*, publiée à Paris en 1544 (Lindemann 1994: 76).

Les nouvelles destinations n'effacent pas les anciennes. Un pénitent hongrois sur le chemin de la Terre Sainte, emprisonné par les infidèles, Bartolomeus Georgiewitz, nous a donné en 1544 un petit manuel français-turc: *Mots et manières de compter en Turquois [...]*, également traduit plusieurs fois en italien aussi (Quemada 1968: 567–571; Cortelazzo 1979: 136; Stein 1990: 45; Lindemann 1994: 75).

L'œuvre d'un anonyme flamand, insérée dans un guide pour pèlerins de Jérusalem et de Rome et conservée dans un manuscrit d'environ 1570, est moins exotique. Le point de départ (les Flandres) et celui de l'embarquement possible (la Provence ou Gênes) justifient parfaitement les langues des dialogues (flamand-français), précédés d'un vocabulaire "sarasin-hollandais" (Riemens 1924: 33–34).

Le plurilinguisme du manuel de Jean Palerne, médecin lyonnais à la cour du roi de France, qui à la fin de son récit de voyage ajoute un recueil lexical et phraséologique en "françois, italien, grec vulgaire, turc, moresque (arabe), esclavon", est analogue à celui d'Arnold von Harff (Banfi 1988: 55–66). En ce qui concerne la structure et la matière, l'œuvre n'est pas originelle: elle reprend de toute évidence le *Vocabulario Nuovo con il quale da se stessi si può benissimo imparare diversi linguaggi, cioè Italiano e Greco, italiano e Turco, Italiano e Tedesco*, dont la première édition que nous connaissons porte la date de 1574. Elle est probablement précédée de plusieurs autres éditions, qui pourraient remonter jusqu'à un manuscrit de 1467 (Rossebastiano 1992: 164–170).

## 3. Venise et l'Orient: les méthodes pratiques entre école et voyage

Avec le *Vocabulario Nuovo*, qui eut un excellent succès, le manuel de conversation montre bien son caractère autonome, prêt è devenir un instrument d'enseignement, surtout pour les autodidactes. Toutefois celui-là n'est pas le produit le plus ancien de la catégorie, ne visant plus un destinataire spécifique comme le voyageur.

Un glossaire italien-arabe (XVe siècle) écrit en Italie du Sud, probablement à Naples, remonte sûrement à une date antérieure. Dans ce cas, la phraséologie est réduite à un seul exemple ("como te chiame"), sur 217 mots (surtout des noms) en ordre méthodique, selon les quatre éléments de l'univers: "aero, terra, aqua, fuocho" (Teza 1893).

Les langues utilisées au Proche Orient apparaissent aussi dans le *Vocabulario Italiano e Arabesco, con alcuni Dialoghi in Turchesco e in Greco Moderno*, conservé dans un ms. du XVe siècle, encore inédit, signalé par M. Cortelazzo (1979: 134). Le thème d'un des dialogues ("salutar, comprar e vendere et numerare in lingua italiana e turchesca") nous indique une possible destination commerciale, mais les allusions au milieu scolaire sont évidentes: "Dov'è il maestro? / Ecome qua".

En ce qui concerne les dialogues *L'opera chi se delettasse de saper domandar ciascheduna cosa in turchesco*, parue entre 1525 et 1530 (Adamović 1975: 217–247; Rossebastiano 1992: 167), est tout à fait originale. Le lieu d'édition est probablement Venise, étant donné le genre linguistique et la présence d'un pamphlet contre les Turcs, les ennemis traditionnels de la Serenissima. Les exemples de conversation montrent que l'œuvre est destinée à un public adulte: "O le belle tette", "Cuore mio chi te feci tanto bella? [...]". Cependant il ne faut pas oublier qu'un bon esprit grivois se répand souvent dans les écoles, surtout dans celles des marchands, bien plongées dans la vie réelle.

Du point de vue de la moralité du contenu, le *Vocabulario Nuovo* est plus contrôlé. Les dialogues ne s'éloignent pas de la banalité, qui ne permet ni de se lever au dessus du quotidien, ni de sombrer dans la trivialité, même quand le contexte en donnerait bien l'occasion: "Fantesca, va e acconcia il letto", "Egli è fatto", "Buona notte [...]".

Dans ce cas, les destinataires sont les voyageurs et les marchands, ainsi que les étudiants. Ces dermiers sont cités dans les exemples de courrier entre un garçon, qui se trouverait à Venise pour suivre ses cours, et son père, résidant à Worms. Le lieu d'élaboration est le même que celui de l'impression, Venise, citée dans le texte italien-allemand, où l'on peut trouver aussi une adresse qui est probablement celle de l'auteur: "Dove è la casa vostra?", "Nella contrà de' Fucari". En ce qui concerne la structure, on peut parler d'un bilingue 'triplique' (c.-à. d., trois langues, 2 à 2), avec différentes combinaisons linguistiques, se trouvant toujours en face de l'italien.

La troisième section (italien-allemand) sera utilisée plus tard (fin XVIIe/commencement XVIIIe siècle) pour donner lieu, avec substitution de la deuxième langue, à un nouveau vocabulaire bilingue, italien-croate, dont nous connaissons une impression datée de 1704. Il y a peu d'additions et de réductions, aussi bien en ce qui concerne le lexique, que les dialogues, point par point copiés du modèle; il y a une seule nouveauté: la section grammaticale (morphologie) des deux langues. L'arrangement semble pouvoir être sorti du milieu franciscain, visant à l'évangélisation de la province de Bosnie, profondément pénétrée par l'expansion des Turcs musulmans (Rossebastiano 1992: 167–170).

On explique ainsi la liaison turc-croate déclarée par la dépendance du *Vocabulario Nuovo*, également évidente dans l'adaptation d'un autre manuel, *L'opera nuova di M. Pietro Lupis Valenciano che insegna a parlar turchescho*, dévenue en 1527 *Opera nuova che insegna a parlare la lingua schiavonesca alli grandi, alli piccoli et alle donne*, parue à Ancone, où les rapports avec la côte dalmate étaient très vivants en général et en particulier grâce à l'importance de la maison des Franciscains de Loreto, juste en face de la plus proche des provinces de la Terre Sainte. L'auteur du manuel 'turchescho' est, toutefois, un juif espagnol, Pedro Lopez de Valencia, expulsé d'Espagne, demeurant à Ancone, mais ayant vécu auparavant dans les pays de l'Est, où les juifs espagnols s'étaient réfugiés après 1496.

Cependant, une autre œuvre, apparemment de type ecclésiastique, mais en réalité d'utilisation populaire, où la combinaison linguistique est italien-croate, s'avère tout à fait originale. Du ms., conservé à la Bodleian Library d'Oxford, on connaît l'édition de Pohl (1976). Dans ce cas les dialogues ont parfois comme objet la vie religieuse ("Andiamo insino alla chiesa"), n'excluant pas la présence de sentiments assez peu chrétiens ("Andiamo a fare vendetta"), ainsi que celle d'éléments de la vie quotidienne ("Andiamo alla merenda") ou, encore, celles des activités des destinataires ("Andiamo alla botega comprare qua/l/che cosa"). La marque dialectale de l'Italie du Nord (en particulier celle de la Vénétie) du texte met encore une fois en relief le rôle de Venise dans les rapports, aussi bien avec le Proche Orient, qu'avec toute la péninsule balkanique.

## 4. Venise et l'Europe du Nord: Georg von Nürnberg et le "Solenissimo Vochabuolista"

Toutefois, Venise était aussi le port principal de la Méditerranée pour les pays du Nord de l'Europe, en particulier pour les Allemands qui durant le Moyen Age y tenaient des magasins économiquement très importants, réunis autour du *Fondaco dei Tedeschi*, près du Campo San Bartolomeo. C'est là qu'un courtier-interprète, Georg von Nürnberg, donnait des cours de sa langue maternelle à ses élèves italiens, destinés aux échanges avec les villes du centre de l'Europe. Le peu de choses que nous savons de ce personnage nous vient des notes de son cours, parvenu jusqu'à nos jours dans plusieurs mss., qui constituent la documentation remarquable d'une méthode conçue explicitement pour l'enseignement des langues vulgaires, c'est à dire, ici, l'italien et l'allemand.

On se trouve ici, il faut bien le dire, dans une tout autre dimension que celle des œuvres précédemment citées: il s'agit cette fois du monde de l'école, et d'une école particulière, celle des marchands, qui ne met pas l'accent sur la théorie de la grammaire, mais sur les exemples du langage parlé de la place. Voilà pourquoi on ne trouve ni règles ni définitions, mais plutôt un grand choix de mots, appliqués à des phrases.

La méthode est rigoureusement structurée et divisée en quatre parties: les substantifs en ordre de matière (à peu près 4.000 mots), alignés sur deux colonnes (italien-allemand), précédés de leur article, parfois les formes du pluriel en opposition au singulier, et enfin la conclusion de l'argument marqué par une phrase, un diction, des calembours, qui soulignent souvent les différences sémantiques des homographes; une riche série d'adjectifs dans les formes du positif, du comparatif, du superlatif; une liste de pronoms, une série de paradigmes verbaux, exemples de conjugaison de verbes; phraséologie. Dans cette dernière section, on trouve des dialogues alertes et piquants, entendus au marché, à l'école, dans les tavernes, portant la marque de toute la richesse du parlé quotidien (Pausch 1972, Rossebastiano Bart 1984, Holtus & Schweickard 1985).

L'œuvre, composée probablement à la fin du XIV$^{e}$ s., mais conservé dans des mss. du XV$^{e}$ (*post* 1422), ouvre vraiment une tradition, qui compte au total 9 témoins, divisés en trois familles, plus ou moins fortement caractérisées. Ce qui change assez visiblement dans le temps est la couleur dialectale du texte italien, qui de 'veneto', parfois plus exactement connoté comme vénitien ou padouan, devient de plus en plus proche de la koiné toscane. Les changements intéressent parfois la combinaison des langues, qui, au nombre de deux (italien et allemand) au début, deviennent quatre (latin, italien, tchèque, allemand) dans uns des mss. suivants (Presa 1975: 166–175; Kresalkova 1984).

La tradition ouverte par les mss. eut beaucoup de succès avec l'invention de la presse.

La méthode se transforme, en abandonnant nombre de ses caractéristiques les plus scolaires, pour en acquérir des nouvelles, valables pour les autodidactes, auxquels elle va s'adresser. Déjà dans la deuxième édition (Bologne 1479), qui suit le prototype d'Adam de Rottweil (Venise 1477; éd. an. Bart Rossebastiano 1971, Giustiniani 1987), on explicite le changement de but: le manuel, privé de la plus grande partie de la phraséologie et de la grammaire, au lexique réduit (même s'il est, de toute façon, encore remarquablement important) est revu pour "artesani et donne", et adapté aux exigences de ceux qui désirent apprendre les langues étrangères "senza andare a schola". C'est de là que s'impose la nécessité d'introduire des règles de prononciation, indispensable en l'absence d'un maître, aussi bien pour l'allemand que pour l'italien. Cette exigence sera perçue au siècle suivant, même pour les nouvelles langues: en 1510 le manuel comprendra quatre langues (lat., it., fr., all.) avec des observations sur la phonétique de l'idiome moderne ajouté.

Entre-temps (éd. de 1502), l'italien avait été remplacé par le catalan, en donnant lieu à un répertoire catalan-allemand (éd. an. Barnils 1916; Colón & Soberanas 1985: 55–59).

Les années suivantes connaissent de nouvelles révisions: de la matière, du format (réduit à 'de poche'), des langues, progressivement plus nombreuses jusqu'à atteindre le nombre de huit, voire, diversement combinés, de douze idiomes européens: l'italien et l'allemand (Venezia 1477), le catalan (Perpignan 1502), le latin et le français (Roma 1510), l'espagnol (probablement Venezia 1513, sinon, Venezia 1526), le tchèque (Nürnberg 1531), le polonais (Kracow 1532), le flamand (Antwerpen 1534), l'anglais (Southwarke 1537), le hongrois (Wien 1538), le grec moderne (Paris 1546). La fortune du manuel décroîtra pendant la deuxième moitié du XVI$^{e}$ siècle, mais il continuera à paraître, une dernière fois en 1636 à Rouen (Rossebastiano Bart 1984a).

L'œuvre sera proposée de nouveau avec la partie finale modifiée, ayant recours au *Vocabulario de Romance en latin* d'Antonio de Nebrija. Le produit, renouvelé par Jan Colin de Thovoyen, aura comme titre *Vocabulario en*

*Español y Flamenco*, Amsterdam 1617 (Hendrik Laurentz; cf. Claes & Bakema 1995: 1929).

L'influence exercée sur le *Thesaurus Linguarum* (1626: lat., it., fr., esp., all.) du basque Juan Angel Sumarán, est moins évidente, mais également sûre; exclusivement en ce qui concerne le choix des thèmes on le remarque également sur la *Nomenclatura* (1629: it., fr., esp.) de Guillaume Alexandre Noviliers Clavel.

Un fragment conservé dans la Biblioteca Vaticana, dont les filigranes datent de 1365–1385 (Scarpa 1991: 59–75), nous confirme que les glossaires italien-allemands sont antérieurs au XV$^{e}$ siècle. C'est d'ailleurs ce siècle qui nous a laissé la documentation la plus riche et la mieux conservée. Il s'agit encore une fois d'un petit manuel didactique, utilisé probablement pour enseigner l'italien aux allemands, vu l'inversion des langues: allemand (bavarois)–italien. L'original de l'œuvre, n'ayant en commun avec le méthode de Georg von Nürnberg que l'idée générale, est encore plus ancien, la copie qui est arrivée jusqu'à nous étant altérée, passée entre les mains d'un grand nombre de copistes. La matière est toujours la même: une liste de termes sur différents thèmes, disposées au hasard, quoique les nombreux rappels par analogie engendrent une sorte de subdivision méthodique. De temps à autre on trouve une phrase, et, à la fin, la série des nombres en allemand. Si l'on compare cette œuvre à l'œuvre précédemment citée, on remarque immédiatement une baisse de niveau, aussi bien en ce qui concerne la structure que la langue, l'allemand étant devenu pratiquement une langue 'macaronique'. Voici quelques exemples: "Hyc bel beitere no(n) mic scina" / "io no[n] voglo stare più co[n] techo"; "Frayta agur disschanchana delpna gamdre bessici sene aura sone" / "figlo de la puctana merdosa sco[n]caçata puççulente". On peut noter aussi la trivialité brutale qui remplace l'ironie aimable de Georg von Nürnberg.

On voit le même combinaison linguistique (allemand-italien) dans un fragment d'incunable conservé à Munich (Bart Rossebastiano 1977: 92–93), non daté et inachevé. On y trouve des paradigmes verbaux et des essais de dialogues, rappelant ceux de Georg von Nürnberg: "Da chi logo vegnì-vui?", "Mi vegna da chaxa". La langue est encore une fois celle de la Vénétie, ce qui confirme que le berceau de ces œuvres est vraiment le 'Fondaco' des Allemands vénetien.

## 5. Anvers: école et marché

Si, en suivant l'évolution des routes commerciales à la fin du Moyen Age, on passe de Venise à Anvers, devenue au XVI$^{e}$ siècle un port fort important et un centre typographique renommé, on trouve un autre manuel, devenu un classique pour l'apprentissage des langues étrangères dans toute l'Europe. C'est l'œuvre de Noël de Berlaimont, *Colloquia et Dictionariolum*.

Même dans ce cas, les antécédents, représentés par les manuels de conversation, sont très anciens et très bien organisés du point de vue méthodologique. Le premier est le *Livre des mestiers* de 1340 (Riemens 1924; Gessler 1931; Mantou 1969: 157–197), français-flamand, composé par un maître d'école, probablement picard. L'auteur vivait à Bruges, ville qu'il aimait comme la sienne, appelée affectueusement dans le texte "une des meilleures villes marchandes qui soit en crestienté" (Gessler 1931: 14), bien connue par l'auteur, même du point de vue topographique.

Le texte est divisé en trois parties: vie domestique, vie sociale, vie religieuse. Les thèmes du répertoire, développés surtout sous forme de dialogues, sont les usuels: "Salutations, parenté, maison, meubles, ustensiles [...], pays". Ensuite on trouve: noms de personnes (par ordre alphabétique approximatif) et de métiers (voilà pourquoi le titre et le motif des dialogues: "Voyage à cheval, achat de vin, préparation de la table [...]"); Dieu et les principaux lieux de pèlerinage, la plupart en France (Riemens 1924: 14–15).

On n'a pas besoin de souligner que cette dernière section confirme explicitement la liaison entre les manuels pour l'étude des langues étrangères et les pèlerinages.

L'œuvre arriva bientôt en Angleterre, où elle fut revue (substitution de l'anglais au flamand, addition et suppression de lemmes et de dialogues, introduction des nombres à la fin de l'œuvre) par William Caxton, marchand anglais vivant à Bruges, centre des échanges anglo-flamands. Elle parut en 1483 avec un nouveau titre: *Dialogues in French and English* (Bradley 1900; Gessler 1931: 31; Lindemann 1994: 17, où l'on mentionne aussi la *Magniere de language*, également franco-anglaise).

La matière du *Gesprächbüchlein*, composé pendant la deuxième moitié du XVI$^{e}$ siècle et arrivé jusqu'à nous dans une copie de 1420, est analogue, mais non identique. L'auteur, anonyme, en partant du *Livre des mestiers*, en tire une œuvre nouvelle. Les thèmes sont à peu près ceux que nous avons déjà cités; il est à souligner toutefois l'introduction des nombres entre deux séries de dialogues. Contrairement au *Livre des mestiers*, conçu aussi bien pour les besoins des marchands et de la bourgeoisie en général, que pour l'éducation des garçons, le destinataire semble être ici plus exactement le public adulte, vues les situations scabreuses souvent commentées. Du point de vue méthodologique, ce qui semble particulièrement intéressant, est le fait que l'auteur se pose le problème de la bonne traduction, en blâmant la simple transposition mot à mot, au profit de l'interprétation du texte, à l'aide des expressions typiques et propres à chaque langue. Voir le passage suivant:

"On dist en romans: 'Comment vous est?' Qui le diroit selonc lez Almans, ilh convenroit dire: 'Comment est ilh aveuc vous?' si qu'il convient tenir le usage et costume de dues parolez" (Gessler 1931: 7). Le français est picard, tandis que le flamand est proche du dialecte du Limbourg.

Un autre témoin de la série est conservé dans un ms. du XV^e^ siècle (Bodleian Lib. d'Oxford), où le dialogue, principe fondamental de la méthode, est remplacé par le monologue de l'auteur, qui donne au lecteur des règles de politesse à l'impératif, selon les thèmes suivants: "[...] saluer ses amis et parents, recevoir des messages, être propre, [...] préparer et servir le dîner, aller à cheval en compagnie de son maître, soigner le cheval" (Meyer 1877: 38–49; Riemens 1924).

Un autre petit manuel français-flamand nommé *Onderrigtingen om de tafel de dienen*, où le dialogue a comme objet les convenances de la table, remonte à la fin du XVI^e^ siècle (Lindemann 1994: 17).

Les titres cités se réfèrent tous au thème de l'école, montrent une volonté d'éducation au sens général, mais font de la politesse le point de départ pour l'apprentissage des langues étrangères.

Les règles de savoir vivre à table, présentées dans le ms. d'Oxford, ont souvent une correspondance point par point dans le *Vocabulair pour apprendre Romain et flameng*, paru à Anvers vers 1500, chez Roland van den Dorpe. On y reconnaît, encore une fois, la marque du *Livre des mestiers*, mais d'autres sources aussi, surtout en ce qui concerne la table, absente jusque là. Il s'agit, plus exactement, de la réduction d'un manuel en trois langues (*Vocabulair pour apprendre Latin, Romain et Flameng*), sorti de l'imprimerie de Adriaen van Liesvelt en 1495 (Riemens 1924: 28–29; Gessler 1931: 43–44; Mantou 1969: 161–162; Claes 1971: 149; Stein 1990: 29–138; Lindemann 1994: 17). Une édition successive en trois langues (remplacement du latin par l'espagnol, ce qui souligne l'importance, à ce moment-là, de cette langue dans les Flandres de Charles I et de Philippe II) est bien connue comme *Vocabulario para aprender Franches Espannol y Flamincq*, Antwerpen 1520, reproposé en 1530 avec peu de modifications.

## 6. Anvers: les *Colloquia* de Noël de Berlaimont

C'est bien à cette date que le plus célèbre des manuels bilingues est imprimé: le *Vocabulare* de Noël de Berlaimont, qui renverse l'ordre traditionnel des langues (français-flamand), en assurant au parlé d'Anvers le rôle principal. La méthode obtiendra un énorme succès tout au long des siècles dans l'Europe entière.

En ce cas, l'auteur est un maître d'école ayant son activité à Anvers, mais d'origine wallonne, qui écrit bien pour ses élèves, mais, plus en général, pour celui qui s'occupe de "mercantie, o prattichi in Corte, o che seguiti la guerra, o che vadi per paesi stranieri" (ed. de 1558).

Les buts sont illustrés dans la deuxième édition, 1536: "Vocabulaire de nouveau ordonne et de rechief recorrige pour aprendre legierment a bien lire escrire et parler François & Flameng lequel est mis tout la pluspart par personnaiges" (Verdeyen 1925: xciv). Ces "personnaiges" sont une nouveauté de l'œuvre, particulière aussi pour ses mesures réduites et pour son format oblong: un livre de poche *ante litteram*, convenant aux voyageurs.

La matière, dans laquelle on perçoit la volonté de former de bons citoyens et de bons croyants, peut être divisée en deux parties. La première est à son tour partagée en quatre chapitres, dont les trois premiers sont des dialogues (banquet, achat, solicitation de paiement), tandis que le quatrième comprend une série de lettres et de documents commerciaux, ce qui confirme la destination fondamentale de l'œuvre. La deuxième partie s'ouvre avec une liste de mots par ordre alphabétique en flamand, continue avec un abrégé de grammaire et de phonologie du français, un certain nombre de prières et de normes fondamentales de la religion chrétienne.

Comme d'habitude, le manuel se modifie au cours des années suivantes, avec une tendance constante à l'expansion, valable aussi pour le nombre des langues: dans sa formule la plus large, on en trouvera huit, tandis que les dialogues seront au nombre de sept. Le développement de la section grammaticale est remarquable aussi. Si l'on considère les langues présentes dans des combinaisons diverses, on peut en compter douze: flamand, français (Anvers 1530), latin, espagnol (Louvain 1551), anglais (Londres 1554), italien (Anvers 1558), allemand (Anvers 1576), portugais (Delft-Amsterdam 1598), tchèque (Leipzig 1602), breton (Morlaix 1626), polonais (Varsovie 1646), suédois (Stockholm–Hamburg vers 1690).

Les élargissements au breton et au suédois sont particulièrement remarquables comme témoins précieux de la circulation européenne de ces langues à une époque assez ancienne.

La formule originale bilingue flamand-français paraîtra encore sous des titres différents (entre-autres: *Cleine Colloquia*; *Cleyn Vocabulaerkens*; *Propos communs ou Colloques*; *Den Kleynen Vocabulaer*), avec révision des thèmes et de la structure, jusqu'en 1703. Toutefois, à partir de 1551 on assistera à un accroissement linguistique remarquable. C'est à ce moment que le manuel devient un répertoire à quatre langues, avec l'addition du latin et de l'espagnol. On apprend de la préface que cette dernière introduction est due à deux auteurs castillans, totalement inconnus.

En revanche, c'est à la plume d'un fameux humaniste, Cornelius Valerius (Wouters) d'Utrecht, professeur à Louvain, qu'on doit la traduction latine. Pendant ce temps, le titre de l'œuvre était devenu *Vocabulaer in vier spraken [...]*, puis (1556) *Dictionarium Quatuor Linguarum*. La remarquable révision intérieure conduira à l'augmentation de la section grammaticale, avec l'insertion d'un "Modus legendi atque scribendi linguae Hispanicae", qui n'est que l'accommodement d'un autre manuel, anonyme, paru l'année d'avant à Louvain: l'*Util y breve institución para aprender los principios y fundamentos de la lengua Hespañola*. La révision du texte à cette occasion semble être due à un certain Francisco de Villalobos, bon connaisseur du flamand, mais "castillien natif de Toledo, homme tres-expert & éloquent en sa langue maternelle (Verdeyen 1925: xxiii; Lope Blanch 1990: 25). L'identité du personnage, ainsi que l'attribution, est douteuse: il pourrait s'agir du médecin personnel de Charles V, Francisco López de Villalobos, qui cependant est né è Valladolid (Gallina 1959: 75).

Une édition bilingue qui n'eut ni succès ni suite (Roberts 1970: 34; Stein 1990: 41) fut compilée en 1554 à partir de l'extension espagnole de 1551, avec l'anglais en plus et les trois autres langues en moins.

En 1558 on voit pour la première fois l'italien dans le manuel: cette langue remplace le flamand dans l'édition d'Anvers de Jan Verwithagen, qui durant la même année l'introduit dans une autre, privée du latin (fl., fr., esp., it.) et publiée jusqu'en 1632. L'auteur de la traduction fut Anton Maria Calabria (Gallina 1959: 75).

Une autre version en quatre langues, dans laquelle l'anglais remplace l'espagnol, dérive de l'édition de 1558, avec le latin. Il s'agirait de la source d'un manuel fr., angl., fl., paru à Londres en 1569, aujourd'hui disparu.

Pendant les années suivantes, les manuels en quatre langues montrent un enrichissement progressif de la matière, avec l'introduction des préceptes moraux, bientôt disparus, mais surtout (éd. G. de Salenson, Gent 1568, avec fl., fr., esp., it.), d'un petit vocabulaire espagnol-flamand et de deux sections grammaticales (conjugaisons et règles phonétiques des quatre langues intéressées), dus à Gabriel Meurier (Vaganay 1906; Bourland 1938: 139–152). Les conjugaisons seront supprimées dans l'édition de 1576, mais les règles de prononciation seront présentes encore dans l'édition De Longhis (Bologna 1692).

Les versions en six langues (addition de l'allemand et de l'anglais, substitution aux "Conjugaisons" de Meurier des seules formes principales d'*être* et *avoir*, réduction des règles de prononciation, suppression des prières et des préceptes moraux) dérivent ensuite des manuels avec fl., fr., esp., it. Le titre aussi va changer, devenant: *Colloques ou Dialogues avec un Dictionnaire en six langues*.

Le même imprimeur, Heyndrickx, introduit deux nouveaux dialogues, d'auteur anonyme, en 1579 et deux autres en 1583. On arrive ainsi à la structure-type des manuels successifs en sept et huit langues.

L'imprimeur qui réunit pour la première fois en une seule œuvre toutes les traductions connues jusqu'à cette époque-là fut Trognaesius. En 1586 il produira à Anvers le *Colloquia et Dictionariolum Septem Linguarum*.

L'adjonction du portugais (1598), réalisée par Schinckel à Delft, donnera lieu à la plus grande extension, mise en vente à Amsterdam (Bart Rossebastiano 1975: 31–85). L'auteur, inconnu, de la traduction portugaise doit être chezché dans le milieu juif d'Amsterdam, qui s'était constitué à partir de 1498, à la suite de l'exode forcé de la péninsule ibérique.

La réduction anonyme italo-portugaise, étudiée par Erilde Reali (1963: 227–276) dérive de cette rédaction.

La réalisation en huit langues n'effaça pas la précédente avec cinq versions, qui parut à Londres chez George Bishop le Jeune en 1578, avec un titre curieux, qui naît de toute évidence d'une superposition: *Dictionnaire, Colloques ou Dialogues en quatre langues: Flamen, Françoys, Espagnol et Italien with the Englishe to be added thereto*. C'est de là que sont tirés, en ajoutant le latin, les *Familiaria Colloquia* (Anvers 1584).

En 1602 la série sera augmentée à Leipzig d'une autre langue, le tchèque, et, en 1646, à Varsovie, du polonais. Les deux éditions portent le titre *Hexaglosson*, qui rappelle celui de l'édition publiée à Bâle par Froeben en 1585.

Pendant ce temps l'œuvre avait été revue encore une fois dans les adaptations en allemand-français (*De new Barlamont*, Cologne 1587, Delf 1645), anglais-français (*The French Schoolmaistr*, imprimé probablement en Angleterre en 1565) de Claude Holyband, alias de Sainliens (Niederehe 1976: 177), anglais-espagnol (*The Spanish Schoolmaster*, Londres, 1591) de William Stepney (Bourland 1933: 238–318; Steiner 1970: 36–37).

La renommée du Berlaimont continue pendant le siècle suivant. En 1626, un remaniement français-breton parait à Morlaix. Il sera proposé de nouveau à Quimper en 1759, puis encore en 1878 et 1885. L'auteur de la traduction bretonne fut Guillaume Quicquer de Roscoff. Dans cette série, le latin est introduit en 1632.

Vers 1690 paraîtra encore une version en quatre langues (lat., fr., all., suéd.), réduction d'une édition en six langues, avec suédois et sans espagnol, italien, anglais.

Entre-temps des remaniements ultérieurs non utilisés dans toute la tradition (ils n'ont pas lieu, par exemple, dans les manuels en sept et huit langues), avaient beaucoup changé l'œuvre. Premièrement l'ordre alphabétique du dictionnaire, plus selon le flamand, mais selon le latin, puis la révision du *Petit Traité* de Meurier, adapté aux exigences de l'apprentissage du français et de l'italien, au détriment de l'espagnol, du flamand et de l'allemand. Voir l'éd. de Stoer (Genève 1652, lat., all, fr., it.).

Après plus d'un siècle et demi d'expansion, le manuel s'achève. Son succès, ouvert à l'enseigne de l'"unicorno d'oro" dans l'éclat de la ville d'Anvers, riche et cultivée à la suite des commerces impériaux, le long des côtes brumeuses de la Mer du Nord, un regard méfiant aussi bien sur l'Europe Centrale que sur la Méditerranée, s'amenuise dans le port de Hambourg, encore à l'affût d'un faible espoir de survie dans le maigre marché suédois. Il jouira d'un dernier regain de vitalité, comme on l'a dit, en Bretagne, où, conduit à servir l'échange local franco-breton, il sera développé et remis à jour jusqu'au moins en 1885.

En Italie, l'œuvre obtiendra peu de succès et sera peu diffusée, comme le montrent la rareté, le retard et la corruption des imprimés. On connaît: un *Sex Linguarum* (Venezia 1634), deux *Septem Linguarum* (Padova 1592 et Venezia 1606), cinq *Octo Linguarum* (quatre à Venezia: 1627, 1646, 1656 (voir éd. Rizza 1996) et 1677, un à Bologna 1692).

L'Espagne, dominatrice des Flandres au moment du projet du manuel, bientôt linguistiquement présente dans l'œuvre, ne sera pas passionnée par le Berlaimont: on ne connaît aucune édition imprimée dans la péninsule ibérique. Il en avait déjà été ainsi pour le *Solenissimo Vochabuolista*.

Pourtant celle-ci n'est que la ligne principale de l'œuvre. Son influence continuera au cours des siècles suivants, en intéressant jusqu'aux langues de l'Asie et de l'Afrique. Voir le manuel de Franciscus de Houtman, *Spraeck ende woordboeck in de Maleysche en de Madagaskarsche talen*, imprimé à Amsterdam en 1603 chez J. E. Cloppenburch: on y utilise les quatre premiers dialogues du Berlaimont! Pareillement, Cornelis Houtman avait publié en 1598 le *Journal du voyageur de l'Inde Orientale faict par les Navires Hollandois*, où l'on pouvait lire les noms et les descriptions de bien des fruits exotiques.

Parmi les dérivés du Berlaimont je cite encore les *Familiar dialogues* de J. Bellot (français-anglais), parus en 1586 (Lindemann 1994: 17).

On retrouve l'empreinte du Berlaimont sur *Den Nieuwen Dictionaris oft Schadt der Duytsche en Spaensche Talen* de A. de la Porte (Anvers 1659) et dans plusieurs autres dictionnaires de langue hollandaise (voir le très important *Thesaurus Teutonicae Linguae* de 1573).

L'idée fondamentale – le dialogue comme base de l'enseignement des langues – se prolongera dans les siècles suivants: voir les œuvres du XIX$^{e}$ siècle, comme le *Manuel du Voyageur* de Madame de Genlis, ou les *Elementi di conversazione in italiano, francese, tedesco, inglese* de Perrin.

A la même période, Gabriel Meurier, dont le traité de grammaire fut introduit dans la structure du Berlaimont, avait publié d'autres méthodes utiles pour l'apprentissage des langues étrangères, toujours basées sur la technique demande-réponse: parmi elles les *Colloques ou nouvelle invention de propos familiers: Non moins utiles que tres necessaires, pour facillement apprendre François et Flameng*, Anvers, 1557 (Mantou 1969: 158–169; Van Selm 1973: 217–225).

Du même il y a également deux petits traités destinés à l'éducation de la jeunesse, un pour les garçons (*Le perroquet mignon des petits enfants françois-flameng*, Anvers 1580), et un autre pour les jeunes filles (*La guirlande des jeunes fulles, en François et Flamen*, Anvers 1564).

Le fait qu'on ait confié aux fameux Plantin, imprimeur de nombreuses publications de ce genre, la rédaction française du chapitre "la typographie" dans l'œuvre de Jean Grévin, *La premiere, et la seconde partie des dialogues françois, pour les jeunes enfans*, imprimée en 1567, nous montre combien d'attention on accordait à Anvers à la compétence linguistique, nécessaire à la précision du vocabulaire, spécialement des technicismes. La traduction flamande du texte français de Plantin fut exécutée par Corneille de Bomberghe et Peter Kerkhof. Ici, outre les dialogues sur les thèmes habituels, on ajoute des sujets nouveaux: l'étude, le livre, la musique.

## 7. Divers

Je ne m'étendrai pas longtemps sur ces derniers manuels, ni sur ceux que je citerai cidessous, car le bilinguisme ne se transforme pas, selon mes informations, en multilinguisme dans les développements successifs.

Je ne citerai donc que l'ouvrage de John Minsheu, *A Dictionarie in Spanish and English*, imprimée à Londres en1599, pour rappeler qu'on trouve là une longue série de dialogues après le vocabulaire et la grammaire: comme dans le mss. de Georg von Nürnberg!

Pour ce qui est de l'espagnol, je cite encore le *Vocabulario de los vocablos que mas comunmente se suelen vsar. Puestos por orden del Abecedario, en Frances, y su declaracion en Español. El estilo de escriuir, hablar y pronunciar las dos lenguas, el Frances en Castellano, y el Castellano en Frances [...] Ahora nueuamente recopilado por Iaques de Liaño criado de la reyna nuestra señora*, imprimé en 1565 par Francisco de Cormellas et Pedro de Robles, qui la même année proposent aussi la *Grammatica con reglas mvy prouechosas y necessarias para aprender a leer y escriuir la lengua Francesa*, de Baltasar Sotomayor. Par la suite, Alcalá de Henares deviendra l'un des centres typographiques de référence pour la production des manuels didactiques.

Juan Sotomayor remaniera l'œuvre, en substituant l'allemand au français et en transformant le titre: *Llave capital con la qual se abre el curioso y rico thesoro de la lengua Castellana [...] la qual Gramatica va en forma de dialogos*, Lipsia 1706 (Garcia Bustillo 1983: 95).

C'est avec beaucoup de regret que je passe sur les *Sinonima variationum sententiarum eleganti stilo constructa ex italico sermone in valentinum* de Jeronimo Amiguet (Valencia, Cristofol Coffman, 1501, it.-cat.), traduction des *Synonyma* de Fieschi (Colón & Soberanas 1985: 79).

Le français et l'anglais sont présents dans les œuvres de Pierre Valence, *Introductions en françois*, de 1528, l'*Esclersissement de la langue françoyse composé par maistre Iehan Palsgraue Angloys natyf de Londres et gradue de Paris* de 1530, pour l'éducation de Mary, sœur du roi d'Angleterre, Henry VIII, en vue de son mariage avec le roi de France, Louis XII (Stein 1985: 121–139). Même objectif dans *An introductorie for to lerne to rede to pronounce and to speke Frenche trewly*, parue en 1532 à Londres. C'est là que sera imprimé en 1553 *A treatise in English and Frenche right necessary and proffitable for al young children [...], made by Peter du Ploiche teacher of the same dwelling in Trinities lane at the signe of the Rose*, composé plus simplement pour les gens du peuple, par un maître, qui, comme Georg von Nürnberg et l'auteur anonyme du *Vocabulario Nuovo*, note son adresse pour diffuser son produit et son travail.

Toujours au XVI$^{e}$ siècle, un traducteur anonyme avait mis en français et en flamand les dialogues latins de l'humaniste espagnol Juan Vives, connus comme *Exercitatio linguae latinae*, déjà imprimés à Bâle en 1539, devenus *Les dialogues de M. Jean Loys Vivès translatés de Latin en François et Flamen, pour la commodité de la jeunesse*, Anvers 1562. Oratio Toscanella en rédigera la version italienne (*Flores Italici, ac latini idiomatis [...] a Horatio Tuscanelle italice interpretati*, Venezia 1570). Ceux-ci furent aussi utilisés pendant longtemps; nous en connaissons une édition datée de 1742, avec changement dans le nom de l'auteur: *Colloqui di Gio. Lodovico Vives latini e italiani tradotti da un sacerdote fiorentino per esercizio dell'una e dell'altra lingua*. Dans cette édition, ainsi que dans l'imprimé florentin de 1585, accru des notes "doctissimi viri Petri Mottae Complutensi", on trouve à la fin un petit vocabulaire lat.-it., qui devient en 1619 lat.-esp., sous la plume de Juan Ramirez.

Les dialogues, qui ont peu à voir avec ceux des œuvres précédemment citées, traiten toutefois les thèmes habituels: les salutations, l'école, les repas, la maison [...]. Ainsi que dans le Berlaimont et le *Livre des mestiers*, les dialogues sont mis dans la bouche de personnages indiqués avec leur nom: ce qui témoigne de la diffusion du système.

On trouve encore une bonne phraséologie utilisée pour l'enseignement du latin dans l'œuvre d'un humaniste de Velletri, Antonio Mancinelli, qui composa le *Latini Sermonis Emporium*, imprimé en 1499. Dans ce cas, le 'magister' prononce la phrase en langue vulgaire, tandis que l'élève la traduit en latin (Giovanardi 1994: 464).

Analogue le recueil de phrases qui complète *Il "glossario Latino-Sabino" di Ser Iacopo Ursello da Roccantica*, de la fin du XV^e^ s. ou commencement du suivant (Vignuzzi 1984: 131).

On trouve une telle phraséologie dans beaucoup de mss. des siècles XIV^e^–XV^e^, dont la plupart encore inédits, comme le latin-catalan conservé à Barcelone (Bibl. Centrale) et d'autres latin-italien. Il serait trop long d'en donner ici la liste (voir Rossebastiano Bart 1986).

Avant de terminer, je voudrais encore citer le *Dictionarium iuventuti studiosae* (latin-portugais) de Jeronimo Cardoso (Coimbra 1551), où le lexique est en ordre méthodique, suivi par une phraséologie rudimentaire.

Les manuels que j'ai mentionnés ne sont que quelques exemples de la très riche production didactique que le XVI^e^ siècle introduit dans le monde moderne comme héritage direct ou indirect du Moyen Âge. Le manque de temps et encore davantage le manque d'espace m'obligent à terminer ici mon exposé.

## 8. Bibliographie


Adamović, Milan. 1975. "Ein italienisch-türkisches Sprachbuch aus den Jahren 1525–1530". *Wiener Zeitschrift für die Kunde des Morgenlandes* 67.217–247.

Banfi, Emanuele. 1985. *Quattro 'lessici neogreci' della turcocrazia*. Milano: Unicopli.

Barnils, Pere. 1916. *Vocabulari català – alemany* de l'any 1502. Barcelona: Institut d'Estudis Catalans.

Bischoff, Bernhard. 1961. "The Study of Foreign Languages in the Middle Ages". *Speculum* 36.209–224.

Bourland, Caroline B. 1933. "The Spanish School-Master and the Polyglot Derivatives of Noël de Berlaimont's Vocabulare". *Revue Hispanique* 81.283–318.

–. 1938. "Algo sobre Gabriel Meurier Maestro de español de Amberes (1521–1597?)". *Hispanic Review* 6.139–152.

Bradley, Henry. 1900. *Dialogues in French and English by William Caxton*. London: Kegan & Co.

Claes, Franz. 1971. "Lijst van Nederlandse Woordenlijsten en Woordenboeken gedrukt tot 1600". *De Gulden Passer* 59.130–229.

– & Peter Bakema. 1995. *A Bibliography of Dutch Dictionaries*. Tübingen: Niemeyer.

Colón, Germà & Amadeu J. Soberanas. 1985. *Panorama de la lexicografia catalana. De les glosses medievals a Pompeu Fabra*. Barcelona: Biblioteca Universitaria.

Cortelazzo, Manlio. 1979. "La conoscenza della lingua turca in Italia nel '500". *Il Veltro* 23.133–141.

Gallina, Annamaria. 1959. *Contributi alla storia della lessicografia italo-spagnola dei secoli XVI e XVII*. Firenze: Olschki.

Gamberini, Silvio. 1970. *Lo studio dell'Italiano in Inghilterra nel '500 e nel '600*. Messina & Firenze: D'Anna.

Garcia Bustillo, Maria Guadalupe. 1983. *Contribución a la bibliografía lingüistica española hasta el siglo XVIII*. Salamanca (Thèse).

Gessler, Jean. 1931. *Le livre des mestiers et ses dérivés*. Bruges: s. e.

Giovanardi, Claudio. 1994. "Il bilinguismo italiano-latino del Medioevo e del Rinascimento". *Storia della Lingua Italiana*, vol. II: *Scritto e parlato*, 435–467. Torino: Einaudi.

Giustiniani, Vito R. 1987. *Adam von Rottweil. Deutsch-Italienischer Sprachführer*. Tübingen: Narr.

Holtus, Günter & Wolfgang Schweickard. 1985. "Elemente gesprochener Sprache in einem venezianischen Text von 1424: das italienisch-deutsche Sprachbuch von Georg von Nürnberg". *Gesprochenes Italienisch in Geschichte und Gegenwart*. Tübingen: Niemeyer.

Kresalkova, Jitka. 1984. *Il vocabolario italiano-latino-ceco-tedesco.* Bergamo: Istituto Universitario di Bergamo.

Lindemann, Margarete. 1994. *Die französischen Wörterbücher von den Anfängen bis 1600.* Tübingen: Niemeyer.

Lope Blanch, Juan M. 1990. *Estudios de Historia Lingüística Hispánica.* Madrid: Arco/Libros.

Mantou, Reine. 1969. "Notes sur quelques manuels de conversation 'français-flamand' du XIV^e^ au XVI^e^ siècle". *Mémoires et Publications de la Société des Sciences, des Arts et des Lettres du Hainaut* 82.157–197.

Meyer, Paul. 1877. "Notice du manuscrit Miscell. 278 de la Bibliothèque Bodléienne, à Oxford". *Bulletin de la Société des anciens textes français* 3.38–40.

Niederehe, Hans-Josef, éd. 1976. *Edmund Stengel. Chronologisches Verzeichnis Französischer Grammatiken vom Ende des 14. bis zum Ausgange des 18. Jahrhunderts.* Nachdruck, mit einem Anhang. Amsterdam: Benjamins.

Pausch, Oskar. 1972. *Das älteste italienisch-deutsche Sprachbuch.* Wien: Bohlaus.

Pohl, Heinz Dieter. 1976. *Das Italienisch-kroatische Glossar Ms. Selden Supra 95.* Wien: Österreichischen Akademie der Wissenschaften.

Pozzi, Mario. 1994. *Antonio Pigafetta. Il primo viaggio intorno al mondo.* Padova: Neri Pozza.

Presa, Giovanni. 1975. "D'un inedito Vocabularium latino, italiano, ceco e tedesco del secolo XV". *Aevum* 49.166–175.

Quémada, Bernard. 1968. *Les dictionnaires du français moderne.* Paris: Didier.

Reali, Ecilde. 1963. "La prima 'grammatica' italo-portoghese". *Annali dell'Istituto Universitario Orientale di Napoli, Sezione Romanza* 5.227–276.

Riemens, Kornelius-J. 1924. *Etude sur le texte fançais du Livre des mestiers, livre scolaire français-flamand du XIV^e^ siècle.* Paris: L'Arnette.

—. 1929. "Bijdrage tot de Bibliografie van Noël van Berlaimont". *Het Boek* 18.11–22.

Rizza, Riccardo, éd. 1996. *Colloquia, et dictionariolum octo linguarum.* Viareggio-Lucca: Baroni.

Roberts, R. J. 1970. "Two Early English-Spanish vocabularies". *The British Museum Quarterly* 34.86–91.

Rossebastiano, Alda. 1992. "Bilinguismo italiano-tedesco nei manuali didattici del Cinquecento per lo studio delle lingue straniere". *Fremdsprachenunterricht 1500–1800* éd. par Konrad Schröder, 157–170. Wiesbaden: Harrassowitz.

Rossebastiano Bart, Alda. 1971. *Jntroito e Porta vocabolario italiano-tedesco "compiuto per Meistro Adamo de Roduila, 1477 adì 12 Augusto".* Torino: Bottega d'Erasmo (rist. an.).

—. 1975. "I 'Colloquia' di Noël de Berlaimont nella versione contenente il portoghese". *Annali dell'istituto Universitario Orientale di Napoli, Sezione Romanza* 17.31–85.

—. 1977. "Antichi vocabolari plurilingui d'uso popolare: la tradizione del 'Solenissimo Vochabuolista'". *De Gulden Passer* 55.67–152.

—. 1983. *Vocabolari veneto-tedeschi del secolo XV.* Savigliano: L'Artistica.

—. 1984. *I 'Dialoghi' di Giorgio da Norimberga.* Savigliano: L'Artistica.

—. 1984a. *Antichi vocabolari plurilingui d'uso popolare: la tradizione del 'Solenissimo Vochabuolista'.* Alessandria: Edizioni dell'Orso.

—. 1986. "Alle origini della lessicografia italiana". *Lexicographie au moyen-âge* éd. par Charles Buridant, 113–156. Lille: Presses Universitaires.

Scarpa, Emanuele. 1991. "Uno sconosciuto glossarietto italiano-tedesco". *Studi di Filologia Italiana* 49.59–74.

Stein, Gabriele. 1985. *The English Dictionary before Cawdrey.* Tübingen: Niemeyer.

—. 1990. "The emerging role of English in the Dictionaries of Renaissance Europe". *Folia Linguistica Historica* 9.29–138.

Steiner, Robert J. 1970. *Two centuries of Spanish and English Bilingual Lexicography 1590–1800.* The Hague & Paris: Mouton.

Teza, Emilio. 1893. *Un piccolo glossario italiano e arabico del Quattrocento.* Roma: Rendiconti della Reale Accademia dei Lincei. Classe di scienze filologiche 5:2.77–88.

Vaganay, Hugues. 1906. "Le vocabulaire français du XVI^e^ siècle et deux lexicographes flamands du même siècle". *Congrès international pour l'extension et la culture de la langue française.* Paris: Klincksieck.

Van Passen, Anne-Marie. 1981. "Appunti sui dizionari italo-francesi apparsi prima della fine del Settecento". *Studi di lessicografia italiana* 3.29–65.

Van Selm, Bert. 1973. "Some early editions of Gabriel Meurier's school-books". *Quaerendo* 3.217–225.

Verdeyen, René. 1925–1935. *Colloquia et Dictionariolum septem linguarum.* Antwerpen & 's Gravenhage: Verreniging der Antwerpsche Bibliophilen.

Vignuzzi, Ugo. 1984. *Il glossario latino-sabino di Ser Iacopo Ursello da Roccantica.* Perugia: Edizioni Università per Stranieri.

*Alda Rossebastiano, Turin (Italie)*

# 95. The teaching of Italian in 15th- and 16th-century Europe

1. 15th-century Venetian-German manuals
2. From the *Solenissimo vochabuolista* to plurilingual dictionaries
3. Italian abroad in the 16th century: Germany and Spain
4. France, Spain and the Slav world
5. Bibliography

## 1. 15th-century Venetian-German manuals

It is a well-known fact that the Italian grammars available in print in the first half of the 15th century were not designed for didactic exploitation and use in schools. Such works were aimed at men of letters and writers. If one is looking for the first texts directed at the practical learning of the Italian language, one must seek elsewhere.

There already existed Venetian-German manuals conceived for a public of merchants in the first half of the 15th century. Such works, which aroused great interest right from the first studies carried out in this area by Mussafia (1873), take us to Venice, a city with a flourishing activity in trade and commerce, an attraction for foreigners, a plurilingual city *par excellence*. The oldest of these small bilingual manuals has been handed down to us in the form of two codices which are preserved respectively in Vienna and in Munich (see Emery 1947; Hoybye 1964 and 1974; Pausch 1972; Zambon 1974; Rossebastiano 1983, 1984a: 25–31 and 1984b). It is attributed to a George of Nuremberg, whether this be a real name or a pseudonym. In the work itself, the writer declares that he taught lessons to young Venetians in the Campo di San Bartolomeo, near the Fondaco dei Tedeschi. There also exist other manuscript versions of this small manual. In these versions, the Italian part of the text, which was heavily Venetian in the original, is written in Tuscan or in the dialect of the Padua-Verona district (see Rossebastiano 1984b). The work, which consists of short bilingual conversations, with a parallel text in German, was principally for Italians who wanted to learn German. Many of the topics of the conversations centre on bargaining, bartering, prices and selling. It is quite obvious that the motivation is eminently practical. Here is a snippet from one of the dialogues: "Egli è una bella cosa sapere tedesco. Per amore del fondaco tu dei imparare forte" ('Knowing German is a good thing. For the love of the 'fondaco' you must learn well') (I quote from Rossebastiano 1984: 28). On the other hand, for those Germans who wished to learn Italian, we presume that a textbook was published for their use before 1500 on the basis of the handful of mutilated copies that have survived. Rossebastiano (1984: 35) quotes a few extracts: a verb paradigm, a number of exemplary phrases or expressions in common use, a few formulaic greetings.

## 2. From the *Solenissimo vochabuolista* to plurilingual dictionaries

In 1477, Adam von Rottwil, a printer who came from Swabia, published in Venice the first edition of a text which was destined to achieve great success, withholding the name of the author. The *Introito e porta, o Solenissimo vochabuolista* (1479) aimed at those "che voleno imparare e comprender todesco a latino cioè italiano, el quale è utilissimo per quele che vadeno a pratichando per el mundo el sia todesco o taliano » ('who want to learn and understand German and Latin, that is Italian, a work which is extremely useful for those who travel round the world practicing both German and Italian') (Rossebastiano 1984: 45). The main objective of the *Solenissimo vochabuolista* is to teach the foreign language, whether it be German or Italian: "Anchora puo' imparare todesco el talian, el todesco puo' imparare talian" ('An Italian may learn German and a German may learn Italian') (ibid). The work is presented as a systematic dictionary, with the addition of fixed expressions, as in a sort of modern phrase book (the comparison was made by Carla Marello 1989: 10). The items are listed under fifty odd categories, such as "de Dio e de la trinità e dela potencia e richeza" ('of god and of the Trinity and of power and of riches'), or "dela citade e deli iudixi e deli offici" ('of the city and of the law and of the offices'), and "del pan e del vin e tute cose che se mangia" ('of bread, of wine and of all things we eat') (Rossebastiano 1984a: 208–212). The *Solenissimo vochabuolista* went through an enormous number of reprints and revisions, becoming one of the most renowned multilingual dictionaries of the 15th century. The early editions, however, included only two languages, Italian and German, in that order, or, to be more precise, with an Italo-Venetian dialect and Bavarian. In the course of time, the importance and tradition of the *Solenissimo vochabuolista* grew, as we stated earlier, and the plurilingual editions appeared (the whole picture may be found in Rossebastiano 1984a). The linguistic format of the Italian section gradually abandoned the dialects of the early 15th century editions. 1526 saw the publication, yet again in Venice, of the first five-language-edition (Latin, Italian, French, Spanish, German). Various editions printed in diverse European cities added new languages, bringing the total to four, five, six, and even eight. Thus the first Italian-German dictionary was transformed into a plurilingual dictionary. Dictionaries of this type constitute one of the important learning devices in use in the 15th and 16th centuries. Take *Calepino*, the Latin dictionary produced by Ambrogio da Calepio (c. 1435–c. 1510), the first edition of which appeared in Reggio Emilia in 1502 and which was reprinted in Venice in 1509. The main objective of this work was to furnish the equivalent of Latin words and examples of use from classical writers. Although achieving this goal in a concise manner, the 1588 Basel edition actually managed to provide the counterpart of the Latin item in a grand total of eleven modern languages. *Calepino* helped people to read classical and modern Latin authors; at the same time, however, it could also be used, albeit in a simplified fashion, as a dictionary for modern idioms, employing Latin (the international language *par excellence*) as the search language. With regard to tools originally planned for the study of Latin and then equipped with foreign languages to increase the possible uses they could be put to and boost their commercial success, we may cite the alphabetically arranged collection of Ciceronian expressions published in 1535 by Mario Nizzoli (1498–1576). The 1606 Venetian edition of the work, which was entitled *Thesaurus ciceronianus*, was furnished with the corresponding expressions in Italian, French and Spanish (see Gallina 1959: 205–218). Space does not permit us to dwell on the plurilingual dictionaries which included Italian. Of those printed in Italy, I will only mention the *Dittionario volgare et latino* by Orazio Toscanella, a polygraph, (the only known edition is Venice 1568: see Gallina 1959: 151–159). This work contains lists of foreign words, almost abbreviated short dictionaries, the richest of which is the Spanish inventory.

Some of the works published outside Italy and including Italian as one of their languages are, as we stated above, extremely important. Italian was sometimes included when producing the revised edition of successful works. Noel de Berlaimont (or Barlaimont, Berlemont etc.), for instance, printed a bilingual Flemish-French dictionary in Antwerp around 1530. The oldest known copy of this work is a revised edition dated 1536. The work was enlarged at the death of the author: the inventory of the editions that have appeared include versions in four or more languages, the maximum being eight, in various combinations (see the outline drawn up by Gallina 1959: 87–91). Hadrianus Junius (1511–1575) published his *Nomenclator omniun rerum propria nomina variis linguis explicata* [...] in Antwerp in 1567. The languages comprised Greek, German, Flemish, French and Italian. Editions of this work with the addition of Italian appeared in Antwerp, Paris, Frankfurt, Cologne, Lyons, Geneva. A survey of the towns in which the above-mentioned works were published gives us an idea of which places were the most active in publishing works concerning languages: to some extent, these were also locations which had a special interest in Italian. Finally, we may refer to instruments of study which were not, strictly speaking, linguistic but which could be adapted to the exigencies of plurilingualism. One of the works of this type which Gallina (1959: 49–55) brings to our attention is the *Historiae animalium* by Konrad von Gesner (1516–1565), which came out in Zurich in 1551–58. These contain the names of the animals in many languages. Moreover, this is what happens in the *Commentari al Dioscoride*, the most important Italian treatise on pharmacy and botany of the 16th century, written by Pier Andrea Mattioli (1500–1577) from Siena: after having dealt with a plant or an animal, a suggestion for the name of that plant or beast is provided in various languages; besides Italian, we find Latin, Greek, Arabic, German, Spanish and French.

## 3. Italian abroad in the 16th century: Germany and Spain

Before examining the tools employed by foreigners to learn Italian in the 16th century, the preliminary observation should be made that Tuscan enjoyed considerable international prestige, not the least reason being that its literature had a high reputation and was the object of imitation, for example through the success of Petrarchism. Migliorini (1978: 379) points out that Charles V could speak Italian, that Francis I conversed with Benvenuto Cellini in Italian, that Elizabeth of England could write letters in Italian (see also Fessia 1939–40: 230–234). To Elizabeth, Michelangelo Florio, father of the more famous John, (see Pellegrini 1954: 88–89 and Agricola 1969) dedicated his Italian translation of *Metallurgia* by Agricola. Jane Grey, the unfortunate 'queen for seven days', had studied Italian under the guidance of Michelangelo himself (see Pellegrini 1954: 91). Finally, as is well known, Montaigne wrote part of his travel journal in Italian. Books were published in Italian in Paris and in London. The knowledge of Italian was fostered by the presence of Italian intellectuals abroad, of exiles who sympathised with the Reformation and who had fled the Inquisition, of princesses who had married into foreign courts, or, vice-versa, of foreigners who had married into Italian courts (see the concise grammar in manuscript form written for Joan of Austria, wife to Francesco de' Medici: see Bonomi 1987).

We will now consider the production of bilingual dictionaries and grammars in the principal European nations, in which Italian is present as a language (see Marello 1989: 10–17; Tavoni 1990: 206–207, 212, 242–245). With regard to Germany, we have already referred to the vigorous tradition of bilingual glossaries. However, the first real Italian-German dictionary to appear was Hulsius's 1605 *opus* (see Tancke 1984 and Bray 1988). Turning to Spain, it is worth remembering that after having published the Sicilian translation of Nebrija's Latin dictionary in Venice in 1519, Christoforo de Escobar published another work in Venice, in 1520, the *Vocabularium ex latino sermone in Siciliensem et hispaniensem denuo traductum*. Escobar was a Spaniard and a pupil of Nebrija's, who later moved to Sicily, and even the 1520 dictionary is built along the lines of Nebrija's model (see Gallina 1959: 17–24). G. M. Alessandri published his *Il paragon della lingua toscana e castigliana* in Naples in 1560. This work stems from the close living proximity of Italians and Spaniards in the Kingdom of Naples. Of greater interest are those works published outside Italy, since these were undoubtedly destined for foreign consumption. An important bilingual dictionary by Cristobal de las Casas came out in Spain in 1570, the *Vocabulario de las dos lenguas Toscana y castellana*. It went through many editions, and was also published in Venice in 1576 (Gallina 1959: 163–180). The dedication written by las Casas presents the work as an instrument which is suitable both for Spaniards who wish to learn Italian and for Italians who desire to study Spanish. He insists most strongly on the interest aroused in Spain by Italian books. The dictionary, which is Italian-Spanish and Spanish-Italian, has an extremely simple structure, especially in the first section: each Italian word is furnished with a Spanish correspondent which almost always consists of a single Spanish word, no distinction of meanings being made. In those cases where a word has more than one meaning, the author prefers to multiply the lexemes; for example, the Italian item *capo* is multiplied by three: 1. *capo* = *cabeza*; 2. *capo* = *principe*; 3. *capo* = *guia*. The Spanish-Italian section, on the contrary, presents a variety of equivalents; for instance *guia* = *capo, condotta, duca, duce, guida, guidamento, scorta*. Example sentences are never provided, nor are examples given either of usage or from authors.

## 4. France, Spain and the Slav world

Those readers interested in France may consult the fundamental bibliography by Bingen (1987), which contains not only didactic works, but also French annotated editions of Italian classics and bilingual editions. The first grammar written in Italian is the one by Jean-Pierre de Mesmes, *La Grammaire italienne composée en françois* , which came out in Paris in 1548 (see Bingen 1984 and 1987: 175). The first Italian-French bilingual dictionaries (without therefore taking multilingual dictionaries into consideration) appeared quite late: Pannonius's *Petit vocabulaire en langue françoise et italienne* (Lyon, 1578) and Giovanni Antonio Fenice's (Phénice, Félis) *Dictionnaire françois et italian* (Morges and Paris, 1584) (see van Passen 1981: 31–32; Bingen 1987: 97–110).

The range of instruments available to English learners of Italian was indeed wide. We need only quote Yates (1983: 164) to bear this point out:

> The learning of languages was more essential to the Elisabethan than to the modern Englishman for the

simple reason that in those days English was a language spoken only in England.

In her work, she quotes one of Florio's mini-dialogues: "English is an language that wyl do you good in England, but passe Douer it is woorth nothing" (Yates 1983: 165). According to Aquilecchia (1953: 167) the Elisabethan aristocracy did not learn Italian to satisfy the needs imposed by commerce but in response to 'the dictates of public life'. In other words, it was a cultural fashion which the upper classes adhered to strongly. Thus, when Giordano Bruno went to England there was no need for him to learn English (see Yates 1983: 165). In the third dialogue of the *Cena delle Ceneri* we learn that after Bruno had been in England a year he could still understand only a few words of English because all the gentlemen with whom he conversed knew Latin or Spanish or Italian. The high quantity and quality of the materials available for the study of Italian are due mainly to John Florio (c. 1553–1625), an author whose prime importance in the history of lexicography is attributable to the publishing of *A Worlde of Wordes, or Most copious, and exact Dictionaire in Italian and English* (London 1598), which contained approximately 45,000 words taken from seventy-two works in Italian declared in the list of authors quoted (Gamberini 1970: 95; reprinted in facsimile: see Florio 1972). The modified version of this work became the *Queen Anna's New World of Words*, London 1611. It comprised approximately 70,000 words, taken from 252 Italian works, and with a significant increase in the number of authors quoted (see Gamberini 1970: 95; O'Connor 1990: 19–44). The two dictionaries by Florio are of enormous importance for Italian lexicography in general, since they are antecedents of the dictionary produced by the Accademia della Crusca in 1612, and their salient feature is their absolute independence of what will become the canon of Florentine lexicography, destined to dominate Italy. The sources which Florio draws from include the oldest dictionaries in existence, both monolingual and bilingual, such as the *Fabrica del mondo* by Alunno (which is, I believe, what inspired the name *A Worlde of Wordes*) and the Spanish dictionary by las Casas. Other sources include practical writers, such as the authors of cookery books, falconry, horse-riding, in addition, obviously, to literary authors, starting with Petrarch, with a dramatic increase in their number in the 1611 *New World*. Florio satisfies the prevailing taste for contemporary works by including the *Cena delle Ceneri* and other works by Giordano Bruno, as well as works of the historian Paolo Paruta and of the preacher Francesco Panigarola. Suffice it to compare Florio's table of authors with that of the Accademia della Crusca to see just how great the difference between these two influential dictionaries is. The equivalents for the Italian words furnished by Florio often take the shape of a real and complete definition, with a great depth of conceptual detail and close scrutiny of the different meanings a lexeme has, without, however, providing grammatical or syntactic information. The authors used as sources are listed in the first table, but examples or quotations never appear in the text, with rare exceptions (for these exceptions, see those given by O'Connor 1990: 40). Later, in 1659, Giovanni Torriano brought out a new edition of the Florio, based on a text the author had revised himself, bearing in mind the 1612 dictionary of the Crusca Academy (see O'Connor 1990: 47–49). The first English-Italian dictionary (in fact, Florio's is only Italian-English) was that contained in *Ductor in linguas*, or *The Guide into Tongues*, by John Minsheu, which is, actually, a plurilingual dictionary (see Gamberini 1970: 145; O'Connor 1990: 58n).

The first attempt at producing an Italian grammar in England was that made by John Clerk (see Gamberini 1970: 58–60). Of far greater interest is William Thomas's *Principal Rules of the Italian Grammar, with a Dictionarie for the better understandynge of Boccace, Petrarcha, and Dante*, London, 1550 (other editions 1562, 1567; a facsimile edition of the 1550 version: Menston, Scolar Press, 1968). The author was Welsh and had published a *Historie of Italie* in 1549. He knew Italy, having stayed in the country (see Griffith 1961: 56–80). One grammar which exists only in manuscript form since it was never published, dating back to the middle of the 16th century, is that by John Florio's father, Michelangelo, in which the author declares he had wanted to complete the work of William Thomas (see Pellegrini 1954, who published it). One of the two remaining manuscripts is dedicated to Jane Grey who was, as we stated earlier, a pupil of Florio's. In 1575 the grammar by Scipio Lentulo, a Neapolitan, was translated into English by H. Grantham with the title *An Italian Grammer*. In Gamberini's opinion, the work is schematic, set out in tables, a collection almost. The original version had come out in Latin (*Italicae Grammatices praecepta, ac ratio. In eorum gratiam quieius linguae elegantiam addiscere cupiunt*: see Bingen 1987: 158) in Geneva in 1567. In 1594 an edition with a French translation was brought out in Frankfurt. Lentulo is well known as an author and his life enables us to gain an insight into the world in which grammars for foreigners were produced. Little is known of Lentulo's origins, apart from his own claim that he is Neapolitan. He was an ex Franciscan friar and preacher who had fled from the Inquisition's prisons in Rome. Having reached Geneva, he was converted to Calvinism. From there he was sent to Piedmont, among the Waldenses. His next stop was Valtellina, which was then in the hands of the reformed Grisons (see Gay 1907). He wrote his grammar for foreigners during his stay in Geneva, and his is not the only case of the spread of Italian through religious refugees. It is also significant that it was precisely these works by antipapist refugees that were used for new editions and translations into other languages. Lentulo's life history has singular analogies with that of Michelangelo Florio (see Pellegrini 1954). Michelangelo had been a friar too, he too had been imprisoned in Rome, he too had fled, though to London, then a "welcome refuge for all Protestants" (Pellegrini 1954: 84), he had joined the Swiss Grisons, not far from Chiavenna, where Ludovico Castelvetro (1505–1571) had sought refuge. Lentulo himself mentions Florio, some time after his death (see Firpo 1969: X–XVI): contacts among religious exiles were frequent and significant (see also Cantimori 1939).

Gamberini points out that Trinity College has numerous manuscripts documenting the teaching of Italian in England, including a work by Simon Haward (1572–1614) which contains 2,000 proverbs arranged by topic (see Gamberini 1970: 143). We will see shortly that the study and collection of proverbs was virtually a must for Italian conversation manuals aimed at English consumers.

As we stated above, didactic mini-dialogues had long been in use in language teaching practice. Claude de Sainliens (Claudius Holyband o Holliband), for example, published *The pretie and wittie Historie of Arnald & Lucedia* in Paris in 1575. The book contained a short story with an Italian-English parallel text, and, to bear out our point, didactic mini-dialogues, of the type *To find a spouse, School-teacher*. The work was later reprinted by Holyband himself with the title *The Italian Scoole-maister* (1583, 1591, 1597) (see Gamberini 1970: 76–78). In this area, however, the most important product was undoubtedly John Florio's celebrated *First Fruites* published in 1578, followed by his *Second Fruites* in 1591. *First Fruites* consists of a set of short conversations with Italian-English parallel texts, which move from everyday topics through to literary topics. *Second Fruites* consists of twelve conversations scattered throughout with proverbs (proverbs were attributed a special pedagogic and linguistic function). Together with *Second Fruites*, Florio published *Il Giardino di ricreazione* (*Garden of Recreation*), an astonishing collection of 6,000 proverbs. Nor are proverbs and conversations wanting in *Il Passagiere* (*The Passenger*) by a Benvenuto Italiano, a work whose subtitle informs the reader of the author's profession: "Già nove anni sono Idiomista ['maestro di lingua'] in Londra" ('I have been an idiomist ['language teacher'] in London for nine years'). The work, which was published in London in 1612, is dedicated to Prince Henry, heir to the throne. Gamberini (1979: 136) defines it "a kind of cocktail made up of a new *Civil conversazione*, courtly language, a book on etiquette, a collection of proverbs, together with an anthology of philosophy and poetics, comic texts, scenes of fashionable behaviour, a primer on morality, gastronomic information, current medical knowledge, and any type of filling imaginable". What is more, Gamberini is flabbergasted by the fact that the text includes a list of Italian names used to refer to prostitutes:

> puttane, arlote, [...] grime, pedrine, cortigiane, amiche, vacche, Troie, donne o femine da partito, zaccare, Zaccarete di Zaccare, putanazze marcie, o ruffiane, già state sfrondate in Roma *etc.* (I quote fro Gamberini 1970: 137).

The fact is that a language school was not for young children but for growing boys and adult males.

After Florio, the most prominent language teacher in England was Giovanni Torriano. In 1642 he published his *Select Italian Proverbs*, 600–700 proverbs in about a hundred pages (see Gamberini 1970: 151): the proverb thus maintained its important role in language teaching. One of Torriano's most outstanding works is entitled *Vocabolario Ital-*

*iano & Inglese*. Dated 1659, it is a re-make of Florio's 1611 work, a fact which is stated in the frontispiece, though with a difference, since it adds the words included in the 1612 *Crusca*. The book also includes a summary of the grammar and 234 proverbs with an English gloss (see Gamberini 1970: 152). In 1666 Torriano also published at his own expense a luxury volume of 500 pages entitled *Piazza universale di Proverbi italiani*, but almost all of the copies were lost in the Great Fire of London. After the fire, he referred to the lost work in the title of the book he published in 1673, *The Italian Reviv'd*.

In 1569 an important treatise on phonetics was published in Padua. The author was a Welsh doctor, Joannes Davides Rhosesus or Rhys (1534–1609) (see Griffith 1961: 10–20; Maraschio 1992).

Those interested in documents from the Slav world may consult the references in Tavoni (1990: 243). Presa-Kresalkova (1975) have studied an unpublished plurilingual 15th century dictionary, in which Czech appears next to Italian, Latin and German. The first Italian grammar designed for use by Croatians was published in the middle of the 17th century in Loreto, a town in the Adriatic coast in Marche and famous for its holy shrine. Its author was Giacomo Micaglia (see Jernej 1979; Marazzini 1993: 38n).

## 5. Bibliography


Agricola, Giorgio. 1969. *L'arte dei metalli tradotto in lingua toscana da Michelangelo Florio fiorentino.* Prefazione di Luigi Firpo. Riproduzione facsimile dell'edizione di Basilea, ca. 1556. Torino: Bottega d'Erasmo.

Aquilecchia, Giovanni. 1953. "L'adozione del volgare nei dialoghi londinesi di Giordano Bruno". *Cultura neolatina* 13.165–189.

Bingen, Nicole. 1984. "Sources et filiations de la 'Grammaire italienne' de Jean-Pierre de Mesmes". *Bibliothèque d'Humanisme et Renaissance* 46.633–638.

–. 1987. *Le Maître italien (1510–1660). Bibliographie des ouvrages d'enseignement de la langue italienne destinés au public de langue française, suivie d'un Répertoire des ouvrages bilingues imprimés dans les pays de langue française.* Bruxelles: E. Van Balberghe.

Bonomi, Ilaria. 1987. "Una grammatichetta italiana per Giovanna d'Austria sposa di Francesco de' Medici" (1565). *ACME – Annali della Facoltà di Lettere e filosofia dell'Università degli Studi di Milano* 40:2.51–73.

Bray, Laurent. 1988. "La lexicographie bilingue italien-allemand / allemand-italien du dixsetième siècle". *International Journal of Lexicography* 1.313–339.

Cantimori, Delio. 1939. *Eretici italiani del Cinquecento. Ricerche storiche.* Firenze: Sansoni.

Emery, Luigi. 1947. "Vecchi manuali italo-tedeschi". *Lingua Nostra* 8.8–12, 35–39.

Fessia, Lina. 1939–40. "A. Citolini, esule italiano in Inghilterra". *Rendiconti dell'Istituto lombardo di scienze e lettere* 73.213–243.

Firpo, Luigi. 1969. "Giorgio Agricola e Michelangelo Florio". Prefazione a Agricola 1969: V–XVI.

Florio, John. 1972. *A Worlde of Wordes.* Facsimile of the edition 1598 from a copy in the possession of the British Museum. Hildesheim & New York: Olms.

Gallina, Annamaria. 1959. *Contributi alla storia della lessicografia italo-spagnola dei secoli XVI e XVII.* Firenze: Olschky.

Gamberini, Spartaco. 1970. *Lo studio dell'italiano in Inghilterra nel '500 e nel '600.* Messina & Firenze: D'Anna.

Gay, Teofilo. 1907. *Vita di Scipio Lentolo*, in Lentolo, Scipione, *Sofismi mondani. Trattato scritto nel 1560, ora copiato alla Biblioteca di Berna ed edito da Teofilo Gay colla biografia dell'autore.* Torre Pellice: Tipografia Alpina, Albarin & Coïsson.

Giustiniani, Vito R., ed. 1987. Adam von Rottweil, *Deutch-italienischer Sprachführer* – Maistro Adamo de Rodvila, *Introito e porta di quele che voleno imparare e comprender todescho o latino, cioe taliano.* Edito di sulle stampe del 1477 e 1500 e corredato di un'introduzione, di note e di indici. Tübingen: Narr.

Griffith, T. Gwynfor. 1961. *Avventure linguistiche del Cinquecento.* Firenze: Le Monnier.

Höybye, Poul. 1974 [1964]. "Glossari italiano-tedeschi del Quattrocento". *Studi di Filologia Italiana* 22.167–204; 32.143–203.

Jernej, Josip J. 1979. "La prima grammatica italiana ad uso dei croati". *Studi di Grammatica Italiana* 7.173–179.

Maraschio, Nicoletta. 1992. *Trattati di fonetica del Cinquecento.* Firenze: Accademia della Crusca.

Marazzini, Claudio. 1993. *Storia della lingua italiana. Il secondo Cinquecento e il Seicento.* Bologna: il Mulino.

Marello, Carla. 1989. *Dizionari bilingui con schede sui dizionari italiani per francese, inglese, spagnolo, tedesco.* Bologna: Zanichelli.

Migliorini, Bruno. 1978. *Storia della lingua italiana.* V edizione. Firenze: Sansoni.

Mussafia, Adolfo. 1873. "Beitrag zur Kunde der Norditalienischen Mundarten im XV. Jahrhunderte". *Denkschriften der Wiener Akademie* 22.103–224.

O'Connor, Desmond. 1990. *A History of Italian and English bilingual Dictionaries.* Firenze. Olschki.

Pausch, Oskar. 1972. *Das Älteste Italienisch-Deutsche Sprachbuch. Eine Überlieferung aus dem Jahre 1424 nach Georg von Nürnberg.* Wien: Böhlaus.

Pellegrini, Giuliano. 1954. "Michelangelo Florio e le sue 'Regole de la lingua thoscana'". *Studi di Filologia Italiana* 12.77–201.

Presa, Giovanni & Jitka Křesálková. 1975. "D'un inedito Vocabolarium latino, italiano, ceco e tedesco del secolo XV". *Aevum* 49.166–204.

Rossebastiano Bart, Alda, ed. 1971. *"Introito e porta". Vocabolario italiano-tedesco compiuto per Meistro Adamo de Roduila*, ristampa anastatica dell'edizione 1477. Torino: Bottega d'Erasmo.

Rossebastiano, Alda, ed. 1983. *Vocabolari veneto-tedeschi del secolo XV.* 3 vols. Savigliano: L'Artistica.

–. 1984a. *Antichi vocabolari plurilingui d'uso popolare: la tradizione del "Solenissimo Vochabuolista".* Alessandria: Edizioni dell'Orso.

Rossebastiano Bart, Alda, ed. 1984b. *I "dialoghi" di Giorgio da Norimberga. Redazione veneziana, versione toscana, adattamento padovano.* Savigliano: Edizioni l'Artistica.

Tancke, Gunnar. 1984. *Die italienischen Wörterbücher von den Anfängen bis zum Erscheinen des 'Vocabolario degli Accademici della Crusca' (1612).* Tübingen: Niemeyer.

Tavoni, Mirko, ed. 1990. "La linguistica rinascimentale". *Storia della linguistica* ed. by Giulio C. Lepschy, vol. II, 167–312. Bologna: il Mulino.

Tavoni, Mirko. 1986. "'Linguistica' italiana del Quattro e Cinquecento. Rassegna di studi 1979–1989". *Bollettino di italianistica* 4: fasc. 1–2.1–28.

Van Passen, A. M. 1981. "Appunti sui dizionari italo–francesi apparsi prima della fine del Settecento". *Studi di lessicografia italiana* 3.29–65.

Yates, Frances Y. 1983. *Renaissance and Reform: The Italian contribution*, vol. II. London, Boston, Melbourne & Henley: Routledge & Kegan Paul.

Zamboni, Albert. 1974. "Un 'libro linguistico' italiano-tedesco del XV secolo". *Scriptorium* 28.311–313.

*Claudio Marazzini, Torino (Italy)*

# 96. Der Unterricht des Deutschen im 15. und 16. Jahrhundert

1. Der Lese- und Schreibunterricht an den Elementarschulen
2. Die Umrisse des späteren Deutschunterrichts
3. Bibliographie

Einen Unterricht des Deutschen, wie ihn der Titel dieses Artikels unterstellt, d. h. einen Unterricht, in dem die deutsche Sprache Gegenstand ist, gab es im 15. und 16. Jh. nicht, und konnte es auch nicht geben (Dolch 1971: 206f.). Denn 'das Deutsche' als übergeordnete, verschiedene Dialekte und Regionalsprachen überdachende Sprachform ist erst später ausgebildet worden, so daß ein Deutschunterricht, wie wir ihn kennen: mit deutscher Sprache und deutscher Literatur als zentralen Gegenständen, erst entstehen konnte, nachdem diese Voraussetzung gegeben war. Das war aber erst gegen Ende des 18. und zu Beginn des 19. Jhs. der Fall (Matthias 1907; Frank 1973; Ludwig 1988).

Wohl aber gab es am Ende des Mittelalters und zu Beginn der Neuzeit einige folgenreiche Veränderungen im kulturellen Leben, in der Praxis des Lesens und Schreibens, im Schulwesen und vor allem auch im Unterricht an den Schulen, die durchaus in einen Zusammenhang mit dem späteren Deutschunterricht gebracht werden können. Die unterrichtlichen Veränderungen fanden sowohl im Sprachunterricht an den weiterführenden Schulen als auch im Lese- und Schreibunterricht an den Elementarschulen statt. Im Mittelpunkt des Unterrichts an den höheren Schulen, den Kloster-, Dom-, Pfarr- und Stadtschulen, stand die lateinische Grammatik. Das Deutsche wurde nur gelegentlich zu Rate gezogen, und wenn, dann nur, um die Verhältnisse im Lateinischen verständlich zu machen. Es war in diesem Zusammenhang nicht mehr als eine Hilfs- oder Erklärungssprache. Doch zeigen einige überlieferte Unterrichtstexte, daß Übersetzungsübungen auch der Eigenart der deutschen Sprache Rechnung tragen sollten und auf diese Weise durchaus auch Regularitäten der deutschen Sprache im Lateinunterricht zur Sprache kommen konnten (Puff 1995, bes. 83ff.).

Für den Elementarunterricht, sei es, daß er an kirchlichen, städtischen oder an eigens für den Elementarunterricht eingerichteten Schulen, den sog. 'deutschen Schulen', erteilt wurde, war die Bindung an die lateinische Sprache im 15. und 16. Jh. nicht mehr verpflichtend. Lesen und Schreiben erfolgten in deutscher Sprache. Damit war zumindest an solchen Schulen das Deutsche etabliert (Wriedt 1983: 166ff.). Doch ein Unterrichtsgegenstand war das Deutsche damit noch lange nicht, auch wenn zwei wichtige Etappen auf dem Weg dahin erreicht worden waren. Das Deutsche war nun die Sprache, in der der Unterricht erteilt wurde (Unterrichtssprache), und es war die Sprache, an der die Kinder lesen und schreiben lernten (Unterrichtsmedium). Die ersten Vorstellungen von einem Unterricht, in dem die deutsche Sprache Gegenstand und Mittelpunkt des Unterrichts ist, kamen im Laufe des 16. Jhs. auf. Mehr als Vorstellungen waren es jedoch nicht.

## 1. Der Lese- und Schreibunterricht an den Elementarschulen

In der grammatischen Tradition wurde zwischen der Form der Buchstaben (*figura* oder auch *forma*), ihren Namen (*nomen*) und ihrer Kraft, d. h. ihrem Lautwert (*potestas*), unterschieden. Die Namen der Buchstaben lernten die Schüler im Zusammenhang mit dem Alphabet kennen. Ihre Form war Gegenstand des Schreib-, ihre Kraft Gegenstand des Leseunterrichts.

### 1.1. Das Alphabet

Der sprachliche Unterricht begann mit dem Alphabet. Die Schüler prägten sich die Buchstabenformen ein und lernten die Namen gleicher Buchstabenformen sowie deren Reihenfolge, wie sie im Alphabet geregelt war, auswendig (Alexandre-Bidon 1989). Das Alphabet war also im 15. und 16. Jh. noch ein eigenständiger Unterrichtsgegenstand, seine Kenntnis gleichermaßen Voraussetzung für den Lese- wie für den Schreibunterricht.

### 1.2. Der Leseunterricht

Der Leseunterricht erschöpfte sich in der Benennung der einzelnen Buchstaben (z. B. ‘be’, ‘ce’, ‘de’, ‘e’ usw.), der Ableitung der entsprechenden Lautwerte (b, c, d, e usw.), der Verbindung der Laute untereinander zu Silben und der Kombination der Silben zu ganzen Wörtern. So heißt es in der Württembergischen Schulordnung von 1559: Der Schulmeister habe die Schüler anzuleiten, “das sie im allweg die Buchstaben recht nennen, die Syllaben deutlich aussprechen, und im letsten die Wörter, syllabatim, underschidlich und verstentlich pronunziren” (Vormbaum 1860: 160). *Littera*, *syllaba* und *dictio* waren die lateinischen Bezeichnungen für die drei konstitutiven Schritte des Leseunterrichtes.

Die Frage stellt sich, warum man sich damals im Leseunterricht mit dem Erlesen von Wörtern zufrieden gab. Die Frage stellt sich um so mehr, als die Praxis, auf die die Schüler vorbereitet werden sollten, weitere Qualifikationen erforderlich machte (Thomas 1985: 100f.). Um Texte lesen zu können, bedurfte es einer flüssigen Artikulation ganzer Sätze. Da mehrere Schriften in Gebrauch waren, gehörte zum Lesen auch die Kenntnis zumindest der gebräuchlichsten Schriftarten. Damit nicht genug. Wer einmal Handschriften aus dieser Zeit eingesehen hat, weiß, daß es oft schon schwierig ist, die Buchstaben zu identifizieren. Das Lesen begann also eigentlich schon mit dem Entziffern. Den höchsten Grad an Literalität wies aber erst der Leser auf, der auch lateinische Texte lesen konnte. Das alles hätte Gegenstand des Leseunterrichtes sein können. Tatsächlich beschränkte sich dieser aber auf das Erlesen einzelner deutscher Wörter. Wenn man nicht gleich von der Annahme ausgehen möchte, daß der Leseunterricht den Ansprüchen, die an ihn gestellt wurden, einfach nicht gerecht wurde, bedarf die Diskrepanz einer Erklärung. Eine Erklärung findet sich in der Lesepraxis der Zeit.

Das ganze Mittelalter hindurch (Saenger 1982; Coleman 1996), wie zuvor schon in der Antike (Balogh 1927) und auch noch später bis ins 18. Jh. (Schön 1987), ist laut gelesen worden. Das laute Lesen ist nicht etwa eine etwas umständlichere Weise des Lesens, sondern grundsätzlich vom leisen Lesen unterschieden. Der Prozeß des Lesens setzt sich aus zwei Schritten zusammen. In einem ersten Schritt werden die Schriftzeichen in die ihnen entsprechenden Laute überführt. Zu einem Verständnis des Gelesenen kommt es zu diesem Zeitpunkt noch nicht. Der Leser beschränkt sich vielmehr darauf, die einzelnen Laute mit dem Mund (oral) zu erzeugen und das Erzeugte über das Ohr (aural) aufzunehmen. Erst indem der Leser die Wörter über das Ohr wahrnimmt und auch nur dann, wenn er sie wahrgenommen hat, vermag er ihnen in einem zweiten Schritt einen Sinn zu geben und sie zu verstehen. Das Verständnis gründete sich also nicht auf das Gesehene (die Schriftzeichen), sondern ausschließlich auf das Gehörte (die aus den Schriftzeichen gewonnenen Laute), und das Problem, das es beim Lesen zu lösen galt, beschränkte sich auf die Gewinnung einer lautlichen Form für die schriftlichen Zeichen. Es war genau das, was die Schüler und Schülerinnen im 15. und 16. Jh. in der Schule lernen konnten.

### 1.3. Der Schreibunterricht

Aufgabe des Schreibunterrichtes war es, die Kinder anzuleiten, "gute deutsche Buchstaben zu machen" (aus der Württembergischen Schulordnung von 1559, vgl. Vormbaum 1860, Bd. 1). Dazu gehörte eine möglichst saubere und klare Handschrift, die Beherrschung nicht nur einer, sondern mehrerer, zumindest der gebräuchlichsten Schriften und darüber hinaus auch eine möglichst schmuckvolle Ausführung einzelner Buchstabenformen. Schreiben in der Schule war weniger, zugleich aber auch mehr, als wir heute darunter verstehen. Es war mehr insofern, als man sich nicht mit der Beherrschung einer einzigen Schrift begnügte und auch auf die kalligraphische Ausführung achtete. Es war erheblich weniger insofern, als die Abfassung oder das Aufsetzen von Texten nicht dazu gerechnet wurde.

Wieder stellt sich die Frage, warum die Abfassung oder das Aufsetzen von Texten nicht als Aufgabe des Schreibunterrichtes begriffen wurde und dieser sich darauf beschränkte, die Kinder 'gute deutsche Buchstaben machen' zu lassen. Die Antwort ergibt sich aus der Art der Rezeption des Geschriebenen. Wenn es beim Lesen nur darauf ankam, den Buchstaben sozusagen wieder eine Stimme zu geben, dann konnte sich das Schreiben auf die Aufzeichnung der Laute oder der Lautgestalt der Wörter beschränken. Die Abfassung oder das Aufsetzen von Texten, also das, was wir heute als Textproduktion bezeichnen, blieb der Rhetorik vorbehalten. So unterschied Fabian Franck (1531) z. B. zwischen dem "recht deutsch schreiben" auf der einen und dem "rein höflich deutsch/ mit geschmückten geblümten worten/ ordentlich und artigk nach dem synn odder meinung eines idlichen dings/ von sich schreiben" auf der anderen Seite (Müller 1882: 95). Jenes zu lernen, war Sache des Schreibunterrichtes, dieses besorgte der Rhetorikunterricht: "welches mehr der redmas und Rhetoriken zuständig/ und derhalb jnn der Redkündiger schule zugehörig" (ebd.). Wenn die Produktion von Texten Aufgabe des Rhetorikunterrichtes war, dann hatte eine solche Zuordnung zu bedeuten, daß die Verfertigung schriftlicher Texte Teil des Lateinunterrichtes war. Texte niederzuschreiben wurde also nicht an deutschen Texten, sondern an lateinischen Vorbildern geübt, nicht in deutscher, sondern in lateinischer Sprache. Einen letzten Rest der Unterscheidung von Schreib- und Rhetorikunterricht finden wir noch heute in unserer Unterscheidung von Schreib- und Aufsatzunterricht.

## 2. Die Umrisse des späteren Deutschunterrichts

Auch wenn im 15. und 16. Jh. selbst an den Schulen, die sich 'deutsche' nannten, die deutsche Sprache nie Gegenstand von Unterricht war, sind in dieser Zeit doch erste Vorstellungen von einem deutschen Unterricht entwickelt worden. Diese stehen in einem direkten Zusammenhang mit der reformatorischen Bewegung und sind als unmittelbare Auswirkungen derselben zu betrachten. Martin Luther war vermutlich der erste, der seine Notwendigkeit erkannte, Valentin Ickelsamer war es dann, der ihm zumindest gedanklich eine überzeugende Form gab.

### 2.1. Luther und die Folgen

Martin Luther, der große Reformator, hat mit seinen Vorstellungen vom allgemeinen Priestertum der Laien, von der religiösen Bildung der Gläubigen und von den Aufgaben der Schulen im Rahmen einer Reform von Kirche und Obrigkeit Bedingungen geschaffen, ohne die eine Unterrichtung in der deutschen Sprache später nicht denkbar ist (Hampel 1980). Mit seiner Erkenntnis der Bedeutung der Sprache im allgemeinen und seiner Überzeugung von dem Wert der deutschen Sprache im besonderen hat er den Grund gelegt, auf dem sich später der Deutschunterricht entwickeln konnte.

In seinen Überlegungen zur Bedeutung von Sprache allgemein ging Luther in Übereinstimmung mit dem gesamten Mittelalter von der Heiligkeit der Bibelsprachen aus: der hebräischen Sprache als der Sprache des Alten und der griechischen als der Sprache des Neuen Testamentes. "Seine gesamte Sprachauffassung ist vom Begriff der Bibelsprache aus bestimmt. Durch sie ist die Sprache überhaupt geweiht und wird zur 'optima Dei creatura, ad optimum usum creata'" (Daube 1940: 33). Die Dignität der dritten Bibelsprache, des Lateinischen, also der Sprache, in der beide Teile der Bibel ihre kanonische Form gefunden hatten, wurde Luther, wie zuvor auch anderen Humanisten, zum Problem. Er löste es, indem er die Würde einer Bibelsprache auf das Hebräische und Griechische, also die Sprachen beschränkte, in der die beiden Teile der Bibel tatsächlich abgefaßt waren, gleichzeitig aber jeder Sprache, in der das Wort Gottes in Erscheinung treten und verkündet werden konnte, eine Bedeutung zusprach, die zuvor nur dem Lateinischen zugesprochen wurde. Als Träger des göttlichen Wortes waren grundsätzlich alle Sprachen geheiligt. "Das neue Modell der religiösen Kommunikation ermöglicht dem einzelnen Gläubigen den unmittelbaren Zugang zum göttlichen Wort, das ihm in seiner eigenen Sprache zugänglich ist" (Ehlich 1993: 194f.). Damit war die Jahrhunderte währende Vorherrschaft der lateinischen Sprache zumindest in der Theorie – und das heißt für die damalige Zeit: theologisch – gebrochen. In seinen Übersetzungen der Bibel, insbesondere des Neuen Testamentes von 1522, des Psalters von 1523 und dann schließlich der ganzen Bibel von 1536, setzte Luther die Idee in die Tat um und wurde damit zu einem entscheidenden Wegbereiter der deutschen Standardsprache. Von nun an konnte das Deutsche in alle Bereiche eindringen, in denen zuvor der Gebrauch der lateinischen Sprache als erforderlich erachtet wurde: in die Liturgie, in die Verkündigung, wo immer sie geschah, in die theologische wie überhaupt in die gelehrte Auseinandersetzung, in den politischen Streit und so schließlich auch in die Schulen. "Das Bewußtsein, daß die deutsche Sprache der zentrale Gegenstand an den deutschen Schulen sei und nicht allein das Medium des Schreib-/Leseunterrichts, trat dabei in gleichem Maße hervor, wie die deutsche Sprache als Medium in der Auseinandersetzung der politischen und religiösen Strömungen, die mehr als je zuvor breite Bevölkerungsschichten erreichte und erfaßte, in der ersten Hälfte des 16. Jahrhunderts Gebrauch fand" (Hampel 1980: 71).

Vielleicht noch bedeutsamer als seine Überlegungen zur Bedeutung von Sprache allgemein dürften seine Vorstellungen von einer deutschen Sprache im besonderen gewesen sein. Schon in der Vorrede zum Alten Testament von 1523 setzte Luther die Existenz einer deutschen Sprache als vorhanden, aber noch nicht verwirklicht voraus: "aber nu sehe ich/ das ich auch noch nicht meyn angeporne deutsche sprach kan/ Ich hab auch noch bis her keyn buch noch brieff gelesen/ da rechte art deutscher sprach ynnen were". Im "Sendbrief vom Dolmetschen" aus demselben Jahre kommt eine solche Auffassung in einer typischen Argumentationsfigur zum Ausdruck: "das ist aber die art vnser deudschen sprache"; "obs gleich die Lateinische odder Griechische sprache nicht thut/ so thuts doch die Deudsche/ und ist jhr art"; "das heist gut deudsch gered" usw. Luther geht hier von einer einheitlichen, über den Dialekten stehenden Sprache der Deutschen aus, auch dann, wenn er sie bisher noch in keinem Buch oder Schriftstück zu Gesicht bekommen hat und überzeugt ist, daß er selbst in seinem Sprachgebrauch ihren Ansprüchen nicht zu genügen vermag. Das Bewußtsein für eine deutsche Sprache hat vielleicht nie wieder eine so mutige gedankliche Form gefunden. Es waren Schulleute wie Fabian Frangk (Götz 1992) und Valentin Ickelsamer (siehe unten), die sich auf der Grundlage von Luthers Entdekkung an die Ausarbeitung einer deutschen Grammatik machten.

In der Wirklichkeit des Unterrichts an den Schulen setzte sich das neue Bewußtsein allerdings kaum oder nur sehr langsam durch. Das Interesse humanistisch gebildeter Lehrer (wie auch einiger Reformatoren) galt in erster Linie der Reform des Lateinunterrichts, so daß es sich "eher hemmend auf die Entstehung deutscher Schulen ausgewirkt" (Hampel 1980: 72) hat. Jedoch hat das Deutsche alsbald auch im Lateinunterricht seine Spuren hinterlassen. In den evangelischen Schulen wurde Latein anhand des Kleinen Katechismus und dessen lateinischer Übersetzung gelernt (Fraas 1971). Auch an den deutschen Schulen, in denen sich das Bewußtsein für die Bedeutung des Deutschen als zentralem Unterrichtsgegenstand am ehesten hätte auswirken können, waren solchen Bestrebungen enge Grenzen gesetzt.

> Daß die Praxis des sprachlichen Unterrichts [...] trotz der auf die Beherrschung der deutschen Sprache gerichteten Zielsetzung nicht sehr weit über die Einübung der Fähigkeiten des Lesens und Schreibens hinauskam, hatte seine Ursache darin, daß die theoretischen Grundlagen der deutschen Sprache hinsichtlich ihrer Struktur noch nicht hinreichend erarbeitet waren und die Entwicklung zu einer deutschen Einheitssprache noch nicht weit genug fortgeschritten war (Hampel 1980: 76).

### 2.2. Valentin Ickelsamer

Die Anregungen, die Luther gegeben hatte, wurden von einigen Gefolgsleuten aufgegriffen und ausgeführt, namentlich von Valentin Ickelsamer (? 1518–? 1542), einem den Schwärmern zugetanen Schulmann aus dem Süden Deutschlands (Giesecke 1992).

Ickelsamer ist als Reformer des Leseunterrichts bekannt geworden. Zwar hat er die Lautiermethode nicht gerade selbst erfunden (Götz 1982: 81f.), doch hat er diese in einer Weise ausgearbeitet und propagiert, daß sie für immer mit seinem Namen verbunden ist (Göckelbecker 1937). Daß er aber auch einen Lehrplan für den Unterricht im Deutschen entworfen hat, der in den entscheidenden Punkten die spätere Entwicklung vorwegnahm, ist bis heute nicht recht gewürdigt worden (Vogel 1894).

Ickelsamer hatte eigentlich nicht mehr beabsichtigt, als die Aufgabe des Elementarschullehrers neu zu definieren. Aus dem Lese- und Schreiblehrer sollte ein Lehrer der deutschen Sprache werden:

> Dann es ist ser unrecht/ das die teutschen schulmaister nitt mehr künden oder thun wöllen/ dann ainen Jungen lesen/ schreiben und rechnen leren/ und jn darnach nit höher im teütschen künnen füren oder leren/ dann was ists anders/ das sich ainer auß thut/ ain teütscher schulmaister zusein/ dann ainen lerer der teütschen sprach zu sein? (Pohl 1971: D4v).

In Wirklichkeit aber hat er ein ganzes Curriculum des Deutschen geschaffen (Ludwig 2000).

Zwei Ziele sind danach dem Unterricht der deutschen Sprache aufgegeben, ein praktisches und ein theoretisches. Die Beherrschung des Deutschen in Wort und Schrift ist das eine: "recht und gut teütsch zu reden/ und schreiben" (Pohl 1971: A2r) und das andere die gründliche Kenntnis der deutschen Sprache: "ain künstlicher verstand der gantzen teütschen wörter sprach art und weis" (Pohl 1971: D4v). Solche Anforderungen an den Elementarunterricht sind ganz neu und hätten, wären sie denn damals realisiert worden, die deutsche Sprache im Unterricht an den Schulen gleichberechtigt an die Seite der klassischen Sprachen gestellt.

Von den beiden Zielen hat Ickelsamer einen Lehrplan für den Unterricht der deutschen Sprache abgeleitet, der für seine Zeit einmalig ist. Ausgangspunkt und Begründung für einen solchen sind lautanalytische Übungen, in denen die Schüler mit dem Lautinventar des Deutschen durch Anleitung und Selbstbeobachtung vertraut gemacht werden. Die lautanalytischen Übungen ersetzen das Alphabet als eigenständigen Unterrichtsgegenstand und liegen nicht nur dem Lese-, sondern auch dem Schreibunterricht zugrunde. Im Leseunterricht führen sie zu einer methodischen Innovation, der sog. Lautiermethode (siehe oben). Die Lautwerte der einzelnen Buchstaben, ihre *potestas*, werden durch Analyse und nicht mehr über das Alphabet erschlossen. Der Schreibunterricht erfährt eine neue Einordnung und damit eine Aufwertung. Er verliert den Charakter der Beliebigkeit, da er die notwendigen Voraussetzungen für den Leseunterricht schafft. Aus eben diesem Grunde muß er diesem vorausgehen. Auf die lautanalytischen Übungen folgt also eine Einführung in das Schreiben, und erst dann kommt es zum Lesen.

Nicht minder bedeutsam als die Transformation des traditionellen Lese- und Schreibunterrichts sind die Erweiterungen, die der Elementarunterricht erfährt. Sie gehen samt und sonders vom Schreibunterricht aus. Ickelsamer begnügt sich nicht mehr damit, die Kinder anzuweisen, wie sie 'gute deutsche Buchstaben machen' können, sie sollen auch lernen, Wörter richtig zu schreiben und Sätze grammatisch korrekt und stilistisch angemessen zu bilden. So folgen auf die Schreib- und Lesestunden orthographische, grammatische und stilistische Übungen. Doch damit nicht genug. Ickelsamer kam es nicht nur auf die Beherrschung des Deutschen in Wort und Schrift an, sondern auch auf eine gründliche Kenntnis der deutschen Sprache als solcher. Dazu dienen Übungen, die her als 'etymologische' deklariert werden, aber doch mehr sind. Es handelt sich um wortsemantische Betrachtungen, die weniger die Herkunft der Wörter als vielmehr ihre Bildung und Bedeutung zum Gegenstand haben (Reynolds 1996: 81ff.).

Wollte man Ickelsamers Verdienste mit wenigen Worten würdigen, dann müßte man wohl feststellen, daß er Anspruch darauf hat, nicht nur als Begründer einer neuen und erfolgreichen Lesemethode, sondern auch als einer der Begründer des Deutschunterrichts zu gelten. Er hat ihn zwar nicht geschaffen. Dazu bedurfte es noch mehr als zwei Jahrhunderte. Doch hat er als erster seine Ziele, Grundlagen und Gegenstände bestimmt.

## 3. Bibliographie


Alexandre-Bidou, Danielle. 1989. "Apprendre a lire a l'enfant au moyen age". *Annales ESC.* 4.953–992.

Balogh, J. 1927. "*Voces Paginarum.* Beiträge zur Geschichte des Lesens". *Philologus* 82.84–109, 202–240.

Coleman, Joyce. 1996. *Public Reading and the Reading in the Public in Late Medieval England and France.* Cambridge: Cambridge Univ. Press.

Daube, Anna. 1970. *Der Aufstieg der Muttersprache im deutschen Denken des 15. und 16. Jahrhunderts.* Frankfurt/M: Diesterweg.

Dolch, Josef. 1971. *Lehrplan des Abendlandes.* 3. Aufl. Ratingen: Heun.

Fraas, Hans-Jürgen. 1971. *Katechismustradition: Luthers kleiner Katechismus in Kirche und Schule.* (= *Arbeiten zur Pastoraltheologie*, 7.) Göttingen: Vandenhoeck & Ruprecht.

Frank, Horst Joachim. 1973. *Dichtung, Sprache, Menschenbildung: Geschichte des Deutschunterrichts von den Anfängen bis 1945.* München: Hanser.

Ehlich, Konrad. 1993. "Rom – Reformation – Restauration". *Homo scribens* hg. von Jürgen Baurmann et al., 177–215. Tübingen: Niemeyer.

Giesecke, Michael. 1980. "Schriftspracherwerb und Erstleseunterricht in der Zeit des 'gemein teutsch' – eine sprachhistorische Interpretation der Lehrbücher Valentin Ickelsamers". *OBST* 11.40–58.

–. 1992. "Alphabetisierung als Kulturrevolution. Leben und Werk V. Ickelsamers (ca. 1500–ca. 1547)". G. M. *Sinneswandel, Sprachwandel, Kulturwandel: Studien zur Vorgeschichte der Informationsgesellschaft.* (= *stw*, 997) 122–185. Frankfurt/M.: Suhrkamp.

Göbelbecker, L. F. 1933. *Entwicklungsgeschichte des ersten Leseunterrichts von 1477–1532.* Kempten & Leipzig: Nemnich.

Götz, Ursula. 1992. *Die Anfänge der Grammatikschreibung des Deutschen in Formularbüchern des frühen 16. Jahrhunderts. Fabian Frangk – Schryfftspiegel – Johann Elias Meichßner.* Heidelberg: Winter.

Hampel, Günther. 1980. *Die deutsche Sprache als Gegenstand und Aufgabe des Schulwesens vom Spätmittelalter bis ins 17. Jahrhundert.* Giessen: Schmitz.

Kiepe, H. 1983. "Die älteste deutsche Fibel. Leseunterricht und deutsche Grammatik um 1486". *Studien zum städtischen Bildungswesen des späten Mittelalters und der frühen Neuzeit.* (= *Abhandlungen der Akademie der Wissenschaften in Göttingen, Phil.-H. 3, 137*) hg. von Bernd Moeller, Hans Platz & Karl Stackmann, 435–461. Göttingen: Vandenhoeck & Ruprecht.

Ludwig, Otto. 1988. *Der Schulaufsatz. Seine Geschichte in Deutschland.* Berlin & New York: de Gruyter.

–. 2000. "Valentin Ickelsamers Beitrag zum Deutschunterricht." *ZGL* 28, 23–40.

Matthias, Adolf. 1907. *Geschichte des deutschen Unterrichts.* München: Beck.

Müller, Johannes. 1882. *Quellenschriften und Geschichte des deutschsprachlichen Unterrichts bis zur Mitte des 16. Jahrhunderts.* Gotha (Repr. Hildesheim: Olms 1969).

Pohl, Karl, Hg. 1971. *Valentin Ickelsamer: Die rechte weis aufs kürtzist lesen zu lernen. Ain Teütsche Grammatica.* Stuttgart: Klett.

Puff, Helmut. 1995. *'Von dem Schlüssel aller Künsten/ nemblich der Grammatica.' Deutsch im lateinischen Grammatikunterricht 1480–1560.* (= *Basler Studien zur deutschen Sprache und Literatur*, 70.) Tübingen & Basel.

Reynolds, Suzanne. 1996. *Medieval Reading: Grammar, rhetoric and the classical text.* Cambridge: Cambridge Univ. Press.

Saenger, Paul. 1982. "Silent Reading: Its impact on late Medieval script and societies". *Viator* 13.367–414.

Schön, Erich. 1987. *Der Verlust der Sinnlichkeit/ oder Die Verwandlungen des Lesers. Mentalitätswandel um 1800.* Stuttgart: Klett-Cotta.

Thomas, Keith. 1986. "The Meaning of Literacy in Early Modern England". *The Written Word* hg. von Gerd Baumann, 97–131. Oxford: Clarendon Press.

Vogel, Theodor M. 1894. *Leben und Verdienste Valentin Ickelsamers. Ein Beitrag zur Geschichte der speziellen Methodik* (Diss.). Leipzig: Oswald Schmidt.

Vormbaum, Reinhold, Hg. 1860. *Die evangelischen Schulordnungen des sechszehnten Jahrhunderts.* (= *Evangelische Schulordnungen*, 1). Gütersloh: Bertelsmann.

Wolf, Herbert. 1996. "Luthers sprachliche Selbstbeurteilungen". *ZfdPh* 115.349–370.

Wriedt, Klaus. 1983. "Schulen und bürgerliches Bildungswesen in Norddeutschland im Spätmittelalter". *Studien zum städtischen Bildungswesen des späten Mittelalters und der frühen Neuzeit.* (= *Abhandlungen der Akademie der Wissenschaften in Göttingen, Phil.-hist. Klasse, 3, Folge Nr. 137*) hg. von Bernd Moeller, Hans Patze & Karl Stackmann, 152–172. Göttingen: Vandenhoeck & Ruprecht.

*Claus Ahlzweig/Otto Ludwig, Hannover (Deutschland)*

# 97. Der Unterricht des Französischen im 16. Jahrhundert

1. Allgemeines
2. Der Französischunterricht in England
3. Der Französischunterricht in den Niederlanden
4. Der Französischunterricht im deutschsprachigen Raum
5. Der Französischunterricht in anderen europäischen Ländern
6. Bibliographie

## 1. Allgemeines

Der nachstehende Überblick informiert schwerpunktmäßig über diejenigen Länder, in denen Französisch im 16. Jh. vorwiegend unterrichtet wurde, d. h. England (vgl. 2.), die Niederlande (vgl. 3.) und Deutschland (vgl. 4.). Für das übrige Europa ist nach dem gegenwärtigen Forschungsstand anzunehmen, daß dort im 16. Jh. nur in sehr begrenztem Umfang Französischunterricht erteilt wurde (vgl. 5.).

Bei der Beschreibung des Französischunterrichts werden, soweit dies hier möglich ist, sozialgeschichtliche Aspekte mit berücksichtigt, vor allem bei der Frage nach den Lehrern und Lernern (vgl. dazu Christ 1988). Weiter wird jeweils kurz auf die verschiedenen Lehrbuchtypen eingegangen, d. h. Grammatik, alphabet. und begriffl. Wörterbuch, Gesprächsbuch und ggf. komplementäre Texttypen wie Briefsteller und Sprichwortsammlungen (zur Frage der Typologie von Fremdsprachenlehrwerken im 16. Jh. vgl. Auroux 1992a; Swiggers 1992; Kaltz 1995). Dabei wird versucht, die vielfältige Verflechtung der verschiedenen Traditionsstränge wenigstens andeutungsweise aufzuzeigen, die sich vor allem im Rückgriff auf die lat. und volkssprachl. Lehrwerke des Mittelalters, im Einfluß der lat. Grammatikographie und Lexikographie des 16. Jhs. auf die Produktion volkssprachl. Lehrwerke in diesem Zeitraum und in der Interaktion von eher theoretisch orientierten, für Franzosen verfaßten Grammatiken und solchen, die für Ausländer bestimmt und primär praktisch orientiert sind, manifestiert (vgl. Giard 1987; Auroux 1992a; Kaltz 1995: 102; Lépinette 1996: 153). Auch das Phänomen der "intertextualité active" (Giard 1987: 64), die von zahlreichen Verfassern von Lehrwerken für Französisch als Fremdsprache praktiziert wird – vieles wird übernommen, bearbeitet, manches auch schlicht abgeschrieben – kann hier nur angedeutet werden.

Die Rahmenbedingungen für eine Ausbreitung des Französischunterrichts sind im Europa des 16. Jhs. äußerst günstig. Nicht nur der Sprache im allgemeinen, sondern auch den Volkssprachen wird nun großes Interesse entgegengebracht (zu den Ursachen vgl. Auroux 1992a; Giard 1992: 206ff.). Wie die anderen Volkssprachen wird Französisch zum "objet de savoir" (Giard 1992: 211); es wird dem Prozeß der "grammatisation" (Auroux 1992a: 28) unterworfen, der in Verbindung mit der Verbreitung des Buchdrucks eine "révolution technico-linguistique" in Europa bewirkt (Auroux 1992a: 25). Zu der "mise en théorie" des Französischen im 16. Jh. (Giard 1987) tragen nicht nur die berühmten Grammatiker (wie Louis Meigret und Petrus Ramus) und Lexikographen (vor allem Robert Estienne) dieser Zeit bei, sondern – in bescheidenerem Umfang – auch die vielen, z. T. kaum bekannten, Verfasser von Lehrwerken für Französisch als Fremdsprache.

Bereits im 16. Jh. erfahren die Französischlehrwerke aufgrund der Drucktechnik erhebliche quantitative und qualitative Veränderungen. So enthalten beispielsweise manche Wörterbücher des 16. Jhs. zehnmal so viele Einträge wie die Vokabularien des Mittelalters. Außerdem ist es nun möglich, den Lehrwerktext visuell zu differenzieren, etwa durch Verwendung verschiedener Druckschriften oder durch Anordnung des Textes in Spalten (vgl. Kibbee 1989b: 18f.). Die Verfügbarkeit gedruckten Lehrmaterials für Französisch als Fremdsprache hat zur Folge, daß der Unterricht durch Haus- und Schullehrer im 16. Jh. nach und nach professionalisiert wird (vgl. Caravolas 1994: 101). Zugleich wächst die Nachfrage nach Französischlehrbüchern für den Selbstunterricht. Insgesamt steigt die Produktion von Französischlehrwerken im 16. Jh. in erheblichem Umfang an.

## 2. Der Französischunterricht in England

Im 16. Jh. wird Französisch hier vor allem aus Prestigegründen gelernt; wer Französisch (mehr oder weniger gut) beherrscht, weist sich als Angehöriger der Oberschicht aus (vgl. Kibbee 1991). Als Rechts- und Verwaltungssprache hat es an Bedeutung verloren (vgl. Droixhe & Dutilleul 1990: 441); es wird aber weiter auch aus praktischen Gründen gelernt, insbesondere in Kaufmannskreisen als internationale Handelssprache (vgl. Kibbee 1991; Caravolas 1994: 94ff.). Neben dem Spracherwerb durch Reisen nach Frankreich (vgl. Caravolas 1994: 98f.) lernt die adlige Jugend Französisch vor allem bei Hauslehrern, von denen einige auch als Lehrbuchautoren bekannt werden, u. a. John Palsgrave, Gilles Du Wes und Claude de Sainliens, der sich in England Hol(l)yband nennt (vgl. Streuber 1963; Reboullet 1992; Caravolas 1994: 96). In öffentlichen Schulen wird Französisch, ebenso wie andere Volkssprachen, zwar noch kaum unterrichtet, doch gibt es zahlreiche Privatschulen, vielfach Gründungen frz. Emigranten (Holyband, du Ploiche u. a.; vgl. Kibbee 1989a: 55, Caravolas 1994: 95). Die Konkurrenz unter den muttersprachlichen und englischsprachigen Französischlehrern führt verschiedentlich zu Konflikten, ebenso wie die Frage der Unterrichtsmethode (vgl. Kibbee 1989a: 55f.).

Die ersten kleinen Lehrwerke für Französisch sind in England bereits im 13. Jh. entstanden (vgl. Lambley 1920; Kibbee 1991); ab dem Ende des 14. Jhs. werden mehrere "manières de langage", d. h. Gesprächsbücher, verfaßt (vgl. Kristol 1995), und schon um 1400 entsteht die erste volkssprachliche Französischgrammatik, der *Donait francois* (vgl. Swiggers 1990: 844f.; Kibbee 1991). Im Laufe des 16. Jhs. gewinnen die Französischlehrwerke deutlich an Umfang und Qualität (vgl. Kibbee 1989a: 62f.). Sie wenden sich weiterhin vor allem an die männliche Jugend; die für junge Mädchen bestimmte *Necessary, fit and convenient Education of a yong Gentlewoman*, eine engl. Bearbeitung eines 1556 in Antwerpen gedruckten frz.-it. Werkes von Giovanni Bruto, erscheint erst 1598 (vgl. Kibbee 1991).

In diesem Zeitraum werden in England zahlreiche Französischgrammatiken veröffentlicht, meist in engl. Sprache, einige zweisprachige mit Französisch (vgl. Kibbee 1991): Palsgrave (1530), ein umfassendes, auch theoretisch bedeutsames Werk mit einem zweisprachigen Wörterbuch (vgl. Kibbee 1985), die kürzere *Introductorie* (1532) von Du Wes (vgl. Schmitt 1979), der *Playne treatise to learne in a short space the French tongve* von Ledoyen de La Pichonnaye (1576), die in Holyband, *Frenche Schoolemaister* (1573) und Holyband (1576) enthaltenen zweisprachigen Kurzgrammatiken (vgl. Streuber 1963; Kibbee 1989a: 68–70) und die *French Grammer* von Jacques Bellot (1578), um nur einige zu nennen (vgl. Streuber 1963; Kibbee 1991; Caravolas 1994: 102–104).

Palsgrave verzeichnet die rund 23.000 Einträge seines engl-frz. Wörterbuches von 1530 nach Wortarten geordnet, innerhalb dieser in alphabet. Folge. Er gehört zu den ganz wenigen engl. Wörterbuchautoren des 16. Jhs., die unabhängig von der lat. Lexikographie sind (vgl. Stein 1985: 121–139; Kibbee 1991). Der *Dictionariolum puerorum* von Jean Veron (1552) ist dagegen lediglich eine Bearbeitung des gleichnamigen Werkes von Robert Estienne, mit engl. Übersetzung der Einträge. Auch der *Dictionarie French and English* (anon., 1570) und John Barets *Alvearie or triple Dictionarie* (1573), ein engl.-lat.-frz. Wörterbuch, sind von Estienne beeinflußt (vgl. Kibbee 1991). Holyband veröffentlicht zwei größere Wörterbücher, 1580 den *Treasurie of the French tong* (1580), eine der Quellen von Cotgraves frz.-engl. Wörterbuch (1611), und 1593 den *Dictionarie French and English* (vgl. Kibbee 1989a: 71ff.).

Der Typus des begrifflichen Wörterbuchs ist u. a. mit den sachlich geordneten Wortlisten in Holyband (1573, 1576) sowie mit dem *Nomenclator, or Remembrancer* (1585) vertreten, einer Bearbeitung von Junius (1567) durch John Higgins (vgl. Kibbee 1991).

Die Tradition der "manières de langage" des späten 14. und des 15. Jhs. (u. a. die dem Drucker Caxton zugeschriebene *Tres bonne doctrine*, um 1483) wird im 16. Jh. fortgeführt, etwa mit dem *Petit livre pour apprendre a parler Francoys, Alemant et Ancloys. Pour apprendre a conter, a vendre & acheter* (anon., ca. 1525; vgl. Kibbee 1991) und den in Du Wes (1532) und Holyband (1576) enthaltenen Gesprächsbüchern. 1563 erscheinen in Antwerpen die *Communications familieres non moins propres que tresutiles a la nation Angloise desireuse du langage Francois* von Meurier (vgl. 3.), der auch der mutmaßliche Verfasser des 1575 in London gedruckten *Plaine pathway to the French Tongue, very profitable for Marchants and also all other which desire the same* ist (vgl. Kibbee 1989a: 69, 1991).

Charakteristisch für die Lehrwerkproduktion des 16. Jhs. in England (wie auch des 17. Jhs.; → Art. 101) ist der Rückgriff auf verschiedene Lehrbuchtypen innerhalb eines Werkes. So werden Grammatik und Wörterbuch assoziiert (z. B. in Palsgrave 1530 und Du Wes 1532); dazu tritt bei vielen Autoren das Gesprächsbuch (u. a. Du Wes 1532; *Plaine Pathway*, 1575; Holyband 1573, 1576). Einige beziehen auch komplementäre Texttypen ein: Musterbriefe (*Plaine Pathway*), Sprichwortsammlungen und religiöse Texte (etwa Holyband 1573, 1576). Besonders erfolgreich waren Holyband, dessen Werke z. T. auch in den Niederlanden bearbeitet wurden (vgl. Streuber 1963: 112), und Guillaume de la Mothe mit seinem *French Alphabet* (1592), in dem Aussprachelehre, Gesprächsbuch und Sprichwortsammlung kombiniert sind (vgl. Kibbee 1989a; 1991; Caravolas, 1994: 105–108).

## 3. Der Französischunterricht in den Niederlanden

Französisch hatte dort schon im ausgehenden Mittelalter eine Vorrangstellung unter den Fremdsprachen, die es auch im 16. Jh. behält (vgl. Droixhe & Dutilleul 1990: 442f.). Es wird nun nicht mehr hauptsächlich durch Reisen, Privat- oder Selbstunterricht gelernt, sondern verstärkt auch in Schulen (vgl. Caravolas 1994: 248f.), häufig wegen seiner besonderen Bedeutung als internationale Handelssprache (vgl. Riemens 1919: 15ff.). Mehrere aus dem Gebiet des heutigen Belgien stammende Sprachlehrer werden weithin als Verfasser von Französischlehrbüchern aller Art bekannt, vor allem Noël de Berlaimont, dessen Werke vielfach bearbeitet und nachgeahmt werden (vgl. Streuber 1964: 60–65; Claes 1988: 22; Aubert 1993), Peeter Heyns (vgl. Streuber 1964: 70–74; Caravolas 1994: 249), Gabriel Meurier (vgl. Streuber 1964: 65–70; de Clercq 1997), Gerard de Vivre (vgl. Kaltz 1988) und Levinus Hulsius (vgl. Hausmann 1984). Einige versuchen ihr Glück im Ausland; so ist de Vivre lange Jahre in Köln tätig, Hulsius in Nürnberg, Heyns zeitweilig in Frankfurt am Main, wo mehrere reformierte Französischlehrer bis zu ihrer Vertreibung 1592 Schulen leiten (vgl. Schröder 1980: 13f., 18). Wie auch in England waren Ansehen und Einkommen dieser Sprachlehrer wohl gering (vgl. Riemens 1919: 15ff.; Reboullet 1992; Caravolas 1994: 249).

Zumindest für die zweite Hälfte des 16. Jhs. deutet einiges darauf hin, daß auch die weibliche Jugend zunehmend Französischunterricht erhält. So gründet Heyns um 1556 eine Schule für junge Mädchen in Antwerpen (vgl. Caravolas 1994: 249), und 1564 erscheint dort Meuriers *Guirlande des Jeunes Filles*, ein Gesprächsbuch für Mädchen, das bis ins 17. Jh. häufig nachgedruckt und bearbeitet wird, u. a. für den Gebrauch in Deutschland (vgl. Streuber 1964: 66–70).

Zu den mehrsprachigen Grammatiken mit frz. und fläm. Komponenten, etwa Meurier (1558), einer frz./it./span./fläm. Kurzgrammatik (vgl. Kaltz 1995: 92), treten die ersten Französischgrammatiken in der Volkssprache: 1571 Heyns, *Cort onderwys van de acht deelen der Françoischer talen* (vgl. Weber 1987: 128), 1576 *Hyperphragme, Formulaire des conjugaisons Flamen-Françoyses* (vgl. Riemens 1919: 223). Heyns' Grammatik, die unter dem Einfluß der 1550 bzw. 1557 erschienenen Grammatiken von Meigret und R. Estienne steht (→ Art. 105 und Weber 1987: 128), zeugt von der Interaktion innerhalb der volkssprachlichen Grammatikographie. In lat. Sprache verfaßte Französischgrammatiken waren vermutlich weniger gebräuchlich; doch wurden etwa die primär für Deutsche bestimmten Grammatiken von Pillot und Caucius (vgl. 4.) auch in den Niederlanden nachgedruckt.

Im Bereich der alphabetischen Wörterbücher stehen ebenfalls sowohl polyglotte als auch zweisprachige Werke zur Verfügung. So enthalten viele der auf Berlaimont zurückgehenden mehrsprachigen Werke einen frz. und fläm. Wörterbuchteil (etwa anon. 1558). Zweisprachige Wörterbücher veröffentlichen u. a. Meurier (1557) auf der Grundlage von R. Estiennes frz.-lat. Wörterbuch (vgl. Claes 1988: 26), Sasbout (1583) mit gesonderten Verzeichnissen für die Fachsprache der Marine und des Jagdwesens (vgl. Kaltz 1995: 84) und Mellema (1592), der die Vorlage für Hulsius (1596) lieferte (vgl. 4.).

Auch bei den begrifflichen Wörterbüchern ist der zweisprachige (z. B. Meurier 1563; vgl. Kaltz 2000) neben dem polyglotten Typus vertreten (etwa Junius 1567; vgl. Claes 1988: 28–30; Hüllen 1992).

Auf das erste, bereits Mitte des 14. Jhs. verfaßte frz.-fläm. Gesprächsbuch, das *Livre des mestiers*, gehen mehrere spätere Werke zurück, u. a. die frz.-engl. *Tres bonne doctrine* (vgl. 2.; Gessler 1931; Streuber 1962). Die zahlreichen im 16. Jh. in den Niederlanden gedruckten zweisprachigen Gesprächsbücher setzen diese Tradition fort, so die *Dialogues françois* (anon. 1567; vgl. Kaltz 1992: 130), die *Dialogues pueriles* von Heyns (1588) oder de Vivre (1574/1581). Viele sind, wie schon aus den Titeln hervorgeht, primär für Kinder und Jugendliche bestimmt, werden aber wohl auch von Erwachsenen benutzt (zur Polyvalenz dieser Lehrwerke vgl. Kaltz 1992: 128); manche (etwa Meurier 1590) richten sich ausdrücklich an Erwachsene, die das Französische aus beruflichen Gründen, vor allem für den Handel, erlernen wollen. Außerdem erscheinen polyglotte Gesprächsbücher mit einem frz. Teil (→ Art. 94).

Ergänzend zu den grammatischen und lexikographischen Werken sowie den Gesprächsbüchern werden schließlich für den Fortgeschrittenenunterricht auch ein- oder zweisprachige Sammlungen von Musterbriefen (insbesondere für die Handelskorrespondenz) und Sprichwörtern sowie kleine Theaterstücke veröffentlicht, etwa de Vivre (1575; vgl. Kaltz 1995: 97f.), die Schulkomödien desselben Autors (vgl. Kaltz 1988: 26ff.), die *Proverbes anciens Flamengs et François* von François Goedthals (1568; vgl. Claes 1970: 365) und die frz.-fläm. Sprichwortsammlung in Meuriers *Guirlande* (vgl. Claes 1974: 76).

## 4. Der Französischunterricht im deutschsprachigen Raum

Auch hier wurde schon im Mittelalter Französisch gelernt (vgl. Streuber 1962: 37f.). Ab dem 16. Jh. wird dem Französischen jedoch erheblich größeres Interesse entgegengebracht. Immer mehr junge Adlige werden zum Erlernen der Sprache nach Frankreich geschickt (vgl. Schröder 1980: 1ff.); die Zahl der in Deutschland tätigen Haus- bzw. Schullehrer für Französisch (darunter viele Hugenotten, auch reformierte Flamen) steigt stetig an, und bereits 1571 wird an der Universität Wittenberg ein Lektor für Französisch eingestellt (vgl. Schröder 1980: 8f.). Die Produktion von Französischlehrbüchern für den deutschen Markt nimmt stark zu (vgl. Streuber 1967; 1968; Caravolas 1994: 149f.).

Hinsichtlich der Grammatik ist die Situation in Deutschland insofern etwas anders als in England und den Niederlanden, als hier eine Reihe lat. geschriebener Französischgrammatiken speziell für dt. Lerner entstehen, insbesondere Pillot (1550), die *Institutio gallicae linguae* von Garnier (1558), die *Grammatica gallica* von Caucius (1570) und das gleichnamige Werk von Serreius (1598) [mit lat.-franz.-dt. Nomenklatur] sowie Cachedenier (1600) [mit Dialogteil] (vgl. Streuber 1967; Padley 1988; Swiggers 1992; Caravolas 1994; Kaltz 1995). Die vielfach nachgedruckte Grammatik von Pillot (1550) beeinflußte u. a. Garnier und Holyband (vgl. Streuber 1967: 236–256; Caravolas 1994: 150f.).

Auch in Deutschland entstehen die ersten Kurzgrammatiken in der Volkssprache, u. a. de Vivre (1566, 1568; vgl. Kaltz 1995: 89) und die in Hulsius (1596) enthaltene knappe Aussprache- und Formenlehre.

Hulsius (1596) gilt als das erste größere frz.-dt. alphabetische Wörterbuch; zuvor waren lediglich ein frz.-dt. alphabetisches Wörterbuch ausgewählter Begriffe (de Vivre 1569; vgl. Kaltz 1988) sowie polyglotte Werke mit einem dt. und frz. Teil erschienen (etwa anon. 1576). Hulsius' Werk ist ein weiteres Beispiel für die "intertextualité active" innerhalb der europäischen Lehrbuchproduktion: die Einträge für den frz.-dt. Teil sind fast wörtlich von Mellema (1592) übernommen (vgl. Hausmann 1984: 308).

Im Bereich der begrifflichen Wörterbücher seien hier besonders das vielfach nachgedruckte lat.-frz.-dt. *Vocabularium* von 1514, die viersprachige *Introductio* von 1516, eine Bearbeitung des ältesten it.-dt. Vokabulars von 1477 (→ Art. 95), sowie Junius (1567) genannt. Das *Vocabularium* enthält auch ein kleines frz.-dt. Gesprächsbuch, das vermutlich älteste für dieses Sprachenpaar (vgl. Kaltz 1995: 95). Weitere frz.-dt. Gesprächsbücher finden sich in den polyglotten Sprachlehrwerken des 16. Jhs. (→ Art. 94).

De Vivres Briefsteller und Schulkomödien (vgl. 3.) entstanden während seiner Tätigkeit als Sprachlehrer in Köln, sind also sicher zumindest dort auch im Französischunterricht für dt. Lerner eingesetzt worden.

## 5. Der Französischunterricht in anderen europäischen Ländern

Aufgrund des Ansehens und der Verbreitung des Italienischen im Ausland ist die Motivation, eine Fremdsprache zu lernen, im Italien des 16. Jhs. gering. Wenn überhaupt eine Fremdsprache gelernt wird, so ist es eher Spanisch oder Deutsch; das Prestige des Französischen ist noch nicht gefestigt (vgl. Mormile 1989: 21; Caravolas 1994: 51f.). Im 16. Jh. erscheinen so gut wie keine Französischlehrwerke in Italien. Zu nennen ist hier allenfalls der *Dittionario volgare et latino* von Orazio Toscanella (Venedig 1568), dessen alphabetisch angeordnete frz. Einträge mit ihren it. Entsprechungen ein kleines frz.-it. Wörterbuch bilden (vgl. Bingen 1987: 231).

Ebenso wie die vielen polyglotten Sprachlehrbücher des 16. Jhs. (→ Art. 94) mögen auch die lat. geschriebenen, außerhalb Italiens gedruckten Französischgrammatiken dort Verwendung gefunden haben (vgl. Mormile 1989: 21); die ersten Französischgrammatiken in it. Sprache erscheinen jedoch erst im 17. Jh. (vgl. Caravolas 1994: 55).

In Spanien wird den Fremdsprachen im 16. Jh. ebenfalls nur vergleichsweise geringes Interesse entgegengebracht, wobei hier allerdings dem Französischen der Vorzug gegeben wird. Doch erscheinen auch dort im 16. Jh. kaum Französischlehrbücher (vgl. Caravolas 1994: 287). Die wohl erste Französischgrammatik in span. Sprache, Sotomayor (1565), illustriert zugleich den im 16. Jh. beliebten Typus der "manuels 'réversibles'" (Reboullet 1992: 3) und – als eine Kompilation der polyglotten Grammatik Meuriers von 1558 (vgl. Lépinette 1996: 151) – das Phänomen der "intertextualité active". Auch in Spanien wurden vermutlich andernorts gedruckte lat. Französischgrammatiken sowie polyglotte Wörterbücher und Dialogsammlungen des 16. Jhs. zum Erlernen des Französischen herangezogen (vgl. Caravolas 1994: 288).

In Schweden ist Französisch im 16. Jh. die beliebteste Fremdsprache, die auch hier hauptsächlich in adligen und kaufmännischen Kreisen von Hauslehrern gelernt wird. Erst im 17. Jh. wird dort jedoch das erste Französischlehrwerk, ein polyglotter Katechismus, gedruckt (vgl. Caravolas 1994: 298). In Dänemark war Französisch im 16. Jh. offenbar kaum verbreitet (vgl. Droixhe & Dutilleul 1990: 443).

In Polen schließlich waren wie in den übrigen europäischen Ländern Hauslehrer für Französisch in adligen Familien tätig; darüber hinaus wurde möglicherweise schon ab Mitte des 16. Jhs. von hugenottischen Emigranten an mehreren Schulen Französischunterricht erteilt (vgl. Caravolas 1994: 302f.).

## 6. Bibliographie

### 6.1. Primärliteratur

Anon. 1514. *Vocabularium latinis Gallicis et Theuthonicis verbis scriptum.* Lyon: J. Thomas.

–. 1516. *Introduction quaedam utilissima.* Augsburg: E. Öglin.

–. 1558. *Vocabvlario, colloqvios o dialogos en qvatro lengvas, Flamengo, Frances, Español, y Italiano.* Antwerpen: I. Verwithagen.

–. 1567. *La premiere et la seconde partie des dialogues francois pour les ieunes enfans. Het eerste ende tweede deel van den Françoische t'samensprekinghen.* Antwerpen: Chr. Plantin.

–. 1576. *Colloquia et dictionariolum sex linguarum, Teutonicae, Latinae, Germanicae, Gallicae, Hispanicae, & Italicae.* Antwerpen: H. Henricx.

Cachedenier, Daniel. 1600. *Introductio ad linguam gallicam [...] in gratiam Germanica iuventutis conscripta.* Frankfurt: M. Becker.

Caxton, William. ca. 1483. *Tres bonne doctrine pour aprendre briefment fransoys et engloys. Ryght good lernyng for to lerne shortly frenssh and englyssh.* London: Caxton.

Hol[l]yband, Claude [de Sainliens]. 1576. *The Frenche Littleton. A Most Easie, Perfect, and Absolute way to learne the frenche tongue.* London: Th. Vautroullier. (Repr. Menston: Scolar Press, 1970).

Hulsius, Levinus. 1614 [1596]. *Dictionaire François-Allemand, & Allemand-François. Avec une brieve instruction de la Prononciation des deux langues en forme de Grammaire.* Oppenheim: H. Galler.

Junius, Hadrianus. 1567. *Nomenclator omnium rerum propria nomina variis lingvis explicata indicans.* Antwerpen: Chr. Plantin.

Mellema, Elcie Edouard Leon. 1592. *Dictionaire ou Promptuaire Francois-Flameng, tres-ample et trescopieux.* Rotterdam: J. van Waesberghe.

Meurier, Gabriel. 1557. *Vocabulaire françois-flameng.* Antwerpen: Chr. Plantin.

–. 1558. *Conjugaisons, Regles, et Instructions, mout propres et necessairement requises, pour ceux qui desirent apprendre François, Italien, Espagnol, et Flamen.* Antwerpen: J. van Waesberghe.

–. 1563. *Petite Fabrique duisante a chacun tyron diseteux du François ou Flamen.* Antwerpen: P. Keerberghen.

–. 1590. *Deviz Familiers propres à tous marchands desireux d'entendre bien lire et naivement parler Françoys et Flamen.* Rotterdam: J. van Waesberghe.

Palsgrave, John. 1530. *Lesclaircissement de la langue francoyse.* London: John Haukyns. (Repr. Menston: Scolar Press, 1969.)

Pillot, Jean. 1550. *Gallicae linguae institutio.* Paris: St. Groulleau.

Sasbout, Mathias. 1583. *Dictionaire francois-flameng, tres ample et copieux, auquel on trouvera un nombre infini de termes & dictions, plus qu'en ceux qui jusques a present sont sortis en lumiere.* Antwerpen: J. van Waesberghe.

Sotomayor, Baltasar. 1565. *Gramatica con reglas muy prochosas para aprender a leer y escrivir la lengua francesa, conferida con la Castellana, con un vocabulario copioso de las mesmas lenguas.* Alcalá: F. de Cormellas y P. Robles.

Vivre, Gerard de. 1566. *Grammaire Françoise, touchant la lecture, Declinaisons des Noms, & Coniugaisons des Verbes.* Köln: M. Cholinum.

–. 1568. *Briefve Institution de la langue françoise, expliquée en Aleman.* Köln: H. von Aich.

–. 1575. *Lettres missives familieres, entresmeslées de certaines confabulations, non moins utiles que recreatives.* Antwerpen: J. van Waesberghe.

–. 1581 [1574]. *Dovze Dialogves, traitants de diverses matieres, tres-propres avx novveauvx apprentifs de la langue Françoise.* Antwerpen: J. van Waesberghe.

## 6.2. Sekundärliteratur

Aubert, Françoise. 1993. "Apprentissage des langues étrangères et préparation au voyage. A propos d'un manuel plurilingue attribué à Berlaimont". *Documents pour l'histoire du français langue étrangère ou seconde* 11.14–20.

Auroux, Sylvain, Hg. 1992a. *Histoire des idées linguistiques.* Tome 2: *Le développement de la grammaire occidentale.* Lüttich: Mardaga.

–. 1992b. "Introduction. Le processus de grammatisation et ses enjeux". Auroux 1992a.11–64.

Bingen, Nicole. 1987. *Le Maître italien (1510–1660). Bibliographie des ouvrages d'enseignement de la langue italienne destinés au public de langue française, suivie d'un répertoire des ouvrages bilingues imprimés dans les pays de langue française.* Brüssel: van Balberghe.

Caravolas, Jean-Antoine. 1994. *La didactique des langues 1450–1700.* Bd. I. Tübingen: Narr & Montréal: Presses de l'Université de Montréal.

Christ, Herbert. 1988. "Pour une histoire sociale de l'enseignement du francais". *Documents pour l'histoire du français langue étrangère ou seconde* 1.6–10.

Claes, Frans. 1970. *De Bronnen van drie woordenboeken uit de drukkerij van Plantin: Het Dictionarium tetraglotton (1562), de Thesaurus Theutonicae Linguae (1573) en Kiliaans eerste Dictionarium Teutonico-Latinum (1574).* Brüssel: Belgisch Interuniversitair Centrum voor Neerlandistiek.

–. 1974. *Lijst van Nederlandse woordenlijsten en woordenboeken gedrukt tot 1600.* Nieuwkoop: de Graaf.

–. 1977. *Bibliographisches Verzeichnis der deutschen Vokabulare und Wörterbücher bis 1600.* Hildesheim & New York: Olms.

–. 1988. "Über die Verbreitung lexikographischer Werke in den Niederlanden und ihre wechselseitige[n] Beziehungen mit dem Ausland bis zum Jahre 1600". *HL* XV:1/2.17–38.

de Clercq, Jan. 1997. "Gabriel Meurier, een XVI$^{e}$-eeuws pedagoog en grammaticus in Antwerpen". *Meesterwerk: Bijdragen van het Peter Heyns Genootschap* 10.29–45.

Droixhe, Daniel & Thierry Dutilleul. 1990. "Französisch: Externe Sprachgeschichte". Holtus, Metzeltin & Schmitt 1990–95. V, 1.437–471.

Gessler, Jean. 1931. *Le Livre des Mestiers de Bruges et ses dérivés.* 6 Bde. Bruges: Imprimerie Sainte-Catherine.

Giard, Luce. 1987. "La mise en théorie du français au XVI$^{e}$ siècle". *Schifanoia* 2.63–76.

–. 1992. "Section 2. L'entrée en lice des vernaculaires". Auroux 1992a. 206–225.

Hausmann, Franz Josef. 1984. "Das erste französisch-deutsche Wörterbuch: Levinus Hulsius' *Dictionaire* von 1596–1607". *ZRPh* 100:3/4.306–320.

Holtus, Günter, Michael Metzeltin & Christian Schmitt. 1990–95. *Lexikon der Romanistischen Linguistik.* Bd. V.1: *Französisch* [1990]. Bd. II,2: *Die einzelnen romanischen Sprachen und Sprachgebiete vom Mittelalter bis zur Renaissance* [1995]. Tübinigen: Niemeyer.

Hüllen, Werner (mit Renate Haas). 1992. "Adrianus Junius on the Order of his NOMENCLATOR (1577)". *Euralex '92* Proceedings I–II. Part II hg. von Hannu Tommola et al. Tampere: Department of Translation Studies.

Kaltz, Barbara, Hg. 1988. *Gerard de Vivre, Synonymes/Synonyma: Nachdruck der Ausgabe Köln 1569 mit einer Einleitung und Bibliographie.* Hamburg: Buske [RomGG 21].

–. 1992. "Etude historiographique des Manières de langage". *Diversions of Galway: Papers on the history of linguistics* hg. von Anders Ahlqvist, 123–133. Amsterdam: Benjamins.

–. 1995. "L'enseignement des langues étrangères au XVI$^{e}$ siècle. Structure globale et typologie des textes destinés à l'apprentissage des vernaculaires". *Beiträge zur Geschichte der Sprachwissenschaft* 5.79–105.

–. 2000. "Die 'Petite fabrique' (1563) von Gabriel Meurier". *Grammaire et enseignement du français 1500–1700* hg. von Jan de Clercq & N. Lioce. Leuven: Peeters Press [im Druck].

Kibbee, Douglas A. 1985. "John Palsgrave's 'Lesclaircissement de la langue francoyse' (1530)". *HL* XII: 1/2.27–62.

–. 1989a. "L'enseignement du français en Angleterre au XVI$^{e}$ siècle". *La langue française au XVI$^{e}$ siècle: Usage, enseignement et approches descriptives* hg. von Pierre Swiggers & Willy van Hoecke, 54–77. Leuven: Leuven Univ. Press.

–. 1989b. "Les manuels anglais du XVI$^{e}$ siècle et l'imprimerie". *Documents pour l'histoire du français langue étrangère ou seconde* 4.18–20.

–. 1991. *For to Speke Frenche Trewely: The French language in England, 1000–1600.* Amsterdam: Benjamins.

Kristol, Andres M., Hg. 1995. *Manières de langage (1396, 1399, 1415).* London: Anglo-Norman Text Society.

Lambley, Kathleen. 1920. *The Teaching and Cultivation of the French Language in England during Tudor and Stuart Times.* Manchester: Manchester Univ. Press.

Lépinette, Brigitte. "Les premières grammaires du français (1565–1799) publiées en Espagne: Modèles, sources et rôle de l'espagnol". *HEL* 18:II. 149–177.

Lindemann, Margarete. 1994. *Die französischen Wörterbücher von den Anfängen bis 1600: Entstehung und typologische Beschreibung.* (= *Lexicographica Series Maior*, 54.) Tübingen: Niemeyer.

Mormile, Mario. 1989. "Les grammaires françaises en Italie dans la première moitié du XVIIe siècle". *Documents pour l'histoire du français langue étrangère ou seconde* 4.31–24.

Padley, G[eorge] A[rthur]. 1988. *Grammatical Theory in Western Europe 1500–1700: Trends in vernacular grammar II.* Cambridge: Cambridge Univ. Press.

Quemada, Bernard. 1967. *Les dictionnaires du français moderne. 1539–1863. Etude sur leur histoire, leurs types et leurs méthodes.* Paris: Didier.

Reboullet, André. 1992. "Hollyband ou l'archétype". *Documents pour l'histoire du français langue étrangère ou seconde* 9.1–4.

Riemens, K[ornelis]-J[acobus]. 1919. *Esquisse historique de l'enseignement du français en Hollande du XVIe au XIXe siècle.* Leiden: A. W. Sijthoff.

Schmitt, Christian. 1979. "La grammaire de Giles Du Wes, étude lexicale". *Revue de Linguistique Romane* 43.1–45.

Schröder, Konrad. 1980. *Linguarum Recentium Annales: Der Unterricht in den modernen europäischen Sprachen im deutschsprachigen Raum*, Bd. 1: *1500–1700.* Augsburg: Universität Augsburg.

Stein, Gabriele. 1985. *The English Dictionary before Cawdrey.* Tübingen: Niemeyer.

Stengel, Edmund Max. 1890/1976. *Chronologisches Verzeichnis französischer Grammatiken vom Ende des 14. bis zum Ausgange des 18. Jahrhunderts nebst Angabe der bisher ermittelten Fundorte derselben.* Neu herausgegeben mit einem Anhang von Hans-Josef Niederehe. Amsterdam: Benjamins.

Streuber, Albert. 1962–64. "Die ältesten Anleitungsschriften zur Erlernung des Französischen in England und den Niederlanden bis zum 16. Jahrhundert". *ZfSL* 72.37–86, 186–211; 73.97–112, 189–209; 74.59–76.

–. 1964–69. "Französische Grammatik und französischer Unterricht in Deutschland während des 16. Jahrhunderts". *ZfSL* 74.342–361; 75.31–50, 247–273; 77.235–267; 78.69–101; 79.172–191, 328–348.

Swiggers, Pierre. 1990. "Französisch: Grammatikographie". Holtus, Metzeltin & Schmitt 1990. I.843–894.

–. 1992. "Les grammaires françaises 'pédagogiques' du XVIe siècle: Problèmes de définition et de typologie; analyse microscopique". *Fremdsprachenunterricht 1500–1800* (= *Wolfenbütteler Forschungen*, 52) hg. von Konrad Schröder, 217–235. Wiesbaden: Harrassowitz.

Weber, Heinrich. 1987. "Die Ausbildung der deutschen Grammatik (einschließlich der niederländischen)". *HEL* XI-1.111–133.

*Barbara Kaltz, Tours (Frankreich)*

# 98. The teaching of Spanish in 16th-century Europe

1. Social and political background
2. 'Vocabularies' or conversation books
3. Grammar books
4. Glossaries and dictionaries
5. Bibliography

## 1. Social and political background

During the Renaissance period, Europe experienced an increase in international travel and an intensification in commercial and cultural exchanges. A vigorous need and desire arose for the learning of foreign tongues, accelerated by the gradual loss in the knowledge of Latin and the prestige acquired by vernacular languages as the result of the discovery of printing and the power gained by emerging new social groups such as tradesmen and merchants. Spanish was studied in those European countries where Spain maintained strong ties such as the Low Countries (under Spain's dominion in the 16th century), Italy, France, England, and Germany. Licentiate Cristóbal de Villalón (1505/10–1558/62?) in his *Gramática castellana* (1558: 9) stated with regard to Spanish: "Y que les aplaze mucho y se preçian de hablar en ella. El Flamenco, el Italiano, Inglés, Francés. Y aun en Alemania se huelgan de la hablar".

The history of the teaching of Spanish as a foreign language began during the reign of Charles V when Spain became a powerful political and commercial power in Europe. The methodology for teaching vernacular languages was similar to that employed earlier with regard to Latin and Greek instruction. The sole difference resided in the type of language being taught. Whereas the study of

Latin was based on the *usus* of classical authors, the corpus utilized for the teaching of the vernaculars generally included the language of artisans, traders, and travelers. Language classes in the 16th century consisted of the practice of dialogs, reading and translation exercises, word memorization, and the study of pronunciation and grammar (cf. Lambley 1920: 179ff.; for primary sources on the topic of this study, consult Niederehe 1995).

## 2. 'Vocabularies' or conversation books

The approach based on the study of dialogs, which included oral practice and the rote learning of words, could be traced back to classical antiquity. This tradition, which continued in the Middle Ages and the Renaissance in connection with Greek and Latin instruction, eventually expanded to the study of the vernaculars. In the Low Countries, as a consequence of the vigorous growth in trade, we observe the development of dialog materials or the so-called *Manière de langage* or *Livres de métiers*. The first dialog book of this kind, known to date, was the *Livre des mestiers* (1349), written by a Bruges schoolteacher. This book with dialogs in French and Flemish covered the various occupations of tradesmen (cf. Gessler 1931: 14).

The first dialog manual to include Spanish, *Vocabulario para aprender Franches, Espannol y Flaminco* (Antwerp 1520) was probably a publication, in which Spanish had been added to the older French-Flemish texts (see Morel-Fatio 1901: 88). The *Vocabulario de quatro lenguas, Tudesco, Francés, Latino y Español* (Louvain 1551) followed closely the one Noël de Berlaimont (died in 1531) had published earlier in French and Flemish. In fact, many early dialog books including French, Flemish, and Spanish were influenced by the Berlaimont *Vocabulaires*, which had become quite popular by the first half of the 16th century. This 1551 edition contained a glossary of common words, the numerals, the days of the week, three dialogs (which increased in number in posterior reissues), letters and documents regarding commerce and trade, several Christian prayers, a few pages on pronunciation and a series of grammatical remarks. Later versions might vary the title or the number of languages, as in *Vocabulario, Colloquios or diálogos en quatro lenguas, Flamenge, Francés, Español, Italiano* (Antwerp 1557). The one whose Latin title began *Colloquia et dictionariolum* (Brussels 1589) had a total of seven languages. These *Colloquia cum dictionariolo*, part of the Berlaimont tradition, went through numerous editions in the Low Countries, Germany, and Italy.

There was no early multilingual *Vocabulaire* including English. Consequently, a need existed for an English-Spanish version of a text similar to Berlaimont's *Vocabulaire*. This gap was fulfilled by *A very profitable boke to lerne the maner of redying, writying & speakying English & Spanish* (London 1554), which was a translation and adaptation into English of the 1551 Louvain edition of the dialog books in the Berlaimont tradition. *A very profitable boke* antedated the presence of the English language in the famous *Vocabulaires* by twenty-two years, since it was not until 1576 that English and German were added to the Berlaimont line of dialogs.

Gabriel Meurier (ca. 1530–1605), a member of the teachers' guild in Antwerp, issued *Coloquios familiares muy convenientes y más provechosos de quantos salieron fasta agora* (Antwerp 1568), in Spanish and French. A resident in the Low Countries, Meurier must have known Berlaimont's *Vocabulaires*, however Meurier's thirty dialogs broke away with the Berlaimont pattern, which never numbered more than seven. These generally focused on the language of trade and commerce, as the author himself stated: "Colloques familiers ... dont l'homme peut à tout heure avoir mestier en toutes se faciendes & negoces, soit en allant, voyageant, vēdant comme en achatant".

William Stepney, a Spanish teacher in England, published *The Spanish Schole-master. Containing seven Dialogues* (London 1591). Stepney made yet another translation and adaptation into English of Berlaimont's 1551 edition of the *Vocabulaire* (see Bourland 1933). This book had a section devoted to proverbs but very little on grammar. Finally, John Minsheu (1570?–1650?), also a Spanish teacher, issued *Pleasant and delightfull dialogues in Spanish and English* (London 1599). Both Stepney and Minsheu included the kind of materials and sections typical of dialog books in those days. Minsheu's dialogs were seven in number following the Berlaimont tradition, although the content was quite original and intermixed with proverbs. It is generally believed that the author of those dialogs was don Alonso de Baeça, a Spaniard who had been taken prisoner by the English after the defeat of the Armada (cf. Ungerer 1956: 51). Minsheu's dialogs, written in both excellent and literary Spanish, were copied by César Oudin (?−1625) and went through numerous editions in subsequent centuries.

## 3. Grammar books

Dialog books were quite useful for artisans and traders interested in studying spoken Spanish. As additional tools for learning Spanish, these dialog books also contained a basic chapter on pronunciation, grammar summaries, and glossaries. However, more complete grammars were needed for certain individuals, social groups, and teachers, who, on account of their position, needed to attain a higher degree of perfection in Spanish. The first Spanish grammar ever to be published was *Gramática de la lengua castellana* (Salamanca 1492) by Antonio de Nebrija (1444−1522). This was the first complete grammar of a vernacular language. The purpose of Nebrija's work was threefold: (1) "fijar" the Spanish language in order to avoid the "muchas mudanzas" it had undergone over the centuries, (2) to facilitate the learning of Latin through the grammatical knowledge of Spanish, and (3) to aid in the teaching of Spanish to foreigners. Nebrija's work was a monolingual grammar, theoretical rather than practical, which was virtually forgotten for a whole century for the simple reason that it had come out too early for its time. Nebrija's third goal, i. e., that his grammar was a tool for teaching Spanish to foreigners, must have occurred to him when his project was nearing completion since this goal does not seem central in the lay-out of his work (for additional information on Nebrija and other writers of Spanish grammars, consult Kukenheim 1932 and Lope 1999).

Just as we observed in connection with the so-called vocabularies or conversation books, it was also in the Low Countries where the first grammars for the teaching of Spanish originated. The anonymous treatise *Util y breve institution para aprender los principios y fundamentos de la lengua Hespañola* (Louvain 1555), written in Spanish, French, and Latin, inaugurated a new trend for the teaching of Spanish to foreigners. Here we find a practical grammar with a brief pronunciation section, an easy and simple morphological study of the parts of speech together with a comprehensive treatment of verbal forms, a note on patronymics, and several Christian prayers similar to those found in dialog books. A second anonymous grammar *Gramática de la lengua vulgar de España* (Louvain 1559) contained an important and long section on pronunciation (21 pages). Based on stylistic clues, a number of scholars have concluded that the authors of those two anonymous grammars were Spaniards (cf. Alonso 1951 and Sánchez 1992: 36−37). *Gramática castellana. Arte breve y compendiosa para saber hablar y escrevir en lengua Castellana congrua y decentemente* (Antwerp 1558) by Licentiate Cristóbal de Villalón differed from the previous two grammars in that it touched upon theoretical questions and reduced the number of examples used in the study of grammatical categories. Villalón wished to promote the knowledge of Spanish among the Flemings, the Italians, the English, the French, and the Germans. This work was written in Spanish and required prior understanding of that language.

Gabriel Meurier, already known for his dialog book, got out an opuscule *Coniugaisons, regles, et instructions, mout propres et necessairement requises, pour ceux qui desirent apprendre François, Italien, Espagnol, & Flamen* (Antwerp 1558), which was followed by *Breve instruction contenante la maniere de bien prononcer & lire le François, Italien, Espagnol, & Flamen.* His main goal here was to make communication easier among the various tradesmen, who exchanged their merchandise in the large port of Antwerp.

In Italy the concern for foreign languages also developed early for political and commercial reasons. During the papacy of Spanish-born Alexander VI (1492−1503), the knowledge of Spanish spread rapidly in Italy. This expansion was further stimulated through the increased political and business contacts between both countries. The first Spanish grammar for Italians, entitled *Il paragone della lingua toscana et castigliana* (Naples 1560) was written by Giovanni Mario Alessandri d'Urbino. Despite its enormous significance, this treatise only went through one edition, indeed it was supplanted by the *Osservationi* of Giovanni Miranda a few years later. Alessandri's *Il paragone* was the first brief attempt at composing a comparative Spanish-Italian grammar. In addition to a section on pronunciation and another on the parts of speech, its author carefully exemplified the points under discussion. Alessandri opened up a new approach in vernacular language instruction; a contrastive approach that had already been present in the teaching of classical languages. He surpassed the grammatical boundaries of the Spanish language and focused on the special difficulties Spanish offered for Italian speakers.

The *Osservationi della lingua Castigliana* (Venice 1565) of Giovanni Miranda can be considered as one of the key, if not they key bilingual grammar in the history of the teaching of Spanish to speakers of other languages. In the 16th century alone, the *Osservationi* went through ten editions in Venice. Miranda's work was the methodological source for the teaching of Spanish in Europe in the following hundred years. The *Osservationi* were indebted to Alessandri's contrastive methodology but had the added value of extending this methodology to a broader corpus (407 pages). This work was clear and easy with regard to the presentation of the subject-matter and contained numerous examples drawn from everyday usage with their corresponding Italian equivalents. With Alessandri and Miranda, foreign language instruction evolved from being a descriptive study with some comparative features to becoming a contrastive approach, in which interference factors stemming from the learner's native tongue were carefully considered (cf. Sanchez 1992: 40–43).

It took some time before grammars for the teaching of Spanish appeared in France; this delay was mainly due to the rivalry and wars existing between Spain and France. This political and religious turmoil hindered cultural and commercial exchanges between both countries in the 16th century. The first Spanish-French grammar worthy of that name was not published until the very end of that century, when N. Charpentier issued *La parfaite méthode pour entendre, escrire et parler la langue Espagnole* (Paris 1596). Charpentier was cautious enough to exclude his name from the title-page, nevertheless he was hanged one year after its publication, having been accused of participation in a pro-Spanish conspiracy. He mentioned Nebrija's and Miranda's names. The latter must have inspired Charpentier, who equally provided numerous examples as well as contrastive discussions useful for native speakers of French. However, Charpentier's grammar was completely eclipsed by that of his successor, César Oudin.

César Oudin was the chief representative of Spanish grammar books for foreigners in France. His *Grammaire et observations de la langue espagnolle, recueillies et mises en François* (Paris 1597), if only for historical reasons, gained a wider readership than that of Miranda and became popular throughout Europe for many years to come. Oudin's treatise (presented as a patriotic undertaking which could help officers in the French army to uncover the war tactics of their Spanish enemy) was an adaptation into French of the comparative methodology displayed by Miranda in his Spanish-Italian grammar. His work was half the size of Miranda's with a chapter on pronunciation, a morphological description of the parts of speech, and a series of usage commentaries with abundant examples. A translation and adaptation of Oudin's grammar into Latin appeared in Cologne (1607), and another translation and adaptation into English came out in London (1662).

In England, Oxford was an important center for learning foreign languages. Here private teachers satisfied the needs of university students concerning foreign language instruction. A Spanish refugee from Seville, Antonio del Corro, had arrived at Oxford in 1569. Del Corro had previously taught Spanish in France, where he composed *Reglas gramaticales para aprender la lengua Española y Francesa* (ca. 1560), which was eventually published at Oxford, in 1586. John Thorius, an Oxford graduate, translated del Corro's work into English as *The Spanish Grammar. With certaine rules teaching both the Spanish and French Tongues … With a Dictionarie* (London 1590) and added a Spanish-English dictionary as indicated in the title. This was not a grammar written for native speakers of English since Thorius simply made a translation of the original with no attempt to resolve the problems faced by English speakers learning Spanish and French.

Richard Percyvall, who had participated in the decipherment of secret documents concerning the Spanish Armada, published *Bibliotheca Hispanica. Containing a Grammar, with a Dictionarie in Spanish, English, and Latine* (London 1591). The most important part of *Bibliotheca Hispanica* was not the grammar (21 pages), but its dictionary (60 pages). John Minsheu was the author of *Spanish Grammar* (London 1599). For this grammar he had drawn heavily on Meurier,

Miranda, and del Corro (see Martín-Gamero 1961 for the teaching of Spanish in England).

At first sight, it seems surprising that in Germany grammars for learning Spanish did not appear until the 17th century, since Charles V was emperor of both Spain and Germany and, as a consequence, close political and trade ties must have existed between the two countries. Cristóbal de Villalón in his *Gramática castellana* (1558: 9) hinted at the fact that Spanish was being studied in Germany when he states "... aun en Alemania se huelgan de la hablar", referring to the Spanish tongue. Therefore, it seems quite likely that those Germans who in the 16th century needed to learn Spanish did so with the help of Latin-Spanish grammars and of Spanish grammars for speakers of other European languages such as Flemish, Italian, French, and English. Bilingual and plurilingual methodologies had been common in 16th-century Europe. In the Renaissance, Greek and Latin were studied simultaneously (following Quintilian's advice in ancient Rome) with the assistance of a third language, which normally was the vernacular tongue of the learner (for Renaissance ideas on classical language instruction, see Breva 1994).

This multilingual methodology extended to the study of vernacular languages. Consequently, it should not shock us if the particular edition of César Oudin's grammar that was conceived for teaching Spanish to the German nobility was not a translation and adaptation of the French original into German (as it happened for English *mutatis mutandis*), but a translation into Latin with the title *Grammatica Hispanica, hactenus gallice explicata, et aliquoties edita* (Cologne 1607). Likewise, Henricus Doergangk's grammar *Institutiones in linguam hispanicam, ad modum faciles, quales ante hac nunquam visae* (Cologne 1614) for teaching Spanish to Germans, which drew on Miranda's and Oudin's ideas, also appeared in Latin (see Sarmiento & Niederehe 1992 for the teaching of Spanish in Germany).

## 4. Glossaries and dictionaries

Small and large polyglot works abounded in the 16th century. We already observed that 16th-century 'vocabularies' or dialog books appended bilingual, trilingual, and multilingual glossaries depending on the number of languages included in them and subsequent *Colloquia* frequently added this kind of glossaries as well. Similarly, grammar manuals sometimes had brief dictionaries. For example, Antonio del Corro's *Spanish Grammer* (1590) contained a dictionary that had been appended by John Thorius.

Before the publication of vernacular bilingual and multilingual dictionaries, the only dictionaries available for foreigners learning Spanish were bilingual lexica that had been written for Spanish students of Latin. In this connection, it was well-known Alfonso González de Palencia's *Universal vocabulario en latín y en romance* (Seville 1490). Antonio de Nebrija was the author of a *Dictionarium latino-hispanum* (Salamanca 1492) and a *Dictionarium hispano-latinum* (Salamanca 1495). Nebrija's lexicographical work was one of the sources of Percyvall's dictionary.

Ambrogio Calepino (1435–1511) published his large (888 pages) monolingual Latin *Dictionarium* at Reggio in 1502. With the passage of time, other languages such as Greek, Hebrew, French, Italian, German, Flemish, Spanish (and up to a total of eleven languages in 1590) were incorporated into the original Latin version. The 1565 Lyons edition contained Latin, Italian, French, and Spanish, while the 1568 Basle edition included Latin, Greek, Italian, French, Spanish, and German.

Cristóbal Escobar issued *Dictionarium trium linguarum* (1512) in Latin, Italian, and Spanish. A popular dictionary with no author was *Quinque linguarum utilissimus vocabulista Latine Tusche, Gallice, Hyspanice & Alemanice* (Venice 1513), with numerous posterior editions in Italy, Germany, and France. According to the 1533 Venice reprinting, this dictionary was written to serve those who, 'without going to school (such as artisans and women)', wished to learn languages. The *Vocabulista* was a topical lexicon in the Medieval tradition (cf. the *Nomenclator* below). Another famous polyglot dictionary was *Septem linguarum, Latinae, Teutonicae, Gallicae, Hispanicae, Italicae, Anglicae, Alemanicae, dilucidissimus dictionarius* (Antwerp 1530), which also went through numerous editions. In fact, the bilingual dictionary *The Boke of Englysshe and Spanysshe* (ca. 1554), published in England, was based on the *Dilucidissimus dictionarius*.

The *nomenclatores*, i.e., lexica in which words were grouped by topics, rather than alphabetically, were not uncommon in the 16th century. Hadrianus Junius (1511–1577) issued a famous *Nomenclator, Omnium rerum propria nomina variis linguis explicata indicans* (Augsburg 1555). Junius's *Nomenclator* had a broad variety of subjects with sections on animals, trees, plants, God, virtues, law, and morals. The Antwerp and Paris 1567 reissues were written in six languages: Latin, Greek, Flemish, French, Italian, and Spanish. This dictionary appeared in unabridged editions of eight, six, four, three, and two languages as well as in abbreviated versions for schools. It went through numerous reprintings in the Low Countries, France and Germany.

Alfonso de Ulloa (?–1580?) wrote several *Glosarios* (1553) for Italian readers in order to help them understand difficult words and idiomatic expressions in Spanish literary works, which he himself had put out in Italy. Gabriel Meurier issued *Recueil de sentences notables, dicts et dictions comuns en adages, proverbes & refrans, traduits la plus part de Latin, Italien & Espagnol* (Antwerp 1568). This volume, as its title suggests, was made up of famous phrases taken from Latin, Italian, and Spanish adages, proverbs, and sayings. Many of these phrases were used by John Minsheu in his dialog book and in his collection of proverbs. Christoval de las Casas got out a bilingual Spanish-Italian dictionary *Vocabulario de las dos Lenguas Toscana y Castellana, con una introducción para la correcta pronunciación de ambas lenguas* (Seville 1570) with a strong influence from Nebrija, which had some bearing on Richard Percyvall's lexicon.

Richard Percyvall's *Bibliotheca Hispanica* (London 1591) gained popularity on account of its 60 page Spanish-English-Latin dictionary. In the preface, Percyvall acknowledged his indebtedness to Thomas Doyley, a friend of the group of Spanish translators at Oxford, who had been writing an English-Spanish-Latin dictionary. Doyley's printer had obtained a licence in 1590 to print it with the title *Spanish grammar conformed to our Englishe Accydence, with a large dictionarye conteyninge Spanish, Latyn, and Englishe wordes*. Even if Percyvall did not say so, it seems that Doyley, a less influential and powerful man than Percyvall, had his trilingual dictionary ready to be sent to the printer (cf. Steiner 1979: 18–19). Up to now no one has researched the magnitude of Doyley's contribution to Percyvall's *Bibliotheca Hispanica*. Finally, John Minsheu issued *A dictionarie in Spanish and English, first published into the English tongue by Ric. Percivale. Now enl. and amplified* (London 1599). What was important about this work was that, to the enlarged Spanish-English dictionary by Percyvall, Minsheu added a Spanish-English dictionary of over one hundred and fifty pages (for additional information on this section, see Collison 1982; Sarmiento & Niederehe 1992; Sánchez 1992: 74–79).

## 5. Bibliography


Alonso, Amado. 1951. "Identificación de gramáticos españoles clásicos". *Revista de Filología Española* 35.221–236.

Bourland, Caroline B. 1933. "*The Spanish Schoole-Master* and the Polyglot Derivatives of Noël de Berlaimont's *Vocabulaire*". *Revue Hispanique* 81.283–318.

Breva-Claramonte, Manuel. 1994. *La didáctica de las lenguas en el Renacimiento: Juan Luis Vives y Pedro Simón Abril.* Con selección de textos. Bilbao: Universidad de Deusto.

Collison, Robert L. 1982. *A History of Foreign-Language Dictionaries.* London: André Deutsch.

Gessler, Jean. 1931. *Le "Livre des Mestiers" de Bruges et ses dérivés. Quatre anciens manuels de conversation.* Bruges: o. Vlg.

Kukenheim, Louis. 1932. *Contribution à l'histoire de la grammaire italienne, espagnole et française à l'époque de la Renaissance.* Amsterdam: N. V. Noord-Hollandsche Uitgevers-Maatschappij.

Lambley, Kathleen. 1920. *The Teaching and Cultivation of the French Language in England during Tudor and Stuart Times.* Manchester: Manchester Univ. Press.

Lope Blanch, Juan M. (1999). "La enseñanza del español durante el siglo de Oro". *Actas de I Congreso Internacional de la Sociedad Española de Historiografía Lingüística. A Coruña, 18–21 de febrero de 1997,* edited by Mauro Fernández Rodríguez et al., pp. 49–73. Madrid: Arcos Libros.

Martín-Gamero, Sofía. 1961. *La eseñanza del inglés en España.* (*Biblioteca Románica Hispánica. II Estudios y Ensayos*). Madrid: Editorial Gredos.

Morel-Fatio, Alfred. 1900. *Ambrosio de Salazar et l'étude de l'espagnol en France sous Louis XIII.* Paris: Picard et Fils.

Niederehe, Hans-J. 1995. *Bibliografía cronológica de la lingüística, la gramática y la lexicografía del español. Desde los comienzos hasta el año 1600.* Amsterdam & Philadelphia: Benjamins.

Sánchez Pérez, Aquilino. 1992. *Historia de la enseñanza del español como lengua extranjera.* (= *Historiografía de la Lingüística Española, Serie Monografías*). Madrid: Sociedad General Española de Librería.

Sarmiento, Ramón & Hans-J. Niederehe. 1992. "Die Verbreitung des Spanischen in Deutschland im Spiegel von Sprachlehrbüchern des 16. und 17. Jahrhunderts". *Beiträge zur Geschichte der Sprachwissenschaft* 2.173–191.

Steiner, Roger J. 1970. *Two Centuries of Spanish and English Bilingual Lexicography (1590–1800).* The Hague & Paris: Mouton.

Ungerer, Gustav. 1956. *Anglo-Spanish Relations in Tudor Literature.* Bern: Francke.

Villalón, Cristóbal de. 1558. *Gramática castellana. Arte breve y compendiosa para saber hablar y escrevir en lengua Castellana.* Amberes: En casa de Guillermo Simon.

*Manuel Breva-Claramonte, Deusto (Spain)*

# 99. Der Unterricht des Englischen im 16. Jahrhundert

1. Der sprachliche und politische Rahmen
2. Frühe Formen des Spracherwerbs und Sprachunterrichts
3. London als Lernort und die Rolle des Stalhofs
4. Frühe Unterrichtsmaterialien
5. Die Grenzen der Ausdehnung des Englischen als Fremdsprache
6. Bibliographie

## 1. Der sprachliche und politische Rahmen

Im Unterschied zum Italienischen gewinnt die englische Sprache in der Form des Frühneuenglischen erst im Verlauf des 16. Jhs. ihre moderne, nationalsprachliche Gestalt. Die politische Aufwertung und Ausgestaltung des Englischen am Beispiel des klassischen Latein ist spätestens seit den 30er Jahren Programm; die mit dem Vorhaben befaßten Gelehrten und Literaten stehen nicht selten dem Hofe nahe, beispielsweise als Prinzenerzieher (Beispiel: Sir Thomas Elyot, Autor des 1531 erschienenen Buches *The Governour*, das Heinrich VIII. gewidmet ist, sowie Übersetzer des 1534 gedruckten *Doctrinal of Princes*) oder als Lehrer an den *Public Schools* (Beispiel: Richard Mulcaster, *Headmaster* der *Merchant Taylor's School* und Autor eines *Elementarie* genannten, 1582 erschienenen Traktats zur Rechtschreibung). Die sprachschöpferische Kraft und Sprachgewalt Shakespeares muß vor dem Hintergrund der sprachpflegerischen Bemühungen zweier vorausgehender Generationen gesehen und gewürdigt werden. (Ausführliche Darstellung bei Baugh 1951 u. ö., Kapitel *The Renaissance, 1500–1650.*)

Unter der Regierung Heinrichs VIII. (England) bzw. Jakobs V. (Schottland) werden England und Schottland im zweiten Viertel des 16. Jhs. Nationalstaaten moderner Prägung, im Falle von England mit eigener nationaler Kirche. Elisabeth I. baut den englischen Nationalstaat konsequent aus, nach ihrem Tode kommt es mit der Vereinigung der Kronen zur Ausbildung des *United Kingdom.* Inzwischen ist auch Schottland ein Staat mit protestantischer, presbyterianisch verfaßter Staatsreligion geworden. Mit dem Sieg über die spanische Armada (1588) verschieben sich in Westeuropa die außenpolitischen, aber auch die wirtschaftspolitischen Gewichte. Forthin ist England die bedeutendste Seemacht Europas; die englische Handelsflotte wird für die Seeschiffahrt der übrigen europäischen Staaten zur empfindlichen Konkurrenz. Englische und schottische Schiffe laufen in verstärktem Maße kontinentale Häfen an; in mehreren Hansestädten längs der Küste bilden sich englische Kapitäns- und Kaufmannsgesellschaften (Beispiel: Hamburg; zur Rolle Hamburgs im Englandhandel des 16. und 17. Jhs. vgl. unter sprachlichem Aspekt vor allem Ehrenberg 1896, aus allgemein wirtschaftsgeschichtlicher Sicht daneben auch Friedland 1960 und Hitzigrath 1907).

## 2. Frühe Formen des Spracherwerbs und Sprachunterrichts

Ein Englischunterricht in schulischem Rahmen ist für das 16. Jh. bisher nicht nachgewiesen, weder in England (Englisch als Muttersprache und Zweitsprache) noch außerhalb (Englisch als Fremdsprache). Auch Lehrer des Englischen als Fremdsprache sind bisher – zumindest außerhalb Londons (siehe unten) – nicht namentlich bekannt. Daraus darf jedoch nicht geschlossen werden, daß es sie nicht gegeben hat. Nach dem Prinzip *Die beste Sprache des Handels ist die des Kunden* werden – in hansischen Kreisen beispielsweise – seit dem 13. Jh. die Volkssprachen der Handelspartner erworben, besonders dort, wo man mit einer internationalen Sprache (in Mittel- und Nordeuropa: Latein, im Mittelmeerraum: Sabir) nicht weiterkommt. Im hansischen Kontor zu Nowgorod darf im ausgehenden Mittelalter nur jener Kaufmann Handel treiben, der über adäquate Russischkenntnisse verfügt. Hansischen Kaufleuten ist es bei Strafe untersagt, Nicht-Hanseaten zu Russischkenntnissen zu verhelfen: Wer die Sprache hat, hat den Handel. (→ Art. 93.) Vor diesem Hintergrund kann davon ausgegangen werden, daß in den kontinentalen Hafenstädten von Cadiz und Lissabon bis Bergen und Riga sowie in den Städten an den für kleinere Seeschiffe passierbaren Unterläufen der Flüsse (Beispiel: Köln) von einzelnen Handelsherren und deren Söhnen im Verlauf des 16. Jhs. oder auch schon früher Englisch gelernt wurde, *ex usu* in direktem Kontakt mit englischen oder schottischen Kapitänen und Kaufleuten oder aber vielleicht auch auf der Basis von Privatunterricht, wobei das Berufsbild des Sprachmeisters, der im städtischen Ambiente seine Dienste anbietet, zu diesem Zeitpunkt noch nicht überall geläufig ist. Dies mag der Grund sein für das Fehlen der Namen von Lehrern. Darüber hinaus ist in den Kaufmannsfamilien der frühen Neuzeit das Auslandspraktikum eine beliebte Etappe des beruflichen Werdeganges: Die Söhne werden in befreundeten Handelshäusern und in Handelkontoren des Auslands untergebracht, wo sie dann auch die Sprache des Landes einschließlich der erforderlichen Fachsprachen erwerben. Eine Verschickung nach Italien, Frankreich oder in die Niederlande und auch in den deutschsprachigen Raum hinein (Hamburg, Leipzig, Nürnberg, Augsburg) ist im 16. Jh. gang und gäbe; es hat mit Sicherheit Fälle gegeben, in denen junge Handelsherren und Kaufmannslehrlinge als Praktikanten und der Sprache wegen nach London oder aber auch in andere englische und schottische Küstenstädte verschickt wurden. Schottland unterhält im 16. und 17. Jh. enge Handelsbeziehungen in den baltischen Raum hinein; in Elbing beispielsweise existiert eine anglo-schottische Kolonie (vgl. dazu Simson 1916, Volckmann 1923).

## 3. London als Lernort und die Rolle des Stalhofs

Im Jahre 1554 erhält das Londoner Hansekontor, der Stalhof, eine neue Kontorordnung. Darin wird festgelegt, daß nur solche Kaufleute zugelassen werden, die über hinlängliche Englischkenntnisse verfügen. Wer den sprachpraktischen Nachweis, daß er sich ein Jahr lang mit der Sprache des Landes befaßt habe, nicht erbringen kann, muß die Zeitspanne bei einem Lakenmeister auf dem Lande zubringen, um die Gemeinsprache und die Fachsprache der Textilproduktion und -vermarktung zu erwerben (Dietze 1927: 10). Die Festlegung erinnert an die Gepflogenheiten im Kontor zu Nowgorod (vgl. Abschnitt 2.). Nach dem Tode Marias der Katholischen (1558) wird England zunehmend eine Zufluchtstätte für protestantische Glaubensflüchtlinge vom Kontinent, wobei die Hugenotten (nach 1572) das größte Kontingent stellen. Gegen Ende der 80er Jahre liegt der Ausländeranteil in London bei über 10% der Gesamtbevölkerung. Hierdurch ergibt sich in der englischen Hauptstadt ein auf das Englische gerichteter Sprachlernbedarf, der die Konzentration von Lernwilligen an jedem anderen Ort der damaligen Welt deutlich übersteigt. Drei Londoner Sprachlehrer aus dem letzten Viertel des 16. Jhs. sind mit Namen überliefert, die neben ihrer Muttersprache (Französisch bzw. Italienisch) auch Unterricht in Englisch für Ausländer erteilt haben: der aus Caen stammende, zunächst mittellose Hugenotte Jacques Bellot, sein Glaubensbruder Claudius Holyband alias Claude de Sainliens aus Moulins (Frankreich) sowie John Florio (ca. 1553–1625), Sohn des aus Italien gebürtigen Pfarrers der Londoner italienischen Gemeinde und einer Engländerin und Italienischlehrer der Königlichen Familie (detaillierte Darstellung zu den Genannten bei Howatt 1984: 12–31; bibliographische Erfassung des auf das Englische bezogenen sprachwissenschaftlichen und sprachpraktischen Œuvre bei Alston 1974, passim; speziell zu Holyband vgl. die Biographie von Farrer 1908; speziell zu Florio vgl. die Biographie von Yates 1934). Bellot, der sich seit den späten 70er Jahren in London aufhält, kommt am ehesten noch dem Prototyp des Sprachmeisters nahe, der – nach Art heutiger Privat-Musiklehrer – einem städtischen Publikum Privatunterricht anbietet. – Holyband, seit Januar 1566 in England und der professionellste unter den drei Lehrern (bereits in Moulins als Lehrer tätig), unterhält in London und der Umgebung der Stadt nacheinander drei Schulen, in denen er den Kindern wohlhabender Handelsherren Französischunterricht erteilt, aber auch das normale Latein-Curriculum anbietet; dennoch bezeichnet er sich auch als "professor of the English tongue". Einer der Schulen, der zu Lewisham, stattet Königin Elisabeth einen Höflichkeitsbesuch ab. Holyband widmet ihr eines seiner Bücher. Zwischenzeitlich erwirbt er sich einen Ruf als Privatlehrer im Haushalt von Lord Buckhurst, der mit der Königin verschwägert ist. Offenbar kehrt er im Anschluß an das Edikt von Nantes (1598) gemeinsam mit seiner zweiten Frau, einer Engländerin, nach Frankreich zurück. – Florio, in Straßburg und der Schweiz aufgewachsen, wohin seine Eltern nach der Thronbesteigung Marias der Katholischen 1553 geflohen waren, eine Zeitlang möglicherweise auch Student an der Universität Tübingen, ist nach seiner Übersiedlung nach England in den frühen 70er Jahren zunächst als Italienisch-Tutor am Magdalen College zu Oxford tätig, an dem er auch studiert. Später arbeitet er in der Londoner französischen Botschaft, von wo aus er als Sekretär und Sprachlehrer in die Haushalte politisch hochrangiger Londoner Adelsfamilien wechselt. Als Mitarbeiter der französischen Botschaft unterhält er mit großer Wahrscheinlichkeit Beziehungen zum elisabethanischen Geheimdienst unter Sir Francis Walsingham. Auch Sir William Cecil, Elisabeths erstem Minister, mag er als Informant gedient haben. In seinen späteren Jahren ist er Privatsekretär der Königin Anna von Dänemark, der Gattin Jakobs I. Als sie 1619 stirbt, verliert Florio seine Kontakte zum Hof; da Jakob die vereinbarten Zahlungen nicht leistet, stirbt er in Armut. Er wird ein Opfer der Pest des Jahres 1625. (Zu den von den drei Sprachlehrern publizierten Lehrmaterialien vgl. Abschnitt 4.)

## 4. Frühe Unterrichtsmaterialien

Bellot publiziert im Jahre 1580 ein für seine hugenottischen Glaubensbrüder und deren Familien gedachtes kleines Lehrbuch mit dem Titel *The English Schoolmaster, containing many profitable precepts for the natural born Frenchmen and other strangers that have their French tongue, to attain the true pronouncing of the English tongue* (London: Purfoote, Dizlie), wobei der Haupttitel an Roger Aschams 1570 veröffentlichtes pädagogisches Traktat *The Schoolmaster* erinnert. Das Buch ist ganz auf die kommunikativen Alltagsbedürfnisse von Einwanderern zugeschnitten, die sich in einer für sie ungewohnten Welt zurechtfinden müssen. Es bietet kaum Bezüge zur Welt des Handels. Eine zweite Publikation, *Familiar Dialogues*, folgt 1586. Im Vorwort beschreibt Bellot sein Anliegen mit den folgenden Worten:

> The experience having in the old time learned unto me what sorrow is for them that be refugiate in a strange country, when they cannot understand the language of that place in which they be exiled, and when they cannot make them to be understood by speech to the inhabiters of that country wherein they be retired [...] I thought good to put into their hands certain short dialogues in French and English. (zitiert nach Howatt 1984: 16)

Den Inhalt des Buches beschreibt Howatt (a. a. O.) wie folgt:

> Bellot's dialogues have a domestic setting with a strong emphasis on shopping. His characters visit the poulterer, the costermonger, the draper, the fishmonger, and the butcher in a lengthy sequence of shop scenes [...] which follows more or less the sequence of a single day. It begins with getting up in the morning and seeing the children off to school. Then comes the shopping and, in the evening, friends call in for dinner, and the conversation gets round to their present depressing predicament [...]. 'There is no other news but of the sickness and the dearth, which be nowadays almost throughout all France.' [...] Later their spirits revive and they play dice and cards. The book ends with some useful travel phrases.

Holybands Unterrichtsmaterialien, *The French Schoolmaster* (1573) und *The French Littleton* (1576), sind auf die Bedürfnisse seiner Schulen und des Französischlernens überhaupt zugeschnitten. Da beide Bücher, die im übrigen viel gemein haben, auf Dialogarbeit großen Wert legen, kommt allerdings auch die englische Sprache angemessen zur Geltung. Im *Littleton* steht die Sprache des Handels im Vordergrund. Dabei sind Holybands Dialoge berühmt für die Echtheit und Liebe zum Detail, mit der sie das tägliche Leben abbilden:

> Held together in a broad thematic context such as 'School', these short, self-contained episodes not only have an artistic impact, they also serve a more prosaic pedagogical purpose which helps to clarify Holyband's classroom methods. Each episode contains enough material for one lesson [...] while the context keeps a situational thread running through from one lesson to the next. This technique has certain advantages not available to modern authors who use either very short dialogues illustraiting a new language point or longer, more discursive 'playlets' which can sometimes be difficult to break down into sections for classroom use. (Howatt 1984: 20)

In seinen Grammatikteilen folgt Holyband einem induktiven Ansatz: Der Lerner soll zunächst "frame his tongue" (S. 2 – zitiert nach Howatt, a. a. O.), indem er mit den Texten arbeitet. Später erwirbt er dann die notwendigen Einsichten in den Sprachbau. Holybands Glossare in den genannten Lehrmaterialien münden ein in sein 1593 erschienenes *Dictionary French and English*, das Randle Cotgrave (ohne Nennung der Quelle) zum Ausgangspunkt für sein englisch-französisches Wörterbuch von 1611 macht.

Florio ist Verfasser zweier für sein adliges englisches Publikum konzipierter italienisch-englischer Dialogsammlungen *First Fruits* und *Second Fruits* (London: Dawson, Woodcock 1578 bzw. London: Woodcock 1591). Schon die Titulaturen deuten an, daß – im Unterschied zu den oben genannten Unterrichtsmaterialien – die ausgefeilte, metaphernreiche Sprache hochgestellter Persönlichkeiten im Mittelpunkt steht: *John Florio His First Fruits, which yield familiar speech, merry proverbs, witty sentences and golden sayings. Also a perfect introduction to the Italian and English tongues as in the table appeareth. The like heretofore never by any man published* bzw. *John Florios Second Fruits, to be gathered of twelve trees, of diverse but delightsome tastes to the tongues of Italians and Englishmen. To which is annexed his Garden of Recreation yielding six thousand Italian proverbs* (Titel nach Alston 1974, Orthographie angepaßt). Im übrigen wird die Intention des Verfassers deutlich, seine Arbeiten auch für den Englischunterricht nutzbar zu machen, wobei er möglicherweise an Mitglieder der Londoner italienischen Gemeinde oder aber an italienische Adlige und Patrizier denkt, die auf ihre Bildungsreise in London Station machen. Wie Holyband, so legt auch Florio gegen Ende des Jhs. ein Wörterbuch vor unter dem Titel *A World of Words, or Most Copious, and Exact Dictionary in Italian and English* (London: Hatfield, Blount 1598), von dem 1611 eine der Königin Anna gewidmete 2. Ausgabe unter dem Titel *Queen Anna's New World of Words* erscheint.

Spezielle Unterrichtsmaterialien für den Erwerb des Englischen als Fremdsprache finden sich im 16. Jh. jenseits der Londoner Publikationen von Bellot, Holyband und Florio offenbar nur in Gestalt einiger anonym erschienener, offenbar nicht sonderlich weit verbreiteter Arbeiten wie *A Very Profitable Book to Learn English and Spanish* (London 1554, Neudruck, herausgegeben von R. C. Alston, 1971, vorgestellt bei Roberts [1970]), *Grammatica anglicana, praecipue quatenus a latina differt* (1594) oder aber *Grammaire anglaise et française* (Rouen: Oursel Witwe), von der, wie der weitere Titel suggeriert, frühere Ausgaben vorgelegen haben müssen: *revue et corrigée tout de nouveau d'une quantité de fautes qui étaient aux précédentes impressions [...], augmentée en cette dernière édition d'un vocabulaire anglais et français* (die drei Titel vorhanden in der *British Library* London). Im deutschsprachigen Raum erscheint das erste Lehrbuch des Englischen, die *Grammatica anglica, in qua methodus facilis bene et succincte anglicae linguae addiscendae continetur* von S. Tellaeus, erst im Jahre 1665 (Straßburg); die erste in London verfaßte und gedruckte English-Grammatik für deutschsprachige Lernende ist Henry Offelens *Double Grammar for Germans to Learn English and for Englishmen to Learn the German Tongue* von 1687. Doch es gibt seit der zweiten Hälfte des 16. Jhs. polyglotte Unterrichtsmaterialien (Gesprächsbücher, Glossare), die als Richtschnur beim Erwerb des Englischen dienen können. (Vgl. dazu → Art. 94.) Frühe Arbeiten dieser Art, die das Englische einbeziehen, sind die zahlreichen auf Noël van Berlemont (Barlaimont) zurückgehenden Wörterbücher. Als frühes Beispiel sei genannt: der anonym erschienene *Sex lingarum, latine, teutonice, gallice, hispanice, italice, anglice, dilucidissimus dictionarius, mirum quam utilis, ne dicam necessarius omnibus linguarum studiosis [...] A Vocabulary in Six Languages, Latin, Dutch, French, Spanish, Italian, and English*, London (Southwark): Nicolson, Renys 1537. Weitere Ausgaben (unter Einbeziehung des Englischen) mit ähnlichem Titel sind: Venedig: Sessa 1541, 1548, Nürnberg: Daubmann 1548, Augsburg: Ulhart, zwischen 1541 und 1557 (2 Ausgaben), Venedig: Bindoni, Pasini 1549, Nürnberg: Daubmann 1549. Zu nennen ist auch der möglicherweise schon 1535 erschienene *Septem linguarum, latinae, teutonicae, gallicae, hispanicae, italicae, anglicae, almanicae dilucidissimus dictionarius [...] A Vocabulary in Seven Languages, Latin, Dutch, French, Spanish, Italian, English and High Allemand* [sic!] (Mittelburg: Peetersen, ohne Jahresangabe, weitere Ausgaben Middelburg, zwischen 1540 und 1551, Antwerpen: Crinitus 1540, Antwerpen: van Ghelen 1569). Für den Verlauf des 16. Jhs. sind mindestens 10 weitere polyglotte Berlemont-Ausgaben mit Englischteil bekannt, wobei auch neue Verlagsorte (beispielsweise Delft und Leiden) hinzukommen. Daneben finden sich seit den 60er Jahren auch Ausgaben des *Nomenclator omnium rerum propria nomina variis linguis explicata indicans* des Adrianus Junius, die das Englische einschließen: Antwerpen (laut Titelblatt: Paris): Plantin 1567 (Sprachen: Latein, Griechisch, Deutsch, Niederländisch, Französisch, Italienisch, Spanisch, Englisch), Antwerpen: Plantin 1577 (gleiche Sprachen), London: Newberry, Denham 1585, letztere Ausgabe unter dem Titel: *The Nomenclator, or Remembrancer of Adrianus Junius [...] divided in two tomes, containing proper names and apt terms for all things under their convenient titles, which within a few leaves follow; written by the said Adrianus Junius in Latin, Greek, French, and other foreign tongues, and now in English, by John Higins. With a full supply of all such words as the last enlarged edition afforded, and a dictional index, containing about fourteen hundred principal words with their numbers directly leading to their interpretations. Of special use for all scholars and learners of the same languages, by Abraham Fleming.*

## 5. Die Grenzen der Ausdehnung des Englischen als Fremdsprache

Trotz der hier skizzierten Ansätze und Materialien ist gegen Ende des 16. Jhs. der Erwerb des Englischen als Fremdsprache, europaweit betrachtet, fast ausschließlich auf küstennahe Handelsstädte beschränkt, und nur wenige Individuen lernen die Sprache, die bis ins späte 19. Jh. ihrer Aussprache und Idiomatizität wegen als extrem schwierig gilt. Die religiöse Neugliederung Europas im Anschluß an die Reformation schafft zusätzliche Barrieren. Im katholischen Binnenland gilt das Englische noch im letzten Viertel des 18. Jhs. – mit den Worten der Kaiserin Maria Theresia – "als gefährliche Sprache wegen religions- und sittenverderblichen Principiis" (Kink 1854: 516); sofern es von diesen Gebieten aus überhaupt England-Kontakte gibt, etwa im Bereich des Handels, werden sie nicht auf direktem Wege wahrgenommen. Daher kommen in der frühesten Zeit allenfalls protestantische oder aber paritätisch ausgerichtete Handelsstädte des Binnenlandes als weitere Lernorte des Englischen in Frage. – Hinzu kommt, daß Englisch um die Wende zum 17. Jh. in keiner Weise als internationale Sprache bezeichnet werden kann, auch wenn eine Handels- und Seemacht im Entstehen begriffen ist, die gut 150 Jahre später, nach dem Siebenjährigen Kriege nämlich, zur Weltmacht aufsteigen wird. Als Sprache der Meere konkurriert Englisch nach wie vor mit Spanisch, Portugiesisch, Italienisch, Niederländisch und Deutsch. Englisch ist auch keine galante Sprache, keine Sprache der Höfe: Selbst am Londoner Hof wird vorwiegend Französisch gesprochen, und Königin Elisabeth selbst verfügt über ausgezeichnete Kenntnisse romanischer Sprachen. Während das Französische europaweit nach 1550 zur Sprache der Prinzenerziehung wird, damit aber auch als aufstrebende internationale Sprache und Latein-Ersatz nach etwa 1570 an den Universitäten und im 17. Jh. dann an den Ritterakademien Fuß faßt, bleibt das Englische zunächst außen vor. Da die Sprache zunächst allenfalls als Medium des Handels von Interesse scheint und eine auf dem Kontinent als lesenswert empfundene englische Literatur zunächst noch nicht vorliegt, scheidet auch das weibliche Geschlecht als Lernergruppe aus. Patriziertöchter lernen im 16. und frühen 17. Jh., wenn sie überhaupt Fremdsprachen lernen, Französisch und Italienisch, dazu vielleicht auch noch etwas Latein.

Doch die Weichen für zukünftige Entwicklungen sind gestellt: Auf den britischen Inseln entsteht in der neuen, nationalen Kirchensprache Englisch eine theologische Literatur, die bald im gesamten protestantischen Raum Wertschätzung genießen wird: In der 2. Hälfte des 17. Jhs. sind es die Theologen der deutschen protestantischen Universitäten, die mit dem Ziel des Erwerbs einer Lese- und Übersetzungskompetenz sich dem Englischen zuwenden und dann auch selbst Studierenden Englischunterricht erteilen. Im süddeutsch-katholischen Raum beispielsweise verbreiten die Englischen Fräulein (*Congregatio Beatae Mariae Virginis*) nach 1626 Englischkenntnisse unter ihren weiblichen Zöglingen: Die Gründergeneration der Kongregation setzt sich fast ausschließlich aus adligen englischen Damen zusammen, die als Glaubensflüchtlinge England verlassen haben und nun der Gegenreformation innerhalb des weiblichen Geschlechts Bahn brechen wollen; Englisch ist Pflichtfach im Noviziat. Die literarisch-belletristische Komponente hingegen spielt erst mit der Abwendung vom französischen Regelgeist und der Hinwendung zu englischem Geschmack und, damit verbunden, zu einem romantisierenden Shakespeare-Kult nach etwa 1770 als Motivation für den Erwerb des Englischen eine Rolle. Die im frühen 17. Jh. populären englischen Komödiantentruppen, die weite Teile des mitteleuropäisch-protestantischen Raumes durchstreifen und auf Marktplätzen spielen, werden von den Zuschauern aufgrund ihrer Mimik und Gestik, nicht aber aufgrund ihrer Sprache verstanden.

## 6. Bibliographie

Alston, Robin C. 1974. *A Bibliography of the English Language from the Invention of Printing to the Year 1800.* Ilkley: Janus Press.

Baugh, Albert C. 1951 u. ö. *A History of the English Language.* London: Routledge & Kegan Paul.

Dietze, Hugo 1927. *Methodik des fremdsprachlichen Unterrichts an Handelsschulen.* Leipzig.

Ehrenberg, R. 1896. *Hamburg und England im Zeitalter der Königin Elisabeth.* Jena.

Farrer, Lucy E. 1908. *La vie et les œuvres de Claude de Sainliens alias Claudius Holyband.* Paris: H. Champion (Genf: Slatkine Reprints 1971.)

Friedland, Klaus. 1960. "Hamburger Englandfahrer, 1512–1557". *Zeitschrift des Vereins für hamburgische Geschichte* 46.1–44.

Hitzigrath, Heinrich. 1907. *Die politischen Beziehungen zwischen Hamburg und England zur Zeit Jakobs I., Karls I. und der Republik, 1611–1660.* Hamburg. Programm der Realschule in Hamm zu Hamburg.

Howatt, Anthony, P. R. 1984. *A History of English Language Teaching.* London: Oxford Univ. Press.

Kink, Rudolf. 1854. *Geschichte der Kaiserlichen Universität zu Wien.* Im Auftrage des k. k. Ministers für Kultus und Unterricht nach den Quellen bearbeitet. 2 Bde. Bd. 1. Wien.

Lambley, Kathleen. 1920. *The Teaching and Cultivation of the French Language in England during Tudor and Stuart Times.* Manchester: Manchester Univ. Press; London: Longmans, Green.

Roberts, J. R. 1970. "Two Early English-Spanish Vocabularies". *The Brtish Museum Quarterly* 34. 16–24.

Schröder, Konrad. 1980a. *Linguarum Recentium Annales. Der Unterricht in den modernen europäischen Sprachen im deutschsprachigen Raum.* Bd. 1: *1500–1700.* (= *Augsburger I & I-Schriften* 10.) Augsburg: Universität.

–. 1980b. "Kleine Chronik zur Frühzeit des Fremdsprachenunterrichts im deutschsprachigen Raum, unter besonderer Berücksichtigung des 16. Jahrhunderts". *Die Neueren Sprachen* 79.114–135.

Simson, Paul. 1916. "Die Handelsniederlassung der englischen Kaufleute in Elbing". *Hansische Geschichtsblätter* 22.87–143.

Staufer, Annegret. 1974. *Fremdsprachen bei Shakespeare. Das Vokabular und seine dramatischen Funktionen.* Frankfurt/M.: Akademische Verlagsgesellschaft.

Volckmann, Edwin. 1923. "Elbing als Residenz der Eastland Company oder Sitz des 'englischen Stapels' ". *Der Grundstein britischer Weltmacht* hg. von E. Volckmann, 172–200. Elbing.

Yates, Frances A. 1934. *John Florio, the Life of an Italian in Shakespeare's England.* Cambridge: Cambridge Univ. Press.

*Konrad Schröder, Augsburg (Deutschland)*

# 100. Der Unterricht des Hebräischen, Arabischen und anderer semitischer Sprachen sowie des Persischen und Türkischen in Europa (bis zum Ende des 18. Jahrhunderts)

1. Allgemeines
2. Hebräisch
3. Arabisch
4. Weitere semitische Sprachen
5. Türkisch
6. Persisch
7. Bibliographie

## 1. Allgemeines

Als Sprache des Alten Testaments war das Hebräische im Abendland seit den Zeiten des Hieronymus nie ganz in Vergessenheit geraten, aber seine Pflege galt im Rahmen christlicher Gelehrsamkeit – trotz der Existenz einzelner Kenner – lange Zeit als nicht notwendig. Das änderte sich in mehreren Etappen: Im 13. Jh. im Rahmen der v. a. von den Dominikanern und Franziskanern angestoßenen Bemühungen um die Mission der Juden, im späten 15. Jh. durch das zunehmende Interesse an der Kabbala (Pico della Mirandola, Johannes Reuchlin) sowie im 16. Jh. durch den Aufschwung der Bibelphilologie im Zuge der Reformation. Erst im Zusammenhang mit der Entstehung protestantischer Lehranstalten (Universitäten, Akademien, Gymnasien) kam es zu einem dauerhaften Unterricht des Hebräischen, dem schon bald die Lehre der anderen, für die Bibelphilologie relevanten semitischen Sprachen (v. a. Bibl.-Aramäisch, Syrisch, Samaritanisch, Äthiopisch, Arabisch) folgte.

Unter ihnen nahm das Arabische insofern einen besonderen Platz ein, als es zugleich die Sakral- und Wissenschaftssprache der islamischen Welt war. Arabisch gelangte erst durch die umfangreichen, in Süditalien und Spanien ab dem 11. Jh. entstandenen Übersetzungen arab. Werke in das Blickfeld europäischer Wissenschaft. Den Anstoß zu erstem organisierten Unterricht gab jedoch auch hier, wie beim Hebräischen, das Missionsinteresse: So entstanden um die Mitte des 13. Jh.s in Murcia und Tunis auf Veranlassung des Dominikaners Ramon de Penyafort († 1275) Sprachschulen für Arabisch. Nach ihrem Vorbild gründete Ramon Llull (Raymundus Lullus; ca. 1232–ca. 1316) um 1276 in Miramar auf Mallorca einen Sprachenkonvent für Missionare. Beiden Unternehmungen war keine Dauer beschieden. Auf Betreiben von Llull beschloß jedoch das Konzil von Vienne (1311/ 12) in seinem can. 11 die Einrichtung von je zwei Lehrstühlen für "Orientalische Sprachen" (genannt waren: Hebräisch, Griechisch (!), Arabisch und Chaldäisch) am Sitz der Kurie sowie in Paris, Oxford, Bologna und Salamanca. Dieser Beschluß wurde nur teilweise und nur für kurze Zeit in die Tat umgesetzt, dauerhafte Gründungen scheiterten v. a. aus finanziellen Gründen. Doch blieb der Konzilsbeschluß von prinzipieller Bedeutung für spätere Lehrstuhlgründungen bzw. als generelle Rechtfertigung für die Lehre orientalischer Sprachen an Universitäten bis ins 20. Jh. Eine universitär fest verankerte Lehre des Arabischen setzte erst ab dem Ende des 16. Jh.s in Frankreich, Holland und England ein.

Mit dem im Sprachenkanon von Vienne genannten Chaldäischen ist die heute Syrisch genannte Sprache gemeint, d. h. die Kirchensprache der Jakobiten, Nestorianer und Maroniten. Im Zusammenhang mit den Kreuzzügen war in der römischen Kirche das Interesse an einer Union mit den verschiedenen orientalischen Kirchen entstanden, die ihrerseits in Rom Konvente gründeten. Im Zeitalter des Humanismus konnten daher christliche Gelehrte in Rom orientalischen Christen begegnen, bei denen sie Arabisch, Syrisch oder Äthiopisch lernen konnten. Es ist bezeichnend, daß die ersten Lehrbücher dieser beiden Sprachen bereits einen ersten Anfang der "vergleichenden" Semitistik markieren, insofern sie das Hebräische und Arabische mitberücksichtigen. Auch später haben orientalische Gelehrte in Rom in verschiedenen Institutionen, so u. a. der 1622 gegründeten "Sacra Congregatio de Propaganda Fide", eine hervorragende Rolle gespielt.

Türkisch und Persisch gelangten erst mit dem Aufstieg des Osmanischen Reiches (1453 Eroberung Konstantinopels) bzw. der Gründung des Safavidenreiches (1501) in den Gesichtskreis der Europäer, und zwar v. a. durch Reiseberichte und darin enthaltene Sprachmitteilungen. Türkisch und Persisch war gemeinsam, daß sie zwar wichtige Verkehrssprachen im islamischen Herrschaftsbereich waren, daß sie andererseits jedoch keine direkte Verbindung zur Bibelphilologie aufwiesen; ihre systematische Erforschung und Lehre begann daher, trotz einzelner Vorarbeiten, erst zu einem Zeitpunkt, als politische Umstände das erforderlich machten, und zwar in den Staaten, die enge Beziehungen zum Osmanischen Reich bzw. zu Persien unterhielten, nämlich Frankreich und Österreich. 1700 wurde in Paris an dem von Jesuiten geleiteten "Collège de Louis-le-Grand" die "École des Jeunes de Langue" gegründet, an der zunächst v. a. Armenier und andere christliche Orientalen, ab 1721 aber nur noch Franzosen zum Missions- bzw. Dolmetscherdienst herangezogen und in Türkisch, Persisch und Arabisch unterrichtet wurden. Ein Teil der Ausbildung fand dabei in Konstantinopel statt. In Wien gründete Kaiserin Maria Theresia 1754 die "Orientalische Akademie" zur Heranbildung von sprachkundigen Diplomaten, deren Ausbildungsgang gleichfalls einen mehrjährigen Aufenthalt in der Türkei vorsah. 1795 wurde in Paris die "École des langues orientales vivantes" gegründet, an welcher der Schwerpunkt der Lehre in bewußtem Gegensatz zur Universität auf den Gegenwartssprachen lag und z. B. eine Stelle für arabische Dialekte eingerichtet wurde. An dieser Einrichtung wirkte seit der Gründung Isaac Silvestre de Sacy (1758–1838), der bedeutendste Lehrer einer neuen Generation von Orientalisten, die das von ihnen betriebene Sprachstudium nicht mehr als theologische Hilfsdisziplin verstand.

## 2. Hebräisch

In weiterem Umfange lehrbar wurde das Hebräische erst zu dem Zeitpunkt, da brauchbare Unterrichtsmittel vorlagen. Eine erste von Konrad Pellikan (1478–1556) verfaßte Fibel (*De modo legendi et intelligendi Hebraeum*. Straßburg: Grüninger 1504) wurde alsbald durch das Grammatik und Lexikon umfassende Werk von Johannes Reuchlin (*De rudimentis Hebraicis*, Pforzheim: Anshelm 1506) überholt, das sich allerdings nicht als Lehrbuch für den Unterricht eignete. Am erfolgreichsten wurden im 16. Jh. die Lehrbücher von Sebastian Münster (1488–1552; u. a. *Grammatica hebraica absolutissima*. Basel: Froben 1525; *Opus grammaticum consummatum*. Basel: Petri 1542, beide in starker Anlehnung an die Werke von Elia Levita, 1469–1549) und Nicolaus Clenardus (Cleynaerts, 1493/4–1542; *Tabula in grammaticen Hebraeam*. Louvain: Martens 1529); im 17. Jh. diejenigen von Johannes Buxtorf (1564–1629; *Epitome Grammaticae hebraeae*. Basel: Waldkirch 1613; *Thesaurus grammaticus linguae sanctae hebraeae*. Basel: Waldkirch 1609), Wilhelm Schickard (1592–1638; *Horologium Hebraeum*. Tübingen: Werlin 1623; von Johann Ernst Gerhard [1621–1668] überarbeitet als *Institutiones Linguae Ebraeae*. Jena: Sengwald & Freyschmid 1647), Jacob Alting (1618–1679; *Fundamenta punctationis linguae sanctae sive grammatica ebraea*. Groningen: p 1654) und Johann Andreas Danz (1654–1727; *Medaqdeq sive Literator Ebraeochaldaeus*. Jena: Bielck 1696); im 18. Jh. diejenigen von Albert Schultens (*Institutiones ad fundamenta linguae hebraeae*. Leiden: Luzac 1737) und Nicolaus Wilhelm Schröder (1721–1798; *Institutiones ad fundamenta linguae hebraeae*. Groningen: Bolt 1766). Die bedeutendsten Lexika stammten von Santes Pagninus († 1541; *Thesaurus linguae sanctae*. Lyon: Gryphius 1529), Johannes Forster (1496–1556; *Dictionarium Hebraicum novum*. Basel: Froben 1557) und, am häufigsten nachgedruckt, Johannes Buxtorf (*Lexicon hebraicum et chaldaicum*, Basel: König 1615).

Schon vor der Reformation wurde an einigen Universitäten vereinzelt Hebräisch gelehrt, so z. B. 1498 in Heidelberg von Reuchlin. Aber erst die Reformation ließ den Hebräischunterricht zum unabdingbaren Bestandteil der protestantischen Theologenausbildung werden. Wittenberg wurde daher maßgebend auch für andere protestantische Lehrstätten. Die ersten bedeutenden Wittenberger Hebraisten waren Johannes Böschenstein (1472–1540), Matthäus Adrianus (?–?), Matthäus Aurogallus (ca. 1470–1543) und Johannes Forster. Weitere Zentren der Hebraistik im 16. Jh. waren Basel – hier wirkten Johannes Oekolampad (1482–1531), Wolfgang Capito (1478–1541) und Sebastian Münster – sowie Zürich. An der von Ulrich Zwingli 1525 eröffneten Hochschule (der sog. "Prophezei") lehrten Jakob Ceporin (1500–1525) und nach ihm Konrad Pellikan. Über den Unterricht an der "Prophezei" liegen genaue Schilderungen vor. Bei der ersten protestantischen Universitätsneugründung in Marburg (1527) war von vornherein eine eigene Professur für Hebräisch in der Theol. Fakultät vorgesehen. Doch auch an katholischen Universitäten wurde Hebräisch unterricht, wie es z. B. für Löwen oder Köln bezeugt ist. – Die Lehre des Hebräischen war im übrigen nicht auf die Universitäten beschränkt, sondern wurde auch an (protestantisch geprägten) Gymnasien angeboten. Eine umfassende Studie dazu fehlt.

Schon im 16. Jh. war der hebr. Unterricht nicht allein auf das Bibl.-Hebr. beschränkt, sondern bezog das Bibl.-Aramäische, das Sebastian Münster erstmals erschlossen hatte (*Chaldaica grammatica* und *Dictionarium Chaldaicum*, beide Basel: Froben 1527), mit in das Studium ein, ebenso wie die nachbiblische Sprache der Juden, oftmals "Rabbinisch" genannt, worunter Mittelhebräisch und Jüdisch-Aramäisch zu verstehen sind, die in der jüdischen Traditionsliteratur (Talmud u. a.) nebeneinander benutzt werden. Die Zeit des 17. Jh.s sowie des frühen 18. Jh.s kann man geradezu als eine Blütezeit der rabbinischen Studien bezeichnen; hervorzuheben sind im deutschsprachigen Bereich Johann Buxtorf d. Ä. und d. J. (1599–1664; beide Basel), Andreas Sennert (1605–89; Wittenberg), August Pfeiffer (1640–1698; Leipzig), Johann Christoph Wagenseil (1633–1705; Altdorf) Esdras Edzard (1629–1708; Hamburg), Johann Andreas Danz (Jena), Johann Christoph Wolf (1683–1739; Hamburg) und Hermann v. d. Hardt (1660–1746; Helmstedt); in England Edward Pocock (1604–1691; Oxford) und John Lightfoot (1602–75; Cambridge); in Holland Joh. Drusius (1550–1616; Leiden), Constantin L'Empereur (†1648; Harderwijk), Joh. Coccejus (1603–69; Leiden), Jacob Alting (Groningen), Joh. Leusden (1624–99; Utrecht), Adrian Reland (1676–1718; Utrecht), und in Frankreich Samuel Bochartus (1599–1667).

Um die Mitte des 18. Jh.s macht sich jedoch deutlich eine Abkehr von der Hochschätzung der "rabbinischen" Tendenz der Hebraistik bemerkbar. Verantwortlich dafür scheint zum einen der durch die Aufklärung verstärkte Impuls kritischer Bibelexegese, der durch das Werk von Richard Simon (1638–1712; *Histoire critique du Vieux Testament*, 1678) initiiert wurde und das Hebräische der Bibel entschieden wieder in den Mittelpunkt der Lehre rückte, zum anderen aber die zunehmende Erforschung des Arabischen, gefördert u. a. durch Albert Schultens (1686–1750; Leiden) und Johann David Michaelis (1717–1791; Göttingen), die der historisch-vergleichenden Semitistik den Weg bereitete.

## 3. Arabisch

Einer der ersten Lehrstühle für Arabisch wurde 1538 am neugegründeten Collège de France in Paris eingerichtet; sein erster Inhaber Guillaume Postel (1510–81), der um 1540 auch eine erste *Grammatica arabica* (Paris: Gromorsus) publizierte, gab die Stelle schon 1543 wieder auf. Erst seit 1587 ist die Stelle permanent besetzt. 1613 wurde Thomas Erpenius (1584–1624), ein Schüler J. J. Scaligers, auf den 1599 eingerichteten, aber lange vakanten Lehrstuhl für Arabisch in Leiden berufen. Erpenius schuf mit seiner *Grammatica arabica* (Leiden: Raphelengius 1613) und mehreren für den Unterricht konzipierten Textausgaben (darunter der auch im Orient als Lehrbuch der Grammatik verwendeten *Âğurrûmiyya*) Werke, die mehr als ein Jahrhundert maßgebend blieben. Das gilt auch für das *Lexicon Arabico-Latinum* (Leiden: Elsevier 1653) von Erpenius' Nachfolger Jacob Golius (Gool, 1596–1667). In England gab es seit 1631 (Cambridge) bzw. 1636 (Oxford) eigene Lehrstühle für Arabisch. Ihre ersten Inhaber Abraham Wheelocke (1593–1653) und Edward Pocock waren Theologen und betrieben das Arabische v. a. im Dienste der Bibelphilologie, wie ihre Beteiligung an der Bibelpolyglotte von Brian Walton (London 1653–1657) beweist. Im Zusammenhang damit erschien das von Edmund Castellus (1606–86) kompilierte *Lexikon heptaglotton* (London: Roycroft 1669), das den für das Verständnis der Polyglotte nötigen Wortschatz des Hebräischen, Aramäischen, Syrischen, Samaritanischen, Äthiopischen und Arabischen vergleichend sowie das Persische separat darbot. Parallel dazu erschienen auch vergleichende Grammatiken der semitischen Sprachen, die zwar die historische Dimension noch unberücksichtigt ließen, aber ebenso wie Castellus' Wörterbuch als in vielem wichtige Vorarbeiten für die moderne Semitistik zu verstehen sind. Zu nennen sind hier u. a. Ludovicus de Dieu (1590–1642; *Grammatica Linguarum orientalium, Hebraeorum, Chaldaeorum, & Syrorum, inter se collatarum*, Leiden: Elsevier 1628), Andreas Sennert (1606–1689; *Arabismus, h. e. praecepta arabicae linguae, in harmonia ad Ebraea ... nec non Chaldaeo-Syra ... conscripta*, Wittenberg: Finzel 1658) oder Johann Heinrich Hottinger (1620–67; *Grammatica Quatuor Linguarum Hebraicae, Chaldaicae, syriacae et Arabicae Harmonica*, Heidelberg: Wyngaerden 1659). Jedenfalls ist aus diesen und weiteren Werken zu entnehmen, daß das Arabische bis gegen Ende des 18. Jh.s stets im Zusammenhang mit anderen semitischen, für die Bibelexegese wichtigen Sprachen und nicht um seiner selbst gelehrt wurde. Daran übte erstmals Johann Jacob Reiske (1716–74) deutliche Kritik, ohne aber zu seiner Zeit Gehör zu finden.

Daher fand der eigentliche Aufschwung der Arabistik und ihre Herauslösung aus dem Lehrzusammenhang der Theologie erst im 19. Jh. statt.

## 4. Weitere semitische Sprachen

Alle im folgenden zu behandelnden Sprachen wurden vor dem 19. Jh. aus rein theologischem Interesse behandelt und stets im Kontext der "Philologia sacra" gelehrt. Welchen Anteil sie im einzelnen im Sprachenangebot der Universitäten hatten, bedarf noch eingehender Untersuchung.

### 4.1. Syrisch

Einer der Pioniere der syrischen Studien war der Italiener Teseo Ambrogio degli Albonesi (1469–1540), der auf dem Laterankonzil 1512 diese Sprache von einem maronitischen Priester erlernt hatte. Seine *Introductio in Chaldaeam linguam, Syriacam atque Armenicam et decem alias linguas* (Pavia: Simoneta 1539) ist die erste grammatische Darstellung des Syrischen (und übrigens auch des Armenischen). Bei Teseo lernte Johann Albrecht Widmanstetter († 1557) Syrisch; neben dem ersten syrischen Neuen Testament (Wien: Zimmermann 1555) veröffentlichte er eine knappe Fibel (*Syriacae linguae ... prima elementa*. Wien: Zimmermann 1555–1556). Einer der Mitarbeiter an der Antwerpener Polyglotte (Plantin 1569–72) war Andreas Masius (1514–73); seine *Grammatica linguae Syriacae* und sein damit zusammen erschienenes Lexikon (*Syrorum Peculium*; Antwerpen:

Plantin 1571) bildeten die Grundlage für die im 17. Jh. v. a. in Deutschland aufblühenden syrischen Studien, wovon zahlreiche Grammatiken, Lexika und Bibelausgaben Zeugnis ablegen. Im 18. Jh. sind die Grammatiken von Christian Benedikt Michaelis (1680–1764; *Syriasmus, id est grammatica linguae syriacae*, Halle: Orphanotrophaeum 1741) und seinem Sohn Johann David (u. a. *Abhandlung von der syrischen Sprache und ihrem Gebrauch*, Göttingen: Barmeier 1768) hervorzuheben.

### 4.2. Äthiopisch (Geez)

Ein Freund Reuchlins, Johannes Potken († 1524), gab 1513 den ersten rein äthiopischen Psalter heraus (Rom: Silber), der im Anhang eine vierseitige Fibel enthielt. Fünf Jahre später publizierte er einen polyglotten Psalter, der neben dem äthiopischen Text den hebräischen, griechischen und lateinischen enthielt (*Psalterium in quatuor linguis*, Köln: Soter 1518). Erst die von dem äthiopischen Priester Tasfâ Sejôn und dem kath. Priester Mariano Vittori (1518–1572) gemeinsam besorgte Ausgabe des Neuen Testaments (Rom 1548/49) schuf die Basis für ausführlichere Beschreibungen, so von Vittori selbst (*Chaldeae seu Aethiopicae linguae institutiones*, Rom: Dorico 1552). Eine wesentlich bessere und ausführlichere Darstellung lieferte erst Hiob Ludolf (1624–1705) in Zusammenarbeit mit dem gelehrten äthiop. Mönch Abba Gregorios (*Grammatica Aethiopica* und *Lexicon Aethiopico-Latinum*, beide London: Roycroft 1661). Doch wandte Ludolf sein Interesse nicht nur der Literatursprache zu, sondern auch der wichtigsten Umgangssprache Äthiopiens, dem Amharischen (*Grammatica Linguae Amharicae* und *Lexicon Amharico-Latinum*, Frankfurt a. M.: Zunner 1698). Ludolfs Werke blieben bis weit ins 19. Jh. maßgebend.

### 4.3. Samaritanisch

Erste Mitteilungen über die Samaritaner nebst einem samaritanischen Alphabet lieferte Guillaume Postel in seinem *Linguarum duodecim … Alphabetum* (Paris: Vidovaeus 1538). Ein von Pietro della Valle (1586–1652) 1616 nach Paris gebrachtes Manuskript des Samaritanischen Pentateuch veröffentlichte Jean Morin (1591–1659) im Rahmen der Pariser Polyglotte (1629–1645) und lieferte dazu auch eine Grammatik (*Grammatica Samaritana*, Paris 1657); der Wortschatz ist in Castellus' *Lexicon Heptaglotton* voll erschlossen. Seither gehörte das Samaritanische zum Kanon der im Rahmen der Bibelphilologie gelehrten Sprachen, fand eine eingehendere Bearbeitung jedoch erst im 19. Jh.

## 5. Türkisch

Trotz intensiver politischer und wirtschaftlicher Kontakte mit den Osmanen kam es im 16. Jh. zu keiner eingehenderen Beschäftigung mit der türkischen Sprache. Die ältesten, noch unvollkommenen türkischen Grammatiken verfaßten Hieronymus Megiser (1553?–1616; *Institutionum Linguae Turcicae Libri Quatuor*, Leipzig: Selbstverl. 1612), André du Ryer (†1688; *Rudimenta Grammatices Linguae Turcicae*, Paris: Vitray 1630) und William Seaman (1606–80; *Grammatica Linguae Turcicae*, Oxford: Hall 1670). Einen bemerkenswerten Fortschritt für die Turkologie bedeutete das Werk von François Mesgnien de Meninski (1623–98). Er verfaßte einen umfangreichen *Thesaurus Linguarum orientalium Turcicae, Arabicae, Persicae* (Wien: Eigenverlag 1680–1687; unter dem Titel Lexicon *Arabico-Persico-Turcicum* 1780 [Wien: Kurzböck] erneut gedruckt), dem er eine grammatische Darstellung vorausschickte (*Linguarum Orientalium Turcicae, Arabicae, Persicae Institutiones, seu Grammatica Turcica*; 2. Aufl. Wien 1756). Im Schatten von Meninski stehen die eigenständigen Arbeiten des Leipziger Orientalisten Johann Christian Clodius (1676–1745; *Compendiosum Lexicon Latino-Turcico-Germanicum, … ac Grammatica Turcica*, Leipzig: Deer 1730), der seit 1720 auch Türkisch unterrichtete. Ob und in welchem Maße es auch an anderen europäischen Universitäten im 18. Jh. Türkischunterricht gab, ist bei dem gegenwärtigen Stand der Forschung schwer zu ermitteln.

## 6. Persisch

Inwieweit Persisch bereits vor der Mitte des 18. Jh.s an Universitäten gelehrt wurde, ist schwer nachweisbar. Schon im 16. Jh. war die 1546 gedruckte (Konstantinopel: Soncino) pers. Pentateuchübersetzung des Jakob Ṭāwûsî bekannt. Anhand dieses Textes wies Bonaventura Vulcanius 1597 (*De literis et lingua Getarum*, Leiden: Plantin) bereits auf die Verwandtschaft zum Germanischen hin. Erste Grammatiken wurden im 17. Jh. verfaßt von Louis de Dieu (*Rudimenta linguae persicae*, Leiden: Elsevier 1639), John Greaves (1602–52; *Elementa Linguae Persicae*, London:

Flesher 1649) und Ignatius a Jesu (1596–1667; *Grammatica linguae Persicae*, Rom: Propaganda fide 1661), im 18. Jh. am bedeutendsten die von William Jones (1746–94; *A Grammar of the Persian Language*, London: Richardson 1771). Lexikalische Sammlungen zum Persischen begann schon Franz Raphelengius; Jacob Golius verfaßte einen ungedruckt gebliebenen *Thesaurus persicus*, der jedoch in den persischen Teil des *Lexicon Heptaglotton* (London: Roycroft 1669; separat gedruckt) von Castellus eingearbeitet wurde.

## 7. Bibliographie

Altaner, Berthold. 1933a. "Die fremdsprachliche Ausbildung der Dominikanermissionare während des 13. und 14. Jh.s". *ZMR* 23.233–241.

–. 1933b. "Raymundus Lullus und der Sprachenkanon (can. 11) des Konzils von Vienne (1312)". *HJ* 53.191–219.

–. 1933b. "Die Durchführung des Vienner Konzilsbeschlusses über die Errichtung von Lehrstühlen für orientalische Sprachen". *ZKG* 52.226–236.

Arberry, Arthur J. 1948. *The Cambridge School of Arabic*. Cambridge: UP.

Babinger, Franz. 1919. "Die türkischen Studien in Europa bis zum Auftreten Josef von Hammer-Purgstalls". *WI* 7.103–129.

Bataillon, Marcel. 1935. "L'Arabe à Salamanca au temps de la Renaissance". *Hespéris* 21.1–17.

Behrmann, D. 1902. *Hamburgs Orientalisten*. Hamburg: Persiehl.

Benfey, Theodor. 1869. *Geschichte der Sprachwissenschaft und orientalischen Philologie in Deutschland*. München: Cotta.

Berthier, André. 1932. "Les Ecoles de Langues Orientales fondées au XIIe Siècle par les Dominicains en espagne et en Afrique". *RAfr* 73.84–103.

Bobzin, Hartmut. 1992a. "Geschichte der arabischen Philologie in Europa". *Grundriß der arabischen Philologie*, Bd. III, 155–187. Wiesbaden: Reichert.

–. 1992b. "Über einige gedruckte und ungedruckte Grammatiken des Arabischen im frühen 16. Jahrhundert und ihre Verfasser". *Fremdsprachenunterricht 1500–1800*, 1–27. Wiesbaden: Harrassowitz.

–. 1993. "Hebraistik im Zeitalter der Philologia Sacra am Beispiel der Universität Altdorf". *Syntax und Text*, 151–69. St. Ottilien: Eos.

–. 1995. *Der Koran im Zeitalter der Reformation. Studien zur Frühgeschichte der Arabistik und Islamkunde in Europa*. Beirut & Stuttgart: Steiner.

–. 1998. "Vom Sinn des Arabischstudiums im Sprachenkanon der Philologia Sacra". *Biographie und Religion,* 21–32. Halle: Universität.

Bourel, Dominique. 1988. "Die deutsche Orientalistik im 18. Jh. Von der Mission zur Wissenschaft". *Historische Kritik und biblischer Kanon in der deutschen Aufklärung*, 113–126. Wiesbaden: Harrassowitz.

Brugman, Jan & F. Schröder, eds. 1979. *Arabic studies in the Netherlands*. Leiden: Brill.

Canard, Marius. 1947. "Les études arabes en Russie. Aperçu historique". *Revue de la Méditerranée* 7.436–65.

Casanova, Paul. 1910. *L'enseignement de l'arabe au Collège de France*. Paris: Geuthner.

*Cent-Cinquantenaire de l'Ecole des langues orientales*. Paris 1948.

Coll, José M.a. 1944–1946/47. "Escuelas de lenguas orientales en los Siglos XIII y XIV". *Analecta Sacra Tarraconensia* 17.115–138; 18. 59–89; 19.217–240.

Colomesius, Paul. 1665. *Gallia Orientalis, sive Gallorum qui Linguam Hebraeam vel alias Orientales excoluerunt Vitae*. Den Haag: Ulacq.

–. 1730. *Italia et Hispania Orientalis sive Italorum et Hispanorum qui Linguam Hebraeam vel alias Orientales excoluerunt Vitae*. Hamburg: Ww. Felgineria.

Diestel, Ludwig. 1869. *Geschichte des Alten Testamentes in der christlichen Kirche*. Jena: Mauke.

Dupont-Ferrier, G. 1922. 1923. "Les Jeunes de Langue ou 'Arméniens' à Louis-le-Grand". *Revue des ét. arméniennes*. 2.189–232; 3.9–46.

Flügel, Gustav. 1834: "Orientalische Studien, Literatur, Hülfsmittel". *Allgem. Encyklop. d. Wissenschaften u. Künste*. III/5, 194–245. Leipzig: Brockhaus.

Fraser, James G. 1988. "Guillaume Postel and Samaritan Studies". *Postello, Venezia e il suo mondo*, 99–117. Firenze: Olschki.

Fück, Johann. 1955. *Die arabischen Studien in Europa bis in den Anfang des 20. Jahrhunderts*. Leipzig: Harrassowitz.

Geiger, Ludwig. 1870. *Das Studium der hebräischen Sprache in Deutschland vom Ende des XV. bis zur Mitte des XVI. Jh.s*. Breslau: Schletter.

Gerson da Cunha, J. 1881. "Materials for the History of oriental Studies amongst the Portuguese". *Atti del IV Congresso internazionale degli Orientalisti* Vol. II, 179–219. Firenze.

Gesenius, Wilhelm. 1973 [1815]. *Geschichte der hebräischen Sprache und Schrift*. Hildesheim: Olms.

Gołuchowski von Gołuchowo, Agenor. 1904. *Die k.u.k. Konsular-Akademie von 1754 bis 1904*. Wien: Innen u. Außenministerium.

Gubernatis, Angelo de. 1876. *Matériaux pour servir à l'histoire des études orientales en Italie*. Paris: Leroux.

Hadas-Lebel, Mireille. 1985. "Les études hébraïques en France au XVIII$^{e}$ siècle et la création de la première chaire d'écriture sainte en Sorbonne". *REJ* 144, 93–126.

Hammerschmidt, Ernst. 1968. *Äthiopistik an deutschen Universitäten.* Wiesbaden: Steiner.

Jenisch, B. v. 1780. *De fatis linguarum orientalium arabicae nimirum, persiacae, et turcicae commentatio.* Wien: Kurzböck.

Juynboll, Wilhelmina M. C. 1931. *Zeventiende-eeuwsche Beoefenaars van het Arabisch in Nederland.* Utrecht (Proefschrift).

Kleinhans, Arduino. 1930. *Historia studii linguae Arabicae et Collegii Missionum ordinis Fratrum Minorum in Conventu ad S. Petrum in Monte Aureo Romae erecti.* Quaracchi: Collegio di S. Bonaventura.

Krajkovskij, Ignatij J. 1950. *Ocerki po istorii Russkoj arabistiki.* Moskva & Leningrad: Akademija Nauk S. S. S. R. [dt.: 1957. Die russische Arabistik. Leipzig: Harrassowitz].

Kreiser, Klaus, ed. 1987. *Germano-Turcica. Zur Geschichte des Türkisch-Lernens in den deutschsprachigen Ländern.* Bamberg: Universitätsbibliothek.

Lewis, Bernard. 1941. *British Contributions to Arabic Studies.* London: Longmans.

Monneret de Villard, Ugo. 1972 [1944]. *Lo studio dell'Islām in Europa nel XII e nel XIII secolo.* Città del Vaticano: Biblioteca Apostolica Vaticana.

Monroe, James T. 1970. *Islam and the Arabs in Spanish scholarship.* Leiden: Brill.

Nat, J. 1929. *De studie van de Oostersche talen in Nederland in de 18e en de 19e eeuw.* Amsterdam (Proefschrift).

Nave, Francine de, ed. 1986. *Philologia Arabica. Arabische studiën en drukken in de Nederlanden in de 16de en 17de eeuw.* Antwerpen: Museum Plantin Moretus.

Perles, Joseph. 1884. *Beiträge zur Geschichte der hebräischen und aramäischen Studien.* München: Ackermann.

Poggi, Vinenzo. 1993. "Arabismo Gesuita nei secoli XVI–XVIII". *Eulogema. Studies in Honor of Robert Taft,* 339–72. Rom: Centro Studi S. Anselmo.

Raphael, Pierre. 1950. *Le rôle du collège maronite romain dans l'orientalisme aux xvii^e^ et xviii^e^ siècles.* Beyrouth: Université St. Joseph.

Richard, Jean. 1976. "L'enseignement des langues orientales en occident au Moyen Age". *REI* 44. 149–64.

Russell, G. A. ed. 1994. *The 'Arabick' Interest of the Natural Philosophers in seventeenth-Century England.* Leiden: Brill.

Schaendlinger, Anton Cornelius. 1963–1964. "Die Turkologie und Iranistik in Österreich". *Bustan* 4/5, 8–11.

Schnurrer, Christianus Fridericus de. 1968 [1811]. *Bibliotheca Arabica.* Amsterdam: Oriental Press.

Smitskamp, Rijk. 1992. *Philologia Orientalis.* Leiden: Brill.

Steinschneider, Moritz. 1973. *Christliche Hebraisten. Nachrichten über mehr als 400 Gelehrte, welche über nachbiblisches Hebräisch geschrieben haben.* Hildesheim: Gerstenberg.

Strothmann, Werner. 1971. *Die Anfänge der syrischen Studien in Europa.* Wiesbaden: Harrassowitz.

Toomer, G. J. 1996. *Eastern Wisedome and Learning. The Study of Arabic in Seventeenth-Century England.* Oxford: Clarendon.

Waardenburg, Jacques D. J. 1992. "Mustashriḳūn". *EI²* VII, 735–753.

Weiss, R. 1952. "England and the Decree of the Council of Vienne on the teaching of Greek, Arabic, Hebrew and Syriac". *BHR* 14.1–9.

Weiss von Starkenfels, Viktor. 1836. *Die kaiserlich-königliche orientalische Akademie in Wien, ihre Gründung, Fortbildung und gegenwärtige Einrichtung.* Wien: Gerold.

Wijnman, H. F. 1952–55. "De studie van het Ethiopisch en de ontwikkeling van de Ethiopische typographie in West-Europa in de 16de eeuw". *Het Boek,* N. R. 31.326–47, 32.225–46

Zenker, J. Th. 1966 [1846–61]. *Bibliotheca Orientalis. Manuel de Bibliographie orientale.* Amsterdam: Oriental Press.

*Hartmut Bobzin, Erlangen (Deutschland)*

# 101. Die Traditionen des Sprachunterrichts im Europa des 17. und 18. Jahrhunderts

1. Vorbemerkung
2. Drei Arten von Sprachunterricht
3. Sprachenwahl und Sprachenfolge
4. Die Lernenden und ihre Motivationen
5. Die Lehrenden
6. Methoden und Lehrwerke
7. Bibliographie

## 1. Vorbemerkung

Der Sprachunterricht des 17. und 18. Jhs. zeichnet sich aus durch eine überraschende Vielfalt der Erscheinungsformen, der Lerner-Typen, der Lerner-Motivationen, aber auch der Lehrerschaft und der Unterrichtsmaterialien. Das Schul-, Hochschul- und Ausbildungswesen ist weniger normiert als heute, und eine Sprachlehrer-Ausbildung im modernen Sinne existiert nicht. Dennoch bilden sich im Verlauf des 16. und 17. Jhs. gewisse Traditionen aus, die dann dem Sprachunterricht des 18. Jhs. einen halbfesten institutionellen Rahmen geben.

## 2. Drei Arten von Sprachunterricht

Zu unterscheiden ist zwischen mutter- bzw. zweitsprachlichem Unterricht, dem altetablierten Unterricht in den 'gelehrten' Sprachen Latein und Griechisch sowie dem damals noch relativ neuen Unterricht in den modernen Fremdsprachen. Beim muttersprachlichen Unterricht ist zu bedenken, daß er bis ins 18. Jh. hinein in einer ausgeprägten Diglossie-Situation stattfindet: Die Lerner sind in aller Regel in sehr viel stärkerem Maße als heute Dialektsprecher. Daher trägt die Unterweisung stärker als heute fremdsprachenunterrichtliche Züge. Hinzu kommt, daß, bedingt durch die paneuropäischen Flüchtlingsströme der nachreformatorischen Zeit (vor allem: Hugenotten, Waldenser) der muttersprachliche Unterricht nicht selten ein 'herkunftssprachlicher' ist: Um das Jahr 1730 beispielsweise ist jeder vierte Berliner frankophon. Bis um die Wende zum 19. Jh. existieren quer durch Europa Hunderte von Hugenottenschulen jedweden Zuschnitts, vom 1687 gegründeten Berliner *Collège français* als einer Pflanz- und Eliteschule (heute: Deutsch-französisches Gymnasium) bis hin zu Küster- und Winkelschulen. An den genannten Anstalten wird zunächst Französisch als Herkunftssprache unterrichtet, im weiteren Verlauf der Geschichte tritt dann Deutsch als Zweitsprache hinzu; später wird Deutsch Erstsprache und Französisch Zweitsprache im Rahmen einer bilingualen Ausgangslage, die sich zunehmend zugunsten des Deutschen verschiebt, bis dann unter dem Eindruck der Napoleonischen Kriege das Französische in vielen Fällen ganz aufgegeben wird. Die Französischlehrer der Hugenotten- und Waldenserschulen sind biographisch erfaßt bei Schröder 1987–99, besonders in den Nachtragsbänden 5 und 6 (1997 und 1999).

Der Unterricht in den alten, den 'gelehrten' Sprachen folgt am ehesten noch einem einheitlichen Muster, nämlich dem eines grammatisierenden, auf Lese- und Übersetzungsfertigkeit hin ausgerichteten Spracherwerbs. Doch ältere Traditionen, innerhalb derer Latein noch als eine lebende Sprache (internationale Sprache des Mittelalters) gelernt worden war, wirken nach. Insofern darf die Methodik des Lateinunterrichts des 18. Jhs. nicht mit der des 19. und 20. Jhs. (Grammatik-Übersetzungsmethode) gleichgesetzt werden. Der im Zeitalter des Humanismus aufgewertete Unterricht im Altgriechischen tritt zum 18. Jh. hin immer stärker zugunsten einer Ausbildung zurück, in der Latein und Französisch die in der Schule einzig gelernten Fremdsprachen sind. Dabei ist zu berücksichtigen, daß die Lateinschulen bis zum Ausgang des 18. Jhs. sechsklassige Anstalten sind; die Scholaren wechseln im Alter zwischen 14 und 16 Jahren zur Universität, wo sie dann zwei bis vier Jahre lang die Artistenfakultät durchlaufen, die den höheren Fakultäten (Jura, Medizin, Theologie) vorgeschaltet ist.

Der Unterricht in den modernen Fremdsprachen findet bis zum Ende des 18. Jhs. fast ausschließlich im Rahmen einer privaten Unterweisung statt, entweder als Individualunterricht oder aber innerhalb von Kleingruppen. Gelegenheit ist an den Lateinschulen, Artistenfakultäten und — in besonders ausgeprägtem Maße — an den Ritterakademien (einer im 17. Jh. entwickelten Konkurrenzform zur klassischen Universität) gegeben, aber auch außerhalb des bestehenden Schulwesens durch sogenannte Sprachmeister, die nach Art heutiger Privat-Musiklehrer ihre Dienste anbieten. (Zum Fremdsprachenunterricht an einer der bedeutendsten Ritterakademien, dem *Collegium Illustre* zu Tübingen, vgl. Rauscher 1957. Zur Geschichte eines fremdsprachlichen Faches [Englisch] an dieser Hochschulform vgl. Aehle 1938.)

## 3. Sprachenwahl und Sprachenfolge

Französisch ist im 17. und 18. Jh. unangefochten die erste moderne Fremdsprache. Im schulischen und akademischen Umfeld wird sie gelernt, nachdem Lateinkenntnisse und zuweilen zumindest Anfangskenntnisse des Altgriechischen vorhanden sind. Selbst in den im 18. Jh. mit Großbritannien dynastisch verbundenen Gebieten Norddeutschlands (Braunschweig-Lüneburg, Hannover) tritt das Englische nicht an die erste Stelle, auch wenn der Sprache aus politischen Gründen besonderes Interesse gilt und die von Georg II. von England in seiner Eigenschaft als

Kurfürst von Hannover gegründete Universität Göttingen nach 1750 eine Pflanzstätte englischer Studien von europäischem Rang und die Stadt selbst ein 'Londres en miniature' werden. – Im 17. Jh. nimmt den zweiten Platz der Rangskala das Italienische ein, gefolgt von Spanisch und Englisch ranggleich auf Platz 3. Im Verlauf des 18. Jhs. verschieben sich die Gewichte insgesamt zugunsten des Englischen, das neben Italienisch auf den Rangplatz 2 rückt. Alle übrigen Sprachen, so das in hansischer Zeit bedeutsame Russisch sowie das im 16. und 17. Jh. aus handelspolitischen Motivationen heraus häufiger erworbene Flämisch (Niederländisch) und schließlich auch das Spanische werden im 18. Jh. weniger gelernt, wobei Spanisch nach 1770 aus literarischen Gründen zumindest im deutschsprachigen Raum einen gewissen Aufschwung erlebt. Dennoch ergeben sich lokal mituner andere Gewichtsverteilungen: In Hamburg wird im Verlauf des 18. Jhs., bedingt durch den Portugal-Handel und die Anwesenheit portugiesischstämmiger Juden in der Stadt, offenbar überdurchschnittlich viel Portugiesisch gelernt: Bereits für die Jahre nach 1720 ist ein Sprachmeister eigens für diese Sprache verzeichnet, und der aus Amsterdam gebürtige, jüdischstämmige Abraham Meldola veröffentlicht 1785 in Hamburg die zweitälteste Portugiesisch-Grammatik des deutschsprachigen Raumes, seine *Nova grammatica portugueza*. (Zur Hamburger Vielsprachigkeit im 17. und 18. Jh., die auch Spanisch und Niederländisch umfaßt, vgl. Schröder 1989.) In Halle werden zu Zeiten des pietistischen Predigers und Theologieprofessors August Hermann Francke die slawischen und baltischen Sprachen, allen voran das Russische, betrieben, wobei missionarische Bemühungen ausschlaggebend sind (vgl. dazu Winter 1954a und Winter 1954b sowie, hinsichtlich der biographischen Details, Eichler et al. 1993 und Schröder 1987–99, hier auch weiterführendes bibliographisches Material). Das Spanische hat am Hofe von Versailles (als potentielle Feindsprache) und in London (ebenfalls zunächst als Feindsprache, später als Handelssprache) einen anderen Stellenwert als beispielsweise am kaiserlichen Hof zu Wien (Spanisch als Hofsprache des kaiserlichen Hauses) oder im italienischen Raum, wo enge kulturelle Beziehungen zu Spanien bestehen. – Trotz der Vormachtstellung des Französischen ist das 17. und 18. Jh. eine Zeit des Sprachen-Sammelns (Vaterunser-Sammlungen) und, global betrachtet, auch des vielfältigen Fremdsprachenerwerbs: Der engagierte Student der Zeit ist in etwa fünfsprachig mit Latein, Altgriechisch, möglicherweise Hebräisch bzw. orientalistischen Grundkenntnissen, Französisch und Italienisch sowie seiner Muttersprache, wozu dann nicht selten auch noch eine gewisse Kenntnis des Spanischen und/oder Englischen (Lese- und Übersetzungsfertigkeit) tritt.

## 4. Die Lernenden und ihre Motivationen

Eine Typologie der Lernenden mit eindeutigen Zuordnungen ist nicht möglich, dennoch gibt es *cum grano salis* quer durch Europa drei Zielgruppen, für die der Fremdsprachenerwerb besonders interessant ist: den Adel, die städtischen Patrizier und großbürgerlichen Familien sowie das akademisch-orientierte städtische Bürgertum, dem auch das protestantische Pfarrhaus, wo immer dieses im Einzelfall angesiedelt sein mag, zuzurechnen ist. In Handwerkerkreisen und im Kleinbürgertum überhaupt sind fremdsprachliche Lernbemühungen weit weniger verbreitet, auch wenn es branchenspezifische und ortsgegebene Ausnahmen gibt (Beispiele: Buchdruck, Nähe eines Hafens).

Der Adel lernt moderne Fremdsprachen in erster Linie aus politischen Gründen: Französisch ist spätestens seit 1648 die Sprache der Diplomatie und seit Ende des 17. Jhs. auch des Offizierskorps, darüber hinaus sind die Sprachen der dynastisch verbundenen Gebiete von Interesse (Polnisch am sächsischen Hofe; Ungarisch und Italienisch, später auch Böhmisch [Tschechisch] am Hofe zu Wien), aber auch die Sprachen feindlicher Mächte (Spanisch wie in Abschnitt 3. angegeben; Türkisch am Hofe zu Wien, im 18. Jh. an der Wiener Theresianischen Ritterakademie unterrichtet). – Die städtischen Patrizier wenden sich in erster Linie aus handelspolitischen Gründen den modernen Fremdsprachen zu. Dabei bestimmen die jeweiligen Handelsbeziehungen die Sprachenwahl. Flämisch beispielsweise ist des Antwerpen-Handels wegen im 17. Jh. quer durch Europa eine von jungen Handelsherren gerne gelernte Sprache. Wer mit Krakau handelt, versucht sich Polnischkenntnisse anzueignen, wobei sich die Inhalte allerdings unterscheiden. Vom Hamburger Portugal- und Spanienhandel und der Rolle des Portugiesischen und Spanischen in der Stadt war schon die Rede (vgl. Abschnitt 3.). – Das akademisch orientierte städtische Bürgertum erwirbt Fremdsprachen, um im Leben voranzukommen, vielleicht eine Anstellung bei Hofe zu finden, sich Zugang zu fremdsprachlicher Fachliteratur (erst gegen Ende des 18. Jhs. auch zu fremdsprachlicher Belletristik) zu verschaffen oder aber gar, um einen Fremdsprachenberuf (Hofmeister, Lateinschullehrer/Pfarrer, Übersetzer) zu ergreifen. In der 2. Hälfte des 18. Jhs. ist angesichts des allumgreifenden Bestrebens, Aufklärung auch mittels übersetzter Texte zu verbreiten, eine breit durch die Sprachen gestreute Translationskompetenz willkommen und gut zu vermarkten. – Innerhalb des Adels und des Patriziertums sind weibliche Lerner keine Seltenheit, im bildungsbürgerlichen Bereich sind Fremdsprachen mehr eine Domäne der Männer: Auch dem aufgeklärten 18. Jh. ist die wissenschaftlich orientierte Frau eher ein Schrecknis als eine Wunschvorstellung. Dennoch sind die Belege für eine auch fremdsprachliche Privaterziehung bürgerlicher Töchter zahlreich, und nicht wenige dieser Töchter nutzen die erworbenen Kenntnisse im späteren Leben, um als Gouvernanten und Lehrerinnen fremdsprachenvermittelnd tätig zu werden. – Das Gros der Lerner ist 16 bis 25 Jahre alt, gerade in Adelskreisen findet daneben jedoch auch eine frühe, teilweise sehr frühe Fremdsprachenunterweisung (durch mehrsprachige Kammerdiener und Gouvernanten) statt. Die Schulform mit dem höchsten Fremdsprachenanteil ist, wie schon angedeutet, die Ritterakademie, in moderner Terminologie zwischen Sekundarstufe II und wissenschaftlichem Grundstudium angesiedelt und, wie der Name sagt, auf eine adlige Klientel hin ausgerichtet, jedoch durchaus auch vom Bürgertum frequentiert.

## 5. Die Lehrenden

Studien des ausgehenden 19. Jhs. zur Frühzeit des Fremdsprachenerwerbs haben die Zeit vor 1800 als *Epoche der Sprachmeister* abqualifiziert. Die Festlegung ist nicht haltbar, denn die modernen Fremdsprachen wurden im gesamten hier interessierenden Zeitraum keineswegs nur von sogenannten Sprachmeistern, den *Maîtres*, unterrichtet. Außerdem umfaßt der Terminus bei näherem Hinsehen Lehrer und auch Lehrerinnen sehr unterschiedlicher Qualifikation und auch unterschiedlicher gesellschaftlicher Akzeptanz. Unter den frühen Fremdsprachenlehrern finden sich Professoren und hochangesehene Prinzenerzieher ebenso wie polyglotte Geistliche, hochgebildete polyglotte Ordensfrauen von Schlage einer Mary Ward ebenso wie geistvolle Aventuriers mit langjähriger Fremdsprachenerfahrung, aber eben auch gestrandete Existenzen, Glaubensflüchtlinge, politische Emigranten, Bankrotteure und mißratene Studierende und sogar Handwerksburschen, die dann als Sprachlehrer mehr Schaden als Nutzen stiften. Die von Schröder 1987–99 zusammengetragenen 3789 (großenteils bruchstückhaften) Biographien zeigen die ganze Bandbreite der Möglichkeiten. (Man vergleiche in diesem Kontext auch die in Kapitel 17, → Art. 99, vorgestellten frühen Londoner Sprachlehrer.) – Ein Berufsbild Fremdsprachenlehrer existiert nicht, Hofmeistertätigkeit ganz allgemein wird in der Regel als wenig attraktives, aber notwendiges Durchgangsstadium auf dem Wege zu einer Stelle als Lateinschullehrer, Pfarrer oder Jurist angesehen. Das 18. Jh. kennt zwar Frühformen der Lehrerausbildung, die aber eher elementarschulorientiert sind und bei denen die modernen Fremdsprachen daher allenfalls eine geringe Rolle spielen. Auch von Sprache zu Sprache ist der Lehrkörper unterschiedlich zusammengesetzt: Die vergleichsweise wenigen Englischlehrer des 18. Jhs. beispielsweise sind in der Mehrzahl akademisch vorgebildet und in der Minderzahl Muttersprachensprecher, dennoch haben sie nicht selten Auslandsaufenthalte in Großbritannien oder gar in den amerikanischen Kolonien absolviert, so daß sie die Sprache wirklich und gerade auch im mündlichen Umgang beherrschen. Die Französischlehrer – zumindest des deutschsprachigen Raumes – hingegen sind in der Mehrzahl Muttersprachensprecher und ohne akademische Ausbildung. Dabei kann man mit aller Vorsicht schätzen, daß auf einen englischen Sprachlehrer im Mitteleuropa des 18. Jhs. mindestens 50 französische Sprachlehrer kommen, worunter sich dann natürlich auch mehrere hervorragende Berufsvertreter befinden. Insgesamt ergibt sich ein facettenreiches Kontinuum, an dessen einem Ende der als Hofmeister tätige Magister Artium steht, der seine Fremdsprachenkenntnisse im Rahmen von Privatunterricht durch polyglotte Professoren oder aber Universitätssprachmeister erworben hat, vielleicht auch schon an der Lateinschule und im Elternhaus mit modernen Fremdsprachen in Berührung gekommen ist, und der die Zielsprachenräume aus eigener Anschauung kennt, während am anderen Extrem der entwurzelte, nicht mit adäquater Schulbildung ausgestattete Muttersprachensprecher angesiedelt ist, der keine andere Möglichkeit des Überlebens sieht, als seine eigene Sprache, die er weder in der Theorie noch in der Praxis grammatisch und stilistisch beherrscht, zu vermarkten. Was beide Prototypen gemein haben, ist dabei vermutlich die Armut: Sie fristen ihr Leben auf unterschiedlichem Bildungsniveau. Und dann ist da noch der hochdotierte Prinzenerzieher, sehr oft selbst adliger Herkunft und zuweilen mit vorgeschalteter politischer Karriere, der als ebenfalls akademisch gebildeter, berufs- und lebenserfahrener Mensch und vielleicht dazu sogar noch als begnadeter Pädagoge ein sicher nicht einfaches, aber doch erfülltes und angemessen remuneriertes Leben bei Hofe führt. Sein weibliches Gegenstück ist im 18. Jh. die Gouvernante oder aber die Erzieherin an einem Mädchen-Philanthropin oder aber die Inhaberin eines großbürgerlich frequentierten Mädchenpensionats. — Erst das ausgehende 19. Jh. bringt, nach einem Jahrhundert des Staatsschulwesens, Fremdsprachenlehrer und später dann auch -lehrerinnen hervor, die eine genormte, fachspezifische Ausbildung erhalten haben. Ob diese dann als berufsadäquat bezeichnet werden kann, ist allerdings eine andere Frage.

## 6. Methoden und Lehrwerke

Der Fremdsprachenunterricht des 15. bis 18. Jhs. ist, gemessen an heutigen Spracherwerbstheorien, erstaunlich modern: Er ist auf klar definierte pädagogische Ziele (Gesprächsfertigkeit oder aber eben Lesefertigkeit und Übersetzungskompetenz) hin ausgerichtet, im weitesten Sinne kommunikationsorientiert, in vielen Fällen im modernen Sinne lernerzentriert, er vermeidet Methodenmonismus und bemüht sich allenthalben um Lebensnähe und situative Einbettung. Welchen Grad der Perfektion methodisches Denken um die Wende vom 17. zum 18. Jh. erreicht hat, zeigen eindrucksvoll die entsprechenden Arbeiten von Matthias Cramer (1696 — dazu Schröder 1992b) und Christian Friedrich Seidelmann (1724). Dabei ist schon den frühesten Fremdsprachenlehrern geläufig, daß es zwei Wege gibt, eine Fremdsprache zu erwerben, *ex usu* und *ex grammaticis, by rote or by rule*. Vor diesem Hintergrund plädieren sie für unterschiedliche Formen einer gemäßigt direkten Methode (in der Terminologie der Reformzeit), die dann auch bis ins späte 18. Jh. hinein den meisten Unterrichtsmaterialien zugrundeliegt. Universitätssprachmeister tendieren insgesamt stärker zu grammatisierenden Ansätzen, wobei sie die Sprachlernerfahrungen der Scholaren in den Schulsprachen Latein, Griechisch und Hebräisch nutzen. Von Interesse ist, daß die Verfahren in jedem Falle kontrastiv ausgelegt sind, und zwar kontrastiv sowohl zur Muttersprache als auch zu den vorher gelernten (auch modernen) Fremdsprachen. Aus Gründen kontrastiver Analyse wird im Unterricht zuweilen auch von der einen in die andere Fremdsprache übersetzt. Bei den minder gebildeten Sprachmeistern und Lehrern ihrer Muttersprache herrschen *ex usu*-Formen bis hin zu einer naiven Naturmethode vor, weil den Lehrern selbst die grammatischen Einsichten in die zu vermittelnden Sprachen und entsprechende Sprachlernerfahrungen fehlen. Das Wirken dieser Lehrer verringert die soziale Akzeptanz des gesamten Sprachmeisterstandes, besonders dann im Anschluß an die Napoleonischen Kriege, als der Begriff Sprachmeister gleichgesetzt wird mit einem ungebildeten, 'hergelaufenen' *maître de langue*, der außer hohlen Phrasen nichts zu bieten habe und seine Scholaren auf die schiefe Bahn bringe. Ihm wird der im Sinne des 19. Jhs. (alt)philologisch ausgebildete Fremdsprachenlehrer gegenübergestellt, der im Idealfall über eine ausgezeichnete grammatische Kenntnis der Zielsprache verfügt, dem aber dafür in vielen Fällen jede kommunikative Kompetenz fehlt. — Da moderne Fremdsprachen oft von Adligen erworben werden, dazu noch in sehr frühem Alter, entwickelt sich durch das Wirken der Prinzenerzieher im fremdsprachlichen Bereich früh eine gewalt- und angstfreie alternative Pädagogik, die modernen Formen bis hin zur projektorientierten Arbeit in nichts nachsteht. — Die frühesten fremdsprachlichen Lehr- und Lernmaterialien sind Gesprächsbücher und Glossare. Beide Gattungen sind aus dem Mittelalter ererbt; durch Hinzufügen neuer Sprachsparten entwickeln sich aus zweisprachigen Formen (nicht selten vom Lateinischen ausgehend) polyglotte Erscheinungsbilder (mit bis zu elf Sprachen). Seit der zweiten Hälfte des 16. Jhs. tritt das Genre Lehrbuch hinzu, häufig als Grammatik bezeichnet, wobei neben der eigentlichen Grammatik (in mehr oder minder didaktisierter Form vorgelegt) ein prosodischer Teil, ein Gesprächsteil (Musterdialoge), mitunter ein Phrasenteil (Sentenzen und Proverbien) sowie kleinere Lesetexte (Anekdoten) und zuweilen auch landeskundliche Informationen eingebunden sind. Die genannten drei Genres bleiben bis ins frühe 19. Jh. bestimmend, spezielle Lesebücher, Übersetzungsbücher usw. sind in der Regel späteren Datums. Die Gesamtzahl der vor 1800 quer durch Europa publizierten Unterrichtsmaterialien liegt, vorsichtig geschätzt, bei etwa 15.000 Ausgaben und Auflagen. Der Markt ist hochgradig parzelliert und wenig übersichtlich, die Auflagen sind mitunter sehr klein. Dennoch determinieren vergleichsweise wenige Autoren weit über die Grenzen der ursprünglichen Verbreitungsräume ihrer Werke hinaus das thematische und methodische Geschehen in den einzelnen Sprachen: 'Der Barlaimont', auf den Antwerpener Sprachmeister Noël van Berlemont (Barlaimont) zurückgehend, ist in ganz Europa verbreitet, der Name des Verfassers wird schließlich zu Parlament verderbt. Komenský's *Orbis pictus* erscheint zwischen 1658 und 1800 in nicht weniger als 145 Ausgaben und in mehr als 20 Sprachen. Andere klangvolle Namen sind beispielsweise Cramer, Franciosini, Mauger, Oudin (Vater und Sohn), Veneroni. – Nach zaghaften, philologisch orientierten Ansätzen im 19. Jh. (etwa: Stengel 1890) sind die Lehr- und Lernmaterialien aus der Zeit vor 1800 erst in neuerer Zeit Gegenstand systematischer bibliographischer Dokumentation und linguistischer sowie fachdidaktischer Recherchen geworden. Einige bibliographische Gesamtdarstellungen sind im Literaturverzeichnis aufgeführt (Alston 1974, Baumann 1969, Bingen 1987, Collison 1982, Gallina 1959, Hammar 1980, Minerva & Pellandra 1997, Mormile 1993, Niederehe 1994, Rossebastiano 1984, Schröder 1975, Stengel & Niederehe 1976). Ein bibliographisches Verzeichnis mit Standortnachweis für einige der weniger gelernten europäischen Sprachen ist in Vorbereitung (Schröder 2000).

## 7. Bibliographie

Aehle, Wilhelm. 1938. *Die Anfänge des Unterrichts in der englischen Sprache, besonders auf den Ritterakademien.* (= *Erziehungswissenschaftliche Studien*, 7.) Hamburg: Buske.

Alston, Robin C. 1974. *A Bibliography of the English Language from the Invention of Printing to the Year 1800.* Ilkley: Janus Press.

Basler, Franz. 1987. *Russischunterricht in drei Jahrhunderten. Ein Beitrag zur Geschichte des Russischunterrichts an deutschen Schulen.* (= *Veröffentlichungen der Abteilung für slawische Sprachen und Literaturen des Osteuropa-Instituts an der Freien Universität Berlin*, 65.) Berlin.

Baumann, Hasso. 1969. *Zur Geschichte der für Deutsche gedruckten Lehrmittel des Russischen, 1731–1945.* 2 Bde. Jena 1969. (Habilitationsschrift, maschinenschriftlich.)

Bingen, Nicole. 1987. *Le Maître italien, 1510–1660. Bibliographie des ouvrages d'enseignement de la langue italienne destinés au public de la langue française, suivie d'un Répertoire des ouvrages bilingues imprimés dans les pays de langue française.* Brüssel: van Balberghe.

Bratt, Ingvar. 1977. *Engelskunder visningens framväxt i Sverige, Tiden före 1850.* (= *Årsböcker i svensk under visningshistoria*, 77.) Stockholm: Föreningen för svensk undervisnings historia.

Busch, Wolfgang. 1983. "Russisch – ein junges Unterrichtsfach mit alter Tradition". *Geschichte der Unterrichtsfächer I* hg. von Anneliese Mannzmann, 118–142. München: Kösel.

Christ, Herbert. 1983. "Zur Geschichte des Französischunterrichts und der Französischlehrer". *Geschichte der Unterrichtsfächer I* hg. von Anneliese Mannzmann, 94–117. München: Kösel.

– & Hans-Joachim Rang, Hg. 1985. *Fremdsprachenunterricht unter staatlicher Verwaltung, 1700 bis 1945. Eine Dokumentation amtlicher Richtlinien und Verordnungen.* 7 Bde. Tübingen: Narr.

Christmann, Hans Helmut. 1992. "Italienische Sprache und Italianistik in Deutschland vom 15. Jahrhundert bis zur Goethezeit". Schröder 1992a. 43–55.

Collison, Robert L. 1982. *A History of Foreign-Language Dictionaries.* London: Deutsch.

Eichler, Ernst et al., eds. 1993. *Slawistik in Deutschland von den Anfängen bis 1945. Ein biographisches Lexikon.* Bautzen: Domowina.

Fabian, Bernhard. 1985. "Englisch als neue Fremdsprache des 18. Jahrhunderts". Kimpel 1985. 178–196.

Fazekas, Tiborc. 1992. "Zur Erforschung und Vermittlung des Ungarischen im 16.–18. Jahrhundert". Schröder 1992a. 125–133.

Folena, Gianfranco. 1983. *L'italiano in Europa. Esperienze linguistiche del Settecento.* Torino: Einaudi.

Gallina, Annamaria. 1959. *Contributi alla storia della lessicografia italo-spagnola dei secoli XVI e XVII.* Firenze: Olschki.

Germain, Claude. 1993. *Evolution de l'enseignement des langues: 5000 ans d'histoire.* Paris: CLE international.

Hammar, Elisabet. 1980. *L'enseignement du français en Suède jusqu'en 1807. Méthodes et manuels.* Stockholm.

–. 1991. *'La Française'. Mille et une façon d'apprendre le français en Suède avant* 1807. Uppsala: Universität.

Kelly, Louis G. 1969. *Twenty-five Centuries of Language Teaching. An inquiry into the science, art, and development of language teaching methodology, 500 B. C. – 1969.* Rowley, Mass.: Newbury House.

Kimpel, Dieter, Hg. 1985. *Mehrsprachigkeit in der deutschen Aufklärung.* (= *Studien zum 18. Jahrhundert*, 5.) Hamburg: Meiner.

Klippel, Friederike. 1994. *Englischlernen im 18. und 19. Jahrhundert. Die Geschichte der Lehrbücher und Unterrichtsmethoden.* Münster: Nodus.

Lambley, Kathleen. 1920. *The Teaching and Cultivation of the French Language in England during Tudor and Stuart Times.* Manchester: Manchester Univ. Press.

Mandich, Anna Maria & Carla Pellandra. 1991. *Pour une histoire de l'enseignement du français en Italie. Actes du Colloque de Parme, 14–16 juin 1990.* (= *Documents pour l'histoire du français langue étrangère ou seconde*, 8.) Paris: SIHFLES.

Mannzmann, Anneliese, Hg. 1983. *Geschichte der Unterrichtsfächer I.* München: Kösel.

Minerva, Nadia. 1996. *Manuels, Maîtres, Méthodes. Repères pour l'histoire de l'enseignement du français en Italie.* (= *HEURESIS* III, *Strumenti* 4.) Bologna: CLUEB.

– & Carla Pellandra. 1997. *Insegnare il francese in Italia. Repertorio analitico di manuali pubblicati dal 1625 al 1680.* (= *HEURESIS* III, *Strumenti*, 5.) Bologna: CLUEB.

Mormile, Mario. 1993. *Storia dei dizionari bilingui italo-francesi. La lessicografia italo-francese dalle origini al 1900.* Fasano: Schena.

Mugdan, Joachim & Wolf Paprotté. 1983. "Zur Geschichte des Faches Englisch als Exempel für eine moderne Fremdsprache". Mannzmann 1983. 65–93.

Niederehe, Hans-Josef. 1992. "Die Geschichte des Spanischunterrichts von den Anfängen bis zum Ausgang des 17. Jahrhunderts". Schröder 1992a. 135–155.

–. 1994. *Bibliografía cronológica de la lingüística, la gramática y la lexicografía del español (BICRES) desde los comienzos hasta el año 1600.* (= *Amsterdam Studies in the Theory and History of Linguistic Science*, 76.) Amsterdam & Philadelphia.

Pellandra, Carla, Hg. 1989. *Grammatiche, grammatici, grammatisti. Per una storia dell'insegnamento delle lingue in Italia dal Cinquecento al Settecento.* Pisa: Editrice Libreria Goliardica.

Rauscher, Gerhard. 1957. *Das Collegium Illustre zu Tübingen und die Anfänge des Unterrichts in den neueren Fremdsprachen, unter besonderer Berücksichtigung des Englischen, 1601–1817.* Tübingen. (Diss. maschinenschriftlich.)

Riemens, Kornelis-Jakobus. 1919. *Esquisse historique de l'enseignement du français en Hollande du XVI^e au XIX^e siècle.* Leiden: A. W. Sijthoff.

Rossebastiano Bart, Alda. 1984. *Antichi vocabolari plurilingui d'uso popolare: La tradizione del 'Solenissimo Vochabuolista'.* Alessandria: Edizioni dell'Orso.

Schmidt, Bernhard. 1931. *Der französische Unterricht und seine Stellung in der Pädagogik des 17. Jahrhunderts.* Halle: Klinz.

Schröder, Konrad. 1969. *Die Entwicklung des Englischunterrichts an den deutschsprachigen Universitäten bis zum Jahre 1850. Mit einer Analyse zur Verbreitung und Stellung des Englischen als Schulfach an den deutschen höheren Schulen im Zeitalter des Neuhumanismus.* Ratingen: Henn.

–. 1975. *Lehrwerke für den Englischunterricht im deutschsprachigen Raum, 1665–1900. Einführung und Versuch einer Bibliographie.* Darmstadt: Wissenschaftliche Buchgesellschaft.

–. 1980–85. *Linguarum Recentium Annales. Der Unterricht in den modernen europäischen Sprachen im deutschsprachigen Raum.* 4 Bde. (= *Augsburger I&I-Schriften* 10, 18, 23, 33.) Augsburg: Universität.

–. 1987–99. *Biographisches und bibliographisches Lexikon der Fremdsprachenlehrer des deutschsprachigen Raumes, Spätmittelalter bis 1800.* 6 Bde. (= *Augsburger I&I-Schriften* 40, 51, 63, 68, 73, 74.) Augsburg: Universität.

–. 1989. "Fremdsprachenunterricht in Hamburg im 17. und 18. Jahrhundert". *Englischdidaktik: Rückblicke, Einblicke, Ausblicke. Festschrift für Peter W. Kahl* hg. von Wilfried Brusch, Wulf Künne & Reiner Lehberger, 11–24. Bielefeld: Cornelsen.

–. Hg. 1992a. *Fremdsprachenunterricht 1500–1800.* (= *Wolfenbütteler Forschungen*, 52.) Wiesbaden: Harrassowitz.

–. 1992b. "Matthias Cramers 'Entretien de la Méthode entre un maître de langues et un écolier' (Nürnberg 1696): Französischunterricht und Fremdsprachendidaktik im Zeitalter Ludwigs XIV.". Schröder 1992a. 171–189.

–. 1994. "Französischunterricht in Berlin im 18. Jahrhundert". *Regards sur l'histoire de l'enseignement des langues étrangères. Actes du colloque de la SIHFLES au Romanistentag de Potsdam du 27 au 30 septembre 1993* hg. von Herbert Christ & Gerda Haßler, 188–209. (= *Documents pour l'histoire du français langue étrangère ou seconde*, 14.) Paris: SIHFLES.

–. 2000. *Die skandinavischen und baltischen Sprachen sowie Jiddisch und Rotwelsch. Ein Verzeichnis der Lehr- und Lernmaterialien 1500–1800 einschließlich der Neudrucke und ausgewählter Sekundärliteratur.* (= *Der Unterricht in den weniger gelernten Sprachen Europas, 1500–1800. Ein bibliographischer Versuch, 1.*) Augsburg: Universität.

Seidelmann, Christian Friedrich. 1724. *Tractatus philosophico-philologicus de methodo recte tractandi linguas exoticas, speciatim gallicam, italicam et anglicam, conscriptus et in usum eorum qui linguas istas exacte nec nimio tempore neque nimio sumtu addiscere cupiunt.* Wittenberg: Gerdesia Witwe. Faksimiliert, übersetzt und herausgegeben von Franz Josef Zapp und Konrad Schröder, mit einer Darstellung der Geschichte des Fremdsprachenunterrichts an der Universität Wittenberg. (= *Augsburger I & I-Schriften*, 30.) Augsburg: Universität, 1984.

Spillner, Bernd. 1985. "Französische Grammatik und französischer Fremdsprachenunterricht im 18. Jahrhundert". Kimpel 1985. 133–155.

Stengel, Edmund. 1890. *Chronologisches Verzeichnis französischer Grammatiken vom Ende des 14. bis zum Ausgange des 18. Jahrhunderts nebst Angabe der bisher ermittelten Fundorte derselben.* Oppeln: Eugen Franck. (Neu herausgegeben mit einem Anhang von Hans-Josef Niederehe. (= *Amsterdam Studies in the Theory and History of Linguistic Science*, 8.) Amsterdam: Benjamins 1976.)

Titone, Renzo. 1968. *Teaching Foreign Languages. An historical sketch.* Washington: Georgetown Univ. Press.

Winter, Eduard. 1954a. *Halle als Ausgangspunkt der deutschen Rußlandkunde im 18. Jahrhundert.* (= *Deutsche Akademie der Wissenschaften zu Berlin. Veröffentlichungen des Instituts für Slawistik*, 2.) Berlin.

–. 1954b. *Die Pflege der west- und südslawischen Sprachen in Halle im 18. Jahrhundert. Beiträge zur Geschichte des bürgerlichen Nationwerdens der west- und südslawischen Völker.* (= *Deutsche Akademie der Wissenschaften zu Berlin. Veröffentlichungen des Instituts für Slawistik*, 5.) Berlin.

*Konrad Schröder, Augsburg (Deutschland)*

# XVIII. The Development of Grammatical Traditions for the Literary Vernaculars in Europe
# Die neuen Literatursprachen und die Herausbildung ihrer grammatischen Tradition
# Le développement des traditions grammaticales concernant les vernaculaires écrits de l'Europe

## 102. Early grammatical descriptions of Italian


1. The *Grammatichetta vaticana*
2. The first Italian grammar in print: Fortunio's *Regole*
3. Bembo's *Prose della volgar lingua*
4. Trissino's *Grammatichetta*
5. Other 16th-century grammars
6. Bibliography


### 1. The *Grammatichetta vaticana*

The oldest known grammar of Italian is the *Grammatichetta vaticana.* It is so called because of its limited proportions and because the only apographal, anonymous transcript, dated 1508, is preserved in the Reginense Latino 1370 codex in the Vatican Library in Rome. The work was, however, written earlier: it dates back to the 15th century, and is now attributed without a shadow of doubt to the distinguished architect and man of letters Leon Battista Alberti (1404–1472) (see Grayson 1964, Alberti 1996). Alberti's Italian grammar (or Tuscan grammar, to be more precise) was well ahead of its times: it was drawn up not long after 1435, probably between 1437 and 1441. It is therefore the first example of a grammar of a modern vernacular in Europe: it antedates Nebrija's Castilian grammar (see Tavoni 1990: 190, 200–210) by over fifty years. Alberti's grammar, however, was not circulated; nor was it afforded any opportunity to become known; nor was it published when the printing press appeared. Thus, it did not gain the prestige it fully deserved (see Colombo 1962; De Blasi 1993: 338). Indeed, its first publication saw the light only at the beginning of this century, and then merely as an appendix to Ciro Trabalza's *Storia della grammatica italiana* (see Trabalza 1908; Poggi Salani 1992: 418–419; 1994: 435–439). Even though the sole copy in our possession is the one which belongs to the Vatican Library, there exists an inventory which demonstrates that Lorenzo il Magnifico's (1449–1492) library possessed an exempar of Alberti's grammar under the Latin title *Regule lingue florentine*, perhaps even bearing the Italian title *Regule della lingua fiorentina* (see Patota in Alberti 1996: XXXI): it therefore constitutes an experiment whose origins lie in the Florentine environment. The extremely succinct premise, just a few lines preceding the "rules" themselves, casts light on the humanist context in which the idea of this kind of work was born: the premise enters into a polemic with those scholars who held that Latin had been the exclusive property of the learned and never a language spoken by the population at large. What emerges here is the main theme of the debates which were held in the course of the famous dispute between Biondo Flavio (1392–1463) and Leonardo Bruni (1369–1444) in 1435. This debate thus constitutes the departure point for the *Grammatichetta Vaticana.* Alberti's short work was born as a sort of challenge: to demonstrate that even the vernacular was equipped, as was Latin, with an orderly structure (see Tavoni 1992a: 63). Over and above this fundamental theoretical commitment, the author's intention was eminently practical: to offer a tool which would teach one "to write and speak without corruptions" (Alberti 1965: 15). The *Grammatichetta* is based on the categories of Latin, in particular, making intensive use of Prisciano's *Institutiones* (see

Vineis 1974; Poggi Salani 1988: 776; Paccagnella 1991: 215); the Tuscan language is described employing the categories noun/article, pronoun, verb, preposition, adverb, interjections, conjunction, even if the compressed structure of this work, which may be defined as a "morphological synopsis", means that the categories are never discussed at a theoretical level, but only put to practical use (Swigers & Vanvonslem 1987: 162). It was inevitable that this first grammar should depend on Latin. Nevertheless, this in no way detracts from its originality. The work is aimed at the living language, that is at contemporary Tuscan. Two pieces of evidence may be cited to demonstrate the point. First, the opening section of the treatise presents a phonetic alphabet (that is, it distinguishes between an open and a closed *e/o*, a voiced and unvoiced *z*, and so forth). Second, some of the morphological indications provided: the choice of the article *el* instead of *il*, and the preference for the imperfect ending in *-o* rather than *-a* (see Patota 1993: 100; Alberti 1996: LVII–LVIII, LXVII–LXVIII). The norm on which the *Grammatichetta* is based is that of 'use' and not on examples from classic 'authors'. Indeed, in contrast to what will be the dominant propensity of the grammarians of the 16th century, Alberti shows no inclination or interest in canonical authors. Alberti's stance may be defined 'synchronic', and the *Grammatichetta* must be given its due for having identified a number of features of the Tuscan language to which scholars still refer today: for instance, when he notes that almost all Tuscan words end in a vowel, or when he observes that Tuscan has a large part of its lexis in common with Latin (see Poggi Salani 1992: 418).

## 2. The first Italian grammar in print: Fortunio's *Regole*

After Alberti's exceptional and precocious attempt, there follows a period of silence. Indeed, the first grammars of the Italian language to be published only appeared in the first half of the 16th century. The grammar included in Book III of the *Prose della volgar lingua* (1525) by Pietro Bembo (1470–1547) is of enormous importance. The *Prose* constituted the theoretical base on which the normative tradition was founded, a tradition which was destined to last for centuries, and which conditioned the development of literary language and of poetic fashion. The extraordinary mix which makes Bembo's treatise so important consists of the union of a strongly charged normative component and its solid aesthetic, rhetorical and historical content. The theoretical framework is perfectly sound and worked out in great detail. So difficult is it to find a work of comparable nature and stature that it may be classified as unique in its field. The first and second books of the *Prose* were already complete by 1512; it was the grammatical part that was missing and which postponed the publication of the entire work for another thirteen years. This delay cost Bembo the honour of being first, for it gave one of his competitors time to beat him to the post: thus it was that in 1516 Giovanni Francesco Fortunio (c. 1471–1517) brought out his *Regole grammaticali della volgar lingua*, the first two volumes of the first grammar of the Italian language to be published, containing the rules of grammar and of orthography. He promised additional volumes in the near future, which would presumably have contained the rules of 'elegance' of the vernacular, inspired perhaps by Lorenzo Valla's *Elegantiarum libri* (see Pozzi, in Fortunio 1972–1973: 152). They would probably have also contained the rules governing versification, the construction of verbs, and lexis. The town in which the two volumes were published in 1516 is Ancona. This town was definitely not a centre where printing and culture flowered. Fortunio, perhaps born in Friuli, and a lawyer, moved there when he was elected *praetor* (Italian *podestà*) and died there in 1517 after having published his grammar, though without having been able to keep his promise of issuing further volumes. The fact that the book came out in central Italy, in a town on the Adriatic, is thus pure coincidence: in acutal fact, Fortunio had received his education elsewhere: Pordenone (where perhaps he was born – instead, until a few years ago, it had been believed he was a Slavon), Trieste, Venice. In other words, he was trained in the Veneto area, as was Bembo, a region in which there flourished a strong and rich humanist culture.

It has been proved that Fortunio was in Venice at the same time as Bembo was publishing his famous Aldine editions. Moreover, the first two grammarians of the Italian language were acquainted with each other, even though their relationship was of a conflictual nature (see Trovato 1994: 91–92). Though they adopt models which are almost identical, yet their grammars constitute a vehicle for conducting a polemic. Fortunio shows quite clearly he cannot abide Bembo's philological analyses carried out on texts written in the vernacular. Thus, on several occasions he criticises the text of the renowned Aldine editions of 1501 and 1502 (respectively, the works by Dante and Petrarch edited by Bembo). In addition, the two scholars provide different evaluations of the language of Dante: Fortunio has no reservations whatsoever as regards the *Divine Comedy*, whereas Bembo is critical of the low and plebeian lexical choices characterising some of the 'realistic' parts of Dante's poem. The terms of this polemic lead us to an important conclusion: unlike the humanist grammar of Alberti, the Italian grammars of the first half of the 16th century take as their object of study not the spoken language, but the language of canonical authors, and their preeminent aim is to solve linguistic problems connected with literature. We are not dealing with synchronic grammars paying careful attention to the living language, but with grammars of literary language, modelled, what is more, on authors belonging to the past, as were Dante, Petrarch and Boccaccio.

Despite the fact that Bembo's grammar had a richer and more complex theoretical framework than that of Fortunio, and was therefore destined to meet which immensely greater cultural success, on a practical level the public continued to appreciate Fortunio's *Regole*, several new editions of which appeared even after 1525. Now exist a modern edition of the *Regole* which is readily accessible to scholars: see Fortunio 1999 (transcription, and anastatic facsimile of 1516 original edition). The anastatic facsimile produced by the publishing company Forni (see Fortunio 1979) is, however, a reproduction of the 1552 reprint and not the original Ancona edition of 1516. The 1516 edition has, instead, been transcribed by Mario Pozzi in an edition which was printed in only a limited number of copies for a university course (see Fortunio 1972–73).

In the presentation to the *Regole*, Fortunio shows he is quite conscious of the innovative value of his work (see Fortunio 1972–73: 7: "discendendo io in campo primo volgare grammatico", 'I am the first to penetrate the field of vernacular grammar') when he explains his intentions and recounts the history of his own work, attributing its genesis to his youthful studies on Dante, Petrarch and Boccaccio. Those three authors, he declares, offer the best grammatical model possible for the vernacular, the only one that assures 'regulated order'. The principle on which Fortunio bases his work is not, as we stated earlier, radically different from that adopted by Bembo, though it must be borne in mind that his evaluation of Dante's artistic production is far more positive than the opinion expressed by Bembo.

We will now examine the structure of the work. The departure point of Fortunio's treatment is the identification of the four parts of speech he deems fundamental ('necessary') to acquire a knowledge of the vernacular: noun, pronoun, verb, adverb. (On the other hand, he devotes but scant attention to participle, conjunction, preposition and exclamation.) He offers no definition of these parts of speech (see Swiggers & Vanvonslem 1987: 164). Rather, he employs them directly to expound the rules, which are presented in a relatively orderly and pedagogically useful form, as well as numbered in sequence, though on the whole (as Tavoni 1992b: 1070 notes) the work is more suited to extensive reading than to use as reference book. Each rule is accompanied by examples, over-abundant at times, *bona fide* teeming extracts from the works of the three great 14th century authors.

The second volume of the *Regole* is devoted entirely to the norms of orthography. This concern for writing may be interpreted in different ways: as a feature which is characteristic of the mode of dealing with problems adopted by a man of letters of the north of Italy, or (the more accurate interpretation, in my view) as the expression of the urgent need to regulate affairs which was then emerging, in the age of the great expansion of printing. The time had come to bring an end to the season in which the Latin-style system of writing had held sway. The rules Fortunio proposed tend to break away from the Latin model (and are thus consistent with the claims he made in the introduction to his work), detaching itself from the etymological writing system. Thus, for instance, Fortunio advises the use of the double *t* in words such as *dotto* ('learned'), *ottuso* ('stupid') etc, in those cases in which some writers, on the contrary, preferred the *t* to be preceded by *c*, *h*, *d*, *p* (see Fortunio 1972–73: 104; 148; Patota 1993: 1040, as for, example, *epso* instead of *esso* ('it') and *scripse* in place of *scrisse* ('wrote') (see Tavoni 1990: 191).

## 3. Bembo's *Prose della volgar lingua*

Bembo's *Prose* is presented in a dialogic form. The conversation is set in 1502. The fiction of a dialogue, therefore, takes us back to a period prior to the publication of Fortunio's *Regole*, almost as if Bembo wished to employ this means too in order to underline the fact that the record of the first grammar was in actual fact his, and did not belong to Fortunio's 1516 *opus* (see Dionisotti in Bembo 1966: 73n). Moreover, in the *Prose*, it was explicitly stated that up to that point in time no one had "delle leggi a regole dello scrivere [...] scritto bastevolmente" ('any laws and rules of writing [...] written adequately') (*Prose*, I,1), despite the fact that the Italian language now had three hundred years of literature behind it: by decreeing its inadequacy, Bembo was indubitably demeaning the work of his competitor Fortunio.

The grammar itself takes up only the last of the three volumes of Bembo's *Prose*. The first two volumes tackle a variety of issues, such as the linguistic situation at the time of Ancient Rome, the history of the Italian language, the debt Italian poetry owed to Provençal poets, the characteristics of courtly language and the linguistic theory of Vincenzo Colli known as Calmeta (c. 1460–1508) which Bembo was averse to, the rights of "natural Florentineness", the concept of literary 'nobility' in contrast to 'popular' culture, the theory of imitation, the formal perfection of the great writers of the 14th century, the defects exhibited by Dante's style, the 'seriousness' and 'pleasantness' of writing, metre, poetry and so forth. In other terms, when the reader reaches volume III, all those theoretical issues which are preliminary to the creation of the norm have already been dealt with.

We shall now examine Book III of the *Prose*, the one which really does contain the grammatical description of literary Italian presented by the author. The first point to note is that Bembo's treatment "è marcatamente non schematica" ('is pointedly non-schematic') (Tavoni 1992b 1077). The dialogic structure itself, which characterises this volume as it did the preceding two, renders it difficult to extract grammatical patterns in the real sense of the term. Thus the text does not have a didactic form, as we intend this concept today. So true is this that it is impossible to even deduce the number of parts of speech that the author employs as his paradigmatic model. There seem to be five (noun, pronoun, verb, participle, adverb), but they are never established in a definitive and explicit list. Nor are the parts of speech ever given a precise definition. At best, a simplified, reduced account is provided. Nevertheless, by including the adjective and the article in the category "noun", Bembo seems to concur with Fortunio's simplification of the categories of Latin. Similarly, the category "adverb" comprises exclamations, conjunctions and prepositions. The Italian grammars that followed these first two grammars, however, tended to reconstruct the Latin model of categories, bringing about an increase in their number.

Taking up another of the observations made by Tavoni (1992b: 1078), it may be noted that just as the grammatical apparatus is shorn almost to the point of dissolving into nothingness, so too the smooth flow of the dialogic form and the exemplification leads to the substitution of technical terminology by expressions drawn from everyday language or which have been invented exhibiting a clear desire to do away with technical language, a tendency which was not destined to find fortune in the grammatical tradition that was to follow. As examples of this process, Tavoni cites *divertimento* for "elisione" ('elision') (*Prose* II: XVII), *maniera* ('manner') for "coniugazione" ('conjugation') (in Bembo's view, verbs exhibit four manners, both in Latin and in Italian, as exemplified by the verbs *amare* ['love'], *valere* ['to be worth'], *leggere* ['read'] and *servire* ['serve']: see *Prose* III: XVII); Bembo never employs the word *coniugazione (conjugation)*; nonetheless, he never furnishes a systematic definition of these *maniere*, he simply takes them for granted; Fortunio, on the other hand, had spoken of only two conjugations, obtained from the variation of the third person singular of the present indicative, which could end in *-a* or in *-e*). Further illustrations are Bembo's use of the term *pendente* for the "imperfect" (*Prose* III: XXXVI, LIII), and of the term *voce senza termine* ('item without an end') for "infinitive" (in the *Prose*, in fact, *infinito* ('infinitive') is used only as an adjective to convey "grande, senza limiti" ('large, having no limits'), never as a grammatical category; Fortunio, of course, employs the term in its traditional grammatical sense). Another observation made by Tavoni (1992b: 1078) with regard to the detechnicalisation process concerns the use Bembo makes of periphrases such as *tempo che corre mentre l'uom parla* ('time which goes by as man talks') for "present" (though Bembo does use the term *present* elsewhere), and *voce che comanda* ('voice which orders') for the "imperative" (the term "imperative" is not to be found in the *Prose*, but it is present in Fortunio's work). In conclusion, with regard to the technical terminology, the *Prose della volgar lingua* represents a break with the existing tradition, which was, obviously, modelled on Latin. This tradition was not, however, interrupted by Bembo's highly idiosyncratic choice.

As our next step is to compare Fortunio's normative system to that of Bembo's, we must again refer to Tavoni's work (1992b: 1079). On various occasions, Bembo identifies those forms that were destined to become standard in Italian: he gives the second person singular of the present indicatives as *ami* and accepts only the form *amiamo* for the first person plural as against *ame* and *amemo* which Fortunio still accepts as correct; for the past simple he prscribes *amammo*, whereas Fortunio proposes *amassimo*; for the conditional, the ending in *-ei* is given as normal, while the alternative in *-ia* is (correctly) defined as not being Tuscan and pertaining exclusively to the domain of poetic usage (*Prose* III: XLIII), in contrast to Fortunio who endorses both variants, though expressing a preference for the former type; Bembo differs from Fortunio on yet another count with reference to the conditional: he rejects the second person singular form *ameressi* and the first person plural ending in *-eressimo*.

As we have seen in the above-mentioned cases, there are choices related to the area of morphology which differentiate the Bembian canon from the more tentative and tolerant tenets of Fortunio, though, as we stated earlier, the models which inspired the work of both scholars are not radically different. Nevertheless, Bembo is more selective and precise in the definition of his model, assigning a subordinate role to Dante, guilty of having allowed himself to be influenced too often by the language of the common people and of having been contaminated by 'low' forms, as when he writes in the *Divine Comedy*

e non vidi mai menar stregghia / a ragazzo aspettato dal segnorso / [...] / e si traevan giù l'unghie la scabbia, / come coltel di scardova le scaglie (And never saw I plied a currycomb / By stable-boy for whom his master waits / Nor by him who keeps awake unwillingly, As everyone was plying fast the bute / Of nails upon himself, for the great rage / Of itching which no other succor had. / And the nails downward with them dragged the scab, / In fashion as a knife the scales of bream.) (*Inferno*, XXIX, vv: 76–83),

lines expressly quoted by Bembo in the third book of the *Prose* in order to demonstrate that Dante had utilised inelegant words. From this standpoint, Petrarch is preferable. It must not be forgotten that in this case poetic theory determines grammatical choice, and that grammar is born to serve an aesthetic ideal. Thus the model of Florentine as the living language has no part to play in the fixing of grammar, because Florentine runs the risk of introducing items originating in 'popular' language. Indeed, in taking this point to its logical conclusion, Bembo goes so far as to say that there is no need whatsoever to know Florentine to become a proficient user of Italian. Grammatical normativity had to be founded on an ancient phase, almost as if Italian were a dead language. When faced with the objection that ignoring linguistic models of use meant that one was not speaking for the living but for the dead, Bembo would turn this polemical perspective on its head, claiming that the living are simply great models of the past, and that one must not write exlusively for one's contemporaries, but, above all, for posterity. Literary and linguistic value must not be such as to please the 'multitudes' but 'the chosen few', the elite of the learned. Bembo's grammar was thus born under the aegis of the most rigourous form of classicism.

## 4. Trissino's *Grammatichetta*

1529 saw the publication of the *Grammatichetta* written by Giovan Giorgio Trissino, a man of letters from Vicenza. This grammar differed from Bembo's, one reason being that he adopted a different solution to the 'language issue', since, inspired by Dante's treatise *De vulgari eloquentia* (translated and published by Trissino himself in 1529), he was a supporter of the so-called 'Italian language'. As are all his works, Trissino's grammar is written in a graphic system which employs those new letters which the author deemed it was necessary to introduce into Italian, namely the Greek letters ε and ω. The treatment of the subject follows the eight-fold division of the parts of speech. Each part is given a concise but clear definition. Exclamations are not construed as an independent class, but form a sub-category of the category of adverbs (see Castelvecchi, in Trissino 1986: LIV). The opening section is devoted to letters (and deals not only with the alphabet, but also with syllables and accents). The subsequent section deals with the article: then follow the noun (which includes adjectives), the verb, the participle, the pronoun, the preposition, with the adverb bringing up the rear. A comparison between this grammar and those published before it unearths an interesting point: it contains no quotations from authors. The book consists of a simple list of forms, with a few patterns as summaries. The terminology is essentially traditional, though the author does contribute some personal innovations. For example, for verb tenses Trissino does not speak of future (Latin *futurum*), but of *tempo che ha da venire* ('time that is still to come') and *l'avenire* ('one's future'), with symmetrical, clear periphrases: *tempo passato indeterminato* ('indeterminate past time') for the Italian tense "passato remoto", *tempo passato (e) non compiuto* ('past [and] unfinished time') for the "imperfect", *tempo passato di poco* ('time which has only just passed') for the "passato prossimo", *tempo passato di molto* ('time which has long since past') for the "trapassato prossimo". Verbs are divided into three conjugations. Following Fortunio, these are identified on the basis of the third person singular. Trissino, however, also employs the criteria of *passato indeterminato* and the *infinito*: thus he singles out the verbs ending in *-are*, *-ere*, *-ire*, a classification which is still used today.

Even if Trissino's theoretical stance on the 'language issue' is different from Bembo's, it must not be believed that this grammatical system differs radically from that expounded in the *Prose*. Although his system was less rigourous, inevitably he was influenced by the model of the *Tre Corone*. Nevertheless, differences between his work and that of his predecessors may be noted here and there. These differences are significant from the point of view of the theoretical choices made by Trissino. By way of illustration, Trissino opts for the form of the conditional in *-ia* in *lieu* of the Tuscan form in *-ei* (Trissino 1986: 145, 148, 151, 153, 154, 156). He also considers the forms *lui*/*lei* to realise the third person singular subject pronoun (Trissino 1986: 164), while Bembo and Fortunio had come down heavily in favour of *egli* to perform the same function. What must be noted, however, is that Trissino never discusses the forms the presents, even less does he motivate or justify his choices. He simply lists his types, without quoting any examples from canonical authors, as stated above, or from common usage, whatever that may mean.

## 5. Other 16th-century grammars

The grammars which followed those we have described so far may be classified under three main headings on the basis of their underlying approach: archaic Tuscan in the style of Bembo, modern Tuscan as in the work of Alberti, or the anti-Bembianism inaugurated by Trissino. If truth be told, Bembo's *Prose* was never more than a work for the few, for a highly cultured elite. Notwithstanding this, the ideas it contained were publicised through other channels, for example through the less expensive and copiously reprinted grammar written by Alberto Acarisio (see Trovato 1994: 116 and Acarisio 1988) or through the *Osservazioni nella volgar lingua* by Ludovico Dolce (1508–1568), a short book with small-sized pages, easy to consult, a work which his contemporaries judged "highly suitable for beginners" (see Trabalza 1908: 127). In 1562 the Venetian publishing firm Sansovino brought out the *Osservazioni della lingua volgare de diversi uomini illustri*, a reprint of five grammars of the first half of the century – those by Fortunio, Bembo, Acarisio, Jacomo Gabriele and by Rinaldo Corso (1525–1580) (see Peirone 1971, Marazzini 1993: 163–166). As may be seen, this collection did not include those grammars which were not in the style of Bembo, for instance Trissino's grammar.

Achieving success was no easy task if one went against the ideas propounded in the *Prose*. The Tuscan opposition to Bembo also found life difficult. The record in the production of normative works continued to be held by Venetian printers. In Florence, under the impetus of the insistent invitations of Duke Cosimo de' Medici (see Nencioni 1983: 221), the Accademia Florentina attempted to produce a grammar of the Tuscan language that would oust Bembo's *opus*. The goal was not achieved, and the only Florentine grammar to come from the pen of one of those academics, Pierfrancesco Giambullari, was the result of a personal effort which did not receive the seal of officialdom. It was published together with an essay by Giovan Battista Gelli (1498–1563) entitled *Ragionamento sopra le difficoltà di metter in regole la nostra lingua*, in which it was explained that the very nature of the parlance of the town of Florence as a living language made it impossible to fix its norms once and for all, an operation which could, however, be successfully carried out for dead languages, as was Latin (see Marazzini 1993: 163–168). Nevertheless, Giambullari's grammar saw the light in 1552, with the title *De la lingua che si parla e scrive in Firenze*, a title which is very apt for describing the author's intentions but of which there is no trace in the original manuscript and which thus led to the selection of a different title for the modern critical edition (see Giambullari 1986). A turning point in Florentine production of grammars came only later with Lionardo Salviati (1540–1589) and with Benedetto Buommattei (1581–1648), whose works were destined to become authoritative (see Manni 1993: 159–161, 190–191; Patota 1993: 111–112).

Finally, also worth citing are some of the grammars which do not toe the line of Bembian orthodoxy and which are extraneous to Florentine Tuscan. These grammars follow the tradition established by Trissino, though not wholeheartedly. They were written by authors who came from geographical areas which were far from the 'centre' constituted by Tuscany. Examples include the *Grammatica volgar* by the Neapolitan Ateneo Carlino (1553) (for which see Trabalza 1908: 108–111; Corti 1969: 217–249), and the curious *Osservationi grammaticali e poetiche della lingua italiana* by Matteo conte di San Martino e di Vische (published in 1555, but according to the author, written in 1535). Matteo conte di San Martino defended the thesis, which though courageous and original was in fact untenable, that the region he came from, Piedmont, had played a part in forming the poetic language of Petrarch (see Marazzini 1992: 18–19).

## 6. Bibliography


Acarisio, Alberto. 1988. *Vocabolario, grammatica et ortographia della lingua volgare* (ristampa anastatica dell'edizione del 1543 ed. by Paolo Trovato). Sala Bolognese: Forni.

Alberti, Leon Battista. 1996. *Grammatichetta e altri scritti sul volgare* ed. by Giuseppe Patota. Roma: Salerno Editore.

Bembo, Pietro. 1966. *Prose e rime* ed. by Carlo Dionisotti. Torino: Utet.

Colombo, Carmela. 1962. "Leon Battista Alberti e la prima grammatica italiana". *Studi linguistici italiani* 3.176–187.

Corti, Maria. 1969. *Metodi e fantasmi.* Milano: Feltrinelli.

De Blasi, Nicola. 1993. "L'italiano nella scuola". *Storia della lingua italiana* ed. by Luca Seriani & Pietro Trifone, I, 383–423. Torino: Einaudi.

Fortunio, Giovanni Francesco. 1972–73. *Regole grammaticali della volgar lingua* ed. by Mario Pozzi (dispense universitarie). Torino: [Tirrenia].

–. 1979. *Regole grammaticali della volgar lingua.* Ristampa anastatica dell'edizione di Venezia 1552. Bologna: Forni.

–. 1999. *Regole grammaticali della volgar lingua* ed. by Claudio Marazzini & Simone Fornara. Pordenone: Accademia San Marco – Propordenone Editore.

Giambullari, Pierfrancesco. 1986. *Regole della lingua fiorentina*, edizione critica ed. by Ilaria Bonomi. Firenze: Accademia della Crusca.

Grayson, Cecil. 1964. *La prima grammatica della lingua volgare.* Bologna: Commissione per i testi di lingua.

Marazzini, Claudio. 1992. "Il Piemonte e la Valle d'Aosta". *L'Italiano nelle Regioni. Lingua nazionale e identità regionali* ed. by Francesco Bruni, 1–44. Torino: Utet.

–. 1993. *Storia della lingua italiana. Il secondo Cinquecento e il Seicento.* Bologna: Il Mulino.

Nencioni, Giovanni. 1983. *Di scritto e di parlato. Discorsi linguistici.* Bologna: Zanichelli.

Paccagnella, Ivano. 1991. "La terminologia nella trattatistica grammaticale del primo trentennio del Cinquecento". *Tra Rinascimento e strutture attuali. Saggi di linguistica italiana* ed. by Luciano Giannelli, Nicoletta Maraschio, Teresa Poggi Salani & Massimo Vedovelli, 119–127. Torino: Rosenberg & Sellier.

Patota, Giuseppe. 1993. "I percorsi grammaticali". *Storia della lingua italiana* ed. by Luca Serianni & Pietro Trifone, 1, 93–137. Torino: Einaudi.

Peirone, Luigi. 1971. "Una raccolta di grammatiche del Cinquecento". *Lingua nostra* 32.7–10.

Poggi Salani, Teresa. 1988. "Storia delle grammatiche". *Lexikon der Romanistischen Linguistik* ed. by Günter Holtus, Michael Metzeltin & Christian Schmitt, IV, 774–786. Tübingen: Niemeyer.

–. 1992. "La Toscana". *L'italiano nelle Regioni. Lingua nazionale e identità regionali* ed. by Francesco Bruni, 402–461. Torino: Utet.

–. 1994. "La Toscana". *L'italiano nelle Regioni. Testi e documenti* ed. by Francesco Bruni, 419–469. Torino: Utet.

Swiggers, Pierre & Serge Vanvolsem. 1987. "Les premières grammaires vernaculaires de l'italien, de l'espagnol et du portugais". *HEL* 9: 1.157–181.

Tavoni, Mirko. 1990. "La linguistica Rinascimentale (L'Europa occidentale)". *Storia della linguistica ed.* by Giulio C. Lepschy, II, 170–245.

–. 1992a. *Storia della lingua italiana. Il Quattrocento.* Bologna: Il Mulino.

–. 1992b. "Prose della volgar lingua di Pietro Bembo". *Letteratura italiana. Le Opere*, I, 1065–1088. Torino: Einaudi.

Trabalza, Ciro. 1908. *Storia della grammatica italiana.* Milano: Hoepli.

Trissino, Giovan Giorgio. 1986. *Scritti linguistici* ed. by Alberto Castelvecchi. Roma: Salerno Editrice.

Trovato, Paolo. 1994. *Storia della lingua italiana. Il primo Cinquecento.* Bologna: Il Mulino.

Vineis, Edoardo. 1974. "La tradizione grammaticale latina e la grammatica di Leon Battista Alberti". *Convegno Internazionale indetto nel V Centenario di Leon Battista Alberti (Roma, Mantova & Firenze, 25–29 aprile 1972)*, 289–303. Roma: Accademia Nazionale dei Lincei.

*Claudio Marazzini, Torino (Italy)*

# 103. Frühe grammatische Beschreibungen des Spanischen

1. Die Anfänge der spanischen Sprachwissenschaft
2. Alfonso X
3. Die literaturbezogene Grammatik
4. Die unmittelbaren Vorläufer Nebrijas
5. Antonio de Nebrija
6. Die kontrastive Methode Latein-Volkssprache
7. Die spekulative Grammatik: Der Einfluß von El Brocense
8. Grammatiken der spanischen Sprache
9. Bibliographie

## 1. Die Anfänge der spanischen Sprachwissenschaft

### 1.1. Grammatische Quellen

Die grammatische Tradition der spanischen Sprachwissenschaft geht auf Donat (4. Jh.) und Priscian (6. Jh.) zurück. Erst ab dem 13. Jh. kommen neue Lehrbücher ins Curriculum, die aber wesentlich in der Tradition des Donat oder des Priscian stehen, sei es nun direkt, wie z. B. die Priscian-Kommentare von Petrus Helie (fl. 1150) oder Robert Kilwardby (1200–1279) oder indirekt, wie das *Doctrinale* des Alexander von Villadei (fl. 1200), der *Graecismus* des Eberhard von Béthune (gest. ca. 1212) oder das *Chatholicon* des Johannes von Genua (gest. ca. 1298).

### 1.2. Mittelalterliche didaktische Methoden und humanistische Grammatik

Bei den mittelalterlichen Lehrwerken lassen sich vier Grundformen unterscheiden: Versgrammatiken, grammatische Kommentare, 'erotematische' Grammatiken und *Grammaticae proverbiandi.*

Verse als mnemotechnische Hilfsmittel wurden schon seit alters her gebraucht. Versgrammatiken waren namentlich in Nordfrankreich verhältnismäßig zahlreich vertreten. Die berühmtesten und umfangreichsten Werke dieser Gattung waren die aus 2645 Verse bestehende Grammatik des Alexander von Villa Dei und der *Graecismus* des Eberhard von Béthune. In Kastilien ist ebenfalls eine Versgrammatik zu finden: das im 13. Jh. erschienene *Verbiginale*.

Die Tradition der Versgrammatiken war ziemlich verbreitet. Gil (1984) rechnet auch Nebrija zu den Anhängern dieser mittelalterlichen pädagogischen Linie, weil er einige Passagen der 2. Bearbeitung seiner *Introductiones latinae* in lateinischen Versen abgefaßt hat.

Kommentare zu Donat und Priscian gab es bereits in der Antike, aber, abgesehen vom Donat-Kommentar des Remigius von Auxerre (10. Jh.), sind erst die ab dem 12. Jh. verfaßten für den Lateinunterricht des Spätmittelalters von Bedeutung. Sie präsentieren sich entweder als separate Ergänzungen bzw. Anmerkungen zur jeweils kommentieren Grammatik oder als in den Text selbst eingesetzte Kommentarblöcke. Das hatte wiederum Folgen für die Kodices. Man ordnete namentlich letztere in Paragraphen, die durch verschiedene Buchstabengrößen gekennzeichnet oder aber in verschiedene Spalten aufgegliedert waren, wobei auf eine klare Unterscheidung zwischen dem Haupttext und dem Kommentar geachtet wurde.

Die Tatsache, daß Nebrija in der endgültigen Version des *Introductiones Latinae* (Salamanca 1495), in der umfangreiche Glossen den grammatischen Textes begleiten, selbst auf diese Präsentationsmethode zurückgreift, spricht nachdrücklich für ihre Relevanz im Lateinunterricht.

Unter 'erotematischen' Grammatiken versteht man Lehrbücher, welche den Stoff in Frage- und Antwortform darbieten. Sie gelten als besonders effizient im Unterricht, vor allem im Anfängerunterricht, und dies nicht nur, was das Latein anbelangt.

Im späten Mittelalter ist diese Gattung besonders häufig vertreten. Donats *Ars minor* liefert hier das Modell, wie bereits schon bei Julian von Toledo (8. Jh.). Zum Teil fließt hierin aber auch die, von einigen so genannte, 'Analysegrammatik' ein, als deren Hauptvertreter der Traktat *Dominus, quae pars?* gilt. Man geht dabei von einem Satz oder Vers aus, dessen einzelne Bestandteile analysiert werden: Aus welchen Redeteilen besteht er?, Welches Genus hat es?, welchen Numerus, Kasus?, Welche syntaktische Funktion? etc.

Das Nachwirken dieser Methode bleibt nicht auf das Mittelalter beschränkt: das 3. Buch der *Introductiones Latinae* von Nebrija entspricht in allen Auflagen ganz diesem Analyseprinzip.

Im 'Herbst des Mittelalters' kommt noch eine weitere Komponente hinzu, die Volkssprache. Sie wird immer häufiger im Unterricht und in der Grammatik selbst eingesetzt, und dies mit klar erkennbarer pädagogischer Zielsetzung. Spätmittelalterliche Grammatiken mit Ergänzungen in der Volkssprache werden damals bereits *grammatica proverbiandi* genannt. Sie bilden den Kern der eigentlichen Grammatikographie des Spanischen.

Texte nach dem Vorbild der *grammatica proverbiandi* hatten in den spanischen Schulen weite Verbreitung gefunden, sowohl im Anfänger- als auch im Fortgeschrittenenunterricht. Durch die in ihnen enthaltenen volkssprachlichen Erklärungen in Kastilisch, Katalanisch, Aragonesisch und Valenzianisch bilden sie eine Art Synthese der oben erwähnten, unterschiedlichen Lehrwerkstypen.

Die Volkssprache erfüllt einen doppelten Zweck: sie begünstigt die Übersetzung aus dem Lateinischen (mittels lateinischer Verblisten und ihren volkssprachlichen Entsprechungen) und die Rückübersetzung ins Lateinische, wobei dann volkssprachliche Ausdrücke dazu dienen, lateinische Konstruktionen zu erklären.

Die Rückübersetzungen sind besonders interessant, wenn damit die unterschiedlichsten Wiedergabemöglichkeiten eines einzigen volkssprachlichen Ausdrucks im Lateinischen demonstriert werden können. Wegen der späteren Nachwirkung sei hier besonders auf die Kommentare über äquivoke Bedeutungen des romanischen Wortes *mas* (vgl. Nebrija, *Gramática Castellana*, S. 30v) oder auf die kastilische Konstruktion *delpor* + *Infinitiv* und das Problem der Übersetzung lateinischer Partizipien verwiesen (vgl. Nebrija, *Gramática Castellana*, S. 40r–v). Im Zusammenhang mit der Übersetzung lateinischer Partizipien bezieht sich Nebrija ein wenig enigmatisch auf "los gramáticos que poco de nuestra lengua sienten" [auf die Grammatiker, die wenig von unserer Sprache verstehen].

Die Autoren *der gramamticae proverbiandi* halten sich an eine sprachlich reduzierte Terminologie, die sich aber im Laufe des 16. und 17. Jhs. als recht wirkungsvoll erweist: 'componer', 'proverbiar', 'romance'... Diese Termini stehen in Beziehung zur sogen. *Supletio*, bei der es darum geht, Konstruktionen der Volkssprache, die so nicht im Lateinischen existieren, doch noch auf Latein wiederzugeben, womit die Volkssprache tatsächlich zum kontrastierenden Hilfsmittel avanciert.

Die *Supletio* begegnet erstmalig in der *grammatica proverbiandi*. Hierbei kommen Hinweise oder Zitate aus anderen Grammatikern kaum vor. Bemerkenswert ist, daß sie normalerweise meistens erst am Ende der Grammatik stehen und damit den Eindruck erwecken, als ob es sich hierbei um einen Nachtrag handelte. Nur bei der *supletio* des Komparativs und des Superlativs stehen sie ausnahmsweise direkt hinter dem entsprechenden Abschnitt. Spätere Beispiele für diesen Analysetypus finden wir in verschiedenen Anhängen zur *Grammatica Brevis* des Gutiérrez de Cerezo (1450–1503) oder in der 2. Überarbeitung der *Introductiones latinae* (1482–1483) von Nebrija.

Die Gliederung des Stoffes der *grammatica proverbiandi* folgt meist einheitlichen Prinzipien; sie entspricht i. G. G. derjenigen, welche sich bereits bei Priscian findet, also der Abfolge 'Orthographie', 'Prosodie', 'Ethimologia' [Lehre von den Worten] und 'Syntax', wozu noch einige Ergänzungen kommen können. M. a. W., der Gebrauch der Volkssprache erlaubt es den Autoren der *grammatica proverbiandi*, Priscians Methode wieder in Kraft zu setzen. Sie wird in der Folgezeit auch von Nebrija und dem Großteil der nachfolgenden Grammatiker aufgegriffen, welche sich der Unterweisung der spanischen Volkssprache verschreiben.

## 2. Alfonso X

Im Werk von Alfonso X el Sabio [der Weise] (1221–1284) begegnen wir den ersten Überlegungen zur Volkssprache. Die Bemerkungen über Natur, Funktion, Ursprung und Entwicklung der Sprachen und Grammatik, welche in seinem Werk eingestreut sind, lassen sich geradezu zu einer Theorie zusammenfassen, welche am Anfang dessen steht, was man Jahrhunderte später in Spanien als die Diskussion um die Nationalsprache bezeichnen wird.

Die 'sprachwissenschaftliche Bibiothek' von Alfonso X, also die von ihm konsultierten sprachwissenschaftlichen Werke (vgl. Niederehe 1987: 147–193), informiert uns über die Traditionen, welche damals in Spanien im Schwange sind und die nachfolgenden Entwicklungen bestimmen. Zu erwähnen wären hier u. a. Eberhard von Béthune, Alexander von Villadei, Papias und Hugucio (Uguggione) von Pisa, welche die logisch orientierte Sprachwissenschaft auf die Iberische Halbinsel repräsentieren, als deren Hauptvertreter der ebenfalls von Alfons X. konsultierte Petrus Hispanus (ca. 1205–1277), Autor des am weitesten verbreiteten logischen Lehrbuches des Mittelalters, gilt. Indem Alfons der Weise sich auf diese (neuen) Autoritäten stützt, nähert er sich mehr und mehr der Lehrmeinung 'von Paris' an, die die folgenden Jahrhunderte bestimmen sollte.

## 3. Die literaturorientierte Grammatik

Trotz der Bedeutung der Traktate aus der Zeit vor Nebrija, die im wesentlichen logisch orientiert sind, darf daneben die Tradition der literaturorientierten Grammatik, also jener Grammatik, welche literarische Texte zu beschreiben sucht, keinesfalls übersehen werden (vgl. Niederehe 1993). Hinsichtlich der Volkssprache beginnt sie mit Enrique de Villena (1384–1434) und setzt sich fort bis Juan del Encina (1468–1529?), auf den Nebrija sich in seiner *Gramática castellana* im Abschnitt über die Prosodie vermutlich bezieht.

Villena, Verfasser einer Poetik (*Arte de trobar*, ca. 1423), bietet den "primer esbozo de una fonética y ortografía castellanas, con certeras observaciones a veces" [die erste Skizze einer Phonetik und Orthographie des Spanischen ...] (vgl. Lapesa 1984: 286). Sie ist in der Volkssprache verfaßt, weil sie sich an den Regelwerken der okzitanischen Minnesänger, den Troubadours, orientiert.

Älter ist wohl noch die Poetik von Don Juan Manuel (1282–1348), von der aber lediglich der Titel (*Arte de trobar o Reglas como se debe trovar*) überliefert ist, so daß nicht gesagt werden kann, ob sie grammatische Regeln enthalten hat. Auch das Werk des Enrique de Villena ist lediglich als Fragment überliefert, weshalb auch hier keine weiterreichenden Schlüsse auf den grammatikalischen Inhalt des Gesamtwerkes möglich sind. Daher könnte hier lediglich noch *La Gaya de consonantes* (1475) des Pero Guillén de Segovia (1413–ca. 1485) genannt werden. Da dieses Werk jedoch keine theoretischen Bemerkungen über Poetik oder Grammatik enthält, kommt es in unserem Zusammenhang auch nicht in näheren Betracht (vgl. noch Viñaza 1893: 791).

Abschließend sei noch festgehalten, daß beide Tradition, die hier knapp skizzierte literaturorientierte Grammatik und die logische (scholastische) grammatische Tradition, geographisch weitgehend getrennt von einander angesiedelt sind. Nur im aragonesischen Kulturraum treffen sie zusammen und führen zu einer nachhaltigen Wirkung.

## 4. Die unmittelbaren Vorläufer Nebrijas

Um die Mitte des 15. Jhs. verstärkt sich die Hinwendung zur Volkssrpache, und die neuen Lehrmeister verknüpfen verschiedene der oben genannten pädagogischen Methoden. So finden sich bei Juan de Patrana (Anfang 15. Jh.), dessen *Compendium grammatice* 1492 gedruckt wurde und von dem ein 30 Jahre früher verfaßtes Manuskript bekannt ist, Anmerkungen in spanischer Sprache zu den Nominal- und Verbalparadigmen, sowie zur Funktionen der Kasus. Seine Grammatik ist nach einem Ordnungsprinzip gestaltet, welche Nebrija in seinen *Introductiones Latinae* später nachahmen wird und das keine sprachlichen Spekulationen in scholastischer Manier mehr enthält. Der gedruckten Version der Grammatik Pastranas ist, als 2. Teil, ein Kommentar von Fernandus Nepos beigegeben, der ganz in der Tradition der *grammatica proverbiandi* steht.

Letzte Spuren dieser Tradition, welche man nicht unbedingt auf Salamanca eingeschränkt sehen darf (vgl. Gómez Moreno 1989), sind in der *Gramática castellana de Palacio* zu finden. Dabei handelt es sich vermutlich um ein Fragment einer umfangreicheren spanischen Grammatik, von der allerdings nur vier Folios mit Anmerkungen zur Orthographie und Prosodie des Spanischen erhalten sind.

Bei der *Grammatica brevis* (1485) des Gutiérrez de Cerezo (1459?–?) und dem *Perutile grammaticale compendium* (1490) des Daniel Sisón (?–ca. 1514) sind schon umfangreichere Passagen in der Volkssprache enthalten. Hier finden sich auch volkssprachliche linguistische Termini, welche als Hilfsmittel zum Verstehen und Übersetzen lateinischer Texte ins Spanische dienen und meistens bloße Adaptationen aus dem Lateinischen darstellen. Als reine Übersetzungen enthalten sie keine präzisierenden linguistischen Vorstellungen, genausowenig wie die ca. 1488 publizierte zweisprachige Version der *Introcutiones Latinae* von Nebrija (vgl. Esparza & Calvo 1996).

## 5. Antonio de Nebrija

### 5.1. Die Besonderheit von Nebrija

In Nebrijas Werk sind allenthalten Spuren früherer grammatischer Traditionen festzustellen (vgl. Esparza 1995). Sowohl in der spanischen Schule, als auch in Italien, wo er einige Jahre verbrachte und wo die *grammatica proverbiandi* besonders lebendig war, konnte er mit den Methoden des mittelalterlichen Lateinunterrichts in Kontakt kommen. Seine Bestrebung aber war es, wesentlich bessere Methoden als alle bis dahin praktizierten zu entwickeln. So veröffentlicht er 1481 seine *Introductiones latinae*, die von da an in immer neuen, überarbeiteten Auflagen erscheinen. Ihnen folgt nicht nur eine zweisprachige Version dieser Grammatik (Salamanca ca. 1488), sondern auch die, mehrfach neu herausgegebenen, lateinisch-spanischen (Salamanca 1492) und spanisch-lateinischen (Salamanca ca. 1495) Lexika, und schließlich auch die *Gramática Castellana* (Salamanca 1492), die erste methodisch rigoros aufgebaute Grammatik einer modernen europäischen Sprache.

Die *Gramática Castellana* ist ganz auf die Neugestaltung des Lateinunterrichts ausgerichtet. Sie geht von einer genauen Beschreibung der Muttersprache aus, um hieran die grammatisch-theoretischen Begriffe des Sprachunterrichts ohne zusätzliche Kommentierungen, Anlagen oder Übersetzungen zu vermitteln. Die kontrastierende Methode des Sprachvergleichs ist damit absolet geworden.

### 5.2. Konzeption und Methode der Grammatik

Bei der Anlage der Grammatik und der im Unterricht zu verwendenden Methoden mußte Nebrija manche Schwierigkeiten überwinden, die im wesentlichen durch die Vorkenntnisse der Schüler bedingt waren.

Was die Grammatikkonzeption anbelangt, so sind für Nebrija sowohl praktische Gesichtspunkte als auch wissenschaftliche Überlegungen maßgebend. Zum einen geht Nebrija von der Auffassung aus, daß Ähnlichkeiten und Übereinstimmungen verschiedener Sprachen mit ein und demselben Instrumentarium beschrieben werden sollten. Das heißt, die Grammatik ist für Nebrija nicht als Sammlung von Regeln anzusehen, mit deren Hilfe eine Einzelsprache beschreiben werden kann, sondern vielmehr als wissenschaftliche Disziplin, welche auf Universalprinzipien beruht. Man kann also feststellen, daß die Vorstellungen der 'Modisten' bei Nebrija deutliche Spuren hinterlassen hat.

Diese Auffassung erlaubt es ihm, die Aufgabe der Grammatik genauer festzusetzen und sie von den übrigen Disziplinen zu unterscheiden. Es ist jene Wissenschaft, welche *circa sermonis congruitate uersat, quemadmodum rhetorica circa ornatum, dialectica circa ueri falsique dissertationem* (*Recognitio*, fol. 6).

Ferner geht er auf die Methoden ein, welcher sich der Grammatiker bedienen sollte: sofern er die Muttersprache behandelt, sei die 'natürliche' Methode am Platze, bei der Fremsprache jedoch die 'kunstgerechte' (*artificialis*).

Die natürliche Methode besteht in einer, von den kleinsten zu den größeren Einheiten der Sprache, von den Buchstaben bis zum Satz, aufsteigenden Darstellungsweise, wobei auch die 'Akzidentien' von Buchstaben, Silbe und Wortart behandelt werden. Dieses Vorgehen ist für ihn nur bei einer Sprache möglich, welche durch Usus erworben worden ist, also bei der Muttersprache.

Der *orden de la doctrina o artificial*, das kunstgerechte Vorgehen, ist namentlich dann am Platz, wenn man 'dem Beispiel derjenigen folgt, welche die Grundzüge und Prinzipien der griechischen und lateinischen Grammatik aufgeschrieben haben' und eine 'knappe näherungsweise Kenntnis von Buchstaben, Silben und Redeteilen, Nomina und Verba vermitteln, nach deren Muster alle anderen gebildet werden könnten' (vgl. *Gramática castellana* fol. 54v).

Die 'natürliche' Methode der Grammatikerklärung könne dagegen nur auf die Muttersprache der Schüler angewendet werdne. Wie schon die grammatische Tradition des Altertums empfahl, war mit der einfachsten Einheit zu beginnen, dem Laut bzw. Buchstaben, der somit den Einstieg in Nebrijas didaktische Methode bildet.

Die Berücksichtigung beider Aspekte, der 'natürlichen' und der 'kunstgerechten' Methode, machen Nebrijas *Gramática* gleichsam zum Gipfel und Endpunkt der traditionellen Schulgrammatik des Mittelalters. Die Notwendigkeit aber, Rhetorik und Metrik in die Volkssprache zu übertragen, führte Nebrija zusätzlich dazu, jene Schemata. welche er zuvor auf das Hebräische, Griechische und Lateinische, den 'Sprachen der Religion, Weisheit und Macht, welche in der Kreuzüberschrift zusammengefaßt sind', auszuweiten. Es ist beinahe überflüssig zu sagen, daß Nebrija auf diese Weise auch an der Tradition der literaturorientierten Grammatik anknüpft, wobei allerdings die von ihm angeführten Autoren von ihm nicht als sprachliche Leitbilder aufgefaßt werden.

## 6. Die konstrastive Methode Latein-Volkssprache

Die Verwendung der Volkssprache im Lateinunterricht, welche schon in der Scholastik hilfsweise zu verzeichnen war, wird bei Nebrija zur neuen Methode erhoben und lange Gültigkeit behalten: Grammatische Texte werden von nun an ganz auf Spanisch abgefaßt, um damit in das Studium der lateinischen Sprache einzuführen.

Es sind zahlreiche Autoren, die hier genannt werden können, auch wenn ihre Beiträge zur eigentlichen spanischen Philologie kaum bekannt sind: Bernabé del Busto (fl. 1/2 XVI), Francisco de Tamara (1500–ca. 1600), Pedro Simón Abril (1530–1600), Luis Pastrana (1540–ca. 1600), Pedro de Madariaga (fl. 2/2 XVI), Juan Sánchez (fl. 2/2 XVI) und Bartolomé Bravo (ca. 1540–1607).

Weitere Autoren lassen sich hier nur mit Einschränkungen anführen, so etwa Palmireno (1514–1580), dessen Werke nicht als grammatische Traktate im eigenlichen Sinne betrachtet werden können, oder das dialogistische Werk von Luis Vives (1493–1540), wenngleich ihre linguistischen Ideen auch durchaus als wichtig sind.

Während die vorgenannten Autoren grammatische Arbeiten und lexikographische Werke teilweise oder ganz in der Volkssprache abfassen, beschränken sich andere Traktate nur auf die Orthographie. Allmählich setzt sich nämlich die Idee durch, daß geeignete Kenntnisse des Spanischen ebenfalls durchaus von Nöten sind. Hier liegt der Ausgangspunkt für eine eigene Grammatikographie des Spanischen (vgl. Esparza 1996: 66).

## 7. Die spekulative Grammatik: Der Einfluß von El Brocense

Die grammatikographischen Aktivitäten des 16. Jhs. enden mit der *Minerva* (1587) des Francisco Sánchez de las Brozas, gen. 'El Brocense' (1527–1600). Obwohl die Orientierung seines Werkes mehr spekulativ als philologisch ist und seine Lehre nicht auf eine Unterweisung in der spanischen sondern der lateinischen Sprache abzielt, trägt es dazu bei, die syntaktische Tradition Spaniens, welche wir heute als 'klassische Lehre' kennen, zu konsolidieren und den volkssprachigen Humanisten das Instrumentarium an die Hand zu geben, die spanische Sprache zu normieren.

Der 'Brocense' stützt sich in seiner *Minerva, sive de causis linguae latinae* auf die Prinzipien 'Ratio' und 'Usus', so wie es in einem Teil der lateinischen Tradition vorgezeichnet ist. Dabei läßt er Vorurteile und Themen seiner Epoche außer Acht und versucht statt dessen, eine Globaltheorie der Sprache zu schaffen, mit der auch Besonderheiten einzelner Sprachen erklärt werden können (vgl. Breva 1983). Der größte Wert seines Werkes besteht allerdings darin, die Syntax, welche in der damaligen Grammatikographie nur eine marginale Rolle spielte, in die Forschungen einbezogen zu haben.

## 8. Grammatiken der spanischen Sprache

### 8.1. Juan de Valdés (1509?–1542)

Das Beispiel von Antonio de Nebrija findet keine Fortsetzer. Man muß vielmehr als ein halbes Jahrhundert warten, bevor neue Überlegungen zur spanischen Sprache erscheinen, welche denjenigen von Nebrija an die Seite gestellt werden können, der *Diálogo de la lengua* (1534–1540?) von Juan de Valdés; hierbei handelt es sich aber, wie der Titel zeigt, nicht um eine Grammatik.

Das Werk des Valdés besitzt unbestreitbare Werte. Es biete einen vorzüglichen Überblick über den Zustand der spanischen Sprache der Zeit: phonetische Eigentümlichkeiten, genaue Beobachtungen zu lexischen und grammatischen Fragen und auch persönliche Kommentare zur Konzeption einer Schriftsprache.

Trotzdem sind die Unterschiede zwischen Nebrija und Valdés aber nicht zu übersehen. Während die Grammatik ein unerläßliches Instrument für Nebrija ist, um die Sprache zu fixieren, glaubt Valdés, es sei unmöglich, eine lebende Sprache grammatikalisch ein für allemal fest zu schreiben.

Außer dieser Einstellung, welche allein schon die große Divergenz zwischen beiden Autoren erkennen läßt, gibt es weitere, welche sich aber in gewisser Weise aus dieser ableiten lassen, so etwa die Möglichkeiten einer Sprachpflege. Nach Valdés beruht sie ausschließlich auf dem Sprachgebrauch und einer geschickten Auswahl innerhalb desselben. Nebrija vertritt dagegen die Meinung, daß der Sprachgebrauch die Sprache der gebildeten Stände widerspiegeln müßte, wobei die beurteilende Stellungnahme nur dem Grammatiker zusteht, wie er immer wieder in seiner Grammatik betont. Weitere Unterschiede zwischen Valdés und Nebrija lassen sich an ihrer abweichenden Einschätzung des Spanischen als Sprache entnehmen. Laut Valdés ist die spanische Sprache als Ausdrucksmittel für Wissenschaften und Literatur dem Lateinischen prinzipiell gleichgestellt, was sich allerdings noch in einer adäquaten schriftlichen Produktion niederschlagen muß, die auf dem allgemeinen Sprachgebrauch basiert und südspanische Dialektalismen und Manierismen vermeidet (vgl. Bustos 1983: 218); Nebrija hält dagegen an einer scharfen Trennung zwischen Wissenschafts- und Alltagssprache fest.

### 8.2. Cristóbal de Villalón

In den ('spanischen') Niederlanden, wo man am ehesten auf das Erlernen des Spanischen angewiesen war, erschien die nächste wichtige Grammatik der spanischen Sprache: die *Gramática castellana* (1558) des *lilcenciado* Cristóbal de Villalón (ca. 1510–ca. 1562): Nach Aquilino Sánchez (1992: 30) handelt es sich dabei, trotz der gegenteiligen Erklärung ihres Autors, nicht um eine Grammatik für Ausländer, sondern um eine Grammatik für Spanischsprechende, deren eigentliches Ziel das Erlernen der lateinischen Sprache ist. Sie stützt sich u. a. auf Nebrijas Unterscheidung zwischen 'Cláusula' und 'Oración' (vgl. Lope Blanch 1990: 103–109; Sarmiento 1989).

### 8.3. Bartolomé Jiménez Patón

Das grammatische Konzept, welches in den *Instituciones de la gramatica española* (1614) von Jimenéz Patón (1569–1640) zum Ausdruck kommt, ist, trotz der auffallenden Kürze des Werkes, bemerkenswert durchdacht und entwickelt. Als Beispiel für seine Begabung als Grammatiker wird immer wieder seine, auf funktionalistische Argumente gestützte, Analyse der Redeteile hingewiesen, die er in fünf Klassen gliedert: Nomen, Verb, Adverb, Präposition und Konjuktion (vgl. Quilis & Rozas 1963).

### 8.4. Gonzalo Correas

Den Höhenpunkt der Grammatikographie des spanischen Goldenen Zeitalters bildet aber der *Arte de la lengua castellana* (1626) von Gonzalo Correas (1570/1571?–1631). Zu den traditionellen Lehrmeinungen und Methoden kommt bei ihm noch eine präzische Sprachtheorie hinzu, welche sich in *prezetos i rreglas para entender i hablar la lengua* '(Vorschriften und Regeln zum Sprachverständnis] niederschlägt, die er aus der aufmerksamen Beobachtung des Sprachgebrauchs und der Untersuchung von *la conformidad i conzierto del hablar natural o usual de las xentes en su lengua* [der Übereinstimmung der natürlichen bzw. gebrauchsgerechten Sprechweise der Leute] herleitet. Correas geht es um eine klare und vollständige Grammatiktheorie, deren Originalität darin besteht, die Eigentümlichkeiten des Usus mit den Prinzipien der Universalgrammatik zu verknüpfen. Genau wie El Brocense ist er der Auffassung, daß alle Sprachen auf universellen Prinzipien basieren, und er plädiert dafür, die acht traditionellen Redeteile auf drei zu reduzieren: Nomen, Verb und Partikel. Die Syntax ist aber für ihn der Hauptgegenstand der Grammatik.

Correas unterscheidet sich von Nebrija besonders hinsichtlich der Identifizierung der Termini *materia* und *forma* mit denen von *uso* und *reglas*. Auch die theoretische Begründung von *presuposición* ('Präsupposition') und *limitación* ('Begrenzung'), welche er auf die Konstruktion der drei Wortarten anwendet, sind wichtig. Speziell der Begriff *limitación* impliziert die Hypothese, daß die grammatischen Beziehungen der Zahl nach begrenzt sind und daß man die übrigen Relationen letztlich mit spezifischen Operationen reduzieren kann; m. a. W., Correas geht von einer regelmäßigen, 'kanonischen' Syntax aus.

Der *Arte* von Correas ist für Sarmiento (1989) daher vor allen Dingen als Grammatik des guten Sprachgebrauchs anzusehen, welche als erster Versuch einer strukturellen Beschreibung des Spanischen gelten könne.

### 8.5. Juan Villar

Etwas später erscheint der *Arte de la lengua española* (1651) von Juan Villar, dessen wichtigster Verdienst in der klaren Formulierung von grammatischen Regeln liegt. In seinem *Arte* sind bereits Vorboten einer rationalistischen Sprachauffassung zu verzeichnen und seine Vorstellungen – etwa die Absicht, 'die Sprache zu reinigen und zu fixieren', seine Hinweise auf sprachliche Fehler, die die Sprache verderben – zeigen eine deutliche Affinität zu dem, was, ein Jahrhundert später, die Spanische Akademie erklären wird (vgl. Lázaro Carreter 1985: 152). Villar zählt damit zu ihren Vorläufern.

## 9. Bibliographie


Breva Claramonte, Manuel. 1983. *Sactius Theory of Language.* Amsterdam: Benjamins.

Bustos, Eugenio de. 1983. "Nebrija, primer lingüista español". *Actas de la Tercera Academia Literaria Renacentista*, 205–222. Salamanca: Universidad.

Esparza, Miguel Ángel. 1995. *Las ideas lingüísticas de Antonio de Nebrija.* Münster: Nodus.

–. 1996. "Die Grammatica proverbiandi in der spanischen grammatischen Tradition des goldenen Zeitalter". *Theorie und Rekonstruktion* hg. von Dutz & Niederehe 75–85. Münster: Nodus.

– & Ramón Sarmiento. 1992 [1492]. *Antonio de Nebrija. Gramática de la lengua castellana.* Estudio y edición. Madrid: S. G. E. L.

– & Vicente Calvo. 1996 [c. 1488]. *Antonio de Nebrija. Introduciones latinas contrapuesto el romance al latín.* [c. 1488]. (= *Materialien zur Geschichte der Sprachwissenschaft und Semiotik* 7.) Münster: Nodus.

Gil, Luis. 1984. "Apuntamientos para un análisis sociológico del humanismo español". *Estudios de Humanismo y Tradición clásica*, 15–40. Madrid: Universidad Complutense.

Gómez Moreno, Ángel. 1989. "La Gramática Castellana de Palacio: un nuncio de Nebrija". *Revista de Literatura Medieval* 1.41–51.

Lapesa, Rafael. 1984. *Historia de la lengua española.* Madrid: Gredos.

Lázaro Carreter, Fernando. 1985 [1949]. *Las ideas lingüísticas en España durante el siglo XVIII.* Barcelona: Crítica.

Lope Blanch, Juan Miguel. 1990. *Estudios de Historia Lingüística Hispánica.* Madrid: Arco/Libros.

Niederehe, Hans Josef. 1987 [1975]. *Alfonso X el Sabio y la lingüística de su tiempo.* Madrid: S. G. E. L.

–. 1993. "Corrientes primarias y secundarias en la prehistoria de la Gramática de la lengua castellana de Nebrija". *Annuario de Letras* 31.265–293.

–. 1995. *Bibliografía Cronológica de la lingüística, la gramática y la lexicografía del español* (bicres). Vol. I: *Desde los comienzos hasta el año 1600.* (= *Studies in the History of The Language Sciencies* 76.) Amsterdam & Philadelphia: Benjamins.

Quilis, Antonio & Juan M. Rozas. 1963. "La originalidad de Jiménez Patón y su huella en el Arte de la lengua del maestro Correas". *Revista de Filología Española* 46.81–95.

Sánchez, Aquilino. 1992. *Historia de la enseñanza del español como lengua extranjera.* Madrid: S. G. E. L.

Sarmiento, Ramón. 1989. "Origen y constitución de la doctrina sintáctica en la época clásica". *Philologica* II.419–438. Universidad de Salamanca.

Viñaza, Cipriano Muñoz y Manzano, Conde de la. 1893. *Biblioteca histórica de la filología castellana.* Madrid: Imprenta y Fundición de Manuel Tello. (Nova ed., Madrid, Ediciones Atlas, 1978.)


*Miguel Ángel Esparza Torres, Vigo (Spanien)*

# 104. Les premières descriptions grammaticales du Portugais

1. Les sources
2. Questions techniques
3. Questions socioculturelles
4. Questions épistémologiques
5. Bibliographie

## 1. Les sources

### 1.1. La première annotation

En janvier de l'année 1536, on publie à Lisbonne la *Gramática da Lingua Portuguesa* de Fernão de Oliveira (1507−1581), prêtre, marin et aventurier. On considère qu'il s'agit de la première grammaire portugaise que l'auteur appelle 'annotation', précisant dès le début: 'Voici la première annotation de la langue portugaise, faite par Fernão de Oliveira' (Oliveira 1975: 37). Et à la fin, 'on vient de terminer l'impression de cette première annotation de la langue portugaise' (ibid., 126). Nous pensons nous trouver en présence de la solution du problème concernant le *primus inventor*, soulevé par les chercheurs et confirmé quatre ans plus tard par João de Barros (1496−1570): le titre de 'Grammaire' sur la page de garde correspond effectivement à un titre générique, dû à la 'consuetudo' de la tradition médiévale qui faisait appeler 'grammaire' toutes les œuvres au contenu linguistique. Fernão de Oliveira prétend faire suivre les premières annotations d'un travail plus vaste et plus ordonné et le fait savoir à plusieurs reprises: 'le langage, dans la jonction des dictions, du style et de la façon de procéder, a ses particularités ou propriétés, comme je la dirai en temps voulu dans une œuvre plus importante, que j'espère réaliser en cette matière' (ibid., 75). Du reste, il répète son intention à deux reprises encore dans son œuvre (ibid., 120, 125).

### 1.2. La première grammaire du Portugais

Toutefois, c'est à João de Barros, une des figures les plus nobles de l'humanisme portugais, historien, penseur et moraliste, que reviendra la place d'auteur de ce que nous considérons être, en fait, la première grammaire du Portugais. En traçant le profil de João de Barros, grammairien, il faut tenir compte de quatre œuvres, publiées en l'espace d'un mois, entre décembre 1539 et janvier 1540: la *Cartinha*, 'pour apprendre à lire', la *Gramática*, le *Diálogo em Louvor da nossa linguagem* et le *Diálogo da Viciosa Vergonha*, qui constituent effectivement un *coprus* pédagogique et didactique relatif à une planification d'ensemble cohérente. Ainsi, la *Cartinha* serait la 'première partie' d'initiation à la lecture et à l'écriture, suivie de la *Gramática*, en tant que 'deuxième partie' et des deux *Diálogos*, qui constituent à la fois la conclusion et les textes complémentaires de lecture (Buescu 1971). L'affirmation réitérée par l'auteur, tout au long de son œuvre, reflète son intention première lors de sa construction: profiter aux jeunes. Elle n'était donc pas destinée en exclusivité à des 'non-Portugais', comme certains critiques l'ont supposé. En effet, une grammaire pour étrangers, par exemple, partant d'une description phonétique (comme l'a essayé Fernão de Oliveira) devrait se baser sur une exemplification simple dans un texte bilingue, processus utilisé nommément dans la *Cartinha em Tamul e Português*, imprimée à Lisbonne en 1554. L'intention strictement pédagogique si souvent soulignée par l'auteur à propos de l'élaboration de la *Gramática*, l'a amené à une rédaction dont la concision délibérée l'a empêché de discuter de façon dialectique la problématique linguistique au-delà de l'encadrement systématique des mécanismes respectifs. Le *Diálogo em Louvor da nóssa linguágem* représente donc le complément, d'une certaine manière spéculatif (bien que parfois pratique), trouvant un espace discursif pour l'abordage, en des termes dialectiques, d'une problématique en même temps épistémologique, culturelle et sociale.

### 1.3. 'Pour les non latins'

La divulgation et la démocratisation culturelle postulée par la presse permettront une diffusion qui dépasse largement les circuits de l'éducation palatine et aristocratique (présupposition de l'œuvre de Barros) dans l'œuvre de Pêro Magalhães de Gândavo (?−1579), *As regras que ensinam a maneira de escrever a Orthographia da Lingua Portuguesa com hum Diálogo* (Lisbonne, 1574). Prenant comme destinataire le 'lecteur discret et curieux', il s'adresse à 'toute personne qui écrit', à qui il convient de 'bien connaître l'orthographe, mettant à la bonne place les lettres et les accents nécessaires au discours des écritures'. C'est ainsi qu'il a eu comme but de les expliquer en peu de mots [...] afin d'en faire profiter tous ceux qui voudraient les suivre'. Plus significatif encore est le fait qu'il écrive 'pour les non latins', c'est à dire ceux qui ne connaissent pas les structures et les systèmes de la langue latine.

## 2. Questions techniques

### 2.1. Le projet alphabétique

Faire correspondre la substance graphique avec la substance phonique, établir, en somme, un alphabet 'nouveau' a été, nous semble-t-il, le souci primordial de Gândavo, son 'projet alphabétique'. Ce but serait atteint en adaptant et élargissant par des diacritiques et des digrammes le vieil alphabet latin.

#### 2.1.1. Vers la norme

L'antinomie entre écriture et lecture, entre graphème et phonème, représente donc l'une des premières questions quand on aborde les problèmes de codification des langues. C'est au problème graphique que vont se heurter non seulement les grammairiens des langues romanes, mais avant eux, les copistes anonymes, scribes et tabellions des XIII^e^, XIV^e^ et XV^e^ siècles, qui disposent d'un alphabet — le latin — déjà longuement et presque parfaitement adapté à la langue latine, mais non approprié et sans correspondance avec les nouveaux systèmes phonologiques des langues romanes. C'est cet alphabet qui sera utilisé pour enregistrer les langues 'barbares' de l'Occident chrétien, hésitantes, fragmentées, non codifiées. C'est à ce moment que vont se résoudre, ou du moins se mettre en question, les problèmes qui pour la plupart seront reconnus par les grammairiens et qui, à partir de la Renaissance, vont donner aux langues respectives une physionomie définitive, quoique passant par des propositions rejetées par l'usage et l'enseignement postérieur. A la fin du siècle, nous pouvons dire que la physionomie orthographique du portugais est esquissée dans sa figure moderne. Finalement se projette l'établissement d'une *norme*, basée sur l'utilisation et l'autorité, à partir de la définition du juste, du légitime et du correct, après la réussite de l'installation des modèles littéraires.

#### 2.1.2. Un nouvel alphabet

Les problèmes graphiques découlant de 'l'insuffisance' de l'alphabet latin concernent en premier lieu le système vocalique et la notation d'ouverture et de fermeture du *a*, du *e* et du *o*. En deuxième lieu, ils concernent la valeur vélaire du *c* et l'utilisation de la cédille (ç); ensuite, le problème de cette lettre 'sans nom et sans voix', le *h* dont la présence va être légitimée par les nouvelles utilisations qui lui sont attribuées et le rendent indispensable: en tant que signe diacritique, en composition dans les digrammes *ch*, *nh*, *lh* et en tant que signe distinctif (*he* = *éle*) ou marque étymologique (*homem*). Enfin la reconnaissance des lettres appelées ramistes, *j* et *v*, et, en consonance, l'abolition du *y* et du *w*. En ce qui concerne le premier problème, à savoir les variations de timbre vocalique, nous vérifions que la façon de les noter varie d'une langue romane à l'autre: le français semble préferer l'utilisation d'accents et, dès 1580, Claude de Sainliens (1565—1597) l'applique dans son *De Pronuntiatione* (Kukenheim 1932: 40), alors que les Italiens dont Trissino et Tolomei proposent comme alternative d'utiliser de nouvelles lettres provenant de l'alphabet grec ou de majuscules. Il faut soligner que ce problème n'a pas été considéré par les grammairiens castillans dont a langue ne possédait pas les variations vocaliques qui, pour les Français et les Italiens, représentaient un problème à résoudre. Pour les Portugais qui préfèrent une solution avec des accents diacritiques, le problème s'étend aussi, abstraction faite du *e* et du *o*, à *a*: *más*/*mas*; *fé*/*lê*; *pode*/*pôde*. Ourtre le problème de la notation du timbre vocalique, le deuxième problème concerne la coexistence de *k*, *c*, *ç* et *q*, dans l'ensemble des lettres de l'alphabet. A la suite de la discussion lancée par Varron, Quintilien, Priscien et Isidore de Séville, la fonction de *k* et *q* serait toujours celle du *c* en tant que consonne vélaire, d'autre part, *ç* serait utilisé dans toute position: *k* et *q* devraient donc être éliminés de l'alphabet proposé. Ainsi: *ca* (*ka*), *ce* (*ke*), *ci* (*ki*), *co* (*ko*), *cu* (*ku*); et en contrepartie *ça*, *çe*, *çi*, *ço*, *çu*. Une telle analyse provoque la discussion analogue et symétrique proposée par les deux grammairiens portugais, par rapport au *g*, indépendamment de la qualité de la voyelle à laquelle il est accolé: *ga*, *ge* (= *gue*), *gi* (= *gui*), *go*, *gu*, exactement comme *ca* (= *ka*), *ce* (= *ke*), *ci* (= *ki*). En ce qui concerne le *h*, bien qu'il soit considéré comme une lettre appartenant à l'alphabet, en réalité le 'pouvoir' qu'il détient ne s'identifie pas au 'pouvoir' des autres lettres: il ne leur est pareil que par la 'figure'. N'ayant pas de voix, il ne se prononce pas tout seul et il est alors pareil en sa fonction au tilde. Pour ces einseignants, Barros et Oliveira, *h* et ~ sont donc des signes diacritiques, ce qui ne veut pas dire qu'ils doivent être supprimés du nombre des lettres de l'alphabet. C'est ainsi que l'on atteint le nombre des trente-quatre lettres qui composent le plus audacieux des alphabets portugais proposés au XVI^e^ siècle: Barros totalise trente-quatre lettres:

a, á, b, c, ç, d, e, ę, f, g, h, I, i, j, y, l, m, n, ó, o, p, q, r, rr, S, s, t, u, v, x, z, ch, lh, nh; Oliveira: α, a, b, c, ç, d, e, ε, f, g, I, j, l, m, n, o, ω, p, q, r, rr, s, ss, t, u, x, z, y, ch, lh, nh, ~.

2.2. Les parties du discours

La tension entre la convention (le modèle ancien) et l'innovation, qui découle du l'observation et de l'analyse des interrogations successives sur une réalité chaque fois plus troublante, vont conduire la pensée des humanistes à concevoir les faits ou les phénomènes humains comme des faits et des phénomènes universels. Ils sont donc sur la voie d'une grammaire universelle, idée suggérée aux Européens par la confrontation avec les langues du Nouveau Monde, toutes capables d'expimer la pensé humaine.

2.2.1. La question théorique

En ce qui concerne le nombre de classes de mots des parties du discours, on remarque, parmi les grammairiens des langues romanes, des divergences qui vont de quatre – Giovan Francesco Fortunio (1470–1517) à dix – António de Nebrija (1441/1444?–1522), en passant par la position classique de huit parties. Quant aux grammairiens portugais, on note que la position de Ferrão de Oliveira n'est pas très nette, car nous avons vu qu'il ne se propose pas de présenter une œuvre systématique, mais simplement des annotations relatives à la langue portugaise. Ainsi, pour lui, la première division correspond à la distinction de Cratyle entre nom et verbe. Il dit: 'dans la voix, les dictions sont différentes car les unes se déclinent et les autres pas' (Oliveira 1975 [1536]: 102). Il est clair que pour lui, le concept de déclinaison recouvre tout le concept de variation flexionnelle pouvant se confondre avec celui de la conjugaison. Il touche donc le *nom et le verbe*: 'ceux qui se déclinent en soi en particulier, comme c'est le cas des noms et des verbes' (Oliveira 1975 [1536]: 103). En ce qui concerne João de Barros, nous reconnaissons ici la supériorité de son œuvre par rapport à celle de ses confrères portugais, là où Magalhães de Gândavo n'aborde pas, dans son bref traité orthographique, la problématique grammaticale. Pour Barros, 'nous pouvons comprendre que notre langage est composé de ces neuf parties: Article [...], Nom, Pronom, Verbe, Adverbe, Participe, Conjonction, Préposition, Interjection'. Ainsi, il est évident que l'auteur cherche à s'en tenir à la tradition classique des huit parties de la grammaire latine – critère qu'il observe dans la grammaire latine dont il est l'auteur, les *Grammatices Rudimenta* (manuscrit enluminé, sans date; BN), ne s'éloignant de cette doctrine que par le fait qu'il y ajoute une nouvelle partie, imposée par la langue même: l'article. Il atteint ainsi le nombre de neuf parties.

2.2.2. Du latin au vernaculaire

D'une façon générale, nous pensons pouvoir assumer le fait que la partie de la grammaire correspondant à la morphologie est élaborée de façon satisfaisante: pour les doctrinaires du XVI^e^ siècle, la morphologie était analogie, proportion et régularité. Du reste, la désignation 'analogie', surtout en ce qui concerne Fernão de Oliveira, recouvre l'étude des formes, intitulée par João de Barros *Da Dicção*. Effectivement, dans ce chapitre, les grammairiens tentent, par un jeu habile et complexe entre tradition et innovation, d'imprimer une certaine régularité. La *syntaxe*, au contraire, est le domaine de l'anomalie, de la disproportion et de l'irrégularité:

'et le cas des noms qui parfois d'échangent les uns avec les autres; parmi les verbes, le résultat est semblable en ce qui concerne les temps et les modes [...]; finalement, si l'on commet beaucoup de disproportions ou d'invraisemblances dans notre langue il n'y en a pas autant que dans d'autres langues'

écrit Fernão de Oliveira (Oliveira 1975: 124). En ce qui concerne João de Barros, dans les divers sous-chapitres qui partagent le chapitre intitulé "Da Construiçam das partes" (Barros 1971: 352), il rend fluides les règles présentées laborieusement par le biais de ce genre de formulation: 'les uns [...] les autres [...] les autres [...]' (Barros 1971: 354). 'Nous avons aussi certains noms [...], Certains régissent [...] d'autres régissent [...] D'autres régissent' (ibid. 349). Ils envisagent la correction de l'anomalie, qui les empêchait de formuler des règles 'universelles', tout en essayant un système d'encadrement morphosyntactique, constitué par les paradigmes de la déclinaison latine. Cette formalisation syntactique va permettre la construction ou 'l'architecture' des grammaires exotiques qui apparaissent au moment où la vieille Europe méditerranéenne et latine s'apperçoit de la multiplicité des langues qui va abolir pour toujours le système triadique (grec, latin, hébraïque). A partir de l'analyse la *Gramática* de João de Barros, en étudiant la flexion (*variaçam*) du singulier au pluriel – *a rainha/as rainhas* – ou du masculin au féminin dans les articles – *o*, *os/a -as*, on constate que la réflexion grammaticale s'insère dans une problématique clairement définie dans la première articulation du langage. Toutefois, en déclinant – *a rainha / da rainha / à rainha / a rainha / ó rainha / da rainha* – le grammairien place le vocable dans un axe syntagmatique virtuel et enveloppe sa réflexion d'une composante syntactique qui, à nos yeux, n'a rien à voir avec le régime flexionnel.

2.2.3. Vers la grammaire universelle

Appliquer aux réalités immédiates des langues vulgaires la 'grille' grammaticale classique, n'englobe pas seulement, à notre avis, une pratique ou une technique pédagogique et didactique, comme on a souvent affirmé à ce propos. Au contraire, cela correspond à un concept abstrait, à une tentative de découverte d'un modèle universel, valable et convenant à "todalas linguágens da terra", pouvant recouvrir tous les mécanismes linguistiques. Nous supposons que ce concept doit représenter la lecture profonde de la métaphore surprenante de João de Barros, lorsqu'il considère que le *nom* et le *verbe* sont les 'rois' du jeu d'échecs auquel il fait allusion à quatre reprises tout au long de son discours grammatical. Effectivement, il s'agit là, plus que d'une métaphore, d'une théorie linguistique implicite qui, à notre connaissance, est particulière à ce grammairien:

'Et comme pour le jeu d'échecs, il faut deux rois, un de chaque couleur, et qu'ils possèdent des pièces, placées dans des cases respectives et ordonnées suivant des règles que chacun doit suivre [...]; de même *todalas linguágens* possèdent deux rois, différents en genre et concordant en action: L'un s'appelle le Nom et l'autre le Verbe. Chacun de ces rois a sa dame: celle du Nom est appelée Pronom et celle du Verbe, Adverbe. Le Participe, l'Article, la Conjonction et l'Interjection sont pièces et capitaines qui commandent les nombreux pions de la diction qui servent en commun ces deux puissants rois, le Nom et le Verbe' (Barros 1971: 293 sq.).

## 3. Questions socioculturelles

### 3.1. La conscience romane. L'usage normatif

Dans la première moitié du XVIe siècle, on passe d'une prise de conscience de la 'romanité' à une conscience nationale ou impériale selon le contexte particulier de chacun des peuples impliqués dans le processus. En dernière instance et après cette double prise de conscience, on passe dans une situation d'une certaine façon polémique et cyclique, dans la mesure où il est possible de rencontrer, tout au long de l'histoire culturelle, plusieurs 'questions de la langue'. Et là, une fois de plus, nous nous trouvons en face d'une formulation différente, en accord avec la spécificité problématique de chaque cas, en Italie, en France, en Castille et au Portugal. S'il nous semble que la conscience romane implique un processus d'une certaine façon lent et pénible, nous voulons dire sourtout que les hommes de la Renaissance se sont trouvés face à un dilemme et à une contradiction radicale qu'ils ont essayé de résoudre en dépassant les risques d'une incohérence de fond. D'une part, ils retrouvent dans les modèles classiques 'leur' propre modèle et d'autre part, ils revendiquent 'leur' propre existence contrastive. L'analyse du texte de Barros nous montre, du point de vue statistique, qu'il se préoccupe davantage de démontrer des différences que des identités. Il se met dans une perspective méthololologique d'opposition, même lorsqu'il adopte le schéma qui pourra servir *todalas linguágens*, non pas uniquement en tant que canevas latin, mais comme schéma virtuellement universel. Cependant – c'est là que se trouve le dilemme et la contradiction – la filiation latine de la langue portugaise et sa conformité ou ressemblance avec la langue mère, ardemment recherchée et toujours soulignée, représentent sans aucun doute des titres de noblesse auxquels il ne veut pas renoncer et qu'il tient même à accentuer. Pour lui, en effet, '[la meilleure et la plus élégante des langues] est celle qui est le plus en conformité avec la langue latine'. (Barros 1971: 397). Déjà vers la fin du siècle, c'est dans la conformité avec la latin que Magalhães de Gândavo centre son apologie de la langue. D'après lui, on commet des fautes 'parce que l'on ne connaît pas le latin (qui est la source de la plupart de nos vocables)' (Gândavo 1574: 3 recto). Bien qu'il s'adresse prioritairement aux 'non latins' à qui, en vérité, il dédie son œuvre, il ne manque pas de formuler son souhait, disant: 'il ne devrait y avoir personne qui se respecte, qui ne travaille à connaître un peu de latin, la condition nécessaire pour bien parler le portugais' (Gândavo 1574: 24 verso). Gândavo voit dans le rapprochement ou la ressemblance avec le latin la plus forte raison, et peut-être l'unique, des perfections et qualités de la langue portugaise et même de son individualité par rapport aux autres langues vernaculaires (en particulier le castillan), différentes, corrompues et éloignées du modèle hiérarchiquement parfait: le latin. João de Barros, de son côté, ne manque pas de reconnaître les spécificités de la langue portugaise par rapport au latin. La conformité apparaît ainsi, suivant deux hypostases, c'est à dire en tant qu'argument apologétique et en tant que référence. Mais le caractère non-conforme ou dissemblable se transforme en une deuxième topique d'apologie, qui postule l'individualité, l'autonomie et surtout l'aptitude expansionniste et créative de la langue portugaise. La conscience nationale se définit, toujours par référence au latin, selon une dialectique entre la conformité / ressemblance et la non conformité / différence; entre la filiation / dérivation et l'autonomie / 'corruption'. Toutefois, la conscience collective qui va assumer la tâche d'élire et d'imposer ensuite une norme linguistique sous la conduite doctrinaire de quelques 'barons savants', va s'emmêler dans une toile de principes contradictoires et conflictuels. Selon la terminologie dispersée tout au long des œuvres étudiées, la norme est 'l'unité habituelle', elle est loi, oreille, mélodie, harmonie, musique, coutume. 'L'oreille [...] juge le langage et la musique et est le censeur des deux, et si un jour on les accepte, elles deviennent perpétuelles' (Barros 1971: 402). Mais elle est aussi 'volonté du peuple' (ibid.). C'est donc 'l'oreille' et la 'volonté du peuple' qui vont produire 'l'unité de la langue', et c'est là le 'bon langage', 'la bonne coutume', 'le bon usage'. Voilà que s'établit un ordre normatif issu d'un jugement de valeur qui, dépendant en principe de l'*auctoritas*, découle aussi d'un concept d'*urbanitas*, ce qui dans le contexte de l'Europe de la Renaissance, correspond au *uso áulico* ou, en ce qui concerne les Italiens, surtout Bembo, à la *lingua cortigiana*.

### 3.2. La question de la langue

Dans l'étude d'introduction à l'édition du *Diálogo em Louvor da nossa linguagem* de João de Barros sur *La Questione della Lingua in Portogallo*, Luciana Stegagno-Picchio (Stegagno 1959) retrace l'itinéraire de la lente conquête d'une individualité propre et définitive de la langue portugaise, depuis les centres laborieux de la culture médiévale, les monastères de Santa Cruz et d'Alcobaça. Lorsque les humanistes mettent l'accent sur la ressemblance avec le latin et l'exaltent, ils cherchent implicitement à souligner la différence par rapport aux autres langues, qu'il considère, à tort ou à raison, comme plus éloignées de la langue mère, surtout le castillan qui par son statut de langue de cour est en concurrence avec le portugais, en tant qu'instrument de l'expression littéraire. S'il est vrai que la 'Question' qui fait s'affronter le portugais et le latin concernait une minorité culturelle, l'élite intellectuelle des humanistes, il n'en reste pas moins que la 'Question' du portugais-castillan, apparemment contraire au binôme latin-portugais, entraîne en fait la neutralisation de ce dernier, dans la mesure où la position par rapport au castillan relève d'une praxis: il montre l'imminence d'un risque pressenti par les humanistes — celui de la prédominance de la langue compétitive, concurrentielle, forme d'expression d'une nation quelque peu rivale et objectivement plus puissante sur le plan politique interne ainsi que sur le plan d'une politique expansionniste et impériale. Cependant, la prise de conscience de la spécificité du portugais et du castillan se développe suivant deux hypostases. Si la différence par rapport au castillan, mise en évidence par la ressemblance du portugais avec le latin, sauvegarde l'individualité du portugais en tant que l'une des langues d'Espagne, cette individualité, anoblie par la dignité de son origine (latine) trouve une fois de plus dans son paradigme latino-romain un stimulant et un modèle: une langue capable de servir en tant qu'instrument d'expansion et de souveraineté. La conscience romane transformée en conscience ibérique subit alors une dernière et douloureuse métamorphose et elle s'assume en tant que conscience impériale. D'après l'opinion des auteurs analysés, la langue portugaises, individualisée, noble, virile, gracieuse, expressive, est riche de telle forme qu'à celui qui ne manque pas de matière ni d'habilité [...], il ne manque pas de vocables'. La langue, donc, sert alors un idéal expansionniste: l'idéal de l'homme portugais du XVI$^{e}$ siècle. La 'Question de la langue', comme instance d'autonomisation et d'affirmation historique se déroule en trois temps qui correspondent en quelque sorte à trois modifications d'une même façon de penser. D'abord, en tant que confirmation d'une conscience nationale par rapport au castillan, la langue devient l'instrument de création d'une littérature et celle-ci permet de dépasser une possible superposition culturelle. Ensuite, dans une deuxième phase, la Question de la Langue, insérée dans un contexte politico-social différent, correspond au concept d'Empire et se transforme en un instrument neuf d'une idée neuve. La courte euphorie expansionniste et la persévérante évangélisation qui, une fois de plus, recherchent leur modèle de justification dans l'exemple latino-romain, font de la langue un de leurs instruments les plus subtils et font du portugais, en Orient, depuis Goa jusqu'au Japon et en Occident, au Brésil, la langue médiatique, par analogie et de la même façon que le latin l'avait été en Europe, en tant que langue de culture.

## 4. Questions épistémologiques

### 4.1. Origine et nature du langage

L'essence, l'origine et la nature du langage en elle-même ne sont que peu abordées par les grammairiens du XVIe siècle, bien que l'on puisse trouver trace de la problématique dans le *Cratyle*, lorsque l'on pose le problème du rapport entre le référent et le signe et dans l'unité de celui-ci, la dichotomie signifié / signifiant, et tant que figures différenciées d'une seule entité. C'est dans ce sens, croyons-nous, qu'il faut interpréter le discours de Fernão de Oliveira: 'ce n'est qu'un moyen (le langage) que Dieu a voulu donner aux âmes rationnelles pour qu'elles puissent communiquer entre elles et avec lequel, si elles sont spirituelles, elles peuvent sentir les corps' (Oliveira 1975: 39). Ces spéculations, issues de la pensée antique, ont trouvé dans le pensée médiévale une formulation théologique inspirée de la tradition biblique. Elles vont être une fois encore motif de réflexion et topique de recherche spéculative, chez les grammairiens de la Renaissance, sans changement jusqu'au XIXe siècle. Partagés entre le dogme et une prise de position critique, ils prennent pour point de départ le passage de la Genèse, selon lequel Adam nomme les objets, assumant la fonction du donneur de noms platonique. Prenant comme point de référence direct le passage biblique mentionné, João de Barros dit:

'comme elle le démontrent [les Saintes Ecritures], après que Dieu a créé Adam, qui fut le premier homme, et qu'il l'a placé en ce lieu délicieux, il lui présente toutes les choses créées à son intention, qu'Adam reconnut et appela par leur nom' (Barros 1971: 394).

Il est donc clair et implicite, selon la tradition autorisée par les textes sacrés, que dans le langage primitif, la première catégorie est effectivement, dans sa spécificité, celle nu nom, et que le caractère dénominatif du langage est ainsi postulé. Par conséquent, il semble qu'à première vue les grammairiens de la Renaissance soient très proches de l'interprétation littérale de la Bible. Ils considèrent ce passages de la Genèse comme un fait historique, lequel postule immédiatement l'identification d'une langue primitive – l'hébreu – celle-ci ayant été probablement la langue d'Adam. Nonobstant, Isidore de Séville (570–636), dans une tirade notable, avait déjà distingué la langue avec laquelle Dieu communiqua avec Adam et les hommes, l'hébreu, seule langue du Paradis, donc monolingue, du langage spirituel servant les esprits et les anges (cf. Isidori *Etymologiarum Lib.* XX,I,11). L'hébreu était également la langue mère des langues ecrites, puisque c'est celle dans laquelle Moïse écrivit la Loi. Et c'est encore Isidore qui fait autorité chez les Grammairiens de la Renaissance. Il est significatif que pour la langue parlée primitivement on dénote une hésitation par omission alors qu'au contraire, en ce qui concerne la langue écrite, le discours est plus explicite. Nebrija, par exemple, débute sa réflexion linguistique dans la Gramática par l'invention de l'écriture chez Moïse, ce qui est significatif de sa double vocation: elle est à la fois un instrument de l'Ordre et de la Loi et aussi de l'incorruptibilité. Adam et Moïse sont donc les inventeurs de la langue dans les deux instances du processus de communication orale et écrite: 'l'hébreu fut la langue de notre père premier, Adam, dans laquelle Moïse écrivit les livres de la loi' (Barros 1971 [1570]: 393). Cependant, si l'hébreu reste indiscutablement, durant de nombreux siècles, la langue primordiale et unique du Paradis, nous ne pouvons qu'identifier dans le discours des savants portugais une certaine réserve, voire une imposition idéologique qui le transforme, dans une certaine mesure, en un discours de contestation. Barros en effet se réfère 'à l'époque de Babylone où le langage était unique'. Selon le grammairien, donc 'à l'époque de l'édification de Babylone', la langue utilisée était née du dialogue Dieu – Adam, complétée par des noms inventés postérieurement: 'Je ne dis pas qu'[Adam] nomma ces choses inventées par les hommes pour leurs besoins et plaisirs, mais celles qui furent créées au début du monde' (Barros 1971: 396).

On va donc vers la coexistence des noms naturels et des noms conventionnels: 'il y avait nombre de choses inventées pour l'usage de cette construction et d'autres besoins auxquels ils ont donné nom et Adam a nommé les choses naturelles (Barros 1971: 395). Don divin, 'figure de la pensée' (Oliveira 1975: 38), le langage est naturel chez l'homme, ce qui amène João de Barros à affirmer avec une concision expressive que: 'la langue est naturelle chez l'homme' (Barros 1971 [1540]: 349). L'homme étant fait de corps et d'esprit, voici selon sa pensée la dualité de l'acte de la parole, provenant, dans son essence, de la divinité:

'(Dieu) a voulu que par le palais, la langue, les dents et les lèvres, un souffle d'air provoqué par une puissance appelée par les Latins *affatus*, émane des poumons et que des mots significatifs se forment, afin que l'ouïe, leur objet naturel, indique à l'entendement différents sens et concepts selon leur disposition [...]' (Barros, *Década II*, "Prologue".

Dans la pensée de ces hommes, nous assistons à la subtile transition de la position théologique vers la position empirique, fondée d'une part sur l'hypothèse de Vitruve et d'autre part, sur la célèbre légende de Psammétik (Hérodote II,2). Quelle que soit la 'langue du Paradis', hébraïque ou araméenne (appelée chaldéenne selon la tradition isidorienne), le problème de l'origine du langage glisse infailliblement vers la diversité des langues. Une fois de plus, la tradition des textes sacrés, à travers la lecture de la Vulgate, transmise et développée à partir d'Isidore de Séville est à son apogée avec le mythe de la Tour de Babel. La version de la Vulgate est présente, de façon explicite, dans le texte de João de Barros et elle est sous-jacente à toute la doctrine linguistique de ses contemporains (Gen., 11,1–9). Ainsi, dans une espèce de profession de foi, João de Barros commence par revendiquer 'le droit' à l'autonomie de la pensée et en s'adressant à António, son fils, il dit: 'nous ne pouvons nier à notre pensée la spéculation de la vérité, car là se trouve tout son plaisir', et il ajoute, comme pour renforcer l'ordre et l'orthodoxie: 'surtout en ce qui concerne les choses qui sont plus de l'opinion que de la foi' (Barros 1971: 343 sq.).

Comment faire coïncider la lettre du mythe avec la raison? Selon la lecture que nous proposons, le texte de João de Barros montre de façon claire et effective qu'il y a une altération du rapport nécessaire entre le signifié et le signifiant: signifiants finis pour des signifiés, potentiellement infinis. En somme, le langage 'naturel' à l'homme, révélé à Adam par Dieu (en tant que signifié) et par lui réduit au statut de signe par le biais de l'alliance primordiale avec le signifiant, s'éloigne de la 'nature': Adam ayant nommé uniquement les choses créées à l'origine du monde et rendues à la nature, il semblerait que l'on puisse postuler une motivation initiale qui se modifie et disparaît définitivement à Babel, brisant la solidarité qui semblait indestructible entre trois relata: référent / signifié / signifiant. Devenu imparfait, le langage n'était plus exactement la forme parfaite et divine de la connaissance de la réalité extralinguistique ou objectuelle. N'étant plus 'naturel' mais se soumettant à la tyrannie de 'l'alphabet de la raison', le pouvoir créateur et gnostique, hypostase primordiale de sa nature originale, lui est retiré.

## 4.2. Le problème de l'étymologie

Si nous prenons pour modèles principaux des grammairiens de la Renaissance, Varron et Isidore de Séville, nous constatons que tous deux – chacun à sa façon – consacrent une part importante de leur recherche linguistique à l'étymologie en tant que 'science' de l'origine des mots. Ils figurent parmi le petit nombre d'auteurs cités par João de Barros dans sa *Gramática*, où l'on s'attendrait à ce qu'un certain espace soit consacré à l'étymologie, étant donné l'influence que ces auteurs-là ont exercé sur nos Humanistes. Toutefois, ce qui se passe, c'est que Barros refuse d'aborder le problème étymologique car d'après lui, rechercher l'origine des dictions (mots) serait plus difficile que de rechercher les sources du Nil. Fernão de Oliveira rejette lui aussi l'étymologie car il la considère comme étant la science d'un petit nombre de savants; mais il n'échappe pas à la tentation de présenter un certain nombre d'étymologies de caractère étiologique. Voici donc, dans son style enlevé et pittoresque, ce que dit Fernão de Oliveira:

'Comme celles-ci (fausses étymologies), nous pourrions nous consacrer à deux cents autres 'galéjades', lesquelles sont toujours excessives et bien souvent fausses et mal acceptées par les hommes de peu de connaissance, acquises avec beaucoup de lecture et de travail et non pas d'imaginations paysannes sans jugement' (Oliveira 1985: 85).

En dernière analyse, il remet la recherche étymologique aux 'femmes ivres'. D'où le fait que l'étymologie soit 'objet de rire', pour l'esprit positiviste 'avant la lettre' d'Oliveira ou qu'elle soit abordée avec précaution, discrétion et réserve, en mettant de côte les 'envols' audacieux et peu prudents (Oliveira 1975: 85 sq.). Pour ces hommes, l'étymologie se présente comme un genre de recherches susceptible de tomber dans le domaine d'ignorants, capables de la manipuler de façon inapte et imprudente: en refusant l'étymologie (João de Barros par un discours d'omission, Oliveira avec ses marques habituelles polémiques et pittoresques), ces deux auteurs refusent d'entrer dans le jeu de Cratyle et rejettent par conséquent la recherche gnoséologique et même la 'manipulation' cabalistique qu'elle pourrait impliquer et dont il est possible de trouver des traces: n'oublions pas l'importance culturelle des catégories de la pensée hébraïque à l'époque de l'Humanisme au Portugal.

## 5. Bibliographie

### 5.1. Sources primaires

Barros, João de. 1539. *Cartinha com os Preceitos e Mandamentos de Santa Madre Igreja.* Lisbonne: Luis Rodrigues.

—. 1540. *Diálogo em louvor da nóssa Linguágem.* (1ère éd. avec la *Gramática.*) Lisbonne: Luis Rodrigues.

—. 1540. *Gramática da Lingua Portuguesa.* Lisbonne: Luis Rodrigues.

—. 1785. "Cartinha com os Preceitos e Mandamentos de Santa Madre Igreja". *Compilaçam de varias obras do insigne portuguez João de Barros.* 2ème éd. Lisbonne: Luis Rodrigues.

—. 1785. "Diálogo em louvor da nóssa Linguágem". *Compilaçam de varias obras do insigne portuguez João de Barros.* 2ème éd. Lisbonne: Luis Rodrigues.

—. 1785. *Diálogo da Viçiosa Vergonha. Compilaçam de varias obras do insigne portuguez João de Barros.* 2ème éd. Lisbonne: Luis Rodrigues.

—. 1785. *Gramática da Lingua Portuguesa. Compilaçam de varias obras do insigne portuguez João de Barros.* 2ème éd. Lisbonne: Luis Rodrigues.

—. 1959. 3ème éd. par Luciana Stegagno-Picchio. Modena: Soc. Tipografica Modenese; 4ème éd. avec la *Cartinha, Gramatica* e *Diálogo em louvor da nóssa Linguágem,* par Maria Leonor Carvalhão Buescu. Lisbonne: Faculté des Lettres.

—. 1971. *Cartinha com os Preceitos e Mandamentos de Santa Madre Igreja.* 3ème éd. avec la *Gramática da Língua Portuguesa, Diálogo em louvor da nóssa Linguágem e Diálogo da viçiosa Vergonha* éd. par Maria Leonor Carvalhão Buescu. Lisbonne: Faculté des Lettres.

—. 1971. *Diálogo da Viçiosa Vergonha.* 3ème éd. avec la *Cartinha, Gramatica e Diálogo em louvor da nóssa Linguágem* éd. par Maria Leonor Carvalhão Buescu. Lisbonne: Faculté des Lettres.

—. 1971. *Gramática de Lingua Portuguesa.* 4ème éd. par Maria Leonor Carvalhão Buescu. Lisbonne: Faculté des Lettres.

—. 1975. *Gramática da Lingua Portuguesa.* 3ème éd. par José Pedro Machado, Lisbonne: s. n.

Gândavo, Pêro Magalhães de. 1574. *Regras que ensinam a maneira de escrever e orthographia da lingua portuguesa com hum Diálogo que adiante se segue em defensam da mesma lingua.* Lisbonne: António Gonsalves.

—. 1590. *Regras que ensinam a maneira de escrever e orthographia da lingua portuguesa com hum Diálogo que adiante se segue em defensam da mesma lingua.* 2ème éd. Lisbonne: Belchior Rodrigues.

—. 1592. *Regras que ensinam a maneira de escrever e orthographia da lingua portuguesa com hum Diálogo que adiante se segue em defensam da mesma lingua.* 3ème Lisbonne: Alexandre Siquira.

—. année. *Regras que ensinam a maneira de escrever e orthographia da lingua portuguesa com hum Diálogo que adiante se segue em defensam da mesma lingua.* 4ème éd. *id.*

—. 1969. *Regras queu ensinam a maneira de escrever e orthographia da lingua portuguesa com hum Diálogue que adiante se segue em defensam de mesma lingua.* 5ème éd. d'aprés la "princeps" par Rolf Nagel in *Aufsätze zur Portugiesischen Kulturgeschichte* 9.

Oliveira, Fernão de. 1536. *Gramática da linguágem portuguesa.* Lisbonne: Germão Galhardo.

—. 1871. *Gramática da linguágem portuguesa.* 2ème éd. Porto: Imprensa Portuguesa.

—. 1933. *Gramática de linguágem portuguesa.* 3ème éd. Lisbonne: s. éd.

—. 1975. *Gramática da linguágem portuguesa.* 4ème éd. Lisbonne: Imprensa Nacional Casa da Moeda.

### 5.2. Sources secondaires

Buescu, Maria Leonor Carvalhão. 1978. *Gramáticos Portugueses de século XVI.* Lisbonne: Instituto de Cultura Portuguesa.

—. 1983. *Babel ou a Ruptura do Signo. A Gramática e os Gramáticos Portugueses do Século XVI.* Lisbonne: Imprensa Nacional Casa da Moeda.

Cesarini, Martinelli. 1980. "Note sulla polemica Poggio-Valla e sulla fortuna delle 'Elegantiae'". *Interpress* III.29–79.

Jespersen, Otto. 1971. *La Philosophie de la grammaire.* Paris: Minuit.

Kukenheim, Louis. 1932. *Contributions à l'histoire de la grammaire italienne, espagnole et française à l'époque de la Renaissance.* Amsterdam: N. V. Noord-Hollandsche Uitgevers-Maatschappij.

Nagel, Rolf. 1971. "Die Einheit der Grammatik des João de Barros". *Iberoromanica* 1.

—. 1969. "Die Orthographieregeln des Pêro de Magalhães de Gândavo". *Aufsätze zur Portugiesischen*

*Kulturgeschichte*, Herausgegeben von Hans Flasche, Aschendorffsche Verlagsbuchhandlung, Münster i. Westfalen, IX.145–160.

Padley, George Arthur. 1976. *Grammatical Theory on Western Europe – 1500–1700. The Latin tradition.* Cambridge: Cambridge Univ. Press.

Révah, Isaac S. 1960. "Deux ouvrages rarissimes de João de Barros à la Bibliothèque Nationale de Rio de Janeiro. (*Gramática e Diálogos com dous filhos*)". *Boletim Internacional de Bibliografia Luso-Brasileira* I.165–190. Rio de Janeiro: Gabinete Português de Leitura.

Stegagno-Picchio, Luciana. 1959. "La questione della lingua in Portogallo". *Diálogo em Louvor de nóssa Lingágem* éd. par João de Barros. Modéna: Soc. Tipografica Modenese.

Teyssier, Paul. 1966. "La prononciation des voyelles portugaises au XVIe siècle d'après le système orthographique de João de Barros". *Annali dell'Instituo Universitario Orientale*, Sez. Romanza, 127–128. Naples.

Tavoni, Mirko. 1984. *Latino, Grammatica, Volgare. Storia di una questione umnistica.* Padoue: Editrice Antenore.

*Maria Leonor Carvalhão Buescu †, Lisbonne (Portugal)*

# 105. Les premières descriptions grammaticales du français

1. Précurseurs
2. Le XVIe siècle anglais
3. La tradition française
4. Vers une 'grammaire de la norme'
5. Bibliographie

## 1. Précurseurs

Les premières tentatives de décrire la grammaire française apparaissent dans le cadre de l'enseignement du français comme langue d'Etat et de culture en Angleterre, à partir du XIIIe siècle (Streuber 1962: 194–211; Kristol 1990). Le plus ancien texte grammatical connu est un petit *Traité de conjugaison française* anonyme, composé vers 1250 (Södergård 1955). Rédigé en latin, il présente les différences caractéristiques entre le système temporel et modal du français et du latin à un public qui est manifestement familiarisé avec la grammaire latine et qui connaît déjà la morphologie verbale du français. L'attention de l'auteur est centrée sur les multiples possibilités de traduire les formes latines en français:

Preteritum perfectum modi indicativi verbi activi duobus modis construitur, verbi gracia: amavi, *jo amai et jo ai amé* [...]. Omnia tempora verbi inpersonalis habent, verbi gracia: amatur, *est amé* et *l'em aime* [...]. (Södergård 1955: 193).

D'autres observations de type grammatical se trouvent dans les *traités d'orthographe française,* également d'origine anglaise, qui paraissent dès la fin du XIIIe siècle (Stengel 1879, Pope 1910, Johnston 1987). En dépit de leur titre, ces opuscules ne se limitent pas à des questions d'orthographe, mais abordent aussi – de manière assez peu systématique – des problèmes de morphologie et de syntaxe:

Item omnia nomina et participia terminancia in *t* in singulari amittent *t* in plurali et scribantur ac sonabuntur cum *s* vel *z* ut *saint*, *faisaunt*, *alant*, in singulari et in plurali *sains*, *faisauns*, *alans* et sic de similibus [...]. (*Tract. orth.*, fin XIIIe siècle, Pope 1910: 192).
Item quando petitis aliquid ab aliquo, potestis diecere *vous pri* sanz *jeo*. (*Orth. Gall.*, XIVe siècle, Johnston 1987: 16).

Les trois traités d'orthographe conservés s'adressent à de futurs clercs anglais qui savent déjà le français, mais se perfectionnent pour leurs besoins professionnels. Leur intérêt particulier réside dans les premières réflexions métalinguistiques qu'ils contiennent. Ainsi, le *Tractatus ortografie* (fin XIVe siècle) fait plusieurs fois allusion à la variation linguistique interne du français. Dans le passage suivant, il commente – sans les comprendre vraiment – les dernières traces de la déclinaison bicasuelle en picard qui n'ont plus d'équivalent en francien et en anglo-normand:

Item Romanica nomina dignitatis aut officii, que sunt singularis numeri, scribunt pluraliter in effectu, ut *lui papes de Rome, l'empereurs d'Alemaigne, lui rois d'Engleter et de France, lui chauncellers du seint peres, lui tresorerers mons. lui duques de Launcastre, lui recevours madame la roigne, lui sainz esperes vous garde*; ubi vero Gallici sine *s* scribunt huiusmodi nomina singulariter, quod pulcrius et brevius est, ut *le pape de Rome, l'empereur de R., le Roy de l'Engleterre* [...]. (Tract. ort., fin XIVe siècle, Stengel 1879: 16).

Les *traités d'orthographe* sont suivis de près par une première véritable grammaire, le *Donait français* de John Barton, rédigé en français pour le même public anglais entre 1400–1409 (Städtler 1988: 128–137). Comme son titre l'indique, le *Donait* est une tentative d'écrire une grammaire française dans la tradition de l'*Ars minor* de Donat, qui fournit un certain cadre à la description. Il comprend trois grandes parties:
(1) Sur la forme traditionnelle de l'*Ars minor*, il commence par une sorte de 'phonétique' du français:

Quantez letters est il? Vint. Quellez? Cinq voielx et quinse consonantez. Quelx sont les voielx et ou seront ils sonnés? Le premier vouyel est *a* et serra sonné en la poetrine [...], le quarte est *o* et serra sonné au palat de la bouche [...]. (Städtler 1988: 128).

(2) Un long chapitre consacré aux différents *accidents* (nombre, genre, cas, comparaison, temps et mode) brasse assez librement différentes parties de l'*Ars minor* (le *Donait* est beaucoup moins systématique que son modèle latin):

Quantez cases est il? Six. Quelx? Nominatif, genitif, datif, accusatif, vocatif, ablatif, et ils sont cognuz par leurs signez. Qui sont ils? Ces trois: *le*, *du*, *au* [...]. (Städtler 1988: 131).

(3) La dernière partie est consacrée à la présentation des huit parties traditionnelles du discours: nom, pronom, verbe, participe; adverbe, conjonction, préposition et interjection. Malheureusement, le manuscrit conservé n'est pas complet: il s'arrête après les chapitres consacrés aux noms, aux pronoms et au verbe.

## 2. Le XVI^e^ siècle anglais

La production d'ouvrages grammaticaux de type didactique s'intensifie du XVI^e^ siècle. En 1521, le poète écossais Alexander Barcley (1475?–1552) donne une adaptation libre en anglais du *Donait* de Barton. En 1528, Pierre Valence (*fl.* 1515–1555), tuteur de français auprès de Henri, comte de Lincoln (Lambley 1920: 80), publie ses *Introductions* (texte anglais avec traduction française en regard). Après un petit chapitre (3 p.) de 'phonétique', la majeure partie (40 p.) s'occupe de morphologie verbale, avec une longue énumération de verbes irréguliers. Tout le reste est brièvement résumé (14 p.): pronoms personnels, adverbes de lieu, de temps, etc.; comparaison; emploi des articles et des prépositions. Valence n'a aucune prétention théorique; il ne croit pas à la possibilité d'écrire une grammaire exhaustive d'une langue vivante (selon lui, il vaut mieux 'lire un bon livre' et suivre l'exemple des bons auteurs). Son attitude est donc *pré-* ou *anti*-grammairienne.

Les deux principaux représentants du courant didactique en Angleterre de la première moitié du XVI^e^ siècle sont Giles du Wes (*c.* 1470–1535), d'origine picarde, et John Palsgrave (1480?–1554), originaire de Londres, tous deux protégés d'Henri VIII, professeurs de français à la cour de Londres. Les conceptions de leurs grammaires partiquement contemporaines – celle de Palsgrave est de 1530, celle de Du Wes de 1532 – sont tout à fait opposées, même si les deux auteurs se sont connus et influencés. La grammaire de Du Wes n'a que 102 p., celle de Palsgrave près de 900. L'ambition de Palsgrave est de donner une grammaire complète et des règles exhaustives pour l'apprentissage du français; c'est la première grammaire 'scientifique' du français. Du Wes se limite aux informations de base.

Pour Du Wes, les connaissances essentielles du français se résument à une bonne connaissance du vocabulaire, et une parfaite maîtrise de la morphologie verbale, présentée nous forme de phrases complètes, à la forme affirmative, négative et interrogative à tous les temps. Dans son enseignement, l'acquisition d'automatismes joue un rôle prépondérant; la théorie grammaticale est secondaire. Comme Valence et le plupart des autres professeurs d'origine française en Angleterre, il ne croit pas à la possibilité d'établir des règles exhaustives pour une langue vivante.

La grammaire de Du Wes se compose d'une petite phonétique (7 règles, 4 p.), d'une vue d'ensemble des parties du discours (40 p.) ainsi que d'une grande morphologie verbale, avec des règles pour la formation des différents temps et modes qui parfois ne manquent pas d'intérêt (presque 100 p.):

Ye shall understande, that all maner verbes in generall ben termyned in their thre persons synguler and plurell nombres after this wayes : *Ray ras ra: rons res ront* : so that ye shall take the verbe in the present and put the *s* away at the later ende: if it be of the seconde or the fyrst coniugation, & adde therto the foresayd termination : as in this worde *Dis*, J saye : ye shall take awaye *s*, and adde *ray* sayeng *Diray*, *diras*, *dira* : *Dirons*, *dires*, *diront*. [...] ("The futer of the indicatiue", Du Wes 1532: f° F.iv r°)

Palsgrave, au contraire, croit dans la valeur des règles grammaticales. Il affirme qu'on peut apprendre le français de manière autodidacte par l'étude des règles qu'il indique. Son ambition est de hisser la description de la grammaire française au niveau atteint par celle du grec et du latin: "We haue [...] by our diligent labours nowe at the last brought the frenche tong under any rules certayn & preceptes grammaticall." (Palsgrave 1530: f° A.iii v°). Sa grammaire n'est pas simplement descriptive; il cherche à comprendre et à classer les phénomènes observés. Palsgrave est aussi le premier grammairien du français à utiliser un riche corpus de citations littéraires (auteurs du XV^e^ siècle surtout) pour étayer ses règles.

A différence de tous ses collègues, Palsgrave étudie la phonétique française de manière détaillée et approfondie. Sur près de 50 p., il décrit la prononciation de toutes les lettres et de tous les digraphes de l'orthographe française, au moyen d'une transcription 'phonétique' avant l'heure, en indiquant les équivalences en anglais (ou en italien) et en essayant de préciser la position des organes de phonation. La langue décrite est celle qu'il a apprise lors de ses études à Paris. Son enseignement est un témoignage précieux pour l'histoire de la prononciation du français.

Pour la morphologie, Palsgrave s'appuie sur la tradition latine, sans en être prisonnier. Capable de voir les divergences entre le latin et le français, il évite de couler le français dans le moule du latin (en général, lorsque le latin ne fournit pas de modèle d'explication satisfaisant pour un phénomène observé, il a recours au grec):

> Partes of reason / if we shall here in take example of the Romayns / they haue thryse .iii. for besydes the .viii. partes of speche commen betwene them and the latines [...] they haue also a nynth part of reason whiche I call article / borowyng the name of the Grekes. (Palsgrave 1530: f° B.iii v°).

Palsgrave est aussi le premier grammairien qui tente une description syntaxique du français, en s'inspirant de la grammaire grecque de Théodore Gaza (1495).

Malgré ses qualités, la grammaire de Palsgrave est restée sans répercussions sur la réflexion grammairienne ultérieure, aussi bien en Angleterre que sur le Continent, où elle est restée inconnue. Aucune grammaire rédigé en Angleterre au XVI^e^ siècle après Palsgrave n'atteint le même niveau théorique. Avec les professeurs-grammairiens de la deuxième moitié du XVI^e^ siècle (Pierre Du Ploiche [*fl.* 1553–1578], Claudius Hollyband [= Claude de Sainliens, Claudius a Sancto Vinculo; *fl.* 1565–† 1597], Jacques Bellot [*fl.* 1580–1590], etc.; cf. Kibbee 1991: 136–138) – ce sont souvent des Hugenots réfugiés qui font de l'enseignement du français leur gagne-pain – on retrouve la tardition de Valence et de Du Wes. Leurs grammaires, composées à la hâte, répondent à des besoins immédiats. Les règles grammaticales sont réduites au strict minimum. Leur principal intérêt pour l'histoire de la grammaire au XVI^e^ siècle est la question des sources qui les inspirent et des normes qu'ils enseignent.

Le plus important de ces auteurs, de Sainliens, s'appuie sur plusieurs grammaires françaises contemporaines (Farrer 1908). Pour la prononciation, sa principale source est le *Dialogue de l'Ortografe e Prononciacion françoese* (1550) de Jacques Peletier du Mans (1517–1582). En outre, il utilise l'*Institutio* (1558) de Jean Garnier (1510–1579) et la *Gramere* (1562) de Pierre de la Ramée (= Petrus Ramus, 1515–1572). Simple vulgarisateur, il illustre une phase au cours de laquelle l'enseignement scolaire ne produit plus sa propre grammaire, mais repose sur les travaux théoriques de la même période.

En ce qui concerne la norme enseignée, de Sainliens rejette à plusieurs reprises certaines variétés régionales du français (picard, normand, bourguignon). Il atteste que dans la deuxième moitié du XVI^e^ siècle, une norme sociolectale et régionale, axée sur le parler cultivé de l'Ile-de-France et de l'Orléanais, commence à s'imposer.

## 3. La tradition française

Au début du XVI^e^ siècle, il n'existe encore aucune grammaire française en France. Certains éléments qui la préfigurent se glissent pourtant dans les manuels de latin (cf. Hausmann 1980: 135–136 pour la période 1526–1530). Le début d'une prise de conscience de la nécessité de décrite (et de régler) la grammaire française se trouve chez Geoffroy de Tory (1480?–1533), considéré parfois comme le 'père' de la linguistique française:

> Pleust a Dieu que quelque Noble cueur semployast a mettre & ordonner par Reigle nostre Langage François! [...] iespere que au plaisir de Dieu quelque Noble Priscian, quelque Donat ou quelque Qintilien Francois naistra de Bref, sil nest desia tout edifie [...] (Tory 1529: f° A.viii).

La première grammaire française écrite sur le continent peu après cet appel est encore en latin et reste dans le moule de la tradition latine (Donat et Priscien): *In linguam Gallicam isagœge una cum eiusdem Grammatica Latinogallica* (1531) de Jacques Dubois (= Sylvius, 1478–1555), originaire d'Amiens et professeur à la Faculté de médecine de Paris. Dans sa préface, Dubois justifie le choix du latin comme métalangue par les besoins des étrangers désireux d'apprendre le français (Lambley 1920: 226 suppose qu'il s'adresse en particulier aux nombreux étudiants étrangers de l'Université de Paris).

Pour Dubois, le latin n'est pas uniquement l'origine du français, mais le modèle idéal vers lequel toute norme du français doit être ramenée (Padley 1988: 333). Pour cette raison, il signale à plusieurs reprises la 'supériorité' du picard par rapport au parisien, lorsque la forme septentrionale est apparemment plus proche du latin:

> Desinant igitur Picardis, puritatem linguae & antiquitatem integrius servantibus illudere Galli, quod dicant mi, ti, si raro: & mè, tè, sè, à mihi vel mi, tibi, sibi, vel ti, si, analogia primae personae. (Dubois 1531: f° 21 r°).

Dans cette optique, la majeure partie de l'*Isagœge* est consacrée à un essai de phonétique historique et d'étymologie. Sa *Grammatica Latinogallica*, par contre, est essentiellement une morphologie française qui reste dans le cadre de la tradition donatienne.

Les langues anciennes restent également le cadre de référence des *Grammaticae* (1544) de Jean de Drosay (*deuxième moitié XV^e^ siècle–*c.* 1550) qui contiennent des grammaires de latin, de grec, d'hébreu et de français. La partie consacrée au français, première grammaire continentale à être rédigée en français, est largement tributaire de celle de Dubois (Padley 1988: 334). Dans sa syntaxe, rédigée en latin, Drosay semble de l'avis qu'elle est 'universelle': pour lui, les constructions latines s'appliquent également au grec, à l'hébreu et au français.

La grammaire française la plus intelligente du XVI^e^ siècle, à côté de celle de Palsgrave, est le *Tretté* (1550) de Louis Meigret (*c.* 1510–*c.* 1558). Même si sa conception d'ensemble est encore assez traditionnelle, Meigret suit souvent des chemins nouveaux – en fait, ses sources, qu'il présente de manière très sommaire, sans jamais nommer ses contemporains, sont encore mal connues. Malheureusement, le *Tretté* est illisible aux yeux de ses contemporains, Meigret ayant adopté une orthographe radicalement 'réformée' qu'il avait lui-même élaborée dans son *Traité touchant le commun usage de l'escriture française* (1542). Pour Meigret, qui s'intéresse à la langue parlée, l'orthographe française n'est qu'un amas de règles biscornues, "un vrai scandale" [Hausmann 1980: 150]: les Français se sont détournés de l'usage clair et logique des anciens qui avaient fait coïncider graphie et phonie:

> Or ęt il q'ao jourdhuy lę' Frãçoęs ont tant etranjé l'ecrittur' ę vne gran' partíe de vocables, de l'uzaje de parler: tant par vne superfluité de lęttres, qe par la cõfuziõ de leur puyssançe [...] q'il n'ęt possible de dressę sur ęlle, aocune façon de grammęre que çe ne fút a notre confuzion. (Meigret 1550, "Ao' lęcteurs, f° 2 v°)

Dans son introduction, Meigret s'oppose à ceux qui croient que la description systématique d'une langue vivante est impossible. Même si le français foisonne de variantes régionales et sociales, même si sa prononciation et sa morphologie ne sont pas stables, le fait est qu'il fonctionne: les Français se parlent et se comprennent. Mieux encore: c'est une langue capable de tout exprimer qui fonctionne aussi bien que le latin et le grec. Il doit donc y avoir un système susceptible d'être décrit. Sur cette base conceptionnelle, Meigret développe une description synchronique du français dans le meilleur sens du terme.

Dans sa phonétique, Meigret décrit les voyelles selon le principe de *l'affinité* (hérité de Priscien) et de *l'opposition*, qui préfigure le principe phonologique des paires minimales:

> Or qant ao' voyęlles je treuue qe la lange Frãçoęz' ęn a juqes ao nombre de sęt, si diuęrses ęntr'ęlles, qe l'une ne peut ę́tre prononçée pour l'aotre, sans manifęst' offęnse de l'oręlle: qoę qe les aocunes ayet ęntr'ęlles vne grand' affinité. Nous auons donc, a, ę ouuęrt, e clós, i, ou, clós (aotremęnt ne l'oze je noter) o ouuęrt, u. (Meigret 1550, "Dę' voyęlles", f° 6 v°).

En développant les recherches de Bovelles (1533), Meigret présente le consonantisme selon un système d'"affinités' dont Hausmann (1980: 159) pense à juste titre qu'on peut l'appeler scientifique. L'ordre proposé est le suivant:

| | | | | | | |
|---|---|---|---|---|---|---|
| B | F PH | C K Q | D | S C | L | M |
| P | V | G | T TH | Z ÇH | Ł | N Ñ |

(Meigret est le premier grammairien du français qui reconnaît l'existence et le statut phonologique de /ʃ/, /ʎ/ et /ɲ/ (ÇH, Ł et Ñ). Le R est traité à part, parce qu'il n'entre dans aucune "affinité". [Meigret 1550, "Dę' Consonantes, f° 13 v°])

Tout en maintenant la terminologie traditionnelle, Meigret est un des premiers (avec Palsgrave) à reconnaître clairement que le nom français n'a pas de système casuel (morphologique):

Or eçhet il ao Nom qatr' acçidęns seulemęnt ęn la lange Frãçoęze: qui sont Espeçe, jęnre, Nombr' ę Figure: ao regard dę' Cazes, la lãge Françoęze ne lę' conoęt point: par çe qe lę' noms Françoęs ne çhanjet point leur fin. (Meigret 1550, "Dęs Noms", f° 20 v°).

Selon Hausmann (1980: 169–171), le chapitre consacré aux pronoms est remarquable. Meigret y explique l'économie que réalisent les pronoms dans le discours et développe une théorie des rapports de dépendance syntaxique: il distingue un *surposé* qui correspond au prime actant, et un *sousposé* qui rassemble tous les autres actants. Cette terminologie lui permet une description pertinente de la diathèse passive: Meigret comprend qu'il ne faut pas confondre sens et fonction syntaxique: le sujet (le surposé) n'est pas toujours l'agent de l'action. Il se révèle ainsi comme un grammairien perspicace et largement indépendant de ses prédécesseurs:

japęlle le nõ surpozé ou appozé, çeluy qi gouuęrne le vęrbe, ę le souspozé ou soupozé, çeluy qi ęt gouuęrné: come Pięrr' eyme Laoręns, la ou Pięrre, ęt le surpozé, ę Laorę̃s, le souspozé, çe qe ne se doęt pas ęntęndre selon l'ordre dę' parolles, męs selon le sęns: car çeluy qi gouuęrn' ęt reputé ę' vęrbes actifs, come ajant, ę çeluy qi ęt gouuęrné, come paçięnt: ę ao contrę́r' ę' vęrbes passifs: car lors le surpozé ęt le paçięnt, ę le souspozé l'ajant, accompaiñé de de, du, ou par, ou dęs. (Meigret 1550, "Dę' cazes ę declinęzons dę' Pronoms", f° 49).

Révolutionnaire à bien des égards par son contenu, le *Tretté* de Meigret a rencontré peu de succès, surtout peut-être à cause de son système orthographique particulier. Néanmoins, il a été attentivement lu et abondamment copié par deux grammairiens importants de la deuxième moitié du XVIe siècle: Robert Estienne (1528–1498) et Ramus. (Dans la première édition de sa *Gramere* [1562], Ramus adapte et développe la graphie de Meigret; les éditions postérieures [1572, 1587] reviennent à l'orthographe traditionnelle [celle de 1572 présente les deux graphies en regard].)

Dans la préface de sa *Gramere* de 1562, Ramus, professeur au Collège Royal, écrit:

La gramerę de ma patrię [...] dę lacelę [...] lę premier auteur a ete Jacę' du Boes [...]. Etienne Dolet a fet celcę treté, comę de' poins e apostrofę: Mes lę batimẽt dę set' euvrę plu' haut e plu' maɲificę, e dę plu' ricę e divers' etofę e' proprę à Loui' Megret. (Ramus 1562: 3–4)

A bien des égards, tout en se référant à Meigret, Ramus revient pourtant en arrière: "What masks his grammatical insight is the customary imposition on the vernacular structural system of the Latin grid of cases" (Padley 1985: 44). Son principal mérite, par contre, à partir de la deuxième édition de sa grammaire (1572), c'est la place qu'il accorde à la syntaxe: Ramus est le premier grammairien qui commence à entrevoir la nature analytique du français, ainsi que les particularités qui y régissent l'ordre des mots (Ramus 1572: 129, 182).

R. Estienne aussi fait explicitement allusion à Dubois et à Meigret. A l'*Isagœge*, il doit ses informations étymologiques; chez Meigret, il a trouvé un modèle de description grammaticale qu'il reprend en partie (sans son système orthographique). Malgré cela, d'un point de vue théorique, la grammaire de R. Estienne est un retour en arrière considérable. Estienne revient p. ex. à la présentation alphabétique des sons à partir des 22 lettres de l'alphabet latin et impose de nouveau le carcan de la grammaire latine aux informations rencontrées chez Meigret: "Et le tout auons mis par ordre, & traicte a la maniere des Grammaires Latines, le plus clerement & facilement qu'auons peu." (Estienne 1557: 3–4). Il est évident que de nombreux progrès réalisés par Meigret n'ont pas été compris par ses successeurs.

La deuxième moitié du XVIe siècle produit un nombre important de grammaires de français pour étrangers autres que anglais, en particulier allemands: Jean Pillot (1510–1570), Jean Garnier (1510–1579), Antoine Cauchie (= Caucius, *c.* 1530–*c.* 1601), Gérard Du Vivier (= De Vivre, *fl.* 1566–1574), etc. (Streuber 1967, 1968, 1969). Parmi leurs ouvrages, le plus intéressant est sans doute la *Grammatica gallica* de Cauchie (1570): comme Meigret, Cauchie est relativement libre des modèles latins; en outre, il commence à développer une syntaxe consistante.

D'une manière générale, en dehors des progrès réalisés dans la description de la syntaxe, cette période se caractérise pourtant plutôt par un recul dans la qualité de l'analyse linguistique en comparaison avec le niveau atteint par Meigret, et un retour au cadre hérité de la grammaire latine.

## 4. Vers une 'grammaire de la norme'

La deuxième moitié du XVI^e^ siècle est marquée par un début de fixation de la norme du français. Dans son *Traicté* de 1557, R. Estienne souligne qu'il a repris de ses prédécesseurs tout ce qui est 'en accord avec ce qu'il a entendu et appris' dans deux milieux sociaux précis: la Cour et les milieux cultivés parisiens:

Nous ayans diligemment leu les deux susdicts autheurs [...], auons faict ung recueil, principalement de ce que nous auons veu accorder a ce que nous auions le temps passé apprins des plus scauans en nostre langue, qui auoyent tout le temps de leur vie hanté es Cours de France, tant du Roy que de son Parlement a Paris, aussi sa Chancellerie et Chambre des comptes: esquels lieux le langage sescrit et se prononce en plus grande pureté qu'en tous autres. (Estienne 1557: 3).

Si Meigret se fait reprocher son orthographe, Dubois est critiqué à cause de son origine picarde: "pourtant que souuent il a meslé des mots de Picardie dont il estoit" (Estienne 1557: 3). R. Estienne est le premier grammairien français qui refuse explicitement tout ce qui n'est pas parisien; son *Traicté* est la première grammaire 'normative' du français dans le sens qu'elle préconise un usage régional et surtout social très précis.

Avec Henri Estienne (1528–1598), fils de Robert, cette tendance s'accentue encore. Dans ses *Hypomneses* de 1582, il n'opère pas seulement un net retour en arrière d'un point de vue théorique. Plus conservateur encore que son père, il parle de nouveau de la 'déclinaison' du français et s'obstine à vouloir y découvrir un neutre. Mais surtout, il n'écrit pas une grammaire systématique, mais une collection de réflexions disparates sur la langue et la norme à suivre, des règles isolées sur différents problèmes grammaticaux. C'est déjà la formule qui fera fortune au XVII^e^ siècle. Il proteste contre le changement de genre que l'usage tend à imposer à des noms comme *navire*, *comté* ou *duché* qui passent au masculin. Il blâme l'omission de pronom sujet, qui est encore possible dans la syntaxe du XVI^e^ siècle. Au nom du 'bon usage', il critique les principaux auteurs de grammaires pour étrangers de son époque (Pillot était Lorrain, Garnier originaire d'Avignon, Du Vivier de Gand et Cauchie Picard): leur principal 'défaut' est de ne pas être parisiens ...

La deuxième moitié du XVI^e^ siècle français prépare ainsi la scission entre une grammaire 'linguistique', théorique ou descriptive, et une grammaire normative, prescriptive.

## 5. Bibliographie

### 5.1. Sources primaires


Barcley, Alexander. 1521. *Introductory to wryte and to pronounce Frenche.* London: R. Coplande.

Bellet, James. 1578. *The French Grammar.* London: T. Marshe.

–. 1588. *The French Method, wherein is contained a perfite order of Grammar for the French Tongue.* London: Robert Robinson. (Repr. Menston: Scolar Press, 1970.)

Bovelles, Charles de. 1533. *Liber de differentia vulgarium linguarum, et Gallici sermonis varietate.* Paris: Robert Estienne.

Cauchie, Antoine [Caucius]. 1570. *Grammatica gallica, suis partibus absolutior, quam ullus ante hunc diem ediderit.* Paris: A. Lithostratei.

Drosay, Jean de [Drosée, Drosaeus]. 1544. *Grammaticae quadrilinguis partitiones.* Paris: C. Wechsel.

Du Ploiche, Pierre. 1553. *A Treatise in English and Frenche right necessary and proffitable for al young children.* London: Richard Grafton.

Du Vivier, Gérard [De Vivre]. 1566. *Frantzösische Grammatica. Wie man die Sprach soll lehren lesen vnd schreiben.* Gesetzt in Frantzösisch und Teutsch durch Gerhardum von Vivier. Gedruckt zu Cöllen durch Maternum Cholinum.

–. 1574. *Les Fondaments de la langue françoise composez en faueur des Allemans.* Gedruckt zu Cöllen bei Heinrich von Ach.

Du Wes, Giles. 1532 [?]. *An introductorie for to lerne to rede to pronounce and to speke Frenche trewly.* London: Thomas Godfray. (Repr. Menston: Scolar Press, 1972.)

Dubois, Jacques. 1531. *Jacobi Sylvii Ambiani in linguam Gallicam Isagœge, una cum eiusem Grammatica Latino-gallica, ex Hebraeis, Graecis et Latinis authoribus.* Paris: Robert Estienne. (Repr. Genève: Slatkine, 1971.)

Estienne, Henri. 1582. *Hypomneses de Gallica lingua peregrinis eam discentibus necessariae, quaedam vero ipsis etiam Gallis multum profuturae.* Genève. (Repr. Genève: Slatkine, 1968.)

Estienne, Robert. 1557. *Traicté de la grammaire françoise.* Paris: Robert Estienne. (Repr. Genève: Slatkine, 1970.)

Garnier, Jean. 1558. *Institutio gallicae linguae in usum iuventutis germanicae ad illustrissimos iuniores *principes Landtgravios Haessiae conscripta.* Genève: Crispin. (Repr. Genève: Slatkine, 1972.)

Hollyband, Claude. 1573. *The French Schoolemaister.* London: Willeam How. (Repr. Menston: Scolar Press, 1972.)

—. 1576. *The Frenche Littleton.* London: Thomas Vautroullier. (Repr. Menston: Scolar Press, 1970.)

Meigret, Louis. 1542. *Traité touchant le commun usage de l'escriture françoise.* Paris: D. Janot. (Repr. Genève: Slatkine, 1972.)

—. 1550. *Le tretté de la grammęre françoęze.* Paris: C. Wechsel. (Repr. Genève: Slatkine, 1972.)

Palsgrave, John. 1530. *Lesclarcissement de la langue francoyse.* Loncon: R. Pynson. (Repr. Genève: Slatkine, 1972.)

Peletier du Mans, Jacques. [1550]. *Dialogue de l'Ortografe e Prononciacion françoese.* Poitiers: Jan et Enguilbert de Marnet. (Repr. Genève: Slatkine, 1964.)

Pillot, Jean. [1550]. *Gallicae lingae institutio latino sermone conscripta per Iohannem Pillotum Barrensem.* Paris: Groulleau. (Repr. Genève: Slatkine, 1972.)

Ramus, Petrus [Pierre de la Ramée]. [1562]. *Gramere.* Paris: André Wechsel. (Repr. Genève: Slatkine, 1972.)

—. [1572]. *Grammaire.* Paris: André Wechsel. (Repr. Genève: Slatkine, 1972.)

Tory, Geoffroy de. [1529]. *Champ fleury.* Paris: Geoffroy Tory et Gilles de Gournaut. (Repr. Genève: Slatkin, 1973.)

Valence, Pierre. 1528. *Introductions in Frensche for Henry the Yonge, erle of Lyncoln.* London: Wynken de Worde [?]. (Repr. Menston: Scolar Press, 1967.)

## 5.2. Sources secondaires

Clément, Louis. 1899. *Henri Estienne et son œuvre française.* Paris: A. Picard.

Demaizière, Colette. 1983. *La grammaire française au XVI^e^ siècle: les grammairiens picards.* Paris: Didier.

Farrer, Lucy E. 1908. *La vie et les œuvres de Claude de Sainliens alias Claudius Holyband.* Paris: Presses universitaires.

Hausmann, Franz Josef. 1980. *Louis Meigret: Humaniste et linguiste.* Tübingen: Narr.

Johnston, R. C. 1987. *Orthographia Gallica.* London: A. N. T. S.

Kibbee, Douglas A. 1991. For to Speke Frenche Trewely. Amsterdam: Benjamins.

Kristol, Andres. 1990. "L'inseignement du français en Angleterre (XIII^e^–XV^e^ siècles): les sources manuscrites". *Romania* 111. 289–330.

Lambley, Kathleen. 1920. *The Teaching and Cultivation of the French Language in England during Tudor and Stuart Times.* Manchester: Manchester Univ. Press.

Neumann, Sven-Gösta. 1959. *Recherches sur le français des XV^e^ et XVI^e^ siècles et sur sa codification par les théoriciens de l'époque.* Lund: Gleerup.

Padley, G. A. 1985–88. *Grammatical Theory in Western Europe 1500–1700: Trends in vernacular grammar.* 2 vols. Cambridge: Cambridge Univ. Press.

Pope, Mildred K. 1910. "The 'Tractatus Orthographiae' of T. H., Parisii studentis". *Modern Language Review* 5. 185–193.

Södergård, Östen. 1955. "Le plus ancien traité grammatical français". *Studia neophilologica* 27. 192–194.

Städtler, Thomas. 1988. *Zu den Anfängen der französischen Grammatiksprache.* Tübingen: Niemeyer.

Stengel, Edmund. 1879. "Die ältesten Anleitungsschriften zur Erlernung der französischen Sprache". *Zeitschrift für neufranzösische Sprache und Literatur* 1. 25–33.

Stengel, Edmund. 1890 ($^2$1976). *Chronologisches Verzeichnis französischer Grammatiken, vom Ende des 14. bis zum Ausgange des 18. Jahrhunderts nebst Angabe der bisher ermittelten Fundorte derselben.* Oppeln: E. Franck. Neu herausgegeben mit einem Anhang von Hans-Josef Niederehe. Amsterdam: Benjamins.

Streuber, Albert. 1962, 1963, 1964. "Die ältesten Anleitungsschriften zur Erlernung des Französischen in England und den Niederlanden bis zum 16. Jahrhundert". *ZFSL* 72. 37–86 et 186–211; 73. 97–112 et 189–208; 74. 59–76.

Streuber, Albert. 1964, 1965, 1967, 1968, 1969. "Französische Grammatik und französischer Unterricht in Frankreich und Deutschland während des 16. Jahrhunderts". *ZFSL* 74. 342–361; 75. 31–50 et 247–273; 77. 234–267; 78. 69–101; 79. 172–191 et 328–341.

Stürzinger, J. 1884. *Orthographia Gallica. Ältester Traktat über französische Aussprache und Orthographie.* Heilbronn: Henninger.

*Andres Max Kristol, Neuchâtel (Suisse)*

# 106. Les premières descriptions grammaticales de l'anglais

1. Introduction: cadre d'étude
2. L'Angleterre de la Renaissance
3. Les objectifs
4. Les méthodes
5. Quelques problèmes et solutions
6. Conclusion: apports classiques
7. Bibliographie

## 1. Introduction: cadre d'étude

L'Humanisme, en introduisant l'anglais dans les classes de latin avec un rôle essentiellement métalinguistique ou instrumental, avait peu à peu accrédité l'idée que ce vernaculaire pouvait être justifiable d'une grammatisation. La seconde étape, celle de la grammatisation elle-même et des premières descriptions de l'anglais pour l'anglais, se produit à la Renaissance, période qu'à la suite de Robins (1967: 108) et Percival (1975: 231) nous ne délimiterons pas par des jalons événementiels, mais identifierons à ses courants de pensée représentatifs, indissociables du contexte culturel, lequel est lui-même tributaire du facteur géographique – ce qui explique que cette Renaissance ait pu se manifester de façon plus ou moins précoce selon la latitude, et bien plus tardivement en Angleterre que dans la plupart des autres pays européens (Auroux 1992: 11–64; Percival 1975: 232, 246–247).

Percival (1975: 232) attire l'attention du chercheur sur la nécessité de s'assurer des sources fiables. Certes, de nombreuses initiatives ont facilité les recherches de ces trente dernières années sur la période: la parution de la très complète bibliographie d'Alston, qui répertorie et localise les sources primaires avec la plus grande précision; la publication par la Scolar Press, à l'initiative de ce même Alston, de fac-similés d'ouvrages essentiels dont l'original n'est guère accessible; sans compter la création de revues telles que *Historiographica Linguistica* (Amsterdam: Benjamins, 1973), *Histoire Epistémologie Langage* (St. Denis: Presses Universitaires de Vincennes, 1979) ou *Beiträge zur Geschichte der Sprachwissenschaft* (Münster: Nodus, 1991): enfin, tout récemment, des informations précieuses ont été mises à la disposition des chercheurs dans le *Lexicon Grammaticorum* (Tübingen: Niemeyer, 1996) et le *Corpus représentatif des grammaires et traditions linguistiques* (Paris: S.H.E.L. et P.U.V, 2000). Bien des documents primaires n'en demeurent pas moins difficiles d'accès. En cette période proche des débuts de l'imprimerie, nombre d'écrits sont restés à l'état de manuscrit ou n'ont survécu qu'à un ou deux exemplaires. Percival met en garde contre la tentation de les négliger dans l'étude d'une époque si fertile d'idées, où chaque auteur apporte son originalité. Ajoutons à cela que plusieurs années se sont parfois écoulées entre la rédaction d'un manuscrit et son impression. La chronologie des œuvres n'est dès lors par toujours facile à établir, et le chercheur soucieux de retracer l'évolution des idées et la genèse d'un courant grammatical se doit d'être très circonspect dans l'élaboration de ses hypothèses. Percival (1975: 232) cite plusieurs exemples de contresens liés à une méconnaissance de cette chronologie. Il évoque enfin les dangers d'une spécialisation excessive qui pourrait nuire à une vision d'ensemble, seule susceptible de permettre une véritable compréhension des phénomènes rencontrés. Cette vision d'ensemble dont il souligne le besoin a été depuis proposée par Padley (1976; 1985) pour la linguistique occidentale des XVI^e^ et XVII^e^ siècles et, à une plus vaste échelle, celle du monde des origines jusqu'à notre XX^e^ siècle, par l'*Histoire des idées linguistiques* éditée par S. Auroux et al. et le présent ouvrage.

## 2. L'Angleterre de la Renaissance

Lorsque, en 1453, la chute de Constantinople fait affluer en Italie des manuscrits qui développent la conscience d'un passé classique et suscitent de l'intérêt pour le grec et l'hébreu, menaçant ainsi l'hégémonie du latin, l'activité littéraire s'en trouve relancée, et un développement de la littérature en vernaculaire favorisé. Les lettrés étrangers – et parmi eux beaucoup d'anglais – sont attirés par l'Italie des belles lettres dont ils importent des idées, par exemple le sonnet qui triomphe dans la poésie anglaise des XVI^e^ et XVII^e^ siècles.

L'ère élisabéthaine connaît à son tour, avec John Lily (c. 1554–1606), Edmund Spenser (c. 1552–1599), Sir Philip Sidney (1554–1586), Christopher Marlowe (1564–1593) et bien sûr William Shakespeare (1564–1616), un remarquable essor de la littérature en vernaculaire favorisé de surcroît par le développement rapide de l'imprimerie après l'installation en 1487 de la première presse de William Caxton (1422–1491). Le nombre des lecteurs potentiels s'en trouve élargi à toute une classe bourgeoise qui émerge, une classe qui aspire à une éducation libérale fondée sur les belles lettres en vernaculaire (Robins 1967: 108). Voilà qui ne peut qu'inciter à faire accéder ce vernaculaire – jusque là essentiellement langue d'oralité – au statut de langue écrite, susceptible de véhiculer le savoir.

Cette promotion du vernaculaire a certainement été freinée quelque temps par la coexistence en Angleterre, après la conquête normande, de deux vernaculaires de statut différent: l'anglais dérivé de l'anglo-saxon, langue du vaincu, associée au peuple, et le français, langue du vainqueur normand, la plus raffinée des deux. Peut-être est-ce là un facteur susceptible d'expliquer que la première description grammaticale du français (John Palsgrave 1531) y ait précédé celle de l'anglais (William Bullokar 1586) de plus d'un demi-siècle? Les rapports entre les deux langues sont tout de même rapidement inversés grâce à la remarquable créativité littéraire qui se manifeste en anglais pendant l'ère élisabéthaine. Y contribuent également le débat théologique de la Réforme et la rupture politique de la monarchie anglaise avec la papauté, par les nombreuses traductions qu'ils suscitent, tant de la Bible (Giard 1992: 207–210; Vorlat 1975: 5) que des grandes œuvres classiques.

Robins (1967: 104) mentionne encore, parmi les caractéristiques de la période, un intérêt marqué pour les travaux de transcription auxquels sont confrontés les missionnaires, et en particulier pour les tons et les caractères chinois. Les grammairiens s'en inspirent pour proposer de nombreux traités de sténographie (Robins 1967: 116–117; Dobson 1957: 384–395), conçus pour servir soit de code secret, soit de code universel susceptible de remplacer le latin – dont le statut diminue d'autant qu'augmente celui du vernaculaire (Robins 1967: 1212).

## 3. Les objectifs

Les objectifs des premiers grammairiens à tenter une description de l'anglais sont longuement développés par Richard Mulcaster (1532–1611) (1582: 77–100).

Ces auteurs sont des amoureux de leur vernaculaire dont ils veulent défendre le nouveau statut de langue écrite sur le plan culturel, artistique, scientifique et patriotique (Vorlat 1975: 4–5) en le comparant éventuellement avec les langues classiques ou d'autres vernaculaires rivaux. Certes, Vorlat (1975: 17) considère les comparaisons de Charles Butler (c. 1560–1647) – qui dans sa préface (1633) relie l'anglais au teutonique, et par là à la tour de Babel – comme une démarche baroque et ridicule, aux arguments pseudo-scientifiques; quant à la comparaison avec le latin qu'en 1594 Paul Greaves (c. 1570–?) annonce dans le titre de sa grammaire (*Grammatica Anglicanae, praecipue quatenus a Latina differt*) elle paraît fallacieuse: comme le note Vorlat (1975: 13), on n'en trouve aucun écho dans son ouvrage; il semblerait que ce ne soit qu'une simple reprise du titre que Petrus Ramus (1515–1572) avait donné à sa grammaire grecque (*Grammatica Graeca, quatenus a Latina differt*), preuve de sa servilité dans l'imitation d'un maître à penser. Il demeure que Ben Jonson (1572–1637) émaille régulièrement ses propos, dans la marge, de remarques contrastives évoquant le grec, le latin et l'hébreu. Et le plus érudit de ces grammairiens, Alexander Gill (1565–1635), procède à des comparaisons pertinentes, solidement étayées par des références à l'origine des langues – peut-être inspirées, comme le suggère Vorlat (1975: 17), par les études anglo-saxonnes amorcées au milieu du XVI^e^ siècle, dont Poldauf (1948: 71) affirme qu'elles constituent les premiers balbutiements de philologie comparative à figurer dans une grammaire de l'anglais.

La langue qu'ils décrivent est essentiellement une langue écrite. Certes, Ben Jonson (1640) ne néglige pas la langue quotidienne: son propos, il l'affirme dans son titre, est de traiter d'une langue 'spoken and in use' [langue vivante parlée], mais il prétend aussi décrire une langue scientifique, et nombreux sont les exemples de sa syntaxe qu'il emprunte à la littérature, à John Gower (c. 1325–1408) ou John Lydgate (c. 1370–C. 1451) par exemple. Paul Greaves (1594) opte pour une description d'une langue du passé littéraire comme le montrent ses *Vocabula Chauceriana*, qui constituent, comme le remarque Poldauf (1948: 69), la première compilation du vocabulaire d'un auteur ancien à être imprimée au XVI^e^ siècle. L'approche de Gill (1619) est tout aussi sélective, privilégiant la langue de l'élite intellectuelle, des savants et érudits: une langue fort littéraire, poétique même. Gill distingue pour la décrire, une syntaxe 'poétique' de la syntaxe 'absolue' et propose à la fin de son ouvrage un traité de versification dans lequel il consacre un chapitre à l'accent et trois chapitres à la métrique.

Cette langue choisie, les auteurs des premières descriptions de l'anglais cherchent à la faire accéder au rang de langue universelle de l'érudition à la place du latin (Robins 1967: 109; Michael 1970: 164). On trouve ce souci chez Gill (1619) dont le titre de l'œuvre *Logonomia* est éloquent – bien qu'il continue encore lui-même à écrire en latin; et on le trouve encore chez Jonson (1640: 465) qui, grâce à l'anglais, prétend assurer la diffusion de travaux et d'études et effectuer toutes sortes de transactions commerciales sans interprète.

Par ailleurs, comme le signale Vorlat (1975: 5–6, 72), le contexte religieux confère aux grammairiens élisabéthains une raison supplémentaire de chercher à améliorer leur langue. Ils la veulent digne du nouveau rôle que lui ont confié la Réforme et leur roi en en faisant la langue officielle de l'Eglise, la langue dans laquelle est appelée à se généraliser la connaissance de la Bible. Cette idée missionnaire est par exemple développée chez le Puritain Gill (Poldauf 1948: 72).

Tout cela suppose un certain degré d'excellence de cette langue, dont les auteurs sont soucieux. Poldauf (1948: 72) note que Gill recommande l'usage d'une langue cultivée aux nobles, ajoutant parfois un légère note prescriptive à sa description lorsqu'il préconise de maintenir le langage écrit à l'écart de la corruption orale, lorsqu'il tente de réguler les emprunts à d'autres langues ou qu'il exclut les auteurs populaires élisabéthains de ses exemples pour ne citer guère que des poètes. Et Jonson après s'être candidement délecté à la description de doubles comparatifs et superlatifs qui lui rappellent d'élégantes tournures grecques, regrette la disparition de la désinence du pluriel des verbes (1640: 62), disparition qu'il assimile à une véritable amputation.

## 4. Les méthodes

Les premiers grammairiens de l'anglais ne sont pas, en général, des professionnels de la grammaire, mais des amateurs éclairés de belles lettres, auteurs d'ouvrages de rhétorique (Butler), voire parfois écrivains eux-mêmes comme Ben Jonson ou John Evelyn (1620–1706). Leur patriotisme et leur passion pour leur langue se nourrissent mutuellement, et ils sont confrontés à un problème toujours actuel: découvrir un mode de grammatisation approprié à la spécificité de la langue maternelle – *a priori* déjà connue et dans laquelle il s'agit d'affiner l'expression – par opposition au mode de grammatisation d'une deuxième langue – qu'il convient de faire découvrir dans son ensemble. Ils cherchent à se libérer de la méthode traditionnelle d'enseignement du latin sans parvenir à échapper totalement à son emprise, tâtonnent et recourent, pour mener à bien la tâche qu'ils ont entreprise, à des méthodes diverses.

En 1586, le premier d'entre eux, William Bullokar (c. 1531–1609), ne semble obéir qu'à une méthode toute personnelle. Funke (1941: 57–58) le décrit à la fois comme un humaniste et un patriote érudit de la Renaissance, un éclectique formé au droit et à l'agriculture, qui partage son temps entre l'armée et l'enseignement. Très conservateur pour l'essentiel, Bullokar tente de prendre du recul par rapport à la méthode de la tradition latine et d'adapter sa description à l'anglais en renouvelant la terminologie ou en proposant quelques modifications occasionnelles, parfois fort inspirées, mais sans véritable cohérence (Poldauf 1948: 59–68; Vorlat 1975: 429–430). Il ne parvient pas par exemple à trancher sur le caractère déclinable ou non déclinable de l'adjectif, du participe ou encore du pronom possessif.

Ses successeurs immédiats ont, pour la plupart, recours au ramisme. Ce mode de pensée mis au point par le protestant français Ramus les séduit par son rejet de la scolastique et de tous les concepts traditionnels de la grammaire latine au profit d'une logique beaucoup plus pratique et surtout d'une rhétorique toute simple, adaptée aux besoins de la bourgeoisie anglaise de robe de l'époque et au souci national de propagande religieuse: le ramisme profite de cette situation de réception très favorable et c'est, comme le note fort justement Ong (1958: 303), avec une orientation nettement rhétorique qu'il est introduit en Angleterre. Land (1974: 81) présente la pédagogie ramiste comme une association de trois facteurs: une nature à observer, une méthode qui sert à traduire ces observations en règles, et enfin la pratique, qui en permet l'acquisition par l'habitude et l'entraînement. Ramus prône effectivement une observation de l'usage comme fondement de toute grammaire, et une démarche procédant du général au particulier, le plus souvent par dichotomies successives établies en fonction de propriétés formelles. C'est, remarque Vorlat (1975: 9) la première approche scientifique du langage qui d'ores et déjà prépare à la méthode rationaliste empirique qu'adoptera la deuxième génération de grammairiens en réponse aux suggestions de Francis Bacon (1561–1626). L'influence de Ramus se manifeste particulièrement dans les universités de St. Andrews et de Cambridge (Padley 1985: 53–83). Elle est très sensible dans les écrits de Greaves (1594) et de Jonson (1640) dont la préface présente un modèle de méthodologie ramiste. Elle est plus diffuse dans ceux de Hume (c. 1617), de Gill (1619) et Butler (1633) où elle est combinée avec d'autres influences.

Alexander Hume (c. 1563–?), par exemple, dans sa préface, se réclame ouvertement de Thomas Linacre (1465–1524) dont il reprend, suivi en cela par Butler, les notions de *personne*, et de *note des cas* (Vorlat 1975: 59–62), sans pour autant en conserver toute la dimension syntaxique originelle.

Chez Jonson (1640), Evelyn (c. 1650) et Gill (1619), les plus cultivés de ces premiers grammairiens de l'anglais, ce sont des traces d'une influence grecque et hébraïque qui apparaissent. Une inspiration aristotélicienne semble par exemple à l'origine de nombre de leurs remarques d'ordre sémantique et également de la catégorie des *consignificativa dictiones* de Gill (Vorlat 1975: 57–58).

Cet éclectisme que l'on note au niveau des méthodes était sans doute prévisible chez des hommes unis par un même projet de grammatisation de l'anglais, certes, mais dotés de sensibilités et de préoccupations si variées. On le retrouve dans leurs réponses aux problèmes que pose cette grammatisation.

## 5. Quelques problèmes et leurs solutions

Le premier problème concerne l'orthographe de l'anglais, très hésitante depuis que l'imprimerie a supplanté le système centralisé des scribes royaux, d'autant plus hésitante, comme le note Poldauf (1948: 55–56), que le vocabulaire anglais provient d'une double source. Avant même l'étape de grammatisation, des théoriciens de l'anglais – Sir Thomas Smith (1513–1577) en 1568 et John Hart (c. 1501–1574) en 1569, bientôt suivis par Bullokar en 1586 et Butler en 1633, proposent de nouveaux caractères jugés plus aptes que les lettres romaines à transcrire les sons. Ce souci d'instituer une orthographe lors de l'accession au statut de langue écrite de la langue d'oralité qu'est initialement le vernaculaire, n'est certes pas spécifique à l'Angleterre (Padley 1985: 28–29). Mais il y est particulièrement sensible, peut-être favorisé par la méfiance nationale vis à vis du papisme qui déteint sur tout ce qui est romain, caractères typographiques inclus. Néanmoins, au nom de l'usage, Mulcaster (1582: 100–108) conteste le côté radical de cette démarche et prône une simple réforme par adjonction de quelques marques diacritiques aux caractères usuels, l'idée étant de respecter à la fois la raison, le son et l'usage: nous en avons un exemple chez Gill ... Toutes ces tentatives avortent. Une graphie se dégage finalement de l'usage, que l'on se contente de fixer, et très vite la démarche s'inverse: c'est dans la description de la prononciation que l'on suit désormais Mulcaster, mais toujours avec le souci de faire correspondre la langue orale et sa transcription écrite (Dobson 1957: 38–198).

Le deuxième point faible de l'anglais était sa pauvreté lexicale, qui imposait un recours fréquent à la dérivation, la composition ou l'emprunt. Thomas Tomkis en 1612 et Gill en 1619, incluent dans leur grammaire, au delà des développements habituels sur la flexion des mots, des considérations – peut-être inspirées par Varron, mais assurément de bon aloi en cette Renaissance – sur leur origine et leur formation, l'enallage, les mutations, les compositions. En répertoriant les procédés de création lexicale, non seulement ils entérinent ces créations, mais surtout ils suggèrent que l'anglais possède une aptitude particulière à l'enrichissement lexical – qui s'oppose à une carence totale de possibilité d'évolution pour le latin, langue morte et désormais stérile.

Enfin, les grammairiens sont confrontés au caractère analytique de l'anglais, cette pauvreté en flexion qui constitue sa lacune essentielle aux yeux des latinistes. Une adaptation des *notes*, *signes* et *tokens* de Thomas Linacre et William Lily (1468–1522) permet de passer d'un concept de signe métalinguistique à un concept de signe qui tient lieu de marque de flexion, un signe qui est érigé en équivalent très souple des terminaisons, que ces dernières soient latines ou anglaises. Gill (1619: 46) est très clair: "Verborum variatio facillima est. Aut enim per signa fit, aut per terminationes.". [La conjugaison des verbes est très facile. Elle s'effectue en effet au moyen de signes ou de terminaisons].

Cela amène à réduire parfois à deux le nombre des cas – *rect* et *oblique* – (Greaves 1594: 34; Butler 1633: 34), et également des temps – *tyme present* et *tyme past* – (Hume c. 1617: 32). Ou bien au contraire, un souci d'analogie peut conduire à généraliser l'utilisation des signes aux dépens des terminaisons, alors considérées comme des modes de construction de second ordre, voire elliptiques. Il en résulte, au prix de quelques accommodements avec la langue, des tableaux très réguliers qui ont permis de parler de courant structuraliste à propos de cette période (Padley 1985: 65). On est ainsi passé d'une grammaire du mot à une grammaire du groupe de mots, lequel est appelé *syntax(e)* (Greaves 1594: 22–23; Jonson 1640: 61–62, 79; Evelyn c. 1650: fol. 95r.), *periphrasin* (Greaves 1594: 21), ou encore *circumlocution* (Evelyn c. 1560–fol. 95v.); on est passé de la nomenclature à la structure, d'une lacune à une originalité féconde. Et toute cette évolution s'est effectuée sans véritable rupture, sans qu'il y ait rejet total de la méthode latine, mais simple adaptation à l'anglais. La méthode très formelle de Ramus, créée pour décrire le latin à partir de ses variations morphologiques, même aménagée, ne règle qu'imparfaitement le grand problème de la description de l'anglais: l'alternance signe / désinence demande à être justifiée. Il manque une composante sémantique qui ne commence à percer que chez Gill (1619: 48–49), lorsque ce dernier oppose les temps formés avec les terminaisons et les temps qui utilisent *do* you *did*:

Cum verbum rem simpliciter fieri significet; haec [do et did] actionis circumstanciam, vehementiam, tarditatem, et similia declarant. [Alors que le verbe signifie que la chose se produit purement et simplement, ces signes expriment les circonstances de l'action, de la véhémence, de la lenteur, etc.] (Gill 1619: 48–49)

Certes beaucoup de problèmes demeurent sans réponse: dès lors que l'on conclut à une moindre importance des flexions, les cadres de description essentiellement formels du ramisme deviennent difficiles à appliquer. Les grammairiens sont presque tous amenés à supprimer la catégorie du genre appliquée au nom dans la grammaire française de Ramus, mais ils se trouvent alors dépourvus de critère formel pour distinguer le substantif de l'adjectif, et contraints de recourir soit à des critères sémantiques tels que l'expression d'une qualité appartenant à un substantif (Butler 1633: 36), soit à un étoffement lexical. Enfin, la syntaxe ne suit pas l'évolution de la description et demeure souvent centrée sur le mot.

## 6. Conclusion: les apports classiques

Sans doute Vorlat (1975: 2–3) a-t-elle raison lorsqu'elle suggère que cette grammatisation a été gênée par le développement parallèle, dans des cadres de description traditionnels, de la grammaire anglaise propédeutique à l'enseignement du latin. Il demeure que la méthode formelle, après avoir porté ses fruits, se révèle vite inadéquate.

Le traitement du vernaculaire qu'elle a introduit connaîtra un nouveau développement grâce à une application de la pensée de Bacon (Brekle 1975: 281–287). Ce dernier conçoit une langue de culture comme une structure hiérarchisée autour des deux éléments fondamentaux que sont le nom et le verbe (Chevalier 1968: 411); cette structure devrait être accessible au terme d'une démarche scientifique, c'est à dire comportant un premier stade d'observation empirique donnant lieu à hypothèses et vérifications, suivi d'un stade d'abstraction et généralisation. Une grammaire selon ses vœux est publiée en 1653 par John Wallis (1616–1703), talentueux mathématicien rompu aux méthodes d'analyse et de classement, dont les contributions majeures à la grammatisation de l'anglais résident dans son refus d'imposer au vernaculaire un cadre grammatical créé pour le latin et dans la méthode scientifique qu'il utilise. Il travaille sur corpus, s'applique à découvrir par induction, à partir d'une étude empirique et rationnelle, des préceptes grammaticaux hiérarchisés propres au vernaculaire: il organise sa description autour du groupe nominal, du groupe verbal et de la dérivation. Il distingue temps grammaticaux et expression des temps, substantifs et adjectifs, verbes absolus et verbes auxiliaires. Il dépasse le stade formel et syntaxique pour se pencher sur la valeur sémantique du message, laquelle sera ensuite développée en 1685 par Christopher Cooper (c. 1646–1698). On peut considérer avec Poldauf (1978: 78–82) ou Padley (1985: 19) les ouvrages de ces deux auteurs comme d'importants jalons dans l'histoire de la grammaire anglaise, comme les premières description authentiques de l'anglais. C'est à partir de là que pourra s'envisager l'étape de normalisation, étape qui marque tout le XVIII$^{e}$ siècle.

## 7. Bibliographie

### 7.1. Sources primaires

Bacon, Francis. 1605. *Of the Proficience and Advancement of Learning.* Londres: H. Tomes.

–. 1623. *De Dignitate et Augmentis Scientiarum.* Londres: J. Haviland.

Bullokar, William. 1586. *Pamphlet for Grammar.* Londres: Edmund Bollifant. (Repr. dans *Palaestra*, LII, cxliv-lii et 339–385, éd. par Max Plessow. Berlin: Myer & Müller, 1906.)

Butler, Charles. 1633. *The English Grammar*, Oxford: Wm Turner.

Cooper, C[hristopher]. 1685. *Grammatica Linguae Anglicanae.* Londres: J. Richardson pour B. Tooke.

[Evelyn, John]. c. 1650. The English Grammar. The First Key (Manuscrit).

Gill, Alexander. 1619. *Logonomia Anglica.* Londres: J. Beale.

G[reaves], P[aul]. 1594. *Grammatica Anglicana, praecipue quatenus a Latina differt ad unicam P. Rami methodum concinnata.* Cambridge: J. Legatt.

[Hart, John]. 1569. *An Orthographie.* (Repr. dans *John Hart's Works on English Orthography and Pronunciation*, 1ère partie, 179–184, éd. par Bror Danielsson. Stockholm: Almqvist & Wiksell. 1955.)

Hume, Alexander. [c. 1617]. *Of the Orthographie and Congruitie of the Britan Tongue.* (Ed. à partir du manuscrit original par H. B. Wheatley), Early English Text Society, Londres: Trübner & Co., 1865.)

Jonson, Benjamin. 1640. *The English Grammar made by Ben Jonson. or the benefit of all strangers, out of his observations of the English language now spoken and in use.* (Repr. dans *The Works of Benjamin Jonson.* Londres: R. Meigham.)

Lily, William. 1549. *A Shorte Introduction of Grammar.* Londres: R. Wolfe.

Linacre, Thomas. [1525?]. *Progymnasmata grammatices vulgaria.* Londres: J. Rastell.

Mulcaster, Richard. 1582. *The First Part of the Elementarie which entreateth chefelie of the right writing of our English tung.* Londres: Th. Vautroullier.

Palsgrave, John [Jehan], 1530. *Lesclaircissement de la langue françoyse.* Londres: Pynson & Haukyns. (Rééd. 1852 Paris: Imprimerie Nationale.)

Ramus, Petrus [Pierre de la Ramée]. 1562. *Gramere*, Paris: A Wechel.

Ramus, P. [Pierre de la Ramée] 1560. *Grammatica graeca, quatenus a latina differt.* Paris: A. Wechel.

Smith, Sir Thomas. 1568. *De Recta et Emendata Linguae Anglicanae Scriptione Dialogus.* Paris: R. Estienne.

Tomkis, Thomas. 1612. De Analogia Anglicani Sermoni liber grammaticus (Manuscrit).

Wallis, John. 1653. *Grammatica Linguae Anglicanae.* Oxford: L. Lichfield.

### 7.2. Sources secondaires

Alston, R. C. 1965. *A Bibliography of the English Language from the Invention of Printing to the Year 1800*, vol. 1: *English Grammars written in English and English Grammars written in Latin by Native Speakers.* Leeds: Arnold & Son.

Auroux, Sylvain. 1992. "Le processus de grammatisation et ses enjeux". *Histoire des idées linguistiques.* Tome 2, éd. par S. Auroux. 11–64. Liège: Mardaga.

Ayres-Bennet, Wendy, J. Noordegraaf, C. Percy, V. Salmon et al. 1994. *La grammaire des dames.* (= *HEL*, 16: 2) 5–7; 95–141.

Brekle, Herbert E. 1975 "The Seventeenth Century". *Current Trends in Linguistics.* Vol. 13: *Historiography in Linguistics* éd. par Thomas A. Sebeok, 277–381. La Hague & Paris: Mouton.

Chevalier, Jean-Claude. 1968. *Histoire de la Syntaxe: Naissance de la notion de complément dans la grammaire française (1530–1750).* Genève: Droz.

Colombat, Bernard, éd. 2000 – *Corpus représentatif des grammaires et des traditions linguistiques*, Tome 2 (= H.E.L. hors série N° 3). Paris: S.H.E.S.L. et Presses Univ. de Vincennes.

Dobson, Eric J. 1957. *English Pronunciation, 1500–1700.* Oxford: Clarendon Press.

Formigari, Lia. 1988. *Language and Experience in 17th-Century British Philosophy.* Amsterdam & Philadelphia: Benjamins.

Funke, Otto. 1940. "Ben Jonson's English Grammar". *Anglia* LXIV. 117–134.

Giard, Luce. 1992. "L'entrée en lice des vernaculaires". *Histoire des idées linguistiques.* Tome 2, éd. par S. Auroux, 206–225. Liège: Mardaga.

Land, Stephen K. 1974. *From Signs to Propositions: The concept of form in eighteenth-century semantic theory.* Londres: Longman.

Michael, Ian. 1970. *English Grammatical Categories and the Tradition to 1800.* Cambridge: Cambridge Univ. Press.

Ong, Walter J. 1958. *Ramus: Method and the Decay of Rhetoric Cambridge.* Cambridge: Harvard, Univ. Press.

Padley, George Arthur. 1976. *Grammatical Theory in Western Europe 1500–1700: The Latin tradition.* Cambridge: Cambridge Univ. Press.

–. 1985. *Grammatical Theory in Western Europe 1500–1700: Trends in vernacular grammar.* Cambridge: Cambridge Univ. Press.

Percival, W. Keith. 1975. "The Grammatical Tradition and the Rise of the Vernaculars". *Current Trends in Linguistics*, vol. 13. *Historiography in Linguistics* éd. par Thomas A. Sebeok, 231–275. La Hague & Paris: Mouton.

Poldauf, Ivan, 1948. *On the History of some Problems of English Grammar before 1800.* Prague: Nákladem Filosofické Fakulty University Karlovy.

Robins, R. H. 1967. *A Short History of Linguistics.* Londres: Longman.

Rousse, Jean & Verrac, Monique. 1992. "Les traditions nationales: Grande Bretagne". *Histoire des idées linguistiques.* Tome 2, éd. par S. Auroux, 339–358. Liège: Mardaga.

Salmon, Vivian. 1979. *The Study of Language in 17th-Century England.* Amsterdam: Benjamins.

Stammerjohann, Harro, ed. et al. éd. 1996. *Lexicon Grammaticorum. Who's Who in the History of World Linguistics.* Tübingen: Max Niemeyer.

Verburg, P. A. 1968. "Ennoësis of Language in 17th-Century Philosophy". *Lingua* 21.558–572. Amsterdam: North Holland Publishing Company.

Vorlat, Emma. 1975. *The Development of English Grammatical Theory 1586–1737 with Special Reference to the Theory of Parts of Speech.* Louvain: Leuven Univ. Press.

Verrac, Monique. 1985. "Des notions de signe et de verbe substantif à la notion d'auxiliaire". *HEL* 7: 2.87–106.

Watson, Foster. 1908. *The English Grammar-Schools to 1660: Their curriculum and practice.* Cambridge: Cambridge Univ. Press.

*Monique Verrac, Pau (France)*

# 107. Frühe grammatische Beschreibungen des Deutschen

1. Einleitung
2. Vorstufen einer Grammatikographie des Deutschen im 15./16. Jahrhundert
3. Die ersten Grammatiken des Deutschen
4. Bibliographie

## 1. Einführung

Die grammatische Beschreibung der deutschen Sprache erfolgt bis über die Mitte des 16. Jh. hinaus nie systematisch und zusammenhängend, sondern zweckgebunden und selektiv. Zählt man Anweisungen über die Verwendung der Sprache außerhalb grammatikographischer Werke hinzu, ergibt sich ein vielfältiges Spektrum von Bemerkungen im Kontext unterschiedlicher Textsorten, die den ersten Grammatiken des Deutschen vorausgehen oder sie zeitlich begleiten.

Reflexionen über die Sprache (an sich) mit Einsichten, die sich auf das Deutsche beziehen lassen, gehen meist explizit oder implizit vom Lateinischen aus. Einige der (meist gelehrten) Autoren haben nicht nur eine genaue Kenntnis der lateinischen Grammatik, sondern durch die direkte oder vermittelte Rezeption führender Grammatikographen und Sprachgelehrter des Altertums und des Humanismus (insbesondere Quintilian, Priscian, Laurentius Valla, Erasmus) ist ihnen auch das Verfahren vertraut, über Sprache und ihr Funktionieren zu reflektieren, das sie auf Äußerungen über das Deutsche übertragen. Im Zentrum des Interesses der Zeit standen folgende Themen: die Beobachtung sprachlicher Phänomene im Hinblick auf ihr Zusammenwirken auf den verschiedenen Sprachebenen (mögliche Wortschatzerweiterung; Ausbau syntaktischer Konstruktionsmöglichkeiten); Sprachenverwandtschaft und -unterschiede sowie deren qualitative Einschätzung, speziell mit Blick auf das Deutsche; Herkunft und Bedeutung der Wörter; historisch bedingte Sprachveränderungen; Möglichkeiten und Grenzen der Sprachreinheit; Fremdwortgebrauch / Latinismen; dialektale Unterschiede und deren Verhältnis zur Idee einer (standardsprachlichen) Norm.

Die genannten Aspekte kristallisieren sich aus einer Fülle von Einzelbemerkungen von unterschiedlicher Abstraktivität und Nähe zum Sprachmaterial heraus. Häufig lassen diese Äußerungen den Bezug zur Sprachverwendung und der dort gewonnenen Erfahrung erkennen. Sie dokumentieren die Vielschichtigkeit der sprachbezogenen Reflexionen und den hohen kulturellen Stellenwert, den die Sprache an sich und die Einzelsprachen (die 'heiligen' sowohl wie die Volkssprachen) in der Zeit hatten. Die entstehenden Grammatiken sind Teilausdruck auf dieser Grundlage und reflektieren des öfteren Spuren der umfassenderen Sprachdiskussion.

## 2. Vorstufen einer Grammatikographie des Deutschen im 15./16. Jahrhundert

### 2.1. Schriften mit sprachbezogener Thematik

(1) Hilfsmittel für den Sprachunterricht: Leselehren, Schreiblehren, Orthographien, Interpunktionslehren (z. B. Frangk, Fuchsperger, Ickelsamer)

(2) Lexikographie: Vokabularien, Lexika, Synonymen- und Fremdwörterbücher (z. B. Maaler, Schwartzenbach)
(3) Brieflehren, Rhetorik und Dialektik (z. B. Riederer, Frangk, Meichßner, Fuchsperger)
(4) Sprachtheorie und Sprachenvergleich (z. B. Bibliander, Gessner)
(5) Historiographie (z. B. Beatus Rhenanus, Aventin)
(6) Verstreute Bemerkungen zu sprachspezifischen Themen in verschiedenartigen Texten, u. a. zur Kunst des Übersetzens (z. B. N. von Wyle, Luther)

Die Äußerungen in Werken der verschiedenen Textsorten überschneiden und ergänzen sich. Sie geben einen Eindruck von der herrschenden Sprachauffassung in der frühen Neuzeit, bes. seit dem Ende des 15. und während des 16. Jhs.
ad 1) Die Lese- und Schreiblehren sowie Orthographien behandeln z. B. sehr genau das Verhältnis zwischen Lautqualität und Buchstaben und üben entsprechend scharfe Kritik an der zeitgenössischen deutschen Orthographie. Regional bedingte Unterschiede in der Realisation eines Phonems werden als dialektale Eigenarten registriert, des öfteren auch als *misbreuche* moniert, als Verstoß gegen eine standardsprachliche Norm, die noch gar nicht definiert ist. Die Vorstellung steht im Zusammenhang mit Ausgleichsvorgängen seit dem 15. Jh., d. h. mit Bemühungen um die Herstellung überlandschaftlicher und übermundartlicher Schreib- und Druckersprachen.
ad 2) In der Lexikographie ist vor allem das erste deutsch-lateinische Wörterbuch, von Josua Maaler (1561), zu nennen, das u. a. zu jedem Lemma (partiell) synonyme Ausdrücke bietet, über grammatische Funktionen informiert und in syntagmatische Verwendungszusammenhänge einführt, z. B. durch Rektionsangaben bei Verben, bei Substantiven durch Anführung geläufiger Attributgruppen und speziell bei Abstrakta durch Auflistung möglicher Verbindungen mit bestimmten Nominalisierungsverben, eine für die frühe Neuzeit zentrale Sprachverwendungseinheit im Übergangsbereich von Lexik und Syntax, deren Behandlung auf dem Wege von Lorenzo Valla über Erasmus in die lat. und deutschsprachige artes-Literatur gedrungen ist.
ad 3) Anleitungen zur Herstellung eines rhetorisch wirksamen Textes sind vorrangig auf die Textsorte Brief ausgerichtet. In Brieflehren und Formularien werden daher besonders gängige rhetorische Tropen und Figuren behandelt. Für die Herstellung eines Textes gelten als Hauptziele: Klarheit, Verständnissicherung und -förderung, Interessenweckung und -erhaltung, Berücksichtigung (sprach)ästhetischer Gesichtspunkte, *zierlichkeit*. Auf die grammatische Korrektheit wird als Voraussetzung nur verwiesen. Als beispielhafte Empfehlungen für den Ausdruckswechsel (*mutatio*, *variatio*) listen z. B. Frangk (1531) und Meichßner (1538) neben Synonymen und Wendungsvarianten auch funktionsidentische grammatische Elemente und syntaktische Fügungen auf. Riederer (1493) hat in seine Brieflehre die Herennius-Rhetorik in freier Übersetzung integriert. Seine konkreten Anweisungen zur Sprachverwendung in bestimmten Situationen zielen auf den sprachlichen Ausdruck im Dienst der sachgerechten und/oder logischen Gedankenordnung und der ansprechenden Wirkung auf den Rezipienten. Das Ergebnis ist u. a. eine Anzahl textsyntaktischer Empfehlungen: Warnung vor Überdehnung der Klammer zwischen Artikel und Substantiv; Empfehlung parataktischer Sequenzen für Berichte oder fortlaufende Sachverhaltsdarstellungen; Empfehlungen einer prosodisch wirksamen Nachtragstechnik statt Überfrachtung eines Einzelsatzes mit Informationen; Hinweis auf mögliche Wortstellungsvarianten; Einschränkung des Ellipsengebrauchs auf eindeutige Fälle; Strukturmuster für Satzgefüge als Korrelate bestimmter Syllogismusformen. — In den Lehrbüchern der Dialektik finden sich besonders zahlreich Anleitungen zum sachgerechten und logisch präzisen Sprachgebrauch im Dienst von Definition und Argumentation. Das erste deutschsprachige Werk, von Fuchsperger (1533), enthält u. a. einen umfassenden Versuch, die Lexik des Deutschen für begrifflich korrekte Aussagen tauglich zu machen, durch Anwendung logischer Kategorien als Ordnungssystem für die Beziehung zwischen Wörtern: Aufstellung und Erörterung der Funktion von wortfeldartigen Begriffshierarchien, Wortfamilien, Synonymien, Antonymien, Konversionen, Periphrasen, Teil-Ganzes-Relationen u. a. Im Bereich der Syntax werden Formulierungen für logische Beziehungen angeführt, die die vielfältigen Variationsmöglichkeiten von Satz- und Wortgruppenstrukturen verdeutlichen sollen.
ad 4) und 5) Historiographische, sprachenvergleichende und sprachtheoretisch ausgerichtete Werke thematisieren u. a. Alter und

Herkunft des Deutschen sowie seine Verwandtschaft mit anderen Sprachen (insbesondere Latein, Griechisch, Hebräisch). Es werden, vor allem anhand von Namen, gesetzhafte Lautentsprechungen festgestellt zwischen der deutschen Sprache in alten Texten und der Gegenwart, dem Deutschen und Lateinischen, verschiedenen deutschen Dialekten, besonders Nd. und Hd. – Zur Kennzeichnung jeder Art der sprachlichen Veränderung/Andersartigkeit dienen vier Kriterien: Hinzufügung, Wegnahme, Umstellung und Austausch (meist von Buchstaben/Lauten eines Wortes). Diese seit der Antike geläufigen Kriterien begegnen bei den Humanisten häufig (z. B. Aventin 1519, m. v; Bibliander 1548, 160f.). Für den Bedarf, sprachbezogene Beobachtungen klassifizierend zu benennen, bieten sie ein zunächst sehr grobes Raster, das in der Folgezeit allmählich verfeinert wird. Das Verfahren ist besonders in der beginnenden Grammatikschreibung des Deutschen wirksam.

ad 6) Kommentare zur Kunst des Übersetzens enthalten einerseits konkrete Empfehlungen, lat. Konstruktionen zu imitieren, um das Dt. geschmeidiger zu machen, z. B. bei N. von Wyle (1478), oder umgekehrt: spezifische Ausdrucksformen des Dt. gezielt zu nutzen, z. B. bei Luther (1530 u. ö.).

### 2.2. Lateinische Schulgrammatiken

Die wichtigste Vorstufe für die Grammatikographie des Deutschen ist die lateinische Schulgrammatik, da sie zunehmend seit der Mitte des 15. Jhs. die deutsche Sprache zur Verständnishilfe der lateinischen benutzt und insofern sie das grammatikographische Rüstzeug grundsätzlich zur Verfügung stellt. Für beide Aspekte gibt es herausragende Beispiele: Eine Handschrift der *ars minor* von Donat (1473) hat neben der vollständigen Glossierung des lateinischen Textes noch einmal in freierer Übersetzung und fortlaufend den Gesamttext der Grammatik: Terminologie, grammatische Darstellung und deutschsprachige Flexionsparadigmen als lexikalische Entsprechungen der lateinischen Flexionsmuster, so daß als Nebenprodukt die "Vorstufe einer kleinen deutschen Sprachlehre" (Ising 1966: 11) entsteht, in der grammatische Sachverhalte zusammenhängend deutsch ausgedrückt werden.

Das erheblich umfassender konzipierte *Exercitium Puerorum Grammaticale*, um 1485 entstanden, setzt die deutsche Sprache sehr differenziert zur Erlernung des Lateinischen ein: durch Übersetzung der lateinischen Beispielsätze, Zuordnung deutscher Konstruktionen zu bedeutungsgleichen lateinischen, verbunden mit Kommentaren, die Einsichten vermitteln in Gemeinsamkeiten und Unterschiede der Struktur beider Sprachen. Besonders eingehend werden die sprachlichen Bedingungen für eine angemessene Übersetzung vom Lateinischen ins Deutsche und umgekehrt abgehandelt. Mehrfach zitierte Empfehlungen L. Vallas für bestimmte lat. Ausdrucksformen erscheinen implizit auch für andere Sprachen, z. B. das Dt., als mustergültig.

Aventins Grammatik, *Rudimenta Grammaticae* (1519), enthält sehr genaue Beobachtungen auf allen Sprachebenen und zeigt einen ausgeprägten Reflexionsstand des Autors als Ergebnis seiner Beschäftigung mit Sprachgelehrten der Antike und seiner Zeit, bes. Erasmus. Aventins Darstellung der lateinischen Grammatik ist ohne direkten Bezug auf das Dt., vermittelt jedoch übereinzelsprachliche Beobachtungen und lenkt auf Funktionen der Sprache schlechthin. Diese bilden die Orientierungsbasis für seine differenzierten Aussagen über die dt. Sprache anhand des Sprachmaterials aus seinen Archivstudien, z. B. in der *Bayerischen Chronik*.

Philipp Melanchthons 1525 erstmals erschienene und in der Folgezeit mehrfach überarbeitete *Grammatica Latina* zeichnet sich, in Verbindung mit der gesondert erschienen *Syntax*, unter den zeitgenössischen lateinischen Schulgrammatiken durch Klarheit und ausgeprägtes grammatikologisches Problembewußtsein ihres Autors aus. Unter seinen zahlreichen Gewährsautoren sind hierfür insbesondere Priscian und Valla von Bedeutung. Als Vorbild für eine kategorial geordnete Darbietung des grammatischen Stoffes ist Melanchthons Werk sehr geeignet. Für die frühe deutsche Grammatikschreibung ist es mehrfach und mit Gewinn benutzt worden.

## 3. Die ersten Grammatiken des Deutschen

### 3.1. Eine frühe Konzeption

Um 1534 ist erstmalig in der Geschichte der deutschen Grammatikschreibung ein Werk mit dem Titel *Grammatik* erschienen: Der Autor, Valentin Ickelsamer, Schulmeister aus Rothenburg ob der Tauber, steht der theologischen Tradition der *devotio moderna* und der oberrheinischen *Freunde-Gottes*-Bewegung nahe sowie den Auffassungen der

Schwärmer. Hieraus erklärt sich sein Bildungskonzept, in dem die Sprache, besonders auch die Muttersprache, und die Didaktik einen hohen Stellenwert haben. Er hatte bereits 1527 eine Leselehre veröffentlicht und diese in der Grammatik weiterverarbeitet. – Als Motiv für die Abfassung seines Werkes nennt der Autor u. a. sein persönliches Interesse an der deutschen Sprache und Grammatik sowie den zeitbedingten Wunsch vieler Laien, lesen zu lernen. Er behandelt die deutsche Grammatik im Hinblick auf ihre Eigenständigkeit. Ihre Beschreibung erfolgt im ständigen Vergleich mit der lateinischen, selten auch mit der griechischen, Sprache. Das zugrundeliegende Verständnis von Sprache ist durch die Rhetorik geprägt. Die Hinwendung zur deutschen Sprache erfolgt mit dem Ziel, das Sprachbewußtsein der Deutschen für ihre Sprache auszubilden. Das Werk verbindet Empfehlungen zur Abfassung einer deutschsprachigen Grammatik des Deutschen für Deutsche, grammatikographische Arbeiten zu Teilgebieten einer solchen Grammatik, didaktische Anweisungen für die Erlernung der deutschen Grammatik, insbesondere des Lesens und Schreibens. Rezipientengruppen sind die potentiellen zukünftigen Grammatikschreiber, -lehrer und Lernenden.

Das Werk bietet Leitlinien für den bewußten Sprachgebrauch. – Die grammatikographisch ausgearbeiteten Kapitel betreffen Benennung und phonetische Beschreibung der Laute des Deutschen, Hinweise auf Mängel in der Korrelation zwischen Lautwerten und -zeichen im Deutschen, zur Silbentrennung, Aussprache, Orthographie, Etymologie und Interpunktion. Hinzu kommen deliberativrhetorisierende Erörterungen über Sinn und Zweck der Behandlung des Gegenstandes, Appelle an die Lehrenden zur Handhabung einer angemessenen Didaktik, Kritik am Verhältnis der Deutschen zu ihrer Sprache, Hinweise auf die Würde der deutschen Sprache, die den Vergleich mit anderen Sprachen nicht zu scheuen brauche, Aufruf an die Gelehrten, die deutsche Sprache zu erforschen. Diese Gedanken wirken in den deutschen Grammatiken der Folgezeit weiter.

Die beiden großen Objektbereiche der Grammatik umfassen nach Ickelsamers Auffassung die acht Redeteile mit ihren Akzidentien und eine darauf aufbauende Syntax. Flexionsparadigmen, wie sie bereits durch frühkindliche unbewußte Spracherlernung angeeignet sind, brauche die Grammatik der Muttersprache nicht (Aj v, 8–20), so seine Kritik an den Donat-Übersetzungen. – Die Übernahme des Kategoriensystems aus der lateinischen Grammatik, dem er universale Gültigkeit zuschreibt, erscheint bei ihm als selbstverständlich, verbunden mit der Forderung angemessener Übersetzung der zugehörigen lateinischen Termini ins Deutsche, einer Erklärung der grammatischen Kategorien und Hinweise zu deren richtigem Gebrauch mit Hilfe von Beispielen. Er verweist hier auf die Funktion, die das Beispiel in den Grammatiken bis weit ins 18. Jh. hat: Es nimmt die Stelle abstrakter Beschreibung der grammatikalischen Sachverhalte ein und repräsentiert regelhaften Sprachgebrauch.

Daß die Syntax einer Grammatik in die richtige und zugleich kunstmäßige Wort- und Satzfügung einführen soll, belegt exemplarisch im Eröffnungsteil die Behandlung des Partizips und im Schlußteil die Funktionserklärung der Interpunktion: Nach Ickelsamer ist die Verwendung von Partizipialkonstruktionen im Deutschen genau so gut möglich wie im Lateinischen, nur bisher ungebräuchlich. Die *zierliche kürtze*, in den lateinischen Grammatiken mit Bezug auf L. Valla verfochten, vergrößere den Ausdrucksreichtum, ohne die Eigenständigkeit des Deutschen zu gefährden. Der Gedanke dringt über Schottelius in die deutschen Grammatiken bis ins 18. Jh. ein. – Mit der Analyse eines komplexen Satzes, nach dem Verfahren der traditionellen Periodenlehre, stellt Ickelsamer im letzten Kapitel als Aufgabe der Interpunktion dar, die interne Gliederung einer Periode so genau wie möglich zu verdeutlichen, um die Verständlichkeit für Lesende oder Hörende zu sichern, und zugleich optimale Wirkung zu erreichen.

Für einen fortschrittlichen Leseunterricht fordert er als erste Phase die phonetische Analyse von Wörtern durch den Lernenden einschließlich der Identifizierung der separierten Laute und der Beschreibung ihrer Artikulation. Er schreibt dieser Methode hohen formalen Bildungswert zu, da sie die Verstandeskräfte auch für andere geistige Tätigkeiten schule.

In der Wortforschung gilt Ickelsamers besonderes Interesse, angeregt durch Beatus Rhenanus, der Herkunft deutscher Wörter und ihrer ursprünglichen Bedeutung. Entsprechend der zeitgenössischen Auffassung von der allgemeinen Sprachenvermischung als Folge des Turmbaus zu Babel, verweist er darauf, daß in der Vorzeit zahlreiche Wörter aus anderen Sprachen ins Deutsche entlehnt worden seien, und leitet daraus die Notwendigkeit des Sprachenvergleichs ab. Orthographie und Worttrennung, besonders der motivierten Komposita, müsse auf etymologischen Kenntnissen basieren. Vorsichtige Empfehlungen für eine konservierende Sprachpflege sind die Folge, und, soweit es die Orthographie betrifft, sogar für die gemäßigte Wiederherstellung ursprünglicher Zustände, allerdings unter Berücksichtigung des Gebrauchs. Die Verwendung von Fremdwörtern, besonders Latinismen, empfiehlt er für den Fall, daß deutsche Bezeichnungen fehlen, die lateinischen aber allgemein verständlich und gebräuchlich sind. – Seine Bemühungen um die deutsche Wortforschung werden von Schottelius fortgeführt.

Der von Ickelsamer angestrebte deutsche Sprachunterricht ist integrierender Bestandteil eines ganzheitlichen Bildungskonzeptes, in dem jeder pädagogische Teilprozeß formal und inhaltlich einen festen Stellenwert hat: Die muttersprachliche Grammatik bereitet auf bestimmte Berufe und auf die Erlernung von Fremdsprachen vor und schult die Verstandeskräfte; die Beschäftigung mit der ursprünglichen Bedeutung der Wörter dient der Erhaltung der Sprache; die Sprachpflege ist zugleich Bewußtseinsbildung, der bewußte Sprachgebrauch die Voraussetzung für ein gottesfürchtiges Leben.

### 3.2. Werke in lateinischer Sprache

Der unkonventionellen Konzeption Ickelsamers stehen die ersten vollständigen deutschen Grammatiken gegenüber, die ein halbes Jahrhundert später geschrieben wurden, von Albertus (1573), Ölinger (1574) und Clajus (1578). Sie sind lateinisch abgefaßt und, trotz notwendiger Abänderungen, streng an der lateinischen Grammatik orientiert, vor allem an Melanchthons *Grammatica Latina*, ergänzt durch die Grammatik des Griechischen und, bei Ölinger, des Französischen. – Die Vielzahl übereinstimmender Regeln erklärt Albertus, der seiner Grammatik eine umfassende theoretisierende Einleitung vorausschickt, mit der Verwandtschaft der Sprachen. Dementsprechend sei selbstverständlich die Gliederung des grammatischen Stoffes (*partes grammaticae*) in allen Sprachen dieselbe, auch für das Deutsche: *Orthographia, Prosodia, Etymologia* (Wortforschung) und *Syntaxis*. Ölinger und Clajus übernehmen die tradierte Aufteilung ebenfalls. – Hauptargumente für den Ausbau einer Grammatik der Muttersprache sind nach Albertus: Die Kenntnis der Grammatik der eigenen Sprache erleichtere das Lernen der Grammatik fremder Sprachen und sei die Voraussetzung dafür, die eigene Sprache richtig und wirkungsvoll zu sprechen. Wer sich in Fremdsprachen gut ausdrücken könne, müsse die eigene Sprache erst recht beherrschen. Ihr Ausbau vermeide unnötige Anleihen bei den anderen Sprachen (besonders Latein und Griechisch).

Daß die vom Lateinischen vorgegebene Kategorienbildung, einschließlich der Anordnung der Flexionsparadigmen, nicht nur Systematisierungshilfe ist, sondern sich häufig für das Deutsche als Problem erweist, zeigt sich, modifiziert, in allen drei Grammatiken. Wie bei gleichem Reflexionsstand die grammatikographischen Entscheidungen wechseln können, belegt z. B. die Diskussion über die Ansetzung eines Ablativs im Deutschen: Albertus entscheidet sich dafür, mit der Begründung, daß den Gelehrten die Zahl von sechs Kasus geläufig sei und, im Unterschied zum Dativ, der Ablativ trotz gleicher Endung notwendig immer mit Präposition plus Artikel verbunden werde. Ölinger ersetzt den Ablativ überall in seiner Grammatik konsequent durch den Terminus *Dativ*. Clajus behält ihn im Paradigma bei, trennt jedoch sonst, besonders in der *Syntax*, nicht scharf zwischen *Ablativ* und *Dativ*. In der Folgezeit bis Gottsched hat das Deklinationsparadigma meist die Kasus Vokativ und Ablativ beibehalten. Erst Aichinger eliminiert sie.

Zur Gewinnung von Deklinationsklassen für das Deutsche orientiert sich Clajus, äußerst beschwerlich, an der lateinischen Grammatik, indem er vom Stammauslaut ausgeht. Und für die Aufstellung von Konjugationsklassen arbeitet er die Silbenstruktur deutscher Verbalstämme rückwärts auf. Es ergeben sich u. a. Beleggruppen, die bei gleichem Stammvokal und gleichartiger Konsonantenumgebung denselben Vokalwechsel für die Tempusbildung aufweisen, wobei sich das Prinzip der Ablautklassen latent abzeichnet, ohne daß die distributionell sauber aufgeteilten Kleingruppen bereits zu größeren Kategorien zusammengeführt werden könnten. Ölingers Ordnungssystem, z. T. auch das von Albertus, ist weniger mühsam und, trotz seiner Vorläufigkeit, ergebnisreicher. – Bei den Verben führt der Versuch, für Genus, Tempus und Modus allen lateinischen Kategorien voll zu entsprechen, bei den Autoren zu zahlreichen periphrastischen Auffüllungen der Paradigmen, z. B. Übertragung einzelner Indikativformen in den Konjunktiv, oder, als Indiz für einen Optativ, Ergänzung einer Form durch vorausgehende Adverbien, Konjunktionen oder kleine Wunschsätze. Viele dieser Entsprechungen gehen zurück auf gängige Übersetzungshilfen, die seit langem in Latein-Grammatiken Funktion und Bedeutung lateinischer Verbformen verdeutlichten. Ölinger zeichnet sich dadurch aus, daß er auf derartige Diskrepanzen zwischen beiden Sprachen deutlich hinweist.

Im Kapitel *Syntax* modifiziert Clajus die lateinische Vorlage sehr differenziert, aber 'stillschweigend': Mehrfach ordnet er den Stoff neu, insbesondere bei Unterschieden des Deutschen und Lateinischen bezüglich Rektion von Verben und Nomina, Kasusforderung freier Angaben, Konstruktion unpersönlicher Verben, Gebrauch von Partizip, Gerundium und Supinum. Vieles stellt er für die folgenden Grammatiken über Schottelius hinaus grundlegend dar. Sein Werk erfährt elf Auflagen und erscheint zuletzt 1720. Als besondere grammatikographische Qualität ist bei Clajus hervorzuheben, daß er bei der Behandlung verschiedener Typen satzinterner syntagmatischer Beziehungen terminologisch sehr genau unterscheidet und die hierbei verwendeten Verben noch stärker differenziert als Melanchthon. – Als Besonderheiten der deutschen Wortstellung behandelt Clajus am Ende der *Syntax* die Rahmenbildung bei Verben mit trennbarem Präfix und bei Prädikaten aus finitem und infinitem Verb, hier und öfter mit Hinweis auf die notwendige Beachtung des Gebrauchs. Ansätze, die deutsche Wortstellung in Regeln zu fassen, bringt auch Albertus, im Kapitel *Etymologie* z. B. für die Zweitstellung des finiten Verbs. Erst- und Endstellung des finiten Hilfsverbs sieht er an das Vorkommen bestimmter Sprechhandlungen geknüpft: Eid, Fluch, Beteuerung, Frage u. a. Im Kapitel *Syntax* erwähnt er mehrfach Erscheinungen der relativen Wortfolge im Satzinnern.

Auf die Wortbildung geht besonders detailliert Albertus ein. Für die Derivation listet er wortartspezifische Suffixe auf, mit Angaben zu deren Funktion und/oder Bedeutung. Für die Komposition stellt er mögliche zwei- und mehrgliedrige Fügungen dar, verbunden mit Angaben über Strukturmerkmale der Glieder sowie zur Funktion des Grundwortes für die Gesamtkonstruktion. Die Wurzel der deutschen Wörter erklärt er wie die der hebräischen Wörter für einsilbig. Albertus bereitet die Wortbildungslehre von Schottelius maßgeblich vor.

Die erwähnten und zahlreiche andere Abänderungen der lateinischen Vorlage kennzeichnen den Anfang eines jahrhundertelangen Prozesses, in dem die Eigenheiten des Deutschen in minutiöser Auseinandersetzung mit dem Lateinischen aufgespürt werden, verbunden mit einer allmählichen, oft kreativen, Umgestaltung des grammatischen Kategorialsystems im Hinblick auf die Belange der deutschen Sprache.

### 3.3. Die erste deutschsprachige Grammatik

Nach dem Versuch einer synoptischen Grammatik des Dt., Lat. und Griech. (Becherer 1596) und einer lat. abgefaßten Grammatik des Dt. für Ausländer (Ritter 1616) erscheint die erste vollständig deutsch abgefaßte Grammatik des Deutschen, von Kromayer (1618). Sie ist thematisch auf wenige Rudimenta reduziert und als Vorbereitung auf den Grammatikunterricht im Lat. konzipiert. Das Werk besteht größtenteils aus Flexionsparadigmen und Beispielreihen für kategoriale Sachverhalte. Darstellender Text, zur Einbettung grammatischer Regeln in einen Zusammenhang, fehlt weitgehend. Das erfaßte Material ist einfacher und übersichtlicher geordnet als bei den Vorgängern, ein deutliches Ergebnis zwischenzeitlicher Bemühungen um Systematisierung der Beobachtungsdaten. So stellt Kromayer vier Konjugationen auf, indem er die Verben gruppiert nach der Art des Stammvokalwechsels bei der Tempusbildung (1.: alle Tempora gleich, 2.: Präsens und Perfekt vs. Imperfekt, 3.: Imperfekt + Perfekt vs. Präsens, 4.: alle Tempora verschieden). Zu 1 gehört, nach Kromayer, ein Perfekt auf *-t*, zu 2 bis 4 auf *-n*. Durch dieses kombinierte Verfahren werden schwache und starke Verben in verschiedene Konjugationen getrennt, ohne Terminologie und ohne daß die klassenbildenden Merkmale bereits vollständig erfaßt sind.

Mit den fast zeitgleich entstandenen Grammatiken von Ratke und Helwig werden neue pädagogische und sprachwissenschaftliche Impulse wirksam, die die vorausgehenden Grammatiken als enger zusammengehörige erste Stufe erscheinen lassen.

## 4. Bibliographie

### 4.1. Primärliteratur

[in Auswahl; ergänzend: Müller (1882), Jellinek (1913–14), Moulin-Fankhänel (1994)].

Albertus, Laurentius. 1895 [1573]. *Teutsch Grammatick oder Sprachkunst* ed. v. Carl Müller-Fraureuth. (= *Ältere deutsche Grammatiken in Neudrukken*, 3.) Straßburg: Trübner.

Aventinus s. Turmair.

Becherer, Johann. 1596. *Synopsis Grammaticae tam Germanicae quam Latinae et Graecae, in usum juventutis scholasticae conscripta.* Jena: Tobias Steinmann.

Bibliander, Theodor (Buchmann). 1548. *De ratione communi omnium linguarum & literarum.* Zürich.

Clajus, Johannes. 1973 [1578]. *Grammatica Germanicae Linguae.* (= *Documenta Linguistica*, Reihe IV.) Hildesheim & New York: Olms.

Donatus, Aelius. 1473. *De octo partibus orationis ars minor.* (lat.-dt.). [s. Ising 1966. 24–207.]

*Exercitium puerorum grammaticale per dietas distributum.* 1491. Hagenau.

*Formulare vnd Tütsch rhetorica.* 1483. Straßburg: Joh. Pruß.

Frangk, Fabian. 1979 [1531]. *Ein Cantzley und Titelbuechlin.* Beigebunden: *Orthographia Deutsch.* (= *Documenta Linguistica*, Reihe IV.) Hildesheim & New York: Olms.

Fuchsperger, Ortholph. 1533. *Ain gründlicher klarer anfang der natürlichen vnd rechten kunst der waren Dialectica.* Augsburg: Alexander Weyssenhorn.

–. 1542. *Leeßkonst.* [s. Müller 1969 [1882]. 166–188.]

Gessner, Konrad. 1974 [1555]. *Mithridates. De differentiis linguarum tum veterum tum quae hodie apud diuersas nationes in toto orbe terrarum in usu sunt.* Hg. v. Manfred Peters. Aalen: Scientia.

Hugen, Alexander. 1528. *Rhetorica vnnd Formularium Teütsch.* Tübingen: Ulrich Morhart.

Ickelsamer, Valentin. 1971 [1527]. *Die rechte weis aufs kürtzist lesen zu lernen.* Hg. v. Karl Pohl. Stuttgart: Ernst Klett.

–. 1971 [1534]. *Ain Teütsche Grammatica.* Hg. v. Karl Pohl. Stuttgart: Ernst Klett.

Kromayer, Johannes. 1986 [1618]. *Deutsche Grammatica. Zum newen Methodo der Jugend zum besten zugerichtet.* (= *Documenta Linguistica*, Reihe IV.) Hildesheim & New York: Olms.

Luther, Martin 1951 [1530]. *Sendbrief vom Dolmetschen.* Hg. v. Karl Bischoff, 6–36. Halle: Niemeyer.

Maaler, Josua. 1971 [1561]. *Die Teütsch spraach. Dictionarium Germanicolatinum novum.* (= *Documenta Linguistica*, Reihe 1.) Hildesheim & New York: Olms.

Meichßner, Johann Elias. 1976 [1538]. *Handtbuechlin grundtlichs berichts Recht vnd wolschrybens der Orthographie vnd Grammatic.* (= *Documenta Linguistica*, Reihe IV.) Hildesheim & New York: Olms.

Melanchthon, Philipp. 1854 [1526]. *Grammatica Latina.* Hg. v. Karl G. Bretschneider & Heinrich E. Bindseil. (= *Corpus Reformatorum*, 20.) 192–335. Braunschweig: C. A. Schwetschke.

Ölinger, Albert. 1975 [1574]. *Vnderricht der Hoch Teutschen Spraach.* (= *Documenta Linguistica*, Reihe IV.) Hildesheim & New York: Olms.

Rhenanus, Beatus. 1531. *Rerum germanicarum libri tres.* Basel: Hieronymus Froben.

Riederer, Friedrich. 1493. *Spiegel der waren Rhetoric.* Freiburg.

Ritter, Stephan M. 1616. *Grammatica Germanica Nova.* Marburg.

Schwartzenbach, Leonhard. 1564. *Synonyma. Formular wie man ainerley rede vnd mainung / mit andern mehr worten / auff mancherley art vnd weise / zierlich reden / schreiben / vnd außsprechen sol.* Frankfurt. [s. Haß 1986.]

*Tractatulus dans modum teutonisandi casus et tempora.* 1451. [s. Müller 1882. 239–242.]

Turmair, Johannes, gen. Aventinus. 1519. *Rudimenta Grammaticae.* Augsburg.

–. 1883–1886 [1566]. *Bayerische Chronik.* Hg. v. Matthias Lexer. (= *Sämmtliche Werke*, 4,5.) München: Christian Kaiser.

Valla, Laurentius. 1527. *De Lingvae Latinae Elegantia Libri Sex.* Köln.

Wyle, Niclas. 1861 [1478]. *Translationen.* Hg. v. Adalbert Keller. (= *Bibliothek des Literarischen Vereins in Stuttgart*, 57.) Stuttgart.

## 4.2. Sekundärliteratur

Besch, Werner, Oskar Reichmann & Stefan Sonderegger, Hg. 1985. *Sprachgeschichte. Ein Handbuch zur Geschichte der deutschen Sprache und ihrer Erforschung.* 2 Bde. (= *Handbücher zur Sprach- und Kommunikationswissenschaft*, 2,2.) Berlin & New York: de Gruyter.

*Deutsche Grammatiken vom Humanismus bis zur Aufklärung. Ausstellung der Forschungsstelle für deutsche Sprachgeschichte der Universität Bamberg in Zusammenarbeit mit der Staatsbibliothek Bamberg.* 1988. Bamberg: Forschungsstelle für Deutsche Sprachgeschichte.

Erben, Johannes. 1989. "Die Entstehung unserer Schriftsprache und der Anteil deutscher Grammatiker am Normierungsprozeß". *Sprachwissenschaft* 14. 6–28.

Fricke, Gerhard. 1933. "Die Sprachauffassung in der grammatischen Theorie des 16. und 17. Jahrhunderts". *Zeitschrift für deutsche Bildung* 9. 113–123.

Götz, Ursula. 1992. *Die Anfänge der Grammatikschreibung des Deutschen in Formularbüchern des frühen 16. Jahrhunderts: Fabian Frangk – "Schryfftspiegel" – Johann Elias Meißner.* (= *Germanische Bibliothek*, Reihe 3.) Heidelberg: Winter.

Grenzmann, Ludger & Karl Stackmann, Hg. 1984. *Literatur und Laienbildung im Spätmittelalter und in der Reformationszeit. Symposion Wolfenbüttel 1981.* (= *Germanistische Symposien, Berichtsbände*, 5.) Stuttgart: Metzler.

Ulrike Haß. 1986. *Leonhard Schwarzenbachs Synonyma. Beschreibung und Nachdruck der Ausgabe Frankfurt 1564. Lexikographie und Textsortenzusammenhänge im Frühneuhochdeutschen.* Tübingen: Niemeyer.

Höchli, Stefan. 1981. *Zur Geschichte der Interpunktion im Deutschen. Eine kritische Darstellung der Lehrschriften von der zweiten Hälfte des 15. Jahrhunderts bis zum Ende des 18. Jahrhunderts.* (= *Studia Linguistica Germanica*, 17.) Berlin & New York: de Gruyter.

Ising, Erika. 1966. *Die Anfänge der volkssprachlichen Grammatik in Deutschland und Böhmen. Dargestellt am Einfluß der Schrift des Aelius Donatus De octo partibus orationis ars minor*, Bd. I: *Quellen.* (= *Deutsche Akademie der Wissenschaften zu Berlin, Veröffentlichungen der Sprachwissenschaftlichen Kommission*, 6.) Berlin: Akademie-Verlag.

Jellinek, Max Hermann. 1913–14. *Geschichte der neuhochdeutschen Grammatik von den Anfängen bis auf Adelung.* Bd. I, II. Heidelberg: Winter.

Moulin-Fankhänel, Claudine. 1994. *Bibliographie der deutschen Grammatiken und Orthographielehren*, Bd. I: *Von den Anfängen der Überlieferung bis zum Ende des 16. Jahrhunderts.* (= *Germanistische bibliothek*, 6,4.) Heidelberg: Winter.

Müller, Johannes. 1969 [1882]. *Quellenschriften und Geschichte des deutschsprachlichen Unterrichtes bis zur Mitte des 16. Jahrhunderts. Mit einer Einführung v. Monika Rössing-Hager.* (= *Documenta Linguistica*, Reihe IV.) Hildesheim & New York: Olms.

Padley, G[eorge] A. 1985 & 1988. *Grammatical Theory in Western Europe 1500–1700. Trends in Vernacular grammar.* Bd. I, II. Cambridge, New York & Melbourne: Cambridge Univ. Press.

Puff, Helmut. 1995. "*Von dem schlüssel aller Künsten / nemblich der Grammatica*". *Deutsch im lateinischen Grammatikunterricht 1480–1560.* (= *Basler Studien zur deutschen Sprache und Literatur*, 70.) Tübingen & Basel: Francke.

–. 1996. "*Exercitium grammaticale puerorum*". *Eine Studie zum Verhältnis von pädagogischer Innovation und Buchdruck um 1500. Schule und Schüler im Mittelalter. Beiträge zur europäischen Bildungsgeschichte des 9. bis 15. Jahrhunderts,* hg. von Martin Kintzinger, Sönke Lorenz & Michael Walter, 411–439. (= *Beihefte zum Archiv für Kulturgeschichte*, 42.) Köln, Weimar & Wien: Böhlau.

Reich, Gerhard. 1972. *Muttersprachlicher Grammatikunterricht von der Antike bis um 1600.* (= *Pädagogische Studien*, 19.) Weinheim: Beltz.

Rössing-Hager, Monika. 1984. *Konzeption und Ausführung der ersten deutschen Grammatik. Valentin Ickelsamer: 'Ein Teütsche Grammatica'.* Grenzmann 1984. 534–556.

–. 1985. *Ansätze zu einer deutschen Sprachgeschichtsschreibung vom Humanismus bis ins 18. Jahrhundert.* Besch, Reichmann & Sonderegger 1985. 1564–1614.

–. 1990. *Leitprinzipien für die Syntax deutscher Autoren um 1500. Verfahrensvorschläge zur Ermittlung spezifischer Qualitätsvorstellungen, ihrer Herkunft und Verbreitung. Neuere Forschungen zur historischen Syntax des Deutschen. Referate der internationalen Fachkonferenz Eichstätt 1989* hg. von Anne Betten. (= *Reihe germanistische Linguistik*, 103.) Tübingen: Niemeyer.

Schmidt-Wilpert, Gabriele. 1985. *Die Bedeutung der älteren deutschen Grammatiker für das Neuhochdeutsche.* Besch, Reichmann & Sonderegger 1985. 1556–1564.

*Monika Rössing-Hager, Marburg (Deutschland)*

# 108. Frühe grammatische Beschreibungen des Niederländischen (ca. 1550–ca. 1650)

1. Die Grammatiken der Triviumperiode
2. Ziele und Probleme der Rechtschreibung
3. Das klassische Modell und die Wortarten
4. Zeugen des Standardisierungsprozesses
5. Bibliographie

## 1. Die Grammatiken der Triviumperiode

Die Periode von etwa 1550 bis etwa 1650 stellt den Anfang des Standardisierungsprozesses des Niederländischen dar, in dem die Kodifizierung der Muttersprache unter anderem in Rechtschreibebüchern und Grammatiken stattgefunden hat. In den Grammatiken werden die Sprachlehrbücher des Lateinischen zum Vorbild genommen, die im Curriculum der lateinischen Schulen in den Niederlanden im Gebrauch sind: insbesondere die *Grammaticæ institutiones* (Paris [1]1550) von Cornelius Valerius (1512–1578), und die *Grammatica latina* (Düsseldorf [1]1575) des Deutschen Ludolffus Lithocomus (?–?), welche sich in der von Gerardus Joannes Vossius (1577–1649) revidierten Ausgabe (Leiden [1]1626) mit bestimmt vierzig neuen Auflagen bis ins neunzehnte Jahrhundert durchgesetzt hat; diese und solche Werke haben zur Nachahmung gedient bei der Hauptgliederung der Grammatiken in Orthographie, Prosodie, Etymologie (die Lehre der Redeteile) und Syntax, bei der Einteilung in Wortarten, der Lehre der Akzidenzien, usw. Einige niederländische Grammatiken gehören zu einer Reihe, die nach dem lateinischen Beispiel des *Trivium* der *Artes liberales* in die Teile Grammatik, Rhetorik und Dialektik gegliedert sind. Deshalb nennt man die Werke dieser Periode häufig *Trivium*grammatiken, und die Historiker der niederländischen Sprachwissenschaft sprechen daher auch gewöhnlich von der *Trivium*periode zur Bezeichnung dieser Zeit (s. Klifman 1983, namentlich 73–114).

Anderswo in Westeuropa entsteht zur Pflege der Muttersprachen zur selben Zeit eine große Zahl von Rechtschreibebüchern und Grammatiken. Nachdem im anonym erschienenen lateinischen Schulbuch *Exercitium puerorum grammaticale* (Antwerpen [1]1485) der Grammatik der Muttersprache schon einige Aufmerksamkeit galt, und Desiderius Erasmus (1466 oder 1469–1536) in *De recta Latini Græcique sermonis pronuntiatione dialogus* (Basel [1]1528) zur Erklärung der fehlerfreien Aussprache des Griechischen und Lateinischen unter anderem auf das Niederländische verwiesen hatte, sind solche Werke auch für das Niederländische realisiert worden. Aber die Ernte ist für diese Periode noch ziemlich gering, besonders was die Sprachlehrbücher anbetrifft:

1584 *Twe-spraack vande Nederduitsche letterkunst.* Leiden: Christoffel Plantijn. (Neudr. Amsterdam, 1614; Amsterdam, 1649; s. Dibbets 1985)

1625 Christiaen van Heule (?–1655?). *De Nederduytsche grammatica ofte spraeckonst.* Leiden: Daniel Roels (s. Caron 1953a)

1633 Christiaen van Heule, *De Nederduytsche spraec-konst ofte tael-beschrijvinghe.* Leiden: Jacob Roels (s. Caron 1953b)

1649 Allard Lodewijk Kók, *Ont-werp der Neder-duitsche letterkonst.* Amsterdam: Johannes Troóst (s. Dibbets 1991)

1653 Petrus Leupenius, *Aanmerkingen op de Neederduitsche taale.* Amsterdam: Hendryk Donker (s. Caron 1958)

Diesen gedruckten Werken kann man noch einige grammatische Betrachtungen hinzufügen, welche als Vorworte in Werke anderer Art aufgenommen sind: *Noodige waarschouwinge aan alle liefhebbers der Nederduijtze tale* (Zwaan 1939: 121–131) von Antonis de Hubert (1583–nach 1643) in seinen *De Psalmen des Propheeten Davids* (Leiden: Pieter Muller, 1624), und *Nederlandsch tael-bericht* / Zwaan 1939: 133–191) von Samuel Ampzing (1590–1632), zum erstenmal erschienen in seiner *Beschryvinge ende lof der stad Haerlem* (Haarlem: Adriaen Rooman, 1628) und im Jahre 1649 mit dem Titel *Taelbericht der Nederlandsche spellinge* (Wormerveer: Willem Symonsz. Boogaert) vom schon erwähnten Christiaen van Heule nochmals publiziert. Auch wenn wir die *Voorreden vande noodich ende nutticheit der Nederduytsche taelkunste* (Bostoen 1984) von Johan Radermacher (1538–1617) mitrechnen, und die *Waernemingen op de Hollandsche tael* (Zwaan 1939: 235–256), welche der namhafte Schriftsteller Pieter Cornelisz. Hooft (1581–1647) für den Eigengebrauch notiert hatte und welche in der ersten Hälfte des 18. Jh. veröffentlicht worden sind, auch dann kann man nicht von einer großen Produktion grammatischer Werke auf dem Gebiet des Niederländischen reden.

Im Herkunftsort der Rechtschreibebücher und Grammatiken spiegelt sich der politische, wirtschaftliche und kulturelle Umsturz, welcher in den Niederlanden etwa 1585 stattgefunden hat, als die südlichen Provinzen von den ehemaligen nördlichen Bündnispartnern getrennt wurden. Die ersten Abhandlungen, welche der Verbesserung der Orthographie des Niederländischen nachstrebten, sind im Süden veröffentlicht worden: die *Néderlandsche spellijnghe* (Gent: Joas Lambrecht, 1550; s. Heremans & Vander Haeghen 1882) stammt aus der Feder des Genter Druckers und Schulmeisters Joas Lambrecht (ca. 1491–1556/7), *De orthographia linguæ belgicæ* (Löwen: Johannes Masius, 1576; s. Goemans 1899–1901) ist von dem Rechtsgelehrten Antonius Sexagius (ca. 1535–1585) aus Mecheln, und die *Nederduitse orthographie* (Antwerpen: Christoffel Plantijn, 1581; s. Dibbets 1972) wird von Pontus de Heuiter (1535–1602), einem in Delft geborenen Priester, der nach 1572 besonders im Süden tätig war, verfaßt.

Die Zahl der südniederländischen Werke kann mit den schon erwähnten *Voorreden* des aus Aachen gebürtigen Antwerpener Kaufmanns Radermacher, und mit zwei orthographischen Abhandlungen die – vielleicht um

1530 – von einem Cornelis van Varenbraken aufgezeichnet überliefert wurden, ergänzt werden: *Die tafele van orthographia* und *Orthographia* (Braekman 1978).

Die erste Sprachkunst des Niederländischen, die *Twespraack vande Nederduitsche letterkunst*, ist im Jahre 1584 – der Exodus aus dem Süden hat sich schon in Gang gesetzt – von der Amsterdamer "Rederijkerskammer" = (etwa "Sprachgesellschaft") *De Eglentier* ("Die Weinrose") veröffentlicht worden, die übrigens das Drucken und Herausbringen des Werkes dem bekannten südniederländischen Drucker und Verleger Christoffel Plantijn anvertraut hatte, der in Leiden innerhalb der neuen *protestantischen* Universität eine Filiale errichtet hatte. In der *Twespraack vande Nederduitsche letterkunst* ("Dialog über die Grammatik der niederländischen Sprache") präsentiert die Kammer die Grammatik in Form einer Wechselrede auf der Straße zwischen Gedeon und Roemer, genau wie Ursus und Leo in Erasmus' *Dialogus* (1528). Zweifellos sind mit diesen Namen Gedeon Fallet (1544–1615) und Roemer Visscher (1547–1620) gemeint, von denen Letztgenannter aus einer Amsterdamer Kaufmannsfamilie stammte, Erstgenannter dagegen aus dem südniederländischen Mecheln gebürtig war: der Nordniederländer bekommt seinen Unterricht in der Grammatik der Muttersprache von einem Gelehrten aus dem Süden.

Diese niederländische Grammatik hat die Grammatikographie des Deutschen (Bornemann 1976: 126) und sogar die des Malaiischen (Kridalaksana o. J.) beeinflußt, nachdem sie in der Edition von 1614 zur ehemaligen Kolonie Indien transportiert worden war. Einige Leute südniederländischer Herkunft haben im 17. Jh. einen Beitrag zur Kodifikation des Niederländischen geleistet, aber diese sind fast alle in der Provinz Holland veröffentlicht worden, wo die Autoren lebten und arbeiteten: Van Heule und Leupenius, schon erwähnt, stammten aus südniederländischen Familien, genau wie der in Meenen geborene Haarlemer Schulmeister Jacob van der Schuere (1576–nach 1643), der anonym eine *Nederduydsche spellinge* publiziert hat (Haarlem: Vincent Kasteleyn, 1612; s. Zwaan 1957), und der Amsterdamer Schulmeister Anthoni Smyters (Antwerpen, ca. 1545–1626), der in seinem *Schryf-kunst-boeck* (Amsterdam: Nicolaes Biestkens, 1612) eine Betrachtung über die Rechtschreibung gegeben hat (Dibbets 1986). Die einzigen Schriften, welche im 17. Jh. im Süden erschienen sind, sind die *Ni'uwe noodeliicke orthographie* (Antwerpen: Jacob Mesens, 1657) des Antwerper Jesuiten Guilielmus Bolognino (1590–1669) und die *Lingua teutonica exexlex* (Hulst: s. n., 1666; s. Ruijsendaal 1993) eines anonymen Autors ("Laco Flandri presbyteri"). Hiernach wird es fast ein Jahrhundert dauern, bis im Süden der nächste Beitrag zur Grammatik des Niederländischen erscheint; im Norden ist da bereits eine große Zahl grammatischer Beiträge veröffentlicht worden (Dibbets 1994).

## 2. Ziele und Probleme der Rechtschreibung

Im allgemeinen wollen die Triviumbücher praktisch, normierend, standardisierend sein: deswegen soll man darin kaum tiefergehende Reflexionen über das Wesen der Sprache, der Funktion der Grammatik usw. erwarten. Trotzdem fehlt es nicht ganz an Tiefgründigkeit. Die *Nederduitse orthographie* vom akademisch ausgebildeten Pontus de Heuiter enthält eine kurze Betrachtung über die Sprache. Für De Heuiter ist sie das Vermögen zu sprechen, Laute mit Bedeutung zu produzieren, nur den Menschen von Gott geschenkt, um einander mitteilen zu können, was in Herz und Sinn lebt. De Heuiter geht auf die Vorteile geschriebener Sprache und der Buchstaben ein: sie sind "unsterbliche schriftliche Bewahrer, welche das Wichtige, das geschehen ist, geschieht und geschehen wird, im Gedächtnis aufbewahren", und er endet mit der Feststellung, daß jeder kultivierten Gesellschaft auch eine geschriebene Form ihrer Sprache zur Verfügung steht, und daß die fehlerfreie Anwendung der Buchstaben, also eine gute Rechtschreibung, von großer Wichtigkeit ist: "keine Gesellschaft, abgesehen von einer, welche unzivilisiert leben will, kann der Buchstaben entbehren, und jeder soll darauf achten, die Buchstaben richtig anzuwenden".

Die Orthographien und Grammatiken des Niederländischen aus der Triviumperiode sind nicht an erster Stelle für Fremdsprachige gedacht, welche sich das Niederländische aneignen wollten. In den ersten Grammatiken des Französischen, *Lesclarcissement de la langue francoise* (London, 1530) von Jehan Palsgrave (1480?–1554) und in *In linguam gallicam isagoge* (Paris, 1531) von Jacobus Sylvius (1478–1555), hatte man sich dagegen an die Ausländer gerichtet. Das war auch der

Fall in den ersten Grammatiken des Deutschen, der *Teutsch Grammatik oder Sprachkunst* (Augsburg, 1573) von Laurentius Albertus (ca. 1540–nach 1583), dem *Underricht der Hoch Teutsche Spraach* (Straßburg, 1574) von Albertus Ölinger (?–?), oder der *Grammatica Germanicæ linguæ* (Leipzig, 1578) von Johannes Clajus (1535–1592), obwohl man daneben lesen kann, daß sie in der Hoffnung verfaßt worden sind, Schüler durch die Einsicht in die Grammatik der Muttersprache leichter in die Grammatik des Lateinischen einzuführen. In seiner Grammatik nennt Clajus auf der ersten Seite "ausländische Völker" als Zielgruppe neben "unseren Einwohnern". In den niederländischen Werken sind die Fremdsprachigen im allgemeinen nur beiläufig erwähnt.

Die Titelseite von Lambrechts *Néderlandsche spellijnghe* kündigt an, daß das Büchlein "zum Unterrichten von Anfängern" gedacht war. Die Kategorie der Schüler (und Lehrer) wird besonders in den Orthographien des 16. und 17. Jahrhunderts mehrere Male genannt. Und nicht umsonst gibt es viele Schulmeister unter den Autoren: Lambrecht, Smyters, Van der Schuere, und Richard Dafforne (1585–1643), Verfasser der *Grammatica ofte leezleerlings steunsel* (Amsterdam: Jan Evertss. Kloppenburgh, 1627); aber auch Priester (De Heuiter, Bolognino, "Laco Flandri presbyteri") und Pfarrer (Ampzing, Leupenius) sind zu erwähnen, welche im Unterricht tätig waren. Das bedeutet, daß diese Autoren sich die Verbesserung des Unterrichts in der niederländischen Sprache zum Ziel gesetzt haben müssen; aber die lateinische Schule räumte für diesen Unterricht kaum einen Platz ein, und so beschränkte es sich im 16. und 17. Jh. in den sogenannten (französisch-)niederländischen Schulen lediglich auf das Erkennen und Reproduzieren von Buchstaben, die zu Silben und zu kürzeren oder längeren Wörtern kombiniert wurden. Der Schreibunterricht ging kaum über die Technik, Linien, Buchstaben und Schnörkel zu zeichnen, hinaus. Aber vielleicht hat es auch Schulmeister gegeben, die ihren Schülern mehr Rüstzeug für den Rest ihres Lebens haben mitgeben wollen als was ihnen die lokalen Schulordnungen auftrugen. Die Triviumgrammatiker sind sich ihres geringen Einflusses wahrscheinlich bewußt gewesen: in der *Twespraack* stöhnt der Schulmeister Gedeon: "Man sollte Hof- und Stadtsekretäre, Drukker und Schulmeister dazu bringen [...], aber wer wird die Initiative dazu ergreifen?" Es gab also einige Zweifel an der Annahmebereitschaft im schulischen Bereich und an der positiven Einstellung bei der Sprachgemeinschaft.

Wem bewußt ist, daß Lambrecht in Gent nicht nur Schulmeister, sondern auch Drukker war, wird nicht erstaunt sein, daß er betroffen war über die Unordnung, die auf dem Gebiet der Orthographie bei Schulmeistern, Autoren und Druckern herrschte. Dieses Chaos ging ihm nicht nur von didaktischen aber auch wirtschaftlichen Gründen gegen den Strich, da der Absatzmarkt eines Buches durch den Gebrauch eines Dialekts eingeengt war. Die Kategorie der Drucker wird auch explizit in einem kurzen Rechtschreibungsvorschlag erwähnt, den die Amsterdamer *Rederijkerskammer* im Jahre 1583 den "Sachverständigen" in den niederländischen Provinzen vorgelegt hat (Dibbets 1985: 32–37). Aber in der *Twe-spraack*, in der die Amsterdamer diese Vorschläge verarbeitet haben, kommen die Drucker nur sehr nebenbei zur Sprache: der Dialog vollzieht sich zwischen einem Schulmeister und einem Erwachsenen, außerhalb der Schule. Coornhert hatte denn auch in seinem Vorwort diese erste Grammatik des Niederländischen als nützlich für die Schuljugend empfohlen, und nur einmal kommen "Ausländer" ins Bild als mögliche Nutznießer der gebotenen Wortartenlehre. In anderen Werken wenden die Autoren sich an nichts näher bestimmte Personengruppen wie "den niederländischen Leser", "den wahrhaften Liebhaber der niederländischen Orthographie", "die Niederländer, die an ihrer Sprache interessiert sind".

Insbesondere mit der Kodifikation der Rechtschreibung und der Lehre von den Wortarten bezweckte man, die Muttersprache auf das Niveau des Griechischen und des Lateinischen zu bringen und sie bestimmt nicht hinter anderen Landessprachen zurücktreten zu lassen:

> Das Niederländische ist eine reine, reiche, zierliche und verständliche Sprache, die man an allen Ecken der Welt hören kann, in vielen Ländern wo täglich gelehrte Männer aufstehen. Also: ist es nicht sehr erstaunlich und bedauerlich, daß diese Sprache kaum auf Niveau gebracht wird und daß sie nur selten verwendet wird, um die Wissenschaften in Worte zu fassen, zuungunsten des Volkes? Dagegen haben die Ägypter, Griechen und Römer ihre Sprachen, obwohl bei weitem nicht so verbreitet, auf bewundernswürdige Weise durch Anstrengung erfordernde Reisen, mühevolle Anstrengungen, sogar finanzielle Investitionen mit allen Wissenschaften,

Kenntnissen und Gelehrtheit ausgestattet und geschmückt. Man kann ja täglich verspüren, daß die Italiener, Spanier, Franzosen und andere ihre Sprachen – Bastardsprachen, mit Verlaub – bereichern, schmücken und ihnen höhere Qualität verleihen.

Der Kern dieser Auffassung von der *Twe-spraack*, die, von einer positiven Attitüde in Hinsicht auf die Muttersprache, inspiriert ist von den – in unseren Augen – manchmal kuriosen Ansichten über die Muttersprache in *Origines antwerpianæ* (Antwerpen: Christoffel Plantijn, 1569) und *Opera* (ibid., 1580; s. Dibbets 1985) des Südniederländers Joannes Goropius Becanus (1519–1572/3), ist auch weiterhin vernehmbar in den niederländischen sprachwissenschaftlichen Schriften des 16. und 17. Jh.: Das Niederländische ist eine Sprache mit hohen Qualitäten, aber es steht auf einem zu niedrigen sprachlichen Niveau und daher ist es notwendig sie mittels einer guten Rechtschreibung und einer guten Wortartenlehre, also einer guten Grammatik, zu zivilisieren.

Es war ein großes Problem, daß in den Niederlanden, namentlich am Anfang der Triviumperiode, keine Rede von einer Kultursprache war, welche überall üblich wäre oder derer man sich bedienen könnte: jedermann verwendete Mundart. Im Verlauf der Periode entwickelt sich – auch unter dem Einfluß der (holländischen) Grammatiken und Rechtschreibebücher – eine von der holländischen Mundart dominierte Standardsprache, die von großen Schriftstellern wie Hooft und Joost van den Vondel (1587–1679) und einer sozial höheren Schicht der Gesellschaft verwendet wird und deren Sprachgebrauch als Norm für die meisten der Grammatiker aus der zweiten Hälfte des 17. und aus dem 18. Jh. gelten wird.

In der ersten gedruckten Orthographie des Niederländischen hat Lambrecht sich an seiner Mundart, der Sprache von Gent, orientiert; dabei hat er den Benutzern anderer Mundarten die Möglichkeit geboten, sich bei der Notierung ihrer Dialekte seiner Notierung anzupassen: "schreibe wie du sprichst", "höre der Sprache zu, welche du sprichst". Dasselbe Wort könnte also auf Grund der unterschiedlichen Aussprache in den Dialekten auf unterschiedliche Weise geschrieben werden (*geen* neben *gien* oder *gein*). Dieselbe Vielfalt hat auch Sexagius zugelassen, der eine Orthographie auf der Grundlage der Mundart von Mecheln, oder besser, von Brabant, entworfen hatte. Dabei wünschte er die Orthographie seines Niederländischen mit der des Lateinischen in Übereinstimmung zu bringen. Der erste der Grammatiker, der versucht, eine überregionale Sprache oder Standardsprache zu schaffen, ist Pontus de Heuiter. In seiner *Nederduitse orthographie* erweist er sich als ein Verteidiger der phonetischen Rechtschreibung, und sein Bestreben, sich einer möglichst geringen Zahl von Buchstaben zu bedienen, führt dazu, daß er *ic* oder *ik* anstatt, wie sonst üblich, *ick* schreibt, ebenso *gelike* und *volx* anstatt *ghelijcke* und *volcks*, usw. Wichtiger war, daß er, unter Anerkennung der Realität der Mundarten, nach "einem ordentlichen Niederländisch" strebt: Wie aus dem Ionischen, Attischen, Dorischen und Æolischen das Griechische geschmiedet worden ist, so muß aus den besten Elementen der niederländischen Mundarten eine *Koine* erstellt werden: "also habe ich im Verlauf von fünfundzwanzig Jahren mein Niederländisch aus den Mundarten von Brabant, Flandern, Holland, Geldern und Kleve gebildet". Die *Lingua communis* entwickelte sich im Laufe des 17. Jhs. tatsächlich, aber nicht so, wie es De Heuiter sich gedacht hatte. Die Sprache einer literarischen holländischen Stadtelite, bei der südniederländische und aus anderen Provinzen stammende Elemente zugelassen waren, vermochte sich zur Standardsprache zu entwickeln (s. Van der Wal 1995: 30–36).

Die Orthographie ist ein wesentlicher und umfangreicher Bestandteil (ca. 35%) der ersten Sprachkunst des Niederländischen, der *Twe-spraack*; in den späteren Grammatiken ist die Rechtschreibelehre (relativ) viel kürzer. Der Kern der Rechtschreibevorschläge der *Twe-spraack* war im Jahre 1582 oder 1583 zur Kommentierung den für Experten Gehaltenen in Holland, Flandern und Brabant (also: im Norden und Süden!) vorgelegt worden. Obwohl Mundartenunterschiede in der *Twe-spraack* einige Aufmerksamkeit finden, stellen die Autoren dies doch dar, als ob es sich um eine einheitliche Sprache handelte. Wichtig ist festzuhalten, daß in der *Twe-spraack* für die Rechtschreibung des Niederländischen einige neue Grundregeln formuliert werden: die vorgeschlagene Orthographie ist traditionell und fußt vor allem auf der Regel der Gleichförmigkeit und der Regelmäßigkeit oder Analogie, Grundregeln, welche wir nicht bei Lambrecht, Sexagius und De Heuiter finden. Die Amsterdamer "Rederijkerskammer" wird in der Triviumperiode (und danach) viele Mitkämpfer unter den Verfassern der

Rechtschreibebücher und Grammatiken (Van der Schuere, De Hubert, Leupenius) gewonnen haben, während andere die phonetische Rechtschreibung weiterhin propagierten (Ampzing, Van Heule). So bevorzugt eine Gruppe die Schreibweise *deugd* wegen der Mehrzahl *deugden*, *ik vind* wegen *wij vinden*, und andere, auf Grund der Aussprache, *deugt* und *vint*. Ein radikaler Vertreter der Gleichförmigkeitsregel ist Leupenius: er schreibt z. B. *paalen* wegen der Einzahl *paal* und *dalen* wegen *dal*.

## 3. Das klassische Modell und die Wortarten

Auch was die Lehre der Wortarten (die *Etymologia*) anbetrifft, haben die Autoren der *Twe-spraack* innovative Arbeit geleistet. Zuallererst mußten sie für diesen Teil der Grammatik eine niederländische Terminologie suchen. Eines der Ziele ist damit realisiert worden, welche den Amsterdamern mit ihrem Trivium vorschwebten, zu zeigen, daß das Niederländische als wissenschaftliche Metasprache geeignet war, und so zeigt sich, daß der Aspekt der Funktionserweiterung – wichtig bei der Standardisierung – im Amsterdamer Trivium verwirklicht wurde. Die niederländischen Fachtermini haben die Amsterdamer zum Teil in fremdsprachlichen Wörterbüchern wie im *Dictionarium tetraglotton* (Antwerpen 1562) von Cornelis Kiliaan (1558–1607) oder in Grammatiken für den fremdsprachlichen Unterricht wie der *Cort onderwys* (Antwerpen [1]1571) vom Schulmeister Peeter Heyns (ca. 1537–1598) aus Antwerpen finden können. Andere Fachausdrücke sind mehr oder weniger wortgetreu übersetzt, unter anderem aus *Donati methodus grammatices* (Straßburg o. J.). Übrigens: diese Terminologie schwankte ziemlich. Christiaen van Heule hat in *De Nederduytsche grammatica ofte spraec-konst* (1625) sehr explizit erklärt, daß er die Terminologie verbessert hatte, und auch andere Autoren haben manchmal andere Fachausdrücke gewählt (s. Ruijsendaal 1989; Dibbets 1995). In der *Twe-spraack* ist das lateinische *verbum* mit *woord* übersetzt, gleichzeitig auch von Heyns und De Hubert, während Van Heule *werkwoord* schrieb, den Terminus, der schließlich Usus geworden ist. Auch der Ausdruck *spraakkunst*, der noch lange mit *letterkunst* konkurrieren sollte, womit anfangs (das ursprünglich griechische) *grammatica* oder (lateinische) *literatura* übersetzt worden war, hat Van Heule (1625) wohlbedacht eingeführt, vielleicht nach dem Vorbild des Deutschen Laurentius Albertus oder der *Sprachkünste* (Giessen, 1619) von Christophor Helwich (1581–1617).

Was die Besprechung der Wortarten anbelangt (s. Dibbets 1995), hat man im Prinzip das klassische Modell übernommen, welches man in den Schulgrammatiken von Valerius und anderen fand, die der Tradition von Donat und Priscian folgten; eine Diskussion über die Frage, ob der Artikel eine eigene Kategorie darstellt – sie war in deutschen, englischen und französischen Grammatiken des 16. und 17. Jhs. aktuell –, hat man in den niederländischen Grammatiken nicht geführt. Also sind in der *Twe-spraack* folgende neun Redeteile unterschieden: die veränderlichen Wörter *lid* (Articulus), *naam* (Nomen), *voornaam* (Pronomen), *wóórd* (Verbum), *deelneming* (Participium), und die unveränderlichen Wörter *bywóórd* (Adverbium), *inwurp* (Interiectio), *kóppeling* (Coniunctio) und *voorzetting* (Præpositio).

Auch diesbezüglich hat Van Heule gezeigt, daß er sich durch die Tradition nicht gebunden fühlte: in *De Nederduytsche spraeckonst ofte tael-beschrijvinghe* (1633) hat er alle unveränderlichen Wörter, gerade wegen dieser ihrer morphologischen Eigenschaft zu einer Kategorie zusammengefaßt, den Adverbien. Zwanzig Jahre später trat Leupenius in Van Heules Fußstapfen. Dem heutigen Sprachwissenschaftler fällt in beiden Ordnungen eher die Anwesenheit des Partizips als einer eigenen Kategorie auf als die Abwesenheit des Zahlwortes, eine Situation die bis zur *Nederduitsche spraakkunst* (Amsterdam: J. Allart, 1805) von Pieter Weiland (1754–1842) andauert. Übrigens hat Van Heule nicht nur die Zahl der Wortarten reduziert: 1625 unterscheidet er noch sechs Fälle, wie im Lateinischen; 1633 sind es dann nur noch vier ("wie im Griechischen"), und dies auf Grund der Tatsache, daß nur vier Kasusformen bei den niederländischen Nomina unterschieden werden können. Vielleicht handelt es sich hier um den Einfluß der *Grammatica Germanica nova* (Marburg, 1616) von Stephan Ritter (1589–nach 1637) oder der *Sprachkünste* von Helwich. Noch weiter geht Leupenius, der zwar für das Niederländische die Funktionen aufzeigt, die von der klassischen Einteilung in sechs Kasus zum Ausdruck gebracht werden, der aber der Meinung ist, nur drei Kasusformen unterscheiden zu können. Aber bis

Ende des 18. Jhs. bleibt das lateinische System mit seinen sechs Kasus in der Grammatik des Niederländischen vorherrschend.

Nicht nur Van Heule hat die Fesseln der Tradition gelöst. Auch in der *Twe-spraack* finden wir originäre Meinungen, zum Beispiel bei der Einteilung der Verben nach Konjugationen. Die Einteilung, wie sie in den lateinischen Grammatiken auf Basis der Konjugation des Indikativs des Präsens (*amo, amas – moveo, moves*, usw.) üblich war, war unbrauchbar für das Niederländische, weil (nahezu) alle Verben die gleiche Konjugationsendung zeigen (*ik speel, jij speelt – ik lees, jij leest*). Wie der Deutschen Ölinger sind die Autoren der *Twe-spraack* bei der Einteilung der Verben vom Verhalten des Stammvokals in den unterschiedlichen Tempora ausgegangen, dem Präsens, dem Präteritum, dem Perfekt. Aber während Ölinger 1. Verben mit *ei* oder *ey* im Stamm (*schreiben*), 2. Verben mit *in* (*trincken*), 3. Verben mit *ie, au, ä* oder *e* (*schiessen, saugen, wärfen, helfen*), und 4. den übrigen Verben unterscheidet, wählen die Amsterdamer die Änderung des Stammvokals zum Maßstab. Sie betrachten die Verben ohne Vokalwechsel als die 'normalen' Verben. Die übrigen werden nach der Zahl der Änderungen eingeteilt, die in den unterschiedlichen Tempora im Stamm festzustellen sind. Ihre Einteilung kann man folgenderweise darstellen (a = Stammvokal im Präsens, b = Stammvokal im Präteritum, c = Stammvokal im Partizip):

1. a = b = c (vat – vatte – gevat; weef – weefde – geweven)
2. a = c ≠ b (lees – gelezen – las; lach – gelacht (!) – loech)
3. b = c ≠ a (schreef – geschreven – schrijf; zocht – gezocht – zoek)
4. a ≠ b ≠ c (spreek – sprak – gesproken; doe – deed – gedaan)
5. $b^1$ oder $b^2$ = c ≠ a (zang/zong – gezongen – zing)

Diese Einteilung ist also auf Formen gegründet. Sie beruht nicht auf dem Vorbild der lateinischen Grammatik, sondern auf dem niederländischen Sprachmaterial, welches *in natura* ('im Grunde') eine eigene Ordnung enthält und diese den Grammatikern anbietet, die nach Gesetzmäßigkeiten der Muttersprache suchen. Die Grammatikregeln des Niederländischen können (und müssen) daher aus dem Sprachgebrauch (*Usus*) erschlossen werden.

Diese Meinung finden wir wiederholt in der Triviumperiode in den grammatikalen Schriften des Niederländischen (Dibbets 1995: 19–21). De Heuiter erklärt, er gründe seine *Koine* auf den "Gebrauch", auf der "Praxis", die Autoren der *Twe-spraack* müssen feststellen, daß es auf dem Gebiet der Wortartenlehre an Vorschriften fehle, daß diese aber aus "dem alten allgemeinen Gebrauch" abgeleitet werden können, und Leupenius meldet unumwunden: "der Brauch soll uns Vorschriften machen, nicht der Brauch eines Individuums oder eines begrenzten Landstrichs, aber der Brauch, den man normalerweise im Druck und im täglichen Verkehr findet und der im allgemeinen akzeptiert worden ist". Reformen sind dabei seines Erachtens akzeptabel, wenn es dazu eine rationale Grundlage gibt. Und nicht umsonst erwähnt Kók auf dem Titelblatt seines *Ont-werp*, daß er sein Buch auf den rationalen Gebrauch und den Usus der guten Schriftsteller gründet.

Nicht einmal zwei Dezennien früher hatte Van Heule – dessen beide Grammatiken auf der Rückseite des Titelblattes nicht von ungefähr die Aussage aus Horaz' *Ars poetica* enthalten, daß "bei dem Gebrauch die Macht, die Entscheidung und der Maßstab für die Sprache liegt" – diese Punkte schon angerührt. Er erwähnt ausdrücklich als die zwei wichtigsten Grundlagen seiner Sprachregeln:

1. der Gebrauch (der sich im Laufe der Zeit verändern kann) ist die wichtigste Norm, und daher gehören ungebräuchliche oder artifizielle Formen und Wendungen nicht in eine Grammatik; 2. der Verstand, die *Ratio*, selektiert aus dem Sprachgebrauch, was für grammatikal oder ungrammatikal gehalten werden soll, oder: was man als regulär in der Grammatik aufzeichnen und was man verwerfen soll.

Also, weil *me* ("mir, mich") von Schriftstellern nur selten verwendet wird, verwirft er diese Form; aber er verteidigt die Einführung des äußerst ungebräuchlichen *him* (Dativ Singular) zur Unterscheidung von *hem* (Akkusativ) mit einem Appell an Ahnen von tausend Jahren zurück. Andererseits ordnet der gesunde Menschenverstand an, auf einem an sich unrichtigen, aber eingebürgerten Gebrauch zu beharren, zum Beispiel auf der Schreibweise *huys*, während man *huus* sagt (s. Dibbets 1989), oder regt es ihn dazu an, *derr, heurr*, usw. im dritten Fall des Singulars im Femininum zu schreiben, um ihn vom Genitiv (*der, heur*, usw.) zu unterscheiden. Genauso artifiziell – und also im Widerspruch zu seiner ersten Hauptregel – ist Van Heules

Vorschlag, in der Schreibweise – nicht in der Aussprache! – die Pluralformen des Indikativs und des Konjunktivs dadurch zu unterscheiden, daß er letztere etwa im Präsens nicht mehr als *wij* oder *zij hebben* notiert, sondern als *wij* oder *zij hebbeën*.

## 4. Zeugen des Standardisierungsprozesses

Die niederländischen Rechtschreibebücher und Grammatiken zwischen ca. 1550–1650 zeugen von dem Standardisierungsprozeß, der in bezug auf die Muttersprache in Gang gesetzt ist. Indem die Grammatiker sich in großer Mehrheit auf die Sprache der literarischen Stadtelite der politisch, militärisch, wirtschaftlich und kulturelle wichtigsten nördlichen Provinz, Holland, stützen, wird das kultivierte Holländisch zur Bezugsgröße für die niederländische Standardsprache. Nicht umsonst hat man die Sprache von zwei ganz verschiedenen Amsterdamer Schriftstellern, dem protestantischen hohen Beamten aus Amsterdam Pieter Cornelisz. Hooft (1581–1647) und dem katholischen notleidenden Unternehmer aus den südlichen Niederlanden Joost van den Vondel (1587–1679) in der zweiten Hälfte des 17. und im 18. Jh. den schreibenden Niederländern als Vorbild hingestellt und zur Erstellung der Sprachregeln in Grammatiken und Rechtschreibebüchern als Basis genommen.

## 5. Bibliographie


Bornemann, Ulrich. 1976. *Anlehnung und Abgrenzung. Untersuchungen zur Rezeption der niederländischen Literatur in der deutschen Dichtungsreform des siebzehnten Jahrhunderts.* Assen & Amsterdam: Van Gorcum.

Bostoen, K[arel]. 1984. "Kaars en bril: de oudste Nederlandse grammatica". *Archief van het Koninklijk Zeeuwsch Genootschap der Wetenschappen*, 1–47 (auch separat erschienen: o. P., 1985: Koninklijk Zeeuwsch Genootschap der Wetenschappen.)

Braekman, Willy L. 1978. "Twee nieuwe traktaten unit de vroege zestiende eeuw over de Nederlandse spelling". *Verslagen en mededelingen van de Koninklijke Academie voor Nederlandse taal- en letterkunde*, 294–387. Gent: Koninklijke Academie.

Caron, W[illem] J. H. 1953a. Christiaen van Heule, *De Nederduytsche grammatica ofte spraec-konst.* (= *Trivium* I: 1). Groningen & Djakarta: Wolters (repr. Groningen, 1971).

–. 1953b. Christiaen van Heule, *De Nederduytsche spraec-konst ofte tael-beschrijvinghe.* (= *Trivium*, I: 2). Groningen & Djakarta: Wolters (repr. Groningen, 1971).

–. 1958. Petrus Leupenius, *Aanmerkingen op de Neederduitsche taale.* (= *Trivium*, II). Groningen: Wolters.

Dibbets, G[eert] R. W. 1972. Pontus de Heuiter, *Nederduitse orthographie.* (= *Trivium*, VI). Groningen: Wolters-Noordhoff.

–. 1985. *Twe-spraack vande Nederduitsche letterkunst.* (= *Studia Theodisca*, 17). Assen & Maastricht: Van Gorcum.

–. 1986. "Anthoni Smyters over de spelling van het Nederlands (a° 1613)". *Tijdschrift voor Nederlandse taal- en letterkunde* 102.104–121. Leiden: Brill.

–. 1989. "*Gebruyc en Reden* in *De Nederduytsche spraec-konst* (1633) van Christiaen van Heule". *Gramma* 13.33–56.

–. 1991. A. L. Kók, *Ont-werp der Nederduitsche letter-konst.* (= *Studia Theodisca*, 14). Assen: Van Gorcum.

–. 1994. "Een nieuw spoor van de Port-Royal-grammatica in Nederland". *Verslagen en mededelingen van de Koninklijke Academie voor Nederlandse taal- en letterkunde*, 250–278.

–. 1995. *De woordsoorten in de Nederlandse triviumgrammatica.* Amsterdam & Münster: Stichting Neerlandistiek VU & Nodus.

Goemans, Leo. 1899–1901. "Antonius Sexagius' *De orthographia linguæ belgicæ*". *Leuvensche bijdragen* 3.167–245; 4.65–123. Antwerpen & Leipzig: De Nederlandsche boekhandel & Otto Harrassowitz.

Heremans, J[acob] F. J. & F[erdinand] Vander Haeghen. 1882. Joas Lambrecht, *Néderlandsche spellijnghe.* Gent: Annoot & Braeckman.

Heuiter, de, siehe Dibbets 1972.

Heule, van, siehe Caron 1953a,b.

Klifman, Harm. 1983. *Studies op het gebied van de Vroegnieuwnederlandse triviumtraditie (ca. 1550–ca. 1650).* Dordrecht: Foris.

Kók, siehe Dibbets 1991.

Kridalaksana, Harimurti. o. J. "Der Beginn der europäiischen Grammatik-Tradition in Indonesien: die Wortarten-Einteilung in der malaiischen Sprache von Joannes Roman (1653)". *Gava. Studies in Austronesian languages and cultures* hg. von Rainer Carle et al., 377–390. Berlin: Reimer.

Leupenius, siehe Caron 1958.

Ruijsendaal, E[lise]. 1989. *Terminografische index op de oudste Nederlandse grammaticale werken.* Amsterdam: Stichting Neerlandistiek VU.

–. 1993. Laconis Flandri Presbyteri, *Lingua teutonica exexlex*. (= *Cahiers voor taalkunde*, 9). Amsterdam & Münster: Stichting Neerlandistiek VU & Nodus.

Twe-spraack, siehe Dibbets 1985.

Wal, M[arijke] J. van der. 1995. *De moedertaal centraal. Standaardisatie-aspecten in de Nederlanden omstreeks 1650*. Den Haag: Sdu uitgevers.

Zwaan, Frederik Lodewijk. 1939. *Uit de geschiedenis der Nederlandsche spraakkunst*. Groningen & Batavia: Wolters (repr. Groningen, 1974.)

Zwaan, F[rederik] L. 1957. Jacob van der Schuere, *Nederduydsche spellinge*. (= *Trivium*, II). Groningen & Djakarta: Wolters.

*Geert R. W. Dibbets, Nijmegen (Niederlande)*

# 109. Frühe grammatische Beschreibungen slawischer Sprachen

1. Einleitung
2. Ostslawische Grammatikschreibung
3. West- und südwestslawische Grammatikschreibung
4. Bibliographie

## 1. Einleitung

Versucht man eine Darstellung der frühen grammatischen Beschreibungen slawischer Sprachen, so sind es mehrere Traditionen, die vor der Epoche der wissenschaftlichen Darstellung slawischer Sprachen festzustellen sind, nämlich außerslawische und slawische Traditionen. Im Bereiche der slawischen Traditionen ist es vor allem die kirchenslawische Überlieferung, die lange Zeit wirksam blieb, bei den außerslawischen Traditionen war es vor allem die 'Donatus-Tradition', die zur Abfassung nicht nur westslawischer, sondern auch ostslawischer Beschreibungen geführt hat. Eine neue Etappe der grammatischen Beschreibung slawischer Sprachen ist erst durch die vergleichenden Sprachuntersuchungen gegeben, wie sie vor allem und zuerst auf den Tschechen Josef Dobrovský (1753–1829) zurückgehen, während gleichzeitig der russische Sprachwissenschaftler A. Ch. Vostokov (1781–1864) eine erste systematische Darstellung der slawischen Lautverhältnisse versucht hatte. Sein *Rassuždenie o slavjanskom jazyke* erschien im Jahre 1820. Von weiterführender Bedeutung war dann die vergleichende Darstellung der Grammatik der slawischen Sprachen des Slowenen Franz Miklosich (1813–1891), die in den Jahren 1852 bis 1875 in Wien erschienen ist. Damit ist das 19. Jh. eindeutig der Zeitraum, für den man nicht mehr von 'frühen grammatischen Darstellungen der slawischen Sprachen' sprechen kann.

In der Neuausgabe der *Wendischen Grammatica* aus dem Jahre 1721 von Georg Matthaei, hat Reinhold Olesch im Jahre 1981 die Frage nach der neuzeitlichen Erforschung nationaler Sprachen und deren grammatischer Darstellung vom 16. bis ins 18. Jh. gestellt und ist dabei u. a. zu folgenden Ergebnissen gekommen:

Seit Dionysius Thrax und seiner *techne grammatiké* zeigte die Grammatik normative Tendenzen in ihren Anweisungen zur konkreten Sprachbeherrschung. Die Römer übernehmen und tradieren grammatische Auffassung und Begriffe der Griechen. Die *ars* des römischen Grammatikers Aelius Donatus bleibt für das Mittelalter bis in die Anfänge der Neuzeit vielverwendetes Lehrbuch des Latein. Das hochdifferenzierte Begriffssystem der antiken Grammatik und dessen Terminologie erwiesen sich als klar durchdacht und fundiert, so daß sie – obwohl für das Griechische und Latein zugeschnitten – auch in der grammatischen Darstellung anderer Sprachen bis in die Gegenwart in sichtbaren Spuren erhalten geblieben sind. In der Antike wie im Mittelalter befand sich die Grammatik im Dienste philosophischer Betrachtungsweisen und Spekulationen, sie war somit hilfswissenschaftlich und auf das Phänomen Sprache nur begrenzt sachbezogen. Einen Wandel schuf erst die beginnende Neuzeit, obwohl die Autorität der lateinischen Grammatik weiterwirkte und deren Musterfunktion für die grammatische Darstellung anderer Sprachen durchaus noch nicht verloren ging. An anderer Stelle heißt es bei R. Olesch, daß sich im 16. Jh. im Bereich der grammatischen Beschreibung Tradition und Neuerung in gegenseitiger Toleranz begegneten, Grammatik, Thesaurus und Diktionar seien typische Erscheinungsformen sprachlicher und beginnender sprachwissenschaftlicher Tätigkeiten.

## 2. Ostslawische Grammatikschreibung

In den Darstellungen zur Entwicklung der russischen Grammatikschreibung wird zuerst auf die älteste Grammatik in einer slawischen Sprache überhaupt hingewiesen, nämlich auf die Übersetzung der griechischen Grammatik des Joann Damaskinos durch den Exarchen Joann im 10. Jh. Überliefert ist jedoch nur der Anfang der Grammatik, der die Lehre von den vier Redeteilen enthält, dem Nomen, dem Verbum, Partizipium und dem Artikel, der in der slawischen Darstellung als *različie* bezeichnet wird, also eine "Unterscheidung", oder "Unterschied" bedeutet. Die Donatus-Tradition erreichte Rußland um die Wende vom 15. zum 16. Jh. im Zuge der Bewegung des Humanismus, der über das Baltikum zunächst nach Novgorod kam. Als erster übertrug Dimitrij Gerasimov, genannt "Tolmač", den Donat aus dem Lateinischen ins Kirchenslawische, eine Arbeit, die im Jahre 1522 beendet war. In den Jahren 1489 bis 1535 wird er in Handschriften erwähnt, die von seiner weitreichenden Tätigkeit nicht nur als Übersetzer, sondern auch als Kommentator berichten. Die Übersetzung des Donat hatte Gerasimov an der Ordensschule in Livland durchgeführt, wo er u. a. auch die deutsche und lateinische Sprache erlernt hatte. Die bereits vorhandenen Darstellungen der Grammatik und der Rechtschreibung des Kirchenslawischen wurden von ihm noch durch eine systematische Darstellung der Formenlehre erweitert. Die Regeln der Herleitung slawischer Formen erfolgte nach den logischen Prinzipien des lateinischen Paradigmas, u. a. *tempus unitum* = Präsens, *perfectum*, *imperfectum* usw. Aelius Donatus war bekanntlich ein römischer Grammatiker, der um 350 v. Chr. lebte. Er war der Lehrer des hl. Hieronymus und verfaßte zwei im Mittelalter vielbedeutende lateinische Grammatiken, nämlich die *Ars minor* und die *Ars maior*, ferner verfaßte er Kommentare zu Terenz und Vergil. Die beiden *artes* wurden im Unterricht des Mittelalters so bevorzugt benutzt, daß die lateinische Elementargrammatik ganz allgemein als "Donat" bezeichnet wurde und ein Verstoß gegen ihre Regeln als "Donatschnitzer" bezeichnet wurde. Entsprechend der Bedeutung dieser Grammatiktradition wurden die Schüler mittelalterlicher Lateinschulen auch als "Donatisten" bezeichnet, wobei es sich durchwegs um Fortgeschrittene in der lateinischen Grammatik handelte. Eine erste lateinisch-polnische Ausgabe der *Elementa Donati* erschien im Jahre 1583 ohne Ortsangabe unter dem Titel: *Donati Vetustissimi Grammatici Elementa. Una cum traductione polonica*. Hierbei handelte es sich um die älteste Donatausgabe in Polen mit einer durchgehenden polnischen Übersetzung. Der *Donatus latino-germanicus* von Johannes Rhenius erschien 1646 in einer Bearbeitung des Textes, der neben den deutschen Übersetzungen der lateinischen Paradigmen und Beispiele auch eine fortlaufende Übertragung ins Polnische aufwies. Der Bearbeiter dieser Ausgabe war Christoph Liebruder, ihr voller Titel lautete: *Donatus latino-germanicus, cum R. Dom. Christoph Liebruderi declinationum versione polonica. Editio nova prioribus ejusdem modi correctior …*

Im Jahre 1591 wurde in L'vov in griechischer und kirchenslawischer Sprache von den Studenten der dortigen Akademie eine grammatische Darstellung auf der Grundlage von Adel'fotes vorgelegt, die für die Erlernung des Griechischen und eigentlich nicht des Kirchenslawischen bestimmt war. Der volle Titel dieser Grammatik lautete: *Grammatika dobroglagolivago Ellinoslovenskago jazyka, soveršennaga iskusstva osmi častej slova. Ko nakazaniju mnogoimenitomu Rossijskomu rodu*. Diese Grammatik umfaßte vier Teile, nämlich *Pravopisanie* (= Rechtschreibung), Pripevanie (= Prosodie), *Nravoslovie* (= Etymologie) und *Săčinenie* (= Koordination, Beiordnung). Der Nutzen dieser Grammatik wird u. a. so beschrieben, daß ein leichterer Zugang zur Dialektik, Rhetorik, Musik, aber auch zur Arithmetik, Geometrie und Astronomie gegeben sei.

Im Jahre 1596 wurde eine weitere Grammatik veröffentlicht, ihr Verfasser war Lavrentij Zizanij, sie wurde in Vilna unter dem Titel *Grammatika Slovenska, săveršennago iskusstva osmi častej slova i innych nuždnych, novosăstavlenna L. Z.* gedruckt. Die Beschreibung der Prosodie mit Hilfe von Zeichen über der Zeile für lange und kurze Silben wurde ganz offensichtlich aus dem Griechischen übernommen. Im Bereiche der *Etymologie* wurden acht *Redeteile* unterschieden, nämlich *Različie* (= Artikel), *Imja* (= Nomen), *Mestoimja* (= Pronomen), *Glagol* (= Verbum), *Pričastie* (= Partizipium), *Predlog* (= Präposition), *Narečie* (= Adverb), *Sojuz* (= Konjunktion). Für den Bereich der Beschreibung der Kasus werden genannt: *Imenovnyj* (= Nominativ), *Rodnyj* (= Genitiv), *Zvatel'nyj* (= Vokativ), *Datel'nyj* (= Dativ), *Tvoritel'nyj* (= Instrumental) und *Vinovnyj*

(= Akkusativ). Für den Bereich der Komparation werden die drei bekannten Kategorien *Položennyj* (= Positiv), *Razsudnyj* (= Komparativ) und *Prevyšnyj* (= Superlativ) angeführt. Von Zizanij werden weiter vier Modi angeführt, nämlich *Izjavitel'nyj* (= Indikativ), *Želatelnyj* (= Wunschform), *Molitvennyj* (= Imperativ) und *Neopredel'nyj* (= Konjunktiv). Es schließen sich dann noch weitere Ausführungen über die Konjugationen, die Redeteile, die Orthographie an, wobei besonders die Wiedergabe der Vokale behandelt wurde.

Im Jahre 1619 erschien die Grammatik des Meletij Smotrickyj, gedruckt in Enju bei Vilna. Diese Grammatik, die weit über den ostslawischen Bereich hinaus Bedeutung erlangte, stellte eine Synthese griechischer, lateinischer, ostslawischer und kirchenslawischer Traditionen dar. Seine wissenschaftliche Ausbildung erhielt Meletij, der bis zur Übernahme der Mönchswürde im Jahre 1616 Maksim hieß, in der orthodoxen Schule von Ostrog. Im Jahre 1601 studierte er Philosophie im Jesuitenkolleg in Vilna, in den Jahren 1605 und 1606 begleitete er den jungen Fürsten Solomireckij auf einer Reise durch Europa. Smotrickij hielt sich u. a. auch an den Universitäten Breslau, Leipzig und Altdorf bei Nürnberg auf, er besuchte auch Wittenberg, das Zentrum der deutschen Reformation. Nach dieser Reise schrieb Smotrickij seine Grammatik nieder, gleichzeitig unterrichtete er die kirchenslawische Sprache an der orthodoxen Brüderschule in Vilna. Smotrickij zitierte griechische Quellen, ebenso auch den Donat, u. a. auch Melanchthon. Die Grammatik Smotrickijs bringt neue Erkenntnisse in der sprachwissenschaftlichen Darstellung des Kirchenslawischen, er berücksichtigt auch die westslawische Grammatiktradition, die Ende des 16. Jhs. durch die polnischen lateinischen Grammatiken entwickelt wurde. Zur Moskauer Ausgabe der Grammatik von Smotrickij im Jahre 1648 wurde ein Vorwort über den Nutzen der Grammatik hinzugefügt, am Ende des Werkes finden sich Anmerkungen von Maksim Grek. Der volle Titel der Grammatik lautete: *Grammatiki Slovenskija pravil'noe sintagma. Potščaniem mnogogrešnago mnicha Meletija Smotrickogo, v koinenii bratstva cerkovnoga Vilenskago, pri chrame Sošestvija presvjatago i životvorjaščago Ducha nazdannom, stranstvujuščago, sniskannoe i prižitoe, leta ot vploščenija Boga Slova 1619.* In der Moskauer Ausgabe tritt nun das Russische mehr in Erscheinung, so erfolgt bei mehreren Flexionen und Formen des Kirchenslawischen eine Ersetzung durch russische. Smotrickij teilt die Grammatik in vier Teile ein, nämlich *Orthographie*, *Etymologie*, *Syntax* und *Prosodie*. Er unterscheidet im Bereiche der Etymologie wie Zizanij acht Redeteile. Über die bekannten Genera der Nomina hinaus werden insgesamt sieben unterschieden, nämlich *Vsjakij* (= Jeglicher), u. a. Von den Deklinationen werden die erste, zweite und fünfte später durch Lomonosov übernommen. Es wird deutlich, daß sich Smotrickij auf die griechische Grammatik stützt, dabei aber die Besonderheiten des Altkirchenslawischen nicht außer acht läßt. Wie noch zu zeigen sein wird, hat Smotrikkij's Grammatik sowohl geographisch als auch chronologisch eine ganz weitreichende Wirkung erlangt.

In direktem Zusammenhang mit Smotrickij steht auch die russische Grammatik von Heinrich Wilhelm Ludolf: *Grammatica Russica, quae continet non tantum praecipua fundamenta Russicae linguae, verum etiam manuductionem quandam ad grammaticam Slavonicam.* Ludolf (1655–1712) war ein deutscher Gelehrter und Reisender, der an den Höfen Dänemarks und Englands tätig war. Seine Reisen erfolgten vor allem im Interesse Englands, längere Zeit verbrachte er in Moskau, nämlich 1692–1694. Die Grammatik Ludolfs erschien im Jahre 1696 in Oxford und war Fürst Boris Golicyn gewidmet. Sie stützt sich vor allem auf Smotrickij, weist jedoch viele Fehler auf, vor allem aber blieb sie auf den Bereich der "Etymologie" beschränkt. Angefügt an diese Grammatik finden sich lateinisch-russische Gesprächstexte mit Übersetzung ins Deutsche, eine Zusammenstellung lateinisch-russisch-deutscher Entsprechungen des Wortschatzes, ferner werden grundlegende Begriffe der Naturgeschichte in lateinischer Sprache geschrieben, einige Anmerkungen wurden jedoch auch in deutscher Sprache abgefaßt. Jedenfalls handelt es sich hierbei um die erste gedruckte russische Grammatik, die die russische Volkssprache in eine grammatische Beschreibung mit einbezieht. Die Vorläufer Ludolfs waren alle vorwiegend oder ausschließlich mit Beschreibungen des Kirchenslawischen hervorgetreten. So ist Ludolfs Grammatik von besonderer Bedeutung für die Geschichte des gesprochenen Russischen, da er den Unterschied zwischen Kirchenslawismen und volkssprachlichen, also echt russischen Elementen erkannte. So gab er

u. a. Verzeichnisse speziell russischer Formen in Gegenüberstellung zu ihren kirchenslawischen Entsprechungen. Daß die Russen damals auch schon diese besondere Eigenart ihrer Sprache kannten, bezeugt der Satz Ludolfs, der sich in seiner Grammatik findet: "Adeoque apud illos dicitur, loquendum est Russisce et scribendum est Slavonice." Ludolf beschreibt das gesprochene Russische des späten 17. Jhs. und gibt auch praktische Hinweise zur Aussprache des Russischen während dieser Zeit. Mit der Grammatik Ludolfs liegt nunmehr eine mehr praktisch ausgerichtete Darstellung vor. Um die aktuelle Kommunikation mit russischen Gesprächspartnern zu erleichtern, wurde auch ein besonderes Kapitel unter dem Titel "Phrases et Modi loquendi communiones" beigefügt, wo sich nützliche Hinweise für eine Konversation finden lassen.

Ebenfalls von Smotrickij beeinflußt erscheint das 1731 bei der Petersburger Akademie der Wissenschaften erschienene *Teutsch-Lateinische und Rußische Lexicon samt deren Anfangsgründen der Russischen Sprache*, das auf das deutsch-lateinische Lexicon von E. Weisman zurückgeht. Bei den *Anfangsgründen der Russischen Sprache* handelt es sich um die erste in deutscher Sprache gedruckte Grammatik des Russischen, möglicherweise auch um die erste Grammatik des Russischen überhaupt. Diese Darstellung berücksichtigt auch die Veränderungen der russischen Literatursprache unter dem Einfluß der Petrinischen Reformen. Verfasser dieser grammatischen Beschreibung des Russischen war mit hoher Sicherheit der Russe Valerij Evdokimovič Adodurov, der sich nicht nur als ein hervorragender Kenner des Russischen, sondern auch als eine Persönlichkeit mit philologischer Vorbildung erwies. Lomonosov bezeichnete die Grammatik Adodurovs zwar als äußerst unvollkommen, greift aber in seiner 1755 fertiggestellten russischen Grammatik immer wieder auf ihn zurück. Auch bei Adodurov liegen Einflüsse Smotrickijs vor, u. a. werden von ihm auch die Hauptformen der russischen und nicht mehr nur der kirchenslawischen Wortveränderungen angegeben. Auch von Ludolf dürfte Adodurov Angaben übernommen haben, so die 41 Grapheme des russischen Alphabetes, wobei neben zehn Vokalbuchstaben auch noch drei Diphthonge angeführt werden, wozu Adodurov auch das 'Jat' rechnet. Allerdings fehlt bei Adodurov eine Übersicht über die grammatische Terminologie des Russischen, während Ludolf diese aus Smotrickijs Grammatik aus dem Jahre 1619 übernommen haben dürfte. Bei Adodurov werden vier Genera genannt, nämlich *Maskulinum*, *Femininum*, *Neutrum* und *Omne*. Der Gebrauch des bereits verfallenen Duals wird von ihm für das Russische abgelehnt. Wie bei Ludolf finden sich auch bei Adodurov Hinweise auf die Funktion des Instrumentals als einem Kasus der Nomina. Auch die Darstellung des russischen Verbums dürfte sich stark an Ludolfs Darstellung ausgerichtet haben.

Erwähnt werden muß in diesem Zusammenhang sicher auch Jurij Križanić (1618–1683), der als Schriftsteller und Politiker, vor allem aber als katholischer Geistlicher sich in Rußland für die Union der russisch-orthodoxen und der römisch-katholischen Kirche eingesetzt hat. In seiner 1663–1668 entstandenen *Politika* trat er für eine gemeinsame slawische Sprache sowie für die Einigung aller slawischen Völker unter der Führung des Zaren ein. Križanić, der als "Vater des Panslawismus" bezeichnet wird, wurde 1661–1676 nach Sibirien verbannt, wo er im Jahre 1666 eine russische Grammatik unter dem Titel *Grammatično izkazanje ob russkom jeziku* verfaßte, der methodisch die slowenische Grammatik von Adam Bohorič aus dem Jahre 1584 sowie die lateinische Grammatik von Emmanuel Alvarus zugrunde lagen.

Zu Beginn des 18. Jhs. traten als Konkurrenten der Jesuiten bei der Missionierung Osteuropas die Pietisten aus Halle auf. Einer von ihnen war Ludolf, der nach einer Reise nach Rußland die bereits erwähnte Grammatik der damaligen russischen Sprache zusammenstellte. Ludolf hat auf die russische Grammatik die beschreibenden Grundsätze der europäischen philologischen Tradition übertragen, u. a. zeigt sich bei ihm auch ein neues Verständnis des Infinitivs, der in der griechischen und lateinischen Tradition sich immer in einer Randposition befand, nunmehr aber zum Ausgangspunkt der Darstellung des Verbums gemacht wurde.

Einen ganz entscheidenden Fortschritt in der frühen Beschreibung des Russischen bedeutete die *Rossijskaja Grammatika* von Michail Lomonosov (1711–1765), gedruckt in St. Petersburg bei der Kaiserlichen Akademie der Wissenschaften im Jahre 1755. Lomonosov war ein russischer Gelehrter, zugleich auch Enzyklopädist, Naturwissenschaftler, Schriftsteller, der u. a. auch die Grundlagen für die gegenwärtige russische Literatursprache schuf. Lomonosov kam zu der Überzeugung, daß die "Reinheit des Stils" vor allem von der grundlegenden Kenntnis der Sprache abhänge, die durch das Studium der grammatischen Regeln der betreffenden Sprache erreicht werden könnte. Die Konzipierung der *Rossijskaja Grammatika* war die erste in dieser Art, die überhaupt den wissenschaftlichen Anforderungen entsprach. Die Ausarbeitung der Grammatik war 1755 beendet, sie erschien jedoch erst 1757 im Druck. Sie stellte eine kritische Zusammenfassung aller damals bekannten Veränderungsregeln der russischen Sprache dar, u. a. wurde auch die russische Wortbildung mit berücksichtigt. Die *Rossijskaja Grammatika* hatte einen deutlich normativen Charakter. Lomonosov hat mit dieser Darstellung wohl einen ganz eigenen Typ russischer Grammatik geschaffen. Seine Grammatik zeichnet sich nämlich durch eine strenge Gliederung aus, ebenso durch Vollständigkeit, Differenziertheit und Durchdachtheit der sprachlichen Belege. Lomonosov verwarf ohne Umschweife veraltete Formen und Kategorien des Russischen und richtete seine ganze Aufmerksamkeit auf die Formen der Flexion des damaligen Russischen. Die *Rossijskaja Grammatika* wurde so zu einem der am weitesten verbreiteten Lehrbücher des Russischen zu ihrer Zeit.

Die Auffassungen Lomonosovs finden sich in späteren Darstellungen wieder, so in der Grammatik von N. Kurganov aus dem Jahre 1769: *Rossijskaja universal'naja grammatika ili vseobščee pis'mennoe, pis'moslovie, predlagajuščee legčajšij sposob osnovatel'nago učenija russkomu jazyku, s sed'm'ju prisovokuplenijami raznych učebnych i poleznozabavnych veščej.* Kurganov wurde 1774 Professor an der Akademie der Wissenschaften in St. Petersburg, wo auch eine weitere Auflage des Werkes erschien. Die nach 1757 erschienenen Grammatiken sind alle mehr oder weniger an Lomonosovs Grammatik ausgerichtet, d. h. die Lehre von den drei Stilen, dem niedrigen, mittleren und hohen Stil, spielt auch in den Veröffentlichungen der Akademie eine Rolle, wo auf den spezifischen Gebrauch von Wörtern innerhalb der drei Stilebenen hingewiesen wird. Der Gebrauch der Lehnwörter sollte auf ein Minimum beschränkt bleiben. Dementsprechend sah auch die Sprachkonzeption der Akademiegrammatik von 1802, der *Rossijskaja grammatika sočinennaja Imperatorskoju Rossii Nacii Akademieju* aus. Diese Akademie-Grammatik behandelte Phonetik und Rechtschreibung des Russischen, die "Rechtschreibung" wurde innerhalb der Etymologie behandelt, verschiedentlich erfolgte auch eine Zuordnung zu den drei Stilen. Russische Grammatiktradition bedeutete aber vor allem die Beschreibung der Verbalformen mit Hilfe logisch-philosophischer Kategorien, nämlich *vremja* (= tempus), *zalog* (= Genus), *naklonenie* (= Modus), *vid* (= species), *lico* (= persona). Damit steht auch die russische Tradition in Beziehung zur Entwicklung wechselnder philosophischer, eigentlich metaphysischer Vorstellungen in Westeuropa.

Ziel der Darstellung der Akademie-Grammatik von 1802 ist ein möglichst vollständiges Regelwerk, wobei die Regeln aber oft ungenau geraten und nicht vollständig sind. Hinzuweisen ist auf die Tatsache, daß die Akzentverhältnisse des Russischen hier ausführlich zur Darstellung gelangen. Die Grammatik ist in folgende Kapitel eingeteilt: Orthographie, Etymologie, Syntax, Prosodie. Diese Einteilung entspricht der traditionellen Behandlung einer Grammatik in vier Teilen, wie sie sich bereits bei Smotrickij findet, ebenso auch bei Sokolov. Lomonosov dagegen gliederte seine *Russische Grammatik* in sechs Teile, nämlich: *O čelovečeskom slove voobšče* (Über das menschliche Wort überhaupt), *O čtenii i pravopisanii rossijskom* (= Über das Lesen und die Rechtschreibung des Russischen), *O imeni* (= Über das Nomen), *O glagole* (= Über das Verbum), *O vspomogatel'nych ili služebnych častjach slova* (= Über Hilfswörter oder Hilfselemente des Wortes), *O sočinenii častej slova* (= Über die Zusammenstellung der Teile des Wortes). Bei Lomonosov fehlt dagegen ein Abschnitt über die Prosodie des Russischen.

Die Beschäftigung mit der russischen Sprache aus wissenschaftlicher Sicht wurde unter Katharina II. wesentlich verstärkt, indem diese eine "Kommissija narodnych učilišč" im Jahre 1782 einsetzte, die sich um die Ausarbeitung von Lehrbüchern und Grammatiken bemühen sollte. Von den vorgelegten Grammatiken wurde der von E. B. Syrejčikov der Vorzug gegeben, die 1787 unter dem Titel *Kratkaja Rossijskaja grammatika, izdannaja dlja narodnych učilišč Rossijskoj Imperii* erschienen war.

Was frühe grammatische Beschreibungen außerhalb Rußlands betrifft, so ist Mark Ridleys *A Dictionarie of the vulgar Russian tongue* aus dem Jahre 1599 zu nennen. Hierbei handelt es sich vor allem um ein Vokabular mit etwa 6000 Einheiten, denen eine siebenseitige grammatische Einführung in das Russische vorangestellt war. Anläßlich eines Besuches Peters des Großen in Frankreich im Jahre 1717 wurde auch die *Grammatica russica* von Heinrich Wilhelm Ludolf aus dem Jahre 1696 von Jean Schiers ins Französische übertragen, sie erschien 1724 unter dem Titel *Grammaire russienne*. Für das Jahr 1716 läßt sich der erste Versuch eines Russisch-Niederländischen Wörterbuches von Jakov Vilimovič Brus anführen, er trug den Titel *Kniga Leksika ili Sobranie Rečej po Alfavitu. S Golandskago na Rossiskoi Jazyk. S Rossiskago na Golandskoj Jazyk*. Anzuführen ist schließlich noch Michael Groening mit seiner *Grammatika Russica, eller Grudelig Handledling til Ryska språket*, erschienen 1750 in Stockholm. Diese Grammatik war für Schweden verfaßt worden, sie enthält Gespräche, kurze Erzählungen und ein Wörterbuch.

In Deutschland war es Johann Severin Vater (1771–1826), der im Jahre 1808 eine *Praktische Grammatik der Russischen Sprache* vorlegte. J. S. Vater wurde 1799 Professor der Theologie und der morgenländischen Sprachen zunächst an der Universität Halle, dann 1809 an der Universität Königsberg. Im Jahre 1813 gab Vater ein *Lesebuch der russischen Sprache* heraus, auf ihn gehen auch Überlegungen zur russischen Syntax zurück. Halle als Ausgangspunkt der deutschen Rußlandkunde im 18. Jh. verfügte nämlich als erste Universität über ein russisches und ein polnisches Sprachlektorat. Hier hatten H. W. Ludolf und S. Todorskij als Lektoren für die russische, J. Henning für die polnische Sprache gewirkt. Beide Lektorate waren von Ch. Francke gefördert worden und bestanden mit Unterbrechungen bis zum Jahre 1735. In der bekannten slawistischen Bibliothek des Waisenhauses in Halle befand sich seit 1745 auch das Manuskript *Rudimenta linguae russicae* von Christoph Stahl. Neben polnischen hatte J. S. Vater auch intensive russische Sprachstudien betrieben, so daß er im Jahre 1808 seine russische Grammatik veröffentlichen konnte, in der sich eine ausführliche Auseinandersetzung mit den russischen Verben findet. Vorbild und Vorlage für dieses Werk Vaters war u. a. die *Russische Grammatik* Lomonosovs, die Vater im russischen Original und in der Übersetzung Stavenhagens kannte. Nach Vater kam keine spätere Veröffentlichung an die Darstellung Lomonosovs heran. So wird von ihm auch die *Russische Sprachlehre für Deutsche* von J. Heym kritisiert und in seiner Einleitung in einer Reihe von Punkten berichtigt. Bei Vater findet sich ein Tabellenanhang mit Deklinationen der Substantiva und Adjektiva sowie der Formenlehre der Verben.

Sozusagen den Abschluß der frühen grammatischen Beschreibungen nicht nur des Russischen, sondern auch der anderen slawischen Sprachen stellt Rasmus Rask (1787–1832) dar, der als der Begründer der vergleichenden Sprachwissenschaft gilt. Rask hielt sich zwei Jahre in Moskau und Petersburg auf, wo er u. a. auch Russisch lernte. Ihm war sehr bald deutlich geworden, daß sowohl die slawischen als auch die baltischen Sprachen eine bedeutende Rolle für das Studium des Indoeuropäischen spielten. In seiner 1814 erschienenen epochemachenden Untersuchung über den Ursprung der "alten Nordischen oder Isländischen Sprache" bezog Rask auch Beobachtungen an slawischen Sprachen mit ein.

## 3. West- und südslawische Grammatikschreibung

Bei den westslawischen Völkern dürfte weitaus mehr als bei den Ostslawen die Tradition des Donatus für die Anfänge grammatischer Darstellungen ausschlaggebend gewesen sein. In Böhmen finden sich lateinisch-tschechische Bearbeitungen des *De octo partibus orationis ars minor* von Aelius Donatus. Eine Übergangsstufe zu den zweisprachigen lateinisch-volkssprachlichen Grammatiken bildeten lateinische Grammatiken mit einzelnen tschechischen Glossen. Hierzu gehörte eine Ausgabe der *Rudimenta grammatices* des italienischen Humanisten Nicolaus Perotti, die 1514 in Wien erschienen war. Mit Ausnahme der *Orthographia Bohemica* des Jan Hus führte jedoch keine dieser Schriften über ein Wortverständnis des Lateinischen hinaus. Nach Jan Hus' *Orthographia* erschien 1533 die *Gramatyka Czeska w dwoyj stánce: Orthographia przedom – Etymologia potom*. Die Verfasser dieser grammatischen Darstellung waren Peter Gzell und Beneš Optát, zwei böhmische Theologen. Das Werk wurde in den Jahren 1548, 1598 und 1643 neu aufgelegt. Hierbei handelte es sich um keine Grammatik des Tschechischen, sondern um sprachliche Beobachtungen der beiden Verfasser bei der Übersetzung des Neuen Testamentes ins Tschechische. Bei der Vermittlung der deutschen humanistischen Grammatiktradition nach Osteuropa spielten sowohl Wittenberg als auch Nürnberg eine herausragende Rolle.

Dabei hatte der Einfluß Melanchthons von Wittenberg aus besonderes Gewicht, während die Donat-Überlieferung vor allem von Nürnberg ausging. Eine Kommentierung des Donat liegt vor von Matthaeus Collinus (1516–1566), der Anhänger des tschechischen Hussitismus war. Auf den Prager Humanisten Martin Bocháček schließlich gehen die 1591 und 1594 erschienenen Abhandlungen *Donati declinationum paradigmata* und *Paradigmata conjugationum Aelii Donati* zurück.

In Polen kam die neue humanistische Sicht der grammatischen Darstellung Anfang des 16. Jhs. an der Universität Krakau erstmals zur Geltung, indem 1519 von Stanisław Zaborowski die *Grammatices rudimenta seu octo partium orationis examen* in Krakau erschienen waren. In dieser Darstellung wurde erstmals die polnische Sprache zur Interpretation der Beispiele herangezogen. Zaborowski war der erste Pole, der der Grammatikschreibung in seinem Lande neue Wege aufzeigte. Zu nennen ist aber auch Franz Mymer als Bearbeiter des polnischen Teils des dreisprachigen lateinisch-deutsch-polnischen Wörterbuches *Dictionarium trium linguarum* aus dem Jahre 1528. Im Jahre 1646 folgte die Veröffentlichung des Erstdruckes des *Donatus latino-germanicus* von Johannes Rhenius, der neben deutschen Übersetzungen der lateinischen Paradigmen und Beispiele eine fortlaufende Übertragung ins Polnische aufweist. Der *Donatus latino-germanicus* wurde erneut von Christoph Liebruder bearbeitet. Er war 1592 in Biała geboren, beendete das Gymnasium in Thorn und studierte dann in Königsberg. Dort wurde er 1620 Prediger an der polnischen Kirche und richtete an dieser mit Genehmigung des Kurfürsten eine polnische Schule ein. Zur Erleichterung des Polnischunterrichtes gab er in Danzig die Donatbearbeitung von Johannes Rhenius heraus, in die er polnische Deklinations- und Konjugationsbeispiele einfügte.

Für Bulgarien ist vor allem Černorizec Chrabăr mit seiner Abhandlung *Za bukvite* über das bulgarische Alphabet und die Lautstruktur des Altbulgarischen anzuführen. Die überlieferten Fragmente dieses klassischen Traktates legen auch Zeugnis ab von der energischen Verteidigung des altbulgarischen Schrifttums gegenüber dem nichtbulgarischen im 9. und 10. Jh. Die ältesten Zeugnisse einer grammatischen Tradition bei den Bulgaren sind bei Ioann Ekzarch, dem Bulgaren, zu finden, der aus dem Griechischen die Lehre von den acht Redeteilen übersetzt hatte, die dann in späteren Abschriften aus dem 14. bis 16. Jh. überliefert sind und auch als eigenständige Grammatik herausgegeben wurde. Diese Übersetzung ist auf der Grundlage der weitverbreiteten *Grammatika Slavenskaja* von Meletij Smotrickij aus dem Jahre 1619 entstanden, später umgearbeitet für Südslawen von dem Serben Avram Mrazović und dann noch mehrfach herausgegeben u. a. als *Rukovodstvo k slavenskej grammatice*, erschienen 1794 in Wien. Sehr populär waren im 14. Jh. und später noch in Bulgarien die Reformen des Patriarchen Evtimij im Bereiche des Stils und der Rechtschreibung für das Schrifttum des Zweiten Bulgarischen Reiches. Die sprachlich-orthographische Problematik wurde von der Schule von Tărnovo weiter verfolgt, zu der u. a. auch Konstantin Kostenec gehörte, Verfasser des *Razjasneno izloženie za bukvite* Anfang des 14. Jhs. Patriarch Evtimij, dessen Schule nach Rußland, Serbien, in die Walachei und Moldau wirkte, kam es vor allem darauf an, daß das Altbulgarische sprachlich neben den anderen klassischen Sprachen, dem Althebräischen, Altgriechischen und Lateinischen bestehen konnte. Anzuführen sind weiter sog. *Bukvari*, wo die damals altbulgarischen volkssprachlichen Merkmale verzeichnet wurden, z. B. *Pervoe učenie chotjaščim učitisja knig pismeni slavjanskimi, nazivaemoe bukvar* ..., herausgegeben 1792 in Wien. Im Jahre 1824 erschien in Brașov das bekannte *Bukvar s različni poučenija* von Petăr Beron. Mit der Epoche von Paisij Chilendarski und Sofronij Vračanski war die Zeit gekommen, wo Lehrbücher und Grammatiken des Bulgarischen eine unumgängliche Notwendigkeit geworden waren. Dies gilt für Neofit Rilskis *Bolgarska grammatika*, erschienen 1835 in Kragujevac und die dazugehörenden *Tablici*, 1848 in Bukarest veröffentlicht.

Zusammenfassend läßt sich feststellen, daß die Entwicklungen der frühen grammatischen Darstellungen je nach dem Bereiche der orthodoxen Slaven bzw. den dem romanisch-germanischen Kulturkreis zugewandten Slawen unterschiedlich aussahen. Im Bereiche der Ostslawen ist die kirchenslawisch-altbulgarische Tradition bis in das 17. Jh. hinein vorherrschende Schriftsprache. Die im Jahre 1619 in Vilna veröffentlichte Slawische Grammatik des Meletij Smotrickij behandelt kirchenslawische Elemente und erfüllt damit ihre Aufgabe vor allem in der Ukraine und in Weißrußland, also in Bereichen, die damals zu Polen gehörten. Im Jahre 1648 wird sie auch in Moskau veröffentlicht und im 18. Jh. wird sie von der Moldau aus den Bulgaren und Serben bekannt gemacht. In Rußland war mit Lomonosovs *Rossijskaja grammatika* erstmals eine nationalsprachliche Grammatik veröffentlicht worden, während bei den Serben und Bulgaren die kirchenslawische Tradition durch volkssprachliche Grammatiken erst im 19. Jh. erfolgte, so durch Vuk S. Karadžićs *Pismenica srbskoga jezika po govoru prostoga naroda*, 1814 in Wien veröffentlicht, ein Jahrzehnt später von Jakob Grimm in deutscher Übersetzung mit einem Vorwort erweitert veröffentlicht.

Bei den Slowenen hatte Adam Bohorič 1584 von Wittenberg ausgehend seine *Articae horulae succesivae de latino-carniolana literatura, ad latinae linguae analogiam accommodata* veröffentlicht, wobei der Einfluß der lateinischen Grammatik von Melanchthon zu bemerken ist. Die slowenische Schriftsprache wurde sowohl durch die Bibelübersetzung Jurij Dalmatins als auch durch die grammatische und orthographische Normierung von Adam Bohorič begründet. Im kroatischen Bereich war es Bartholomaeus Cassius, der nach Aufenthalten in Italien im Jahre 1604 seine *Institutiones linguae Illyricae* veröffentlichte und dabei keine Rücksicht auf kirchenslawische Traditionen nehmen mußte wie dies in Serbien bei Vuk Karadžić der Fall war, so daß seine Rechtschreibreform erst mit großer Verzögerung wirksam werden konnte.

Im westslawischen Bereich war bei den Tschechen nach Jan Hus' *Orthographia Bohemica* im Jahre 1406 oder 1412 die tschechische Grammatik von Optát und Gsell im Jahre 1543 erschienen, gefolgt von der im Jahre 1571 von Jan Blahoslav (1523–1571) geschriebenen *Grammatica česká*, die jedoch erst 1857 im Druck erscheinen konnte. 1577 erschien die auf Donatus fußende *Grammatica bohemica studiosis eius linguae utilissima* von Matthaeus Benešovský, während in der darauffolgenden Zeit bis Josef Dobrovský den *Grammaticae ad leges naturalis methodi conformatae et notis numerisque illustratae ac distinctae libri duo* von Laurentius B. Nudožerský eine führende Rolle zukam.

Auch bei den Polen war es die Frage der orthographischen Normierung, die wie bei den Tschechen zu ersten grammatischen Versuchen wie bei Jakób Parkoszowic in Krakau im Jahre 1440 führten. Bereits 1568 folgte die erste polnische Grammatik, verfaßt von Petrus Statorius (polnisch Stojeński) unter dem Titel *Polonicae grammaticae institutio*, fertiggestellt im Jahre 1568. Wesentlich später als bei den Polen entstand bei den Sorben in der Lausitz eine Grammatiktradition. Im Zuge der Reformation im 16. Jh. waren auch grammatische Bearbeitungen des Ober- und Niedersorbischen notwendig geworden. Im Jahre 1679 erschien in Prag eine Grammatik von Jacobus Ticinus mit dem Titel *Principia linguae Venedicae, quam aliqui Vandalicam vocant*. Vorangegangen war im Jahre 1673 die Darstellung *Rudimenta grammaticae Sorabico-Vandalicae idiomatis Budissinatis* von Georgius Ludovici. Die von Georgius Matthaei im Jahre 1721 in Bautzen veröffentlichte *Wendische Grammatica* folgte im wesentlichen den Prinzipien des *Donatus latino-germanicus*, soweit er in der Orthographie und Prosodie der Viergliederung von Rhenius folgte.

Ganz offensichtlich wurde in der Zeit des Humanismus die Grammatik als die Kunst der Anleitung zur Abfassung von Texten betrachtet, damit hatte die Grammatik eine zentrale Aufgabe der Theologie übernommen. Hierbei ging es in erster Linie auch um eine möglichst angemessene Übersetzung von Texten. So ist verständlich, daß die in Südwestrußland entstandenen kirchenslawischen Werke sich vor allem mit Methoden einer möglichst genauen Wiedergabe der grammatischen Information eines Textes befassen, denn grammatische Genauigkeit bedeutete zugleich auch Exaktheit in der Formulierung kirchlicher Dogmen. So wie im übrigen Europa auch beteiligten sich die ukrainischen Gelehrten an Diskussionen, innerhalb derer theologische Fragen ebenso eine Rolle spielten wie grammatische. Erst mit der Überwindung der dominierenden Rolle des Kirchenslawischen im Osten und Südosten, des Lateinischen im Westen der slawischen Völker, konnten sich mit den neuen Literatursprachen auch neue grammatische Traditionen herausbilden.

## 4. Literatur

Bojič, Vera. 1977. *Jacob Grimm und Vuk Karadžić. Ein Vergleich ihrer Sprachauffassung und ihre Zusammenarbeit auf dem Gebiet der serbischen Grammatik.* München: Sagner.

Bulič, Sergej Konstantinovič. 1904. *Očerki istorii jazykoznanija v Rossii 1.* St. Petersburg.

Davydov, I. I. 1856. "Predislovie k novomu izdanije Rossijskoj grammtiki", in: *Rossijskaja grammatika Michaila Lomonosova.* St. Petersburg, I–XLVI.

–. *Spisok slavjanskich i russkich grammatik, izdannych na slavjano-russkom i russkom jazykach.* XLVII–LXXXVI.

Glück, Johann Ernst. 1984. *Grammatik der russischen Sprache.* 1704. Herausgegeben und mit einer Einleitung versehen von H. Keipert, B. Uspenskij, V. Živov. Köln–Weimar–Wien: Böhlau.

Horbatsch, Olexa. 1964. *Die vier Ausgaben der kirchenslavischen Grammatik von M. Smotryc'kyj.* Wiesbaden: Harrassowitz.

–, Hrsg. 1591. *Adelphotes. Die erste gedruckte griechisch-kirchenslavische Grammatik.* L'viv-Lemberg: München Sagner.

Ising, Erika. 1966. *Die Anfänge der volkssprachlichen Grammatik in Deutschland und Böhmen: Dargestellt am Einfluß der Schrift des Aelius Donatus de octo partibus orationis ars minor.* Berlin: Akademie-Verlag.

Olesch, Reinhold, Hrsg. 1981. *Georgius Matthaei: Wendische Grammatica. Buddissin 1721.* Köln–Wien: Böhlau.

Zachar'in, D. B. 1965. *Evropejskie naučnye metody v tradicii starinnych russkich grammatik* (XV–XVIII v.) München: Sagner.

Zasadkevič, K. 1883. *Meletij Smotrickij kak filolog.* Odessa.

*Helmut W. Schaller, Marburg (Deutschland)*

# 110. Early grammatical descriptions of the Celtic languages

1. Background
2. Grammars of Welsh, 1567 to 1621
3. Grammars of Breton, 1659 to 1738
4. Lhuyd's grammar of Cornish, 1707
5. Grammars of Irish, c. 1610 to 1728
6. Shaw's grammar of Scottish Gaelic, 1778
7. Kelly's grammar of Manx, 1804
8. Bibliography

## 1. Background

The Welsh grammars of Gruffydd Robert (1567–1594) and Siôn Dafydd Rhys (1592) as well as the Irish grammars of the Louvain school, foremost among them Bonaventura O'Hosey's (c. 1610), are the first comprehensive works on Celtic languages to correspond to a Latin-based concept of grammaticography. Their approach is significantly different from earlier works in that the formative influence of Renaissance teaching is readily discernible, and all were written by authors who for at least a certain time of their lives, lived abroad and outside their native learned contexts. Earlier works in both Wales and Ireland originated in a native context and were specifically addressed to members of the learned classes of poets; they were not intended as comprehensive grammars, but were "remarkably independent efforts to grapple with peculiarities of the Celtic linguistic and metrical systems" (Matonis 1990: 273) relevant for the poets' professional training and practice (see also Ó hAodha 1991, Ó Cuív 1973). But these tracts too were susceptible to revisions under the influence of Renaissance ideas, Matonis (1990: 273) and Lambert (1987: 28–29) point up the case of Simwnt Fychan's Welsh bardic tract of c. 1575, *Pum Llyfr Kerddwriaeth* ("The Five Books of Poetry") (Williams and Jones 1934: 89–142). Chapters on metrics remained a feature of many grammars of the post-medieval time, in O'Hosey's case significantly written in Irish rather than in Latin as are the other chapters of his grammar (Mac Aogáin 1969: 82–106).

Separate rudimentary descriptions of the Welsh and Irish sound systems respectively are already found in the humanist lexicographer William Salesbury's (1520–1584?) *A briefe and playne introduction how to pronounce the letters in the British tong* of 1550 and in Seaán Ó Cearnaigh's Irish catechism *Aibidil Gaoidheilge & Caiticiosma* of 1571 (Ó Cearnaigh 1994: 58–67, 13–14, 161–163). The grammaticographical tradition in the other Celtic countries (Brittany, Cornwall, Scotland, Mann) emerges after the Renaissance and is motivated mainly by didactic, religious, philological, and antiquarian interests.

## 2. Grammars of Welsh, 1567 to 1621

The humanists' project to apply to the vernaculars the model of Latin grammar proved problematical due to many structural differences between Latin and the objects of their descriptions, in the case of Welsh e. g. the absence of case-forms of nouns and the existence of synthetic and analytic verbal forms. With regard to these two areas Poppe (1991, 1995) has shown that a first phase of experimentation came to an end with John Davies's *Antiquae linguae Britannicae rudimenta* of 1621. His analysis of the literary language has been characterised as 'final' by Morris Jones (1913: v), and Watkins (1963: 145) agrees that "there are very few important differences between Davies's grammar and a good modern Welsh grammar", of the normative and descriptive Latinate mould. However, in the case of the verbal paradigms his description is not comprehensive – it does not provide the analytic formations with a place in the paradigm, but neither did Morris Jones (1913) – and it was "neither immediately nor universally accepted, at least as grammaticographical theory, though it influenced the actual format of the paradigms" of most later grammars (Poppe 1995: 31).

The humanist influence on Gruffydd Robert (pre-1532/post-1598) is obvious from his biography: He left Wales for religious reasons after the Acts of Supremacy and Uniformity in 1599 and lived in Italy for the rest of his life; in 1567 he published his *Dosparth Byrr ar y rhann gyntaf i ramadeg Cymraeg* ("A short exposition of the first part of a Welsh Grammar") in Milan – three further parts were published between 1584 and 1594 (Robert 1939) – in his native tongue and the form of a learned dialogue, and both choices have parallels in works of contemporary Italian humanists (Hays 1988). Robert describes and analyses the structure of Welsh with success (Williams 1973–74: 204); he realizes, for example, that the Latin concept of declensions cannot be applied – though he suggested an alternative solution based on differences in the syllabic structure of the singular and plural of nouns. Williams (1973–74: 204) has stressed that his motivation was

> to show how the living language could be adapted to meet the needs of the times, how it could be enriched, and how its vocabulary could be enlarged so that Welsh poets and writers could translate the Greek and Roman classics in order that they could write treatises on all the subjects that interested the cultured classes in the new world which had been created by the revival of learning.

Siôn Dafydd Rhys (1534–c. 1619), the author of *Cambrobrytannicae Cymraecaeve linguae institutiones et rudimenta* (1592), also spent some time in Italy, between 1556/57 and the early 1570s, where he may have had contact with Gruffydd Robert (Griffith 1953–58: 15–16) and where he published a grammar of Greek, now lost, and treatises on Latin syntax and Italian pronunciation (De Clerq & Swiggers 1991). On the title page Rhys places his grammar into the context of the recent translation of the Bible into Welsh and thus indicates his emphasis on its literary register. His analysis of Welsh has been rightly called "often confused and perplexing" (Watkins 1963: 145), despite, or because of, his attempts at systematising and tabulating the data. He is, however one of the very few Welsh grammarians who systematically tried to accomodate into the paradigms the analytic verbal forms. Poppe (1995: 27–28, 35) has suggested some possible contemporary influences on Rhys's doctrines of tense and mood, as well as the possible inspiration of Greek grammar here and in his orthographic innovations, e. g. *bh* for /v/, instead of *f*.

Henry Salesbury's (1561–1637?) *Grammatica Britannica* (1593) betrays its author's acquaintance with Rhys's grammar, but the formative influence on his approach, and on many details of definition and classification, was Petrus Ramus's Grammatica, first published in 1559 (Poppe 1997). Salesbury participates in what Poppe (1991) has called the Welsh paradigm of declensions. In contrast to Rhys he admits forms of the spoken register. His aim is to provide an introduction to the structure of the language "in usum ejus linguae studiosorum", and it is significant here that unlike Roberts and Rhys he does not treat of metrics. In his preface he points up the qualities of Welsh "quae cum antiquissimis totius Europae linguis lepore, argumento & regularum certitudine certare possit (Salesbury 1593: vii), and the humanists' emphasis on the vernacular is expressed in his addition to the standard definition of grammar: "Grammatica est ars bene loquendi: ut Britannis Britannicè" (Salesbury 1593: 1). Salesbury also attempted to introduce some orthographic innovations, e. g. to abolish consonantal digraphs. His grammatical analysis is not always successful, e. g. his attempt to differentiate verbal phrases with and without pronominal subjects (Poppe 1995: 28–30).

John Davies (1570–1637?), author of a monumental Welsh dictionary and collaborator in the Welsh translation of the Bible, succeeded to solve a majority of the descriptive problems of Welsh grammaticography in his *Antiquae Linguae Britannicae [...] Rudimenta* (1621) within a traditional Latinate framework; Williams (1973–74: 207) has indicated his achievements in the analysis of Welsh syntax. The enhancement of the vernacular's status by drawing constant parallels between Welsh and Hebrew is a characteristic feature of the *Rudimenta*. This focus and his preoccupation with the status and the antiquity of Welsh places the grammar firmly within a Renaissance antiquarian ideology which need to be balanced against his undoubted achievements on the level of descriptive adequacy. Lambert (1976–79: 237) has stressed that his orientation at an Hebrew model was "un antidote à la latinisation" of the dominant grammaticographical tradition.

## 3. Grammars of Breton, 1659 to 1738

Breton grammaticography, which has been discussed comprehensively by Lambert (1976–79), owes its emergence mainly to religious and antiquarian motifs. The first grammar is part of Julien Maunoir's work of religious instruction *Le sacré Collège de Jésus* (1659), which is more readily accessible in M. Williams's close English translation in Lhuyd's *Archaeologia Britannica* (Lhuyd 1707: 180–194; Lambert 1976–79: 232–233). Maunoir's practical sketch was intended "a aider a connoistre aimer & louer Dieu en cette langue" (quoted Lambert 1976–79: 230), but this didactic purpose is lost in the philological context of the *Archaeologia Britannica*. Lambert (1987: 37) has drawn attention to Maunoir's originality and his analytic insights with regard to the syntactic distribution of verbal forms, but he also indicates that the chapter on syntax follows closely the Latin syntax of Despauterius (c. 1460–1520) (Lambert 1976–79: 231). The unpublished grammar of Louis Le Pelletier (1663–1733) as well as his tract "Des Lettres et leur Changement", which also covers the initial mutations, were written between 1716 and 1725 as an appendix to his *Dictionnaire de la langue bretonne* (Le Pelletier 1975: 27–100). The grammar is a revision of Maunoir with only slight changes (Lambert 1967–77); the following remark, however, indicates the direction of Le Pelletier's special etymological and antiquarian interests:

> une Grammaire Bretonne dont la quelle je donne une espece d'etymologies toute nouvelle, dont je n'ai jamais vu d'examples. (Le Pelletier 1975: 16)

This places him into the emerging philological and comparative tradition in the study of language which is concerned not only with describing the grammatical, or lexicographical, system of a language, but also with ideological and antiquarian arguments about its age, its history and relations, and ultimately, its relative status within the hierarchy of languages.

Grégoire de Rostrenen's *Grammaire Françoise-Celtique* (1738) is aimed at French-speaking learners, as are the works of his predecessors Maunoir and Le Pelletier, but unlike them, he was a native speaker and supplies rich data on dialectical variations. His motivation is religious, didactic, and antiquarian. He refers to the potential interest of Breton etymologies to French. His emphasis on "usage", "raison", and "autorité" in his definition of grammar (de Rostrenen 1738: v) places him in a French intellectual tradition. He followed Maunoir in many details, but was also the first Breton grammarian to transcend the Latin/French grammaticographical mould by using Davies's *Rudimenta* (1621). He based the structure of his work and much of his terminology on Davies, and although he may not have been entirely successful in his description, his grammar is a "succès mérité" (Lambert 1976–79: 236) and marks the beginning of a grammaticographical tradition for Breton which was continued in the nineteenth century by Le Gonidec's *Grammaire Celto-Bretonne* (1807).

## 4. Lhuyd's grammar of Cornish, 1707

Edward Lhuyd's (1660?–1709) "Cornish Grammar" in his *Archaeologia Britannica* (1707: 222–253; on Lhuyd's Cornish contacts see Murdoch 1993: 131–140) is the only grammar of Traditional Cornish, which ceased to exist about 1800 as a living community language. All later work was done either by academic philologists or by revivalists as, for example, Henry Jenner in his *Handbook of the Cornish Language* (1904). Lhuyd's work is contemporary with Late Cornish, and he quotes a "Specimen of the Cornish as it's now spoken" (Lhuyd 1707: 251–253), a version of the tale "The Servant's Good Counsels" (Murdoch 1993: 133–134). The numerous comparisons with Welsh in his grammar indicate his philological focus (Williams 1973–74: 209–213). For the description of the Cornish sound system he devised a special system (Lhuyd 1707: 251; Jenner 1904: 54–67). Although Lhuyd knew grammaticographical descriptions of the other Celtic languages and compared the grammatical systems of Welsh and Breton to that of Cornish, his description did not systematically benefit from these models, compare, for example, his treatment of the Cornish case system (Lhuyd 1707: 241; for Breton see Lhuyd 1707: 181), his definition of nominal declensions by characteristic plural endings (Lhuyd 1707: 242–243), or his list of verbal forms (Lhuyd 1707: 246–247; for a possible Breton model see Lhuyd 1707: 186).

## 5. Grammars of Irish, c. 1610 to 1728

The early phase of the post-medieval grammaticographical codification of Irish was dominated by scholars associated with the Louvain school, culminating in Hugh Mac Curtin's *Elements of Irish Grammar* (1728), "in which an attempt at a synthesis of grammatical doctrine is made" (De Clerq & Swiggers 1992: 87). Charles Vallancey (1773) followed their model, and after a period of experimentation in the early nineteenth century John O'Donovan's *Grammar of the Irish Language* (1845) provided a model for most later grammaticography. Ó Briain (1933: 107) has emphasised

> that grammatical work of the Louvain Franciscans was only part of a very big scheme that included the production of an exhaustive dictionary and grammar worthy of the Irish language, undertaken, however, for the practical purpose of helping those missionaries of Anglo-Irish origin, whose knowledge of the language was not adequate to the missionary labours awaiting them in Ireland.

Brother Bonaventura O'Hosey (alias Giolla Brighde Ó hEaghasa/Ó hÉosa, d. 1614) was the first of the Louvain grammarians (for background see De Clerq & Swiggers 1990). His *Rudimenta Grammaticae Hibernicae* (Mac Aogáin 1968: 3–106) was written in Latin, with the exception of the chapter on metrics, and circulated in manuscript only. Modern scholarship agrees that it shows "a combination of the native tradition of the bardic schools and the classical learning of the continental schools" (Ó Cuív 1956: 99–100). He introduced a system of five declensions which became, with slight modifications, the dominant model in Irish grammaticography, and broke "new ground in this attempt to synthesize where his forerunners [the bardic tracts] had analysed" (Ó Cuív 1956: 104). De Clerq & Swiggers (1992: 88–89) have identified his classification of the parts of speech and finite verb forms as further areas in which a Latin-based model is used to supplant a native descriptive paradigm. A short description in Irish of the sound-system and prosodic rules is found in a tract associated with Tuileagna Ó Maolchonaire (Mac Aogáin 1968: 109–142); and both this tract and O'Hosey's grammar were used by Lhuyd (1707: 299–309). The same sources were also exploited by Francis(cus) O'Molloy (alias Froinsias Ó Maolmhuaidh) for his *Grammatica Latino-Hibernica* (1677), published in Rome under the imprint of the Congregatio de Propaganda Fide, with the addition of a work from a Continental learned tradition, Justus Lipsius's *De recta pronunciatione Latinae linguae* (Egan 1955–56). Its grammatical discussion is predominantly discursive and cursory, and lacks paradigmatic organisation (De Clerq & Swiggers 1992: 93–95). Hugh Mac Curtin's (1680?–1755) *Elements of the Irish Language* (1728) continued the Louvain tradition with the intention to codify Irish at a time when its written standard had come under threat and, additionally and in line with contemporary intellectual pursuits, "to render it more familiar to […] lovers of Antiquity" (Mac Curtin 1728: ii). De Clerq & Swiggers (1992: 98–99) have stressed that although O'Hosey's, O'Molloy's and Mac Curtin's grammar originated within the Louvain tradition, they vary subtly in terms of their audience, scope, and intention.

## 6. Shaw's grammar of Scottish Gaelic, 1778

William Shaw's (1749–1831) *Analysis of the Galic Language* (1778) was the first grammar of Scottish Gaelic; his work gained little acceptance, mainly because of his association with Samuel Johnson and his role in the debate about the authenticity of the poems attributed to Ossian (Cram 1996), and was superseded early in the 19th century by Alexander Stewart's *Elements of Galic Grammar* (1801), which was reprinted and revised until 1896. Shaw wanted to codify Scottish Gaelic in "a rational account", "for it has hitherto been left to the caprice and judgment of every speaker, without the steadiness of analogy or direction of rules" (Shaw 1778: xx, xvi), but he also stresses its fashionable antiquarian appeal as "the mother-tongue of all the languages in the west" (Shaw 1778: xxiii). Cram (1996) has described the grammar as 'a characteristically eighteenth-century work'. Although Shaw (1778: xviii–xix) singles out Vallancey's grammar as the most satisfactory of the closely related Irish language, he does not partake in the Irish grammaticographical tradition of five declensions, but, like Stewart after him, set up two declensions, the first characterised by the identity of the nominative plural with the genitive singular, the second by the occurrence of a suffix in the nominative plural.

## 7. Kelly's grammar of Manx, 1804

John Kelly (1750–1809) states in the "Dedication" to his Manx grammar that he wrote it in 1766, i. e. before the publication of Vallancey's Irish grammar, mainly "to assist and direct my fellow-labourers and myself in that arduous and important work, the translation of the Manks Bible" (Kelly 1859: xliv), at a time when the use of Manx as a community language had begun to decline. Thomson (1969: 186–202), in his comprehensive account of the textual history and the characteristics of Kelly's grammar, has stressed Vallancey's influence on the printed edition in "a considerable amount of direct, though unacknowledged, quotation" (Thomson 1969: 188). Kelly (1859: 19) set up five declensions, perhaps following the Irish model, "though there is no similarity in the membership of the proposed declensions" (Thomson 1969: 188). William Gill, the editor of the 1859 reprint of Kelly's *Grammar*, has emphasised the formative influence of a Latinate model on this work and contrasted this with the "modern rule [...] to have just as many cases, and as many moods and tenses, as there are actual variations of the words" (Kelly 1859: iv). It is this tension between a dominant Latinate grammaticographical model and the requirements of descriptive adequacy that characterises the early grammars of the Celtic vernaculars surveyed here.

## 8. Bibliography


Cram, David. 1996. "William Shaw's *Analysis of the Galic Language* (1778): Text and Context", *Linguistics and their diversions. A Festschrift for R. H. Robins on his 75th birthday* ed. by Vivian Law & Werner Hüllen, 245–274. Münster: Nodus.

Davies, John. 1621. *Antiquae Linguae Britannicae, nunc communiter dictae Cambro-Britannicae, à suis Cymraecae vel Cambricae, ab alijs Wallicae, Rudimenta.* Londini: Iohannem Billium. (Repr. in *English Linguistics 1500–1800.* Ed. by R. C. Alston, 70. Menston: Scholar Press, 1968.)

De Clerq, J. & P. Swiggers. 1990. "Het Sint-Antoniuscollege van Leuven". *Museumstrip Leuven* 17.69–75.

–. 1991. "Le *De Italica Pronunciatione et Orthographia Libellus* (1559) de John David Rhys". *Studies in Renaissance Linguistics*, 19–33. Leuven: Department Linguistiek, Katholike Universiteit.

–. 1992. "The Hibernian Connection: Irish grammaticography in Louvain". *Diversions of Galway: Papers on the history of linguistics from ICHoLS* ed. by A. Ahlqvist in collaboration with K. Koerner, R. H. Robins & I. Rosier, 85–102. Amsterdam & Philadelphia: Benjamins.

de Rostrenen, Grégoire. 1738. *Grammaire Françoise-Celtique ou Françoise-Bretonne, qui contient tout ce qui est nécessaire pour apprendre par les Règles la Langue Celtique, ou Bretonne.* Rennes: Julien Vatar.

Egan, Bartholomew. 1955–56. "Notule sur les sources de la *Grammatica Latino-Hibernica* du Père O'Molloy". *Études Celtiques* 7.248–436.

Griffith, T. Gwynfor. 1953–58. "Italian Humanism and Welsh Prose". *Yorkshire Celtic Studies* 6.1–26.

Hayes, Heledd. 1988. "Claudio Tolomei: A major influence on Gruffydd Robert". *The Modern Language Review* 83: 1.56–66.

Jenner, Henry. 1904. *A Handbook of the Cornish Language.* London: David Nutt.

Kelly, John. 1859. *A Practical Grammar of the Antient Gaelic, or Language of the Isle of Man, usually called Manks.* Ed. by William Gill. Douglas: The Manx Society.

Lambert, Pierre-Yves. 1976–79. "Les grammaires bretonnes jusqu'en 1914". *Études Celtiques* 15.229–288, 16.233–236.

–. 1987. "Les premières grammaires celtiques". *Histoire Épistémologie Langage* 9: 1.13–45.

Le Gonidec, J.-F.-M.-M.-A. 1807. *Grammaire Celto-Bretonne.* Paris: Rougeron.

Le Pelletier, Dom Louis. 1975. *Dictionnaire de la langue bretonne suivi de textes littéraires et de quelques études.* Vol. 4. Rennes: Bibliothèque Municipale.

Lhuyd, Edward. 1707. *Archaeologica Britannica.* Vol. 1: *Glossography.* Oxford: At the Theatre. (Repr. with Introduction by Anne and William O'Sullivan. Shannon: Irish Univ. Press, 1971.)

Mac Aogáin, Parthalán. 1968. *Graiméir Ghaeilge na mBráthar Moinúr.* Baile Átha Cliath: Institiúid Ard-Leinn.

Mac Curtin, Hugh. 1728. *The Elements of the Irish Language, Grammatically explained in English.* Louvain: Martin van Overbeke. (Repr. in *English*

*Linguistics 1500–1800*. Ed. by R. C. Alston, 351. Menston: Scholar Press, 1972.)

Maunoir, Julien. 1659. *Le Sacré Collège de Jésus, divisé en cinq classes où l'on einseigne en langue armorique les leçons chrestiennes avec les trois clefs pour y entrer, un Dictionnaire, une Grammarie et Syntaxe en même langue.* Quimper: Jean Hardouyn.

Matonis, A. T. E. 1990. "Problems Relating to the Composition of the Welsh Bardic Grammars". *Celtic Language, Celtic Culture: A Festschrift for Eric P. Hamp* ed. by A. T. E. Matonis & Daniel F. Melia, 273–291. Van Nuys: Ford and Bailie.

Morris Jones, John. 1913. *A Welsh Grammar Historical and Comparative.* Oxford: Clarendon Press.

Murdoch, Brian. 1993. *Cornish Literature.* Cambridge: Brewer.

Ó Briain, Felim. 1933. "The Louvain Grammarians". *Irish Book Lover* 21.107–109.

Ó Cearnaigh, Seaán. 1994. *Aibidil Gaoidheilge & Caiticiosma.* Ed. by Brian Ó Cuív. Dublin: Dublin Institute for Advanced Studies.

Ó Cuív, Brian. 1956. "Grammatical Analysis and the Declension of the Noun in Irish". *Celtica* 3.86–125.

–. 1973. "The Linguistic Training of the Mediaeval Irish Poet". *Celtica* 10.114–140.

O'Donovan, John. 1845. *A Grammar of the Irish Language.* Dublin: Longman.

Ó hAodha, Donncha. 1991. "The First Middle Irish Metrical Tract". *Metrik und Medienwechsel. Metrics and Media* ed. by Hildegard L. C. Tristram, 207–244. Tübingen: Narr.

O'Molloy, Franciscus. 1677. *Grammatica Latino-Hibernica.* Romae: Congregatio de Propaganda Fide.

Poppe, Erich. 1991. "Latin Grammatical Categories in the Vernacular: The case of declension in Welsh". *HL* 18: 2/3.269–280.

–. 1995. "Tense and Mood in Welsh Grammars, c. 1400 to 1621". *Cylchgrawn Llyfrgell Genedlaethol Cymru. The National Library of Wales Journal* 29.17–38.

–. 1997. "Henry Salesbury's *Grammatica Britannica* (1593) and Ramist Linguistic Method". *Studia Celtica Japonica* 9.35–49.

Rhys, Siôn Dafydd. 1592. *Cambrobrytannicae Cymraecaeve linguae institutiones et rudimenta.* Londini: Thomas Orwinus.

Robert, Gruffydd. 1939. *Gramadeg Cymraeg yn ol ar argraffiad y dechreuwyd ei gyhoeddi ym Milan yn 1567.* Ed. by G. J. Williams. Caerdydd: Gwasg Prifysgol Cymru.

Salesbury, Henry. 1593. *Grammatica Britannica in usum ejus linguae studiosorum.* Londini: Thomas Salesburius. (Repr. in *English Linguistics 1500–1800.* Ed. by R. C. Alston, 189. Menston: Scholar Press, 1969.)

Salesburg, William. 1550. *A briefe and a playne introduction, teachyng how to pronounce the letters in the British tong.* London: Roberte Crowley. (Repr. in *English Linguistics 1500–1800.* Ed. by E. C. Alston, 179. Menston: Scholar Press. 1969.)

Shaw, William. 1778. *An Analysis of the Galic Language.* London: Printed for the Author by W. and A. Strahan. (Repr. in *English Linguistics 1500–1800.* Ed. by R. C. Alston, 356. Menston: Scholar Press, 1972.)

Stewart, Alexander. 1801. *Elements of Galic Grammar.* Edinburgh & London: Peter Hill, Vernon & Hood.

Thomson, R. L. 1969. "The Study of Manx Gaelic". *Proceedings of the British Academy* 55.177–210.

Vallancey, Charles. 1773. *A Grammar of the Iberno-Celtic or Irish Language.* Dublin: G. Faulkner, T. Ewing & R. Moncrieffe.

Watkins, T. Arwyn. 1963. "Language and Linguistics". *Celtic Studies in Wales: A survey* ed. by Elwyn Davies, 143–182. Cardiff: Univ. of Wales Press.

Williams, G. J. 1973–74. "The History of Welsh Scholarship". *Studia Celtica* 8/9.195–219.

–. & E. J. Jones. 1934. *Gramadegau'r Penceirddiaid.* Caerdydd: Gwasg Prifysgol Cymru.

*Erich Poppe, Marburg (Germany)*

# 111. Early grammatical descriptions of Finno-Ugric

1. The rise of the Finno-Ugric literary languages
2. The Hungarian pioneers of vernacular grammar
3. The first grammars of the Balto-Finnic languages
4. The early descriptions of Lappish
5. The emergence of comparative linguistics
6. The great research journeys
7. The establishment of the modern comparative research into the Finno-Ugric languages
8. Bibliography

## 1. The rise of the Finno-Ugric literary languages

The peoples speaking Finno-Ugric languages have always constituted a peripheral zone on the linguistic map of the Europe. All these languages are spoken in a vast out-of-the-way territory stretching from the northeast Baltic across Russia to east of the Ural mountains (Sinor 1988). The only exception is Hungarian, whose speakers came from the east and occupied the Carpathian Basin at the end of the ninth century. Nonetheless, in terms of both the length of the tradition and its quality, the comparative linguistic study of Finno-Ugric matches the Indo-European standard, and in some respects it has even been of a pioneering nature.

The Finno-Ugric languages were relatively late in acquiring a written culture. The oldest continuous text written in Hungarian, a funeral sermon and a prayer, dates from around 1200. The second oldest literary language was ancient Zyryan, which was established in the 14th century by Bishop Stephen of Perm. The first texts written in Finnish and in Estonian appeared in the 16th century, in Lappish in 17th century and in other Finno-Ugric languages only later. In all cases, the overwhelming majority of the oldest records were closely connected with religious activities.

In the Middle Ages, there was hardly any demand for linguistic descriptions of illiterate vernaculars spoken by uneducated minority populations, as was the case with most of the Uralic languages. The 'Lingua Franca' of the Catholic Church and of the universities was Latin. In practice, it must have been impossible to avoid the use of vernaculars on certain occasions, e. g. in missionary preaching or when hearing confessions, but these activities could be performed orally only. The grammatical tradition of the vernaculars traces its origins in most cases to practical needs, and those needs did not emerge until a written language had evolved. Variation is a typical and well tolerated phenomenon in spoken language, but in the written form it can cause problems and irritation. The grammatical tradition, especially for normative grammar, is closely connected with the rise of a literary language.

Towards the end of the Middle Ages, the growth of Humanism and the Reformation aroused new interest in vernaculars. The Protestant churches adopted the languages of the ordinary people as their liturgical languages, and thus made it necessary to create a written language, where none already existed, in order to translate sacred texts into the vernacular. At the same time the new invention of printing spread over civilized Europe and made books available for a wider circle of readers.

## 2. The Hungarian pioneers of vernacular grammar

The pioneer of Finno-Ugrian grammars was János Sylvester (1504?–1551?), an university teacher, translator and poet (Szathmári 1968). In the 1520s he studied at the University of Cracow, Poland, participating in a Humanist circle inspired by the ideas of Erasmus Roterodamus, and contributed to the publication of two popular elementary Latin textbooks, *Rudimenta grammatices Donati* (Hegendorf 1527) and *Puerilium colloquiorum formulae* (Heyden 1527), by translating the paradigms, examples, explanations and terms into Hungarian. In the spirit of Humanism it was allowed and even recommended to resort to the native language of the students when teaching Latin, and for this reason the schoolbooks mentioned here contained explanations in German, Polish and Hungarian. As a byproduct, these efforts brought about the first outlines of a Hungarian grammar. Some of the linguistic terms invented by Sylvester are still in use in present-day Hungarian, e. g. *köznév* "noun, common name") and *tulajdonnév* ("proper noun, own name").

In 1536 Sylvester completed his *Grammatica Hungaro-Latina*, which was published in

1539. The explicit intent of this grammar, too, was to teach Latin; and to assure a complete understanding of the peculiarities of Latin, Sylvester illustrated the differences by means of contrast and comparison. In the phonological section, he listed the letters necessary for writing Hungarian in addition to the Latin ones. He also pointed out the opposition of short and long vowels as well as the three different sibilants in Hungarian. In describing pronominal attributives, he emphasized how rich the Hungarian system was: instead of the inflected pronouns one could choose an uninflected definite article, too. In verb inflection, he extended the traditional paradigms by adding the forms with a built-in accusative, i. e. the objective conjugation, which is typical of the Ugric languages.

In the 16th century, written Hungarian was still very heterogeneous, since each author tended to use his own regional vernacular. With his contrastive grammar, Sylvester laid a general foundation for all those writing in Hungarian, and thereby contributed to unifying and standardizing written Hungarian. About the same time, the orthographic rules were codified by Mátyás Dévai Bíró, a Protestant preacher, in his *Orthographia Ungarica.* The political situation was not especially favourable for the development of a uniform standard language, however: the central part of Hungary, including the capital Buda, was occupied by the Turks, the western and the northern parts belonged to the Hapsburgian empire, and only the Transylvanian regions constituted an independent Hungarian realm. On the other hand, it was precisely this geopolitical disintegration that created space for the Hungarian language to be used to a certain extent in literature and in public life.

The first grammar strictly intended as a description of the Hungarian language was *Nova Grammatica Ungarica* by Albert Szencsi Molnár (1574–1634), a Reformed preacher whose literary career (much of it under very difficult circumstances) won respect in Germany and in Hungary. Unlike Sylvester's work, Molnár's Grammatica was not a contrastive description but rather a typological one. Obviously, there were no other Hungarian sources available for him but his own writings, among them a Latin-Hungarian-Latin Dictionary and an improved edition of the Hungarian Bible. His models seem to have been some German vernacular grammars, and the French and Latin Grammars of Pierre de la Ramée (Ramus).

Initially, Latin grammar provided the principal model for any vernacular grammar, and for Sylvester's work, this holds true literally. The model was not inappropriate; basically, the word and paradigm description widely used for Latin was easy to apply to the Uralic languages with their rich morphological system. The problem was that the specific paradigms available within this model did not correspond to the type and the number of categories and subcategories typical of the Finno-Ugric languages. At its worst, the Latin scheme forced grammarians to create artificial categories or to collapse others together in order to make the grammar analogous with the "universal" Latin model.

Sylvester had already commented in his text on this mismatch, but Molnár was bold enough to introduce changes in categorization: the number of cases in his Hungarian grammar was seven, in contrast to the six in Latin grammar. The additional case was the *mutativus*, expressing various kinds of transformations. Molnár displayed the declension table in both the absolute and possessive paradigms, the latter including possessive suffixes in addition to the case endings, as is typical of the Uralic languages. Under numerous "Observatio" headings, Molnár pointed out other characteristics of Hungarian which have only later found their final place in the grammatical system. Significant improvement in the mode of description of Hungarian was to come only in the beginning of the 19th century, with the work of Ferenc Verseghy (1757–1822).

## 3. The first grammars of the Balto-Finnic languages

The next Finno-Ugric language to be described grammatically was Estonian. The author was Heinrich Stahl (c. 1600–1657), a church superintendent in northern Estonia. The language of administration in Estonia at that time was German, which also held a strong position within the Lutheran Church, as the educated class of people was entirely German-speaking. The literary Estonian used for liturgical purposes was thus also deeply influenced by German. For practical reasons, German-speaking clergy and civil servants needed to learn some Estonian, and to help this, the Council of Reval (Tallinn), the capital, commissioned Stahl to produce an elementary description of Estonian. Stahl was born in Estonia, but he knew German better than Estonian and the basis for his grammar was the German grammatical system, which he assumed would be familiar to his readers (Haarmann 1976; Paul 1999: 229–234).

*Anführung zu der Esthnischen Sprach* by Stahl came out in 1637. The text was written in German, but using Latin grammatical terminology, e. g. "Die Consonantes der Ehsten; von der pronunciation und aussrede" (1637: 1). The orthography of Estonian was thus also strongly influenced by German, and for this reason, the written form failed to render the quantitative opposition of short and long phonemes. For declension, the case system was stated to be the same as in German, although the system of six cases used ultimately originated from the Latin grammar. A strange detail was that the genitive (now: *jumala*) and ablative (*jumalast*) were allocated exactly the same form in the singular: *jummalast* "God's; of/from God", presumably due to the potentially identical German translation of both forms using *von*. Stahl's grammar also included a German-based word list of 100 pages, a feature which was often followed in later grammars of Estonian.

In theoretical terms, Stahl's grammar was a rather modest achievement, and his most important work was the bilingual *Hand- und Hauszbuch Für die Pfarherren und Hauszväter* written in German and Estonian (1632–1638). Although this was not the first book printed in Estonian, it was the first time that such an extensive collection of texts had been published in a relatively standardized form for a wider reading public. Thanks to his publications, Stahl is generally respected as the creator of literary Estonian.

The linguistic situation in Estonia was not that simple, however. Dialectal differences between northern and southern Estonian were and still are very significant. Stahl used the northern dialect, spoken in Tallinn and its surroundings, but the southern form of the language had its supporters, too. Religious literature was published in both dialects. In 1648 Johann Gutslaff (?–1657), a German-born minister of the church, published the first grammar of South Estonian, under the name *Observationes Grammaticae circa linguam Esthonicam.* The book was written in Latin, apart from the German-Estonian word list, which has not been preserved in complete form.

Gustlaff had thus studied Estonian as a foreign language, and very successfully. Although he largely followed the patterns established by Stahl, in certain cases he managed to improve the description to do more justice to the real character of Estonian. In his grammar, the number of cases was five: the vocativus was omitted, and the ablativus was replaced by a new case, the rectivus, which Gustlaff had modeled on Hebrew grammar. The name rectivus was chosen to refer to the fact that this case was governed by all the adpositions. In addition, further cases could be formed by attaching supplementary endings (*l*, *lt*, *n*, *nt*, *e*, *st*, *tte*, *to*) to the rectivus. These extra cases were not included in the paradigmatic system, but merely illustrated by means of syntactical examples.

Since the first grammar of northern Estonian had come under sharp contemporary criticism, efforts were made to improve on Stahl's work. Heinrich Göseken, in his *Anführung Zur Öhstnischen Sprache* (1660) was hardly more successful with the grammatical system, but the appendix, *Farrago Vocabulorum*, a four hundred-page German-Estonian dictionary, provided the most extensive lexis written for Estonian in the 17th century. Johann Hornung, in his *Grammatica Esthonica* (1693), improved the orthographic system and brought description closer to contemporary usage by taking his syntactical examples from the vernacular. He also tried to formulate rules for object marking, which is one of the most problematic syntactic features of the Balto-Finnic languages from the learner's point of view.

The earliest grammars of Finnish were written in the first half of the 17th century, although some initial work may have been undertaken in the late 16th century (Korhonen 1986: 12–13). The first completed grammar was a manuscript compiled by Henricus Crugerus (the years of life unknown), the curate in Naantali. This grammar was never printed, and even the manuscript has been lost, but it is mentioned or cited in some linguistic works, e. g. Erik Pontoppidan's *Grammatica Danica.* Crugerus seems to have been relatively successful in escaping from Latin formulas in describing the Finnish case system. The number of cases in his grammar was twelve (modern grammars recognize 14 or 15). He analyzed derived words and tried to give etymological explanations for the suffixes; he also described alternative ways for adapting loanwords, and the metrical form of Finnish traditional poetry (Mark 1949).

Some interesting observations about the structure of Finnish are also included in the key to the map *Orbis arctoi nova et accurata delineatio* published by the Swedish cartographer, Andreas Bureus, in 1626. Bureus noted that there was no grammatical gender in Finnish, that words may not begin with consonant clusters, and that prepositions were positioned after their headwords, i. e. postpositions were used instead of prepositions.

In 1640, the first university in Finland was founded, in Åbo (Turku), *Academia Aboensis*. At that time Finland was a part of Sweden, and the official language of administration was Swedish only. There was no chair or other permanent teaching post in Finnish or Finno-Ugric languages, but the study of Finnish was nevertheless motivated for practical reasons: civil servants and clergymen of Swedish origin who came to work in Finland needed to learn some Finnish and for that purpose they needed grammars and dictionaries. Count Per Brahe, the Governor General of Finland and the founder of the university, instructed the professors to compile some handbooks, and at his request, Aeschillus Petraeus (1539–1657), the professor of theology wrote a Finnish grammar entitled *Linguae Finnicae brevis institutio* in 1649.

Petraeus forced Finnish into the Latin mold, however, and the result was no better than Stahl's achievement in applying the German/Latin model to Estonian. It is clear that Petraeus did not use Stahl's grammar as a model, but had based his description directly on the school grammar of Latin, familiar to any educated person in Finland at that time (Vihonen 1978). The Finnish language described in Petraeus' grammar was the same as that used in the first Finnish Bible, published in 1642, Petraeus being the chief editor, and was based on the southwestern dialects spoken in the surroundings of Turku, the capital. Apocope and shortening of long vowels in non-first syllables are peculiar to these dialects, and these features are for the most part reflected in the written form, resulting in relatively short and compact word forms.

The next attempt to describe Finnish grammatically was *Hodegus Finnicus* by Matthias Martinius (1655–1728), a native speaker of Finnish from Häme, in 1689. Martinius made efforts not merely to copy Petraeus' work, even if the frame remained identical. He slightly improved the orthography and presented many new examples, including elements reflecting his own dialectal background. He also added Swedish translations and explanations.

The first grammarian of Finnish who successfully broke free from the restriction of applying Latin grammar was Bartholdus Vhael (1667–1723), a teacher and clergyman in Ostrobothnia, whose *Grammatica Fennica* came out posthumously in 1733. Using his own dialectal background as a base, he presented the inflectional suffixes and suffix combinations in a more non-reduced form than had been usual before, and made notes on "variationes ex Dialectis" (1733: 92–94). The number of cases was expanded to fourteen. Unfortunately, he included no syntax section; the modern grammatical tradition of Finnish syntactical description started only with Reinhold von Becker's *Finsk grammatik*, published in 1824.

## 4. The early descriptions of Lappish

Lappish had also become an object of linguistic interest in the 17th century, when foundations were laid for language affinity studies. From the beginning, it was taken for granted that Lappish was related to Finnish, and this was adequately demonstrated in 1650 by Michael Wexionius (1609–1670), the professor of history at Academia Aboensis, using a method very similar to the comparative linguistics properly established only much later. The best known description from that time, however, was included in Johannes Schefferus' *Lapponia* (1673), in which one chapter is devoted to the Lappish language.

The Lapps had remained heathens until the 17th century, and in Christian Europe this could not be tolerated. Missionary work was organized by the Scandinavian Lutheran churches, supported by the Swedish and Danish-Norwegian Governments, eager to establish their authority in the remote wilderness. In connection to these efforts, the first grammars of Lappish were written by clergy in northern parishes. The Revd Petrus Fiellström in Lycksele, Sweden, published a grammar and a dictionary of Ume-Lappish in 1738, and a number of religious works, and thus became the founder of the southern Lappish literary language. In 1743 the Revd Henricus Ganander, in Enontekiö, wrote a grammar of Torne Lappish, a subdialect of

Norwegian Lappish. Fiellström's and Ganander's works, both entitled *Grammatica Lapponica*, were basically built on Vhael's model. For Norwegian Lappish, however, a more important contribution was *En Lappisk Grammatica* (1748) by Knud Leem, the principal of the missionary seminary in Trondheim. The material in this copious and rather complex work was later reorganized and published by Rasmus Rask.

## 5. The emergence of comparative linguistics

In 1799, Sámuel Gyarmathi (1751–1830) attested the linguistic affinity of the Finno-Ugric languages by means of grammatical comparisons. As shown above, the western parts of the language family were well documented grammatically, but most of the languages spoken in Russia were still beyond the reach of scholarship. The only exceptions were Cheremis and Votyak, the first grammars of which had been published in St. Petersburg in 1775, entitled *Sočinenija prinadležaščija k grammatike čeremiskogo* vs. *votskago jazyka*. It is not known for sure who the author was, but the most plausible candidate is Veniamin Pucek-Grigorovič (1706–1782), the principal of the seminary at Kazan. A third, analogous grammar was also written for Chuvas, a Turkic language spoken in the neighbourhood of Cheremis and Votyak. In Kiev, Pucek-Grigorovič had studied Latin, and become familiar with the western grammatical tradition. The university library at Kazan held a copy of Donatus' grammar of Latin, translated into Church Slavonic in the 16th century, which may have also served as a model. (Stipa 1990: 204–205.)

The next grammar of Cheremis, *Grammatika gornogo čeremisskogo jazyka*, appeared in 1837, written by Bishop Andrej Al'binskij. Basically, it did not differ greatly from the first one, but it contained a complete representation of the alphabet, which had not been provided earlier. Al'binskij's grammar was based on the western group of dialects, Hill Cheremis, which is the minor of the two main dialects, the other being East Cheremis. Each has subsequently developed its own literary standard form. These main dialects were compared with each other in the article by Hans Conon von der Gabelentz, *Vergleichung der beiden Tscheremissischen Dialekte* (1841b). He also wrote a modest grammar of Zyryan, *Grundzüge der syrjänischen Grammatik* (1841a).

In the early 19th century, the Finno-Ugric language family became the object of systematic comparative study. The starting signal was Rasmus Rask's visit to Turku in 1818. There Rask met Finnish linguists, and spoke warmly in favour of historical studies and created enthusiasm for more effective research into the Finno-Ugric languages. He emphasized how important it was to study the languages in their natural environment. A year later, Rask was in St. Petersburg, where he made contact with Count Nikolaj Petrovič Rumjancev, who had started a research project in Eastern Russia. Rumjancev wanted to have Finnish scholars join the expedition, and Rask recommended a young graduate, Anders Johan Sjögren, who had written a letter to Rask, inspired by his visit to Finland, saying that he wished to devote himself to the historical and linguistic study of Finnish.

In 1824 Sjögren set out on his first expedition, a journey of c. 20,000 kilometres that was to last five years. He travelled to Novgorod, Finnish Karelia, Lapland, and Archangel'sk, and collected materials for Balto-Finnic and Lappish. He was the first researcher to study Vepsian, a minor Balto-Finnic language, and made notes on the Lapp dialect in Kemijärvi, soon to become extinct. He continued eastwards to the Zyryan and Votyak regions, to study the Permic languages. In the Volga area he also made notes about Cheremis. En route, he collected and copied masses of information about languages, folklore, history, geography and archaeology etc. (Branch 1973.) He also revised grammatical manuscripts of some local writers, e. g. the Samoyed grammar of Archimandrite Venjamin and the Permyak grammar of Fedor Ljubimov (Sjögren 1955: 207–208, 213). The latter was printed in 1838.

The most important publication by Sjögren was *Die Syrjänen, ein historisch-statistisch-philologischer Versuch*, which was published only posthumously in 1861. The language section of this book, however, *Über den grammatischen Bau der Sürjänischen Sprache mit Rücksicht auf die Finnische*, had already appeared in 1832 and proved to be much more satisfactory than the first Zyryan grammar, which had been published in 1813. This has been attributed to "A. Flerov" (probably a pseudonym), but in reality, the author may have been Aleksandr Šergin, the pioneer of the New Zyryan literary language (Stipa 1990: 344–345). In his *Zyrjanskaja grammatica* the number of cases recognized was, in the traditional fashion, six, whereas Sjögren distinguished 13 cases. Sjögren's Livonian material was later edited and published by Ferdinand Johann Wiedemann: *Livische Grammatik nebst Sprachproben* came out in 1861, providing the first thorough description of this language.

## 6. The great research journeys

The research undertaken by Sjögren laid the foundations for a totally new era of study, the great expeditions to the Finno-Ugric peoples in Russia, which continued until Russia became the Soviet Union and the frontier between Russia and Finland (since 1809 a Grand Duchy under the Russian Tsar) was closed. In 1827 Sjögren was invited to become a corresponding member of the Academy of Sciences in St. Petersburg, and in 1844 he was appointed permanent academician for Finno-Ugrian and Caucasian languages and ethnology. In this high position, Sjögren was able to help other linguists to organize and finance their journeys; and thus it became the common practice that almost every linguist started his career by undertaking field work among linguistic kin.

The most successful of those explorers was Mathias Alexander Castrén (1813–1852), who set out on his first expedition in 1841, the Samoyed being his main interest of study. He travelled through eastern Lapland and through the regions of European Russia into Siberia, was taken ill with tuberculosis, tried to continue, but was finally forced to return to Finland in 1844. On his route, he studied several languages besides the Samoyed. *Elementa grammatices Syrjaenae* was published in 1844, and the same year he wrote an article on the common origins of the Finno-Ugric and Samoyed languages and managed to prove their linguistic relationship. The next year he published *Elementa grammaticae Tscheremissae*, the manuscript of which he completed in Kazan in 1845.

In Finland Castrén had started to compile a grammar of the Samoyed languages, which he hoped to complete on his next expedition to Siberia in 1845–1849. On the journey he spent a few weeks in Surgut studying Ostyak. The result was *Versuch einer ostjakischen Sprachlehre*, published in 1849. On his journey Castrén investigated all the Samoyed languages (Tundra and Forest Yurak, Yenisey Samoyed, Tavgi, Selkup and Kamassian) but he was unable to publish the grammar himself. In 1852 his health finally failed, and his scholarly remains were left in the care of his friend Franz Anton Schiefner, who edited Castrén's works in a twelve-volume series entitled *Nordische Reisen und Forschungen*. Number 7 in this series, *Grammatik des samojedischen Sprachen*, came out in 1854.

The first grammar of Mordvin was written by Pavel Ornatov, a teacher at the seminary in Tambov, in 1838. The language in this book represented Moksha, one of the two main dialects of Mordvin. Both dialects, Erza and Moksha, have subsequently developed literary languages of their own. Russian grammar was taken as a pattern for Ornatov's grammar, which was not particularly successful in scholarly terms, but useful as a textbook, though strangely enough, this grammar was characterized by A. J. Sjögren as "dangerous rather than useful" (Stipa 1990: 354). Obviously, the level of expectations had risen following the advances in historical and comparative linguistics. The next year, a modest grammatical sketch of Erza was given out by Hans Conon vor der Gabelentz (1839).

## 7. The establishment of the modern comparative research into the Finno-Ugric languages

The first real linguistic research into Moksha was launched by August Ahlqvist (1826–1889), better known as a promoter of written Finnish. On his expedition he collected materials for a study of the verb system in Moksha and a grammar, *Versuch einer Mokscha-Mordwinischen Grammatik* (1861). Prior to this, Ahlqvist had published a concise grammar of Vote, *Wotisk grammatik* (1856), which was the first scholarly investigation of this Balto-Finnic language. Ahlqvist also studied the Ob-Ugrian languages, but the manuscript of the Vogul grammar was published only posthumously in 1894. His Ostyak grammar is still unpublished.

While Finnish linguists kept travelling to the east, Ferdinand Johann Wiedemann remained as a schoolmaster teaching Greek in Tallinn, and studied the Finnish-related languages on the basis of the increasing range of refrence literature available. He also made use of Finno-Ugric informants stationed at the Russian naval base in the city. In 1847 he published a Cheremis (1847b) and a Zyryan grammar (1847a), the latter of which he expanded later with comparisons to Votyak (1884). The material for the Cheremis grammar was taken from the New Testament translated into Hill Cheremis. The grammar of Votyak appeared in 1851, and the grammar of Erza Mordvin was published in 1864. Both dialects of Mordvin were described in a grammar by József Budenz, *Moksa- és erza-mordvin nyelvtan*, published in Hungary in 1877. A little earlier in 1864–1865, Budenz had published a study of Cheremis, *Cseremisz tanulmányok* (Reguly 1864–1865). The first native Cheremis linguist to describe his mother tongue grammatically was Fedor Vasil'ev, whose textbook appeared in 1887.

The Ob-Ugrian branch of the Finno-Ugric languages, especially Vogul (the nearest linguistic kin of the Hungarians), remained in grammatical obscurity until the end of the 19th century. The first linguistic explorer to enter the Vogul area was a Hungarian, Antal Reguly, about the middle of the century, but he concentrated on collecting folk tradition. His compatriot, Pál Hunfalvy, who published a significant part of Reguly's collections, wrote a grammar of the Vogul dialect of Konda based on Georg and Grigorij Popov's biblical translations, in 1872. A more adequate achievement was the morphological description of six different dialects by Bernát Munkácsi (1894), *A vogul nyelvjárások szóragozásukban ismertetve*, the material for which he had collected himself. His Finnish rival collector, Artturi Kannisto, did not even make plans for a grammar. By the end of the century, linguists were increasingly turning their attention to the history of sounds and lexicology, and synchronic grammatical description was no longer accorded status as real linguistic research.

## 8. Bibliography


Ahlqvist, August. 1856. *Wotisk grammatik jemte språkprof och ordförteckning.* (= *Acta Societatis Scientiarum Fennicae*, V: 1–62; 1858.) Helsingfors.

–. 1861. *Versuch einer Mokscha-mordwinischen Grammatik nebst texten und Wörterverzeichniss.* St. Petersburg.

Al'binskij, [Andrej]. 1837. *Grammatika gornogo čeremisskogo jazyka.* Kazan'.

von Becker, Reinhold. 1824. *Finsk grammatik.* Åbo.

Branch, Michael. 1973. *A. J. Sjögren, studies of the North.* Helsinki: Société Finno-Ougrienne.

Budenz, József. 1877. "Moksa- és erza-mordvin nyelvtan". *Nyelvtudományi Közlemények* 13. 1–134.

Bureus, Andreas. 1626. *Orbis arctoi nova et accurata delineatio.* Stockholmiae.

Castrén, M[athias] A[lexander.] 1844. *Elementa grammatices Syrjaenae.* Helsinforsiae.

–. 1845. *Elementa grammaticae Tscheremissae.* Kuopio.

–. 1849. *Versuch einer ostjakischen Sprachlehre nebst kurzem Wörterverzeichniss.* St. Petersburg: Die Kaiserliche Akademie der Wissenschaften.

–. 1853–58. *Nordische Reisen und Forschungen* 1–12. Ed. by Anton Schiefner. St. Petersburg: Die Kaiserliche Akademie der Wissenschaften.

–. 1854. *Grammatik der samojedischen Sprachen.* (= *Nordische Reisen und Forschungen*, VII.) St. Petersburg: Die Kaiserliche Akademie der Wissenschaften.

Dévai Biró, Matthias. 1538. *Orthographia Ungarica.* Krakkó.

Fiellström, Petrus. 1738a. *Dictionarium Sueco-lapponicum.* Stockholm.

–. 1738b. *Grammatica Lapponica.* Holmiae.

Flerov, A. [pseudonym.] 1813. *Zyrjanskaja grammatika.* V Sanktpeterburge.

von der Gabelentz, H[ans] C[onon.] 1839. "Versuch einer Mordwinischen Grammatik". *Zeitschrift für die Kunde des Morgenlandes* Band 2, Heft 2–3. 235–284. Göttingen.

–. 1841a. *Grundzüge der syrjänischen Grammatik.* Altenburg: Pierer.

–. 1841b. "Vergleichung der beiden tscheremissischen Dialekte". *Zeitschrift für die Kunde des Morgenlandes* Band 3, Heft 1. 122–139. Göttingen.

Ganander, Henricus. 1743. *Grammatica Lapponica.* Holmiae.

Gösekenius, Henricus. 1660. *Manuductio ad Linguam Oesthonicam. Anführung Zur Öhstnischen Sprache.* Reval.

Gutslaff, Johannes. 1648. *Observationes Grammaticae circa linguam Esthonicam.* Dorpati.

Haarmann, Harald & Anna-Lisa Värri Haarmann. 1976–77. *Die estnischen Grammatiken des 17. Jahrhunderts I–II.* Hamburg: Buske.

Hegendorf, [Christophorus]. 1527. *Rudimenta grammatices Donati.* Cracoviae.

Heyden, [Sebald]. 1527. *Puerilium colloquiorum formulae.* Cracoviae.

Hornung, Johannes. 1693. *Grammatica Esthonica brevi. Perspicuâ tamen methodo ad dialectum Revaliensem.* Riga.

Hunfalvy, Pál. 1872. "A kondai vogul nyelv". *Nyelvtudományi Közlemények* 9. Budapest.

Korhonen, Mikko. 1986. *Finno-Ugrian Language Studies in Finland 1828–1918.* Helsinki: Societas Scientiarum Fennica.

Leem, Knud. 1748. *En Lappisk Grammatica Efter den Dialect, som bruges af Field-Lapperne udi Porsanger-Fiorden. Samt Et Register over de udi samme Grammatica anførte Observationers Indhold.* Kjøbenhavn.

Ljubimov, Fedor. 1838. *Kratkija grammatičeskija pravila prinadležaščija znaniju Permjatskogo jazyka.* [Sine loco.]

Mark, Julius. 1949. "Die finnische Grammatik von Henricus Crugerus". *Finnisch-Ugrische Forschungen* 30. 55–146. Helsinki.

Martinius, Matthias. 1689. *Hodegus Finnicus, eller Finsk Wägwijsare.* Holmiae.

Molnár Szencsiensis, Albertus. 1604. *1: Dictionarium Latinohungaricum. 2: Dictionarium Ungaro-Latinum.* Norimbergae.

–. 1610. *Novae grammaticae Ungaricae, succincta methodo comprehensae et perspicuis exemplis illustratae Libri duo.* Hanoviae.

–. 1969 [1610/1866]. *Nova Grammatica Ungarica.* With an Introduction by Gyula Décsy. The Hague: Mouton.

Munkácsi, Bernát. 1894. *A vogul nyelvjárások szóragozásukban ismertetve.* (= *Ugor füzetek*, 11; separatum ex *Nyelvtudományi Közlemények*, 21–24, 1890–1894.) Budapest.

Ornatov, Pavel. 1838. *Mordovskaja grammatika, sostavlennaja na narečii Mordvy mokši.* Moskva.

Paul, Toomas. 1999. *Eesti piiblitõlke ajalugu. Esimestest katsetest kuni 1999. aastani.* Eesti Teaduste Akadeemia. Emakeele Seltsi toimetised nr. 72. Tallinn.

Petraeus, Aeschillus. 1649. *Linguae Finnicae brevis institutio.* Aboae.

Pontoppidanus, Ericus Ericii. 1688. *Grammatica Danica.* Hauniae.

[Pucek-Grigorovič, Veniamin.] 1775a. *Sočinenija prinadležaščija k grammatike čeremiskago jazyka.* V Sanktpeterburge: pri Imperatorskoj Akademii nauk.

–. 1775b. *Sočinenija prinadležaščija k grammatike votskago [!] jazyka.* V Sanktpeterburge: pri Imperatorskoj Akademii nauk.

Reguly, Antal. 1864–65. "Cseremisz tanulmányok". Hrsg. József Budenz. *Nyelvtudományi Közlemények* 3. 397–470; 4. 48–105. Budapest.

Schefferus Argentoratensis, Ioannes. 1673. *Lapponia: Id est, regionis Lapponum et gentis nova et verissima descriptio.* Francofurti: Christian Wolff, Anno 1674.

Sinor, Denis, ed. 1988. *The Uralic Languages. Description. History and Foreign Influences.* (= *Handbuch der Orientalistik. Achte Abteilung, 1.*) Leiden: Brill.

Sjögren, Anders J. 1832. *Ueber den grammatischen Bau der Sürjanischen Sprache mit Rücksicht auf die Finnische.* (= *Mémoires de l'Académie Impériale des Sciences de Saint-Pétersbourg*, 6,1.) St.-Pétersbourg.

Sjögren, Joh. Andreas. 1861a. *Livische Grammatik nebst Sprachproben.* (= *Joh. Andreas Sjögren's Gesammelte Schriften*, Band II.) St. Petersburg: Kaiserliche Akademie der Wissenschaften.

–. 1861b. *Die Syrjänen, ein historisch-statistisch-philologischer Versuch.* (= *Joh. Andreas Sjögren's Gesammelte Schriften*, I: 233–459.) St. Petersburg: Die Kaiserliche Akademie der Wissenschaften.

Sjögren, A[nders] J[ohan]. 1955. *Tutkijan tieni.* Käsikirjoituksesta suomentanut Aulis J. Joki [from a Swedish manuscript translated into Finnish by Aulis J. Joki.] Helsinki: Suomalaisen Kirjallisuuden Seura.

Stahl, Henricus. 1632–1638. *Hand- und Hauszbuch Für die Pfarherren und Hauszväter Ehsthischen Fürstenthumbs 1–4.* Riga/Revall.

–. 1637. *Anführung zu der Esthnischen Sprach.* Revall.

Stipa, Günter Johannes. 1990. *Finnisch-ugrische Sprachforschung von der Renaissance bis zum Neupositivimus.* (= *Mémoires de la Société Finno-Ougrienne. 206.*). Helsinki: Société Finno-Ougrienne.

Sylvester Pannonius, Ioannes. 1539. *Grammatica Hungarolatina in usum puerorum recens scripta Ioanne Syluestro Pannonio autore.* Neanesi.

–. 1968 [1539.] *Grammatica Hungaro-Latina.* With a Foreword by Thomas A. Sebeok. (= *Indiana University Publications, Uralic and Altaic Series*, 55.) The Hague: Mouton.

Szathmári, István. 1968. *Régi nyelvtanaink és egységesülő irodalmi nyelvünk.* Budapest: Akadémiai Kiadó.

Vasil'ev, Fedor. 1887. *Posobie k izučeniju čeremisskogo jazyka na lugovom narečii.* Kazan'.

Vhael, Bartholdus. 1733. *Grammatica Fennica.* Aboae.

Vihonen, Sakari. 1978. *Suomen kielen oppikirja 1600–luvulla.* (= *Studia philologica Jyväskyläensis, 11.*) Jyväskylä: Jyväskylän yliopisto.

Wexionius, Michael O. 1650. *Epitome descriptionis Sueciae, Gothiae, Fenningiae et subiectarum provinciarum.* Aboae.

Wiedemann, Ferdinand Joh. 1847a. *Versuch einer Grammatik der syrjänischen Sprache nach dem in der Übersetzung des Evangelium Matthäi gebrauchten Dialekte.* Reval.

–. 1847b. *Versuch einer Grammatik der tscheremissischen Sprache nach dem in der Evangeliumübersetzung von 1821 gebrauchten Dialekte.* Reval.

—. 1851. *Grammatik der wotjakischen Sprache nebst einem kleinen wotjakisch-deutschen und deutsch-wotjakischen Wörterbuche*. Reval.

—. 1865. *Grammatik der ersamordwinischen Sprache nebst einem kleinen mordwinisch-deutschen und deutsch-mordwinischen Wörterbuche.* (= *Mémoires de l'Académie Impériale de Sciences de Saint-Pétersbourg*, 7,9,5.) St. Petersburg: Akademie der Wissenschaften.

—. 1884. *Grammatik der syrjänischen Sprache mit Berücksichtigung ihrer Dialekte und des Wotjakischen.* St. Petersburg.

*Kaisa Häkkinen, Turku (Finland)*

# XIX. The Normative Study of the National Languages from the 17th Century Onwards
# Das normative Studium der Nationalsprachen ab dem 17. Jahrhundert
# L'étude normative des langues nationales à partir du fin du XVIe siècle

## 112. Die Accademia della Crusca und die Standardisierung des Italienischen


1. Situierung
2. Theoretisch-pragmatischer Rahmen
3. Etappen der Entwicklung
4. Das *Vocabolario*
5. Wege der Standardisierung
6. Bibliographie


### 1. Situierung

Als Anfang moderner Sprachstandardisierung in Europa kann mit guten Gründen das Erscheinen des *Vocabolario dell'Accademia della Crusca* (1612) angesehen werden: nicht dass dieses als lexikalische – und damit wohl einprägsamste – Realisierung plötzlich und von einem Moment zum andern eine neue kulturelle Zielsetzung gebracht und damit den Wunsch nach vermehrter sprachlicher Einbindung der Individuen in nationale und gesellschaftliche Zugehörigkeit erfüllt hätte – solche Tendenzen bestanden schon lange –, sondern weil nun modellhaft, in Wirkung und Gegenwirkung, erst in Italien, dann in Frankreich und Europa überhaupt, nicht mehr weg zu denkende Folgen sich zeigen sollten. So wurde das *Dictionnaire de l'Académie française* (1694), trotz Unterschieden im Resultat, zuerst einmal in Anlehnung an die Methoden der *Crusca* konzipiert, und bis heute folgt der Typ der grossen Sprachwörterbücher – auch der französischen und grosser Dialekte, (wie der romanischen in der Schweiz, des Venezianischen in Boerio und des Neuprovenzalischen Mistrals) – ihrem Prozedere der Definitionen, Belege und Distinktion der Sinne.

Wie, aus welchen Wurzeln und in welchem theoretischen Paradigma das Wörterbuch der *Crusca* in Italien entstanden ist, wie es in seiner Geisteshaltung derjenigen der französischen Klassik entgegenstand, wie damit zwei Sprach- und Kulturverständnisse sich entwikkelten, wie beide auch in Italien sich entgegenstehen, sei unser enger umrissenes Thema.

### 2. Theoretisch-pragmatischer Rahmen

Das Sprachverständnis der *Crusca* ist auf dem Hintergrund römischer Rhetorik und Grammatik, verflochten mit Mythisch-Biblischem und philosophischer Reflexion der Griechen gewachsen. Hinzugekommen war für die Sprachen der Romania die Problematik der mindestens den Gebildeten erfassbaren Nähe eines genetisch verwandten Lateins. Das Italienische hatte in diesem Spannungsfeld ein schwer entwirrbares Durch- und Gegeneinander lateinischer wie vulgärer Rede- und Schreibpraxis entwickelt, das theoretisch als Opposition von Kunst und Natur, Regel und Ungeregeltem, Vorbestimmtem und Vergänglichem gedeutet wurde, und sich terminologisch in der Synonymie *Grammatica* "Grammatik" wie auch "Latein" (der in Italien *Volgare* "Volkssprache" wie "vulgär" zur Seite trat) abzeichnete. Zur Überwindung dieser Konzepte kam es mit Albertis *Prima grammatica* des Florentinischen (± 1440) und der Gleichstellung ein Jahrhundert später der Sprachen (und Dialekte) in Speronis *Dialogo delle lingue* (± 1535). Den Strukturalismus des 20. Jhs. vorausnehmend wendet sich die Aufmerksamkeit der Gelehrten den Eigenheiten (*proprietà*) der Sprachen zu.

Theorie und Pragmatik trafen sich: Donats Grammatik und Ciceros Rhetorik wurden auf mittelalterliche Verhältnisse, Sprach- und Stillehre auf die neuen Idiome übertragen (Heinimann 1987); Guido Faba schuf für Bolognas Studenten gleichlaufende Briefmuster in Latein und *Volgare* (± 1243); Guido d'Arezzo spickte *Rime* und Briefe mit kunstvollen Figuren (Baehr 1957); volkssprachliche Grammatiken nach lateinischem Vorbild lehren das Provenzalische und seine Regeln der Dichtung (Uc Faidit 1225–1246, Raimon Vidal 1190–1213): noch im Cinquecento, nachdem Bembo der Sprache der Trobardors ein Buch der *Prose* gewidmet hatte, wird Varchi Uc Faidit übersetzen. Auch Neuerungen trugen bei, die Kluft zwischen Latein und *Volgare* zu überbrücken, so der *Cursus*, ein an der Kurie entstandener und im Briefstil genutzter Komplex rhythmischer Satzschlüsse, der auf die volkssprachliche Literatur übergriff: die Werke Dantes wie Boccaccios, ob lateinisch oder in *Volgare*, sind damit durchsetzt (Parodi 1957; Schiaffini 1973). Anderseits etablierte sich um Dante, Boccaccio, Petrarca nun bald, wie um die Texte der *aurea latinitas*, das philologische Sammeln nachzuahmender Ausdrücke und Stileme (*Elegantiae*) und der Buchdruck: Die Editionen des *Decamerone*, in Restitution von Sprache und Text, sind eine direkte, im *A' lettori* denn auch explizit genannte Vorstufe des Wörterbuchs der *Crusca*.

## 3. Etappen der Entwicklung

Retrospektiv treten uns Etappen einer Entwicklung vor Augen, die vielleicht als solche im Moment nicht zu erkennen waren. In einer allgemein als "Anfänge" (*Origini*) bezeichneten Zeit kamen neben Religion und Polis (Angleichung des Ausdrucks zwischen der Handelsmacht Venedig und ihren Korrespondenten, Eindringlichkeit der Akzente umbrischer *Laudi* und der Predigt Barsegapès) vor allem zwei sprachbildende Prozesse zur Wirkung: der Siegeszug der sizilianischen Lyrik, unter direktem Einfluss des Provenzalischen (seiner *Razos de trovar* und seiner Stileme) durch Italien, konvergent zu dem des altfranzösischen Epos und höfischen Romans, die Attraktivität Bolognas und seiner Universität als Schmelztigel studentischer Nationen und Idiome. Aus Bologna sind, neben Fabas *Epistole* und *Parlamenta* (Gaudenzi 1889), die Vertragskompendien (*Memoriali*), deren offen bleibende Räume Notare mit der Niederschrift zeitgenössischer sizilianischer und toskanischer Lyrik füllten; dort entstand jener *Dolce stil novo*, der von Guicciardini auf Dante und auf Florenz, die andere Handelsmacht und Stätte aufblühender Kultur, übergehen sollte.

### 3.1. Dante

In einer für die damalige Zeit einmaligen Synthese überführte Dante die überkommenen Traditionen und die neue Praxis in eine explizite Theorie. Wie er im *Convivio* die Philosophie der Antike mit der christlichen versöhnte und das "Brot seines Wissens" muttersprachlich denen eröffnete, die des Lateins nicht kundig waren, so vermittelte er zwischen Latein und *Volgare*, jedem seine Stellung zuweisend. Im *De vulgari eloquentia* entwarf er auf der biblischen Grundlage der Namensgebung Adams und der babylonischen Verwirrung eine Klassifikation der Sprachen der damals bekannten Welt; die romanischen ordnete er in Erkennung lexikalischer Identitäten zum Latein; für Italien breitete er in umfassendem Panorama konkrete dialektale Daten aus. Latein und *Volgare* treten nun in die Gegensätze 'Universal-Diversifiziert' und 'Artifiziell-Natürlich'; er strebt eine immer noch natürliche aber für Italien universale Sprache an, Ausdruck der Menschen in ihrem Denken und Fühlen. Selbstredend beinhaltet dieses Ziel eine erste Normierung: die ideale Sprache ist eine komposite Vereinigung des Besten aller verschiedenen *Volgari*. In Hinsicht auf Stil und Kunst überführt er zugleich den aus provenzalisch-sizilianischer Tradition stammenden Konzeptualismus der Dichtung – abschreckendes Beispiel in Dantes Sicht Guittone d'Arezzo – ins Individual-Emotive. Die Vorzugsstellung des Lateins wird auf dieser Grundlage im muttersprachlichen *Convivio* umgestürzt und das ganze Gebäude im *Paradiso* (XXVI 130ss) zeichentheoretisch – nicht ohne Rückgriff auf Horaz (*Ars poetica* 58ss.) – abgestützt: Natürlichkeit der Sprachkraft, Konventionalität und Mutabilität der Sprachen sind die Themen: Varchi wird sich dessen im *Ercolano* erinnern.

### 3.2. Die Sprachenfrage

Damit hatte Dante schon zu Anfang des 14. Jahrhunderts den Grund für die 'Sprachenfrage' (*Questione della lingua*) gelegt, gegen das Latein einen Entscheid zu Gunsten der Volkssprache gefällt – weder in Frankreich noch in Spanien wäre derartiges denkbar gewesen (Marzys 1996: 127; Eberenz 1996: 143) – und recht eigentlich auch den Streit um deren zu wählende Variante vorprogrammiert, nachdem er sich theoretisch für die Mischsprache entschieden hatte, in der Praxis aber sein grösstes Werk, die *Divina Commedia*, florentinisch schrieb. Es ging in der nächsten Etappe folgerichtig um die Wahl zwischen *lingua cortigiana* – in *intercourse* gewachsene, von Castiglione im *Cortigiano* ($^{3}$1524) propagierte Sprache des Hofs –, Florentinisch der *Tre corone* (Bembo 1525) – Gegenstück der *latinitas aurea* –, oder der Zeit (Machiavelli 1525; Gelli, Giambullari 1550).

### 3.3. Die Medici

Die nächste Etappe ist nicht so sehr linguistisch als politisch bestimmt: Cosimo I. de' Medici, Herzog von Florenz 1537–1574, Grossherzog der Toscana nach der Eroberung Pisas 1569, sucht die Vormacht in Italien. Er wirft das Prestige der florentinischen Schriftsteller, Kunst und Sprache in die Wage, gründet die *Accademia Fiorentina*, ruft den exilierten Varchi nach Florenz zurück und begünstigt ihn über alle Massen, macht ihn zu seinem Sprachrohr. Seinem Sohn Francesco überreichte 1548 Giambullari das Manuskript *De la lingua che si parla e si scrive in Firenze*; wohl auf das hin gibt Cosimo 1550 der Akademie den Auftrag, eine Grammatik und ein Wörterbuch zu verfassen; das führt nicht weiter als zur Einsetzung einer Kommission und zur Publikation der genannten Schrift Giambullaris mit einem vorangeschickten *Ragionamento infra M. Cosimo Bartoli & Giovan Batista Gelli sopra le difficoltà di mettere in regole la nostra lingua*; 1564 nimmt Salviati in einer akademischen Rede,

> nella quale si dimostra la fiorentina favella e i fiorentini autori essere a tutte l'altre lingue, cosí antiche come moderne, e a tutti gli altri scrittori di qual si voglia lingua di gran lunga superiori,

das Thema auf, 1572 wiederholt Cosimo sein Verlangen nach "Regeln der [wie es fortan heissen sollte] toskanischen Sprache"; 1583 vermittelt Salviati einer unter dem Namen *Crusca*, "Kleie", gebildeten "Akademie" – deren Ziel vorerst war, in spielerischen Diskursen und Polemik 'Spreu und Korn' zu trennen – die Aufgabe neu; ihr Augenmerk richtet sich bald mehr auf die Erstellung eines Wörterbuchs (eine Art Grammatik hatte Salviati unterdessen mit den *Avvertimenti della lingua sopra'l Decamerone* selbst an die Hand genommen); 1612 erschien endlich das *Vocabolario degli Accademici della Crusca*. In Siena war inzwischen ein Lektorat für Toskanisch geschaffen worden, in dem 1589 Diomede Borghesi zu wirken begann.

### 3.4. Varchi, Borghini, Salviati

Allgemein ist bekannt, dass Speronis *Dialogo delle lingue* auf Du Bellays *Défense et Illustration de la langue française* (1548) wirkte, und wie Du Bellay Speronis philosophisch-linguistische Thesen auf die literarische Kreation und das Vorhaben der *Pleiade* ummünzte. Wenig damit verknüpft wurde der eben genannte, vergleichbare Ruf zur Aufwertung der nachmaligen "italienischen" Sprache Salviatis in der *Accademia fiorentina*. Inspirator war – wie wohl auch das einleitende Stilem *Tutte le cose* zeigen sollte (Bascetta 1969) – Benedetto Varchi, der mit Speroni von Padua (und einer gemeinsamen Mitgliedschaft bei den *Infiammati*) her befreundet war, dahinterstehende Autorität natürlich Cosimo de' Medici. Varchi (1503–1565) kann als einer der bemerkenswertesten Theoretiker der Zeit angesehen werden, der in seinem 1570 veröffentlichten aber durchaus schon zu Lebzeiten bekannten *Ercolano* nicht nur die *Questione della lingua* differenziert behandelt, sondern auch allgemeinsprachliche Distinktionen (wie *Sprachkraft, Sprache, Rede*) formuliert hat, die Gabelenz und Saussure nahe kommen (Engler 1975, 1982–83). Seine Position ist die der kultivierten, zeitgenössischen Variante des Florentinischen, der latinisierend-philologischen Tradition noch durchaus verbunden, aber essentiell auf den mündlichen Sprachgebrauch einer von "Stadtgraben und Mauern umschlossenen" Bevölkerung abstellend. Wobei dieser Gebrauch normierend dem "Missbrauch" des Pöbels (*infima plebe*) entgegengestellt und auch von der Sprache der Ungebildeten (*idioti*) abgehoben wird; er setzt als Sprache der *non-idioti* und *letterati* den möglichen Rückgriff auf Latein und Griechisch voraus.

Ein Gespann mit Varchi bildete Vincenzio Borghini (1513–1580), Prior des *Ospedale degli Innocenti*. Historiker und Philologe, wie jener sehr um die Probleme der Sprache bemüht, zu welchen er bemerkenswerte Notizen hinterliess (Woodhouse 1971), vertrat, was die *Questione* angeht, auch er die Linie des gesprochenen Florentinischen, schaffte aber zugleich mit seiner sprach- und textkritischen Ausgabe des *Decamerone* (erste *Rassettatura*, 1572) und den *Annotazioni* dazu (Deputati 1574) eine sichere Basis zur literarischen Sprachimitation.

Lionardo Salviati endlich (1540–1589), unbemittelter, aus der Nebenlinie einer mächtigen, mit den Medici mehrfach verschwägerten Familie stammender Gelehrter, markiert laut Trabalza den Höhe- und Endpunkt der damaligen Sprachenfrage. Einzig Buommattei und seine Grammatik fügen Neues hinzu. Früh Sekretär Varchis, dessen literarisch-sprachliche Autorität – Guarini und Tasso unterbreiteten ihm ihre Werke – nicht aber die Gunst des Fürsten er erben sollte, trat er auf seine Art in die Nachfolge Borghinis ein, dessen ersten *Rassettatura* des *Decameron* er 1582 eine zweite folgen liess, ihrerseits von sprachlichen *Avvertimenti* (1584–86) begleitet. Die Eigenheit seiner Stellung ist, eine grundlegende Identität der Sprache des Trecento und des Cinquecento zu postulieren; zwei Gebrauchsebenen, als *uso* des Volks und *buon uso* der Schriftsteller, anzunehmen, wobei der "gute Gebrauch" eine Abschöpfung und Perpetuierung des jeweils besten Teils des naturgemäss flüchtigen mündlichen "Gebrauchs" (*uso*) des Volks darstellt; den *uso* nicht mehr den *letterati* sondern den *idioti* zuzurechnen, die Latein und dergleichen nicht können und damit die Eigenheiten der Muttersprache unverdorben bewahren; im Gegenzug (am Beispiel Boccaccios) eine künstlerische Gestaltungskraft der Schriftsteller anzuerkennen, die selbst das an sich Schlechtere (so die vielen Latinismen) annehmbar machen und adeln kann; eine daraus resultierende komplexe Sprachentwicklung, die das neu im Volk Erwachsende und das durch den Schriftsteller Gestaltete kombiniert; eine Triplizität von drei semiologischen Prinzipien im Sinne a) der Eigengesetzlichkeit einer von Ursprung an dem Volk und seinem Belieben anheimgestellten Sprache, b) der Forderung nach purem Abbild-Charakter der Schrift, die nur und getreu die Lautung wiederzugeben hat, c) der Anerkennung einer Kreativität der Kunst im ästhetischen Streben (Wohlklang, Rhetorik, Poetik).

## 4. Das *Vocabolario*

Das *Vocabolario degli Accademici della Crusca* erschien 1612 versehen mit den Privilegien des *Sommo Pontefice*, des *Re Cattolico*, der *Serenissima repubblica di Venezia*, der Fürsten und Potentaten in- wie ausserhalb Italiens, der *Maestà Cesarea*, des *Re Cristianissimo* und des *Arciduca Alberto*. Papst und Kaiser also, die Könige Spaniens und Frankreichs, Venedig, Italien, Oesterreich und Europa standen an seiner Wiege. Gewidmet war das Werk *Concino Concini, Primo Gentil'huomo della Camera del Re Cristianissimo, Governatore di Perona, Roye, e Mondidir, e della Città, e Cittadina d'Amiens, e Luogotenente generale di S. Maestà in Piccardia*, einem durch die Gunst Marias de'Medici und ihres königlichen Gatten vom Abenteurer zum mächtigsten Mann Frankreichs emporgestiegenen (nach Henris Tod dann gleichfalls ermordeten) Florentiner. Schon elf Jahre später erschien eine zweite "durchgesehene und erweiterte" Ausgabe, "unter Beifügung vieler Wörter der Autoren des guten Jahrhunderts und einer bedeutenden Anzahl solcher des Gebrauchs", dem Kardinal Barberino, *nipote di Urbano VIII.*, gewidmet.

### 4.1. Die Einführung *An die Leser*

Salviati war 1589 gestorben. In seinen *Avvertimenti* hatte er auf ein bereits von ihm begonnenes Wörterbuch hingewiesen. Was, wenn das wahr sein sollte, daraus geworden ist, entzieht sich unserer Kenntnis. Dass er aber eine bestimmende Kraft in der Ausrichtung des *Vocabolario della Crusca* gewesen ist, bestätigt die der ersten wie auch der zweiten Ausgabe fast gleichlautend vorangesetzte Einführung "*A' lettori*", wo die Grundsätze dessen, was wir als erste Sprachnormierung im modernen Eurpa ansehen, formuliert sind. Die einstimmige Meinung Bembos, der Deputierten zur Korrektur des *Decamerons* 1573 und die Salviatis – in der Form des Kompromisses, den die *Avvertimenti* geben – ist angerufen, wonach die Sprache ihren Höhepunkt zwischen 1250 und 1350 erlebt habe; danach sei der Niedergang gefolgt; doch wie der alte "*buon uso*" aus dem "*uso*" des Volks erstanden sei, so sei Wertvolles wiederum im modernen Gebrauch entstanden, was das Wörterbuch nützen müsse, ansonst die Sprache verarme. So bestätige sich auch die Einheit des alten und neuen *Volgare*, die Salviati (Anhang *Avv.* Band I [Buch 1–3]) über das Experiment der modernen Nacherzählungen des *Re di Cipri* [*Decamerone* I 9]) bewiesen habe. Die gemeinsame Einschätzung der Schriftsteller wird angeführt und fürs Detail auf Salviatis Beurteilung in *Avv.* 2. Buch Kap. 12 verwiesen; zur Orthographie beruft man sich auf das dritte Buch, dessen Richtlinien (nicht von ungefähr) analog zum Vorwort der zweiten *Rassettatura* wiedergegeben sind; in Fragen der Grammatik ist Band II zuständig.

In der Struktur des Wörterbuchs sind alphabetische Ordnung der Lemmen, Sinndefinition und Textbelege – fürnehmlich aus Werken des guten Jahrhunderts – das oberste Prinzip. Wohl eine Anspielung auf die doppelte Forderung Cosimos de'Medici nach Wörterbuch und Grammatik ist die nicht selbstverständliche Behauptung, das *Vocabolario* stelle dieserart das beste Mittel dar, die Sprache zu fördern, indem es "leicht und vergnüglich deren vollkommene Kenntnis" vermittle. Mit anderen Worten: dadurch, dass das Wörterbuch Beispiele paradigmatischer Wahl, syntagmatischer Zuordnung und stilistischen Gebrauchs der Wörter vermittle, sei es eben Grammatik. Gleichsetzung von Grammatik und Texten ist übrigens auch in Salviatis akademischer Rede von 1564 zu belegen. Für "Sprache" steht "la nostra lingua" und "questo idioma", im zweiten Fall also ein rein deiktischer Ausdruck, ohne explizite Antwort darauf, ob es sich nun um Italienisch, Toskanisch oder Florentinisch handle, um gesprochene Rede oder literarische Kunst, um aktuellen oder traditionellen Gebrauch. All das ist letztens auch dem Prozess der Normierung innewohnend und eher final resultierendes als zu Grunde gelegtes Objekt. Für das zeitgenössische Verständnis wird zudem in der Namensfrage auf Varchis Klarstellung zurückzugreifen sein, wonach Florentinisch, Toskanisch und Italienisch sich gleich zueinander verhalten, wie Individuum, Spezies, und Gattung (im Beispiel "Cesare-Mensch-Lebewesen"); die Epochenfrage löst sich für die Akademiker der *Crusca* in der Annahme einer überdauernden Synchronie, welche den Akzidenzien, denen Sprechweisen (*linguaggi*) im Laufe der Zeit unterliegen, nicht Rechnung zu tragen braucht; Gebrauchsebenen werden, wo für nötig empfunden, durch Kennzeichnung (*modo basso, qui è metafora, voce latina*) spezifiziert, und ausdrücklich wird betont, plebejische und burleske Sprechweisen habe man nicht ausschliessen wollen, da

> auch sie zur Perfektion der Sprache beitragen und die Bequemlichkeit jener sie erfordert, die ihrer für ihre Schriften bedürfen.

Eigentümlich ist endlich die Lösung, die für zeitgenössische Wörter und Redensarten gefunden wurde: sie sind dadurch kenntlich, dass sie ohne Autorenzitat oder [nur] mit dem Zitat eines modernen Autors stehen, und sind so weit als möglich ausserhalb der alphabetischen Ordnung (aber mit Verweis aus ihr) an den Schluss verwandter Lemmen des traditionellen Gebrauchs gestellt (was eine paradigmatische Rehabilitierung des hierarchisch Ausgeschlossenen darstellt) und ihre in den Augen der Kompilatoren doch erhebliche Zahl wird im Sinne der Supplementarität *uso/buon uso* folgendermassen gerechtfertigt:

> Es ist [...] zu bemerken, dass wir neben den in den Autoren jenes guten Jahrhunderts gefundenen Wörtern sehr viel andere im Gebrauche haben, die jene Schriftsteller vielleicht nicht Gelegenheit hatten [!], zu brauchen; uns aber schien es gut, davon Kunde zu geben, damit unsere Sprache hierin nicht verarme; so haben wir einige von ihnen registriert und zu ihrer Bestätigung haben wir zuweilen das Beispiel einiger von uns als die besten erachteten modernen Autoren hingesetzt [...]. Noch haben wir es vermieden, diese auch dort zu zitieren, wo das Wort alter Autoren arm an Belegen war, oder wo das moderne Beispiel die Kraft jenes Wortes lebendiger ausdrückte oder dieses in abgewandeltem Sinne gebraucht worden ist.

Besondere Beachtung wird endlich der jeweiligen Sinndefinition und der Unterscheidung der Sinne geschenkt. Letztere ist für die Zitate Ordnungsprinzip. Die Definition soll nicht gelehrt sondern volksnahe sein; wo solche in den exzerpierten Texten gefunden wurden, sind sie in der Beispielreihe (jeweils an erster Stelle) mitzitiert. Spezieller Gebrauch – wie oben hinsichtlich der Metapher erwähnt – wird angezeigt. Fragen der Grammatik werden mit angegangen. Die Umfänglichkeit dessen, worüber das *A' lettori* sich Gedanken macht, und das Beabsichtigte (wenn auch nicht immer Erreichte) beeindruckt.

### 4.2. Zur Tradition der Wörterbücher

Über "die italienischen Wörterbücher von den Anfängen bis zum Erscheinen des *Vocabolario della Crusca*" hat Tancke 1984 berichtet. Seine Bestandesaufnahme ein- und zweisprachiger Wörterbücher (S. 11–88) und Analyse der sprachgeschichtlichen Entwicklung im 16. Jh. (S. 91–156) schliesst die *Crusca* ein. Es findet sich so (S. 102s.) eine Aufstellung der 'Schwerpunkte' unter den von Pier della Vigna (1249) bis Tasso (1595) exzerpierten Autoren im *Vocabolario*, in Luna (1536), Alunno (1543), Porcacchi (1584), Montemerlo (1566) und Pergamini (1602–17). In einem Anhang (S. 157–230) vergleicht Tancke zudem die Erhebungen des

Wortfelds Pflanzenbezeichnungen in der *Crusca* mit den englisch-italienischen (1598–1611) des seiner Einschätzung nach bedeutendsten Verfassers zweisprachiger Wörterbücher des 16./17. Jhs., Florio. Den archaischen Charakter der *Crusca* sieht er insbesondere bestätigt, wenn man bedenke,

> dass zusätzlich zu den in der Tabelle verzeichneten Autoren die *Tavolo dei citati* [sic!] [...] noch über 100 weitere Namen und Titel von Dichtern und Werken des 13. und 14. Jahrhunderts aufweist, die bis zu diesem Zeitpunkt noch von keinem Lexikographen exzerpiert worden waren (S. 104).

Er muss aber S. 369 auch anerkennen, dass

> erst der Aufbau des Wörterbuchs der Crusca [...], was Gliederung und Übersichtlichkeit betrifft, eher Anforderungen, wie sie auch an ein heutiges Wörterbuch gestellt werden, [entspricht],

und zu den Pflanzenbezeichnungen schreibt er:

> Im Vergleich untereinander gehen die einsprachigen Wörterbücher vor Florio von einer sehr schmalen Basis aus: Boccaccio, Petrarca und Dante. Der Bereich der Botanik und damit die Zahl der verzeichneten Pflanzen nimmt erst mit den Werken Pergaminis und v. a. der Crusca zu. Die Akademiker exzerpieren nach Pergamini als erste auch naturwissenschaftliche Arbeiten in grösserem Umfang [...]. Im wesentlichen ist der verzeichnete Umfang jedoch literarisch ausgerichtet. Diese Tendenz in den italienischen Sprachwörterbüchern hat sich bis in die Neuzeit weitgehend erhalten. Der überwiegend literarische Charakter kennzeichnet auch die heutigen Sprachwörterbücher der italienischen Schriftsprache. So bleibt mancher Fachterminus auch in einem als umfassend geltenden Wörterbuch des 20. Jahrhunderts, wie dem Grande Dizionario della Lingua italiana von Salvatore Battaglia, unberücksichtigt, trotz unbestreitbarer Fortschritte des Werkes in dieser Hinsicht (S. 160).

Selbst in Verkennung des unterliegenden Sprachmodells der *Crusca* – das, wie hier dargelegt, weniger Bembo zuzuordnen ist, als meistens angenommen wird –, ist ihr also ein fortschrittlicher Charakter nicht abzusprechen; nicht abzusprechen ist ihr auch ihr Vorbildcharakter, wobei die starke Beachtung der Realia – trotz expliziter literarischer Bestimmung – geradezu erstaunlich scheint. Das nicht literarische sondern auf gesprochene Sprache ausgerichtete *Dictionnaire de l'Académie française* hat demgegenüber die Realia ausgeschlossen und in ein *Dictionnaire des arts et métiers* verbannt.

Aus dem gleichen Blickwinkel heraus hat Bielfeld 1996 die "Methoden der Belegsammlung für das *Vocabolario della Crusca* exemplarisch vorgestellt am lexikographischen Werk Francesco Redis" dargestellt. Die Untersuchung betrifft hauptsächlich die dritte und die vierte Ausgabe des Wörterbuchs, Ausgangspunkt sind aber natürlicherweise – Zannoni 1848, Marconcini 1910 und Parodi 1974/83 zugrunde legend) – die erste (*Entwicklung der Richtlinien zur Sammlung von Belegen bis 1612*, S. 2–6). Besondere Beachtung verdienen hierbei Tagebuchblättern des *Archivio della Crusca* (A-3) entnommene Regeln, welche sich die Akademiker gaben. Darin wird die Stossrichtung der *Crusca* weiter deutlich gemacht, so (14. April 1597):

> 6. I termini dell'arte si dichiarino tanto che comporta il vocabolario. 7. Allegare in pro dell'uso Bembo, Casa, Poliziano, Lorenzo de'Medici e simili, secondo il giudicio de'deputati. 8. Il mettere i proverbi si rimette al giudicio de'deputati, purche s'usini parcamente. 9. L'uso si metta quello che può abbellire e arricchire la lingua, secondo la discrezione di chi scrive (S. 4, N. 13).

Im Gegensatz zur vergangenheitsgerichteten Rückschau kann hier auch ein gegenwarts- und zukunftsträchtiger Geist herausgelesen werden. In den Richtlinien zur Neubearbeitung des *Vocabolario* (2. Ausgabe) wurde schliesslich auch eigene Kreativität ermutigt:

> Faccisi diligenza di metterci tutte le voci del nostr'uso, con l'esempio d'autori moderni, trovandosi in essi. E, non si trovando, dopo la definizione data, si aggiunga qualche esemplo composto di fantasia, per maggior dichiarazione (S. 5: *Archivio della Crusca*, cod. VII, Bl. 68).

### 4.3. Gestaltung der Artikel

In der *Einführung an die Leser* der *Crusca* sind zur Verdeutlichung des Vorgehens Beispiele von Artikeln angesprochen. Solche näher anzusehen lohnt sich. So etwa MANEGGIARE und MANGIARE. Der Eintrag zieht jeweils eine Definition und eine "Etymologie" nach sich: keine Etymologie natürlich im heutigen Sinn sondern eine bedeutungsmässige, nur unter Umständen auch historisch-lautlich nahekommende Entsprechung. Hier sind es "*Toccare, e trattar con le mani.* Lat. *tractare, attractare*" und "*Pigliar cibo, e mandarlo masticato allo stomaco.* Lat. *edere, vesci*". Es folgen die Belege: für MANEGGIARE "Amm[aestramenti] ant[ichi]. *Meglio è maneggiare i suoi mali, che gli altrui*" und als *uso*-Zusätze "Di qui MANEGGIO nome. Lat. *negotium. Flos 32. Onde essere in un gran maneggio, essere in un gran traffico, e negocio di grande affare*" Das *Flos Italicae linguae* ist eine Sprichwort- und Redensartsammlung, auf welche die *Crusca* sich eingestandenermassen gerne beruft. Nach einem Paragraphenzeichen, immer als Beleg modernen Gebrauchs: "Maneggiare un cavallo, è l'ammaestrarlo, che fa il cavalcatore: e MANEGGIO il luogo deputato, per maneggiarlo". Man erkennt das heutige deutsche Lehnwort *Manege*, französisch *manège*. 'Am alphabetischen Platz', das heisst in diesem Falle unmittelbar folgend, vor MANELLA, erscheint der 'eigene Eintrag' "MANEGGIO Vedi MANEGGIARE". Seinerseits hat MANGIARE vier Belege aus dem *Decameron*, einen aus Dantes *Purgatorio*, einen aus dem *Volgarizzamento* der *Genesis*. Nach dem Paragraphenzeichen kommt "*Per metaf[ora]*" eine längere Stelle aus Villani, in der *mangiare* im Sinn von "*consumare, togliendo le facoltà*", also "auszehren, der Habe berauben" zu nehmen ist. Dann RIMANGIARE "*di nuovo mangiare*" als *uso*, belegt im *Morgante*. Auch hier alphabetischer Verweis (unter R). Ihren eigenen Eintrag haben (morphologisch gesondert) substantivisches MANGIARE, und MANGIAFERRO, MANGIATA, MANGIATOIA, MANGIATORE. Der monumentale *Tommaseo-Bellini*, des 19. Jhs., verfährt gleich, ist überhaupt – bis in die Beispiele – stark von der *Crusca* abhängig. Battaglia nützt die Errungenschaften der modernen Etymologie und präsentiert ein stupendes Material, eigenartigerweise freilich in einer Illusion aesthetischer Durchdringung, die der Identifikation von Sprache und Literatur, wie sie sich das Cinquecento vorstellte, gar nicht so fremd ist (vgl. Heinimann 1964 und Tankkes oben zitierte Bemerkung zu seinem 'literarischen' Charakter).

Lange epilogieren liesse sich über die Definitionen des Sinns. Ein in die Nachzeit der *Crusca* weisender Vergleich liefert bei Battaglia als generellste Bestimmung von MANEGGIARE/MANEGGIO "Uso, impiego manuale di qualcosa (in particolare di utensili, di attrezzo, di strumenti, ecc.) secondo una determinata tecnica, per lo più applicata con perizia, con abilità". Das auf Manzoni ausgerichtete *Novo Vocabolario* Broglios hat "Tenere in mano e tra le mani una cosa girandola e rigirandola prolungatamente". Das selbe gab für MANGIARE "Dell'omo e di tutti gli animali, Introdurre nel corpo gli alimenti, facendoli passare dalla bocca allo stomaco". Die Katze war für die *Crusca* ein "bekanntes Tier, das man im Haus hält, der speziellen Feindschaft wegen, die es gegen die Mäuse hegt, auf dass sie sie töte"; Broglio spricht gelehrt von einer "Art Karnivoren aus der Familie der Feliden" um sich gleich noch über Herkunft, Aussehen, Trächtigkeit usw. auszulassen (14 Zeilen!). Viel kritisiert wurde die *Crusca* wegen SPECCHIO "Einseitig bleiunterlegtes Glas, in das man schaut, um darin durch Reflex das eigene Bild zu sehen". – SPEGLIO "Specchio":

> perchè il Vocabolario non serve solamente per i toscani, ma i romani, i milanesi, i napoletani, i franzesi, gli svizzeri, e gl'indiani ancora, come sapranno questi che si può dire *datemi lo specchio*, e non si dee dire *datemi lo speglio*, quando troveranno che *speglio* e *specchio* è tutt'uno? (Magalotti, Brief an Redi, 7. 11. 1677, zit. Migliorini 1961, S. 452).

Für ihre Zeit und ihr Vorhaben hatten die Akademiker von 1612 freilich eine Antwort bereit:

> Non s'è dato giudicio quali sien le voci del verso, e quali sien della prosa, se non di rado: stimando potersi ciò lasciare alla discrezione altrui, e all'uso, arbitro di simil cose (*A'Lettori*).

## 5. Wege der Standardisierung

Was bis hierher geschildert wurde, kann, es ist angedeutet, als die gerade Linie zur Standardisierung des Italienischen hin aufgefasst werden; nun kann es auch wichtig sein, Abweichungen ins Auge zu fassen, die da und dort ansetzten um sich wieder zu verlieren, oder im Gegenteil untergründig weiterzuleben und später oder anderswo wieder zu erscheinen. Im Spiel und Widerspiel von Kommunikation und Selbstbehauptung – Saussures *Intercourse* und Kirchturmgeist – war in Florenz ein 'italienisches' Idiom entstanden, an dessen Silbenfluss und Lautungen sich die Redenden und Schreibenden höherer Kultur, von den sizilianischen Gestaden des Meers bis zum Wall der Alpen, zu halten begannen; die Anhänger einer Mischtheorie (*Intercourse*) taten das praktisch so gut wie die Puristen, und nicht zu Unrecht sah Machiavelli in der typologischen Angleichung auch fremder Elemente recht eigentlich einen Stempel des Florentinischen (Wunderli 1985). Das aufstrebende Idiom wurde als 'Sprache' erkannt, die gleich dem Latein 'Regeln' besass und die ein Gefäss der alten Kultur wie auch das Instrument neuer menschlicher Intelligenz sein konnte. Hier trafen sich der Philosoph Speroni und Galilei, der Forscher. Die Regeln wurden von Alberti noch rein empirisch gefunden; Bembo sah im Florentinischen ein Analogon zum Latein, eher zum Zeitvertreib (*nu-*

*gae* Petrarcas) und Ausdruck der Gefühle bestimmt; selbst für Varchi bleibt es unter der Obhut des Latein und Griechischen; erst mit Salviati wird stolz verkündet, die Regeln des Lateins bänden die florentinische Sprache nicht, ja die Kenntnis des Lateins könne ihre Reinheit trüben und machten sie ihrer Eigenheiten (*proprietà*) verlustig. Woraus ein 'Antilatinismus' Salviatis konstruiert wurde (Sozzi 1955; Brown 1966), der so nicht zutrifft; im Spiel war die reelle Verschiedenheit zweier Sprachen und – in dieser Erkenntnis – ein vorzeitiger Strukturalismus.

Mit dem Erscheinen des *Vocabolario* sind aber die Probleme der Sprache noch längst nicht vorbei. Zum einen kommen schon vorher divergierende Ansätze bei Salviati selbst und in seinem Kreise zum Vorschein. Zum andern entsteht natürlicherweise eine Gegenbewegung in Form von 'Anticrusca' und 'Antiakademismus'. Schliesslich geht die im Kern literarisch-schriftsprachlicher Tradition verpflichtete Standardisierung der *Crusca* – was ein wesentlicherer Vorwurf sein könnte als der 'Archaismus' – an der mündlichen Sprache vorbei. Ansätze, wie wir sie bei Machiavelli und in den Komödien des Ariost finden, werden erst in Goldoni wirksam, zu einer Zeit in der Englisch und Französisch Vorbild sprachlichen Ausdrucks werden, der Illuminismus mit seinen rationellen Schemen die Geister erfüllt und die Hinwendung Manzonis zum Modell Paris und französische Schreib- und Sprechkompetenz bevorsteht.

### 5.1. Divergente Ansätze der frühen Zeit

Salviati war ein versatiler Geist, der sich auch sprachlich nicht mit der Imitation Boccaccios begnügte. Unter den ihm zugeschriebenen Werken ist ein *Discorso sopra le prime parole di Cornelio Tacito "Urbem Roman a principio reges habuere"* [1582], der nach Browns glücklicher Formulierung (1960: 23) "Machiavelli in 'pure' archaic Tuscan" ist, also im Gegensatz zu Boccaccios Stil, der "ganz Reinheit, ganz Flor, ganz Süsse" ist, "Klarheit, Effizienz und Kürze" darstellt (Avv. I 1 XII [279]); in seinem Theater und in Gedichten stösst man auf den komischen Stil eines Berni, vor dessen Imitation er in den *Avvertimenti* warnt; es ist wahrscheinlich, dass ein *Discorso di M. Ridolfo Castravilla*, der ein Verriss Dantes ist und zu dessen Verteidigung er mitsamt seinen Freunden prompt aufmarschiert, sein Machwerk ist (*Castravilla* Anagramm von *Cav[alie]r L. Salviat*); aus der gleichen Lust am Streit und Polemik heraus greift er als Mitglied der damals noch in burlesken Spielen und Paradoxie sich ergehenden *Crusca* mit unseliger Wirkung Tasso an, nachdem der Neapolitaner Pellegrino ihn über Ariost gestellt hatte. Dabei wäre er bereit gewesen, Tasso zu rühmen und zu verteidigen, wie er es nach Einsicht in dessen *Gerusalemme* versprochen hatte und wie er es auch später noch in einem Brief an Pellegrino andeutet ("an anderer Stelle hätte das Urteil verschieden ausfallen können"). Was er in der Polemik als Missgriffe Tassos angreift, hätte er effektiv ebensogut wie im Falle Boccaccios als durch die Kunst geadelt hinstellen können (*Avv.* 2 XII [264–286]). Noch bedeutsamer ist vielleicht, dass ein naher Freund von ihm, dem er nichts weniger als den zweiten Band der *Avvertimenti* gewidmet hatte, der Franziskaner Panicarola (1548–1594; Studien der Rechte in Pavia und Bologna, der Philosophie und Theologie in Padua, Pisa und – 1571–73 – Paris; Bischof von Asti 1587, Mitstreiter des Carlo Borromeo, Begleiter 1589–90 – wieder in Paris – Papst Sixtus des V.) auf der Basis eben dieser *Avvertimenti* und des "commune uso" des modernen Florentinischen einen pragmatischen Begriff des Gemeinitalienischen als für den Prediger wohlverstanden gesprochene Sprache, entwickeln konnte (De Angelis 1995).

### 5.2. Anticrusca und Antiakademismus

Es ist Paolo Beni, der schon 1612, also im Jahr des Erscheinens, die Diskussion um das *Vocabolario* mit *L'Anticrusca ovvvero il paragone dell'Italiana lingua, nel qual si mostra chiaramente che l'antica sia inculta e rozza: e la moderna regolata e gentile* eröffnete; ihm antwortete im gleichen Jahr Orlando Pescetti, was Beni (unter dem Pseudonym Michelangelo Fonte) 1614 seinerseits zu einer Replik führte. 1615 mischte sich Traiano Boccalini in den *Ragguagli del Parnaso* in den Streit ein. 1623 erscheint die zweite Ausgabe des *Vocabolario*; 1691 die dritte, mit Tasso, Pallavicini (dessen Belege aber aus der vierten Ausgabe 1729–38 wieder verschwanden!), und mit zahlreichen vulgären Elementen der vergnüglichen florentinischen Literatur (Buonarroti, *Fiera*; Lippi, *Malmentile*). Diese in verschiedenen Kompendien benutzte und schon 1741 neu aufgelegte vierte Ausgabe rief neuer Polemik; heftige Angriffe richtete Giuseppe Barretti in der *Frusta letteraria* gegen sie und eine Sprache, die – ungleich dem Englischen und Französischen – nicht der natürlichen Ordnung des Gedankens folge;

Alessandro Verri schwor ihr sogar im Namen der Aufklärer und des Mailänder Kreises im *Caffè* ab (*Rinuncia avanti nodaro al vocabolario della Crusca*, 1764). Schliesslich hob 1783 der letzte Medici, Grossherzog Pietro Leopoldo, die Eigenständigkeit der *Accademia della Crusca*, sie mit der *Accademia fiorentina* verschmelzend, auf. Vittorio Alfieri setzte ihr in einem bewegenden Sonett (*L'idioma gentil sonante e puro*) ein Epitaph.

5.3. Der französische Weg

Die Begegnung des Italienischen mit dem Französischen ruft einer weiteren Bemerkung: wie erinnerlich hat die Entwicklung, die letztlich zum *Vocabolario della Crusca* führte, eine Parallele in Frankreich. Du Bellay, der lange in Rom weilte, hatte seine *Défense et illustration de la langue française* unter dem Einfluss von Sperone Speroni geschrieben (wie übrigens Juan de Valdés den spanischen *Diálogo de la lengua* unter dem Bembos). Sicher auch infolge der französischen Heiraten Caterinas und Marias de'Medici bestanden in der uns interessierenden Zeit spezielle Beziehungen zwischen Florenz und dem französischen Hof: der Provenzalist und Dantist Jacopo Corbinelli, verhasster Rivale Salviatis, von dessen Clique mit Schmähgedichten (*I Corbi*) verfolgt, fand in Paris Zuflucht; Panicarola gilt auch für Frankreich als Inspirator religiöser Eloquenz; Salviatis Konzeptionen von 'Gebrauch' und 'gutem Gebrauch' finden sich ähnlich bei Vaugelas wieder (Marzys 1984, Engler 1995); Glanz und Elend Concinis, dem das Los des Wörterbuchs in Frankreich anvertraut wurde, haben wir berichtet: und dieses wurde dann ja auch anfänglich zum Modell und Mass des zu planenden *Dictionnaire de l'Académie française* genommen. Nur dass die Lage sehr anders war: Die *Crusca* konnte die goldene Zeit ihrer Sprache in der Vergangenheit wähnen und sich auf die *Tre corone* Dante, Boccaccio, Petrarca beziehen; Frankreich hatte nach dem Bruch mit der Vergangenheit, den die Pléiade darstellt, keine solchen Vorbilder mehr. Seine goldene Zeit war die Gegenwart, seine Sprache die der zeitgenössischen guten Gesellschaft, deren Belege die aktuelle Rede am Hof eines sich zunehmend zentralisierenden modernen Staats. So wurde das *Dictionnaire de l'Académie française* ein Wörterbuch der gesprochenen Sprache, für das die Regeln der gesprochenen Sprache gelten: – einer Sprache, die der Ordnung des Gedankens folgt, wo zuerst hingestellt wird, wovon man spricht und dann erst kommt, was man darüber sagt, wo das Verb dem Subjekt folgt, Objekt und Komplement dem Verb. Der Schriftsteller hat sich daran zu halten: Anstand, nicht raffinierte Ästhetik, Klarheit, nicht rhythmische Verschlungenheit sind gefragt. Und ein einziges Wort, sagt Vaugelas, das nicht der Konvention des Hofs entspricht, kann ein Werk unwürdig machen. Weit sind wir von der Auffassung Salviatis, dass die Kunst eines Autors selbst die Fehler seiner Sprache adelt.

5.4. Gegenwirkung auf Italien

Der so herausgestellte Gegensatz ist nicht nur ein Gegensatz zweier partikulärer (wenn auch noch so sehr für die Kulturgeschichte bedeutender) Wörterbücher. Er reiht sich in die ganze Typologie der zwei Sprachen ein. Das französische Wort, durch die lautgeschichtliche Entwicklung weitgehend seiner morphologischen Differenzierungen beraubt und oft homonym, ist fest in syntaktische Folgen eingebettet und hängt semantisch vom paradigmatischen Zusammenschluss ab; die Rede ist in der Determination der Elemente sozial auf den Hörer eingestellt, dem stets das *was* vor dem *wie* geboten ist, nicht wie im Deutschen, das von den Emotionen und Gewichtungen des Sprechers ausgeht; das Italienische nimmt eine Mittelstellung wahlweisen Vorgehens ein. Die beiden extremen Ausrichtungen wurden schon von Condillac erkannt und richtig eingeschätzt; eine gesamthafte Ergründung der typologischen Strukturen ist vor allem Bally (1944) und Segre (1963) zu verdanken. Gerade aus der Mittelstellung des Italienischen heraus erklärt sich die Kehrtwendung der italienischen Aufklärung. Die rationell soziale Redeweise war ihm so gut offen, wie die emotionell künstlerische, und im Aufbau einer gemeinitalienischen gesprochenen Sprache war es verlockend, darauf hinzustreben. Nur rasch sei darauf hingewiesen, wie benachteiligt nun wiederum das Französische ist: nicht ohne tieferen Grund konnte so Rimbaud in der *Lettre du voyant* ihm vorwerfen, nichts anderes mehr als Prosa sei seit der Klassik in ihm geschrieben worden.

Der Standard einer italienischen gesprochenen Sprache und der ihr nahen Prosa hat sich also logisch und ideologisch, zur Zeit der Aufklärung, am Französischen und am Englischen, das ihm typologisch nahe stand, ausrichten können; in der Praxis, über das Mittel des Theaters, das landesweit alle Volksschichten berührt, gab vor allem Goldoni ein Vorbild, der ja des Französischen derart mächtig war, dass er in später Zeit einen *Bourru bienfaisant* für die *Comédie française* zu schreiben vermochte – auch die *Memoiren* sind in Französisch – wobei freilich auch die untergründige italienische Tradition des Cinquecento (Machiavelli und Ariost) hineinspielt und er drittens von der dialektalen Kraft des Venezianischen zehren konnte: es ist nicht zu vergessen, dass seine venezianischen Komödien wohl die lebensnahesten sind. Im Roman schaffte Manzoni den Durchbruch: Varchis Modell der zwischen "Graben und Mauern" eine Stadt gesprochenen Sprache aufnehmend (Florenz wie Paris) "wäscht er seine Tücher im Arno" und formt aus einem sprachlich eher heterogenen *Fermo e Lucia* das florentinische Meisterwerk der *Promessi Sposi*. Damit begann in Italien aber auch wieder das Spiel von Mischsprache (*Intercourse*) und Kirchturm (*Clocher*). Manzonis Sprachtheorie weitert sich auf ein pädagogisches Projekt aus, nach dem die Italiener alle Florentinisch zu lernen haben, so wie für Frankreich nur das Idiom der *Ile de France* massgebend ist. Schulbücher und Wörterbücher – darunter das hochoffizielle Broglios – entstehen danach. Als Widersacher Manzonis erhebt sich der Linguist und Dialektologe Ascoli, der die Sprache als gemeinsames Werk einer ganzen Nation, im Mitwirken aller Regionen und Dialekte versteht, freilich auch er in Anerkennung der historisch entstandenen Vorgabe toskanisch-florentinischer Tradition – er, und beileibe nicht Manzoni, ist es, der das florentinisch-hochsprachliche *-ie-* und *-uo-* als die schönste Blüte der italienischen Sprache preist (Ascoli 1873). Modell für Ascoli ist die "Werkstatt des deutschen Volks", in der um Luthers Bibelübersetzung herum Sprache überregional entstand. Daran hat dann in einer "italienischen *officina*" unter andern auch Pirandello gewirkt, wie Verga (aber in explizitem linguistischem Bekenntnis) sizilianische Mündlichkeit beisteuernd und Goldoni gleich dialektale Dramen seinen italienischen entgegenstellend. Und die tatsächliche Weiterentwicklung, über Radio und Television, ist dann auch Ascolis Modell, nicht dem Manzonis, gefolgt. Pasolinis Illusion einer industriellen Sprache konnte hingegen nirgends bestehen – pikant in unserem Zusammenhang und paradoxal, dass er mit der *Nuova questione della lingua* sich auf einen Bally-Segre beruft, der in sein ideologisches Konstrukt auf keine Art hineinpasst – und führte höchstens (was dann auch Pasolinis persönlicher Rückzug ins bereits früher geübte friulanische Schrifttum belegen sollte) zur Verstärkung dialektaler Verfremdungserscheinungen.

## 6. Bibliographie


Alberti, Leon Battista. 1964. *La prima grammatica della lingua volgare* [± 1440]. Hg. von Cecil Grayson. Bologna: Commissione per i primi testi di lingua.

Ascoli, Graziadio Isaia. 1873. "Proemio". *Archivio glottologico italiano* 1, V–XLI. (Manzoni-Ascoli 1974.)

Baehr, Rudolf. 1957. "Studien zur Rhetorik in den 'Rime' Guittones von Arezzo". *Zeitschrift für romanische Philologie* 73.193–258; 357–413.

Bally, Charles. 1965 [1944]. *Linguistique générale et linguistique française*. 4. Aufl. Hg. von Siegfried Heinimann. Berne: Francke.

–. 1963. *Linguistica generale e linguistica francese.* Introduzione e appendice di Cesare Segre. Milano: Il Saggiatore.

Bascetta, Carlo. 1969. "Tutte le cose". Lingua nostra 30: 2.37–39.

Battaglia, Salvatore. 1961ss. *Grande dizionario della lingua italiana* [Bd. 8, 1996.] Torino: Utet.

Bembo, Pietro. 1931 [1525]. *Prose della volgar lingua.* Hg. von Carlo Dionisotti-Casalone (= *Collana di classici italiani con note.*) Torno: Utet.

Beni, Paolo. 1982s. [1612]. *L'Anticrusca overo.il paragone dell'italiana lingua: nel qual si mostra chiaramente che l'antica sia inculta e rozza: e la moderna regolata e gentile.* Anastatische Ausgabe und kritischer Text hg. von Gino Casagrande. 2 Bde. Firenze: Accademia della Crusca.

Bielfeld, Antje. 1996. *Methoden der Belegsammlung für das 'Vocabolario della Crusca'.* Exemplarisch vorgestellt am lexikographischen Werk Francesco Redis (= *Beihefte zur Zeitschrift für romanische Philologie*, 261.) Tübingen: Niemeyer.

Bonomi, Ilaria. 1985. "Giambullari e Varchi grammatici nell'ambiente linguistico fiorentino". *La Crusca nella tradizione letteraria e linguistica italiana.* (= IV *Centenario dell'Accademia della Crusca*), 65–79. Firenze: Accademia della Crusca.

Borghini, Vincenzio. 1857. *Annotazioni e discorsi sopra alcuni luoghi del 'Decamerone' di G. Boccaccio fatte dalli molto magnifici Deputati di loro Altezze serenissime sopra le correzioni di esso Boccaccio stampato l'anno MDLXXIII.* Firenze: Giunti.

Broglio, Emilio. 1897. *Novo vocabolario della lingua italiana secondo l'uso di Firenze* ordinato dal ministero della pubblica istruzione sotto la presidenza del comm[issario] Emilio Broglio. Firenze: Celini.

Brown, Peter M. 1960. "Lionardo Salviati and the 'Discorso sopra le prime parole di Cornelio Tacito'". *Italian Studies* 15, 1960. 50–64.

–. 1966. "The Conception of the Literary 'volgare' in the Linguistic Writings of Lionardo Salviati". *Italian Studies* 21, 1966. 57–90.

–. 1971. "Jacopo Corbinelli and the Florentine 'crows'. *Italian studies* 26, 1971. 69–89.

–. 1974. *Lionardo Salviati.* A critical biography. London: Oxford University.

Buommattei, Benedetto. 1720 [1643]. *Della lingua toscana.* Firenze & Verona: Berno.

Castiglione, Baldesar. 1906 [1524]. *Il Cortigiano.* Hg. von Vittorio Cian. Firenze: Sansoni.

Castravilla, Rudolfo. 1608 [1571–72]. "Discorso nel quale si mostra l'imperfettione della 'Commedia' di Dante contro al 'Dialogo delle lingue' del Varchi". *Annotazioni ovvero chiose marginali* hg. von Bellisario Bulgarini. Siena: Bonetto.

Condillac, Etienne Bonnot de. 1973 [1746]. "Essai sur l'origine des connoissances humaines". *Condillac, Essai sur l'origine des connoissances humaines; Jacques Derrida, L'archéologie du frivole* hg. von Charles Porset, 97–298. Auvers-sur-Oise: Galilée.

Corti, Maria. 1982. *Dante a un nuovo crocevia.* Firenze: Casa editrice Le Lettere: Libreria commissionaria Sansoni.

Crusca 1612. *Vocabolario degli Accademici della Crusca* con tre indici delle voci, locuzioni, e proverbi latini, e greci, posto per entro l'opera, con privilegio del sommo pontefice, del re cattolico, della serenissima Repubblica di Venezia, e degli altri principi, e potentati d'Italia, e fuor d'Italia, della maestà cesarea, del re cristianissimo, e del sereniss. arciduca Alberto. Venezia MDCXII. Appresso Iacopo Sarzina.

–. 1623. *Vocabolario degli Accademici della Crusca* in questa seconda impressione da'medesimi riveduto, e ampliato, con aggiunta di molte voci degli autor del buon secolo, e buona quantità di quelle del uso [...]. Venezia MDCXXIII. Appresso Iacopo Sarzina.

Dante Alighieri. 1921. Le Opere. Testo critico della Società dantesca italiana. Firenze: Bemporad.

De Angelis, Simone. 1995. *Francesco Panicaloras Begriff des Gemeinitalienischen auf der Basis des 'commune uso' des modernen Florentinischen.* Manuskript. (Seminararbeit im Fach Romanische Philologie.)

Battaglin, Deanna. 1964–65. "Leonardo Salviati e le 'Osservazioni al Pastor Fido' del Guarini". *Atti e memorie dell'Accademia patavina di scienza, lettere ed arti (già Accademia dei Ricovrati)* 77,3.249–284.

*Dictionnaire (Le) de l'Académie françoise*, 1694, dédié au Roy. A Paris, chez la Veuve de Jean Baptiste Coignard, Imprimeur du Roy & de l'Académie françoise, ruë S. Jacques, à la Bible d'Or: et chez Jean Baptiste Coignard, Imprimeur ordinaire du Roy & de l'Académie françoise, ruë S. Jacques, près S. Severin, au Livre d'Or. M. DC. LXXXXIV. Avec privilège de sa Majesté.

Du Bellay, Joachim. 1969 [1549] La deffense et illustration de la langue françoyse. Kritische Ausgabe von Henri Chamard. Genève: Slatkine. (Nachdruck der Ausgabe Paris 1904.)

Engler, Rudolf. 1964. [Besprechung von] Segre 1963. *Cahiers Ferdinand de Saussure* 21.139–143.

–. 1972. *Studien zu Lionardo Salviatis 'Avvertimenti della lingua sopra'l Decamerone'.* Manuskript. (Habilitationsschrift Bern.)

–. 1975. "I Fondamenti della favella in Lionardo Salviati e l'idea saussuriana di 'langue complète'". *Lingua e stile* 10.17–28.

–. 1982a. "Lionardo Salviati e la linguistica cinquecentesca". *Atti del XIV° congresso di linguistica e filologia romanza* 5.625–633. Napoli: Macchiaroli & Amsterdam: Benjamins.

–. 1982b. "Philologia linguistica: Lionardo Salviatis Kommentar der Sprache Boccaccios (1584/86)". *Historiographia linguistica* 9.299–319.

–. 1988. "Tra teoria e pratica: considerazioni su Lionardo Salviati e la sua polemica tassesca". *Prospettive di storia della linguistica: lingua, linguaggio, comunicazione sociale* hg. von Lia Formigari & Franco Lo Piparo, 97–112. Roma: Editori riuniti.

–. 1993. "La discussion italienne sur la norme et sa réception en Europe". *Ecriture, langues communes et normes: formation spontanée de koinès et standardisation dans la Galloromania et son voisinage.* (*Université de Neuchâtel, Recueil de travaux publiés par la Faculté des Lettres*, 42), 205–225. Neuchâtel: Faculté des Lettres & Genève: Droz.

Eberenz, Rolf. 1996. "¿Qué tipo de español escribe Nebrija? El gramático como usuario y teórico de la lengua". *Vox Romanica* 55.143–159.

Faba, Guido. 1889 [± 1243]. "Parlamenta et epistole". *I suoni, le forme e le parole dell'odierno dialetto della città di Bologna* hg. von Augusto Gaudenzi. Torino: Loescher.

Gelli, Giovan Battista. 1855 [1552]. "Ragionamento infra M. Cosimo Bartoli & Giovan Batista Gelli sopra le difficoltà di mettere in regole la nostra lingua". *Opere* hg. von Agenore Gelli, 290–324. Firenze: Le Monnier.

Giambullari, Pierfrancesco. 1985 [1552]. *De la lingua che si parla e scrive in Firenze.* Firenze: Accademia della Crusca.

Heinimann, Siegfried. 1963. [Besprechung Battaglia, vol. 22.] *Kratylos* 8.59–63.

–. 1987. *Romanische Literatur- und Fachsprachen in Mittelalter und Renaissance. Beiträge zur Frühgeschichte des Provenzalischen, Französischen, Italienischen und Rätoromanischen.* Wiesbaden: Reichert.

Krömer, Wolfram. 1967. "Die Ursprünge und die Rolle der Sprachtheorie in Du Bellays Deffence et illustration de la langue françoyse". *Romanische Forschungen* 79.589–602.

Machiavelli, Niccolò. 1976 [1525]. *Discorso o dialogo intorno alla nostra lingua.* Kritische Ausgabe hg. von Bertolo Tommaso Sozzi. (= *Piccola biblioteca Einaudi.*) Torino: Einaudi.

Manzoni, Alessandro. 1972. *Scritti linguistici.* Hg. von Ferruccio Monteresso. Milano: Ed. Paoline.

– & Graziadio Isaia Ascoli. 1974. *Scritti sulla questione della lingua.* (= *Classici italiani commentati*). Torino: Loescher.

Maraschio, Nicoletta. 1998. "Il pensiero linguistico tra tradizione classica e innovazione". *Vox Romanica* 57. 101–116.

Marconcini, Cartesio. 1910 (1612). *L'Accademia della Crusca dalle origini alla prima edizione del Vocabolario.* Pisa: Valenti.

Marzys, Zygmunt. 1996. "La codification du français à l'époque de la Renaissance: une construction inachevée". *Vox Romanica* 55.120–142.

Mazzacurati, Giancarlo. 1965. *La questione della lingua italiana dal Bembo all'Accademia fiorentina.* Napoli: Liguori.

Migliorini, Bruno. 1975. *Cronologia della lingua italiana.* (= *Biblioteca del Saggiatore,* 38.) Firenze: Le Monnier.

–. 1961. *Storia della lingua italiana.* Firenze: Sansoni.

Musarra, Franco. 1982. "L'orazione in lode della fiorentina lingua e de' fiorentini autori: un momento cruciale della storia della lingua del Rinascimento". *Il Rinascimento. Aspetti e problemi attuali. Atti del X congresso dell'Associazione Internazionale per gli Studi di Lingua e Letteratura Italiana* hg. von Vittore Branca et al., 553–565. Firenze: Olschki.

Panicarola (bzw. Panigarola), Francesco. 1609. *Predicatore overo parafrasi, commento, e discorsi intorno al libro dell'Elocutione di Demetrio Falereo.* Onde vengono i precetti, e gli esempi del dire, che già furono dati a'Greci, ridotti chiaramente alla pratica del ben parlare in prose italiane [...]. *Venezia* MDCIX, appresso Bernardo Giunti, Giovan Battista Ciotti & Compagni.

Parlangeli, Oronzio. ²1974. *La nuova questione della lingua.* Saggi raccolti da O. Parlangeli. Brescia: Paideia.

Parodi, Ernesto Giacomo. 1957. *Lingua e letteratura.* Studi di teoria linguistica e di storia dell'italiano antico. Mit einer Einleitung von Alfredo Schiaffini hg. von Gianfranco Folena. 2 Bde. Venezia: Pozza.

Parodi, Sevrina. 1983. *Quattro secoli di Crusca 1883–1983.* Firenze: Accademia della Crusca.

Pasolini, Pier Paolo. 1964. "Nuove questioni linguistiche." *Rinascita*, 26 dic.

Pellegrino. Camillo. 1584. *Il Carrafa o vero della epica poesia dialogo.* Firenze: Sarmatelli.

Pirandello, Luigi. 1973. "Scritti varii, 1: Prose letterarie [Prosa moderna (1890), Per la solita questione della lingua (1899), Come si parla in Italia (1895); 4. Teatro in dialetto. Teatro siciliano? (1909), Dialettalità (1921, 'U Ciclopu (1918)]". *Opere*, vol. 6. (= *I Classici contemporanei italiani*), 878–891, 1205–1224. Verona: Mondadori.

Pozzi, Mario. 1974. "Il pensiero linguistico de Vincenzio Borghini". *Giornale storico della letteratura italiana* 148.216–294.

Ramon Vidal: s. Stengel 1878.

Rossi, Mario 1897. "Il Castravilla smascherato". *Giornale dantesco* 5, n. s. 2.1–18.

Salviati, Lionardo. 1564. *Orazione nella quale si dimostra la fiorentina favella e i fiorentini autori essere a tutte l'altre lingue, cosí antiche come moderne, e a tutti gli altri scrittori di qual si voglia lingua di gran lunga superiori.* Da lui pubblicamente recitata nella Fiorentina Academia il di ultimo d'aprile 1564 nel consolato di M. Baccio Valori.

–. 1582. *Il Decamerone di messer Giovanni Boccacci cittadin fiorentino,* di nuovo ristampato e riscontrato in Firenze con testi antichi & alla sua vera lezione ridotto. Firenze: Giunti.

–. 1584. *Degli Avvertimenti della lingua sopra 'l Decamerone* volume primo del cav. L. S. Venetia: Guerra.

–. 1586. *Del secondo volume degli Avvertimenti della lingua sopra il Decamerone libri due* del cav. *L. S.* Firenze: Giunti.

–. 1810. *Opere.* 5 Bde. Milano: Soc. tip. de' Classici italiani.

Sansone, Mario. 1954. "Le polemiche antitassesche della Crusca". *Torquato Tasso.* Comitato per le celebrazioni di Torquato Tasso, 527–574. Ferrara.

Saussure, Ferdinand. 1916. *Cours de linguistique générale.* Lausanne & Paris: Payot.

Schiaffini, Alfredo. ³1973. "Avviamenti di storia della prosa del secolo XIII". *Momenti e storia della lingua italiana.* (= *Cultura*, XI), 71–89. Roma: Studium.

Sozzi, Bertolo Tommaso. 1955. "Leonardo Salviati nella questione linguistica cinquecentesca". *Aspetti e momenti della questione linguistica nel Cinquecento* (= *Guide di cultura contemporane.*) Padova: Liviana.

Speroni, Sperone. 1975 [1542]. *Dialogo delle lingue.* Hg., übersetzt und eingeleitet von Helene Harth (= *Humanistische Bibliothek,* II: 11.) München: Fink.

Stengel, Edmund. 1878. *Die beiden ältesten provenzalischen Grammatiken*: Lo Donatz proensals *und* Las Rasos de trobar. Marburg: Elwert.

Tommaseo, Nicolò & Bernardo Bellini. 1865–79. *Dizionario della lingua italiana.* Torino: Società L'Unione tipografica-editrice.

Tancke, Gunnar. 1984. *Die italienischen Wörterbücher von den Anfängen bis zum Erscheinen des 'Vo-*

*cabolario della Crusca' (1612).* (= *Beihefte zur Zeitschrift für romanische Philologie*, 198.) Tübingen: Niemeyer.

Trabalza, Ciro. 1908. *Storia della grammatica italiana.* Milano: Hoepli.

Uc Faidit: s. Stengel 1878.

Varchi, Benedetto. 1859 [1570]. "Ercolano ovvero Agli Alberi Dialogo" nel quale si ragiona generalmente delle lingue e in particolare della fiorentina e della toscana. *Opere*, 2, 1–202. Trieste: Sezione letteraro-artistica del LLoyd austriaco.

Vaugelas, Claude Favre de. 1994 [1647]. *La préface des 'Remarques sur la langue françoise'.* Mit Einleitung und Anmerkungen hg. von Zygmunt Marzys (= *Université de Neuchâtel, Recueil de travaux publiés par la Faculté des Lettres*, 37.) Neuchâtel: Faculté des Lettres, Genève: Droz.

Viscardi, Antonio. 1959. "Introduzione". Viscardi & Vitale. 25–74.

Viscardi, Antonio, M. Vitale, A. M. Finoli & C. Cremonesi. 1959. *Le prefazioni ai primi grandi vocabolari delle lingue europee, I: Le lingue romanze: (Vocabolario degli Accademici della Crusca, Dictionnaire de l'Académie françoise, Vocabolario portuguez e latino, Diccionario de la lengua castellana).* (= *Testi e documenti di letteratura moderna*, 5.) Milano & Varese: Istituto editoriale cisalpino.

Vitale, Maurizio. 1959. "La I[a] edizione del Vocabolario della Crusca e i suoi precedenti teorici e critici". Viscardi & Vitale. 8–23.

Woodhouse, John R. 1967. "Vincenzio Borghini and the Continuity of the Tuscan Linguistic Tradition". *Italian Studies* 22.26–42.

Wunderli, Peter. "Machiavelli linguista". *Vox romanica* 44.33–58.

Zannoni, Giambattista. 1848. *Storia dell'Accademia della Crusca.* Firenze: Piatti.

*Rudolf Engler, Worb (Schweiz)*

# 113. Die Sprachgesellschaften und die Entstehung eines literarischen Standards in Deutschland

1. Sprachgeschichtliche Situation
2. Kulturpatriotismus nach europäischen Vorbildern
3. Die wichtigsten Sprachgesellschaften
4. Ziele und Argumente
5. Fremdwortverdeutschung
6. Wirkungen
7. Bibliographie

## 1. Sprachgeschichtliche Situation

1.1. Unter *Sprachgesellschaften* im engeren Sinne (im folgenden als *SG* abgekürzt) versteht man in der germanistischen Forschung verschieden benannte private Sozietäten, die in der Zeit von 1617 bis 1658 in deutschsprachigen Territorien gegründet worden sind und meist noch im 17. Jh. zu bestehen aufgehört haben. Entsprechend ihren Zielen und Tätigkeiten sind aber zu ihren Nachwirkungen auch meist *Deutsche Gesellschaft* benannte Gesellschaften der Aufklärungszeit hinzuzurechnen, die bis in die Gottsched-Zeit (um 1750) an der Entstehung eines literarischen dt. Standards Anteil hatten. Eine gewisse, z. T. einseitig mißzuverstehende Kontinuität führt schließlich von den SG zu dt. Sprachvereinen des 19. und 20. Jh.

Unter *literarischem Standard* ist hier ein vielfältiger, allmählicher Prozeß der Sprachkultivierung in der Sprachbewußtseinsgeschichte zu verstehen, der in den SG und bei mehr oder weniger mit ihnen in Verbindung stehenden Einzelpersonen als interpersonaler, intertextueller und sozietärer Diskurs zur Theorie- und Ideologiebildung zu wirken beginnt und durch publizistische, literarische und organisatorische Tätigkeiten ab Ende des 17. Jh. in die Phase der Kodifizierung übergeht, die erst im Laufe des 18. Jh. zu einer allgemeinen, noch elitärgesellschaftlichen Konsensbildung (nicht Normsetzung) über dt. Schriftsprachnormen geführt hat.

Diese schrittweise, durch Bewußtseinsbildung, konkretes Handeln und soziales Verhalten vorbereitende Entwicklung erklärt sich aus der sprachgeschichtlichen Situation im 16. und 17. Jh.: Die von der absolutistischen Fürstenherrschaft geprägte Epoche bedeutete für die kulturelle Entwicklung der dt. Sprache zunächst eine folgenreiche Behinderung, Verzögerung und Verengung aus folgenden Ursachen:

– Das Alte Reich zerfiel von der Mitte des 16. Jh. bis zum Ende des 18. Jh. zu einem fast anarchischen System zahlreicher quasi-souveräner Territorialfürstentümer, so daß für die Vereinheitlichung und Kultivierung der dt. Sprache mehr denn je ein nationalstaatlicher Rahmen und Mittelpunkt fehlte.

- Der wirtschaftliche und politische Aufstieg bürgerlicher Schichten in Deutschland war stärker eingeschränkt als etwa in Frankreich, England, Italien oder in den Niederlanden, wo schon im 16. Jh. von Paris, London, Florenz und Amsterdam aus die Nationalsprachen als Literatur- und Öffentlichkeitssprachen erfolgreich kultiviert werden konnten.
- Zum alten Bildungsmonopol des Lateins in Staat, Kirche und Wissenschaft kam das Französische als schriftliche und mündliche Oberschichtsprache in Politik, Wissenschaft und höfischem Gesellschaftsleben erschwerend hinzu, so daß der dt. Sprache gesellschaftliches und kulturelles Prestige vorenthalten wurde und ihr einige kulturell wichtige Kommunikationstypen und Textsorten verschlossen blieben.

1.2. Das 16. Jh. war – im Geist der Renaissance ebenso wie noch dem der universalistisch-übernationalen katholischen, kaiserlichen und territorialfürstlichen Politik – in Mitteleuropa von einer weitgehenden Mehrsprachigkeit gekennzeichnet, die mit entsprechenden Kleidermoden und Umgangsformen der Oberschichten einherging (vgl. v. Polenz 1994: 49ff.). Staats-, Kirchen- und Wissenschaftssprache war im Alten Reich, seit der Humanistenzeit verstärkt, das Latein der Geistlichen und Gelehrten, stark dominierend neben Deutsch, auch im lutherischen höheren Bildungswesen. Am Wiener Kaiserhof wurde im Bereich von Zeremonien, Geselligkeit und Kultur viel Spanisch und Italienisch gesprochen. Im Fernhandel spielten Ital. oder Ndl., im Militärwesen Franz. eine große Rolle. Für das gesellschaftliche Renommieren in höfischen Kreisen setzte sich, besonders an den Territorialfürstenhöfen mit antikaiserlicher Tendenz, seit dem frühen 17. Jh. das Franz. als vorbildgebende Herrschafts- und Kultursprache immer mehr durch, teils mit partiellem (nur für bestimmte Sachdomänen und Rollenregister beherrschtem) Bilinguismus der aristokratischen Oberschicht, teils mit hemmungsloser Interferenz franz., ital. usw. Wörter, Routineformeln und Phraseologismen ins Dt., was bereits vor der Dominanz des Franz. im frühen 17. Jh. als *Alamodisch, Sprachmengerey, Fremdgierigkeit, Nachäfferey* usw. verspottet und kritisiert wurde.

Entgegen späterer nationalistischer Kulturideologie sind die Ursachen dieser extremen Offenheit für fremde Kultureinflüsse nicht nur im Sprachenkontakt der Bevölkerung mit fremden Truppen während des 30jährigen Krieges zu suchen, sondern für die Oberschichten vor allem in den ökonomischen Folgen der überseeischen Entdeckungen und Kolonialisierungen, an denen die deutschsprachigen Territorien kaum Anteil hatten, auch in der spanisch-westeuropäischen Orientierung des habsburgischen Kaiserhauses und in der merkantilistischen Fortschrittlichkeit Frankreichs, die das Luxusbedürfnis dt. Fürstenhöfe schon vor der Ausstrahlungskraft des Versailler Königshofes Ludwigs XIV. provozierte (Hattenhauer 1987: 8; Brunt 1983: 1ff.; Brunot 1934).

1.3. Die Angewöhnung franz. Sprechens und franz. Lehnwörter geschah meist in der Alltagspraxis auf Auslandsreisen dt. Adliger (*Cavalierstouren*), durch *Hofmeister* und *Gouvernanten*, durch Kriegsdienst, Handel, Handwerkerwanderung, durch ausländische Reisende und Emigranten, nicht zuletzt durch Zeitungskorrespondenten aus dem Ausland (Kinnemark 1964) und in allen mit dem höfischen Leben verbundenen Dienstleistungsberufen, in der Aufklärungszeit mehr auf literarischem Wege (Übersetzungen, Lektüre). Zu Art, Textsortenverteilung, Chronologie und Ausmaß des franz. Lehneinflusses im 17./18. Jh. s. Jones 1976; Brunt 1983; v. Polenz 1994: Kap. 5.4. Die Erstbelege für franz. Wörter stiegen seit der Zeit um 1600 von etwa 1% auf etwa 40% (1650) und 60% (um 1800) der Gesamtzahl von Entlehnungen aus anderen Sprachen. Die besonders in den 1640er Jahren parodistisch hergestellten fremdwortüberladenen dt. Texte (s. unter dem Stichwort 'Sprachsatire' bei Jones 1995: 675) sind aber ebenso Übertreibungen wie die Wehklagen und Warnungen über eine Gefahr der Verdrängung des Dt. durch das Franz. von Leibniz bis Herder oder die geschmeichelten Äußerungen frankophoner Gäste an dt. Höfen, man spräche dort nur Franz. und das Dt. sei nur für Soldaten, Pferde und die Gasse (s. v. Polenz 1994: 49f., 66f.).

1.4. Die Kultivierung der dt. Sprache befand sich um 1600 noch in einem unbefriedigenden Stadium (vgl. v. Polenz 1991: Kap. 4.4–4.6, 4.8): Zwar war Luthers Bibelübersetzung als hervorragende sprachliche Leistung weithin anerkannt, auch bei katholischen Gegnern und Nacheiferern, ebenso der Schreibgebrauch von Reichsinstitutionen (Reichstagsabschiede, Reichskammergericht); und die Verdrängung der niederdt. Schriftsprache durch die hochdt. war unter ostmitteldt.-lutherischem Einfluß in ihrem Endstadium (v. Polenz 1991: 279ff.). Von einem festen überregionalen Sprachstandard kann jedoch bis zur Mitte des 18. Jh. noch keine Rede sein. Regionale Varianten, vor allem im Süden und Westen, waren in allen Sprachbereichen noch stark. Die Vorbilder und Normprinzipien schwankten noch sehr und waren heterogen (Josten 1976; v. Polenz 1994: Kap. 5.6). Die noch unsicher konsolidierte dt. Schriftsprache wurde nur von einer kleinen Schicht mit kirchlich/akademischer und professioneller Bildung aktiv beherrscht, die zunehmend mit Spott oder Verachtung auf die meist weit davon entfernte *Provinz-, Land-* oder *Pöbelsprache*, also den Dialekt der noch kaum alphabetisierten großen Mehrheit der Bevölkerung herabschaute, obwohl Phonemik und Morphemik in der Sprechsprache auch bei Gebildeten noch bis ins 19. Jh. stark dialektal waren (außer in Norddeutschland). In der später *belletristisch* genannten Literatur galt noch um 1600 das gelehrte Neulatein mehr als das Dt.; späthumanistisch-gelehrsame Poesie erhob sich darum seit Martin Opitz (1597–1639) weit über volkstümliche Literatur (v. Polenz 1994: 300ff.). Wissenschaftssprache war noch bis Ende des 17. Jh. stark vom Latein dominiert, Gesetzessprache noch bis Ende des 18. Jh. (v. Polenz 1994: Kap. 5.11, 5.12).

## 2. Kulturpatriotismus nach europäischen Vorbildern

2.1. Im Unterschied zu Frankreich, England, den Niederlanden und skandinavischen Ländern gab es im Alten Reich noch kein staatlich orientiertes allgemeines Nationalbewußtsein. Man war Untertan eines Fürsten- oder Stadtstaates; *Vaterland* und *Patriotismus* bezogen sich auf so etwas wie Bayern, Kursachsen, Mainz oder Frankfurt. Der altständische 'Reichspatriotismus' wurde immer illusorischer. Bei akademisch Gebildeten hatte sich aber seit den Tacitus-Studien einiger dt. Humanisten (Celtis, Hutten, Aventin) ein historisierend-abstrakter 'Nation'-Begriff im Sinne eines Kulturpatriotismus entwickelt (v. See 1970; Krapf 1979; Huber 1984; Jones 1993), mit dem, gegen die universale Latinität von Kirche und Reich und die volkssprachfeindliche Rezeption des Römischen Rechts, das kulturkritisch geschönte Germanenbild des Tacitus auf die Deutschsprachigen übertragen und, in einer von Sprachloyalität getragenen Haltung, gemeinsame Sprache als Kriterium für den Begriff 'Nation' genommen wurde (v. Polenz 1998). Auch eine "Krisenerfahrung" förderte die späthumanistische Hinwendung zu den Volkssprachen (Kleinschmidt 1990: 192ff.): Das Erlebnis der Erstarrung des Lateins seit seiner philologischen Konservierung nach ciceronianischem Entwicklungsstand machte Intellektuelle, die auf gesellschaftliche Nützlichkeit und Modernisierung hin orientiert waren, sensibel für "entbundene Sprache" als funktionsfähiges System mit kreativer, sprachkultivierender Weiterentwicklung. Nicht ohne Einfluß war auch das frühe Engagement für die Volkssprachen in Italien und Böhmen im Rahmen der nationenbildenden Identitätsfindung (Dante, Hus).

2.2. Die deutschen SG sind im Sinne dieses Kulturpatriotismus im Rahmen einer späthumanistisch-frühaufklärerischen Sozietätsbewegung in einem europäischen Zusammenhang zu sehen, in dem sie Vorbilder hatten, obwohl sie sich in mancher Hinsicht anders entwickelt haben als diese:

In Italien gab es in den meisten Städten seit dem 15. Jh. hochkulturell-städtebürgerliche Institutionen, die sich *Akademien* nannten, mit dem kulturpatriotischen Ziel, die ital. Sprache als Wissenschafts- und Literatursprache zu entwickeln und durchzusetzen (Otto 1972a: 7ff.; Weinrich 1988). Die 1582 gegründete *Accademia della Crusca* (→ Art. 112) war nachweislich durch einen längeren Florenz-Aufenthalt Fürst Ludwigs v. Anhalt (der seit 1600 ihr Mitglied war) in mehreren Merkmalen Vorbild für die *Fruchtbringende Gesellschaft* (s. 3.1.), die aber einen loseren Zusammenhalt hatte, mehr aristokratisch war, es nicht bis zu einem eigenen Wörterbuch gebracht hat und noch keine eigentliche Akademie war (Flamm 1994: 23; 48ff. gegen Bircher & Cornermann 1991ff.).

Die niederländischen *rederijkers*-Kammern ('Rhetorikvereine') waren populäre bürgerlich-kaufmännische Geselligkeits- und Kulturvereine seit dem 14./15. Jh., in denen geistliche Spiele, Kirchengesang und die Kunst des Redens und Schreibens, von Religion,

Politik und Wissenschaften bis zur Poesie praxisbezogen betrieben und gelehrt wurden. Ndl. Einfluß auf dt. SG und einzelne dt. Sprachkultivierer im 17. Jh. ist sehr wahrscheinlich, aber nur indirekt durch Aufenthalte in den Niederlanden nachzuweisen (Engels 1983; van Ingen 1987; Trunz 1937): Fürst Ludwig hatte seine Studienreise in den Niederlanden begonnen; mehrere seiner Gesellschafter waren ebenfalls dort, vor allem Philipp v. Zesen (1619–1689), Gründer einer Hamburgischen SG. Fürst Ludwigs Eintreten für den Abbau von Standesschranken kann ebenso wie Zesens eifrige Fremdwortverdeutschung (s. 5.2.) von den Niederländern angeregt sein. Justus Georg Schottelius (1612–1676) hat in Leiden studiert und ist theoretisch von Niederländern beeinflußt (Gützlaff 1988; Kiedroń 1991; Klijnsmit 1993). Diese von Italien und den Niederlanden herkommende Bewegung für 'Sprachenlegitimation' hat sich auch bis nach Schweden fortgesetzt (Blume 1978b).

2.3. Die westeuropäische Sozietätsbewegung (Garber & Wismann 1995; Hardtwig 1989) hatte, ebenso wie die dt. SG (Bircher & van Ingen 1978: 53ff.) über Sprache und Literatur weit hinausgehende Ziele, so daß sie als Vorläuferin der späteren Akademien, aber auch der bildungsbürgerlichen Aufklärungs- und Lesegesellschaften um 1800 anzusehen ist. Es gab viele solcher Sozietäten in Deutschland: *Orden der Temperanz, Civitas Solis, Tugendliche Gesellschaft* usw.; ihre Interessen waren Sittlichkeit, Geselligkeit, Bildung, Wissenschaft, Dichtung, einige mehr aristokratisch (Ritterorden und -akademien), andere mehr bürgerlich-zünftisch, z. T. mit kaiserlichen Dichterkrönungen, mit Adelsnachahmung als *nobilitas mentis*. Sie hatten mehr alternativ-höfische als antihöfische Tendenzen (Huber 1984: 255). Viele waren motiviert durch die stärker werdende adelige Konkurrenz bei Verwaltungsämtern in den absolutistischen Territorialstaaten (van Ingen 1978: 14ff.). Von daher spielte auch in den dt. SG das Bemühen um *deutschgesinnten Tugendmut, teutsche Aufrichtigkeit und Frömmigkeit* eine Rolle, z. T. mit puritanischer protestantischer Ethik, sowohl gegen die modisch-unaufrichtige Hofberedsamkeit (*conversatio*), Kavaliers- und Klerikermoral West- und Südeuropas gerichtet als auch gegen *grobianischen, pöbelhaften* Sittenverfall (auch beim Adel), besonders während des 30jährigen Krieges.

Von den kulturpatriotischen Zielen her sind auch einige sprachpolitische Ausdrucksformen bei den dt. SG zu verstehen: Wolfgang Ratke/Ratichius (1571–1635) richtete 1612 sein sprachreformerisches *Memorial* an den Reichstag, wenn auch ohne Erfolg; Christian Gueintz (1592–1650) rechtfertigte 1641 die Sprachkultivierung mit *Erhaltung Deutscher Hoheit*; Zesen rühmte die dt. Sprache 1656 als *Sprachenkeiserin*; Schottelius forderte 1663 die Obrigkeiten auf, über Sprachreformer, die die *"grundrichtigkeit"* der dt. Sprache nicht beachteten, eine Zensur auszuüben; Georg Philipp Harsdörffer (1607–1658) stellte solche Sprachneuerer '*denen Aufrührern die das Regiment zuverändern gedenken*' gleich. Die beliebte Formulierung *Haupt- und Heldensprache* erhob die Sprachpflege sozusagen zur 'staatlichen Aufgabe' (Huber 1984: 53; 248ff.). Der Jurist Schottelius berief sich für seine gelehrte Spracharbeit auf ndl. Naturrechtstheorien, also auf eine philosophische Grundlage des rationalisierten Verwaltungsstaats der Frühaufklärung: "*Auf die Enderung der Sprache folget eine Enderung der Sitten*". Hier kündigt sich der Sprach-Realismus oder Panlinguismus mancher moderner Sprachkritiker an. Mit der frühaufklärerischen, moralisch-pädagogischen Motivation verband sich teilweise noch eine religiöse: Sprachpflege als Buße für den als Strafe Gottes empfundenen Sprachverfall.

## 3. Die wichtigsten Sprachgesellschaften

3.1. Den Ausdruck *Sprachgesellschaft* gab es erst seit Leibniz (1697 für die Florentiner Akademie), seit 1824 für die besonders mit Sprache und Dichtung befaßten dt. Sozietäten; sie selbst nannten sich nur *Gesellschaft, Genossenschaft* oder *Orden*, mit meist symbolischen Attributen. Aus einer größeren, nicht mehr genau nachweisbaren Zahl werden in der germanistischen Forschung folgende vier in den Vordergrund gestellt (Otto 1972a; Engels 1983; Moser 1984; Bircher & van Ingen 1978).

– *Fruchtbringende Gesellschaft* [*FG*] (später auch: *Palmenorden*), begründet 1617 in Weimar von Fürst Ludwig v. Anhalt-Köthen auf Anregung des Weimarischen Hofmarschalls v. Teutleben; Sitze und Tagungsorte: Weimar, Köthen, Halle; bestehend bis nach 1680; insgesamt 890 nachgewiesene Mitglieder, auch in Süddeutschland und Österreich; die bedeutendsten: Fürst Ludwig, Herzog Anton Ulrich v. Braunschweig-Lüneburg, Sigmund v. Birken (1626–1681), August Buchner (1591–1661), Gryphius, Gueintz, Harsdörffer, Friedrich v. Logau (1604–1655), Johann Michael Moscherosch (1601–1669), Opitz, Johann Rist (1607–1667), Schottel, Caspar Stieler (1632–1707), Zesen.

– *Deutschgesinnte Genossenschaft* [*DG*]: begründet um 1642 in Hamburg von Zesen nach Vorbild der *FG*, aber in mehrere Zünfte gegliedert; stark christliche Ideale; insgesamt 207 nachgewiesene Mitglieder, zu denen auch Harsdörffer, Birken, Johann Klaj (1616–1656), Moscherosch, Joost van den Vondel (1587–1679) gehörten.
– *Pegnesischer Blumenorden* [*PB*]: gegründet 1644 in Nürnberg von Harsdörffer und Klaj; bis ins 18. Jh. insgesamt 117 nachgewiesene Mitglieder, darunter Birken, Rist, Schottel und die Dichterinnen Maria Katharina Stockfleth und Katharina Regina von Greiffenberg (1633–1694); anfangs mehr eine Literatenvereinigung; sehr tolerant, pietistisch orientiert; erst durch Birken sprachlich interessiert.
– *Elbschwanenorden* [*ES*]: gegründet 1658 in Wedel bei Hamburg von dem dortigen Pastor Rist auf Anregung fürstlicher *FG*-Mitglieder, in Konkurrenz und bald Feindschaft zu Zesen und seiner *DG*; bestehend bis zu Rists Tod 1667; 45 Mitglieder nachweisbar, z. T. bis nach Ostpreußen, Brandenburg, Obersachsen; für Sprache und Dichtung nur nebenbei interessiert.

Weniger ist über weitere Sprach- und Dichtergesellschaften bekannt: z. B. in Straßburg, Leipzig, Dresden und Königsberg.

Die weitaus bedeutendste SG nach Alter, Mitgliederzahl, Prestige und Wirkung war die *FG*, die den meisten anderen Vorbild war und um deren Mitgliedschaft sich die meisten Dichter und Sprachgelehrten der Barockzeit eifrig bewarben. Ihre Aktivitäten spielten sich, unter ständiger Einwirkung und Kontrolle des Fürsten Ludwig, mehr durch Briefwechsel, Begutachtungen und Vereinstraktate als auf Tagungen ab, von denen nur wenige bezeugt sind und auf denen immer nur wenige Mitglieder anwesend sein konnten. Auch bei den anderen SG hing die Vereinstätigkeit meist vom persönlichen Engagement der Gründer bzw. Oberhäupter ab. Es gab viele Doppel- und Mehrfachmitgliedschaften; die Oberhäupter anderer SG waren meist Mitglieder in der *FG*.

3.2. Die soziale Zusammensetzung war verschieden (Otto 1972a; 1977; Moser 1984; Hattenhauer 1987: 18f.): Bei der *FG* waren mit 75% Fürstlichkeiten und Adel tonangebend, entsprechend der kulturpatriotischen Motivation und dem im absolutistischen Deutschland relativ geringen politischen Prestige bürgerlicher Schichten. Das fürstliche Interesse an SG wird (auch von Zeitgenossen) am Bedarf mittlerer und kleiner Landesherren an Lobgedichten erklärt, während sich große Potentaten distanziert verhielten. Allerdings waren Fürst Ludwig als Übersetzer und Herzog Anton Ulrich als Dichter selbst literarisch produktiv. Ansonsten waren Mitglieder des Bildungsbürgertums (darunter später geadelte wie Zesen und Birken), z. T. auch aus dem Patriziat, die eigentlichen Träger der SG-Arbeit, vielfach Inhaber niederer Hofämter (Sekretäre, Hofmeister, Bibliothekare), während sich Räte und andere höhere Juristen meist ablehnend verhielten.

Katholische Mitglieder gab es kaum. In der *FG* wurden Geistliche meist abgelehnt, um konfessionelle und theologische Streitereien fernzuhalten. Aus politischen Gründen wurden auch einige Ausländer aufgenommen. Frauen waren in der *FG* nur als Ehefrauen von Mitgliedern zugelassen. Die Sitzordnung bei Tagungen der *FG* richtete sich nach dem Alter der Mitgliedschaft; die allegorischen Vereinsnamen (z. B. *der Nährende, der Suchende, der Schmackhafte* usw.) sollten Standesgleichheit und Gruppensolidarität fördern. Die Hamburger und Nürnberger SG waren ganz überwiegend bürgerlich, auch mit Geistlichen, und ließen z. T. auch Frauen als gleichberechtigt zu.

## 4. Ziele und Argumente

4.1. Soweit die reich überlieferten Dokumente (Vereinssatzungen, Programme, Festgedichte, Briefe usw.) schon ediert und ausgewertet sind (Jones 1995; Bircher 1970; Bircher & Conermann 1991ff.) läßt sich die Argumentationsentwicklung der dt. Sprachkultivierer des 17. Jh. wie folgt skizzieren (vor allem nach Huber 1984 und Josten 1976):

Im Sinne des alten rhetorischen Begriffs *puritas* war neben der Vermeidung / Verdeutschung *ausländischer* Wörter meist auch die Vermeidung bestimmter intralingualer Varianten gemeint: anstößiger, zweideutiger, veralteter, vulgärer, *provinzieller* Wörter, Wendungen und Formen, sowie bessere (konsequentere, einfachere) Orthographie, gute Aussprache, immer im Rahmen der oben angedeuteten allgemeinen moralischen und kulturpatriotischen Ziele. Zwischen *Reinheit* und *Richtigkeit* der Sprache unterschied man oft nicht.

4.2. Noch vorideologisch war zunächst das Bemühen um Nützlichkeit des Sprachgebrauchs für bestimmte praktische Zwecke wie Rhetorik und *Conversation*, so bei dem Reformpädagogen Ratke (E. Ising 1959), der ab 1610 breiten Erfolg bei der Verbesserung des muttersprachlichen Schulunterrichts vor allem in Anhalt-Köthen, Sachsen-Weimar, Hessen und England hatte. Solche zeitgemäß-pragmatischen Ziele spielten auch bei der *FG*, später bei dem Schul- und Rhetorikreformer Christian Weise (1642–1708) und bei den dt. Lexikographen des 17./18. Jh. eine Rolle.

4.3. Sprachideologisch, aus religiöser Wurzel (von Luther her), war dann das Argument der Gleichwertigkeit der deutschen Sprache mit den drei *Heiligen* Sprachen Hebräisch, Griechisch, Latein, also die Gleichstellung des Deutschen als *Hauptsprache* neben Ital. und Franz. gegen das Latein, so bei Ratke und den Poetikern Opitz, Zesen und Harsdörffer. Die Gleichwertigkeit wurde aus dem Wortreichtum (*copia verborum, völligkeit*) des Dt. begründet, womit sein reicher Vorrat an alten *Stammwörtern* und Wortbildungsmöglichkeiten gemeint war. So erklärt sich das starke Interesse für Probleme der Wortbildung, vor allem bei Gueintz, Zesen und Schottel.

4.4. Ein mehr historisierendes sprachideologisches Argument war das philologisch entdeckte oder sprachmythologisch angenommene hohe Alter der dt. Sprache, vor allem bei Opitz, Gueintz, Zesen, Schottel, Harsdörffer: Nach der Sprachursprungstheorie des bayerischen Humanisten Aventin (Johannes Turmair, 1477–1534) hielt man das Dt. für älter als die roman. Sprachen und glaubte, daß es direkt aus dem Hebräischen abstamme und nach der Babylonischen Sprachverwirrung durch *Tuiscon*, den angeblichen ersten deutschen König und seinen Sohn *Mannus* nach Deutschland gebracht worden sei (Jones 1993). In einer Radikalisierung des Kulturpatriotismus wurde der Gedanke der Gleichwertigkeit zur Überlegenheit der dt. Sprache über andere lebende Sprachen gesteigert; und nach der kulturkritisch-tendenziösen Behauptung des Tacitus, die Germanen seien 'unvermischt', forderte man mit dem Verweis auf die roman. Sprachen und das Englische als 'Mischsprachen' die Erhaltung der *Unvermischtheit* des Dt.

4.5. Eine mehr späthumanistisch-gelehrte Richtung erhielt die dt. Sprachkultivierung vor allem durch den am Wolfenbütteler Herzogshof wirkenden Sprachgelehrten Schottelius, besonders in seiner *Ausführlichen Arbeit von der Teutschen Haubt-Sprache* (1663). Seine Berufung auf Karls d. Gr. Bemühungen um eine dt. Grammatik und auf die Förderung des Dt. durch Könige und Kaiser bis hin zu Maximilian I. sind ebenso historisch fundiert wie sein Hinweis auf Luther "*als ein rechter Meister Teutscher Wolredenheit und beweglicher Zier*". Schottels auf Sprachkultivierung des Dt. für *Künste und Wissenschaften* gerichtete Theorie der *Sprachreinheit* beruhte auf seiner Forderung nach *Grundrichtigkeit* (gemäß dem historisch nachweisbaren älteren oder 'ursprünglichen' Gebrauch) und *Kunstrichtigkeit* (Regelhaftigkeit) gegen Beliebigkeit, Unregelmäßigkeit, Undeutlichkeit und bloßen Sprachgebrauch (Huber 1984: 48 ff.; Barbarić 1981; Takada 1985; Neuhaus 1991; v. Polenz 1994: 111 ff., 152 ff.).

In der Entwicklungslinie von späthumanistischer niederländischer Naturrechtstheorie (Hugo Grotius, Justus Lipsius) und Jakob Böhmes Ursprachentheorie zu aufklärerischem Rationalismus erscheint bei Schottelius der Gegensatz zwischen *Natur* und *Kunst* aufgehoben: Sprache sei *Natur* vom Ursprung her, mit *saftvollen Wurtzelen*. Aber zugleich habe sie aufgrund ihrer natürlichen Ordnung *tieffe Vernunfft* in ihrem gesetzmäßigen Aufbau, sei zugleich *Sprachnatur* und *Sprachkunst, Kunstgewächs* und *Kunstgebäu*.

Mit dem Standesbewußtsein der Späthumanisten, die sich dem absolutistischen Verwaltungsstaat andienen mußten, gilt Schottelius der allgemeine Sprachgebrauch (*mancherley Landarten*) nicht viel; er hält vielmehr die *Meister* und *gelehrten Männer*, die die *ars grammatica* beherrschen und anwenden, für fähig, durch Erforschung der älteren, ursprünglichen Sprachformen und durch Anwendung der *Analogie* als sprachliches Strukturprinzip die *Sprachrichtigkeit* festzustellen. Schottelius wurde für mehr als ein Jahrhundert zum Vorbild für systematische, rationalistische Grammatikforschung und für die Idealvorstellung 'Hochsprache', die sich nicht nach einem bestimmten Sprachusus (z. B. *Meißnisches Deutsch*) zu richten habe, sondern nach einem abstrakten schreibsprachlichen Auswahlprinzip aus überregionalem Sprachgebrauch, wissenschaftlich kontrolliert nach Regelhaftigkeit und Ursprünglichkeit, entstehen müsse.

4.6. Der Begrifff *Sprachreinheit* war noch bei Schottel, ebenso wie in der *FG*, erst in zweiter Linie als Kampf gegen die *alamodische* Sprachmischung zu verstehen. Die konkrete Wörterarbeit war *Sprachreinigung* in einem weiteren Sinne, auch in bezug auf indigene Wörter.

In den Vereinssatzungen wurde gefordert, daß in der dt. Sprache "*alles eingeschlichene Unreine, Ungesetzmäßige und Ausheimische abgeschaffet und in ein besseres, wo immer thunlich, verändert werde*"; "[...] *soll sich ein jeder der neuen, unbekannten Wörter, der wunderbaren und widrigen Zusammenfügungen, auch der verworfenen und undeutlichen Arten im Vortrag* [...] *enthalten* [...] *nicht nur neue Wörter selber erfinden, sondern zuerst in den älteren Schrifften nach passenden deutschen Ausdrücken suchen, sie lernen und benutzen*" [...] "*sich so wol der besten aussprache im reden als der reinesten im schreiben und Reime=dichten befleissigen*; [...] *entweder durch Schriften oder durch andere Mittel*; [...] *der hochsteigenden Poesie so mündlich als schriftlich.*"

Auch die Fremdwortverdeutschung verstand Schottel nicht als Selbstzweck; sie sollte vielmehr der besseren Ausnutzung der Sprachpotenz dt. Wortbildung dienen, für die Schottel methodisch grundlegend wurde (Gützlaff 1989). Die "Freilegung des durch das Fremde zugeschütteten Wortbildungspotentials" war ein innersprachliches Motiv für Fremdwortverdeutschung, weshalb sich spätere Fremdwortpuristen immer wieder auf Schottel (und Leibniz) beriefen (Kirkness 1984: 292). Während die *puritas* der Sprache in der *FG* anfangs noch im Zusammenhang mit der rhetorischen *conversatio* als überständische Tugend verstanden wurde, um durch *Sprachrichtigkeit* niemanden sozial zu benachteiligen oder zu bevorzugen, wurde der *puritas*-Gedanke bei Schottel und seinen Nachfolgern von praktischer Nützlichkeit isoliert und zum abstrakten philologischen Prinzip gesteigert, zur *Sprachkunst* für Gebildete im repräsentationsbedürftigen absolutistischen Staat (Huber 1984: 259ff.). Dieser gelehrten Richtung zwischen Späthumanismus und Aufklärung ist es auch zuzuschreiben, daß die Sprachkultivierungsbemühungen des 17. und 18. Jh. vorwiegend und primär der Schriftlichkeit des Dt. zugute kamen und das Dt. schon ab Ende des 18. Jh. sprachkritisch als *papieren* und *pedantisch* (d. h. 'gelehrt'), also politisch unbrauchbar galt (Schiewe 1989).

## 5. Fremdwortverdeutschung

5.1. Nur ein Teil der Aktivitäten der SG, aber weitaus mehr als nur Nebenprodukt ihrer Übersetzungsarbeit, war die Bekämpfung, Vermeidung und Verdeutschung fremdsprachlicher Wörter, also der Fremdwortpurismus als Sprachreinigung im engeren Sinne (zusammenfassend vor allem Jones 1995; Kirkness 1975; 1984). In den Programmen der SG stand die Erwähnung der *Gemenge-* oder *Flickwörter*, der *Sprachmengerey* oft erst an zweiter oder letzter Stelle. Im *PB* und im *ES* stand er in der ersten Zeit nicht im Vordergrund. Warnungen vor Sprachverderb durch Sprachmischung gab es schon im 16. Jh. bei einigen Schriftstellern (Jones 1995: 17ff.). Für SG und Dichter der Barockzeit war Martin Opitz' Aufruf zur Vermeidung von Fremdwörtern im hohen poetischen Stil vorbildlich (*Aristarchus sive de contemptu linguae Teutonicae*, 1617; *Deutsche Poeterey*, 1624).

5.2. Eine erste Radikalisierung der Fremdwortkritik zeigt sich in dem guten Dutzend satirischer und parodistischer Schriften zwischen 1642 und 1652 mit Titeln wie *Rettung der Edlen Teutschen Hauptsprache, Unartig Teutscher Sprach-Verderber*, in denen meist in Form fingierter Briefe oder Reden Texte mit Häufung fremdsprachlicher Wörter der Lächerlichkeit preisgegeben wurden. In der gleichen Zeit steigerte Zesen seine Spracharbeit zum übertriebenen Fremdwortpurismus (Otto 1972b; Blume 1967; 1972; van Ingen 1970). Im Rahmen der allgemeinen kulturkritischen Welle der Satiren und Parodien jener Jahre muß Zesens Übereifer als durchaus zeitmodisch erklärt werden. Er berief sich für die Fremdwortverdeutschung auf die *FG*, auf

Vorgänger seit den Römern und Zeitgenossen, auch auf Niederländer (Jones 1995: 198ff.). Sein Engagement bei diesem Bemühen muß von den Niederlanden angeregt sein, wo die Ersetzung oder Nachprägung fremdsprachlicher Wörter eine alte frühbürgerliche Tradition war (Kirkness 1975: 41; Engels 1983: 128; 136). Etwa 15% von Zesens Verdeutschungen hatten ndl. Vorbilder (Trunz 1937; Blume 1967).

Viele von Zesens Verdeutschungen sind — wenn auch oft mit Bedeutungsdifferenzierung neben dem Lehnwort — bis heute erfolgreich geblieben. Meist sind es semantisch durchsichtige, aber recht speziell motivierte Determinativkomposita: *Augenblick (Moment), Gesichtskreis (Horizont), Grundstein (Fundament), Jahrbücher (Annalen), lustwandeln (spazieren), Rechtschreibung (Orthographie), Trauerspiel (Tragödie)* usw.; aber auch Ableitungen nach produktiven Wortbildungsmustern: *Bücherei (Bibliothek), Leidenschaft (Passion), Entwurf (Projekt), Abstand (Distanz), Vertrag (conventio)* usw. Seine Verdeutschungsarbeit ist schon damals als *Wortschöpferey, Wortschmiederey, Neuerungssucht* verspottet worden, mit Beispielen, die, aus dem Zusammenhang gerissen, mit sehr einseitiger Wortmotivierung lächerlich wirken, von Zesen aber nur als Gelegenheitsvorschläge in bestimmten, oft poetisch-metaphorischen Kontexten, nicht als Normsetzungen, gemeint waren, z. B. *Gesichtserker (Nase), Tageleuchter (Fenster), Zeugemutter (Natur)* usw.

Wegen seiner kühnen, die Wortbildungskreativität anregenden Verdeutschungsarbeit muß Zesen das Verdienst zugeschrieben werden, ein sprachkritisches Bewußtsein in Deutschland provoziert zu haben, mit dem bis ins 20. Jh. die semantische Motiviertheit von Wörtern und der Wortgebrauch überhaupt besonders wichtig genommen wurde. — Zum Sprachpurismus allgemein s. Rechtmann 1953; Jernudd & Shapiro 1989; Thomas 1991 (s. 6.4. und 6.5.).

## 6. Wirkungen

6.1. Im Unterschied zur vorbildgebenden Florentiner Akademie (Flamm 1994) erscheinen die tatsächlichen Leistungen der SG auf den ersten Blick als gering. Als offizielles Produkt der *FG* kann allenfalls die *Deutsche Rechtschreibung* von Christian Gueintz (1645) bezeichnet werden, da sie von Fürst Ludwig in Auftrag gegeben war und der Verfasser sie als Mitglied vor der Publikation von der *FG* hat überprüfen lassen. Der Wörterbuchplan der *FG* kam offiziell nie zustande. Aber Caspar Stieler hat sein Wörterbuch noch 1691 — als die *FG* eigentlich nicht mehr bestand — unter seinem Gesellschaftsnamen *Der Spate* veröffentlicht und als Publikation der *FG* gelten lassen. Andere bedeutende sprachwissenschaftliche, poetologische oder rhetorische Werke von Gesellschaftsmitgliedern wie Opitz, Schottel, Harsdörffer, Buchner, Zesen sind meist vor der Zeit ihrer Mitgliedschaft entstanden, dienten z. T. als Voraussetzung für die Aufnahme in die *FG*, können also als Arbeiten im Umkreis der SG gelten. Praktische Wirkung im Rahmen der Bemühungen, die dt. Sprache literaturfähig zu machen, hatten die SG vor allem mit ihrer Übersetzungsarbeit, die meist auch programmatisch als Vorübung für eigene literarische Werke gefordert wurde. Einige Dutzend Mitglieder von SG sind als Übersetzer bekannt, auch Nichtmitglieder, die Übersetzungen mit dem Ziel der Mitgliedschaft einreichten. Zweck dieser Sprachübungen war vor allem das Experiment der Nachahmung bestimmter (ausländischer) Stilformen. Übersetzungen aus modernen Fremdsprachen, vor allem Franz., überwogen solche aus dem Lat. und Griech. Bedeutend waren die SG auch als Zentren des literarischen Lebens im 17. Jh. (Moser 1984: 130f.).

Die vom Pfälzer Hof stammende, teilweise am Braunschweiger Hof erzogene Herzogin Elisabeth Charlotte von Orleans hat, jahrzehntelang durch Briefeschreiben um die Bewahrung ihrer dt. Sprachkompetenz in fremdsprachiger Umgebung eifrig bemüht, noch um 1700 einmal brieflich nach jemandem aus der '*fruchtbringenden Gesellschaft zu Franckfort*' gefragt, der ihr in einer Frage des dt. Wortgebrauchs Rat geben könne (Mattheier 1990). Indirekt von der *FG* und anderen SG angeregt sind die zahlreichen *Deutschen Gesellschaften*, die es im 18. Jh. in vielen Städten gab. Johann Christoph Gottscheds (1700—1766) Erfolg in Österreich beruhte z. T. auf der um sprachlichen Rat gefragten Leipziger *Deutschen Gesellschaft*.

6.2. Die mit der Übersetzungstätigkeit zusammenhängende praktische und metasprachlich-diskursive Wortschatzarbeit hat viel dazu beigetragen, daß beim Aufbau und bei der Weiterentwicklung dt. Fach-, Wissenschafts- und Verwaltungsterminologien neben der Entlehnung von Internationalismen und der Lehnwortbildung die Tendenz zur Lehnprägung mit indigenen Lexemen und Wortbildungsmitteln relativ stark geblieben ist. Das kulturpatriotische Ziel der Literatur- und Wissenschaftsfähigkeit der dt. Sprache erforderte den Nachweis und den Ausbau des Wortschatzreichtums im Rahmen der *Grundrichtigkeit, Kunstrichtigkeit* und des *Fortwachses* nach Schottels Sprachtheorie: "[...] *daß die Stammwörter wollauten / und jhr ding / dessen Namen sie sind / eigentlich austrükken*". Die vielgelästerten Übertreibungen, Pedanterien und Mißerfolge bei Verdeutschungen (nicht nur bei Zesen) sind deshalb eher als philologische Experimentierübungen früher 'Germanisten' zu verstehen, aus einer "Art intensiver Laboratoriumssituation, deren Paradigmatik darin besteht, daß der Weg einer Sprache aus einer nur umgangswertigen Gebrauchsfunktion zur vollen und differenzierten Verwendung auf allen Textgebieten verfolgt werden kann" (Kleinschmidt 1990: 204).

Mit der sprachstrukturellen Bevorzugung der Wortbildung, vor allem der determinativen Komposita, und der damit zusammenhängenden semantischen Motiviertheit von Wörtern ('durchsichtige' Wörter als 'wesenhafte Abbilder' der Dinge) konzentrierte sich die frühe Sprachkultivierung des Dt. – anders als in Frankreich, dessen Literatursprache bereits konsolidiert war – auf Wortbildung, Morphemik und Wortschatz, während sie auf dem Gebiet des Satzbaus kaum etwas tat oder erreichte (Blume 1978a: 46). Die Motiviertheitsideologie wirkt bis heute bei dt. Sprachkritikern und bei 'semantischen Kämpfen' und Bezeichnungskonkurrenzen in der Politiksprache nach, von Friedrich Engel's Kritik an den Bezeichnungen *Arbeitgeber/-nehmer* bis zu *Atommülldeponie* statt *Entsorgungspark* in der Ökobewegung.

6.3. Eine indirekte Wirkung der SG war auch eine gewisse Kontinuität in der dt. Lexikographie von der Wortschatzarbeit und darauf bezogenen Diskussionen in der *FG* zu den verschiedenen Wortschatzkodifikationen des späten 17. und des 18. Jh. (G. Ising 1956; Henne 1968; Reichmann 1989; Kühn & Püschel 1989; v. Polenz 1994: Kap. 5.7): Angeregt von der Entstehung des italienischen Akademiewörterbuchs durch Fürst Ludwig, wurde in der *FG* ein dt. Wörterbuchprogramm im kulturpatriotischen Sinne diskutiert: Reichtum und Gleichwertigkeit/Überlegenheit der dt. Sprache sollten nachgewiesen werden, möglichst nach dem Wortstammprinzip und mit Wortbildungsfreudigkeit über den bereits nachweisbaren Usus hinaus, so in den Wörterbüchern von Georg Henisch (1616), Caspar Stieler (1691), Matthias Kramer (1700–1702), Christoph Ernst Steinbach (1734); s. v. Polenz 1994: 183–186. Bei Stieler war die Bindung an den Geist der FG nur noch formale Traditionsbezeugung; als erster dt. Publizistikwissenschaftler hat er die lexikographische Sprachkultivierung schon im praktisch-aufklärerischen Sinne verstanden, indem er, im Bewußtsein der wichtigen Volksbildungsfunktion der Zeitung, seinem Buch *Zeitungs Lust und Nutz* (1695) ein alphabetisches Verzeichnis *Erkärung Derer in den Zeitungen gemeiniglich vorkommenden fremden und tunklen Wörter* beigab, womit er die Tradition der Zeitungslexika und Konversationslexika begründete (Wilke 1985).

In der zweiten, von franz. und engl. Vorbildern beeinflußten Phase der frühen dt. Lexikographie, von Leonhard Frisch (1741) bis Johann Christoph Adelung (1774–86) und Joachim Heinrich Campe (1807–13), ging es im Sinne der Aufklärung, aufgrund einer u. a. von Leibniz angeregten Lexikographiediskussion, mehr um gesamtsprachliche Dokumentation (Kodifizierung) des literarisch belegbaren Wortschatzes, ohne Wortneubildungen, ohne Zwang zur Fremdwortverdeutschung. Ziel war vor allem Sprachrichtigkeit und Sprachdeutlichkeit, mit systematischen Bedeutungsdifferenzierungen und -definitionen, um die dt. Sprache für Wissenschaften, abstraktes Denken und andere Erfordernisse modern-rationalistischer Sprachkultur leistungsfähiger zu machen.

Die dt. Lexikographen haben von Henisch bis Campe (und darüber hinaus bis zu den Brüdern Grimm) über Generationen hinweg miteinander kooperiert, indem sie voneinander gelernt und abgeschrieben, einander kritisiert haben. Dies und die Benutzung von Wörterbüchern durch Schriftsteller in der Zeit um 1800 entspricht dem Geist und den Zielen der alten SG.

6.4. Die Weiterentwicklung des Fremdwortpurismus war zwar ebenfalls kontinuierlich, aber mehr von Widersprüchen, Mißverständnissen und Einseitigkeiten gekennzeichnet. Während Gottsched und Adelung der Fremdwortverdeutschung reserviert gegenüberstanden, hat Campe vor seinem Allgemeinwörterbuch mit theoretischen Schriften über *Reini-*

*gung* und *Bereicherung* der dt. Sprache und seinem zweibändigen *Wörterbuch zur Erklärung und Verdeutschung der unserer Sprache aufgedrungenen fremden Ausdrücke* (1801), mit großem Eifer an die Tradition der SG, vor allem Zesens, angeknüpft und mit zahlreichen teils erfolgreichen, teils nicht akzeptierten Verdeutschungen viel Spott, aber auch ernsthafte Diskussion provoziert (Daniels 1979; Kirkness 1975: 78ff.; 139ff.; v. Polenz 1994: 126ff.).

Im Gegensatz zur nationalistischen Vereinnahmung Campes bei den Sprachpuristen und Germanisten des 19. Jh. war Campes Verdeutschungsarbeit nachweislich und ausdrücklich volksaufklärerisch und demokratisch motiviert. Sie war die Ersatzaktivität eines durch die restaurative Verhinderung der Revolution in Deutschland gescheiterten Reformpädagogen und Journalisten: Nur durch Verbreitung des gelehrten Aufklärungswissens in alle Bevölkerungsschichten, mit aus sich heraus verständlichen Begriffswörtern, könne allmählich eine Veränderung der gesellschaftlichen Verhältnisse herbeigeführt werden, ähnlich wie der lange Zeit ignorierte spätaufklärerische Sprachkritiker Carl Gustav Jochmann (1789–1830) die politikunfähige, elitäre, akademisch-schreibsprachliche dt. Sprachkultur der Zeit um 1800 beurteilt hat (Kirkness 1984: 294; Schiewe 1988ab; 1989).

6.5. Die nationalistische Art von Fremdwortpurismus, von der sich bereits bei Klopstock Ansätze erkennen lassen, begann im wesentlichen in der Napoleonischen Zeit und wirkte sich in immer neuen Wellen sprachideologischer Unterstützung politischer Bewegungen aus: vom romantischen Nationalismus der Befreiungskriege über den Nationalchauvinismus der Wilhelminischen Zeit bis zur deutschtümelnden Begleitbewegung des Nationalsozialismus (Kirkness 1975; 1985; v. Polenz 1967; Lutzebäck 1991; Ameri 1991; Olt 1991). In mancher Hinsicht bedeutete der 1885 gegründete *Allgemeine deutsche Sprachverein* eine Anknüpfung und Fortsetzung der SG des 17./18. Jh. Seine Fremdwortkritik und -verdeutschung hat sich Ende des 19. Jh. auch als umfangreiche staatliche Terminologieänderung des Bismarckreiches (ohne die anderen deutschsprachigen Staaten) ausgewirkt, in der frühen NS-Zeit als sprachideologischer *Gleichschaltungs*-Beitrag, im Zweiten Weltkrieg mitunter als nationalsozialistische Personenverfolgung, z. B. im Elsaß und in Luxemburg gegen den Gebrauch des Franz. und franz. Wörter (Simon 1979; 1989; Bernsmeier 1983). Daneben, und in seiner Nachfolgeorganisation *Gesellschaft für deutsche Sprache* (nach 1945) hat man sich, eher im Geiste der alten SG, in der Zeitschrift *Muttersprache* und in zahlreichen lokalen Zweigvereinen und ähnlichen Vereinen in Österreich und in der Schweiz, um sprachpraktische Fragen wie Fachwortschatz, Rechtschreibung, guten Stil, regionale und soziale Varietäten und Sprachberatung gekümmert (Blume 1991; Olt 1991; Bernsmeier 1977; 1980; Greule & Ahlvers-Liebel 1986: 23ff.).

6.6. Indirekte Nachwirkungen der SG sind, im Sinne frühaufklärerischer Ziele der Sprachkultivierung, bei den dt. Grammatikern und Orthographielehrern des 17. und 18. Jh. (→ Art. 107, → Art. 114) nachzuweisen, die zunehmend zur Konsolidierung der dt. Schriftsprachnormen, aber auch zur entsprechenden Sprachbewußtseinsbildung beigetragen haben (Jellinek 1913–14; Schmidt-Wilpert 1985; Nerius 1967; Reichmann 1978; Gardt 1994; Gardt et al. 1991). Sie waren keine eigenwilligen Theoretiker, keine Normsetzer oder Stubengelehrte; sie waren eher systematisierende Vermittler, Multiplikatoren und Ratgeber für eine engagierte, in der Sprachreflexion bereits voranschreitende Schicht literarisch Gebildeter und Interessierter. Sie hatten ähnliche berufliche Tätigkeiten wie die meisten Mitglieder der SG: Gelehrte, Pädagogen, Bibliothekare, Übersetzer, Publizisten usw. und standen in einem Generationen und Regionen übergreifenden persönlichen Diskurszusammenhang der bildungsbürgerlichen Sprachbewußtseinsgeschichte, wie sich aus neueren Forschungen ergibt (Bergmann 1982; 1995; Brekle et al. 1992ff.; Erben 1989; v. Polenz 1984; Kap. 5.6):

In meist *Deutsche Sprachkunst/-lehre* genannten, z. T. in mehreren Auflagen oder Nachdrucken erschienenen Grammatikbüchern bzw. Orthographielehren, von den mit der FG verbundenen Ratke 1619, Gueintz 1641 und Schottel 1642 bis zu Gottsched 1748, Aichinger 1753 und Adelung 1781 sind grammatikalische und orthographische Regularitäten beschrieben, erklärt und diskutiert worden, die im wesentlichen nachträgliche Kodifikationen bereits weithin üblicher und akzeptierter Variantenpräferenzen darstellen (s. v. Polenz 1994: 149–168). Diese Konsensbildung ist, ganz nach Art der SG, durch intellektuelle Kooperation zustandegekommen, durch persönliche Beziehungen, Besuche, Briefwechsel, Begutachtungen, literarische und publizistische Arbeiten, Belehrung, Diskussion und Polemik in Zeitschriften, verlegerische Aktivitäten, vor allem durch Kenntnis und Benutzung der Vorgänger sowie Mitgliedschaften oder Beziehungen zu mehreren lokalen *Deutschen Gesellschaften.* Dies gilt auch für Süddeutschland und Österreich, wo anfangs widerstrebend, später sprachwissenschaftlich und sprachpolitisch bewußt sich anpassend, die von Gottsched propagierten mittel- und norddeutsch orientierten, aber im Süden längst überregional geläufigen neuhochdt. Schriftsprachnormen im Laufe der zweiten Hälfte des 18. Jh. übernommen wurden, in einigen Fällen auch mit literarischen Verweisen auf die Arbeit und Ziele der *FG* und Schottels (Reiffenstein 1988; 1989; 1995; Mattheier 1989; Wiesinger 1985; 1995; v. Polenz 1994: 171 ff.).

Diese im wesentlichen vorpolitische, noch nicht staatlich institutionalisierte, vorwiegend privat-sozietäre Konsensbildung der dt. Schriftsprachstandardisierung hat im 19. Jh. (und in konservativer Haltung bis ins 20.) charakteristische Merkmale der in der Schule gelehrten und gesellschaftlich erwarteten Sprachnormen zur Folge gehabt: bildungssprachlich, konservativ-belletristisch, schreibsprachlich, seriös, pedantisch, puristisch, mehr an Richtigkeit und gehobenem Stil orientiert als an Allgemeinverständlichkeit, praktischer Nützlichkeit und Weltoffenheit.

6.7. Alle Versuche, nach dem Vorbild der *Académie Française* (→ Art. 115) eine dt. Sprachakademie als nationale sprachkultivierende und -normierende Institution zu gründen, sind gescheitert (Flamm 1994): Ansätze dazu in Form von Empfehlungen, Denkschriften, Vorträgen, Eingaben hat es z. B. von Leibniz, Gottsched, Klopstock, Herder, Uhland, v. Ranke, Sanders gegeben, bis zur Reichsgründung (1871) mit traditionell kulturpatriotischer Motivation, im 19. Jh. mit dem Ziel, ein breites dt. Nationalbewußtsein für die Gründung eines dt. Nationalstaats zu fördern, nach 1871, als dieses Ziel erreicht war, mehr mit verschiedenen speziellen praktischen und wissenschaftlichen Zielen (Fremdwortgebrauch, Rechtschreibung, Literatenvereinigung, Deutsch im Ausland).

Davon sind nur zustandegekommen: eine *Deutsche Akademie* in München als eingetragener Verein (1925–1945), das *Goethe-Institut* (ab 1932), in der NS-Zeit ein *Sprachpflegeamt* (1941–45), in der Nachkriegszeit die *Deutsche Akademie für Sprache und Dichtung* (ab 1949) in Darmstadt, abgesehen von rein wissenschaftlichen Zentralinstituten wie dem *Deutschen Sprachatlas* in Marburg, dem DDR-*Zentralinstitut für dt. Sprache* an der Ostberliner Akademie der Wissenschaften und dem *Institut für deutsche Sprache (IdS)* in Mannheim (seit 1964).

Versuche, eine autoritäre Sprachakademie nach franz. Vorbild zu gründen, sind (nach Flamm 1994) mißlungen oder nicht zustandegekommen, weil die dt. Fürstenstaaten daran nicht interessiert waren, der Wiener Kaiserhof des Alten Reiches sich stets ablehnend verhielt, territoriale Zersplitterung, konfessionelle Gegensätze, später nationalstaatliche Eigeninteressen (Schweiz, Österreich) entgegenstanden. Außerdem waren die Interessenten und Experten sich stets über die Ziele uneinig und niemand hat einen voll ausgearbeiteten Plan vorgelegt. Von Anfang an, im Grunde seit Schottels Theorie von *Grund-* und *Kunstrichtigkeit*, ließen sich wissenschaftliche Forschungs- und praktische Sprachpflegeziele kaum miteinander vereinbaren, vor allem seit Herders Lehre vom natürlichen Wachsen von Sprache, das keine normativen Eingriffe verträgt. So hat sich für die dt. Sprache ein kaum organisiertes, konfliktreiches System der Sprachstandardisierung entwickelt, das hauptsächlich auf private Gruppen-, Institutions- und Verlagsinitiativen angewiesen ist, z. B. bei der Rechtschreibung, der Lautnormung, der technischen Terminologisierung. Dies entspricht auch den schlechten Erfahrungen der Deutschsprachigen mit autoritärem Zentralismus und ihren guten mit kulturellem Liberalismus, Föderalismus und flexibler Pragmatik.

## 7. Bibliographie


Ahlzweig, Claus. 1994. *Muttersprache – Vaterland. Die deutsche Nation und ihre Sprache.* Opladen.

Ameri, Sussan Milantchi. 1991. *Die deutschnationale Sprachbewegung im Wilhelminischen Reich.* New York etc.: Lang.

Barbarić, Stjepan. 1981. *Zur grammatischen Terminologie von J. G. Schottelius und K. Stieler, mit Ausblick auf die Ergebnisse bei ihren Vorgängern.* Bern etc.: Lang.

Barthold, Friedrich Wilhelm. 1969 [1848]. *Geschichte der Fruchtbringenden Gesellschaft.* Berlin. (Neudruck Hildesheim: Olms.)

Bergmann, Rolf. 1982. "Zum Anteil der Grammatiker an der Normierung der neuhochdeutschen Schriftsprache". *Sprachwissenschaft* 7.261–281.

Berns, Jörg Jochen. 1977. *Justus Georg Schottelius 1612–1671. Ein Teutscher Gelehrter am Wolfenbütteler Hof.* (= *Ausstellungskataloge der Herzog August Bibliothek*, 18.) Wolfenbüttel.

Bernsmeier, Helmut. 1977. "Der Allgemeine deutsche Sprachverein in seiner Gründungsphase". *Muttersprache* 87.369–395.

–. 1980. "Der Allgemeine Deutsche Sprachverein in der Zeit von 1912 bis 1932". *Muttersprache* 90.117–140.

–. 1983. "Der Deutsche Sprachverein im 'Dritten Reich'". *Muttersprache* 93.35–58.

Besch, Werner, Oskar Reichmann & Stefan Sonderegger, Hg. 1984–85. *Sprachgeschichte. Ein Handbuch zur Geschichte der deutschen Sprache und ihrer Erforschung.* Berlin & New York: de Gruyter. (HSK 2.1, 2.2.). 2., erw. Aufl. 1998 ff.

Bircher, Martin, Hg. 1970. *Die Fruchtbringende Gesellschaft. Quellen und Dokumente in 4 Bänden.* München: Kösel.

– & Klaus Conermann, Hg. 1991. *Die deutsche Akademie des 17. Jahrhunderts. Fruchtbringende Gesellschaft. Kritische Ausgabe der Briefe, Beilagen und Akademiearbeiten, Dokumente und Darstellungen.* Tübingen: Niemeyer.

– & Ferdinand van Ingen, Hg. 1978. *Sprachgesellschaften, Sozietäten, Dichtergruppen.* Hamburg: Hauswedell.

Blackall, Eric. 1966. *Die Entwicklung des Deutschen zur Literatursprache 1700–1775. Mit einem Bericht über neue Forschungsergebnisse 1955–64 von Dieter Kimpel.* Stuttgart: Metzler & Poeschel.

Blume, Herbert. 1967. *Die Morphologie von Zesens Wortneubildungen.* Clausthal-Zellerfeld.

–. 1972. "Zur Beurteilung von Zesens Wortneubildungen". van Ingen 1972.253–273.

–. 1978a. "Sprachgesellschaften und Sprache". Bircher & van Ingen 1978.39–52.

–. 1978b. "Sprachtheorie und Sprachenlegitimation im 17. Jh. in Schweden und in Kontinentaleuropa". *Arkiv för nordisk filologie* 93.205–218.

–. 1980. "Deutsche Literatursprache des Barock". *Lexikon der germanistischen Linguistik* hg. von Hans Peter Althaus, Helmut Henne & Herbert E. Wiegand, 719–725. 2. Aufl. Tübingen: Niemeyer.

–. 1991. "Die Sprachgesellschaften des 17. Jahrhunderts in der Sicht des Allgemeinen Deutschen Sprachvereins". *Europäische Barock-Rezeption* hg. von Klaus Garber, 605–616. Wiesbaden: Harrassowitz.

Braun, Peter, Hg. 1979. *Fremdwort-Diskussion.* München: Fink.

Brekle, Herbert E. et al. 1992 ff. *Bio-bibliographisches Handbuch zur Sprachwissenschaft des 18. Jahrhunderts. Die Grammatiker, Lexikographen und Sprachtheoretiker des deutschsprachigen Raums mit Beschreibung ihrer Werke.* Tübingen: Niemeyer.

Brunot, Ferdinand. 1934. *Histoire de la langue française des origines à 1900*, vol. VIII,1: *Le français dans les divers pays d'Europe.* Paris: Colin.

Brunt, Richard James. 1983. *The Influence of the French Language on the German Vocabulary (1649–1735).* Berlin & New York: de Gruyter.

Cherubim, Dieter. 1995. "Schottelius. Justus Georg". *Lexicon grammaticorum*, hg. von H. Stammerjohann et al. Tübingen: Niemeyer.

– & Siegfried Grosse & Klaus J. Mattheier, Hg. 1998. *Sprache und bürgerliche Nation. Beiträge zur deutschen und europäischen Sprachgeschichte des 19. Jahrhunderts.* Berlin & New York: de Gruyter.

Daniels, Karlheinz. 1979. "Erfolg und Mißerfolg der Fremdwortverdeutschung. Schicksal der Verdeutschungen von J. H. Campe". Nachdruck von 1959. Braun 1979: 145–181.

Engels, Heinz. 1983. *Die Sprachgesellschaften des 17. Jahrhunderts.* Gießen: Schmitz.

Erben, Johannes. 1989. "Die Entstehung unserer Schriftsprache und der Anteil deutscher Grammatiker am Normierungsprozeß". *Sprachwissenschaft* 14.6–28.

Flamm, Traugott. 1994. *Eine deutsche Sprachakademie. Gründungsversuche und Ursachen des Scheiterns (von den Sprachgesellschaften des 17. Jahrhunderts bis 1945).* Frankfurt/M. etc.: Lang.

Flood, John L. et al. Hg. 1993. *'Das unsichtbare Band der Sprache'. Studies in German language and linguistic history in memory of Leslie Seiffert.* Stuttgart: Heinz.

Garber, Klaus & Heinz Wismann, Hg. 1995. *Europäische Sozietätsbewegung und demokratische Tradition. Die europäischen Akademien der Frühen Neuzeit zwischen Frührenaissance und Spätaufklärung.* 2 Bde. Tübingen: Niemeyer.

Gardt, Andreas. 1994. *Sprachreflexion in Barock und Frühaufklärung. Entwürfe von Böhme bis Leibniz.* Berlin & New York: de Gruyter.

–. 1999. *Geschichte der Sprachwissenschaft in Deutschland vom Mittelalter bis ins 20. Jahrhundert.* Berlin & New York: de Gruyter.

Gardt, Andreas et al. 1991. "Sprachkonzeptionen in Barock und Aufklärung. Ein Vorschlag für ihre Beschreibung". *ZPSK* 44.17–33.

Gardt, Andreas, Klaus J. Mattheier & Oskar Reichmann, Hg. 1995. *Sprachgeschichte des Neuhochdeutschen. Gegenstände, Methoden, Theorien.* Tübingen: Niemeyer.

Greule, Albrecht & Elisabeth Ahlvers-Liebel. 1986. *Germanistische Sprachpflege. Geschichte, Praxis und Zielsetzung.* Darmstadt: Wissenschaftliche Buchgesellschaft.

Gützlaff, Kathrin. 1988. "Simon Stevin und J. G. Schottelius – Spuren der deutsch-niederländischen

Beziehungen im 17. Jh.". *Sprache in Vergangenheit und Gegenwart* hg. von Wolfgang Brandt & Rudolf Freudenberg, 91–108. Marburg: Elwert.

Gützlaff, Kathrin. 1989. *Von der Fügung Teutscher Stammwörter. Die Wortbildung in J. G. Schottelius' "Ausführlicher Arbeit von der Teutschen HaubtSprache"*. Hildesheim: Olms.

Hardtwig, Wolfgang. 1989. *Sozietäts- und Vereinswesen in Deutschland 1500–1870.* Stuttgart.

Hattenhauer, Hans. 1987. *Zur Geschichte der deutschen Rechts- und Gesetzessprache.* (= *Joachim-Jungius-Gesellschaft d. Wiss.*, 5,2.) Hamburg & Göttingen: Vandenhoeck & Ruprecht.

Hausmann, Franz Josef et al., Hg. 1989. *Wörterbücher/Dictionaries/Dictionnaires.* Berlin & New York: de Gruyter. (HSK 5).

Henne, Helmut. 1968. Deutsche Lexikographie und Sprachnorm im 17. und 18. Jahrhundert". *Wortgeographie und Gesellschaft* hg. von Walther Mitzka, 80–114. Berlin: de Gruyter.

Huber, Wolfgang. 1984. *Kulturpatriotismus und Sprachbewußtsein. Studien zur deutschen Philologie des 17. Jahrhunderts.* Frankfurt/M. usw.: Lang.

Ingen, Ferdinand van. 1970. *Philipp von Zesen.* Stuttgart: Metzler.

Ingen, Ferdinand van, ed. 1972. *Philipp von Zesen 1619–1689. Beiträge zu seinem Leben und Werk.* Wiesbaden: Steiner.

–. 1978. "Die Erforschung der Sprachgesellschaften unter sozialgeschichtlichem Aspekt". Bircher & van Ingen 1978: 9–26.

–. 1987. "Die Rhetorik-Kammern in den Niederlanden und die Sprachgesellschaften in Deutschland". *Res Publica Litteraria* hg. von Sebastian Neumeister & Conrad Wiedemann, 111–130. Wiesbaden: Harrassowitz.

Ising, Erika. 1959. *Wolfgang Ratkes Schriften zur deutschen Grammatik (1612–1630).* Berlin: Akademie-Verlag.

Ising, Gerhard. 1956. *Die Erfassung der deutschen Sprache des ausgehenden 17. Jahrhunderts in den Wörterbüchern Matthias Kramers und Kaspar Stielers.* Berlin: Akademie-Verlag.

Jellinek, Max Hermann. 1913–1914. *Geschichte der neuhochdeutschen Grammatik von den Anfängen bis zu Adelung.* 2 Bde. Heidelberg: Winter.

Jernudd, Björn H. & Michael J. Shapiro, Hg. 1989. *The Politics of Language Purism.* Berlin & New York.

Jones, William Jervis. 1976. *Lexicon of French Borrowings in the German Vocabulary (1575–1648).* Berlin & New York: de Gruyter.

–. 1993. "König Deutsch zu Abrahams Zeiten: Some perceptions of the place of German within the family of languages from Aventinus to Zedler". Flood et al. 1993. 189–213.

–, Hg. 1995. *Sprachhelden und Sprachverderber. Dokumente zur Erforschung des Fremdwortpurismus im Deutschen (1478–1750), ausgewählt und kommentiert.* Berlin & New York: de Gruyter.

Josten, Dirk. 1976. *Sprachvorbild und Sprachnorm im Urteil des 16. und 17. Jahrhunderts. Sprachlandschaftliche Prioritäten, Sprachautoritäten, sprachimmanente Argumentation.* Frankfurt/M. & Bern: Lang.

Kiedroń, Stefan. 1991. *Niederländische Einflüsse auf die Sprachtheorie von Justus Georg Schottelius.* Wroclaw: Wydawnictwo Uniwersytetu Wroclawskiego.

Kimpel, Dieter, Hg. 1985. *Mehrsprachigkeit in der deutschen Aufklärung.* Hamburg: Meiner.

Kinnemark, Karin. 1964. "Studien zum Fremdwort in deutschen Zeitungen in der 1. Hälfte des 17. Jahrhunderts". *Publizistik* 9.359–363.

Kirkness, Alan. 1975. *Zur Sprachreinigung im Deutschen 1789–1871. Eine historische Dokumentation.* 2 Bde. Tübingen: Narr.

–. 1984. "Das Phänomen des Purismus in der Geschichte des Deutschen". Besch et al. 1984–85. 290–299.

–. 1985. "Sprachreinheit und Sprachreinigung in der Spätaufklärung. Die Fremdwortfrage von Adelung bis Campe". Kimpel 1985: 85–104.

Kleinschmidt, Erich. 1990. "Entbundene Sprache. Zur intellektuellen Formierung des Deutschen im 17. Jahrhundert" *Zeitschrift für deutsches Altertum und deutsche Literatur* 119.192–211.

Klijnsmit, Anthony. 1993. "Schottel and the Dutch". Flood et al. 1993: 215–235.

Kramer, Johannes & Sabine Kowallik. 1992. *Das Französische in Deutschland. Eine Einführung.* Stuttgart: Steiner.

Krapf, Ludwig. 1979. *Germanenmythos und Reichsideologie. Frühhumanistische Rezeptionsweisen der taciteischen 'Germania'.* Tübingen: Niemeyer.

Kühn, Peter & Ulrich Püschel. 1989. "Die deutsche Lexikographie vom 17. Jahrhundert bis zu den Brüdern Grimm ausschließlich". Hausmann et al. 1989: 2049–2077.

Lutzebäck, Rolf. 1991. *Das Fremdwortproblem in der deutschen Sprach- und Kulturkritik von 1918 bis 1945. Eine sprachhistorische Abhandlung.* Frankfurt/M.: Sauerländer.

Mattheier, Klaus J. 1989. "'Gemeines Deutsch – Süddeutsche Reichssprache – 'Jesuitendeutsch'. Bemerkungen über die Rolle Süddeutschlands in der Geschichte der neuhochdeutschen Schriftsprache". *Bayerisch-österreichische Dialektforschung* hg. von Erwin Koller et al., 160–166. Würzburg: Königshausen & Neumann.

Mattheier, Klaus J. 1990. "Liselottes Sprache. Bemerkungen zum Sprachgebrauch Elisabeth-Charlottes von Orléans". *Pathos, Klatsch und Ehrlichkeit. Liselotte v. d. Pfalz am Hofe des Sonnenkönigs* hg. von Klaus J. Mattheier & Paul Valentin, 217–232. Tübingen: Stauffenburg.

Moser, Hans. 1984. "Sprachgesellschaften". *Reallexikon der deutschen Literaturgeschichte* hg. von Klaus Kanzog & Achim Masser, 122–132. 2. Aufl. Bd. 2. Berlin & New York: de Gruyter.

Nerius, Dieter. 1967. *Untersuchungen zur Herausbildung einer nationalen Norm der deutschen Literatursprache im 18. Jahrhundert.* Halle: VEB Niemeyer.

Neuhaus, Gisela M. 1991. *Justus Georg Schottelius: Die Stammwörter der Teutschen Sprache Samt dererselben Erklärung / und andere die Stammwörter betreffende Anmerkungen. Eine Untersuchung zur frühneuhochdeutschen Lexikologie.* Göppingen: Kümmerle.

Olt, Reinhard. 1991. *Wider das Fremde? Das Wirken des Allgemeinen Deutschen Sprachvereins in Hessen 1885–1944. Mit einer einleitenden Studie über Sprachreinigung und Fremdwortfrage in Deutschland und Frankreich seit dem 16. Jahrhundert.* Darmstadt & Marburg: Historische Kommission für Hessen.

Otto, Karl F. 1972a. *Die Sprachgesellschaften des 17. Jahrhunderts.* Stuttgart: Metzler.

–. 1972b. *Philipp von Zesen. A bibliographical catalogue.* Bern: Francke.

–. 1977. "Soziologisches zu den Sprachgesellschaften: Die Deutschgesinnte Genossenschaft". Bircher & van Ingen 1978: 151–161.

Padley, G. Arthur. 1985–1988. *Grammatical Theory in Western Europe 1500–1700: Trends in vernacular grammar.* 2 Bde. Cambridge: Cambridge Press.

Polenz, Peter von. 1967. "Sprachpurismus und Nationalsozialismus. Die 'Fremdwort'-Frage gestern und heute". *Germanistik eine deutsche Wissenschaft* hg. von Eberhard Lämmert et al. Frankfurt/M.: Suhrkamp. 111–165. *Nationalismus in Germanistik und Dichtung* hg. von Benno v. Wiese. Berlin: Schmidt. 79–112.

–. 1991–99. *Deutsche Sprachgeschichte vom Spätmittelalter bis zur Gegenwart.* Bd. I: *Einführung, Grundbegriffe, Deutsch in der frühbürgerlichen Zeit.* Bd. II: *17. und 18. Jahrhundert.* Bd. III: *19. und 20. Jahrhundert* Berlin & New York: de Gruyter.

–. 1998. "Zwischen 'Staatsnation' und 'Kulturnation'. Deutsche Begriffsbesetzungen um 1800." Cherubin et al. 1998: 55–70.

Rechtmann, Heinrich. 1953. *Das Fremdwort und der deutsche Geist. Zur Kritik des völkischen Purismus.* Köln.

Reichmann, Oskar. 1978. "Deutsche Nationalsprache. Eine kritische Darstellung". *Germanistische Linguistik* 2–5.389–423.

–. 1989. "Geschichte lexikographischer Programme in Deutschland". Hausmann et al. 1989: 230–246.

Reiffenstein, Ingo. 1988. "Der 'Parnassus Boicus' und das Hochdeutsche. Zum Ausklang des Frühneuhochdeutschen im 18. Jahrhundert". *Studien zum Frühneuhochdeutschen* hg. von Peter Wiesinger, 27–45. Göppingen: Kümmerle.

–. 1989. "Gottsched und die Bayern". *Soziokulturelle Kontexte der Sprach- und Literaturentwicklung. Festschrift für Rudolf Große* hg. von Sabine Heimann et al. Stuttgart: Heinz.

–. 1995. " 'Oberdeutsch' und 'Hochdeutsch' in Bayern im 18. Jahrhundert". Gardt et al. 1995: 307–317.

Schiewe, Jürgen. 1988a. *Sprachpurismus und Emanzipation. Joachim Heinrich Campes Verdeutschungsprogramm als Voraussetzung für Gesellschaftsveränderungen.* Hildesheim: Olms.

–. 1988b. "Joachim Heinrich Campes Verdeutschungsprogramm. Überlegungen zu einer Neuinterpretation des Purismus um 1800." *Deutsche Sprache* 16.17–33.

–. 1989. *Sprache und Öffentlichkeit. Carl Gustav Jochmann und die politische Sprachkritik der Spätaufklärung.* Berlin: Schmidt.

–. 1998. *Die Macht der Sprache. Eine Geschichte der Sprachkritik von der Antike bis zur Gegenwart.* München: Beck.

Schmidt-Wilpert, Gabriele. 1985. "Die Bedeutung der älteren deutschen Grammatiker für das Neuhochdeutsche". Besch et al. 1984–85: 1556–1563.

Schröter, Walther. 1985. "Die Bedeutung der älteren deutschen Lexikographen für das Neuhochdeutsche". Besch et al. 1984–85: 1520–1533.

See, Klaus von. 1970. *Deutsche Germanen-Ideologie vom Humanismus bis zur Gegenwart.* Frankfurt/M.: Athenäum.

Simon, Gerd, Hg. 1979. *Sprachwissenschaft und politisches Engagement. Zur Problem- und Sozialgeschichte einiger sprachtheoretischer, sprachdidaktischer und sprachpflegerischer Ansätze in der Germanistik des 19. und 20. Jahrhunderts.* Weinheim: Beltz.

Simon, Gerd. 1989. "Sprachpflege im 'Dritten Reich' ". *Sprache im Faschismus* hg. von Konrad Ehlich, 58–86. Frankfurt/M.: Suhrkamp.

–. 1989. *Muttersprache und Menschenverfolgung.* Stuttgart.

Stoll, Christoph. 1973. *Sprachgesellschaften im Deutschland des 17. Jahrhunderts.* München: List.

Takada, Hiroyuki. 1985. "J. G. Schottelius, die Analogie und der Sprachgebrauch. Versuch einer Periodisierung der Entwicklung des Sprachtheoretikers". *ZGL* 13.129–153.

Thomas, George. 1991. *Linguistic Purism.* London & New York.

Trunz, Erich. 1937. *Dichtung und Volkstum in den Niederlanden im 17. Jahrhundert. Ein Vergleich mit Deutschland und ein Überblick über die niederländisch-deutschen Beziehungen in diesem Jahrhundert.* München: Reinhardt.

Volland, Brigitte. 1986. *Französische Entlehnungen im Deutschen. Transferenz und Integration auf pho-*

*nologischer, graphematischer, morphologischer und lexikalisch-semantischer Ebene.* Tübingen: Niemeyer.

Weinrich, Harald. 1988. "Die Accademia della Crusca als Lehrmeisterin der Sprachkultur in Deutschland". H. Weinrich. *Wege der Sprachkultur*, 85ff. Stuttgart: Deutsche Verlagsanstalt.

Wiesinger, Peter. 1985. "Die Entwicklung des Verhältnisses von Mundart und Standardsprache in Österreich". Besch et al. 1984–85: 1939–1949.

–. 1995. "Die sprachlichen Verhältnisse und der Weg zur allgemeinen deutschen Schriftsprache in Österreich im 18. und frühen 19. Jahrhundert". Gardt et al. 1995: 319–368.

Wilke, Jürgen. 1985. "Zeitungssprache und Zeitungslexika im 17. und 18. Jahrhundert". Kimpel 1985: 69–84.

*Peter von Polenz, Trier (Deutschland)*

# 114. Entwicklungen in Deutschland im 17. und 18. Jahrhundert außerhalb der Sprachgesellschaften

1. Sprache, Sprachnorm und Sprachnormierung in der Sprachtheorie des 17. und 18. Jahrhunderts
2. Sprachstreite: Zum Maßstab der Normen
3. Entwicklungen der normativen Sprachforschung auf dem Weg zur deutschen Standardsprache
4. Schlußbemerkungen
5. Bibliographie

## 1. Sprache, Sprachnorm und Sprachnormierung in der Sprachtheorie des 17. und 18. Jahrhunderts

Unter *Sprachnorm* wird im folgenden eine Konfiguration bzw. ein Bündel konventioneller Regeln verstanden, die relativ zu außersprachlichen Bedingungen der Kommunikation die Auswahl und den Gebrauch sprachlicher Mittel steuern (vgl. grundsätzlich dazu Gloy 1980, Hartung 1977, Nerius 1967: 9ff.). Aufgrund dieser Vermittlungsfunktion sind Sprachnormen für die Herausbildung, Etablierung und Entwicklung von Varietäten verantwortlich, wie beispielsweise die der Varietät 'Deutsche Standardsprache' im 17. und 18. Jh. Die Frage, die sich für diese beiden Jahrhunderte in erster Linie stellt, ist die nach dem Anteil der Sprachforscher an der Formung dieser Varietät im Wege der Sprachnormierung, d. h. im Wege der (sprachlenkenden, sprachreinigenden, sprachkritischen, sprachpflegerischen usw.) Kodifikation und erfolgreichen Etablierung von Sprachnormen. Denn auf welche Sprachbeschreibungsebene die sprachwissenschaftlichen Normierungshandlungen in diesem Zeitraum auch immer bezogen waren – Grammatik, Lexik, Orthographie, Stilistik –, und von welcher Existenzweise von Sprache die Versuche der Normierung auch immer ihren Ausgang nahmen – Sprachverkehr, Sprachgebrauch, Sprachkompetenz oder Sprachsystem –, stets waren sie auf das System einer zu etablierenden deutschen Standardsprache als Bezugsgröße ausgerichtet.

Dieses gemeinsame Ziel der normativ orientierten Sprachforschung im 17. und 18. Jh. zeigt sich schon terminologisch: Gleichermaßen für die in der modernen Sprachwissenschaft diffus gebrauchten Termini 'Regel', 'Norm' und 'Normierung' wird in den meisten Texten dieser Zeit relativ unterminologisch der Begriff der 'Regel', zeitgenössisch oft noch latinisierend 'Regul', gebraucht, daneben auch 'Lehrsatz' (Schottelius 1663: 11 beispielsweise spricht von "Haubtregulen und Lehrsetzen") sowie, vor allem im Bereich der Orthographie, auch 'Gesetz', gar 'Grundgesetz'. Johann Christoph Adelung definiert am Ende dieses Zeitraums "Sprachregeln" als "allgemeine Vorschriften, nach welchen die Wörter einer Sprache gebildet, gesprochen, gebeuget, verbunden und geschrieben werden" (1782d I:91) und bilanziert damit den normativen Charakter der Arbeit seiner Zunft.

Sind die Gründe und Rechtfertigungen für die normierenden Eingriffe in den Bau der deutschen Sprache auch von Sprachforscher zu Sprachforscher unterschiedlich, so lassen sich doch gemeinsame Stränge bei den einzelnen Sprachforschern ermitteln. Gardt (1994: 21f.) gruppiert die Sprachforscher des 17. und beginnenden 18. Jhs. zwar noch in drei Richtungen der Sprachreflexion (einzelsprachlich-transzendental, rational-universalistisch und ontologisierend-patriotisch), doch seien sie alle vereint im Ziel, "den Zugriff auf Wirklichkeit mittels Sprache zu optimieren", und d. h., die Einzelsprache so zu formen, daß sie diesen Zugriff ermöglicht. Im Zusammenhang mit außersprachlichen Antrieben für eine solche Formung der deutschen Sprache – die Leidenszeit des Dreißigjährigen Krieges, das Fehlen eines kulturellen, ökonomischen, politischen und nationalen Zentrums und damit einhergehend die territoriale und sprachliche Zerfaserung (vgl. im Überblick v. Polenz 1994: 49ff.; Nerius 1967: 27ff.) – stehen sprachenpolitische, philosophische, ideologische und soziologische Motive für die Sprachnormierung im 17. und 18. Jh. (vgl. Henne 1975a: 10ff.; Josten 1976): die Verwirklichung des Anspruchs der deutschen Sprache auf Anerkennung als eine der Hauptsprachen, die Gleichstellung der deutschen Sprache mit anderen europäischen Sprachen – und dazu war ein gewisses Maß sprachlicher Einheit Voraussetzung – sowie die Etablierung einer deutschen Wissenschafts- und Literatursprache als Sprache der Gelehrten im Unterschied zur (gesprochenen) "altages Rede", gar zum "Pöbelgebrauche" (Schottelius 1663: 168).

Für eine große Gruppe der Sprachforscher im 17. Jh. waren Eingriffe in die Sprache und in den Sprachgebrauch des weiteren vom Wesen der deutschen Sprache her legitimiert. Im Rahmen einer "ontologisierend-patriotischen Sprachreflexion" (Gardt 1994: 129ff.) wurde dem Deutschen eine geradezu abbildhafte, in zeitgenössischer Termonologie: 'eigentliche', 'deutliche', 'grundrichtige' Nähe zu den Gegenständen und Sachverhalten der außersprachlichen Wirklichkeit zugesprochen: Die deutsche Sprache galt als 'grundrichtig', weil ihre Stammwörter "jhr ding / dessen Namen sie sind / eigentlich austrükken" (Schottelius 1663: 62). Mit dem 1643 von Schottelius als Verdeutschung für *Analogie* in die Diskussion gebrachten Terminus *Grundrichtigkeit* war über dieses referentielle Verhältnis zwischen Sprache und außersprachlicher Wirklichkeit hinaus eine durchgehende, analogischen Prinzipien folgende Regelmäßigkeit und Strukturiertheit der Sprache gemeint, die nur den *Hauptsprachen*, d. h. den originären, nicht von anderen abgeleiteten Sprachen zugesprochen wurde. Ein Ziel der Sprachnormierung vor allem im 17. Jahrhundert war es daher, die deutsche Sprache überhaupt erst als "HaubtSprache" (so Schottelius 1663) auszuweisen. Erst dann konnten deren Grundrichtigkeit behauptet und alle Versuche der Sprachnormierung, diese Grundrichtigkeit mit wissenschaftlichen Mitteln (also 'kunstrichtig') zu rekonstruieren, sprachenpolitisch legitimiert werden (vgl. Takada 1998: 29ff.; Gardt 1994: 368ff.).

Im 18. Jh. verschob sich die sprachtheoretische Grundlegung der Normierung merklich weg von solch einem rückblickend hypostasierenden und hin zu einem gegenwarts- und gesellschaftsbezogenen Sprachbegriff. So findet sich zwar bei den oberdeutschen Grammatikern Friedrich Carl Fulda und Johann Nast noch ein der Schottelschen Grundrichtigkeit vergleichbarer Begriff der "Sprachgründe" (vgl. Nerius 1967: 48ff.), doch obsiegten auch bei ihnen schließlich, wie im 18. Jh. im Zeichen von Bildungsbürgertum und Volksaufklärung vorherrschend, außersprachliche, nämlich soziale und geographische Kriterien bei der Normierung der deutschen Standardsprache. Hierin fanden so unterschiedliche Arbeiten normativer Sprachforschung ihren gemeinsamen Bezugspunkt, wie beispielsweise Gottscheds synonymisches Wörterbuch (1758), das auch als Wegweiser zum treffenden Ausdruck zu lesen ist, Freyers Orthographie (1722) und Adelungs *Deutsche Sprachlehre* (1781), die beide dem Schulunterricht zugedacht waren, sowie Campes Ansatz von Sprachreinigung zum Zwecke der Volksbildung. Normativ orientierte Sprachforschung im 17. und 18. Jahrhundert sollte also beides leisten: eine deutsche Standardsprache formen und für den deutschen Sprecher lernbar machen.

## 2. Sprachstreite: Zum Maßstab der Normen

Die deutsche Standardsprache wurde jenseits dieser sprachtheoretischen Grundlagen und der sprachenpolitischen wie der sprachsoziologischen Ziele gleichwohl eher traditionell definiert: sprachsoziologisch im engeren Sinn (als deutsche Sprache der Höfe, Gelehrten und Literaten) und sprachgeographisch (unter Hervorhebung des Obersächsischen). Traditionell deshalb, weil diese herkömmlichen Kriterien lediglich einen Ersatz der fremdsprachigen Schichten (französisch und lateinisch) durch deutsche Wissenschafts-, höfische Umgangs- und Literatursprache und eine Überdachung der mundartlichen Varietäten durch eine überregionale Varietät bewirken konnten und nicht, wie es die Sprachtheorie gefordert hatte, die 'richtige' deutsche Nationalsprache originär aus einer Grundrichtigkeit schöpften. Galt das Lob der deutschen Sprache und die Behauptung ihrer Vorbildlichkeit als einer Hauptsprache als Grundlage und Legitimation der Versuche der Sprachnormierung, so führte diese ernüchternde Erkenntnis des Fehlens einer 'grundrichtigen' Vorlage zur Suche nach Maßstäben für die Sprachnormierung. Beschreibung und Normierung gingen deshalb Hand in Hand. Damit war freilich auch die Verantwortlichkeit für dieses 'wahre Hochdeutsch' einer sprachimmanenten Grundrichtigkeit genommen und den Sprachforschern zugewiesen worden.

Der berühmteste und umstrittenste Vorschlag war, das Meißnische als Standardsprache zu etablieren. Obersachsen war schon im 16. Jh. als geographische Verortung des Hochdeutschen angesehen worden, und da selbst Luther diese Varietät zur Nationalsprache erhoben hatte, folgten ihm einflußreiche Sprachforscher wie Wolfgang Ratke, sodann – etwas unentschlossen – Johann Christoph Gottsched und – unerbittlich – Johann Christoph Adelung. Der Gegenentwurf, vertreten sowohl vom Norddeutschen Johann Bödiker wie vom Süddeutschen Carl Friedrich Aichinger, vom Analogisten Justus Georg Schottelius wie vom Volksaufklärer Joachim Heinrich Campe, favorisierte eine sprachwissenschaftlich konstruierte, geographisch unabhängige und vornehmlich sprachsoziologisch definierte Mischung – Campe nannte es "Aushub" – des Hochdeutschen aus schriftlichen Texten von Literaten, Kanzleischreibern und Gelehrten (ausführlich zu den berühmten Streiten ums Meißnische Jellinek 1913, passim; Eichler & Bergmann 1967; Henne 1968.

Zu den Maßstäben der Normierung gehören jedoch nicht nur die Vorbilder – also etwa die Sprache Luthers, die Sprache der Gelehrten oder eben die ‚chursächsische' Mundart –, sondern auch die Kriterien, die in konkreten Fällen die Entscheidung für oder gegen die Normierung einer sprachlichen Einheit als 'grundrichtig', 'richtig', 'hochdeutsch' usw. leiten sollten. Die im 17. und 18. Jh. erstellte Liste dieser Kriterien folgt Mustern der antiken Rhetorik (vgl. Haas 1980: 57ff.) und ist zugleich ein Zeugnis der wechselseitigen Kenntnisnahme der prachforscher und ihrer Schriften – modern: der Intertextualität – im Dienste der Sprachnormierung: Schottelius gab eine Reihenfolge insofern vor, als mit seiner Postulierung des Konzepts der Grundrichtigkeit der deutschen Sprache die sprachsystematische Analogie an die Spitze der normgebenden Prinzipien gestellt wurde. Die Etymologie ('Wortforschung') war ihr zu Diensten und damit ebenfalls zum wissenschaftlichen Nachweis des Richtigen befähigt, während der Sprachgebrauch als sprachsoziologisch orientierte Richtschnur der Normierung von Schottelius erst 1663 anerkannt und zunehmend der Analogie an die Seite gestellt wurde (vgl. ausführlich Takada 1998: 29ff.). Schottelius setzte also am Sprachsystem an und versuchte, über eine Normierung desselben auch den Sprachgebrauch zu normieren.

Gottsched gewichtete diese Liste zugunsten seiner Theorie vom Hochdeutschen anders: Demnach waren "Regeln einer Sprache fest zu setzen" 1) "nach der besten Mundart" eines Volkes, 2) nach dem "Gebrauch der besten Schriftsteller" und schließlich 3) nach der Analogie als "Aehnlichkeit in den Ableitungen und Verwandelungen der Wörter" (Gottsched 1762: 1ff.). Gemäß dieser Reihenfolge ist ein regional und sozial begrenzter Sprachgebrauch Maßstab für die Normierung des Systems des Hochdeutschen. Der am Ende dieser Epoche der Sprachforschung wirkende Adelung setzte diese Reihenfolge mit leicht verschobener Gewichtung fort und formulierte vier Instanzen für die Normierung des Hochdeutschen: 1) der "Sprachgebrauch, als die höchste und unumschränkteste Macht" – womit freilich der Sprachgebrauch der "obern Classen" gemeint war; 2) die "Analogie oder Sprachähnlichkeit", 3) die "Etymologie oder Abstammung" und 4) der "Wohllaut" (Adelung 1782d: I 109ff.). Wenngleich auch Adelung unter Sprachgebrauch nur den Sprachgebrauch einer bestimmten Sozialschicht Obersachsens versteht, wird man angesichts der seit Schottelius vorgenommenen Umkehrung der Reihenfolge weg vom Sprachsystem und hin zum Sprachgebrauch als Autorität für die Sprachnormierung den deskriptiven Zug der normativen Sprachforschung bei einer Gesamtbeurteilung der Herausbildung der neuhochdeutschen Standardsprache in Rechnung zu stellen haben.

## 3. Entwicklungen der normativen Sprachforschung auf dem Weg zur deutschen Standardsprache

### 3.1. Grammatik(ographie)

Die wissenschaftsgeschichtliche Erforschung der Grammatikschreibung im 17. und 18. Jh. wird zwar kontinuierlich vorangetrieben, doch kann von einer abschließenden Aufbereitung der Quellen oder gar von abschließenden Ergebnissen zu einzelnen Entwicklungen noch keine Rede sein; Standardwerk ist nach wie vor Jellinek 1913–1914, zu dessen alphabetischer Quellenliste als chronologische Ergänzung Leser 1914: 94ff. und Poppe 1982: 416f. herangezogen werden können.

Die wichtigsten grammatischen Gegenstände, die immer wieder im Lauf der zwei Jahrhunderte Normierungsversuchen zugeführt wurden, stammten aus den Bereichen der Orthographie, der Wortbildung, der Morphosyntax (Deklination und Konjugation) sowie der Syntax (vgl. zusammenfassend Jellinek 1914: 1ff.; Poppe 1981: 337ff.). Schottelius etwa widmete den größten Teil seiner *HaubtSprache* der "Wortforschung" (Etymologie und Wortbildung) und der "Wortfügung" (Syntax) der Stammwörter. Bei Bödiker (1701) ist es ähnlich: "Recht=Schreibung", "Wort=Forschung", "Wort=Fügung" und "Thon=Sprechung"; auch Aichinger bietet neben Orthographie und Orthoepie vor allem "Wortforschung" und "Syntaxe" in seinem *Versuch einer teutschen Sprachlehre* (1754), und fast ebenso gliedert Adelung sein *Umständliches Lehrgebäude* (1782d).

Umstrittene Versuche der grammatischen Normierung sind vornehmlich im morphosyntaktischen Bereich zu finden (vgl. Semenjuk 1972), wie z. B. das 'lutherische *-e*' in der Flexion der Substantive, Adjektive und Verben, das im süddeutschen Raum bereits apokopiert war und nach der Reformation aus ostmitteldeutschen Mundarten sowohl nicht-flexivisch (*die Sprach – die Sprache, der Knab – der Knabe*) wie auch als Flexionsendung (z. B. in der Deklination des Femininums attributiver Adjektive) für die Leitvarietät wieder eingeführt wurde (vgl. z. B. Jellinek 1913: 296ff.; Penzl 1978; v. Polenz 1994: 251ff.). In diesem Zusammenhang führte vor allem die Normierung der Plural-Flexive, insbesondere Schottelius' Forderung nach einem Plural-*e* bei sonst endungslosen Pluralformen auf *-el* und *-er* (z. B. *die Himmel – die Himmele, die Bürger – die Bürgere*) zu tiefschürfenden Auseinandersetzungen.

Daß für einen guten Teil dieser grammatikographischen Bemühungen weniger das "Deskriptionsproblem und seine präskriptive Lösung" (Donhauser 1989) als das Präskriptions- bzw. Normierungsproblem und seine deskriptive Lösung festzustellen ist, darf indes nicht übersehen werden. Besonders deutlich zeigt sich dies bei Gottsched, der sich immer wieder in Widersprüche verstrickt und neben normativen Forderungen sogleich deren Ausnahmen vermerkt (etwa bei den Flexionsformen der 2. und 3. Pers. Sg., bei denen er die vollen Formen fordert und zugleich die synkopierten mit aufnimmt; vgl. Semenjuk 1972: 113); oder bei Aichinger, der zwar Entscheidungen nicht scheut, gleichwohl keinen Zweifel daran läßt, daß nicht alles in klarer Eindeutigkeit entschieden werden kann: Das Phänomen Sprache, schreibt er, erfordere viel zu oft, daß "man nun hierinnen fünf muß gerad seyn lassen" (1754: 122). Wenn Grammatiker Varianten anführen, kann von präskriptiver Normierung im strengen Sinn keine Rede sein. Adelung hat dies klar formuliert, wenngleich seine Bemerkungen auch als Selbstschutz zu dienen vermochten: Insofern Sprachregeln für ihn abstrakte "Erfahrungssätze" sind, die "in der Sprache gesammelt und abgezogen werden müssen", nimmt der Grammatiker lediglich die Rolle des ordnenden Moderators zwischen Sprache und Sprachbenutzer ein; er "entscheidet nie, sondern sammelt nur die entscheidenden Stimmen der meisten." (1782d I: 112ff.).

### 3.2. 'Wortforschung' und Lexikographie

Deutsche Lexikologie erscheint im Zuge der normativen Sprachforschung im 17. Jh. als Etymologie ("Uhrankunften") und Wortbildungslehre ("Ableitungen und Verdoppelungen"; Schottelius 1663: 181). Das lexikologische Kernstück bildet dabei die von Schottelius grundlegend entwickelte Stammworttheorie, die insofern gerade Richtschnur der Normierungen werden sollte, als sie die "Grundrichtigkeit" der deutschen Sprache theoretisch, d. h. 'kunstrichtig', zu erfassen suchte (vgl. Schottelius 1663: 50f., 1270ff.; Gützlaff 1989; Neuhaus 1991: 90ff.

Insofern die deutschen Stammwörter nicht nur in wortbildnerischer und orthographischer (s. u.), sondern auch in semantischer Hinsicht als 'grundrichtig' galten, und zudem 'deutlich', möglichst sogar 'eindeutig' (im Sinne von monosem) zu sein hatten, wurde lexikalische Bedeutung im 17. Jh. als Abbild der Dinge in der Sprache eines Volkes begriffen – also als *physei*, wie Schottelius mehrfach darlegt (z. B. 1663: 59). – Die Bedeutungstheorie im 18. Jh. stellte demgegenüber das, was modern als Arbitrarität und Konventionalität des Sprachzeichens bezeichnet wird, in den Vordergrund. Dadurch brachte sie, insofern damit der *physei*-These eine Absage erteilt war, wiederum den Sprachforscher als Normverfasser stärker in Erscheinung (zur Lexikologie im 18. Jh. vgl. Henne 1972: 66ff.)

Die gesamte Epoche ist in lexikographischer Hinsicht jedoch eher theoretisch und programmatisch denn praktisch ausgerichtet. So lassen sich die Erzeugnisse der normativ orientierten Lexikographie im 17. und 18. Jh. rasch überblicken: Es sind dies die lexikographischen Abschnitte in Schottelius' *Haubt-Sprache* (1663: 1269ff.), sodann die Bedeutungswörterbücher von Matthias Kramer (1700–1702), Christoph Ernst Steinbach (1734), Johann Leonhard Frisch (1741), Johann Christoph Adelung (1774–1786 bzw. 1793–1801) und – ebenfalls noch ein Werk des 18. Jhs. – Joachim Heinrich Campe (1807–1811). Schließlich sind hier noch Gottscheds normative lexikographische Streifzüge zu nennen (1758), in denen er in alphabetischer Ordnung semantische und stilistische, onomasiologische und semasiologische sowie phraseologische Kommentare zu bedeutungsverwandten Wörtern bietet. Normativ war vor allem die lexikographische Theorie, wie sie in den Vorreden entworfen wurde und in der "die Theoretiker die 'kunstrichtige' Verfassung der deutschen Sprache garantiert sahen durch die grammatische Analyse und Fixierung des Wortmaterials sowie durch die wortbildnerische Zergliederung" (Henne 1975a: 27). – Die lexikographische Praxis hingegen ging oft eigene Wege, und es scheint sogar fraglich, ob die Charakterisierung dieser Wörterbücher als 'normativ' hinreichend ist. Das der Normierung dienende Stammwortprinzip etwa findet sich nur bei dem sprachgesellschaftlich verpflichteten Kaspar Stieler (1691), sodann bei Kramer (1700–1702) und Frisch (1741) lexikographisch umgesetzt und wurde schließlich vom alphabetischen Prinzip verdrängt. Des weiteren erscheinen deutsche Paraphrasen, die eine Normierung des Gebrauchs stützen, zuerst bei Gottsched 1758, systematisch bei Adelung 1774ff. Im Sinne einer Vorschrift von Wortbedeutungen und Gebrauchsweisen können die Wörterbücher also allenfalls eingeschränkt normative Kraft entfaltet haben. Adelung selbst wiederum war innerhalb des von ihm abgesteckten Kreises der 'Hochdeutschen Mundart' keineswegs strenger Normsetzer, im Gegenteil sei "in der deutschen Sprache nur zu viel entschieden worden; es ist Zeit, daß man einmal anfange, zu prüfen und zu untersuchen" (Adelung 1774: XIII).

Erst durch den Bezug zur Herausbildung der deutschen Standardsprache kommt diesen Wörterbüchern ein normierender Zug insofern zu, als makrostrukturell durch die Aufnahme oder Nicht-Aufnahme von Wörtern eine positive und negative Sprachlenkung betrieben wurde, und mikrostrukturell der Akt der Bedeutungserklärung sowie die Setzung von Sonderzeichen, ferner grammatische Angaben und stilistische Kommentare normativ wirkten. Was die Auswahl des zu lemmatisierenden Wortschatzes anbelangt, waren die Wörterbücher notwendigerweise synchronisch-gegenwartsbezogen und zudem auf die sprachsoziologischen und sprachgeographischen Begrenzungen der zugrunde liegenden Sprachtheorie ausgerichtet. Der Einsatz diakritischer Sonderzeichen und stilistischer Kommentare zur sprachsoziologischen Normierung des gebuchten Wortschatzes wurde von Steinbach bis Campe zunehmend perfektioniert (vgl. Steinbach 1734, Praefatio; Adelung 1774: XIV; Campe 1807: XXf.). Insoweit die Lexikographie bei den normativen Beschreibungen jedoch zeitgenössischem Gebrauch folgte, schrieb sie lediglich bereits etablierte Normen nieder und versuchte, sie wissenschaftlich zu systematisieren. Die Aufgaben der normativ orientierten Sprachforschung hatten sich damit an der Wende zum 19. Jh. grundlegend gewandelt (vgl. Adelung 1774: XII).

### 3.3. Exkurs: Sprachpurismus und Lexikographie

Die Fremdwortlexikologie und -lexikographie im 17. und 18. Jh. ist präskriptiv-normativ im engeren Sinn, soweit sie im Dienste der Sprachreinigung und -bereicherung stand (was bei weitem nicht für alle Fremdwörterbücher dieser Epoche zutrifft). Eine Fremdwortlexikographie in diesem Sinn hat es im 17. Jh. noch nicht gegeben, und auch im fremdwortlexikographisch produktiveren 18. Jh. sind in erster Linie die Verdeutschungslisten Kinderlings (1795) und Campes (1790) sowie schließlich Campes Verdeutschungs-Wörterbuch (1801) anzuführen (vgl. Takada 1981, Kirkness 1975, Schiewe 1988), die gleichsam den Auftakt zur puristischen Fremdwortlexikographie in Deutschland bilden. Zur Unterscheidung der dabei maßgeblichen sprachenpolitischen Intentionen des 17. und 18. Jhs. von den späteren nationalistischen Antrieben ist es üblich geworden, hier von "kulturpatriotischen" (Huber 1984), für das 18. Jh. mehr noch von "volksaufklärerischen" (Schiewe

1988) Ansätzen des Sprachpurismus zu sprechen, die auch als "aufklärerische Sprachkritik" (v. Polenz 1994: 123) begriffen werden können. Übereifrigen Puristen hatte überdies schon Schottelius eine Absage erteilt, indem er das, was als fremdes Wort gelten sollte, sprachsoziologisch und textsortenspezifisch definierte (1663: 1273). Gut einhundertdreißig Jahre später bot Campe (1790) dafür ein sprachwissenschaftlich fundiertes System, indem er die fremden Wörter nach semantischen Kriterien in 'sinnliche', 'unsinnliche' und 'übersinnliche' einteilt, sie auf der Grundlage sprachstruktureller Kriterien (phonologische und morphologische Assimilation) beschreibt und sie schließlich nach sprachsoziologischen Kriterien (Sprechergruppen und Varietäten) bewertet (1790: XII ff.)

Mit Campes *Wörterbuch zur Erklärung und Verdeutschung der unserer Sprache aufgedrungenen fremden Ausdrücke* (1801) findet dieser fremdwortpuristische Strang der normativ orientierten Sprachforschung im 18. Jh. seinen Abschluß. Dabei zeigt schon die für ein Wörterbuch mit über einhundert Seiten ungewöhnlich lange Einführung über "Grundsätze, Regeln und Gränzen der Verdeutschung", daß es sich hierbei noch um sprachwissenschaftlich reflektierte Sprachpflege handelte. Doch wiederum: Der Volksaufklärer Campe schoß schließlich übers Ziel hinaus und zwängte durch übereifrige sprachlenkende Verdeutschungen die deutsche Sprache in ein zu enges Kleid.

### 3.4. Orthographie und Orthoepie

Nachdem bereits im 16. Jh. einzelne orthographische Regeln ungeordnet aneinandergereiht worden waren, im großen und ganzen jedoch der jeweils landes- bzw. druckereiübliche Gebrauch die Richtschnur abgegeben hatte, setzten Versuche der orthographischen Normierung verstärkt um 1640 ein (vgl. Moulin 1992: 28 ff.). Orthographische Fragen wurden in fast jedem sprachwissenschaftlichen Werk dieser Epoche behandelt, galt die Rechtschreibung doch als ein Gebiet, auf dem der Fortschritt der Vereinheitlichung besonders deutlich zutage treten mußte. So steht die Orthographie bei Schottelius als "AnfangsStükk der Wortforschung" (1663: 181) an zentraler Stelle, an der er seine Ansichten in sieben "gemeine Lehrsätze" bringt, die eine "grundrichtige Gewisheit wegen Rechtschreibung" liefern sollen (ebd. 186). Vergleichbar präsentiert sich die Orthographie zum Beispiel in Gottscheds *Deutscher Sprachkunst* (1762), in der ihr nicht nur ein umfangreiches "Hauptstück" nebst einem "Verzeichniß gewisser zweifelhafter Wörter" gewidmet wird, sondern auch ein beträchtlicher Anhang "Erörterung der orthographischen Frage: Ob man Deutsch oder Teutsch schreiben solle?" Diesem Werk, das sich in orthographischer Hinsicht im wesentlichen den von Freyer formulierten Normen anschloß, darf man aufgrund seiner weiten Verbreitung Einfluß auf die Vereinheitlichung der Schreibung zuweisen.

Neben den allgemeinen Sprachlehren aber erschienen auch orthographische Regelbücher, die einzig dem Zweck der orthographischen Normierung dienten und zumeist mit alphabetischen Wortlisten versehen waren (z. B. Sattler 1607, Bellin 1657, Freyer 1722, Adelung 1788).

Mit Takada (1998: 60) lassen sich folgende Prinzipien der Orthographienormierung im 17. und 18. Jh. unterscheiden, die im wesentlichen noch heute Gültigkeit beanspruchen und die Einzel(wort)regeln überdachen: das phonologische Prinzip ("daß man schreibe/ wie man geredet" (Olearius), "Schreibe, wie du sprichst" (Adelung)), das graphiegeschichtliche Prinzip (Beibehaltung der überkommenen Schreibung guter Autoren), das morphologische (Stammwort-)Prinzip, das semantische Prinzip (Homonymiedifferenzierung) und das grammatische Prinzip (vgl. Jellinek 1914: 49 ff.; Moulin 1992: 28 ff.).

Das phonologische Prinzip wurde verständlicherweise in erster Linie von denjenigen propagiert, die eine existierende Aussprachepraxis, eben das Meißnische, zur Norm erheben wollten (vgl. Jellinek 1913: 329 ff., 1914: 68 ff.). Adelung verband dieses Prinzip schließlich mit weiteren zu einem 'Grundgesetz':

> Schreib das Deutsche und was als Deutsch betrachtet wird, mit den eingeführten Schriftzeichen, so wie du sprichst, der allgemeinen besten Aussprache gemäß, mit Beobachtung der erweislichen nächsten Abstammung, und, wo diese aufhöret, des allgemeinen Gebrauches. (1788: 17)

Indem Adelung "Aussprache", "Abstammung" (also Etymologie) und "allgemeinen Gebrauch" als Kriterien anführt, stellt er sich in eine Tradition der orthographischen Normierung: Gueintz hatte 1645 bereits 1) "Ursprung und Stamm der Wörter", 2) "Aussprechung" und 3) "Gewonheit" als Richtlinien der Orthographienormen angegeben (Gueintz 1645; vgl. Jellinek 1914: 55). Freyer hatte das darauf folgende Kriteriengestrüpp systematisch nach Prinzipien und Einzelregeln geordnet und den Prinzipien die Reihenfolge "Pronunciation" ("Aussprache"), "Derivation" ("Herleitung"), "Analogie" ("Gleichheit und Ubereinstimmung") und "Usus scribendi" ("gemeine Weise und Gewohnheit im schreiben") zugewiesen (Freyer 1722: 1–23), wobei jedoch faktisch dem "Usus scribendi" Vorrang gegeben wurde. Diese Reihenfolge übernahm sodann auch Adelung nur nominell; in praxi kehrte auch er sie um insofern, als er dem Gebrauch die erste Stimme zuwies (vgl. Nerius 1989: 84f.; Ewald 1992: 75ff.). Unter der Hand wird dadurch sein Prinzipiengefüge ("Grundgesetz") dominiert von dem Prinzip: Schreibe, wie allgemein geschrieben wird – freilich in den 'obern Classen' Obersachsens. Was die einzelnen Gegenstände der orthographischen Normierung anbelangt, so stand in beiden Jahrhunderten die Normierung der Phonem-Graphem-Beziehung eindeutig im Zentrum des Interesses, wie beispielsweise die orthographische Tilgung der "stummen" Konsonanten nach *m* (*kompt, Lamb*), die von Schottelius erfolgreich normierte Unterscheidung zwischen vokalischen *i* und *u* versus konsonantischen *j* und *v*; ferner etwa die graphische Wiedergabe von Vokallänge und Vokalkürze (Dehnungszeichen und Konsonantengemmination).

Insofern schon die Bezeichnung *Orthographie* das normative Element betont, erscheint eine rein deskriptive Orthographielehre als *contradictio in adjecto.* Gleichwohl wurde auch hier nicht alles bis ins Detail entschieden (vgl. z. B. Aichinger 1754: 91), oft wurde gar von vornherein versucht, das strenge Anführen von Regeln durch Zusammenstellung von Wortlisten zu ersetzen (ebd. 39–85).

Was schließlich die Wirkung der orthographischen Normen anbelangt, so wird in neueren Forschungen deutlich, daß die Versuche der orthographischen Normierung im 17. und 18. Jh. in den seltensten Fällen wirklich Neuerungen einzuführen vermochten. Ihr Verdienst liegt vielmehr darin, die Schreibpraxis in systematische und vor allen Dingen lehr- und lernbare Ordnungen gebracht zu haben; ihre normative Wirkung besteht darin, daß sie die Rechtschreibung nachschlagbar machten und auf diesem Wege vereinheitlichten.

Die Herausbildung und Normierung der deutschen Standardsprache war in allererster Linie schriftsprachlich orientiert, und es ist kein Zufall, daß die Orthographie eine so wichtige Rolle im 17. und 18. Jh. spielte. Folgte die orthographische Normierung dem phonologischen Prinzip, dann stand sie gleichwohl in enger Beziehung zur orthoepischen Normierung. Das Prinzip 'Schreibe, wie du sprichst' führte hier jedoch zu dem Problem, daß die gesprochene Sprache selbst erst zu normieren war – und zwar nach Möglichkeit gemäß den Normen für die geschriebene Sprache. Morhof hatte diesen Zirkel schon 1682/1700 erkannt und deutlich gemacht (1700: 426; Repr. 1969: 232); er wird gleichwohl bei Adelung noch einmal besonders sinnfällig, insoweit nicht die Aussprache der "chursächsischen Landen", sondern auch bei ihm die Schriftsprache den Maßstab der orthoepischen Normen abgibt, kurz: Adelungs orthographischer Vorsatz 'Schreibe, wie du sprichst' erfährt in seinen orthoepischen Ausführungen die Umkehrung: 'Sprich, wie du schreibst'.

Die Normierung der Orthoepie unterlag somit ebenfalls den Auseinandersetzungen über das wahre Hochdeutsch, also der Frage, ob eine konstruierte Abstraktion oder das Meißnische die Norm abgeben sollte. Und in bezug darauf standen sich im großen und ganzen wieder dieselben Parteiungen und Personen mit denselben Normierungskriterien gegenüber, wie im Rahmen der orthographischen Normierung (vgl. Eichinger 1983, Penzl 1977).

### 3.5. Pragmatik und Stilistik

Eine Sprachkunst, so heißt es bei Gottsched, ist nicht nur eine Anweisung, wie man "richtig", sondern auch, wie man "zierlich, sowohl reden als schreiben, solle" (1762: 1). Indem Adelung die "Sprachlehre" mit der "Logik" verknüpft und den "Schmuck" der "Redekunst" zuweist (1782d I: 91), formuliert er demgegenüber die übliche Ansicht der Sprachforschung im 17. und 18. Jh., die das Pragmatisch-Stilistische den Rhetoriken, Briefstellern und Poetiken überlassen wollte. Dies war nur folgerichtig, führte das Pragmatisch-Stilistische doch vom 'grundrichtigen' und (ana)logischen Sprachsystem weg zum Sprachgebrauch, gar der Wirkung des Sprachgebrauchs. Als genuin pragmatisch-stilistische Normkriterien außerhalb von Rhetorik und Poetik heben sich im 18. Jh. allenfalls 'Deutlichkeit' – im stilistischen, weniger im darstellungsfunktionalen und erkenntnistheoretischen Sinn – und 'Wohllaut' heraus (vgl. z. B. Aichinger 1754: XLII*f.), und da es bei diesen Kriterien "ganz allein auf den Geschmack und die eigene Empfindung ankommt" (Adelung 1774: XIV), stießen Normverfasser hier an ihre Grenzen – und widersprachen einander kräftig, wie z. B. im Fall der verbalen Satzklammer, die u. a. die gefürchteten 'Schachtelsätze' erzeugt: Der Auffüllung des Satzrahmens zwischen finitem und infinitem Prädikatsteil maß Schottelius (1663: 743) durchaus "einen sonderlichen Wollaut" zu, während Bödiker (1701: 240f.) und Stieler (1691: 203) die Tendenz zu Schwerverständlichkeit und Überspannung des Rahmens beklagten. Der Satzrahmen blieb gleichwohl erhalten und wurde im Laufe des 17. und 18. Jhs. sogar endgültig zur Norm. Diese Entwicklung fand aber ohne wesentliches Zutun der Grammatiker statt, und dies belegt einmal mehr, daß sie in ihren Werken zu einem Gutteil lediglich den herrschenden Gebrauch a posteriori via Beschreibung normiert haben (vgl. Konopka, 1996: 24ff.; Takada 1998: 231).

## 4. Schlußbemerkungen

In bezug auf den Forschungsstand sind nach wie vor viele Lücken zu beklagen; zugleich ist aber auch ein seit etwa 1980 einsetzendes verstärktes Forschungsinteresse an der Sprachforschung des 17. und – wenn auch etwas schwächer – des 18. Jhs. unübersehbar. Um mit den Desiderata zu beginnen: Im Bereich der Geschichte der Grammatikographie ist es fast schon ein Topos, eine Neubearbeitung des 'Jellinek' einzuklagen. Dieses Standardwerk ist bislang unübertroffen in bezug auf die Materialfülle und systematische Ordnung der in den Grammatiken beschriebenen Gegenstände, doch stellte Jellinek die Geschichte der Grammatikinhalte in den Vordergrund und ließ die Geschichte der Grammatikschreibung, der Sprachforschung und ihrer Wirkungen nur nebenbei einfließen. Sein Urteil ist zudem durch seine Orientierung an den Sprachnormen des frühen 20. Jhs. ahistorisch, oft gar verzerrt. Die in den letzten Jahren erstellten Studien zu einzelnen Grammatikern und ihren Werken (z. B. Poppe 1982, Diederichs 1983, Heinle 1982) oder zu einzelnen Regionen (z. B. Tauber 1993) harren der Zusammenfassung in einer neuen Überblicksdarstellung (ausführlich dazu Bergmann 1982: 270ff. mit weiterer Lit.). Die Quellen dafür und für weitere Forschungen werden erfreulicherweise in einer bibliographischen Reihe zur deutschen Orthographietheorie und Grammatik zusammengestellt (Moulin-Fankhänel 1994 u. 1997). Das *Lexicon Grammaticorum* eröffnet erste biographische Zugänge zu einzelnen Sprachforschern (Stammerjohann 1996); für das 18. Jh. ist zudem das im Entstehen begriffene, bislang auf sechs Bände angewachsene *Bio-bibliographische Handbuch* (BBHS) eine Fundgrube für weiterführende Forschungen. Durch diese Hilfsmittel erhöhen sich die Chancen, daß auch einmal die normativen Bemühungen der weniger bekannten Sprachforscher, etwa Johann Nasts, Abraham Gotthelf Mäzkes oder Christian Pudors, zu Forschungsgegenständen werden.

Für die Geschichte der (normativ orientierten) Lexikographie gibt es bedauerlicherweise immer noch keinen 'Jellinek'. Die mit Einleitungen und Bibliographien versehenen Neudrucke der auf die deutsche Standardsprache bezogenen Wörterbücher (vgl. Henne 1975) sowie neuere Spezialuntersuchungen (Tauchmann 1993), Überblicksdarstellungen (Kühn & Püschel 1990) und Einzeluntersuchungen (Dill 1992) bieten indes Bausteine auch für eine Geschichte der lexikographischen Sprachnormierung im 17. und 18. Jh.

Die Erkenntnisinteressen all dieser Untersuchungen divergieren je nach Sprachbeschreibungsebene und Quellenauswahl. In bezug auf die Normierung einer überregionalen Varietät des Deutschen im 17. und 18. Jh. ist die große Anzahl von Quellenwerken ein Indikator für eine Phase des sprachgeschichtlichen Umbruchs, an dessen Abschluß die deutsche Standardsprache als Leitvarietät des Deutschen stand. Die Frage, inwiefern dieser Umbruch lediglich Ergebnis eines "Invisible-hand-Prozesses" (Keller) war oder aber durch Eingriffe von Sprachforschern maßgeblich gestaltet wurde, harrt nach wie vor einer Antwort. So gibt es im Hinblick auf den Ertrag der Versuche der Sprachnormierung im 17. und 18. Jh. im Zusammenhang mit der Herausbildung der deutschen Standardsprache zunächst einmal große Lücken in der Sprachgeschichtsforschung (vgl. Schmidt-Wilpert 1985: 1557; Konopka 1996: 41ff.), und dies, obwohl gerade der *Einfluß / der Anteil / die Rolle der Grammatiker / Lexikographen / Orthographen* usw. *auf die Herausbildung und Normierung der deutschen Standardsprache* – so oder ähnlich lautet eine ganze Reihe von Titeln in diesem Forschungsbereich – immer wieder Gegenstand von Untersuchungen gewesen ist. Die Crux der Beantwortung dieser Wirkungsfrage scheint darin zu bestehen, daß sie auf einer höheren Abstraktionsebene unbeantwortbar ist. Ergiebiger sind Arbeiten, in denen empirisch die Frage nach den Wirkungen einzelner Sprachforscher oder aber mehrerer Sprachforscher in bezug auf einzelne Gegenstände zu beantworten gesucht wird. Des weiteren ist es notwendig, sich der Frage zuzuwenden, welche Wege der Wirkung von Versuchen der Sprachnormierung zu einer gegebenen Zeit überhaupt zur Verfügung standen. Ein Blick auf die Sprachpraxis von Multiplikatoren scheint hier erfolgversprechender als ein Vergleich von Sprachnorm und Sprachpraxis bei den Grammatikern selbst (Erben 1989: 15ff., 22f.).

Vorliegende Detailergebnisse zusammenfassend darf die normativ orientierte Sprachforschung des 17. und 18. Jhs. als vielschichtige Abfolge von Normierungsversuchen und Irrtümern, Postulierungen und Rücknahmen, Entwürfen und Gegenentwürfen begriffen werden, die sich zur Normierung einer Standardvarietät verdichteten, und zwar allein schon aufgrund ihrer Existenz in Textsorten, die gemeinhin in Schriftsprachgesellschaften als normativ gelten. Insoweit diese Form der Sprachnormierung als deskriptive beschrieben werden muß, ist die Ermittlung des Bindeglieds zwischen metasprachlichen Kodifikationen und objektsprachlichen Umsetzungen der Schlüssel zur Beantwortung der Wirkungsfrage. Empirische Arbeiten dazu sind dringend notwendig; die bereits erwähnten Untersuchungen Konopkas 1996 und Takadas 1998 haben in bezug auf die Wirkung der Grammatiker neue Ergebnisse vorgelegt und dürften für weitere Untersuchungen auch methodologisch anregend sein.

## 5. Bibliographie

### 5.1. Primärliteratur


Adelung, Johann Christoph. 1781. *Deutsche Sprachlehre. Zum Gebrauche der Schulen in den Königl. Preuß. Landen.* Berlin: Voß.

–. 1774–1786. *Versuch eines vollständigen grammatisch-kritischen Wörterbuches Der Hochdeutschen Mundart [...].* Leipzig: Breitkopf.

–. 1793–1801. *Grammatisch-kritisches Wörterbuch der Hochdeutschen Mundart [...].* 2., verm. u. verb. Aufl. Leipzig. (Repr. mit einer Einführung und Bibliographie von Helmut Henne. Hildesheim & New York: Olms, 1970.)

–. 1782–84. (zit.: 1782a, b, c) *Magazin für die Deutsche Sprache.* 2 Bde. Leipzig. (Repr., Hildesheim: Olms, 1969.)

–. 1782. (zit.: 1782d) *Umständliches Lehrgebäude der deutschen Sprache, zur Erläuterung der deutschen Sprachlehre für Schulen.* 2 Bde. Leipzig. (Repr., Hildesheim: Olms, 1971.)

–. 1788. *Vollständige Anweisung zur Deutschen Orthographie, nebst einem kleinen Wörterbuche für die Aussprache, Orthographie, Biegung und Ableitung.* Frankfurt & Leipzig: Weygand.

Aichinger, Carl Friedrich. 1754. *Versuch einer teutschen Sprachlehre. [...].* Wienn 1754. (Repr. mit einem Vorwort von Monika Rössing-Hager. Hildesheim & New York: Olms, 1972.)

Antesperg[er], [Johann] Balthasar von. 1747. *Die Kayserliche Deutsche Grammatik [...].* Wien: Heyinger.

Bellin, Johann. 1657. *Hochdeudsche Rechtschreibung; darinnen die ins gemein gebräuchliche Schreibart [...] unforgreiflich gezeiget würd.* Lübeck 1657. (Repr., Hildesheim & New York: Olms, 1973.)

Bödiker, Johann. 1701. *Neu=vermehrte Grund=Sätze Der Deutschen Sprachen Im Reden und Schreiben [...].* Berlin: Nicolai.

Campe, Joachim Heinrich. 1794. *Ueber die Reinigung und Bereicherung der Deutschen Sprache. Dritter Versuch welcher den von dem königl. Preuß. Gelehrtenverein zu Berlin ausgesetzten Preis erhalten hat. [...].* Verbesserte und vermehrte Ausgabe. Braunschweig: Schulbuchhandlung.

–. 1801. *Wörterbuch zur Erklärung und Verdeutschung der unserer Sprache aufgedrungenen fremden Ausdrücke [...].* 2 Bde. Braunschweig: Schulbuchhandlung.

–. 1807–11. *Wörterbuch der Deutschen Sprache [...].* Braunschweig. (Repr. mit einer Einführung und Bibliographie von Helmut Henne. Hildesheim & New York: Olms, 1969.)

Freyer, Hieronymus. 1722. *Anweisung zur Teutschen Orthographie.* Halle: Waisenhaus.

Frisch, Johann Leonhard. 1741. *Teutsch-Lateinisches Wörter-Buch [...].* 2 Bde. Berlin. (Repr. mit einer Einführung und Bibliographie von Gerhardt Powitz. Hildesheim & New York: Olms, 1977.)

Fulda, Friedrich Carl. 1788. *Grundregeln der deutschen Sprache.* Stuttgart: Metzler.

Gottsched, Johann Christoph. 1758. *Beobachtungen über den Gebrauch und Misbrauch vieler deutscher Wörter und Redensarten.* Strassburg & Leipzig. (Repr., [im Rahmen der "Academisch Proefschrift" von Johannus Hubertus Slangen]. Heerlen: Winants, 1955.)

–. 1762. *Vollständigere und Neuerläuterte Deutsche Sprachkunst, Nach den Mustern der besten Schriftsteller [...].* 5. Aufl. Leipzig 1762. (Repr., Hildesheim: Olms, 1970.)

Kinderling, Johann Friedrich August. 1795. *Über die Reinigkeit der Deutschen Sprache [...].* Berlin. (Repr., Leipzig: Zentralantiquariat, 1977.)

Kramer, Matthias. 1700–02. *Das herrlich-Grosse Teutsch-Italiänische Dictionarium [...].* Nürnberg (Repr. mit einer Einführung und Bibliographie von Gerhard Ising. Hildesheim: Olms, 1982.)

Morhof, Daniel Georg. 1700. *Unterricht von der Teutschen Sprache und Poesie [...].* Von den Erben herauß gegeben, Lübeck, Franckfurt. (Repr., Bad Homburg, Berlin & Zürich: Gehlen, 1969.)

Nast, Johann, ed. 1777–78. *Der teutsche Sprachforscher. allen Liebhabern ihrer Muttersprache zur Prüfung vorgelegt.* 2 Bde. Stuttgart: Metzler.

[Olearius, Tilmann:]. 1630. *Deutsche Sprachkunst [...].* Halle: Oelschlegeln.

Ratke [Ratichius], Wolfgang. *Sprachkunst* (1612–1615), *Allgemeine Sprachlehr* (1619), *Distinctionslehr* (1628), *SchreibungsLehr* (um 1629), *WortschikkungsLehr* (um 1630), *WortbedeutungsLehr* (nach 1639). Texte zitiert nach Erika Ising: Wolfgang Ratkes Schriften zur deutschen Grammatik (1612–1630), Teil II: Textausgabe. Berlin: Akademie-Verlag, 1959.

Schottelius, Justus Georg. 1663. *Ausführliche Arbeit Von der Teutschen HaubtSprache [...].* Braunschweig 1663. (Repr., hg. von Wolfgang Hecht. 2., unveränderte Aufl. Tübingen: Niemeyer, 1995.)

Steinbach, Christoph Ernst. 1734. *Vollständiges Deutsches Wörter=Buch [...].* Breßlau 1734. (Repr. mit einer Einführung von Walther Schröter. Hildesheim & New York: Olms, 1973.)

Stieler, Kaspar. 1691. *Der Teutschen Sprache Stammbaum und Fortwachs / oder Teutscher Sprachschatz [...].* 3 Bde. Nürnberg. (Repr. mit einer Einführung und Bibliographie von Gerhard Ising. Hildesheim: Olms, 1968.)

## 5.2. Sekundärliteratur

BBHS: *Bio-bibliographisches Handbuch zur Sprachwissenschaft des 18. Jahrhunderts. Die Grammatiker, Lexikographen und Sprachtheoretiker des deutschsprachigen Raums mit Beschreibung ihrer Werke* hg. von Herbert E. Brekle, Edeltraud Dobnig-Jülch, Hans Jürgen Höller und Helmut Weiß, bisher 6 Bde. Tübingen: Niemeyer, 1992–98.

Bergmann, Rolf. 1982. "Zum Anteil der Grammatiker an der Normierung der neuhochdeutschen Schriftsprache". *Sprachwissenschaft* 7.261–281.

Blume, Herbert. 1978. "Sprachtheorie und Sprachenlegitimation im 17. Jahrhundert in Schweden und in Kontinentaleuropa". *Arkiv för nordisk filologi* 93.205–218.

Cherubim, Dieter, 1993. "Elias Caspar Reichard. Sprachwissenschaft und Sprachkritik im frühen 18. Jahrhundert". *Sprachwissenschaft im 18. Jahrhundert. Fallstudien und Überblicke* hg. von Klaus D. Dutz, 23–46. Münster: Nodus.

Dill, Gerhard Johann. 1992. *Christoph Adelungs Wörterbuch der 'Hochdeutschen Mundart'. Untersuchungen zur lexikographischen Konzeption.* Frankfurt/M., Bern, New York & Paris: Lang.

Donhauser, Karin. 1989. "Das Deskripitionsproblem und seine präskriptive Lösung. Zur grammatikologischen Bedeutung der Vorreden in den Grammatiken des 16. bis 18. Jahrhunderts". *Sprachwissenschaft* 14.29–57.

Eichinger, Ludwig M. 1983. "Der Kampf um das Hochdeutsche. Zum zweihundertsten Todestag des Oberpfälzer Sprachforschers C. F. Aichinger (1717–1782)". *Sprachwissenschaft* 8.188–206.

Eichler, Ingrid & Gunter Bergmann. 1967. "Zum Meißnischen Deutsch. Die Beurteilung des Obersächsischen vom 16. bis zum 19. Jahrhundert". *PBB* (H) 89.1–57.

Erben, Johannes. 1989. "Die Entstehung unserer Schriftsprache und der Anteil deutscher Grammatiker am Normierungsprozeß". *Sprachwissenschaft* 14.6–28.

Ewald, Petra. 1992. "Das 'Grundgesetz der Deutschen Orthographie' bei Johann Christoph Adelung. Darstellung und Wertung". *Studien zur Geschichte der deutschen Orthographie* hg. von Dieter Nerius & Jürgen Scharnhost, 61–89. Hildesheim: Olms.

Gardt, Andreas. 1994. *Sprachreflexion in Barock und Frühaufklärung. Entwürfe von Böhme bis Leibniz.* Berlin & New York: de Gruyter.

Gloy, Klaus. 1980. "Sprachnorm". *LGL* 2.363–368. Vollst. neu bearb. und erw. Aufl. Tübingen: Niemeyer.

Greule, Albrecht & Elisabeth Ahlvers-Liebel. 1986. *Germanistische Sprachpflege. Geschichte, Praxis und Zielsetzung.* Darmstadt: Wissenschaftliche Buchgesellschaft.

Gützlaff, Kathrin. 1989. *Von der Fügung Teutscher Stammwörter. Die Wortbildung in J. G. Schottelius' "Ausführlicher Arbeit von der Teutschen HaubtSprache".* Hildesheim: Olms.

Hartung, Wolfdietrich. 1977. "Zum Inhalt des Normbegriffs in der Linguistik". *Normen in der sprachlichen Kommunikation* hg. von Wolfdietrich Hartung, 9–69. Berlin: Akademie-Verlag.

Henne, Helmut. 1968. "Das Problem des meißnischen Deutsch oder "Was ist Hochdeutsch" im 18. Jahrhundert". *Zeitschrift für Mundartforschung* 35.109–129.

–. 1972. *Semantik und Lexikographie. Untersuchungen zur lexikalischen Kodifikation der deutschen Sprache.* Berlin & New York: de Gruyter.

–. Hg. 1975. *Deutsche Wörterbücher des 17. und 18. Jahrhunderts. Einführung und Bibliographie.* Hildesheim & New York: Olms.

–. 1975a. "Deutsche Lexikographie und Sprachnorm im 17. und 18. Jahrhundert." Henne 1975. 1–37.

–. 1984. "Johann Christoph Adelung – Leitbild und Stein des Anstoßes. Zur Konstitutionsproblematik gegenwartsbezogener Sprachforschung". *Sprache und Kulturentwicklung im Blickfeld der deutschen Spätaufklärung. Der Beitrag Johann Christoph Adelungs* hg. von Werner Bahner, 98–108. Berlin: Akademie-Verlag.

Huber, Wolfgang. 1984. *Kulturpatriotismus und Sprachbewußtsein. Studien zur deutschen Philologie des 17. Jahrhunderts.* Frankfurt/M., Bern, New York & Nancy: Lang.

Ising, Erika. 1959. *Wolfgang Ratkes Schriften zur deutschen Grammatik (1612–1630)*, Teil I: *Abhandlung.* Berlin: Akademie-Verlag.

Jellinek, Max Hermann. 1913–1914. *Geschichte der neuhochdeutschen Grammatik von den Anfängen bis auf Adelung.* 2 Bde. Heidelberg. (Repr., Heidelberg: Winter, 1968.)

Kirkness, Alan. 1975. *Zur Sprachreinigung im Deutschen 1789–1871. Eine historische Dokumentation.* Tübingen: Narr.

Konopka, Marek. 1996. *Strittige Erscheinungen der deutschen Syntax im 18. Jahrhundert.* Tübingen: Niemeyer.

Kühn, Peter & Ulrich Püschel. 1990. "Die deutsche Lexikographie vom 17. Jahrhundert bis zu den Brüdern Grimm ausschließlich". *HSK* 5: 2.2049–2077. Berlin & New York: de Gruyter.

Leser, Ernst. 1914. "Fachwörter zur deutschen Grammatik von Schottel bis Gottsched. 1641–1749". *ZDW* 15.1–98.

Moulin, Claudine. 1992. "'Aber wo ist die Richtschnur? wo ist die Regel?'. Zur Suche nach den Prinzipien der Rechtschreibung im 17. Jahrhundert". *Studien zur Geschichte der deutschen Orthographie* hg. von Dieter Nerius & Jürgen Scharnhost, 23–60. Hildesheim: Olms.

Moulin-Fankhänel, Claudine. 1994 u. 1997. *Bibliographie der deutschen Grammatiken und Orthographielehren*, bisher 2 Bde. Heidelberg: Winter.

Naumann, Bernd. 1983. "Die zwei Grammatiken des C. F. Aichinger". *Sprachwissenschaft* 8.277–290.

Nerius, Dieter. 1967. *Untersuchungen zur Herausbildung einer nationalen Norm der deutschen Literatursprache im 18. Jahrhundert.* Halle: Niemeyer.

–. 1989. "Die Rolle J. Ch. Adelungs in der Geschichte der deutschen Orthographie". *Sprachwissenschaft* 14.78–96.

Neuhaus, Gisela M. 191. *Justus Georg Schottelius: Die Stammwörter der Teutschen Sprache Samt dererselben Erklärung / und andere die Stammwörter betreffende Anmerkungen. Eine Untersuchung zur frühneuhochdeutschen Lexikologie.* Göppingen: Kümmerle.

Penzl, Herbert. 1977. "Gottsched und die Aussprache des Deutschen im 18. Jahrhundert". *Sprachwissenschaft* 2.61–92.

–. 1978. "Gottsched und das 'Lutherische e': Zur deutschen Aussprache im 18. Jahrhundert". *Deutsche Sprache: Geschichte und Gegenwart. Festschrift für Friedrich Maurer zum 80. Geburtstag* hg. von Hugo Moser, Heinz Rupp & Hugo Steger, 135–145. Bern & München: Francke.

Polenz, Peter v. 1994. *Deutsche Sprachgeschichte vom Spätmittelalter bis zur Gegenwart*, Bd. II: *17. und 18. Jahrhundert.* Berlin & New York: de Gruyter.

Poppe, Erich. 1982. *C. F. Aichingers "Versuch einer teutschen Sprachlehre". Untersuchungen zur Geschichte der deutschen Grammatikschreibung im 18. Jahrhundert.* Hildesheim, Zürich & New York: Olms.

Schiewe, Jürgen. 1988. *Sprachpurismus und Emanzipation. Joachim Heinrich Campes Verdeutschungsprogramm als Voraussetzung für Gesellschaftsveränderungen.* Hildesheim, Zürich & New York: Olms.

Schmidt-Wilpert, Gabriele. 1985. "Die Bedeutung der älteren deutschen Grammatiker für das Neuhochdeutsche". *HSK* 2: 2.1556–1564. Berlin & New York: de Gruyter.

Semenjuk, Natalia N. 1972. "Zustand und Evolution der grammatischen Normen des Deutschen in der 1. Hälfte des 18. Jh. am Sprachstoff der periodischen Schriften". *Studien zur Geschichte der deutschen Sprache* hg. von Günter Feudel, 79–166. Berlin: Akademie-Verlag.

Stammerjohann, Harro, Hg. 1996. *Lexicon Grammaticorum. Who's Who in the History World of Linguistics.* Tübingen: Niemeyer.

Takada, Hiroyuki. 1981. "Zum aufklärerischen Begriff der Sprachreinheit – aufgrund einer Abhandlung von J. F. A. Kinderling (1795)". *Sprache und Kultur* 15.55–65.

–. 1997a. "Orthographische Vorschrift und Praxis im Barock. Zum Anteil der Grammatiker an der schriftsprachlichen Norm". *ZdPh* 116.68–89.

–. 1998. *Grammatik und Sprachwirklichkeit von 1640–1700. Zur Rolle deutscher Grammatiker im schriftsprachlichen Ausgleichsprozeß.* Tübingen.

Tauber, Walter. 1993. *Mundart und Schriftsprache in Bayern (1450–1800). Untersuchungen zur Sprachnorm und Sprachnormierung im Frühneuhochdeutschen.* Berlin & New York: de Gruyter.

Tauchmann, Christine. 1992. *Hochsprache und Mundart in den großen Wörterbüchern der Barock- und Aufklärungszeit.* Tübingen: Niemeyer.

*Jörg Kilian, Braunschweig (Deutschland)*

# 115. La langue et l'État: l'Académie française


1. Introduction
2. La tradition des descriptions de la langue
3. Une commande d'État
4. Le *Dictionnaire de l'Académie* dédié au Roy
5. Le sentiment de l'unité de la langue
6. Bibliographie


## 1. Introduction

Pour la conscience linguistique française, pour l'école, pour le discours ordinaire, il semble qu'existe une langue française, commune, 'la' langue française. Une et indivisible comme la République, dit-on à la Révolution. L'école conforte l'idée qu'il s'agit de la langue de Racine et Molière, donc de la seconde moitié du XVII^e^ siècle, même si cette langue semble difficile à faire comprendre aux élèves, et le parler ordinaire, en faisant du dictionnaire un véritable 'juge de paix', véhicule l'idée que cette langue est tout entière contenue dans 'le' dictionnaire, sans référence d'auteur ou d'éditeur. Si 'ce n'est pas dans le dictionnaire', ce n'est pas français. Ceci explique qu'on centre cet article sur l'événement à la fois linguistique et politique responsable de cet état de fait: en 1694, la production par l'Académie française, fondée par Richelieu, du *Dictionnaire de l'Académie.*

L'Académie, qui continue aujourd'hui de travailler à 'son' dictionnaire (9^e^ édition), n'a pas cessé de proposer sinon d'imposer ses arbitrages. Son engagement aux côtés des services du Premier Ministre lors de la dernière tentative de réforme de l'orthographe, en 1989–1990, témoigne de sa place dans les questions de politique langagière. Cependant, elle n'est plus un instrument de politique linguistique à proprement parler. Ses récentes remarques (1998) sur le féminin des noms de métier, qui tentaient de maintenir une distinction entre sexe et genre, en particulier quand il s'agit de titres (doit-on dire *le/la haut (e) fonctionnaire*?) n'ont pas prévalu contre les revendications féministes des ministres. Depuis la fin du XVIII^e^ siècle et sa suppression par la Révolution en 1794 (elle sera rétablie en 1803), mais surtout depuis la grande entreprise de l'académicien (tardif) Émile Littré (1801–1881) dont le dictionnaire a détrôné le sien, tout en s'en inspirant, elle a cessé de faire figure de corps d'état engagé dans la construction d'une langue nationale comme ce fut le cas au XVII^e^ siècle, lors de la constitution du premier dictionnaire de langue monolingue en France, outil maître de la formation du sentiment linguistique français.

Dans la première moitié du XVII^e^ siècle, l'État se stabilise par la construction d'un pouvoir royal centralisé. Dans la même période, les discussions sur l'excellence des langues vernaculaires, et sur la nécessité de les 'fixer', quittent les cercles de lettrés pour devenir un véritable phénomène mondain, intéressant imprimeurs, traducteurs, voyageurs, pédagogues, mais aussi la Cour et la Ville, en particulier les salons. Ce sera la conjonction réussie entre les nécessités de construire un État unifié et le désir de fixation de la langue comme espace de communication normalisant des pratiques langagières, littéraires ou techniques, qui fera du français du XVII^e^ siècle le début du français moderne. La création de l'Académie Française par Richelieu, ministre de Louis XIII, en 1635, peut alors se lire comme le petit événement historique qui va permettre, en fin de siècle et en pleine gloire de Louis XIV et des lettres, l'imposition, critiquée mais incontestable, d'une langue d'état. En radicalisant le propos, on pourrait dire que l'état, par 'arrêté' pris sur la commande d'un produit linguistique (un dictionnaire), a arrêté une idée systématisée de l'unité du français, et que cet événement singulier n'est pas sans conséquence pour les discussions actuelles touchant aux concepts de langue, de langage et d'hyperlangue dans l'espace linguistique français. Mais pour comprendre comment un simple outil linguistique a pu agir sur une langue au point d'assurer un sentiment linguistique, de soutenir une politique nationale culturelle, scientifique et d'enseignement, il convient de ne pas le traiter comme un simple dictionnaire ayant les caractéristiques du genre et ses particularités, mais comme une construction complexe (cf. 4), insérée à la fois dans le mouvement des études sur la langue (cf. 2), et dans une politique monarchique, expansionniste dans l'espace, et réductrice au plan symbolique (cf. 3).

## 2. La tradition des descriptions de la langue

### 2.1. Grammaire et dictionnaire

Même si la mémoire scolaire retient plutôt les querelles normatives d'écrivains et les *Défenses*, puis les *Ramarques*, les *Observations* et les *Doutes* sur la langue, dont la densité de publication va croissant jusqu'à la fin du XVIIe siècle, on sait que la grande grammaire du XVIIe siècle est la *Grammaire Générale et raisonnée* de Port-Royal. Il s'agit d'une grammaire générale dont le français est seulement une des langues d'illustration. Mais elle inspire tout le plan du *Dictionnaire de l'Académie* et nombre de ses définitions (Delesalle & Mazière 1998), quand l'Académie pratique la définition 'raisonnée', celle qui tient compte des liaisons entre forme des mots (les traditionnelles 'parties du discours') et sens, par le jeu des dérivations. Cependant l'Académie se fait aussi le secrétaire de l'usage des mots, de leurs appariements (les collocations) comme faisant le 'génie' de la langue. C'est par cette activité double sur la langue qu'elle va se distinguer: mise en place d'une définition de tous les termes d'une langue particulière selon la raison générale et selon l'usage particulier, et non par un traité de rhétorique, ou par une grammaire, pourtant commandés (Chevalier 1998).

### 2.2. Les recueils

L'héritage lexicographique, en France, n'est pas alors unifié. On peut rappeler plusieurs types d'ouvrages déjà anciens: les nomenclatures et lexiques spécialisés, les bi ou plurilingues de langues vernaculaires accédant à l'autonomie, les latin-français, de thèmes et de version, en général rendus nécessaires par les difficultés d'un enseignement qui ne se fait pas en langue maternelle, nettement dominés par le dictionnaire latin-français, puis français-latin de Robert Estienne (1539), développé par Nicot (*Thresor de la langue française*, 1606). Mais existent aussi des recueils et florilèges rhétorico-lexicaux: dictionnaires des *synonymes*, des *meilleures épithètes*, des *dictons dorés*, des *illustres proverbes*, des *curiosités* etc. Ce sont des recueils de 'marguerites et fleurs du bien dire', 'façons de parler' 'comiques', 'familières', 'burlesques', 'triviales', 'communément admises', c'est-à-dire des sortes d'enquêtes linguistiques pragmatiques dont les académiciens sont très proches, quand ils "recueillent les façons de parler" (*Préface*) et privilégient les collocations, c'est à dire les appariements convenus de mots, à la limite de la locution figée. Livrant un 'prêt-à-parler', la langue française commune (Collinot & Mazière 1997), l'Académie n'est pas l'héritière des grands bilingues mais bien plutôt de ces recueils, reflets de l'usage.

### 2.3. Le bon usage

Dès le XVIe siècle on cherche la référence du 'bon usage' de la langue (Danièle Trudeau 1992): Peuple, bourgeoisie, aristocratie, courtisans, poètes, ont tour à tour été réclamés comme modèles. Au début du XVIIe siècle, la nouveauté vient du fait que le rapport critique aux productions littéraires et courtisanes se double d'une sensibilité aux productions conversationnelles (les femmes, les salons) comme image sociale valorisée et d'un engouement des conversations pour un sujet déjà à la mode depuis un siècle, la réflexion linguistique sur le bien parler. L'Académie arrivera donc dans un espace français investi par une discussion généralisée sur le langage, mais aussi balisé par des ouvrages dont le succès est considérable. Dans le contexte d'interrogations sur une stabilisation du dire et des façons de dire rappelé ici, une injonction politique va pouvoir entraîner la production française autour de la notion de 'langue commune', nationale.

## 3. Une commande d'État

### 3.1. Langue et État

Richelieu, grand ordonnateur de la centralisation monarchique, fait entrer l'unité de la langue dans ses préoccupations d'efficacité politique dès 1632 et la fondation de l'Académie date de 1635.

L'Académie Française est donc créée dans le grand mouvement de mise en exclusion, à l'intérieur, des particularismes et des pouvoirs locaux au profit d'un centralisme étatique et, sur le plan extérieur, l'année de l'entrée en guerre contre l'Espagne, la puissance dominante dont le castillan est nettement mieux outillé que le français.

Il s'agit aussi d'un moment très particulier de la production des idées (Saint Cyran deviendra directeur de Port Royal en 1636) et de la production littéraire. Pour faire très vite, au moment où va s'affirmer ce que l'histoire littéraire étiquettera comme 'classissisme'. Deux événements se préparent: *Le Cid* en 1636, et surtout, en 1637, *Le Discours de la Méthode* de Descartes, premier ouvrage philosophique écrit en français. C'est le début du 'grand siècle', quand l'Italie, l'Espagne, l'Angleterre, (Dante, Cervantes, Shakespeare) ont terminé leur entrée dans la modernité en langue vulgaire. La production littéraire française dite 'classique', qui stabilise le foisonnement baroque, est donc postérieure à la création de l'Académie, si l'on s'en tient aux dates, mais tous les premiers travaux de l'Académie accompagnent (mêmes acteurs, quasi consensus sur la langue) le classicisme. Elle n'est pas née de lui, elle ne le crée pas, elle y participe et l'accompagne par une convergence du sentiment linguistique et des pratiques, au sein d'une protection (puis de pensions) d'état.

Il fallut quatre lettres de cachet pour que le Parlement accepte l'Académie. Cependant les interventions directes de Richelieu, même après la création, ont été rares; il a refusé de pensionner les Académiciens (seul Vaugelas sera pensionné pour le dictionnaire); il n'a même jamais attribué de lieu de travail à l'Académie, malgré le projet de l'installer dans une future *Place Ducale.* Séguier, à la mort de Richelieu, l'accueille et la sauve de la dispersion. C'est Colbert qui l'installera au Louvre, en 1672 seulement.

L'important est donc simplement que Richelieu ait eu l'idée d'une telle assemblée, et qu'il ait pesé sur elle par son projet même, c'est à dire qu'il ait créé tout à la fois un lieu de représentation, une scène, et un observatoire pour la langue française. Et, surtout, qu'il ait fait de ce lieu, par contrat, un observatoire officiel en même temps qu'un lieu de régulation pour l'espace communicationnel national. Si construire un état moderne, c'est unifier une communauté de sujets en l'administrant de façon efficace, ceci suppose toutes sortes d'outils administratifs, qui se compliquent au fur et à mesure que l'autorité se renforce, c'est à dire que l'état s'établit et diversifie ses fonctions. Contre les appropriations de la langue et les éloquences locales, fussent-elles religieuses ou juridiques, est en marche la machine à forger 'la langue commune' par l'ordre (le sens) des mots.

### 3.2. Fondation et principes

La création de l'Académie se fait par étapes. Un groupe obscur d'amis se réunit pour parler des œuvres qui paraissent. Richelieu lui propose sa protection si celui-ci accepte de se constituer en Corps. Cette proposition ne fut pas d'abord acceptée. Il fallut deux ans de contre-propositions et d'élaboration (1633–35) pour que soient rédigés des *Statuts* puis des *Lettres Patentes.* Richelieu signa et fit signer le Roi. Puis il fallut deux ans encore, et une intervention directe de Richelieu, pour que le Parlement de Paris accepte d'enregistrer la création de l'Académie Française. Dernière officialisation: afin que la Compagnie puisse sceller les actes qui émaneront d'elles, Richelieu lui attribue un sceau à son effigie portant au revers la fameuse inscription: "A l'Immortalité".

Là où avaient échoué toutes les entreprises du XVI^e^ siècle initiées par des auteurs (qui se souvient d'une *Académie Française* instituée en 1568 par *Lettres Patentes* de Charles IX, œuvre de Baïf, soutenue par Ronsard, et qui fonctionna jusqu'en 1585?), le pouvoir, par la volonté de deux ministres centralisateurs, Richelieu puis Colbert, va réussir, à partir d'un groupe de remarqueurs protestants, sans éclat.

Dans un contexte de réflexion sur le français, dans un contexte de constitution d'un état français, la démarche de Richelieu s'apparente à ce qu'on appellerait aujourd'hui une politique linguistique. En l'absence de textes privés émanant des protagonistes (la correspondance de Richelieu est très dispersée mais témoigne de son intérêt jusqu'à sa mort, en 1642), nous disposons essentiellement des textes fondateurs, statuts et lettres patentes et de l'*Histoire de l'Académie* de Pélisson complétée par d'Olivet (Livet 1858).

Le nom *Académie Française* avait été arrêté dès 1634 par le groupe d'origine. C'est aussi ce groupe qui, pour l'essentiel, rédigea les statuts. De ces *Statuts et Règlements*, on a l'habitude de citer les articles 24, 25 et 26 qui fixent les "fonctions" de l'assemblée:

> 24: La principale fonction de l'Académie sera de travailler avec tout le soin et toute la diligence possible à donner des règles certaines à notre langue et la rendre pure, éloquente et capable de traiter les arts et les sciences;
> 25: Les meilleurs auteurs de la langue française seront distribués aux Académiciens pour observer tant les dictions que les phrases qui peuvent servir de règles générales et en faire rapport à la Compagnie qui jugera de leur travail et s'en servira aux occasions;
> 26: Il sera composé un Dictionnaire, une Grammaire, une Rhétorique et une Poétique sur les observations de l'Académie.

Régler, observer, composer sur les observations, on a souvent rassemblé ces trois commandements pour limiter le rôle de l'Académie à une entreprise réductrice. *Régler* reprend pourtant un programme de plus d'un siècle, une exigence des littérateurs désireux que la rapidité des changements ne nuise pas à leur lecture postume, mais aussi des grammairiens soucieux de "raisonner" la langue. Cependant, il est ici question également des arts en général et des sciences. Les descriptions des naturalistes, puis des 'savants' comme Fontenelle, les écrits philosophiques comme le *Discours de la Méthode* mais aussi toute la querelle des Anciens et des Modernes suppose ces *règles* que les grammairiens du siècle précédent avaient déjà tenté d'établir et que l'injonction du pouvoir va permettre d''arrêter'. La position d'observatoire semble particulièrement intéressante. Elle aussi est traditionnelle; elle relève de la soumission à 'la tyrannie de l'usage'. Mais l'important est dans l'objet proposé: *dictions* et *phrases*, en vocabulaire de l'époque, désignent les collocations, les appariements figés, les locutions, les constructions, c'est à dire des unités qui ne coïncident pas avec le mot graphique tel que nous l'entendons. Est programmée ainsi la description du lexique par ses emmplois, ses assemblages discursifs, et non plus ses possibles synonymes, ou substituts latins ou romans. Quant à la commande d'outils, elle témoigne de l'intuition de la valeur interventionniste des ouvrages métalinguistiques sur l'usage langagier (Auroux 1994). En fait, ni la rhétorique ni la poétique ne seront envisagées au XVIIe siècle. Les lectures critiques, les discours, les harangues, les prix et surtout les Conférences font toute la régulation, et semblent suffire à assurer le passage de l'éloquence religieuse et civile (l'Académie est, par statut (article 21), interdite de sujet religieux et (article 22) contrôlée par le gouvernement pour les sujets moraux et politiques) à celle des Belles Lettres (Fumaroli 1980: 654). Mais l'absence de grammaire sera ressentie comme un manquement, auquel il sera remédié en 1705 par le *Traité* de Regnier-Desmarais (Il faudra attendre le XXe siècle pour que sorte une grammaire officielle de l'Académie, très critiquée). Cela s'explique si l'on revient à l'appréhension particulière du lexique que supposent les *Remarques* et surtout la *Grammaire Générale et Raisonnée* de Port-Royal, et à leur influence sur le *Dictionnaire*.

Pour les *Lettres Patentes*, signées de Louis XIII, elles articulent essentiellement le parallèle entre les armes et les lettres, pour la gloire d'un état.

On s'est peu soucié d'analyser ces textes, préférant les stigmatiser comme trop interventionnistes et trop peu soucieux de la richesse baroque. Mais le programme pragmatique n'est pas trivial. Commander des outils linguistiques, c'est à dire des ouvrages qui, en organisant les observations, les posent en corps de savoir et, par officialisation, en corps de prescription, c'était anticiper sur l'idée même de langue comme langue commune, et la projeter sur l'idée de langue efficace. A plus long terme, tous les dévelopements qui suivront sur la langue universelle ou sur la langue de la raison sont ici en germe. On s'étonnera beaucoup, jusqu'à nos jours, de la 'synchronie' de référence du *Dictionnaire*, unique en son genre. Mais il était programmé pour cela, dès lors qu'il devait être l'outil d'une langue d'état historiquement définie et revendiquée. On peut donc relire les textes fondateurs de l'Académie française comme 'modernes' autant ou plus que 'puristes'. Beaucoup d'académiciens, dans la querelle des Anciens et des Modernes, en fin de siècle, seront Modernes. En particulier ceux qu'intéresse le dictionnaire, comme Charpentier qui défendait le français contre le latin pour les inscriptions sur les médailles et les monuments, ce qui était aller très loin dans l'idée de fixation de la langue. En effet, le latin dit 'de Cicéron' était vanté pour sa stabilité incorruptible. La position de Charpentier sera que le français est entré dans cette stabilité sémantique d'une langue digne des monuments et médailles.

### 3.4. Langue et pouvoir

Sous Colbert s'ouvre une deuxième époque. Ministre le plus célèbre de Louis XIV, et ministre d'après les désordres et violences de la Fronde, Colbert entend utiliser l'Académie (il s'y fait admettre en 1667) comme un des rouages de la politique hégémonique de la France. Ce n'est plus le temps de la construction mais de l'exploitation du centralisme monarchique, ce n'est plus le temps de la composition avec les particularismes en vue de l'harmonie mais de la radicalisation de l'uniformité. La politique culturelle qu'il met en œuvre participe d'une ambition d'ordre universel, la même que celle qui présidera à la construction de Versailles. Voulant des compagnies d'artisans, de savants, d'artistes, créant des académies des sciences, de peinture, d'architecture, une Académie de France à Rome, il visait l'universel par l'universelle raison politique et par le concours des talents, d'où qu'ils soient, contre l'événement et la mode.

Il est ainsi conduit à régenter le fonctionnement de l'Académie Française par de nombreuses réformes, afin d'en hâter les travaux. Il incite Louis XIV à devenir lui-même protecteur de l'Académie et à lui donner un lieu permanent de réunion (1672). Ce sera le Louvre, lieu hautement symbolique (Fumaroli 1986), même si le gouvernement se transporte alors à Versailles. Il place son homme de confiance, Charles Perrault, au sein de l'Académie afin d'encourager la progression du *Dictionnaire* et prend des mesures en ce sens: institution des jetons de présence (1673), c'est à dire d'une forme de rémunération, instauration d'horaires stricts, ouverture des *Registres des procès-verbaux* (1672–81), constitution d'une bibliothèque (1674), et enfin obtention du privilège d'impression en juin 1674. Ce privilège était particulièrement avantageux car il faisait expressément défense à qui que ce soit de publier aucun dictionnaire avant la publication de celui de l'Académie non plus que pendant les vingt ans qui suivraient sa publication. Les publications commencèrent en 1678. Si l'on ajoute quelques marques d'honneur comme le droit de haranguer le roi dans les circonstances solennelles au même rang que les grands corps de l'État, celui de s'adresser à lui sans passer par l'intermédiaire d'aucun ministre, on comprend que l'assemblée fondée par Richelieu ait sous Colbert changé de statut, sans avoir à changer ses statuts. Elle est un corps d'état et en a les pouvoirs. L'irritation de certains s'accroît alors d'autant que, parallèlement à cette agrégation dans la politique royale, l'Académie se popularise du côté mondain. La cérémonie des réceptions en est l'occasion. C'est Charles Perrault qui, devant le succès de sa harangue le jour de sa réception, suggère d'accueillir le public (en 1702, les dames à leur tour seront admises aux séances de réception).

L'almanach de l'année 1676 peut représenter *L'Alliance de Mars et de Minerve ou la Gloire des armes, des sciences et des arts soubs l'heureux règne de Louis XIV* (gravure de Livens, reproduite dans le remarquable Catalogue de l'exposition de Langeais, 1994).

Le parallèle des armes et des lettres, qui structure les *Lettres patentes* de 1635 sous forme de projet, est donc une réalité en 1676. Rappelons que c'est entre 1676 et 1678 (Paix de Nimègue) que Louis XIV est partout victorieux et en 1678 que sont publiés les premiers textes du dictionnaire, détruits, et que l'*Epistre au Roy* de 1694 reprendra encore le parallèle, mais dans une logique d'expansion et non plus de gloire: "Tandis que nous nous appliquons à l'embellir [la langue française], vos armes victorieuses la font passer chez les Etrangers, nous leur en facilitons l'intelligence par notre travail et vous la leur rendez nécessaire par vos Conquetes". Bien que depuis 1689 les armes soient moins glorieuses, le français sera effectivement la langue de l'Europe au XVIIIe siècle.

## 4. Le *Dictionnaire de l'Académie* dédié au Roy

Cette œuvre, parue en 1694, qui ne peut valoir que par son anonymat, donne dans son titre son nom d'auteur et dit sa justification par le destinataire royal.

De son lien au pouvoir, elle tire au moins deux caractères décisifs: c'est un dictionnaire en synchronie, c'est le dictionnaire de la 'langue commune' des Français. De là son allure d'événement historique. De son insertion dans le mouvement grammatical elle tire son caractère 'raisonné', qui en fait un événement linguistique.

Ces traits ne lui ont été reconnus que de façon négative par la critique contemporaine jusqu'à ces derniers temps, malgré deux siècles d'encensement des diverses éditions (l'Académie a pour tradition de beaucoup remanier). Pour apprécier ce double événement, historique et linguistique, il faut donc le replacer dans un espace discursif très encombré, d'autant que du projet à l'édition il s'écoule plus de 50 ans.

### 4.1. Les acteurs

Les critiques ont pu d'abord porter sur les acteurs, cohorte des 'pensionnés' du pouvoir. Livet tente de justifier quelques grands absents de l'Académie: Ménage, trop critique, Descartes, résidant à l'étranger, Molière, qui s'obstinait à vouloir monter sur les planches. Le poids du pouvoir s'affirme dès le premier article des statuts:

> Personne ne sera reçu dans l'Académie qui ne soit agréable à Monseigneur le Protecteur et qui ne soit de bonnes mœurs, de bonne réputation, de bon esprit et propre aux fonctions académiques. (*Statut et règlements de l'Académie Françoise*, 1635, Premièrement).

Si Richelieu se contenta d'intervenir pour une affaire de mœurs, Colbert fut beaucoup plus pesant. Il y eut des pressions à propos des élections de Corneille, de Boileau, de La Fontaine. L'histoire retient essentiellement, parmi les Académiciens, des noms d'écrivains, mais, jusqu'à aujourd'hui, la présence de généraux ou d'archevêques ou d'anthropologues, sans préséance d'ordre sous l'ancien régime, de titre aujourd'hui, montre que ce corps représente plus qu'une simple assemblée de gens de lettres. La liste des quarante premiers montre combien certains nous restent inconnus comme Antoine Godeau, Evèque de Grasse, qui se trouve être à l'orgine de la constitution de l'Académie ou Philippe de Habert, issu de la Robe et Commissaire de l'artillerie, qui participa à l'examen du projet présenté à Richelieu.

Mais les Académiciens du XVII$^{e}$ siècle ont quelques traits dominants: ils sont de la Cour, et fréquentent souvent l'Hotel de Rambouillet; même d'origine provinciale, ils doivent séjourner à Paris; ils sont polyglottes, comme en témoignent leurs activités de traducteurs, leur fréquentation quasi professionnelle des villes étrangères, surtout Lisbonne, Madrid et Rome, leur production en langue étrangère (Voiture en espagnol, Vaugelas en italien etc.).

Cependant, classicisme oblige, dès 1675, nous trouvons des noms beaucoup plus connus: Bossuet, Colbert, Corneille, Fléchier, Furetière, Perrault et Racine. La liste de 1694, date de publication du *Dictionnaire*, comprend en outre: Boileau, La Fontaine, Fontenelle, La Bruyère.

Ce taux de notoriété ne sera dépassé qu'au XIX$^{e}$ siècle: Victor Cousin, Lamartine, Royer-Collard, Scribe, Chateaubriand, Nodier, Casimir Delavigne, Bonald, Thiers, Guizot, Lamartine, Hugo, Vigny, Musset, Pasquier, Berryer, Mgr Dupanloup, Villemain, Tocqueville, Montalembert, Mérimée, Sainte-Beuve ...

Mais il faut signaler surtout les académiciens engagés dans le *Dictionnaire* (désormais *DA*). Quelques hommes ont marqué l'entreprise, là encore, ce ne sont pas les plus connus. Il s'agit des premiers 'secrétaires perpétuels': Conrart (1634–1675), Mézeray surtout (1675–1683), Régnier-Desmarais (1683–1713), des artisants du dictionnaire: Chapelain, qui dès la deuxième assemblée, le 20 mars 1634, "représenta qu'à son avis [la fonction de l'Académie] devait être de travailler à la pureté de la langue et de la rendre capable de la plus haute éloquence [...] que pour cet effet il fallait premièrement en régler les termes et les phrases par un ample dictionnaire" (Livet, 28), Vaugelas, remarqueur plus connu, qui est chargé en 1639 de 'composer' le dictionnaire. Il termine la lettre A en octobre de la même année. Il fournit la matière aux trois bureaux qui se tiennent chaque semaine, en dehors des assemblées ordinaires. Quand il meurt en 1650 le travail est arrivé à la lettre *I*. Les manuscrits de Vaugelas seront saisis pour dettes, et en grande partie perdus, si l'on en croit Furetière (*Factum*). Mézeray assurera le travail jusqu'à la lettre *S*. En 1674, il est relayé par Charpentier. Les écrivains sont moins actifs. Corneille rédige quelques définitions. Racine n'aimerait pas que sorte un mauvais dictionnaire mais participe peu. La Fontaine acceptera de réviser les lettres F à P de l'édition de 1687 et s'engage dans la querelle contre Furetière. Bossuet intervient pour défendre une othographe historique.

### 4.2. Options

En second lieu, les critiques atteignent les options de l'Académie, qui heurtent des traditions lexicographiques, dans et hors de l'Académie.

Si le *DA* ne paraît qu'en 1694, les premières définitions imprimées datent de la fin des années 1670, et les querelles aussi. L'Académie n'assume pas ses premiers travaux et, mis à part un exemplaire imprimé contrefait à Francfort en 1687, nous ne possédons pas de témoignage des premiers tirages. Ces hésitations, mais surtout les options sur la langue et la structure du dictionnaire, partout discutées, irritent certains membres de la Compagnie qui vont inspirer des ouvrages concurrents. La commande de Richelieu aura initié une querelle de méthode qui va s'éclairer à travers la production de deux dictionnaires qui témoignent d'autres positions sur la langue, et d'autres positionnements sociaux. Il s'agit d'abord du *Dictionnaire français, contenant les mots et les choses, plusieurs nouvelles remarques sur la langue françoise. ses expressions propres, figurées et burlesques, la prononciation des mots les plus difficiles, le genre des noms, le régime des verbes [...]* de Pierre Richelet qui parait en 1680, à l'étranger par nécessité, à cause du privilège dont jouit l'Académie (l'imprimeur genevois qui voulut malgré l'interdiction l'introduire en France fut ruiné par la saisie de 1500 exemplaires, qui furent brulés). Dictionnaire sensible aux styles, proposant des définitions plus fines que linguistiquement stabilisées, il est en grande partie inspiré par le courant académique des traducteurs (d'Ablancourt), des puristes (Patru), et aussi des étymologistes comme Ménage, hors de l'Académie. C'est un ouvrage tout à fait intéressant et dont la postérité est importante (Bray 1986) mais pris dans la problématique des dictionnaires dits 'd'Autorités', qui s'appuient sur 'nos meilleurs auteurs', comme les grands monolingues espagnol et italien, l'auteur ayant plus de personnalité que de notoriété pour imposer un discours sur le sens. En 1690, parait le *Dictionnaire Universel contenant généralement tous les mots françois tant vieux que modernes de toutes les sciences et des arts, sçavoir [...]* d'Antoine Furetière, lui aussi contraint de paraître à l'étranger (il sera édité à Amsterdam deux ans après la mort de l'auteur avec une importante préface de Bayle). Ce beau travail à tendance encyclopédique (A. Rey, introduction à la réimpression, 1978), très largement ouvert aux langues des métiers, très systématique dans l'organisation de ses définitions et qui ne néglige pas de donner l'origine des mots, vaut à son auteur d'être exclu de l'Académie et condamné pour non respect du privilège. En effet, Furetière avait obtenu puis perdu le privilège royal l'autorisant à éditer les seuls mots des arts exclus par l'Académie. Il reconnaît d'ailleurs que "les termes des Arts et des Sciences sont tellement engagés avec les mots communs de la langue, qu'il n'est pas plus aisé de les séparer que les eaux de deux rivières à quelque distance de leur confluent" (Premier factum, ed 1694: 32). Au contraire, les académiciens sépareront résolument les termes, faisant paraître en 1694 un *Dictionnaire universel des termes des arts et des sciences*, en deux volumes, signé de Thomas Corneille. L'Académie opère donc en toute lucidité cette distinction entre dictionnaire de langue et dictionnaire de choses que théorisera Diderot dans l'*Encyclopédie*.

Les positions de l'Académie sont en rupture avec l'héritage comme avec la concurrence sur trois points majeurs: la synchronie absolue, la 'langue commune', l'invention d'une définition 'raisonnée' qui conduit à promouvoir une organisation stricte des entrées et des sens en usage.

#### 4.2.1. La synchronie

Au contraire des académiciens de la Crusca et de Covarrubias, les rédacteurs ne construisent pas des définitions philologiques, ils ne prennent pas appui sur les 'Autorités' littéraires, ils ne décrivent pas des emplois préjustifiés par de grands noms. Le fait qu'ils ne citent pas interdit qu'ils définissent à partir d'un corpus d'écrits forcément datés: ils débattent du sens (cf. la séance sur *ami* en présence de Colbert rappelée dans la *Préface*) à partir de leur propre usage, et "dans la vie civile et dans le commerce ordinaire du monde" (Vaugelas, *Remarques*, p. 19), "dans le commerce ordinaire des honnêtes gens, des orateurs [c'est à dire des hommes politiques] et des poètes" (Préface au *Dictionnaire*). Soulignons que cette option découle directement de la commande du pouvoir: il faut fixer la langue dans le degré d'excellence qui est présentement le sien, et que la technique adoptée (ne pas citer), ne sera plus tenable en lexicographie passé ce moment historique de coïncidence entre volonté politique et légitimité assumée par les acteurs.

#### 4.2.2. La 'Langue Commune'

Par politique linguistique, les académiciens posent la notion de *Langue Commune* comme modèle et frontières de la *Langue Française*, ainsi conçue comme la langue d'échange des Français qui fréquentent salons et Louvre. Ce n'est pas seulement la population de référence mais aussi les lieux de référence qui circonscrivent l'usage. D'où le rejet des jargons (langue d'un petit groupe), des termes spécialisés et plus particulièrement des termes d'arts et métiers dans le dictionnaire de Thomas Corneille. Ils insistent dans la *Préface* sur cette curieuse spécificité de leur tâche: ne pas s'arrêter à la définition des mots simples à définier comme *téléscope* mais devoir définir jusqu'aux termes que la philosophie de l'époque (Descartes, Pascal), et la *Logique* de Port-Royal classent comme indéfinissables, et ils disent la difficulté de cette entreprise nouvelle:

> Elle [l'Académie] a donné la Définition de tous les mots communs de la Langue dont les Idées sont fort simples; et cela est beaucoup plus malaisé que de définir les mots des Arts et des Sciences dont les Idées sont fort composées; Car il est bien plus aisé, par exemple, de définir le mot de Télescope, qui est une Lunette à voir de loin, que de définir le mot de voir; Et l'on éprouve même en définissant ces termes des Arts et des Sciences, que la Définition est toujours plus claire que la chose définie; au lieu qu'en définissant les termes communs, la chose définie est toujours plus claire que la Définition. (*Préface*).

Corrélativement, les académiciens rejettent régionalismes (Corneille est dans un premier temps refusé comme trop provincial dans son parler) et archaïsmes (auxquels on était plus sensible qu'aujourd'hui, et que défendaient les plus 'classiques' comme Ménage, mais aussi Furetière, jusque dans son titre) mais non les populismes parisiens. Le *Dictionnaire des Halles*, ouvrage anonyme (attribué à Artaud), paru à Bruxelles en 1696, le leur reproche assez, qui repère avec indignation près de mille "expressions basses qui ne conviennent qu'à la lie du peuple, sans pouvoir entrer dans aucun genre d'écriture raisonnable, ni même dans le discours familier des honnêtes gens", réservées, dit le présentateur anonyme, aux "harengères, gadoûard, goujats d'armée [...]" comme *river le clou à quelqu'un, il a chié dans ma malle* ou *il est glorieux comme un pet* (*Dictionnaire des Halles* ou Extrait du Dictionnaire de l'Académie Françoise, 1696). Mais Vaugelas n'avait-il pas prévenu, évoquant le style de la conversation? "un langage composé de mots et de phrases du bon usage peut être bas et familier et du bon usage tout ensemble" (*Remarques*, p. 20) et, distinguant bon et bel usage: "Un dictionnaire reçoit toutes sortes de mots, pourvu qu'ils soient français, encore qu'ils ne soient pas du bel usage et qu'au contraire ils soient bas et de la lie du peuple" (*Remarques*, p. 19).

L'hétérogénéité exclue est donc diachronique et régionale, mais aussi 'particulière' (Richelieu ne supportait pas la langue du Palais de Justice), confirmant le parti pris de recueil d'une langue écrite et parlée en synchronie, par le commun de l'élite politique. C'est ce 'retranchement' dans la langue commune (Collinot, 1985) qui affecte la nomenclature du dictionnaire (18 000 mots seulement), et que l'on désigne de façon péjorative comme purisme, sans prendre garde que là n'est pas une censure de pédant (Vaugelas préfère l'opinion des femmes à celle des savants) ou une option sociale, comme en témoigne l'accueil complaisant des mots bas, mais une normalisation politique de la langue de communication, pensée comme langue de pouvoir restreinte et unifiée. Chaque fois que les honnêtes gens, les orateurs et les poètes emploient *La Langue Commune*, ils rendent visible *La Langue Française* (Collinot & Mazière 1994).

Excellence présente, méfiance contre les particularismes langagiers, voici donc deux traits inspirés par la commande du pouvoir, et respectés, malgré de graves querelles. Le fait de ne pas citer a été attaqué jusque dans les années 60 et Richelet sera engagé vers les 'Dictionnaires d'Autorités' à l'espagnole, alors qu'il s'agit d'une position directement inspirée par la nécessaire et stricte synchronie. Quant à la limitation de la nomenclature, il s'agit sans doute d'un des points les plus controversés. Il y avait jusque là des dictionnaires spécialisés, très nombreux, qui ne posaient pas le problème de la langue commune. Il y avait des définitions philologiques qui donnaient les sens chez tel ou tel auteur reconnu. Il y a maintenant la nécessité de forger des définitions 'en langue', pour une 'entrée' qui n'est en rien une citation: ni citation d'auteur, ni citation d'artisan, ni citation de provincial etc.

Si la commande du pouvoir a conduit l'Académie à innover pour ses options quant aux mots à définir comme constituant le français (c'est à dire au niveau de la nomenclature), elle l'a conduit à inventer beaucoup plus radicalement pour tout ce qui touche à la forme de la définition elle-même:

### 4.2.3 L'invention d'une définition 'raisonnée' et d'une définition par et pour l''usage'

Les académiciens traitent la langue française comme une langue particulière, mais aussi comme une manifestation générale de la faculté de langage, et donc comme un ensemble "raisonné", capable de dire notre pensée, au sens de Port-Royal (Mazière 1996: 1; Delesalle & Mazière 1998). D'où le choix de construire une entrée en regroupant les dérivés autour de la base morphologique (à condition qu'elle soit française et non latine), la systématisation d'une définition morphologique respectueuse de la formation grammaticale des mots, la mise en place de la métalangue de l'usage dans le texte de l'article, en particulier par l'invention d'un traitement de la polysémie issu directement des collocations autant que des domaines, la prise en compte de la collocation comme unité de sens de la langue en emploi (ou de l'hyperlangue au sens de Auroux 1997), c'est à dire le listage de ce que l'usage autorise comme appariement des mots (par exemple, *homme d'armes, homme de mer*, mais non *homme de terre*), l'usage donné par un exemple forgé et non littéraire ou didactique, aussi près que possible de la collocation, donc pris dans le discours ordinaire. Furetière ne suit pas, qui choisit des entrées alphabétiques, recueille peu de collocations, et propose la solution du nom composé et non de l'appariement de termes pour traduire des façons ordinaires de nommer (Mazière 1996: 2), qui néglige la systématicité morphologique dans la définition, qui double l'exemple d'usage par la citation, qui adopte un parti pris descriptif et fait suivre la définition en langue d'une définition de chose. Et son continuateur *Trévoux* s'intitulera *Dictionnaire français-latin* revenant à la traduction comme l'un des modes traditionnels de définir en langue, par la synonymie simple.

L'injonction de Richelieu aboutit donc à ce considérable évènement linguistique: la sélection d'un lexique 'expliqué' par la grammaire et encodé par la rhétorique du discours mondain, et donc une organisation des sens d'un mot qui va donner ses lettres de noblesse au dictionnaire de langue et expliquer qu'il soit beaucoup plus populaire que n'importe quelle grammaire pour l'ensemble des Français.

#### 4.2.4. La langue française

Le résultat de cet ensemble de contraintes et de choix est alors la fixation, pour trois siècles, de l'unité imaginaire de 'la' langue française.

Par politique linguistique toujours, les académiciens reprennent la mise en parallèle entre la langue vulgaire et une mythique Langue Latine, celle de Cicéron. L'Académie sépare le français du latin en théorisant la langue vernaculaire par calque imaginaire, parallèlement à une langue latine reconnue et arrêtée par l'histoire, déclarée 'à son plus haut degré d'excellence'. C'est le geste le plus idéologique, cause la plus nette de l'impression normative. Le plus efficace aussi sans doute pour la constitution du sentiment linguistique. Dans le parallèle *La Langue Françaíse / La Langue Latine*, le latin cicéronien est présenté comme image virtuelle d'une langue française apte à être la langue dans laquelle seraient formulées les inscriptions sur les arcs de triomphe. C'est pourquoi le *DA* arrive à son heure pour monumentaliser une langue parvenue à sa dernière perfection. Monument lui-même, le *DA* est bien une entreprise de construction, par normalisation sur un usage centralisé de la langue, de l'imaginaire langagier français.

Si on se reporte à la typographie originale de la *Préface* (1694), on remarquera l'usage de la majuscule dans l'écriture de l'expression *La Langue Françaíse*, l'Académie donnant ainsi au syntagme une valeur institutionnelle que corrobore l'incipit de la préface: "[...] Le Cardinal de Richelieu lui proposa [à l'Académie Française] de travailler à un Dictionnaire de la Langue Française [...]". Par la suite le syntagme "un Dictionnaire de la Langue Française" se réécrira sous forme de titre *Le Dictionnaire de l'Académie Française* (Collinot & Mazière 1995).

Afin que nul n'en ignore, l'État, c'est à dire le Roy, reçoit donc en 1694, et institue par sa réception, la commande de 1635. Et peu importe qu'il préfère le Furetière 'en son particulier'. Le corps du Roy, maître de la scène politique comme de la scène théâtrale, reçoit le corps de la langue, le dictionnaire étant un repère d'unification, un repère d'espace, un repère de communication. C'est le début d'une longue carrière. Huit rééditions: 1718, 1740, 1762, 1798, 1835, 1878, 1932–35. (la neuvième est en cours), bien des modifications, mais, jusqu'au XIX^e^ siècle au moins, une référence constante pour toute la lexicographie française, et parfois étrangère, de Lisbonne à Saint Petersbourg.

## 5. Le sentiment de l'unité de langue

On conçoit que la position académicienne irrite notre époque sensible aux variations et régionalismes. Les académiciens sont alors les défenseurs d'une langue française dont l'unité n'existe pas mais qu'ils proclament, font exister et aussi se pérénniser par la fixation, surtout au niveau des graphies et constructions. Tout en le reconnaissant (en soixante ans, la langue a changé), ils minimisent le changement et souhaitent le limiter, voire l'entraver, adhérant sans état d'âme passéiste à la perfection présente qui se perpétuera 'à jamais', donnant l'immortalité aux œuvres du Roy et de ses poètes (*Épître au Roy*). Aussi fort qu'ils aient pu être moqués au XVII^e^ siècle dans leurs prétentions de 'docteurs' de la langue, leur position politique sur la langue leur survivra dans la mémoire collective.

Elle sera retravaillée, autrement, par les continuateurs lexicographes comme Féraud au XVIII^e^ siècle (Branca Rosoff 1995) mais surtout par une nouvelle institution, celle de la littérature qui, dans les années 1740–1760, essentiellement à travers l'académicien Voltaire, va tenter de prévenir le changement, de fixer la fixation à travers les œuvres, devenues le garant de la langue. D'où les nouvelles querelles pour faire entrer les citations dans le dictionnaire et ce véritable triomphe de la citation que sera le Littré. Politiquement, elle sera retravaillée par la Révolution (Guilhaumou 1995), qui renforcera encore le désir d'unité et permettra qu'il soit reconduit dans toute la lexicographie française jusqu'à une date très récente. Le dictionnaire est l'outil linguistique normatif, de préférence anonyme, qui a sans doute le plus contribué à faire intérioriser par les locuteurs francophones l'idée d'une langue française pour tous. Cela consacre l'avènement de la conscience linguistique et constitue un véritable événement historique. En France [à partir du XVIII^e siècle] la question d'une unification linguistique ne se posera jamais vraiment. L'unité indivisible de la langue – comme celle du Royaume –, est un préalable indépassable de l'analyse linguistique (Auroux 1992: 372). Le travail du *DA* et sa postérité jusqu'au XIX^e siècle n'y ont pas peu contribué. Il y avait déjà eu des productions linguistiques émanant de grammairiens et d'écrivains illustres, des rois législateurs de la langue et favorables à la traduction des œuvres anciennes en langue vulgaire, mais jamais un pouvoir à visée centralisatrice puis hégémonique auquel aurait prêté la main l'ensemble des gens de lettres, d'art, de science, de religion, de justice, un Etat en résonance d'intérêts avec un corps d'état constitué de lettrés, divers dans leurs origines et leurs fonctions mais rassemblés sur et par une tâche ciblée.

Pour singulier que cela puisse paraître par rapport à nos attentes implicites, c'est en autonomisant non pas une description grammaticale, ni même une rhétorique qui aurait pu tenter de "concilier la tradition du Palais, celle de l'Eglise gallicane et celle de la Cour" (Fumaroli 1980: 658) mais un choix de mots, étendu à leur construction, à leur valeur de contrôle, que s'institutionnalise l'ultime phase de la 'grammatisation' du français (Auroux 1994).

Au delà de l'événement, considérable pour l'histoire linguistique et sociale du français, ceci pose la question du rôle des dictionnaires en tant qu'outils linguistiques. Ce sont apparemment des objets essentiellement sociolinguistiques, à même de réfléchir la langue en tant que pratique langagière (donc dans les moments de son histoire), le vocabulaire comme fait (ce qui est une autre façon de dire comme usage) et non comme 'domaine linguistique', et de poser comme bon ou mauvais cet usage, confondant règle normative et description, sans que la réputation de l'objet puisse en pâtir. Pour n'être pas un lexique au sens grammatical du terme, la nomenclature du dictionnaire constitue la langue en langue utile et utilisable, en 'prêt à parler'. Mais tout dictionnaire n'en vaut pas un autre, et un 'bon' dictionnaire de consultation n'est pas forcément un événement linguistique, c'est à dire un événement fondateur. Pour intéressantes et riches que soient les production de Richelet et de Furetière, elles sont limitées par leur honnêteté référentielle. L'un dérive ses définitions des auteurs, l'autre des métiers. Ils travaillent, en quelque sorte, dans l'empirie, sur corpus attesté. L'Académie est une et anonyme. Elle est compétente de par le roi et son domaine de compétence fait son corpus. Certes, son travail est marqué au coin de l'histoire, mais, s'apparentant en cela (et c'est le seul dictionnaire intéressant à ce niveau) à une grammaire de 'la' langue, elle travaille à faire oublier que la langue a une histoire.

Décréter l'excellence des langues vulgaires, puis la précellence de l'une d'elle, c'était tout à la fois donner corps à l'imaginaire de l'unité linguistique (Littré, au XIX^e siècle, parlera encore du 'corps de la langue', constitué d'un corpus qui va du XVII^e au début du XIX^e siècle) et repousser sur des marges, fussent-elles littéraires, les rapports de force mais aussi les rapports de sens entre langage et histoire, langage et société. Même si le geste peut paraître dérisoire, l'interdiction de l'Académie sous le Révolution explicite que, dès la constitution de la langue à travers la constitution du sentiment linguistique, les discours – les discours politiques en l'occurrence – aient été dérangés par l'idée de langue.

C'est le discours d'injonction sur la langue d'état qui a permis d'instituer la langue d'état comme certains discours sur la valorisation des particularismes permettent de donner valeur symbolique aux variations identitaires. Le *Dictionnaire de l'Académie* ne dit pas l'identitaire particulier, concret, il crée l'identitaire national, abstrait. Il pose le mode d'enregistrement des actes politiques et des œuvres mémorables, universellement. Malgré qu'on en ait, il demeure comme une ombre portée sur le paysage linguistique français.

Le colloque international *Le Dictionnaire de l'Académie et la lexicographie institutionnelle européenne*, qui s'est tenu les 17, 18 et 19 novembre 1994, à Institut de France, et dont les actes viennent de paraître, a permis de rendre compte de cette dimension historique.

## 6. Bibliographie

### 6.1. Sources primaires

Arnauld, Antoine & Lancelot Claude. 1660. *Grammaire générale et raisonnée [...].* Paris: Pierre Le Petit. (Rééd. Paris, Republications Paulet, 1969. Introd. de M. Foucault.)

Arnauld, Antoine & Nicole Pierre. 1662. *La Logique ou l'Art de penser.* Paris: E. Savreux (autre éd., 1690; Rééd. Paris, Flammarion coll. Sciences de l'Homme, 1970.)

Catalogue de l'exposition *Le dictionnaire de l'Académie française*, 16 avril–3 juillet 1994. Paris: Institut de France.
*Dictionnaire des Halles ou Extrait du Dictionnaire de l'Académie françoise.*

Estienne, Robert. 1539–49. *Dictionnaire François-latin, autrement dit les mots françois avec les manières d'user d'iceulx, tournés en latin.* Paris: Robert Estienne.

Furetière, Antoine. 1690. *Dictionnaire Universel [...].* 2 vol. La Haye & Rotterdam: Arnout et Reinier Leers.

*Le dictionnaire de l'Académie.* Première partie. 1687. Paris: Le Petit.

*Le grand dictionnaire de l'Académie.* Première partie. 1687. Francfort: F. Arnaud.

*Le Dictionnaire de l'Académie françoise, dédié au Roy.* 1694. 2 vol. Paris: veuve Jean-Baptiste Coignard & Jean-Baptiste Coignard.

*Dictionnaire Universel françois et latin*, dit de Trévoux (six éditions). 1704. Trévoux: E. Ganeau.

*Les Préfaces du Dictionnaire de l'Académie française. 1694–92.* Textes, introductions et notes. Sous la direction de Barnard Quémada, 1997. Paris: Honoré Champion.

Nicot, Jean. 1606. *Thrésor de la langue françoyse tant ancienne que moderne auquel [...].* Paris: David Douceur.

*Nouveau recueil des factums du procès d'entre défunt M. L'abé Furetière, l'un des quarante de l'Académie françoise, et quelques uns des autres membres de la même Académie [...]. Tome I*, 1694. Amsterdam: Henry Desbordes, anon.

Richelet, Pierre. 1680. *Dictionnaire français contenant les mots et les choses [...].* Genève: Jean Herman Widerhold.

Vaugelas, Claude Favre de. 1647. *Remarques sur la langue françoise.* Paris: Augustin Courbé et Vve Camusat. (rééd: 1981 Paris, Editions Champ Libre.)


## 6.2. Sources secondaires


Actes du colloque *Le Dictionnaire de l'Académie française et la lexicographie institutionnelle européenne*, publ. par Bernard Quémada avec la collaboration de J. Pruvost. Paris: Champion.

Auroux, Sylvain. 1992. *Histoire des idées linguistiques.* Tome 2. Liège: Mardaga.

–. 1994. *La révolution technologique de la grammatisation.* Liège: Mardaga.

–. 1997. "La réalité de l'hyperlangue". *Langage, praxis et production de sens* éd. par Paul Siblot, 110–121. (= *Langages* 127.) Paris: Larousse.

Branca Rosoff, Sonia. 1995. "La construction de la norme lexicographique à la fin du XVIIIe siècle: Féraud le médiateur" dans *La genèse de la norme.* Archives et Documents. Seconde Série 11, juin 1995.

Bray, Laurent. 1986. *César-Pierre Richelet (1626–1698), biographie et œuvre lexicographique.* Tübingen: Niemeyer.

Chevalier Jean-Claude. 1998. *Le Dictionnaire de l'Académie française (1694) et la grammaire.* Actes du colloque *Le Dictionnaire de l'Académie française et la lexicographie institutionnelle européenne* publiés par Bernard Quémada avec la collaboration, de J. Pruvost. Paris: Champion.

Collinot, André. 1985. *L'ouverture des Dictionnaires. Lexique* 3, Lille.

– & Mazière Francine. 1994. "Une autre lecture du *Dictionnaire de l'Académie*". *Parcours linguistiques de discours spécialisés* éd. par S. Moirand et al. Berne: Lang.

–. 1997. *Un Prêt à parler: le dictionnaire.* Paris: PUF.

Delesalle, Simone & Francine Mazière, 1998. "Raison, foi et usage. Les modes de la signification dans le *Dictionnaire de l'Académie* (1694), la *Grammaire Générale et Raisonnée* et la *Logique* de Port-Royal". *Semiotique nº 14, Sens, figures, signaux. Quelques enjeux historiques de la sémantique.* Paris: CNRS-INALF, Didier érudition.

Fumaroli, Marc. 1980. *L'age de l'éloquence.* Genève: Droz. IIIe partie tome 3. 321–388.

–. 1986. *La Coupole dans Les lieux de mémoire II La Nation* *** sous la direction de Pierre Nora. Paris: Gallimard.

Guilhaumou, Jacques. 1989. *La langue politique et la révolution française.* Paris: Méridien Klincksieck.

Livet, Charles L., éd. 1858. *Histoire de l'Académie française par Pellisson et d'Olivet avec une introduction, des éclaircissements et des notes.* Paris: Didier.

Mazière, Francine. 1996a. "Un événement linguistique: La définition des noms abstraits dans la première édition du *Dictionnaire de l'Académie* (1694)". *Les noms abstraits, histoire et théories* Actes du Colloque international "*Les noms abstraits*", Dunkerque, septembre 92. Lille: PU Septentrion.

–. 1996b. "Élaboration d'un dictionnaire de langue: *Le Dictionnaire de l'Académie* (1694) et la préédition de 1687". *Histoire de la grammaire et du sens*, ed. par Sylvain Auroux, Simone Delesalle & Henri Meschonnic, 124–139. Paris: A. Colin.

–. 1998 à paraître. "Le dictionnaire de l'Académie et la consitution de la langue commune". *Actes du Colloque international "Les dictionnaires et l'histoire de la langue française au sein de la francophonie"*, 18 mars 1998. Cergy-Pontoise.

Mesnard, Pierre. 1857. *Histoire de l'Académie française depuis sa fondation jusque 1830.* Paris: Charpentier.

Rey, Alain. 1978. Intruduction au *Dictionnaire Universel.* Furetière, *Dictionnaire Universel* réimpression. Paris: Le Robert.

Trudeau, Danielle. 1992. *Les inventeurs du bon usage (1529–1647).* Paris: éditions de Minuit.


*Francine Mazière, Paris (France)*

# 116. Die Königliche Spanische Akademie und die Pflege der Nationalsprache

1. Einleitung
2. Die historische Bedeutung der Akademiegrammatik
3. Der Entwurf eines kollektiven, multisäkularen Werkes: Das Projekt der Grammatik von 1741
4. Welches deskriptive Schema wird zugrunde gelegt?
5. Welches Verfahren wählt die Akademie, um die spanische Norm zu kodifizieren und modellhaft zu beschreiben?
6. Weshalb ist ein kollektives, multisäkulares Werk notwendig und bleibt es auch in unserer Zeit?
7. Bibliographie

## 1. Einleitung

Die Grammatik der Königlichen Spanischen Akademie (*Real Academia Española*, abgekürzt RAE) (1771–1973) stellt eines der interessantesten Kapitel in der (noch zu schreibenden) Geschichte der spanischen Sprachwissenschaft dar. Im Folgenden möchte ich die Bedeutung der Akademiegrammatik als Instrument der normativen Gestaltung des modernen Spanisch über fast drei Jahrhunderte nachzeichnen. In diesem Sinn werde ich aufzeigen, worin der Wert der Grammatik der königlichen Akademie besteht, welches die wissenschaftlichen Voraussetzungen waren, die sie inspirierten, welches das verwendete Beschreibungsschema war, auf welche Art und Weise vorgegangen wurde, um die sprachliche Norm zu kodifizieren und zu gestalten, und schließlich, warum ein Kollektivwerk zur Sprachpflege, an dem man über mehrere Jahrhunderte gearbeitet hat, selbst heute noch notwendig ist und wissenschaftliche Gültigkeit besitzt.

## 2. Die historische Bedeutung der Akademiegrammatik

Die Gründung der *Real Academia Española* (1713) ist das herausragendste Ereignis der Geschichte des modernen Spanisch. Dank dieses Umstandes erlebte die spanische Sprache eine noch nie dagewesene Zeit der Blüte und Pflege (Lapesa 1980: 419–421). Die spanische Sprache erhält ein lexikalisches Repertorium, welches auf den Autoritäten des Sprachgebrauchs beruht und somit die spanische Literatur auf eine Höhe mit den kulturell am weitesten entwickelten europäischen Ländern stellt, und man legt die Prinzipien fest, auf denen alle künftigen Reformen basieren und die 1815 schließlich zur Erarbeitung der einfachsten Orthographie unter allen romanischen Sprachen führen sollten. Dessenungeachtet, und obwohl das Wörterbuch und die Orthographie zwei außerordentliche und ausschlaggebende Werke in der Entwicklung der Sprache waren, wären die Anstrengungen der Akademie bezüglich der Kodifizierung der panhispanischen Norm weder so verdienstvoll noch so entscheidend gewesen, hätte man nicht gleichzeitig auf das Instrument der Grammatik von 1771 zählen können, welche, in späteren Ausgaben (1796, 1854, 1870, 1917–1920–1924, 1973) verbessert, in allen Schulen des Reiches verpflichtend verwendet werden mußte (Gesetze von 1780 und 1857), wodurch sie zum unverzichtbaren Requisit aller geisteswissenschaftlichen Studien bis hin zu unseren Tagen avancierte.

Die große Bedeutung der Akademiegrammatik beruht auf zwei historischen Fakten, einem wissenschaftlichen und einem politischen. In den historischen Bereich gehört die Tatsache, daß zum erstenmal eine Beschreibung der schriftlichen und mündlichen Norm des Spanischen vorgelegt wird, welche auf klaren linguistischen und pädagogischen Prinzipien beruht, im Unterschied zu früheren Beschreibungen, welche lediglich auf einer Zusammenstellung von Beobachtungen zu einzelnen, weitgehend unverbundenen, Aspekten des Sprachgebrauchs beruhten; in den politischen gehören jene Entscheidungen, welche dazu beitrugen, zum ersten Mal auch die Sprachlehre Gesetzen zu unterwerfen, welche ausdrücklich von der Akademie sanktioniert waren. In einem für dirigistische und aufgeklärte Politiken günstigen historischen Moment diente somit die Grammatik der *Real Academia Española* zur Gestaltung einer hispanischen *koine*, und es konnte in diesem Bereich das kulturelle Vakuum aufgehoben werden, das durch die Vertreibung der Jesuiten aus Spanien entstanden war (López Alonso 1998). Im Prolog der Grammatik von 1870 (p. XI) wird dies ausdrücklich anerkannt:

desde 1739 no se ha publicado en nuestro país *Diccionario*, ni después *gramática*, cuyos autores no hayan tenido muy á la vista el *Diccionario* y la *Gra-*

*mática* de la Academia Española. [seit 1739 hat man in unserem Land weder Wörterbuch noch Grammatik publiziert, bei dem man nicht ständig das Wörterbuch bzw. die Grammatik der Spanischen Akademie vor Augen gehabt hätte].

## 3. Der Entwurf eines kollektiven, multisäkularen Werkes: Das Projekt der Grammatik von 1741

Nachdem die Akademie die ehrenvolle Position erreicht hatte, das *opus magnum* der spanischen Lexikographie nach der Renaissance verfaßt zu haben, ein Werk, welches unter dem Namen *Diccionario de autoridades* bekannt wurde (Lázaro Carreter 1972), nahm sie die Redaktion einer Grammatik in Angriff, welche sich dadurch auszeichnen sollte, daß sie "perfecta y completa, siguiendo a Nebrija y a Gerardo Vosio, príncipes de los gramáticos" sein solle, also 'vollkommen und vollständig und den Fürsten der Grammatikographie, Nebrija und Gerhard Vossius, nacheifern sollte', so wie es im Projekt von 1741 zu dieser Grammatik heißt. Dieses Dokument, welches nicht nur eine vollständige Übersicht über den Stand der Grammatikographie zur Mitte des 18. Jh. bietet, enthält Definitionen und Inhaltsanalysen von mehr als 70 Grammatiktraktaten, und zwar sowohl zu alten als auch zu neueren Sprachen, darunter das Hebräische, Griechische, Lateinische, Arabische, Deutsche, Italienische, Französische, Englische, Portugiesische, Mexikanische und Spanische. Insgesamt gesehen bildet diese Liste so etwas wie die Zusammenstellung der direkt benutzten Quellen, auf denen die Grammatik von 1771 basiert, heißt es doch hierzu in besagtem Dokument, diese Werke "sirvieron de dirección y de luz para trabajar con más acierto la gramática española" [diese Werke dienten als Vorbild und Leitstern für die Arbeit an der Grammatik des Spanischen]. Die erste Feststellung, zu der sich die Mitglieder der Akademie genötigt sahen, war enttäuschend, mußten sie sich doch klar machen, daß andere Sprachen über zahlreiche Grammatiken verfügten – die Französische allein über 27 –, die Spanische dagegen nur über den *Arte Castellano* [1627] des Meisters Gonzalo de Correas (1571–1631. "Todas las demás gramáticas como las de L. Franciosini (m. 1645), F. Sobrino (m. 1732) y P. Billet (c. 1688), y otras que se podía ver, lo eran solamente en el nombre, y en realidad unas cuantas observaciones sobre la lengua" [Alle anderen Grammatiken, wie z. B. die von L. Franciosini, F. Sobrino und P. Billet u. a. waren Grammatiken nur dem Namen nach bzw. eigentlich nur Bemerkungen zur Sprache] (*Proyecto* de 1741).

Dank dieses Dokuments wissen wir, daß die Akademie von Anfang an die Absicht hegte, eine *perfekte* und *vollständige* Abhandlung über die Sprache zu verfassen, welche den zeitgenössischen Anforderungen voll und ganz entsprach. In den Akademieakten ist die Rede von "la conveniencia de escribir una gramática uniendo las reglas y los fundamentos en cuya virtud se establecían" [der Notwendigkeit, eine Grammatik zu verfassen, welche die Regeln mit den Prinzipien verband, aus denen heraus sie aufgestellt wurden]. Folglich mußten die Grammatiker von 1771, gemäß der damals gültigen wissenschaftlichen Terminologie, zwischen einer 'praktischen' und einer 'gelehrten' Grammatik wählen. Der erste Typus setzte den Primat des Sprachgebrauchs voraus und reihte sich ein in die Linie der didaktisch orientierten Grammatiken, deren eigentlicher Zweck es war, den Sprachgebrauch zu vermitteln und die Regeln aufzuzeigen, denen er gehorchte. Der zweite Typus entsprach mehr der Auffassung des Humanismus, der entdeckt hatte, daß die Regeln des Sprachgebrauchs nicht ausreichend waren, um eine Sprache zu erlernen, weil sie eben nicht auf theoretisch begründbaren Prinzipien basierten. Das Resultat all dieser Überlegungen war eine 'gelehrte' oder 'philologische' Grammatik, nach lateinischem (deskriptivem) Vorbild à la Nebrija (1481) bzw. Gerard Voss (1577–1649), bei der die Logik dazu diente, konkrete Probleme des Sprachgebrauchs abzuklären.

Nachdem der theoretische Rahmen und das angestrebte Ziel feststanden, um die Wertschätzung des Publikums zu erwerben, entschloß sich die Akademie, eine abhandlungsorientierte (philologische) Grammatik zu verfassen, die zudem weder allzu kurz noch allzu weitschweifig konzipiert sein sollte, sondern dazu dienen sollte, eine Norm des Spanischen aufzuzeigen, wie sie im Unterricht präsentiert werden konnte. Das spanische 18. Jh. verfügte über einen breiten Fächer grammatischer Traditionen, welcher aber alles andere als uniform war (Niederehe 1997). Da war einerseits die graecolateinische Tradition und andererseits die des Rationalismus der Renaissance. Für den heutigen Forscher erscheint es als Sammelsurium von Widersprüchen, welches die Erstellung jeglichen grammatischen Traktats erschwert. Ignacio de Ceballos berichtet der Akademie hierüber in der Sitzung vom 27. September 1742, und ähnliches kann dem "Prólogo" zur Ausgabe von 1771 entnommen werden; auf S. V heißt es da:

Oxalá que como es fácil probar la utilidad de la gramática lo fuera su composición. [Wäre es doch genau so leicht, die Redaktion einer Grammatik zu beschreiben, wie den Beweis ihres Nutzens anzutreten.]

Die Akademie hatte sich nämlich vorgenommen, nicht nur lediglich einige kurze, konzise Bemerkungen zum Sprachgebrauch zu präsentieren, sondern sprachliche Prinzipien und Grundannahmen so darzulegen, daß das erstaunliche Kunstwerk Sprache sichtbar wird. Gleichzeitig wollte sie zeigen, wie die Wörter derart verbunden werden, daß das Redegefüge entsteht. Aber dies setzt ein konstantes Studium und eine fortwährende Analyse der Sprache als kontingentes, variables Produkt des Sprachgebrauchs und der ihn bestimmenden Regeln und der Bedeutungen voraus, welche die Wörter im Laufe der Zeit annehmen.

Eine wissenschaftlich zufriedenstellende Grammatik hatte demzufolge ebenfalls komplett zu sein, d. h. sie mußte aus den vier kanonischen Teilen bestehen, als da sind *Prosodie, Ethimologia* [Lehre von den Wortarten], *Syntax, Orthographie.* Sie mußte also sowohl der geschriebenen als auch der gesprochenen Sprache gerecht werden. Überdies war die Akademie sich bewußt, daß ein allzu umfangreiches Werk, welches der Sprachlehre diente, auch allzu sehr das Gedächtnis der lernenden Jugend belasten und manche Kenntnisse vorwegnehmen würde, die im Laufe der Zeit und gleichsam nebenbei, durch Lektüre und Studium, erlernt würden. Es sollte also eine bereinigte, wohldurchdachte Grammatik sein, welche gleichermaßen Kindern wie Erwachsenen nützlich sein konnte. Von Anfang an war die Akademie deshalb davon überzeugt, daß sie, angesichts der Veränderlichkeit des schriftlichen bzw. mündlichen Sprachgebrauchs, das Werk notwendigerweise immer wieder revidieren, vervollkommnen und anpassen mußte, genau so wie der Sprachgebrauch sich ja auch beständig neuen Gegebenheiten anpaßt. Im Prolog der Grammatik von 1870 heißt es dazu [S. XII]:

... [la RAE era consciente] de que es una necesidad ir ajustando los preceptos á la lenta, pero continua, variacion, que experimentan las lenguas vivas y escritas. Pruebas de ese convencimiento son las modificaciones y novedades que va introduciendo, cada vez que reimprime su *Diccionario* y su *Gramática.* [Die kgl. Akademie war sich der Notwendigkeit bewußt, die Vorschriften den sich langsam, aber beständig vollziehenden Veränderungen anzupassen, welche lebende (und verschriftete) Sprachen erfahren. Belege dieser Überzeugung bieten jene Veränderungen und Neuerungen, welche sie regelmäßig einführt, wenn sie das Wörterbuch oder die Grammatik neu auflegt.]

Auf diese Weise ließ sich die Akademie auf ein, auf mehrere Jahrhunderte angelegtes, Unternehmen ein, bei dem es um eine Überwachung der Sprache und der sie (be)nutzenden Autorenschaft ging, also auf ein Unternehmen, welches den Stolz und den Ruhm des Schrifttums ausmachen sollte. Das grammatische Werk der Akademie wurde so bis in die Gegenwart zu einem nützlichen Werk des Sprachunterrichts, war es gleichzeitig doch auch ein Modell an Klarheit und Einfachheit, denn sowohl das Regelwerk als auch die Ausnahmen wurden und werden beispielhaft erläutert, aber ohne 'metaphysische Subtilitäten'.

[Porque] este Cuerpo literario – como se lee en la *GRAE* (1870: XIII) – no puede ni debe guiarse por el prurito de *filosofar*; no puede proponerse extender innovaciones poco maduras, ni fundar sus reglas en *teorías* más ó menos depuradas, sino que ha de limitarse a consignar el estado real y presente del idioma, á registrar las leyes instintivas á que obedece en su curso y desenvolvimiento, y á sancionar con su autoridad las prácticas regulares y constantes del *buen uso.* [Denn das literarische Korpus – so liest man in der *GRAE* (1870: XIII) – darf dem *philosophischen* Kitzel nicht nachgeben und kann sich auch nicht erlauben, halbreife Neuerungen zuzulassen und seine Regeln auf mehr oder minder purifizierte Theorien aufzubauen, sondern muß sich darauf beschränken, den wirklichen, aktuellen Sprachzustand zu verzeichnen und die intuitiven Regeln zu registrieren, denen die Sprache in ihrer Entwicklung folgt und die üblichen Praktiken des *guten Sprachgebrauchs* mit der ihr zugestandenen Autorität zu besiegeln.]

Der Akademie steht bei ihrem Tun also eine moralische Verantwortung zu. Als offizieller Einrichtung unterliegt ihr die Überwachung der Sprache. Daher darf die Akademie sich auch nicht darauf einlassen, wie Rafael Lapesa bereits 1956 hervorgehoben hat, eine 'rein wissenschaftliche' Grammatik zu erarbeiten, also eine nicht-normative Grammatik, welche sich jeglichen Urteils über den Sprachgebrauch enthält.

La incorporación de puntos de vista nuevos – dijo Rafael Lapesa (1956: 84) – habrá de hacerse tras cuidadosa meditación, sin olvidar cuál es el cometido de la Gramática académica: no nos está encomendado encajar el estudio de nuestra idioma en el esquema teórico de una escuela, ni analizar los hechos del lenguaje independientemente de la estima que gocen. Lo que se nos pide es que presentemos el sistema de la lengua española según los usos admitidos entre gentes cultas; por lo tanto, una Gramática a la vez científica y práctica, descriptiva y normativa, que, atenta a registrar y comprender el funcionamiento de la lengua hablada y escrita, ponga en guardia contra incorrecciones y vulgarismos. [Neue Gesichtspunkte – so sagte Lapesa (1956: 84) – dürften nur nach sorgfältigen Überlegungen aufgenommen werden, wobei keinesfalls die eigentliche Zielsetzung der Akademiearbeit aus dem Auge verloren gehen darf: Uns steht es nicht zu, das Studium unserer Sprache in das theoretische Schema einer Schule zu pressen, noch sprachliche Fakten unabhängig von der Wertung zu betrachten, welche sie allgemein genießen. Was man von uns fordert, ist, das System der spanischen Sprache so zu beschreiben, wie es von gebildeten Leuten verwendet wird. Eine Grammatik, welche sowohl wissenschaftlich als auch praktisch ist, welche sowohl deskriptiv als auch normativ ist, sollte gleichzeitig das Funktionieren der gesprochenen und geschriebenen Sprache registrieren und verständlich machen und gegen Inkorrektheiten und Vulgarismen aufmerksam machen.]

Dies führt, wie schon zu anderen Zeiten, dazu, einen Mittelweg zwischen der Sprachforschung einerseits und den normativ-didaktischen Zielen andererseits zu suchen, um dadurch die zentrale Idee aufrechtzuerhalten, mit diesem Werk zur Normbildung des Spanischen beizutragen.

## 4. Welches deskriptive Schema wird zugrunde gelegt?

Bei dem Versuch, die systematischen Regularitäten des Spanischen zu beschreiben und seine sprachlichen Formen zu kategorisieren, verfügten die Autoren von 1771, genauso wie ihre Nachfolger im 19. und 20. Jh., über keine andere Methode oder keine andere Theorie als diejenigen, welche sie aus der traditionellen Lateingrammatik der Renaissance ererbt hatten, das Schema der *partes orationis*. Die Zahl der Redeteile galt 1741 als eines der dornenreichsten Kapitel der Grammatikographie, sahen die Autoren sich hierbei doch konfrontiert mit einer größeren Zahl von 'störenden Faktoren', etwa die Klassifikation des Artikels oder die der Interjektion, und so erschienen ihnen manche der bislang angewandten definitorischen Kriterien als nicht mehr länger haltbar. Im *Proyecto de gramática* von 1741 lesen wir entsprechend:

En el orden a las partes de la oración que se comprehenden debaxo del nombre de etymología es tanta la inconstancia de los gramáticos que ni los antiguos ni los modernos han convenido hasta ahora en el número cierto. [Hinsichtlich der Anordnung der Redeteile, welche unter der Rubrik 'Etymología' angeführt werden, herrscht unter den Grammatikern eine derartige Uneinigkeit, daß sich bislang weder die alten noch die modernen auf eine einheitliche Zahl geeinigt haben.]

Trotzdem konnten sich die Autoren von 1771 dahingehend einigen, die Zahl der Wortarten auf neun festzulegen, ein Beschreibungsschema, welches fruchtbringend bis hin zu *El Esbozo de una nueva gramática* (1973) angewandt wurde.

Es ist offensichtlich, daß diese Verschiedenheit der Meinungen über die Anzahl der Satzteile von der Unterschiedlichkeit der Kriterien herrührt, die für die Definition der besagten Klassen verwendet wurden, was zwangsläufig einige Grammatiker dazu verleitete, das Pronomen und das Partizip als unabhängige Kategorien zu betrachten, den Artikel vom Pronomen zu unterscheiden, das Adverb von der Interjektion zu trennen, und schließlich – das ist der Fall von Julius Cæsar Scaliger (1484–1558) in *De Causis Linguae Latinae* (1541) – die Interjektion als ersten und wesentlichen Satzteil zu zählen. Francisco Sánchez de las Brozas (Sanctius) (1523–1601) folgt dagegen logischen Kriterien, wenn er in seiner *Minerva* (1581) das auf das Lateinische anzuwendende Beschreibungsschema, so wie es Aristoteles und andere Autoren gemacht hatten, insbesondere Arabisten und Hebraisten, auf lediglich drei Teile reduziert: Nomen, Verb und Partikel. Bei der Definition des Nomens und des Verbs mußte er sich dabei allerdings auf ein formales Kriterium berufen, ein Kriterium, welches an Petrus Ramus (1515–1572) erinnert, die Unterscheidung zwischen deklinablen und indeklinablen Redeteilen.

Diese Ansicht wurde im 17. Jh. von vielen geteilt, fiel sie doch mit dem Descarteschen Rationalismus zusammen und seiner Anwendung auf eine Grammatik wie die *Nouvelle Méthode* von Lancelot (1616–1695), welche von Ignacio de Luzán (1702–1754) mit "der neuen Methode Port-Royals" identifiziert wurde. Trotzdem unterscheidet sich die Auffassung der Akademie hinsichtlich der Definition der Redeteile von der Methode Port-Royals. Denn anstatt Sánchez de las Brozas zu folgen, schloß sie sich dem französischen Jesuiten C. Buffier (1661–1737) an, welcher lehrte, daß eine gute Methode der Grammatikographie es erforderte, von den allgemeinsten und einfachsten Wahrheiten auszugehen, um dann erst zu den weniger allgemeinen und analytisch komplexeren vorzugehen.

Das bezeichnendste Beispiel dieser Vorgehensweise war die Überprüfung der sechzehn Definitionen des Nomens, die die Autoren von 1771 durchführten: Sie kamen zu dem Schluß, daß man sie alle problemlos auf drei reduzieren konnte, je nachdem, ob das Kriterium begrifflicher, formaler oder begrifflich-formaler Natur war (Akten vom 9. März 1745):

El nombre, assí en español como en qualquiera otra lengua puede considerarse de dos modos, o con relación a su essencia o con respecto a los accidentes o propiedades sujetas a la gramática, y de aquí nace que, sin ser contrarias las opiniones de algunos autores, sean diferentes las definiciones que han dado del nombre, porque unos las consideraron de un modo, otros de otro y algunos de ambos modos, incluyendo en una sola definición lo essencial y lo accidental. [Das Nomen, gleichgültig ob es nun der spanischen oder einer anderen Sprache angehört, kann auf zwei unterschiedliche Weisen betrachtet werden: hinsichtlich seiner Wesenheit oder seiner Akzidentien bzw. hinsichtlich der Eigenschaften, die es in der Grammatik aufweist, und daraus resultiert, daß manche Definitionen des Nomens, je nach Autor, unterschiedlich ausfallen, haben die einen es doch nach der einen Weise, die anderen nach der anderen, und einige weitere schließlich auf beide Weisen aufgefaßt, wobei in ein und derselben Definition Wesentliches und Akzidentelles gemeinsamen erfaßt werden.']

Mit dieser wissenschaftlichen Vorentscheidung mußte die Definition des Nomens notwendigerweise zu Gunsten einer synthetischen Methode ausfallen, was nicht nur der Tatsache entgegen kam, daß es sich um ein kollektives Werk handelte, sondern auch dem klaren Interesse der Akademiemitglieder. Hierin beruht ein Teil der Originalität der Grammatik von 1771. Denn bei der Anwendung des begrifflichen Kriteriums, demzufolge das Nomen als Wort definiert wurde, 'welches dazu dient, Dinge zu bezeichnen', ging man von allgemeinen, einfachen Wahrheiten aus, und angesichts der Tatsache, daß man dies als begriffliche Definition einstufte, stellte man sich auf eine gemeinsame Ebene mit vielen Grammatikern, wobei die Vagheit und die Allgemeinheit ihrer Extension es überdies erlaubte, die gesamte Nominalklasse zu erfassen: Substantive, Adjektive und Pronomina. Dies unterstrich ein Akademiemitglied in einem Vortrag über das Thema: 'Obwohl die Grammatik das Nomen nicht mit derselben Extension wie die Logik charakterisiert, so hört sie deswegen doch nicht auf, es hinsichtlich seiner Funktionalität zu betrachten, welche in allen Sprachen dieselbe ist: Gegenstände bzw. Sachen zu bezeichnen'.

Bei dem Überblick vom Allgemeinen zum Einzelnen gewann die Logik eine beachtliche Bedeutung als Analyseinstrument, um konkrete idiomatische Probleme zu lösen. Dieses Vorgehen unterscheidet die erste Akademiegrammatik (von 1771) und die zweite (von 1854) von weiteren, weniger logisch orientierten Ausgaben, wie die von 1870 oder von 1917–20–24, oder der, noch sehr viel deskriptiver eingestellten, Ausgabe von 1973. Bei all diesen Zugangsweisen galt aber stets das Prinzip, daß die Akademie sich nicht von allgemeinen Sprachtheorien bestimmen lassen wollte, sondern die beobachtbaren Fakten in den Vordergrund stellte, nicht aber widerstreitende (wenn auch nicht uninteressante) Theorien, welche ein 'moderner Aristarch' der Akademie durchaus hätte formulieren können.

## 5. Welches Verfahren wählt die Akademie, um die spanische Norm zu kodifizieren und modellhaft zu beschreiben?

Man hört oder liest häufig, die Akademie sei als Bollwerk gegen die Invasion von Gallizismen oder gegen eine allzu barocke Ausdrucksweise entstanden. Diese Auffassung von R. Lapesa (1980: 419–420) oder von F. Lázaro (1972) sind aber alles andere als Gemeingut geworden. Daher sei mit aller Klarheit festgehalten, auch gegen Lehrmeinungen wie die hier angeführten, daß die Akademie eine der wenigen historisch gewachsenen Institutionen ist, auf die wir stolz sein können. Es ist die einzige Forschungsgruppe – wie man heutzutage zu sagen pflegt – welche sich beinahe drei Jahrhunderte lang der Festlegung und Modellierung der Norm des Spanischen verschrieben hat. Bereits in der 'Widmung' (*Dedicatoria*) der Erstauflage der Grammatik liest man so etwas wie Vorboten dieser Idee (*GRAE* 1771, 2–2v):

Todas las naciones deben estimar su lengua nativa, pero mucho mas aquellas que abrazando gran número de individuos gozan de un lenguaje comun, que los une en amistad e interés (2–2v). [Alle Völker sollen ihre Muttersprache schätzen, besonders aber jene, welche aus einer großen Zahl von Individuen bestehen und über eine gemeinsame Sprache verfügen, die sie in Freundschaft und gemeinsamem Interesse verbindet.]

Trotzdem hat die Akademie in ihrer Eigenschaft als Körperschaft nie öffentliche Erklärungen über normative Prinzipien abgegeben. Sicher, es gibt Äußerungen von einzelnen Mitgliedern, welche aber nicht als repräsentativ für die gesamte Körperschaft angesehen werden können. Indessen, wenn wir uns auf die systematische Überprüfung der akademischen Grammatik beschränken, kann man entdecken, wie die akademische Norm konzipiert ist und woraus sie besteht (Fries 1989). Tatsächlich greift die Akademiegrammatik (1771 – 1973) grundsätzlich auf drei Vorgehensweisen der Kodifizierung der besagten Norm zurück: die 'Beschreibung', die 'Vorschrift' und die 'Modellgebung'.

Auf die erste Vorgehensweise greift die Akademie immer dann zurück, wenn es um den allgemeinen Sprachgebrauch geht, der aufgrund seines modellhaften Charakters keine Schwierigkeiten in sich birgt. Bei der zweiten Vorgehensweise geht es um die Absicherung eines idiomatischen Sprachgebrauchs, der vielleicht im Wettstreit mit anderen, abweichenden Ausdrucksweisen steht. Hierbei werden drei verschiedene Vorgehensweisen unterschieden: Im ersten Falle bedient man sich positiver Vorschriften, welche einen Sprachgebrauch bzw. eine sprachliche Form ausdrücklich bestätigen. So lesen wir beispielsweise, 'man müsse folgende Regel berücksichtigen ...' [*hay que observar la regla siguiente* ...]; 'man müsse ... verwenden' [*se ha de usar* ...]; 'es sei ... zu verwenden' [*es preciso usar* ...]; 'man müsse ... verwenden' [*debe emplearse* ...]; 'es sei zwingend vorgeschrieben ...' [*será forzoso usar* ...]; 'es wäre nötig ... zu sagen' [*fuera preciso decir* ...]; etc. Im zweiten Falle bedient man sich negativer Vorschriften, etwa der ausdrücklichen Negation vorstehender Anweisungen oder Formen, welche als von der Norm abweichend angesehen werden. Die dabei verwendeten Ausdrucksweisen lauten: 'man sagt eigentlich nicht ...' [*no se dirá con propiedad* ...]; 'man sagt so nicht ...' [*no se dirá bien* ...]; 'unpassend ...' [*sería impropiedad* ...]; 'unerträglich ...' [*intolerable* ...]; 'unkorrekter Sprachgebrauch ...' [*es un uso incorrecto* ...]; 'schlechter Sprachgebrauch ...' [*es un mal uso* ...], etc. (*GRAE* 1854). Im dritten Falle pflegt man diasystematische Markierungen anzuführen, um über den eingeschränkten Gebrauch eines sprachlichen Phänomens aufzuklären, das nur einer regionalen oder sozialen Varietät, einem Register, etc., angehört. Dabei wird dann angemerkt 'bewahrt in der Umgangssprache, Literatursprache ...' [*se conserva bien en el habla oral y literaria* ...]; 'charakteristisch für eine bestimmte Gegend, im Unterschied zur spanischen Standardsprache ...' [*son características de aquellas regiones, contra el uso general del español.* ...]; 'in Lateinamerika vorwiegend verwendet ...' [*en gran parte de Hispanoamérica predomina absolutamente sobre* ...]; 'in der Madrider Umgangssprache vornehmlich verwendet für ...' [*el habla vulgar madrileña muestra cierta inclinación a favor de* ...] (*EGRAE* 1973). Das dritte und letzte Verfahren, die Modellgebung, wird stets dann verwendet, wenn es keinen etablierten bzw. allgemein verbreiteten Sprachgebrauch gibt, sondern verschiedene, regional unterschiedene Ausdrucksweisen.

Nachdem die Gebräuche von den Experten untersucht worden sind, formuliert die Akademie in diesem Fall die Regeln, die, in Einklang mit einigen sprachlichen und stilistischen Prinzipien, einen regulierenden Einfluß auf denjenigen Gebrauch ausüben sollen, von dem die Akademie glaubt, daß er der Wesensart der Sprache am nächsten kommt. Zum Beispiel sagt man, daß "debe evitarse el uso del pronombre como enclítico cuando, uniéndose al verbo, pueda originar cacofonía o combinaciones de sílabas repugnantes al oído; v. gr.: *encaraméme, acatéte, duélele, señalólo*" ['der Gebrauch des Pronomens als enklitisches Element ist zu vermeiden, wenn es in Verbindung mit dem Verb Kakophonien hervorruft, wie z. B. ...'] (*GRAE* 1924, 201).

Im Licht dieser Überlegungen ergibt sich unschwer, daß die Akademiegrammatik nicht nur normativ ist; sie ist eher deskriptiv als normativ. Nachdem das gesagt ist, muß man aber auch zur Kenntnis nehmen, daß sie so weder in dem einen noch in dem anderen Aspekt frontal mit den grundlegenden Lehrmeinungen der modernen Sprachwissenschaft bzw. der Fremdsprachendidaktik kollidiert. Jedoch erwarten weder die Benutzer noch die Adressaten von der Akademiegrammatik an erster Stelle eine wissenschaftliche Beschreibung, sondern eine möglichst umfassende Information über sprachliche Besonderheiten, wobei viele dieser Besonderheiten den Analysen der Sprachwissenschaft immer noch widerstehen. Sie erwarten einen Leitfaden, der in der Lage ist, ihnen die größte Anzahl an Kombinationsmöglichkeiten zu zeigen, seien es literarische oder umgangssprachliche, und Lösungsvorschläge in schwierigeren Fällen (Fernández Ramírez 1960 und 1968a, 412).

## 6. Weshalb ist ein kollektives, multisäkulares Werk notwendig und bleibt es auch in unserer Zeit?

Viele Argumente sind es, die man für die Beharrlichkeit der Akademie bei der hier skizzierten normativen Arbeit anführen kann. Es gibt historische, aber auch wissenschaftliche Argumente. Schon in den Gründungsdokumenten kann man sehen, daß die Grammatik ein Teil des Programms der Gestaltung der Norm und der Sprachpflege war, aber, als dieses Programm in die Praxis umgesetzt wurde und auf zahlreiche unvorhergesehene Probleme stieß, wurde der Text der Grammatik zum wirksamsten Instrument der Modellbildung (Lapesa 1980; Lorenzo 1974). Die jahrhundertealte Konzeption einer grammatisch-rhetorischen Ausbildung in zwei Stufen wies der Grammatik im 18. Jh. die Funktion zu, vor allem den korrekten Gebrauch der Sprache zu fördern, was als unverzichtbare Bedingung für das Studium der Geisteswissenschaften und die Erlangung anderer gesellschaftlicher Vorteile angesehen wurde. Diese ursprüngliche Konzeption war in allen Auflagen des Werks präsent, den *Esbozo* von 1973 eingeschlossen, aber es scheint, daß sie im Lauf der Zeit aus vielen Gründen aus dem Denken der Akademiemitglieder verschwand. Übrig blieb die Überzeugung, daß eine normative Grammatik notwendig war und der Benutzer der Sprache diese Art von Hilfsmittel brauchte, um seine sprachlichen Zweifel zu lösen. Das historische Argument ist unbestreitbar: Die Grammatik ist ein wirksames Instrument zur Kodifizierung der Norm gewesen, und nun ist sie es bei der Modellgebung.

Von einem wissenschaftlichen Standpunkt aus ist es fast unmöglich, ein Werk wie das der Akademiegrammatik zu diskreditieren. Heute kann niemand mehr, der etwas von Grammatik versteht, die am Anfang des Jahrhunderts gegen die 'traditionelle' Grammatik vorgebrachten Einwände nachvollziehen (Sarmiento 1995: 104). In den früheren Grammatiken gab es Beschreibungen und Formalismen, aber sie basierten auf anderen Voraussetzungen als den heutigen. In den zeitgenössischen, deskriptiven Grammatiken, die vorgeblich 'wissenschaftlicher' sind, wäre auch der Frage nachzugehen, wo die Grenzen des Deskriptivismus oder des Formalismus liegen. Beim gegenwärtigen Zustand der sprachwissenschaftlichen Forschung ist man jedenfalls zu der Überzeugung gelangt, daß eine Grammatik, teilweise zumindesten, normativ sein muß, da sie gleichzeitig doch auch eine Grammatik des Sprachgebrauchs sein muß, d. h. der gebräuchlichen (häufigsten) und von einer großen Zahl von Benutzern akzeptierten (normalen) Strukturen. Somit konzentriert sich das Problem auf den Unterschied zwischen 'gebräuchlich' und 'normativ'.

Kurz und gut, die Akademiegrammatik, die wir gerade charakterisiert haben, war nicht nur ein wirksames Instrument zur Gestaltung der hispanischen Norm, sondern sie ist auch weiterhin notwendig und vom wissenschaftlichen Standpunkt aus gesehen gültig. Wenn es sie nicht schon gäbe, müßte man sie erfinden.

## 7. Bibliographie

Correas, Gonzalo de. 1625. *Arte de la lengua Española Castellana.* Edición y prólogo de Emilio Alarcos García. (= *Revista de Filología Española: Anejo*, 56.) Madrid: Consejo Superior de Investigaciones Científicas & Patronato "Menéndez y Pelayo" & Instituto "Miguel de Cervantes", 1954.

EGRAE 1973 = Real Academia Española (Comisión de Gramática), ed. 1973. *Esbozo de una Nueva Gramática de la Lengua Española.* Madrid: Espasa-Calpe.

Fernández Ramírez, Salvador. 1960. *Lengua literaria y norma lingüística.* Discurso leído el día 29 de mayo de 1960 en su recepción pública, por ... Madrid: Imprenta Aguirre Torre.

–. 1968a. "Anticipos de la nueva gramática". *Boletín de la Real Academia Española* 48.401–417.

–. 1968b. "Cuatro capítulos de fonología". *Boletín de la Real Academia Expañola* 48.419–479.

Fries, Dagmar. 1989. *"Limpia, fija y da esplendor". La Real Academia Española ante el uso de la lengua (1713–1973.)* Madrid: Sociedad General Española de Libros.

GRAE 1771 = Real Academia Española, ed. 1771. *Gramática de la Lengua Castellana, compuesta por la Real Academia Española.* Madrid: Ibarra, Impresor de Cámara de S. M.

GRAE 1854 = Real Academia Española, ed. 1854. *Gramática ... por la Real Academia española.* Nueva Edición. Madrid: Imprenta Nacional.

GRAE 1870 = Real Academia Española, ed. 1870. *Gramática ... por la Real Academia Española.* Nueva Edición, corregida y aumentada. Madrid: Imprenta y estereotipia de M. Rivadeneyra.

GRAE 1917–1920–1924 = Real Academia Española, ed. 1917; 1920; 1924. *Gramática ... por la Real Academia Española.* Nueva Edición Reformada. Madrid: Perlado.

Lapesa Melgar, Rafael. 1956. "Sugestiones relacionadas con la futura edición de la gramática de la Real Academia Española. Conveniencia de tener en cuenta otras gramáticas de mérito notable". *Memorias del II Congreso de las Academias de Lengua Española, celebrado del 22 de abril al 2 de mayo de 1956*, 83–88. Madrid: Imprenta Aguirre.

–. 1980. *Historia de la lengua española.* Prólogo de Ramón Menéndez Pidal. Octava edición refundida y muy aumentada. (= *Biblioteca Románica Hispánica:* III. *Manuales*, 45.) Madrid: Gredos.

Lázaro Carreter, Fernando. 1972. *Crónica del Diccionario de Autoridades (1713–1740).* Discurso leído el día 11 de junio de 1972, en el acto de su recepción, por el Exmo. Sr. Don Fernando Lázaro Carreter y contestación del Exmo. Sr. Don Rafael Lapesa Melgar. Madrid: Real Academia Española.

López Alonso, Covadonga. 1998. "El ejemplo literario como autoridad en la 'Gramática Castellana' de 1771". Aparecerá en el Homenaje a la Profesora Elena Catena, Universidad Complutense de Madrid.

Lorenzo Criado, Emilio. 1974. "Descripción y norma en dos lenguas supranacionales". *FilM.* 14.173–202.

Niederehe, Hans-Josef. 1997. "La gramaticografía del siglo XVIII entre tradición y reorientación". *Historiographia Linguistica* 24.41–55.

Sarmiento González, Ramón. 1977. *La gramática de la lengua Castellana de 1771: Aportación a la Historia de la Real Academia Española.* Universidad Autónoma de Madrid. Inédita.

–. 1995. "La investigación gramatical mediante corpus: el Corpus Cumbre". *Corpus Lingüístico del Español Contemporáneo. Fundamentos, Metodología y Aplicaciones* hg. von Aquilino Sánchez Pérez 83–114. Madrid: Sociedad General Española de Libros.

–. 1996. "Tres modelos de gramática tradicional en España". *Theorie und Rekonstruktion: Trierer Studien zur Geschichte der Linguistik* hg. von Klaus D. Dutz & Hans-Josef Niederehe, 25–54. Münster: Nodus Publikationen.

–. 1998. "De la norma hispánica de la GRAE (1924) a la norma panhispánica del EGRAE (1973)". Aparecerá en el Homenaje al Prof. Germán de Granda, Universidad de Valladolid.

*Ramón Sarmiento Gonzales, Madrid (Spanien)*

# 117. L'Académie des Sciences de Lisbonne

1. Origines et modèles
2. La 'vie associative' de la Renaissance
3. Les premières institutions académiques
4. L'*Arcádia Lusitana*
5. De l'Académie Royale des Sciences à l'Académie des Sciences de Lisbonne
6. Bibliographie

## 1. Origines et modèles

L'Académie des Sciences de Lisbonne a eu pour modèles l'Accademia della Crusca (→ Art. 125) et l'Académie Française (→ Art. 128). Toutefois, on doit considérer l'expansion du mouvement antérieur, nommé arcadien, (désignation qui renvoie à l'œuvre de Sannazzaro *Arcadia*, paradigme de la poésie renaissante) comme un point de départ plus ou moins éloigné. L'idéal associatif (littéraire et culturel) fut l'origine et la cause de la création des Académies, dont le pic de l'expansion se situe au XVIIIe siècle; elle remonte surtout au Moyen Âge et aux Jeux Floraux (→ Art. 87) ou défis poétiques entre troubadours. Nous pouvons trouver trace de cette activité dans la littérature portugaise des XIIIe et XIVe, dans diverses polémiques sur le 'droit à la création poétique', qui opposa troubadours et jongleurs. Toutefois, c'est dans le *Cancioneiro Geral* de Garcia de Resende, publié en 1516, énorme compilation de plus de trois cents poètes, correspondant à la deuxième moitié du XVe siècle, que ces 'defis et débats' montrent l'existence d'une activité associative à la Cour: le débat entre Jorge de Silveira (1460–1513) et Nuno Pereira (1450–?), concernant la meilleure façon d'aimer, organisé formellement comme un jugement, avec accusation, défense, avocats, témoins et un juge, Dona Leonor da Silva (?–1528), belle dame de la Cour, montre, quoique de façon indirecte, une forme de fonctionnement évocatrice de ce que seront, plus tard, les séances académiques.

## 2. La 'vie associative' de la Renaissance

Le XVI$^{e}$ siècle, surtout à partir de 1526 ou 1527, assiste avec enthousiasme à la réception, dans le cadre de la création littéraire portugaise, des prestigieux modèles de la poésie classique à la mode italienne. Francisco Sá de Miranda (1481–1558) est généralement considéré comme le fondateur de la Renaissance au Portugal. En effet, après un voyage en Italie et en Castille, il introduit le sonnet, ainsi que d'autres formes poétiques classiques ou italiennes, tels que l'épître, l'ode, la chanson, l'églogue. Il attire immédiatement un grand nombre de poètes qui adoptent les nouveaux modèles; s'instaure alors le mouvement que Carolina Michaelis de Vasconcelos (1851–1925), philologue d'origine allemande et première femme à obtenir une chaire à l'Université portugaise, appellera *Arcádia de Entre Douro e Minho*, renvoyant aux nobles gentilhommes originaires de la région Nord-Ouest du pays, le 'nid' de la culture nationale. Les membres de cette 'Académie' avant la lettre, sans statuts, mais active et productive, qui s'appellent entre eux les 'Bergers de l'Estrémadure (allusion aux 'bergers' italiens de Sannazzaro), s'adressent mutuellement de façon régulière, mais surtout au Maître, Sá de Miranda, leurs écrits pour qu'ils soient loués ou critiqués, afin de s'améliorer. Nombre de ces productions sont remises au petit-fils de Dom Manuel, le Prince des Indes (1469–1521), au jeune prince Dom João (1537–1554), empêché de régner par une mort prématurée. En tant que Président Honoraire de cette 'Académie', le Prince est incité à devenir le Mécène Portugais. A la même époque, on découvre nettement une véritable Académie 'féministe' à la Cour, autour de la noble personne qu'est l'Infante Dona Maria (1521–1577), fille de Dom Manuel, et sœur du roi de Portugal, Dom João III (1502–1557). Lors des soirées littéraires de son palais de Santa Clara, on pouvait rencontrer des poètes, des savants et des artistes. Les poètes y présentaient leurs compositions: notamment Luis de Camões (1524–1580), et, avec les Dames de cette Cour, ils formaient une véritable Académie, toutefois sans aucun statut. Il convient de mentionner, entre autres, Dona Léonor de Noronha (1488–1563) et Luisa Sigea (?–1569), auteur d'un texte sous forme de Dialogue de deux jeunes filles, où se confrontent deux modes de vie: la *Vita aulica* et la *Vita rustica*. C'est Carolina Michaelis qui, dans son ouvrage, *A Infanta Dona Maria e as suas Damas* (Coimbra: à l'ordre de l'Université, 1902) fait une étude sérieuse à partir de documents historiques de cette véritable association littéraire et culturelle. Toujours dans ce même siècle, il faut faire référence à l'Academia Bracarense, fondée à Braga en 1581 par l'Archevêque Dom Frei Bartolomeu dos Mártires (1514–1590). Aussi bien cette Académie que le couvent de Santa Cruz à Viana do Castelo (1571), dont il tire son origine, sont le point de départ des centres d'einseignement et de réflexion théologique, religieuse et morale, bien davantage que les Académies du siècle postérieur. La vocation de celles-ci était surtout poétique et oratoire, sans toutefois refuser d'autres problèmes d'ordre moral, esthétique, etc., se rapprochant du modèle italien à la manière des Académies Pontaniana, Platonique, Crusca et d'autres.

## 3. Les premières institutions académiques

C'est toutefois au XVII$^{e}$ siècle que s'instaurent, au Portugal, les Académies dans les petites villes de province et dans les colonies, en partiuclier au Brésil, où la pensée et l'activité littéraire se forma à l'ombre du mouvement académique. Très souvent éphémères mais laborieuses, leur étude approfondie reste à faire, les écrits provenant de leur activité étant toujours inédits. Entretemps, le poète Francisco Rodrigues Lobo (1528–1620) publie à Lisbonne (1619, chez Pedro Craesbeeck) un livre en prose intitulé *Corte na Aldeia ou Noictes de Inverno* ('La Cour au village ou soirées d'hiver'). Comportant des implications politiques et autonomistes dont nous ne parlerons pas ici, ce livre apparaît comme la publication des 'actes avant-lettre' des séances d'une Académie qui se réunit régulièrement, a son siège propre et un règlement interne, accepté par ses participants: discuter tous les sujets sauf ceux qui touchent la religion et les livres sacrés. Ainsi, lors de toutes les séances-soirées, les participants (cinq permanents et certains assistant sporadiquement) abordent, discutent, argumentent sur les sujets les plus divers: la poésie, les langues, les romans de chevalerie, les modes d'aimer, la courtoisie, les bonnes manières et le protocole, l'art épistolaire, etc. La modération et la convivialité aristocratiques, le cérémonial des modèles de comportement évoquent le fonctionnement d'une Académie. L'*Academia dos Singulares de Lisboa dedica-*

*dos à Apolo* est fondée en 1628 mais ce n'est qu'en 1655 et 1668 que sont publiés les deux tomes qui contiennent ses productions, chez Antoine Craesbeeck de Melo. Ils témoignent de son activité et consignent les contributions poétiques et critiques de ses associés. Chacun des tomes a un schéma identique: 18 séances avec présidence tournante, la première s'étant faitee en novembre 1663 et la dernière en février 1665. Le contenu de ces séances est constitué de compositions poétiques de valeur variable et de dissertations théoriques et normatives présentant un caractère satirique et polémique, souvent très accentué. Il y a quelques compositions en italien, en castillan et en latin. L'emblème de cette Académie est une pyramide de livres de grands poètes et philosophes grecs, latins, portugais et castillans, ornée d'une guirlande de lauriers, au sommet de laquelle se trouve le Soleil; sa légende ou sa devise est: *Solaque non possunt haec monumenta mori*. Dom António Alvares da Cunha, Grand Ecuyer Tranchant (1626–1690) puis Conservateur des Archives Nationales du Royaume (Torre do Tombo), fonde en 1685, à son initiative privée, l'*Academia dos Generosos* dont l'emblème est une bougie allumée et la légende "Non extingetur". Elle fonctionna par intermittences et fut approuvée officiellement en 1687, et rénovée en 1693 par Dom Francisco Xavier de Menezes, 4ème Comte d'Ericeira (1673–1743). Trois ans après, cependant, ce dernier fonde les *Conferências Discretas e Eruditas* qui sont la continuation de l'Academia dos Generosos, désignation qui sera maintenue jusqu'à 1703. Ces conférences, issues directement de celles des Generosos, avaient, pur siège des réunions, la librairie du Comte d'Ericeira où se réunissait, tous les dimanches soir,

> la plus illustre et érudite noblesse du Royaume, afin d'examiner et résoudre des problèmes physiques et moraux et en vue d'améliorer l'élégance de la prose et de la poésie nationale (Rafael Bluteu, *Preâmbulo Breve na Renovação da Academia dos Generosos, na casa do Conde da Ericeira*, Lisboa, 1717, p. 4).

En 1714 elle réapparaît grâce au Comte d'Ericeira, sous le nom de l'*Academia dos Anónimos*. En 1717, la vielle *Academia dos Generosos*, à l'instar de l'Académie Française, prend le nom d'*Academia Portuguesa*. Les membres d'autres Académies contemporaines (*A. dos Unicos* et *A. dos Ilustrados*) vont grossir les rangs de cette Académie, à laquelle le roi Dom João V accorde la protection royale en 1720 et attribue le nom d'*Academia Real de História Portuguesa*. Il s'agit donc de la première institution académique soutenue par des instances officielles. Il existe deux gros volumes manuscrits concernant l'activité de l'*Academia dos Generosos*. Le premier contient des compositions et des dissertations de la première séance de 1686 à la quatorzième séance. La plupart des membres se présentent sous un pseudonyme (épigraphe), ces épigraphes représentent les témoignages d'un certain 'savoir' social: Académico Peregrino, Académico Indigno, Ermitão da Serra de Ossa, etc. Le deuxième manuscrit contient du matériel qui semble être une partie des séances d'une autre académie, celles des *Ocultos*, dont le contenu semble se confondre avec celui des *Generosos*. Tout ce fonds est inédit (et le reste toujours) et n'a pas fait l'objet d'études, bien qu'une partie significative de ces œuvres ait été publiée sous le nom de leurs auteurs respectifs, l'un des plus importants étant l'écrivain et polygraphe Dom Francisco Manuel de Melo (1608–1666). A la différence du ton polémique et parfois populaire du matériel recueilli par les *Singulares*, les *Generosos* et leurs successeurs gardent un niveau de sociabilité intellectuelle rigoureusement aristocratique et leur production manifeste une nette évolution courtisane.

## 4. L'*Arcádia Lusitana*

Le phénomère associatif en tant que création d'un territoire à la fois vaste et réservé, marqué d'obligations, de solidarités et de compromis mutuels, prend racine dans une société envahie, on peut le dire, par une inspiration bourgeoise. C'est cet espace qui rend propice l'anoblissement par les lettres, l'aristocratie de la culture, la création d'un nouveau jeu du pouvoir, le pouvoir culturel fonctionnant parfois comme contre-pouvoir. Dans l'ensemble du mouvement académique, les Arcádias se consacraient exclusivement aux Belles-Lettres et à la langue. Parmi elles, la plus importante a été l'*Arcádia Lusitane* ou *Ulissiponense*, fondée en 1756, et dont furent membres fondateurs António Dinis da Cruz e Silva (1731–1799), Manuel Esteves Negrão (?–1874) et Teotónio Gomes de Carvalho (1728?–1800). La plus notoire et importante des académies littéraires a tenu vingt ans, à la suite de quoi elle fut réorganisée sous la désignation de *Nova Arcádia*. Son but, comme il apparaît dans ses statuts, était de réformer le goût détérioré et de rallumer l'intérêt des nouvelles générations pour les arts littéraires; elle prétendait donc

> former une école de bons sentiments et de bons exemples en matière d'éloquence et de poésie, servant de modèle aux jeunes étudiants et diffusant [...] la chaleur à restaurer l'ancienne beauté de ces Arts oubliés (Braga 1899: 189–205).

Toutefois, elle se transforma rapidement en un espace de polémiques personnelles. Les bases sur lesquelles les membres de l'Arcádia fondaient leur intervention réformatrice et disciplinaire, consistaient surtout, et selon les statuts composés par Cruz e Silva, en une critique mutuelle, objective et sans ombre, des productions littéraires présentées lors des séances de l'Arcádia par ses membres, à qui il était demandé beaucoup de rigueur quant aux critères esthétiques et littéraires de leur 'censure'; il fallait revenir à l'imitation des classiques de l'Antiquité en tant que sources les plus pures de la perfection littéraire, tout en les adaptant au goût moderne, selon la leçon du français Nicolas Boileau, de l'italien Ludovico Antonio Muratori, de l'espagnol Luzán; les thèmes du quotidien devaient montrer une bourgeoisie agréable et aimable ce qui représentait un des aspects du renouveau de l'Arcádia. Selon les Arcadiens, les véritables causes de la décadence littéraire venaient donc de l'abandon des purs classiques et de la recherche d'inspiration dans l'imitation répétée de la Renaissance. Les membres de l'Arcádia, c'est-à-dire les Arcadiens qui signaient leurs productions sous des pseudonymes littéraires, avaient pour emblème une main empoignant une faux et pour légende, la devise de l'Arcádia: *Inutilia truncat.* Son but principal était en effet de restaurer la sobriété et l'équilibre du classicisme, fuyant les excès du gongorisme; ils préconisaient aussi la libération de la rime, qui d'après eux, empêchait la libre expression de la pensée. Outre ses fondateurs, ont fait partie de l'Arcádia, Domingos dos Reis Quita (1728–1770), Francisco José Freire (1719–1773), Manuel de Figueiredo (1725–1801), le célèbre Cândido Lusitano, et, en tant que principal théoricien du néo-classicisme (c'est-à-dire de cette tentative de retour à la pureté des modèles classiques), Pedro António Correia Garção (1724–1772), considéré comme le plus noble exemple de ces doctrines. Nous citerons comme principaux documents de cette théorie littéraire, la célèbre *Sátira Sobre a Imitação dos Antigos* adressée au Comte de S. Lourenço, et *l'Epistola a Olino*, sans oublier les textes qui constituent les *Dissertações da Arcádia*, la plupart ayant pour auteur Garção. Bien que les objectifs de ses membres n'aient pas été totalement atteints, il n'en reste pas moins vrai que le néo-classicisme et les modèles de l'Arcádia se maintiennent bien après l'apparition de l'école Romantique (1825).

## 5. De l'Académie Royale des Sciences à l'Acádemie des Sciences de Lisbonne

A la suite de l'intense activité des académies des XVII$^{e}$ et XVIII$^{e}$ siècles et en corollaire, après l'étiolement de l'Académie Royale de l'Histoire Portugaise, naît l'Académie Royale des Sciences, une fois de plus sur une initiative privée, mais réussissant très vite à avoir l'agrément et le soutien de la Reine. C'est cette Académie qui existe aujourd'hui, toujours fidèle à l'idéal culturel fixé à l'origine de sa fondation, en 1779, par le Duc de Lafões, Dom João Carlos de Bragança (1719–1808), par l'Ábbé Correia da Serra (1750–1823), par l'érudit Vandelli et par le Vicomte de Barbacena. Issue d'une initiative à l'origine nettement aristocratique, cette Académie va être préservée du destin polémique, fondé sur des rivalités et des inimitiés personnelles qui présidaient à l'évolution des académies auxquelles nous avons fait référence; toutefois, elle ne sera pas immunisée contre le conventionnalisme artificieux qui réglera les rapports entre ses membres. A Dom João Carlos de Bragança, personnage cultivé ayant parcouru toute l'Europe, de Paris à la Mer Noire, la Grèce, Constantinople, la Laponie, arrivant jusqu'en Egypte, revient l'honneur de sa fondation. A son retour, il fut nommé ministre, conseiller et maréchal. La reine Dona Maria approuva ses statuts, par un décret royal, le 24 décembre 1779 et lui concéda le titre de Royal en 1783. Le Duc de Lafões fut élu président à vie et on décida que la présidence soit donnée, par la suite, à un prince de la Maison de Bragance. Cette situation s'est maintenue jusqu'en 1910, date de l'implantation du régime républicain et du bannissement de la Maison de Bragance. Ses premiers membres venaient de la Real Academia de História Portuguesa, entre-temps supprimée. Parmi eux, nous nommerons les plus importants, dont le père Joaquim de Foios (1733–1811), auteur de nombreux poèmes (dont celui sur le tremblement de terre qui détruisit Lisbonne en 1755 et auquel Voltaire consacra lui aussi un poème) et d'un Mémoire sur la poésie bucolique es poètes portugais, publié dans les *Memórias da Literatura da Academia* (Tome I); Teodoro de Almeida (qui prononça l'allocution d'ouverture lors de la première séance le 4 juillet 1780); Dom Miguel du Portugal, Domingos Mascarenhas, marquis de Penalva, et bien d'autres encore. Au départ, l'Académie était composée de membres effectifs, honoraires, étrangers, libres, de correspondants et de vétérans. Elle était subventionnée par son fondateur, le duc de Lafões et par le Tiers du Revenu Annuel de la loterie de la Santa Casa da Misericordia. Ce régime dura jusqu'en 1910, date de l'implantation de la République au Portugal et de l'abolition de la Monarchie. L'épithète de *Real* (Royale) fut alors supprimée du nom de l'Académie. En 1780, cette dernière possédait déjà une typographie propre et une bibliothèque importante. En 1789, elle est exemptée de la censure et en 1790 affranchie des droits de douane pour ce qui est du papier nécessaire à ses publications. D'abord installée au *Palácio das Necessidades*, L'Académie fonctionne ensuite dans divers locaux de la ville de Lisbonne, et en 1836 elle siège dans le bâtiment du vieux Couvent de Jesus, qui lui est octroyé et où elle se tient encore aujourd'hui. La Bibliothèque ainsi que le Musée, prévus par les statuts, sont installés dans une pièce magnifique, construite à cet effet, d'après les ordres de l'érudit Frei Manuel de Cenáculo (1744–1814). Elle possède un plafond merveilleusement peint, des étagères ornementées de bustes d'hommes célèbres dans le domaine des sciences, des arts et des lettres. C'est là qu'aujourd'hui encore, se tiennent les séances solennelles de l'Académie. Il s'agit d'une des Bibliothèques les plus riches du pays, avec ses 250 000 volumes, 112 incunables et plus de 200 manuscrits uniques. L'Académie se composait de trois classes: les Sciences Exactes (Mathématiques); les Sciences Naturelles et les Belles Lettres. Ensuite, ces trois classes se réduiront à deux: les Sciences et les Lettres (voir ci-dessous. Les mêmes statuts déterminent que le développement des lettres et de la langue portugaise est prioritaire. C'est ainsi que l'Académie a commencé la réalisation du *Dicionário da Língua portuguesa* (1793) dont le premier volume est paru (A–AZ) en 1793, sous le nom d'auteurs érudits comme Pedro José da Fonseca (1737–1815), et José Costa de Macedo (1777–1867). Bien qu'inachevé, le *Dicionário* n'en reste pas moins un modèle lexicographique, rendant compte d'éléments et d'informations, d'après un vaste tableau de réponses à une enquête auprès d'un ensemble d'écrivains, élaborée par les auteurs: on a donc là un document paradigmatique d'une culture supérieure. Il faut aussi souligner l'importance des *Memórias da Literatura* publiées à Lisbonne par la Typographie de l'Académie et sous ses auspices, une des premières tentatives pour établir un corpus d'auteurs portugais, ainsi que la collection des *Livros inéditos da Históriae Portugusa*, les volumes de *Portugaliae Monumenta Historica* (1856–1888) (publiés aussi à Lisbonne), compilés par le célèbre écrivain et historien Alexandre Herculano (1810–1877), membre correspondant de l'Académie en 1844, et qui exhuma les textes des chroniques jusqu'alors enfouies dans les archives portugaises, publiques et privées. Il faut encore rappeler la *Colecção dos principais autores da História Portuguesa*, les *Monumentos inéditos para a História das Conquistas dos portugueses, l'História e Memórias*, le *Boletim de Segunda Classe*, les *Monumentos de Literatura dramática, Corpo diplomático*, etc.

Durant tout le XX^e siècle, nous retrouvons à la présidence, qui est de trois ans, des noms de la culture et de la science nationales, d'écrivains et d'hommes poliltiques, parmi lesquels Henrique Lopes de Mendonça (1856–1931), Braamcamp Freire (1849–1921), Egas Moniz (1874–1955) (prix Nobel de Médecine) – ce dernier ayant rempli trois mandats comme président (1928, 1932, 1940) –, etc. Les statuts de l'Académie, qui en 1851 prévoyaient l'existence de trois classes, les Sciences Naturelles, les Sciences Exactes et les Belles Lettres, ont été modifiés en 1912 et 1928. Les membres ont alors été regroupés en deux classes: Les Sciences Mathématiques, Physiques et Naturelles et les Sciences Morales, Politiques et Belles-Lettres. Chaque classe est composée de vingt membres perpétuels, trente correspondants nationaux et le même nombre d'étrangers. Cette disposition a de nouveau été réglementée en 1946 et son premier article est rédigé de la façon suivante: 'L'académie des Sciences de Lisbonne a pour but la culture, la diffusion et le développement des Sciences et des Lettres, la défense de l'unité et le perfectionnement de la langue portugaise, ainsi que la consécration du mérite de ceux qui se sont distingués par leur travail scientifique et littéraire' (1945, *Academia das Ciências de Lisboa. Estatutos*, p. 5). Du point de vue institutionnel, l'Académie dépendait alors du Ministère de l'Education. Aujourd'hui elle est rattachée au Ministère de la Culture. Le nouveau règlement (1946, avec addenda en 1955, 1961 et 1966) prévoit que chacune des classes soit composée de vingt académiciens perpétuels, trente correspondants nationaux et soixante étrangers.

## 6. Bibliographie

### 6.1. Sources primaires


Academia das Ciências de Lisboa. 1945. *Estatutos e Regulamentos Internos.* Lisbonne: Acadêmia das Ciências.

*Academia das Singulares de Lisboa, dedicada a Apolo.* 1655–1668. Lisbonne: Antonio Craesbeck de Melo.

*Boletim da Segunda Classe da Academia.* 1898–1929. Lisbonne: Acadêmia Real das Ciências.

Braga, Teofilo. 1892–1902. *Documentos das Chancelarias Reais Anteriores a 1531; História da Universidade de Coimbra.* 4 tomes. Lisbonne: Acadêmia Real das Ciências.

*Colecção de Livros Inéditos da História Portuguesa.* 1790–1824, en 5 volumes. Lisbonne: Acadêmia Real das Ciências.

Colecção de Opúsculos réimprimés concernant *l'História das Navegações, Viagens e Conquistas dos Portugueses,* 1844–1875. Lisbonne: Acadêmia Real das Ciências.

*Ephemerides Nauticas.* 1788–1862, en 65 tomes. Lisbonne: Acadêmia Real das Ciências.

*História e Memórias da Real Academia das Ciências de Lisboa.* 1797–. Lisbonne,

*Memórias da Literatura da Academia.* 1792–1839. Lisbonne: Acadêmia Real das Ciências.

*Memórias Económicas.* 1792–1814, en 5 tomes.

*Mémórias de Agricultura.* 1788–1791, en 2 tomes. Lisbonne: Acadêmia Real das Ciências.

*Os Livros das Menções.* 1880–1893. 4 tomes. Lisbonne: Acadêmia Real das Ciências.

*Quadro Elementar das Relações Políticas de Portugal com as diversas Potências du Mundo.* 1842–1876. Lisbonne: Acadêmia Real das Ciências.

Sousa Viterbo. 1899–1922. *Dicionário Histórico e Documental dos Arquitectos, Engenheiros e Construtores Portugueses ao serviço de Portugal.* 3 tomes. Lisbonne: Acadêmia Real das Ciências.


### 6.2. Sources secondaires


1920, 1922, 1924, 1926. *Catálogo Geral das Publicações da Academia das Ciências de Lisboa.* Lisbonne: Academia das Ciências.

Agudo, Fernando Dias. 1972. "A Academia des Ciências de Lisboa e as Relações Internacionais". *Memórias da Academia das Ciências,* Classe de Ciências, tomo XXIII.139–152. Lisbonne.

Aguiar e Silva, Vitor Manuel. 1988. » Classicismo e Neoclasscismo". *Teoria da Literatura.* Coimbra: Almedina.

Aires, Cristóvão. 1927. *Para a História da Academia das Ciências de Lisboa.* Coimbra: Imprensa da Universidade.

Almeida, Carlos Marques de. 1996. *O Elogio do intelectual: a figura do "Sabo Christão" nas Prosas Portuguesas de D. Rafael Bluteau.* Lisbonne: Universidade Nova de Lisboa.

Braga, Teófilo. 1899. *A Arcádia Lusitana.* Porto: Liv. Chardon.

Branco, Fernando Castelo. 1973. "Significado cultural das Academias de Lisboa no século XVIII". *Portugaliae Historica* I. 175–201. Lisbonne.

Ferrão, António. 1932. *A Academia das Ciências de Lisboa e o Movimento Filosófico, Científico e Económico do século XVIII.* Coimbra: Imprensa da Universidade.

Ferreira, João Palma. 1982. *Academias Literárias dos Séculos XVII e XVIII.* Lisbonne: Biblioteca Nacional.

Ferreira, M$^a$ Natália Almeida. 1992. *Certames poéticos realizados em Lisboa nos séculos XVII e XVIII.* Lisbonne: Universidade Nova de Lisboa.

Figueiredo, Fidelino de. 1931. *Historia da Literatura Clássica. 3$^a$ época.* 2$^a$ ed. Lisbonne: Liv. Clássica

Monteiro, Ofélia Paiva. 1964. "No alvorecer do 'iluminismo' em Portugal: D. Francisco Xavier de Menes, 4° Conde da Ericeira". *Revista da História Literária de Portugal* I.73–89. Lisbonne.

Pimentel, António Augusto. 1958. "A Academia das Ciências e os estudos farmacêuticos em Portugal". *Revista Portuguesa de Farmácia* 8, 195.135–152. Lisbonne.

Pimentel, António Forjaz. 1960. "As Academias, História e Renovação". in *Memórias da Academia das Ciências,* Classe de Ciências VIII.27–43. Lisbonne: Academia das Ciências.

*Recapitulação da Historia da Literatura.* 1918. Porto: Os Árcades.

Rossi, Giuseppe Carlo. 1941. *L'arcadia e il Romanticismo in Portogallo.* Firenze: Le Monnier.

Sampaio, Albino M. Forjaz de. 1929–42. "As Academias". *História Literária de Portugal Ilustrada* III.283 sqq. Paris: Aillaud.

Toscano, Maria Margarida. 1994. *Racionalidade Communicativa, expaço público e antecedentes da emergência duma esfera pública literária em Portugal.* Lisbonne: Universidade Nova de Lisboa.

Veloso, José Queirós. 1929–42. "A Academia Real de História Portuguesa". *História Literária de Portugal Ilustrada* III.291 sqq. Paris: Aillaud.

Vicente, António Pedro. 1996. "Academia de Ciências". *Dicionário de História do Estado Novo,* dir – de Fernando Rosas e J. M. Brandão de Brito I.9–11. Lisboa: Círculo de Leitores.


*Maria Leonor Carvalhão Buescu †, Lisbonne (Le Portugal)*

# 118. Normative studies in England

1. Introduction
2. Codification and prescription
3. The 17th century
4. The 18th century
5. Prescriptive grammar
6. Norms of correctness
7. Effectiveness of prescriptive grammar
8. Conclusion
9. Bibliography

## 1. Introduction

One month after the publication of his grammar (1762), Robert Lowth (1710–1787) wrote to his publisher: "I am very glad to find the Public has so good an Appetite for Grammer [sic]" (Tierney 1988: 461). The public's appetite for grammar was indeed so great that a year later, a second edition came out. Alston (1965: 42–48) lists 48 editions and reprints of the grammar until 1838, published mostly in London but also in the Unites States. In 1790 the grammar was translated into German, while in 1794 an English edition came out in Basel.

The reception of Lowth's grammar had been very favourable (Tierney 1988: 461n; Percy 1997:130). Within a year, however, a reprint came out of a grammar subtitled "an easy introduction to Dr. Lowth's English grammar". The author was John Ash (1724?–1779), a minister at Pershore (Michael 1970: 550). Originally, the grammar had borne the title *Grammatical Institutes: Or Grammar, Adapted to the Genius of the English Tongue* (1760). The question arises what made Ash change the title.

Lowth's grammar, despite its favourable reception, had been criticised as being difficult (Percy 1997: 131); a schoolmaster friend of Ash's decided to adopt Ash's book as an introductory text for his school (Michael 1970: 278). Because of Lowth's popularity, Ash must have sensed a market for his own grammar as well, so much so that in 1766 he called his grammar *The Easiest Introduction to Dr. Lowth's English Grammar.*

Alston (1965) lists 50 editions and reprints of Ash's grammar, published in England, Scotland, Ireland and America. The grammar was even translated into German in 1775, and again in 1789. It is therefore striking that Ash is not mentioned in *The Oxford Companion to the English Language* (1992; *OCEL*): only Lowth is discussed in any detail, while one other 18th-century grammarian, Noah Webster (1758–1843), is mentioned briefly with the comment that "his grammar was influenced by Robert Lowth and in later editions by Horne Tooke" and that it "was criticized as being too advanced for schoolchildren" (1992, 'Webster'). Lindley Murray (1745–1826) is not referred to at all, despite the many editions and reprints of his grammars (1795, 1797) (Tieken 1996a). *OCEL* notes that Lowth's "name has become synonymous with prescriptive grammar" (1992, 'Lowth'); his name does indeed feature prominently in most accounts of English prescriptive grammar, often coupled with Joseph Priestley (1733–1804) because of their contrasting attitudes to the importance of usage (Crystal 1988: 206–207). Another popular grammar published around the same time as Lowth (1762), Ash (1760–1763) and Priestley (1761) is *The British Grammar* by James Buchanan (fl. 1753–1773).

There was much more grammatical activity during the 17th and 18th centuries than appears from surveys like *OCEL* and Crystal (1988). While Baugh and Cable (1993 [1951]: 269–281) provide a lucid account of 18th-century grammars, much further information has become available since the book was originally published. As a result of publications such as Alston's bibliography (1965), his reprint series (1974), Michael (1970, 1987), Vorlat (1975, 1979) and Sundby et al. (1991), it is now possible to give a more detailed description of the latter stages of the standardisation process of the language.

In what follows, I will deal with two of the stages in this process, codification and prescription (Milroy & Milroy 1985: 27). During both stages, normative grammars of English were written, though with a different outlook on language and different aims vis-à-vis their users. I intend to analyse the normative nature of the grammars, what norms they describe, and who and what their authors were. Moreover, I will try to define the differences between normative and prescriptive grammar, terms which are often regarded as more or less synonymous (e. g. Chalker & Weiner 1994, 'normative'). I will also demonstrate that, though the prescription stage is still in force today, attitudes to correct usage have changed in time. For full details of the works referred to below, see Alston (1965) and Michael (1970: 547–587). Many of the grammars and other early works on the English language have been reprinted by Alston (1974).

## 2. Codification and prescription

The publication of Priestley (1761), Buchanan (1762), Ash (1760/63), and Lowth (1762) marks the early 1760s as an active period. In this respect the second half of the 18th century presents a marked contrast with the first: from the publication in 1586 of the first grammar of English by William Bullokar (ca. 1530–ca. 1590), Alston (1965) lists only 43 grammars until 1750, while the second half of the century saw the publication of nearly four times as many. Many dictionaries were compiled as well (Osselton 1995: 1); Osselton even argues that the early 18th century witnessed the emergence of the professional lexicographer. All this activity was part of the codification process the English language was undergoing – as were other Western European languages around the same time (see Baugh & Cable 1993: 198, 258–259). While attempts had been made to monitor efforts at codification through the founding of an Academy – pleas for an Academy were made by Dryden, Defoe, Swift, Addison and others – no such institution ever came about, in contrast to Italy (1582), France (1635) and Spain (1713). The need for an academy was gradually felt less strongly as a result of the increasing number of grammars and dictionaries which appeared.

Robert Baker's (fl. 1770) call for an Academy therefore comes rather late in the day, according to Alston in his introduction to the microfiche reprint of Baker's *Reflections on the English Language* (1770). Leonard (1929: 35) describes the work as "the ancestor of those handbooks of abuses and corrections which were so freely produced in the nineteenth century". The book in fact belongs to a later stage in the standardisation process of the English language, the prescription stage, a stage which continues to the present day, leading to a regular output of such publications as Simon (1980). Though writing more than 200 years later, Simon still calls for an Academy (1980: 12) to purify and fix the English language, which puts him into the same category of purists like Baker.

Purists believe in the prescription of good usage and the proscription of bad usage – terms associated with normative grammar (Baugh & Cable 1993: 273). By contrast, modern linguistics is regarded as 'descriptive', as representing a more truly scientific, objective approach to language. As a result, "the term is generally used pejoritatively" (Chalker & Weiner 1994, 'prescriptive'). Vorlat (1979: 129) argues that the dichotomy between a descriptive and a prescriptive approach does not work for grammars produced before the 18th century; nor does it hold for the 18th century (Tieken 1987: 221; Peters 1996: 126). Vorlat's threefold distinction is more useful:

> (1) descriptive registration of language, without value judgments and including ideally [...] all language varieties; (2) normative grammar, still based on language use, but favoring the language of one or more social or regional groups and more than once written with a pedagogical purpose; (3) prescriptive grammar, not based on usage but on a set of logical (or other) criteria (Vorlat 1979: 129).

However, these are not discrete categories: prescriptive and proscriptive comments can even be found in modern handbooks professing to be of a purely descriptive nature. At the same time, certain 17th-century grammars like those by Ben Jonson (1572–1637) and John Wallis (1616–1703) are more descriptive than might have been expected (Pullum 1974: 65–66). The early grammars tend to be either of a more descriptive or more prescriptive nature, while they are all strongly normative in the sense that they set out to describe a norm of correctness in their attempts to codify the language. This may be based on ideals of correctness, which some grammarians feel more at liberty to shape by any available means than others. As the 18th century progresses, notions of correctness are increasingly influenced by actual usage, a development which gives rise to a more clear-cut split into descriptive and prescriptive grammars. It is then that we embark on the next stage of the standardisation process, the prescription stage.

## 3. The 17th century

Prescriptive grammar starts with Christopher Cooper's (ca. 1655–1698) grammar of 1685, called *Grammatica Linguae Anglicanae* (Vorlat 1979: 137). There were two earlier attempts at descriptive grammar writing, Jonson (1640) and Wallis (1653). While Jonson's has been rated "a poor grammar", it is original in that it contains a section on syntax based on quotations ranging from Chaucer to Sir Thomas More. In taking actual usage as a starting point, Jonson is more than a century ahead of his time (Osselton 1982: 208). In the kind of usage he describes, Jonson shows his outlook to be normative at the same time: his norm is not the language of the common people but that of the educated classes. Jonson was thus not only "a pioneer among descriptive grammarians" (Osselton 1982: 212), but his treatment of syntax makes him look forward to a grammarian like Lowth.

Wallis (1653) was "the first to analyze English grammar by framing and testing hypotheses based on formal criteria derived from his observations on sentence structure" (Subbiondo 1992: 184). He did so in order to break away from the grammar of Latin which until then had been used as a model for English grammar (Subbiondo 1992: 186). Typical features of English had previously attracted the notice only of authors of bilingual grammars, such as John Palsgrave (d. 1554) and James Bellot (fl. 1580) published in 1530 and 1580 (Tieken 1987: 203).

Wallis was thus not the first to break away from the example of Latin. In his rigorous scientific approach, however, he goes further than any of his predecessors, even developing his own metalanguage (Subbiondo 1992: 187). His grammar is therefore not prescriptive; nor is his approach purely normative, as he was aware of the existence of different registers in the standard language of the time and accepted variation in usage. Furthermore, he used common English as a basis for his grammar (Subbiondo 1992: 188). Subbiondo regards Wallis's grammar as "the first structural grammar of English" (1992: 183).

## 4. The 18th century

In writing his grammar (1711), James Greenwood (d. 1737) owed much to Wallis (Lehnert 1937/38, 193–196), a debt he acknowledges in his introduction (1711, A4^r). Parts of the grammar were translated from Wallis; even the layout is often identical. Samuel Johnson (1709–1784) also borrowed from Wallis in the grammar prefixed to his *Dictionary* (1755). Greenwood nevertheless did not follow Wallis quite slavishly, occasionally showing a more proscriptive approach to language than his source. He more firmly than Wallis marks off standard from nonstandard English, disfavouring the language of certain social and regional groups of speakers.

The most popular grammars in the 18th century were Brightland (1711), Fisher (1750 [1745?]), Ash (1760), Lowth (1762), Harrison (1777), Webster (1784), Bingham (1785) and Murray (1795, 1797). Of all these, ten or more editions and reprints are listed by Alston (1965). In addition, there are 59 titles in Alston which were reprinted at least once in the course of the 18th century. All this shows that there was a considerable market for grammars of English at the time. While one of these grammars was by a woman, Ann Fisher, two of them, by Webster and Caleb Bingham (1757–1817), were published only in America. The title of Bingham's grammar is significant: *The Young Lady's Accidence.* Thus, grammars were written by men and women, in Britain and America, and some of them were particularly addressed to women.

### 4.1. The grammarians

With codification in the air at the time, it seemed as if every educated person felt he could try and write a grammar: Priestley was a scientist, Webster and Murray were lawyers, and J. Nicholson (fl. 1793) was a mathematician; Benjamin Martin (1704–1782) is best known as an inventor of microscopes. There was even a printer who wrote a grammar in 1796 (Alston 1965: 98). Mostly, however, the authors were schoolmasters, such as Thomas Dyche (fl. 1735), John Collyer (fl. 1735), Daniel Fenning (fl. 1756–1771) and Peter Walkden Fogg (fl. 1792–1796), or ministers, such as Daniel Turner (1710–1798), John Kirkby (1705–1754), John Wesley (1703–1791), Ash, Ralph Harrison (1748–1810) and John Fell (1735–1797) (Michael 1970: 549–587). Even Webster (1784) and Johnson (1755) had been teachers in their early days (Monaghan 1983: 23; Clifford 1955: 154–155). Those listed as school-masters often taught subjects other than English or in addition to English, such as elocution and geography, mathematics, rhetoric and writing. It is not until the early 1770s that authors advertise themselves as teachers of English only.

It is not hard to see how ministers might turn into grammarians. Many of them found employment as private tutors, teaching the grammar of Latin. From Latin it was a small step to English, which was often described in terms of Latin terminology anyway. A good example is Kirkby, who is listed by Michael as "Tutor to Edward Gibbon, 1744–1745" (1970: 569). Kirkby's grammar was published in 1746, but was probably written while Kirkby was still with the Gibbons (Tieken 1992: 161).

While the early half of the 18th century witnessed the birth of the professional lexicographer (Osselton 1995: 1), the same claim cannot be made for the grammarians of the period. The 19th century presents a different situation, as the abundance of English grammars then published suggests (Michael 1991). In the course of the 18th century we do see the rise of specialist studies, such as the monographs on the English verb published in 1761 and 1789 by James White (d. ca. 1812) and James Pickbourn (fl. 1789), and of corpus-based studies, such as White's and William Ward's (1708–1772) of 1765. These arose out of a greater interest in actual usage which characterised the period in which they were written. Around the same time another new phenomenon emerges, that of the so-called textbook writer, such as Webster and Murray (see below).

### 4.2. Grammars by and for women

Among the 18th-century grammarians there were seven women (Sundby & al. 1991: 10). The female grammarian is of interest in a society which lacked intellectual opportunities for women. That so many women wrote grammars is significant in its own right – by contrast, there appears to have been only a single female grammarian in Holland at the time, Johanna Corleva (1698–1752) (Noordegraaf 1994). It is also an indication of a growing attention to the educational needs of women, as most of the grammars in question were meant for girls as well as boys. This change in attitude is one of the reasons for the explosive growth in the number of grammars published during the second half of the century (Michael 1970: 517).

The first female grammarian was Ann Fisher (1719–1778). The first edition of her grammar has not come down to us (Alston 1965: 25), but on 29 June 1745 an advertisement for the book appeared in the *Newcastle Journal* (Alston, introd. facs. repr.). Fisher's grammar was plagiarised by Kirkby, whose grammar came out in 1746 (Tieken 1992: 166–167). As a schoolmistress (*DNB*, 'Fisher'), she must have developed her own method of teaching English grammar, and being the wife of the Newcastle printer Thomas Slack (Michael 1970: 562) she may not have found it hard to find a publisher.

Fisher's grammar is important, not only because it was popular – Alston lists 31 numbered editions – but also because it was the first to contain exercises of false grammar. The idea to confront the pupil with examples of bad English was taken from Latin grammar. Exercises like Fisher's became very popular, and they are found throughout the rest of period (Michael 1970: 196, 473).

Like many other grammars of the time (e. g. Greenwood 1711; Buchanan 1762; Fenning 1771; Webster 1784), Fisher's grammar is presented in the form of question and answer. Her discussion of the category mood, for example, illustrates her aim in describing English for its own sake, rather than in terms of Latin. In denying the existence of mood in English Fisher was part of a minority of grammarians at the time (Michael 1970: 426). She also adopted a native metalanguage, such as the word "time" for "tense" and "helping Verb" for "auxiliary". Though she was indeed continuing in a direction begun by Wallis (1653) and passed on through e. g. Greenwood (1711) and Johnson (1755), Fisher's attitude in the matter may have been determined by the fact that she wrote for a reading public which included women as well. At the time, knowledge of Latin was still predominantly a male prerogative.

Percy (1994: 123) suggests that Loughton's grammar (1734) was "calculated chiefly for the fair sex" but Loughton was not the first to include women among his readers: one of Greenwood's aims in writing his grammar was "to oblige the *Fair Sex* whose *Education* perhaps, is too much neglected in this Particular" (1711, A3$^{v}$). While Gough (1712–1780) aimed his grammar (1754) at anyone lacking knowledge of Latin, hence also women, Ussher's grammar (1785) was the first to be "Designed particularly for the use of ladies' boarding schools" (title-page). Ussher argues that "a grammatical knowledge of English is become essentially necessary in the education of ladies" (1785: vi). The education of women was thus becoming a matter of general concern during the 18th century.

There were six more female grammarians (Percy 1994: 122), though not until the last decades of the century: Ellin Devis (fl. 1775–1782), Mrs. M. C. Edwards (fl. 1796), Lady Eleanor Fenn (1743–1813), Jane Gardiner (1799), Blanch Mercy (fl. 1799–1808) and Mrs. Eves (fl. 1800) (Alston 1965). There may well have been more: many anonymous titles in Alston may have been from the hand of women. More women contributed to the grammars published at the time, as appears from the title-page of Mackintosh (1797), which reads "Duncan Mackintosh and his two Daughters".

The titles of some of these grammars by women, such as Fenn's *The Child's Grammar. Designed to Enable Ladies who may not have Attended to the Subject themselves to Instruct their Children* (1799), inform us that their reading public consisted of children, who were to be taught by their mothers. Fenn's grammars were extremely popular: Alston records 21 editions of *The Mother's Grammar* and 26 editions of *The Child's Grammar* until 1820. A 50th edition of the latter booklet was advertised as late as 1876 (Michael 1987: 453). The grammar was intended for girls only, as appears from many of the example sentences given. Percy (1994: 127) notes that Fenn's grammars are "conventional in content", but her distinction into nouns, adjectives, pronouns, verbs, adverbs, conjunctions, prepositions and interjections was not a very common classification at the time (Michael 1970: 228). Fenn's definitions of the parts of speech are remarkably similar to those in Murray (1795). In view of Murray's reliance on his predecessors (Vorlat 1959), it would be hard to prove that Fenn depended on him rather than on any other grammar. Even so, the simplified definitions and the adaptation of the examples and of the treatment of grammar to her audience suggests that her aim was the same as that of Ash before her: to offer an easy introduction to the grammar currently most popular.

### 4.3. English grammars in America

Bingham's grammar (1785), published in Boston, seems to have been written with a similar aim in mind as Fenn and Ash: its subtitle, "a short and easy introduction to English grammar", suggests a link with Lowth's, which had been reissued in America ten years before. Lowth's grammar was not the first British grammar to be published in America: before the Declaration of Independence, two grammars were published in New York, by Samuel Johnson in 1765 and by Thomas Byerly in 1773 and one in Dresden, Vt., by Abel Curtis (1779) (cf. Finegan 1980: 34–35). Only Curtis's grammar met with any success: Alston (1965: 68) records four numbered editions between 1779 and 1785. The absence of any further reprints of the work may have to do with the publication of Webster's grammar one year before the last edition of Curtis's work came out.

Webster's grammar (1784) was part of a series consisting of a spelling book (1783) and a reader (1785). With this series, Webster envisaged the creation of "a standard American speech that would serve as a unifying force in the new Republic" (Monaghan 1983: 13) and that would be independent from the former mother tongue (Finegan 1980: 37). The beginnings of the codification process of American English must therefore be traced to Webster.

Webster's grammar was successful despite the competition of rival schoolbooks such as those by Ash, Lowth and Buchanan. Altogether, Alston records twenty-three editions and reprints of Webster's grammar and a further eleven under different titles. After 1843, the grammar drops out of circulation.

### 4.4. Murray's English grammar

Webster met his ultimate rival in Murray, who produced a similar educational programme (Austin 1996). Though Murray's books were all first published in Britain, his two grammars (1795, 1797), the *English Exercises* (1797), the readers (1799, 1800, 1801) and the speller (1804) quickly made it to America. In 1800, the first American edition of the *English Grammar* came out, establishing itself as a serious rival to Webster. Ten years later, Murray's books were published in most major cities of the United States (Monaghan 1996: 32).

Murray's grammars were a worldwide success. Alston (1965: 92–96, 99–102) records 65 numbered editions of the grammar and 133 of the abridgement which came out in 1797. Numerous other editions and reprints appeared in America, Ireland, India, Germany, France, Portugal and Japan (Tieken 1996a). Moreover, Alston notes that the *English Grammar* was translated into French, German, Dutch, Swedish, Spanish, Russian and Japanese. Murray's popularity must have contributed to the spreading of English as a world language, though a demand for English grammars had already begun to make itself felt earlier, as the German translations of Ash (1775, 1789) and Lowth (1790) indicate. 'Murray' became "a household word for 'Grammar'" (Wales 1996: 209), and he was to remain so for three quarters of a century and more.

Murray owes much of his success to the way in which he arranged his material. In writing his grammar he merely presented his readers with a judiciously arranged "compilation" (Murray 1795: iii). That he refrained from mentioning his sources earned him the reputation of a plagiarist (Tieken 1996b), though this did nothing to impede the sales of his book. Immediately after the accusation, he provided a list of the sources he had used: Harris, Johnson, Lowth, Priestley, Beattie, Sheridan, Walker, and Coote (1818 [1795]: 5).

Murray's grammar is subtitled "Adapted to the different classes of learners", and though many other grammarians made similar claims, Murray is perhaps the only one who put it into practice. His grammar is a graded grammar, with the basic rules and principles of the language printed in normal type and additional information for the more advanced student in smaller type (Murray 1795: iv). His rules can easily be committed to memory; that this actually happened appears from numerous references to Murray in 19th-century literature (Tieken 1996a: 18). The additional information concerns further grammatical details, such as different classes of adverbs, the derivation of adverbs from nouns and the like (Murray 1795: 75–77). The grammar is distinguished by its learnability, an important requirement in a teaching grammar.

## 5. Prescriptive grammar

While Lowth came to be the embodiment of prescriptive grammar (*OCEL* 1992, 'Lowth'), Murray's improvement on Lowth makes his grammars even more deserving of this title. Vorlat (1996: 163) argues that the grammar's prescriptiveness is caused by a combination of factors: "the limited references to usage, the pages and pages of 'false grammar' with proposals for correction, the labelling of so-called ungrammatical patterns, Murray's ideas on linguistic variation, and the overwhelming use of deontic and related patterns". She argues that Murray's prescriptive attitude to language is dated at the end of the 18th century (Vorlat 1996: 180). Even so, the sales figures of his grammars indicate that a prescriptive grammar like his was just what people wanted (Michael 1991: 12–13). Murray's grammars gave those wishing to improve themselves by improving their command of grammar as well as those wishing to learn English as a second language the opportunity for doing so.

As a prescriptivist Murray looks forward to purist writings of the present century, such as Gowers's *Complete Plain Words* (1954), Fowler's *Dictionary of Modern English Usage* (1965), and Simon's *Paradigms Lost* (1980). An important change had occurred during the 18th century: from codifying the English language, grammarians had shifted their attention to the prescription of the rules previously drawn up – the final stage in the standardisation process.

The beginning of the prescription stage cooccurs with a greater attention to usage, which is usually attributed to Priestley (Leonard 1926: 14; Baugh & Cable 1993: 278) though it starts some time earlier. Previously, a doctrine of correctness had prevailed, adherents of which set out to "mold linguistic practice according to selected patterns of grammar; they attempt to retard the pace of language change or halt it altogether" (Finegan 1980: 10). To achieve this, the grammarians had three aims in mind: "(1) to reduce the language to rule and set up a standard of correct usage; (2) to refine it – that is, to remove supposed defects and introduce certain improvements; and (3) to fix it permanently in the desired form" (Baugh & Cable 1993: 252).

There were many "supposed defects" in the language – most of these concerned matters of syntax, which was characterised then as now by variation. Was it *different to, different from, different than?* Was *than* in *taller than I* a conjunction or a preposition, in which case *me* would be the correct form? In setting up a standard by "reducing the language to rule" only one of these possibilities could be correct. The major question was how to decide between the variants currently in use.

In doing so, the grammarians resorted to means alien to language in general or the English language in particular, such as principles of logic and analogy with the classical languages. A good example is the proscription of multiple negation (Tieken 1982), though the only grammarian to explain the principle was Martin (1748), who was more than familiar with the discipline referred to:

"[...] our ordinary use of two negatives (in which the force of the first is much more than merely destroyed by the latter) corresponds to the multiplication of two negative quantities in Algebra, the product of which is always affirmative; as mathematicians very well know" (1748: 93).

### 5.1. Rules of syntax

Syntax was an aspect of English grammar which had not always been taken for granted as such. Many grammarians believed that if relations between words in a sentence were expressed through inflections as in Latin and Greek, English, as an analytical language, did not have a syntax (Michael 1970: 467). Thus, Wallis (1653) does not provide any rules of syntax; but Greenwood, despite having based his grammar on Wallis, does, though he notes that because "the *Syntax* or Construction of the Noun, [is] chiefly perform'd by the help of the *Prepositions*, and I having in every Chapter given an account of what more particularly relates to each part of Speech, there is not much left for me to say on this Head" (1711: 209). The same applies to Johnson's grammar prefixed to the *Dictionary* (1755). Johnson has been criticised for treating syntax in only twelve lines. In omitting a separate syntax, Johnson, missed an important opportunity in that he could have produced the authoritative grammar published by Lowth (Sledd & Kolb 1955: 179). But as in the case of Greenwood, there is more syntax in the *Dictionary* (Nagashima 1968: 223n).

Johnson was aware of the fallacy of the old belief that the English language, once it had been refined, could be fixed. Instead, he believed that rules of the language should be distilled from usage "by the best authors", or that not the grammarians but actual usage should be the basis of grammatical description. This attitude must have originated from the set-up of his *Dictionary*, the entries of which are all illustrated by quotations. For all that, Johnson's attitude to usage was not new. Martin's discussion of double negation, for example, shows that the new approach was already evident several years before the publication of Johnson's *Dictionary*:

> We use but one negative, though the Saxons used two [...] which method of negation is also in the French tongue [...] We on the contrary affirm by two negatives, as, *It is not unpleasant*, for, *it is pleasant; it is not impossible*, i. e. *it may be so*. (1748: 93).

Martin thus takes usage into account rather than merely proscribing double negation as others did. The same attitude is found in Kirkby's (1746) adaptions of some of the rules from Fisher (1745?).

### 5.2. Correctness in usage

There was at the time no universal agreement as to what was correct usage. Leonard (1929) provides a survey of the constructions which called for comment from 18th-century grammarians and other writers on the English language, listing those for and those against each instance. More recently, Sundby *et al.* (1991) listed all those usages which were commented on adversely in the grammars.

Fisher (1789 [1745?]: 118) asserts that her rules of syntax are such as are "observed by our best Writers", and Fogg (1796: iii) claims that his examples "have been generally extracted from approved authors" (Tieken 1990: 484). Yet who the "approved" writers were is not always clear. Johnson considers the best authors to be those writing "before the restoration, whose works I regard as the *wells of English undefiled*" (1755: C1r). In practice, however, he regularly quoted from contemporary writings, including his own.

Some grammarians are more specific in this matter. Thomas Dilworth (fl. 1740–1780) and James Gough (1712–1780) mention the authors of the *Spectator*, the *Tatler* and the *Guardian* in the prefaces to their grammars (1751: ix; 1754: xvi), while Fell (1784: xv) lists "the Holy Scriptures, Shakespeare, Chillingworth, Algernon Sidney, Locke, Tillotson, and Addison" (Tieken 1990: 485–486). In the second half of the 18th century we see the birth of corpus-based grammars. White's study of the English verb (1761) is the first, and he is followed by Ward (1765), Baker (1770) and Fogg (1792, 1796) (Tieken 1990: 486–487; Wright 1994: 244). Lowth (1762) likewise drew on a corpus, though one primarily consisting of instances of grammatical errors. His standard of correctness was the Bible, which he quotes from most and criticises least.

### 5.3. Incorrect usage

The list in Sundby *et al.* (1991: 35–37) of authors criticised by the grammarians is headed by Swift, and followed by the New Testament, Hume, Addison and Pope. Lowth's criticism of contemporary writers, found in the footnotes which litter his grammar, serves to show that the study of English grammar is indispensable to prospective authors (1762: ix). The kind of 'error hunting' Lowth engaged in is a typical characteristic of the prescription stage. After the codification stage is completed, it must next be seen to that the rules which were formulated are adhered to. Lowth was thus the first prescriptivist proper. Baker (1770), whose book has many of the characteristics of a usage guide, professes a totally unbiased view in the matter: "I have censured even our best Pen-men, where they have departed from what I conceive to be the Idiom of the Tongue, or where I have thought they violate grammar without Necessity" (1770: iv).

There are striking parallels between Baker and the book by Simon (1980): both call for an Academy well after the primary needs for one, the publication of an authoritative grammar and dictionary, had been fulfilled, and both boast of a complete lack of relevant education in their fields (Baker 1770: 11; Simon 1980: x–xi). Being a non-specialist in 1980 put Simon on the opposite side to the generative linguists who looked "with disdain upon prescriptive grammar, because of its unscientific or prescientific paradigm" (Vorlat 1996: 179–180). In this context we must interpret Pullum (1974) and Subbiondo (1975), who argue that neither Lowth (1762) nor Ward (1765) deserved the treatment they received from the American structuralists, but that they must be seen for what they set out to provide: accurate, if normative, descriptions of the English of their time.

## 6. Norms of correctness

Leonard (1929: 169) claims that the grammarians based their norms of correctness on the language of gentlemen, the kind of upper-class educated English used in 'polite' London circles. In particular, he writes, the grammarians warned their readers against "contamination with the language of the vulgar". Apart from the language of the lower classes, 'provincial' English was criticised as well. Thus, Scotsmen and Irishmen were criticised for mistakes in their usage of *shall* and *will* (Webster 1789: 236–237; Fogg 1796: 129). Boswell's linguistic insecurity is well-known, and Sheridan's pronouncing dictionary (1780) was considered as "too Hibernian" (Sledd & Kolb 1955: 176). In his *Philosophy of Rhetoric* (1776), Campbell defined good English as present, national and reputable. Even so, many grammarians illustrated constructions with examples from previous centuries (Tieken 1990: 488), by which they ran the risk of describing out-of-date usage. The lack of an historical awareness in matters of grammar led, for example, to the persistence of the archaic pronouns *thou* and *ye* in English grammars well into the 19th century (e. g. Murray 1818 [1795]: 62; Percy 1997: 135).

As shown in 5.2., the written language took priority over the spoken, which led to tag questions and other constructions typical of 18th-century speech failing to attract the grammarians' attention (Tieken 1987: 221, 216). Often, however, a distinction is made between poetic and non-poetic use, as in Bayly (1772: 39), who notes that "The Verb Substantive and Auxiliaries are often omitted, particularly in poetry" (see also Percy 1997: 137–142).

### 6.1. Actual usage

With the greater attention to usage during the second half of the 18th century, the spoken language becomes the focus of attention, too. After proscribing the use of double negation and providing a series of examples, Kirkby observes: "And yet these are all found to be common Expressions in Conversation" (1746: 126–127). Webster (1784) also looked at other registers and dialects (Finegan 1980: 39), but merely to reject deviant usage, as with the rule for *shall/will* (Tieken 1985: 129). This attitude, however, was part of his ideal of a single, national language for the new America. Finegan refers to Webster's concern over the language of immigrants who might "retain their respective peculiarities of speaking; and [...] may imperceptibly corrupt the national language" (Webster 1789: 19).

One important adherent of what Baugh and Cable refer to as the doctrine of usage was Priestley (1761). Priestley may have picked up his concern with usage from Kirkby (1746), who was possibly one of his teachers (Tieken 1992, 168) – both in any case adopt the same, as yet unusual division of parts of speech. In contrast to Campbell, who defined 'good' usage without keeping to his own principles (Baugh & Cable 1993: 279), Priestley did live up to them, and strictly so, too (1993: 279–280).

In his opposition to the idea of an Academy, Priestley shows himself averse from the imposition of a linguistic norm. The belief in "custom" providing the norm explains Priestley's disapproval of Lowth (Swiggers 1994: 34). What the two men did have in common, like most other 18th-century grammarians, was their desire to rid the language of unwanted variants (Percy 1997: 132). It is only their approaches in which they differed. Priestley, as a scientist, believed that language first had to be observed before it could be described (Swiggers 1994: 35). In this respect, he was closer to Wallis than to any of his predecessors.

Priestley's adherence to the principle of usage may have warned off buyers looking for a more traditional approach to grammar – even so, his grammar reached nine editions until 1798, and two reprints (1826, 1833). The grammar never made it to the United States, unlike those by Ash, Lowth and Buchanan; this seems due to the fact that at the time Americans strove to improve their status by improving their language (Tieken 1996a: 15). In this aim they sooner needed a normative, prescriptive grammar than one which, by its tolerance of actual usage, they must have feared might perpetuate errors. This attitude also explains Murray's popularity thirty years later.

Baugh and Cable (1993: 279) claim that Priestley stood alone in his "unwavering loyalty to usage", but Subbiondo (1975: 36) argues that for Ward (1765) "custom" was important, too. Ward's grammar consists of two parts, "the one SPECULATIVE, being an Attempt to investigate proper Principles" and "the other PRACTICAL, containing Definitions and Rules deduced from the Principles, and illustrated by a Variety of Examples from the most approved Writers" (title-page). The first part of the grammar belongs to the tradition of the speculative grammar, adherents of which, such as James Harris (1709–1780), Lord Monboddo (1714–1799) and James Beattie (1735–1803), were concerned with the nature and origin of language. The "Practical" part of Ward's grammar deals with the usual subjects: orthography, etymology, syntax and prosody (Ward 1765: 297). The book was meant for use in schools, and it offers rhymes – usually poorly written – to facilitate memorising the rules of grammar. The use of rhymes to his end was, as far as I know, unique, and it shows that Ward had the interests of his reading public very much at heart. Alston (1965) records seven editions and reprints of the work, which shows that the grammar enjoyed a moderate success. Despite the rhymes, the grammar seems to have been too learned to make it truly popular.

### 6.2. The language of women

In any grammar which claimed to take usage into account, whether written or spoken, prose or verse, it was, as Leonard (1929: 169) observes, the language of gentlemen only: among the many authors referred to by the grammarians as authoritative there is not a single woman. Women did write at the time, and not only literature: there are, to mention a few of the more outstanding examples, Elisabeth Elstob (1683–1756), who wrote a grammar of Old English, the female grammarians discussed above, Lady Mary Wortley Montagu (1689–1762), who published a political journal, Sarah Fielding (1710–1768), who besides writing novels published a translation from Xenophon, Hannah More (1745–1833), who is recorded as "poet, playwright and religious writer" (*Oxford Guide to British Women Writers* 1993, 'More'), and the Bluestocking women, who were widely respected by men and women alike. Even so, women's writings are neither held up as examples of good usage in the grammars, nor (with only a few exceptions) criticised for any linguistic mistakes they might have made (Tieken 1990: 492; Sundby et al. 1991: 35–37).

Women's language was, however, the subject of criticism outside the grammars. Thus, Horace Walpole (1717–1797) called pronominal mistakes as in *they don't mind you and I* a "female inaccuracy" (Leonard 1929: 188). The grammatical problem in question was a recurrent subject in the grammars of the time (cf. Leonard 1929: 262). My analysis of a number of 18th-century writers, male and female, revealed the inaccuracy of Walpole's observation (Tieken 1994: 219–223). What his comment does illustrate is the androcentricity of the linguistic norm of the period: the language of men constituted the only acceptable norm of usage. The same attitude gave rise to the rule that the pronoun *he* is to be used when the sex of the antecedent is unknown. This rule, which was even passed by Act of Parliament in 1850 (Bodine 1975: 135), was first formulated by Kirkby (1746: 167), though he had actually copied it from Fisher (Tieken 1992: 167). Bodine (1975: 131–133) demonstrated that singular *they* was current at the time as well. The selection of either *he* or *they* as a sex-indefinite pronoun would have violated a concord requirement, of gender in the case of *he* and of number in the case of *they*. In view of the then current norm of correct usage such an option would never even have been considered. Today, singular *they* is gaining ground, despite usage guides like Gowers (1973: 197) advising "the official writer" to use either *he or she* or *he* and "not to be tempted by the greater convenience of [singular *they*]".

## 7. Effectiveness of prescriptive grammar

The preference among many speakers today of singular *they* to sex-indefinite *he* raises the question of the effectiveness of prescriptive grammar. Many of the items tested by Mittins et al. (1970) were also subject to variation during the 18th century. Two hundred years of prescriptivism has led to the creation of a clear sense of what standard English entails – or should entail. Thus, speakers of standard English know it is 'wrong' to end a sentence with a preposition, that it should be *whom* not *who* in direct object position and that the pronoun *I* should not follow a preposition like *between*. Mistakes in these matters betray the speaker's lack of education. In the importance attached to the use of "correct" grammar we see the development of what Milroy and Milroy call "the ideology of standardisation", the belief that the standard consists of "a set of abstract norms to which actual usage may conform to a greater or lesser extent" (1985: 23). In reality this ideology reflects an imperfect understanding of how language works, in that rules of grammar are believed to apply irrespective of the medium (speech or writing) or the formality of the utterance. As different media, speech and writing each range stylistically from formal to informal, each style being characterised by a different set of grammatical rules. Thus, in formal written utterances a preposition may not occur at the end of a sentence, and *whom* is obligatory in direct object position. In informal spoken utterances, these rules may be relaxed, so that *he is older than me* is more appropriate than *he is older than I*. Even *between you and I* might not be wholly out of place: Honey (1995: 5) has shown that this usage is current even among supposedly authoritative speakers like Mrs. Thatcher.

The ideology of the standard has created language guardians who see it as their duty to keep the standard alive and well. One way in which such purists express their concern for the state of the language is by writing to the media to complain about a particular linguistic mistake they encountered. The comments sent to the BBC led Burchfield to compile a booklet for the use of broadcasters (Ilson 1985: 168). The booklet deals with usage problems in the field of pronunciation, vocabulary and grammar. Despite the fact that many of these usage problems can be traced to the 18th century, attitudes to these problems have to some extent changed since then. Even in the 18th century Webster came to accept *who* for *whom* in object position between the publication of his two works on the English language in 1784 and 1789 (Finegan 1980: 41). In their survey of user attitudes conducted thirty years ago, Mittins et al. (1970) note an increased acceptance rate, irrespective of the style of the utterance, of most of the items investigated. Nevertheless, Honey's (1995) article, which showed that *between you and I* is now very common, stirred up a lot of criticism in the national press. This indicates that the ideology of the standard is still very much alive today.

While prescriptive writing has contributed to the creation of a standard ideology, it has also had its effect by retarding linguistic change. The distinction between subject and object pronominals might have blurred even further if it had not been for the insistence of grammarians and usage guides upon correct application of the original rules (Tieken 1994: 234).

## 8. Conclusion

According to Sundby et al., the fact that prescriptivism is still flourishing in Britain and the United States has "helped normative grammar to assert itself as a serious object of study" (1991: 1). Twenty years ago, Pullum (1974) still had to defend his interest in Lowth by demonstrating that his neglect was due to the modern approach of grammar as a science, a requirement Lowth's grammar could not meet. Similarly, Subbiondo (1975) had to argue that Ward was worthy of study because he could be interpreted as a precursor of modern scientific views on language. Recent publications such as Vorlat (1979), Finegan (1980), Michael (1987), Sundby et al. (1991), Percy (1994), and Tieken (1996) suggest that the tide has turned and that normative grammar can be studied as a subject in its own right.

In 1975, Subbiondo wrote that "a better understanding of the notion of prescriptivism" is needed (1975: 42). He worked within a framework which designates grammars as either prescriptive, which does not reflect a scientific approach to grammar, or descriptive, which does. Vorlat (1979) proposed a threefold distinction instead, into descriptive, normative and prescriptive grammars, though this distinction does not quite work either, as it is often impossible to place the 17th- and

18th-century grammars discussed into a single category. Instead, the grammars tend to be either more descriptive or less so, but they are usually normative irrespective of their rather more or less descriptive nature. Thus, Jonson (1640) and Wallis (1653) are both descriptive and yet have a norm of standard English as their basis which is determined by the language of the educated classes in Jonson's case and of non-dialect speakers in Wallis's case. In time, grammars become more prescriptive due to the greater attention to usage rather than relying on an artificial doctrine of correctness which marks off the grammars produced during the first half of the 18th from those of the second half: by then grammarians have become aware of a discrepancy between the rules of grammar — mostly matters of syntax, and of concord at that — and actual usage.

The development of prescriptive grammar marks the final stage in the standardisation process of the English language. The rules having been formulated, they subsequently had to be adhered to. By looking at actual usage the grammarians saw that the rules of grammar were frequently broken; Lowth cited usage errors in order to press home the need for a grammar like his own. Around the same time we see the birth of usage guides like Baker (1770) which could be consulted in order to learn to avoid grammatical pitfalls. The popularity of Murray's grammars (1795, 1797) may be explained by the need for a reference grammar which could be used in school but also at home by adults to improve their grammar — and their social status. Murray's grammar similarly served an important purpose abroad in the study of English as a second language. It cannot therefore be said that Murray's prescriptivism came late in the day. It was precisely what people wanted at a time when correctness of language and social class membership were closely linked and when English had begun to develop as a world language. Nor was Murray alone responsible for perpetuating prescriptivism as such, as has been shown by Michael (1991). Murray's prescriptivism and that of his 18th- and 19th-century fellow grammarians was a natural consequence of the standardisation process affecting the English language. Once the language had been codified, the prescription stage followed. And as a living language can never be fixed to such an extent as to become a standard in the strictest sense of the word, the prescription stage, and with it prescriptive writings such as handbooks or usage guides, will be there to stay.

## 9. Bibliography


Alston, R. C. 1965. *A Bibliography of the English Language from the Invention of Printing to the Year 1800.* Vol. 1. Leeds: Arnold and Son.

—, ed. 1974. *English Linguistics 1500—1800.* Menston: Scolar Press.

Austin, Frances. 1996. "Lindley Murray's 'little code of elementary instruction'". Tieken 1996. 45—61.

Baugh, Albert C., & Thomas Cable. 1993 [1951]. *A History of the English Language.* 4th ed. London: Routledge.

Bodine, Ann. 1975. "Androcentrism in Prescriptive Grammar: Singular 'they', sex-indefinite 'he', and 'he or she'". *Language in Society* 4.129—146.

Chalker, Sylvia, & Edmund Weiner. 1994. *The Oxford Dictionary of English Grammar.* Oxford: Clarendon Press.

Clifford, James L. 1955. *Young Samuel Johnson.* London etc.: Heinemann.

Crystal, David. 1988. *The English Language.* London: Penguin.

*DNB: The Compact Edition of the Dictionary of National Biography.* London: Oxford Univ. Press.

Finegan, Edward. 1980. *Attitudes toward English Usage.* New York & London: Teachers College Press.

Fowler, H. W. 1965. *A Dictionary of Modern English Usage.* 2nd ed. Oxford: Oxford Univ. Press.

Gowers, Sir Ernest. 1954. *The Complete Plain Words.* Harmondsworth: Penguin. (1973; repr. 1976.)

Honey, John. 1995. "A New Rule for the Queen and I?". *English Today* 11.3—8.

Ilson, Robert F. 1985. "Usage Problems in British and American English". *The English Language Today* ed. by Sydney Greenbaum. Oxford etc.: Pergamon Press. 166—182.

Lehnert, Martin, 1937/38. "Die Abhängigkeit frühneuenglischer Grammatiken". *Englische Studien* 72.192—206.

Leonard, S. A. 1929. *The Doctrine of Correctness in English Usage, 1700—1800.* Madison: Univ. of Wisconsin.

Michael, Ian. 1970. *English Grammatical Categories and the Tradition to 1800.* Cambridge: Cambridge Univ. Press.

—. 1987. *The Teaching of English: From the sixteenth century to 1870.* Cambridge: Cambridge Univ. Press.

–. 1991. "More than Enough English Grammars". *English Traditional Grammars* ed. by Gerhard Leitner 11–26. Amsterdam & Philadelphia: Benjamins.

Milroy, James, & Lesley Milroy. 1985. *Authority in Language: Investigating language prescription and standardisation.* London: Routledge & Kegan Paul.

Mittins, W. H., Mary Salu, Mary Edminson & Sheila Coyne. 1970. *Attitudes to English Usage.* London: Oxford Univ. Press. (Repr. 1975.)

Monaghan, Charles. 1996. "Lindley Murray, American". Tieken 1996. 27–43.

Monaghan, E. Jennifer. 1983. *A Common Heritage. Noah Webster's blue-back speller.* Hamden, Conn.: Archon Books.

Nagashima, Daisuke. 1968. "Mutual Debt between Johnson and Lowth: A contribution to the history of English grammar". *Studies in English Literature* (Japan) 44.221–232.

Noordegraaf, Jan. 1994. "Women and Grammar: The case of Johanna Corleva". *Histoire Epistémologie Langage* 16.169–190.

*OCEL: The Oxford Companion to the English Language* ed. by Tom McArthur. 1992. Oxford & New York: Oxford Univ. Press.

Osselton, N. E. 1982. "Ben Jonson's Status as a Grammarian". *DQR* 12.205–212.

–. 1995. *Chosen Words: Past and present problems for dictionary makers.* Exeter: Univ. of Exeter Press.

*The Oxford Guide to British Women Writers* ed. by Joanne Shattock. 1993. Oxford & New York: Oxford Univ. Press.

Percy, Carol. 1994. "Paradigms for their Sex? Women's grammars in late eighteenth-century England". *Histoire epistémologie langage* 16.121–141.

–. 1997. "Paradigms Lost: Bishop Lowth and the 'poetic dialect' in his English Grammar". *Neophilologus* 81.129–144.

Peters, Hans. 1996. "Early Modern English *who*: Discourse function and standardization". *NOWELE* 27.67–135.

Pullum, G. K. 1974. "Lowth's Grammar: A reevaluation". *Linguistics* 137.63–78.

Simon, John. 1980. *Paradigms Lost.* Harmondsworth: Penguin.

Sledd, James H., & Gwin J. Kolb. 1955. *Dr. Johnson's Dictionary.* Chicago: Univ. of Chicago Press.

Stein, Dieter, & Ingrid Tieken-Boon van Ostade, eds. 1994. *Towards a Standard Language 1600–1800.* Berlin & New York: Mouton de Gruyter.

Subbiondo, Joseph L. 1975. "William Ward and the Doctrine of Correctness'". *Journal of English Linguistics* 9.36–46.

–. 1992. "John Wallis' *Grammatica Linguae Anglicanae* (1653): The new science and English grammar". *Diversions of Galway. Papers on the History of Linguistics* ed. by Anders Ahlqvist. Amsterdam & Philadelphia: Benjamins. 183–190.

Sundby, Bertil, Anne Kari Bjørge & Kari E. Haugland. 1991. *A Dictionary of English Normative Grammar 1700–1800.* Amsterdam: Benjamins.

Swiggers, Pierre. 1994. "Joseph Priestley's Approach to Grammatical Categorization and Linguistic Diversity". *Perspectives on English* ed. by Keith Carlon, Kristin Davidse & Brygida Rudzka-Ostyn, 34–53. Leuven: Peeters.

Tieken-Boon van Ostade, Ingrid. 1982. "Double Negation in the Eighteenth Century". *Neophilologus* 61.278–285.

–. 1985. "'I Will Be Drowned and No Man Shall Save Me': The conventional rules for *shall* and *will* in eighteenth-century English grammars". *English Studies* 66.123–142.

–. 1987. *The Auxiliary Do in Eighteenth-Century English: A sociohistorical-linguistic approach.* Dordrecht: Foris.

–. 1990. "Exemplification in Eighteenth-Century English Grammars". *Papers from the 5th International Conference on English Historical Linguistics* ed. by Sylvia Adamson, Vivien Law, Nigel Vincent & Susan Wright. Amsterdam & Philadelphia: Benjamins. 481–496.

–. 1992. "John Kirkby and *The Practice of Speaking and Writing English:* Identification of a manuscript". *Leeds Studies in English* n. s. 23.157–179.

–. 1994. "Standard and Non-Standard Pronominal Usage in English, with Special Reference to the Eighteenth Century". Stein & Tieken. 1994. 217–242.

–, ed. 1996. *Two Hundred Years of Lindley Murray.* Münster: Nodus.

–. 1996a. "Two Hundred Years of Lindley Murray: An introduction". Tieken 1996. 9–25.

–. 1996b. "Lindley Murray and the Concept of Plagiarism". Tieken 1996. 81–95.

Tierney, James, E. ed. 1988. *The Correspondence of Robert Dodsley (1733–1764).* Cambridge etc.: Cambridge Univ. Press.

Vorlat, Emma. 1959. "The Sources of Lindley Murray's 'The English Grammar'". *Leuvense Bijdragen* 48.108–25.

–. 1975. *The Development of English Grammatical Theory, 1586–1737.* Leuven: Univ. Press.

–. 1979. "Criteria of Grammaticalness in 16th and 17th-Century English Grammar". *Leuvense Bijdragen* 68.129–140.

–. 1996. "Lindley Murray's Prescriptive Canon". Tieken 1996. 163–182.

Wales, Katie. 1996. "'With Apologies to Lindley Murray': The narrative method of the 'Eumaeus' episode in *Ulysses*". Tieken 1996. 207–216.

Wright, Susan. 1994. "The Critic and the Grammarians: Joseph Addison and the prescriptivists". Stein & Tieken 1994. 243–284.

*Ingrid Tieken-Boon van Ostade, Leiden (The Netherlands)*

# 119. Normative studies in the Scandinavian countries

1. Introduction
2. The 18th century
3. The 19th century
4. The 20th century
5. Bibliography

## 1. Introduction

A prominent part of linguistic studies and linguistic debate after the Renaissance in Denmark and Sweden was devoted to orthography and the standardization of the two written languages of Denmark and Sweden. The standardization of the other Scandinavian languages (Faroese, Finnish, Icelandic and Norwegian) first started in the 19th century. The standardization of the Saami language did not start until the 20th century. Some of the basic problems of language standardization in Scandinavia in this period were:

- how to construct a literary norm for a community with many different dialects with equal social and political status
- how to write sounds that had no orthographic correspondence in the Latin alphabet.

The main question was, however, to what extent the orthography should reflect or correspond to the spoken language and this problem was in many cases linked to both theological aspects (to preserve the orthography of the Bible) and practical pedagogical ones (how to make it easier for people to master writing and reading). Another important point was an increasing purist nationalistic attitude concerning both the use and the spelling of loan-words.

Until 1800 the discussion concerning language norms and standardized orthographies was mainly the province of school teachers and independent intellectuals. Except for Sweden, it was not until the end of the 19th and early 20th century that there were official organizations (academies, committees, etc.) devoted to language planning in the Scandinavian countries.

## 2. The 18th century

### 2.1. Danish

At the end of the 17th century, the two leading Danish grammarians Peder Syv (1631–1702) and Erik Pontoppidan (1616–1678), started the tradition of Danish normative studies. They advocated a moderate application of Julius Cæsar Scaliger's rule that one should write as one speaks. In addition to advocating orthographic reforms, Syv was interested in purifying the vernacular by ridding it of foreign loans, particularly items originating from French and Latin.

One area of linguistic purification with which both Syv and Pontoppidan were preoccupied was that of grammatical terminology. They both suggested a native terminology. Almost all of their terms are translations from Latin, some of which have been clearly mediated by way of German.

The first public orthographic debate in Denmark was set in motion by Henrik Gerner (1629–1700) in his *Orthographia Danica* (Gerner 1678). Indirectly he attacked the spelling reforms proposed by his personal friend and scholarly opponent, Peder Syv. Gerner wanted nothing to do with the spoken language, insisting instead that orthographic norms should be based on previously established written usage, even at the expense of uniformity. After a period of silence in Denmark, orthographic questions were taken up again by Peder Schulz (ca. 1691–1773) whose discussion of the orthography of the vernacular (Schulz 1724) was purposely written so that it could be understood by the common man. He was interested in bringing the written language closer to the spoken language, and his ideas concerning the correct orthography for Danish differed only slightly from those of Pontoppidan and Syv.

A renewed orthographic debate began when Niels von Hauen (1709–1777) published a brief treatise on orthography along with a spelling dictionary (Hauen 1741). His views on questions like refraining from the use of initial capital letters for nouns and the banning of plural verbal forms provoked an intensive discussion.

### 2.2. Swedish

A heated discussion about the proper way of spelling Swedish started in the last decades of the 17th century and continued until the first decades of the 20th century. The conservative line wanted to maintain spellings which had been more or less established, e. g. the abundant use of *ch* (still existing in *och*, "and")

and the use of *f* and *fv* for *v* in final and medial word positions, respectively.

The most vehement defender of the older spelling was the bishop Jesper Swedberg (1653–1735) who wanted to restore the language of the first Bible translation. In Swedberg (1716) he argued for a conservative and purist attitude. As an example of his argumentation, we can take one of his objections to writing long vowels as double vowels: "The Hebrews and Greeks whose languages the Holy Spirit used to compose our bliss, the holy Bible, do not know double vowels." (Swedberg 1716: 59)

Abraham Sahlstedt (1716–1776) worked as a secretary in the state archives, but after 1756 he was not expected to do any work but "to publish useful books". Following the French ideas about language normalization taking the language spoken by educated people as the norm, he played an important role in the standardization of Swedish both through his dictionary (Sahlstedt 1773) and his grammar (Sahlstedt 1769) which only covers orthography and morphology. Both the dictionary and the grammar were officially accepted by the Royal Academy of Sciences.

Sven Hof (1703–1786) was a lector and partly rector at a high school who strongly advocated a phonological orthography: "Let the spelling as closely as possible follow a correct Swedish pronunciation" (Hof 1753: 263) and "Write the words according to correct pronunciation" (Hof 1753: 254). Hof also wanted a grammar free from the disturbing influence of Latin and he had no interest in, or respect for, etymological and diachronic aspects. His main preoccupation was with the modern language.

In 1786 the Swedish Academy was founded and it was soon to take part in the discussion of spelling through various contributions by its members.

## 3. The 19th century

The position of orthography and the needs to regulate orthography were very different concerning the new literary languages of Finland and Norway as well as Faroese and Icelandic on the one hand, and the well established literary languages of Denmark and Sweden on the other.

### 3.1. Danish

Although there was great interest in questions of orthography on the part of a number of Danish grammarians, educators, and editors during this period, most of what was produced had no real influence on the written standard.

Rasmus Rask (1787–1832) attempted to formulate what he termed a scientific orthography (Rask 1826). The basis for Rask's orthography was the pronunciation of educated speakers of the language, which meant, in principle, that there should be only one single letter for each individual sound. Where the vowels were concerned he set up a system of 10 vowels, each with its own corresponding letter, including *å* for *aa*, and he distinguished between an open *ö* and a closed *ø*. He insisted that there were no diphthongs and wrote *v* for *u* in words like *Evropa* and *j* for *i* (or *y*) in words like *Vej* "road"; furthermore, he saw no need to write long vowels with a double vowel as long as this did not result in ambiguity. Otherwise he recommended the use of diacritics to distinguish vowel length (*Dûg* "tablecloth": *Dug* "dew"). Like many of his predecessors, he found the letters *c*, *q*, *x* and *z* superfluous.

Those in more official positions completely rejected Rask's system, and when Rask refused to change the orthography in his own works, The Academy of Science, The Danish Society and The Scandinavian Literary Society all refused to publish his works.

Some years later Niels Matthias Petersen (1791–1862), from 1845 the first appointed professor of Scandinavian languages in Copenhagen, proposed his own orthography based on Rask's ideas, but influenced by the pan-Scandinavian movement. His orthography, often referred to as the Rask–N. M. Petersen orthography, deviated from Rask's original proposal only on minor points. It won fairly widespread acceptance, and was adopted in pro-Scandinavian circles and by educators and scholars. When Johan Ludvig Madvig (1804–1886), as Minister of Education, was required to take a stance on the use of the new orthography in the schools, he was conservative on some points and accepted reform with respect to others. As a result, there was confusion in the schools as to whether certain reforms were acceptable or not, but no immediate steps were taken to remedy this problem.

In the 1860s many people were interested in a greater uniformity in the orthography of the two Scandinavian languages (Danish and Dano-Norwegian were considered as one language). A meeting was held for this purpose in Stockholm in 1869, and the result for

Danish was not too far from the Rask-N. M. Petersen orthography. The Stockholm meeting was widely publicized, and several famous authors such as Ibsen quickly announced that they would follow its recommendations.

A spelling dictionary was quickly produced adhering precisely to the rules set down at the meeting. With the printing of this dictionary, however, the reforms became extremely visible. The dictionary was a provocation to some and an aid to others. Under pressure from those who advocated reform, a government commission was appointed to arrive at official rules for spelling, which it issued in 1888.

Although there was a strong opposition to this official language reform, it could not persuade the government to abandon its reforms, which after a proclamation of 1889 were to be followed in the schools.

The result of this first official orthography for Danish resembled Rask's to a great extent. Capital letters were retained in nouns, but the letter *å* and Rask's extra *ö*-sound were not included. With a few exceptions, the plural forms of verbs were also retained, not being abolished until a proclamation of 1902, which also did away with the plural forms of participles after *være* and *blive*.

The government also commissioned an official spelling dictionary, which appeared in 1891.

### 3.2. Faroese

Venceslaus Ulricus Hammershaimb (1819–1909) is considered the founder of the Faroese literary language. Hammershaimb (1854) is a grammar of Faroese covering both the phonology and morphology, and including a short syntax. Hammershaimb's grammar was important for the standardization of Faroese in that it introduced a relatively uniform Faroese orthography, based in part on Old Norse. Jens Christian Svabo (1746–1824), who was the first to record Faroese oral literature, used a spelling which was quite orthophonic. Hammershaimb was originally in favor of such a solution too, but N. M. Petersen (cf. above) persuaded him to alter the orthography in the direction of Old Norse. Petersen's main argument, besides an aesthetic one, was to preserve the basic unity of the Scandinavian languages by letting the literary languages reflect the older language as much as possible.

The resulting orthography made Faroese rather easy to read for other Scandinavians, but it created a number of orthographic problems for the Faroese children. Owing to the great dialectal diversity of the Faroe Islands, not the least in the phonology, this was probably the only possible solution.

### 3.3. Finnish

Gustav Renvall (1781–1841), who was influential in many respects on Finnish linguistics, as a teacher as well as in official positions, laid down several fundamental principles for Finnish orthography in his insightful work, written in Latin, from 1810–1811:

> All letters that do not represent a specific sound in the language to which they are transferred should immediately be excluded from it. On the other hand, no sound which is distinct from the others should lack its own letter. (Renvall 1810: 4)

When Reinhold von Becker (1788–1858) introduced a few eastern dialect elements and excluded a number of Swedishisms in his grammar of Finnish (1824), he ignited a debate concerning the morphological and orthographic normalization of the Finnish literary language. This fiery discussion came to be known in Finnish linguistics as the 'Dialect Battle' (*murteiden taistelu*) and it lasted until the 1850s. Renvall was very much in favour of a standard based purely on West Finnish, and in 1840 he published a Finnish grammar based on the Western dialects. By then, however, the matter had already been settled. The final solution for a unified literary language was given in Lönnrot's publication of the national poem *Kalevala* in 1835 in which the orthography is based on the western dialects, but which is also full of words and grammatical features from the eastern dialects. From that time on, there were only minor controversies regarding Finnish orthography.

Volmari Kilpinen [= Wolmar Styrbjörn Schöldt] (1810–1893) proposed a number of orthographic changes in Finnish, like writing a long vowel not as a sequence of two vowels, but as a single vowel with a circumflex, e. g. *â* = *aa*, *ê* = *ee*, etc., and writing *æ* and *œ* instead *ä* and *ö*. The old orthography was, however, too well established to be changed. By 1860 or so, Finnish orthography basically had the appearance it has today.

Volmari Kilpinen and Elias Lönnrot (1802–1884) were the most influential creators of neologisms in Finnish, having both invented several thousand words that are in common use today. Their favorite method was to use the rich derivative and compounding capabilities of Finnish or coining the new words.

In the course of the stabilization of Standard Finnish, there also developed towards the end of the 1800s a tradition of strict normativity which was to dominate the use and teaching of Finnish for decades.

### 3.4. Icelandic

The first attempt to give a normative survey of Icelandic orthography is Jónsson (1856) written by the later pastor Magnús Jónsson (1828–1901). His orthographic principles were according to the author based on Gíslason (1846). A more extensive treatment of the same matter is Friðriksson (1859) which is also based on Konrað Gíslason's (1808–1891) works. Gíslason himself had first been in favor of a more phonetically oriented orthography, but had later on changed his mind and advocated a spelling closer to the way older stages of the languages were written.

An interesting feature of Icelandic language norms is a strong lexical purism, but also a cultivation of morphological archaisms which are quite uncommon. This resulted in the actual reintroduction of older and outdated inflectional forms and even complete paradigms into the modern language. The main instigator of the reintroduction of such morphological archaisms was Konrað Gíslason, professor of Scandinavian languages in Copenhagen 1862–1886.

### 3.6. Norwegian

The orthographic debate in Norway in the 19th century was completely focus on the two new emerging literary languages: *landsmål* (later *nynorsk*) and *riksmål* (later *bokmål*) which since 1885 have both been official literary languages with equal status. But the intense and bitter orthographic debate that is so characteristic of Norway in the 20th century was mostly absent in the 19th century.

When Ivar Aasen (1813–1896) established his norm for *landsmål*, he was attacked for not placing it closer to Old Norse and not selecting the most archaic dialect forms. However, he undoubtedly made a wise choice in keeping the language much closer to a general consensus of the living dialects. The natural growth of *landsmål* as a written language and a school language took place without the strong engagement of either linguists or politicians. It was not until the end of the century that the signs of the coming linguistic dispute became visible.

The development of *riksmaal* as a literary language distinct from Danish took place in a similar natural way and was strengthened by the strong position of Norwegian literature in *riksmål* in the last part of the century (Henrik Ibsen, Bjørnstjerne Bjørnson, etc.). The orthographic characteristics of *riksmål* – distinct from Danish – were mainly developed through the work of Knud Knudsen (1812–1895). Knudsen was not so much interested in linguistics as in pedagogy, and his main aim with his spelling reforms which were widely accepted was to facilitate the task of the pupils in learning to write the vernacular. His main principle advocated already in Knudsen (1845) was that the orthography should be based on "the most common pronunciation of the words in the mouth of educated people." He wanted, for example, to replace *b*, *d*, and *g* in the Danish orthography in cases in which the Norwegians pronounced unvoiced stops by *p*, *t*, and *k* and to drop letters that were no longer pronounced.

### 3.7. Swedish

The publication of 'The treatise of the Swedish Academy concerning Swedish orthography' *(Svenska Akademiens Afhandling om svenska stafsättet)* (Leopold 1801) marks the opening of a new interest in the Swedish language.

The preface makes it clear that the Swedish Academy sided with the French Academy in having good authors as the ideal and norm rather than the usage of the people. It states that grammarians and lexicographers cannot institute laws and rules, only collect examples, and formulate the rules on the basis of the examples.

As expected, the book met with some criticism and a long debate followed. There were especially three points on which the discussion focused:

(a) The etymological principle which has as the basic tenet that the spelling of morphemes should change as little as possible and readily supersede pronunciation.
(b) The use of gemination of consonants in the spelling which has been used in order to mark a long consonant and distinguish, for example, *tal* "speech" from *tall*, "fir". The vowel is long in the first

word and short in the second. The natural orthographic rule would then be to spell long (or geminated) consonants by doubling the consonant disregarding the length of the vowel in the spelling. Leopold decided to use double consonant in all these cases except where the consonant is *n* or *m* and this rule is on the whole still followed in Modern Swedish.

(c) The spelling of loanwords by which the academy recommended that the ending *-eur* as in *directeur* "director" be rendered by *-ör* and that *lieutenant* "lieutenant" was rendered by *löjtnant*, although those who moved in French circles found it abominable.

Due to Leopold's good intuition and common sense most of his proposals have survived. The public seems to be willing to accept a number of exceptions and irregularities and disregard for principles.

## 4. The 20th century

In the 20th century governmental committees and institutions have gradually taken over the field. With the exception of Norway, there have been few significant orthographic or morphological changes in the standard literary languages of Scandinavia, just minor orthographic changes. In Norway, both of the two official languages underwent numerous and partly profound orthographic and morphological changes in their norms. The changes in the official rules for orthography which were all instigated and supervised by the government took place in 1901 (*landsmål/nynorsk*), 1907 (*riksmål/bokmål*), 1910 (*landsmål/nynorsk*), 1917 (both languages), 1938 (both languages) and 1959 (both languages). Even today 'The Norwegian Language Council' (*Norsk Språkråd*) is continually proposing new smaller changes in the orthography of both of the two official norms.

In Finland language planning has in this century to a large degree focused on the relationship between Finnish and Swedish, especially the position and rights of Swedish as a minority language. The cultivation of the Finnish standard language has largely followed the very normative and conservative attitude dominant already in the 19th century.

In the 20th century, the question of standardizing the Saami language has also become prominent. The Saami language is spoken in various variants (dialects and languages) in Norway, Finland, Sweden, and Russia. There existed nomerous orthographies, some dating back to the early 19th century, based on dialectal as well as political criteria. There have been numerous attempts at standardizing the orthography on a national or dialectal area level. In 1979 a norm for writing standard northern Saami was accepted in Finland, Norway, and Sweden.

A main problem for all the Scandinavian languages in the second part of the 20th century has been the great number of loanwords from English, and how to spell them or how to replace them by indigenous words.

## 5. Bibliography


Becker, Reinhold von. 1824. *Finsk grammatik.* Åbo. Bibel-sällskapets tryckeri.

Friðriksson, Halldór Kr. 1859. *Íslenzkar rjettritunarreglur.* Reykjavík: Gefnar út af Hinu íslenzka bókmentafjelagi.

Gerner. Henrich Thomaesøn. 1678. *Orthographia Danica eller Det Danske Sprogs Skrifvericktighed.* Kiøbenhaffn: Christian Geertsøns Boghandler.

Gíslason, Konrád. 1846. *Um frum-parta íslenzkrar túngu í fornöld.* Kaupmannahöfn: Á kostnað Hins íslenzka bókmenntafjelags.

Hammershaimb, V. U. 1854. Færøisk Sproglære. *Annaler for nordisk Oldkyndighed og Historie. Udgivne af Det kongelige nordiske Oldskrifts-selskab.* 1854: 223–316. Kjöbenhavn: J. D. Qvist.

Hauen, Niels von. 1741a. *Et lidet orthographisk Lexicon eller Ord-Bog.* Kjœbenhavn: Johan Christoph Groth.

Hof, Sven. 1753. *Swänska Språkets Rätta Skrifsätt Med Sina Bevis Föreställt Och till Kongl. Swänska Wettenskaps Academien Framgifwit.* Stockholm: Jacob Merkell.

Jónsson, Magnús. 1856. *Stuttur leiðarvísir fyrir alpýðu til pess að skrifa íslenzku rjett og greinilega.* Reykjavík.

Kilpinen, V. 1857. "Sananen Suomen kilen ulkomuodosta, sanoja." *Suomi* 16: 81–84.

[Leopold, C. G. af,] 1801. *Svenska Akademiens Afhandling om svenska stafsättet.* Svenska Akademiens Handlinghra Ifrån 1796. I. Stockholm.

Rask, Rasmus Kristian. 1826. *Forsøg til en videnskabelig dansk Retskrivningslære.* Kjøbenhavn.

Renvall, Gustavus. 1810–11. I–II. *De orthoëpia et orthographia linguæ Fennicæ.* Aboæ. Typis Franckellianis.

Sahlstedt, Abraham. 1769. *Svensk grammatik.* Upsala: Johan Edman.

–. 1773. *Svensk ordbok Med Latinsk Uttolkning/ Dictionarium Svecicum Cum interpretatione Latina.* Stockholm. Carl Stolpe.

[Schulz, Peder.] 1724. *Danskens Skriverigtighed.* Kjøbenhavn: Povel Joh, Phoenixbergs Bogtrykkeri.

Swedberg, Jesper. 1716. *Shibboleth. Swenska Språkets Rycht och Richtighet. Skara. Tryckt hos sal. Kiellbergs Änckia.*

*Even Hordhaugen, Oslo (Norway)*

# 120. Normative studies in the Low Countries

1. Introduction
2. Towards a Dutch Trivium: The 16th and 17th centuries
3. The 18th century
4. The 19th century: The codification of written Standard Dutch
5. The 20th century
6. Towards the end of the standard language?
7. Bibliography

## 1. Introduction

Of the Dutch national language (*Nederlands*), *Algemeen Beschaafd Nederlands* (*ABN*, 'General Cultured Dutch') is the standard version. It has taken several centuries to reach its present form; it may be noted that grammarians have played a crucial role in this process of standardisation. Without a host of language teachers and their prescriptive works, sometimes even written at the behest of the Dutch government, the constitution of an elaborate standard language would not have been possible. Note that in this contribution the term 'Dutch' will be used to refer to the language that has become standard in both the Netherlands and the northern part of Belgium.

General overviews of both the external and internal history of Dutch are given in de Vooys 1970, van der Wal 1992 [$^2$1994] and van den Toorn et al. 1997 (with much recent literature). Although written in a more popular fashion, de Vries et al. 1993 also provides many pertinent references. The history of linguistics, including lexicography, is presented in Bakker & Dibbets 1997, Noordegraaf, Versteegh & Koerner 1992 being its English counterpart and updated to a certain extent. Van der Wal 1995 presents an excellent description of the process of language regulation around 1650. Gillaerts 1989 gives, among other things, a concise discussion of language norms and the authority of Dutch dictionaries. Van Bree & van Santen 1996 is a recent collection of papers on various aspects of language standardisation.

In addition, a search under the heading 'normatieve studies' in the current multivolume *Bibliografie van de Nederlandse taal- en literatuurwetenschap* (*BNTL*, Bibliography of Dutch linguistic and literary studies), which can nowadays also be consulted on-line in both an English and a Dutch version, may yield a host of valuable references concerning language standardisation in the Netherlands and Flanders. Not only studies of a general character are listed, but also works on spelling and pronunciation, morphology, syntax and the correct use of various words. The historical dimension of normative linguistics is dealt with in a separate section of the *BNTL*.

The study of the mother tongue within a normative framework has always been an integral part of the study of language in the Low Countries. Problems which had to be dealt with included where to find the proper norm for a good language, and the relationship between spoken language and its orthography. Other perennial issues were those concerning case and gender.

Following a chronological line, I shall focus here on several major normative works and episodes which were crucial as to the rise of Dutch as a standardised written language in the Northern part of the Low Countries, leaving out, however, the rather complicated 'Flemish' question (cf. de Jonghe 1967, Suffeleers 1979, Willemyns 1987; Wilmots & Vromans 1986 includes a list of selected 20th-century normative studies with regard to Flanders. See also Haeseryn 1999).

## 2. Towards a Dutch *Trivium*: The 16th and 17th centuries

Following the manifest rise of interest in the vernacular (van den Branden 1967), Dutch grammarians were actively engaged in creating a standard language from the second half of the 16th century (Stellmacher 1992, van der Wal 1992b, Rizza 1996). 17th-century Dutch grammarians were mainly interested in spelling and prescriptive grammar, the Latin grammatical tradition playing a major role in their considerations. The system and categories of Latin grammar were assumed to have a more or less universal character; in addition, the Latin system was used as a universal tool of analysis not only to describe the vernacular language in a systematic way, but also to order and to develop it.

In general, this process of 'language building' (Peeters 1989) is considered to span the period from approximately 1550 to 1650. It was in London, in 1568, that the merchant Johannes Radermacher (1538–1617) wrote his brief treatise on the necessity and the utility of the Dutch language. The year 1584 saw the publication of the first comprehensive Dutch grammar, the *Twe-spraack vande Nederduitsche letterkunst* ('Dialogue of Dutch grammar'). This grammar, presented in the form of a dialogue between a teacher and his pupil, was written by members of the Amsterdam Chamber of Rhetoric, *De Eglantier.* It was soon followed by a Rhetoric and a Logic, also in Dutch and by the same Chamber. This series represents the first Dutch 'trivium'; the last 'trivium' appeared in 1648–1649 (Klifman 1992).

In the first half of the 17th century the codification process prompted the publication of various grammars and other linguistic writings. Thus, the *Twe-spraack* was followed by a series of other works on grammar and orthography (cf. Dibbets 1992, and in particular Ruijsendaal 1991 for an extensive description), Petrus Leupenius's (1607–1670) *Aenmerkingen op de Neederduitsche taale* ('Comments on the Dutch language') of 1653 closing the series. The period till 1700 is generally regarded as a transitional period. These grammatical works were not written by university teachers, but by merchants, schoolmasters and so on. A debate on orthography, made urgent by the needs of the movable-type press, was a necessary preliminary to the standardisation of grammar (Rizza 1996: 74). In the *Twe-spraack*, for instance, 'orthographia' takes the largest part, some 35%. The final chapter of this book discusses the mother tongue itself, this 'Duyts' being regarded as the oldest language, and its richness, which is supported by 'etymological' evidence borrowed from and inspired by the works of Goropius Becanus (1519–1572). As such, the *Twe-spraack* follows the well-known tradition of extolling the mother tongue (van den Branden 1967).

The compilation of a dictionary can throw useful light on the process of language building. For instance, in his Dutch-Latin dictionary, *Dictionarium Teutonico-Latinum* (1st ed. 1574) Cornelis Kiliaan (1528/9–1607) did his best to present the Dutch vocabulary as completely and clearly as possible "ne obscuritatem brevitas, nauseam prolixitas moveat" (Claes 1992: 31). In the second edition (1588), Kilaan banished Roman loan words, whose use he depreciated, to an appendix (Claes 1977: 211). By so doing, he showed himself an proponent of language purism, which has been a constant feature in Dutch linguistic thought (van der Wal 1992a: 193–195).

Due to political circumstances (cf. Israel 1995) the dialect of the province of Holland, the most powerful of the provinces of the Dutch Republic, formed the basis of the standard language, although elements from some prestigious southern dialects were also included as important constituents. In their quest for grammatical norms and rules Dutch grammarians, fell back on the criteria which were already used in classical Antiquity; among other things, they assumed that the *natura* of each language could be discovered by practicing the *ars grammatica, natura* being conceived of as systematic and characterized by regularity and analogy (Klifman 1992: 73–75). The authors of the *Twe-spraack*, for instance, sought to arrange the vernacular according to its *natura*, which was to be found in the linguistic usage (*usus*) through an inventory of its own 'natural' declension and conjugation to a system of rules. Later grammarians stress the fact that they base themselves on the *natura* of Dutch, on the *consuetudo* that is based on the reason (*ratio*), and on the linguistic usage of the 'ghoede Schrijvers', the good authors. Leupenius, too, maintained in 1653 that linguistic usage should lay down the norm, and in 1633 Christiaen van Heule (c. 1655) explicitly referred to Horace's "usus, quem arbitrium est, et jus et norma loquendi", the second important criterion being reason (*ratio*).

In the second half of the 17th century the standardisation and regulation continued mainly on the basis of writings of a different character, such as discussions of poetical practise. For example, in his long poem "Aen de Nederduitsche schryvers" (1678) the reverend Joannes Vollenhove (1631–1708) proposed language rules and discussed linguistic problems. Referring to grammarians such as van Heule and Leupenius, and showing his admiration for authors such as Hendrik Laurensz. Spiegel (1549–1612), Simon Stevin (1548–1620) and Hugo Grotius (1583–1645), he was mainly trying to follow the *usus*. Obviously, the norm had already been fixed. He considered Joost van den Vondel (1587–1679) and P. C. Hooft (1581–1647), great authors from Holland's 'Golden Age', as authorities, whom he also recommended to others (Dibbets 1991). The last decades of the 17th century saw, as van der Wal (1995: 103) has argued, a slackening of the influence of 16th-century views, and the rise of the demanding task of language standardisation and regulation on the basis of the 'boni autores'. This shift may be regarded as the end of a phase in the development of the Dutch language.

## 3. The 18th century

The 18th century was largely dominated by discussions of spelling and language norms. It can be argued that the regulation of the mother tongue was the major aim of Dutch linguistic activity throughout the century. The demand for strict regulations increased, especially in the period after 1760. However, during the era of the federal Republic of the Seven United Provinces there was no central authority qualified to proclaim official rules for spelling and grammar (Knol 1977: 70–78).

In principle, the answer to the question 'where to find the rules' could be found in three ways. First and foremost, the 'usus', i. e. the usage of great authors, could be chosen as a standard; second, one could search for norms in the linguistic past, taking the language of an older period as an example, and, third, the spoken language could be taken as a starting point. This last way, however, was never followed: not only did the written language hold sway in contemporary linguistic thought, but also the spoken language did not possess the uniformity language regulation could be based upon.

An example of the first method was the *Nederduitsche Spraekkunst* ('Dutch grammar', [$^{1}$1706, $^{5}$1751]) by Arnold Moonen (1644–1711). This book can be considered to be a summa of Dutch grammatical thinking from the late 16th century onwards. Note, however, that Moonen's work is not longer presented within the framework of a trivium. Grammar is now regarded as an independent entity, a new feat within the Dutch grammatical tradition. Like all Dutch grammars published in this century, Moonen's work was set up after the classical 'partes' model.

Moonen's intentions are clear: his grammar was written "to provide the rules according to which the Dutch language is to be properly spoken and written from now on", as it was stated in the introduction (Knol 1977: 71). To Moonen, the language of the great 17th-century writer, Joost van den Vondel, constituted the norm. Most of Moonen's sample sentences can be traced back to prose texts written by Vondel. Thus, just as in the Latin tradition, the language by the great, classical authors provided the standard. Moonen's work had a considerable impact; for almost a century "gehörte sie zu den tonangebensten Sprachlehren des Niederländischen" (Schaars 1988: 375).

It was, amongst others, Balthasar Huydecoper (1695–1778) who preferred the historical way, as is shown by his *Proeve van Taal- en Dichtkunde; in vrijmoedige aanmerkingen op Vondels Vertaalde Herscheppingen van Ovidius* ('Specimen of Philology and the Art of Poetry; in frank comments on Vondel's Translation of Ovid's Metamorphoses', [$^{1}$1730, 1782–91]). The *Proeve* seeks to establish that even Vondel had sinned against the grammatical rules and purity of the Dutch language. Although Huydecoper was of the opinion that the most elegant Dutch could be found in the works of great authors, the purest form of Dutch was to be found in the writings of the so-called "Ouden", the 'Ancients', who lived before Spanish troops under the leadership of the Duke of Alva occupied the Netherlands (1567). Huydecoper felt that Dutch had fallen into decay after this time of turmoil. Consequently, he argued that the proper forms of language and spelling were to be found in the Middle Ages: it was only the "Ouden" who could teach us what is Dutch and how one ought to speak and write it (cf. Knol 1977: 76–77). It is hardly surprising, then, that Huydecoper became a pioneer in the study of Middle Dutch.

Huydecoper's 'comments' gained a considerable authority among his contemporaries. It has been concluded that Huydecoper had an important share in 18th-century language regulation (van der Wal 1992: 235–238). Later generations of linguists called him "a language despot from the Regency period", his reflections on language being regarded as the consequences of a *grammaire raisonnée* doctrine. Within the numerous literary societies which flourished in the years 1750–1800 (cf. Singeling 1991), many members followed in Huydecoper's footsteps by publishing 'linguistic comments' on their own poems – "polissez-le et repolissez", as Boileau's notorious rule went.

At any rate, the second half of the 18th century witnessed a growing interest in Dutch as a standard language. Among other things, the foundation, in 1766, of the Leiden *Maatschappij der Nederlandsche Letterkunde* ('Dutch Literary Society'), set up after the example of the *Académie française* and similar societies, can be seen as a sign of this change in intellectual and cultural attitude. Another striking fact is that both in the letters and conversations of contemporary Dutch classical philologists Latin began to lose ground to Dutch. This meant an expansion of the use of the mother tongue by scholars who had a perfect command of Latin. Dutch Graecists launched several initiatives to bring Dutch to a higher standard, at the same time challenging the overestimation of Latin. The first academic Dutch language courses, for example, were given by classicists. As one of them argued in 1765: "the mother tongue needs to be cultivated and taught with great care, [...] to enhance the glory of our people" (Gerretzen 1940: 342). Thus, eloquence in the mother tongue is a matter of national interest.

The fact that many prestigious classical scholars were members of the Leiden Society enhanced its status, and secured the connection between the age-old classical philology, which had for centuries held the unchallenged position of constituting language study κατ' ἐξοχήν, and the study of the mother tongue which was carried out within the framework of the Maatschappij, a liaison which eventually lead to the establishing of a chair in Dutch language and literature at Leiden in 1797, Matthijs Siegenbeek (1774–1854) becoming "professor Eloquentiae Hollandicae extraordinarius". The same year also saw the appointment of Everwinus Wassenbergh (1742–1826), Professor of Greek at the University of Franeker, as a Professor of 'Dutch linguistics'. It will not come as suprise that both Siegenbeck and Wassenbergh taught from grammatical textbooks of a clearly normative character (cf. Noordegraaf 1985: 215 sqq.).

## 4. The 19th century: The codification of written Standard Dutch

The establishment of chairs in Dutch language and literature was in part due to altered political circumstances. From 1795 till 1813, the Netherlands were closely allied with and for some years even part of the French empire. This 'French period' saw many political and cultural changes, leading to administrative and educational reform. These reforms included a government regulation concerning the written language, something which had never existed before in the former federalist Republic of the Seven United Provinces. The efforts in the field of spelling and grammar were explicitly meant to serve the unitarian aims of the new régime: one state, one language. They proved to be successful.

The early 19th century saw a continuation of the main linguistic trend in the preceding century. At the behest of the government of the so-called Batavian Republic, the reverend Pieter Weiland (1754–1842) composed a *Nederduitsche Spraakkunst* ('Dutch Grammar'), published in 1805, and Matthijs Siegenbeek devised a spelling system in 1804. Both authors repeatedly refer to the German scholar J. C. Adelung (1732–1806). Weiland's book was the first important Dutch grammar that appeared after Moonen's 1706 *Spraekkunst*; it even included a number of phrases borrowed from Moonen. So, on the one hand, Weiland 1805 can be seen as the summa of 18th-century normative Dutch grammar. On the other hand, having been authorised by the government, Weiland's grammar remained the most authoritative one until the middle of the 19th century (Noordegraaf 1985: 257 sqq.; van Driel 1992: 225–228). As numerous schoolbooks and textbooks were largely based on Weiland's *Spraakkunst*, it may be considered to be the beginning of the final phase of the codification of the Dutch written standard language.

Siegenbeek's treatise on orthography, his *Verhandeling over de Nederduitsche spelling*, provided official rules for spelling in the Netherlands for the very first time. In 1847, Siegenbeek edited a 'List of words and phrases which are incompatible with the Dutch idiom'. He did so at the behest of the Dutch Literary Society, which sought to contribute to "the purging of the mother tongue from loan words". This puristic trend in the second half of the 19th century must be seen as the expression of a defensive attitude towards

German language and German culture, which was based on non-linguistic considerations and inspired by the 'Volksgeist' concept, and was to be continued until the middle of the 20th century. This normative, nationalistic trend can also be found in *Woordenboek der Nederlandsche Taal* ('Dictionary of the Dutch Language'), a huge project which was set up in 1851 by Matthias de Vries (1820–1892), amongst others. De Vries saw his dictionary as a weapon in the battle against the 'corruption' of Dutch, fighting the manifold 'barbarisms' that threatened the very heart of the language.

During the years 1855–1858 a discussion on spelling took place in the Royal Netherlands Academy of Arts and Sciences. In 1855, the orientalist Taco Roorda (1801–1874) delivered a lecture there in which he proposed a reform of the written language as much as possible in the direction of the spoken language. His proposals immediately provoked sharp criticism from more traditionally minded scholars, his principal opponent being de Vries, now a professor of Dutch language at the University of Leiden. In 1858, Roorda published his *Verhandeling over het onderscheid en de behoorlijke overeenstemming tusschen spreektaal en schrijftaal* ('Treatise on the difference and the appropriate conformity between spoken and written language'), in which he presented his views in a more elaborate fashion. Roorda lost the battle: the primacy of the written language remained untouched for several more decades (Noordegraaf 1996).

In the early 1890s, a new generation of linguists and schoolmasters founded the periodical *Taal en Letteren* ('Language and Letters', 1891–1906), a "new, heretical revolutionary journal" (cf. Noordegraaf 1991: 269), which was to breathe new life into philology and to revolutionise native language education in the Netherlands under the slogans 'language is sound' and 'language is individual'. They saw Roorda, amongst others, as their forerunner in the battle against the dominance of the written language, and founded their linguistic norms on contemporary spoken language, which they called "Algemeen Beschaafd Nederlands", *ABN*. Thus, it can be concluded that in the course of the 19th century a standard pronunciation had developed on which one of the members of the *Taal en Letteren* movement, Roeland Anthonie Kollewijn (1857–1942), could base his far-reaching proposals for a simplification of Dutch spelling. He became the leader of a national reform movement which only saw most of its proposals finally realized in 1947. By joint order of the Belgian and Dutch governments an official *Woordenlijst van de Nederlandse taal* ('Word list of the Dutch language') was published in 1954, Molewijk 1992 presents a highly critical survey of the vicissitudes of Dutch spelling reform, providing its reader with many useful references.

## 5. The 20th century

The last phase of the process of standardisation started around 1900. This comprised the further diffusion of the standard language in its spoken form, a process which had its definitive break-through only after World War II.

The ideals of the 'Taal en Letteren' group were propagated in the new periodical *De Nieuwe Taalgids* ('The New Language Guide', 1907–1995), edited by Cornelis G. N. de Vooys (1873–1955), a professor of Dutch at Utrecht and an ardent proponent of spelling reform. On the one hand, the 1930s saw an initial victory for the adherents of spelling reform, and in 1941 an official report concluded that the promotion of *ABN* had been succesful. On the other hand, however, in the 1930s a call was heard from several sides for more discipline in matters of language (Noordegraaf 1991).

In 1931, the society *Onze Taal* ('Our Language') was founded by a number of interested laymen who were concerned about the increasing 'impurity of the Dutch language'. It was decided to fight these impurities, a fight which 'in this very era' should be directed against Germanisms in particular. Note, however, that already at an early date, *Onze Taal* was aiming at the general cultivation and protection of Dutch. To that end, the society was assisted by a Board of Experts, mainly university professors of Dutch, who managed to guard this society of laymen against excessive diffuseness, and the riding of hobby-horses in their discussions. As from 1932, the society has published a periodical of the same name, providing its members with a forum for public discussion on matters concerning spelling and proper language use. This periodical long remained a source of normative studies. In cases of doubt, the Board of Experts was asked to decide the issue. Another authority which was often called in was the renowned *Woordenboek der Nederlandse Taal* (1883–1998). A monthly periodical, *Onze Taal* had some 5 000 subscribers in 1952; it has some 45 000 now. The current contents of this popular periodical differ dramatically from these from the 1930s: no normative discussions *re* barbarisms for example, but advice on how best to write comprehensible Dutch. As such, the periodical *Onze Taal* reflects the turn that linguistic advices have taken from the 1960s onwards: from guidelines for writing 'proper' Dutch to guidelines for writing 'comprehensible' Dutch (cf. Maureau 1983 for a discussion of this phenomenon). A convincing specimen of this shift is Jan Renkema's best seller *Schrijfwijzer* (1st ed. 1979; 3rd rev. ed. 1995). The history of both the society and the periodical was recorded in Veering 1966, and Burger & de Jong 1991.

The year 1980 saw an important development towards a common language policy in the Netherlands and Belgium. The two countries concluded a treaty by which the so-called Dutch Language Union was called into being, an institution which aims at a Dutch-Flemish integration in the field of language and literature in the widest sense. The *Nederlandse Taalunie* supports a wide variety of activities, not only by promoting the Dutch language abroad and, more recently, guarding its position within the European Union, but also by initiating and stimulating common Dutch-Flemish projects concerning grammar and spelling. For instance, it subsidized the last phase of a common Dutch-Flemish project on a practical grammar of contemporary Dutch, which had started in 1977. In 1984, a nearly 1300 page comprehensive standard grammar of Dutch appeared, exactly four hundred years after the first Dutch grammar of 1584. The *Algemene Nederlandse Spraakkunst* (*ANS*, 'General Dutch Grammar', cf. Geerts et al. 1984) can be considered as a rather traditional grammar following a structuralist approach in certain areas of description. Furthermore, it is an implicitly normative grammar which does not provide clear rules: the manifold varieties of *ABN* are all mentioned, but, as the editors emphasized, it is up to the user to make his own choice. For this reason, among other things, the grammar was criticized for being an 'ANS tolerans' in the many reactions that followed its publication. In particular in Flanders disappointment was voiced from various sides. One of the editors, however, vigorously defended the position taken by the editorial team (Geerts 1987). A completely revised edition of this major Dutch grammar appeared in 1997 (Hasereyn et al. 1997).

At the behest of the *Taalunie* a new (moderate) spelling reform was devised, which resulted in a new version of the official *Woordenlijst Nederlandse taal* (1995). After a brief, though fierce discussion this spelling was sanctioned by the Dutch and Belgian governments.

## 6. Towards the end of the standard language?

As to the written language, in the course of the last quarter of the 20th century norms have definitively shifted from 'proper language' to 'effective language'. With regard to the spoken language, on which as a matter of fact the *Algemeen Beschaafd Nederlands* is based from the 1890s onwards, it has been suggested that tolerance within the Dutch speaking linguistic community has increased to such a degree that the *ABN* is now in a state of transition to various colloquial languages which are bound to exist alongside one another (Stroop 1992). Thus, 'norms' and 'normativity' will become even more relative concepts than they are at the moment.

## 7. Bibliography

### 7.1. Primary sources


Geerts, Guido et al. 1984. *Algemene Nederlandse Spraakkunst.* Groningen & Leuven: Wolters-Noordhoff.

Haeseryn, Walter et al. 1997. *Algemene Nederlandse Spraakkunst.* 2nd rev. ed. Groningen: Martinus Nijhoff; Deurne: Wolters Plantyn.

van Heule, Christiaen. 1633. *De Nederduytsche spraec-konst ofte taelbeschrijvinghe.* Leyden: Jacob Roels. (New ed. by W. J. H. Caron. Groningen & Djakarta: J. B. Wolters, 1953.)

Huydecoper, Balthasar. 1730. *Proeve van Taal- en Dichtkunde: In vrymoedige aanmerkingen op Vondels Vertaalde Herscheppingen van Ovidius.* Amsterdam: E. Visscher & J. Tirion.

Kiliaan, Cornelis. 1574. *Dictionarium Teutonico-Latinum.* Antwerpiae: Christophorus Plantinus. (Repr., with an introduction by F. Claes. Hildesheim & New York: Olms, 1975.)

Leupenius, Petrus. 1653. *Aanmerkingen op de Neederduitsche taale.* Amsterdam: Hendryk Donker. (New ed. by W. J. H. Caron. Groningen: J. B. Wolters, 1958.)

Moonen, Arnold. 1706. *Nederduitsche Spraekkunst.* Amsterdam: F. Halma.

Radermacher, Johannes. 1568. *Voorreden vanden noodich en nutticheit der Nederduitscher taelkunste.* Ms., printed in Bostoen 1985, 25–34.

Renkema, Jan. 1979. *Schrijfwijzer. Handboek voor duidelijk taalgebruik.* 's-Gravenhage: Staatsuitgeverij.

Roorda, Taco. 1858. *Verhandeling over het onderscheid en de behoorlijke overeenstemming tusschen spreektaal en schrijftaal.* Leeuwarden: G. T. N. Suringar.

Siegenbeek, Matthijs. 1804. *Verhandeling over de Nederduitsche spelling, ter bevordering van eenparigheid in dezelve.* Amsterdam: J. Allart.

–. 1810. *Syntaxis, of woordvoeging der Nederduitsche taal.* Leyden: D. du Mortier; Deventer: J. H. de Lange; Groningen: J. Oomkens.

–. 1814. *Grammatica of Nederduitsche spraakkunst.* Leyden: D. du Mortier; Deventer: J. H. de Lange; Groningen: J. Oomkens.

–. 1847. *Lijst van woorden en uitdrukkingen, met het Nederlandsch taaleigen strijdende.* Leiden: S. & J. Luchtmans.

*Twe-spraack vande Nederduitsche letterkunst.* 1584. Leyden: Christoffel Plantyn. (New ed. by Geert R. W. Dibbets. Assen & Maastricht: van Gorcum, 1985.)

Vollenhove, Joannes. 1678. "Aan de Nederduitsche schryvers". *J. Vollenhoves Poëzy.* Amsterdam: Henrik Boom en wed. Dirk Boom, 1686, 564–577. (Repr. in Dibbets 1991, 67–111.)

de Vries, Matthias, L. A. te Winkel et al. 1882–1998. *Woordenboek der Nederlandsche Taal.*

Weiland, Pieter. 1805. *Nederduitsche Spraakkunst.* Amsterdam: J. Allart.

*Woordenlijst van de Nederlandse taal. Samengesteld in opdracht van de Nederlandse en de Belgische regering.* 1954. 's-Gravenhage: Staatsdrukkerij- en Uitgeverijbedrijf.

*Woordenlijst Nederlandse taal. Samengesteld door het Instituut voor Nederlandse Lexicologie in opdracht van de Nederlandse Taalunie.* 1995. Den Haag: Sdu Uitgevers; Antwerpen: Standaard Uitgeverij.

### 7.2. Secondary sources

Bartsch, Renate. 1987. *Norms of Language. Theoretical and practical aspects.* London & New York: Longman.

Bakker, Dirk Miente & Geert R. W. Dibbets, eds. 1977. *Geschiedenis van de Nederlandse taalkunde.* Den Bosch: Malmberg.

Bostoen, Karel. 1985. *Kaars en bril: de oudste Nederlandse grammatica.* [Middelburg]: Koninklijk Zeeuwsch Genootschap der Wetenschappen.

van den Branden, Lode. 1967. *Het streven naar verheerlijking, zuivering en opbouw van het Nederlands in de 16de eeuw.* Arnhem: Gysbers & van Loon. (Reprint of the 1st ed., Gent 1956.)

van Bree, Cor & Ariane van Santen, eds. 1996. *Leidse mores. Aspecten van taalnormering.* Leiden: SNL.

Claes, Frans. 1977. "De lexicografie in de zestiende eeuw". Bakker & Dibbets 1977. 205–217.

–. 1992. "Über die Verbreitung lexicographischer Werke in den Niederlanden und ihre wechselseitige Beziehungen mit dem Ausland bis zum Jahre 1600". Noordegraaf, Versteegh & Koerner 1992: 17–38.

Dibbets, Geert R. W. 1991. *Vondels zoon en Vondels taal. Joannes Vollenhove en het Nederlands.* Amsterdam: Stichting Neerlandistiek VU.

–. 1992. "Dutch Philology in the 16th and 17th Century". Noordegraaf, Versteegh & Koerner 1992: 39–61.

van Driel, L[odewijk] F[rans.] 1992. "19th-Century Linguistics: The Dutch development and the German theme". Noordegraaf, Versteegh & Koerner 1992: 221–251.

Geerts, Guido. 1987. "De ondergrond van rekkelijk en precies inzake de ANS". *Algemene Nederlandse Spraakkunst.* Special issue of *Forum der Letteren* 28.59–68.

Gerretzen, Jan Gerard. 1940. *Schola Hemsterhusiana.* Nijmegen & Utrecht: Dekker & Van de Vegt.

Gillaerts, Paul. 1989. *Handboek normatieve taalbeheersing.* Leuven & Amersfoort: Acco.

Haeseryn, Walter. 1999. "Normatieve studies". *De Nederlandse taalkunde in kaart* ed. by W. Smedts & P. C. Paardekooper, 237–247. Leuven & Amersfoort: Acco.

de Jong, Jaap & Peter Burger. 1991. *Onze Taal! Zestig jaar strijd en liefde voor het Nederlands.* 's-Gravenhage: SDU Uitgeverij.

Israel, Jonathan. 1995. *The Dutch Republic: Its rise, greatness, and fall.* Oxford: Clarendon Press.

de Jonghe, A. 1967. *De taalpolitiek van Willem I.* Sint Andries/Brugge: Darthet.

Klifman, Harm. 1992. "Dutch Language Study and the Trivium: Motives and elaborations". Noordegraaf, Versteegh & Koerner 1992: 63–83.

Knol, Jan. 1977. "De Nederlandse taalkunde in de achttiende eeuw". Bakker & Dibbets 1977: 65–112.

van Leuvensteijn, J. A. & J. B. Berns, eds. 1992. *Dialect and Standard Language, Dialekt und Standardsprache in the English, Dutch, German and Norwegian Language areas.* Amsterdam: North Holland.

Maureau, J. H. 1983. *Goed en begrijpelijk schrijven. En Analyse van 40 jaar schrijfadviezen.* 2nd rev. ed. Muiderberg: Coutinho.

Molewijk, C. G. 1992. *Spellingverandering van zin naar onzin (1200–heden).* 's-Gravenhage: SDU Uitgeverij.

Noordegraaf, Jan. 1985. *Norm, geest en geschiedenis. Nederlandse taalkunde in de negentiende eeuw.* Dordrecht & Cinnaminson: Foris Publications.

–. 1991. "'Taal en Letteren' honderd jaar later. Een tijdschrift tegen de schrijftaalcultuur". *Forum der Letteren* 32.269–280. (Repr. in *Voorlopig verleden. Taalkundige plaatsbepalingen, 1797–1960* by J. Noordegraaf, 110–124. Münster: Nodus 1997.)

–. 1996. "Trends in 19th-Century Linguistics and the Debate in the Royal Netherlands Academy (1855–1858)". *The Dutch Pendulum. Linguistics in the Netherlands 1740–1900* by J. Noordegraaf, 56–71. Münster: Nodus.

–, Kees Versteegh & Konrad Koerner, eds. 1992. *The History of Linguistics in the Low Countries.* (= *Studies in the History of Language Sciences*, 64.) Amsterdam & Philadelphia: Benjamins.

Peeters, Leopold. 1989. *Taalopbouw als Renaissance-ideaal. Studies over taalopvattingen en taalpraktijk in de zestiende en zeventiende eeuw.* Ed. by G. R. W. Dibbets, J. Noordegraaf & M. J. van der Wal. Amsterdam: Buijten & Schipperheijn.

Rizza, Riccardo. 1996. "The Birth and Development of the Standard Language in the Low Countries". *Italia ed Europa nella linguistica del Rinascimento / Italy and Europe in Renaissance Linguistics* ed. by Mirko Tavoni, I, 69–87. Modena: Panini.

de Rooij, Jaap, ed. 1987. *Variatie en Norm in de Standaardtaal.* Amsterdam: Meertens-Instituut.

Ruijsendaal, Els. 1991. *Letterkonst. Het klassieke grammaticamodel en de oudste Nederlandse grammatica's.* Amsterdam: VU Uitgeverij.

Schaars, Frans. 1988. *De Nederduitsche Spraekkunst (1706) van Arnold Moonen (1644–1711). Een bijdrage tot de geschiedenis van de Nederlandstalige spraakkunst.* Wijhe: Uitgeverij Quarto.

Singeling, C. B. F. 1991. *Gezellige schrijvers. Aspecten van letterkundige genootschappelijkheid in Nederland, 1750–1800.* Amsterdam & Atlanta, Ga.: Rodopi.

Stellmacher, Dieter. 1992. "Die Niederländische Grammatikforschung im Überblick vom 16. bis 19. Jahrhundert". *Studia Neerlandica et Germanica* ed. by Stanislaus Predota, 405–418. (= *Acta Universitatis Wratislaviensis*, 1356.)

Stroop, Jan. 1992. "Towards the End of the Standard Language in the Netherlands". Van Leuvensteijn & Berns 1992, 162–177.

Suffeleers, Tony J. 1979. *Taalverzorging in Vlaanderen. Een opiniegeschiedenis.* Brugge: Orion; Nijmegen: Gottmer.

van den Toorn, M. C. et al., eds. 1997. *Geschiedenis van de Nederlandse taal.* Amsterdam: Amsterdam Univ. Press.

Veering, Jan. 1966. *Mogelijkheden en moeilijkheden van taalverzorging.* Delft: Van Markens Drukkerij. (Doctoral dissertation, Univ. of Amsterdam.)

de Vooys, Cornelis G. N. 1970. *Geschiedenis van de Nederlandse taal.* Groningen: Wolters-Noordhoff. (Repr. of 5th rev. ed., 1953.)

de Vries, Jan, Roland Willemyns & Peter Burger. 1993. *Het verhaal van een taal. Negen eeuwen Nederlands.* Amsterdam: Prometheus.

van der Wal, Marijke. 1992a. *Geschiedenis van de Nederlandse taalkunde.* Met medewerking van Cor van Bree. Utrecht: Het Spectrum. (2nd ed. 1994.)

–. 1992b. "Dialect and Standard Language in the Past: The rise of Dutch standard language in the sixteenth and seventeenth centuries". Van Leuvensteijn & Berns 1992: 119–129.

–. 1995. *De moedertaal centraal. Standaardisatieaspecten in de Nederlanden omstreeks 1650.* Den Haag: Sdu Uitgevers.

Willemyns, Roland. 1987. "Norm en variatie in Vlaanderen". De Rooij 1987: 143–164.

Wilmots, J. & J. Vromans. 1986. "Normatieve studies". *De Nederlandse taalkunde in kaart* ed. by P. C. Paardekooper, 84–87. Leuven: Departement Linguïstiek Katholieke Universiteit Leuven.

*Jan Noordegraaf, Amsterdam (The Netherlands)*

# 121. Les approches normatives en Russie (XVIIIᵉ siècle)

1. Introduction
2. Alphabet
3. Orthographe
4. Morphologie
5. Lexique et dictionnaires
6. Rhétorique
7. Bibliographie

## 1. Introduction

La fixation de la norme linguistique en Russie, définissant ce qu'il est convenu d'appeler *russkij literaturnyj jazyk* (que l'on traduira par *langue russe normée* et non par *langue russe littéraire*) est l'un des grands enjeux du XVIIIᵉ siècle. Elle vient se greffer sur l'existence d'un cadre terminologique et conceptuel slavon, élaboré à partir de la grammaire grecque principalement, latine secondairement, dans une suite de grammaires slavonnes (*Donat slavon* 1522; 'Αδελφότης 1591–1596; Lavrentij Zizanij 1596, *Hrammatika slovenska [...]*; Meletij Smotrickij 1618–1619, *Grammatiki Slavenskija [...]*). Ces grammaires, décrivant la langue des textes religieux, accordent à ce titre une place réduite aux faits de langue vernaculaire. Ceux-ci sont en revanche largement pris en compte dans les descriptions élaborées par des étrangers soucieux de promouvoir la langue parlée vivante, dans des buts commerciaux, diplomatiques ou religieux.

Ainsi, la distinction du slavon et du russe est-elle affirmée dans le manuel de Tönnies Fenne (1607; *Tonnies Fenne's Low German Manual of Spoken Russian*), puis dans la grammaire du diplomate Wilhelm Ludolf, proche des milieux piétistes allemands *Grammatica Russica* ... (1696), ou encore dans la *Grammaire et Methode Russes et Françoises* (1724) de l'interprète auprès de la bibliothèque royale de Paris Jean Sohier. Quelle langue russe décrivent ces étrangers? Ainsi que l'affirme Sohier (1724 [1987]: i), il s'agit du russe de chancellerie:

> C'est donc du stile de chancellerie que j'ay entendu traiter icy, [...] comme étant le seul le plus utile, et le plus necessaire à sçavoir pour l'écriture, la correspondance et l'intelligence des livres.

Le russe de chancellerie est depuis le XVIᵉ siècle la langue officielle de Moscou; c'est une langue administrative dont la fonction est avant tout pratique et qui doit, pour rester intelligible, suivre l'évolution de la langue parlée (Unbegaun 1935: 15–22).

C'est ce double mouvement de fidélité à la langue d'église et de promotion du russe de chancellerie, révélateur tantôt d'un centrage sur un modèle, tantôt d'une ouverture aux standarts étrangers qui déterminera les conditions d'émergence de la norme, au moment où la Russie fait le choix d'entrer dans le concert des pays européens, à l'instigation du Tsar Pierre le Grand (1672–1725), entraînant du même coup la langue russe dans le concert des langues européennes.

## 2. Alphabet

La rénovation de l'alphabet constitue un ample chantier, souhaité et suivi par Pierre le Grand lui-même. Dès 1698, il a envoyé en Hollande Elie Kopiewicz, traducteur et érudit, pour se former à l'imprimerie. Celui-ci travaillera un moment avec Tessing, puis seul, voyageant à travers l'Europe centrale et orientale avec son imprimerie (les vicissitudes de son activité sont rapportées chez Ďurovič, 1987).

Les textes sacrés disponibles ont été rédigés pour la plupart en alphabet cyrillique (Kirillica), quelques textes antérieurs au Xᵉ siècle en alphabet glagolitique (Glagolica), (très peu représenté en Russie), les deux alphabets offrant une correspondance dans l'ordre des graphèmes et dans les sons qu'ils représentent, mais de profondes disparités dans la calligraphie. De 44 graphèmes répertoriés dans les textes des Xᵉ–XIᵉ siècles, l'alphabet cyrillique s'est simplifié, par élimination des graphèmes représentant les voyelles iodisées entre autres. C'est cet alphabet qui subsistera comme alphabet religieux.

L'alphabet dit laïque n'est pas une création. Il prend appui sur l'alphabet de la langue de chancellerie, que Fenne décrivait dès 1607. La mention de deux graphèmes distincts correspondant au même contenu phonétique atteste qu'au début du XVIIᵉ siècle, l'écriture cursive propre au russe de chancellerie est constituée comme un ensemble ordonné de graphèmes. Fenne assigne à chacun des alphabets une fonction stylistique: les graphèmes slavons sont employés pour 'des choses de Dieu', 'de l'Empire ou du seigneur', les graphèmes russes pour parler des 'choses basses' (cf. Uspenskij 1994: 63).

C'est donc cette écriture cursive qui servira de base au nouvel alphabet. L'imprimerie est appelée à connaître un puissant développement au XVIII^e^ siècle: de fait, le nombre des imprimeries en Russie passera durant le siècle de 1 à 80, on avancera une motivation technologique pour justifier l'adoption de l'alphabet civil. L'allègement de l'alphabet slavon, avec ses 44 graphèmes aux dessins complexes qui boivent l'encre, doit accompagner l'expansion de l'imprimerie. Mais l'impératif technique vient se doubler d'une motivation culturelle: le nouvel alphabet ne doit pas comporter de signes prosodiques (ce qui le rapproche de l'alphabet latin), contrairement à l'alphabet slavon (qui était proche de l'alphabet grec). Si l'on a pu insister sur la filiation que souhaitait ainsi affirmer Pierre le Grand avec les empereurs romains, une telle motivation culturelle masque à son tour une motivation religieuse: la promotion d'un alphabet dit civil (*graždanskij šrift*) est censée limiter, voire contrer, l'influence de la religion orthodoxe dans la vie sociale, et au premier chef dans l'éducation. La laïcisation de l'éducation passe aussi par la laïcisation de l'alphabet. Le dessein de Pierre le Grand a même été de supprimer purement et simplement l'alphabet slavon, comme en témoigne la demande de transcrire en alphabet civil une prière, en l'espèce le 'Notre Père' (Correspondance de l'année 1708).

En fin de compte, le décret de 1727 stipule que l'alphabet civil servira à l'édition de tous types de textes, y compris spirituels, alors que l'alphabet religieux sera réservé à l'impression de textes religieux, dans les murs de l'imprimerie synodale de Moscou exclusivement. L'alphabet est une métaphore de la Russie: les nouveaux livres, édités en nouvel alphabet, seront édités dans la nouvelle capitale, les livres du passé resteront à Moscou, capitale du passé.

Cependant, il y a loin de la volonté réformatrice à l'entrée en vigueur des décisions. Si l'emploi du nouvel alphabet est impérieusement recommandé aux typographes et imprimeurs en 1733, il mettra tout le XVIII^e^ siècle pour s'imposer véritablement. Dans la seconde moitié du siècle, l'apprentissage de la lecture se faisait encore à travers la récitation par cœur du Psautier et lorsque Catherine II mit en chantier sa réforme de l'instruction dans les années 60, elle souhaita que l'apprentissage de la lecture se fît à parité d'après les livres religieux et la norme laïque. Les directives de Catherine ne furent pas appliquées, ainsi que le note Živov (1996: 24).

Aux confins des problèmes soulevés par l'alphabet, et des considérations liées à la phonétique, l'orthographe fera l'objet d'une attention particulière de la part des codificateurs de la langue, Vasilij Adodurov (1709–1780) et de Vasilij Trediakovskij (1703–1768) en tout premier lieu.

## 3. Orthographe

Une part importante de la réflexion sur l'orthographe a été menée dans le cadre de la société savante fondée en 1735 à l'instigation de Vasilij Trediakovskij, la Société russe (*Rossijskoe Sobranje*), hébergée par l'Académie des Sciences. Cette assemblée se fixe pour tâche d'élaborer la norme de la langue civile, au travers d'outils linguistiques divers: grammaire, dictionnaire, traduction des grands auteurs, rhétorique [...]; elle se donne pour modèle l'Académie de Leipzig (→ Art. 114), et au delà, l'Académie française (→ Art. 115).

Concernant précisément l'orthographe, outre une répartition rigoureuse des emplois des deux graphèmes *i* (*i* devant voyelle, *u* dans les autres cas), la répartition du *φ* et du *θ* selon le principe étymologique, l'éviction de graphèmes jugés surnuméraires, l'assemblée accordera une grande attention à l'élaboration d'une orthographe cohérente pour la langue moderne, basée sur un principe phonétique. L'orthographe des désinences suscite un vif débat, Adodurov et Trediakovskij préconisant des variantes uniques *-ij/yj* pour le nominatif accusatif masculin singulier, et une variante *-ija/yja* pour le génitif féminin singulier. Trediakovskij reproche à Sumarokov d'employer la désinence *-oj* (*zloj*, et non *zlyj*), au nominatif-accusatif masculin singulier. Ces formes relèvent selon lui d'un registre *campagnard grossier*, Trediakovskij se montrant, sur ce point précis, plus puriste que Sumarokov.

## 4. Morphologie

La classification morphologique et l'établissement des paradigmes au XVIII^e^ siècle sont largement redevables aux travaux des étrangers. Ďurovič & Sjöberg (1987: 255–278; 1991: 171–211) ont montré que la doctrine grammaticale élaborée au sein du Lycée de l'Académie, fondé à partir d'un collège allemand ouvert par le pasteur Johann Ernst

Glück, prisonnier de guerre, en 1703, a nourri toute la réflexion grammaticale de la première moitié du XVIIIe siècle. Glück est luimême l'auteur d'une grammaire récemment publiée *Grammatik der russischen Sprache* (1704). Ďurovič et Sjöberg ont par ailleurs fait la découverte de tables de déclinaisons et de conjugaisons, dans le fonds étranger des archives suédoises, rédigées sous forme d'un manuscrit qu'ils ont baptisé Extranea, et qu'ils considèrent, démonstration à l'appui, comme la source de la 'paradigmatique russe'.

L'étude de ces textes produits à l'orée du XVIIIe a contribué à ruiner l'idée longtemps accréditée par l'historiographie russe et soviétique d'un Lomonosov premier codificateur de la langue russe, au travers de sa *Rossijskaja grammatika* de 1755 (parue en 1757).

Tant la grammaire de Glück que les tables du manuscrit Extranea reprennent le cadre de Smotrickij (1618), et montrent tout à la fois une permanence des exemples et une modernisation des flexions.

Les paradigmes flexionnels amorcent une nette séparation entre cas et désinence. Chez Glück, ils comportent 6 cas, mais 7 désinences. Ces 6 cas sont présentés dans l'ordre suivant: Nom., Gen., Dat., Acc. Voc., Abl. A l'ablatif correspondent deux désinences: celle du prépositionnel (selon le terme que donnera plus tard Lomonosov, mais que n'ignorait pas le Suédois Sparwenfeld (1655–1727) dans son *Lexicon Slavonicum*) et celle de l'instrumental. (Notons une hésitation, dûe à la fidélité au modèle latin, concernant le prépositionnel, regroupé avec un génitif après préposition sur le mode de l'ablatif (*ot vody, ot zemli*). Le traitement distinct des animés et des inanimés est ici affirmé, représenté par deux paradigmes différents. L'Extranea prend acte de la marginalisation, dans la langue vivante, du vocatif, désigné *Voc S* (*vocativus slavonicus*).

Cas et désinence, autrement dit fonction et forme étaient, dans la tradition slavonne, étroitement liés. Chez Smotrickij "le cas est la modification de la terminaison en déclinaison" (1619 [1974]: 29). Dans les textes du début du siècle, la distinction s'amorce, mais les fonctions des cas n'étaient pas décrites. Elles le sont chez Lomonosov (1952: 411); les variations affectant les mots répercutent la réalité extralinguistique, sont dotées d'exemples, et enfin nommées.

Actes et objets peuvent se rapporter aux choses diversement, d'où les variations suivantes affectant les noms: 1) lorsqu'une chose est simplement présentée ou nommée, par exemple, un bras puissant, une bruyante victoire; 2) lorsque la chose est présentée dans son appartenance à une autre chose, par exemple, l'œuvre d'un bras puissant, le son d'une bruyante victoire [...] Ces variations sont appelées cas: 1) nominatif, 2) génitif, 3) datif, 4) accusatif, 5) vocatif, 6) instrumental (1755 [1952]: 411 § 56).

Il y ajoute un septième cas, le prépositionnel *predložnyj*.

Dans sa vaste entreprise de présentation raisonnée de la grammaire russe (*Rossijskaja Grammatika*, 1981 [1783–1788]), Anton Barsov différenciera radicalement cas et désinence: "Pour ce qui est de l'étude des cas, on remarque que si la langue russe en possède sept, elle ne connaït que cinq désinences" (Barsov 1981: 100–101). Il franchit un pas vers la suppression du vocatif, en notant à sa place la mention 'comme le nominatif'. Il théorise également la distinction animés: inanimés:

Pour bien comprendre les déclinaisons, il importe de distinguer les choses animées ou les animaux des inanimés, parce que les noms des choses animées dans toutes les déclinaisons ont l'accusatif identique au génitif (1981: 103).

Dans les différentes grammaires du XVIIIe siècle, la présentation de la morphologie du verbe accuse d'importantes modifications, sur deux points sensibles dans toute la tradition grammaticale russe, l'identification des paradigmes (tantôt à partir de la voyelle thématique du présent, tantôt à partir de la terminaison de l'infinitif), et la présentation du système des temps (Archaimbault 1999: 84–153).

Dans sa grammaire slavonne, Smotrickij avait opté pour un système simple, qui retenait 2 grands types de conjugaison en fonction de la voyelle thématique prise à la deuxième personne du singulier du présent (*e* ou *i*). Les formes de 1ère personne étaient ensuite réparties en terminaisons 'pures' et 'impures', ces dernières présentant une alternance consonantique à la première personne, qui disparaît ensuite aux autres.

Ludolf et le manuscrit suédois reprenaient les deux conjugaisons, Glück les abandonne, au profit de 5 conjugaisons, identifiées grâce à l'infinitif (*-ati*, *-eti*, *-iti*, *-oti*, *-uti*), complétées du verbe substantif *esm'*, ce qui constitue une importante innovation. Lomonosov reviendra à un classement par voyelle thématique, qu'il complètera néanmoins par l'indication conjointe de l'infinitif. Il sera d'ailleurs violemment critiqué sur ce point par les auteurs de la première grammaire de l'Académie (1802, 1809), qui lui imputent des nombreuses fautes commises par les locuteurs russes. Constatant la difficulté d'enseigner et d'appliquer les règles de conjugaison à partir de la voyelle thématique, l'Académie préconisait en effet, dans un but pédagogique, un regroupement par type d'infinitifs:

Dans toutes les grammaires du slavon ou du russe publiées à ce jour, les verbes sont divisés en deux conjugaisons, essentiellement selon la terminaison de la deuxième personne du singulier du présent; les verbes, terminés à la dite personne en *-eš'* appartenant à la première conjugaison ceux en -iš' à la seconde. L'Académie, ayant confronté de nombreux verbes aux exemples proposés, a noté qu'une grande majorité de verbes font, à des temps divers, exception aux modèles [...]. C'est pourquoi l'Académie de Russie, dans le but d'alléger l'apprentissage de la langue russe et de réduire le nombre des verbes irréguliers ou dissemblables a jugé utile de diviser les verbes en quatre conjugaisons selon l'infinitif (Gram. de l'Académie, éd. 1809: 167).

Les Académiciens ne mentionnent pas la grammaire de Glück, peut-être en ignoraient-ils l'existence? Il est remarquable que cette primauté accordée à l'infinitif favorisera l'identification de la catégorie de l'aspect, grâce à la mise en rapport de critères morphologiques (dérivation verbale) et de valeurs sémantiques associées.

En ce qui concerne les temps, la grammaire de Glück et l'Extranea reprennent un système allégé chronologiquement, tel qu'avait pu le représenter Ludolf, avec trois temps de l'indicatif, le présent, le passé et de futur, l'infinitif étant placé dans les formes nominales du verbe. La présentation est somme toute assez proche de celle que connaît le russe moderne aujourd'hui, à la notable différence que ces deux grammaires n'identifiaient pas le couple aspectuel. *Extranea* enregistre cependant le rôle du préfixe dans la formation du futur, le préverbe étant nettement séparé de la préposition, en raison justement du rôle particulier qu'il joue dans la composition verbale.

Un fossé sépare ce système de celui de Lomonosov, qui reviendra à 10 temps, cherchant ainsi à réactiver d'anciens temps tombés en désuétude, dans une fidélité excessive au modèle slavon, mais aussi certainement dans la volonté de rivaliser avec les autres langues européennes, dont les nombreux temps savent exprimer des rapports chronologiques complexes.

## 5. Lexique et dictionnaires

Les dictionnaires antérieurs au XVIIIe siècle répertoriés sont assez rares. Citons parmi ceux-ci le *Leksis* de Lavrentij Zizanij (1596), et le *Leksikon slavenorossijskij* de Pamva Berynda (1627) ainsi que l'important *Lexicon Slavonicum*, dictionnaire slavon-latin en quatre tomes, rédigé par le Suédois Johan Gabriel Sparwenfeld (1655–1727) et pour lequel des prisonniers de guerre de haut rang avaient pu être utilisés comme informateurs (Birgegård 1992: 42 sq.).

Au XVIIIe siècle, la production des dictionnaires est importante en Russie, comme en témoignent les 277 titres recensés par Vomperskij (1986). Ceux-ci regroupent aussi bien des dictionnaires monolingues – thématiques ou alphabétiques –, des dictionnaires plurilingues, que des concordances (*konkordacija*), listes de mots ou de locutions employés dans les textes religieux. En outre, un grand nombre de dictionnaires étrangers sont publiés en Russie dans leur langue d'origine, ou traduits.

L'emprunt de termes étrangers constitue un point sensible au regard de la norme. Le premier dictionnaire renfermant exclusivement des emprunts avait été rédigé sous la commande expresse de Pierre le Grand, qui avait noté ses corrections sur le manuscrit. Ce *Leksikon vokabulam novym po alfavitu* (Smirnov 1910), dont la date de rédaction est incertaine, contient des termes techniques de divers registres (juridique, militaire, architectural). On citera également le dictionnaire bilingue néerlandais-russe, rédigé par J. Brus (1717) *Kniga leksikon ili Sobranie rečej po Alfavitu*. Il s'agit au départ d'une liste de termes hollandais présentant des particularités grammaticales, donnée en annexe de la grammaire néerlandaise de Sewel, grammaire dont la traduction en russe avait été commandée à Brus par Pierre le Grand. Cette liste deviendra un dictionnaire bilingue inverse, le russe apparaissant comme langue des définitions, la langue décrite étant le hollandais (Biržakova 1980). Les mots hollandais ne sont pas systématiquement accompagnés de leur traduction russe. Le terme hollandais est en outre proposé en transcription lorsqu'il n'est pas d'équivalent russe, ce qui favorise de fait l'emprunt, ainsi: "Gaft, imenovanie moškam na vozduxe živuščim tokmo edinoj den'". Haft. ['Gaft, appellation des moucherons éphémères. Haft'].

Ce lexique fera l'objet d'une première édition séparée en avril 1717, puis en novembre de la même année, en annexe à la grammaire de Sewel.

Le début du XVIII^e siècle se caractérise, dans le domaine du lexique comme dans celui de la grammaire, par une ouverture et une volonté d'enrichissement par intégration. La seconde moitié du siècle verra au contraire bien souvent une volonté de stabiliser une langue 'pure', et privilégiera le néologisme construit sur des racines russes.

Ainsi le *Slovar' inostrannyx slov, kotorye naprasno starajutsja vvodit'* [Dictionnaire des mots étrangers que l'on essaie en vain de faire entrer en russe], publié dans le journal *To i sjo* en 1769, recommande-t-il 269 mots russes à employer en lieu et place des emprunts.

En 1774 est fondée la Société Russe libre de l'université de Moscou qui se consacre à

> La correction et la perfection de la langue russe [qui] doit constituer l'objet particulier de cette assemblée, et la composition d'un dictionnaire alphabétique russe correct [pravil'nyj] doit être le premier travail des participants. Les œuvres et les traductions des langues étrangères en russe ne pourront être publiées qu'elles n'aient été visées et corrigées par notre assemblée (Opyt trudov [...] 1774: 3–4).

Dès lors, un important travail lexicographique est mis en chantier, auquel sera donnée une nouvelle impulsion en 1783, avec la fondation de l'Académie de Russie, et qui aboutira à la rédaction du premier Dictionnaire de l'Académie russe (1789–1794).

Une fois intégrées les techniques lexicographiques occidentales, qui allaient permettre la mise en œuvre même du Dictionnaire, les Académiciens prônèrent – sans que l'unanimité se fît sur cette question – le rejet de l'emprunt au nom de "l'épuration et l'enrichissement de la langue", comme l'a relevé Sara Biensan (1994). Les termes techniques empruntés firent l'objet d'un renvoi à un calque russe, e c'est à cette entrée qu'était donnée la définition, sur le modèle suivant: "Antidot", Greč.: Zri Protivujadie ('Antidote, Grec: voir contrepoison').

La position adoptée vis à vis de l'emprunt devait privilégier les mots russes mais aussi, plus largement, slaves (surtout polonais ou tchèques), ce qui eut pour effet de limiter à un cinquantième de l'ouvrage les termes empruntés aux langues non slaves (dont 342 au grec, 107 au latin, 92 au français, 74 à l'allemand [...]), selon le décompte de Suxomlinov (1888, VIII: 129). S'il s'agissait d'emprunter une méthode, il ne fallait pas que, subrepticement, les mots en profitassent pour polluer le vivier lexical.

## 6. Rhétorique

C'est par la Pologne et l'Ukraine que l'enseignement de la rhétorique s'est répandu en Russie au XVII^e siècle. Renate Lachmann (1984: 140 sq.) a étudié comment la *Ritorika* de Makarij (1619), composée dans la région de Vologda, combine l'adaptation d'un modèle polonais (par la traduction massive de termes rhétoriques polonais, eux-mêmes traduits du latin) au service de l'exaltation d'une culture locale, la fonction cérémoniale (*genus sublime*) étant prioritairement visée.

A la charnière des deux siècles, l'enseignement de Feofan Prokopovič (1681–1736), professeur puis recteur de l'Académie Mohila de Kiev, exerce une large influence, notamment grâce à son cours de poétique donné en latin dès 1705, ainsi qu'à son syllabaire. Plusieurs cours et écrits *De arte rhetorica, De arte poetica* ont été édités au XVIII^e siècle. Vomperskij (1988: 80) a insisté sur sa volonté d'égaler, dans la langue vivante moderne, les langues de la littérature antique et en conséquence, sur le caractère normatif de ses recommandations linguistiques et stylistiques. Souhaitant prolonger l'expérience d'une *lingua rustica* telle qu'elle avait pu se développer aux XVI et XVIII^e siècles en Ukraine et Biélorussie (langue non dialectale, écrite, normée, désignée par les termes *prosta mova* ou *ruska mova*) et considérant que le slavon russe a su rester proche du vieux slave des premières traductions, Prokopovič tente de revivifier le slavon d'église dans sa version russe, en le reliant à la tradition écrite antérieure d'une part, et en l'enrichissant de tout un vocabulaire parlé de l'autre, ce dans le but de l'imposer comme langue de culture.

Il n'est pas indifférent que Prokopovič, ouvert aux doctrines luthériennes, fût conseiller ecclésiastique de Pierre le Grand, auprès duquel il fit valoir la nécessité de traduire les écritures dans une langue accessible à tous. Sur la base d'une prose religieuse, dont les modèles avaient été élaborés dans les Académies de Pologne et d'Ukraine, Prokopovič développa l'arsenal d'une rhétorique politique, dans lequel viendront puiser largement les auteurs du siècle entier, à commencer par Georgij Danilovskij, professeur de rhétorique au monastère de la Laure Alexandre Nevskij de Saint-Pétersbourg, dont la *Ritorika* (ca. 1720) vise la normalisation de la parole religieuse autant que publique.

Pour reprendre le classement que propose Françoise Douay (1992: 495) des positions que définit la Rhétorique en Europe aux XVIIe et XVIII siècle, nous dirons que les Russes sont, par la force de choses, rénovateurs: il s'agit, dans une langue nouvelle qui s'élabore simultanément, de développer une nouvelle esthétique, de nouvelles méthodes scientifiques, de nouveaux rapports de citoyenneté, ceux-ci passant par la redéfinition des deux sphères religieuse et laïque. C'est dans cette optique qu'il convient de considérer la réforme des trois styles telle que la conçoit Lomonosov.

Contrairement à Vasilij Trediakovskij, qui, dans son traité *Novyj i kratkij sposob k složeniju rossijskix stixov* [...] (1735) [Nouvelle méthode brève pour la composition des vers russes] déplaçait l'étude vers la langue poétique et posait l'opposition de principe entre les 'mots et formes de la langue slavonne religieuse', et du 'discours russe' vivant, tout en dressant le répertoire des licences poétiques (variantes phonématiques, accentuelles, morphologiques, slavonismes [...]), Lomonosov recherche une position de compromis, selon le terme de Boris Uspenskij (1994: 140). En effet, les trois styles, intimement liés au choix du lexique, reposent certes sur l'opposition du style élevé et bas, mais aussi et surtout sur un vaste style moyen 'œcuménique', regroupant des mots des trois registres, à la restriction près qu'il est déconseillé de faire voisiner trop étroitement slavonisme et mot du registre populaire.

## 6. Bibliographie

'Αδελφοτ ησ. 1591 [1973]. *Grammatika Dobroglagolivavo Ellinoslovenskavo Iazyka, sover-šennago iskustva osmi častej slova* [...] [Grammaire de la langue helléno-slave bien parlée, de l'art achevé des huit parties du discours [...]] Lvov', Imp. de la confrérie. (Horbatsch, Olexa, ed. München: Kubon & Sagner.)

Adodurov, V[assili]. 1731. *Anfangs-Gründe der Russischen Sprache.* (voir Unbegaun 1969.)

Archaimbault, Sylvie. 1999. *Préhistoire de l'aspect verbal. L'émergence de la notion dans les grammaires russes.* Paris: CNRS Editions.

Barsov, A[nton] [Alexejevič.] 1783–88. *Rossijskaja Grammatika* [Grammaire russe]. (Newman, Lawrence W., éd. 1980. *The Comprehensive Grammar of A. A. Barsov.* Chelsea, Mich.: Slavica Publishers Inc.; Uspenkij, B[oris] [Alexejevič] & Tobolova, éds. 1981. *Rossijskaja grammatika A. A. Barsova.* Moskva. Izd. Moskovskogo Universiteta.)

Biensan, Sara. 1994. *Les sources étrangères de la première édition du Dictionnaire de l'Académie de Russie.* Diplôme d'Etudes Approfondies: Université de Paris-Sorbonne.

Birgegård, Ulla. 1992. "Sparvenfel'd o russkom jazyke". *Dolomonosovskij period russkogo literaturnogo jazyka, The pre-Lomonosov Period of the Russian Literary Language* éd. par Sjöberg, Anders, Ďurovič & Birgegård. Stockholm: Slavica Suecana. (= *Series B – Studies,* 1.)

Biržakova. 1980. *Slovari i slovarnoe delo v Rossii.* Sankt Petersburg: Izd. Akad. Nauk SSR.

Brjus, Ja. V. 1717. *Kniga leksikon ili Sobranie rečej po alfavitu s Rossijskogo na Gollandskij jazyk* [Lexique, ou Recueil alphabétique de mots traduits du russe en hollandais.] Sankt Peterburg (Appendice à la grammaire de Sevel. Vilim: *Iskusstvo nederlandskogo jazyka* [Art de la langue néerlandaise].)

–. 1717. *Leksikon gollandsko-russkij* [Lexique hollandais-russe.] Sankt Peterburg.

Donat 1522. *Donatus, sireč gramatika i azbuka perevedenaja Dimitriem Tolmačem s latinskago jazyka* [Le Donat, à savoir grammaire et alphabet traduits du latin par Dimitri l'Interprète.] (voir Jagič, 1885–1895 [1968] et Worth, 1983)

Douay, Françoise. 1992. "La rhétorique en Europe à travers son enseignement". *Histoire des Idées Linguistiques* éd. par Sylvain Auroux, tome 2, 467–507. Liège: Mardaga.

Ďurovič, Lubomir. 1991. "Grammatika Akademičeskoj gimnazii". *Dolomonosovskij period russkogo literaturnogo jazyka, The pre-Lomonosov period of the russian literary language.* Slavica Suecana. (= Series B, Studies, 1: 171–211.) Stockholm: [La grammaire du Lycée de l'Académie.]

– & Sjöberg, Anders. 1987. "Drevnejšij istočnik paradigmatiki sovremennogo literaturnogo jazyka" [Aux sources de la paradigmatique du russe moderne]. *Russian Linguistics* 11: 2, 3.255–278.

Fenne Tonnis. 1607. *Tönnies Fenne's Low German Manual of Spoken Russian.* Éd. par Hammerich & Jakobson, 1970. Copenhagen: A. H. van den Baar.

Glück, Johann Ernst. 1704. *Grammatik der russischen Sprache.* Éd. par Helmut Keipert, B. Uspenskij & V. Živov, 1994. Köln, Weimar & Wien: Böhlau.

Jagič, Vatroslav, éd. 1885–95. *Razsuždenija južnoslavjanskoj i russkoj stariny o cerkovno slavjanskom jazyke.* Issledovanija po russkomu jazyku. Sankt Peterburg.

Kutina, L. L. & É. É. Biržakova. 1980. *Slovari i slovarnoe delo v Rossii XVIII v.* [Dictionnaires et dictionnairique en Russie au XVIIIe siècle.] Leningrad: Nauka.

Lomonosov, M[ixail] V[asiljevič]. 1755. *Rossijskaja grammatika* [Grammaire russe.] Sankt Peterburg. (Ed. utilisée, voir Lomonosov. OC. 1952.)

—. 1951—52. *Polnoe sobranie sočinenij.* Tome 7: *Materjaly k trudam po filologii.* Moskva & Leningrad: Izd. Akademii Nauk. (Œuvres Complètes, Tome 7: Travaux de philologie.)

Ludolf, Wilhelm Henry. 1696. *Grammatica russica, quæ continet non tantum præcipua fundamenta Russicæ Linguæ, verum etiam Manuductionem quandam ad Grammaticam Slavonicam.* Oxonii: E Theatro Sheldoniano. Éd. par Boris Unbegaun. 1959. Oxford: Clarendon Press.

Pamvo Berinda. 1627. *Leksikon" slavenorosskij i imen" tl "kovanie.* Kiev. Éd. par Vasyl' Vasyl'ovič Nimčuk. 1961. Kiev: Academija Nauk Ukrainskoj RSR.

Sparwenfeld, Johan Gabriel. ca. 1700. *Lexicon Slavonicum*, 4 tomes. Éd. par Ulla Birgegård. 1987, 1988, 1989, 1990. Upsalla.

Smirnov, N. A. 1910. *Zapadnoe vlijanie na russkij jazyk v Petrovskuju epoxu.* Sankt Peterburg: Tip. Imp. Akademii Nauk.

Smotrickij, Meletij. 1618—1619. *Grammatiki Slavenskija pravilnoe Syntagma osmi častij potščaniem mnogogrešnago mnixa Meletija Smotrickogo* [Composition correcte des huit parties de la grammaire slave par le soin du pécamineux moine Meletjus Smotrickij.] Éd. par Olexa Horbatsch, 1974. Frankfurt/M.: Kubon & Sagner.

Stankiewicz, E. 1984. *Grammars and Dictionaries of the Slavic Languages from the Middle Ages up to 1850.* An annotated Bibliography. Berlin, New York & Amsterdam: Mouton de Gruyter.

Suxomlinov, M[ixail] I[vanocič.] 1874. *'Istorija Akademii Nauk' v Sbornike otdelenija russkago jazyka i slovesnosti Imperatorskoj Akademii Nauk.* Vol. 1, Tome XI. Sankt Peterburg. ["Histoire de l'Académie des Sciences" in Recueil de la section de langue russe et philologie de l'Académie impériale des Sciences.]

Unbegaun, Boris. 1935. *La langue russe au XVI^e^ siècle (1500—1550)*, vol. I, *La flexion des noms.* Paris: Honoré Champion.

Unbegaun, Boris O., éd. 1969. *Drei russische Grammatiken des 18. Jahrhunderts.* Nachdruck der Ausgaben von 1706, 1731 und 1750 mit einer Einleitung von B. O. Unbegaun. München: Fink.

Uspenskij, B[oris] A[leksandrovič.] 1994. *Kratkij očerk istorii russkogo literaturnogo jazyka* [Abrégé d'histoire de la langue russe normée.] Moskva: Gnosis.

Vomperskij, V[alentin] P[avlovič.] 1986. *Slovari XVIII veka* [Les dictionnaires du XVIII^e^ siècle.] Moskva: Nauka.

Vomperskij, V[alentin] P[avlovič]. 1988. *Ritoriki v Rossii XVII—XVIII vv.* [Rhétoriques en Russie aux XVII^e^ et XVIII^e^ siècles.] Moskva: Nauka.

Zizanij Lavrentij. 1591 & 1596. *Grammatika slovenska soveršennago iskustva osmi častij slova i inyx nuždyx sostavlena L. Z.* [Grammaire slave de l'art parfait des huit parties du discours et autres choses utiles.] Éd. par Gerd Freidhof, 1972. München: Kubon & Sagner, Specimina Philologiæ Slavicaæ.

Živov, V[iktor] M[arkovič.] 1996. *Jazyk i kul'tura v Rossii XVIII veka* [Langue et culture dans la Russie du XVIII^e^ siècle.] Moskva: Škola "Jazyki russkoj kul'tury".

*Sylvie Archaimbault, Paris (France)*

# 122. Normativ orientierte Sprachforschung zum Tschechischen

1. Der Begriff der Literatursprache
2. Die älteste Periode
3. Die Anfänge des Purismus
4. Humanistische Philologie
5. Die Barocke Periode
6. Die Entstehung der modernen Literatursprache
7. Der Prager Strukturalismus
8. Die neueste Entwicklung
9. Bibliographie

## 1. Der Begriff der Literatursprache

Die Literatursprache (Standard) als ein funktionales System, das den Bedürfnissen der Sprachgemeinschaft im Bereich der intellektuellen und kulturellen Verständigung dient, ist nicht nur das Ergebnis einer eigenen Entwicklung, sondern auch der Kultivierung der Sprache durch die Benutzer.

Diese regulative, normative Tätigkeit ist eingestellt auf das Erreichen der Funktionalität und Stabilität der einzelnen Sprachmittel. Ziel dieser Regulierung ist die Funktionalisierung der Literatursprache als "Trägerin und Vermittlerin von Kultur und Zivilisation durch einen möglichst großen Umfang ihres territorialen und ethnischen Verbreitungsgebiets" (Havránek in: Horálek et al. 1975: I.106).

In der tschechischen Literatursprache haben sich seit ihren Anfängen im 13. Jh. drei aus der Antike stammenden Kriterien der Regulierung der Sprache geltend gemacht: der Sprachgebrauch der Zeitgenossen, *usus*, das

Vorbild der anerkannten Autoren, *auctoritas*, und die Übereinstimmung der Philologen, *consensus eruditorum* (Quint. *I. o.* 1,6,45).

## 2. Die älteste Periode

Als älteste Literatursprache auf böhmischen Gebiet ist seit der 2. Hälfte des 9. Jh. die kirchenslawische Sprache verwendet worden; sie diente als Sprache der Liturgie, des Kirchenrechtes und der Legenden. Das Verbot der kirchenslawischen Liturgie und die Auflösung der slawischen Mönchgemeinde (1097) bedeutete das Ende der kirchenslawischen Kultur in Böhmen. Die Funktion der Literatursprache wurde jetzt vom Lateinischen, Tschechischen und Deutschen übernommen.

Die tschechische Literatursprache war seit den ältesten Zeiten durch die Zugehörigkeit zum Prager kulturellen Zentrum gekennzeichnet. Dadurch wurden die liturgische und allgemein religiöse Funktion der Literatursprache um die Funktionen der dichterischen, fachbezogenen und administrativ-rechtlichen Sprache ergänzt. Während der Reformation und Gegenreformation haben sich Genres des persuasiven Stils der Sprache entwickelt (Predigten, Manifeste, etc.).

Die Entwicklung der Literatursprache war nicht geradlinig. Perioden des Aufschwungs wechselten mit Perioden, die durch eine Einschränkung der Rolle der Literatursprache markiert waren. Die Einheitlichkeit der Literatursprache wurde durch den Schulunterricht in der Muttersprache verstärkt, seit dem Anfang des 16. Jh. auch durch die schnelle Verbreitung des Buchdruckes.

Die normative Rolle der ältesten schriftlichen Dokumente entstammt dem Bedürfnis, die Literatursprache zu stabilisieren und ihre stilistische Differenzierung zu vertiefen. Das Anfangsstadium der Sprachbeschreibung repräsentieren die terminologischen Wörterbücher, die sogenannten *Mamotrekte*, Erläuterungen zur Bibel, welche thematisch, nach der Abfolge der Bücher der Bibel, oder alphabetisch angeordnet waren.

## 3. Die Anfänge des Purismus

Der Höhepunkt dieser Periode bilden drei thematische Nomenklatoren des Bartholomeus von Chlumec (Klaret) († 1379), in denen viele Neologismen eingeführt werden: *Vokabulář gramatický, Bohemář* und *Glosář*.

Neben dem Wortschatz wird auch die Grammatik (unter Einschluß der Orthographie) zum Objekt der normativen Sprachbeschreibung. Eine besondere Stellung hat die *Orthographia Bohemica* (1406 oder 1412), welche dem Magister der Karlsuniversität Jan Hus (1370?–1415) zugeschrieben wird. Hus kodifiziert hierin die sogenannte diakritische Regelung der lateinischen Schrift, um sie dem tschechischen Lautsystem anzupassen. Diakritika (z. B. *č, š, ř, ž*) beseitigen die Nachteile der älteren Schreibsysteme.

Hus war auch einer der ersten Verfechter der Sprachreinigung (Purismus). Seine Zeitgenossen kritisiert er für den Gebrauch der Wörter deutscher Abstammung; in dem Wortschatz seiner Schriften und Predigten entwickelt er die Wortbildungsmöglichkeiten der Literatursprache. Er lehnt sich an den Gebrauch des Prager Kulturzentrums an (wovon er sich andererseits durch einen gewissen Konservativismus wieder unterscheidet).

Die Sprache von Hus und das Tschechische der ältesten Bibelübersetzungen (aus dem 15. Jh. sind 20 Manuskripte der tschechischen Bibel und mehr als 100 Übersetzungsfragmente erhalten) wurden zu den ältesten Mustern der national einheitlichen Literatursprache.

## 4. Humanistische Philologie

Der tschechische Humanismus, der in einem intensiven Kontakt mit den Zentren der europäischen Kultur entwickelt wurde, zeichnet sich durch eine philologische Orientierung aus. Verbreitet ist besonders das Genre der mehrsprachigen Wörterbücher (*Silva quadrilinguis vocabulorum et phrasium bohemicae latinae, grecae et germanicae linguae* (1598) von Daniel Adam von Veleslavín (1546–1599), das durch seine tschechische Komponente Aktualität bis zur 'Periode der nationalen Wiedergeburt' behält). An der Grenze zwischen Wörterbüchern und Schriften zu Stilfragen entwickelt sich das Genre der sogenannten Eleganzen, die neben den grammatischen Lehrsätzen auch Listen von Phrasen, Sprichwörtern und Redewendungen enthalten (nach Valla und Erasmus), so die *Dicteria seu proverbia bohemica* (1582) von Jakub Srnec von Varvažov (?–1586), die *Elegantissimae colloquiorum formulae* (1550) von Pavel Vorličný und die Auswahl der Redewendungen aus der antiken Literatur mit tschechischen Äquivalenten von Veleslavín (1591).

Auf Vallas Auffassung, daß das höchste Kriterium der Richtigkeit der Usus der Zeitgenossen ist, berufen sich die Autoren des Versuchs der tschechischen Grammatik (1533) von den Mährern und Mitgliedern der Unitas fratrum, Beneš Optát, Petr Gzel und Václav Philomates, geschrieben wurde. Die Grammatik enthält eine Rechtschreibungs- und Aussprachekodifikation, stilistische Erläuterungen und eine Verteidigung der Grundsätze, nach denen sich die Autoren bei der Übersetzung der Bibel (die sogenannte *Bible kralická*) richteten. Die 'Brüderrechtschreibung' (*bratrský pravopis*) hatte sich bis zum Anfang des 19. Jhs. erhalten. Die Sprachnorm der Bibel von Kralice wurde weitgehend durch die *Grammatika česká* (1571, neue Ed. 1991) von Jan Blahoslav (1523–1571) übernommen. In seiner Auffassung von der Literatursprache ist Blahoslav konservativ.

Die Sorge um die 'Kultur der Muttersprache' (*cultura idiomatis*) charakterisiert die Schrift *Grammaticae bohemicae libri duo* des Slowaken Vavřinec Benedikt Nudožerin (1603, neue Ed. 1999).

## 5. Die Barocke Periode

Nach der Niederlage der Reformation im Jahre 1620 mußten die Mitglieder der Brüdergemeinde das Land verlassen. Der Hauptrepräsentant der tschechischen Exilliteratur Jan Ámos Komenský (1592–1670) hat einen Thesaurus des Tschechischen verfasst, der jedoch einem Brand in Lešno zum Opfer fiel. Sein pädagogisches Werk ist vor allem auf den Unterricht der Muttersprache konzentriert, welche er ständig mit Fremdsprachen konfrontierte (*Janua linguarum reserata*, 1637). In den Grammatiken von Komenský kommt seine normative Bestrebung zum Ausdruck, die Übereinstimmung zwischen Wörtern und bezeichneten Phänomenen zu festigen (was mit dem Projekt einer künstlichen internationalen Sprache zusammenhängt).

Die inländische Lage war für die Entwicklung der tschechischen Sprache nicht günstig. Sie hatte aufgehört, Sprache des höheren Adels und der reichen Bürger zu sein. Die Sprache der Wissenschaften wurde das Lateinische und das Deutsche. Die Rolle der Amtssprache teilten sich das Tschechische und das Deutsche seit 1627 (infolge dessen wurde in den Manuskripten bis zur ersten Hälfte des 19. Jh. die ältere humanistische Schrift durch die einheimische Variante der deutschen neogotischen Kursive, die Kurrentschrift, ersetzt).

Tschechisch geschriebene Dramen beschränkten sich auf Schul- und volkstümliche Szenen; höhere Dichtung wird nur ausnahmsweise in Tschechisch geschrieben (Kadlinský, Bridel). Die Barockzeit hat jedoch einen Aufschwung des tschechischen Predigens und des geistigen Liedes gebracht. In Tschechisch wurden auch Dorf- und Stadtchroniken geschrieben. Seit der theresianischen Reform des Grundschulwesens (1774) verbreitet sich der tschechische Unterricht und entsprechende Lehrbücher. Seit 1786 werden tschechische Zeitungen, aber auch Unterhaltungswerke und Bücher belehrenden Inhalts herausgegeben.

Die Konkurrenz des Tschechischen mit Fremdsprachen führte zu puristischen Tendenzen. Eine Bemühung um eine Verbesserung des Sprachgebrauchs macht sich bemerkbar in der Grammatik von Jan Drachovský *Grammatica bohemica in V libris divisa*, herausgegeben von Václav Matěj Šteyer (1660). Šteyer selbst hat im Jahre 1668 ein Kodifikationshandbuch *Žáček* (Der kleine Schüler, 1668) in Form eines Dialogs zwischen Lehrer und Schüler herausgegeben. Die antike Tradition des 'Sprachpolierens' reflektiert *Lima linguae bohemicae, to jest Brus jazyka českého* ('Das Wetzmittel der tschechischen Sprache', 1667) von dem Jesuiten Jiří Konstanc. Mehr radikal puristisch-neologistisch orientiert ist *Čechořečnost seu Grammatica linguae bohemicae* (Tschechischrederei [...], 1672, neue Ed. 1991) von Václav Jan Rosa (1620–1689). In den angeführten Paradigmen spiegelt sich der uneinheitliche Usus der Epoche wider. Ein Fortschritt in der Beschreibung der Sprache und ein Ausgangspunkt für die späteren Kodifizierungen war die *Grammatica Slavico-Bohemica* (1746) des Slowaken Pavel Doležal, die sich auf das biblische Tschechisch, wie es in der Slowakei verbreitet wurde, stützte. Im 18. Jh. wurde zum siebtenmal die *Grammatica linguae Bohemicae* von Václav Jandyt (1704) herausgegeben, in der die damalige Schwankung der Standardnorm erfasst wurde. Befürchtungen über das Schicksal des Tschechischen kamen zum Ausdruck in patriotischen Apologien der Muttersprache (z. B. in der lateinischen Apologie des Jesuiten Bohuslav Balbín aus dem Jahre 1672–1673).

Die steigende Anzahl der tschechisch gedruckten Bücher sowie die Forderungen der Schule haben die Notwendigkeit, die Standardnorm zu konsolidieren, mit sich gebracht. Zum Sprachmuster wurde die modifizierte Ausgabe der Sankt-Wenzeslaus Bibel (1715), die von der Bibel von Kralice ausgeht. Zwischen 1775 und 1825 wurden 28 tschechische Grammatiken und 14 Wörterbücher gedruckt.

Durch Konservativismus sind die *Grundsätze der böhmischen Grammatik* (1796) von František Martin Pelcl (1734–1801) gekennzeichnet; dagegen zeichnet sich *Böhmische Sprachlehre* (1782) von František Jan Tomsa (1753–1814) durch eine Bevorzugung des mündlichen Sprachgebrauchs aus.

## 6. Die Entstehung der modernen Literatursprache

Bei der Stabilisierung der Literatursprache im 19. Jh. spielte jedoch – dank seiner Systematik und der sorgfältigen Bearbeitung der Fakten – das 'Ausführliche Lehrgebäude der böhmischen Sprache' von Josef Dobrovský (1809, 1819) eine wichtige Rolle. Dobrovský stützt sich darin auf die Sprache der Humanisten vom Anfang des 16. Jh. Er verweist gewisse Erscheinungen in das Gebiet der Volkssprache und führt die sogenannte analogische Rechtschreibung, d. h. die Differenzierung zwischen *y* und *i* in den Flexionsendungen, ein.

Nach der sogenannten 'zusammenşetzenden' Modifikation von Pavel Josef Šafařík i. J. 1849 (z. B. *v* statt *w*, *ou* statt *au*) wurde die tschechische Orthographie für lange Zeit stabilisiert. Eine wichtige Folge des Rückgriffs auf die humanistische Norm ist die Unterscheidung zwischen Literatursprache und Alltagssprache. Als Klassizist lehnt Dobrovský Neologismen ab (er zählt die Erfindung neuer Wörtern nicht zu den Aufgaben der Grammatiker); er empfiehlt statt dessen, nach vergessenen Wörtern zu suchen oder Wörter aus slawischen Sprachen zu übernehmen.

Die Entwicklung des Wortschatzes wird eine Aufgabe für folgende Generationen. Autorität gewinnt das fünfbändige *Česko-německý slovník* (Tschechisch-deutsches W., 1835–1839) von Josef Jungmann und die terminologische Tätigkeit des Jungmann-Kreises.

In der zweiten Hälfte des 19. Jh. steht die normative Einstellung zur Sprache ganz im Zeichen des Purismus. Zum Muster der sprachlichen Richtigkeit wird nach den Autoren des *Matiční brus* ('Muttersprachenwetz', 1877) – zahlreiche Autoren lassen ihm ähnliche Handbücher folgen – die Sprache der älteren Autoren, der Volksgebrauch, ferner Analogien mit anderen slawischen Sprachen und die Bemühung, das Tschechische von wirklichen sowie vermuteten Einflüssen des Deutschen freizumachen.

"Die Gräber, die den Weg des neuzeitlichen Tschechischen Purismus säumen" (Mathesius in: Horálek et al. 1975: 92) gehen auf das Konto des Strebens nach historischer Reinheit und Regularität der sprachlichen Formen. Mit Recht hat der berühmte, mit Sprachgeschichte sich beschäftigende Grammatiker Jan Gebauer (1838–1907), Autor der normativen Schulbücher des Tschechischen, in der Einleitung zu der ersten Ausgabe der Orthographieregeln (*Pravidla pravopisu*, 1902) diese zwei Prinzipien abgelehnt: "Was die Formen betrifft, so halten wir uns streng an das, was sich in der Literatursprache von sich selbst entwickelt und eingelebt hat" (Mathesius in: Horálek et al. 1975: 93).

Nach Gebauers Tode verstärkten sich trotzdem die archaisierenden Tendenzen, deren Hauptförderer die Redaktion der 1916 gegründeten Zeitschrift *Naše řeč* (Unsere Sprache) war. Ihre puristische Orientierung wurde in den zwanziger Jahren durch die Arbeit der Linguisten Josef Zubaty und Václav Ertl gemildert. Ertl sieht die organische Grundlage der literatursprachlichen Norm im heutigen Usus, der aber keine Auslese aus der Alltagssprache darstellt, sondern auf der sprachlichen Praxis der guten Autoren beruht, welche in den letzten 50 Jahren publiziert haben.

## 7. Der Prager Strukturalismus

Als nach der Gründung des tschechoslowakischen Staates im Jahre 1918 die nationale und die kulturelle Selbständigkeit errungen wurde, wurden an die tschechische Literatursprache neue Ansprüche gestellt. In dieser Lage wandte sich eine Gruppe von Linguisten (Mathesius, Havránek, Jakobson usw.), die unter der Bezeichnung Prager Linguistenkreis, PLK, auftrat, Fragen der gegenwärtigen Sprache zu. Die neue Einstellung zu der sprachlichen Realität, die das Programm des PLK bildete, wurde erstmals in kollektiven *Thesen* (Horálek et al. 1975: 43f.) formuliert, die dem in Prag stattfindenden I. internationalen Slawistenkongress (1929) vorgelegt wurden. Besondere Aufmerksamkeit wurde hierin Problemen der Norm der Literatursprache und ihrer Kultivierung gewidmet.

Fragen der Norm und der Sprachkultur wurden zum festen Bestandteil der Prager Sprachtheorie. Die Kodifizierung der Literatursprache sollte aus dem Gebrauch, der als bedeutende, aber nicht einzige Quelle ('der oberste Schiedsrichter') gilt, hervorgehen. In dem Sammelband *Spisovná čeština a jazyková kultura* (Die tschechische Literatursprache und die Sprachkultur, 1932) betonte Havránek, daß der Gebrauch alleine die Norm der Literatursprache nicht hervorbringen kann. Sie entwickelt sich unter dem Einfluß verschiedener Tendenzen, worunter auch die Theorie zu zählen ist.

Eingriffe in die Literatursprache müssen auf der Grundlage sicherer Kenntnisse der bestehenden Normen und ihrer Tendenzen erfolgen. Zur Theorie der Norm genügt also nicht das einfache Erfassen, die bloße Feststellung des Gebrauchs, sondern es ist dazu vor allem notwendig, in das Sprachsystem und seine funktionale Schichtung einzudringen und die Regelmäßigkeiten zu erkennen, die der heutigen Norm zugrundeliegen. Die Kultivierung der Sprache und die Kodifikation der Standardnorm müssen sich nach dieser Erkenntnis richten. Die Aufgabe der Linguisten ist es, innerhalb der möglichen systembedingten Entwicklung der Norm die tatsächlichen Tendenzen herauszufinden und Veränderungen nicht zu hemmen, sondern durch geeignete Kodifizierung zu fördern.

Das neunbändige *Příruční slovník jazyka českého* (Handwörterbuch der tschechischen Sprache, 1935–1957) ist deskriptiv, enthält allerdings auch einige bewertende Angaben wie 'unrichtig', 'unangemessen', etc. Das vierbändige *Slovník spisovného jazyka českého* (W. der tschechischen Sprache, 1960–1971), Ergebnis der Tätigkeit des im Jahre 1946 gegründeten Instituts für die tschechische Sprache (vorher, seit 1911, Büro des tschechischen Wörterbuches), befasste sich schon mit der Bewertung des Sprachsystems. Das dritte der akademischen Wörterbücher, *Slovník spisovné češtiny pro školu a veřejnost* (W. der Literatursprache für Schule und Öffentlichkeit, 1978, überarbeitete Ausgabe 1994) kodifiziert ein ganzes Gefüge von Normen – lexikalische, orthographische, orthoepische, morphologische und syntaktische.

## 8. Die neuste Entwicklung

Nach der 'Samtrevolution' 1989 konzentriert sich das erhöhte Interesse der Öffentlichkeit auf die Kultur des Tschechischen (das mit dem neu entstandenen Patriotismus und der Kritik an der Sprache des Totalitarismus verknüpft ist), besonders auf die Sprache der Medien, des Rechtes und der Staatsverwaltung. Dieses Interesse gerät manchmal in Konflikt mit dem gleichzeitig betonten Bedürfnis nach Toleranz für Alternativen bzw. Randerscheinungen, auch auf dem Gebiet der Sprache. Widersprüche ergeben sich in den Diskussionen über das Verhältnis von Literatursprache und Alltagssprache (vgl. z. B. Eckert 1993), über die Orthographiereform des Jahres 1993 sowie über die Möglichkeiten und Grenzen der Kodifikation der Literatursprache im allgemeinen.

## 9. Bibliographie

Eckert, Eva, Hg. 1993. *Varieties of Czech: Studies in Czech sociolinguistics.* Amsterdam & Atlanta: Rodopi.

Havránek, Bohuslav. 1979. *Vývoj českého spisovného jazyka* [Die Entwicklung der tschechischen Literatursprache.] Praha: Státní pedagogické nakladatelství.

Horálek, Karel, Jaroslav Kuchař, Jürgen Scharnhorst & Erika Ising, Hg. *Grundlagen der Sprachkultur. Beiträge der Prager Linguistik zur Sprachtheorie und Sprachpflege.* Teil 1. Berlin: Akademie Verlag, 1975. Teil 2. Berlin: Akademie Verlag, 1982.

Sgall, Petr, Jiří Hronek, Alexandr Stich & Ján Horecky, Hg. 1992. *Variation in Language.* Amsterdam & Philadelphia: Benjamins.

Vachek, Josef. 1966. *The Linguistic School of Prague.* Bloomington: Indiana Univ. Press.

–, Hg. 1964. *A Prague School Reader in Linguistics.* Bloomington: Indiana Univ. Press.

*Jiri Kraus, Prag (Tschechien)*

# 123. Normative studies in Poland

1. Normative studies from the Middle Ages to the second half of the 18th century
2. Care for language from the Enlightenment to regaining independence
3. Normative studies between the wars; new institutions and conceptions
4. After World War II
5. Bibliography

## 1. Normative studies from the Middle Ages to the second half of the 18th century

### 1.1. The first 15th century document of thought on language

The need of translating into and writing in Polish — in the cases of historical, theological and legal documents which should be intelligible to everyone — is for the first time acknowledged in the anonymous Latin introduction to Jakub Parkoszowic [Treatise on Polish Orthography] (ca. 1450; cf. Taszycki, 1953: xiv–xv, 3–9), preserved in manuscripts, as well as in the later pronouncements of Polish humanists of the 16th century.

### 1.2. The 16th century: the period of conscious cultivation of the language

The 16th century, later recognized as the 'Golden Age' of the Polish Renaissance culture, brings the first grammar books, dictionaries and other writings confirming the emergence of thinking about the Polish linguistic norm. Piotr Statorius (born about 1530), of French origin, in his *Polonicae grammatices institutio* (1568), aims at describing 'elegant' Polish. Statorius frequently warns against dialectal forms, thus complying with the requirement of the Polish 16th century humanists to create a literary standard of Polish. Two competing attitudes towards the literary language become explicit in the linguistic debate among the Lutheran translators of the Bible in the forties of the 16th century (cf. Klemensiewicz 1974: 388–399). The first approach favours archaisms and accepts Czech borrowings, while the other — open to German and Latin impact — advocates colloquialisms. The latter attitude is more popular in the discussed period: in the 16th century Latin borrowings together with neologisms are considered indispensable for vocabulary enrichment necessary to match the rapid cultural advancement.

### 1.3. The Baroque grammarians and dictionary compilers against Latin influences

In the 17th century, when the literary language standard becomes relaxed and the influence of the Baroque poetics and of the Latin language on Polish become more pronounced, Grzegorz Knapski (Cnapius, 1564–1639), an eminent lexicographer, strongly objects to the growing number of Latin loanwords and to the ornate style. His dictionary: *Thesaurus Polono-Latino-Graecus* (Kraków 1621) is clearly normative in character. Among the numerous grammarians of the period, Jan Karol Woyna (1665–1693), the author of *Compendiosa linguae Polonicae Institutio* (Gdańsk 1690) — an explicitly normative grammar containing a fairly extensive list of words described as 'obsoleta, barbara et inusitata' — is especially sensitive to foreign influences.

## 2. Care for language from the Enlightenment to regaining independence (1918)

### 2.1. The thought on language as an element of the general task of the nations enlightenment

The second half of the 18th century is the time of the Enlightenment in Poland. It is also the time of patriotic revival and attempts at reforming the declining state. Grammarians, authors of poetics, tutors of rhetoric, writers and essayists point to the necessity of cultivating the native language in pursuit of knowledge, interpersonal communication and 'general enlightenment'. The need of establishing an academy or another 'learned society' that could pass judgements in linguistic matters became more and more pronounced. In 1773, the Committee for National Education and a primary school system are set up. Onufry Kopczyński (1735–1817), the most respected linguist of the period prepares a normative grammar for the schools. — The Enlightenment writers, beginning with a forerunner of the Polish Enlightenment, Stanisław Konarski (a Piarist; 1700–1773) — the author of the Latin works *De emendandis eloquentiae vitiis* (Warszawa 1741) and *De arte bene cogitandi ad artem dicendi bene necessa-*

*ria* Warszawa 1767) – and Michał Abraham Troc (1703–1769) – the author of the *Nowy dykcjonarz, to jest mownik polsko-niemiecko-francuski* [A new dictionary, that is a new Polish-German-French lexicon] (Leipzig 1764) – postulate clarity and spontaneity of language in opposition to the ideals of the Baroque poetics. Konarski introduces a sharp distinction between written and spoken language on the one hand and between the languages of poetry and prose on the other (cf. Mayenowa 1958: 39, 45). According to many Enlightenment writers, the written language should be free of dialectal and foreign (Latin, French) loanwords, with the exception of those that had already been assimilated. There is a need – especially in scientific terminology – to coin neologisms which, however, should meet specific requirements. The ideal Polish is the Polish of the 16th century, hence the latter should be used in the fight against loanwords and colloquialisms.

### 2.2. The period of the nation's bondage; alttempts at preserving pure and unified Polish

In the early decades of the 19th century, i. e. during the Polish Neo-classicism, the ideal of language purity becomes even more emphasized. Until the November Uprising in 1830, the Society of the Friends of Sciences develops its activities in Warsaw. They are important for advancing and spreading knowledge about the Polish language and its cultivation. In 1830 a branch of the Society comes up with the Studies on and Recommendations for Polish Orthography, the most important of the studies on Polish orthography in that period. The work was also recognized by the Polish Academy of Skills, when in 1890 it proclaimed its rules for Polish orthography (Bajerowa 1986: 154). – The leaders of the Enlightenment and the members of the Society of the Friends of Sciences suggested that a great normative dictionary of Polish, similar to those of French or Russian, should be compiled. However, Samuel Bogumił Linde's (1771–1847) six volume *Słownik Języka Polskiego* [The dictionary of the Polish language], published in the years 1807–1814 did not satisfy their needs. The dictionary was historical and comparative with few stylistic and prescriptive notes. Troc's dictionary from the 18th century contained many more remarks about pure, elegant and stylistically diversified Polish (cf. Walczak 1988: 417–418). Troc's normative thinking is continued in the 19th century by the authors of the so called Vilna Dictionary (published by Maurycy Orgelbrand in 1861), who introduce a fully modern, extensive system of qualifiers including the stylistic and prescriptive ones. – For Poland, the 19th century is a period of national bondage. In the first half of the century, there is a strong influence of Western European Romanticism, especially in its German version, according to which the spirit of the language determines the expression of national identity. Poles perceived 'the spirit of the language' as an important factor in surviving the 'night of slavery'. – In the first half of the 19th century many authors of Polish grammars – beginning with O. Kopczyński, T. Szumski, J. N. Deszkiewicz and others – advocate introducing archaic language norms, with the Polish of the 16th century remaining the ideal. They perceive the influences of the languages of the three partitioners (Russian and German) and of the upper classes (French) as especially dangerous for Polish (cf. Urbańczyk 1958: 495–496). Apart from grammar, many works focus on linguistic mistakes and inaccuracies. They are written by both linguists and non-linguists such as Władyslaw Bentkowski – a deputy to the Prussian Parliament, or Franciszek Skobel – a professor of medicine in the Jagiellonian University. The authors are convinced that preserving a pure and unified language – in spite of the partitions – constitutes the foundation of the Polish culture endangered by the occupants' persecution. – At the beginning of the 20th century, the linguists such as Aleksander Brückner (1856–1939) or Artur Pussendorfer (1964–1936) write in a similar vein. In 1901, the journal *Poradnik Językowy* [Advising on language] comes into existence. In 1913 its title changes to *Język Polski* [The Polish language] and eminent linguists of the period (Jan Łoś (1860–1928), Kazimierz Nitsch (1874–1958), Jan Rozwadowski (1867–1935)) turn it into a more general linguistic periodical. – Jan Baudouin de Courtenay's (1845–1929) attitude to normative linguistics had undergone a change: in the seventies of the 19th century his views were close to those of the Young Grammarians, when he claimed that "all discussions on how one should [...] speak [...], which forms one should use [...] are worthless from a purely scientific perspective" (Baudouin 1904: 274); in 1888, however, he recognized as one of the goals of linguistics "preserving the continuity and purity of the literary language" (ibid., 46). Similarly to other Polish linguists of the 20th century, Baudouin believes that language correctness requires at least some linguistic knowledge among language users.

## 3. Normative studies between the wars; new institutions and conceptions

In between the wars, normative linguists aimed at unifying the language of Poles, who had lived in three different states until regaining independence (cf. Szober 1937: 63). The linguists also realized that a Polish terminology in sciences, crafts, and social life needed creation or extension. Finally, they knew that language and style awareness among the citizens of the new Polish state needed deepening. Two societies: the Society of the Friends of the Polish Language in Cracow and the Society for Advancing Language Correctness and Culture (now: the Society of Language Culture) in Warsaw were to help in the process. Moreover, in the thirties, the journal *Poradnik Językowy* reappeared and has been published ever since. – In the 20th century, the view (reflected in the title of the journal) that the function of normative linguistics is only advisory becomes well established: linguists should provide synchronic and diachronic descriptions of languages and justifications of linguistic norms, which (outside schools and orthography) should be treated as guidelines rather than prescriptive rules (cf. e. g. Szober 1913; Brückner 1917: 6). However, this approach has not been reflected in the two subsequent orthoepic dictionaries which have had many printings so far (Szober 1937a; Doroszewski & Kurkowska 1973). Similarly, the great post-war dictionaries of the Polish language edited by W. Doroszewski (1958–1969) and M. Szymczak (1978) are clearly normative in character.

## 4. After World War II

### 4.1. Criteria of language correctness; influences of structuralism

Witold Doroszewski (1899–1976) is the author of, among others, the work on language correctness criteria, which he divides into: formal and logical, national, aesthetic, geographical, literary and historical. Depending on their views on the evolution and functions of language, other Polish theoretical normative linguists have modified the criteria and restructured their hierarchy, preserving, however, the tendency (present since the Enlightenment) to treat the language of the educated members of the society as the standard, although the very identification of the members has caused problems. – In the post-war period, the fundamental normative work, the two-volume *Kultura Języka Polskiego* [The culture of the Polish language] (Buttler, Kurkowska & Satkiewicz 1973, 1982) assumes the framework of the European structuralism, especially of the Prague School. The authors focus on the correctness of the language code, at the same time accepting Coseriu's distinctions among system, use and norm. The latter, which is of the greatest interest to the authors, is understood as a set of language units and rules of their combinations (called 'the natural norm' as opposed to the 'codified norm') accepted by the language community. The authors consider as ideal the language which "satisfies all the communicative needs of its users at their least effort" (Buttler, Kurkowska & Satkiewiez 1973: 22). Consequently, the criteria of "evaluating innovations in language" comprise not only the educated language users' standard but also the language internal criterion of sufficiency and economy. – Halina Kurkowska (1977: 24) introduced to the Polish normative linguistics the problem of the language norm diversification. Accordingly, authors of subsequent works accept two separate codifying norms: colloquial and standard (cf. Markowski 1999: X). J. Miodek (1983: 79) and A. Furdal (1971: 69) emphasize the need of establishing different norms for different language varieties and styles.

### 4.2. Linguistic normative studies interacting with sociolinguistics, pragmatics and cultural anthropology

The latest development of normative linguistics in Poland has been influenced by sociolinguistics, pragmatics and cultural anthropology. Sociolinguistics has helped in drawing clear social distinctions among language users and in approaching the issues of language policy (cf. Lubaś 1977; Bugajski 1989). Pragmatics and text grammar have brought to the attention of normative linguists the whole area of communicative acts (cf. Puzynina 1990: 157) and text structure (Gajda 1995: 58–59). Austin's notion of speech act felicity conditions, Grice's theory of conversational maxims and Robin Lakoff's 'politeness grammar' have led to the incorporation in normative linguistics of some elements of speech ethics: the truth of the message and respect for the addressee (cf. Pajdzińska & Puzynina 1996: 36). The issues have shown their significance and complexity in Poland — a, then, socialist country, in which authorities, mass media and many representatives of culture and science used Orwell's 'newspeak'. — Since the twenties of the 20th century, the Polish normative linguistics has taken on the label "the culture of language". The very wording of the phrase applies both — to the 'culture' of language constituting a branch of applied linguistics and to the way people use their language — correctly and fluently but also 'culturally', i. e. in agreement with a person's individual culture, which roots 'the culture of language' in culture as such (cf. Puzynina 1990: 154—157; Markowski & Puzynina 1993: 54—55). — Works written within cultural studies lead to similar conclusions: language is one of the most important components of culture. Together with other factors, it is open to conscious modifications introduced by human communities.

## 5. Bibliography


Bajerowa, Irena. 1986. *Polski język ogólny XIX wieku. Stan i ewolucja.* Katowice: Uniwersytet Sląski.

Baudouin de Courtenay, Jan. 1904. *Szkice językoznawcze.* Warszawa: P. Laskauer i Ska.

Bralczyk, Jerzy. 1996. *Język na sprzedaż.* Warszawa: Business Press.

Brückner, Aleksander. 1917. *Walka o język.* Lwów: Książnica Polska.

Bugajski, Marian. 1989. *Podstawowe zagadnienia lingwistyki normatywnej.* Wrocław: Wydawn. Uniwersytetu Wrocławskiego.

Buttler, Danuta, Halina Kurkowska & Halina Satkiewicz. 1973 [1982]. *Kultura języka polskiego.* Vol. 1—2. Warszawa: PWN.

Doroszewski, Witold. 1950. *Kryteria poprawności językowej.* Warszawa: Państw. Zakłady Wydawnictw Szkolnych.

—. 1962, 1968. *O kulturę słowa. Poradnik językowy.* Warszawa: Państwowy Instytut Wydawniczy.

— & Halina Kurkowska. 1973. *Słownik poprawnej polszczyzny* PWN. Warszawa: PWN.

Furdal, Antoni. 1971. "Ważniejsze zasady językoznawstwa normatywnego". Rozprawy Komisji Językowej. Wrocławskie Towarzystwo Naukowe 8.63—73.

Gajda, Stanisław. 1995. "O pojęciu kultury języka dziś". *Kultura języka dziś.* 54—62. Poznań: Wyd. Kurpisz.

Glowiński, Michal. 1990. *Nowomowa po polsku:* Wydawnictwo PEN.

Karaś, Mieczyslaw, Maria Madejowa, eds. 1977. *Slownik wymowy polskiej PWN.* Warszawa: PWN.

Klemensiewicz, Zenon. 1947. "Poprawność i pedagogika językowa". *Język Polski* 27.38—46.

—. 1974. *Historia języka polskiego.* Warszawa: PWN.

Kurkowska, Halina. 1977. "Polityka językowa a zróżnicowanie społeczne współczesnej polszczyzny". *Socjolingwistyka* 1.17—25. Katowice: Uniwersytet Śląski.

Lubaś, Władysław, ed. 1977. *Socjolingwistyka* 1. *Polityka językowa.* Katowice: Universytet Śląski.

Markowski, Andrzej, ed. 1999. *Nowy slownik poprawnej polszczyzny PWN.* Warszawa: Wydawnictwo Naukowe PWN.

— & Jadwiga Puzynina. 1993. "Kultura języka". *Encyklopedia kultury polskiej XX wieku. Współczesny język polski* ed. by Jerzy Bartmiński, 53—72. Wrocław. Wiedza o kulturze.

Mayenowa, Maria Renata, ed. 1958. *Ludzie oświecenia o języku i stylu.* Vol. 1. Warszawa: państwowy Instytut Wydawniczy.

Mazur, Jan, ed. 1999. *Polska polityka językowa na przelomie tysiącleci.* Lublin: Wydawn. Uniwersytetu M. Curie-Sklodowskiej.

Miodek, Jan, ed. 1996. *O zagrożeniach i bogactwie polszczyzny.* Wrocław: Towarzystwo Przyjaciół Polonistyki Wrocl.

Miodunka, Władysław, ed. *Edukacja językowa Polaków.* Kraków. "UN-O".

Pajdzińska, Anna & Jadwiga Puzynina. 1996. "Etyka słowa". *O zagrożeniach i bogactwie polszczyzny* ed. by Jan Miodek, 35—45. Wrocław: Towarzystwo Przyjaciół Polonistyki Wrocławskiej.

Pisarek, Walery, ed. 1999. *Polszczyzna 2000. Orędzie o stanie języka na przełomie tysiącleci.* Kraków: Ośrodek Badań Prasoznawczych UJ.

Pisarek, Walery & Halina Zgółkowa, eds. 1995. *Kultura języka dziś.* Poznań: Wydawnictwo Kurpisz.

Polański, Edward, ed. 1999. *Nowy slownik ortograficzny PWN z zasadami pisowni i interpunkcji.* Warszawa: Wydawnictwo Naukowe PWN.

Puzynina, Jadwiga. 1990. "O pojęciu kultury języka". *Poradnik Językowy.* 153—162.

Szober, Stanisław. 1913. *O poprawności języka.* Warszawa: M. Arct.

—. 1937. *Na straży języka. Szkice z zakresu poprawności i kultury języka polskiego.* Warszawa: Nasza Księgarnia.

—. 1937a *Słownik ortoepiczny.* Warszawa: M. Arct.

Taszycki, Witold. 1953. *Obrońcy języka.* Biblioteka Narodowa I. Wrocław: Ossolineum.

Urbańczyk, Stanisław. 1959. "Językoznawstwo polskie 1. połowy XIX wieku". *O języku Adama Mickiewicza*, 487–519. Warszawa: PWN.

Walczak, Bogdan. 1988. "Kwalifikatory w słownikach języka polskiego". *Wokół języka. Rozprawy i studia poświęcone pamięci Profesora Mieczysława Szymczaka*, 413–422. Wrocław: Ossolineum.

*Jadwiga Puzynina, Warsaw (Poland)*

# 124. Normativ orientierte Sprachforschung in Ungarn

1. Gesellschaftliche Rahmenbedingungen
2. Der Anschluß an die europäische Sprachwissenschaft: von Sylvester bis Szenczi Molnár
3. Pragmatische Bestrebungen in der Sprachnormierung und Sprachpflege
4. Bibliographie

## 1. Gesellschaftliche Rahmenbedingungen

Obwohl der erste ungarische Text bereits um 1192 aufgezeichnet wurde, spielte im eigenen Land das Ungarische bis zum 15. Jh. nur eine sehr untergeordnete Rolle. Im Vergleich zu den indogermanischen Sprachen fehlte auch das Bewußtsein irgendeiner Verwandtschaft mit anderen Sprachen, und daher hat man sich auch nicht an vergleichbaren Beispielen in der Kulturgeschichte und Sprachgestaltung anderer Völker orientieren können.

Die Sprachgelehrten hatten daher zwei Aufgaben parallel zu lösen: das Ungarische zu beschreiben, also eine eigene Grammatik zu erarbeiten, und zugleich das Ungarische in der Schrift zu fixieren. Bei der Lösung dieser Herausforderungen diente naturgemäß das Lateinische als Vorbild, wobei allerdings die Grenzen dieses Vorgehens schnell klar wurden, stimmte das Ungarische doch in seiner Struktur mit dem Latenischen nicht überein, und auch die 25 Buchstaben des Lateins waren ungenügend, um die damaligen etwa 35 Laute des Ungarischen in der Schrift korrekt wiederzugeben. Somit begann ein langer Prozeß des Vergleichens, des Gleichstellens und der Abgrenzung, sowohl was die grammatikalische Darstellung als auch die Orthographie des Ungarischen anbelangt. Dieser Prozeß fand auf unterschiedlichen Wegen statt, mal mehr, mal weniger koordiniert.

Als die lateinischsprachige zentrale Macht des Königs und der Kirche zunehmend schwächer wurde, nahm im Schrifttum die Zahl und die Formenvielfalt der ungarischsprachigen Texte zu. Die zwischen 1420 und 1441 geschriebene erste ungarische (hussitische) Bibelübersetzung bezeugt in ihrer Schreibweise emanzipatorische und vereinheitlichende Bestrebungen in der Sprache. Wegen der Verfolgung der Hussiten war ihre Wirkung jedoch nicht so stark, daß sie zu einer einheitlichen ungarischen Schreibweise hätte führen können. Am Anfang des 16. Jhs. sind die Bibelübersetzungen und die Reformation weiterhin die treibenden Kräfte der kulturellen Entwicklung.

Die ersten Grammatiken des Ungarischen verdanken wir den beiden ungarischen Gelehrten János Sylvester (c. 1504–*post* 1551) und Albert Szenczi Molnár (1574–1634). Sie gehen darin auch auf Fragen der Orthographie ein, aber die definitive Normierung der Schreibweise benötigte noch mehr Zeit.

## 2. Der Anschluß an die europäische Sprachwissenschaft: von Sylvester bis Szenczi Molnár

Die Kontakte zu Wittenberg und namentlich zu Melanchton haben János Sylvester angeregt, fast zeitgleich zu der Grammatik auch das Neue Testament ins Ungarische zu übersetzen. In seiner *Grammatica Hvngarolatina* (Neanesi, 1539) versucht er zum ersten Mal, eine Systematisierung des Ungarischen nach dem Muster des Lateinischen vorzunehmen, wobei er sich, wie der Titel sagt, hauptsächlich um die grammatische Beschreibung des Ungarischen bemüht. Ohne eine eigene Schreibtradition (die seit dem späten 12. Jh. gebrauchte Kanzleischrift hat nach 1526, dem Zerfall des Landes, keine normierende Wirkung ausüben können), stützt sich Sylvester dabei auf die autoritäre Rolle der Grammatik und faßt "zahlreiche Erscheinungen des zeitgenössischen ungarischen Sprachgebrauchs" (Molnár 1977: ix) in Regeln zusammen. Da die grammatische Terminologie in der Tradition des Donatus (4. Jh.) und auch die Struktur des Lateins zur Beschreibung einer finnisch-ugrischen Sprache nicht sonderlich geeignet erschienen, war Sylvester gezwungen, manche Formen des Ungarischen mit dem Griechischen oder dem Hebräischen zu erklären. Seine *Grammatica* wird dadurch zu mehr als bloß einer Beschreibung des Ungarischen; sie stellt den Anfang der ungarischen deskriptiven Sprachforschungen dar.

Mit seiner Lehre von der Orthographie weicht er deutlich von der mittelalterlichen Schreibweise ab; "he takes over, with slight modification, the version of the Hussite orthography [...] he uses *o, u*, of German origin, to denote *ö, ő, ü, ű*, and *ß* also derived from German, to render *sz*." (Abaffy 1970: 39) Obwohl Sylvesters Versuch seinerzeit kaum zur Kenntnis genommen wurde, stellt er den Anfang einer bis heute andauernden Entwicklung dar, die darauf abzielt, das Ungarische zu festigen (zu normieren) und gleichzeitig auch fortzuentwickeln (reformieren).

Die sich zunehmend ausbreitende neue Technik des Buchdrucks, aber auch die religiösen Auseinandersetzungen der Zeit verlangten geradezu danach, Texte für die Allgemeinheit verständlich abzufassen. Daher spielte die Normierung der Schrift eine zentrale Rolle in dieser Zeit. Aus dem Jahre 1549 ist die zweite Auflage der (wahrscheinlich 1538, also noch vor der *Grammatica Hvngarolatina* von Sylvester veröffentlichten) *Orthographia Vngarica*, das erste Regelheft der ungarischen Rechtschreibung, von Mátyás Dévai Bíró (c. 1500–c. 1545), erhalten geblieben.

Dieses Werk befaßt sich mit allen wichtigen Problemen des Lautbestandes bzw. mit der Lautbezeichnung im Ungarischen und ist bemüht, die aufgestellten Regeln im Sinne einer Sprachpflege anzuwenden. Sylvester und Dévai Bíró haben die Rolle der Bildung und die Aufgaben der Schule in ihren Werken sehr stark berücksichtigt; mit diesen beiden Arbeiten beginnt die Entstehung eines gebildeten lese- und schreibkundigen ungarischen muttersprachlichen Publikums.

Ende des 16. Jhs. (Vizsoly, 1590) erscheint die erste vollständige Fassung der protestantischen Bibelübersetzung von Gáspár Károli (c. 1530–1591), was wesentlich zur Entwicklung und Normierung des Ungarischen beiträgt. Sie dient als sprachliches Vorbild für die vielfältigen Publikationen von Albert Szenczi Molnár. Nach dem *Dictionarivm Latinovngaricum [...]* und dem, im selben Band publizierten, *Dictionarivm Vngaricolatinvm* (Nürnberg 1604) sowie dem *Psalterium Ungaricum* (Herborn 1607) veröffentlicht er schließlich die lateinisch-sprachige *Novæ Grammaticæ Ungaricæ libri duo* (Hanau 1610). Diese umfangreiche Abhandlung zum Ungarischen befindet sich "zwar durchgängig im Prokrustesbette der lateinischen Kategorien" (Szinnyei 1907: 1), aber erst dadurch wird das System des Ungarischen – anhand eines allgemein bekannten Sprachsystems – für die Gelehrten Europas zugänglich. Szenczis Ziele werden bereits im ersten Kapitel ("De etymologia") klar formuliert: "Grammatica est ars bene loquendi, idque Ungaris Ungarice." (Décsy 1960: 29)

Daher möchte Szenczi das Ungarische in die Regeln der Grammatik zwingen:

> [...] ut linguam patriam, quam Dictionarii et Psalterii editione excolere tentassem, etiam praeceptis Grammaticis, quoad ejus fieri possit, brevibus includerem, et praecepta exemplis perspicuis illustrarem. (Décsy 1969: 21)

Er folgt hier den grammatikalischen Traditionen Europas.

> His models may have been the German vernacular grammars of A. Ölinger, L. Albertus, and J. Clajus, as well as the French and Latin grammars of the Frenchman Pierre d[e la]Ramée. Especially do his grammatical terminology and the plan of his syntax recall Ramée's Latin grammar (published under the Latin form of his name, Ramus), which is based on the grammatical tradition established by Apollonios Dyscolos. (Décsy 1969: xv–xvi)

Seine detaillierte Grammatik folgt einerseits der soeben erwähnten 'Schule' der Volkssprachenbeschreibung, aber auch der ungarischen philologischen Tradition. Szenczis Lebenswerk ist die erste zeitgenössische Zustandsbeschreibung des Ungarischen, welche zugleich die Grundlagen zur Entstehung einer als 'Rechtschreibung der reformierten Kirche' bezeichneten Orthographie sowie des normativen Kerns der ungarischen Hochsprache geliefert hat.

## 3. Pragmatische Bestrebungen in der Sprachnormierung und Sprachpflege

Nach den bahnbrechenden Arbeiten von Sylvester und Szenczi Molnár wurde das System des Ungarischen zugänglicher und verständlicher, ja vergleichbar. In dieser Situation stellte sich die Regulierung, die Normierung des Sprachgebrauchs als nächste Aufgabe. Denn die ungarische Sprache wurde in dieser Epoche sowohl mündlich als auch schriftlich deutlich mehr verwendet. Wanderprediger, Liedermacher, Feldherren, Gelehrte, Verleger, alle benutzten ihre eigene ungarische Sprach- und Schreibvariante. Aus diesem Grund konzentrierte sich die Sprachpflege des 17. Jhs. besonders auf die Fragen der Orthographie. In seiner *Magyar Grammatikatska A' vagy, az igaz magyar irasban és ſzollásban kévántato néhány szűkséges Observatiok* [Kleine Ungarische Grammatik oder einige in der rechten ungarischen Schrift und Rede erforderlichen und notwendigen Observationes] (Gyulafehérvár, 1645) faßt István Geleji Katona (1589–1649), der reformierte Bischof Siebenbürgens, seine Ansichten über die Rechtschreibung, die Wortbildung und den Sprachgebrauch zusammen. Besonders wichtig sind in dieser nicht systematisierend zusammengestellten Arbeit die Beobachtungen zu den Rechtschreibungsregeln im Ungarischen, in der Geleji Katona – ebenso wie die heutige ungarische Rechtschreibung – die phonematischen, wortanalysierenden und etymologischen Prinzipien (also *mond-ja* [er/sie sagt es] statt der bloßen Wiedergabe der Lautung des Wortes [*mongya*] in der Schrift) gleichzeitig anwendet. Die großen Unterschiede im Gebrauch des Ungarischen veranlassen Geleji Katona "[...] vor allem praktische Ratschläge und Regeln des Schriftstellers und Predigers, der sich sehr bewußt um die Pflege seiner Muttersprache kümmerte [...]" (Szathmári 1965: 323) zu erteilen. Auch seine Bemühungen, den ungarischen wissenschaftlichen Fachwortschatz zu erweitern, haben ihn als Vorbild wirken lassen. Insbesondere János Apáczai Csere (1625–1659) hat in seiner *Magyar Encyclopædia* [Ungarische Enzyklopädie] (1654) auf Geleji Katonas Feststellungen zurückgegriffen. Nach deutschem Muster hat Geleji Katona darüber hinaus in Siebenbürgen eine Art 'Sprachgesellschaft' gegründet, welche den historischen Keim der ungarischen Spracherneuerung Ende des 18. Jhs. darstellt.

Die nächste bedeutende Arbeit, die *Hungaria Illustrata* (Utrecht 1655) von György Komáromi Csipkés (1628–1678), möchte zwar das Ungarische (vor allem den Deutschen) zugänglicher machen – daher verfaßte er sein Buch auf Latein – aber genauso wichtig war es ihm, daß damit auch die Ungarn richtig schreiben und sprechen lernten, denn "[...] multos Hungaros non esse rectos Hungaros." (Toldy 1866: 339). In seiner Sprachbetrachtung schlägt Komáromi Csipkés einen neuen Weg ein und versucht das Ungarische ohne Hilfe der traditionellen Lateingrammatik zu beschreiben. Seine Grammatik folgt in ihrem Aufbau (Einleitung und drei Bücher) eher dem Beispiel des Hebräischen, beschäftigt sich jedoch nur mit Fragen der Orthographie und der Morphologie. Ein neues sprachliches Bewußtsein zeigt sich in seinen Feststellungen, daß das Ungarische keinen Abkömmling oder Dialekt anderer Sprachen, sondern eine *lingua cardinalis* darstellt. Der Struktur nach gehört es sogar zu den 'reinen' Sprachen ("lingua Hungarica [...] casta est et pura"; Toldy 1866: 342).

Die *Hungaria Illustrata* ist ein wichtiges Glied in der Reihe der Beschreibungen des Ungarischen, weil sie auch in stilistischen und in die Sprachnorm betreffenden Fragen deutlich Stellung bezieht und – ohne die Werke von Sylvester und Szenczi Molnár näher gekannt zu haben – ihre Tradition fortsetzt.

Der normative Charakter der Grammatiken wird auch in der *Grammatica Lingvæ Vngaricæ* (Tyrnaviae 1682), einer offensichtlich für die Jesuitenschulen zusammengestellten Arbeit von Pál Pereszlényi (1631–1689), gestärkt. Sie faßt zwar die Regeln der 'katholischen Rechtschreibung' zusammen, stützt sich dabei aber auch stark auf die 'protestantische' Tradition seit Szenczi Molnár. Wie wichtig die Rolle der Schulen inzwischen geworden war, zeigt sich an der steigenden Zahl der Grammatiken für praktische Unterrichtszwecke.

Die *Elementa Linguæ Hungaricæ* (Leutschoviæ 1686) von Pál Kövesdi (?–1682) sind eine zu diesem Zweck zusammengestellte, gekürzte Fassung früherer Grammatiken (besonders der von Szenczi Molnár). Miklós Misztótfalusi Kis (1650–1702) verlangt schon die ungarisch-sprachige Schulbildung für alle. Seine *Apologia Bibliorum: Rationatio de Orthographia* (Claudiopoli 1697) ist der radikalste und konsequenteste Bruch mit dem lateinischen grammatikalischen Gerüst. Da Misztótfalusi auch als Drucker einen Ruf hatte, konnte er seine orthographischen und sprachpflegerischen Prinzipien direkt in die verlegerische Praxis umsetzen.

Seine normierende Wirkung ist durch die Herausgabe von entsprechend gestalteten Büchern deutlich stärker als die vieler früherer Grammatiken. In den Arbeiten von Misztótfalusi erscheint zum ersten Mal die Muttersprache als höchster Wert, weil sie über eigene Regeln und über eine eigene Ästhetik verfügt, welche geschützt und gelehrt werden muß.

Ähnliche Ansichten werden auch von János Tsétsi (1650–1708) vertreten. Sein *Observationes Orthographico-Grammaticæ* sind als Addendum zum *Dictionarium* von Ferenc Pápai Páriz (1649–1716) (Lőcse 1708) erschienen. Das ist ein ausschließlich die Regeln des Ungarischen beschreibendes Buch, das die schriftliche und sprachliche Norm festhält und zugleich verbreitet. Das Ungarische wird durch die geschilderte Entwicklung zunehmend als eine Sprache angesehen, die den anderen gleichwertig ist. Damit sind die Voraussetzungen zu seiner vollen Emanzipation durch die Spracherneuerung im 18. Jh. geschaffen.

## 4. Bibliographie

Molnár, József. 1977. *Corpus Grammaticorum Hungarorum.* (= *Fontes ad historiam linguarum populorumque Uraliensum*, 4.) Budapest: Eötvös Loránd Tudományegyetem.

Szinnyei, Joseph. 1907. *Die ungarische Sprache.* Straßburg: Trübner.

Abaffy, Elisabeth. 1970. *On Sylvester's two Systems of Orthography.* (= *Annales Universitatis Scientiarum Budapestinensis de Rolando Eötvös nominatæ*, 1.), 35–39.

Décsy, Gyula. 1969. *Albertus Molnár Szencziensis Nova Grammatica Ungarica.* Indiana University Publications. (= *Uralic and Altaic Series*, 98.) The Hague: Mouton.

Sylvester, János. 1539. *Grammatica Hvngarolatina.* Neanesi.

Szathmári, István. 1965. *István Geleji Katona und die deutschen Sprachgesellschaften des 17. Jahrhunderts.* (= *Acta Linguistica Academiæ Scientiarum Hungaricæ*, 15.) 323–330.

Toldy, Ferenc. 1866. *Corpus Grammaticorum Linguæ Hungaricæ Veterum.* Pest: Eggenberger.

*Tiborc Fazekas, Hamburg (Deutschland)*

# 125. Normative studies in Malta

1. The Maltese language
2. The earliest Maltese word lists
3. The first Maltese dictionaries
4. The earliest Maltese manuscript grammars
5. The first Maltese grammarians
6. Francis Vella and Fortunato Panzavecchia
7. Maltese 19th-century academies and scholars
8. The first half of the 20th century
9. Joseph Aquilina (1911–1997) and Erin Serracino Inglott (1904–1983)
10. The contemporary period (till 1995)
11. Bibliography

## 1. The Maltese language

Maltese, born and developed during the Arab domination of Malta between AD 870 and AD 1091, is the only national language in Europe which is of Semitic origin. The end of the Arab period and the consequent gradual re-absorption of the island into the Western world – Malta was conquered by Roger of Normandy in 1091 – marked the beginning of an influx of romance lexes, particularly from Sicily. The linguistic ties with Malta's Mediterranean neighbour, and with the Italian peninsula in general, were further strengthened during the rule of the *Hospitaller Knights of St John of Jerusalem* (1530–1798).

By the time the British came to Malta in 1800, Maltese already had an identity of its own. However, as time passed, and especially during the latter stages of Britain's 164-year rule, Anglo-Saxon terminology, in particular in the technical and scientific fields, became part and parcel of the Maltese language, which was thus defined as a *mixed language* (Aquilina 1985: 42–62).

The evolutionary process of the language is still under way; a process which has been so intense that Maltese words of non-Semitic origin now outnumber those of Semitic origin (Brincat 1992).

## 2. The earliest Maltese word lists

Although foreign visitors to Malta in the 16th and 17th centuries had given their impressions of the island's language (Cassola 1992a), the first attempted codification of Maltese is to be found in the 17th century word lists of Hiernoymus Megiser (ca. 1553–1618) and Philip Skippon.

Megiser, a professor of history at the University of Leipzig, visited Malta in 1588. Fifteen years later, in 1603, he published his *Thesaurus Polyglottus*, a multilingual dictionary comprising four hundred languages.

The 9 words gathered in Malta and included in this work constitute the first printed list of Maltese words (Cassola 1988: 78). In 1606, Megiser published an entire text about Malta, the *Propugnaculum Europae*, which contains a German-Maltese word-list of 121 words belonging to what he described as the 'parlata africana o moresca' spoken by the island's population (Cowan 1964; Cassola 1988).

Englishman Philip Skippon, who had already travelled through much of Europe between 1664 and 1680, visited Malta in 1684. His description of the island, its inhabitants and its customs is contained in Churchill 1732: 618–616. As regards language, Skippon noted that "the natives of the country speak little or no *Italian*, but a kind of *Arabick*, like that the *Moors* speak; but in the cities, most speak *Italian* very well" (Churchill 1732: 624). In the final part of his description, Skippon lists 381 Latin words and gives the Maltese equivalent. The list is preceded by the words: *The curious will be pleas'd with the following specimen of the language of Malta.*

Both Megiser and Skippon resorted to the use of the Latin alphabet to transcribe the Maltese words.

## 3. The first Maltese dictionaries

The first published dictionary of the Maltese language is Michele Antonio Vassalli's *Ktyb yl Klym Malti* (Vassalli 1796). The volume contains an appeal entitled *Alla Nazione Maltese*, a *Discorso Preliminare* and a Maltese-Latin-Italian dictionary in 682 columns on 341 pages. Vassalli utilises an alphabet made up of 21 Roman letters, the Greek letter *y*, and another 10 newly created characters denoting the Semitic sounds of Maltese.

The significance of Vassalli (1764–1829) and his works lies not only in his giving us the first published dictionary of Maltese, based on sound scientific study, but also, and more importantly, in the fact that he was the first intellectual to come up with the concept of *Maltese nationality* and with the idea of Maltese as a dignified *national language*.

Manuscript dictionaries of the Maltese language did exist prior to Vassalli's publication. The most worthy of mention are the 17th century *Regole per la lingua maltese* (Cassola 1992b), Gian Pietro Francesco Agius de Soldanis's mid-18th century *Damma tal Kliem Kartaginis mscerred fel fom tal Maltin u Ghaucin*, whose four volumes are written in Latin alphabet, and the c. 1750–1770 anonymous *Mezzo Vocabolario*, which has only recently been brought to light (Cassola 1996).

## 4. The earliest Maltese manuscript grammars

Although the first published grammar of the Maltese language was Agius de Soldanis's *Della lingua punica presentemente usata da maltesi*, which appeared in 1750, various attempts had been made previously at compiling a grammar of the language. Amongst these, one finds those of the Bishop of Epifania, Xiberras, the French Knight Tournon (Agius de Soldanis 1750: 61) and Commendatore Francesco Bardon (Mifsud 1764: 325). None of these manuscript grammars have, however, survived.

The one pre-de Soldanis grammar that did survive is the 17-page one contained in the *Regole per la lingua Maltese* manuscript, presumably compiled in the 17th century by the Provençal knight, Thezan (Cassola 1992b: 3r–11r). This somewhat skimpy grammatical description focuses mainly on the article, numbers, pronouns, possessive pronouns, the verbs *to be* and *to have*, and on the formation of the various tenses of Maltese verbs. The most notable feature of Thezan's grammar and dictionary is that the author made use of a mixed Latin-Arabic alphabet, with nine Arabic characters and the Persian letter *cim* to denote the Semitic sounds of Maltese. Folios 3r to 4v of the grammar are devoted to a description of these ten characters, with examples.

## 5. The first Maltese grammarians

The first grammar of the Maltese language was, then, the one published in Rome in 1750 by Agius de Soldanis (1712–1770), a priest from the island of Gozo. Following the example of the German scholar Henricus Majus, Agius de Soldanis accepts the theory on the Punic origin of Maltese, a theory overtly publicised in the volume's title. Agius de Soldanis's main intention behind his *Grammatica* was "per agevolmente apprendere la lingua punica-maltese agli studenti Maltesi, e forestieri, abitanti in Malta" (Agius de Soldanis 1750: 65). To this purpose, and since he believed that the Latin script was the easiest medium to convey written Maltese, Agius de

Soldanis formulated a 26-letter alphabet exclusively made up of Latin characters.

The defect in Agius de Soldanis's work is that, having been built on the model of Italian grammars, it sheds very little light on word building and verb roots which, in Maltese, are strongly associated with Arabic forms.

In 1791, Michele Antonio Vassalli published in Rome his Maltese grammar (Vassalli 1791), written in Latin. Like Agius de Soldanis, Vassalli subscribes to the theory on the Punic origin of Maltese too. He divides his grammar into three main parts (*De Elementis, De Dictionibus* and *De Syntaxi*) and describes the constituent parts of the Maltese language in great detail. His 33-letter *Novum Melitensis linguae alphabetum* was to form the basis of all his future works (cf. 3.).

Thirty six years later, Vassalli published an Italian version of his grammar. In this edition, which is divided into five main chapters (*Dell'Ortografia Maltese, Delle Dizioni Correlative, Del Verbo, Del Nome* and *Della Sintassi Maltese*), Vassalli drops his theory on the Punic origin of Maltese. His intention, in fact, is to carry out some comparative analyses, establishing "un parallelo fra la nostra e la lingua Arabica del sesto secolo dell'Egira, con altre erudizioni analoghe alla Fonografia e Costruzione d'ambe le lingue" (Vassalli 1827: vii). His perception of Maltese as an offshoot of Arabic is, therefore, now quite clear.

## 6. Francis Vella and Fortunato Panzavecchia

From Thezan's times onwards, at least another seven authors made use of a mixed Latin-Arabic script to transcribe Maltese (Cassola 1992b: x–xvi); an approach which met with opposition from different quarters, including the educationalist Salvatore Cumbo (1810–1877) and the Arabist George Percy Badger (1815–1888) (Cassola 1992b: xiii). But perhaps the fiercest opposition came from Francis Vella.

Vella published his *Maltese Grammar for the Use of the English* in 1831, opting for a 26-letter alphabet based on the Latin script. In describing the Maltese language, Vella states that:

> the Maltese tongue, as well as the English, has nine parts of speech, viz. [...] The Noun, The Adjective, The Article, The Pronoun, The Verb, The Adverb, The Preposition, The Conjunction, The Interjection (Vella 1831: 19).

He then goes on to describe these various linguistic features in detail. In his preface, Vella writes that the semi-oriental alphabetical method devised by Vassalli is confusing to those who want to learn Maltese.

> On the other hand, if we follow the rules, and the Italian method, we do not only facilitate the means of learning our own language, but by these we afford great advantage to such of the Maltese as are obliged to learn the European ones; the root of the Maltese verbs, tho' it is at the third person of the past tense, will be no obstacle to them, as we intend to prove by facts (Vella 1831: 5).

For Vella, the lack of a proper alphabet is the main obstacle in the teaching of the Maltese language. In his words, "many causes have contributed to render abortive the efforts of Vassalli towards making literary the maltese language, and his employing the *Semi-oriental* system has been the principal." (Vella 1831: 4).

Vella's theories are reinforced in his successive works, including his *Dizionario Portatile*, where the author reiterates that the Latin alphabet is "l'unico alfabeto che concilia l'ortografia italiana, e maltese [e] mi giovò per scrivere quest'ultima." (Vella 1843: *Preface* entitled *Concittadini!*). Vella ends his preface by expressing the hope that his choice of orthographic system will end a fifty year crisis and solve the "interminabile questione alfabetica" (Vella 1843: *Preface*).

A couple of years later, Vella's hopes were dashed when Fortunato Panzavecchia (?–1850) published his *Grammatica della lingua maltese* (Panzavecchia 1845) and proposed some innovations, with the addition of codas to certain letters. The aim was to combine the Semitic features of Maltese with Italian orthography. Despite the fact that hardly anybody followed Panzavecchia's orthographic system, his grammar was to be considered the best since Vassalli's times owing to the fact that the author based his grammatical rules on the Arab morphology, a constituent part of the Maltese language (Cremona & Vassallo 1924: xv).

## 7. Maltese 19th century academies and scholars

During the 19th century, various academies and societies played a part in keeping alive the debate on the Maltese language. In 1840, the *Società Medica* appointed a commission chaired by Stefano Zerafa to draw up an alphabet for the Maltese language. The orthographic system which the commission published in 1841 met with little success.

In 1843, the *Accademia Filologica* presented its own 33-letter alphabet, based on the Italian system. This system was adopted in Maltese schools between 1850 and 1883 (Aquilina 1985: 87) and actually turned out to be the most popular until the current one was introduced in 1924 (Cremona & Vassallo 1924).

A 'phonetic' alphabet meant to include a different letter for each sound was devised by the *Xirka Xemija* in 1882. The *Xirka*'s orthographic rules, considered quite simple and effective, actually provided the basis for the modern Maltese alphabet.

Many were the Maltese writers of the 19th century and early 20th century who, through their works, contributed to the debate on the Maltese language. The most noteworthy of these are Giovanni Battista Falzon (1813–1884), author of a *Dizionario Maltese-Italiano-Inglese* (1845) and a *Dizionario Italiano-Inglese-Maltese* (1882), Antonio Emanuele Caruana (1839–1907), who wrote *Sull'origine della lingua maltese* (1896), and the *Vocabolario della lingua maltese* (1903), and Annibale Preca (1832–1901) with his *Malta Cananea* (1904). Caruana and Preca revived the theory on the Punic origin of Maltese.

## 8. The first half of the 20th century

With the publication of the *Għaqda tal-Malti*'s grammar in 1924 (Cremona & Vassallo 1924), one can safely state that most of the problems relating to the standardisation of a Maltese alphabet were solved, and that the era of grammars based on a scientific approach was about to begin. G. Vassallo's *Il-Muftieh tal-Chitba Maltija* [The key to Maltese writing] (1901) had already paved the way for modern grammar writing by highlighting the fact that solving problems connected with the alphabet was not enough; proper grammatical rules were also required. The 1924 *Għaqda* grammar further emphasised this principle and thus managed to reproduce a system that, as well as being phonetic, with one symbol for each sound, "had also to be etymological to make the teaching of Maltese grammar as rational as possible." (Aquilina 1985: 78).

The most complete and detailed Maltese grammar of the first half of this century was, however, published in 1936 by Edmund Sutcliffe (1886–1963). Sutcliffe considered that, prior to his publication, "no adequate [grammar] book has been attempted for nearly a hundred years" (Sutcliffe 1936: v). In fact, as far as Sutcliffe was concerned, the most ambitious Maltese grammars, like Vella's, had:

> failed to grasp the grammatical structure of the language. This is especially noticeable in the verb. Not one of the Grammars enumerated in the bibliography presents a correct scheme of the verb. These remarks are made only to show the need of a new attempt to present the grammar and syntax of this most interesting Semitic language (Sutcliffe 1936: v).

The novelty in Sutcliffe's grammar is that it highlights the workings of Maltese syntax, with paragraphs on the syntax of the article, nouns, the adjective, verbs, pronouns, and the sentence as a whole. Moreover, Sutcliffe's grammar is of a comparative nature; his frequent comparisons between Maltese, Arabic and Hebrew making it easier to focus on the structure of Maltese.

## 9. Joseph Aquilina (1911–1997) and Erin Serracino Inglott (1904–1983)

The end of World War II brought with it the end of fascism in Italy. In Malta, this meant that the strong prejudices against anything Italian, which had first appeared with the *Language Question* (c. 1880) (Hull 1993) and had continued throughout the fascist period, no longer had any reason to persist. From a linguistic point of view, this brought about the beginning of a more balanced appraisal of the Maltese language in its entirety, with both romance and Semitic elements being given equal dignity in the study of the language.

Joseph Aquilina's *The Structure of Maltese* (Aquilina 1959) marked the beginning of this new and scientific trend in the study of the Maltese language and thus "has for long been regarded as the classical description of Maltese" (Mifsud 1995: 3). Aquilina aims at a comprehensive phonomorpho-syntactical description of both the Semitic and the romance elements in the language, and reaffirms his approach in *Teach yourself Maltese*, where he states that excluding the Romance element would be "as absurd as writing a grammar of the English language including only the lexical and morphological Anglo-Saxon element, leaving out all the linguistic

Romance element." (Aquilina 1965: vi). Aquilina is also the author of a *Maltese-English Dictionary* (1987–90), the most complete bilingual dictionary to date.

Erin Serracino Inglott is the author of the nine-volume *Il Miklem Malti* [The Maltese dictionary] (1975–89), the foremost Maltese monolingual dictionary. The last volume of the work also contains Serracino Inglott's *Grammatika Umanizzata ta' l-ilsien Malti* [Humanised grammar of the Maltese language]. Serracino Inglott's intention was to produce an easy to understand, "humanised" grammar. Apart from demonstrating 'how' Maltese works, he also aimed at explaining 'why' it works in such a way. This attempt at explaining 'why' the language works as it does can be considered an innovative feature of the Serracino Inglott grammar.

## 10. The contemporary period (till 1995)

Pedagogical grammars apart, the latest additions to the study of the language by Maltese authors are Borg 1988 and Cachia 1994. While the former work limits itself to a synchronic description of what is basically known as *Malti pulit* [Standard Maltese], the latter is divided into three main sections: orthography and phonology; morphology; verbs. A chapter on "Verbs and nouns and their pronominal suffixes" and another one on the "Orthography of Anglo-Saxon and Romance neologisms" are appended to the text.

What characterises the contemporary period, however, is the publication of a number of excellent works which analyse particular features of the language. Prevaes 1993, for example, is a historical study of Maltese, its origins and early Maltese texts. In particular, there is a chapter entitled *The Standardisation of Maltese* which deals with the codification of grammatical rules from Vassalli's times onwards.

Vanhove 1993 may be considered the major work on the study of Maltese syntax. The author's approach is essentially a synchronic one, even though the work is intended to focus on the evolution of the varying forms and sentence constructions in the course of time. Vanhove studies the morphology of the verb and compares the Maltese verbal system with that of other Semitic languages. Most of the work looks at auxiliaries, verb particles and verb prefixes. The author concludes that it would be useful in future to develop a parallel study on Sicilian, Italian, English and dialectal Arabic in order to try and pinpoint the degree of influence of other linguistic families on Maltese syntax, and to determine the internal dynamics of the evolutions recorded in Arabic and the Semitic languages in general (Vanhove 1993: 430).

The latest publication on a particular aspect of the Maltese language is Mifsud 1995, an in-depth analysis of loan verbs in Maltese.

> The immediate aim of this work is to analyse this continuum [of morphological types] and propose a typological classification of these morphological verb types, which moves from maximum to minimum integration with the native morphology. [...] A secondary aim of this work is to provide future grammarians with a ratonal and systematic grammatical classification of loan verbs, thus helping to complete the pedagogical description of Maltese. [...] This work could also help in an assessment of the productiveness of select morphological features, leading eventually to a more realistic pedagogical approach to Maltese grammar (Mifsud 1995: 8).

Mifsud has certainly succeeded in achieving his declared aims. Indeed, his pioneering work, together with that of others like Aquilina and Vanhove, should open up new pastures to future scholars, who will undoubtedly benefit from the great progress made in the field of scientific normative studies in Malta during the latter part of this century.

## 11. Bibliography

Agius de Soldanis, Giovanni Pietro Francesco. 1750. *Della lingua punica presentemente usata da Maltesi.* Roma: appresso Gregorio Roisecco mercante Libraro in Piazza Navona.

Aquilina, J[oseph]. 1959. *The Structure of Maltese.* Malta: Progress Press Co. Ltd.

–. 1965. *Teach Yourself Maltese.* London: The English Univ. Press Ltd.

–. 1985 [1961]. *Papers in Maltese Linguistics.* Malta: Malta Univ. Press.

Borg, Albert. 1988. *Lsienna.* Malta: Has-Sajjied.

Brincat, Joseph. 1991. *Malta 870–1054. Al Himyarī's Account.* Malta: Said International.

–. 1992. "Maltese Words". *The Sunday Times* (Malta) 31/5/1992. 48.

Cachia, L[awrenz], *Grammatika Ġdida tal-Malti* [A new grammar of Maltese]. Malta: L-Awtur, 1994.

Cassola, Arnold. 1988. "Una edizione diversa della lista di voci maltesi del seicento di Hieronymus Megiser". *Incontri Siculo-Maltesi. (= Journal of Maltese Studies*, 17–18). 72–86.

–. 1992a. “La lingua maltese nel ’500 attraverso i resoconti di scrittori e viaggiatori stranieri”. *Journal of Maltese Studies* 21–22. 79–90.

–. 1992b. *The Biblioteca Vallicelliana “Regole per la lingua maltese”*. Malta: Said International.

–. 1996. *Il Mezzo Vocabolario Maltese-Italiano del ’700.* Malta: Said International.

Churchill, Awnsham & John Curchill. 1732. *Collection of Voyages and Travels.* London: John Walthoe.

Cowan, William. 1964. “An Early Maltese Word-List”. *Journal of Maltese Studies* 2. 217–225.

[Cremona, Ninu] & [Ganni Vassallo]. 1924. *Tagħrif fuq il-kitba Maltija* [Directions on writing in Maltese]. Malta: Stemperija tal-Gvern.

Hull, Geoffrey. 1993. *The Malta Language Question.* Malta: Said International.

Mifsud, Ignazio Saverio. 1764. *Biblioteca Maltese.* Malta: nel Palazzo e Stamperia di S. A. S.

Mifsud, Manwel. 1995. *Loan Verbs in Maltese. A Descriptive and Comparative Study.* Leiden, New York & Köln: Brill.

Panzavecchia, Fortunato. 1845. *Grammatica della lingua maltese.* Malta: Tipografia di M. Weiss.

Prevaes, Mathias Hubertus. 1993. *The Emergence of Standard Maltese. The Arabic factor.* Nijmegen: Univ. of Nijmegen.

Sutcliffe, Edmund F[elix]. 1936. *A Grammar of the Maltese Language: with Chrestomathy and Vocabulary.* Oxford: Oxford Univ. Press.

Vanhove, Martine. 1993. *La langue maltaise. Études syntaxiques d’un dialecte arabe “peripherique”.* Wiesbaden: Harrassowitz Verlag.

Vassalli, Michele Antonio. 1791. *Mylsen Phoenico-Punicum sive Grammatica Melitensis.* Roma: Antonio Fulgoni.

–. 1796. *Ktyb yl klym Malti ’mfysser Byl-Latin u Byt-Taljan sive Liber Dictionum Melitensium, ecc.* Roma: Antonio Fulgoni.

–. 1827. *Grammatica della lingua maltese.* Malta: Stampata per l’Autore.

Vella, Francis. 1831. *Maltese Grammar for the Use of the English.* Leghorn: Printed by Glaucus Masi.

–. 1843. *Dizionario Portatile delle lingue Maltese, Italiana, Inglese.* Livorno: Stamperia degli Artisti Tipografi.

*Arnold Cassola, University of Malta (Malta)*

# XX. The Study of 'Exotic' Languages by Europeans
# Die Europäer und die 'exotischen' Sprachen
# La connaissance des langues 'exotiques'

## 126. The Great Travellers and the studies of 'exotic languages'


1. Introduction
2. The early explorers
3. The great explorers
4. Bibliography


### 1. Introduction

When Europeans started on their far-reaching exploratory expeditions at the end of the 15th century, collecting linguistic material was not one of their aims. Their interests in the people they met comprised their religion, social organization, morals and, above all, natural resources and economic status. From the very first moment, however, language turned out to be a practical problem of great significance. To establish contact with the people they met and to obtain maximal benefit from the encounter, a certain amount of communication was necessary.

As a rule, from the very beginning and increasingly so until the end of the 18th century, the languages of 'primitive' people were considered to be poor in words (and even more so in grammar) by the explorers, a view that was rather different from what the missionaries held (Hovdhaugen 1996). Accordingly, the explorers started from the very beginning to collect short word lists from the natives. These word lists, which continued to be a favorite linguistic occupation of explorers until the 18th century, were, however, usually not very helpful. Owing to their lack of any knowledge of phonology and phonetics, the explorers wrote the words they heard as well as they could in the orthography of their native tongue. In case this native tongue was Spanish, the result was not that bad since Spanish after all has a fairly good correspondence between orthography and pronunciation. However, in cases where the vocabulary writer was French or English, the result was usually of little use to anybody but the writer himself. A modern linguist may have a hard time figuring out what the writer actually intended to write. Anyhow, to learn the languages was a time-consuming and laborious task. Accordingly, many of the first explorers (and, it must be added, some merchants and even missionaries, too) found another and easier way to achieve satisfactory communication: they simply kidnapped a few natives and took them for a long trip on the ship or back to Europe for some time in order for them to learn the language of their captors and later function as interpreters (Naro 1978, Greenblatt 1991). Although the death rate among these kidnapped language students was very high, a few managed to survive. This practice which is very old and probably originated with the Portuguese voyages to West Africa in the 15th century (Naro 1978: 315–329), was in continual use until at least 1800 (Bougainville and Cook) although at the end set in a scientific frame and with the kidnapping more voluntarily.

Many interpreters, however, became so under less dramatic circumstances or of their own free will. They were frequently misfits or castaways, natives who for various reasons joined the foreigners or Europeans going native, cf. Karttunen (1994) for some moving biographies of such interpreters.

Linguistic material collected by travelers in Africa and Asia did not create the same interest among either lay people or scientists as similar material from the Americas and later on from the Pacific. The scanty lexical material on Iroquois languages from Jacques Cartier's (1491–1557) travels and from his successors in Canada was, for example, very important for European philosophers of language in their search for the prototypical primitive language, cf. Schreyer (1996).

## 2. The early explorers

Already on Ferdinand Magellan's (ca. 1480–1521) first voyage around the world in 1519–1521, short vocabularies of various languages were collected. The purpose was not primarily scientific but more of potential future practical value. An interesting and strange aspect of all the explorers from Columbus to Cook is their enormous self-confidence in their own ability to communicate with the 'savages' and to understand them. One of the survivors from Magellan's journey tells about the meeting with the Patagonians that one of them "raised one finger on high, thinking that we came from heaven" (Alderley 1874: 50).

About the people on the Philippine island of Samar, he says that "[t]hese people became very familiar and friendly with us, and explained many things to us in their language" (Alderley 1874: 73). This self-confidence in one's own abilities and intellectual superority including the ability to interpret on the spot communication in a 'primitive' language was a part of the general European self-confidence that enabled the feats of Cortés and Pizzaro and their numerous followers.

There are few detailed and trustworthy descriptions of what happened when the explorers and the natives met. One of the earliest and best ones in Álvaro de Mendaña's (1541–1595) description from his visit to the island Santa Isabel in the Solomon Islands 1567–1568:

> I made him [a chief on Santa Isabel] sit down, and began to ask him what they called the sun, the moon, the sky, and other things; and he named them all in his tongue, which is such that it may easily be learned by us, as ours by them, for they speak very distinctly, and without the affection (*de papo*) of the people of Peru. They seemed very eager to learn our words, and asked us to teach them, at which we were greatly rejoiced [...] (Hackney & Thomson 1901: 113)
>
> As I had given him to understand before how vast was the territory of His Majesty, and what a great chief he was, I repeated the same thing on this occasion, and showed him on the map the part that represented the sea, to which he listened very attentively; then I told him that everything that I pointed out as land was under the dominion of the King of Castille, and I showed him a small island marked upon the chart, and said that this was his own country; he was much amazed, and assured me that his island was very large, but I said that it was no larger than that which I pointed out. All this conversation was carried out in a few words of his language, and by signs, which they were very quick at understanding. (Hackney & Thomson 1901: 130)

Later on there were even cases in which the Europeans admitted that they understood nothing at all, like one of the crew on H. M. S. Dolphin wrote when the Europeans first had contact with Tahitians (June 19, 1767):

> all of them appeard chearful and talkt a good dale but non of us could understand them, but to pleas them we all seemd merry and said something to them, their language is not Guttural but they talkd so very fast that we could not distinguish one word from another. The neares resemblance that I know too it, is the patagonians Language [...] (Carrington 1948: 136).

We also find expeditions that were completely uninterested in language, e. g. the Dutch expedition of Jacob Roggeveen (1659–1729) to the Pacific (Easter Island and other Polynesian islands) in 1721–1722. From a linguistic point of view, the most influential of these early expeditions was the Dutch one of Jacob Le Maire (1585–1617) (together with Willem Cornelisz Schouten) which in 1616 visited numerous Polynesian islands both in the east and the west and collected a short vocabulary from the dialect on the northern Tongan island Niutoputapu which together with Le Maire's account of the journey was published in Herrera (1622). This word list was sufficient to establish the relationship of this language to Malay (Reland 1708) and it was used later by practically all the great explorers to show the widespread affinity of the Polynesian languages.

## 3. The great explorers

The great explorers (Captain Cook, Bougainville, Bligh, La Pérouse, etc.) and their scientific expeditions just before 1800 were explicitly instructed to study the people they discovered and their culture, but language was never specifically mentioned as a topic of investigation (cf. the instructions to Captain Cook's first voyage, Beaglehole 1955: cclxxix–cclxxxiv). And when the explorers studied the language of the people they encountered, they did so in the framework of natural sciences and rationalism, that is, they collected and classified languages just like plants, fish and birds in a Linnean world of hierarchical categories. Some quotations from the journal of the scientist Johan Reinhold Forster (1729–98) on Captain Cook's second voyage 1772–1775 is revealing: "We collected just a couple of plants. I collected likewise a good many words into my Vocabulary" (Hoare 1982: 589); "I collected some plants & some words of the Language of the Natives; & returned on board to dinner." (Hoare 1982: 654).

The great explorers collected these word lists to establish the relationship among the languages they encountered. Furthermore, there were frequent comments about the beauty of the languages as well as their poverty of vocabulary and lack of grammar. Nobody expressed it more clearly than Commerçon, the botanist on Bougainville's expedition, who in an influential letter of February 25, 1769, which was published in November of the same year in *Mercure de France*, stated the following about the Tahitian language:

Une langue très-sonore, très-harmonieuse, composée d'environ quatre ou cinq cens mots indéclinables & inconjugables, c'est-à-dire sans aucune syntaxe, leur suffit pour rendre toutes leurs idées, & pour exprimer tous leur besoins. (Corney 1915: 462)

But Banks, Cook, and the others were no different, just a bit less poetic, mixing aesthetic characterization with negative evaluation of the more intellectual aspects of the language; compare Joseph Bank's characterization of Tahitian (August 1769):

Their Language appeared to me to be very soft and tuneable, it abounds much with vowels and was very easy pronoun'd by us when ours was to them absolutely impracticable. [...]

I cannot say that I am enough acquainted with it to pronounce whether or not it is copious. In one respect however it is beyond measure inferior to all European languages, which is its almost total want of inflexion both of Nouns and verbs, few or none of the former having more than one Case or the latter one tense. (Beaglehole 1962 I: 370)

The aesthetic evaluation of language was a prominent feature of the linguistic fieldwork of the explorers, and frequently the main information (beside word lists) that we get of a language is that it, for instance, is "remarkably harsh and guttural many of their Words not to be pronounced by Europeans" (Beaglehole 1967: 1103).

Although the journals from the first visits to the Polynesian islands give the impression that the explorers almost from the first moment on could converse without serious problems with the natives, at least some of them like Cook and Bougainville later on realized that this had been a self-deceptive impression and that they probably had understood very little of the languages and what was going on in the places they visited (Beaglehole 1961: 234, n. 5. To the explorers and their colleagues at home, the main interest in the natives focused on the exotic aspects of their culture and language and when a famous language scientist like Lord Monboddo met Joseph Banks after Banks' return from Tahiti his main concern was whether Banks' informants had tails like other beasts or not and not aspects of the grammatical structure of their language (Beaglehole 1962: 52, n. 4).

The French explorer Louis Antoine Bougainville (1729–1811) made his famous journey around the world in 1766–1769. The expedition was mainly interested in natural history and had no linguist in the crew. With the exception of Tahitian, there are just a few scattered words from other languages noted and they mostly communicated with signs with the natives. The observation on Tahitian was not so much based on the few days they stayed on the island as on information from a young Tahitian, Aotourou, who went with them on the ship back to France and stayed there for some time until he died on his return home. Bougainville's remarks on the language are almost exclusively focused on its pronunciation and on language as a phenomenon of natural science:

La langue de Taiti est douce, harmonieuse & facile à prononcer. Les mots n'en sont presque composés que de voyelles sans aspiration; on n'y recontre point de syllables muettes, sourdes ou nasales, ni cette quantité de consonnes & d'articulations qui rendent certaines langues si difficiles. Aussi notre Taitien ne pouvoit-il parvenir à prononcer le François. Les mêmes causes qui font accuser notre langue d'être peu musicale, la rendoient inaccessibles à ses organes. On eût plutôt réussi à lui faire prononcer l'Espagnol ou l'Italien.

M. Pereire, célebre par son talent d'enseigner à parler & bien articuler aux sourds & muets de naissance, a examiné attentivement & plusieurs fois Aotourou, & a reconnu qu'il ne pouvoit physiquement prononcer la plûpart de nos consonnes, ni aucune de nos voyelles nasales.

Au reste la langue de cette île est assez abondante; j'en juge par ce que, dans le cours du voyage, Aotourou a mis en strophes cadencées tout ce qui l'a frappé. C'est une espece de récitatif obligé qu'il improvisoit. Voilà ses annals, & il nous a paru que sa langue lui fournissoit des expressions pour peindre une multitude d'objects tous nouveaux pour lui. (Bougainville 1771: 231)

Bougainville (1771: 389–402) also gives a vocabulary of about 300 words.

The first exploratory expedition that had someone on board with some linguistic qualifications was Captain Cook's second expedition (1772–1775). The person in question was the German scholar Johann Reinhold Forster (1729–1798). Forster "reputedly mastered seventeen languages, living and dead; he was learned in philology, ancient geography and Egyptology to an uncommon degree" (Hoare 1982: 2). He was also a well-versed naturalist. His vocabularies from the journey, many of them unpublished, were used by W. von Humboldt and formed a basis for his comparative works (Hoare 1982: 114). A main linguistic contribution by Forster is his "A comparative table of the various languages in the isles of the South-Sea" (Forster 1778: 284) where he convincingly showed the relationship of the Polynesian languages, a relationship that both Bougainville and especially Captain Cook had observed. To Forster this relationship became more and more obvious as he travelled from island to island. Forster had studied both philology and theology, but the main inspiration for his comparative linguistic studies is probably botany and medicine, and especially the professor of surgery in Berlin, Simon Pallas whose son, the botanist Peter Simon Pallas (1741–1811) should be the editor of the great systematized lexical compilation planned by Catherine II. Forster visited the Pallas family frequently during his stay in Berlin 1745–1748, cf. Hoare (1982: 5).

The most ambitious French exploratory expedition was the one headed by Jean-François de Galaup de la Pérouse (1741–1788) in the years 1785–1788; it had several natural scientists on board. Linguistic research was not a main objective of the expedition, but it was stated in the instructions for the expeditions that they should "have observations made on the characteristics, character, customs and practices, temperament, language, form of government and number of the inhabitants" (Dunmore I: cxlv) for the places they visited.

The most interesting linguistic observations on board were made by Jean-Honoré-Robert de Paul, Chevalier de Lamanon (or La Manon) (1752–1787) killed by Samoans in Tutuila. He was a typical scientist of the enlightment with interests ranging from natural history and physics to philology and philosophy. He did not only collect word lists, but gave numerous interesting typological observations on the languages he studied. Similar insightful linguistic observations were not found in any of the earlier exploratory expeditions. As an example, we can take his observations of the Tlingit language of West North America. After presenting a short word list and several observations on pronunciation, phonological system and phontactics (Dunmore 1994 I: 141–143) he adds:

> I do not think that they have articles, as I did not find words that recurred frequently and served to link their parts of speech. They are aware of numbers and have words for them, without however distinguishing between singular and plural either by a change in the endings or by articles; I showed them the tooth of a seal – they called it *kaourré*, and gave the same name, unchanged in any way, to several teeth shown together. (Dunmore 1994 I: 143)

He also gave the following very accurate description of the language situation in California:

> [...] there is perhaps no country where there are more dialects than in northern California; this country is divided among several nations who, although quite close to each other, live in isolation and have their own language. (Dunmore 1994 I: 198)

The last of the great exploratory expeditions and scientifically the most thorough and successful was the famous U. S. Exploring Expedition of 1838–1842 under the equally famous Commander Charles Wilkes (1798–1877). This was, moreover, the first of these expedition that had a philologist in the staff, the young but very gifted Horatio E. Hale (1817–1896) who became the real founder of Polynesian scientific linguistics (Hale 1846), cf. Mackert (1994).

## 4. Bibliography

Alderley, Lord Stanley of, ed. 1874. *The First Voyage round the World by Magellan*. Translated from the accounts of Pigafetta and other contemporary sources. Works issued by The Hakluyt Society. No. LII. London. The Hakluyt Society.

Beaglehole, John, ed. 1955. *The Journals of Captain James Cook on his Voyages of Discovery*. Vol. I. (= *Hakluyt Society, Extra Series*, 34.) London: Cambridge Univ. Press.

–, ed. 1961. *The Journals of Captain James Cook on his Voyages of Discovery*. Vol. II. (= *Hakluyt Society, Extra Series*, 35.) London: Cambridge Univ. Press.

–, ed. 1962. *The Endeavour Journal of Joseph Banks 1768–1771*. 2 vols. Sydney: Angus & Robertson.

–, ed. 1967. *The Journals of Captain James Cook on his Voyages of Discovery.* Vol. III. (= *Hakluyt Society, Extra Series*, 36.) London: Cambridge Univ. Press.

Bougainville, Louis Antoine. 1771. *Voyage autour du monde, par la frégate du roi La Boudeuse et la flûte l'Étoile; en 1766. 1767, 1768 & 1769.* Paris: Saillant & Nyon.

Carrington, Hugo, ed. 1948. *The Discovery of Tahiti.* A Journal of the second voyage of H. M. S, Dolphin round the world, under the command of Captain Wallis, R. N., in the years 1766, 1767 and 1768 written by her master George Robertson. Works issued by The Hakluyt Society. Second Series No. XCVIII. London. The Hakluyt Society.

Corney, B. G. 1915. *The Quest and Occupation of Tahiti by Emissaries of Spain during the Years 1772–76.* Vol. II London: The Hakluyt Society.

Dunmore, John, ed. 1994. *The Journal of Jean-François de Galaup de la Pérouse 1785–1788.* Vols. I–II. Works issued by the Hakluyt society. Second Series No. 179. London: The Hakluyt Society.

Forster, John Reinhold. 1778. *Observations made during a Voyage Round the World, on Physical Geography, Natural History, and Ethnic Philosophy.* London: G. Robinson.

Greenblatt, Stephen. 1991. *Marvelous Possesions. The wonder of the New World.* Oxford: Clarendon Press.

Hackney, Lord Amherst of & Basil Thomson, eds. 1901. *The Discovery of the Solomon Islands by Alvaro de Menndaña in 1568.* Translated from the original Spanish Manuscripts. 1–2. Works issued by The Hakluyt Society. Second Series. No. VII. London. The Hakluyt Society.

Hale, Horatio. 1846. *United States Exploring Expedition under Charles Wilkes.* Vol. VII: *Ethnography and Philology.* Philadelphia: C. Sherman.

Herrera, Antonio de. 1622. *Novus orbis sive Descriptio Indiæ Occidentalis.* Amstelodami: Apud Michael Colinium.

Hoare, Michael E., ed. 1982. *The Resolution Journal of Johann Reinhold Forster 1772–1775.* I–IV. London. The Hakluyt Society.

Hovdhaugen, Even, ed. 1996. *... and the Word was God. Missionary linguistics and Missionary Grammar.* Münster. Nodus.

Kattunen, Frances. 1994. *Between Worlds. Interpreters, guides, and survivors.* New Brunswick. Rutgers Univ. Press.

Mackert, Michael. 1994. "Horatio Hale and the Great U. S. Exploring Expedition." *Anthropological Linguistics* 36: 1.26.

Naro, Anthony J. 1978. "A study on the origins of pidginization." *Language* 54: 314–347.

Reland, H. 1708. *Dissertatio de linguis insularum quarundam orientalium.* Hadriani Relandi dissertationum pars tertia et ultima, 55–139. Trajecti ad Rhenum.

Schreyer, Rüdiger. 1996. "Take your Pen and Write. Learning Huron: A documented historical sketch". Hovdhaugen, ed. 1996, 77–121.

*Even Hovdhaugen, Oslo (Norway)*

# 127. Missionary linguistics and the description of 'exotic' languages

1. Introduction
2. The global expansion of Roman Catholicism
3. Roman Catholic missionaries in Asia, 1500–1700
4. Roman Catholic missionaries in the Americas, 1500–1700
5. Protestant missionaries in the Americas, 1600–1900
6. Conclusion
7. Bibliography

## 1. Introduction

1.1. To properly understand the experiences and contributions of missionary linguists, one must abandon the impulse to search among their writings for the seeds of modern language science. This is not to diminish the many and real contributions of Christian missionaries to the growth of the scientific study of language. Rather, it is to suggest that in order to have any meaningful historical understanding of the sources of those contributions, we must move beyond the all too common tendency among historians of linguistics to be satisfied with simply identifying the antecedents of their own discipline. The goal of what follows, then, is not so much to explore the ways in which early missionary linguists were somehow ahead of their time – or whose work seems, from our present-day perspective, to have been somehow modern. Rather, it is to do just the opposite: to understand them as figures of their times, figures whose experience as linguists and missionaries tells us much not just about their contributions to language science, but more importantly, about the broader cultural and historical forces that made those contributions possible.

1.2. While the experiences of Christian missionaries have varied widely in time and place, one generalization can be made with confidence: until the 19th century, their language studies were a means to an end, namely the salvation of souls. The result of this was, on the whole, a highly utilitarian approach to the study of language. Only in exceptional cases does one find among the vast corpus of early missionary writings elaborate morphological analyses or philosophical ruminations on the nature of language. Instead, those writings reveal a persistent struggle to comprehend foreign languages in familiar, Western terms. This does not reflect some sort of impediment imposed by Christian dogma. Rather, it is indicative of the fact that for most Christian missionaries language-acquisition, not language *tout court*, has been the primary concern. The emergence of Protestant missions, beginning in the 17th century, brought a new emphasis on the translation of Christian texts into non-European tongues, and while this forced missionaries to move beyond simple language acquisition, it did not diminish the utilitarian approach of missionary language study.

## 2. The global expansion of Roman Catholicism

2.1. Christianity was, until the beginning of the 16th century, a religion whose geographic scope was – compared with that of the other world religions – relatively small. Christians occupied much of Western Europe, but Muslims – their chief competitors for converts – occupied a vast arc of territory from North Africa and southern Europe through central Asia. The area of Christian influence began to grow significantly only after the beginning of the 16th century, as Portuguese and Spanish seafarers extended European commerce and culture to include isolated portions of West Africa, the West Indies, and portions of South and Southeast Asia. In addition to transforming peripheral nations into true global powers, the seaborne expansion of Spain and Portugal provided the critical conduit for extending the global reach of Roman Catholicism. Nearly all early Spanish and Portuguese exploratory and trading expeditions included Catholic clergy among their crew members. These representatives of the Pope were to serve as emissaries for the Catholic Church in faraway lands. But they also constituted a sort of moral conscience for conquistadors and traders, serving as an ever-present reminder that the overseas activities of Spain and Portugal required the support of the Church, and that that support was forthcoming only so long as the agents of imperialism facilitated the primary goal of the Church: the saving of souls.

## 3. Roman Catholic missionaries in Asia, 1500–1700

3.1. By Papal decree, the Asian trading routes were given to the Portuguese, and because Portugal was primarily a trading power (as opposed to a colonizing power), its presence in Asia was generally confined to seaports. For missionaries, this meant that activity was limited to trading centers, cities with abundant linguistic resources, including cosmopolitan merchants and seafarers, some hailing from the Levant or other regions long acquainted with Europeans and their languages. For this reason, there was little need for missionaries to study local languages. They could, instead, rely for interpretation on the many multilinguals who lived in these trading centers.

3.2. The initial seat of Roman Catholicism in Asia was the port city of Goa, on the western coast of India. In 1557, Goa became the archbishopric for the Church in all of East Asia, encompassing sees as far south as Malacca and as far east as Macao. The predominant missionary order in these cities was the Society of Jesus (Jesuits), and indeed, the order – founded in 1534 by Ignatius Loyola – grew in influence in almost precise proportion to the growth of the Portuguese empire. The first significant Jesuit overseas mission was to Goa and southern India, where it was led by none other than the greatest of all Jesuit missionaries, the Basque Francis Xavier (1506–52). Contrary to popular myth, Xavier's linguistic skills appear to have been rather poor. He never acquired more than a crude knowledge of Tamil, and relied heavily on local interpreters. While Xavier and a small number of other Jesuits and Spanish Franciscans expanded their missionary activities as far East as Japan, from a linguistic standpoint, by far the most important 16th-century Asian mission was to China.

3.3. China, much like Japan, had strongly resisted any form of Western intrusion. But unlike Japan, China had an independent merchant community whose wealth depended on European trade. For this reason, the Portuguese were able to establish the small trading outpost of Macao, a Christian enclave at the mouth of the Canton River. There, a young Italian Jesuit prepared for one of the greatest spiritual and linguistic journeys in recorded history. That Jesuit was the famous Matteo Ricci (1552–1610).

3.4. Unlike the missions of Xavier and most other previous Jesuits in Asia, Ricci's was shaped by a fundamental and pervasive quest to accommodate and emulate the customs of the people he sought to convert – and that meant, among other things, mastering their language. In large measure, this strategy resulted from the simple practical problem of penetrating a Chinese society suspicious of foreigners of all sorts, let alone those seeking to alter traditional religious beliefs. But it also reflects a reorientation of Jesuit thinking.

Jesuits in India had come to see that if they were to have any significant impact on the population, they would have to begin not by attempting to convert all classes, but rather by focusing their limited resources on members of the social elite – an often cosmopolitan group captivated by aspects of European thought and technology. To this end, they impressed these figures with astronomical predictions (including the prediction of eclipses), the use of magnets, clocks, telescopes, and various feats of memory and learning, not the least important of which was the mastery of local languages. And they did all this while offering little resistance to indigenous cultural mores – something that earned them the contempt of other missionary orders and some European governments, all of whom thought that the Jesuits' permissive ways inhibited the growth of Christianity and European hegemony. Ricci – who had initially been sent to Goa – vigorously applied this strategy of cultural accommodation in China. Very early on in his mission he discovered that by adopting elements of the dress and manners of Confucian intellectuals, he could more readily gain the trust of local officials and other elites. One should acknowledge, though, that this was not an entirely novel impulse. As early as the 13th century, the scholar and courtier, Ramon Lull had argued that the Church ought to embrace the study of foreign languages. Doing so, Lull suggested, would afford Catholics the ability to publicly challenge leaders of rival faiths.

Ricci first entered mainland China in 1583, and from that time expanded his social ties to include an increasingly elite and exclusive group until he finally entered the imperial capitol of Peking in 1601. While there, he insinuated himself into the upper echelons of the imperial court as the maintainer of the Chinese royal clocks – the latter being gifts Ricci himself had presented to the emperor. Ricci's language skills appear to have evolved along with his social ties. Sometime in the 1580's, Ricci and Father Michele Ruggieri produced a Chinese/Portuguese dictionary, and in 1595, he wrote in Chinese a book of maxims on friendship, based on the writings of various Christian and classical scholars. In addition to these works, Ricci produced a series of letters and reports that contain much information concerning his experience as a language-learner.

In 1583, writing from Macao, Ricci explained to his rhetoric teacher, Martino de Fornari,

> I have recently given myself to the study of the Chinese language and I can promise you that it's something quite different from either Greek or German. In speaking it, there is so much ambiguity that there are many words that can signify more than a thousand things, and at many times the only difference between one word and another is the way you pitch them high or low in four different tones. Thus when [the Chinese] are speaking to each other they write out the words they wish to say so that they can be sure to understand – for all the written letters are different from the other. As for these written letters you would not be able to believe them had you not both seen and used them, as I have done. They have as many letters as there are words and things, so that there are more than 70,000 of them, every one quite different and complex. (Spence 1983: 136–37)

Ricci was obviously most struck with the sheer abundance of Chinese characters. But he also recognized the potential impediment posed by the distinct tonality of Chinese. Without any means of dicriminating between words whose pronunciation differed only in tone – something not indicated in Chinese script – Ricci had to invent his own phonetic alphabet. For the same reason that Ricci found Chinese difficult to learn, he also recognized what was to be the primary allure of the language in 17th-century Europe: namely the seeming universality of its written characters. Precisely because written Chinese was largely non-phonetic, it could be understood by speakers with a wide range of distinct native tongues. In the same letter to Fornari, Ricci marveled at the way Chinese ideographic script allowed "all the countries that use this kind of writing [to] understand each other's correspondence and books even though the languages are different, something which is not at all the case with our letters" (Spence 1983: 137). Indeed, in the universality of their written script, it appeared that the Chinese were able to do what no Christian had ever done: counter the ill-effects of Babel.

The universality of written Chinese partly explains why Ricci's discussions of Chinese are limited almost exclusively to phonetics and writing. Aside from its apparent power to transcend human difference, Chinese writing promised to facilitate the missionary's ambition by giving him easy access to the souls of speakers of a wide range of languages. But there was another reason Ricci's descriptions were limited to writing: in a society that placed the highest premium on powers of memory, Ricci's memorization of thousands of Chinese characters earned him much esteem among the intellectual elite. And his willingness to teach European mnemonic techniques – techniques Chinese could use to improve their grasp of their own language – only further raised his status.

3.5. In addition to India, China, and Japan, another notable area for Catholic missionaries in 16th century Asia was the Philippines. In 1579, the Pope created the bishopric of Manila, which, largely because of Spanish trading ties, was incorporated into the holy see of Mexico. Very much unlike those elsewhere in Asia, missionaries in the Philippines faced little concerted resistance to their presence. There was simply no large-scale, imperial structure to unite the people against foreigners. Yet, to some degree because of this fact, the missionaries' burden was all the more difficult to bear. Without any sort of overarching governing apparatus, there was no extrinsic force to bring unity to Philippine culture and language. Missionaries could not, therefore, rely on a single elite lingua franca such as Mandarin in China, or Nahuatl in Mexico. Similarly, without the clear social hierarchies of China or India, there was no far-reaching imperial elite to disseminate Catholic learning.

These circumstances left missionaries with no choice but to master various local languages and dialects, and to this end, they produced numerous grammars and dictionaries. Among these were the Dominican Tomas Pinpin, Blancas de San José's *Arte y reglas de la lengua tagalag*, first published in 1610, and Father Augustín de Magdalena's *Arte de la lengua tagala sacado de diversos artes* (1679). Much like other missionary grammars of the era, these works relied on a Latin grammatical standard. The use of a Latin standard, as numerous scholars have observed, was perhaps the single trait that unified all pre-modern missionary grammars. And while one familiar explanation for this is the absence of a relativistic world view, there is another less often recognized explanation. Far from being dispassionate scientific treatises, missonary grammars were textbooks, designed first and foremost to aid missionaries in the expedient acquisition of local languages. It only made sense, then, to present these languages in familiar terms. And for Jesuits, Dominicans, and Franciscans, all of whom had spent time learning Latin, and many of whom had taught Latin, it made even more sense to employ a Latin standard.

## 4. Roman Catholic missionaries in the Americas, 1500–1700

4.1. The first Roman Catholic missionaries to the Americas were members of the Franciscan and Dominican orders. In Central and parts of South America, these groups benefited from the presence of imperial lingua francas – in Mexico, Nahuatl, and in Peru, Quechua. But beyond this, from very early in the Spanish conquest of Mexico, Spanish missionaries had the extraordinary advantage of having printing presses at their disposal. In Mexico, a press was established in the 1530's, under the auspices of the first bishop of Mexico, Don Antonio de Mendoza, and the first book printed on the press was a bilingual catechism entitled *Breve y más compendiosa doctrina Christiana en lengua castellana y mexicana*. This work was followed in 1555 by the first Spanish-Nahuatl dictionary, written by the Franciscan Alonso de Molina. The first printing press in Peru was established in 1580, and soon it too was issuing religious works in Quechua and Aymara. The first of these was the *Doctrina Christiana y catecismo para instrucción del los Indios* (1584), a fully trilingual work in Spanish, Quechua, and Aymara. In addition to yielding various grammars and dictionaries, by the end of the 16th century, these presses had produced dozens of indigenous-language religious texts – including catechisms, biblical passages, confessionals, and prayer manuals. One scholar has estimated that in Mexico, between the years 1524 and 1572, no fewer than sixty-six such books were published in Nahuatl; thirteen in Tarascan; six in Otomí; five in Prinda; five in Mixtec; five in Zapotec; four in Huaxtec; two in Totonac; one in Zoque; and one in the dialect of Chilapa (Ricard 1966: 49).

Given the absence of indigenous alphabetic writing in the Americas, it is not surprising to find that the various examples of American languages printed by the Spanish were composed in a modified Roman alphabet. This should not, however, lead one to conclude that missionaries ignored indigenous writing systems. By the middle of the 16th century, Spanish missionaries had been employing native Nahua painters to reproduce passages from the Bible in Nahua pictographs. Missionaries' did not only produce Christian texts in indigenous media. They also employed Nahua painters to codify Indian accounts of recent Mexican history. By far the most celebrated surviving example of this practice is what has come to be known as the *Florentine Codex*. This work is a combination of Aztec pictographs and alphabetic writings – the latter being commentaries, written initially in a phonetic Nahuatl and later in Spanish by the Franciscan missionary Bernardino de Sahagún (1499?–1590). Aside from exemplifying the degree to which Spanish missionaries used native writing systems, the work offers a vivid demonstration of the collaborative nature of linguistic activity in the colonial world: rarely did missionaries work alone. On the contrary, it is difficult to find a case in which a translated work, grammar, or dictionary was not the result of some sort of collaboration between missionaries and indigenous speakers.

It should also be said that although missionaries in early Mexico tended to emphasize the study of Nahuatl – the imperial lingua franca – they did not do this to the exclusion of the multitude of other regional languages. For instance, in addition to Nahuatl, most Dominicans also studied Mixtec and Zapotec. The Augustinians and Franciscans, because of the greater linguistic variation in the terrotories assigned to them, learned even more languages. Members of the Augustinian order, for instance, are known to have studied (in addition to Nahuatl) Otomí, Tarascan, Huaxtec, Pirinda, Totonac, Chichimec, Tlapanec, and Ocuiltec. While most missionaries knew one or two indigenous languages, there were exceptional cases, such as that of Fray Andrés de Olmos who preached and wrote catechisms in ten different Indian languages. Missionaries' willingness to learn regional languages reflected the growing Catholic awareness that by assimilating elements of local cultures they could gain influence in indigenous societies.

Catholic missionaries began arriving in New France – the region adjoining the St. Lawrence Seaway, the Great Lakes, and the Canadian maritime provinces – in the early 17th century. And they too produced grammars, dictionaries, prayer books, and catechisms in various indigenous languages. But significantly, they were never able to do this on any kind of large scale. Although Jesuits requested a printing press in 1665, the request was never granted. Works such as Sagard's *Dictionaire de la langue huronne* (1632) or the many treatments of American-Indian speech in Jesuits' *Relations* had to be printed in France, and rarely circulated in America. As a consequence, missionaries depended on the hand-written grammars and vocabularies of their predecessors to aid their language studies, and much of this material has long since been lost or destroyed. Furthermore, as in the Philippines, in North America there were no readily identifiable lingua francas.

In addition to this limitation, few obstacles frustrated French missionaries as much as the scarcity of willing translators and language instructors. There were French fur traders who had some knowledge of American languages, but given the corrupt and immoral qualities missionaries generally attributed to these figures, they hardly seemed like suitable conduits for Christian wisdom. The only option was to turn to the Indians themselves for language instruction. This resulted in a total reversal of the usual channels of authority in Jesuit education. Far from being the teacher, the priest in this case, found himself acting as the pupil. For Jesuits, many of whom had served as teachers of Latin in their native France, to find themselves abandoned to the whims of Indian teachers must have been to experience the deepest humiliation and confusion.

Once again, a brief survey of French missionary writings on Amerindian languages reveals a continued reliance on a Latin standard, and, in turn, the persistence of the Christian utilitarian approach to language study. In terms of describing American languages, Jesuits and Recollects (the other missionary order represented in New France) generally derided the languages, characterizing the polysynthetic character of American languages as a symptom of social decay. In keeping with their heathen character, missionaries widely assumed, Indians had failed to impose grammatical discipline on their languages. But by far the most prevalent complaint about Huron, Iroquois, and the various Algonquian languages with which French missionaries had contact, concerned their seeming lexical failures. French missionaries endlessly bemoaned the difficulty of providing a spiritual education to peoples who lacked such essential abstractions as "belief", "spirit", and "soul", let alone less generic terms such as "angel", "saint", "grace", etc. To be sure, this was not a problem unique to the missionaries of colonial North America. Nonetheless, the French missionaries seem to have been more concerned with the problem than others. Perhaps they had simply recognized that the earlier practice of introducing European terms to foreign speech produced dangerous confusions. While in Japan, Francis Xavier, for instance, had employed the Portuguese *Deos*, but this was equated by Japanese priests with the term *Dajuzo*, which meant "a great lie" (Ricard 1966: 55). In New France, a striking example of the problem is contained in the Jesuit Father Jean Brébeuf's 1636 *Relacion.* Struggling to convey to his superiors the difficulties involved in bringing Huron speakers into the Church, Brébeuf observed that one cannot say in Huron, "In the name of the Father, the Son, and of the holy ghost". Huron simply has no easily identified definite articles to which "father", "son", and "ghost" could be attached (Schreyer 1996: 99–100).

## 5. Protestant missionaries in the Americas, 1600–1900

5.1. Until the 19th century, Protestant missionary work was – in comparison with that of the Roman Catholic Church – distinctly paltry. Nonetheless, there were a number of important initiatives, particularly in North America. Again, like the early Catholic missions, these Protestant missions depended for their existence on the maritime expansion of Europe. In this case, the most important nations were the two great Protestant powers: Holland and, later, England.

Dutch missionaries worked in 17th-century New York, Surinam, Ceylon, and Indonesia. For the most part, they followed the Catholic model, and hence their linguistic work tended to be similarly utilitarian. To some extent this was true of all Protestant missions. But there were certain significant differences in the ways Protestants approached non-European languages. One might, for instance, look at the Tupinamba vocabulary prepared by the French Huguenot missionary to Brazil, Jean de Léry. This work takes the missionaries' utilitarian ethos one step further: beyond simply diagramming the language in terms of a Latin standard, Léry prepared what amounted to a traveler's phrase book. One is struck by the similarities between this and another Protestant work, that of the 17th-century New England religious radical, Roger Williams. Williams' *A Key Into the Language of America* (1643) is much more a traveler's phrase book than a systematic grammar. Chapters include "Of Salutation", "Of Eating and Entertaiment", "Concerning Sleepe and Lodging", "Of Buying and Selling", and "Of Sicknesse". Each of these chapters consists of a series of Eastern Algonquian terms, arrayed next to appropriate English terms, and embellished with Williams' observations about indigenous culture.

5.2. The most remarkable of the early Protestant missions to the Americas was that of the New England minister, John Eliot (1604–1690) who spent the second half of the 17th century pursuing the conversion of a small group of Algonquian-speaking Indians in Eastern Massachusetts. Much like the Catholic missionaries in New Spain, Eliot had a printing press at his disposal, but Eliot's use of print differed profoundly from that of these Catholic missionaries. If, for the latter, printed works in indigenous languages were intended to serve the missionaries themselves, for Eliot they were intended to serve the Indians.

Eliot's greatest achievement was thus his translation of the entire Bible into Massachusett, a member of the Eastern Algonquian family of American Indian languages. This gesture, far more than either Eliot's success as a missionary (which was minimal) or his strictly linguistic writings (limited to one work) marks Eliot's mission as a turning point in the history of missonary linguistics: Eliot was the first to apply to a non-European peoples the Protestant doctrine that every Christian should have ready and immediate access to Scripture. His translation, entitled *Mamusee Wunneetapanatamwe Up-Biblium God* (1663) not only marked the beginning of an extraordinary trend in missionary linguistics, but also foreshadowed a stunning development in European cultural expansion: the global dissemination of a single, canonical text.

While Eliot wrote little about the languages of America, we can gain some insight into his perspective by examining his theology. Eliot was a member of a zealous sect of English Protestants, labeled "Puritans" by their opponents. But even within this group, Eliot was radical. He believed fervently in the millennialist notion that the second coming of Christ was imminent, and that humans had much to do to prepare the way for Christ's return. Most importantly, they had to reconstruct an early "primitive" church of Christians that resembled the morally uncorrupt world before original sin. In Eliot's view, the only acceptable way to do this was to begin with persons devoid of the corrupt habits of mind endemic to the Old World. The American Indians seemed the ideal subjects for such an experiment. They appeared untouched by European greed and immorality, and (in Eliot's view) may even have been one of the Ten Lost Tribes of Israel.

Eliot recognized that the best way to inoculate Indians against the corrupting ways of Europeans was to preserve the barrier imposed by linguistic difference. Thus, there was a clear practical reason he elected to give his Indian charges a Bible in their own language. But beyond this, unlike Catholic missionaries to New France, Eliot expressed almost no doubt that Christian knowledge could be conveyed in indigenous Indian languages. He appears to have had complete faith that whatever lexical disparities there were between Massachusett and English constituted no serious barrier to the transmission of Christian knowledge. Again, if we look at the broader intellectual world of which Eliot was a part, this makes considerable sense.

There was, in the mid-17th century Anglo-American world, something of a millennialist-linguistics, shaped by the thinking of Puritan educational reformers and millennialist theologians who generally regarded Christ's return as imminent. These figures increasingly accepted the notion that language learning could be founded on experience and the study of students' own vernacular tongues rather than a labored and tedious study of Latin grammar. This revisionist pedagogy was driven by the fundamental Protestant desire to make Scripture accessible to all souls. To think that the Word was better understood in one language than another was merely to perpetuate the fundamental fallacy – according to radical Protestants – perpetuated by the Roman Catholic Church: namely, that God's word could be shaped and distorted by mortal human speech. To think this, in the minds of Puritans of Eliot's strain, was to think that humans had the power to subvert the Word of God – an utterly unacceptable notion in a world whose moral order is secured by the ultimate and indisputable superiority of an arbitrary and capricious God. Thus what ultimately distinguished this millennialist language philosophy was the belief that no language could claim superior expressive power and hence that there was no reason for Divine wisdom not to be conveyed in the Indians' language.

Eliot revealed this conception of language in his approach to translation. Far from depending on a systematic understanding of the grammar of Massachusett, he relied on a combination of phonetics and Indian experience. He would read a passage from the Bible to an Indian translator, and would then reproduce the Indians' words in a modified Roman alphabet. There was nothing in this process that suggested a desire or a need to understand Massachusett in European terms. Having said this, one must acknowledge that Eliot did produce a Massachusett grammar (1666) that was based on a Latin standard. Eliot suffered from an enduring fear that he would not live to finish his Bible translation. As part of an effort to secure the project against his death, he thus produced a grammar to assist subsequent Anglophone translators.

5.3. After Eliot, another complete Bible was not to be produced in an American Indian language until 1862, when Canadian missionaries translated the Bible into Western Cree.

In part this reflects the diminution of Eliot's fanatical brand of Protestantism; but more importantly, it reflects the prevalence of an Enlightenment language philosophy that presupposed a connection between language and social condition. This doctrine made it difficult to justify the creation of Christian texts in the languages of peoples who appeared to be culturally and socially backward.

Nonetheless, there were significant Protestant linguistic initiatives in North America, particularly those of the Moravian Brethren in Western Pennsylvania and the Ohio River Valley. Very much unlike the Puritan missionaries, or any of the Catholics, the Moravians did not set out to provide Indians with a spiritual education. Instead they sought to convert through example. This meant that Moravians lived among the Indians for ten, sometimes twenty years, engaging in various charitable activities and addressing strictly religious matters only at occasional, carefully chosen moments. It also meant that they had an unusually thorough knowledge of Indian customs and languages.

The two most notable linguists in this group were David Zeisberger (1721–1808) and John Heckewelder (1743–1823). Zeisberger is best known for producing a highly detailed Delaware grammar, first published by the American Philosophical Society in 1827, while Heckewelder is best known for his rich collaborations with the Philadelphia linguist, Peter Stephen Duponceau (1760–1844), published in 1819, also by the American Philosophical Society. Heckewelder's correspondence with Duponceau – most of which remains in the Archives of the American Philosophical Society – constitutes by far the most detailed and thorough analysis of a North American Indian language then produced. And it very much reinforced Duponceau's own strikingly modern perspective on the indigenous languages of North America. Duponceau's chief concern was to overturn the Enlightenment assumption that "primitive" peoples necessarily spoke "primitive" languages. To this end, he and Heckewelder discussed at length the alleged lexical deficiencies of American Indian languages. Was it true, Duponceau wanted to know, that these tongues lacked a capacity to express abstract thoughts? Heckewelder provided the empirical evidence (drawn from his extensive knowledge of Delaware) that in fact this was a groundless hypothesis, perpetuated by European philosophers with no first-hand knowledge of American languages. It would be no exaggeration to say that it was the former Moravian missionary Heckewelder who gave the Philadelphia lawyer-linguist, Duponceau, the empirical foundation for his extraordinarily novel and modern theories about American Indian languages.

## 6. Conclusion

The growth of linguistic knowledge over the past century and a half has been unprecedented in human history, and missionary linguists are responsible for much of this. One need only peruse *The Book of a Thousand Tongues* (1972), published by the United Bible Societies, to grasp the extraordinary geographic scope of modern missionary linguistics. Hundreds of languages in Asia, Africa, and the Americas, many spoken by only a handful of speakers, have been mastered by missionary linguists engaged in translating the Bible. It is not coincidental that the modern proliferation of Bibles, and the growth of a modern, post-Darwinian conception of language have been concurrent historical phenomena. The middle-class society that funds most modern missionary linguistics has fully assimilated the notion that a language's expressive power has nothing to do with the social condition of its speakers. It must be said that the basic premise of this modern linguistic relativism has been integral to Protestantism since the time of Eliot – and was vigorously defended by John Heckewelder. What distinguishes their eras from our own, however, was the degree to which that position was accepted in society at large. In the end, their's were isolated views. The history of Christian missionary linguistics, one must conclude, has always been shaped by a complex interplay of secular and non-secular influences. At present, that interplay is revealed in the computer equipment and secular university degrees missionary linguists take with them into the field. At the same time, secular linguists have found themselves collaborating most notably with members of the Wycliffe Bible Translators, and its sister organization, the Summer Institute of Linguistics. While this group was founded for the purposes of disseminating Scripture, over the past half-century it has become increasingly dedicated to descriptive linguistics. Linguists such as the Americans Kenneth Pike and Eugene Nida who began their careers as Bible translators, but subsequently contributed significant scholarly work to secular linguistics, exemplify this trend.

## 7. Bibliography

Nida, Eugene A. 1972. *The Book of a Thousand Tongues.* Rev. ed. London: United Bible Societies.

Ricard, Robert. 1966. *The Spiritual Conquest of Mexico: An Essay on the Apostolate and the Evangelizing Methods of the Medicant Orders in New Spain: 1523–1572.* Berkeley, Cal.: Univ. of California Press.

Schreyer, Rüdiger. 1992. *The European Discovery of Chinese (1550–1615) or The Mystery of Chinese Unveiled.* Amsterdam: Stichting Neerlandistiek VU.

–. 1996. "Take Your Pen and Write: Learning Huron: A documented historical sketch", in Even Hovdhangen, ed. ... *and the Word was God. Missionary linguistics and missionary grammar.* Münster: Nodus Publikationen.

Spence, Jonathan D. 1984. *The Memory Palace of Matteo Ricci.* New York: Viking Penguin Inc.

*Edward G. Gray, Tallahassee, Fl. (USA)*

# 128. Das Studium der autochtonen Sprachen Zentralamerikas: Nahuatl

1. Einführung
2. Die Entdeckung Amerikas und seiner Sprachen
3. Das Jahrhundert der Eroberung
4. 'Gegen die Fallstricke des Teufels'
5. Das Zeitalter der Aufklärung
6. Die Studien zum Nahuatl im 19. Jahrhundert
7. Die aktuelle Linguistik des Nahuatl
8. Bibliographie

## 1. Einführung

Vor zehn Jahren veröffentlichte Ascensión H[ernández] de León Portilla (1988) *Tepuztlahcuilolli*, ein Werk, das eine Bibliographie mit fast 3000 Einträgen ausschließlich über Drucke in oder bezüglich des Nahuatl enthält, die zwischen 1546 und 1980 erschienen sind, darüber hinaus eine historische Untersuchung, welche auf diesem reichhaltigen bibliographischen Material basiert. Wenn man sie auf zwölf Seiten zusammenfaßt, wird man einer Geschichte nicht gerecht, die mehr als 450 Jahre alt ist, denn wenn auch das älteste bekannte Druckwerk aus dem Jahr 1546 stammt, so gab es doch Werke, die in handschriftlicher Form mindestens seit 1532 unter den Interessenten zirkulierten, wenngleich sie erst viel später in Druck gegeben wurden.

Viele der in diesen viereinhalb Jahrhunderten auf Nahuatl verfaßten Werke sind aus 'praktischen' Gründen geschrieben worden; es sind keine rein linguistischen Studien – obwohl anzunehmen ist, daß an ihrem Beginn eine Untersuchung der Sprache oder zumindest ihr gewissenhaftes Erlernen steht – aber bei anderen handelt es sich ganz offensichtlich um Sprachanalysen, die ein außerordentliches sprachliches Verständnis und ein Interesse am Nahuatl an sich erkennen lassen, selbst wenn sie gleichzeitig auch einen praktischen Zweck beim Unterrichten desselben haben. Bei den ältesten dieser Werke kann man nur selten zwischen den 'theoretischen' und den 'praktischen' Absichten unterscheiden.

In der Geschichte der Studien zum Nahuatl gibt es keinen Bruch oder abrupten Richtungswechsel (wie es ihn in der Geschichte allgemein nicht gibt). Die Periodisierung ist in gewisser Hinsicht künstlich, aber nützlich, um die Richtung anzuzeigen, die die Mehrheit der sich langsam verändernden Untersuchungen in dem jeweiligen Zeitabschnitt einschlagen, was nicht selten mit dem Namen bestimmter herausragender Persönlichkeiten verbunden ist, die wir hier zwar nicht mit der gebotenen Sorgfalt untersuchen können, die wir aber auch nicht unerwähnt lassen können.

## 2. Die Entdeckung Amerikas und seiner Sprachen

Am Ende des 15. Jhs. wußten die Europäer von der Vielfalt der Volkssprachen der verschiedenen Regionen der Welt, wo sie Handel betrieben oder Krieg führten – darüber hinaus kannten sie natürlich die heiligen klassischen Sprachen Latein, Griechisch und Hebräisch – aber so wie ihnen die Geographie Asiens und Afrikas unbekannt war, so wußten sie genausowenig von der dort existierenden Sprachenvielfalt. Andererseits dienten

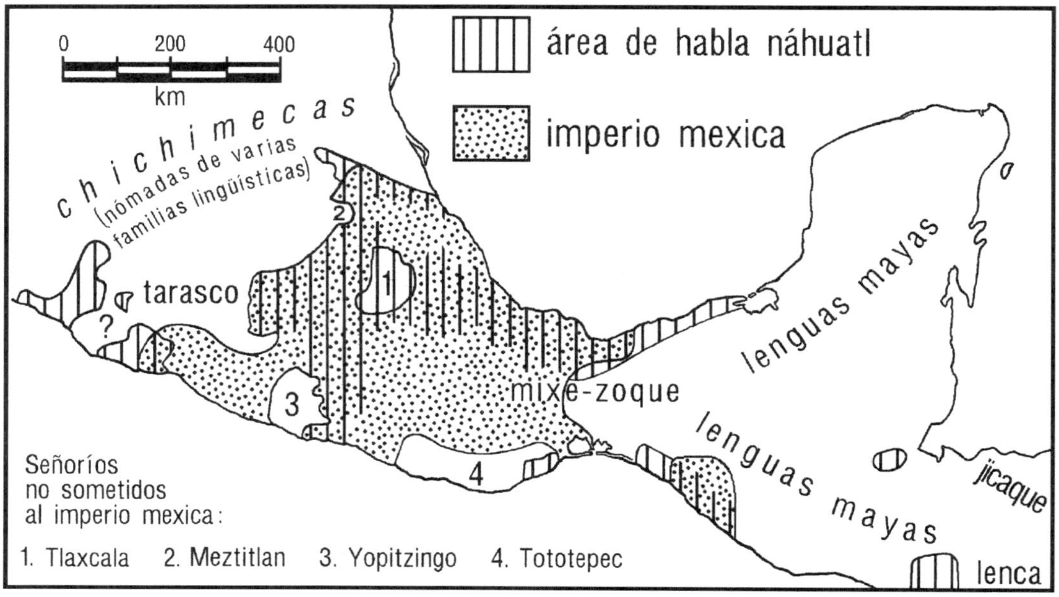


Abb. 128.1.: Verbreitung des Nahuatl und des Aztekischen Reiches

ihnen das Arabische und das Syrische dazu, mit den Händlern zu verkehren, die die Produkte, die sie in den entlegenen Gebieten jener Kontinente erwarben, zu den außereuropäischen Küsten des Mittelmeeres brachten. So ist es nicht verwunderlich, daß Christoph Kolumbus auf seiner ersten Reise nach Indien den *faraute* und *lengua* (Vermittler und Zwischenhändler) Luis de Torres mitnahm, der Hebräisch, Chaldäisch und etwas Arabisch beherrschte.

Die Ankunft auf den Inseln brachte die Europäer mit völlig unbekannten Sprachen in Kontakt und sorgte alsbald dafür, daß sie einheimische Wörter in das Spanische übernahmen, vor allem solche, die Tiere und Pflanzen der Region bezeichneten. Eines dieser Wörter, *canoa*, erscheint schon im *Vocabulario español-latino* (1495?) von Nebrija, aber viele andere fanden Eintritt in das Spanisch der Eroberer der Antillen, um dann später sowohl nach Spanien als auch auf das amerikanische Festland zu gelangen.

Die Expeditionen, die, von Kuba ausgehend, im Gebiet des heutigen Mexiko landeten, brachten die Spanier mit dem Maya der Halbinsel Yucatán und später mit dem Nahuatl in Kontakt, dessen Sprecher in Tabasco sehr zahlreich waren und die mit den Maya Handel trieben.

Die Sprache des Reiches der Mexica – oder Azteken – war das Nahuatl (häufiger 'mexikanisch' genannt), eine Sprache, die seit mehreren Jahrhunderten im Zentrum des Landes präsent war und deshalb auch die Sprache von Herrschaftsgebieten war, die niemals von den Azteken unterworfen wurden (Manrique 1988); sie wurde im Laufe der Zeit zur *lingua franca* vieler Völker mit unterschiedlicher Sprache:

Esta [lengua] mexicana corre por toda la Nueva España, que el que la sabe puede ir desde Zacatecas hasta el cabo de Nicaragua, que son más de seiscientas leguas, y en todas ellas hallar quien le entienda, porque no hay pueblo ninguno [...] en donde no haya indios mexicanos [= nahuas] o quien sepa aquella lengua, que cierto es cosa grande. (Ciudad Real 1976: 55) [Diese mexikanische Sprache ist in gesamt Neuspanien verbreitet, so daß derjenige, der sie beherrscht, von Zacatecas bis zum Kap von Nicaragua gehen kann, was mehr als sechshundert Meilen sind, und er kann überall jemanden treffen, der ihn versteht, weil es kein Dorf gibt [...], in dem es keine mexikanischen Indios [= Nahuas] gibt oder in dem niemand diese Sprache beherrscht, was wirklich eine große Sache ist.]

## 3. Das Jahrhundert der Eroberung

Die spanische Eroberung zerstörte fast auf einen Schlag die politischen Strukturen, die soziale und administrative Organisation, sowie die Religion der indianischen Nationen, beginnend mit denen des Aztekenreiches, und ersetzte sie – manchmal an die Gegebenheiten angepaßt – allmählich durch die europäischen politischen, administrativen und religiösen Institutionen, wobei sich die religiösen Vorstellungen und Strukturen aufgrund ihrer Natur lange Zeit noch halbverborgen in ihrem ursprünglichen Zustand erhalten konnten.

Die Spanier, deren Könige Isabel und Fernando wegen ihres Eifers, den Katholizismus auf Kosten der Moslems und Juden auszudehnen, 'die Katholischen' genannt wurden, waren zutiefst religiös, so daß die Evangelisierung der Indios eines ihrer fundamentalen Interessen war, zugleich aber auch als Rechtfertigung für die wirtschaftliche Ausbeutung während der Kolonialzeit diente. Cortés bat Karl V., ihm Franziskanermönche zu schikken, um diese Aufgabe in Angriff zu nehmen. Indem sie die Zahl der Apostel imitierten, kamen zwölf von ihnen im Jahr 1524; vorausgegangen waren ihnen nur einige Geistliche, die die spanischen Heerscharen als Kapläne begleiteten, und drei flämische Franziskaner (einer von ihnen, Fray Pedro de Gante [Gent], war ein Verwandter Karls V.).

Diese Missionare besaßen eine humanistische Bildung, die stark durch die Schriften des Erasmus beeinflußt und an der Reform orientiert war, die Kardinal Cisneros, Beichtvater der Königin, Gründer der Universität von Alcalá, Inspirator der *Biblia políglota complutense* und später Regent des Reiches, ihrem Orden gegeben hatte. Nahuatl zu erlernen war eine praktische Notwendigkeit, aber die Missionare folgten auch der humanistischen Maxime, in der religiösen Praxis und in der Verbreitung der Heiligen Schriften die Volkssprachen zu gebrauchen.

Die flämischen Missionare, die zuerst nach Mexiko gelangt waren, gründeten eine Schule für Kinder, in der sie ihnen lesen, schreiben, Gesang und Katechismus beibrachten und zugleich von ihnen die mexikanische Sprache lernten. Die zwölf machten das gleiche:

> se ponían a jugar con ellos [...] y traían siempre papel y tinta en las manos, y en oyendo un vocablo [nuevo] lo escribían y [por qué se] dijo (Torquemada 1977, V: 61) [Sie begannen, mit ihnen zu spielen [...] und hatten immer Papier und Tinte zur Hand, und wenn sie ein neues Wort hörten, schrieben sie es auf und auch wofür man es verwendete].

Um in die Feinheiten des Nahuatl einzudringen, in die alten religiösen Ideen – die sie auslöschen wollten – und allgemein in die Kenntnisse, die die Kinder nicht haben konnten, griffen die Missionare auf die Alten zurück, vor allem auf die *temachtiani* oder Weisen. Zuerst machten sie es beiläufig, aber seit 1533 wurde die Befragung systematisch im *Imperial Colegio de Santa Cruz de Tlatelolco* (1536 offiziell in Tlatelolco, einem Viertel von Mexiko-Stadt, gegründet) durchgeführt. In dieser Schule, welche die aufgrund ihrer Ausbildung (in Sprachen, Theologie, etc.) herausragensten Mönche und diejenigen alten Indios zusammenführte, die am besten wußten, was in dem alten *calmecac* (vorspanische Schule, wo die adeligen Nahuas alles über Religion, Regierung, Kunst, Militärwesen und Wissenschaften erlernten) unterrichtet wurde, unterwiesen beide Gruppen zusammen die jungen indianischen Adeligen im neuen Katechismus, in spanischen Sitten und Gebräuchen und auch im *trivium* und im *quatrivium* und gebrauchten dazu die drei Sprachen Spanisch, Nahuatl und Latein.

Die Missionarschronisten sagen, daß die Mönche, sobald sie genügend Kenntnisse im Nahuatl erworben hatten, in dieser Sprache predigten und einige Jugendliche dahingehend unterwiesen, selbst das Christentum zu verbreiten. Sie setzten großes Vertrauen in das geschriebene Wort und bereiteten Schriftstücke vor, die die Neugetauften, denen sie aus diesem Grund das Lesen und Schreiben beigebracht hatten, mit sich führen konnten. Vielleicht leitet sich von diesen Manuskripten die *Doctrina christiana en lengua mexicana* ab, von der gesagt wird, daß Fray Pedro de Gante sie 1528 in Antwerpen drucken ließ (Von dieser Ausgabe ist kein Exemplar bekannt, sondern nur von der, die 1553 in Mexiko erschien. Der erste neuspanische Druck, von dem man sichere Kenntnis hat, ist eine *Breve y más compendiosa doctrina christiana*, im Auftrag des ersten Bischofs von Mexiko 1539 angefertigt, teilweise auf Nahuatl geschrieben.).

Bei ihrer Ankunft in Mexiko beherrschten die Franziskaner bereits mehrere Sprachen: Alle sprachen sie Latein und mehr oder weniger Griechisch, einige waren des Hebräischen mächtig, und jeder von ihnen sprach seine Muttersprache – wobei es sich um Spanisch, Niederländisch, Italienisch, Französisch oder Deutsch handeln konnte – und war sich bewußt, daß seine Ordensbrüder oftmals eine andere Muttersprache hatten. Gelegentliche Verweise in ihren Schriften zeigen, daß ihnen die grammatikalischen Ideen der Antike und des Mittelalters bekannt waren, genauso wie die *Introductiones latinae* (1481) von Nebrija, die für den Unterricht bestimmt waren, und

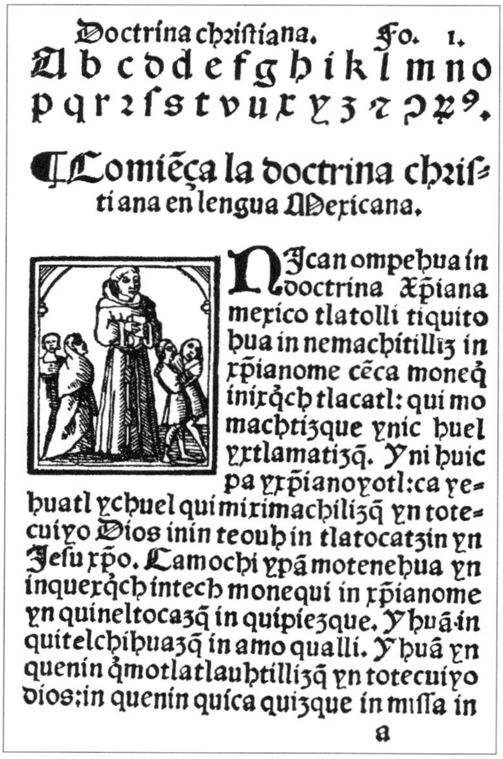
Doctrina christiana. Fo. 1.
Abcdefghiklmno
pqrꝛſstvuxyz

Comiença la doctrina christiana en lengua Mexicana.

Nican ompehua in doctrina xpiana mexico tlatolli tiquito hua in nemachitilliz in xpianome cēca moneq inixqch tlacatl: qui mo machtizque ynic huel yxtlamatizq. Yni huic pa yxpianoyotl: ca ye huatl ychuel quimiximachilizq yn totecuiyo Dios inin teouh in tlatocatzin yn Jesu xpo. Camochi ypā motenehua yn inquexqch intech monequi in xpianome yn quineltocazq in quipiezque. Y huā in quitelchihuazq in amo qualli. Y huā yn quenin qmotlatlauhtillizq yn totecuiyo dios: in quenin quica quizque in missa in a

Abb. 128.2.: Erste Seite der *Doctrina Christiana en Lengua Mexicana* von Fray Pedro de Gante [Gent]

seine *Gramática castellana* (1492), die einen eher präskriptiven Charakter besaß. Somit waren sie auf die Beschäftigung mit den fremden Volkssprachen, die sie bei der Evangelisierung verwenden sollten, vorbereitet. Sie versuchten sehr bald das, was sie in der Praxis gelernt hatten, zu systematisieren. Es gibt Zeugnisse darüber, daß schon im Jahr 1531 handschriftliche *Artes* existierten (H. de León Portilla 1988: 12). Es ist möglich, daß einer dieser Traktate der erste ist, von dem Fray Andrés de Olmos vorgibt, ihn geschrieben zu haben, und da diesem Traktat "faltarle mucho en el corte [vieles in der Gestaltung fehlt]", "[a] esta segunda [terminada en 1547] pareció darle la orden y traça que lleva" [schien es [i. e. Olmos] angemessen, ihm in dieser zweiten Auflage [1547 beendet] die Anordnung und Form zu geben, die er hat].

Es paßt nicht in den Rahmen einer kurzen Geschichte der Linguistik des Nahuatl, die Werke im Detail zu analysieren, aber ich muß einige Zeilen der Beschreibung der auffälligsten Kennzeichen einiger dieser Werke widmen, weil sie die Grundlage für alle nachfolgenden Arbeiten und Studienmodell für andere 'exotische' Sprachen, das heißt, für die Entwicklung des sprachwissenschaftlichen Denkens, sind.

Wie der Titel *Arte para aprender la lengua Mexicana* schon andeutet, hat Olmos sein Werk mit einer didaktischen Absicht geschrieben. Deshalb ist es nur natürlich, daß er dazu neigt, sich an Nebrija zu orientieren:

En el arte de la lengua latina creo que la mejor manera y orden que se ha tenido es la que Antonio de Lebrixa sigue en la suya; pero porque en esta lengua [mexicana] no quadrara la orden que él lleva, por faltar [...] las declinaciones, supinos y las especies de los verbos [...] no seré reprehensible si en todo no siguiere la orden de la Arte de Antonio" (1993: 15) [Bezüglich der lateinischen Sprache ist die beste Art und Weise und Reihenfolge in der Beschreibung die, die Antonio von Lebrixa in der seinigen verwendet hat; da diese aber für die Beschreibung dieser [mexikanischen] Sprache ungeeignet ist, weil ihr [...] die Deklinationen, Supina und die Verbarten fehlen [...] wird man mich nicht tadeln, wenn ich die Reihenfolge der Beschreibung von Antonio nicht im ganzen einhalte].

Und tatsächlich hält er eine ganz andere Reihenfolge ein: Er läßt die Modelle (Deklinationen und Konjugationen) aus, die dem Text vorausgehen, ebenso wie das Wörterverzeichnis am Ende; er faßt nicht alle 'Satzteile' in einem "Ersten Teil" zusammen, wie es Nebrija tut, der den "Zweiten Teil" der Syntax, den "Dritten Teil" der Orthographie, etc. widmet, sondern der erste Teil bei Olmos handelt nur von den "nombres y pronombres y lo que a ellos pertenece" [Nomina und Pronomina und das, was zu ihnen gehört], der zweite beschränkt sich auf die "conjugación, formación y pretéritos y diversidad de verbos" [Konjugation, Morphologie, Vergangenheitsformen und Verschiedenheit der Verben] und im dritten Teil faßt er die "partes indeclinables y parte de la ortografía, una plática de los naturales, con otras maneras de hablar" [undeklinierbaren Satzteile und einen Teil der Orthographie, eine Unterhaltung der Einheimischen, mit anderen Ausdrucksweisen] zusammen. Als ob das nicht genug wäre, beginnt er den *Arte* nicht mit dem Nomen, sondern mit "Las diferencias que hay de pronombres" [Die Unterschiede, die es bei den Pronomina gibt]. (In vier Kapiteln werden vier Klassen von Pronomina behandelt, in den folgenden beiden die Form und die Regeln der Verbindung mit Nomina, Verben und Präpositionen.).

Den Text hindurch stellt Olmos das Nahuatl dem Latein gegenüber, manchmal auf implizite Weise: "los comparativos y superlativos en esta lengua no los tienen propios, sino usan de rodeos" [Die Komparative und Superlative dieser Sprache haben sie in ihrer nicht, sondern sie gebrauchen Umschreibungen], "fuera del infinitivo, en todos los otros modos no hay sino dos tiempos [...]" [Außer dem Infinitiv gibt es in den anderen Modi nur zwei Zeiten[...]), "en esta lengua de otra manera tomamos los neutros que en la latina" [In dieser Sprache werden die Neutrumformen anders als im Lateinischen gebildet], "en la langua latina no se hallan partículas assí encorporadas o juntas con el verbo, las quales denoten la persona [gramatical] que padece" [In der lateinischen Sprache gibt es keine solchen Partikel, die in das Verb inkorporiert sind oder bei ihm stehen und die [grammatische] Person anzeigen, die die Handlung erleidet]. Es ist klar, daß Pater Olmos die tiefgreifenden Unterschiede zwischen dem Latein und dem Mexikanischen wahrgenommen und sich die linguistischen Konzepte seiner Zeit zunutze gemacht hat, indem er sie erweiterte und veränderte, so daß sie die Wirklichkeit des Nahuatl widerspiegelten.

Dieser *Arte* gelangte seiner Zeit nicht in den Druck, wurde aber in handschriftlichen Exemplaren benutzt (Rémi Siméon fand zwei davon und benutzte sie für seine erste Ausgabe [1875] und León-Portilla & León-Portilla erwähnen andere Exemplare [Olmos 1993]). Zwei andere Werke, die man aufgrund ihrer Wichtigkeit mit einer gewissen Ausführlichkeit betrachten muß, sind ebenfalls um die Mitte des 16. Jhs. entstanden: dasjenige, welches man gemeinhin als "Vocabulario de Molina" kennt und die monumentale Arbeit von Sahagún.

Fray Alonso de Molina veröffentlichte 1555 ein *Vocabulario en lengua Castellana y mexicana.* Er war als kleines Kind nach Neuspanien gelangt, erlernte Nahuatl fast so gut wie spanisch und half den Mönchen beim Erlernen der Sprache; er trat in den Orden ein und studierte Latein und die grammatikalischen Konzepte, die europäischen ebenso wie die neuen Ideen, die hier entwickelt worden waren, wozu er selbst zweifellos beigetragen hat. Dieses Wörterbuch wurde 1571 erneut aufgelegt und hatte dann als zweiten Teil, wenn auch mit eigenem Titelblatt, ein viel ausführlicheres *Vocabulario en lengua Mexicana y Castellana* (Der erste Teil hat mehr als 17.000 Artikel, der zweite fast 25.000.). Die Experten bezeichnen in abgekürzter Form die beiden Teile zusammen als "Vocabulario de Molina".

Am Wörterbuch von Molina ist nicht nur der Umfang bemerkenswert, sondern ebenfalls die verschiedenen in ihm enthaltenen expliziten und impliziten Neuerungen. Die ersten bestehen aus 22 "avisos" [Hinweisen] (12 im spanisch-mexikanischen und 10 im mexikanisch-spanischen Teil), in denen der Autor die Charakteristika seines Werks erklärt. Angesichts der Unmöglichkeit, sie hier alle wiederzugeben, führe ich die interessantesten in gekürzter Form und modernisierter Graphie an.

Im ersten Teil gibt es "algunos romances que en nuestro Castellano [no] se usan mucho, y esto se hace por dar a entender mejor la propiedad de la lengua de los indios" [einige Formen, die in unserer kastilischen Sprache nicht häufig verwendet werden, und ich führe sie hier an, damit man die Eigenart der Sprache der Indios besser verstehen kann]; "se pone *lo mesmo* o *idem* [cuando] los naturales no tienen otro vocablo proprio en su lengua, sino que usan del mismo que nosotros [adaptándolo]" [es steht *lo mesmo* [= dasselbe] oder *idem*, [wenn] die Indios kein eigenes Wort in ihrer Sprache haben, sondern dasselbe, wie wir verwenden [indem sie es anpassen]; "Por faltar los nombres verbales [del latín o el español] proprios en la lengua, algunas veces los suplen por los pretéritos perfectos del verbo [...]" [Da die Verbalsubstantive [des Lateins oder des Spanischen] in ihrer Sprache fehlen, ersetzen sie sie manchmal durch die Perfektformen des Verbs [...]].

In zwei langen "avisos" des zweiten Teils erklärt und rechtfertigt Molina die von ihm gewählte alphabetische Reihenfolge, "que no es totalmente el [...] que otros vocabularios suelen llevar, [aunque se asemeja al del] vocabulario del Antonio" [die nicht genau der in anderen Wörterbüchern verwendeten entspricht, obwohl sie der des Wörterbuchs von Antonio ähnelt]. Ebenso sagt er, daß "los verbos activos en esta lengua nunca se [...] hallan absolutos, sino siempre acompañados con pronombres o partículas que denoten la persona que padece y la que hace" [die aktiven Verben in dieser Sprache sich niemals in absoluter Stelle befinden, sondern immer von Pronomina und Partikeln begleitet werden, die die Person anzeigen, die die Handlung erleidet und diejenige, die sie ausführt], aber um sie nicht aus der richtigen alphabetischen Reihenfolge herauszunehmen "pongo el cuerpo [= radical] del [...] verbo y luego la partícula, quitándosela de delante" [setze ich zuerst den Körper [= die Wurzel] und danach die Partikel, indem ich sie von vorne wegnehme]. Andere Neuerungen stellen das Auflisten der spanischen Wörter dar, die die Nahuas [= Azteken] schon in ihre Sprache übernommen haben, sowie die Kreation neuer Wörter mit mexikanischen Elementen für christlich-biblische Konzepte, z. B.:

bautismo [Taufe] = *nequatequiliztli*
confesarse [die Beichte ablegen]= *nino, yolmelaua*
lagar [Kelterpresse] = *xocomecaquequeçaloyan*

Eine weitere Neuerung besteht im Notieren von dialektalen Varianten (wie er in einem seiner "avisos" erklärt) und im Registrieren einiger Wörter der alten Religion, wie *teteu* "dioses" [Götter], *techcatl* "piedra sobre que se sacrificaban y mataban hombres delante de los ídolos" [Stein, auf dem Menschen getötet und den Götzen geopfert wurden] und andere mehr.

Ebenfalls im Jahre 1571 ließ Molina seinen *Art de la lengua Mexicana y Castellana* drukken, welcher als Komplement zum *Vocabulario* gedacht war (im *Arte* wird mehrmals auf das *Vocabulario* verwiesen). Darin ist er weniger kühn als Olmos, da er die acht "partes de la oración" [Satzteile] in der konventionellen Reihenfolge der lateinischen oder spanischen Grammatik behandelt und das im Nahuatl jeweils Äquivalente angibt, und zwar sogar für die Kasus (wenngleich er darauf hinweist, daß "propiamente no tienen" [es sie eigentlich nicht gibt]). Der zweite Teil behandelt die "Declaración de algunas dicciones dificultosas" [Erklärung einiger schwieriger Diktionen], wo er, dem Beispiel Olmos folgend, einige Beispiele und ausgewählte Stücke verwendet, um "el phrasis y manera de hablar que esta lengua tiene" [die Phrase und Art, diese Sprache zu sprechen] zu erklären. Für die Konjugation kreiert er Begriffe auf Nahuatl: *De la voz activa : tepan tlachihualiz caquiztli : Activa vocis.*

Bernardino de Sahagún war, wie Olmos und Molina, Franziskaner. Im Jahr 1547 stellte er traditionelle Reden über "La retórica y filosofía moral que estos naturales usaban" [Die Rhetorik und Moralphilosophie, die die Ureinwohner verwendeten] zusammen. Später bereitete er, inspiriert durch die *Historia Naturalis* des Plinius, eine Art Führer vor, um so systematisch Texte auf Nahuatl zu bekommen, die, auf Spanisch übersetzt und glossiert, es ihm erlaubten, "sacar a luz todos los vocablos desta lengua con sus propias y metafóricas significaciones y todas sus maneras de hablar y las más de sus antiguallas buenas y malas" [alle Vokabeln dieser Sprache mit ihren eigenen und metaphorischen Bedeutungen und alle Ausdrucksweisen und alle alten Gegebenheiten und Sachverhalte, die guten und die schlechten, ans Licht zu bringen (Sahagún 1979,1, "Prólogo", 2)]. Er versuchte, etwas ähnliches wie den Calepinus zu machen – er bedauerte aber, nicht, wie dieser, alte Schriften zu haben, von denen er ausgehen könnte – was dazu dienen würde, "los pecados de la idolatría y ritos [...] y agüeros [...] [que] no son aun perdidos del todo". [die Sünden des Götzendienstes und der Riten [...] und der Omen [...] [die] noch nicht ganz verlorengegangen sind] zu verstehen und "Para predicar contra estas cosas" [gegen sie zu predigen]. Dieses Werk wurde zu seiner Zeit nicht gedruckt. Als *Codex Florentinus* ist eine Endversion in Nahuatl und Spanisch, ohne Glossen, bekannt; in mehreren Archiven werden partielle Exemplare (veröffentlicht in diesem Jahrhundert) aufbewahrt, die den langen Prozeß der Ausarbeitung deutlich machen.

Die Absicht Sahagúns, das Buch mit drei Spalten pro Seite zu drucken, die erste Spalte mit den Texten auf Nahuatl, die spanische Übersetzung in der zweiten und in der dritten Glossen und Anmerkungen, wurde nicht verwirklicht. Das aus zwölf "libros" bestehende Werk ist eine sehr reichhaltige Quelle, um die Sprache und das soziale und natürliche Umfeld des vorspanischen Nahuavolks kennenzulernen. Bei dieser Aufgabe hatte Sahagún die Hilfe vieler Indios, besonders von Studenten des *Colegio de Santa Cruz*.

Im 16. Jh. wurden viele Katechismen, Predigtsammlungen und Beichtspiegel für die Christianisierung und Verwaltung der Indios auf Nahuatl (oder auf Nahuatl und Spanisch, um die Arbeit der Missionare zu erleichtern) geschrieben, denn das war das eigentliche Ziel der linguistischen Studien. Einige wurden in der zweiten Hälfte jenes Jahrhunderts herausgegeben, andere blieben in handschriftlicher Form erhalten, bis sie gegen Ende des vergangenen oder in diesem Jahrhundert gedruckt wurden.

## 4. 'Gegen die Fallstricke des Teufels'

Während des Übergangs vom 16. zum 17. Jh. war der Streit zwischen Katholiken und Protestanten nichts Neues mehr. Seit einem hal-ben Jahrhundert folgte ein Religionskrieg auf den anderen, und so sollte es auch noch fünfzig Jahre weitergehen; zu den religiösen Streitigkeiten im engeren Sinne (Bibelinterpretation, Papsttum, Transsubstantiation, Jungfräulichkeit Mariens, etc.) hatten sich wirtschaftliche und politische Motive dazugesellt, die sich teilweise auf die Konzeptionen der Reformatoren stützten.

Reformation und Gegenreformation hatten ihre gegenseitige Intoleranz und ihr gegenseitiges Mißtrauen verstärkt und sie intern auf das Aufspüren und die Verfolgung derjenigen ausgedehnt, die sich vom Teufel vom rechten Weg abbringen ließen. Weder die Verfolgung Andersdenkender noch der Kampf gegen den "Herrn der Finsternis" waren etwas grundsätzlich Neues, aber es steht außer Zweifel, daß im 17. Jh. – im Vergleich zum vorigen und zum folgenden Jahrhundert – die Verbrennung von Hexen und Ketzern zunahm. Wie nicht anders zu erwarten, griffen die neuen Tendenzen auf die Neue Welt über.

Der Verdacht, daß der Teufel immer auf der Lauer läge, schlägt sich in allen Chroniken der religiösen Orden in Mexiko nieder. In diesem Klima ist es nur natürlich, daß die Werke zunehmen, die versuchen, dem Teufel seine Maske zu nehmen, genausso wie diejenigen, welche die Konzeptionen des Katholizismus zu verbreiten und zu bestätigen suchen. Im ersten Drittel des 17. Jhs. wurden zwei Bücher geschrieben, um die abergläubigen Vorstellungen, die sich bei den mexikanischen Indios noch bewahrt hatten, zu bekämpfen. Dieselbe Absicht hatte Sahagún gehabt, aber im 16. Jh. wurde dieses Festhalten an den alten Praktiken als Unschuld verstanden, während man es im 17. Jh. eher als eine böswillige, vom Teufel inspirierte Tat ansah.

1629 beendete der Priester Hernando Ruiz de Alarcón (Bruder des Dramaturgen Juan) seinen *Tratado de las supersticiones y costumbres gentílicas que hoy viven entre los indios naturales de esta Nueva España* [Traktat über die abergläubigen Vorstellungen und heidnischen Gebräuche, die heutzutage unter den Indios Neuspaniens weiterleben]. Er stellt eine große Anzahl von 'heidnischen' Texten in Nahuatl zusammen, die er ins Spanische übersetzt und kommentiert, um die anderen Geistlichen vor den Praktiken des Götzendienstes zu warnen, in die viele ihrer Gläubigen zurückfielen, damit sie sie bekämpfen konnten. Er klassifiziert die Texte in sechs große Gruppen: 1. Über Hexer und "nahuales" (eine Art Schutzpatron des rituellen Kalenders in Tiergestalt) und die Gottheiten der Sonne, der Berge, des "Amarantsamens"; 2. Beschwörungsformeln, damit verschiedene tägliche Aktivitäten gut gehen; 3. Anrufungen, damit die Aussaat gedeiht; 4. Liebesmagie; 5. Verschiedene Formen der Wahrsagung; 6. Anrufungen und Beschwörungsformeln, welche die 'abergläubischen Ärzte' für die Heilung verwenden.

Dieser Traktat, der ein Beispiel für die Sorgen der Geistlichen in jener Zeit ist, gelangte damals nicht in den Druck, aber wir wissen, daß andere Priester ihn kannten und einen Teil seines Inhalts sich zunutze machten, als sie Bücher mit einer ähnlichen Orientierung schrieben, die ebenfalls zu ihrer Zeit nicht gedruckt wurden, da die kirchlichen Zensoren es vermutlich für nicht sehr klug hielten, diese Formeln unter anderen Indios zu verbreiten.

Die Beichtspiegel aus dem besagten Jahrhundert hatten da mehr Glück. Fast zwei Drittel derjenigen, von denen man weiß, daß sie auf mexikanisch (oder in Nahuatl und Spanisch und einer in diesen Sprachen und in Latein) veröffentlicht wurden, wurden zwischen 1599 und 1692 herausgegeben. Mehrere davon enthalten Fragen bezüglich der abgelehnten Praktiken, wie *Luz y método de combatir idólatras y destierro de idolatrías* (Villavicencio 1692), der außer dem Beichtspiegel eine ausgedehnte Abhandlung über das Thema enthält.

Auch die Predigtsammlungen (Mijangos 1624) – Diskurse, die, besonders anläßlich der Sonntagsfeierlichkeiten oder der Heiligenfeste, einen Punkt des katholischen Katechismus oder der Moral behandeln – sind in diesem Jahrhundert sehr häufig, ebenso wie Heiligenviten, moralische Beispiele, die außerhalb des Katholizismus völlig undenkbar sind (Medina 1605). Von besonderem Interesse ist in dieser Gruppe von Veröffentlichungen die von Bautista (ungefähr 1600) über die vorspanischen "huehuetlatolli", die Olmos aufgezeichnet hatte und die jetzt zur moralischen Erbauung der katholischen Indios verwendet wurden.

Aus diesem Jahrhundert datieren bestimmte, von adligen Nahuas in ihrer Sprache geschriebene Werke historischen Charakters, mit denen sie die Erinnerung an die glorreiche Vergangenheit ihrer Völker einforderten, indem sie sie in den Rahmen der offiziellen spanischen und europäischen Geschichte einfügten (Tezozomoc 1949). Sie blieben bis

Ende des 19. Jhs. oder bis ins 20. Jh. hinein als Manuskripte erhalten.

Es gibt Hinweise darauf, daß schon im 16. Jh. Theaterstücke mit unterweisender oder erbauender Absicht aufgeführt wurden (Horcasitas 1974), aber gerade im 17. Jh. hatte man einen besonderen Gefallen an ihnen; sogar das Mysterienspiel Calderóns *El gran teatro del mundo* [Das große Welttheater] wurde ins Nahuatl übersetzt. Kürzlich wurden diese Werke, die nur dazu gedacht waren, aufgeführt zu werden, in Druck gegeben.

Die erste Grammatik dieser Periode wurde am Ende des vorherigen Jahrhunderts von dem Jesuiten Antonio del Rincón (1595) veröffentlicht. In ihren ersten beiden Teilen folgt er, bei einigen Unterschieden, den ersten beiden Teilen des *Arte* von Olmos, behandelt aber die Derivation (3. Teil) und die Komposition (4. Teil) getrennt, und er ist der erste, der sich detailliert mit "la pronunciación y acento de la sílaba" [Der Aussprache und dem Silbenakzent] beschäftigt (5. Teil), die Olmos und Molina der Praxis der Lernenden überlassen hatten. Rincón schlägt eine Reihe von Akzenten vor, um die Vokalquantität und die Existenz des silbenschließenden *saltillo* – des Glottisverschluss – zu verdeutlichen; er bietet sogar eine Liste von "dicciones que mudan la significación solamente por la variación del acento" [Wörter, die die Bedeutung nur aufgrund der Variation des Akzents verändern], um auf diese Weise seine Wichtigkeit für das Nahuatl hervorzuheben.

Im Jahre 1640 wurde der Lehrstuhl für Mexikanisch an der Königlich-Päpstlichen Universität von Mexiko eröffnet, dessen Besuch für bestimmte Studiengänge obligatorisch war. So wurde das, was die Missionare schon seit dem Jahrhundert zuvor praktizierten, in der höchsten Bildungseinrichtung formalisiert, und es wurde dem Rechnung getragen, was verschiedene königliche Verfügungen seit 1580 (und mit noch mehr Beharrlichkeit im ersten Viertel des 17. Jhs.) über die Unterrichtung der *lengua general* [Hauptsprache] anordneten.

Fray Diego de Galdo Guzmán gewann das Auswahlverfahren sowohl für den Lehrstuhl für Nahuatl als auch für den für Otomí. Als Hilfe für die Studenten veröffentlichte er zwei Jahre später einen *Arte mexicano* (Galdo 1942), der auf den ersten Blick einen Rückschritt gegenüber vorherigen *Artes* zu sein scheint, da er sich sehr eng an die lateinische Grammatik anlehnt. In Wirklichkeit scheint dies einen didaktischen Zweck zu haben: Wenn die Struktur die des Lateins ist – das die Studenten kennen sollten – gibt er die Entsprechungen im Nahuatl an, und zwar mit ausführlichen Anmerkungen, die erklären, was dieser Sprache eigen ist.

Im Jahre 1645 wurde das Sprachlehrwerk des Florentiners Horacio Carochi gedruckt, der sich im Vorwort dafür entschuldigt, daß es überflüssig erscheinen könnte "habiendo salido a luz tres artes" [da schon drei Lehrwerke erschienen sind] (Es waren die von Molina, Rincón und Galdo, die wir erwähnt haben). Seine Absicht war, daß man das Mexikanische ohne die Hilfe eines guten Lehrers erlernen könne, so wie der seinige Rincón war, dem er größtenteils folgt; Carochi aber fügt ein ganzes Buch – ein Drittel des Werks – über die Adverbien hinzu, deren Gebrauch er mit ausführlichen Beispielen illustriert, weil "éstos son lo que los nervios en un cuerpo" [diese wie die Nervenstränge in einem Körper sind]. Bemerkenswert ist, daß er in absolut allen Wörtern des Nahuatl den Akzent anzeigt, eine Praxis, die nach ihm fast niemand mehr anwendet, ausgenommen Linguisten unseres Jahrhunderts.

Die anderen drei Lehrwerke, die im 17. Jh. gedruckt wurden, tragen größtenteils nichts Neues zur Entwicklung der Linguistik des Nahuatl bei, wenngleich auch sie ihren Wert haben. In diesem Jahrhundert gibt es keine lexikographischen Arbeiten, da der *Vocabulario manual de las lenguas mexicana y castellana* (Arenas 1611) ausführlich angemessene Ausdrücke für die Anrede und die Konversation über bestimmte Themen präsentiert.

## 5. Das Zeitalter der Aufklärung

Anfang des 18. Jhs. übernimmt die Bourbonen-Dynastie, Förderin der Künste, der Wissenschaften und der für den aufgeklärten Absolutismus typischen administrativen Reformen, die Herrschaft in Spanien (und somit auch in Neuspanien). Der entsprechende Zeitabschnitt in der Geschichte der Linguistik des Nahuatl beginnt jedoch ein Jahrzehnt zuvor und dauert bis in die ersten Jahre des 19. Jh. fort, als die spanische Herrschaft über dieses Gebiet endet.

Wenn bis zu diesem Punkt der Geschichte bestimmte Autoren erwähnt und punktuell ihre Beiträge zur Kenntnis des Nahuatl gezeigt wurden, werden wir uns im folgenden darauf beschränken müssen, auf die allgemeineren Strömungen und die wirklich neuen Beiträge hinzuweisen.

In dem Zeitraum zwischen 1693 und 1810 erschienen zehn grammatische Studien. Sie nutzen alle die Analysen der ihnen vorausgehenden Werke, wenngleich sie in manchen Aspekten gewisse Neuheiten bieten; zum Beispiel behandeln drei von ihnen Varietäten des Nahuatl, die sich von der des Zentrums des Landes (geringfügig) unterscheiden, und ein Werk – um 1775 von einem vertriebenen Jesuiten geschrieben – spiegelt klar den Geist der Aufklärung wider, indem es den Ausdrucksreichtum des Nahuatl aufzeigt, um so die Meinung vieler Europäer über Amerika und seine Sprachen zu widerlegen (Clavijero 1974).

Neuigkeiten gibt es ebenfalls bei den auf Nahuatl geschriebenen Werken religiösen Charakters. Es gibt weiterhin Beichtspiegel und Predigtsammlungen, aber jetzt – in Einverständnis mit dem wachsenden Rationalismus der Epoche – legt man weniger Interesse auf die Suche nach 'Götzendienern' und ihre Bekehrung. Im Gegensatz dazu gibt es mehr Veröffentlichungen über die Sakramentenspendung (Pérez 1713) und zur Förderung der religiösen Praktiken (Paredes 1758). Sie alle implizieren die Übersetzung auf Nahuatl von Fachausdrücken für katholische Konzepte oder ihre Aufnahme als Lehnwörter in die mexikanische Sprache.

Dieselbe Rationalität empfiehlt der vizeköniglichen Verwaltung, die öffentlichen Erlasse auf mexikanisch herauszugeben (zum Beispiel, derjenige, der mit *Intlenonotzalistli S. M. Intlacaquini* [...], vom 2. Februar 1762, beginnt), damit sie von denen verstanden würden, an die sie gerichtet waren –Teile der Bevölkerung (z. B. die indianischen Autoritäten) konnten lesen und schreiben – und obwohl im Jahre 1772 in Mexiko die königliche Verordnung verbreitet wurde, die festlegte "desterrar de estos sus dominios los diferentes idiomas que usan sus naturales y que sólo se hable el castellano" [aus allen Gebieten die Sprachen, die Einwohner gebrauchen, zu verbannen und daß nur noch kastilisch gesprochen werden solle], sind vizekönigliche Erlasse auf mexikanisch aus der Zeit danach bekannt.

Eine Annonce aus dem Jahr 1774 über die therapeutischen Vorzüge eines bestimmten Präparats zeigt sehr gut, wie man versuchte, den wissenschaftsgläubigen und merkantilistischen Geist der Epoche unter den Sprechern des Nahuatl zu verbreiten: *Netemachtiliztli. In itechpa in ce yancuican pahtli* [...] [Hinweis. Über eine neue Medizin [...]].

Am Ende dieser Periode wurde in Madrid der *Catálogo* von Hervás (1800–1805) veröffentlicht. Er ist hier von Interesse, weil er eine Sektion dem Mexikanischen widmet, welches, gemäß seiner, einer Vorläuferin der vergleichenden Sprachwissenschaft gleichkommenden Vision, eine der "lenguas matrices" [Hauptsprachen] ist. Hervás bekam Information von anderen vertriebenen Jesuiten und versorgte seinerseits damit, auf dessen Bitten hin, Wilhelm von Humboldt.

## 6. Die Studien zum Nahuatl im 19. Jahrhundert

Die Bourbonen-Monarchie mit den Formen, die sie der öffentlichen Verwaltung gab (einschließlich des Versuchs, die Eingeborenensprachen durch das Spanische zu ersetzen), der Förderung der Wissenschaft und der Künste, der Kolonialwirtschaft, etc., erlitt im Jahr 1810 einen Bruch, als der Krieg um die Unabhängigkeit begann, welche im Jahr 1821 erklärt wurde.

Auf die elf Jahre des Kampfes – die die Wirtschaft des Landes zerstörten – folgten etwa drei Jahrzehnte mit politischer Instabilität, Militärputschen, Zwangsrekrutierungen und Unordnung in der Verwaltung, Bedingungen, die für keine Art von Studien förderlich waren. Der nationalistische mexikanische Geist der ersten Hälfte des 19. Jhs. war vor allem politisch und nicht akademisch, wie er es später sein sollte.

Das was in diesem Zeitabschnitt gedruckt wurde, hat religiösen Charakter: Handbücher, um die Arbeit der Priester zu erleichtern (Sáenz 1642), kurze Katechismen, die zur Unterweisung der Kinder bestimmt waren – da es nach zwei Jahrhunderten Evangelisierung keine 'götzendienerischen' Erwachsenen mehr gab – und Werke katholischer Frömmigkeit (Kreuzwege, Gebete zum Heiligen Herzen, geistige Exerzitien). Bezeichnend für die Haltung gegenüber dem Protestantismus ist, daß die Übersetzung von Bibeltexten ins Nahuatl außerhalb des Landes gedruckt werden mußte (Anónimo 1833), welches offiziell katholisch war; als die *Leyes de Reforma* [Reformgesetze] (unter ihnen das über die Religionsfreiheit) erlassen wurden, konnte sie in Mexiko herausgegeben werden.

Während der zweiten Jahrhunderthälfte (und bis 1910, dem Beginn der Revolution) begünstigen verschiedene Faktoren die Studien zum Nahuatl, von Einheimischen ebenso wie von Ausländern. 1848 verlor Mexiko die Hälfte seines Territoriums, dessen sich die Vereinigten Staaten bemächtigten; als Reaktion darauf nahm der Nationalismus zu, gestützt auf Studien zur grandiosen indigenen Vergangenheit und zu den Eingeborenensprachen. Von 1862 bis 1867 erlitt das Land die französische Invasion und das kurzlebige Imperium Maximilians von Österreich (zum großen Teil durch das französische Heer gestützt); verschiedene europäische Forscher waren damals in Mexiko, und in Europa kam das Interesse an mexikanistischen Studien auf. Zuletzt kann man sagen, daß die Regierung unter Porfirio Díaz (1876 bis 1911) von den französischen Vorbildern inspiriert wurde, aber gleichzeitig die Studien zur indigenen Vergangenheit förderte, um einen Mexikanismus zu verherrlichen, der jene fremden Vorbilder ausgleichen sollte.

In jener Zeit wurde didaktische Grammatiken entsprechend dem traditionellen Modell geschrieben (Chimalpopoca 1869; Palma 1886). Andererseits sind die neuspanischen *Artes*, die das Museo Nacional von 1885 bis 1904 neu herausgab – gemäß dem Vorbild Siméons (1875) – eher Dokumente für die Geschichte und die Forschung.

Andere Studien über das Nahuatl aus der zweiten Hälfte des 19. Jh. schlagen eine ganz neue Richtung ein. 1869 studierte Buschmann die systematischen Ähnlichkeiten zwischen dem Nahuatl und den Sprachen des mexikanischen Bundesstaates Sonora. Er wurde von Pimentel (1874) überboten, der mit den Verfahrensweisen und der Theorie der Vergleichenden Sprachwissenschaft die genetische Beziehung der Sprachen bewies, die jetzt als utoaztekische Familie bekannt sind (ebenso die anderer Familien). Nicht alle vergleichenden Studien waren so exakt, wie diese, da sie auf unbekümmerte Weise das Nahuatl mit Sprachen der Alten Welt verglichen (Sanskrit, Griechisch und andere), so wie es fast 'Mode' auch unter einigen europäischen Forschern war.

Als Gegenpart zu der vergleichenden Forschung mit ihrer notwendigen großen Ausdehnung erscheint eine Reihe von Studien über einige Wortfelder (Pflanzen-, Tier- und Metallnamen, etc.) oder Ortsnamen, die häufig in den *Anales del Museo Nacional* erschienen.

Um diese Sektion abzuschließen, kann man noch über die Rolle spekulieren, die das Nahuatl in den linguistischen Theorien Wilhelm von Humboldts spielte, der eine *Mexicanische Grammatik* (Nansen 1984) hinterließ, in der er, in Einklang mit seinen Ideen, die Materialien und die Information auswertete, die er von Hervás erhalten hatte. Der Beitrag der europäischen Forscher, speziell der französischen (Grasserie 1903) und deutschen (Preuss 1968), für die mexikanistischen Studien ist offensichtlich, ebenso wie der Einfluß, den das Studium des Nahuatl auf die Entwicklung ihrer Ideen hatte.

## 7. Die aktuelle Linguistik des Nahuatl

Wenn man über die wichtigsten Tendenzen der Studien zum Nahuatl im 20. Jh. sprechen will, ist es angemessen, dieses in drei Zeitabschnitte zu unterteilen, ohne dabei die Grenzen allzu scharf zu setzen. Die Anzahl der Veröffentlichungen – als Gradmesser für das Aufkommen der Nahuatlstudien – ist in dieser Periode so groß, daß wir in den bibliographischen Hinweisen nicht einmal zu jedem Modell zumindest ein Beispiel geben können. Dakin (1994) kann der Liste von H[ernández] de León Portilla (1988) noch 700 Titel – mehr als 300 Wiederholungen – hinzufügen, von denen sich mehr als die Hälfte auf andere utoaztekische Sprachen oder vergleichende und rekonstruierende Arbeiten beziehen.

Das erste Drittel (von 1910 bis 1933) entspricht dem Triumph der Mexikanischen Revolution und ist durch einen intensiven indigenistischen Nationalismus charakterisiert, der sich in den Künsten (Musik, Wandmalerei, Literatur), in der Bildung (Landschule, kulturelle Missionen) und in der Forschung (Archäologie, Ethnologie, Linguistik) zeigt. Mexikaner und Ausländer – besonders aus den Vereinigten Staaten – sammelten auf dem Land Material (Boas 1917) und werteten es zuhause aus (Kroeber 1934).

Die Zeitschrift *El México Antiguo*, von Hermann Beyer 1919 als Organ der Deutschen Mexikanistischen Gesellschaft gegründet, bezog fünf Jahrzehnte lang Beiträge von mexikanischen und auswärtigen Forschern, von denen einige in Mexiko, andere aber in ihrem Heimatland wohnten. Viele der veröffentlichten Artikel beziehen sich nicht auf die Sprache und Kultur der Nahuas, verwenden aber in ihrer Interpretation archäologischer Daten, historischer Informationen oder ethnographischen Materials verschiedener Gruppen, mexikanische Vokabeln, und das ist ein typischer Zug der Studien dieser Zeit.

Die Paradigmen der strukturalistischen Linguistik sind charakteristisch für eine Anzahl von Studien über das Nahuatl aus dem zweiten Drittel unseres Jahrhunderts (Pittman 1954), ohne daß die philologische Strömung – etwas mehr den in den neuspanischern *Artes* entwickelten Analysen und Kategorien verbunden, wenngleich modernere Konzepte mit einbezogen werden – verschwand (Durand-Forest 1960). Auch zu dieser Zeit werden alte Werke, die häufig als Manuskripte erhalten geblieben waren, in kritischen Ausgaben (neu)aufgelegt.

Viele dieser Arbeiten wurden in akademisch-periodischen Publikationen veröffentlicht, die während dieser Periode begründet wurden (in Klammern das Gründungsjahr): *Anales del Instituto Nacional de Antropología e Historia* (Name, den seit 1938 die ehemaligen *Anales del Museo Nacional* führen), *Tlalocan* (1944), *Archivos nahuas* (von 1954 bis 1958, Jalapa, Ver.), *Anales de Antropología* (1964), *Estudios de Cultura Náhuatl* (1959).

Diese letzte ist das Organ des *Seminario de Cultura Náhuatl*, welches Ángel María Garibay und sein Schüler Miguel León Portilla 1957 an der Universidad Nacional Autónoma de México gründeten. Ihnen beiden und dem 'Seminario' sind viele Studien (ungefähr 40 dem ersten [Garibay 1940, 1992], bisher mehr als 70 dem zweiten [León Portilla 1956, 1992] und die Förderung der Studien zum Nahuatl in der ganzen Welt zu verdanken, denn viele der mexikanischen und ausländischen (aus Frankreich, Deutschland, Schweden, den Vereinigten Staaten, etc.) Forscher haben das 'Seminario' besucht, das León Portilla seit 40 Jahren leitet.

Das zweite Drittel dieses Jahrhunderts ist durch die nachdrücklich revolutionäre politische Orientierung gekennzeichnet, die ihm der Präsident Lázaro Cárdenas (1934–1940) zu Beginn gegeben hat: Organisierung der Arbeiter, Nationalisierung des Erdöls, intensive Agrarreform, Indigenismus. In dieser Atmosphäre erschienen verschiedene Zeitungen auf Nahuatl oder zum Teil zweisprachig: *Mexicayotl/Mexicanismo* (1946, Organ der Sociedad pro Lengua Náhuatl), *Izcalotl* (1960, von dem Movimiento Confederado Restaurador de Anahuak), *Mexicatl Itonalma/El periódico del mexicano* "periódico semanal de divulgación en lengua náhuatl" [populärwissenschaftliche Wochenzeitung auf Nahuatl] (nur 34 Nummern, 1950), von Roberto Barlow, einem nordamerikanischen, in Azcapotzalco wohnenden Mexikanisten gegründet.

Im letzten Drittel des 20. Jhs. haben sich die Studien zum Nahuatl in Mexiko und in anderen Ländern verbreitet. Zum Teil wurden die etablierten Praktiken fortgeführt: Neuauflage alter Werke, kritische Ausgaben von Manuskripten (Werke und Dokumente unterschiedlicher Wesensart: Testamente, Gerichtsdossiers, etc.), von Untersuchungen begleitete Faksimileausgaben der allgemein "códices" genannten piktographischen Dokumente, Beschreibungen von Dialekten – Grammatiken und Wörterbücher – Sprachenvergleich bzw. Sprachenrekonstruktion (Miller 1967).

Es ist von Interesse, festzustellen, daß diese Studien häufig auf das begriffliche Instrumentarium zurückgreifen, das als Hilfsmittel für die jüngsten linguistischen Theorien entwickelt wurde, was somit eine 'Probe' derselbigen darstellt und gleichzeitig die Kenntnis der mexikanischen Sprache vertieft (Launey 1984). Jetzt gibt es eine verläßliche Dialektologie (Lastra 1986), anstelle der vorherigen impressionistischen. Keines der jüngeren lokalen Wörterbücher reicht an das von Molina (1571) heran – zum Beispiel, Brewer & Brewer (1979) hat 1/7 des Umfangs des von Molina – oder an das von Siméon (1885, der das von Molilna erweitert, indem er aus anderen Quellen spickt), vielleicht, weil viele Elemente der alten Kultur verlorengegangen sind; sie sind aber nützlich, um das aktuelle Nahuatl kennenzulernen.

In jüngster Zeit ist eine Gruppe von jungen Muttersprachlern des Nahuatl mit linguistischer Ausbildung auf den Plan getreten, was bedeutet, daß ihre Arbeiten technisch gesehen wie die eines jeden anderen Linguisten sind, wenngleich sie den Vorteil (der gelegentlich ein Nachteil sein kann) haben, daß sie ihre Muttersprache analysieren (García de León 1976, Ramírez Celestino 1995). Für sie, für andere Anthropologen und allgemein für die Nahua-Indios ist die mexikanische Sprache ein Pfeiler im Kampf um die Verteidigung und Neubewertung der Sprache und Kultur ihres Volkes (Torre 1987).

Heutzutage gesellt sich zu Studium und Erforschung des Nahuatl der Vergangenheit und in seinen zeitgenössischen Varietäten durch Mexikaner – einige von ihnen Muttersprachler – das literarische Schaffen und Wirken. Es gibt Dichter, Erzähler, Romanciers und Übersetzer von großer Qualität, die durch ihre persönlichen Erlebnisse, die zeitgenössischen Formen der Sprache und ihre Kenntnis der alten Sprache inspiriert wurden.

Die bibliographischen Referenzen, die diesen Artikel begleiten, geben nur ein sehr schwaches Bild des bestehenden enormen Reichtums an linguistischen Studien zum Nahuatl (sie stellen nur ein Hundertstel der registrierten Titel dar); trotzdem habe ich immer ein Beispiel ausgewählt, das die Charakteristiken der Forschung in jedem historischen Moment verdeutlicht, sodaß die Leser meine Ausführungen ausgiebig überprüfen können.

## 8. Bibliographie


Anónimo. 1833. *El Evangelio según San Lucas, del latín al mexicano o mejor náhuatl.* Londres: The Bible Society. (1889 erneut aufgelegt als *El Evangelio según San Lucas. Yancuic iyec tenonetzaltzin Jesucristo.* México: Imprenta Evangélica.)

Arenas, Pedro de. 1611. *Vocabulario manual de las lenguas castellana y mexicana. En que se contienen las palabras, preguntas y respuestas más comunes y ordinarias que se suelen ofrecer en el trato y comunicación entre españoles e indios.* México: Imprenta de Henrico Martínez.

Bautista, Juan, Fray. 1600?. *Huehuetlatolli. Pláticas morales de los indios para doctrina de sus hijos, en lengua mexicana.* (Datum und Verleger unbekannt, da das Titelblatt verlorengegangen ist.)

Boas, Franz. 1917. "El dialecto mexicano de Pochutla, Oaxaca". *International Journal of American Linguistics* 1.9–44.

Brewer, Forrest & Jean. 1979. *Vocabulario mexicano de Tetelcingo, Morelos.* (= *Vocabularios Indígenas "Mariano Silva y Aceves"*, 8.) México: Instituto Lingüístico de Verano.

Buschmann, Johann Carl Eduard. 1859. *Die Spuren der aztekischen Sprache im nördlichen Mexiko und höheren amerikanischen Norden. Zugleich eine Musterung der Völker und Sprachen des nördlichen Mexico's und der Westseite Nordamerika's von Guadalaxara an bis zum Eismeer.* Berlin: Königliche Akademie der Wissenschaften.

Carochi, Horacio. 1645. *Arte de la lengua mexicana con la declaración de los adverbios della.* México: Juan Ruiz.

Chimalpopoca Galicia, Faustino. 1869. *Epítome o modo fácil de aprender el idioma náhuatl o lengua mexicana.* México: Tipografía de la viuda de Murguía.

Ciudad Real, Antonio de. 1976. *Tratado curioso y docto de las grandezas de la Nueva España.* (= *Serie de Historiadores y Cronistas de Indias*, 6.) 2 vols. México: Universidad Nacional Autónoma de México. Instituto de Investigaciones Históricas.

Clavijero, Francisco Xavier. 1974. *Reglas de la lengua mexicana, con un vocabulario.* (= *Monografías*, 16.) Edición, introducción, paleografía y notas de Arthur J. O. Anderson. México: Universidad Nacional Autónoma de México. Instituto de Investigaciones Históricas.

Dakin, Karen. 1994. "La familia Yutoazteca, una visión de lo que hay y de lo que falta hacer". *Panorama de los estudios de las lenguas indígenas de México* hg. von Lastra de Suárez, Yolanda, Manrique Castañeda, Leonardo & Bartholomew, Doris, 1.36–136. (= *Biblioteca Abya-Yala*, 16–17.) Quito: Abya-Yala.

Durand-Forest, Jacqueline de. 1960. "Discours de la mère aztéque a sa petite fille". *Estudios de Cultura Náhuatl* 2.149–161. México: Universidad Nacional Autónoma de México. Instituto de Investigaciones Históricas.

Galdo Guzmán, Diego de, Fray. 1642. *Arte Mexicano.* México: viuda de Bernardo Calderón.

García de León, Antonio. 1976. *Pajapan, un dialecto mexicano del Golfo.* (= *Colección Científica*, 43.) México: Instituto Nacional de Antropología e Historia.

Garibay Kintana, Ángel María. 1940. *Llave del Náhuatl: Colección de trozos clásicos con gramática y vocabulario, para utilidad de los principiantes.* Otumba. (ohne Druckvermerk.)

–. 1965. "Romántico náhuatl". *Estudios de Cultura Náhuatl* 5.9–14. México: Universidad Nacional Autónoma de México. Instituto de Investigaciones Históricas.

Grasserie, Raoul de la. 1903. *Le Nahuatl, langue des Aztèque, conquérants du Mexique précolumbien: Grammaire, vocabulaire, textes avec analyse et traduction interlinéaire.* (= *Bibliothèque Linguistique Americaine*, 25.) Paris: E. Guilmoto.

H[ernández] de León Portilla, Ascensión. 1988. *Tepuztlahcuilolli, Impresos en Náhuatl: Historia y Bibliografía.* (= *Serie de Cultura Náhuatl: Monografías*, 27.) 2 vols. México: Universidad Nacional Autónoma de México. Instituto de Investigaciones Históricas & Instituto de Investigaciones Filológicas.

Hervás y Panduro, Lorenzo. 1800–05. *Catálogo de las lenguas de las naciones conocidas y numeración, división y clases de éstas según la diversidad de sus idiomas y dialectos.* Madrid: Imprenta de la Administración del Real Arbitrio de Beneficencia.

Horcasitas, Fernando. 1974. *El teatro náhuatl: Épocas novohispana y moderna.* México: Universidad Nacional Autónoma de México. Instituto de Investigaciones Históricas. (Der Studie sind 30 Theaterstücke auf Nahuatl, übersetzt und kommentiert, beigefügt.)

Kroeber, Alfred L. 1934. *Uto-Aztecan languages of Mexico.* (= *Ibero-Americana*, 8.) Berkeley: Univ. of California Press.

Lastra de Suárez, Yolanda. 1986. *Las áreas dialectales del náhuatl moderno.* México: Universidad Nacional Autónoma de México. Instituto de Investigaciones Antropológicas.

Launey, Michel. 1984. "Fonctions et categories dans l'opposition verbo-nominales: l'exemple du Nahuatl". *Modèles linguistiques* 6.133–147. Nancy: Presses Universitaires.

León Portilla, Miguel. 1956. *La filosofía náhuatl, estudiada en sus fuentes.* México: Instituto Indigenista Interamericano. (5 Auflagen auf spanisch und Übersetzungen in mehrere Sprachen.)

León Portilla, Miguel. 1992. "Have we really translated the Mesoamerican 'Ancient word'?". *On the Translation of Native American Literature* hg. von Brian Swann. Washington: Smithsonian Institution Press.

Manrique Castañeda, Leonardo. 1989. "La historia del idioma de los mexica y sus congéneres". *Primer Encuentro nahua: los nahuas de hoy* hg. von Dora Sierra Carrillo. (= *Subdirección de Etnografía: Cuadernos de Trabajo*, 7.13–26.) México: Museo Nacional de Antropología.

Medina, Francisco de, Fray. 1605. *La vida y milagros del glorioso San Nicolás de Tolentino, de la Orden de San Augustín, Doctor de la Iglesia.* Traducida en Lengua Mexicana por [...] México: Pedro López Dávalos.

Miller, Wick R. 1967. *Uto-Aztecan cognate sets.* (= *University of California Publications in Linguistics*, 48.) Berkeley & Los Angeles: Univ. of California Press.

Mijangos, Juan de, Fray. 1624. *Primera parte del Sermonario y Sanctoral en lengua Mexicana.* México: Imprenta de Juan Alcázar.

Molina, Alonso de, Fray. 1571a. *Arte de la lengua Mexicana y Castellana.* México: Pedro Ocharte.

– . 1571b. *Vocabulario en lengua Castellana y Mexicana [...]* [y] *Vocabulario en lengua Mexicana y Castellana* [...] México: Antonio de Spinosa. [Ediciones facsimilares: 1944. Madrid: Instituto de Cultura Hispánica (= *Colección de Incunables Americanos*; 6.), 1970. México: Porrúa (Biblioteca Porrúa; 44), con estudio preliminar de Miguel León Portilla.]

–. 1605. *Rosario o Psalterio de Nuestra Señora. Teocuitlaxochicozcatl inic tlahpalo in cemihca tlahtoca ichpuchtli Sancta María* [...] México: Imprenta de Diego López Dávalos.

Motolinia, Toribio de Benavente, Fray. 1996. *Memoriales: Libro de Oro MSJGI/31.* (= *Biblioteca Novohispana*; 3.) Edición crítica, introducción, notas y apéndice de Nancy Joe Dyer. México: El Colegio de México. Centro de Estudios Lingüísticos y Literarios.

Nansen, Eréndira. 1984. *Die Mexicanische Grammatik von Wilhelm v. Humboldt: Textedition und historisch-kritische Einleitung.* Dissertation. Tübingen: Universität.

Olmos, Andrés de, Fray. 1885. *Arte para aprender la lengua Mexicana.* México: Museo Nacional de México.

–. 1993. *Arte de la lengua Mexicana.* Edición facsimilar del ms. en la Biblioteca Nacional de Madrid, con estudio introductorio, transliteración y notas por Ascención [Hernández de] Léon Portilla & Miguel León Portilla. Madrid: Ediciones de Cultura Hispánica.

Palma, Miguel Trinidad. 1886. *Gramática de la lengua azteca o mejicana escrita con arreglo al programa oficial para que sirva de texto en las escuelas normales del Estado.* Puebla: Imprenta de M. Corona.

Paredes, Ignacio. 1758. *Nican motenehua in quenami. Motempohuaz in Santíssimo Rosario* [...] (= Aquí se refiere cómo se rezará el Santísimo Rosario.) México: Imprenta del Real y más antiguo Colegio de San Ildefonso.

Pérez, Manuel, Fray. 1713. *Farol Indiano y guía de Curas e Indios. Suma de los cinco Sacramentos que administran los Ministros Evangélicos en esta América. Con todos los casos morales que suceden entre los Indios. México: Francisco Rivera Calderón.*

*Pimentel, Francisco. 1974. Cuadro descriptivo y comparativo de las lenguas indígenas de México.* 3 vols. México: Sociedad Mexicana de Geografía y Estadística.

Pittman, Richard S. 1954. *A Grammar of Tetelcingo (Morelos) Nahuatl.* (= *Language Dissertation: Supplement to Language*, 50.) Baltimore: Linguistic Society of America.

Preuss, Konrad Theodor. 1968–76. *Nahua Texte aus San Pedro Jícora in Durango.* 3 Bde. (= *Quellenwerke zur Alten Geschichte Amerikas*, 10–12.) Berlin: Iberoamerikanisches Institut. (Gesammelt 1907, herausgegeben von Elsa Ziehm.)

Ramírez Celestino, Cleofas. 1995. *Etnobotánica náhuatl de Xalitla, Guerrero.* México: Centro de Investigaciones y Estudios Superiores en Antropología Social.

Rincón, Antonio del. 1595. *Arte mexicana.* México: Pedro Balli.

Sáenz de la Peña, Andrés. 1642. *Manual de los Santos Sacramentos. Conforme al Ritual de Paulo Quinto. Formado por mandado del Rever$^{mo}$ Ilustriss$^{mo}$ y Excll$^{mo}$ Señor D. Juan de Palafox y Mendoça, Obispo de la Puebla de los Angeles.* México: Francisco Robledo Impressor. (auf Nahuatl, kastilisch und Otomí geschrieben; in verschiedenen Druckereien und Städten – zumindest 1671, 1691, 1712, 1789, 1809, 1826, 1847, 1864, 1894 – wieder von Neuem gedruckt.)

Sahagún, Bernardino de, Fray. 1979. *Códice Florentino.* Edición facsímil del manuscrito 218–20 de la Colección Palatina de la Biblioteca Medicea Laurenciana. 3 vols. México: Gobierno de la República.

Siméon, Rémi. 1875. *Grammaire de la Langue Nahuatl ou Mexicaine: Composée en 1547, par le Franciscain Andrés de Olmos et publiée avec notes, éclaircissements, etc. par Rémi Siméon.* Paris: Imprimerie Nationale.

–. 1885. *Dictionnaire de la Langue Nahuatl ou Mexicaine: Rédigé d'après les documents imprimés et manuscrits les plus authentiques et précédé d'une introduction.* Paris: Imprimerie Nationale.

Tezozomoc, Fernando Alvarado. 1949. *Crónica Mexicayotl.* (= *Primera Serie Prehispánica*, 3.) Con traducción directa del náhuatl por Adrián León. México: Universidad Nacional Autónoma de México. Instituto de Investigaciones Históricas.

Torquemada, Juan de, Fray. 1977. *Monarquía indiana.* (= *Serie de Historiadores y Cronistas de Indias*, 5.) Edición preparada [...] bajo la Coordinación de Miguel León Portilla. 8 vols. México: Universidad Nacional Autónoma de México. Instituto de Investigaciones Históricas. (1. Auflage 1615.)

Torre, Rodrigo de la. 1987. "Lengua y communidad indígena: un caso en el municipio de Tepoztlán, Morelos". *Papeles de la Casa Chata* 2.44–57.

Villavicencio, Diego Jaymes Ricardo. 1692. *Luz y Méthodo de combatir idólatras, y destierro de idolatrías debajo del tratado siguiente: Tratado de avisos, y puntos importantes, del abominable Seta de la Idolatría; para examinar por ellos al penitente en el fuero interior de la conciencia, y exterior judicial. Sacados no de los Libros; sino de la experiencia en las aberiguaciones con las Rabbies de ella.* Puebla de los Ángeles: Imprenta de Diego Fernández de León.

*Leonardo Manrique, México (Mexiko)*

# 129. Das Studium der Eingeborenensprachen Südamerikas: Ketschua

1. Einleitung
2. Frühzeit (Vorgeschichte)
3. Neuere Sprachwissenschaft
4. Bibliographie

## 1. Einleitung

### 1.1. Verbreitung

Das Ketschua (im Folgenden *K.*), die Sprache des ehemaligen Inka-Reiches, ist heute über sechs Andenrepubliken, von Kolumbien im Norden über Ekuador, Peru und Bolivien bis nach Chile und Argentinien verbreitet. Die Ketschua-Bevölkerung konzentriert sich auf Peru (4,4 Mill.), Ekuador (2,2 Mill.) und Bolivien (1,4 Mill.) und entspricht dort knapp 30% der Gesamtbevölkerung. Cerrón (1987: 76ff.) gibt die Gesamtzahl der Sprecher mit ca. 8,3 Millionen an; andere Schätzungen gehen bis auf 10 Millionen. Der Anteil der Zweisprachigen in Ketschua und Spanisch nimmt ständig zu, während die k. Einsprachigkeit abnimmt. Wegen seines niedrigen gesellschaftlichen Status wird das K. bei Volkszählungen oft verschwiegen. Dreisprachigkeit von K. und Spanisch mit dem benachbarten Aimara ist im Umkreis des Titicacasees verbreitet, gelegentlich auch mit anderen einheimischen Sprachen, wie z. B. dem Guarani in Bolivien. Der historische Ursprung des K. ist das Thema vieler (mehr oder weniger wissenschaftlicher) Arbeiten gewesen. Es ist jedoch ziemlich sicher, daß sein Ursprungsgebiet ins heutige Peru fällt, wahrscheinlich in Küstennähe, und daß es erst nach Aufspaltung des Inkareiches kurz vor der *Conquista* nach Ekuador gekommen ist. Seine örtliche Verbreitung beschränkt sich heute nicht mehr auf die ruralen andinischen Hochebenen, die *puna*. Es wird nicht nur in den Städten des Hochlandes gesprochen, sondern hat infolge der Landflucht die Großstädte, wie z. B. die Elendsviertel der sieben-Millionen-Stadt Lima und die Satellitenstadt El Alto bei La Paz erreicht.

### 1.2. Rahmenbedingungen

Die Hauptaufgabe dieses Kapitels, den Beitrag europäischer Forscher zur K.-Linguistik herauszustellen, ist nicht unproblematisch. Selbst wenn wir uns auf Europäer konzentrieren, müssen nicht nur aus Fairneß, sondern wegen ihrer bedeutenden Rolle und der zunehmenden internationalen Zusammenarbeit besonders in der neueren K.-Forschung wenigstens einige wichtige nord- und südamerikanische Linguisten erwähnt werden. Die Zuordnung nach Autorennamen birgt nicht nur im Spanischen einige Schwierigkeiten, wie z. B. bei Xavier Albó, gebürtigem Katalanen und nationalisiertem Bolivianer, sondern auch bei Auslandseuropäern wie dem Auslandsdeutschen Co-Autor dieses Kapitels, W. Wölck. Bei der Auswahl der Sachgebiete wurden die rein linguistischen Arbeiten – im klassischen wie gegenwärtigen Sinne unseres Faches, d. h. Beschreibungen der Sprachstruktur, des Sprachgebrauchs und des Sprachwandels – in den Vordergrund gestellt. Zu unserer Kenntnis des K., seiner Sprecher und ihrer Welt haben jedoch nicht nur Linguisten beigetragen, deren Disziplin sich ohnehin erst vor etwa 50 Jahren selbständig zu machen begann, sondern ebenso die Laienforscher des 19. Jhs., sowie viele Anthropologen, Ethnologen und Pädagogen. Ohne die Ausgabe und Erläuterung von

Texten, ganz besonders in einer Sprache mit nur beschränkter schriftlicher Überlieferung, wüßten wir kaum etwas von der Sprachkultur des Inkareiches und seiner Nachfahren; und ohne die Arbeit von Sprachsoziologen und -pädagogen wären die Überlebenschancen des K. noch fragwürdiger.

In der andinen Linguistik wird das Ketschua oft mit seiner Nachbarsprache, dem Aimara, der drittgrößten einheimischen Sprache Amerikas, in einem Atemzug genannt. Die Diskussion der genetischen Verwandtschaft und gegenseitigen Beeinflussung der beiden in neuerer Zeit, ihre gemeinsame Behandlung in frühen Grammatiken und Wörterbüchern sowie das Fehlen eines dem Aimara gewidmeten Kapitels in diesem Handbuch erlaubt uns wohl auch einen gelegentlichen Hinweis auf diese wichtige Sprache. Letztlich spielten bei der Auswahl der hier erwähnten Beiträge noch zwei Kriterien eine Rolle: ihr Umfang und ihre Zugänglichkeit. Büchern und Monographien gaben wir den Vorrang vor Artikeln und (Buch-)Kapiteln, vor allem vor solchen, die in weniger verbreiteten Zeitschriften erschienen sind, denn Ziel eines jeden Handbuchs ist auch die Bereitstellung einer zugänglichen Auswahl-Bibliographie für den interessierten Leser und Benutzer.

## 2. Frühzeit (Vorgeschichte)

Den Beginn der K.-Linguistik können wir sicher mit dem Erscheinen von Domingo Sto. Tomas' Grammatik und Wörterbuch der Ketschua-Sprache im Jahre 1560 ansetzen; genauer genommen, schon mit dem Beginn seiner K.-Forschungen unmittelbar nach der "Eroberung" Perus. Sto. Tomas ist zugleich auch der Taufpate des Namens unserer Sprache. Er gebrauchte die spanische Schreibung *quechua*, die sich zumindest im hispano- und anglophonen Raum bis heute behauptet hat. In diesem Kapitel wird die der deutschen Lautung angepaßte Schreibung verwandt, durch die jedenfalls die Verwechslung des Anlauts unserer Sprache mit dem Anlaut in dt. 'Quatsch' vermieden wird. Phonologisch korrekter wären Schreibungen wie 'qechwa' oder 'qeshwa', oder selbst 'quichua' für Dialekte mit dem ekuatorianischen Vokalsystem. Andere Bezeichnungen, wie *Inca* oder (ekuatorianisch) *Inga* und selbst die einheimische Alternative, die vor allem von der Sprachgemeinschaft selbst verwandt wird, nämlich k. *runa simi* (dt. "Sprache oder Mundart des Volkes"), haben sich nicht durchgesetzt. In der internationalen Linguistik wird die spanische Form *Quechua* immer häufiger verwandt.

Die Wissenschaftsgeschichte der K.-Linguistik läßt sich grob in drei große Perioden einteilen: die Kolonialzeit, die Zeit der Entdeckungsreisen, und die moderne Epoche der Sprachwissenschaft.

### 2.1. Die Kolonialzeit

Die Geschichte der K.-Linguistik beginnt mit der Christianisierung der einheimischen Anden-Bevölkerung. Die ersten schriftlichen Zeugnisse sind Übersetzungen von biblischen oder katechistischen Texten ins K., verfasst von Mitgliedern des spanischen Klerus, insbesondere des Jesuitenordens. Ihre Beiträge zur Literatur und Linguistik der einheimischen Sprachen (Süd)-Amerikas sind auch als erste schon im 17. Jh. bibliographisch erfaßt worden (s. Ribadeneira & Alegambe 1643). Das erste große Werk der K.-Linguistik verdanken wir allerdings einem Dominikaner aus Sevilla. Santo Tomás' Grammatik und Wörterbuch der 'Allgemein-Sprache' (Sp. *lengua general*) der Indianer Perus von 1560 hat bis heute kaum an Bedeutung verloren. Es wurde wiederholt als Faksimile neu herausgegeben. Die jüngste Neuausgabe stammt vom derzeit führenden K.-Spezialisten Perus und enthält eine ausgezeichnete Einführung und ausführliche Kommentare (Cerrón-Palomino 1995a). Sto. Tomás' Ziel war weit mehr als nur linguistisch: er wollte mit seiner Grammatik, die kategorisch, wie damals und (fast) bis in unsere Zeit üblich, am Lateinischen orientiert war, zeigen, daß diese 'Indianer' eine Sprache sprechen, die sich an Differenziertheit und Ausdrucksfähigkeit durchaus mit dem Lateinischen messen kann; und im besten Humboldtschen und Sapir-Whorfschen Sinne folgerte er daraus, daß es sich deshalb bei diesen Indianern um ein hochentwickeltes Kulturvolk und nicht um unzivilisierte Wilde handelt. Vor allem war sein Ziel pädagogisch: seine Grammatik cum Wörterbuch war als Lehr- und Handbuch des K. für den spanischen Klerus geschrieben. Anfang des 17. Jhs. erschien die erste Grammatik-*cum*-Wörterbuch, welche das K. mit seiner großen Nachbarsprache, dem *Aimara*, zusammenstellt: eine in Rom erschienene *Gramatica y vocabulario en lengua quichua, aymara y español.* Sie wird dem berühmten spanischen Jesuiten Diego de Torres Rubio (1603) zugeschrieben und erschien im gleichen Jahre wie die erste umfassendere Beschreibung des Aimara des Italieners Ludovico Bertonio. Auch Torres Rubio (1616) verfaßte kurz danach zuerst eine sog. 'Arte' des Aimara, und wenig später (1619) dann eine ähnliche des K. Diese 'Artes' waren zumeist Übersetzungen in die einheimischen Sprachen von Teilen des Katechismus, begleitet von oft nur kurzen zweisprachigen Wortlisten.

Nach Sto. Tomás das nächste größere und bis heute wissenschaftlich bedeutende Werk der K.-Forschung war und ist González Holguín's großes Wörterbuch (1608), derzeit am besten zugänglich in der Ausgabe von Porras Barranechea (1952). Es blieb bis zum Erscheinen in Argentinien von J. Liras k.-spanischem Wörterbuch von 1944 das umfangreichste. Dem Wörterbuch vorausgegangen war 1607 eine Grammatik, neu herausgegeben mit einer kurzen Einleitung 1975 von Bernard Pottier, die im dritten Kapitel auf SS. 110ff. eine ausführliche alphabetische Liste der Suffixe und Partikel des K. enthält. Kapitel VI, betitelt "Elegancia" gibt wichtige syntaktische Information über Wortstellung und Suffixfolgen. Eine weitere Grammatik der Kolonialzeit ist erwähnenswert: die *Arte Breve* von Alonso de Huerta (1616), deren Ms. in der New York Public Library bewahrt wird und weil sie jüngst (1993) von Ruth Moya mit einer Einleitung neu herausgegeben wurde.

Das Erscheinen von Missionsgrammatiken ist keineswegs auf die Kolonialzeit beschränkt. Gegenwärtig beschäftigen sich vor allem protestantische Missionare und Bibelübersetzer mit den einheimischen Sprachen Amerikas und haben nicht nur wissenschaftliche Grammatiken, sondern auch viel Unterrichtsmaterial verfaßt.

### 2.2. Frühe historische Sprachwissenschaft

Schon seit Beginn der historisch-vergleichenden Sprachwissenschaft Anfang des 19. Jhs., als Fragen nach dem Ursprung der menschlichen Sprache und nach Sprachverwandtschaften in den Mittelpunkt des Forschungsinteresse rückten, wird das K. und seine Beziehung zu anderen Sprachen diskutiert, und zwar von den bedeutendsten Köpfen jener Zeit. In Johann Chr. Adelungs und J. S. Vaters (1806–1817) dreibändigem Klassiker des Sprachvergleichs, *Mithridates*, finden sich unter den fast fünfhundert behandelten Sprachen auch das K. und das Aimara. Zwei ganze Teilbände des dritten Bandes sind den amerikanischen Sprachen gewidmet. Dieser enthält u.a. eine kurze Liste von Wortentsprechungen zwischen K. und A. (Bd. 3, 1813, 2. Teil, S. 547). Adelung stellt fest, daß die beiden Sprachen sehr ähnlich sind, hält sich jedoch vor der Annahme einer engeren Verwandtschaft zurück. Die auch heute noch ernstgenommene Besiedlungstheorie des amerikanischen Kontinents von Asien über die Behring-Straße motivierte einige Forscher, wie z.B. Platzmann (1871), eine Verbindung zwischen dem K. und asiatischen Sprachen zu finden. Wenige Jahre nach Johann Chr. Adelung hat Friedrich Adelung in seiner kataloghaften *Übersicht aller bekannten Sprachen und ihrer Dialekte* (1820) das K. erstmalig in fünf Dialekte unterteilt: den von Quito, von Lamas, des Chinchaysuyo, den von Cuzco und Calchaqui. Nach dem ersten internationalen Amerikanisten-Kongreß in Paris 1875 nimmt das Interesse an den einheimischen Sprachen Amerikas zu. 1878 veröffentlicht Lucien Adam in Paris seine vergleichende Studie von sechs bekannten Sprachen Nord-(Dakota), Mittel-(Maya, Nahuatl, Quiché) und Südamerikas (K., Chibcha), über die er zuvor auf dem Amerikanistenkongreß vorgetragen hatte. Noch vor der Jahrhundertwende erscheint das erste große Werk zur Klassifikation aller amerikanischen Sprachen und Stämme des amerikanischen Ethnolinguisten Daniel Brinton (1891).

### 2.3. Die Forschungsreisenden

Um die Mitte des 19. Jhs. wird Südamerika als Forschungsreiseziel für europäische Akademiker attraktiv, vor allem die Regionen der 'alten Kulturen', darunter das Reich der Inkas, die Andenrepubliken. Gründe dafür sind auf der europäischen Seite die revolutionären Unruhen, in Südamerika das Ende des Kolonialismus, d.h. die politische Unabhängigkeit der neugegründeten Staaten, aber auch der Beginn einer neuen Wissenschaftlichkeit, nicht nur in den Naturwissenschaften. Alle uns Sprachwissenschaftlern bekannten Namen tauchen zuerst als Autoren von Reiseberichten und kulturgeographischen Studien auf. Einer der ersten dieser Epoche ist der Schweizer Arzt und Naturwissenschaftler Johann Jakob von Tschudi, der schon in seinen *Reiseskizzen* über Peru (1846), die auch bald ins Englische übersetzt wurden, mehrere Seiten dem K. widmet. Nebst einer kurzen Sprachbeschreibung gibt er auch einige Textproben. Das erste größere und immer noch bedeutende Werk dieser Epoche ist jedoch seine K.-Grammatik von 1853, veröffentlicht zusammen mit ausführlichen Sprachproben im ersten Band, gleichzeitig mit einem Wörterbuch als zweitem Band. Er nennt seine Grammatik "Sprachlehre" und unterteilt sie in die klassischen Abschnitte: Lautlehre, Formenlehre, Wortbildung und Syntax. Letzterer widmet er volle hundert Seiten. Die Grammatik schließt mit einigen Seiten von "Bemerkungen" über den Chinchaysuyu-Dialekt. Für den K.-Forscher interessant geblieben ist bis heute der erste bekannte Abdruck des seither so berühmt gewordenen K.-Dramas *Ollantay* als bedeutendste der 'Sprachproben'. Auch das Wörterbuch hat bis heute noch gewisse Bedeutung behalten. 1876 erschien Tschudis philologische Studie mit deutscher Übersetzung des *Ollanta*-Dramas. 1884 gab er eine wesentlich verbesserte und berichtigte Auflage seiner Grammatik heraus, jedoch ohne die Sprachproben. In ähnlicher Weise trat auch der britische Geograph Clements Markham in die K.-Forschung ein. Auch er begann mit historisch-politischen Reiseberichten, in denen sich schon längere Einschübe zur Inkasprache und -literatur, u. a. auch zu *Ollanta*, finden, dessen vollen Text er 1871 in einer k.-englischen zweisprachigen Ausgabe veröffentlichte. Kurz davor erschienen seine *Beiträge* zur K.-Grammatik und Lexik (Markham, 1864). Sein K.-Wörterbuch ist dreisprachig: K.-Englisch-Spanisch. In einer späteren, leicht verbesserten Neuausgabe (1907) sind dem Wörterbuch eine Anzahl Entsprechungen aus dem Aimara hinzugefügt. Unter seinen englischen Übersetzungen peruanischer Mythen (Markham 1873) findet sich auch schon ein Stück aus dem berühmten Werk von Francisco de Avila aus Huarochiri (s. u.).

Der bedeutendste Ketschuologe der älteren Epoche ist zweifellos Ernst Wilhelm Middendorf, dessen Grammatik seit ihrem Erscheinen (1890) zu den Klassikern der Ketschuistik gehört. Sie war der erste Band in seinem sechsbändigen Werk über *Die einheimischen Sprachen Perus*; ein Wörterbuch des K. war der zweite und eine ins Deutsche übersetzte und kommentierte Ausgabe des *Ollanta*-Dramas der dritte Band. Band IV (1891) enthält dramatische und lyrische Poesie auf K., der fünfte Band (1891) ist eine Beschreibung des Aimara, und der sechste und letzte (1892) des Muchik (span. *mochica*), der Chimu-Sprache. Obwohl Middendorfs Sprachstudien ursprünglich auch durch die Frage nach dem Ursprung der einheimischen Sprachen Südamerikas und deren mögliche Verwandtschaft mit asiatischen Sprachen angeregt waren, sah er offenbar bald die Fruchtlosigkeit oder zumindest die Unbeweisbarkeit solcher Vergleiche ein und konzentrierte sich auf die reine Sprachbeschreibung. Middendorf kannte und benutzte fast alle bisherigen Beschreibungen des K., von Holguín bis Markham und Tschudi (nur die Grammatik von Sto. Tomas war ihm leider nicht zugänglich) und zitiert die Klassiker der damaligen Sprachwissenschaft (z. B. W. von Humboldt und Ponçeau). Ob die Junggrammatiker ihn auch beeinflußt haben, ist nicht sicher; sein sprachpsychologischer und -vergleichender Ansatz läßt es zumindest vermuten. In seiner Einleitung gibt M. als erster moderner Grammatiker klare Auskunft über seinen 'Haupt-Informanten' aus Cuzco, der ihm während der fünfjährigen Datenerhebung zur Seite stand als wichtigste, lebende, wenn auch nicht als einzige Quelle seines Sprachmaterials. Er betont, daß er das 'runa simi', d. h. die Volkssprache, und nicht das 'inca simi', die Hof- oder Adelssprache beschreibt. Von allen bisherigen (und vielen späteren) Grammatiken wird M.'s der wahren Struktur des K. am gerechtesten. Er stellt klar, daß seine Struktur grundverschieden von der europäischer Sprachen ist und versucht, nicht immer mit Erfolg, latein-europäische Kategorien zu vermeiden. Abgesehen von einigen wenig sinnvollen Systematisierungsversuchen, wie z. B. der Einteilung von Nomina nach auslautendem Vokal, sind seine Analysen nicht nur zutreffend, sondern immer noch wegweisend; wie z. B. die der Verbalsubjekt und -objekt verbindenden Suffixe. Wichtige Einsichten in die Eigenheiten nominalisierender, d. h., nicht satzsubordinierender Sprachen, wie z. B. das Fehlen von Relativ- oder Passivkonstruktionen im K., stehen zum erstenmal bei Middendorf. Der fünfte Band seiner Peru-Reihe beginnt mit einer klugen Diskussion zum Verwandtschaftsverhältnis von Aimara und K., welche er für sehr verschiedene und nur entfernt verwandte Sprachen hält.

Erwähnenswert am Ende jener Epoche ist noch die erste umfassende Beschreibung des argentinischen K.-Dialekts von Mossi (1889), einmal weil dieser Dialekt selten beachtet wird und weil, abgesehen von einigen (abwegigen) Vergleichen mit europäischen Sprachen, Mossis Analyse recht zuverlässig ist und immer noch zitiert wird (vgl. Adelaars neue (1994b) Untersuchung desselben Dialekts).

## 3. Neuere Sprachwissenschaft

### 3.1. Strukturelle Linguistik

Während die ethno-philologischen und historischen Studien des K. regelmäßig, wenn auch langsam fortschritten, begann die nächste und neueste wichtige Epoche der K.-Linguistik nach dem zweiten Weltkrieg unter Einfluß des amerikanischen Strukturalismus. Die mehr praktische Motivation zum amerikanischen Studium des K. kam vornehmlich aus zwei Richtungen: vom *Peace Corps* und den Missionaren des *Summer Institute of Linguistics*. Ersteres brauchte Sprachkurse für seine 'volunteers', die zum Einsatz in die Andenrepubliken entsandt wurden, letzteres Sprachbeschreibungen für die Übersetzung religiöser Texte sowie zur Ausbildung seiner Missionare. Unter Leitung von D. F. Solá wurden an der Cornell Universität nicht nur Lehrmaterialien für verschiedene Dialekte – Cuzco, Ayacucho, Cochabamba – vorbereitet, sondern entsprechende Strukturbeschreibungen als Dissertationen ausgearbeitet (Solá 1958/1967; Lastra 1968; Parker 1969). Sie sind zumeist morphologische Konstituentengrammatiken, durchaus adäquat für das polysynthetisch agglutinierende K., das recht wenig Allomorphie hat. Hervorzuheben ist, daß die Autoren durchweg mit guten muttersprachlichen Informanten zusammenarbeiteten und damit der K.-Linguistik neuen Auftrieb gaben. In den phonologischen Studien wurde jetzt besonderes Augenmerk auf Dialektunterschiede gelenkt, deren bestes Resultat eine Einteilung des K. in zwei große Dialektgruppen war. Die beiden fast gleichen und immer noch gültigen und auf gründlichen synchronischen und diachronischen Studien fußenden Klassifikationen erschienen in kurzer Reihenfolge nacheinander; Parker (1963) nannte die südlichen Dialekte K. A, die nördlichen Dialekte K. B, der in Paris ausgebildete Peruaner Alfredo Torero (1964) die nördlichen K. I und die südlichen K. II. Büttner (1983) interpretiert und erweitert ihre Klassifikation. Eine weniger wünschenswerte Folge der detaillierten strukturalistischen Dialektphonologie war die Überbetonung und starre Festlegung von Dialektgrenzen, die zur Aufspaltung der K.-Sprache nicht nur in Dialekte, sondern in der Interpretation einiger Kollegen sogar in verschiedene 'Sprachen' führte, wodurch den Lebens- und Verbreitungschancen des K. kein guter Dienst erwiesen wurde.

Die Generativistik erhöhte das Interesse an der Syntax des K. Nicht nur amerikanische Kollegen erarbeiteten gute syntaktische Analysen von bisher weniger beachteten Dialekten (Cole 1892: Imbabura, Ekuador; Weber 1984, 1989: Huallaga/Huanuco, Peru). In den Niederlanden, die die Führung in der gegenwärtigen europäischen Linguistik übernommen hatten, trat eine Forschergruppe um Willem Adelar und Pieter Muysken unübersehbar in die K.-Studien ein. Adelaar selbst verfolgte traditionellere Richtungen und beschränkte sich nicht nur auf die Beschreibung mehrerer Dialekte (Tarma 1977; Santiago del Estero 1994b, s. o.) sondern machte auch dialektphilologische Studien am Huarochirí-Manuskript (1994a; s. u.). Sein Kollege Pieter Muysken analysierte, mehr im generativistischen Paradigma, (morpho-)syntaktische Eigenheiten von Verbalphrasen im ekuatorianischen K. (1977) und, zusammen mit seiner französischen Kollegin Lefebvre, die Nominalisierungsprozesse des K. (1988). Mit Louisa Stark ist er zudem der Autor des umfangreichsten Wörterbuchs des gegenwärtigen K. Ekuadors (1972). Die Arbeit seines Schülers Simon van de Kerke (1996) über die Morphosyntax der Suffixe im bolivianischen K. ist der jüngste größere Beitrag der holländischen Ketschuistik. Der seit langem in Paris arbeitende Australier Gerald Taylor ist ein weiterer bedeutender Vertreter der europäischen K.-Forschung, der uns besonders zu den 'periphären' nördlichen Dialekten des K. wichtige Einsichten verschafft hat (Taylor 1975, 1979, 1982) und einen wichtigen Beitrag zur K.-Textlinguistik geleistet hat (1980, s. u.). Den ersten Versuch einer pragma-linguistischen Diskurs-Analyse des K. hat Calvo Pérez (1993) gemacht. Seit den 70er Jahren haben sich zunehmend Kollegen aus dem einheimischen Sprachraum der Anden der K.-Linguistik gewidmet. Alfredo Torero und Rodolfo Cerrón sind zweifellos die bedeutendsten. Beispielhaft für die erfolgreiche Zusammenarbeit zwischen Peruanern und 'Ausländern' wurde 1976 A. Escobar mit der Herausgabe von Grammatiken und Wörterbüchern der sechs Hauptdialekte des peruanischen K. Alle folgen dem gleichen theoretischen Prinzip und schufen die Vergleichsbasis für Wölcks (1987) synthetisierende Analyse der Gemeinsamkeiten und Differenzen innerhalb dieser Gruppe als linguistische Grundlage für die Ausarbeitung eines überregionalen oder Standard-K. (Wölck 1991).

### 3.2. Klassifikation und historische Linguistik

Die derzeit gültige Klassifikation der einheimischen Sprachen Südamerikas stammt von dem Tschechen Č. Loukotka (1968). Ähnlich der der nord-amerikanischen Sprachen ist sie, wegen fehlender schriftlicher Zeugnisse, unzureichender mündlicher Überlieferung und nur weniger zuverlässiger Beschreibungen früherer Varianten, keine klassisch historisch-genetische, sondern eine areal-anthropologische, fußend auf Vergleichen oft spärlicher Wortlisten. K. gehört danach mit Aimara zur "South Central Andean Division" (S. 264ff.). Die dem Buch beigefügte Sprachenkarte zeigt u. a. den gewaltigen Unterschied zwischen der (vermutlichen) Ausbreitung des K. vor der Eroberung und seiner post-kolonialen, fast dreimal so großen 'Expansion'.

Die gründlichsten Arbeiten zur Rekonstruktion eines Proto-K. aufgrund umfangreicher Dialektvergleiche hat Parker (1969–1971) geleistet. Die Beziehungen des K. zu seinen Nachbarsprachen (Aimara, Haqaru, Muchik, Puquina) hat Torero (1974) in seiner einsichtsvollen soziohistorischen Studie zur Sprachentwicklung im Andenraum gezeigt. Im Mittelpunkt von Mannheims (1991) wichtiger sprach- und kulturhistorischer Arbeit steht die Entwicklung des Konsonantensystems des K. Die auffallende Ähnlichkeit zwischen K. und Aimara hat während mehr als hundert Jahren die Ketschuologen zu Annahme oder Ablehnung, jedenfalls zur Erwägung und Untersuchung dieses möglichen Verwandtschaftsverhältnisses bewogen. Als offenbar erster hielt Steinthal schon 1888 auf dem Amerikanistenkongreß einen Vortrag zu dieser Frage. Es gibt zwischen südlichem K. und nördlichem Aimara starke phonologische und lexikalische Entsprechungen, die schon früh zur Prägung des Gemeinschaftsnamens "Quechumara" für beide Sprachen führte. Dennoch ist bis heute ein genetisches Verwandtschaftsverhältnis nicht beweisbar, so jedenfalls ist die Schlußfolgerung in L. Campbells (1995) Zusammenfassung und auswertender Diskussion zu diesem Thema.

### 3.3. Sprache und Literatur; Ethnolinguistik

Trotz der immer wiederkehrenden Hypothesen auf den Kongressen für Altamerikanistik über ein Ketschua-Schriftsystem (s. Barthel, 1970), gibt es bislang keine etwa dem Nahua vergleichbare historische Evidenz. Die oft erwähnten Knotenschnüre ("Khipus") deuten vielmehr auf ein buchhalterisches Hilfsmittel zur Güterverwaltung und -verteilung. Die schriftlichen Quellen, die zu Beginn der postkolonialen Phase entstehen, sind begrenzt und qualitativ funktional ausgerichtet: religiöse Texte, Anweisungen zur Missionierung, Katechismen und Übersetzungen der Bibel, teilweise auch Theaterstücke und Lyrik. Erst der Indigenismo zu Beginn des 20. Jhs. fördert eine Aufwertung der K. Alltagskultur in der gesellschaftspolitischen Diskussion. Prominentester literarischer Vertreter in spanischer Sprache ist sicherlich José María Arguedas dank seiner Zweisprachigkeit und profunden Kenntnis der K.-Lebenswelt.

Im Zentrum des ethno-philologischen Interesses steht zweifellos das seltene und bislang wichtigste K.-Manuskript, die Mythen der Bewohner von Huarochirí, ca. 80 km nördlich von Lima, aufgezeichnet von Francisco de Avila um 1600. Hermann Trimborn, der auf dieses so wertvolle Manuskript in Madrid aufmerksam gemacht wurde, hat es 1938 durch die erste Übersetzung und den Kommentar dem deutschsprachigen Raum zugänglich gemacht. Er ergänzte es 1944 mit "Nachträgen" und gab es, zusammen mit einigen Märchen und Gedichten, 1967 neu heraus (Trimborn-Kelm 1967). Eine ausführliche Bewertung der Übersetzungen des Huarochirí-Textes in andere Sprachen – ins Lateinische durch Hippolito Galante (1942), ins Spanische durch José Maria Arguedas (1966), auf English von Jorge Urioste (1983) und ins Französische von Gerald Taylor (1980) – ist in Hartmann (1981) enthalten. Die Verschriftung oder Transkription oraler Tradition, von Märchen, Mythen, Rätseln und Erzählungen, gewinnt durch die neuen Dokumentationsmedien (Tonband, Kassette, Video) eine neue Dimension. Sie wird authentischer und basiert nicht mehr ausschliesslich auf dem Langzeitgedächtnis der Feldforscher, wohl aber der Informanten. Eine langjährige Sammlung ethnologisch sehr aufschlussreicher Erzählungen mit Ratschlägen zur Bewältigung des Alltags hat Gutmann (1998) vorgelegt.

Die akademische Interpretation und Übersetzung andiner Literatur wurde in Deutschland vorrangig an der Universität Bonn fortgesetzt; nach Trimborn und Hartmann (s. o.) jetzt von Dedenbach-Salazar (1990); in Frankreich sind neben Taylors Arbeiten (s. o.) die von Itier und Duviols (1993) zu beachten. In England hat Rosaleen Howard-Malverde (1981, 1997) ihre ethnolinguistische Arbeit von Sprachtexten auf den semiotischen Kontext von Textilien und Webmustern ausgedehnt.

3.4. Kontaktlinguistik und Sprachpädagogik

Die Sprachkontaktforschung Ketschua-Spanisch befasst sich traditionell mit dem vermuteten Einfluss der K. Varietäten auf die spanische Sprache, mit der Lehnwortbildung und mit grammatischen und phonologischen Interferenzprozessen. Hier sind besonders die Entdeckung und Beschreibung der 'Chaupi Lengua', eines hybriden K.-Spanisch, von Muysken (1978) zu nennen sowie die Untersuchungen von Büttner (1993) zur 'media lengua', betrachtet aus der Perspektive der linguistischen Identität. Die grammatischen Besonderheiten des zweisprachigen Spanisch beschreibt A. M. Escobar (1990, 1999). Die Verwendung des Ketschua als Mutter- und Unterrichtssprache in zweisprachigen Pilotschulen von Bolivien über Ekuador, Kolumbien und Peru bis nach Argentinien hat zu vielen praxisorientierten Forschungen geführt. Eine der gründlichsten empirischen Untersuchungen stammt von Hornberger (1988). Der umfangreichste Beitrag im Bereich der Herstellung von Unterrichtsmaterialien, von Handbüchern für Lehrer, von Anthologien, Wörterbüchern und pädagogischen Grammatiken, wird von Entwicklungshilfsinstitutionen in Kooperation mit einheimischen Wissenschaftlern und k.-sprachigen Lehrern geleistet. Vorrangig unterstützt die Deutsche Gesellschaft für Technische Zusammenarbeit (GTZ) seit Mitte der 70er Jahre in allen Andenländern zweisprachige Forschung und Erziehung; Terra Nova aus Italien arbeitet in Ekuador, die Fundación Patiño aus der Schweiz vorwiegend in Bolivien; amerikanische Missionare vom Summer Institute of Linguistics in Peru.

Eine weitere sprachpädagogische Aktivität ist die Lehre und Verbreitung des Ketschua als Fremdsprache. Der Hauptzweck der ersten K.-Grammatiken des spanischen Klerus als Lehrbücher wurde schon erwähnt. Das Erlernen von K. als obligatorischer Fremdsprache für das Studium der andinen Kulturen hat nicht nur in der deutschen Ketschuistik der Gegenwart einen hohen Stellenwert: '60 Jahre Quechua Lehre und Forschung am Seminar für Völkerkunde der Universität Bonn' konnten 1996 gefeiert werden, erstmalig unterrichtet von Hermann Trimborn im Jahre 1936. 1985 erschien nach einer Serie von Testkursen ein eigenes Lehrbuch unter Bonner Federführung von Roswith Hartmann, nunmehr in 3. erweiterter Auflage (1994), an dem auch C. Soto, Peruaner, K.-Sprecher und Linguist mitarbeitete, der zuvor sein eigenes Lehrbuch für Spanisch-Sprecher in Lima veröffentlicht hatte (Soto 1979). Das bekannteste K.-Lehrbuch für Anglo-Amerikaner stammt von G. Bills et al. (1969). Neuerdings gibt es technisch, linguistisch und pädagogisch wunderbare Lehrprogramme auf Laserdisketten.

3.5. Sprachsoziologie und Soziolinguistik

In engem Zusammenhang mit der politischen Absicht der gesellschaftlichen Aufwertung der indigenen Sprachen als Schul- und Unterrichtssprachen in den andinen Ländern ist ein neuer Forschungsbereich zu nennen, die Sprachsoziologie und Soziolinguistik, die zu Beginn der 60er Jahre in Lateinamerika die gesellschaftlichen Beziehungen zwischen den einheimischen Sprachen und den dominanten überregionalen Verkehrssprachen, Spanisch und Portugiesisch, erstmalig in die wissenschaftliche Diskussion in den Andenländern einbringt. Prominentestes Beispiel und Wegbereiter aller nachfolgenden Studien ist die grosse Survey-Untersuchung des k.-spanischen Bilinguismus in Peru, eine Studie der San Marcos Universität in Zusammenarbeit mit der State University of New York in Buffalo, entworfen und begonnen durch W. Wölck (1975). Die soziolinguistische Analyse einer Teilstichprobe von Ayacucho wurde als Langzeitstudie von Utta von Gleich (1982) fortgeführt und 1996 in einer dritten gemeinsamen Untersuchungsphase nach 30 Jahren durch beide abgeschlossen (von Gleich, 1992; von Gleich und Wölck, 1995). Die erste Einzeluntersuchung zum K. Sprachgebrauch unternahm Xavier Albó in Cochabamba, Bolivien (1970). Empirisch ebenso gut fundiert ist der soziolinguistische Beitrag von Inge Sichra (1986) zum Nachweis der ethnolinguistischen Vitalität der Ketschuas in derselben Region. Zu den wenigen Migrationsstudien der Ketschuas mit Bezug auf ihr Sprachverhalten gehören die Arbeit von Eva Gugenberger in Arequipa (1995) und die Untersuchung zu Sprachwahl zwischen K. und Spanisch von Gnaerig in Peru (1981).

Die methodologischen Ansätze der Gemeinschaftsprofiluntersuchungen nach Wölck (1976) wurden in adaptierter Form in den soziolinguistischen Studien zur Vorbereitung bilingualer Grundschulprojekte und Programme eingesetzt, wie z. B. bei der soziolinguistischen Diagnostik des Departement Puno (1979), in Kooperation von deutschen und spanischen Fachleuten. Die zahlreichen aus diesen Projekten stammenden Publikationen einschliesslich der später erstellten Unterrichtsmaterialien in K. sowohl in Bolivien, Peru, Ekuador und begrenzt auch für die Ingas in Kolumbien verwerten nationale und internationale ethno-kulturelle Forschungsergebnisse.

Nachüberlegungen zum Projektverlauf sind eine neue Kategorie in der interdisziplinären Zusammenarbeit zwischen Pädagogik und Sprachwissenschaft. Dazu gehören die Studien von Abram (1992), von Valiente-Catter und Küper (1996) und von Jung (1989), die das bilinguale Projekt in Puno (Peru) analytisch und deskriptiv als Auseinandersetzung zwischen Sprachen- und Kulturkonflikt im Kontext der Erziehungspolitik darstellt. Von Gleich (1989) gibt einen umfassenden Überblick über die zentralen bilingualen Primarschulprojekte und Programme in ganz Lateinamerika.

Abschließend muß noch einmal betont werden, daß unser Kapitel auf seinem beschränkten Platz nur einen kurzen Einblick in die Geschichte der K.-Studien geben konnte. Rivets und Créqui-Monforts vierbändige Bibliographie aller Veröffentlichungen auf und über Aimara und K. vom 16. Jh. bis zu ihrem Erscheinen im Jahre 1956 enthält über 4000 Titel, von denen der weitaus größte Teil dem K. gewidmet ist. Zusammenfassungen speziell der deutschen K.-Forschung wurden erstellt von R. Hartmann (1987), der neueren Strömungen der Ketschuistik von Cerrón-Palomino (1995b).

## 4. Bibliographie

Abram, Matthias. 1992. *Lengua, cultura e identidad. El Proyecto EBI 1985–1990.* Quito: Abya-Yala.

Adam, Lucien. 1878. *Etude sur six langues américaines: Dakota, Chibcha, Nahuatl, Kechua, Quiché, Maya.* Paris: Maisonneuve.

Adelaar, Willem. 1977. *Tarma Quechua: Grammar, texts, dictionary.* Lisse: de Ridder.

–. 1994a. "La procedencia dialectal del manuscrito de Huarochirí en base a sus características lingüísticas". *Revista Andina* 12.1.

–. 1994b. "Raices lingüísticas del quichua de Santiago de Estero". *Actas de las Segundas Jornadas de Lingüística Aborigen.* Universität Buenos Aires.

Adelung, Johann Christoph. 1806–1817. *Mithridates. oder allgemeine Sprachenkunde mit dem Vater Unser als Sprachprobe in beynahe fünfhundert Sprachen und Mundarten.* (beendet von J. S. Vater.) 3 Bde. Berlin: Voss.

Adelung, Friedrich. 1820. *Übersicht aller bekannten Sprachen und ihrer Dialekte.* Petersburg: Gretsch.

Albó, Xavier. 1970. *Social Constraints on Cochabamba Quechua.* Ithaca, NY: Cornell Univ. Press.

Arguedas, José María et al. (Übers. und Hg.) 1966. *Dioses y hombres de Huarochirí.* Lima: Instituto de Estudios Peruanos.

Barthel, Thomas. 1970. "Gab es eine Schrift in Alterperu?". *Verhandlungen des 38. Internationalen Amerikanistenkongresses,* Stuttgart 1968, II.237–242.

Bertonio, Ludovico. 1603. *Arte y grammatica mvy copiosa dela lengua aymara.* Rom. Faksimile Ausgabe 1879. Leipzig: Teubner.

Bills, Garland et al. 1969. *Introduction to Spoken Bolivian Quechua.* Austin, TX: Univ. of Texas Press.

Brinton, Daniel. 1891. *The American Race: A linguistic classification and ethnographic description of the native tribes of North and South America.* New York: N. D. C. Hodges.

Büttner, Thomas Th. 1983. *Las lenguas de los Andes Centrales. Estudios sobre la clasificación genética, areal y tipológica.* Madrid: Ed. Cultura Hispánica.

–. 1993. *Uso del quichua y del castellano en la sierra ecuatoriana.* Quito: Abya-Yala.

Calvo Pérez, Julio. 1993. *Pragmática y gramática del quechua Cuzqueño.* Cuzco: Bartolomé de las Casas.

Campbell, Lyle. 1995. "The Quechumaran Hypothesis and Lessons for Distant Genetic Comparison". *Diachronica* 12,2.157–200.

Cerrón-Palomino, Rodolfo. 1987. *Lingüística quechua.* Cuzco: B. de las Casas.

–, Hg. & Komm. 1995a. *Grammatica o arte de la lengua general de los indios de los reynos del Peru, por el maestro Fray Domingo de Santo Tomas.* Cuzco: B. de las Casas.

–. 1995b. "Tendencias actuales de la lingüística quechua". *Actas de las Segundas Jornadas de Lingüística Aborigen,* 51–77. Buenos Aires: Instituto de Ling.

Cole, Peter. 1982. *Imbabura Quechua.* Amsterdam: North-Holland Publishing Co.

Dedenbach-Salazar, Sabine. 1990. *Inca pachaq llamanpa willaynin. Uso y crianza de los camelidos en la época incaica.* (*Amerik. Studien* 16.) Bonn.

Duviols, Pierre & César Itier. 1993. *Relación de antiguedades deste reyno del Piru (Joan de Santa Cruz Pachacuti.)* Lima: Institut Français d'Etudes Andines.

Escobar, Alberto, Hg. 1976. *Gramáticas referenciales y diccionarios de consulta de la lengua quechua.*

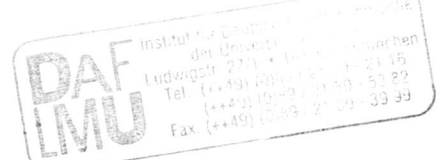

Lima: Ministerio de Educación & IEP. (Grammatiken und Wörterbücher für die folgenden Dialekte: Junín-Huanca, von R. Cerrón Palomino; San Martín, von D. Coombs et al.; Cuzco-Collao, von A. Cusihuaman; Ancash-Huaylas, von G. Parker; Cajamarca-Cañaris, von Felix Quesada; und Ayacucho-Chanca, von C. Soto Ruiz.)

Escobar, Anna María. 1990. *Los bilinǵes y el castellano en el Perú.* Lima: IEP.

–. 1999. *Contacto social y lingüístico: El español en contacto con el quechua en el Perú.* Lima: P. U. Católica.

Galante, Hippolito (transkr. und übers.) 1942. *De priscorum haruchiriensium origine et institutis.* Madrid: Instituto Oviedo.

Gleich, Utta von. 1982. *Die soziale und kommunikative Bedeutung des Quechua und Spanischen bei Zweisprachigen in Peru (1968–1978).* Hamburg: Universität.

–. 1989. *Educación primaria bilingüe intercultural en América Latina.* Eschborn: GTZ.

–. 1992. "Changes in the Status and Function of Quechua". *Status Change of Languages* hg. von Ulrich Ammon & M. Hellinger, 43–65. Berlin: de Gruyter.

– & W. Wölck. 1995. "Changes in Language Use and Attitudes of Quechua-Spanish Bilinguals in Peru". *Language in the Andes* hg. von Peter Cole et al, 27–51. Newark, DE: Latein American Studies Program.

Gnärig, Burkhard. 1981. *Zwischen Quechua und Spanisch. Sprachwahl und -verwendung als Momente kultureller Konkurrenz. Zwei Beispiele aus Peru.* Frankfurt.

González Holguín, Diego. 1607. *Gramática y arte nueva de la lengua general de todo el Perú llamada lengua qqichua o lengua del Inca.* (Neuausgabe mit Vorwort von B. Pottier. Vaduz, 1975.)

–. 1608. *Vocabulario de la lengua general de todo el Peru llamada lengua qquichua o del Inca.* Neu hg. und eingeleitet von Raul Porras Barrenechea (1952). Lima: Instituto de Historia.

Gugenberger, Eva. 1995. *Identitäts- und Sprachkonflikt in einer pluriethnischen Gesellschaft.* Wien: Universitätsverlag.

Gutmann, Margit. 1998. *El qanchi machu aún vive: Cuentos de Pomacanchi.* Cuzco/Lima: B. de las Casas.

Hartmann, Roswith. 1981. "El texto quechua de Huarochirí, una evaluación crítica de las ediciones a disposición". *Historica* 5.167–208.

–. 1987. "Quechua Forschung". *Deutsche Iberoamerika-Forschung in den Jahren 1930–1980* hg. von W. Stegman, 99–136. Berlin: Colloquium Verlag.

– et al. 1985. *'Rimaykullayki'. Unterrichtsmaterialien zum Quechua Ayacuchano.* Bonn: Dietrich Reimer. (3. Aufl. 1994.)

Hornberger, Nancy. 1985. *Bilingual Education and Language Maintenance: A southern Peruvian Quechua case.* Berlin: Mouton.

Howard-Malverde, Rosaleen. 1981. *Dioses y diablos. Tradición oral de Cañar, Ecuador.* Paris: Ass. de Ethnolinguistique Amerindienne.

–, Hg. 1997. *Creating Context in Andean Cultures.* New York: Oxford Univ. Press.

Huerta, Alonzo de. 1616. *Arte breve de la lengua quechua.* Hg. und eingeleitet von Ruth Moya (1993). Quito: Corp. Editora Nacional.

Jung, Ingrid. 1989. *Das Zweisprachenprojekt in Puno, Peru. Erziehungspolitik im Sprachen- und Kulturkonflikt.* Berlin.

Kerke, Simon van de. 1996. *Affix Order and Interpretation in Bolivian Quechua.* Meppel: Krips.

Lastra, Yolanda. 1968. *Cochabamba Quechua Syntax.* Den Haag: Mouton.

Lefebvre, Claire & Pieter Muysken. 1988. *Mixed Categories: Nominalizations in Quechua.* Dordrecht: Kluwer.

Lira, Jorge A. 1944. *Diccionario kkechuwa-español.* Tucuman: Universidad Nacional (2. Auflage 1982, Bogotá: SECAB.)

Loukotka, Čestmír. 1968. *Classification of South-American Indian Languages.* Los Angeles: Univ. of California Press.

Mannheim, Bruce. 1991. *The Language of the Inca since the European Invasion.* Austin: Univ. of Texas Press.

Markham, Clements R. 1864. *Contributions towards a Grammar and Dictionary of Quichua. The Language of the Yncas of Peru.* London: Trübner. (Neuausgabe 1907. *Vocabularies of the General Language of the Incas of Peru or runa simi.* London: Ballantyne.)

–. 1873. *Narratives of the Rites and Laws of the Yncas.* London: Hakluyt Society.

Middendorf, Ernst Wilhelm. 1890–1892. *Die einheimischen Sprachen Perus.* Leipzig: Brockhaus, Bd. I: *Das Runa-Simi oder die Keshua-Sprache, wie sie gegenwärtig in der Provinz Cuzco gesprochen wird*; Bd. II: *Wörterbuch des Runa-Simi oder der Keshua-Sprache*; Bd. III: *Ollanta, ein Drama der Keshua-Sprache*, Bd. IV: *Dramatische und lyrische Dichtungen der Keshuasprache*; Bd. V: *Die Aimará-Sprache*; Bd. VI: *Muchik oder die Chimu-Sprache.*

Mossi, Miguel Angel. 1889. *Manual del idioma general del Peu. Gramática razonada de la lengua qichua.* Cordoba: Minerva.

Muysken, Pieter. 1979. "La mezcla de quechua y castellano. El caso de la 'media langua' en el Ecuador". *Lexis* 3.41–56.

–. 1977. *Syntactic Development in the Verb Phrase of Ecuadorian Quechua.* Lisse: de Ridder.

Parker, Gary J. 1963. "La clasificación genética de los dialectos quechuas". *Revista del Museo Nacional* 32.241–252.

–. 1969. *Ayacucho Grammar and Dictionary*. Den Haag: Mouton.

–. 1969–71. "Comparative Quechua Phonology and Grammar I–V." *University of Hawaii Working Papers in Linguistics* 1 (1969).1–61, 65–87, 123–147, 149–204; 3 (1971).45–109.

Platzmann, Julius. 1871. *Amerikanisch-asiatische Etymologien via Behring-Strasse, from the East to the West*. Leipzig: Teubner.

Ribadeneira, Pedro & Felipe Alegambe. 1643. *Bibliotheca Scriptorum Societatis Iesu*. Antwerpen. (Neue und erw. Aufl. 1676.)

Rivet, Paul & Georges de Créqui-Montfort. 1951–1956. *Bibliographie des langues aymará et kičua*. 4 Bde. Paris: Institut d'Ethnologie.

Santo Tomás, Domingo de. 1560. *Gramática o arte de la lengua general de los indios de los reynos del Perú*. Valladolid.

–. 1560. *Lexicon, o vocabulario de la lengua general del Perú*. Valladolid (Facsimile Ausgaben: Leipzig 1891, J. Platzmann, Hg.; Quito 1947, J. M. Vargas, Hg.; Lima 1951, R. Porras Barrenechea, Hg.; Quito 1992, R. Moya, Hg.)

Sichra, Inge. 1986. *Nachweise der ethnolinguistischen Vitalität einer Minderheit in ihrer Sprache. Empirische Untersuchung zweier Quechua-Gemeinden in Cochabamba, Bolivien 1979–1980*. Wien: Universität.

Solá, Donald F. 1958. *Huanuco Kechua: the Grammar of Words and Phrases*. Diss. Cornell; (Span. Übers. 1967: *Gramática del quechua de Huánuco*. Lima: Plan de Fomento Lingüístico.)

Soto Ruiz, Clodoaldo. 1979. *Quechua: manual de enseñanza*. Lima: Instituto de Estudios Peruanos.

Stark, Louisa & Pieter Muysken. 1972. *Diccionario español-quichua, quichua-español*. Quito: Banco Central del Ecuador.

Steinthal, Hermann. 1890. "Das Verhältnis, das zwischen dem Keschua und Aimara besteht." *Akten des 7. Internationalen Amerikanistenkongresses*, Berlin 1888.462–465.

Taylor, Gerald. 1975. *Le parler quechua d'Olto, Amazonas (Pérou)*. Paris: CNRS.

–. 1979. *Diccionario normalizado y comparativo quechua: Chachapoyas-Lamas*. Paris: L'Harmattan.

–, Hg. 1980. *Rites et traditions de Huarochirí*. Paris: L'Harmattan (span. Übers. 1987, Lima: IEP.)

–. 1982. *Aspectos de la dialectología quechua I: Introducción al quechua de Ferreñafe*. Paris: Chantiers Amerindia.

Torero, Alfredo. 1964. "Los dialectos quechuas". *Anales Científicos de la Universidad Agraria* 2.446–478.

–. 1974. *El quechua y la historia social andina*. Lima: Univ. Ricardo Palma.

Torres Rubio, Diego de. 1603. *Gramática y Vocabulario en lengua Quichua, Aymara y Española*. Rom.

–. 1616. *Arte de la lengua aymara*. Lima.

–. 1619. *Arte de la lengua qvichva*. Lima.

Trimborn, Hermann. 1944. "Dämonen und Zauber im Inkareich. Nachträge zum Khetschua-Werk des Francisco de Avila". *Zeitschrift für Ethnologie* 73.146–162.

Trimborn, Hermann & Antje Kelm, Hg. 1967. *Francisco de Avila. Quellenwerke zur alten Geschichte aufgezeichnet in den Sprachen der Eingeborenen*. Berlin: Ibero-Amerik. Institut.

Tschudi, Johann J. von. 1846. *Peru: Reiseskizzen aus den Jahren 1838–42*. St. Gallen: Scheitlin & Zollikofer.

–. 1853. *Die Kechua-Sprache*, Bd. I: *Sprachlehre und Sprachproben*; Bd. II: *Wörterbuch*. Wien: Akademie der Wissenschaften. Neuausgabe der *Sprachlehre* 1884: *Organismus der Ketsua-Sprache*. Leipzig: Brockhaus.

–. 1876. *Ollanta. Ein altperuanisches Drama, aus der Kechuasprache übersetzt und commentirt*. Wien: Akademie d. Wiss.

Urioste, Jorge (übers. und transkr.) 1983. *Hijos de pariya qaqa: la tradición oral de Waru Chiri*. Syracuse, NY: Foreign Studies P.

Valiente Catter, Teresa & W. Küper. 1996. *Sprache, Kultur und Erziehung in Ecuador*. Eschborn: GTZ-Verlagsgesellschaft Rossdorf.

Weber, David. 1984. *Relativization and Nominalized Clauses in Huallaga (Huanuco) Quechua*. Berkeley: Univ. of Calif. Press.

–. 1989. *A Grammar of Huallaga (Huanuco) Quechua*. Berkeley: Univ. of California Press.

Wölck, Wolfgang. 1975. "El Proyecto BQC: metodología de una encuesta sociolingüística del bilingüismo quechua-castellano". *Lingüística e indigenismo moderno en América* hg. von R. A. Matos & R. Ravines, 337–359. Lima. IEP.

–. 1976. "Community Profiles". *IJSL* 9.43–57.

–. 1987. *Pequeño breviario quechua*. Lima: Instituto de Estudios Peruanos.

–. 1991. "The Standardization of Quechua: Problems and suggestions." *Standardization of National Languages* hg. von U. von Gleich & E. Wolff, 43–54. Hamburg: UNESCO.

*Wolfgang Wölck, Buffalo (USA)*
*Utta von Gleich, Hamburg (Deutschland)*

# 130. Das Studium der Eingeborenensprachen Südamerikas: Guaraní

1. Einleitung
2. Das Tupinambá in Brasilien
3. Das Guaraní in Paraguay
4. Heutige Bedeutung der Amerindianistik
5. Bibliographie

## 1. Einleitung

Von den zahlreichen eingeborenen Sprachen Südamerikas sind nur relativ wenige in der Zeit der spanischen und portugiesischen Kolonisierung von sprachlich interessierten Europäern beschrieben worden. Dies liegt zum einen naturgemäß daran, daß die Besiedlung zunächst noch nicht alle Gebiete erfaßte, besonders in Brasilien, wo die riesigen und durch stark zersplitterte Stämme bewohnten inneren Teile z. T. bis ins 19. Jh. unentdeckt blieben, zum anderen aber an der Art des Kontaktes, den die Europäer mit den Eingeborenen pflegten. Bei der starken Vermischung der europäischen Siedler mit indianischen Frauen behielten zwar häufig zunächst die einheimischen Sprachen gegenüber dem Spanischen und besonders gegenüber dem Portugiesischen in Brasilien die Oberhand (Rodrigues 1986: 101), aber diese Verbreitung der Kenntnis indianischer Sprachen drang aufgrund der 'Indianisierung' dieser Europäer nicht ins Bewußtsein der Gebildeten, die solche Kenntnisse nach Europa hätten vermitteln können. Solches konnte außer durch Reiseberichte in größerem Umfang nur durch die Missionierung der Indios geschehen. Angesichts der Sprachenvielfalt mußten sich jedoch die Missionsorden auf einige wenige Sprachen beschränken.

Hierbei kam ihnen einmal der Umstand zu Hilfe, daß die beiden großen Reiche des mexikanischen bzw. peruanischen Hochlandes, die die Conquista zuerst vernichtet hatte, selbst ihre Sprachen, Nahuatl (→ Art. 128) und Quechua (→ Art. 129), schon vor der spanischen Eroberung über große Flächen ausgedehnt hatten, diese Sprachen also schon weit verbreitete Verkehrssprachen waren, die von der Mission nur noch konsequent sprachlich ausgebaut und in der geographischen Verbreitung zementiert werden mußten. Daneben wurden jedoch im spanischen Amerika auch andere, kleineren territorialen eingeborenen Reichen entsprechende Sprachen wie etwa das Mapuche in Chile und zeitweilig das Muisca in Kolumbien für die regionale Mission gebraucht und daher in Grammatiken analysiert und ab 1580 auf Lehrstühlen für die Priesterausbildung in Lima, Quito und Bogotá (neben Mexiko) gelehrt. Die anfängliche Aufgeschlossenheit für die Vielzahl der Eingeborenensprachen wich nach manchem Hin und Her zwischen Offenheit gegenüber den Indianersprachen als Instrumenten der Mission und dem Zweifel daran, ob diese überhaupt fähig seien, die Wahrheiten des christlichen Glaubens adäquat auszudrücken, dem Bestreben, nur das Spanische durchzusetzen (Tovar & Larrucea de Tovar 1984: 191 f.). Dennoch hielt sich neben dem Aztekischen in Mexiko vor allem das Quechua in Peru, während das Guaraní in Paraguay erst seit dem 17. Jh. für die Mission benutzt wurde (vgl. unten 3.). Im spanischsprachigen Raum wurden diese für die Mission gebrauchten und kodifizierten Sprachen sehr schnell 'lenguas generales', d. h. allgemein verwendete und damit herausgehobene Sprachen genannt, die alle anderen tribalen Sprachen aus dem Blickwinkel der Europäer bis zur Vertreibung der Jesuiten aus Amerika und dem erwachenden Interesse für die Sprachen der Welt gegen Ende des 18. Jh. (vgl. Hervás y Panduro 1785) verbannte.

In Brasilien dagegen war praktisch an der gesamten Küste, welche allein zunächst kolonisiert wurde, eine einzige Sprache in nur geringen dialektalen Varianten verbreitet, die heute unter der Bezeichnung Tupinambá zusammengefaßt werden. Unter den verschiedenen Namen sind die bekanntesten die Tupinambá der Küste von Bahia, die südlich anschließenden Tupiniquim oder Tupinakín, die Tamoyos der Gegend um Rio de Janeiro und die Tupi (oder auch Tupiniquim) der Küste bei São Paulo (Rodrigues 1997: 374). Alle diese nahestehenden Dialekte sind ebenfalls nahe Verwandte des Guaraní, dessen Zentrum im heutigen Ostparaguay lag (vgl. unten 3.)

Neben dem für die Mission verwendeten Tupinambá der Eingeborenen entwickelten sich im 17. Jh. zwei verschiedene daraus abgeleitete vereinfachte Verkehrssprachen der missionierten, akkulturierten Indios und der Mestizen, die 'línguas gerais' genannt wurden. Die 'língua geral' des Südens war die der 'Bandeirantes' (ins Landesinnere vorstoßende Siedler, Goldsucher und Sklavenjäger) von São Vicente und São Paulo, während sich im Norden von der Provinz Maranhão aus bei der Erschließung des Amazonasbeckens die 'língua geral amazônica' herausbildete, die als 'nheengatú' "gute Sprache" bis ins 19. Jh. im gesamten Norden vorherrschte und heute noch am oberen Rio Negro gesprochen wird (Rodrigues 1986: 99–103).

'Língua geral' hat also in Brasilien eine andere Bedeutung ("vereinfachte Verkehrssprache") als 'lengua general' in Hispanoamerika ("reine indianische Missionssprache mit weiter Verbreitung"). Die im 18. Jh. ausgestorbene 'língua geral paulista' ist nie beschrieben worden, das Nheengatú erst zu Beginn des 20. Jhs., allerdings nur lexikalisch.

## 2. Das Tupinambá in Brasilien

### 2.1. Erste Analysen durch Jean de Léry

Abgesehen von den häufig anonymen Missionaren sind Nachrichten über das Tupí Brasiliens auch von Reisenden und Abenteurern überliefert. Einer der ersten ist Hans Staden (1525/28–?) aus Straubing, der 1554 ein Jahr lang bei den Tupinambá in Ubatuba (nördl. von São Paulo) gefangen war und in seinem Bericht (Staden 1557) etwa 150 Wörter, aber auch ganze Sätze in Tupinambá mit Übersetzung, aber ohne weitere sprachliche Analyse liefert. Der aus Burgund stammende Jean de Léry (1534–1613), der, als Calvinist in den Religionsstreit seiner Zeit verwickelt, 1557/58 an einer der erfolglosen französischen Kolonisationsversuche unter Villegaignon in der Bucht von Guanabara (Rio de Janeiro) teilnahm und ein Jahr unter den Tupinambá und Tupinakín lebte, kann dagegen als einer der ersten ethnographischen und linguistischen Beobachter bezeichnet werden.

Sein Reisebericht (Léry 1578) enthält eine Fülle Bezeichnungen des täglichen Lebens in Tupinambá. Das ganze 20. Kapitel ist aber eine Musterkonversation ("Colloque de l'entrée ou arrivée en la terre du Brésil") mit zahlreichen Beobachtungen zur Sprachstruktur, obwohl die Transkription in französischer Orthographie (z. B. *augé-pé* für [oʒe'pe] "eins" oder *iendé* für [ja'nde] "wir (inklusiv)") nur bedingt sichere lautliche Analysen zuläßt und hinter der Stadens zurückbleibt. Sicher ohne Kenntnis der ersten Quechua-Grammatik von Domingo de Santo Tomás (Rodrigues 1997: 383) hat er als erster im Tupinambá die in den Tupí-Guaraní-Sprachen ebenso wie im Quechua bekannte Unterscheidung zwischen einer ersten Person Plural, die den Dialogpartner einschließt ('inklusiv', als Pronomen *jandé*), und einer, die ihn ausschließt ('exklusiv', *oree*), angesprochen, indem er einen gelehrten Vergleich mit dem griechischen Dual zieht (Léry 1972: 242), wohl, weil es um die Zweiheit der Dialogpartner ('wir' = 'ich' und 'du') geht. Er beschreibt die Personenmarkierung der Substantive ('possessif', Léry 1972: 247f.), einiges der Flexion der Verben, der Modi und der syntagmatischen 'Tempus'-Bildung, wenn auch nicht sehr systematisch (Léry 1972: 249f.).

### 2.2. Die Grammatik von José de Anchieta

Die einzige originelle Grammatik des Tupinambá der Kolonialzeit ist die des Begründers der Jesuitenmission in Brasilien, des von den kanarischen Inseln stammenden, in Portugal ausgebildeten und ab 1554 in Brasilien missionierenden José de Anchieta (1533–1597). Neben der reichen ekklesiastischen Literatur über ihn stammen die meisten linguistischen Untersuchungen über ihn aus der Feder des besten Kenners des Tupinambá, Aryon Rodrigues. Sie sind neben Pottier 1998 die Grundlage für die folgenden Ausführungen (Rodrigues 1997). Nach Rodrigues' Einschätzung war die Grammatik des Anchieta, die schon um 1560 konzipiert war, aber erst 1595 gedruckt wurde, in ihrer konzisen und linguistisch genialen Beschreibungsweise für die praktischen Zwecke der jesuitischen Missionare wenig geeignet und wurde daher bis zum 19. Jh. ignoriert (Rodrigues 1997: 392) und durch das umfangreichere, aber kaum originelle Werk von Figueira (1621, 1687, 1795) ersetzt. Befremdlich wirkt in der Tat die Form des knappen Werkes von Anchieta (16 Kapitel, 82 Seiten), das keinerlei Vorwort enthält, in dem etwaige Zielsetzungen oder grundsätzliche Gedanken über die Verschiedenheit der amerikanischen und der europäischen Sprachen verzeichnet wären, und in der Regel auch die Beispiele unübersetzt läßt, was voraussetzt, daß es ein Wörterverzeichnis gab, anhand dessen zusammen mit den grammatischen Beschreibungen die Bedeutung der Beispiele klar werden sollte. Als Wörterbuch war ein in wohl mehreren Abschriften vervielfältigtes Manuskript Portugiesisch-Tupinambá im Umlauf, das seit dem 18. Jh. als *Vocabulário na língua brasílica* bekannt war und an dessen ursprünglicher Abfassung vielleicht auch Anchieta beteiligt war (Drumond 1952–53; Dietrich 1991).

Anchieta, der zuerst einige Jahre im Gebiet von São Paulo wirkte und sich zunächst das dortige Tupí aneignete, bevor er in Salvador da Bahia die dortige Variante des Tupinambá lernte, äußert sich zu Beginn, bei der Beschreibung der Laute des Tupinambá, auch über die regionale Gliederung: Das Tupinambá kenne Wörter, die auf Konsonant enden, wie z. B. *apâb* "ich beendete / bin ans Ende gelangt", während die südlichen Tupí (wie die paraguayischen Guaraní)

"nunqua pronuncião a última consoante no verbo affirmativo, ut pro *Apâb*, dizem, *Apâ*, pro *Acêm*, & *Apên, Acẽ, Apẽ, pronunciando o til somente, pro Aiúr*, Aiú" (Anchieta 1595: 2). ['sprechen bei der Bejahungskonjugation niemals den auslautenden Konsonanten aus, wie z. B. daß sie statt *apáb apá* sagen, statt *asém* ("ich kam an") und *apén* ("ich zerbrach, intr.") *asẽ* und *apẽ*, indem sie nur den Nasalvokal aussprechen, statt *ajúr* "ich kam") *aju'*.]

Wie auch Rodrigues (1997: 358f.) betont, erkannte Anchieta (1595: 24) sehr klar, daß die Verneinung des Prädikats nicht einfach durch eine hinzugesetzte Partikel syntagmatisch ausgedrückt wird, sondern durch ein Verfahren, das, da nicht in allen Tempora gleich, durchaus als morphologische affirmative und negative Konjugation angesehen werden kann (z. B. *ajucâ* "ich töte(te)" *versus najucái* "ich töte(te) nicht", aber *ajucáne* "ich werde töten" *versus najucaixoéne* "ich werde nicht töten" (1595: 24f.), ein Darstellungsverfahren, das sowohl Figueira (1795: 14ff.) als auch Montoya (1640: 13ff.) befolgt haben.

Anchieta hat, wie auch Rodrigues (1997: 396) betont, alle wesentlichen morphologischen und syntaktischen Strukturen des Tupinambá erkannt und in erstaunlicher Unabhängigkeit vom Modell der lateinischen Grammatik beschrieben. Recht lakonisch teilt er mit, daß die Nomina dieser Sprache keine Kasus haben, daß viele Adjektive durch Nominalkomposition ausgedrückt werden (was in heutiger Terminologie eher als augmentative, diminutive, intensivierende, meliorisierende oder pejorisierende usw. Derivation bezeichnet würde), daß die Grundform des Verbums neben dem Präsens auch die Tempusbedeutungen des Imperfekts, Perfekts und Plusquamperfekts einschließe und nur das Futur einen eigenen morphologischen Ausdruck habe, daß auch die Nomina Tempora haben (nach heutiger Vorstellung eher Aspekte wie 'perfektiv', z. B. *mbaêpoéra* "gewesene, nicht mehr existente oder zugehörige Sache", *versus* 'destinativ', z. B. *eimeéng xepinda-ráma* "gib 1.P.Sg.-Angelhaken-DEST", "gib mir die Angelhaken (die bestimmt sind, meine Angelhaken zu werden)", Anchieta 1595: 47) usw.

Er unterscheidet aktive, d. h. transitive, und neutrale, d. h. intransitive Verben, die als Personenmarkierung Präfixe ('Artikel' in seiner Terminologie) tragen, und bemerkt, daß auch Nomina wie intransitive Verben konjugiert werden können, jedoch mit der nominalen Personenkennzeichnung durch präfigierte Personalpronomina (z. B. *xemaenduâr* "ich erinnere mich", aber auch "meine Erinnerung", und *naxemaenduári* "ich erinnere mich nicht, ich habe keine Erinnerung"). Daneben stellt er eine intransitive reflexive synthetische Konjugation (*neutro reciproco*, mit dem Präfix *-yè-* nach dem 'Artikel') fest, z. B. *ayejucâ* "ich töte(te) mich", die, wie er sagt, auch in passivischem Sinne gebraucht werde, z. B. *oyeû* "comeditur, comestibilis est" (Anchieta 1595: 49). Damit ist er nicht nur ein Vorläufer der heute üblichen Verwechslung von Passiv und unpersönlicher bzw. medialer Handlung (vgl. span. *esto se come* "man ißt es"; siehe auch Quesada 1997), sondern bringt auch einen ersten Beleg für die frühe Verwendung dieser Diathese im Tupí-Guaraní, die man sonst in ihrem heutigen Gebrauch im paraguayischen Guaraní für einen Hispanismus halten würde. Auch die reziproke Diathese mit *-yo-* (*reciproco mutuo*, z. B. *oroyo jucâ* "wir töte(te)n uns gegenseitig", Anchieta 1595: 49f.) ist erkannt und korrekt beschrieben. Somit kommt, wie Rodrigues (1997: 396ff.) und Pottier (1998: 176) dargelegt haben, Anchieta in der Geschichte der Erforschung einer historisch herausragenden Tupí-Guaraní-Sprache wie dem Tupinambá sowohl chronologisch als auch in der linguistischen Analysefähigkeit eine Pionierrolle zu.

### 2.3. Die Grammatik von Luis Figueira

Auch diese Grammatik der 'língua do Brasil', wie Luis Figueira (1573–1643) sie schon nennt, geht ohne Vorwort gleich *medias in res*. Sie folgt in ihrem Aufbau im wesentlichen Anchieta, ist aber in der Darstellung ausführlicher, gleichzeitig aber auch schulmeisterlicher. Im phonischen Bereich erkennt er ebenso wenig wie irgendeiner der Zeitgenossen, auch nicht Montoya (1640), die Existenz des Glottisverschlusses vor Vokal, z. B. in [ʃembaˈʔe] "meine Sache". Trotz der Aussage, daß die Sprache ebenso wie das Portugiesische keine Kasus habe, gibt er dann in kontrastiver Übersetzungsmanier an, wie jeder lateinische Kasus auszudrücken sei (Figueira 1795: 4f.). Unter den Modi nennt er immer noch einen – allerdings nur syntagmatisch zu bildenden – Optativ, gibt jedoch den Terminus 'Konjunktiv' Anchietas für den morphologisch in Opposition zum Indikativ stehenden Modus auf und benennt ihn richtiger als 'Permissiv' (z. B. *t-o-jucà* "soll er [ihn/sie/es] doch töten!", Figueira 1795: 11). Etwas überraschend wird in der Mitte der Grammatik, nach der ersten Beschreibung der Nomina und Verben, wie wenn eine neue, aber eigentlich traditionellere Richtung der Analyse einsetzte, festgestellt, daß die Sprache acht Wortarten aufweise (Figueira 1795: 48). Diese werden anschließend behandelt, allerdings in einer geschickten Weise, die zum einen zwar die klassischen Wortarten Nomen, Pronomen, Verb, Partizip, Präposition, Adverb, Interjektion und Konjunktion aufführt, diese aber wiederum eher als Kategorien der Ausgangssprache behandelt, indem Figueira darunter die Zielsprache in ihren eigenen Strukturen beschreibt, z. B. 'Präpositionen' als Postpositionen oder Suffixe oder etwa innerhalb der Nomina weitere Unterscheidungen trifft, wie z. B. Adjektive, nominale Verbalformen mit ihren jeweiligen Tempusmarkierungen usw.

Der abschließende Teil der Grammatik ist – eine Neuheit gegenüber Anchieta – der Syntax gewidmet (Figueira 1795: 92–102). Hier werden Fragen der Konstruktion der pronominalen Objekte und der abhängigen Sätze, immer ausgehend vom Portugiesischen, behandelt. Nur bei den Bemerkungen zur Stellung der Satzglieder zueinander (1795: 101–102) steht das Tupinambá im Vordergrund.

## 3. Das Guaraní in Paraguay

### 3.1. Soziale und sprachliche 'Reduktion'

Seit 1601 waren die Jesuiten in Asunción tätig und mit dem Studium des östlich davon verbreiteten Guaraní beschäftigt. In den zahlreichen überlieferten Korrespondenzen und der Geschichtsschreibung der Missionare ist bezeugt, daß sie selbstverständlich die Grammatik Anchietas kannten und daß darauf aufbauend verschiedene Mönche Grammatiken und Wörterbücher des Guaraní verfaßten, darunter besonders Fray Luis Bolaños, dessen schon vor 1611 verfaßten Werke allerdings nicht erhalten sind (Montoya 1993: 24f.). Am bedeutendsten ist hier Montoya (1640), dessen Hauptwerke jedoch seine Wörterbücher sind (vgl. Dietrich 1991). Er, der aus Lima stammte, dort 1606 in den Orden eintrat und eine Ausbildung erhielt, in die auch die Erfahrungen des Padre Diego González Holguín aus der Beschreibung des Quechua einging (→ Art. 129), kam 1612 über Asunción in die Mission Loreto im Guairá-Gebiet, auf halbem Wege zwischen Asunción und São Paulo gelegen, im heutigen brasilianischen Bundesstaat Paraná. Montoyas Sprachbegabung wird allenthalben gerühmt, außer dem gründlich erlernten Guaraní soll er auch Yvyjára (eine Guaraníbezeichnung für das Kaingáng aus der Jê-Familie in Paraná gelernt haben (Montoya 1993: 26f.). Um 1616 waren seine Guaraní-Grammatik und das Wörterbuch Spanisch-Guaraní ("Vocabulario") im wesentlichen fertig (Montoya 1993: 28), der "Tesoro", das Wörterbuch Guaraní-Spanisch als wertvollster und reichster Teil der Beschreibung erst später. Alles wurde erst 1639/40 gedruckt, nachdem in den zwanziger Jahren schon eine weitere Kurzgrammatik im Manuskript in den Missionen um den Río Uruguay kursierte, die erst vor kurzem im Druck erschienen ist (Aragona 1979, Manuskript der Grammatik 1629).

Die spanischen wie die portugiesischen Siedler des Guairá-Gebietes übten in ihrer Suche nach indianischen Sklaven von 1620 an einen derart verstärkten Druck auf die Jesuitenmissionen aus, daß diese unter Montoyas Leitung aufgegeben und mitsamt einer großen Schar von Indios im ruhigeren Südparaguay als befestigte Siedlungen, sogenannte 'Reduktionen' neu gegründet wurden. So, wie die Missionare unter 'Reduktion' die Indios durch den Zusammenschluß in großen Dörfern aus der Vereinzelung des Waldlebens zu wahrhaft 'politischem' und menschlichem Leben bringen wollten, so wollten sie auch die Sprache grammatisch 'reduzieren', d. h. die Redeweise der Indios zu neuen thematischen und stilistischen Ausdrucksformen führen, indem sie ihr mythisches Denken zugunsten christlichen und rationalen Argumentierens aufgeben sollten. Oberflächlich morphologisch und syntaktisch bleiben die von Anchieta, Montoya und allen anderen beschriebenen Sprachen die orginalen, sozio-, pragma- und textlinguistisch gesehen aber werden sie von tribalen zu europäisierten, mestizischen. Dies zeigt sich nicht in der morphologischen und syntaktischen Beschreibung der Grammatiken, sondern in den Wörterbüchern, die den Sprachausbau im christlichen

Sinne widerspiegeln, z. B. durch die Schaffung von Termini wie *abaré*, wörtl. "Nach-Mensch, Übermensch" für "Priester", *ai-mo-jasuk* "1.P.Sg.-CAUS-sich baden" für "taufen" (Drumond 1952: 53, s. v. *bautizar*), *a-mo-Tupã-raý* "1.P.Sg.-CAUS-Gott-Sohn", "zum Sohn Gottes machen, taufen" (Montoya 1876: 105, s. v. *baptizar*), die aber auch den Ausbau in den neuen sozialen Verhältnissen dokumentieren, indem z. B. das Konzept *yoguá* "sich zum Herrn machen von etwas" umgedeutet wird zu "kaufen" oder *poria-hú* "Korb-sich (be)finden", "sich in unangenehmer Lage befinden" bewußt für "arm" eingesetzt wird (vgl. auch Morínigo 1990: 89–99). So kann man im lexikalischen Bereich des jesuitischen Guaraní durchaus von einer Plansprache sprechen, ein Verfahren, das augenblicklich auch beim modernen Ausbau des paraguayischen Guaraní angewandt wird, z. B. *ysypó mbyrý* "Fern-Liane" oder *pumbyrý* "Fern-Ton" für "Telefon".

### 3.2. Die Grammatikbeschreibung des Antonio Ruiz de Montoya (1585–1652)

Systematisch hat Montoya das Guaraní der Guairá-Region in seiner Grammatik beschrieben, die reichhaltigsten Informationen finden sich aber – noch unaufgearbeitet (vgl. Montoya 1993: 35) – in seinem *Tesoro*, dem guaraní-spanischen Wörterbuch. Die 100 Seiten umfassende Grammatik beginnt mit einer sehr knappen phonetischen Beschreibung der vom Spanischen abweichenden Laute im "Preludio" und geht dann in 20 von den insgesamt 23 Kapiteln die üblichen acht Wortarten durch, ersetzt jedoch die 'Präposition' Figueiras gleich durch 'Postposition'. Kap. 1–4 sind dem Nomen, Kap. 5–15 der Morphologie und Syntax des Verbums, Kap. 16 den Fragekonstruktionen, Kap. 17 den Postpositionen, Kap. 18 dem Adverb, Kap. 19 der Interjektion, Kap. 20 den Konjunktionen gewidmet, deren Bedeutung und Gebrauch sich jedoch nur aus dem *Tesoro* erschließen läßt. In Kap. 21 versucht Montoya eine syntaktische Typologie der Verben, die er wie seine Vorgänger in aktive (mit direktem Objekt), neutrale (mit Postpositional- bzw. Suffixrektion) und absolute (intransitive, ohne Ergänzung) gliedert. Die letzten beiden Kapitel betreffen lautliche und orthographische Fragen und behandeln auch die sehr wichtigen morphonologischen Prozesse bei der Flexion und Derivation.

Grundsätzliche Neuerungen in der linguistischen Analyse sind gegenüber Figueira, mit dem er sich am ehesten vergleichen läßt, nicht zu erkennen. Freilich ist nicht ausgemacht, daß Figueira nicht etwa von Montoya als dem damals berühmteren Sprachlehrer gelernt hat und nicht umgekehrt Montoya sich hat von Figueira inspirieren lassen. Montoya benutzt die vorgegebenen Wortarten nur als traditionelle Muster der Ausgangssprache, um die dem Guaraní eigenen Kategorien durchaus hervortreten zu lassen (inklusive und exklusive 1. P. Pl.; reflexive ('reziproke') und nicht-reflexive ('relative') Possessivmarkierung des Nomens, z. B. *ç-oó* "Fleisch", *h-oó* "sein / dessen Fleisch", *gu-oó* "sein (eigenes) Fleisch"; die reflexive und reziproke Diathese des Verbs (vgl. oben 2.2.), die auch schon von Anchieta (Kap. 15) beschriebenen Formen der Reduplikation des Verbstammes zum Ausdruck der frequenten Verbalhandlung oder zur Intensivierung des Objekts (z. B. "viel essen", Montoya 1640, Kap. 12) usw.). Montoya erkennt auch das Fehlen der Temporalität beim Verbum und den im wesentlichen durch 'Partikeln' oder 'Adverbien' geleisteten syntagmatischen Ausdruck von Tempus und Aspekt (1640: 18).

Montoya beschreibt die Valenzerhöhung des Verbs ('Bildung aktiver aus neutralen Verben', Kap. 10) mit *m(b)ɔ-* "faktitiv" ("se refiere solo al paciente" ['bezieht sich nur auf das Patiens'], wie z. B. *a-mbo-bahẽ* "ich lasse kommen, ohne daß ich mitkomme)" gegenüber *ro-* "soziativ-faktitiv", wie *a-ro-bahẽ* "ich lasse kommen, indem ich mitkomme", "ich begleite", *versus* *-ucá* "kausativ (bei schon transiven Verben)", wie etwa *y-apó-ucá* "ich lasse (es) machen" ("haze hazer la cosa por una tercera persona" ['läßt die Sache durch einen Dritten machen'], Montoya 1640: 48f.).

Das in der jesuitischen Tradition verfestigte Wissen über das Guaraní, das auf Ruiz de Montoya (1640) und Aragona (1979 [1629]) aufbauend vor allem in zahlreichen Katechismen von Kennern der Sprache wie dem akkulturierten Indio Nicolás Yapuguay und dem Padre Simón Bandini angewendet worden war, wird in der Grammatik Restivos (1724) vor allem in Form von ausführlichen Anmerkungen und Zusätzen ausgebreitet. Ihre moderne Fortsetzung finden sie in den Grammatiken des heutigen Paraguay-Guaraní, z. B. von Guasch (1976) und Ayala (1989). Von weitaus größerem linguistischen Interesse sind jedoch die Werke Anchietas und Montoyas selbst.

## 4. Heutige Bedeutung der Amerindianistik

Nach den Sprachbeschreibungen durch die frühen Missionare und die Ethnologen des 19. und frühen 20. Jh. haben die Eingeborenensprachen Südamerikas seit etwa 1960 die Beachtung der modernen Linguistik gefunden, vor allem von nordamerikanischer, zunehmend aber auch von europäischer Seite. Im Rahmen der Erforschung syntaktischer Strukturen und Universalien, aber auch genetischer und klassifikatorischer Fragestellungen spielen die südamerikanischen Sprachen zunehmend eine größere Rolle, darunter auch diejenigen der Tupí-Guaraní-Familie und des Tupí-Stammes, vor allem jedoch die tribalen Sprachen (Rodrigues 1986: 41–46; Kakumasu 1986; Dietrich 1986; Jensen 1989, 1998, 1999; Cabral 1995; Schleicher 1998).

## 5. Bibliographie

Anchieta, Joseph de, S. J. 1595. *Arte de grammatica da lingoa mais usada na costa do Brasil.* Coimbra: Antonio de Mariz. Novamente dada áluz por Julio Platzmann, Lipsia: Teubner, 1874. (Faksimile-Ausgabe durch Platzmann, Leipzig: B. G. Teubner, 1876.)

–. *Arte de gramática da língua mais usada na costa do Brasil.* 1990. Edição facsimilar, obras completas, 11° volume. Apresentação do Prof. Dr. Carlos Drumond, aditamentos do Padre Armando Cardoso, S. J. São Paulo: Loyola.

Aragona, Alonso de. 1979. "Breve introducción para aprender la lengua guaraní por el P. Alonso de Aragona. Presentación, edición y notas por Bartomeu Melià, S. J.". *Amerindia* 4.23–61.

Ayala, Valentín. 1989. *Gramática guaraní.* Corrientes: Cícero Impresiones.

Cabral, Ana Suelly de Arruda Câmara. 1995. *Contact-induced Language Change in the Western Amazon: The Non-genetic Origin of the Kokama Language.* Diss. University of Pittsburgh.

Dietrich, Wolf. 1986. *El idioma chiriguano. Gramática, textos, vocabulario.* Madrid: Instituto de Cooperación Iberoamericana.

–. 1991. "Die Lexikographie des Tupí-Guaraní". *Wörterbücher / Dictionaries / Dictionnaires. Ein internationales Handbuch zur Lexikographie* hg. von F. J. Hausmann, O. Reichmann, H.-E. Wiegand & L. Zgusta, Art. 276, Bd. III, 2670–2676. Berlin: de Gruyter.

Drumond, Carlos, Hg. 1952–53. *Vocabulário na língua brasílica.* 2ª edição revista e confrontada com o Ms. fg., 3144 da Bibl. Nacional de Lisboa, Bd. 1: *A–H*, Bd. 2: *I–Z*. São Paulo: Faculdade de Filosofia, Ciências e Letras, Boletim 137 & 164.

Figueira, Luis. [1621]. *Arte da lingua brasilica.* Lisboa: Manuel da S. Menescal. (3. Aufl. *Arte da grammatica da lingua brasilica.* Lisboa: Miguel Deslandes, 1687; 4. Aufl. Lisboa: Off. Patriarcal, 1795.)

Guasch, P. Antonio, S. J., 1976. *El idioma guaraní: Gramática y antología de prosa y verso.* 4ª ed. refundida y acrecentada. Asunción: Loyola.

Hervás y Panduro, Lorenzo. 1785. *Catalogo delle lingue conosciute e notizia della loro affinità e diversità.* Cesena: G. Biasini.

Jensen, Cheryl Joyce S. 1989. *O desenvolvimento histórico da língua Wayampi.* Campinas: Editora da UNICAMP.

–. 1998. "Comparative Studies: Tupí-Guaraní". *Handbook of Amazonian Languages*, Bd. IV, hg. von Desmond C. Derbyshire & Geoffrey K. Pullum, 487–618. Berlin–New York: Mouton de Gruyter.

–. 1999. "Tupí-Guaraní". *The Amazonian Languages*, hg. von R. M. W. Dixon & Alexandra Y. Aikhenvald, 125–163. Cambridge: Cambridge University Press.

Kakumasu, James. 1986. "Urubu-Kaapor". *Handbook of Amazonian Languages*, Bd. I, hg. von Desmond C. Derbyshire & Geoffrey Pullum, 326–402. Berlin–New York–Amsterdam: Mouton de Gruyter.

Léry, Jean de, 1578. *Histoire d'un voyage fait en la terre du Bresil, autrement dite Amerique* [...]. [La Rochelle]: Antoine Chuppin. (Moderner Nachdruck der Ausgabe Genf 1580: Lausanne: Bibliothèque Romande, 1972.)

Montoya, Antonio Ruiz de, S. J. (1639). *Tesoro de la lengua Guaraní.* Madrid: Iuan Sanchez. (Faksimile-Ausgabe durch Julius Platzmann, Leipzig: Teubner, 1876.)

Montoya, Antonio Ruiz de, S. J. 1640. *Arte, y bocabulario de la lengua guarani.* Madrid: Iuan Sanchez. (Faksimile-Ausgabe durch Julius Platzmann, Leipzig: Teubner, 1876. *Arte de la lengua guaraní. 1640;* Edición facsimilar con introducción y notas por Bartomeu Meliá, S. I. Asunción del Paraguay: Centro de Estudios Paraguayos "Antonio Guasch", 1993.)

Morínigo, Marcos Augusto. 1990. *Raíz y destino del guaraní.* Asunción: Universidad Católica.

Pottier, Bernard. 1998. "La gramática del Padre Ioseph de Anchieta". *Suplemento Antropológico* (Asunción/Paraguay) 33.155–176.

Quesada, J. Diego. 1997. "Die spanische *se*-Fügung ist kein Passiv". *ZRPh* 113: 1.65–81.

Restivo, Paulo, S. J. 1724. *Arte de la lengua guaraní por el P. Antonio Ruiz de Montoya* [...] *con escolios, anotaciones y apéndices del P. Paulo Restivo.* Pueblo de Santa Maria la Mayor [heute Misiones / Argentinien]. (Neuausgabe durch Christian Friedrich Seybold. 1892. *Linguae Guarani Grammatica Hispanice* [...]. Stuttgart: Kohlhammer.)

Rodrigues, Aryon Dall'Igna. 1986. *Línguas brasileiras: para o conhecimento das línguas indígenas.* São Paulo: Edições Loyola.

Rodrigues, Aryon D. 1997. "Descripción del tupinambá en el período colonial: El *Arte* de José de Anchieta". *La descripción de las lenguas amerindias en el período colonial* hg. von Klaus Zimmermann. 371–400. Frankfurt/M.: Vervuert, Madrid: Iberoamericana.

Schleicher, Charles Owen. 1998. *Comparative and Internal Reconstruction of the Tupi-Guarani Language Family.* Diss. Madison: University of Wisconsin (published by UMI: Ann Arbor, 1999).

Seki, Lucy. 2000. *Gramática do kamaiurá – língua tupi-guarani do Alto Xingu.* Campinas: Editora da UNICAMP.

Staden, Hans. 1557. *Warhaftige Historia eyner Landschafft der wilden nacketen grimmigen Menschenfresser-Leuthen in der Newenwelt America gelegen.* Marburg: Andreas Kolben.

Tovar, Antonio & Consuelo Larrucea de Tovar. 1984. *Catálogo de las lenguas de América del Sur.* Nueva edición refundida. Madrid: Gredos.

*Wolf Dietrich, Münster (Deutschland)*

# 131. The study of the native languages of North America: The French Tradition

1. Early exploration
2. Early settlement
3. Missionary linguistics
4. Geographical realities
5. Missionary attitudes
6. The orthographic traditions
7. The Micmac hieroglyphics
8. 19th-century studies
9. 20th-century studies
10. Conclusion
11. Bibliography

## 1. Early exploration

Among the most important of the early explorers of North America was the Frenchman Jacques Cartier who sailed from St. Malo in 1534 and explored the Northeast coast of Newfoundland and the Gulf of St. Lawrence. Cartier recorded the names of birds from Newfoundland, a sentence possibly in Montagnais from the north shore of the Gulf, and a sentence in Micmac from Bay des Chaleurs on the south shore. He also took with him on his return two boys from an Indian village on the tip of the Gaspé Peninsula, and at the end of the narration of his voyage recorded a vocabulary of "the newly found land, called New France" (Biggar 1924: 80–81), probably taken down from these boys. The language is Iroquoian, inidicating that the Iroquois, who controlled the St. Lawrence River valley at the time of the early contacts, moved down as far as the Gulf of St. Lawrence in the summertime.

The next year he returned and ascended the St. Lawrence River valley as far as the Iroquoian village of Hochelaga (modern Montreal), where the Lachine Rapids prevented any further progress to ocean-going vessels.

This early contact with two different linguistic families, Algonkian (Montagnais and Micmac) and Iroquoian (Huron and possibly Mohawk) was predictable, since speakers of these two major linguistic groupings occupy most of Northeast North America, the only other group being the Inuktitut who occupy the Labrador coast, the northern part of the Labrador peninsula, and the Arctic islands.

## 2. Early settlement

The first settlement in Canada was Samuel de Champlain's 1604 establishment on the East coast, close to what is now the US border. Champlain soon moved to Port Royal in Nova Scotia, where he made an allliance with the Micmac chief Membertou, a remarkable individual who in 1610 became the first aboriginal to be baptized on the North American continent. The missionaries that came with Champlain were the forerunners of those who would accompany all the early explorations, and would devote themselves to the study of the Iroquoian and Algonkian languages they encountered in order to translate the scriptures and the liturgy, and to instruct their new allies in the Christian faith.

There is also a most interesting and perceptive narrative of the early days of the early Port Royal settlement from the pen of Marc Lescarbot (1609 [1866]), a lawyer who accompanied the expedition. It is from him that we have the detailed narratives of Membertou, shaman, chief, healer, strategist, orator, a leader who encouraged his people to learn from the Europeans, and insisted that the European boats entering Port Royal harbour should fire a 21 gun salute in his honour, a courtesy reserved for royalty among European nations. Lescarbot also gives us descriptions of dances, speeches, preparations for war, and the numbers 1–10 in Micmac and Abenaki.

## 3. Missionary linguistics

The voyages of discovery led to a world wide missionary activity that has gone on from 1500 to the present day, accompanied by a great deal of linguistic analysis and description resulting in the production of large numbers of grammars, dictionaries, and other linguistic works. Hovdhaugen (1996: 14–15) gives the following definition of a missionary grammar;

> [...] a description of a particular language created as part of missionary work by non-native missionaries. It is a pedagogical, synchronic grammar covering phonology, morphology and syntax based on data mainly from an oral corpus (in a few cases from religious – mostly translated – texts).

Grammars were pedagogical because the missionaries were endeavouring to pass on to their colleagues and successors the knowledge that they had gained in a very hard school, by dint of listening, thinking, analysing, and finally understanding, over a long period, usually a minimum of five to seven years of continuous endeavour. Hanzeli's detailed documentation of the work of the French missionaries in North America (1969), a fine work of scholarship based upon a meticulous survey of manuscripts in archives, is also an engrossing read because it describes the daily lives and careers of those who set themselves to study in this hard school, in which several of them lost their lives.

The first missionaries were Recollects, a sub-order of Franciscans, one of whom, Chrétien Leclercq, in 1691 published a book, *La nouvelle relation de la Gaspésie*, describing his life among the Micmac, and his struggles to learn the language. He also tells of how he began, about 1677, to develop a system of hieroglyphic writing, based on native patterns, to help his catechists learn their prayers.

He had noted that they themselves would often make marks on birchbark, using shapes and forms that were employed in decoration, such as the typical Algonkian double scroll motive, and he adapted these native marks, used as an *aide-mémoire*, to compose a rudimentary orthographical system of hieroglyphics, that Father Maillard, in the next century would adapt to create an aboriginal prayer book (see section 7).

The Recollects were soon followed by Jesuits, who, in their annual reports to their Superiors in Europe have left us a very complete picture not only of the missionary endeavors but also of the linguistic studies of the missionaries themselves. The missions were centrally controlled by the Archdiocese of Quebec, established in the 1640's: the Archbishop's library and the Archives of the Séminaire de Québec are today storehouses of valuable manuscripts, grammars, dictionaries, prayer books, catechisms, written in Amerindian languages by missionaries who lived for years among the Huron, the Micmac, the Montagnais, the Algonkins, and the Abenaki, and whose work, when they died, was deposited in these centralized archives.

There are many works in other archives in Montreal, Ottawa, and Nicolet, as well as works that found their way to the Bibliothèque Nationale in Paris. These are listed by Hanzeli in his Appendix D (1969: 125–128), which gives an overview of the archives and their manuscripts. There are also items not listed by Hanzeli that found their way to other destinations in France: the Treasury of the cathedral at Chartres, for example, has on display a 17th century manuscript written in Abenaki.

## 4. Geographical realities

Before contact times the Iroquois, enemies of the Algonkians, and feared by the latter because of their superior technology and organization, had driven northwards into the St. Lawrence River valley, and divided the speakers of Algonkian languages into two groups: those who lived to the west and north of the St. Lawrence (Central Algonkians, e. g. Algonkins in the south and Montagnais in the north), and those who lived to the east of the river and its estuary and south of the Gulf of St. Lawrence (Eastern Algonkians, e. g. Abenaki in the south and Micmac in the north). The Jesuits recognized that there were two major linguistic groupings, that they referred to vaguely as "Huron-Iroquois and Algonkin-Montagnais"; they normally sent out two missionaries to explore new areas, one with competence in an Iroquoian language, and one competent in an Algonkian language (Hanzeli 1969: 53). Central Algonkian languages, however, are sufficiently different from languages of the Eastern group that a knowledge of Abenaki (from Eastern Algonkian) would be all but useless for missionary work among the Montagnais, for example.

## 5. Missionary attitudes

The early missonaries, reared on a diet of Latin and Greek, used the linguistic tools of the ancient grammarians that had become a part of the tradition of European linguistic scholarship. Their first reaction was to note what was missing from the native languages they studied: Hanzeli (1969: 59) quotes Father Brébeuf (one of the ablest of the Jesuit linguists – fluent in both Huron and Montagnais) writing about Huron in the 1636 *Relation*, for example: "Ils ne cognoissent point de B. L. F. M. P. X. Z et jamais I. E. V. ne leur sont consonnes. La plupart de leurs mots sont composés de voyelles. Toutes les lettres labiales leur manquent." (A notable feature of Iroquoian languages is their lack of labials, so that *Marie*, for example, turns up as *Ouarie*, /w/ being the closest approximation to /m/).

A later reaction was the admiration that they expressed for grammatical categories that for them were completely exotic, and for the representational possibilities, especially derivational possibilities that these languages provided (see Section 9) which were not available to the same degree in Indo-European languages (see, for example, Hanzeli 1969: 45).

As well as the commentaries from the Jesuit Relations, we have extensive commentaries from Fr. Pierre Maillard, a Spiritain (Order of the Holy Spirit) who worked among the Micmac in Nova Scotia from 1735 to 1762. Maillard expresses his admiration for Micmac: "a language extremely rich and expressive". He himself was a master of spoken Micmac, admired by the Indians as being the equal of their most distinguished orators.

Maillard in his grammar, written in the middle of the 17th century, now lost, but published from a copy in 1864, gives as an example of the subtleties of Algonkian languages the difference between the first person plural inclusive in Micmac (*kinu*) and the first person plural exclusive (*ninen*) (1864: 9–10):

> There is a notable difference between kinu and ninen. The Indians speaking to the French will say *ninen l'nuiek, we Indians*: because those to whom they speak are not included in this *we*. But talking among Indians they will say *kinu l'nui'kw*. The verbal inflections also mark the difference, in both dual and the plural. One would be hard pressed to find, in scholarly and polite languages, a distinction at once so delicate and so logical. (Translated, with Micmac words transcribed into the modern orthography, where the apostrophe marks a syllabic sonorant or a long vowel).

Maillard produced a massive documentation in Micmac. He drafted all the liturgical offices, the usual prayers, the catechism, numerous passages of Scripture, long sermons and other instructions, and finally a detailed questionnaire for confession (130 pages) in French and in Micmac, which could be used for the study of the language as well as for the ministry. In 1755 he wrote a long letter (published in 1863) to M. de Lalanne, his Superior, of the Foreign Missions, in which he commented:

> What it costs, Sir, in work, in struggle, and in burning the midnight oil, to learn these sorts of languages by oneself, and to finally manage to pronounce the words: I dare not say the number of years spent on this work. Eight years devoted almost solely to this have not been enough (qu. Pacifique 1939: 4, translated JH).

## 6. The orthographic traditions

Maillard's Micmac orthography was also obviously influenced by the practices of the Jesuits in developing scripts for Amerindian languages; it is clear that he had access to their works in the central archives of the missions. Working on Algonkian and Iroquoian languages, the Jesuits had noticed that the high back vowels [o] and [u] were not distinctive, and that both allophones alternated with [w]. Sometimes they would use their own French spelling *ou* for a high back vowel, which is a digraph because in the history of French /u/ was fronted to /y/, and consequently the *u* spelling in French has represented /y/ for about a thousand years. A similar digraph has been used in Greek for over two thousand years, and for the same reason: the fronting of the high back vowel. Consequently, in Medieval and Modern Greek the only vowel that is normally spelled with a digraph is /u/. Aware that the medieval Greek scribes had written this digraph vertically, with the *u* written over the *o*, the Jesuits borrowed this Medieval Greek digraph to represent [u], [o], [w], all allophones of /o/. They also used it for the long vowels [u:] and [o:], allophones of /o:/, and even began to use it for the French glosses in their dictionaries: Hanzeli, noting that this ligature first appeared in print "in Brébeuf's account of Huron in the Relations of 1636", comments that "most missionaries occasionally lapsed into using *ŏ* in French words for *o* or *ou*, e. g., *sŏlier, cŏper, cŏteau* [...]" (1969: 73). Maillard also used this digraph in writing Micmac to represent /u:/, /u/, and /w/, and writing *o* for Micmac /o:/ and /o/. Like the other missionaries, he also occasionally lapsed into using *ŏ* for French /u/, writing the letter with a single stroke, much like an 8 open at the top.

On p. 10 of his grammar (published by John Gilmary Shea in 1864) he gives us his explicit reason for using this symbol: having just written the Micmac word n'ouschiou-oouak (for which the text has no gloss) he comments "Mais comme je m'apperçois que la diphtongue *ou* rend ces mots difficiles à lire, j'y suppléerai à l'avenir par le caractère grec *ŏ* (ou par un 8 caractère des chiffres), et on dira alors: nŏschiŏoŏak, *nos pères*". (This appears to be a miscopying of *kujjiwowaq* "your (pl) late father", and the gloss "nos pères" may have been added by Fr. Bellenger, who made the copy from which the printed version was made).

One of the features that distinguishes Montagnais from other dialects of Cree is the palatalization of /k/ before front vowels: Moose Cree *kikiske:limitin* "I know you" is heard as /čičisse:nimitin/ in the *n*-dialect of Montagnais on the North Shore of the Gulf of St. Lawrence. Although a similar palatalization (k > ts) had occurred in the passage from Latin to French, (L. *caelum* > Fr. *ciel*) the resulting affricate had been reduced to /s/ in French (*ciel* = *[sjɛl]*) and there was no simple way of spelling /č/ in French. The situation was complicated by the fact that all the variants from /k/ to /č/ could be heard among the Montagnais informants, as shows from the glosses in the dictionaries of Fabvre (1679–93/1970) and Silvy (1678–84/1974). Brébeuf's use of *Khi* to represent this phoneme in his report of 1636 in the *Relations* indicates a palatalized /k/, but he says it was also used by the Algonkins, where it would have been the /č/ that is common to Algonkian languages and has been reconstructed for Proto-Algonkian. Both are written *tsh* in the orthography that developed among the 19th century French missionaries: Lemoine (see Section 8) spells this root *tshiselim* in his 1901 dictionary based on the l-dialect from Lac St-Jean, 150 miles north of Quebec City. Here we note an odd mixture of English and French orthographical traditions: *sh* instead of French *ch* for /š/, but *tsh* for /č/ instead of English *ch*. Maillard, by contrast used *tch* for the /č/ in Micmac.

Maillard also used a capital *K*, normally with a bar across the top and an acute accent, to mark the post-velar /q/ of Micmac. This sound does not occur in European languages, but Maillard noted the phonemic contrast with /k/, and the consequent necessity for a distinctive orthographic representation. He also follows the pattern of the older missionaries of using *k* instead of c; k is very rare in French: it was not part of the Latin alphabet (it is from Greek). Consequently it had not suffered from the Late Latin palatalization of velars before front vowels, and kept the same value before all vowels, unlike French *c*, *g*. Sometimes however Maillard used *g* when /k/ was voiced in intervocalic position (voicing being non-contrastive in all Algonkian languages), writing *meguidèdemek* for *mekite't-mek* [megide:dm̩ek] "we (exclusive) honour it", the *u* being added in the French orthographic tradition to make the *g* "hard" before front vowels. In passing we may note that Maillard has marked the long vowel (*è*), but does not distinguish the schwa from the front vowel in his spelling *-emek* (he would have heard the syllabic /m/ as schwa + /m/; in fact, in his day the /m/ may not have been phonologically syllabic). This is entirely consistent with the rules of French orthography: the first *e* would be in an open syllable (automatically schwa, as in Fr. *ce*), and the second in a closed syllable (automatically low mid front vowel as in Fr. *cette*).

## 7. The Micmac hieroglyphics

One of the most remarkable orthographic products of all this missionary industry was a Micmac prayer book with an entirely hieroglyphic script. Maillard obviously had access to the work of the Franciscan Leclercq from the previous century, and adapted and expanded Leclercq's hieroglyphics (see Section

3. above) to create a complete hieroglyphic Prayer Book of which the Indians made their own personal copies on birch bark, and later, in the 19th century, on paper. In the British Library in London there are two birch bark manuscripts (Additional MS 11038 – probably the only birch bark in the whole collection!) which show samples of the hieroglyphics collected in Newfoundland in the summer of 1791 by John Thompson, a midshipman on HMS Fly, on summer duty in Newfoundland waters. Thompson sent these two pieces of birch bark, one of which has the *Our Father*, the other the *Hail Mary* in Maillard's hieroglyphics to Sir Joseph Banks, President of the Royal Society, the great antiquarian who was interested (among other things) in the writing systems of the world. Thompson's accompanyinig letter, dated 13 September 1791, reporting that the Indians wrote with "a stick in the shape of a pen", is in the same folder, and Banks must have replied since there is a further letter from Thompson dated 10 December 1791 which informs Banks that every Micmac household has a birch bark prayer book. Thompson offered "any prize for one of these books" but the Micmac "would not part with them upon any account".

There appear to be no extant copies of the birch bark books of hieroglyphics, but there are copies on paper from the next century: there is one in the Princeton University Library, for example, with the paper watermarked with the date 1825, and fragments of such a book in the Houghton Library at Harvard. There is also a somewhat tattered example, bound in caribou skin in the possession of the Conne River Band in Newfoundland, dating from before 1830.

In the second half of the 19th century this hieroglyphic Prayer Book was eventually set in print, through the services of Father Christian Kauder, a Redemptorist priest from Luxemburg, who had settled in Nova Scotia, was intrigued by the Micmacs' attachment to their hieroglyphic prayer book, and through influential friends in the Austrian court had an edition printed in Vienna in 1866 (Lenhart 1922). The total number of types, specially cast, was 5703, and after the printing they were never used again. Even worse, almost all of this first edition was lost in a shipwreck at sea, and never reached Canada. A second edition, organized by Father Pacifique, (see below, section 9) was finally published in Canada in 1922. Both first and second editions are extremely rare and consequently sought after by collectors.

There has been little study of the Micmac hieroglyphics. An early article by Shea (1861) led to their inclusion in Pilling's massive Algonkian bibliography (1891), which devotes a page to the subject and prints a version of the Our Father in hieroglyphics. Marie Battiste has given us an interesting commentary on the ability of some dozen Micmacs still literate in the hieroglyphic tradition, who have passed down the two hundred and fifty year tradition to their juniors (1983: 106–108). Recently David Schmidt and Murdena Marshall have published (1995) a selection of prayers and readings from the hieroglyphic prayer book, with the Micmac text (in the new orthography) interlined with the hieroglyphics, so that native speakers may renew contact with the hieroglyphic script.

Obviously, this form of writing is not very profitable, since it would take a long time to master, and one needs to know the text first, so that the hieroglyphics are only a reminder of a text that is already known: it would be difficult to read a text that had not been known before. Since word formation in Micmac, as in all Algonkian languages, is quite complex, it would be also difficult to create simple ideograms to represent complex words, since account would have to be taken of the many formative elements in such words. It was inevitable with the passage of time that such a ponderous writing system should be replaced by a much simpler alphabetic system, and eventually the Micmac did develop a modified Latin alphabet which is, ironically, much the same as that used by Maillard in in his own manuscript prayer book and grammar designed for the missionaries. Maillard did not teach this simplified alphabet because of a paternalistic desire to shield his flock from secular literature (Johnson 1970: 83; Battiste 1983: 118–119).

## 8. 19th-century studies

By the end of the 18th century the Jesuits had disappeard from the missionary scene, and in the 19th century a new order of missionaries, the Oblate Fathers, took up missionary endeavours in the Canadian north, where they are still to be found today. They continued the linguistic work of their predecessors, and many of their linguistic manuscripts can be found in the Archives Deschâtelets, Scolasticat St. Joseph des Oblats, in Ottawa. The Foreword of the *Dictionnaire français-montagnais* (1901) of Father Lemoine, omi, tells us that the work was put together to further the work of the missionaries, to interest linguists by opening new horizons for their studies, and for the temporal and spiritual benefit of the native people themselves.

The 19th century also saw the beginning of the publication of manuscripts that had lain for decades in the archives. The American Academy of Arts and Sciences, as well as publishing works by English and German missionaries, published, for example, the substantial and impressive French-Abenaki dictionary of Fr. Sebastian Rasles (or Râle), a Jesuit missionary who had settled among the Abenaki at Nanrantsouack (modern day Norridgewock), on the Kennebec River about 200 miles east of Boston. This is a splendid work, and was until recently the only dictionary of Abenaki that was available. It is done in the style of the early missionaries with entries around a centre of interest: if one wants the word for *bear, moose,* or *beaver*, for example, the appropriate place to look is under the gloss "Animal".

## 9. 20th-century studies

The Oblate fathers have continued their missionary endeavours up to the present day with occasional publications such as Fr. Lemoine's second dictionary (1911), this time of Algonkin, and Fr. Schneider's impressive *Dictionnaire esquimau-français du parler de l'Ungava*, describing a dialect of Inuktitut from the Labrador peninsula where there is a phonological reduction of alternate consonant clusters in the process of word formation that is known to Eskimologists as "Schneider's Law", since he was the first to give an accurate description of the phenomenon.

The 20th century also saw the foundation of linguistics departments in the major francophone universities in Quebec, and the growth of academic interest in the aboriginal languages. Jean-Paul Vinay, who founded the Département de Linguistique at the Université de Montréal, did field work on Montagnais, and published, among his many other interests, occasional papers on Algonkian linguistics. The Centre d'Etudes Nordiques de l'Université Laval, in Quebec City, was also active in the latter half of the century in research on Montagnais and Inuktitut, producing grammars, dictionaries and texts, not only of the languages and dialects of Eastern Canada, but also of Inuktitut dialects of the North West Territories. The interest in aboriginal studies also spead to the new universities, especially to the various branches of the Université du Québec, which have grown up across the Province since the 1960's.

These new departments and research centres also continued the 19th century tradition of transcription and publication of older missionary manuscripts. The *Racines montagnaises* of the Jesuit Father Bonaventure Fabvre, who arrived in Quebec in 1679 and died in 1693, stored in the Archives of the Séminaire de Québec, was published in 1970 by the Centre d'Etudes Nordiques at Laval. Subsequently, the *Dictionnaire montagnais-français* of the Jesuit Antoine Silvy, preserved in the Public Archives of Canada at Ottawa, was transcribed by scholars from the Université du Québec à Chicoutimi, and published by the Presses de l'Université du Québec in 1974. In the closing years of the 20th century the universities, research centres, and research councils have sponsored a great range of research projects, field work, and publications, on the present state, history, and prehistory of the native languages of North America.

In the older missionary tradition there is also a remarkable Micmac grammar (1939) by Father Pacifique, ofmcap, a Capuchin (i. e. Franciscan) who worked among the Micmac of the Atlantic Provinces and Quebec from 1895 until his death in 1940. He was the last of a long line of missionary priests in the tradition of Leclercq and Maillard (see Sections 3 and 5 above), who spoke the Micmac language fluently, and worked assiduously on the documentation left by his distinguished predecessors. Fr. Pacifique's grammar is an extensive reference grammar, which traces in the Introduction the 250 year old tradition of missionary linguistic work on the Micmac language.

After some 27 chapters dealing with the basics of phonology, and the paradigms of noun morphology and verb morphology, Pacifique has a chapter on verb classification that illustrates the extraordinary capacity for derivation of verbal forms that so captivated the early missionaries when they gained proficiency at these languages. Nouns in Algonkian languages have two genders, called *noble* and *ignoble* by the early Jesuits and Maillard, but today called animate and inanimate. Intransitive verbs agree with their subjects, their morphology being either AI (animate intransitive) or II (inanimate intransitive). Transitive verbs agree with the gender of the patient, being either TA (transitive with animate goal) or TI (transitive with inanimate goal). The cumulative markers of these four categories are suffixed to the lexical stem, and are called *finals*. If we take a simple stem such as Micmac *wel(i)-* "good", for example, we may add a stative AI final to get *welei* "I am well", or a progressive AI final to get *weliey* "I am happy". Such verbs can then be transformed into TA verbs: *weleyaq* "I treat him well", or TI verbs: *welo'tm* "I treat it well". These transitive verbs can then be recycled as AI middle voice forms with final /-si/: *weleyasi* "I treat myself well", and *welo'tasi* "I do well for myself". Alternatively an "inverse" final may be added to produce a passive: *weleyuksi* "I am well treated", *welo'tmuksi* "I am blessed in my affairs". Or, in the case of the TI, a further TA final may be added to give a two-goal TA verb: *welo'tmaq* "I look after his interests for him", where the goal is primarily animate (him), but secondarily inanimate (his interests). Alternatively an indefinite object AI final may be added to the TI: *welo'tekey* "I do (things) well, I make progress". Or the two-goal TA may be made into an AI middle voice: *welo'tmasi* "I look after my own interests". In this latter form we have a combination of TI + TA + AI finals. In two brief pages, Pacifique gives 45 different verbal derivations from this one simple lexical stem *wel(i)-*.

But this is not the end of the possiblities. If one adds the indefinite subject marker *-imk* to *welo'tmasi*, the form *welo'tmasimk* "one looks after one's interests" can then be turned into a noun by the addition of the noun final *-ewey* (which can be added to any indefinite subject form): *welo'tmasimkewey* "something that looks after things for one (e. g. wax for the car)". This in turn can be made into a noun plural: *welo'tmasimkewe'l*, which could be used of tools for the car. Given this range of derivation, which is exploited to the hilt by native speakers, it is no small wonder that the early missionaries, linguists and students of these exotic vernaculars, expressed admiration for languages that offered such a range of expressive possibilities.

## 10. Conclusion

From the earliest voyages of discovery onwards, the Europeans who came to the North American continent were interested in the languages and culture of the native peoples. Many people learned a smattering of these languages, for the purpose of communication and trade, and some, such as the French *coureurs des bois* lived among the natives, adopted their lifestyle, became fluent speakers and served as strategic interpreters when such important matters as treaties were to be discussed between the European authorities and the native chiefs. But the real students and scholars of these languages were the European missionaries, many of them men of deep learning, who not only immersed themselves in these languages so that they could master them and use them for the purposes of evangelization, but left large quantities of written records: grammars, dictionaries, texts, important tools destined for those who would follow in their missionary endeavours. Not until the 20th century, and the foundation of linguistics departments in most major universities of the North American continent, would others take on the tasks of linguistic research, of field work, and of the writing of grammars and dictionaries.

## 11. Bibliography


Biggar, H. P. 1924. *The Voyages of Jacques Cartier.* Ottawa: King's Printer.

Fabvre, Bonaventure, SJ. 1696/1970. *Racines montagnaises.* Québec: Presses de l'Université Laval.

Hanzeli, Victor. 1969. *Missionary Linguistics in New France.* The Hague: Mouton.

Hewson, John. 1996. "An Eighteenth-century Micmac Grammarian". *Historiographia Linguistica* 221.65–76.

Hovdhaugen, Even. 1996. "... *and the Word was God.*" *Missionary Linguistics and Missionary Grammar.* Studium Sprachwissenschaft Beiheft 25. Münster: Nodus.

Johnson, Micheline. 1970. *Apôtres ou agitateurs.* Trois-Rivières: Le Boréal Express.

Leclercq, Chrétien, ofm. 1866 [1691.] *La nouvelle relation de la Gaspésie.* Paris: A. Auroy.

Lenhart, John, ofmcap. 1921. "History of the Ideographic Manual of the Micmacs". Maillard 1921 [1866.] (Later published separately: *History Relating to Manual of Prayers, Instructions, Psalms and Hymns in Micmac Ideograms Used by Micmac Indians of Eastern Canada and Newfoundland.* Sydney & Nova Scotia: Cameron Print, 1932.)

Lescarbot, Marc. 1866 [1609.] *Histoire de la Nouvelle-France.* Paris: Tross.

Maillard, Pierre-Antoine, cssp. 1863 [1755.] "Lettre de M. l'abbé Maillard sur les missions d'Acadie et particulièrement sur les missions micmaques". *Les soirées canadiennes*, 290–426. Québec: Brousseau Frères.

–. 1863. *Grammaire de la langue micmaque.* New York: Cramoisy Press of John Gilmary Shea. (Repr. New York: AMS Press, 1970.)

–. 1921 [1866]. *Manual of Prayers, Instructions, Psalms and Hymns in Micmac Ideograms.* 2nd ed. by R. P. Pacifique. Restigouche: The Micmac Messenger. (Earlier ed. by Christian Kauder, cssr, with the title *Buch das gut enhaltend den Katechismus, Betrachtung, Gesang.* Vienna: Ludwig-Missionsverein, 1866.)

Pacifique, Rév. Père, ofmcap. 1939. *Traité théorique et pratique de la langue micmaque.* Restigouche.

–. 1990. *The Micmac Grammar of Father Pacifique.* Translated and retranscribed with an Introduction by John Hewson and Bernard Francis. Winnipeg: Algonquian and Iroquoian Linguistics, Memoir 7.

Pilling, James C. 1891. *Bibliography of the Algonquian Languages.* Washington D. C.: Bureau of American Ethnology Bulletin 13.

Schmidt, David & Murdena Marshall. *Mi'kmaq Hieroglyphic Prayers.* Halifax: Nimbus.

Schneider, L., omi. 1970. *Dictionnaire esquimau-français du parler de l'Ungava.* Québec: Presses de l'Univ. Laval.

Shea, John G. 1861. "Micmac or Recollect Hieroglyphics", *The Historical Review* V.289–292.

Silvy, Antoine, sj. 1974. *Dictionnaire montagnais-français.* Montréal: Presses de l'Université du Québec.

*John Hewson, St. John's (Canada)*

# 132. First descriptive approaches to Indigenous Languages of British North America

1. The background
2. First encounters
3. Keys to mind and soul
4. Missionary grammars
5. The genius of the languages
6. The aftermath of missionary linguistics
7. Bibliography

## 1. The background

To discuss the history of linguistic approaches to North American languages is to discuss the history of European dealings with these languages. Colonial expansion and appropriation, as well as missionary zeal, shaped the individual histories of indigenous nations and the languages spoken by them. Scholarly investigation of native languages began only late in the history of contact and remained marginal until the second half of the 19th century. Governmental policies, i. e. coordinated, planned, and administered actions, with respect to native languages were equally late in coming. Until very recently these steps more often than not were disastrous. I will primarily be concerned with the areas later called 'New England' and Canada, i. e., the area which has been predominately shaped by colonial dominance of the British Empire.

In the 18th century, the Inuit (Eskimo) lived as far south as the northern shore of the Gulf of St. Lawrence and northern Newfoundland (Dorais 1980: 1). The Eskimo-Aleut language family extends from eastern Greenland to the northeasterly tip of Asia. It covers a variety of distinct languages, most of which are closely related and which today are spoken by roughly 100,000 people. To the south and west, the Algonquian language group constitutes the largest family in the area, as far as geographic extension, number of different languages, and, today, number of speakers is concerned. Cree with approx. 70,000 speakers, and Ojibwa with 50,000 speakers are among those few languages which might still have a future. In the first century of contact, a crucial role was played by the Iroquoian nations (Jennings 1984). All Iroquoian languages still spoken are severely threatened, as are the languages of the Siouan, Salishan, Wakashan, Tsimshian, and Athabascan stocks to the west and north, and the Tlingit, Kutenai, and Haida isolates (Kinkade 1991; Morrison & Wilson 1995: 28–30).

## 2. First encounters

The oldest documented account of a North American language is to be found in Davis' (1550–1605) journals of his voyages 'in search of the Northwest Passage and Cathay' in the years 1585–1588 (Nowak 1999b). Thomas Harriot collected a list of Algonquin words during his stay in 'Virginia' in 1585–86 (Salmon 1992: 28ff.); John Smith's *Map of Virginia* (1612) contains a vocabulary of the language of the Indians of Virginia, just to mention the oldest. In addition to the French, who will not be discussed here, other European nations contributed too, such as the Dutch (Johannes de Laet (1630); Adriaen van der Donck (1655)) and the Swedish (Thomas Campanius Holm (1702)). Reports of exploring expeditions such as Carver (1778) or Mackenzie (1801), to name just those most often quoted, saw several editions and were translated into other European languages. The information on languages contained in these books of travel in many cases was limited to scanty word lists and impressionistic characterizations. They nevertheless provided an important source for further study and consideration, carried out in the seclusion of European, and American studies. Adelung and Vater's *Mithridates* (1806–1816) provides ample evidence, as does Gallatin's *Table of North American Native Languages* (1826) and, most comprehensively, Pillings bibliographies, compiled for the Smithonian Institution and its Bureau of Ethnology in the years 1887–1894 (see also Andresen 1990: 69). Equally important was the political value of such accounts, since they greatly influenced public opinion and could easily be exploited to strengthen the changing attitude against the Indian nations and their rights in the 18th century. Not all of these descriptions pictured the native Americans unfavorably, others did and most characteristically, it was just these which "traveled well across the Atlantic" (Andresen 1990: 88). So the stage was set ideologically when in the later 18th century good relationships to the Indians were no longer needed by the whites. The situation of the European settlements, which had been established in the early 17th century, had remained rather precarious for many years, and the population small in numbers. In 1650 the Pilgrim colony comprehended only 2,500 people in ten 'towns' (Handy 1976: 19). But, in the Northeast Indian hostility was not the reason for the disappearance of European colonies: the small Swedish colony was captured by the Dutch in 1655, who in turn surrendered to the English in 1664. By the Treaty of Paris (1763) France ceded all territory west of the Mississippi to Spain, but all other claims to the British. In contrast to the tightly ruled, homogeneous French colony, the other colonies were remarkable heterogeneous with respect to their political, economical and especially religious life. Although they were predominantly Protestant, i. e., not Catholic, the familiar mosaic of a multitude of congregations, separated or not separated from the Church of England, of churches and evangelical movements is to be observed right from the start (Grant 1984: 112ff.; Beaver 1988: 430ff.; Handy 1976: 45ff.). In the different colonies which developed into different states, religious matters were handled differently, as was the relationship to the native population (Beaver 1988: 435ff.). With the consolidation of British rule, the Anglican Church gained increasing influence, which played no small role in the movement towards independence. Quebec had remained predominantly French-speaking and Catholic under British rule, but after the War of Independence, English-speaking Protestants and Anglicans swept into the country. In 1791 Quebec was divided into 'Upper' and 'Lower Canada', paying tribute to the wishes of the immigrants (Handy 1976: 132ff.).

## 3. Keys to mind and soul

Taking into account that in Europe the time was one of extreme religious excitement, which to no small degree initiated emigration to America and the search for religious freedom, it also must be recognized that the political and economic consequences of Christianization were clearly invisaged by people such as Richard Hakluyt right from the beginning (Salmon 1992: 29; Beaver 1988: 430; Jennings 1984: 176–77). Aiming at conversion meant aiming at 'civilization'. In the end, however, this aim was rendered superfluous in what might be called the final stage of colonization: marginalization, the pushing back of native Americans by an ever expanding 'frontier' (Beaver 1988: 439–441; Miller 1996: 151–376; Grant 1984: 154ff., 196ff.). Some missionaries and church officials believed that the best way to christianize the natives would be via interpreters and instruction in English (Grant 1984: 110f.; Beaver 1988: 435), but the native language proved to be the key to mind and soul. Although general conduct may prove a Christian life, it is the linguistic act of convincing a person which is essential and prior to all conversion. Conversion implies conviction of Christian values and beliefs on the part of the convert.

For the missionary then, especially the evangelical missionary, translation of the Bible and other religious texts into the respective tongue is an integral part of the conversion process. To accomplish such a task, an elementary vocabulary and a rudimentary ability to make oneself understood would not suffice. The oldest printed book on a North American language, the Algonquian language Narraganset, addresses just this need to familiarize oneself with an unknown language: Roger William's *Key into the language of America*, printed in 1643, deals with a variety of topics in thirty chapters, each containing short vocabularies and dialogues, a method not uncommon at that time. It is important to note that all of the grammars written later on were intended exclusively for use by missionaries, not by the native population. For the natives, translations of religious texts, intended for instruction and the teaching of reading and writing, were composed, many of them by Indian converts (Miller 1996: 61–88). The oldest is John Eliot's Catechism in the Massachusetts language of 1654 (Pilling 1891: 127). Eliot translated extensively into Massachusetts, including gospels, primers, and the whole Bible. Grammars were few and far between. In 1666 Eliot's grammar of Massachusetts was printed, titled *The Indian Grammar begun*; it remained the only printed grammar for years. Pilling mentions an unspecified grammar of Huron dating to 1699 (Pilling 1888: 192), and Foertsch (1988: 70) lists fifteen grammars produced by Jesuits before 1773, but none of these grammars was printed. As a matter of fact, the next grammar to be printed in English was Zeisberger's posthumously published Delaware grammar of 1827. The grammars of Greenlandic by Paul Egede (1760) and Otho Fabricius (1791) were both published in Copenhagen, the first being written in Latin and Danish, the latter exclusively in Danish. Grammars of Ojibwa (Summerfield 1834; Baraga 1850), and Cree (Howse 1844) followed, but all in all, a survey of titles listed in Pilling (1887–1894) and the Native Studies Collection (1993) shows that the total production of grammars as compared to the amount of translation work done remained astonishingly small, and by no means all of the languages received such a description. This underlines the primary objectives of missionary efforts, which only in rare cases were supplemented by more intellectual interests, independent of religious instruction.

## 4. Missionary grammars

It may be assumed that among those missionaries who had become fluent in the language, only a few understood the importance of a grammar and were able to attempt writing one. Grammars emerged out of notebooks, as a by-product of the acquisition process; they were initially meant to help memorizing, or to help others learn the language. Especially in Protestant missionary strategies, exegesis of the Bible played (and still plays) a highly important role. Consequently, translation of the Bible into the respective language and the ability of potential converts to read were essential. Translation demands a thorough understanding of the language and its grammatical principles, a basic writing standard, and uniformity of terminology and phrasing. In the case of North American languages, these standards had to be developed first. Grammars written by missionaries reflect this process of initial codification. They are not to be confused with scientific descriptions of languages, e. g., reference grammars. The missionaries' only goal was to attain command of the respective language and to hand this knowledge down to fellow missionaries; it was just a means to a well-defined end. It is this attitude which clearly separates missionary grammars from genuine scientific work (Nowak 1996b, 1999c, 1999a). Although there are important exceptions to the rule, such as Zeisberger, Kleinschmidt or Petitot, missionaries generally were not interested in theoretical issues or meticulous description, let alone discussion relating these two aspects of linguistic work. Two highly idiosyncratic factors are critical for the scientific standard achieved and the quality of the grammars written: (1) the individual capabilities of the missionary at work and (2) the differences between the missionary societies, churches or denominations and the specific training provided by them. It is this more than anything else which makes it close to impossible to draw a homogeneous picture and to make generalizations about 'missionary linguistics' or 'missionary grammar writing'. Catholic as well als Anglican and Protestant priests and pastors were members of official churches, even state churches; they had completed a strictly regulated higher education, including university training. They had learned Latin, Greek, and Hebrew and consequently had experienced differences in grammar and alien writing systems at a quite conscious level. They knew how to deal with foreign languages – if not on a professional scale, then at least in a well-educated manner. The members of the small congregations, in contrast, were often laypersons who had received little or no formal education. Many of them had learned how to read and write only when they joined the congregations. The early grammatical collections by Moravian brethren in Greenland clearly reflect their helplessness and lack of knowledge, and in many respects can be viewed as desperate attempts to come to grips with a totally alien subject matter (Nowak 1992). Within the Moravian Society, all the notes taken were compiled and systematically scanned for further use (Nowak 1999a). Brinton in his edition of a Lenape-English dictionary "from an anonymous Ms. in the Archives of the Moravian Church at Bethlehem, Pa," (1888), identifies the author as Christian Friedrich Dencke, who must have used Zeisbergers older dictionary, which again underlines the purely practical purpose of these manuscripts (Brinton 1888: ivff.). This practice did not aim at improvement in the sense of descriptive adequacy, let alone scientific progress. Sometimes, as in the case of Samuel Kleinschmidt and his grammar of Greenlandic (1851), this was achieved too; however, it cannot be attributed to research efforts or strategies fostered by the Moravian Society, but must be exclusively credited to the individual. Individual genius, interest in and affection for linguistic investigation played an outstanding role with respect to the quality of the work done. To present the actual peculiarities of the grammars is beyond the scope of this paper (but see the detailed studies by Bergsland & Rischel 1986; Bergsland 1994: viii–xliv; Nowak 1987; 1996a; 1999a). Quite generally, the structural differences between Indo-European languages, from which the template of grammar was derived, and all North American languages is enormous. It covers very basic assumptions such as the distinction between nouns and verbs, and between words and phrases, plus the nature of the basic sentence structure, just to name the most spectacular ones. While features, especially those of inflectional paradigms, were more or less recognized as long as they matched familiar ones, others were set aside or misrepresented as soon as they encoded unknown aspects. Examples are the so-called fourth person in Inuktitut (Eskimo) or the obviative marking in Algonquian languages, both indicating disjoint reference morphologically. Another is the identification of discourse-establishing verbal inflection as 'infinitives', 'gerunds', or 'supina' (Nowak 1999a). The relation of the exceedingly rich morphology to larger speech units, traditionally called syntax, did not receive any attention. But it is only fair to state that questions in this area are only today being raised.

## 5. The genius of the languages

Of course it was just this being different in an obviously fundamental way which attracted scholary attention – the structure named polysynthetic by Duponceau and the abundantly rich inflectional paradigms accompanying it (Haas 1969: 239, 241). Pickering identified it as the common link of all American languages (Pickering 1834: 2,4,9). In the light of the ongoing evaluation of grammatical structures, it was the complexity of inflection compared to that of classical European languages which caused some stir. The prevailing opinion that languages reflected the level of culture was repeatedly and ever more urgently questioned by American scholars like Pickering and Duponceau (Robins 1987; Haas 1969: 239). They called upon others as witnesses, respectable people like David Zeisberger and John Heckewelder, both Moravians, both having lived with the Indians for many years (see the introduction to Pickering 1834: 3; Heckewelder 1821: iv–vii, ix–xviii; Howse 1844: v–xv). The debate on the nature and value of American languages was a hot topic in the early 19th century, with obvious political and economic implications. The concept of superiority, and the categories 'lack' and 'absence', were so strongly rooted in scholarly European thought that the notion of equality between languages or an unbiased understanding of unfamiliar language structures was hardly possible – even with scholars of the stature of Wilhelm von Humboldt. The debate among Humboldt, Pickering, and Duponceau (Müller-Vollmer 1974; Andresen 1991: 87, 93ff.) marks a new quality in scholarly discussion of hitherto unknown grammatical structures and features. Zeisberger's grammar of Lenape (Delaware) was translated into English and published posthumously by Duponceau in 1827; a comparative dictionary by Zeisberger was published by Eben Norton Horsford in 1887.

Daniel Brinton edited another valuable manuscript by a Moravian brother, a *Lenâpé-English Dictionary* (1888), John G. Shea a French-Onondaga dictionary "from a manuscript of the seventeenth century" (1860). James Trumbull collected a Natick Dictionary from Eliot's bible, which was hoped to be the first volume in a series of vocabularies of native languages (Trumbull 1903: ix). The fact that American scholars took the effort to edit such manuscripts illuminates yet two more interesting aspects. First, the manuscripts were perceived as documents of historical value even at the beginning of the 19th century, and much more so by the end of the century. Second, the reliability of information circulating in Europe, "the random words taken down in a few hours by a traveller" (Shea 1860: vii), was questioned. The way information had been collected and the competence of the collector began to play a more and more important role. The evolution of descriptive linguistics from prescientific grammar writing undertaken by people in need of a manual, represented by the missionaries' approach, to a science based on "the process of induction" (Pickering 1836, in Mackert 1994: 2) – the quest for a scientific method of investigation had begun. As a consequence, the relation between anthropology, as an emerging science, and linguistics, as an empirical enterprise was established. As can be inferred from the works of Heckewelder, Howse, Petitot or Rand (Grant 1984: 169), the anthropological interest in the people and their culture, as well as the method of collecting and comparing specimens, of classification, gained increasing importance and also marked a changed attitude in some missionaries. A kind of turning point was reached when Horatio Hale, the first linguist ever to be appointed for such a research task, took part in the US Exploring Expedition of 1838–42 (Mackert 1994). During the next decades, explicit instructions for the elicitation of language data were developed, and by the end of the century, fieldwork had become an institutionalized part of American linguistics.

## 6. The aftermath of missionary linguistics

To return to the linguistic efforts of missionaries, the most influential and consequential of their activities certainly was their putting down the respective language in writing. As for the spelling, it is not only the educational background of the missionaries and their individual capability, but equally their mother tongue that is mirrored by the representation of the respective language. The missionaries of different denominations did not necessarily cooperate, but to some extent even engaged in a kind of competition (see, e. g., Grant 1984: 104ff., 156). As a consequence, very similar or even one and the same language ended up being written with different spellings based on the orthographies of different European languages. To give an example, with Inuit languages even today the domains of the different missions can be identified by the different writing systems, namely, syllabics, introduced by Anglican missionaries, and at least four different orthographies using the Roman alphabet originating with Moravian, Danish, and Catholic missionaries, not to mention the Alaskan variants (Nowak 1996a).

Until the middle of the 19th century the opinion was voiced that American languages were lacking certain sounds. By the rather naive procedure of checking a language against the alphabet, the missionaries failed to recognize the actually existing sound pattern fully and correctly. First and foremost, translations into and transliteration of a language was intended as an aid for preaching and teaching. Many missionaries were not very proficient in the language but could at least try to read to the people if its representation was familiar to them. For use by the natives, the Roman alphabet was considered to be too difficult – in the light of the fact that the spelling modes of European languages with all their idiosyncrasies and irregularities were of course employed, a not altogether unrealistic consideration. As a consequence, a number of distinct spelling systems were invented by missionaries (see Grant 1984, appendix), one of which actually became a success and today is widespread in northern Canada: the syllabic writing created by the Methodist missionary James Evans (1801–1846) for Cree. The first book in syllabics, a version of St. John's Gospel, was printed at Norway House, Manitoba, in 1846. Other Missionary Societies such as the British and Foreign Bible Society came to use the syllabary too. John Hordon and E. A. Watkins, missionaries belonging to the Church Mission Society, adopted it for Inuktitut (Eskimo) in the 1850s. Today it is in general use throughout the Canadian Eastern Arctic. In the mid-19th-century, the need for a "standard alphabet for reducing unwritten languages and foreign graphic systems to a uniform orthography in European letters" (Lepsius 1863) was increasingly felt, and in 1863, the second, enlarged edition of the English translation of Lepsius' treatise of 1855 was "recommended for adoption by the Church Mission Society" (Lepsius 1863, title page). Pickering's earlier attempt at a "Uniform orthography for the Indian Languages of North America" (Pickering 1820) had not caught on (Andresen 1991: 98–101). For the peoples concerned the translations were very important, not just because they influenced their spiritual life, but also because they set writing standards which today are perceived as heritage and which have gained considerable emotional value. Especially in remote areas such as Labrador or the North, languages were thus sheltered against the increasing influence of English. But this did not preclude the fact that later on the missionaries were instrumental in the forceful implementation of English as language of instruction in residential schools run by them all over North America. Despite the laudable efforts of individuals, the contribution of missionaries to the study of North American languages, as well as to their preservation remains a rather ambiguous one.

## 7. Bibliography


Andresen, Julie Tetel. 1990. *Linguistics in America 1769–1924.* London & New York: Routledge.

Baraga, Frederic. 1850. *A Theoretical and Practical Grammar of the Otchipwe Language.* Detroit: Jabez Fox.

Beaver, R. Pierce. 1988. "Protestant Churches and the Indians". *Handbook of North American Indians* 4.430–458. Washington: Smithonian Institution.

Bergsland, Knut. 1994. *Aleut Dictionary.* Fairbanks: Alaska Native Language Center.

– & Jørgen Rischel. 1986. *Pioneers of Eskimo Grammar.* Copenhagen: Linguistic Circle of Copenhagen.

Brinton, Daniel. 1888. *A Lenâpé-English Dictionary. From an anonymous MS. in the Archives of the Moravian Church at Bethlehem, PA.* Philadelphia: The Historical Society of Pennsylvania.

Carver, Jonathan. 1778. *Travels Through the Interior Parts of North-America in the Years 1766, 1767, and 1768.* London: J. Walter.

Donck, Adriaen van der. 1655. *Beschryvinge van Nieuvv-Nederlant.* Amsterdam: Evert Nieuwenhof.

Dorais, Louis-Jacques. 1980. *The Inuit Language in Southern Labrador From 1694–1785.* National Museum of Man. Mercury Series. Canadian Ethnology Service Paper No. 66. Ottawa.

Egede, Paul. 1760. *Grammatica Grönlandico-Danico-Latina.* Copenhagen.

Eliot, John. 1666. *The Indian Grammar Begun: Or, an essay to bring the Indian language into rules.* Cambridge: Marmaduke Johnson.

Fabricius, Otho. 1791. *Forsøg til en forbedret Grønlandsk Grammatica.* Copenhagen: Schubart.

Foertsch, Henrike. 1998. "Missionare als Sprachensammler". *Wege durch Babylon. Missionare, Sprachstudien und interkulturelle Kommunikation* ed. by Reinhard Wendt, 43–73. Tübingen: Narr.

Gallatin, Albert. 1826. *A Table of the Indian Tribes within the United States, East of the Stony Mountains Arranged According to Languages and Dialects.* Broadside.

Grant, John Webster. 1984. *Moon of Wintertime. Missionaries and Indians of Canada in Encounter.* Toronto: Univ. of Toronto Press.

Haas, Mary. 1969. "Grammar or Lexicon? The American Indian side of the question from Duponceau to Powell". *IJAL* 35.239–255.

Handy, Robert, T. 1976. *A History of the Churches in the United States and Canada.* Oxford: Clarendon Press.

Heckewelder, John. 1821. *Nachricht von der Geschichte, den Sitten und Gebräuchen der Indianischen Völkerschaften, welche ehemals Pennsylvanien und die benachbarten Staaten bewohnten.* Göttingen: Vandenhoeck & Ruprecht.

Holm, Thomas Campanius. 1702. *Kort Beskrifning om Provincien Nya Sverige uti America, som nu fortjden af the Engelske Pensylvania.* Stockholm: J. H. Werner.

Horsford, Eben Norton, ed. 1887. *Zeisberger's Indian Dictionary, English, German, Iroquois – the Onondaga and Algonquian – the Delaware. Printed from the original manuscript in Harvard College Library.* Cambridge: Wilson.

Howse, Joseph. 1844. *A Grammar of the Cree Language with which is Combined an Analysis of the Chippeway Dialect.* London: Rivington.

Jennings, Francis. 1984. *The Ambiguous Iroquois Empire.* New York & London: Norton.

Kinkade, Dale. 1991. "The Decline of Native Languages in Canada". *Endangered Languages* ed. by Robert H. Robins & Eugenius M. Uhlenbeck, 157–176. Oxford & New York: Berg.

Kleinschmidt, Samuel. 1851 [1991.] *Grammatik der grönländischen Sprache mit teilweisem Einschluß des Labradordialekts.* Berlin: Reimer [Hildesheim: Olms.]

Laet, Johannes de. 1630. *Beschrijvinghe van West-Indien.* Leyden: Elzeviers.

Lepsius, Richard. 1863 [1981.] *Standard Alphabet for Reducing Unwritten Languages and Foreign Graphic Systems to a Uniform Orthography in European Letters.* London: Williams & Norgate [Amsterdam: Benjamins.]

Mackenzie, Sir Alexander. 1801. *Voyages from Montreal, on the River St. Laurence, through the Continent of North America, to the Frozen and Pacific Oceans; In the years 1789 and 1793.* London: R. Noble.

Mackert, Michael. 1994. "Horatio Hale and the Great U. S. Exploring Expedition". *Anthropological Linguistics* 36.1–26.

Miller, J. R. 1996. *Shingwauk's Vision. A history of native residential schools.* Toronto: Univ. of Toronto Press.

Morrison, R. Bruce & C. Roderick Wilson. 1995. *Native Peoples: The Canadian experience.* Toronto: McClelland & Stewart.

Müller-Vollmer, Kurt. 1974. "Wilhelm von Humboldt und der Anfang der amerikanischen Sprachwissenschaft: Die Briefe an John Pickering". *Universalismus und Wissenschaft im Werk und Wirken der Brüder Humboldt* ed. by Klaus Hammacher, 259–334. Frankfurt: Klostermann.

*Native Studies Collection.* 1993. The Early Canadiana Microfiche Series. Canadian Institute for Historical Microreproductions.

Nowak, Elke. 1999a. The "Eskimo Language" of Labrador: Moravian missionaries and the description of Labrador Inuttut 1733–1891. Études/Inuit/Studies 23.173–197. Université Laval: Québec.

–. 1999b. "tempora sunt tria ... Über die Begegnung mit fremden Menschen und fremden Sprachen". *Sprachdiskussion und Beschreibung von Sprachen im 17. und 18. Jahrhundert* ed. by Gerda Haßler 41–52. Münster: Nodus.

–. 1999c. "Investigating Diversity. Descriptive grammars, empirical research and the science of language". *History of Linguistics 1996* ed. by David Cram, Andrew Linn & Elke Nowak. Vol. 1, 147–164. Amsterdam: Benjamins.

–. 1996a. "A Mission for Grammar Writing. Early approaches to Inuit (Eskimo) languages". *Geschichte der Sprachtheorie*, vol. 6. ed. by Peter Schmitter. Tübingen: Narr (forthcoming).

–. 1996b. "Considering the Status of Empirical Research in Linguistics. Approaches and attitudes since 1800". *"... and the Word was God". Missionary linguistics and missionary grammars* ed. by Even Hovdhaugen, 23–44. Münster: Nodus.

–. 1992. "How to 'Improve' a Language: The case of eighteenth century descriptions of Greenlandic." *Diversions of Galway. Papers on the History of Linguistics* ed. by Anders Ahlqvist. 157–167. Amsterdam: Benjamins.

–. 1987. *Samuel Kleinschmidts "Grammatik der grönländischen Sprache".* Hildesheim: Olms.

Petitot, R. P. E. 1876. *Dictionnaire de la Langue Dène – Dindjié. Dialectes Montagnais ou Chippewayan, Peaux de Lièvre et Loucheux. Renfermant en outre un grand nombre de termes propres a sept autres dialectes de la memes langue. Précédé d'une monographie des Dènè-Dindjié d'une Grammaire et de Tableaux synoptiques des conjugaisons.* Paris: Ernest Leroux, Editeur; Maisonneuve. San Francisco: Bancroft.

Pickering, John. 1834. *Über die indianischen Sprachen Amerikas.* Leipzig: Vogel.

–. 1820. *An Essay on a Uniform Orthography for the Indian Languages of North America.* Cambridge: Cambridge Univ. Press.

Pilling, James. 1887–1894 [1973.] *Bibliographies of the Languages of the North American Indians.* 9 Parts in 3 Vols. Washington D. C. 1887–1894. Washington: Government Printing Office [New York: AMS Press.]

Robins, Robert. 1987. "Duponceau and Early Nineteenth-century Linguistics". *Papers in the History of Linguistics* ed. by Hans Aarsleff et al., 435–446. Amsterdam: Benjamins.

Salmon, Vivian. 1992. "Thomas Harriot (1560–1621) and the English Origins of Algonkian Linguistics". *HL* 19.25–56.

Shea, John Gilmary. 1860. *French-Onondaga Dictionary, from a Manuscript of the Seventeenth Century.* New York: Cramoisy Press.

Smith, John. 1612. *A Map of Virginia. With a description of the covntrey, the commodities, people, government and religion.* At Oxford, Printed by Joseph Barnes.

Summerfield, John (Sahgahjewagahbahweh). 1834. *Sketch of the Grammar of the Chippeway Language, to which is added a Vocabulary of the Most Common Words.* Cazenovia: Fairchild.

Trumbull, James Hammond. 1903. *Natick Dictionary.* Washington: Government Printing Office.

Vater, Johann Severin 1816 [1970]: *Mithridates oder allgemeine Sprachkunde* [...] von Johann Christoph Adelung, [...] fortgesetzt [...] von Dr. Johann Severin Vater. Dritter Theil, Dritte Abteilung. Berlin: Vossische Buchhandlung [Hildesheim: Olms.]

Williams, Roger. 1643. *A Key into the Language of America.* London: Gregory Dexter.

Zeisberger, David. 1827. *Grammar of the Language of the Lenni Lenape or Delaware Indians by David Zeisberger.* Translated from the German manuscript of the author by Peter Stephen Du Ponceau. (= *Transactions of the American Philosophical Society,* III.1.) Philadelphia: Kay.


*Elke Nowak, Leipzig/Berlin (Germany)*

# 133. Das Studium der schwarzafrikanischen Sprachen

1. Vorbemerkung
2. Vorkoloniale Epoche
3. Koloniale Epoche
4. Postkoloniale Epoche
5. Gegenwärtige Trends in der Forschung
6. Bibliographie

## 1. Vorbemerkung

Die wissenschaftliche Beschäftigung mit den in Afrika heimischen Sprachen, deren Zahl auf etwa 1500 geschätzt wird, setzte erst im 19. Jh. ein. Erste Aufzeichnungen von Wortlisten und Redewendungen, sogar der Versuch einer monographischen Beschreibung nach dem lateinischen Grammatikmodell neben Übersetzungen christlich-religiöser Texte stammen jedoch schon aus dem 16. Jh. (Heine, Schadeberg & Wolff 1981: 19ff.). Missionare und Reisende sind die Autoren. Die Entwicklung zu einer eigenständigen Disziplin, für die sich seit Beginn dieses Jahrhunderts die Bezeichnung Afrikanistik (Jungraithmayr & Möhlig 1983: 22f.) eingebürgert hat, vollzog sich in enger Abhängigkeit zur Weltgeschichte der letzten 200 Jahre. Mit jedem ihrer Abschnitte sind auch grundlegende Änderungen in der wissenschaftlichen Ausrichtung der afrikanischen Sprachwissenschaften verbunden, so daß es sinnvoll ist, sich in dieser Abhandlung der historisch vorgegebenen Gliederung anzuschließen und folgende drei Epochen zu unterscheiden: eine vorkoloniale, eine koloniale und eine postkoloniale. Nachdem die Afrikanistik in ihren ersten Phasen weitgehend auf die europäischen Kernländer Deutschland, England und Frankreich beschränkt war, hat sich das Interesse an den afrikanischen Sprachen seit der Unabhängigkeit der afrikanischen Staaten weltweit ausgebreitet. Nicht zuletzt in den Universitäten, die seither auf dem afrikanischen Kontinent entstanden sind, ist ein Interesse für die eigenen Sprachkulturen erwacht. Wir werden hierauf eingehen, den Schwerpunkt in der Beschreibung jedoch auf die deutsche Afrikanistik legen. Ein abschließender Paragraph ist den gegenwärtigen Trends in der Disziplin gewidmet. Wer sich einen zusätzlichen Eindruck verschaffen möchte, sei auf die zusammenfassenden Darstellungen von Köhler (1975), Heine, Schadeberg & Wolff (1981) sowie Jungraithmayr & Möhlig (1983) verwiesen. Wir haben uns bemüht, im Literaturverzeichnis die unterschiedlichen Arbeitsrichtungen zusätzlich zu repräsentieren.

## 2. Vorkoloniale Epoche

Die frühen Afrika-Sprachforscher suchten vor allem aus humanitären Gründen den sprachlichen Umgang mit der afrikanischen Bevölkerung. Es ging ihnen um christliche Mission und um die Abschaffung des Sklavenhandels bzw. um der Resozialisierung befreiter Sklaven. Ehe den Afrikanern die christliche Basisliteratur (Bibel, Katechismus) in ihre eigenen Sprachen übersetzt werden konnten, mußten ihre zumeist schriftlosen Sprachen zuvor grammatisch und lexikalisch analysiert werden. Die intensive Befassung mit den afrikanischen Sprachen führte die ersten Pioniere in Missionsdiensten unausweichlich auf die Spur zu dem reichen Schatz an Mythen, Märchen und Fabeln, den fast jede afrikanische Sprachkultur damals noch besaß. Auf diese Weise entstanden im 19. Jh. aus allen Teilen Afrikas nicht nur zahlreiche sprachmonographische Beschreibungen, sondern auch viele Anthologien von sogenannter Oralliteratur. Während die Sprachmonographien auch aus heutiger Sicht beachtliche analytische Leistungen darstellen, deutlich von der Absicht getragen, in den Wesenskern der afrikanischen Sprachen vorzudringen, sind die oralliterarischen Anthologien aus wissenschaftlicher Perspektive zumeist nur anspruchslose Dokumentationen mit Übersetzungen in eine europäische Sprache ohne weitere Erschließung ihres Inhaltes oder ihrer kunstvollen Gestaltung. Die entsprechenden analytischen Werkzeuge wurden von der Afrikanistik erst in jüngster Zeit aus anderen Disziplinen rezipiert bzw. entwickelt.

Unter den frühen Afrika-Sprachforschern ragen vier Persönlichkeiten hervor, die wir heutzutage als Gründerväter der Afrikanistik ansehen. Es sind dies Johann Ludwig Krapf (1810–1881), Heinrich Barth (1821–1865), Sigismund Wilhelm Koelle (1823–1902) und Wilhelm Heinrich Immanuel Bleek (1827–1875). Krapf ist der Begründer der modernen Swahiliforschung (1850, 1882), der wohl bedeutendsten Sprache Afrikas (Miehe & Möhlig 1995). Barth bereiste zwischen 1851 und 1856 weite Teile des westlichen Sudan und sammelte neben ethnographischen, historiographischen und geographischen Daten auch eine Fülle von Sprachmaterial (Barth 1862–1866). Seine akribischen Methoden der Materialerhebung, der Aufbereitung und der Darstellung eilten den Standards seiner Zeit weit voraus. Die moderne Sprachforschung in Zentral-Westafrika baut nach wie vor auf dem von ihm gelegten Fundament auf. Koelle verdanken wir vor allem eine Synopse von 300 Wörtern und Sätzen aus über 200 afrikanischen Sprachen (1854a), die er unter befreiten Sklaven in Freetown (Sierra Leone) sammelte. In dem Werk ist auch ein erster Gliederungsversuch der afrikanischen Sprachen enthalten. Koelle eröffnete damit ein Forschungsfeld, dessen Thematik auch heute noch die Afrikanistik intensiv beschäftigt. Darüber hinaus befaßte er sich mit dem Vai (1853) und dem Kanuri (1854b), zu dem er uns auch eine oralliterarische Sammlung hinterließ (1854c). Bleek, auf den der Terminus Bantu zurückgeht, verfaßte eine vergleichende Grammatik dieser so bezeichneten Unterfamilie afrikanischer Sprachen. Obwohl davon wegen seines vorzeitigen Ablebens nur zwei Teile (1862, 1869) erscheinen konnten, bildet dieses Werk bis heute eine wichtige Grundlage der modernen Bantuistik, jener Teildisziplin, die sich mit den annähernd 600 Sprachen im Südteil des afrikanischen Kontinents befaßt.

In dieser frühen Phase wurde die wissenschaftliche Beschäftigung mit den afrikanischen Sprachen als ein Teil der Orientalistik angesehen. Obwohl die Afrikanistik schon seit vielen Jahrzehnten im Kanon der Geisteswissenschaften als eigenständige Disziplin neben der Orientalistik anerkannt ist, besteht im Rahmen der Deutschen Morgenländischen Gesellschaft eine organisatorische Klammer zwischen Afrikanistik und Orientalistik fort, die auf jene Zeit zurückgeht.

## 3. Koloniale Epoche

Der Beginn der kolonialen Epochen läßt sich unmittelbar mit der Berliner Konferenz von 1884/85 in Verbindung bringen. Unter dem Vorsitz Bismarcks teilten damals die europäischen Mächte Afrika untereinander auf. Nach dem Erwerb der Kolonien ergab sich für Deutschland, England und Frankreich gleichermaßen die praktische Notwendigkeit, eine möglichst reibungslose Kolonialverwaltung aufzubauen. Dazu mußte man die kulturellen und gesellschaftlichen Grundstrukturen, insbesondere die Rechtsanschauungen der afrikanischen Völker näher kennenlernen. Die Ausbildung der zukünftigen Kolonialbeamten in afrikanischen Sprachen erschien aus dieser Perspektive nicht nur nützlich, sondern unabdingbar. Auch Kaufleute und Missionare entwickelten zunehmend ein Interesse am Erwerb von Kenntnissen in afrikanischen Verkehrssprachen (vgl. dazu Meinhof 1910). Um den Erfordernissen der kolonialen Alltagspraxis zu entsprechen, schuf man in Deutschland zwei Institutionen: 1888 wurde an der Berliner Friedrich-Wilhelms-Universität (später Humboldt-Universität) das Seminar für Orientalische Sprachen mit einer großen Afrika-Abteilung gegründet. 1908 entstand das Hamburgische Kolonialinstitut (später Universität Hamburg), ebenfalls mit einer Abteilung für Afrikanische Sprachwissenschaft. An der Wiener Universität entwickelte sich etwa gleichzeitig ohne kolonialen Bezug um den Orientalisten Leo Reinisch (1832–1919) herum der kuschitistische Zweig der Afrika-Sprachforschung. Seine Vertreter befassen sich mit den sogenannten hamitosemitischen bzw. afroasiatischen Sprachen, die im Ost-Sudan, in Äthiopien, Somalia, Erythräa, Nord-Kenia und Nord-Zentral-Tansania gesprochen werden. Reinisch beschrieb nach mehreren Feldforschungen viele dieser Sprachen zum ersten Mal (Übersicht siehe Jungraithmayr & Möhlig 1983: 201f.) und schuf so ein solides Fundament, auf dem die moderne Kuschitistik immer noch aufbaut. Die mehr philologisch orientierte Richtung der Österreichischen Afrikanistik wurde von seinem Nachfolger, dem Ägyptologen Wilhelm Czermak (1889–1953) konsequent fortgeführt.

In England sind die Anfänge der Afrikanistik mit dem Namen von Alice Werner (1859–1935) verbunden. Seit 1896 erteilte sie in London zunächst Privatunterricht in afrikanischen Sprachen, bis ihr Unterricht 1901 offiziell in das Lehrprogramm des King's College in London übernommen wurde. Von 1917 an lehrte Werner afrikanische Sprachen an der neugegründeten School of Oriental and African Studies. An dieser vor allem in der Epoche nach dem Zweiten Weltkrieg wohl bedeutendsten Institution der Afrikanistik wurde 1937 unter der Leitung von Ida C. Ward (1880–1949) eine Abteilung für afrikanische Sprachen und Kulturen eingerichtet. Schon zuvor war 1926 in London aufgrund privater Initiative unter deutscher und französischer Mitwirkung das International African Institute gegründet worden. Über ein halbes Jahrhundert lang gab es durch seine Unternehmungen und Veröffentlichungen der europäischen Afrikaforschung auf sprachlichem und kulturellem Gebiet bedeutende Impulse.

In Frankreich entstand die Afrikanistik ähnlich wie in Deutschland als eigenständige Disziplin aus der Orientalistik. Da aber die französischen Kolonialbehörden aus ihrer kulturpolitischen Perspektive einer konsequent betriebenen Frankophonie wenig Einfluß auf die afrikanische Sprachforschung nahmen, verlief die institutionelle Entwicklung dort sehr viel langsamer als in Deutschland. Erst in der postkolonialen Epoche nahm sie Gestalt an. Die afrikanistische Forschung war zunächst an Einzelpersonen geknüpft. Insbesondere Maurice Delafosse (1870–1926) und Henri Labouret (1878–1959) erlangten wegen ihrer westafrikanischen Sprachstudien internationale Anerkennung.

Unbeschadet der politischen Entwicklungen während und nach dem Ersten Weltkrieg wurde die internationale Afrikanistik während der kolonialen Epoche maßgeblich von den beiden deutschen Afrikanisten Carl Meinhof (1857–1944) und Diedrich Westermann (1875–1956) bestimmt. Sie verstanden es, die Afrikanistik über angewandte Aufgaben hinaus zu einer eigenständigen Wissenschaft mit überwiegend akademischen Zielsetzungen zu entwickeln. Insbesondere Fragen der Sprachgliederung und der Rekonstruktion historischer Sprachzustände standen im Mittelpunkt ihres Interesses. Aus Mangel an geeigneten Sprachdenkmälen bediente man sich für die historischen Rekonstruktionen einer komparativistisch-induktiven Methode, die von rezenten, empirisch gewonnenen Sprachdaten ausging und aus der Perspektive der Einzelsprachen die linguistischen Merkmale der gemeinsamen Ursprache zu erschließen versuchte. Meinhof schuf nach dieser Methode für die Bantuistik grundlegende Werke (1899; 1906). Abgesehen von einer Fülle sprachmonographischer Werke mit Lehrbuchcharakter trat er mit einer Hamitentheorie hervor (1912), die mehrere Jahrzehnte lang die internationale Fachdiskussion beschäftigte und vor allem auch von benachbarten Disziplinen mehr oder weniger kritiklos übernommen wurde. Die Idee eines hamitischen Sprachstammes in Afrika war zwar nicht ganz neu, als Meinhof sie aufgriff. Er glaubte ihn jedoch linguistisch nachweisen zu können. Anders als bei der Rekonstruktion des Urbantu, wo den Rekonstruktionen das Prinzip der regelmäßigen Lautentsprechung zugrunde lag, ließ sich Meinhof hier auf typologische Vergleiche ein. Hinzu kamen rassische und theologisch-exegetische Erwägungen. Der Kern seiner Theorie besagt, daß es sich bei den Hamiten um Träger hochentwickelter Wirtschaftsformen und Technologien bis hin zu höheren Sprachformen handelt. Alles, was seiner Meinung nach in Afrika diesen Merkmalen entsprach, führte er deshalb historisch auf die Hamiten zurück. Daß Meinhofs Studie methodologisch völlig unhaltbar war und seine Konzepte eigentlich in das Reich der Science Fiction gehörten, hätte damals nur jemand aus dem inneren Kreis des Faches nachweisen können. Dieser Akt der Selbstreinigung unterblieb jedoch, zum einen weil die Theorie dem heraufziehenden rassistischen Zeitgeist entsprach, zum anderen weil eine Auseinandersetzung mit Meinhof für jeden anderen Afrikanisten seiner Zeit ein berufliches Risiko bedeutet hätte. In ähnlich evolutionistischer Weise formulierte Meinhof auch eine allgemeine Sprachentwicklungstheorie (1910–11, 1936), deren Stufen er sämtlich in Afrika vertreten sah. An der Spitze der Evolution stehen dieser Theorie zufolge die flektierenden Genussprachen vom Typ eben jener hypothetischen Hamitensprachen und der indogermanischen Sprachen. An der Basis findet man die isolierenden Sprachen vom Typ der Kwa-Sprachen in Westafrika, den 'eigentlichen Negersprachen'. Im mittleren Bereich der Evolutionsleiter ordnete Meinhof die agglutinierenden Klassensprachen vom Typ der Bantusprachen ein. Seiner Meinung nach waren sie das Ergebnis eine Sprachmischung von "hamitischem Vater und nigritischer Mutter" (1910–11: 164f.). Beide Theorien sind niemals ausdrücklich widerlegt worden. Sie wurden zu Beginn der nachkolonialen Phase vielmehr stillschweigend zu den Akten gelegt. Von bleibendem Wert erwies sich indessen die 1910 erfolgte Gründung einer afrikanistischen Fachzeitschrift. Sie erschien bis zum 9. Band unter dem Titel *Zeitschrift für Kolonialsprachen*, wurde ab 1919 in *Zeitschrift für Eingeborenen-Sprachen* umbenannt und trägt seit 1952 mit Band 36 den Namen *Afrika und Übersee.*

Westermann betätigte sich, von Meinhof angeregt, sprachhistorisch im Bereich der sogenannten Sudansprachen (1911; 1927). Seine Studien dienten zum Teil später Greenberg (1955, 1963) für eine umfassende Sprachgliederung. Auch Westermann verfaßte viele sprachmonographische Arbeiten, die aber im Gegensatz zu Meinhofs Arbeiten größtenteils auf eigenen Feldforschungen in Afrika beruhten. Ein Denkmal schuf er sich mit seinen Studien zum Ewe (1905–06, 1907, 1930, 1954). Sie bilden die Grundlage des modernen Schrift-Ewe in Togo. Während sich die von Meinhof begründete Hamburger Schule der Afrikanistik vor allem der sprachhistorischen Forschung unter den Bantusprachen widmete, unterschied sich die Berliner Schule um Westermann nicht nur regional durch ihren Schwerpunkt auf die Sudansprachen, sondern auch methodologisch. Die gelegentlich als Gesamtafrikanistik bezeichnete Berliner Richtung untersuchte Sprache als kulturellen Gegenstand, der im Kontext mit anderen kulturellen Phänomenen untersucht werden mußte. Den fachlichen Grenzen der ersten Hälfte dieses Jahrhunderts entsprechend, suchte die Berliner Afrikanistik ihren Standort auf der Schnittstelle zwischen Sprachwissenschaft und Völkerkunde. Dieser Forschungsansatz, der den pragmatischen Aspekt sprachlicher Phänomene zum Mittelpunkt macht, hat sich in der Gegenwart durch die Schaffung dreier interdisziplinärer Sonderforschungsbereiche (s. u.) als besonders tragfähig und fruchtbar erwiesen.

In Deutschland ging die koloniale Epoche nach dem Ersten Weltkrieg mit dem Verlust der Kolonien keinesfalls zu Ende. Noch bis in die vierziger Jahre hinein gab es ernsthafte Bestrebungen, den Wiedereinzug in die ehemaligen Kolonien vorzubereiten (Wolff 1943; Lukas 1944). Es ist nicht zu verhehlen, daß unter dieser politischen Vorgabe die afrikanistische Sprachforschung vor Ende des zweiten Weltkriegs nochmals einen gewissen Auftrieb erfuhr. Zwar überlebten die afrikanistischen Einrichtungen in Berlin und Hamburg das Ende des Kriegs, sie waren jedoch durch personelle Verluste so geschwächt, daß sie während der spätkolonialen Phase in den fünfziger und Anfang der sechziger Jahre international keine Rolle mehr spielten. Die Führung der Disziplin ging hinfort auf die School of Oriental and African Studies in London über. Es fanden sich dort Experten für nahezu alle Sprachgruppen Afrikas zusammen, was nicht nur zu einer gegenseitigen wissenschaftlichen Befruchtung führte, sondern vor allem zu einer Fülle von monographischen und vergleichenden Studien, durch welche die Kenntnis der afrikanischen Sprachen ganz entscheidend gefördert wurde. Insbesondere wurden dort erstmals die modernen strukturalistischen Methoden der Linguistik rezipiert. Dies hatte sprachadäquate Analysen zur Folge, die in ihrem Aufbau weitgehend vergleichbar waren. Die erheblich erweiterte Kenntnis der afrikanischen Sprachen während der strukturalistischen Phase führte schließlich zu Übersichten und referenziellen Gliederungen, die aufgrund ihres pragmatischen Ansatzes unverändert Gültigkeit haben. In Fragen der Sprachgliederung gingen die bisher nachhaltigsten Impulse allerdings von dem amerikanischen Außenseiter Joseph H. Greenberg aus (1955, 1963). Wenn auch nicht unangefochten (Fodor 1966, 1982), so wird seine umfassende genetische Klassifikation der Sprachen Afrikas in der Afrikanistik und in benachbarten Disziplinen bis heute als umfassendes Referenzsystem verwendet. Greenberg ordnete im Prinzip alle Sprachen Afrikas, auch die noch unerforschten, vier genetischen Großfamilien zu: (1) Niger-Kordofanisch, (2) Afroasiatisch, (3) Nilo-Saharanisch und (4) Khoisan. Für jede Großfamilie stellte er mehr oder weniger verzweigte Stammbäume auf. Das wohl augenfälligste Ergebnis dieser Gliederung ist darin zu sehen, daß die Masse der Bantusprachen, die im gesamten südlichen Subkontinent verbreitet sind, einem einzigen Unterzweig des Niger-Kordofanischen angehören sollen. Auch dieser Teil seines unilinear-genealogischen Abstammungsmodels ist inzwischen in Zweifel gezogen worden (Bennett & Sterck 1977; Möhlig 1981). Die von Greenberg angewandte Methode weicht bewußt vom historisch-vergleichenden Prinzip der regelmäßigen Lautentsprechung ab und stellt stattdessen das Ähnlichkeitsprinzip in den Vordergrund, dies allerdings kombiniert mit dem Prinzip des Massenvergleichs, um zufällige Ähnlichkeiten oder solche, die auf Entlehnung beruhen, auszuschließen.

## 4. Postkoloniale Epoche

Der Übergang in die postkoloniale Epoche setzte in der europäischen Afrikanistik zu Beginn der sechziger Jahre mit der Unabhängigkeit der afrikanischen Staaten ein. Bedingt durch die Ost-West-Teilung und infolge des kulturellen Partikularismus der Länder entstanden auf deutschem Boden sechs neue Afrika-Institute, so daß die deutsche Afrikanistik mit den beiden in der Kolonialzeit gegründeten Instituten heute insgesamt über acht Forschungsstätten an folgenden Universitäten verfügt: Bayreuth, Berlin (Humboldt), Frankfurt, Hamburg, Köln, Leipzig, Mainz und München. In der Lehre, etwa bei der Vermittlung der großen afrikanischen Sprachen wie Swahili, Hausa, Bambara und Somali gibt es Überschneidungen, in den Forschungsschwerpunkten sind die deutschen Institute jedoch weitgehend komplementär.

Die Londoner School of Oriental and African Studies mußte aufgrund mangelnder politischer Unterstützung in den achtziger Jahren ihr ehemals breites Angebot in Forschung und Lehre erheblich einschränken, während zur gleichen Zeit in Frankreich die afrikanischen Sprachstudien erstmals in der Geschichte ausgebaut wurden.

In Paris entstanden mehrere Forschungseinrichtungen, die sich mit unterschiedlicher regionaler Gewichtung auf afrikanische Sprachkulturen konzentrieren, wobei die ehemals französischen Kolonialgebiete den größten Anteil ausmachen. In der Lehre führend ist die Afrika-Abteilung der École Pratique des Hautes Études in Paris. Die Forschung ist nach bestimmten thematischen Schwerpunkten auf mehrere selbständige Arbeitsgruppen des Nationalen Forschungsrats C. N. R. S, sogenannte Werkstätten (Laboratoires) verteilt. So befaßte sich die Gruppe "Langues et Civilisations à Tradition Orale" bis vor kurzem mit sprachanalytischen Forschungen vor allem in Kamerun, in Ostafrika und in der Zentralafrikanischen Republik, während die Forschergruppe "Langage et Culture de l'Afrique de l'Ouest" sich regional auf Westafrika und thematisch auf ethnolinguistische Fragen konzentriert, sich vor allem aber mit oraler Literatur befaßt. Aber selbst im Rahmen des entwicklungspolitisch orientierten Inisitituts "ORSTOM" [Office de la Recherche Scientifique et Technique d'Outre-Mer] werden Forschungsthemen bearbeitet, die in die fachliche Zuständigkeit der Afrikanistik fallen, z. B. Sprachatlanten, Sprachprofile bestimmter Länder oder sprachsoziologische Erhebungen. Neben den in Paris konzentrierten Institutionen bestehen weitere afrikanistische Forschungseinrichtungen in Nizza und Lyon. Letztere Einrichtung ist insbesondere auf dem Gebiet der Bantuistik tätig.

In Italien wird afrikanische Sprachforschung und Lehre vor allem an der Universität von Neapel betrieben. Das dortige Seminario di Studi Africani befaßt sich mit kuschitischen Sprachen und mit dem Swahili unter linguistischen sowie literaturwissenschaftlichen Aspekten.

In Spanien und Portugal ist man über Ansätze, die Afrikanistik zu etablieren, nicht hinausgekommen, obwohl beide Länder, bezogen auf Europa, am längsten Kolonialinteressen in Afrika verfolgt haben. Es besteht eine afrikanistische Fachvereinigung, die ihren Sitz an der Madrider Universität im Colegio Mayor Universitario "Nuestra Señora de África" hat.

In Belgien werden seit etwa 1925 an den Universitäten Gent und Leuven afrikanische Sprachen gelehrt und erforscht. Entsprechend den ehemaligen Kolonialinteressen handelt es sich dabei vor allem um Sprachen aus Zaire und dem ostafrikanischen Zwischenseengebiet. Der Anteil an Forschern in Missionarsdiensten ist hier besonders hoch. Eine hervorragende Rolle in der afrikanistischen Forschung spielt die 1950 eingerichtete Sprachabteilung am Königlichen Museum für Zentral-Afrika [Musée Royal de l'Afrique Centrale] in Tervuren. Von hier gingen zahlreiche Impulse aus, die sowohl thematisch als auch methodologisch die moderne Afrikanistik befruchteten.

Zu einem besonders wichtigen Partner im europäischen Netzwerk afrikanistischer Sprachforschung hat sich seit den sechziger Jahren die Fachgruppe für afrikanische Sprachwissenschaft [Vakgroep Afrikaanse Taalkunde] an der Universität Leiden entwickelt. Seit 1979 wird dort das international renommierte *Journal of African Languages and Linguistics* herausgegeben. Es widmet sich allen Aspekten der afrikanischen Sprachen, ihren Strukturen und ihrer Geschichte ebenso wie ihrer Rolle in Gesellschaft und Erziehung. Außerdem wird seit über einem Vierteljahrhundert von den Leidener Afrikanisten jährlich eine Fachtagung veranstaltet, die regelmäßig Afrika-Linguisten aus aller Welt für mehrere Tage zu einem regen Gedankenaustausch vereinigt.

Unter den skandinavischen Staaten haben sich Dänemark, Schweden und Finnland in jüngerer Zeit afrikanischen Sprachstudien zugewandt. Seit neuestem gibt es auch in der Schweiz an der Züricher Universität Bestrebungen, Afrikanistik im Rahmen der allgemeinen Linguistik zu betreiben.

Traditionsreiche afrikanistische Institute, die allerdings schwer unter Finanznot leiden und daher in der Forschung eher als rezeptiv bewertet werden müssen, bestehen an den Universitäten von Warschau und Krakau, St. Petersburg und Moskau.

In Afrika gibt es afrikanistische Lehr- und Forschungseinrichtungen, die in ihrer Entstehung zum Teil noch auf die koloniale Epoche zurückgehen, wie das "Institut de l'Afrique Noire" in Dakar (Senegal), die Afrika-Institute an der ghanaischen Universität von Legon, Accra und den Universitäten in Makerere (Kampala, Uganda), in Harare (Simbabwe) und in Südafrika. Die meisten Einrichtungen in Afrika, die sich mit afrikanischen Sprachen befassen, sind jedoch erst nach der Unabhängigkeit der betreffenden Staaten entstanden, wobei europäische Afrikanistik-Institute im Wege von Paten- und Partnerschaften zum Aufbau wesentlich mit beitrugen. So wurde etwa das Department of African Languages and Linguistics an der Universität Nairobi in den siebziger Jahren von Köln aus intensiv unterstützt, wobei sich die Hilfe vor allem auf die Entsendung von Hochschullehrern und die Betreuung von Doktor- und Magisterarbeiten konzentrierte. Bemerkenswert ist in diesem Zusammenhang, daß an der ältesten Universität auf afrikanischem Boden, dem altehrwürdigen Fourah Bay College in Sierra Leone, erst 1984 auf massive ausländische Einflußnahme hin eine afrikanistische Abteilung eingerichtet wurde, während dort zur gleichen Zeit mehrere Lehrstühle für Latein, Hebräisch und Griechisch bestanden.

In Nord-Amerika und Kanada beruhte die Beschäftigung mit afrikanischen Sprachen bisher weitgehend auf dem wissenschaftlichen Interesse einzelner, die sich zumeist im Rahmen der allgemeinen Linguistik diesem Bereich zuwandten, um bestimmte Theorien zu überprüfen oder zu entwickeln. Sie sind entsprechend den Möglichkeiten des Arbeitsmarktes über viele Universitäten verstreut. Ein bedeutenderes afrikanistisches Zentrum hat sich lediglich an der University of California in Los Angeles – UCLA – gebildet. Dort wird auch seit 1970 die betont linguistisch ausgerichtete Fachzeitschrift "Studies in African Linguistics" herausgegeben. Eine besondere Rolle für die Erforschung und Verschriftlichung afrikanischer Sprachen spielt das weltweit arbeitende Summer Institute of Linguistics. Wie schon die Gründerväter Kenneth L. Pike und Eugene Nida haben die mit einer christlich-religiösen Zielsetzung vereinigten Mitglieder des Summer Institutes einerseits die allgemeinen Linguistik-Theorien stark beeinflußt, andererseits aber in vielen Gebieten Afrikas durch akribische monographische Arbeiten erheblich zur heutigen Kenntnis der dort gesprochenen Sprachen beigetragen.

In Asien interessieren sich die beiden Länder Süd-Korea und Japan für afrikanische Sprachen. Die Korean Association of African Studies gibt seit 1986 eine Fachzeitschrift heraus, die neben allgemein afrikanologischen auch afrikanistische Themen behandelt. An der Universität Kyoto besteht seit 1966 ein Afrika-Zentrum, das die Zeitschrift "Kyoto University African Studies" herausgibt und sich auch durch seine intensiven Feldforschungen in Afrika inzwischen einen internationalen Ruf erwerben konnte.

## 5. Gegenwärtige Trends in der Forschung

In ihren Anfängen wurde die postkoloniale Epoche zunächst durch eine massive Rezeption moderner linguistischer Methoden amerikanischer Provenienz geprägt. Es bildeten sich unter den deutschsprachigen Afrikanisten in den siebziger Jahren zwei antagonische Richtungen heraus, die jeweils die Disziplin Afrikanistik unterschiedlich definierten. Die einen faßten sie als Afrika-Linguistik auf, die anderen in Fortentwicklung der alten These Westermanns 'durch die Sprachen zu den Kulturen' als eine Afrika-Kulturwissenschaft, deren wesentliches Erkenntnismittel die afrikanischen Sprachen sind. Afrika-Kulturwissenschaft umfaßt nicht nur die Sprachen, d. h. ihre historischen und typologischen Zusammenhänge, ihre geographischen und soziologischen Rahmenbedingungen, ihre semantischen und syntaktischen Strukturen, sondern auch ihre Literaturen. Darunter wird zum einen die bis in dieses Jahrhundert tradierte Wortkunst Afrikas (Mythen, Märchen, Fabeln, Sprichwörter, Rätsel, Preislieder, Poesie usw.) verstanden, zum anderen aber auch die sogenannte Dokumentarliteratur (Geider 1994). Dieser Begriff faßt afrikasprachliche Texte verschiedenen Inhalts zusammen, deren gemeinsames Ziel darin besteht, bestimmte Sachverhalte der afrikanischen Kulturen zur Wissensbewahrung und als Identifikationsgrundlage für zukünftige Generationen schriftlich niederzulegen. Darunter fallen beispielsweise Chroniken, Biographien, Autobiographien und auto-ethnographische Berichte von afrikanischen Autoren. Die Übergänge zur Wortkunst sind fließend. In der Mehrheit handelt es sich um Texte, die im Berichtsstil verfaßt sind. Ausnahmen sind Texte in gebundener Sprachform wie die Gedichte des Swahili-Gelehrten Nabhany über den traditionellen Bootsbau (Miehe & Schadeberg 1979) oder den Anbau von Kokospalmen (El-Maawy 1985). Gelegentlich kann die Dokumentarliteratur sogar die Gestalt von ethnographischen Romanen annehmen, wie die auch ins Deutsche übersetzten Werken des Ost-Afrikaners Aniceti Kitereza (Kitereza 1980, Kitereza & Möhlig 1991, 1993) zeigen.

In Abhängigkeit von individuellen Forschungsinteressen lassen sich zur Zeit folgende Themenbereiche ausmachen, die in afrikanistischen Veröffentlichungen und auf internationalen Fachtagungen diskutiert werden, bzw. zu denen Forschungsprojekte bestehen:

(1) Sprachmonographische Arbeiten nehmen nach wie vor die erste Stelle ein. Trotz beachtlicher Fortschritte in der Kenntnis afrikanischer Sprachen während der letzten dreißig Jahre, gelten viele Sprachen linguistisch immer noch als unbearbeitet. Die 'weißen Flecken' auf der Sprachenkarte Afrikas sind aus kolonialhistorischen Gründen allerdings ganz unterschiedlich verteilt. Man kann wohl sagen, daß die Sprachen der ehemals britischen Gebiete am besten erforscht sind. Besonders große Wissenslücken ergeben sich hingegen in den früheren Kolonien Portugals, vor allem in Angola und Moçambique. Die Motivation, afrikanistische Grundlagenforschung zu betreiben, nährt sich auch aus dem Phänomen, daß viele Sprachen mit einer geringeren Sprecherzahl inzwischen von den großen Verkehrs- und Nationalsprachen verdrängt werden. Sprachentod (Brenzinger 1992) ist allenthalben erkennbar. So wurden beispielsweise Anfang der sechziger Jahre auf dem Staatsgebiet des heutigen Tansania noch 124 afrikanische Sprachen gezählt. Durch die konsequente und letztlich auch erfolgreiche Swahilisierungspolitik des ehemaligen Staatspräsidenten Julius Nyerere werden diese Sprachen heutzutage, wenn überhaupt, nur noch von Menschen im höheren Lebensalter gesprochen. Die ehemaligen Erzähler und Erzählerinnen oral überlieferter Texte befinden sich als Greise zwar noch unter den Lebenden. Da man sie aber schon seit langem nicht mehr einlädt, ihre Geschichten zu erzählen, fallen ihre Texte zunehmend in Vergessenheit, womit wichtige Elemente der sprachkulturellen Identität untergehen. Beide Faktoren, Wegfall der kommunikativen Funktion und Untergang des traditionellen Erzählgutes, werden in naher Zukunft viele afrikanische Sprachen aussterben lassen, noch ehe man ihre Inventare und Strukturen erforschen konnte. Restsprachenforschung ist darum in Afrika ein vorrangiges Ziel.

(2) Die seit den Anfängen der Afrikanistik verfolgte Frage, wie die Fülle der afrikanischen Sprachen zu gliedern sei, ist ebenfalls nach wie vor aktuell. Es geht weniger um die Definition von sprachgenetischen Großfamilien im Sinne Greenbergs (1963) als vielmehr darum, die historischen Zusammenhänge in kleineren Arealen anhand bestimmter Sprachmerkmale aufzuklären (Mukarovsky 1976–77; Wolff 1981; Rottland 1982; Vossen 1982; Gerhardt 1983; Miehe 1991; Cyffer 1995; Jungraithmayr 1994; Jungraithmayr & Ibriszimow 1995; Kastenholz 1996). Auf diese Weise entsteht zusätzliches Quellenmaterial für die Rekonstruktion der überwiegend schriftlosen Ethnohistorie in den betreffenden Gebieten. Der Schritt zwischen Sprachgeschichte und Völkergeschichte stellt ein methodologisches Problem dar, das zwar erkannt ist (Vansina 1985, 1990), zu dem befriedigende Lösungen jedoch nach wie vor gesucht werden. Vorherrschend in den Überlegungen zur Rekonstruktion der Sprachgeschichte sind immer noch unilinear-genetische Modelle. Man versucht zumeist, die Verwandtschaft zwischen mehreren verglichenen Sprachen, die aktuell noch gesprochen werden, mit ihren rezenten Inventaren auf eine gemeinsame Protosprache zurückzuführen. Als Vorbild dienen die Arbeiten Meinhofs (1899, 1906) und in Fortentwicklung dazu vor allem die von Malcolm Guthrie (1967–71). Das im Kontrast dazu entwickelte Stratifikations-Modell (Möhlig 1981; Winter 1981; Weier 1985) konnte sich bisher noch nicht durchsetzen.

(3) Da die historische Perspektive empirisch weitgehend von rezenten Daten abhängt, kommt es auf deren möglichst genaue Erfassung an. Das früher bei der Erhebung des Vergleichsmaterials angewandte Stichproben- bzw. Testsprachenprinzip (Guthrie 1967–1971) wurde durch das dialektologische Prinzip abgelöst. Dieses besagt, daß bei der Erhebung des Vergleichsmaterials zwischen den Belegsprachen kein undokumentiertes Gebiet zugelassen werden darf (Heine & Möhlig 1980: 38). Veranlaßt durch diese methodologische Prämisse, wurden seit Anfang der siebziger Jahre dialektologische Methoden von der Afrikanistik rezipiert und auf die afrikanischen Verhältnisse angepaßt (Möhlig 1974).

Als deutsch-französisches Gemeinschaftsprojekt entwickelte man zur Messung dialektaler Distanzen eine eigenständige Methode, die sogenannte Dialektometrie (Möhlig 1983; Guarisma & Möhlig 1986). Deren Ergebnisse dienen nicht nur der historischen Zielsetzung, sondern vor allem auch angewandten Fragestellungen, wie sie von Sprachpolitik und Sprachplanung in den einzelnen afrikanischen Staaten vorgegeben werden.

(4) Ein typologisch-historischer Themenbereich der allgemeinen Linguistik, der durch Arbeiten über afrikanische Sprachen befruchtet wurde, ist der der Grammatikalisierung. Es geht dabei um die Frage, wie sich bestimmte grammatische Kategorien, z. B. das Tempus-Aspekt-Modus-System oder Präpositionen, entwickelt haben (Heine 1976; Heine & Reh 1984; Heine & Traugott 1991).

(5) Auf semantischem Gebiet werden seit einigen Jahren Untersuchungen zur Konzeptualisierung ganzer Wortfelder durchgeführt. Im Mittelpunkt stehen vor allem Pflanzentaxonomien (Heine 1985; Heine & König 1987; Heine & Heine 1988; Heine & Legère 1995). Zur Zeit werden aber auch Projekte zur Erforschung kulturhistorisch indikativer Wortfelder wie der Eisenherstellung und Töpferei (Reinhard Klein-Arendt) oder der traditionellen Architektur (Axel Fleisch) durchgeführt.

(6) Ein vergleichsweise junges Arbeitsgebiet, das sich die Afrikanistik erschlossen hat, liegt im Bereich der Text-Linguistik. Es konzentriert sich derzeit auf zwei Schwerpunkte. Zum einen werden Diskurse in ihrer Struktur und ihren spezifischen sprachlichen Gestaltungsmitteln untersucht (Klein-Arendt 1992; Bearth 1993, 1995), zum anderen geht es um die Architektur von Erzähltexten, die der traditionellen Wortkunst zuzurechnen sind (Paulme 1972, 1976; Bremond 1980; Möhlig 1986, 1995).

(7) Bereits in der ersten Hälfte des 19. Jhs. waren die wenigen Wissenschaftler, die sich mit afrikanischen Wortkulturen befaßten, von deren Reichtum an oraler Literatur beeindruckt. Dementsprechend intensiv wurden Beispiele dieser Wortkunst gesammelt und veröffentlicht. Von der europäisch dominierten Folklore-Forschung wurden jedoch diese Kompendien und Anthologien weitgehend ignoriert. So berücksichtigt auch der international anerkannte Typen-Katalog von Stith Thomson kaum afrikanisches Erzählgut. Außer daß man die afrikanischen Erzähltexte verschriftlichte und in eine europäische Sprache übersetzte, wurden sie wissenschaftlich selten bearbeitet (Finnegan 1970, 1992; Derive 1975). Sprichwörter wurden besonders eifrig gesammelt und publiziert, ihre sinngebende Abhängigkeit vom jeweiligen situativen Kontext blieb jedoch weitgehend unerkannt und deswegen in den Dokumentationen auch unberücksichtigt. Es gibt nur wenige Abhandlungen über afrikanische Sprichwörter, die diesen Gesichtspunkt berücksichtigen (vgl. Messenger 1959; Möhlig 1994). Erst seit den achtziger Jahren hat man sich auf Initiative deutscher und französischer Oralisten der Analyse von afrikanischen Erzähltexten und der damit verbundenen Problematik verstärkt zugewandt. Zumeist werden thematische Schwerpunkte gewählt, indem man sich einzelnen Figuren (Paulme 1988; Steinbrich 1982, 1988; Geider 1990) oder Erzähltypen (Seydou & Paulme 1972; Görög-Karady 1980, 1992; Görög-Karady et al. 1980; Seydou 1985; Schott 1988) bzw. ganzen Erzählkulturen (Schott 1993; Wolff 1994) oder gar dem Motivvergleich (Schmidt 1989; Schott 1990) widmet. Um das vom Untergang bedrohte Erzählgut Afrikas für die Nachwelt zu bewahren, kommt es jetzt darauf an, dieses rechtzeitig zu dokumentieren und der Öffentlichkeit zugänglich zu machen. Ein entsprechendes Projekt wurde kürzlich in Namibia begonnen (Wilfred Haacke & W. J. G. Möhlig).

Das gesamtafrikanistische Konzept hat in Deutschland zur Bildung dreier Sonderforschungsbereiche (SFB) geführt, in deren multi- bzw. interdisziplinäre Netzwerke die afrikanistische Sprachforschung jeweils fest integriert ist. Im folgenden sollen die einzelnen Forschungsvorhaben kurz vorgestellt werden:

(1) Der älteste SFB mit einer Orientierung auf Afrika wurde bereits 1983 an der damals neu gegründeten Universität Bayreuth eingerichtet. Er widmet sich dem Thema der Identität in Afrika, insbesondere den Prozessen ihrer Entstehung und Veränderung. Im Kontext von Gesellschafts-, wirtschaftswissenschaftlichen und kulturwissenschaftlichen Disziplinen einschließlich der Human- und Wirtschaftsgeographie befaßt man sich unter drei verschiedenen Perspektiven mit afrikanischen Sprachen. Eine Gruppe von Wissenschaftlern untersucht mit sprach-soziologischen Methoden die Identitätsproblematik am Phänomen des Sprachgebrauchs, insbesondere des Sprachwechsels. Eine andere

Gruppe befaßt sich mit Fragen der Konzeptualisierung von Identität im Bereich der Verwandtschaft und allgemein von Gesellschaft und Umwelt, wobei auch die Auswertung von oralliterarischen Texten und von Dokumentartexten eine Rolle spielt. Eine dritte Gruppe untersucht die Identitätsthematik an der kolonialsprachlichen Literatur Afrikas mit literaturwissenschaftlichen und komparatistischen Methoden.

(2) Seit 1988 besteht an der Universität Frankfurt am Main ein weiterer Afrika-SFB zum Thema 'Kulturentwicklung und Sprachgeschichte im Naturraum Westafrikanische Savanne'. Es ist das Ziel dieses SFB, die historische Entwicklung in der westafrikanischen Sahelzone von den frühesten noch faßbaren Anfängen bis zur Gegenwart im Wechselspiel zwischen Mensch und Natur zu untersuchen. Der Anteil der Sprachwissenschaftler im Verbund mit Ethnohistorikern, Ethnologen verschiedener Spezialgebiete, Archäologen, Ethnobotanikern und Geographen konzentriert sich zum einen auf historisch orientierte Untersuchungen des Kulturwortschatzes, zum anderen auf die sprachhistorische Aufarbeitung des Forschungsareals, wobei in den ersten Phasen naturgemäß die Dokumentation und Beschreibung bisher noch unbekannter Sprachen im Vordergrund stand.

(3) Der zunächst jüngste Afrika-SFB wurde 1995 an der Universität Köln ins Leben gerufen. Er befaßt sich im Kern ebenfalls mit den Wechselwirkungen zwischen Mensch und Natur in Afrika, allerdings unter der Prämisse einer bereits seit Jahrtausenden fortschreitenden Austrocknung des Kontinents. Wodurch auch für den afrikanischen Frühmenschen schon der Zwang bestand, sich ständig neue Lebensräume und Ressourcen erschließen zu müssen. Aus logistischen Gründen wurden zunächst zwei regionale Forschungsschwerpunkte gebildet, einer in Namibia, ein anderer in Nordost-Afrika (Ägypten und Sudan). Die beteiligten Disziplinen sind neben der Afrikanistik Ägyptologie, Archäologie, Botanik, Ethnologie, Geographie und Geschichtswissenschaft. Die afrikanistische Sprachforschung ist mit mehreren methodischen Ansätzen am SFB beteiligt, die sich insbesondere in Namibia überlappen und ergänzen. Angesichts der historisch rezenten Überschichtung von wenigstens zwei verschiedenen Bevölkerungsstraten, Bantu und Khoisaniden, geht es darum, Wesen und Ausmaß dieses Prozesses anhand von Konzeptualisierungen in bestimmten, kulturhistorisch relevanten Wortfeldern sichtbar zu machen. Hinzu kommt die Arbeit mit oral tradierten Texten, soweit sie historische Sachverhalte enthalten. Auch Typen- und Motivvergleich spielt eine Rolle. Ein in der Afrikanistik bisher wenig bearbeitetes Gebiet ist die Ortsnamenforschung. Sie soll erstmals in Namibia angewandt werden, um Völkerverschiebungen sowie ethnische Übersichten und Mischungsprozesse aufzudecken. Daneben kommen die üblichen sprachhistorisch-dialektologischen Methoden zum Einsatz.

Insgesamt haben die Sonderforschungsbereiche die Entwicklung der deutschen Afrikanistik sehr gefördert, so daß sie heute wieder wie zu Beginn des Jahrhunderts führend in der Welt ist.

## 6. Bibliographie

Barth, Heinrich. 1862–66. *Sammlung und Bearbeitung Central-Afrikanischer Vokabularien.* Gotha: Justus Perthes.

Bearth, Thomas. 1993. "Satztyp und Situation in einigen Sprachen Westafrikas". *IX. Afrikanistentag. Beiträge zur afrikanischen Sprach- und Literaturwissenschaft* hg. von Wilhelm J. G. Möhlig, Siegmund Brauner & Herrmann Jungraithmayr, 91–104. Köln: Köppe.

–. 1995. "Wortstellung, Topik und Fokus". *Swahili-Handbuch* hg. von Gudrun Miehe & Wilhelm J. G. Möhlig. Köln: Köppe.

Bennett, T. L. & J. P. Sterk. 1977. "South Central Niger Congo: A reclassification". *Studies in African Linguistics* 8.240–273.

Bleek, Wilhelm Heinrich Immanuel. 1862. *A Comparative Grammar of South African Languages*, Teil I: *Phonology*. London: Trübner.

–. 1869. *A Comparative Grammar of South African Languages*, Teil II: *The Concord.* Section I: *The Noun.* London: Trübner.

Bremond, C. 1980. "Morphologie d'un conte africain". *Cahiers d'Études Africaines* 73–76. 485–494.

Brenzinger, Matthias, Hg. 1992. *Language Death: Factual and theoretical explorations with special reference to East Africa.* Berlin & New York: Mouton de Gruyter.

Cyffer, Norbert. 1995. "Die Saharanischen Sprachen: Innere und äußere Beziehungen". *Sprachkulturelle und historische Forschungen in Afrika* hg. von Axel Fleisch & Dirk Otten, 103–118. Köln: Köppe.

Derive, Jean. 1975. *Collecte et traduction des littératures orales: Un exemple négro-africain: les contes ngbaka-ma'bo de RCA.* Paris: SELAF.

El-Maawy, A. A. A., Hg. 1985. *Umbuji wa mnazi* [Die elegante Schönheit des Palmbaums] by Ahmed Sheikh Nabhany. Nairobi: East African Publishing House.

Finnegan, Ruth. 1970. *Oral Literature in Africa.* Oxford: The Clarendon Press.

–. 1992. *Oral Traditions and the Verbal Arts. A guide to research practices.* London & New York: Routledge.

Fodor, István. 1966. *The Problems in the Classification of the African Languages. Methodological and theoretical conclusions concerning the classification system of Joseph H. Greenberg.* Budapest: Center for Afro-Asian Research of the Hungarian Academy of Sciences.

–. 1982. *A Fallacy of Contemporary Linguistics. J. H. Greenberĝs classification of the African languages and his "Comparative Method".* Hamburg: Buske.

Geider, Thomas. 1990. *Die Figur des Oger in der traditionellen Literatur und Lebenswelt der Pokomo in Ost-Kenya.* 2 Bde. Köln: Köppe.

–. 1994. "Indigene Ethnographien in der Swahilisprachigen Dokumentarliteratur". *Sprachen und Sprachzeugnisse in Afrika. Eine Sammlung philologischer Beiträge Wilhelm J. G. Möhlig zum 60. Geburtstag zugeeignet* hg. von Thomas Geider & Raimund Kastenholz. Köln: Köppe.

Gerhardt, Ludwig. 1983. *Beiträge zur Kenntnis der Sprachen des nigerianischen Plateaus.* Glückstadt: Augustin.

Görög-Karady, Veronika. 1980. "Les deux filles. Conte bambara". *Recueil de littérature manding,* 18–33. Paris: ACCT.

–. 1992. *Le mariage dans les contes africains: Études et anthologie.* Paris: Karthala.

–, Suzy Platiel, Diano Rey-Hulman & Christiane Seydou, Hgg. 1980. *Histoires d'Enfants Terribles* (*Afrique Noire*): *Études et anthologie.* Paris: Maisonneuve & Larose.

Greenberg, Joseph H. 1955. *Studies in African Linguistic Classification.* Brandford, Ct.: Compass. (Repr. from the *South Western Journal of Anthropology.*)

–. 1963. *Languages of Africa.* Den Haag: Mouton.

Guarisma, Gladys & Wilhelm J. G. Möhlig, Hgg. 1986. *La méthode dialectométrique appliquée aux langues africaines.* Berlin: Reimer.

Guthrie, Malcolm. 1967–71. *Comparative Bantu: An introduction to the comparative linguistics and prehistory of the Bantu langues,* 4 Bde. Farnborough: Gregg Press.

Heine, Bernd. 1976. *A Typology of African Languages Based on the Order of Meaningful Elements.* Berlin: Reimer.

–. 1985. "Concepts of Plant Taxonomy among the Samburu (Kenya): Some preliminary observation". *Afrikanistische Arbeitspapiere AAP* 3.5–36.

– & Wilhelm J. G. Möhlig, Hgg. 1980. *Language and Dialect Atlas of Kenya,* Bd. I: *Geographical and Historical Introduction. Language and Society. Selected bibliography.* Berlin: Reimer.

–, Thilo C. Schadeberg & Ekkehard Wolff, Hgg. 1981. *Die Sprachen Afrikas.* Hamburg: Buske.

– & Mechthild Reh. 1984. *Grammaticalization and Reanalysis in African Languages.* Hamburg: Buske.

– & Christa König. 1987. "On the Taxonomic Status of Folk Botanic Categories among the Samburu". *Afrikanistische Arbeitspapiere AAP* 10.31–52.

– & Ingo Heine. 1988. *Plants of the Chamus (Kenya).* (= *Plant Concepts and Plant Use,* III.) Saarbrücken & Fort Lauderdale: Breitenbach.

– & E. C. Traugott, Hgg. 1991. *Approaches to Grammaticalization,* Bd. I: *Focus on Theoretical and Methodological Issues.* Amsterdam & Philadelphia: Benjamins.

– & Karsten Legère. 1995. *Swahili Plants.* Köln: Köppe.

Jungraithmayr, Herrmann. 1995. "Was ist am Tangale noch tschadisch/hamitosemitisch?". *Sprachkulturelle und historische Forschungen in Afrika* hg. von Axel Fleisch & Dirk Otten, 197–205. Köln: Köppe.

– & Wilhelm J. G. Möhlig, Hg. 1983. *Lexikon der Afrikanistik.* Berlin: Reimer.

– & D. Ibriszimow. 1994. *Chadic Lexical Roots.* 2 Bde. Berlin: Reimer.

Kastenholz, Raimund. 1996. *Sprachgeschichte im West-Mande. Methoden und Rekonstruktionen.* Köln: Köppe.

Kitereza, Aniceti. 1980. *Bwana Myombekere na Bibi Bugonoka. Ntulanalwo na Bulihwali.* Dar es Salaam: Tanzanian Publishing House.

– & Wilhelm J. G. Möhlig. 1991. *Die Kinder der Regenmacher: Herr Myombekere und Frau Bugonoka. Eine afrikanische Familiensaga.* Wuppertal: Hammer.

– & Wilhelm J. G. Möhlig. 1993. *Der Schlangentöter. Ntulanalwo und Bulihwali.* Wuppertal: Hammer.

Klein-Arendt, Reinhard. 1992. *Gesprächsstrategien im Swahili.* Köln: Köppe.

Koelle, Wilhelm Sigismund. 1853. *Outlines of a Grammar of the Vei Language, together with a Vei-English Vocabulary.* London: Kegan Paul.

–. 1854a. *Polyglotta Africana.* London: Church Missionary House.

–. 1854b. *Grammar of the Bornu or Kanuri Language.* London: Church Missionary House.

–. 1854c. *African Native Literature, or Proverbs, Tales, Fables, and Historical Fragments in the Kanuri or Bornu Language* [...]. London: Church Missionary House.

Köhler, Oswin. 1975. "Geschichte und Probleme der Gliederung der Sprachen Afrikas: Von den Anfängen bis zur Gegenwart". *Die Völker Afrikas und ihre traditionellen Kulturen*, Teil I: *Allgemeiner Teil und südliches Afrika* hg. von H. Baumann. Wiesbaden: Steiner.

Krapf, Johann Ludwig. 1850. *An Outline of the Elements of the Kisuaheli Language with Special Reference to the Kinika Dialect.* Tübingen: Ludwig Friedrich Fuchs.

—. 1882. *A Dictionary of the Suahili Language With Introduction Containing an Outline of the Grammar.* London: Trübner.

Lukas, Johannes. 1944. "Neue Beiträge zur Kolonialforschung". *Studien zur Auslandskunde, Afrika* 3.9–18.

Meinhof, Carl. ²1910 [1899]. *Grundriß einer Lautlehre der Bantusprachen nebst einer Anleitung zur Aufnahme von Bantusprachen.* Berlin: Reimer.

—. ²1948 [1906]. *Grundzüge einer vergleichenden Grammatik der Bantusprachen.* Berlin: Reimer.

—. 1910. *Die moderne Sprachforschung in Afrika.* (= *Hamburgische Vorträge.*) Berlin: Berliner ev. Missionsgesellschaft.

—. 1910–11. "Sudansprachen und Hamitensprachen". *Zeitschrift für Kolonialsprachen* 1.161–166.

—. 1912. *Die Sprache der Hamiten.* Hamburg: Friederichsen.

—. 1936. *Die Entstehung flektierender Sprachen.* Berlin: Reimer.

Messenger, J. C. 1959. "The Role of Proverbs in a Nigerian Judicial System". *Southwestern Journal of Anthropology* 15.64–73.

Miehe, Gudrun. 1991. *Die Präfixnasale im Benue-Congo und im Kwa.* Berlin: Reimer.

— & Thilo C. Schadeberg, Hg. 1979. *Sambo ya Kiwandeo. The Ship of Lamu-Island.* Leiden: Africa-Studiecentrum.

— & Wilhelm J. G. Möhlig, Hg. 1995. *Swahili-Handbuch.* Köln: Köppe.

Möhlig, Wilhelm J. G. 1974. *Die Stellung der Bergdialekte im Osten des Mt. Kenya: Ein Beitrag zur Sprachgliederung im Bantu.* Berlin: Reimer.

—. 1981. "Stratification in the History of the Bantu Languages". *Sprache und Geschichte in Afrika SUGIA* 3.251–316.

—. 1983. "Dialektometrie in Afrika: Methoden zur Messung synchroner sprachlicher Nähe". *Sprache, Geschichte und Kultur in Afrika: Vorträge gehalten auf dem III. Afrikanistentag, Köln, 14./15. Oktober 1982* hg. von Rainer Voßen & Ulrike Claudi, 209–242. Hamburg: Buske.

—. 1986. "Grundzüge der textmorphologischen Struktur und Analyse afrikanischer Erzählungen". *Afrikanistische Arbeitspapiere AAP* 8.5–56.

—. 1994. "Semantische und pragmatische Analyse von Sprichwörtern im situativen Kontext: Beispiele aus dem Kerewe". *Perspektiven afrikanistischer Forschung: Beiträge zur Linguistik, Ethnologie, Geschichte, Philosophie und Literatur. X. Afrikanistentag* hg. von Thomas Bearth et al., 247–258. Köln: Köppe.

—. 1995. "The Architecture of Bantu Narratives: An interdisciplinary matter: Analysis of a Dciriku text". *The Complete Linguist: Papers in memory of Patrick J. Dickens* hg. von A. Traill, R. Vossen & M. Biesele. Köln: Köppe.

Mukarovsky, Hans G. 1976–1977. *A Study of Western Nigritic.* 2 Bde. Wien: Afro-Pub.

Paulme, Denise. 1972. "Morphologie du conte africain". *Cahiers d'Études Africaines* 45.131–163.

—. 1976. *La mère devorante: Essai sur la morphologie des contes africains.* Paris: Gallimard.

—. 1988. "Contes nzakara du décepteur". *Die Oralliteratur in Afrika als Quelle zur Erforschung der traditionellen Kulturen* hg. von W. J. G. Möhlig, H. Jungraithmayr & J. F. Thiel, 39–49. Berlin: Reimer.

Rottland, Franz. 1982. *Die Südnilotischen Sprachen: Beschreibung, Vergleichung und Rekonstruktion.* Berlin: Reimer.

Schmidt, Sigrid. 1989. *Katalog der Khoisan-Volkserzählungen des südlichen Afrikas – Catalogue of the Khoisan Folktales of Southern Africa.* 2 Bde. Hamburg: Buske.

Schott, Rüdiger. 1988. "Les histoires d'enfants terribles chez les Bulsa (Ghana du Nord) et les Mossi (Burkina Faso) commes sources ethnographiques". *Die Oralliteratur in Afrika als Quelle zur Erforschung der traditionellen Kulturen* hg. von W. J. G. Möhlig, H. Jungraithmayr & J. F. Thiel, 125–138. Berlin: Reimer.

—. 1990. "Project of Comparative Analysis of Motifs and Themes in African Tales". *Asian Folklore Studies* 49.140–142.

—, Hg. 1993. *Bulsa Sunsuelima. Folktales of the Bulsa in Northern Ghana.* Münster & Hamburg: LIT.

Seydou, Christiane. 1990. "La fille recluse. Variations sur un thème". *D'un conte … à l'autre* hg. von V. Görög-Karady, 503–522. Paris: CNRS.

— & Denise Paulme. 1972. "Le conte des 'Alliés animaux' dans l'Ouest African". *Cahiers d'Études Africaines* 45.76–108.

Steinbrich, Sabine. 1982. *Gazelle und Büffelkuh. Frauen in Erzählungen der Fulbe und Haussa.* München: Renner.

—. 1988. "Femmes dans les contes ouest-africains. Une variante lyela du conte de 'l'enfant chez l'ogre' (Burkina Faso)". *Die Oralliteratur in Afrika als Quelle zur Erforschung der traditionellen Kulturen* hg. von W. J. G. Möhlig, H. Jungraithmayr & J. F. Thiel, 139–153. Berlin: Reimer.

Vansina, Jan. 1985. *Oral Tradition as History.* London: Currey.

–. 1990. *Paths in the Rainforest: Toward a history of political tradition in Equatorial Africa.* London: Currey.

Vossen, Rainer. 1982. *The Eastern Nilotes: Linguistic and historical reconstructions.* Berlin: Reimer.

Weier, Hans-Ingolf. 1985. *Basisdemonstrativa im Bantu.* Hamburg: Buske.

Westermann, Diedrich. 1905–06. *Wörterbuch der Ewe-Sprache.* Berlin: Reimer.

–. 1907. *Grammatik der Ewe-Sprache.* Berlin: Reimer.

–. 1911. *Die Sudansprachen: Eine sprachvergleichende Studie.* Hamburg: Friederichsen.

–. 1927. *Die westlichen Sudansprachen und ihre Beziehungen zum Bantu.* (= *Beiheft zu den Mitteilungen des Seminars for Orientalische Sprachen,* Jahrgang XXX.) Berlin: de Gruyter.

–. [4]1965 [1930]. *A Study of the Ewe Language.* London: Oxford Univ. Press.

–. 1954. *Wörterbuch der Ewe-Sprache.* Berlin: Reimer.

Winter, Jürgen Christoph. 1981. "Bantu Prehistory in Eastern and Southern Africa: An evaluation of D. W. Phillipson's archaeological synthesis in the light of ethnological and linguistic evidence". *Sprache und Geschichte in Afrika SUGIA* 3.317–356.

Wolff, Ekkehard. 1981. "Die omotischen Sprachen". *Die Sprachen Afrikas* hg. von Heine et al., 217–224. Hamburg: Buske.

–. 1994. *Our Peoples Own. (Ina Lamang): Traditions and specimens of oral literature from Gwad' Lamang speaking peoples in the Southern Lake Chad Basin in Central Africa.* Hamburg: Research and Progress.

Wolff, Günther, Hg. 1943. *Beiträge zur Kolonialforschung.* Tagungsband I: *Koloniale Völkerkunde, koloniale Sprachforschung, koloniale Rassenforschung. Berichte über die Arbeitstagung im Januar 1943 in Leipzig.* Berlin: Reimer.

*Wilhelm J. G. Möhlig, Köln (Deutschland)*

# 134. Das Studium der Eingeborenensprachen des indischen Ozean: Frühe Kontakte mit dem Sanskrit und den dravidischen Sprachen

Redaktioneller Hinweis: Aus terminlich-technischen Gründen muß der an dieser Stelle vorgesehene Artikel leider entfallen.

Editorial note: Due to circumstances beyond our control, the article originally scheduled to be published here had to be omitted.

Avis de la rédaction: En raison d'impératifs de fabrication et de prescription de délais l'article prévu ici ne peut être publié.

# 135. Das Studium der Sprachen des Fernen Ostens: Chinesisch

1. Einführung
2. Warum und zu welchem Zweck wurde die chinesische Sprache studiert?
3. Die Forschung im einzelnen
4. Literatur

## 1. Einführung

Die Sinologie, die Erforschung der chinesischen Kultur und Zivilisation anhand überlieferter schriftlicher Quellen, bedarf als ihrer Grundlage des Studiums der Sprache, in welcher diese Quellen verfaßt sind. In diesem Sinne beginnt die Geschichte der europäischen Sinologie mit dem Studium der chinesischen Sprache durch Europäer, d. h. am Ende des 16. Jhs. durch Matteo Ricci (1552–1610), einen der ersten Missionare Europas in China und einen der genialsten dazu; er ist der eigentliche Ahnvater der europäischen Sinologie (Demiéville 1966: 58).

Als im 19. Jh. die ersten Lehrstühle für Sinologie in Europa entstanden, konnte die neue Disziplin somit bereits auf mehr als zwei Jahrhunderte des Studiums der chinesischen Sprache durch Missionare, zumeist Jesuiten, und – in geringerem Umfang – durch weltliche Gelehrte zurückblicken. Diese Gelehrten, die sich meist eher nebenbei, dabei mit mehr Enthusiasmus als Sachkenntnis, mit China befaßten, gründeten all ihre philologischen Forschungen zur chinesischen Sprache auf Informationen, die sie mittel- oder unmittelbar von Missionaren erhalten hatten und die sie oft nicht richtig verstehen konnten. Dies hielt sie jedoch in vielen Fällen nicht davon ab, sich in den überraschendsten Spekulationen über Wesen und Geschichte von chinesischer Schrift und Sprache zu versuchen. Man darf jedenfalls sagen, daß für den hier in Rede stehenden Zeitraum, vom Ende des 16. bis zum Beginn des 19. Jhs., christliche Missionare das Monopol auf das Studium der chinesischen Sprache besaßen.

Überhaupt ist das Interesse am Chinesischen außerhalb des kirchlichen Bereichs, verglichen mit dem an den Sprachen des Vorderen Orients oder Indiens, erst spät erwacht; mögliche Gründe hierfür können darin gesehen werden, daß keine Beziehung zur biblischen Überlieferung und kein Zusammenhang mit indo-europäischer Linguistik bestanden sowie generell kein Ertrag für die damals vielerorts betriebene Forschung über die Grundprinzipien menschlicher Sprache erwartet wurde (Zurndorfer 1995: 6).

Generell läßt sich sagen, daß das 17. Jh. das Jahrhundert der Sammlung von Informationen über China (und somit auch über die chinesische Sprache) und ihrer beginnenden Popularisierung war, das 18. das Jahrhundert ihrer weiteren Verbreitung und Bearbeitung durch Dilettanten und das 19. schließlich ihrer zunehmenden wissenschaftlichen Erarbeitung und Verarbeitung. Die erste Grammatik der chinesischen Sprache (J. P. Abel-Rémusat, *Elémens de la grammaire chinoise*, Paris 1822), die auch für nicht in China lebende Gelehrte brauchbar und zugänglich war, und auch das erste größere Wörterbuch (C. L. J. de Guignes Fils (1749–1845), *Dictionnaire chinois, français, latin*, Paris 1813) sind erst im 19. Jh. veröffentlicht worden; beide fußen weitestgehend auf Vorarbeiten sprachlich interessierter Missionare.

## 2. Warum und zu welchem Zweck wurde die chinesische Sprache studiert?

Das Studium des Chinesischen im Sinne des Erwerbs der Fähigkeit, Chinesisch zu sprechen und chinesische Texte zu lesen, war natürlich für die Mission von zentraler Bedeutung, zum einen, um in chinesischer Sprache das Evangelium verkünden bzw. religiöse Texte übersetzen zu können, zum andern im Zusammenhang mit der von Matteo Ricci für China entwickelten Missionsmethode, die eine Synthese chinesisch-konfuzianischer und christlicher Traditionen versuchte; zu diesem Zweck mußten die Missionare in die schriftlich überlieferte chinesische Tradition eintauchen und sich den Bildungshintergrund der Elite, auf die sich die Missionsbemühungen zunächst richten sollten, aneignen. Die erforderliche sprachliche Ausbildung geschah oft in einführenden Lektionen von bereits sprachkundigen Mitbrüdern auf der Reise nach Fernost, nach der Ankunft dann auch im Austausch mit Muttersprachlern und immer mehr auch unter Zuhilfenahme von mehr oder weniger dilettantisch zusammengestellten Lehrbüchern, mehrsprachigen Wortlisten und Textsammlungen. Daß unter diesen Umständen viele Missionare nie richtig Chinesisch lernten, verwundert nicht (s. Lundbaek 1991: 73). Jedenfalls liegt hier ein wichtiger Grund für die Entstehung von Wörterbüchern und Grammatiken, neben dem theoretischen philologischen Interesse einiger weniger Missionare.

Weiter sind es – besonders gegen Ende des 18. und am Beginn des 19. Jhs. – diplomatische und ökonomische Erfordernisse, die die Erforschung des Chinesischen voranbringen. So hatte für die Macartney-Mission Englands von 1792, den ersten größeren diplomatischen westöstlichen Kontakt, kein Dolmetscher gefunden werden können. Auch bedurfte der immer stärker wachsende Handel Europas, insbesondere Frankreichs, mit China eines für Kaufleute leicht zugänglichen und benutzbaren Wörterbuchs. Die Bemühungen um die Abfassung eines umfangreichen europäisch-chinesischen Wörterbuchs der chinesischen Sprache stellen das verbindende Element zwischen der Proto-Sinologie des 18. und der Sinologie des 19. Jhs. dar (Cordier 1918–19: 62).

Es gab aber auch eher wissenschaftlich geprägte Interessen an China, seiner Sprache und kulturellen Überlieferung. So ließ Ludwig XIV. seinen Minister Colbert einem bekannten Jesuiten-Gelehrten gegenüber äußern, er wünsche, daß die Missionare neben der Verkündigung des Evangeliums Zeit finden mögen, vor Ort Informationen zu sammeln und diese nach Frankreich zu übermitteln, zur Vervollkommnung der Künste und Wissenschaften; später machte sich in diesem

Sinne auf königlichen Befehl hin eine aus sechs Jesuiten bestehende Mission nach Fernost auf (Demiéville 1966: 61).

Neben dem hier zur Wirkung kommenden enzyklopädischen Interesse ließen Gelehrte in Europa in ihrer Beschäftigung mit dem Chinesischen Forschungsinteressen erkennen, die damals die gesamte intellektuelle Welt prägten, z. B. die Suche nach einer universellen Sprache (*lingua universalis*), wobei das Chinesische ein aussichtsreicher Kandidat schien; des weiteren die Untersuchung der Natur und angenommenen logischen Struktur von Sprache überhaupt, in deren Rahmen die Suche nach einem Generalschlüssel zur Enträtselung der chinesischen Schrift und Sprache (*clavis sinica*) fruchtbar schien; sowie schließlich auch den Versuch, das Chinesische in die Entwicklung der europäischen Sprachen mit einzubeziehen, als Teil eines allgemeinen Versuchs, den Schock der Begegnung mit einer bis dahin so gut wie unbekannten Hochkultur durch ihre Einbindung ins christlich-europäische Weltbild zu überwinden. Gleichzeitig entstand in Reaktion auf die Nachrichten aus China eine bis zur zweiten Hälfte des 18. Jhs. andauernde Sinophilie in Europa, die nicht zuletzt auf der Bewunderung der Aufklärer für die chinesische Philosophie/Ethik und das scheinbar auf rationalen Grundlagen basierende — und damit für Europa vorbildhafte — chinesische Staatswesen fußte.

## 3. Die Forschung im einzelnen

Die Forschungen zur chinesischen Sprache durch europäische Missionare und weltliche Gelehrte des 17. und 18. Jhs. lassen sich im wesentlichen unter folgenden Themen fassen:

Lehrbücher, Schriftkunde und Grammatiken,
Lexikographie und Lauttranskription,
das Chinesische als Quelle und Ziel von historischen und philosophischen Spekulationen.

Naturgemäß verließen sich die Missionare in China für ihre Berichte nach Europa zunächst auf das, was sie mit eigenen Augen sahen, bzw. — soweit sie Chinesisch zu sprechen und lesen gelernt hatten — auf Arbeiten chinesischer Gelehrter, deren Beschäftigung mit Schriftgeschichte und Lexikographie, weniger mit Grammatik, eine lange Tradition besaß. Bereits sehr früh gab es aber auch Missionare, die trotz ihrer Überlastung mit missionarischen u. a. Aufgaben Zeit fanden, eigene Sprachforschung zu betreiben.

Die Informationen über die chinesische Sprache finden sich zum einen in enzyklopädischen Werken über China, zum andern in eigenständigen Werken über einzelne Themen, Wörterbüchern u. a.; einige von diesen konnten erst lange Zeit nach ihrer Entstehung oder überhaupt nicht im Druck erscheinen und liegen nur in Manuskriptform vor.

Beide, Sammelwerke und Monographien, waren für weltliche Gelehrte dann die Quelle für ihre proto-sinologischen Bemühungen, — neben umfangreichen Gesprächen mit Missionaren, die manche suchten, während diese in Europa weilten.

### 3.1. Enzyklopäische Werke: Allgemeine Darstellungen der chinesischen Sprache

Die wichtigsten Darstellungen der chinesischen Sprache in enzyklopädischen Werken finden sich in:

de Mendoza, Juan Gonzales, *Historia de las cosas, ritos y costumbres, del gran reyno de la China*, Rom 1585 (viele Übersetzungen im 16. Jh.)
Ricci, Matteo & Trigault, Nicolas, *De Christiana Expeditione apud Sinas*, Lyon 1616
Semedo Alvaro, *Imperio de la China*, Madrid 1642
Kircher, Athanasius, *China monumentis qua sacris profanis, nec non variis naturae & artis spectaculis, aliarumque rerum memorabilium argumentis illustrata*, Rom 1667 (viele Übersetzungen)
Magalhaes, Gabriel de, *Nouvelle relation de la Chine contenant la déscription des particularitez les plus considérables de ce grand empire*, Paris 1690
Le Comte, Louis, *Nouveaux mémoires sur l'état présent de la Chine*, Paris 1696
Du Halde, Jean Baptiste, *Déscription de l'Empire de Chine*, Paris 1735 (viele Übersetzungen im 18. Jh.).

Während die Darstellung in de Mendoza und Ricci-Trigault eher knapp gehalten ist, dabei jedoch wesentliche Eigenarten der chinesischen Sprache schon völlig richtig erkennt (z. B. die Monosyllabilität und den Unterschied zwischen Schriftsprache und Umgangssprache), ist Semedo erheblich umfangreicher.

Er spricht vom hohen Alter der chinesischen Sprache, stellt die Bedeutung der Schriftsprache für den Zusammenhalt des riesigen chinesischen Reiches heraus und betont die Monosyllabilität, wie auch die grammatikalische Einfachheit (besonders im Vergleich mit dem Lateinischen); von seiner Sachkenntnis zeugt der Hinweis, die Knappheit der chinesischen Sprache sei verantwortlich für einen Mangel an Präzision; dabei denkt er wohl eher an die Schriftsprache. Allerdings fehlen Hinweise auf die Polysyllabilität der

Umgangssprache und ebenso auf die Bedeutung der Partikel und der Wortstellung für die Strukturierung des Satzes.

Seine Ausführungen zur chinesischen Schrift sind aus gängigen chinesischen Abhandlungen entnommen; sie enthalten Informationen zur Geschichte der Schrift, den verschiedenen Schriftstilen, dem formalen und semantischen Aufbau der Schriftzeichen, wobei z. B. die Funktion der Radikale als bedeutungstragender Elemente richtig gesehen ist. Er bewundert die chinesische Drucktechnik mit Holzplatten und erwähnt die Verehrung für beschriebene Blätter. Schließlich weist er darauf hin, daß diese Schrift auch für andere asiatische Sprachen geeignet sei (Mungello 1985: 76ff.).

Magalhaes, der auch einen heute verlorenen Traktat über die chinesische Sprache und Schrift verfaßt hat, betont besonders die Tatsache, daß die Schriftzeichen Bilder sind bzw. aus solchen entstanden sind; bei der Darlegung ihrer Etymologie vermengt er allerdings bisweilen Schriftform und Lautform des jeweiligen Wortes.

Besonders wichtig ist es ihm, die Einfachheit der chinesischen Sprache zu betonen; sie sei dies einmal wegen des Bildcharakters ihrer Schriftzeichen, des weiteren aufgrund der geringen Zahl unterscheidbarer Silben und schließlich, weil sie keine Flektion kenne. Er weist besonders auf die Tonalität hin und widmet sich ausführlich phonetischen Fragen. Ans Ende seiner Darstellung stellt er zur Illustration ein chinesisches Textfragment, das er dann übersetzt (Mungello 1985: 96ff.).

Kircher, den man schon als Proto-Sinologen bezeichnen könnte (Mungello 1985: 134ff.), ist in seiner Darstellung (einer reinen Schreibtischarbeit, er verstand so gut wie kein Chinesisch) auf der Höhe des zeitgenössischen Wissens, stellt jedoch die Tonalität besonders klar heraus (fünf Töne, mit Hilfe von sechs musikalischen Tönen darstellbar), geht auf die Tatsache der sehr unterschiedlichen Dialekte ein und weiß vor allem, daß sich auch andere asiatische Völker, wie z. B. die Japaner, Koreaner und Vietnamesen, der chinesischen Schrift bedienen.

Im übrigen aber ist seine Darstellung dominiert von der Absicht, nachzuweisen, daß die chinesischen Schriftzeichen aus ägyptischen Hieroglyphen abgeleitet sind, was sich vor allem an formalen Übereinstimmungen und am Bildcharakter beider Schriften zeige. Seine umfangreiche Darlegung von 16 Typen von Schriftzeichen, die jeweils verschiedenen Ursprungs seien, ist durchsetzt von schwer nachvollziehbaren Spekulationen und nicht identifizierbaren Schriftzeichen (Mungello 1985: 143ff.).

Le Comte bietet vor allem die beste Behandlung der Schrift. Er war der Meinung, es sei besser für China, das europäische Alphabet zu übernehmen; die Ignoranz vieler chinesischer Intellektueller habe ihren Grund in der Notwendigkeit, übermäßig viel Zeit für das Erlernen der enormen Menge chinesischer Schriftzeichen zu verschwenden (Mungello 1985: 340ff.).

### 3.2. Lehrbücher, Schriftkunde und Grammatiken

Schon Matteo Ricci versuchte sich an einer Grammatik der chinesischen Sprache, die allerdings nie gedruckt wurde; die Notwendigkeit, Lehr- und Lernmittel, d. h. zusammenfassende Darstellungen der grammatikalischen Strukturen des Chinesischen, Textsammlungen, Vokabellisten, Hilfen zum Schrifterwerb u. ä. zu erstellen, prägt die diesbezüglichen, meist nur in Manuskriptform überlieferten Texte (s. z. B. auch Lundbaek 1980).

Gelehrte in Europa wiederum konnten diese Texte nicht richtig verstehen: sie hatten keine Vorkenntnisse, es fehlten ihnen andere Hilfsmittel; man kann sagen, daß es im 17. und 18. Jh. viele Versuche gab, in Europa eine wissenschaftlichen Ansprüchen genügende Darstellung der Grammatik und Schrift der chinesischen Sprache zu schreiben (vgl. z. B. die Suche der beiden Gelehrten Andreas Müller und Christian Mentzel nach einer *clavis sinica*, einem Schlüssel zur Entschlüsselung der chinesischen Sprache, Mungello 1985: 198ff.), dies aber damals einfach noch nicht möglich war.

Der Dominikaner Francisco Varo (1627–1687) verfaßte 1682 das Werk *Arte de la lengua mandarina* (gedruckt erst 1703 in Kanton im Holzdruckverfahren), ein einfaches Lehrbuch der chinesischen Umgangssprache, mit beigefügten Vokabellisten Chinesisch – Lateinisch/Spanisch/Portugiesisch/Französisch, alles dargeboten ohne chinesische Schriftzeichen, nur in Umschrift. Dieses Buch, Vorbild für viele ähnliche Lehrbücher, das kaum als Grammatik bezeichnet werden kann, – damals in Europa so gut wie unbekannt (Lundbaek 1980: 264, n. 6) – wurde von dem französischen Orientalisten Etienne Fourmont (1683–1745), der selbst offensichtlich keine Kenntnis des Chinesischen besaß, als Grundlage für eine Grammatik mit dem Titel *Lin-*

*guae Sinarum mandarinicae hieroglyphicae grammatica duplex* (ersch. 1742 in Paris) benutzt; dieses mangelhafte Werk zeigt das Niveau des Wissens über die chinesische Sprache in europäischen Gelehrtenkreisen noch im 18. Jh.

Auch das Buch des Proto-Sinologen Gottlieb Siegfried Bayer (1694–1738) *Museum Sinicum in quo Sinicae Linguae et Litteraturae ratio explicatur* (St. Petersburg 1730), das erste in Europa gedruckte Textbuch der chinesischen Sprache, ist ein Dilettanten-Werk, das manches Richtige und viel Ungereimtes über das chinesische Schriftsystem und grammatikalische Strukturen enthält, dazu eine Chrestomathie als Anhang. Am wichtigsten ist heute seine Einleitung, die eine Geschichte der europäischen Beschäftigung mit der chinesischen Sprache, Schrift und Literatur, also der Proto-Sinologie, von den Anfängen bis in Bayers Tage bietet, insgesamt vor allem ein Bericht über die vergeblichen Bemühungen, fundiertes Wissen zusammenzutragen (s. Lundbaek 1986).

Zweifellos das bedeutendste Werk zur chinesischen Grammatik, im strengen Sinn auch das einzige, vor dem 19. Jh. ist Joseph Henri-Marie de Prémare (1666–1736), *Notitia linguae sinicae* von 1728; es war auch die Hauptquelle für die o. g. Grammatik J. P. Abel-Rémusats. Daß es erst 1831 in Malacca erscheinen konnte, lag nicht zuletzt daran, daß es vorher praktisch unmöglich war, einen Text mit Tausenden von chinesischen Schriftzeichen in Europa zu drucken.

Dieses Werk, das vielfach gewürdigt wurde (s. v. d. Gabelentz, 1878: 604–606; s. a. Lundbaek 1991), stellt ein umfassendes Textbuch zur chinesischen Sprache und Literatur dar. Es enthält umfangreiche Abschnitte zu den Themen: Literaturgattungen und -beispiele, chinesische Wörterbücher, Schriftzeichen, Lautformen u. a. Es unterscheidet zum ersten Mal klar zwischen der Umgangssprache (Teil 1) und der Klassischen Schriftsprache (Teil 2); die Beispiele sind allerdings alle aus der Literatur genommen, im Falle der Umgangssprache aus den Dialogen der Dramen der Yuan-Zeit und den berühmten Romanen.

Prémare war der Auffassung, die damals viele Missionare teilten, daß die chinesische Sprache nicht auf Regeln zurückzuführen sei, insbesondere die Regeln des Lateinischen nicht auf sie anwendbar seien; man könnte sagen, daß sein Werk eine geordnete Sammlung von Beispielen darstellt, anhand derer man die Eigenarten des Chinesischen studieren kann. Er folgt chinesischen Vorbildern, indem er die Partikel einzeln vorstellt, ebenso, indem er Stilistik und Rhetorik einen besonderen Platz einräumt und damit ihre Bedeutung für die sprachlichen Strukturen des Chinesischen anerkennt.

### 3.3. Lexikographie und Lauttranskription

Wir haben Kenntnis von einer Fülle von chinesisch-europäischen Wörterbüchern, die von Missionaren verfaßt sind (vgl. Theunissen 1943), die teilweise in Manuskriptform oder gar gedruckt erhalten sind; die Mehrheit allerdings dürfte nie im Druck erschienen sein.

Bereits in der Mitte des 16. Jhs. gab es Wörterbücher, so z. B. Martin de Radas (1533–1578) *Arte y Vocabulario de la lengua China* (erwähnt in de Mendoza, s. o.), Matteo Ricci verfaßte mit Mitbrüdern ein unvollendet gebliebenes Portugiesisch-Chinesisches Wörterbuch; der Hauptzweck dieser Werke war natürlich ihre Verwendung in der Missionsarbeit im weitesten Sinne. Es gab aber auch schon Gedanken an Handelserfordernisse: So schreibt zum Beispiel der protestantische Missionar Justius Heurnius, der 1628 ein Chinesisch–Holländisch/Lateinisches Wörterbuch verfaßte, er hoffe, es werde für die Nachwelt von großem Nutzen sein, sobald der China-Handel eröffnet sei (s. Duyvendak 1936: 318).

Oft wurden auch chinesische Texte zusammen mit Übersetzungen in verschiedene europäische Sprachen als eine Art Vokabellisten benutzt, so z. B. der in Chinesisch geschriebene Katechismus des João Soerios (1566–1607), zuerst gedruckt 1601 in Shaozhou. So erscheint auch die erste in Europa gedruckte chinesische Wortliste, mit Schriftzeichen, Transkription (mit Anzeige der Töne) und lateinisch/französischen Entsprechungen, im Zusammenhang der Präsentation eines gesamten Textes, nämlich einer nestorianischen Inschrift in Athanasius Kirchers *China [...] illustrata*, Rom 1667.

Generell gilt, daß all diese Wörterbücher eigentlich mehr Vokabellisten waren, in ihrer Auswahl zufällig und unzureichend, dazu schwer zugänglich. Es gab daher bis zum 19. Jh. ständig Versuche europäischer Gelehrter, ihren eher – oder zumindest auch – säkularen wissenschaftlichen Interessen entsprechende Wörterbücher zu verfassen, die überdies auch von Laien sollten benutzt werden können; diese Versuche waren nicht von Erfolg gekrönt.

In der 2. Hälfte des 18. Jhs. wurde dieser Mangel immer klarer gespürt. So arbeitet z. B. ein Chinese namens Arcadius Huang (?–1716) an einem Wörterbuch (s. Elisséeff 1985); diese Arbeit wurde dann auf königlichen Befehl von Etienne Fourmont (s. o.) fortgesetzt, ohne Erfolg. Auch das von dem Jesuiten Joseph Amiot (1718–1793) verfaßte Wörterbuch *Dictionnaire polyglotte sanskrit-tibétain-mandchou-mongol-chinois* erfüllte nicht die neuen Erfordernisse. Es dauerte noch bis 1813, als dann das auf Befehl von Napoleon zusammengestellte große Wörterbuch des C. L. J. de Guignes Fils (1749–1845) *Dictionnaire chinois, français, latin* (mehr als 14 000 Zeichen) in Paris erschien. Sehr schnell erwies sich, daß es sich dabei um die nur leicht modifizierte Kopie eines Wörterbuches in Manuskriptform des Franziskaners Basilio Brollo de Glemona (1648–1704) handelte (Cordier 1918–19: 91 ff.)! Erst im Verlauf des 19. Jhs. wurden dann einigermaßen brauchbare Wörterbücher veröffentlicht, aber bis in unsere Tage ist ein Mangel an ausreichend umfangreichen, den verschiedenen Bedürfnissen von Wirtschaft, Wissenschaft und moderner Gesellschaft gerecht werdenden chinesisch-europäischen Wörterbüchern spürbar.

Mehr als Kuriosum ist das erste deutsch-chinesische Wörterbuch des Jesuiten Florian Bahr (1706–1771) zu erwähnen, das – 1748 in Peking kompiliert – erst 1937 in der Zeitschrift *Sinica*, Frankfurt, gedruckt erschien. Es enthält ca. 2200 Wörter und Ausdrücke; es gibt die Laute der aufgenommenen deutschen Wörter mit Hilfe lautlich verwendeter chinesischer Schriftzeichen wieder (Franke 1968: 7 f.).

Die Transkription der Lautformen chinesischer Wörter bzw. der Lesungen der Schriftzeichen stellte natürlich für die Mission ein ganz besonderes Problem dar. Zunächst gab es verschiedene Transkriptionssysteme, bei welchen die Lautwerte der jeweiligen Muttersprachen der Missionare in Ansatz kamen; schon früh gab es Versuche zur Vereinheitlichung.

Auch hier kommt der Vorarbeit von Matteo Ricci entscheidende Bedeutung zu. Er versuchte bereits 1588, ein Transkriptionssystem zu entwickeln, zunächst ohne Anzeige der Töne. Später verfaßte er zusammen mit – auch chinesischen – Mitbrüdern das verlorengegangene Werk *Vocabularium sinicum, ordine alphabetico europaeorum more concinnatum et par accentus suos digestum*, in welchem bereits die Töne bezeichnet waren. Schließlich legte er in dem chinesischsprachigen Buch *Xizi qiji* ("Das Wunder der westlichen Buchstaben") von 1605 (Peking) seine theoretischen Auffassungen über die Entwicklung eines systematischen chinesischen Lauttranskriptionssystems dar (Ladstätter 1971: 368 f.).

1626 erschien dann die epochemachende Abhandlung *Xiru ermuzi* ("Hör- und Seh-Hilfe für die westlichen Gelehrten") von Nicolas Trigault (1577–1628) in Hangzhou (vgl. hierzu Chen 1987). Sie bringt Riccis Transkription in leicht vereinfachter und verbesserter Form, unter Verwendung diakritischer Zeichen zur Bezeichnung der 5 Töne. Das Buch diskutiert in einem Einleitungsband den Stand der chinesischen Lautforschung und begründet seine eigene Vorgehensweise und bringt in zwei weiteren Bänden über 20 000 Schriftzeichen in graphischer und phonetischer Anordnung, wobei es zum einen die Aussprache der Zeichen angibt und zum andern die Zeichen nach Aussprachegruppen zusammenfaßt. Es rief eine ungeheure Resonanz unter chinesischen Gelehrten hervor und belebte auch die eigene chinesische Tradition phonologischer Studien. Es wurde zum Standard-Umschriftswörterbuch der Mission und ist bis heute für die katholische Kirche bei Transkriptionsfragen maßgebend.

Ricci-Trigaults Transkriptionssystem gilt heute noch – auch für die Volksrepublik China – als Orientierungspunkt und hat die heute dort benutzte Umschrift bis in die – wenn auch modifizierte – Übernahme der diakritischen Zeichen für die Bezeichnung der Töne hinein beeinflußt. Es ist darüberhinaus von großer Bedeutung für die Untersuchung des Lautbestandes des Chinesischen am Übergang vom 16. zum 17. Jh.

### 3.4. Das Chinesische als Quelle und Ziel von historischen und philosophischen Spekulationen

Die Spekulationen über die chinesische Sprache, ihren Charakter und ihre Geschichte haben ihr Hauptmotiv in dem Versuch, durch Synchronisierung der biblischen Chronologie mit bekannten oder vermuteten historischen Ereignissen in China diese plötzlich ins Blickfeld gebrachte Hochkultur in das damalige europäisch-christliche Weltbild zu integrieren; sie kreisen im wesentlichen um Fragen der Verwandtschaft des Chinesischen mit europäischen Sprachen und seiner inneren Logik bzw. der seines Schriftsystems, d. h. seiner

Anwartschaft auf die Stellung und Bedeutung einer 'Ursprache' bzw. 'universellen Sprache'.

So behauptete A. Kircher in seinem Werk *Oedipus Aegyptiacus* von 1652 (Rom), die Chinesen hätten ihre Sprache von weisen ägyptischen Priestern erhalten, wie überhaupt für ihn die chinesische Kultur, ihre religiösen Riten usw. ihren Ursprung in Aegypten hatten (s. Mungello 1985: 143, 185ff.). Noch im 18. Jh. findet sich diese Auffassung in Joseph de Guignes' Buch *Mémoire dans laquelle on prouve, que les chinois sont une colonie égyptienne*, Paris 1759 (s. Zurndorfer 1995: 7).

Auch die erste umfangreiche Einzelveröffentlichung über die chinesische Sprache überhaupt, die Abhandlung *The Antiquity of China, or an Historical Essay, Endeavouring a Probability That the Language of the Empire of China is the Primitive Language Spoken Through the Whole World Before the Confusion of Babel* von John Webb (1611–1672), 1669 in London erschienen, versuchte zu beweisen, daß Chinesisch die Sprache Adams, also die 'Ursprache' sei, die Noahs Nachkommen nach China gebracht hätten; sie erfülle die entsprechenden Kriterien nach Genesis 11: 1, wie hohes Alter, Einfachheit, Bescheidenheit im Ausdruck, Kürze u. a. (s. Mungello 1985: 178ff.).

Im Jahr 1713 veröffentlichte ein gewisser Philippe Masson (lebte um 1700), unterstützt von Adrianus Reland (1676–1718), einem bekannten Orientalisten, die These, die chinesische Sprache habe sich aus dem Hebräischen, das von vielen als die 'Ursprache' angesehen wurde, entwickelt; er versuchte, dies mit der Kürze und der lautlichen Ähnlichkeit vieler Wörter beider Sprachen, die er in langen Listen deutlich machte, zu beweisen (s. Duyvendak 1936: 329ff.).

Schließlich kommt dem Chinesischen im Rahmen der Suche des 17. Jhs. nach einer 'universellen Sprache', die das Lateinische ersetzen sollte, als Anwärter eine besondere Bedeutung zu; seiner Schrift und seinen grammatikalischen Strukturen lag ein angeblich rationales, nichtkonventionelles, mathematisch explizierbares Schema zugrunde, das es nur zu entdecken galt (s. o. die Suche nach einer 'clavis sinica'). Vgl. hierzu auch den Briefwechsel zwischen dem Jesuiten-Missionar Joachim Bouvet (1656–1730) und G. W. Leibniz (Mungello 1985: 16, 288 et passim).

## 4. Literatur

Barrett, T. H. 1989. *Singular Listlessness: A Short History of Chinese Books and British Scholars.* London: Wellsweep.

Brou, Alexander, S. J. 1934. "Les jesuites sinologues de Pekin et leurs editeurs de Paris". *Revue d'histoire des missions* 11.551–566. Amis des missions.

Bold, J. & John Webb. 1981. "Composite Capitals and the Chinese Language". *Oxford Art Journal* 4.9–17. McWilliam & Wrigley.

Chen, Liang-chi. 1988. *Eine funktionell-strukturelle und historisch-vergleichende Untersuchung des Xiru ermuzi (1626, Hangzhou)*, eine vergleichende Studie zur traditionellen chinesischen Lexikographie. Trier: Diss. Universität Trier.

Ch'en, Shou-yi & John Webb. 1935. "A Forgotten Page in the Early History of Sinology in Europe". *The Chinese Social and Political Science Review* 19.295–330. Peking: Chinese Social and Political Science Association.

Cordier, Henri. 1895. "Fragments d'une histoire des études chinoises au XVIII$^{e}$ siècle". *Centenaire de l'Ecole des Langues orientales vivantes 1795–1895.* Paris: Imprimerie nationale.

–. 1920. "Les études chinoises sous la Révolution et l'Empire". *T'oung Pao* 19.59–103. Leiden: Brill.

Demieville, Paul. 1966. "Aperçu historique des études sinologiques en France". *Acta Asiatica* 11.56–110. Tokyo: Tôhô Gakkai.

Duyvendak, J. J. L. 1936. "Early Chinese Studies in Holland". *T'oung Pao* 32.293–344. Leiden: Brill.

–. 1950. *Holland's Contribution to Chinese Studies.* London: China Society.

Elisséeff, Danielle. 1985. *Moi, Arcade, interprète chinois du Roi-Soleil.* Paris: Arthaud.

Franke, Herbert. 1968. *Sinologie an deutschen Universitäten.* Wiesbaden: Steiner.

Gabelentz, Georg von der. 1878. "Beitrag zur Geschichte der chinesischen Grammatiken und zur Lehre von der grammatischen Behandlung der chinesischen Sprache". *Zeitschrift der Deutschen Morgenländischen Gesellschaft* 32.601–664. Stuttgart: Steiner.

Goodman, H. & Grafton, A. 1990. "Ricci, the Chinese, and the Toolkits of Textualists". *Asia major* 3: 2.95–184. Princeton: Princeton Univ. Press.

Kraft, Eva S. 1976. "Frühe chinesische Studien in Berlin". *Medizinhistorisches Journal* 11.92–128. Stuttgart u. a.: Fischer.

Ladstätter, Otto. 1971. "Nicht-ideographische Schriftsysteme zur Darstellung der chinesischen Sprache seit Matteo Ricci". *Asien – Tradition und Fortschritt*, 368–388. Wiesbaden: Harrassowitz.

Li Jian-jun. 1990. *Lettres édifiantes et curieuses de Chine: de l'édification à la Propaganda.* Cambridge, Mass.: Harvard Univ. Diss.

Lundbaek, Knud, ed. 1991. *Joseph de Prémare (1666–1736) S. J.: Chinese Philology and Figurism.* Aarhus: Aarhus Univ. Press.

–. 1988. *The Traditional History of the Chinese Script – from a Seventeenth Century Jesuit Manuscript.* Aarhus: Aarhus Univ. Press.

–. 1986. *T. S. Bayer (1694–1738), Pioneer Sinologist.* London & Malmö: Curzon Press.

–. 1980. "Une grammaire espagnole de la langue chinoise au XVIIIe siècle". *Actes du IIe Colloque de Sinologie,* 259–269. Paris: Les Belles Lettres.

Mungello, David E. 1985. *Curious Land: Jesuit Accomodation and the Origins of Sinology.* Wiesbaden: Steiner.

Pfister, Louis. 1932–1934. *Notices biographiques et bibliographiques sur les Jesuites de l'ancienne mission de Chine 1552–1773.* Shanghai: Mission catholique.

Schafer, Edward H. 1990–91. "What and How is Sinology?". (neu abgedruckt in: *T'ang Studies* 8–9.33–44. Boulder 1990–1991: T'ang Studies Society.)

Simon, Walter. 1959. "The Attribution to Michael Boym of two Early Achievements of Western Sinology". *Asia major* 7.165–196. Princeton: Princeton Univ. Press.

Spence, Jonathan. 1984. *The Memory Palace of Matteo Ricci.* London: Faber.

Stifler, Susan Reed. 1938. "The Language Students of the East India Company's Canton Factory". *Journal of the North China Branch of the Royal Asiatic Society* 69.46–83. Shanghai: Kelly & Walsh.

Szczesniak, Boleslaw. 1947. "The Beginnings of Chinese Lexicography in Europe with Particular Reference to the Work of Michael Boym (1612–1659)". *Journal of the American Oriental Society* 67.160–165. Ann Arbor: American Oriental Society.

–. 1949–1955. "The Writings of Michael Boym". *Monumenta Serica* 14.481–538. Tokyo: Steyler.

–. 1969. "The First Chinese Dictionary Published in Europe". *Semi-centennial volume, American Oriental Society (Mid West Branch)* 2.17. Bloomington: Indiana Univ. Press.

Theunissen, P. Beatus. 1943. "Lexicographia missionaria linguae Sinensis 1550–1800". *Collectanea Commissionis Synodalis* 16.220–224. Peking: Commissio Synodalis in Sinus.

Weingartner, Friedrich F. 1975. "El primo diccionario europeo-chino". *Boletin de la Asociacion Espanola de Orientalistas* 11.223–227. Madrid: Asociación Española de Orientalistas.

Widmaier, Rita. 1983. *Die Rolle der chinesischen Schrift in Leibniz' Zeichentheorie.* Wiesbaden: Steiner.

Zurndorfer, Harriet T. 1995. *China Bibliography.* Leiden: Brill.

*Wei Chiao, Trier*
*Magnus Kriegeskorte, Trier*
*(Deutschland)*

# 136. La connaissance du malais et des langues de l'Océanie

1. Introduction
2. La zone insulindienne et le malais
3. Les expéditions espagnoles du XVIe siècle et les langues mélanésiennes
4. Le XVIIe siècle et la découverte du polynésien par les Hollandais
5. Les grandes expéditions du XVIIIe siècle et les premières théories sur les langues océaniennes
6. Bibliographie

## 1. Introduction

Dans l'histoire de l'expansion européenne, la découverte du Pacifique et de ses populations s'échelonne sur environ trois siècles. La connaissance des langues océaniennes progresse lentement au long de cette période dont il convient de rappeler d'abord les principales étapes.

A l'aube du XVIe siècle, Portugais et Espagnols atteignent les rives du Pacifique. Les premiers investissent l'aire insulindienne cependant que les seconds, venus par l'ouest, colonisent les Amériques. Les uns et les autres recherchent l'Extrême-Orient, pour s'enrichir de son commerce. En 1521, Magellan contourne le continent américain et découvre le Pacifique. Dans son sillage, l'Espagne explore l'Océanie jusqu'à la fin du XVIe siècle.

Espagnols et Portugais sont supplantés au siècle suivant par la Hollande. L'emprise de cette nation s'exerce sur les voies maritimes et commerciales reliant l'Europe à l'Insulinde. Par le biais de la Compagnie des Indes Orientales fondée en 1602, l'Océanie se trouve alors sous son contrôle. Au XVIIIe siècle prennent place les grandes expéditions de la France et de l'Angleterre. Les deux puissances rivales parcourent les zones inexplorées d'un monde où elles s'apprêtent à s'implanter.

Voyageurs, commerçants et scientifiques de divers pays d'Europe visitent donc l'aire Pacifique au long de ces trois siècles. A la fin de cette période, le bilan des connaissances dans le domaine des langues est contrasté: riche à la périphérie de cette vaste zone, dans l'aire insulindienne, mais limité en ce qui concerne les îles de la Mélanésie, de la Micronésie et de la Polynésie.

## 2. La zone insulindienne et le malais

Au terme de son voyage transpacifique, Magellan atteint les Philippines où son esclave sumatranais peut, grâce au malais, faire office d'interprète. Pigafetta, chroniqueur de l'expédition, recueille quelques centaines de mots de cette *lingua franca* dans la région des îles Moluques. A quelques temps de là, les missionnaires jésuites parviennent aussi, grâce à cette langue véhiculaire, à surmonter l'obstacle que constituent les nombreuses langues de l'Insulinde. Toutefois, leur œuvre linguistique parait avoir été réduite, alors qu'à cette époque, Jésuites et Franciscains en poste au Nouveau Monde décrivent déjà les langues qu'ils utilisent (nahuatl, quechua ...).

Il faut attendre la venue des Hollandais pour qu'un savoir d'ordre linguistique se constitue. En effet les *predikant* ne se contentent pas d'utiliser le malais pour leur apostolat, ils étudient aussi cette langue, dans ses niveaux d'usage et ses variantes. En 1623, les pasteurs Kaspar Wiltens et Sebastian Danckaerts publient leur dictionnaire puis, dans la seconde moitié du siècle, Melchior Leijdecker (1645–1701) mène à bien une traduction de la bible en haut malais (elle ne paraîtra qu'en 1733).

Ces différents travaux sont devancés par le *Spraeckende Woord-boeck* du voyageur Frederick de Houtman, paru dès 1603 à Amsterdam. Sorte de traité de malais à usage des voyageurs et commerçants, cet ouvrage propose, sur le modèle des colloques multilingues alors en vogue, l'enseignement de près d'un millier de phrases sur des sujets usuels (commerce, demande de renseignements ...). Organisé en saynètes, doté d'un lexique néerlandais-malais, l'ouvrage connaît plusieurs éditions et traductions qui popularisent la langue malaise et l'exotisme de l'Insulinde. L'édition de Batavia, parue en 1707, est enrichie d'indications grammaticales (prépositions, conjonctions, conjugaisons ...) montrant qu'à cette époque, grâce aux travaux des missionnaires, le lexique et la syntaxe de cette langue sont déjà bien étudiés. Textes religieux et monographies sur le malais ou les grandes langues de la région (soundanais, javanais) continuent de paraître au XIX$^e$ siècle, sous l'impulsion de la *Société biblique des Pays-Bas* et de la *Bataviaasch Genootschap*, société savante fondée à Batavia en 1778 (Lombard 1990). Grâce à son rôle véhiculaire dans l'archipel insulindien, le malais suscite donc très tôt l'intérêt des voyageurs, commercants et missionnaires. Ces derniers ont joué un rôle prépondérant, quoique non exclusif, dans l'édification d'un corpus d'études sur cette *lingua franca*.

## 3. Les expéditions espagnoles du XVI$^e$ siècle et les langues mélanésiennes

Orientés vers les Philippines et les Moluques, les voyages transpacifiques du XVI$^e$ siècle infléchissent aussi leur cours vers l'hémisphère austral. Les espagnols y recherchent le continent *nondum cognita*, censé recéler en abondance des métaux précieux, des terres à conquérir et des âmes à convertir.

Dans la seconde moitié du XVI$^e$ siècle, les expéditions d'Alvaro de Mendaña (1567, 1595) et de Pedro Fernandez de Quiros (1595, 1605) pénètrent au cœur de la Mélanésie. Ils y découvrent successivement l'archipel des Salomon (1567), les Santa-Cruz (1595), les îles Banks et Espiritu Santo (1605). La préoccupation première de ces navigateurs *misioneros* n'est pas, comme on s'en doute, l'investigation des langues locales. Certes, des éléments de vocabulaire leur sont utiles pour les besoins de la communication et l'obtention de denrées, ou pour le repérage des îles et des populations dont ils font la découverte. Mais leur satisfaction est à son comble lorsque les 'Indiens' répètent les gestes et les prières qu'on entreprend de leur inculquer, prononcent de l'espagnol ou du latin et manifestent ainsi, aux yeux de leurs interlocuteurs, leur prédisposition à devenir chrétiens. A l'occasion, quelques-uns de ces insulaires sont enlevés de force afin qu'on parachève leur instruction et qu'ils puissent être utilisés comme auxiliaires et interprètes.

Quelques dizaines de mots figurent ici et là dans les relations du premier voyage de Mendaña aux Salomon. Rassemblés et commentés par différents auteurs (Amherst 1901; Ray 1926), ils constituent les plus anciens témoignages dont on dispose sur les langues mélanésiennes. Recueillis au sud de Santa Isabel (îles Salomon) en langues gao, bugotu et gela, ils sont notés de façon correcte et mettent en évidence, à plusieurs siècles d'intervalle, la stabilité des langues et de leurs frontières dans cette région (Codrington 1903).

Quiros et Mendaña perçoivent la diversité humaine et linguistique de la Mélanésie, sans que cette diversité les décourage dans leurs projets de colonisation et d'évangélisation. Des Franciscains les accompagnent dans ces voyages de reconnaissance mais leur projet de mission mélanésienne, prêt de se réaliser vers 1577, est ajourné au bénéfice des Philippines que l'Espagne vient d'annexer. Seule l'implantation de telles missions aurait sans doute fourni de substantiels apports à la connaissance des langues mélanésiennes, effleurées seulement au long de ce siècle.

## 4. Le XVII^e siècle et la découverte du polynésien par les Hollandais

En 1616, Jacques Le Maire et William Cornelius Schouten délaissent la route des Indes Orientales et se dirigent vers les mers du sud, pour tenter d'y découvrir le continent austral et y faire 'gros commerce'. Le progrès des connaissances concernant l'aire océanienne fait partie des préoccupations de Le Maire, dont on sait qu'il s'informe aussi bien sur les îles de la Sonde que sur celles de la Mélanésie (le plus célèbre des Mémoires de Quiros est traduit en hollandais en 1612).

L'expédition découvre la civilisation polynésienne aux Tuamotu, au nord des îles Tonga ("îles Cocos" ) et enfin à Futuna ("île Horn") où les relations avec les insulaires se stabilisent, sous la double autorité des étrangers et des notables locaux. Au cours de ce séjour de près de deux semaines, Le Maire transcrit 118 mots en langue de Futuna, auxquels s'ajoutent quelques dizaines de mots recueillis précédemment aux îles Cocos. Ce premier échantillon de langue polynésienne est constitué pour l'essentiel de substantifs, de quelques verbes (manger, dormir, danser) et de numéraux. La simplicité de la langue facilite l'enquête, d'autant que Le Maire, comme la plupart de ses continuateurs, ne note ni la consonne glottale ni la longueur des voyelles (*la'aa* "soleil" est noté *la*).

La proximité de cette langue et du malais est certainement perçue dès cette époque, puisque la relation de l'expédition — qui connait un vif succès dans toute l'Europe — est faite par un de ses membres qui 'entendait le malais'. Le rapprochement n'est pourtant fait qu'en 1706 par Hadrian Reland qui, dans sa *Dissertatio de linguis insularum quarandam orientalium*, croit déceler l'influence de la langue malaise sur le malgache comme sur le polynésien.

## 5. Les grandes expéditions du XVIII^e siècle et les premières théories sur les langues océaniennes

Les voyages d'exploration commandités par la France et l'Angleterre se multiplient dans la seconde moitié du siècle. La collecte méthodique d'observations et de renseignements figure parmi les objectifs de ces voyages; mais l'étude des langues et des populations n'est encore, à cette époque, qu'un chapitre à part des sciences de la nature, laissé aux hommes instruits, savants, officiers ou voyageurs qui participent à ces expéditions.

### 5.1. Les expéditions françaises

Elles sont marquées par le passage de Louis Antoine de Bougainville à Tahiti (1768), l'échec de Jean-François de La Pérouse en Mélanésie (1788), puis par l'expédition d'Antoine Raymond d'Entrecasteaux envoyé à sa recherche en 1791. Elles se prolongent pendant le XIX^e siècle avec les voyages de Louis-Claude de Freycinet (1817) et de Jules Sébastien Dumont d'Urville (1822, 1826, 1836). Là encore, parmi une documentation considérable, la part réservée aux langues reste modeste: Bougainville ramène de Tahiti une liste de 300 mots cependant que l'expédition de d'Entrecasteaux recueille deux listes au nord de la Nouvelle-Calédonie. Mais les observations réalisées ne sont pas sans incidence sur les débats philosophiques et linguistiques de cette époque.

Aux yeux de Philibert Commerson, naturaliste de l'expédition, les Tahitiens possèdent toutes les vertus des peuples restés proches de "l'état de nature". Leur langue elle-même, dans sa simplicité morphologique et phonétique, lui semble l'illustration parfaite du langage à ses débuts selon Rousseau: elle est sonore, musicale, capable de moduler l'expression directe de notions et de sentiments simples (Rensch 1991). Plus prosaïque, Bougainville n'entend qu'une langue 'harmonieuse', dont le vocabulaire présente des points communs avec celle dont Le Maire a rapporté des témoignages au siècle précédent. Mais c'est à la sagacité d'un savant de son temps, Antoine Court de Gébelin (1725–1784), qu'il doit d'apprendre "que la langue de Taïti a la plus grande analogie avec le Malais, et conséquemment que la plupart des isles de la Mer du Sud ont été peuplées par des émigrations sorties des Indes Occidentales" (cité par Auroux 1981: 29). En effet, très attentif aux découvertes de son époque, Court de Gébelin esquisse, dès 1771, les contours de la famille Malayo-Polynésienne même si, au delà des regroupements qu'il échafaude, le but ultime de ses études demeure, pour lui aussi, "la langue universelle et primitive" (Auroux 1981: 55).

### 5.2. Les expéditions anglaises

Elles sont dominées par les trois voyages que James Cook (1728–1779) conduit, de manière exemplaire, entre 1768 et 1780. Il met un terme définitif au mythe du continent austral et, en sciences naturelles comme en géographie humaine, met en œuvre des méthodologies nouvelles. Pour la première fois, le relevé des langues devient une procédure courante. Plusieurs dizaines de vocabulaires sont collectés dans les archipels océaniens, mais aussi en Australie, en Nouvelle-Guinée et le long des côtes américaines (Lanyon-Orgill 1979). Sept langues sont échantillonnées dans l'aire polynésienne, parcourue pendant ces trois expéditions. La Mélanésie, visitée au cours du second voyage, suscite l'intérêt du naturaliste Johann (*alias* John) Reinhold (1729–1798) Forster qui recueille huit vocabulaires, en Nouvelle-Calédonie et dans différentes îles de l'actuel Vanuatu. Toutes ces enquêtes amènent quelques savants de l'époque à rapprocher les listes collectées et stimulent le développement des recherches comparatives. Elles confirment la ressemblance des langues polynésiennes entre elles et mettent en évidence, à l'inverse, l'étonnante diversité des langues mélanésiennes.

Elles conduisent Forster à supposer que l'Océanie a été peuplée depuis la frange maritime de l'Extrême-Orient par une race à peau claire, dont les Polynésiens sont les actuels représentants, mais aussi, à partir de la Nouvelle-Guinée, par une race à peau plus sombre présente dans la Mélanésie (Forster 1778). Quoique formulées de façon prudente, ses idées sont immédiatement reprises (Lorenzo Hervas y Panduro, 1735–1809) et répercutées pendant le XIXe siècle (Johann Christoph Adelung (1732–1806), William Marsden (1754–1836), John Crawfurd (1783–1858)). La coupure hypothétique entre langues mélanésiennes et malayo-polynésien alimente pendant longtemps les débats entre linguistes océanistes. Il faut attendre les monographies des missionnaires, catholiques et protestants (cf. Hovdhaugen & Mosel. A paraître), et l'essor de la linguistique comparative pour que soit mise en évidence, vers la fin du XIXe siècle, l'appartenance de ces deux groupes au même ensemble austronésien.

## 6. Bibliographie

Amherst, Lord of Hacknney & Basil Thompson. 1901. *The Discovery of the Solomon Islands By Alvaro de Mendaña in 1568.* London: Hakluyt Society.

Auroux, Sylvain & Anne Boes (avec la collaboration de Charles Porset). 1981. "Court de Gebelin (1725–1784) et le comparatisme, deux textes inédits". *HEL* 3: 2.21–65.

Codrington, Robert Henry. 1903. "On the Stabiliy of Unwritten Languages". *Man*, 1903.25–26. Royal Anthropological Institute of Great Britain and Ireland. London.

Forster, John Reinold. 1778. *Observations made during a Voyage Round the World.* London: printed for G. Robinson.

Hovdhaugen, Even & Ulrike Mosel. A paraître. "Some Early Grammars of Oceanic Languages". *Geschichte der Sprachwissenschaft*, vol. 6. Tübingen: Gunter Narr Verlag.

Lanyon-Orgill, Peter A. 1979. *Captain Cook's South Sea Island vocabularies.* London: the author.

Lombard, Denys (avec la collaboration de Winarsih Arifin et Minnie Wibisono). 1970. *Le "Spraeck Ende Woord-Boek" de Frederick de Houtman.* Paris: Publication de l'EFEO.

Lombard, Denys, avec la collaboration de Winarsih Arifin & Minnie Wibisono. 1990. *Le Carrefour Javanais 1. Les limites de l'occidentalisation.* Paris: EHESS.

O'Reilly, Patrick. 1963. "Le Maire et Schouten à Futuna en 1616". *Journal de la Société des Océanistes* 29: 38.69–100.

Ray, Sidney Herbert. 1926. *A Comparative Study of the Melanesian Island Languages.* Cambridge: Cambridge Univ. Press.

Rensch, Karl. 1991. "The Language of the Noble Savage: Early European perceptions of Tahitian". *Currents in Pacific Linguistics: Papers in Austronesian languages and ethnolinguistics in honour of George W. Grace* éd. par Robert Blust, 403–414. Canberra: Pacific Linguistics C-117.

*Jean-Claude Rivierre, CNRS Paris (France)*

# XXI. Theories of Grammar and Language Philosophy in the 17th and 18th Centuries
# Grammatiktheorien und Sprachphilosophie im 17. und 18. Jahrhundert
# Théories grammaticales et philosophie de langage aux XVII$^{e}$ et XVIII$^{e}$ siècles

## 137. Les transformations de l'héritage médiéval dans l'Europe du XVII$^{e}$ siècle


1. Position du problème
2. Grammaires 'scientifiques'
3. Nouvelles configurations épistémologiques
4. Bibliographie


### 1. Position du problème

#### 1.1. Entre rupture et continuité

La Renaissance s'est définie en réaction à la scolastique et, plus globalement, à la spéculation médiévale dans son ensemble. Mais celle-ci a durablement influencé la tradition grammaticale occidentale qui en a recueilli l'héritage dès avant le XVII$^{e}$ siècle. Rien ne laisse présager d'ailleurs qu'il y ait véritablement eu rupture, si l'on tient compte des diverses productions grammaticales de l'époque. Aussi peut-il être préférable de parler simplement de 'résurgences', tout en restant attentif aux possibles évolutions. Si la *grammatica speculativa* constitue le "genre" grammatical dominant du Moyen-Âge, et ce notamment à partir du XIII$^{e}$ siècle, il convient de souligner l'extrême variété des positions théoriques défendues par ses représentants (cf. les questions de fond discutées dans le *Proœmium* ouvrant les traités *De modis significandi*). La complexité des thématiques abordées et la connaissance encore insuffisante des textes rendent souvent bien difficile d'identifier avec certitude les sources de telle ou telle conception, ou encore d'en suivre l'évolution, d'autant que les influences croisées ne sont pas à exclure.

#### 1.2. Une situation de diglossie en évolution

Durant le Moyen-Âge, l'Europe est caractérisée au point de vue linguistique, dans les trois zones romane, germanique et slave qui la constituent, par la variété de ses parlers régionaux. C'est alors une situation de diglossie qui est la plus fréquente: on écrit en latin (langue de l'Eglise, du savoir et de l'enseignement, mais également langue véhiculaire entre les pays), tandis qu'on parle, pour les besoins de la communication courante, le dialecte de sa région. Le morcellement linguistique est néanmoins tempéré par les mouvements d'uniformisation qui se font jour, assez tôt en France (du fait de la situation politique notamment) et plus tardivement en Allemagne (XVI$^{e}$ siècle seulement). Une tendance analogue se manifeste de manière généralement beaucoup plus nette pour la langue écrite: dans la majorité des pays apparaissent à partir des XII$^{e}$–XIII$^{e}$ siècles des langues écrites sinon communes, du moins supra-régionales qui sont à l'origine le moyen d'expression de la poésie épique et de la littérature chevaleresque. Cette avancée des langues vernaculaires peut, comme en Angleterre ou en France ultérieurement (Lusignan 1992), être favorisée par le pouvoir central et conduire à introduire le vernaculaire dans des domaines jusque là réservés au latin (pour un panorama exact de la situation dans les différents pays, voir Haarmann 1993).

A cet égard, les traductions ont joué un rôle non négligeable: de même que par le truchement du latin s'est opérée la *translatio studii* de l'antiquité à la chrétienté médiévale

(Curtius 1948: 36–38; 1986: 70–73; van Hoof 1991: 25–29), de même la traduction en vernaculaire de textes latins d'ordre religieux d'abord, puis relevant de divers horizons culturels (littérature, science, philosophie, histoire, etc.) contribue-t-elle, notamment dès la seconde moitié du XV^e^ siècle (chute de Constantinople et développement de l'imprimerie), à enrichir les possibilités expressives de ces mêmes vernaculaires. L'enrichissement est d'ailleurs mutuel, car les œuvres littéraires étrangères en langue vernaculaire suscitent, à un degré variable selon les pays, l'intérêt des traducteurs, amplifiant un courant initié au Moyen-Âge avec la poésie courtoise par exemple.

Une évolution peut d'ailleurs être observée quant à la manière de traduire: si les premières traductions latines, comme celles de G. de Moerbeke (1220–1286), restent très proches de la formulation grecque de l'original (ce sont les premières qui ne recourent pas à une version arabe intermédiaire), les traductions effectuées à la Renaissance prennent en compte la dimension esthétique et s'attachent à restituer un latin 'éloquent' (Lardet 1989). Elles servent ainsi de version de référence au XVII^e^ siècle, lequel n'apporte guère de nouvelles traductions latines des textes antiques (Schmitt 1992: 107).

Le latin 'classique' remis à l'honneur par les humanistes conserve une position déterminante dans l'Europe des XV^e^ et XVI^e^ siècles – et même encore au XVII^e^ siècle dans certains pays comme l'Allemagne ou la Pologne. Langue savante, riche d'un long passé culturel, le latin reste, par-delà les clivages religieux et idéologiques, le lien privilégié qui unit l'ensemble des lettrés au sein d'une même *Respublica litteraria*. En contre-point s'affiche, comme déjà par le passé avec Dante (1265–1321), la conscience d'une culture nationale, dont le lieu naturel d'expression est le vernaculaire (Gerighausen 1963). Ces deux aspirations apparemment inverses ne sont cependant pas obligatoirement exclusives l'une de l'autre, elles manifestent en réalité un même culte de la langue (Lorch 1991: 157): l'*elegantia* prônée par Cicéron (*Rhétorique à Herennius* II, 17) et revendiquée par Valla (v. 1440), qui est à la fois pureté, clarté et beauté, est une qualité vers laquelle doivent tendre toutes les langues qui veulent échapper à l'état de barbarie (Chomarat 1981: 234). Cette attention portée au style, par laquelle les humanistes entendent se démarquer des médiévaux, se reflète dans les grammaires de l'époque: elles ont pour objet la description du latin des bons auteurs et intègrent à ce titre une théorie des figures (dites de construction). Celle-ci survit, réinterprétée et articulée dans une *épistémè* différente, dans maintes grammaires du XVII^e^ siècle.

### 1.3. Aristotélismes et rejet de la scolastique

Contrairement à une idée communément répandue, l'aristotélisme reste, jusqu'à une période avancée du XVII^e^ siècle, la philosophie dominante en Europe. Si, dès la seconde moitié du XIV^e^ siècle, des critiques se font réellement entendre (Valla, Ramus, etc.), il ne s'agit pas là d'un fait intrinsèquement nouveau. Simplement, les arguments avancés concernent désormais moins le contenu de cette philosophie qu'ils ne relèvent d'un point de vue philologique, et les auteurs mêmes de ces critiques restent le plus souvent à leur insu fortement imprégnés de la philosophie qu'ils entendent combattre. L'enseignement contribue encore largement à la diffusion des idées scolastiques, même si à ses méthodes se mêlent parfois celles des humanistes: il n'est pas rare que le savoir nouveau soit inséré dans le cadre ancien (Schmitt 1992: 25; 127–130). En réalité, l'aristotélisme de la Renaissance est tellement éclectique qu'il convient de parler avec Charles Schmitt d'aristotélismes au pluriel, tout en remarquant que déjà au Moyen-Âge, il existait plusieurs courants aristotéliciens et qu'ils recelaient déjà des conceptions parfois totalement étrangères à la philosophie d'Aristote.

L'histoire de la grammaire illustre parfaitement cette intrication des théories: en 1332, peu après la parution de la *Grammatica speculativa* de Thomas d'Erfurt, Johannes Aurifaber, dans sa *Determinatio*, conteste les fondements logiques et métaphysiques de la théorie des *modi significandi*, visant de ce fait à ruiner l'ensemble de l'édifice (Biard 1989: 239–288). En effet, parmi les textes fondateurs sur lesquels prend appui la réflexion modiste figure en bonne position le *De interpretatione* (16a 3–8), où est indiquée la relation de continuité qui associe l'être, la pensée et le langage. C'est dans ce cadre que les modistes définissent les éléments linguistiques, les parties du discours étant notamment distinguées les unes des autres par la différence de leurs modes de signifier. Ceux-ci sont l'objet de diverses réfutations émanant principalement de logiciens terministes, les humanistes (Alexander Hegius 1503) enchérissant sur le caractère artificiel et barbare du latin, objet de l'étude et métalangage. Or nonobstant ces attaques, le système modiste survit partiellement, et ce jusqu'au-delà du XVIIe siècle: à la fin du XVIe siècle, Sanctius, qui à bien des égards s'inscrit dans le prolongement de la pensée modiste, recourt à la suite de Ramus aux accidents formels des parties du discours pour en permettre l'identification, évitant ainsi toute définition qui renverrait explicitement à la manière dont elles signifient, cette question étant délibérément abandonnée à la philosophie. De cela il ne faudrait pas conclure que Sanctius récuse les conceptions modistes en la matière. Il serait également erroné d'en induire que le grammairien s'interdit de philosopher. Bien au contraire, il semble que le principal apport des grammaires médiévales, qui réside précisément dans leur spéculation philosophique, nourrisse encore largement les réflexions de l'âge classique. Mais les analyses s'inscrivent alors dans des problématiques différentes, une pondération autre des disciplines au sein du trivium pouvant cantonner le discours grammatical dans des limites plus étroites (Linacre fol. 53v).

## 2. Grammaires 'scientifiques'

### 2.1. La rationalité de l'usage

La réaction humaniste à la scrutation médiévale du latin avait suscité l'apparition de manuels parfois plus brefs, mais généralement descriptifs et accordant la plus large place aux citations tirées de la latinité classique. Ils répondaient ainsi de manière plus adéquate à un apprentissage qui n'était plus une propédeutique à l'enseignement de la philosophie, mais dont le but était une efficacité pratique, d'orientation rhétorique et philologique. La redécouverte des textes grammaticaux anciens, expurgés de leurs commentaires médiévaux, ainsi que la confrontation des langues vernaculaires, souvent ressenties comme peu stables, posait un nouveau défi: dévoiler la rationalité de l'usage. Ce sont les grammaires du latin (rédigées en latin) qui, prenant appui sur leurs précédents médiévaux, donnent lieu aux théorisations les plus consistantes. Initié au XVIe siècle par Linacre (1524), puis par Scaliger (1540), l'effort de rationalisation se poursuit avec Sanctius (1587) dont l'analyse ne connaîtra de réelle diffusion qu'au XVIIe siècle, après que Scioppius, en ayant assuré la réédition, en aura remanié la présentation pour la rendre accessible à un public scolaire (Lecointre 1985). De nouvelles approches seront élaborées au cours du XVIIe siècle, prenant appui sur d'autres sources médiévales. La plus connue à ce jour est sans nul doute la *Grammaire Générale et Raisonnée* (Arnauld & Lancelot 1660, désormais *GGR*), à côté de laquelle il convient de mentionner la *Grammaire Philosophique* de Campanella (1638) ainsi que la *Grammatica audax* de Caramuel (1654).

### 2.2. La recherche d'une explication par les 'causes'

Ainsi que le titre retenu par Scaliger l'indique clairement, c'est dans le cadre de la théorie aristotélicienne de la science qu'il entend situer ses investigations. Comme déjà pour les médiévaux, la grammaire est définie par Scaliger comme une science, *recte seu pure loquendi scientia*. Par-delà la distinction établie par Quintilien (I, 6: 27) entre un parler grammatical et une expression idiomatique, Scaliger identifie la correction à l'usage et se fixe pour objectif d'atteindre cette *cognitio certa per causas*, c'est-à-dire de parvenir à une connaissance certaine en cherchant au-delà de la grammaire les principes qui assurent l'organisation rationnelle de la langue: l'analyse du latin s'appuie sur celle de la réalité. Ainsi Scaliger peut-il rejeter une conception anomaliste de la langue et, même si pour les aristotéliciens il n'y a de science que de l'universel, chercher un fondement stable à la diversité linguistique (Lardet 1990: 268 sv.; Jensen 1990: 103–109). Le *De causis* peut d'ailleurs être lu comme construit autour de l'examen des différentes causes (Jensen 1990). Organisation que Sanctius, en dépit d'une référence appuyée à Scaliger (cf. le titre complet de la *Minerve*), ne reprend pas à son compte.

Scioppius, en revanche, rétablit explicitement l'assise philosophique de l'ouvrage et, mettant en balance les mérites de la grammaire sanctienne et les défauts des grammaires purement descriptives, compte au nombre des critères qui font la valeur de la grammaire sanctienne ceux de brièveté et de simplicité, de généralité, de fondement en raison et d'adéquation à l'usage (et celui-ci parce que celui-là). C'est l'enracinement dans l'être, dans la réalité des choses qui assure la sémanticité de l'énoncé, le grammairien devant montrer comment le discours s'articule sur le réel. Un argument de ce type intervient par exemple pour la rection du génitif: de par sa nature de 'terme relatif' – en l'occurrence, 'chose possédée' –, le génitif est nécessairement régi par un nom qui exprime le possesseur. Quel que soit donc l'environnement syntaxique dans lequel apparaît le génitif, il faut admettre qu'il est structurellement régi par un substantif. L'analyse de la construction des verbes actifs à l'aide de la théorie aristotélicienne du *motus*, qui réhabilite une conception médiévale, en fournirait un autre exemple (Kelly 1977; Lecointre 1993: 774–778), tout comme le recours à la théorie de la participation pour rendre compte de la constitution de l'*oratio* (proposition) (Schmitt 1992: 114; Lecointre 1993: 756–759). Pour Scioppius, le *fundamentum in re* présente le degré maximum de certitude, l'attestation de l'usage n'apportant à la validité de la théorie qu'une confirmation extérieure, supplémentaire, mais en tout état de cause secondaire.

En bref: selon Scioppius, une théorie grammaticale c'est vraiment puissante que si elle découvre derrière la diversité des expressions linguistiques la régularité dont elles procèdent. L'*oratio*, en tant qu'expression douée de sens, ne se réduit pas à la succession des mots qui la composent, elle résulte d'un ensemble de relations. La théorie grammaticale a donc pour objet de démontrer de quelle manière est effectuée la construction du sens dans la phrase. Pour cela, le grammairien doit dans un premier temps s'éloigner de l'expression d'usage: seul ce 'détour' met en mesure d'expliquer ce qui fait que le donné observable est tel (problème que les scientifiques ont également à résoudre: Scioppius est l'exact contemporain de Galilée, de Kepler et d'Harvey). Le "concept théorique" (Hempel) fondamental sur lequel repose l'édifice sanctien trouve son origine dans une conception plus globale du langage développée au Moyen-Âge.

### 2.3. Le *verbum mentis*

La théorie grammaticale élaborée par Sanctius et prolongée par Scioppius ne peut être comprise qu'en référence à une conception du langage encore largement répandue aux XVI<sup>e</sup> et XVII<sup>e</sup> siècles, et dont Sanctius a donné un aperçu dans un fragment (resté manuscrit) intitulé *De verbo mentis* (cf. Lecointre 1993: 661–669). Cette conception prend appui sur la doctrine augustinienne du "Verbe" (cf. *De Trinitate*) ainsi que sur certains des différents développements auxquels cette dernière a donné lieu par la suite, notamment dans son application thomiste à la connaissance humaine. Evoquant le passage déjà mentionné du *De Interpretatione*, Thomas d'Aquin (*De differentia divini verbi, et humani*) en conclut que "ce qui est à l'intime de notre âme et est exprimé avec notre voix extérieure par notre verbe, doit nécessairement être appelé 'verbe'" (*De necessitate ergo sequitur, quod illud intrinsecum animæ nostræ, quod significatur voce exteriori cum verbo nostro, verbum vocetur*). Le *verbum interius* est ensuite identifié à "ce qu'élabore celui qui conçoit tandis qu'il conçoit" (*illud [...] quod intelligens intelligendo format*). Le verbe intérieur encore appelé *verbum cordis* ou *verbum mentis* (Arens 1980) et qui est au terme de la connaissance, est à distinguer du verbe extérieur (cf. *De Veritate* IV, q. 1) qui l'exprime et est donc second par nature. Par rapport au verbe extérieur, le verbe intérieur est à la fois cause efficiente (parce que l'homme exprime ses pensées grâce à la voix) et cause finale (parce que le *verbum exterius* ne se comprend que comme effectuation du *verbum interius*, faute de quoi il ne serait plus *significativum*), tout comme l'image que le peintre a dans l'esprit avant de peindre l'est du tableau. Enfin, le *verbum exterius* peut être envisagé en tant que pensé (*quod habet imaginem vocis*) ou en tant que proféré, distinction que Sanctius reprend par les termes de *locutio interior/exterior*. Il enrichit enfin ce modèle en distinguant à son tour au sein du verbe mental (= v. m.) le v. m. proprement dit, qui est le v. m. i(nterius), commun à tous les hommes [?] et non verbalisé, et le v. m. e(xterius), bien connu des logiciens de la fin du Moyen-Âge, et qui aurait déjà une signification conventionnelle. Il aboutit ainsi à une double distinction 1) entre v. m. i. et v. m. e. 2) entre l. i. [*locutio interior*] et l. e. [*locutio exterior*] (ces dernières présentant des structures rigoureusement parallèles). Aucune relation de successivité n'est postulée selon un axe v. m. i. [verbe mental intérieur] – v. m. e. [verbe mental extérieur] – *oratio*, car v. m. i. et v. m. e. sont de nature totalement différente. Le v.m.i., en tant qu'il est en deçà de toute langue particulière, ne peut être atteint en lui-même, mais le sens qui le constitue peut-être reconstruit de manière analytique (lexématiquement) à partir de la *locutio*: c'est le v. m. e. Ce modèle permet au grammairien de résoudre le problème de la rationalité inhérente à toute expression (l. i./l. e. = *oratio*) usuelle.

### 2.4. La théorie de la figure et la méthode de résolution

Pour autant que l'*oratio* est combinaison de mots entre eux, elle ne le peut être qu'en tant qu'elle est douée de sens, c'est-à-dire achèvement du v. m. qui lui est consubstantiel: il n'y a pas davantage d'*oratio* sans v. m. [verbe mental] que de v. m. sans l'*oratio* qui en est la formulation linguistique. Toute *oratio* sera donc analysée en fonction du v. m. qui l'informe et non comme pure concaténation de mots. De là découle dans la *GP* [*Grammatica Philosophica* de Scioppius] le dédoublement de la syntaxe en "régulière" (mode exclusivement analytique d'expression) et "figurée" (avec variation formelle par rapport au mode régulier, par conformité à l'usage de ceux qui parlent bien), à l'instar de la division établie par Linacre environ un siècle plus tôt, et qui définissait la "construction juste" comme celle "qui révèle simplement le concept mental" (1524, VI, fol. 22v°), soit encore "à qui, en quelque manière que ce soit, rien ne manque, ni n'est redondant, ni n'est déplacé, ni n'est altéré" (III, fol. 50r°). (Sur le schéma déjà ancien de la *quadripertita ratio*, cf. Desbordes 1983). Si Linacre accorde une très large place à l'enallage, c'est que la construction figurée reste pour lui encore en marge de la construction régulière. Il n'en va plus de même pour Sanctius et Scioppius qui refusent toute *immutatio*, parce que ce serait méconnaître la valeur fonctionnelle des formes dans le système linguistique et finalement, revenir à une conception de la figure comme écart. En effet, les deux syntaxes ne s'opposent pas (Scioppius propose une formulation commune des règles): la sémanticité du discours figuré repose sur son homologie fondamentale avec la construction régulière. C'est ce que confirme le fait que l'ellipse soit dans la grammaire sanctienne la figure la plus fréquente: les voies de l'expression sont le plus souvent synthétiques. La régularité de la construction figurée n'apparaissant pas d'emblée, la résolution ou reconstruction à partir d'une *oratio* d'usage d'une formulation linguistique intégrant tous les éléments constitutifs du sens, de telle manière qu'à un sémantème corresponde un et un seul vocable (relation biunivoque entre le sens et l'expression), permet de mettre en évidence l'identité foncière des deux constructions: ainsi, parce que le sens de l'oratio *plenus vino* est complet, même si l'expression ne l'est pas, il est possible de rétablir une forme complète *plenus de vino* (plein ⟨de⟩ vin) où la régularité, condition de sémanticité, est directement lisible. Cette problématique prolonge les débats médiévaux sur la complétude *ad sensum* (c'est-à-dire une complétude perceptible par les sens) et la complétude *ad intellectum* (c'est-à-dire perceptible par l'esprit, cf. Rosier 1983), bien que la notion même de complétude (*perfectio*) ne constitue plus au XVII^e siècle l'une des trois dimensions de la syntaxe. La complétude sémantique étant considérée comme nécessairement réalisée, c'est par rapport à la résolution qu'il est possible de parler d'énoncé incomplet, pléonastique ou, plus généralement, figuré. Il convient toutefois de souligner que la résolution n'est en aucun cas un énoncé d'usage. Elle est une reconstruction de grammairien, visant à rendre transparente la composition du sens. Résolution et énoncé (usuel) ne se situent pas au même niveau épistémique, et en ce sens la pertinence de la résolution ne peut être jugée sur sa qualité stylistique (elle n'est pas *locutio*, mais v. m. e.). Elle est une sorte d'auto-explicitation du langage.

## 3. Nouvelles configurations épistémologiques

### 3.1. La notion de signe

Si dans la *Nouvelle Méthode pour apprendre la langue latine* Lancelot se montre encore disposé à admettre avec Sanctius que

> la rationalité de la grammaire nous oblige aussi à comprendre beaucoup de mots qui, s'ils étaient ajoutés, ruineraient l'élégance de la latinité, ou rendraient le sens douteux. [...] Nous voyons manquer d'autres mots qui ne peuvent être restitués sans une incorrection et que pourtant la nécessité grammaticale suppléera (p. 278),

il n'en va plus de même des auteurs de la *GGR*, pour qui "on n'a aucun fondement de dire qu'un mot est sous-entendu, lorsqu'il n'est jamais exprimé, et qu'on ne le peut même exprimer sans que cela paraisse absurde" (II, 21). L'explication par l'ellipse n'est admissible que si elle est attestée par l'usage, ce qui invalide l'ensemble de la théorie sanctienne, laquelle avait cependant tenté par le biais de la figure de surmonter l'héritage médiéval d'une syntaxe centrée sur le mot, où les relations syntaxiques étaient envisagées sur le mode binaire. En définissant le langage comme servant à exprimer la pensée (II, 1), la *GGR* – tout en abandonnant la perspective médiévale relayée par Sanctius du *fundamentum in re* – renouait avec les courants médiévaux logicisants. D'où le recours à la notion de signe, dont la *LAP* [*la Logique ou l'art de penser* de Port-Royal] (1683⁵, I, 4) note qu'il "renferme deux idées, l'une de la chose qui représente, l'autre de la chose représentée, et sa nature consiste à exciter la seconde par la première". Cette conception trouve probablement son origine chez Augustin (*De Doctrina christiana*, II, 1, 1: "le signe est une chose qui, en plus de l'impression qu'elle produit sur le sens, fait venir, d'elle-même, une autre idée à la pensée"), elle a été reprise notamment par les modistes (cf. Thomas d'Erfurt, *Grammatica Speculativa*, chap. 45, qui fait des *voces significativæ* (sons vocaux doués de sens) les signes des concepts mentaux — les signes sont dits tels car (chap. 6) ils possèdent la faculté de représenter quelque chose en termes absolus). La pensée est au cœur de la réflexion linguistique de la *GGR*, elle est envisagée dans le cadre d'une théorie de la connaissance selon laquelle nos idées ne proviennent pas de l'expérience sensible (contrairement à ce que pensent aristotéliciens et thomistes) mais, quand elles ne sont pas innées, de l'activité de l'intelligence (ainsi que le suggère la philosophie cartésienne). Tandis que Sanctius intègre en une vaste synthèse le processus de production langagière, envisageant — dans un mouvement d'ensemble — l'intellection jusqu'à son achèvement dans le langage, la *GGR* semble distendre langage et pensée. Le signe linguistique (tel qu'il est présenté *LAP* I, 4) consisterait en une relation binaire reliant la *vox* (son) à l'idée (d'une chose), la jonction étant effectuée au niveau des représentations mentales (cf. *LAP*, 1683[5], II, 1). Arnauld identifie l'idée (de l'objet représenté dans le signe) au concept objectif, qu'il distingue du terme d'une pensée qui ne tend plus intrinsèquement vers une expression nécessaire (cf. *Des vraies et des fausses idées*, V). La pensée connaît comme un achèvement propre (cf. Pariente 1985: 112), qui instaure une rupture par rapport au processus de verbalisation tel que le concevaient encore Sanctius et Scioppius. Pour Arnauld, l'idée préexiste en quelque sorte à son expression. D'où en particulier, la plus grande distance constatée dans l'analyse des parties du discours selon Port-Royal entre l'ordre de la pensée et celui du langage, tandis que Sanctius et ses disciples maintiennent une plus forte cohésion entre *verbum mentis* et *locutio*. A la différence de ce que professeront les théories empiristes ultérieures, la prise en compte, dans le signe, du concept objectif, n'implique pas, pour les Solitaires, l'abandon de leurs positions réalistes. La relation du signe aux objets extra-mentaux reste bien partie prenante des rapports de signification, comme l'illustrent, par exemple, les développements de la *GGR* relatifs à la division des noms en substantif et adjectif ou à l'emploi du génitif adnominal (cf. Pariente 1975: 47). La pensée subsiste indépendamment des signes, qui n'ont d'utilité qu'en vue de la communiquer. Cette autonomie de la pensée par rapport au langage permet aux Messieurs de développer un véritable calcul des idées, qui est la mesure à laquelle sont rapportés les faits de langage.

### 3.2. Synthèses

Au début du XVIIe siècle apparaissent divers projets concernant la grammaire et les langues. Les premiers ont cela de commun entre eux qu'ils subdivisent la grammaire, ce qui revient en pratique à associer dans un projet d'ensemble les divers types de grammaires, avec leurs finalités respectives, hérités du passé.

Ainsi Campanella (1568—1639) dominicain italien, distingue-t-il dans sa *Philosophiæ rationalis pars prima continens grammaticalium libros tres* (1638) deux types de grammaire: la *grammatica civilis*, ou grammaire d'usage, qui s'appuie sur l'autorité des bons auteurs, et à laquelle il rattache la *GP* de Scioppius (lequel aurait conservé par devers lui pendant une dizaine d'années le manuscrit de la *Philosophia rationalis* que Campanella, alors emprisonné, lui avait confié), et la *grammatica philosophica* qui, théorique (elle est dite science), prend appui sur la raison. Sa propre grammaire philosophique s'apparente à la grammaire modiste (Padley 1976: 160—178).

Quelques années auparavant, Francis Bacon (1561—1626), avait esquissé dans le *De dignitate et augmentis scientiarum* la distinction entre une *grammatica literaria* (qui est un manuel d'apprentissage), une *grammatica philosophica* (qui étudie la relation des mots aux choses) et une *grammatica nobilissima* qui, comparant les diverses langues entre elles, les enrichit mutuellement et crée par là même une langue parfaite.

Le besoin d'une langue internationale de communication autre que le latin (que beaucoup de personnes ne maîtrisent pas), la découverte de langues exotiques, la publication d'ouvrages savants en vernaculaires, toutes ces raisons favorisent dès la première moitié du XVIIe siècle l'émergence de projets de langue universelle. Campanella, dans sa *Philosophia rationalis*, évoque brièvement la question et conseille par exemple de nommer les objets en fonction de leurs propriétés, de bannir tous les synonymes et homonymes, etc. Divers projets seront développés en Europe jusqu'à nos jours.

## 4. Bibliographie

### 4.1. Sources premières

Arnauld & Lancelot. 1660[1]. *Grammaire Générale et Raisonnée* contenant les fondements de l'art de parler expliqués d'une manière claire et naturelle, les raisons de ce qui est commun à toutes les langues, et des principales différences qui s'y rencontrent, etc. (Reprint de l'édition de 1830, 1969, Paris, Republications Paulet.)

Campanella, Tommaso. 1638. Philosophhiæ *rationalis pars prima continens grammaticalium libros tres.* Paris. (Rééd. Milan 1954).

Lancelot, Claude. 1644[1]. *Nouvelle méthode pour apprendre facilement la langue latine.* Paris: Pierre Le Petit (1677[7].)

Linacre, Thomas. 1524. *De emendata structura Latini sermonis libri sex.* London: R. Pynson.

Quintilien. Vers 93. *Institution Oratoire.* (Paris: Garnier, 1954.)

Sanctius, Franciscus. 1587. *Minerva, seu de causis linguæ latinæ.* (*Minerve ou les causes de la langue latine.* Introduction, traduction et notes par par Geneviève Clérico. Lille: Presses Universitaires, 1982.)

Scaliger, Jules César. 1540. *De causis linguæ Latinæ libri tredecim.* Lyon: S. Gryphius.

Scioppius, Gasparus. 1628. *Grammatica Philosophica*, Milan: J. B. Bidellius.

### 4.2. Sources secondaires

Arens, Hans. 1980. "'Verbum cordis': Zur Sprachphilosophie des Mittelalters". *Historiographia Linguistica* VII.13–27.

Biard, Joël. 1989. *Logique et théorie du signe au XIVe siècle.* Paris: Vrin.

Chomarat, Jacques. 1981. *Grammaire et rhétorique chez Erasme.* Paris: Société d'édition "Les belles lettres".

Curtius, Ernst-Robert. 1948. *Europäische Literatur und lateinisches Mittelalter.* Bern: Francke. (Traduction française *La littérature européenne et le Moyen-Âge latin.* Paris: PUF, 1956; Presses Pocket & Agora 1986.)

Desbordes, Françoise. 1983. "Le schéma 'addition, soustraction, mutation, métathèse' dans les textes anciens". *HEL* V, 1.23–30.

Gerighausen, Josef. 1963. *Die historische Deutung der Nationalsprache im französischen Schrifttum des XVI. Jahrhunderts.* Bonn: Romanisches Seminar der Universität.

Haarmann, Harald. 1993. *Die Sprachenwelt Europas, Geschichte und Zukunft der Sprachnationen zwischen Atlantik und Ural.* Darmstadt: Wissenschaftliche Buchgesellschaft.

Jensen, Christian. 1990. *Rhetorical Philosophy and Philosophical Grammar. Julilus Caesar Scaliger's Theory of Language.* München: Fink.

Kaczmarek, Ludger. 1984. "Modi significandi and their Destructions". *Matériaux pour une histoire des théories linguistiques* éd. par Auroux & al., 1984. Villeneuve d'Asq: PULille III.

Kelly, Louis G. 1977. "La physique d'Aristote et la phrase simple dans les ouvrages de grammaire spéculative". *La Grammaire générale des modistes aux idéologues* éd. par André Joly & Jean Stéfanini, 1977. Villeneuve d'Ascq: PULille III.

Lardet, Pierre. 1989. "Les traductions de la *Rhétorique* d'Aristote à la Renaissance". *Traduction et traducteurs au Moyen-Âge*, 15–30. Paris: Editions du CNRS.

–. 1990. "Grammaire et philosophie chez Jules-César Scaliger". *History and Historiography of Linguistics.* (= *Studies in the History of the Language Sciences*, 51) éd. par Hans-Josef Niederehe & Konrad Koerner, 261–271. Amsterdam & Philadelphia: Benjamins.

Lecointre, Claire. 1985. "Caspar Schoppe et les écoles pies: un exemple de collaboration scientifique au 17e siècle". *Archivum Scholarum Piarum* IX.275–306.

–. 1993. *La "Gramatica Philosophica" de Caspar Schoppe.* Thèse de doctorat d'Etat, Université de Paris X – Nanterre, à paraître Genève, Droz.

Lorch, Jennifer. 1991. "Aspiriting to a National Language: The case of fifteenth century Florentine". *Langues et nations au temps de la Renaissance* éd. par M. T. Jones-Davies, 153–167. Paris: Klincksieck.

Lusignan, Serge. 1992. "Le latin était la langue maternelle des Romains". *Préludes à la Renaissance*, Aspects de la vie intellectuelle en France au XVe siècle éd. par Carla Bozzolo & Ezio Ornato, 265–282. Paris: Editions du CNRS.

Padley, Georges A. 1976. *Grammatical Theory in Western Europe 1500–1700. The Latin Tradition.* Cambridge Univ. Press.

Rosier, Irène. 1983. "Roger Bacon et le problème du sujet sous-entendu". HEL V, 1.31–42.

Pariente, Jean-Claude. 1985. *L'analyse du langage à Port-Royal.* Paris: Minuit.

Schmitt, Charles. 1992. *Aristote et la Renaissance*, traduit de l'anglais et présenté par Luce Giard. Paris: PUF.

Van Hoof, Henri. 1991. *Histoire de la traduction en Occident.* Paris–Louvain-la-Neuve: Duculot.

*Claire Lecointre, Nancy (France)*

# 138. Les origines de la didactique des langues en tant que discipline autonome

1. Introduction
2. Juan Luis Vivès (1492–1540)
3. William Bathe, S. J. (1564–1614)
4. Jan Amos Coménius (Komenský)
5. Bibliographie

## 1. Introduction

Au 17e siècle, les philosophes (Francis Bacon, René Descartes, Thomas Hobbes, John Locke, Baruch Spinoza, Wilhelm Gottfried Leibniz) exercent sur la linguistique une influence croissante et finissent par la dominer (Malmberg 1991: 183). Ils s'intéressent en général aux mêmes questions que les grammairiens du siècle précédent: les rapports entre les 'mots et les choses', l'origine du langage et la standardisation de la langue vernaculaire, mais en les abordant chacun sous un angle différent. "No novelties in the seventeenth century, but looked at again from a fresh viewpoint" (Salmon 1976: 72). Dans le domaine de la didactique des langues, toutefois, la situation est toute autre. Sous l'influence de la révolution scientifique qui commence et de la ruée de la jeunesse européenne vers les études, nombre de pédagogues du début du 17e siècle jugent surannée la méthode dominante d'enseignement des langues et proposent toutes sortes de solutions susceptibles de rendre leur apprentissage plus efficace. Ce mouvement de renouveau culmine, vers 1650, avec l'élaboration par Jan Amos Komenský ou Coménius (1592–1670) de la première théorie générale de la didactique des langues.

Coménius cependant n'aurait jamais pu réussir cet exploit sans les travaux de ses grands prédécesseurs, par exemple Juan Luis Vivès (1492–1540), ainsi que ceux des plus petits, tel William Bathe (1564–1615). C'est pourquoi cet article traite précisément de la contribution de ces trois pédagogues à la constitution de la didactique des langues en discipline autonome.

## 2. Juan Luis Vivès (1492–1540)

### 2.1. L'homme

L'Espagnol Juan Luis Vivès est né à Valence en 1492, dans une famille juive aisée, convertie au christianisme. Après des études au gymnase de sa ville natale et au Collège de Montaigu à Paris, il va, en 1512(?), s'établir à Bruges. C'est là, probablement, qu'en 1516, il rencontre Érasme de Rotterdam (v. 1469–1536) dont il devient l'ami, le disciple et le collaborateur. Vivès gagne alors sa vie comme précepteur de personnes de qualité (princesse Marie Tudor), comme professeur (Université de Louvain, Université d'Oxford) ou comme écrivain. Auteur prolifique, admiré de ses contemporains pour sa science et son art de la communiquer, il est entré dans l'histoire comme le 'second Quintilien'. Il expose ses idées pédagogiques dans *De ratione studii puerilis* (1523), *De disciplinis* (1531), *De ratione dicendi* (1532), *De conscribendis epistolis* (1536), *Exercitatio linguae latinae* (1538), et ses opinions sur les fonctions de l'âme dans *De Anima et Vita* (1538), premier traité moderne de psychologie (Watson 1913: cxxi; Riber 1947). Tous ces ouvrages se trouvent dans ses *Opera omnia* I–VIII, 1782.

### 2.2. La conception de la langue

Vivès considère la langue comme le pilier le plus solide de la société. C'est avec des mots que l'on éveille les sentiments, que l'on contrôle les passions et que l'on gagne l'appui des autres. Cet immense pouvoir de la langue ne peut laisser indifférent un homme tel que lui, entièrement dévoué au service du bien public. Aussi son information sur tout ce qui concerne la langue est-elle impressionnante. Il connaît aussi bien les textes des grammairiens de l'Antiquité et du Moyen Âge que ceux des grammairiens humanistes: Nicolo Perotti (1430–1480), Antonio de Nebrija (1444–1522), William Lilly (v. 1468–1522), Philippe Mélanchthon (1497–1560), Jean Despautère (v. 1460–1520), Aldo Manuzio (1449–1515), etc. Vivès lui-même a, sur le sujet, des idées fort intéressantes qu'il développe dans nombre de ses écrits, notamment dans *De Disciplinis* et *De anima et Vita*. Pourtant il reste à ce jour un des théoriciens les moins connus de la linguistique de la Renaissance (Coseriu 1977: 62).

Pour Vivès le langage est un don de Dieu, au contraire des langues qui sont des créations humaines, 'un produit de l'art' (1785 VI, 298). Il affirme que si la faculté de parler est naturelle à l'homme, la capacité de parler une langue, quelle qu'elle soit, s'acquiert. Il constate que toutes les langues possèdent des traits communs: elles servent principalement d'instrument de communication ("instrumentum societatis et communionis", 1782: I. 36); se composent d'un corps (les mots) et d'une âme (le sens) (1782: II. 94); évoluent lentement; présentent plusieurs variantes; et surtout, elles reflètent toute l'âme ("animi index lingua" (1785: VI. 298), c'est-à-dire les pensées, les émotions, la volonté et l'intelligence de ceux qui la parlent. Cela rend la communication plus riche, mais aussi plus difficile. Le moyen le plus sûr, selon Vivès, de la rendre plus aisée serait que tous les peuples utilisent une langue commune, de préférence le latin, à cause de ses qualités et de sa large diffusion. L'emploi généralisé du latin accélérerait également l'évangélisation des païens et la conversion au christianisme des Juifs et des Musulmans. L'idée d'une langue universelle est vieille (Eco 1994), mais à la Renaissance et, surtout, au 17$^{e}$ siècle, elle devient particulièrement populaire, grâce, entre autres, au prestige de Vivès.

### 2.3. La théorie de la connaissance

Selon Vivès, l'homme vient au monde avec le désir et la volonté d'apprendre, équipé des instruments d'apprentissage et même avec dans l'esprit des semences 'qui sont les débuts et les origines des arts, de la prudence, de toutes les sciences' (1782: III. 357). Le devoir de chaque individu est de les faire germer, car, contrairement à ce qu'affirment les théologiens fanatiques, sans connaissances il n'y a ni bonheur matériel réel ni vraie piété. Les outils d'apprentissage sont: les sens (extérieurs et intérieurs), l'esprit et la raison. Les sens extérieurs (la vue, l'ouïe, etc.) sont 'nos premiers maîtres'. Ils nous renseignent sur les choses sensibles et les sentiments. Cette connaissance est concrète mais rudimentaire et pas toujours fiable. Les sens intérieurs, esprit ou pénétration intellectuelle, sont: l'imagination, la mémoire, la fantaisie et l'évaluation. On s'en sert afin de saisir par des opérations rationnelles l'essence des choses connues, ce qui en elles est universel. On y parvient rarement, la puissance de la raison humaine n'étant pas illimitée et les données fournies par les sens extérieurs pas toujours précises. Quant à nos jugements, ils sont influencés par notre talent intellectuel, (esprit ou *ingenium*) et par nos passions, notre tempérament et notre caractère. La nature approximative de nos connaissances, insiste Vivès, ne nous empêche pas toutefois d'agir sur nous-mêmes et sur le monde avec une grande mesure d'efficacité (Noreña 1970: 254–274).

Dans *De Disciplinis* et *De Anima et Vita* Vivès analyse les différents types d'ingenium, son *action* (la grandeur, la durée, la rapidité des opérations intellectuelles) et sa *matière* (inclination pour les opérations manuelles ou intellectuelles) ainsi que la variété des aptitudes, des tempéraments et des caractères qui en résultent. Si les parents et les maîtres ne tiennent pas compte de l'ingenium des enfants, leurs efforts échoueront. Pour le connaître, Vivès leur conseille de les observer pendant un ou deux mois en classe, au jeu et à la maison et de se rencontrer régulièrement pour échanger leurs observations et coordonner leurs démarches (Vivès 1785 VI, 278). Cette partie de sa théorie psychologique est la plus originale et constitue la base de sa théorie d'apprentissage.

### 2.4. La conception de l'apprentissage des langues

La connaissance des langues représente pour Vivès 'la porte d'entrée à toutes les disciplines et à tous les arts' (1785: VI. 345). Il désire pour cela transformer la pédagogie des langues en une discipline qui, comme la médecine, soit aussi bien un art qu'un science. 'Dans l'enseignement des arts nous collecterons plusieurs expériences et observerons l'expérience de beaucoup de maîtres, afin d'en former des règles générales' (1785: VI. 296). Il s'agit d'un projet audacieux, difficile à réaliser à l'époque où la science expérimentale (alchimie, anatomie, botanique) se trouve encore dans un état embryonnaire.

Selon Vivès on apprend à parler d'abord par l'imitation puis, si nécessaire, par l'étude. Les enfants ressemblent aux singes et imitent facilement les paroles qu'ils entendent, surtout celles des personnes qu'ils admirent ou en qui ils ont confiance (1785: VI. 280). Le sens par excellence de l'apprentissage est l'ouïe. La rétention par la mémoire de nouvelles connaissances ou leur oubli dépend toutefois des sentiments éprouvés par celui qui écoute. Sans mémoire il n'y a pas d'apprentissage. Il faut donc la cultiver. Le meilleur exercice reste la pratique abondante et quotidienne. 'Rien n'est aussi important pour assimiler une langue que de l'utiliser; si quelqu'un a honte de le faire, on peut désespérer de son talent' (1785: VI. 312). Les parents et les maîtres, dans leurs conversations avec les enfants, choisiront leurs mots avec prudence et n'oublieront pas de corriger instantanément les défauts de prononciation ou d'élocution des enfants. Mais l'action de corriger fait partie de l'enseignement.

### 2.5. La conception de l'enseignement des langues

Au temps de Vivès, les garçons étudient, pendant trois ans au collège ou école latine, dans des classes souvent de plus de cent élèves, la grammaire latine et la grammaire grecque, les humanités pendant deux autres années et la philosophie dans les deux dernières classes, habituellement très peu fréquentées. La méthode d'enseignement consiste en l'explication de la leçon par le maître, la mémorisation par les élèves des règles de grammaire, du vocabulaire et des textes expliqués ainsi qu'en l'imitation orale et écrite des modèles classiques.

Contrairement aux collèges humanistes, dont le but principal est la culture du goût et/ou de l'éloquence, Vivès souhaite que l'enseignement des langues serve à l'acquisition des connaissances nécessaires à la satisfaction des besoins matériels et spirituels des élèves. C'est pourquoi il attache plus d'importance à la connaissance des *choses* que des *mots*, au contenu plus qu'à la forme du discours. 'Quelle importance y a-t-il à connaître le latin, le grec, le français ou l'espagnol si la connaissance des choses contenues dans ces langues est enlevée' (1785: VI. 417)?

Dans son projet d'une Académie idéale (1786: VI. 279), un établissement qui combinerait les écoles secondaire et supérieure, les jeunes de sept à quinze ou seize ans reçoivent une instruction encyclopédique. Le programme d'études se divise en trois cycles: au premier, on étudie les choses sensibles et les rudiments du latin, au second, la grammaire et les auteurs et au troisième le grec, l'hébreu et surtout la philologie (le contenu et le style des ouvrages des auteurs anciens). Quant à la méthode d'enseignement, elle imite 'l'ordre de la vie et de la nature', qui 'va des sens à l'imagination, de là à l'intelligence' (1782: III. 373).

L'enseignement de toutes les matières à l'Académie de Vivès étant dispensé en latin le progrès des élèves est lié à leur maîtrise de cette langue. Une des conditions fondamentales pour l'acquisition du latin, et de toute autre langue étrangère est la connaissance solide de la langue maternelle (*lingua patria*), autre originalité de la didactique des langues de Vivès. Enseigner la langue maternelle est de la responsabilité de la mère, ce qui suppose des femmes instruites, évidence que tous les hommes de la Renaissance étaient loin d'admettre. L'apprentissage de la langue maternelle se poursuit à l'école, non seulement durant la première année quand l'élève ne peut encore communiquer en latin, mais aussi dans les classes supérieures, son usage correct et élégant étant une préoccupation permanente des maîtres.

Toutefois, Vivès s'oppose à l'apprentissage de la langue nationale de manière formelle, même quand il existe déjà un bon manuel de grammaire, comme la *Grammatica de la lengua Castellana* (1492) de Nebrija pour l'espagnol. Il est convaincu que pour apprendre une langue vivante (maternelle ou étrangère) l'usage seul suffit. Il refuse pour cela aux grammairiens le droit de dicter à la population comment parler sa langue. 'L'arbitrage en matière de langue appartient au peuple, maître de sa parole' (1785: VI. 78). Il admet cependant que la connaissance du latin rend plus aisée l'acquisition des langues vivantes, en particulier des langues romanes (1785: VI. 300). Seules les langues anciennes seront donc étudiées à l'Académie suivant les règles, leur apprentissage par l'usage n'étant plus possible.

### 2.6. Enseigner les quatre habiletés linguistiques

Comme tous les pédagogues humanistes Vivès s'inspire de l'*Institution oratoire* de Quintilien, mais l'adapte à sa théorie de la connaissance. Dans l'Académie qu'il propose, tous les élèves doivent maîtriser le programme du premier cycle. Seuls, ceux qui sont capables et désireux de continuer leurs études suivent ensuite des cours supérieurs, en accord avec leurs dispositions naturelles. Enseigner, comme on fait dans les collèges, les mêmes matières à tous et exiger le même rendement de tous, c'est, dit-il, pratiquer l'égalitarisme le plus inéquitable. Indépendamment de leur talent, tous les disciples doivent acquérir les quatre habiletés linguistiques, au moins de manière élémentaire. La première habilité qu'ils auront à posséder est la *compréhension.* Comprendre une langue étrangère est facile pour les enfants qui entendent normalement, d'une part parce qu''aucun sens ne fait comprendre plus vite que l'audition' (1782: I. 13) et d'autre part, parce que le maître peut toujours intervenir et fournir l'explication dans la langue maternelle.

Pour enseigner à *lire* et à prononcer le latin, Vivès recommande aux maîtres de suivre l'approche analytique et d'utiliser pour manuel le petit Donat. Les garçons apprendront ainsi en un seul temps et la lecture et les flexions. Une fois les rudiments assimilés ils passent à la lecture des dialogues de l'*Exercitatio linguae latinae* (1782: I) – le manuel composé par Vivès pour enseigner aux débutants à converser sur les sujets de la vie quotidienne – des *Distiques* de Caton, des comédies de Térence, des *Épitres* de Cicéron, etc.

Au deuxième cycle les disciples étudient la *grammaire* de manière systématique. Vivès, comme Mélanchthon, considère la connaissance des règles indispensable si l'on veut éviter les fautes tant à l'oral qu'à l'écrit et comprendre les auteurs. Il ne partage point l'opinion de ceux qui, comme son ami et mécène Georges de Halluin (v. 1470–v. 1536) ou Nicolas Clénard (1493–1542), prônent un enseignement du latin par le seul usage (la conversation).

L'usage, dans l'enseignement des langues anciennes, est pour Vivès synonyme de lecture des auteurs grecs et latins. L'emploi de leurs livres à l'école pose toutefois d'énormes problèmes. Non seulement les sujets et le style dépassent-ils l'intelligence des enfants mais encore le message s'oppose-t-il souvent aux principes de la religion chrétienne. Il refuse néanmoins de les rayer du programme, comme le conseillaient les fanatiques religieux ou de les remplacer par des épitomés, ce type de publications n'offrant qu'un 'semblant de science'. La solution qu'il propose est la sélection des textes classiques avec la plus grande prudence; la suppression des passages osés comme des 'branches mortes'; la mise en garde des élèves contre le fait qu'en prenant ces textes en main ils entrent dans 'un champ empoisonné' et l'invitation à ignorer tout ce qui dans l'ouvrage s'oppose à la piété chrétienne.

L'habileté à *écrire* la langue étrangère s'acquiert, selon Vivès, en lisant les bons auteurs à haute voix et en imitant leur style oralement et par écrit. Il ne peut imaginer un élève lisant sans la plume à la main. Il souhaite que les garçons s'habituent à écrire dans des cahiers et des dossiers les remarques du maître, le nouveau vocabulaire, les expressions intéressantes, les proverbes, les maximes, etc. Non seulement parce que les dictionnaires sont encore rares et chers, mais également parce qu'en écrivant on apprend aussi à parler la langue. Surtout parce que, comme l'avait déjà remarqué Quintilien, l'usage simultané de l'œil, de la langue, de l'oreille et de la main, renforce la mémoire. Bref 'c'est une pratique très utile d'écrire ce dont nous voulons nous souvenir' (1785: VI. 310–311).

En ce qui concerne la *graphie* il recommande, comme pour la lecture, la méthode analytique (les lettres, les syllabes, les mots) et que l'on copie des phrases et des passages. Pour la composition libre, il conseille de l'introduire graduellement et seulement après un très long entraînement méthodique. Un des exercices écrits les plus usités à la Renaissance était la rédaction de lettres. Vivès offre des modèles de correspondance pour toutes les circonstances de la vie, en un latin élégant mais simple, dans le *De conscribendis epistolis* (1782: 263–314).

Du fait de sa propre expérience de polyglotte, Vivès sait que *parler* une langue étrangère est bien plus difficile que la comprendre (1782: III. 371). La compétence orale dépend, selon lui, en grande partie de la mémoire 'Celui qui jouit d'une bonne mémoire maîtrise les langues avec facilité, les parle aisément' (1782: III. 370–371). Il accorde, à cause de cela, une place considérable dans ses écrits aux différents types de mémoire et aux exercices qui fortifient cette dernière. Les pages qu'il consacre dans *Anima et Vita* aux associations d'idées et à leur importance dans l'apprentissage des langues (1782: III. 345–352) sont parmi les plus intéressantes de cet ouvrage. Pour acquérir l'habileté de parler la langue étrangère, Vivès suggère que les élèves répètent, d'abord dans leur langue maternelle puis en latin, ce qu'ils ont entendu et compris en classe. Au début ils entremêleront inévitablement les mots des deux langues, mais le maître habile ne corrigera que les fautes les plus grossières et cela avec beaucoup de prudence pour ne pas décourager les garçons.

### 2.7. Le maître et l'élève

Vivès exige des maîtres de son Académie idéale des qualités et des vertus hors du commun: posséder de vastes connaissances dans plusieurs disciplines, maîtriser parfaitement les langues anciennes et la langue vernaculaire, être bon psychologue, avoir de la méthode, être diligent, de nature affable, d'humeur stable, et aussi se distinguer par sa piété. Dans le *De Disciplinis* il écrit que 'l'homme n'apprend rien de la nature mais que tout arrive par l'instruction, le dur travail, l'habitude et la diligence' (1785: VI. 316). Pourtant il ne dit pas un mot sur la formation des enseignants. Probablement croyait-il que le talent pédagogique et la lecture de son traité ou de l'*Institution oratoire* de Quintilien suffisent.

Vivès ne s'intéresse à l'éducation, l'érudition et la science que pour autant qu'elles servent la pratique:

Hic est ergo studiorum omnium fructus, hic scopus, ut quaesitis artibus vitae profituris, eas in bonum publicum exerceamus, unde merces immortalis consequitur, non ad pecuniam, non ad praesentem gratiam aut delicias, quae fluxae et momentaneae sunt [...] (*Voici donc le fruit de toutes ces études, voici leur but: être utiles à la vie. Nous devons les utiliser pour le bien public, afin de mériter une récompense éternelle, non pas de l'argent, non pas des plaisirs ou des délectations passagères et momentanées* [...]. 1785: VI. 423).

Il encourage donc les disciples à observer, à réfléchir, à étudier et à appliquer ce qu'ils apprennent à leurs exercices, leurs jeux, leurs rapports avec les autres. Il s'attend à ce que les élèves brillants aident leurs camarades moins doués et à ce que les forts protègent les faibles, sans espérer d'autre récompense que de plaire à Dieu. Il s'oppose à l'émulation sous toutes ses formes, car plutôt qu'un aiguillon tout puissant de l'apprentissage, elle est un moyen sûr de former 'de petits ambitieux et orgueilleux', péchés graves pour un chrétien. Vivès surestime le sens moral et le bon sens des enfants.

Ce défaut il le partage avec tous les pédagogues humanistes. Cependant, il les surpasse tous sur le plan théorique et il en est conscient. Il sait qu'il est un pionnier, mais aussi que personne ne peut poser les fondements d'un art nouveau et qu'il soit parfait dès ses débuts ("nulla ars simul et inventa est, et absoluta" (1785: VI. 7) et à cause de cela, il prie ses lecteurs de lui pardonner ses omissions. Ses contemporains reconnurent vite la sagesse de ses conseils et l'influence du maître 'melliflue', comme beaucoup l'appelaient, se répandit rapidement d'un bout à l'autre de l'Europe. Les idées pédagogiques de François Rabelais, Paul Baduel, Roger Ascham, Richard Mulcaster, Joseph Webbe, Jean Sturm, Jan Amos Coménius et des Jésuites portent la marque de ce grand humaniste espagnol.

## 3. William Bathe, S. J. (1564–1614)

### 3.1. L'homme

Selon une rumeur persistante (Watson 1913, Mir 1968) Ignace de Loyola décida de créer les collèges de la Société de Jésus (1540) après sa rencontre, en 1529, à Bruges avec Vivès. Il est généralement connu que ces collèges gagnèrent instantanément les faveurs du public et se répandirent rapidement dans toute l'Europe, en Amérique et en Asie. Ce succès extraordinaire est souvent attribué à la discipline rigoureuse des 'soldats de Jésus' et à l'homogénéité de leur programme d'études et de leur méthode d'instruction. En réalité, à aucun moment de son histoire la Compagnie de Jésus n'a formé un corps parfaitement monolithique. L'exemple de William Bathe, un parmi des centaines, est là pour le prouver.

Bathe naquit à Dublin en 1564 dans une grande famille irlandaise. Il étudie les humanités avec des précepteurs privés au château paternel, la philosophie à Oxford et le droit à Londres. Après quatre ans à la cour royale, il se rend à Louvain étudier la théologie. En 1595 il entre dans la Société de Jésus, enseigne un peu, participe à des missions diplomatiques et est nommé finalement, en 1605, au collège irlandais de Salamanque. Il passe alors le reste de sa vie à mettre au point une nouvelle méthode d'enseignement des langues, conçue au temps de ses études à Oxford, à remplir ses fonctions de père spirituel du collège, à s'occuper d'actes de charité et à travailler à sa sanctification. Épuisé, il meurt au cours d'une retraite spirituelle à Madrid en 1614, à l'âge de cinquante ans.

### 3.2. La conception de la langue

Petit garçon, Bathe avait appris à Dublin le latin, le grec, le français et probablement aussi l'italien. Il continua d'étudier les langues vivantes à Oxford, mais elles ne l'intéressaient que comme moyen de communication. Les questions théoriques ne commencent à le préoccuper, qu'au moment où il s'applique à la rédaction de la *Janua Linguarum* (1611), son seul ouvrage de caractère linguistique. Même alors il ne semble pas avoir trop consulté les travaux des grammairiens ou des pédagogues des langues du passé. Dans la préface de son ouvrage il ne cite ni Quintilien, ni Vivès, ni Varron, ni Priscien, ni Scaliger, ni Ramus, mais Calepin pour son *Dictionnaire* et Manuzio pour son édition des *Adages* d'Érasme. On notera cependant qu'il ne mentionne pas non plus le *Ratio Studiorum* (1599) de la Société de Jésus qu'il devait pourtant très bien connaître.

Sur sa conception de la langue nous ne savons que ce qu'il écrit dans l'avant-propos de la *Janua Linguarum*. C'est très peu et cela ne concerne que ce qu'il appelle le 'noyau' de la langue: le lexique, l'analogie, les phrases (idiotismes, expressions) et le style (Avant-propos: ch. 1). Le dictionnaire, écrit-il, fournit le vocabulaire; les manuels de grammaire expliquent l'analogie; on trouve les phrases dans les œuvres des bons auteurs: on apprend les règles du style dans les traités de rhétorique. Presque toutes les observations d'ordre linguistique qui suivent se rapportent au lexique. Les sections qui devaient concerner l'enseignement de la grammaire, des phrases et du style, et qu'il avait promises dans l'avant-propos (ch. 3, 7) n'ayant jamais été rédigées, ses commentaires sur ces branches sont extrêmement laconiques. À propos de la grammaire il écrit qu'elle a un but pratique: enseigner à parler correctement les langues anciennes, et un but scientifique: formuler des règles pour l'usage de ces langues (Avant-propos ch. 6). Ses observations su la phraséologie et le style sont traitées en trois phrases (Avant-propos ch. 7) dont la plus importante est que de la même manière qu'on ne peut comprendre le sens d'un mot que dans une phrase, on ne peut comprendre le sens d'une expression que dans un discours continu et bref.

3.3. La théorie de la connaissance et de l'apprentissage des langues

Bathe n'explique nulle part comment l'homme apprend et donne très peu de précisions sur sa conception de l'apprentissage des langues. Dans l'Avant-propos il écrit seulement qu'il existe deux méthodes pour apprendre les langues: la 'régulière', qui utilise la grammaire pour enseigner la concordance (*congruitates*) et l''irrégulière', employée par ceux qui enseignent les langues modernes par la conversation et la lecture. La première mène à une plus grande correction grammaticale, la seconde à une plus grande facilité d'expression. 'Si seulement une troisième méthode pouvait être élaborée qui égalerait la première en précision et la deuxième en facilité de parole, elle serait alors supérieure aux deux autres' (Avant-propos ch. 2). C'est à la construction d'une telle méthode idéale ou de moyen terme (*via tertia media*) que Bathe consacrera vingt ans de sa vie d'adulte, sans parvenir à la compléter. Sous la pression de ses admirateurs il accepte cependant de publier la première section de sa méthode, un mince volume intitulé *Janua Linguarum*.

Bathe compose son manuel alors qu'en Europe fait rage la *guerre de grammaire* ('bellum grammaticale'), le débat sur le rôle de la grammaire dans l'apprentissage des langues (voir Watson 1908: 276–287). La Société de Jésus exigeait de tous ses professeurs qu'ils enseignent la grammaire latine de manière systématique pendant les trois premières années d'études au collège, d'après le *De Institutione Grammatica* (1575) du père Emmanuel Alvarez (*Ratio Studiorum* 1599 VIII, 12). Bathe, dont le but est de créer une méthode qui enseigne toutes les habiletés linguistiques dans toutes les langues, avec précision et facilité et en peu de temps (Avant-propos ch. 1), ne se rallie ni aux didacticiens traditionalistes ni aux réformistes, et, surtout il ne tient aucunement compte des règlements de son Ordre.

3.4. La méthode des langues de Bathe

Bathe pense que le moyen le plus efficace pour apprendre à *comprendre* une langue étrangère, quand l'occasion de converser avec les natifs ne se présente pas, est de s'appuyer sur la langue maternelle et de se servir de publications bilingues. Sur l'acquisition de l'aptitude à *lire* il ne dit rien. Peut-être comptait-il y revenir dans un autre volume. De même, il se tait sur la procédure à suivre pour apprendre à *écrire*. La seule compétence sur laquelle il s'étend quelque peu est l'aptitude à *parler*. Il est convaincu que la meilleure façon d'acquérir rapidement la compétence orale dans une langue étrangère, savante ou vivante, est de mémoriser des phrases dans la langue étrangère que l'on veut apprendre, traduites à partir de la langue maternelle ou d'une autre langue connue (Avant-propos ch. 10).

Dans sa méthode de 'moyen terme' la mémoire joue un rôle particulièrement important. Nous savons que, jeune, Bathe se passionnait pour la mnémonique, discipline qu'il enseigna même à la reine Elisabeth 1re, qu'il ne cessa jamais de s'intéresser à la mémoire artificielle, que dans le ch. 10 de la Préface de la *Janua Linguarum* il recommande sans réserve les astuces de cet *art divin* ('divina arte memoriae localis'), et que son frère et collaborateur John était connu en Espagne comme le "Don Juan de la gran memoria" (O'Mathuna 1986: 155) à cause de son extraordinaire mémoire.

3.5. Les sentences de la *Janua Linguarum*

Jusqu'ici Bathe n'apporte rien de nouveau. L'approche bilingue est connue depuis le temps des Sumériens, et des manuels de phrases avec leur traduction interlinéaire ou parallèle existent en grand nombre à la Renaissance. Bathe les rejette tous comme de 'grossières et confuses collections de sentences'. Son ouvrage sera méthodique et aura un objectif précis: servir d'accès aux langues étrangères aux missionnaires, aux confesseurs des visiteurs étrangers, aux étudiants autodidactes d'âge mûr, aux commerçants, pèlerins et autres voyageurs, aux hauts fonctionnaires d'état, aux valets de grands seigneurs, et dans une certaine mesure aux collégiens et à leurs professeurs aussi.

Chaque groupe de ce public hétérogène a cependant des intérêts bien spécifiques et les satisfaire représente pour Bathe, dès le départ, un défi impossible. Il se résoud à une solution de compromis: il composera en priorité des sentences morales, nécessaires aux missionnaires et aux religieux, et les complétera de quelques centaines de phrases d'intérêt général, utiles à tous.

Choisir les mots avec lesquels rédiger les sentences était une tâche bien plus hardie. C'est l'épisode du déluge dans la Bible qui lui inspirera la solution. Si, pour reconnaître tous les animaux de la Terre, il suffisait d'en voir un couple de chaque espèce dans l'arche de Noé, il devrait être possible d'apprendre tous les mots d'une langue en réunissant dans un seul volume tous les mots radicaux combinés dans des phrases (Avant-propos ch. 10).

Afin d'éviter les défauts de ses prédécesseurs et donner à son ouvrage un caractère scientifique, Bathe s'impose une série de règles si rigides qui rendent la rédaction des sentences extrêmement lente et pénible.

Les phrases latines, par exemple, et leur équivalent espagnol seront brèves, indépendantes les unes des autres, mais unies librement en centuries autour d'un thème moral ('de la vertu et des vices', 'de la prudence et de l'imprudence', 'de la modération et de l'intempérance', etc.). En outre, les sentences seront composées uniquement de mots latins 'familiers' (sans mots rares), plus exactement de mots familiers 'fondamentaux' (sans mots dérivés). Enfin, et pour mieux mettre en évidence leur signification première, aucun vocable ne pourra figurer dans le texte plus d'une fois, à l'exception des mots outils, tels que *et, qui, esse,* etc.

Si Bathe s'était arrêté là, sa *Janua Linguarum* ne serait qu'un manuel curieux de plus parmi les dizaines d'autres qui virent le jour au temps de la 'guerre de grammaire'. Heureusement, il a l'idée d'établir des critères précis pour la sélection lexicale, critères d'une modernité tout à fait impressionnante. Il y en a sept: le temps (à quelle époque le mot était-il utilisé?); le lieu (où? dans quelle partie du pays?); le statut social du locuteur (qui parle? un médecin? un artisan?); le contexte (le mot est-il utilisé dans toutes les circonstances ou seulement dans certaines situations?); le style (le mot est-il utilisé plus souvent en poésie? rarement dans une oraison?); le mode d'utilisation (s'agit-il d'un mot de la langue écrite ou orale?); l'opinion (qui considère ce mot familier? commun? rare?).

### 3.6. Le contenu de la *Janua Linguarum*

Armé de ces critères, il sélectionne 5,302 mots latins familiers fondamentaux et se met à composer des phrases et à les grouper en centuries, le texte latin sur la page de gauche, la traduction espagnole sur la page de droite. Son plan réussit jusqu'à la sentence 454, quand il se voit obligé d'abandonner, provisoirement, le principe de phrases isolées et de terminer la cinquième centurie par un hymne sur la *Passion du Christ* en discours continu. Mais le vocabulaire se plie toujours plus difficilement à ses exigences et après la phrase 1041 il arrête la rédaction. Il lui reste toutefois une centaine d'adverbes et autres mots indéclinables qu'il tient absolument à inclure dans son manuel, mais avec lesquels il lui est impossible de composer de nouvelles phrases indépendantes. Mis au pied du mur il laisse la onzième centurie inachevée et rédige, tant bien que mal, la dernière, *Contre Zoile*, en un discours continu.

Voici quelques exemples des sentences de Bathe:

297. Copia fastidium generat. *L'abondance engendre le dégoust.*
450. Meticulosus umbram veretur suam. *Le timide a peur de son ombre.*
963. Calo hispidus, hirsuti aeneatoris thorum, in porticu, temeravit. *L'esclave pelu viola le lict du trompette velu, au portail.*
1029. Vespam terebrasse vesicam fortè figmentum est. *C'est peut estre une feinte, qu'une guespe ait percé la vessie.* (Trad. fr. de J. Barbier, 1617).

### 3.7. Le sort de la *Janua Linguarum*

L'ouvrage de Bathe est bientôt après sa publication à Salamanque traduit en plusieurs langues (anglais, français, portugais, italien) et connaît une trentaine d'éditions bilingues ou plurilingues. Des didacticiens de marque du 17e siècle (Johann Rhenius, Isaac Habrecht, Caspar Schoppe, Coménius) saluent le manuel comme un événement important de l'histoire de l'enseignement des langues. *Janua Linguarum* est aussi introduite comme manuel auxiliaire dans nombre d'écoles en Allemagne, au Portugal, en Espagne, en Angleterre et en Italie, mais pas dans les collèges jésuites. Puis, dans la deuxième moitié du siècle, on l'oublie, ainsi que son auteur.

Il y a plusieurs raisons à cela. *Janua Linguarum* n'est pas la méthode idéale que Bathe avait promise. L'invention d'une méthode des langues qui combine la solidité de l'appprentissage par les règles à la facilité de l'acquisition par l'usage reste à ce jour du domaine du rêve. Le titre du manuel de Bathe, *Porte des langues*, ne correspond ni à son contenu ni à sa forme. Il ne peut pas servir d'entrée dans une langue ancienne ou moderne, ni aux enfants ni à la majorité des adultes auxquels il est destiné. Le fait que certains individus, notamment Schoppe (1576–1649), affirment en avoir grandement profité ne peut être considéré comme une preuve suffisante de l'efficacité de la méthode. Il est même difficile de parler ici de méthode.

### 3.8. La contribution de Bathe

En effet, l'auteur ignore complètement les principes les plus fondamentaux de la pédagogie des langues, en particulier celui de la répétition et celui de la progression. Il rédige et assemble ses sentences selon ses propres règles. Il n'explique même pas comment il faut utiliser *Janua Linguarum* pour apprendre à parler la langue étrangère, ce qui est le but avoué de son ouvrage. Lui-même a conscience de certaines lacunes de son texte, et en plusieurs endroits de l'avant-propos il s'en excuse et en appelle à la compréhension de ses lecteurs.

Pourtant le fier Irlandais mérite bien une place dans l'histoire de l'enseignement des langues. Il n'est certainement pas 'un pionnier de la linguistique' comme le dit O'Mathuna (1986), ni un très bon didacticien, mais il a compris le besoin d'une 'porte' dans les langues, rôle que ne peuvent pas jouer les chefs-d'œuvre littéraires, même les plus faciles. Il lui revient aussi l'honneur d'avoir conçu l'idée de réunir tout le lexique fondamental dans un manuel unique et de présenter chaque mot, non séparément, comme dans un dictionnaire, mais dans des phrases. Sa plus grande contribution à la didactique des langues reste toutefois d'avoir établi des critères pour la sélection du vocabulaire fondamental et de les avoir appliqués, avec plus ou moins de succès, dans le choix du lexique latin. La lexicométrie et la statistique lexicale n'atteignent pas aujourd'hui des résultats bien plus satisfaisants ou scientifiquement plus valables (Laforge 1972: 74).

## 4. Jan Amos Coménius (Komenský)

### 4.1. L'homme

Le Tchèque Jan Amos Komenský (Coménius) est né en 1592 à Nivnice en Moravie, dans une famille qui appartient à l'Unitas Fratrum Bohemorum, importante Eglise réformée tchèque. Après des études de théologie an Allemagne, à Herborn et à Heidelberg (1611–1614), il retourne dans son pays et enseigne à l'école latine où il avait été élève peu d'années auparavant. Après son ordination (1616), il se marie (1618) et part pour Fulnek, où il est nommé pasteur et directeur de la petite école locale. Mais la guerre de Trente Ans éclate (1618–1648), le royaume de Bohême perd son indépendance (1620), les réformés sont persécutés et Coménius s'exile à Leszno (1628), en Pologne. Là, il enseigne au gymnase, exerce ses fonctions de pasteur et prépare la réforme des écoles de sa patrie, qu'il espère voir bientôt libre. Dans ce but il se familiarise avec la littérature philosophique et pédagogique, découvre Francis Bacon, lit Juan Luis Vivès et William Bathe, écrit des traités sur l'éducation et compose *Janua linguarum reserata* (1631), un petit manuel de latin de 1000 phrases, inspiré en partie de la *Janua Linguarum* de Bathe, qui le rend immédiatement célèbre.

Considéré comme le grand spécialiste européen en matière de pédagogie des langues, il est invité au nom du cardinal Richelieu à venir en France ouvrir une école pansophique et, semble-t-il, par les Américains à prendre la direction du Collège Harvard qui vient d'être fondé, mais préfère se rendre en Angleterre (1641–1642), en Suède (1642–1648) et en Transylvanie (1650–1654). Finalement, il s'établit à Amsterdam (1656) où il publie ses *Opera didactica omnia* (1657), dans lesquelles figurent, outre la *Janua* (1631), *Didactica Magna* (v. 1638), *Methodus linguarum novissima* (1648), *Schola Ludus* (1656) et beaucoup d'autres ouvrages intéressants, dont *Pansophiae Praeludium* (1637). Il termine aussi *Orbis sensualium pictus* et le publie à Nuremberg en 1658.

Coménius cependant souhaite pouvoir se consacrer entièrement à des tâches plus 'élevées': compléter sa 'philosophie chrétienne' qu'il appelle 'pansophie' et terminer la rédaction de la *De Rerum humanarum emendatione consultatio catholica*, à laquelle il travaillait depuius 1643. Mais cet ouvrage monumental restera inachevé et le manuscrit, oublié jusqu'en 1934 à la bibliothèque de l'orphelinat piétiste de Halle, ne sera publié pour la première fois qu'en 1966.

4.2. La conception de la langue

L'intérêt des Coménius pour les langues date du temps de ses études à Herborn, comme le montrent les thèses qu'il y défend en 1611 et en 1612. C'est à la même époque aussi qu'il commence à rédiger le *Trésor de la langue tchèque*, dont le manuscrit périra dans les flammes à Leszno, en 1656. Son premier ouvrage publié est une grammaire (*Grammaticae facilioris praecepta*, 1616). Tous ses livres pédagogiques et philosophiques (*Didactica Magna, Pansophiae Praeludium, Via lucis*, 1668) accordent une grande place aux questions de la langue. Toutefois, c'est dans *Methodus Linguarum Novissima* qu'il expose de la manière la plus systématique et la plus détaillée sa conception de la langue. On consultera aussi avec profit la *Panglottie* et le *Lexicon reale pansophicum* dans *De Rerum humanarum* [...] (1966: II. 147–204; 803–1275).

Selon Coménius le langage est un don divin, les langues une des création humaines, donc imparfaites. Des douze caractéristiques de la langue énumérées dans le *Methodus* (1657: I. 2.21–23) rappelons les trois suivantes: La langue est l'image des choses reflétée par les sens dans l'esprit ("Primo, sermonem esse pictam Rerum imaginem" (1657: I. 2.21). Elle est le moyen de communication entre les hommes réalisé avec des mots – 'signes extérieurs' de la langue. Pour remplir sa fonction communicative elle a besoin d'une nomenclature, d'un code sémantique et d'une grammaire. Ces trois composantes présentent, dans toutes les langues connues, de graves lacunes qui engendrent confusion et malentendus, d'où la nécessité d'une langue universelle. Provisoirement, ce rôle pourrait être joué par le latin, comme l'avait suggéré Vivès, un siècle plus tôt. L'idéal serait d'inventer une langue philosophique, parfaite, simple et facile à apprendre, qu'il appelle 'panglottie'. Il consacre beaucoup de temps à élaborer les bases théoriques de cette langue artificielle et révèle les résultats de ses efforts dans la *Panglottie*, le cinquième livre du *De Rerum humanarum* [...]. C'est la partie de son œuvre linguistique la mieux connue aujourd'hui. Une analyse sérieuse de ses grammaires latines, de ses dictionnaires et nomenclatures, et surtout du *Methodus*, démontrerait que la contribution du grand penseur tchèque à la linguistique est bien plus riche (Šabršula 1992).

4.3. L'apprentissage ou *mathetica*

Selon Coménius les hommes, créatures d'un même Dieu, ont tous la même nature (1657 I, 2.199). Un des traits caractéristiques de cette nature est la présence en tout être humain d'un certain nombre d'idées, de dispositions et d'instincts innés. C'est ce qui explique l'universalité des règles générales appliquées à penser, apprendre et agir: 'ni un Indien ni un Éthiopien n'a besoin d'autres règles de pensée qu'un Européen' (1657: I. 2.29). Pour apprendre, l'homme utilise ses sens, sa raison et sa foi. Les sens sont la porte par laquelle les choses hors de nous pénètrent dans l'âme. Coménius aime répéter qu''il n'y a rien dans l'intellect qui n'ait d'abord été dans les sens' (1658: Préface). La raison permet de comprendre les choses que les sens ont perçues, de les juger et de les garder en mémoire. Là où on ne peut connaître une chose de manière sensible ou rationnelle, on se fie au témoignage d'autrui (d'une personne ou d'un livre). Dans le processus intellectuel on se sert généralement de l'analyse et de la synthèse. Coménius recommande d'y ajouter la *syncrise.* Il compare l'analyse au microscope, la synthèse au télescope et la syncrise au miroir. L'addition de la syncrise lui paraît nécessaire parce qu'à son avis on ne comprend pleinement une chose que lorsqu'on sait en quoi elle ressemble aux autres choses et en quoi elle diffère d'elles. Le savoir cependant est vain si les connaissances ne sont pas retenues par la mémoire et associées aux notions parentes qui y sont emmagasinées. Bref, sans mémoire et association d'idées on ne peut rien apprendre et surtout pas les langues. Coménius illustre sa conception de l'apprentissage des langues par l'exemple suivant:

Si, aujourd'hui je voulais apprendre la langue persane, je serais en présence d'une chose inconnue. Afin de l'apprendre, j'ai besoin de la médiation d'une chose connue, c'est-à-dire d'un interprète vivant (un homme) ou mort (un dictionaire) qui maîtrise cette langue ainsi que ma langue maternelle, et je dois fournir un effort intensif (*opus labore & studio*) pour interpréter une chose après l'autre et, par une répétition fréquente, acquérir la connaissaince de la langue auparavant inconnue de moi, par l'intervention de la langue connue de moi auparavant. Supprime un des ces éléments et l'apprentissage sera nul (1657: I. 2.95. *Trad. J. C.*).

### 4.4. La conception de l'enseignement ou *didactica*

Les prédécesseurs de Coménius, à l'exception peut-être de Vivès, considéraient la pédagogie des langues comme une affaire de bon sens, de talent et d'expérience, un art. Aujourd'hui encore, "à peu près tout ce que recouvre ce domaine des méthodes de langues, fait l'objet d'expressions d'opinions, plutôt que d'analyses factuelles et objectives" (Mackey 1972: 194). Komenský, témoin de la révolution scientifique, est convaincu qu'il existe des règles sûres, *scientifice canones*, pour traiter les intelligences, pour enseigner et faire apprendre les langues ("Ingenia tractandi, ars certa est" 1657: I. 2.98). Celles qu'il croit avoir découvert s'élèvent à plusieurs dizaines. Nous n'en retiendrons que deux à titre d'exemple:

(1) L'âme de la didactique est la capacité du maître à adapter son enseignement au niveau de l'intelligence de l'élève (1657: I. 2.132). Hélas, les maîtres oublient souvent qu'un enfant n'est pas un adulte en miniature et que son intelligence se développe lentement. Coménius en distingue quatre étapes: dans la petite enfance se forment les sens externes; dans l'enfance (six à douze ans) les sens internes: l'imagination, la mémoire; dans l'adolescence (12 à 18 ans) le raisonnement; dans la jeunesse (18 à 24 ans) la volonté et la capacité d'abstraction (1657: I. 2.132). Chaque âge demande une autre forme d'instruction, une autre école: l'école du giron maternel pour les tout petits; l'école nationale, avec un enseignement dans la langue maternelle qui s'adresse aux sens, pour les enfants; l'école secondaire (latine) avec accent sur le raisonnement, pour les adolescents; l'Académie (Université) pour les jeunes hommes, capables d'abstraction. Personne avant Coménius n'avait pensé à structurer les études en rapport avec le développement des facultés intellectuelles, avec l'âge des élèves et leurs connaissances préalables.

(2) La règle d'or de la didactique coménienne est de tout enseigner par des exemples, des règles et des exercices. Plus exactement: présenter la chose qu'on enseigne, l'expliquer, montrer comment la faire ou l'imiter et la faire faire ou imiter par les élèves, jusqu'à ce qu'ils la sachent parfaitement. 'Sans exemples, préceptes et exercices on n'enseigne et on n'apprend rien ou rien correctement' (1657: I. 2.102). De ces trois facteurs le plus important est l'exercice ('praxis'). Le maître divisera pour cela la période d'enseignement en trois parties et accordera 'une fraction du temps à la démonstration de la chose, trois fractions aux règles et leur explication et neuf fractions du temps aux exercices' (1657: II. 1.787). Comme il écrit ailleurs: "Fabricando fabricamur" ('En fabriquant nous nous fabriquons nous-mêmes.' 1657: I. 2.X-129).

### 4.5. Enseigner les quatre habiletés linguistiques

Pour Coménius l'école est un 'atelier d'humanité'. L'enseignement des langues n'est qu' une des matières du programme de formation générale des jeunes. Parce qu'en éducation tout se tient, comme dans la nature, on ne peut prétendre bien enseigner une matière, p. ex. une langue, sans tenir compte des autres matières. 'Nul ne peut être parfaitement instruit dans une science particulière s'il n'a pas des connaissances dans les autres disciplines' (1657: I. 1.74). À l'époque de l'autonomisation des sciences, Coménius prône l'interdisciplinarité. Il affirme qu'on ne peut résoudre aucun problème de la didactique des langues si on l'isole de l'ensemble dont il fait partie:

> [...] les Didacticiens que nous avons entendus ont vu quelque chose de pertinent, mais personne [n'a vu] le tout (*totum*). Parce que le tout n'a pas été et ne sera pas découvert, tant que les observations ne seront que partielles et dispersées. Il faut avoir recours à une théorie universelle (1657: I. 2.90).

C'est cette approche interdisciplinaire et globaliste qui distingue Coménius de tous ses prédécesseurs et fait de lui "un précurseur de l'écologie du langage" (Mackey 1992: 236).

Pour Coménius le but, le contenu, la méthode d'enseignement, les outils didactiques, ainsi que le rôle du maître et celui de l'élève doivent découler de la théorie de la didactique des langues. Si la méthode est fondée sur des bases théoriques solides, les résultats de l'enseignement le seront aussi. Le but de la théorie didactique coménienne des langues est de former la bouche (parler), la main (écrire) et la raison de l'élève (penser), de contribuer au développement de toute sa personnalité. Un homme éduqué doit connaître plusieurs langues: la langue maternelle parfaitement; les langues des peuples voisins suffisamment bien pour communiquer avec eux ('les Polonais, par exemple, apprendront l'allemand, le hongrois, le valaque et le turc' 1657: I. 1.127); le latin pour lire les livres savants; enfin le grec, l'hébreu et l'arabe, si la profession envisagée l'exige.

Connaître une langue signifie pour Coménius la maîtriser 'entièrement', c'est-à-dire être capable de l'utiliser, dans toute sa pureté et promptement quand on parle et lorsqu'on écrit (1657: I. 2.152). Par 'entièrement' il entend posséder le lexique fondamental (les mots primaires), les principales formes linguistiques (règles de grammaire) et les structures essentielles (syntaxe) prévus pour chaque niveau d'études et, en outre, ce qui appartient à la future profession de chacun; par exemple, le médecin doit connaître les termes médicaux.

On peut apprendre toutes les langues par le seul usage, mais une telle connaissance 'est quelque chose d'occasionnel, long, superficiel, quelque chose d'imparfait' (1657: I. 2.VII–70). Il faut connaître aussi les règles 'pour éclairer et confirmer l'usage' et cela même quand on apprend une langue vivante, car 'l'italien, le français, l'allemand, le tchèque, le hongrois peuvent être soumis à des règles déjà explicitement formulées' (1657: I. 1.129). Coménius est l'un des rares pédagogues de son temps à demander la connaissance des règles de la langue maternelle et des langues vivantes.

Les choses qu'il faut savoir dire et écrire, dans la langue maternelle comme dans la langue étrangère, sont les mêmes à tous les niveaux de l'apprentissage: celles qui se rapportent à la nature, à la société et à Dieu, celles que tous doivent connaître pour vivre heureux dans ce monde et mériter le salut. Coménius propose de présenter ce contenu encyclopédique en quatre étapes, appelées d'après les titres de ses manuels de latin: étape *vestibulaire, januale, atriale* et littéraire.

Le niveau *vestibulaire* est réservé aux débutants. Ils y apprennent à 'balbutier' la langue étrangère: prononcer, lire, écrire ainsi que les rudiments de la grammaire. Au niveau *janual* ils étudient le système ou la structure de toute la langue et apprennent aussi à parler la langue; au niveau *atrial* ils se familiarisent avec les finesses et les élégances de la langue et apprennent à s'exprimer de manière soignée. Ce n'est qu'après avoir maîtrisé le contenu de ces trois niveaux qu'ils commencent à lire les auteurs et s'entraînent à parler selon les règles de l'art oratoire.

Comme pour Vivès, la lecture des auteurs de l'Antiquité représente pour Coménius un problème presqu'insoluble. Le théologien en lui voudrait qu'on imite les Éphésiens ("Ephesii imitandi") et qu'on brûle les ouvrages des anciens 'afin que disparaissent plus facilement les ténèbres de la confusion subsistant encore du paganisme' (1657: I. 1.153. Trad. Piobetta). Le pansophe toutefois ne peut se passer complètement de la culture antique, et c'est ainsi que Coménius n'est pas entré dans l'histoire comme un nouveau Érostrate. Cela explique, en partie, pourquoi l'étape littéraire est restée la moins élaborée de sa méthode.

### 4.6. La méthode

La méthode d'enseignement des langues de Coménius est bilingue: '[...] notre méthode proclame qu'il ne convient pas d'enseigner le latin à qui ignore la langue nationale parce qu'elle a établi que la seconde doit servir la première' (1657: I. 1.173. Trad. Piobetta). Elle est aussi universelle:

VIII. Toutes les langues peuvent donc s'apprendre par une même et unique méthode.
16. On peut les apprendre par l'usage, en ajoutant seulement les règles très faciles qui montrent les différences d'avec les langues déjà connues' (1657: I. 1.130. Trad. Piobetta).

Surtout, elle est active ("practica Methodus"): 'Que cette méthode vraiment pratique (qui enseigne tout par *autopsie, autolexie et autopraxie*), soit observée en tout, afin que les élèves s'habituent à devenir maîtres en tout' (1657: II. 1.787). Les élèves doivent donc s'exercer à tout observer méthodiquement (en classe, au cours des excursions aux champs ou les visites dans les manufactures), et à dire, répéter, écrire, découvrir et faire tout par eux-mêmes, sous la direction et la surveillance du maître, car l'école doit les préparer à la vie réelle (1657: I. 1.112).

Dans la préface du *Methodus Linguarum Novissima* Coménius résume sa méthode d'enseignement des langues en trois principes fondamentaux: le *parallélisme* exact des mots et des choses, la *progression* par degrés sans brûler les étapes, et la *pratique*, moyen et critère de la réussite. Par réussite il entend la maîtrise des quatre habiletés linguistiques autant qu'il le faut pour communiquer et obtenir des connaissances utiles.

*Comprendre* la langue étrangère est la compétence la plus facile et s'acquiert par l'écoute attentive du maître (dans les classes supérieures également par des sessions hebdomadaires d'écoute des nouvelles des gazettes en latin), la traduction dans la langue maternelle, la répétition fréquente des mots, expressions, phrases, règles et textes déjà appris par cœur, l'enseignement visuel (la présentation par le maître d'objets, de leur modèle, ou de dessins). Un de plus grands titres de gloire de

Coménius comme didacticien des langues est la publication, en 1658, d'*Orbis sensualium pictus*, un manuel illustré bilingue (latin-allemand) qui enseigne tout le vocabulaire qui se rapporte au monde visible (environ 4000 mots) en 150 chapitres, composés de quelques petites phrases chacun. Les images servent à inspirer aux petits enfants l'amour des livres et parallèlement jouent un rôle sémantique et mnémonique. Le livre connut un succès extraordinaire (plus de 250 éditions), fut traduit dans presque toutes les langues et servit longtemps d'exemple pour la rédaction des manuels de langues.

Komenský souhaite que les enfants apprennent à *lire* et à *écrire* simultanément, et cela de manière analytique, comme le recommandait déjà Quintilien. Dans l'*Orbis pictus* il a même créé pour les jeunes commençants un alphabet symbolique en quatre colonnes:

(1) l'image d'un animal (un agneau pour enseigner la lettre *b*),
(2) son nom, en latin et en allemand, et le nom du son qu'il produit (*l'agneau bèle*),
(3) la syllabe *bé*,
(4) la lettre *B-b*).

Les garçons lisent un chapitre de leur manuel après l'autre, le traduisent et l'analysent (lecture intensive). Les élèves avancés lisent en outre des livres choisis par le maître pour s'instruire ou se divertir (lecture extensive). Tous font une variété d'exercices écrits dans lesquels ils ne leur est permis d'utiliser que des mots qu'ils connaissent et qu'ils comprennent exactement. La lecture et la composition libres sont réservées aux élèves des dernières classes qui ont maîtrisé parfaitement la matière du programme.

Coménius sait que *parler* la langue étrangère est la compétence la plus difficile à acquérir en milieu scolaire. Il suggère que les élèves soient encouragés à ne parler que des choses qu'ils comprennent et qu'ils savent nommer et écrire, à lire à haute voix, à réciter par cœur, à traduire oralement, à convertir les leçons du manuel en textes dialogués et à les présenter en classe. Surtout il conseille la pratique du théâtre scolaire, non seulement comme moyen idéal pour apprendre à parler les langues, mais aussi pour la formation générale des jeunes. 'Sans les jeux scéniques on espérerait en vain que l'esprit soit complètement instruit' (1657: II. 1.33). Aussi est-il particulièrement fier du succès de la représentation, en 1654, de *Schola ludus* – L'école de jeu ou par le jeu – (1657: II. 1.831–1040) par les élèves de son école pansophique à Saros Patak, en Hongrie. Il considère même cette pièce comme une de ses plus précieuses contributions au progrès de la didactique des langues. N'a-t-il pas enfin réalisé le vieux vœu de Quintilien: 'que l'étude soit donc un amusement' (*Institutio Oratoria* I. 1.20)?

### 4.7. Les outils didactiques

Pour Coménius il n'a pas d'enseignement ni d'apprentissage sans manuels pour les élèves et pour les maîtres. Il est probablement le premier didacticien à avoir esquissé une théorie cohérente du manuel scolaire (*Didactica Magna, Methodus Linguarum Novissima*) et à en avoir composé des dizaines pour la langue maternelle, les langues étrangères et les sciences (la métaphysique, la physique naturelle, l'astronomie, etc.). Les plus célèbres sont toutefois *Janua linguarum reserata* et *Orbis sensualium pictus.* Voici quelques exemples du premier:

484. En quelque lieu que tu sois, pren garde avec qui tu es; observant finement ce qu'on fait en cachette.
485. Car es voyages toutes choses sont mal asseurées, (dangereuses, il n'y a rien d'asseuré.) Les brigands tuent, les voleurs detroussent, les pirates (escumeurs de mer) emmenent ceux qu'ils ont pris. Il te faut donc donner garde d'estre rencontré des ces brigands & voleurs. Es hosteleries memes principalement ches les taverniers, l'hoste n'est pas asseuré de son hoste. (Trad. fr. de E. Courcelles, 1643).

et voici quelques autres du second:

LXXV. Le barbier
Le barbier[1] / dans son échoppe[2], / taille / les cheveux et la barbe / avec des ciseaux[2]; /ou bien il rase/ avec un rasoir que de sa cassette[4]/ il tire/, et lave [les cheveux]/ au-dessus d'un bassin[5],/ avec de l'eau bouillie qui coule d'une aiguière[6], comme aussi avec du savon[7], et les essuie avec une serviette[8]. Il peigne avec un peigne[9], frise avec un fer à friser[10]. Parfois, il coupe une veine, à l'aide d'une lencette[11], là où le sang gicle[12]. En tant que chirurgien il soigne les blessures. [Les chiffres renvoient à l'image au dessus du texte.] (Trad. fr. J. C.)

Les manuels de lecture de Coménius, complétés des manuels de grammaire et des lexiques qui les accompagnent, marquent un tournant dans l'histoire de la didactique des langues, le début du passage de la pédagogie humaniste à la pédagogie 'réaliste'. Les élèves n'y apprennent plus la langue des auteurs anciens mais le vocabulaire et les structures de la langue parlée soignée. Le but visé n'est pas l'éloquence ni la culture du goût, mais la communication (orale et écrite) sur les sujets les plus divers et l'acquisition de connaissances utiles. Ce sont des manuels pansophiques. La lecture des textes classiques n'occupe dans la méthode des langues coménienne qu'une place secondaire.

### 4.8. Les maîtres et les élèves

Coménius exige des maîtres érudits ('bibliothèque ambulante'), méthodiques, diligents, affables et pieux. Leur rôle principal est de mener la classe avec assurance, celui des élèves de travailler avec ardeur. Pourtant il ne prévoit pas de formation spéciale pour les maîtres: on naît pédagogue ou bien on s'en tient au manuel et on suit scrupuleusement les instructions du concepteur de la méthode. Le rôle du 'Collège didactique' ou universel qu'il envisage dans *Didactica Magna* est de réunir des savants qui 'approfondiraient les sciences par leurs travaux' (1657: I. 1.125), non de former des spécialistes de l'enseignement des langues.

### 4.9. Conclusion

Coménius réussit à faire la synthèse de l'expérience de ses prédécesseurs, y compris Vivès et Bathe, à l'enrichir de ses propres observations et réflexions et à l'organiser en un ensemble cohérent, si riche en idées qu'il reste, encore aujourd'hui, une source intarissable d'inspiration. Maître d'école rompu, linguiste respecté, théoricien génial de l'enseignement et de l'apprentissage, aucun des didacticiens des langues qui l'ont précédé ne peut lui être comparé. Il exerça sur cette discipline une influence profonde, surtout dans les pays réformés (Allemagne, Angleterre, Nouvelle Angleterre). Son œuvre, en dépit des hésitations, contradictions et erreurs, qu'il reconnaît d'ailleurs avec beaucoup de candeur (1657: II. 2.41–64), représente 'un saut historico-épistémologique' (Titone 1987: 148). En effet, c'est avec Coménius que commence le long processus qui aboutit à la constitution de la didactique des langues en une discipline moderne autonome.

## 5. Bibliographie

### 5.1. Sources premières

Alvarez, Emmanuel. 1575. *De Institutione Grammaticae. Venetiis.*

Bathe, William. 1611. *Ianua linguarum.* Salamanticae: Apud Franciscum de Cea Tesa. (Trad. fr. de Jean Barbier dans *Ianua Linguarum Quadrilinguis or A Messe of Tongues.* Londini, excudebat R. F. impensis Matthaei Lownes, MDCXVII.)

Coménius (Komenský), Jan Amos. 1657. *Opera didactica omnia.* Amsterdami: Excuderunt Christophorus Cunradus & Gabriel à Roy (Édition en facsimilé. Prague: ČSAV, 1957.)

–. 1631. *Janua Linguarum Reserata.* Leszno (Trad. fr. É. Courcelles, Amstelodami, Apud Ludovicum Elzevirum, 1643.)

–. 1658. *Orbis sensualium pictus.* Norimbergae, Typis & Sumptibus Michaelis Endteri. (Trad. fr. de Blaise Teppati dans *Orbis sensualium pictus quadrilinguis.* Nuremberg: Endter, 1666.)

–. 1966. *De rerum humanarum emendatione consultatio catholica.* 2 vol. Prague: ČSAV.

–. 1952. *La Grande Didactique.* Paris: P. U. F. (Traduction française de la *Didactica Magna* par J.-B. Piobetta.)

Nebrija, Antonio de. 1492. *Grammatica de la lengua Castellana.* Salamanca: s.n.

Quintilien. 1975. *Institution oratoire.* Texte [latin] établi et traduit par Jean Cousin. Paris: Les Belles Lettres.

–. *Ratio atque institutio studiorum Societatis Jesu.* 1599. Rome: Tarquinius Longus. (Trad. fr. André Paquet. Montréal: Éditions de l'Entr'aide, 1940.)

Vivès, Juan Luis. 1782–90. *Opera Omnia I–VIII* Éd. par Gregorio Mayans y Siscar. Valentiae: in officina Benedicti Monfort. (Republished London: The Gregg Press, 1964.)

### 5.2. Sources secondaires

Caravolas, Jean. 1984. *Le Gutenberg de la didacographie ou Coménius et l'enseignement des langues.* Montréal: Guérin.

Coseriu, Eugenio. 1972. "Acerca de la teoria del lenguaje de Juan Luis Vives". *Tradicion y novedad en la ciencia del lenguaje. Estudios de historia de la linguistica*, 62–85. (= *Biblioteca Romanica Hispanica.*) Madrid: Editorial Gredos.

Laforge, Lorne. 1972. *La sélection en didactique analytique.* Québec: Les Presses de l'Université Laval.

Mackey, Francis W. 1972. *Principes de didactique analytique.* Traduit en français par Lorne Laforge. Paris: Didier.

–. 1996. "La philosophie et la linguistique de Coménius dans le cadre des idées écologiques de notre siècle". *Jan Amos Coménius (1592–1670). Aspects culturels, philosophiques, pédagogiques et didactiques de son œuvre.* Actes du colloque international Coménius 11–12–13 juin 1992 éd. par Jean A. Caravolas avec l'aide de Gilles Bibeau, 235–242. Montréal: Université de Montréal. Publications de la Faculté des sciences de l'éducation.

Malmberg, Bertil. 1991. *Histoire de la linguistique. De Sumer à Saussure.* Paris: P. U. F.

Mir, Gabriel Godina. 1968. *Aux sources de la pédagogie des Jésuites: Le "Modus Parisiensis".* Roma: Institutum Historicum S. I.

Noreña, Carlos G. éd. 1970. *Juan Luis Vives.* The Hague: Martinus Nijhoff.

O'Mathuna, Sean. 1986. *William Bathe S. J., 1564–1614. A Pioneer in Linguistics.* Amsterdam & Philadelphia: Benjamins.

Riber, Lorenzo, trad. *Juan Luis Vives Valenciano: Obras Completas I–II.* Madrid: M. Aguilar, 1947.

Salmon, Vivian. 1976. *The Works of Francis Lodwick: A study of his writings in the intellectual context of the seventeenth century.* London: Longman.

Šabršula, Jan. 1992. *La linguistique dans les écrits latins de Coménius.* Praha: Listy filologické. Ústav pro klasická studia ČSAV.

Titone, Renzo. 1987. "La glottodidattica al crocevia delle scienze". *La glottodittatica oggi* éd. par R. Titone, 2–13. Milano: Oxford Institutes Italiani, 7° Convegno, 30° Anniversario.

Watson, Foster. 1971 [1908]. *The English Grammar Schools to 1660, their Curriculum and Practice.* Cambridge: Univ. Press.

–. 1913. *Vives on education.* Cambridge: Univ. Press. (Repr., Totowa, N. J.: Rowman and Littlefield, 1971.)

*Jean Antoine Caravolas, Montréal (Canada)*

# 139. Port-Royal et la tradition française de la grammaire générale

1. La première grammaire théorique moderne
2. La théorie des idées
3. Les parties du discours
4. La théorie de la phrase
5. Conclusions
6. Bibliographie

## 1. La première grammaire théorique moderne

La *Grammaire générale et raisonnée* publiée en 1660 par le philosophe Antoine Arnauld et le grammairien Claude Lancelot est incontestablement l'un des textes linguistiques les plus célèbres de l'âge classique. Il le doit sans doute à ses auteurs et au fait qu'il représente l'un des grands textes pédagogiques des fameuses Petites écoles de Port-Royal, le berceau du jansénisme. Il le doit surtout au fait qu'il répond avec élégance et originalité au problème théorique et pratique le plus difficile que la Renaissance ait suscité: comment dominer la diversité des langues du monde? On sait, en effet, qu'à partir, d'une part, de la dissolution du monde médiéval et de la naissance des Etats-nations et, d'autre part, du début de la conquête du monde par les Occidentaux, la connaissance des langues se développe sous la forme de la multiplication exponentielle des grammaires des différents vernaculaires: ceux de l'Europe, bien sûr (chaque Nation entend disposer d'une langue policée qu'elle impose à ses conquêtes), mais aussi celles des autres familles linguistiques. On n'insistera jamais assez sur la révolution culturelle, technique et scientifique que constitue ce mouvement de *grammatisation* (v. Auroux 1994). Contemporain de la révolution galiléo-cartésienne dans la conception de l'univers et des lois de la physique, il a des conséquences tout aussi fondamentales pour l'avenir de l'humanité.

On peut concevoir la situation de l'accès aux langues tel que la Renaissance l'a mis empiriquement en place sous la forme d'un graphe dont les sommets sont les langues et les arcs les grammaires (ou les dictionnaires) d'un vernaculaire dans une autre langue. On dominera la diversité des langues si on trouve un sommet d'où atteindre tous les autres (mathématiquement, il s'agit de disposer d'un graphe fortement connexe). Le latin n'est pas en mauvaise position. Mais, pratiquement, on se heurte à la capacité forcément limitée des polyglottes.

Pour dominer la diversité, on peut donc songer à lister le multiple comme le font les dictionnaires multilingues, en le ramenant à une mesure commune. Sans être totalement inutile, la solution est largement illusoire: on n'atteindra jamais la totalité des éléments dans son exhaustivité. L'une des astuces théoriques profondes de Port-Royal, c'est de choisir la totalité distributive, plutôt que la totalité additive: s'intéresser aux éléments présents dans toutes les langues, plutôt qu'à tous les éléments de toutes les langues. C'est ce choix qui se traduit lexicalement par l'usage du qualificatif de "général" plutôt que celui d'"universel", que l'on rencontrera rarement dans la tradition française (Court de Gébelin 1774 est une exception, sans doute inspirée par la tradition anglaise et *l'Hermes de* J. Harris). Si l'on parvient à trouver une liste de tels éléments, on aura fourni une introduction à l'étude de toutes les langues. La grammaire générale est une propédeutique à valeur pédagogique. Tout comme le *Discours de la méthode* (1637) de Descartes était une introduction à des traités particuliers (la géométrie, l'optique et les météores), la *Grammaire générale* est une propédeutique à la grammaire des langues particulières (notamment l'espagnol et l'italien dont Lancelot est un excellent spécialiste qui a rédigé des manuels pour les petites écoles). D'autres solutions étaient possibles. En 1689, le britannique G. Hickes fait paraître ses *Institutiones grammaticae anglo-saxonicae et moesogothicae* par lesquelles il entend faire une œuvre symétrique à celle de Port-Royal (qu'il considère limitée à une introduction aux langues romanes) pour les langues germaniques. Il choisit de décrire la langue de la Bible d'Ulphila (le "moeso-gothique") et de décrire les "règles" par lesquelles on passe à l'anglo-saxon. Un arbre généalogique est aussi un graphe fortement connexe: la grammaire historique et comparée est une réponse au même problème que celui auquel s'attaque la grammaire générale! Le pari théorique est toutefois très différent. La grammaire générale suppose que le noyau commun, dont elle fait la racine de l'étude de toutes les langues, corresponde à la nature même du langage humain.

Il y a très peu de "grammaires générales" au sens propre. Après Port-Royal, il faut attendre presqu'un siècle pour retrouver un ouvrage qui reprenne le titre. Il s'agit de l'œuvre de Beauzée (1767), dont le volume est presque dix fois supérieur à celui (relativement modeste, une centaine de pages) d'Arnauld et Lancelot. La tradition française de grammaire générale est essentiellement le produit des Lumières. L'élément fondamental, ce sont les articles grammaticaux de l'*Encyclopédie* de d'Alembert et Diderot (à partir de 1751), rédigés principalement par Dumarsais (jusqu'à la lettre G), puis, après sa mort, par Nicolas Beauzée: ils constituent quantitativement le plus vaste traité de grammaire générale jamais publié (trois forts volumes *in quarto* lorsqu'ils sont repris, corrigés et complétés sous forme séparée dans l'*Encyclopédie Méthodique,* 1782–1786), et, véritablement, le premier grand ouvrage de linguistique théorique. Dans le dernier quart du siècle, la densification des grammaires générales correspond au mouvement des idéologues, philosophes empiristes, disciples critiques de Condillac. Ils jouèrent un rôle politique important entre 1785 et 1803 et créèrent des chaires de grammaire générale dans les Ecoles Centrales qui disparurent avec la création des lycées napoléoniens.

La grammaire générale, telle que l'initie Port-Royal, est la théorie des éléments communs à toutes les langues. Cette vaste perspective est peut-être ce qui explique la rareté des tentatives. Beauzée en fera un programme empirique exigent qui suppose le dépouillement de quantité de grammaires particulières, comme celles du lapon ou du quechua. L'influence de Port-Royal se lit également dans la façon d'aborder les phénomènes linguistiques. Il ne s'agit pas simplement d'en faire des listes comme dans les grammaires pédagogiques, nombreuses pour le français dès le 16ème siècle, mais de donner une explication. L'aspect raisonné et méthodique est la partie du programme initial qui assure le succès et l'influence théorique fondamentale de l'œuvre des Messieurs. On tente principalement une application au français et la grammaire raisonnée devient le programme de recherche majeur de la grammaire. Ce changement de perspective n'est pas sans précédent, comme en témoigne la *Minerve* de Sanctius et l'idée d'aborder les *causes* de la langue latine. Les auteurs de Port-Royal ont toujours su bénéficier de leurs prédécesseurs; on le voit notamment à l'évolution que marquent les différentes éditions de la *Nouvelle Méthode pour apprendre facilement et en peu de temps la langue latine* (1644) de Lancelot. On a récemment montré (v. Colombat 1996) que ce manuel reprenait les *Commentarii Grammatici* de Despautères (1537), eux-mêmes inspirés du *Doctrinale* (*circa* 1200) d'Alexandre de Villedieu, tout en prenant progressivement davantage à Sanctius. Contrairement à la grammaire spéculative médiévale, la grammaire générale représente un programme scientifique développé par des grammairiens fortement engagés dans la connaissance empirique de différentes langues. C'est pourquoi il correspond véritablement à la naissance de la grammaire moderne (v. Dominicy 1994).

## 2. La théorie des idées

Les langues disposent d'éléments que l'on ne retrouve nulle part ailleurs dans l'ordre des choses; ce sont eux que la tradition linguistique occidentale a entrepris de décrire avec un vocabulaire propre, lentement élaboré depuis

Platon et Aristote. On dispose ainsi de termes théoriques comme "nom", "verbe", "particule", "cas", etc. Leur référence est directement constituée par les phénomènes linguistiques. Ils servent déjà à formuler des règles générales qui font de la grammaire une entreprise de représentation relativement abstraite (par exemple, "le verbe s'accorde en nombre avec le nominatif"). Le projet explicatif produit par la grammaire générale est largement réductionniste dans son esprit même. Il s'agit rien moins que de rendre compte des catégories linguistiques par des catégories non-linguistiques. Toute la tradition occidentale va dans ce sens: dès Aristote, le signe linguistique est défini comme le "symbole des affections de l'âme". Port-Royal ne change pas fondamentalement cette définition du langage: il est "l'image de la pensée". On en conçoit vite l'intérêt pour le programme généraliste. Les langues sont différentes; nul ne peut nier cette simple constatation empirique, mais on peut imaginer que la pensée est une caractéristique indépendante des langues et propre à l'espèce humaine. Dès lors ce que les langues ont de commun provient de la nécessité où elles se trouvent toutes de traduire la même pensée. C'est dans la relation de l'élément linguistique à ce qu'il exprime de la pensée que doit se trouver l'explication de sa nature et de son fonctionnement. La rationalité de la grammaire générale provient de ce qu'elle repose sur une théorie de l'entendement, c'est-à-dire du fonctionnement cognitif. La grammaire spéculative médiévale avait globalement le même fondement, mais elle dépendait d'une tout autre théorie cognitive.

On doit concevoir le cartésianisme – qui va servir de fondement initial à la grammaire générale – comme une représentation digitale de l'esprit par opposition à la conception analogique qui a prévalu d'Aristote à la fin du Moyen-Age. Pour la théorie ancienne, les choses ont des formes (des modes d'être) que la perception transmet à l'esprit (modes de compréhension) et qui sont éventuellement identiques aux modes de signification des mots. Avec le dualisme cartésien l'esprit et les choses n'ont plus de contenu commun (l'idée de cercle n'est pas ronde, notera Spinoza); comme le langage appartient à l'ordre des choses (sous forme de son ou de figure), il n'est qu'une image arbitraire qui ne vaut qu'autant que respectant les distinctions des éléments et des fonctions de la pensée qu'il traduit, il est apte à restituer dans la pensée d'autrui ce qui se passe dans la pensée du locuteur. Il importe pour être grammairien de connaître ces éléments et ces fonctions. C'est pourquoi la *Logique*, qui paraît deux ans après la *Grammaire générale* et est considérablement plus développée, revêt autant d'importance pour tous les travaux ultérieurs. Arnauld et Nicole ont largement innové par rapport à la logique aristotélicienne et scolastique (v. Auroux 1993, Dominicy 1984, Pariente 1985), et une grande partie des découvertes linguistiques ultérieures (chez Beauzée, notamment) auront leur source dans ces innovations.

La pensée est de nature substantielle et se décompose en "idées". L'idée – "cette forme de nos pensées par laquelle nous avons conscience de ces mêmes pensées", disait Descartes – est en quelque sorte un terme primitif. Penser, c'est faire des opérations sur les idées: les concevoir, les additionner, les soustraire, les comparer, etc. L'essentiel de la théorie cognitive classique peut se résumer à la conception d'un univers d'idées douées de lois de compositions interne de nature algébrique. Une idée est composée d'autres idées qui constitue sa compréhension (en d'autres termes une idée $a$ est définie par l'addition d'autres idées, par exemple $b + c$ ); cette composition instaure une relation d'ordre entre les idées, de la plus particulière à la plus générale. Une idée possède aussi une extension composée, selon Port-Royal, des idées de la compréhension desquelles elle fait partie. Il en résulte que l'extension et la compréhension d'une idée varient en sens inverse (loi dite de Port-Royal). Lorsque l'on ajoute une idée à une autre idée, on obtient par conséquent une idée de compréhension supérieure et d'extension moindre. Beauzée fera de l'extension un ensemble d'individus (ou d'idées d'individus), à peu près ce que l'on entend aujourd'hui par classe. La loi de Port-Royal n'est plus valable dans ce cas (on peut restreindre l'extension sans changer la compréhension), aussi distingue-t-il entre la latitude d'étendue (définie par la compréhension) et la quantité d'individus auxquels on applique l'idée, distinction qui sera capitale pour la théorie des parties du discours. On remarquera la nature quasi-booléenne de l'ensemble des idées, dotée d'une relation d'ordre ($<$) et d'une relation de composition interne ($+$). Toutefois ce calcul des idées perd son isomorphie avec une algèbre des classes dès que l'on introduit la négation (la négation n'est pas une opération interne sur les idées) et l'identité (identité en extension et identité en compréhension ne se recouvrent pas). En développant la logique des idées les théoriciens de la grammaire générale (et de la logique classique) mettent au jour les limites de tout calcul intensionnel.

La pensée n'est pas limitée à la conception, sa fonction essentielle est le jugement susceptible d'être vrai ou faux. Port-Royal en fait un acte spécifique de l'esprit qui se traduira dans le langage par la copule. On reprend donc, d'une certaine façon, la théorie de la proposition mise en place par Aristote dans le *Peri Hermeneias*. La structure élémentaire est donc *Sujet (S) est Prédicat (P)*. Ce qui peut s'interpréter comme le fait que l'idée qui est le sujet est dans l'extension de l'idée qui est le prédicat, ou, ce qui revient au même que l'idée qui est le prédicat est dans la compréhension de l'idée qui est le sujet. D'autres interprétations sont possibles: la copule représente une identité (entre l'extension considérée des deux idées) ou encore l'affirmation de l'existence intellectuelle de l'idée du sujet sous le rapport déterminé par l'idée du prédicat (autrement dit dans le jugement, on vise quelque chose dont la représentation est une idée composée des deux idées $S + P$). On comprend immédiatement que ces interprétations ne sont pas sans incidence sur les théories linguistiques. Mais plus globalement, puisque le jugement est une séquence élémentaire de pensée, le rôle de la théorie des idées dans la théorie linguistique impose que le langage ait pour séquence élémentaire l'image du jugement. La proposition, dans la configuration ainsi décrite, devient la structure de base de l'analyse grammaticale, ce qui permettra ultérieurement (notamment chez l'abbé Girard, dans les *Véritables principes de la langue française*, 1747) une analyse fonctionnelle de ses éléments.

On ne notera jamais assez l'importance de cette conception opératoire du fonctionnement de l'esprit, même si les analogies conduisent parfois à des rapprochements qui ne sont guère évidents. Ainsi la séquence (($S$ (= Nom) + (qui + est $P$ (= Adjectif)) dont la relative doit contenir une représentation de jugement (présence de la copule) est-elle conçue comme équivalente à une séquence (Nom + Adjectif). La structure opératoire conduit également à mettre en lumière des phénomènes qui n'étaient pas répertoriés dans les grammaires. La loi de Port-Royal conduit ainsi à admettre que lorsque l'on additionne à une idée une idée qui est déjà contenue dans sa compréhension on obtient la même idée (autrement dit $a + b = a$, si $a < b$). Cette contrainte est à l'origine, dans la théorie de la connaissance, de la différence entre jugement synthétique et jugement analytique et, dans la théorie linguistique (dans la *Logique* de Port-Royal et dans la grammaire à partir de Girard 1747), de la distinction entre relative explicative et relative déterminative.

Le rôle de la théorie des idées dans l'explication grammaticale peut faire penser que la logique comme discipline précède nécessairement la grammaire. Que la logique de Port-Royal soit parue après la grammaire semble purement contingent et, au reste, n'est qu'un embryon de théorie que de nombreux passages de la logique viennent compléter après coup. Beauzée fera de la précédence de la logique un point doctrinal essentiel; c'est que, pour ce rationaliste, la structure de la pensée est indépendante du langage. Il en va autrement avec la saveur nominaliste de la philosophie empiriste qui va dominer à partir de Condillac. Ce dernier n'hésite pas à écrire que la grammaire est la première partie de l'art de penser. Cela ne remet pas en question le rôle de la théorie cognitive (ce que Destutt de Tracy nommera l'idéologie) dans l'explication grammaticale, simplement, d'une part le langage est nécessaire à la formation de la représentation constituée, d'autre part, la théorie du raisonnement (la logique proprement dite) suppose un langage déjà bien formé. Contrairement à ce qu'on lit chez de nombreux commentateurs et historiens modernes, le programme scientifique de la grammaire générale n'est pas lié à la philosophie rationaliste, proche du cartésianisme, qui, lors de son origine, est celle des jansénistes, puis, à son sommet, encore celle de Beauzée. Les choix philosophiques en matière de théorie de la connaissance ont naturellement des incidences sur des points particuliers de doctrine, ils ne suffisent pas à déterminer un programme de recherche scientifique.

## 3. Les parties du discours

La grammaire générale doit accorder une place essentielle à la théorie des catégories grammaticales les plus générales que sont les parties du discours. L'enjeu est double. D'abord, il s'agit de les définir à partir des catégories cognitives, c'est-à-dire soit des opérations de la théorie des idées, soit des éléments les plus généraux des parties de représentation (les contenus sémantiques). Ensuite, il importe absolument que les catégories retenues assument vis-à-vis des éléments de toutes les langues la fonction même de généralité qui est le cœur du programme scientifique. Cette dernière contrainte n'est pas simple et elle conduira à un certain affaiblissement de la pensée linguistique lorsque les grammairiens post-kantiens de langue allemande (Bernardhi, par exemple, dans sa *Reine Sprachlehre*, 1801), voudront déduire, en dehors de tout contexte empirique (c'est-à-dire de façon *a priori* au sens kantien), les catégories linguistiques universelles de la table des catégories de l'entendement que l'on trouve dans la *Critique de la raison pure.* Il n'a jamais été question d'un tel programme, même chez les rationalistes, dans la tradition française qui restera toujours largement étrangère à ce type de problématique. Pour le rationaliste Beauzée la grammaire générale est une théorie empirique: "Les différents usages des langues sont (...) les phénomènes grammaticaux de l'observation desquels il faut s'élever à la généralisation des principes et aux notions universelles". La théorie des parties du discours est une théorie falsifiable empiriquement parce qu'elle doit pouvoir être confrontée à la diversité des langues. Depuis que les Latins ont adapté la grammaire des Grecs ont sait bien que les langues n'ont pas les mêmes catégories grammaticales (contrairement au grec, la latin n'a pas d'article et ne possède pas le même nombre de cas). Il n'est pas question de nier cette diversité. Mais on doit trouver un niveau de généralité qui, non seulement, ne la remette pas en question, mais au contraire puisse l'expliquer. De fait, face à ce problème, on trouve deux variantes quant au statut épistémologique de la théorie:

- *variante rationaliste* (Beauzée): les parties du discours générales (interjections, noms, pronoms, adjectifs, verbes, prépositions, adverbes, conjonctions) sont des *éléments nécessaires* dans toute langue; si on ne les retrouvait pas dans une langue, ce ne serait pas une véritable langue.
- *variante empiriste* (Condillac): les parties du discours générales (noms substantifs, adjectifs, verbe substantif (copule), prépositions) sont des *éléments suffisants* dans toute langue ; du moment qu'on les retrouve, on a affaire à une véritable langue.

Dans les deux cas on respecte bien l'axiome de généralité: les catégories doivent être attestées dans toutes les langues connues ou inconnues. L'exhaustivité des connaissances dont on dispose n'est pas nécessaire pour assurer la validité de l'axiome. La structure théorique de Beauzée est celle d'une classification au sens strict; si on découvre une nouvelle catégorie dans une langue inconnue, pour que la théorie demeure valable, il suffit qu'elle puisse se brancher quelque part sous l'une des catégories générales. Celle de Condillac s'apparente à une combinatoire. Il suffit que toute nouvelle catégorie soit virtuellement décomposable dans toute combinaison possible des quatre catégories générales. On peut même envisager qu'une langue manque en apparence de l'une des quatre catégories. Imaginons une langue sans copule; il faudra alors qu'elle possède des verbes, lesquels seront analysés comme une combinaison (verbe substantif + adjectif). La structure combinatoire n'est pas compatible avec la structure classificatoire qui exige des dichotomies strictes. Il s'agit cependant d'une technique explicative à laquelle Beauzée n'hésite pas à recourir également: "ce qui distingue l'adverbe des autres espèces de mots, c'est que l'adverbe vaut autant qu'une préposition et un nom".

On peut voir sur un exemple simple l'apport de la théorie des idées à la classification des parties du discours. Revenons à la distinction entre compréhension et extension (latitude d'étendue dans la terminologie de Beauzée). Dans une séquence comme *le chat noir,* nous disposons de trois éléments *a, b c.* L'expression linguistique correspond à une composition des idées signifiées par les mots: $a + b + c$. Admettons qu'on prenne *b* comme premier élément parce qu'il est susceptible de référer à des individus du monde (il désigne "déterminément" note Beauzée), critère distinctif de la classe des noms. La fonction des deux autres éléments est évidemment de réduire l'extension de l'idée générale signifiée par le nom. On tient le critère de définition de la catégorie des "adjectifs". Toutefois les deux éléments ne le font pas de la même manière: celui de droite ajoute à la compréhension du substantif (il change la latitude d'étendue); celui de gauche ne change que la quantité actuelle des individus auxquels l'idée de "chat noir" est appliquée. On a donc une division de la classe des adjectifs. Beauzée donne à la première branche le nom d'"adjectif métaphysique"; à la seconde celle d'"article" 'plus exactement celle d' "article indicatif", la catégorie d'article correspond chez lui au nœud immédiatement supérieur (nos déterminants). C'est la nature des opérations cognitives qui explique la distinction entre classes de mots. La hiérarchie classificatoire quant à elle rend compte de la variabilité entre les langues: "Notre *le*, *la*, *les* et les correspondants qu'il peut y avoir dans d'autres idiomes, ne forme donc point une partie d'oraison distinguée de toute autre; c'est simplement un individu d'une espèce nécessaire partout, quoique cet individu ne soit absolument pas nécessaire à l'intégrité de l'espèce, puisqu'on s'en passe dans bien des langues". Pour la grammaire générale toutes les langues ont des articles (des déterminants), toutes n'ont pas d'articles indicatifs.

On ne peut guère faire le reproche à la grammaire générale d'être incapable d'accueillir la diversité des langues. Il n'est cependant pas certain que la structure théorique mise en place ne bénéficie pas d'une stratégie qui lui permette d'être pratiquement intouchable par d'éventuelles falsifications empiriques. Prenons le cas du chinois. On sait parfaitement au 18$^{ème}$ siècle qu'aucun mot n'est susceptible d'y être affecté distinctivement de marques temporelles. N'y aurait-il pas de verbe en chinois? La réponse de Beauzée est claire: "La vérité est qu'il y a des *Verbes* dans tous les idiomes; que, dans tous ils sont caractérisés par l'idée générale de l'existence intellectuelle d'un sujet indéterminé sous une relation à une manière d'être; que, dans tous, en conséquence, la déclinabilité par temps est une propriété essentielle; mais qu'elle n'est qu'en puissance dans les uns, tandis qu'elle est en acte dans les autres". La distinction acte/puissance possède toute l'apparence d'une hypothèse *ad hoc* susceptible d'éliminer tous les contre exemples. En fait, la théorie est profondément orientée par la structure des langues européennes. Les éléments dont elle assume la généralité sont toujours des *mots*. Il lui est dès lors difficile d'aborder de façon satisfaisante les langues dont la structure morphologique est assez éloignée du modèle européen. C'est une question sur laquelle Beauzée reviendra dans l'*Encyclopédie Méthodique*. Il rédigera, par exemple, un article *affixe* (catégorie empruntée aux grammairiens de l'hébreu) pour traiter "des particules qui se mettent à la fin d'un mot, pour y ajouter l'idée accessoire de rapport à l'une des trois personnes" et qu'il retrouve en hébreu, lapon et quechua. Dans le même ordre d'idée, il remarquera que la langue basque "n'a point de prépositions; elle a un certain nombre de terminaisons qu'elle adopte à la fin des mots énonciatifs du second terme d'un rapport". Dans les deux cas les éléments sont identifiés par leur équivalence en traduction: les terminaison du basque font l'"effet " des prépositions, les affixes "tiennent lieu des adjectifs possessifs". "Particule", "affixe" sont des catégories qui n'ont pas de statut théorique dans la grammaire générale, tandis que "préposition" est une partie du discours à statut universel, dont on doit reconnaître qu'une langue en manque. Malgré tous les efforts, la grammaire générale n'est pas vraiment adaptée au traitement des langues non indo-européennes.

## 4. La théorie de la phrase

La structure de la théorie des idées conduit la grammaire à faire une place essentielle à la notion de proposition, ce qui est une innovation profonde et conduit à plusieurs conséquences importantes. Tout d'abord, dès Port-Royal on assiste à une généralisation de la notion, qui devient une catégorie susceptible de divisions. La nouveauté est due à la notion de "proposition incidente" qui a pour fonction de modifier un élément linguistique. Les relatives sont incidentes au nom (elles déterminent ou expliquent l'antécédent). Mais une proposition peut aussi être incidente au verbe, ce qui correspond à ce que nous appelons aujourd'hui des "attitudes propositionnelles" (*Copernic croit* QUE la terre tourne autour du soleil). Il en résulte une autre catégorie de proposition, celle de principale. La grammaire générale se trouve ainsi à l'origine des distinctions ultérieures entre différents types de propositions qu'affectionnera la grammaire scolaire. On notera qu'elle a permis de dépasser l'analyse du seul énoncé élémentaire (la proposition minimale) en abordant celle de la phrase en générale et qu'elle contient en germe l'abandon de la définition logique de la proposition comme énoncé vrai ou faux.

La théorie des idées n'a pas que des conséquences heureuses. La structure propositionnelle élémentaire *S est P* est extrêmement limitée et peu adéquate. De même qu'elle ne permet pas à la logique d'aborder le fonctionnement des relations (et donc de comprendre le raisonnement mathématique), elle n'offre pas à la grammaire de cadre adéquat pour aborder les objets du verbe. Enfin, elle n'a pas d'intérêt immédiat pour l'étude de la structure intrinsèque du syntagme. C'est pourquoi la grammaire générale va mettre en place la théorie (largement *ad hoc*) de la distinction entre la composition logique de la proposition (la distinction sujet, copule, prédicat) et la composition grammaticale de ces parties logiques. Une phrase comme *Le chat noir est sur le paillasson* dispose ainsi d'un sujet (*Le chat noir*) et d'un prédicat (*sur la paillasson*) composés. Il s'agit de la mise en place d'un dispositif d'analyse qui régnera dans la grammaire scolaire jusqu'à la seconde moitié du 20ème siècle.

La stratégie théorique élaborée pour aborder la structure proprement grammaticale de la phrase est de même nature que celle que l'on a vu en œuvre dans la théorie des parties du discours. On identifie une catégorie linguistique, largement décrite par la tradition (la concordance ou le régime) et on tâche de mettre en face d'elle une opération cognitive ou, plus généralement, un élément sémantique dont elle est le signe. Le mécanisme cognitif est universel, la catégorie linguistique ne l'est pas nécessairement (des cas ou l'ordre des mots peuvent signifier les mêmes opérations en fonction des langues). Le phénomène répertorié par la catégorie linguistique est l'*explicandum* et l'opération cognitive l'*explicans*. La concordance (l'accord morphologique, par exemple entre le substantif et l'adjectif) s'explique par l'identité. "La concordance indique (...) l'application du sens vague d'une espèce au sens précis de l'autre, et l'identité, si j'ose dire, très physique, du sujet énoncé par les deux espèces de mot sous des aspects différents" (Beauzée). Le régime est plus complexe et faisait dire à Port-Royal que "la syntaxe de régime est presque toute arbitraire". Dans l'article "gouverner" de l'*Encyclopédie* Beauzée parvient à le ramener aux mécanismes de la théorie des idées. "Les noms appellatifs, les prépositions et les verbes relatifs ont essentiellement une signification vague, qui doit être déterminée (...). Cette détermination se fait communément par des noms que l'on joint aux mots déterminés (...). Or, ce sont les mots indéterminés qui, dans le langage des grammairiens, gouvernent ou régissent les mots déterminants" (v. Auroux 1979).

Une large partie des progrès apportés par la grammaire générale tient à son programme explicatif susceptible de s'appliquer à de nombreux domaines. La théorie des temps verbaux bénéficie de ce dépassement de la morphologie pour se concentrer sur la constitution même des valeurs temporelles. Les auteurs utilisent des repères linéaires, eux-mêmes repérés sur le repère de l'énonciation (par exemple: i) le moment de l'énonciation auquel on rapporte ii) le temps d'un événement qui peut lui-même être rapporté à iii) un autre événement). Ainsi l'imparfait est-il un temps concernant un événement simultané à un autre événement antérieur à l'énonciation. La pratique classificatoire, par critères abstraits permet, à Beauzée d'offrir un tableau qui dispose de plus de cases que le français ne possède de formes différentes. Destutt définit le conditionnel français non comme un mode, mais comme un temps l'"imparfait du futur", ce qui permet à l'analyse notionnelle de rejoindre la morphologie et d'en rendre compte (terminaison en *-ais* du conditionnel comme pour l'imparfait, présence du *-r* — comme dans le futur).

## 5. Conclusions

La grammaire générale est incontestablement un programme de recherche riche et fécond. En deux siècles la théorie grammaticale a fait des progrès considérables et l'on peut dire que jamais auparavant un tel effort théorique abstrait n'avait été fourni dans les sciences du langage. Jamais auparavant on ne s'était intéressé à la diversité des langues. Pourtant, au début du 19ème siècle le programme marque le pas, au point que l'on a parfois parlé de la fin des grammaires générales et raisonnées auxquelles aurait succédé la grammaire historique et comparative comme nouveau programme de recherche. Assurément, on peut constater que la grande période créative est achevée. Mais, d'une part, les acquis ont été largement conservés dans la grammaire scolaire, voire dans la grammaire comparée qui conservera la définition des catégories. D'autre part, on assistera à la fin du 19ème siècle à un renouveau certain des préoccupations de grammaire théorique dont on peut considérer qu'ils reprennent le même projet (et se rangent parfois explicitement sous la bannière de la grammaire générale). Enfin, le comparatisme, qui constitue la grande affaire du siècle du positivisme, ne correspond pas à un véritable changement de paradigme, puisqu'il n'a pas les mêmes objets et qu'il ne vise pas les mêmes phénomènes. Il s'agit plutôt de l'invention d'un nouveau domaine. Alors pourquoi ce relatif désintérêt pour un champ de recherche qui a bénéficié, avec l'*Encyclopédie,* de la plus vaste synthèse et de la plus grande diffusion dont aucune théorie linguistique ait jamais bénéficié auparavant sur un temps aussi court? De fait, le 19ème siècle français voit se développer la grammaire scolaire dans des proportions considérables et de façon relativement anarchique. Chaque responsable d'institution y va de son manuel et de sa théorie. Aucun grand théoricien n'émerge, mais il s'agit davantage d'une dégénérescence par éclatement que d'une disparition. En quelque sorte les raisons sont avant tout sociales. D'un côté, les idéologues ont perdu politiquement la partie dans le domaine de la rénovation pédagogique. De l'autre, les sophistications théoriques de la grammaire générale ne sont guère productives pédagogiquement, malgré les efforts de Sicard pour la mettre à la portée des enfants. Théorie scientifique qui atteint son sommet chez Beauzée, la grammaire générale n'est pas plus utile à l'apprentissage des langues que ne le sera le *Cours* de Saussure. Elle n'a pas développé le rôle propédeutique que lui assignait Port-Royal. Faute de recherche universitaire, elle ne trouve pas de lieu où se développer dans la France moderne. On n'en conclura pas que sa mise en sommeil relative ne correspond à aucune faille du programme. Comme théorie linguistique, elle a le défaut considérable de négliger la morphologie.

## 6. Bibliographie

### 6.1. Sources primaires

Arnauld, Antoine et Lancelot, Claude. 1969. *Grammaire générale et raisonnée* (1660). Ed. critique par Herbert Brekle. Stuttgart-Bad Cannstatt: Friedrich Frommann Verlag.

Arnauld, Antoine et Nicole, Pierre. 1965. *La logique ou l'art de penser* (1662). Ed. critique par Herbert Breckle et le baron von Freytag Löringhoff. Stuttgart-Bad Cannstatt: Friedrich Frommann Verlag.

Beauzée, Nicolas. 1767. *Grammaire générale ou exposition raisonnée des éléments nécessaires du langage pour servir de fondement à l'étude de toutes les langues*. Paris: Barbou.

Condillac, Etienne Bonnot de. 1775. *Grammaire. = Cours d'étude pour l'instruction du prince de Parme.* Vol. I: *Grammaire.* Parme: Imprimerie royale. (Nouvelle impression en facsimile de l'édition de Parme 1775 avec une introduction par Ulrich Ricken. Stuttgart-Bad Cannstadt: Fromman-Holzbog, 1986.)

Court de Gébélin, Antoine. 1774. *Grammaire universelle et comparative.* (*Monde Primitif*, t. 2). Rééd. en 1776 sous le titre *Histoire naturelle de la parole.* Paris: l'Auteur.

Destutt de Tracy, Antoine-Louis-Claude. 1803. *Éléments d'idéologie. Seconde partie. Grammaire.* Paris: Courcier.

Domergue, Urbain. 1799. *Grammaire générale analytique.* Paris: C. Houel.

Silvestre de Sacy. 1799. *Principes de grammaire général mis à la portée des enfants, et propres à servir d'introduction à l'étude de toutes les langues.* Paris: J.-J. Fuchs.

Thiébault, Dieudonné. 1802. *Grammaire philosophique, ou la Métaphysique, la logique et la grammaire reunies en un seul corps de doctrine.* Paris.

### 6.2. Sources secondaires

Auroux, Sylvain. 1979. *La sémiotique des encyclopédistes*. Paris: Payot.

–. 1993. *La logique des idées.* Montréal: Bellarmin. Paris: Vrin.

–. 1994. *La révolution technologique de la grammatisation.* Liège: Mardaga.

Chevalier, Jean-Claude. 1968. *Histoire de la syntaxe. Naissance de la notion de complément dans la grammaire française (1530–1750).* Genève: Droz.

Colombat, Bernard. 1996. "Archéologie de la *Nouvelle méthode latine* de Port-Royal". *Histoire et grammaire du sens* éd. par Sylvain Auroux, Simone Delesalle et Henri Meschonnic, 59–71. Paris: Armand Colin.

Dominicy, Marc. 1984. *La naissance de la grammaire moderne.* Liège: Mardaga.

Donzé,, Roland. 1967. *La grammaire générale et raisonnée de Port-Royal.* Berne: Francke.

Pariente, Jean-Claude. 1985. *L'analyse du langage à Port-Royal. Six études logico-grammaticales.* Paris: Minuit.

Tsiapera, Maria & Wheeler, G. 1993. *The Port-Royal Grammar, Sources and Influences.* Münster: Nodus.

*Sylvain Auroux, Lyon (France)*

# 140. Universal language schemes in the 17th century

1. Introduction
2. The intellectual context
3. Proposals for a universal character
4. Proposals for a philosophical language
5. Dalgarno
6. Wilkins
7. Leibniz
8. Bibliography

## 1. Introduction

During the 17th century there was a widespread concern with the construction of artificial languages intended to provide a universal means of communication and a philosophically adequate representation of knowledge. A large number of projects emerged, ranging from extremely tentative proposals to fully-developed universal language schemes. These projects link up with various longstanding traditions in logic, grammar and philosophy. Further, they are connected with a series of ideas and trends specific to the 17th century. The complexity of the subject is reflected in the variety of approaches from which these projects have been studied in the present century (see the book-length treatments by Rossi 1960, Salmon 1972, Knowlson 1975, Slaughter 1982, Strasser 1988, Hüllen 1989, Eco 1995, Stillman 1995, and the anthology of articles in Subbiondo 1992). The present article sketches some crucial characteristics of the intellectual context, treats the majority of schemes briefly, and focuses on Dalgarno and Wilkins. Finally, the work of Leibniz in this area will be considered. Though constituting a new departure, this work was firmly rooted in the intellectual movement outlined here.

## 2. The intellectual context

### 2.1. Attitudes towards language

A strong belief in human intellect and craftsmanship as instruments for improving the world is a prominent trait of the intellectual climate in the 17th century. Within the mechanistic world picture engendered by the new science, language was basically looked upon as a tool, or device, which can be judged for efficacy in achieving the goals it was made for, and which may be replaced by better tools if necessary. Rather than being viewed as either a natural phenomenon or a divine gift, organically interwoven with our personal and social identity, language was considered, as Ian Michael once tellingly put it, as "something external, which hence, like teeth, could be artificial" (unpublished lecture, Leyden 1992). Further, the position of Latin as a lingua franca was being undermined both by increasing contacts with peoples and cultures beyond Europe and the Middle East, and by the rise of the European vernaculars. The changing linguistic situation caused a great interest in problems concerning language and language teaching. In addition, it was widely felt that the time devoted to the study of languages was ultimately wasted, since it reduced the time available for the more rewarding study of the world of nature. In reaction to the humanist ideal of literary education, the 17th-century mainstream emphatically preferred knowledge of things to knowledge of words. Accordingly, the many idiosyncrasies and irregularities of existing languages were considered to be so many defects. Nevertheless, the 17th century was deeply concerned with semiotics. Acquaintance with Chinese script and hieroglyphics stimulated a fascination with symbol systems in general, and subjects such as cryptography, shorthand, and methods for communication with the deaf and dumb were intensively studied. An especially important source of inspiration was mathematics, in which new methods of notation were recognised as having paved the way for new paradigms of thought.

### 2.2. The contribution of the Bible

17th-century theorizing about language was to a considerable extent determined by a biblical framework, two elements of which are of special importance. Firstly, the question of language origin was treated in the context of the account in Genesis of Adam giving names to all creatures: "So the Lord God formed of the earth every beast of the field, and every foule of the heaven, and brought *them* unto the man to see how he would call *them*: for howsoever the man named the living creature, so was the name thereof" (Genesis II 19). On the basis of this account, it was beyond doubt that all mankind originally spoke one and the same language, which was created by Adam. However, the nature of this language was controversial. Some believed that it was irrecoverably lost, others assumed that one of the languages currently in existence could be identified with, or at least be considered as the most direct descendant of the Adamic language, most scholars opting for Hebrew. Further, many believed that the names given by Adam in his pre-lapsarian state of perfect knowledge were not arbitrarily chosen, but somehow expressed the essence of the things named. Although it was a matter of speculation and debate how this could have been done, the Adamic language was thus viewed not only as the first and universal, but also as the best possible language. Secondly, the diversity of languages was accounted for by the confusion of tongues at Babel. Accordingly, the existence of language barriers was seen as a curse inflicted on human kind. Although this curse was a punishment for human pride, it is characteristic of 17th-century secularisation and optimism that it was generally believed to be both legitimate and feasible for the curse of Babel to be reversed by the invention of a new universal language.

### 2.3. The logical tradition

However great the differences between medieval and early modern ways of viewing the world, the study of language had been connected with logic for many centuries. In the 17th century, the influence of the logical tradition was still far-reaching. One ingredient of this tradition was particularly important for the shape the universal language schemes eventually took, namely the categories, or as they were commonly called, the 'predicaments'. Aristotle's short treatise on categories, together with his *De Interpretatione* and some commentaries from late antiquity formed the core of the so-called 'old logic'. It was not until the 12th century that Aristotle's other logical writings were rediscovered by the Western world. In the scholastic period, the predicaments formed the standard paradigm of knowledge representation, functioning as the most general heads of an all-embracing classification of reality, and serving as an inventory of the basic concepts and subject areas of the various special sciences. Although the value of the theory of predicaments was seriously challenged during the 17th century, the language planners naturally turned to it when looking for a general and systematic catalogue of 'things and notions'.

Another component of the logical tradition is the distinction of various levels in the analysis of both linguistic meaning and thought, namely terms, propositions, and syllogisms. These levels are ordered by increasing degrees of complexity. The basic level is that of terms or words, which correspond to concepts, forming the object of the theory of categories. Terms are combined into propositions, which correspond to sentences expressing judgements. Propositions in their turn are combined to form syllogisms, i. e. a series of sentences constituting an argument. Since logic books were typically organized according to these levels, and logic was a standard part of 17th-century education, the compositionality of meaning and of knowledge was generally taken for granted. Consequently, many language planners shared the notion that ideally the primitive symbols of a language ought to correspond to the primitive elements of knowledge, and that complex expressions ought to mirror the composition of their referents.

### 2.4. The tradition of philosophical grammar

Western grammatical theory as inherited from the classical period, and described in the works of Priscian and Donatus, acquired a new branch of investigation during the later Middle Ages. In the 12th century, Peter Helias tried to provide philosophical explanations for the rules of grammar laid down by Priscian. Thereafter the field of grammar became divided into a descriptive part, primarily concerned with the exposition of grammatical rules to schoolboys on the one hand (grammatica positiva), and a theoretical part on the other hand, which aimed at supplying a philosophical basis for grammar in general (grammatica speculativa). The latter type of grammar culminated in the work of the Modistae, who sought to establish a correspondence between the structure of reality, the workings of the human mind and the basic concepts of grammar. Opposed by the humanists in the post-medieval period, philosophical grammar was revived in the 16th century by the works of Scaliger and Sanctius, the latter of whom was a major source for the famous 17th-century rationalist grammarians of Port Royal. Though differing in orientation, the Modistae and their post-medieval successors shared the supposition that linguistic expressions should be considered as specific realizations of underlying universal principles of grammar, which are intimately connected with the principles of human thought. The 17th-century language planners worked within this atmosphere, postulating a universal logical form underlying all languages, and using this form as a standard which determined the characteristics a language ought to have.

## 3. Proposals for a universal character

### 3.1. A 'Real Character'

The later philosophical language schemes grew out of earlier attempts to devise an auxiliary notational system which was to serve primarily as a bridge between pairs of languages. Acquaintance with Chinese script was a major factor in the emergence of this idea, which was articulated by a series of writers, but most influentially by Francis Bacon (1561–1626) in *The Advancement of Learning* (1605). A crucial element of this programme was the supposed possibility of reversing the order holding between spoken and written language, grammatical tradition maintaining that the latter was secondary to and parasitic upon the former. Such a reversal would result in a so-called 'real character', which designates things rather than words. Though largely mistaken, the conviction became widespread that such a real character could be 'read off' in different languages, just as it was reported that Chinese logographs could be read off into various mutually incomprehensible varieties of Chinese. It was also observed that real characters such as astronomical signs and Arabic numerals are written and understood, though differently pronounced, by speakers of different languages. A comprehensive system of real characters would, it was believed, if not reverse the curse of Babel at one stroke, at very least push back the diversity of languages to the level of spoken language alone.

### 3.2. Lost or incomplete schemes

A large number of universal writing schemes are referred to by contemporary writers, but some of these are now lost and others were never completed and survive only as fragments. A rich source of references to such schemes is to be found in the diary and correspondence of Samuel Hartlib, who emigrated from Germany to England and who maintained a network of contacts between scholars all over Europe. Among the lost or incomplete schemes are proposals by Champagnolles, Le Maire, Douet and Des Vallées made in the 1620s in France, a scheme by Johnson in Ireland in the 1630s, and schemes drawn up by Kinder, Morley and Beale in England.

### 3.3. Wilkins' *Mercury*

John Wilkins's *Mercury, or the Secret Messenger* (1641) was an early work devoted to diverse aspects of communication, ranging from cryptography to a prototype for semaphore. Wilkins presents arguments in favour of a universal language in the context of a discussion of the multiplicity of human languages resulting from the confusion of tongues at Babel, and justifies the practicability of such a project by reference to the logographic system of characters used by the Chinese. He also refers to symbols such as numerals, musical notes and astronomical and chemical signs. No further details concerning the structure of such an invention are given in this work.

### 3.4. Lodwick

Francis Lodwick (1619–1694) was engaged with universal language schemes throughout his life, being associated with the Hartlib circle in the 1650s, and later on with the Royal Society committee set up to improve Wilkins's *Essay*. In a *Common Writing* (1647) he outlines a system of non-phonetic symbols by which concepts could be represented, and which could be read off in any language. These, he claimed, would function in the same way as already instituted universal characters such as the symbols for the planets. He goes on to propose a dictionary of 'radical' words, together with a set of diacritics by which semantically related words can be represented. This latter feature is elaborated in greater detail in a subsequent work *The Groundwork, or foundation laid for the framing of a new perfect language* (1652), in which he argues that in an ideal language the structure of the symbol would display the qualities of the object represented, thereby anticipating the aim of a fully philosophical language. Lodwick also pays some attention to the need to reduce the multiplicity of grammatical rules in the instituted languages, and suggests the possibility of providing a spoken counterpart to his written character.

### 3.5. Bermudo

It is reported by Caspar Schott (1664: 483) that when he was in Rome in 1653, a Spanish Jesuit promoted a universal writing scheme which was called *Arithmeticus Nomenclator.* Schott does not mention the author by name, but modern scholarship assumes that he was called Pedro Bermudo (Strasser 1988: 134–135). The only description of the scheme that is extant is Schott's detailed account (1664: 483–505). The scheme consists of over 1,200 words which are arranged into 45 classes. Some of these classes coincide with distinctions traditionally made within the framework of Aristotelian science, such as elements, beasts and parts of animals. Others seem to reflect more practical viewpoints, such as the class of 'things having to do with travel', which includes both 'road' and 'oats'. Further, some classes consist of linguistic items, such as the class of 'adjectives' and that of 'proper names'. The writing system boils down to a numerical code: each class is assigned a number, and so is each item within classes. In order to write the words listed, a numerical expression is used consisting of the number of the class and of the number of the item within that class. Various dots placed around the numerals indicate grammatical categories such as number, tense and case. The scheme closely resembles those of Beck (3.6.) and Becher (3.7.), though it differs in that the words codified by numerals are arranged thematically rather than alphabetically.

### 3.6. Beck

One of the early schemes to reach print as a publication in its own right was by the Ipswich schoolmaster Cave Beck (1623–1706), appearing under the title *The Universal Character* in 1657. In his preface, Beck refers to the programmatic calls for such an invention issued by Bacon (3.1.) and by Wilkins (3.3.), and outlines the features of a universal character. His own scheme, although worked out in some detail, is an extremely simple one. It amounts to little more than an alphabetic listing of English words, to each of which a numerical value is assigned. An 'inverse' dictionary of some other language (a French version being promised here, and others to follow), with identical numbers assigned to semantic equivalents, would allow these numbers to function as real characters. Grammatical elements, including inflectional and derivational categories, were to be represented by alphabetic signs.

### 3.7. Becher

In 1661, Johann Joachim Becher (1635–1682) published his *Character, pro notitia linguarum universali.* Becher provides a list of 10,283 Latin words, which are consecutively numbered. The universal writing system consists in writing the numbers rather than the words. For each language, two dictionaries are to be produced, an alphabetical one and a numerical one, enabling translation into and from the universal character respectively. In addition, Becher presents a table of 173 'variations of the sense', in which grammatical inflections for indicating number, various cases, moods, tenses and persons are provided with a number. Each expression of Becher's character consists of at least two numbers, one designating a lexical item and the other or others designating inflections. Since Arabic numerals are not universally used, Becher devised a special character by means of which numbers can be expressed.

### 3.8. Kircher

The *Polygraphia Nova et Universalis* (1663) by the Jesuit Athanasius Kircher (1602–1680) is as much concerned with cryptography as it is with a universal writing system. Its aim is to 'reduce all languages to one', and it tries to execute this program for 5 languages: Latin, German, French, Italian and Spanish. The method used is similar to that of Beck and Becher: an alphabetical list of Latin words is numbered so that equivalents from other languages can be expressed by numbers. Kircher uses a Roman numeral to refer to the page on which a word is printed, and an arabic numeral to identify one of the 40 words listed on every page. Kircher prints word lists in numerical order of all 5 languages mentioned. Further, he devised special characters for indicating grammatical inflections.

## 4. Proposals for a philosophical language

### 4.1. Universal character vs philosophical language

Modern authors have commonly divided 17th-century artificial language schemes into two categories: on the one hand projects of the kind mentioned in section 3., on the other hand philosophical languages such as those created by Dalgarno (5.) and Wilkins (6.). Although the latter projects differ from the former ones in important respects, attempts to draw a sharp dividing-line between the various schemes must fail. Couturat and Leau (1903) proposed a distinction between a priori vs. a posteriori schemes: a posteriori schemes are based on existing languages, a priori ones on a language-independent model either of reality or of knowledge. The same distinction was made by 17th-century writers: thus Wilkins indicated that his early scheme propounded in his *Mercury* (1641) differed from his philosophical language published in 1668 in that the former proposed to take the vocabulary of Hebrew as a basis, whereas the latter was founded on 'a regular enumeration of things and notions'. However, a dichotomy of this kind unsatisfactorily cuts across continuities, as in the case of Dalgarno's philosophical language, which gradually developed from his early, a posteriori scheme. Further, it fails to distinguish between rudimentary sketches of a 'real character', which are in essence a priori, and the sophisticated schemes of Dalgarno, Wilkins and Leibniz. Moreover, the schemes characterized as a priori are modelled on existing languages in various respects.

A number of modern writers regard the use of a classification scheme in the construction of the lexicon of the artificial language as characteristic of philosophical languages. This criterion is equally unsatisfactory: first, it overlooks the fact that both Dalgarno and Leibniz attached relatively minor importance to classification, and second, it leads one to include a rudimentary scheme like that of Bermudo, which closely resembles such uncontroversially unphilosophical schemes as those of Beck and Becher, in the group of philosophical projects. A third criterion focuses on aims rather than method: philosophical languages, unlike merely universal ones, are aimed at modelling the structure of reality, or of thought, in addition to providing a means of international communication. Unfortunately, schemes of all kinds were claimed by their authors to constitute a considerable improvement on existing languages, and often so for being more congruent with either reality or thought. Nevertheless, this criterion was important in the period. Descartes mentioned it when criticising an early universal writing scheme (see 4.2.), and Leibniz used a similar criterion to distinguish his own plans from what Dalgarno and Wilkins had achieved, which shows that similar criteria may lead to quite different dividing lines. In sum, although it is hard to make a satisfactory classification of the various 17th-century artificial language projects, the criteria mentioned reflect important characteristics of these projects. In particular, the concept of a philosophical language was a central one. The following sections explore how this concept was handled by a number of influential writers.

### 4.2. Descartes

The topic of a philosophical language was not of central concern to René Descartes (1596–1650). Nonetheless, he put forward some seminal ideas on the subject in a 1629 letter to Mersenne, in which Descartes contrasted the idea of a philosophical language with that of a universal character. Criticising a proposal of the latter kind as theoretically straightforward and practically of little use, he suggested the construction of a language built on an orderly series of simple ideas, out of which everything people think is composed. If such a series could be established, it would be possible to construct an easy-to-learn universal language, capable of helping the understanding by representing everything so distinctly that it almost could not go wrong. However, this language is unattainable as long as a perfect theory of knowledge does not exist. Although he believed that such a perfect theory could be found, Descartes emphasized that it would still not be realilstic to imagine the philosophical language depending on that theory ever to be in use.

### 4.3. Mersenne

In *Harmonie Universelle* (1636) Marin Mersenne (1588–1648) affirms that a 'Musicien Philosophe', who both masters the science of sounds and has the capacity to assign names to things, is able to invent "the best of all possible languages". In principle, the best language is characterized by a natural connection between the words and the things they designate, so that the meaning of words can be understood by everyone without a previously established convention. However, since even the names Adam assigned to animals depend on his arbitrary decision rather than nature, such a language does not seem possible. Thus for a language to be the best, it is enough that it expresses the thoughts of the mind and the desires of the will in the clearest and briefest way. Further, the most excellent language is also the most simple, i. e. consisting of fewest words, which by combinatorial variation are fit to designate a huge number of things. Mersenne's approach is for the most part quantitative. Discussing such questions as whether the number of possible words is larger than the number of things, he concludes, on the basis of combinatorial tables, that the letters of the alphabet are quite sufficient to form a distinct word for each individual thing, including grains of sand and hairs. He further observes that it is theoretically possible to derive a name for a kind of thing, such as water, from its relative properties, e. g. how much lighter it is than gold. Hence the number of ways to form names for individual things and kinds of things is astronomical. Mersenne did not make any specific proposals, but he contributed to the development of the idea of a philosophical language in approaching the subject in an abstract manner, disseminating the proposal to invent an entirely new language from scratch, and establishing standards determining the quality of every thinkable language.

### 4.4. Campanella

In a work published in 1638, Tommaso Campanella (1568–1639) treats grammar as the first of five parts of 'rational philosophy'. Reviving the distinction between ordinary and philosophical grammar, he continued the Modistic tradition in using an Aristotelian metaphysical framework as a theoretical basis for philosophical grammar. Unlike the Modistae, Campanella viewed this type of grammar as a suitable framework for the construction of a new philosophical language: in a brief appendix he indicates that his treatment of the various parts of speech should be taken as a guideline for anyone wishing to establish a new language in a philosophical manner. Further, he states that words should be formed according to the nature of things and that ambiguous words, synonyms and metaphors should be abolished. Campanella's grammar was a major source for Wilkins's 'natural grammar' (cf. 6.).

### 4.5. Comenius

In the *Via Lucis*, written in 1641 but not published until 1668, Jan Amos Comenius (J. A. Komensky, 1592–1670) sketches an ambitious program for the improvement of education and learning, directed towards universal peace and harmony. A major obstacle for achieving this goal is the "multiplicity, diversity and confusion of languages". Comenius therefore proposes the institution of a universal language, the most important function of which is to be an antidote against the vagueness of ideas. This requires that the language "parallels things", i. e. that it contains exactly as many words as there are things, that words are joined in the same way as things are joined, and that the sounds express the nature of things. Further, the language should be completely regular and free from meaningless elements. It should also be easier, more agreeable and more perfect than any other language in that knowing this language will greatly enhance the understanding of things themselves. In the *Panglottia*, which was never published during his lifetime, Comenius argues at length for the necessity, possibility and facility of a new universal language once more, and he adds a first tentative outline. As to the lexicon, he points out that sound symbolism should be used as much as possible in order to present the meaning of a word directly to the imagination. Thus the letter 'a' should signify largeness, the letter 'i' something small or thin, the letter 'o' something round, and so on. Comenius estimates that a set of 300 monosyllabic root words, if combined into polysyllabic ones and enlarged by means of various affixes, will suffice to build a lexicon which is complete and free from redundancy. For example, the number of words can be reduced by expressing 'cow' as 'bull + female'. As for the grammar, he specifies a series of rules borrowed from the standard Latin framework, but aimed at simplifying and regularizing this. For instance, gender is only used if it is relevant to indicate male or female sex, but is equally applied to nouns and verbs. Further, each verb should indicate by its form whether being, making or becoming is expressed with respect to what is designated by the root word. Again, the main purpose of this rule is to reduce the size of the lexicon: e. g. 'to show' can be expressed by 'to make appear'. Comenius believed that if the precepts he set forth in *Panglottia* would be put into practice, a universal language would result which was both more compendious and easier to learn than any existing one.

### 4.6. Kinner

Early in the 1640's, the Silesian scholar Cyprian Kinner (d. 1649) experimented with various ways of creating a 'remedy against the Babylonic confusion of tongues' (letter from Kinner to Hartlib, June 1647, reproduced in DeMott 1958: 11–13). He coined what he called 'technical words' for various plants, such that the various syllables were indicative of various qualities of the plant. He imagined that the same method could be used for signifying other things as well. Later he decided that, rather than the letters of the Latin alphabet, newly contrived symbols should be used that could be quickly written and understood by everyone, and which could not be confused. The 'radical words' of this system were to designate simple things, that is, elements, while very complex things such as animals and man were to be designated by symbols of equal complexity. He foresaw that the problem would be to identify the radical words. Further, it would be necessary to express derivations, inflections and syntactic connections. Kinner thought this could be done by means of diacritics around a major symbol that expresses the radical. Kinner also insisted that mnemonic aids should be devised for learners of the system.

4.7. Urquhart

Thomas Urquhart (1611–?1660) was a Scot, and it is perhaps significant that both he and Dalgarno received their university education at Aberdeen (at King's College and Marischal College respectively). He is best known as the translator of Rabelais. A staunch royalist, he survived the rout following the disastrous Battle of Worcester, although in the course of the campaign his papers were lost, at least according to his own dramatic, but clearly embellished account of the events. It is unclear whether the detailed workings of his own universal language scheme ever in fact existed, but Urquhart tells us that he managed to salvage his proposed preface. Whether in fact rescued from the battlefield, or more likely written in his subsequent period of imprisonment in the Tower of London, this was published, together with an outline sketch, as part of the work *Ekskubalauron*, in 1652. Urquhart's description of his language, presented as a simple listing of its characteristics, does not allow us to reconstruct the scheme as a whole. Nevertheless, his proposals are explicit enough to make clear his understanding of a philosophical language; e. g. the nature of 'real character' (item 1, cf. item 104), the nature and number of his 250 radicals (item 73) and the role of the predicaments in their organisation (item 72).

4.8. Ward

Seth Ward (1617–1689) was a noted mathematician and theologian who was associated with some of the central language planners of the mid-17th century. In a joint publication with John Wilkins, written in a defence of university education, *Vindiciae Academiarum* (1654), he addresses, among other current issues, the desirability of a universal language and the prospects for its construction. Although sketchy, his proposals are more sophisticated than those previously offered by Wilkins in his *Mercury*. We know that he was for a while engaged in active work on this topic, for he subsequently handed over to Dalgarno some tables of substantives which he had drawn up towards the project for a real character. Dalgarno acknowledged his assistance, but the tables appear to be no longer extant. In the debate between Dalgarno and Wilkins (cf. 5.2.; 6.1.), Ward is known to have played a mediating role, unsuccessfully as it turned out. Ward was not active on the Royal Society Committee set up after Wilkins's death to investigate the improvement and implementation of the *Essay*, but his views were ascertained by Paschall, who set them out in a letter to Hooke dated 21 February 1679/80 (cf. Cram 1994). He reports that Ward has arrived at the conclusion that a real character need not itself be constructed in order to achieve the goals set out by the language planners; these could equally well be met by the use of a natural language in accordance with the current developments in algebraic notation and argumentation. Thus although Ward never himself produced a universal language, he was important as a contributor to the development of both Dalgarno's and Wilkins's proposals and he also offered critical speculations on the subject from the perspective of newer mathematical and philosophical understanding which were in due course to render such schemes obsolete.

4.9. Newton

It was probably in the early 1660s that Isaac Newton (1642–1727) drafted a scheme for a universal language in his notebook (Elliott 1957). A universal language, Newton notes, can be best deduced from "the natures of things themselves". Taking a classification of notions as a starting point, one could mark each category by distinctive letters "as of Instruments with s, beasts with t, the Souls passions with b" and so on. Newton further sketches an elaborate system of modifications designed to indicate comparisons, degrees, circumstances and relations among things.

## 5. Dalgarno

### 5.1. The development of Dalgarno's scheme

The ideas of George Dalgarno (1616?–1687) which saw print finally in *Ars Signorum* developed through a number of distinct preliminary stages (cf. Salmon 1966, Cram 1980, Cram & Maat forthcoming). When he first chanced upon a universal character he was preoccupied solely with the development of a shorthand system, or system of brachygraphy as it was then called. Since the representations of English words he was using were not phonetic, they could, it was pointed out to him, be equally well read off into some other language, and what had been devised as a shorthand could thus also serve as a universal character. Contemporaries report that Dalgarno's skills at shorthand were well known and respected in Oxford circles, as were his first attempts at a universal character. His project soon came to the attention of Samuel Hartlib, who records in his diary for April 1657 that Seth Ward and John Wallis were assisting a Scotsman (unnamed, but undoubtedly Dalgarno) in the enterprise. Dalgarno's scheme at these early stages was presented, in broadsheet advertisements, as having multifarious advantages and uses, not all of which turned out to be compatible. Another central preoccupation, alongside shorthand, was that of constructing a mode of representation which would serve as a system of artificial memory. To this end the scheme which was publishied as a broadsheet in 1657 was provided with a set of mnemonic verses which could be learned off by heart and by means of which the form of the words in the universal character could be recalled. The needs of both mnemonics and of shorthand receded in importance as Dalgarno developed his invention in new directions, notably by the addition of a phonetic component which transformed a 'dumb character' into a spoken language.

### 5.2. Dalgarno's debate with Wilkins

Although Dalgarno was but a humble schoolmaster in Oxford, his activities brought him into increasingly close contact with leading intellectuals in university spheres, and in particular with John Wilkins (cf. 6.) who himself was already speculating about the construction of a real character. Wilkins, who was then Warden of Wadham College, was generous to Dalgarno, inviting him to 'battel' (i. e. dine) at the college so that they could more readily have conversation, and embarking on a collaborative venture to develop what would be a truly philosophical language. In a very short time, however, it emerged that their respective ideas of what would constitute such a language were diametrically different, and this led to an abrupt parting of the ways. Wilkins's scheme is most easily characterised as being encyclopedic in scope; it aimed to provide for the fullest possible coverage of human notions. Dalgarno, by contrast, was intent upon a strict logical analysis of ideas, such as would reduce all complex notions to their simple constituents, these non-decomposable elements being perhaps few enough in number to be an 'alphabet of simple notions'. In this, Dalgarno's views were perhaps closest to those of Seth Ward (Cram 1994). As a result of Dalgarno's difference of views with Wilkins, the two men became estranged and their schemes saw light as separate publications.

### 5.3. Dalgarno's *Ars Signorum*

Dalgarno's book, as befits the nature of his scheme, is a small and densely-argued work, written "ad solos doctos" who would be able to supply the necessary inferences. Just as the author had prided himself in his earlier broadsheet publication that the essential elements of his scheme could be presented on one side of a single sheet, so too in *Ars Signorum* the set of primitives or 'radicals' of the language were presented on a single fold-out sheet, entitled *Lexicon Grammatico-Philosophicum.* This is printed in columns, but organised in a hierarchical tree structure. The essence of the scheme is that the highest categories are represented by simple letters/sounds (thus giving flesh to the idea of an alphabet of simple notions), while subordinate categories are represented by sequences of letters/sounds, such that each component element was significant in its own right. For example, the radical word meaning 'heat' is 'gam'. The initial 'g' indicates that this is a sensible quality. The combination 'ga' consistently refers to sensible qualities perceived by touch, just as radical words beginning with 'gi' refer to qualities perceived by the ear, and words beginning with 'go' to qualities that can be seen, i. e. colours. The final 'm' affixed to 'ga' designates 'heat', while other final consonants designate other sensible qualities of the same kind, such as 'gan', which means 'humidity', and 'gab', which means 'hardness'. Dalgarno employed insertion of 'r' as a device indicating opposites. For instance, since 'gam' means heat, the radical for 'cold' is 'gram'. Similarly, 'gran' means 'dryness' and 'grab' means 'softness'. Thus the structure of the sign constitutes a partial 'definition' of the thing or object signified, by virtue of indicating the position of the concept in the hierarchical framework. For this reason, the system qualified as a philosophical language: as Dalgarno points out on the title page, those learning his language are not just acquiring the means for communication between speakers of different languages, but they are thereby "imbibing the true principles of philosophy".

However, the internal structure of the radical words is just one of two different strategies Dalgarno uses to accomplish his primary objective, namely that complex notions will always be represented by complex signs, and simple by simple (Maat 1995a). In Dalgarno's view, the hierarchical classification could not be but very arbitrary and should not be so comprehensive as to include species of plants and animals. This was one of the major issues in the debate with Wilkins, who on the contrary was convinced that as many items as possible should be subsumed under the classification scheme. Dalgarno thought that this would lead to an impracticably large lexicon, which was to be almost impossible to memorize. Instead, he resorted to combination of radical words as a means of expressing compound concepts, a method which in his view is philosophically more adequate. For instance, Dalgarno's word for 'university' is composed of two radicals, one meaning 'place' and the other 'intellectual act'. Likewise, the word meaning elephant is composed of a radical word meaning 'whole-footed beast' and another meaning 'largest'. Dalgarno emphasized that in his language several alternative compound words may be used to express a certain concept. Thus 'university' may also be rendered as 'place art', or 'house art'.

The grammar of Dalgarno's language is very simple, although like the lexicon it resulted from a compromise between various methods. Theoretically speaking, Dalgarno preferred the whole grammatical content of his language to be expressed by means of his radical words. For instance, since the copula designates the act of confirming that the predicate and the subject belong together, the copula should be expressed by the radical word meaning 'affirmation'. In practice, Dalgarno borrowed a number of grammatical inflections from existing languages, so that various affixes in his language are used to indicate distinctions between substantives and adjectives, and various moods and tenses.

## 6. Wilkins

### 6.1. Assisting Dalgarno

John Wilkins (1614–1672) was a leading figure in intellectual life in 17th-century Britain. Apart from the Mercury (cf. 3.3.), he wrote a number of popular works on natural science and mechanics, as well as on religious matters, and was the first Secretary of the Royal Society. According to Wilkins's own retrospective account in his Essay (6.2.), it was Seth Ward who showed him the right path to be followed in creating a universal character: rather than the lexicon of some existing language, a regular enumeration of things and notions should be the foundation of a new means of communication. Accordingly, while collaborating with Dalgarno in the 1650s (cf. 5.2.), Wilkins drew up classificatory tables of the kind known from the logical theory of predicaments. Starting with the category of substance, Wilkins classified a large number of stones, animals and plants, intending to coin names for the enumerated items which were to be indicative of the classification. In Dalgarno's judgement however, these tables were far too elaborate to be suitable as a basis for the lexicon. The collaboration ended, and Wilkins pursued the design which in his view was the only viable one.

### 6.2. The *Essay*

Wilkins expounded his scheme in the *Essay towards a Real Character and a Philosophical Language* (1668). The publication of this book was delayed when a large part of the manuscript was destroyed in the Great Fire of London in 1666. In writing the *Essay*, Wilkins was assisted by experts in various fields. Although the *Essay* is an impressive work, Wilkins emphasized its tentative character, urging for the institution of a committee for its revision. On the other hand, in an appendix he compares his invention with existing languages and concludes that it surpasses both Chinese writing and Latin in facility. Wilkins's scheme consists of two independent but equivalent sign systems: a written symbolism called the 'real character', and a language capable of being both written and spoken, the 'philosophical language'. Both the character and the language are based upon extensive classificatory tables, which take up the largest part of the book. The *Essay* further contains an introductory chapter dealing with issues like language change and the defects of existing languages, and a large chapter on 'Natural Grammar', that sets out the principles underlying a language structured according to 'the philosophy of letters and speech in the general' (p. 297). Finally, a dictionary refers several thousands of English words to expressions of Wilkins's character and language.

6.3. Aims

As Wilkins explains, the main purpose of his scheme is to provide 'a Real universal Character', i.e. a writing system which signifies things and notions rather than words, and which consequently can be read off by everyone in their own language (*Essay* p. 13). The philosophical language is conceived as a way of pronouncing the character. Thus it appears that Wilkins viewed the scheme described in the *Essay* as a specimen of the kind of symbol system he outlined in the *Mercury* (cf. 3.3.), though it had two features that were unforeseen in the early work and which he clearly saw as improvements. First, a spoken language was added, and secondly, the symbols of the character and the words of the language represented to some extent the nature of things, by reflecting the classificatory tables. At one point, Wilkins describes the latter improvement as an 'advantage superadded' to the principal aim of providing a real character (*Essay*, p. 21), though at another point (the Epistle to the reader) he suggests that the tables are the most valuable part of his scheme, stating that even if the character and the language were to prove unsuccessful, the tables still provided the best course available for instructing men in the knowledge of things. Despite low expectations of success, Wilkins foresaw many advantages should his character and language be generally accepted. This would facilitate international commerce, improve knowledge of nature and be helpful in spreading Christian faith. Further, it could be instrumental in settling religious disputes that arise from the use of 'affected insignificant phrases'.

6.4. The Tables

Wilkins's enumeration of "all things and notions to which names are to be assigned" is systematic in that all items listed are arranged into a comprehensive classification scheme, consisting of three types of categories. At the highest level there are 40 genera. Each genus is subdivided into at most 9 'differences', most genera having 6 of them. Differences in their turn are subdivided into species, usually 9. In all, the classification contains 2,326 categories. To each of these a 'radical' corresponds, which in the tables is expressed by an English word. In many cases, pairs of radicals rather than single ones are associated with a place in the classification, and sometimes three radicals occupy a single place. Since either pairs or triads of radicals correspond to a single category in 1,781 cases, more than 4,100 radicals are listed in the tables. Pairs of radicals are formed on the basis of either antonymy or affinity. Thus both 'good' and 'bad' are assigned the same place on the classificatory tables (antonymy), and so are 'sheep' and 'goat' (affinity). Apart from the classificatory arrangement, the tables provide ample further information on the items listed. For instance, 'sheep' is listed as the second species of the difference 'cloven footed' under the genus 'beast'. The tables further tell us that cloven footed beasts are viviparous, that some of them are horned, and that among these both sheep and goats are smaller than cows, besides being useful for their meat (*Essay*, pp. 156–157).

Wilkins's tables were inspired by the theory of predicaments inherited from Scholastic logic (cf. 2.3.). He indicates that 14 out of his 40 genera belong to the traditional category of 'substance'. These were the ones he started with and which were rejected by Dalgarno. The tradition subsumed the other 9 Aristotelian categories under the heading of 'accidents'. Wilkins follows the tradition in this, but he deviates in retaining only 4 categories of accidents: 3 of his genera are concerned with 'quantity', 5 with 'quality', 4 with 'action' and 8 with 'relation'. Further, the notions traditionally called 'transcendentals', that is, concepts which cannot be classified under one of the predicaments, were usually considered to be few. In Wilkins's scheme, they are so numerous as to fill 6 genera. In expanding the number of classified items to an unprecedented degree, and in providing elaborate descriptions of the things and notions classified by his scheme, Wilkins turned the rudimentary classifications of the logical tradition into an encyclopedic overview of contemporary learning.

### 6.5. The lexicon

The radicals defined and described in the tables are systematically represented in both the character and the language. Each of the 40 genera is represented by a basic symbol of the real character and a word of the language. The symbols are formed by a horizontal line having some curved part or by a horizontal line which is crossed by a second line at a certain angle, or to which a little hook or circle is attached. Differences are indicated by strokes added to the left end of the horizontal line, and species by strokes on the right. The words for genera consist of a consonant and a vowel, and differences are indicated by adding a consonant to the word indicating the genus. Species are represented by adding a vowel to the word for the difference to which it belongs. For instance, the word for 'sheep' is 'zida', where 'zi' means 'beast' and 'zid' means 'cloven footed beast'. The final a indicates the second species. Using the second consonant as an ending indicates the radical word joined by virtue of affinity: thus 'zidad' means 'goat'. In this way, the symbols of Wilkins's character and the words of his language reflect the classification expounded in the tables. Yet only part of the information provided by the tables is encoded in the character and the language. Thus there is no indication that beasts fall under substance, nor can it be inferred from the symbol or the word for 'sheep' that sheep are viviparous, horned and useful because of the meat.

In order to provide equivalents to all or most of the words of existing languages, Wilkins enlarges his basic vocabulary of more than 4,100 radicals by means of so-called 'transcendental particles', of which he distinguishes 48. These particles are expressed by diacritics added to the characters and by affixes to the radical words. One of these particles expresses 'aggregate'. If combined with the radical for 'sheep' it means 'flock', and if combined with 'cow' it means 'herd'. In thus using a uniform expression for similar kinds of things, Wilkins amended what he considered to be redundancies in existing languages. Further, the transcendental particles considerably reduce the number of basic expressions required: the same particle added to 'ship' expresses 'fleet', and its combination with 'tree' signifies 'wood'.

### 6.6. The grammar

Wilkins professes that the grammar of his character and language uses abstract rules derived from nature rather than from existing languages (Essay, pp. 297–298). Thus there are no verbs in Wilkins's language, because 'natural' or 'philosophical' grammar teaches us that verbs consist of the copula and an adjective. However, all the other word classes traditionally distinguished by grammarians are retained. Wilkins first makes a major distinction between 'integrals', comprising substantives, adjectives and (derived) adverbs on the one hand, and 'particles', comprising copula, pronouns, interjections, prepositions, adverbs and articles on the other hand. He further creates an elaborate morphological system to indicate whether integrals are active, passive or neuter. Finally, he makes provisions to mark imperative mood, modal verbs and three tenses: past, present and future.

## 7. Leibniz

### 7.1. The ideal language

Unlike most philosophers of his day, Gottfried Wilhelm Leibniz (1646–1716) was deeply concerned with the construction of a philosophical language. Indeed, from the earliest stages of his career until the end of his life he was convinced that a successful implementation of his ideas on the subject would constitute one of the greatest achievements human kind is capable of. In Leibniz's view, a philosophical language is both a convenient means of international communication and an adequate and unambiguous representation of knowledge. But the most important characteristic of the language he envisaged is that it provides us with a powerful tool for thinking. The Leibnizian ideal language guides our thought, making it both more comprehensive and more reliable. In addition to this, the language leads us to the discovery of new truths. This picture of an ideal language proceeds firstly, from Leibniz's specific view on the relationship between language and thought (cf. 7.2.) and secondly from his taking mathematics as a model (cf. 7.3.). Further, his atomistic epistemology (cf. 7.4.) and his analytical theory of truth (cf. 7.5.) are essential in this context.

### 7.2. Language and thought

Descartes and his followers were inclined to regard thought as in principle independent from language. Pure thinking consists of contemplating concepts, a process which is quite distinct from any representation of these concepts either by pictures or by words. By contrast, the tradition represented by such writers as Bacon and Locke maintained that our thinking is largely contaminated by language, as we are often unable to separate our concepts from the words we use to designate them. Leibniz reconciles these views by recognizing on the one hand that much of human thinking is in fact of a linguistic nature, and on the other hand by emphasizing that such so-called 'blind' thought may be efficient and reliable, provided that the language is sound.

### 7.3. Mathematics as a model

In Leibniz's view, the ideal language is exemplified by the rules for using algebraic and arithmetical symbols: it is possible and easy to solve algebraic equations by the methodical application of rules for the substitution of symbols by others, regardless of what these symbols stand for, i. e. 'blindly'. The rules guarantee that the outcome is correct. The challenge of constructing a philosophical language consists in accomplishing in everything what has been partly achieved in the limited field of numbers. Although he was impressed by the powers of formal deductive systems, Leibniz never doubted that these powers depend essentially on the interpretation of the symbols used in such systems. Hence the philosophical language as he conceived it was both a formal language and a specific representation of the basic elements of all knowledge.

### 7.4. Atomistic epistemology

Leibniz took it for granted that knowledge consists of concepts, and that most of these concepts are complex, that is, that they are an aggregate of other, less complex concepts. These in turn may be analyzed further into less complex concepts until the process of analysis must stop because the primitives are reached. Thus everything we know is ultimately built up out of a set of primitive notions, which Leibniz often calls 'the alphabet of human thoughts'. If a symbol is assigned to each of these primitive notions, then every statement can be written in terms of these symbols. A mechanical test applied to the resulting expression will reveal whether the statement is true or not. The latter point follows from Leibniz's theory of truth.

### 7.5. Analytical theory of truth

Assuming that each proposition is basically of the form 'A is B', consisting of a subject term (A), a predicate term (B) and the copula (is), Leibniz maintains that if a proposition is true, the concept expressed by the predicate term is contained in the concept of the subject term. Thus the proposition 'man is rational' is true, because the concept 'rational' forms part of the concept 'man'. All that is required for a formal proof of this, is analysis of the concept 'man' into some less complex components, i. e. 'rational animal'. The sentence 'rational animal is rational' is obviously true, since the expression in predicate position is identical with one of the expressions in subject position. If a statement is written in terms of symbols designating primitive concepts, its truth or falsity can be mechanically decided by testing whether the expression symbolizing the predicate is identical with some part of the expression of the subject. However, as the 'man is rational' example shows, it is not always necessary to completely analyze the concepts occurring in a proposition in order to establish its truth.

### 7.6. Method

Leibniz was aware that his ideal language could not be easily realized, as we are generally unable to resolve our concepts into primitives. Whereas Descartes had rejected any endeavour to construct a philosophical language before such an analysis had been successfully completed, Leibniz emphasized that we should start from the knowledge we have, and from an investigation of the basic operations we use in thinking. Since most of our thinking is linguistic, such an investigation is best carried out by means of analysis of existing languages. Thus the Leibnizian project for a philosophical language does not entail replacing existing languages, in one go, by a newly constructed one, but rather aims at extracting an ideal language from existing ones. This process has two major components, a lexical (7.7.) and a grammatical one (7.8.).

### 7.7. The lexicon: Definitions

Among Leibniz's papers a considerable number of word lists are preserved, on which the words are provided with a definition of their meaning. Leibniz produced such lists over an extended period of time. Apparently, the work was broken off and resumed time and again. Leibniz sometimes borrowed the lists from dictionaries. He also used the tables of radical words of both Dalgarno and Wilkins as a starting point (cf. Maat 1995b). In all cases, the definitions he produced were his own. It is generally, and quite justifiably, assumed that these definitions were part of Leibniz's philosophical language project. Since definitions are analytically more explicit than the words they define, they provide insight into the components of the concept designated by the defined word. Ideally, a definition, or a chain of definitions, gives a complete enumeration of all ingredients of the concept designated by the word defined. Though Leibniz was convinced that humans are seldom if ever capable of producing such a perfect definition, he emphasized that partial definitions may contribute to the improvement of our knowledge (cf. 7.5.).

### 7.8. Rational Grammar

Whereas the lexical part of Leibniz's project is concerned with the decomposition of specific concepts, the grammatical part has a more general aim: to characterize the operations that are basic in human thinking and to identify the means that are necessary for the expression of these operations. On the face of it, most sentences of existing languages do not fit the restricted 'A is B' pattern Leibniz takes as a starting point. Rational grammar tries to show how these sentences can nevertheless be reduced to this pattern. To this end, Leibniz examines the various parts of speech, which leads to the following results: Firstly, there is only one genuine substantive, namely the concept 'being, thing' (ens, res); all other substantives can be reduced to 'ens + adjective'. For instance, 'man' is short for 'human being'. Secondly, verbs are reduced to the copula 'is' plus an adjective, e. g. 'Peter writes' is equivalent to 'Peter is writing'. Thirdly, as to adverbs, Leibniz reaches various conclusions. On the one hand, he maintains that adverbs relate to verbs just as adjectives relate to substantives. For example, 'amat sincere' (he loves sincerely) means the same as 'amicus sincerus' ((he is) a sincere friend). On the other hand, he observes that adverbs may serve to abbreviate several propositions into one. E. g., 'Peter stands beautifully' is to be reduced to 'Peter is beautiful in so far as he is standing'.

Substantives, adjectives, verbs and adverbs are termed 'material words' by Leibniz. Of these, the only parts of speech necessary for the expression of thought are the single substantive noun 'ens' or 'res', the copula 'is' and adjectives. Apart from the material words Leibniz distinguishes a class of 'formal words' or 'particles', by means of which the logical structure of thought is predominantly expressed. Formal words are conjunctions, formal adverbs, prepositions and pronouns. Unlike the material words, every single formal word requires special analysis in the context of rational grammar. Leibniz produced several texts in which he undertakes such an analysis, which is apparently aimed at sorting out the particles that are indispensable for the philosophical language.

## 8. Bibliography


Aristotle. 1949. *Categoriae et Liber de Interpretatione.* Ed. by L. Minio-Paluello. Oxford: Oxford Univ. Press. [Trans. *Aristotle's Categories and De Interpretatione, translated with Notes by J. L. Ackrill.* 1963. Oxford: Clarendon Press.]

Bacon, Francis. 1887–1901. *The Works of Francis Bacon. Philosophical Works. Edited by James Spedding*, et al. London: Longmans.

Becher, Johann Joachim. 1661. *Character, pro Notitia Linguarum Universali.* Frankfurt.

Beck, Cave. 1657. *The Universal Character.* London.

Campanella, Tommaso. 1638. *Philosophiae Rationalis partes quinque, videlicet: Grammatica, Dialectica, Rhetorica, Poetica, Historiographia.* Paris.

Comenius, Jan Amos. 1668. *Via Lucis.* Amsterdam.

–. 1966. *Panglottia. De Rerum Humanarum Emendatione Consultatio Catholica* ed. by J. Červenka and V. T. Miškovská, vol. II, 147–204. Prague: ČSAV.

Couturat, Louis & Léopold Leau. 1903. *Histoire de la langue universelle.* Paris: Hachette.

Cram, David. 1980. "George Dalgarno on *Ars Signorum* and Wilkins' *Essay*". *Progress in Linguistic Historiography.* (= *Studies in the History of Linguistics*, vol. 20) ed. by Konrad Koerner. Amsterdam: Benjamins.

–. 1994. "Universal language, specious arithmetic and the alphabet of simple notions". *Beiträge zur Geschichte der Sprachwissenschaft* 4.213–233.

– & Jaap Maat. (forthcoming). *George Dalgarno on Universal Language: The Art of Signs (1661), the Deaf and Dumb Man's Tutor (1680), and the unpublished papers.* Oxford: Oxford Univ. Press.

Dalgarno, George. 1657. *Tables of the Universal Character, so contrived, that the practice of them exceed's all former wayes of short hand writing, and are applicable to all languages.* [Oxford: Leonard Lichfield].

–. 1661. *Ars Signorum, vulgo character universalis et lingua philosophica.* London: J. Hayes.

Descartes, René. 1897. *Œuvres de Descartes. Tome I: Correspondance.* Charles Adam & Paul Tannéry (eds.). Paris: Léopold Cerf.

Dolezal, Frederick. 1985. *Forgotten but Important Lexicographers: John Wilkins and William Lloyd.* Tübingen: Niemeyer.

Eco, Umberto. 1995. *The Search for the Perfect Language.* Oxford: Blackwell.

Elliott, Ralph W. V. 1957. "Isaac Newton's 'Of an Universall Language'". *Modern Language Review* 52–1. 1–18.

Hüllen, Werner. 1989. *'Their Manner of Discourse': Nachdenken über Sprache im Umkreis der Royal Society.* Tübingen: Narr.

Kircher, Athanasius. 1663. *Polygraphia Nova et Universalis.* Rome.

Knowlson, J. R. 1975. *Universal Language Schemes In England and France 1600–1800.* Toronto & Buffalo: Toronto Univ. Press.

Leibnitz, Gottfried Wilhelm. 1999. *Sämtliche Schriften und Briefe. Herausgegeben von der Berlin-Brandenburgischen Akademie der Wissenschaften und der Akademie der Wissenschaften in Göttingen. Sechste Reihe. Philosophische Schriften. Herausgegeben von der Leibniz-Forschungsstelle der Universität Münster. Vierter Band, Teil A und B.* Berlin: Akademie Verlag.

Lodwick, Francis. 1647. *A Common Writing.* London: for the author. (Facsimile in Salmon 1972.)

–. 1652. *The Groundwork, or Foundation laid (or so intended) for the Framing of a New Perfect Language.* (Facsimile in Salmon 1972.)

Maat, Jaap. 1995a. "The Logic of Dalgarno's 'Ars Signorum'". *History of Linguistics* 1993 ed. by Kurt R. Jankowsky. Amsterdam & Philadelphia: Benjamins.

–. 1995b. "Leibniz on Wilkins and Dalgarno". *Beiträge zur Geschichte der Sprachwissenschaft* 5.169–183.

Mersenne, Marin. 1636. *Harmonie vniverselle, contenant la theorie et la pratiqve de la mvsiqve.* Paris: Sebastien Cramoisy.

Risse, Wilhelm. 1964. *Die Logik der Neuzeit.* Stuttgart & Bad Cannstatt.

Rossi, Paolo. 1960. *Clavis Universalis: Arti mnemoniche e logica combinatoria da Lullo a Leibniz.* Milan & Naples: Riccardo Ricciardi.

Salmon, Vivian G. 1966. "The evolution of Dalgarno's 'Ars Signorum'". *Studies in Honour of Margaret Schlauch*, 353–71. Warsaw: Polish Scientific Publishers. (Repr. in Salmon 1988: 157–175.)

–. 1972. *The Works of Francis Lodwick: A Study of his writings in the intellectual context of the seventeenth century.* London: Longman.

–. 1988. *The Study of Language in Seventeenth-Century England.* Amsterdam: Benjamins.

Schottus, Gasparus. 1664. *Technica Curiosa, sive Mirabilia Artis.* Nuremburg.

Shapiro, Barbara J. 1969. *John Wilkins 1614–1672: An intellectual biography.* Berkeley & Los Angles: Univ. of California Press.

Slaughter, Mary M. 1982. *Universal Languages and Scientific Taxonomy in the Seventeenth Century.* Cambridge: Cambridge Univ. Press.

Stillman, Robert E. 1995. *The New Philosophy and Universal Languages in 17th-century England.* Lewisburg: Bucknell University Press/London: Associated University Presses.

Strasser, Gerhard F. 1988. *Lingua Universalis. Kryptologie und Theorie der Universalsprachen im 16. und 17. Jahrhundert.* Wiesbaden: Harrassowitz.

Subbiondo, Joseph L., ed. 1992. *John Wilkins and Seventeenth-Century British Linguistics.* Amsterdam: Benjamins.

Urquhart, Thomas. 1652. *Ekskubalauron, or the discovery of a most exquisite jewel.* London.

Ward, Seth. 1654. *Vindiciae Academiarum, containing, some briefe animadversions upon Mr Websters Book, stiled, The Examination of the Academies.* Oxford: Leonard Lichfield.

Wilkins, John. 1641. *Mercury, or the Secret and Swift Messenger.* London: John Maynard & Timothy Wilkins. (Facsimile edition of the third edition, 1707, with an introductory essay by B. Asbach-Schnitker, Amsterdam & Philadelphia: Benjamins, 1984.)

–. 1668. *An Essay towards a Real Character and a Philosophical Language.* London: Samuel Gellibrand & John Martyn.



*Jaap Maat, Amsterdam (The Netherlands)*
*David Cram, Oxford (Great Britain)*

# 141. Die 'Allgemeine Sprachwissenschaft' um die Wende zum 19. Jahrhundert

1. Einleitung
2. Grammatikschreibung, Sprachunterricht und 'Allgemeine Sprachwissenschaft'
3. 'Allgemeine Sprachwissenschaft' um 1800
4. Schluss: 'Allgemeine Sprachwissenschaft' als Historisch-Vergleichende Sprachwissenschaft
5. Bibliographie

## 1. Einleitung

Nicht lange vor der Wende zum 19. Jh. dachte der damals sechsundzwanzigjährige Georg Michael Roth über den "reinen Begriff der menschlichen Sprache" nach:

> Es läßt sich eine allgemeine Grammatik von gedoppelter Art denken, je nachdem der Sinn ist, in welchem man den Begriff des Allgemeinen faßt. In weniger strengem Sinne heißt schon das allgemein, was sich durch die bisherige Erfahrung als allgemein bestätigt hat; im strengsten Sinne nur dasjenige, was nicht nur durch alle wirkliche Erfahrung als allgemein bestätigt worden, sondern was selbst außerdem unabhängig von aller möglichen Erfahrung als allgemein und folglich als nothwendig bestimmt ist. (1795: 3)

Hier klingen die wichtigsten Motive an, um die sich 'Allgemeine Sprachwissenschaftler' von jeher Gedanken gemacht haben und noch immer machen. Gibt es so etwas wie eine Universale Grammatik? Und wenn ja, wie kommt sie zustande, durch Erfahrung und Abstraktion oder durch Spekulation a priori? Was sind essentielle und was empirische Universalien? Wie verhält sich das Allgemeine zum Speziellen jeder Sprache? (Siehe dazu etwa Haßler 1990, Schreyer 1990 und zahlreiche Beiträge in Dascal et al. HSK 7.1/2, 1996). Das Gemeinsame am Beispiel des Individuellen aufzuspüren und zu zeigen, dass alles Individuelle letztlich Spiegel des Allgemeinen ist, wenn auch oft nur schwach erkennbar, war und ist seit jeher die Aufgabe aller 'Allgemeinen Sprachwissenschaftler' von Aristoteles bis Chomsky. Auch die 'Allgemeinen Sprachlehrer', um 1800, Antoine Sylvestre de Sacy (1758–1838), Johann Severin Vater (1771–1826) und James Beattie (1735–1803), um jetzt nur je einen Vertreter aus Frankreich, Deutschland und England zu nennen, arbeiteten an dieser Aufgabe, jeder auf seine Weise.

Der hier gesteckte Zeitrahmen "um die Wende zum 19. Jh." bedeutet einen Spielraum eher nach rückwärts als nach vorne, also so etwa 1775 bis 1810. Ausgeschlossen sein sollen die Arbeiten der ersten Hälfte des 18. Jhs., wiewohl auch in diesem Zeitraum eine ganze Reihe Allgemeiner Grammatiken geschrieben wurden, vor allem in Frankreich. Im 19. Jh. war diese Art der Sprachwissenschaft ein Auslaufmodell, das zwar nie ganz verschwand (Wilhelm von Humboldt 1767–1835, Karl Ferdinand Becker 1775–1849, Karl Wilhelm Ludwig Heyse 1797–1855 und Heymann Steinthal 1823–1899 seien als herausragende Vertreter genannt), aber sehr bald von den Arbeiten der Historisch-Vergleichenden Sprachwissenschaft in den Schatten gestellt wurde.

Vor der Darstellung der Allgemeinen Sprachwissenschaft um 1800 in Mitteleuropa soll kurz auf einen Aspekt eingegangen werden, der sehr eng mit diesem Thema zu tun hat, auf Grammatikschreibung und Sprachunterricht.

## 2. Grammatikschreibung, Sprachunterricht und 'Allgemeine Sprachwissenschaft'

In den meisten Ländern Europas hatten sich bis um 1800 überregionale Schriftsprachen ausgebildet, deren Beherrschung in Wort und Schrift auf unterschiedlichen Ebenen in Schulen gelernt werden musste. Dazu benötigte man normative Grammatiken, mehr oder minder umfangreiche Beschreibungen des Sprachgebrauchs der jeweiligen Gegenwart. Da sich dieser von Zeit zu Zeit änderte, mussten derartige Beschreibungen etwa jede Generation angepasst werden. Mit zunehmendem allgemeinem Schulbesuch erhöhte sich die Menge dieser Art von sprachlicher Gebrauchsliteratur, die in den meisten Fällen keinen Anspruch auf Wissenschaftlichkeit stellte. Generelles Vorbild für alle derartigen Grammatiken in Europa waren die beiden Fassungen der *Ars Grammatica* (die ausführlichere *Ars Maior* für den Fortgeschrittenenunterricht und die kürzere *Ars Minor* für den Elementarunterricht) des römischen Grammatikers Aelius Donatus (Mitte des 4. Jhs.). Im Zentrum stand dabei die systematische Darstellung der Wortarten, der Deklination und der Konjugation. Wie traditionsmächtig diese Gliederungsvorgabe war, zeigt sich auch in den Allgemeinen Sprachlehren um 1800: Die meisten von ihnen stellen die Redeteile, die Wortarten in den Mittelpunkt ihrer Darstellung und behandeln unter diesem Aspekt die Morphemkategorien der Grammatik.

Vorbilder korrekten Sprachgebrauchs waren für Donatus die klassischen römischen Schriftsteller. Die Grammatiker der Sprachen, die in Europa um 1800 gesprochen wurden, verließen sich für die Regularitäten der geschriebenen Sprache ebenfalls auf den Gebrauch der jeweils anerkannten Schriftsteller und für den mündlichen Sprachgebrauch auf das Vorbild der großen Höfe.

Im 18. Jh., im Zeitalter des Rationalismus und der Aufklärung, wurde Grammatikschreibung zunehmend von der Tradition der Philosophischen Grammatik beeinflusst, und Philosophische Grammatik wurde mit pädagogischen Argumenten begründet. Einen ersten Höhepunkt erreichte diese Entwicklung gegen Ende des Jahrhunderts bei Johann Christoph Adelung (1732–1806). Durch die Reflexion über die Grundlagen der grammatischen Kategorien wurde die Gebrauchsgrammatikschreibung so zu einer Wissenschaft:

> Man bahnet dadurch der Sprachlehre den Weg, sich zu einer Wissenschaft zu erheben, da sie bisher mit dem niedrigsten Rang einer freyen Kunst zufrieden seyn mußte, und eine der verächtlichsten unter denjenigen war, je weniger sie auf Verstand, Ordnung, und deutliche Begriffe gegründet war (1781: Vorrede unpaginiert).

Seitdem können Grammatiken den Anspruch der Wissenschaftlichkeit erheben und seitdem erhebt der Muttersprachunterricht mit den Lernzielen möglichst vollkommener Sprachbeherrschung in Wort und Schrift auch Schulung im logischen Denken zu sein. Noch einmal Adelung:

> Die Erlernung der Sprache wird dadurch angenehmer. Nichts ist dem menschlichen Geiste unangenehmer und ekelhafter, als sich Jahre lang mit Wörtern zu plagen, von welchen man keinen Begriff hat, und mit Regeln, von welchen man keine Ursache weiß. Und was ist unser bisheriges ganzes Sprach-Studium anders, als ein solches elendes und langweiliges Gedächtnißwerk (1781: Vorrede unpaginiert).

Aus diesem Grunde haben vor allem die deutschen und französischen Allgemeinen Sprachwissenschaftler um 1800 theoretische Werke und zugleich Arbeiten für den Schulunterricht geschrieben, und die, die dies nicht taten, wie etwa Johann Werner Meiner, oder in Frankreich Nicolas Beauzée und Sylvestre de Sacy, haben ihre Arbeit von vornherein auch für den Schulunterricht konzipiert. Selbst der Engländer James Beattie schrieb im "Advertissement" seiner Allgemeinen Grammatik von 1788: "A Philosophical Examination of the principles of Grammar is a profitable exercise to the mental powers of Young People" (1788: A). Sprachunterricht sollte entsprechend den pädagogischen Intentionen der Aufklärung der Emanzipation des Individuums von allen nicht durch die Ratio bestimmten Zwängen dienen. Im ersten Drittel des 19. Jhs. nannte man diese Richtung in Deutschland dann oft und gerne "Sprachdenklehre".

Bis heute ist die Maxime, dass Sprachunterricht zugleich Unterricht im logischen Denken sei, als Prinzip des schulischen Muttersprachunterrichts erhalten geblieben (siehe dazu für das 19. Jh. Matthias 1907: 202–278; für die erste Hälfte des 20. Jhs. Frank 1973: 155–213).

## 3. 'Allgemeine Sprachwissenschaft' um 1800

Um 1800 verstand man den deutschen Terminus *Allgemeine Grammatik* bzw. *Allgemeine Sprachlehre* als Philosophische Grammatik in der Tradition der *Grammaire générale et raisonnée* [...] der französischen Sprachlehrer Antoine Arnauld und Claude Lancelot aus dem Jahre 1660, die vielfach aufgelegt und in mehrere Sprachen übersetzt worden ist (siehe dazu etwa die Arbeiten von Auroux 1973, 1982, 1991 u. a.) und mit der in der Neuzeit die wissenschaftliche Beschäftigung mit Sprache beginnt. Weil viele europäische Sprachwissenschaftler um 1800 an diese Tradition anknüpften, weisen ihre Arbeiten Ähnlichkeiten und Gemeinsamkeiten auf, die oft stärker ins Auge fallen als die Unterschiede. In Frankreich, dem Ursprungsland des Rationalismus, wurden in der Folgezeit die meisten Philosophischen Sprachlehren verfasst. Von Frankreich aus ging die Entwicklung nach Deutschland und nach England, in eingeschränktem Umfang auch in andere europäische Länder, etwa in die Niederlande (siehe dazu Noordegraaf 1996), nach Italien, Spanien und Russland (siehe dazu Ricken et al. 1990). In keinem Land Europas erreichte die Beschäftigung mit Philosophischer Grammatik allerdings den Umfang wie in den genannten drei Ländern, deshalb wird sich die folgende Darstellung darauf beschränken.

### 3.1. Frankreich

Philosophische Grammatik der Neuzeit wird nicht nur in Frankreich oft als "linguistique cartésienne" bezeichnet, d. h. als Sprachwissenschaft in der Nachfolge von René Descartes (1596–1650): Chomsky (1966) nannte eines seiner früheren Werke *Cartesian Linguistics* (zum Terminus *Cartesianische Linguistik* siehe Amorowa u. a. 1980: 184–187). Auch Arnauld und Lancelot lehrten cartesianischen Rationalismus ("cogito ergo sum"), der in manchen Punkten im Gegensatz zum Aristotelischen Empirismus ("sum ergo cogito") stand (und wurden deshalb, wie Descartes selber, von der Römischen Kirche verfolgt). Cartesianer teilen die Welt dualistisch in zwei finite Substanzen (Gott ist danach die dritte, infinite Substanz), in Materie und in Geist. Das lässt sich auf Sprache übertragen, und man hat es wieder und wieder auf Sprache übertragen, auf den Dualismus zwischen jeweils individuellen und historisch bedingten, materiellen Sprachformen und den allgemeinen, zeitlosen, rationalen Funktionen der sprachlichen Kategorien. Die französische Tradition im allgemeinen hat Dominicy (1996) in einem, seine zahlreichen früheren Arbeiten zusammenfassenden Artikel dargestellt. Hier sollen deshalb nur die beiden bedeutendsten Vertreter um 1800 behandelt werden, Nicolas Beauzée (1717–1789) und der schon eingangs genannte Sylvestre de Sacy. In Darstellungen der Sprachwissenschaft in der französischen Aufklärung werden meistens auch die folgenden Namen genannt: Rousseau (1712–1778), Condillac (1715–1780), Maupertius (1698–1759), Diderot (1713–1784), de Brosses bzw. Debrosses (1709–1777), Duclos (1704–1772) und du Marsais bzw. Dumarsais (1676–1756). Ganz abgesehen davon, dass sie alle ihre Arbeiten z. T. lange vor 1775 verfassten und deshalb ganz oder zumindest mit der Abfassung ihrer Hauptwerke außerhalb des hier gesetzten Zeitlimits fallen, waren die bekannteren unter ihnen eher an den allgemeinen Bedingungen des Sprachursprungs interessiert, an der notwendigen physiologischen Grundausstattung des Menschen dazu und an den sozialen und sozialpolitischen Implikationen des Sprechens als an den universalen Kategorien der Allgemeinen Grammatik. In Deutschland steht ihnen als bekanntester, ähnlich interessierter Vertreter der etwas jüngere Herder (1744–1803) gegenüber (siehe Ricken et al. 1990, Niederehe & Koerner 1990 und Gessinger 1994).

#### 3.1.1. Nicolas Beauzée

Nicolas Beauzée starb im Jahr der Französischen Revolution, gehörte also auch, wie die meisten der oben genannten, noch zu den Vertretern des Ancien Régime. Sein Hauptwerk entstand zwar noch kurz vor dem hier gesetzten Zeitrahmen, im Jahr 1767, es war aber wirksam bis in die 20er Jahre des 19. Jhs. Er war Mitarbeiter der großen Französischen Encyclopédie, deren sprachwissenschaftliche Artikel er nach dem Tode von Du Marsais redigierte und z. T. selber verfasste. Für seine *Grammaire générale* [...] erhielt er einen Orden der österreichischen Kaiserin Maria Theresia und eine Professur für Sprachwissenschaft an der École Royale Militaire. Die Einladung Friedrichs II., der in Potsdam schon eine Reihe bedeutender französischer Gelehrter der Aufklärung versammelt hatte, schlug er aus. Beauzée betrachtete sich als Nachfolger von Du Marsais, der in der ersten Jahrhunderthälfte in Frankreich die Tradition der Allgemeinen Grammatik vertreten hatte. Der bisher letzte Herausgeber von Beauzées Hauptwerk, Barrie E. Bartlett, hebt besonders sein kontinuierliches Bestreben nach einer zutreffenden grammatischen Metasprache und nach Präzision des Ausdrucks hervor:

> Un de plus grands mérites de Beauzée en tant que théoricien du langage provient de ses efforts continus pour améliorer sa métalangue et pour la rendre plus précise, en écartant tout critère qui ne soit de fondement linguistique (1974: 11*).

Er definierte sprachwissenschaftliche Termini neu, etwa die Fachwörter *complement*, *concordance*, *détermination*, *régime*, *ellipse*, *inversion* (siehe dazu Bartlett 1974: 25*–34*). Allerdings war Beauzée damit nicht immer erfolgreich. Bartlett diskutiert ausführlich Beauzées verwirrenden Gebrauch des zentralen Terminus "mot".

In seinem Vorwort greift Beauzée in guter cartesianischer Tradition die Unterscheidung zwischen einer "grammaire générale" und einer "grammaire particulière" auf:

> La grammaire, qui a pour objet l'enonciation de la pensée par le secours de la parole prononcée ou écrite, admet donc deux sortes de principes. Les uns sont d'une vérité immuable & d'un usage universel, ils tiennent à la nature de la pensée même,

ils en suivent l'analyse, ils n'en sont que le résultat: les autres n'ont qu'une vérité hypothétique, & dépendante des conventions fortuites, arbitraires, & muables, qui ont donné naissance aux différents idiômes. Le premiers constituent la Grammaire générale, les autres sont l'objet des diverses Grammaires particulières (1767/I: IX f.).

*Grammaire générale* ist danach das, was wir heute Sprachtheorie nennen würden, die Erarbeitung von Maximen, die universalen Geltungsanspruch erheben. Ihren konkreten Niederschlag finden diese allgemeinen Postulate dann in den jeweiligen Objektsprachen unterschiedlicher Zeiten. Das Postulat, dass Sprache aus artikulierten Lauten besteht, ist universal, die individuelle Auswahl aus dem Inventar menschlicher Sprachlaute trifft jede Sprache zu jeder Zeit etwas anders.

An Beauzée lässt sich gut darstellen, wie der Dualismus des Descartes'schen Denkens in die Praxis umgesetzt wurde: So gut wie alles in seiner Allgemeinen Grammatik von 1767, die schon im Titel an das Werk von Arnauld und Lancelot erinnert (*Grammaire générale ou exposition raisonnée* [...]) ist Teil einer Dichotomie auf einer von vielen Ebenen. Diese Methode des kontinuierlichen Dichotomisierens hat sich mindestens bis zu den sprachwissenschaftlichen Strukturalisten moderner Prägung gehalten. Auch für Beauzée ist Grammatik etwas Universales, weil alle individuellen Sprachformen letztlich Spiegel menschlicher Denkmöglichkeiten, einer universalen Logik seien. Um diese allgemeinen Prinzipien zu finden, beschritt er allerdings, wie viele andere auch, einen empirischen Weg: Er konsultierte alle Grammatiken aller Sprachen, die er finden konnte, um so etwas herauszufinden, was man heute (etwa Coseriu) "empirische Universalien" nennen würde.

Er teilt seine sehr umfangreiche Grammatik in drei Abschnitte: 1. Des Éléments de la Parole, 2. Des Éléments de l'Oraison und 3. Des Éléments de la Syntax. Die beiden ersten Großkapitel bilden den ersten von zwei im Umfang gleich starken Bänden seiner Grammatik, die Syntax nimmt einen eigenen Band ein. Im ersten Abschnitt geht es im weitesten Sinne um Aspekte der Phonetik, um Artikulation, um Silbenbau, um Akzent und Intonation, um Prosodie, auch um Orthographie und ums Lesen. Im zweiten Kapitel, dem Hauptkapitel jeder Grammatik in der abendländischen Tradition, geht es um die Teile der Rede, um die Rolle der Wortarten beim Denken des Menschen, neun auch bei Beauzée, "ui sont, comme on le verra dans la suite, les seuls & véritables éléments de l'Oraison" (1767, I: 234): Nomen, Pronomen, Adjektiv, Artikel, Verb, Präposition, Adverb, Konjunktion, Interjektion. Es gilt der Grundsatz der Allgemeinen Grammatik: "L'Oraison, dans le langage des grammairiens, c'est l'exercice actuel de la faculté de la parole appliqué à la manifestation des pensées" (1767, I: 233). Das Syntaxkapitel, das sich an vielen Stellen mit der Allgemeinen Grammatik von Du Marsais auseinandersetzt, setzt ähnlich ein wie das zu den Wortarten: "L'objet du langage est l'énonciation de la pensée" (1767, II: 1). Es geht auf vielen hundert Seiten um alle grammatischen Bestandteile des Satzes, der 'proposition' und ihre Funktionen. Die Morphologie der Hauptwortarten und die Kategorien der Grammatik werden hier eingebracht, nicht im Kapitel der Redeteile, wie man zunächst vermuten würde. Oberste Dichotomie ist die zwischen Subjekt und Attribut, ihr wird alles andere untergeordnet: "La matière grammaticale de la Proposition, c'est la totalité des parties intégrantes dont elle est composée, & que l'analyse réduit à deux, savoir *le sujet & l'attribut*." (1767, II: 7). Die Terminologie Beauzées ist für deutsche Sprachbenutzer erklärungsbedürftig. Was er unter *attribut* versteht, geht aus seinem ersten Mustersatz hervor: "Dieu est juste". In dieser Proposition wäre der Teil "Dieu" das Subjekt, der Teil "est juste" das "Attribut". Diese Terminologie hatte auch James Harris (1709–1780) gewählt, auch andere haben sie übernommen. In der deutschen Tradition würde man eher sagen das "Prädikat". Ähnlich wie sehr viel später Fillmore betrachtet Beauzée die Funktion der Fälle in Analogie zur Funktion der Präpositionen, d. h. als Mittel zur vielfältigen Relationierung von Sachverhalten.

Beauzées Arbeit wurde etwa dreißig Jahre nach seinem Tode noch einmal aufgelegt (1819), auch eine verkürzte Fassung für den Schulunterricht erschien (1826 von Rouget-Beaumont).

### 3.1.2. Antoine Sylvestre de Sacy

Der Baron Antoine Sylvestre de Sacy war zu seiner Zeit ein hoch angesehener und sehr bekannter Wissenschaftler. Er lernte schon in seiner Jugend eine ganze Reihe von europäischen und orientalischen Sprachen. Nach seiner Ausbildung arbeitete er als Sprachlehrer für Arabisch an der neu gegründeten École Spéciale des Langues Orientales Vivantes in Paris. Später wurde er (zusammen mit Abel

Remusat und Julius Heinrich Klaproth) Gründungspräsident der berühmten Société Asiatique. Auch ihn führten umfangreiche Sprachenkenntnisse dazu, 1803 eine Allgemeine Grammatik zu veröffentlichen, die das Grundprinzip der Allgemeinen Sprachwissenschaft in neuer Variation illustrierte, das Prinzip, dass alle Sprachen der Welt Manifestationen eines universalen logischen Modells seien. Er konzipierte sie (wie schon der Titel besagt) als Lehrwerk für den Sprachunterricht und widmete sie seinem Sohn ("C'est pour toi, mon cher Fils, que ce petit ouvrage a été entrepris; c'est à toi que je le dédie." (1803: III). Für Frankreich war dieses Werk etwa fünfzig Jahre lang die repräsentative Variante einer Allgemeinen Grammatik (so Baggioni 1996: 901). Bislang hatte man Allgemeine Grammatik nur an den großen klassischen und kontemporären Sprachen Europas, ab und zu auch am Hebräischen betrieben. Sylvestre de Sacy bezog nun auch weitere orientalische Sprachen ein, vor allem das Arabische.

Sylvestre de Sacys Allgemeine Grammatik war überaus erfolgreich. Bis zur Mitte des 19. Jhs. (1852) erlebte sie sechs Neuauflagen. Wie die Arbeit seines Vorgängers Beauzée hat sie drei Teile: 1. Funktionen der Redeteile in der Syntax. Er beginnt mit der Grundstruktur des Satzes, der "proposition": "Elle est essentiellement composée d'un Sujet, d'un Attribut et d'un Verbe, et toujours accompagnée d'un Compellatif exprimé, ou sous-entendu." (1803: 1). Das ist kein wesentlicher Unterschied zu Beauzées Zweiteilung, Sylvestre de Sacy benennt lediglich die Kopula "est" separat als "le verbe". "Compellatif" nennt er die Anreden, also etwa im Satz "Seigneur, je suis votre créature" das Element "seigneur". Im Anschluss daran folgt fast so etwas wie Pragmatik, ein Hinweis auf non-verbale Kommunikation: "Tout discours suppose un Compellatif, mais il arrive fréquemment que le Compellatif est sous-entendu, parce que les circonstances, le geste, l'attitude de celui qui parle, ou la disposition de ceux qui écoutent, y suppléent parfaitement" (1803: 8). Dieser Ansatz wird dann aber nicht weiter verfolgt. Das 2. Kapitel behandelt die Morphemkategorien (Numerus, Kasus, Tempus, Modus etc.), 3. "Syntaxe" und "Construction". Sylvestre de Sacy unterscheidet wie Beauzée zwischen einer *grammaire générale* und einer *grammaire particulière* und differenziert zwischen den beiden Grundfunktionen der Syntax, nämlich Regularitäten bereitzustellen, die den Satz als Ausdruck des logischen Urteils geeignet machen (*syntaxe*), und die Wortfolge festlegen (*construction*).

### 3.2. Deutschland

Die Deutschen Allgemeinen Grammatiker des 18. Jhs. stehen alle unter dem Einfluss französischer Vorbilder. Nur in bezug auf ihre Überlegungen zur Konstruktion einer künstlichen Universalsprache knüpfen sie an Ideen von Gottfried Wilhelm Leibniz (1646–1716) und an die von John Wilkins (1614–1672) an. Aber diese Richtung war um 1800 eine eher periphere Erscheinung. Das Jahrzehnt davor und danach war die Blütezeit der Allgemeinen Grammatik in Deutschland. Es galt geradezu als schick, sich zumindest mit dem Gedanken zu tragen, ein derartiges Werk zu verfassen, und Akademien setzten Preise dafür aus (worüber sich Jacob Grimm 1819 in der Vorrede zum ersten Band seiner großen Grammatik bitter beklagt). Die meisten, die dann auch tatsächlich durchhielten und eine entsprechende Veröffentlichung vorlegten, blieben allerdings ohne sichtbaren Einfluss auf die Sprachwissenschaft (für einen Überblick über die zu dieser Zeit in Deutschland vorgelegten Arbeiten siehe Naumann 1966b). Hier sollen deshalb nur die bedeutenderen Arbeiten vorgestellt werden, die Arbeit von Johann Werner Meiner (1723–1789), des Nestors dieser Bewegung, die Arbeiten von Georg Michael Roth (1769–1817), die von August Ferdinand Bernhardi (1769–1820) und die von Johann Severin Vater (1771–1826).

#### 3.2.1. Johann Werner Meiner

Meiner war zeit seines Lebens Sprachlehrer und lehrte *Griechisch*, *Lateinisch*, *Hebräisch* und *Französisch* (am renommierten Gymnasium von Langensalza). Die Beschäftigung mit Allgemeiner Grammatik war für ihn deshalb nicht Endzweck, sondern – getreu der Forderung Adelungs – Mittel zum Zweck eines effektiveren und interessanteren Sprachunterrichts:

> Der Nutzen der philosophischen Sprachlehre ist von sehr weitem Umfang. Denn außerdem, daß ich mir 1) keine vollkommenere praktische oder auch sinnliche Logik denken kann, als die philosophische Sprachlehre wirklich ist, weil sie alles das, was sie an der menschlichen Sprache findet aus der Denkungsart des menschlichen Verstandes erkläret; so zeiget sie ihren Nutzen auch hauptsächlich 2) in der großen Erleichterung, die sie uns in Erlernung einer jeden Sprache verschaffet (1781: LXII).

Meiner übersetzte die seit Arnauld und Lancelot geltende Unterscheidung zwischen *grammaire générale* und *grammaire particulière* als "philosophische" versus "harmonische" Sprachlehre. Auch seine Grammatik besteht aus drei Hauptkapiteln, die allerdings anders geordnet sind als bei Beauzée oder Sylvestre de Sacy. Das erste Großkapitel behandelt Phonologie und Graphematik, das zweite Morphologie, die Redeteile und Syntax, das dritte Periodenbau. Im Zentrum steht natürlich das zweite Kapitel: "Von derjenigen Verknüpfung, in welcher die vollkommenen und vernehmlichen Töne unseres Mundes mit den Begriffen und Vorstellungen unserer Seele stehen." Er arbeitet morphosyntaktisch, d. h. er integriert alle grammatischen Kategorien in die Syntax. Zwar ging auch er grundsätzlich von der Subjekt-Prädikat-Dichotomie aus, aber dadurch, daß er das Prädikat an die oberste Stelle aller satzhierarchischen Beziehungen stellte, entwickelte er einen Ansatz, der dem der Dependenzgrammatik Tesnières sehr nahe kommt:

Das Prädikat ist der vornehmste Theil des Satzes; denn aus ihm entwickelt sich der ganze Satz. Es gleichet einer vollen Frühlingsknospe. Wie diese bey ihrer Entwickelung aus sich einen ganzen Zweig sammt Nebenzweigen und Blättern hervor treibet; also liegen auch in dem einzigen Prädikat nicht nur alle Hauptheile, sondern auch Nebentheile des Satzes verschlossen, die sich daraus herleiten lassen (1781: 127).

Damit tritt das, was wir heute Valenz nennen, in das Zentrum der syntaktischen Analyse. Nach Meiner können Prädikate "einseitig=unselbständig", "zwoseitig=unselbständig" oder "dreyseitig=unselbständig" sein. "Einseitig=unselbständig" ist dasjenige Prädikat, welches nur an einem einzigen selbständigern Dinge gedacht zu werden braucht" (1781: 132). Das sind also Verben, die wir heute einwertig nennen würden, Verben wie *sitzen*, *liegen*, *gehen*, *stehen* (Meiners eigene Beispiele!). Aber er führt hier auch Konstruktionen mit Verbum Substantivum an, *weiß*, *schwarz*, *roth ... weise*, *vorsichtig*, *treu ... seyn*. Das heißt, Meiner ordnet die Wortart Adjektiv in Verbindung mit dem Verbum Substantivum unter syntaktischen Aspekten mit zu den Verben. Er führt dazu aus, dass das, was im Deutschen auf diese Weise ausgedrückt wird, in anderen Sprachen rein verbal ausgedrückt werden kann, etwa im Lateinischen *pallere* = *weiß seyn* oder *rubere* = *roth seyn*. Die reine Form ist also sekundär. "Zwoseitig=unselbständige" Verben sind entsprechend zweiwertige (*setzen*, *legen*, *stellen* ... aber eben auch *begierig seyn*) und "dreiyseitig=unselbständige" sind dreiwertige (*beschuldigen*, *anklagen*, *lossprechen*, *überführen* etc.). Meiner kennt auch schon den Unterschied zwischen dem, was wir heute kategoriale versus lexikalische Valenz nennen würden: Die Gradation der Adjektive macht alle einwertigen Adjektive zu zweiwertigen. Alle seine Entscheidungen und Überlegungen begründet Meiner sehr ausführlich und mit vielen Beispielen aus den fünf Sprachen, die er beherrschte.

Adelung hat Meiners Arbeit ausführlich rezensiert (1782 in seiner eigenen Zeitschrift *Magazin für die Deutsche Sprache*) und rezipiert. Ihn beeindruckte Meiners Konzeption des Sprachunterrichts als Reflexion über den Zusammenhang zwischen Sprechen und Denken. Für Meiners zentrale syntaxorientierte Neuerungen hat er allerdings kein Verständnis gefunden. Die waren ihm wohl zu revolutionär (siehe dazu Naumann 1990). Außerdem war Adelung grundsätzlich eher an Morphologie interessiert als an Syntax. Vielleicht ist das der Grund, warum Meiners Arbeit zu seiner Zeit wenig Einfluss hatte und erst heute in ihrer Bedeutung erkannt wird.

### 3.2.2. Georg Michael Roth

Roth war Theologe, Philosoph, Jurist und Gymnasialprofessor. Er verfasste eine Allgemeine Grammatik und zwei Schulgrammatiken nach diesem Muster. Seine nur knapp über hundert Seiten starke Allgemeine Grammatik trägt den polemischen Obertitel *Antihermes* in Anspielung an die Arbeit des Engländers James Harris, dessen *Hermes* im Jahr 1751 erschienen war, ein Buch, das im Ausland, besonders in Deutschland mehr Beachtung fand als im Ursprungsland England. Harris ging in Platonischer Tradition von angeborenen Ideen aus, einer Art mentaler Universalien, die auch unser Wissen über Sprache dominierten. Roth dagegen leitete sein Sprachverständnis aus seiner Kantlektüre ab, aus Kants "Kritik der reinen Vernunft" (1781), aus der Erkenntnis a priori:

Die innern Merkmale der Vorstellung sind *reine*, von der Erfahrung unabhängige *Merkmale*, in wie ferne sie durch das Vorstellungsvermögen als Bestandtheile der Vorstellung *a priori*, d. h. vor aller Erfahrung, vor aller Vorstellung selbst, bestimmt sind; *nothwendige Merkmale*, in wie ferne sich ohne sie keine Vorstellung überhaupt denken läßt; *allgemeine Merkmale*, in wie ferne sie allen Vorstellungen ohne Ausnahme zukommende Merkmale sind (1795: 37).

Das Adjektiv "rein" begegnet in vielen deutschen Allgemeinen Grammatiken nach Kant 1781. Der Gegenbegriff dazu ist "empirisch" oder auch "auf Erfahrung gegründet". Harris wirft er immer wieder vor, in seiner Arbeit nicht deutlich zwischen einer "reinen allgemeinen Sprachlehre" und einer "empirisch allgemeinen Sprachlehre" unterschieden zu haben, also zwischen dem, was die Franzosen oder auch Meiner auch ohne Kantkenntnisse mit *grammaire générale* und *grammaire particulière* bezeichnet haben. Das zeige sich an Harris' unsauberer Trennung zwischen dem sprachlichen Zeichen und dem damit Bezeichneten. Besonders deutlich wird Roths Abhängigkeit von Kant in der Kategorienlehre. Roth übernimmt Kants erkenntnistheoretische Kategorien, die vier Hauptkategorien und die ihnen zugeordneten Prädikabilien, insgesamt zwölf an der Zahl, vollständig für seine "Im Verstande a priori bestimmte Darstellungsweisen der Sprache" (1795: 78f.). Natürliche Sprachen müssen nicht Formen für alle (Kantschen) Kategorien ausgebildet haben, aber sie können keine Formen ausbilden, die nicht aus diesen Kategorien ableitbar sind, sagt Roth.

In seinen beiden Schulgrammatiken, für die er wie Adelung Wissenschaftlichkeit beansprucht (Roth bezieht sich ausdrücklich auf Adelung und auf Meiner), hat Roth dann versucht, seine von Kant abgeleiteten Ansichten konkret auf die *deutsche* Grammatik anzuwenden. Auch Roth geht dabei strikt dichotomisch vor. Oberster Knoten ist Sprachwissenschaft/Sprachkunst, nur erstere wird weiterverfolgt: dann folgt die Unterteilung in logische/ästhetische Sprachwissenschaft, auch hier geht es zunächst wieder nur links weiter: Form/Materie, die Wissenschaft, die sich mit der Form befasst, heißt Sprachlehre oder Grammatik, sie wird wieder subklassifiziert in allgemeine und in besondere, und beide "zerfallen" wiederum in zwei Möglichkeiten:

"Alle Gedanken sind entweder Begriffe oder Urtheile. Erstere werden durch einzelne Wörter, letztere aber durch Verknüpfung der Wörter zu einem Ganzen bezeichnet. Daher zerfällt die Sprachlehre in zwey Theile; in die Etymologie, oder die Lehre von einzelnen Wörtern, so ferne durch sie Begriffe bezeichnet werden, und in den Syntax, oder die Lehre von der Bezeichnung der Urtheile durch die Verknüpfung der Wörter zu einem Ganzen" (1799: 10).

Alle Einheiten der Sprache werden "formal" und "material" analysiert, nach ihrer Funktion im logischen Urteil und nach ihrem Ausdruck. Dadurch erhält seine Sprachlehre etwas Mechanistisches, Schematisches, was Spätere ja bekanntlich nicht ganz zu Unrecht der ganzen Richtung vorgeworfen haben. Roth selber ist davon überzeugt, dass der menschliche Geist so funktioniert:

Ich nenne diese systematische Sprachlehre eine Sprachlehre für Schulen. Mancher wird sie vielleicht zu philosophisch für diesen Gebrauch finden; mir scheint dieß anders. Soll die Sprachlehre die Denkkraft wecken und üben, so muß sie deutlich seyn, welches im Grunde in dieser Beziehung mit dem Philosophischen Einerley ist. Sonst wird die Denkkraft durch das Gedächtniß verkümmert (1799: XL).

### 3.2.3. August Ferdinand Bernhardi

Wie die meisten seiner akademischen Zeitgenossen studierte Bernhardi Theologie und Philosophie, bevor er in Berlin Gymnasiallehrer, später Rektor (des Friedrich-Werderschen Gymnasiums) wurde. Vor seiner deutschen Sprachlehre verfasste Bernhardi eine *lateinische* und eine *griechische* Grammatik. Bereits hier hat er die Möglichkeiten einer Allgemeinen Grammatik diskutiert, in die Tat umgesetzt hat er sie dann erst in seiner *deutschen* Sprachlehre von 1801/3 (nach Gessinger 1990: 562 "streckenweise [...] wie ein sprachphilosophischer und erkenntnispsychologischer Kommentar zu Fichtes 1795 erschienenem Aufsatz 'Von der Sprachfähigkeit und dem Ursprung der Sprache'") und in der Arbeit von 1805. Von allen Allgemeinen Grammatikern der Zeit war Bernhardi vielleicht der unsystematischste, das genaue Gegenteil von Roth: Das Inhaltsverzeichnis seiner Sprachlehre vermittelt nur einen vagen Eindruck dessen, was abgehandelt wird. Man muss die beiden Bände gewissermaßen am Stück lesen, um zu wissen, was drin steht. Drei Bücher des ersten Bandes (1801) erarbeiten den theoretischen Rahmen, das, was auch Bernhardi "reine Sprachlehre" nennt. Hier werden die erkenntnistheoretischen Grundlagen der Sprachwissenschaft abgehandelt, die grammatischen Kategorien als Korrelate logischer Begrifflichkeit, die syntaktischen Relationen und die Wortarten. Dies ist eine philosophische Sprachlehre im eigentlichen Sinne. Damit müsste sich Bernhardi als Allgemeiner Grammatiker im strengen Sinne zufrieden geben. Aber im Einklang mit der idealistischen Philosophie lässt er dieser Darstellung eine weitere folgen: Im zweiten Band, der "angewandten Sprachlehre" (1803) geht es um Sprachgebrauch in Poesie,

Kunst und Wissenschaft, und um Musik. (Bernhardi war literarisch interessiert, er war Schwager Ludwig Tiecks, verkehrte mit Schelling und anderen Schriftstellern in der Berliner Szene). Schon der erste Satz seiner Sprachlehre schlägt eher romanhafte als systematische Töne an:

Wenn wir Wesen annehmen, um eine Stufe über die Menschen erhöhet, aber der Natur derselben verwandt; Geschöpfe, welche gegen unser Geschlecht in demselben Verhältnisse stehen, als wir gegen das der Thiere; und wenn wir glauben, daß jene Wesen uns mit eben der unermüdeten Sorgfalt beobachten, als wir die uns untergeordneten thierischen Naturen: so müßte nach unsern Begriffen, das Geschlecht der Menschen der interessanteste Gegenstand ihrer Beobachtungen sein. Am wenigstens aber würde ihnen wohl jenes Murmeln, Zwitschern und Zischen auffallen; jene dem Anscheine nach so wenig verschiedenen Töne, diejenige Erscheinung, welche wir unter dem Nahmen Sprache begreifen (1801: 3; vgl. dazu Gessingers Kommentar 1990: 563).

Bernhardis Sprachlehre basiert in gewisser Weise auch auf der Philosophie Kants, aber längst nicht mehr so direkt wie die Grammatiken von Roth, er hat viel von der idealistischen Philosophie Fichtes übernommen und dessen Konzeption einer "absoluten Vernunft", die allen menschlichen Bedürfnissen zur Kommunikation zugrundeliegt. Seine Arbeit von 1805 ist strenger gegliedert und systematischer aufgebaut. Auch sie basiert auf der von Kant und Fichte ausgearbeiteten Methode der strengen Deduktion aller relevanten Elemente. In seiner Syntax geht es vorrangig um das Begriffspaar Substanz–Akzidenz, das er in Anlehnung an Fichte definiert, und damit zusammenhängend um Inhärenz und Dependenz, worunter Bernhardi die semantischen Relationen zwischen den Hauptwortarten (Inhärenz) und die durch Präpositionen oder Kasus bewerkstelligten Abhängigkeiten (Dependenz) versteht (siehe dazu Höller 1992: 244 f.).

Bernhardis Wirkung war viel stärker als die von Roth. Man hat seine für den Unterricht ungeeigneten, weil für Schüler viel zu komplizierten Sprachlehren in didaktisch verwertbare Form gebracht (Georg Reinbeck), und man hat ihn als Anreger rezipiert, nicht nur andere Allgemeine Grammatiker, sondern sogar Jacob Grimm und über fünfzig Jahre später noch August Pott. Außerdem hat er durch zahllose pädagogisch-organisatorische Beiträge zum preußischen Unterrichtswesen und durch seine engen Kontakte zur preußischen Kultusbehörde viel Einfluß in den Schulen des Landes gehabt.

### 3.2.4. Johann Severin Vater

Der Theologieprofessor Vater beherrschte ähnlich viele Sprachen wie Sylvestre de Sacy, beste Voraussetzung für jeden Allgemeinen Grammatiker. (Er hat Sylvestre de Sacys Allgemeine Grammatik auch ins Deutsche übertragen). Neben den meisten europäischen beherrschte er arabische, semitische und slavische Sprachen, er besaß sogar Kenntnisse einiger Sprachen nordamerikanischer Indianer. Am bedeutendsten war er aber wohl als Orientalist. Diese Sprachkenntnisse prädestinierten ihn dazu, Adelungs angefangenen *Mithridates* nach dessen Tod zu vollenden und eine Bibliographie der gesamten sprachwissenschaftlichen Literatur seiner Zeit (1815) zu verfassen. Seine Allgemeine Sprachlehre erschien im selben Jahr wie die von Bernhardi, 1801. Durch ihre undogmatische Art und den auf reicher Erfahrung beruhenden Aussagen zu allem, was mit Sprache verbunden ist, hebt sie sich wohltuend von den stark spekulativen Arbeiten Roths und Bernhardis ab. "Sprache ist ein in der Erfahrung gegebener Gegenstand. Der Begriff derselben kann nur auf dem Wege der Erfahrung gefunden werden" (1801: VII). Das klingt ganz unkantisch und ist zumindest ansatzweise auch so gemeint. Vater leitet sprachliche Kategorien nicht aus dem Denken a priori ab, sondern fragt, in wieweit die von der Logik vorgegebenen Denkmöglichkeiten für die zutreffende Beschreibung der vielen verschiedenen Sprachen nutzbar gemacht werden können: "Eben da Sprache ein in der Erfahrung gegebener Gegenstand ist: so muß gezeigt werden, wie und in wiefern derselbe sich durch die allgemeine und philosophische Uebersicht wirklich übersehen läßt." (1801: VIII). Allgemeine Sprachlehre ist demnach für Vater auch kein Spiegel der Logik, sondern ihre Erweiterung:

Sie unterscheidet sich [...] von der Logik, von welcher sie eher eine Fortsetzung (eine Fortsetzung des logischen Verfahrens) zum Behufe der möglichen Uebersicht eines in der Erfahrung gegebenen Gegenstandes, als eine Anwendung ist, welche von gewissen, aus der Erfahrung abgeleiteten Datis ausgienge (1801: 157).

Vaters Sprachlehre beginnt zunächst mit Überlegungen zum Ursprung und zur Geschichte der Sprache(n). (Schon Bernhardi hatte ja in seiner "Angewandten Sprachlehre" einige Kapitel dazu). Erst im dritten Abschnitt, überschrieben "Eigentliche Prolegomenen" kommt Allgemeine Grammatik im gewohnten Sinn: "Ueber den Begriff und die Begründung der allgemeinen Sprachlehre". Hier geht es ihm zunächst um die Natur des sprachlichen Zeichens, um das Verhältnis zwischen Bezeichnung und Bezeichnetem. Er geht das Thema grundsätzlich an:

> Man kann diese Begriffe also festsetzen, daß man 1) den, welcher bezeichnet, 2) den, für welchen man bezeichnet, 3) den Zweck der Bezeichnung, 4) den Erfolg, die Erreichung dieses Zwecks, 5) das Zeichen, das Mittel, und 6) das, was bezeichnet wird, betrachtet (1801: 137).

Sehr viel umfassender kann die Fragestellung zu einer Theorie des sprachlichen Zeichens nicht sein. Die Antworten fallen allerdings weniger umfassend aus, die hier gestellten Fragen werden im Verlauf seiner Arbeit eher implizit beantwortet und auch nicht besonders ausführlich: Das vierte Kapitel, der "Entwurf der allgemeinen Sprachlehre", das eigentliche Hauptkapitel, ist vom Umfang her eher bescheiden. Es geht um die systematische Darstellung der Funktionen der Redeteile. Im Anhang, "Anwendung der allgemeinen Sprachlehre bei den Grammatiken einzelner Sprachen" postuliert er abschließend, dass sich die hier erarbeiteten allgemeinen Prinzipien auf jede Sprache anwenden lassen müssten und dass jede Sprache damit besser und zutreffender erklärt werden könne. "Vergleichende Sprachlehre" sei nur sinnvoll, wenn das tertium comparationis die allgemeine Sprachlehre sei.

Gezeigt hat er das dann vier Jahre später in seinem Lehrbuch für "höhere Schul=Classen".

> Dem reifenden Zögling, der sich an Speculation gewöhnen soll, bietet sich kein anderes Geschäft dar, zu welchem er mehr vorbereitet wäre und mehr angezogen würde, als das Nachdenken über die Sprachen, deren Einrichtungen er durch mehrjährige Unterweisung und Uebung kennen gelernt hat (1805: 3f.).

Vater sagt bewusst nicht "Nachdenken über Sprache", sondern "Nachdenken über die Sprachen", und er geht davon aus, dass die von ihm angesprochenen Schüler zunächst Sprachen auf konventionellem Wege lernen müssen (sie müssen "die Data der Spracheinrichtungen" kennen), bevor sie darüber im Rahmen einer allgemeinen Grammatik spekulieren dürfen.

Auch diese Arbeit stellt die Wortarten in den Mittelpunkt und ordnet sie funktional den Teilen des Urteils zu, dem Subjekt, dem Prädikat und der Kopula. "Ob die einzelnen Sprachen jeden dieser Theile des Urtheils in dem Satze durch ein eigenes, abgesondertes Wort ausdrücke, darauf kommt Nichts an" (1805: 17). Besonders ausführlich geht Vater deshalb auf die Sprachen ein, wo dies eben nicht so ist. Der letzte Abschnitt, die Syntax, besteht nur aus zwei Seiten: "Die allgemeine Sprachlehre hat keine besondere Syntax, sondern handelt alles dahin Gehörige bei den einzelnen Redetheilen ab" (1805: 202). Adelung hätte dem zugestimmt, Meiner und die anderen Allgemeinen Grammatiker sicher nicht.

### 3.3. England

In England nahm die Allgemeine Sprachlehre eine etwas andere Entwicklung als auf dem Kontinent. Die Tradition bis 1700 hat Padley (1985 und 1988) ausführlich dargestellt, den Zeitraum danach Aarsleff (1967). Im 18. Jh. ist vor allem James Harris von Bedeutung. Etwa gleichzeitig mit ihm hat Adam Smith seine Vorstellungen über den Ursprung der Sprache veröffentlicht (1761) und Joseph Priestley seine Arbeit über Universale Grammatik (1762), beides lange vor dem hier gesteckten Zeitrahmen. Innerhalb des Zeitrahmens fällt Lord Monboddos monumentales Werk (1773–1792) über Ursprung und Entwicklung der Sprache und vor allem die Arbeiten von James Beattie (1783/1788) und John Horne Tooke (1786/1798 und 1805).

#### 3.3.1. James Beattie

Beattie war Professor für Moralphilosophie und Logik in Aberdeen. Auch er war der festen Überzeugung, dass Sprache und Denken zusammen gesehen werden müssen, und dass es eine allgemeine Grammatik gebe: "Shall we unfold the principles of Universal Grammar, by tracing out those powers, forms, or contrivances, which, being essential to language, must be found in every system of human speech that deserves the name" (1788: 126). Allgemeine Grammatik ist nach ihm nicht der kleinste gemeinsame Nenner der Grammatiken aller natürlichen Sprachen, sondern der notwendige Rahmen für die Regularitäten in allen Sprachen. Der erste Teil seiner Sprachlehre ist überschrieben "Of the Origin and General Nature of Speech". Hier erarbeitet Beattie so etwas wie eine Kulturgeschichte der Sprache vom Urmenschen (der vor allem Gesten zur Kommunikation benutzte, was Südeuropäer z. T. noch heute täten, sogar die gebildeten Franzosen) bis zum zeitgenössischen Engländer ("people of a graver turn [...] who have words for all their ideas [and] trust to language alone for a full declaration of their mind" 1788: 11). Der zweite Teil *Of Universal Grammar* bietet dann das, was man von einer Allgemeinen Sprachlehre der Zeit erwartet. Hier stehen die Redeteile im Mittelpunkt der Darstellung. Sie werden, getreu der Tradition, in notwendige, essentielle und in entbehrliche aber nützliche unterschieden. Allgemeines Fazit: "The Noun, Pronoun, Verb, Participle, Adjective, Preposition, and Conjunction, seem to be essential to language: the Article, Interjection, and most of the Adverbs, are rather to be called useful, than necessary, Parts of Speech" (1788: 39). Beattie unterscheidet zwischen mentalen und formalen Kategorien, nur die mentalen seien universal und notwendig und in jeder Sprache vorhanden: Elemente zum Ausdruck von Temporalität sind nach ihm notwendig, nicht aber die Tempusflexive in der Verbkonjugation, weil Temporalität formal auch anders ausgedrückt werden könne, etwa auch durch selbständige Wörter, durch temporale Adverbien.

3.3.2. John Horne Tooke

"Though he lived on into the second decade of the 19th century, Tooke was essentially a man and scholar of the 18th century; his life, his style, and his scholarship should be understood and judged in the context of that century" (Robins 1996: 927). Sein eigentlicher Name war John Horne, sein Freund und Gönner hieß William Tooke und besaß ein Landgut in Purley/Surrey. John Horne nahm den Namen seines Freundes zusätzlich zu seinem eigenen an und den Namen des Landguts in den Titel seines Hauptwerks auf: "Επεα πτεροεντα" (epea pteroenta), d. h. geflügelte Worte, "or the diversions of Purley". Damit spielt Horne auf die Anlage seines Buches an, Kaminplaudereien zwischen drei Freunden, dem Autor selber, William Tooke und Richard Beadon, Master of Jesus College, Cambridge. Sie unterhielten sich über das Naturrecht des Menschen, über Sprachursprung und Entwicklung, über Etymologie, über Sprachtypologie, über Allgemeine Grammatik und die englische Sprache im besonderen (siehe dazu ausführlich Aarsleff 1967: 44–114). Im ersten Band werden eingangs die philosophischen Ansichten von John Locke besprochen (zustimmend) und die Allgemeine Grammatik von Harris (ablehnend). Danach stehen auch bei Horne die Redeteile im Mittelpunkt der Darstellung. Er teilt alle Wortarten in zwei Großklassen: "Words necessary for the communication of our thoughts" und zweitens "Abbreviations, employed for the sake of dispatch". (1798: 45). Notwendig in diesem Sinne und deshalb auch universal seien lediglich Substantive und Verben. Alle anderen Wortarten würden nur als "signs for other words" fungieren, d. h. für die syntaktische Organisation benötigt werden, angenehm und nützlich für jeden Sprecher, aber eigentlich nicht notwendig und auch nicht universal: "B: Do you mean then that, without using any other sort of word whatever, and merely by the means of the Noun and Verb alone, you can relate or communicate any thing that I can relate or communicate with the help of all others?". Darauf die Antwort von H: "Yes. It is the great proof of all I have advanced [...]" (1798: 49). Im zweiten Band übernimmt Francis Burdett Beadons Rolle als Gesprächspartner. Es geht auch hier um die Verteidigung seiner These, dass letztlich nur Substantive und Verben notwendig und universal seien, und es geht um viele Etymologien, ein Versuch, Philologie und Philosophie zu kombinieren. Horne Tooke erweist sich als sprachenkundiger und gelehrter Mann und genoss bei seinen Zeitgenossen hohes Ansehen und noch mehr bei seinen Nachfolgern. Noch etwa vierzig Jahre nach dem ersten Erscheinen des ersten Bandes seines Werkes gab John Fearn (1768–1837) einen 800seitigen *Anti-Tooke* heraus, der voller Missverständnisse ist, weil Fearn offenbar inzwischen sehr weit weg von den Grundsätzen der Allgemeinen Sprachlehre des 18. Jhs. war (siehe dazu Aarsleff 1967: 79–81).

The reputation of Tooke's *Diversions* is one of the most remarkable phenomenons in the intellectual and scholarly life of England during the first third of the nieneteenth century. For thirty years it kept England immune to the new philology until the results and methods finally had to be imported from the continent in the 1830's, and even then they met with strong opposition (Aarsleff 1967: 73).

## 4. Schluss: 'Allgemeine Sprachwissenschaft' als Historisch-Vergleichende Sprachwissenschaft

Die Sprachwissenschaft nach 1800 wird zunehmend dominiert von der Historisch-Vergleichenden Methode. Vergleichend-universalistisch arbeiteten schon Forscher des 17. und 18. Jhs. Man stellte Grundwörter oder Grundtexte (beliebt war das Vaterunser) nebeneinander und stellte Wörterlisten in allen möglichen europäischen und vor allem außereuropäischen Sprachen zusammen, um daraus allgemeine Schlüsse zu ziehen. Man sammelte Sprachmaterial aus antiquarischem Interesse, so wie Steine, Versteinerungen und Merkwürdigkeiten der Natur (siehe dazu etwa Naumann 1996a). Da Sprachwissenschaft als eigene Disziplin vor dem 19. Jh. nicht existierte, betrachtete es jeder allgemein kulturhistorisch interessierte Wissenschaftler als Herausforderung, auch sprachforschend tätig zu werden, etwa der Vater der deutschen Geologie, Abraham Gottlob Werner (1750–1817) in Freiberg, der umfangreiche Wörterlisten aus allen möglichen Sprachen zusammenstellte (sie allerdings nie veröffentlichte). Um 1800 war der bekannteste Europäer, der sich damit befasste, Peter Simon Pallas (1741–1811), auch er zunächst Geologe und Naturforscher. In den 60er und 70er Jahren des 18. Jhs. bereiste er im Auftrag der Zarin Katharina II. die Länder Russlands und sammelte zahlreiches Wortmaterial aus den östlichen Provinzen des russischen Imperiums, das er, zusammen mit Wörterlisten aus anderen Sprachen, in vier dicken Bänden veröffentlichte. Über das reine Sammeln kamen derartige Unternehmungen aber kaum hinaus, die Vergleichsarbeit überließen sie anderen, späteren, denn ihnen fehlte jedes sprachwissenschaftliche Rüstzeug. Die letzte Arbeit Johann Christoph Adelungs versuchte gerade dieses und erreichte dadurch einige Berühmtheit, wenn auch nicht in jeder Beziehung im positiven Sinne. Adelung, der immer ein offenes Ohr für Zeitströmungen hatte, versuchte, das zu initiieren, was dann im 19. Jh. als "Allgemeine Grammatik" verstanden wurde und wie noch heute zumindest z. T. Lehrstühle für "Allgemeine Sprachwissenschaft" an deutschen Universitäten sich verstehen, die historisch-vergleichende Untersuchung von Gemeinsamkeiten und Unterschieden in Phonologie und Morphologie als Mittel zur Sprachtypologie. Er hatte erkannt:

daß eine bloße historische Nachricht von dem Eigenen dieser und jener Sprache [...] bei weitem nicht hinreicht, weil sie nicht anders als sehr allgemein und trocken gerathen kann, sahe man bald ein; daher kam man auch schon frühe auf den Gedanken, diese Kenntniß auf wahre aus den Sprachen selbst hergenommene Proben zu gründen. Werden diese Proben aus mehrern Sprachen auf eine gewisse gleichförmige Art gewählt, so können sie, wenn sie neben einander gestellt, schon für sich allein zu einiger Beurtheilung der Verwandtschaft und des Unterschiedes der Sprachen dienen (1806: IV).

Als Material, das "eine gewisse gleichförmige Art" hatte, wählte auch er Versionen des Vaterunsers aus 500 europäischen und außereuropäischen Sprachen, "weil man keine Formel in so vielen Sprachen haben kann als diese" (1806: IX). Gradmesser für den kulturellen Status einer Sprache und des diese Sprache sprechenden Volkes war für ihn und für die meisten seiner Zeitgenossen, auch für Wilhelm von Humboldt, die mehr oder weniger komplexe Morphemstruktur der jeweiligen Sprache (was ihn bekanntlich zu dem oft zitierten, grotesken Fehlurteil über das Chinesische führte).

Etwa ab 1800 dringt mehr und mehr Historisches in die Arbeiten der Allgemeinen Grammatiker ein. Vater und Bernhardi haben historische Abschnitte in ihren Arbeiten, Beattie und Horne Tooke beschäftigten sich zumindest z. T. mit Sprachgeschichte und Etymologie. Friedrich Schmitthenner versuchte noch 1826 Sprachgeschichte und Allgemeine Grammatik zu verbinden, fand zu seiner Zeit damit aber nur noch wenig Resonanz – und Wilhelm von Humboldt ist in jeder Hinsicht ein Kapitel für sich.

## 5. Bibliographie


Aarsleff, Hans. 1967. *The Study of Language in England 1780–1880.* Minneapolis: Univ. of Minnesota Press.

–. 1982. *From Locke to Saussure: Essays on the study of language and intellectuaql history.* Minneapolis: Univ. of Minnesota Press.

Adelung, Johann Christoph. 1781. *Deutsche Sprachlehre. Zum Gebrauche der Schulen in den Königl. Preuß. Landen.* Berlin: Christian Friedrich Voß und Sohn.

–. 1806. *Mithridates oder allgemeine Sprachenkunde, mit dem Vater Unser als Sprachprobe in bey nahe fünf hundert Sprachen und Mundarten.* Berlin: Vossische Buchhandlung.

Amirova, T. A., B. A. Ol'chovikov & J. V. Roždestvenskij. 1980. *Abriß der Geschichte der Linguistik.* Ins Deutsche übersetzt von Barbara Meier. Leipzig: VEB Bibliographisches Institut.

Arens, Hans. 1969. *Sprachwissenschaft. Der Gang ihrer Entwicklung von der Antike bis zur Gegenwart.* 2 Bde. Frankfurt: Fischer.

Arnauld, Claude. 1662. *La Logique ou L'Art de penser, contenant, outre les Règles communes, plusieurs observations nouvelles, propres à fermer le judgement.* Sixième Édition revue et de nouveau augmentée. Amsterdam: Chez Abraham Wolfgang. (Faksimile Neudruck mit einer Einleitung von B. Baron von Freytag-Löringhoff u. Herbert E. Brekle. 1965. Stuttgart Bad Cannstatt: Friedrich Frommann.)

Arnauld, Antoine & Claude Lancelot. 1660. *Grammaire générale et raisonnée contenant les fondements de l'art de parler; expliquez d'vne maniere claire & naturelles; Les raiseons de ce qui est commun à toutes des langues, & des principales differences qui s'y recontrent; Et plusieurs remarques nouvelles sur la Langue Françoise.* Paris. (Faksimile Neudruck mit einer Einleitung von Herbert E. Brekle 1966. Stuttgart Bad Cannstatt: Friedrich Frommann.)

Auroux, Sylvain. 1973. *L'Encyclopédie. 'Grammaire' et 'Langue' au XVIIIe siècle.* Paris: Mame.

–. 1982. "General Grammar and Universal Grammar in Enlightenment France". *General Linguistics* 23. 1–18.

–. 1991. "Innovation et sytème scientifique: le temps verbal dans la grammaire générale". *Hommage à J. T. Desanti*, 55–86. Mauvezin: Editions T. E. R.

Baggioni, Daniel. 1996. "Sylvestre de Sacy, Baron Antoine-Isaac". *Lexikon Grammaticorum* hg. von Harro Stammerjohann, 901f. Tübingen: Niemeyer.

Beattie, James. 1783. *Dissertations moral and critical.* London & Edinburgh: A. Strahan, T. Cadell & W. Creech. (Darin "The Teory of Language", 231–502; separat erschienen 1788. The Theory of Language in two parts. London & Edinburgh: A. Strahan, T. Cadell and W. Creech. Repr. 1968 Menston: Scolar Press.)

Bernhardi, August Ferdinand. 1801–03. *Sprachlehre.* 2 Theile. Berlin: bei Heinrich Fröhlich.

–. 1805. *Anfangsgründe der Sprachwissenschaft.* Berlin: bei Heinrich Fröhlich. (Faksimile Neudruck 1973. Hildesheim & New York: Olms).

Beauzée, Nicolas. 1767. *Grammaire générale ou exposition raisonnée des éléments nécessaires du langage, pour servir de fondement à l'étude de toutes langues.* 2 Bde. Paris. (Faksimile Neudruck mit einer Einleitung von Barrie E. Bartlett 1974. Stuttgart Bad Cannstatt: Friedrich Frommann.)

Brekle, Herbert E. 1975. "'Syntaxe et construction' in Silvestre de Sacys 'Principes de Grammaire Générale' 1803". *Akten der 1. Salzburger Frühlingstagung für Linguistik* hg. von Gabarell Drachman, Bd. 1, 267–272. Tübingen: Narr.

Chomsky, Noam. 1966. *Cartesian Linguistics.* New York: Harper & Row.

Dascal, Marcello et al., eds. 1996. *Sprachphilosophie/Philosophy of Language/La philosophie du langage. Ein internationales Handbuch zeitgenössischer Forschung/An International Handbook of Contemporary Research/Manuel international des recherches contemporaines.* (= *Handbücher zur Sprach- und Kommunikationsforschung*, Bd. 7.1./2.) Berlin & New York: de Gruyter.

Dominicy, Marc. 1996. "La grammaire générale et sa survie dans les traditions de langues romanes: Une esquisse méthodologique". *Geschichte der Sprachtheorie*, Bd. 5: *Sprachtheorien der Neuzeit* hg. von Peter Schmitter, II. 3–23. Tübingen: Narr.

Fearn, John. 1824–27. *Anti-Tooke; or an Analysis of the Principles and Structures of Language exemplified in the English Tongue.* London (Facsimile Edition of the London ed. 1824–1827, 1972. Stuttgart Bad Cannstatt: Frommann.)

Frank, Horst Joachim. 1973. *Geschichte des Deutschunterrichts. Von den Anfängen bis 1945.* München: Hanser.

Gessinger, Joachim. 1990. "August Ferdinand Bernhardi". Niederehe & Koerner 1990. II. 561–575.

–. 1994. *Auge & Ohr. Studien zur Erforschung der Sprache am Menschen. 1700–1850.* Berlin & New York: de Gruyter.

Haßler, Gerda. 1990. "Die Erkenntnisfunktion der Sprache – ein Diskussionsthema an der Wende vom 18. zum 19. Jh.". Niederehe & Koerner 1990. II. 529–540.

Horne Tooke, John. 1786 und 1805. Επεα πτεροεντα *or, The Diversions of Purley.* 2 Bde. London: Johnsons (printed for the author.) 2. Aufl. d. 1. Bandes 1798. (Repr. 1968. Menston: Scolar Press.)

Höller, Hans Jürgen. 1992. "Bernhardi, August Ferdinand". *Bio-Bibliographisches Handbuch [...]* hg. von Herbert E. Brekle et al., 1 (A–Br). 241–248. Tübingen: Niemeyer.

Matthias, Adolf. 1907. *Geschichte des Deutschen Unterrichts.* München: Beck.

Meiner, Johann Werner. 1781. *Versuch einer an der menschlichen Sprache abgebildeten Vernunftlehre oder Philosophische und allgemeine Sprachlehre.* Leipzig: Johann Gottlob Immanuel Breitkopf. (Faksimile Neudruck mit einer Einleitung von Herbert E. Brekle 1971. Stuttgart Cannstatt: Frommann.

Naumann, Bernd. 1990. "Die 'dependenzgrammatischen' Überlegungen Johann Werner Meiners (1723–1789)". Anne Betten, hg. *Neuere Forschungen zur historischen Syntax des Deutschen* hg. von Anne Betten, 439–450. Tübingen: Niemeyer.

–. 1992. "Adelung, Johann Christoph". *Bio-bibliographisches Handbuch zur Sprachwissenschaft des 18. Jahrhunderts. Die Grammatiker, Lexikographen und Sprachtheoretiker des deutschsprachigen Raums mit Beschreibungen ihrer Werke* hg. von Herbert E. Brekle, Edeltraud Dobnig-Jülch, Hans Jürgen Höller & Helmut Weiß, 1 (A–br). 16–42. Tübingen: Niemeyer.

–. 1996a. "Die Rolle des Antiquars in der Geschichte der Sprach- und Geowissenschaften: Johann Ernst Immanuel Walch". *A Science in the Making. The Regensburg Symposia on European Linguistic Historiography* hg. von Herbert E. Brekle, Edeltraud Dobnig-Jülch & Helmut Weiß, 181–195. Münster: Nodus Publikationen.

–. 1996b. "Die Tradition der Philosophischen Grammatik in Deutschland". *Geschichte der Sprachtheorie* hg. von Peter Schmitter, Bd. 5, *Sprachtheorien der Neuzeit* II. 24–43. Tübingen: Narr.

–. 1998. "Meiner, Johann Werner". *Bio-Bibliographisches Handbuch zur Sprachwissenschaft des 18. Jahrhunderts. Die Grammatiker, Lexikographen und Sprachtheoretiker des deutschsprachigen Raums mit Beschreibung ihrer Werke* hg. von Herbert E. Brekle, Edeltraud Dobnig-Jülch, Hans Jürgen Höller & Helmut Weiß, Bd. 6 (M–Pa). 59–68. Tübingen: Niemeyer.

Niederehe, Hans-Josef & Konrad Koerner, Hg. 1990. *History and Historiography of Linguistics*, 2 Bde. Amsterdam: Benjamins.

Noordegraaf, Jan. 1996. "General Grammar in the Netherlands, 1670–1900". *Geschichte der Sprachtheorie*, Bd. 5. *Sprachtheorien der Neuzeit* hg. von Peter Schmitter, Bd. II. 94–121. Tübingen: Narr.

Padley, G. Arthur. 1985 und 1988. *Grammatical Theory in Western Europe 1500–1700. Trends in Vernacular Grammar.* 2 Bde. Cambridge: Cambridge Univ. Press.

Pallas, Peter Simon. 1790–91. *Linguarum totius orbis vocabularia.* 2. Aufl., 4 Bde. St. Petersburg.

Priestley, Joseph. 1762. *A Course of Lectures on the Theory of Language and Universal Grammar.* Warrington. (Repr. 1970. Menston: Scolar Press.)

Ricken, Ulrich et al. 1990. *Sprachtheorie und Weltanschauung in der europäischen Aufklärung. Zur Geschichte der Sprachtheorien des 18. Jahrhunderts und ihrer europäischen Rezeption nach der Französischen Revolution.* Berlin: Akademie-Verlag.

Robins, Robert H. 1996. "Tooke, John Horne". *Lexikon Grammaticorum* hg. von Harro Stammerjohann, 926 f. Tübingen: Niemeyer.

Roth, Georg Michael. 1795. *Antihermes oder philosophische Untersuchung über den reinen Begriff der menschlichen Sprache und die allgemeine Sprachlehre.* Frankfurt/M. & Leipzig: in der neuen Buchhandlung.

–. 1799. *Systematische deutsche Sprachlehre für Schulen.* Giessen: bey Georg Friedrich Heyer.

Schmitthenner, Friedrich. 1826. *Ursprachlehre. Entwurf zu einem System der Grammatik mit besonderer Rücksicht auf die Sprachen des indisch-teutschen Stammes: das Sanskrit, das Persische, die pelasgischen, slavischen und teutschen Sprachen.* Frankfurt/M.: Verlag der Hermannschen Buchhandlung. (Faksimile Neudruck mit einer Einleitung von Herbert E. Brekle 1976. Stuttgart & Bad Cannstatt: Frommann.)

Schreyer, Rüdiger. 1990. "Of General Terms on Language and Mind in 18th-century Linguistic Theory". Niederehe & Koerner 1990. II. 399–414.

Sylvestre de Sacy, Antoine-Isaac. 1799. *Principes de Grammaire générale mis à la portée des enfans et propres à servir d'introduction à l'étitude de toutes les langues.* Paris: Chez Delance et Lesueur. (Nouvelle impression en facsimilé de l'édition de 1803 avec un commentaire par Herbert E. Brekle et Brigitte Asbach-Schnitker 1975. Stuttgart Bad Cannstatt: Frommann.)

Vater, Johann Severin. 1801. *Versuch einer allgemeinen Sprachlehre. Mit einer Einleitung über den Begriff und Ursprung der Sprache und einem Anhange über die Anwendung der allgemeinen Sprachlehre auf die Grammatik einzelner Sprachen und auf Pasigraphie.* Halle: in der Rengerschen Buchhandlung. (Faksimile Neudruck mit einer Einleitung von Herbert E. Brekle 1970. Stuttgart Bad Cannstatt: Frommann.

–. 1804. *A. J. Silvestre de Sacy's Grundsätze der allgemeinen Sprachlehre in einem allgemein faßlichen Vortrage, als Grundlage alles Sprachunterrichts, und mit besonderer Rücksicht auf die französ. Sprache bearbeitet.* Nach der zweiten Ausgabe übersetzt, und mit Anmerkungen und Zusätzen, besonders in Rücksicht auf die deutsche Sprache herausgegeben von J. Sev. Vater. Halle & Leipzig: Rengeresche Buchhandlung.

–. 1805. *Lehrbuch der allgemeinen Grammatik besonders für höhere Schul-Classen mit Vergleichung älterer und neuerer Sprachen.* Halle: in der Rengerschen Buchhandlung.

*Bernd Naumann, Erlangen (Deutschland)*

# XXII. Ideas on the Origin of Language and Languages from the 16th to the 19th Centuries
# Vorstellungen vom Sprachursprung und vom Ursprung der Sprachen (16.–18. Jahrhundert)
# Conceptions de l'origine des langues et du langage du XVI au XVIIIe siècle

## 142. Les conceptions du changement et de la parenté des langues européennes aux XVIIe et XVIIIe siècles

1. Introduction
2. Les crises de l'hébreu langue-mère
3. Vers un autre prototype
4. Leibniz
5. Vico
6. Turgot
7. La mécanique des langues
8. L'expansion comparative au XVIIIe siècle
9. Le sanskrit: les détours de la découverte
10. Bibliographie

### 1. Introduction

La linguistique de la Renaissance a légué au classicisme deux thèmes à partir desquels vont s'organiser les idées sur l'histoire et la parenté des langues européennes. D'une part, la nomination originelle des choses par Adam sous l'inspiration divine fondait une recherche postulant un principe de relative continuité de l'évolution. S'y associait un principe d'unité dans la mesure où l'épisode de Babel avait épargné le parler d'Heber et se comprenait comme la 'division' d'un archétype en idiomes susceptibles de conserver quelque chose de la parole primitive. L'harmonisation des langues du monde fut d'abord fondée sur la théorie de la monogenèse hébraïque, qui traversa dès le XVIe siècle différentes crises appelées à s'amplifier considérablement au siècle suivant. D'autre part, l'épisode de Babel était propre à symboliser la brutalité des ruptures affectant une évolution qui s'apparentait davantage à une révolution perpétuelle. L'anarchie des variations historiques trouvait son équivalent spatial dans l'infinie diversité des idiomes.

Les XVIIe et XVIIIe siècles résolurent les tensions essentielles qu'induisaient les thèmes d'Adam et de Babel en élaborant des modes originaux de conciliation, qui mirent en évidence le 'génie', la 'mécanique' ou la structuration grammaticale des langues (Coseriu 1970–72). On se limitera ici aux investigations portant sur l'origine et l'organisation des familles indo-européenne et finno-ougrienne.

### 2. Les crises de l'hébreu langue-mère

#### 2.1. Le regain des rivalités

La théorie de la monogenèse hébraïque, dénuée de fondement explicite dans les Écritures, avait été contestée dès l'époque de sa cristallisation, du IIIe au Ve siècle, par des Pères dissidents. Pour Théodoret, les premiers noms propres mentionnés dans la Bible appartiennent au syriaque, qui désigne par *Adam* la "terre rouge", par *Abel* le "deuil", etc. Le nom d'*Heber* signifierait "qui traverse le fleuve": en quoi il traduit la nature foncière des juifs, imigrés ayant progressivement abandonné le privilège de la langue élue en même temps que leur patrie. La thèse de la primauté syriaque sera ravivée dans la littérature maronite des grammairiens Georges Amira (1596) et Jean Gaspard Myricaeus (1620). Certains orthodoxes chercheront la conciliation. Claude Duret, dans son *Trésor de l'histoire des langues de cet univers* de 1613, et l'érudit Athanase Kircher, dans son *Oedipus aegyptiacus* de 1652–54, considèrent hébreu et syriaque comme deux formes d'un même idiome: la première, 'doctrinale', est instrument sacré de la Révélation; la seconde, 'usuelle', servait à la communication courante.

Ailleurs, et particulièrement en Italie, "on soutient désormais que la langue araméenne est l'idiome à partir duquel les branches hébraïques et chaldéennes se sont différenciées, c'est-à-dire que l'hébreu n'a pas été la première langue" (Demonet 1992). On rappelle qu'au XVIe siècle déjà, Giambullari avait présenté l'hébreu et l'étrusque comme des langues soeurs remontant à l'araméen.

D'une façon générale, l'exploration des langues sémitiques aura pour conséquence de réduire le caractère privilégié de l'hébreu par la comparaison avec le phénicien, le copte ou l'éthiopien, dont l'antiquité suprême sera défendue par Mariano Vittori au milieu du XVIIe siècle.

### 2.2. Joseph Scaliger: haro sur les monogénèses

On doit à Joseph-Juste Scaliger d'avoir ouvert l'ère du soupçon méthodique, en matière de changement et de parenté linguistiques. Comme Théodoret, il situe en Assyrie le berceau indiscutable de l'humanité. "Là demeura la postérité d'Adam, avant le déluge" (Scaliger 1627, correspondance de 1607–1608 avec Richard Thomson et Stéphane Ubertus). Dégénérée dans le pays même, "par le commerce et le négoce avec des populations extérieures", la langue fut exportée en Phénicie, avant d'être adoptée et corrompue davantage encore par les juifs de Palestine. Leur parler n'offre ainsi qu'un rapport éloigné avec l'idiome primitif puisqu'il résulte d'une série de mélanges.

La *Diatriba de Europaeorum linguis* de 1599, publiée en 1610, étend la critique à tout monogénétisme. Scaliger y écrit par défi – en dépit des évidences apportées par le comparatisme de la Renaissance – qu'"aucune parenté" n'unit les quatre familles majeures et les sept groupes mineurs de langues qu'il inventorie (Zeller 1967: 30–31). Qu'il n'existe *nulla cognatio* entre les parlers slaves qui disent *boge* pour "Dieu" et les langues germaniques qui ont des formes de *godt*, passe encore. Le Praguois Gelenius, avait pourtant établi dès 1537 *la concorde de quatre langues européennes familières, à savoir le grec, latin, germanique et slavon.* Qu'aucun apparentement ne lie grec et latin était, par contre, quasiment insoutenable. L'*Hellenismos* d'Angelo Canini avait parfaitement dégagé, dès 1555, des correspondances lexicales donnant lieu à des règles précises. L'actualité linguistique du début du XVIIe siècle fournissait maint démenti au paradoxe de Scaliger. En 1609, Christian Becmann compare grec et latin en soulignant des correspondances phonétiques du type *huper-super* et en dirigeant l'attention vers la morphologie (*De originibus latinae linguae*).

Le refus même de la *cognatio*, tel qu'exprimé par Scaliger, trahissait la conscience de l'appareil comparatif qui se mettait en place. La *Diatribe* récusait à juste titre de trop faciles apparentements *in verbis*, dans le vocabulaire. Mais elle y joignait un type de rapprochement plus sophistiqué, en enveloppant dans sa critique les correspondances *in analogia*, orientées vers la morphologie et la grammaire.

## 3. Vers un autre prototype

### 3.1. Cluvier: origine perdue et reconstruction

Philipp Clüver écrit dans la *Germania antiqua* de 1616: "La langue primitive qui existait avant le déluge ne subsiste aujourd'hui nulle part; par contre, elle reviendra dans une vie future et heureuse" (*Index*). Une déclaration analogue, également célèbre, figure dans les *Annotations sur le Vieux et le Nouveau Testament* de Grotius, 1644.

Chez Cluvier, la contestation invoquait avec une force nouvelle l'*originarité* foncière des parlers germaniques. Les concordances depuis longtemps observées entre ceux-ci et le latin ne peuvent résulter d'un simple transfert, d'un emprunt. Une langue adopte des dénominations étrangères quand il s'agit d'aromates, d'oiseaux exotiques ou "d'autres choses qui viennent de loin" (Cluvier 1616: 73 sv.). Mais on ne va pas chercher ailleurs les noms des "choses et actions présentes dans une nation dès le commencement de celle-ci". "Qui se hasarderait à imaginer que les Germains n'avaient pas de mots pour de telles réalités, jusqu'à ce qu'ils les reçoivent de quelque peuple extérieur?". Et "croira-t-on, s'ils avaient des mots à eux, qu'ils les aient par la suite changé pour d'autres?".

Il faut donc bien que ces rapports entre *deus*, *theos* et le *dan* des Germains, entre *oculus*, l'allemand *Auge* et le russe *oko*, renvoient à un prototype non formellement identifiable à telle ou telle langue, mais devant faire l'objet d'une vaste entreprise de comparaison.

Cluvier ne pousse pas très loin l'enquête: les exemples limités qu'il fournit font d'autant mieux ressortir la part d'ombre, et pour ainsi dire de mystère, qui entoure la secrète logique de l''harmonie des langues'. La morphologie, à nouveau, y occupe la place la plus haute, la plus significative – car les conjugaisons, à la différence du nom du safran ou du colibri, ne voyagent pas. Certains avaient fait remarquer l'analogie unissant l'allemand *sein* et le grec *einai*. Suivons la randonnée des ressemblances. "A *eimi* est semblable le *sum* des Latins", comme aussi l'anglais *am*, "encore plus proche", tandis que "le *sum* latin est *gsem* chez les Sarmates" (Cluvier 1616: *ibid.*). D'ailleurs, "*es* se dit chez eux *sy* et *jestes*". Curieuse, aussi, cette analogie entre *sunt* et le polonais *sa*, surtout si on observe que le mot "sonne presque comme *son*". Impératifs, subjonctifs multiplient les échos.

L'archéologie des langues avait jusqu'alors obéi, pour l'essentiel, au souci d'identifier la langue primitive avec tel parler déterminé. Chez Cluvier se dessine véritablement le principe d'une participation multiple à la reconstruction de l'ancêtre commun. En même temps se met en place, dans la définition d'un nouveau prototype d'homme européen, un dispositif d'émulation ou de rivalité dirigé contre le modèle culturel méditerranéen, et au delà contre les privilèges de l'Hébreu. Ceci donnera lieu aux relations ambiguës qu'entretiendront familles sémitique et 'aryenne', au sein de ce que M. Olender a appelé un "couple providentiel".

La dualité pourrait être prolongée en direction d'une opposition, plus profonde encore, entre la logique de la filiation et celle de l'invention de soi. La concurrence traverse tout l'âge classique, en associant notamment linguistique et droit. Comme dit Bodin, il y a deux façons, pour les peuples, de valoriser leurs origines: en remontant à un dieu ou à un héros législateur, ou en revendiquant l'autochtonie intégrale, une pure naissance à partir du sol – à partir d'un degré zéro où la nation construit la totalité de son être et fonde sur ce dynamisme la légitimité de son destin, de ses conquêtes, etc.

En Italie, les deux options se refléteraient dans les apologies de la filiation romaine, d'une part, et les théories dites "de la catastrophe", qui privilégient des origines liées aux irruptions barbares, principe d'une régénération libératrice (Marazzini 1992; Vanwelkenhuyzen 2000). Un contraste analogue caractérise au XVIII^e siècle la polémique opposant les 'romanistes', partisans d'un enracinement foncièrement latin du *peuple* français et de sa langue, l'autorité royale remontant à l'Empire, et les 'germanistes', pour qui la *nation* et son aristocratie trouvent leur fondation dans la rupture que constitue la conquête de l'empire par les Francs. Dans ce cas, la filiation implique adaptation et changement, tandis que la théorie de la régénération tend à préserver la pureté retrouvée de l'origine. L'abbé Dubos, défenseur des vertus du métissage, qui fait les peuples forts, se fait l'interprète du 'romanisme'; Levesque de La Ravalière, porteur de l'idéologie nobiliaire, récuse l'origine latine du français.

### 3.2. La parenté germano-persane

Des témoignages de voyageurs faisaient périodiquement état, depuis le moyen âge, des curieuses ressemblances unissant des langues de l'Orient aux parlers germaniques. A la fin du XVI^e siècle, un collaborateur de l'imprimeur Christophe Plantin à Anvers, François Ravlenghien, ou Raphelengius, découvre les correspondances unissant à leur équivalent flamand les noms persans de la "dent", de la "lune", du "frère", etc. Il communiqua sa trouvaille à Juste Lipse, qui la popularisa en 1602 dans la *troisième centurie* de ses *Lettres aux Belges* (n° 44). L'idée d'un apparentement se répandit comme traînée de poudre. Au milieu du siècle, un orientaliste, Andreas Müller, prétendait par boutade que "tout vers écrit par un Persan peut être compris d'un Germain" (Leibniz 1718: 152).

Certains entreprirent avec enthousiasme la chasse aux analogies. Le plus connu fut Johann Elichmann, médecin de Leyde. Une brigade internationale d'érudits – philologues, astronomes, théologiens – se mit à déchiffrer des concordances qui n'étaient pas sans toucher aux matières de foi, quand ces similitudes redoublaient celles que découvrait l'histoire comparée des religions. Ce n'est donc pas un hasard si l'interrogation sur la parenté germano-persane est notamment illustrée dans des dissertations traitant de *Frea et Wodan*, la Vénus et le Mars des Germains (par Christophe Arnold, 1651), ou dans des ouvrages comme l'*Histoire religieuse des anciens Perses* de Thomas Hyde (1700).

### 3.3. La thèse scythique en personne: Boxhorn

C'est également à propos d'une question de mythologie que Marc-Zuer Boxhorn, professeur à Leyde, rédige la dissertation cristal-lisant l'hypothèse d'une commune origine 'irano-européenne' des langues occidentales (Fellman 1974). En 1645 apparaissent sur les plages de Zélande, suite à un retrait des eaux, plusieurs stèles représentant la déesse celto-germanique Nehalennia. Boxhorn interprète son nom par une racine communes à diverses langues européennes. Embrayant sur l'hypothèse de leur commune origine, il lui consacre en 1647 une dissertation, en flamand, qui traite notamment des questions suivantes: *Quels éléments montrent que grec, latin et germanique viennent des Scythes? Comment expliquer qu'une si grande différence sépare ces langues si Grecs, Romains et Germains utilisent en fait un seul et même idiome?*

La démonstration d'apparentement est en tous points remarquable. Aux concordances lexicales, Boxhorn joint résolument les correspondances morphologiques. Il souligne l'unité profonde de ces langues en matière de finales d'infinitif ou de formation des participes présents, comparatifs et diminutifs "Que les peuples en question aient appris leur langue d'une seule mère, c'est ce qui ressort également de leur manière ordinaire de varier les mots et les noms, comme dans les *déclinaisons*, les *conjugaisons*, etc.; et même dans les anomalies" (1647: 80–85). Cette 'mère' ne pouvait être qualifiée que de 'scythique', conformément à une tradition remontant au moins à Isidore de Séville.

Collègue de Boxhorn à Leyde, Claude Saumaise publia en 1643 un *De hellenistica commentarius* où il proposait des formes hypothétiques rendant compte de la ressemblance entre les noms de nombre, en grec, allemand et perse. Mais l'alliance avec Boxhorn, qui aurait pu devenir décisive, fit naufrage, pour de sourdes raisons d'appartenance clanique où s'entremêlaient divergences idéologiques et rivalités professorales. Ces idées, pourtant, revinrent périodiquement sur le devant de la scène. Dans les *Discussions mensuelles* de Wilhelm Ernst Tentzel, un interlocuteur déplore en 1690 les errements étymologiques de Boxhorn, mais un autre lui répond que "son opinion principale n'en demeure pas moins juste, quand il prétend que la langue des Scythes, c'est-à-dire le gothique ou vieux germanique, est langue-souche" (Droixhe 1989: 377).

## 4. Leibniz

Wilhelm Gottfried Leibniz se voit traditionnellement réserver une place importante dans l'histoire des idées sur l'évolution et la parenté des langues. Volney écrivait déjà en 1819, dans son *Discours sur l'étude philosophique des langues*: "Ce ne fut que vers 1710 qu'un homme d'un esprit simple et droit, sortant de la route commune, émit les premières idées judicieuses sur la manière de poser la question de l'étude des langues; cet homme fut Guillaume Leibniz" (Volney 1826: t. 1, 467–469).

On invoque souvent, à la base, un rejet ou une mise en cause radicale de l'hébreu langue-mère. Leibniz montre en fait une attitude pour le moins diplomatique. Recevant le *Glossarium universale hebraicum* du P. Thomassin (1697), qui répète la thèse monogénétique, il écrit à ses correspondants: "Je n'arrive pas à me persuader que l'hébreu est la langue primitive" (Schulenburg 1973: 69–70). La balance paraît pencher dans l'autre sens, dans un de ses principaux écrits linguistiques, le *Bref essai sur l'origine des peuples principalement déduite des indications fournies par les langues* (*Brevis designatio meditationum de originibus gentium, ductis potissimum ex indicio linguarum*, 1710). On y concède: "il se peut que l'hébreu conserve mieux que les autres langues les vestiges les plus archaïques, puisque nous ne possédons d'aucun peuple de livres plus anciens" (Jacob 1973: 46 sv.).

C'est que le rêve d'une conciliation universelle est têtu. R. Schwab traduisait sans doute un peu brutalement l'intervention de Leibniz quand il écrivait que celui-ci évince l'hébreu 'au profit de l'allemand'. Disons qu'une sorte de légitimité scientifique se trouve désormais conférée à la rivalité. Cette "scientificité" sera notamment fondée sur la capacité des langues à délivrer des vues importantes concernant l'histoire de l'humanité, ce que va autoriser une conception renouvelée du signe linguistique.

### 4.1. La nébuleuse celto-germanique

On peut considérer que la recherche de Leibniz sur l'harmonie des langues s'ordonne en une série de cercles concentriques ayant pour noyau un agrégat celto-germanique de caractère mal différencié. Que grec, latin et langues germaniques dérivent d'une même source 'japhétique' est une évidence que son ami Ludolf n'a pas besoin de lui rappeler au début des années 1690. Leibniz en fait la matière d'une lettre au P. Verjus, publiée dans l'*Otium hanoveranum* de 1718.

L'intégration des langues celtiques à cet ensemble relève d'une tradition qui traverse le XVII^e^ siècle. Celle-ci trouvait son origine dans la nuit des textes, et en particulier dans la *Germanie* de Tacite. Cluvier, en 1616, considère que Celtes et Germains parlent deux formes d'une même langue. Justus Georg Schottel imprime à la conception un nouveau tournant à partir des années 1640, en caractérisant cette unité par une structure spécifique de base (*fundamina, Eigenschaft*) que les Allemands, malgré le changement et la décadence qui menace toute langue, ont dans une large mesure maintenue (Metcalf 1953b). Ceux-ci, par l'observance de la *Grundrichtigkeit*, "conformité aux fondements", se distinguent des héritiers du latin, qui apparaissent très éloignés de leurs origines. Au groupe germanique se trouvent ainsi réunis, chez Schottel, l'écossais, l'irlandais et le gallois, qui montrent des racines analogues ou le même régime d'articles et d'auxiliaires. La fidélité linguistique est consacrée devoir national. Tacite n'avait-il pas souligné chez les Germains un vif attachement à l'intégrité physique de l'ethnie, hostile à l'altération par mélange avec d'autres tribus?

Leibniz se montre quelque peu embarrassé, sur la question des rapports entre langues celtiques et germaniques. D'un côté, quand il considère, dans ses *Nouveaux essais sur l'entendement humain* de 1704 (publiés en 1765), la célèbre version gotique de la Bible rédigée au IV^e^ siècle par l'évêque Ulfilas, il doit constater que cette langue, "très différente du germanique moderne", l'est "encore plus" de ce qu'on sait du gaulois ou de ce que montre l'irlandais d'aujourd'hui. "Cependant ces langues viennent toutes d'une source et peuvent être prises pour des altérations d'une même langue, qu'on pourrait appeler la *Celtique*" (Leibniz 1966: 240).

Dans les *Nouveaux essais*, Leibniz adopte et module un système de 'cercles d'apparentement' assez souple pour intégrer, en quelque sorte, les zones d'ombre ou de confusion que présente le savoir du temps. La notion de celtique regroupe plutôt ce qui serait commun aux Celtes, Latins et Germains. Un cercle 'scytho-celtique' étend la parenté vers l'est en ajoutant au noyau celto-germanique le domaine slave. Une aire plus proprement orientale comprend sous l'étiquette de 'scythique' le grec – détaché de sa traditionnelle fraternité méditerranéenne avec le monde romain. Ce dispositif, qui n'est pas sans analogie avec le mode d'organisation comparative de la 'théorie des ondes' ou d'Ascoli, maintenait une sort d'équilibre entre ses composantes, même si l'élément germanique y appraissait en position de pivot face au démembrement des langues classiques.

Le poids du centre celto-germanique s'alourdit brutalement dans le *Bref essai sur l'origine des peuples*. On y rejette vers la frontière orientale la notion de 'scythique', qui perd son avantageux caractère de concept prototypique pour désigner plus particulièrement un obscur conglomérat rassemblant les langues slaves, les parlers turco-tartares et l'ensemble finno-ougrien.

### 4.2. A la recherche du berceau européen

La nébuleuse celto-germanique laissait apercevoir chez Schottel l'unité d'un plus vaste domaine, qui engloberait l'étrusque, base du latin, ou le vieux 'moscovite', tandis que l'on maintient le perse, un peu trop étranger, à la porte de la famille. La question se pose en effet, désormais, avec une acuité nouvelle: qui est Européen? Ou autrement dit: qui est digne de se réclamer, historiquement, intellectuellement, racialement, des pères fondateurs?

Circonscrire l'espace privilégié des descendants de Japhet, fils de Noé, c'est d'abord tracer l'itinéraire suivi par ceux qui repeuplèrent le vieux continent après le déluge. Le chapitre IX de la Genèse, qui dénombre ces premiers descendants et les peuples auxquels ils donnèrent naissance, demeure chez beaucoup d'érudits l'inévitable grille de référence commandant la réflexion. A. Borst a consacré une grande partie de son magnifique *Turmbau von Babel* aux argumentations généalogiques privilégiant tel ou tel héritier de Japhet. Ceux auxquels on rattachait la famille germanique étaient les mieux placés: Gomer, le fils aîné, Gog, Magog et Aschkenaz, petit-fils et ancêtre traditonnel des Goths. La localisation du berceau de ceux-ci, qui implique progressivement l'origine des Européens, déchaîne une intense et complexe polémique. La thèse allemande et 'orientale', représentée par Cluvier, situe du côté de Gdansk et de la vieille Prusse, vers le delta de la Vistule, le premier siège des Goths avant qu'ils migrent vers la mer Noire. La thèse scandinave fait au contraire valoir la mystérieuse antiquité des runes, mise en évidence par Olaus Worm (1636), et l'archaïsme de l'islandais. Celui-ci permet à des auteurs comme Runolphus Jonas ou Olof Verelius d'éclairer tout le passé des langues du nord par la description grammaticale *in vivo* d'un parler moderne et par l'édition des eddas.

Deux auteurs développent la thèse scandinave à l'époque de Leibniz et suscitent chez lui polémique ou ironie. Olaus Rudbeck l'ancien a eu le tort, dans son *Atlantica* de 1675, d'élever l'idée du berceau nordique au niveau du mythe: la conscience de l'origine septentrionale aurait donné lieu au récit de l'Atlantide. L'adversaire n'est pas trop redoutable, même s'il montre une certaine méthode en matière de comparaison des langues. Georg Stiernhielm est d'une autre trempe. Président du Collège des antiquités suédoises, il a donné une exemplaire édition parallèle des Evangiles, dans le gotique d'Ulfilas et en version 'svéo-gothique, norroise ou islandaise' (1671). Lui aussi réclame pour son pays la primauté historique, dans son *Anticluverius* de 1685.

Ces idées retentissent dans deux dissertations universitaires illustrant de manière typique, comme l'a montré G. Metcalf, l'idée du prototype européen: le *De lingua vetustissima Europae scytho-celtica et gothica* du Suédois Andreas Jäger (1686) et le *Parallelismus et convenientia XII. linguarum ex matrice scytho-celtica Europae* de Michael Hepp (1697). On peut ici parler d'une 'école de Wittenberg' puisque ces traités furent présentés aux savants de la 'blanche Académie' sous la direction d'un même patron, le philologue Georg Kaspar Kirchmaier.

Non moins patriote, Leibniz s'oppose fermement à la thèse scandinave. Mythe contre mythe, le principe d'une origine située aux environs de la mer Noire caresse le plus l'imagination. Leibniz montrera donc les premiers Européens gagnant l'ouest suivant 'la course du soleil', comme s'ils forgeaient dans le devenir du voyage de conquête leur identité essentielle. Le philosophe de l'harmonie volontariste séparait ainsi de la 'nature' des langues la part de l'action et de la culture, accordant de façon magistrale donné brut et idéologie.

### 4.3. La tentation du primitif

Alos qu'il commençait à s'intéresser à la question des langues et à leur histoire, Leibniz était entré en relation avec deux érudits dont les entreprises et les découvertes hanteront sa correspondance (notamment avec Hiob Ludolf, spécialiste de l'éthiopien).

Le Suédois Bengt Skytte est mentionné avec Stiernhielm en tête de ceux qui "ont — vainement — cherché l'harmonie de quantité de langues" (lettre à Ludolf du 19 déc. 1687; dans Leibniz 1923–70: t. 5, 28–33; Waterman 1978: 19–21; Aarsleff 1982: 954). Cet homme politique en disgrâce occupait ses loisirs par la rédaction d'un grand ouvrage intitulé *Sol praecipuarum linguarum*, qui demeurera inédit. Il y alignait d'interminables listes de mots apparentés, dans des parlers aussi divers que le polonais, le lette ou le breton.

Leibniz fut aussi impressionné par les recherches du Hambourgeois Martin Fogel, qui établit la parenté finno-ougrienne dans son *De finnicae linguae indole observationes* de 1669, également resté inédit. Aux analogies lexicales, cette dissertation ajoutait la recherche d'autres types d'arguments, de nature grammaticale.

Malgré toutes les réticences et prudences auxquelles se sent tenu Leibniz, soucieux de ne pas *goropiser* comme Becanus, le souvenir de ces deux érudits entretenait l'espoir, ou le rêve, d'un élargissement comparatif touchant aux origines de l'homme, ce que H. Aarsleff a appelé l'*adamisme* de Leibniz.

Il s'agissait, dans une première étape, de tenter d'harmoniser les deux grandes familles linguistiques européennes, et donc de considérer l'éventualité d'un berceau commun. La correspondance avec le jésuite Adam Kochanski paraît localiser celui des Finno-Ougriens dans le pays des Bachkirs, de langue tchérémisse, là où l'imagination vient buter contre l'Oural, après avoir traversé le désert des Tartares. Un pont est lancé vers la Tatarie Crimée où ont longtemps survécus les héritiers des anciens Goths. "Chaque fois que l'on rencontre une sonorité identique ou quelque peu modifiée qui soit commune aux Bretons, aux Germains, aux Latins, aux Grecs, aux Sarmates, aux Finnois, aux Tartares, aux Arabes (ce qui n'est pas rare du tout), on est en présence d'une survivance de l'ancienne langue commune" (*Bref essai sur l'origine des peuples*; Jacob 1973: 46sv.). Un exemple est emprunté à Fogel: "tête" se dit "en finnois *pææ* [*pää*], en hongrois *fæ* ou *foe* [*fö*, *fej*], en gallois *peh*" (*Leibnitiana*, art. 46).

Les rapprochements s'enhardissent dans dans la correspondance avec La Loubère comme dans le *Bref essai*, quand l'enjeu devient celui de l'unité religieuse. Pour "ciel", le siamois dit *savang*, terme qui "pourrait avoir du rapport à *Taiwan* dieu des Finnois (si je ne me trompe)" (Leibniz 1923–70: t. 7, 553–554), tandis que l'harmonie providentielle éclate dans les autres désignations européennes: "le *debbessis* des Livonois; le *nebesit* des Esclavons, *nubes* et *nefelê* des Latins et Grecs, *nefoedd* du pays de Wales, le *menyegbe* des Hongrois". "Il existe un grand nombre de mots qui s'étendent de l'Océan atlantique jusqu'aux mers du Japon".

### 4.4. L'histoire des signes

Si le comparatisme semble nous conduire vers un langage commun et donc relativement naturel, comment concilier ceci avec l'extrême diversité des idiomes et l'arbitaire du signe qu'ils mettent en évidence? Comment, dans une perspective de progrès, unir cette puissance fonctionnelle de l'arbitraire, qui caractérise la seule parole humaine, et la mimesis des essences que doit établir la langue rationnelle, la 'langue parfaite'? Telles sont les questions que rencontre nécessairement Leibniz en dialoguant avec Locke dans les *Nouveaux essais sur l'entendement humain.*

Maintenir une primauté du signe naturel à la manière de l'ancien "adamisme" n'était plus possible. Le dépassement du cartésianisme linguistique implique un "renversement de la hiérarchie fondative entre signes de convention et signes naturels, l'arbitraire se trouvant privilégié en ce qu'il fournit une *grille d'analyse* et un *espace combinatoire à travers lesquels la nature va se donner en ce qu'elle est*" (Courtine 1980: 390). Ce "déplacement d'accent vers la priorité historique des signes" (Borsche 1990: 105–106) doit dès lors affronter le *casus*, le "hasard" qui produit la variation. Mais celle-ci garde l'empreinte d'un *affectus* qui a déterminé ou conditionné "les différentes modalités par lesquelles le réel se réfracte dans l'esprit des individus ou des communautés" (Gensini 1995: 65).

Une autre notion, émergeant dans des travaux du temps, médiatise l'opposition entre "naturel" et "arbitraire". Alors que Babel symbolisait plutôt l'avènement de la contingence dans le langage, une dissertation présentée à Wittenberg en 1664 par le professeur Johann Meisner et son élève August Zobell, *Sur la confusion des langues à Baylone*, réévalue l'épisode en refusant son caractère "privatif". L'intervention divine eut au moins cet aspect positif qu'elle produisit "différents tours d'esprit, correspondant aux différentes langues". Au même moment, Heinrich Kipping, dans un *Essai sur la première langue*, défendait de son côté la valeur intrinsèque de tout idiome, et par voie de conséquence de l'allemand, "très parfait" puisqu'il "exprime à sa manière les dispositions de l'âme" (Borst 1957–63: 1365sv.). Cet *habitus* que l'on nommera bientôt "génie des langues" sert non seulement chez Leibniz à motiver le signe lors de son institution, mais le langage dans sa phase "dérivative". Les ressorts de la primitivité se déplacent vers l'histoire et notamment – à nouveau – vers "la langue germanique", qui peut en effet "passer pour primitive" puisqu'elle conserve des "racines primordiales" dictées par "l'instinct naturel". Celui-ci apparaît aussi à l'œuvre, sous une autre forme, dans la pratique quotidienne où les mots sont d'abord, comme dans l'origine, les instrument d'une "pensée sourde et vuide d'intelligence" (Leibniz 1875–90: t. 5, 265). Ce sont l'échange et la communication qui instituent intégralement la signification, puisque l'on commence par "ranger les mots selon la coutume des autres, se contentant de croire qu'on pourrait en apprendre le sens au besoin" (Leibniz 1966: 246). L'expérience présente du *consensus* vient à son tour féconder le statut historique du signe.

Audacieuse entreprise "d'harmonisation totale", la linguistique de Leibniz sut "maintenir une rigoureuse correspondance entre la double *mimesis* (celle que retrouve l'étymologie et celle qu'instaure la langue rationnelle), entre le spectacle des choses et la langue des affects d'une part, et l'intuition de l'essence et la *lingua rationalis* d'autre part, entre le perspectivisme ou la scénographie des langues *vulgaires* et le géométral de la langue universelle" (Courtine 1980: 390). On ne peut mieux dire.

## 5. Vico: Pour un autre comparatisme

Comparé à Leibniz, et même par rapport à des exaltés comme Becanus, à des occultés comme Boxhorn ou des philologues spécialisés comme Stiernhielm, Giambattista Vico n'a pratiquement joué aucune rôle dans la constitution de la linguistique historique et comparée telle qu'elle se présente au XIX$^{e}$ siècle. N'a-t-il pour autant pas sa place dans l'évolution des conceptions sur la parenté des langues?

Sa célèbre théorie des trois stades et formes archaïques du "language", compris au sens large de "systèmes de discours" sur le monde, concerne plutôt l'histoire des théories de l'origine (voir la section adéquate). Mais la vision du primitif qu'approfondissent les trois versions de sa *Scienza nuova* (1725, 1731–1733 et 1744) implique à l'évidence, comme chez Leibniz, une révolution sémiotique engageant à son tour tout le passé des langues.

### 5.1. Les aménagements de la tradition religieuse

On a pu dire de la linguistique de Vico qu'elle demeurait foncièrement attachée à la tradition religieuse, sur les plans théorique et factuel. J. Derrida a opposé la persistance de la théorie de 'l'origine divine' chez Vico à la désacralisation à l'œuvre chez Condillac et Rousseau. D'autre part, le chapitre 23 de la première *Scienza nuova* réaffirme que l'hébreu conserve quelque chose d'une telle origine, puisqu'il "se distingue des idiomes des nations païennes en ce qu'il fut au départ et demeura par la suite le langage d'un Dieu unique, tandis que ces nations, bien qu'ayant aussi, à l'origine, conçu l'idée d'un Dieu unique, en vinrent à sa monstrueuse multiplication". Le chapitre 39 confirme ce privilège: comme on peut penser que la première langue fut chantée, ce dont on aperçoit des traces dans les tons du chinois ou dans la manière dont les sourds-muets essaient de prononcer les voyelles, les "vers héroïques" du livre de Job, plus ancien que celui de Moïse, "attestent à la fois la vérité de ce saint livre et l'antiquité de la langue sainte".

Les deux thèmes hérités de la tradition chrétienne connaissent néanmoins chez Vico des modulations plus ou moins sensibles. S'il maintient une adhésion formelle à la thèse de la révélation linguistique, au point de ne "même pas proposer un essai de médiation entre le récit biblique et l'histoire désacralisée de l'humanité" (Trabant 1989), le chapitre 23 de la première *Scienza nuova* lie l'apparition de la communication à l'amorce d'une 'conception commune de quelque divinité', de sorte que le langage, peut-on dire avec ellipse, a dû se développer d'une 'manière divine'.

Par ailleurs, son interprétation de Babel fait éclater le cadre de la monogenèse. Réécrivant la *Scienza nuova* en 1731–33, Vico distingue deux types de punition infligée aux bâtisseurs de la tour. Parce qu'ils sont demeurés monothéistes, les Sémites ont gardé leur caractère d'humanité et la faculté de parler, même s'ils ont perdu l'unité linguistique. Les descendants de Cham et de Japhet ont dégénéré dans le polythéisme et la bestialité. Aussi durent-ils, après avoir erré "à travers la grande forêt vierge" du monde occidental, pendant "au moins deux siècles", réinventer le langage par eux-mêmes selon le plan établi par la théorie des trois âges. Les étymologistes ayant favorisé l'hébreu se sont donc trompés sur toute la ligne (*Annotazioni alla tavola cronologica*, 1744). La langue sainte ne peut plus organiser autour de sa 'pureté' disparue la généalogie sémitique. Celle des parlers européens est à reconstruire indépendamment de toute référence orientale, puisque "les choses ont marché différemment".

Cet affranchissement des enfants de Japhet ne s'accompagne chez Vico d'aucune indulgence particulière pour les pionniers de la désacralisation. Becanus et son 'cimbrique' primitif, Rudbeck et la généalogie scandinave de l'Europe sont renvoyés à leurs chimères (livre II, section 2, chap. 4). Tout ici est *boria*: pure arrogance.

### 5.2. Du langage civil au discours des mythes

On voit que Vico partage avec Leibniz plusieurs positions caractéristiques d'une époque de transition, en 'rupture douce' avec l'âge précédent. Leur cousinage est peut-être plus intime, comme l'ont souligné G. Modica, A. Pennisi et d'autres, dans la mesure où une relation dialectique unit également ce qu'E. Coseriu a considéré comme les deux tendances fondamentales dominant l'histoire de la philosophie du langage: la discussion sur le rapport entre mots et référents, et la réflexion sur la fonction communicative de la parole. Pour Vico, la vérité du *logos*, que recherche l'*étymologie*, n'est saisissable que quand la représentation du monde se trouve testée dans la société, pour prendre la forme d'un *dialogos*. Comme toute vérité, celle du langage obéit à la loi quasi existentialiste du faire et du vécu social. L'historien a dès lors pour tâche de retrouver à travers les 'universaux fantastiques' que véhiculent les langues les principes d'action collective régissant les systèmes culturels qu'elles reflètent, notamment en matière d'organisation juridique des fonctions productives. La communauté des besoins humains refonde une autre convergence universelle des langues, dont les différentes manières (*guise*) d'appréhender et de construire la réalité dessinent à l'horizon un un même *dizionare mentale*. Les archives de la parole nous restituent ainsi le scénario idéal des débuts de l'humanité. Par d'autres voies, Vico retrouvait l'essentiel de l'historicisme de Leibniz, ici infléchi vers le questionnement structurel des mythes, au prix d'un abandon du comparatisme strictement linguistique.

## 6. Turgot

### 6.1. Théorie du signe et primitivisme

Avec Leibniz et Vico, Turgot fut peut-être le plus important théoricien d'un étymologisme conçu comme instrument privilégié de la connaissance des cultures anciennes. Cette histoire des signes appliquée à déchiffrer les systèmes de pensée qu'elles recouvrent, Turgot l'appelle 'métaphysique expérimentale'.

De telles conceptions participent évidemment de la sémiotique sensualiste développée en France par Condillac. On sait comment le fameux *Essai sur l'origine des connaissances* de 1746 (voir la section suivante) décrivit l'émergence du langage comme une conquête strictement progressive et pour ainsi dire 'holistique' mettant en œuvre une capacité séminale de fixer par les mots les éléments fuyants du réel. Parmi les premiers commentateurs de Condillac, Maupertuis radicalisa un procès d'objectivation qui laissait se constituer, dans les différentes langues, divers 'plans d'idées' par une combinatoire de notions simples, de type mathématique, où pouvait subsister quelque chose des 'essences' d'autrefois. Turgot poussa plus loin le principe d'une absolue solidarité dialectique entre formation de l'idée et genèse du signe. Le mot, dans l'origine n'était pour lui qu'une sorte de marque approximative appartenant à un réseau dynamique, mobile, constitué d'autres marques aux contours incertains. La définition du mot devenait le produit d'une histoire.

Pareille plasticité fonctionnelle des premiers systèmes linguistiques s'accordait bien à l'image d'un précieux jaillissement de représentations sauvages. En 1760 paraissaient les poèmes d'Ossian, dans lesquels Turgot trouva la confirmation d'une idée chère, à savoir que 'l'air' et 'la situation du pays' sont invoqués à tort dans la différenciation des cultures et des langues. Il écrira dans les *Discours sur l'histoire universelle*, qui datent des environs de 1751: "Ce langage métaphorique qu'on nous donne comme un effet de la plus grande proximité du soleil était celui des anciens Gaulois et des Germains, au rapport de Tacite et de Diodore de Sicile", et "il est encore celui des Iroquois au milieu des glaces du Canada". "Tous les peuples grossiers" ont versifié "leurs actions les plus mémorables". "Tels sont les chants des sauvages de nos jours, ceux des anciens bardes, les rimes runiques des habitants de la Scandinavie, quelques anciens cantiques insérés dans les livres historiques des Hébreux, le *Chou-king* des Chinois, et les romances des peuples modernes de l'Europe" (Turgot 1913–23: t. I, 304–6).

La conception de la 'métaphore primitive' intervient dans un contexte assez différent chez Rousseau, dont le fameux *Essai sur l'origine des langues* met en œuvre la climatologie de Montesquieu en empruntant surtout ses références linguistique au monde méditerranéen et à la Bible.

### 6.2. L'invention de la loi phonétique

En soustrayant l'étude historique des langues à toute forme de psychologisme ou de sociologisme sommaires, Turgot renfermait le principe de leur diversité dans leur évolution. Le changement devenait l'objet essentiel de l'interrogation sur leur passé. Aussi Turgot était-il le mieux placé pour écrire l'article *Etymologie* de l'*Encyclopédie* (1756), dont la rédaction avait d'abord été confiée au président de Brosses, naturellement porté à traiter de l'origine plutôt que de l'évolution proprement dite.

Appliquant au changement linguistique le principe leibnizien de continuité, Turgot en dériva des règles méthodiques d'immédiateté et de proximité. Une étymologie doit prendre en compte les relations internes de la langue en question avant de chercher l'origine d'un mot loin de sa patrie, et notamment dans des parlers exotiques. Il s'agit ensuite de reconstituer la 'chaîne des altérations' en considérant que celles-ci sont fondamentalement particulières, sur les plans croisés de la géographie et de la chronologie. "Chaque langue, et dans chaque langue chaque dialecte, chaque nation, chaque siècle changent constamment certaines lettres en d'autres lettres, et résistent à d'autres changements aussi constamment adoptés par leurs voisins" (Turgot 1961; Zumthor 1958). On trouverait l'amorce ou l'illustration pratique de ce principe dans des écrits contemporains d'un extrême intérêt: le traité *Über die Grundsätze und den Nutzen der Etymologie* de Johann Nicolaus Tetens (1765–66) et les *Elementos etimológicos según el método de Euclides* de M. Sarmiento (1758–66).

L'exemple de Turgot fait bien apparaître la différence entre genèse de l'historicisme et constitution de la grammaire comparée. Sur ce second terrain, son apport est pratiquement inexistant, notamment parce qu'il tend à attribuer certaines correspondances à l'emprunt et au contact, au détriment de l'apparentement. Ceci n'est sans doute pas sans rapport avec la place occupée, chez le théoricien du libéralisme, par la notion polymorphe de 'commerce' (linguistique, économique). Une certaine idéologie bourgeoise doit aussi marquer sa conception du signe comme appropriation comportant une "valeur ajoutée" à la réalité brute. Turgot retrouve ainsi spontanément la fonction de transformation 'poétique' assignée par Vico aux désignations primitives et par Tetens à la créativité naturelle ou *bildendes Dichtungsvermögen* du langage.

## 7. La mécanique des langues

Dans ses *Discours sur l'histoire universelle*, Turgot utilise l'image de la 'mécanique' à propos des changements réglés qui affectent la parole. On se demandera d'abord dans quelle mesure cette idée de 'mécanique' a pu aussi conditionner les modalités de l'enquête comparative ou généalogique.

En 1751, l'abbé Pluche avance l'idée que la Providence, après avoir inspiré le langage à l'homme, ne peut que préserver un tel don en ménageant quelque chose de sa nature première (*Mécanique des langues*). "Ce qu'il était dans les premiers temps du genre humain, il l'est encore aujourd'hui" (Pluche 1751: 1–2, 42). La conviction chrétienne d'une relative permanence des formes primitives du langage, par lesquelles s'est transmise la Révélation, s'affirme également, peu après, chez Johan Peter Süssmilch (*Essai de démonstration que la première langue ne tient pas son origine de l'homme mais du seul Créateur*, 1756). On y invite à chercher dans les méthodes de création lexicale, déclinaisons et conjugaisons le reflet d'un "ordre divin" et "une preuve impressionnante de la perfection du langage". *Les éléments primitifs des langues* de l'abbé Nicolas-Sylvestre Bergier (1764) développent des idées analogues, tout en engageant – sous la bannière de l'hébreu – un projet comparatiste qui se fonde aussi sur la "mécanique des langues" pour affirmer l'absolue régularité de la variation.

L'année suivante paraissait un ouvrage qui accrédita beaucoup plus largement le principe d'une histoire du langage intégralement soumise à des 'lois' de type physique. La *Mécanique des langues* du président de Brosses décompose le passé de la parole en deux temps magistralement harmonisés. Le temps de l'origine est investi d'une rationalité phonomimétique ou phonostylistique débordant largement sur la vie ultérieure du langage. Le système d'explication de la naissance des mots étend son optimisme sur leurs 'dérivations' et changements, en repoussant l'apparent arbitraire des signes. La 'faute heureuse' de la théorie génétique légitime un projet d'*archéologue universel* constitué selon les règles d'une science expérimentale.

Sans ajouter grand-chose du point de vue de la comparaison positive des langues du monde, le *Monde primitif* d'Antoine Court de Gébelin (1773–82) servit surtout de caisse de résonance à cette annonce d'une science possible. Celle-ci est nommée au titre du volume II du *Monde primitif*: ce sera la *grammaire universelle ou comparative*, qui réclame des 'principes' et le 'flambeau de l'analyse', pour guider dans ce 'chaos' le chercheur 'environné de doutes, d'incertitudes et d'erreurs'.

Jacques Le Brigant fait chorus. Mais dans quel concert de chimères! Si tout n'est pas faux chez lui, presque tout est faussé par la celtomanie. Attentif à la réalité parlée, au langage enfantin, il soumet le galibi, pour le ramener au patois de Pontieux, à des jeux de 'transposition de lettres' qui feraient croire qu'il n'a pas la moindre idée de la linéarité naturelle de la parole. Il conçoit qu'il faille établir la généalogie des langues en tenant compte du fait qu'elles changent graduellement, par un mouvement 'lent et successif', mais il n'en tire pas davantage de leçon dans la pratique. Sa rêverie s'offre même la coquetterie d'entrevoir l'importance d'un mystérieux 'Hanscrit' – mais vu comme clef de la parenté entre celtique et chinois …

## 8. L'expansion comparative au XVIIIe siècle

### 8.1. Le domaine slave et l'Europe

L'unité de la famille slave se trouve bien établie, sur une base foncièrement lexicale, dans le *Dialogue de deux amis sur l'utilité des sciences et des écoles* de Vasilii Nikitich Tatishchev (1733). On y souligne à la manière de Leibniz l'importance de l'étude linguistique pour celle de l'origine des peuples. La comparaison grammaticale sera utilisée par le grand savant Mikhaïl Lomonossov sur fond de réflexion typologique relative aux diminutifs ou au genre des mots (notes pour une *Lettre sur la similitude et l'évolution des langues*, 1755). L'identification de la famille slave y progresse en direction des parlers "courlandais" des Lettons et Lithuaniens.

Le projet leibnizien d'exploration systématique des parlers de l'empire, tel qu'il avait été soumis à Pierre le Grand, ne cessera de hanter les esprits. En 1775, Chr. Bacmeister publiait à Saint-Pétersbourg un vaste plan d'enquête linguistique. Catherine II, qui avait dès auparavant eu l'idée de composer un dictionnaire universel, prit à son compte l'entreprise. Elle s'adjoignit la collaboration de F. Nicolai et de Peter Simon Pallas, le premier préparant une liste des langues du monde, le second se chargeant du classement des mots recensés. Le *Linguarum totius orbis vo-*

*cabularia comparativa*, limité au lexique, parut de 1787 à 1789 sous le nom de Pallas et par les *soins de l'Augustissime*.

8.2. Un modèle: la famille finno-ougrienne

La recherche sur les langues en Russie devait nécessairement, en dépassant le cadre des parlers slaves, mettre en éveil une extrême attention aux règles et conditions d'apparentement. L'inventaire produisit en particulier une image plus riche et plus complexe de la famille finno-ougrienne. Philip von Strahlenberg donnerait le ton dès 1730 dans son *Das nord- und ostliche Theil von Europa und Asia*, en pressentant "l'unité ouralo-altaïque affirmée avec éclat au milieu du XIXe siècle par Bunsen et Max Müller" (cité par J. Deny dans Meillet & Cohen 1952: 274). Cette unité se construit également, peu après, chez Tatishchev et G. F. Müller, dans des travaux qui resteront en leur temps inédits. On y agrège au noyau finno-ougrien l'océan de langues venant buter contre l'Oural, pour le surmonter ensuite et se perdre dans les plaines de la Sibérie: le mordvine des collines de la Volga, importé au début de l'ère chrétienne par des pêcheurs et agriculteurs finnois; l'archipel *mari* des Tchérémisses; au nord de celui-ci, les langues permiennes, avec les parlers zyriènes du pays *komi*; puis, derrière l'apparente cassure de l'Oural, les parlers "ougriens" du bassin de l'Ob. Quel espace ouvert à l'imagination, quand on constate en outre les ressemblances unissant cette famille à celle des Samoyèdes sibériens! Johann Eberhard Fischer, qui voyage au Kamtchatka dans les années 1740, rédige "le premier dictionnaire étymologique finno-ougrien de niveau scientifique" (Gulya 1974: 262–663): un *Vocabularium sibiricum* pareillement demeuré inédit, mais utilisé dans des ouvrages qui parurent vers 1770.

Cette année-là, le Hongrois Janos Sajnovics, publiait sa célèbre *Demonstratio idioma Ungarorum et Lapponum idem esse*, qui mettait en œuvre de manière exemplaire la comparaison grammaticale. Trente ans plus tard, Samuel Gyarmathi adopta la même méthode dans son *Affinitas linguae hungaricae cum linguis fennicae originis grammatice demonstrata*, sans guère recevoir plus d'écho que son prédécesseur. Ceci s'explique sans doute par la technicité et l'abord quelque peu vieillot de ces dissertations – typiquement rédigées en latin – à quoi s'ajoute le faible attrait que la fierté magyare pouvait trouver dans des rapprochements avec des 'mangeurs de poisson'.

8.3. La continuité scandinave

Le chauvinisme le moins raisonné continua de faire de nombreux émules de Rudbeck dans les pays du Nord. Le danois, dont Otto Sperling avait exalté en 1694 l'*antique gloire et les prérogatives sur les autres langues septentrionales*, se présente comme l'origine de l'allemand chez Erik Pontoppidan (1740–41). A la même époque, Johan Göransson fait remonter l'*Edda* de Snorri à des tables de cuivres gravées trois siècles avant la fondation de Troie.

Johan Ihre sut se dégager de ces excès. Ce professeur d'Uppsala publie en 1769 un *Glossarium suiogothicum* qui réaffirme l'intime parenté unissant grec, latin, langues germaniques, celtiques, slaves et persan. Il limite cependant l'ambition comparative au groupe 'moesogothique' (non sans une incartade du côté du gallois et du breton), parce que la méthode exige des faits rigoureusement situés dans le temps et des règles phonétiques pour les relier entre eux. Ce n'est pas Ihre, constate Charles Pougens dans son *Essai sur les antiquités du Nord*, qui prostituerait "son érudition à comparer avec les langues de l'Europe le chinois, le siamois, le péruvien" (1799: 75).

8.4. En Italie et en Espagne: Hervás

En dehors de l'auteur dont il va être question, l'Italie et l'Espagne des XVIIe et XVIIe siècles n'ont pas produit d'érudit qui se soit spécialement attaché, sur un plan technique et à certain niveau de généralité, à la question de l'unité historique des langues européennes.

G. Bonfante l'avait souligné. Ayant montré "une intelligence et une curiosité merveilleuses dans tous les domaines du savoir", les Italiens "abandonnèrent le leadership quasi exclusif, en la matière, aux pays du Nord", de sorte qu'ils "ne contribuèrent pratiquement en rien à une investigation tellement fascinante" (1953–54: 683). En seraient responsables: la focalisation sur la 'questione della lingua', qui conduisit néanmoins à "de nombreuses et importantes découvertes dans le domaine de la linguistique historique, du changement phonétique, de la dialectalisation"; l'emprise du modèle antique, qui concentrait l'intérêt sur la langue comme instrument littéraire; et la permanence d'une indifférence classique pour les parlers 'barbares'. Ajoutons-y que l'Italie ne fut pas aiguillonnée par la rivalité anti-hébraïque animant particulièrement l'érudition allemande, peut-être parce que l'opposition aux juifs n'y atteint pas le degré d'organisation consciente que connurent d'autres pays.

On doit notamment à Max Müller l'idée selon laquelle l'œuvre de Lorenzo Hervás y Panduro, né en 1735 à Horcajo de Santiago (Cuenca), constitue 'l'aurore de la linguistique moderne'.

Ceci résulte d'abord de l'étendue de la documentation. A la fin du XVII^e^ siècle, le plus grand inventaire de langues du monde, l'*Oratio orationum* d'Andreas Müller (1680) fournissait une centaine de spécimens du *pater*. L'*Orientalische und occidentalische Sprachmeister* publié en 1748 chez Chr. Fr. Gesner double le chiffre. Atteint en 1767 par l'ordre de Charles III expulsant la Compagnie d'Espagne, Hervás se réfugia successivement à Rome et à Cesena, où furent publiés en italien, de 1778 à 1787, son *Idea dell'universo*, qui met en œuvre plus de trois cents idiomes. Le *Mithridates* d'Adelung et Vater (1806–17) portera le nombre de langues recensées à près de 450.

Des vingt-et-un volumes que comporte l'*Idea dell'universo*, les cinq derniers, prenant en quelque sorte la relève des questions suscitées dans les tomes précédents par la création de l'homme et la population du globe, sont consacrés au langage. Le tome XVII, paru en 1784 s'intitule *Catálogo delle lingue conosciute e notizia della loro affinitá e diversitá*. Le volume suivant nous rappelle certaines étapes du développement du comparatisme antérieur, en traitant *de l'origine, formation, mécanisme et harmonie des idiomes* (1785). Le tome XIX (1786) envisage comment l'histoire du langage ouvre sur les formes les plus archaïques de la culture, en ce qui concerne la numération ou les divisions du temps. Une version espagnole du *Catálogo* parut de 1800 à 1805, sans que l'œuvre fût achevée.

Si les matériaux rassemblés par Hervás offrent pour la première fois un caractère 'vraiment universel', comme l'a souligné Antonio Tovar, l'essentiel serait ailleurs: dans la mise en évidence du critère grammatical pour l'établissement des parentés linguistiques. Les recueils antérieurs, en effet, n'avaient pas suffi à produire des acquis sûrs. Le vertige de la diversité avait plus souvent égaré que mis sur le droit chemin. Au début du *Catálogo* espagnol de 1800, Hervás résume ce que lui a appris l'expérience, à savoir que la classification des langues s'éclaire particulièrement par l'observation de l'*artificio gramatical*, "principal moyen dont je me suis servi pour connaître leur affinité ou différence, et pour les réduire à des classes déterminées".

Il en résulte une image assez 'moderne' des langues européennes. On crédite Hervás, en particulier, d'une identification du groupe celtique séparant opportunément la branche brittonique des parlers continentaux, même si le cornique se trouve mal placé dans le rameau gaélique. Le rôle des Celtes d'Espagne est également reconnu. La romanité du roumain est établie (Coseriu 1981). Hervás prit par ailleurs conscience de l'importance du sanskrit grâce au P. Paulin de Saint-Barthélemy, auteur d'une dissertation *De antiquitate et affinitate linguae zendicae, samscradamicae et germanicae* parue à Padoue en 1799 – un peu tardivement pour que Hervás en exploite les possibilités.

D'autres aspects de son travail apparaissent nettement moins tournés vers la modernité. Son classement des langues prétend répondre, même si c'est de manière formelle, à la question posée par l'épisode de Babel. Mais on ne peut nier que la rémanence religieuse produise ici encore un effet positif, puisque l'idée d'un noyau primitif inaltérable abrite, comme dans la longue tradition mentionnée plus haut, le principe de la priorité de la structure grammaticale. Plus étonnante est l'absence du principe et de la pratique de la 'loi phonétique', qu'avait si heureusement élaborés son compatriote Sarmiento, sans remonter à Nebrija ou Aldrete.

## 9. Le sanskrit: les détours de la découverte

On sait comment le marchand Filippo Sassetti, à la fin du XVI^e^ siècle, mentionna certaines analogies unissant italien et sanskrit, dans une correspondance qui n'est pas restée inédite jusqu'au XIX^e^ siècle, comme on l'écrit souvent. En 1725, le missionnaire protestant Benjamin Schultze relève le caractère 'purement latin' des termes de numération dans le parler *Kirendum*. Peu après, le P. Pons adresse à ses supérieurs, de la côte de Tanjavûr, un autre courrier soulignant l'intérêt que présente la "langue *samskrète* ou *samskroutan*", "la plus riche du monde" (d'après Beauzée 1786: 355 sv.). Publiée en 1743, la description d'un idiome à la structure grammaticale aussi parfaite donna lieu de croire, dans les milieux éclairés, qu'il s'agissait d'une "langue inventée par les brahmines pour être l'enveloppe mystérieuse de leur religion", comme l'écrit l'Ecossais Alexander Dow dans son *History of Hindostan* (1768: 23 sv.).

Ni la *Mécanique des langues* du président de Brosses, ni l'article *Samskret* de l'*Encyclopédie méthodique*, par Beauzée, n'inscriront l'ancien idiome dans une véritable interrogation historico-comparative. Le premier y voit l'illustration d'un principe régissant 'la fabrique du langage': "les hommes appliquent un petit signe vocal à toute une classe d'idées, à toute une manière de considérer les choses", avant de se démultiplier sémantiquement en "une infinité de dénominations des objets extérieurs", et ce signe, dénué de référence phyique, ne peut "exister séparement du sujet dont il n'est que la forme" (1765: art. 241, t. 2, 523–525). Fonctionnalité bien abstraite et sévère, par rapport aux mimétismes immédiatement convaincants dont nous instruit l'éternelle nature. Laissons cet appareillage technique "hors de la portée de nos recherche", solennellement "enseveli pour nous dans les ténèbres de l'oubli". Beauzée ne songe à l'en tirer que pour faire servir cette langue qu'il croit artificielle de "moyen de communication entre les savants de tout l'univers" (1786: troisième partie, II, 3). Voltaire, qui aime l'idée selon laquelle le christianisme aurait emprunté aux régions du Gange une partie de sa culture la plus archaïque, accentuera l'image d'un parler fabriqué par la malignité sacerdotale, et donc dénué de rapport généalogique avec les langues européennes.

On a souvent raconté comment le P. Coeurdoux adresse à son tour de Pondichéry, en 1767, un mémoire faisant état de 'curieuses analogies' entre celles-ci et la 'langue sanscroutane'. L'Académie des Inscriptions enterrera la communication, publiée quarante ans plus tard. Aussi bien est-ce en Angleterre que l'attention à la vieille langue de l'Inde va profiter de l'intérêt primitiviste dont Blackwell, Lowth et Warburton avaient été les initiateurs européens, dans la première moitié du siècle. Lord Monboddo ne peut manquer de mentionner le sanskrit dans une réflexion consacrant une séparation entre des idiomes 'primitifs' dénués de généalogie et des langues 'de civilisation' ou 'd'art' qui offrent l'image d'une "construction intentionnelle due semble-t-il, en vérité, non aux peuples en question mais à des groupes d'individus particulièrement doués" (*Of the origin and progress of language*, 1773 sv.). Comme le fera Carlo Denina dans sa *Clef des langues* de 1804, Monboddo se souvient par ailleurs de Saumaise, relevant l'analogie de certains termes "en teutonique, en persan, en grec et dans le dialecte grec le plus ancien, c'est-à-dire le latin" (1773: t. 1, 419 et 1774: t. 2, 531; Gusdorf 1973: 281–282). Rosane Rocher a rappelé comment Monboddo était un des auteurs favoris de William Jones, avec lequel il dîne en 1780. L'intérêt pour la question des origines linguistiques de l'Europe sera entretenue dans l'Angleterre de la seconde moitié du siècle par James Parsons (*Survivances de Japhet*) et John Pinkerton (*Recherches sur l'origine et les divers établissements des Scythes ou Goths*).

Ami de William Jones à Oxford, Nathaniel Brassey Halhed 's'étonne' dans sa *Bengal grammar* de 1778, de la 'similitude' unissant sanskrit, latin et grec "dans l'organisation fondamentale de la langue, les monosyllabes, les noms de nombres", etc. (Aarsleff 1967: 131, note 53). Une lettre de Jones au prince Czartoryski noue au même moment le bouquet des diverses découvertes et des courants profonds qui traversent les deux siècles.

> En réponse à vos questions concernant le point de savoir comment tant de mots européens se sont glissés dans la langue perse, je ne le sais pas avec certitude. Procope fait état, je pense de rapports considérables qu'entretinrent les Perses et les peuples du Nord de l'Europe et de l'Asie, que les anciens désignaient sous le nom général de Scythes. Bien d'érudits connaisseurs de l'Antiquité sont pleinement persuadés qu'une très vieille langue, presque primitive, était en usage chez les nations nordiques (Droixhe 1984: 13).

Volney conclura: "la langue de cette nation scythique" dont des générations d'exaltés nous ont battu les oreilles annonce évidemment celle "retrouvée par nos savants européens dans les livres sacrés de l'Inde" (*Discours sur l'étude philosophique des langues*, 1819; Marazzini 1984: 126).

## 10. Bibliographie

Aarsleff, Hans. 1967. *The Study of Language in England, 1780–1860.* Princeton: Princeton Univ. Press.

–. 1982. *From Locke to Saussure.* Minneapolis: Univ. of Minnesota Press.

Beauzée, Nicolas. 1786. "Samskret". *Encyclopédie méthodique.* T. 3. Paris–Liège: Panckoucke-Plomteux.

Bonfante, Giuliano. 1953–54. "Ideas on the Kinship of the European Languages from 1200 to 1800". *Cah. d'hist. mondiale* 1. 679–699.

–. 1956. "A Contribution to the History of Celtology". *Celtica* 3. 17–34.

Borsche, Tilman. 1990. "Die Säkularisierung des tertium comparationis. Eine philosophische Erörterung der Ursprünge des vergleichenden Sprachstudiums bei Leibniz und Humboldt". *Leibniz, Humboldt, and Comparativism* éd. par Tullio De Mauro et al., 103–118. Amsterdam: Benjamins.

Borst, Arno. 1957–53. *Der Turmbau von Babel.* Stuttgart: Hiersemann.

Coseriu, Eugenio. 1978. "Lo que se dice de Hervás". *Estududios ofrecidos a Emilio Alarcos Llorach* III. 35–58. Oviedo: Universidad.

Courtine, Jean-François. 1980. "Leibniz et la langue adamique". *Revue des sciences philososophiques et théologiques* 64. 373–391.

Dan, Robert. 1977. "The Age of Reformation versus 'Linguam sanctam hebraicam'. A survey". *Annales Universitatis Scientiarum Budapestinensis. Sectio linguistica* 8. 131–144.

Demonet, Marie-Luce. 1992. *Les voix du signe. Nature et origine du langage à la Renaissance (1480–1580).* Paris: Champion.

Diderichsen, Paul. 1974. "The Foundation of Comparative Linguistics: Revolution or continuation?". *Studies in the History of Linguistic* éd. par D. Hymes, 277–306. Bloomington. (égal. dans *Ganzheit und Struktur*, 288–319. München: Fink, 1976.)

–. 1976. *R. Rask und die grammatische Tradition.* München: Fink.

Droixhe, Daniel. 1978. *La linguistique et l'appel de l'histoire (1600–1800).* Genève: Droz.

–. 1984. "Avant-propos". *Genèse du comparatisme indo-européen.* N° spéc. de *HEL* 6. 5–16.

–. 1989. "Boxhorn's Bad Reputation". *Speculum historiographiae linguisticae* éd. par K. Dutz, 359–384. Münster: Nodus.

Eco, Umberto. 1993. *La ricerca della lingua perfetta.* Rome & Bari: Laterza.

Fellman, Jack. 1975. "On Sir William Jones and the Scythian Language". *Language Science* 34. 37–38.

Formigari, Lia. 1990. "Philosophies of Language in the Heyday of Comparativism". *Understanding the Historiography of Linguistics* éd. par W. Hüllen, 277–285. Münster: Nodus.

*Genèse du comparatisme indo-européen.* N° spéc. de *HEL* 6. 1984.

Gensini, Stefano. 1990. *Leibniz: dal segno alle lingue.* Casale Monferrato: Marietti.

Gusdorf, Georges. 1973. *Les sciences humaines et la conscience occidentale.* T. 6. *L'avènement des sciences humaines au siècle des Lumières.* Paris: Payot.

Gulya, János. 1974. "Some Eighteenth-Century Antecedents of Nineteenth-Century Linguistics: The discovery of Finno-Ugrian". *Studies in the History of Linguistic* éd. par D. Hymes, 258–276. Bloomington.

Haßler, Gerda. 1989. "Hervás et les théories linguistiques des Lumières". *Actes du 18e Congrès international de linguistique et philologie romane* éd. par D. Kremer, t. VII. 148–155. Tübingen: Niemeyer.

Hiersche, Rolf. 1985. "Zur Etymologie und Sprachvergleichung vor Bopp". *Festschrift J. Knobloch* éd. par H. M. Ölberg et al., 157–165. Innsbruck: Inst. f. Sprachwissenschaft.

Jacob, André. 1973. *Genèse de la pensée linguistique.* Paris: Colin.

Lakó, György. 1969. "M. Fogelius' Verdienste bei der Entdeckung der finnougrischen Sprachverwandtschaft". *UAJb* 41: 1–4. 3–13.

–. 1970. "J. Sajnovics und seine *Demonstratio*". *ALASH* 20: 3–4. 269–289.

Leibniz, Gottfried Wilhelm. 1875–90. *Die philosophischen Schriften* éd. par C. I. Gerhardt. Berlin: Weidmann.

–. 1718. *Otium Hanoveranum.* Leipzig.

–. 1923–70. *Sämtliche Schriften und Briefe. Allgemeiner politischer und historischer Briefwechsel*, 8 t. Éd. par Deutsche Akad. d. Wiss. z. Berlin. Berlin: Akademie-Verlag.

–. 1966. *Nouveaux essais sur l'entendement humain.* Paris: Garnier-Flammarion.

Marazzini, Claudio. 1984. "Langue primitive et comparatisme dans le système de Carlo Denina". *HEL* 6. 117–129.

–. 1992. "Carlo Denina e il paleocomparativismo europeo del Sei e Settecento". *Storia, problemi e metodi del comparativismo linguistico* éd. par Mario Negri & Vincenzo Orioles, 20–48. Pisa: Giardini.

Meillet, Antoine & Marcel Cohen. 1952. *Les langues du monde.* Paris: CNRS.

Metcalf, George J. 1953a. "Abraham Mylius on Historical Linguistics". *PMLA* 68. 535–554.

–. 1953b. "Schottel and Historical Linguistics". *The Germanic Review*, 113–125.

–. 1974. "The Indo-European Hypothesis in the 16th and 17th Centuries". *Studies in the History of Linguistic* éd. par D. Hymes, 233–276. Bloomington.

Modica, Giuseppe. 1986. "Sulla fondazione del linguaggio in Vico". *Bolletino del Centro di Studi Vichiani* 16. 335–344.

Muller, Jean-Claude. 1986. "Early Stages of Language Comparison from Sassetti to Sir William Jones (1786)". *Kratylos* 31. 1–31.

Olender, M. 1989. *Les langues du paradis. Aryens et Sémites: Un couple providentiel.* Paris: Gallimard & Le Seuil.

–. 1993. "Europe, or How to Escape Babel". *Proof and Persuasion* éd. par Anthony Grafton & Suzanne L. Marchand, 5–25. Wesleyan Univ. Press.

Pennisi, Antonino. 1987. *La linguistica dei mercatanti. Filosofia linguistica e filosofia civile da Vico a Cuoco.* Napoli: Guida.

Poppe, Erich. 1986. "Leibniz and Eckhart on the Irish Language". *Eightenth-century Ireland* 1. 65–79.

Pougens, Charles. 1799. *Essai sur les antiquités du Nord et les anciennes langues septentrionales.* 2e éd. Paris: Pougens.

Rocher, Ludo. 1961. "Paulinus a Sancto Bartholomeo on the Kinship of the Languages of India and Europe". *The Adyar Library Bull.* 25. 321–352.

Rosiello, Luigi. 1987. "Turgot's *Etymologie* and Modern Linguistics". *Speculative Grammar, Universal Grammar and Philosophical Analysis of Language* éd. par D. Buzzetti et al., 75–84. Amsterdam.

Scaliger, Joseph Juste. 1927. *Epistolae.* Leyde.

–. 1967. *Diatriba de Europaeorum linguis.* Dans *Opuscula varia.* Paris. 1610. (dans Zeller 1967.)

Schulenburg, Sigrid von der. 1973. *Leibniz als Sprachforscher.* Frankfurt: Klostermann.

Setälä, Emil Nestor. 1891. *Lisiä suomalais-ugrilaisen kielentutkimuksen historiaan* [Essai sur l'histoire de la linguistique finno-ougrienne.] Helsinki.

Simone, Raffaele. 1990. "Seicento e Settecento". *Storia della linguistica* éd. par G. Lepschy, t. II. 313–395. Bologna: Il Mulino.

Stehr, Alfred. 1957. *Die Anfänge der finnisch-ugrischen Sprachvergleichung (1669–1771).* Diss. Göttingen.

Stipa, G. J. 1974. "Sprachverwandtschaftsprobleme zur Zeit von Comenius und Stiernhielm". *ALH* 24. 351–358.

Swiggers, Pierre. 1990. "Le fondement cognitif et sémantique de l'étymologie chez Turgot". *Cahiers Ferdinand de Saussure* 43. 79–89.

Tavoni, Mirko. 1990. "La linguistica rinascimentale". *Storia della linguistica* éd. par G. Lepschy, t. II. 169–312. Bologna: Il Mulino.

Tovar, Antonio. 1982. "Mayans y la filología en España en el siglo XVIII". *Mayans y la Ilustración,* t. I. 379–408. Valencia: Publ. del Ayuntamiento de Oliva.

Trabant, Jürgen. 1989. "*Parlare scrivendo:* Deconstructive remarks about Derrida's reading of Vico". *New Vico Studies* 7. 43–58.

Turgot, Anne-Robert-Jacques. 1913–23. *Œuvres* éd. par G. Schelle. Paris: Alcan.

Vanwelkenhuyzen, Nadine. 2000. *L'étymologie romane en France et en Italie à l'âge classique.* Thèse de l'Univ. Libre de Bruxelles.

Veenker, Wolfgang, éd. 1986. *Memoriae Martini Fogelii Hamburgensis (1634–1675).* Hamburg: Mitteilungen der Soc. Uralo-Alataica.

Volney, Constantin-François de Chassebœuf, comte de. 1826. *Œuvres.* Paris: Parmantier & Froment.

Waterman, J. T. 1978. *Leibniz and Ludolf on Things Linguistic.* Berkeley.

Zeller, Otto. 1967. *Problemgeschichte der vergleichenden (indogermanischen) Sprachwissenschaft.* Osnabrück: Biblio Verlag.

*Daniel Droixhe, Bruxelles et Liège (Belgique)*

# 143. Vorstellungen über den Ursprung von Sprachen im 16. und 17. Jahrhundert

1. Rahmenbedingungen
2. Klassifikation und Binnengliederung
3. Beschreibung
4. Bibliographie (in Auswahl)

## 1. Rahmenbedingungen

Bei der Betrachtung der Vorstellungen über den Ursprung von Sprachen im 16. und 17. Jh. müssen mehrere, sich überschneidende Parameter in Betracht gezogen werden. Zum einen läßt sich die terminologische Grenze 'Sprache' vs. 'Sprachen' wissenschaftshistorisch gesehen in diesem Zeitraum nicht ziehen. Die Frage nach dem Ursprung von Sprachen stellt sich immer auch als Frage nach dem Sprachursprung; ontogenetische und phylogenetische Sichtweisen werden zumeist nicht methodologisch getrennt. Zum anderen wird, in Zusammenhang mit der beginnenden neuzeitlichen Reflexion über Sprache, nicht nur über verschiedene Ansätze der Spracherklärung nachgedacht, sondern auch, im gesellschaftshistorischen Zusammenhang, die Ursprungserklärung instrumentalisiert. Hinzu tritt die in Folge der Regression des Lateins als Wissenschaftssprache veränderte Erfahrung national begriffener Einzelsprachen, deren Anwendung legitimationsbedürftig erscheint. Des weiteren spiegeln sich in den Auseinandersetzungen mit der Frage nach dem Sprach(en)ursprung auch Primigenitätsdiskussionen einzelner Nationalsprachen, sowie Versuche, der eher konservativistischen Suche nach der Ursprache eine rekonstruktive Projektion auf eine *lingua uni-*

*versalis* entgegenzusetzen. Bei Betrachtung der jeweiligen Äußerungen zu dem gestellten Problem ist immer auch der Motivationshintergrund der Forscher zu beachten, denn, wenn auch die damalige Wissenschaft nicht in so streng unterschiedene Sparten wie die moderne Forschung eingeteilt wurde, so gibt es philosophisch, sprachvergleichend, politisch (irenisch oder bellistisch), religiös oder schwärmerisch begründete Folien, vor deren Hintergrund die einzelnen Äußerungen immer in ihrem über die sprachwissenschaftlichen Aspekte hinausgehend im größeren geisteswissenschaftlichen Kontext betrachtet und bewertet werden sollten (vgl. Dutz 1989).

## 2. Klassifikation und Binnengliederung

Grob lassen sich die verschiedenen Auffassungen über den Ursprung der Sprache wie folgt klassifizieren – ausführlicher bei Kaczmarek (1989: 69 ff.) –: Man findet zwei Hauptthesen, (I) "Der Ursprung der Sprache ist erklärbar" oder (II) "Der Ursprung der Sprache ist nicht [mehr] erklärbar". Unter der Hauptthese (I) müssen nun verschiedene Denkansätze unterschieden werden, die, je vor philosophischem, aber auch diastratischem Hintergrund, davon ausgehen, daß (a) der Ursprung der Sprache Gottes Werk sei, daß (b) der Ursprung der Sprache ein Werk der Natur darstelle, und daß (c) der Ursprung der Sprache Menschenwerk sei.

Ausgehend von der Annahme (a) wird diskutiert, ob Sprache von Gott dem Menschen vollständig entweder anerschaffen, geschenkt, eingeflößt (inditum-Theorien), eingegossen (infusio-Theorien), eingehaucht ([in]spiratio-Theorien), offenbart (revelatio-Theorie) worden sei oder ob er sie rational gelehrt (instructio-Theorien) habe. Daneben steht in diesem Interpretationsschema der Ansatz, Gott habe dem Menschen eine rudimentäre Sprache gegeben, die dieser erst entwickelt hat. Des weiteren wird gedacht, Gott habe den Menschen die Sprache unter seiner Anleitung oder auf seine Anweisung hin erfinden lassen (inventio-Theorien); oder aber Adam habe die Sprache unter Gottes Aufsicht erfunden; oder letztlich, Gott habe dem Menschen nur Sprachfähigkeit gegeben und die Einzelsprachen erlerne der Mensch.

Die Theorie, der Ursprung der Sprache sei Werk der Natur, differenziert sich in Überlegungen, ob entweder Sprache aus der Nachahmung der Natur oder aus Onomatopoesie, oder nur die Sprechfähigkeit der Natur entstamme.

Die Frage nun, ob der Ursprung der Sprache auf Menschenwerk beruhe, stellt verschiedene epistemische Implikationen zur Disposition. Zum einen wird angenommen, daß die Modalitäten des Sprachursprungs in der rationalen Psyche des Menschen begründbar sind, wobei der Mensch die Sprache entweder zufällig, willkürlich, genötigt oder vernünftig schuf. Zum anderen denkt man über den Ursprung der Sprache aus der Eigenschaft des Menschen, Sozialwesen zu sein, nach. Die Parameter der Entstehung sind hier das Individuum, die Gemeinschaft, das Gespräch, die Konvention (Vereinbarung), oder die absichtlose Gewohnheit. Des weiteren finden sich eklektische Auffassungen, die die Frage nach dem Sprach*ursprung* durch die nach dem Sprach*erfinder* ersetzen. Als mögliche Kandidaten treten hier Adam, spezielle Denker oder Dichter und auch Herrscher auf. Die jeweilige Auswahl kennzeichnet zugleich auch die Nähe oder Ferne zum Christentum.

Etwas abgeschieden von der obigen Strukturierung lassen sich Überlegungen nachweisen, in denen der Sprachursprung nicht mehr mit *Gen* 1,3 ("Dixitque Deus: Fiat lux") bzw. *Gen* 2,19 ("Appellavitque Adam nominibus suis cuncta animantia ...") in Verbindung gebracht wird oder nur am Rande eher beiläufig erwähnt wird, wesentlich, um sich davon abzusetzen. Frühere Bezüge wie auf das "Pfingstwunder" (*Apg* 2,1–15; noch einschlägig behandelt von theologisch interessierten Autoren, die in den einhundert Jahren zwischen 1530 und 1630 publizieren, wie Martin Luther (1483–1546); Jean Calvin (1509–1564); Rudolph Walther (Gwalther, 1519–1586), Pierre de La Primaudaye (*c. 1545), Gervase Babington (c. 1550–1610), Thomas Lodge (c. 1558–1625), Nicolas Gibbens (fl. 1601), Henry Ainsworth (1571–1622/23), Jacob Böhme (1575–1624), Godfrey Goodman (1583–1656) und John Mayer (1583–1664)) entfallen völlig, hingegen wird desweilen *Gen* 11,1–9 ("Turmbau zu Babel") instrumentalisiert (programmatisch etwa in Athanasius Kirchers (1602–1680) *Turris Babel, sive Archontologia* (Amsterdam 1679); dazu Leinkauf 1993) in Erwägung gezogen. Unter diese Gruppierung fallen Auffassungen, es gäbe elementare Zeichensysteme als Vorstufen zur Sprache, oder die Sprachentstehung sei synchron diastratisch verteilt oder die Sprachentstehung wiederhole sich ontogenetisch innerhalb des kindlichen Spracherwerbs (zu den in den Berichtszeitraum fallenden Isolationsexperimenten mit Kindern, die der schottische König James IV. (1473–1513) durchführen ließ, vgl. Campbell & Grieve 1982: 49–53).

Mit der obigen Gliederung überschneiden sich nun die jeweiligen Auffassungen nicht nur darüber, *wie* Sprache, sondern *was* im "Sprachlichen Urknall", genauer betrachtet, entstanden sei. In den meisten Fällen tritt die Sprache nach dem *Ursprung*, abgehandelt in den Vorwörtern und einleitenden Traktaten, zurück hinter der bestimmten Absicht, entweder phylogenetisch oder ontogenetisch, physikalisch oder epistemisch über Sprache instrumentalisiert zu reden. Kulminationspunkte in der Instrumentalisierung sind dann Übertragungen im Sinne sogenannter Nachweise, die jeweilige eigene Nationalsprache, oder die 'drei heiligen Sprachen' (Griechisch, Latein, Hebräisch), oder sogar das Chinesische, Phyrgische etc. zu Ursprachen zu erklären. Der Legitimationsanlaß hierzu findet sich in der Rezeption der Schriften von Flavius Magnus Aurelius Cassiodorus (ca. 485–580) und des Isidor von Sevilla (ca. 560–636), die der von den Kirchenvätern in ihrer eurozentristischen Bibelexegese vorgenommenen Sprach(en)beschreibung eine nationale Dimension zur Seite stellte, die in Utopien über die Ursprünge Europas ihren Ausdruck fand (vgl. hierzu Olender 1996: 944ff.).

## 3. Beschreibung

Obwohl schon Dante Alighieri (1265–1321) Ursprachtheorien und Sprachursprungstheorien verspottete (*De vulgari eloquentia*, I, vi, 2) und auch der 1664 exilierte Schwede Anders (Andreas) Pederson Kempe (1622–1689) in seinen *Die Sprachen des Paradises* [sic], *das ist Gegebene Anleitung der Natur zu erkennen, was vor Sprachen im ersten Anfange der Welt im Paradiese [...] geredet worden* von 1683 (Elert 1978 nennt das Jahr 1688) eine später viel beachtete Polemik (im Paradies sprach Gott Schwedisch, Adam Dänisch und die Schlange Französisch; dazu sowie zur Existenz des Textes Elert 1978) gegen die national-sprachlich orientierten Versuche vorlegte, finden sich besonders zwei Kernbereiche, in der die Frage des Sprachursprungs politisch instrumentalisiert wurde. Zum einen in Schweden, in Korrelation zu der damaligen Stellung dieses Landes als europäische Großmacht mit entsprechenden Ansprüchen. Als erster wäre hier Georg Stiernhielm (1598–1672) zu nennen, der schon vor der Zeit der babelischen Sprachverwirrung eine Entwicklung der sogenannten Ursprache annimmt und somit die Dignität dieser relativiert. Dies führt dazu, daß er das Hebräische dem Schwedischen gleichstellt. Das unterschwellig immer vorhandene eigentliche Interesse, die Aufwertung der Nationalsprache, wird bei ihm besonders deutlich. Allerdings erklärt schon Peter Bang (1633–1696) mit Hilfe pseudo-wissenschaftlicher Argumente die Schweden zu den ältesten unter allen nachsintflutlichen Völkern (vgl. Borst 1957–63, *s.v.*). Den Abschluß der Reihe der schwedischen Gelehrten mag Olof (Olaus) Rudbeck (der Ältere; 1630–1702) bilden, der seinen Zweifel an der hebräischen Ursprache mit dem interessanten Argument begründet, daß man dieser, wenn sie keinem Wandel unterlegen wäre, auch nicht den Rang eines historischen Dokuments zuschreiben könne, da sich die Urgeschichte der Völker in der Geschichte ihrer Sprache(n) abbilde. Im folgenden verfällt auch Rudbeck in absonderliche Etymologien, um seine These der Vorherrschaft der schwedischen Sprache und (eigentlich) Nation zu erläutern.

Eine besondere Variante dieser "autochthonen Linguistik" (Olender 1996: 945) verdeutlichte sich in den spanischen, später dann (1648) unabhängigen Niederlanden. Auch hier bildete der kulturell politische Hintergrund (Spannungen zwischen der Flämisch sprechenden Bevölkerung und der Vorherrschaft des Spanischen und Französischen im 'offiziellen' Gebrauch) und, zusammen mit religiösen Fraktionierungen (theologische Auseinandersetzungen zwischen den Protestanten bzw. Kalvinisten und den Katholiken), den Anlaß und später Hintergrund für die Heranziehung der Sprachursprungsfrage innerhalb der linguistischen Diskussion, die dann wiederum instrumentalisiert in den Vordergrund trat (vgl. Olender 1996: 945–947; Dutz 1989: 210–212), ein Diskurs, der sich bis in das 19. Jh. fortsetzte (vgl. Noordegraaf 1996). Die speziell niederländische Variante der Sprachursprungsdiskussion bezog sich vorderhand auf *Gen* 9,19; 10,20 – die Aufteilung der Menschen in drei Stämme, "ab his divisae sunt insulae gentium in regionibus suis, unusquisque secundum linguam suam et familias suas in nationibus suis" (*Gen* 10,5). Diese Aufteilung unter den drei Söhnen

Noahs, Sem, Cham und Japhet, wurde in der frühen Kirchengeschichte zugleich auf die griechische Mythologie (Kronos, Titanos und Iapetos) projiziert, wobei Japhet/Iapetos als kriegerischer Sohn des Uranos und der Gaia ohne weiteres als Vorfahr einer Sippe von Rebellen empfunden wurde. Vor diesem Hintergrund entwickelte Joannes Goropius Becanus (Jan van Gorp van Hilvarenbeek; 1519–1572) in seinen *Origines Antwerpianae* (1569) und in den *Hermathena* (1580) die nicht unumstrittene These, der Vorläufer des Niederländischen sei als das 'Kimbrische' zu identifizieren. Dies parallelisierte sich zugleich mit der Doppelbezeichnung des 'Japhetischen' als der Sprache, die nach Noahs Aufteilung im kalten Norden (sprich: Europa) gesprochen wurde. Goropius Becanus dreht die Argumentation bezüglich der Dignitität des Hebräischen einfach um, indem er zum einen behauptet, nur diejenigen, die am Turmbau zu Babel beteiligt waren, seien auch der Ursprache verlustig geworden. Da aber, so seine Interpolation, den Niederländern schon vorher durch Noah ihr europäisches Erbteil zugewiesen worden war, hatten sie schließlich auch keinen Anlaß, sich an diesem häretischen Unterfangen zu beteiligen. Mehr noch, Goropius griff ein Moment der Auffassung auf, daß der Ursprung der Sprache Menschenwerk sei ("Una igitur prima lingua fuit & ea quidem a viro, uti a capite, facta", *Hermathena* II,24): Die Ursprache ist einheitlich, einsilbig und präzise ("Perfectissimam autem eam dicimus quae quam apertissime, & quam brevissime, una cum sono convenientissimo, imagines animi, & carum compositionem dat intelligendas" (*Hermathena* II,25), und dies träfe in höherem Maße für das Niederländische denn für das Hebräische zu (*Hermathena* II,25). Folglich impliziert er den Schluß, daß das Niederländische auch der sogenannten Ursprache näher zu stellen sei, oder – auf die Spitze getrieben – die *lingua Adamica* darstelle, von der alle anderen Sprachen abgeleitet seien. Die Babel-Erzählung war hiermit eigentlich überflüssig geworden. Goropius hält an ihr jedoch, wohl auch aus legitimativen Gründen, fest. Zudem verfällt er in ein spekulatives Etymologisieren, was von den Zeitgenossen distanziert betrachtet wurde, jedoch zugleich, nicht sach- sondern formbezogen, eine bestimmte Methodik der lexikalischen Untersuchung initiierte, die später Anregungen für die Komparatistik lieferte.

Wie Olender (1996:947–948) ausführt, läßt sich auf diese Situation ein weiteres 'Paradigma' projizieren: Adriaan van Schrieck, Seigneur de Rodorne (Scrieckius Rodorn[i]us, 1560–1621/23) – dessen monumentale und heftig umstrittenen *Originum rerumque Celticarum et Belgicarum libri XXIII* (1614) von Morhof (1747: I,739) mit den Worten "in quibus bona multa sunt" qualifiziert wurden – begründete zusammen mit Abraham van der Myl[e] (Mylius; 1558/63–1637), Claude Saumaise (1588–1635), Jean De Laet (1593–1649), Marcus Zuerius Boxhorn (1602–1653), Georg Stiernhielm (Stjernhjelm; 1598–1672) und Andreas Jäger (gest. 1730) eine neue Forschungstradition, die die Annahme einer gemein-indogermanischen Sprachenwurzel praejudizierte. Olenders These ist so einfach nicht haltbar, da sowohl der Lebens(zeit)raum der Genannten stark divergiert, als auch deutlich wird, daß im Kontext vieler (aber nicht aller) Autoren es der Van Gorp'sche Terminus 'Japhetisch' war, der durch den Terminus 'Skythisch' ersetzt wurde. Es trifft den methodologischen Kern der Sache, wenn er schreibt: "Als Kunstprodukt spekulativen Forschergeistes konnte das 'Skythische' zukünftig beliebige begründungstheoretische Aufgaben erfüllen – der *bloße Name* genügte mehreren Wissenschaftlergenerationen als Rechtfertigung dafür, eine gemeinsame Wurzel der griechischen, lateinischen, germanischen und persischen Sprache annehmen zu dürfen" (Olender 1996: 948), es ist aber zu kurz gegriffen, da er übersieht, daß spätestens zum Ausgang des 17. Jhs. ernsthafte Überlegungen über die Sprachenverwandtschaften vorgenommen wurden, die durch gerade derartige Spekulationen überhaupt erst angeregt wurden und in den Ergebnissen der Sprachvergleichung des 19. Jh.s gleichsam münden.

Wichtig in diesem Zusammenhang ist festzuhalten, daß mit der instrumentalisierten Sprachursprungsdebatte in sämtlichen europäischen Ländern sprachvergleichende Studien angeregt, wenn nicht zur Mode geworden waren (vgl. die Überblicke bei Allen 1947; Bonfante 1954; Metcalf 1974). Die primäre Frage, die des *Ursprungs* von Sprache(n), trat zurück hinter die Frage nach dem (auf unterschiedlichem wissenschaftlichen Niveau) Vergleich der *Eigenschaften* von Sprachen. Dabei sind, ganz im Zusammenhang mit den oben schon beschriebenen nationalen Tendenzen auch unterschiedliche Tendenzen und Intensitäten zu beobachten.

Die Situation im deutschsprachigen Bereich stellt sich in diesem Zusammenhang differenzierter und komplizierter dar. Es gibt bedeutende Probleme, die einschlägige Literatur zu gliedern (Borst 1957–63,III.1: 1342; einen guten Einstieg bietet immer noch Morhof [1687] 1747: I,733–743). Auffällig ist, daß hier die Sprach(en)ursprungsfrage stärker als in den restlichen europäischen Ländern religiös motiviert oder legitimiert ist. Zudem läßt sich dieser Bereich diastratisch nicht als homogen beschreiben, so daß eher von Einflüssen über die jeweiligen Landesgrenzen zu sprechen wäre.

Eine Reflexion über die nationalsprachliche Legitimation der Sprachenursprünge setzt erst 1648, nach Abschluß des Westfälischen Friedens, ein und wird anfangs schnell auch mit den beginnenden rationalistischen und sprachvergleichenden Reflexionen verbunden. Die philosophischen Rahmenvorgaben der frühen Aufklärung (hierzu weiter unten) drängen das Interesse an dem Ursprung von Sprachen zu Gunsten der Beschäftigung mit der 'inneren' Konsolidierung und Normierung der jeweiligen Sprachform in den Hintergrund. Diachrone Aspekte werden im Abschluß dieser Entwicklung weniger legimativ denn 'philologisch' beigeführt. Man denke in diesem Zusammenhang auch an Joseph Justus Scaligers (1540–1609) *Diatriba de Europaerorum linguis* (1610; abgefaßt 1599; vgl. hierzu auch Dutz 1989: 212; Olender 1996: 948), an Georg Crucigers (gest. 1637) *Harmonia linguarum quatuor cardinalium Hebraicae* (1616) und an Franciscus Mercurius Helmonts (1614–1698/99) *Alphabeti vere rationalis hebraici delineatio* (1657; dt. 1667; vgl. Coudert 1996:9). Zu den distanzierten Betrachtern zählte auch Samuel von Pufendorf (1632–1694; vgl. Ricken 1985: 32–33).

In einer kurzen selektiven Aufzählung läßt sich die Entwicklung skizzieren. So knüpft der lutheranische Mystiker Jacob Böhme (1575–1624; 1955–61 [1730]) an die Idee einer Ursprache an, die er in Anlehnung an Paracelsus (Theophrast von Hohenheim; 1493–1541; 1976) *"Natur-Sprache"* nennt (vgl. Haferland 1989: bes. 115ff.). Böhme denkt sich die Sprache zugleich mit der Natur gleichsam in einer alchemischen Spekulation simultan entstanden, wobei die Elemente der Sprache nicht aus arbiträren Zeichen bestehend zu begreifen wären. Vielmehr kennzeichnet er 'arbiträres Bezeichnen' als "Resultat eines Vergessens, wie die Vielzahl der Sprachen das Produkt einer Verfallsgeschichte" (Haferland 1989: 89) seien. Böhme steht unter starkem Einfluß der Renaissance-Auffassungen über den Mikro- und Makrokosmos, in Folge z. B. des Giovanni Pico della Mirandola (1463–1494) und des Marsilio Ficino (1433–1499), aber auch der Lehre vom 'inneren Menschen' des Valentin Weigel (1533–1588) (vgl. Willard 1989: 146; zu weiteren Details der Böhmeschen Sprachauffassung vgl. Bayer 1977: 170–201; Benz 1936: 340–357; Konopacki 1979; Mendels 1953; Moulton 1952; kritisch zu Böhme auch Feinhals 1731). Ähnlich schwärmerisch äußerten sich der für andere Veröffentlichungen berühmtere Johannes Kepler (1571–1630), der Theologe Johann Valentin Andreä (1586–1657) sowie dessen Lehrer Christoph Besold (1577–1638).

Selbstverständlich lassen sich weniger spekulative Versuche zur Beantwortung der Frage nach dem Sprach(en)ursprung aufweisen. Sie sind, im Gegensatz zu den eher an der Ursprungshypothese von 'Sprache' orientierten Traktaten, als Studien konzipiert, die die Ursprünge einer einzelnen Sprache oder Sprachengruppe zu untersuchen versuchen, weniger deren "Ursprünglichkeit", obwohl eine derartige Auseinandersetzung sich in wesentlichen Teilen mit der Primigenität des Hebräischen auseinandersetzen mußte (zur Situation im 16. Jh. vgl. Percival 1984; Dán 1977; bereits der französische Arabist und Hebraist Guillaume Postel (1510–1581; vgl. auch Dubois 1994) stellte in seinen *De originibus seu de Hebraicae linguae et gentis antiquitate* [Paris 1538] erste Überlegungen zu einer typologischen Betrachtung der Sprachen an). Zu nennen wären hier in aller Kürze die *Ars etymologica Teutonum e philosophiae fontibus derivata* (1663) des Johann Clauberg (1622–1665) und der *Praecursor Logicus complectens Grammaticam audacem* (1654) von Juan Caramuel y Lobkowitz (1606–1682); Johann Heinrich Alsted (1588–1638; vgl. Flint 1904: 113–118) sammelt auf der einen Seite Sprachenlisten zur Eruierung der Sprachenverwandtschaft, vertritt andererseits die These von der hebräischen Ursprache. Auch für Justus Georg Schottel (1612–1676) ist das Hebräische die 'Ursprache', allerdings die *zweit*älteste aller Sprachen. Für Schottel stellt sich ähnlich wie bei Goropius Becanus die angebliche 'Monosyllabität' als Kriterium für deren Ursprünglichkeit dar. Von der Monosyllabität zur Affektentheorie, in der einfache 'emotive' Ausdrücke (vgl. Jakob Böhme)

Anlaß zur Sprachbildung sind, besteht nur ein kleiner Schritt, der – spekulativ – Morphologie in Semantik transformiert. Skeptischer ist da schon der "Apokalyptiker" Quirinus Kuhlmann (1651–1689), der den beginnenden rationalistischen Wandel von der historischen Ursprache über den Sprachenvergleich zur künstlichen Weltsprache zu ahnen beginnt, wobei sich bei ihm, wie bei Böhme, kabbalistische, mystische und ekstatische Elemente verbinden (zur Kabbalah vgl. Coudert 1996; Kilcher 1998; Lenoble 1943: 96–103; Skolem 1974: 196–203).

Zwar mit diesem schwärmerischen Denken verbunden und dennoch quer dazu zu interpretieren ist die Bewegung der 'Rosenkreuzer', die um 1614/15 auftrat. Diese historisch nicht unproblematische Bezeichnung verweist, je nach Interpretation, entweder auf eine okkulte Sekte der Spätrenaissance, die möglicherweise niemals existierte, oder fungiert pauschal als 'umbrella term' für Geheimbünde jedwelcher Färbung. In den unterstellten gemeinsamen Äußerungen läßt sich eine bestimmte Nähe zum Neoplatonismus (vgl. Coudert 1978; 1996) und zu Ficino wie Pico della Mirandola feststellen (vgl. Willard 1989: 135). Eine weitere Quelle stellt *De Occulta Philosophia* des Heinrich Cornelius Agrippa von Nettesheim (1486–1535) dar. Auffällig ist die protestantische Ausrichtung der diesen Zirkeln zugeschriebenen Sprachauffassung, zugleich ergab sich ein Streit zwischen den anonymen Verfassern rosenkreuzerischer Manifeste und den Anhängern des Paracelsus über die Herkunft und Originalität der Signaturlehre, die wiederum die Basis für die Arbitraritätsauffassung der Wörter in den Volkssprachen legte: Die Dignität der Sprachen bestimmt sich nicht mehr aus ihrem Ursprung, sondern aus der Art der Bezeichnungs- und Formungsweise, die sich stereotyp auch in den Sprachqualitäten 'Reichtum', 'Reinigkeit' und 'Glanz' (oder verwandten Formulierungen von Schottel bis hin zu Gottfried Wilhelm Leibniz (1646–1716)) wiederfindet. Des weiteren aber wurde mit dem Streit zwischen Rosenkreuzern und Paracelsisten die (teilweise kabbalistische Sprach-) Diskussion nach England (zur Situation dort vgl. Grazia 1978; 1980) übertragen. Robert Fludd (1574–1637) ergriff in verschiedenen Schriften die Partei der Rosenkreuzer, die er auch gegenüber kritischen Nachfragen Johannes Keplers und Marin Mersennes (1588–1648) beibehielt. Überhaupt wurde, wie das Beispiel Isaac Newtons (1643–1727) zeigt, der sich sehr wohl auch mit Alchemie wie kabbalistischen Sprachexperimenten beschäftigte, die Grenze zwischen rationalistischer und mystischer Sprachursprungsauffassung nie klar gezogen (vgl. dazu auch Webster 1982). Einflüsse auf Thomas Vaughan (1622–1666) und John Webster (1610–1682) sind vorhanden. Dagegen wurde von Seth Ward (1617–1689) und John Wilkins (1614–1672) gegen rosenkreuzerische Tendenzen und die darin enthaltenen platonischen Denkansätze polemisiert und als antipodisches, aristotelisches, Konzept das der künstlich geschaffenen Universalsprache favorisiert (vgl. Dutz 1989: 220ff.; Slaughter 1982). Als ein Beispiel für den aristotelischen Standpunkt finden sich ebenfalls schon die Auffassungen bei Pietro Pomponazzi (1462–1525; vgl. Nuchelmans 1992: 113–114), die auf ein frühaufklärerisches Bildungsideal hinauslaufen.

Zudem lassen sich Rezeptionsstränge zwischen Fludd und dem oben genannten Andreä nachweisen. In dessen Auseinandersetzung mit Theophilus Schweighar[d]t (*fl.* Konstanz 1618–20) gewann im Rahmen der Sprachenursprungsdiskussion ein bestimmter Terminus an Bedeutung, den der italienische Philosoph Francesco da Cherso Patrizi (Franciscus Patritius; 1529–1597) popularisiert hatte: Pansophia.

Hier ist vor allem Jan Amos Komenský (Comenius; 1592–1670) zu erwähnen. Comenius gelingt der Übergang von der konservatistischen Vorstellung einer Ursprache wie dem Hebräischen zur Determinierung einer utopistischen Vorstellung einer *lingua universalis*, indem er den jeweiligen, aus der Betrachtung der Sprachursprungsfrage gewonnenen Einsichten bestimmte Aufgabenbereiche zuweist. Neben der Sprachdidaktik (und damit der Vermittlung der derzeit gültigen *Verkehrssprache*) propagiert er die Rekonstruktion *sowie* die Entwicklung eines vollständigeren Sprachsystems. Zwar finden sich weiterhin Bezüge auf die Sprachursprungsfrage hinsichtlich *Gen* 2,19 – Comenius dialektisiert die Problemstellung jedoch durch die Feststellung, Adam habe ja eine simple 'Benennung' durchgeführt, was erweise, wie unvollständig diese Sprache war. Comenius begreift die Sprache als ein lebendiges System, in der eine simple Nomenklaturthese keinen Platz hat (vgl. Comenius 1648; 1681 [=1966]; zur Nomenklaturthese Rijlaarsdam 1978).

Das Problem in der methodischen Beschreibung der divergenten Sichtweisen über den Ursprung von Sprachen im 16. und 17. Jh. spiegelt das Defizit an *Konsistenz* an theoretischem Denken der zeitgenössischen Autoren, das nur in seltenen Fällen sachorientiert, sondern instrumentalisiert auftrat (zur Rekonstruktion der verschiedenen leitenden 'Wort'-Begriffe der Zeit vgl. Klein 1992). Es sind nun im wesentlichen zwei philosophische Denkansätze, die das spekulative Denken über den Ursprung der Sprachen 'rationalisieren': Es war zum einen der Rationalismus des René Descartes (1596–1650), zum anderen die vor allem von John Locke (1632–1704) speziell vertretene Form des Sensualismus.

In Folge von Descartes gewann die zu Beginn aufgeführte These, der Sprach(en)ursprung beruhe auf der Schöpfung des mit voller Denkfähigkeit ausgestatteten Menschen, immer mehr Raum. Die Frage der göttlichen Beteiligung an der Entstehung von Sprachen wird – lange vor der Herder/Süßmilch-Debatte – zudem von Sprache auf die Denkfähigkeit verlagert (vgl. Gaier 1992: 351–358). Damit ist die menschliche Erkenntnisfähigkeit zwar in das Zentrum der philosophischen Diskussion gerückt, die Instanz der Bibel aber bei weitem noch nicht in Frage gestellt. Dies reflektiert im *Thresor de l'histoire des langues de cest univers* (1607; 1613; 2. Aufl. 1619) von Claude Duret (1565–1611), worin die damaligen Meinungen über Sprache(n) und ihren Ursprung zusammengestellt sind (vgl. Dear 1985: 204f.; Droixhe 1978: 46; zum romanischen Hintergrund vgl. auch Dubois 1970; Demonet 1992; Demonet-Launay 1993). Auch Duret bevorzugt die monogenetische Sprach(en)ursprungsthese und weist dem Hebräischen die Primigenität zu. Darüber hinaus verweist er auf die kabbalistische Tradition (vgl. Duret 1619: 42f.; Skolem 1974; Lenoble 1943). Die Sprachsetzung Adams mittels Eigennamen impliziert, in dem damals gängigen neoplatonischen, hermetischen oder kabbalistischen Kontext, eine sehr spezifische Beziehung zwischen Benennung und Natur der benannten Sache, die in der Feststellung mündet, Wörter einer 'ursprünglicheren' Sprache besäßen notwendig Eigenschaften, die mit der von ihnen bezeichneten Sache zusammenfallen (oder sie zumindest à la Paracelsus, 'signieren'). Damit ist der onomatopoetischen Spekulation der damaligen Zeit ein breiter, meist spekulativ genutzter Spielraum gegeben.

Marin Mersenne (1588–1648), Korrespondent von Descartes, sah in solchen Überlegungen den Mißbrauch platonischer Auffassungen und kritisierte die kabbalistische Tätigkeit als Zeitverschwendung (vgl. Dear 1985: 227, der auch auf die Kontroverse mit Robert Fludd hinweist). Mersenne unterstellt zwar ebenfalls den Wahrheitsgehalt der biblischen Erzählungen, bestreitet aber in seinen *Quaestiones celeberrimae in Genesim* (1623) die Möglichkeit, zeitgenössisch die Verbindung von Wörtern und Sachen nach derartigem Muster herzustellen. Hingegen verlegt er die Herkunft der ausgezeichneten Wörter wiederum in den Rahmen göttlicher Imposition, so daß die Wörter Adams in ihrer Ausgezeichnetheit nicht menschliche, sondern göttliche Fähigkeit repräsentieren (Mersenne 1623: 71). Unter dem offensichtlichen Einfluß von Descartes verschärft er seine Auffassung insofern, als er prinzipiell abstreitet, Wörter bezeichneten Substanzen. Descartes räumte zwar ein, nichtintentionelle Lautungen wie Lachen und Weinen seien in allen Sprachen gleich und könnten somit als natürliche Bezeichnungen aufgefaßt werden. Die Verbindung von ursprünglicher Benennung und benannter Sache sei zumindest nach dem 'Sündenfall' entfallen (vgl. den Brief von Descartes an Mersenne v. 18. 12. 1629; Mersenne 1932ff., II: 352). Mersenne übernimmt den Zweifel an der natürlichen Bezeichnung der Wörter (vgl. Mersenne 1636 [= 1963: 65]). Notgedrungen führen solche Überlegungen auch zu Reflexionen über die Wahrscheinlichkeit oder Möglichkeit einer *lingua philosophica*, wie Universalsprachentwürfe zeitgenössisch häufig betitelt wurden (vgl. Descartes an Mersenne; Mersenne 1932ff, II: 328). Sprach(en)ursprungstheorien und Universalsprachpläne bedingen sich im behandelten Zeitraum mutuell und müssen reflektiv betrachtet werden.

In seinem *An Essay Concerning Human Understanding* (1690; [= 1961]) geht John Locke auf den Sprach(en)ursprung *als Problemstellung* nicht ein (vgl. Dutz 1989: 218–219; Polk 1989). Er folgt der Hypothese der rationalen Begründung von Sprache durch den Menschen, der ab ovo mit der Fähigkeit der Reflexion ausgestattet ist und gerät somit nicht in Konflikt mit der Ursprungsthese *Gen* 2,19, verweist vielmehr darauf, daß durch die Schöpfung des Menschen *als Sozialgeschöpf* Gott ihn nicht nur mit der Bestimmung, gesellschaftliches Wesen zu sein, sondern auch mit dem Instrument *Sprache*, Grundlage der

Sozialität, ausgestattet habe (*Essay* III.1.1 = 1961,2: 9). Locke interpretiert die 'Adamische Sprache' weniger als konkretes Idiom denn als Sprach*fähigkeit*. Folglich nennt er (*Essay* III.1.1. – 3) die Voraussetzungen für die Ausübung der Sprachfähigkeit: "to be fit to frame articulate sounds", "[to] be able to use these sounds as signs of internal conceptions", "[those signs should] be made use of as to comprehend several particular things". An die letztere Bedingung schließt sich dann, in konsequenter Verlagerung der Ursprungsproblematik in epistemologische Fragestellungen, Lockes sensualistische Prämisse an: "we having [...] no *ideas* at all, but what originally come either from sensible objects without, or what we feel within ourselves, from the inward workings of our own spirits, of which we are conscious to ourselves within" (*Essay* III.1.5 = 1961,2: 10). Mit diesen Thesen hat Locke sich argumentativ nicht nur völlig von dem göttlichen Anteil an der Sprache des Menschen entfernt, sondern auch den sprachphilosophischen Kern der Wortsemantik angesprochen. Er ist somit frei, die Relation zwischen Wörtern und den Ideen als menschengeschaffene Signifikationsleistung zu begreifen: die fehlende Ur- oder Universalsprache liefert sogar die Begründung, warum eine 'natürliche', i.e. isomorphische Verbindung zwischen Wörtern und Ideen abzulehnen sei (vgl. *Essay* III.2.1 = 1961,2: 12).

Gottfried Wilhelm Leibniz, der philosophische Widerpart Lockes, hat bedeutende Bedenken, sich mit den zeitgenössischen Auffassungen zur Sprach(en)ursprungsdebatte so wie Locke auseinanderzusetzen. Seine Beschäftigungen mit Sprache zeichnen einen großen Bogen von den eher jugendlichen Interpretationen kabbalistischer Ansätze, der Entwicklung einer *ars combinatoria* im Gefolge des Ramon Llull (1232 – 1315) über die sprachphilosophischen Reflexionen im ausgehenden 17. Jh., die zugleich mit immer umfangreicheren sprachvergleichenden Studien begleitet werden. Sein Standpunkt zur Debatte war von ausdrücklicher methodologischer Skepsis geprägt, ihn konnte keine der damals kursierenden Theorien überzeugen und ihm waren neben den bekannteren Namen sehr wohl auch randständigere Diskussionsteilnehmer wie Ferencz Foris (Franciscus Foris Otrokocsi, 1648 – 1718), Matthaeus Praetorius (c. 1640 – 1707) und Giovanni Pietro Erico (Ericus, Johann Peter Erich, fl. 1697) geläufig. Zugleich hatte er ein distanziert interessiertes Verhältnis zu den Thesen von Descartes und Locke. Für Leibniz war die *Geschichtlichkeit* von Sprache(n) zentral, so konnte er die philosophisch determinierten Äußerungen der Genannten nur differenzieren. Auf der anderen Seite stand er der damals grassierenden These, das Hebräische (oder aber irgendeine andere Nationalsprache) sei die Ursprache, ablehnend gegenüber. Seine Ablehnung erreichte einen Höhepunkt, als er 1697 das postum herausgegebene *Glossarium universale Hebraicum* (1697) des Ludovicus Thomassin (1619 – 1695) erhielt (vgl. Dutz 1989: 220 – 222) und resultierte in der programmatischen Äußerung: "Lingua Adamica vel certe vis ejus, quam quidam se nosse et in nominibus ab Adamo impositis essentias rerum intueri posse contendunt, nobis certe ignota est" (Leibniz 1688/89 [= 1987: 1204]).

Zusammenfassend läßt sich folgendes bemerken: Die Betrachtung der Sprach(en)ursprungsfrage im 16. und 17. Jh. zeigt einen bemerkenswert vielfältigen, aber auch verworrenen akademischen Diskurs. Die Anlässe für diese Debatten sind nicht zu Beginn des betrachteten Zeitraums anzusetzen, sondern führen zurück bis in die antike und klassische Tradition und fußen zudem auf (mehr oder weniger ausgesprochenen oder gar bewußten) Prämissen der mittelalterlichen Auseinandersetzung im Spannungsfeld zwischen biblischer Exegese und Wirklichkeitserfahrung – einmündend in Großversuche wie etwa Samuel Bocharts (1599 – 1667) *Geographia sacra* (Caen 1646) oder Isaac de La Peyrères (1596 – 1676) *Praeadamitae* (Amsterdam 1655) (worin auch die These diskutiert wird, daß es bereits *vor* Adam eine Sprachenvielfalt gegeben habe) über Richard Simons (1638 – 1712) *Histoire critique du Vieux Testament* (Paris 1680ff.) bis hin zu Brian Waltons (c. 1600 – 1661) Versuchen zum Sprachursprung in seiner *Biblia sacra polyglotta* (London 1655 – 57 [u. ö.]). Die Debatten sind mit Abschluß des Betrachtungszeitraums ebenfalls nicht beendet, wenngleich die philosophisch motivierte Sprachbetrachtung der Rationalität mehr Raum gewährt und gleichzeitig die Agglomeration des Wissens zu weniger spekulativen denn vergleichenden Sprachstudien führt, bzw. die Spekulationen in den methodischen Bereich der Details verlegt. Es war aber immer noch Zeit genug, daß noch 1765 Nicolas Beauzée (1717 – 1789) den einseitigen Thesen Thomassins in seinem Artikel "Langue" für die *Encyclopédie* von Diderot und d'Alembert den

Vorzug gab und die berühmte Preisfrage der Berliner Akademie von 1772 den (oft mißverstandenen) Gegensatz zwischen Süßmilch und Herder evozierte. Vor dem Hintergrund der hier vorgeführten 'eurozentrischen' Perspektive – die hier leider nicht auf interessante Gebietsüberschreitungen wie (z. B.) bei Hugo Grotius (1583–1645), *De origine gentium Americanarum dissertatio* (Paris 1642), oder bei dem Architekten und Inigo-Jones-Schüler John Webb (1611–1672), *The Antiquity of China or [...] a Probability that the Language of China is the Primitive Language* (London 1669; 1678), ausgedehnt werden kann – darf nicht vergessen werden, daß es außerhalb des enger betrachteten Bereichs auch zu Ende des 20. Jahrhunderts zahlreiche Beispiele für legitimatives und instrumentalisiertes Umgehen mit Sprache(n) hinsichtlich der angeblichen 'Dignität', 'Würde', etc. gibt, was die Betrachtung der damaligen Argumentation historiographisch aktualisiert.

## 4. Bibliographie (in Auswahl)

Allen, Don Cameron. 1947. "Some Theories of the Growth and Origin of Language in Milton's Ages". *Philological Quarterly*. 28: 5–16.

Bayer, Hans. 1977. "Die empraktischen Sprachkategorien von Jacob Böhmes Weltdeutung". *Zeitschrift für deutsche Philologie*. 96: 170–201.

Benz, Ernst. 1936. "Zur metaphysischen Begründung der Sprache bei Jacob Böhme". *Euphorion*. 37: 340–357.

Böhme, Jacob. 1955–61. *Sämtliche Schriften. Bde. 1–11. Faksimile-Neudruck der Ausgabe von 1730*. Hrsg. v. August Faust, Will-Erich Peukert. Stuttgart: Hiersemann.

Bonfante, Giuliano. 1954. "Ideas on the Kinship of the European Languages from 1200 to 1800". *Cahiers d'Histoire Mondiale / Journal of World History / Cuadernos de Historia Mundial*. 3: 679–699.

Borst, Arno. 1957–63. *Der Turmbau zu Babel. Geschichte der Meinungen über Ursprung und Vielfalt der Sprachen und Völker*, 4 vol. in 6. Stuttgart: Hiersemann. [Nachdr. München: Dt. Taschenbuch Verlag 1995].

Campbell, Robin N. & Grieve, Robert. 1982. "Royal Investigations of the Origin of Language". *Historiographia Linguistica. 9: 43–74.*

*Caramuel y Lobkowitz, Juan. 1654. Caramuelis Praecursor Logicus. Complectens Grammaticam audacem, cuius partes sunt tres, Methodica, Metrica, Critica*. Francofurti, Sumptibus Iohan. Godofredi Schönwetteri.

Clauberg, Johann. 1663. *Ars etymologica Teutonum e philosophiae fontibus derivata, id est, Via Germanicarum vocorum & origines & praestantiam detegendi, cum plurimum tum harum vernunft/suchen/ ausspruch exemplis, atque exinde enatis regulis praemonstrata. Deutsch von Deutschem*. Duisburgi ad Rhenum, prostant apud D. Asendorp.

Comenius, Johannes [Komenský, Jan Amos]. 1648. *Novissima linguarum Methodus. Fundamentis Didacticis solide superstructa: Latinae L[inguae] exemplo realiter demonstrata: Scholarum usibus jam tandem examussim accomodata. Ante tamen Eruditorum judicio publico exposita, seriisque ac severis censuris submissa*. S. l. [Leszno].

Comenius, Johannes [Komenský, Jan Amos]. 1681. "Panglottia. In qua De Aperiendo vi Sapientis Linguarum Culturae Gentium Commercium Universali consultantur: Reique tantae haud infeliciter tentatae et tentandae specimina exhibentur", 147–204. *De Rerum Humanarum Emendatione Consultatio Catholica. Editio princeps, Tomus II*. Moderante Otokar Chlup. Pragae, in Academia h. e. in Aedibus Academiae Scientiarum Bohemoslovacae 1966.

Coudert, Allison P. 1978. "Some Theories of Natural Language from the Renaissance to the Seventeenth Century". *Magia Naturalis und die Entstehung der modernen Naturwissenschaften. Symposion der Leibniz-Gesellschaft Hannover, 14. und 15. November 1975*. (= Studia Leibnitiana. Sonderheft. 7). Hrsg. v. Albert Heinekamp, Dieter Mettler, 65–114. Wiesbaden: Steiner.

Coudert, Allison P. 1996. "Leibniz, Knorr von Rosenroth, and the *Kabbalah Denudata*". *Im Spiegel des Verstandes. Studien zu Leibniz*. Hrsg. v. Klaus D. Dutz, Stefano Gensini, 9–28. Münster: Nodus Publikationen.

Dán, Róbert. 1977. "The Age of Reformation versus 'Linguam sanctam Hebraicam' – A Survey". *Annales Universitatis Scientiarum Budapestiensis, Sectio Linguistica*. 8: 131–144.

Dante Alighieri. 1968. *De vulgari eloquentia*, vol. I, ed. Pier Vincenzo Mengaldo. Bari: Laterza.

Dear, Peter. 1985. "Mersenne and the Language of Philosophy". *Rekonstruktion und Interpretation. Problemgeschichtliche Studien zur Sprachtheorie von Ockham bis Humboldt*. Hrsg. v. Klaus D. Dutz, Ludger Kaczmarek, 197–241. (= Tübinger Beiträge zur Linguistik. 264). Tübingen: Narr.

Demonet, Marie-Luce. 1992. *Les voix du signe: nature et origine du langage à la Renaissance (1480–1580)*. (= Bibliothèque littéraire de la Renaissance, Série 3. 29). Paris: Champion.

Demonet-Launay, Marie-Luce. 1993. "Du mythe à l'hypothèse: les changements méthodiques dans les recherches sur l'origine des langues au XVIe siècle". *La linguistique entre mythe et histoire. Actes des journées d'étude organisées les 4 et 5 juin 1991 à la Sorbonne en l'honneur de Hans Aarsleff*. Ed. par Daniel Droixhe, Chantal Grell, 11–30. Münster: Nodus Publikationen.

Droixhe, Daniel. 1978. *La linguistique et l'appel de l'histoire (1600–1800). Rationalisme et révolutions positivistes*. (= Langue et Cultures. 10). Genève: Droz.

Dubois, Claude-Gilbert. 1994. *La mythologie des origines chez Guillaume Postel: de la naissance à la nation.* (= Collection Varia. 19). Orléans: Paradigme.

Dubois, Claude-Gilbert. 1970. *Mythe et langage au seizième siècle.* (= Collection Ducros. 8). Bordeaux: Ducros.

Duret, Claude. 1619. *Thresor de l'histoire des langues de cest univers. Contenant les origines, beautés, perfections, decadences, mutations, changements, conversions et ruines des langues*. 2e éd. Yverdon: Impr. de la Société helvetiale caldoresque.

Dutz, Klaus D. 1989 "'Lingua Adamica nobis certe ignota est'. Die Sprachursprungsdebatte und Gottfried Wilhelm Leibniz". *Theorien vom Ursprung der Sprache*. Hrsg. v. Joachim Gessinger, Wolfert von Rahden, vol. I, 204–240. Berlin, New York: de Gruyter.

Elert, Claes-Christian. 1978. "Andreas Kempe (1622–89) and the Languages Spoken in Paradise". *Historiographia Linguistica*. 5: 221–226.

Feinhals, Johann Jakob. 1731. *Die Orchideen des Bösen, oder über die All-Gegenwart des Teufels.* Cölln a. d. Rh. [= Köln; o. D.; ggf. apud Joachimum Liebigensis].

Flint, Robert. 1904. *Philosophy as Scientia Scientiarum and A History of Classifications of the Sciences*. London: William Blackwood and Sons.

Gaier, Ulrich. 1992. "Johann Gottfried Herder (1744–1803)". *Sprachphilosophie / Philosophy of Language / La philosophie du langage*. Hrsg. v. Marcelo Dascal, Dietfried Gerhardus, Kuno Lorenz, Georg Meggle, vol. I, 343–362. Berlin, New York: de Gruyter.

Goropius Becanus, Joanes [Jan van Gorp]. 1569. *Origines Antwerpianae, Sive, Cimmerriorum Becceslana. Novem Libros Complexa*. Antverpiae: Ex officina Christophori Plantini.

Goropius Becanus, Joanes [Jan van Gorp]. 1580. *Hermathena, Hieroglyphica, Vertumnus, Gallica, Francica, Hispanica*. Antverpiae: Excudebat C. Plantinus.

Grazia, Margreta de. 1978. "Shakespeare's View of Language: An Historical Perspective". *Shakespeare Quarterly*. 29: 374–388.

Grazia, Margreta de. 1980. "The Secularization of Language in the Seventeenth Century". *Journal of the History of Ideas*. 41: 319–329.

Haferland, Harald. 1989. "Mystische Theorie der Sprache bei Jacob Böhme". *Theorien vom Ursprung der Sprache*. Hrsg. v. Joachim Gessinger, Wolfert von Rahden, vol. I, 89–130. Berlin, New York: de Gruyter.

Helmont, Franciscus Mercurius. 1667. *Kurtzer entwurff des eigenthlichen natur-alphabets der heiligen sprache; nach dessen anleitung man auch taubgebohrne verstehend und reden machen kan*. Ans liecht gegeben durch F. M. B. Helmont. Sulzbach.

Kaczmarek, Ludger. 1989. "Aspekte scholastischer Sprachursprungstheorien. Dionysius der Karthäuser über den Ursprung der Sprache. Mit einem chronobibliographischen Anhang". *Theorien vom Ursprung der Sprache*. Hrsg. v. Joachim Gessinger, Wolfert von Rahden, vol. I, 65–88. Berlin, New York: de Gruyter.

Kilcher, Andreas B. 1998. *Die Sprachtheorie der Kabbala als ästhetisches Paradigma. Die Konstruktion einer ästhetischen Kabbala seit der Frühen Neuzeit*. Stuttgart, Weimar: Metzler.

Klein, Wolf Peter. 1992. *Am Anfang war das Wort. Theorie- und wissenschaftsgeschichtliche Elemente frühneuzeitlichen Sprachbewußtseins*. Berlin: Akademie Verlag. [Diss. FU Berlin 1991].

Konopacki, Stephen A. 1979. *The Descent into Words. Jakob Böhme's Transcendental Linguistics*. (= Linguistica Extranea, Studia. 7). Ann Arbor/Mich: Karoma.

Leibniz, Gottfried Wilhelm. 1999 [1688]. "Fundamenta calculi ratiocinatoris". *Gottfried Wilhelm Leibniz, Philosophische Schriften*. Hrsg. v. d. Leibniz-Forschungsstelle der Universität Münster. *Vierter Band. 1677–Juni 1690*, 917–922. Berlin: Akademie-Vlg.

Leinkauf, Thomas. 1993. *Mundus combinatus. Studien zur Struktur der barocken Universalwissenschaft am Beispiel Athanasius Kirchers SJ (1602–1680)*. Berlin: Akademie Verlag.

Lenoble, Robert. 1943. *Mersenne ou la naissance du mécanisme*. Paris: Vrin.

Locke, John. 1961. *An Essay Concerning Human Understanding*. In Two Volumes. (= Everyman's Library 332, 984). London, New York: Heineman.

Mendels, Judy. 1953. "Jacob Boehme's 'R'". *Journal of English and Germanic Philology*. 53: 559–562.

Mersenne, Marin. 1623. *Quaestiones celeberrimae in Genesim, cum accurata textus explicatione; in hoc volumine athei et deistae impugnantur et expugnantur, et Vulgata editio ab haereticorum calumniis vindicatur, Graecorum et Hebraeorum musica instaurantur, Francisci Veneti cabalistica dogmata fuse refelluntur*. Lutetiae Parisiorum: Sebastianus Cramoisy.

Mersenne, Marin. 1932ff. *Correspondance de P. Marin Mersenne, religieux minime*. Publ. par Mme Paul [i.e. Marie] Tannery, éd et ann. par Cornelis de Waard, avec la collaboration de René Pintard, Bernard Rochot. Paris: Beauchesne [vol. 1]; Presses Universitaires de France [vols. 2–4]; Centre National de la Recherche Scientifique [vols. 5ff.].

Mersenne, Marin. 1963. *Harmonie universelle contenant la théorie et la pratique de la musique* [1636]. Éd. facs. de l'exemplaire conservé à la Bibliothèque des Arts et Métiers et annoté par l'auteur. Introduction par François Lesure. Vols. 1–3. Paris: Éditions du Centre National de la Recherche Scientifique.

Metcalf, George J. 1974. "The Indo-European Hypothesis in the Sixteenth and Seventeenth Centuries". *Studies in the History of Linguistics. Traditions and Paradigms*. Ed. by Dell Hymes, 233–257. Bloomington/Ind., London: Indiana University Press.

Morhof, Daniel Georg. 1747. *Polyhistor literarius, philosophicus et practicus* [1687]. Cum accessionibus a Johannes Frick et Johannes Moller. Ed. quarta, cui praefationem praemisit Johann Albert Fabricius [...], nunc autem et ad a. 1747 continuatam a J. Joachim Schwab. 3 tom. in 2. Lubeca [= Lübeck]: Boeckmann. [Neudruck Aalen: Scientia 1970].

Moulton, William. 1952. "Jacob Boehme's Uvular 'r'". *Journal of English and Germanic Philology*. 51: 83–89.

Noordegraaf, Jan. 1996. "Dutch Linguists and the Origin of Language. Some Nineteenth-Century Views", *ders.*, *The Dutch Pendulum. Linguistics in the Netherlands 1740–1900*, 72–85. Münster: Nodus Publikationen.

Nuchelmans, Gabriel. 1992. "Renaissance Philosophy of Language". *Sprachphilosophie / Philosophy of Language / La philosophie du langage*. Hrsg. v. Marcelo Dascal, Dietfried Gerhardus, Kuno Lorenz, Georg Meggle, vol. I, 104–116. Berlin, New York: de Gruyter.

Olender, Maurice. 1996. "Der arisch-semitische Streit zu Beginn der modernen Sprachwissenschaft". *Sprachphilosophie / Philosophy of Language / La philosophie du langage*. Hrsg. v. Marcelo Dascal, Dietfried Gerhardus, Kuno Lorenz, Georg Meggle, vol. II, 943–952. Berlin, New York: de Gruyter.

Paracelsus (Theophrast von Hohenheim). 1965. *Studienausgabe. Bd. 1–5.* Ausgew. u. hrsg. v. Will-Erich Peukert. Basel: Schwabe & Co.

Percival, W. Keith. 1984. "The Reception of Hebrew in Sixteenth-Century Europe: The Impact of the Cabbala". *Historiographia Linguistica*. 11: 21–38.

Polk, James. 1989. "From Locke to Hume. The Radicalization of the Sensualistic Premisses in the Empirical Interpretation of the Origins of Speech". *Theorien vom Ursprung der Sprache*. Hrsg. v. Joachim Gessinger, Wolfert von Rahden, vol. I, 183–203. Berlin, New York: de Gruyter.

Ricken, Ulrich. 1985. *Probleme des Zeichens und der Kommunikation in der Wissenschafts- und Ideologiegeschichte der Aufklärung*. (= Sitzungsberichte der Sächsischen Akademie der Wissenschaften zu Leipzig, Phil.-hist. Klasse. Band 125,6). Berlin: Akademie-Verlag.

Rijlaarsdam, Jetske C. 1978. *Platon über die Sprache. Ein Kommentar zum Kratylos. Mit einem Anhang über die Quelle der Zeichentheorie Ferdinand de Saussures*. Utrecht: Bohn, Scheltema & Holkema.

Scaliger, Joseph Justus. 1610. "Diatriba de Europaeorum linguis". *Jos. Justi. Scaligeri Opuscula varia, antehac non edita*, 119–122. Parisiis, apud Hadrianum Beys.

Skolem, Gershom. 1974. *Kabbalah*. (= Library of Jewish Knowledge). Jerusalem, New York.

Slaughter, Mary M. 1982. *Universal Languages and Scientific Taxonomy in the Seventeenth Century*. Cambridge, London, New York, New Rochelle, Melbourne, Sydney: Cambridge University Press.

Thomassin, Louis. 1697. *Glossarium universale Hebraicum, quo ad Hebraicae linguae fontes linguae et dialecti pene omnes revocantur*. Auctore Ludovico Thomassino, [Éd. par C. Bordes, N. Barat], Parisiis, E Typographia regia.

Webster, Charles. 1982. *From Paracelsus to Newton. Magic and the Making of Modern Science*. Cambridge: Cambridge University Press.

Willard, Thomas. 1989. "Rosicrucian Sign Lore and the Origin of Language". *Theorien vom Ursprung der Sprache*. Hrsg. v. Joachim Gessinger, Wolfert von Rahden, vol. I, 131–157. Berlin, New York: de Gruyter.

*Klaus D. Dutz, Münster (Deutschland)*
*Ludger Kaczmarek, Borgholzhausen (Deutschland)*

# 144. Die großen Sprachensammlungen vom frühen 18. bis frühen 19. Jahrhundert

1. Einleitende Bemerkungen
2. Vorarbeiten zu den Sprachensammlungen seit der Renaissance
3. Gottfried Wilhelm Leibniz und seine methodischen Sondierungen umfassender Sprachensammlungen
4. Johann Eberhard Fischers *Vocabularium Sibiricum* und damit assoziierte Sammlungen
5. Die *Vocabularia comparativa* von Peter Simon Pallas
6. Die Sprachenenzyklopädie von Lorenzo Hervás y Panduro

7. Die Sprachensammlungen von Johann Christoph Adelung und Johann Severin Vater
8. Ausblick
9. Bibliographie

## 1. Einleitende Bemerkungen

Unberechtigterweise spielen die großen Sprachensammlungen des 18. und 19. Jhs. in den historiographischen Gesamtdarstellungen unserer Zeit lediglich eine Statistenrolle, zudem fehlt eine substantielle Verknüpfung dieser Tradition mit der historisch-vergleichenden Sprachbetrachtung. Die allgemeinen Hinweise auf die Sprachensammlungen, die sich seit den sechziger Jahren finden, sind oberflächlich, lückenhaft und vermitteln zum Teil falsche Informationen (z. B. Tagliavini 1968: 46ff.; Ivić 1971: 27f.; Arens 1980: 102; Morpurgo Davies 1992: 160; Seuren 1998: 62f.). Ausgewogener ist die Behandlung der Sprachensammlungen bei Gipper und Schmitter (1975: 490ff.).

Die allgemeine Unsicherheit bei der Einordnung der polyglotten Kompilationen in die Geschichte der Sprachwissenschaft liegt zum einen daran, daß die Leistungen der Sprachensammlungen, gemessen an ihrem Inhalt und ihren methodischen Ansprüchen, erst in einigen neueren Spezialstudien herausgearbeitet worden sind, und diese Erkenntnisse warten noch darauf, in allgemeinere Darstellungen eingebracht zu werden (u. a. Haarmann 1976a, 1979c; Coseriu 1978a, b; Fodor 1982; Lüdtke 1978; Sarmiento 1990). Zum anderen steht die linguistische Historiographie in einer Tradition, die den Wert einzelner Sprachensammlungen mit Vorliebe für philologische Einzeldisziplinen (z. B. Indogermanistik, Finno-Ugristik, Afrikanistik) aufzeigt, wobei ein interner Vergleich der Kompilationen unterbleibt.

Die Epoche der Aufklärung war eine Zeit, in der die Fürsten antike und exotische Kunstschätze und die Gelehrten Sprachen sammelten. Konsequenterweise hat das 18. Jh. Dutzende von Entwürfen für Sprachensammlungen hervorgebracht, von denen allerdings nur ein Bruchteil konkret ausgeführt wurde. Von diesen wiederum sind die wenigsten von historischem Wert für die linguistische Historiographie. Auf diese Sammlungen beziehe ich mich hier.

## 2. Vorarbeiten zu den Sprachensammlungen seit der Renaissance

Die im 18. Jh. intensivierte Aktivität, Sprachen zu sammeln und zu beschreiben, geht letztlich auf Impulse der Renaissance zurück, als die Volkssprachen als Medien der Literaten an Prestige gewannen, und sich die Bildungselite daran gewöhnte, die Pflege und Erforschung ihrer Muttersprachen ebenso zu schätzen wie die der klassischen Bildungssprachen Latein und Griechisch. Äußeres Zeichen der Aufmerksamkeit für die Volkssprachen war die Entstehung einer bis dahin unbekannten Gattung von Schrifttum: grammatische Traktate über die Muttersprache.

Die ersten Grammatiken der europäischen Volkssprachen entstehen im 15. Jh., und zwar des Italienischen von Leon Battista Alberti (um 1450, ungedruckt) und des Spanischen von Antonio de Nebrija aus dem Jahre 1492. Im 16. Jh. erweitert sich das Spektrum der grammatischen Literatur, die nicht nur europäische Sprachen (Grammatik des Italienischen von 1516, des Französischen von 1521, 1530, 1531), sondern auch "exotische" Sprachen (Grammatik des Taraskischen von 1558, des Nahuatl von 1571) einschließt (Percival 1975).

Die sich erweiternde Kenntnis natürlicher Sprachen und die Einblicke in Verschiedenheiten des Sprachbaus vermitteln die wesentlichen Impulse, sich mit der Frage der genealogischen Sprachverwandtschaft auseinanderzusetzen. Die Bibeltradition dominiert die Diskussion insofern, als die frühen sprachvergleichenden Versuche (z. B. Guillaume Postels *De originibus* von 1538, Theodor Biblianders *De ratione communi omnium linguarum* von 1548, Conrad Gesners *Mithridates* von 1555) davon ausgehen, daß das Hebräische die Mutter aller Sprachen der Erde sei (lingua matrix). In seinem *Mithridates*, einer Kompilation des größten Teils der damals bekannten Sprachen (Coseriu 1975: 206f.), bietet Gesner Sprachproben in einer Weise an, wie sie bei den Vertretern nachfolgender Generationen von Sprachenkundlern populär geblieben ist: mit Übersetzungen des Vaterunser.

## 3. Gottfried Wilhelm Leibniz und seine methodischen Sondierungen umfassender Sprachensammlungen

Im Gesamtwerk (Traktate, Korrespondenz) des Universalgelehrten Gottfried Wilhelm Leibniz (1646–1716) finden sich theoretische und praktische Ausführungen über Sprache und Sprachen. Die Leibnizschen Bemühungen um eine 'universale Charakteristik' (characteristica universalis) von Sprache mit ihren inhaltlichen Bezügen zu modernen formalen Sprachtheorien sind wohlbekannt (s. Heinekamp 1972). Erörterungen von Problemen natürlicher Sprachen bei Leibniz beinhalten "questions of the origin and diversity of human languages, the natural or conventional basis of meaning, and the semantics of natural language expressions" (Rutherford 1995: 240).

Die Überlegungen zur Organisation von Sprachensammlungen und zur historisch-vergleichenden Sprachforschung, die Leibniz anstellt, sind ebenso verdienstvoll, obwohl bislang wenig beachtet. Für die großen Sprachensammlungen des 18. Jhs. wird Leibniz damit ein wichtiger Impulsgeber. Seine Ausführungen über historische Sprachverwandtschaft finden sich hauptsächlich in zwei Essays, und zwar *Brevis designatio* ... von 1710 sowie *Epistolaris de Historia Etymologica Dissertatio* von 1712, die unvollendet blieb und bislang nicht veröffentlicht ist (s. Hinweis bei Rutherford 1995, 262, Fn 47). Mit seinen Gedanken zur vergleichenden Methode in seiner *Brevis designatio* nimmt Leibniz die Essenz dessen, was die Sprachenkunde des 18. Jhs. entwickeln sollte, in gedrängter Form vorweg. Dies macht den historischen Wert des Essays aus (Jacob 1973: 45).

In der Annäherung von Leibniz an das Phänomen Sprache über seine Methode der "universalen Charakteristik" drückt sich sein ursprüngliches Erkenntnisinteresse und ursächliches Forschungsanliegen aus. Die Aufmerksamkeit, die derselbe Leibniz später dem Studium der natürlichen Sprachenvielfalt entgegenbringt, erklärt sich zum Teil aus seiner Biographie (Stipa 1990: 159ff.; Ariew 1995). Das Quellenstudium des Projekts einer Geschichte des Welfenhauses, mit dem Herzog Johann Friedrich von Hannover Leibniz beauftragt hatte, machte zahlreiche Reisen erforderlich.

Während einer dieser Reisen führt Leibniz in Frankfurt Gespräche mit dem Orientalisten J. Ludolf (1663–1737) über die semitisch-hamitischen Sprachen (s. Waterman 1978 zum akademischen Gedankenaustausch zwischen Leibniz und Ludolf) und in Rom, wo sich Leibniz von 1687 bis 1690 aufhält, mit dem Jesuiten C. F. Grimaldi, dem damaligen Präsidenten des Tribunale mathematicum in Peking. Die Gespräche mit Grimaldi regen Leibniz zur Ausarbeitung eines detaillierten Fragebogens (mit Musterwörtern für verschiedene Wortfelder) zum Zweck des Sammelns von Sprachproben an, den er im Juli 1689 Grimaldi übermittelt. Mit Hilfe des Fragebogens – so die Leibnizsche Vorstellung – könnten Missionare auf ihrem Weg von Europa in den Fernen Osten Sprachproben sammeln.

Besonders wichtig für Leibniz sollte sein Kontakt zu Nicolaes Witsen (1641–1717), dem Bürgermeister von Amsterdam, werden. Dieser hatte sich im Jahre 1664 einer holländischen Gesandtschaft nach Moskau angeschlossen und dort begonnen, Informationen zur Geschichte und den Sprachen der Völker Rußlands zu sammeln (Stipa 1990: 164f.). Witsens Werk *Noord en Oost Tartarye*, das im Jahre 1692 erscheint, beeindruckt Leibniz, der Witsen animiert, die Sammeltätigkeit von Sprachproben (und zwar Texte des Vaterunsers) sowie von Musterwörtern fortzusetzen. Seit 1694 gibt Witsen den Leibnizschen Anregungen in seiner Korrespondenz mit Freunden in Moskau Ausdruck. Leibniz erhält von Witsen etliche Vaterunserversionen über die persönliche Korrespondenz, u. a. verschiedener samojedischer Sprachen, des Wogulischen, Syrjänischen und Tscheremissischen (s. Abb. 144.1.). In seinen letzten Lebensjahren widmet sich Leibniz mehr denn je dem Versuch, die Ursprünge der Sprachen mit Hilfe vergleichender Wortforschung und der Entdeckung von Wurzelwörtern zu erschließen. Leibniz war der Ansicht, daß 'die meisten Sprachen auf einem großen Teil der den Alten bekannten Welt aus irgendeiner gemeinsamen Quelle geflossen sind' (Leibniz, *Epistolaris de Historia Etymologica Dissertatio*, § 26, zitiert nach Stipa 1990: 162). Die Aufdeckung von sprachverwandtschaftlichen Gruppierungen ist nach Leibniz gleichsam eine Art Zwischenstufe, um zur "gemeinsamen Quelle", der Ursprache, vorzudringen (Rutherford 1995: 241f.).

Leibniz hat in seinen letzten Lebensjahren sein Hauptaugenmerk auf Rußland und seine Sprachenvielfalt gelenkt. Die Anregungen zu Sprachsammlungen großen Umfangs finden ihren sublimen Ausdruck in einem Brief, den Leibniz an den russischen Zaren Peter den Großen (reg.: 1689–1725) schreibt. Dieser Brief (s. Wortlaut bei Adelung 1815: v–vi), vom 26. Oktober 1713 datiert, führt drei Hauptpunkte an, die das Studium der Sprachen Rußlands wichtig machen: die Verschriftung bislang schriftloser Sprachen, die Ver-

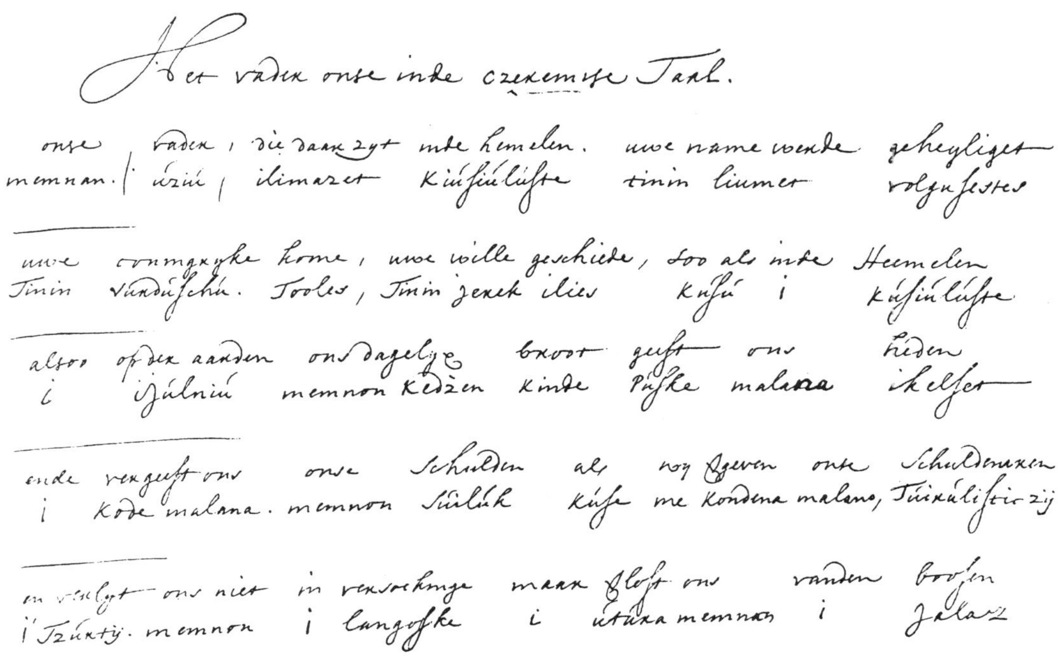

Het vader onse inde czeremise Taal.

onse vader, die daar zyt inde hemelen. uwe name werde geheyliget

uwe coningryke kome, uwe wille geschiede, soo als inde Heemelen

alsoo op der aarden ons dagelyx broot geeft ons heden

ende vergeeft ons onse schulden als wy vergeven onse schuldenaren

en verleyt ons niet in versoekinge maar verlost ons van den boosen

Abb. 144.1: Ein von Witsen 1699 an Leibniz übersandtes tscheremissisches Vaterunser mit niederländischer Interlinearversion (Stipa 1990, Abb. 23)

breitung christlicher Lehre und Schrifttums bei den Vertretern von Naturreligionen und die Vergleichung des gesammelten Sprachmaterials zur Feststellung 'des Ursprungs der Nationen'.

## 4. Johann Eberhard Fischers *Vocabularium Sibiricum* und damit assoziierte Sammlungen

Die Anregungen von Leibniz werden aufgegriffen und grundsätzlich beachtet. Gipper und Schmitter (1975: 490) heben hervor, daß es zwar keine direkte Beziehung zwischen den Leibniz'schen Impulsen und dem monumentalen Wörterbuch von Pallas (s. unter 5.) gibt, daß aber die von Leibniz an Peter den Großen vermittelten Ideen zu Sprachensammlungen ihre Langzeitwirkung entfalteten. In der Mitte des 18. Jhs. macht sich diesbezüglich auch der Einfluß Michail Vasil'evič Lomonosovs (1711–1765) bemerkbar, der die grammatische Tradition in Rußland mit seiner 1755 erschienenen *Rossijskaja Grammatika* (Russische Grammatik) prägt (Kononov 1972: 84).

Sehr aktiv engagiert sich V. N. Tatiščev (1686–1750), Leiter des Oberbergamtes im Ural, für die Ausarbeitung eines Fragebogens zum Zweck des Sammelns von Sprachmaterial. Sein Entwurf, den er der 1725 gegründeten Petersburger Akademie der Wissenschaften anbietet, wird abgelehnt. Auch weigert sich die Akademie, Tatiščevs Rezension des Werkes von Philipp Johann von Strahlenberg (1676–1747) (*Das nord- und ostliche Theil von Europa und Asia* ..., Leipzig & Stockholm 1730) zu veröffentlichen. "Die deutschen Gelehrten an der Akademie wollten den russischen, im Staatsdienst tätigen Autodidakten nicht zum Zuge kommen lassen" (Stipa 1990: 183).

Tatiščev wird indes von Regierungsseite unterstützt. Kopien seines Fragebogens werden an alle Kanzleien in den Gouvernements Sibirien und Kazan verteilt. Die von lokalen Stellen durchgeführten Sammlungen von Sprachmaterial werden wichtige Bausteine in der sibirischen Sprachensammlung des aus Württemberg stammenden Johann Eberhard Fischer (1697–1771). Fischers *Vocabularium Sibiricum* aus dem Jahre 1747 ist eine von insgesamt 28 Schriften, die der aus Sibirien zurückgekehrte Forscher der Petersburger Akademie übergibt.

Dieses Werk mit seinen 737 etymologischen Vergleichen und 2432 gesammelten

Wörtern ist lange Zeit nur als Originalmanuskript zugänglich gewesen. Der Inhalt des Manuskripts ist von Gerhard Doerfer (1965: 40–182) im Facsimiledruck herausgegeben worden. Einen Abdruck des gesamten etymologischen Teils hat János Gulya (1995) vorgenommen. Die Gelegenheit für seine Sammlungen erhält Fischer eigentlich durch Zufall. In die Dienste der Petersburger Akademie tritt der Kenner der klassischen Sprachen (Griechisch, Latein) gerade zu der Zeit ein, als der Historiker Gerhard Friedrich Müller (1705–1783), Leiter der zweiten großen Kamtschatka-Expedition (heute als 'Große Nordische Expedition' bekannt), seine Forschungsreise wegen Erkrankung abbrechen muß.

Fischer setzt Müllers Arbeit fort und reist zwischen 1740 und 1746 durch das zentrale und östliche Sibirien. Immerhin kommt Fischer bis Jakutsk im heutigen Saxa (Jakutische Republik in der Russischen Föderation). Auf seiner Reise wertet Fischer die mit Hilfe des Fragebogens von Tatiščev bereits gesammelten Sprachproben aus und sammelt selbst weitere. Die in Kyrillica transkribierten Wörter transliteriert Fischer in Lateinschrift.

Fischer übergibt sein Originalmanuskript des *Vocabularium Sibiricum* der Akademie, die aber nicht für eine Veröffentlichung sorgt. Im Jahre 1767 vertraut Fischer die Unterlagen August Ludwig Schlözer (1735–1809) in der Hoffnung an, daß dieser das Werk zum Druck bringen würde. In den Archiven der Akademie verbleibt eine von Fischer überarbeitete Fassung des Vocabulariums. Schlözer nimmt das *Vocabularium* mit nach Göttingen, wo das Manuskript seither in der Universitätsbibliothek aufbewahrt wird. Entgegen Fischers Hoffnung publiziert Schlözer das *Vocabularium* nicht, veröffentlicht allerdings dessen Materialien in Auszügen (unter Nennung von Fischers Namen) in seinen eigenen Werken (*Probe russischer Annalen* 1768, *Nestor* 1802–09).

Das Exemplar der Petersburger Akademie ist verschollen. Adelung (1815: 21) merkt an, daß er Fischers Manuskript nicht finden konnte. Fischer hat seine Sammlungen in den Jahren nach seiner Rückkehr nach St. Petersburg ergänzt und bearbeitet. Außer dem *Vocabularium* verfaßt er eine Studie über die Sprachverwandtschaft des Ungarischen (*De origine Ungrorum, mit einer Tabula harmonica linguarum*, Ms. 1756), die Schlözer 1770 in seinen *Quaestiones* abdruckt. Schlözer macht Fischers Manuskripte später Sámuel Gyarmathi (1751–1830) anläßlich von dessen Besuch in Göttingen zugänglich. Auf diese Weise werden Fischers Sammlungen für die Tradition der finnisch-ugrischen Sprachforschung rezipiert, ihr Nachklang findet sich in Gyarmathis bahnbrechendem Werk *Affinitas lingvae hvngaricae cum lingvis fennicae originis grammatice demonstrata* (Göttingen 1799).

## 5. Die *Vocabularia comparativa* von Peter Simon Pallas

In der zweiten Hälfte des 18. Jhs. organisiert die Petersburger Akademie das von Peter Simon Pallas (1741–1811) bearbeitete Großprojekt eines monumentalen vergleichenden Wörterbuchs (*Linguarum totius orbis vocabularia comparativa*, 2 Bde, 1786 u. 1789), das wegen der aktiven Beteiligung der Zarin Katharina II. (reg.: 1762–1796) und ihres Mäzenatentums auch 'Wörterbuch Katharinas' genannt wird. Im Hinblick auf seine Gesamtleistung ist das Werk als 'Krönung der Sprachwissenschaft des 18. Jahrhunderts' (Doerfer 1965: 15) gewürdigt worden. Über dieses Werk und seine Sammlungen, die Vorgeschichte seiner Entstehung und die Rezeption in der Fachwelt hat Friedrich von Adelung (1768–1843) einen Forschungsbericht verfaßt (Adelung 1815). F. von Adelung war der Neffe des Sprachforschers Johann Christoph Adelung, des Bearbeiters des *Mithridates*, an dessen Sammlungen er nach dem Tod seines Onkels auch mitwirkt (s. unter 7.; *Allgemeine Deutsche Biographie* 1, 1875: 80).

Katharina II. zeigte bereits in jungen Jahren reges Interesse für Literatur, Sprachstudium und aufklärerisches Gedankengut. Die Zarin sendet auch Expeditionen zur Erforschung des asiatischen Rußland aus. Diese werden in den Jahren 1768 und 1774 durchgeführt und ihre Ergebnisse innerhalb von zwei Jahren publiziert. Als Mäzenatin einer neuen Generation von Literaten sammelt die Herrscherin Literatur aus Westeuropa und fördert die Wissenschaften (Cronin 1995: 272f.). Von dem Verleger Christoph Friedrich Nicolai (1733–1811) in Berlin läßt sich Katharina eine Übersicht aller bekannten Sprachen anfertigen (s. Nikolai 1785).

Peter Simon Pallas (s. Rudolphi 1812: 1–78 sowie Wendland 1992 zu Biographie und Werken), der seit 1766 eine Professur für Naturgeschichte in Berlin bekleidete, beruft sie an die Akademie nach St. Petersburg und beauftragt ihn mit der Ausarbeitung eines "Universal-Glossariums" (Kononov 1972: 86f.). Die Zarin übergibt Pallas eine von ihr selbst zusammengestellte Liste von Musterwörtern, die dem Projektleiter als Orientierung dient. Adelung (1815: 41f.) erwähnt zwei Dokumente in der Handschrift Katharinas, die von Pallas als authentisch bestätigt wurden. In dem einen sind 277 Wörter in russischer Sprache aufgeführt, von denen später 274 in das Vokabular aufgenommen werden. In dem anderen findet sich ein Verzeichnis von 159 Sprachen.

Einen wichtigen Rückhalt findet Pallas in den handschriftlichen Sprachensammlungen von Hartwig Ludwig Christian Bacmeister (1730–1806), der 1773 einen Fragebogen entworfen und an zahlreiche Forscher verschickt hatte (Kononov 1972: 85f.). Das Echo darauf war beachtlich (s. Adelung 1815: 26ff.). Bacmeister wählt als Mustertexte Redensarten aus, die nach ihrem Inhalt weitgehend kulturunabhängig sind, d. h. allgemeine Lebensweisheiten reflektieren. Auf diese Weise erhoffte er sich Informationen über die grammatischen Strukturen fremder Sprachen.

Bacmeister selbst aber verlor das Interesse an seinem Projekt und gab die Materialien, vielleicht einem Vorschlag Katharinas folgend, an Pallas weiter. Außer den Aufzeichnungen von Bacmeister gehören dazu auch Materialien, die F. v. Adelung beigesteuert hat (Kononov 1972: 75ff.). Ein Modellentwurf des Wörterverzeichnisses (*Modèle du vocabulaire, qui doit servir à la comparaison de toutes les langues*, gedruckt 1786) wird von der Zarin abgesegnet, durch entsprechende Kabinettsanweisungen autorisiert und an die Kanzleien aller Gouvernements, an Gesandtschaften und Gelehrte im Ausland verschickt mit der Bitte, die angeforderten Materialien umgehend zu beschaffen.

Das eintreffende Material wird von Pallas redigiert und katalogisiert (Gulya 1959, Kononov 1972: 79ff.). Das Endergebnis, die zweibändigen *Linguarum totius orbis vocabularia comparativa*, sind ohne die Aufnahme amerikanischer und afrikanischer Sprachen (s. u.) Stückwerk geblieben. Zusammen mit den erst in der zweiten Ausgabe von 1790–1791 veröffentlichten neuen Materialien sind die *Vocabularia* die umfangreichste Sprachenkompilation des 18. Jhs. Der erste Band enthält auch eine kurze Einleitung in lateinischer Sprache (Pallas 1786: xi–xv). Dieses Monumentalwerk führt insgesamt 200 Sprachen und Dialekte auf, von denen 63 in Europa, 137 in Asien (einschließlich des Pazifik) verbreitet sind. Lexikalisches Material ist jeweils für 285 Begriffe gesammelt worden, wobei 130 Eintragungen auf den ersten Band, 155 auf den zweiten Band verteilt sind.

Ein entscheidender Nachteil der *Vocabularia* ist der Umstand, daß die Namen der Sprachen in Russisch aufgeführt werden, und die Beispiele aus den verschiedenen Sprachen sämtlich – auch für bekannte Sprachen mit Lateinschrift (z. B. Französisch) – in kyrillischer Schrift transkribiert sind. In den Besprechungen der *Vocabularia* (s. u.) wird die Verwendung der Kyrillica scharf kritisiert, und auch Adelung (1815: 84), der dem Pallas'schen Projekt sehr gewogen ist, räumt ein, daß die Wahl der Kyrillica ein Hindernis für die Benutzung des Werks im westlichen Ausland und damit insgesamt ein empfindlicher Nachteil ist.

Die *Vocabularia comparativa* erwecken Aufsehen in der gelehrten Welt, allerdings ist die Verbreitung des Werks dadurch stark eingeschränkt, daß außer den Exemplaren, die die Zarin an Gesandtschaften und Gelehrte verschenkt, nur etwa vierzig zum Verkauf kommen, die übrigen im sogenannten 'Kaiserlichen Cabinet' verbleiben und erst zu Beginn des 19. Jhs. im Buchhandel erhältlich sind (Adelung 1815: 93). Die meisten Exemplare der *Vocabularia*, die sich heute in westeuropäischen Bibliotheken finden, haben daher eine ganz persönliche Geschichte, die mit der Schenkung durch Katharina II. oder durch den Kompilator Pallas beginnt, wie etwa das Exemplar der Hamburger Staatsbibliothek, nach dem der moderne Nachdruck besorgt worden ist (Haarmann 1979a: 11ff.). Pallas hat vermutlich die *Vocabularia* dem Fürsten Zubov, dem damaligen Günstling der Zarin, geschenkt, und über den Pastor der Petersburger evangelischen Kirche gelangte das Exemplar in den Besitz von Friedrich Gottlieb Klopstock (1724–1803), der es 1803 weiterverschenkte.

Aus den meisten Besprechungen des Werks erhellt, daß Pallas bei der Auswahl des Sprachmaterials nicht das nötige Geschick besessen hat und Material aus so mancher obskuren Quelle unkritisch und ungeprüft übernommen hat. Die schärfste und zugleich inhaltlich gewichtigste Kritik wird von dem Königsberger Geschichtsprofessor Christian Jakob Kraus (1787) vorgetragen, der den ersten Band der *Vocabularia* rezensiert. Kraus moniert die Anwendung der Kyrillica, das Fehlen grammatischer Strukturvergleiche und die fehlende Unterscheidung von Begriff und Wort. Nach seiner Ansicht haben diese grundsätzlichen Mängel dazu geführt, daß bei der Aufzeichnung von Sprachmaterial (Sprachstoff) einerseits phonetische Besonderheiten nicht berücksichtigt werden konnten, andererseits die Wortvergleiche vielfach willkürlich sind, da der grammatische Bau (Sprachbau) unberücksichtigt bleibt.

Was die Feststellung der genetischen Sprachverwandtschaft (Sprachkreis) betrifft, äußert sich Kraus skeptisch, daß die Befragung von Einzelpersonen nicht notwendigerweise repräsentative Ergebnisse für die Zusammensetzung des Wortschatzes einer Sprachgemeinschaft bietet, und daher individuelle Ausdrucksweisen das Bild einer möglichen Verwandtschaft der Sprachen erheblich verzerren können. In der Tat zeigt die Kraus'sche Stellungnahme, daß den *Vocabularia* eine verfeinerte Methodik fehlt. Allerdings das gesamte Werk mit Arens (1980: 102) als "dilettantisch" abzutun, bedeutet wohl, das Kind mit dem Bade auszuschütten. Und wenn Arens (1969: 136) den eigentlichen Wert der *Vocabularia* darin sieht, daß sie die Kraus'sche Kritik veranlaßt haben, so ist ihm offenbar der Tatbestand verborgen geblieben, daß das Werk erstmals Sprachproben vieler schriftloser Sprachen bietet (z. B. samojedischer, tungusischer, paläoasiatischer, kaukasischer und afrikanischer Sprachen), deren sprachhistorische Erforschung ohne diese Sammlungen wesentlich erschwert wäre (Vdovin 1954; Fodor 1975: 35ff.; Haarmann 1979c).

Die sachliche Kritik der *Vocabularia* von Kraus, die von Adelung (1815: 111) als "meisterhafte Recension" hervorgehoben wird, findet in der deutschen gelehrten Welt große Beachtung und wird auch in St. Petersburg aufmerksam zur Kenntnis genommen. Die Zarin sendet Kraus einen Brillantring mit der Versicherung ihres Respekts (Adelung 1815: 111). Bedingt durch die von Kraus und anderen vorgebrachte Kritik – wozu auch Joseph Dobrowsky, Johann Christian Christoph Rüdiger und Volney (Constantin François de Chasseboeuf) gehören (Nachdruck ihrer Besprechungen bei Adelung 1815: 138ff.) – verzichtet man auf die Publikation des geplanten dritten Bandes der *Vocabularia*, der Materialen aus amerikanischen und afrikanischen Sprachen enthalten sollte.

Stattdessen gibt die Zarin Anweisung, die Materialien neu zu redigieren und die Sammlungen durch die Aufnahme amerikanischer und afrikanischer Sprachen zu erweitern. Mit der Neuausgabe wird der Direktor der Normalschulen, Theodor Jankiewitsch de Miriewo (1741–1814), betraut, der die Kompilation in wenigen Jahren umarbeitet. Unter dem Titel *Sravnitel'nyj Slovar' vsech jazykov i narečij po azbučnomy porjadku raspoložennyj* (Vergleichendes Wörterbuch aller Sprachen und Mundarten in alphabetische Ordnung gebracht) erscheint das vierbändige Werk in den Jahren 1790 und 1791 in St. Petersburg. Ergänzt wurde die Zahl der Sprachen durch 23 amerikanische und 30 afrikanische (s. Fodor 1975: 35f. zum wissenschaftshistorischen Wert der afrikanischen Sammlungen). Die Zweitausgabe der *Vocabularia* durch Jankiewitsch de Miriewo findet allerdings wenig Verbreitung, und die meisten Exemplare der insgesamt Tausenderauflage verbleiben im "Kaiserlichen Cabinet" (Adelung 1815: 95).

## 6. Die Sprachenenzyklopädie von Lorenzo Hervás y Panduro

Die gelehrte Welt Europas pflegt im 18. Jh. einen regen Informationsaustausch über die Grenzen der Nationalkulturen hinweg. Daher bleibt kein größeres Projekt zur Sprachensammlung den Interessenten im Ausland unbekannt. Dies gilt auch für das umfassende enzyklopädische Werk von Lorenzo Hervás y Panduro (1735–1809).

Der Haupttitel seines einundzwanzigbändigen Monumentalwerkes ist der Mentalität von Universalgelehrten wie Leibniz oder Diderot verpflichtet: *Idea dell'Universo, che contiene la Storia della vita dell'uomo, elementi cosmografici, viaggio estatico al mondo planetario, e Storia della terra, e delle lingue.* Hervás wird im September 1785 von den Vorbereitungen zu den *Vocabularia* von Pallas unterrichtet, als bereits zwei Bände seiner Sprachensammlungen erschienen sind. Später steht ihm offenbar ein Exemplar der *Vocabularia* zur Verfügung, über deren Materialsammlung Hervás später sagt, daß sie umfangreicher sei als die in seinem eigenen polyglotten Wörterbuch (Hervás 1800/I: 64f.).

Als Mitglied des Jesuitenordens, dem er als Novize im Jahre 1749 beitritt, hat Hervás später Zugang zu den bedeutendsten Informationsquellen der damaligen westlichen Welt, insbesondere die Bibliothek des Vatikan und des Quirinalpalastes in Rom sowie das Archiv der Krone von Aragón in Barcelona. Nach Abschluß seiner Studien im Colegio de Alcalá verbringt Hervás einige Jahre als Missionar in den spanischen Kolonien Amerikas. Angeregt durch die Vorschläge zu Sprachensammlungen, die Leibniz seinerzeit dem Jesuiten Grimaldi übermittelt hatte (s. unter 3.), legt Hervás das Fundament für seine Sammlungen amerikanischer Sprachen während seines dortigen Aufenthaltes.

Ereignisse der zeitgenössischen Kirchengeschichte mit einschneidenden Folgen für die Biographie des Jesuiten Hervás prägen die Entstehungsphase des Enzyklopädieprojekts. Nach der Auflösung des Jesuitenordens im Jahre 1767 wird Hervás zusammen mit anderen Jesuiten aus Spanien expatriiert. Als Flüchtling findet er Aufnahme in Italien, zunächst in Forlí und wenige Jahre später, als der Jesuitenorden 1773 auch in Forlí verboten wird, in Cesena. Dort kann Hervás seine Pläne für eine Universalenzyklopädie unter dem Mäzenatentum der Familie Ghini verwirklichen. Das einundzwanzigbändige Werk wird zwischen 1778 und 1787 gedruckt. Nach elfjährigem Aufenthalt in Cesena siedelt Hervás nach Rom über. Insbesondere für die Bearbeitung der beiden letzten, auf die Sprachenvielfalt konzentrierten Bände seiner Enzyklopädie profitiert Hervás von den Quellen der Vatikanbibliothek.

Aufgrund einer Amnestie für Einzelpersonen kehrt der ehemalige Jesuit Hervás im Jahre 1798 nach Spanien zurück. Nach einem Aufenthalt von mehreren Monaten in Barcelona, den er vor allem zu Studien im Archivo de la Corona de Aragón nutzt, kehrt Hervás in seinen Geburtsort Horcajo de Santiago (Cuenca) zurück. König Carlos IV. (reg.: 1788–1808) widerruft die Amnestie, und Hervás wird 1801 erneut des Landes verwiesen. In Rom lebt Hervás bis zu seinem Tod als Bibliothekar des Quirinalpalastes.

Die letzten Jahre seines Lebens widmet Hervás der Redaktion einer erweiterten spanischen Ausgabe seiner Enzyklopädie, zu deren Bearbeitung er bereits 1789 konkrete Schritte unternommen hatte. Die spanische Fassung stellt eine erhebliche Erweiterung der Bände XVII bis XXI der italienischen Originalausgabe dar. Die größere Materialfülle der spanischen Ausgabe geht aber auf Kosten der Systematik, der Kohärenz und der Klarheit (Coseriu 1978a: 48, Fn 29). Die sprachenkundliche Essenz des Werkes von Hervás findet sich in den fünf letzten Bänden (XVII bis XXI) der italienischen Ausgabe (Tovar 1986: 13).

Als das Werk einer Einzelperson bleibt die Enzyklopädie von Hervás bis heute nach seiner Themenvielfalt einmalig und nach seiner Materialfülle unerreicht. Das Gesamtwerk des spanischen Enzyklopädisten ist indes weitaus umfangreicher als die im Druck erschienenen Bände der *Idea dell'Universo* (bzw. *Catálogo*). In der Nationalbibliothek von Madrid sind zahlreiche Manuskripte aufbewahrt, u. a. eine mehrbändige Geschichte der Schrift (*Historia del arte de escribir*, 2 Bde; *Paleografia universal*, 3 Bde), grammatische Beschreibungen von 25 Sprachen aus verschiedenen Teilen der Welt, die *Biblioteca jesuítico-española* (2 Bde) und der 'äußerst wertvolle' (Correa Rodríguez 1981: 734) *Catálogo de manuscritos españoles y portugueses en Roma*.

Entgegen der Auffassung von Leibniz, der nach der einen (und einzigen) Ursprache der Menschen forscht und das vergleichende Studium der natürlichen Sprachen in den Dienst der Suche danach stellt, geht Hervás davon aus, daß es keine einzige Ursprache gegeben habe, sondern daß sich die modernen Sprachen aus mehreren Ursprachen entwickelt hätten. Den Begriff der Ursprache bezeichnet Hervás im Italienischen als *lingua matrice*, im Spanischen als *lengua matriz*. Vor der Sintflut, so seine Bibelinterpretation, hätten die Menschen verschiedene Sprachen, eben die Matrices, gesprochen. Die Sprachverwirrung anläßlich des Turmbaus von Babel sei eine sekundäre Entwicklung. Die eigenwillige Interpretation der biblischen Texte verschafft Hervás Spielraum für Gedanken, womit sich bis heute die Vertreter der linguistisch orientierten Anthropologie beschäftigen, nämlich die Hypothese von der Affiliation aller natürlichen Sprachen in einer begrenzten Anzahl von Sprachfamilien (Ruhlen 1994: 12f.).

Auf gleicher Linie mit Leibniz liegt Hervás mit seinem Postulat, wonach das Studium der Geschichte natürlicher Sprachen den Weg zur Geschichte der sie sprechenden Völker bahnt. Hervás hebt – wie Leibniz Jahrzehnte vorher – hervor, daß die schriftliche Aufzeichnung von Sprache sekundär sei, während die gesprochene Sprache der eigentliche Schlüssel ist, um zu den historischen Ursprüngen zu gelangen. Hervás setzt die sprachliche mit der volklichen (= ethnischen) Geschichte gleich: 'Die Geschichte der Sprachen ist die der Nationen, die sie sprechen' (Hervás 1787b: 24). Diese Auffassung entspricht dem Zeitgeist des 18. Jhs., dessen Tradition ihrerseits über die Brücke der Sprachauffassung zur Zeit der Renaissance bis ins frühe Mittelalter zurückreicht (Haarmann 1993: 144ff., 1995: 32ff.).

Ebenso sorgfältig durchdacht wie seine Hypothesen über ursprachliche Verschiedenheiten sind die methodischen Überlegungen, die Hervás zur Vergleichbarkeit der Sprachen anstellt. Entgegen der Mehrzahl der zeitgenössischen Forscher, die sich – wie Pallas und die meisten Petersburger Akademiemitglieder – primär auf lexikalische Vergleichungen verlassen, nimmt Hervás das Primat der historisch-vergleichenden Sprachwissenschaft des 19. Jhs. vorweg: 'Die Ähnlichkeiten der Sprachen in der Struktur sind das sicherste Zeichen ihrer Verwandtschaft' (Hervás 1785: 174). Der grammatische Bau wird von Hervás *artifizio grammaticale* (bzw. *artificio gramatical* im Spanischen) genannt, und dies ist der Bereich, auf den sich der Sprachvergleich vorrangig richten soll.

Dem Strukturvergleich, der einen Vergleich phonetischer Äquivalenzen einschließt, mißt Hervás in seinem gesamten Werk mehr Bedeutung für die Auffindung der Matrices bei als den Wortvergleichungen, obwohl in seinen Publikationen und Manuskripten enorm umfangreiche Wörtersammlungen in Verzeichnissen und Vergleichstabellen angehäuft sind. In seinem polyglotten Wörterbuch hat Hervás 63 Wörter aus insgesamt 154 Sprachen gesammelt (Hervás 1787a). Zusätzlich finden sich Wörtersammlungen in anderen Werken, beispielsweise in den Traktaten über Arithmetik und Zeitmessung (Hervás 1785–86).

Für die Zwecke des grammatischen Vergleichs stützt sich Hervás auf eine Sammlung von Vaterunsertexten in 300 damals bekannten Sprachen (Hervás 1787b). Im Unterschied zu den bis dahin angestellten Sammlungen solcher Texte – eine Tradition, die ihren Anfang zu Beginn des 16. Jhs. nimmt (s. die erste größere Sammlung in der zwischen 1515 und 1517 erschienenen *Biblia Políglota Complutense*) – versieht Hervás die Originaltexte mit einer wörtlichen Übertragung, um auf diese Weise den Satzbau und den Formenschatz der untersuchten Sprachen besser zu verstehen. Dieses Verfahren ermöglicht es ihm, beispielsweise die Position von Pronomen und Adjektiven entweder vor oder nach dem Nomen festzustellen (s. Abb. 144.2.).

Beeindruckend ist das Geschick, mit dem Hervás Sprachen genealogisch gruppiert. Die indoeuropäische Sprachverwandtschaft ist bei ihm ebenso vermerkt wie die genetische Zusammengehörigkeit der finnisch-ugrischen Sprachen, von denen er das ihn besonders interessierende Ungarische mit dem Lappischen und Finnischen vergleicht (Hervás 1787a). Bis dahin unerkannt war die Sprachverwandtschaft der malayo-polynesischen Sprachen, die Hervás als erster zu gruppieren versucht. Seine Klassifizierung der amerikanischen Indianersprachen ist die erste Übersicht mit wissenschaftlichen Ansprüchen (Landar 1975: 1360f.).

Da die Vergleichung der Sprachen nach Hervás der Auffindung ihrer Ursprünge dient, beschäftigen ihn in erster Linie historische Aspekte des Sprachwandels durch Kontakteinflüsse. Wie Leibniz, so sieht auch Hervás in den Ortsnamen einen stabilen Faktor für Hinweise auf ältere Besiedlung einer Region, als Relikte von verschollenen Sprachen. Für das Fortbestehen einer Sprache ist nach Hervás der Alltagswortschatz maßgebend, und dies ist der beständigste Teil des Lexikons, der sich unter Fremdeinfluß weniger leicht verändert als andere lexikalische Bereiche (Hervás 1787a: 14ff.).

Im Fall einer Überlagerung einer Sprache durch eine Kontaktsprache verändern sich nach Hervás die Bereiche in folgender Reihenfolge: Wortschatz, Grammatik, Phonetik (Hervás 1785: 162f.). Die neu angenommene Sprache wird nach den Aussprachegewohnheiten der verdrängten Sprache gesprochen: 'Von der alten Sprache bleiben im allgemeinen die Aussprache und einige Wörter erhalten' (Hervás 1787a: 128).

Gegründet auf diese methodischen Überlegungen untersucht Hervás ältere Sprachschichten und findet sie in vielen Fällen dort, wo spätere Generationen von Substratforschern sie auch diskutiert haben. Nach Coseriu (1978b: 523) hat Hervás "eine ausführliche Theorie des Substrats entwickelt". Für das Spanische nimmt Hervás ein baskisches Substrat an, u. zw. im Hinblick auf den Wandel von anlautendem f- zu h- (lat. *filia* > span. *hija*); (Hervás 1784: 219f., 1785: 66f.). Hinsichtlich des Französischen erkennt Hervás Einflüsse des Festlandkeltischen (Hervás 1784: 188f., 1785: 163). Das keltische Substrat ist nach Hervás (1785: 163, 1787b: 33) ebenfalls ausschlaggebend für die Verschiedenheit der norditalienischen Dialekte von den übrigen lokalen Sprachvarianten Italiens. In der Toskana glaubt Hervás, Relikte des Etruskischen zu entdecken (Hervás 1785: 142).

*Vilela*
tate-kis = padre-nostro
lauè-l-àt = altezze-le-in
yasit = stante
hüat-mi = nome-tuo
ilchubè-p = baciato-il
puop = sia

*Guaraní*
Oreruba = Nostro-padre
ibape éreibae = cielo-in-tu-stante
imboyerobiaripiramo = il riverito
ndèrera = tuo-nome
toico = sia

*Kichua*
Yaya-icu = padre-nostro
hanac-pachacuna-pi = alti-luoghi-in
cac = stante
suti-iqui = nome-tuo
muchasca = adorato
càchun = sia

Abb. 144.2: Der Anfang des Vaterunsers in drei Sprachen Lateinamerikas mit grammatischen Analysen nach Hervás (1787b)

Mit voller Berechtigung hat Sarmiento (1990: 476) Hervás als einen Sprachforscher bezeichnet, der zwischen Tradition und Moderne steht, 'der es fertigbrachte, eine Entwicklungsphase der Sprachenkunde zu begraben und eine andere neue und weitreichende auszuleuchten: die der historisch-vergleichenden Sprachwissenschaft'. Eine direkte Berührung mit deren Vertretern führt über die persönliche Bekanntschaft zwischen Hervás und Wilhelm von Humboldt (1767–1835). Hervás schenkt Humboldt eines seiner Manuskripte (*Gramáticas abreviadas de las diez y ocho lenguas principales de América*), dem später Adelung und Vater Materialien für den Mithridates entnehmen (s. unter 7.).

Die Priorität, die Hervás dem grammatischen Strukturvergleich zur Aufdeckung der Sprachverwandtschaft einräumt, ist allerdings in der Folgezeit nicht gebührend gewürdigt worden, weder in Friedrich Adelungs (1801) Besprechung der italienischen Ausgabe der Hervás'schen Enzyklopädie noch in Friedrich Max Müllers (1861) berühmten *Lectures on the science of language*.

## 7. Die Sprachensammlungen von Johann Christoph Adelung und Johann Severin Vater

Das letzte Monumentalwerk seiner Art, das den Anspruch erhebt, Textproben und Wörtersammlungen aus allen bekannten Sprachen der Welt zu bieten, ist der vierbändige *Mithridates oder allgemeine Sprachenkunde* (1806–17), dessen Titelwahl an Gesners Werk von 1555 erinnert (s. unter 2.). Der *Mithridates* wird von Johann Christoph Adelung (1732–1806) konzipiert und begonnen, mehr als die Hälfte des Monumentalwerks wird von Johann Severin Vater (1771–1826) redaktionell ausgeführt (s. *Allgemeine Deutsche Biographie* 1, 1875: 80–84 und Sickel 1933: 7–98 zur Biographie Adelungs, *Allgemeine Deutsche Biographie* 39, 1895: 503–508 zur Biographie Vaters).

An dem Plan einer Gesamtübersicht aller Sprachen der Erde hat Adelung bereits bald nach der Drucklegung seines Werks *Versuch eines vollständigen grammatisch-kritischen Wörterbuchs der hochdeutschen Mundart* (5 Bde, 1774–1786) gearbeitet. Das Projekt des *Mithridates* wird verzögert durch die Arbeiten an der zweiten, erweiterten und verbesserten Auflage des deutschen Wörterbuchs (1793–1801). Als schließlich die Drucklegung des ersten Bandes der Sprachensammlungen im Jahre 1806 abgeschlossen ist, wird Adelung bewußt, daß er durch sein Alter zu geschwächt ist, um das Gesamtwerk allein weiterzuführen.

Auf Vater, der zwischen 1799 und 1806 als Professor der Theologie und der orientalischen Sprachen in Halle wirkte, war Adelung durch dessen Studien zur Semitistik (insbesondere das Hebräische) und allgemeinen Grammatik aufmerksam geworden (Vater 1799, 1801, 1805). Adelung bittet den später als Bibliothekar in Königsberg tätigen Vater, das Projekt des *Mithridates* mit ihm zusammen zu Ende zu bringen. Als Adelung stirbt, ist ein Teil des zweiten Bandes im Druck. Die Materialien des dritten und vierten Bandes muß Vater im wesentlichen selbst zusammenstellen.

Im *Mithridates* finden sich Sammlungen und Beschreibungen von annähernd 500 Sprachen. Bd. 1 enthält eine Übersicht der asiatischen Sprachen, Bd. 2 der europäischen, Bd. 3 der afrikanischen und Bd. 4 der amerikanischen Sprachen. Für jede Sprache wird eine Version des Vaterunser als Textprobe gegeben, der in einem analytischen Teil grammatische und lexikalische Erläuterungen folgen. Der Konzeption des *Mithridates* sieht man es an, daß Vertreter verschiedener Generationen daran gearbeitet haben. Adelung, fast vierzig Jahre älter als Vater, ordnet die Materialien im ersten, von ihm besorgten Band, in der Konvention der Sprachenkunde des 18. Jhs. nach geographischen Kriterien.

Ab dem zweiten Band wird der Einfluß Vaters deutlich, der sich verstärkt um grammatische Vergleiche und genealogische Gruppierungen bemüht. In die Ausarbeitung des *Mithridates* bringt Vater seine Erfahrungen als Grammatiker ein. Vater hat "unter Betheiligung Wilhelm v. Humboldt's und Friedrich Adelung's" (*Allgemeine Deutsche Biographie* 1, 1875: 82) die von Adelung hinterlassenen Materialien verwendet und außerdem die *Vocabularia* von Pallas sowie die Werke von Hervás ausgewertet. Gabelentz (1901: 28) stellt treffend fest, daß der *Mithridates* von Adelung und Vater im Vergleich zur Sprachenenzyklopädie von Hervás "weniger selbständig aber reichhaltiger ist".

Betrachtet man den *Mithridates* nach Konzeption und Inhalt im Zusammenhang mit den anderen Schriften Adelungs, so stellt man erhebliche methodische Diskrepanzen fest (Arens 1969: 149f.). In seiner Schrift *Über den Ursprung der Sprachen* (1781) spricht sich Adelung ausdrücklich für die Bedeutung des grammatischen Sprachenvergleichs aus. In der Vorrede zum ersten Band des *Mithridates* (1806: viii) hebt er den gleichen Aspekt hervor, indem er Bedenken gegen rein lexikalische Vergleichungen erhebt. In der Durchführung des Sprachenvergleichs stützt sich Adelung allerdings in der Hauptsache auf lexikalische Ähnlichkeiten, während die grammatische Vergleichung nur eine marginale Rolle spielt.

Andererseits finden sich im *Mithridates* wichtige Gedanken zur genetischen Sprachverwandtschaft, wobei entsprechende Stellungnahmen in anderen Schriften Adelungs verworrener erscheinen. Im *Mithridates* (1806, I: 279) äußert Adelung die Vermutung, daß Germanen und Perser vielleicht "gleichzeitig aus einer und derselben Sprachquelle geschöpft" hätten. In seiner *Älteste(n) Geschichte der Deutschen* (1806: 350) dagegen nimmt Adelung eine Sprachmischung von "deutschen Bestandtheile(n) im Persischen" an, die wahrscheinlich zur Zeit der Völkerwanderung stattgefunden habe.

Obwohl durch Vaters Bemühungen, dem grammatischen Sprachvergleich größeres Gewicht einzuräumen als Adelung, die Präsentation der Sprachensammlungen in den letzten Bänden des *Mithridates* ausgewogener ist als in dem von Adelung betreuten ersten Band, zeigen sich in der genetischen Klassifikation beider Forscher deutliche Mängel. Obwohl William Jones 1786 anhand seines Vergleichs von Verbstammformen und grammatischen Formantien den methodischen Weg für die Erforschung der Verwandtschaft des Sanskrit mit dem Griechischen und Lateinischen gewiesen hatte, führt Adelung den Vergleich nicht weiter aus. Stattdessen assoziiert er mit dem Sanskrit auch Sprachen, die keinem genealogischen Vergleich standhalten (z. B. Hebräisch, Syrisch, Türkisch oder Ungarisch).

Benfey (1869: 355) spricht von einem "Rückschritt" im Vergleich zu den bereits von Jones erreichten Erkenntnissen. Vater seinerseits gelingt es nicht, die finnisch-ugrischen Sprachen zu gruppieren, und dies trotz der bahnbrechenden grammatischen Vergleiche von Sajnovics (1770) und Gyarmathi (1799). Im zweiten Band des *Mithridates* wird das Ungarische als "Balkansprache" aufgeführt, ohne Verbindung mit den übrigen finnisch-ugrischen Sprachen.

## 8. Ausblick

Geradezu symbolisch überschneiden sich die Publikation des letzten Bandes des *Mithridates* (1817), mit dem die "Vorgeschichte" der Sprachwissenschaft ausläuft, und der bahnbrechenden Studie von Franz Bopp (1791–1867) *Über das Conjugationssystem der Sanskritsprache* … (1816), die den Beginn der eigentlichen "Geschichte" der historisch-vergleichenden Sprachwissenschaft markiert. Mit dem Abschluß des von Adelung begonnenen und von Vater weitergeführten Monumentalwerks endet eine ganze Epoche, die der großen Sprachensammlungen.

Bei Berücksichtigung der neueren Erkenntnisse über Inhalt und Konzeption der großen Sprachensammlungen, über die Intentionen und methodischen Ideale ihrer Bearbeiter, ist ohne Übertreibung festzustellen, daß diese Werke nicht als Fossilien der linguistischen Historiographie zu betrachten sind, deren Erwähnung einen Statistenplatz in einer Gesamtdarstellung der Geschichte der Sprachwissenschaft wert ist, sondern daß sie Wegbereiter für eine wissenschaftliche Betrachtungsweise von Sprachproblemen waren, deren Entwicklung ohne die Sprachensammlungen erheblich verzögert worden wäre.

Das Verfahren des Vergleichs grammatischer Strukturen war den Komparativisten nicht fremd. Als methodisches Desiderat ist der grammatische Sprachenvergleich allen bewußt. Während sich aber die konkrete Ausführung der Sprachklassifikation bei Bacmeister, Pallas und Adelung (im ersten Band des *Mithridates*) weitgehend auf lexikalische Vergleichungen stützt, und bei Vater (*Mithridates*, Bd. 2–4) der grammatische Vergleich keine durchgängige Berücksichtigung findet, ist Hervás der einzige, in dessen Werk das Primat des grammatischen Vergleichs auch praktisch aufrecht erhalten wird.

## 9. Bibliographie


Adelung, Friedrich v. 1801. "Nachricht von den Werken des spanischen Exjesuiten Don Lorenzo Hervás über die Sprachen". *Allgemeine Geographische Ephemeriden* VII, 543–554.

–. 1815. *Catherinens der Grossen Verdienste um die Vergleichende Sprachenkunde.* St. Petersburg: Friedrich Drechsler (Nachdruck mit einer Einleitung und einem biobibliographischen Register von H. Haarmann). Hamburg: Buske.

Adelung, Johann Christoph. 1806. *Älteste Geschichte der Deutschen, ihrer Sprache und Litteratur, bis zur Völkerwanderung.* Leipzig: Göschen.

Adelung, Johann Christoph & Johann Severin Vater. 1806–17. *Mithridates oder allgemeine Sprachenkunde mit dem Vater Unser als Sprachprobe in beynahe fünfhundert Sprachen und Mundarten*, 4 Bde. Berlin: Vossische Buchhandlung.

Althaus, Hans Peter et al., Hgg. 1980. *Lexikon der Germanistischen Linguistik.* Tübingen: Niemeyer (2. Aufl.).

Arens, Hans. 1969. *Sprachwissenschaft: Der Gang ihrer Entwicklung von der Antike bis zur Gegenwart.* 2. Aufl. Freiburg & München: Alber.

–. 1980. "Geschichte der Linguistik". Althaus et al. 1980. 97–107.

Ariew, Roger. 1995. "G. W. Leibniz, Life and Works". Jolley 1995. 18–42.

Batllori, Miguel. 1951. "El archivo lingüístico de Hervás en Roma y su reflejo en W. von Humboldt". *Archivum Historicum Societatis Jesu* XX. 59–116.

Benfey, Theodor. 1869. *Geschichte der Sprachwissenschaft und orientalischen Philologie in Deutschland seit dem Anfange des 19. Jahrhunderts mit einem Rückblick auf die früheren Zeiten.* 2. Aufl. München: Cotta.

Bopp, Franz. 1816. *Über das Conjugationssystem der Sanskritsprache in Vergleichung mit jenem der griechischen, lateinischen, persischen und germanischen Sprache.* Frankfurt: Andreäische Buchhandlung.

Bright, William, Hg. 1992. *International Encyclopedia of Linguistics.* 4 Bde. New York & Oxford: Oxford Univ. Press.

Coseriu, Eugenio. 1975. "Andrés de Poza y las lenguas de Europa". *Studia Hispanica in Honorem R. Lapesa*, Bd. III, 199–217. Madrid: Editorial Gredos.

–. 1978a. "Lo que sabemos de Hervás". *Estudios ofrecidos a Emilio Alarcos Llorach*, Bd. III, 35–58. Oviedo: Universidad de Oviedo.

–. 1978b. "Hervás und das Substrat". *Studii şi cercetări lingvistice* 5, 523–530.

Cronin, Vincent. 1995. *Katharina die Große.* 2. Aufl. Hildesheim: Claassen.

Doerfer, Gerhard. 1965. *Ältere westeuropäische Quellen zur kalmückischen Sprachgeschichte (Witsen 1692 bis Zwick 1827).* Wiesbaden: Harrassowitz.

Dutens, L. L., Hg. 1768. *G. G. Leibnitii Opera Omnia.* 6 Bde. Genf.

Fischer, Johann Eberhard. 1747. *Vocabularium continens trecenta vocabula triginta quatuor gentium, maxima ex parte Sibiricarum.* (= *Vocabularium Sibiricum*; Cod. ms. philol. Göttingen 261, 4 Bl. + 143 S.); s. Gulya 1995.

Fodor, István. 1975. *Pallas und andere afrikanische Vokabularien vor dem 19. Jahrhundert. Ein Beitrag zur Forschungsgeschichte.* Hamburg: Buske.

–. 1982. "The Redaction of the Vocabulary of Pallas". *Studia Slavica Hungarica* 28. 229–245.

Gabelentz, Georg v. d. 1901. *Die Sprachwissenschaft, ihre Aufgaben, Methoden und bisherigen Ergebnisse.* 2. Aufl. Leipzig. (Nachdruck Tübingen: Narr, 1969).

Gipper, Helmut & Peter Schmitter. 1975. "Sprachwissenschaft und Sprachphilosophie im Zeitalter der Romantik". Sebeok 1975. 481–606.

Gyarmathi, Sámuel. 1799. *Affinitas lingvae hvngaricae cvm lingvis fennicae originis grammatice demonstrata.* Göttingen.

–. 1983. *Grammatical Proof of the Affinity of the Hungarian Language with Languages of Fennic Origin.* (Engl. Übersetzung des lat. Originals von V. E. Hanzeli). Amsterdam & Philadelphia: Benjamins.

Gulya, János. 1959. "Pallas szótárának kéziratos forrása". *Magyar Nyelv* 55. 95–106.

–, Hg. 1995. Johann Eberhard Fischer: *Vocabularium Sibiricum* (1747). Der etymologisch-vergleichende Anteil (bearbeitet und herausgegeben von János Gulya). Frankfurt/M., Berlin & New York: Lang.

Haarmann, Harald. 1976a. "Die Klassifikation der romanischen Sprachen in den Werken der Komparativisten aus der zweiten Hälfte des 18. Jahrhunderts (Rüdiger, Hervás, Pallas)". Niederehe & Haarmann 1976. 221–243. (Überarbeitete und erweiterte Fassung in Haarmann 1979c, 45–69; = 1979b.)

–. 1976b. *Die estnischen Grammatiken des 17. Jahrhunderts I.* Hamburg: Buske.

–. 1979a. "Vorwort". Haarmann 1979c. 7–16.

–. 1979b. – s. Haarmann 1976a.

–, Hg. 1979c. *Wissenschaftsgeschichtliche Beiträge zur Erforschung indogermanischer, finnisch-ugrischer und kaukasischer Sprachen bei Pallas.* Hamburg: Buske.

–. 1993. *Die Sprachenwelt Europas. Geschichte und Zukunft der Sprachnationen zwischen Atlantik und Ural.* Frankfurt/M. & New York: Campus.

–. 1995. "Europeanness, European Identity and the Role of Language. Giving profile to an anthropological infrastructure". *Sociolinguistica* 9. 1–55.

Heinekamp, A. 1972. "Ars Characteristica und natürliche Sprache bei Leibniz". *Tijdschrift voor Filosofie* 34. 446–488.

Hervás y Panduro, Lorenzo. 1778–87. *Idea dell'Universo, che contiene la Storia della vita dell'uomo, elementi cosmografici, viaggio estatico al mondo planetario, e Storia della terra, e delle lingue.* 21 Bde. Cesena: Gregorio Biasini. I–VII: *Storia della vita dell'uomo* 1778–80; VIII: *Notizia dell'uomo* 1780; IX–X: *Viaggio estatico al mondo planetario* 1781; XI–XVI: *Storia della terra* 1781–84; XVII: *Catalogo delle lingue conosciute e notizia della loro affinità, e diversità* 1784; XVIII: *Trattato dell'Origine, formazione, meccanismo ed armonia dell'Idiomi* 1785; XIX: *Trattato I. Aritmetica di quasi tutte le nazioni conosciute; Trattato II. Divisione del tempo fra le nazioni Orientali* 1785–86; XX: *Vocabolario poligloto* 1787a; XXI: *Saggio pratico delle lingue* 1787b.

–. 1800–05. *Catálogo de las lenguas de las naciones conocidas, y numeracion, division, y clases de estas segun la diversidad de sus idiomas y dialectos.* 6 Bde. Madrid: Imprenta de la Administración del Real Arbitrio de Beneficencia. (Nachdruck Madrid: Ranz 1979.) I: *Lenguas y Naciones americanas* 1800; II: *Lenguas y naciones de las islas de los mares Pacífico, e Indiano austral* 1801; III: *Lenguas y Naciones europeas. Parte I. Naciones europeas advenidizas, y sus lenguas* 1802; IV: *Lenguas y naciones europeas. Parte II. Naciones europeas primitivas: sus lenguas matrices y dialectos de estas* 1804a; V: *Continuacion del Tratado III. Lenguas y Naciones europeas: y de su parte II. Naciones primitivas: sus lenguas matrices y dialectos de estas* 1804b; VI: *Continuacion del Tratado III. Lenguas y Naciones europeas: y de la parte II: Sus lenguas matrices y dialectos de estas* 1805.

Ivić, Milka. 1971. *Wege der Sprachwissenschaft.* München: Hueber.

Jacob, André. 1973. *Genèse de la pensée linguistique.* Paris: Armand Colin.

Jolley, Nicholas, Hg. 1995. *The Cambridge Companion to Leibniz.* Cambridge: Cambridge Univ. Press.

Kononov, Andrej Nikolaevič. 1972. *Istorija izučenija tjurkskich jazykov v Rossii. Dooktjabr'skij period.* Leningrad: Nauka.

Kraus, Jakob. 1787. Rezension von Pallas 1786. *Allgemeine Literatur Zeitung* 1787, 235–237 (abgedruckt mit Kommentierung bei Adelung 1815, 112ff.).

Landar, Herbert. 1975. "Native Ibero-America". Sebeok 1975. 1359–1377.

Leibniz, Gottfried Wilhelm. 1710. "Brevis designatio meditationum de originibus gentium, ductis potissimum ex indicio linguarum". *Miscellanea Berolinensia* 1710, 1–16 (ediert in Dutens 1768, IV.ii 186–198.)

–. 1712. *Epistolaris de Historia Etymologica Dissertatio* (Niedersächsische Landesbibliothek, Handschriftenabteilung, Manuskript IV 469; Hannover).

Lüdtke, Jens. 1978. *Die romanischen Sprachen im "Mithridates" von Adelung und Vater. Studie und Text.* Tübingen: Narr.

Malkiel, Yakov. 1973. "Adelung-Vater's Pioneering Survey of Romance Languages and Dialects (1809)". *Studii şi cercetări lingvistice* 24. 589–593.

Morpurgo Davies, Anna. 1992. "Comparative-Historical Linguistics". Bright 1992/2. 159–163.

Müller, F. Max. 1861. *Lectures on the Science of Language, delivered at the Royal Institution of Great Britain in April, May and June 1861.* London.

Niederehe, Hans-Josef & Harald Haarmann, Hgg. 1976. *In Memoriam Friedrich Diez, Akten des Kolloquiums zur Wissenschaftsgeschichte der Romanistik (Trier, 2.–4. Okt. 1975).* Amsterdam: Benjamins.

Niederehe, Hans-Josef & Konrad Koerner. Hgg. 1990. *History and Historiography of Linguistics. Papers from the Fourth International Conference on the History of the Language Sciences (ICHoLS IV), Trier, 24–28 August 1987.* Amsterdam & Philadelphia: Benjamins.

Nikolai, Christoph Friedrich. 1785. *Tableau général de toutes les langues du monde avec un catalogue préliminaire des principaux dictionnaires dans toutes les langues et des principaux livres qui traitent de l'origine de toutes les langues, de leur étymologie et de leur affinité, fait par ordre de S. M. l'Impératrice de toutes les Russes* (Manuskript, fertiggestellt im Januar 1785).

Pallas, Peter Simon. 1786–89. *Linguarum totius orbis vocabularia comparativa.* 2 Bde. St. Petersburg.

(Nachdruck: Hamburg: Buske 1977–78, mit einem Vorwort von H. Haarmann.)

Percival, W. Keith. 1975. "The Grammatical Tradition and the Rise of the Vernaculars". Sebeok 1975. 231–275.

Rudolphi, K. A. 1812. *Beyträge zur Anthropologie und allgemeinen Naturgeschichte*. Berlin.

Ruhlen, Merritt. 1994. *On the Origin of Languages. Studies in linguistic taxonomy*. Stanford: Stanford Univ. Press.

Rutherford, Donald. 1995. "Philosophy and Language in Leibniz". Jolly 1995. 224–269.

Sajnovics, János. 1770. *Demonstratio Idioma Ungarorum et Lapponum idem esse*. Kopenhagen.

–. 1972. *Beweis, daß die Sprache der Ungarn und Lappen dieselbe ist* (dt. Übersetzung des lat. Originals von M. Ehlers). Wiesbaden: Harrassowitz.

Sarmiento, Ramón. 1990. "Lorenzo Hervás y Panduro (1735–1809): Entre la tradición y la modernidad". Niederehe & Koerner 1990. 461–482.

Schlözer, August Ludwig 1768. *Probe russischer Annalen*. Bremen & Göttingen.

–, Hg. 1770. *Quaestiones Petropolitanae*. Göttingen & Gotha.

–. 1771. *Allgemeine nordische Geschichte*. Halle.

–. 1802–09. *Nestor. Russische Annalen in ihrer slavonischen Grundsprache verglichen und erklärt*. 5 Bde. Göttingen.

Sebeok, Thomas A., Hg. 1975. *Current Trends in Linguistics*. Bd. 13: *Historiography of Linguistics*. Den Haag & Paris: Mouton.

Seuren, Pieter A. M. 1998. *Western linguistics. An historical introduction*. Oxford: Blackwell.

Sickel, Karl-Ernst. 1933. *Johann Christoph Adelung: Seine Persönlichkeit und seine Geschichtsauffassung* (Diss.). Leipzig: Gerhardt.

Sobolevskij, S. 1866. *Filologičeskie zanjatija Ekateriny II-j. Russkij Archiv izdavaemyj pri Čertkovskoj Biblioteke Petrom Bartenevym*, 1863, Bd. 1. 2. Aufl. Moskau.

Stipa, Günter Johannes. 1990. *Finnisch-ugrische Sprachforschung. Von der Renaissance bis zum Neupositivismus*. Helsinki: Suomalais-ugrilainen seura.

Tagliavini, Carlo. 1968. *Panorama di storia della linguistica*. 2. Aufl. Bologna: Pátron.

Tovar, Antonio. 1986. *El lingüista español Lorenzo Hervás (Estudio y selección de obras básicas). I. Catalogo delle lingue*. Madrid: S.G.E.L.

Vater, Johann Severin. 1799. *Uebersicht des Neuesten, was für Philosophie der Sprachen in Deutschland gethan worden ist*. Gotha.

–. 1801. *Versuch einer allgemeinen Sprachlehre*. Halle (Faksimile mit Einleitung und Kommentar von H. E. Brekle; Stuttgart-Bad Cannstatt 1970.)

–. 1805. *Lehrbuch der allgemeinen Grammatik*. Halle.

Vdovin, I. S. 1954. *Istorija izučenija paleoaziatskich jazykov*. Moskau & Leningrad: Nauka.

Waterman, J. T. 1978. *Leibniz and Ludolf on Things Linguistic: Excerpts from their Correspondence (1688–1703)*. Berkeley.

Wendland, Folkwart. 1992. Peter Simon Pallas (1741–1811). Materialien einer Biographie. 2 Bde. Berlin & New York: Walter de Gruyter.

Witsen, Nicolaes. 1692. *Noord en Oost Tartarye*. 2 Bde. Amsterdam. (2. Aufl. 1705, Neuaufl. 1785; deutsche Übersetzung der 2. Aufl. in Auswahl von T. Mikola 1975.)

*Harald Haarmann, Helsinki (Finnland)*

# Publications from Mouton de Gruyter

## Atlas of Languages of Intercultural Communication in the Pacific, Asia, and the Americas

Stephen A. Wurm, Peter Mühlhäusler and
Darrell T. Tyron (Editors)

Two text volumes, one map volume (299 maps on 151 A3 map sheets).
1996. 29,7 x 22 cm. XXXVIII, 1642 pages (text volumes);
XXIV, 151 pages (map volume) in a boxed set.
Cloth. DM 1.098,– /€ 561,40 /öS 8.015,– /sFr 977,–/approx. US$ 549.00
• ISBN 3-11-013417-9

The two text volumes cover a large geographical area, including: Australia, New Zealand, Melanesia, South-East Asia (Insular and Continental), Oceania, the Philippines, Taiwan, Korea, Mongolia, Central Asia, the Caucasus Area, Siberia, Arctic Areas, Canada, Northwest Coast and Alaska, United States Area, Mexico, Central America, South America.
The Atlas is a detailed, far-reaching handbook of fundamental importance, dealing with a large number of diverse fields of knowledge, with the reported facts based on sound scholarly research and scientific findings, but presented in a form intelligible to non-specialists and educated lay persons in general.

"The Atlas [...] deserves to be in every university library."
Gerhard Leitner in *Newsletter Gesellschaft für Australienstudien e.V.*

Price is subject to change

WALTER DE GRUYTER GMBH & CO. KG
Genthiner Straße 13 · 10785 Berlin
Telefon +49-(0)30-2 60 05-0
Fax +49-(0)30-2 60 05-251
www.deGruyter.de

Mouton
de Gruyter
Berlin · New York